AF597455

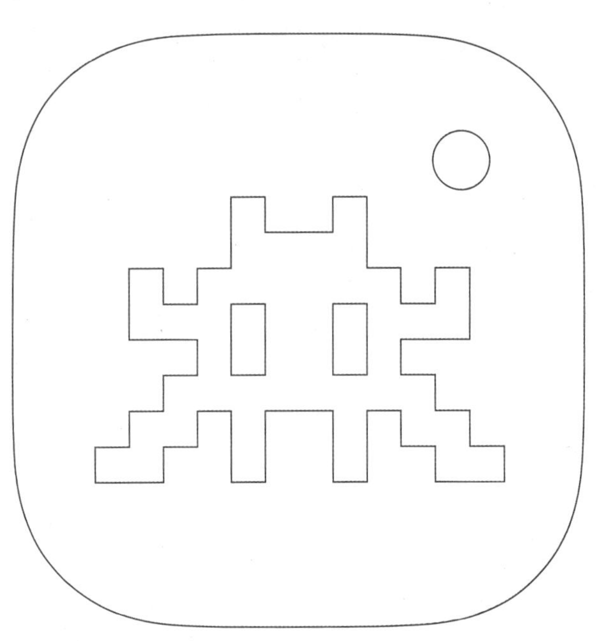

@invaderwashere

Ten Years on Instagram
#Invader #instabook #2013-2023

Table of contents

Foreword

ENG I created my Instagram account on October 22, 2013. I was about to present the film Art4Space in a New York arthouse cinema but, a week before, I realized there had been no communication around the event!
At that time Instagram was a new, fast-growing social network, and a few days before leaving for NY, I created an account on the app to inform my fanbase in the City of the screening. Up until then I'd been absent from all social media platforms, and this was the perfect opportunity to try one. I chose the username @invaderwashere because @invader was already taken and ultimately 'Invader Was Here' was perfect for what I had in mind for the account: allow people to follow my movements with a slight time lag, particularly when it came to my urban invasions, since, to ensure anonymity and security,

I only intended to make my posts once I'd left the scene. In the following years, Instagram spread like wildfire and became the top global social media of the moment, both addictive and time-consuming for millions of users seeking to unravel the mysteries of its algorithm and reach maximum visibility. I've reproduced almost all my posts in this book plus some of the stories* I still find interesting even when stripped of animation or sound. For me, this catalogue is like a time capsule that will still exist when Instagram, smartphones and even the Internet have disappeared and been replaced by other technologies. We'll then be able to browse through this 'insta-book' and discover a decade of an artist's work on the great social media of an era.

* Still images or video displayed in vertical format that are only visible for 24 hours after publication, and which first appeared on Instagram in August 2016.

Urban installations, exhibitions, projects in progress, studio photos or images of my everyday life, I kept my account updated myself and, like a logbook, it charted my activities from October 22, 2013 to October 22, 2023. I like the idea of having once more given a physical form to digital data, and in doing so allow people to read it in a new light.

Greetings from space,
Invader
10-2023

FR J’ai créé mon compte Instagram le 22 octobre 2013. J’étais alors sur le point de présenter le film Art4Space dans un cinéma d'art et d'essai new-yorkais mais, une semaine avant la projection, j’ai réalisé qu’aucune communication n’avait été faite à son sujet ! Instagram était alors un tout jeune réseau social émergent et, quelques jours avant mon départ pour NY, j’y ai créé un compte afin d’informer ma fan base locale de l’évènement. J’avais jusque-là été absent de tous les réseaux sociaux et c’était l’occasion pour moi de tenter l’expérience. J'ai choisi le pseudo @invaderwashere, @invader étant déjà pris, et finalement *Invader Was Here* traduisait très bien l’idée que je me faisais de ce compte : permettre aux gens de suivre mes pérégrinations avec un léger décalage temporel, particulièrement en ce qui concernait mes invasions urbaines, puisque, pour des raisons d'anonymat et de sécurité, je ne devais publier mes posts qu'après avoir quitté les lieux d'intervention. Dans les années qui ont suivi, Instagram s'est répandu comme une traînée de poudre et est devenu le grand réseau social planétaire du moment, addictif et chronophage pour des millions d'utilisateurs cherchant à percer le mystère de son algorithme et à obtenir un maximum de visibilité.

En plus de la quasi-totalité de mes posts, j'ai reproduit ici certaines *stories** en choisissant celles qui gardent encore leur intérêt une fois privées d'animation ou de son.

Ce livre est donc comme une *time capsule* qui restera consultable quand Instagram, les smartphones ou même Internet auront disparu et auront été remplacés par d'autres technologies.

* Images fixes ou vidéos affichées en format vertical qui ne sont visibles que pendant 24 heures après leur publication et qui ont fait leur apparition sur Instagram en août 2016.

Alors on pourra parcourir cet « insta-book », témoignage de dix années d'activité d'un artiste sur le grand réseau social d'une époque.
Installations urbaines, expositions, projets en cours, photos d'atelier ou images de mon quotidien, j'ai personnellement tenu ce compte qui, à la manière d'un journal de bord, retrace mes activités du 22 octobre 2013 au 22 octobre 2023.
J'aime l'idée d'avoir, à nouveau, apporté une matérialité physique à des données numériques et d'en proposer ainsi une nouvelle lecture.

Salutations de l'espace,
Invader
10-2023

2013

INVADERWASHERE 

9	23k	29
Posts	Followers	Following

Edit your profile 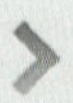

Invader

I finally opened an instagram. Follow my Invasions...

www.space-invaders.com

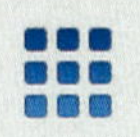  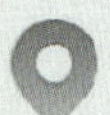 

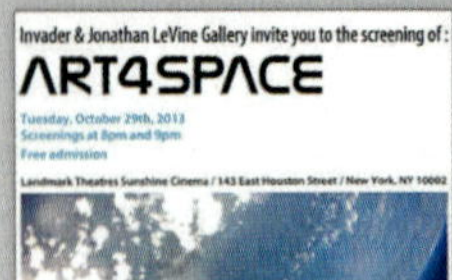

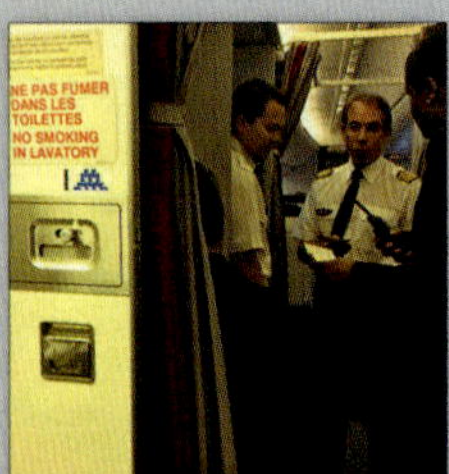

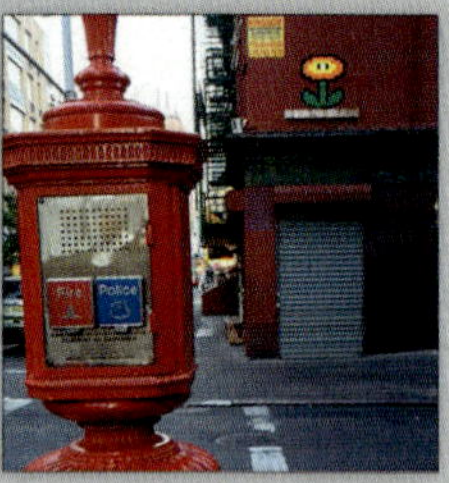

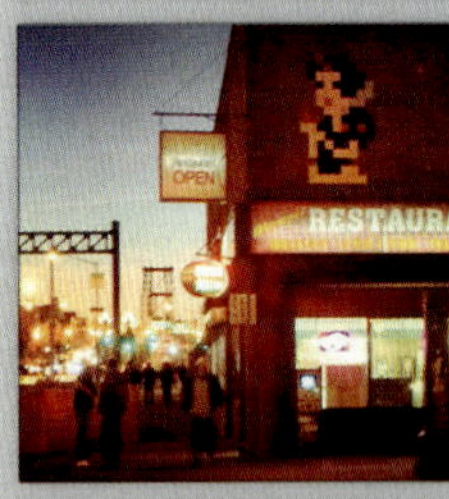

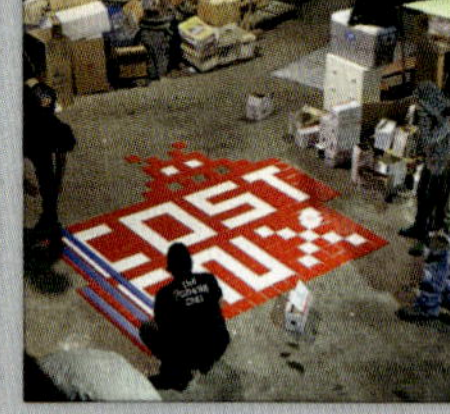

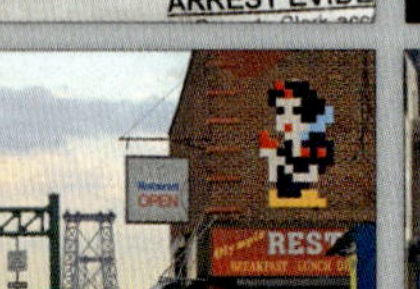

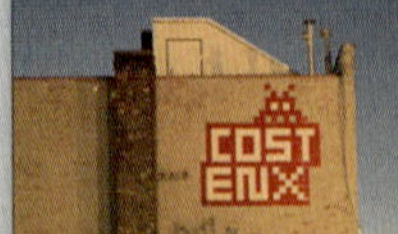

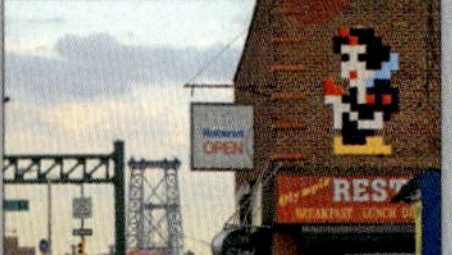

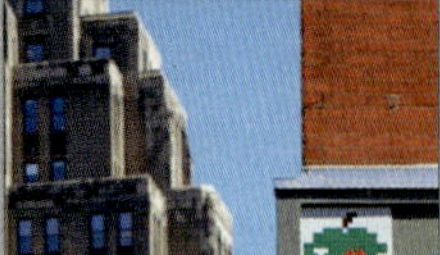

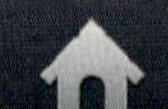 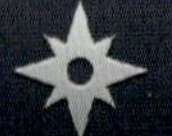 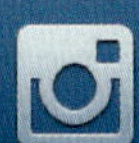  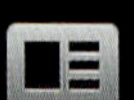

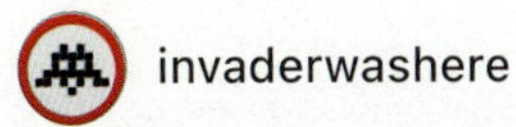

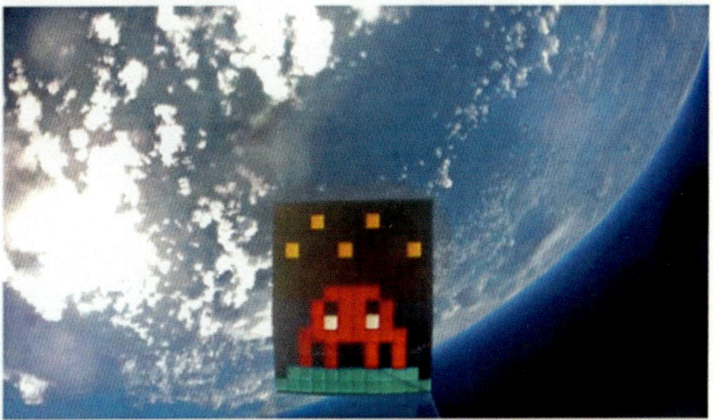

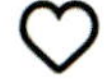   

821 likes

invaderwashere Art4space the movie / NY screening / Oct-29th 2013 / Save the date / More info: art4space.com #invader #art4space #movie #spaceart

View all 71 comments

22 October 2013

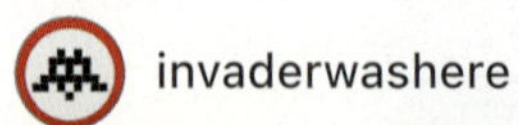
invaderwashere ...

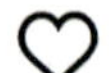 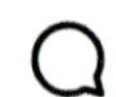  

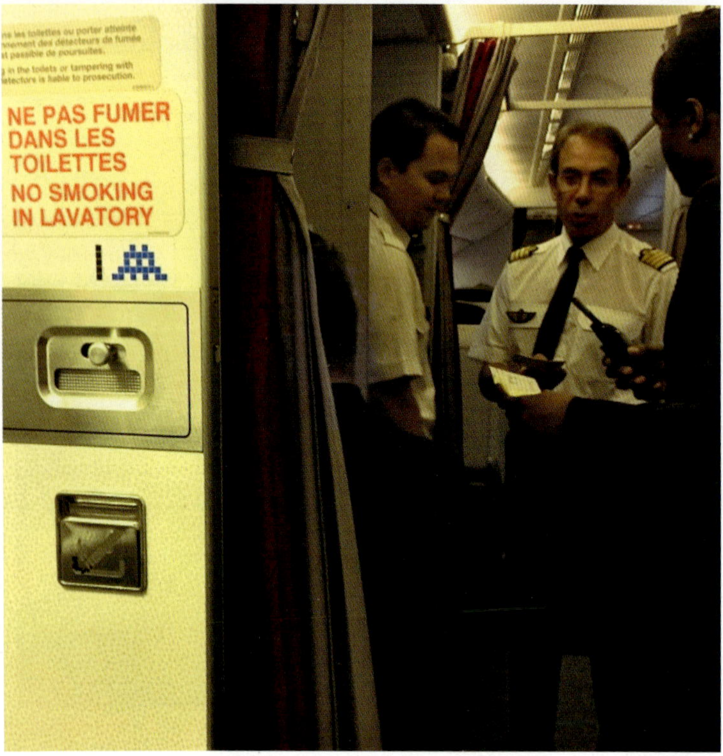

1602 likes

invaderwashere On the road... #onair #airfrance #I-Invade #sticker #placement

View all 39 comments

25 October 2013

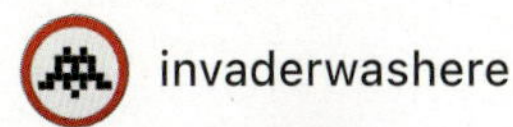

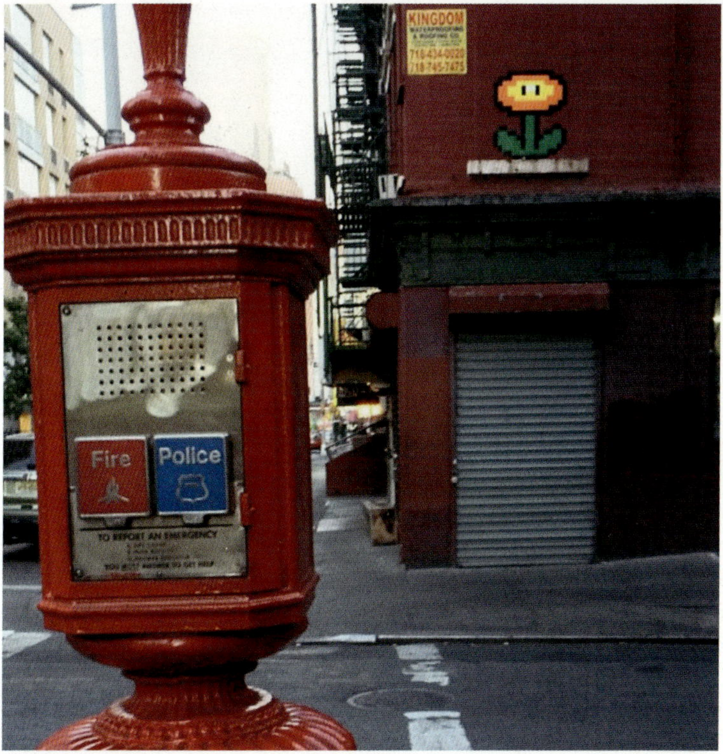

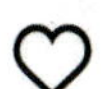   

2 273 likes

invaderwashere 7:16 am. 6th invasion of the night
#backinNYC #invaderwashere 👾👾👾👾👾👾

View all 99 comments

27 October 2013

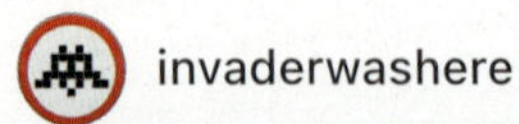

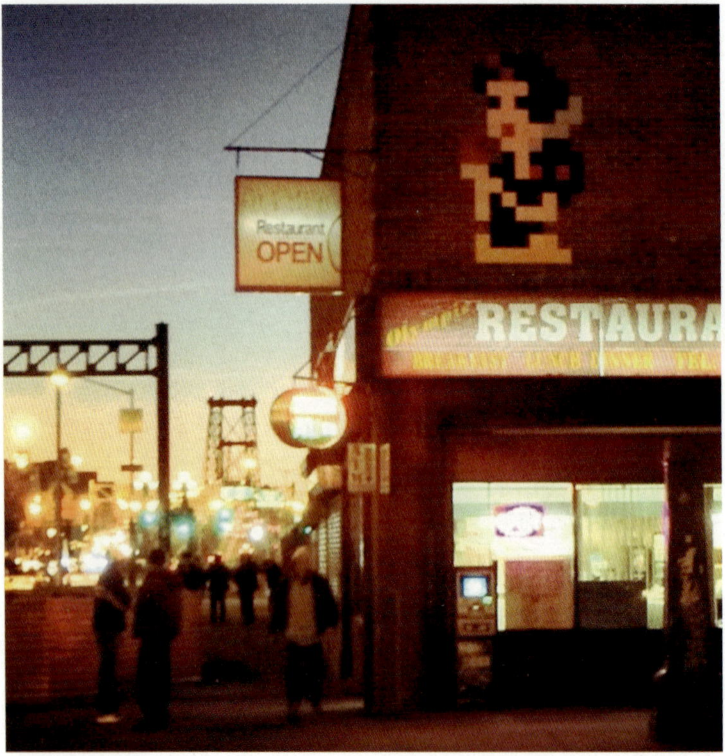

1828 likes

invaderwashere 6:38 am. Snow White crunching the (big) apple #snowwhite #justdone #sunrise #williamsburgbridge #invaderwashere #NYC

View all 103 comments

28 October 2013

invaderwashere

1410 likes

invaderwashere GO TO JAIL! They kept my phone and wasted my time, but I'm out now and the game is not over... You can't stop an artist from creating! #NYinvasion #artrrested #nypd

5 November 2013

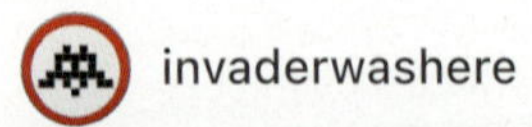

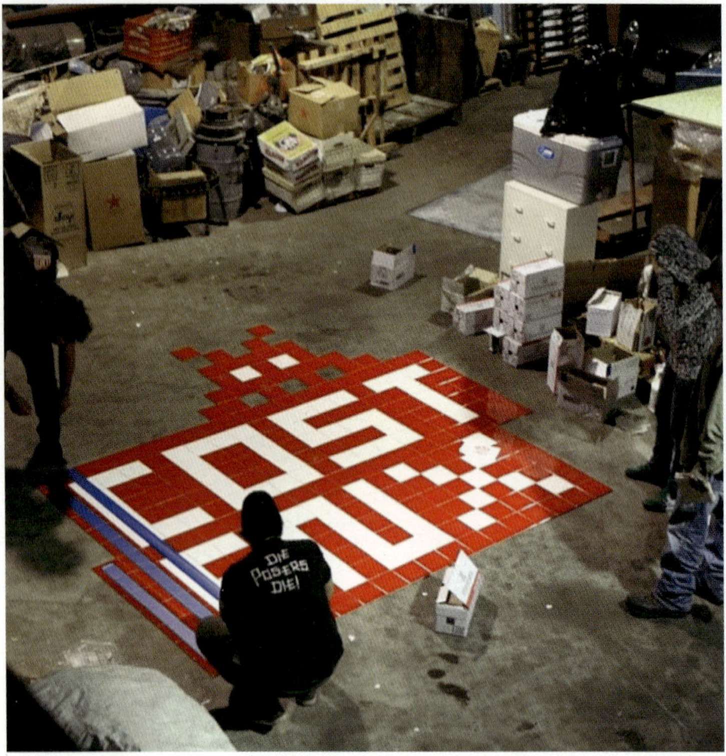

1863 likes

invaderwashere Back to work... Preparing a piece with COST & ENX #graffitilegends #NY2013 #bushwick #invadercostenx @costkrt @enx108

View all 58 comments

9 November 2013

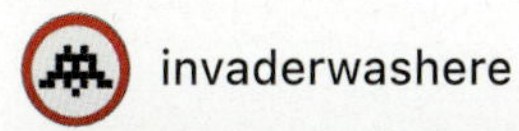

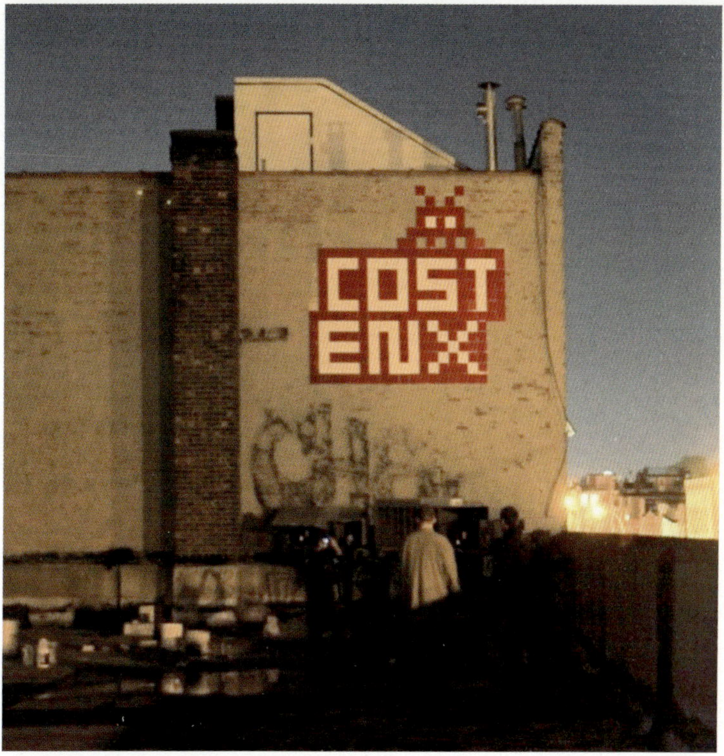

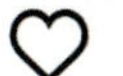   

2466 likes

invaderwashere Just done with COST & ENX #NY136 #COST #ENX #graffitiles #NY2013 #bushwick @costkrt @enx108

View all 42 comments

9 November 2013

invaderwashere

  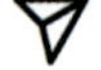 

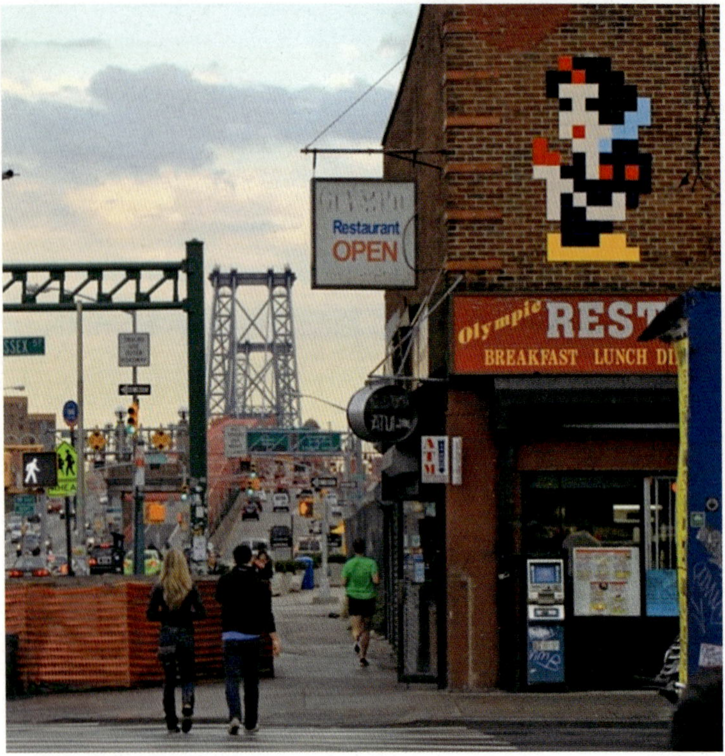

3 912 likes

invaderwashere NY_130 / Snow White #NY2013 #NYwave05 #snowwhite #williamsburgbridge #topspot #daytime

View all 190 comments

9 November 2013

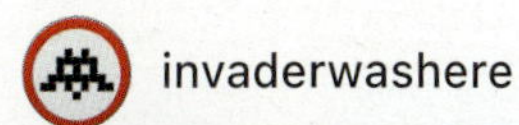

•••

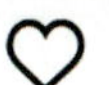   

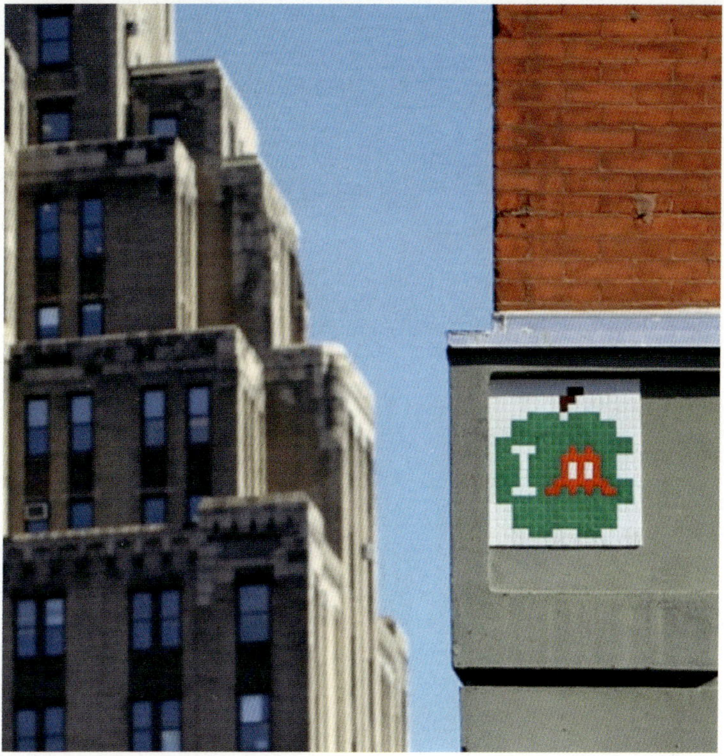

3 220 likes

invaderwashere 🍏 👾 NYC Wave05 completed / 25 new pieces in #NYC #bigapple #spaceinvaders #pixelart #NY133

View all 83 comments

9 November 2013

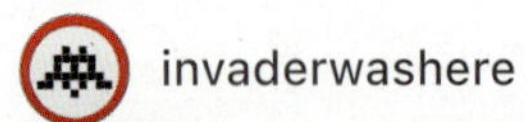

invaderwashere

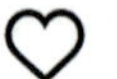   

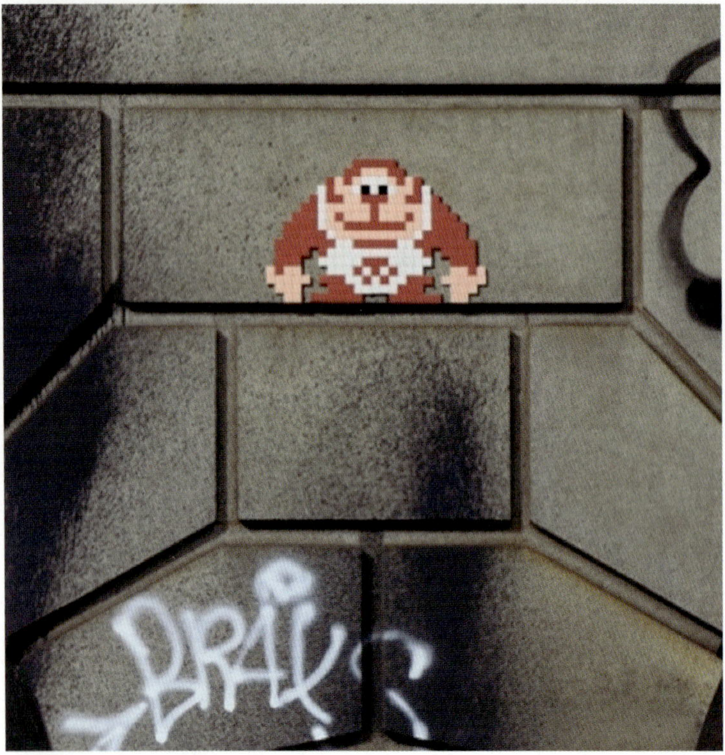

4954 likes

invaderwashere Donkey Kong Jr is in NY #NY122 #bowery #NYC

View all 71 comments

10 November 2013

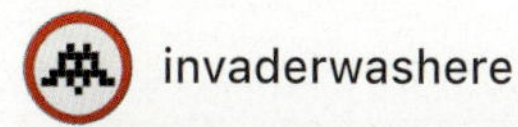

•••

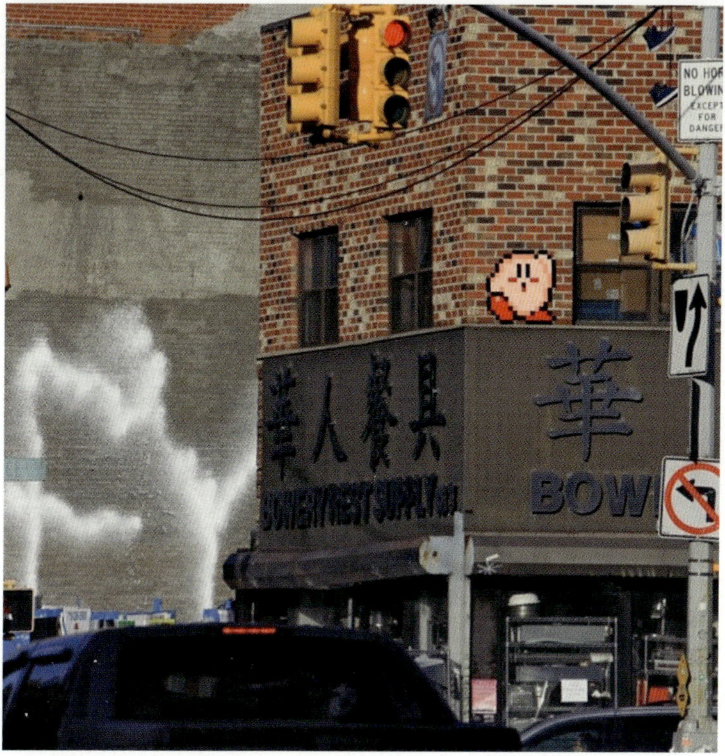

4928 likes

invaderwashere Kirby is in NY... #invader #NY129 #kirby #bowery #hotspot 🔥🔥🔥

View all 79 comments

13 November 2013

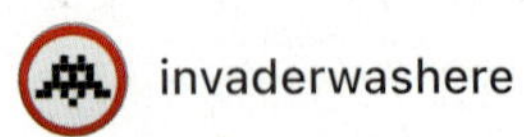

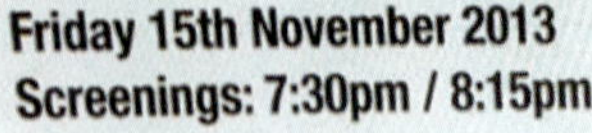

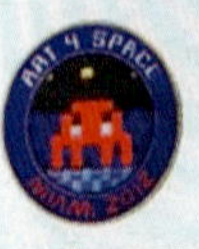

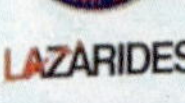

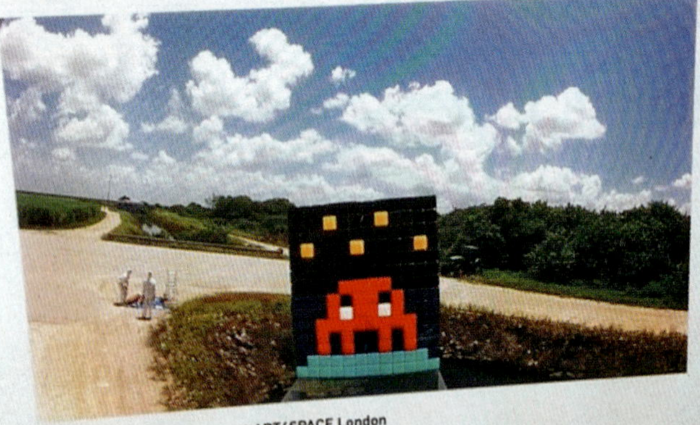

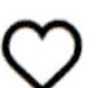

1429 likes

invaderwashere Art4space / London screening / next Friday #art4space #movie #lazarides #sohohotel #screening

View all 30 comments

13 November 2013

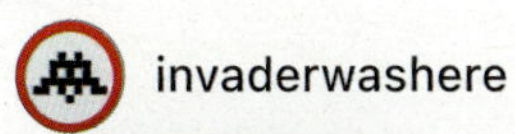

Photographe : Karl Lagerfeld
Photo en couleur
Dimension : 45 x 60 cm
Signée au dos

6fruits by Space Invader

Depuis plus de 10 ans, un artiste parisien fait revivre les "space invaders", ces créatures échappées du jeu vidéo éponyme de la fin des années 70' qui préfigurait l'avènement du pixel et de la technologie numérique.

Pour la vente cette artiste a offert à l'APREC cette oeuvre intitulée 6fruits.

Details
Nom : 6fruits
Artiste : Space Invader
Dimensions : 21 X 29,7 cm
Caractéristique : Encre sur papier, signée et datée, titrée au dos
Année : 2013

Guitare Gibson du groupe électro Justice

Justice est un groupe de musique électro connu dans le monde entier. Formé par Gaspard Augé et Xavier de Rosnay, Justice a offert à l'APREC cette magnifique Gibson, notamment utilisée dans le clip "Audio, Video, Disco".

Details

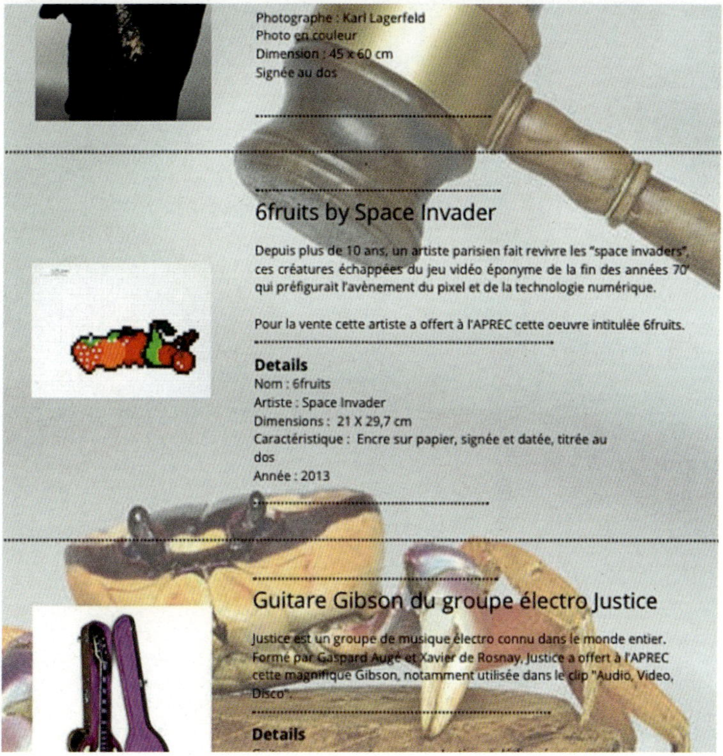

685 likes

invaderwashere 6fruits / Ink on paper / 2013, this drawing will be for sale this Monday at Hotel Meurice in Paris / www.venteauxencheres-aprec.com #charityauction #againstcancer

View all 12 comments

14 November 2013

invaderwashere

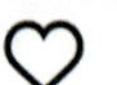

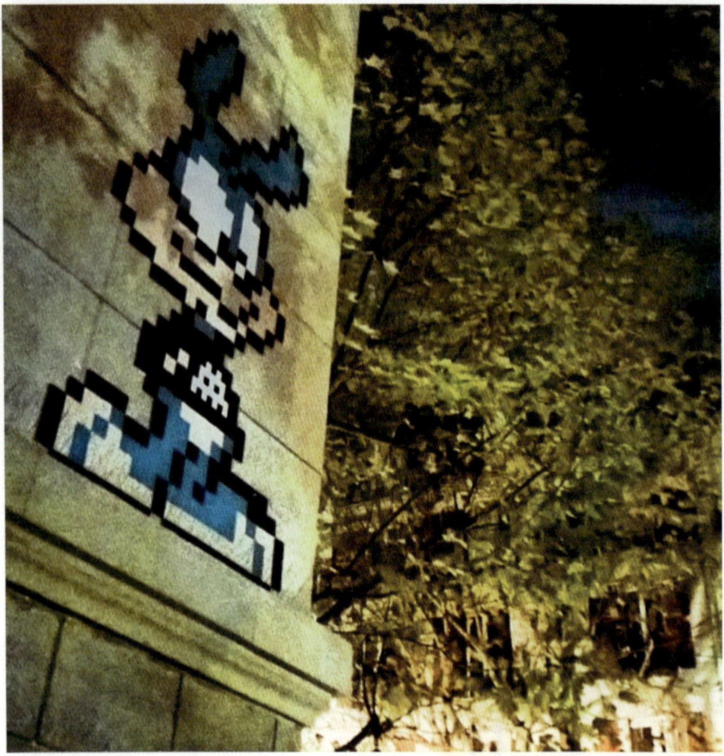

4 317 likes

invaderwashere Just done! #PA1083 #busterbunninvader #tinytoons

View all 53 comments

20 November 2013

invaderwashere •••

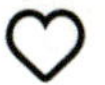   

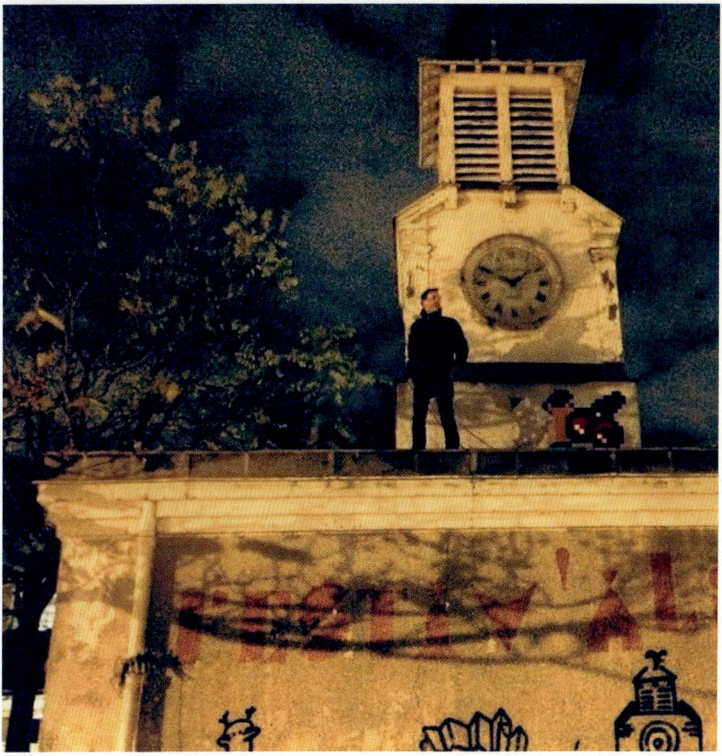

2 570 likes

invaderwashere Installing a new piece... #invasionofParis #aligre #marchedaligre #invaderwashere

View all 17 comments

21 November 2013

invaderwashere

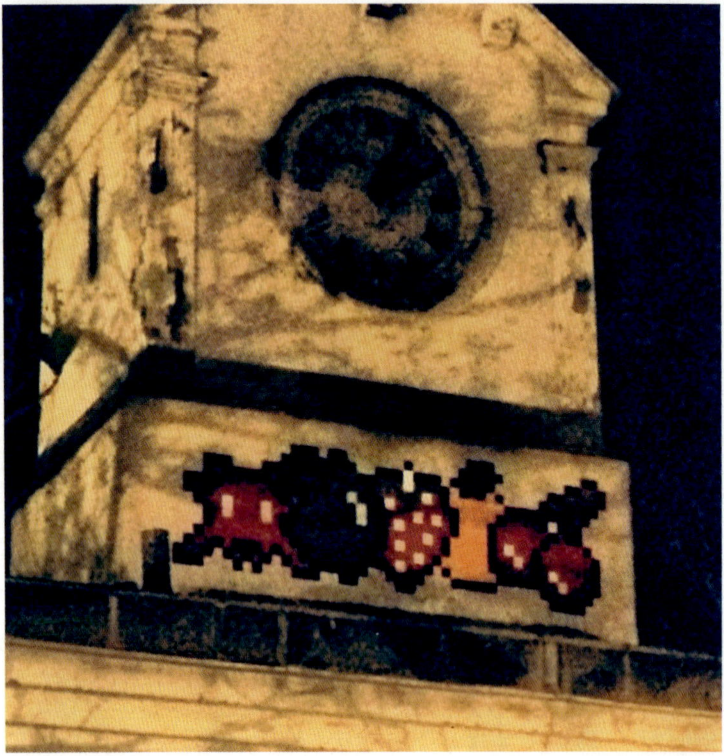

•••

4 219 likes

invaderwashere Just done! #invasionofParis #aligre #marchedaligre #aligremarket

View all 57 comments

21 November 2013

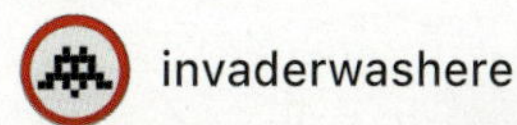

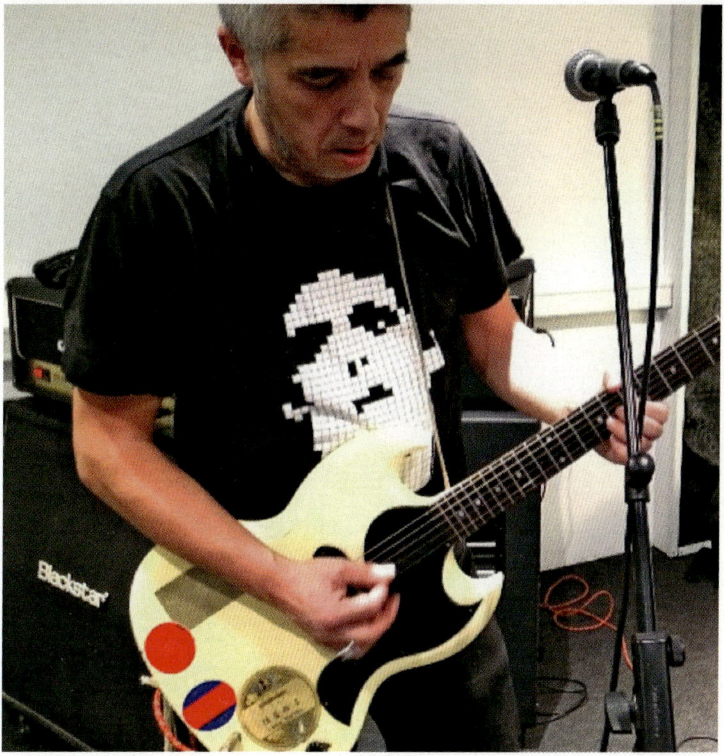

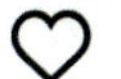   

1183 likes

invaderwashere Tai-luc, lead singer of La Souris Déglinguée is wearing the Lou Reed Tshirt I did few years ago for #lesinrockuptibles #tailuc #lasourisdeglinguee #lsd #loureed #transformer

View all 29 comments

28 November 2013

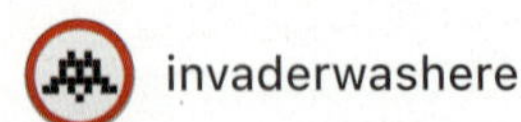

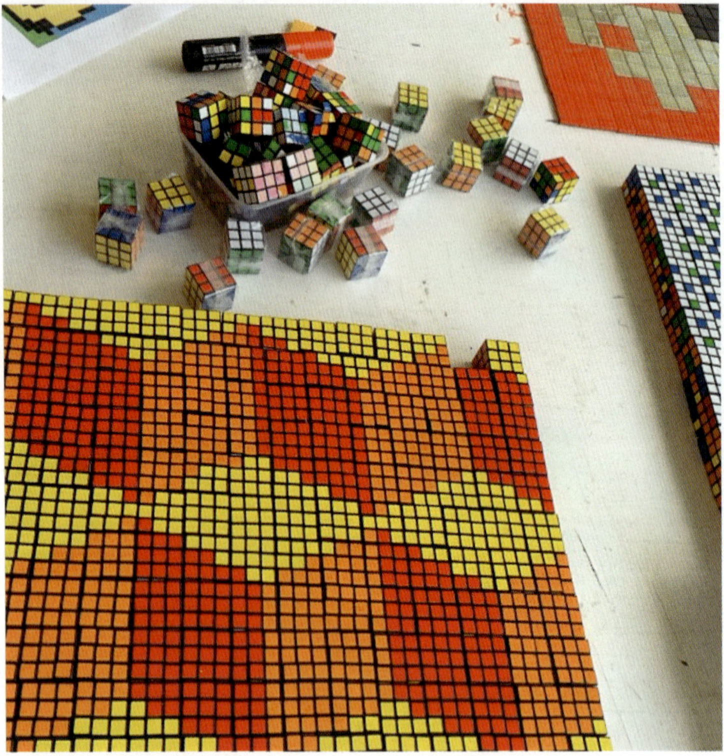

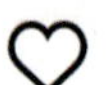   

3 533 likes

invaderwashere Studio detail #rubikcubism #rubikcubisme #tinycubes #abstract #geometric #afterEscher

View all 76 comments

3 December 2013

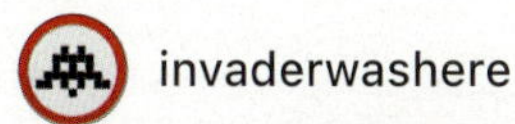

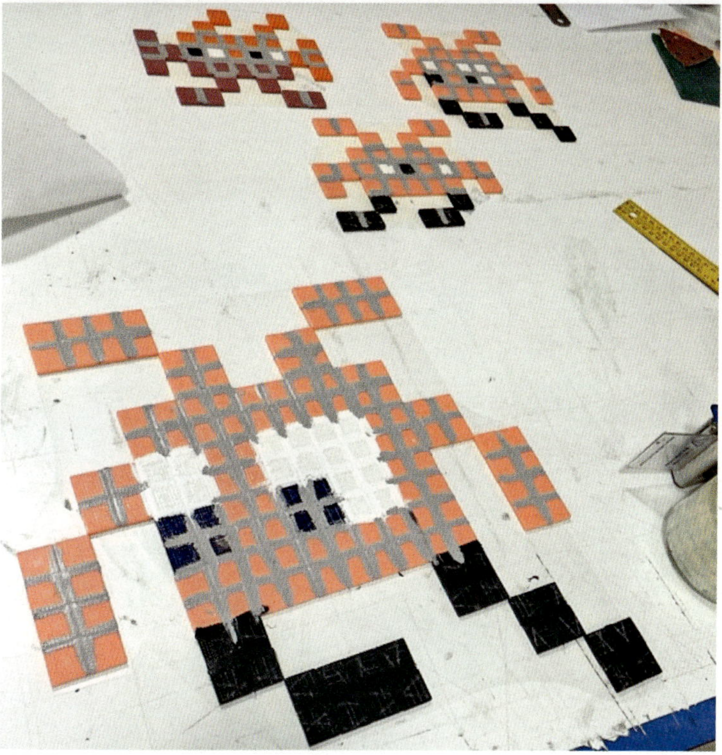

2490 likes

invaderwashere Studio detail #spaceinvaders #insidethemothership

View all 22 comments

3 December 2013

invaderwashere

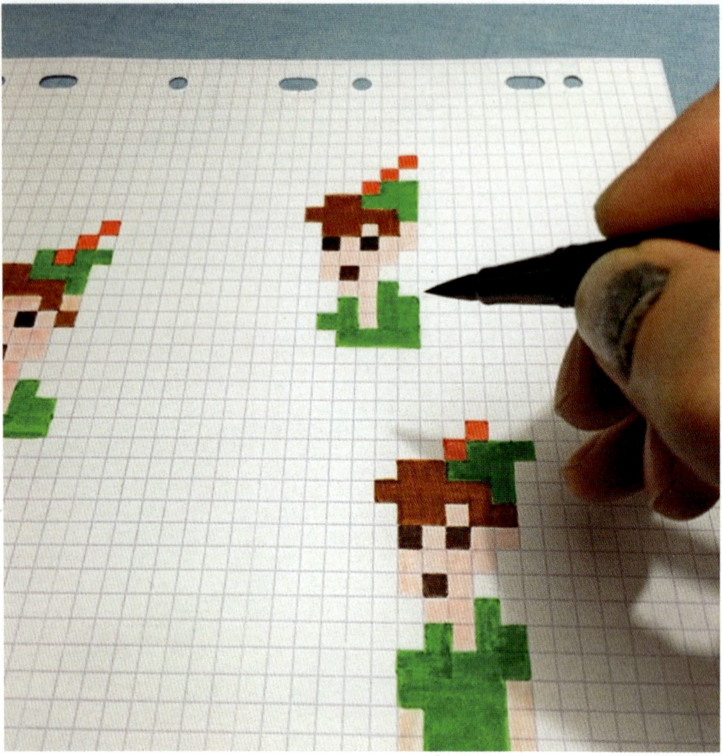

4 205 likes

invaderwashere Drawing on paper #8bits #pixelart #lowres #peterpan #blacknail

View all 82 comments

3 December 2013

invaderwashere

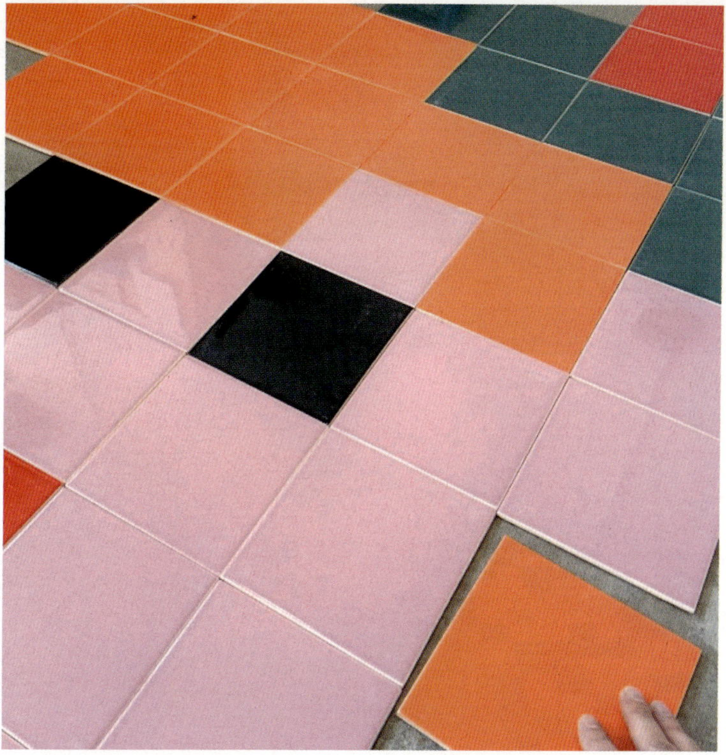

2 997 likes

invaderwashere Studio detail. Working on low-res Peter Pan #bigtiles #workinprogress

View all 46 comments

3 December 2013

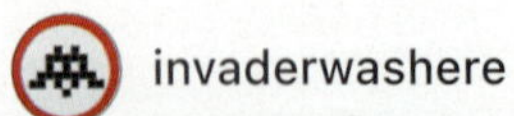

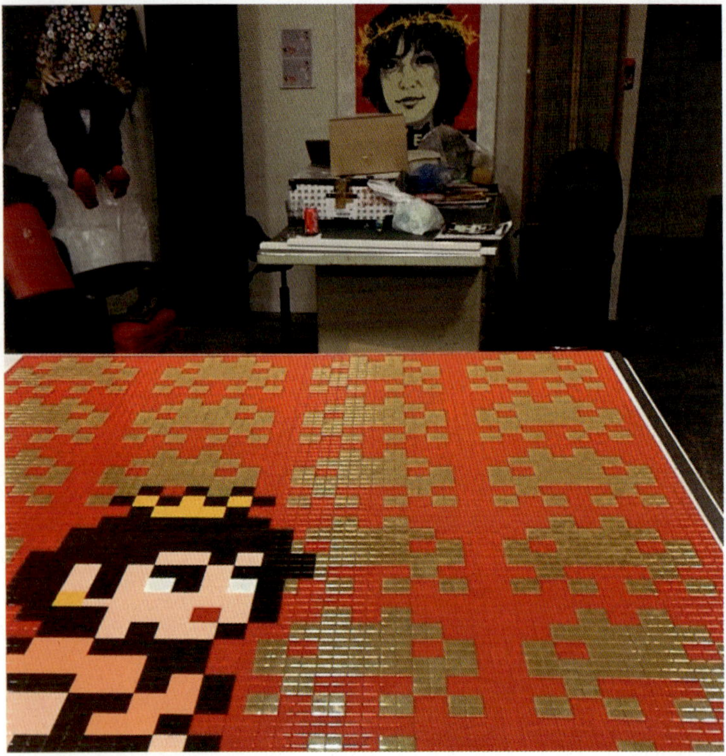

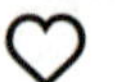   

4229 likes

invaderwashere Studio detail #workingprogress #clandestineculture #princesspeach #red #gold

View all 72 comments

10 December 2013

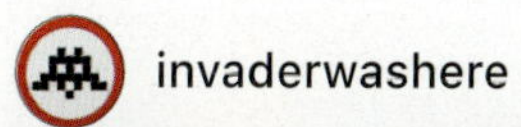

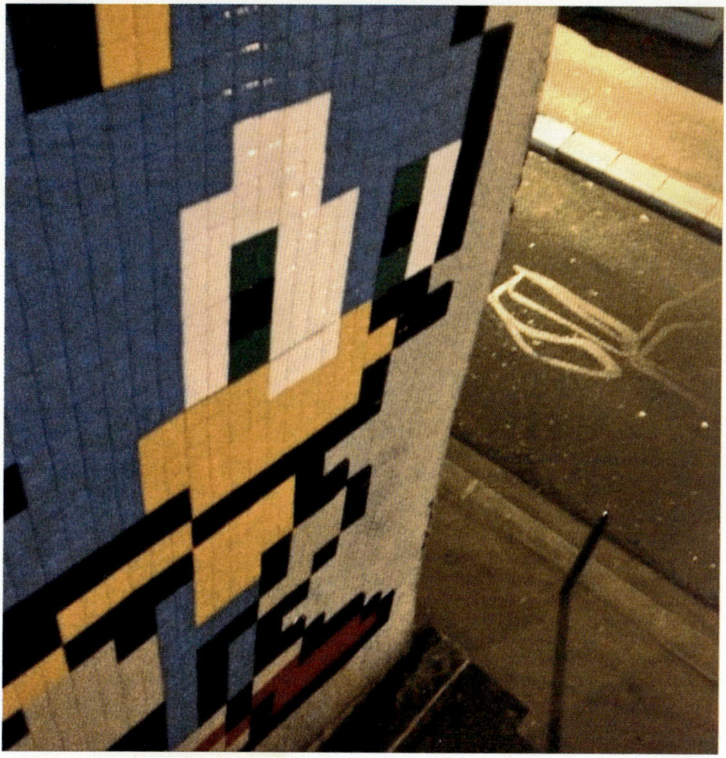

3885 likes

invaderwashere Installing Sonic #paris #invasion

View all 70 comments

11 December 2013

invaderwashere •••

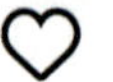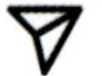

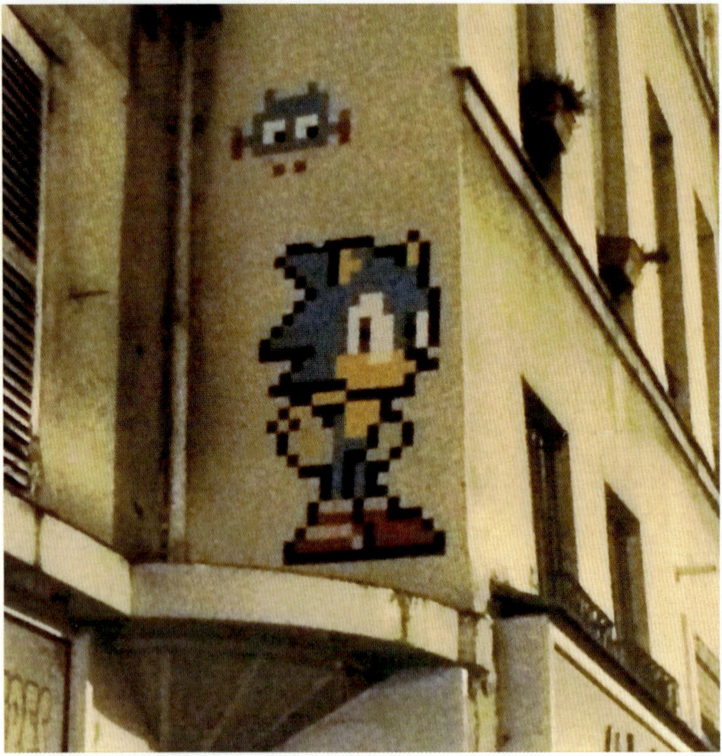

5908 likes

invaderwashere Just done! #sonic #PA1084
#invaderwashere

View all 103 comments

11 December 2013

invaderwashere

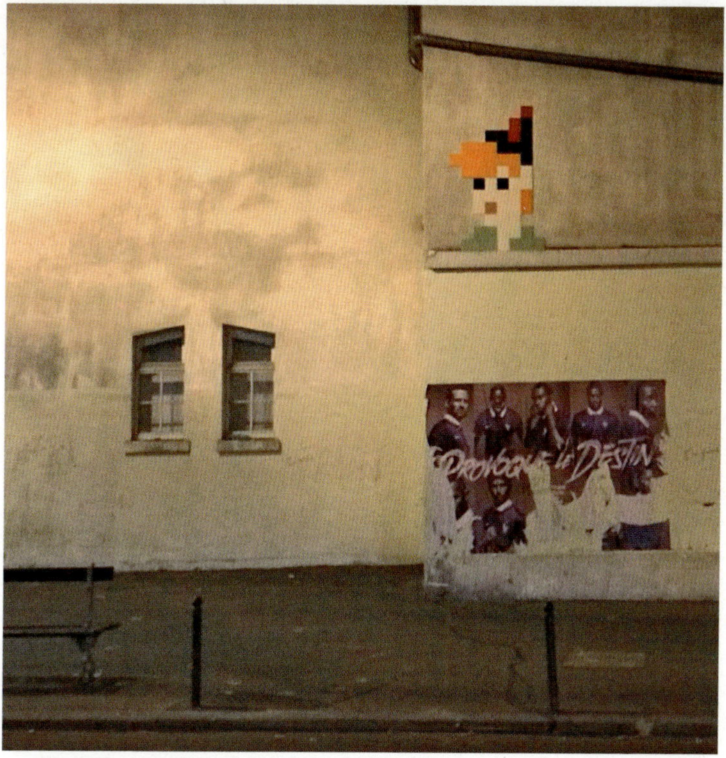

4141 likes

invaderwashere Low-res Peter Pan #justdone #peterpan #PA1085 #paris #invasion #invaderwashere

View all 68 comments

11 December 2013

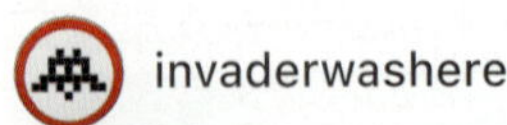

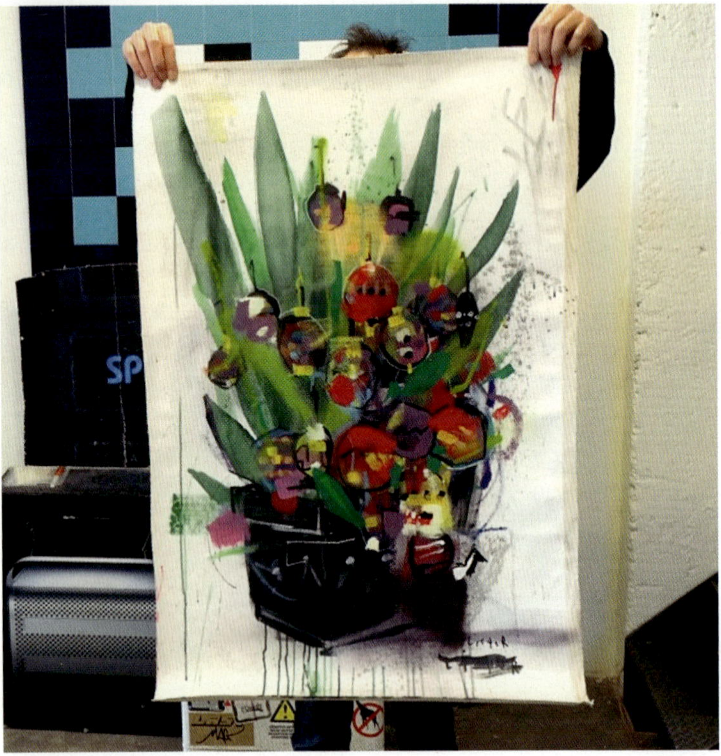

2 009 likes

invaderwashere Xmas tree painting by artist Anthony Lister #studiodetail Thank's @anthonylister 🐺

View all 13 comments

13 December 2013

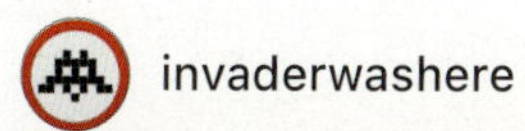
invaderwashere

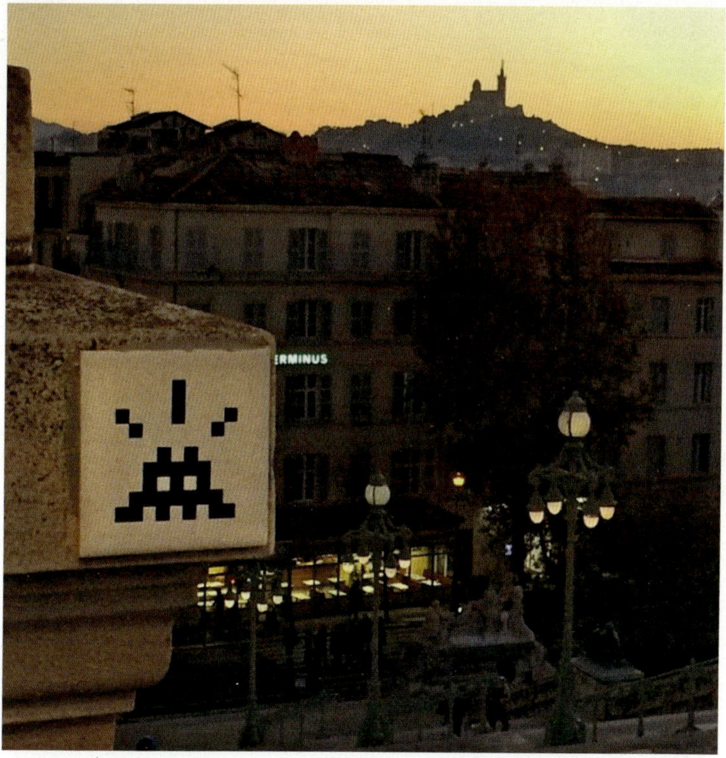

4586 likes

invaderwashere Good night Marseille #printedtile #spaceinvader #marseille #bonnemere

View all 30 comments

15 December 2013

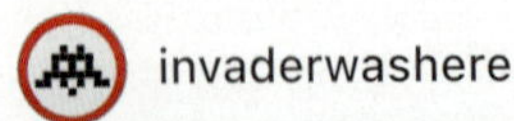

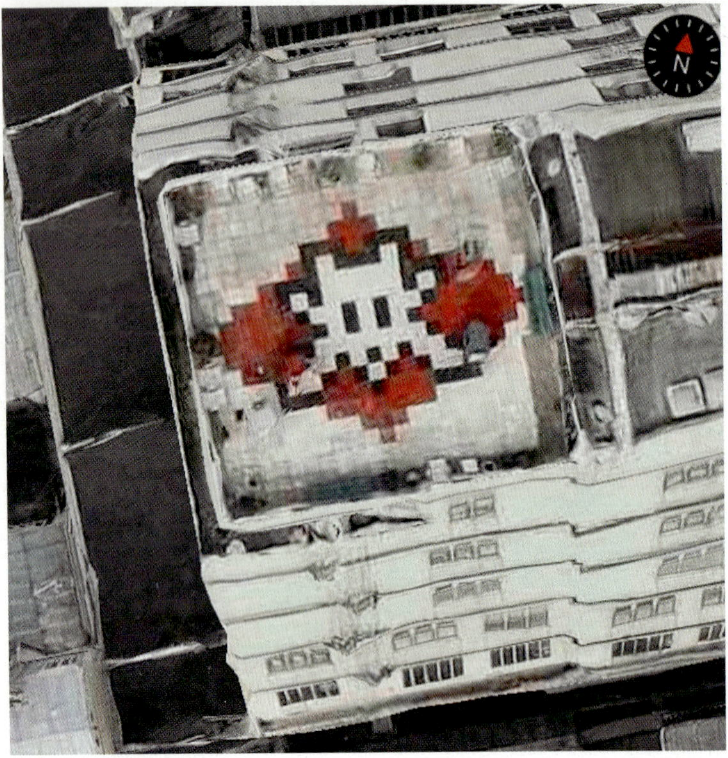

3 385 likes

invaderwashere Screenshot from Maps app / This painting has been made in 2011 on the roof of Liberation newspaper office #paris #Maps #closeup @liberationfr #libe #spaceinvader #paintingvisiblefromspace

View all 33 comments

16 December 2013

invaderwashere •••

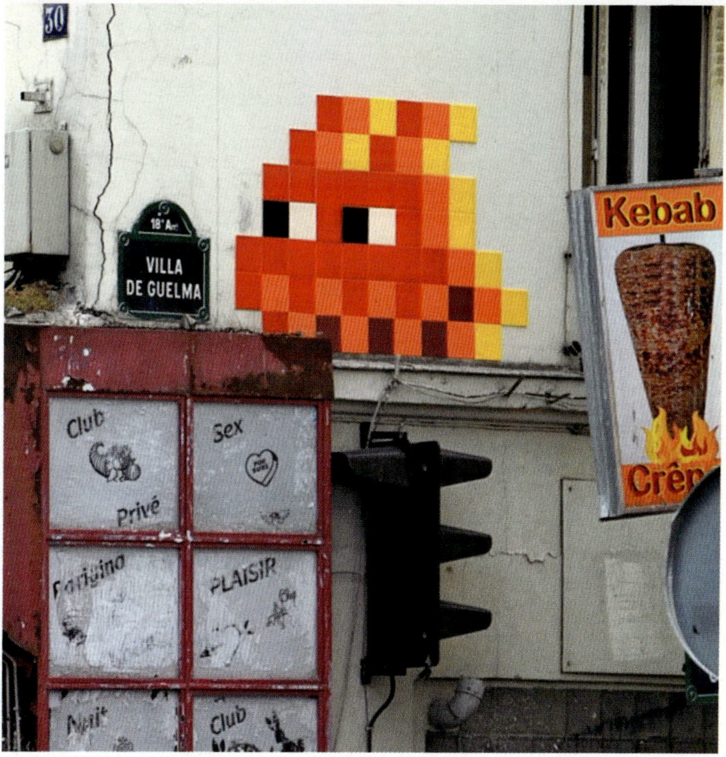

4094 likes

invaderwashere PA_1060 / Sex, kebab & space invader
#paris #pigalle

View all 36 comments

20 December 2013

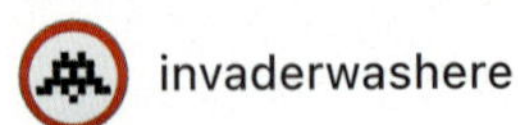

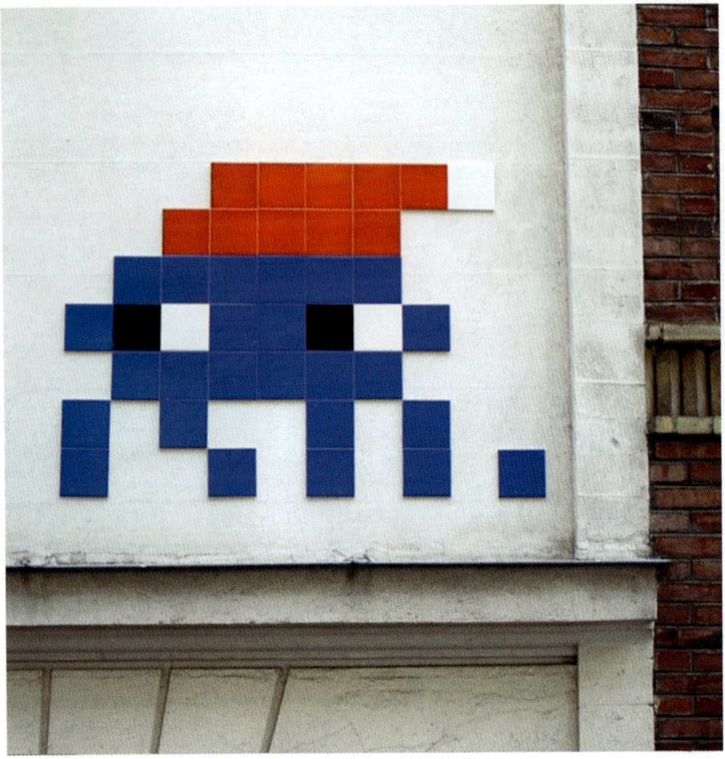

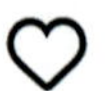

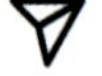

5 364 likes

invaderwashere Merry Xmas!

View all 61 comments

25 December 2013

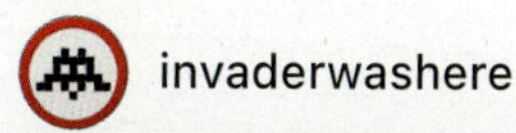

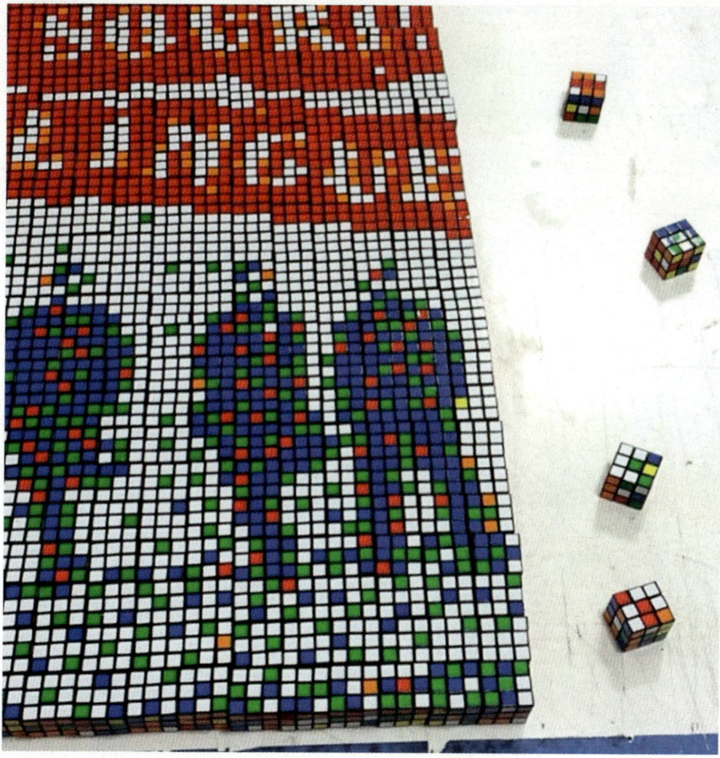

3 220 likes

invaderwashere Making of a rubikcubist piece to illustrate the cover of the new album of the French band La Souris Déglinguée #lasourisdeglinguee #lsd #punkrock #rubikcubism #lestoitsdupalace

View all 63 comments

26 December 2013

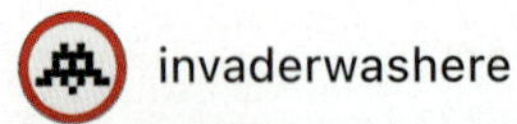

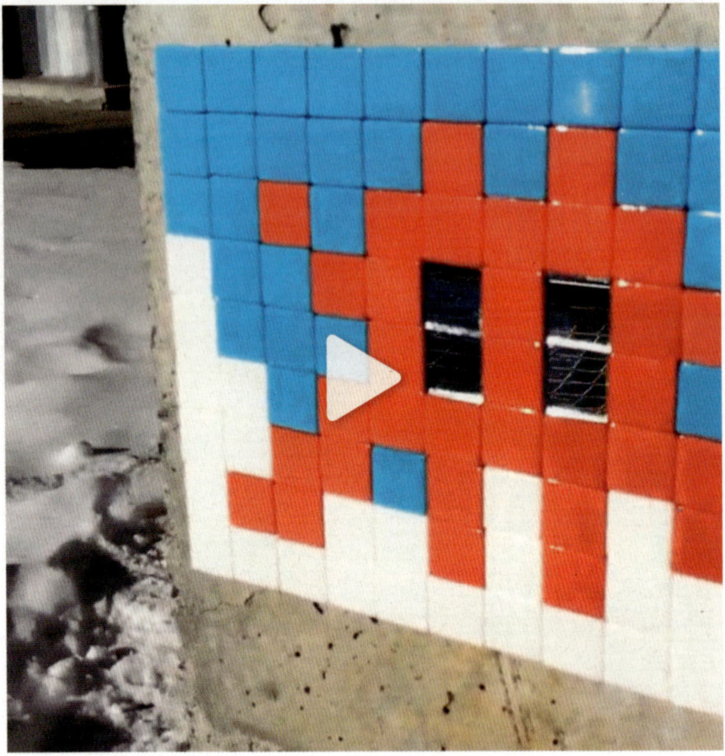

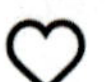   

3 998 likes

invaderwashere 2362 m above sea level, must be the higher space invader on Earth #switzerland #spaceinvader #skilift #mountain

View all 122 comments

30 December 2013

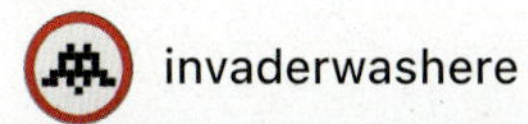

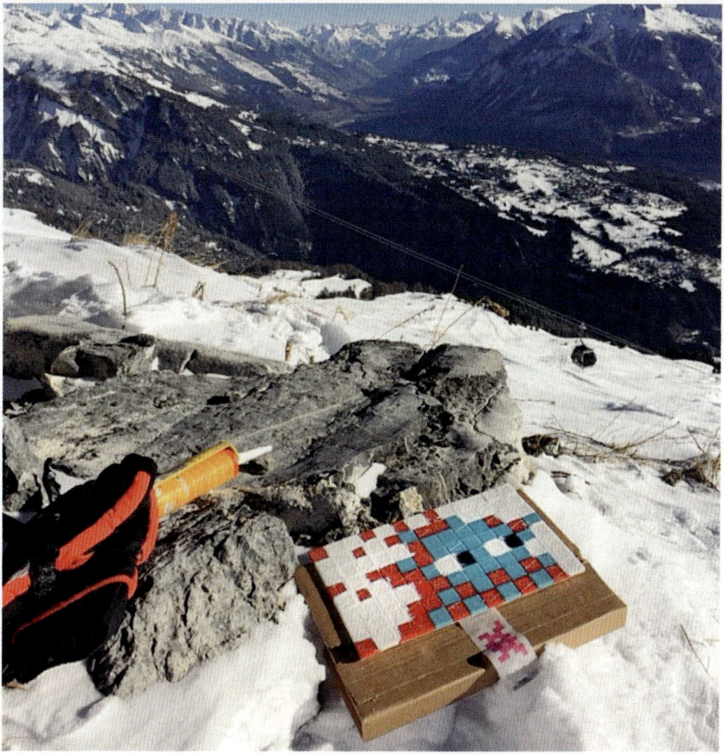

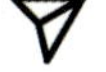

3 742 likes

invaderwashere Preparing a new piece... #mountains #invasion #snow #lastdayof2013

View all 77 comments

31 December 2013

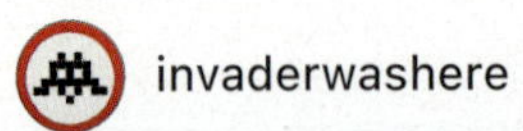

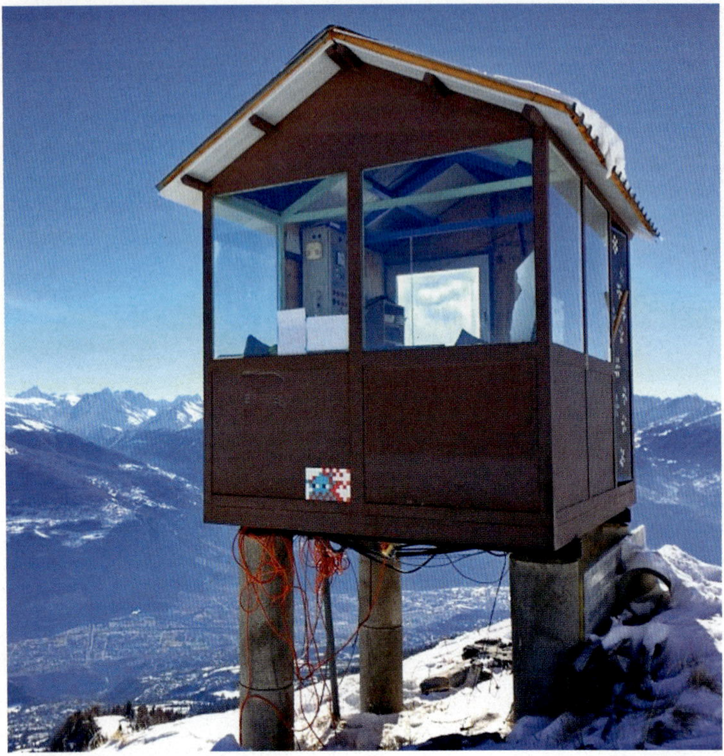

3728 likes

invaderwashere Done! Enjoy the view... #invaderwashere

View all 56 comments

31 December 2013

2014

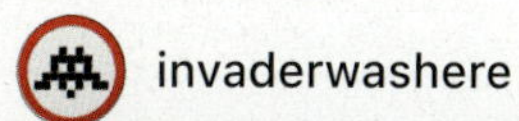

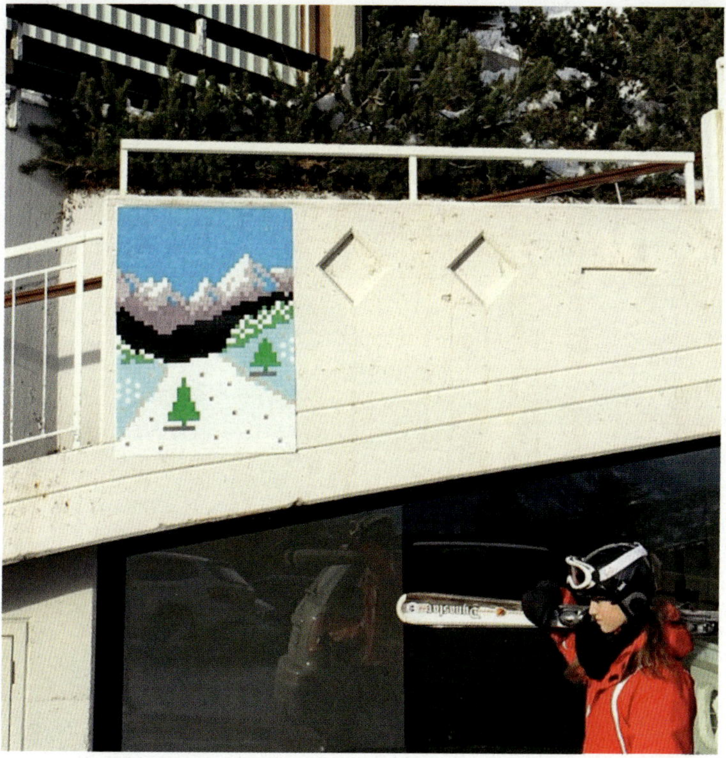

4 387 likes

invaderwashere Pixel mountains! #slalum #nintendo #ski #snow

View all 44 comments

2 January 2014

invaderwashere

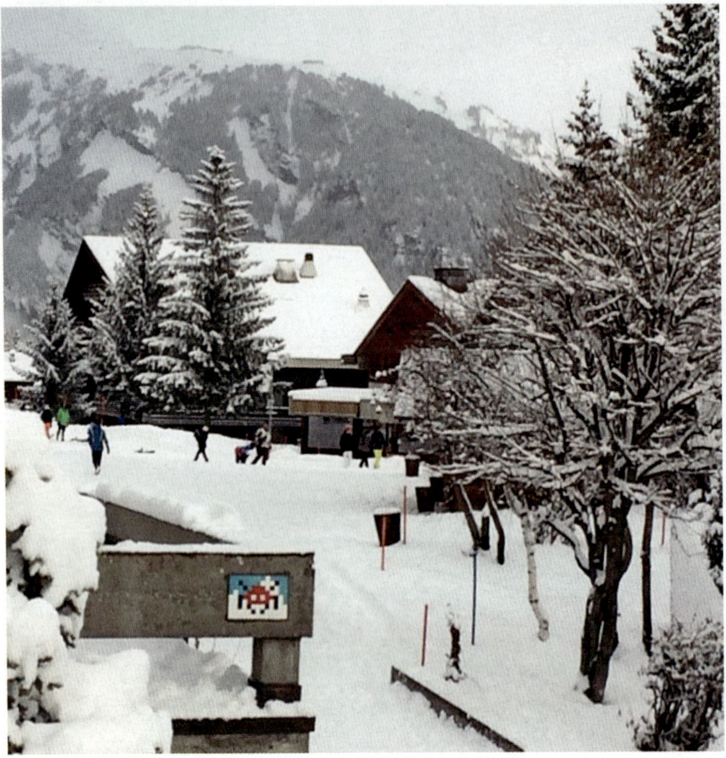

3 390 likes

invaderwashere Place du village #anzère #mountains #snow #spaceinvader

View all 20 comments

3 January 2014

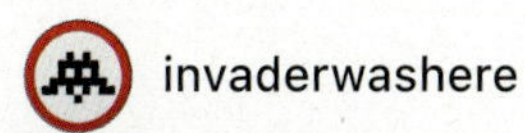

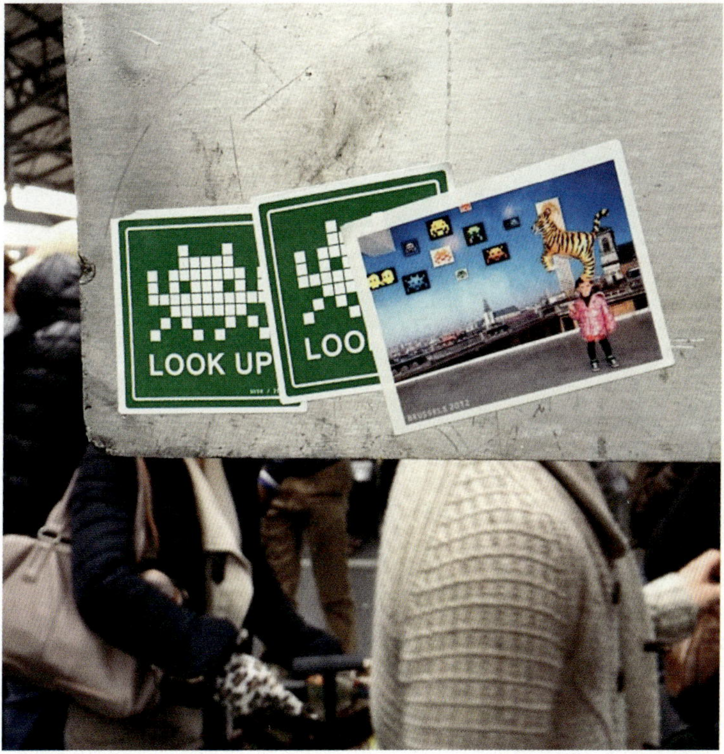

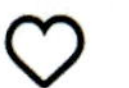  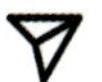 

2495 likes

invaderwashere #stickers #lausanne #trainstation

View all 18 comments

5 January 2014

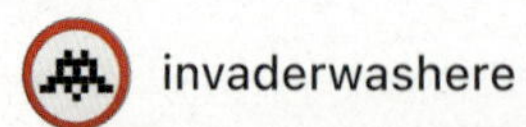

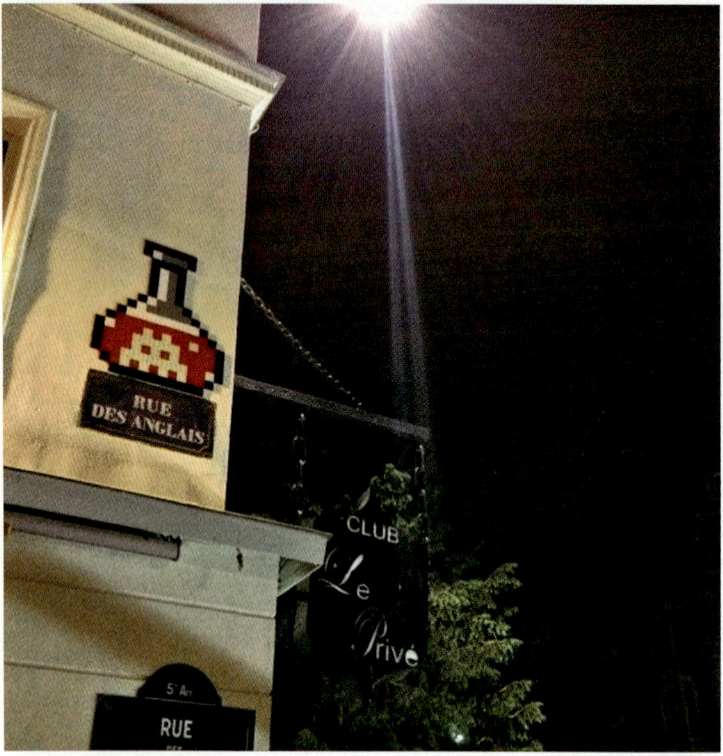

4 513 likes

invaderwashere Just done! #PA1086 #paris #magicpotion

View all 49 comments

8 January 2014

invaderwashere ...

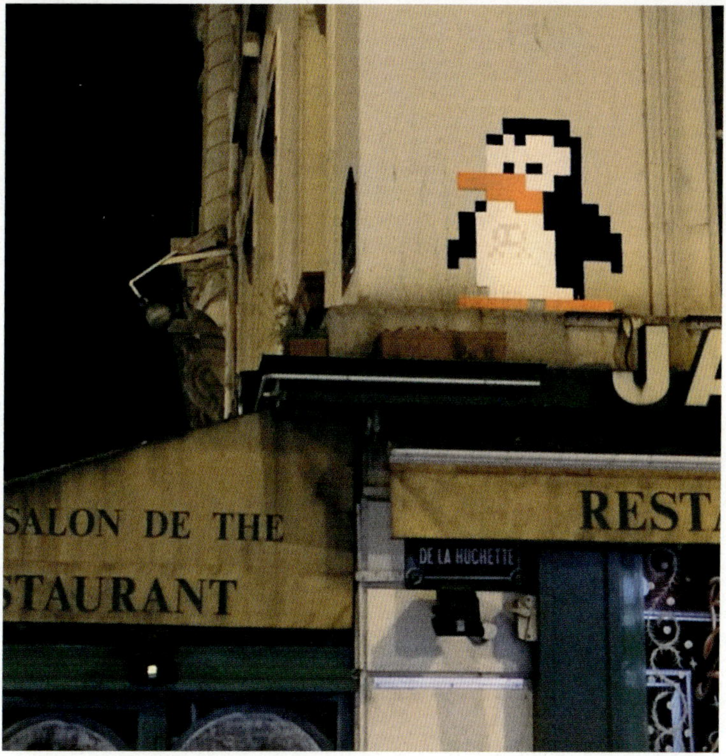

5430 likes

invaderwashere Just done! #PA1087 #paris
#pinguinvader

View all 102 comments

8 January 2014

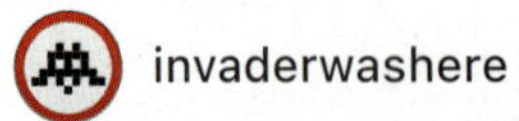

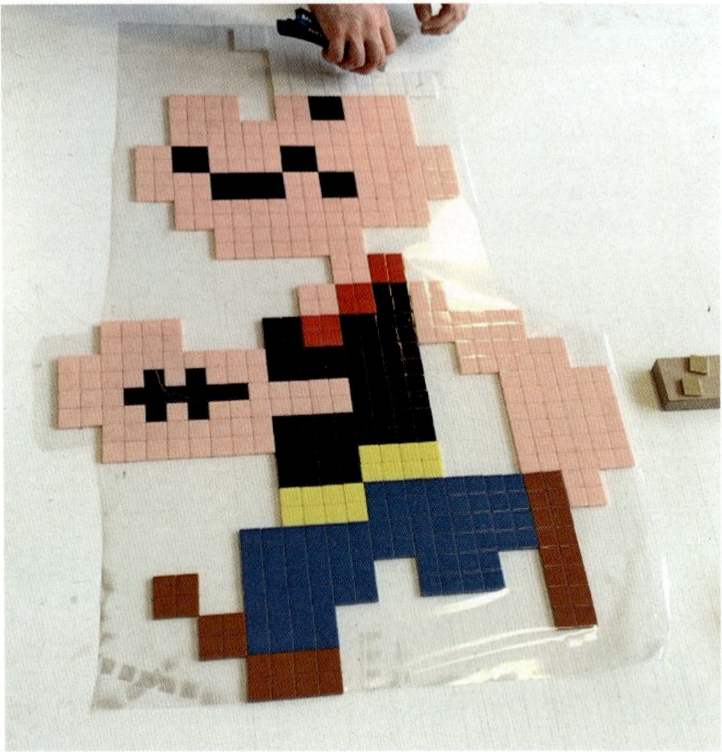

5453 likes

invaderwashere Studio detail / new piece for the street...
#impopeyethesailorman #pixelart to be continued...

View all 118 comments

9 January 2014

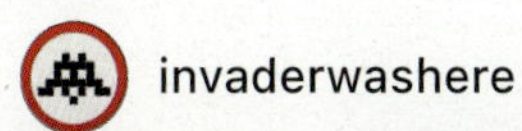

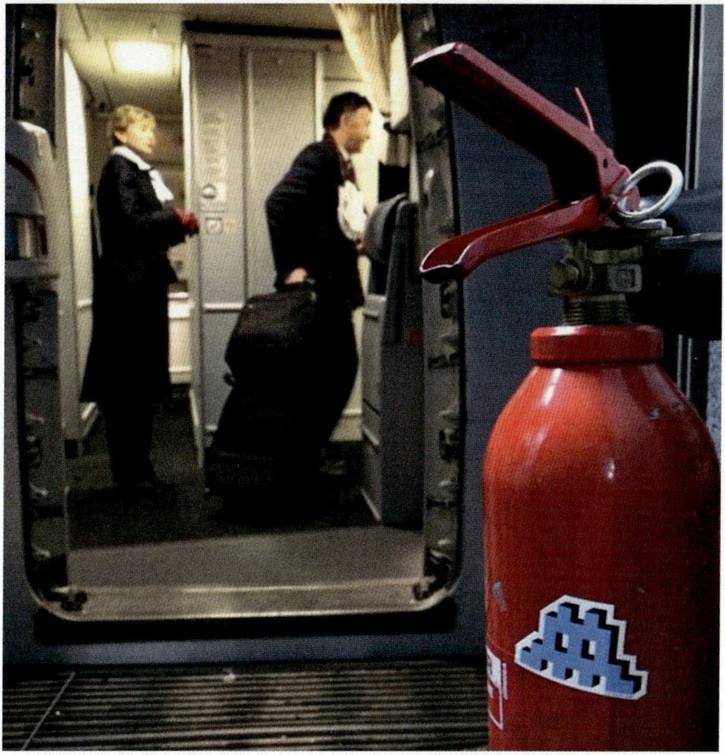

3 825 likes

invaderwashere On the road... #airfrance #sticker

View all 38 comments

13 January 2014

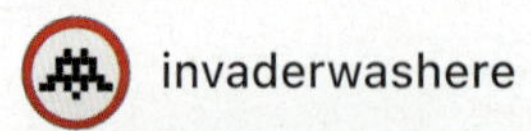

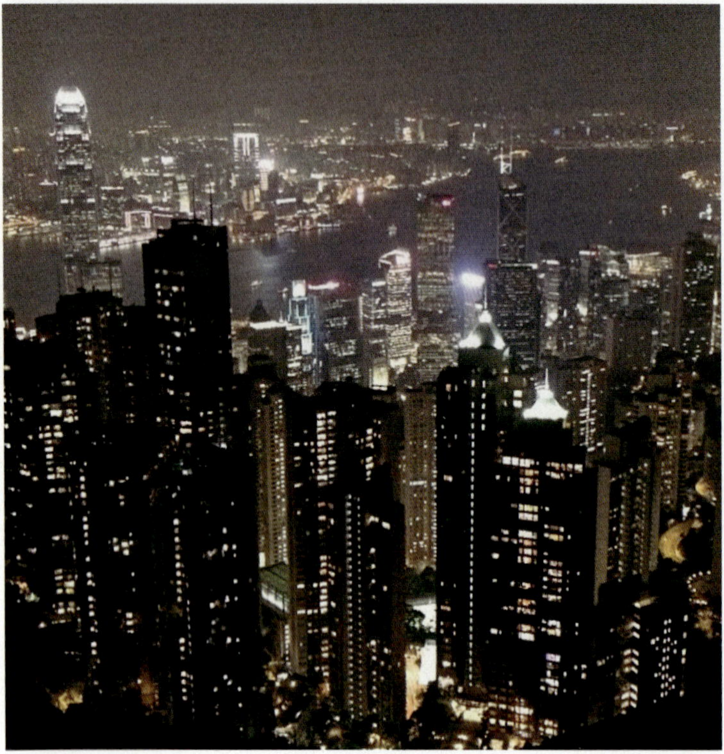

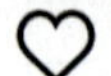 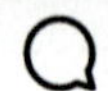  

2 896 likes

invaderwashere New playground... guess where?

View all 82 comments

16 January 2014

invaderwashere

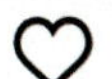   

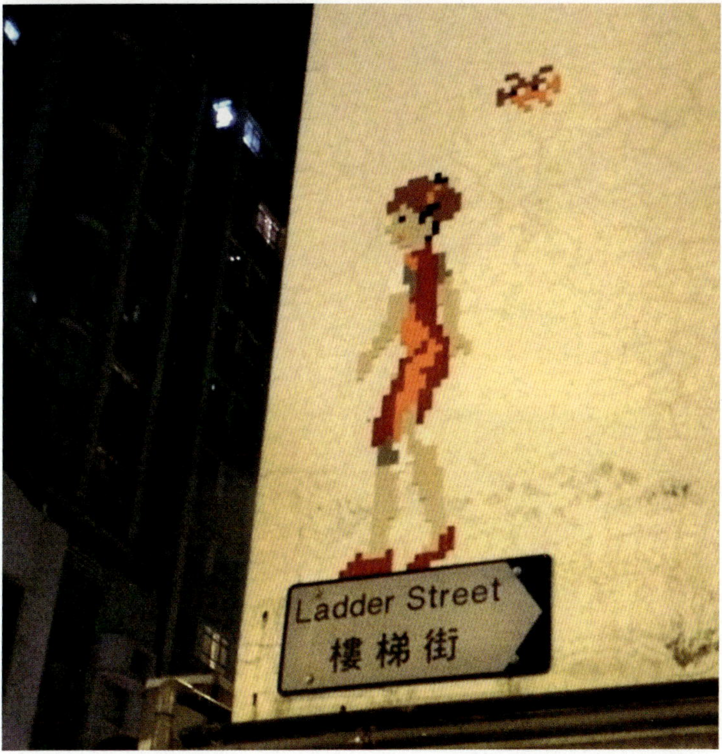

4 227 likes

invaderwashere Hong Kong 2014 #justdone #sylvia #kungfu #nes #nintendo #invaderwashere

View all 60 comments

20 January 2014

invaderwashere ...

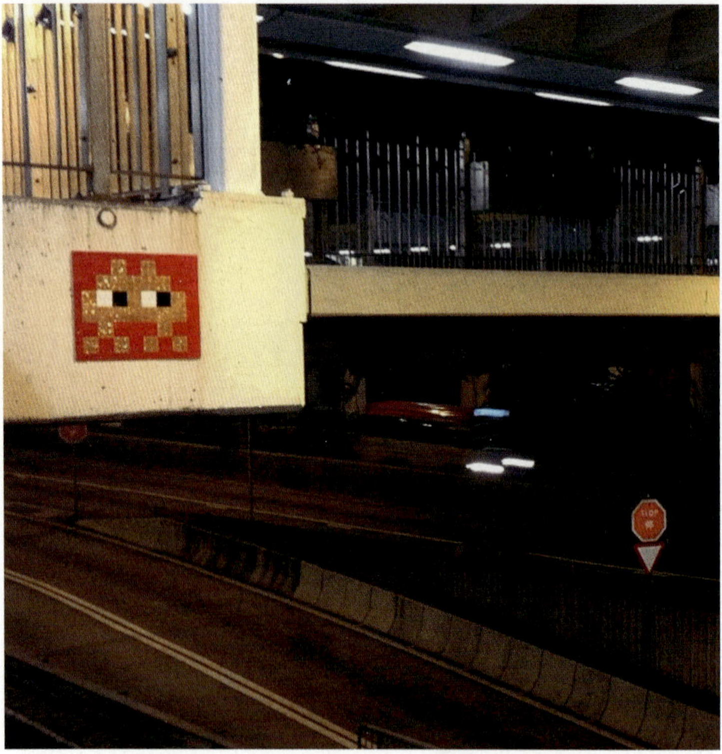

3 342 likes

invaderwashere Just done / Red & gold #HK36

View all 28 comments

20 January 2014

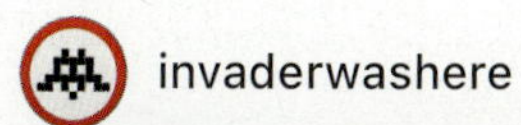

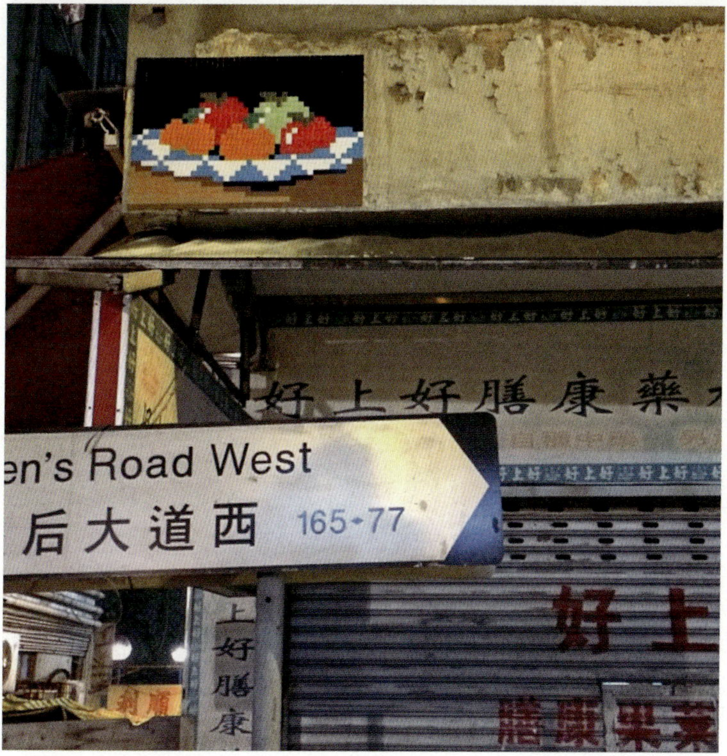

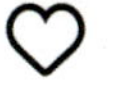   

3 369 likes

invaderwashere The owner heard some noise and thought we were robbing his place. So he called the police and I could escape but they caught my guys and brought them to jail 😬 #dangerousfruits #stilllife #HK38 #justdone #invaderwashere #gotojail

View all 29 comments

20 January 2014

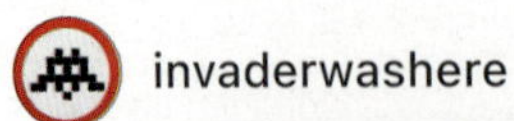

invaderwashere •••

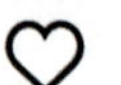   

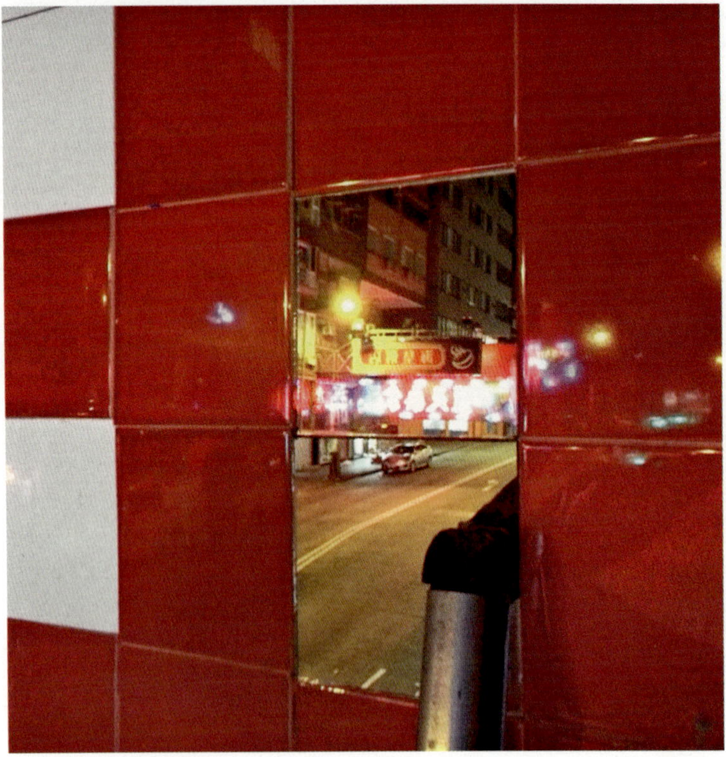

1843 likes

invaderwashere Up of the ladder! Hong Kong 2014
#mirroreyes #reflection

View all 25 comments

20 January 2014

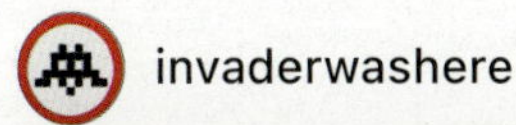

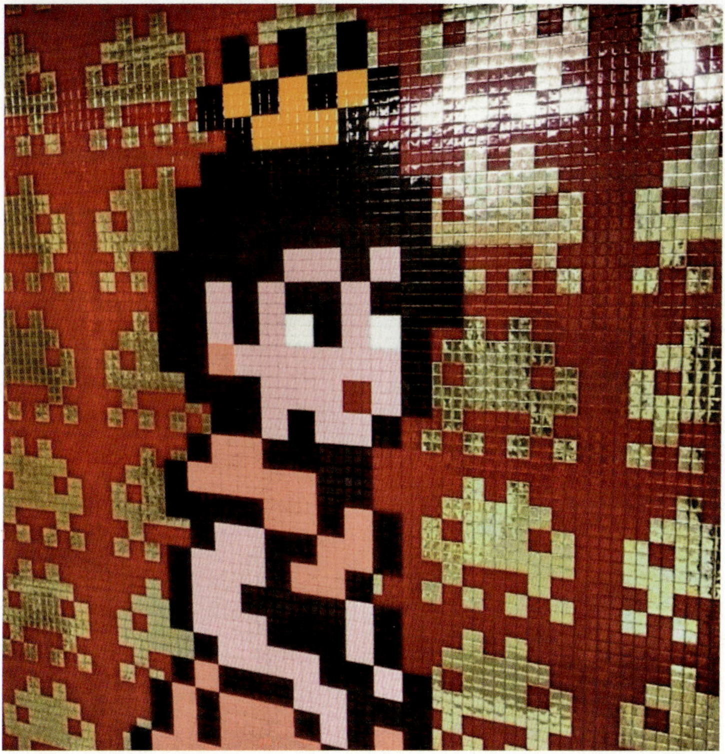

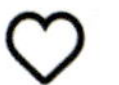  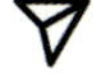 

4959 likes

invaderwashere Somewhere in Hong Kong...
#princessbibo #spaceinvaders #biborestaurant

View all 82 comments

21 January 2014

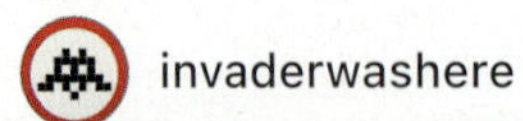

•••

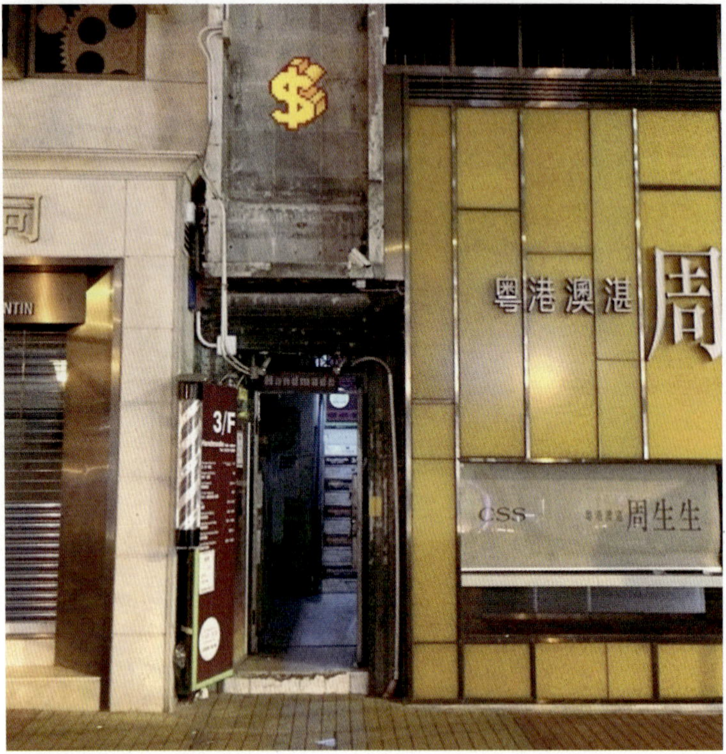

3 062 likes

invaderwashere Hong Kong $ I #hongkong #causewaybay #3am

View all 20 comments

22 January 2014

invaderwashere ...

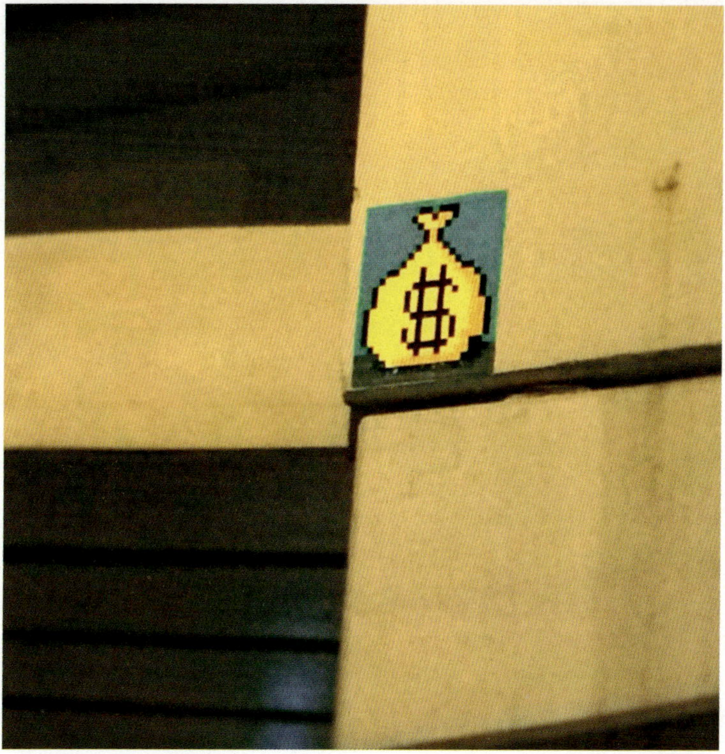

3 817 likes

invaderwashere Hong Kong $ II #hongkong #bankdistrict #4am #HK40

View all 23 comments

22 January 2014

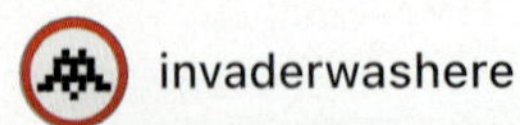

invaderwashere ...

 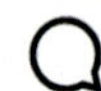  

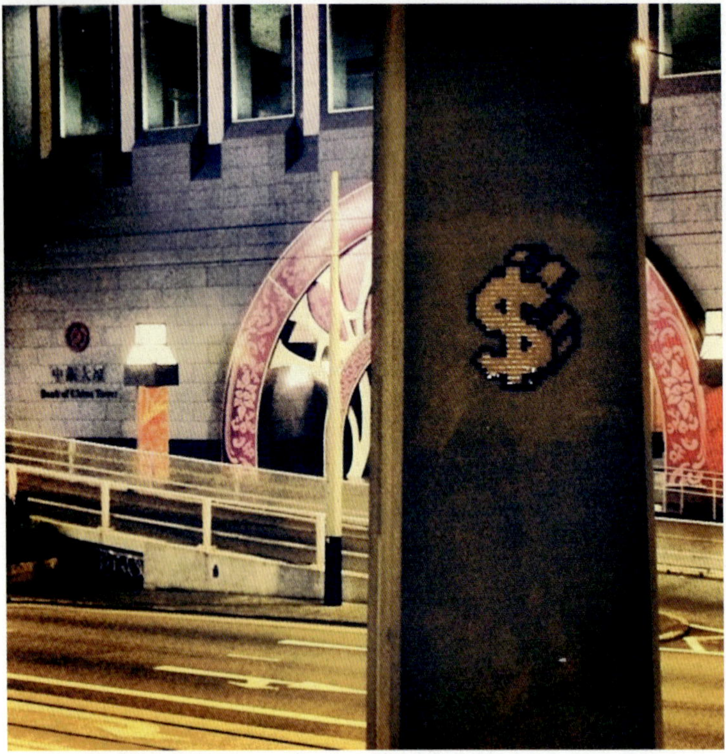

4031 likes

invaderwashere Hong Kong $ III #hongkong #bankdistrict #5am #HK42

View all 32 comments

22 January 2014

invaderwashere

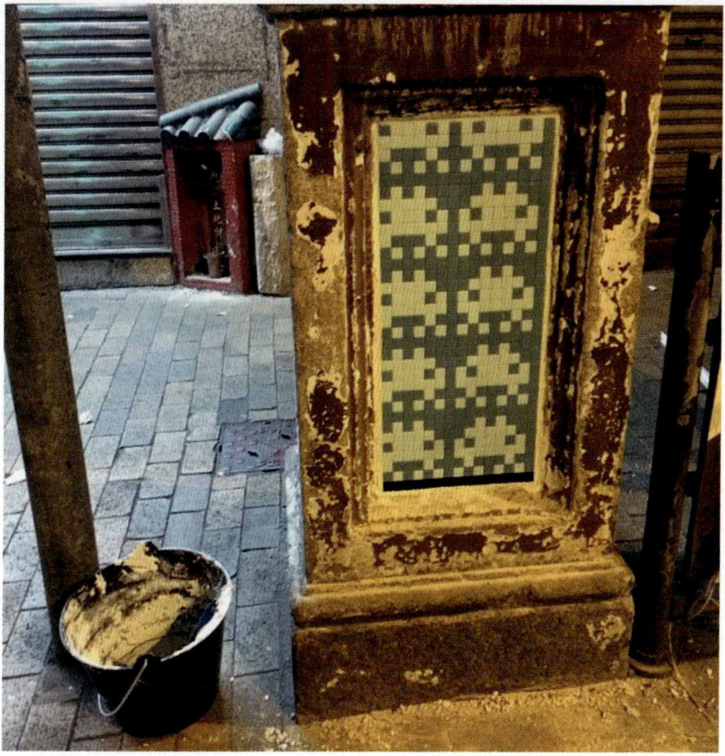

•••

4 501 likes

invaderwashere HK_46 inside the pillar #justdone #invaderwashere

View all 49 comments

22 January 2014

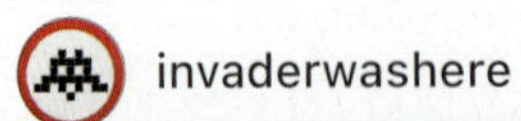

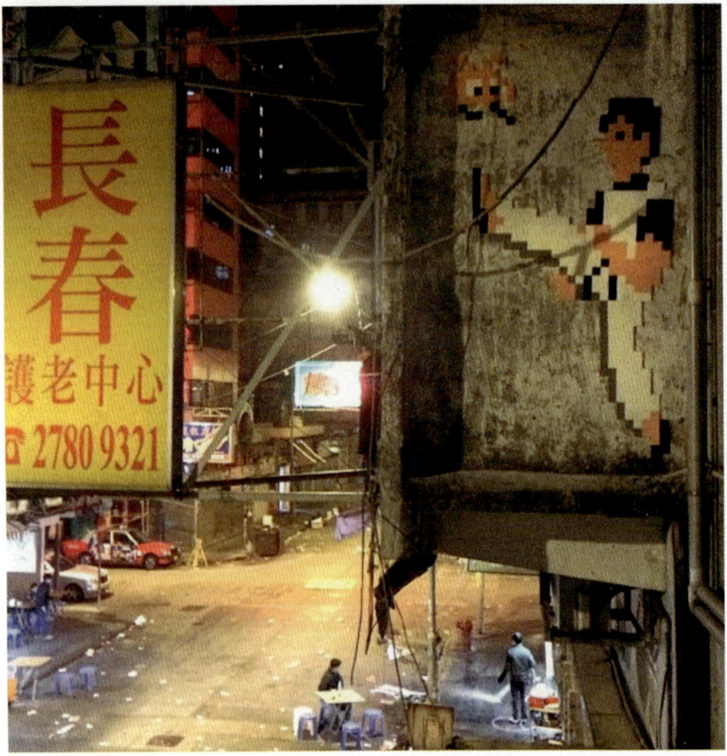

  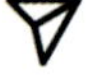 

4 414 likes

invaderwashere HK_32 was not easy to install #justdone #templestreet #kungfumaster #hongkong

View all 83 comments

23 January 2014

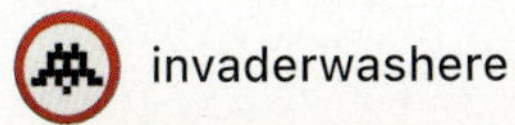

invaderwashere •••

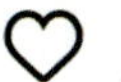  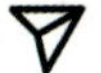 

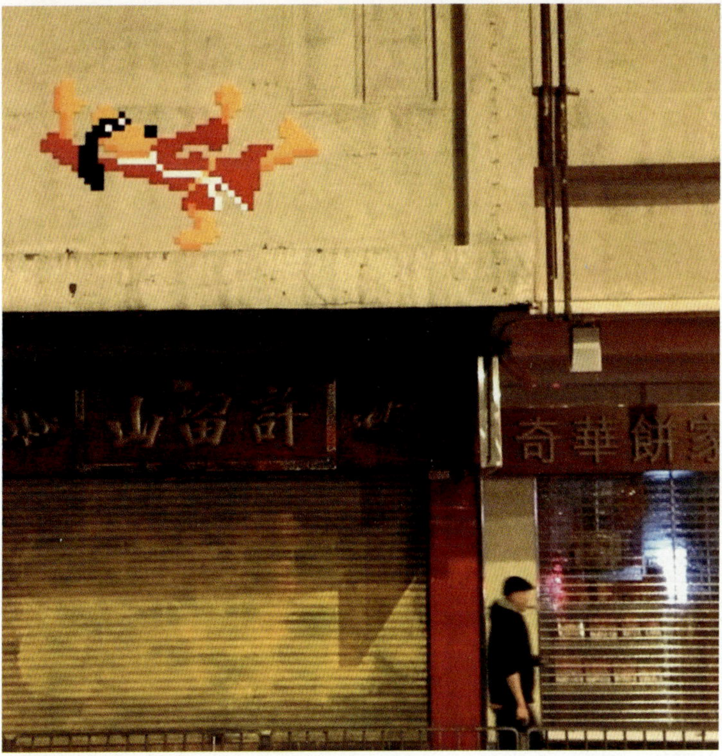

5105 likes

invaderwashere 8bit Hong Kong Phooey #justdone #hongkongphooey #hongkongfoufou #kowloon #HK54

View all 109 comments

23 January 2014

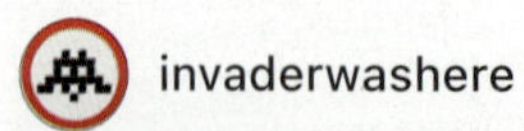

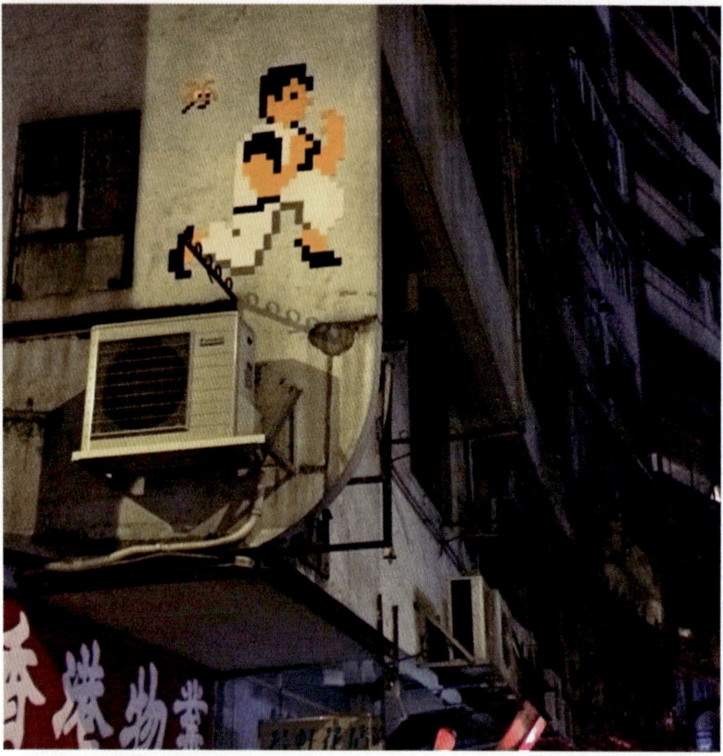

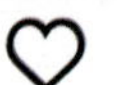  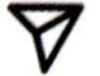 

3 935 likes

invaderwashere More Kung Fu in Hong Kong! #justdone

View all 63 comments

23 January 2014

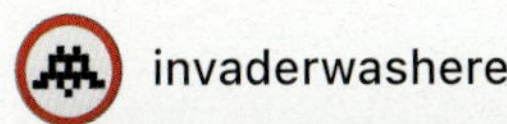

invaderwashere

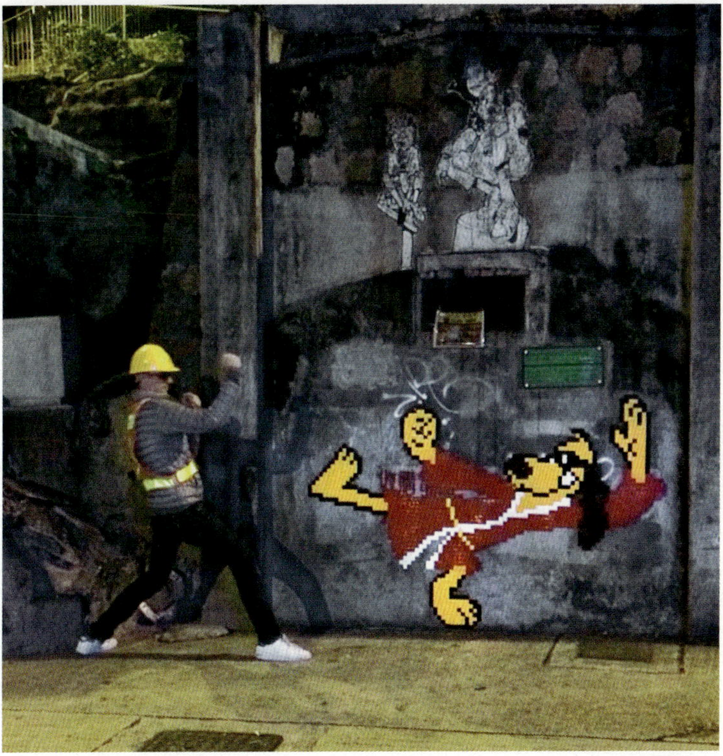

4 441 likes

invaderwashere Street fighters! Hong Kong Phooey II
#hongkongfoufou #hongkongphooey #invader #fight
#justdone

View all 74 comments

24 January 2014

invaderwashere •••

 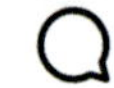  

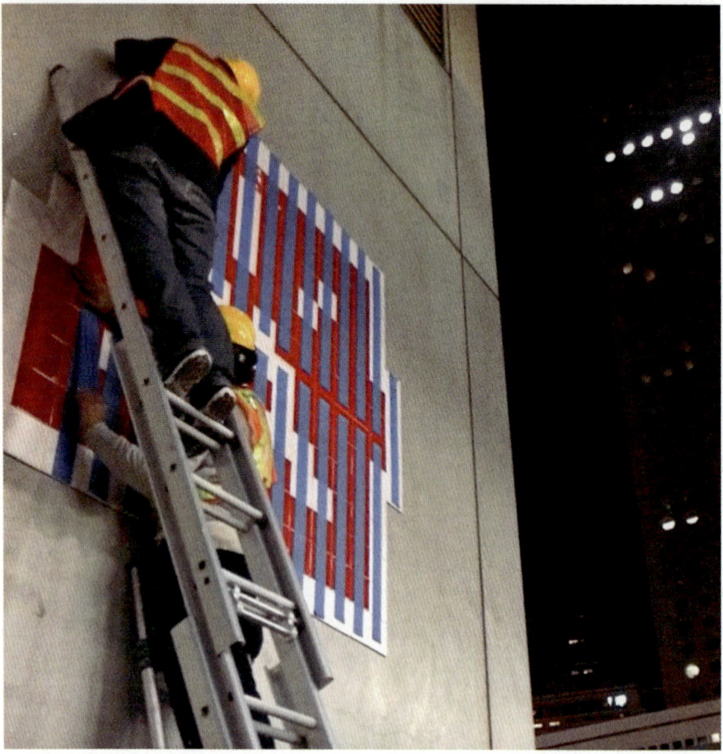

2904 likes

invaderwashere Going big in Hong Kong #greatspot #spaceinvader #macos7 #extension #HK59

View all 53 comments

24 January 2014

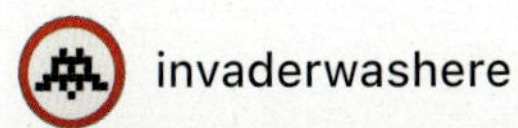

•••

HONG KONG

Campaign to educate helpers on their rights

STOP-WORK ORDER ON HISTORIC HOUSE SITE

Ladder Street
樓梯街

Artistic invader of the urban space covers the city

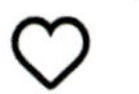  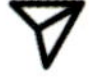 

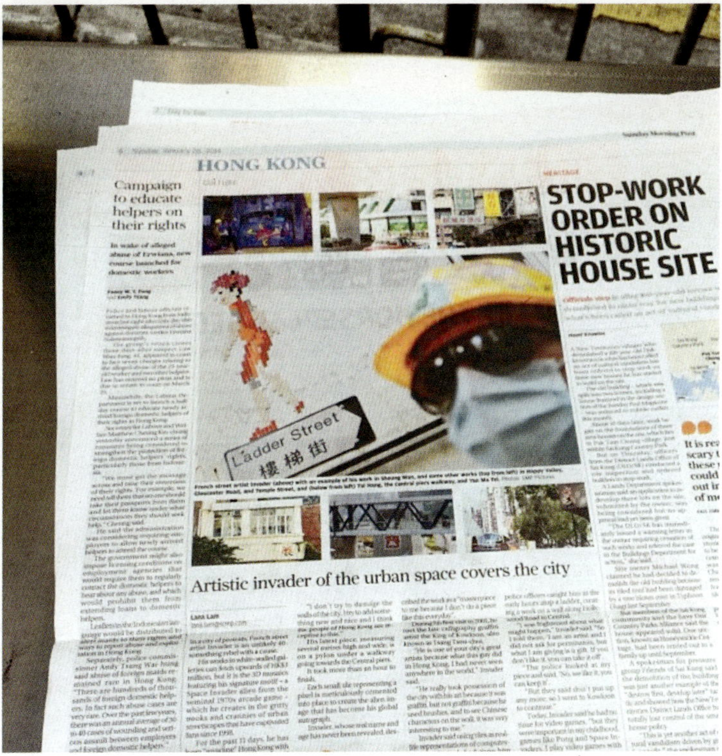

2708 likes

invaderwashere Media Invasion in South China Morning Post of today #scmp #invader #hongkong #mediainvasion

View all 33 comments

26 January 2014

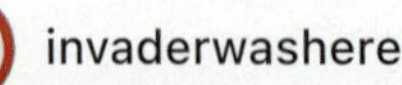

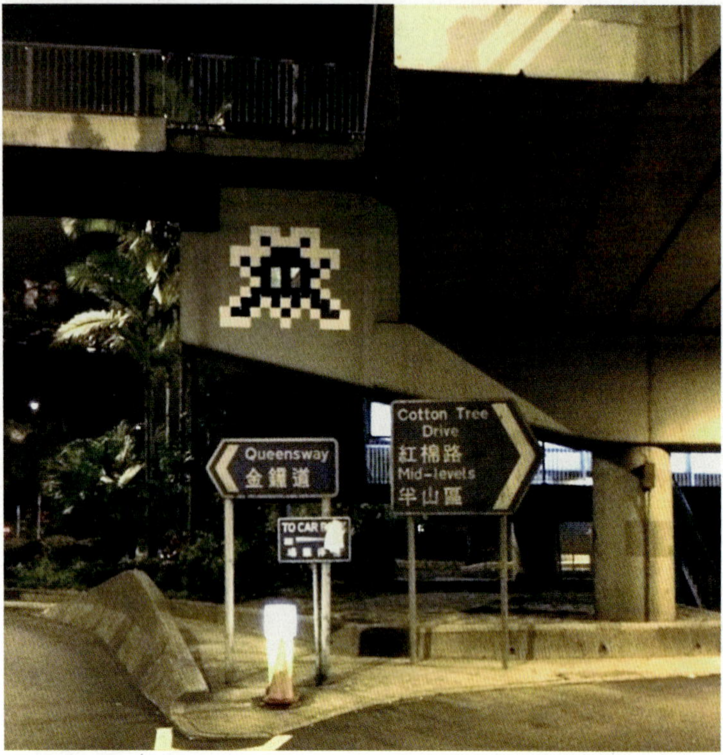

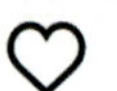   

3 914 likes

invaderwashere Great spot #justdone #hk64

View all 31 comments

26 January 2014

invaderwashere ...

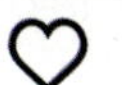

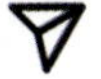

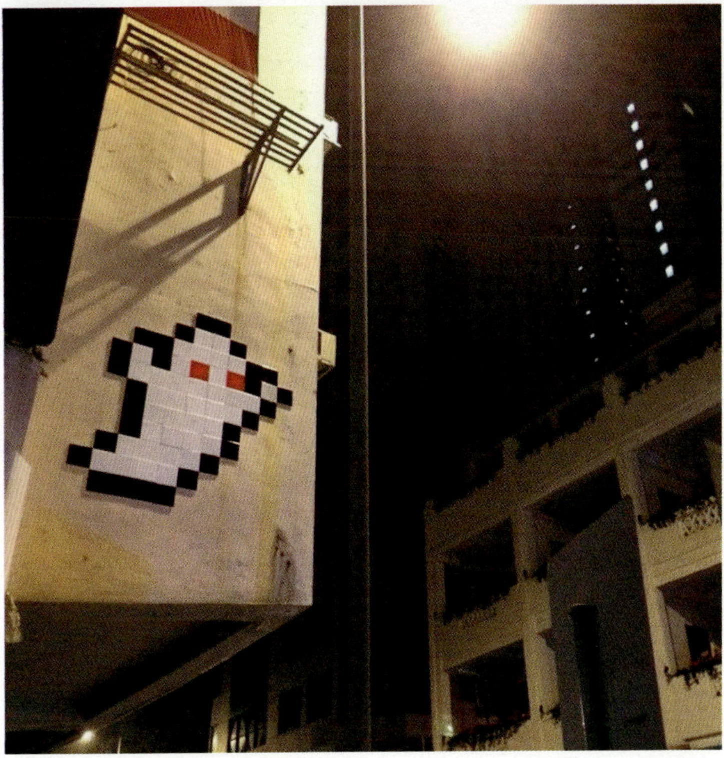

4159 likes

invaderwashere Ghost of Wanchai! 3:45 am #justdone

View all 46 comments

27 January 2014

invaderwashere •••

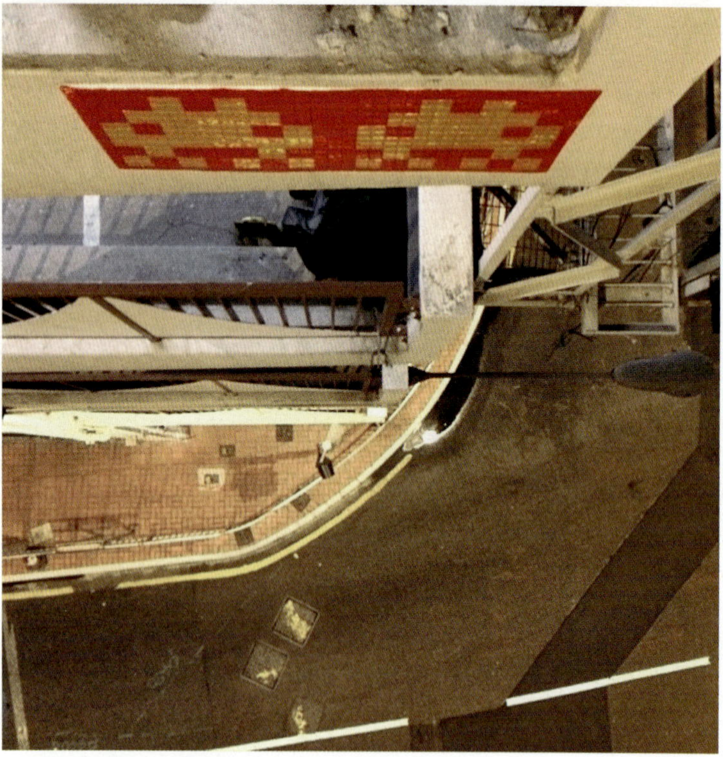

2683 likes

invaderwashere Super hard to reach but super good spot!
#invaderwashere

View all 14 comments

27 January 2014

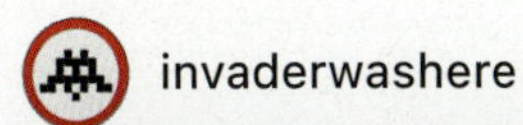

...

  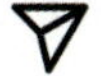 

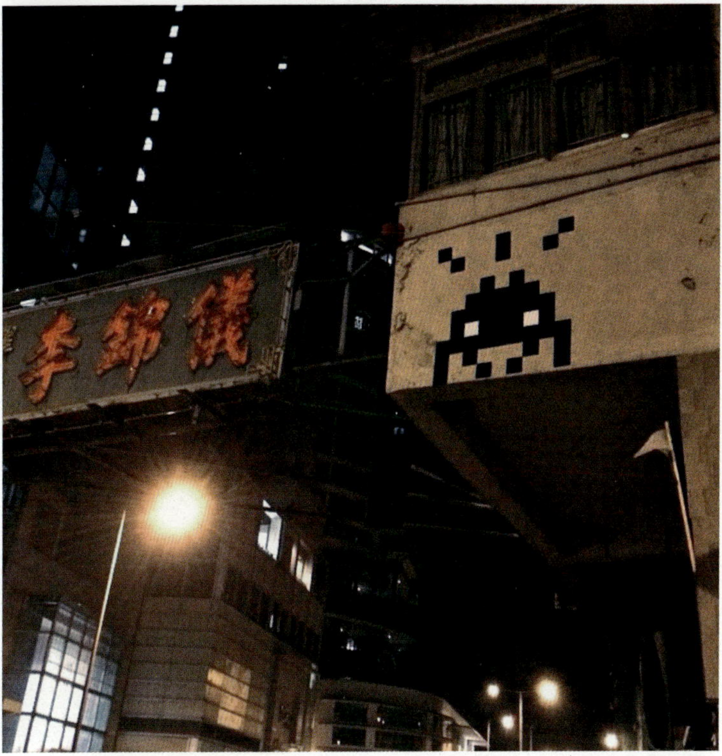

3 595 likes

invaderwashere Wanchai #HK47

View all 32 comments

27 January 2014

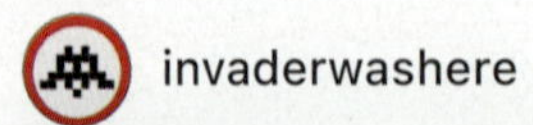

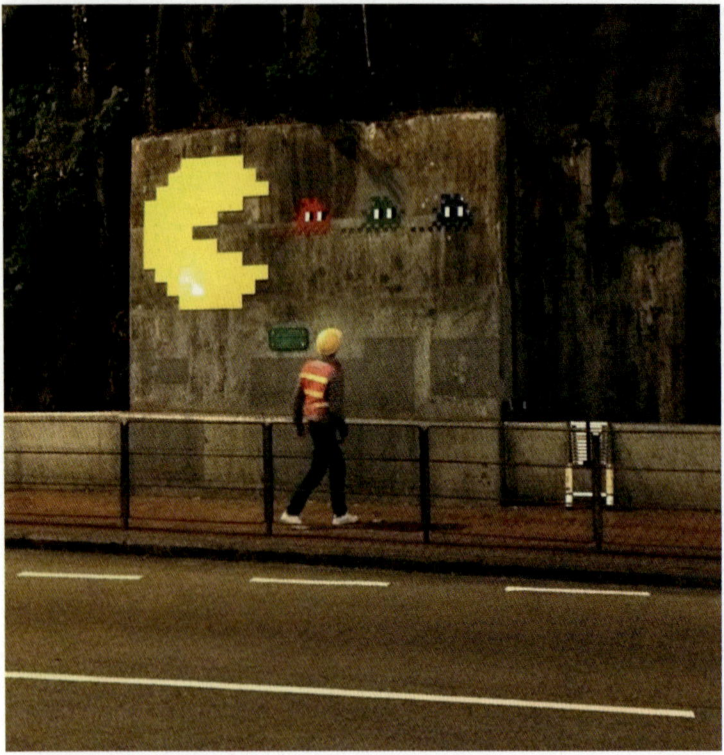

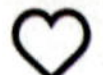 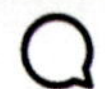  

6 195 likes

invaderwashere Good morning Hong Kong #pacman #justdone #HK72 #5:08am

View all 130 comments

28 January 2014

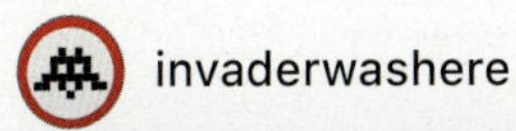

invaderwashere

 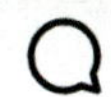  

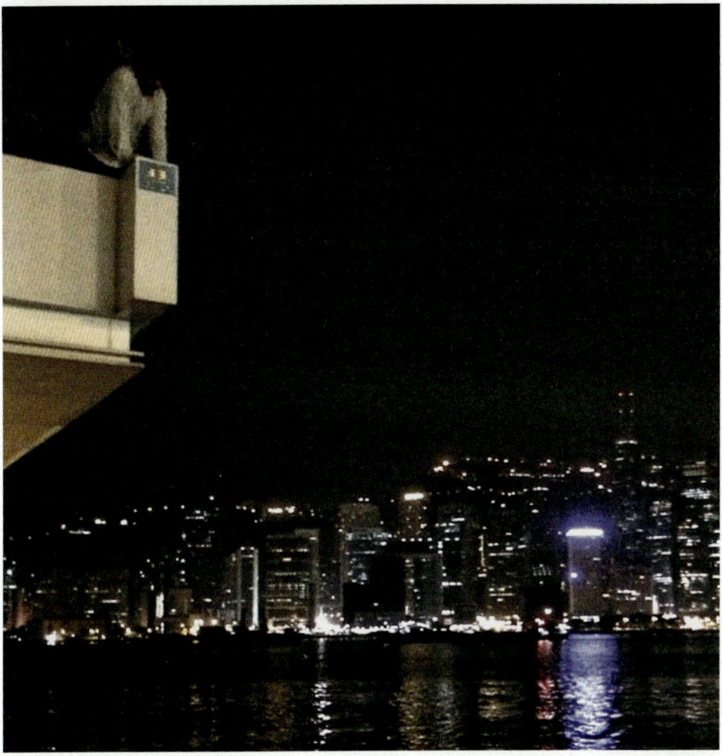

2 344 likes

invaderwashere Tsim Sha Tsui #hongkong #spaceinvader
Enjoy the view

View all 23 comments

29 January 2014

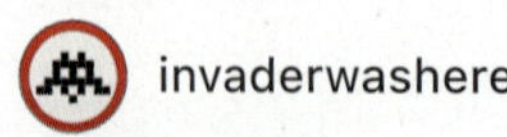
invaderwashere

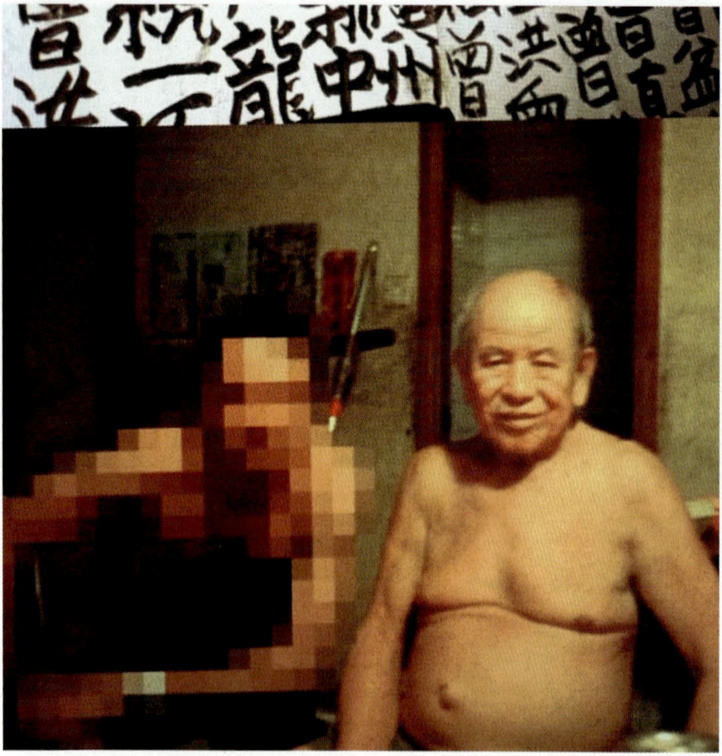

...

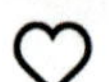   

1868 likes

invaderwashere Back in 2001 with Tsang Tsou Choi "the king of Kowloon" #kingofkowloon #invader #hongkong

View all 33 comments

31 January 2014

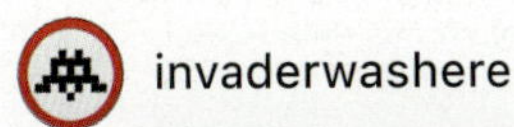

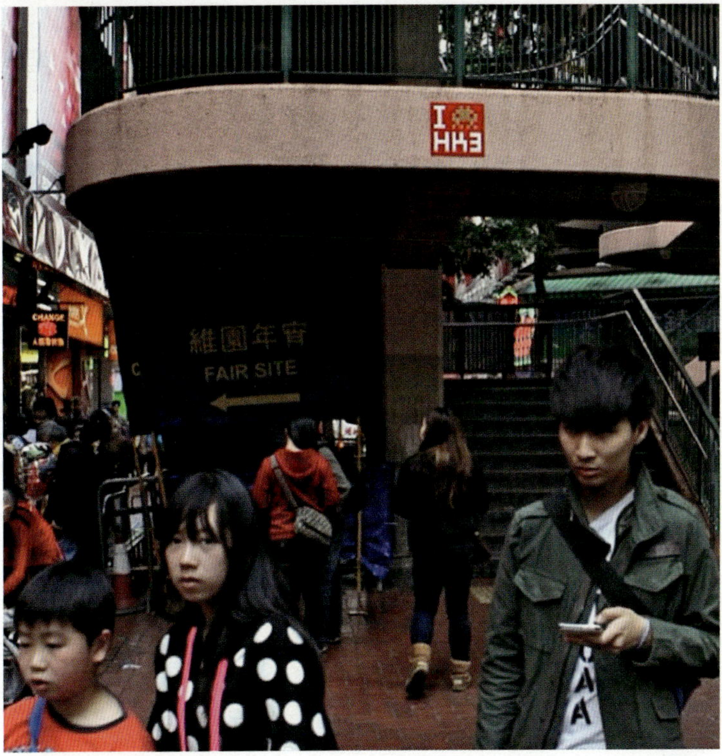

2 614 likes

invaderwashere Wave 03 of the Invasion of Hong Kong:
Successful, 48 new pieces: 2180 Points
Total in Hong kong: 74 pieces / 2630 Points
#HongKongInvasion #wave3 #latest #HK74

View all 43 comments

31 January 2014

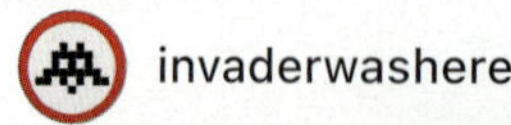

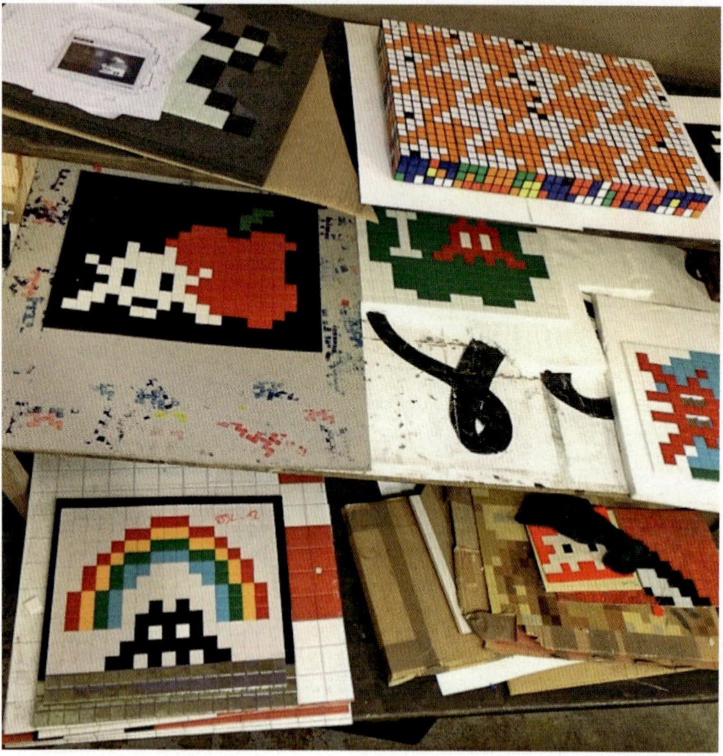

3 560 likes

invaderwashere Back to the studio #mothership #paris #mess

View all 54 comments

11 February 2014

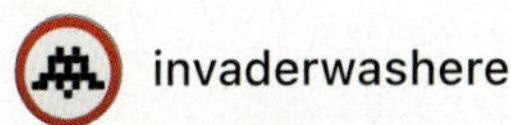

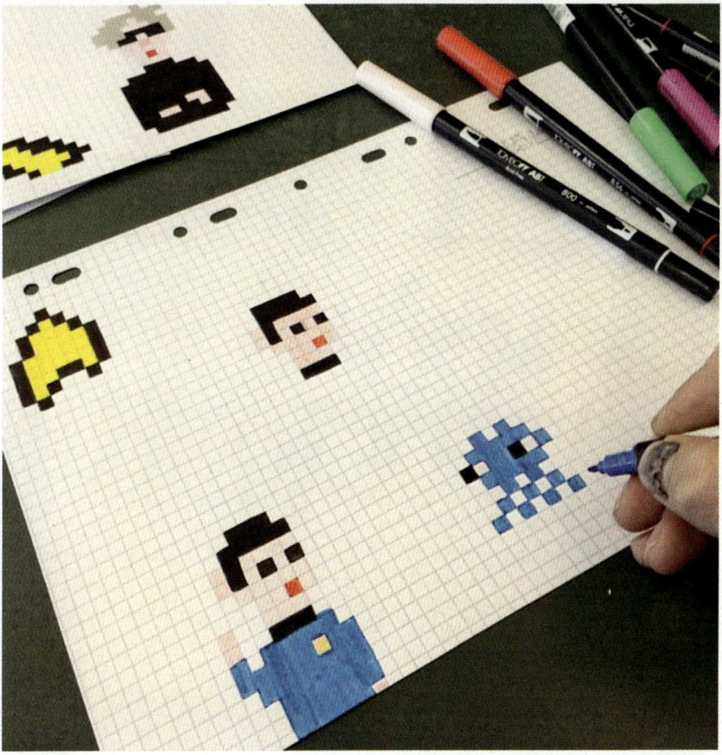

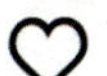   

4 597 likes

invaderwashere Spock to Enterprise! #Studiodetail #invader #blacknail #spock #warhol #drawings

View all 81 comments

11 February 2014

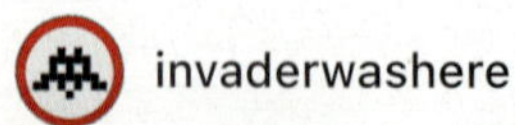

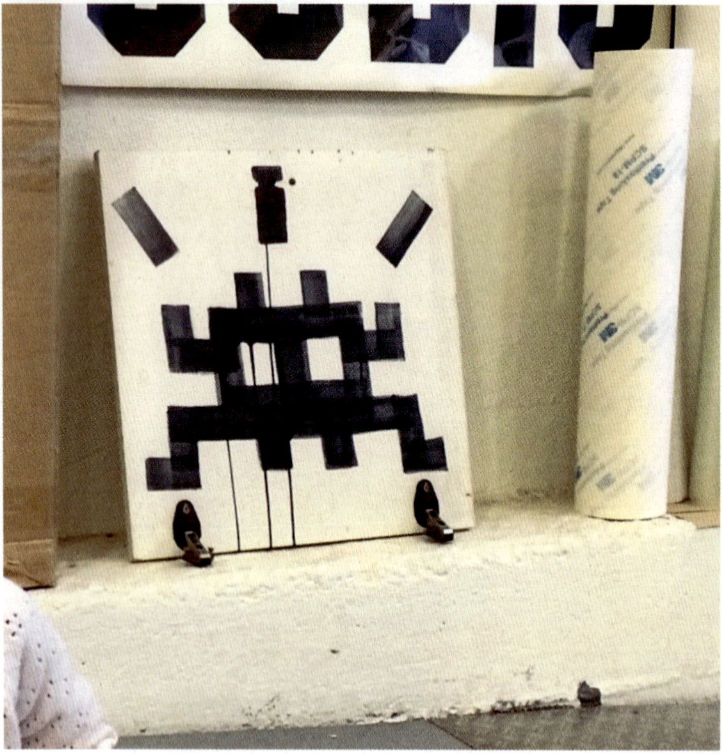

2623 likes

invaderwashere #Studiodetail Ink on closet door, an old piece from 2001 #spaceinvader #invader #blackink #marker

View all 13 comments

11 February 2014

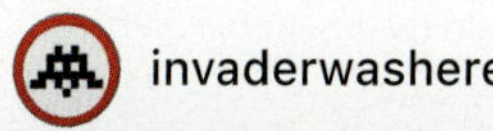
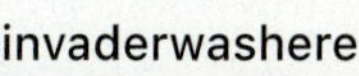

invaderwashere

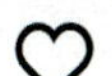 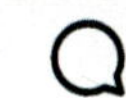  

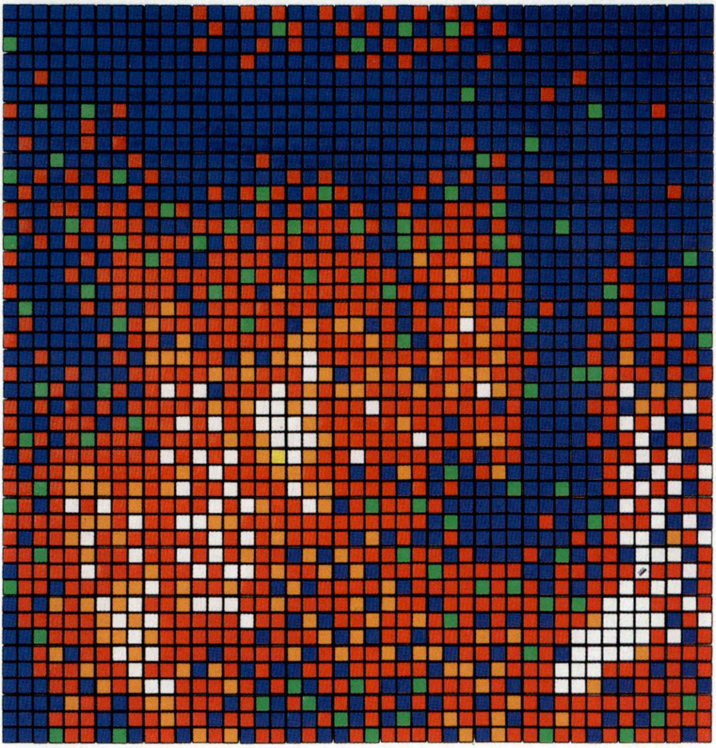

2 240 likes

invaderwashere My rubikcubist version of Pornography album made with 325 Rubik's cubes #thecure #rubikcubism #lowfidelity #abstraction #figuration

View all 16 comments

12 February 2014

invaderwashere •••

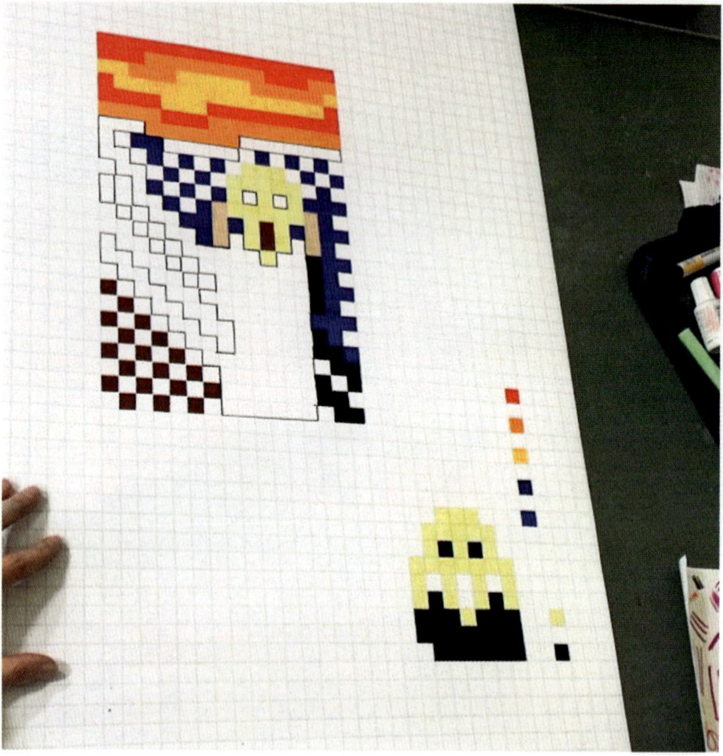

3163 likes

invaderwashere My drawings on paper are becoming bigger... 😱✍️ #thescream #aftermunch #spaceinvaderhead #inkonpaper #drawingonsilkscreenprintedgrid

View all 66 comments

13 February 2014

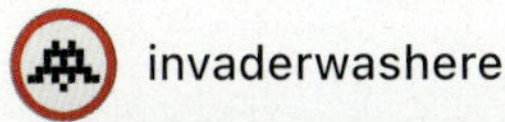

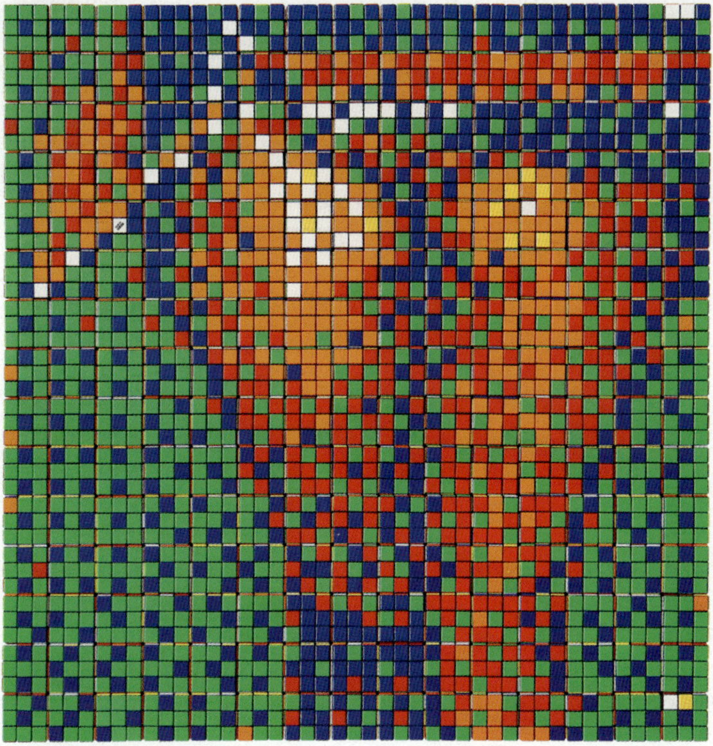

2 472 likes

invaderwashere One of my top10 album #live1969 #velvetunderground #rubikcubism #Lowfidelity #albumcover #invader

View all 31 comments

17 February 2014

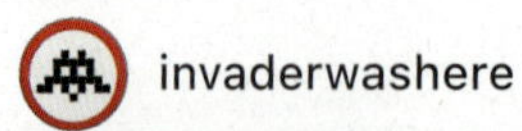

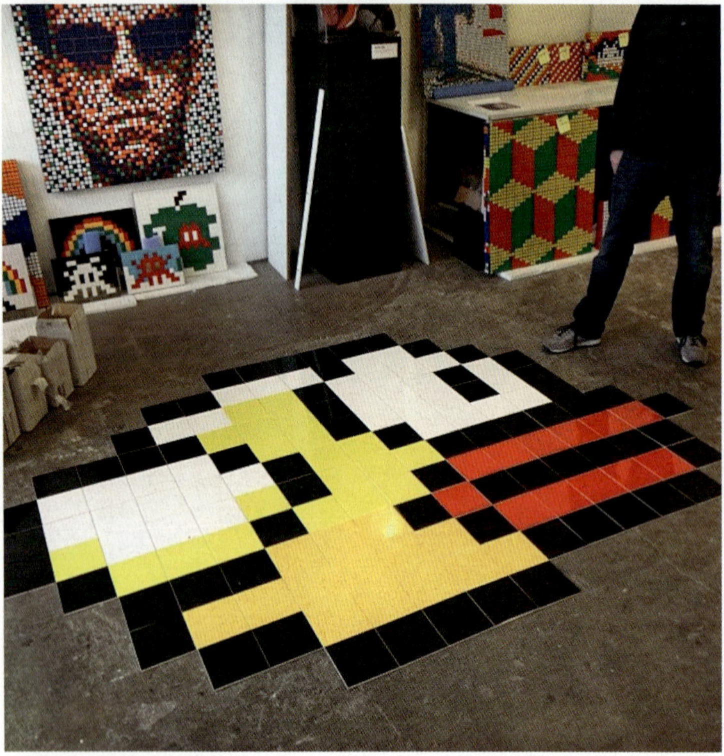

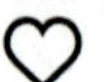   

5 891 likes

invaderwashere Studio detail / making of Flappy bird. Soon in the street... #flappybird #rubiksmithagent #matrix #spaceinvaders

View all 203 comments

19 February 2014

invaderwashere •••

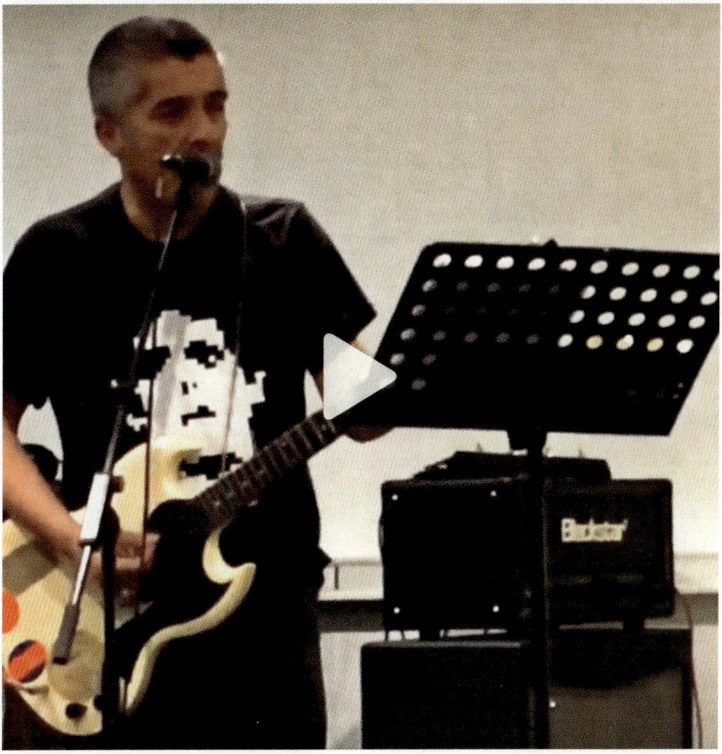

548 likes

invaderwashere Tai Luc wearing my Lou Reed Tshirt #tailuc #leadsinger #lsd #Lasourisdeglinguee #frenchrock #yasminaPA

View all 8 comments

22 February 2014

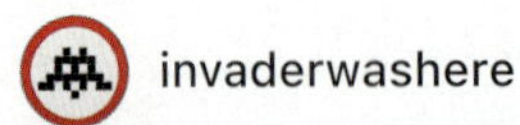

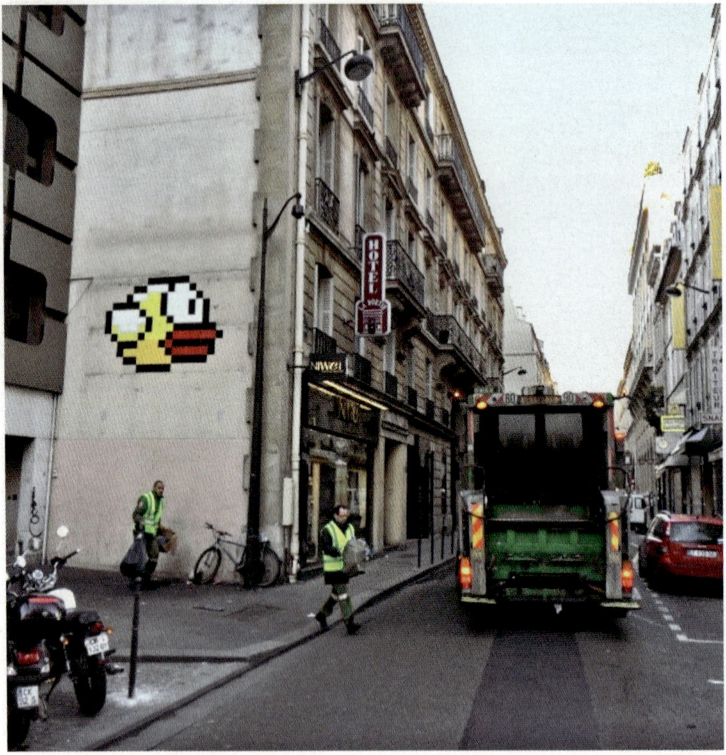

8145 likes

invaderwashere PA_1088 #Paris #earlymorning #BigFlappyBird #Justdone

View all 244 comments

2 March 2014

invaderwashere

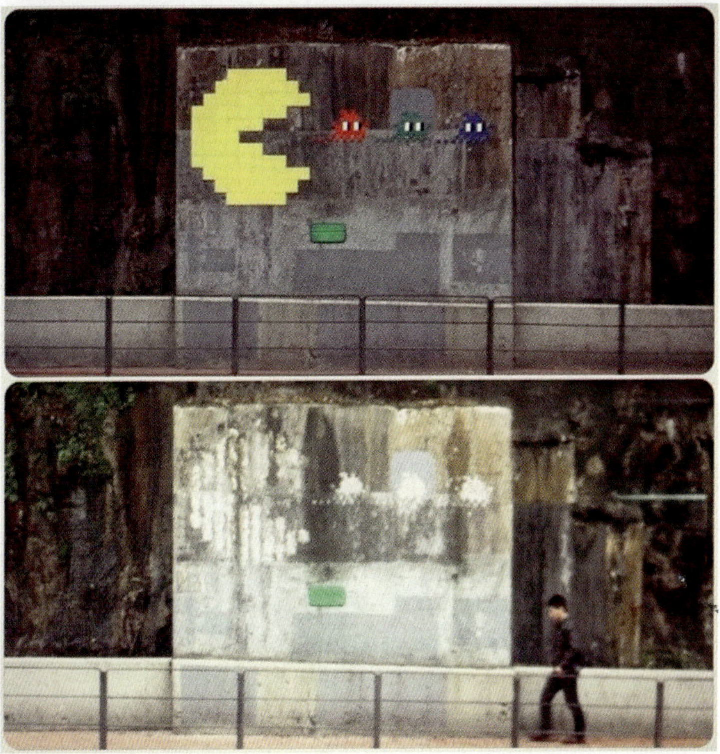

3175 likes

invaderwashere I made this piece in Hong Kong one month ago. Two weeks later it was removed by the Highways Department with many others of my new pieces. To be continued in my next post... #hongkongstory photo by @christesio

View all 60 comments

6 March 2014

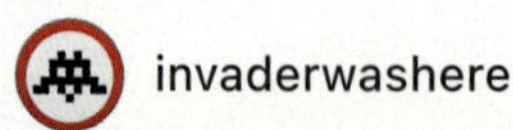

invaderwashere

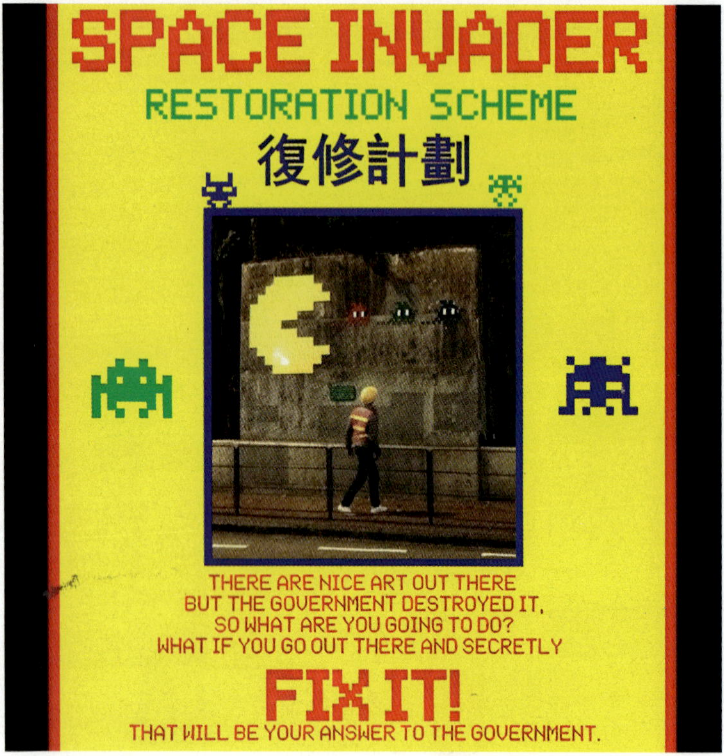

SPACE INVADER
RESTORATION SCHEME
復修計劃

THERE ARE NICE ART OUT THERE
BUT THE GOVERNMENT DESTROYED IT,
SO WHAT ARE YOU GOING TO DO?
WHAT IF YOU GO OUT THERE AND SECRETLY
FIX IT!
THAT WILL BE YOUR ANSWER TO THE GOVERNMENT.

 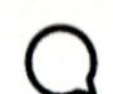  

2132 likes

invaderwashere Then a local artist created this poster. To be continued on my next post... #kaceywong #hongkongstory

View all 31 comments

6 March 2014

invaderwashere ...

 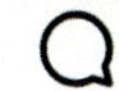  

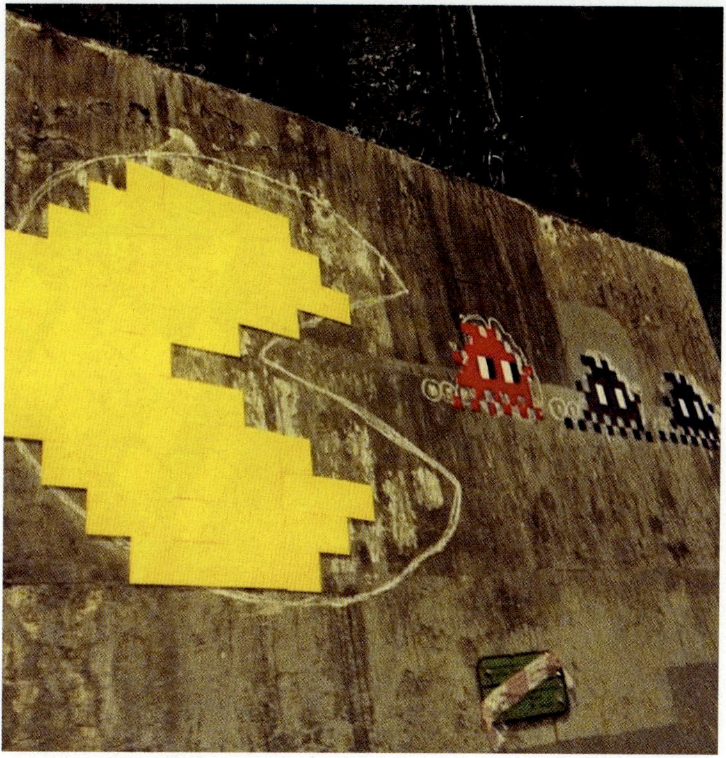

4258 likes

invaderwashere This morning I had the surprise to discover that some people have recreated the piece! Thanx guys! 🙏 #hongkongstory #happyend photo @kensomepoon For more infos about this hong kong story, check the articles of Vivienne Chow on the South China Morning Post

View all 81 comments

6 March 2014

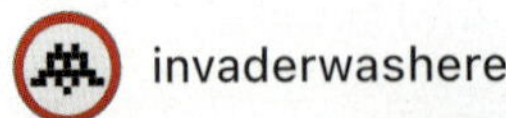

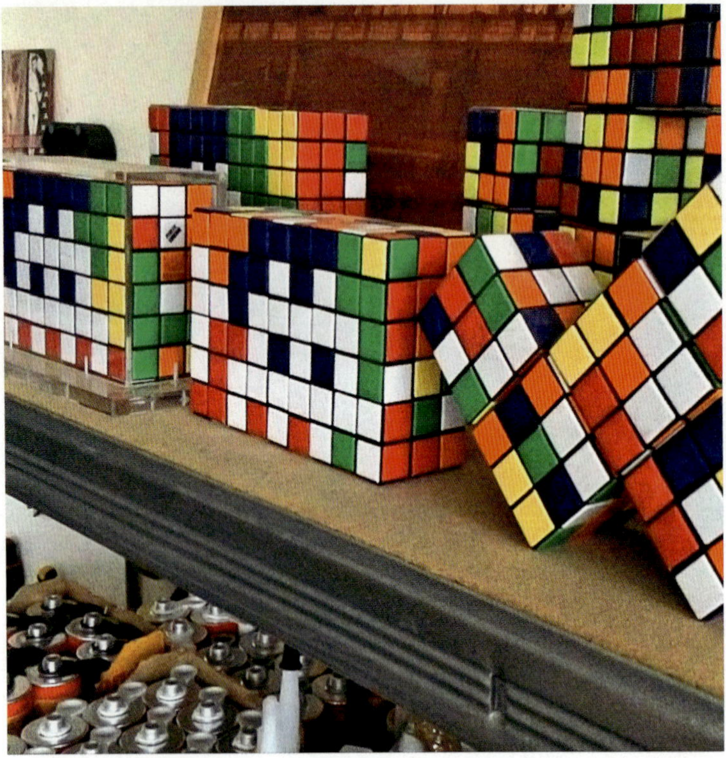

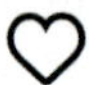   

3 296 likes

invaderwashere What interests me in Rubikcubism is the possibility of revisiting a ludoscientific object and transforming it into an artistic medium #rubickubism #spaceinvaders #studiodetail #6cubesmatrix

View all 51 comments

7 March 2014

invaderwashere

  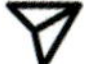 

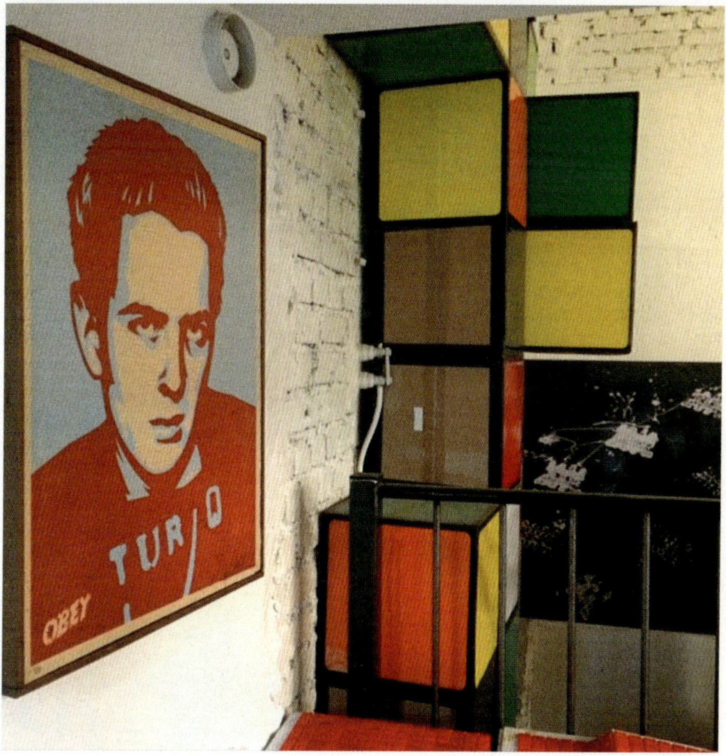

2063 likes

invaderwashere #Studiodetail with #JoeStrummer portrait by @obeygiant

View all 17 comments

8 March 2014

invaderwashere

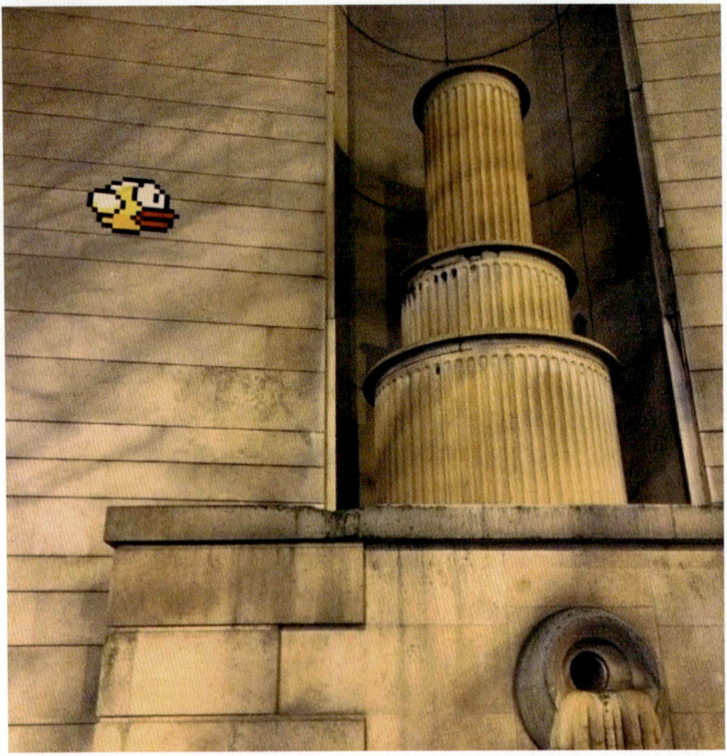

5 568 likes

invaderwashere Found a great spot for a new #flappybird / Paris 2:45am #justdone #invaderwashere

View all 91 comments

12 March 2014

invaderwashere

 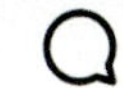  

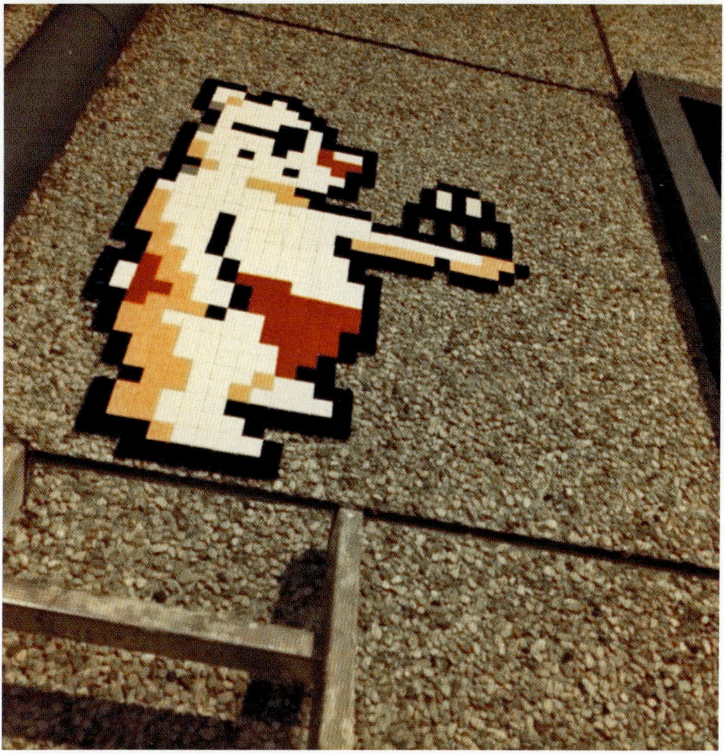

5089 likes

invaderwashere 4:05am / third piece of the night
#iceclimber #PA1092 #justdone

View all 60 comments

12 March 2014

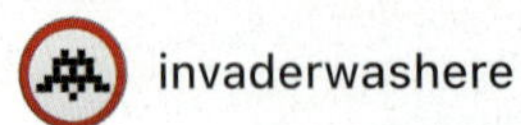

•••

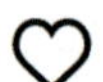   

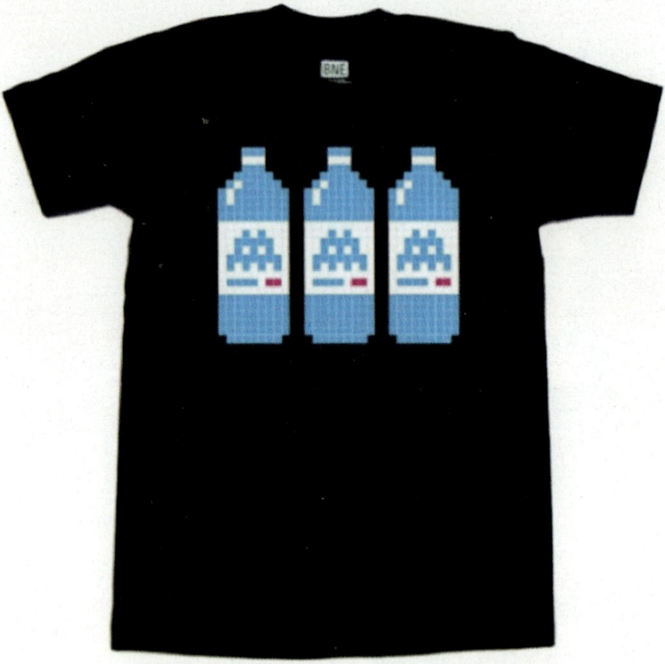

3 284 likes

invaderwashere I did a limited edition, organic cotton Tshirt with BNE to raise funds + awareness for @charitywater Limited to 100 pieces. Release: Tomorrow, Thursday, 3/13, 10AM PST at BNE.org. An @ObeyGiant tee will also be available. Follow @bnedotorg #collaboration #charity #tshirts

View all 58 comments

12 March 2014

invaderwashere •••

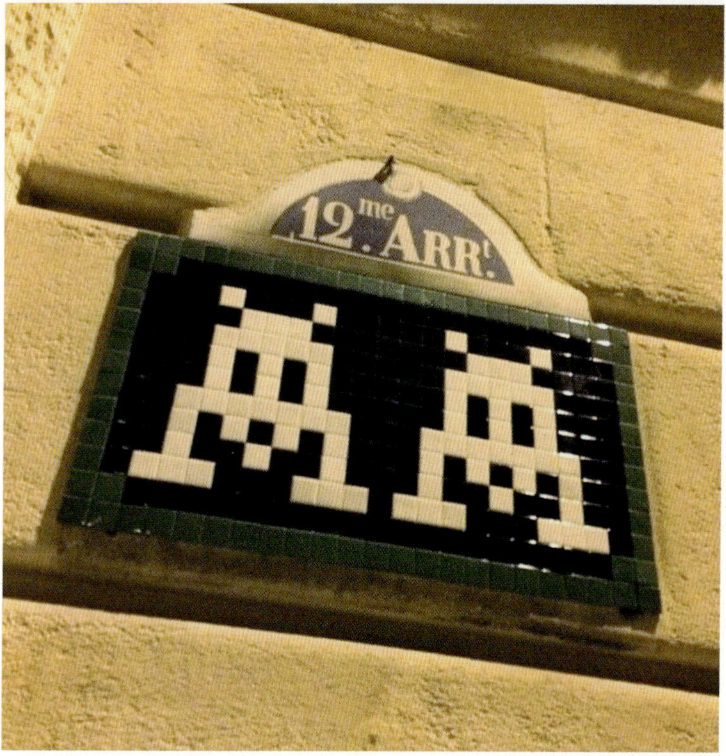

5204 likes

invaderwashere 5:18am / PA_1095 / third piece of the night #justdone #spaceinvaders #75012

View all 56 comments

20 March 2014

invaderwashere

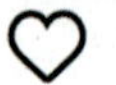  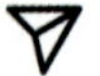 

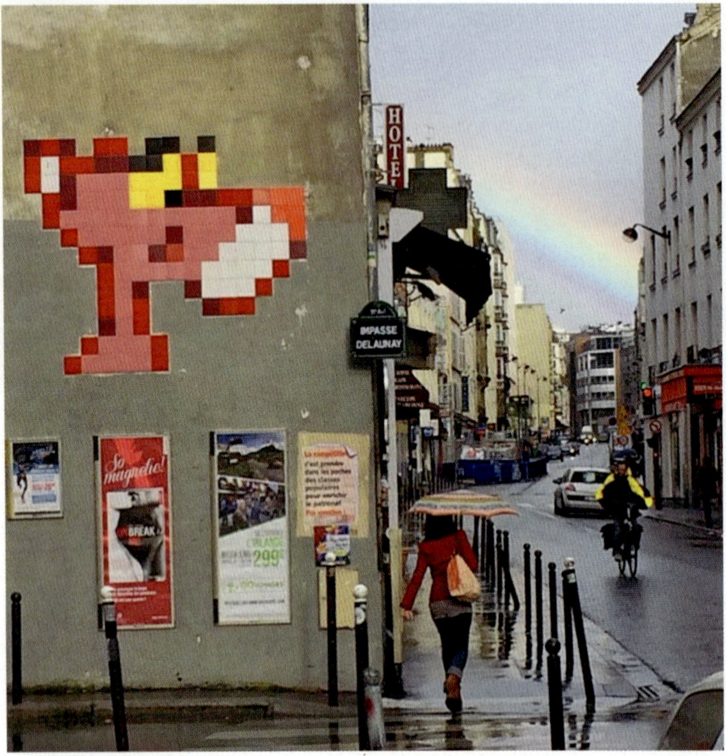

8 027 likes

invaderwashere Sunday rainbow #PA1039 #paris #pinkpanther

View all 124 comments

23 March 2014

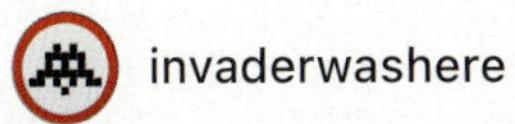

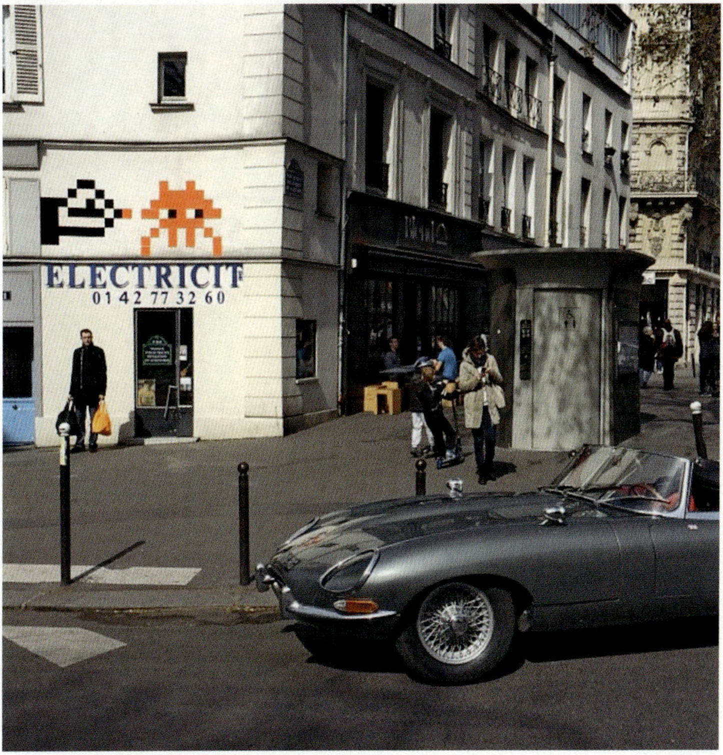

  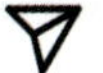 

5175 likes

invaderwashere Beautiful day in Paris #paris

View all 58 comments

29 March 2014

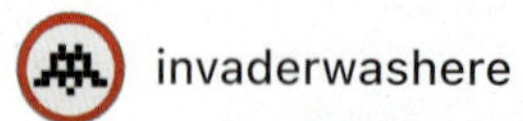

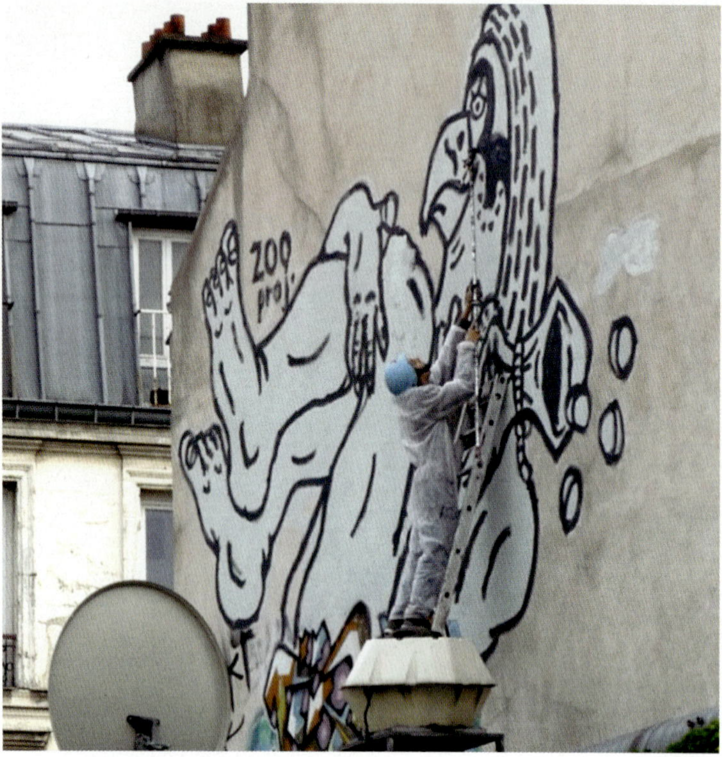

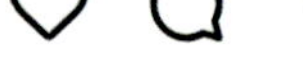

2 526 likes

invaderwashere I'm so sad today to learn the terrible death of Bilal aka #ZooProject. I met him and took this picture in 2009. He was so young, so talented, so real and had such a great heart. RIP Brother, we miss you.

View all 21 comments

31 March 2014

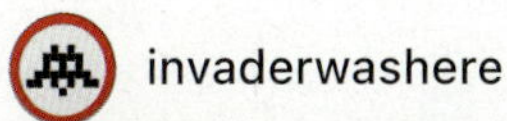

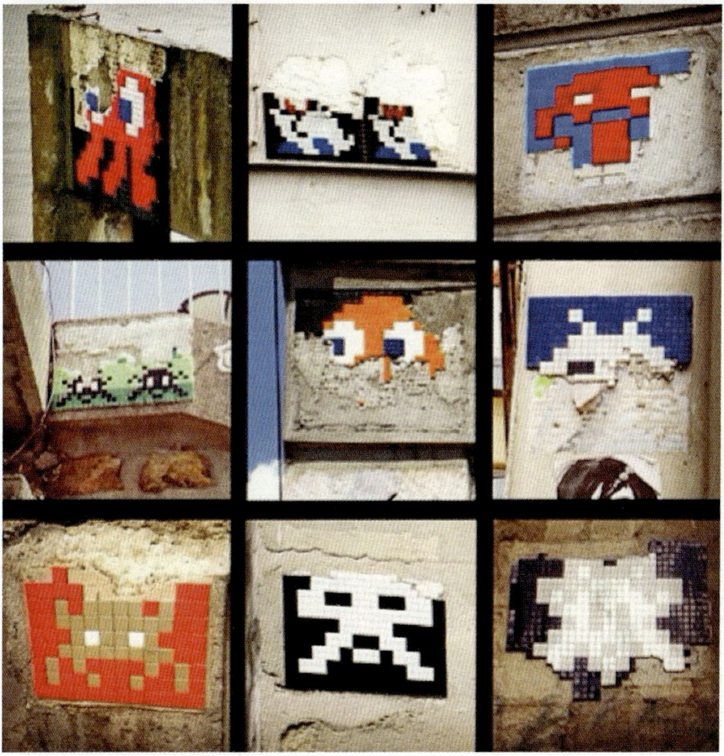

 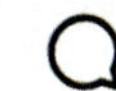  

3 261 likes

invaderwashere Broken by fuckin thieves... Check my blog for more details: space-invaders.com/cheersfromspace #spaceinvaders #thieves

View all 86 comments

3 April 2014

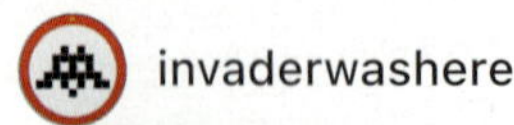

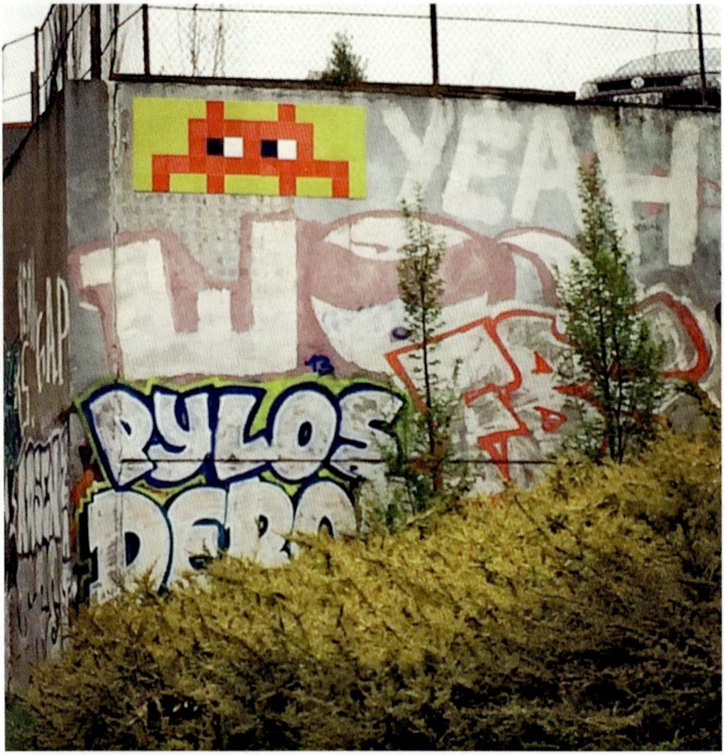

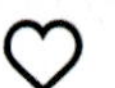   

3 528 likes

invaderwashere PA_1096 Brand new... #YEAH #50points #paris #highway

View all 39 comments

4 April 2014

invaderwashere

 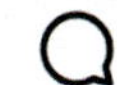 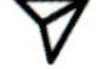 

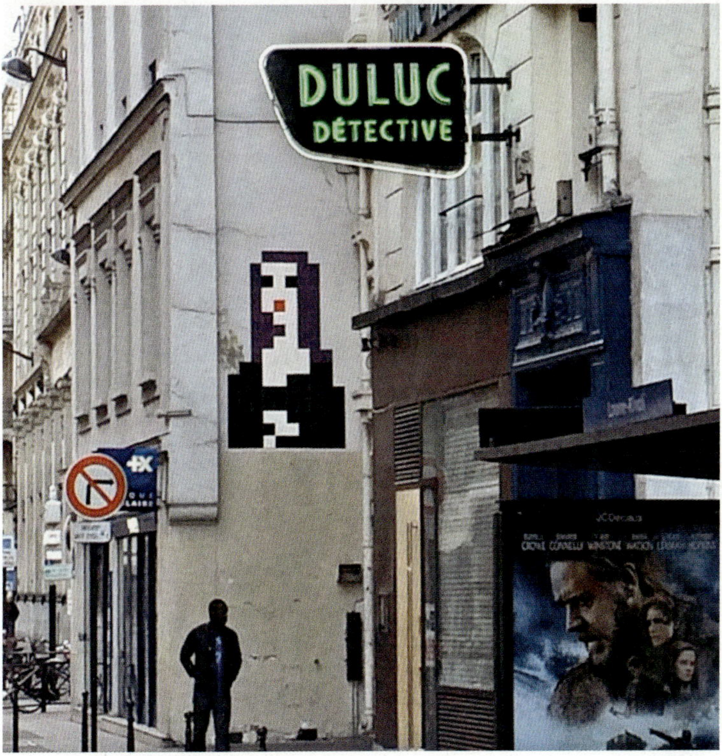

6306 likes

invaderwashere 6:45am Paris / Rue du Louvre! #MonaLisa #LaJoconde #PA1097 #justdone #invaderwashere

View all 126 comments

6 April 2014

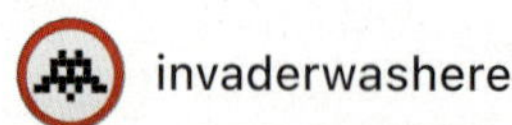

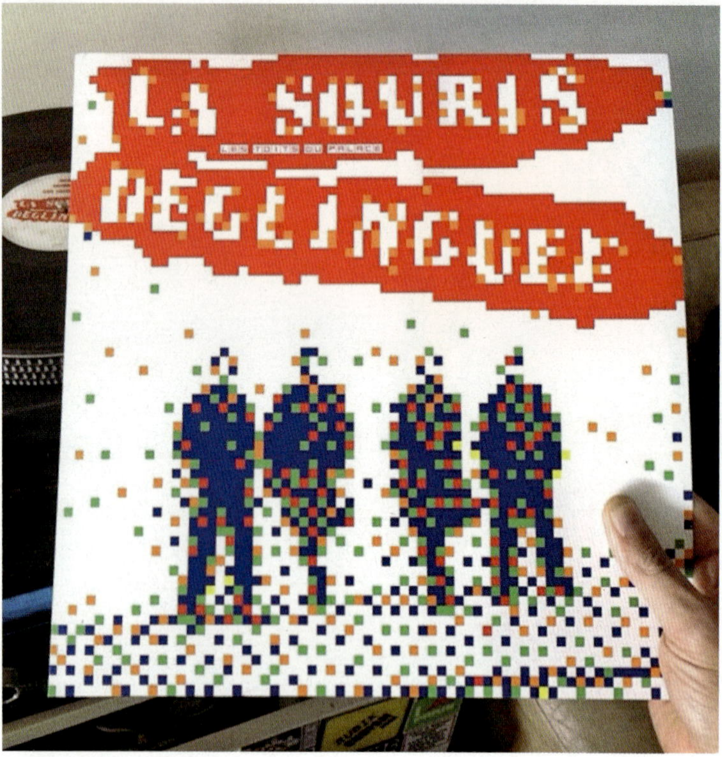

2 713 likes

invaderwashere The new album of the French band La Souris Déglinguée will be released tomorrow with a print and a rubikcubist work. The album and the print will be available on lasourisdeglinguee.fr and the artwork will be auctioned on ebay. All the profits will go to LSD to pay the production of the album and its promotion. #LaSourisDeglinguee #albumcover #punkrock #indie #designbyinvader

View all 25 comments

14 April 2014

invaderwashere ...

 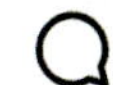 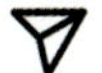 

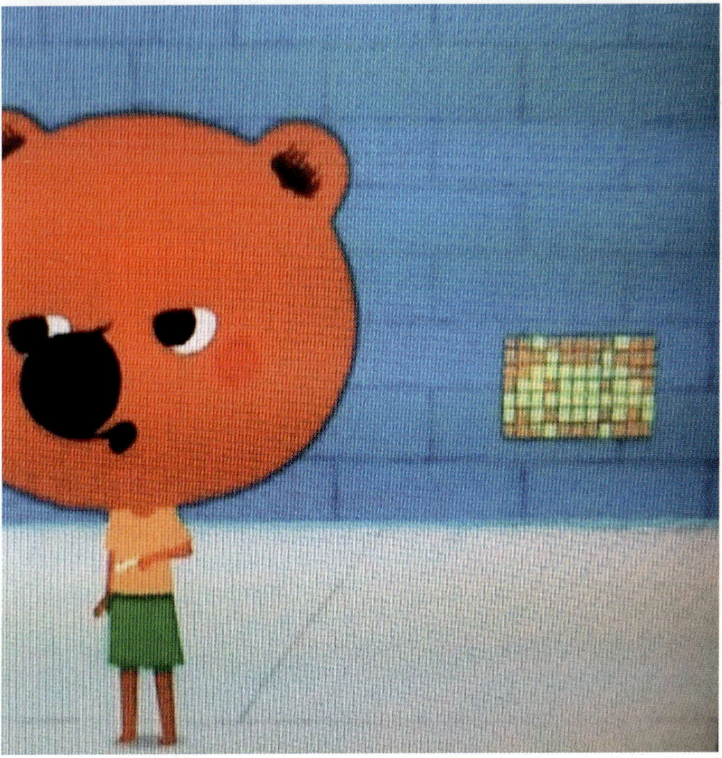

2 491 likes

invaderwashere Invasion of Mouk cartoon, thanks to #marcBoutavant #mouk #seenonTV

View all 23 comments

19 April 2014

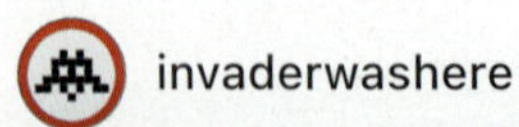

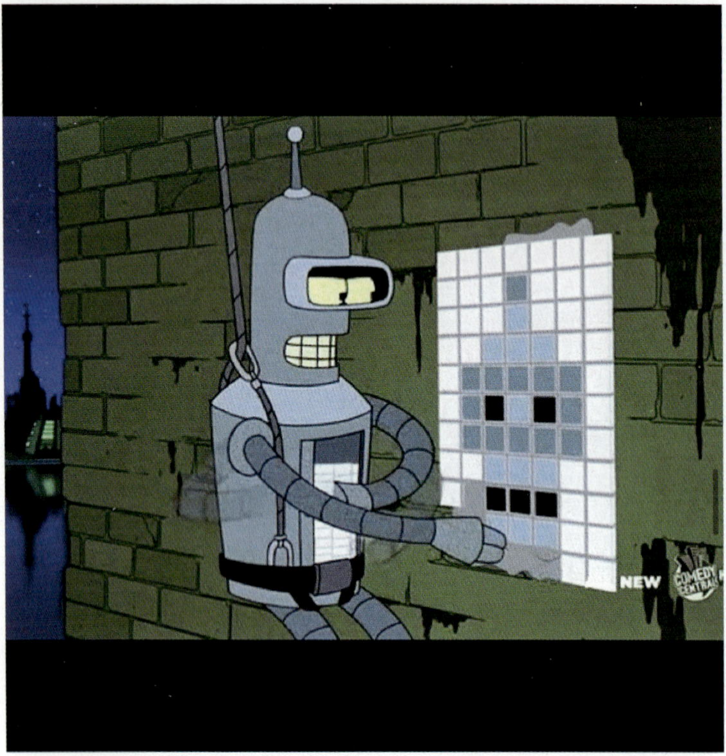

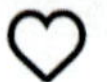   

7617 likes

invaderwashere An other cartoon invaded: Futurama S06E04 with Bender playing Invader!
Thanks #mattgroening #2010 #futurama #bender

View all 123 comments

21 April 2014

invaderwashere

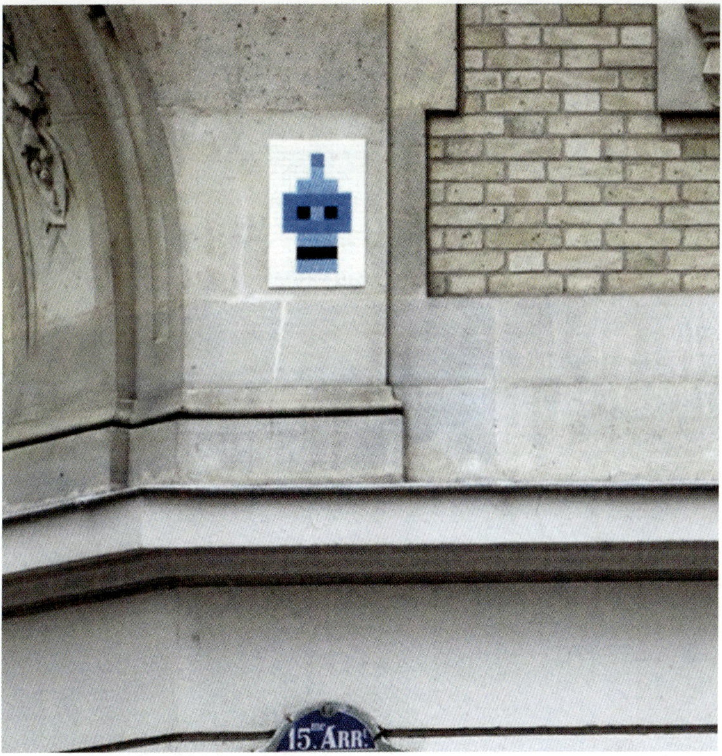

4 573 likes

invaderwashere ... Then few weeks later, I made 2 Bender portraits, like the one in the cartoon, and I put them in the streets. The circle is complete ! PA_882 & PA_901 #bender #futurama

View all 64 comments

21 April 2014

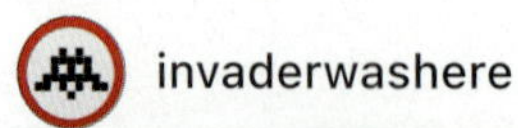

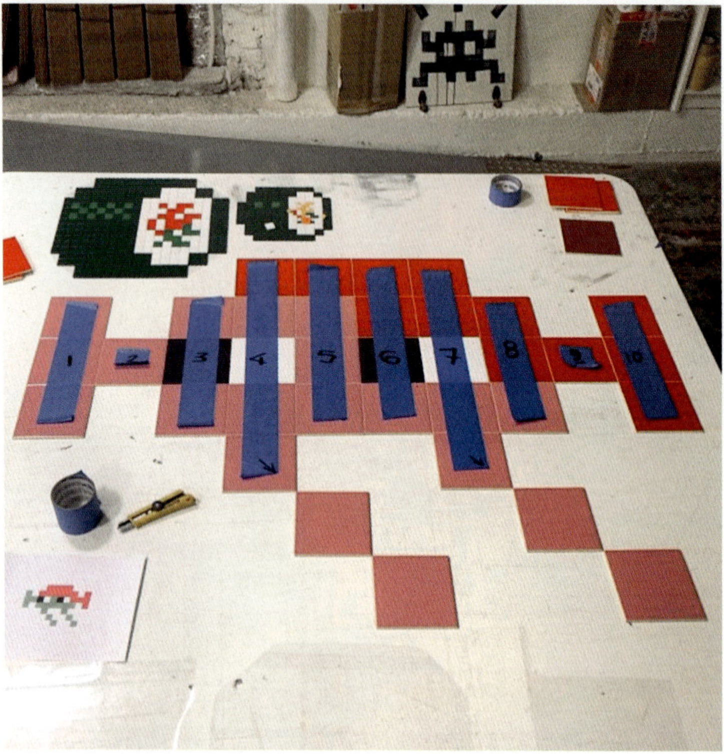

3 337 likes

invaderwashere #studiodetail #pink&red

View all 43 comments

22 April 2014

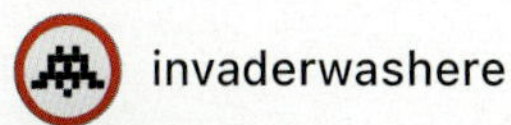

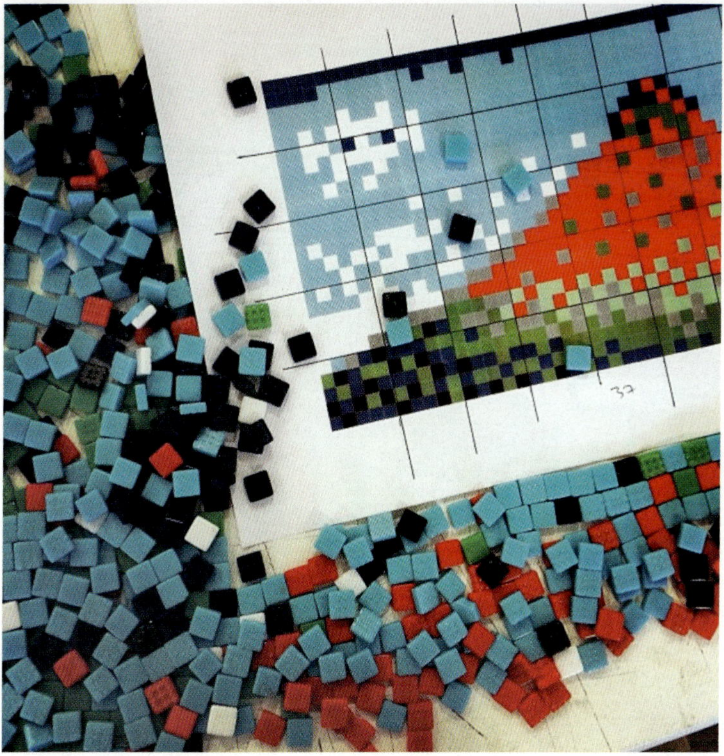

 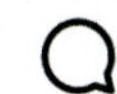 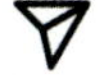 

4955 likes

invaderwashere Studio detail #workinprogress #spaceinvader #fuji

View all 54 comments

7 May 2014

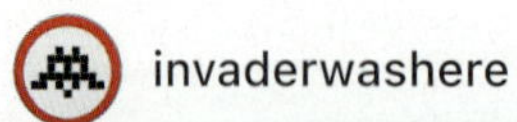

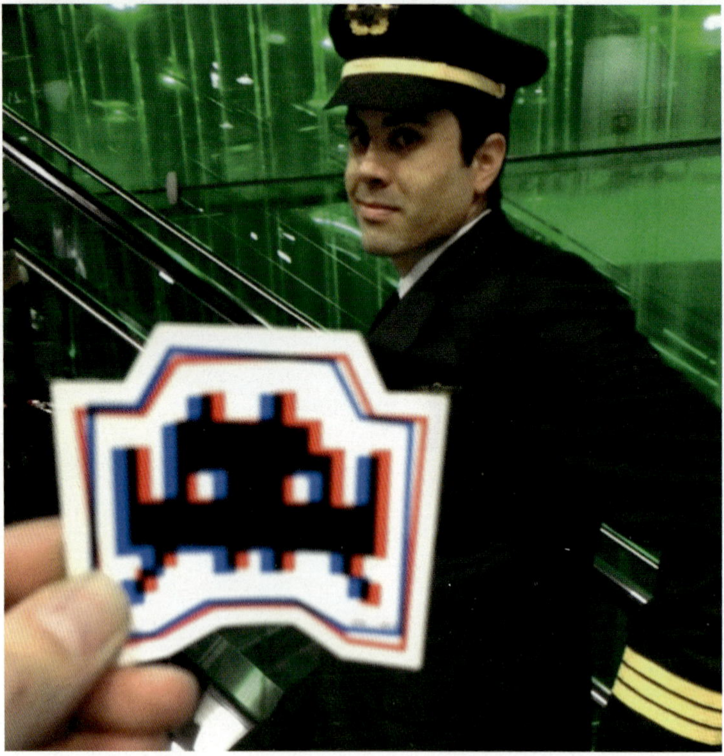

3 514 likes

invaderwashere On the road again #airport

View all 32 comments

9 May 2014

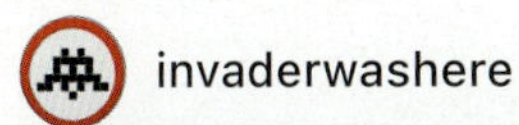

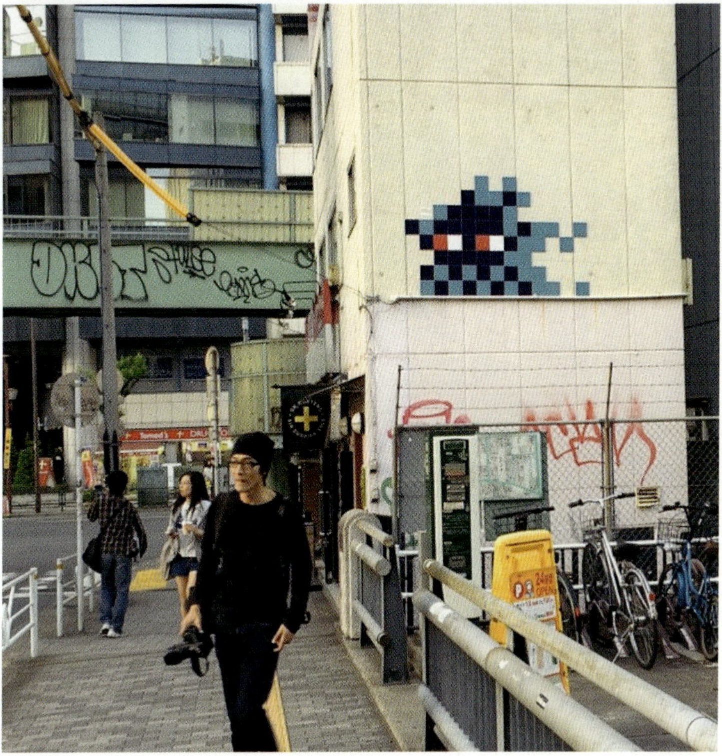

  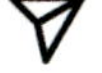 

5076 likes

invaderwashere Guess where...

View all 74 comments

11 May 2014

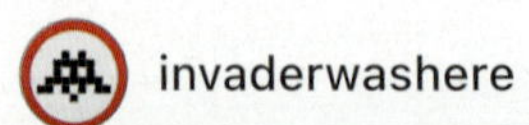

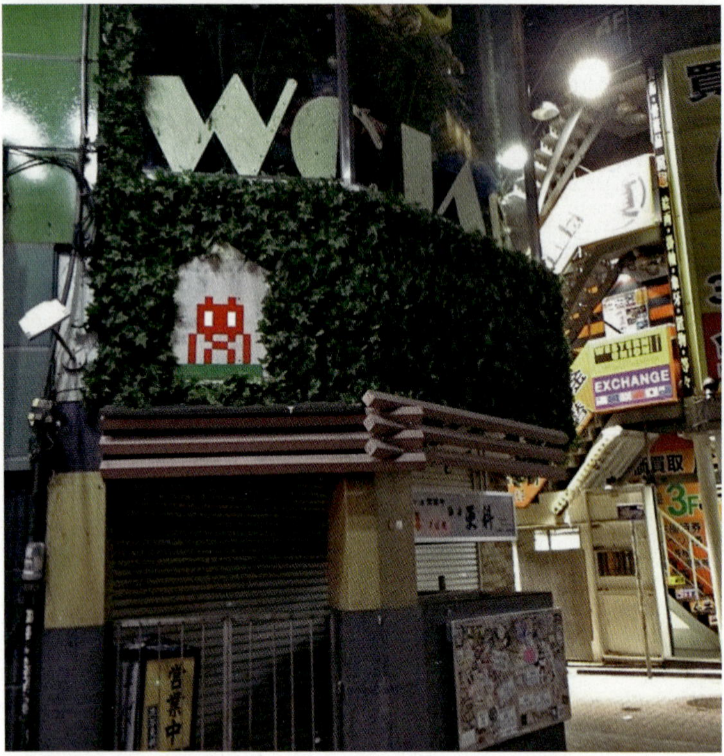

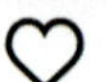   

4 017 likes

invaderwashere 6th invasion of the night... #justdone #shibuya #tokyo #invaderwashere

View all 36 comments

11 May 2014

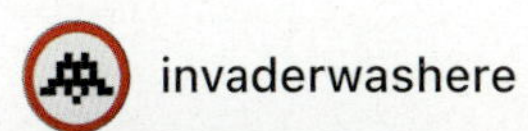

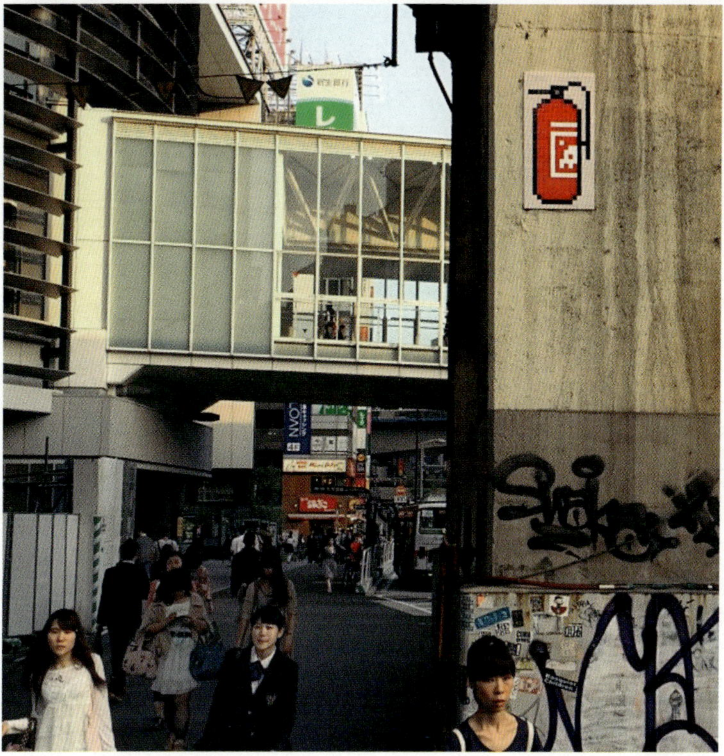

4065 likes

invaderwashere TK_92 #shibuya #fireextinguisher

View all 33 comments

13 May 2014

invaderwashere •••

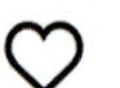   

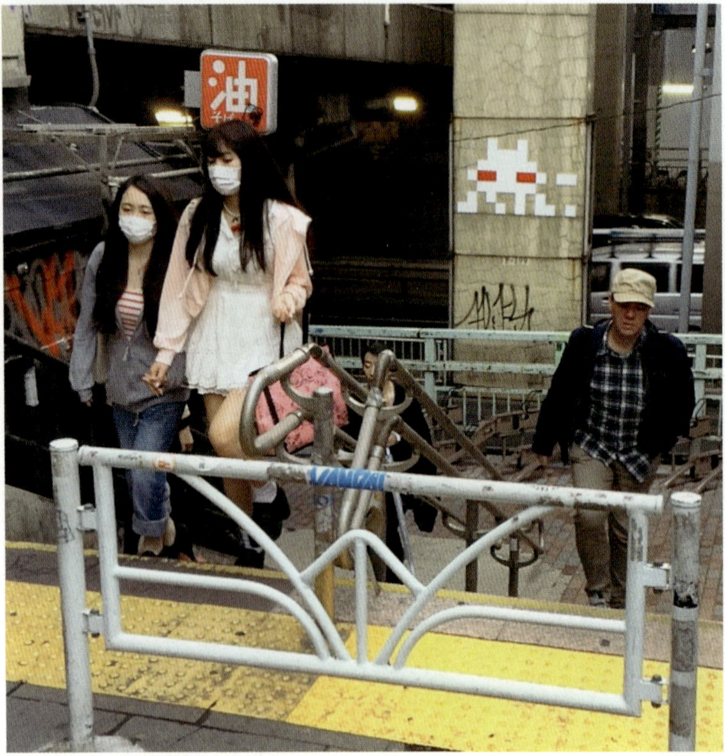

3623 likes

invaderwashere TK_95

View all 29 comments

13 May 2014

invaderwashere •••

 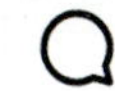  

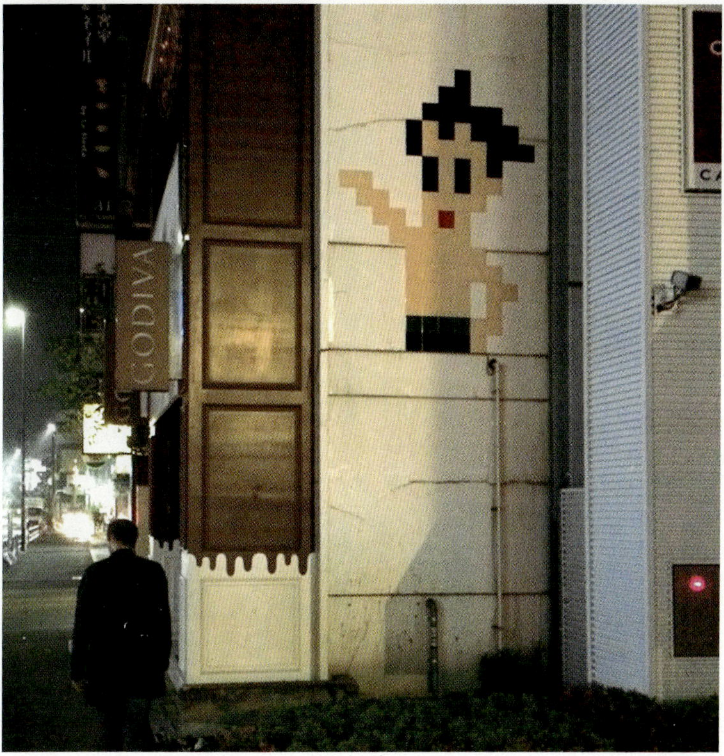

4669 likes

invaderwashere 3:15am #AstroBoy, #justdone #tokyo #鉄腕アトム #東京

View all 57 comments

13 May 2014

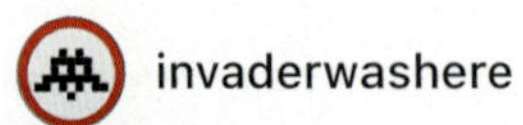

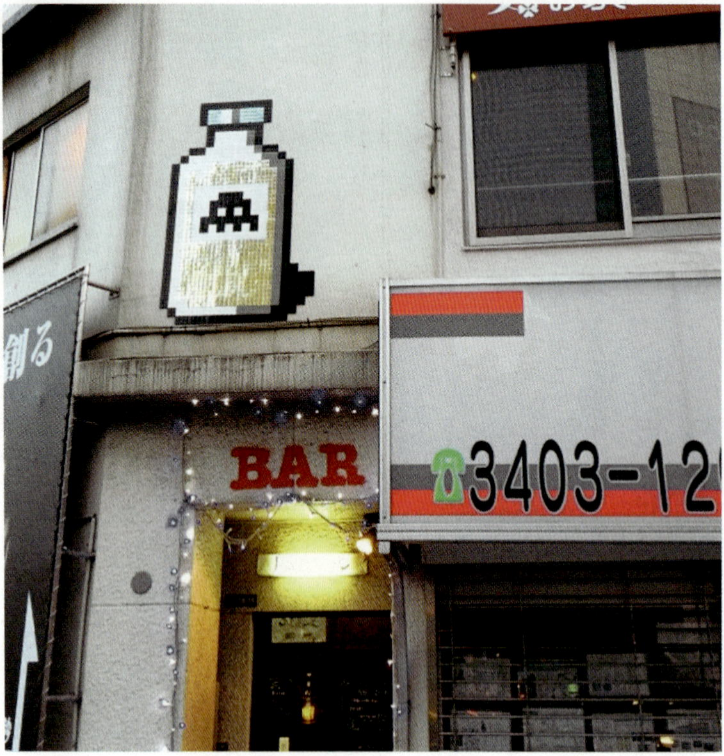

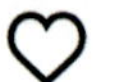   

5951 likes

invaderwashere 4:30am Show me the way to the next whiskey bar...

View all 76 comments

13 May 2014

invaderwashere

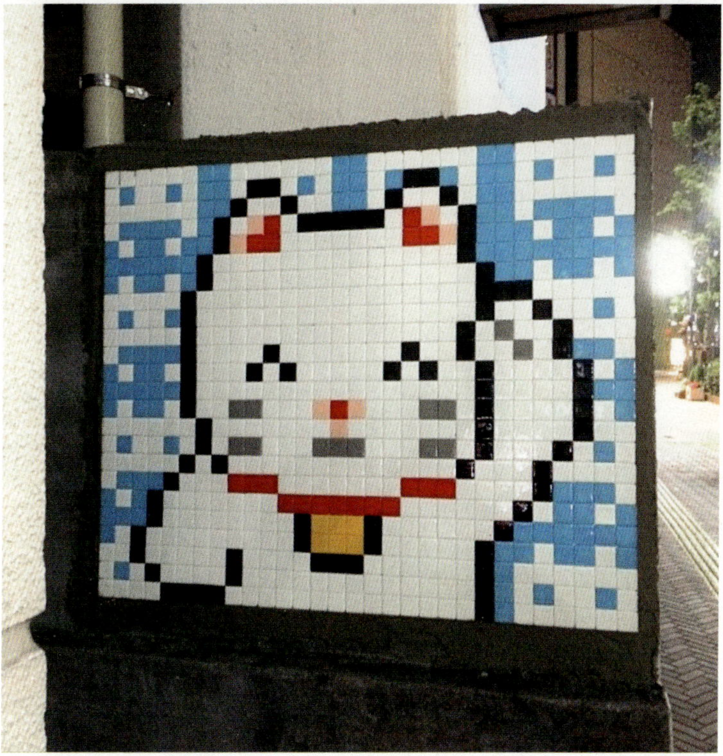

•••

5782 likes

invaderwashere #manekineko #justdone in #shibuya #tokyo 2:45am #invaderwashere

View all 160 comments

14 May 2014

invaderwashere

  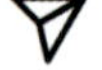 

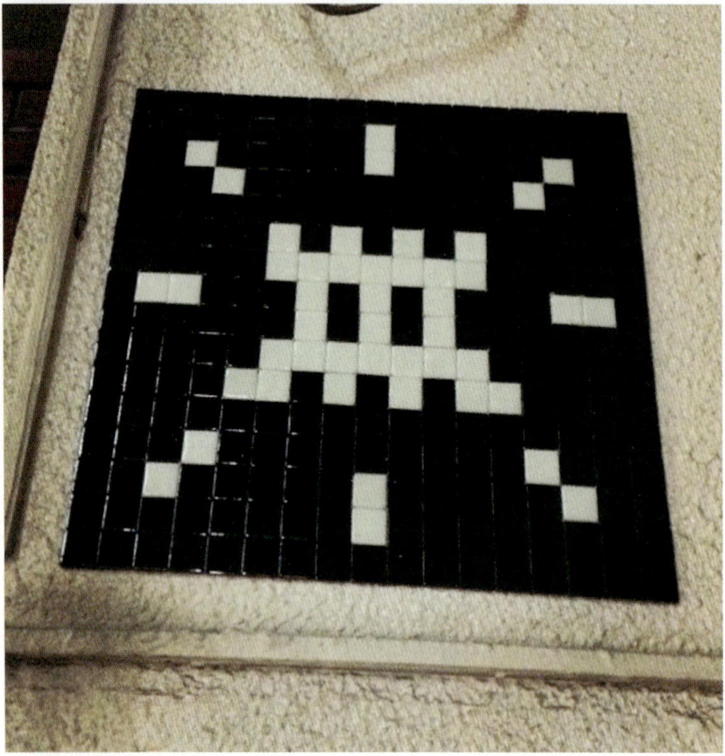

3 676 likes

invaderwashere Radiant space invader #glowinthedark #afterfukushima

View all 25 comments

14 May 2014

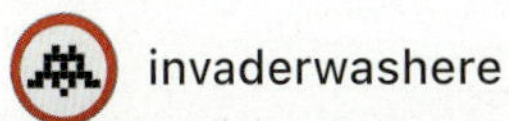

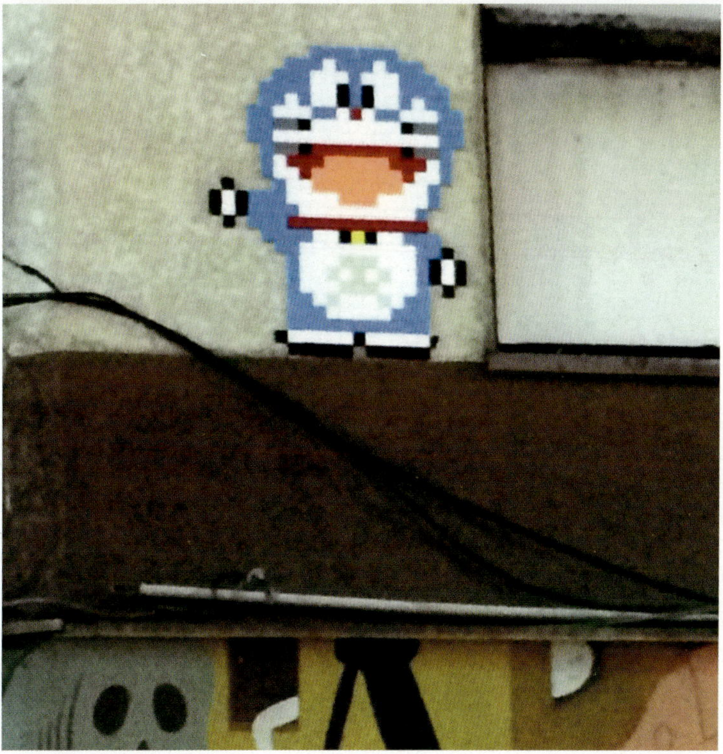

5 356 likes

invaderwashere Invaded #Doraemon in #Ebisu

View all 108 comments

15 May 2014

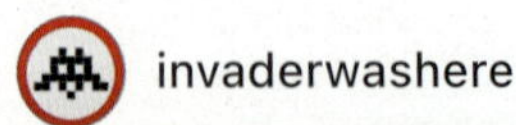

INVADER & GALLERY TARGET invite you to the Japan Premiere of:
ART4SPACE
Saturday, May 17th, 2014
18:30 / 19:30 / 20:30 / 21:30
Free admission

UPLINK
Totsune Building 1F
37-18 Udagawa Cho
Shibuya-ku, Tokyo
T: 03.6825.5503

ローソン
UPLINK
セブンイレブン
メガネスーパー
東急本店
ドンキホーテ
109
Q-front
渋谷駅

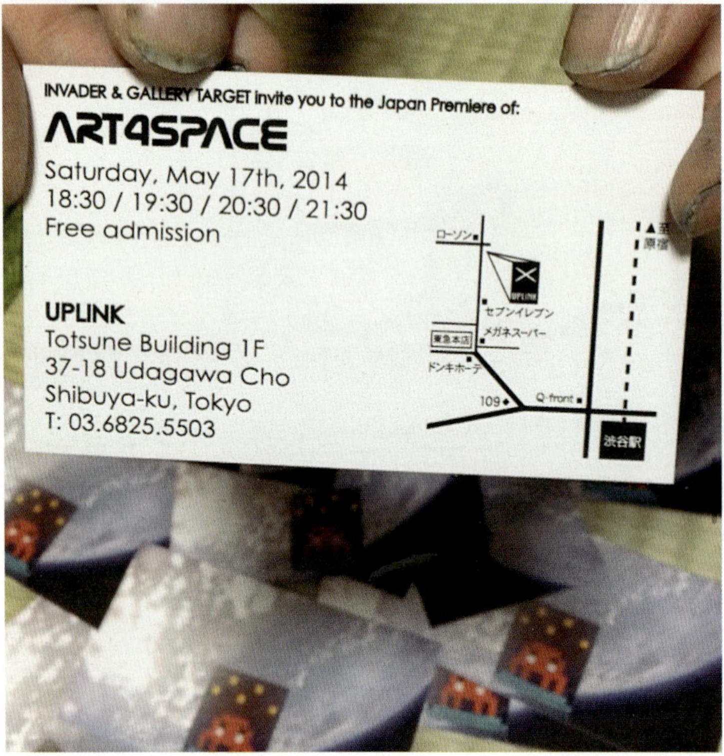

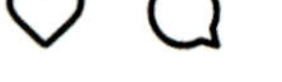

1522 likes

invaderwashere #Art4Space movie / Tokyo screening / next Saturday / more info: www.uplink.co.jp and www.gallery-target.com

View all 34 comments

15 May 2014

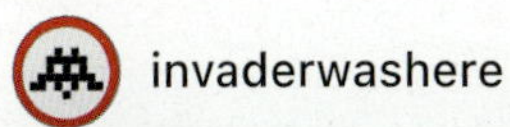

invaderwashere

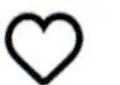   

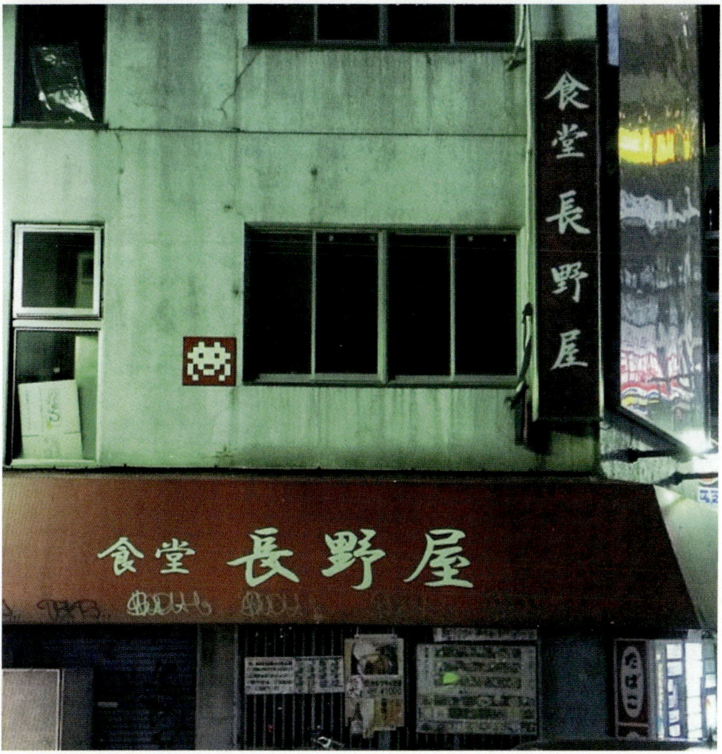

3 446 likes

invaderwashere TK_114 #justdone in #shinjuku

View all 37 comments

15 May 2014

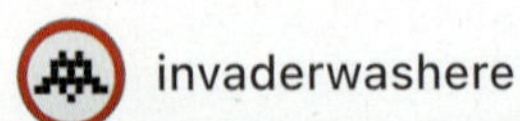

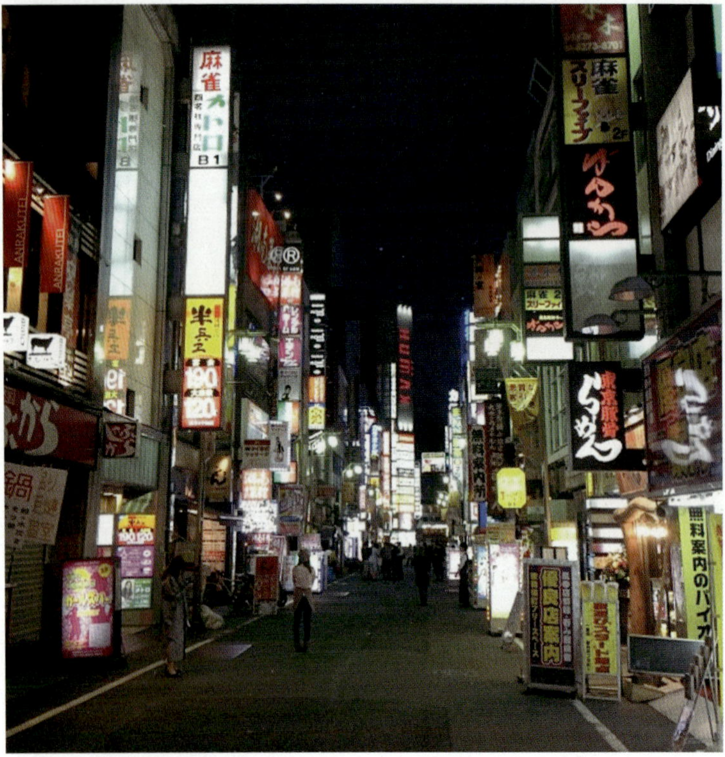

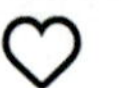   

3 072 likes

invaderwashere #Tokyo la nuit... #tokyoatnight

View all 32 comments

15 May 2014

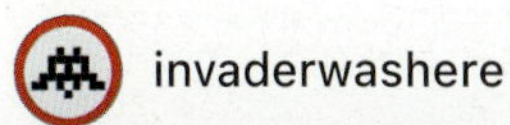

invaderwashere •••

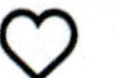   

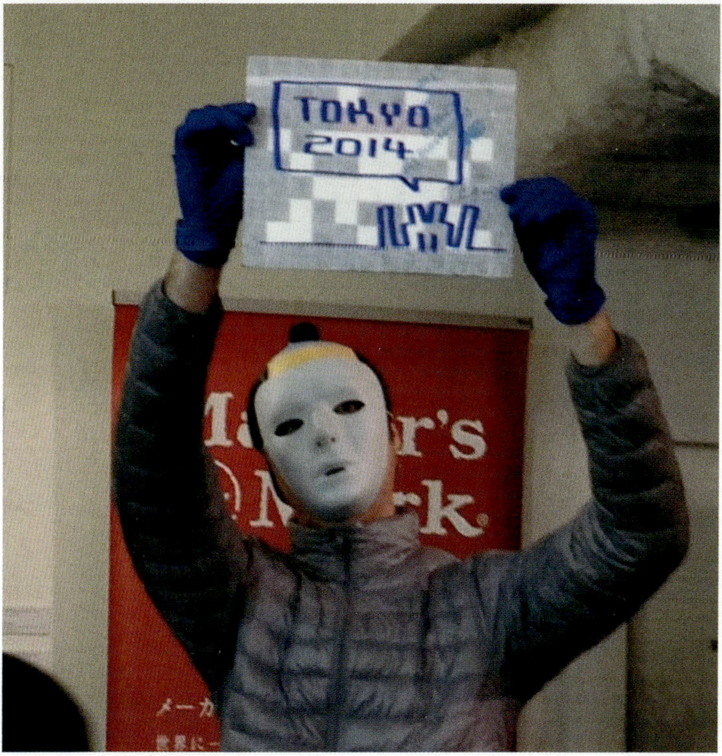

2 464 likes

invaderwashere Screening of #Art4Space & Happening at Uplink / #Invader 2014 / photo by @takazui #uplink

View all 29 comments

17 May 2014

invaderwashere

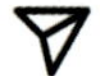

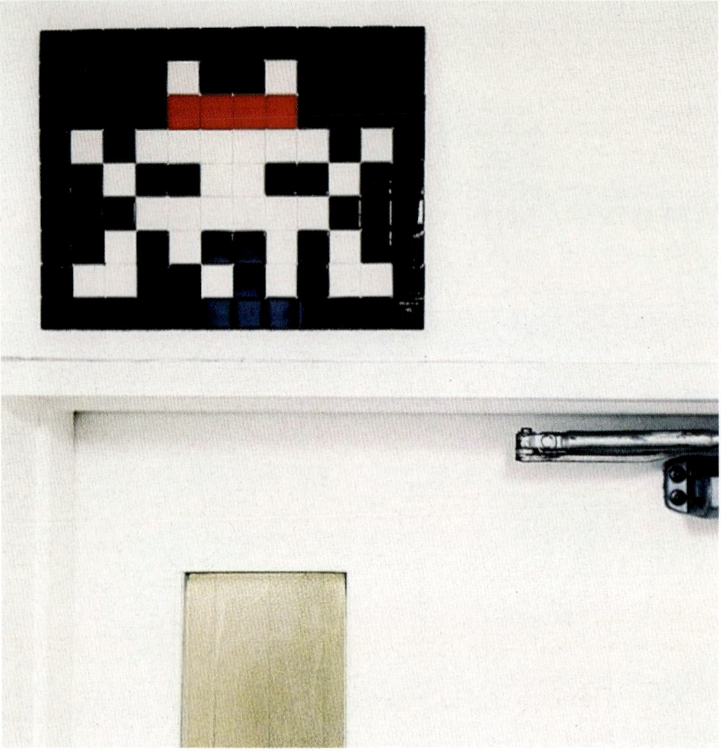

3146 likes

invaderwashere TK_115 #uplink #tokyo / photo by @hkdtmy

View all 17 comments

17 May 2014

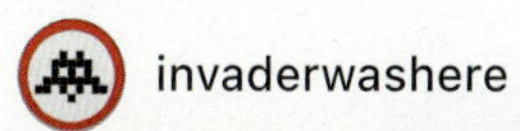

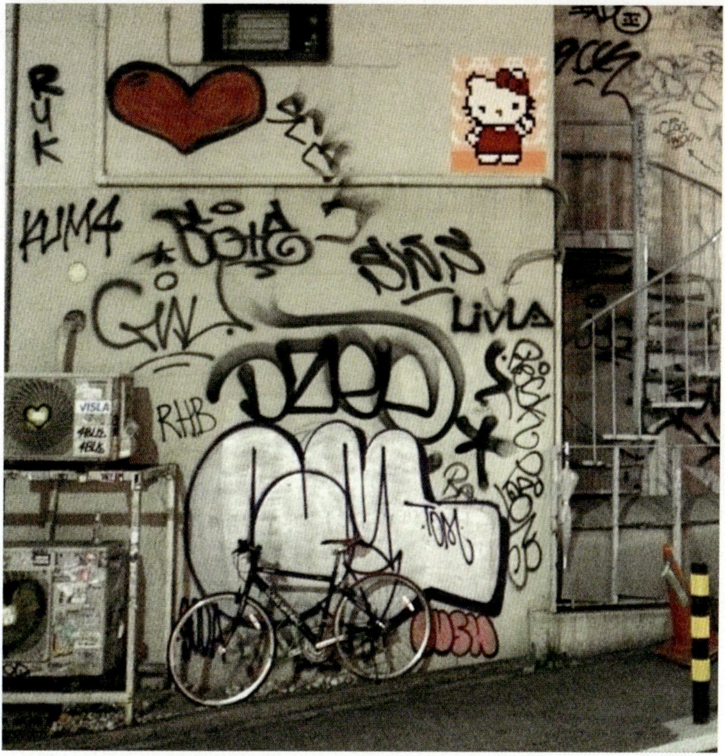

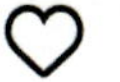   

4 434 likes

invaderwashere Invaded #HelloKitty and #Tokyo graffities / just made in Harajuku

View all 144 comments

18 May 2014

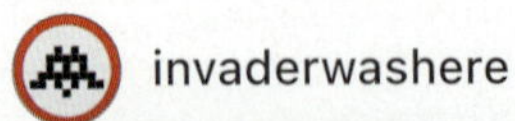

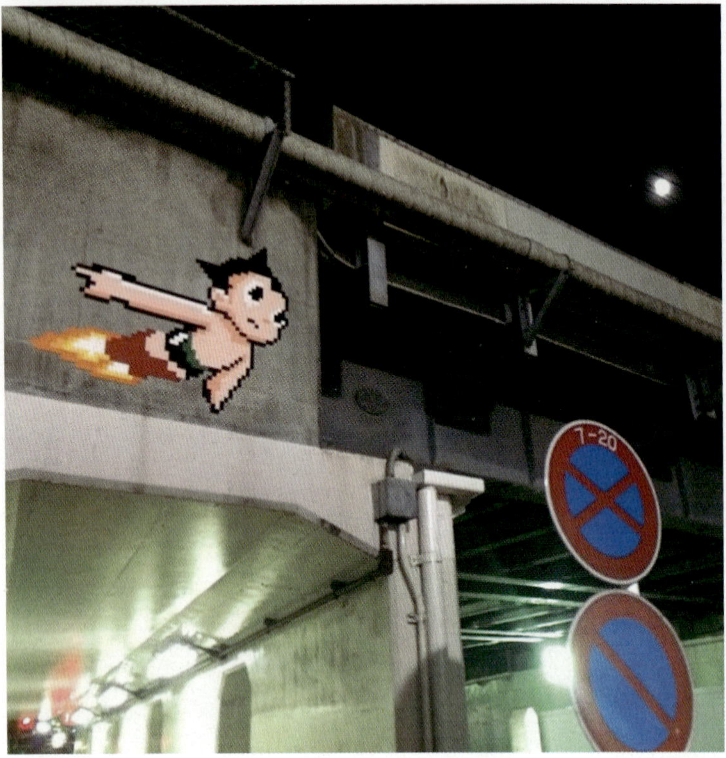

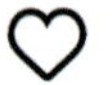   

7796 likes

invaderwashere Fly me to the moon #Astroboy / Just made in #Tokyo #masterpiece

View all 203 comments

18 May 2014

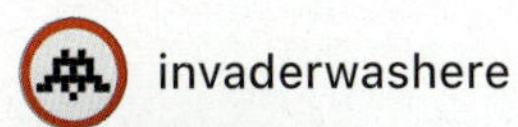

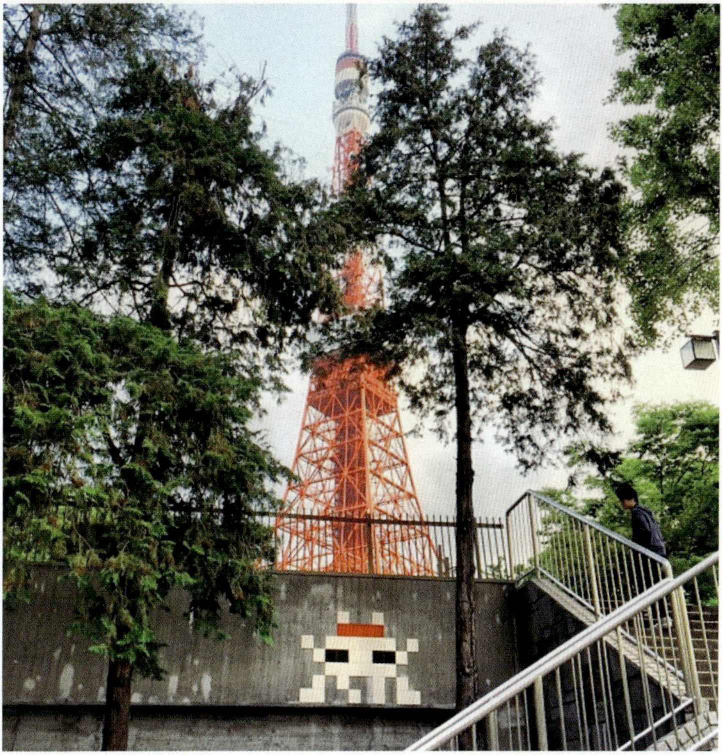

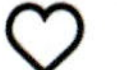 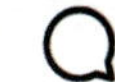  

3652 likes

invaderwashere 4:30am #Sunrise in #Tokyo / 9th
#SpaceInvader of the night... #ninja #tokyotower

View all 29 comments

18 May 2014

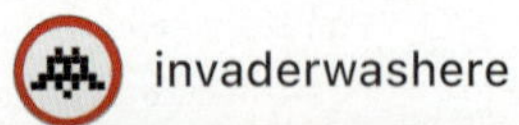

invaderwashere •••

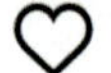   

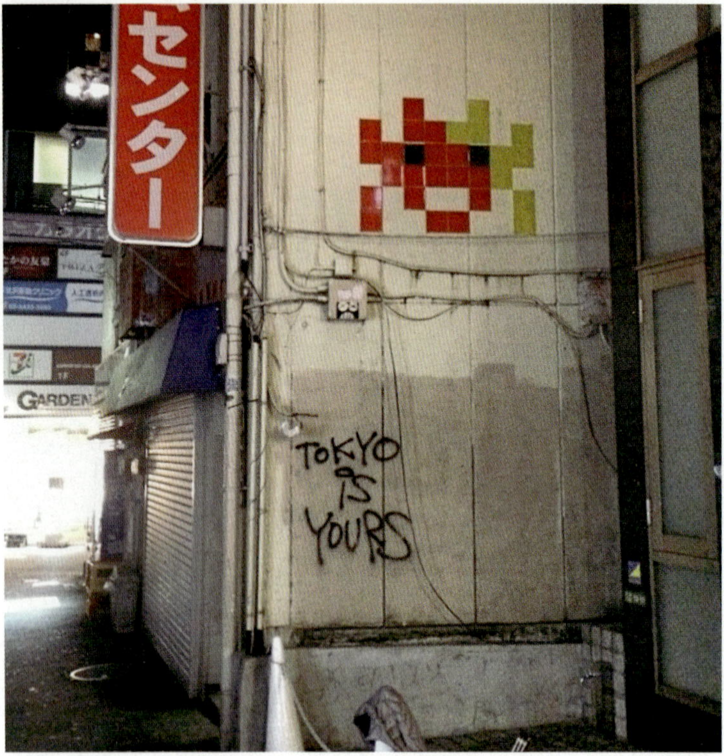

3752 likes

invaderwashere Tokyo is mine! #tuna #wasabi #spaceinvader #shimokita

View all 34 comments

19 May 2014

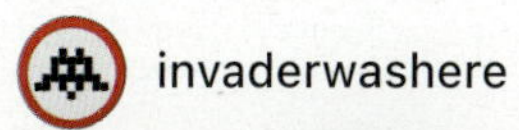

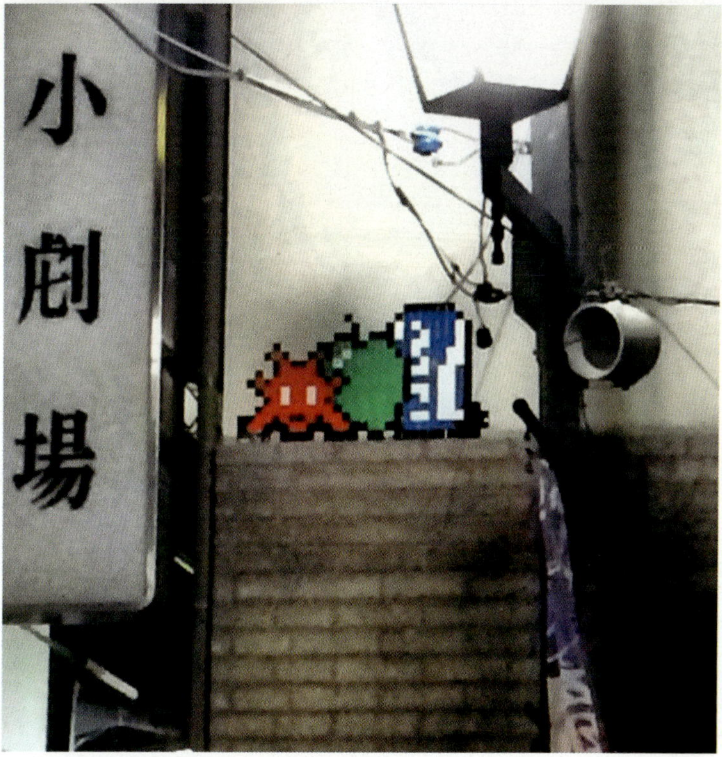

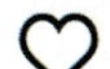   

3721 likes

invaderwashere Still life with #Pocari can / fresh from last night #tokyo

View all 30 comments

19 May 2014

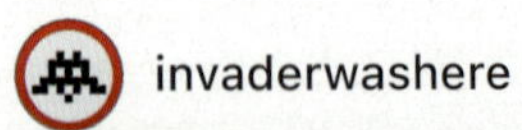

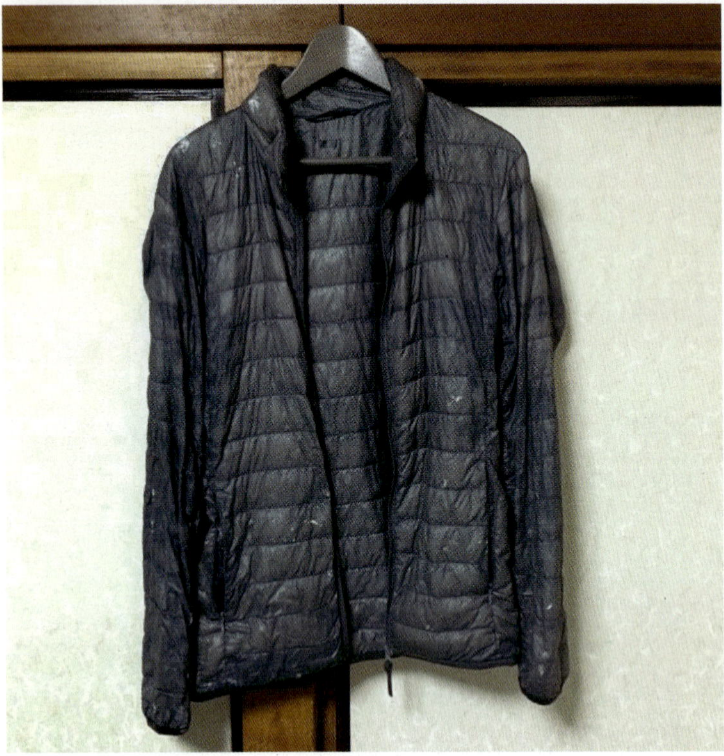

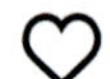   

969 likes

invaderwashere Wet coat after a big rain 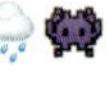
#backtothebase

View all 18 comments

21 May 2014

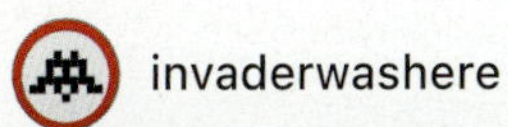

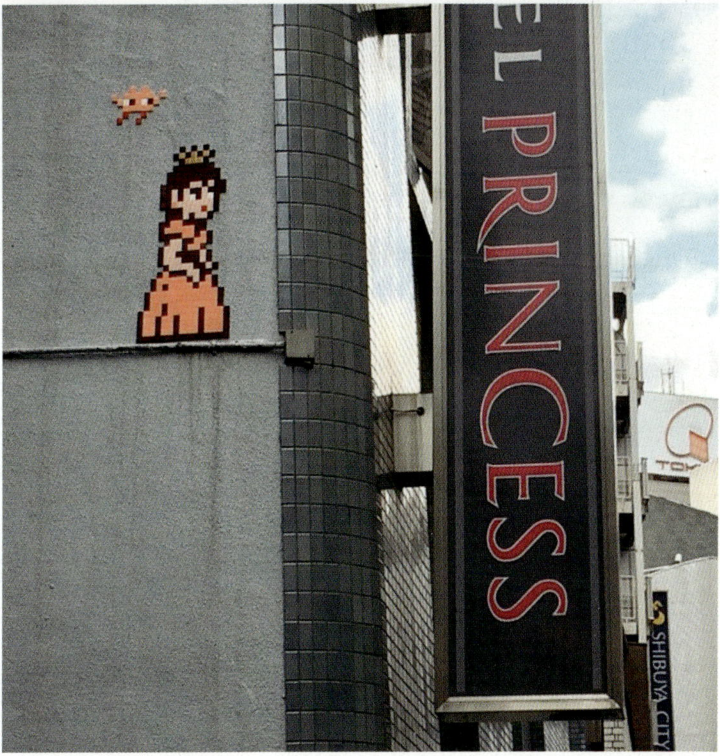

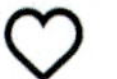   

6165 likes

invaderwashere TK_121 Hotel Princess #lovehotel #shibuya #peachyprincess #tokyo 2014

View all 152 comments

22 May 2014

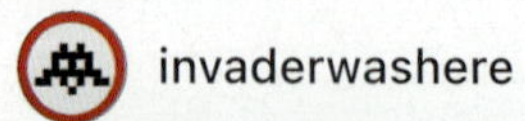

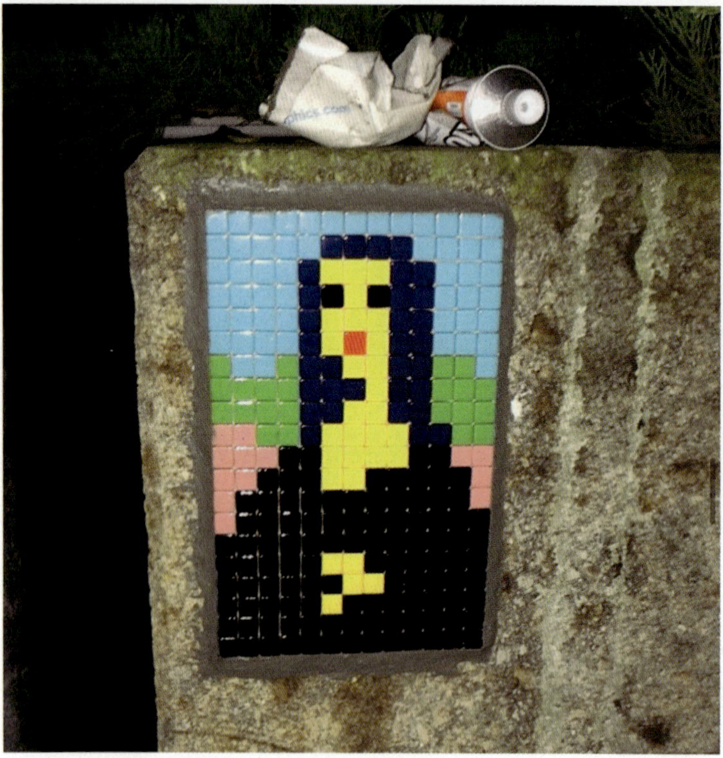

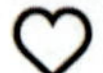 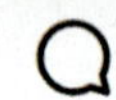  

7180 likes

invaderwashere Life and death of Low-res Mona Lisa... It was removed in the morning! 😢😢😢 #daykanyamagarden

View all 131 comments

23 May 2014

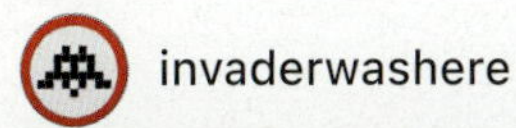

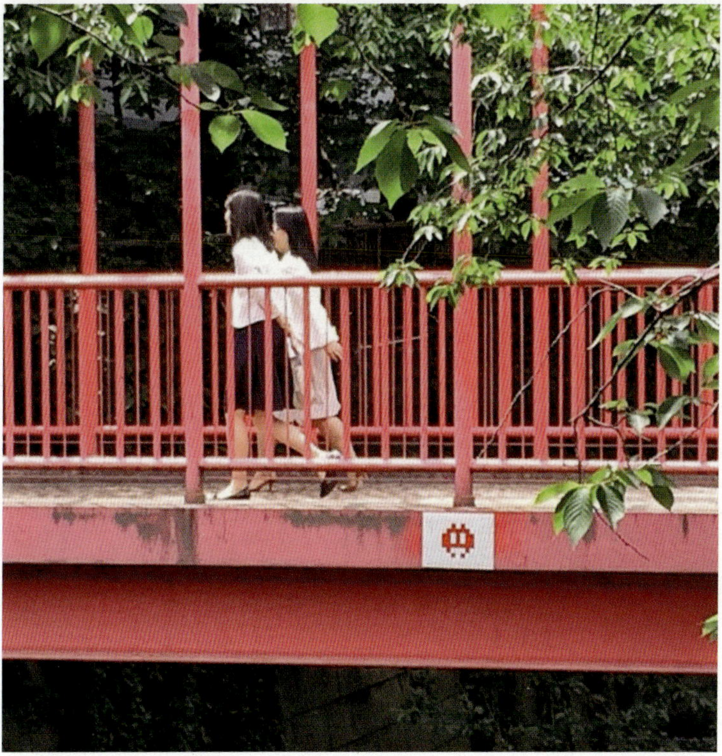

3182 likes

invaderwashere TK_96 / Naka meguro / Invaded Japanese flag #tokyo

View all 22 comments

23 May 2014

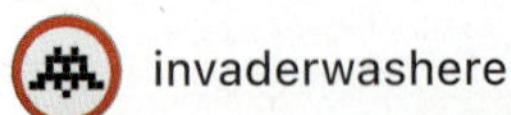
invaderwashere

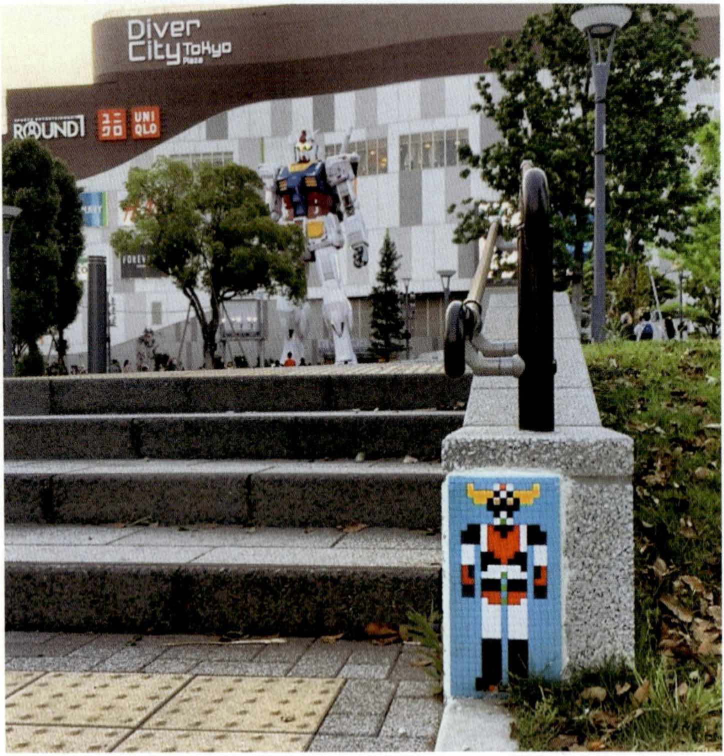

•••

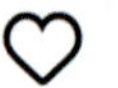  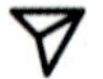 

6 749 likes

invaderwashere #grendizer & #gundam #robots #japan

View all 120 comments

24 May 2014

invaderwashere •••

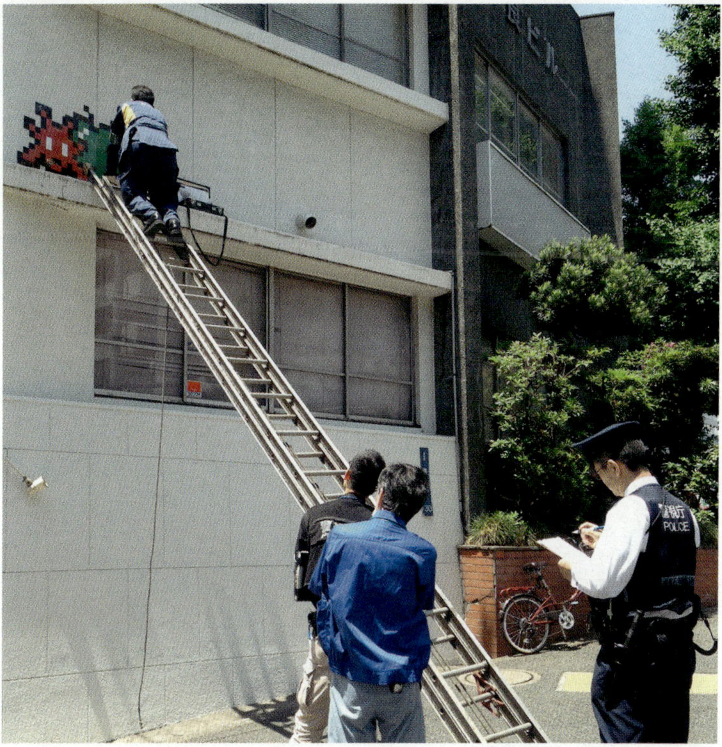

5 992 likes

invaderwashere Tokyo police looking for my finger prints! Time to leave soon... Photo by @sasu_lyri

View all 46 comments

25 May 2014

invaderwashere ...

 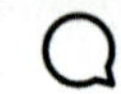  

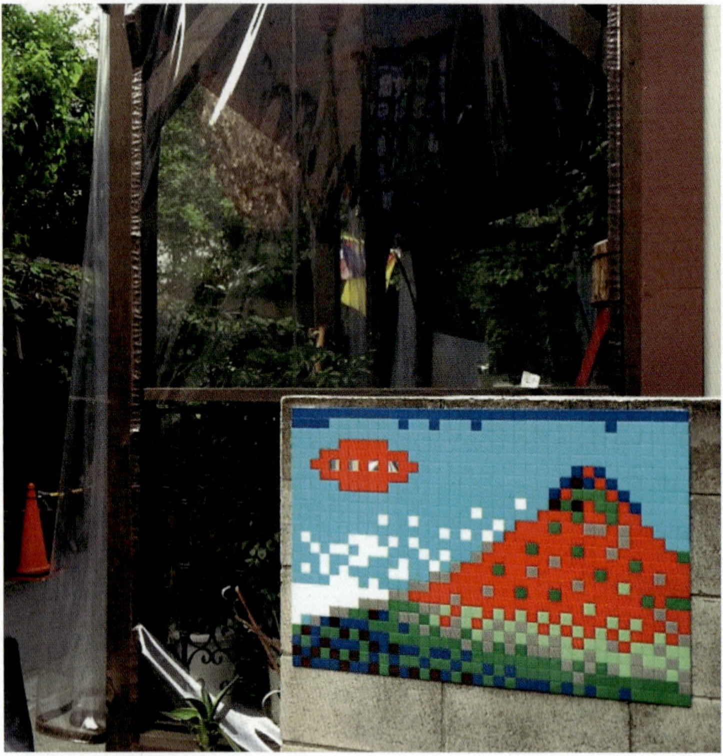

5019 likes

invaderwashere 4:48am last of the night #fuji #fujiyama #mothership #hokusai #tokyo

View all 76 comments

25 May 2014

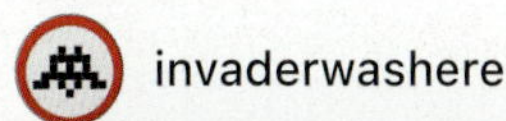

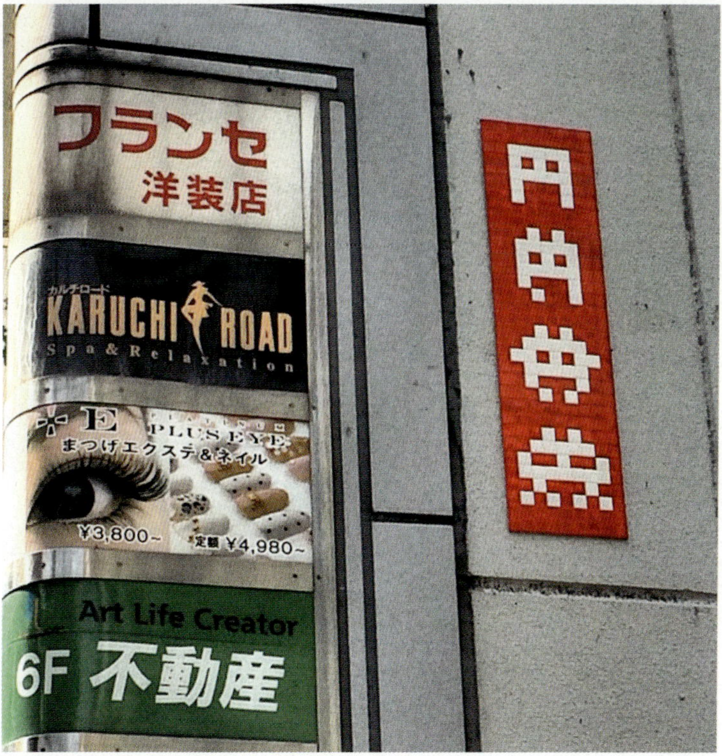

5236 likes

invaderwashere From #Yen to #spaceinvader

View all 68 comments

27 May 2014

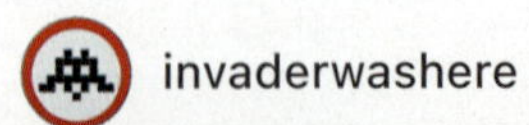

•••

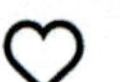   

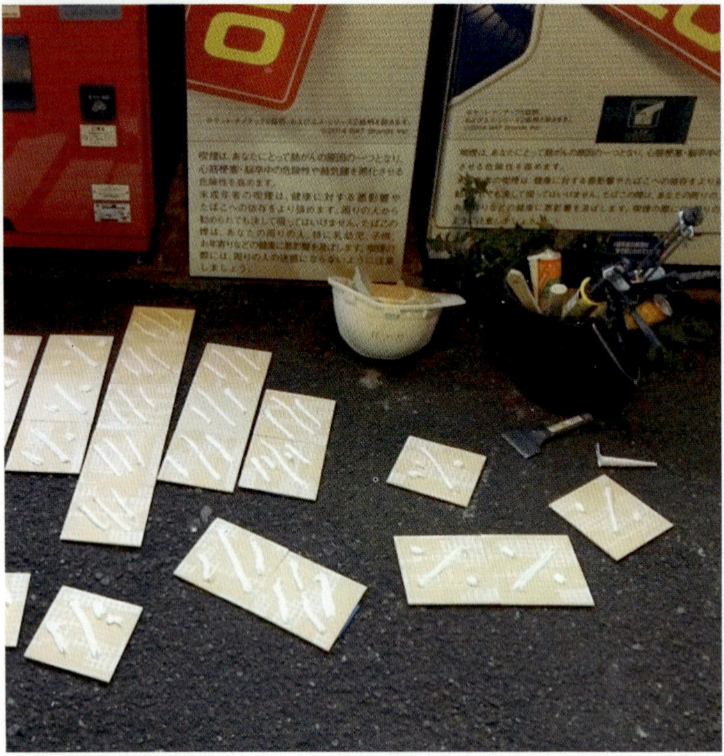

2 002 likes

invaderwashere Making of TK_112 #Ebisu #Tokyo #Japan

View all 16 comments

28 May 2014

invaderwashere

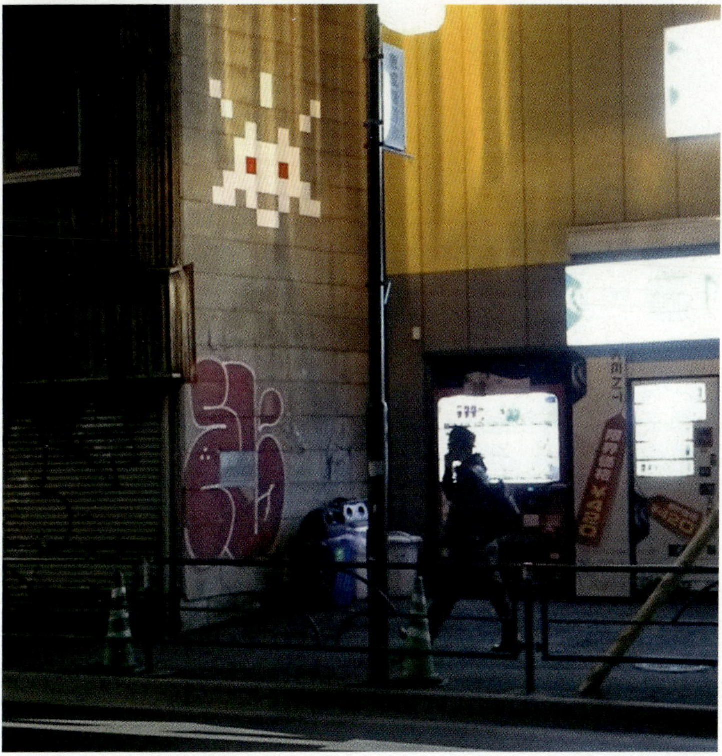

4121 likes

invaderwashere TK_112 made in #Ebisu #Tokyo

View all 31 comments

28 May 2014

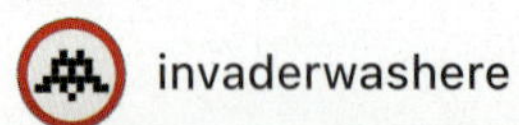
invaderwashere •••

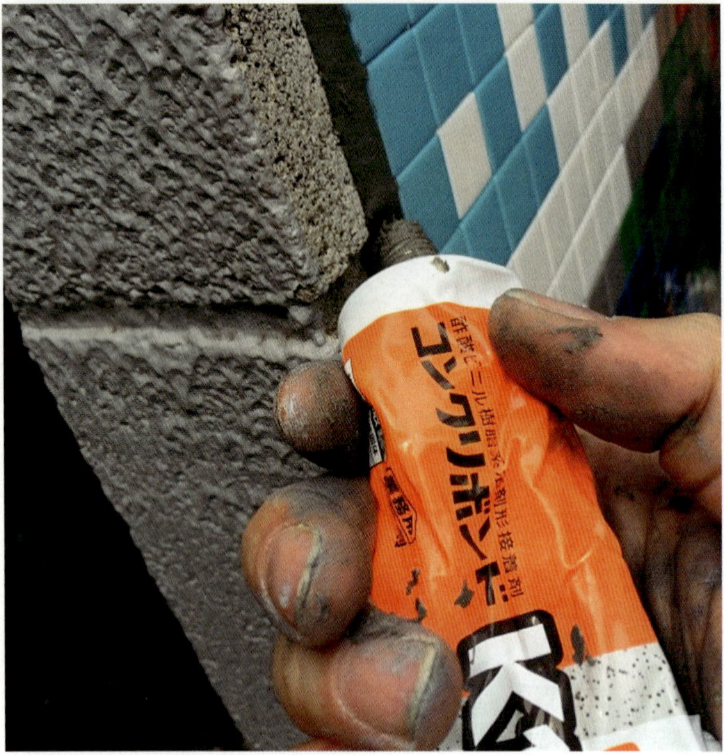

4 224 likes

invaderwashere Finishing TK_136 using japanese glue
#K10 #dirtyhands

View all 46 comments

29 May 2014

invaderwashere •••

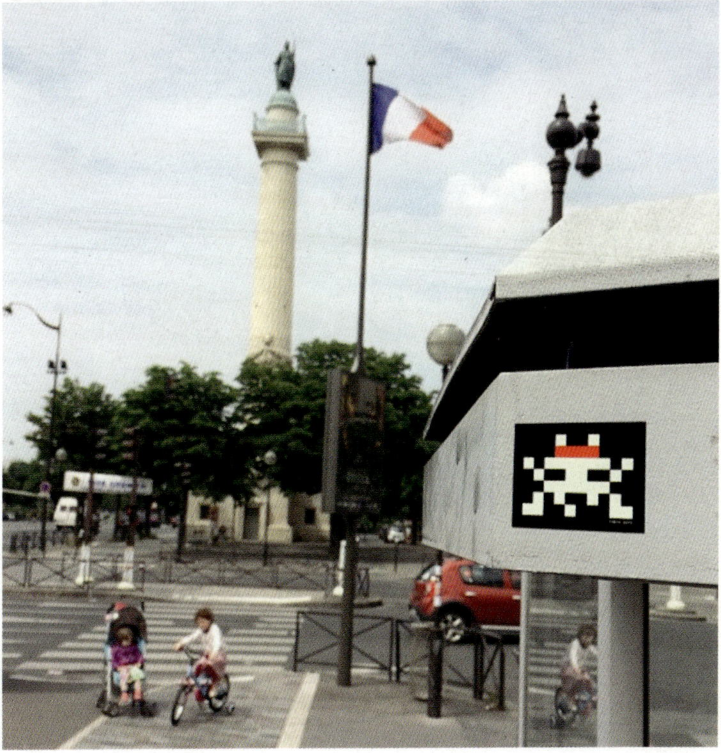

4269 likes

invaderwashere Back in #Paris #spaceNinja #Sticker #glowinthedark #nation

View all 55 comments

1 June 2014

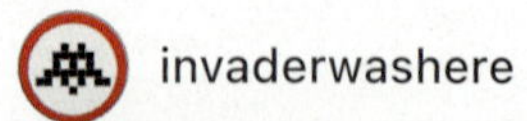

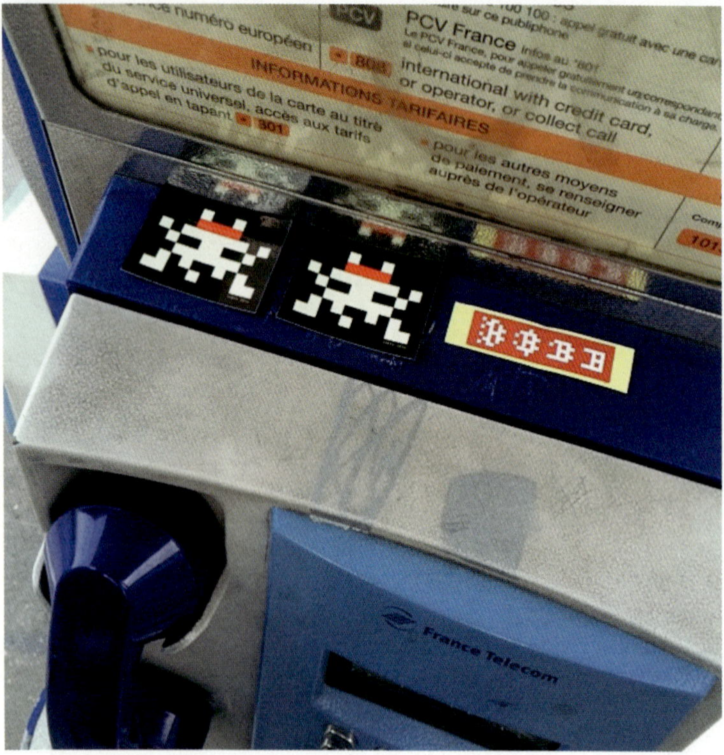

 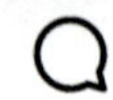  

3 595 likes

invaderwashere Je viens de déposer 3 stickers japonais dans la cabine téléphonique de mon post précédent. A vos marques, prêts... #jeu #stickers #forfree #paris

View all 53 comments

2 June 2014

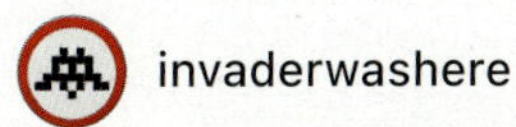

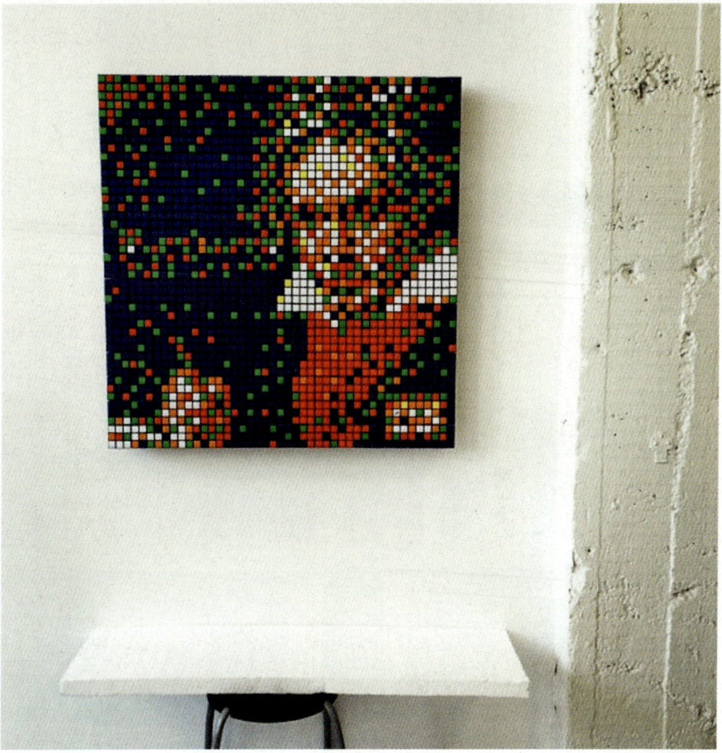

4 858 likes

invaderwashere Unlike vinyl albums recorded in high fidelity, Rubikcubism degrades images by lowering their resolution and restricting their palette to six colours, hence this series of album covers is called: Rubik Low Fidelity. Rubik Von Beethoven #studiodetail #beethoven #rubikcubism #rubikcubisme #lowfidelity

View all 84 comments

6 June 2014

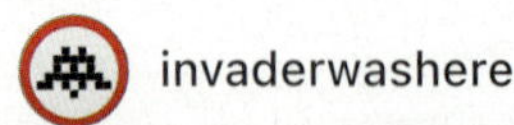

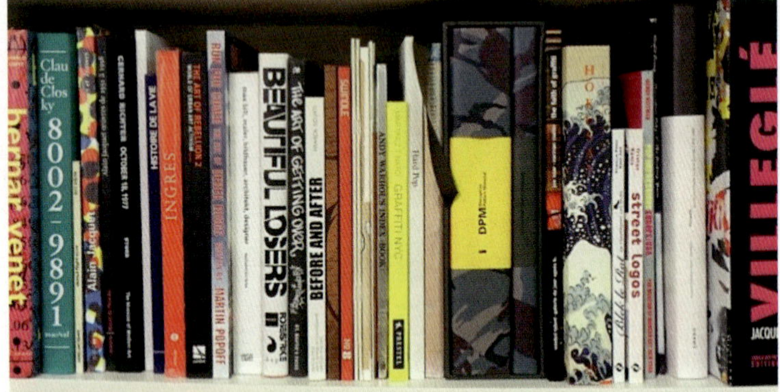

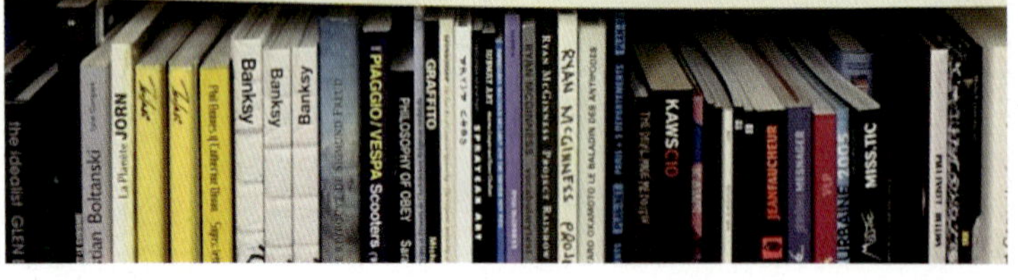

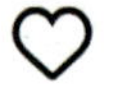

2 259 likes

invaderwashere I 🧡 artbooks #shelfie #detail

View all 32 comments

8 June 2014

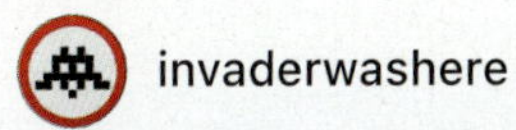

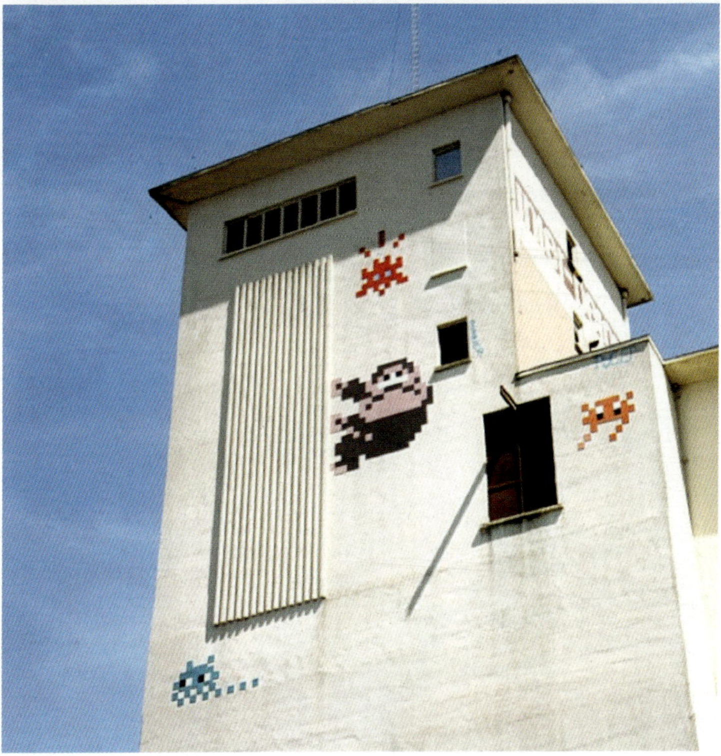

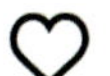 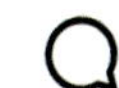  

6 531 likes

invaderwashere A new piece from my 1% legal! #publiccommission #charleroi #belgium #asphaltBiennale #Alicegallery #donkeykong & #spaceinvaders

View all 92 comments

18 June 2014

invaderwashere

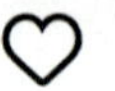

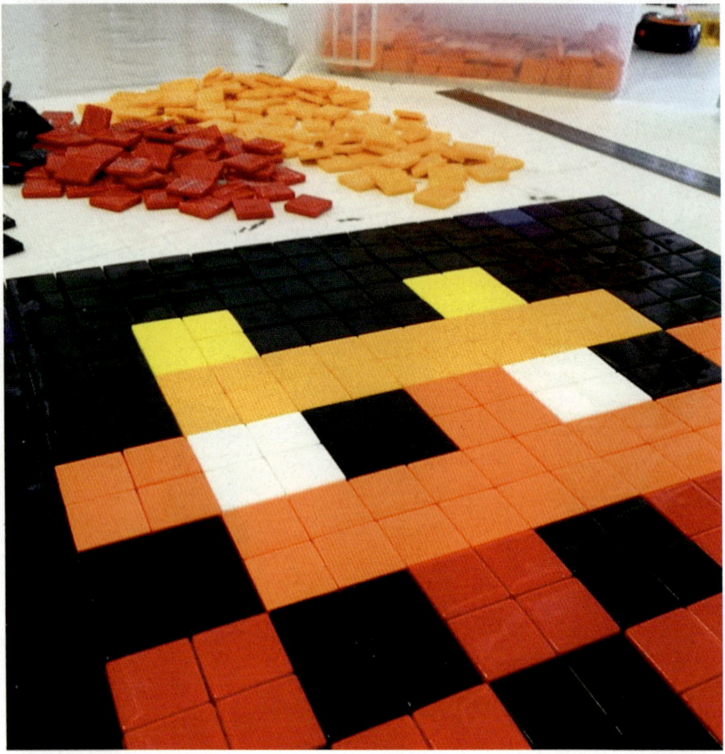

4901 likes

invaderwashere Studio detail

View all 52 comments

26 June 2014

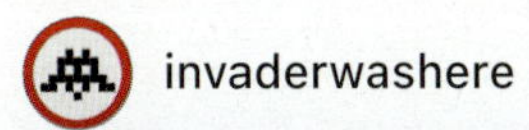

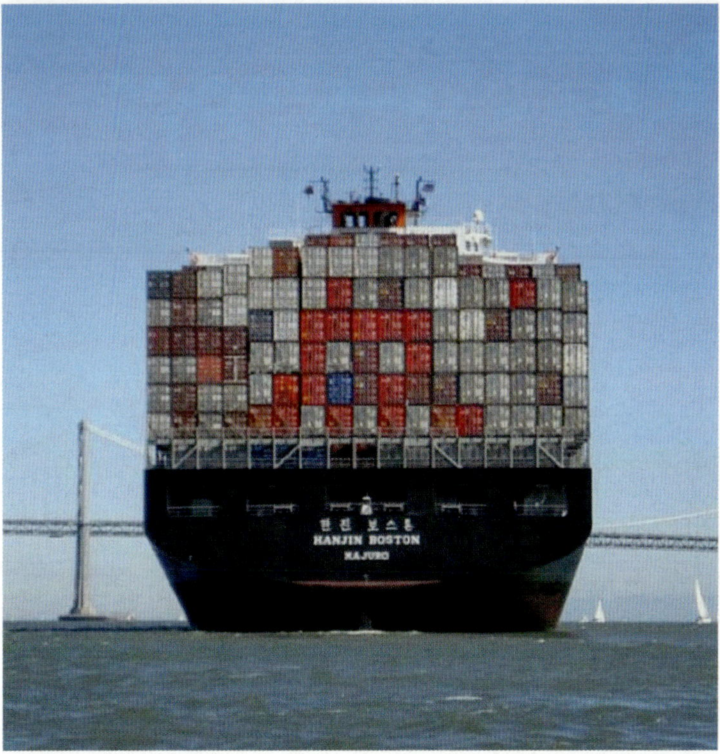

10 319 likes

invaderwashere An old project from 2010 #pixel #containers #spaceinvader #bucketlist

View all 307 comments

29 June 2014

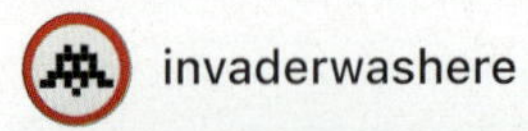

•••

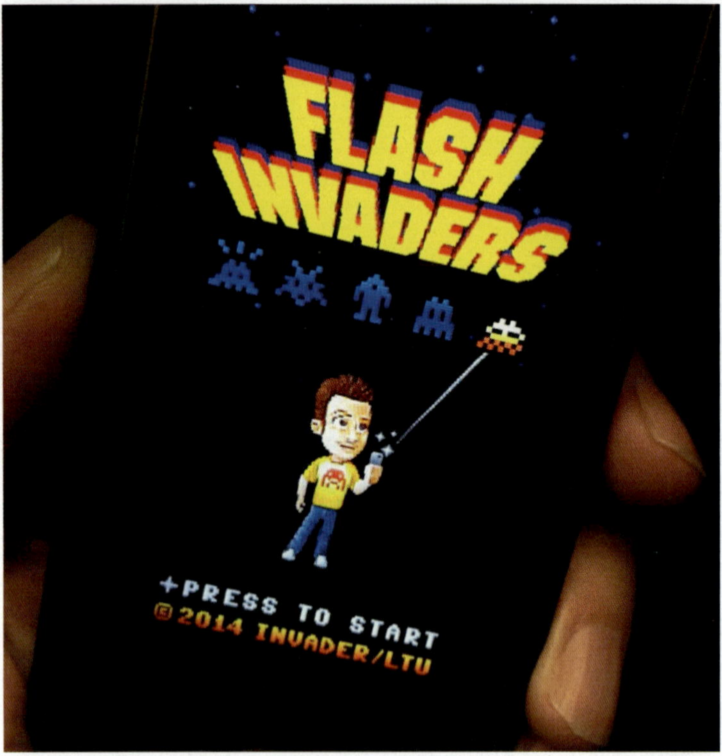

3 199 likes

invaderwashere FlashInvaders for iOS and Android. Coming soon... #flashinvaders #invader #app #realitygame #smartphone

View all 68 comments

1 July 2014

invaderwashere •••

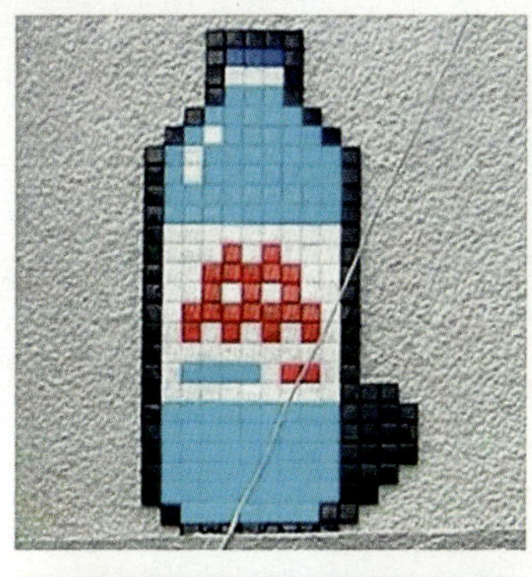
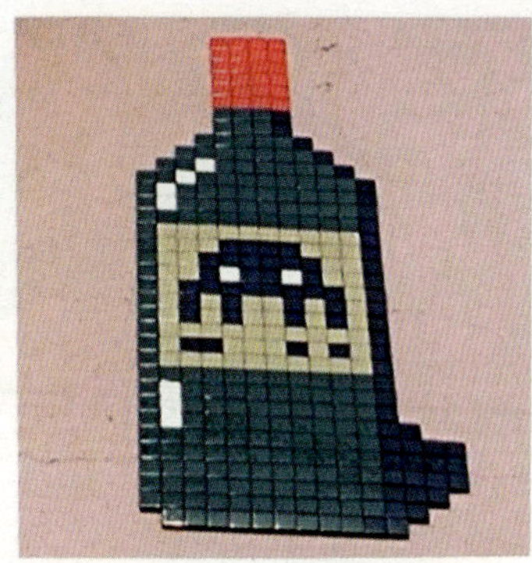
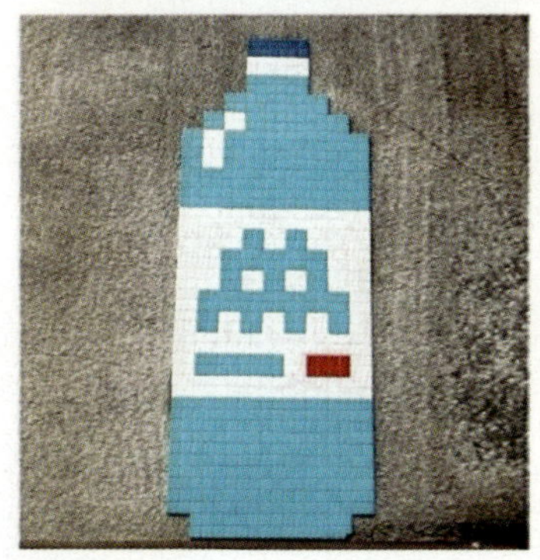
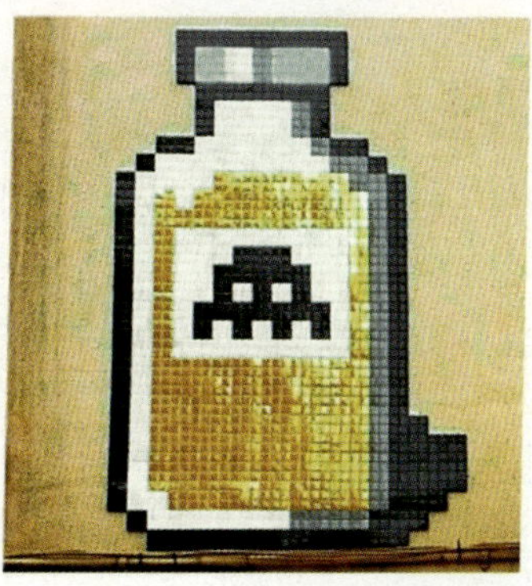

7197 likes

invaderwashere Pictures by @cocainsta123 #spacebottles #tokyo #8bits

View all 59 comments

4 July 2014

invaderwashere 

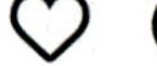 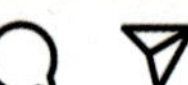  

2 379 likes

invaderwashere Signing a new print for The Provocateurs curated by Shepard Fairey #chicago #artalliance #silkscreenprint @obeygiant

View all 27 comments

10 July 2014

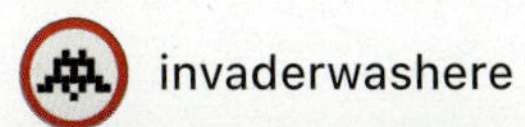

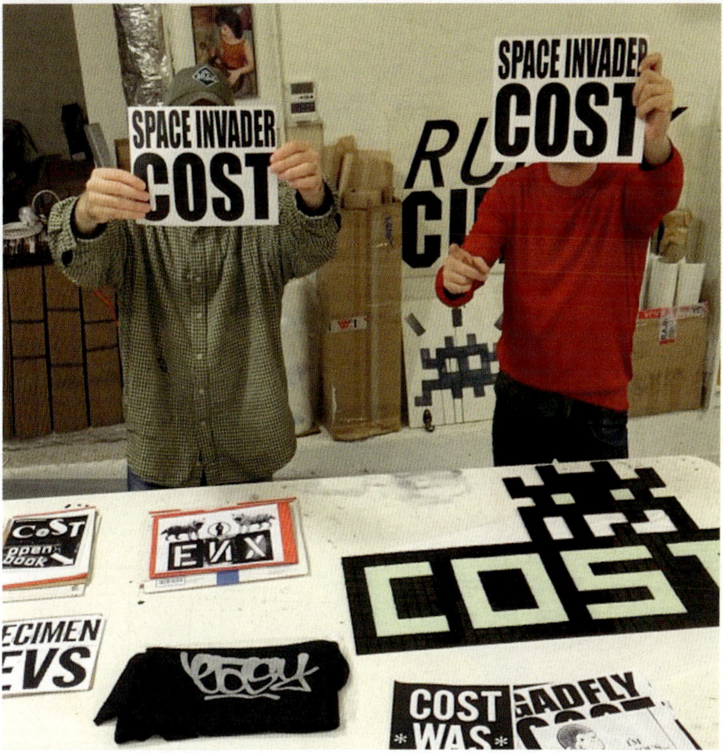

 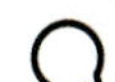  

2 674 likes

invaderwashere Cost is in the place... #paris #studio #cost #enx #revs @costkrt

View all 43 comments

13 July 2014

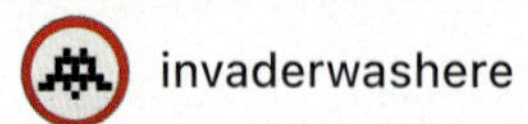

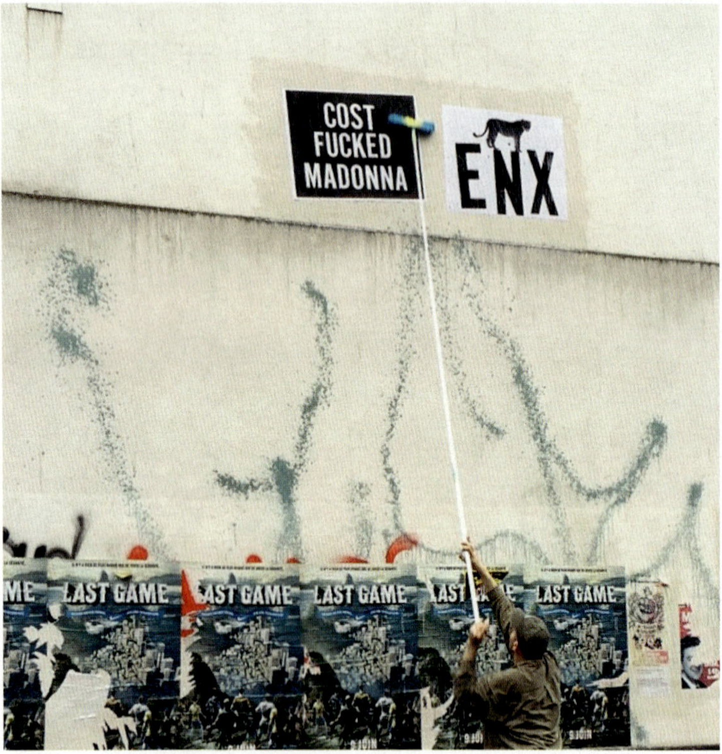

2 615 likes

invaderwashere Cost at work #paris #6am @enx108 @costkrt #costfuckedmadonna

View all 22 comments

13 July 2014

invaderwashere ...

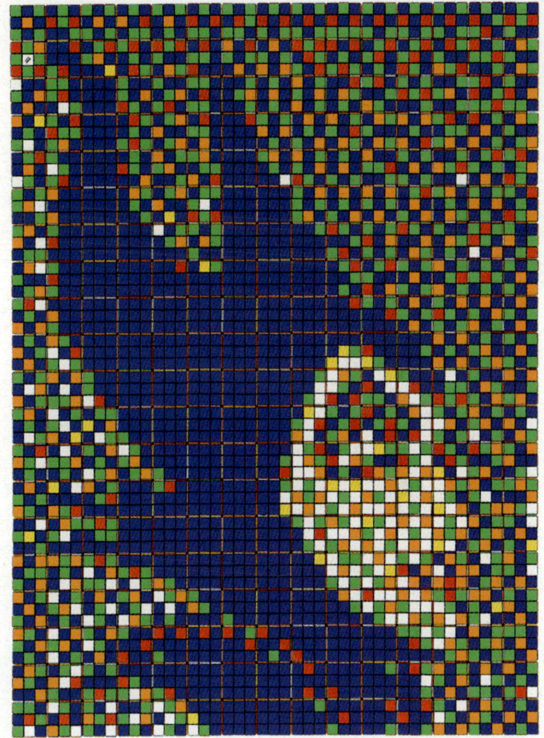

5840 likes

invaderwashere The Rubik Bad Men series is a collection of portraits of real-life or fictional villains. I particularly like the contrast between the dark nature of the subject matter and the flashy pop colours of the Rubik's Cubes. Rubik Maleficent / 2005 #rubikcubism #maleficent #rubikbadmen #rubikcubism

View all 173 comments

15 July 2014

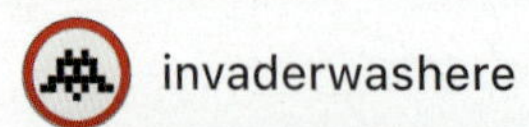

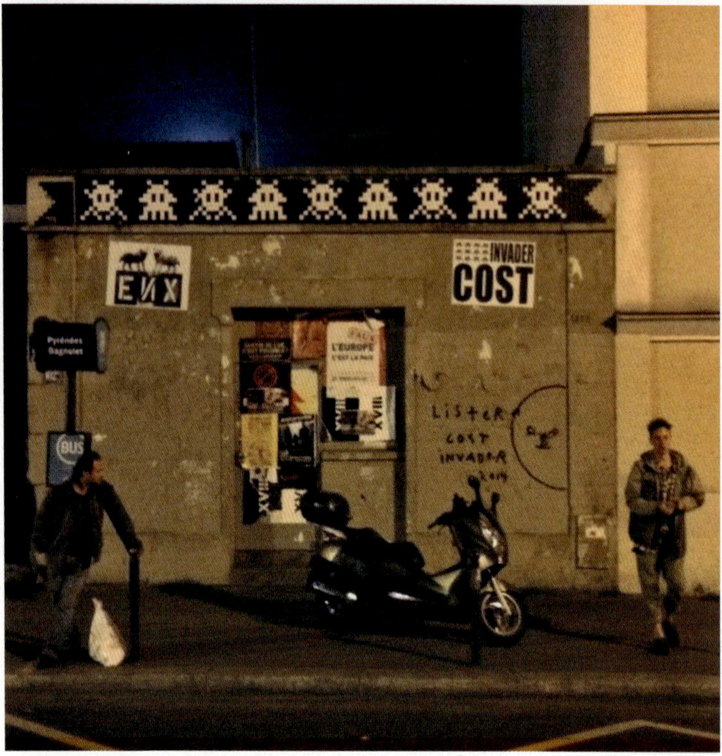

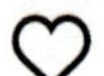   

3 553 likes

invaderwashere International gang of vandals 🌗
@anthonylister @costkrt @enx @invaderwashere
#streetbombers #paris July 15th 2014

View all 26 comments

15 July 2014

invaderwashere ...

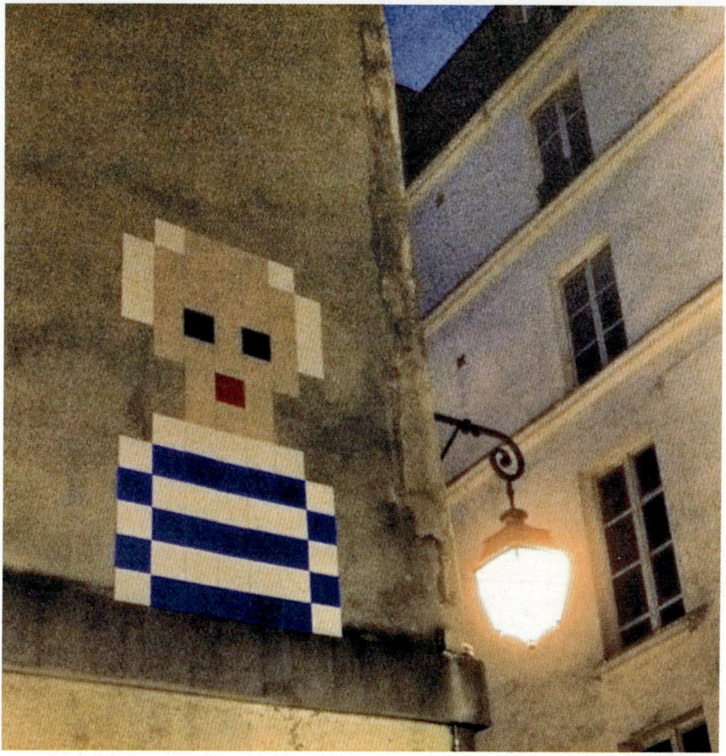

6729 likes

invaderwashere Low-res #Picasso / In front of musée Picasso / Paris / 4th piece of the night

View all 115 comments

16 July 2014

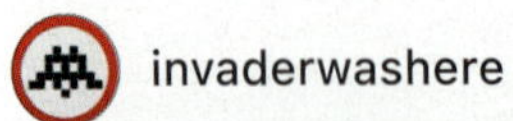

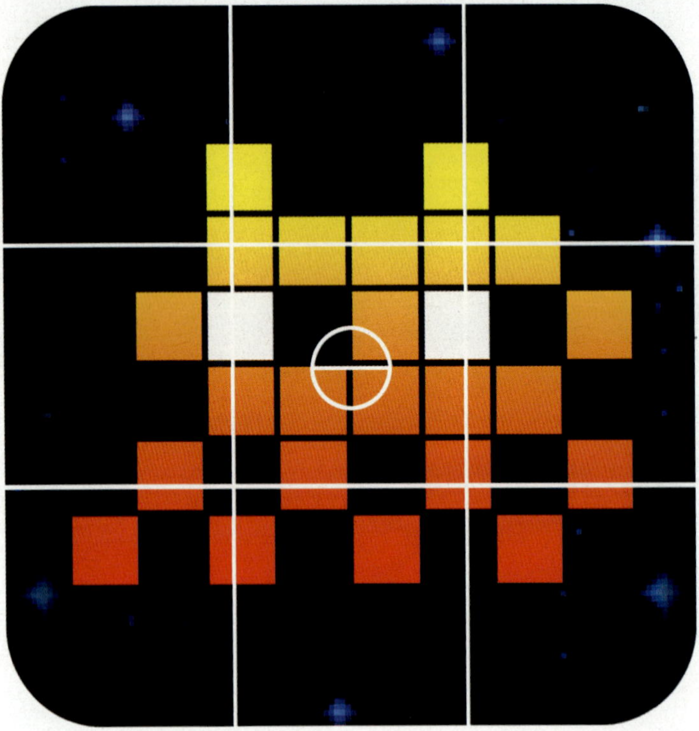

2480 likes

invaderwashere Flashinvaders is now available on Appstore and Googleplay. This free app combines virtual technologies and the real world in a global game to track down my mosaics. Good luck & have fun. #freeApp #realitygame #iphone #android #LTUtechnologies #interactivart

View all 50 comments

20 July 2014

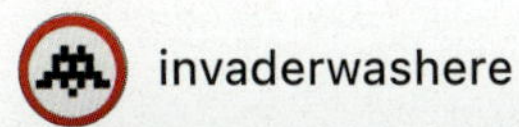

HIGHSCORES

RANK	PLAYER	FOUND	SCORE
01	OLIVIERTOF	94	2860
02	RIEN_DE_NO···	78	2670
03	NALICE_MAL···	62	2140
04	COCA123	55	1980
05	UN OEIL QUI···	55	1700
06	ADRIEN	45	1630
07	PAUL (STREE···	36	1340
08	TIDENIS TOF···	45	1230

1295 likes

invaderwashere A very good start for #flashinvaders. More than 1000 downloads in 24 hrs and some amazing players.

View all 50 comments

21 July 2014

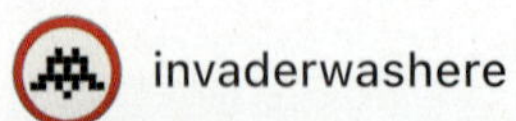

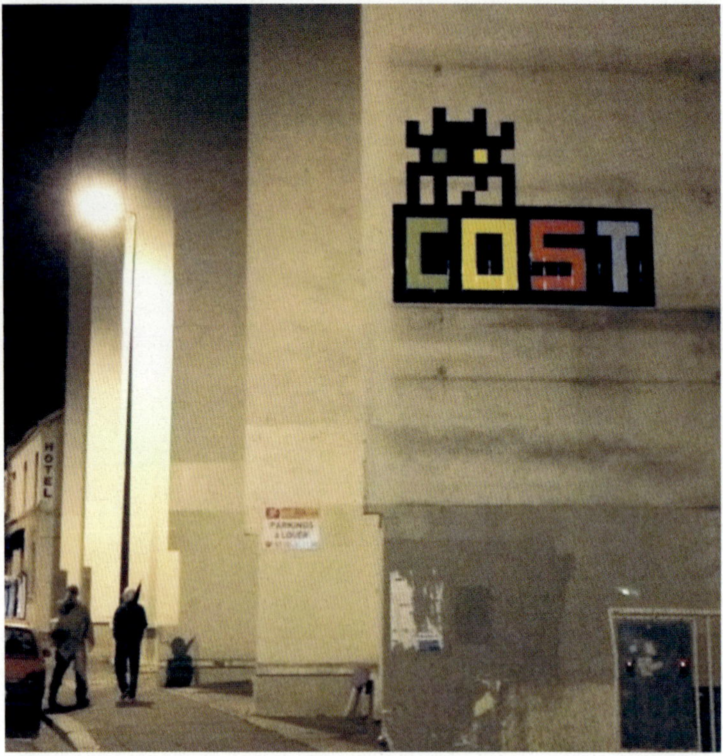

5403 likes

invaderwashere Just done with Cost / 100pts! #Paris #collab #legend @cost

View all 59 comments

24 July 2014

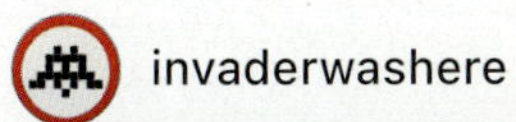

•••

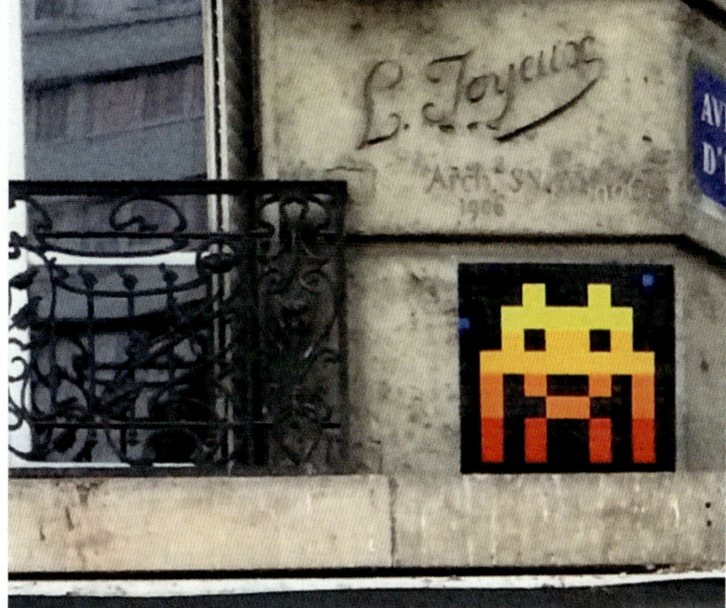

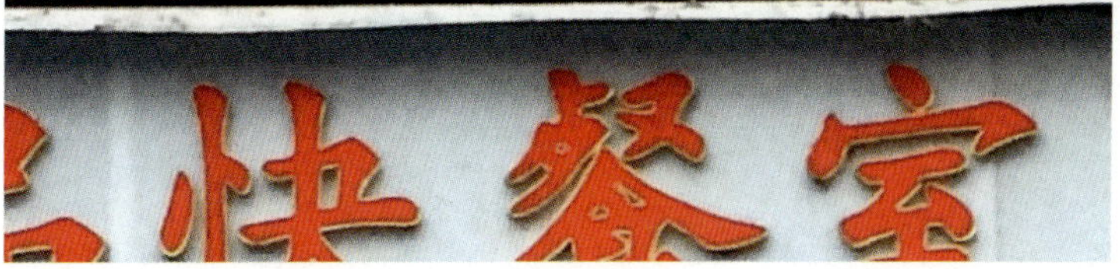

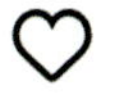   

5125 likes

invaderwashere 5 new pieces last night. #paris

View all 84 comments

25 July 2014

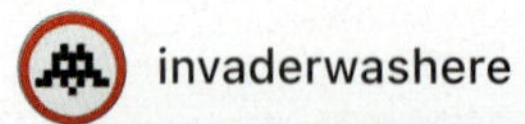

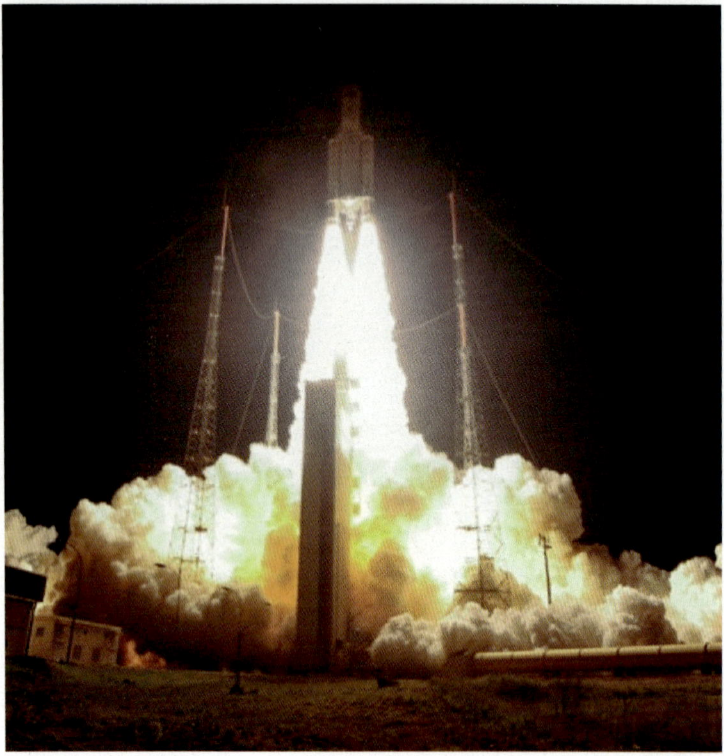

2682 likes

invaderwashere Europe's Spaceport in Kourou, French Guiana, 3 days ago. One of my mosaic is on board!!!! Follow this Spacecraft... Photo: ESA #GeorgesLemaitre #ATV #AutomatedTransferVehicle #SpaceTwo #art4space

View all 31 comments

1 August 2014

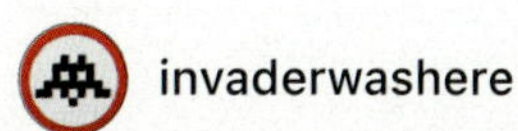
invaderwashere

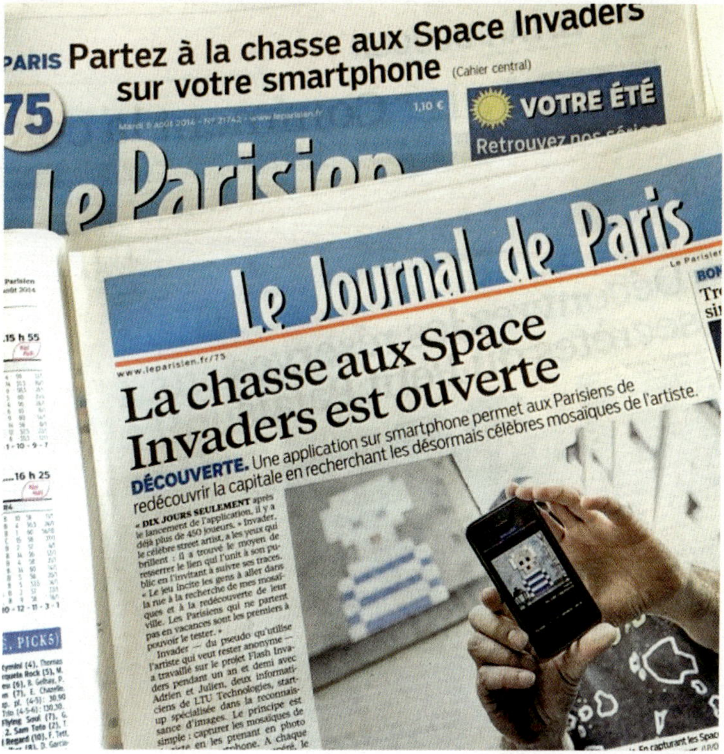

PARIS Partez à la chasse aux Space Invaders sur votre smartphone (Cahier central)

75

Le Parisien

VOTRE ÉTÉ

Le Journal de Paris

www.leparisien.fr/75

La chasse aux Space Invaders est ouverte

DÉCOUVERTE. Une application sur smartphone permet aux Parisiens de redécouvrir la capitale en recherchant les désormais célèbres mosaïques de l'artiste.

« DIX JOURS SEULEMENT après le lancement de l'application, il y a déjà plus de 450 joueurs. » Invader, le célèbre street artist, a les yeux qui brillent : il a trouvé le moyen de resserrer le lien qui l'unit à son public en l'invitant à suivre ses traces. « Le jeu incite les gens à aller dans la rue à la recherche de mes mosaïques et à la redécouverte de leur ville. Les Parisiens qui ne partent pas en vacances sont les premiers à pouvoir le tester. »

Invader — du pseudo qu'utilise l'artiste qui veut rester anonyme — a travaillé sur le projet Flash Invaders pendant un an et demi avec Adrien et Julien, deux informaticiens de LTU Technologies, start-up spécialisée dans la reconnaissance d'images. Le principe est simple : capturer les mosaïques de

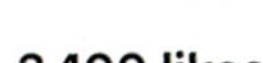

3499 likes

invaderwashere #FlashInvaders in #leParisien newspaper of today...

View all 79 comments

5 August 2014

invaderwashere •••

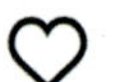   

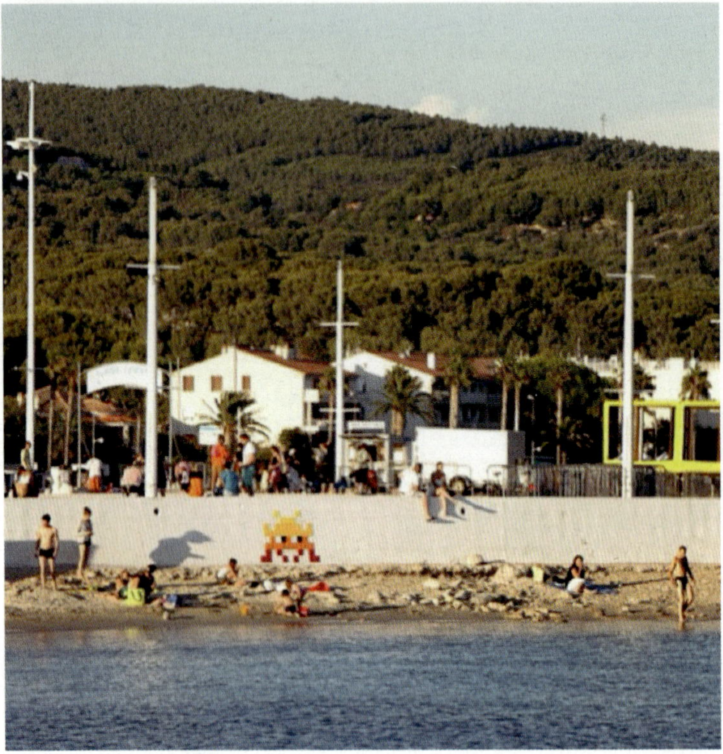

4038 likes

invaderwashere Summer Invader

View all 33 comments

19 August 2014

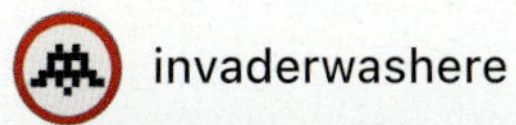

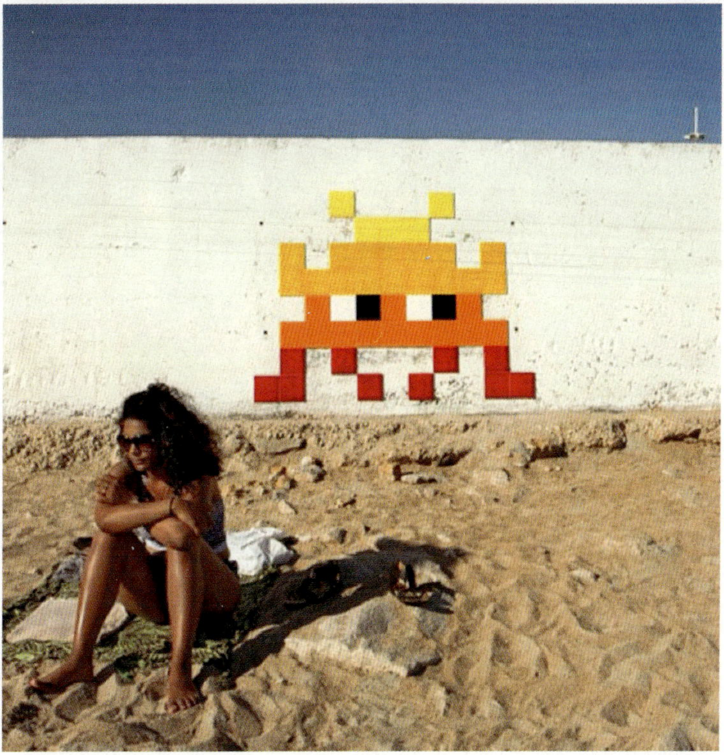

 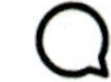 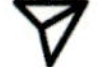 

7428 likes

invaderwashere Summer Invader / Close-up #beach #playa #laCiotat

View all 71 comments

19 August 2014

invaderwashere •••

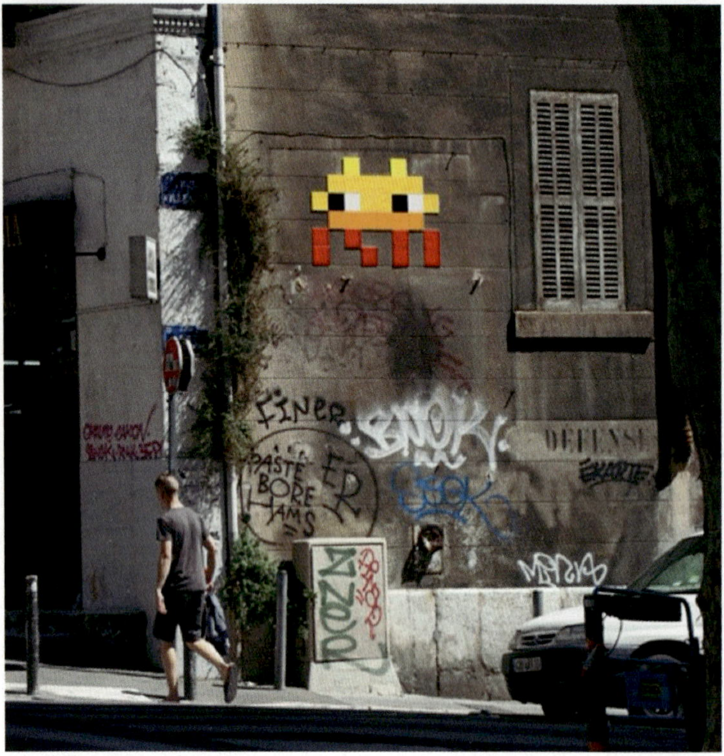

7037 likes

invaderwashere New piece in #Marseille

View all 86 comments

20 August 2014

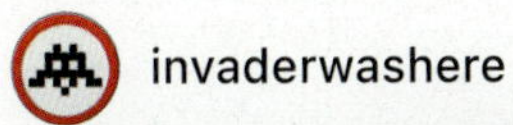

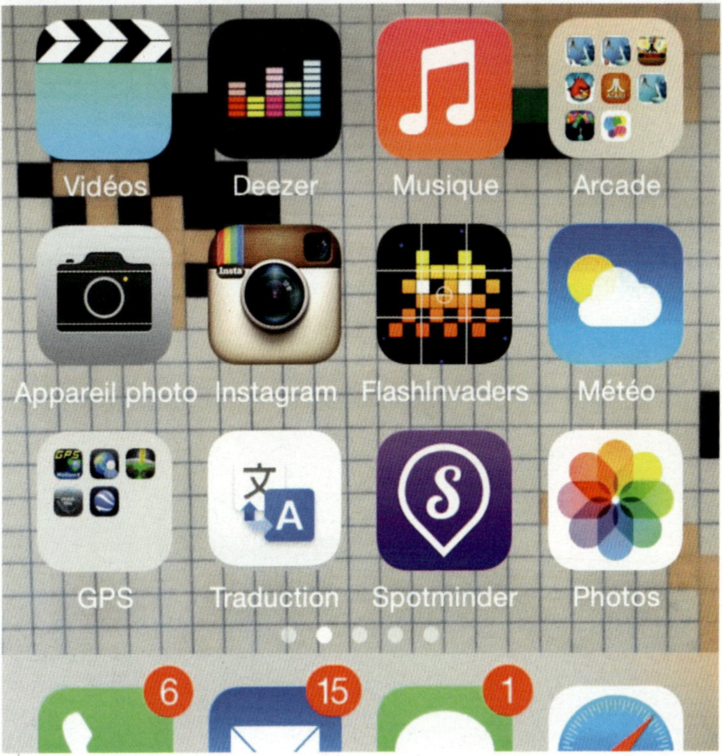

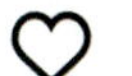   

2 124 likes

invaderwashere #Flashinvaders free app for #iOS and #android

View all 62 comments

30 August 2014

invaderwashere •••

  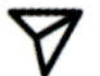 

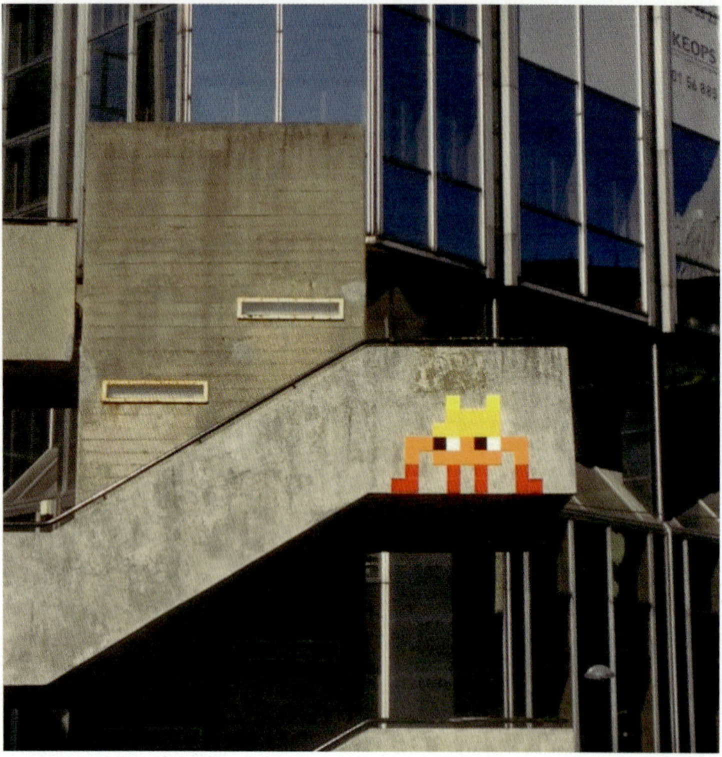

6139 likes

invaderwashere PA_1112 / Fresh from last night #paris #ladefense

View all 51 comments

10 September 2014

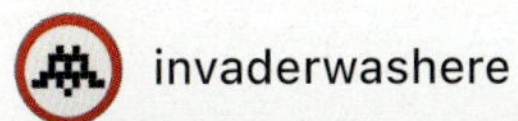

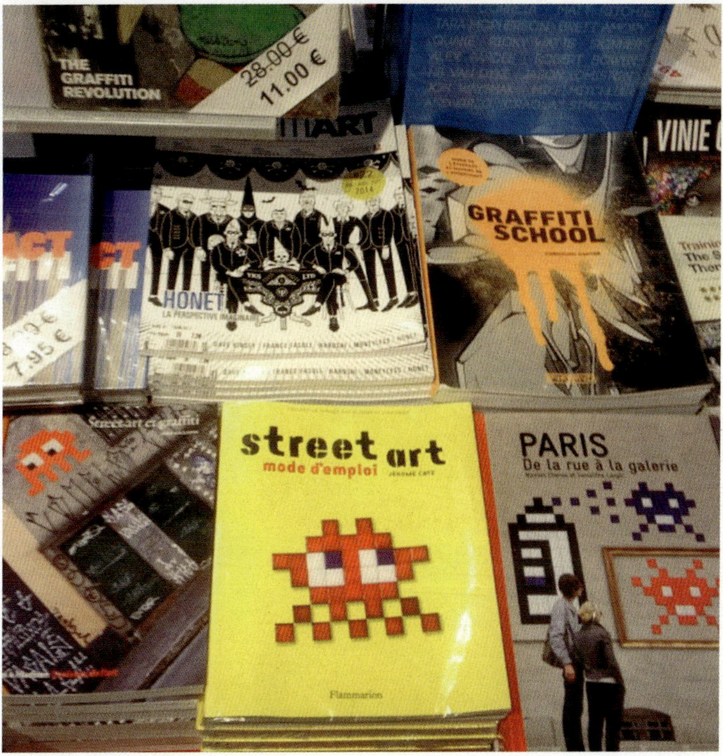

 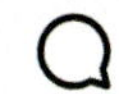 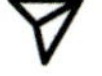 

4707 likes

invaderwashere Pompidou center bookstore Invaded!!! #streetart #books #beaubourg #paris #horribleyellowcover

View all 44 comments

13 September 2014

invaderwashere

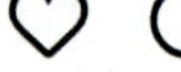
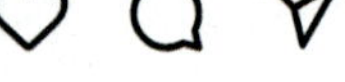

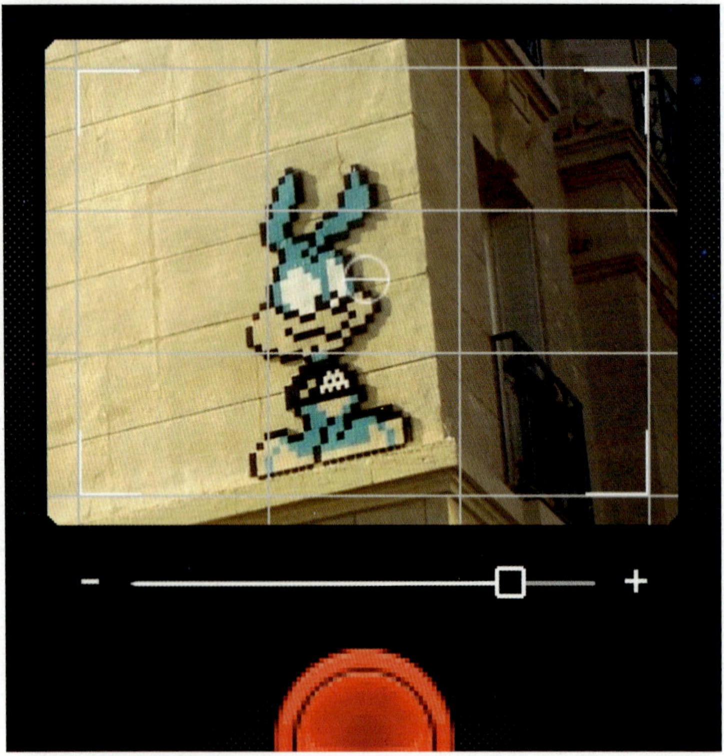

5708 likes

invaderwashere Flashing PA_1083 BunnInvader... 50 Pts #flashinvaders #freeapp

View all 50 comments

13 September 2014

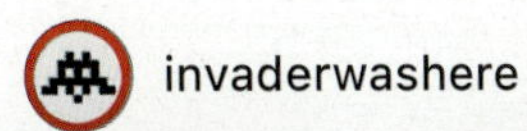

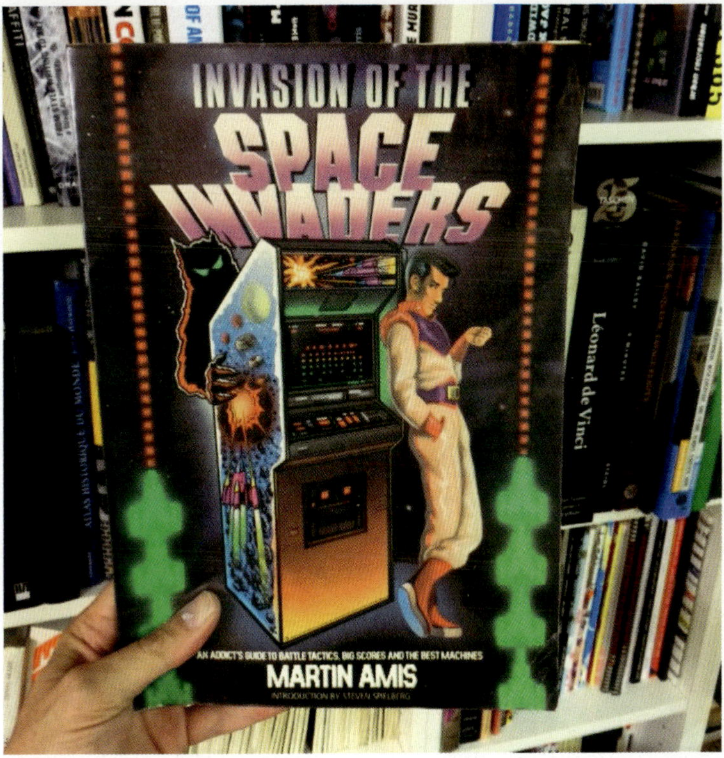

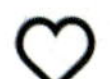   

3 341 likes

invaderwashere Invasion of the space invaders / Martin Amis 1982. A premonitory book...

View all 12 comments

16 September 2014

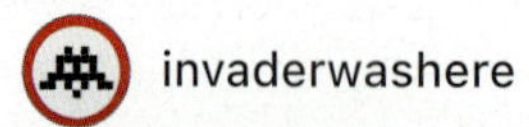
invaderwashere

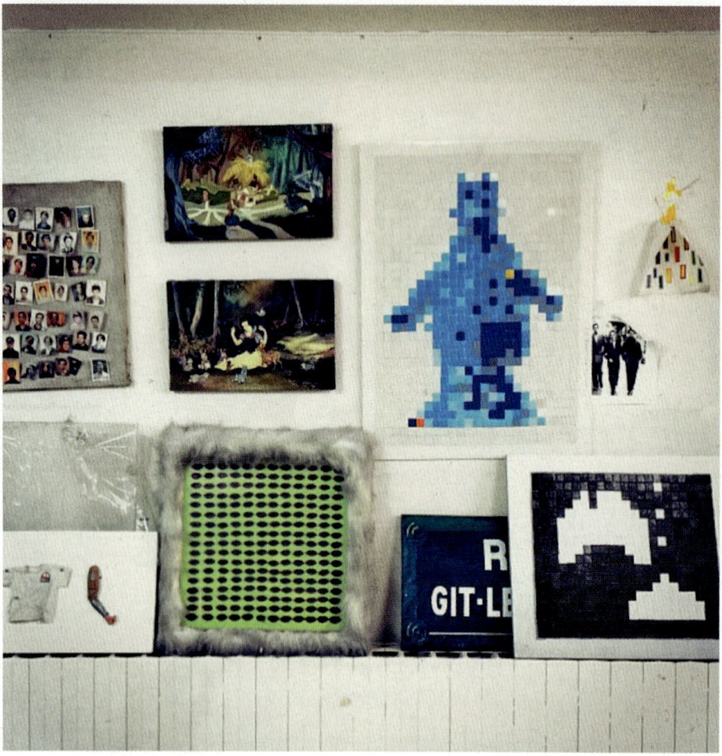

3 751 likes

invaderwashere My studio in 1998 #studioDetail #throwback #archive

View all 14 comments

16 September 2014

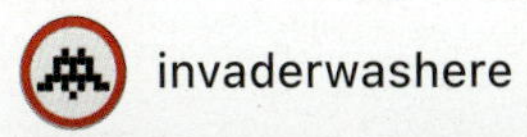

WYNWOODMAP.COM & THE OLYMPIA THEATER PRESENT

ART4SPACE

A FILM BY INVADER

Art Days 2014, Downtown Miami

The Olympia Theater at the Gusman Center
174 E. Flagler St. / Miami, FL. 33131

Showtimes: Sept. 19, 2014 11 am & 1 pm | Sept. 20, 2014 11 am & 1 pm | Sept. 21, 2014 11 am & 1 pm

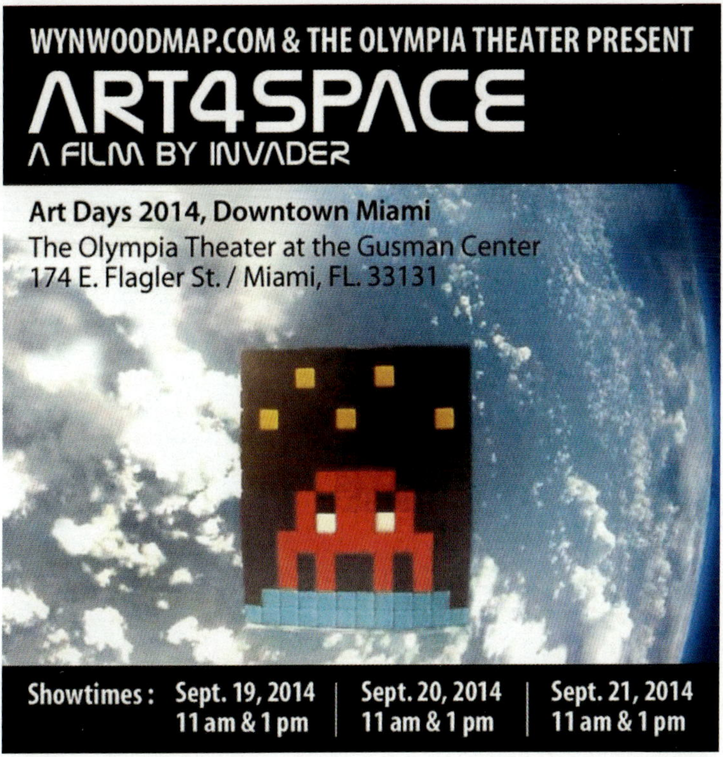

1744 likes

invaderwashere If you are in Miami next weekend don't miss the screening of #Art4Space at #OlympiaTheater #freeEntrance #DowntownArtDays #WynwoodMap

View all 111 comments

17 September 2014

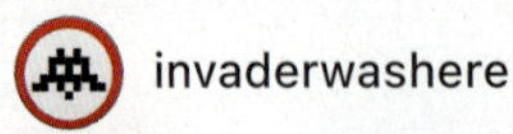
invaderwashere

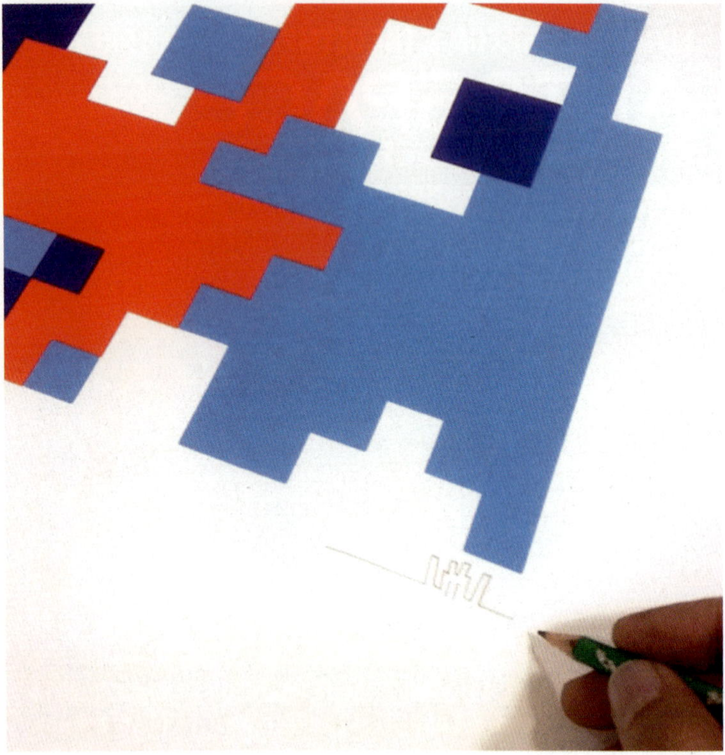

4 130 likes

invaderwashere Prints signing... #InkyAladdinSane #comingsoon #POW #PicturesOnWalls

View all 76 comments

20 September 2014

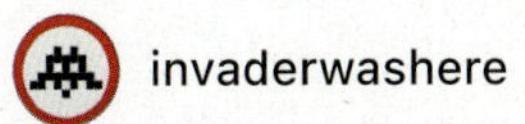

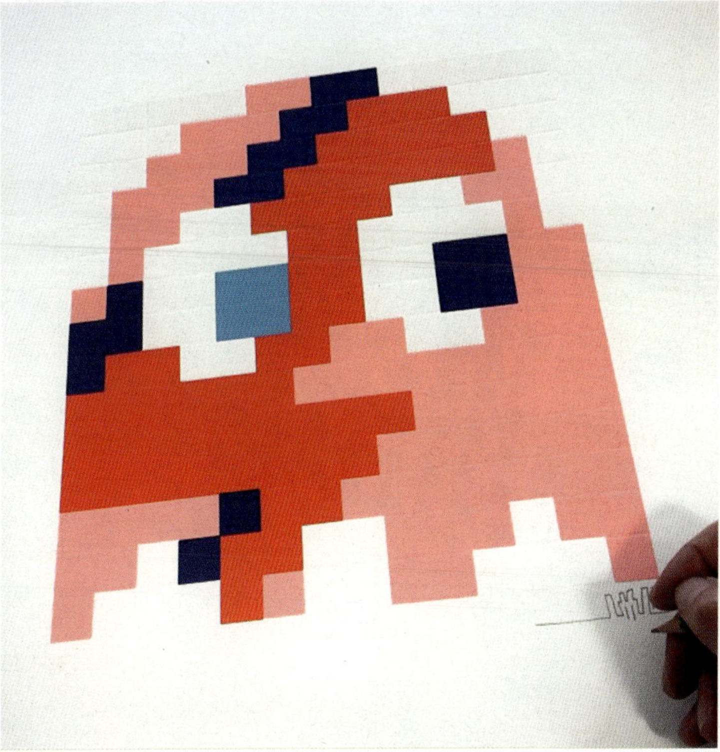

7009 likes

invaderwashere Pinky Aladdin Sane #comingsoon #pow #prints #bowie #pacman

View all 137 comments

24 September 2014

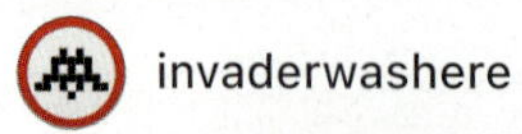

...

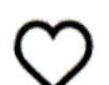 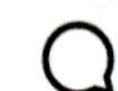  

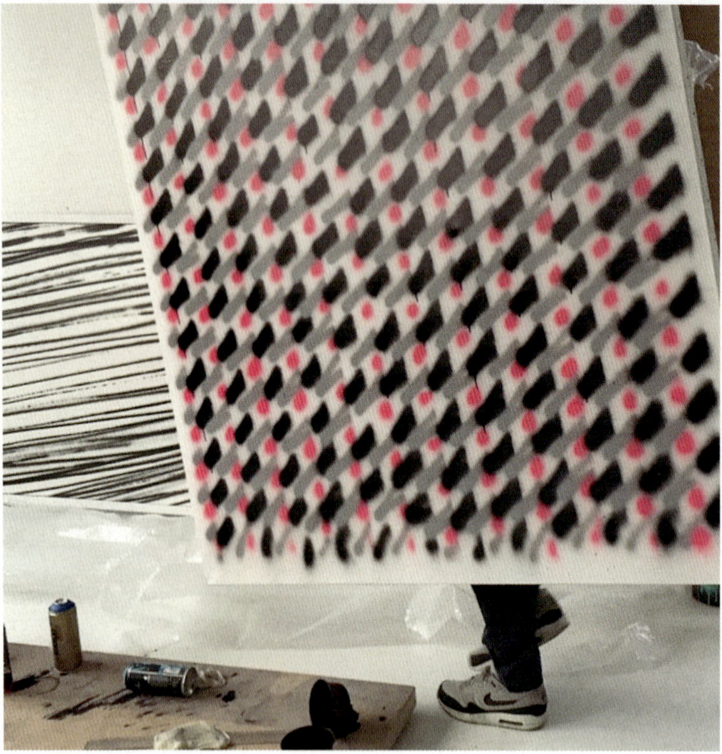

2759 likes

invaderwashere Visiting @tanc1979 #studio #tanc #paris

View all 12 comments

24 September 2014

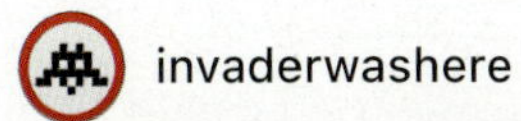

•••

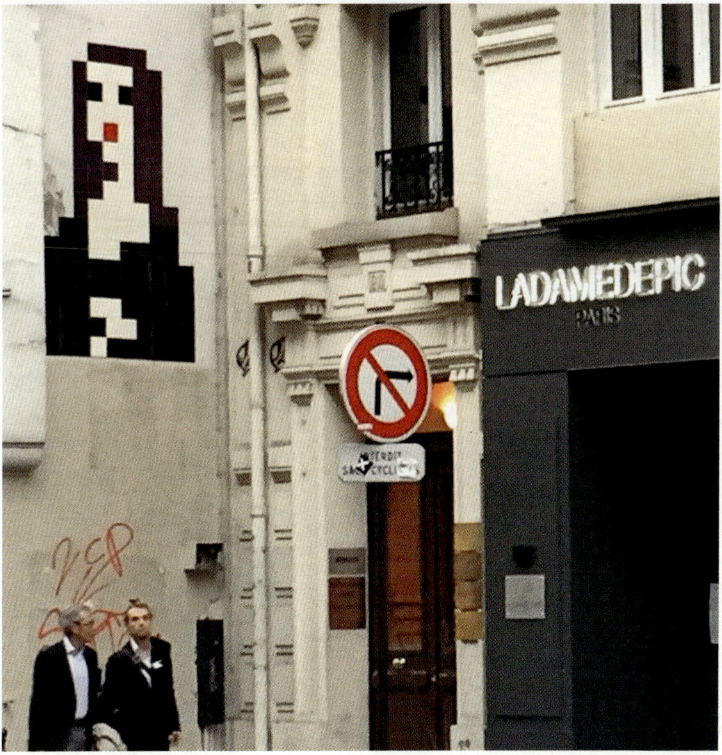

7178 likes

invaderwashere Art is useless... but it's vital! #paris #pa_1097 #MonaLisa #laJoconde #lowRes

View all 137 comments

29 September 2014

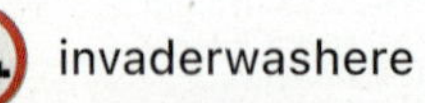

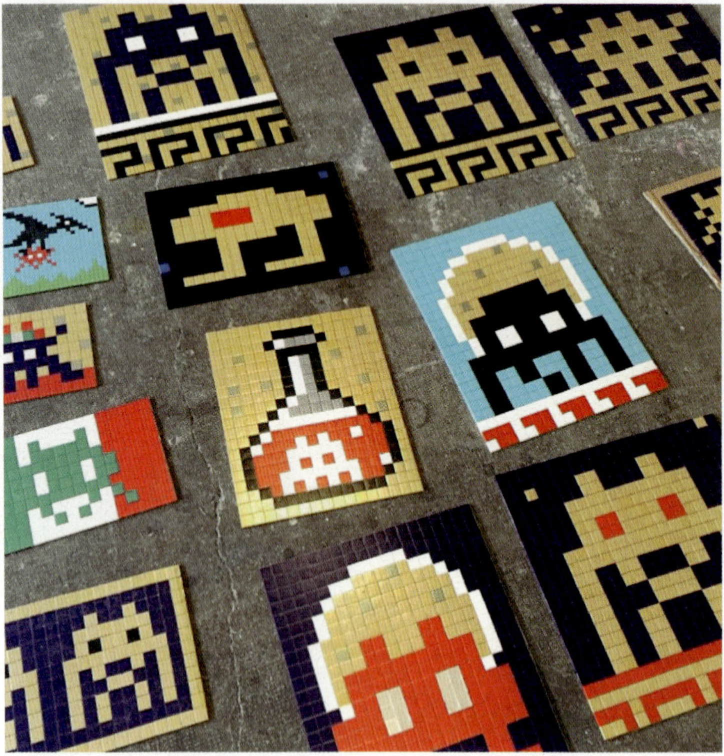

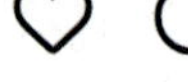  

7 914 likes

invaderwashere New pieces for a new destination...

View all 205 comments

1 October 2014

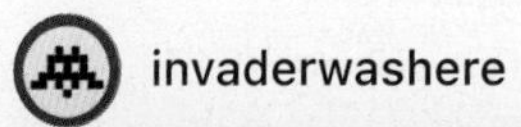

3192 likes

invaderwashere On the road...

View all 31 comments

3 October 2014

invaderwashere

  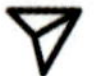 

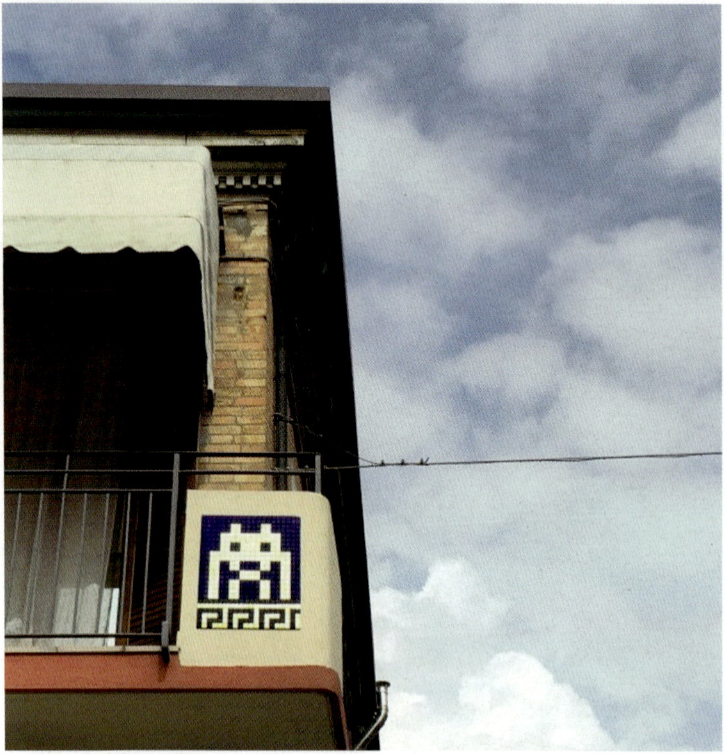

5201 likes

invaderwashere Sky of Italy...

View all 45 comments

6 October 2014

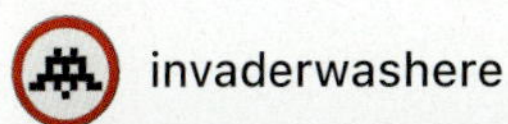

...

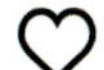  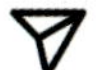 

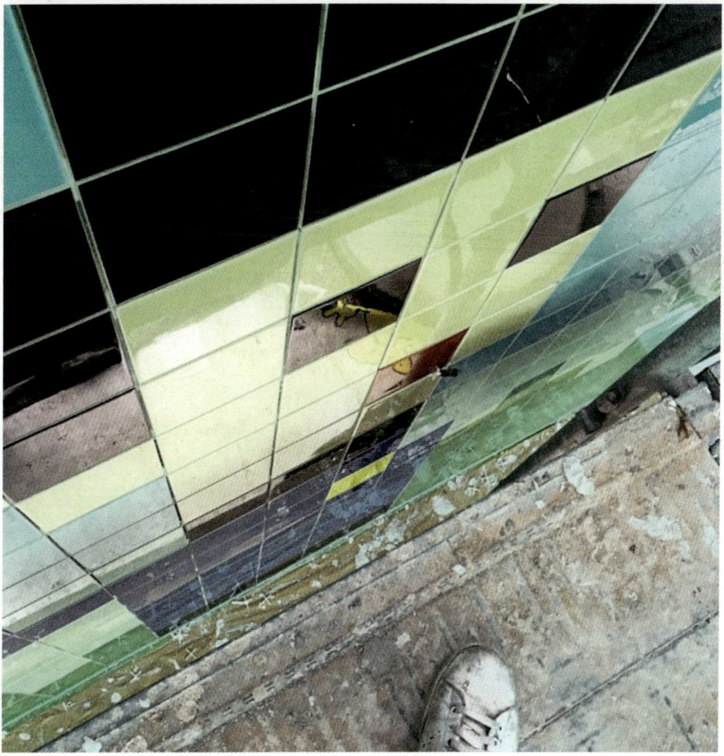

3 745 likes

invaderwashere This one is legal and big!
#publiccommission #ravenna #observatory #italy #detail
#workinprogress

View all 37 comments

6 October 2014

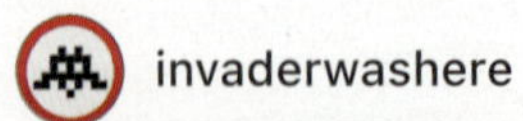

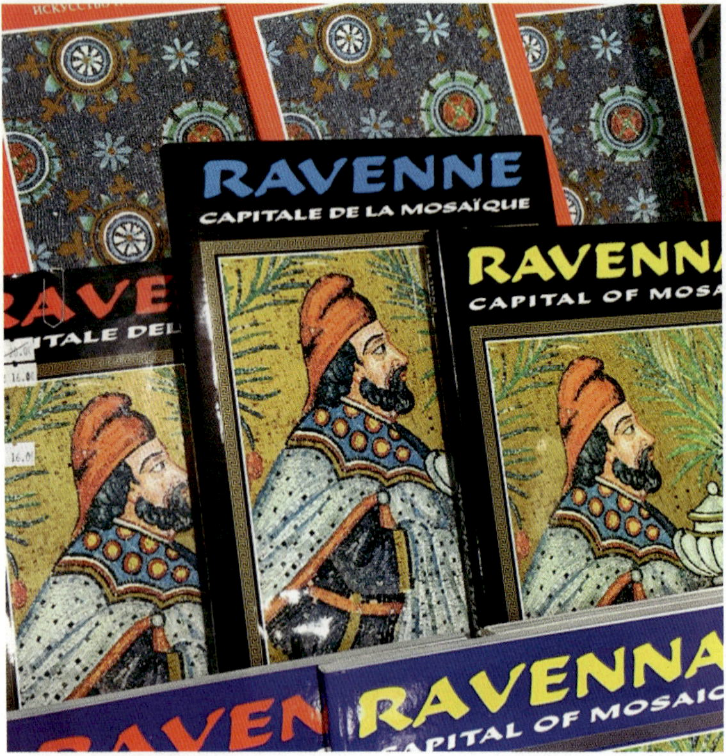

  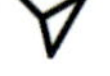 

1703 likes

invaderwashere Ravenna: The world capital of mosaic owns some space invaders now...

View all 28 comments

6 October 2014

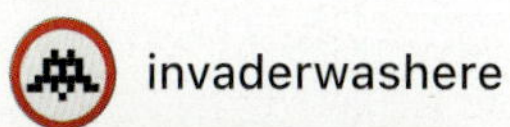

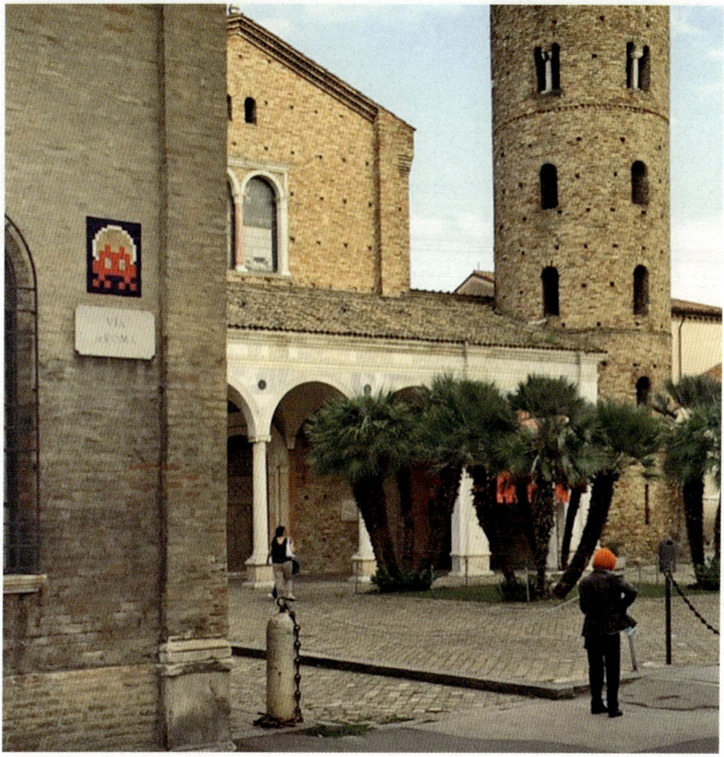

4 018 likes

invaderwashere Great spot in #Ravenna #basilicaStApollinareNuovo #santoInvader

View all 54 comments

6 October 2014

invaderwashere •••

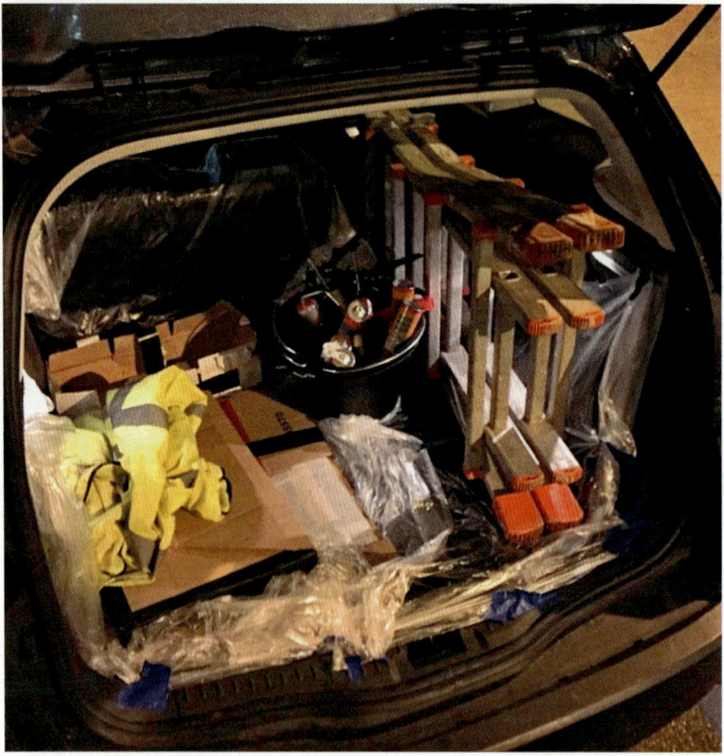

2 420 likes

invaderwashere At night in Ravenna... #spacemobile #toolboxcar #invasioninprogress

View all 29 comments

7 October 2014

invaderwashere

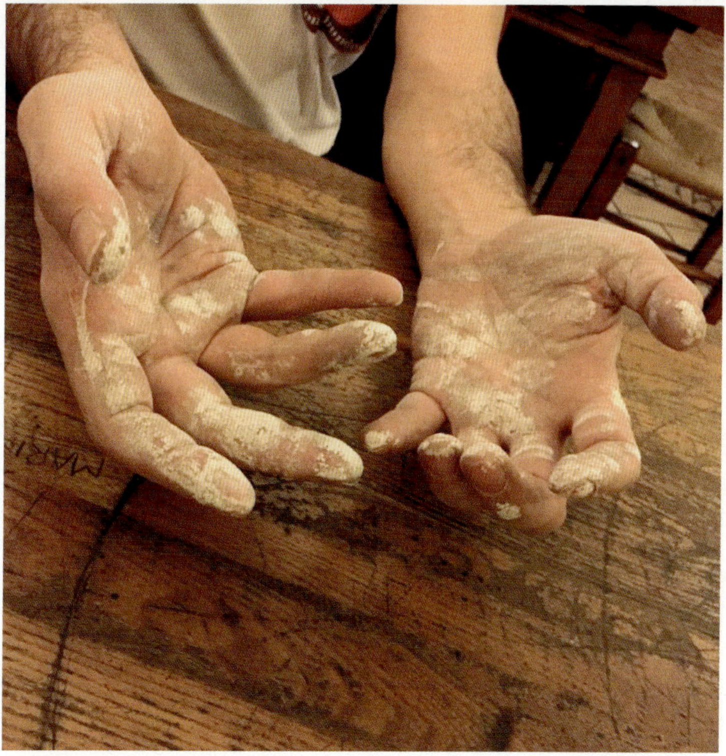

2 258 likes

invaderwashere Dirty hands!

View all 20 comments

7 October 2014

invaderwashere ...

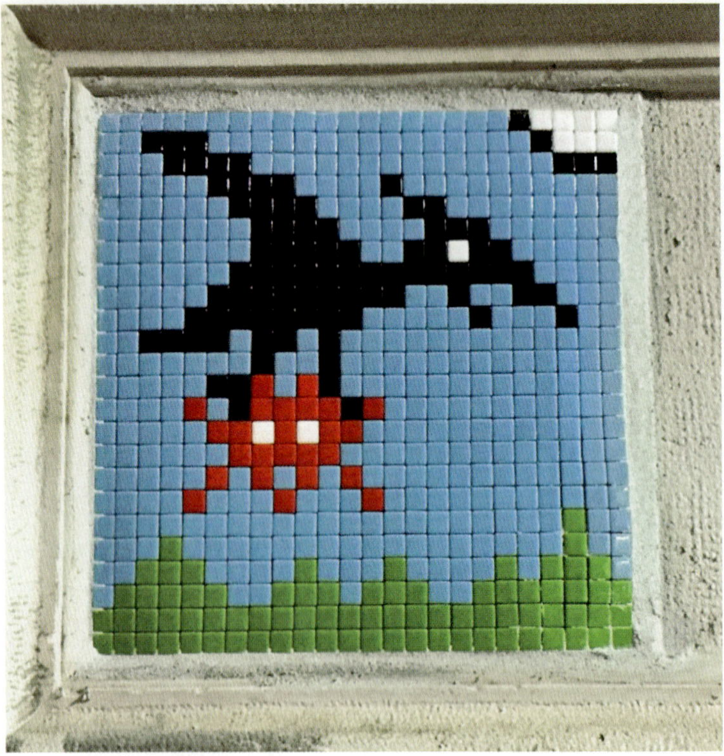

6 837 likes

invaderwashere RA_16, Just made in Ravenna, prehistory of mosaic #Dinorun

View all 69 comments

7 October 2014

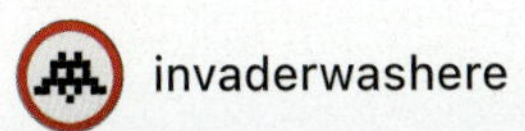

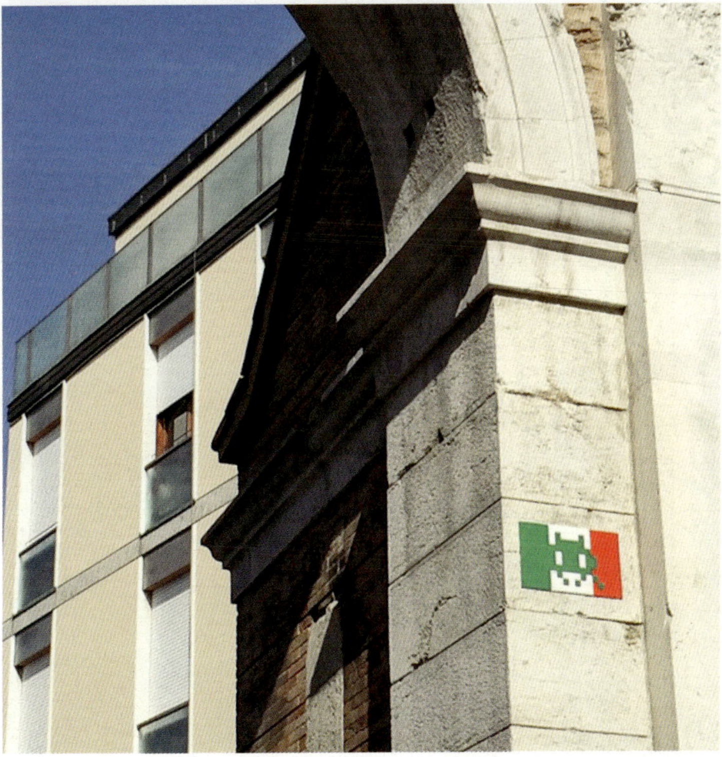

4 863 likes

invaderwashere Sky of Italy.

View all 73 comments

7 October 2014

invaderwashere ...

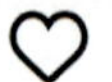   

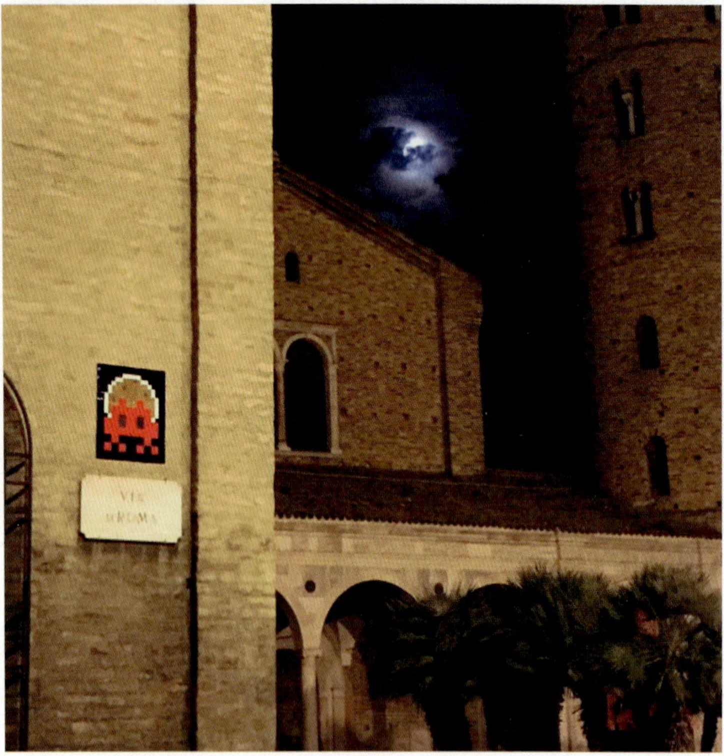

5024 likes

invaderwashere RA_09 by night #Ravenna #fullMoon

View all 48 comments

8 October 2014

invaderwashere

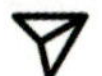

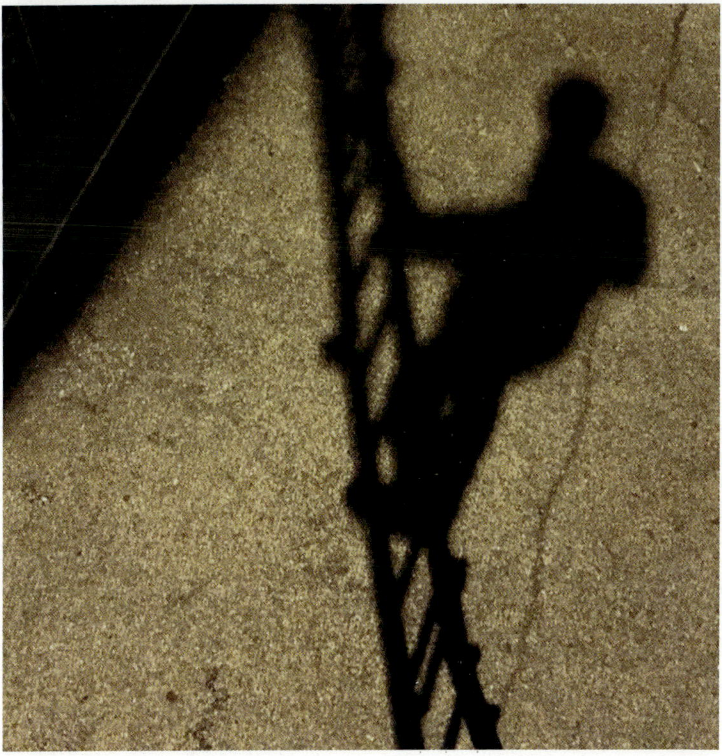

4 398 likes

invaderwashere Selfportrait at work / 4:08am

View all 41 comments

8 October 2014

invaderwashere

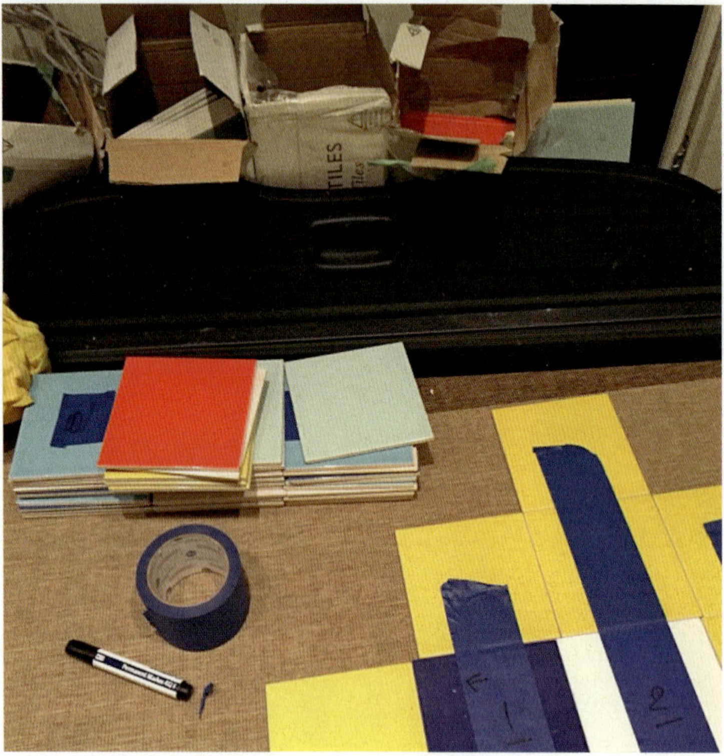

2 515 likes

View all 15 comments

8 October 2014

invaderwashere

 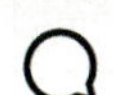  

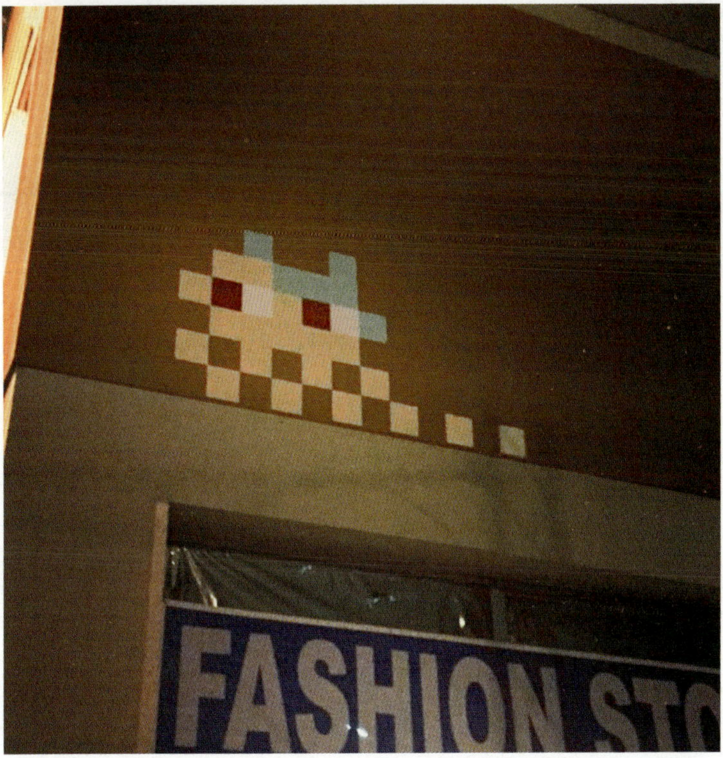

5207 likes

invaderwashere RA_21 #justdone #ravenna

View all 31 comments

8 October 2014

invaderwashere

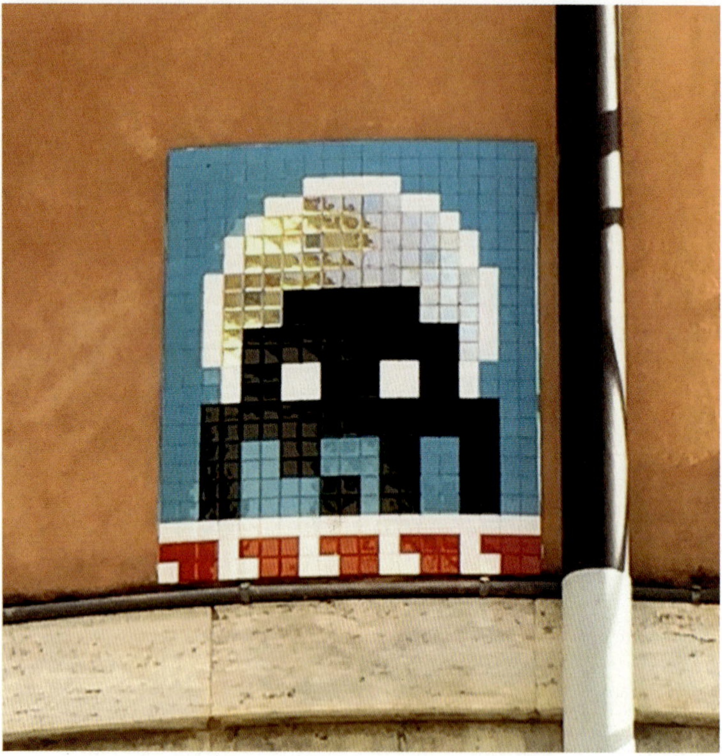

5649 likes

invaderwashere #Ravenna #italy

View all 46 comments

10 October 2014

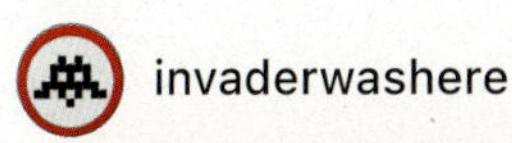

invaderwashere •••

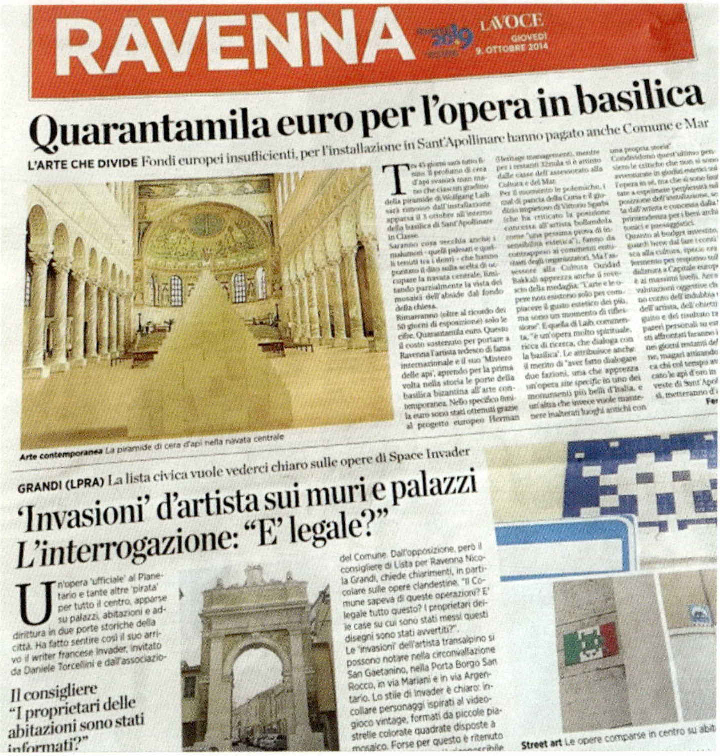

RAVENNA

LA VOCE GIOVEDÌ 9 OTTOBRE 2014

Quarantamila euro per l'opera in basilica

L'ARTE CHE DIVIDE Fondi europei insufficienti, per l'installazione in Sant'Apollinare hanno pagato anche Comune e Mar

Tra 45 giorni sarà tutto finito. Il profumo di cera d'api svanirà man mano che ciascun gradino della piramide di Wolfgang Laib sarà rimosso dall'installazione apparsa il 3 ottobre all'interno della basilica di Sant'Apollinare in Classe.

Saranno cosa vecchia anche i malumori - quelli palesati e quelli tenuti tra i denti - che hanno puntato il dito sulla scelta di occupare la navata centrale, limitando parzialmente la vista dei mosaici dell'abside dal fondo della chiesa.

Rimarranno (oltre al ricordo dei 50 giorni di esposizione) solo le cifre. Quarantamila euro. Questo il costo sostenuto per portare a Ravenna l'artista tedesco di fama internazionale e il suo 'Mistero delle api', aprendo per la prima volta nella storia le porte della basilica bizantina all'arte contemporanea. Nello specifico 8mila euro sono stati ottenuti grazie al progetto europeo Herman (Heritage management), mentre per i restanti 32mila si è attinto dalle casse dell'assessorato alla Cultura e del Mar.

Per il momento le polemiche, i mal di pancia della Curia e il giudizio impetuoso di Vittorio Sgarbi (che ha criticato la posizione concessa all'artista bollandola come "una pessima prova di insensibilità estetica"), fanno da contrappeso ai commenti entusiasti degli organizzatori. Ma l'assessore alla Cultura Ouidad Bakkali apprezza anche il rovescio della medaglia: "L'arte e le opere non esistono solo per compiacere il gusto estetico dei più, ma sono un momento di riflessione". E quella di Laib, commenta, "è un'opera molto spirituale, ricca di ricerca, che dialoga con la basilica". Le attribuisce anche il merito di "aver fatto dialogare due fazioni, una che apprezza un'opera site specific in uno dei monumenti più belli d'Italia, e un'altra che invece vuole mantenere inalterati luoghi antichi con una propria storia".

Arte contemporanea *La piramide di cera d'api nella navata centrale*

GRANDI (LPRA) La lista civica vuole vederci chiaro sulle opere di Space Invader

'Invasioni' d'artista sui muri e palazzi L'interrogazione: "E' legale?"

Un'opera 'ufficiale' al Planetario e tante altre 'pirata' per tutto il centro, apparse su palazzi, abitazioni e addirittura in due porte storiche della città. Ha fatto sentire così il suo arrivo il writer francese Invader, invitato da Daniele Torcellini e dall'associazio-

Il consigliere "I proprietari delle abitazioni sono stati informati?"

del Comune. Dall'opposizione, però il consigliere di Lista per Ravenna Nicola Grandi, chiede chiarimenti, in particolare sulle opere clandestine. "Il Comune sapeva di queste operazioni? E' legale tutto questo? I proprietari delle case su cui sono stati messi questi disegni sono stati avvertiti?".

Le 'invasioni' dell'artista transalpino si possono notare nella circonvallazione San Gaetanino, nella Porta Borgo San Rocco, in via Mariani e in via Argentario. Lo stile di Invader è chiaro: incollare personaggi ispirati al videogioco vintage, formati da piccole piastrelle colorate quadrate disposte a mosaico. Forse per questo è ritenuto

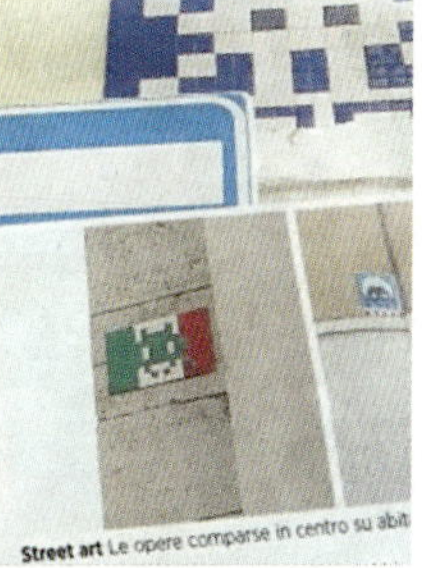

Street art Le opere comparse in centro su abit

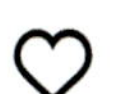   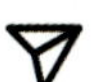 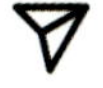 

2 420 likes

invaderwashere Media invasion in Ravenna. « E' legale? »

View all 56 comments

10 October 2014

invaderwashere •••

 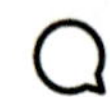  

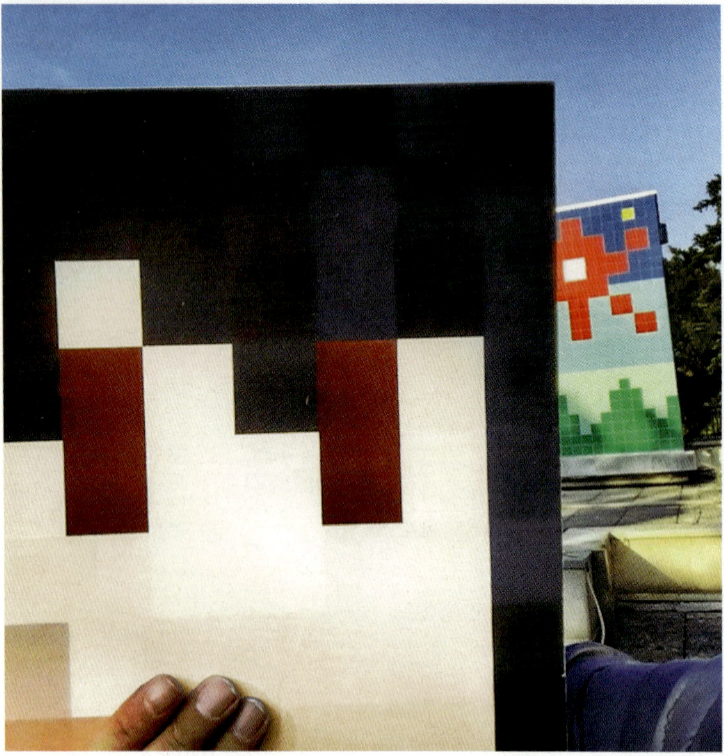

3150 likes

invaderwashere Selfie / Observatory of Ravenna. With a detail in the background of the piece wich will be unveiled tomorrow.

View all 12 comments

10 October 2014

invaderwashere •••

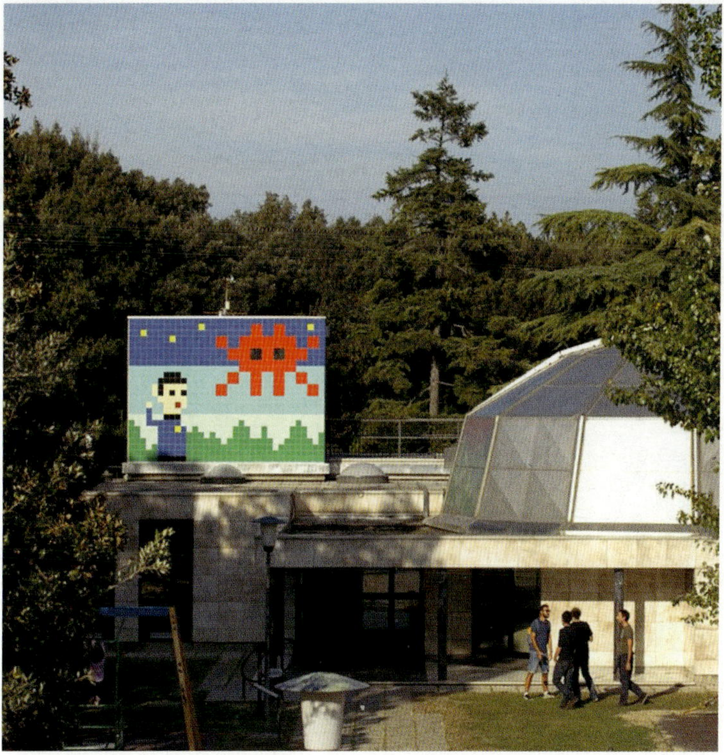

5698 likes

invaderwashere This is RA_01 the official piece on the planetarium of Ravenna. If you visit the city you can also find 23 unofficial pieces around... Big thanx to Daniele, Luca, Marte and Arti team.

View all 71 comments

11 October 2014

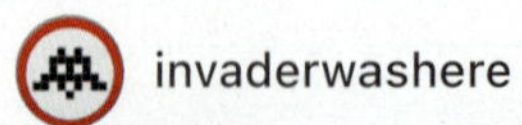

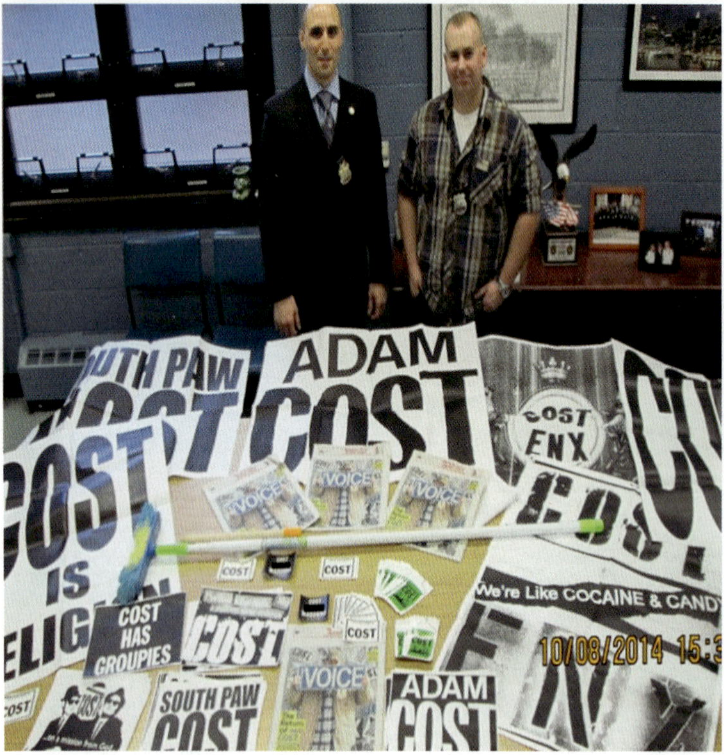

2190 likes

invaderwashere Looks like Cost is in trouble 😬
#FREECOST #costarrested #nypd

View all 183 comments

13 October 2014

invaderwashere

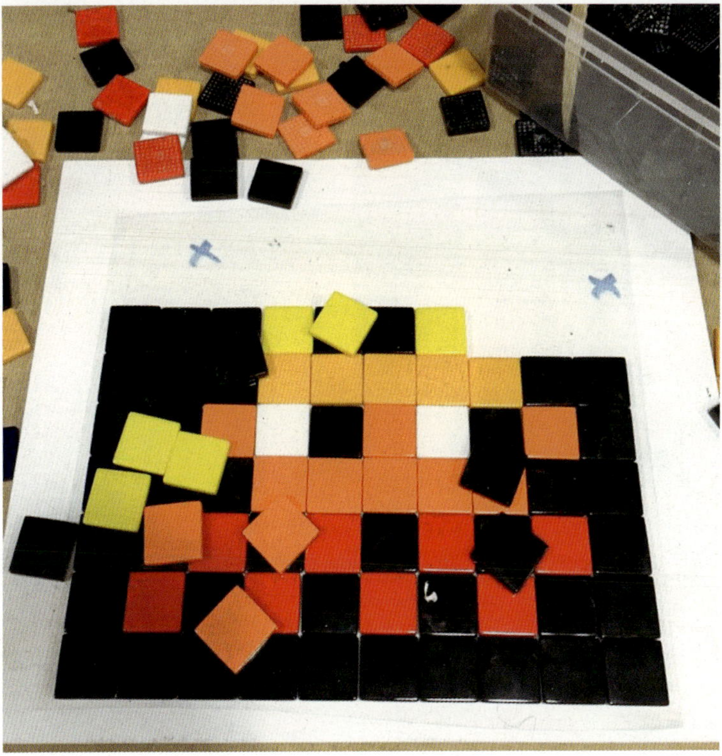

...

4 299 likes

invaderwashere #studiodetail Working on a new #InvasionKit #flashinvaders #handmade #studiodetail Coming next November

View all 87 comments

16 October 2014

invaderwashere ...

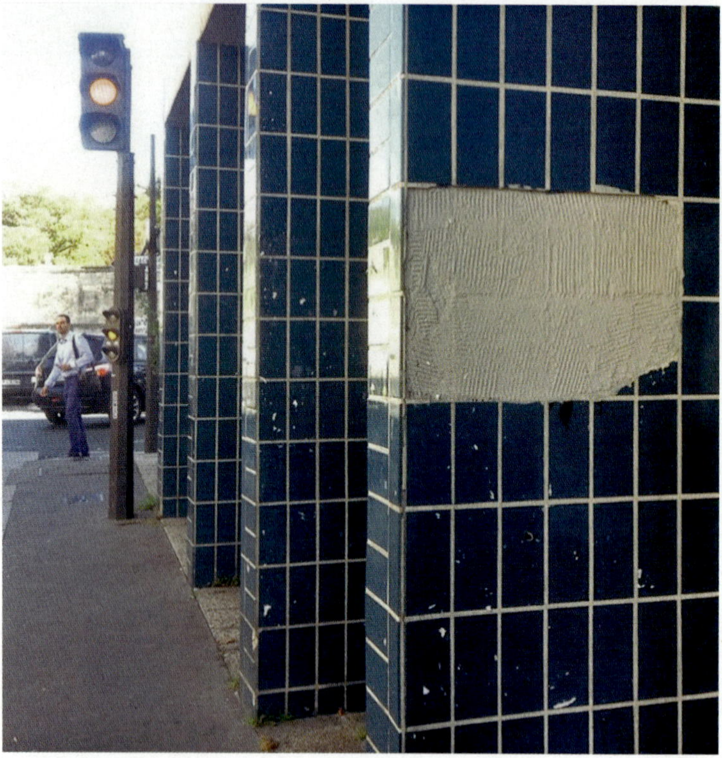

2 441 likes

invaderwashere BEFORE / Front of Pere Lachaise cimetery / Paris #brokenwall #missingtiles

View all 21 comments

24 October 2014

invaderwashere ...

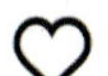

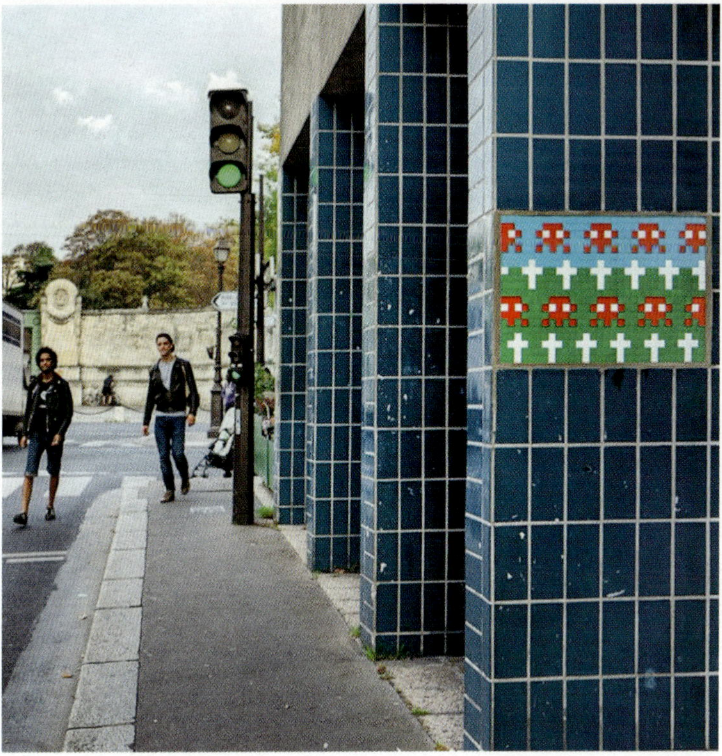

7145 likes

invaderwashere AFTER / Front of Pere Lachaise cimetery / Paris / PA_1115 #fixedwall

View all 90 comments

24 October 2014

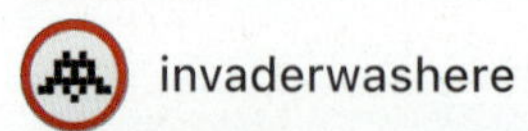

WORLD INVASION MORE PROJECTS

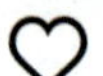  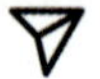 

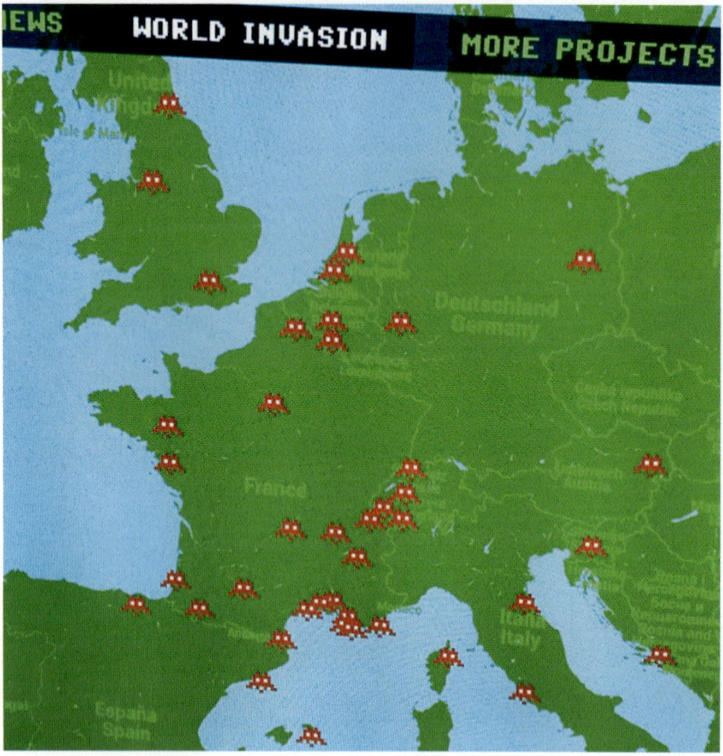

5409 likes

invaderwashere Working on my new website, coming soon ... space-invaders.com #worldInvasionpage

View all 193 comments

25 October 2014

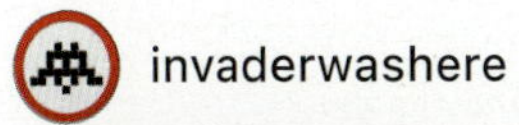

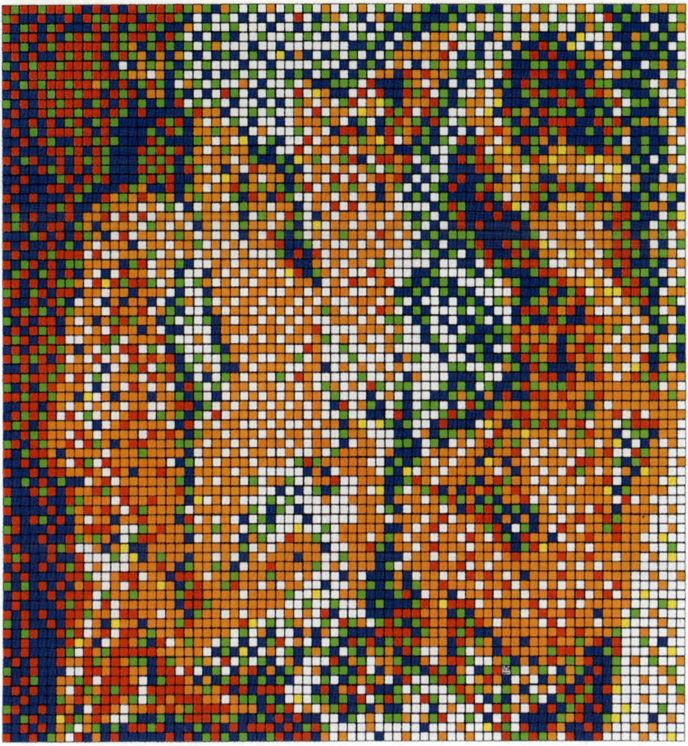

5500 likes

invaderwashere Happy birthday Pablo! Here is my Rubikcubist version of your first and most famous Cubist painting #picasso #birthday #demoisellesdavignon #cubism #rubikcubism #rubikmasterpiece

View all 77 comments

26 October 2014

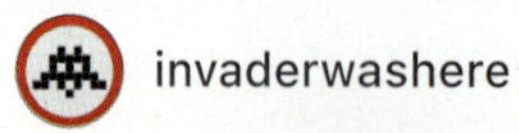

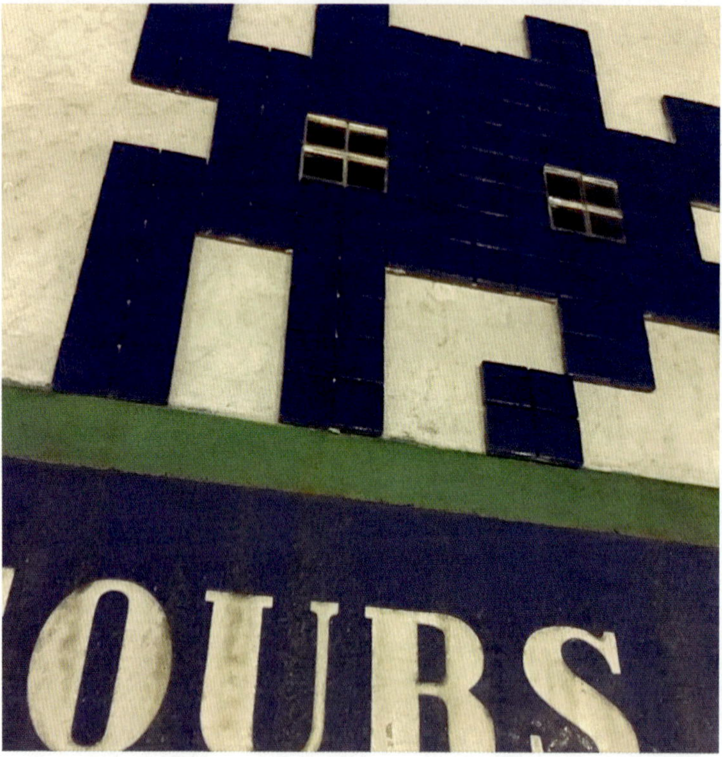

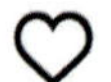   

3892 likes

invaderwashere Just made in #Paris

View all 41 comments

26 October 2014

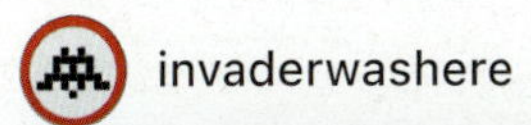

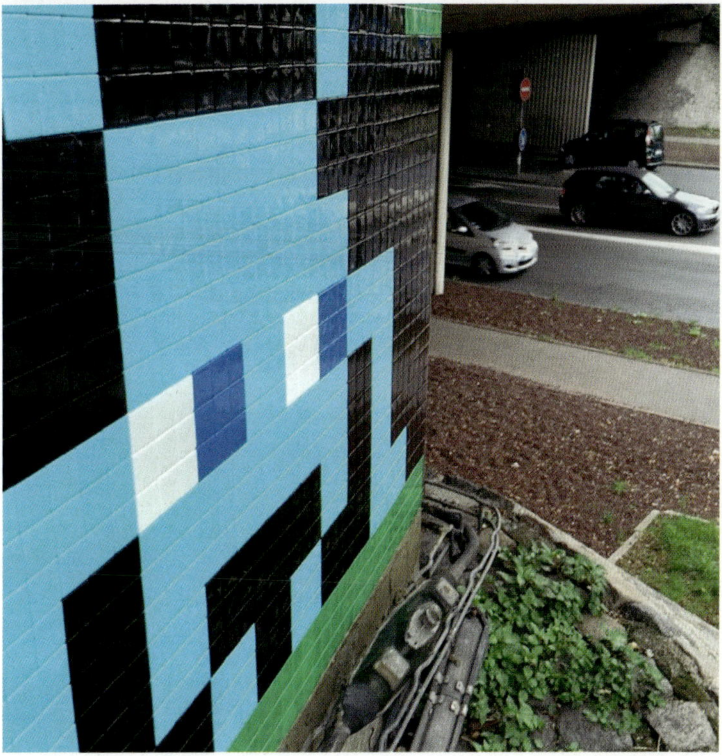

5409 likes

invaderwashere New born #Paris #suburb #invaderwashere

View all 75 comments

28 October 2014

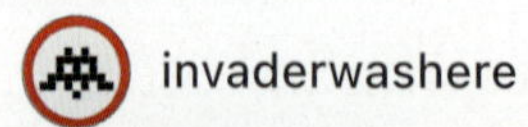

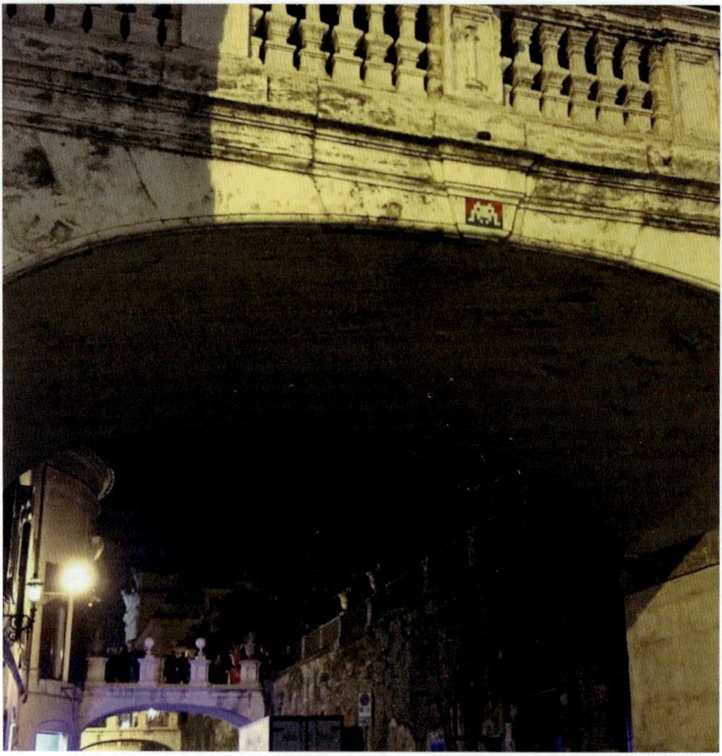

4 224 likes

invaderwashere Rom_43 #untouchable

View all 39 comments

30 October 2014

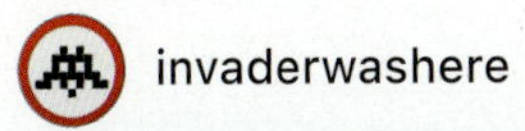

...

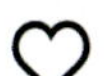  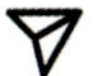 

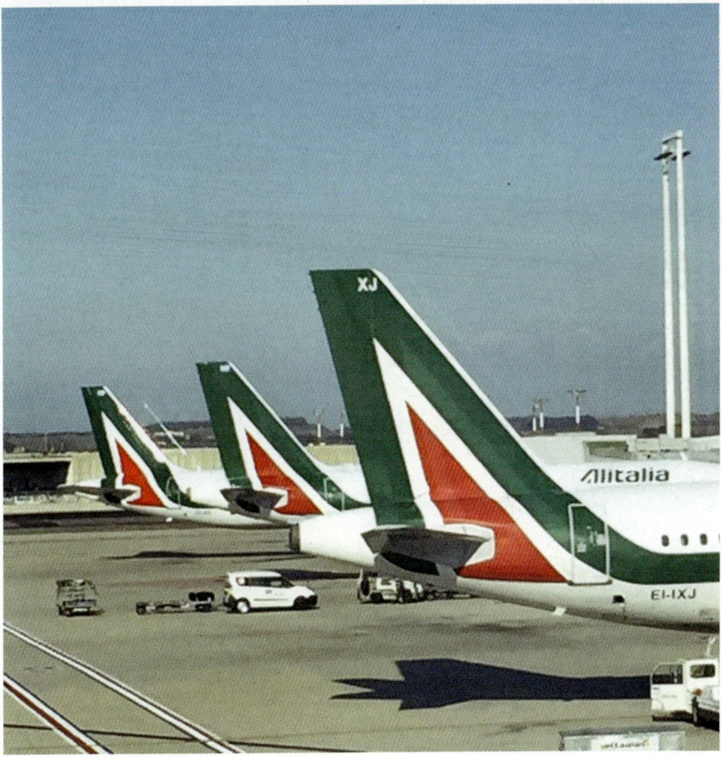

2 567 likes

invaderwashere Ciao Roma

View all 28 comments

30 October 2014

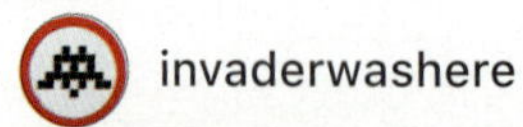

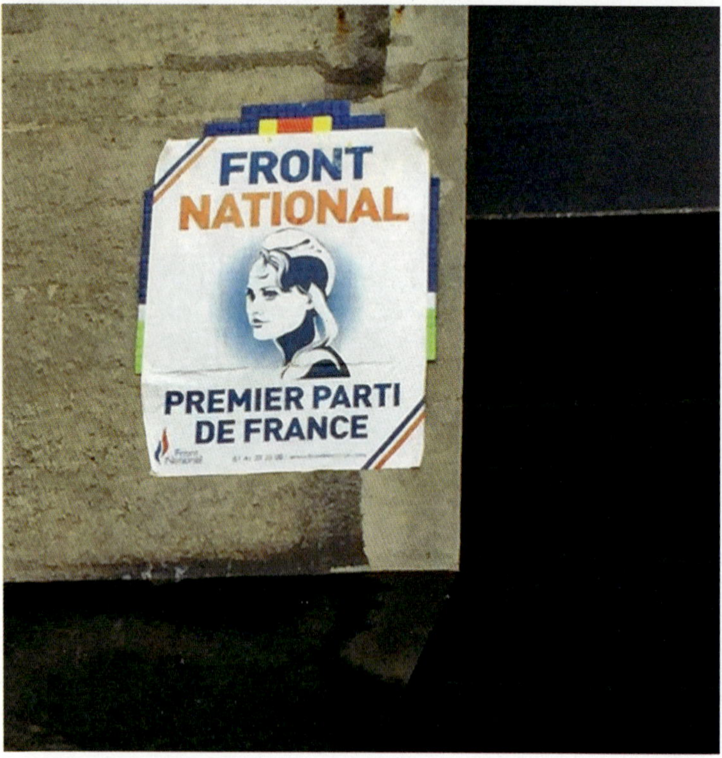

2808 likes

invaderwashere Obviously National Front does not like my work! #idontlikethemeither

View all 128 comments

2 November 2014

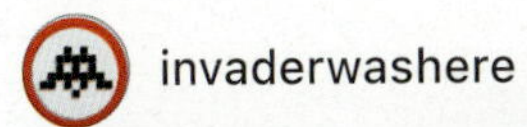

•••

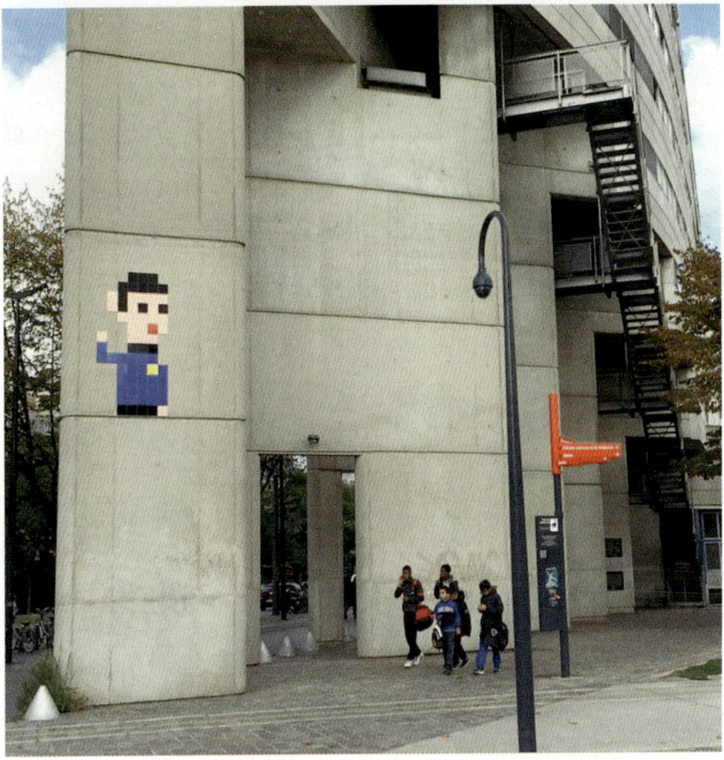

7797 likes

invaderwashere Cheers from Vulcan! #spock #citedessciences #paris

View all 100 comments

2 November 2014

invaderwashere •••

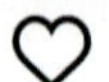   

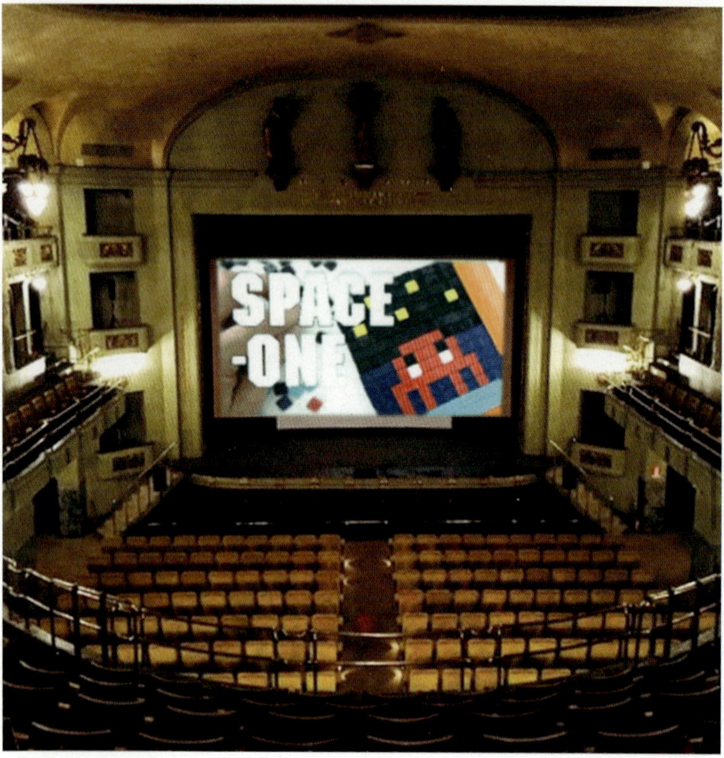

3668 likes

invaderwashere Screening of Art4Space tomorrow 22.45 pm at Cinema Odeon Florence / Italy / lo schermo dell'arte Film Festival #art4space #schermodellarte.org

View all 35 comments

10 November 2014

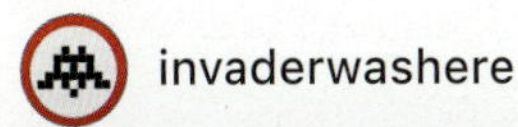

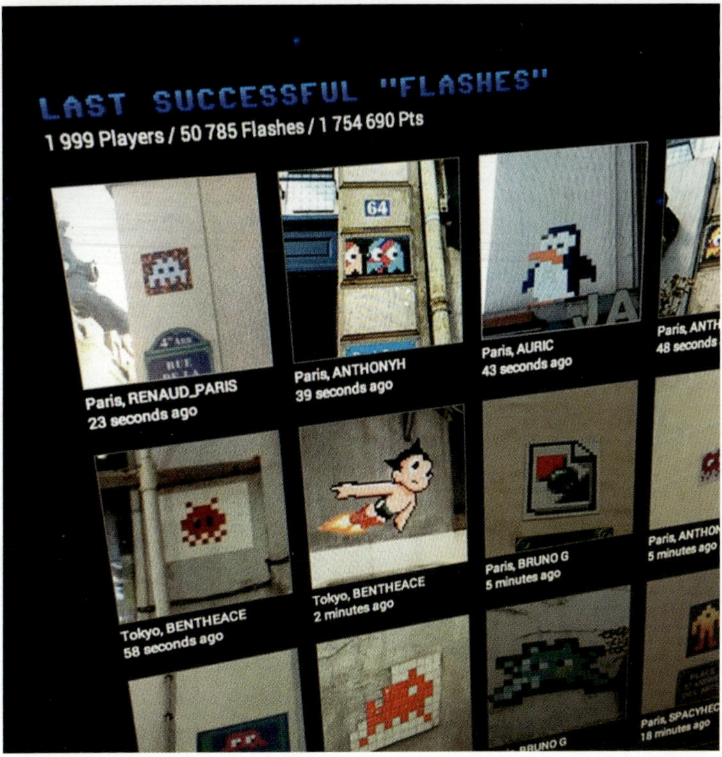

 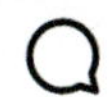  

3649 likes

invaderwashere Soon 2000 players and more than 50.000 successful flashes on FlashInvaders. Big thanx to the 1999 players & congrats to the top 100 #flashinvaders

View all 62 comments

12 November 2014

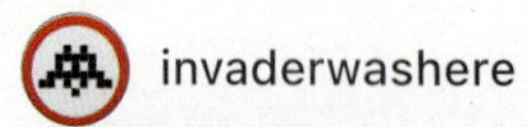

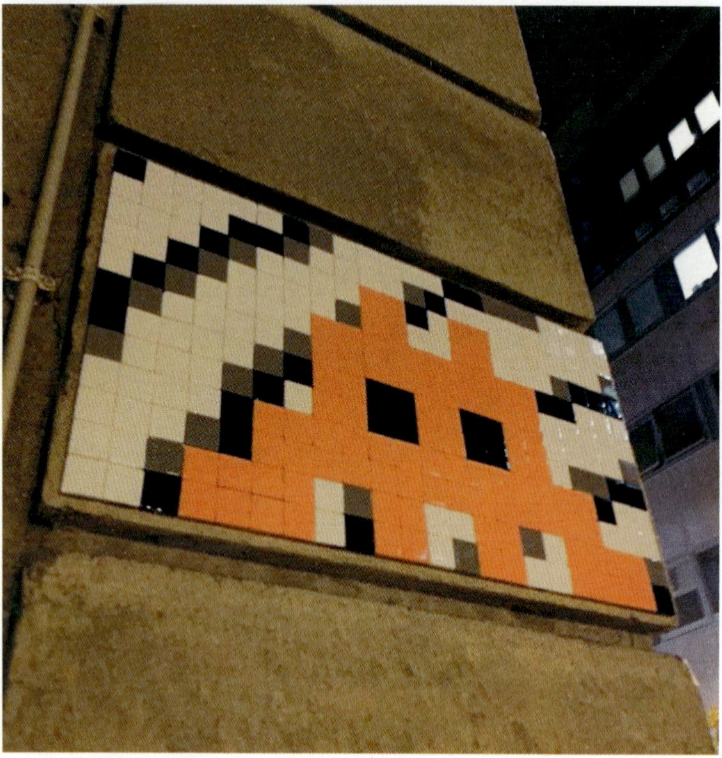

 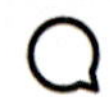  

6 997 likes

invaderwashere 4:42am Just made in #paris

View all 90 comments

14 November 2014

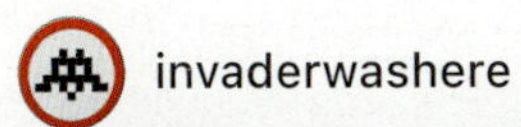

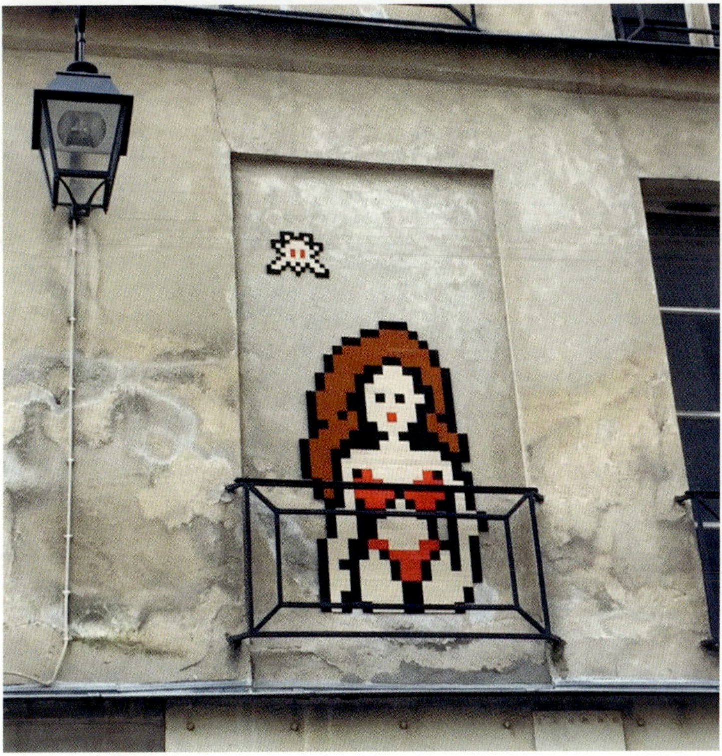

 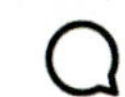  

10 389 likes

invaderwashere Find the girl... #paris #newpiece #PA1127

View all 197 comments

16 November 2014

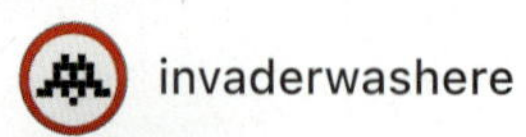

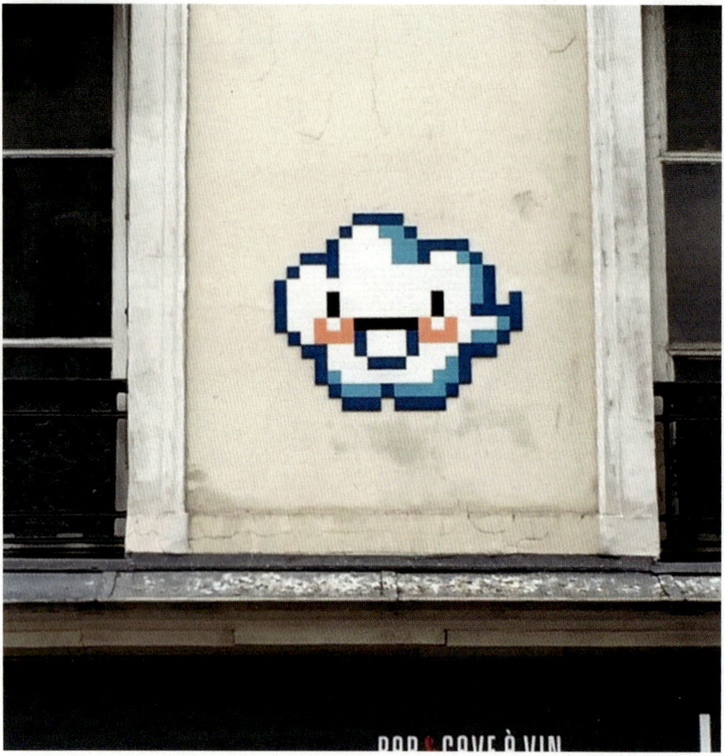

8633 likes

invaderwashere PA_1124 New born #paris

View all 108 comments

17 November 2014

invaderwashere

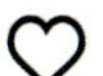

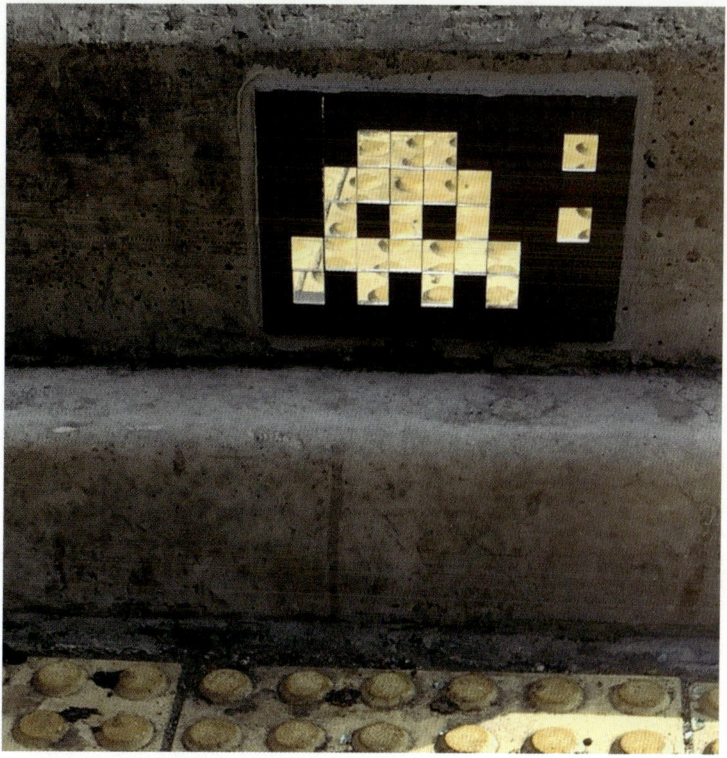

7252 likes

invaderwashere HK_20 reloaded #reactivation #closeup #mirrors #hongkong #2014

View all 73 comments

29 November 2014

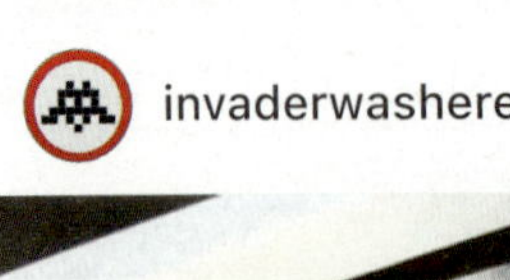

Jenni Marsh

SOMETHING NEW Olivia Rosenman

Space odyssey

Attention *Space Invaders* fans: reality just got a little closer to the 1970s arcade game thanks to FlashInvaders – an app invented by Invader, the anonymous creator of street art inspired by the characters of old games.

Earlier this year, the Frenchman "re-invaded" Hong Kong, adding more than 40 Pac-Mans, Space Invaders and aliens to the 34 murals he had gifted to the city's walls since 2001. The app is a treasure hunt for these creations.

Using FlashInvaders is simple: when you find a mosaic, turn on your GPS and snap a

The app will verify your "flash" using

onfirmed as genuine, your

scoreboard and you'll

Kong.

discover about 3,000 Invader mural

including Tokyo and Osaka, in Jap

in Thailand; and Dhaka, in Bangl

hasn't yet made it into the mainl

could change.

"When I invade a new city i

new level to the game," he say

The art is not without con

Invader was arrested in New

a mural in the East Village.

more than 50 of his works w

Hong Kong government.

While he says he expect

art to be removed, he has

Kong wipeout a "massacr

another reinvasion.

Given that Hong Kon

difficulty level, surely sp

here should be worth b

The app is free and

store and for Android.

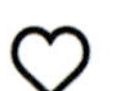  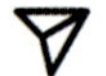 

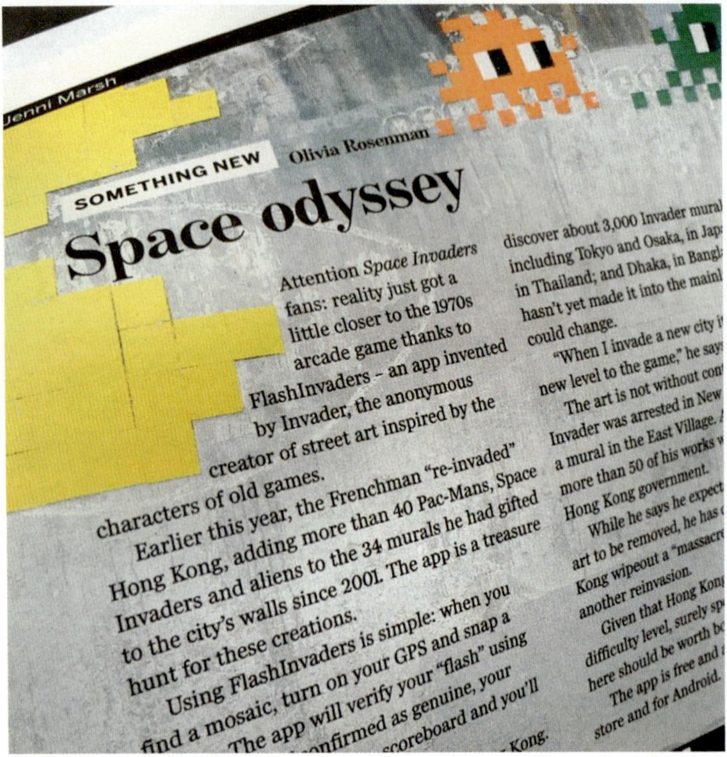

3 239 likes

invaderwashere Sunday Morning Post of today #scmp #hongkong #flashinvaders #spaceinvaders #mediainvasion

View all 22 comments

30 November 2014

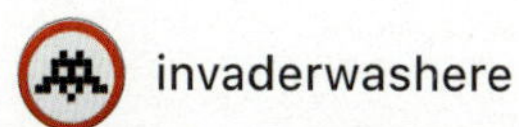

invaderwashere

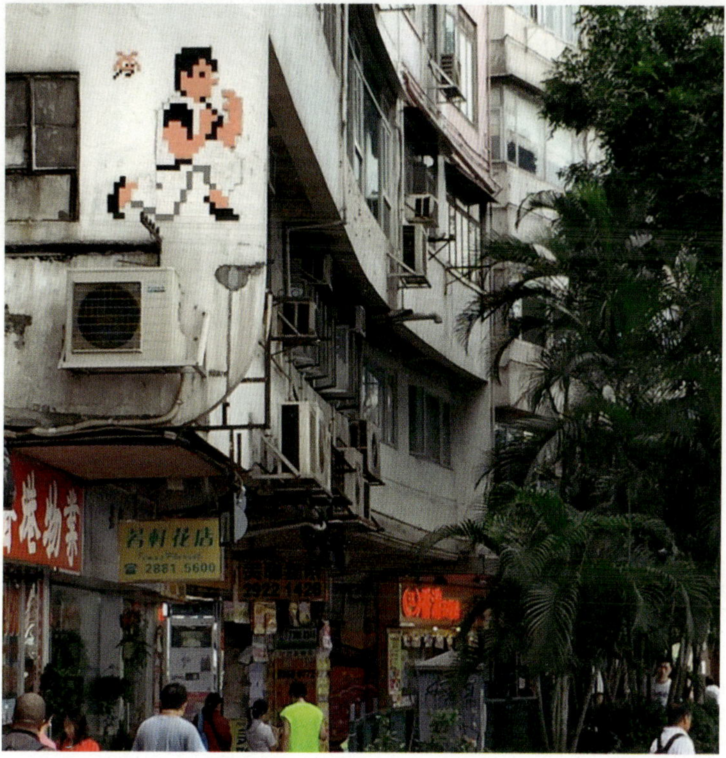

8 273 likes

invaderwashere HK_56 #survivor #hongkong #causewaybay

View all 100 comments

30 November 2014

invaderwashere •••

  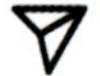 

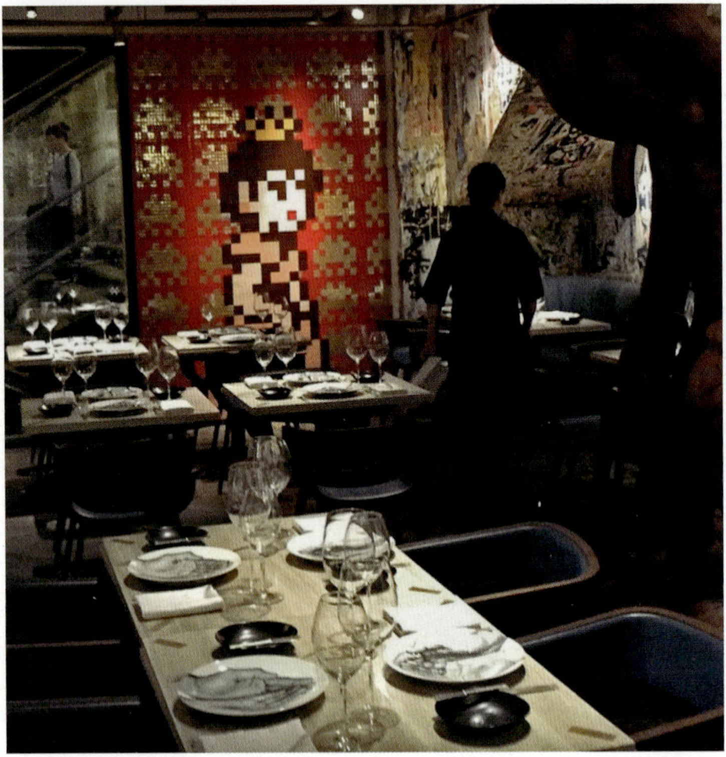

6793 likes

invaderwashere Lunch at #Bibo restaurant #hongkong #gastronomy #BiboPrincess #HK32 #100pts

View all 69 comments

30 November 2014

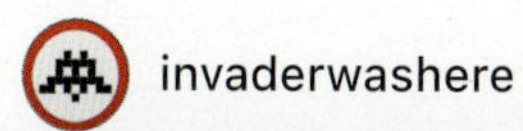

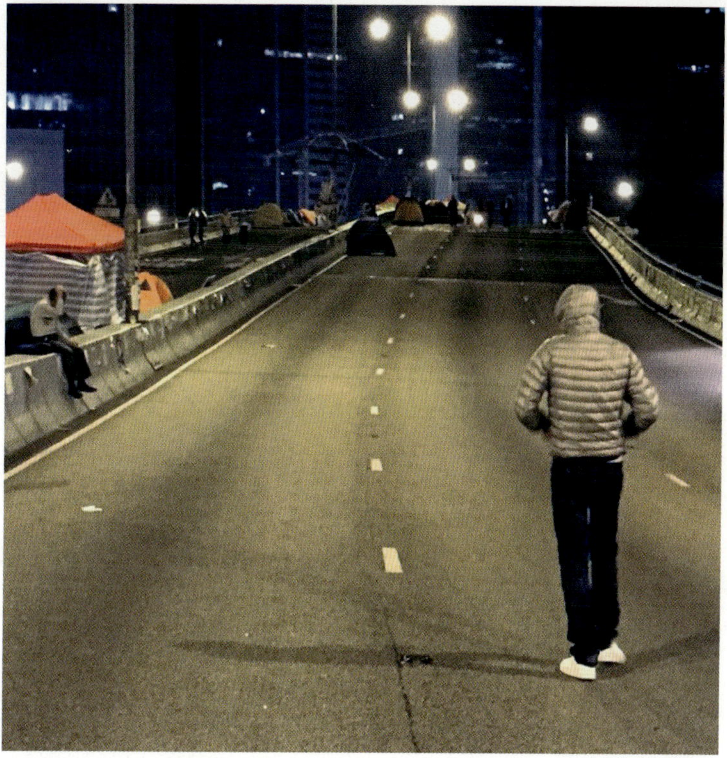

5194 likes

invaderwashere Bye bye Hong Kong, I'll be back soon...

View all 57 comments

30 November 2014

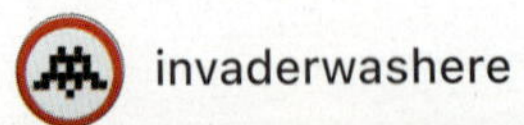

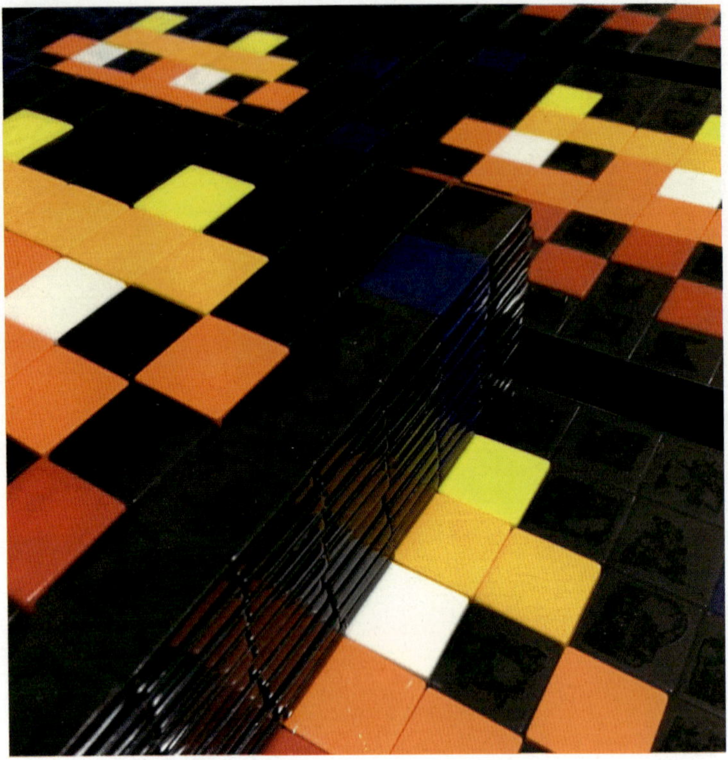

 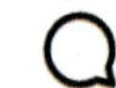 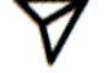 

5 576 likes

invaderwashere A new #Invasionkit is coming soon / more infos next Monday on my new website...

View all 153 comments

3 December 2014

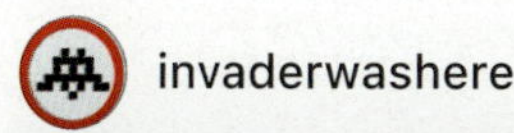

•••

 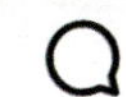  

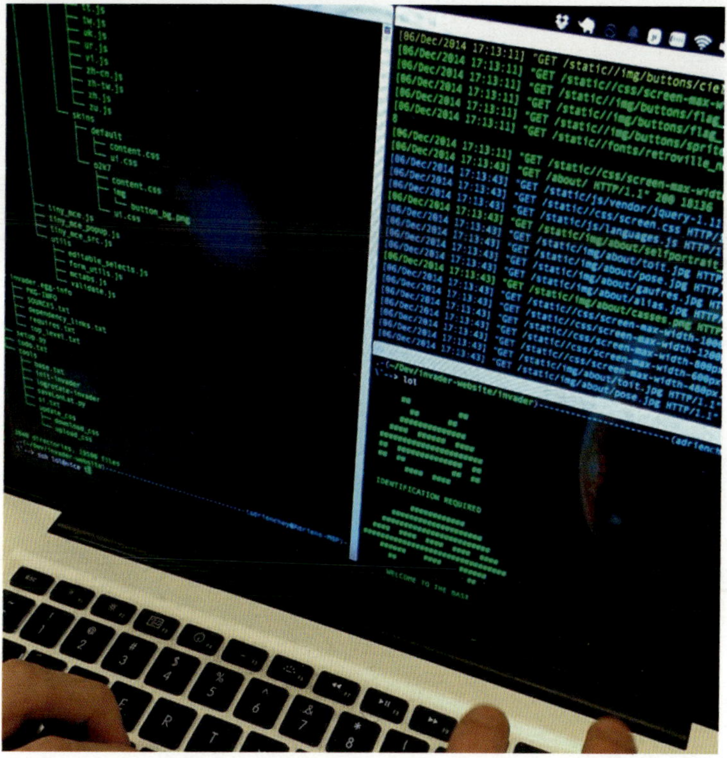

4573 likes

invaderwashere Break the code, solve the crime! Last touches on my new website. Launch Monday #space-invaders.com #geekfingers #ascii

View all 61 comments

6 December 2014

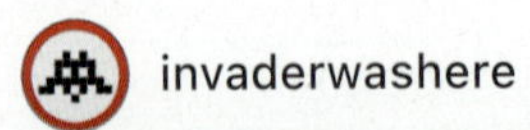

invaderwashere ···

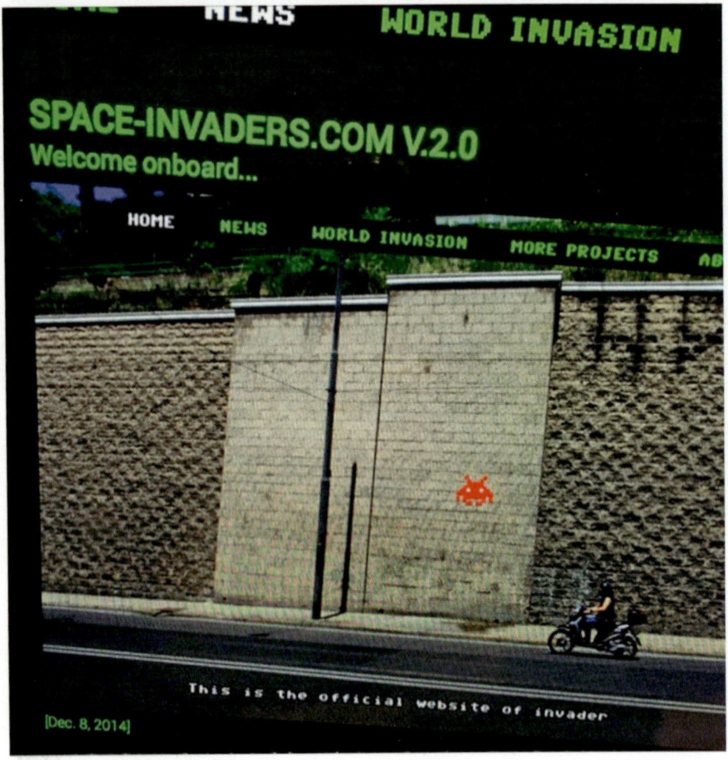

3 294 likes

invaderwashere www.space-invaders.com is out / new website / online now...

View all 55 comments

8 December 2014

invaderwashere •••

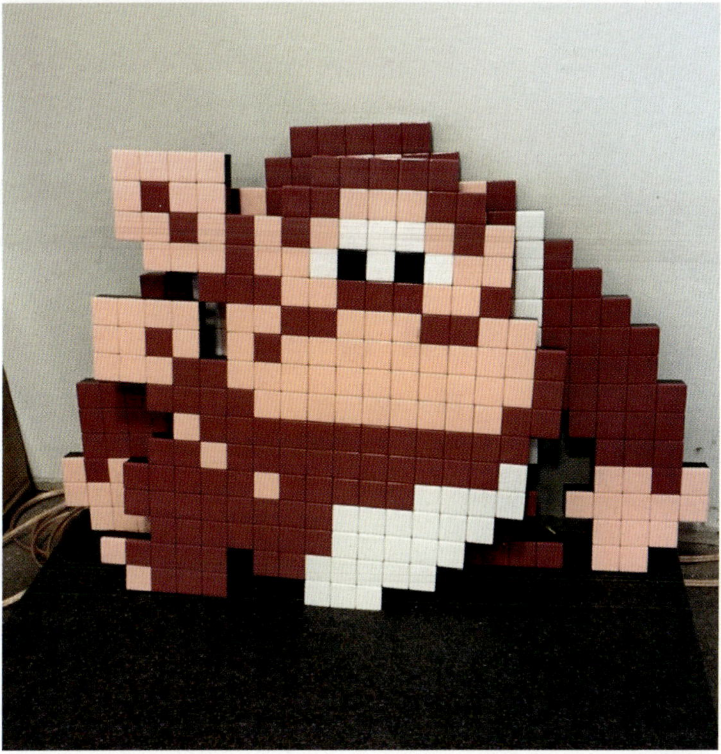

7658 likes

invaderwashere Studio detail #donkeykongbabies #alias #mosaics #pixelart

View all 94 comments

10 December 2014

invaderwashere

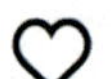   

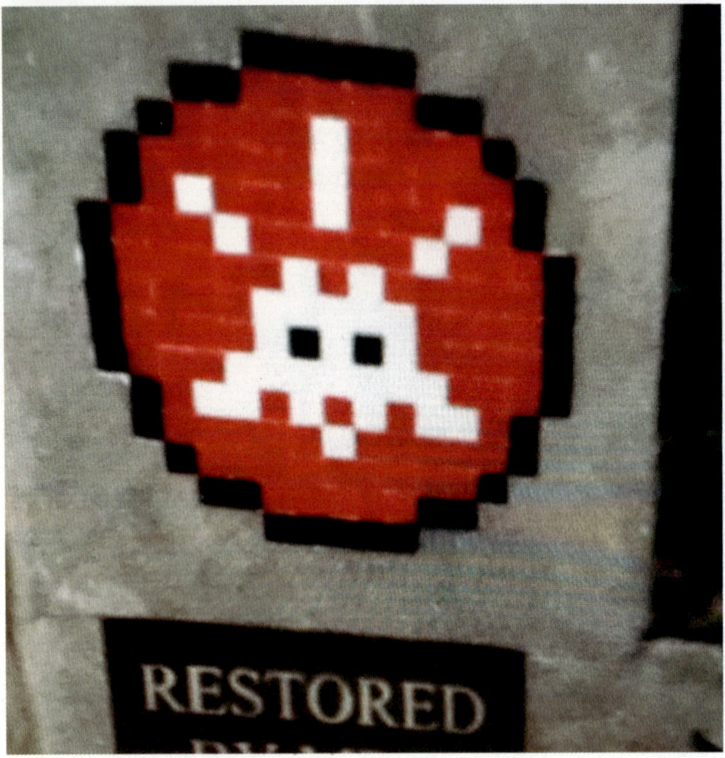

3 913 likes

invaderwashere LCT_04 is back to life! Thanks to @mdr_mosaiquesderue for putting it back 🙂🙏 #laciotat #reactivation

View all 33 comments

19 December 2014

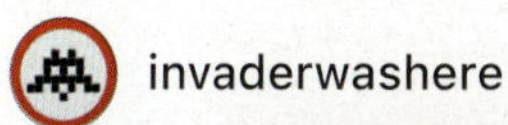

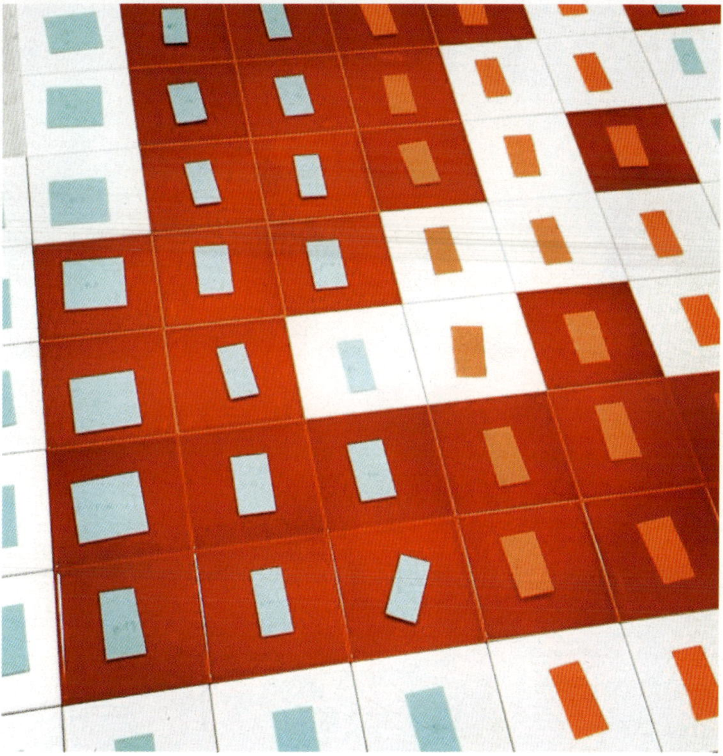

 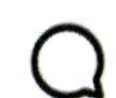 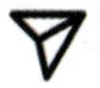 

3 197 likes

invaderwashere Studio detail

View all 21 comments

24 December 2014

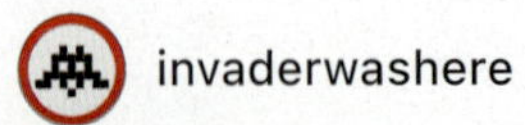

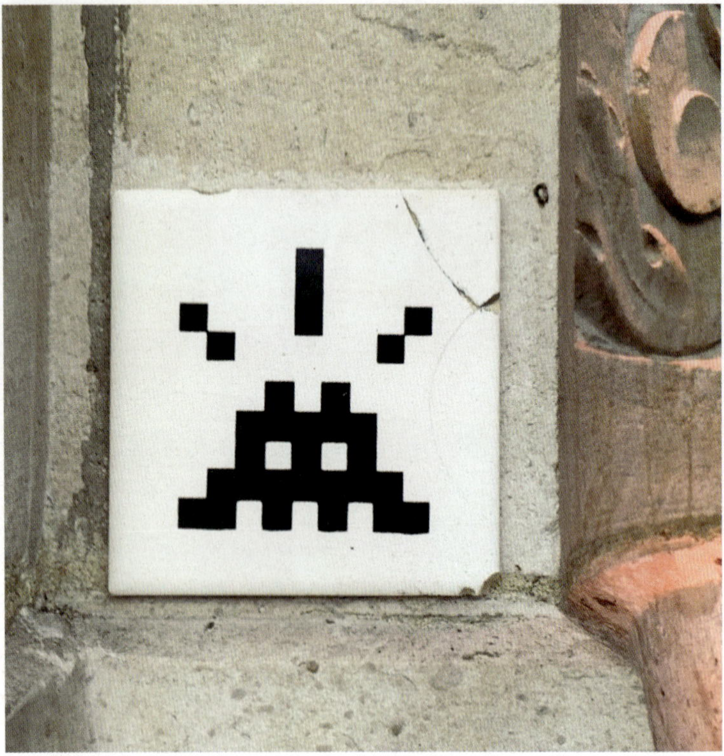

 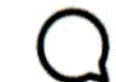  

6 313 likes

invaderwashere Just bumped into one of my old printed tiles #paris #stickertile #2003 #12yearsold

View all 41 comments

28 December 2014

2015

invaderwashere

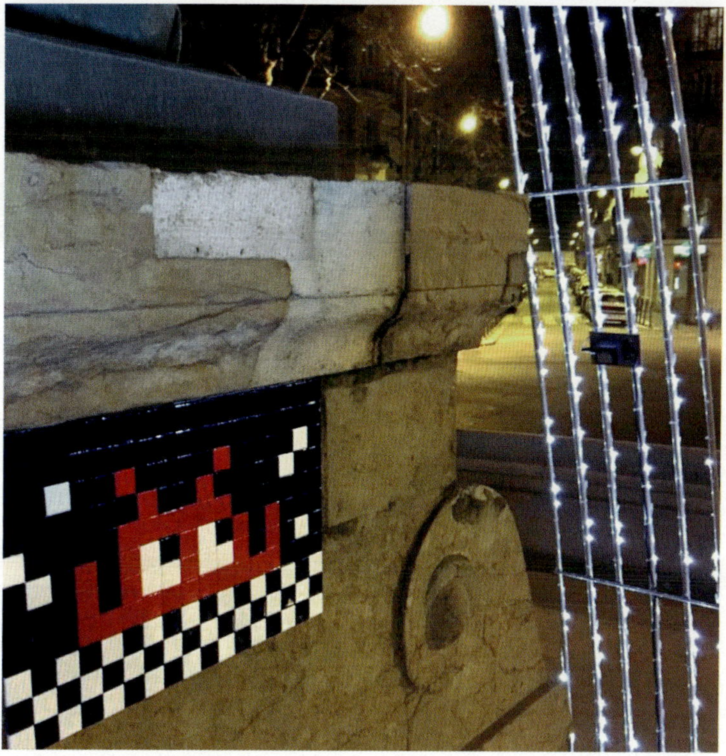

6135 likes

invaderwashere PA_1131 first piece of the year! Happy new year to all of you #paris #fountain #01012015

View all 66 comments

1 January 2015

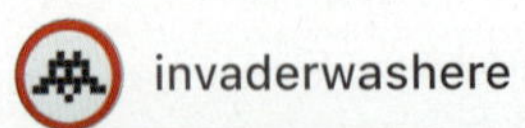

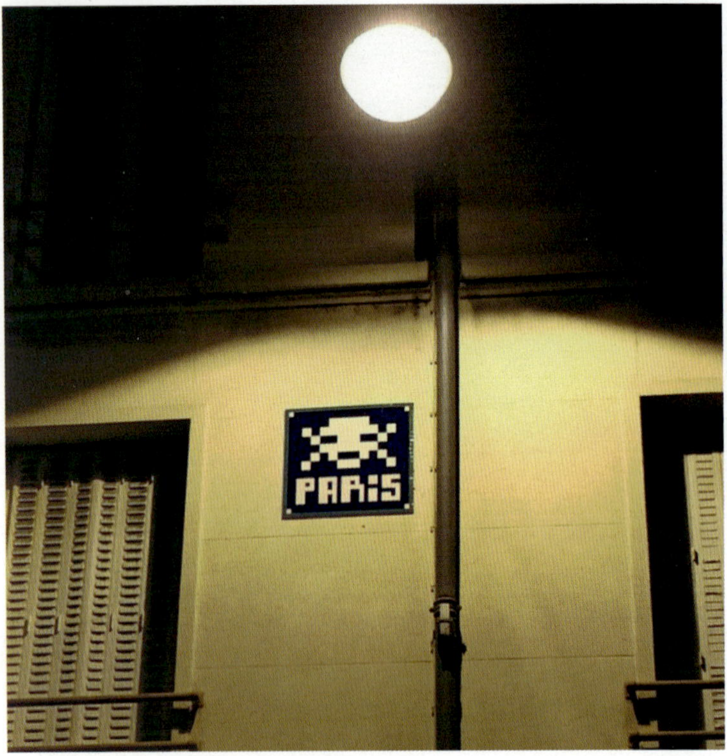

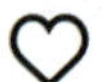   

7696 likes

invaderwashere PA_1132 Hello Paris 5:45 am #justdone better view from trains #garedelyon

View all 65 comments

6 January 2015

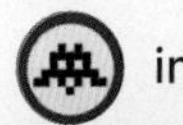
invaderwashere

•••

3 010 likes

invaderwashere Charlie Hebdo #blackday

View all 72 comments

7 January 2015

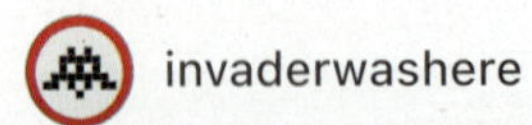

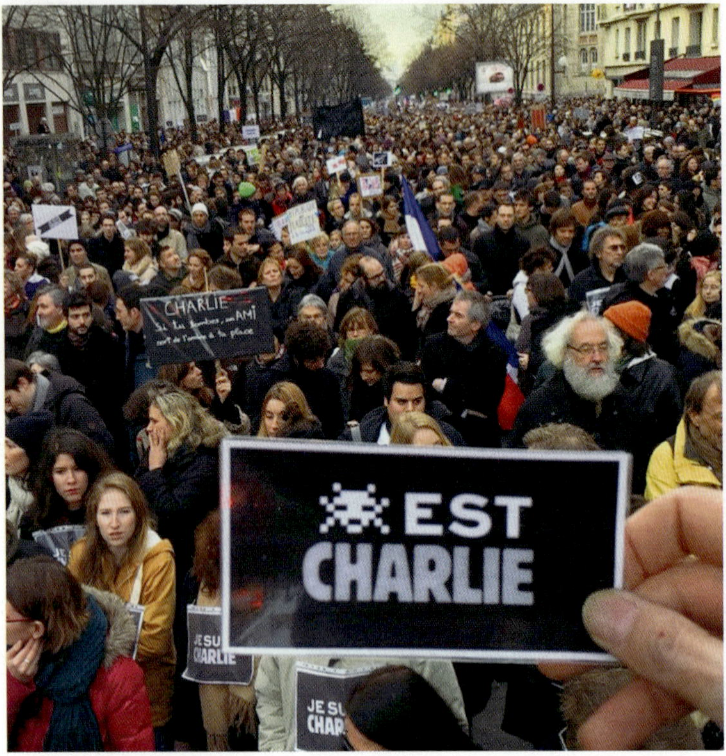

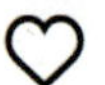   

10 011 likes

invaderwashere #paris #now #jesuischarlie #invaderwashere #againstbarbarism #forfreedomofexpression

View all 125 comments

11 January 2015

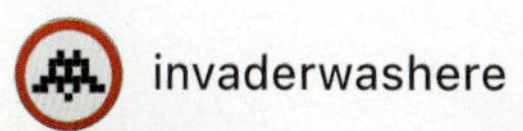

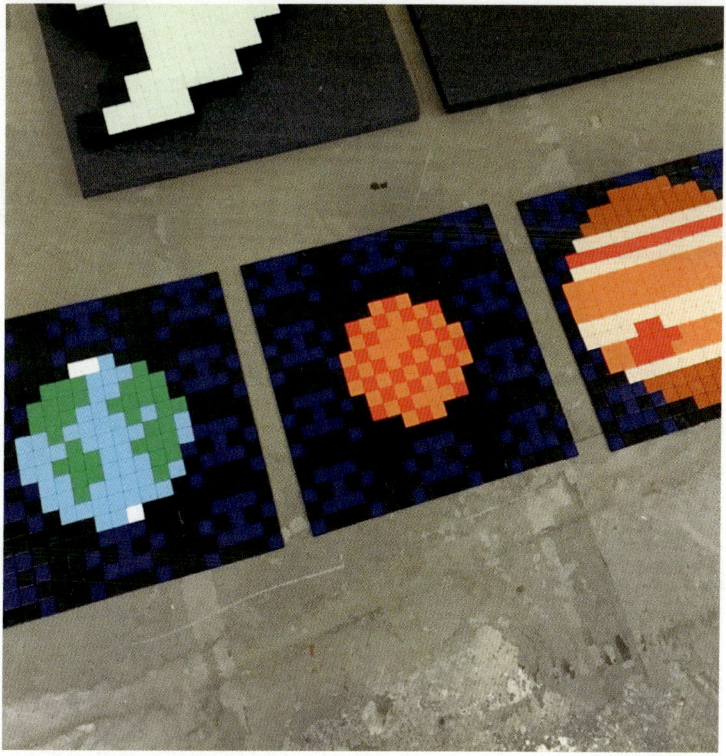

6930 likes

invaderwashere Studio detail / working on #space2 project
Stay tuned... #solarsystem #planets #esa #iss #space

View all 99 comments

14 January 2015

invaderwashere •••

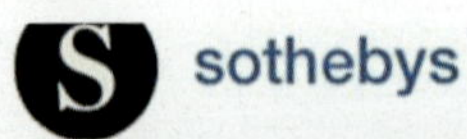

5h

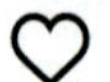   

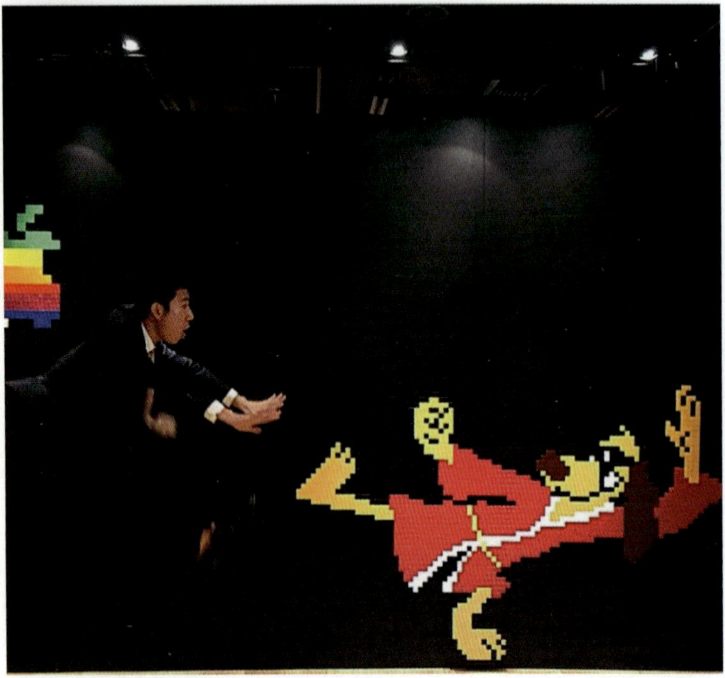

5920 likes

invaderwashere HK_58 - Hong Kong Phooey - seems to drive Sothebys'staff crazy 👊💥✨ @sothebys #hongkong #kungfu #brucelee #invader #alias

View all 53 comments

15 January 2015

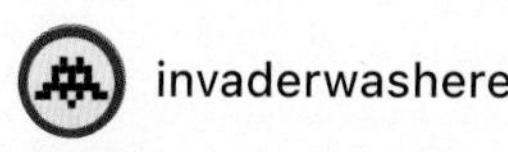
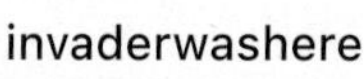

invaderwashere •••

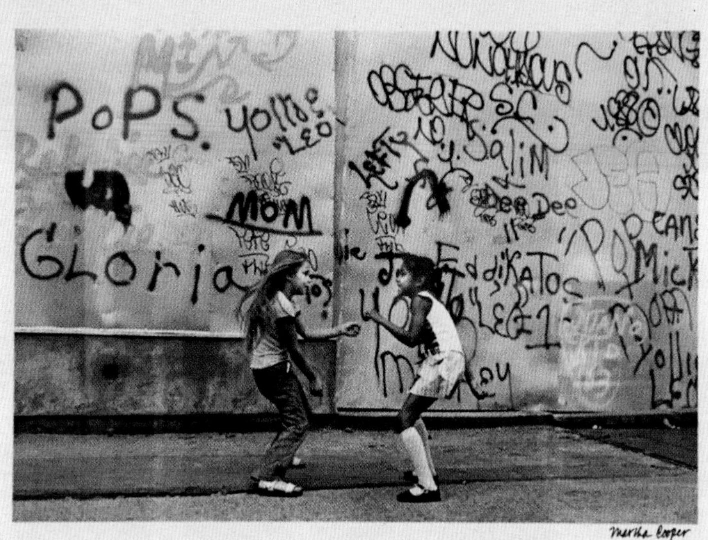

5425 likes

invaderwashere New York late 70's by @marthacoopergram / Thank's Martha

View all 33 comments

18 January 2015

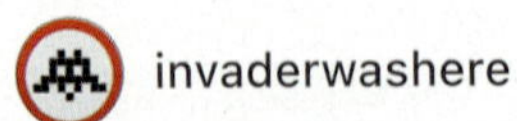

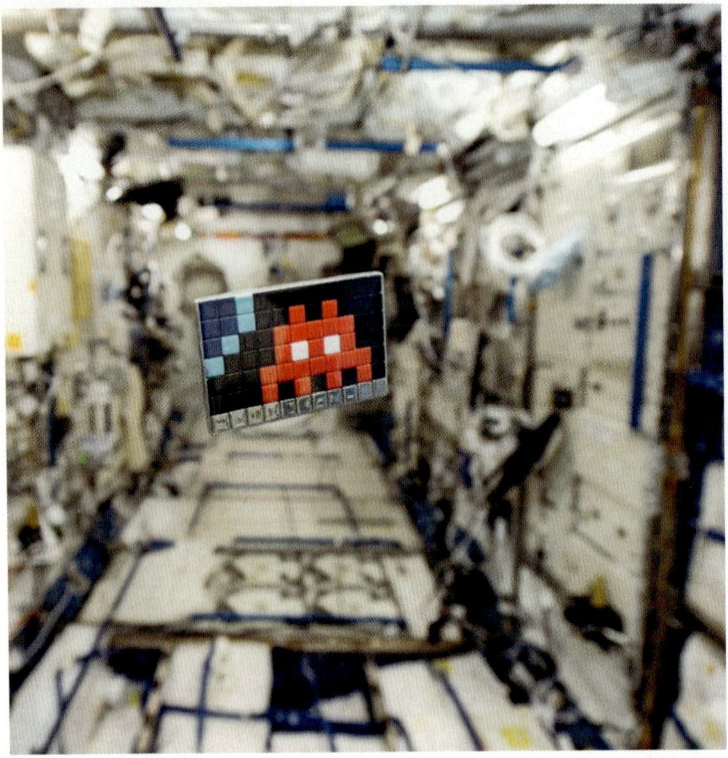

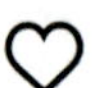   

8 429 likes

invaderwashere Floating is so fun!
#space2iss #spaceinvader #esa #futura42 #space
#0gravity #internationalspacestation #iss

View all 178 comments

21 January 2015

invaderwashere ...

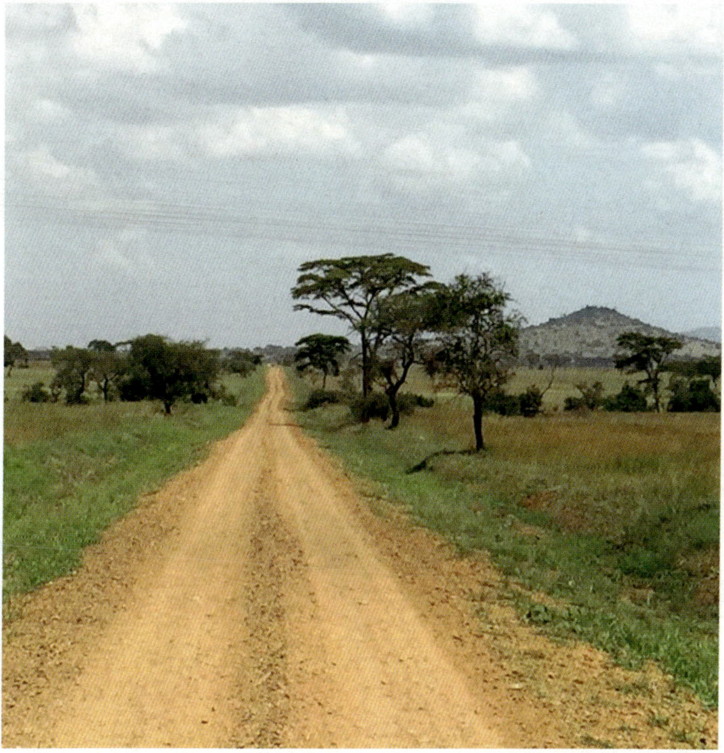

3739 likes

invaderwashere On the road...

View all 29 comments

23 January 2015

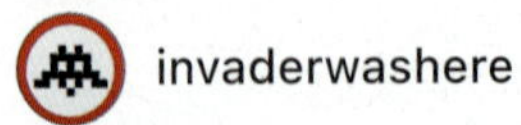

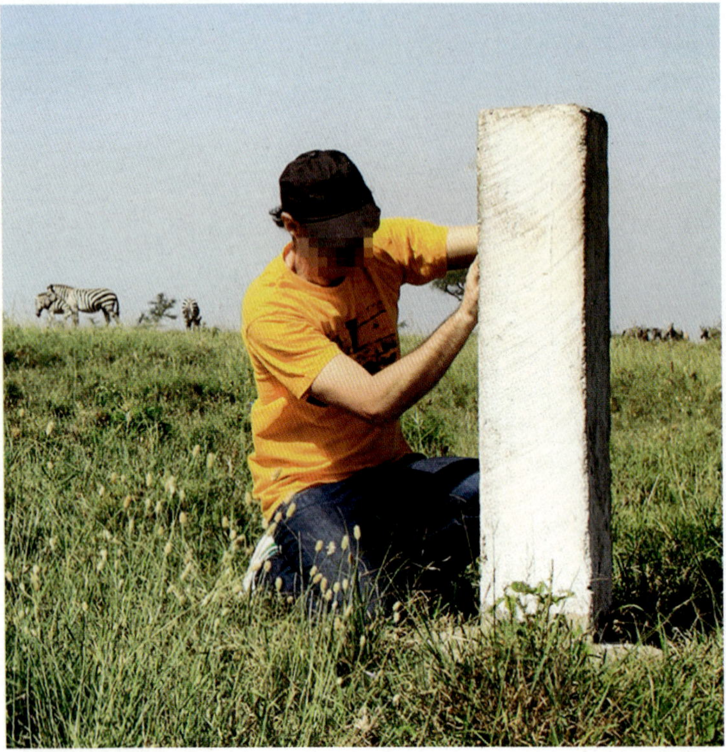

 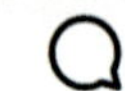  

3753 likes

invaderwashere #Invader at work #savana #tanzania #serengeti #grumeti #zebras

View all 39 comments

24 January 2015

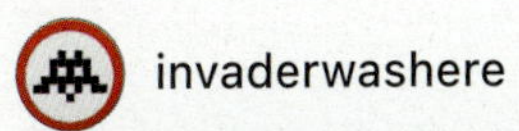

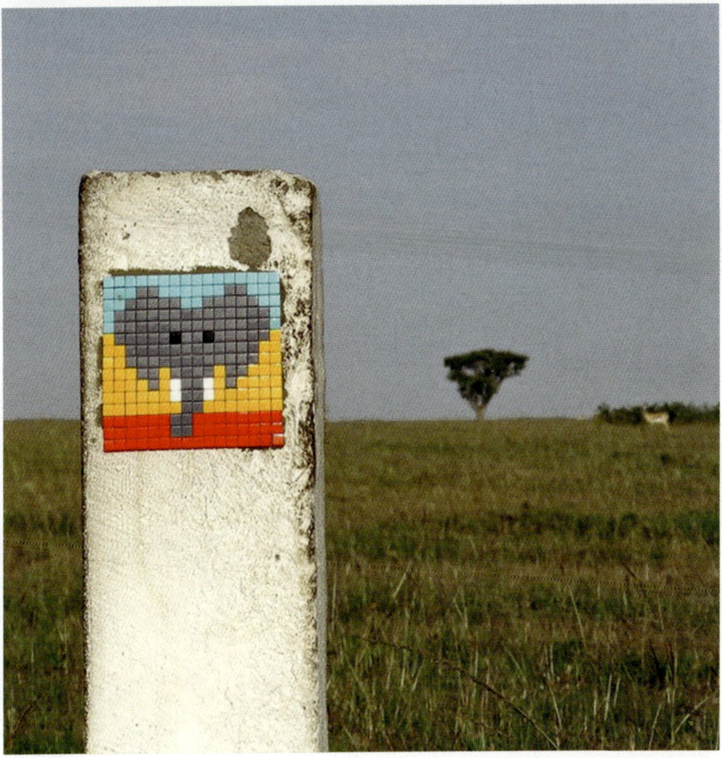

12 186 likes

invaderwashere Elephant in the savana #grumeti natural reserve #Tanzania #GRTI01 #elephant #impala

View all 265 comments

24 January 2015

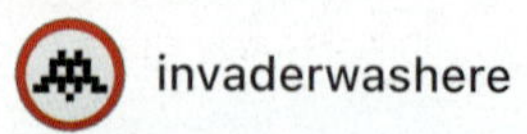

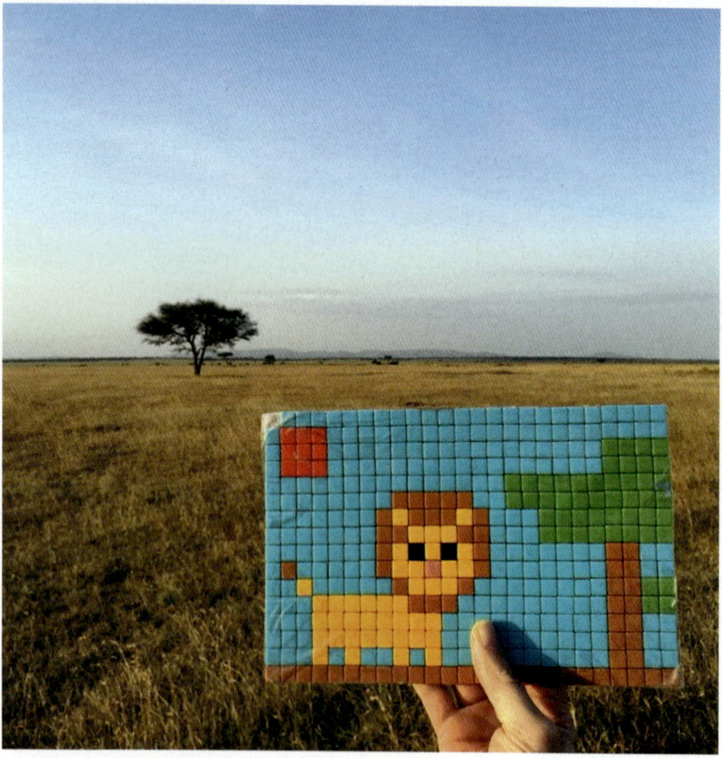

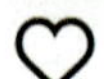   

11513 likes

invaderwashere Not easy to find a spot around there!
#Tanzania #Savana

View all 216 comments

24 January 2015

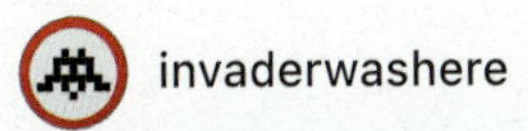

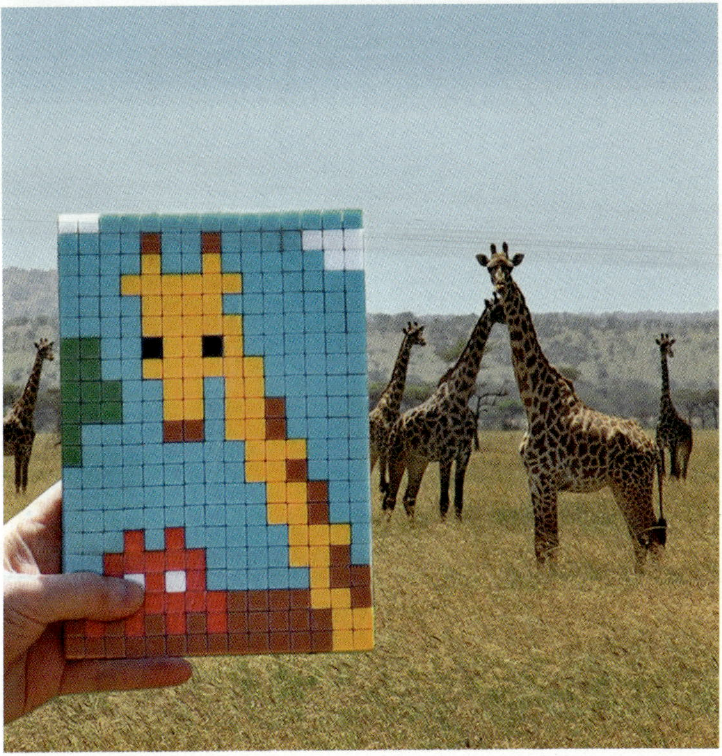

 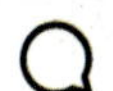  

12 577 likes

invaderwashere Low-res portrait

View all 285 comments

26 January 2015

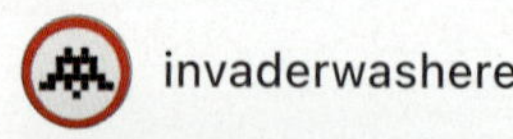

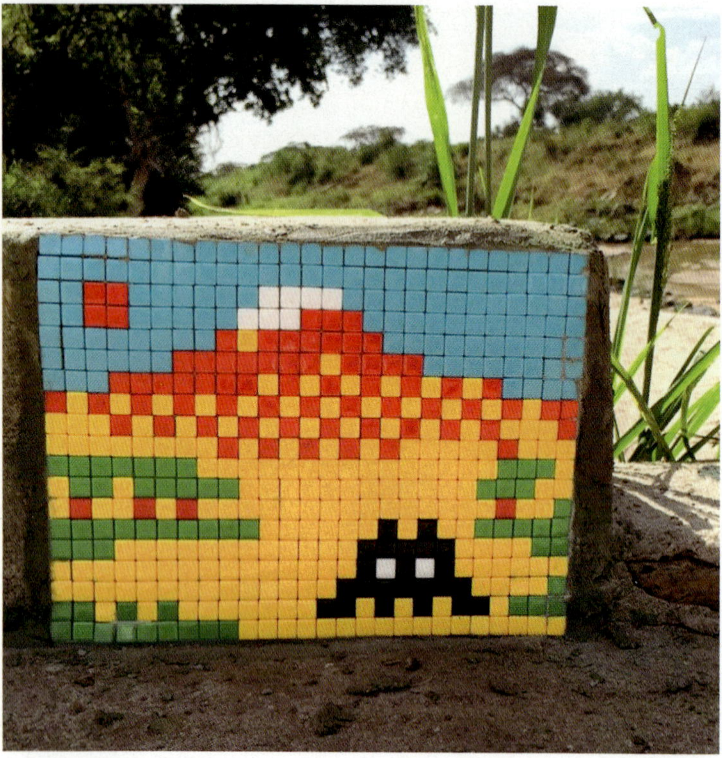

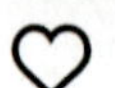

7686 likes

invaderwashere I took advantage that crocodiles were not here this day #Kilimanjaro #river #bushArt #savana #africa

View all 73 comments

27 January 2015

invaderwashere

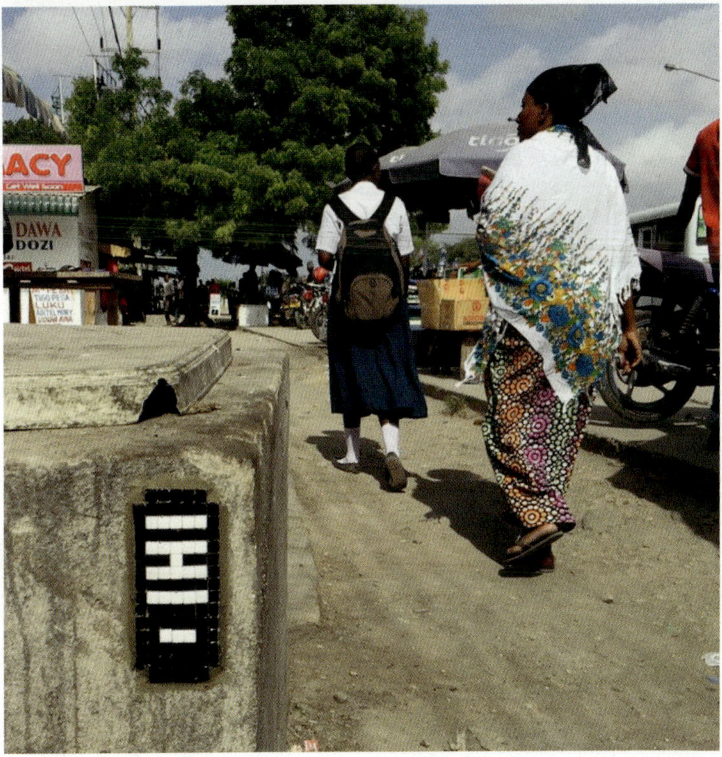

4620 likes

invaderwashere I wanna go to Africa to the black jah rastaman, to the black culture... #africanmask #africanreggae #tanzania #invaderswashere

View all 32 comments

27 January 2015

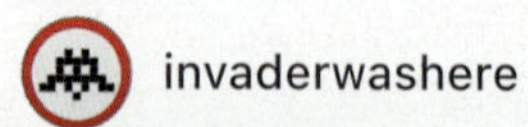

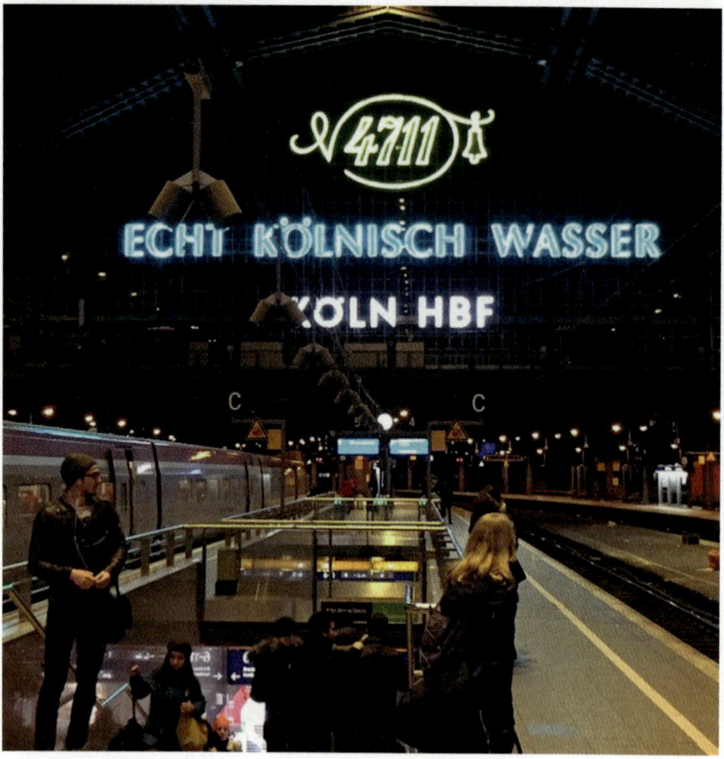

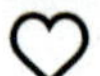 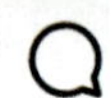  

2 641 likes

invaderwashere Back in Europe and on the road again
#cologne #germany #trainstation

View all 46 comments

30 January 2015

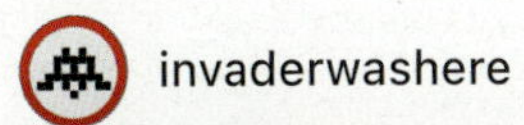

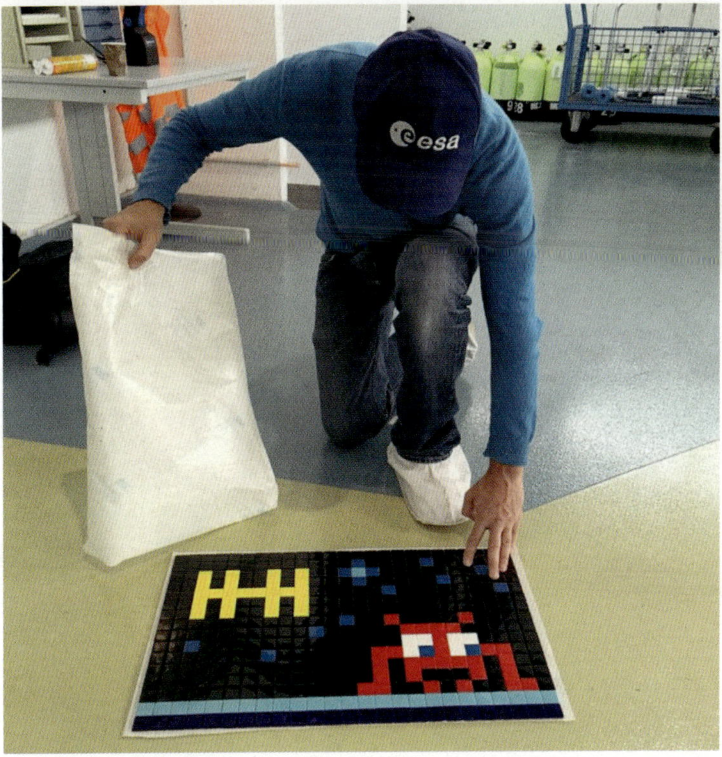

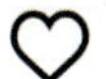 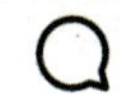  

6 889 likes

invaderwashere Installing a piece at the European Astronaut Centre #EAC #ESA #space2iss project #ISS #spaceinvader #cologne #koln #invader at work

View all 52 comments

31 January 2015

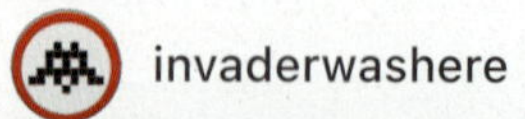

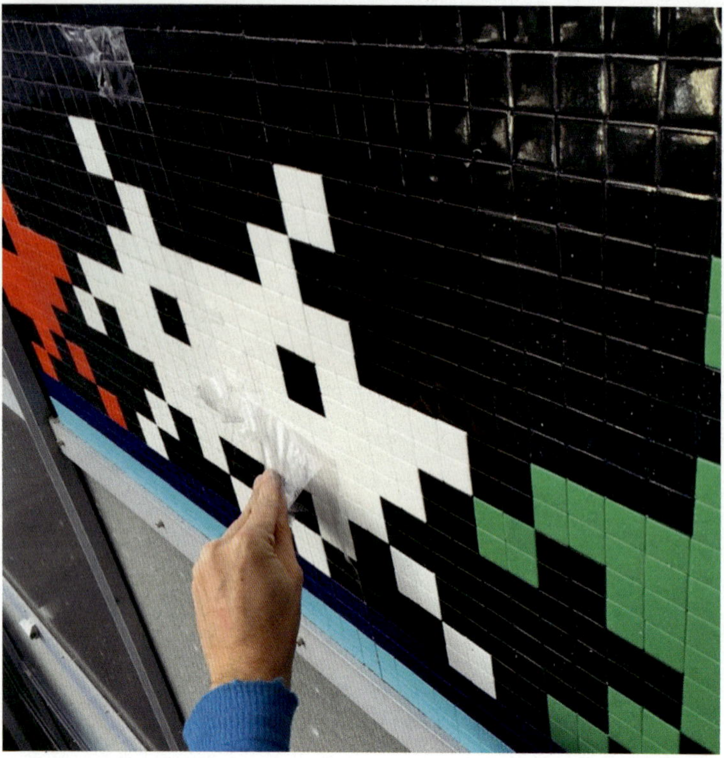

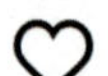   

6 232 likes

invaderwashere Making of KLN_26 #EAC entrance #esa #astronauts #cologne #germany #space2iss

View all 32 comments

31 January 2015

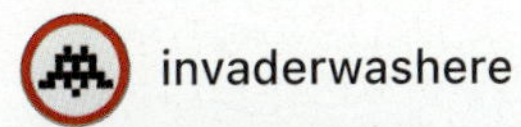

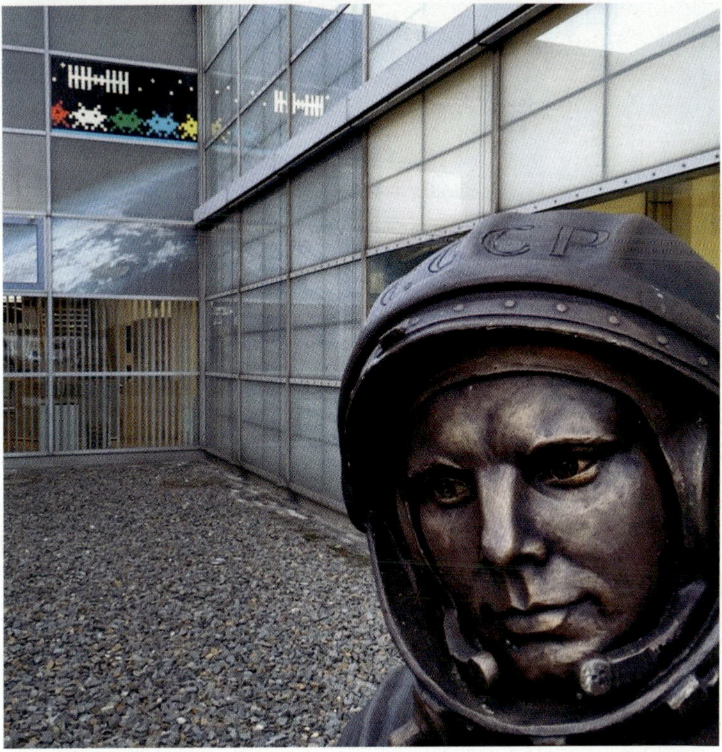

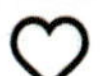   

6 246 likes

invaderwashere Made under the eyes of Youri Gagarine at the European Astronaut Centre entrance #EAC #astronauts hand in hand #ISS #space2iss #cologne #germany

View all 65 comments

1 February 2015

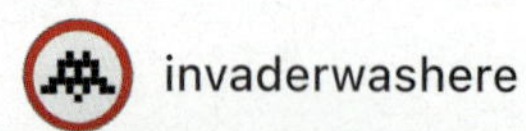

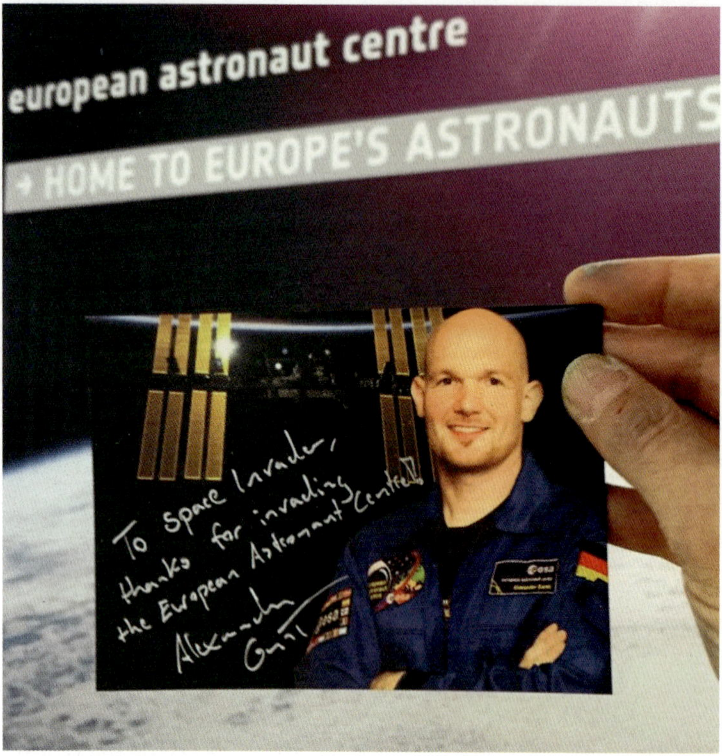

3625 likes

invaderwashere Invasion of the European Astronaut Centre successful. Thank you to #AlexanderGerst and to the #EAC team. #cologne #germany #astronauts #ESA #space2iss

View all 38 comments

3 February 2015

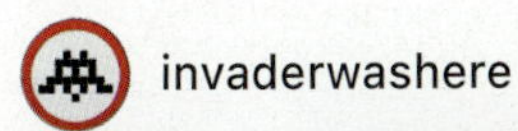

•••

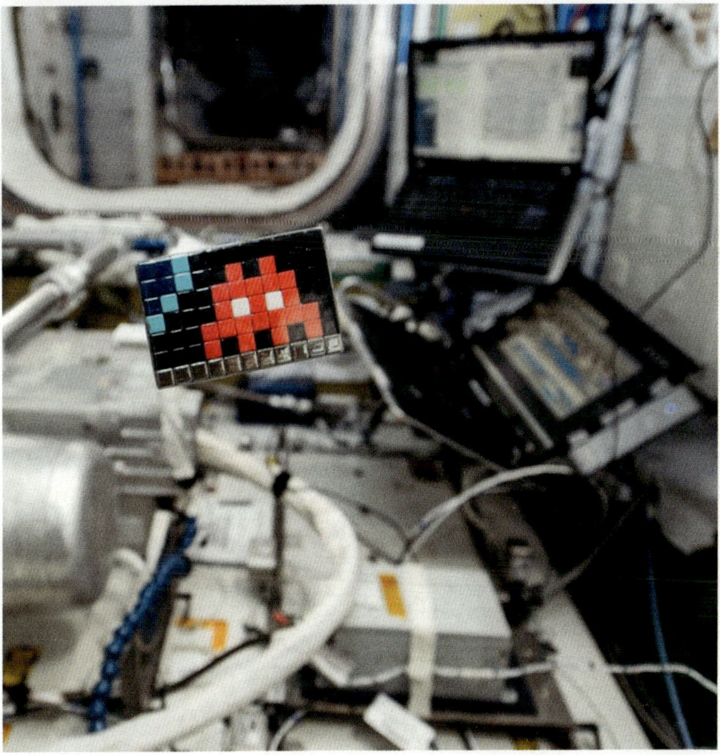

8065 likes

invaderwashere Meanwhile in space... #Space2 floating!
#0gravity #esa #iss #space2iss #spaceinvader #laptops

View all 114 comments

4 February 2015

invaderwashere

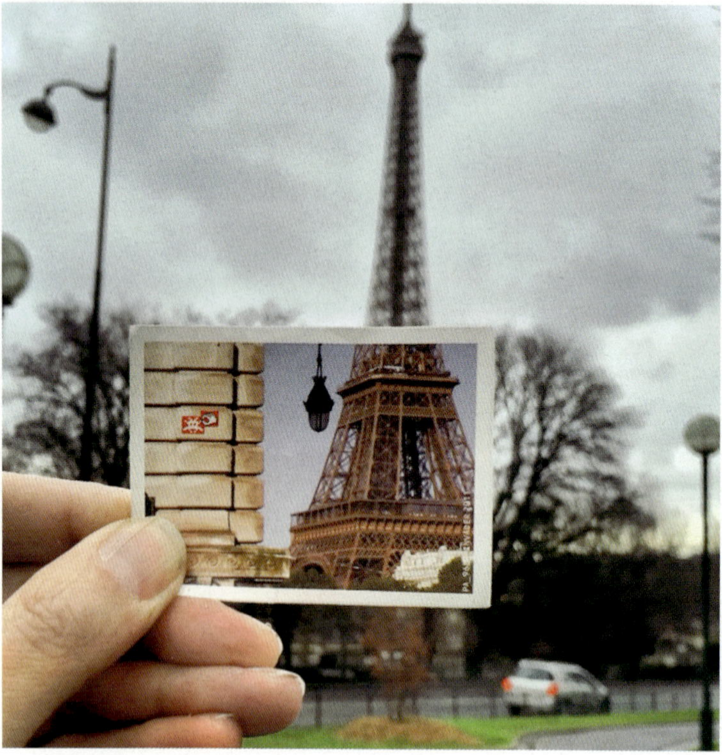

...

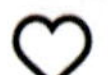   

8 349 likes

invaderwashere Back in #paris #sticker #eiffeltower

View all 61 comments

8 February 2015

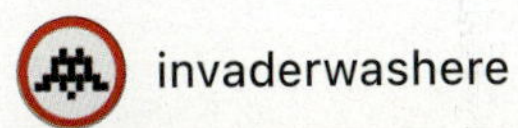

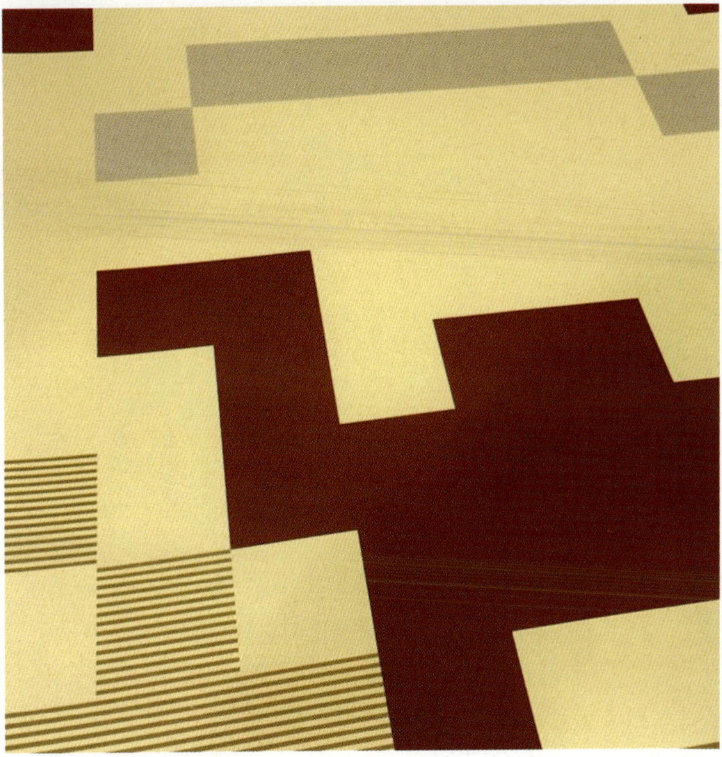

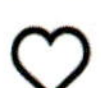 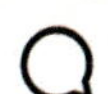  

3 231 likes

invaderwashere Just get my new print from the silk screen printer #detail #camel #smokingkills

View all 41 comments

13 February 2015

invaderwashere

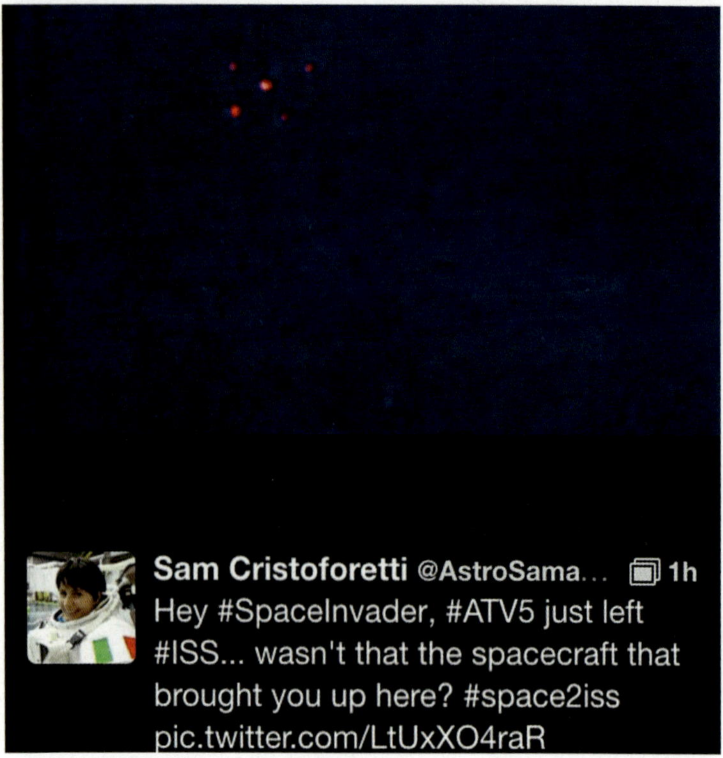

Sam Cristoforetti @AstroSama... 1h
Hey #SpaceInvader, #ATV5 just left #ISS... wasn't that the spacecraft that brought you up here? #space2iss pic.twitter.com/LtUxXO4raR

2 209 likes

invaderwashere New tweet from my astro friend #SamanthaCristoforetti #ISS #ATV5 #ESA #futura42 #space2iss #space #invader

View all 18 comments

14 February 2015

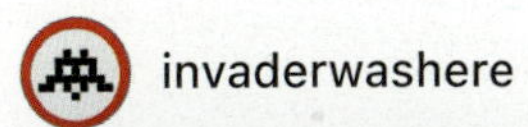

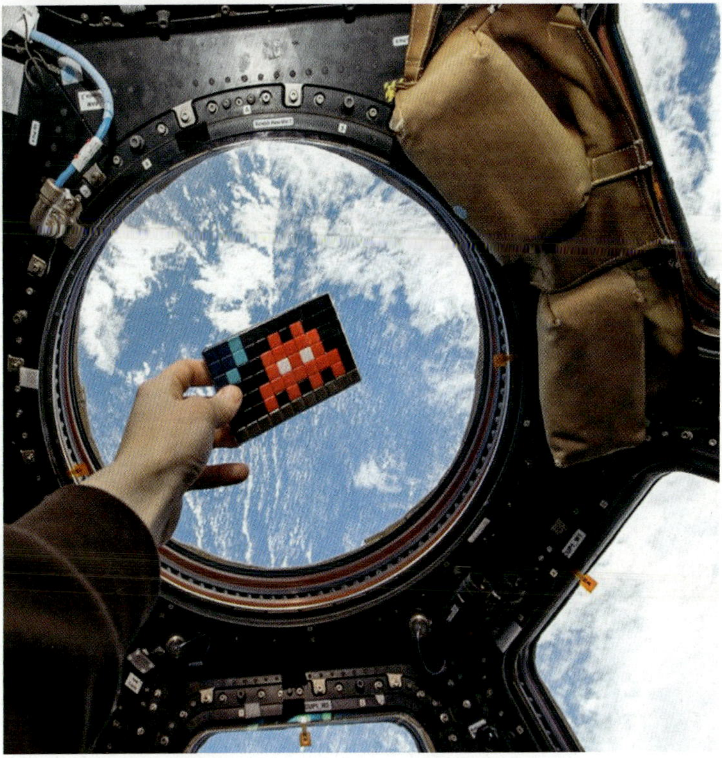

10 073 likes

invaderwashere Goodbye Earth! Space2 stays in the International Space Station. The International Space Station (ISS) unites USA, Russia, Japan, Canada and Europe in one of the largest partnerships in the history of science. Crews of up to six astronauts conduct research into life and physical sciences and applications, and prepare for future human exploration missions. The Station is the biggest object ever flown in space, it covers an area as big as a football pitch. The ISS flies at the altitude of 260 mi high (400 km) at the speed of 17.700 mph. It only takes 90 minutes for the weightless laboratory to make a complete circuit of Earth. Astronauts working and living on the Station experience 16 sunrises and sunsets each day. #SPACE2ISS #astronaut #ISS #ESA #NASA

View all 267 comments

14 February 2015

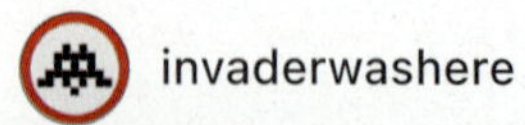

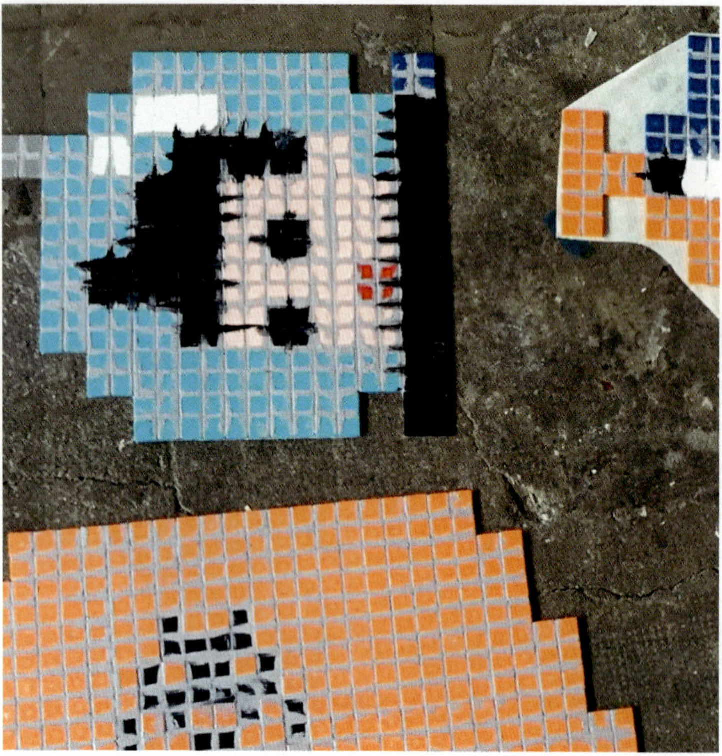

5147 likes

invaderwashere Studio detail / Backside of a new piece for the European Space Agency #ESA #SPACE2ISS

View all 35 comments

22 February 2015

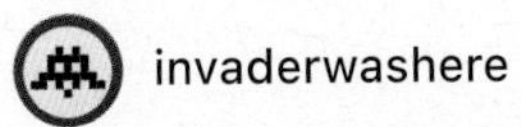
invaderwashere

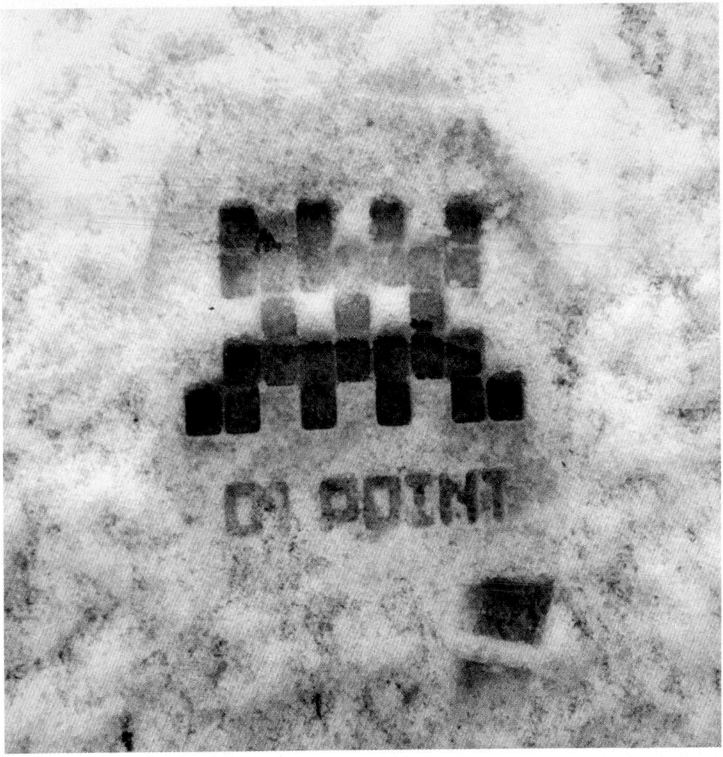

5456 likes

invaderwashere It's snowing here... #footprint #snow #R-Invader #Belgium

View all 37 comments

23 February 2015

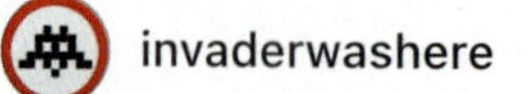

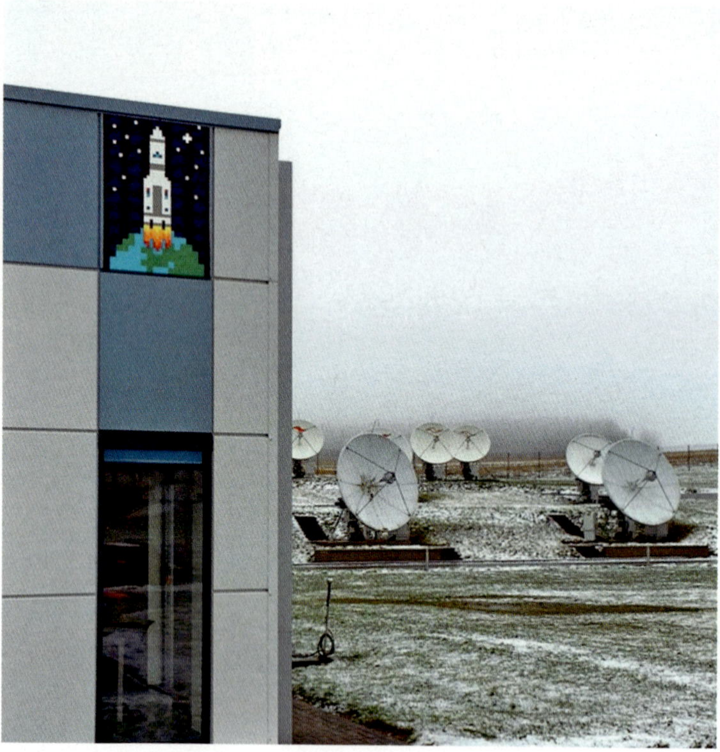

  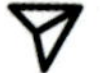 

6 878 likes

invaderwashere RDU_01 #Redu #Belgium #ESA #Ariane5 #antennas #SPACE2ISS

View all 41 comments

24 February 2015

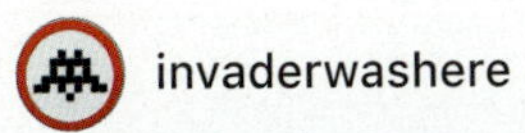

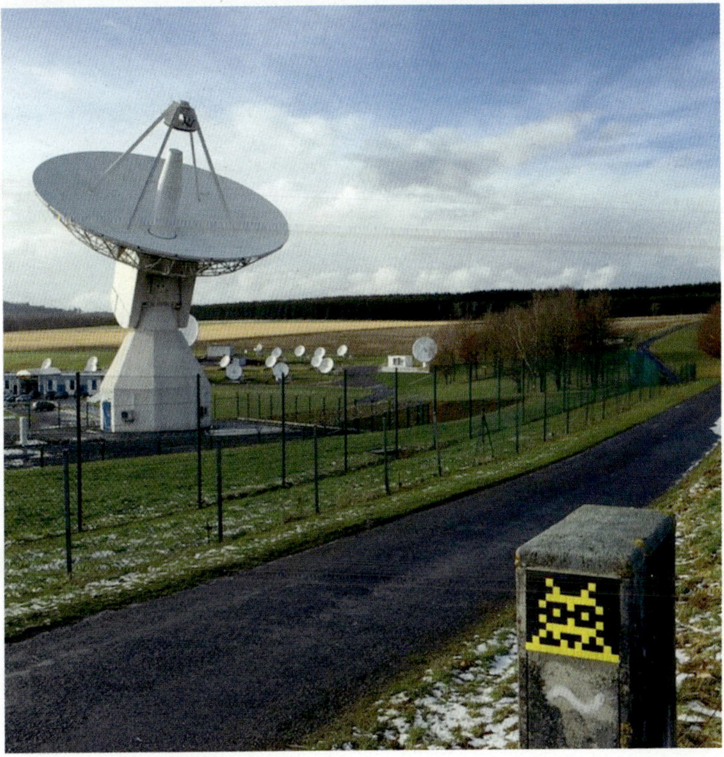

5052 likes

invaderwashere RDU_04 #Redu #Belgium European Space Center #ESA #antennas #SPACE2ISS #spaceArt

View all 29 comments

24 February 2015

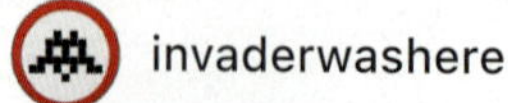

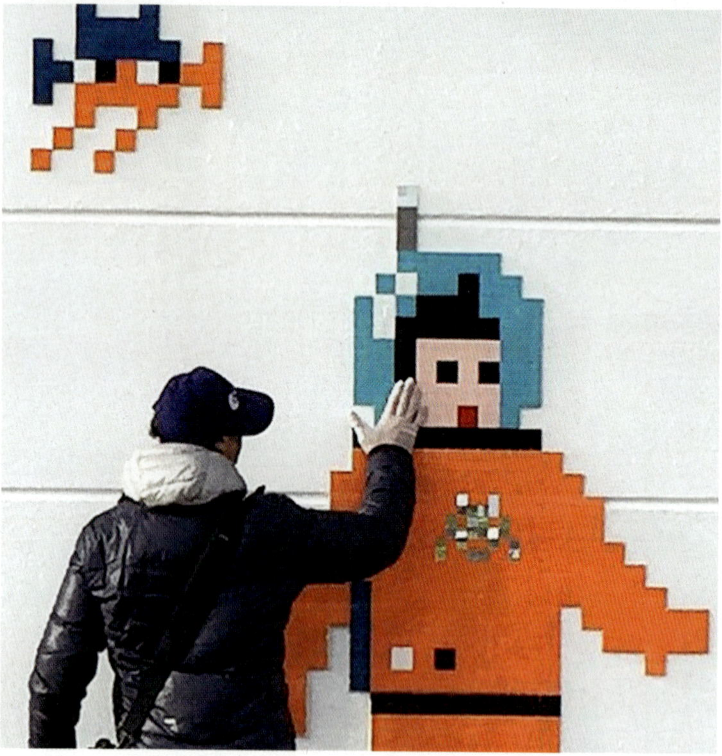

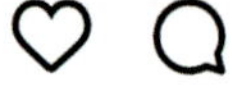 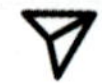  

6975 likes

invaderwashere Installing RDU_02 #astronaut #spaceinvader #Redu #Belgium #ESA #SPACE2ISS

View all 49 comments

24 February 2015

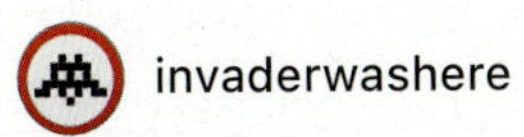

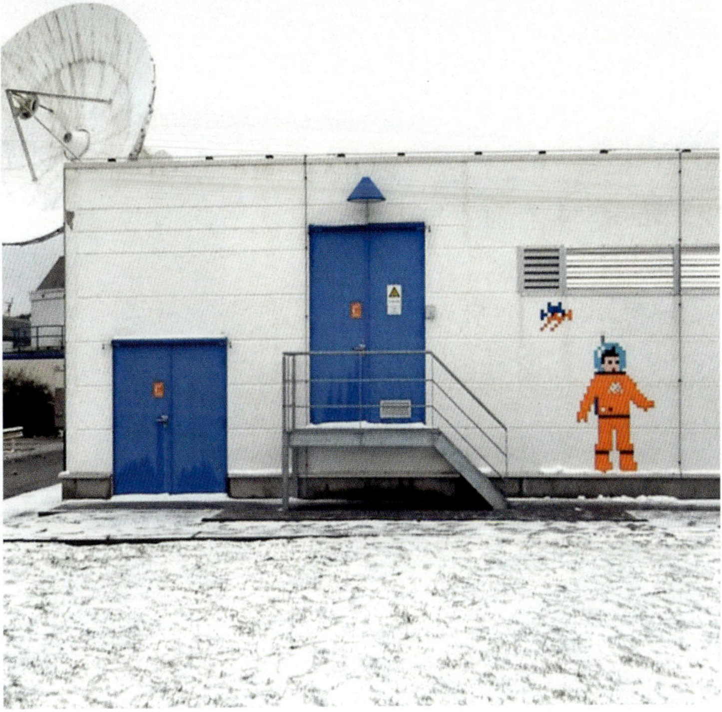

6 309 likes

invaderwashere RDU_02 #Redu #Belgium European Space Agency #ESA #SPACE2ISS #astronaut

View all 46 comments

24 February 2015

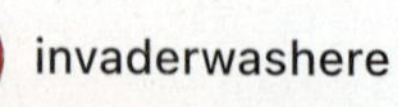

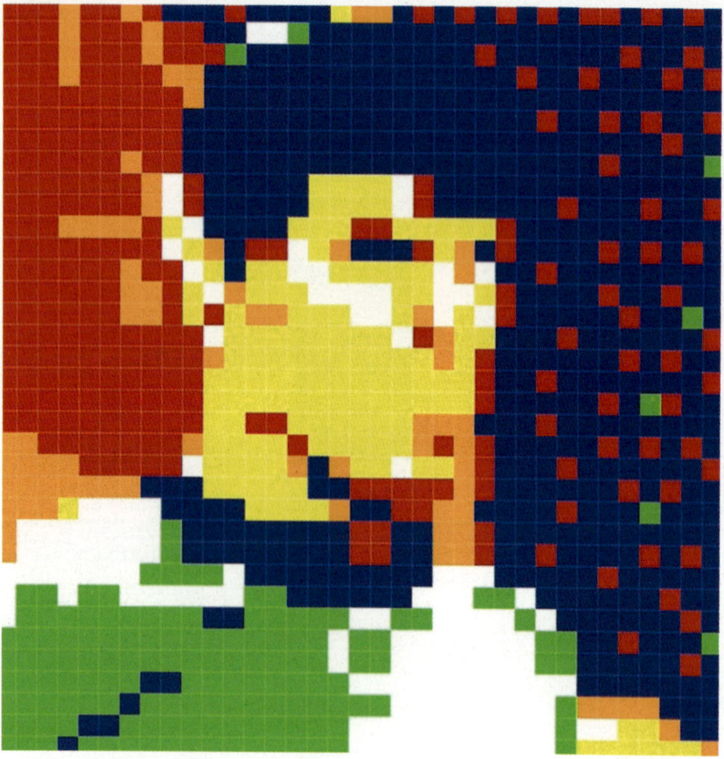

7153 likes

invaderwashere You've been a great source of inspiration, RIP #LeonardNimoy #Spock #rubikcubism Rubikcubist study from 2005

View all 54 comments

1 March 2015

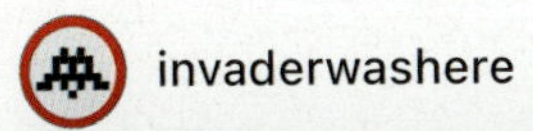

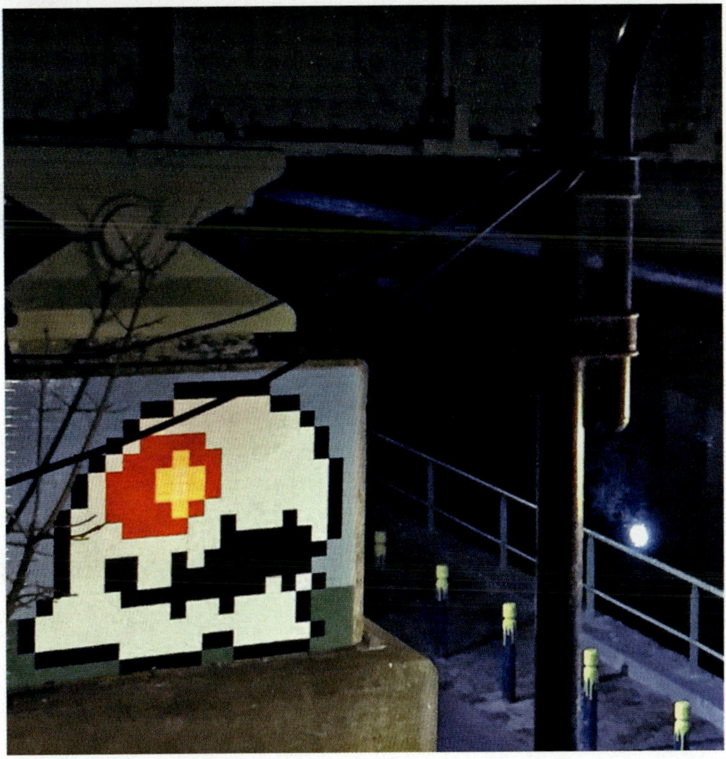

7627 likes

invaderwashere Creature from the black lagoon / Paris / 3:52am

View all 68 comments

10 March 2015

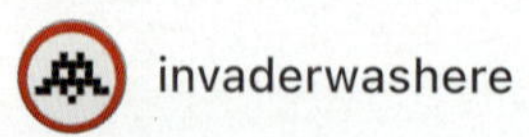

→ EUROPEAN SPACE AGENCY | ABOUT US | OUR ACTIVITIES | CONNECT WITH US | FOR MEDIA | FOR EDUCATORS | FOR KIDS

space for europe

esa

HOME

→ SPACE INVADERS

Our Universe is the canvas as iconic Space Invader mosaics link the International Space Station and ESA establishments

Archive

LATEST NEWS

All News

11 March 2015
Hot water activity on icy moon's seafloor

09 March 2015
Testing astronauts' lungs in Space Station airlock

09 March 2015
Galileo satellites ready for fuelling as launcher takes s...

06 March 2015
Scanning Earth, saving lives

06 March 2015
Have you ever used a camera on board an interplanetary cr...

04 March 2015
ESA experts assess risk from exploded satellite

26 February 2015
CubeSats offered deep-space ride on ESA asteroid probe

25 February 2015
Improved vision for James Webb Space Telescope

Search here

ESA IN YOU

LATEST PRESS RELEASE

previous

25 February 2015 European Data Relay System confirms services for Copernicus in cooperation with the European Commission

→ SPACE IN IMAGES

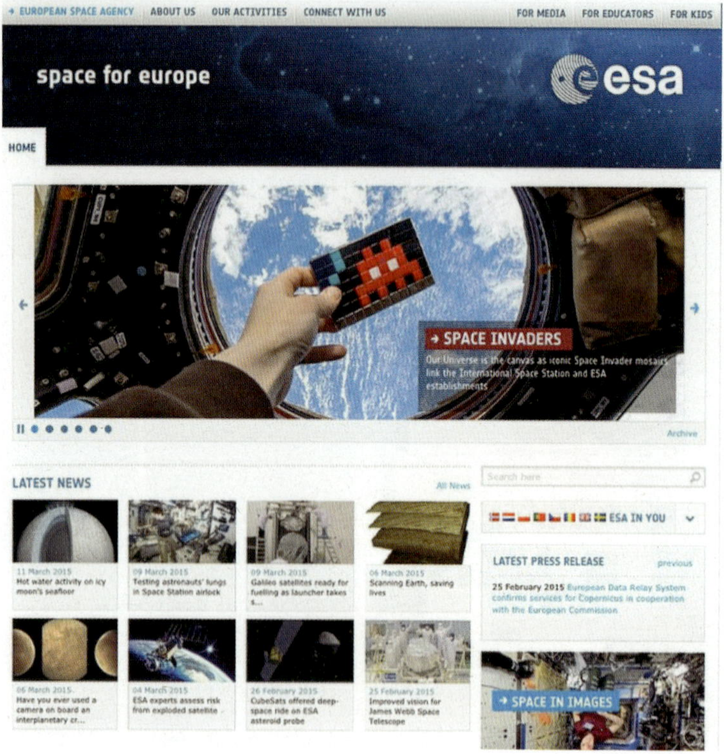

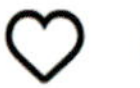

2 921 likes

invaderwashere Checkout www.esa.int #SPACE2ISS #ESA / more tomorrow...

View all 24 comments

11 March 2015

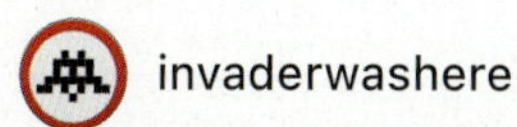

•••

 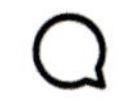  

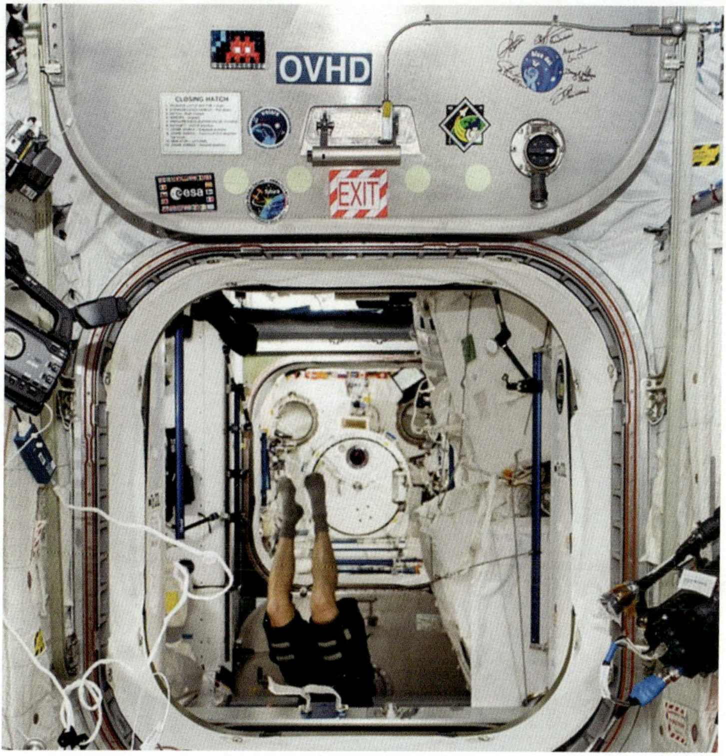

6163 likes

invaderwashere Invasion of the #ISS successful!!! Space2 has just found a permanent spot in the Colombus module aboard the ISS.

I would have never imagined that my Space Invaders project might take me that high! What looked like an unrreachable dream has come true as the mosaic Space2 is the first piece of art ever installed on a spaceship among real astronauts living in zero gravity and with Earth and the universe as a background. Art, Science, space conquest: a great move! #ESA #astroSamantha #SPACE2ISS #spaceart #internationalspacestation

View all 143 comments

12 March 2015

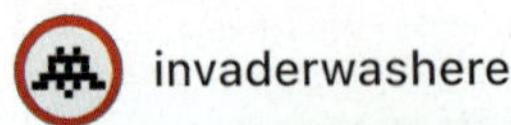

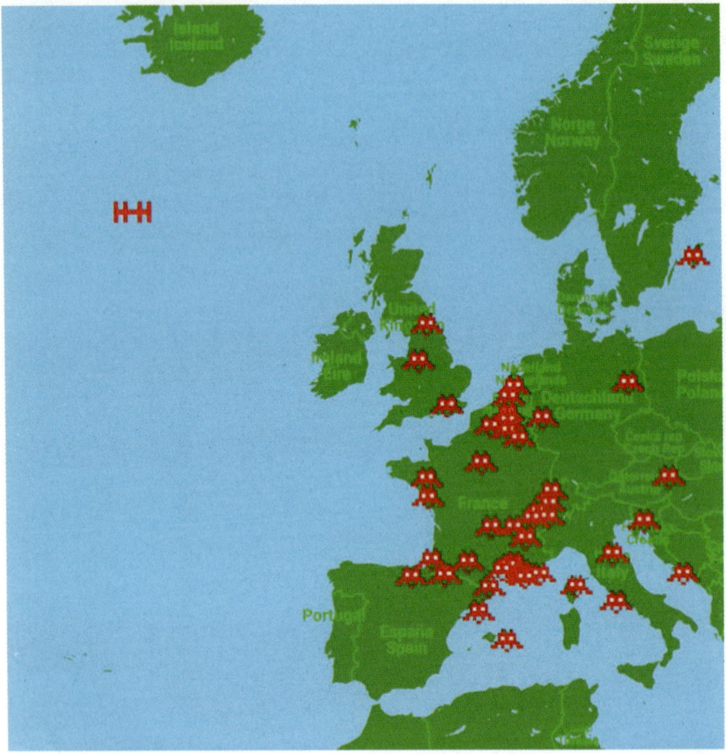

5 441 likes

invaderwashere You can now follow the position of the #ISS and #Space2 in real time on the World Invasion map page of my website #SPACE2ISS #ESA #futura42

View all 114 comments

12 March 2015

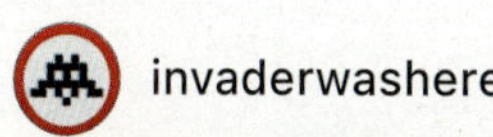

...

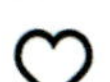   

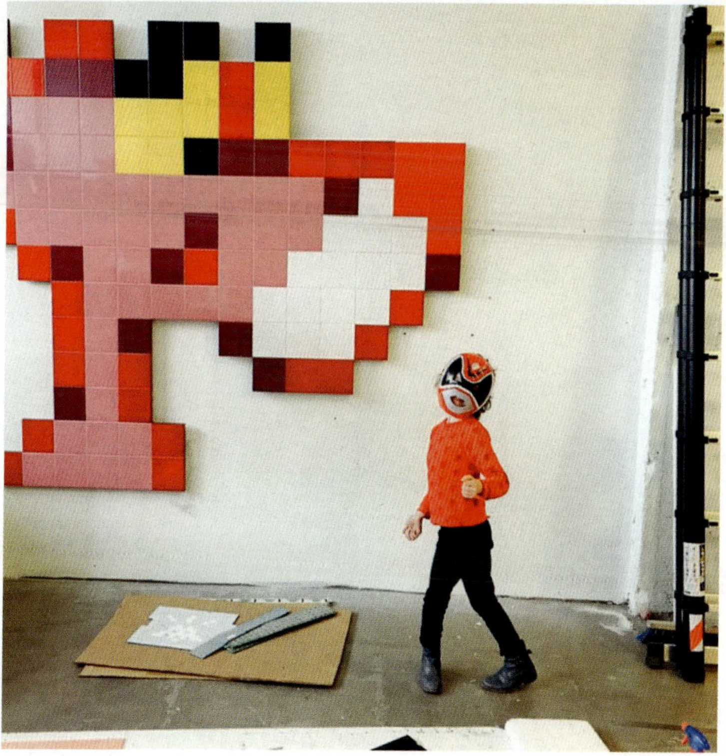

8 279 likes

invaderwashere Studio detail / Force rose / alias PA_1039

View all 72 comments

15 March 2015

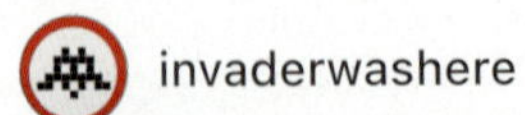

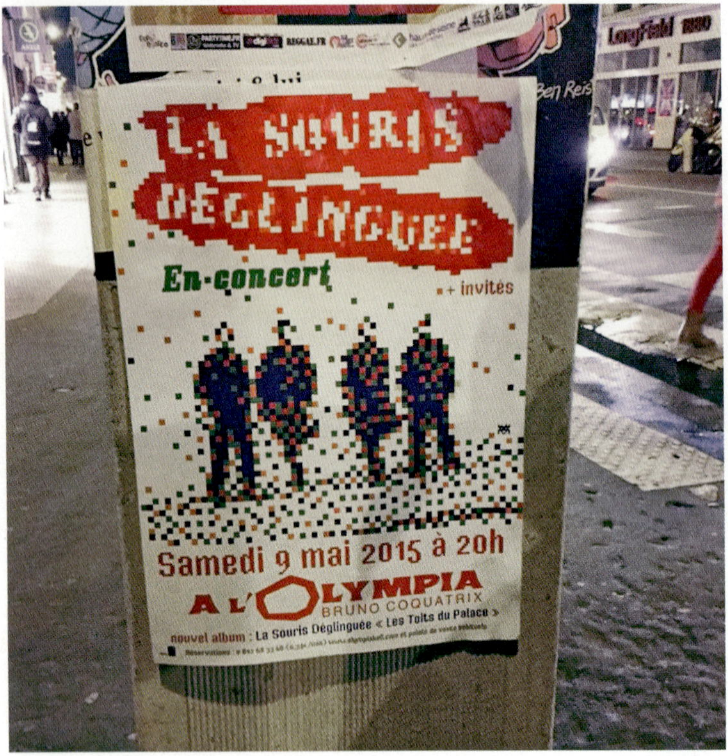

2777 likes

invaderwashere Just bumped into this poster in Paris #poster #live #lasourisdeglinguee #lsd #Olympia 9 mai 2015

View all 12 comments

17 March 2015

invaderwashere

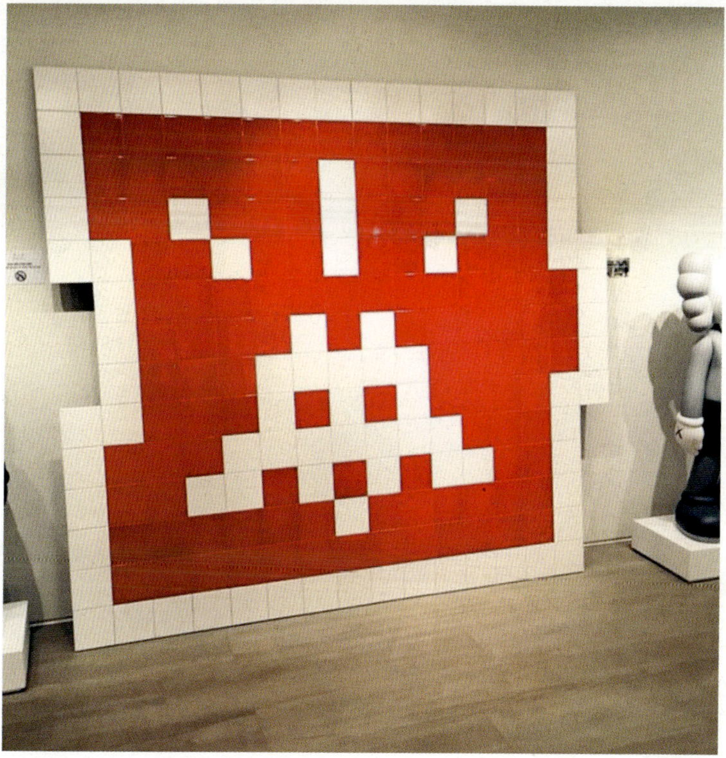

6 887 likes

invaderwashere My 1st piece at #Christies / photo by @Eyllme

View all 83 comments

22 March 2015

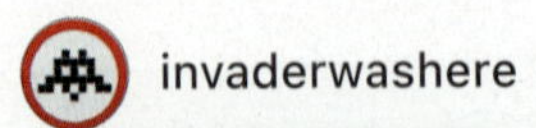

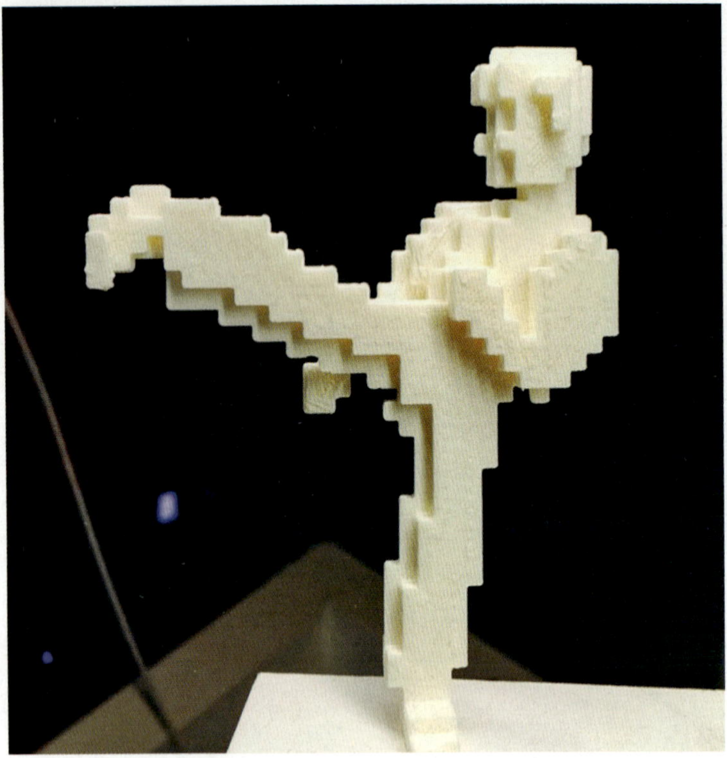

 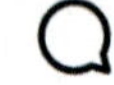 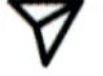 

6 099 likes

invaderwashere 3D printing / Test 18 #KungFuFighter #BruceLee #3D #pixel

View all 101 comments

24 March 2015

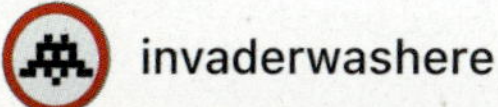

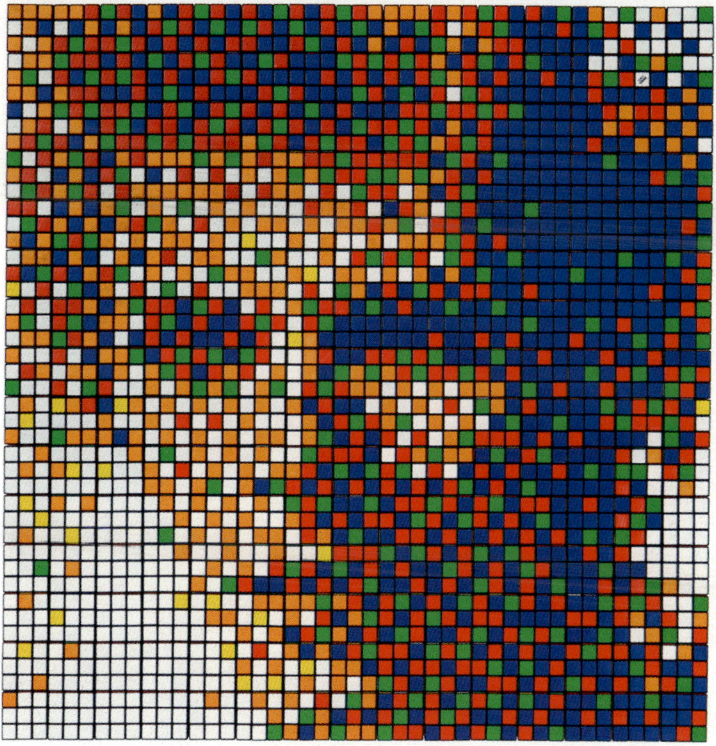

6 546 likes

invaderwashere Rubik Space oddity #bowie 2nd album #rubikcubism #lowFidelity #2011 private collection

View all 96 comments

27 March 2015

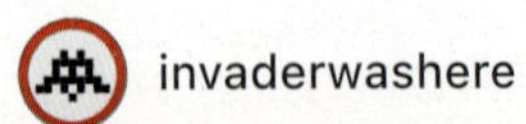
invaderwashere •••

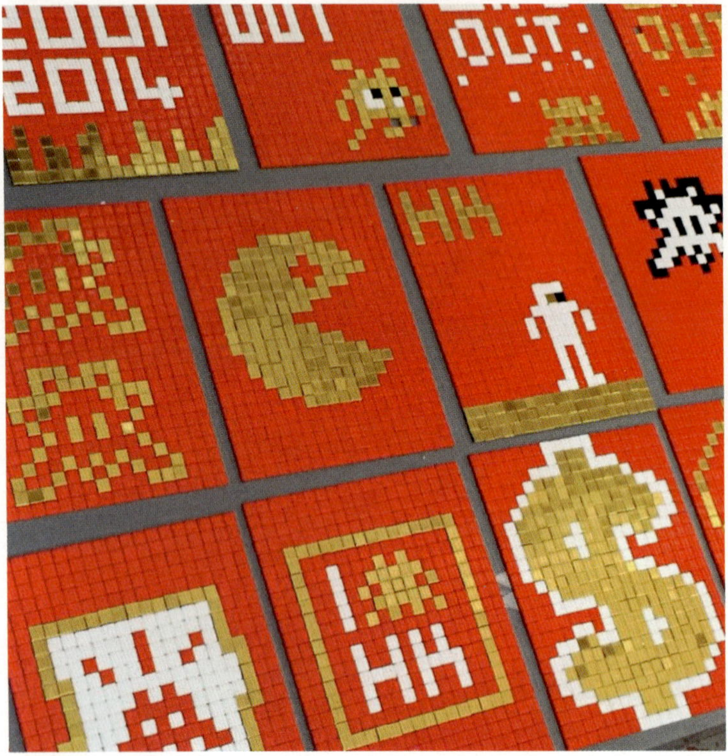

6 557 likes

invaderwashere Preparing the tile covers for my next Invasion Guide #456tiles #red&gold #WipeOut #invasionguide06 Coming soon...

View all 121 comments

2 April 2015

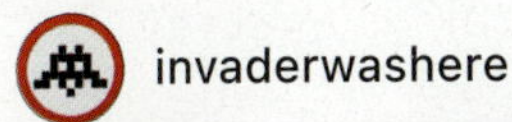

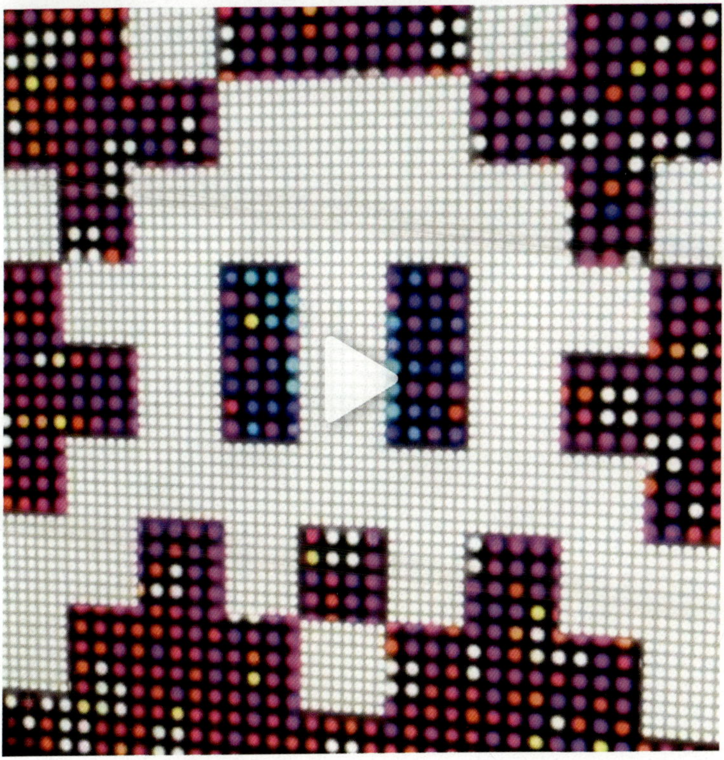

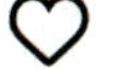 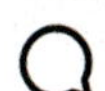  

4570 likes

invaderwashere Working on new pieces #Led #WipeOut
🔴🟢🔵 Stay tuned...

View all 91 comments

3 April 2015

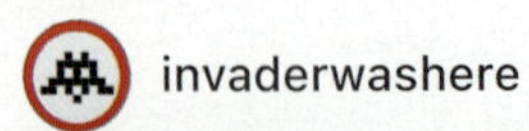

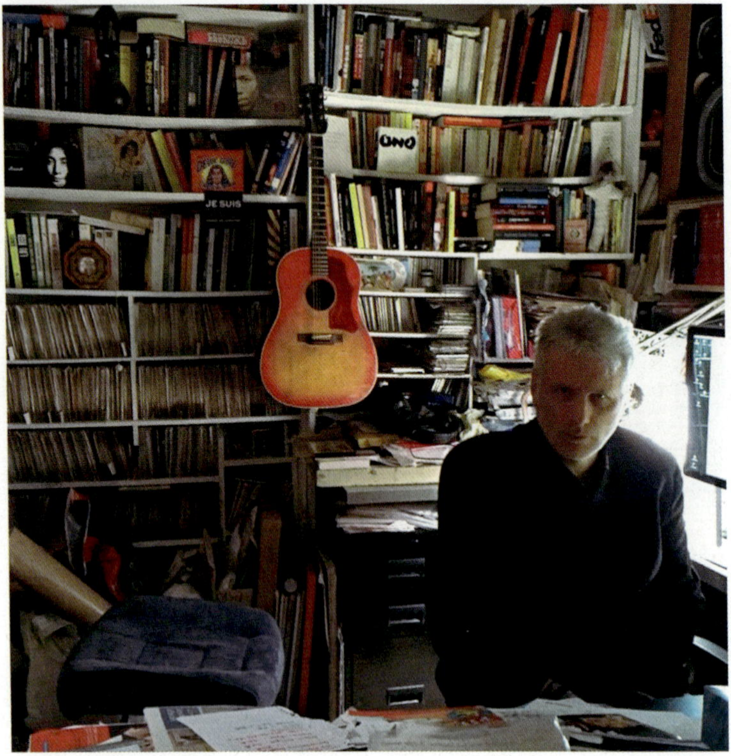

2 568 likes

invaderwashere Visiting Bruno Blum in his office. BB is a talentuous #musician #singer #producer #writer #thinker #biographer #reggaehistorian #rockcritic #vegan #activist and much more...

View all 3 comments

4 April 2015

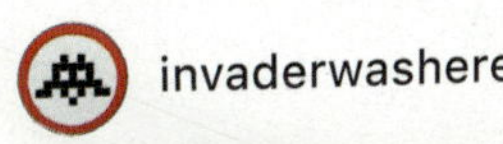

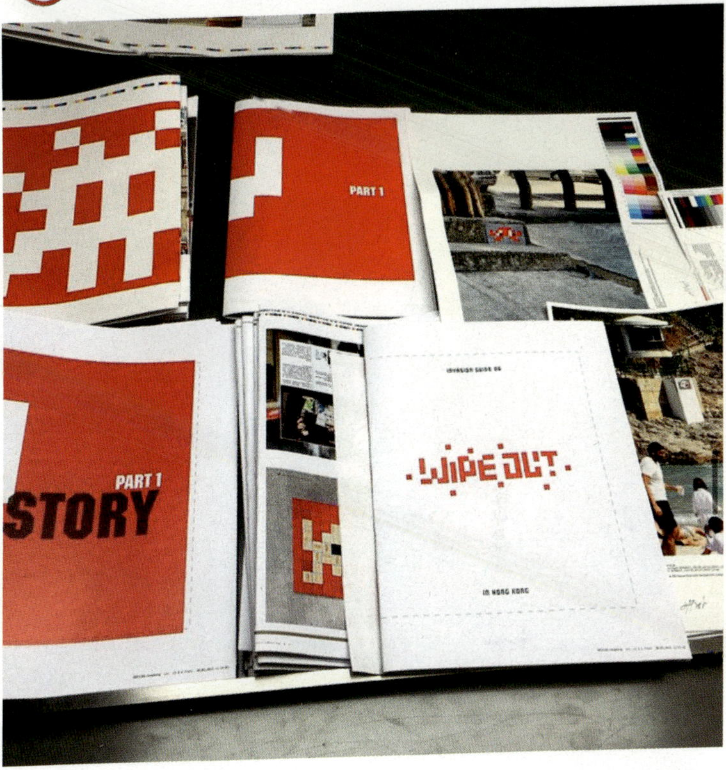

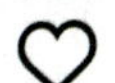   

3 242 likes

invaderwashere The Invasion Guide 06, Wipe Out in Hong Kong, is under printing. My books are an integral part of my art. They are entirely designed in my studio, and I dedicate as much care and attention to them as I do to the rest of my work. #wipeOut #hongkong #invasionguide06 published by #HOCA

View all 37 comments

4 April 2015

invaderwashere ...

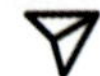

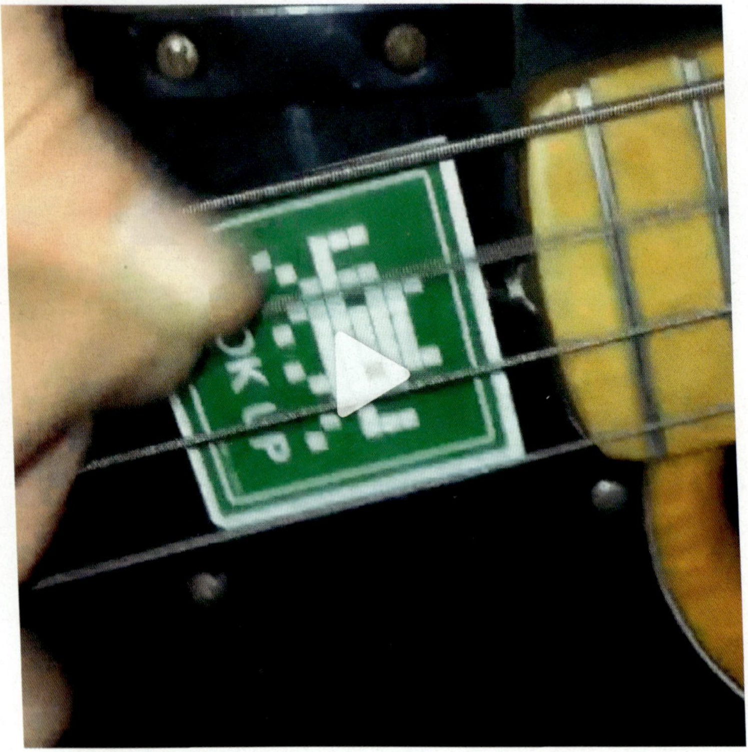

2 829 likes

invaderwashere Shot02 WapambeWapabelula #live #juliecolere #sticker #goodspot #BassInvasion #HappyEaster

View all 20 comments

5 April 2015

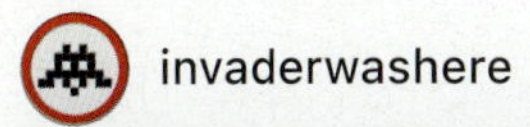

invaderwashere

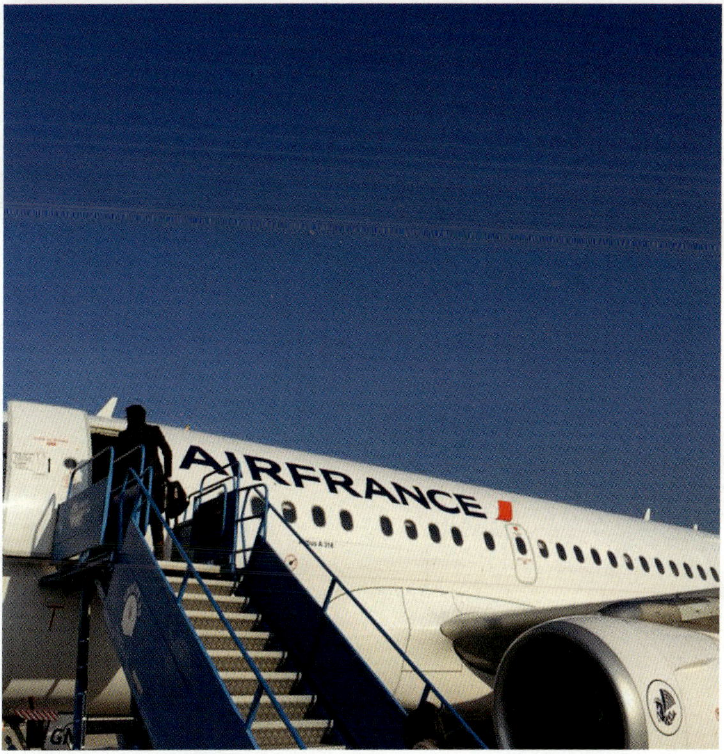

2 487 likes

invaderwashere On the road...

View all 21 comments

8 April 2015

invaderwashere ...

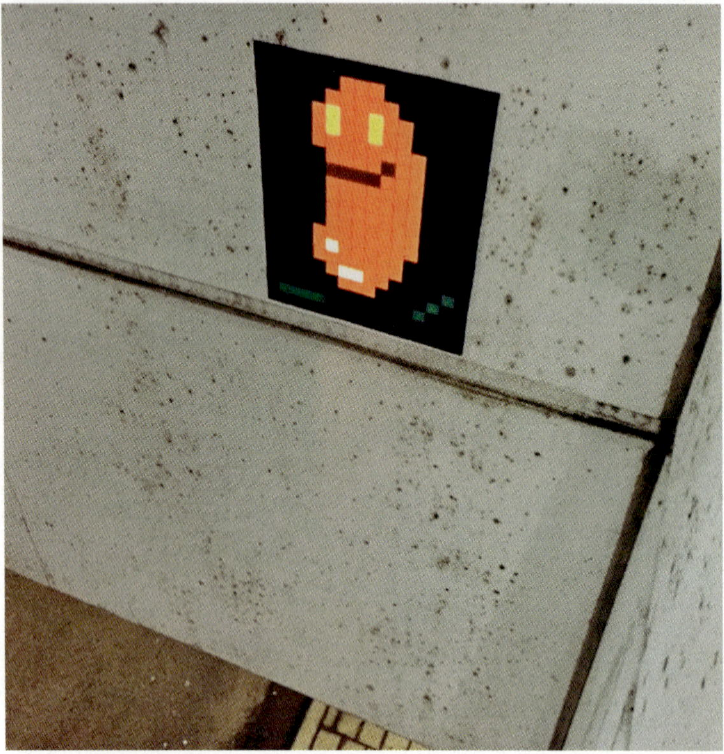

5 513 likes

invaderwashere 2nd piece of a new city...

View all 46 comments

9 April 2015

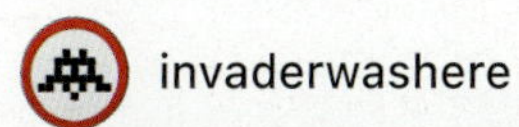

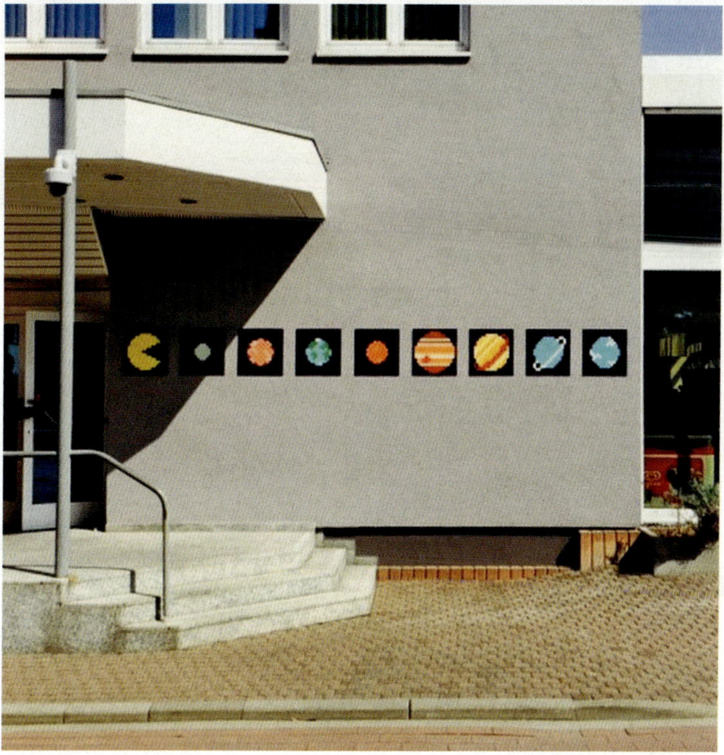

 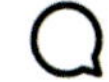  

9136 likes

invaderwashere Pac-Man gobbling the solar system #mercury #venus #earth #mars #jupiter #saturn #uranus #neptune at #esoc #esa #space2iss

View all 183 comments

9 April 2015

invaderwashere

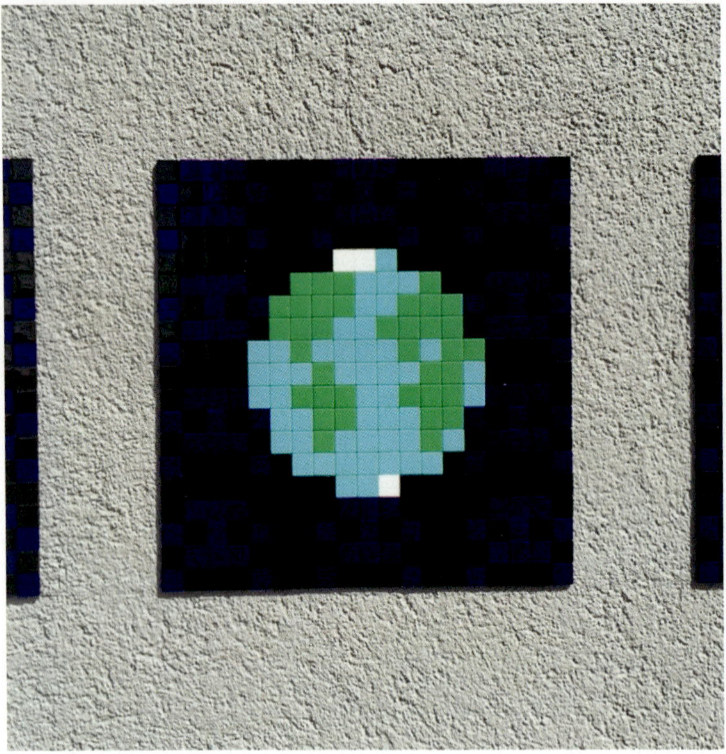

•••

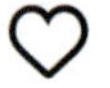

6030 likes

invaderwashere You are here!

View all 45 comments

9 April 2015

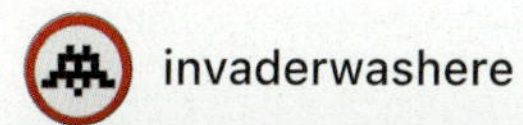

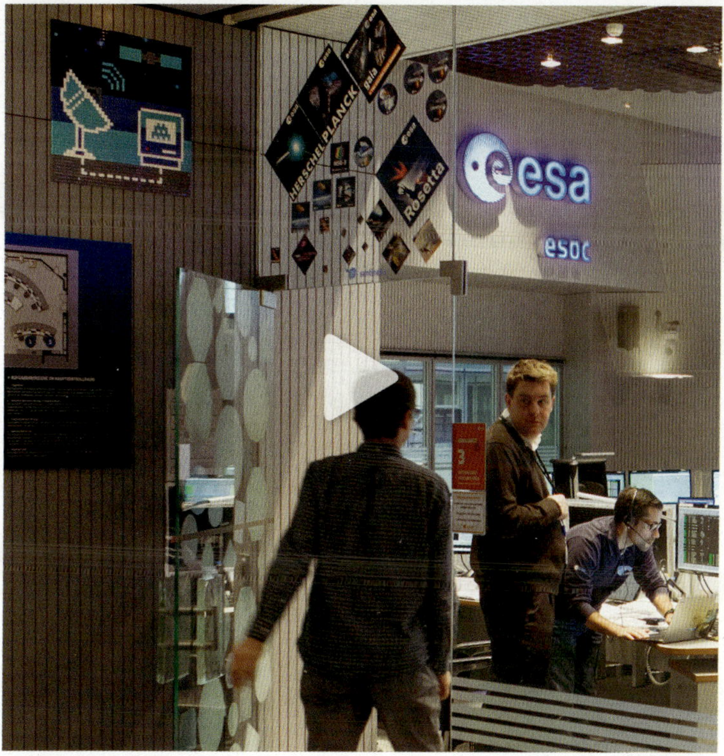

4 693 likes

invaderwashere Main control room at The European Space Operations Centre #ESOC #ESA #Darmstadt #Germany #space2iss

View all 74 comments

9 April 2015

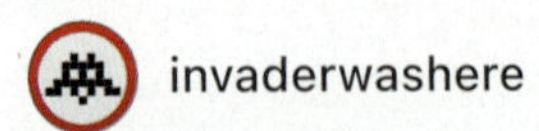
invaderwashere ...

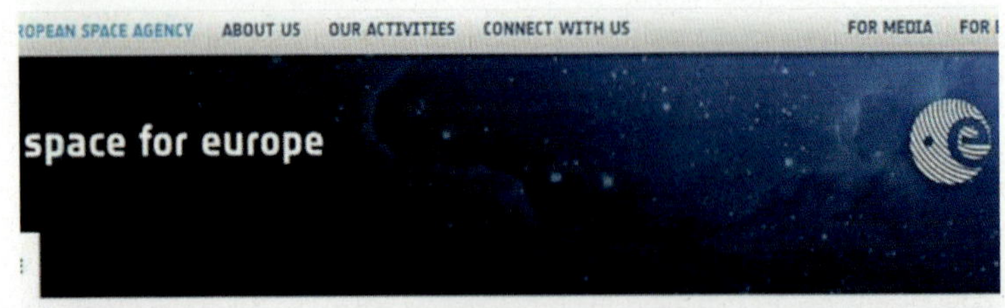

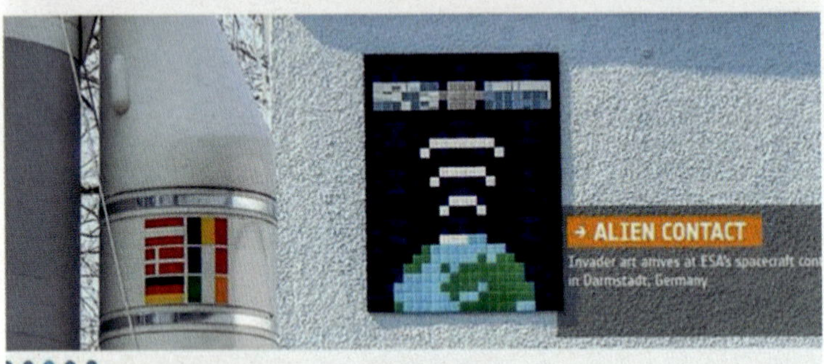

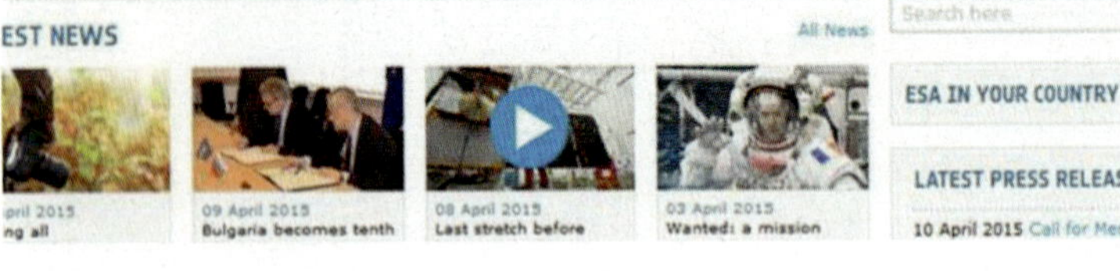

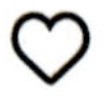

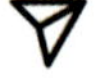
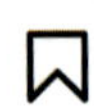

2 590 likes

invaderwashere Today #ESA's homepage / Showing FKF_04 installed last week at #ESOC #Frankfurt #Darmstadt #Germany #space2iss #EuropeanSpaceAgency

View all 7 comments

13 April 2015

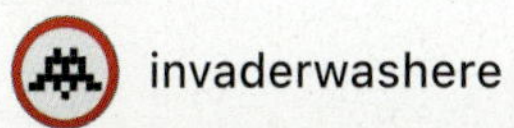

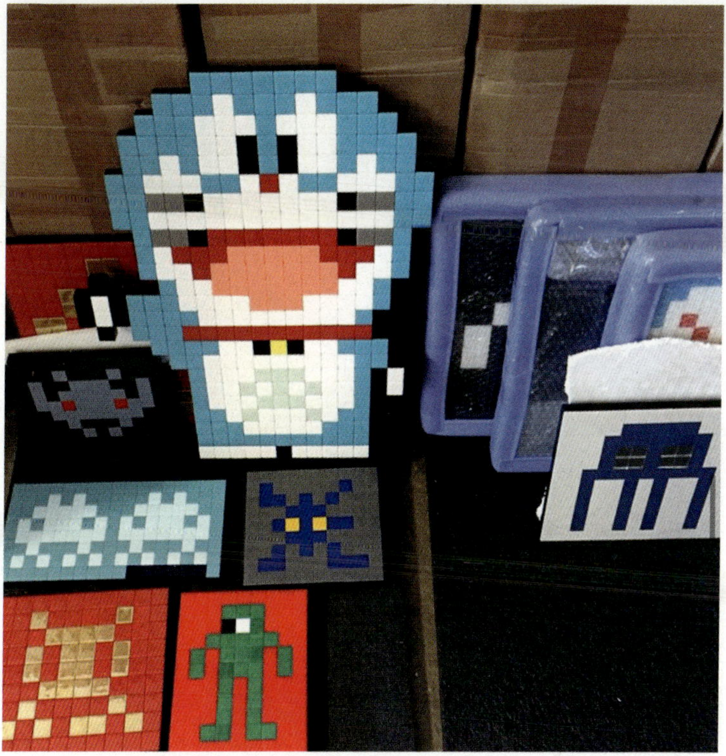

  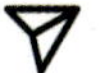 

6946 likes

invaderwashere Studio detail / #Alias #Doreamon #Spaceinvaders for #WipeOut in #HongKong #HOCAfoundation

View all 112 comments

13 April 2015

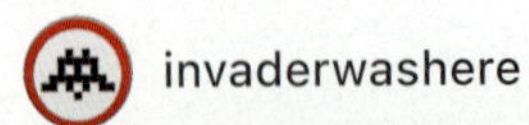

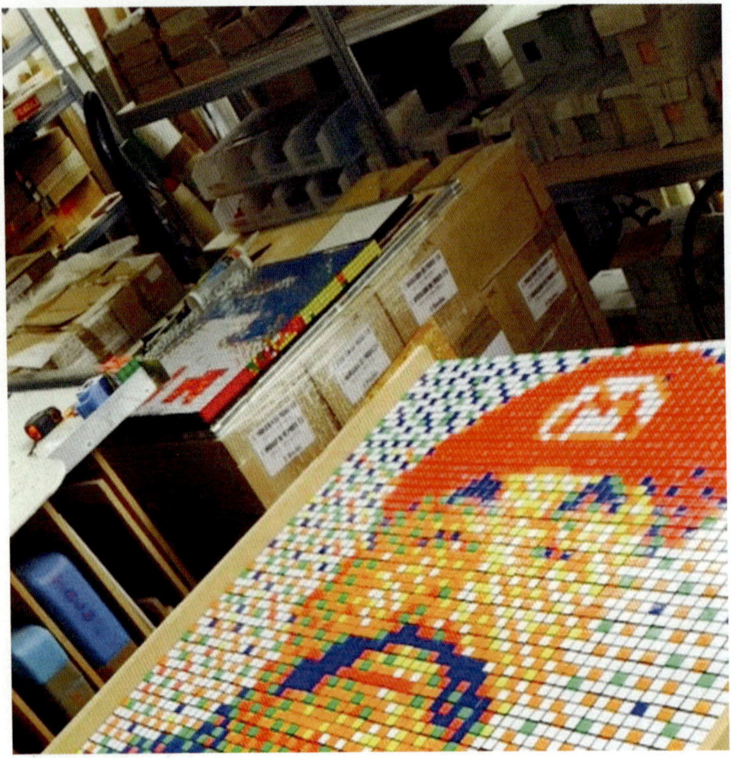

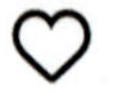  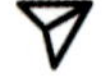 

6069 likes

invaderwashere #Studio view / preparing #WipeOut / my next solo show #rubikcubism #MarioZedoung #HongKong #HOCAfoundation

View all 62 comments

14 April 2015

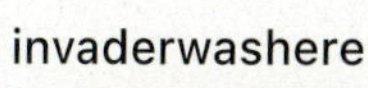
invaderwashere

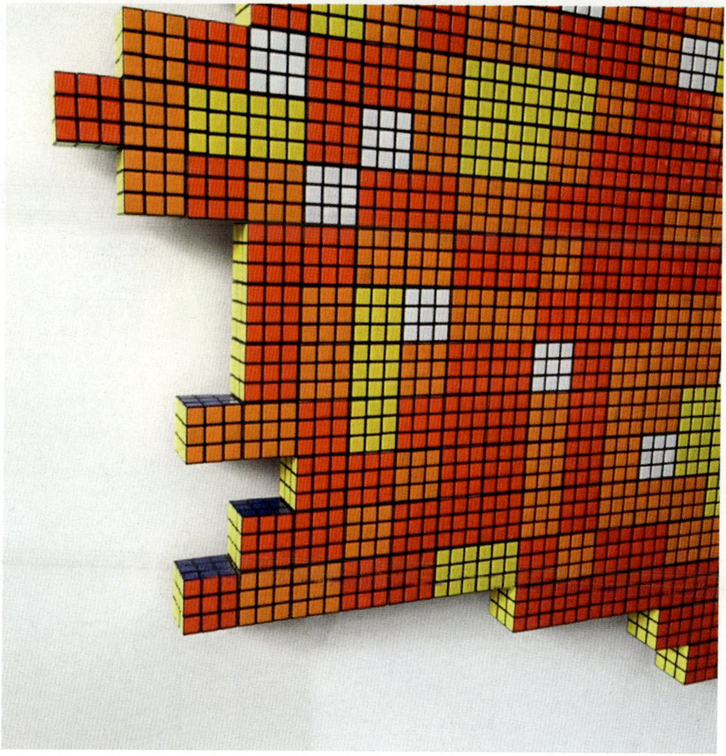

5634 likes

invaderwashere Detail of Rubik Wipe Out for #WipeOut #exhibition #HongKong may 2015 #HOCAfoundation

View all 64 comments

14 April 2015

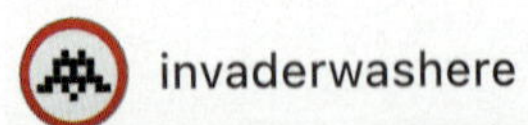

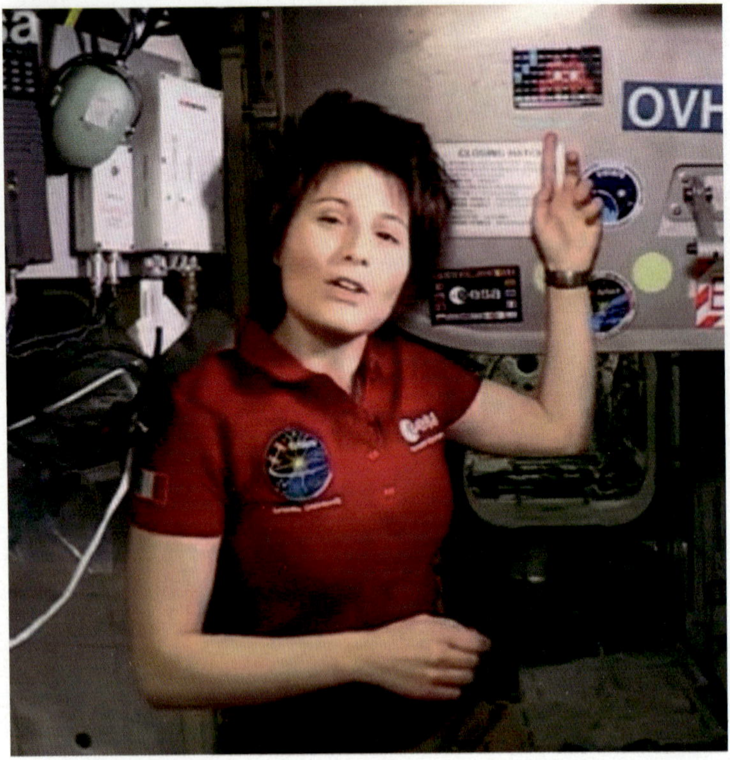

3 614 likes

invaderwashere Astronaut #SamanthaCristoforetti presents, from the #ISS, "Create Your Own Mosaic!" a competition for kids / more infos: www.esa.int/esaKIDSen #space2iss #ESA

View all 38 comments

16 April 2015

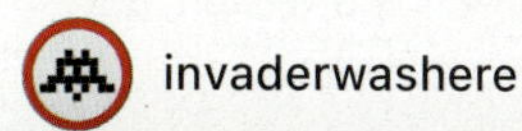

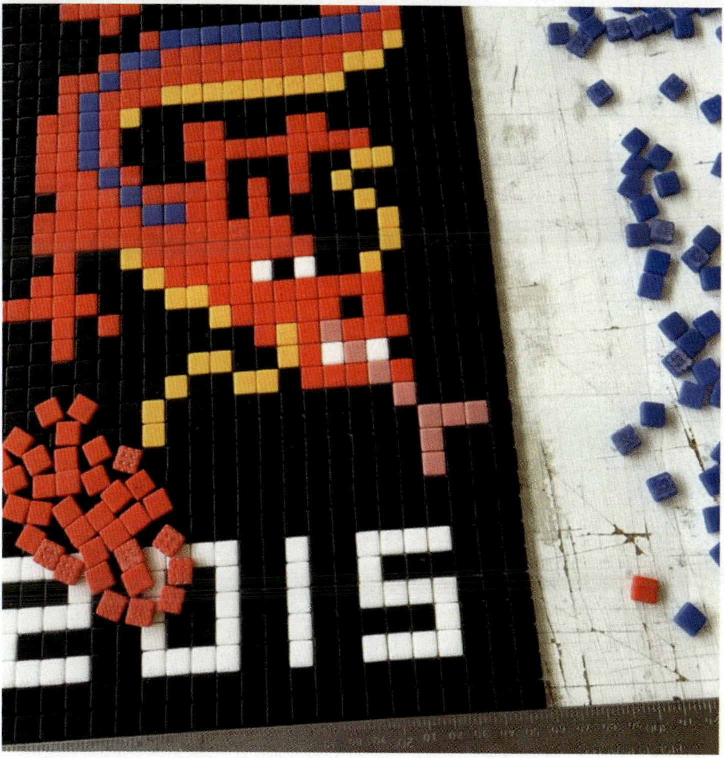

 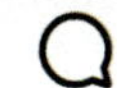  

4706 likes

invaderwashere Working on a small red dragon for the streets of #HongKong #tinytiles

View all 45 comments

17 April 2015

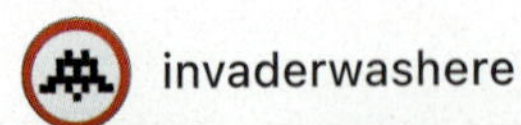

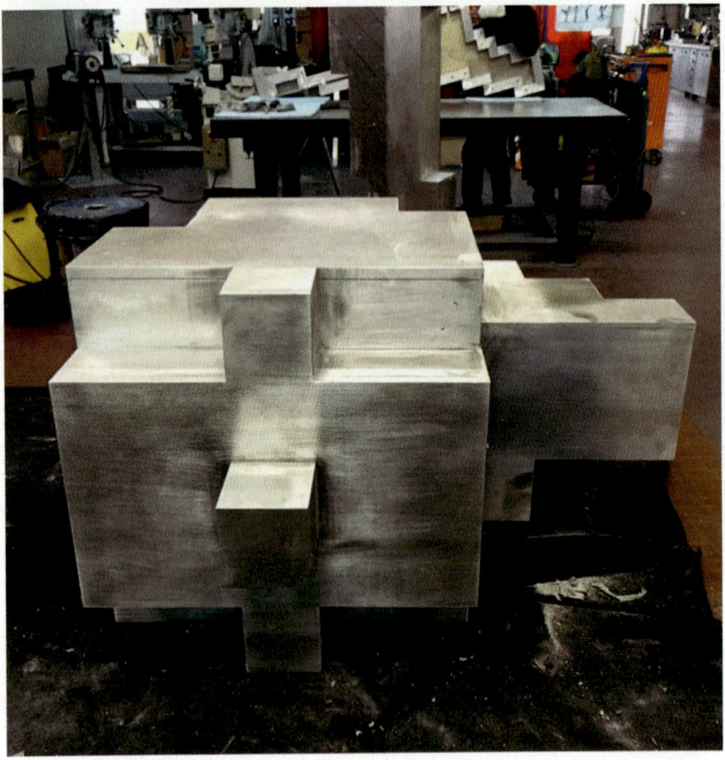

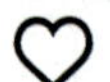   

3 936 likes

invaderwashere Detail of a new sculpture. Has to be painted now... #HongKong #WipeOut #HOCAfoundation #BruceLee #head

View all 31 comments

19 April 2015

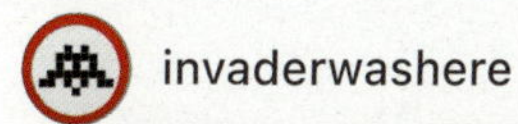

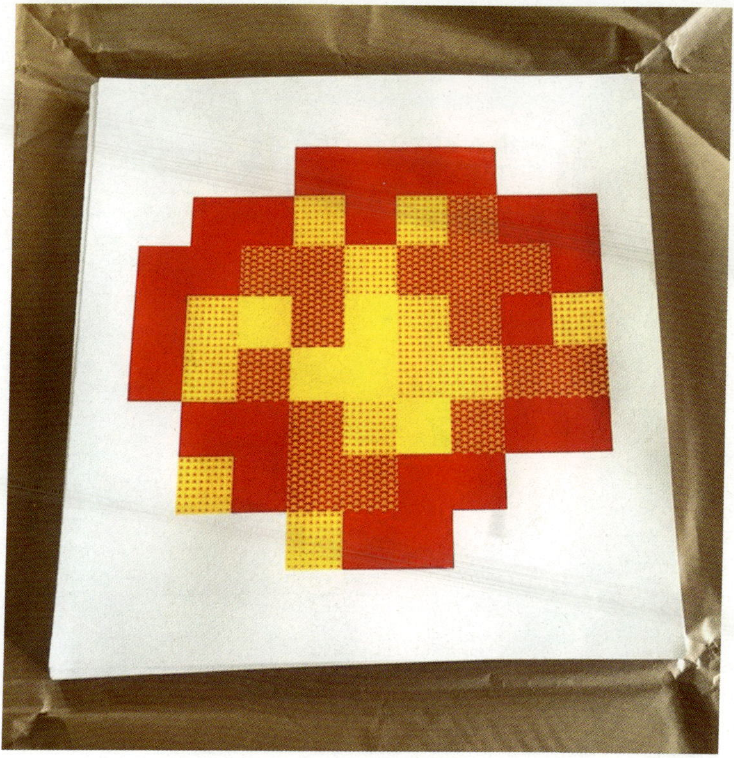

4433 likes

invaderwashere One of the 3 prints I've made for my coming exhibition #WipeOut in H💥NG K💥NG at PMQ #HOCAfoundation #silkscreen #boum!

View all 55 comments

20 April 2015

 invaderwashere •••

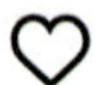   

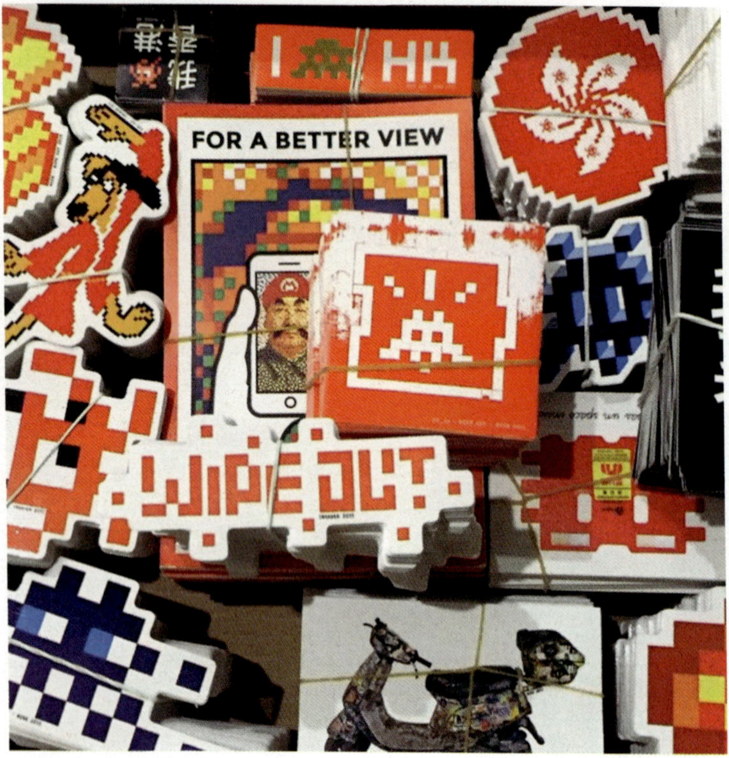

4 873 likes

invaderwashere New stickers for the vending machines of my new show #WipeOut #HongKong #HOCAfoundation

View all 102 comments

24 April 2015

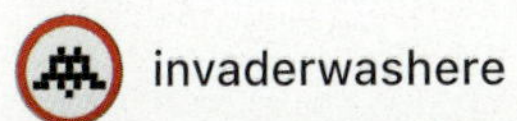
invaderwashere

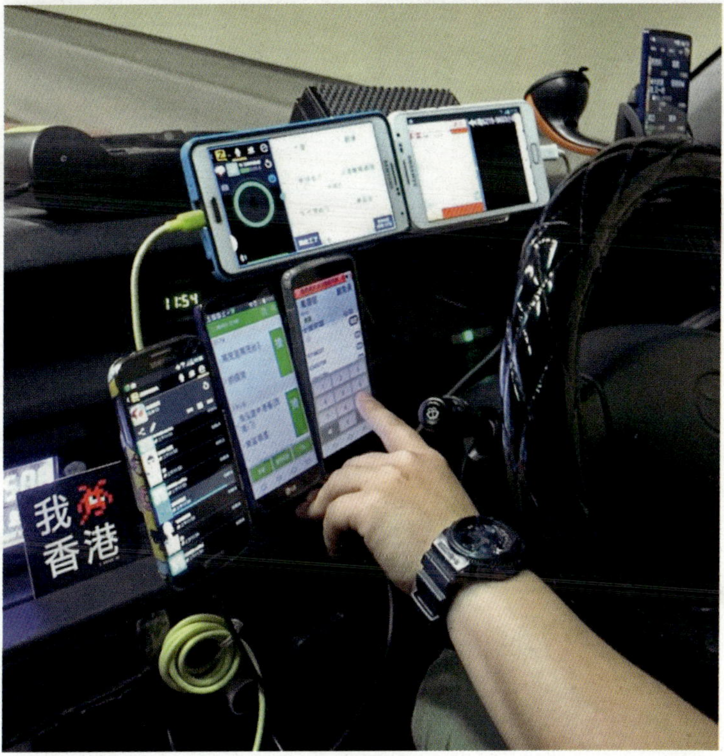

5656 likes

invaderwashere Back to Hong Kong #connected #taxidriver

View all 220 comments

25 April 2015

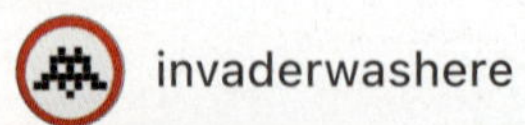

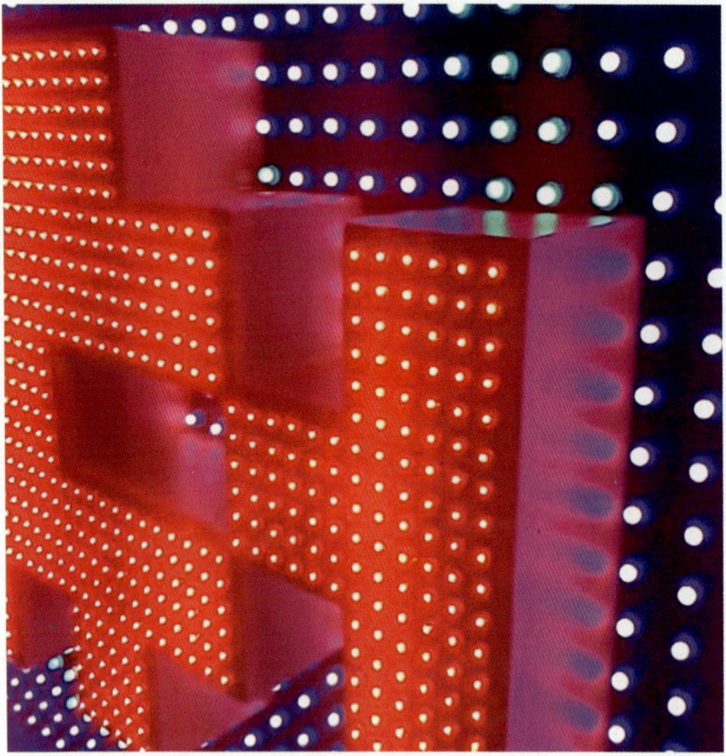

3651 likes

invaderwashere Close up of my new works made with leds for #WipeOut #HongKong #HOCAfoundation #thefrenchmay #PMQ

View all 15 comments

26 April 2015

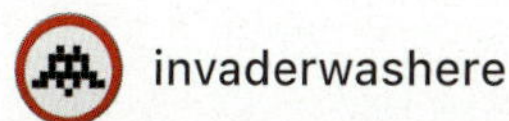

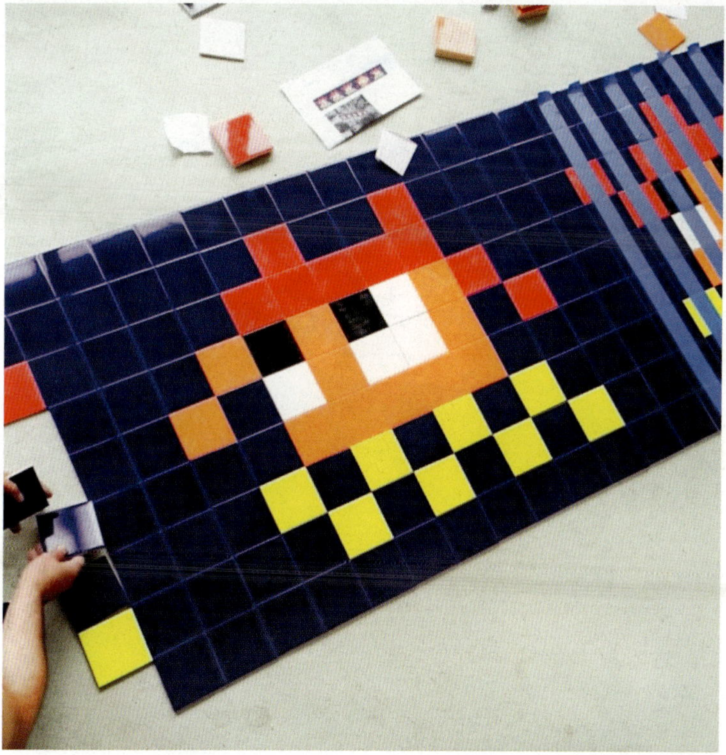

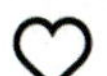   

5226 likes

invaderwashere Preparing a street piece... #HongKong #invasion #wave5

View all 58 comments

26 April 2015

invaderwashere ···

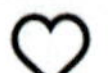   

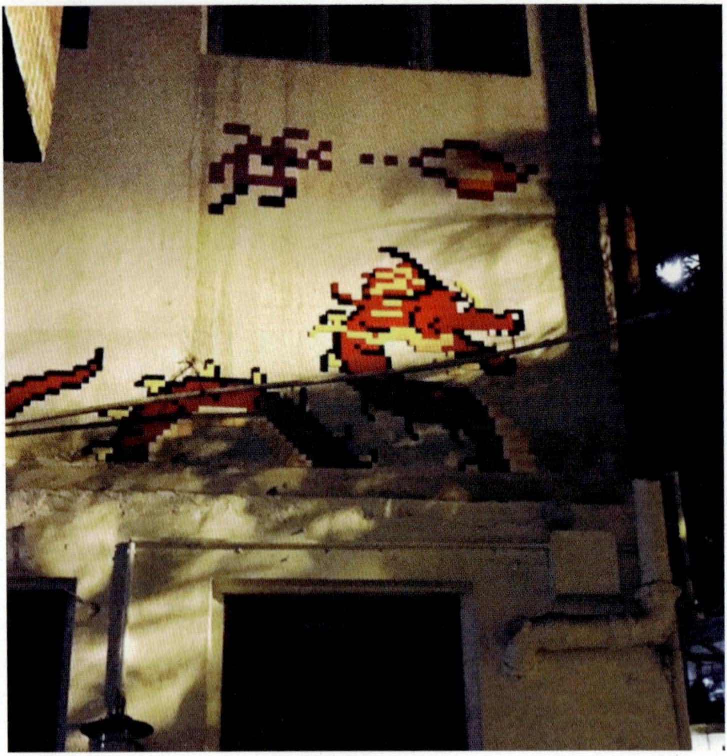

5 937 likes

invaderwashere Streets of Hong Kong #wave5 #HK_78 #100Points

View all 61 comments

26 April 2015

invaderwashere

 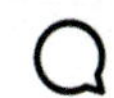  

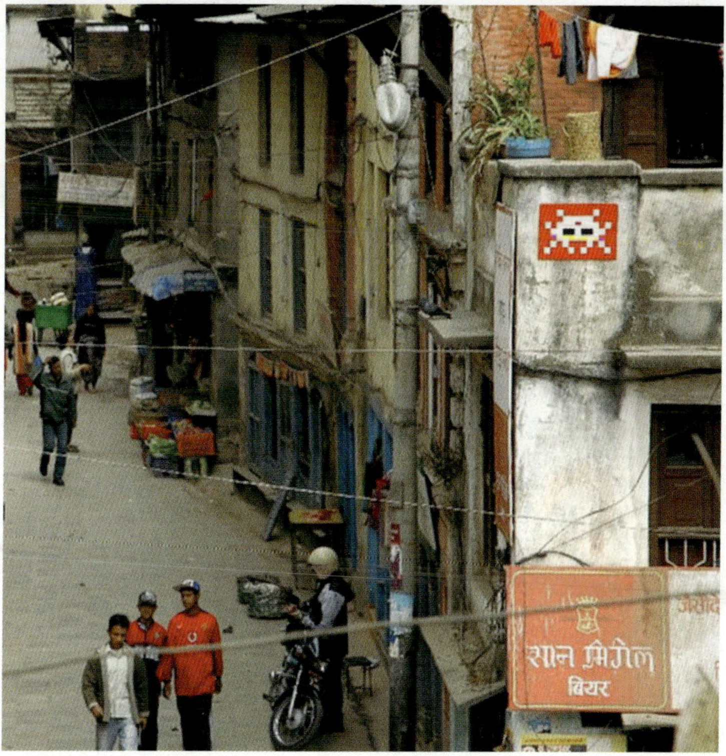

6147 likes

invaderwashere A thought for Nepal #kathmandu #earthquake KAT_11 #2008

View all 30 comments

27 April 2015

invaderwashere

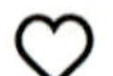   

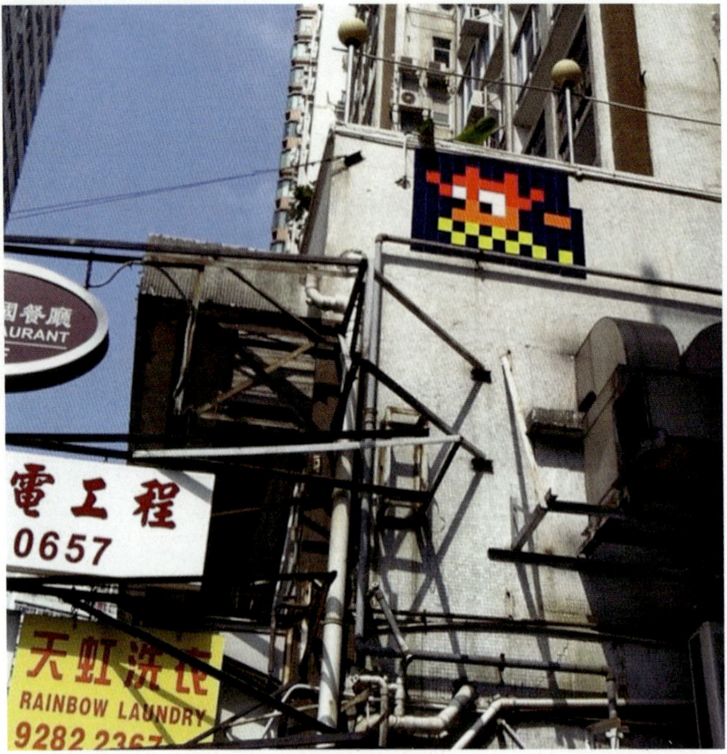

5 528 likes

invaderwashere HK_77 #HongKong #NorthPoint #50points #2015

View all 51 comments

28 April 2015

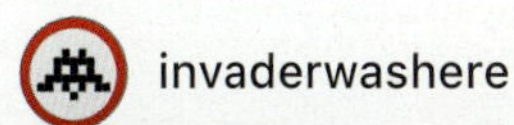

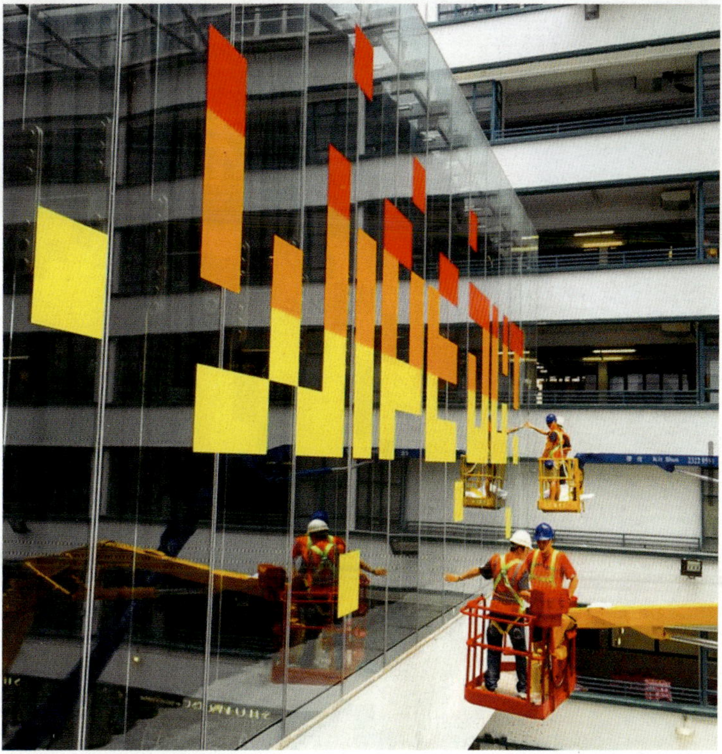

 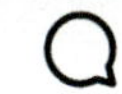  

4770 likes

invaderwashere Started to install #WipeOut in #HongKong #HOCAfoundation #PMQ #thefrenchmay opening on May 2nd

View all 54 comments

29 April 2015

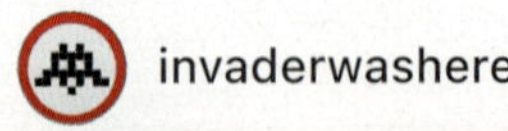
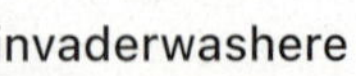

invaderwashere

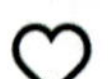
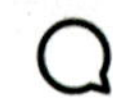

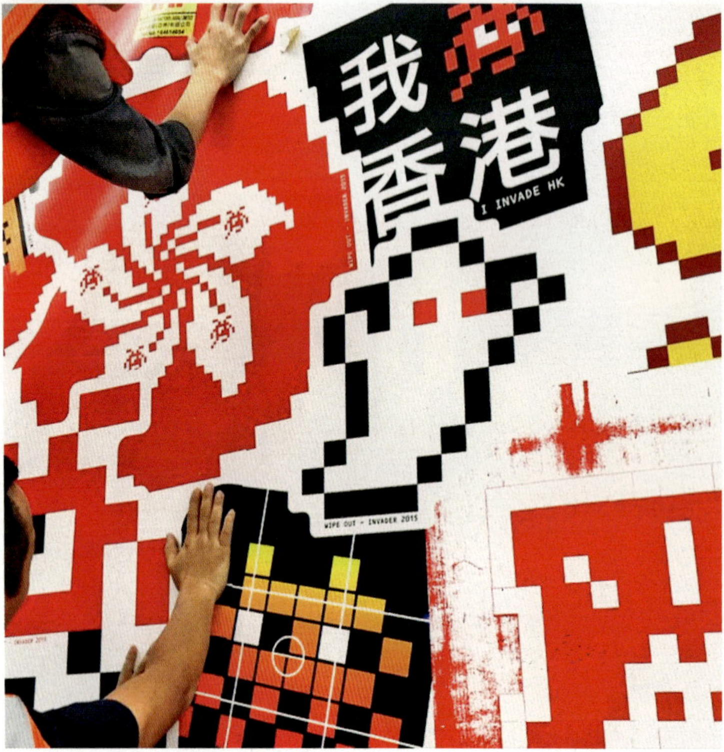

5 376 likes

invaderwashere Installing the Stickers Corner at Wipe Out exhibition / opening on May 2nd #hongkong

View all 54 comments

29 April 2015

invaderwashere

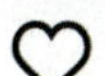 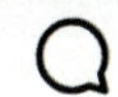  

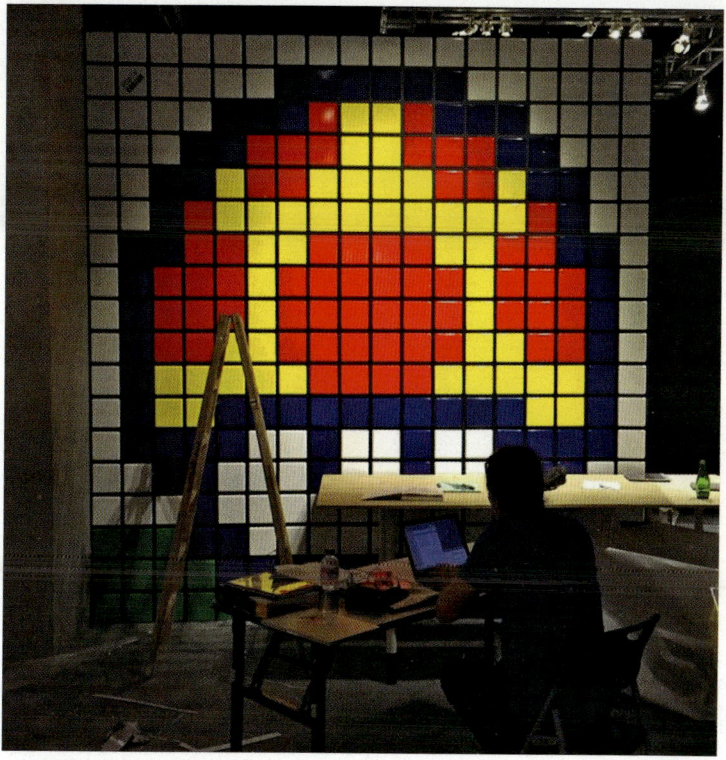

6 338 likes

invaderwashere Working late on the installation of #WipeOut #rubikcubism #mario #mushroom #big!

View all 66 comments

29 April 2015

invaderwashere

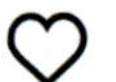

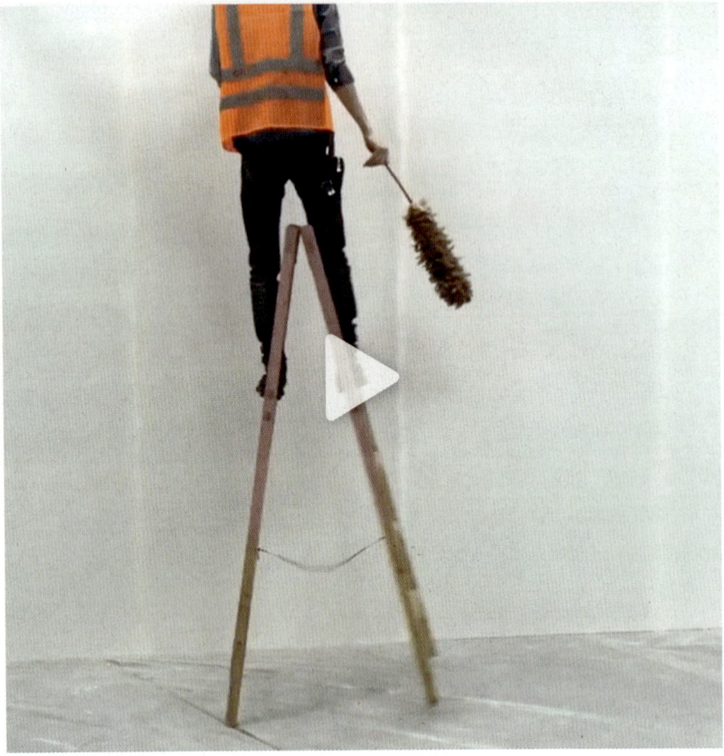

4734 likes

invaderwashere Walk like an Invader! #HongKongStyle #ladderWalk preparing #WipeOut

View all 125 comments

1 May 2015

invaderwashere

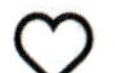   

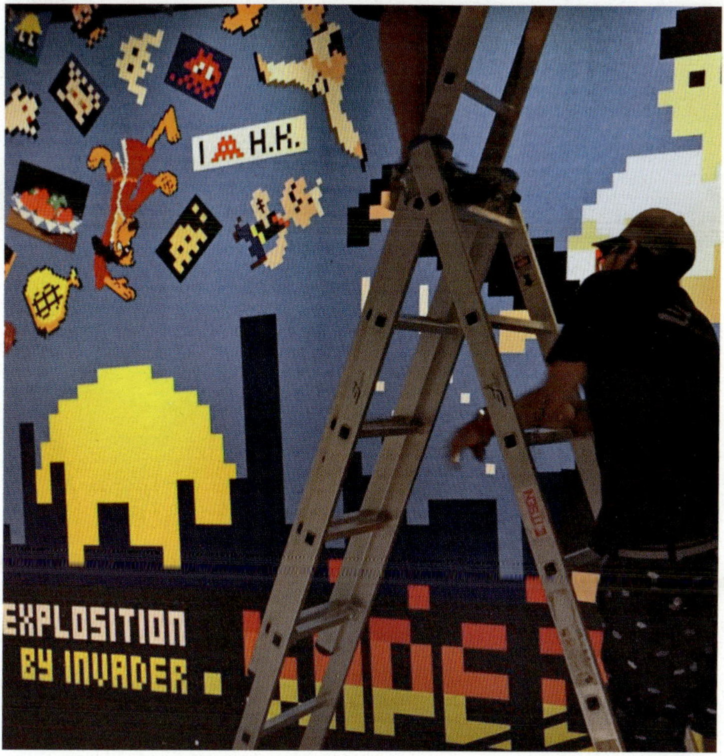

4 432 likes

invaderwashere Lighting #WipeOut for the tomorrow opening... #HongKong #HOCAfoundation #PMQ

View all 29 comments

1 May 2015

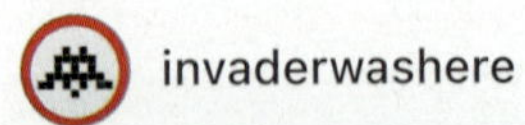

WIPE OUT CINEMA
ART & SPACE
TOP10, FUTURAMA, INVADER WALK (TRAILER)

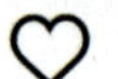  

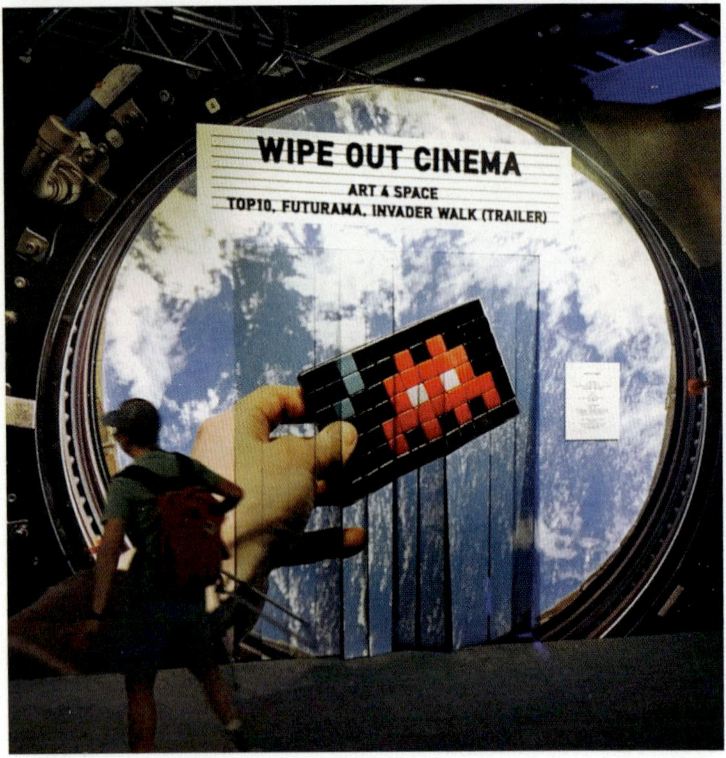

3626 likes

invaderwashere Final touches on #WipeOut

View all 17 comments

1 May 2015

invaderwashere •••

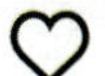 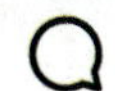  

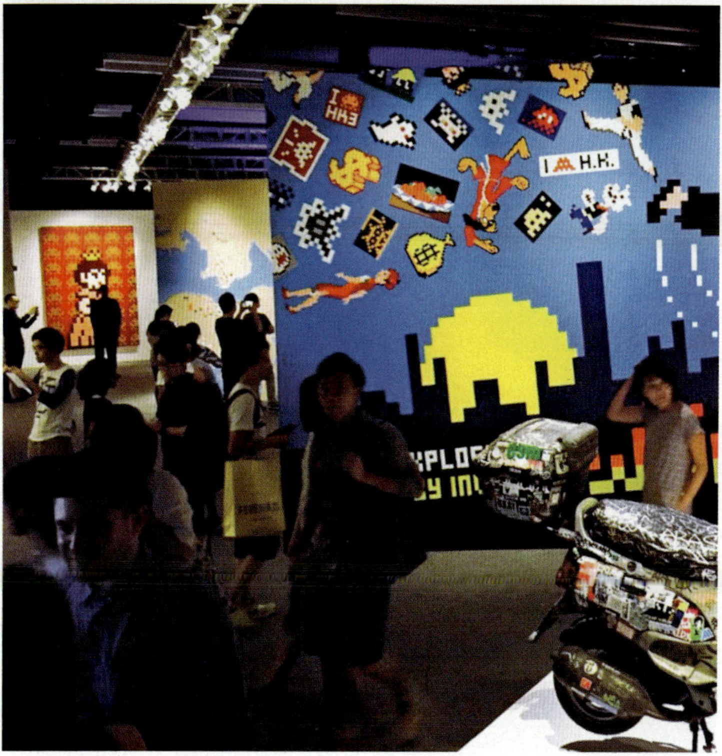

3855 likes

invaderwashere #WipeOut is open now! An explosition with #HOCAfoundation at #PMQ #theKube Aberdeen St & Hollywood Rd #HongKong Don't miss it...

View all 61 comments

2 May 2015

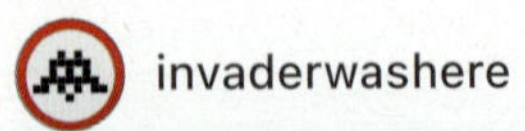

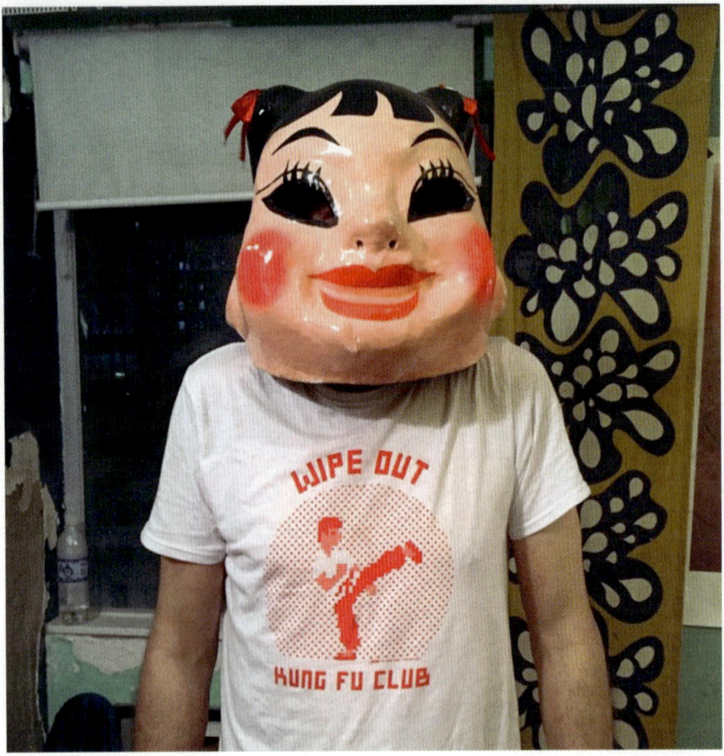

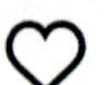   

3 440 likes

invaderwashere Hello my name is Invader... #mask #wipeout #Tshirt #wmhostel #hongkong

View all 38 comments

3 May 2015

invaderwashere •••

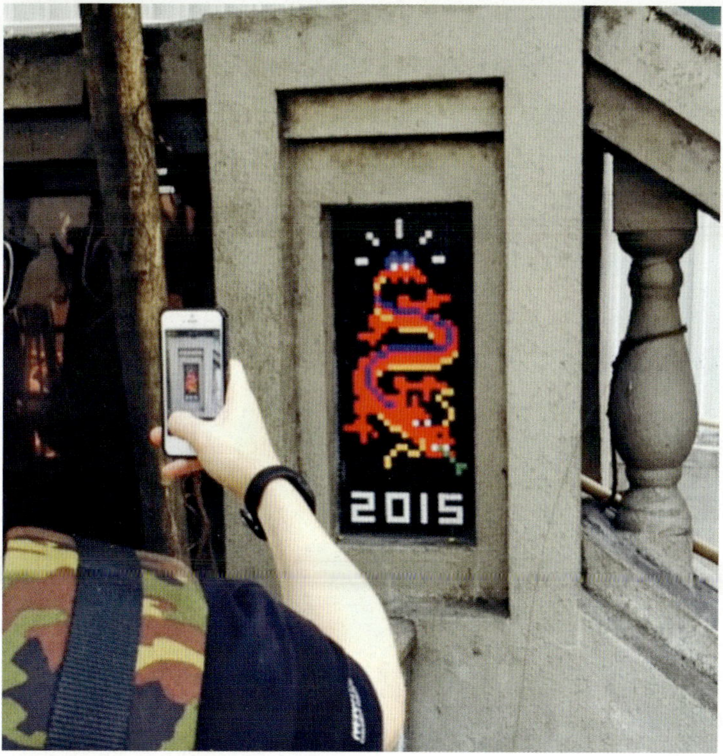

6795 likes

invaderwashere Hunting the Dragon in #HongKong HK_76 new street piece

View all 33 comments

3 May 2015

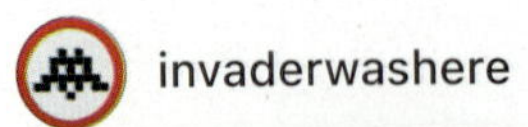

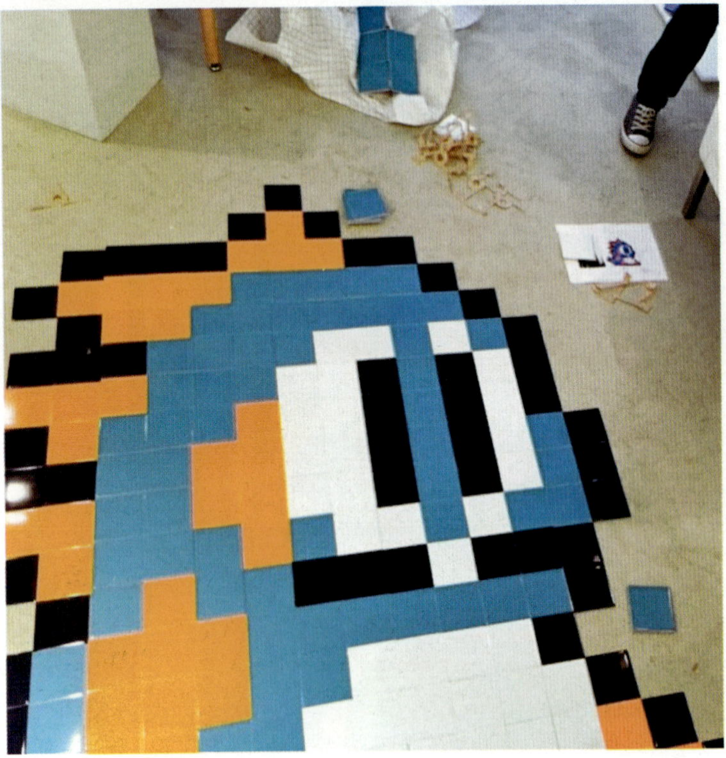

6937 likes

invaderwashere Clandestine studio in #HongKong preparing #BobbleBubble soon in the streets...

View all 98 comments

3 May 2015

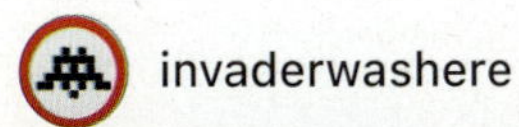

SORRY,
WE ARE OUT OF STICKERS!
WE WILL BE REFILLED AS SOON AS POSSIBLE.
THANK YOU FOR YOUR PATIENCE!

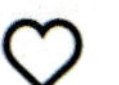   

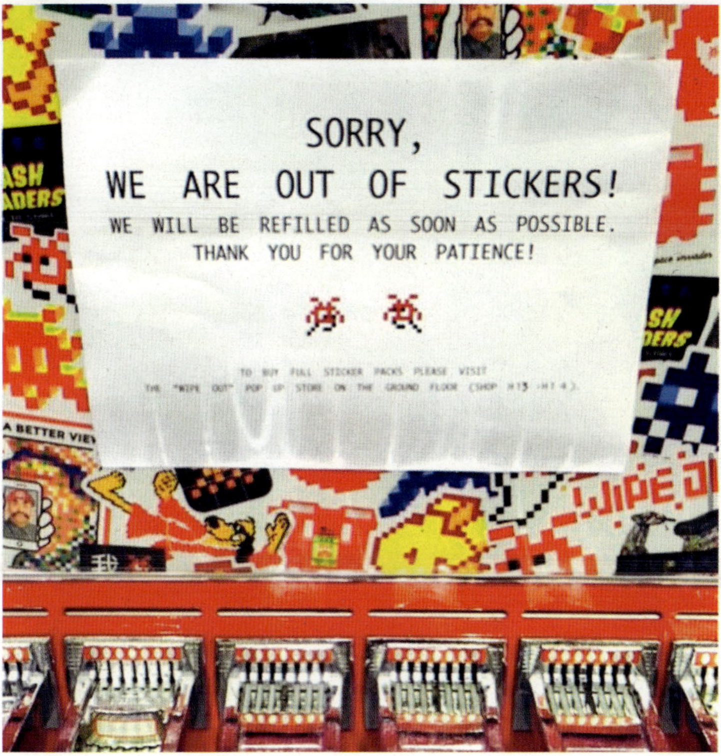

3849 likes

invaderwashere Huge success for #Wipeout this weekend. 5000 stickers have been sold! The machines will be refilled tomorow #charity #stickers

View all 54 comments

3 May 2015

invaderwashere

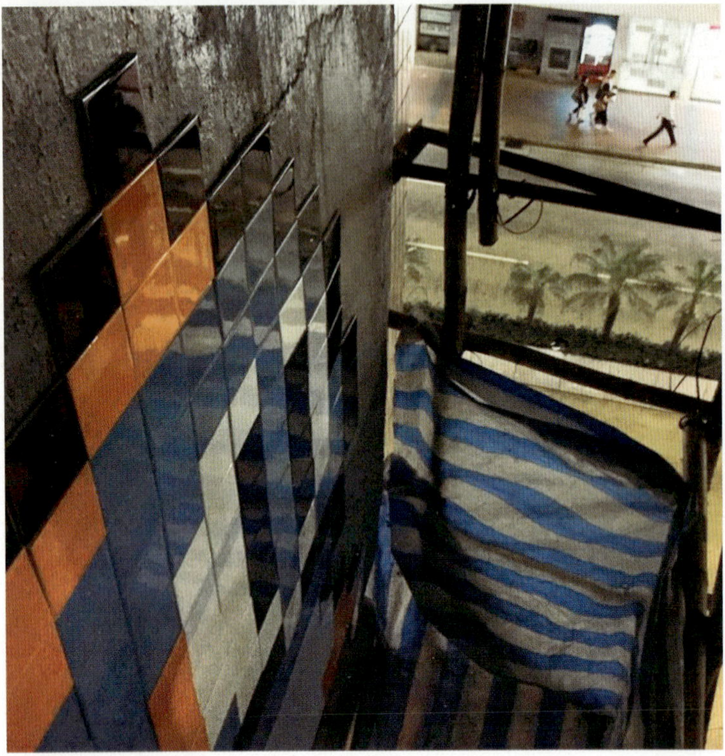

3 589 likes

invaderwashere #BubbleBobble just installed #kowloon #bambooscaffolding big and high!

View all 41 comments

3 May 2015

invaderwashere •••

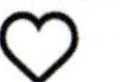   

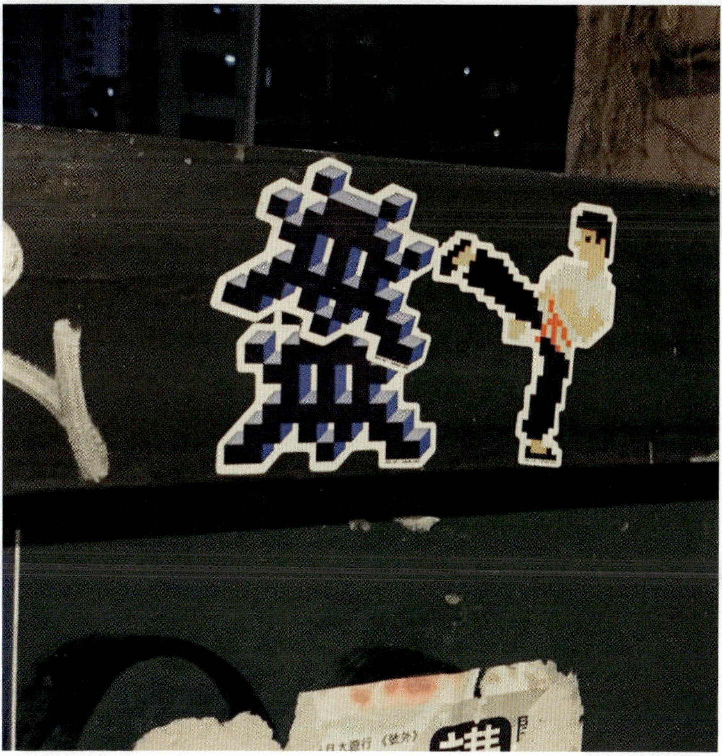

4934 likes

invaderwashere Even if less noble than mosaics, stickers have always seems to me as a great artistic and invasion tool. I always have some in my pockets and I've stuck them up in every town I've ever been to.

View all 15 comments

3 May 2015

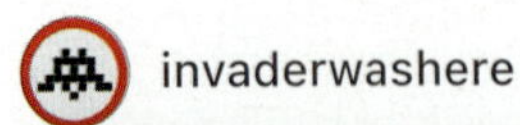

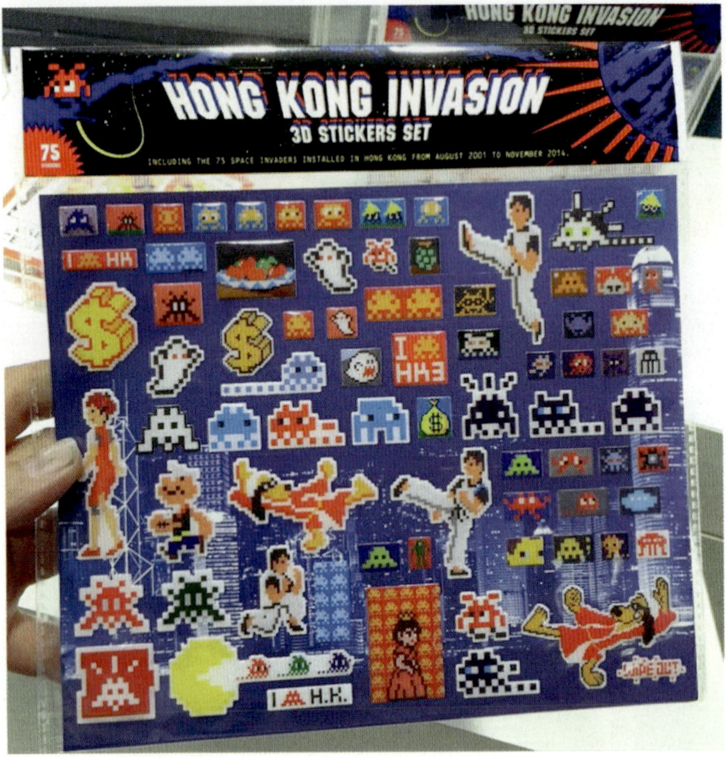

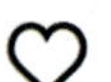

5492 likes

invaderwashere 3D sticker pack / 75 #puffy #stickers / 1000 copies / Available at #wipeout #popupstore #kapok #PMQ

View all 152 comments

4 May 2015

invaderwashere •••

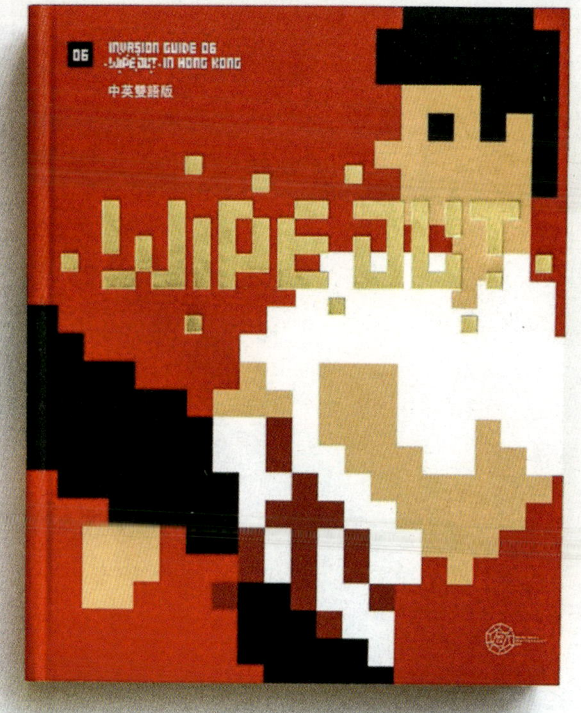

4 512 likes

invaderwashere Wipe Out in Hong Kong / 316 pages / Invasion guide 06 / available at #wipeout #popupstore #PMQ #kapok #HOCAfoundation

View all 55 comments

4 May 2015

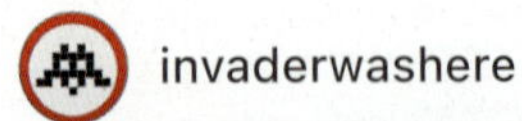

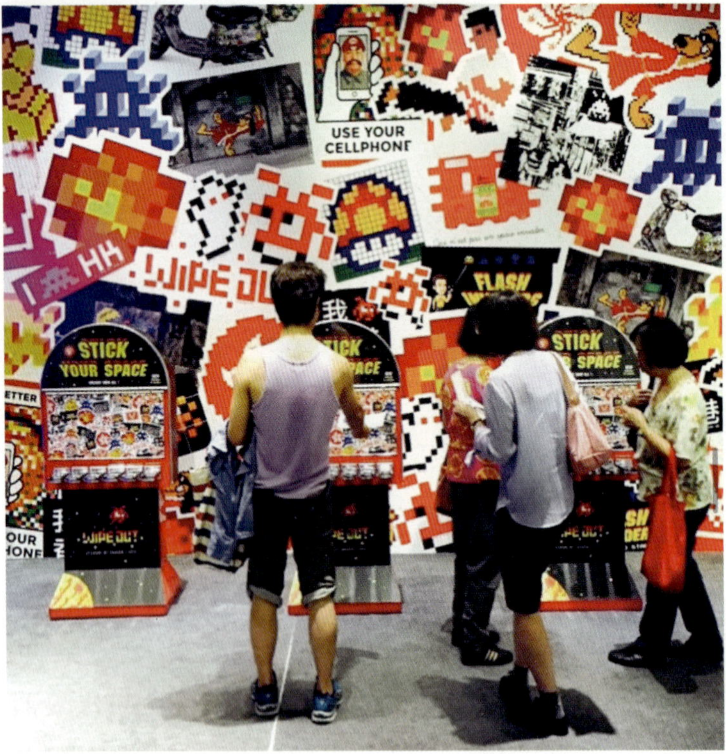

5102 likes

invaderwashere The stickers vending machines are refilled #Wipeout #charity #stickers #PMQ #HongKong #HOCAfoundation

View all 79 comments

5 May 2015

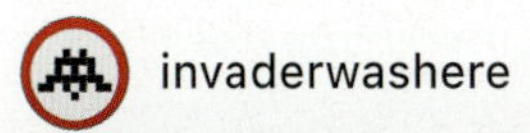

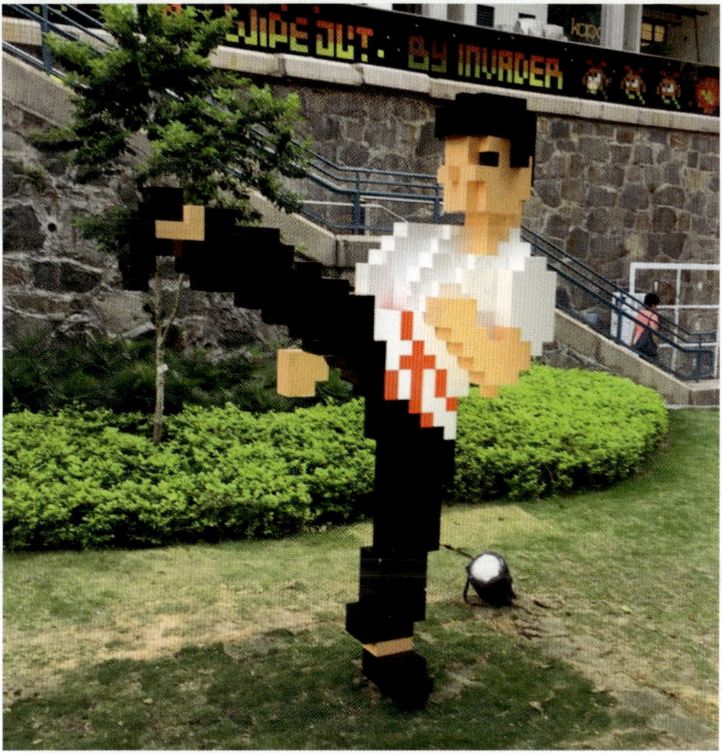

8015 likes

invaderwashere 👊💥👊💥👊💥 #3D #Bruce / painted metal / 3m high #sculpture #Wipeout #PMQ garden

View all 123 comments

5 May 2015

invaderwashere •••

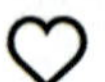   

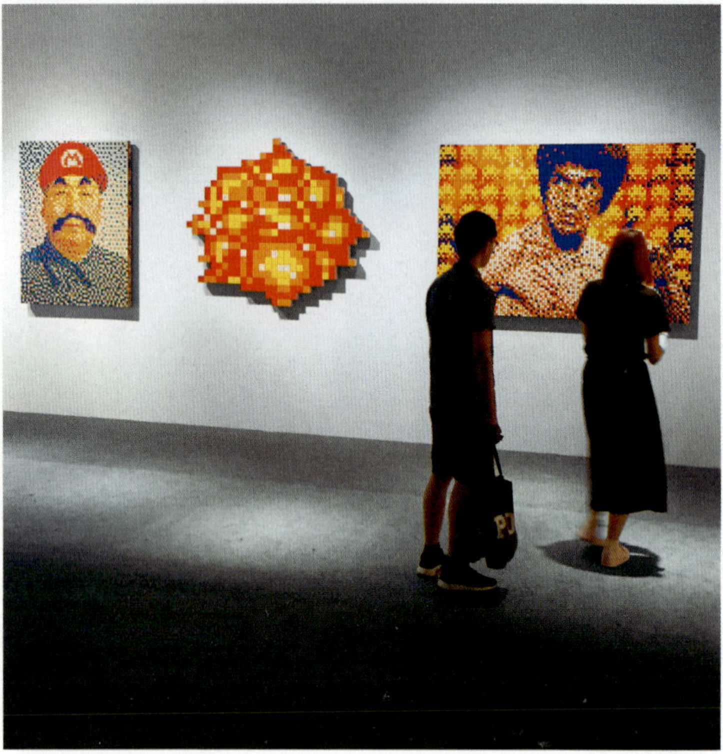

5854 likes

invaderwashere #Rubikcubism #Wipeout #HOCAfoundation

View all 38 comments

5 May 2015

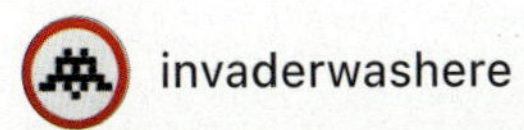

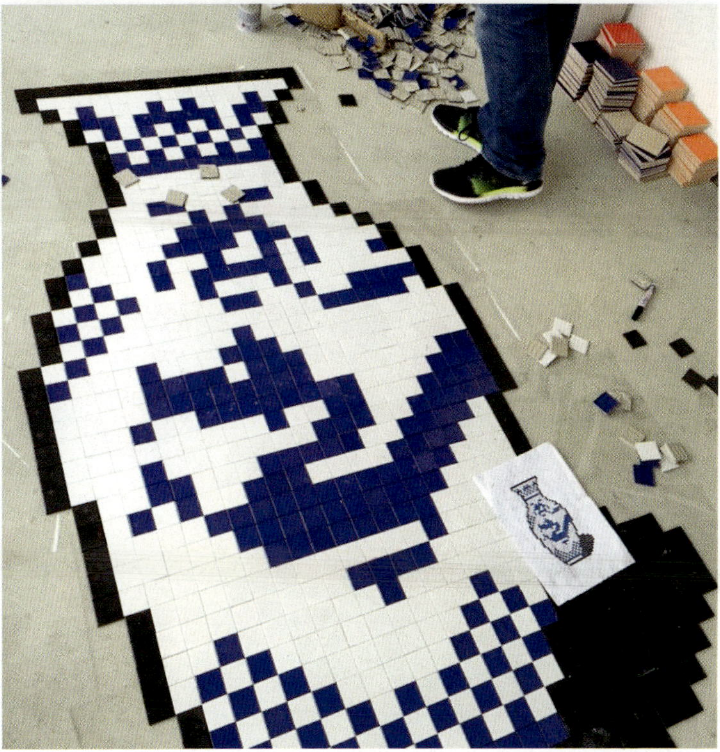

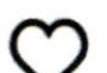 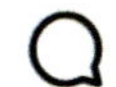  

5 540 likes

invaderwashere Clandestine studio #HongKong #streetpiece #Dragon #Mingvase

View all 54 comments

6 May 2015

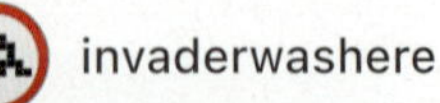

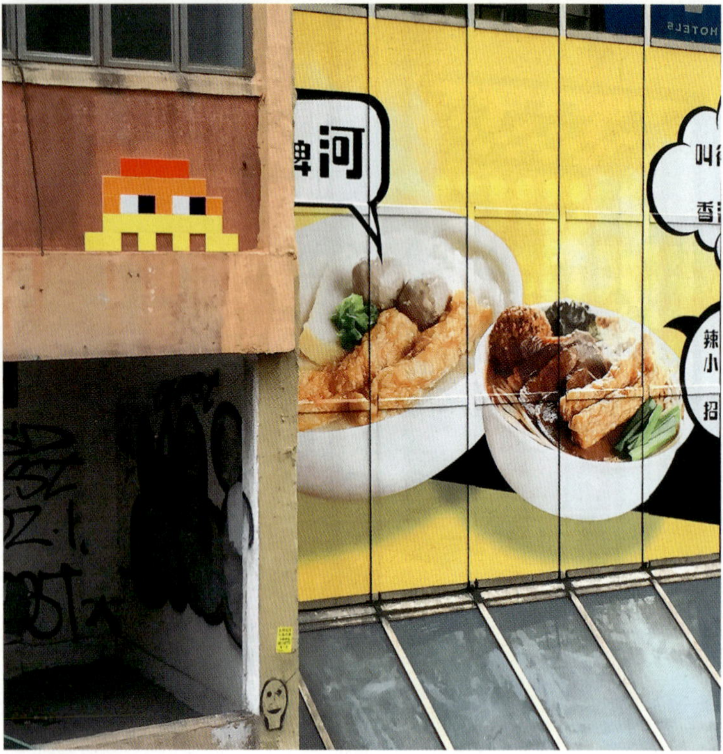

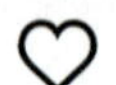   

3 248 likes

invaderwashere HK_84 just made in #HongKong

View all 36 comments

6 May 2015

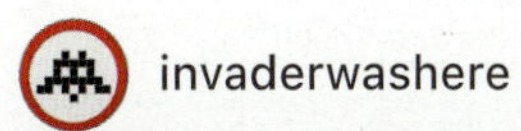

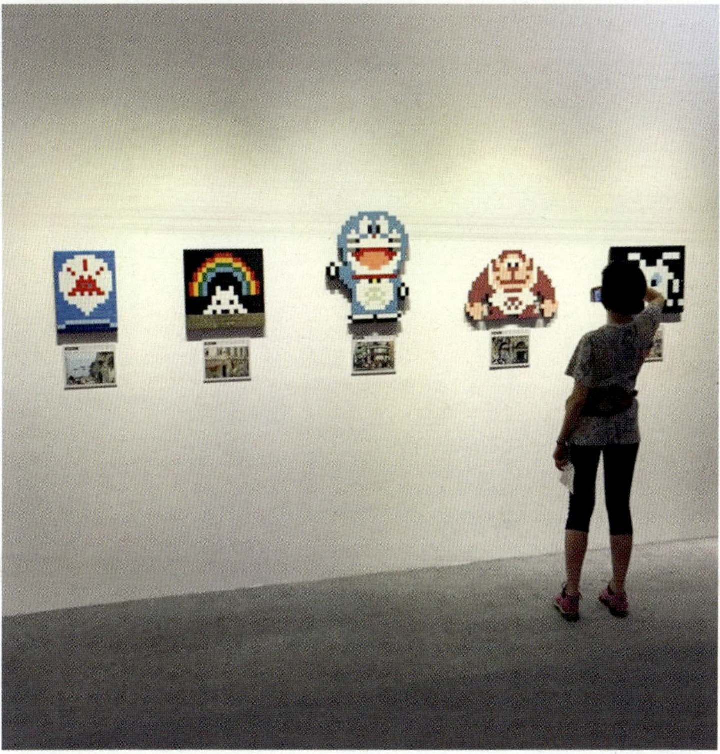

8113 likes

invaderwashere Aliases are a direct link between my urban work and the galleries. Each Alias is a unique replica of a mosaic installed in the street and contains all the metadata of the work in situ in its ID card #Aliases #Wipeout #HongKong

View all 73 comments

6 May 2015

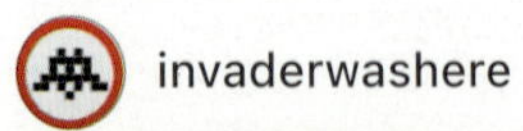

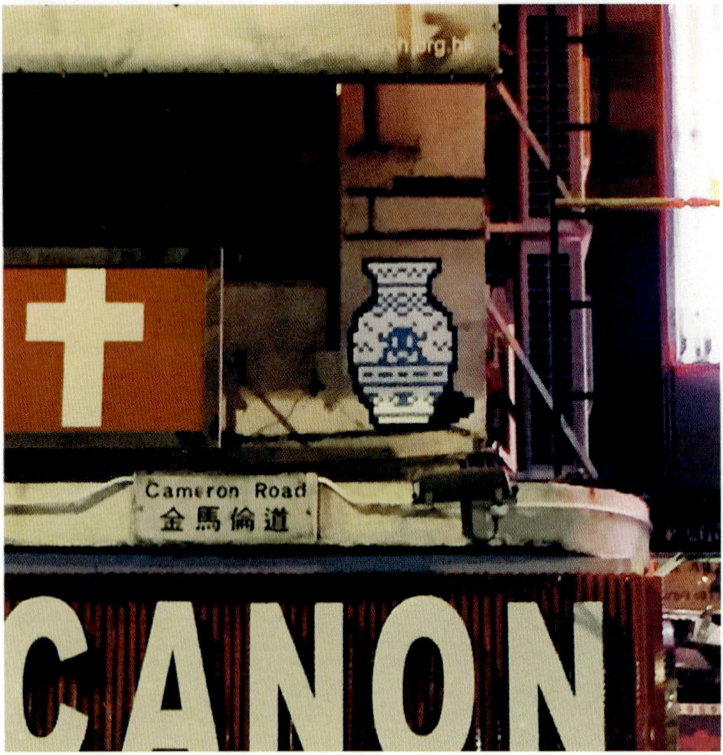

  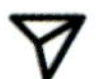 

4 599 likes

invaderwashere Strike 💥💥💥 3:20 am #HongKong #HK86 #perfectspot

View all 48 comments

6 May 2015

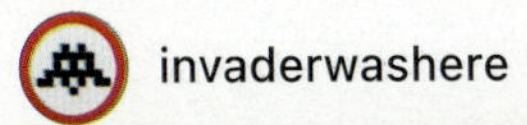

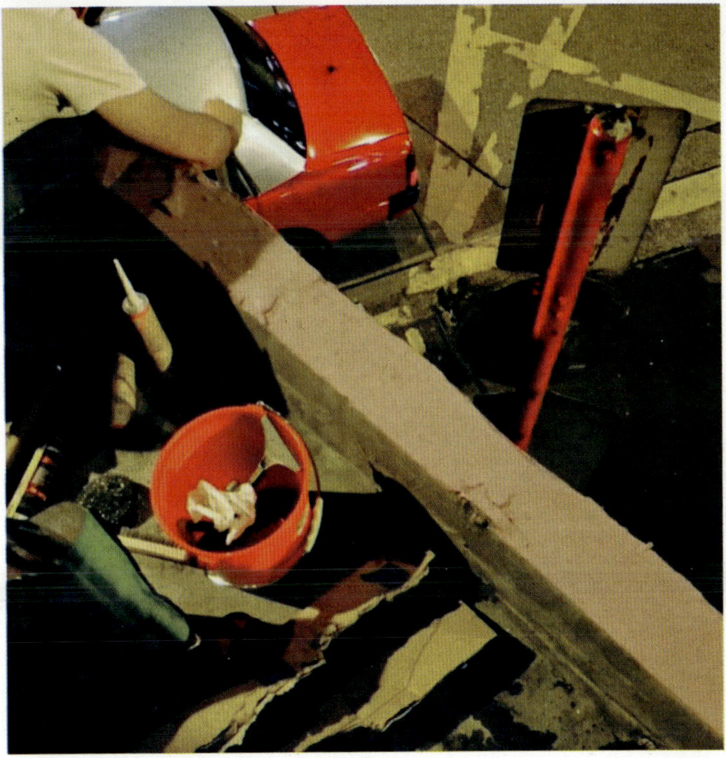

2 315 likes

invaderwashere Going down the rooftop...

View all 8 comments

7 May 2015

invaderwashere •••

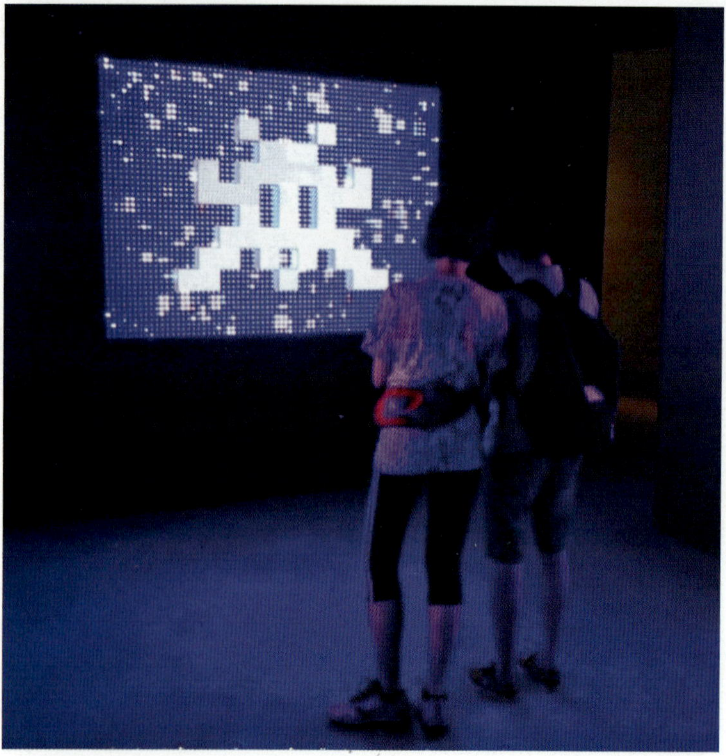

3 426 likes

invaderwashere #LEDpieces room #Wipeout #PMQ #HOCAfoundation #HongKong

View all 13 comments

7 May 2015

invaderwashere •••

 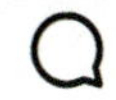  

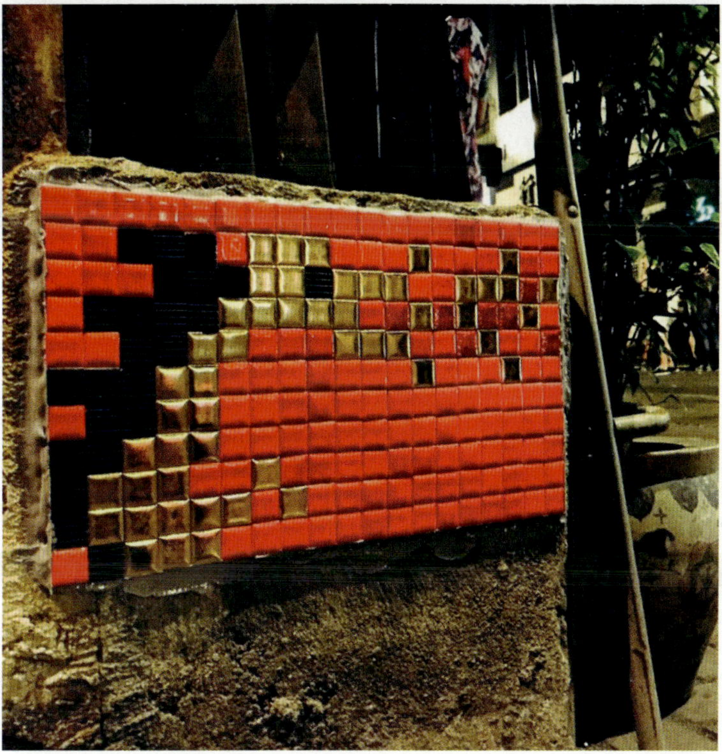

3 959 likes

invaderwashere Just made HK_92, the Golden Dragon #HongKong 2:48 am

View all 46 comments

8 May 2015

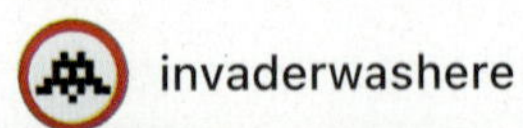

•••

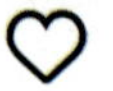  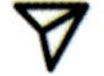 

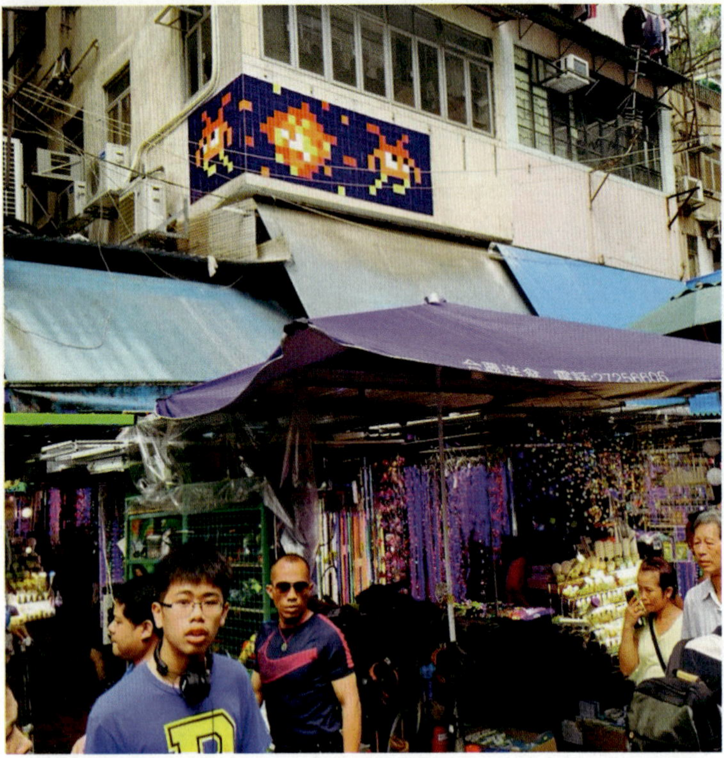

4953 likes

invaderwashere HK_88 new born #WipeOut in #HongKong

View all 50 comments

9 May 2015

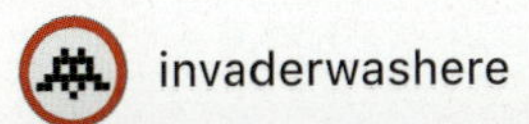

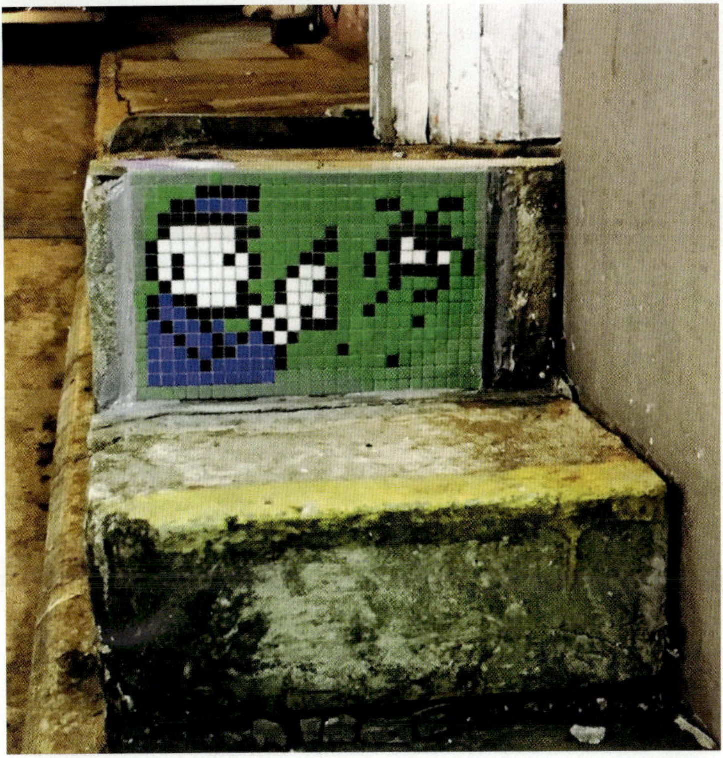

7053 likes

invaderwashere HK_94 Go to Jail! #HongKong #wipeout street piece

View all 47 comments

11 May 2015

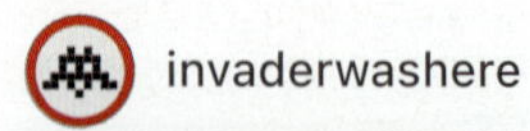

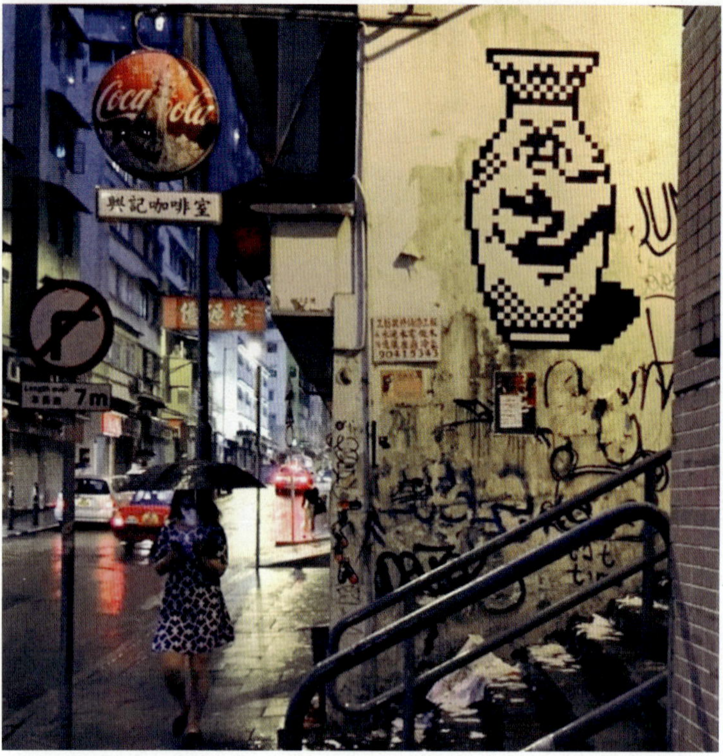

6563 likes

invaderwashere HK_98 made under a big rain! #Mingvase #HongKongInvasion

View all 69 comments

11 May 2015

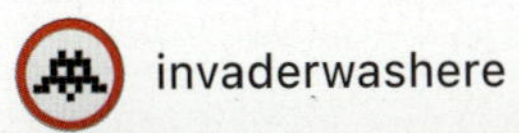

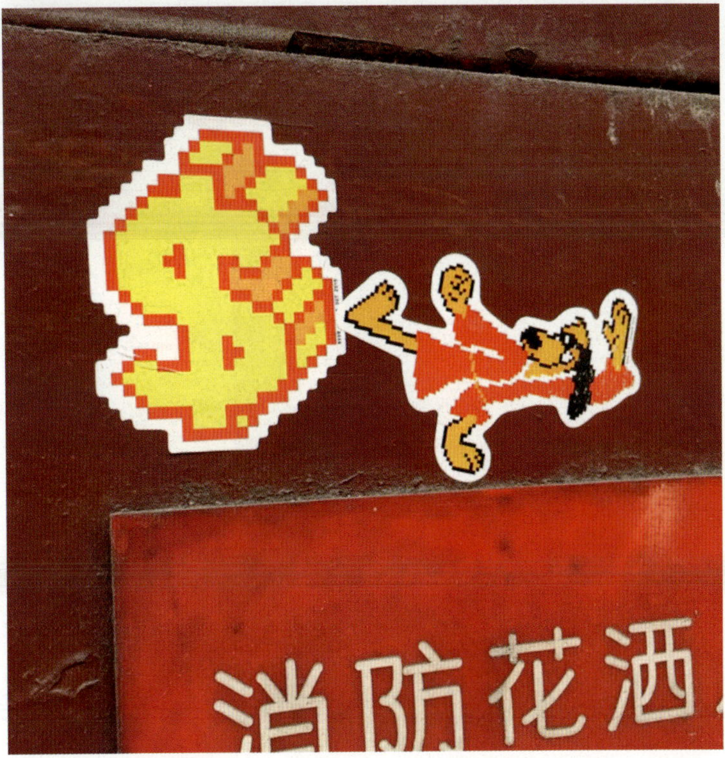

4 277 likes

invaderwashere Hong Kong $ vs Hong Kong Phooey
#stickerArt

View all 23 comments

13 May 2015

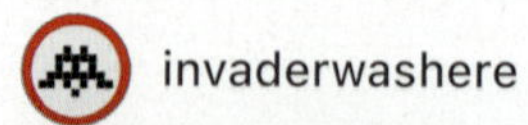

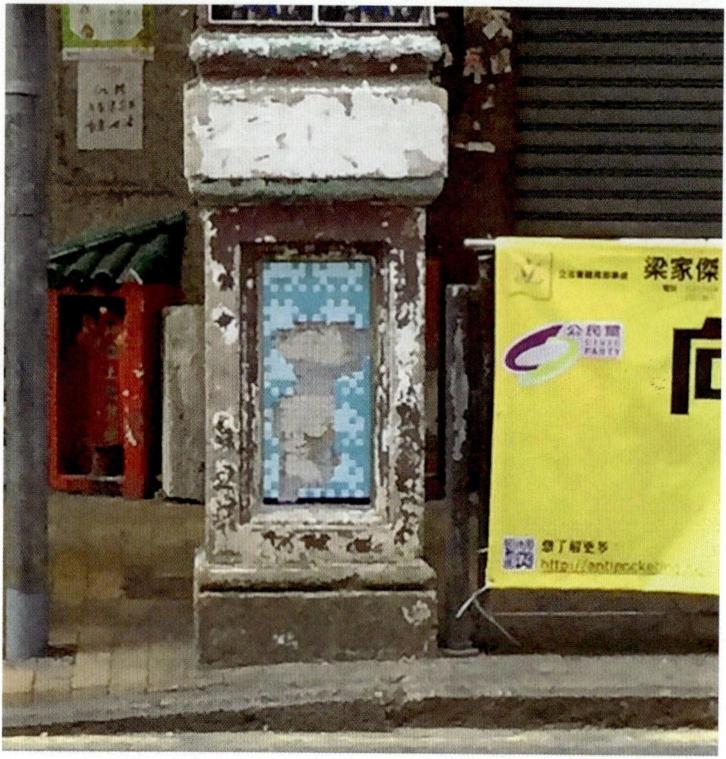

3 499 likes

invaderwashere This is what happens when someone tries to steal my street works #brokentiles #badkarma

View all 148 comments

14 May 2015

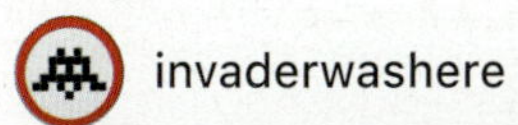

invaderwashere

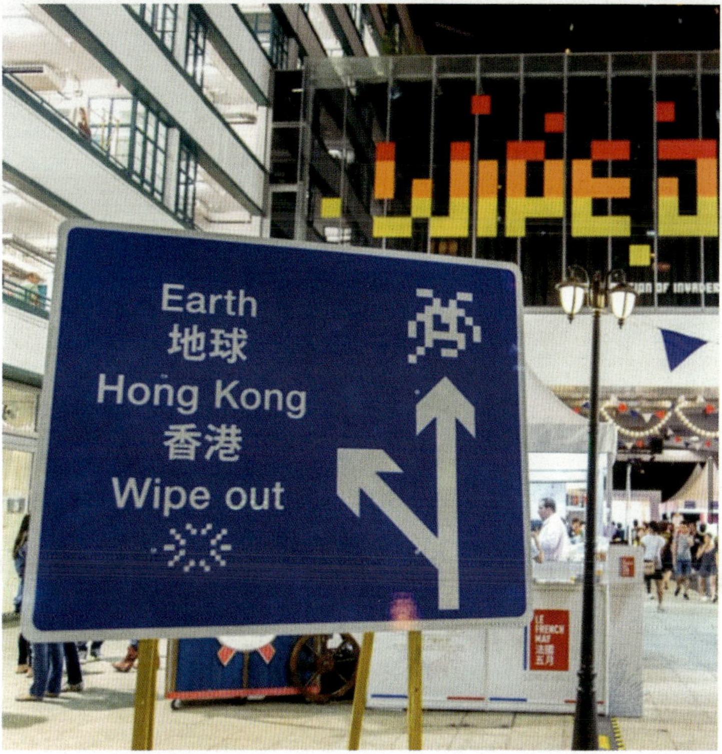

3746 likes

invaderwashere #Wipeout last week end!!! #PMQ #central #HongKong #freeEntrance @HOCAfoundation photo: @unoeilquitraine

View all 23 comments

14 May 2015

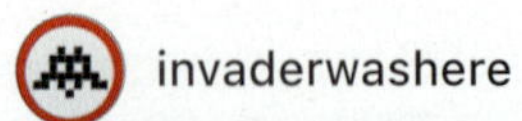
invaderwashere

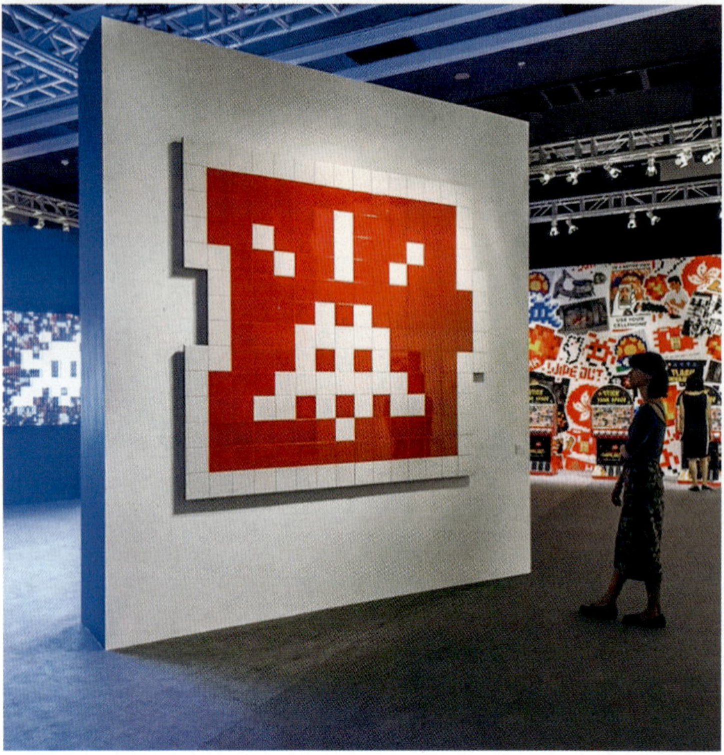

3 816 likes

invaderwashere #Wipeout last week end!!! #PMQ #central #HongKong #freeEntrance photo: @kitminlee courtesy #HOCAfoundation

View all 19 comments

14 May 2015

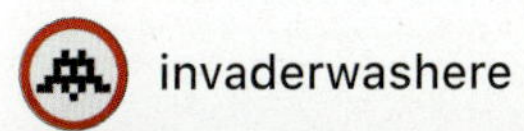

invaderwashere

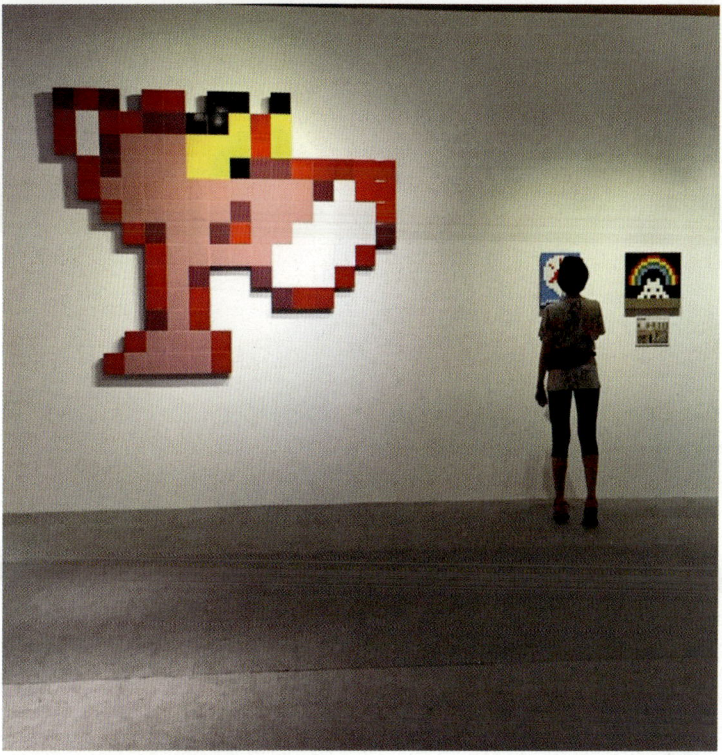

6960 likes

invaderwashere #Wipeout last week end!!! #PMQ #central #HongKong #freeEntrance #HOCAfoundation

View all 78 comments

14 May 2015

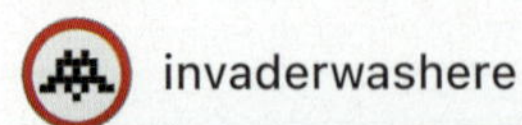

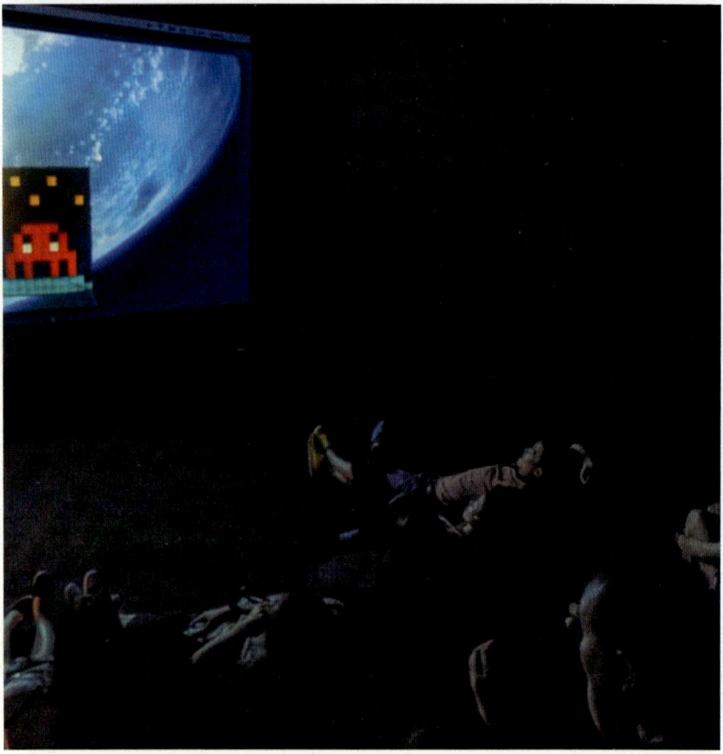

1932 likes

invaderwashere #Wipeout last week end!!! #PMQ #central #HongKong #freeEntrance @HOCAfoundation photo: @unoeilquitraine

View all 4 comments

14 May 2015

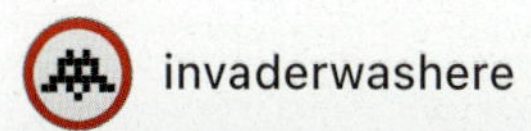

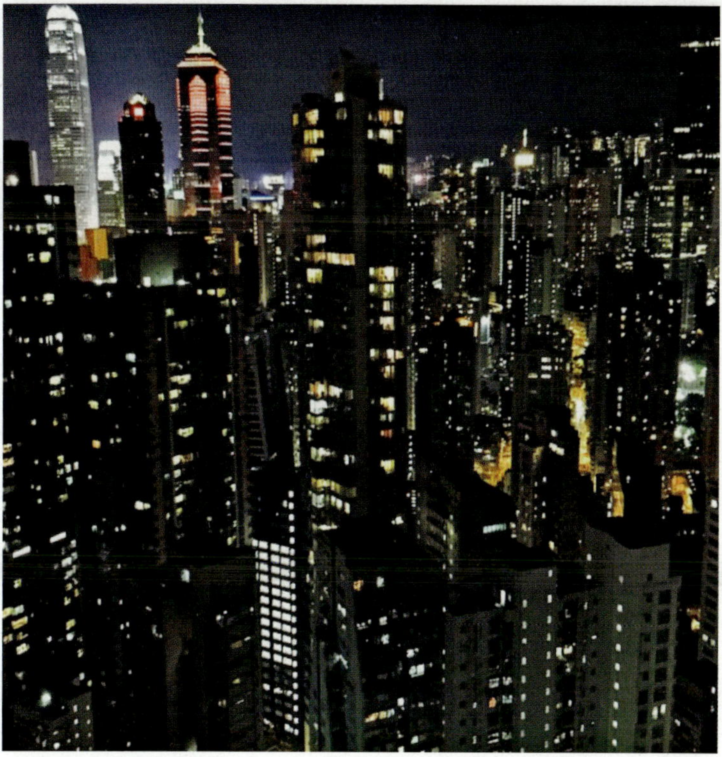

3 234 likes

invaderwashere Good night #HongKong

View all 9 comments

14 May 2015

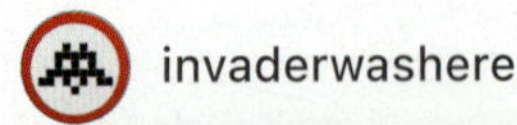

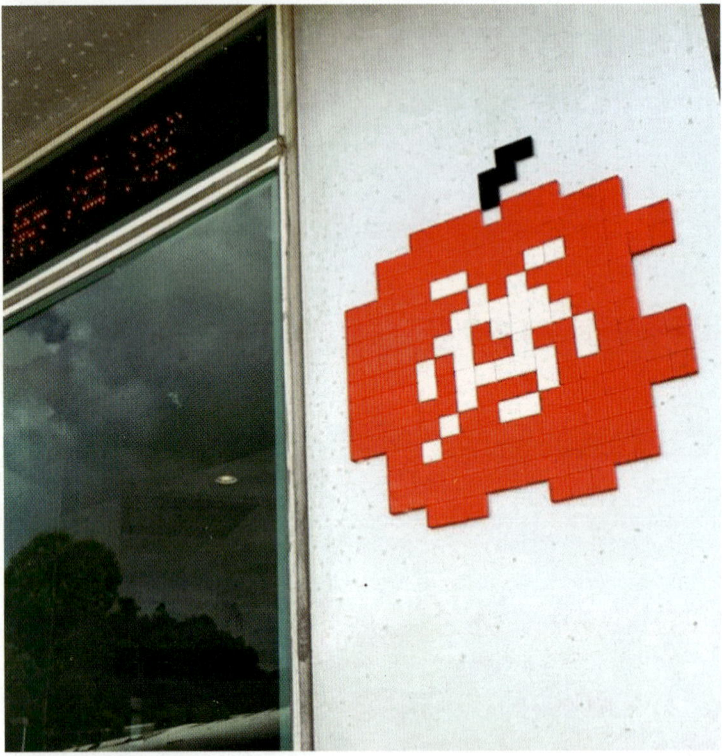

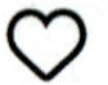   

4888 likes

invaderwashere Just put HK_99, the last piece of my 5th Invasion wave of #HongKong / The whole story in @AppleDailyHK newspaper of tomorrow

View all 43 comments

14 May 2015

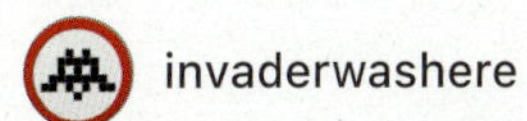

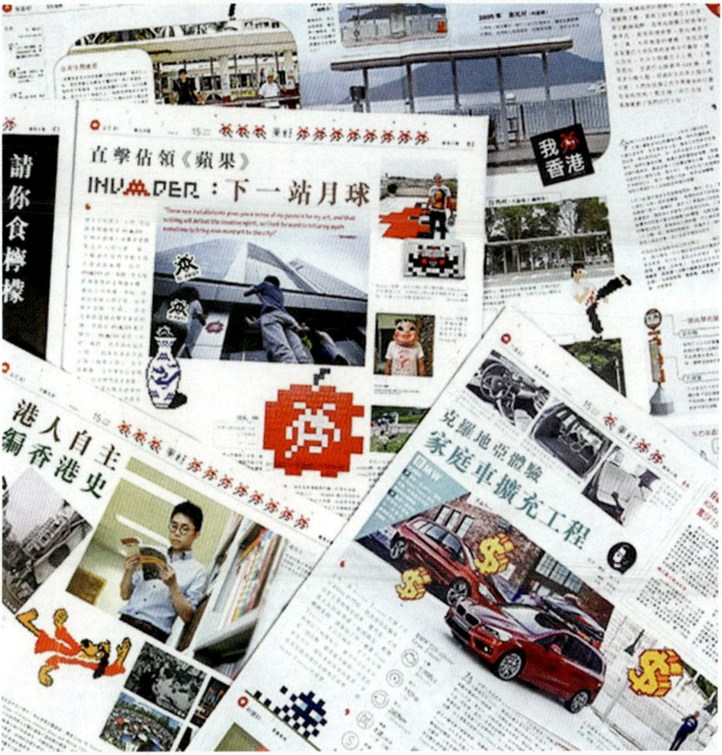

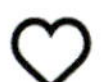

2610 likes

invaderwashere Today: Special issue of @appledailyhk newspaper / 8 Invaded pages! Don't miss it! #invader #appledaily may15 #2015

View all 25 comments

15 May 2015

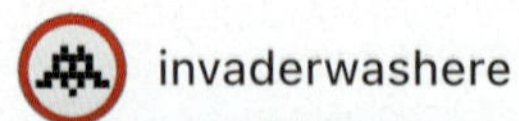

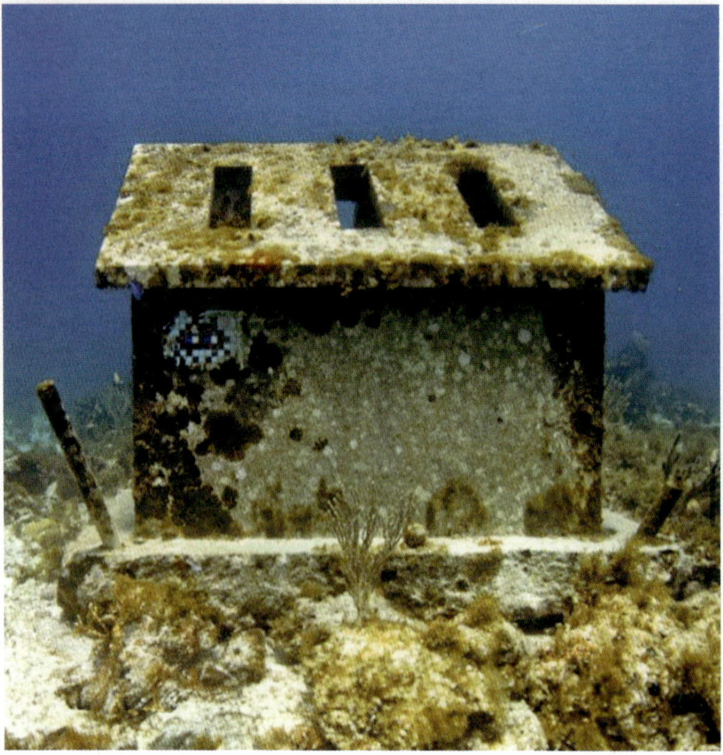

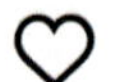   

5635 likes

invaderwashere In 2007, I was planning to create underwater sculptures and five years later, when I was technically ready to embark on such a project, I discovered the amazing underwater sculptures of artist Jason de Caires, who had just joined one art gallery I was working with. I decided not to venture into his territory and wrote him an e-mail about the coincidence. He replied that he was currently working on a series of new sculptures and that I was welcome to join in. This is how three space invaders ended up at the bottom of the Cauncun Bay on Jason sculptures! CCU_01 is still under water. #CancunBay #mexico photo: @musamuseo Thank you #JasondeCaire

View all 87 comments

18 May 2015

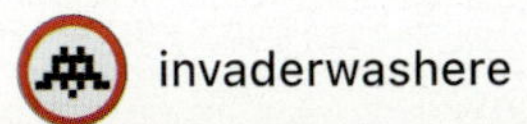
invaderwashere

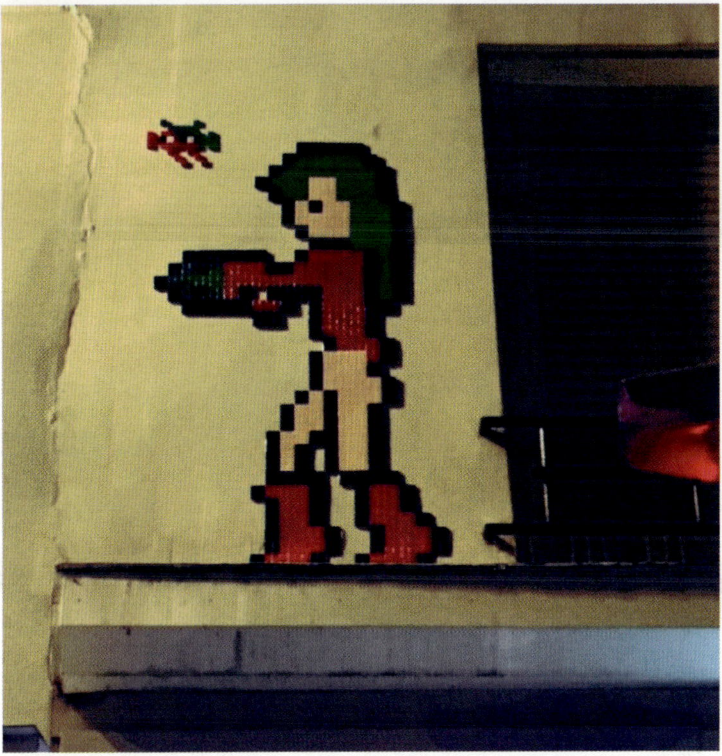

6729 likes

invaderwashere PA_1139 #justdone #Paris 3:55 am
#justinbailey

View all 70 comments

20 May 2015

invaderwashere •••

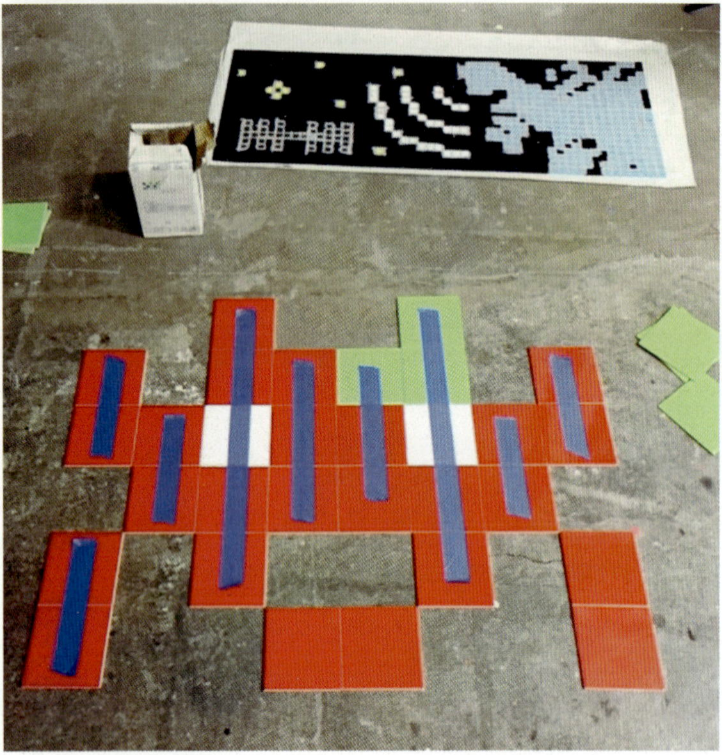

3 428 likes

invaderwashere PA_1140 and PA_1141 just before being installed #Paris #HelloSushi #tunaWasabi #Space2iSS #HQ #ESA #studio

View all 17 comments

28 May 2015

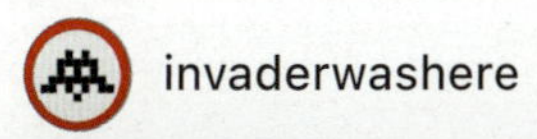

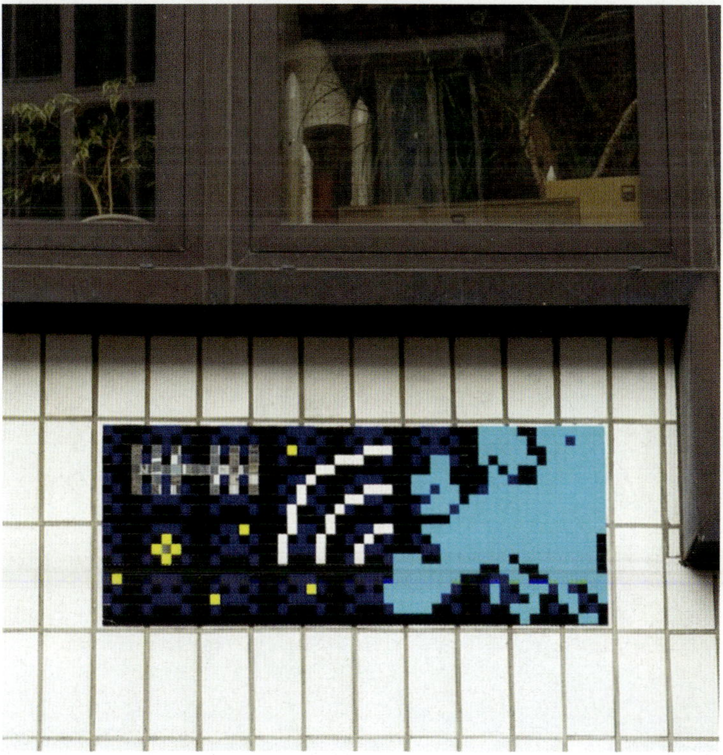

4 872 likes

invaderwashere PA_1141 is in the place! #ESA #HQ #Paris #Space2iSS

View all 27 comments

29 May 2015

invaderwashere •••

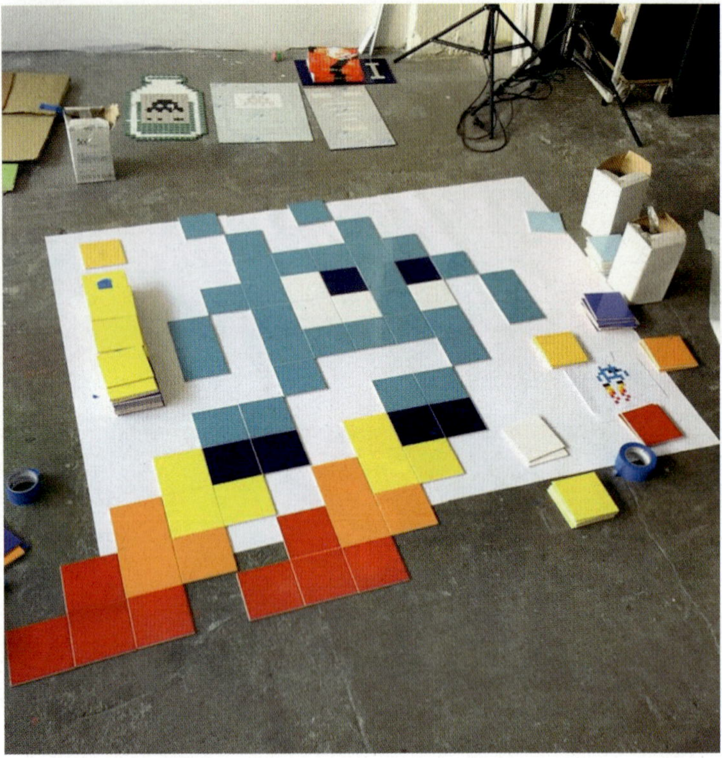

5 551 likes

invaderwashere Soon on Earth... #studio #makingof #rocket #spaceInvader #invader

View all 36 comments

1 June 2015

invaderwashere 

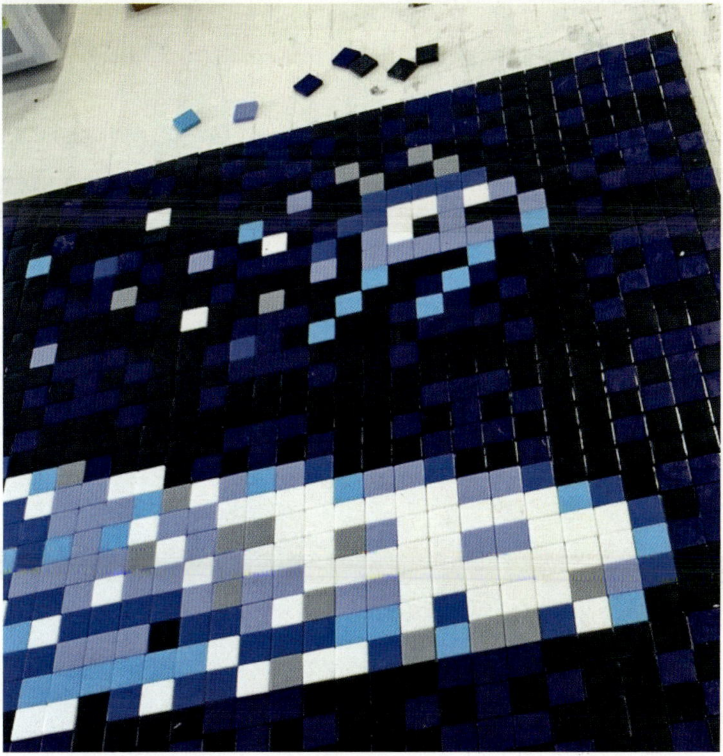

4703 likes

invaderwashere #spaceInvader flying over the #comet
Soon on Earth #detail #makingof #studio

View all 30 comments

2 June 2015

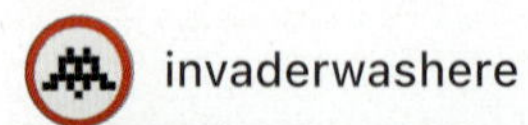

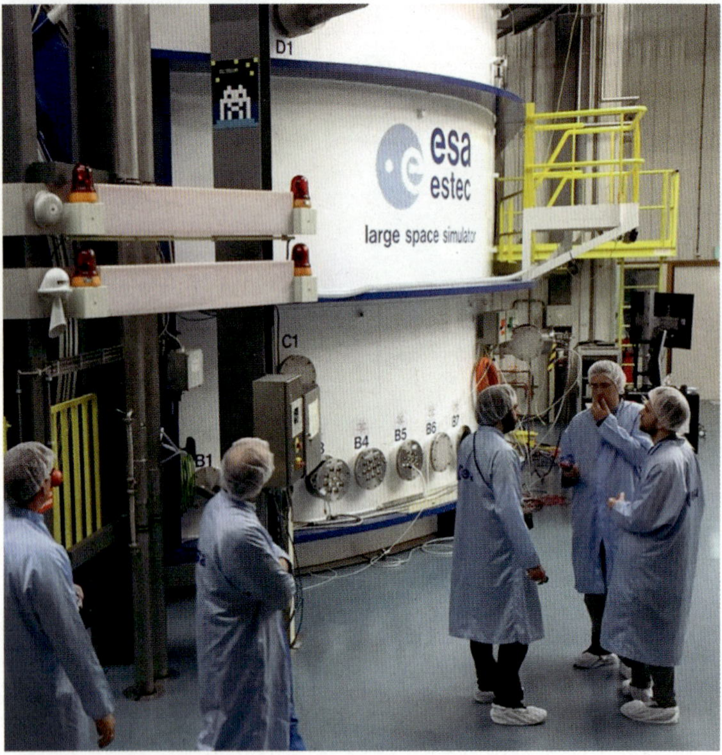

3 544 likes

invaderwashere Large Space Simulator invaded!
100 Points / #ESTEC #Noordwijk #Holland #ESA
#SpaceArt

View all 30 comments

3 June 2015

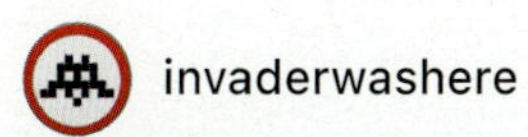

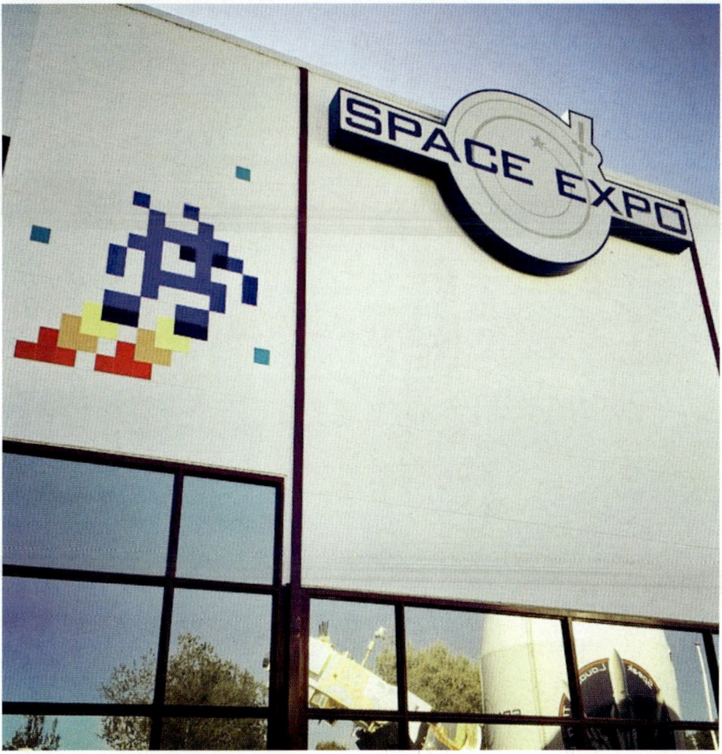

4 713 likes

invaderwashere #invasion of the #SpaceExpo façade #Noordwijk #Holland #ESTEC #ESA #Space2iSS #space #art

View all 26 comments

3 June 2015

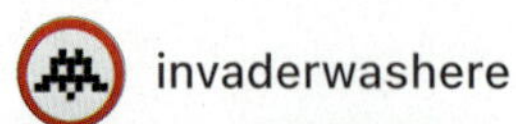

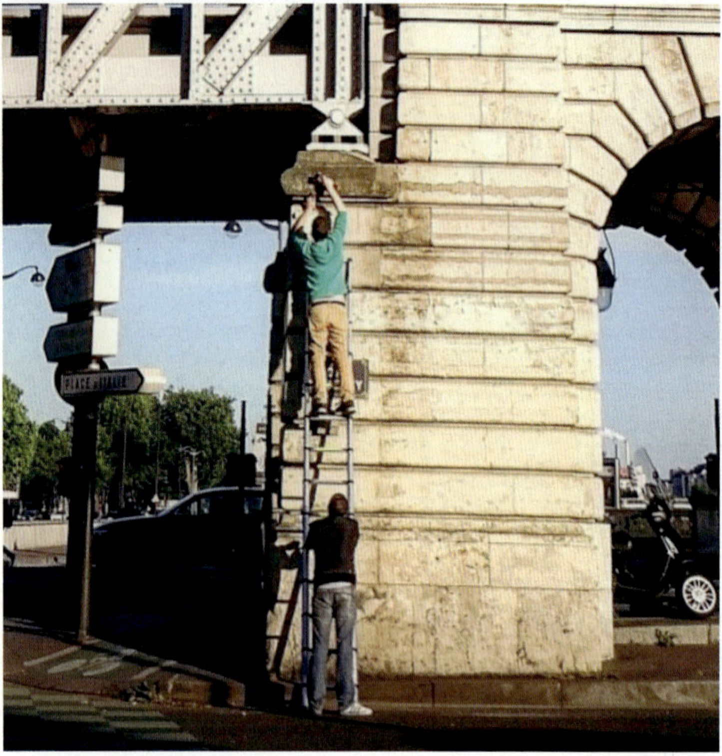

3669 likes

invaderwashere #Warning! Don't be fool! Some people are trying to steal my pieces in the streets but as they can't, they end with smashing them to make and sell replicas on black market. Here is a list of brands and places where to find the same tiles that I use. You can easily make perfect copies of my #spaceinvaders for less that 10€ without destroying any street pieces #spaceInvaders #thieves #hammer #destruction #tiles #opiocolor #briare #pointP #LeroyMerlin #homeDepot Photo: @fredmery

View all 75 comments

4 June 2015

invaderwashere •••

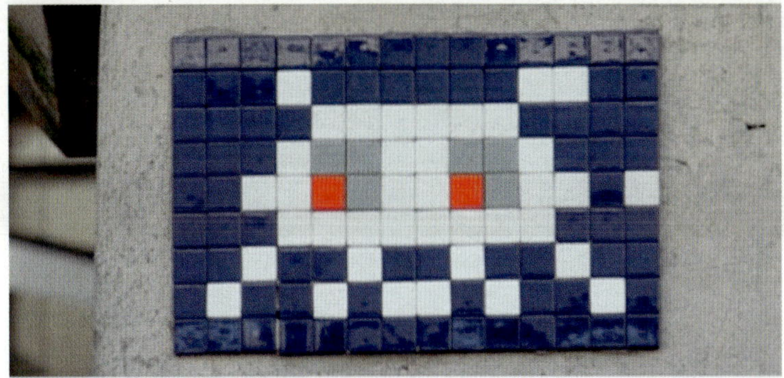

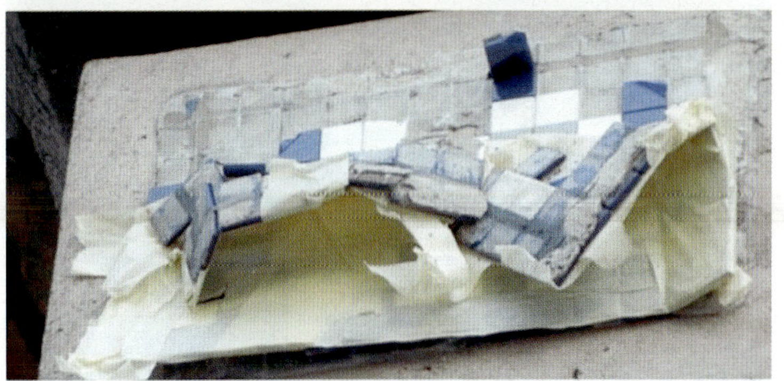

5336 likes

invaderwashere #Warning! Don't be fool! Some people are trying to steal my pieces from the streets but as they can't, they end with smashing them to make and sell replicas on black market. Here is a list of brands and places where to find the same tiles that I use. You can easily make perfect copies of my #spaceinvaders for less that 10€ without destroying any street pieces #before #after #thieves #destruction #tiles #copy #replicates #opiocolor #briare #pointP #LeroyMerlin #homeDepot Photo: @street_art77

View all 224 comments

4 June 2015

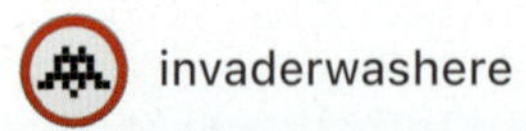

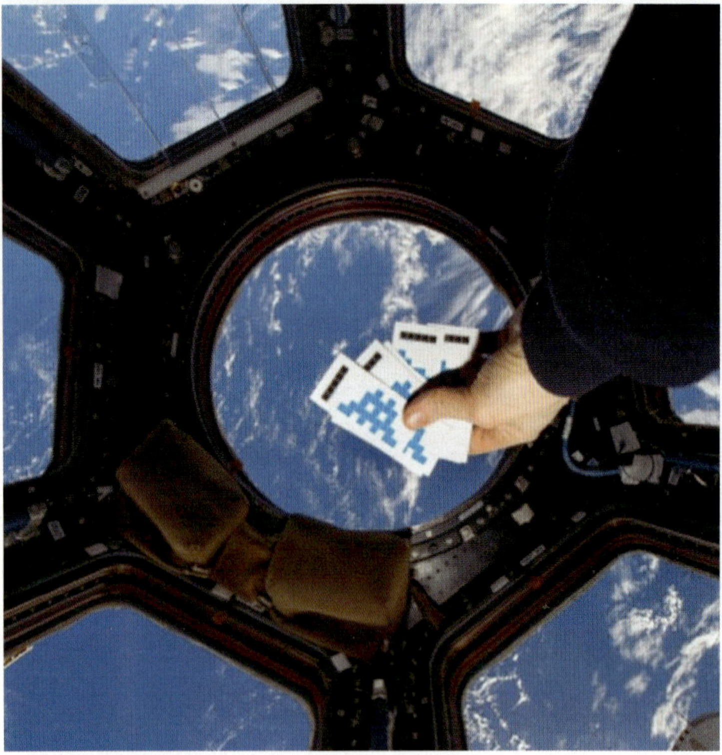

 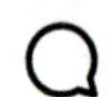  

6 278 likes

invaderwashere Just got this shot from the International Space Station #ISS #SPACE2ISS #ESA #invader #stickers #astroSamantha #cupola

View all 84 comments

10 June 2015

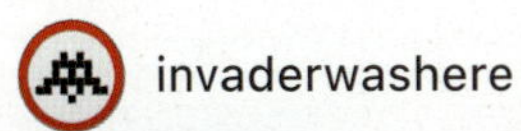

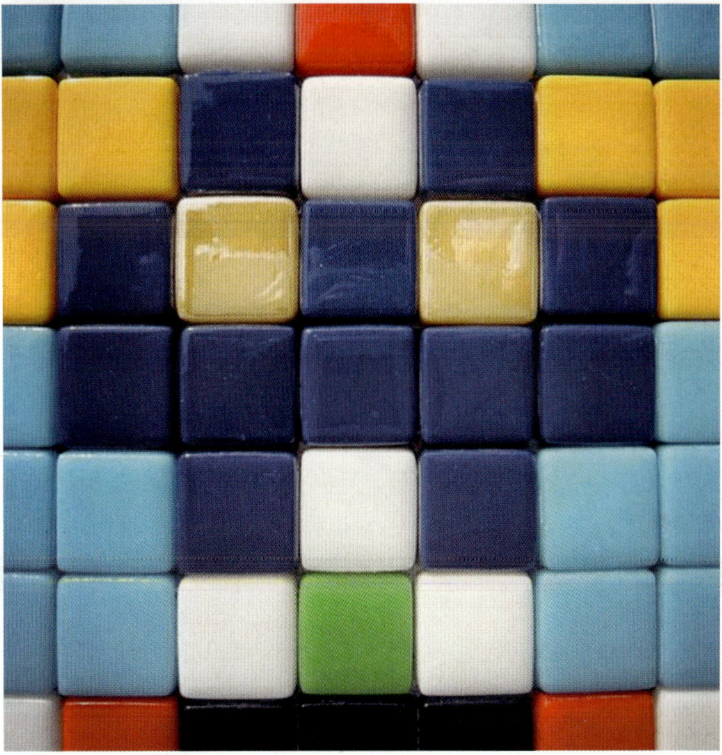

5479 likes

invaderwashere Close-up of TK_132 / #Tokyo #Gundam #Grendizer #goldorak Photo: @Doraebon

View all 22 comments

13 June 2015

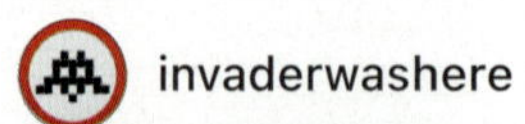

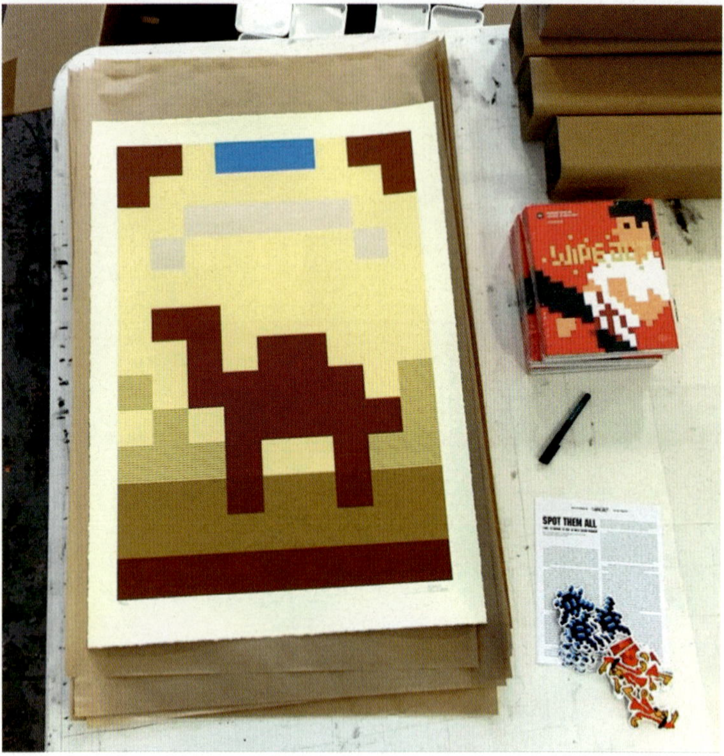

4767 likes

invaderwashere A new print featuring a wild animal in the Egyptian desert and my new book #wipeoutinHK are available online today #spaceshop #silkscreenprint #invasionguide06

View all 95 comments

15 June 2015

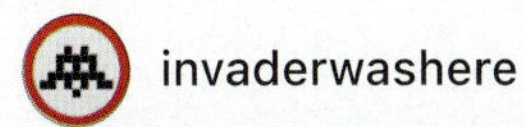

•••

 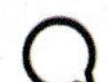  

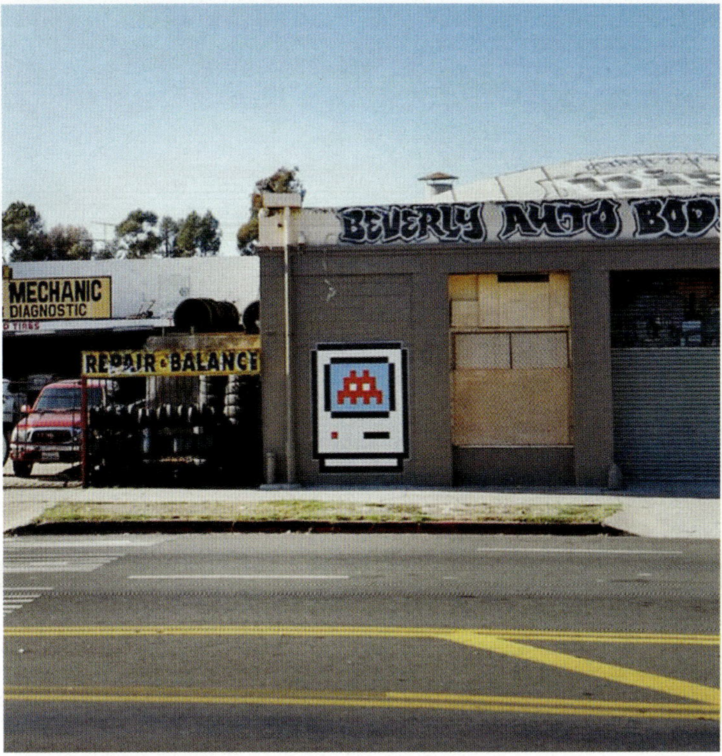

5532 likes

invaderwashere For a little while some of my removed mosaics have come back to life 🙌 That wonderful LA_134 has just been reactivated in L.A. by an anonymous.
Those kind of « reactivations » can be noticed in Paris, Bastia, London, La Ciotat, Lyon, Basel and L.A.
A huge thank's to all the people who are making this awesome job. Photo: @detroitdennis #reactivation #backtolife

View all 53 comments

17 June 2015

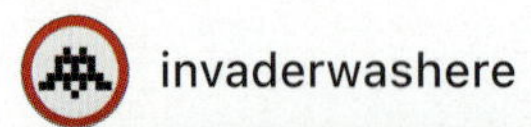

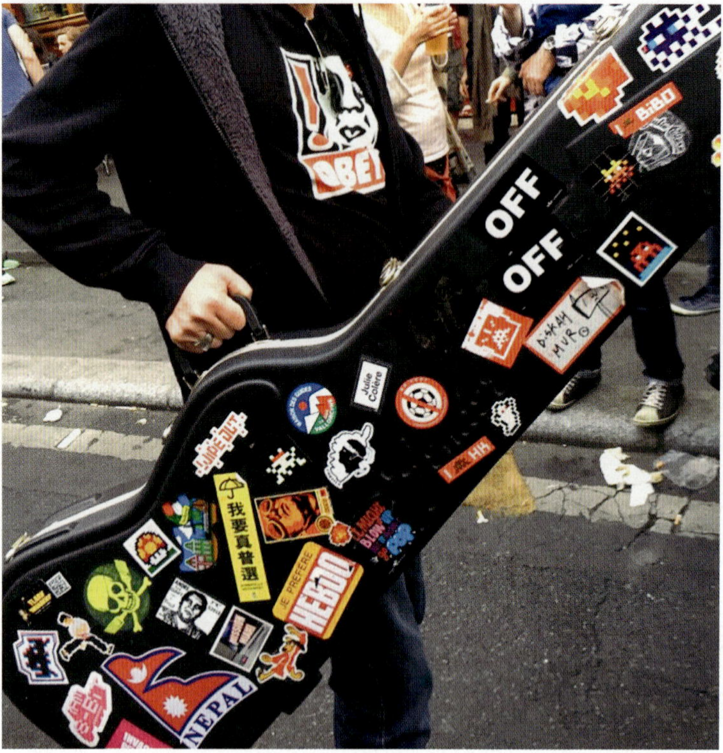

 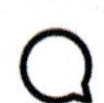  

3 684 likes

invaderwashere Fête de la musique #21juin #paris #juliecolere #guitarebass #stickers

View all 40 comments

21 June 2015

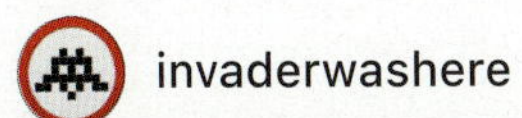

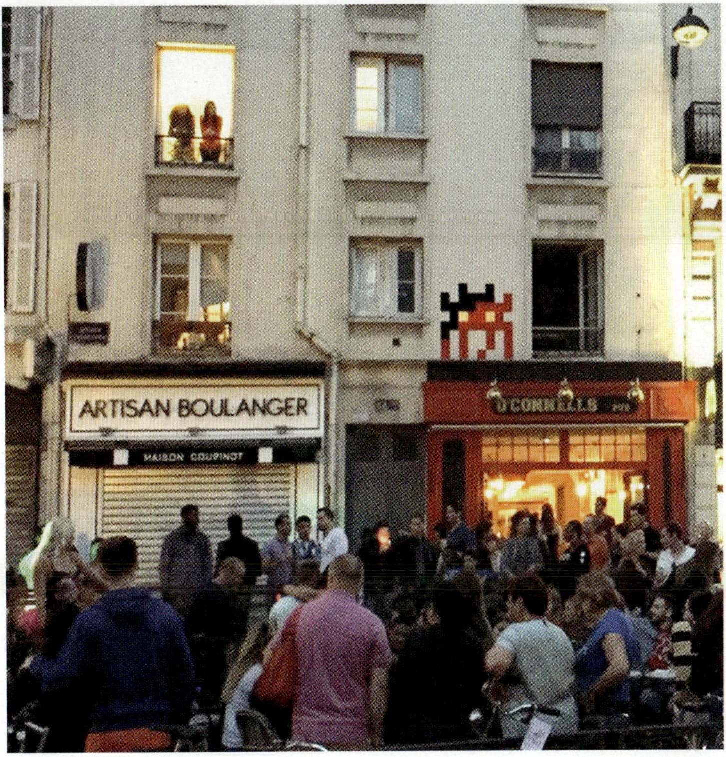

5446 likes

invaderwashere Fête de la musique #21juin #paris
PA_1047

View all 34 comments

22 June 2015

invaderwashere ...

  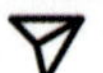 

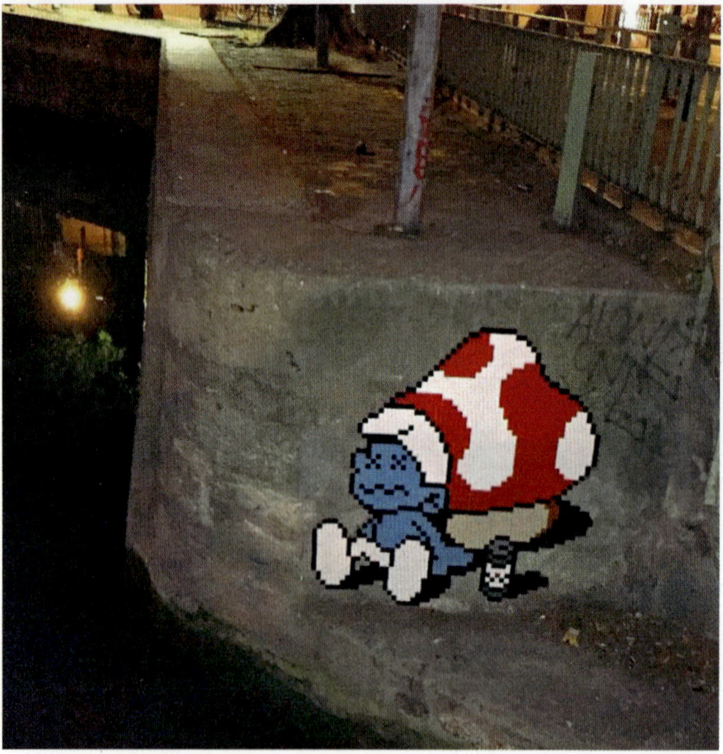

10 144 likes

invaderwashere PA_1147 the drunk Smurf #100Pts

View all 143 comments

25 June 2015

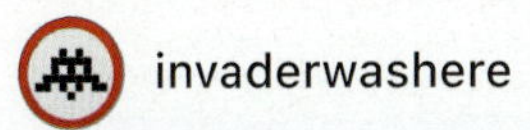

invaderwashere •••

  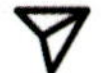 

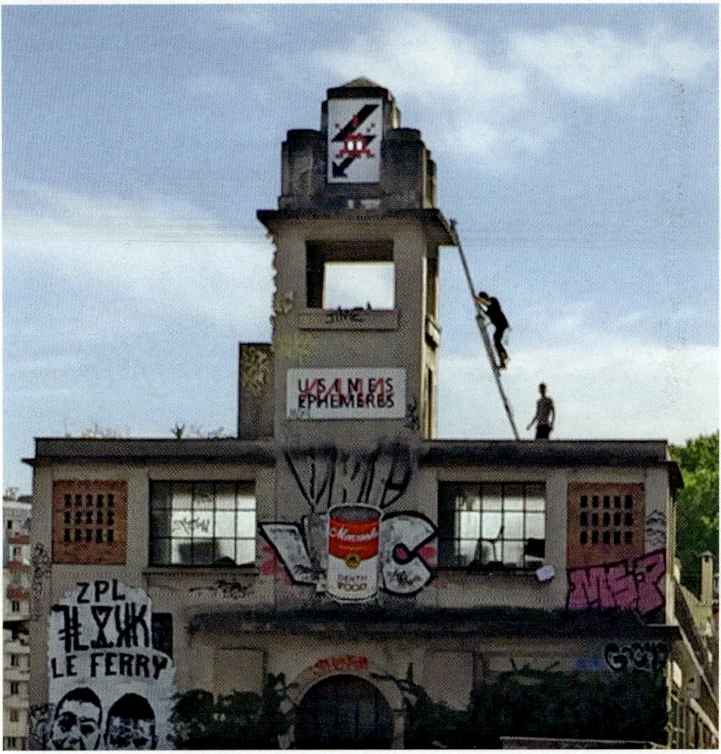

4099 likes

invaderwashere Making of PA_1148 today in #paris #PointEphemere #sideB

View all 43 comments

26 June 2015

invaderwashere

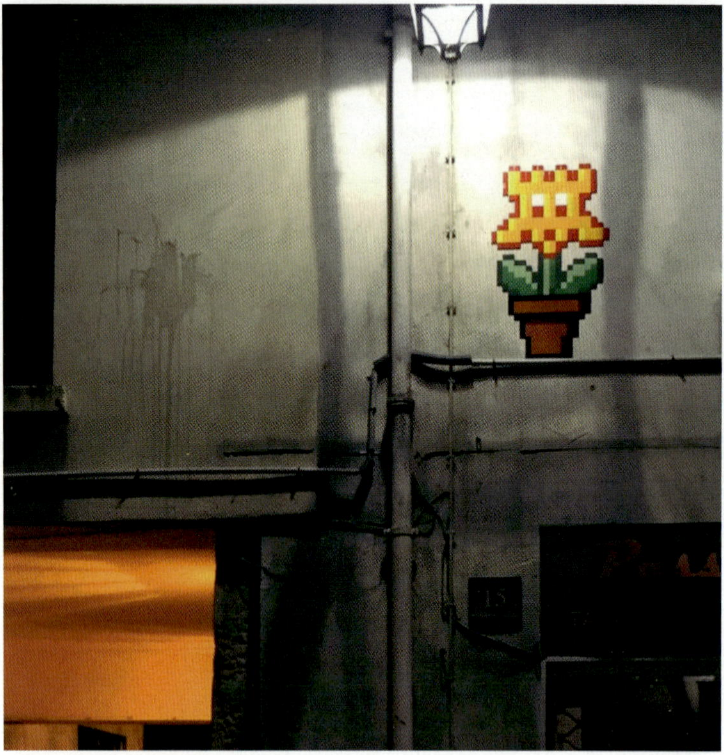

7 471 likes

invaderwashere PA_1152, a new Space Flower in Paris 4:21 am

View all 51 comments

1 July 2015

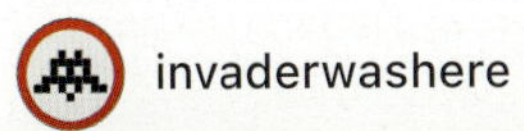

•••

 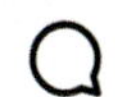  

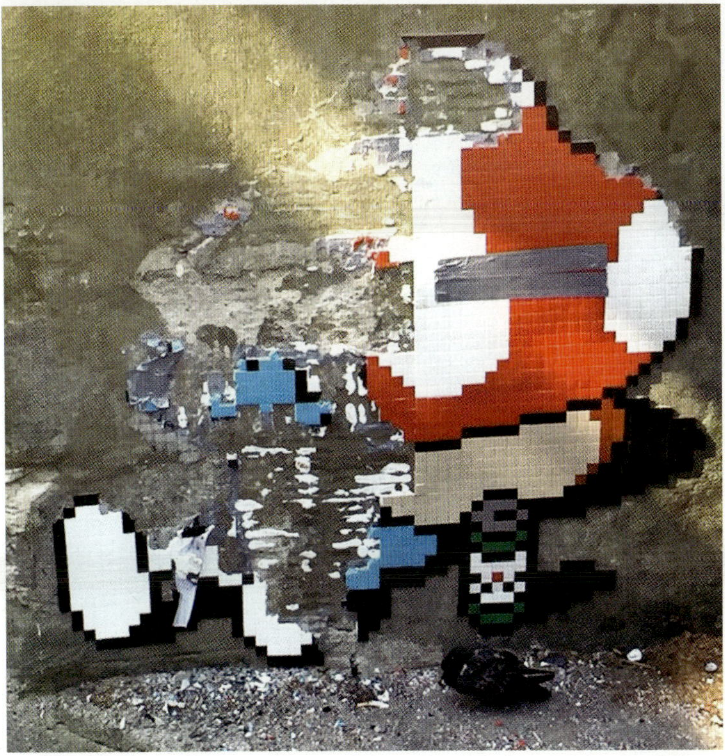

4743 likes

invaderwashere PA_1147, 5 days old and already totaly fucked up by a theft attempt. Just silly and sad! #theSmurfisDead #adhesivetape #streeArtThieves #brokenTiles #noRespect #totalwaste #badkarma

View all 464 comments

1 July 2015 ·

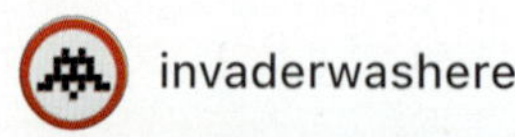

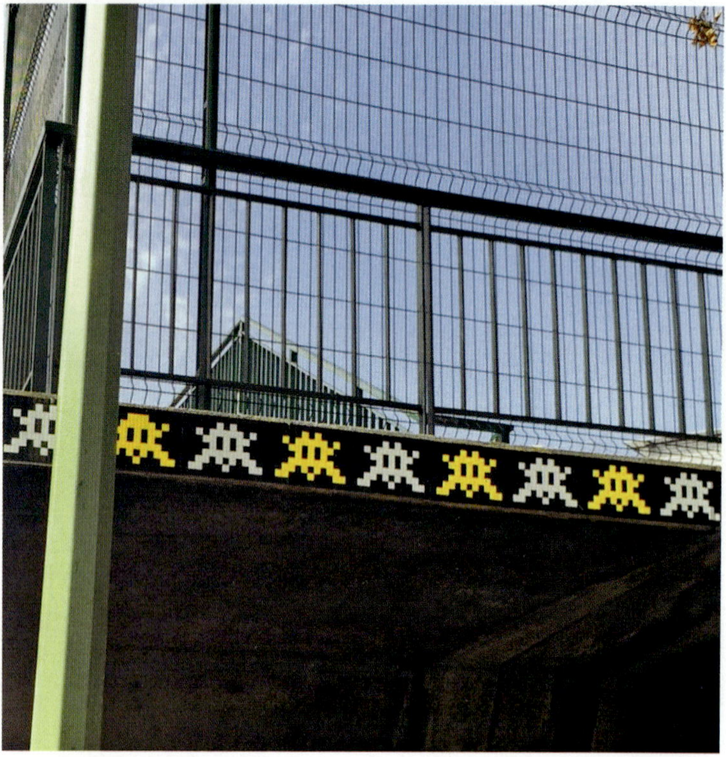

6 293 likes

invaderwashere A black, white & yellow composition just appeared along the ring of Paris / PA_1155 #spaceinvaders #frieze #peripherique Millions of viewers everyday! 👀🚗

View all 38 comments

5 July 2015

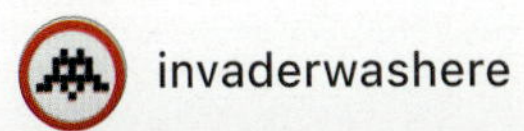

invaderwashere

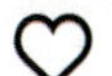   

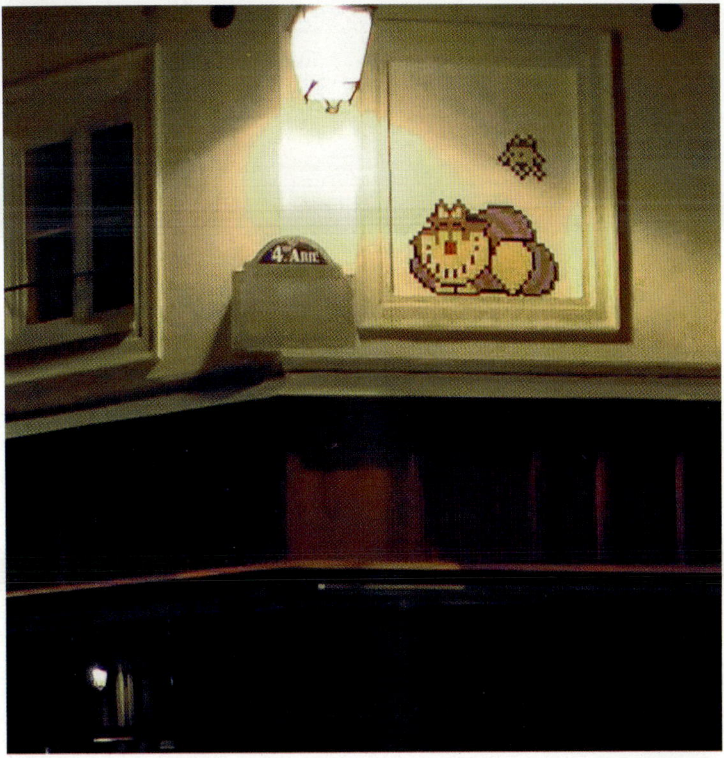

7547 likes

invaderwashere Last night, the Cheshire cat showed up in Paris PA_1156

View all 125 comments

10 July 2015

invaderwashere •••

 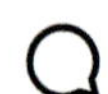  

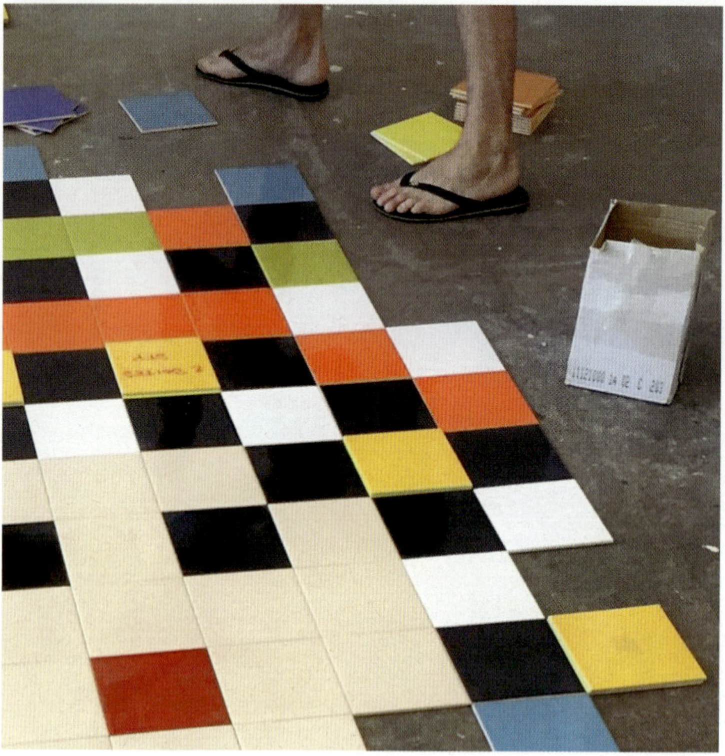

3 674 likes

invaderwashere #Summertime working at the studio #work #flipflops #tongs #sooninthestreets

View all 32 comments

16 July 2015

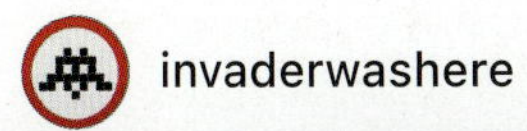

...

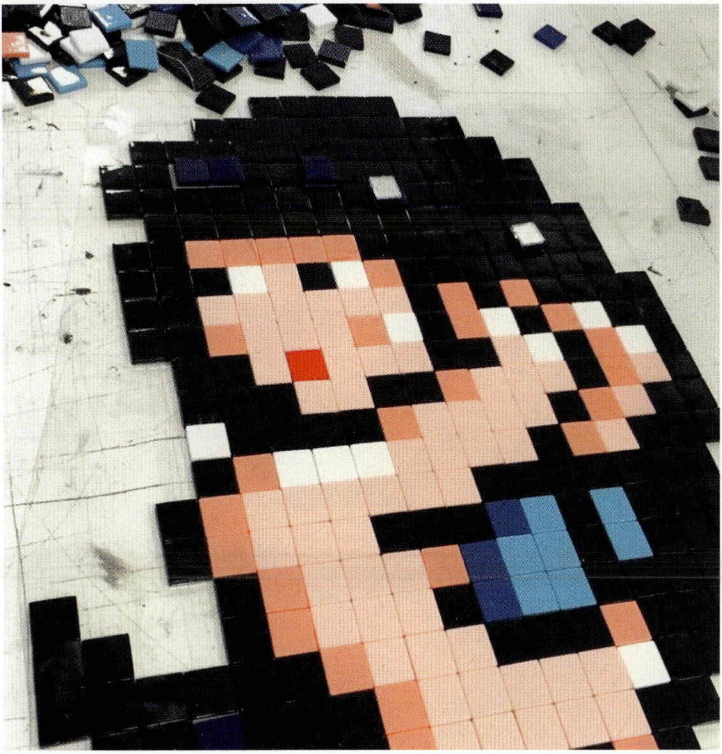

5 859 likes

invaderwashere Summer piece #mermaid #workinprogress stay tuned...

View all 34 comments

20 July 2015

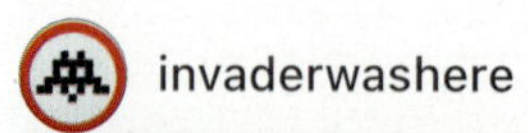

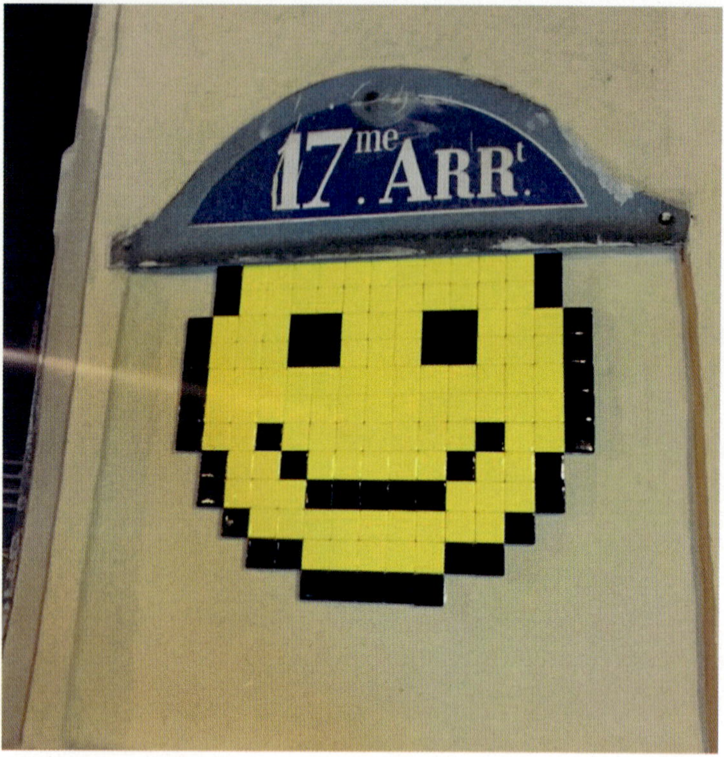

 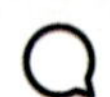  

7158 likes

invaderwashere PA_1159 4:18 am 🙂+🎩=🤠

View all 72 comments

21 July 2015

invaderwashere

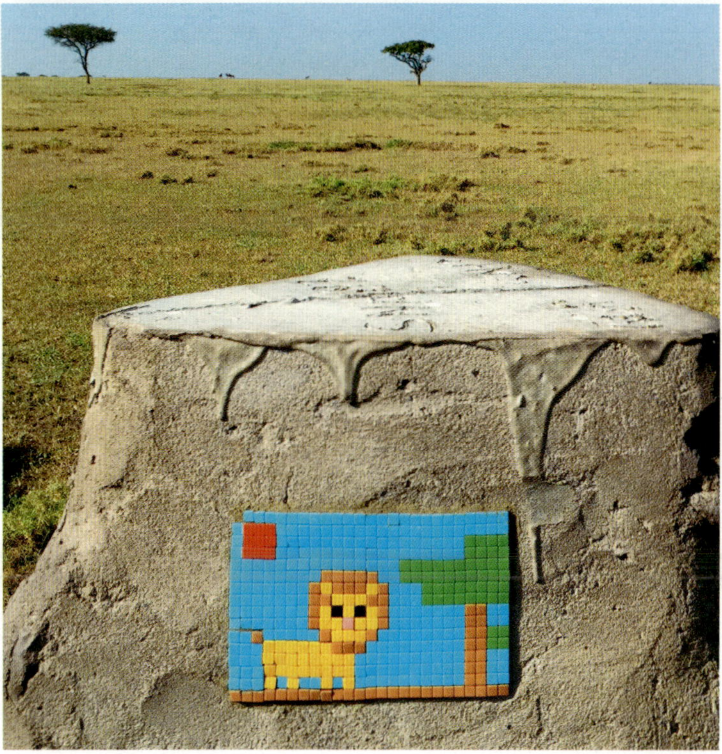

8748 likes

invaderwashere "We can judge the heart of a man by his treatment of animals" E.Kant #protectwildlife #freeanimals #cecilthelion #shot Hunt with a camera not a gun 😡 GRTI_02 #Grumeti #Tanzania 01-2015

View all 160 comments

30 July 2015

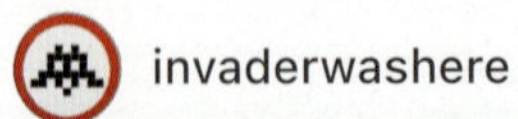

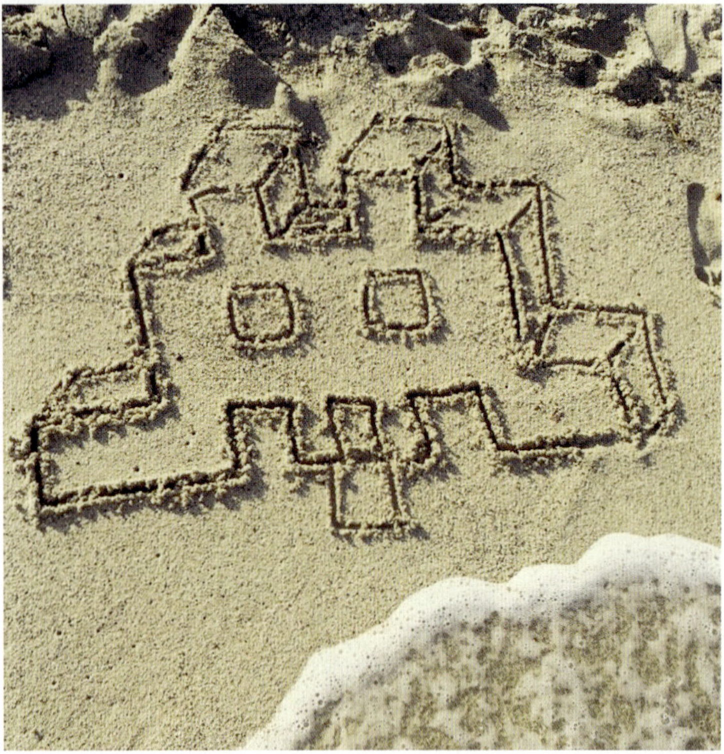

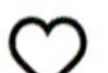 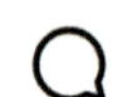  

6626 likes

invaderwashere Ephemeral #holidaysinthesun #beachDrawing

View all 42 comments

1 August 2015

invaderwashere •••

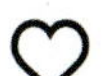 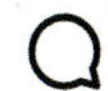  

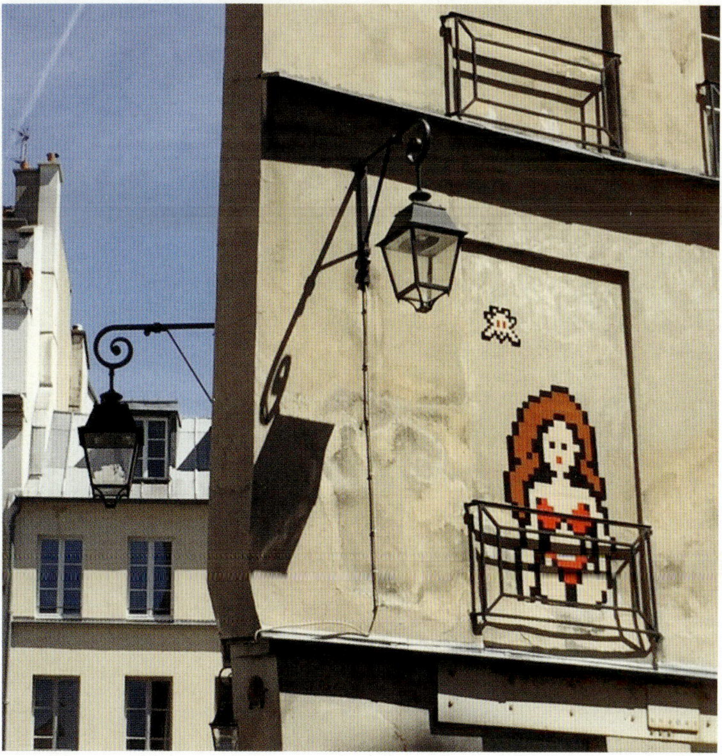

9 385 likes

invaderwashere PA_1127 #paris #summertime

View all 83 comments

2 August 2015

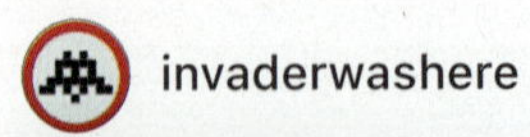

HIGHSCORES

RANK	PLAYER	FOUND	SCORE
01	OLIVIER	1001	30000
02	VIVIANE 64	945	29120
03	OLIVIERTOF	963	28760
04	CHASSEUR D···	932	27850
05	JULES	921	27830
06	PAUL (STREE···	890	27580
07	JOETHECRAB	933	27510
08	USA69	881	27100

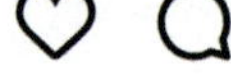 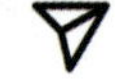 

1787 likes

invaderwashere 🏆🏆🏆 to the top player at #FlashInvaders who just rose above 1000 flashed mosaics #spaceinvaders #august2015 #30000points #app #freeapp #cellphones #android #iOS #searchandflash

View all 59 comments

4 August 2015

invaderwashere

 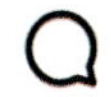  

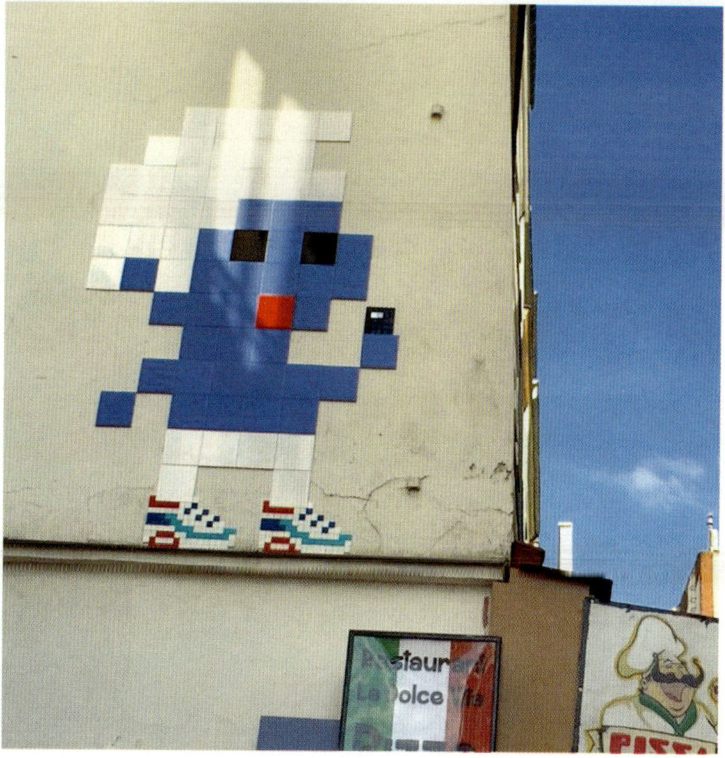

8482 likes

invaderwashere Le Schtroumpf des Halles #newpiece #paris #lesHalles #smurf #schtroumpf #sneackers #cellphone #lowres

View all 169 comments

6 August 2015

invaderwashere ...

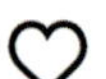

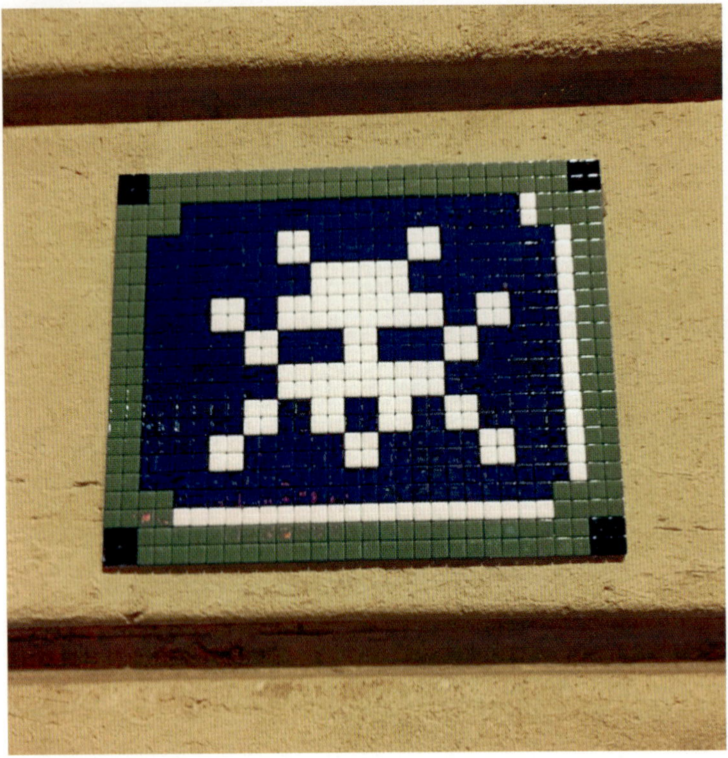

6045 likes

invaderwashere Just made in #paris 4:45 am

View all 54 comments

7 August 2015

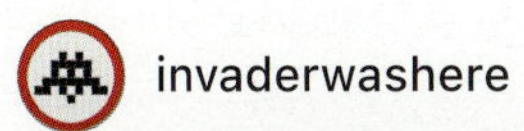

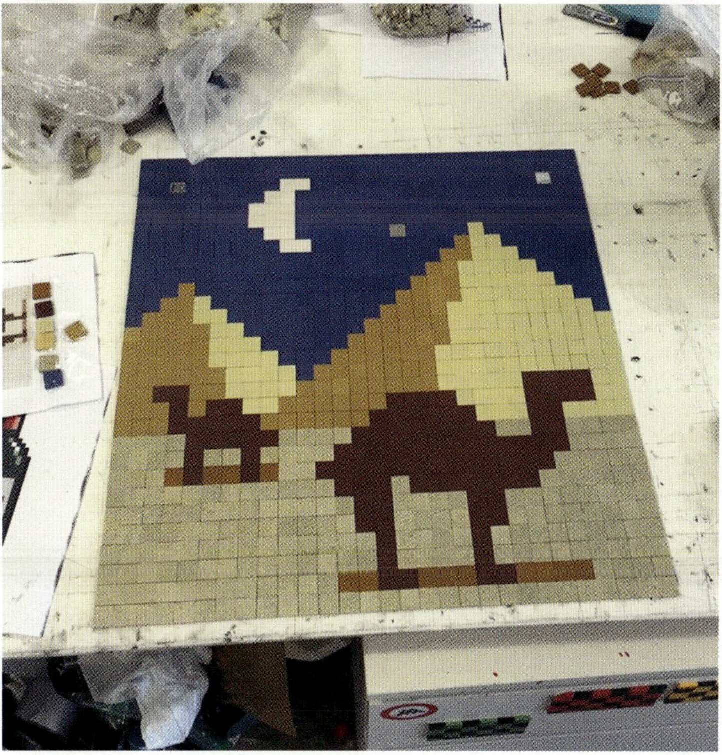

7098 likes

invaderwashere Making of a new piece for Paris...

View all 71 comments

7 August 2015

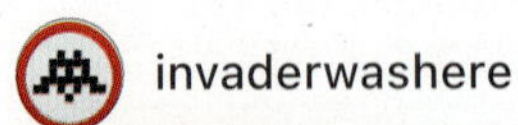

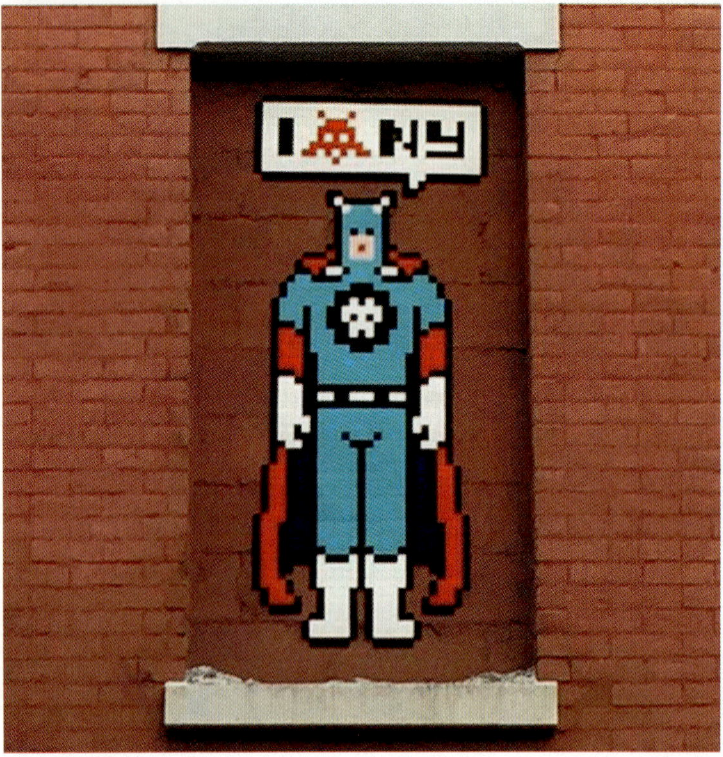

8091 likes

invaderwashere New Invasion in NY. Big thanks to @LoManArtFest and @thelisaprojectnyc for making it happen #50points

View all 89 comments

9 August 2015

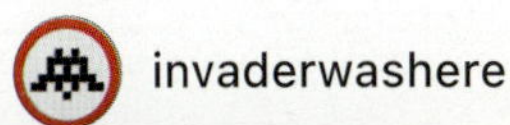

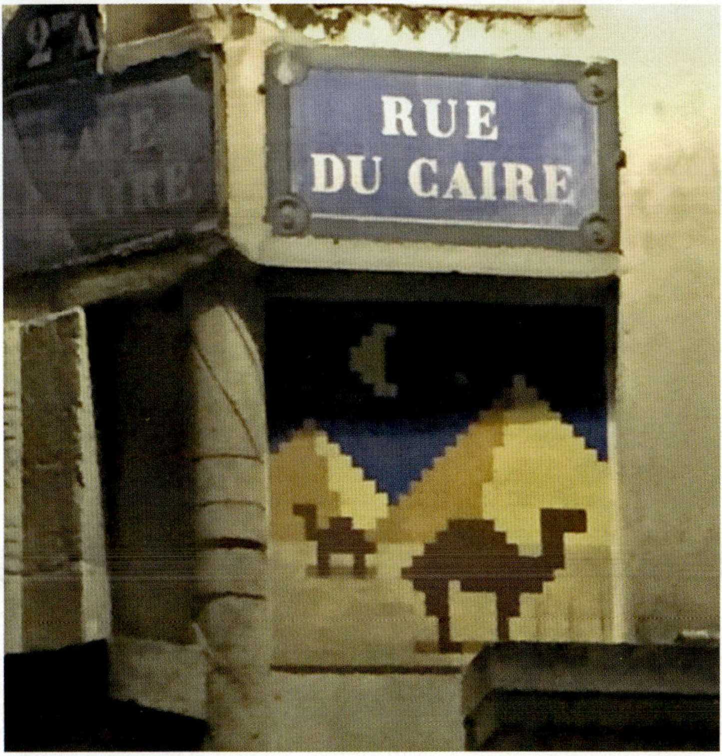

6 626 likes

invaderwashere Egyptian night in Paris #rueducaire #PA1165 #justdone #invaderwashere

View all 70 comments

10 August 2015

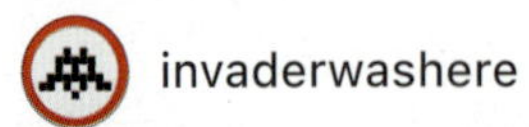

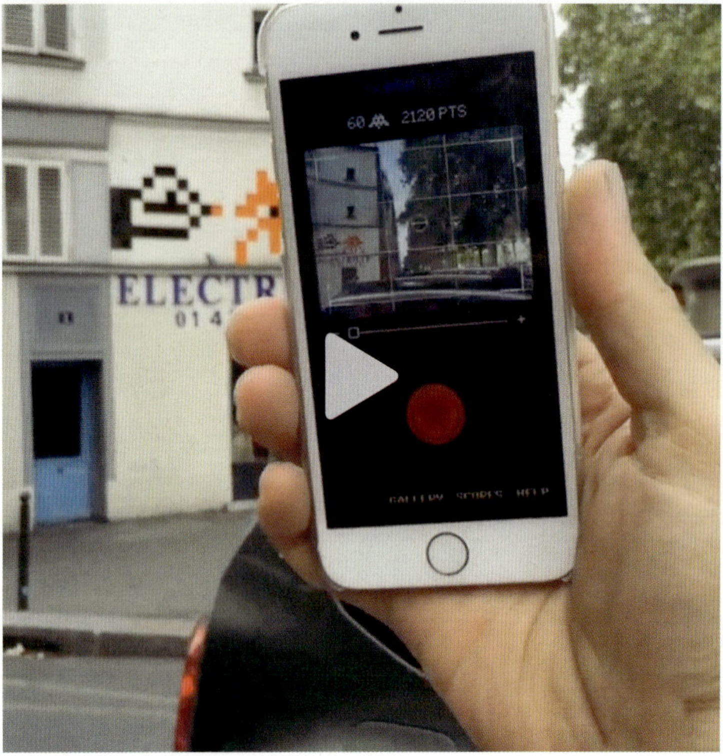

 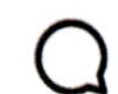 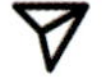 

4326 likes

invaderwashere Flashing PA_1033 #flashinvaders

View all 264 comments

11 August 2015

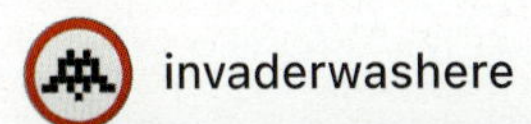

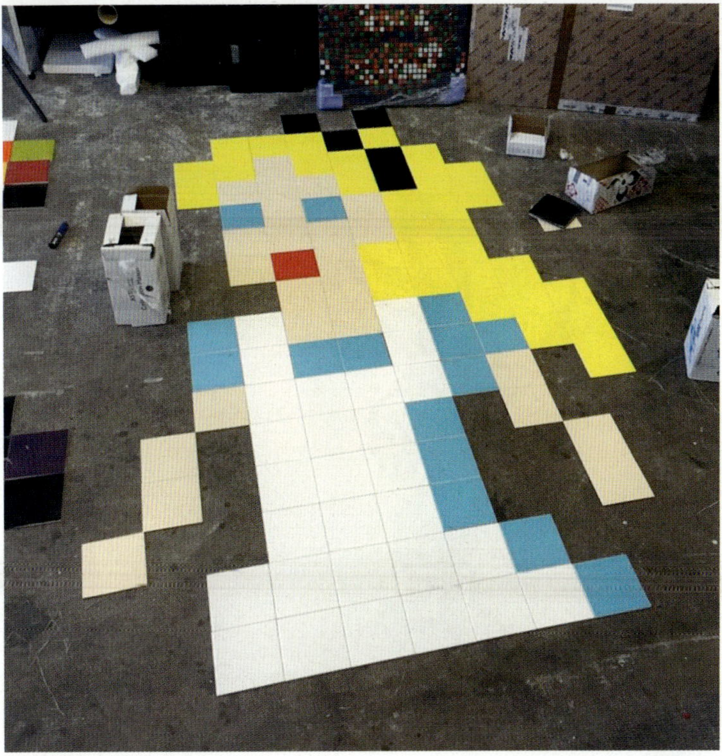

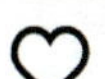 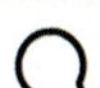  

8286 likes

invaderwashere Making of #lowresAlice #studiodetail

View all 129 comments

17 August 2015

invaderwashere ...

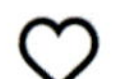   

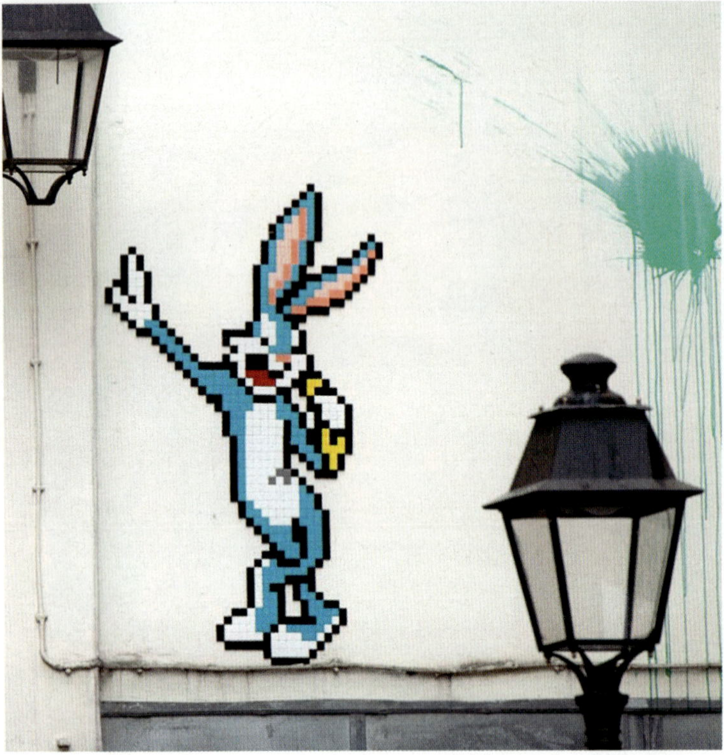

13 541 likes

invaderwashere Bugs Bunny eating a banana / Le Marais Paris

View all 209 comments

16 August 2015

invaderwashere

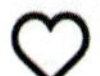   

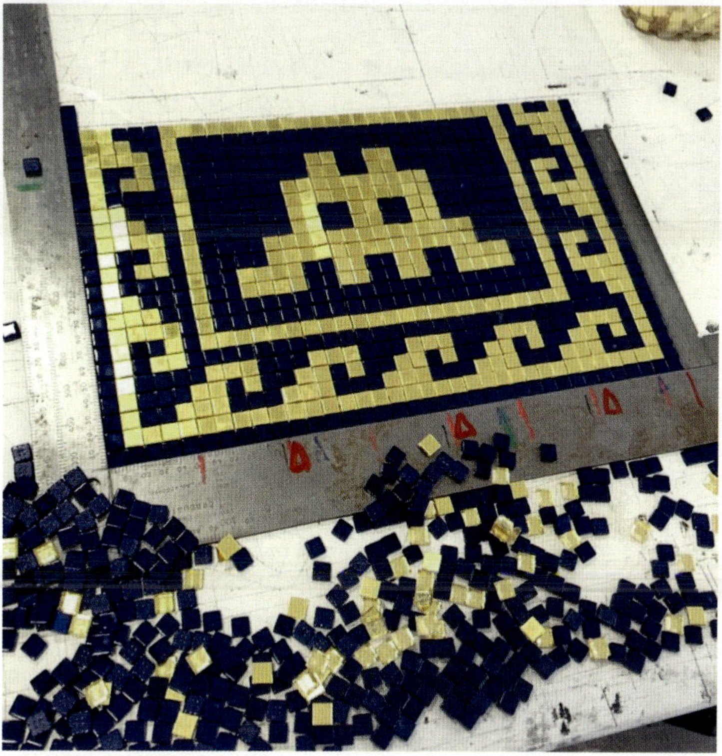

8 436 likes

invaderwashere Making of a new piece for my next destination #studiodetail #blue&gold

View all 87 comments

17 August 2015

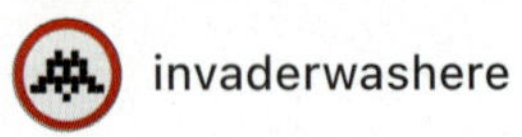

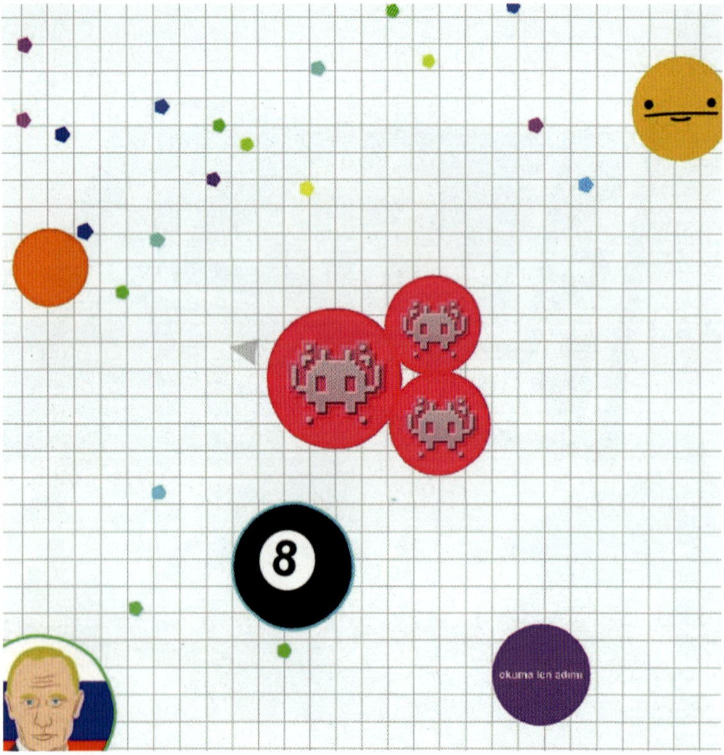

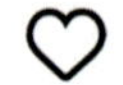 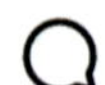  

2 965 likes

invaderwashere Invasion of Agar.io! A very addictive game! #AgarIO #hungrycells #screensot

View all 31 comments

18 August 2015

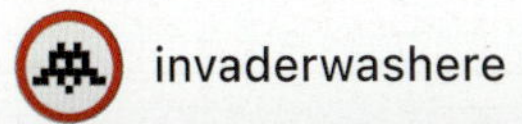

invaderwashere

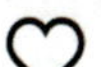   

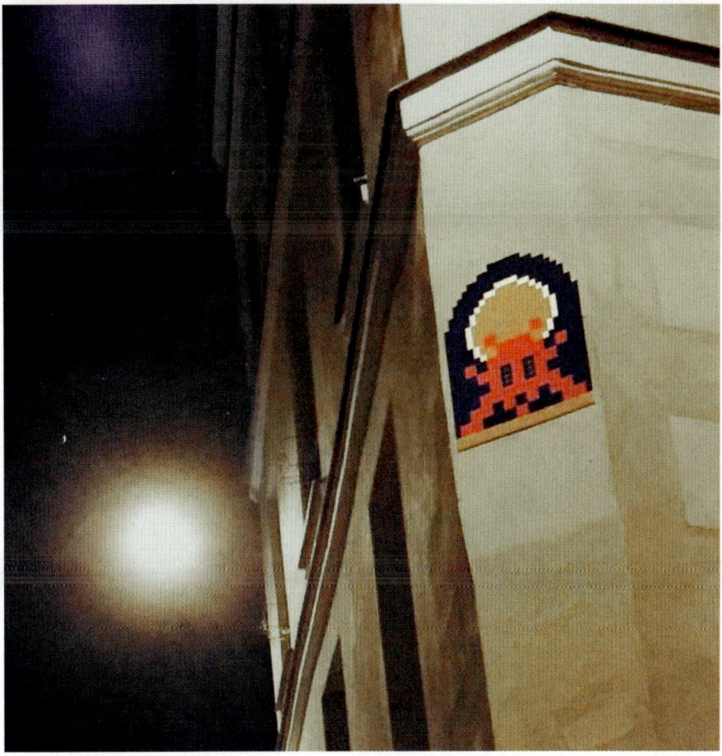

5489 likes

invaderwashere Saint Invader! #Paris

View all 30 comments

18 August 2015

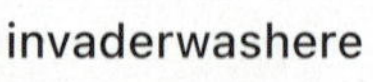

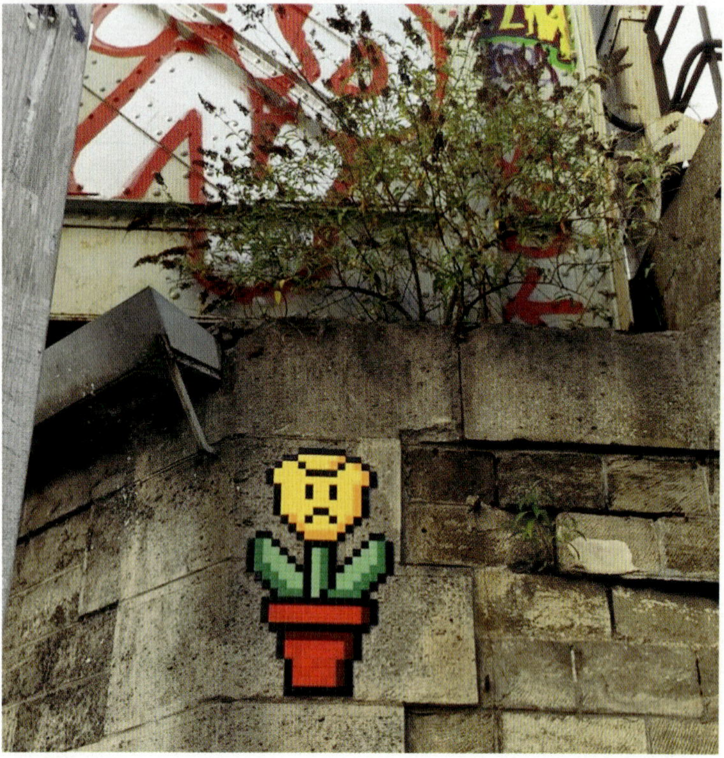

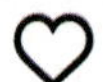   

8 510 likes

invaderwashere New space flower #paris #north #pollution #unhappy

View all 61 comments

22 August 2015

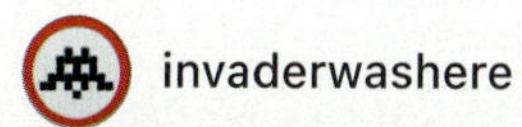

...

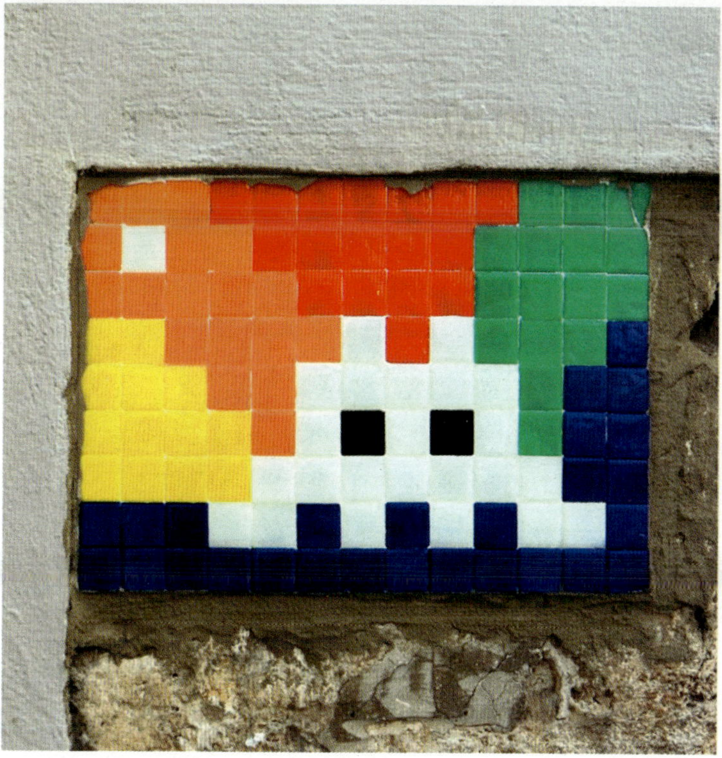

4 898 likes

invaderwashere Rom_48 and many others are back to life! Thank you Joethecrab ;) #reactivations #awesome #Roma

View all 23 comments

25 August 2015

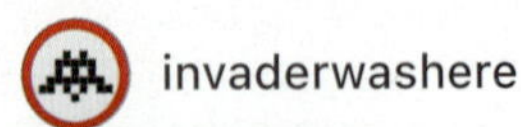

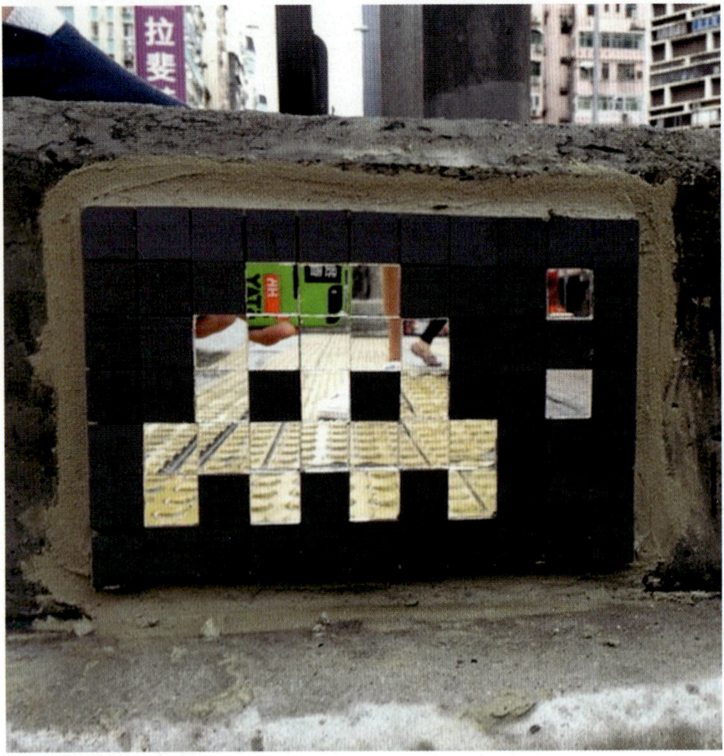

6 821 likes

invaderwashere HK_20 and many others are back to life! Thank you to the reactivation teams 👏👏🙏🙏 photo: @streetartww #reactivation #flashinvaders #hongkong

View all 65 comments

25 August 2015

invaderwashere 

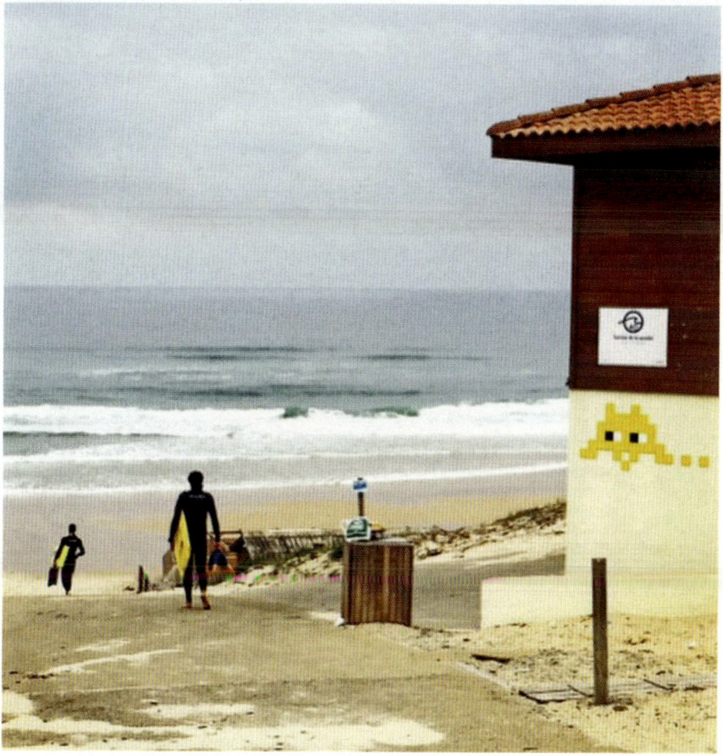

4 889 likes

invaderwashere CON_01 and many others are back to life! 👾👏👏🙏🙏 #reactivations #contisplage photo: @oliviertof

View all 34 comments

25 August 2015

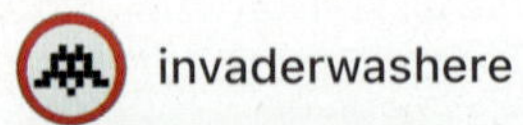

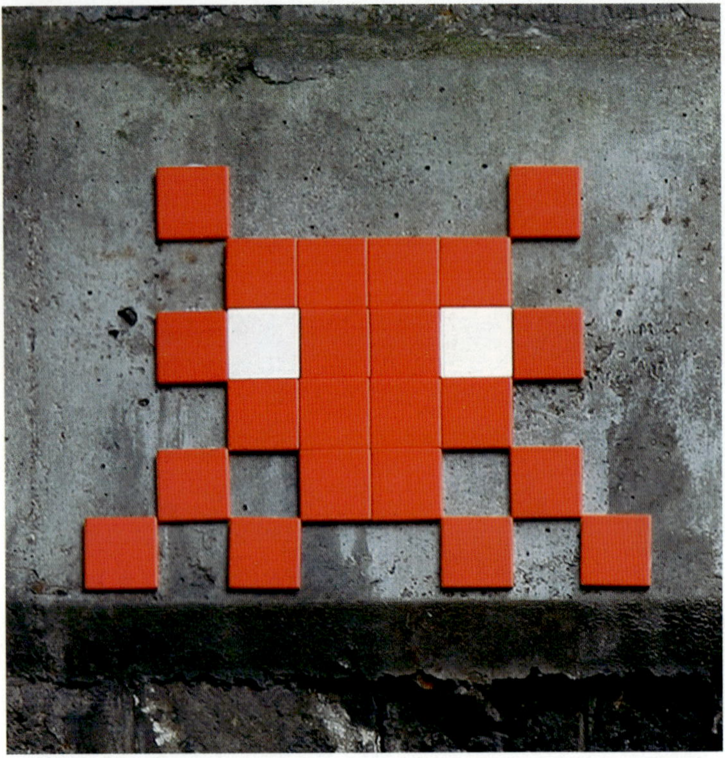

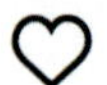   

5541 likes

invaderwashere PA_830 and many others are back to life! 👾👏👏🙏🙏 to #reactivators #reactivationteams #flashinvaders #paris Flash it!

View all 33 comments

25 August 2015

invaderwashere ...

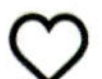   

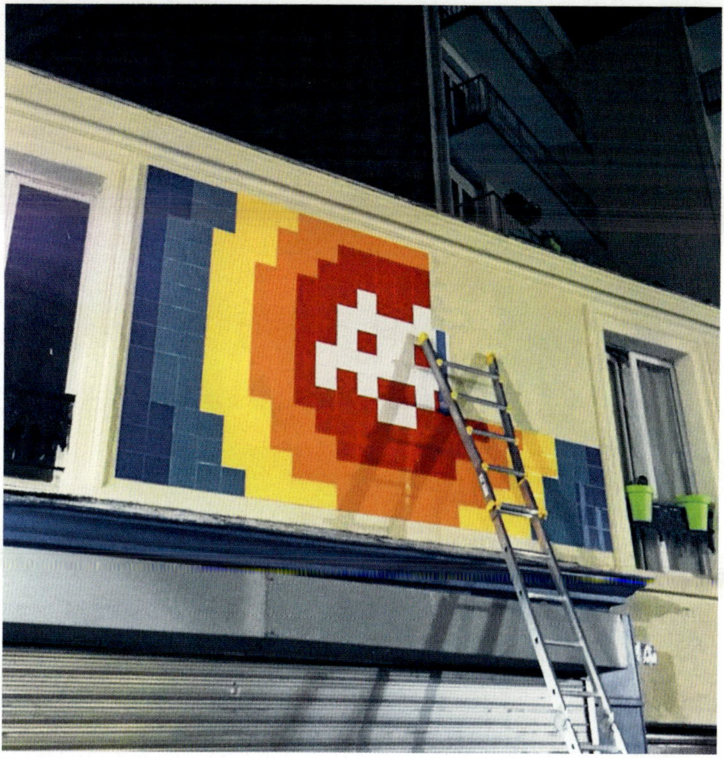

6623 likes

invaderwashere Making of PA_1174 / that's all Folks!
#Paris 4:03am #big #100pts

View all 70 comments

27 August 2015

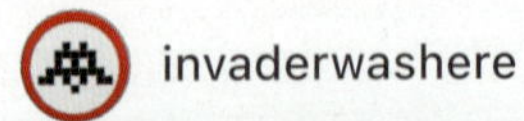

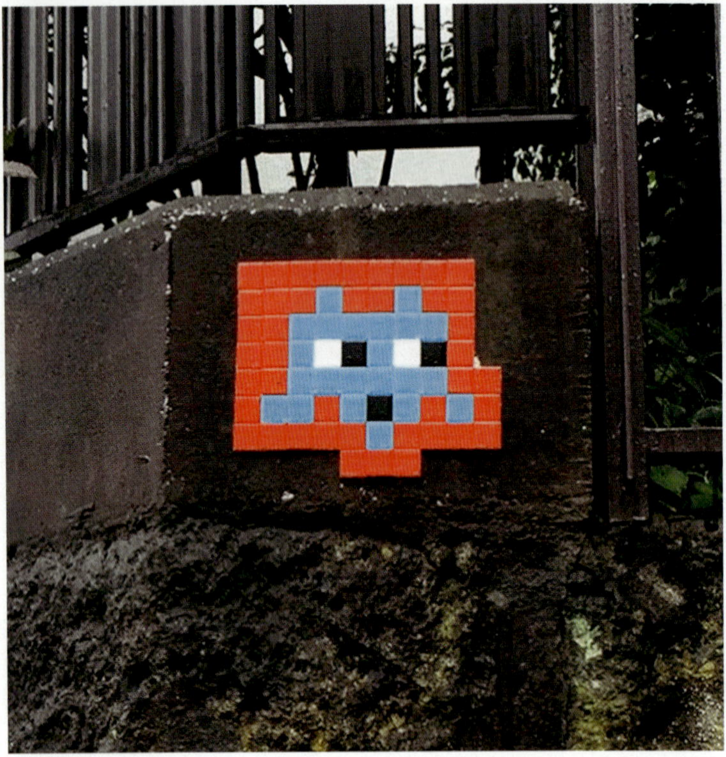

5038 likes

invaderwashere TK_02 and many others are back to life! 👾👏👏🙏🙏 to #reactivators #reactivation #flashinvaders #awesome #Tokyo photo: @nico_funato

View all 36 comments

27 August 2015

invaderwashere

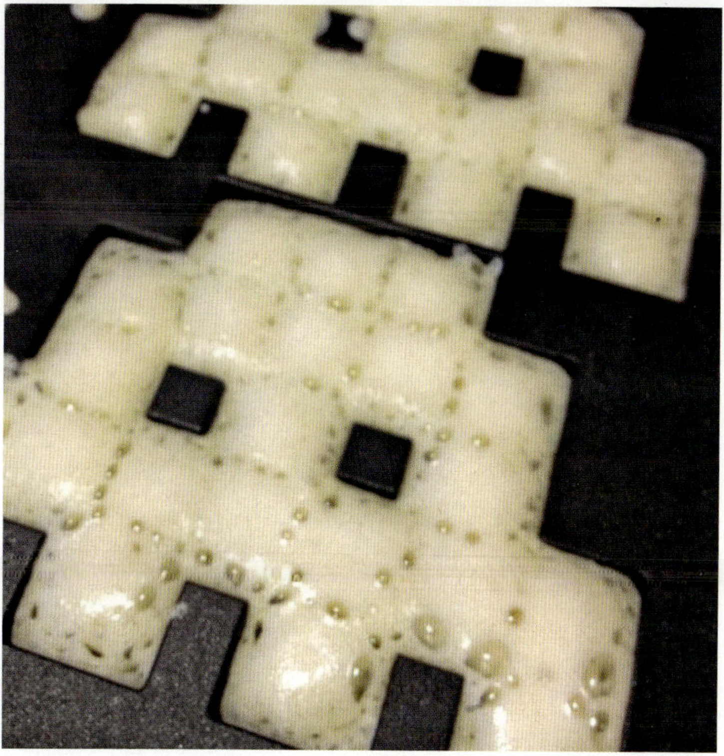

6198 likes

invaderwashere Cooking space waffles! #yumyum #waffles #spacewaffles

View all 97 comments

31 August 2015

invaderwashere

  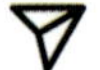 

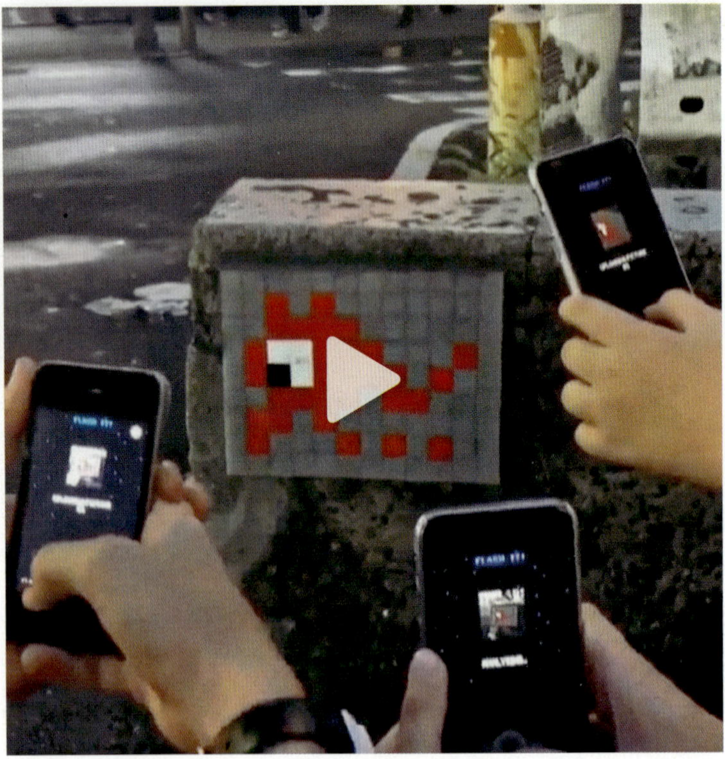

4 350 likes

invaderwashere Young Flashers in Tokyo!!! Shot by @jinkinoko Turn the sound on!!! #flashinvaders #happyflashers #Tokyo #shibuya #TK62

View all 59 comments

3 September 2015

invaderwashere

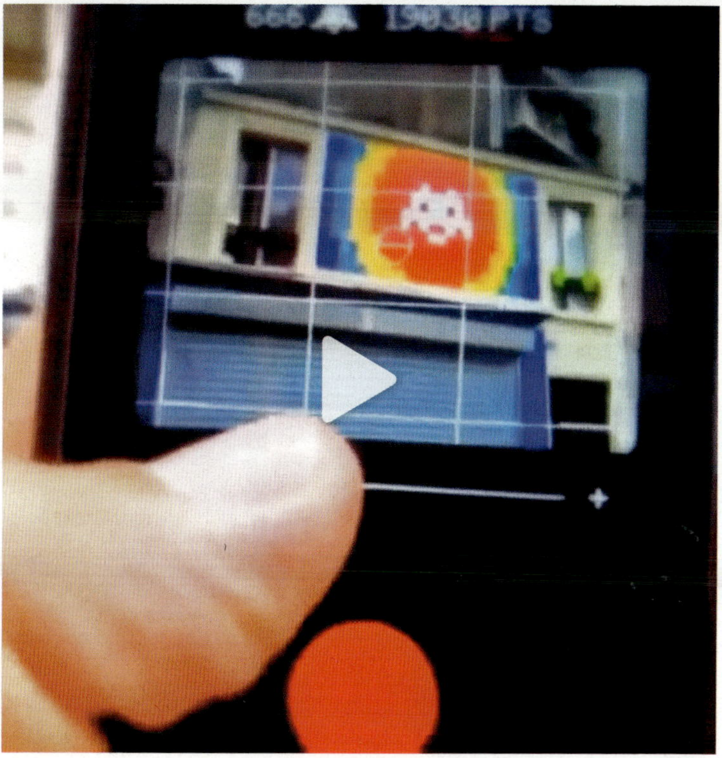

3 395 likes

invaderwashere Flashing PA_1174 / shot by @unoeilquitraine 👏👏👏 Put the sound on!!! #flashinvaders #flasher #Paris

View all 140 comments

3 September 2015

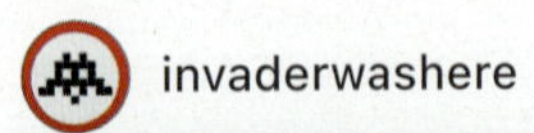

LAST SUCCESSFUL "FLASHES"
4 997 Players / 152 114 Flashes / 5 379 940 Pts

Bastia, OLIVIERTOF
8 minutes ago

Paris, KUMI.....
11 minutes ago

Hong-Kong, INVADERSA
14 minutes ago

Paris, AGC 173
15 minutes ago

Ljubjana, THE JJ
19 minutes ago

Tokyo, EBATARUI
19 minutes ago

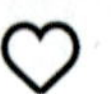  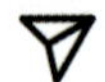 

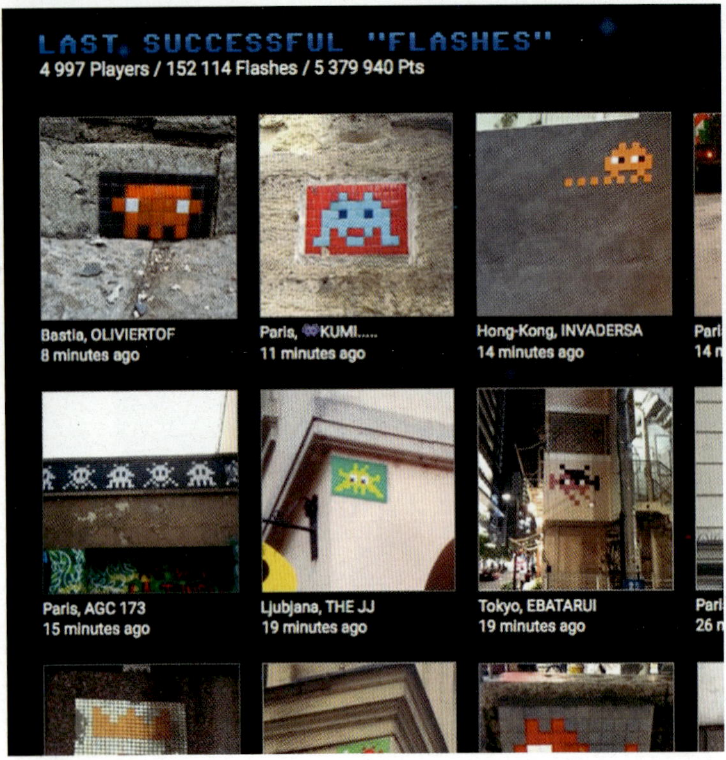

3 004 likes

invaderwashere Not far to reach 5000 players on #flashinvaders #freeapp #ios #android #artgame flashinvaders.com

View all 48 comments

4 September 2015

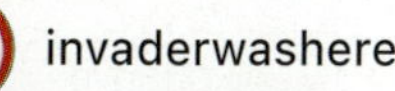

invaderwashere

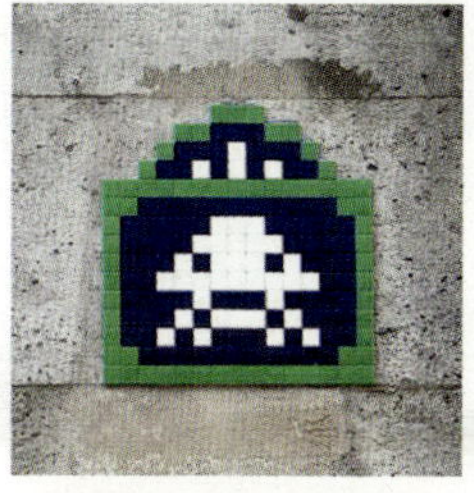

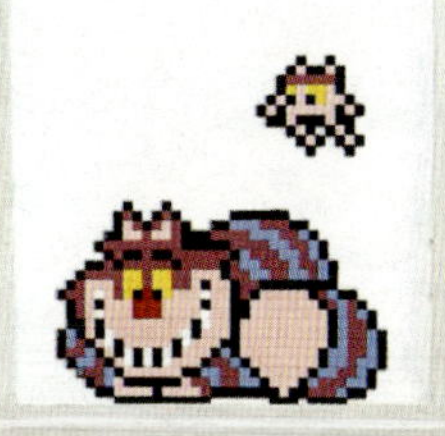

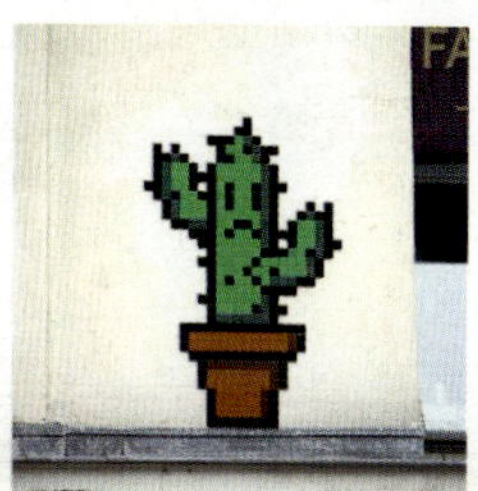

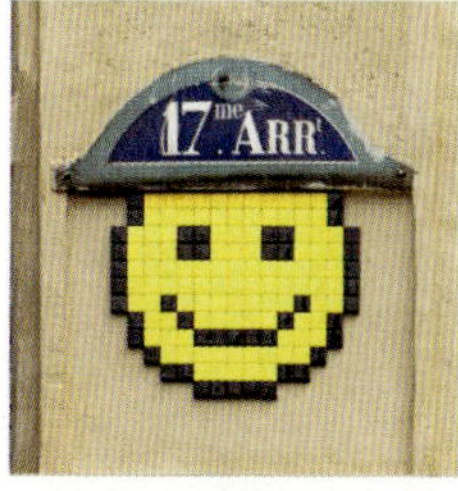

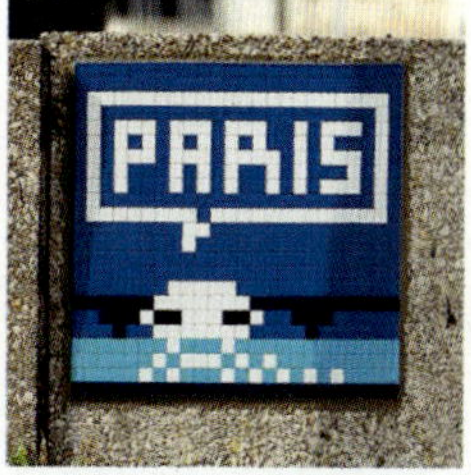

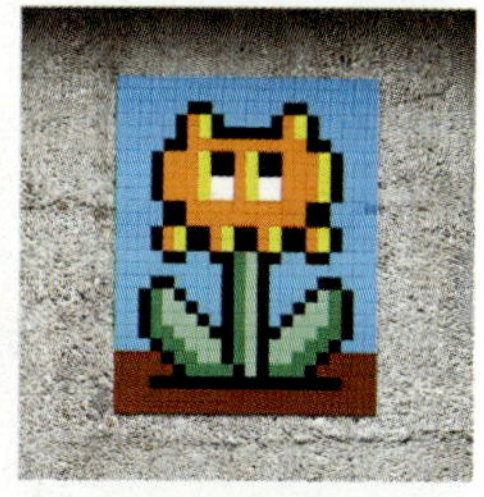

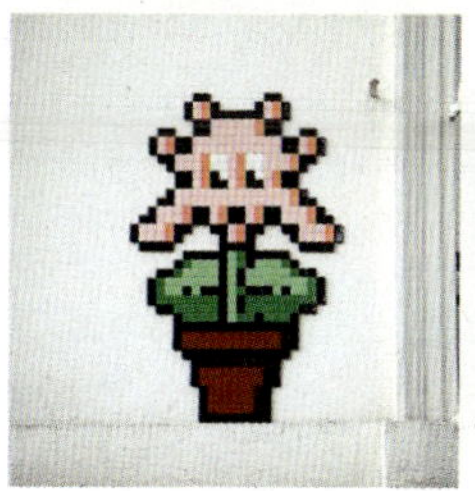

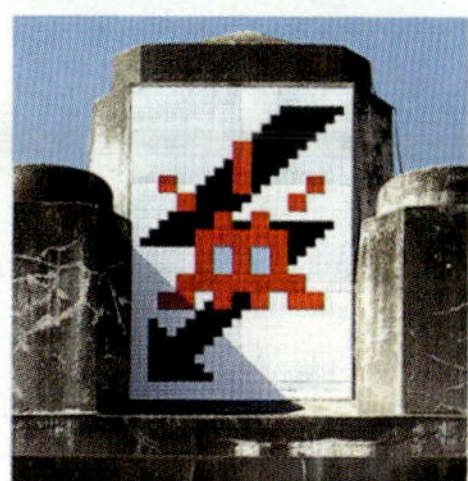

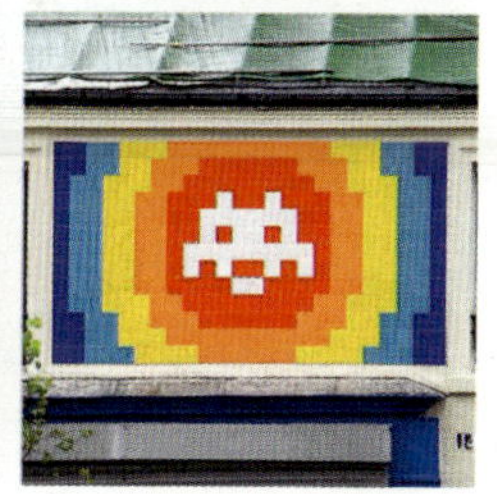

9 571 likes

invaderwashere Summer is a perfect time to invade Paris: the streets are empty and the nights are mild. I took advantage of this to add more than 30 new pieces to the city. More info and photos on the News of my website #paris #invasion

View all 157 comments

7 September 2015

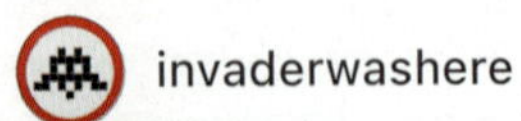

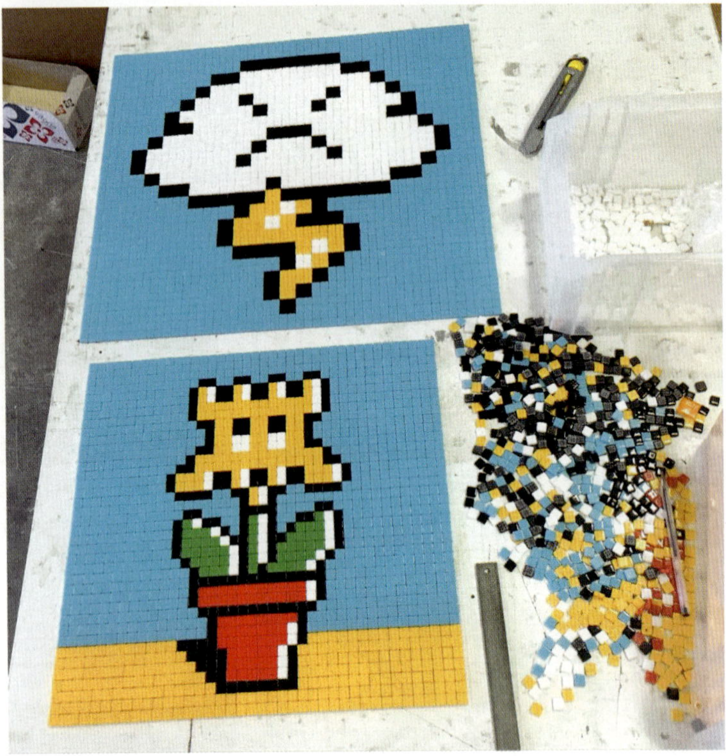

7 474 likes

invaderwashere Preparation of cloud and space flower.
Now in the streets of Paris.

View all 75 comments

8 September 2015

invaderwashere

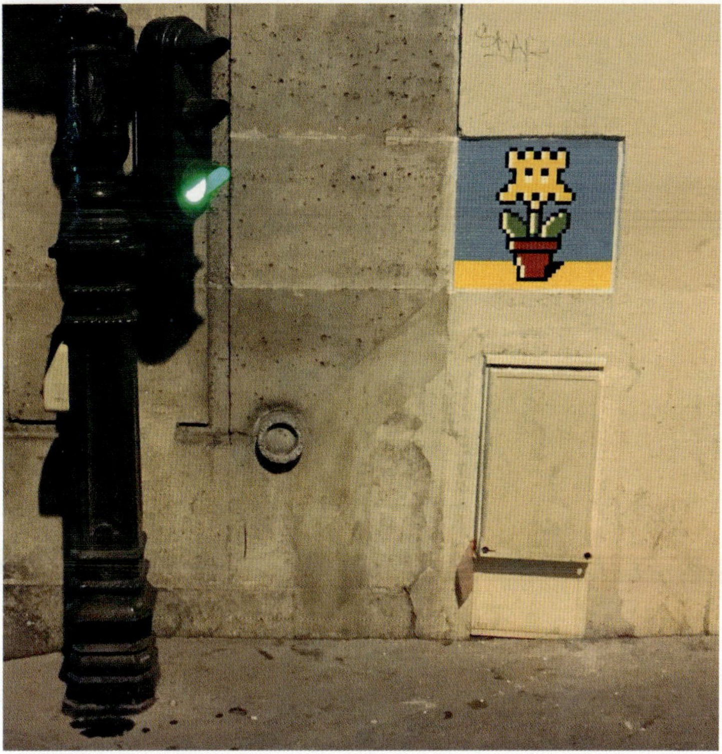

7784 likes

invaderwashere #justdone in #Paris 5:20 am #spaceflower part2 of a diptych...

View all 62 comments

8 September 2015

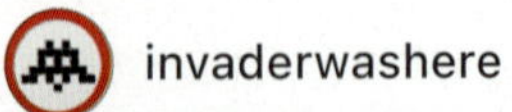

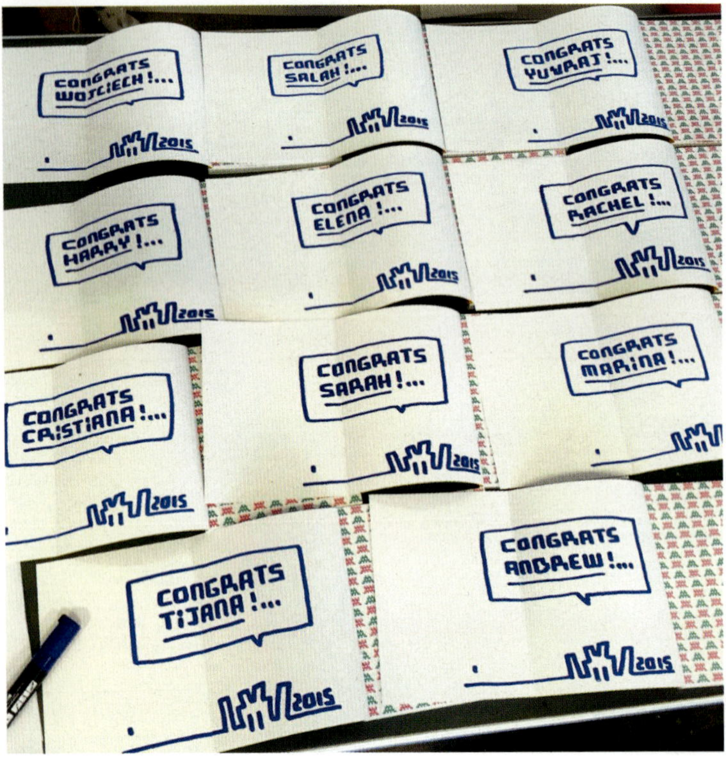

3192 likes

invaderwashere Signing books for the 11 young winners of the ESA kids mosaic competition #esa esa.int #space2iss #art4space #congrats

View all 22 comments

10 September 2015

invaderwashere ...

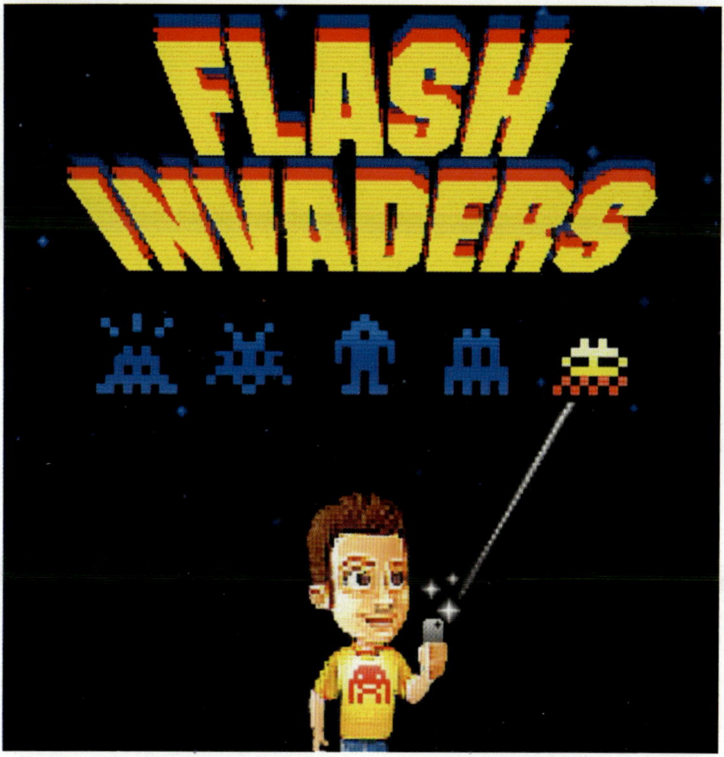

FLASH INVADERS

3 029 likes

invaderwashere An Update of #flashinvaders is available / Download it to fix the bug of last week 😁 #debug #flashinvaders #freeapp #artgame #android #ios

View all 29 comments

12 September 2015

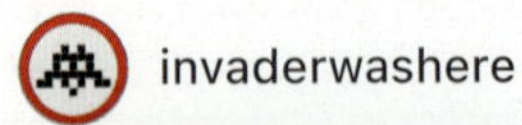

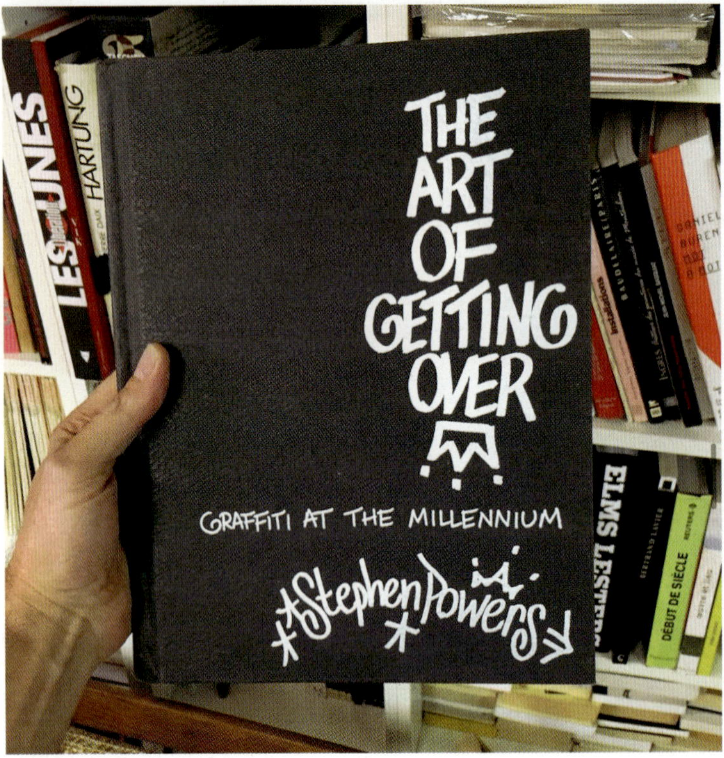

4714 likes

invaderwashere One of my favorite book about graffiti. Written by @steveespopowers in 1999 featuring #revs #reas #kr and many more... #shelfie #books #nygraffiti

View all 48 comments

13 September 2015

invaderwashere

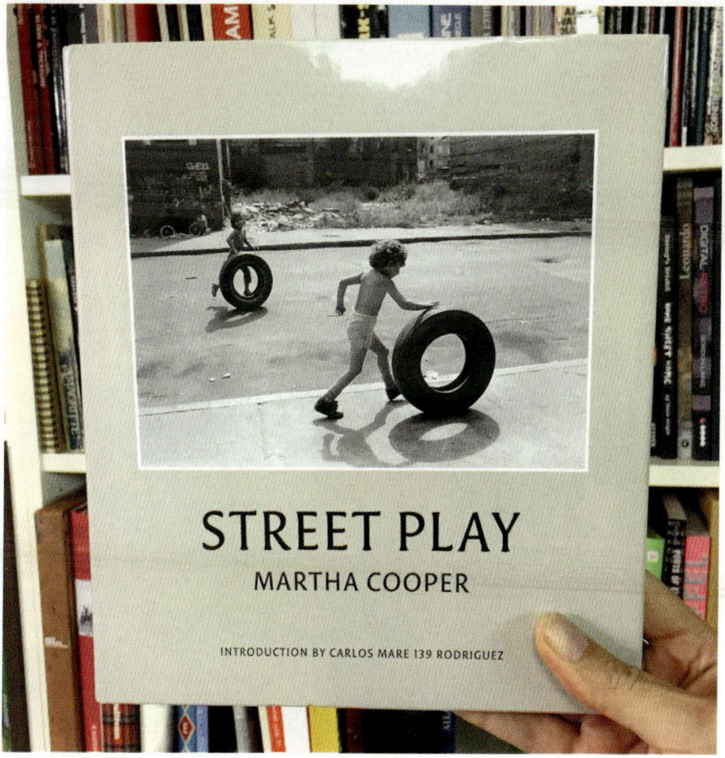

STREET PLAY
MARTHA COOPER
INTRODUCTION BY CARLOS MARE 139 RODRIGUEZ

2 574 likes

invaderwashere Street play by @marthacoopergram NY in #blackandwhite #70s #80s #shelfie

View all 14 comments

13 September 2015

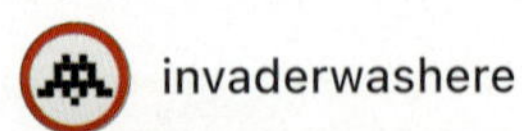

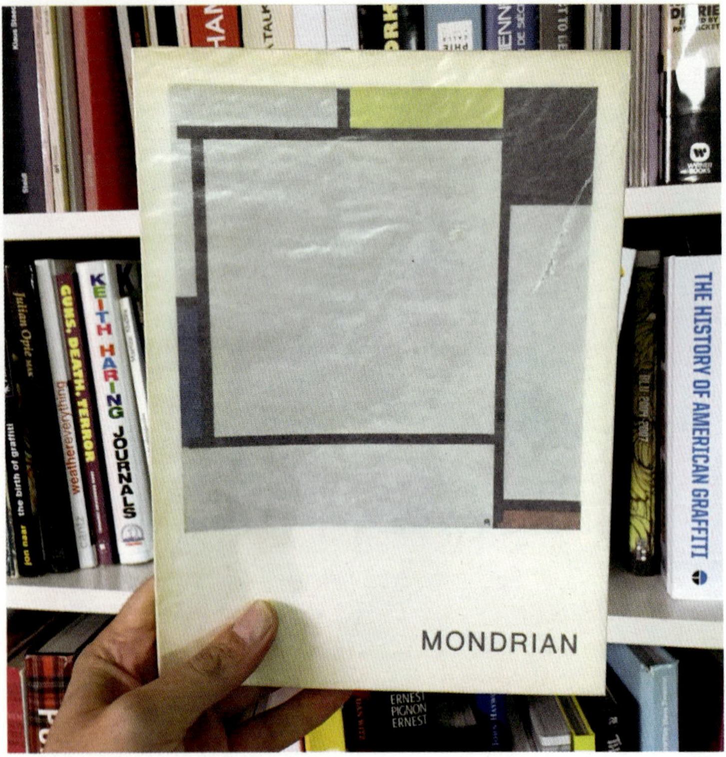

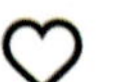   

3 281 likes

invaderwashere #Mondrian catalog from 1969 #shelfie

View all 16 comments

13 September 2015

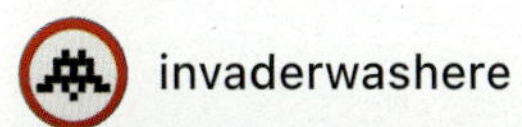

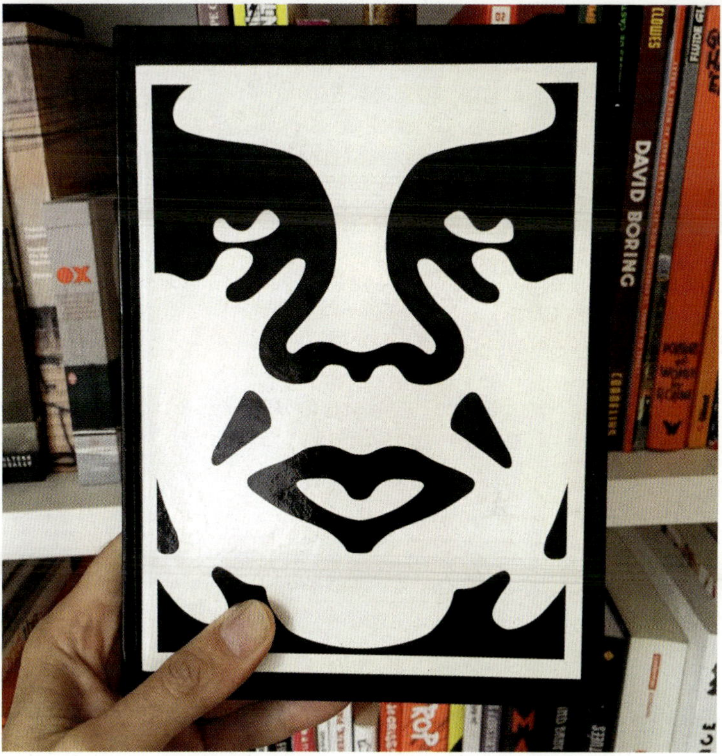

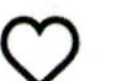   

6 291 likes

invaderwashere I've published this Obey Giant prints catalog in 2003 @obeygiant #collector #book

View all 29 comments

13 September 2015

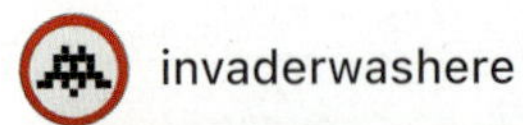

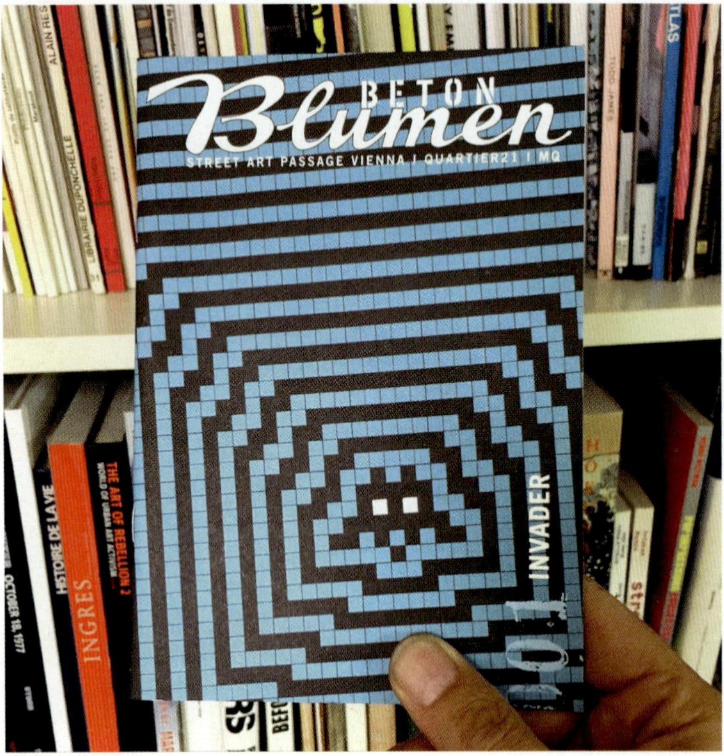

3925 likes

invaderwashere Invasion of Vienna 2008 #betonblumen #booklet #smallinvasionguide #rarebook

View all 20 comments

13 September 2015

invaderwashere

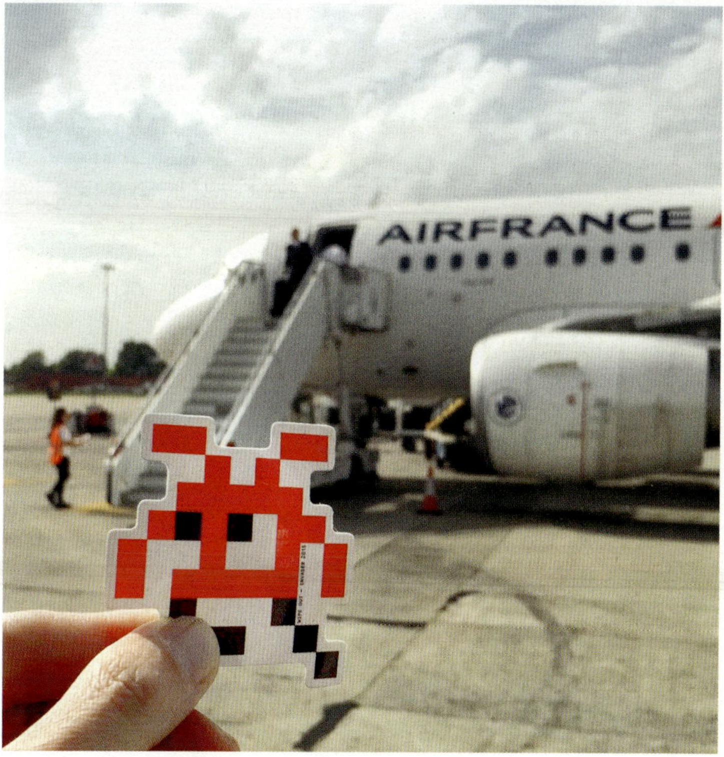

•••

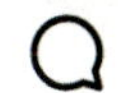

5730 likes

invaderwashere On the road...

View all 35 comments

18 September 2015

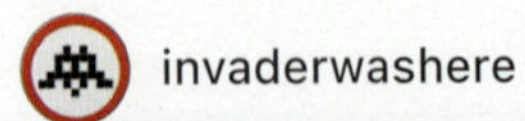

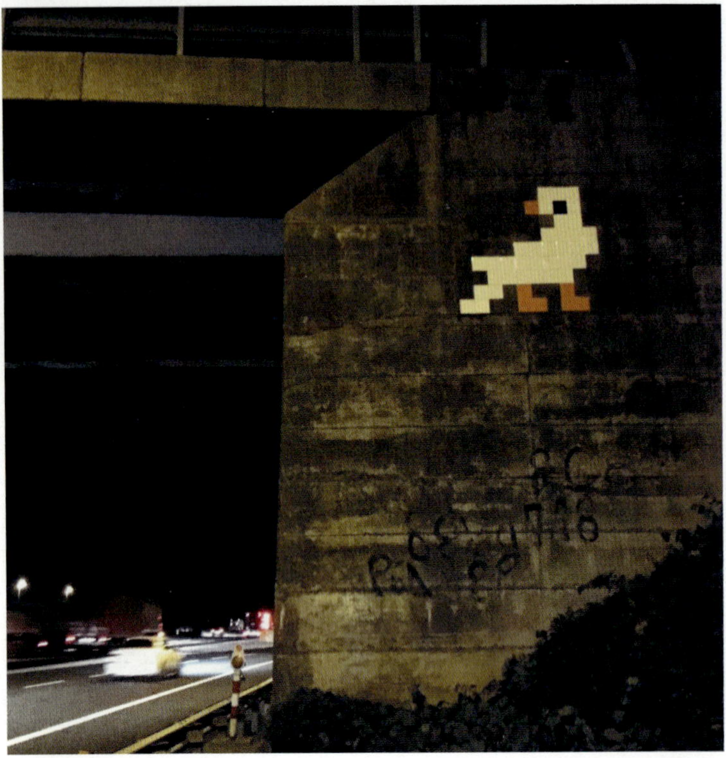

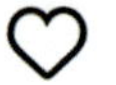   

6601 likes

invaderwashere That one was not easy to install...
#Justdone #dove #colombe #lowRes #highway
#invaderwashere

View all 42 comments

18 September 2015

invaderwashere

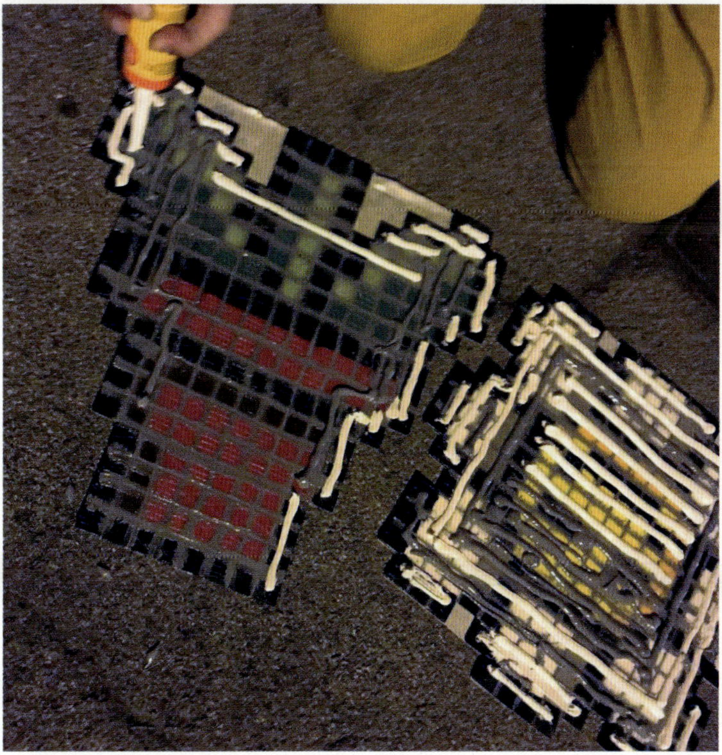

5 443 likes

invaderwashere Invasion in progress... #makingof

View all 67 comments

19 September 2015

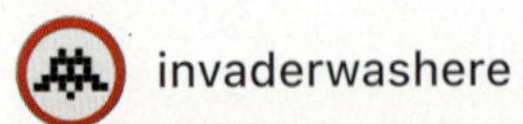

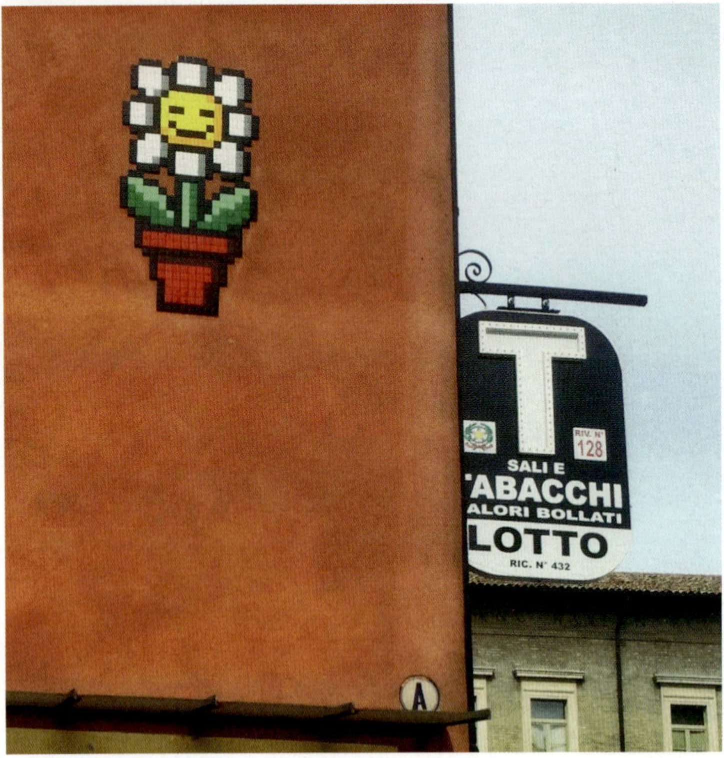

7897 likes

invaderwashere Done! #flower #power

View all 65 comments

19 September 2015

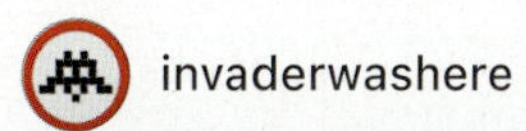

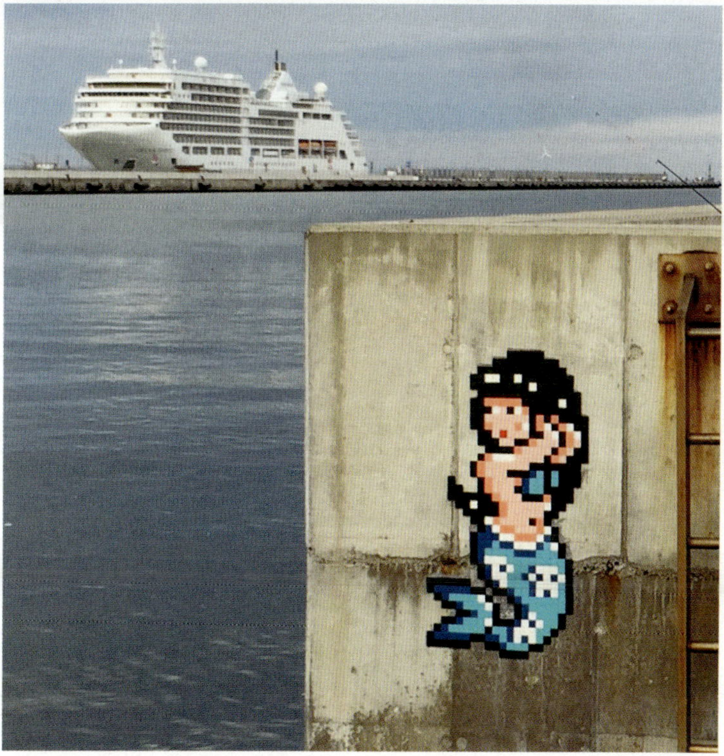

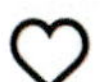   

10 854 likes

invaderwashere Italian #mermaid

View all 194 comments

19 September 2015

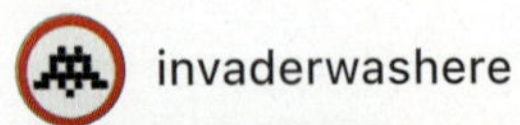

•••

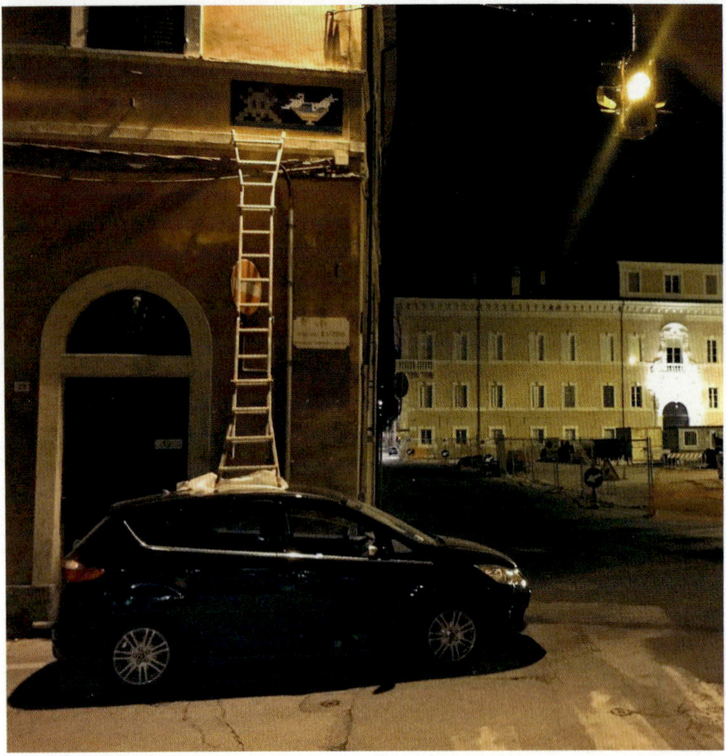

5282 likes

invaderwashere Reach the spot! #Ladder on rental car. Thanks to Avis for supporting the #invasion 😂

View all 77 comments

20 September 2015

invaderwashere

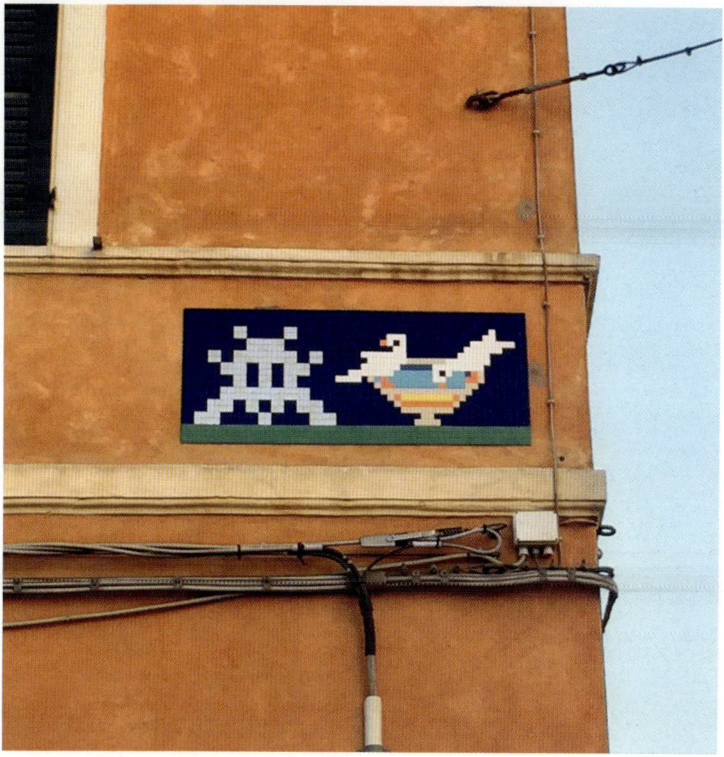

6944 likes

invaderwashere Done! #spaceinvader & #doves #ravenna #classic #remake #bizantinemosaic #italy

View all 28 comments

20 September 2015

invaderwashere ...

 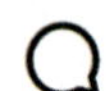  

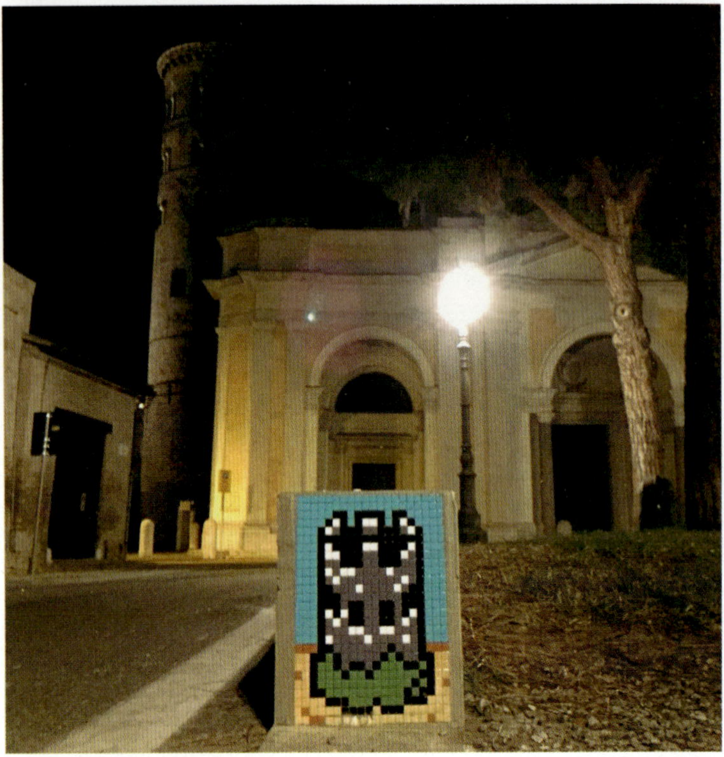

6169 likes

invaderwashere Model & 8bit representation #antictower #justdone

View all 31 comments

21 September 2015

invaderwashere ...

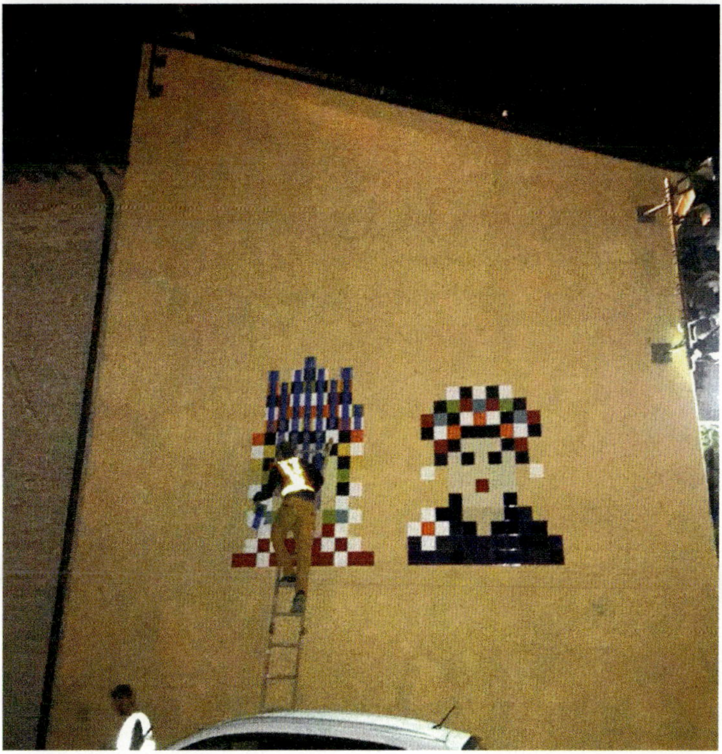

6 331 likes

invaderwashere Making of RA_38 / Empress and emperor #theodora & #justinian #byzantine #mosaic #remake #lowres #portraits #big #Ravenna 5:08 am

View all 64 comments

21 September 2015

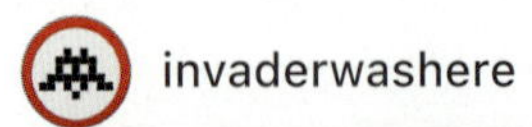

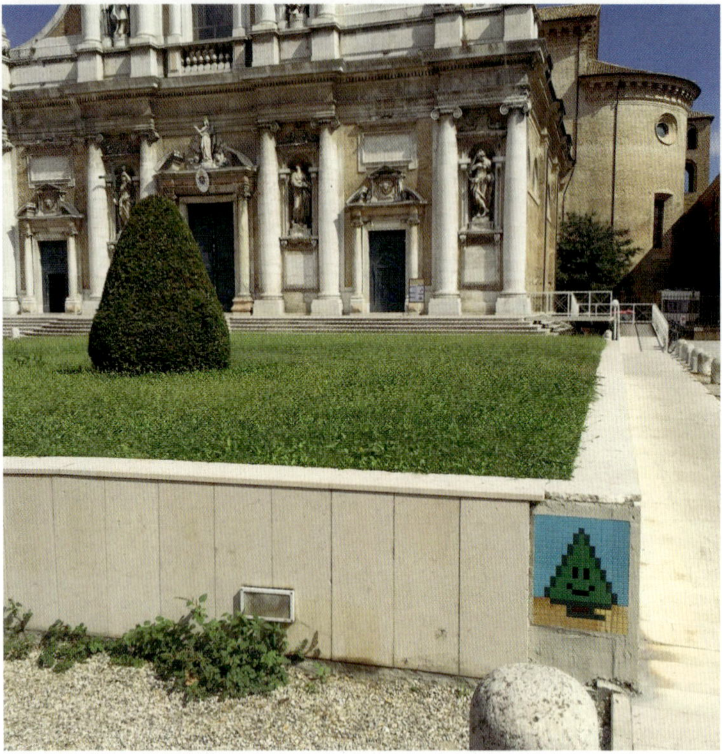

 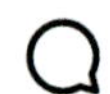  

5 271 likes

invaderwashere Model & 8bit representation #firtree #Ravenna #2015

View all 38 comments

21 September 2015

invaderwashere

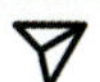

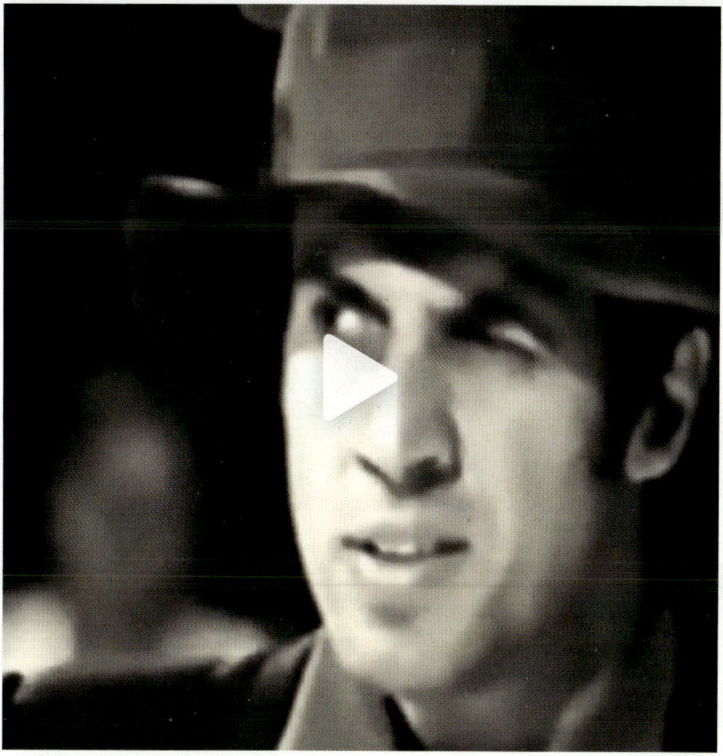

1539 likes

invaderwashere #adriano #celentano #italy #yuppidu

View all 42 comments

22 September 2015

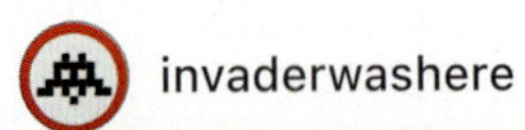

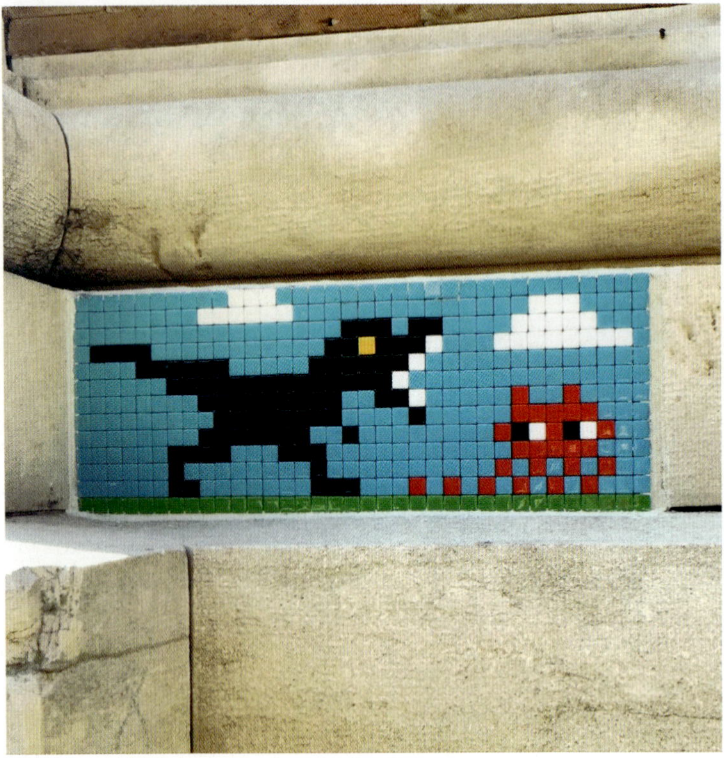

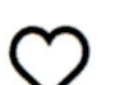   

7738 likes

invaderwashere #Jurassic #mosaic in #ravenna

View all 74 comments

23 September 2015

invaderwashere ...

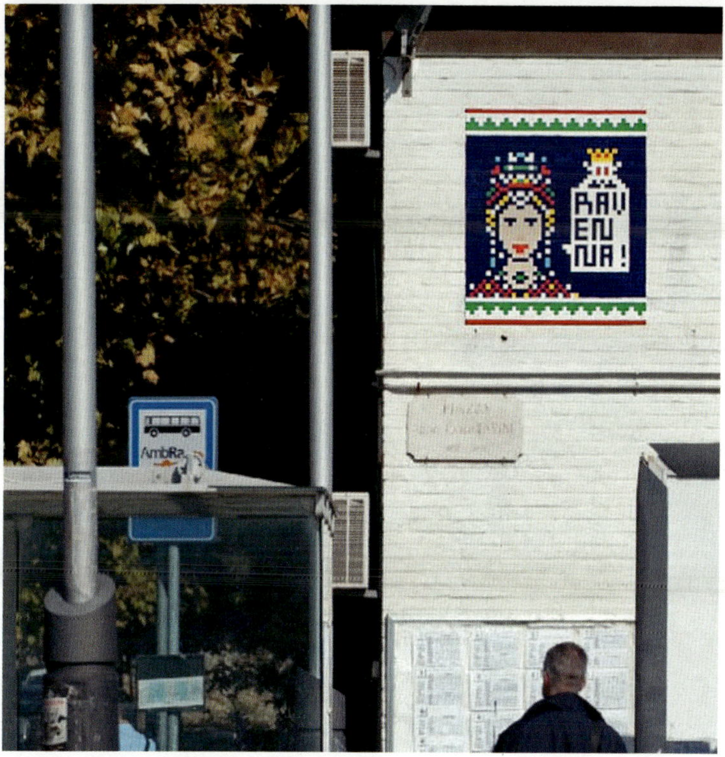

5 257 likes

invaderwashere #Ravenna train station

View all 38 comments

23 September 2015

invaderwashere •••

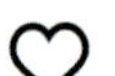   

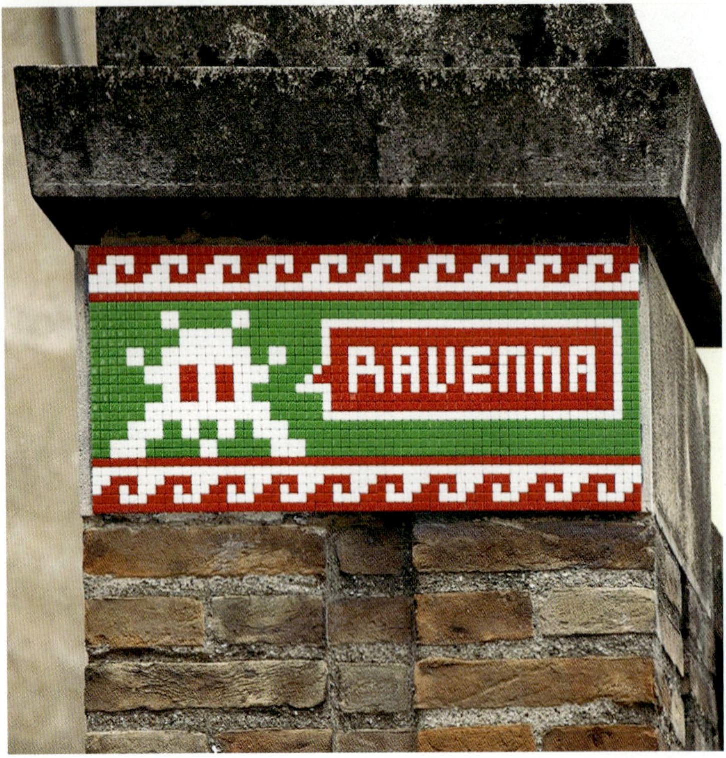

5655 likes

invaderwashere Invasion of Ravenna Wave II: successful! 15 new pieces have just appeared in the world capital of mosaic / A new #invasionMap & #InvasionGuide are under preparation / More info on my website #mosaics #Ravenna #italy 🇮🇹

View all 56 comments

24 September 2015

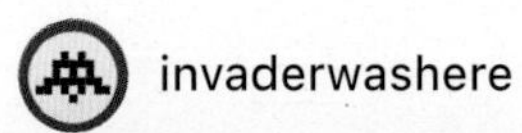

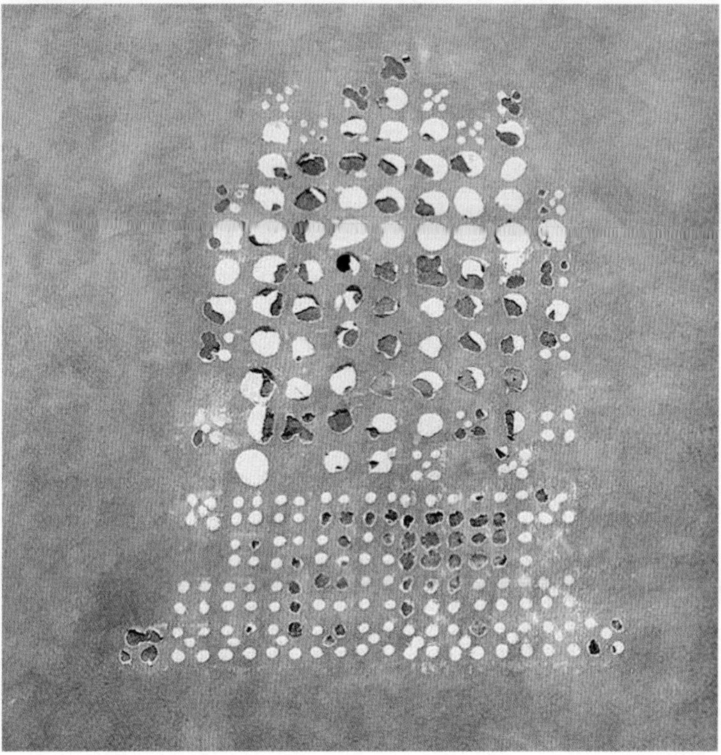

3 288 likes

invaderwashere It seems that the owner of this wall did not appreciate my work... RIP #theodora and #justinien #ravenna photo by @samskeyti79

View all 105 comments

28 September 2015

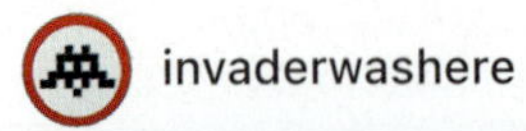

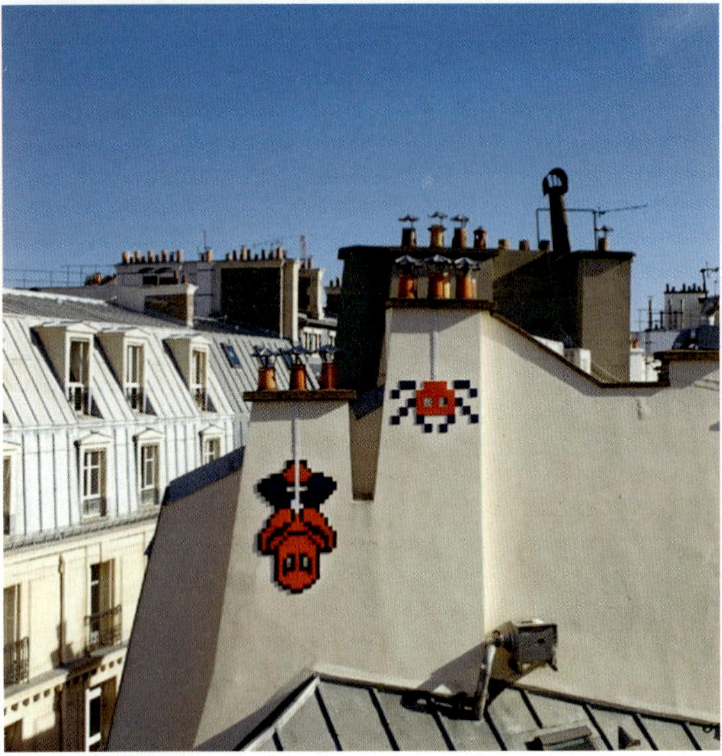

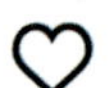  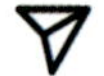 

13 279 likes

invaderwashere PA_1040 #Paris #today #bluesky

View all 260 comments

28 September 2015

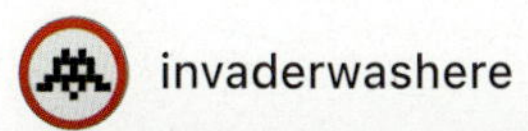

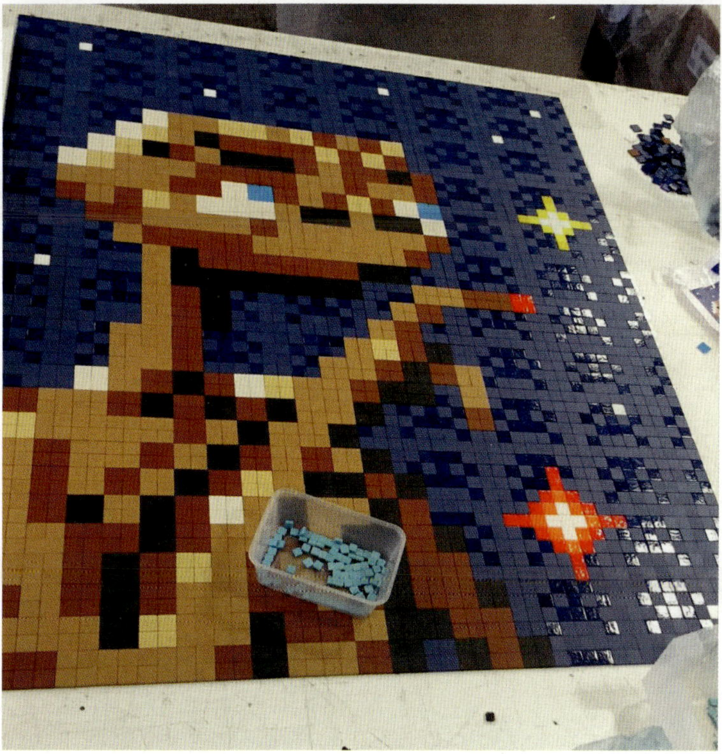

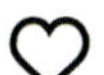   

10 225 likes

invaderwashere Studio detail #diptych #Leftside

View all 243 comments

29 September 2015

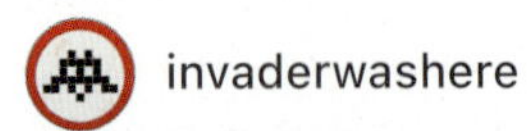

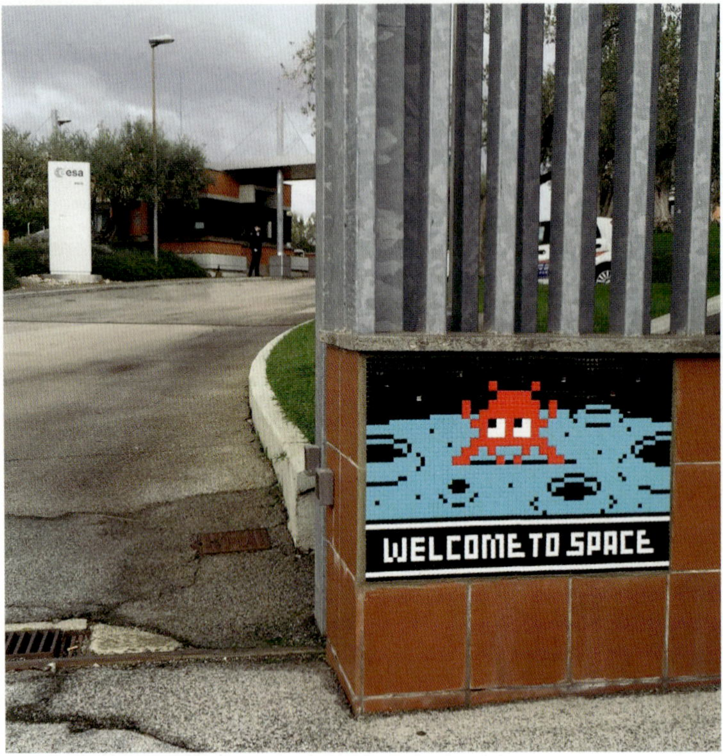

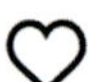   

6 320 likes

invaderwashere Welcome to space... #esrin entrance #esa #italy #space2iss #justdone

View all 29 comments

2 October 2015

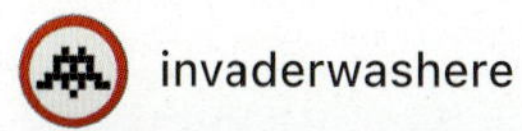

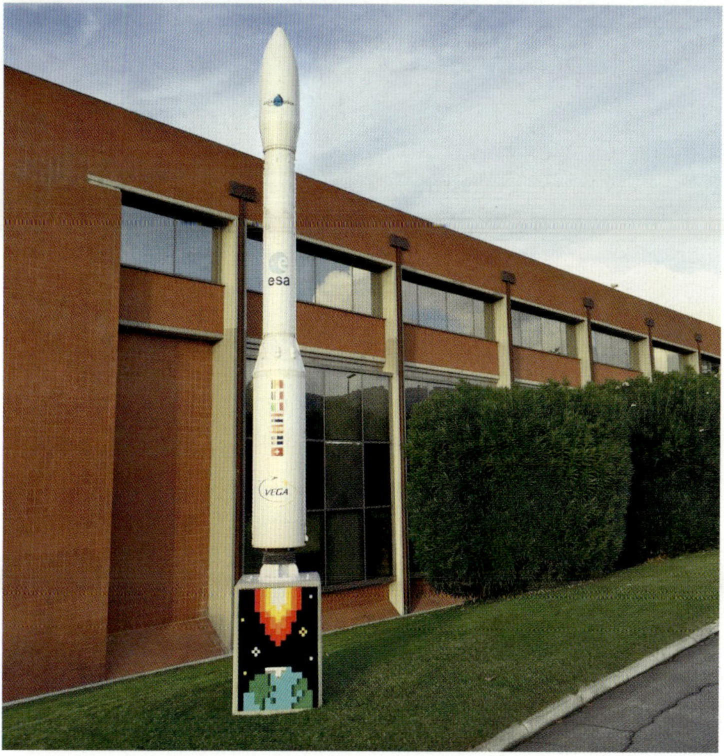

 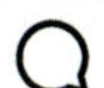  

5729 likes

invaderwashere 3, 2, 1, Take off #vega #esrin #esa #italy #roma #space2iss

View all 38 comments

2 October 2015

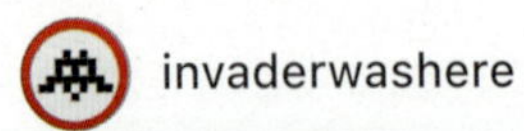

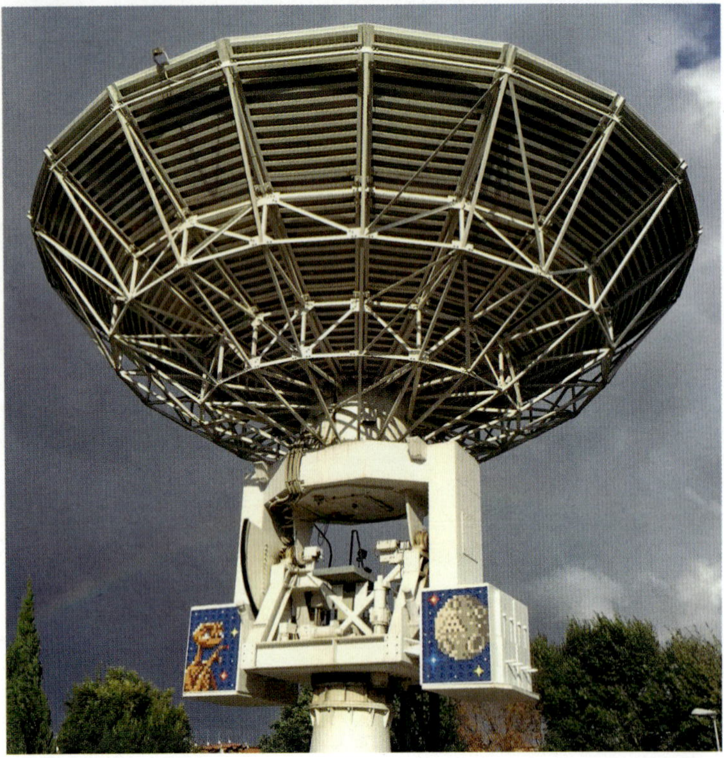

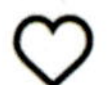  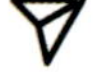 

5446 likes

invaderwashere E.T. phone home... #esrin #esa #antena #space2iss #justdone

View all 79 comments

2 October 2015

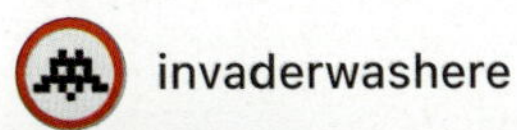

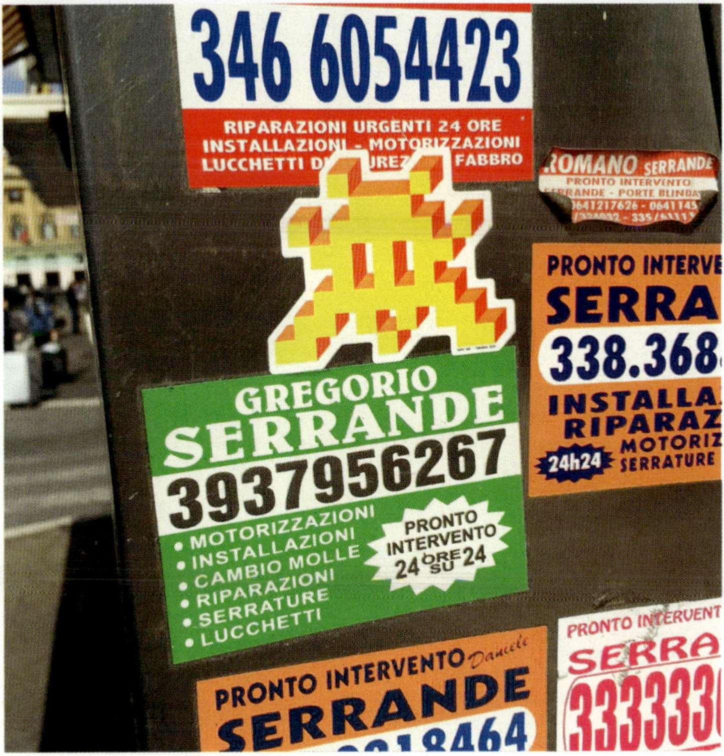

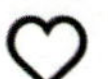   

3 546 likes

invaderwashere Pronto intervento #stickers of #roma

View all 17 comments

3 October 2015

invaderwashere

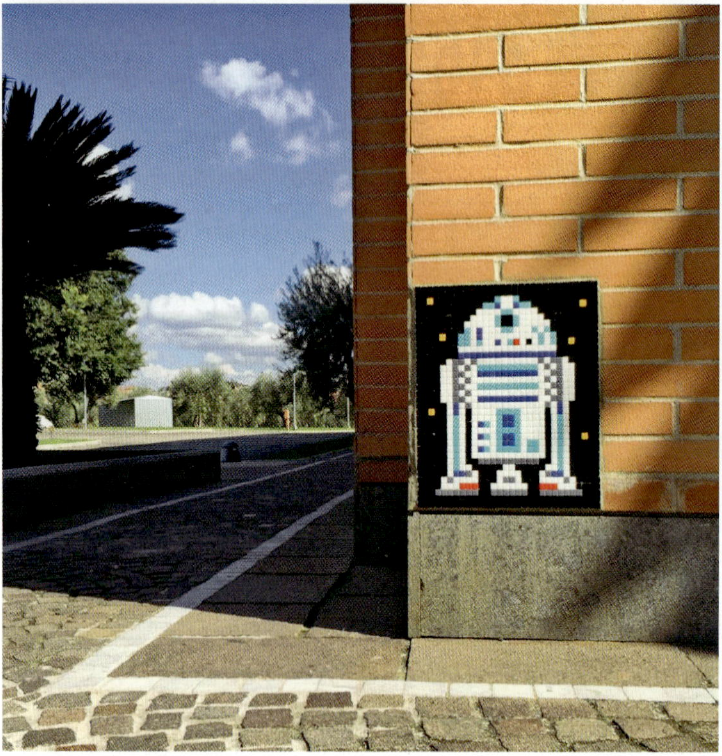

10 361 likes

invaderwashere #r2d2 just landed at #esrin #esa #italy #roma #space2iss

View all 218 comments

3 October 2015

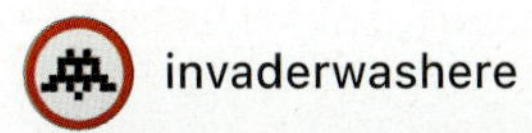

...

→ EUROPEAN SPACE AGENCY ABOUT US OUR ACTIVITIES CONNECT WITH US FOR MEDIA FOR EDUCATORS FOR KIDS

space for europe

esa

HOME

WELCOME TO SPACE

→ ALIENS OBSERVED

Space Invader art has arrived at ESA's Earth observation centre in Italy

Archive

LATEST NEWS

All News

08 October 2015
Astronaut brains as beacons for researchers

30 September 2015
Fifth mission for Ariane 5 this year

30 September 2015
SMOS meets ocean monsters

28 September 2015
How Rosetta's comet got its shape

25 September 2015
Space for safer cars

25 September 2015
Galileo satellites handed over to operator

24 September 2015
Forty years of European space tracking

23 September 2015
Rosetta reveals comet's water-ice cycle

Search here

LATEST PRESS RELEASE

previous

5 October 2015 Agreement paves the way for MetOp Second Generation

  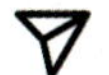 

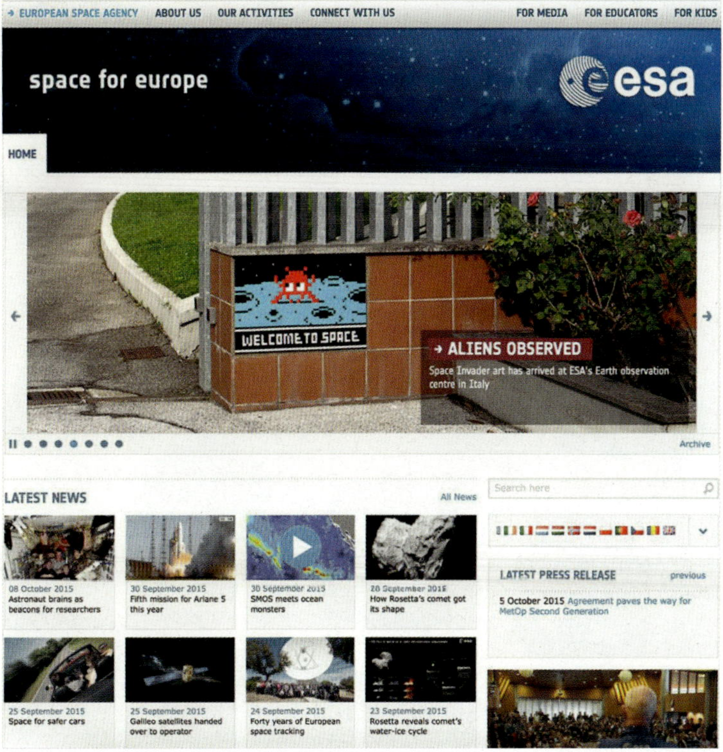

2 263 likes

invaderwashere ALIENS OBSERVED... from the european space research institute #esrin #esa www.esa.int #space2iss @europeanspaceagency #homepage

View all 10 comments

8 October 2015

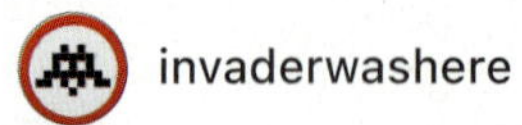

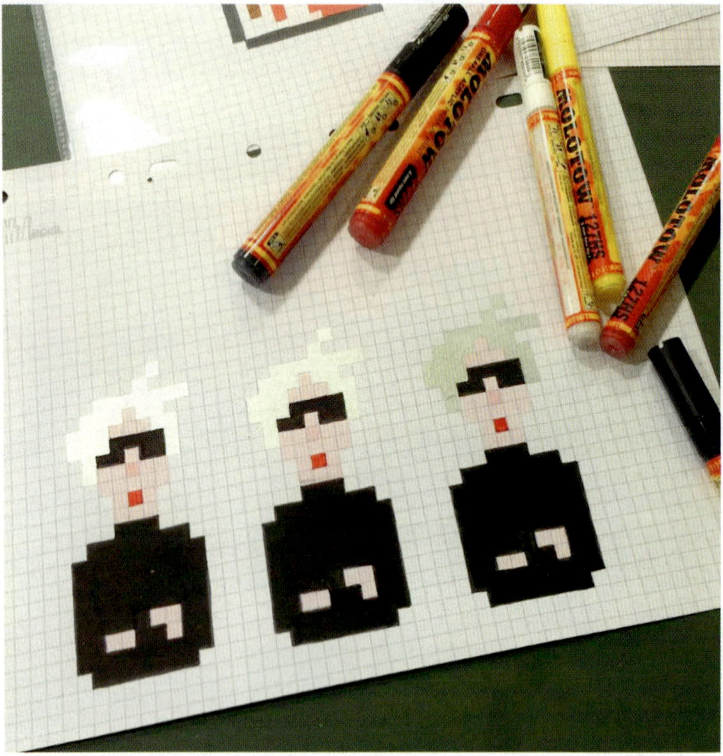

8486 likes

invaderwashere 3 times Andy Warhol #acrylic + #silverink on #paper

View all 163 comments

13 October 2015

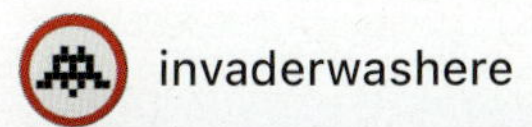

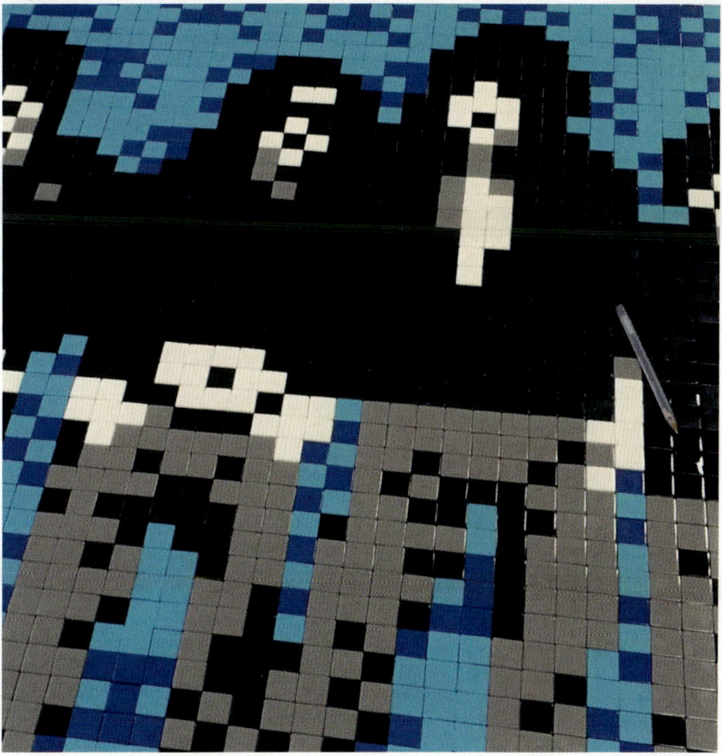

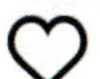   

6 035 likes

invaderwashere #gabbagabbahey #newyorkers studio detail

View all 68 comments

19 October 2015

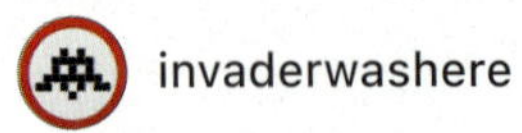

Artists for Syria

featuring artwork donated by:

Above
Aza
Borf
Bustart
Cept
dmstff
Faile
Fake
Invader
Jeremy Geddes
Jimmy C
John Dolan
JJ Adams
Kunstrasen
Laura Keeble
Liam Snootle
Louis Masai
Mark Petty
Martin Whatson
Mr. Cenz
Non-conformist
Nick Smith
Opie
Pablo Delgado
Pure Evil
POGO
Raffaella Bertolini
Scout
Skurk
Simon Mathewson
Snik
Thierry Noir
VLong
1743

to benefit:

REFUGEE COUNCIL
PROTECTING REFUGEES FOR 60 YEARS
Syria Relief
Hand in Hand for Syria

special thanks to the following galleries for donating:

HOWARD GRIFFIN GALLERY
BLACK APPLE
Cg

begins October 13th
for links to auctions and raffles visit:
notbanksyforum.com

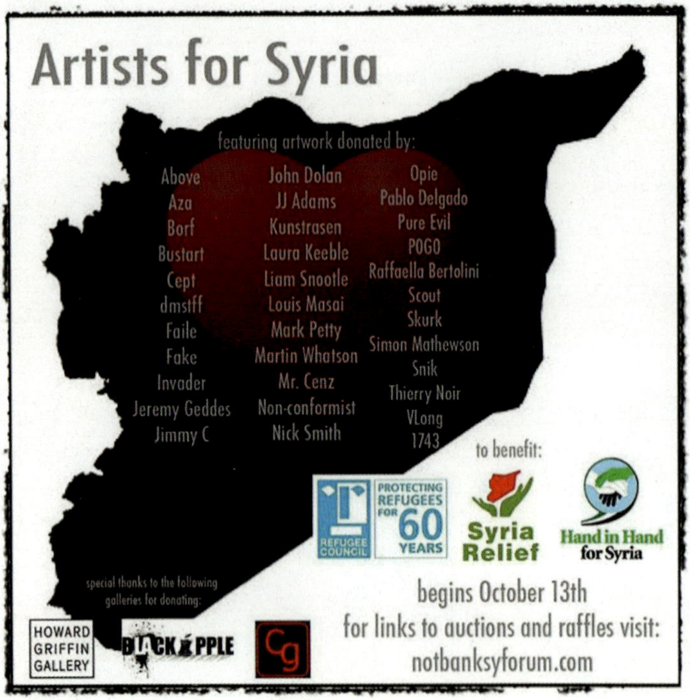

1344 likes

invaderwashere Artist for Syria, last day @notbanksyforum

View all 17 comments

22 October 2015

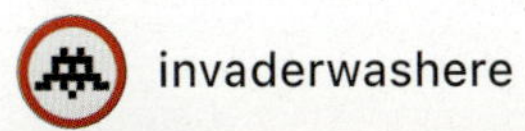

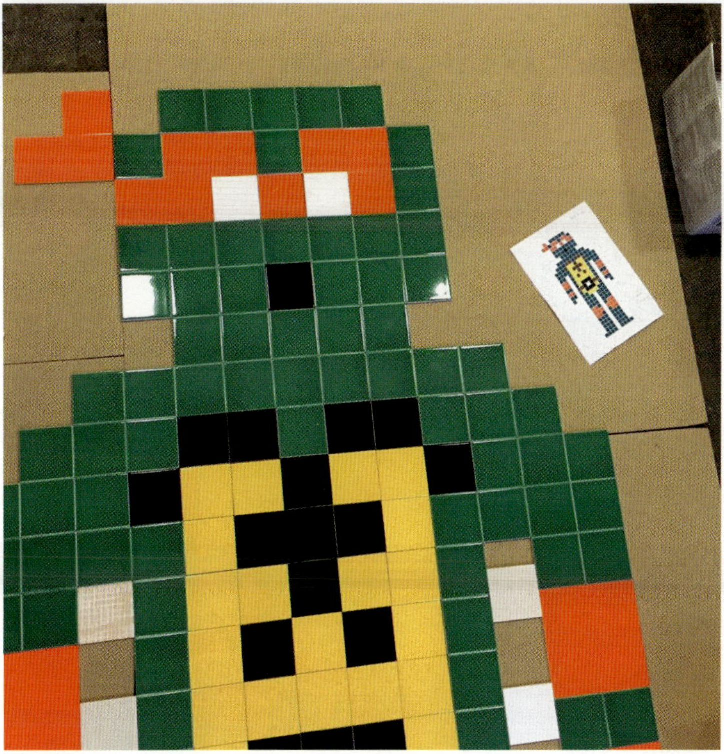

7155 likes

invaderwashere Studio detail #michelangelo #ninjaturtles #newyorkers #makingof

View all 127 comments

23 October 2015

invaderwashere

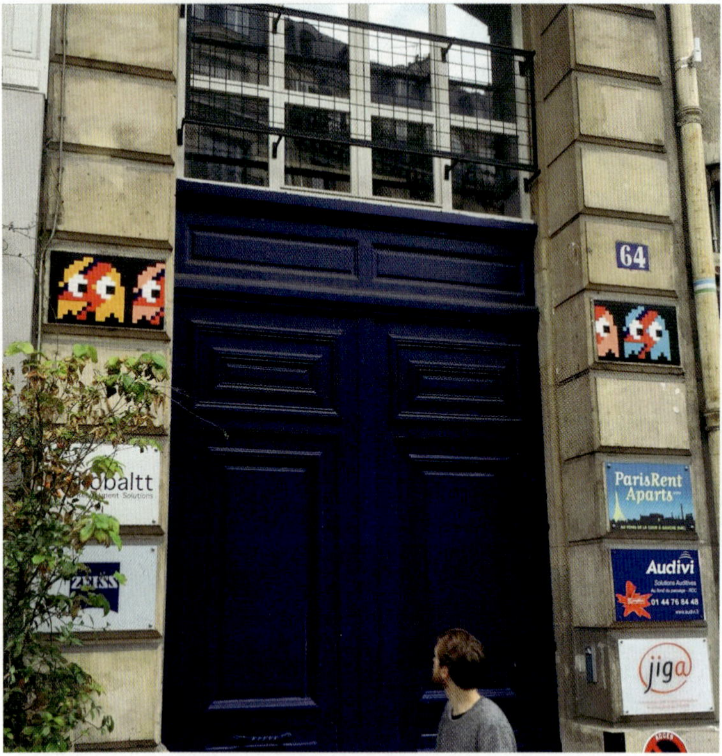

6 555 likes

invaderwashere PA_1057 & PA_1062 #paris #pacman #bowie #aladdinsane #passemuraille #wallpass

View all 60 comments

24 October 2015

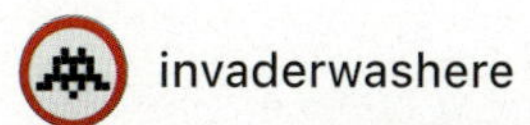

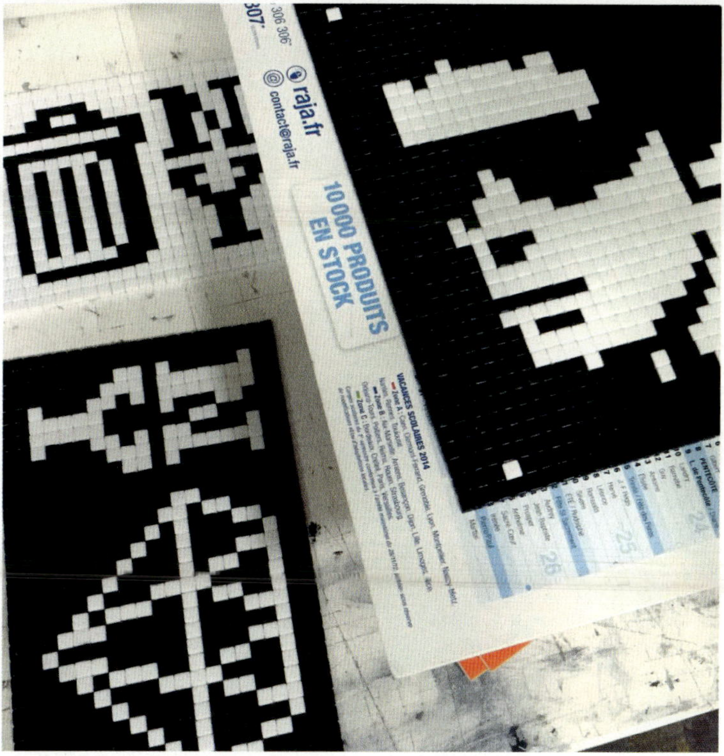

5226 likes

invaderwashere #studiodetail #workinprogress

View all 68 comments

28 October 2015

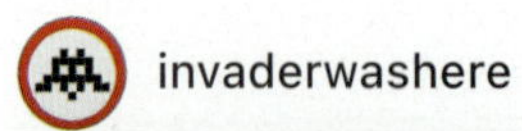

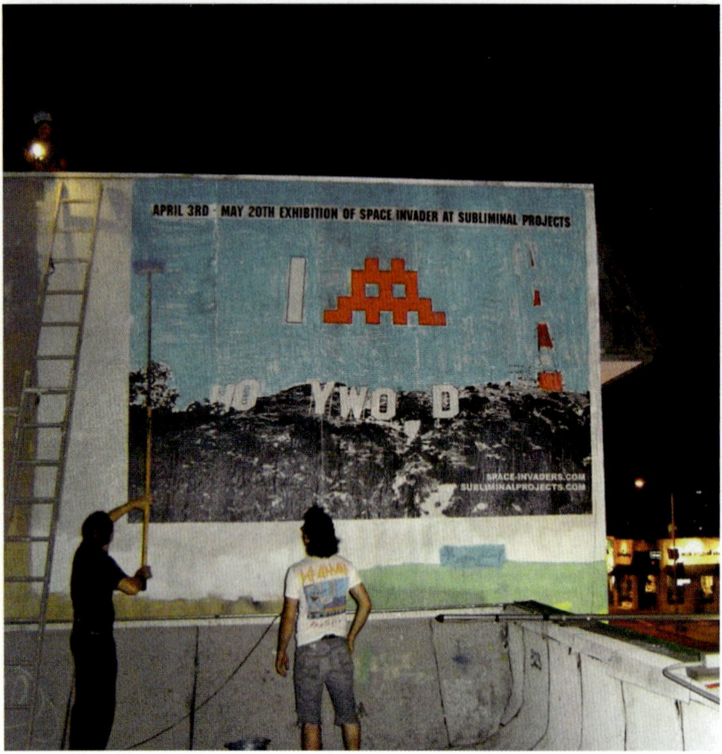

4616 likes

invaderwashere I invade HO__YW_OD #throwback with @mrbrainwash @obeygiant and @thecobrasnake #posterpasring #LA #2003

View all 37 comments

29 October 2015

invaderwashere

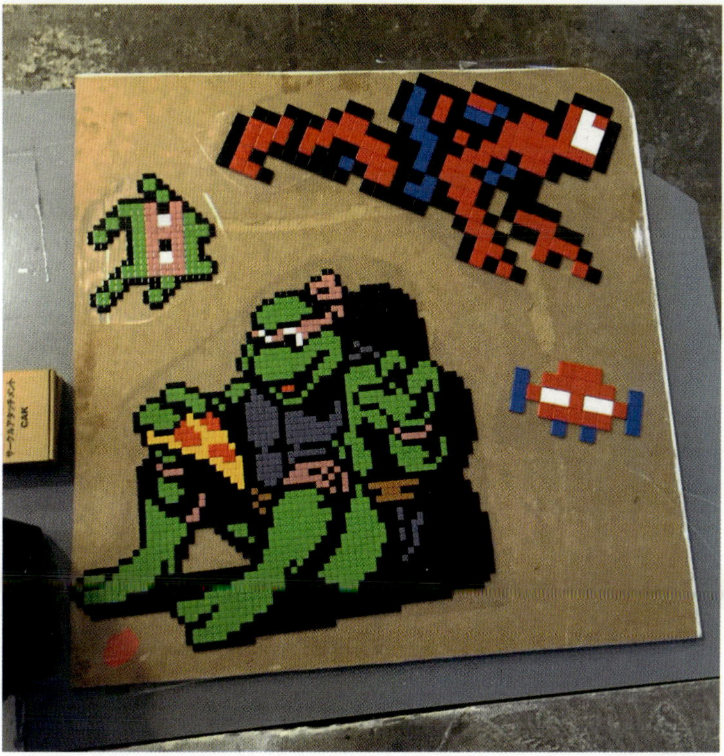

9 389 likes

invaderwashere Studio detail #newyorkers

View all 172 comments

3 November 2015

invaderwashere

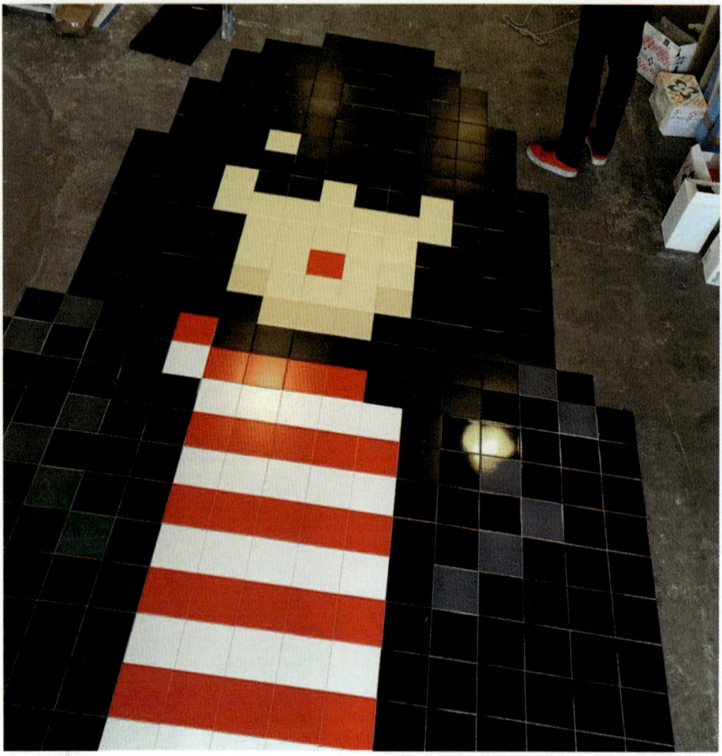

7770 likes

invaderwashere Studio detail #newyorkers

View all 153 comments

3 November 2015

invaderwashere

…about what I'm doing" there, he said. "I am seen not as a vandal but as an artist."

a Phantom Street Artist Returns

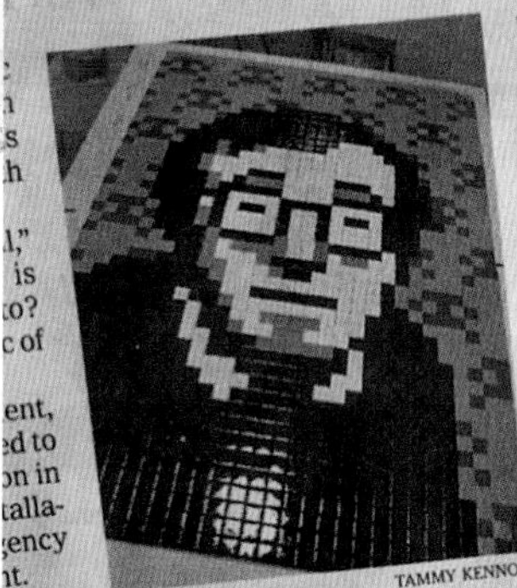

TAMMY KENNON

Invader's pixel portrait of a certain New York auteur.

Gates mask. In Banksy's 2010 documentary "Exit Through the Gift Shop," his face was pixelated.

"Usually the anonymous want fame, and famous people seek anonymity," he said. "I have both. I feel free, both inside and outside from the art world."

popular with collectors. In March, a large piece sold at auction for almost $350,000 at Christie's in Hong Kong.

"He could transition fine," Mr. McCormick said. "He could have a museum or gallery or fine art practice. But his passion lies elsewhere. "He just can't stop doing the illegal work on the street."

In Paris, Invader has reached an unspoken détente with that city's gendarmes, who allow him to go about his business. In general, he feels embraced there.

"Police don't see me as a threat," he said. "After 15 years, nobody is complaining about what I'm doing," he said. "I am seen not as a vandal but as an artist."

Other cities are often less welcoming. So Invader has opted for a new tactic in New York, putting out a call on Instagram to building owners to determine who might be willing to let him install some of his mosaics legally. In exchange, the owners would acquire valuable Invader works at no charge. This will allow him to work on those pieces without fear of ar-

rest, although stil… hours to protect hi…

But authorizatio… price: He has to … the works thems… building owners. "… for me," he said.

These legal wo… be out of reach t… thieves. To thw… might take down … own profit, he sa… out sites with na… al recesses or f… By installing a … size and shape … leaves little wig… one who might t…

In recent ye… used larger, th… jimmy them o… apart rather th… tact.

After his Ne… plans to retur… on his next in… anonymity.

"I have ne… reveal my ide… "What I do a… portant than…

7434 likes

invaderwashere Today's #newyorktimes

View all 136 comments

9 November 2015

invaderwashere •••

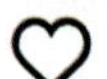

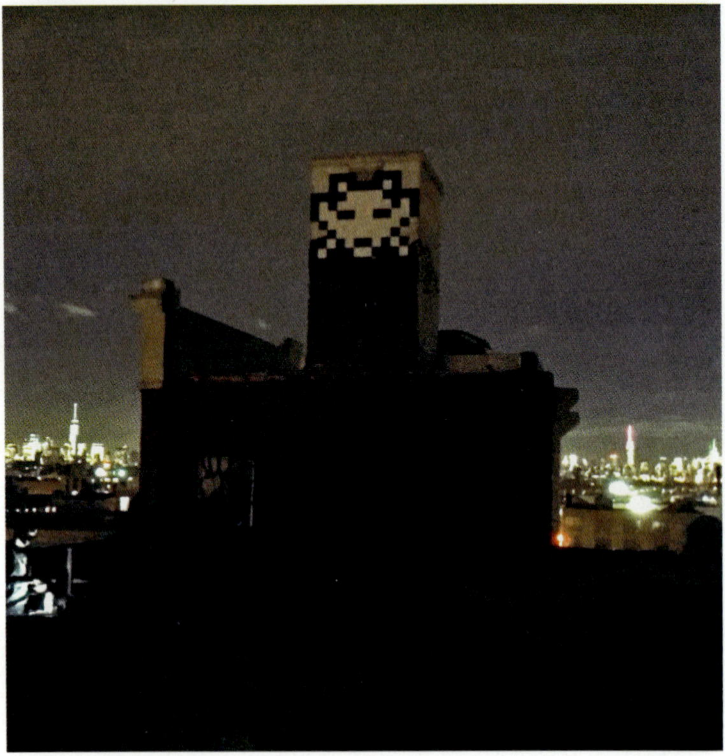

7952 likes

invaderwashere High in NY #brooklyn #bushwick @thebushwickcollective NY_150

View all 93 comments

10 November 2015

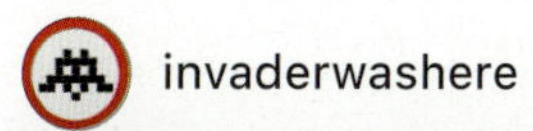

invaderwashere

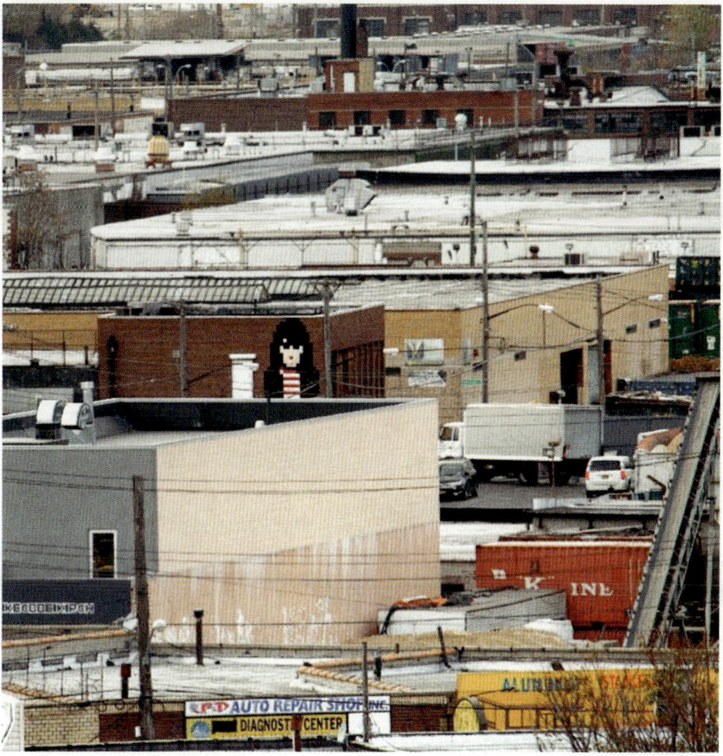

7354 likes

invaderwashere Low-res Joey is in the place! #newyork #bushwick @thebushwickcollective NY_149 #ramones #newyorkers

View all 141 comments

11 November 2015

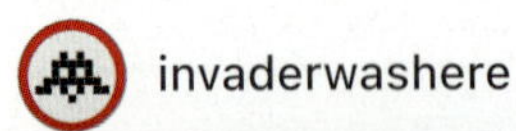

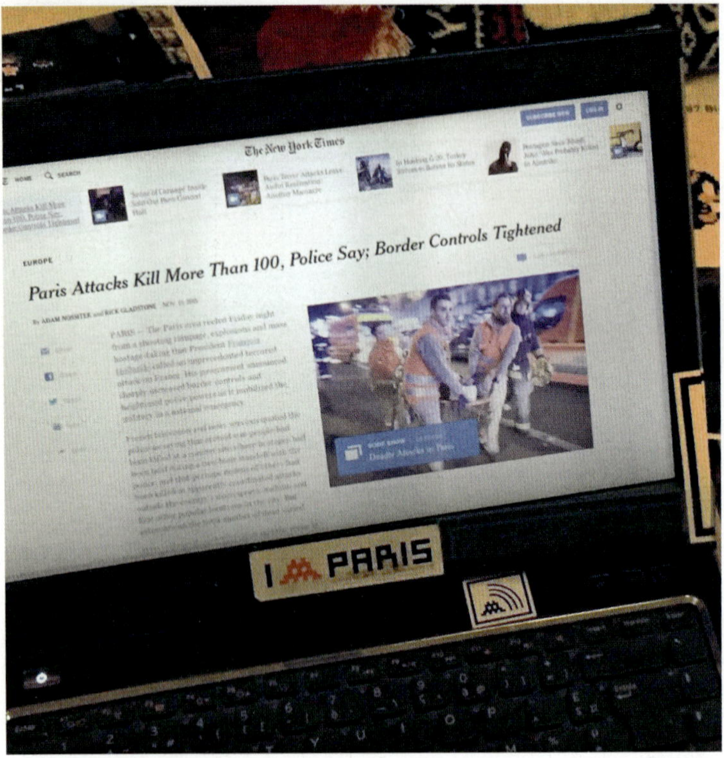

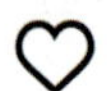   

4 500 likes

invaderwashere Following the terrible news in Paris from my NY base... Courage Paris! #tragedy #barbary #shocked #blackfriday

View all 66 comments

14 November 2015

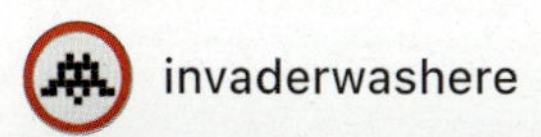

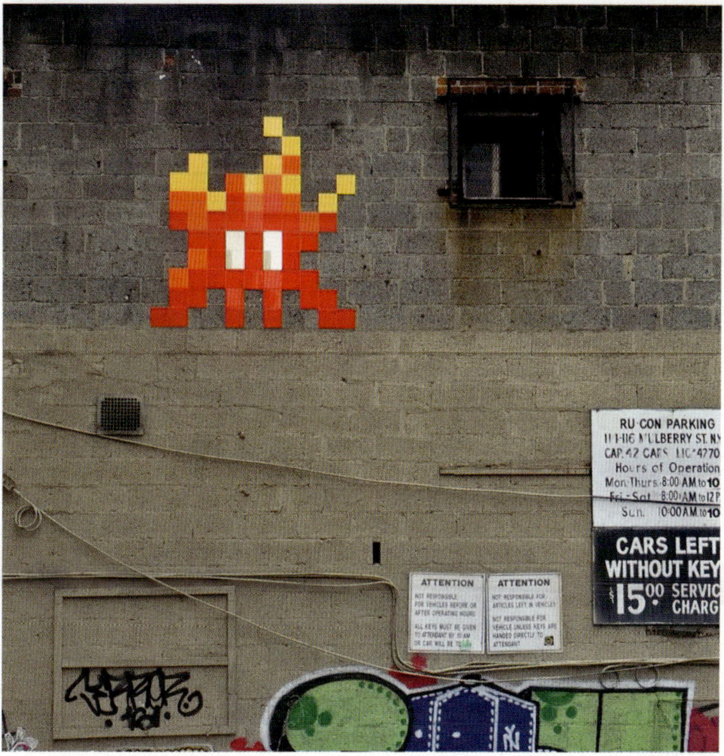

8777 likes

invaderwashere NY_152 burning @thelisaprojectnyc

View all 78 comments

16 November 2015

invaderwashere •••

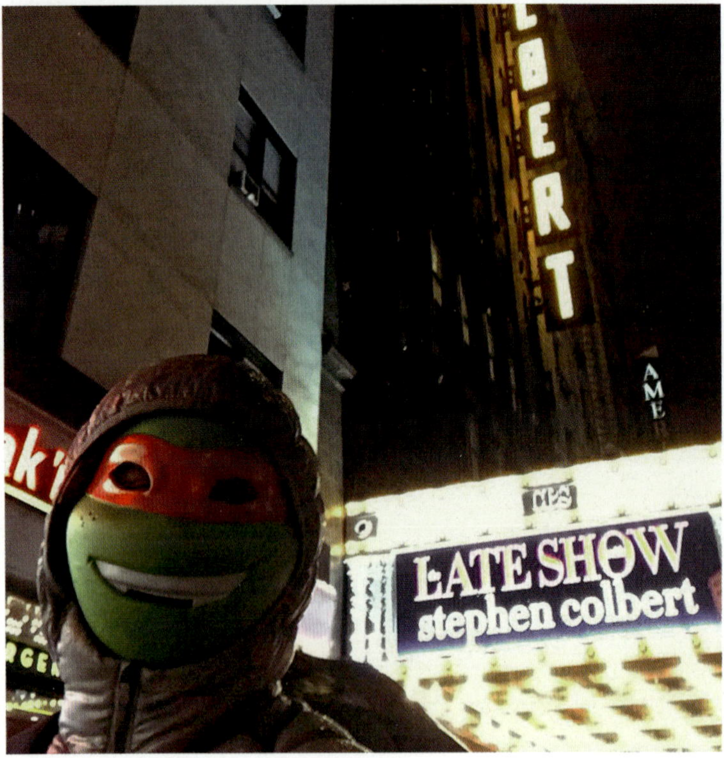

6 548 likes

invaderwashere Special appearance tonight in #thelateshow #stephencolbert #cbs #newyork @colbertlateshow

View all 78 comments

20 November 2015

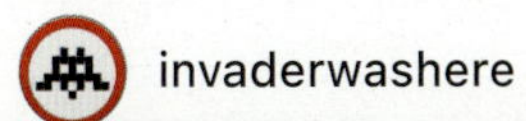

•••

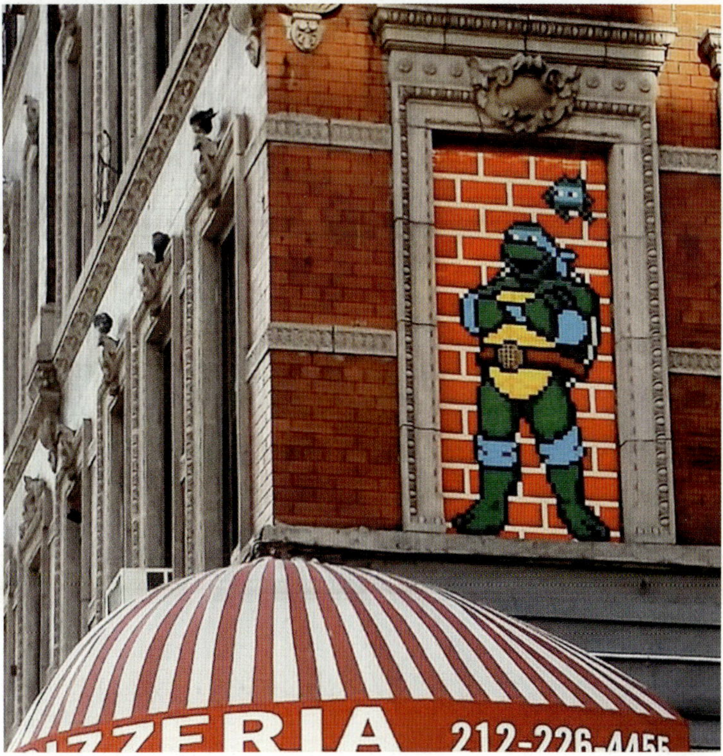

10 649 likes

invaderwashere Pizza time! #Leonardo NY_156 photo by @deniseeeo

View all 196 comments

20 November 2015

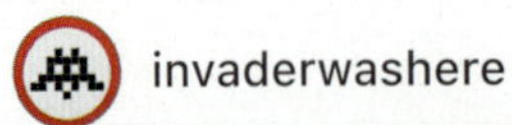

•••

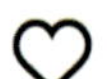   

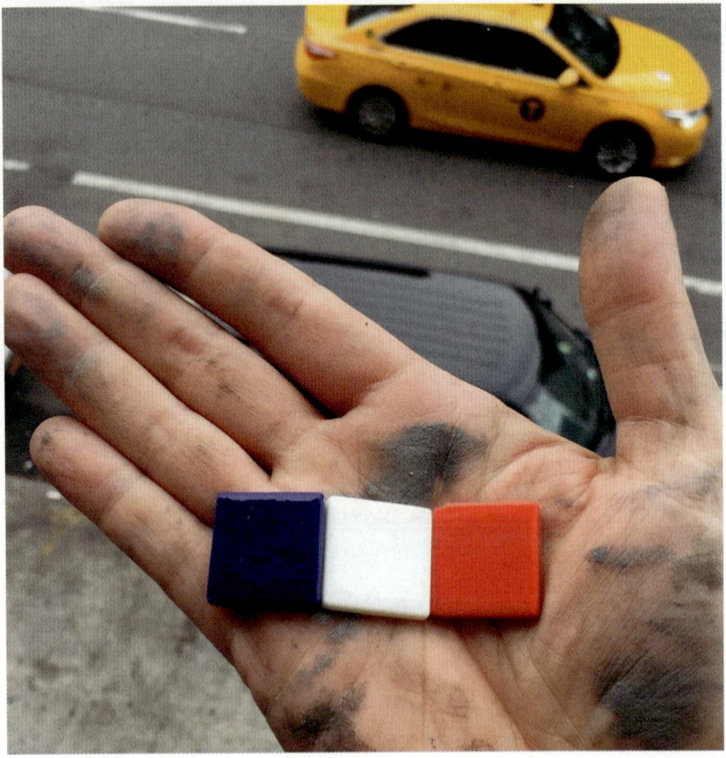

9826 likes

invaderwashere Thoughts for Paris #attentat #attacks

View all 73 comments

22 November 2015

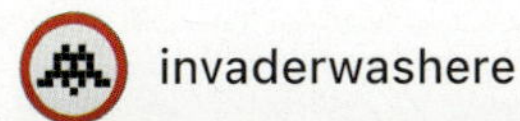

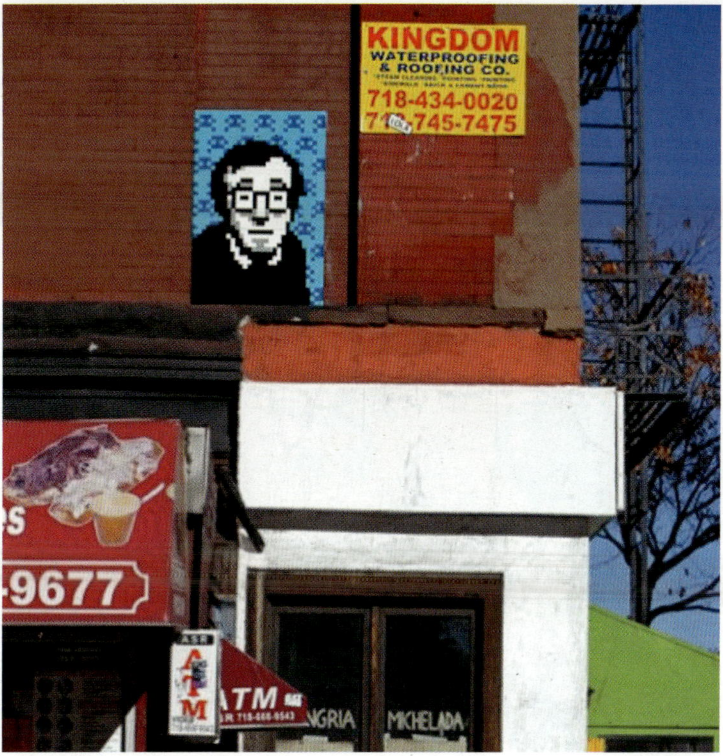

9761 likes

invaderwashere Woody is in the place! #newyork2015 #woodyallen #newyorkerseries

View all 170 comments

23 November 2015

invaderwashere

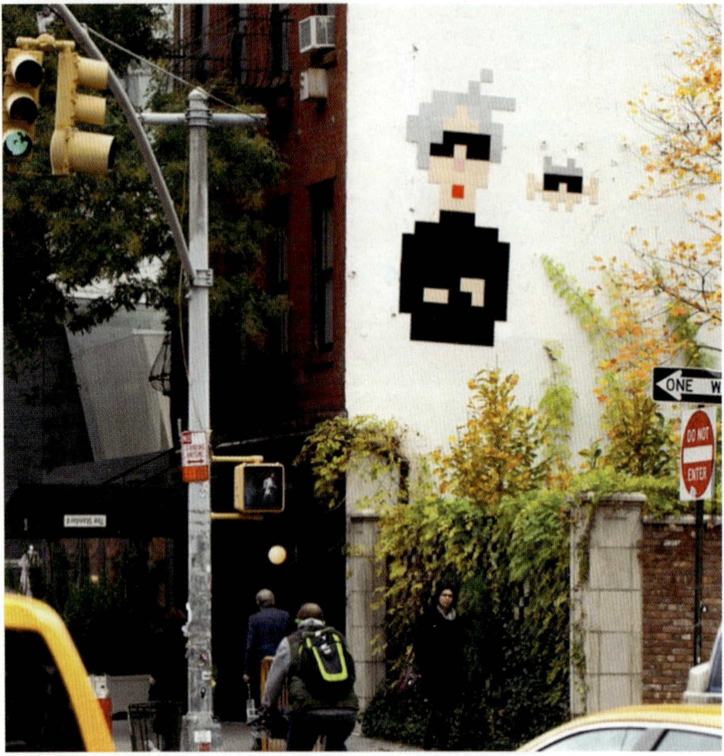

9492 likes

invaderwashere Andy is in the place! #newyork2015 #newyorkers thanks to the Standard hotel and @thelisaprojectnyc

View all 142 comments

23 November 2015

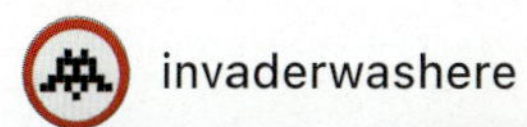

invaderwashere

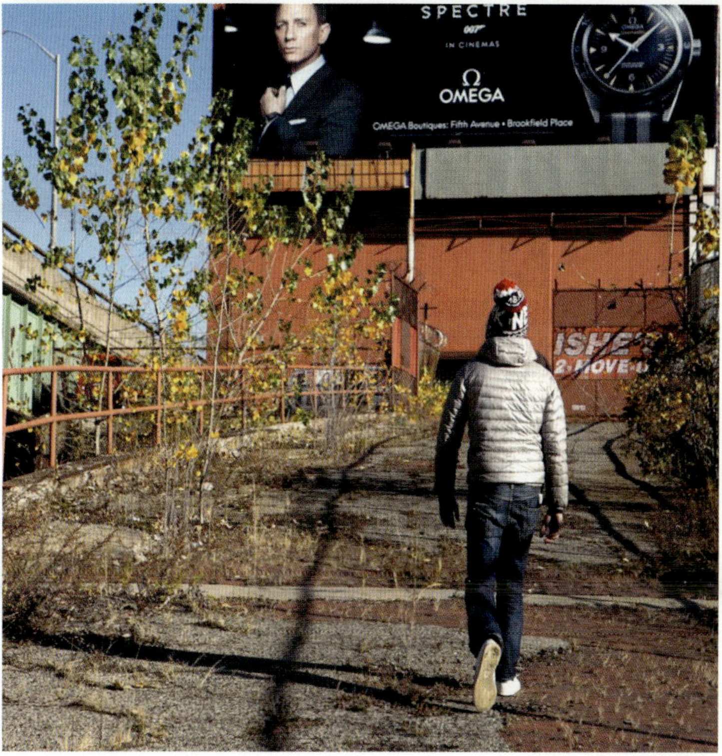

3 267 likes

invaderwashere On the way to the new spot...

View all 38 comments

23 November 2015

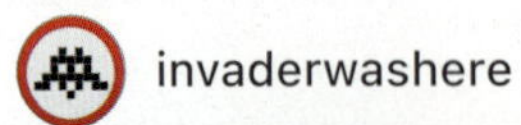

invaderwashere ...

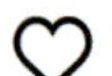 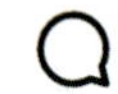  

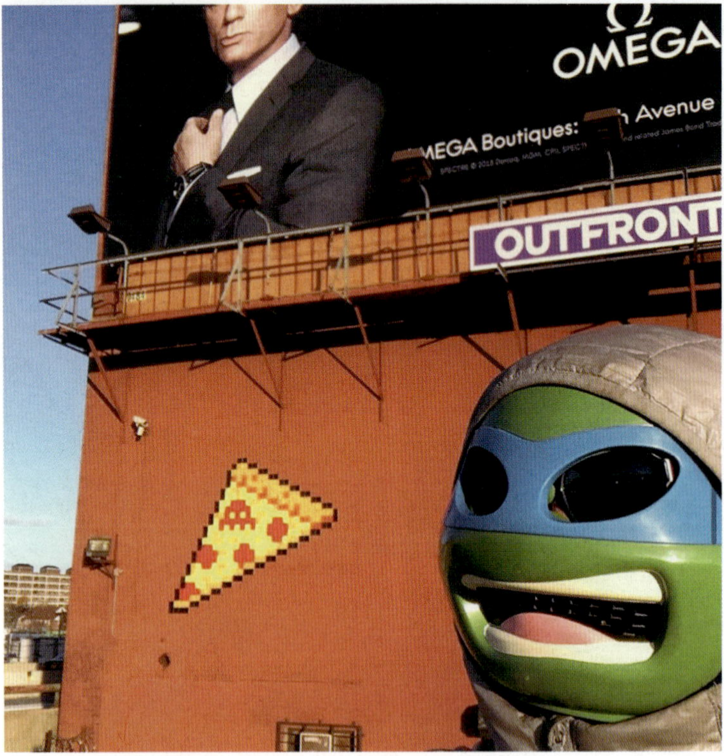

8729 likes

invaderwashere Selfie with NY_179 🍕🍕🍕 Thanks to @manaurbanartsprojects @manacontemporary @thebushwickcollective

View all 148 comments

23 November 2015

invaderwashere •••

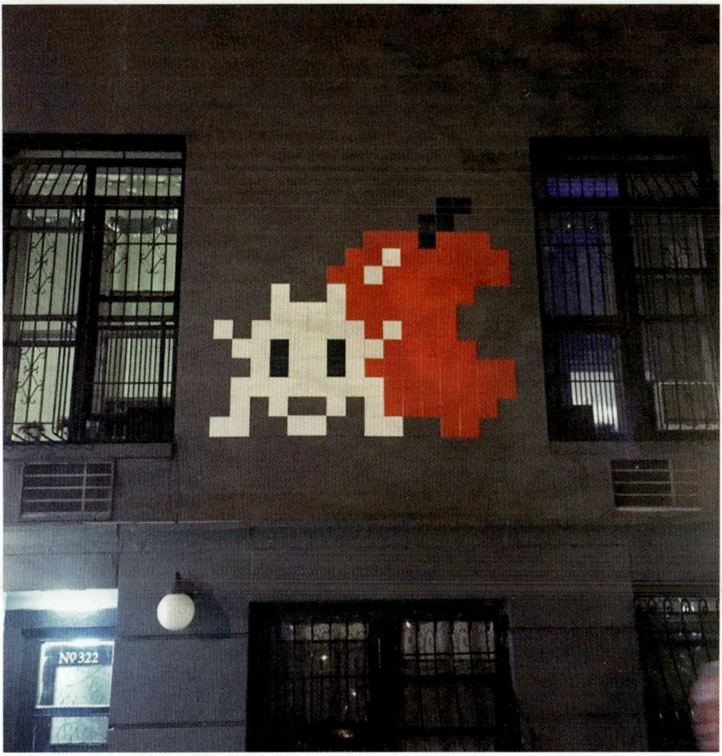

8 560 likes

invaderwashere Big apple!

View all 119 comments

24 November 2015

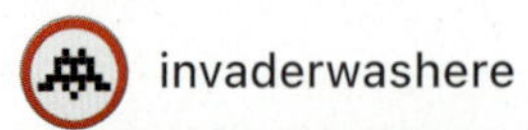

...

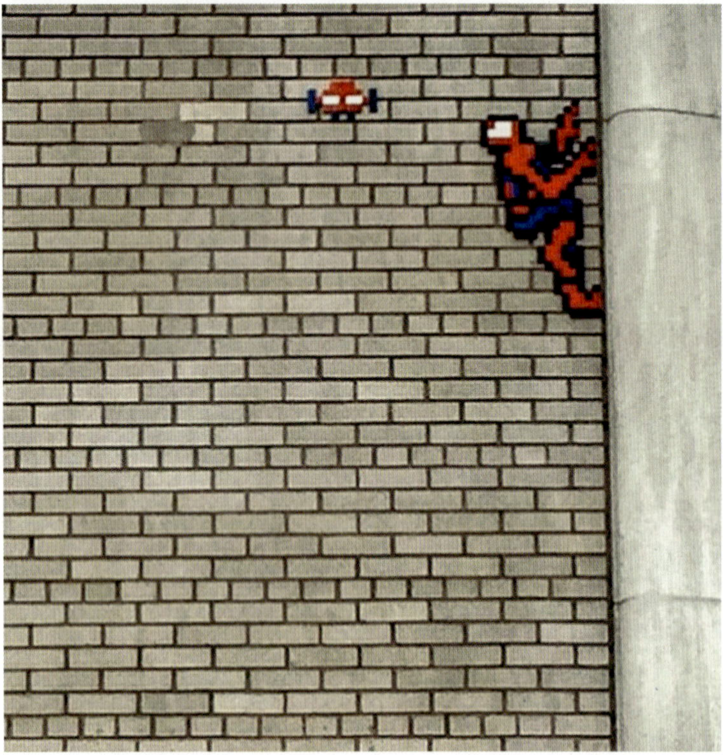

10 872 likes

invaderwashere Here comes the Spider-Man...
#Newyorkerseries #newyork2015 photo by @lostkaws

View all 122 comments

24 November 2015

invaderwashere •••

  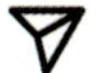 

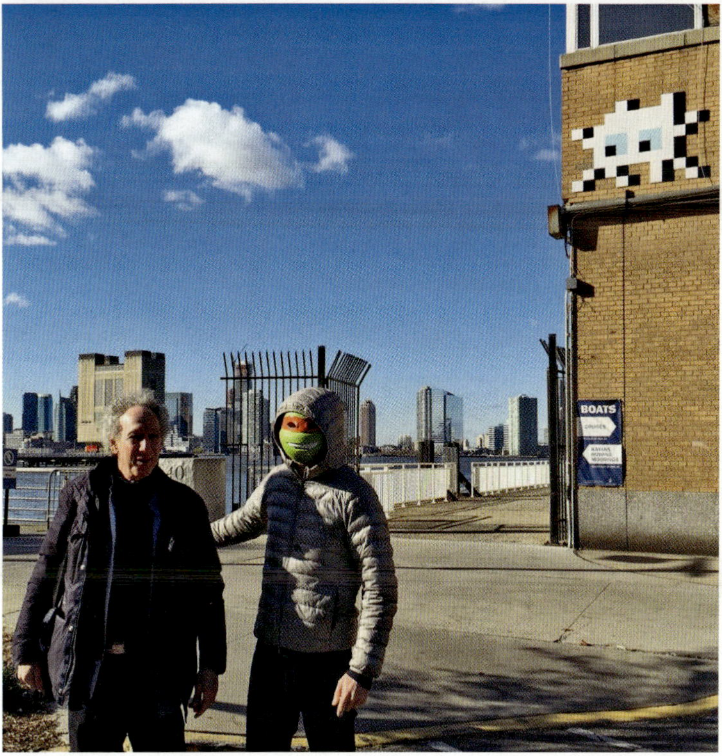

5620 likes

invaderwashere Posing with @bob_gruen & NY_169
#pier40 #NYC

View all 36 comments

24 November 2015

invaderwashere •••

  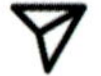 

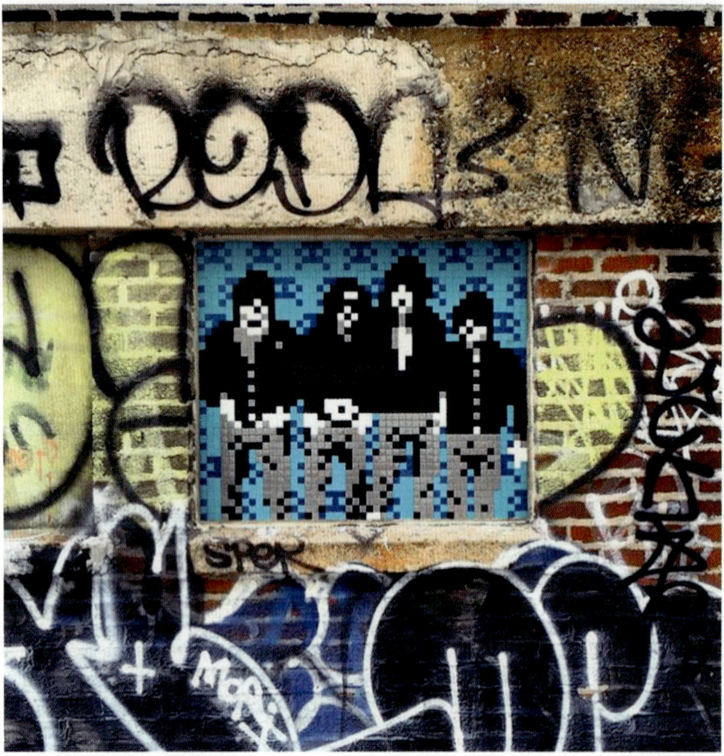

8 412 likes

invaderwashere Hey ho let's go #ramones #newyorkers
photo: @crystinue

View all 141 comments

25 November 2015

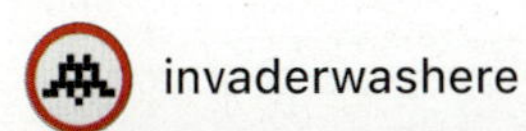

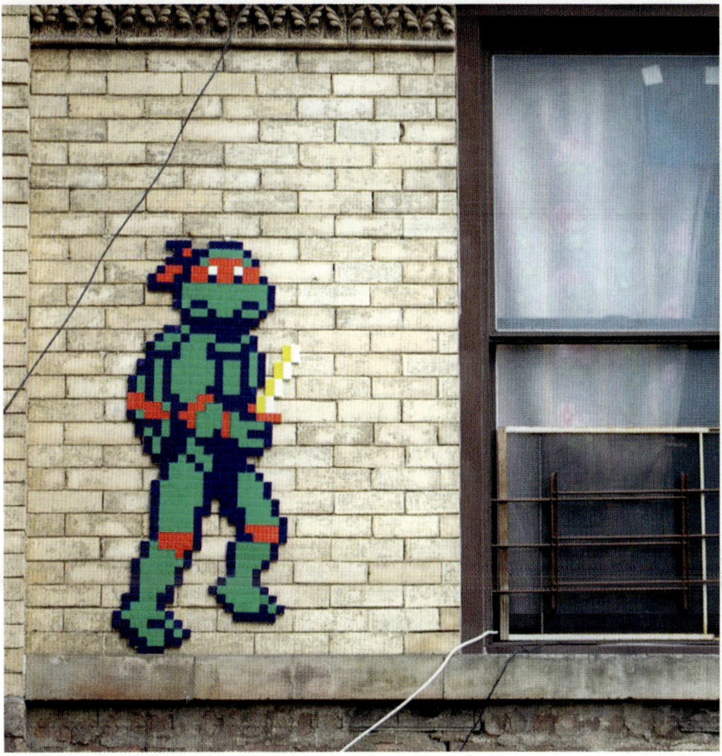

10 251 likes

invaderwashere #Raphael somewhere in NY #newyorkers #ninjaturtles #newyork2015

View all 167 comments

26 November 2015

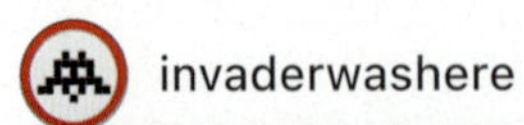

invaderwashere

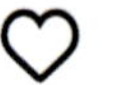   

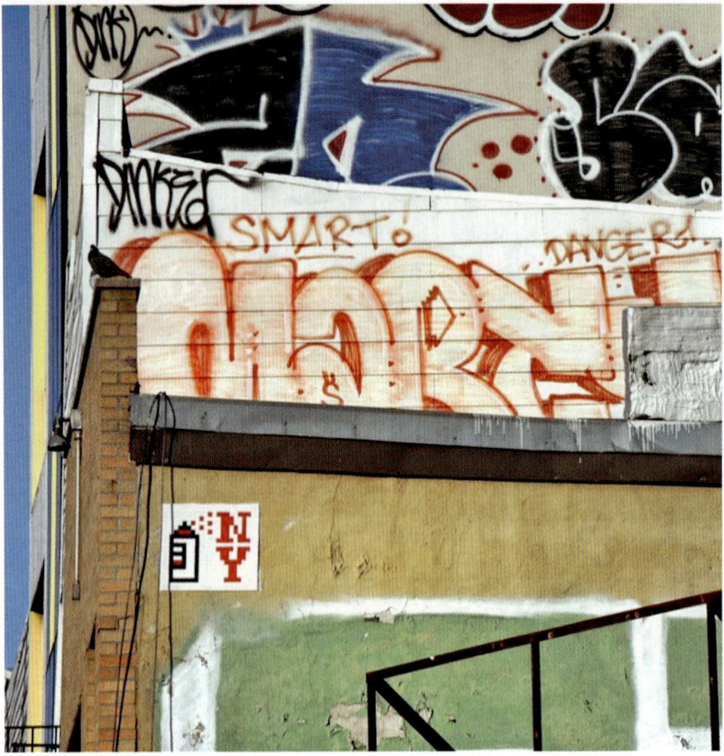

4197 likes

invaderwashere NY_186 #ny #brooklyn #newyork2015 #wave6

View all 50 comments

25 November 2015

invaderwashere

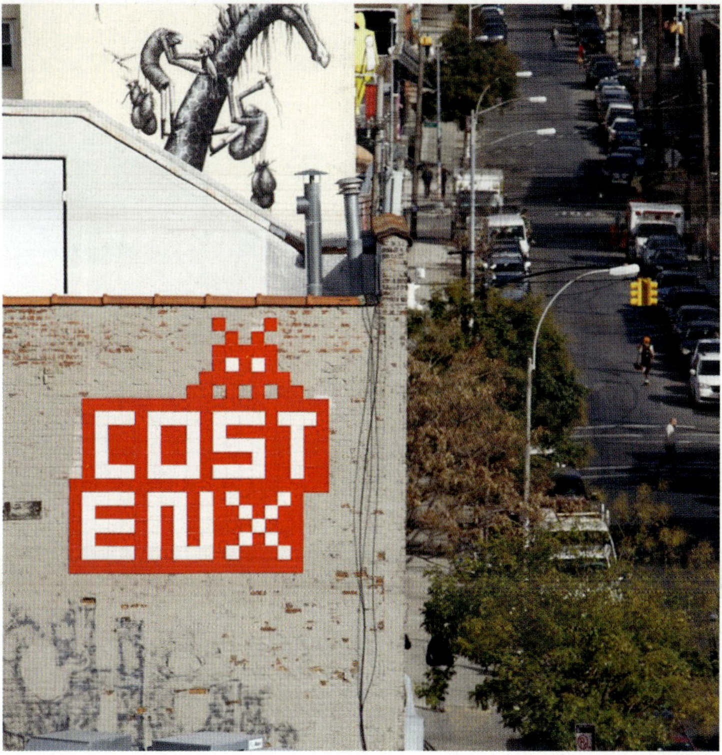

4685 likes

invaderwashere NY_136 Collab from 2013 with @costkrt and @enx108 #throwback #nyc #bushwick

View all 22 comments

26 November 2015

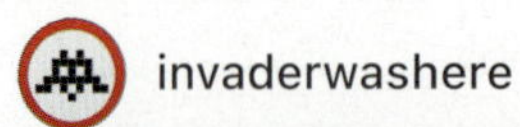

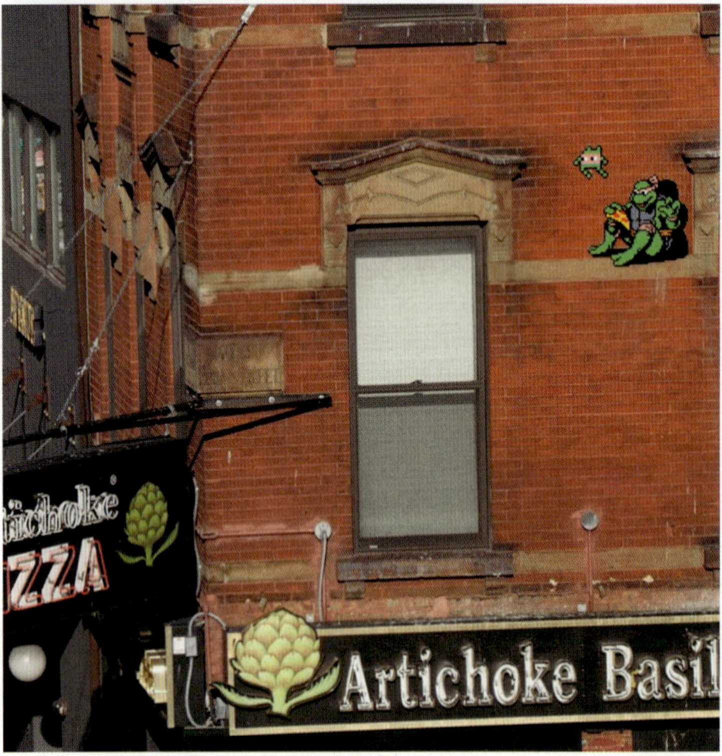

 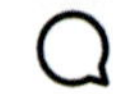  

7298 likes

invaderwashere Donatello is in the place! #newyork2015 #newyorkers #highline #artichokepizza

View all 213 comments

26 November 2015

invaderwashere

  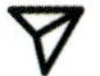 

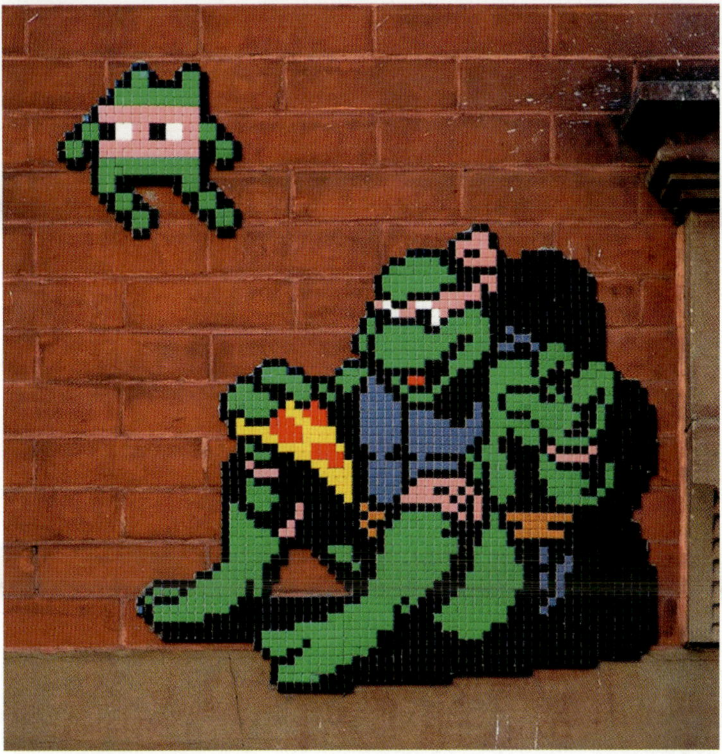

14 055 likes

invaderwashere NY_163 close up

View all 293 comments

26 November 2015

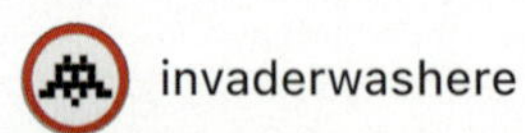
invaderwashere ...

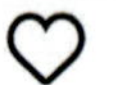   

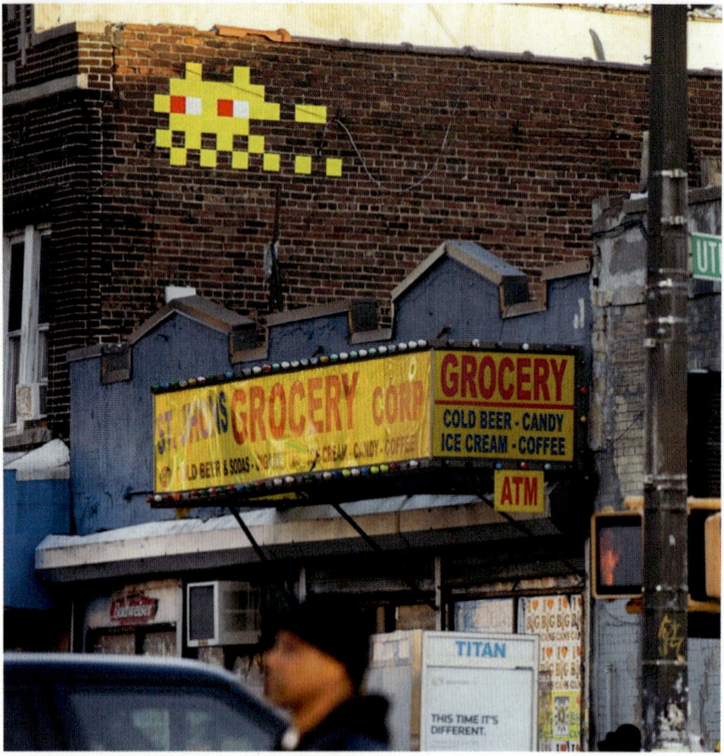

6633 likes

invaderwashere NY_160 lost in Brooklyn

View all 38 comments

27 November 2015

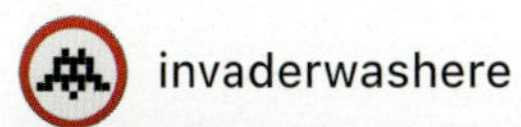

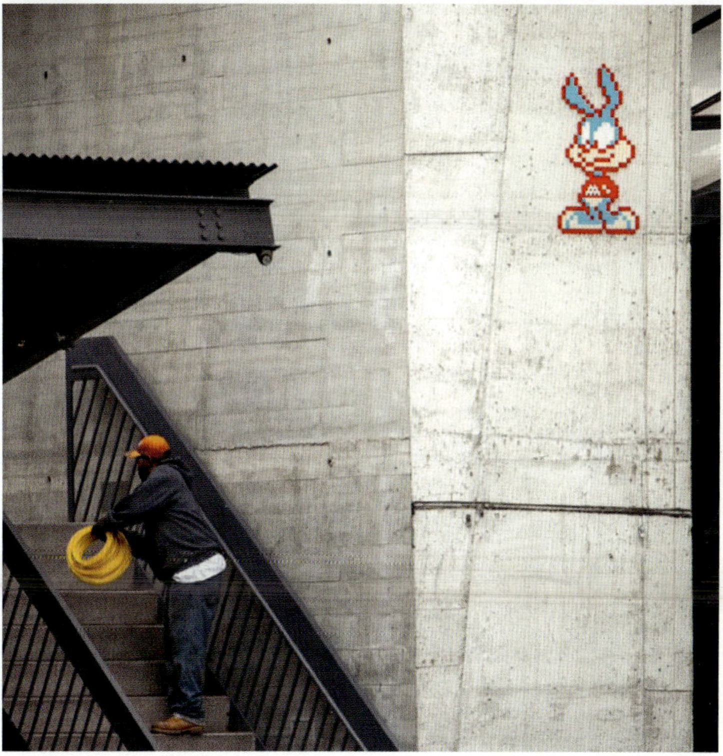

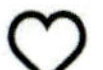   

8946 likes

invaderwashere NY_172 #meatpacking #highline #nyc #glowinthedark

View all 70 comments

28 November 2015

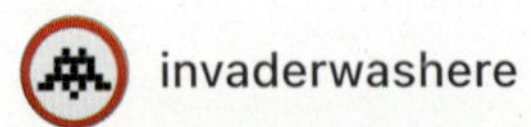

invaderwashere ...

  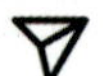 

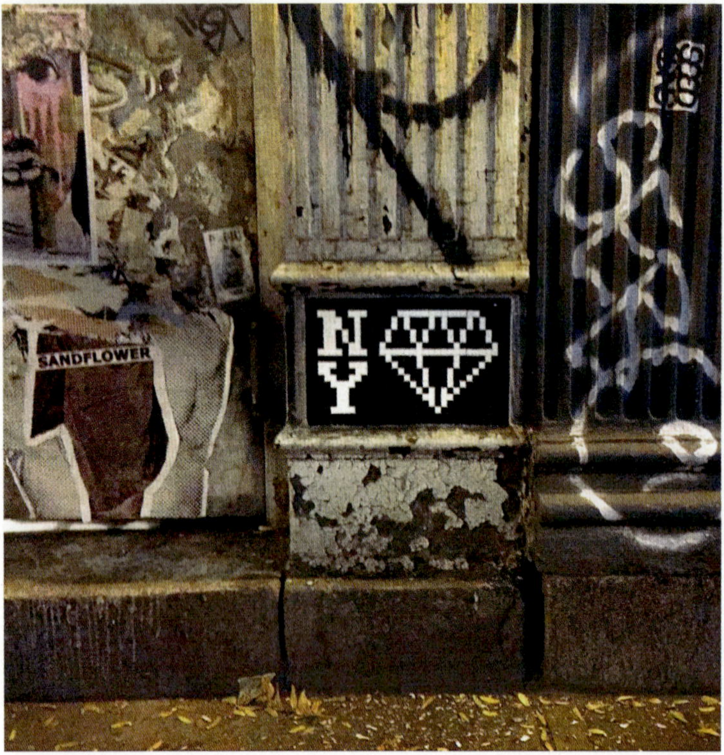

6749 likes

invaderwashere NY_188 NYC Jewel

View all 59 comments

29 November 2015

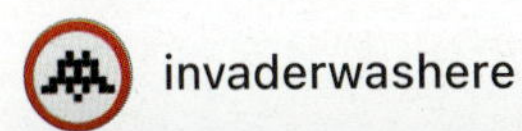

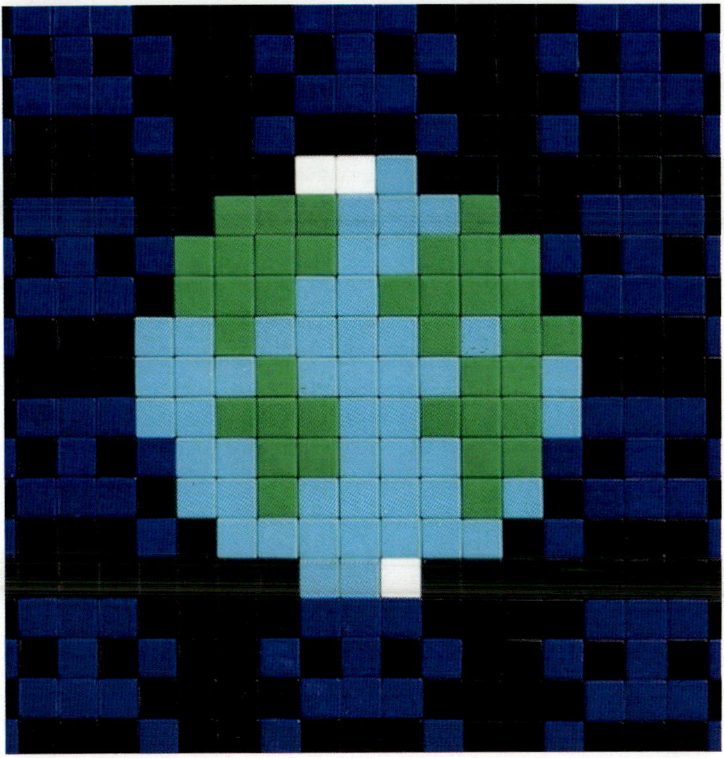

6834 likes

invaderwashere Humans, don't fuck the Earth!!! #cop21
FKF_08

View all 45 comments

30 November 2015

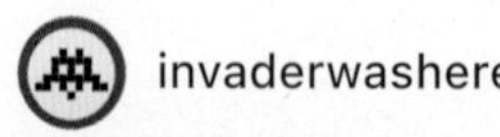

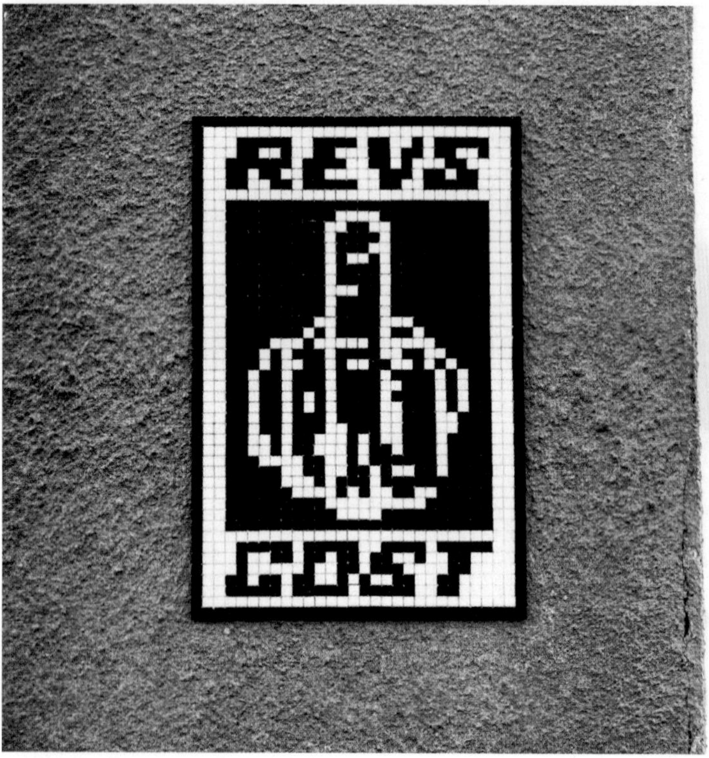

6189 likes

invaderwashere NY_185 #Revs #Cost #sticker #tribute #IloveNYpd

View all 59 comments

2 December 2015

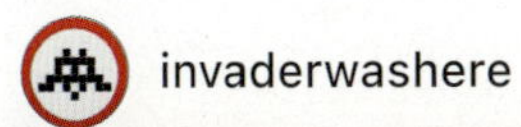

•••

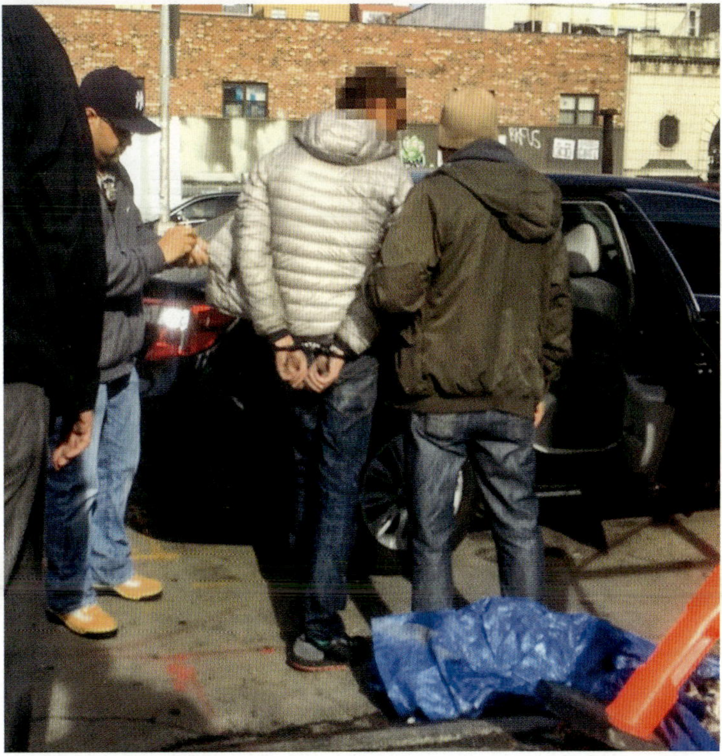

10 751 likes

invaderwashere It is awesome how NYPD appreciates my work. Each time I go to NYC they offer me a free drive + a free room with food included and some nice roommates... Thank you #NYPD #undercovers #nyc #gotojail

View all 725 comments

2 December 2015

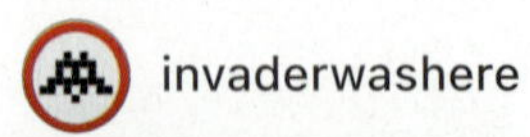

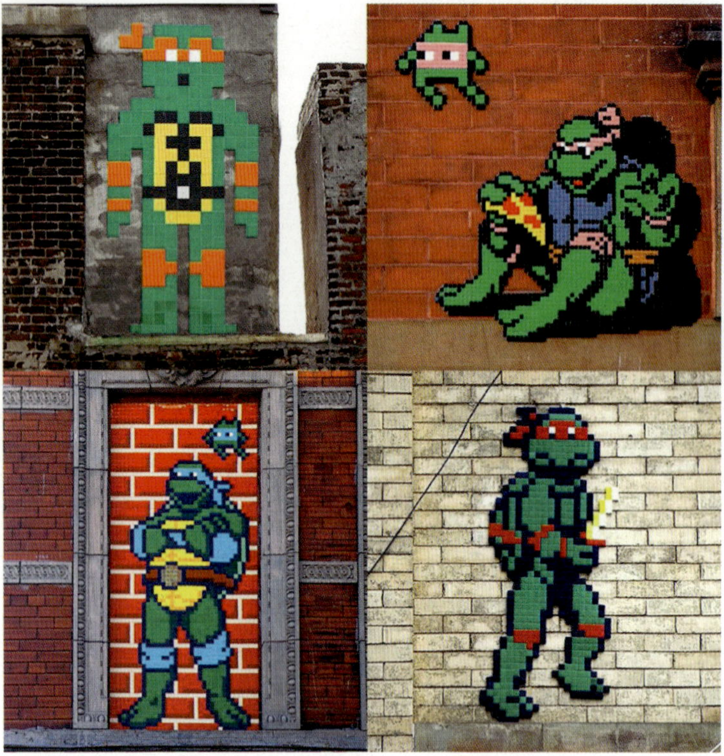

 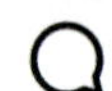  

12 495 likes

invaderwashere #ninjaturtles #nyc2015 Wave 06 in NYC completed: 42 new pieces / 2090 Points. More info soon on my website.

View all 404 comments

2 December 2015

invaderwashere

 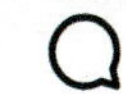  

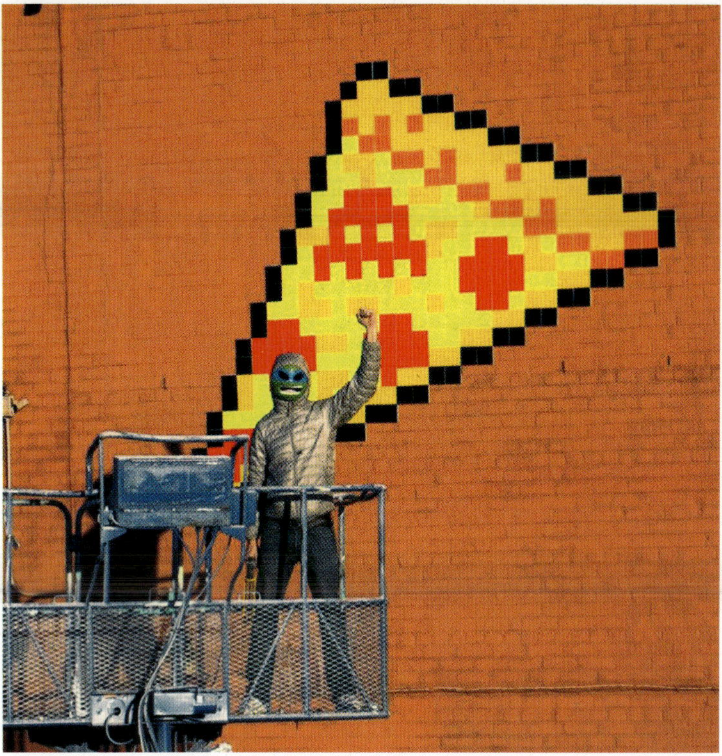

12 977 likes

invaderwashere Pizza power!

View all 497 comments

3 December 2015

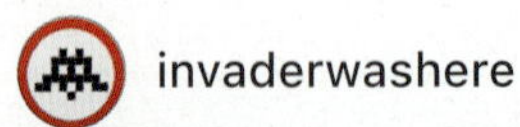

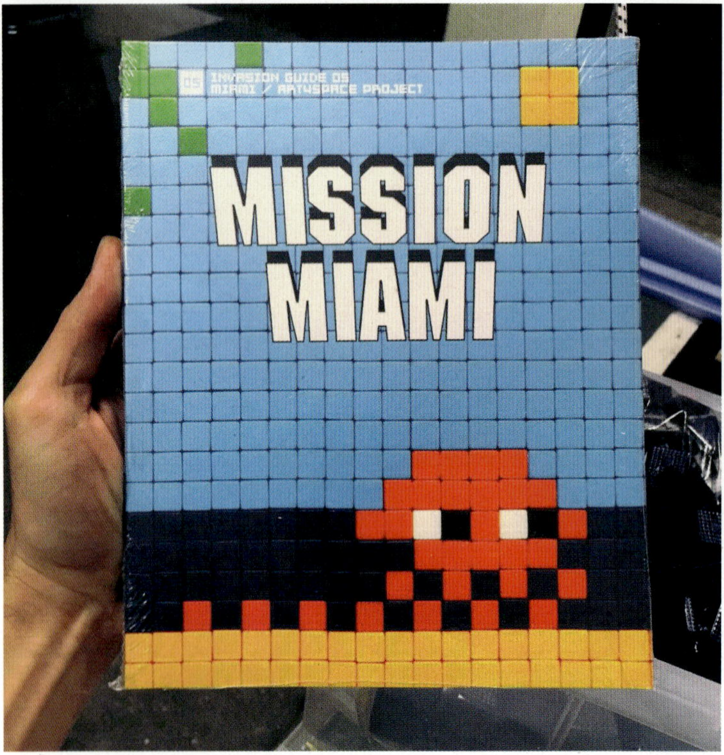

4752 likes

invaderwashere MISSION MIAMI / Invasion Guide 05 / Last copies online. When I produced my first book, "L'invasion de Paris", in 2003, no publisher agreed to publish it. So I did it on my own, and since then, with around 20 books to my credit, I've continued to publish them independently. #Miami #book #art4space #invader #invasionguide space-invaders.com

View all 57 comments

4 December 2015

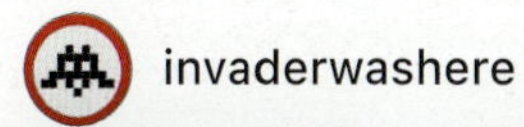

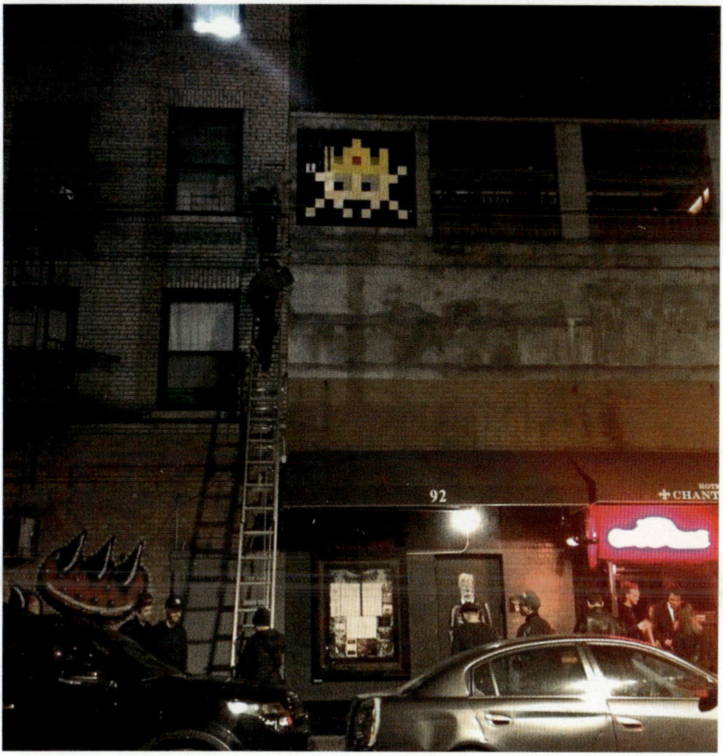

7354 likes

invaderwashere Putting up NY_157 #newyork2015 #gofast
photo by @enx108

View all 64 comments

6 December 2015

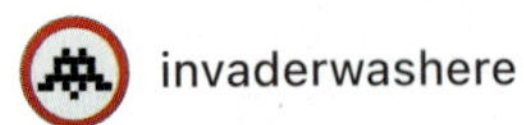

•••

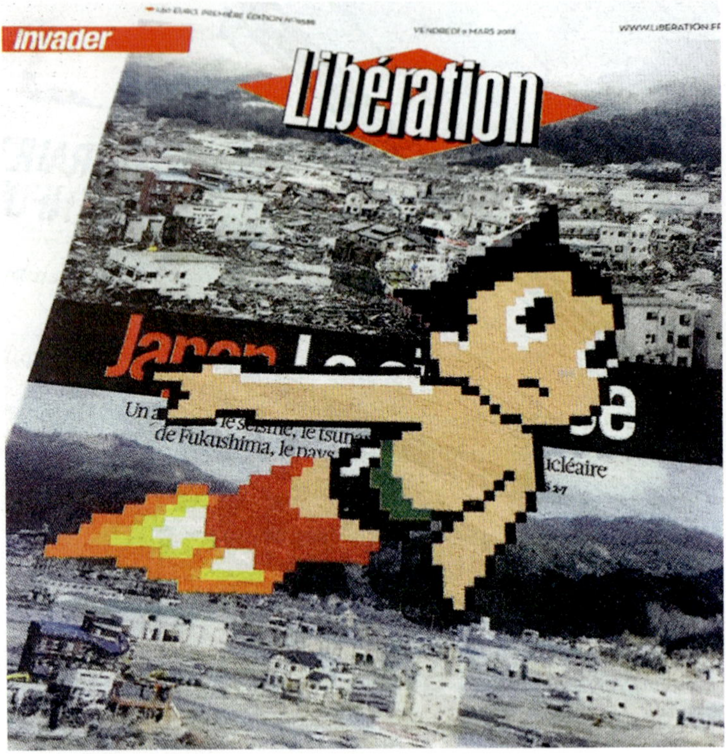

5700 likes

invaderwashere Hand painting on Libération front page for « Artistes à la une » to be exhibited at Le Palais de Tokyo this week-end. The artwork will be auctioned off in January, with all the proceeds donated to Reporters sans Frontières. More info on today's Libération newspaper #artistesalaune #fukushima #atom #atomicpower @palaisdetokyo @liberationfr @reporterssansfrontieres

View all 44 comments

11 December 2015

invaderwashere

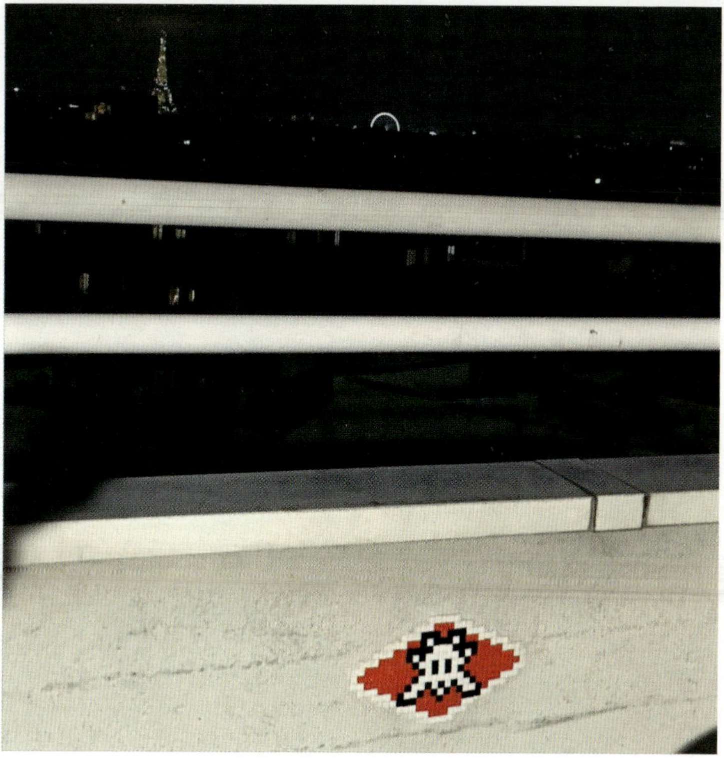

5 353 likes

invaderwashere PA_992 view with Eiffel Tower 😻
@liberationfr #rooftop #paris

View all 18 comments

20 December 2015

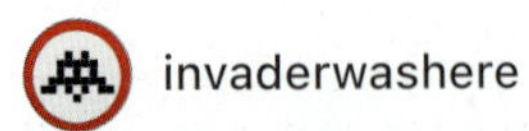

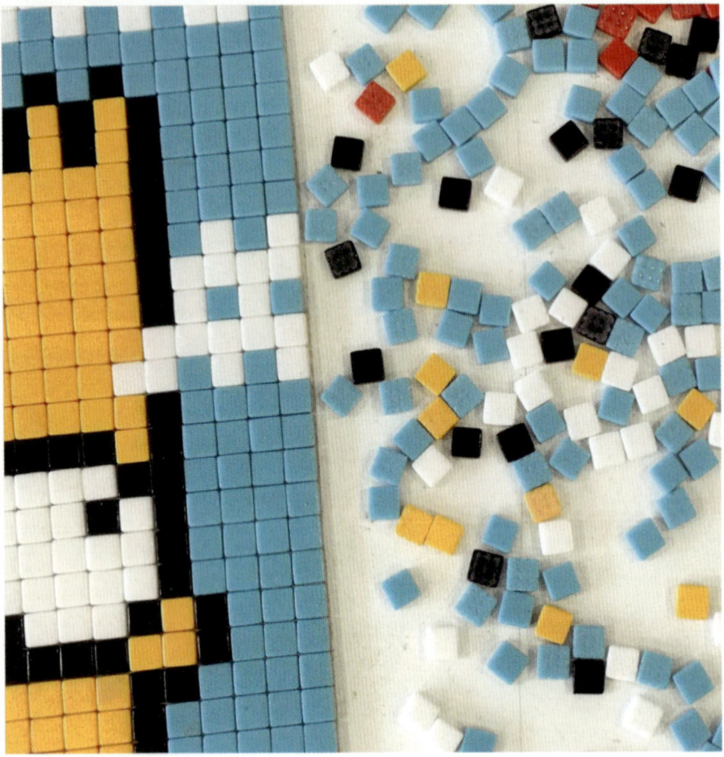

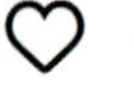  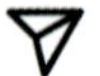 

7 842 likes

invaderwashere #studiodetail

View all 81 comments

24 December 2015

invaderwashere

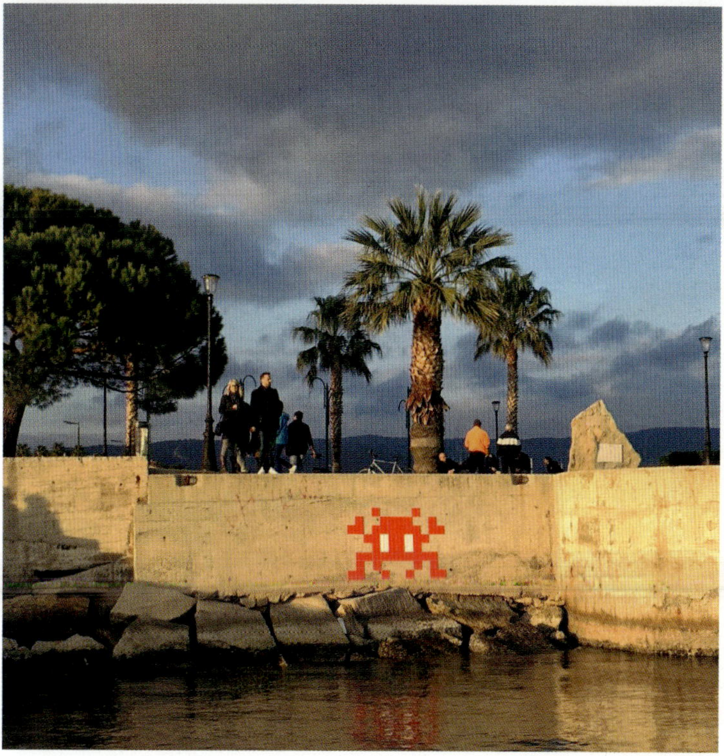

9029 likes

invaderwashere LCT_09 / South of France / Thank you assoduvieuxport for the boat tour 📸 #Laciotat

View all 58 comments

27 December 2015

invaderwashere

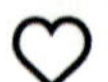

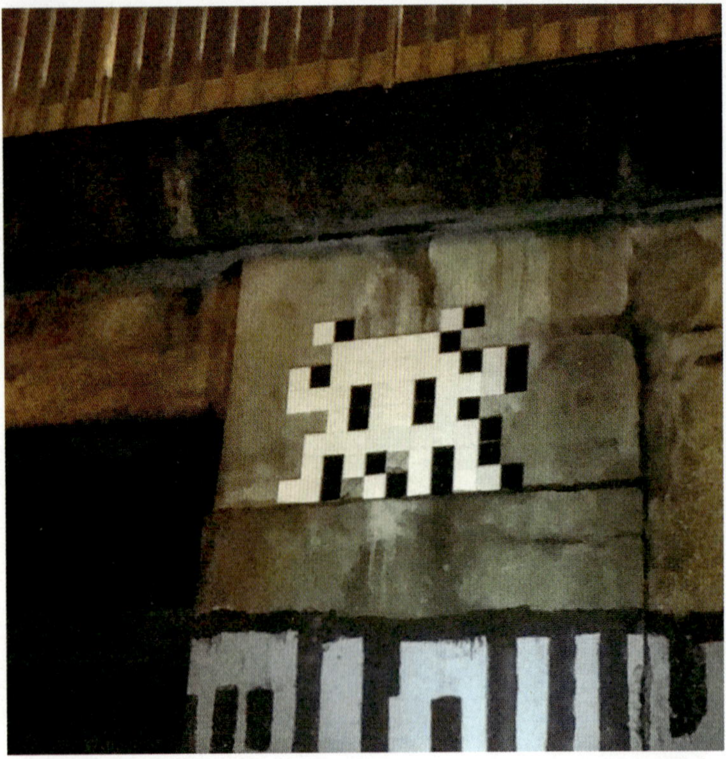

6954 likes

invaderwashere Last piece of 2015, B&W mood #justmade #highway #invaderwashere #Paris

View all 39 comments

30 December 2015

2016

invaderwashere •••

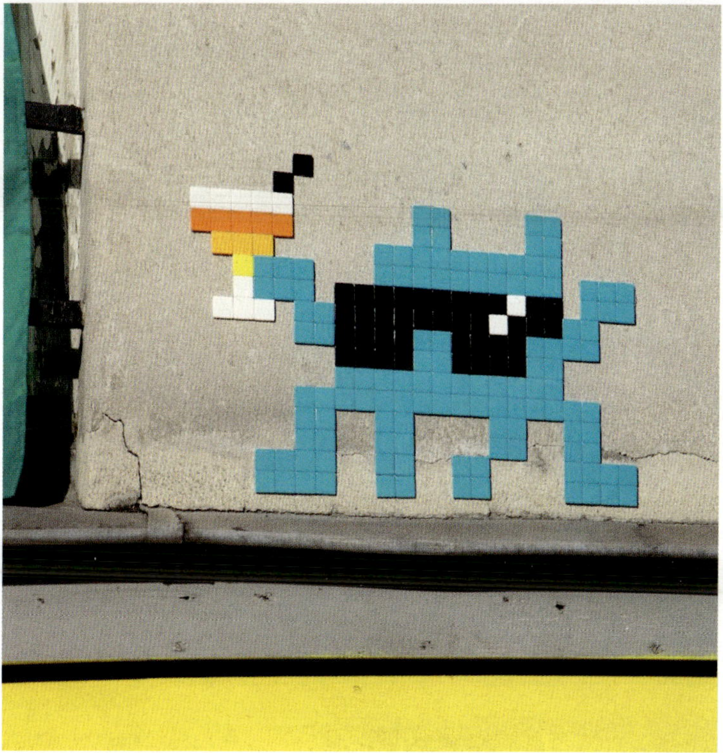

10 326 likes

invaderwashere Happy New year 🎈 #2016 #newpiece #paris

View all 122 comments

1 January 2016

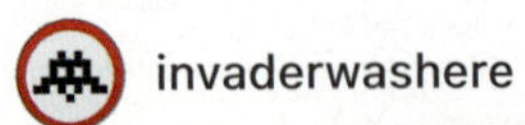

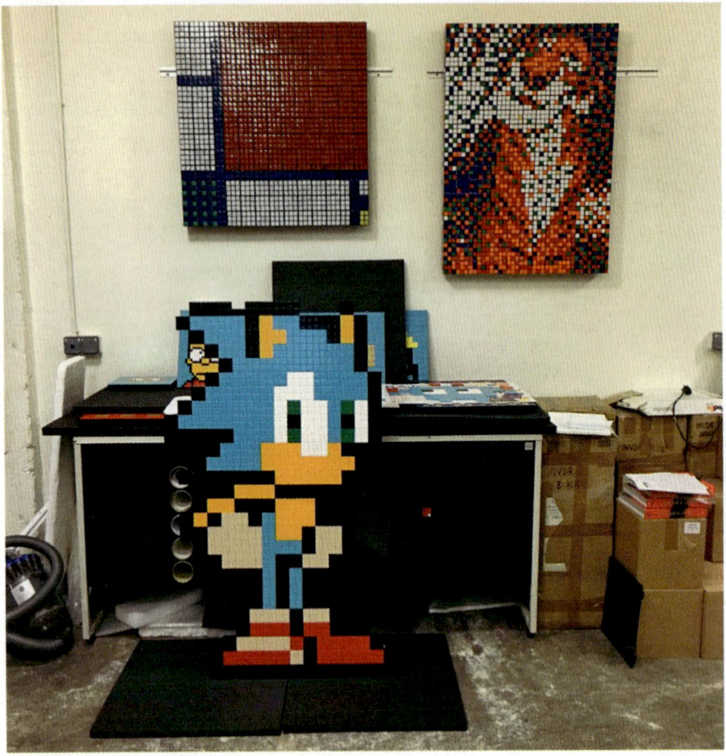

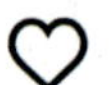   

11777 likes

invaderwashere Mondrian, Sherkhan & Sonic at the studio

View all 169 comments

4 January 2016

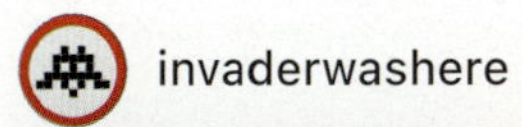

invaderwashere •••

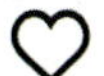 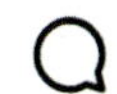  

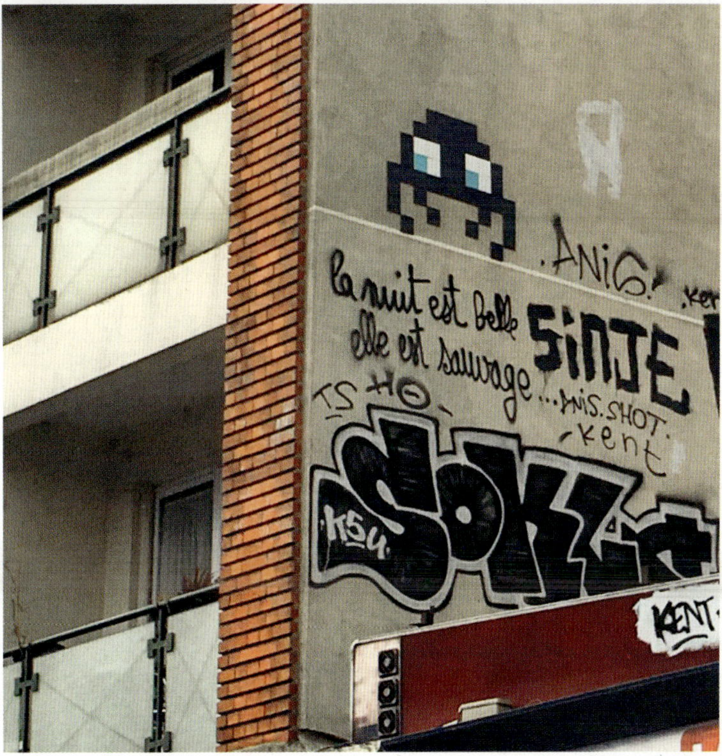

6709 likes

invaderwashere #paris graffitis & PA_1009

View all 39 comments

6 January 2016

invaderwashere ...

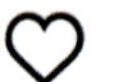   

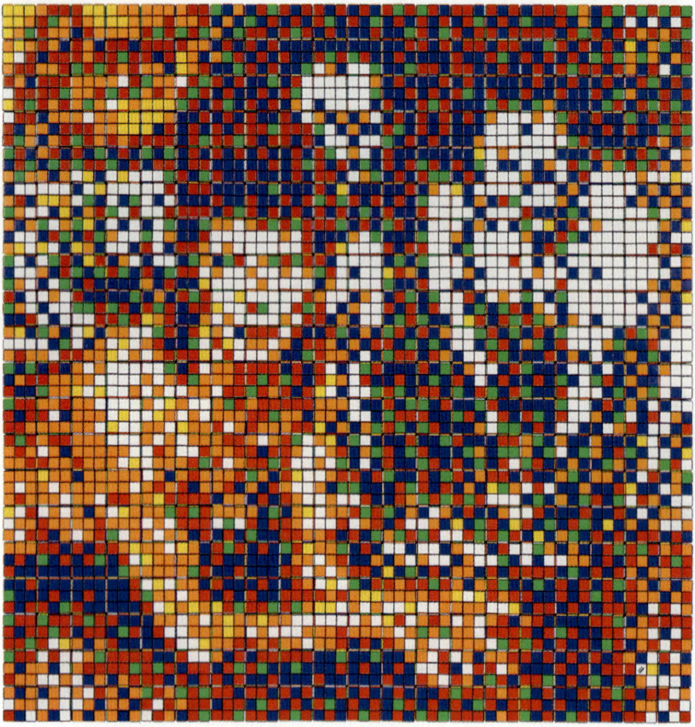

11048 likes

invaderwashere RIP David Bowie ⚡ #diamonddogs #rubikcubism #lowfidelity #bowie

View all 91 comments

11 January 2016

invaderwashere

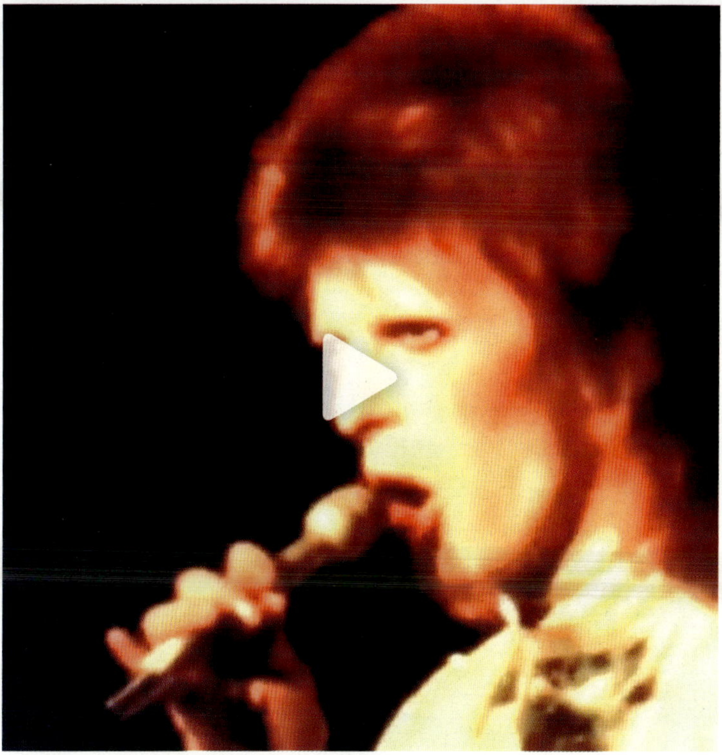

29 031 views

invaderwashere I'm a mama-papa coming for you, I'm the Space Invader... #moonagedaydream #ziggystardust #davidbowie

View all 47 comments

11 January 2016

invaderwashere •••

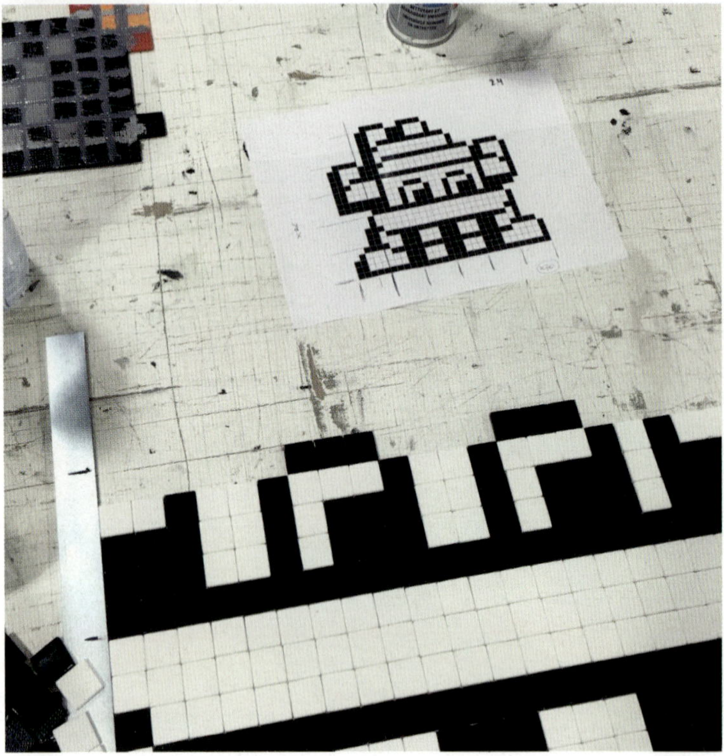

5456 likes

invaderwashere Preparing a new city invasion...  
#studiodetail #makingof

View all 30 comments

18 January 2016

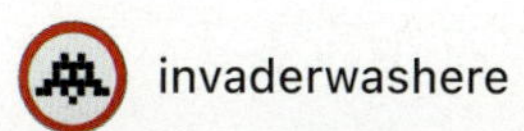

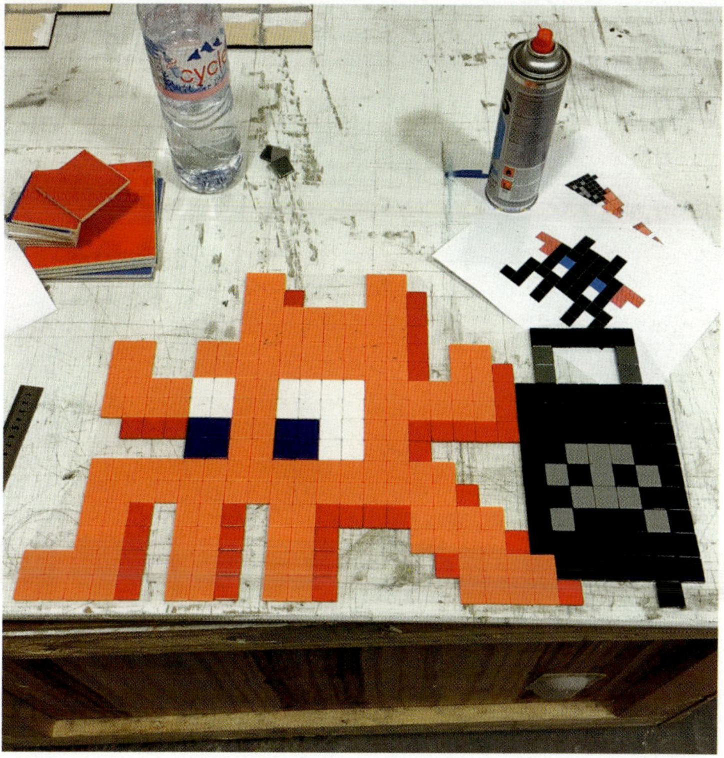

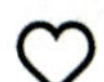  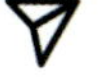 

8106 likes

invaderwashere Space invaders getting ready for an imminent invasion 👾🚀🌍

View all 73 comments

19 January 2016

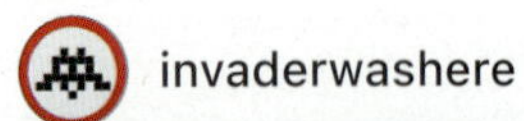

invaderwashere •••

  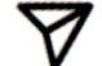 

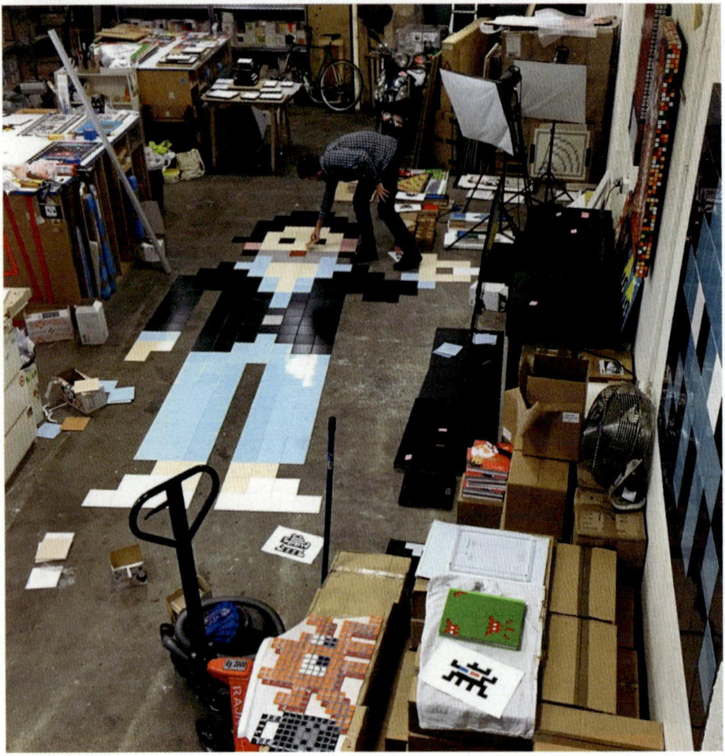

7954 likes

invaderwashere Final touch of the 8bit Gainsbourg in the mothership

View all 106 comments

19 January 2016

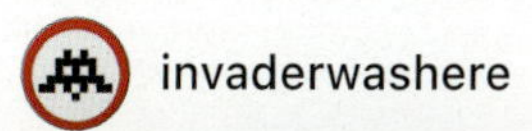

•••

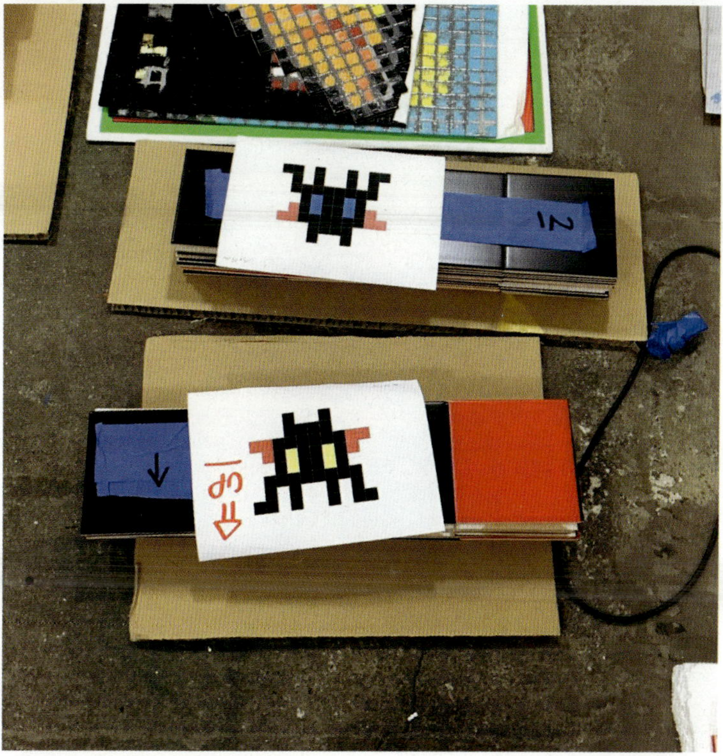

4924 likes

invaderwashere Packing some Bat-Invaders !

View all 42 comments

20 January 2016

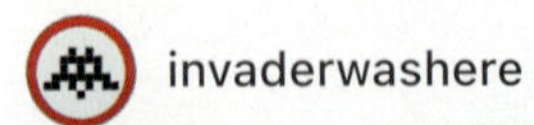

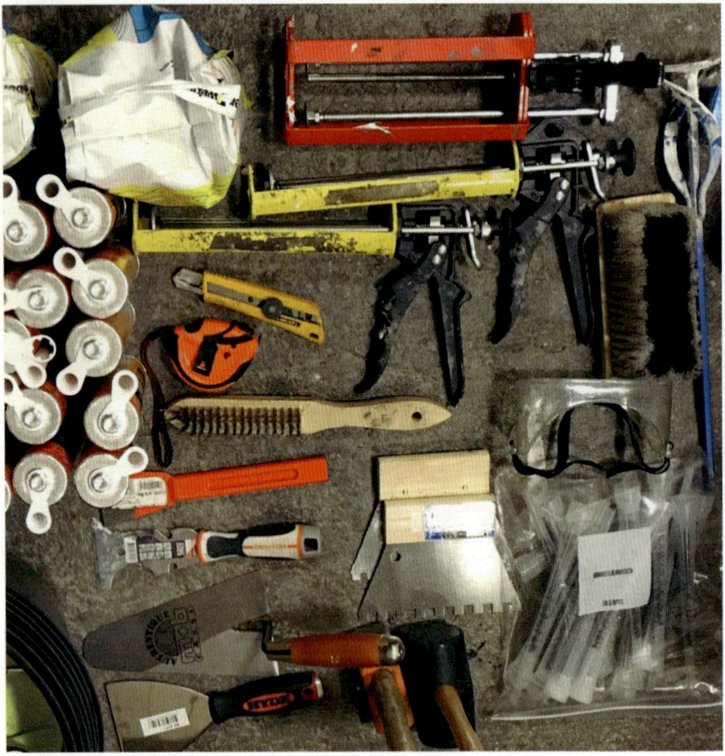

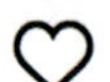   

3 927 likes

invaderwashere Ready to tile the bathroom :)

View all 37 comments

21 January 2016

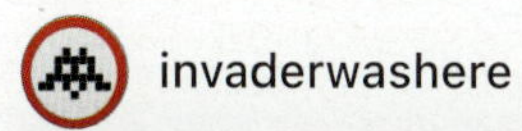

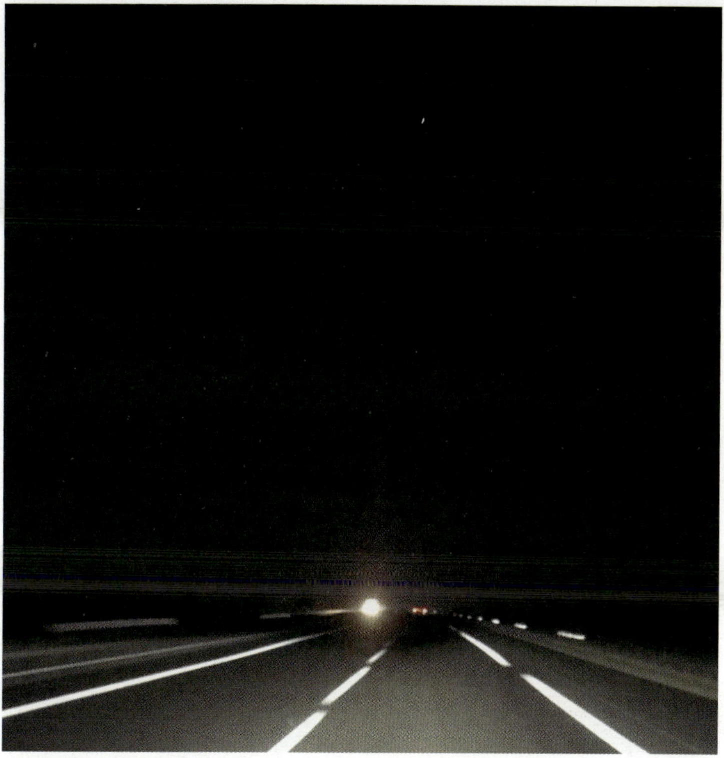

3139 likes

invaderwashere More than an artistic practice, my Space Invaders project is a real commitment, even a way of life. For over twenty years, my modus operandi has been to travel the world, invading it with my mosaics. #ontheroad

View all 28 comments

22 January 2016

invaderwashere

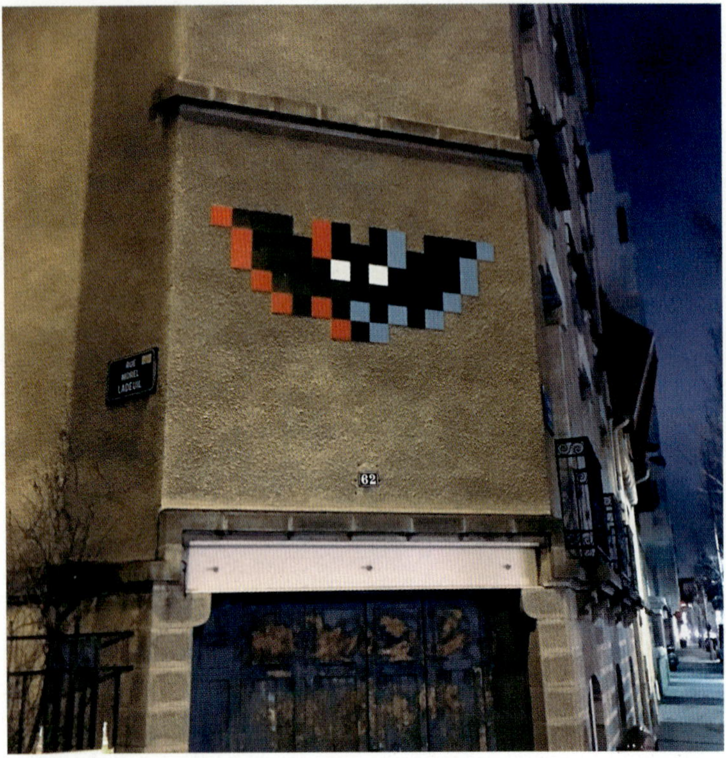

10 443 likes

invaderwashere 3D Bat-Invader!!!

View all 100 comments

24 January 2016

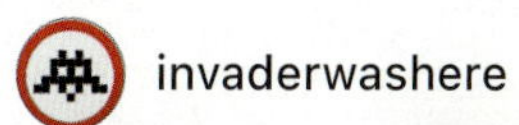

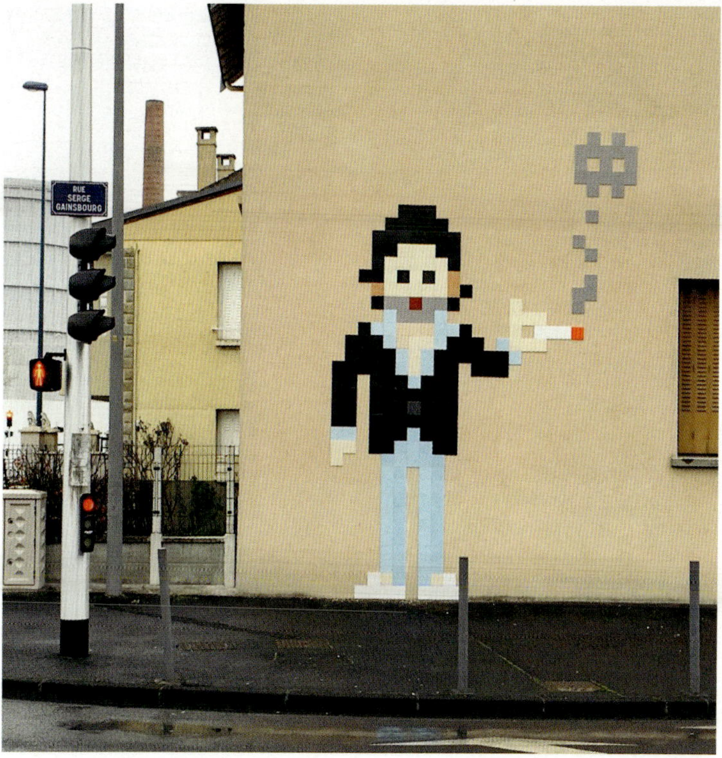

14 014 likes

invaderwashere Serge Gainsbourg is in the place!
#ruesergegainsbourg

View all 254 comments

24 January 2016

invaderwashere

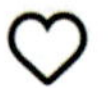   

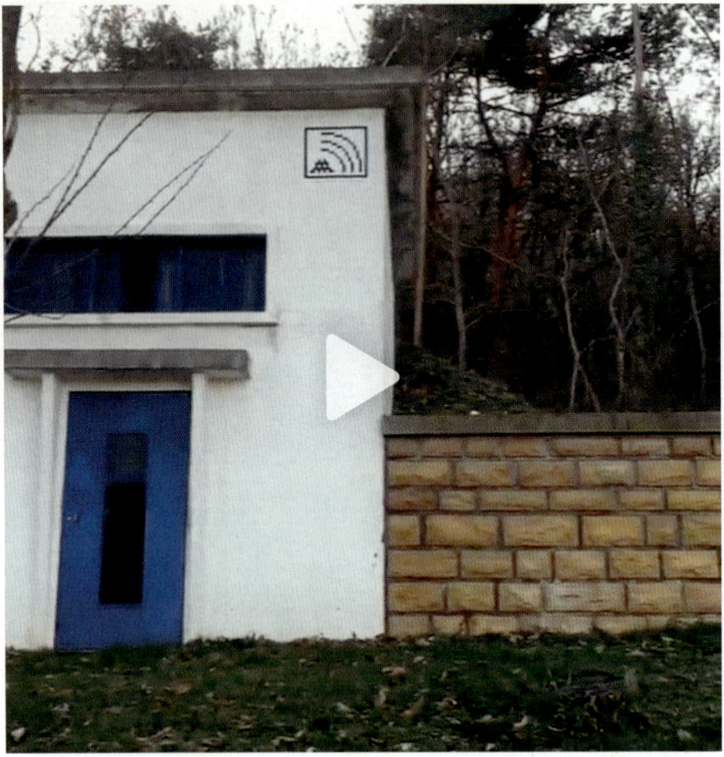

22 661 views

invaderwashere Well hidden... #forest

View all 41 comments

24 January 2016

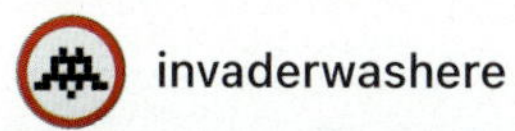

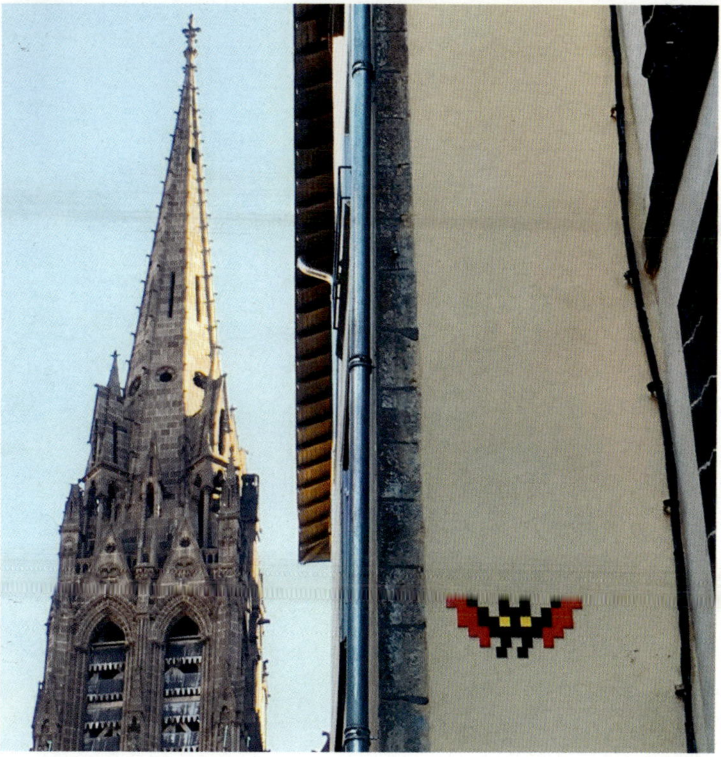

8 808 likes

invaderwashere Clermont Ferrand is a city located in the center of France. It is well known for its volcano black stone, its International short film festival and its gothic cathedral.

View all 81 comments

25 January 2016

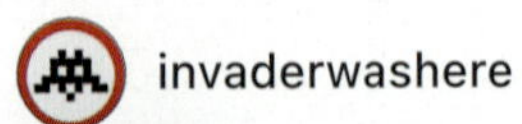

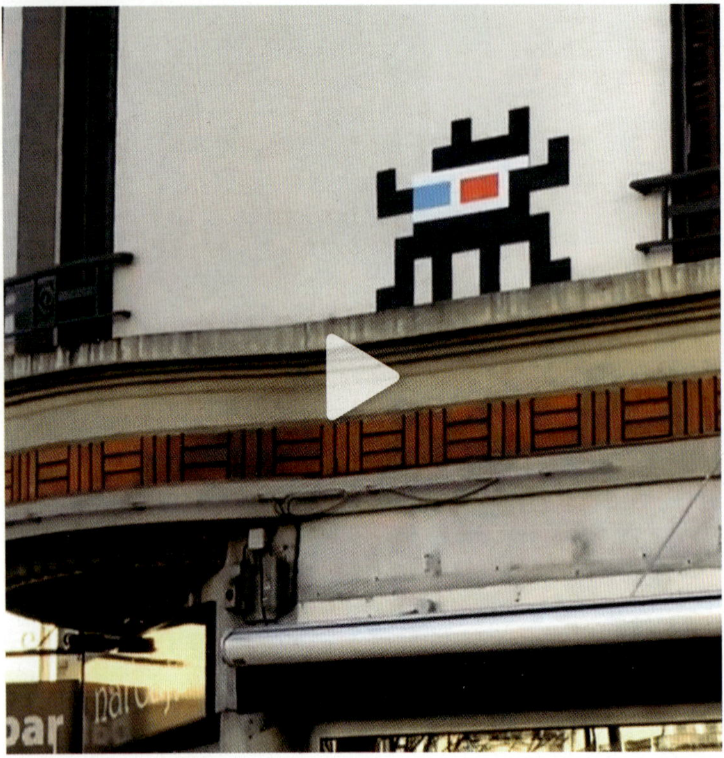

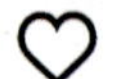   

27 940 views

invaderwashere 3D street scene #clermontferrand

View all 145 comments

25 January 2016

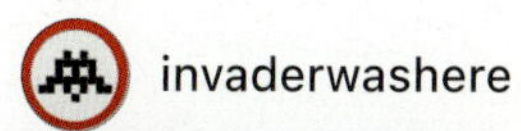

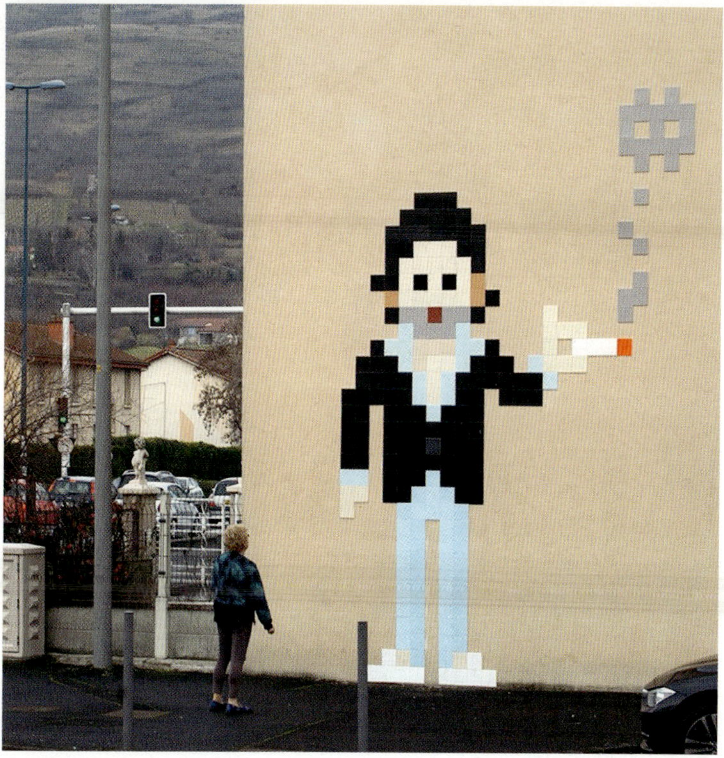

 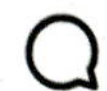  

12 217 likes

invaderwashere The owner of the house wondering what has happened on her wall during the night!!! #gainsbourg #ruesergegainsbourg #clermontferrand

View all 260 comments

25 January 2016

invaderwashere ...

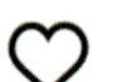  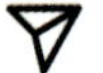 

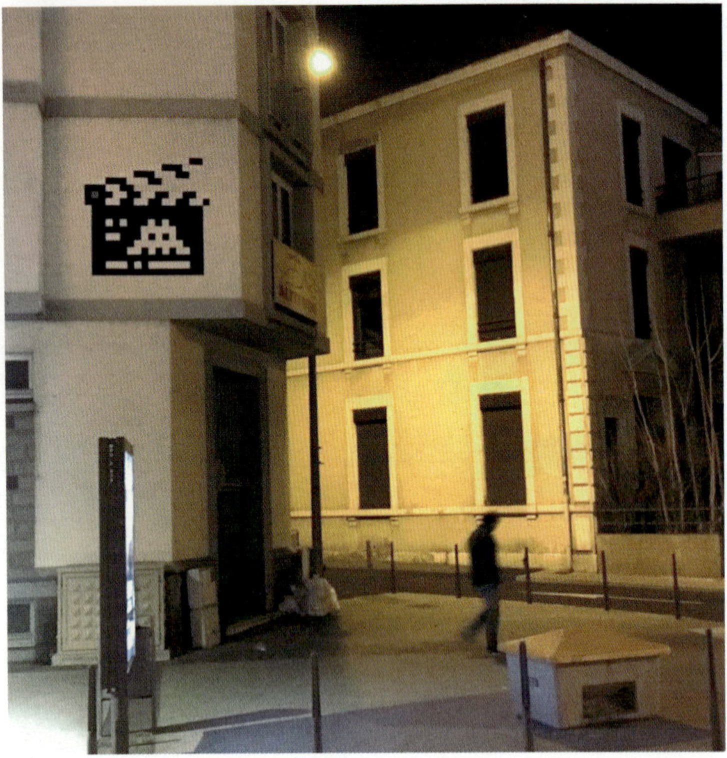

7 535 likes

invaderwashere Action! Just made in #clermontferrand

View all 40 comments

26 January 2016

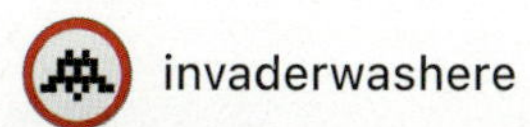

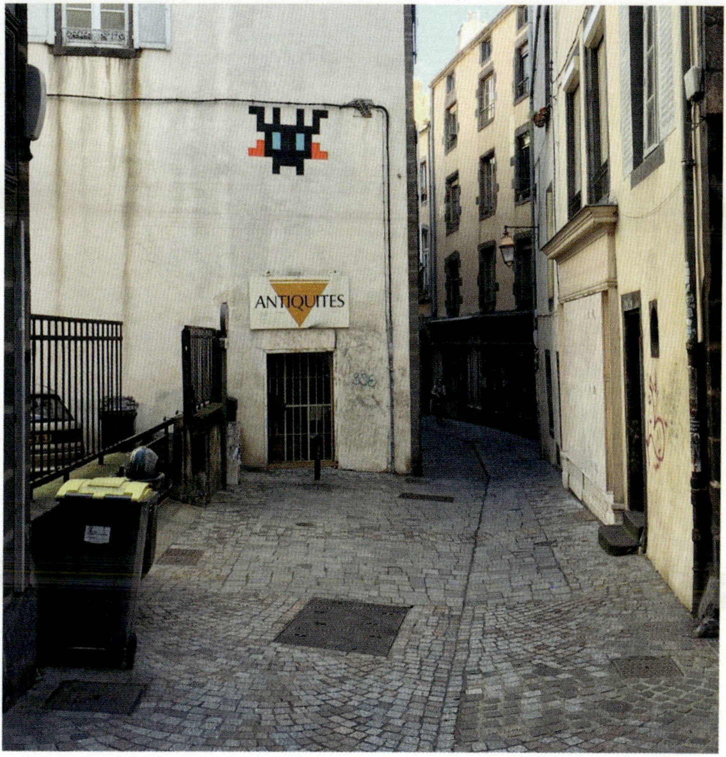

7142 likes

invaderwashere Bat-Invader #clermontferrand

View all 44 comments

26 January 2016

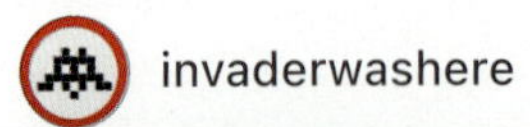

invaderwashere

  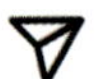 

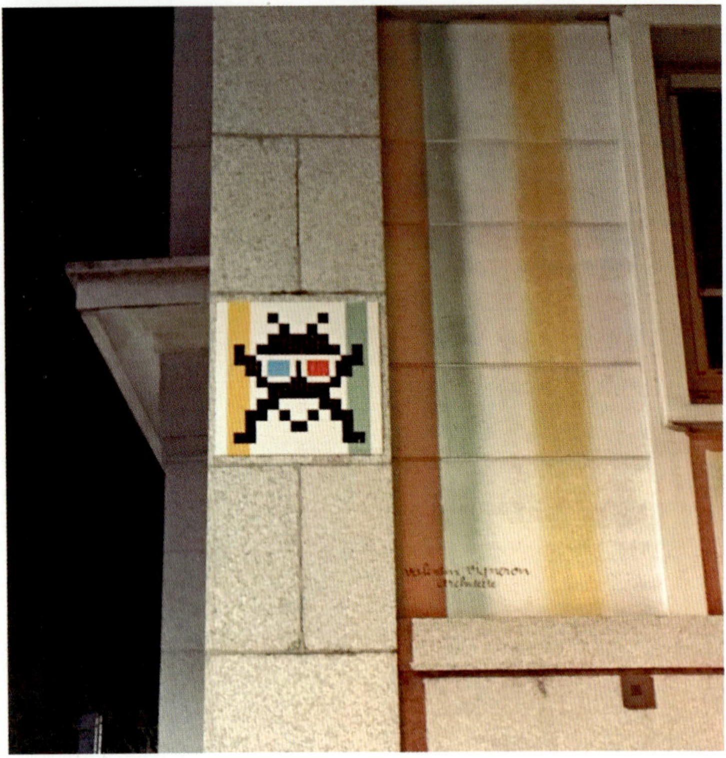

6 926 likes

invaderwashere Architectonic

View all 35 comments

27 January 2016

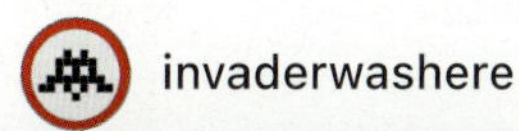

invaderwashere

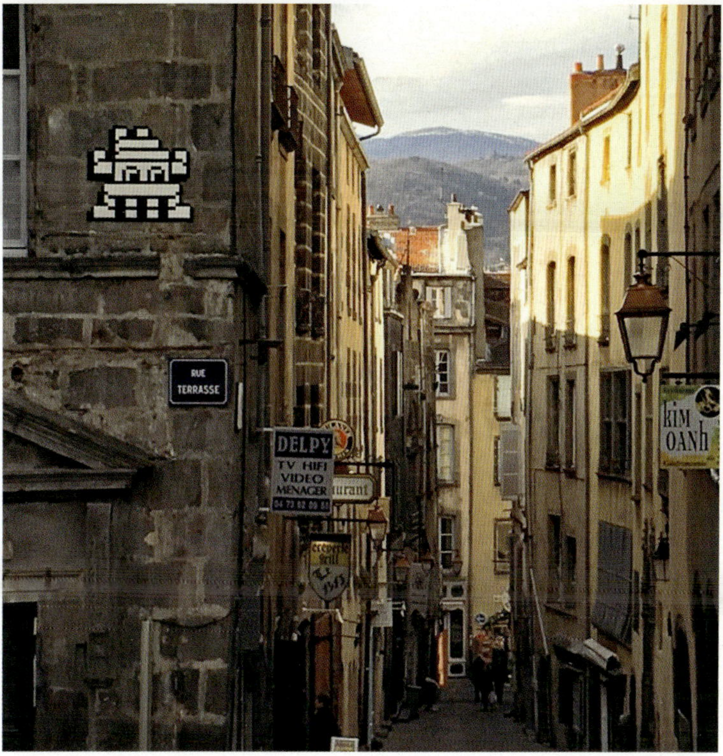

7751 likes

invaderwashere Bibendum style

View all 42 comments

27 January 2016

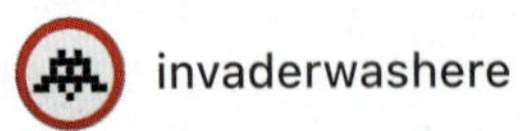

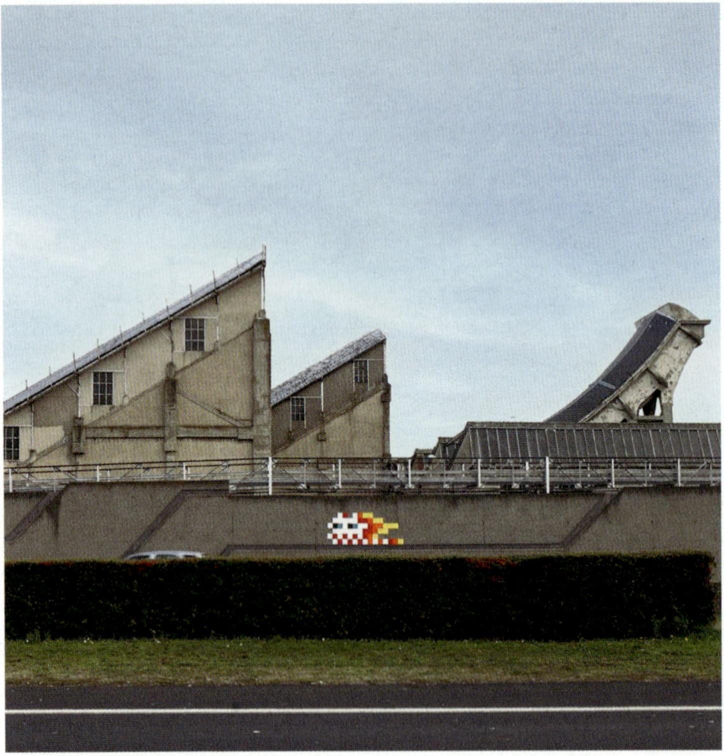

6700 likes

invaderwashere CLR_35 on the former Michelin's testing tracks wall #clermontferrand

View all 48 comments

28 January 2016

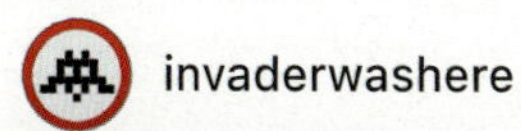

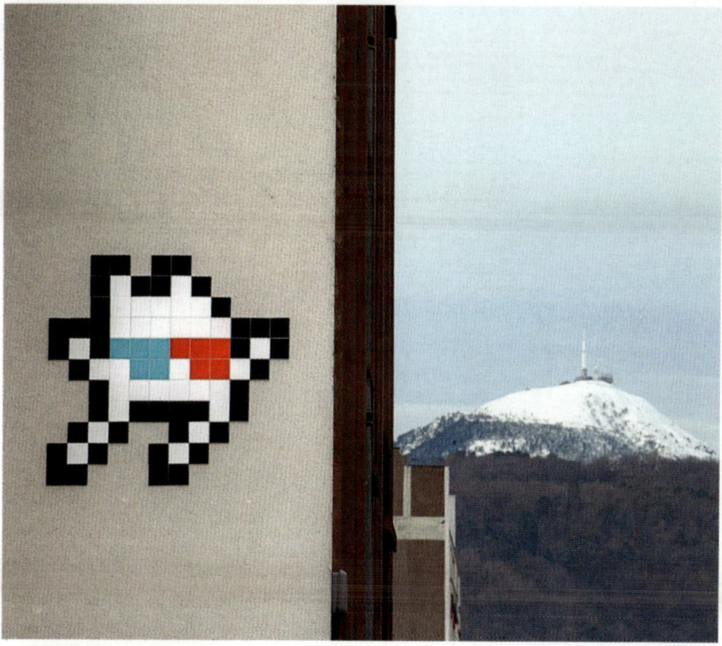

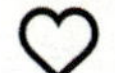 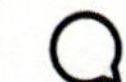  

7563 likes

invaderwashere Invasion of Clermont Ferrand successful more images on space-invaders.com #news #clermontferrand #puydedôme

View all 37 comments

2 February 2016

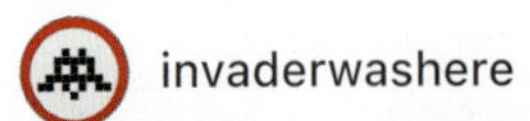

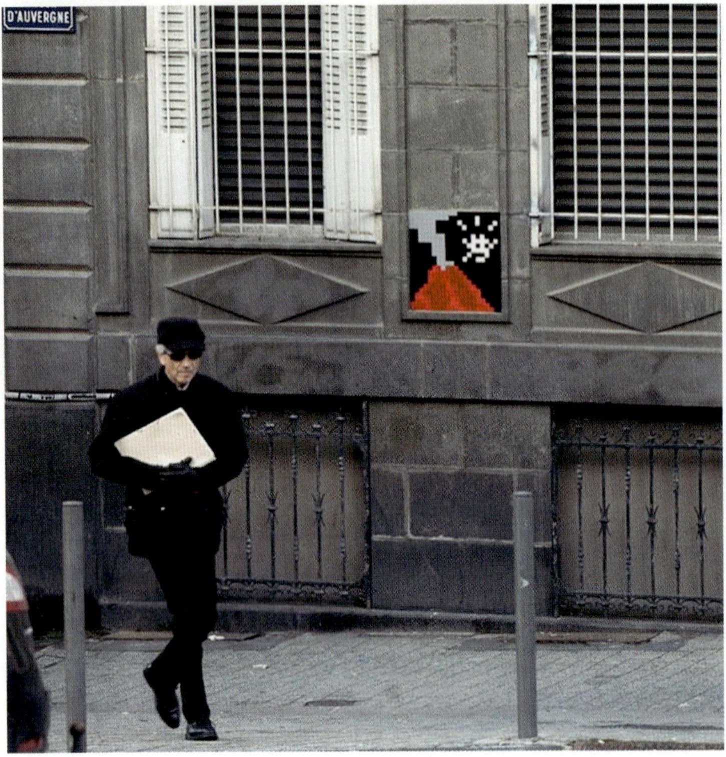

 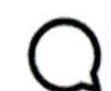  

6 287 likes

invaderwashere CLR_39

View all 26 comments

2 February 2016

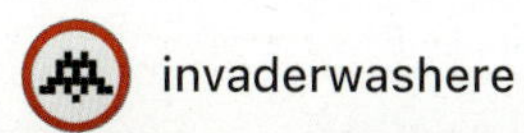

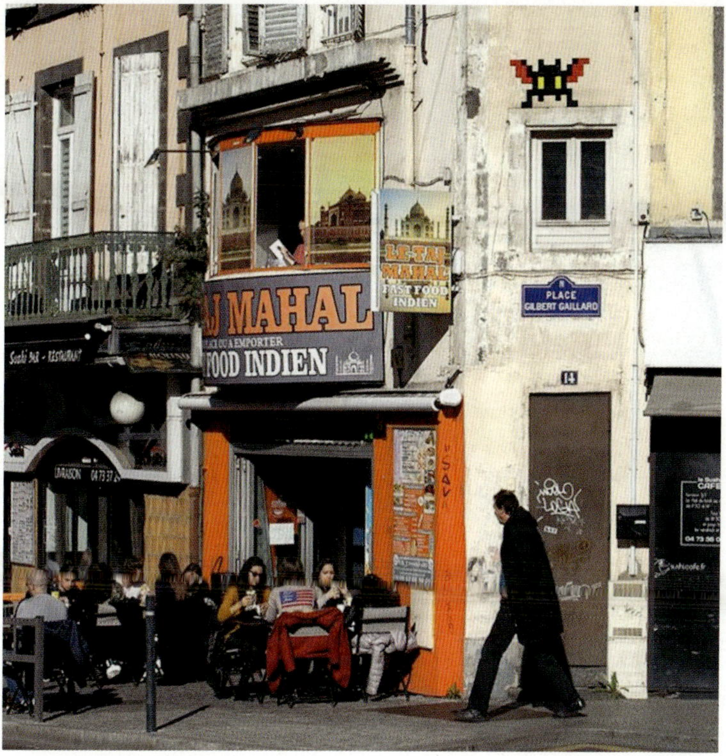

5 547 likes

invaderwashere Vampire of Clermont Ferrand / space-invaders.com #news

View all 17 comments

2 February 2016

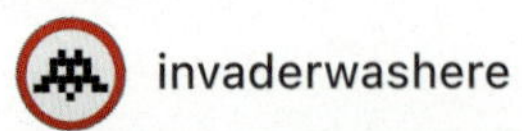

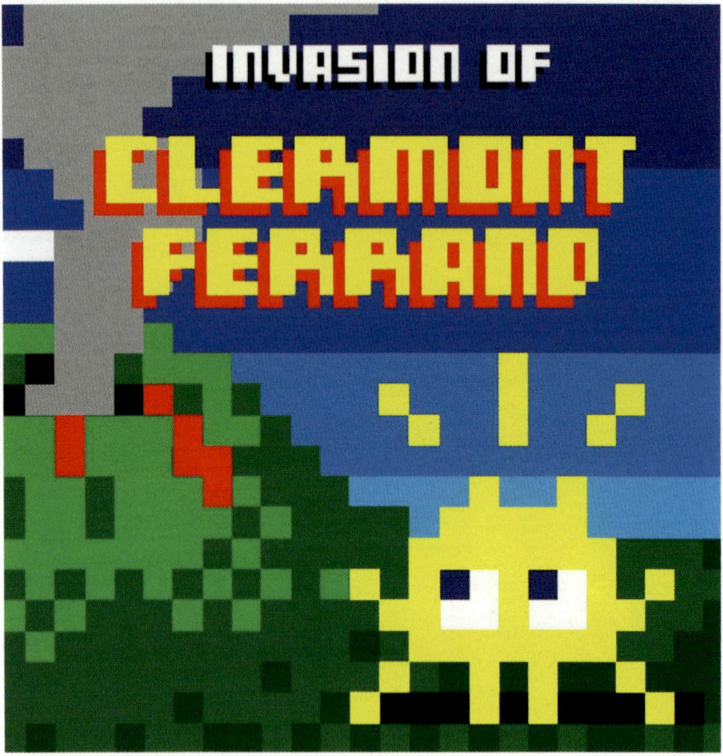

 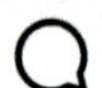  

3230 likes

invaderwashere Invasion of Clermont Ferrand completed / Waves: 03 SpaceInvaders: 39 Score: 1480 Pts.

View all 36 comments

3 February 2016

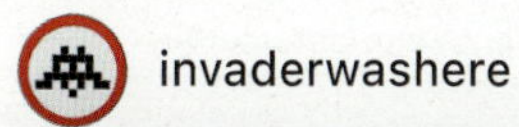

CLERMONT
FERRAND 2016
SHORT FILM FESTIVAL

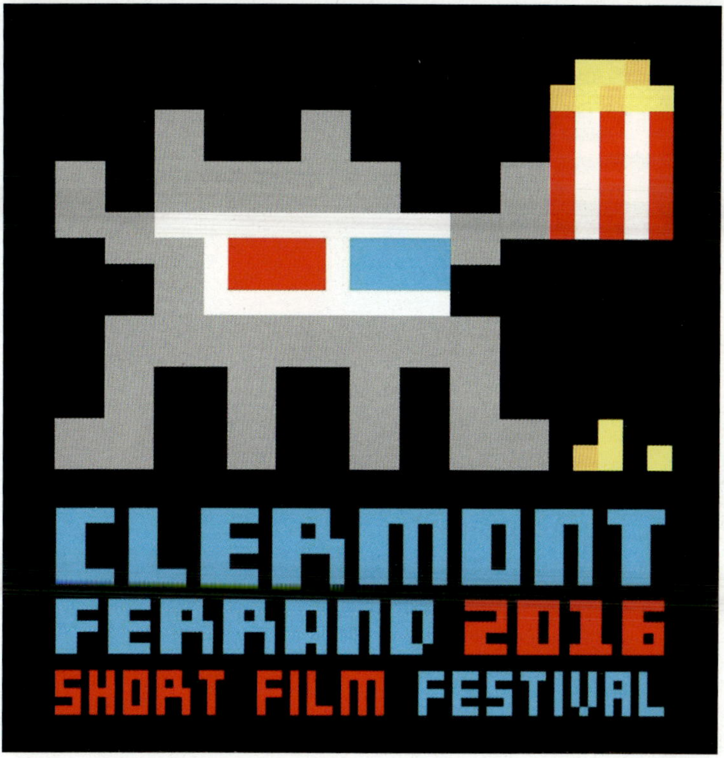

3 272 likes

invaderwashere Art4Space will be screened everyday, from today to next Friday, at the International Short Film Festival of Clermont Ferrand #art4space @clermontfilmfest

View all 22 comments

6 February 2016

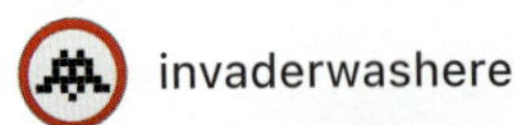

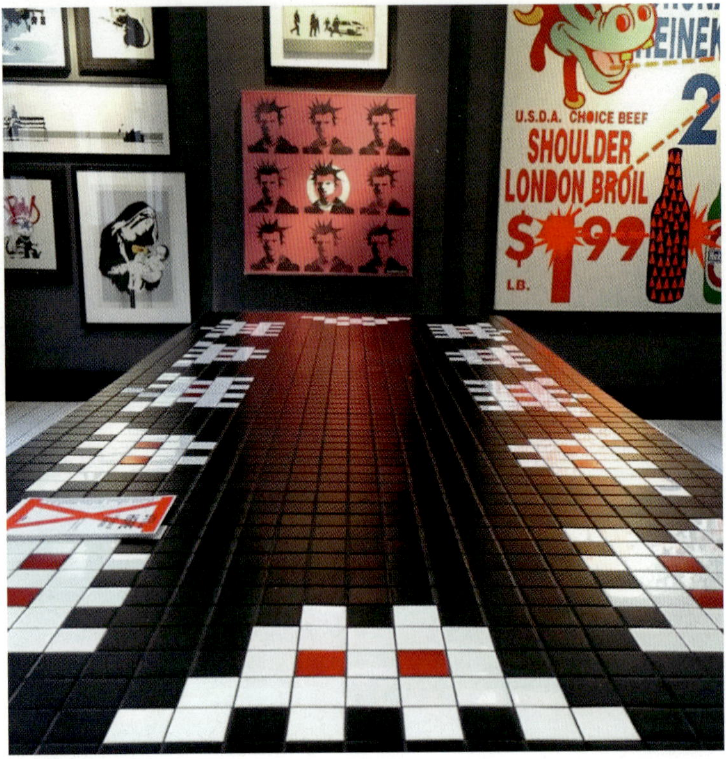

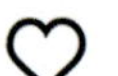   

5899 likes

invaderwashere A decade of Lazarides #groupshow @lazarides #london #table #notforsale regram from @_ekap_

View all 31 comments

14 February 2016

invaderwashere

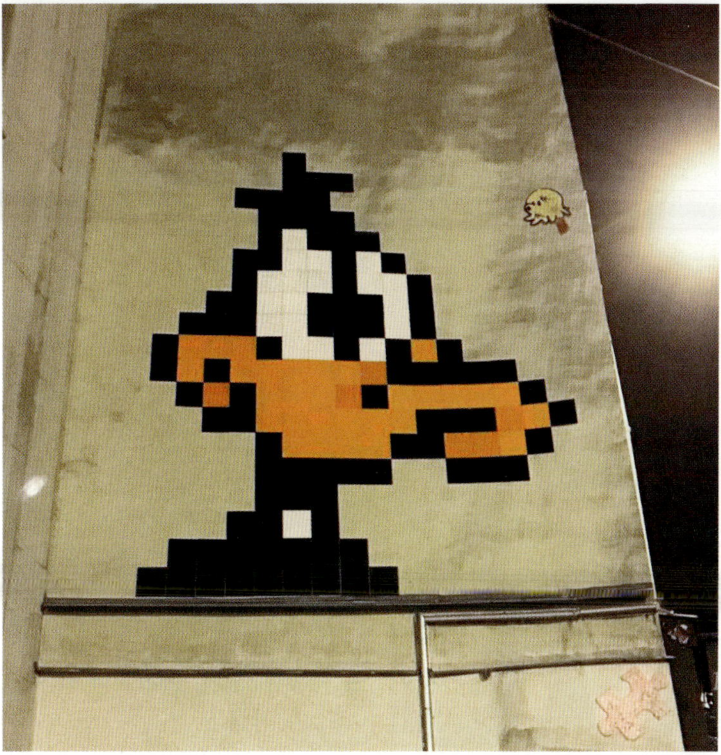

12 522 likes

invaderwashere Paris 3:53 am #justdone #Daffy #big

View all 150 comments

18 February 2016

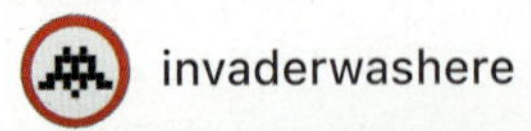

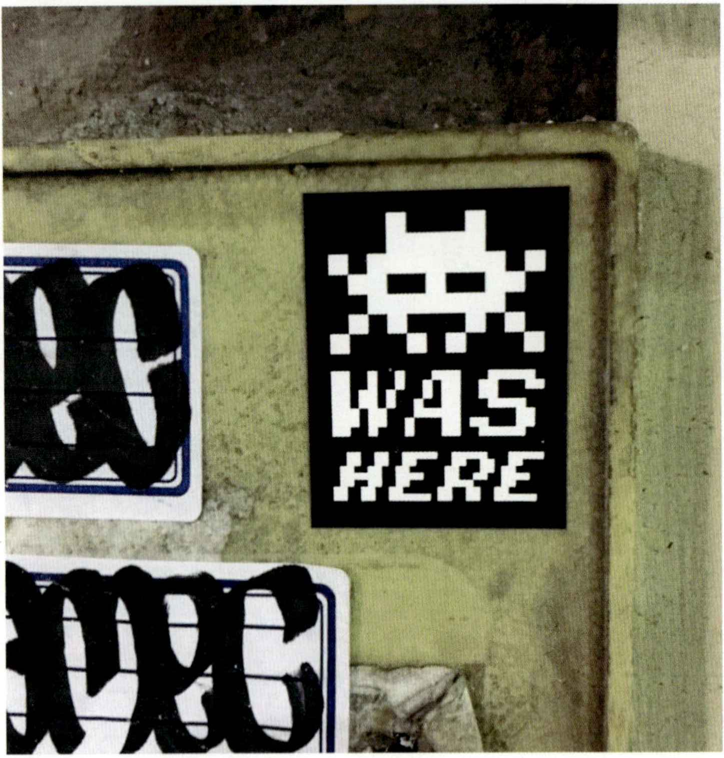

 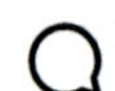  

7834 likes

invaderwashere InvaderWasHere!!!

View all 29 comments

22 February 2016

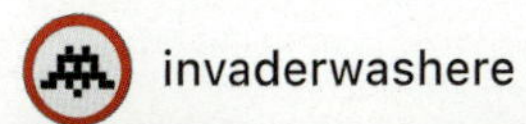

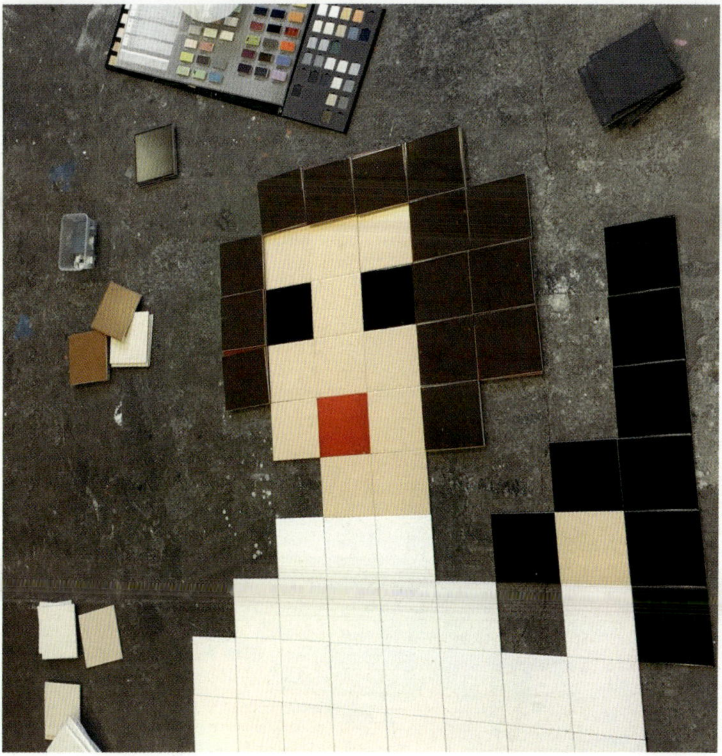

8 467 likes

invaderwashere Making of princess Leia ✨ #studiodetail

View all 82 comments

24 February 2016

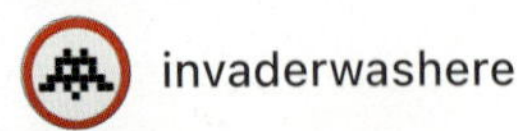

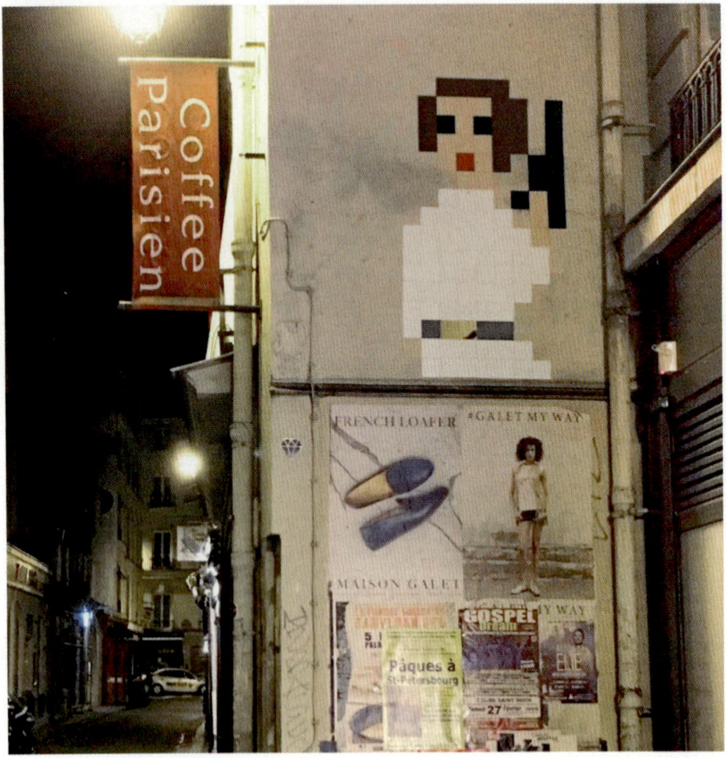

12 017 likes

invaderwashere 5:12 am / rue princesse / Paris

View all 231 comments

24 February 2016

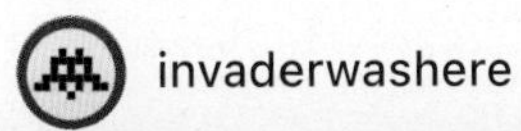

invaderwashere •••

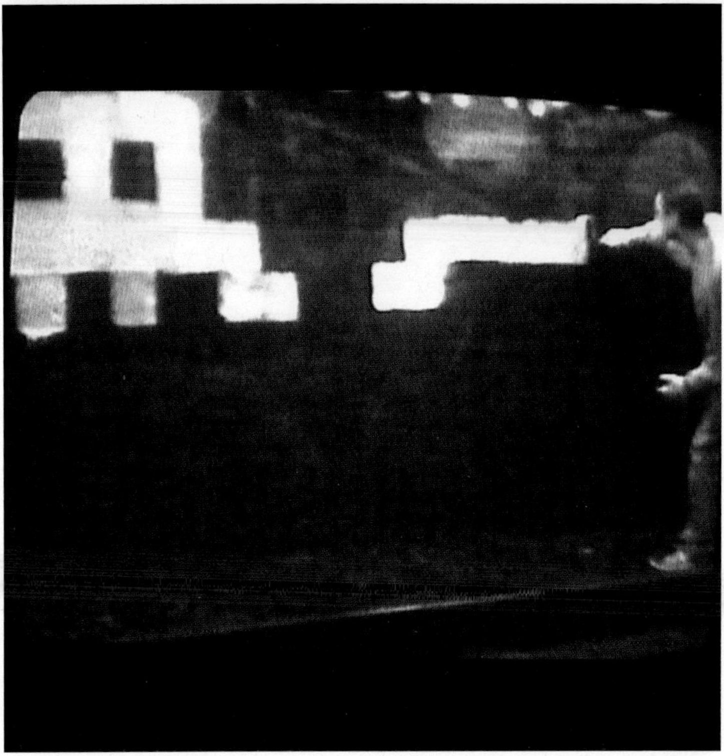

5133 likes

invaderwashere #throwback #Paris #1999 #subway #tunnels #underground #roller #fatPen shot by #oclock

View all 37 comments

3 March 2016

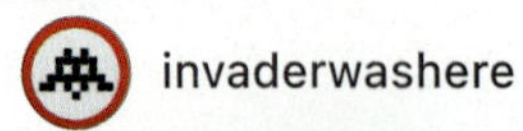
invaderwashere

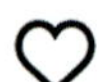   

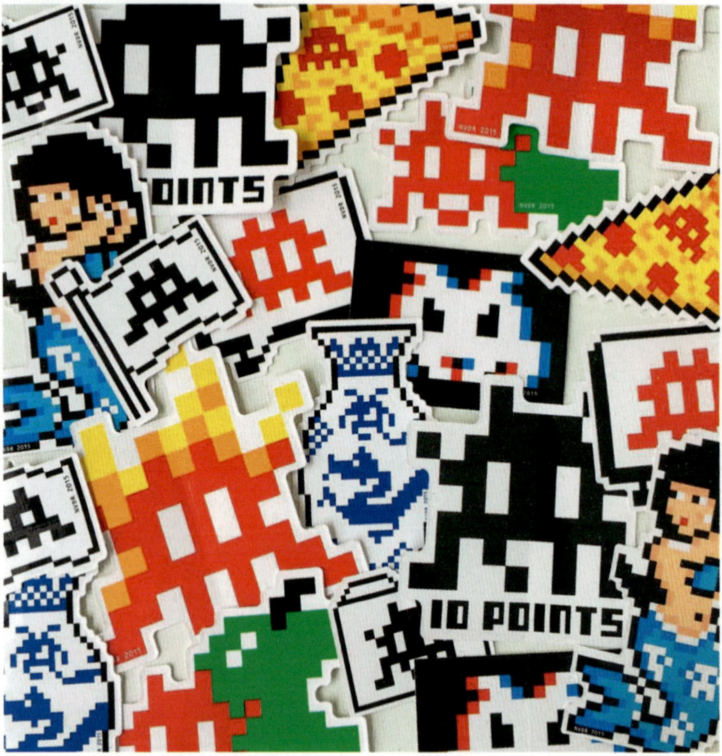

7846 likes

invaderwashere I've always thought of my stickers as little works of art. I've just created a new set, soon available online, stay tuned... #silkscreened #stickers

View all 85 comments

5 March 2016

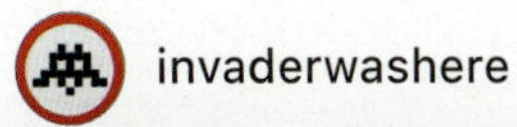

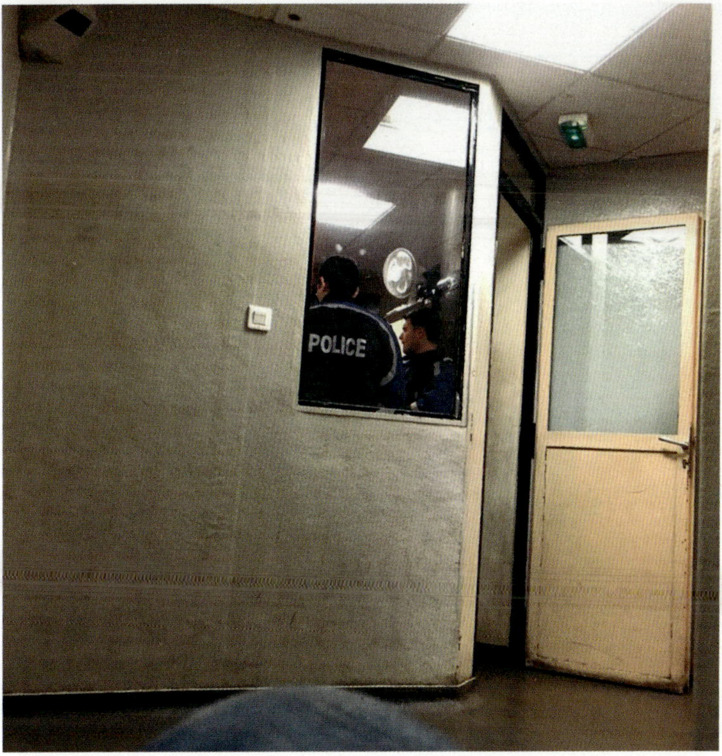

7529 likes

invaderwashere Wrong move! Street art is like Monopoly you sometimes end up in the "go to jail" corner space. But no worries, I'm out now 😁

View all 189 comments

10 March 2016

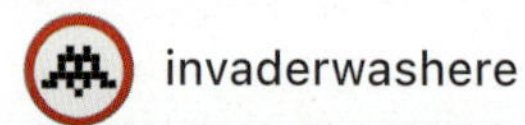

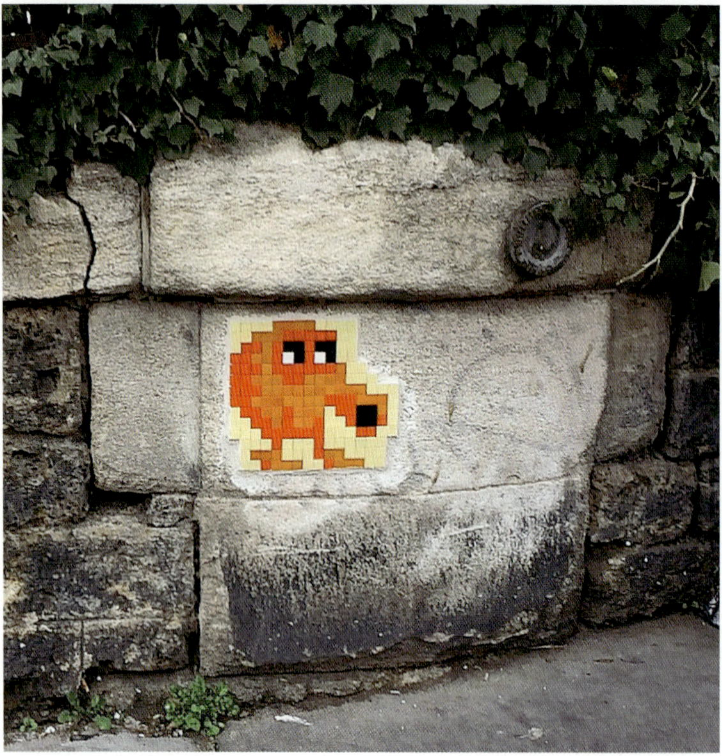

9 277 likes

invaderwashere PA_307 : One of the numerous reactivations in Paris, Tokyo, LA etc... Thank you guys 👍🙏👏👍🙏👏 #reactivationTeam #flashers #flashinvaders

View all 94 comments

11 March 2016

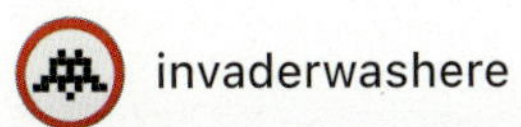
invaderwashere

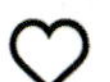 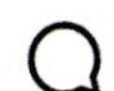  

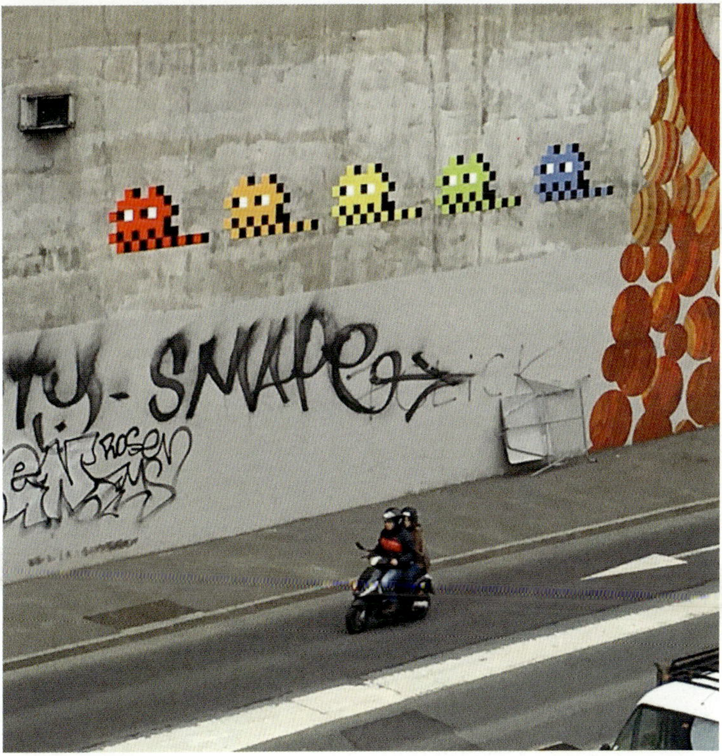

9 552 likes

invaderwashere Fresh from last night!!! 🌞 🏍️ 👫 ❄️
#paris #autoroutedusoleil #rideintothesun

View all 95 comments

16 March 2016

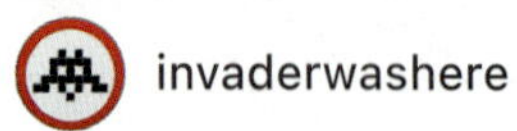

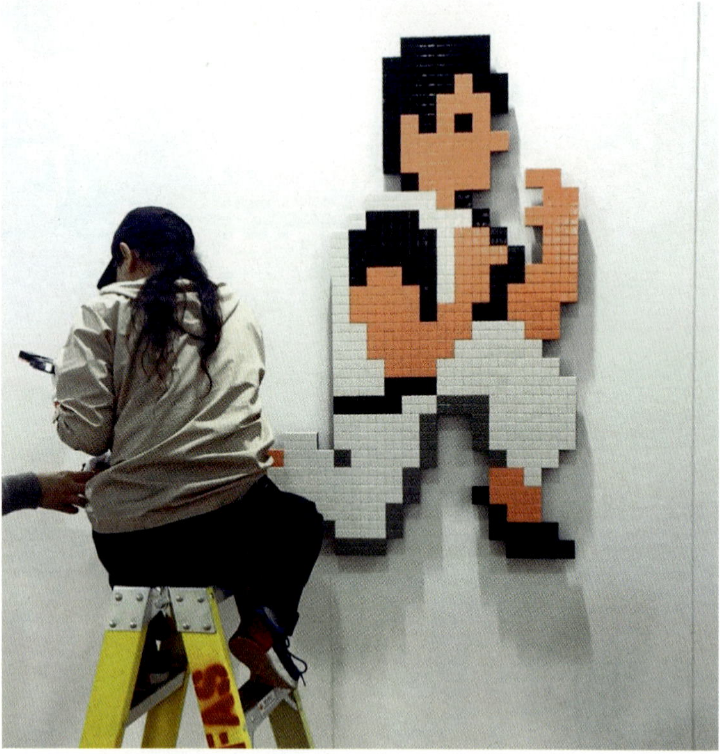

8 828 likes

invaderwashere Over The Influence installing booth B14 at Art Cental in Hong Kong #Alias #Aliases #artcentral #artfair #soloShow @overtheinfluence_hk

View all 105 comments

20 March 2016

invaderwashere

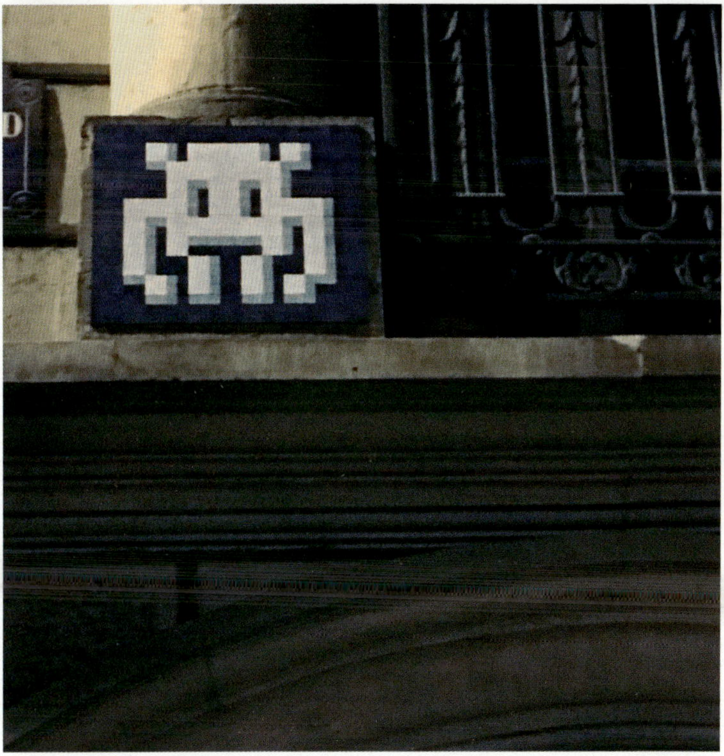

6631 likes

invaderwashere PA_1198 from last night #Paris #artdeco #spaceinvader

View all 25 comments

23 March 2016

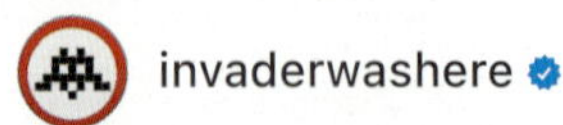

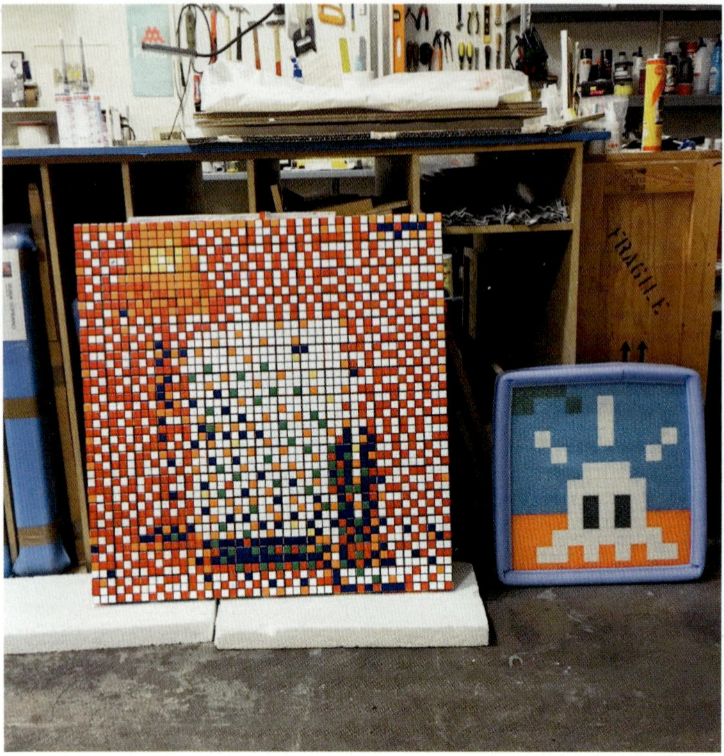

5960 likes

invaderwashere 10:15 on a Sunday night at the studio / Rubik three imaginary boys & Mia_12 #rubikubism #lowfidelity #Alias #studio

View all 48 comments

28 March 2016

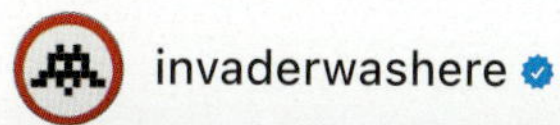

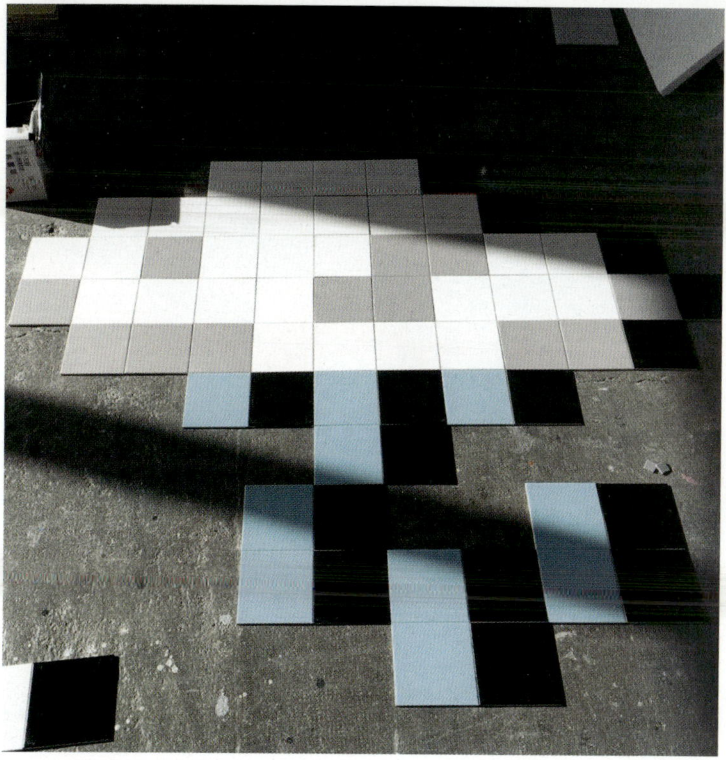

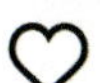   

5459 likes

invaderwashere Preparing the next city invasion
#itgonnarain

View all 20 comments

29 March 2016

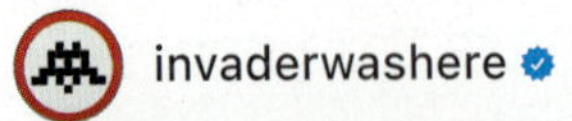

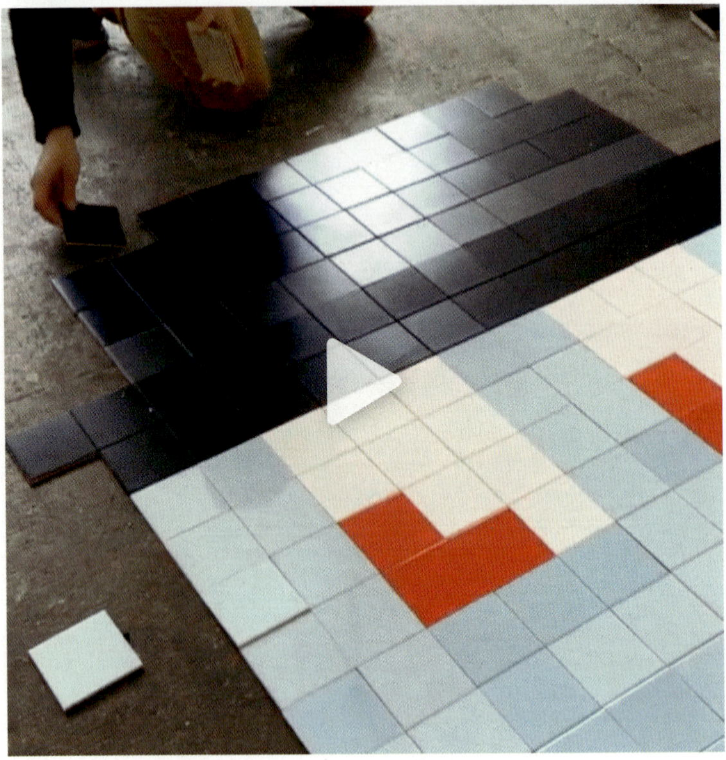

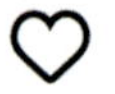   

42 292 views

invaderwashere Clandestine pixel factory!!!

View all 52 comments

30 March 2016

invaderwashere

 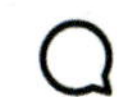  

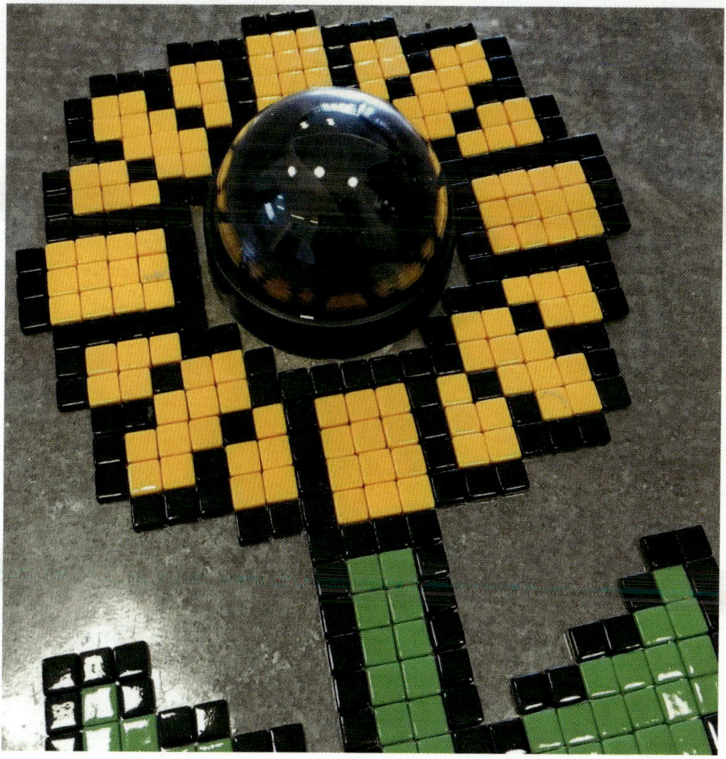

8 391 likes

invaderwashere Working on CCTV flowers, soon in the streets... #bigbrotheriswatchingyou

View all 105 comments

31 March 2016

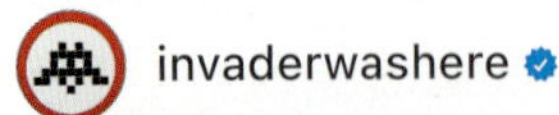

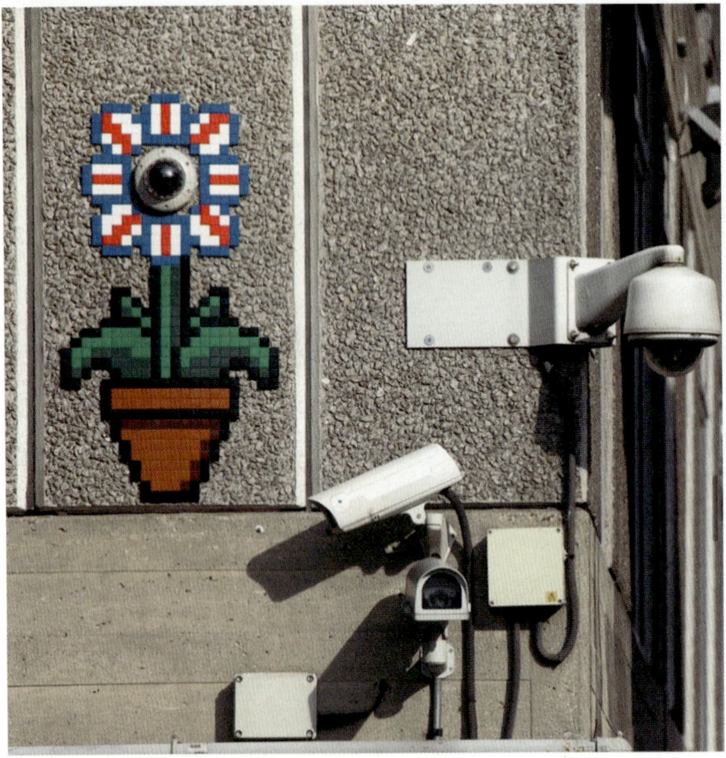

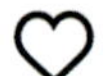   

12 869 likes

invaderwashere One of the 12 new pieces in London! #wave18 #invasionoflondon 1999-2016 #cctvFlower #thisislondon

View all 152 comments

2 April 2016

invaderwashere

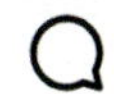

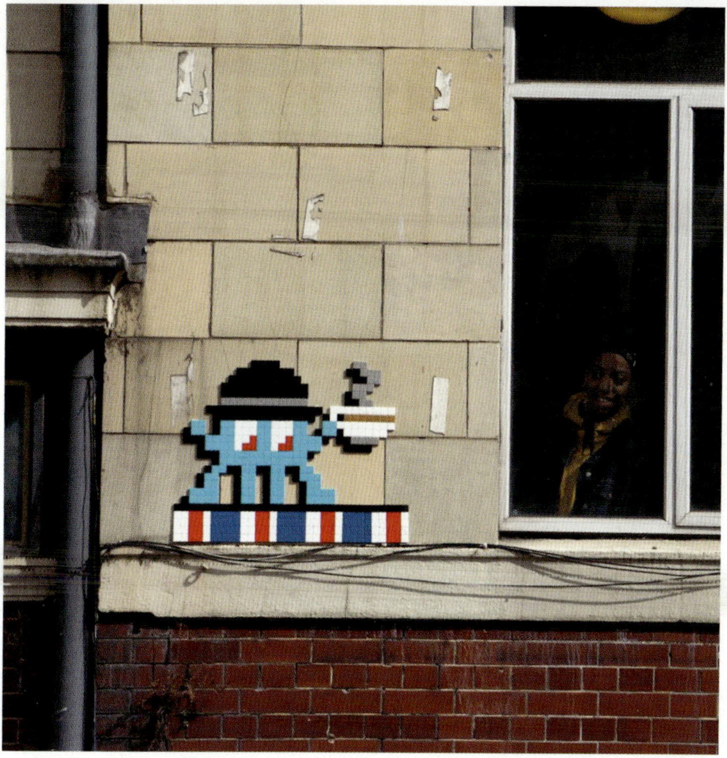

10 334 likes

invaderwashere Tea time! New piece in #london

View all 100 comments

3 April 2016

invaderwashere ...

  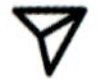 

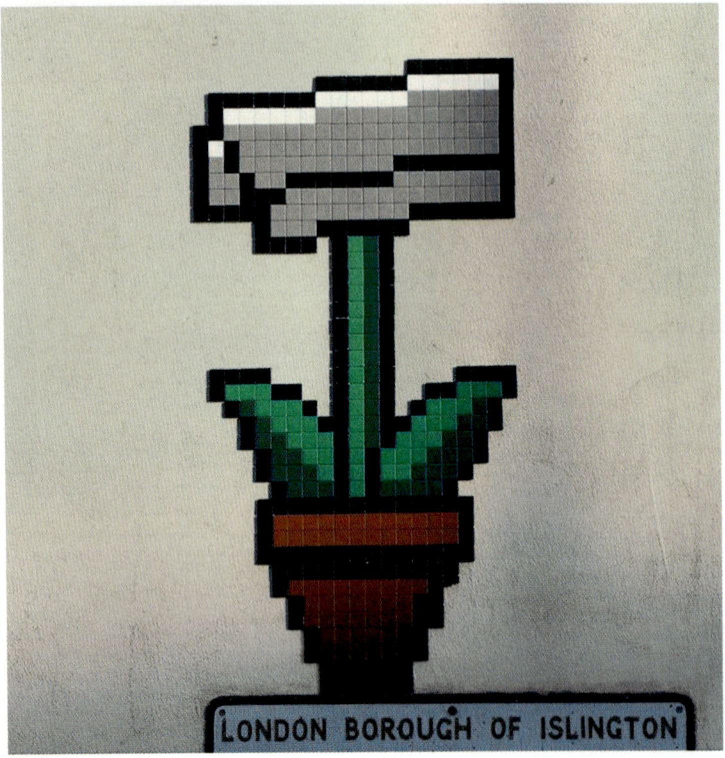

8 222 likes

invaderwashere An other CCTV flower in London

View all 42 comments

3 April 2016

invaderwashere

 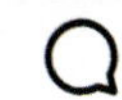  

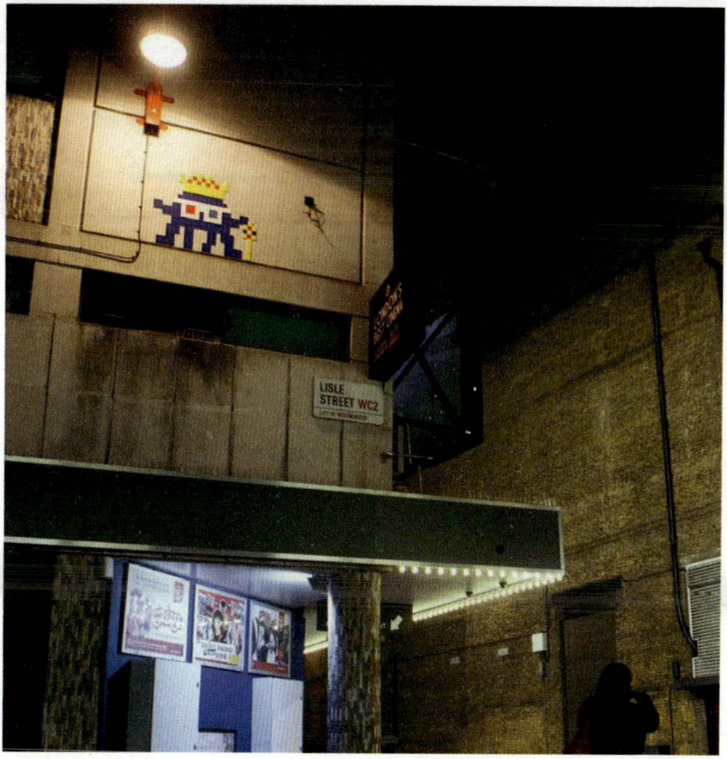

6 234 likes

invaderwashere LDN_143 on the Prince Charles Cinema 👑 Thank you #londongamesfestival for the spot and @globalstreetart for the help and the ladder #london #invasion

View all 22 comments

4 April 2016

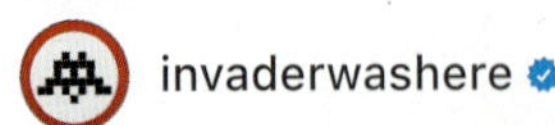

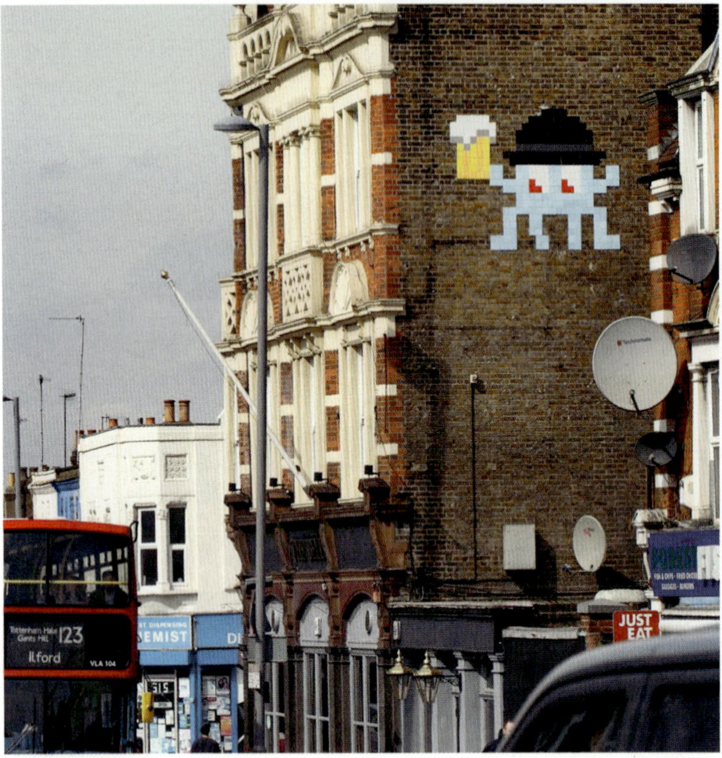

9920 likes

invaderwashere Beer time! Big thanx to @londongamesfest @woodstreetwalls and #giveartistsspace #walthamstow #london

View all 117 comments

4 April 2016

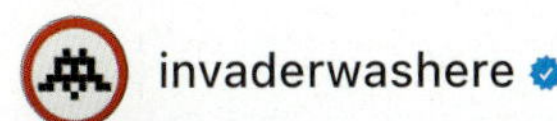

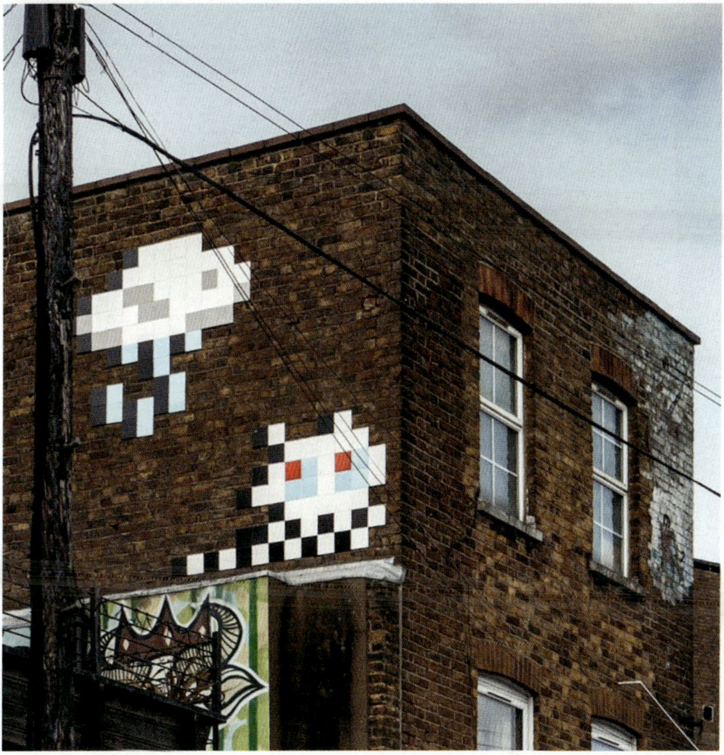

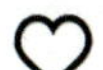 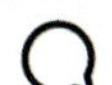  

7406 likes

invaderwashere Rainy London... Time to leave #london #2016

View all 58 comments

6 April 2016

invaderwashere

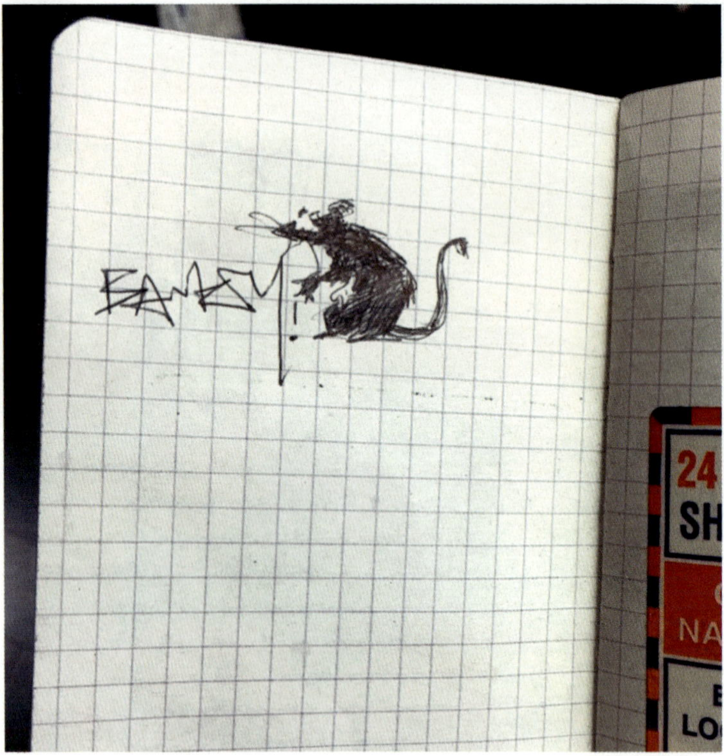

10 033 likes

invaderwashere I have just found back this little rat in my old "London invasion notebook" #throwback #london #archives #b

View all 122 comments

7 April 2016

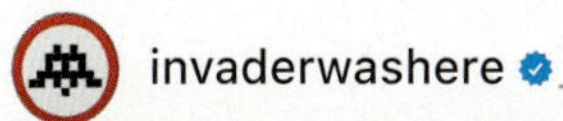

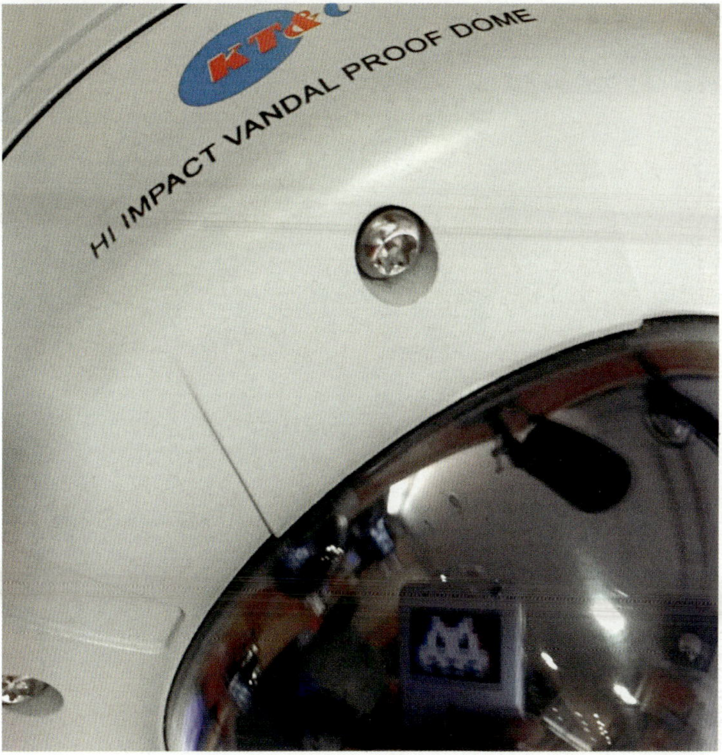

   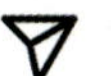 

3 253 likes

invaderwashere Eye of a CCTV flower #studiodetail

View all 21 comments

7 April 2016

invaderwashere ...

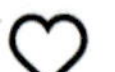   

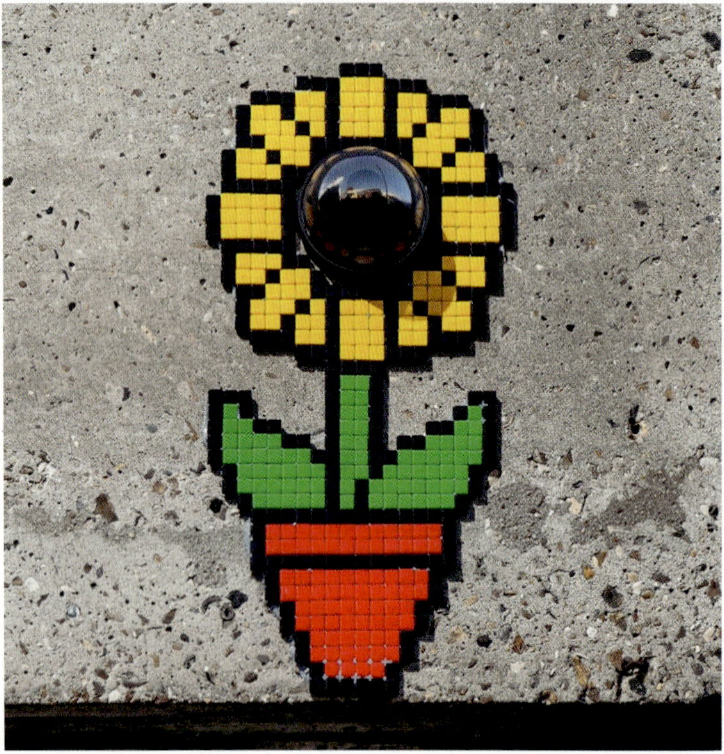

10 070 likes

invaderwashere London is full of CCTV cameras. They're ubiquitous on the streets, so I decided to incorporate them into my pieces. LDN_145 #viciousflower #bigbrotheriswatchingyou

View all 97 comments

7 April 2016

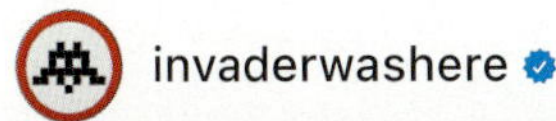

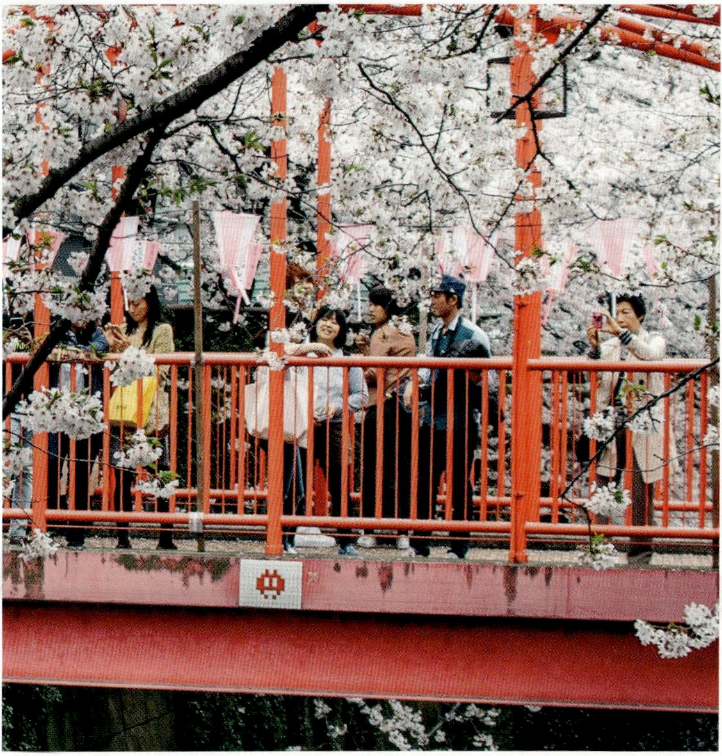

7033 likes

invaderwashere Sakura & TK_96 #tokyo photo by @nalice_malice

View all 73 comments

8 April 2016

invaderwashere

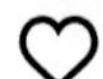   

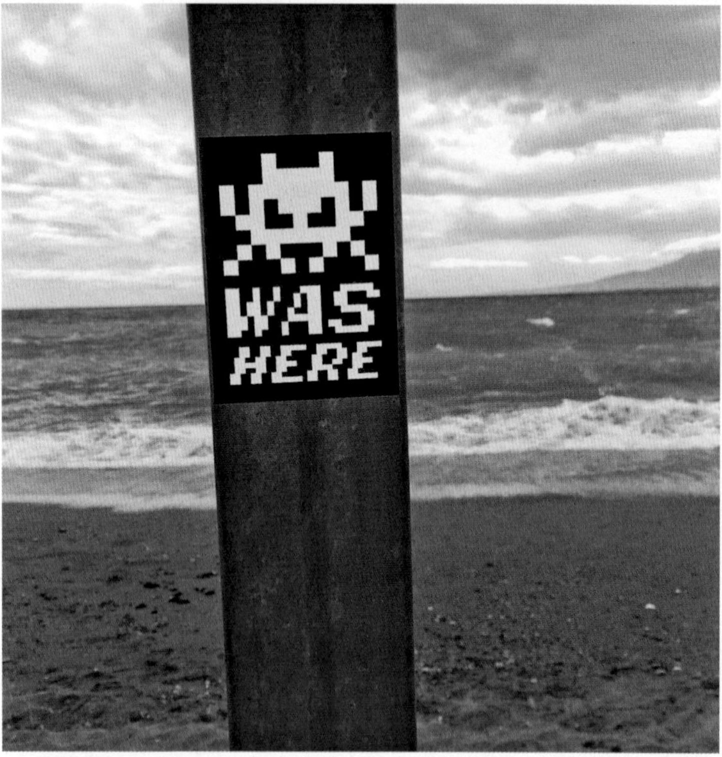

8 836 likes

invaderwashere Scouting in a new city #somewhere

View all 80 comments

10 April 2016

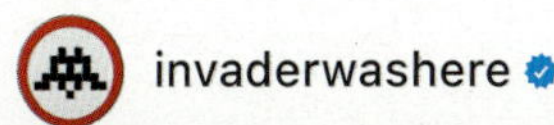

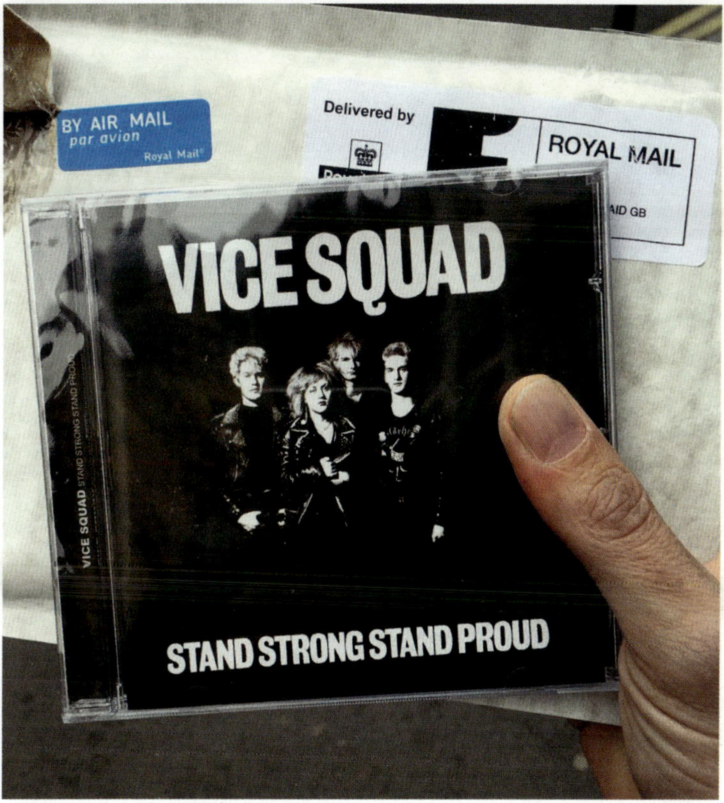

1923 likes

invaderwashere #mailbox Vice Squad was founded by the songwriter and vocalist #bekiBondage in 1978 #punkrock

View all 36 comments

12 April 2016

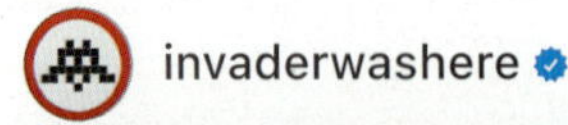

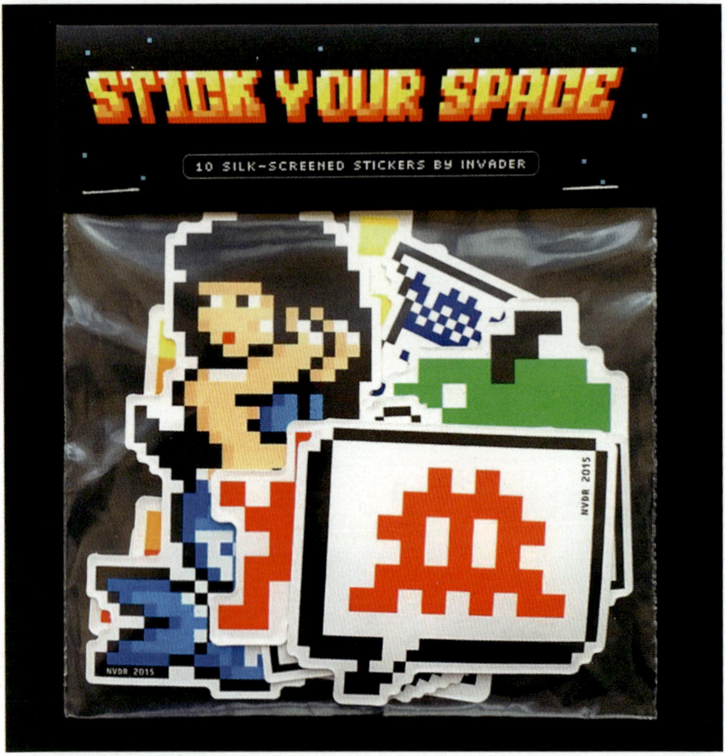

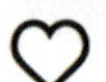   

5384 likes

invaderwashere New #stickers online now

View all 148 comments

18 April 2016

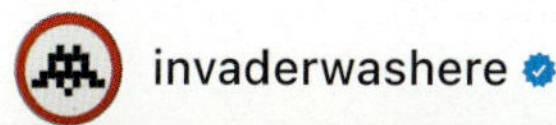

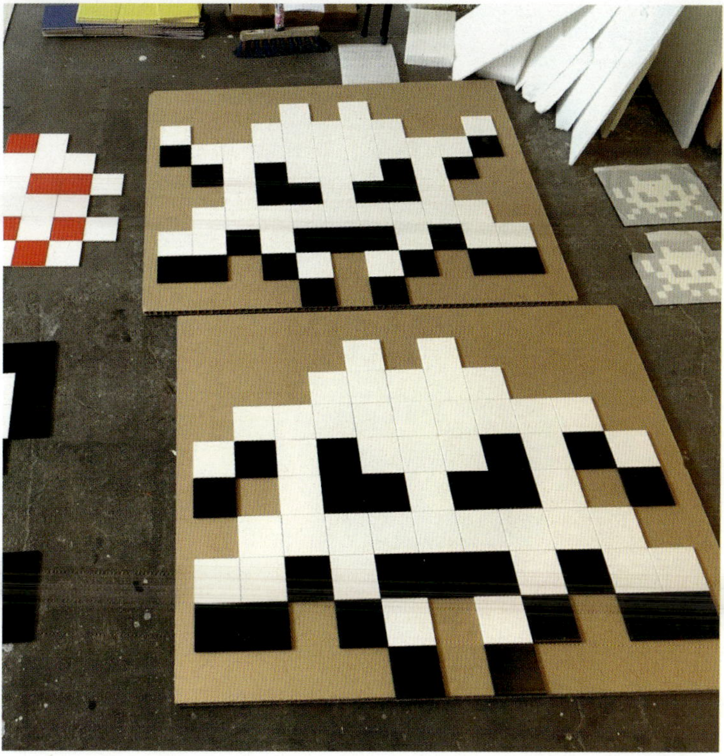

7 551 likes

invaderwashere Soon on Earth...

View all 68 comments

26 April 2016

invaderwashere

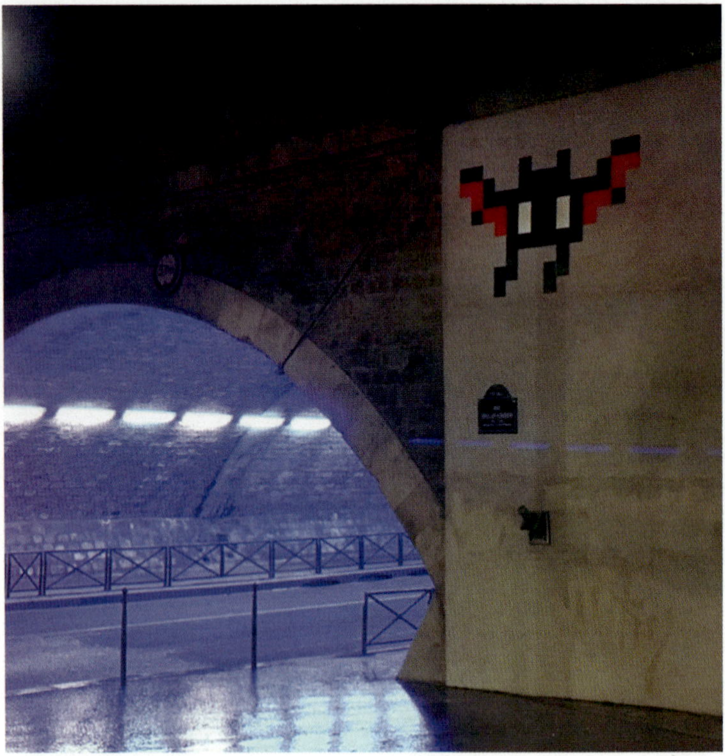

8820 likes

invaderwashere PA_1199 A bat is born! #batinvader #justborn #paris

View all 71 comments

27 April 2016

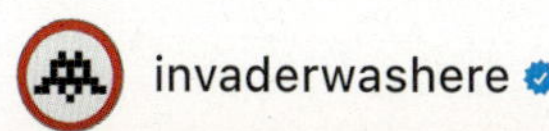

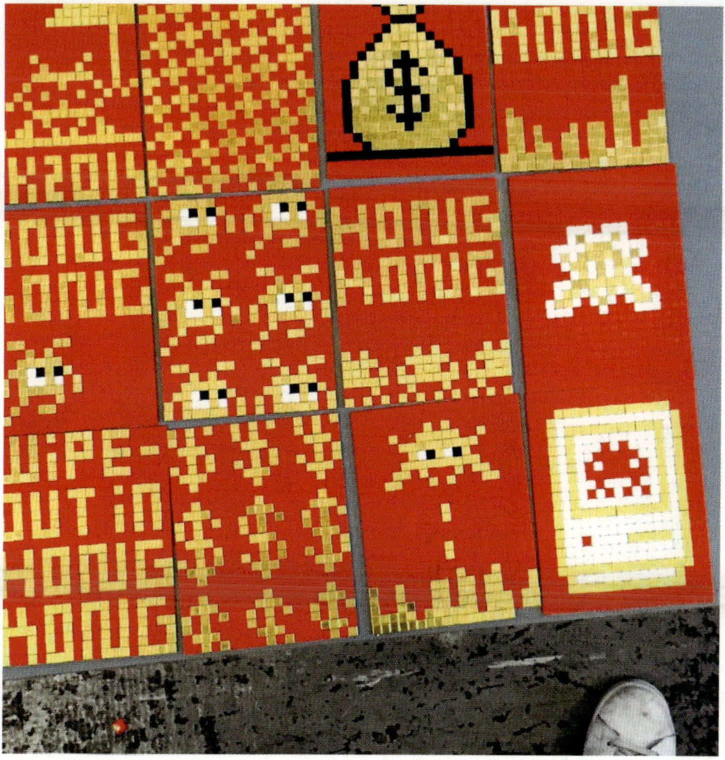

7057 likes

invaderwashere Preparing the mosaic covers for WipeOut in Hong Kong book #throwback #2015

View all 64 comments

3 May 2016

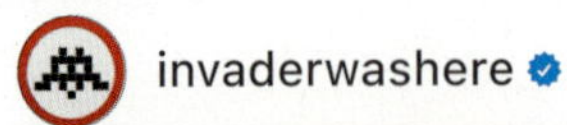

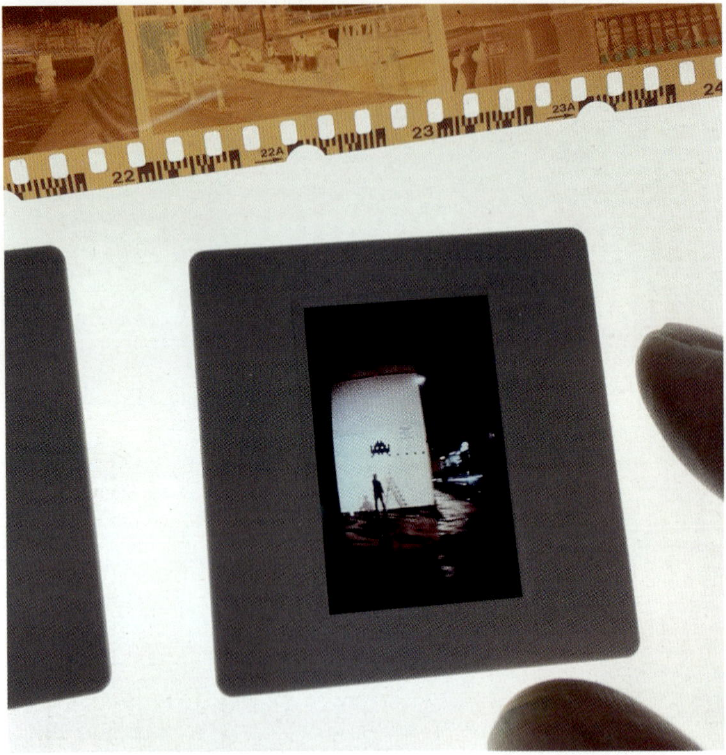

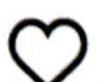  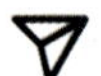 

3 368 likes

invaderwashere Scanning archives

View all 14 comments

3 May 2016

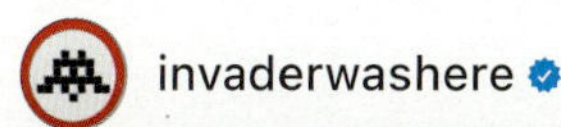

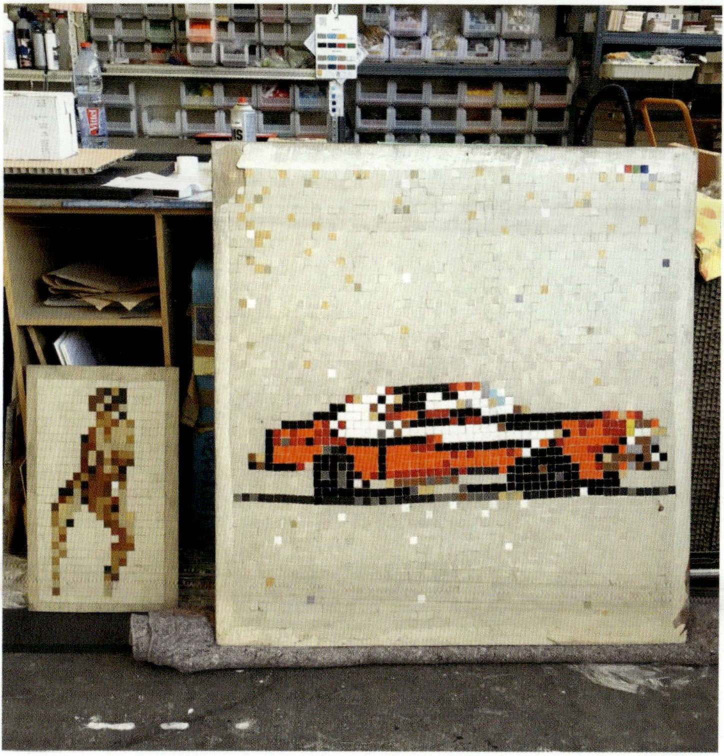

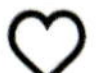

7364 likes

invaderwashere Found back those antiquities from 1997!
#lostArt #19yearsOld

View all 53 comments

4 May 2016

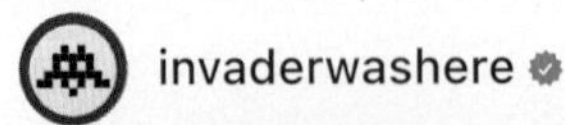

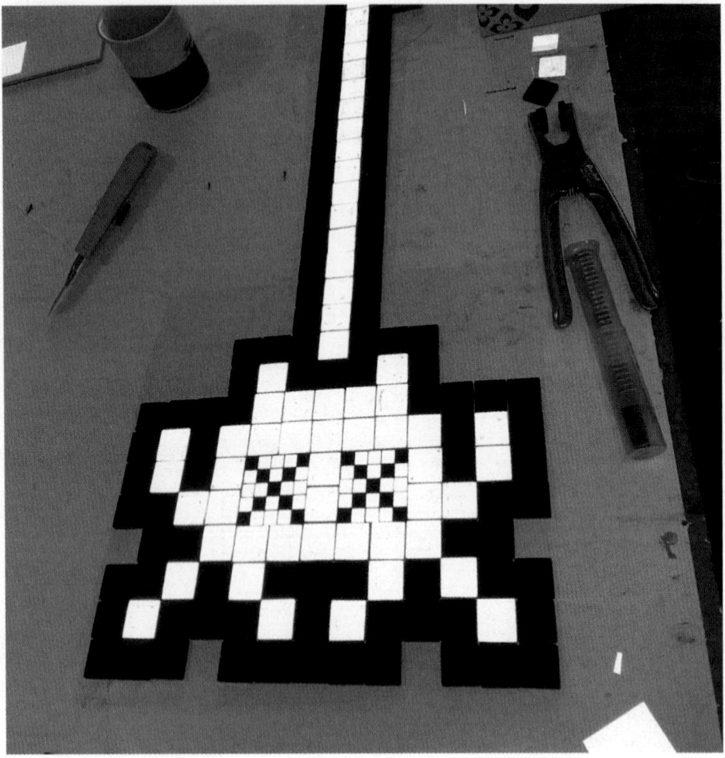

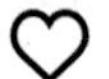   

8624 likes

invaderwashere Hanged invader with reflective tiles for the next city invasion

View all 55 comments

12 May 2016

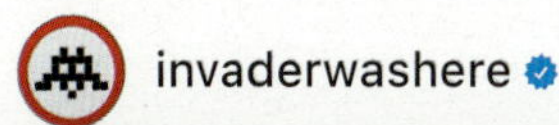

11 226 likes

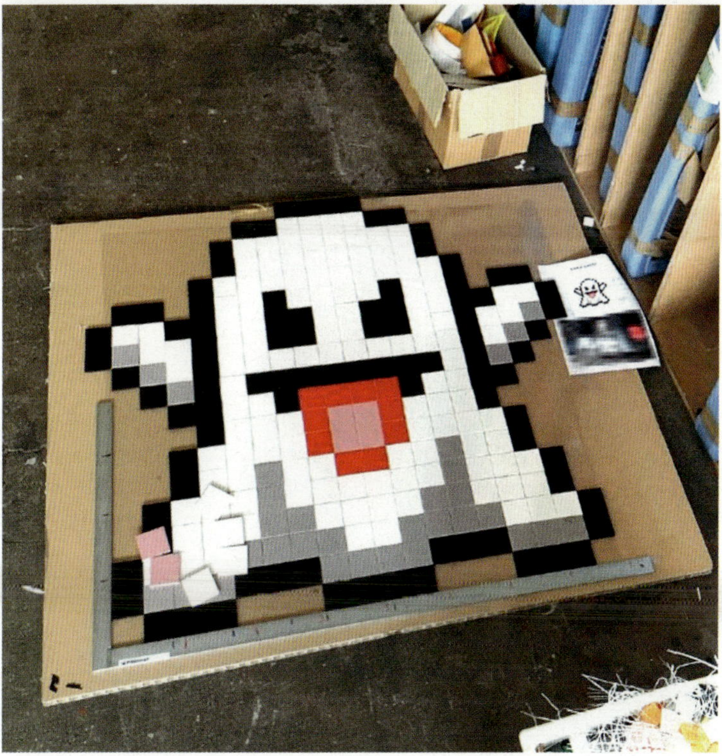

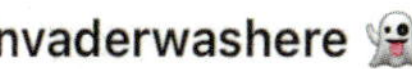

View all 93 comments

14 May 2016

invaderwashere •••

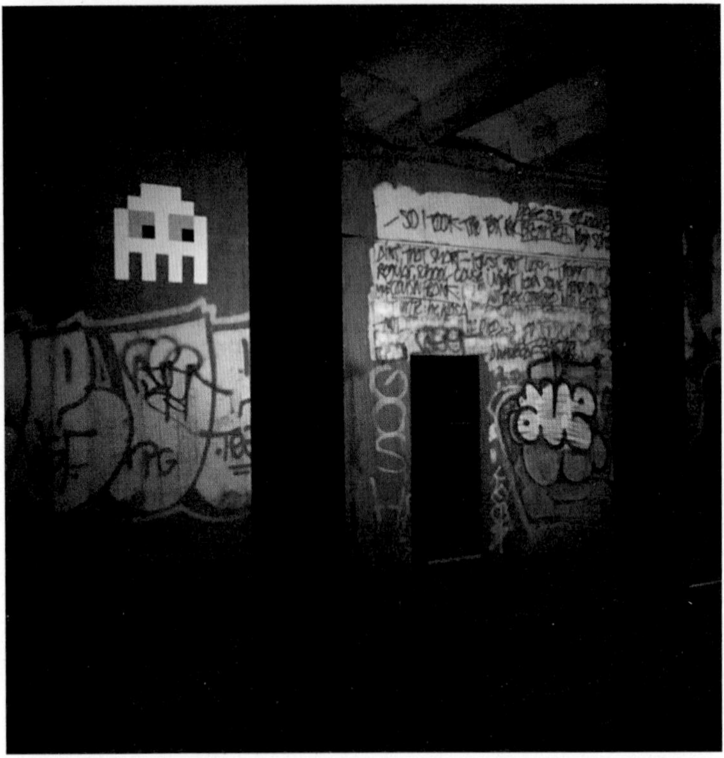

6151 likes

invaderwashere Into the darkness...

View all 63 comments

23 May 2016

invaderwashere

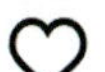 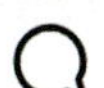  

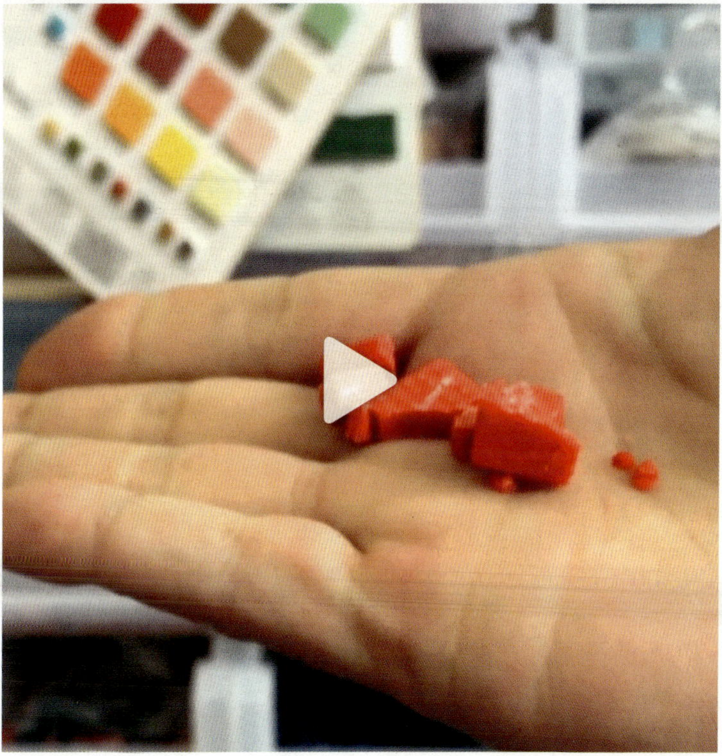

28 596 views

invaderwashere ⚠️ Crumble like a cookie ⚠️ The glue that I use is strong and the tiles are fragile, so people who sell some street pieces are just fooling you, they break them and sell you replicas. #pixel #tiles #fragile

View all 61 comments

25 May 2016

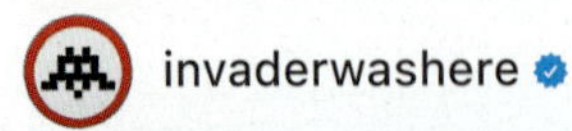

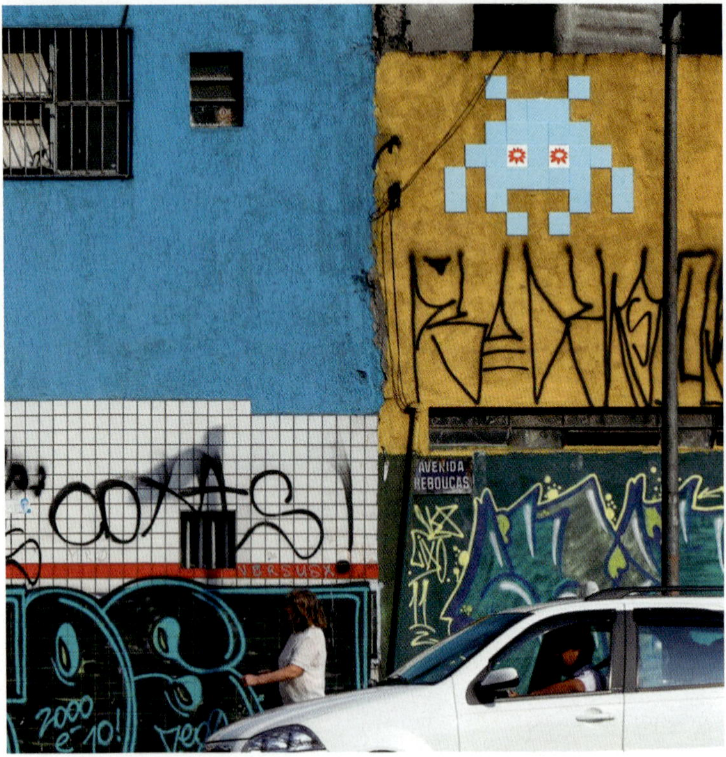

 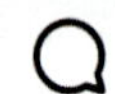  

7657 likes

invaderwashere SP_21 & pichaçaos #saopaulo #throwback #2011 #50pts

View all 40 comments

1 June 2016

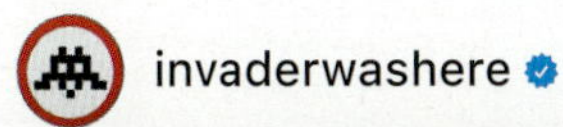

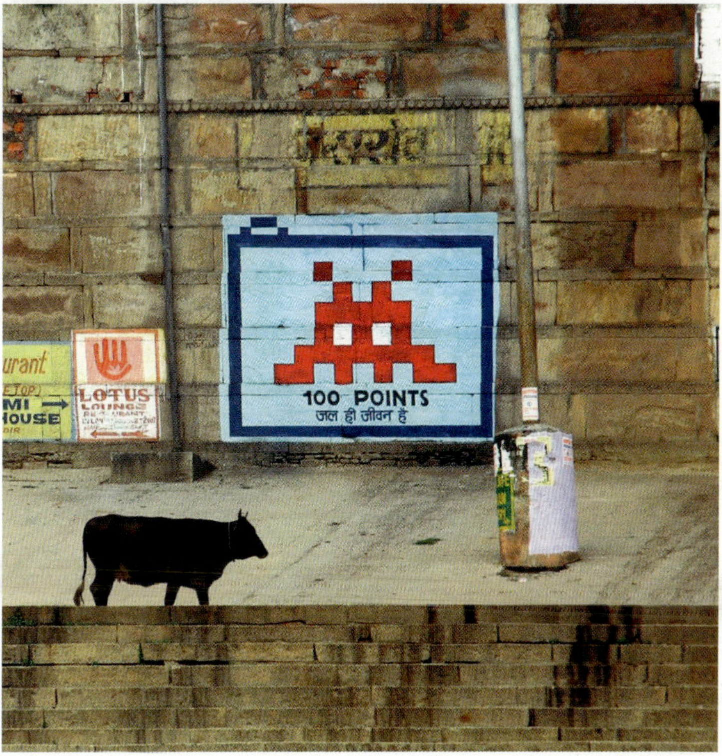

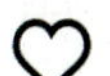

6 377 likes

invaderwashere Varanasi in India is the only city where I have painted on the walls in addition to my mosaics. All kind of painted advertisements can be found all along the Ganges River. With the help of one of the local wall painter, I added my own touch. #varanasi #benares #ghat #india #throwback #2008

View all 29 comments

2 June 2016

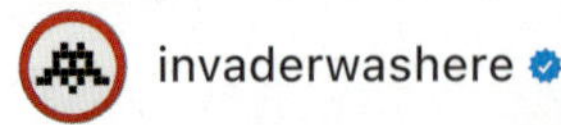

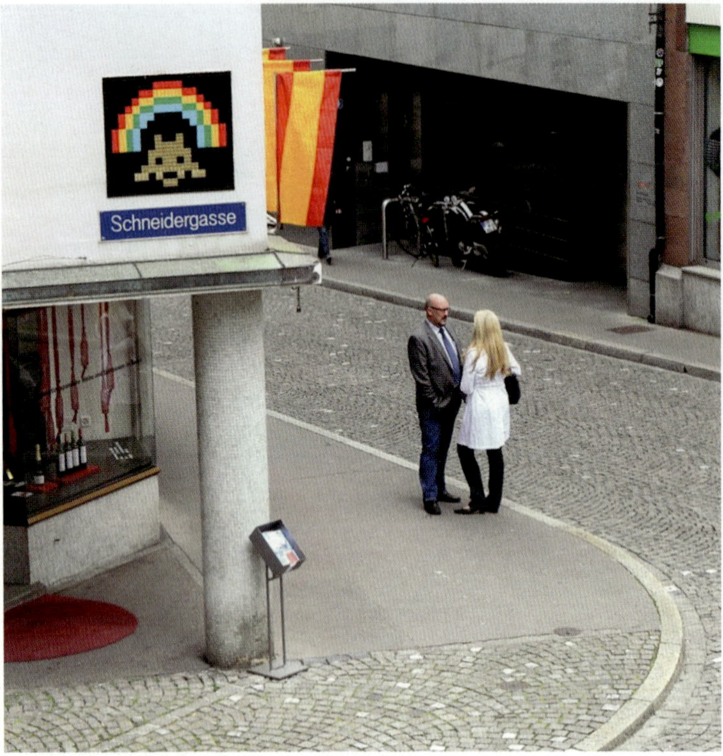

7267 likes

invaderwashere BSL_03 #Basel #throwback #2013

View all 40 comments

3 June 2016

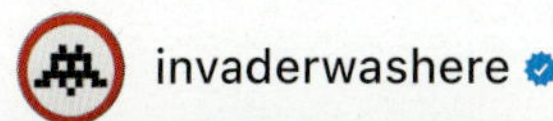

invaderwashere

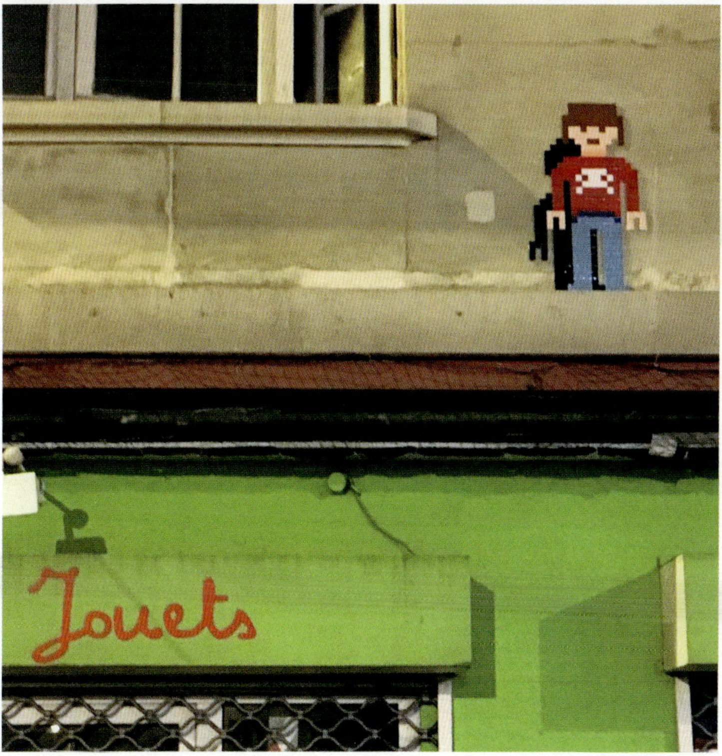

9729 likes

invaderwashere PA_1201 3:25 am #justmadeinParis

View all 74 comments

8 June 2016

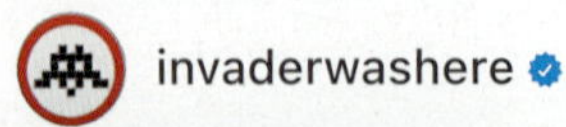

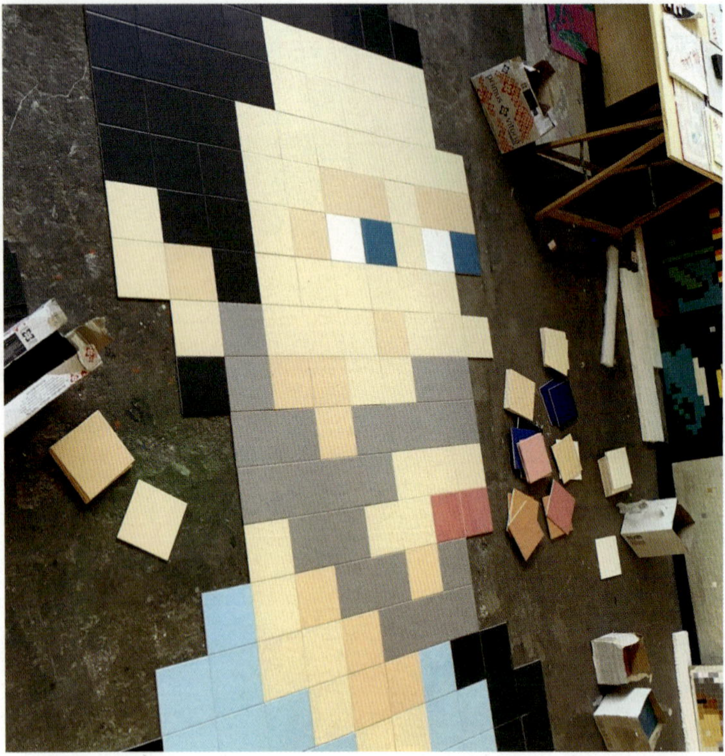

  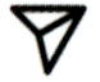 

7 501 likes

invaderwashere Work in progress #studio

View all 60 comments

8 June 2016

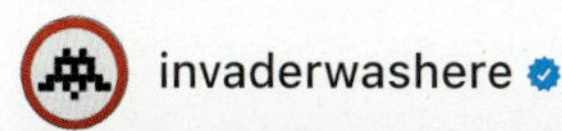

•••

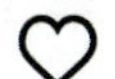   

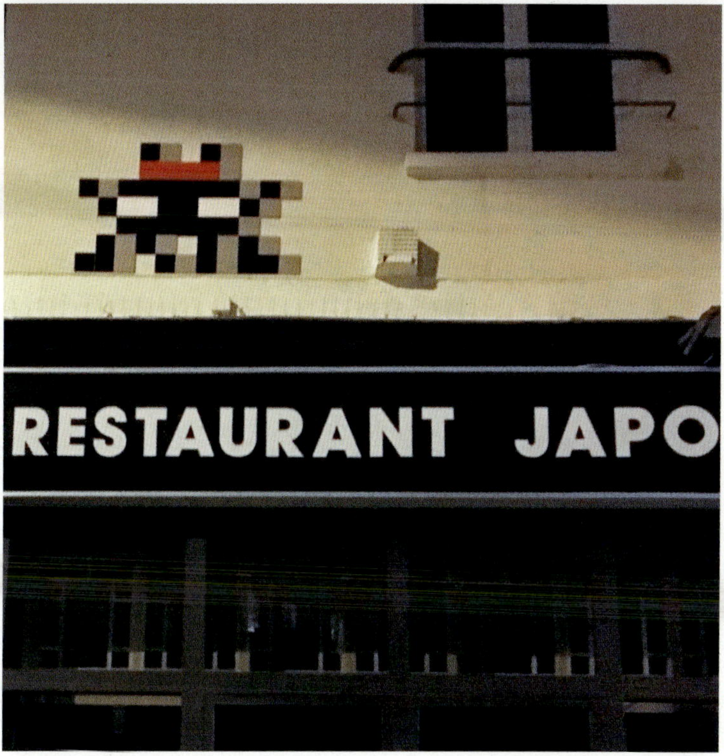

6894 likes

invaderwashere PA_1203 4:14 am #justmadeinParis

View all 43 comments

9 June 2016

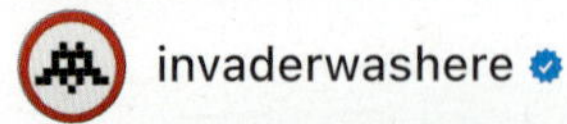

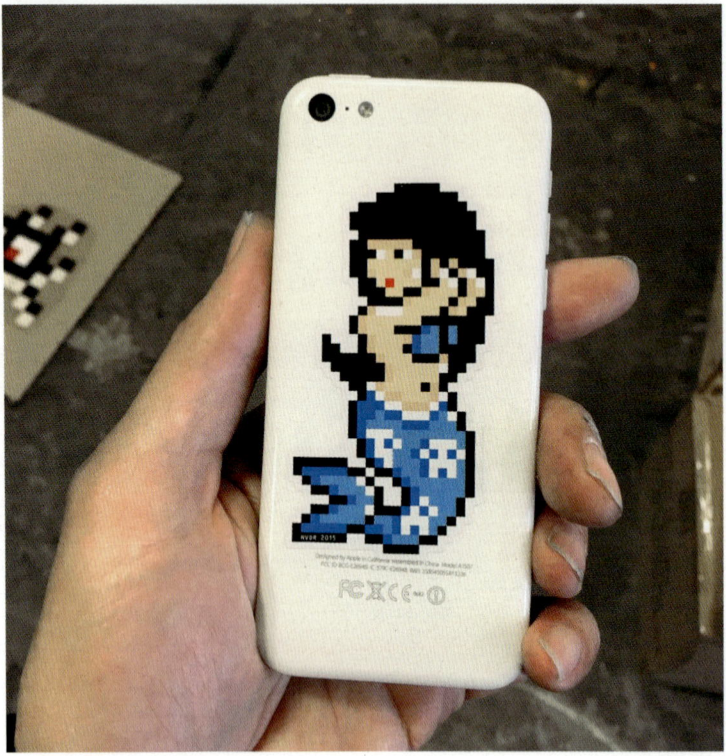

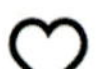   

6 487 likes

invaderwashere Sticked!

View all 69 comments

10 June 2016

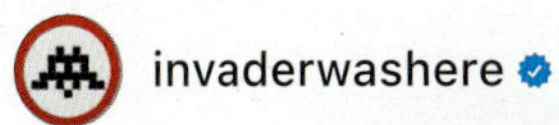

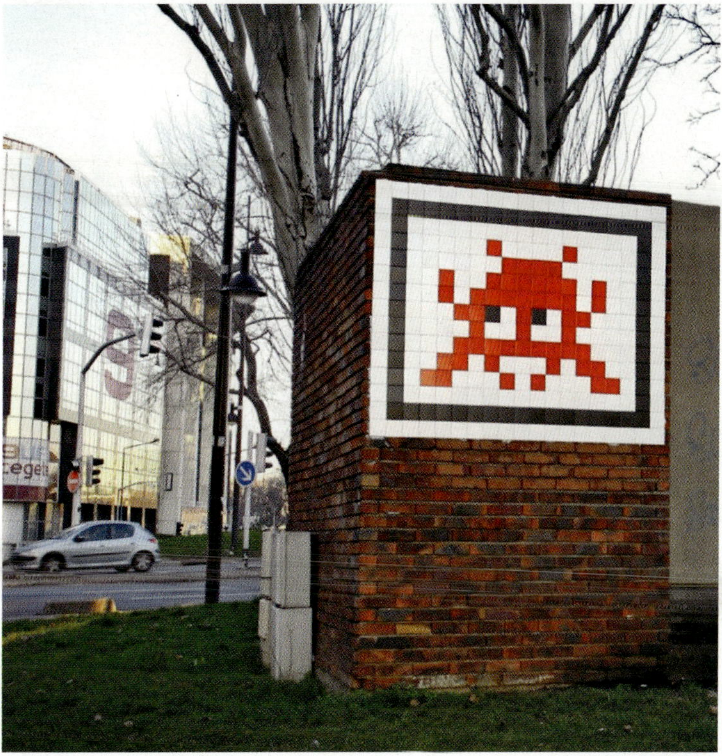

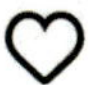   

8 203 likes

invaderwashere Reactivation Team goes big! #rteam #reactivationteam #paris #PA758 #50points

View all 44 comments

11 June 2016

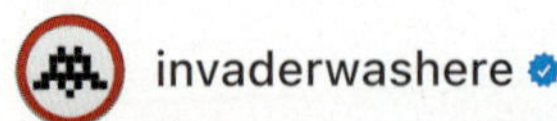

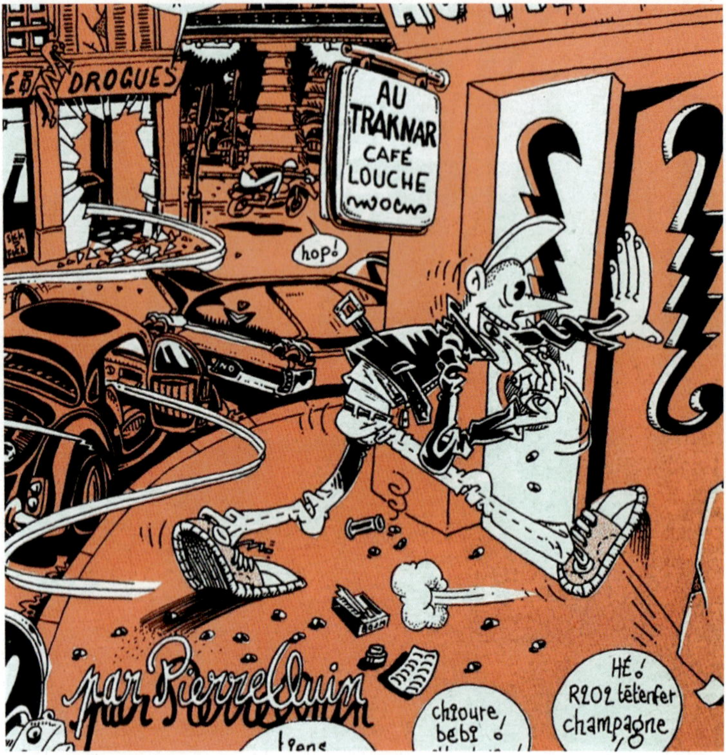

 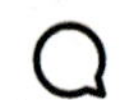  

3 613 likes

invaderwashere C'est avec une immense tristesse que je viens d'apprendre (tardivement*) la disparition de l'auteur de bande dessinée Pierre Ouin, figure incontournable de la BD underground parisienne. *Pas une seule ligne sur sa vie et son oeuvre dans les grands media hexagonaux, c'est effarant... RIP #PierreOuin #bloodi #frenchcomics @lemondefr @liberationfr @lesinrocks

View all 14 comments

14 June 2016

invaderwashere

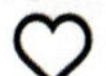
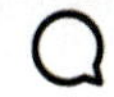

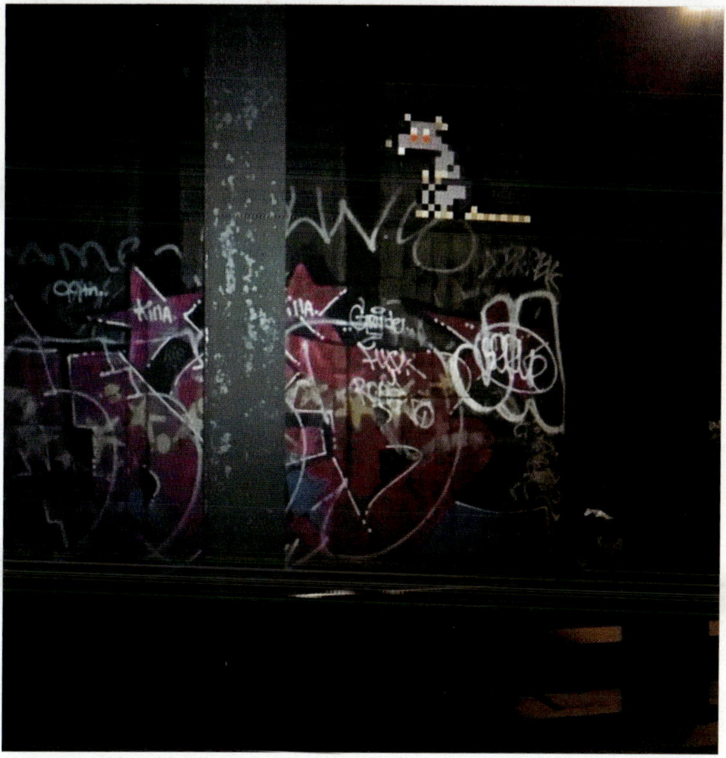

6280 likes

invaderwashere Deep underground! #adertherat

View all 63 comments

19 June 2016

invaderwashere

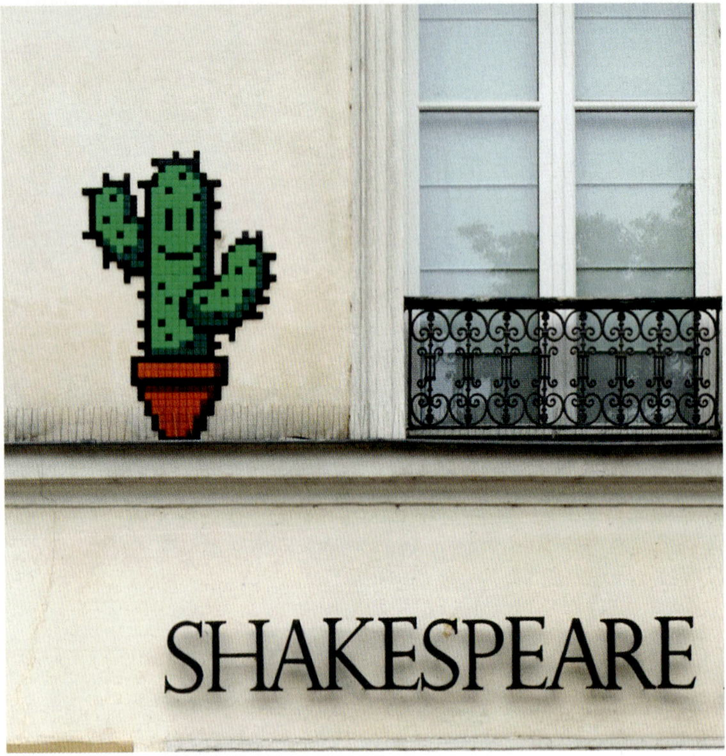

SHAKESPEARE

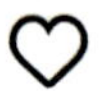  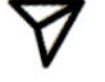

17 462 likes

invaderwashere PA_1200 To 🌵 or not to 🌵?

View all 161 comments

21 June 2016

invaderwashere

 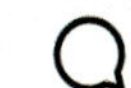 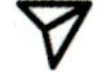 

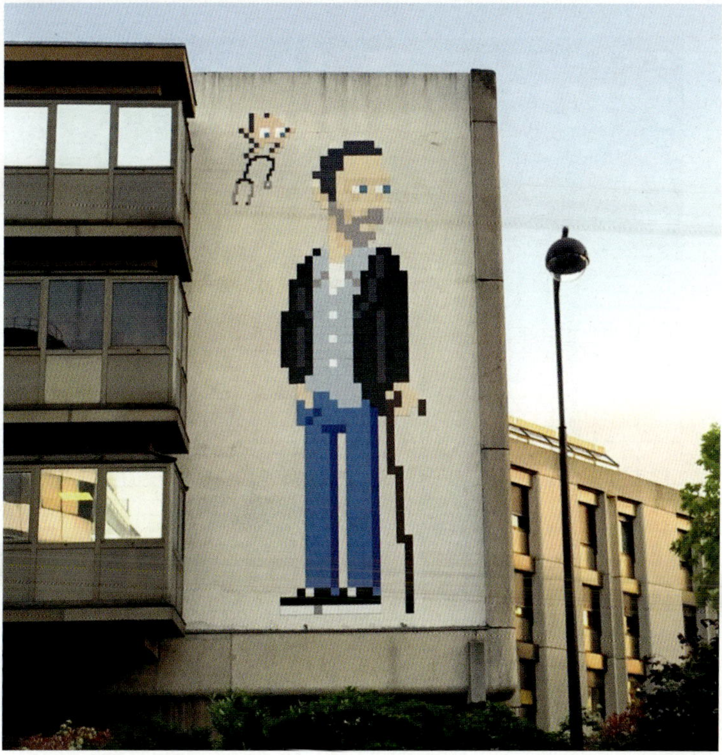

16 065 likes

invaderwashere Dr House is on da house! #lapitié #hospital #Paris #75013 #madelastnight #huge #100pts

View all 242 comments

23 June 2016

invaderwashere •••

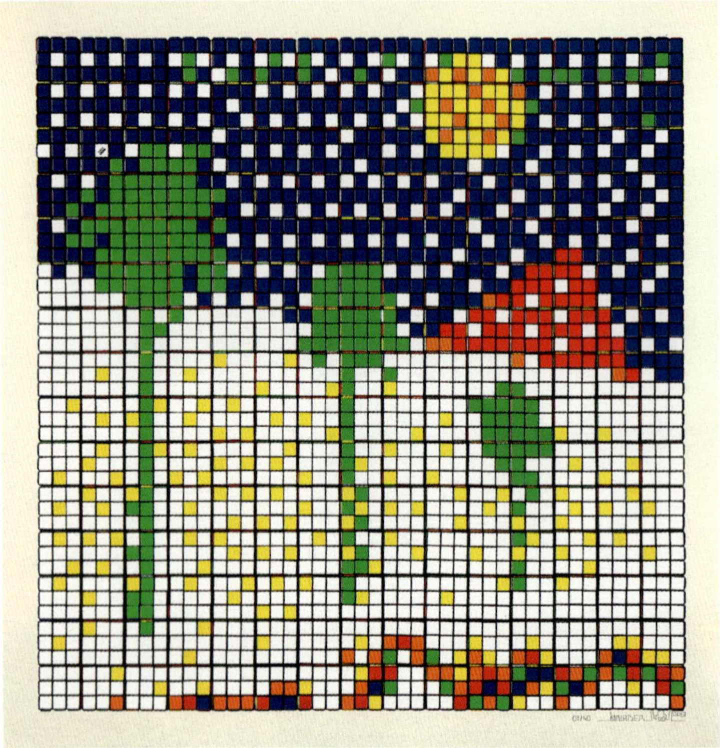

4 395 likes

invaderwashere Rubik Boys don't cry / silkscreen print 7/40 from 2009 #unicef #charity #auction last day: www.3wallsauction.com

View all 17 comments

24 June 2016

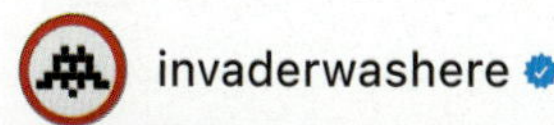

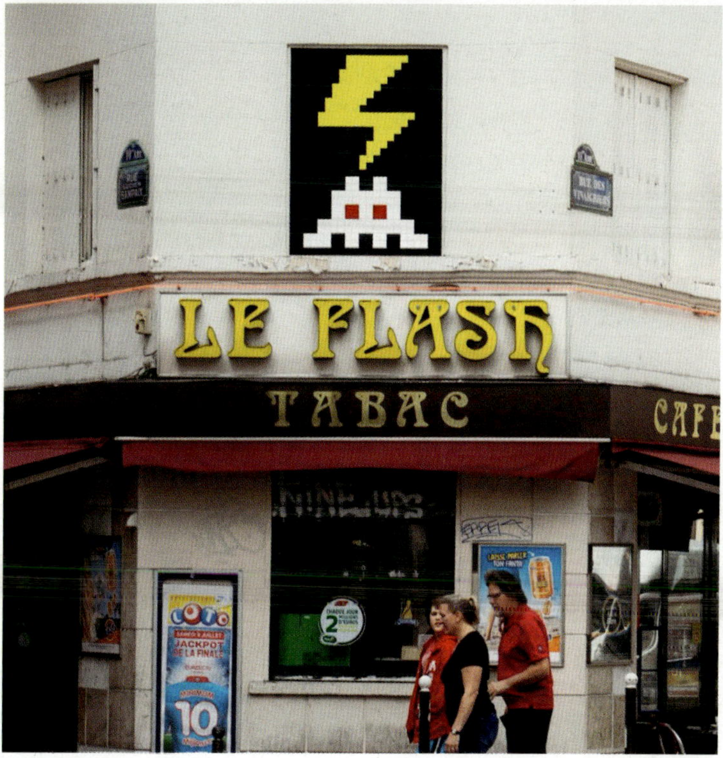

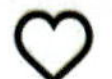
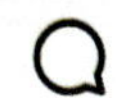

11681 likes

invaderwashere Fresh from last night... PA_1207 ⚡
#leFlash #Paris #flashinvaders

View all 97 comments

29 June 2016

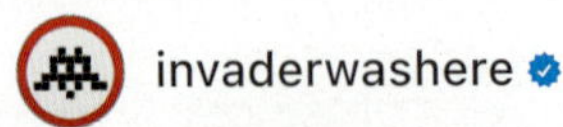

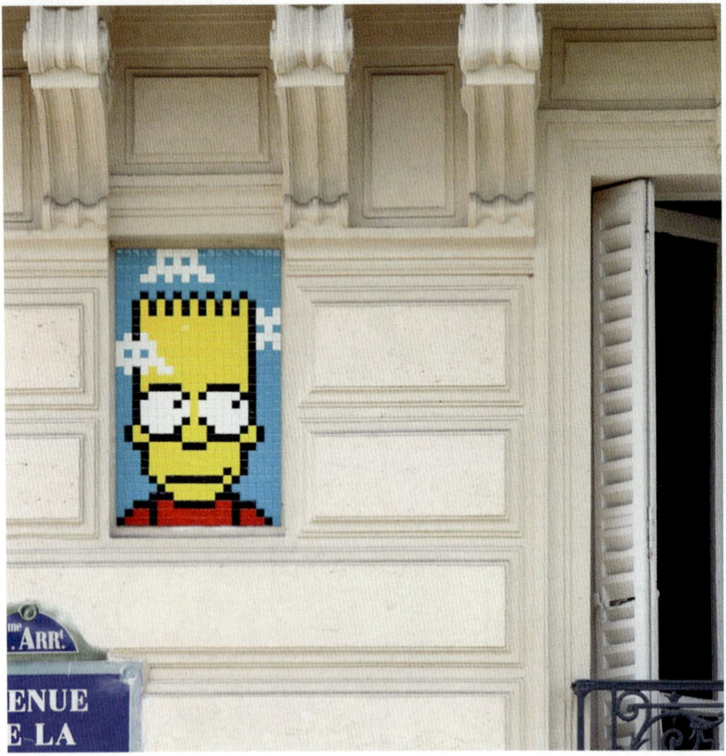

19 274 likes

invaderwashere PA_1206 

View all 210 comments

30 June 2016

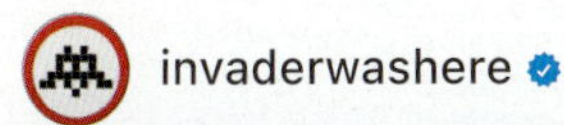

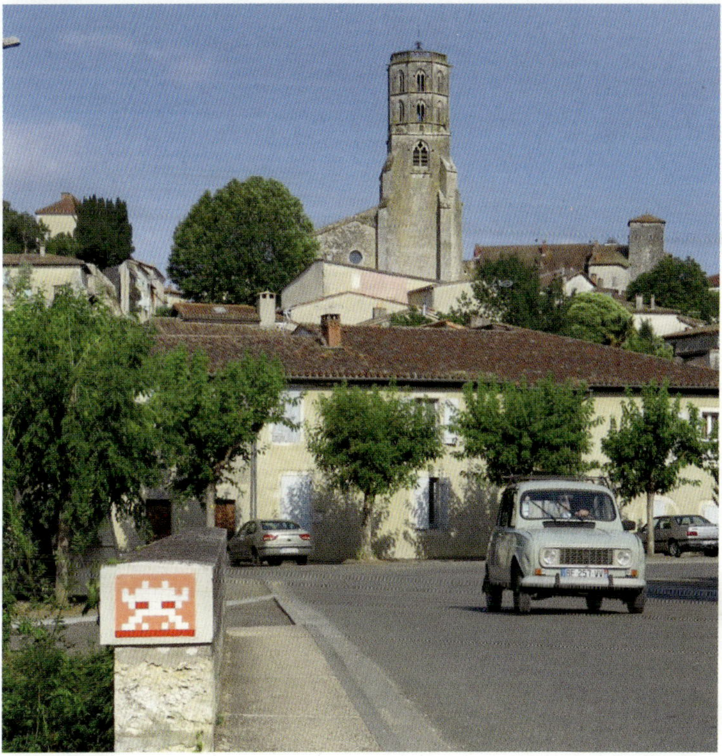

8 366 likes

invaderwashere Just made the 3333rd space invader in the 66th invaded city!!! #numbers

View all 84 comments

8 July 2016

invaderwashere

  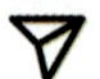 

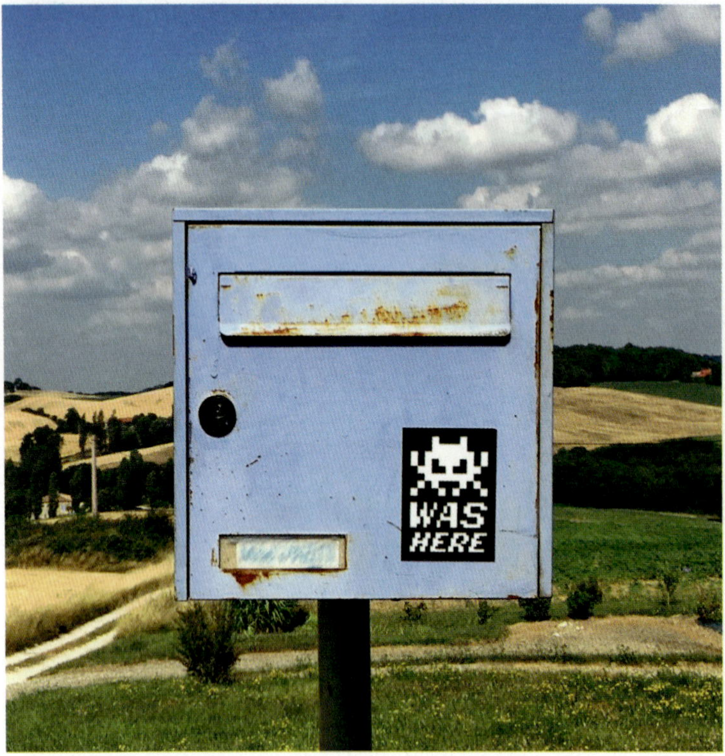

9099 likes

invaderwashere 👾 WAS HERE #invaderwashere

View all 40 comments

11 July 2016

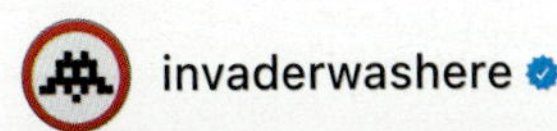

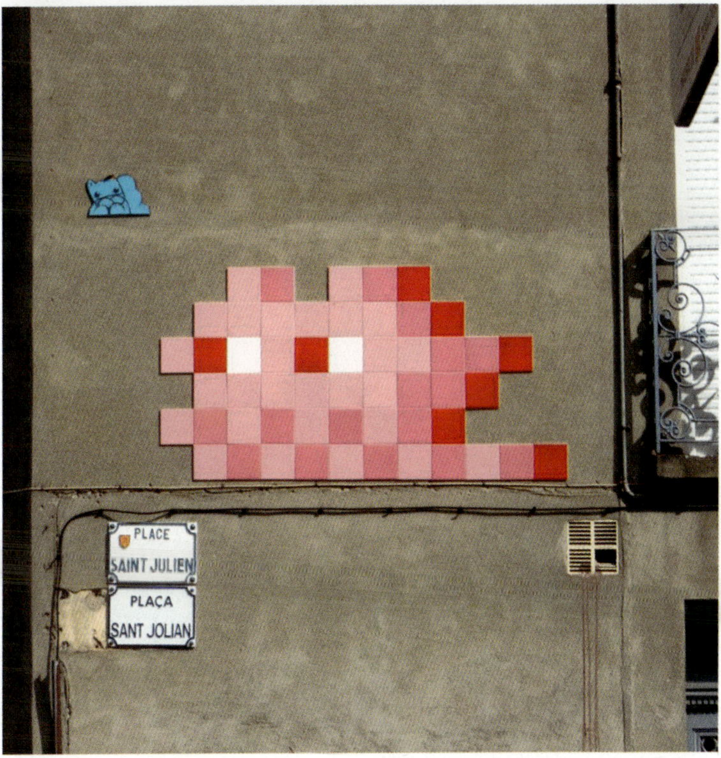

 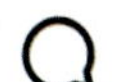  

11342 likes

invaderwashere Pink in Toulouse

View all 50 comments

15 July 2016

invaderwashere

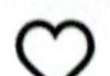   

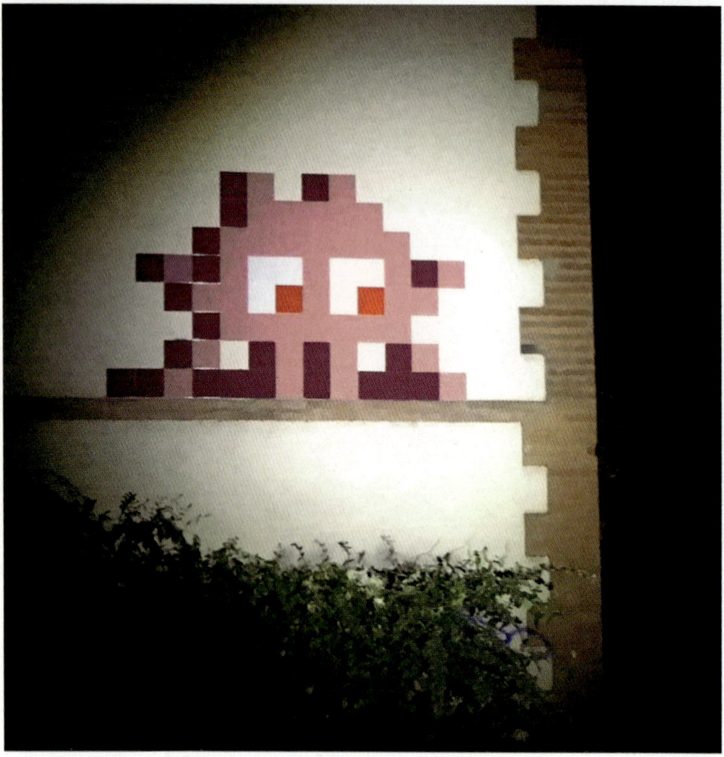

8 365 likes

invaderwashere TSL_10 just installed #toulouse

View all 30 comments

18 July 2016

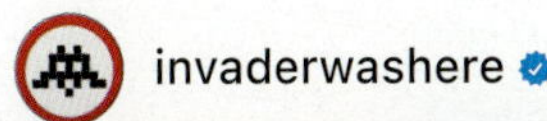

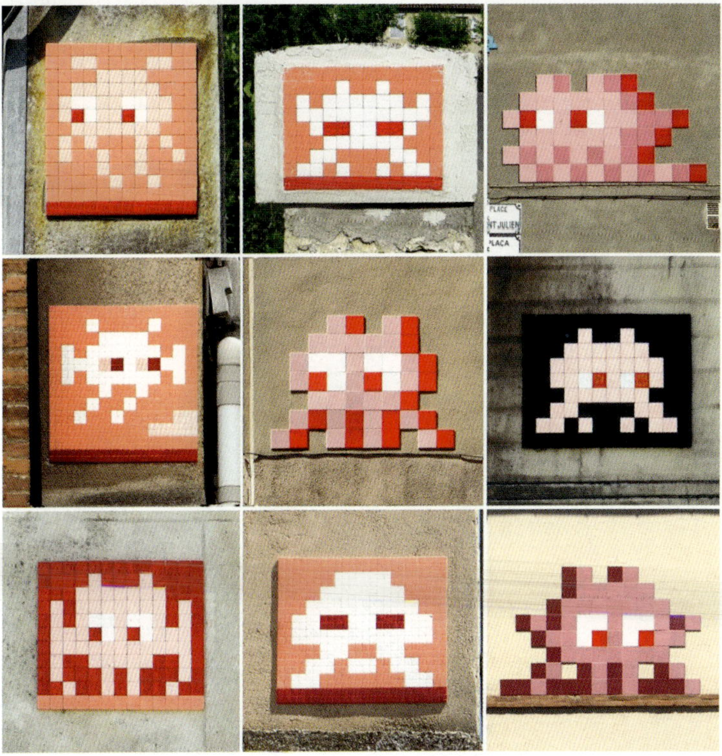

11 360 likes

invaderwashere The first wave of the Invasion of Toulouse is completed. More photos online in the News section. #toulouse #pinkcity #pinkinvasion

View all 76 comments

19 July 2016

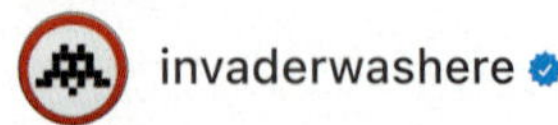

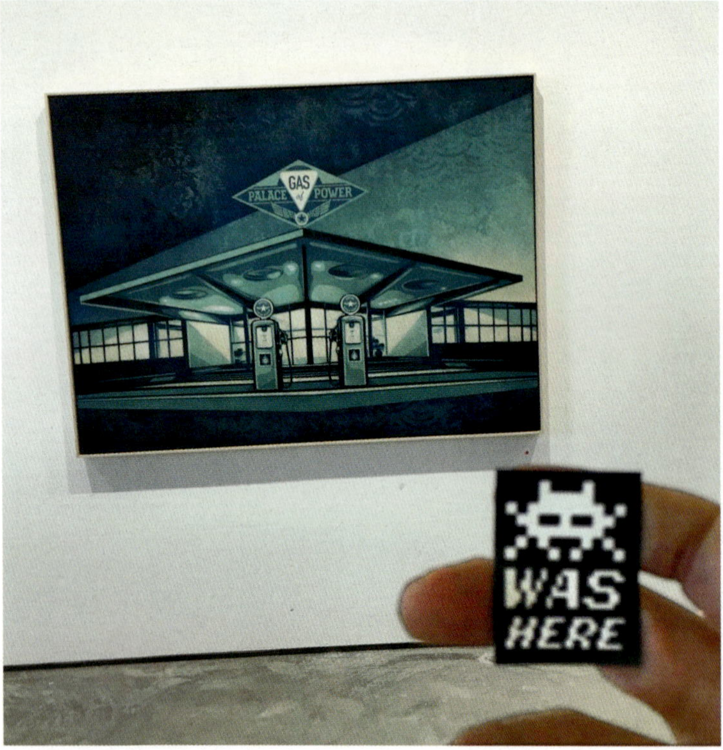

6748 likes

invaderwashere Last days to visit the exhibition of Shepard Fairey in Paris @galerie_itinerrance @obeygiant #earthcrisis #invaderwashere

View all 17 comments

24 July 2016

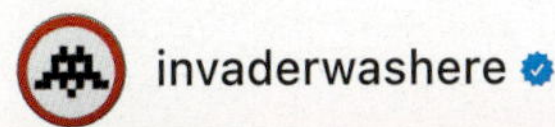

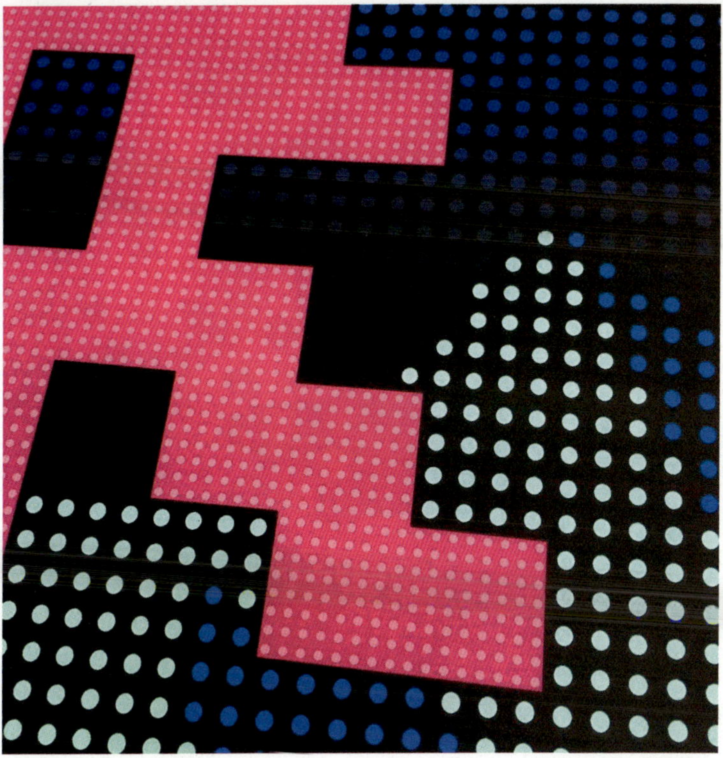

3 678 likes

invaderwashere Working on a new print for @lazarides #silkscreened #detail #led

View all 34 comments

25 July 2016

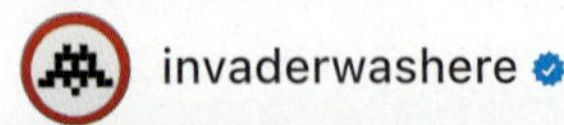

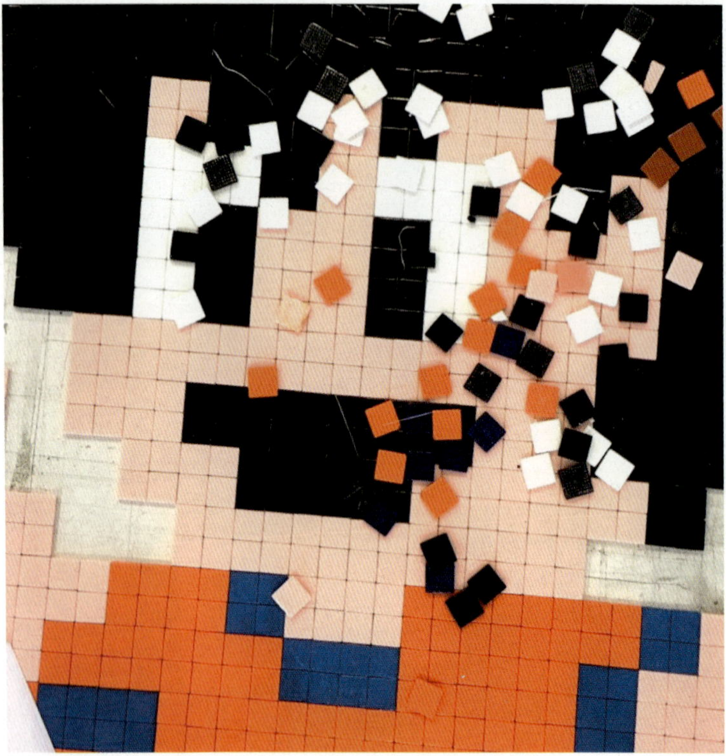

6149 likes

invaderwashere Studio detail

View all 55 comments

26 July 2016

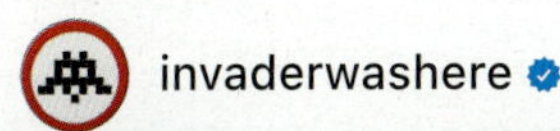

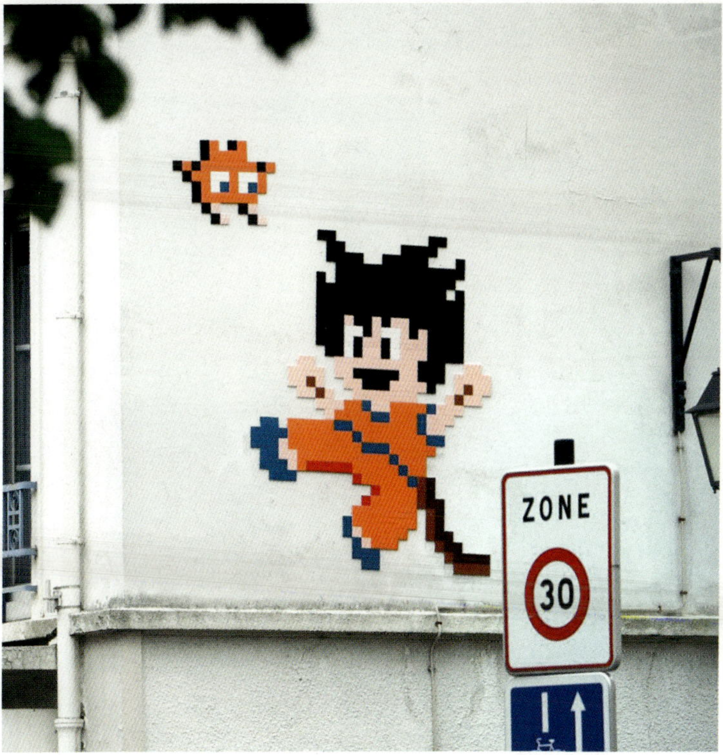

18 919 likes

invaderwashere Kamehameha!!! #goku #dragonball #nes #paris #new

View all 259 comments

27 July 2016

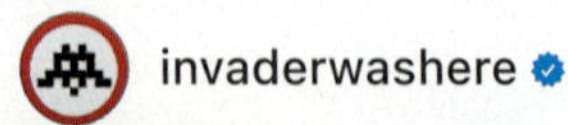

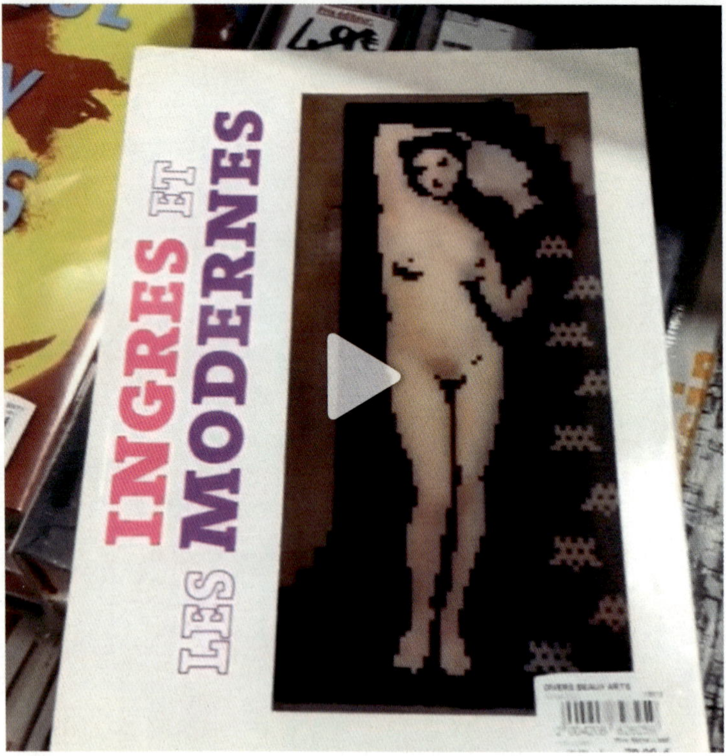

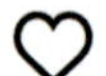  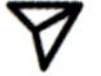 

32 804 views

invaderwashere Chillin in a book store… #catalogcover #2009 #Ingres #alainjacquet #invader

View all 51 comments

31 July 2016

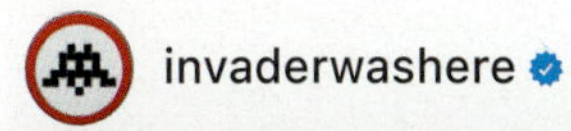

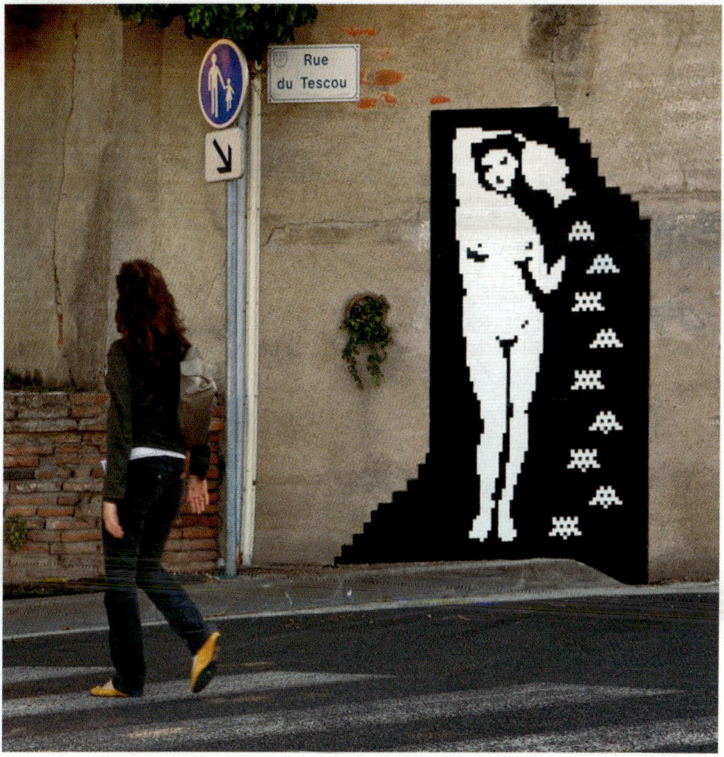

13 898 likes

invaderwashere MTB_09 La source de l'Invasion
#montauban #afterIngres #throwback #2009

View all 84 comments

31 July 2016

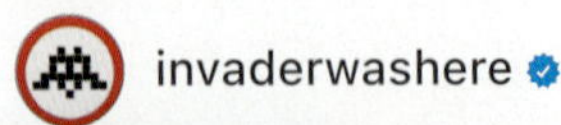

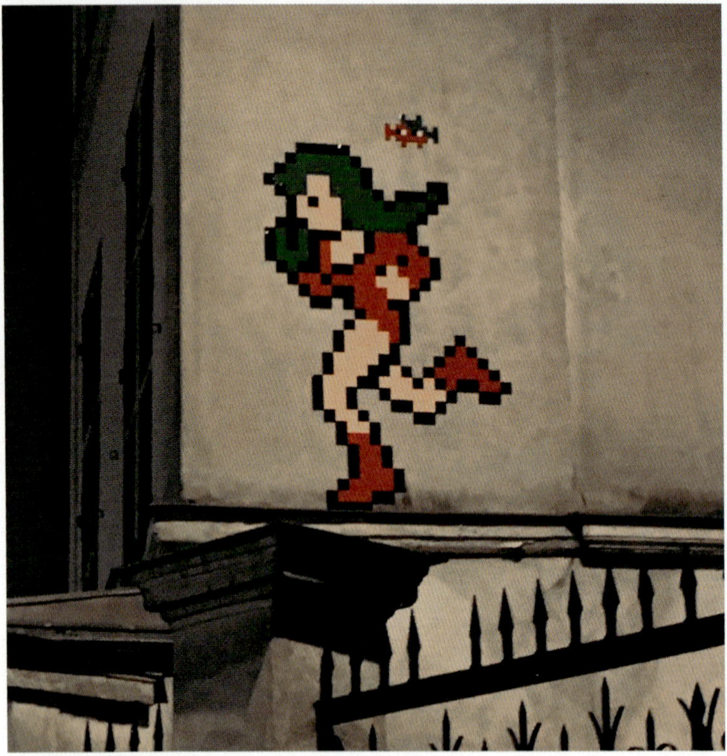

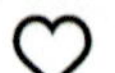   

11973 likes

invaderwashere PA_1219 #new #paris #metroid #invaderwashere

View all 53 comments

3 August 2016

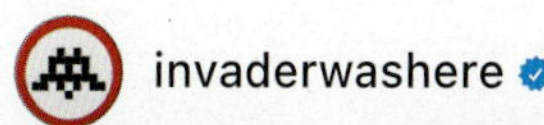

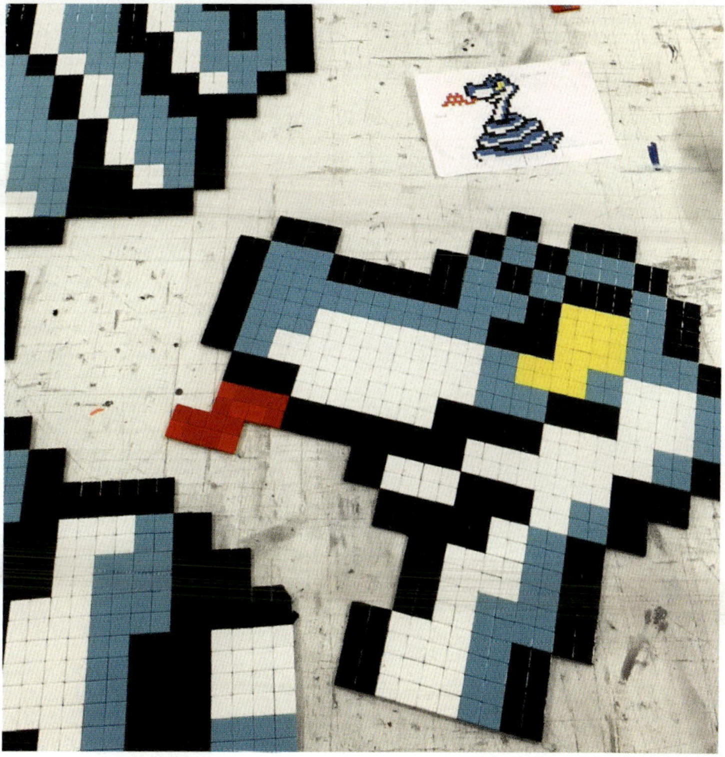

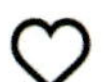

7878 likes

invaderwashere Studio detail

View all 36 comments

3 August 2016

invaderwashere

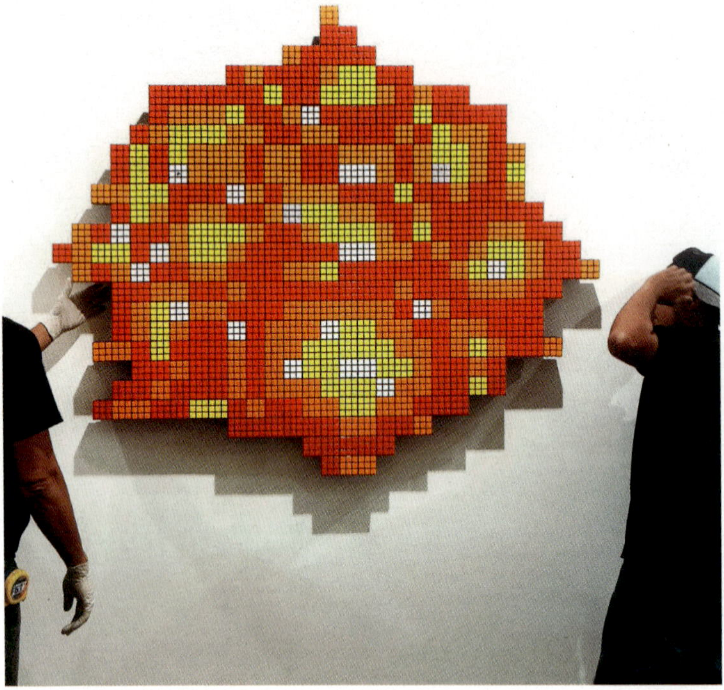

7697 likes

invaderwashere 💥 in Jakarta / Presented by @overtheinfluence_hk at Art Stage Jakarta - Sheraton Grand - booth C7 Hall B #rubikcubism #artfair #jakarta #indonesia

View all 38 comments

5 August 2016

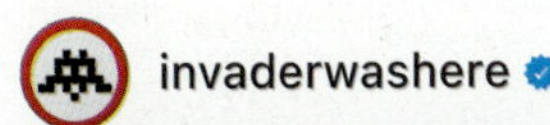

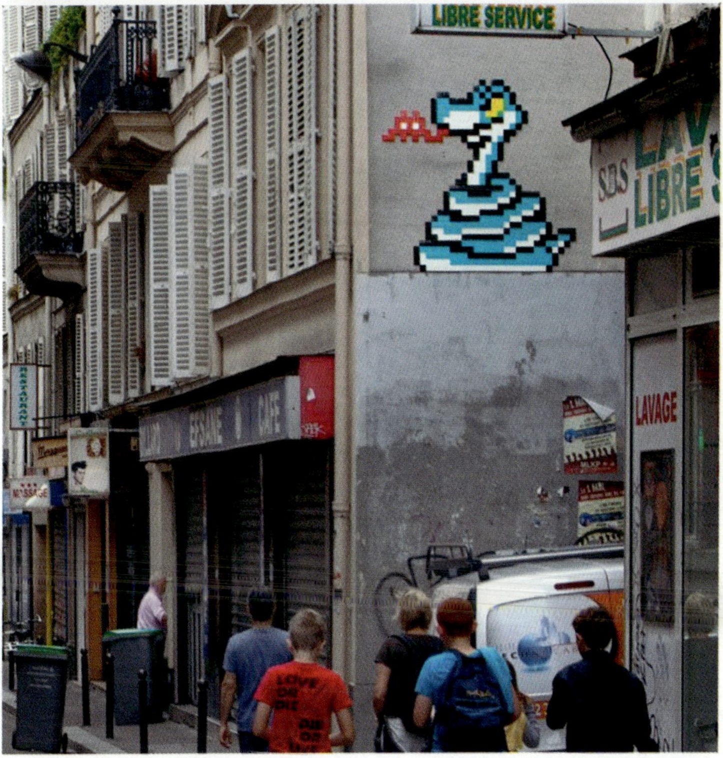

15 135 likes

invaderwashere Be careful kids!!! #new #paris

View all 83 comments

7 August 2016

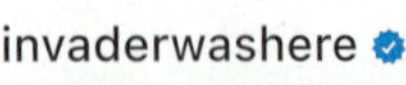

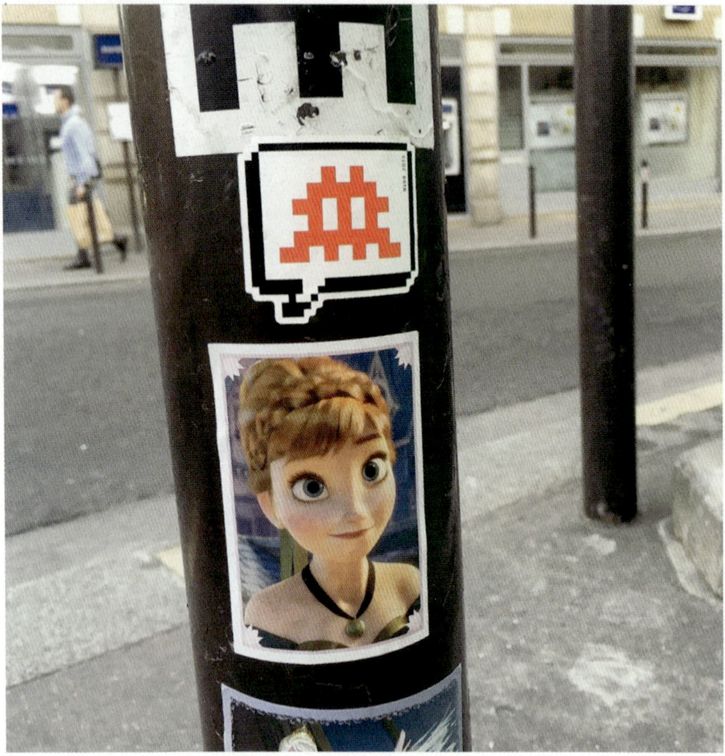

7689 likes

invaderwashere Street #stickers

View all 27 comments

9 August 2016

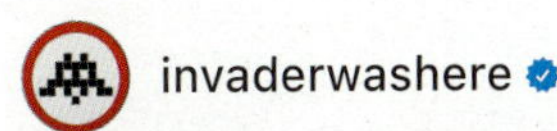

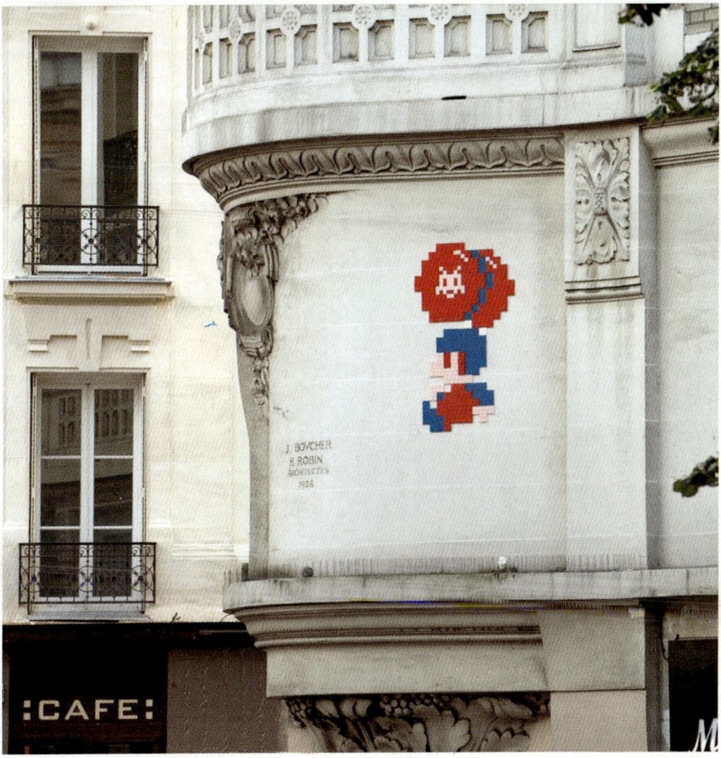

 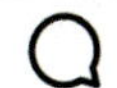  

10 567 likes

invaderwashere PA_1222 new piece in #paris #baloonfight

View all 49 comments

11 August 2016

invaderwashere

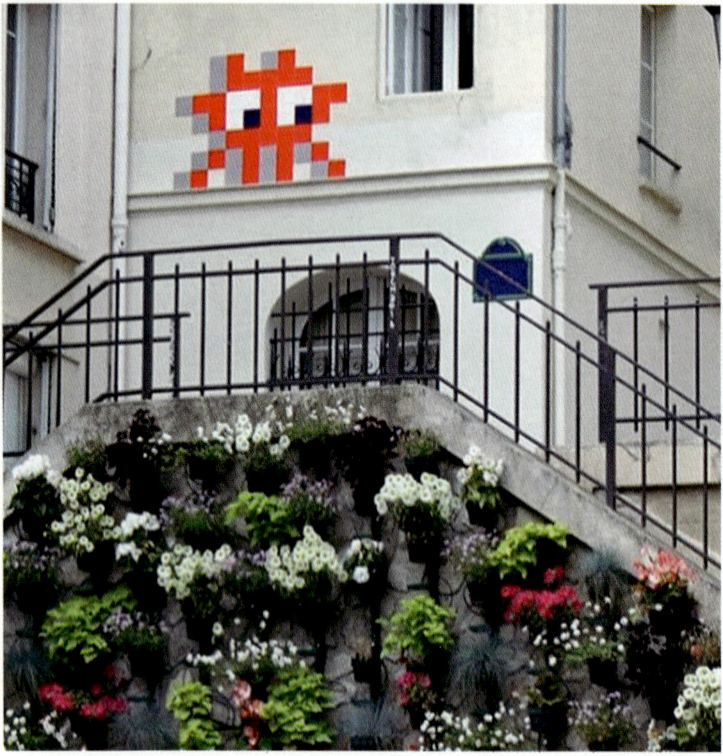

8 420 likes

invaderwashere PA_1221 classic! Photo: @street_art77

View all 42 comments

12 August 2016

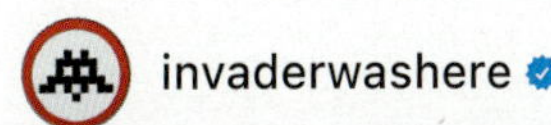

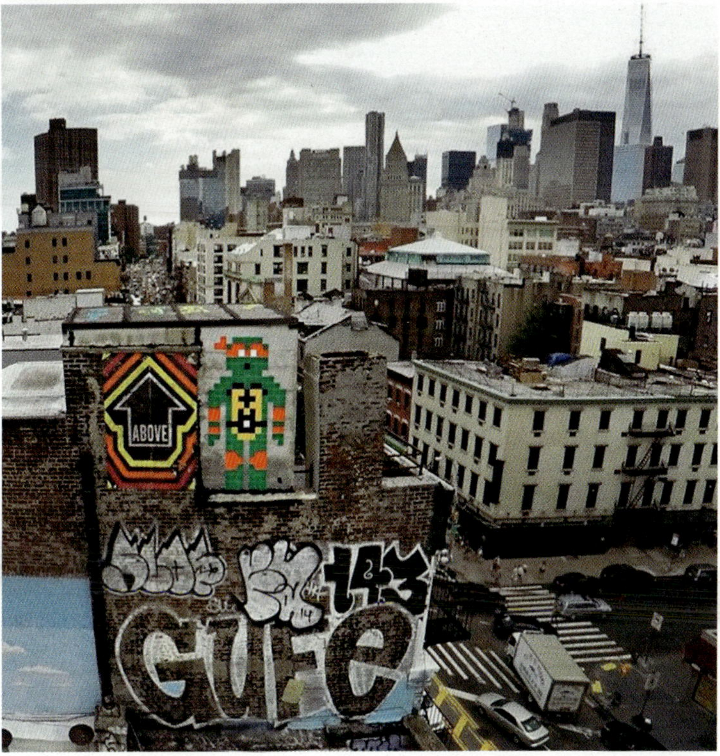

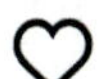   

13 663 likes

invaderwashere Thank you @abovestudio for this great photo of NY_153 shot by @streetartdrone #rooftop #drone #bowery #nyc #michelangelo

View all 96 comments

12 August 2016

invaderwashere

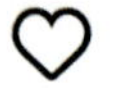  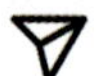 

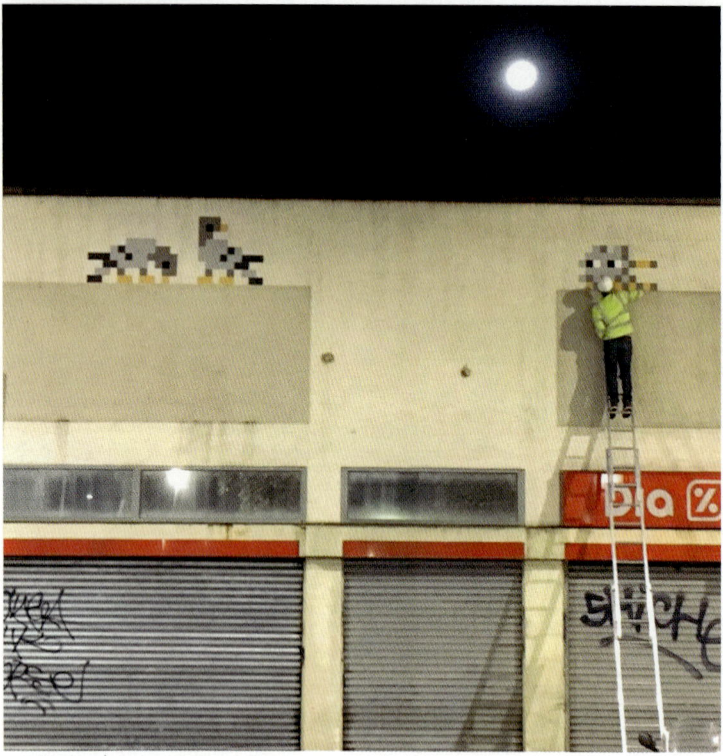

11772 likes

invaderwashere Under the full moon  

View all 82 comments

17 August 2016

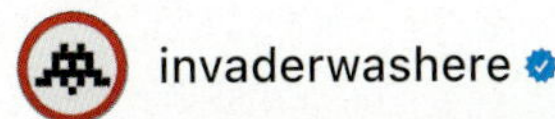

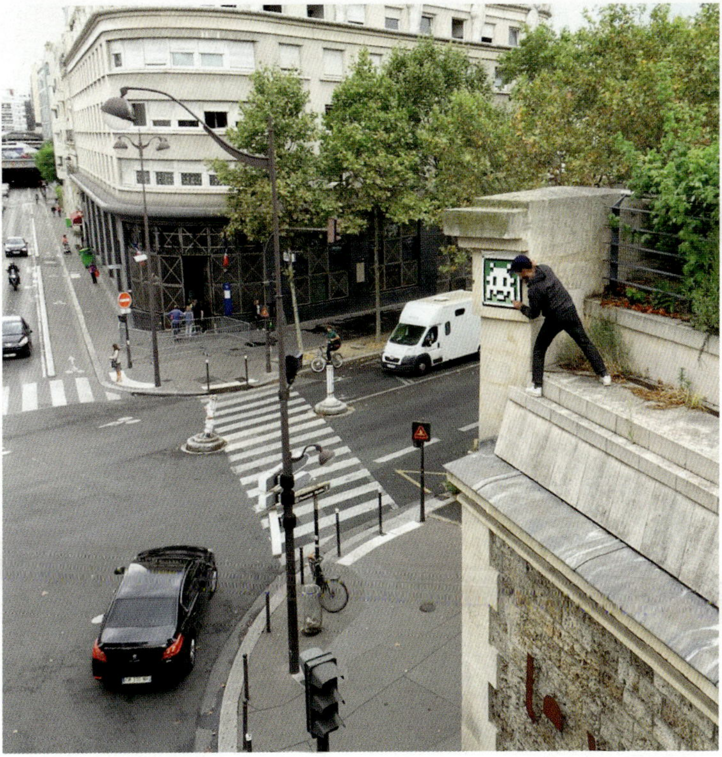

21066 likes

invaderwashere Sunday morning physical activities

View all 132 comments

21 August 2016

invaderwashere

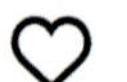   

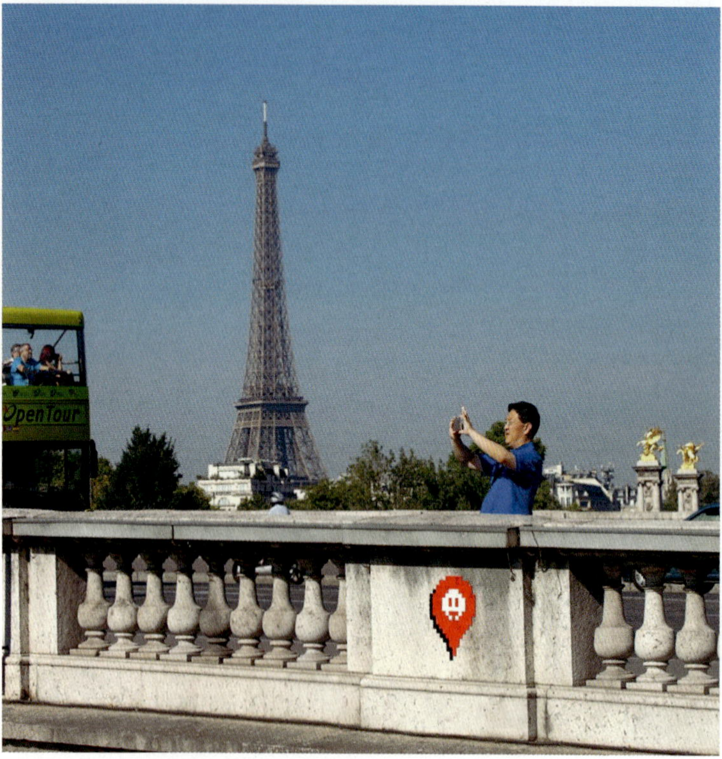

11907 likes

invaderwashere Point of Interest

View all 55 comments

25 August 2016

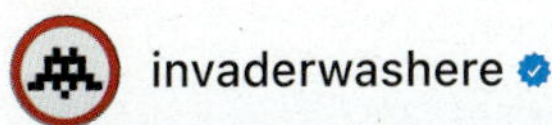

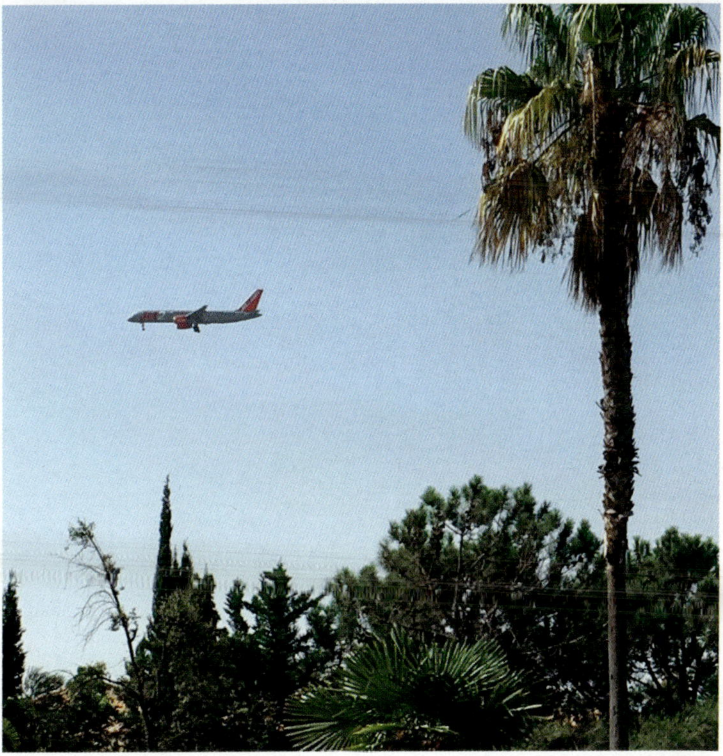

3084 likes

invaderwashere On the road... A bit of #vacation a bit of #invasion 👾 🌞

View all 25 comments

27 August 2016

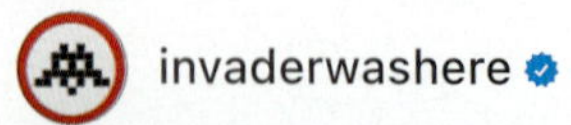

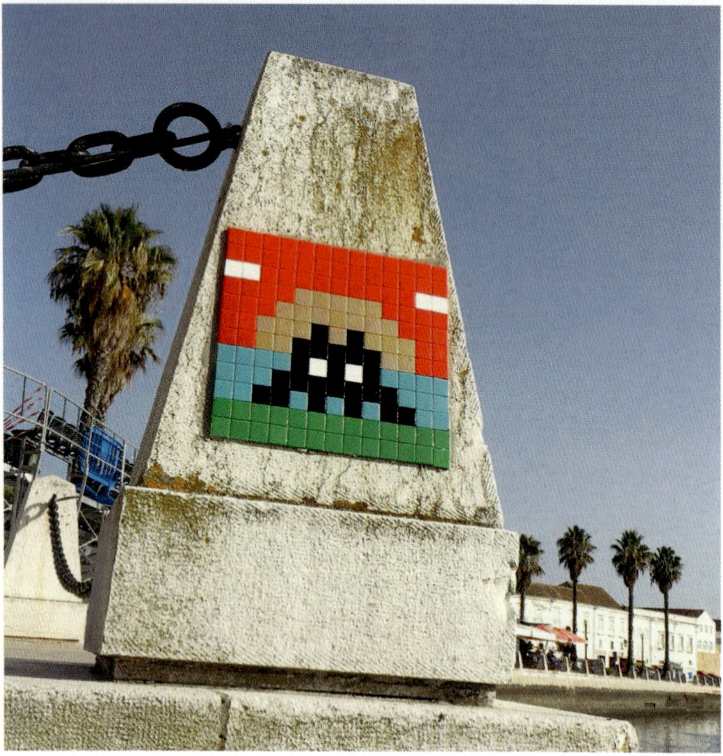

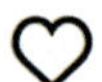  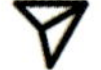 

11765 likes

invaderwashere First space invader in Portugal 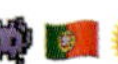 

View all 116 comments

28 August 2016

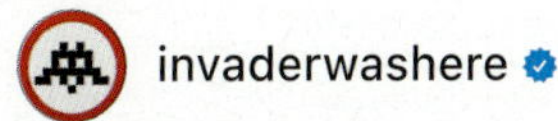

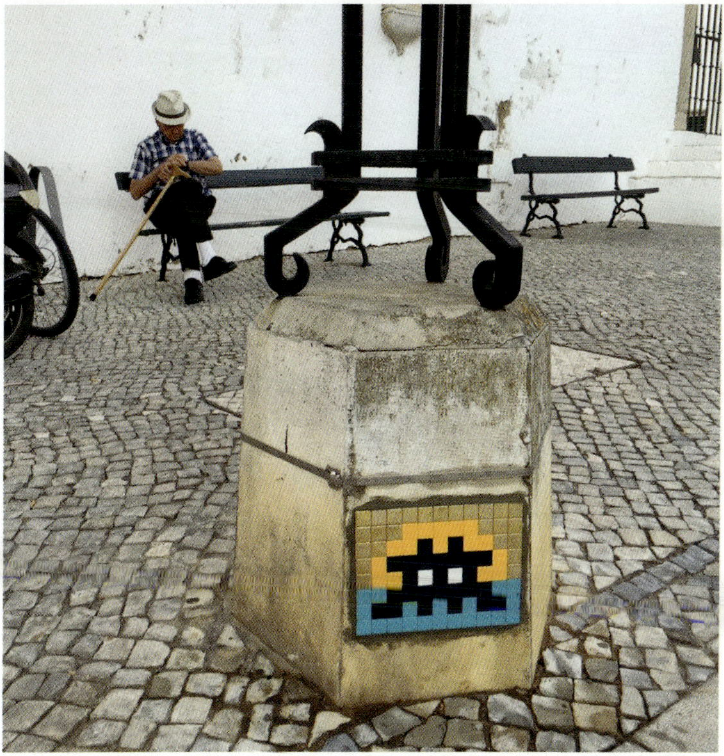

10 522 likes

invaderwashere 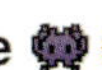 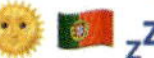

View all 52 comments

29 August 2016

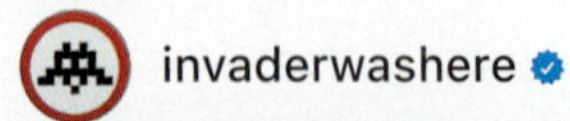

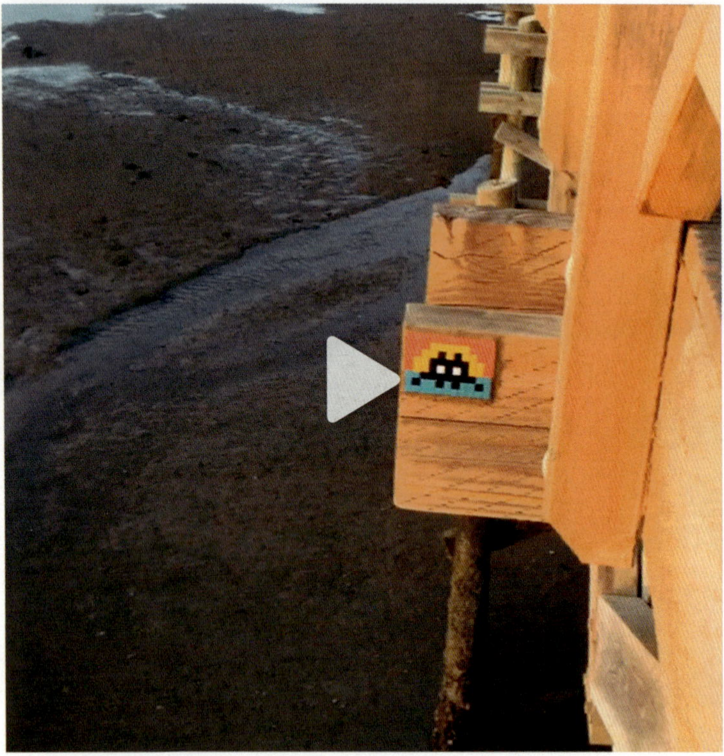

  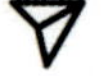 

36 259 views

invaderwashere 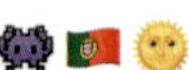

View all 87 comments

30 August 2016

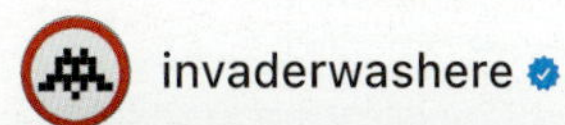

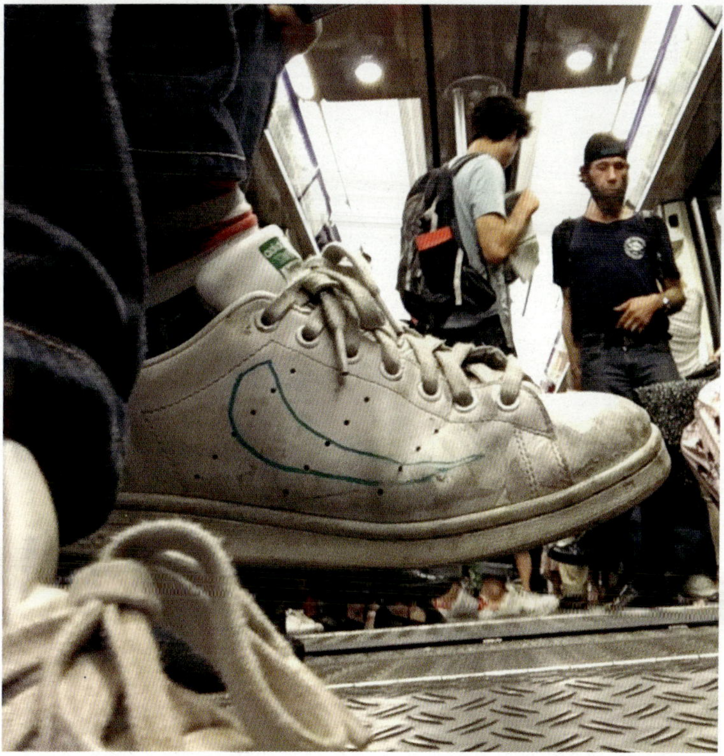

7542 likes

invaderwashere Back to the civilization! #metro #paris #customstansmith #adinike

View all 78 comments

31 August 2016

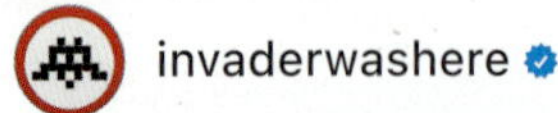

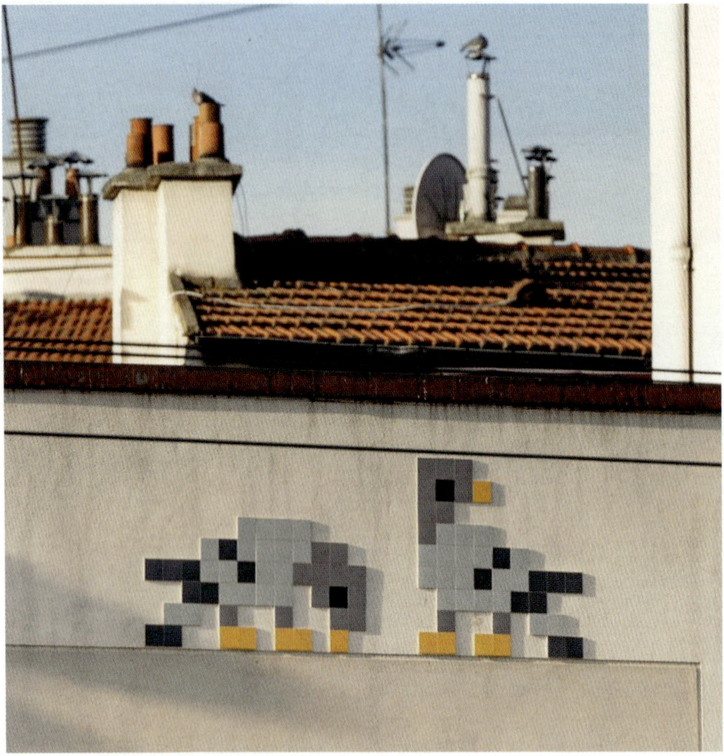

14 577 likes

invaderwashere PA_1225 close up in the daylight

View all 126 comments

2 September 2016

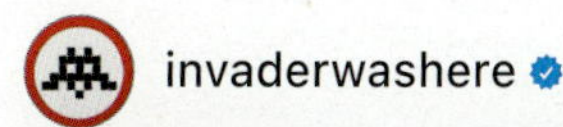

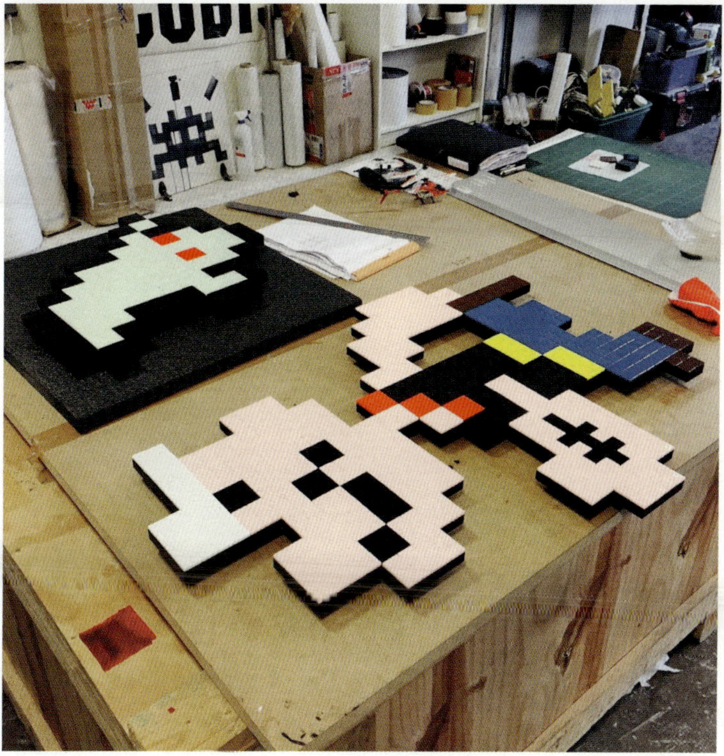

11542 likes

invaderwashere Studio detail #mothership #aliases

View all 66 comments

4 September 2016

invaderwashere

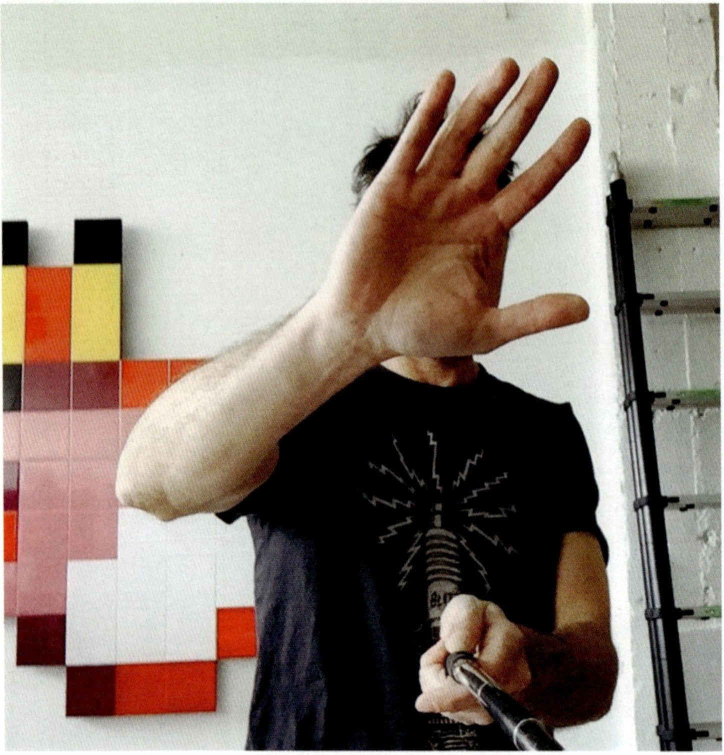

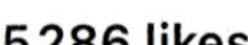

5286 likes

invaderwashere #selfiestick #studio #2015

View all 35 comments

5 September 2016

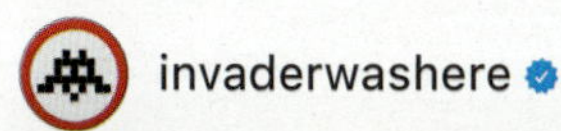

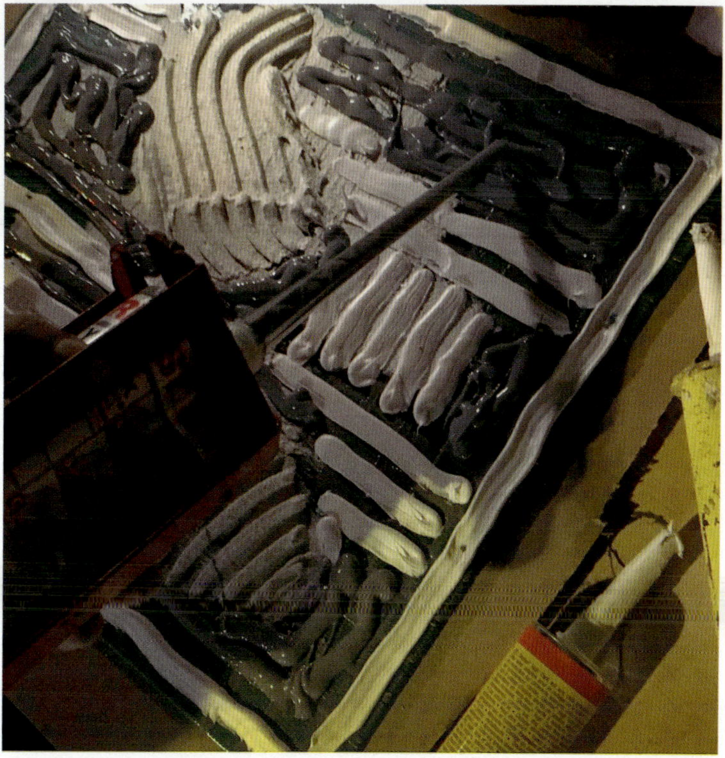

 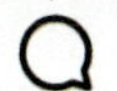  

4083 likes

invaderwashere B side

View all 43 comments

7 September 2016

invaderwashere

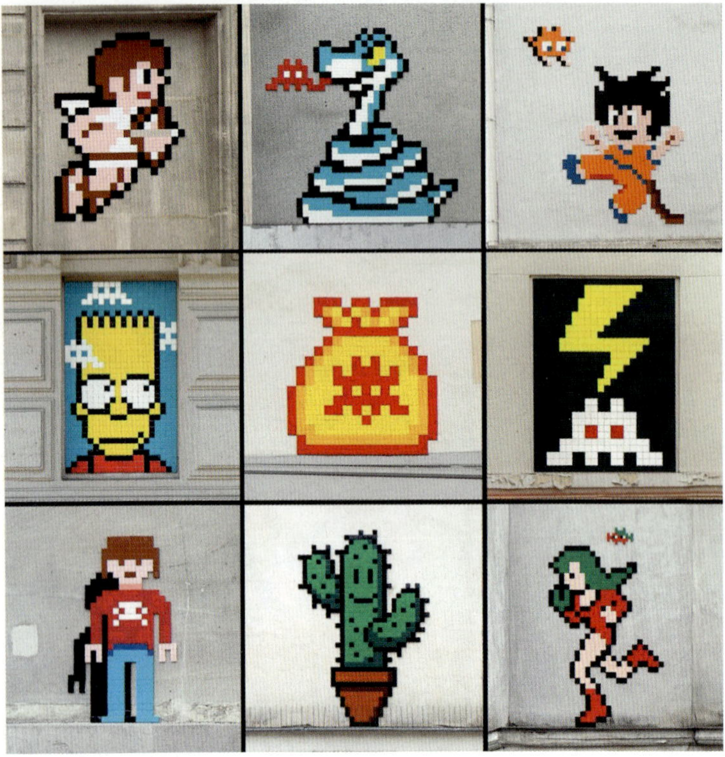

18 020 likes

invaderwashere 9 of the 30 new summer pieces in Paris
#paris #invasion #summer2016

View all 187 comments

8 September 2016

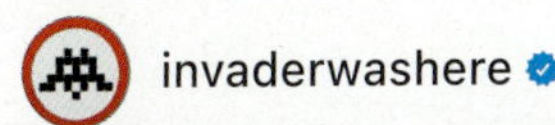

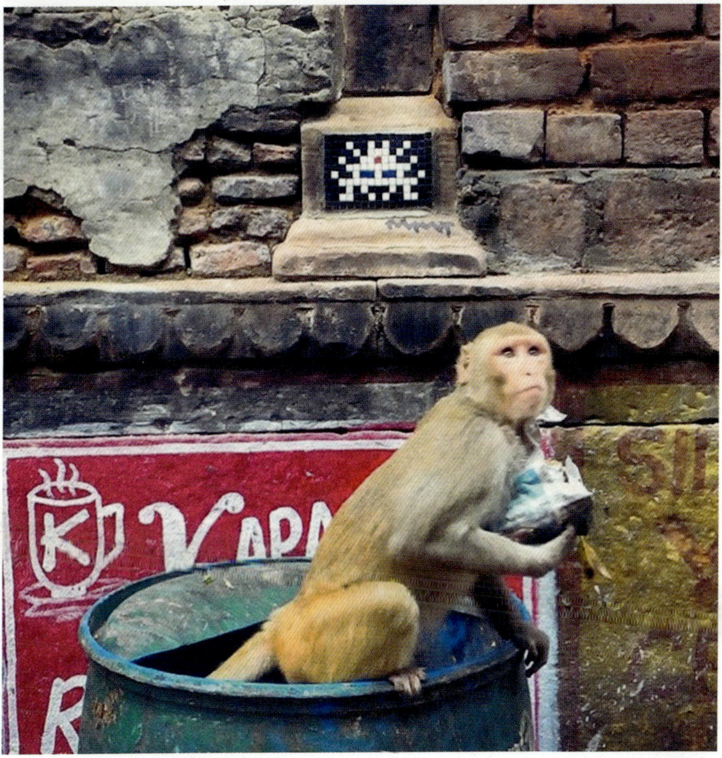

7612 likes

invaderwashere VRN_03 and friend #varanasi #benares #india 8 years old! photo by @sherefj

View all 34 comments

9 September 2016

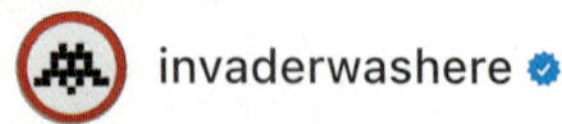

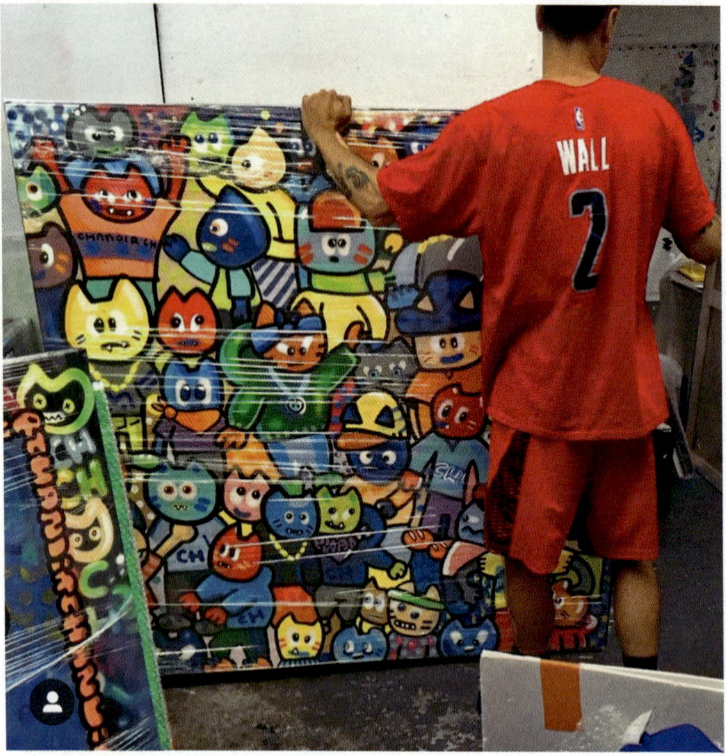

5 697 likes

invaderwashere Visiting @chanoir1980 studio #lavidaloca #catsinvasion

View all 15 comments

10 September 2016

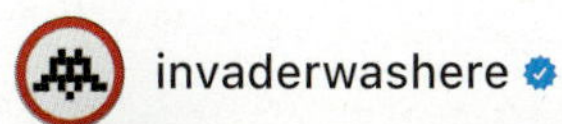

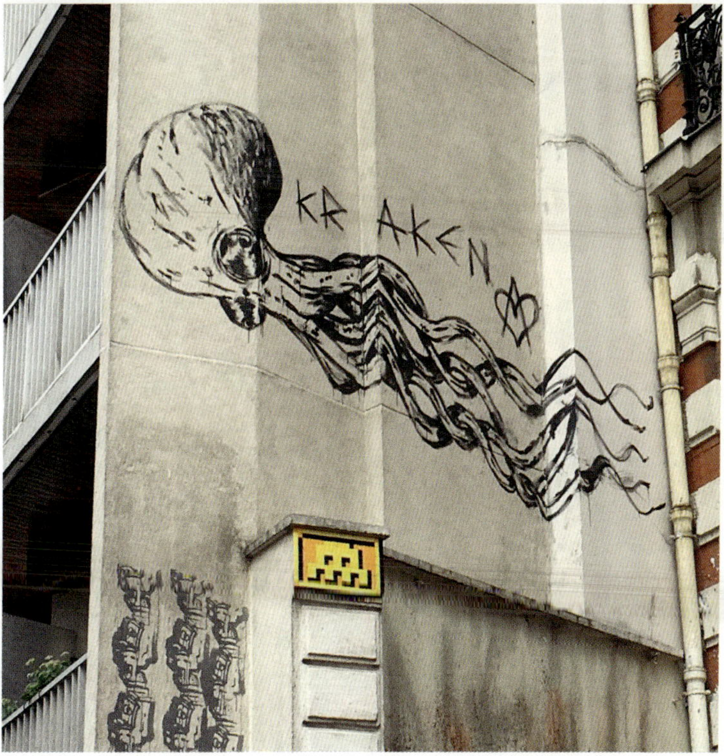

11238 likes

invaderwashere PA_1212 #paris #kraken #invader

View all 53 comments

11 September 2016

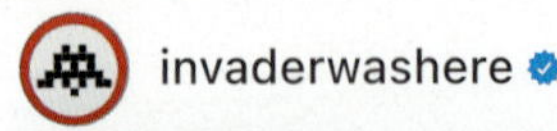

invaderwashere Detail of Rubik 9-11 #memorial #neverforget #history #disaster #rubikcubism #2005

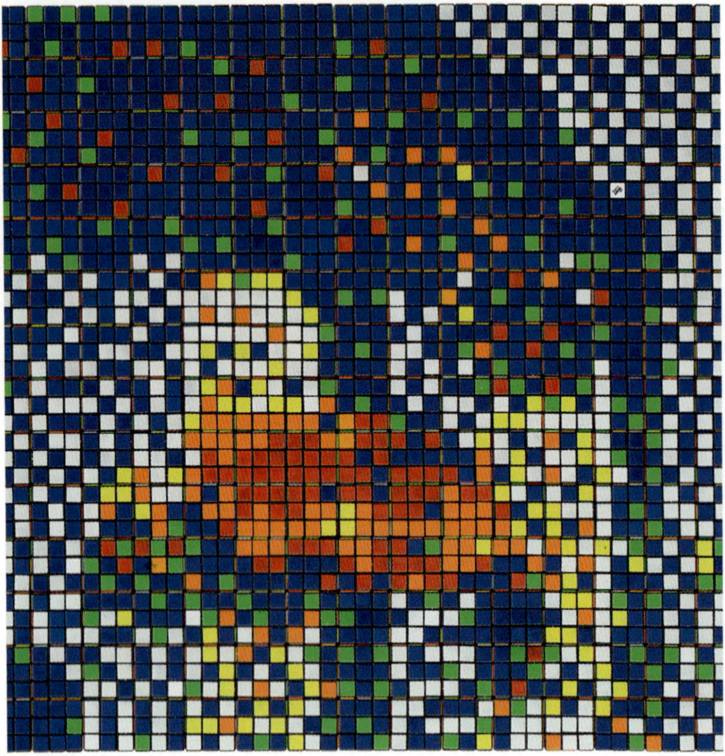

View all 25 comments

11 September 2016

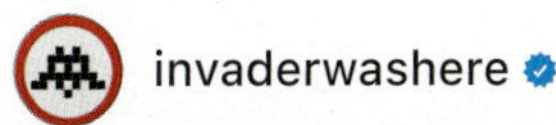

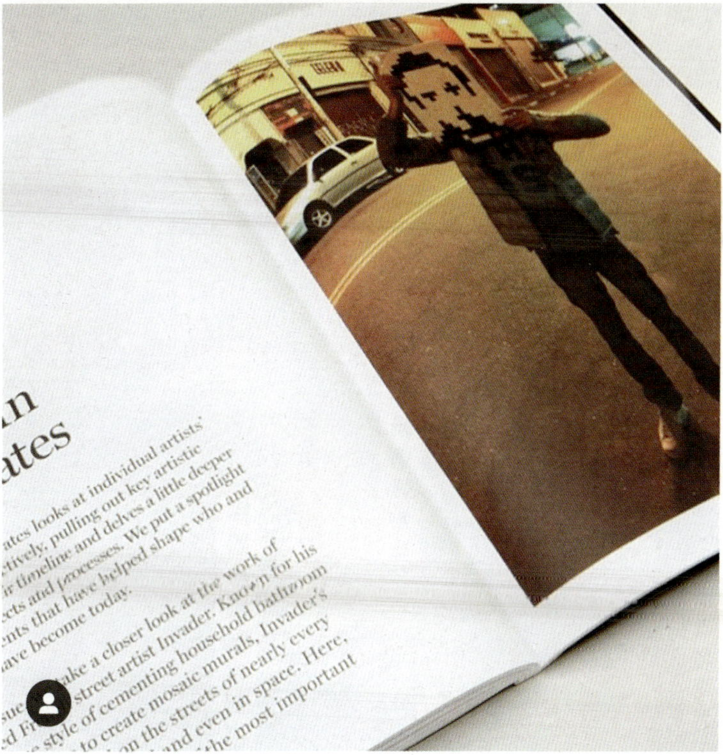

4092 likes

invaderwashere Uk based and independent, @vnamagazine is certainly one of the most beautiful graffiti/street art magazine in the world. I'm honored to be part of their new issue featuring @marthacoopergram #keithharing and many more... #vna #verynearlyalmost #34

View all 19 comments

15 September 2016

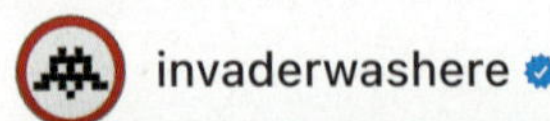

invaderwashere

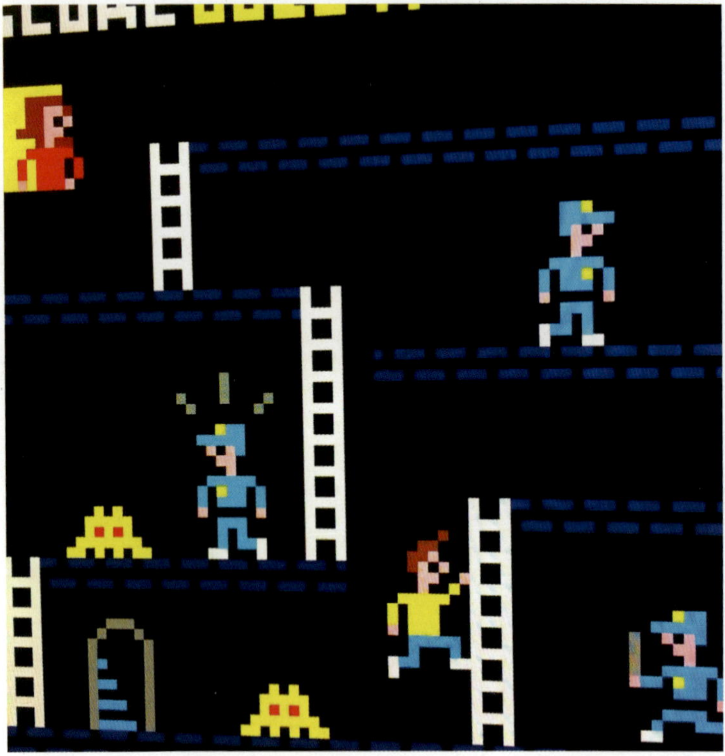

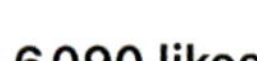

6 090 likes

invaderwashere Image of the day

View all 27 comments

16 September 2016

invaderwashere

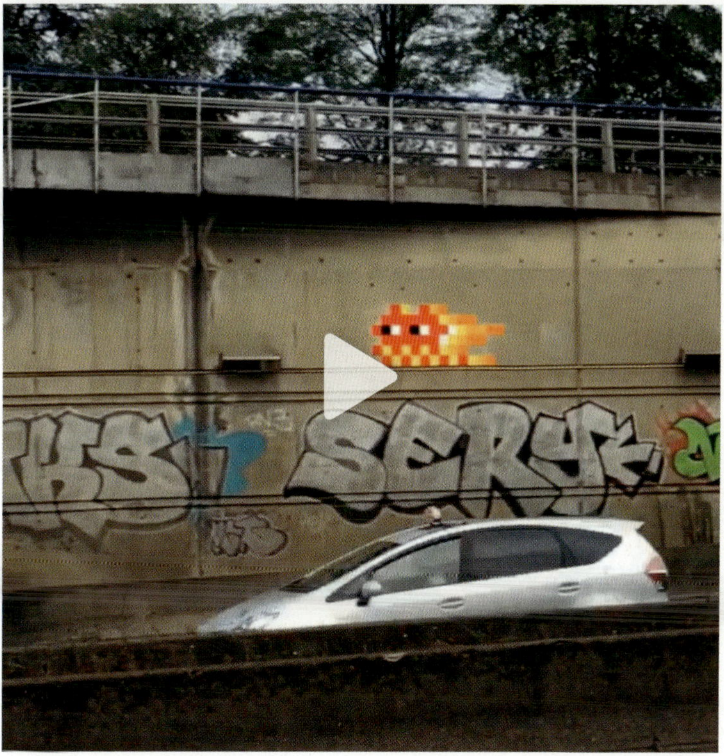

33 053 views

invaderwashere Children, don't do that at home! Let your mama papa do it #newborn #goodspot #highway #paris

View all 54 comments

18 September 2016

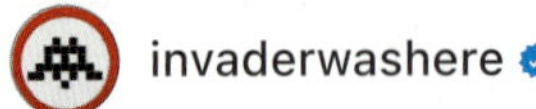

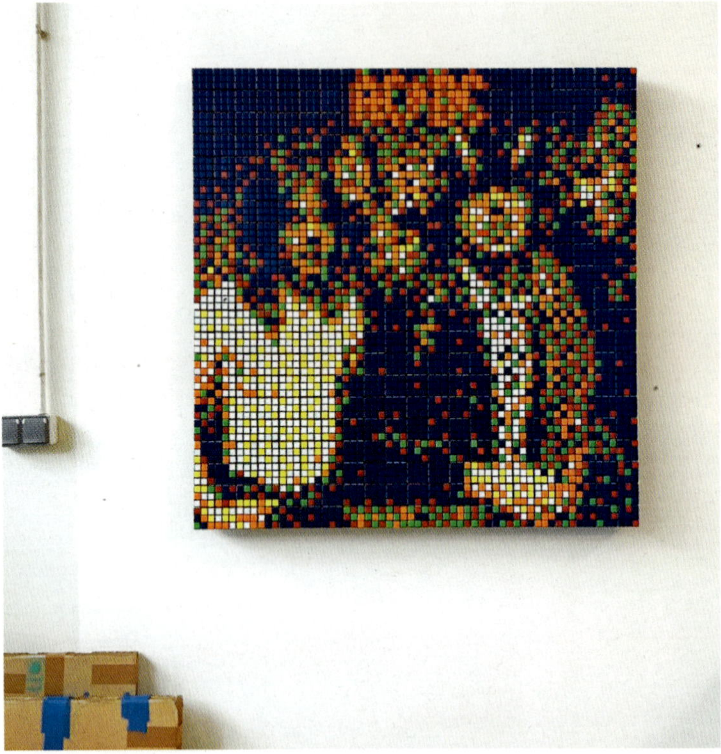

7192 likes

invaderwashere 🤘 Rubik Highway to Hell is back at the studio #restauration #studiodetail #acdc #2009 #lowfidelity #rubikcubism

View all 51 comments

19 September 2016

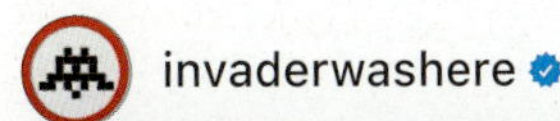

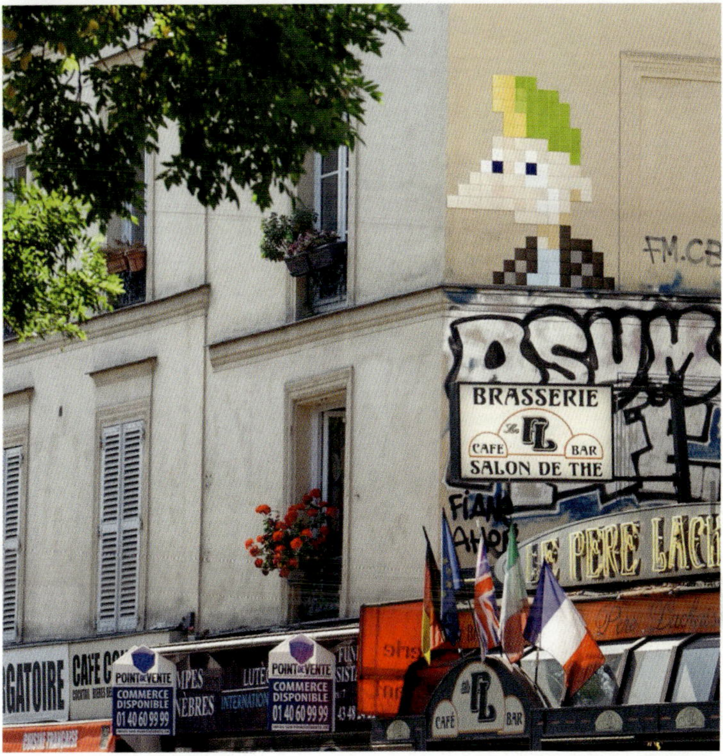

9627 likes

invaderwashere Latest invasion from the night... A tribute to Bloodi, comic's character by parisian cartoonist Pierre Ouin #bloodi #pierreouin #perelachaise #rip

View all 59 comments

21 September 2016

invaderwashere

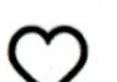   

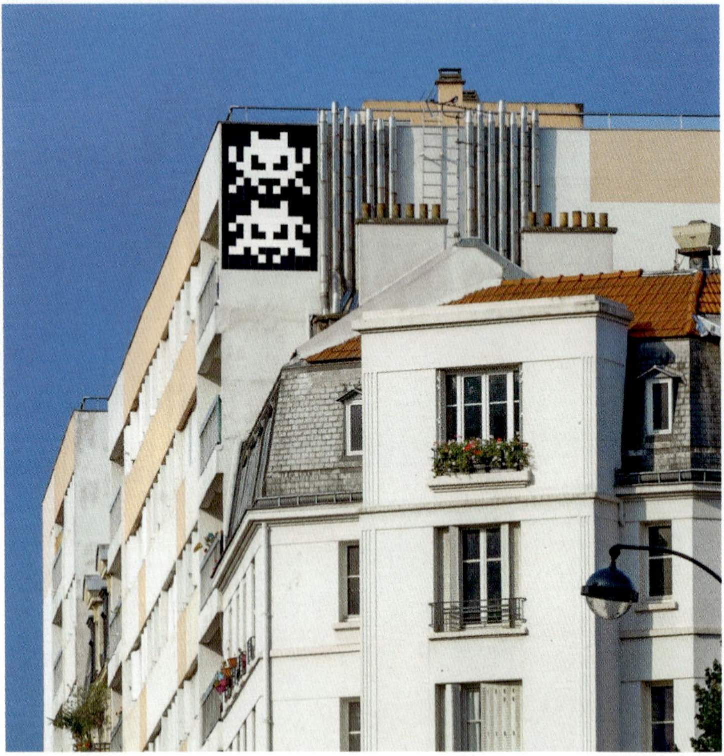

10 794 likes

invaderwashere PA_1240 from the ground

View all 46 comments

24 September 2016

invaderwashere

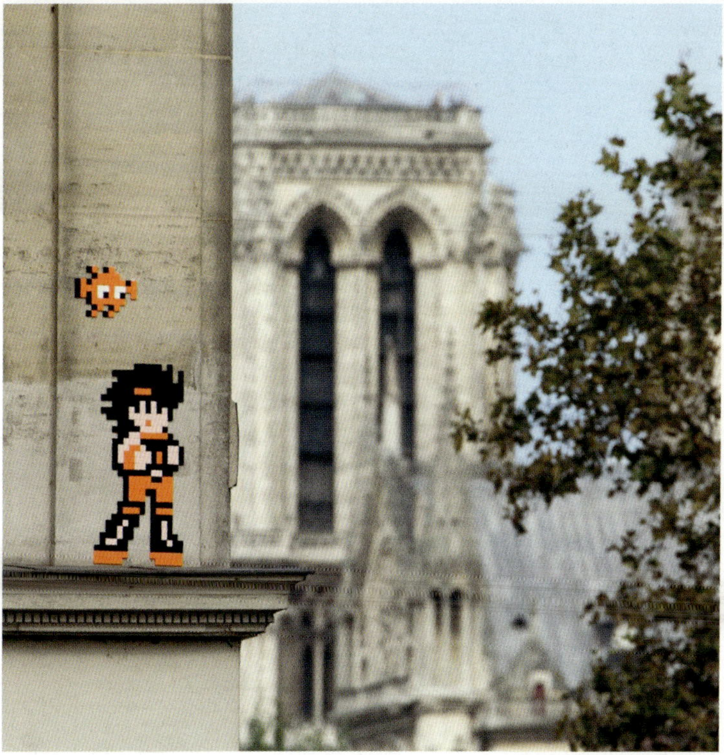

13 819 likes

invaderwashere PA_1241

View all 57 comments

25 September 2016

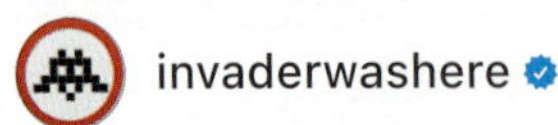

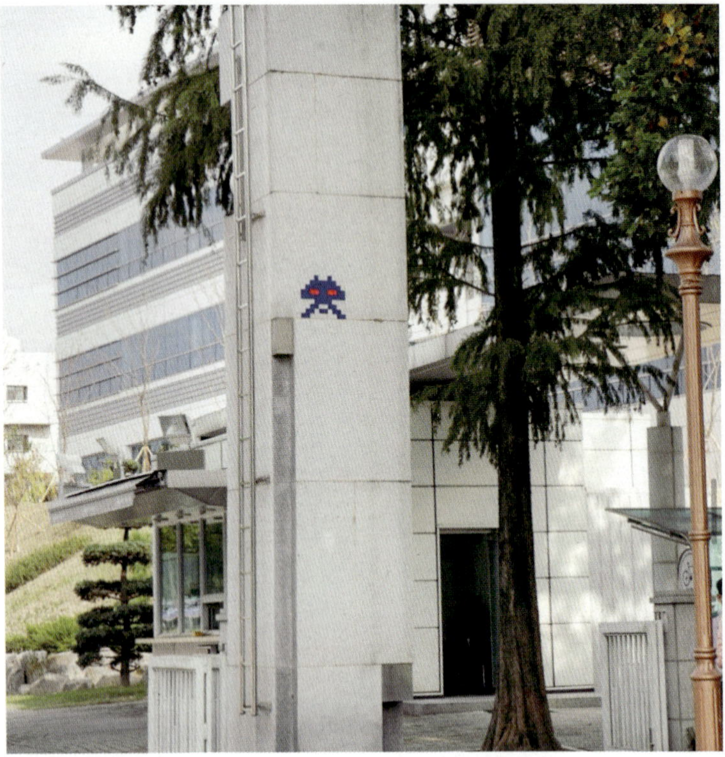

 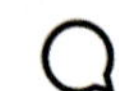  

7206 likes

invaderwashere Can someone help me to find the exact location of this mosaic? No google streetview in Daejeon 😅 #help #lostinvader #DJN19 #daejeon #southkorea #thankyou

View all 27 comments

27 September 2016

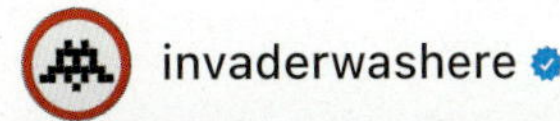

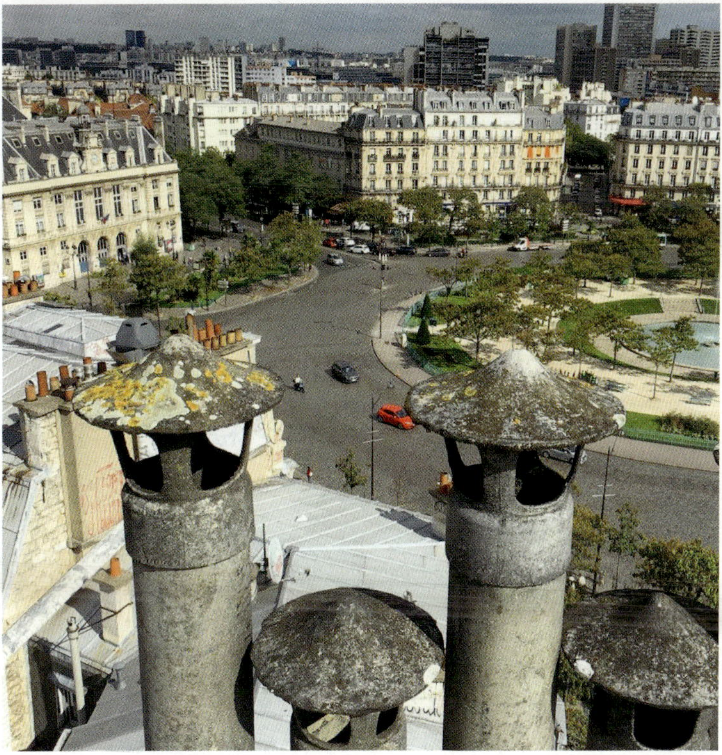

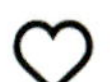 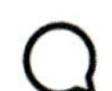  

4 324 likes

invaderwashere Scouting of the day #paris #rooftops

View all 23 comments

28 September 2016

invaderwashere ...

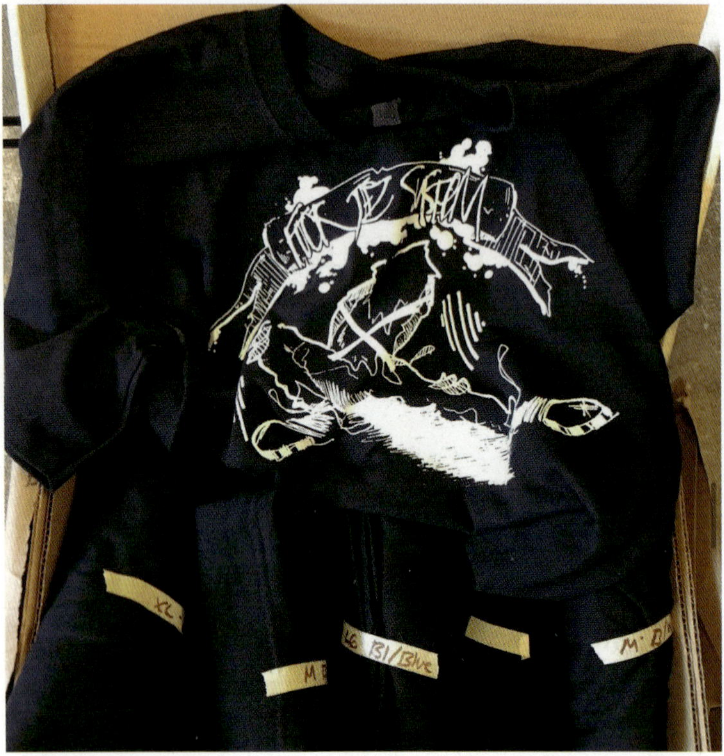

2 046 likes

invaderwashere Arrival of the day: Fuck the System / Designed by Revs for The Deacons / 100 copies / Available on the Space Shop #revs #fuckinrevs #thedeacons #m13 #madeinbrooklyn

View all 11 comments

29 September 2016

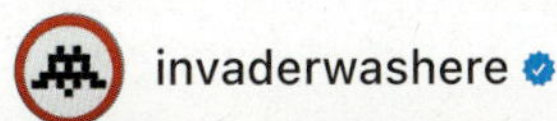

invaderwashere

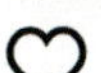   

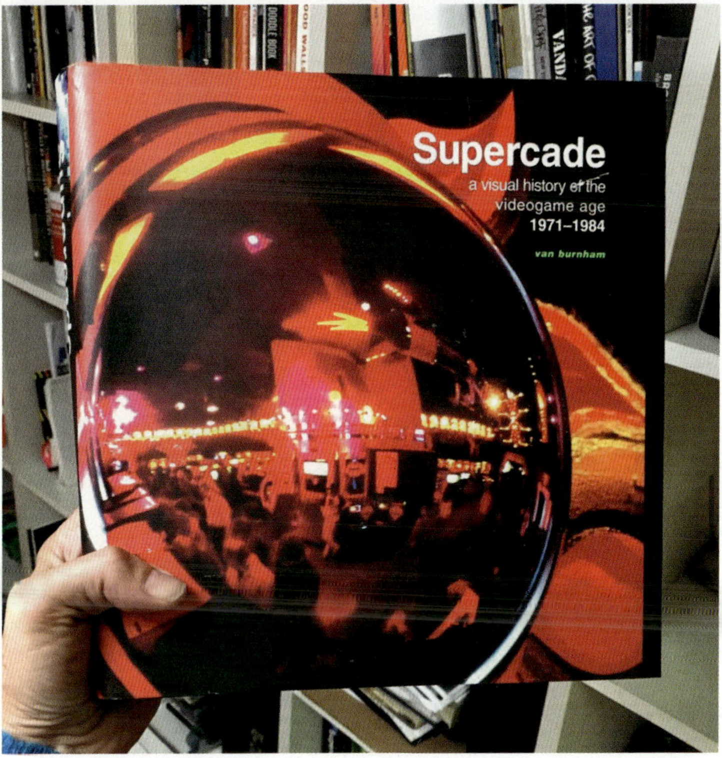

2 827 likes

invaderwashere Definitely the best book about vintage videogames / Supercade by @thevanburnham #supercade #MITpress Got this copie for 15 years!

View all 25 comments

2 October 2016

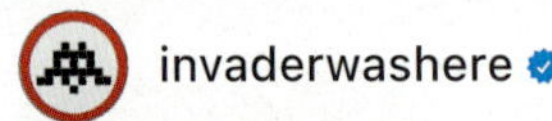

invaderwashere

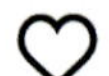   

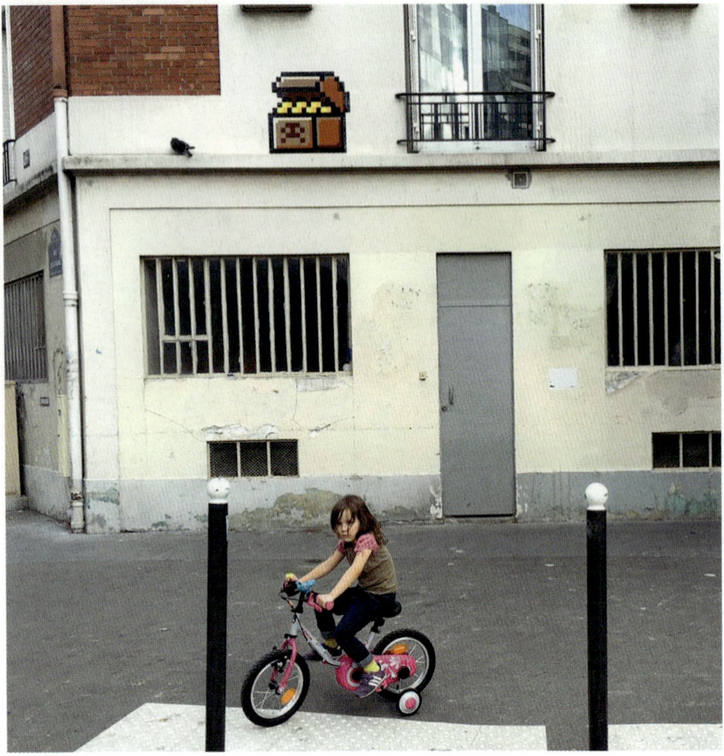

8 213 likes

invaderwashere Looks like the treasure is well guarded!!!
#newpiece #pa1242 #treasure #biker

View all 52 comments

3 October 2016

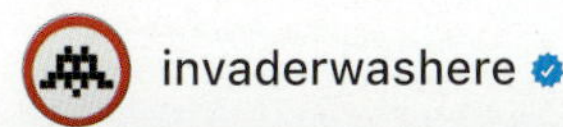

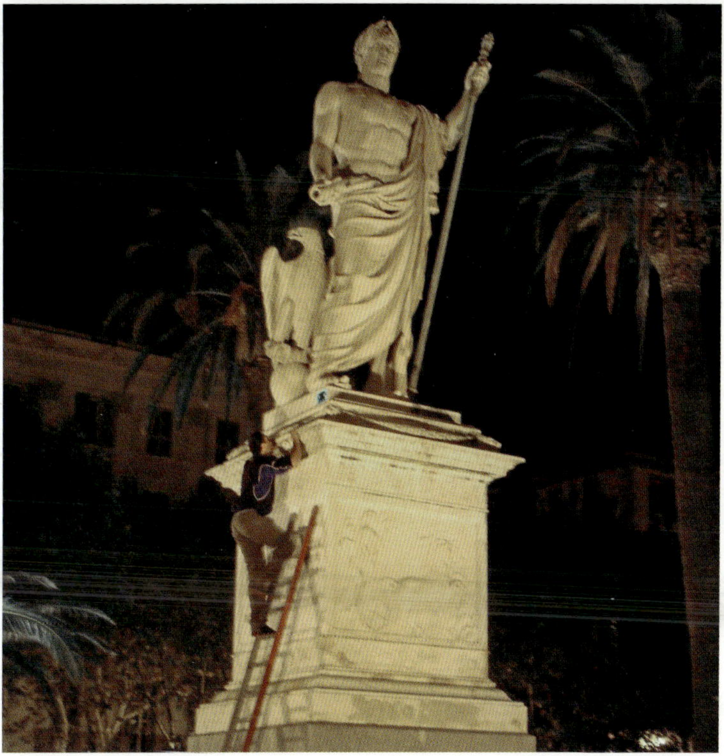

 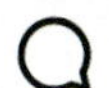  

3 827 likes

invaderwashere Invading Napoleon! Bastia #corsica #bta31 #throwback #2005

View all 40 comments

5 October 2016

invaderwashere

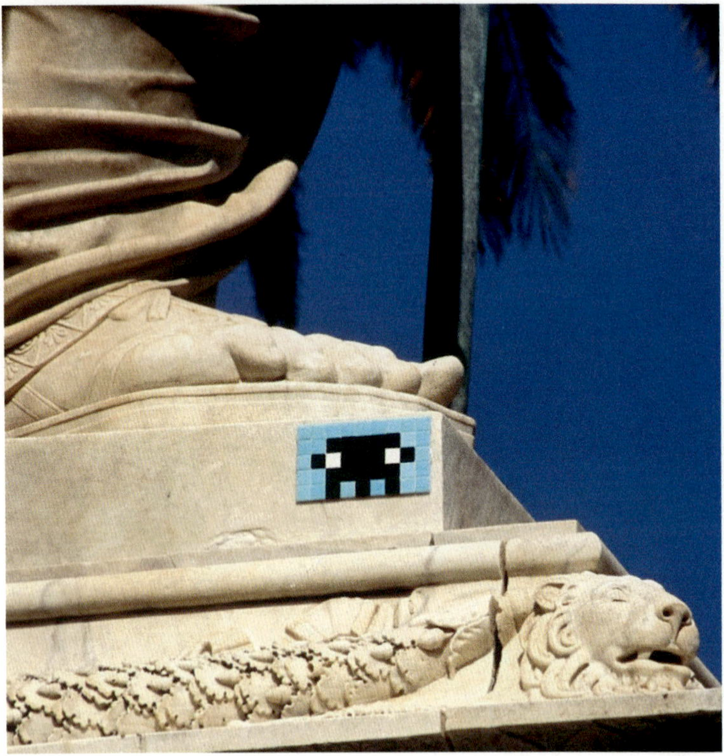

8 422 likes

invaderwashere BTA_31 close up #corsica #bastia #throwback #2005

View all 37 comments

5 October 2016

invaderwashere

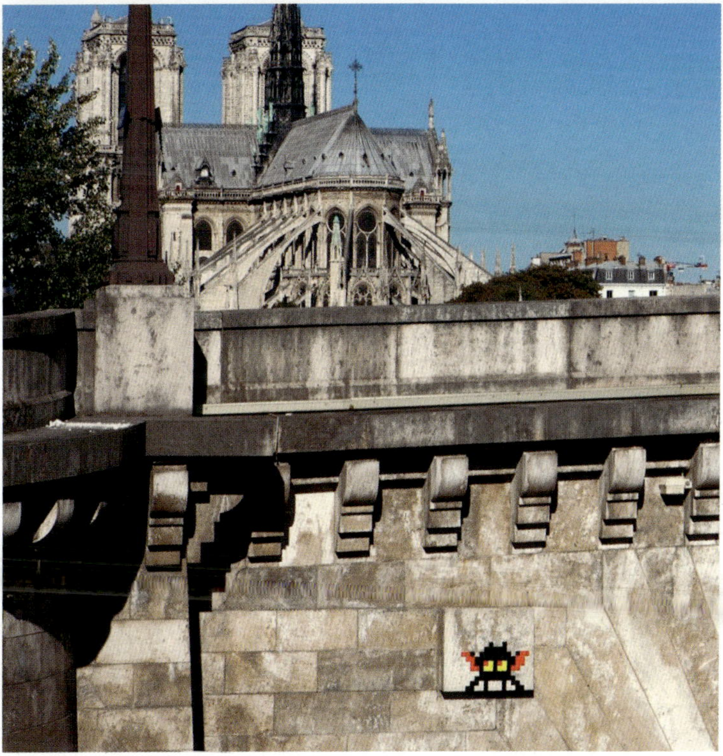

7667 likes

invaderwashere PA_1245 #justlanded #batinvader #notredame

View all 35 comments

7 October 2016

invaderwashere

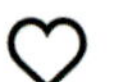   

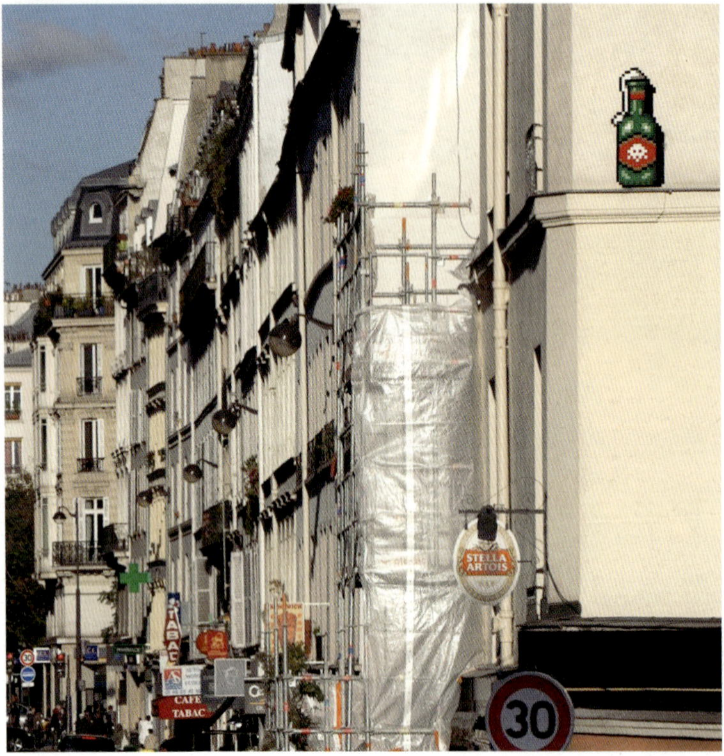

8892 likes

invaderwashere Oberkampf street is well known for its bars and its night life 👾 🍺 #spacebeer #newpiece #paris

View all 43 comments

8 October 2016

invaderwashere

 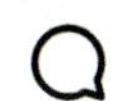  

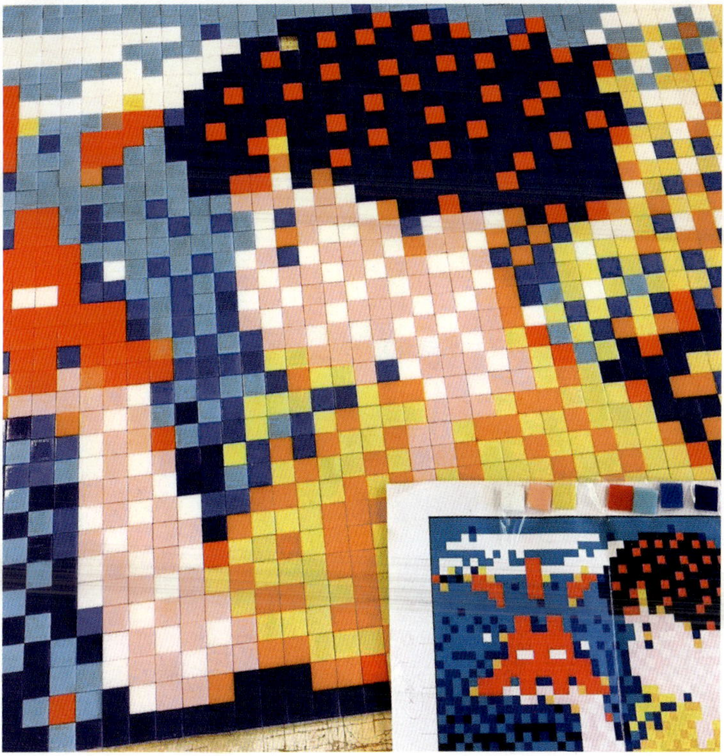

8 372 likes

invaderwashere Studio detail #ponyo

View all 48 comments

13 October 2016

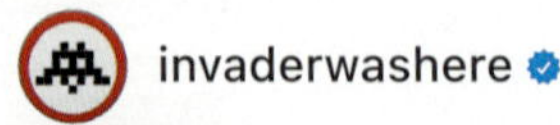

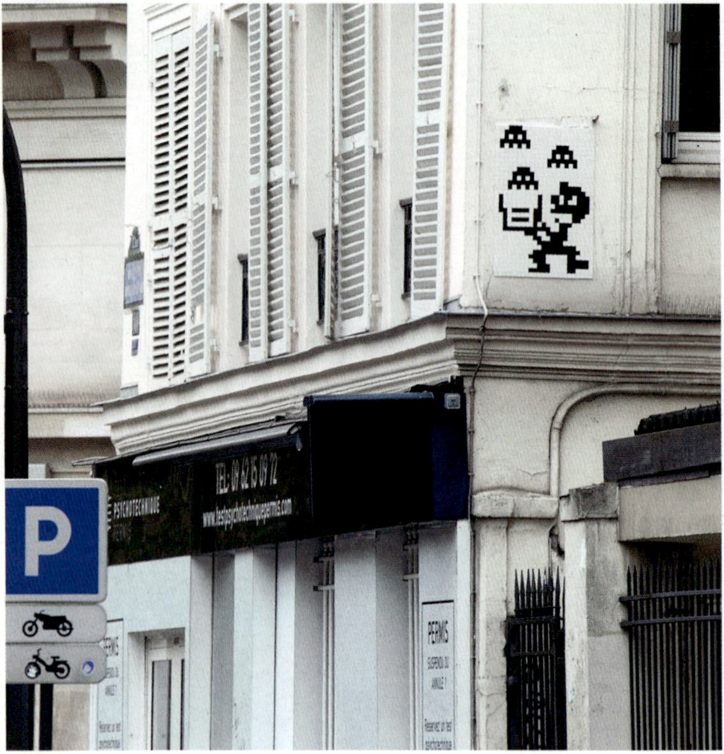

10 182 likes

invaderwashere Brand new PA_1248

View all 56 comments

19 October 2016

invaderwashere

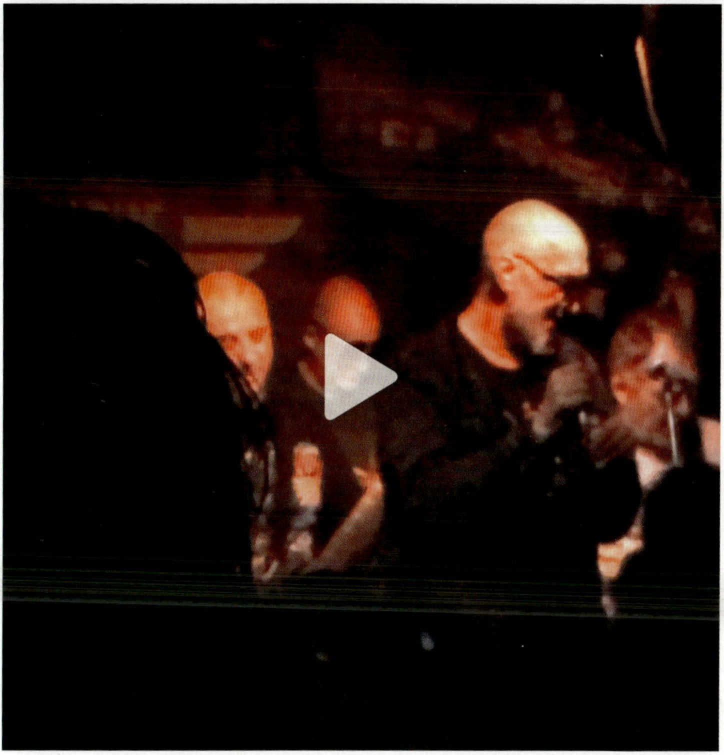

13 462 views

invaderwashere Warum Joe live #paris #warumjoe #ventdivin

View all 9 comments

20 October 2016

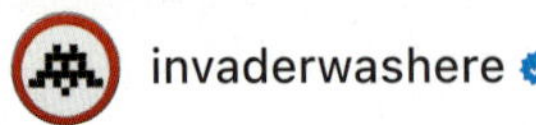

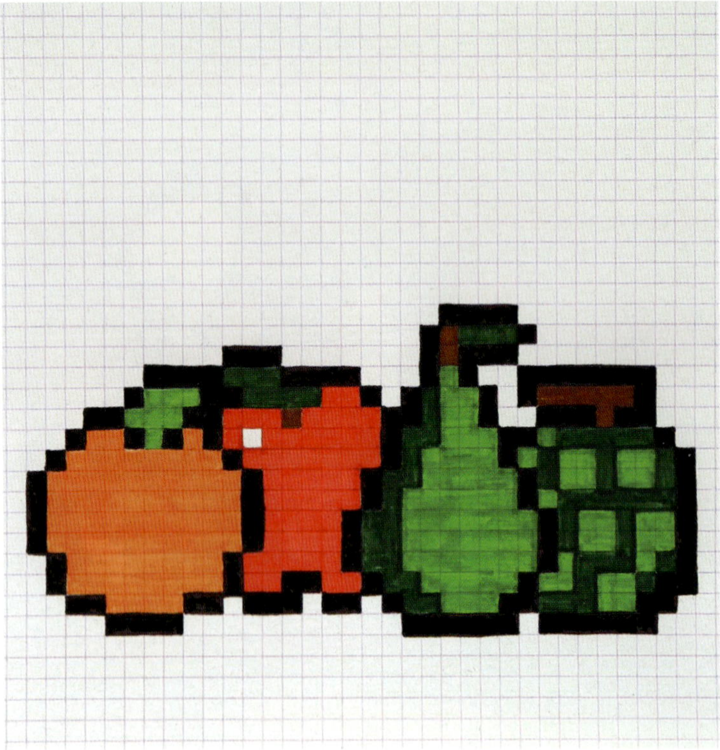

7095 likes

invaderwashere Hand drawing for the vegan cause
#stilllife #fruits #vegan #brunoblum #cabaretvegan
@artcurial__

View all 48 comments

20 October 2016

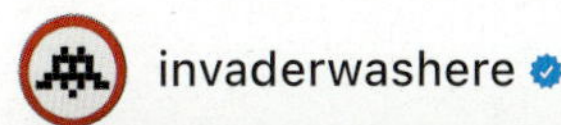

invaderwashere

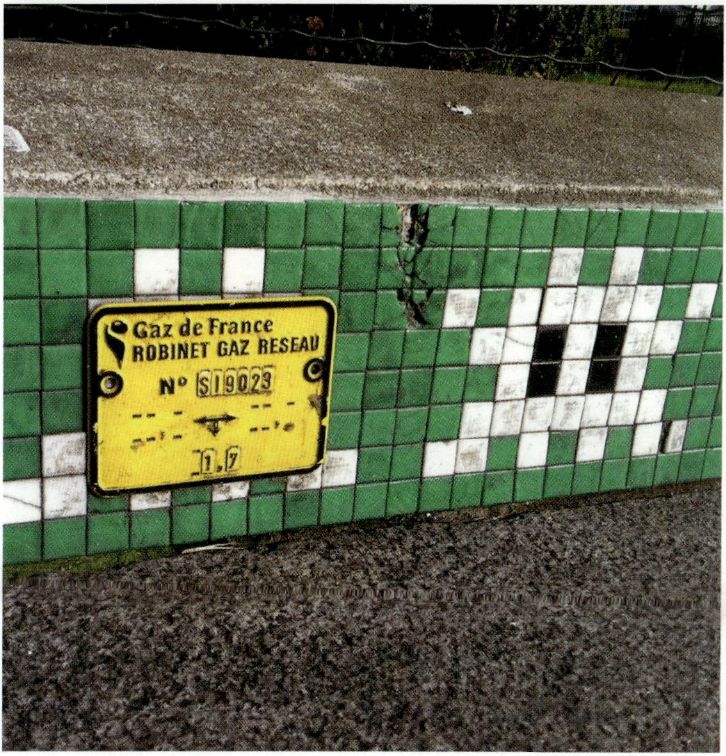

7 515 likes

invaderwashere Detail of PA_689 #throwback #gazdefrance

View all 39 comments

21 October 2016

invaderwashere

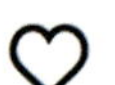   

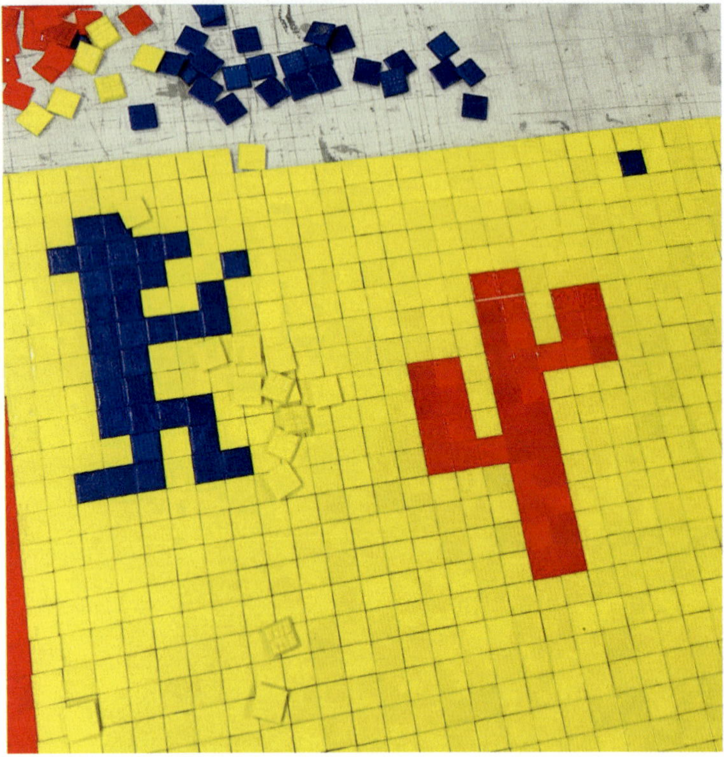

6613 likes

invaderwashere Bang Bang 🔫💥🌵 #outlaw #atari2600

View all 38 comments

23 October 2016

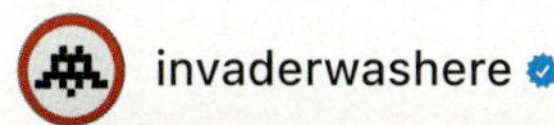

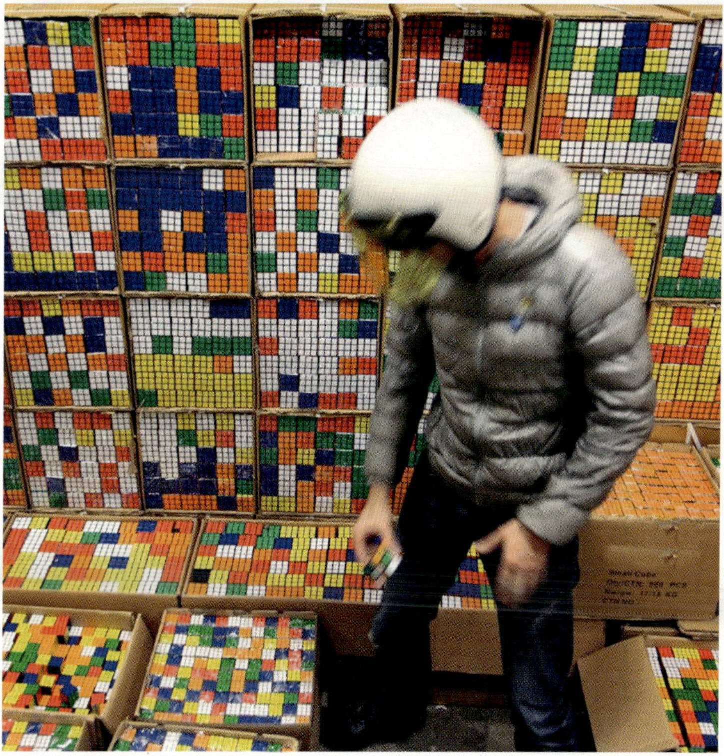

9831 likes

invaderwashere Delivery of the day #rubikscubes #studiodetail

View all 79 comments

25 October 2016

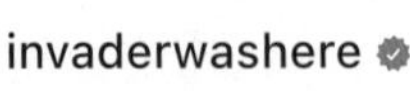

•••

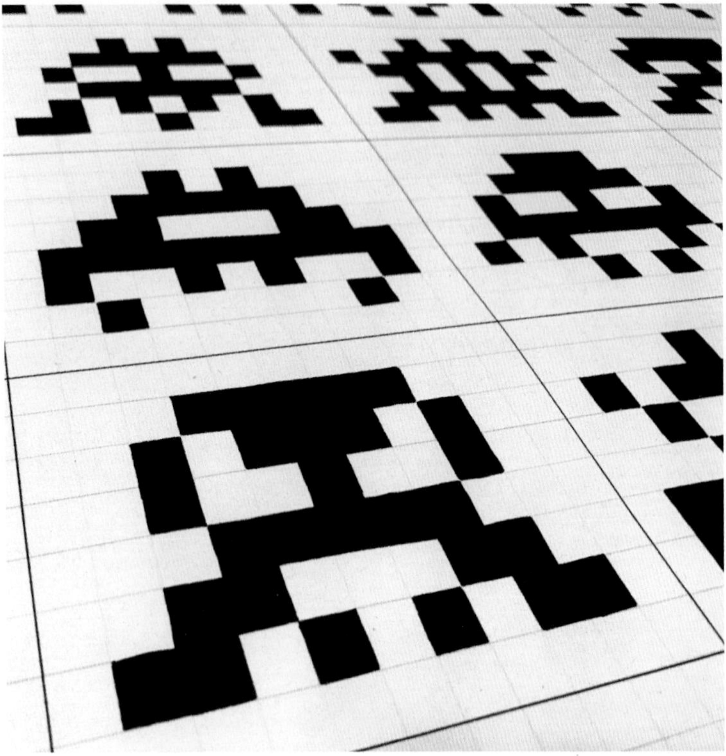

7949 likes

invaderwashere Ink on Paper #spaceinvaders #variations #detail #workinprogress

View all 45 comments

28 October 2016

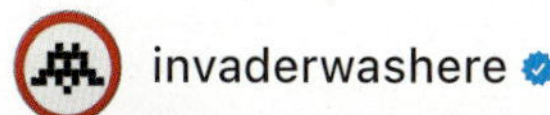

•••

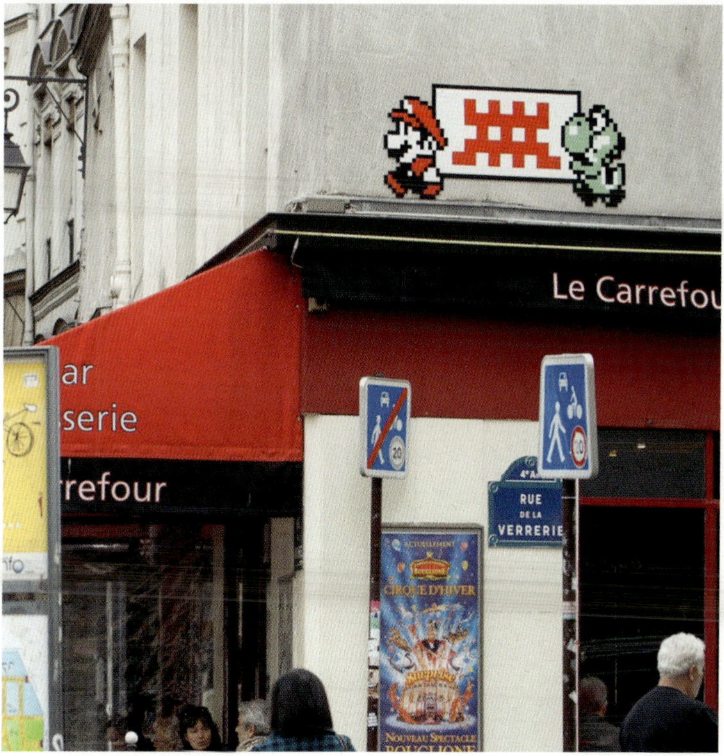

13 091 likes

invaderwashere By working in the streets and public space I bring art into life, everywhere and for everyone / PA_1249 #lecarrefour

View all 85 comments

30 October 2016

invaderwashere

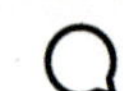

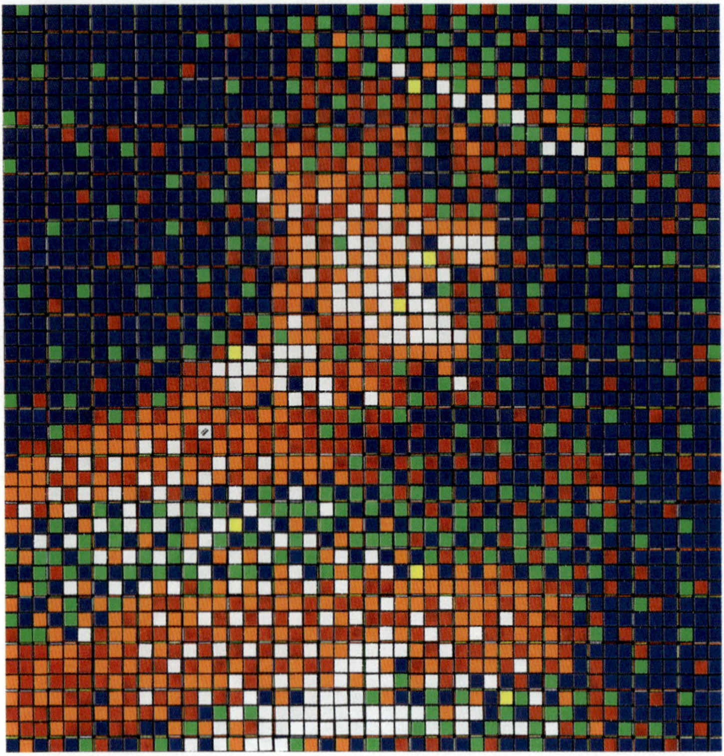

6 223 likes

invaderwashere Happy Halloween 🎃🎃🎃
#rubikfreddykrueger #rubikcubism #detail #2007

View all 34 comments

1 November 2016

invaderwashere

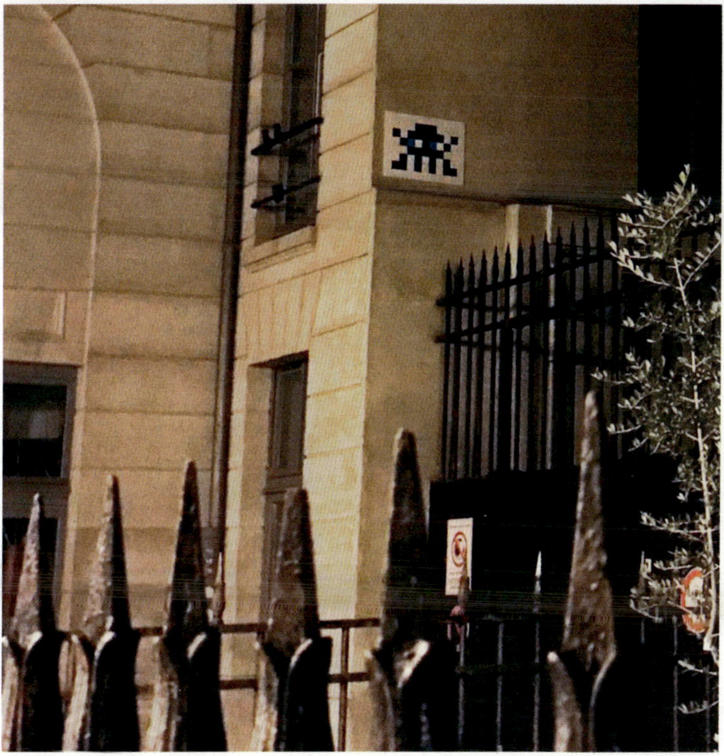

8782 likes

invaderwashere Just done

View all 54 comments

4 November 2016

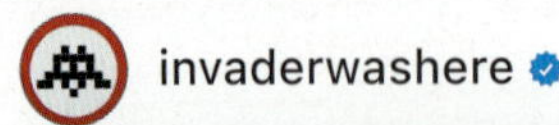

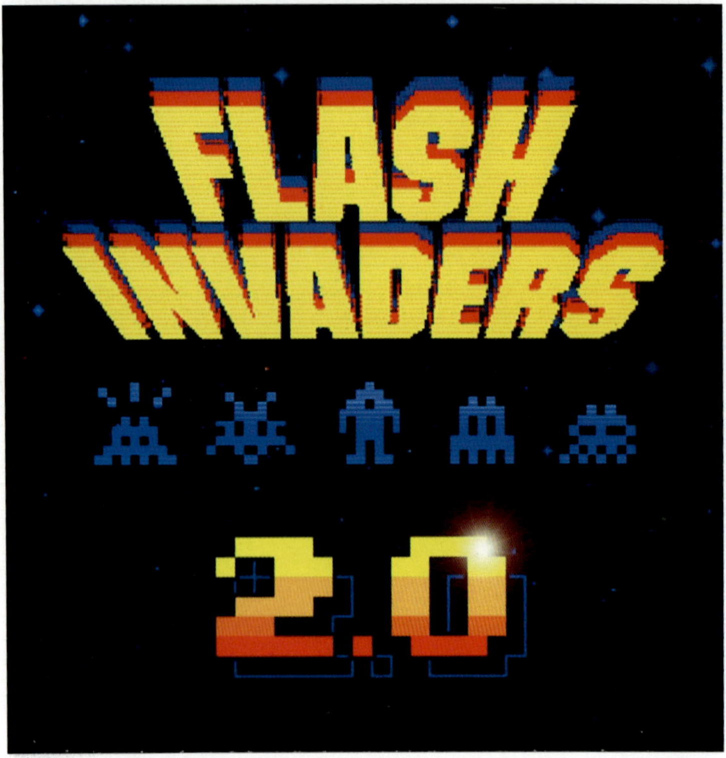

4002 likes

invaderwashere Flashinvaders 2.0 is now available on #applestore and #googleplay #freeapp #havefun

View all 41 comments

10 November 2016

invaderwashere

 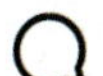   

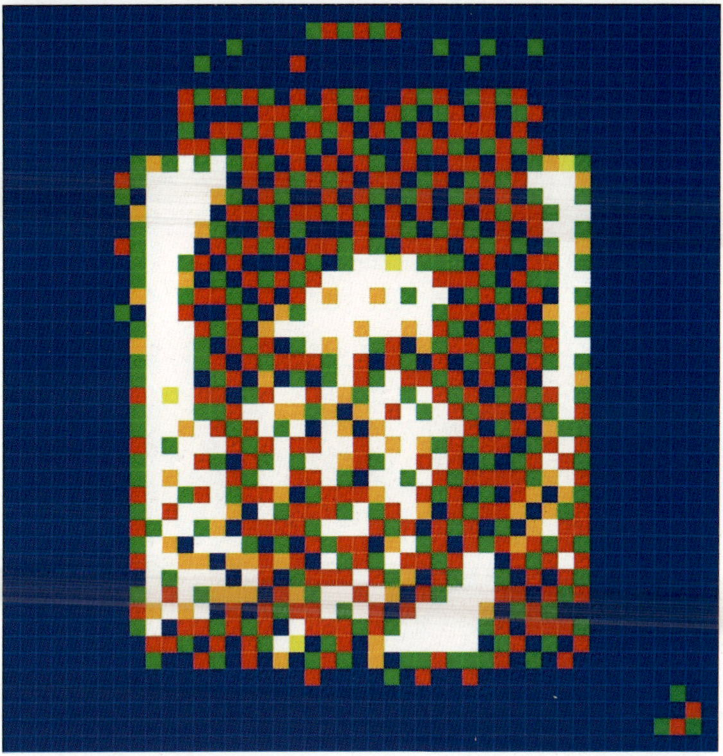

6 223 likes

invaderwashere So long Leonard 🌹 Thank you for the poems and songs / Study for Rubik Songs of #LeonardCohen 2010

View all 32 comments

11 November 2016

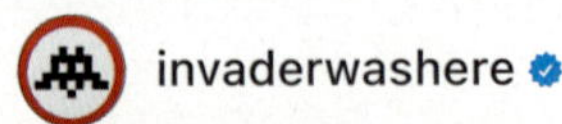

Invader, play again

Les mosaïques de l'artiste français qui ont envahi les rues depuis la fin des années 90 sont au cœur d'un jeu de pistes grandeur nature. Une chasse au niveau mondial qui mobilise des milliers de joueurs exaltés.

Par STÉPHANIE AUBERT

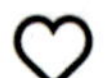   

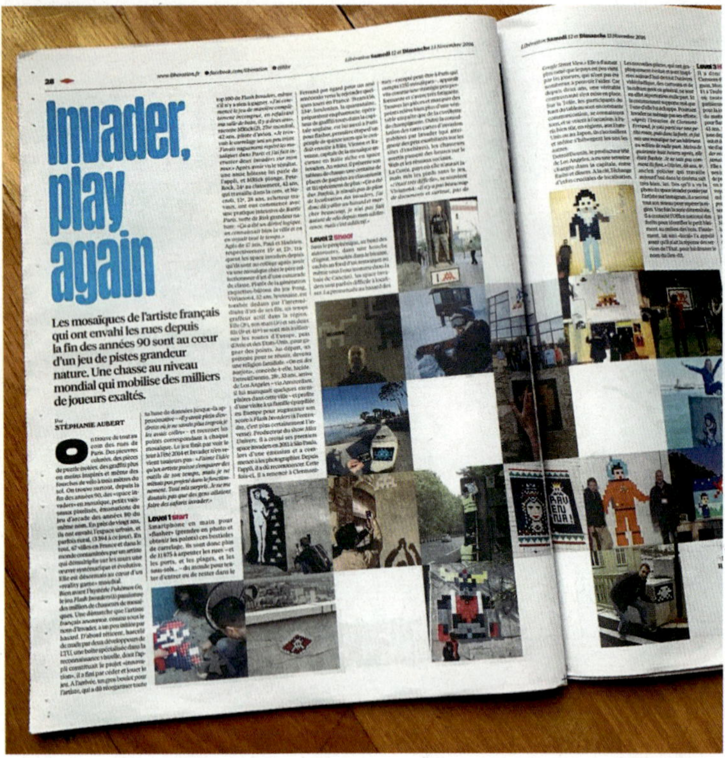

4225 likes

invaderwashere Thank you Liberation newspaper for this great article about Flashinvaders and the players @liberationfr #today #flashinvaders by Stephanie Aubert

View all 26 comments

12 November 2016

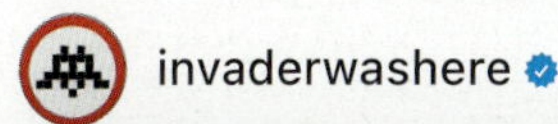

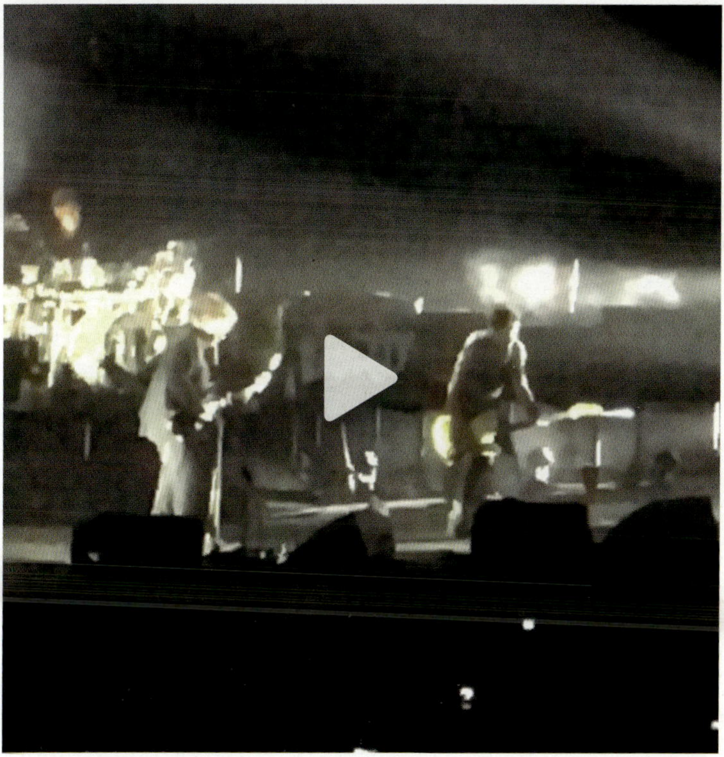

25 706 views

invaderwashere 🙌🙌🙌 #thecure #bercy #paris #legend

View all 42 comments

16 November 2016

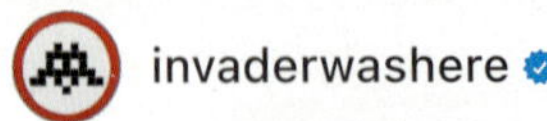

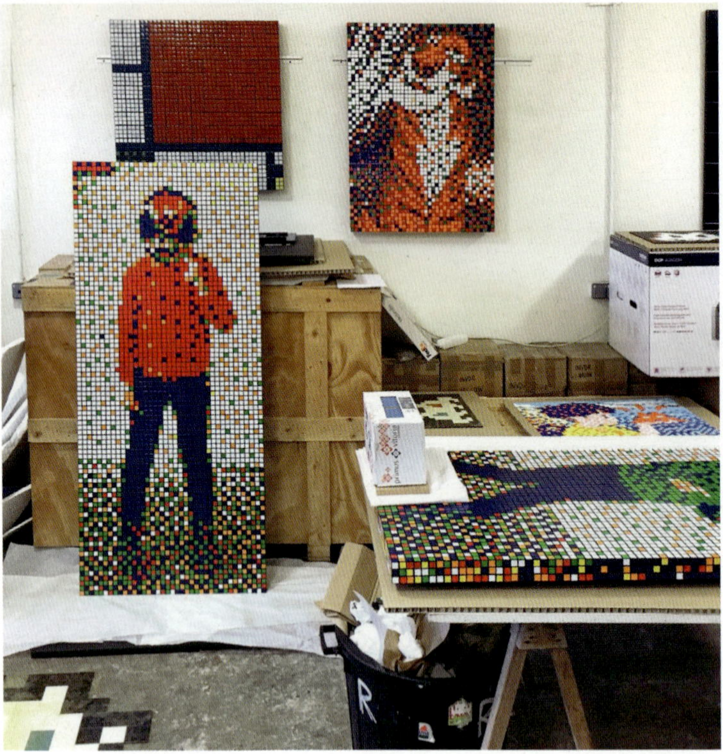

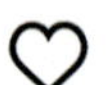   

9932 likes

invaderwashere #sunday #studio working on my next show...

View all 75 comments

20 November 2016

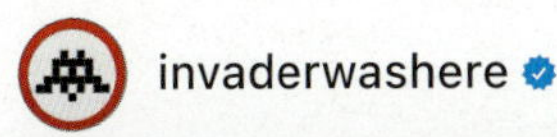

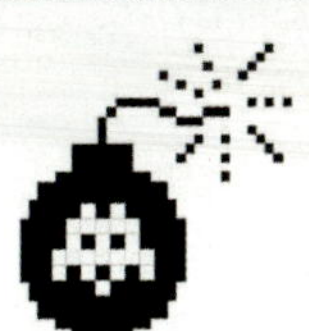

Sorry, a system error occurred.

All the flashs of this past week-end have been lost !

Flash Again

 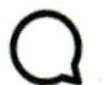  

4 238 likes

invaderwashere 😬 #hostcrash #errorsystem #flashinvaders #blackweekend

View all 61 comments

21 November 2016

invaderwashere

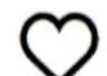   

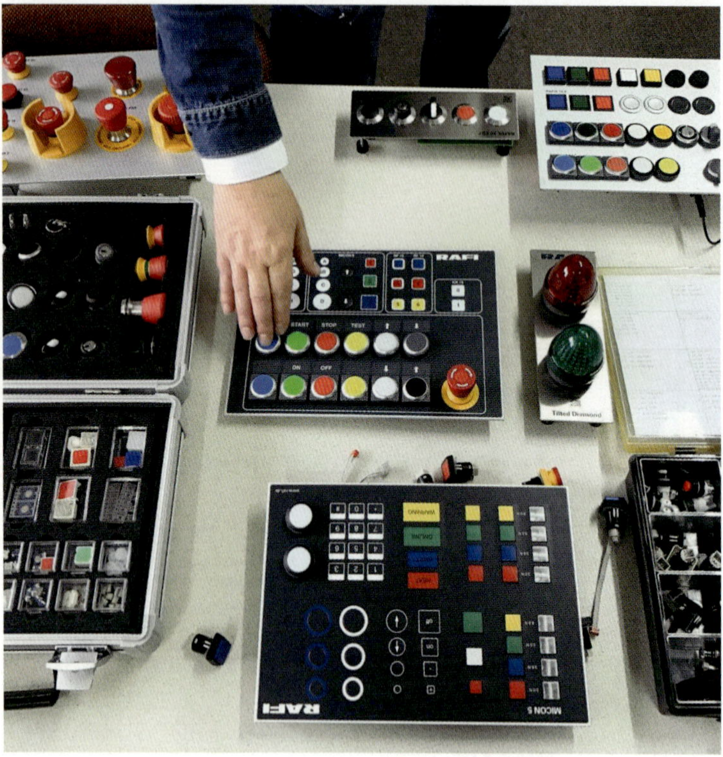

4949 likes

invaderwashere Clic clic, working on my next show...
#studiodetail #buttonschoice

View all 33 comments

25 November 2016

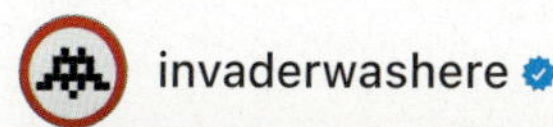

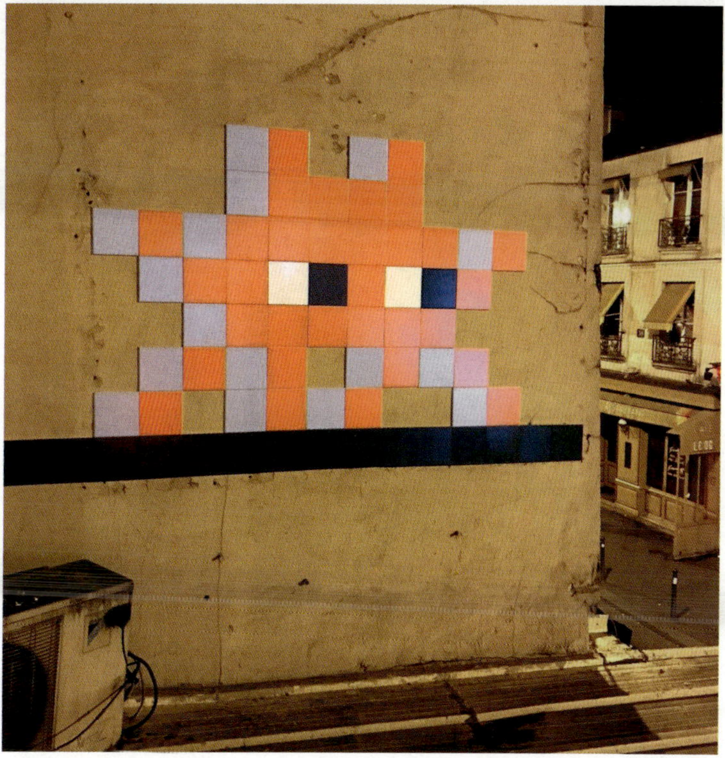

 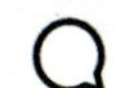  

12 000 likes

invaderwashere It was not supposed to go there... but it is a good spot! PA_1258 #paris #bastille 4:15 am

View all 67 comments

30 November 2016

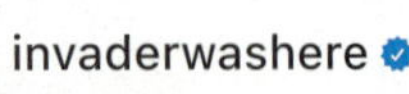

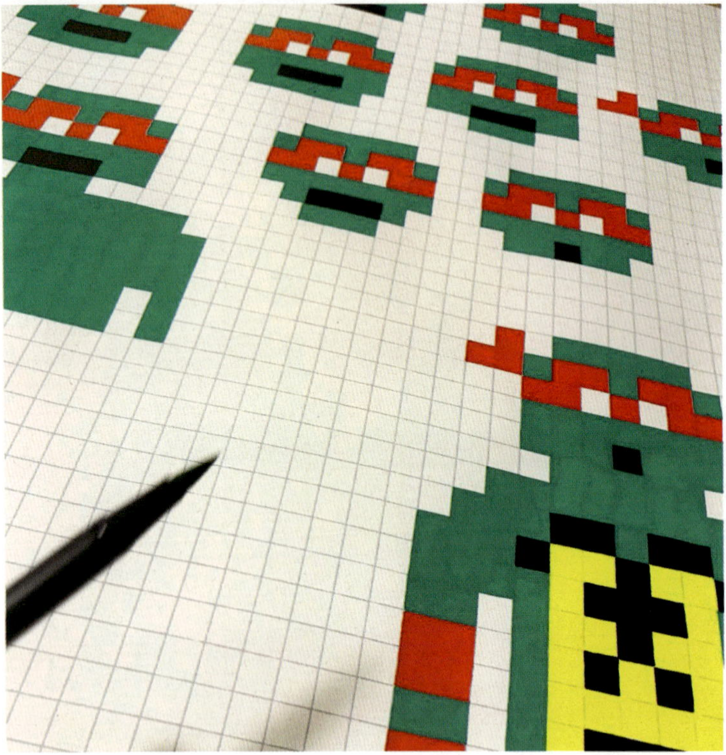

  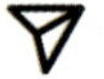 

9 966 likes

invaderwashere 🐢 👾 #raphael #study #graphpaper

View all 92 comments

2 December 2016

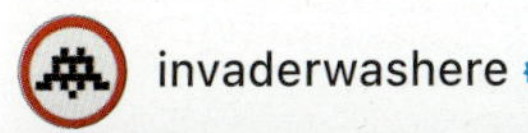

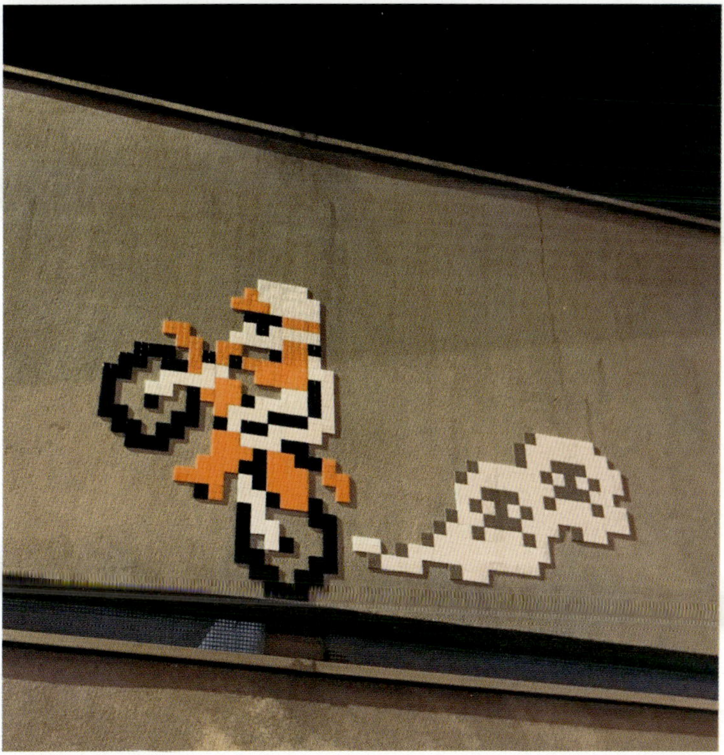

 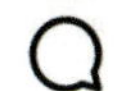  

19138 likes

invaderwashere 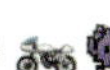 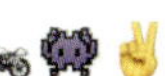

View all 239 comments

7 December 2016

invaderwashere 

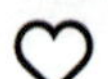   

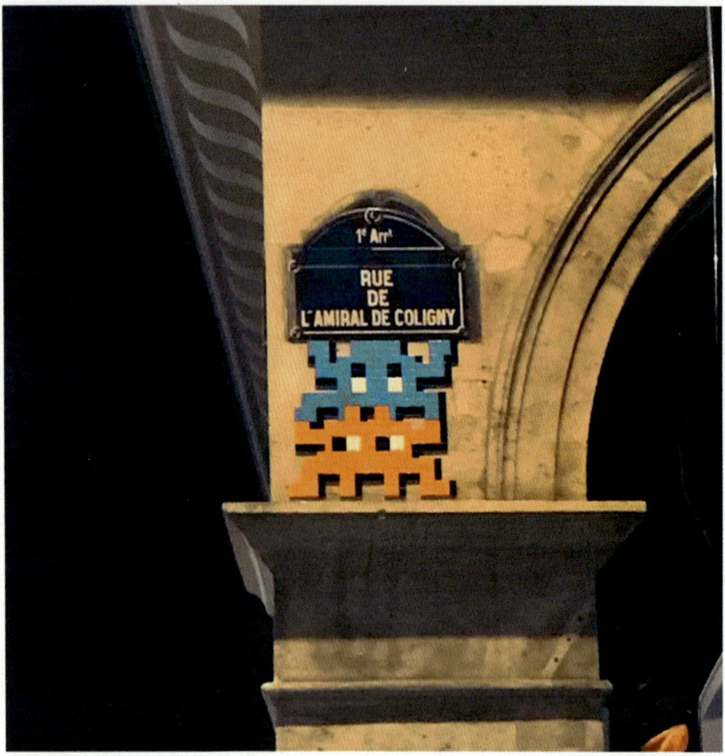

9 353 likes

invaderwashere PA_1260 #equilibrium

View all 43 comments

8 December 2016

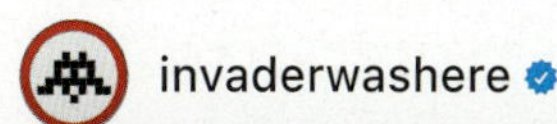

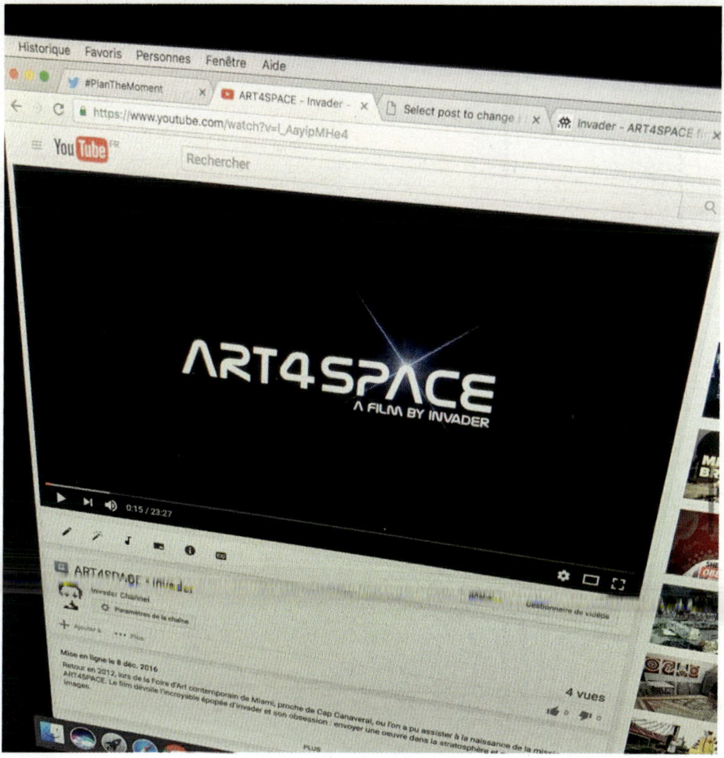

2028 likes

invaderwashere ART4SPACE online now!!! Link in bio / French & English / full version #art4space #youtube #themovie 👾 🚀

View all 54 comments

13 December 2016

invaderwashere

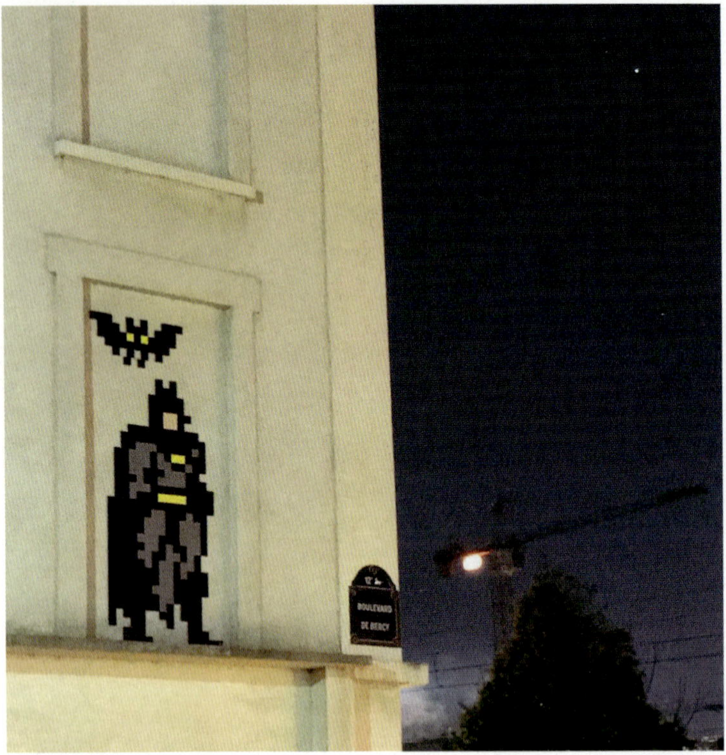

23 108 likes

invaderwashere Another night creature / Paris 3:03 am
#batinvader

View all 252 comments

14 December 2016

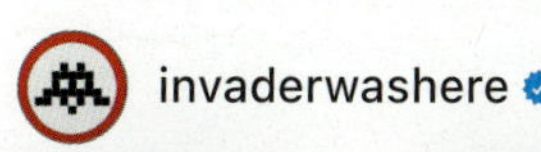

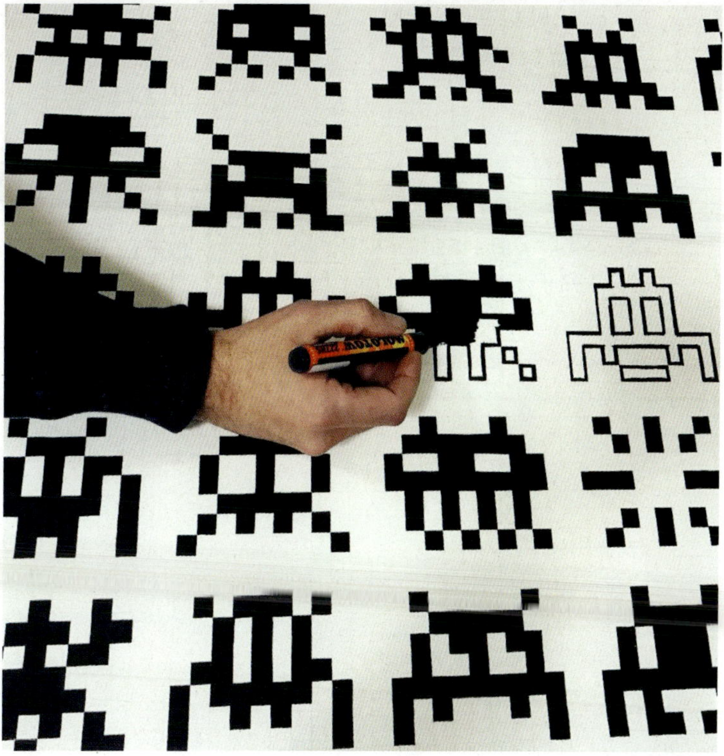

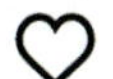 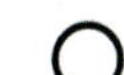  

10 954 likes

invaderwashere Ink on paper #repetitions #variations #mutations

View all 54 comments

18 December 2016

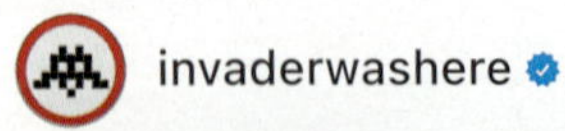

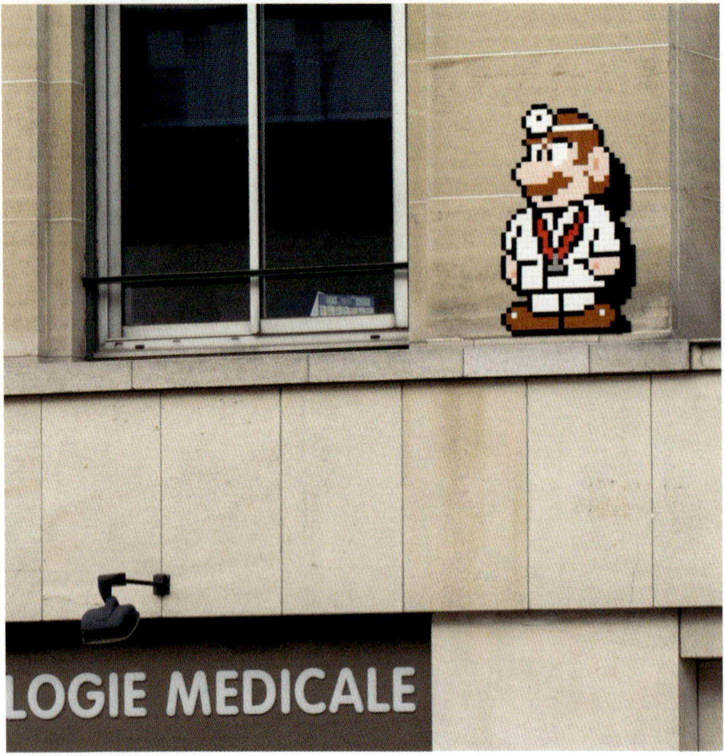

16 426 likes

invaderwashere Fresh from last night!!! PA_1262 #DrMario #paris

View all 126 comments

21 December 2016

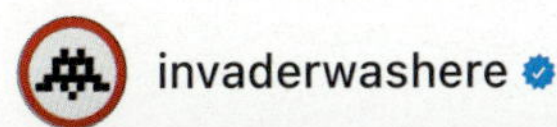

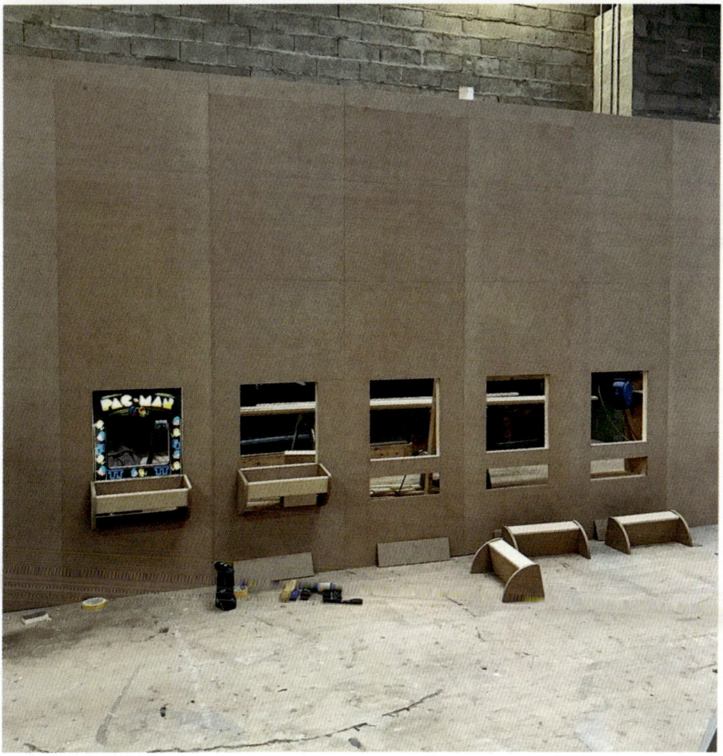

5 570 likes

invaderwashere Starting to install my next show... Stay tuned...

View all 58 comments

23 December 2016

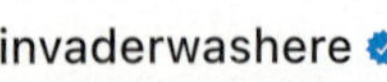

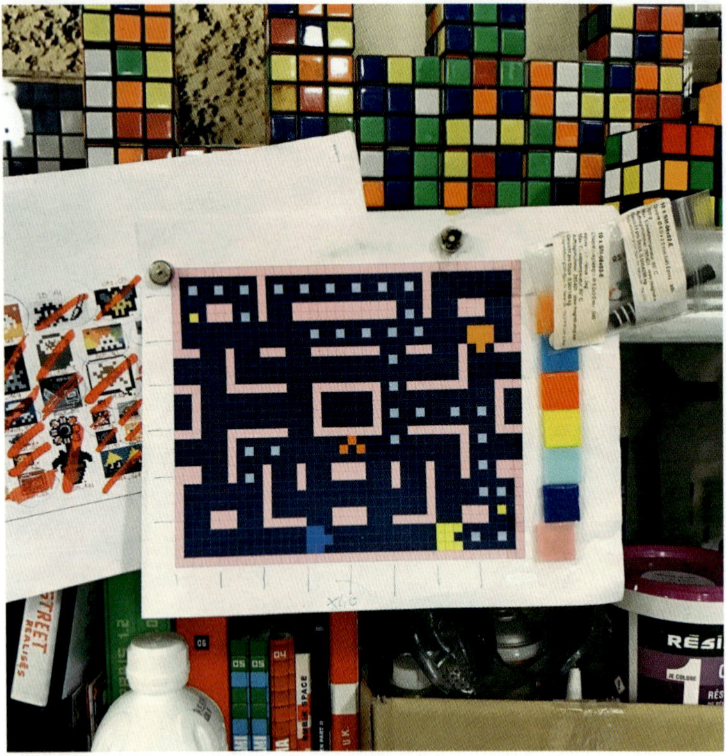

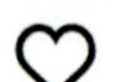 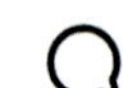  

5634 likes

invaderwashere Studio detail

View all 44 comments

23 December 2016

invaderwashere

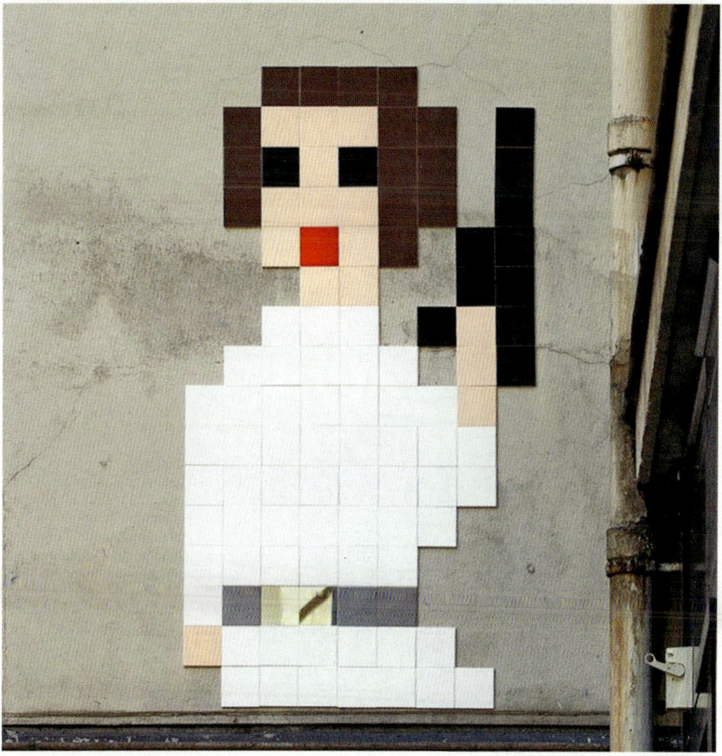

39 329 likes

invaderwashere RIP Carrie Fisher ✨ #princessLeia #ruePrincesse #paris #PA1190

View all 302 comments

27 December 2016

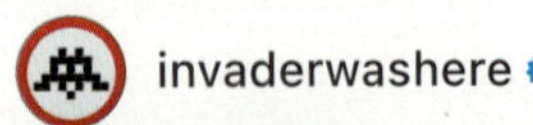

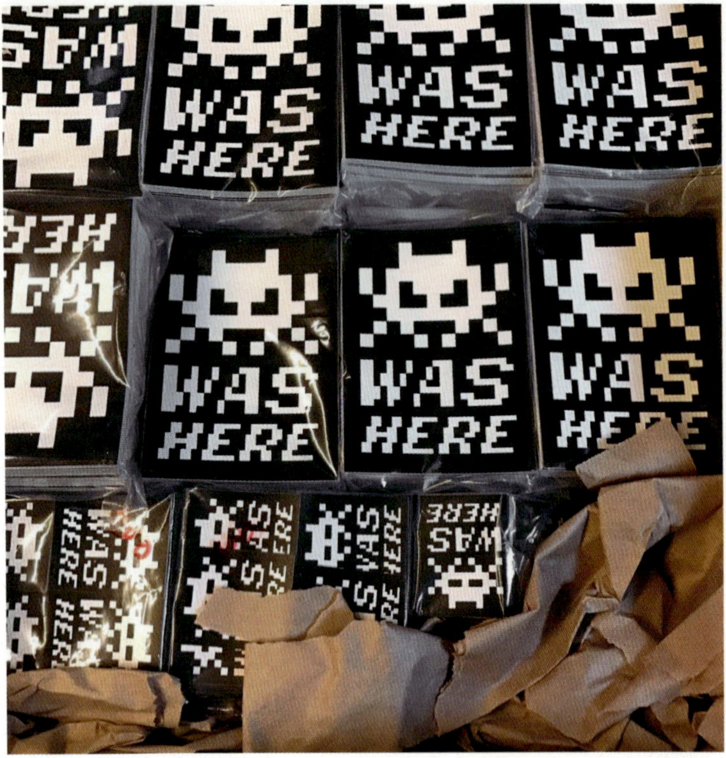

9586 likes

invaderwashere Delivery of the day... #ammunitions 😁 #stickers

View all 148 comments

31 December 2016

2017

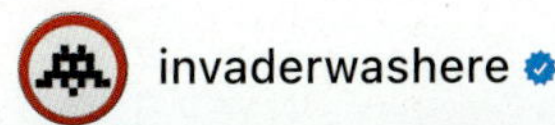

invaderwashere ...

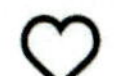   

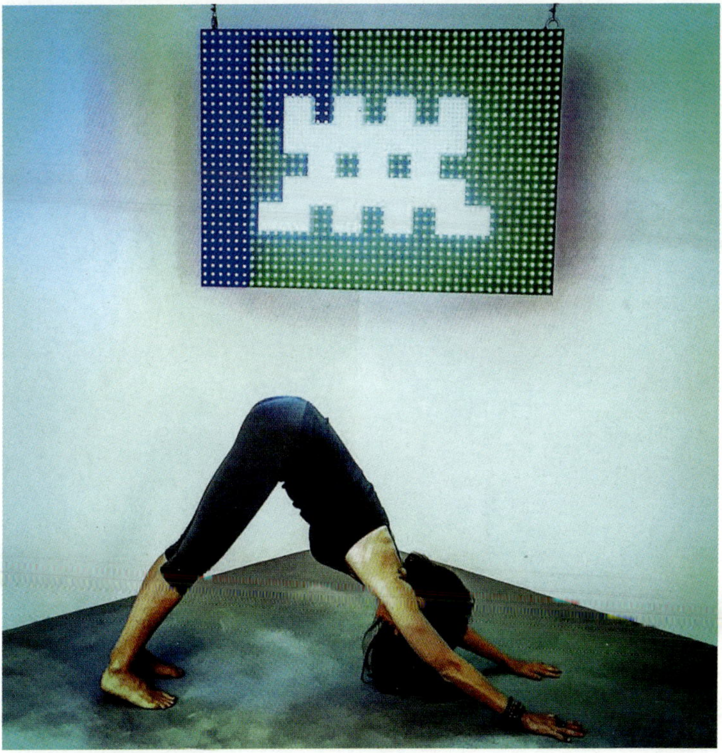

5 439 likes

invaderwashere #happynewyear 👾🙌👯2️⃣0️⃣1️⃣7️⃣
#ledpainting #overtheinfluence Photo by
@withgraceandjoy

View all 37 comments

3 January 2017

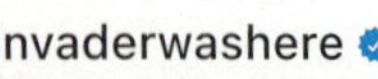

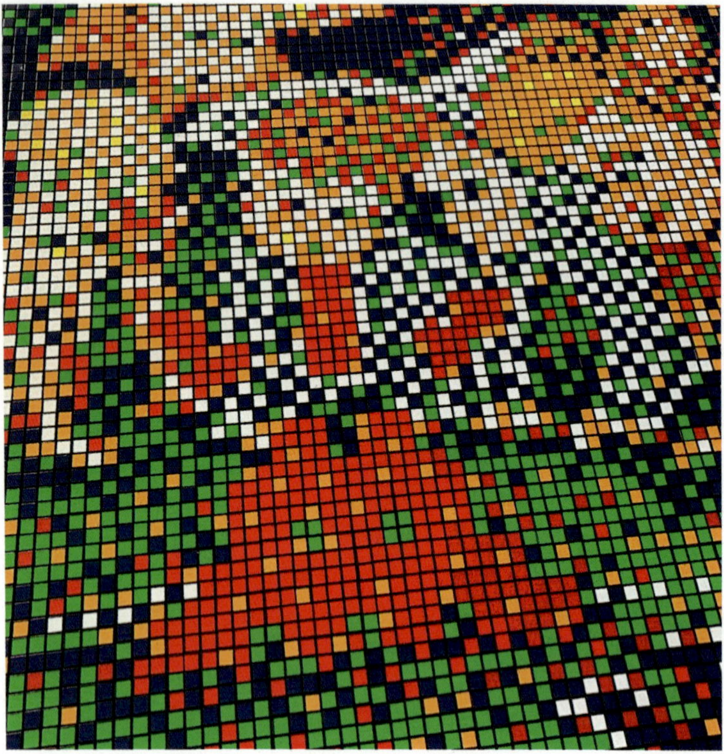

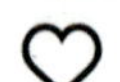

7 568 likes

invaderwashere Finishing the last pieces for my coming show #studio #detail #rubikcubism stay tuned...

View all 53 comments

12 January 2017

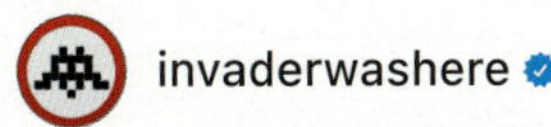

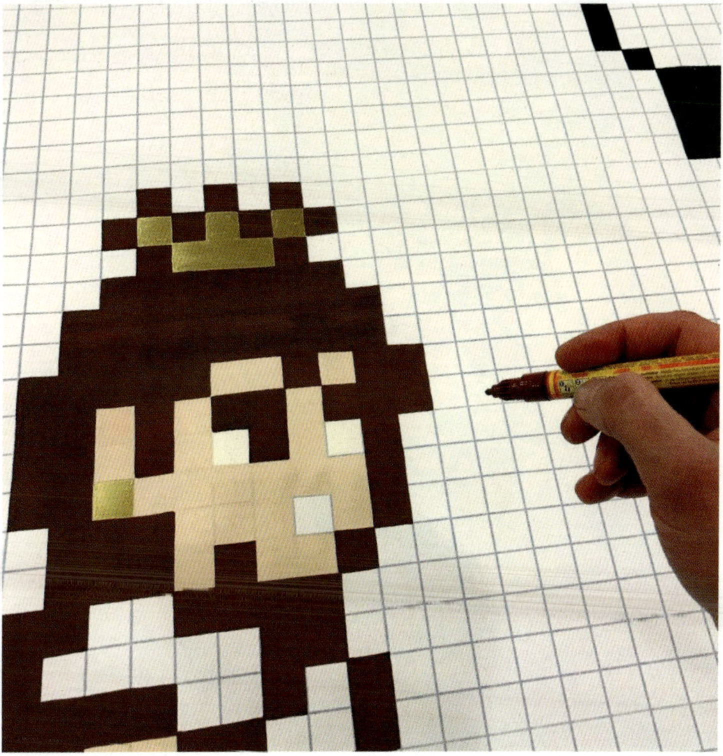

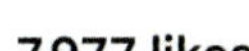

7 977 likes

invaderwashere Before lipstick 

View all 31 comments

15 January 2017

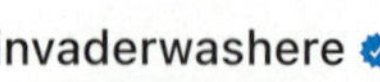

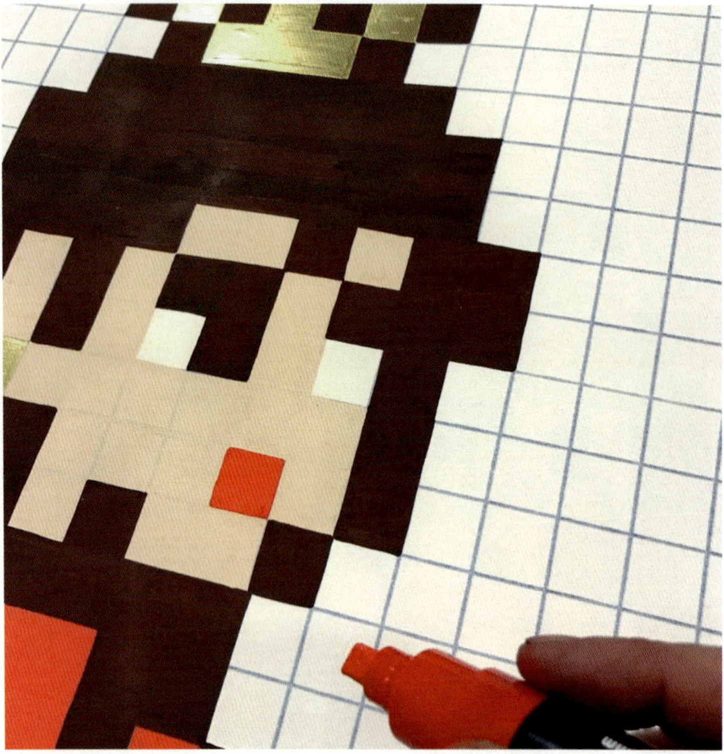

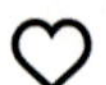 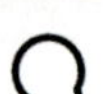 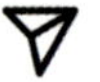 

7268 likes

invaderwashere Lipstick on  

View all 45 comments

16 January 2017

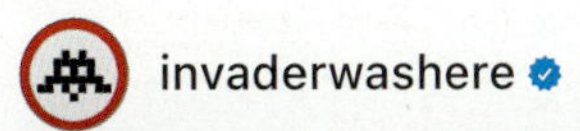

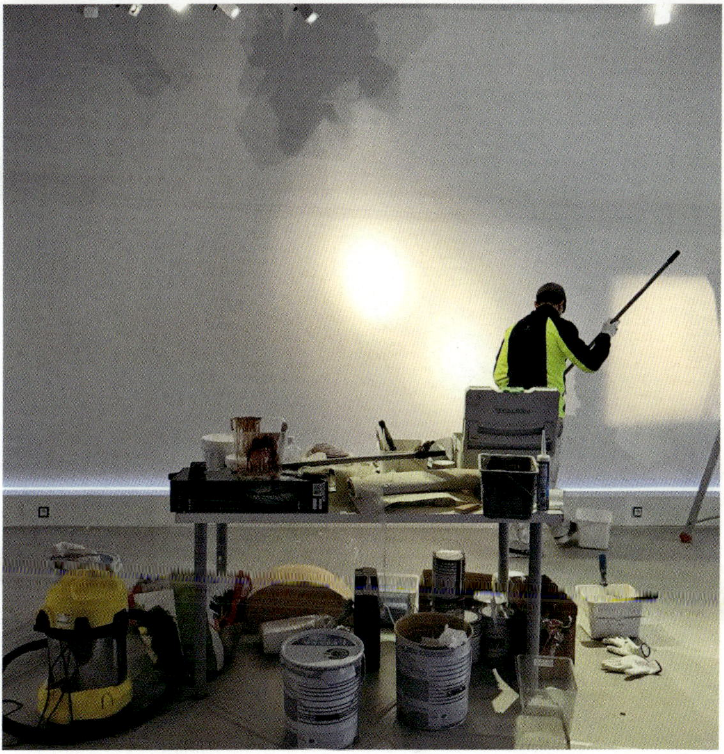

2655 likes

invaderwashere J-10 #hellomygameis @museeenherbe #whitecube

View all 27 comments

16 January 2017

invaderwashere

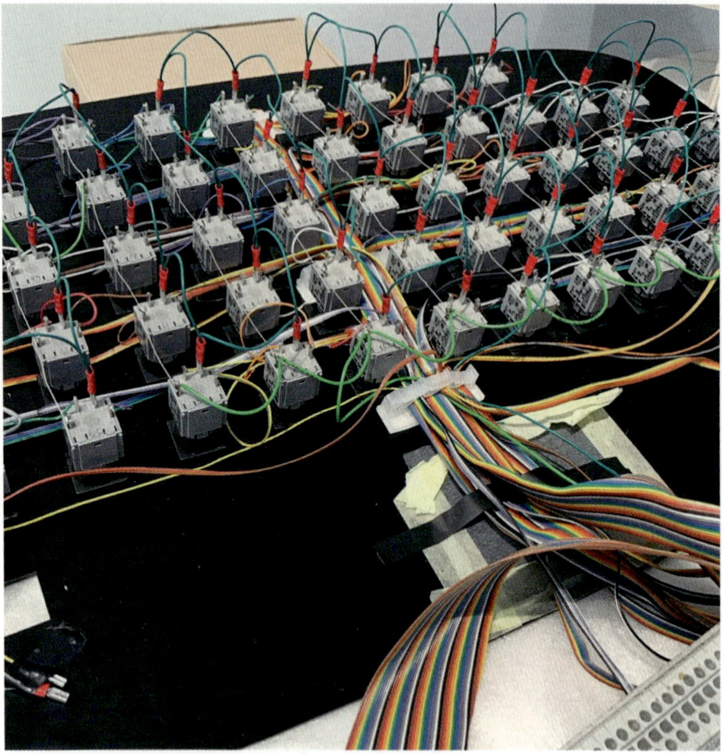

4106 likes

invaderwashere J-9 #hellomygameis @museeenherbe #wiring

View all 35 comments

17 January 2017

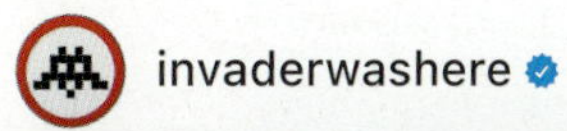

invaderwashere

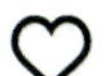   

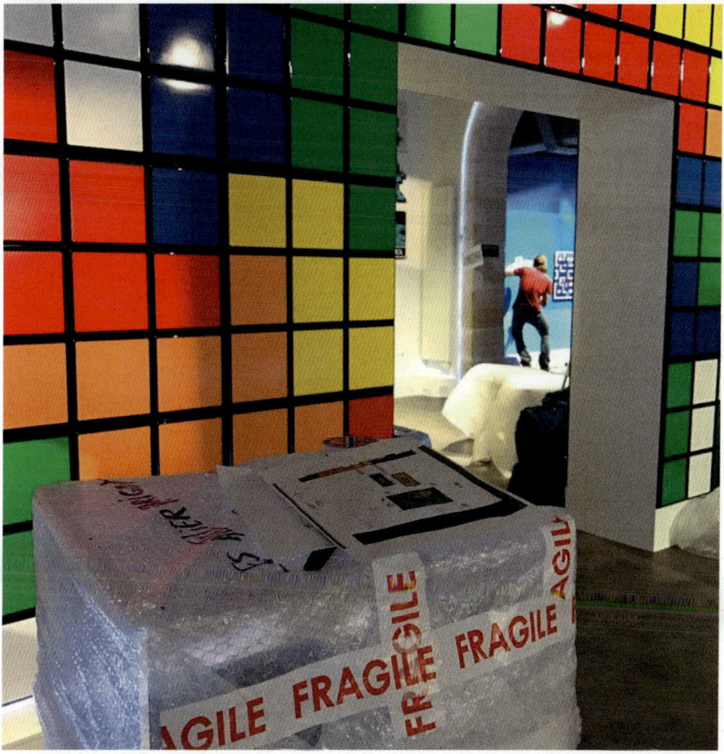

5849 likes

invaderwashere J-8 #hellomygameis @museeenherbe

View all 47 comments

18 January 2017

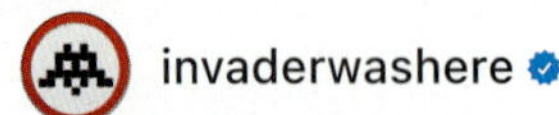

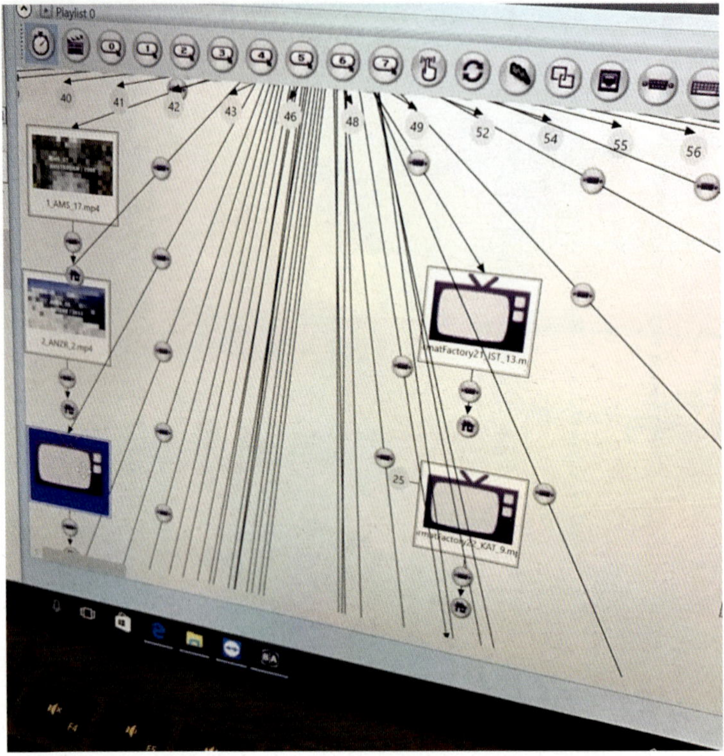

2 188 likes

invaderwashere J-6 #hellomygameis @museeenherbe #installation

View all 21 comments

20 January 2017

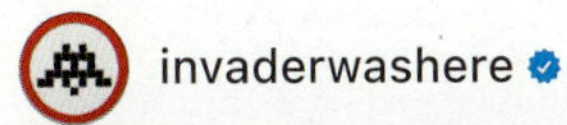

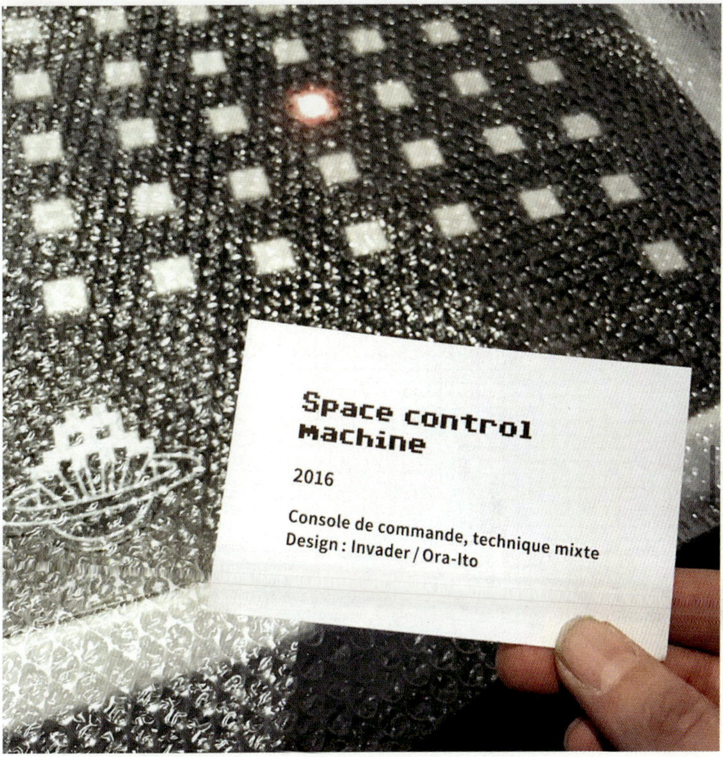

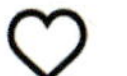  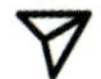 

3 670 likes

invaderwashere J-5 #hellomygameis @museeenherbe #detail thank you @ora_ito for the design of the #spacecontrolmachine

View all 15 comments

21 January 2017

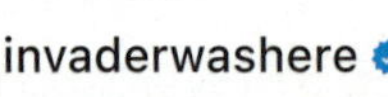

invaderwashere

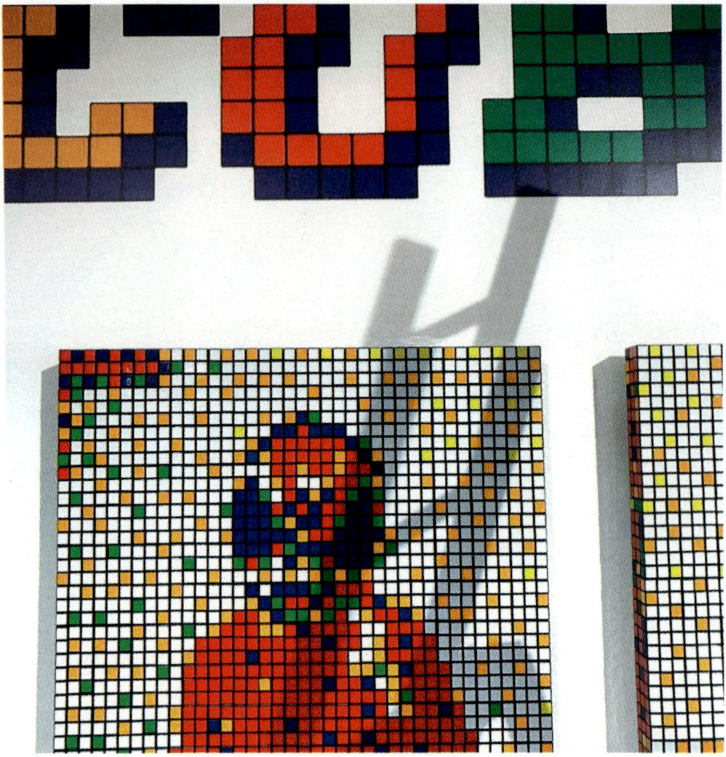

6 073 likes

invaderwashere J-4 #hellomygameis @museeenherbe #installation

View all 20 comments

22 January 2017

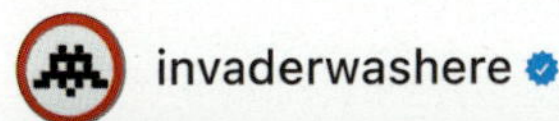

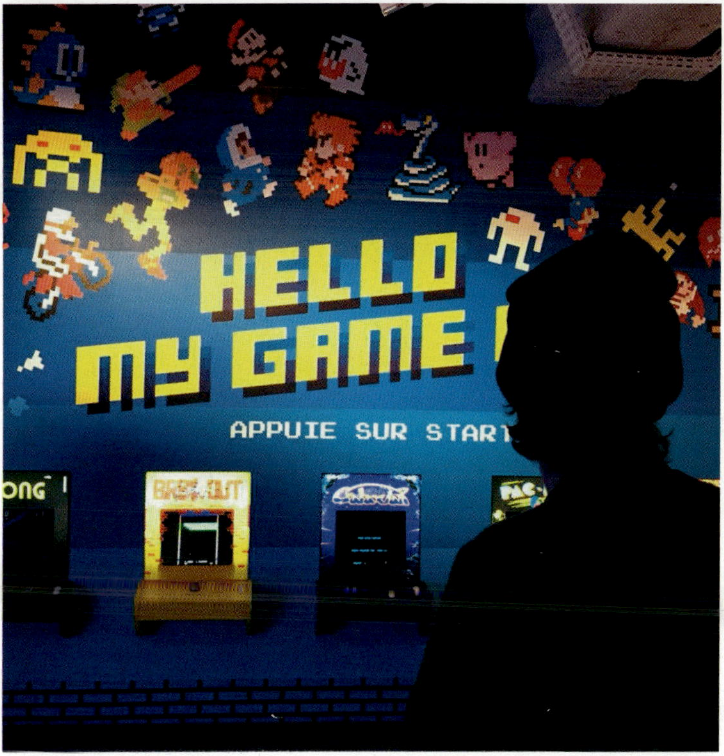

4 899 likes

invaderwashere J-3 #hellomygameis @museeenherbe #lighting

View all 37 comments

23 January 2017

invaderwashere

 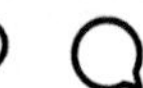 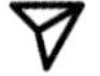 

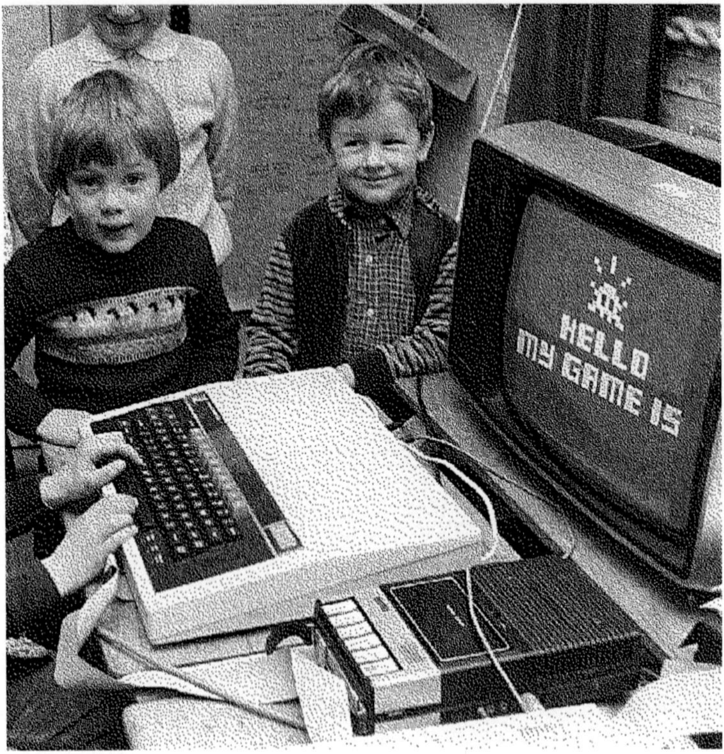

7785 likes

invaderwashere J-1 #Hellomygameis @museeenherbe #onlyforchildren

View all 40 comments

25 January 2017

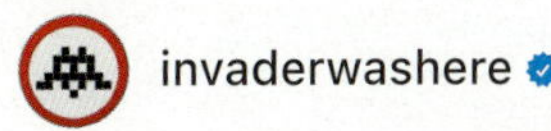

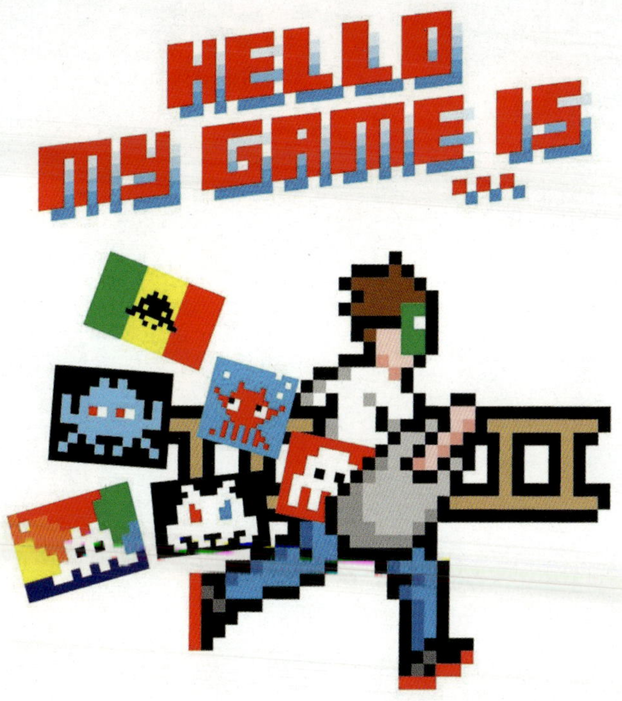

 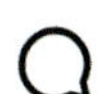  

5672 likes

invaderwashere #HELLOMYGAMEIS from today until September 3rd @museeenherbe / An exhibition for children from 3 to 103 years old! #museum #invasion #paris

View all 73 comments

26 January 2017

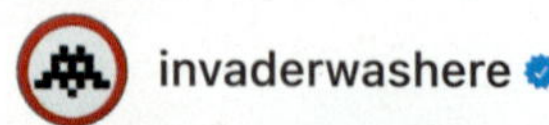

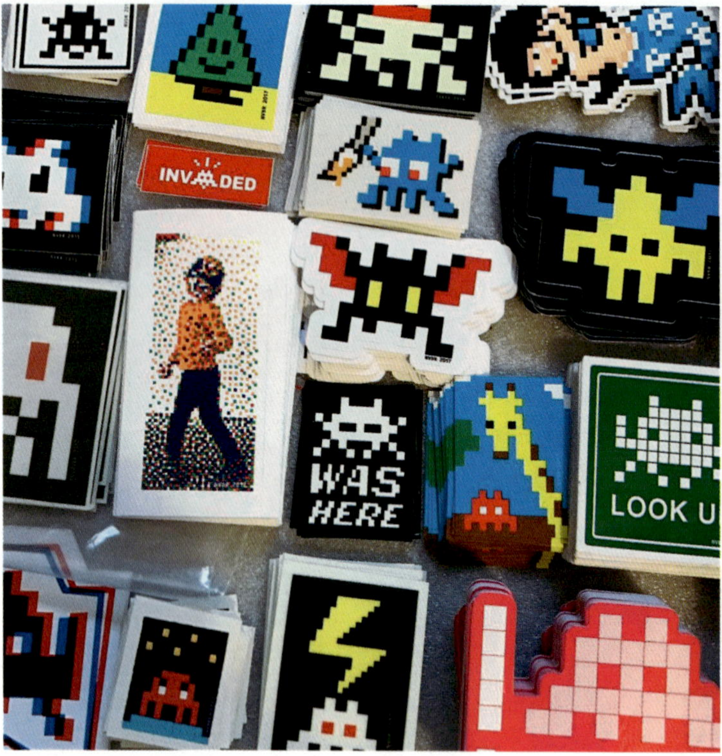

12 437 likes

invaderwashere Got to fill the stickers machines...
#stickers #candies #hellomygameis

View all 197 comments

2 February 2017

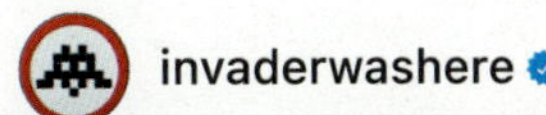

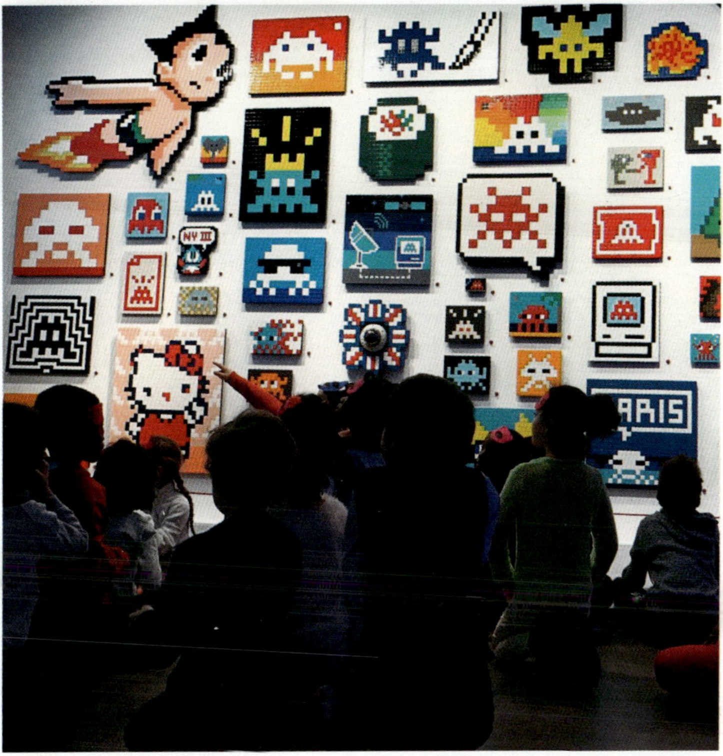

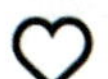   

19 573 likes

invaderwashere Morning school visit @museeenherbe #hellomygameis

View all 166 comments

3 February 2017

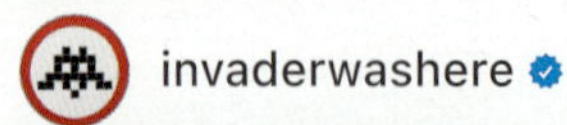

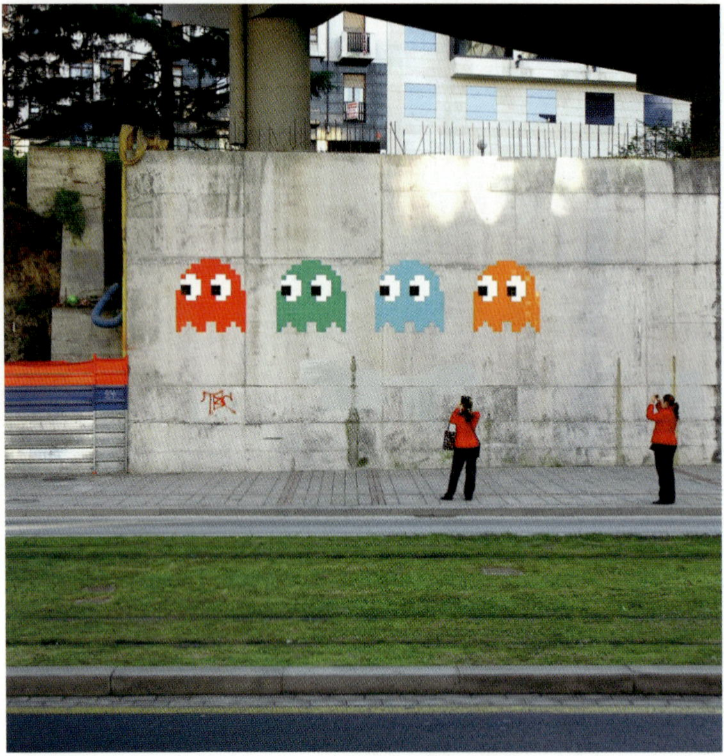

19 390 likes

invaderwashere RIP Masaya Nakamura father of Pac-Man
#pacman #namco #bbo23 #bilbao

View all 88 comments

4 February 2017

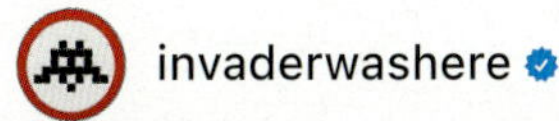

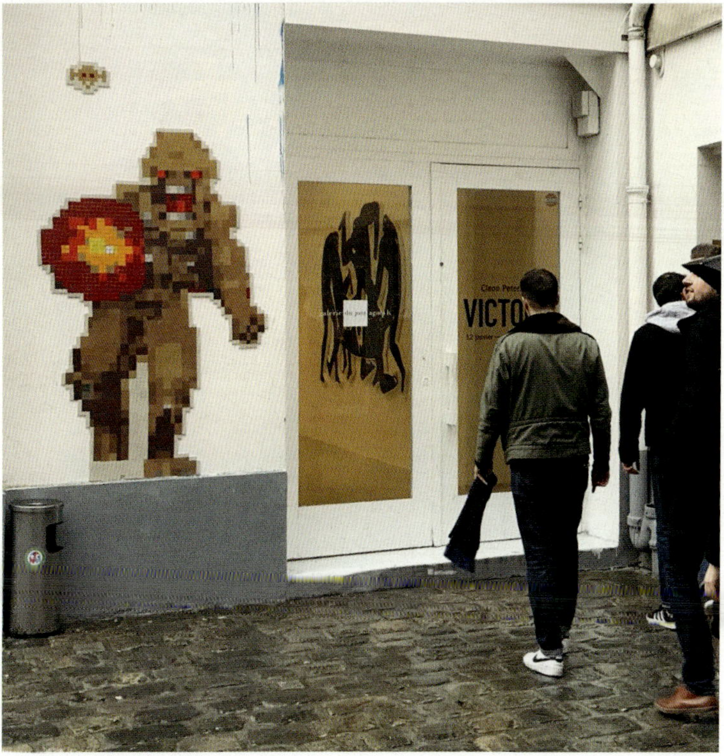

 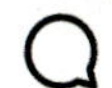  

12 112 likes

invaderwashere INVADER X CLEON PETERSON #doom #16yearsold #PA436 This piece has been hidden for years behind a wood panel, it has just reappeared during the @cleonpeterson exhibition at #galeriedujour

View all 123 comments

5 February 2017

invaderwashere

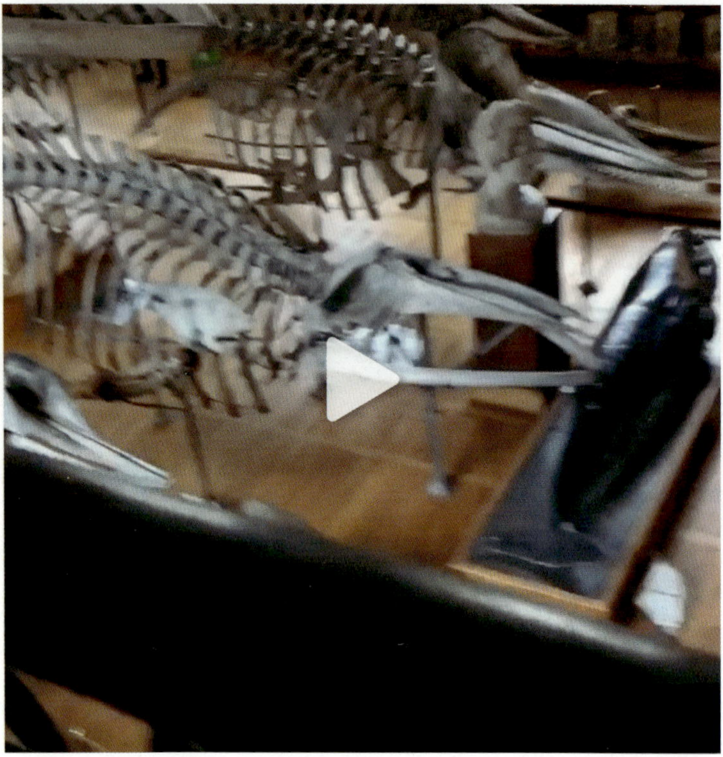

35 928 views

invaderwashere Invasion not successful ! A witness called the security guard who took off the piece 🙁

View all 174 comments

5 February 2017

invaderwashere

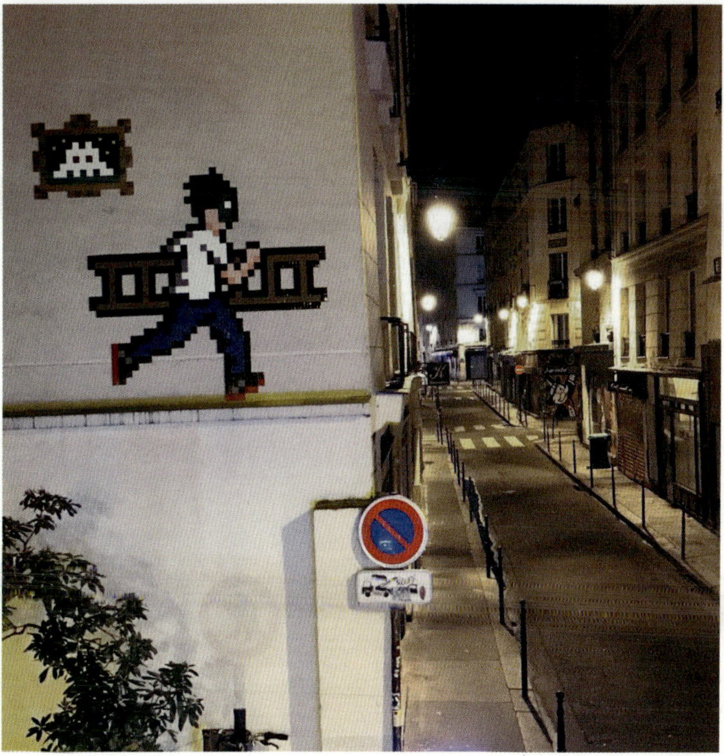

21 238 likes

invaderwashere Back to the streets / PA_1266 3:33 am
#hellomygameis #selfportrait #paris #invaderwashere

View all 139 comments

8 February 2017

invaderwashere

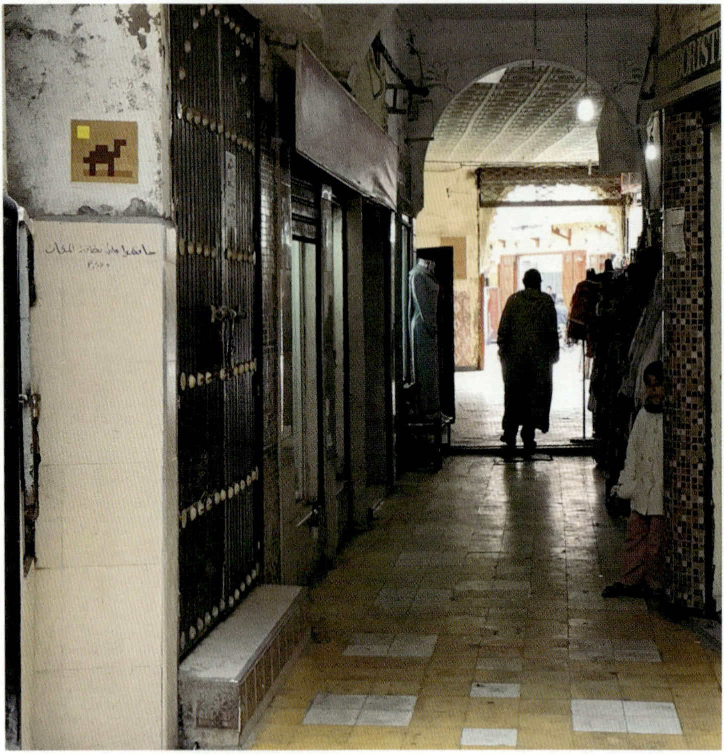

8020 likes

invaderwashere Just made in #Marrakech #mrak01 #camel #souk

View all 60 comments

11 February 2017

invaderwashere

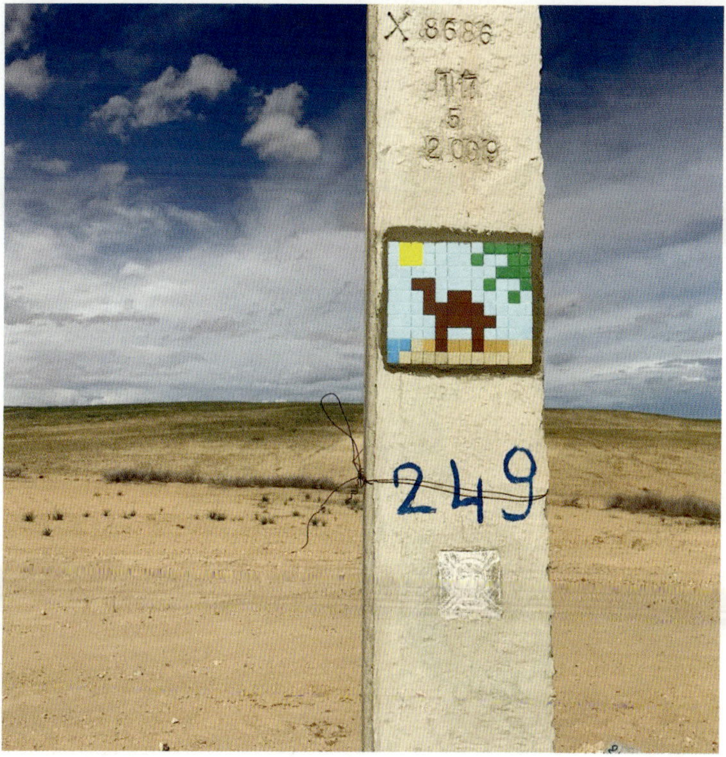

15 315 likes

invaderwashere Daytime invasion, no witness! 👾🐪
#spacecamel #desert #marrakech #invaderwashere
#triptyque #part1

View all 89 comments

12 February 2017

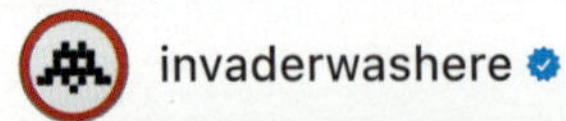

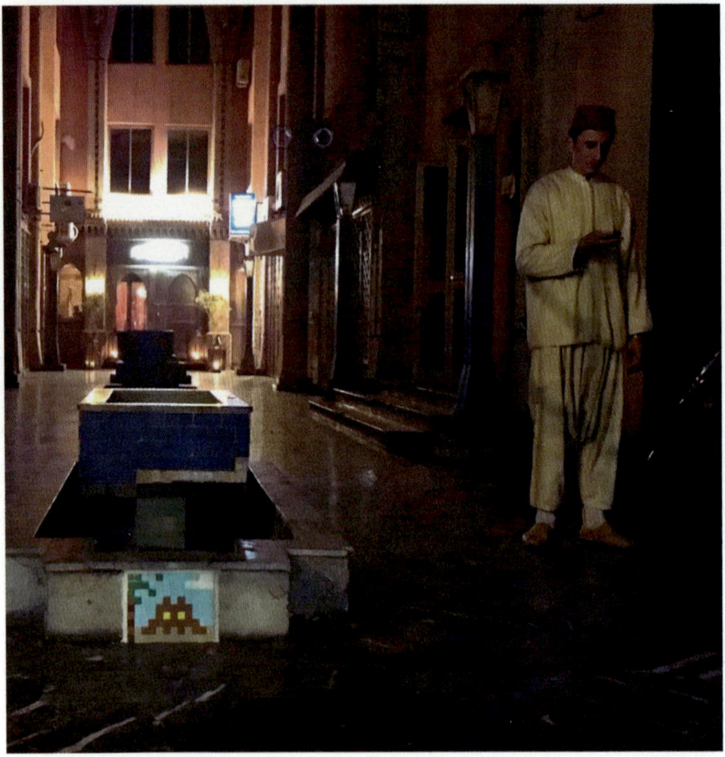

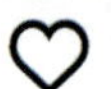   

7 398 likes

invaderwashere 👾🌙 #marrakech #triptyque #part2

View all 41 comments

16 February 2017

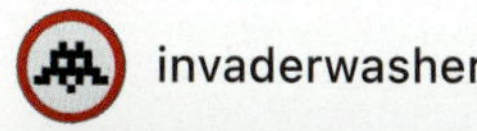

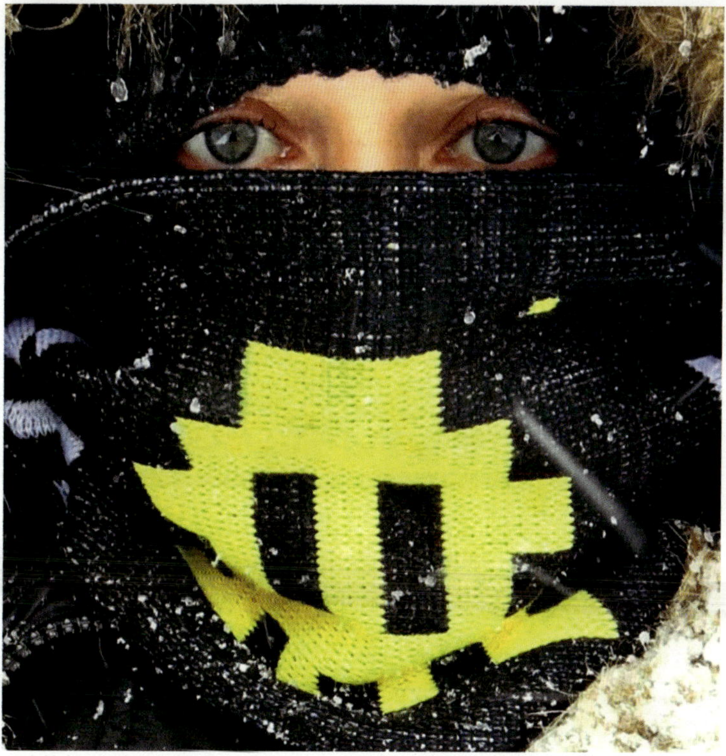

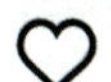   

6166 likes

invaderwashere Great photo by @julesandregulations @vnamagazine #scarf 👾❄️👱‍♀️

View all 46 comments

16 February 2017

invaderwashere

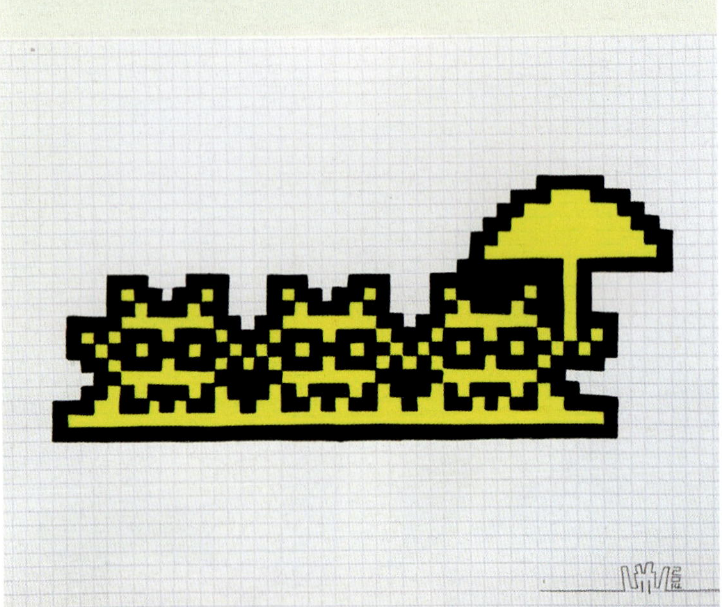

7122 likes

invaderwashere I am proud to support Amnesty international by donating this original drawing for their online auction: http://carnival.amnesty.org.hk @amnestyhk @amnesty #humanrights "Umbrellas of Hong Kong" Acrylic on graphic paper, 21 x 29.7 cm, 2014

View all 55 comments

17 February 2017

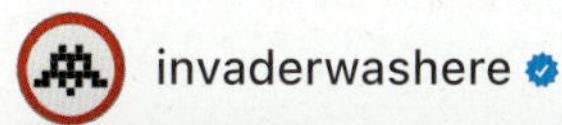

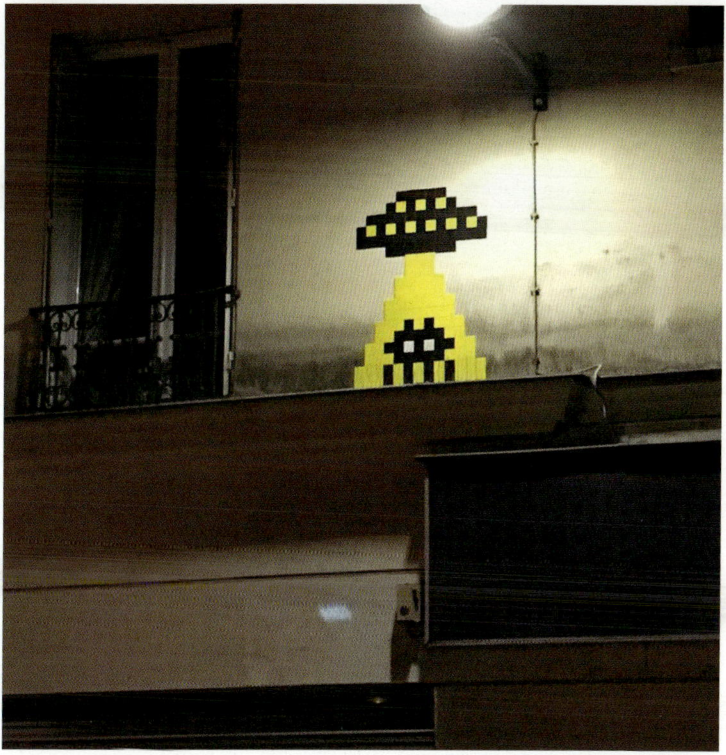

12 726 likes

invaderwashere Just made Pa_1267 and 2 more... #paris
4:08 am

View all 62 comments

22 February 2017

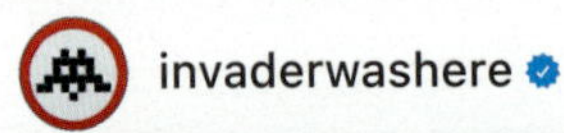

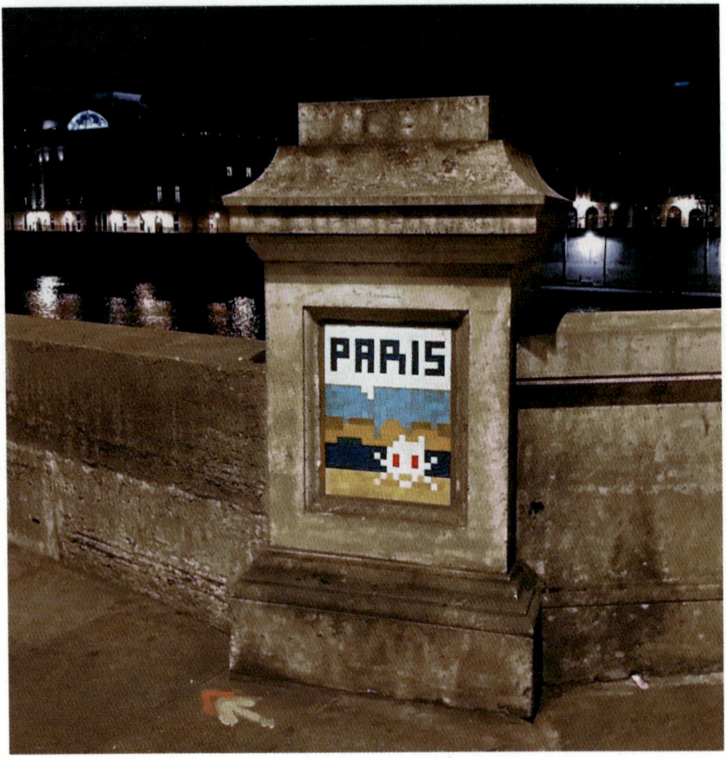

  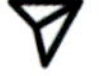 

18 418 likes

invaderwashere Fresh from last night #paris

View all 109 comments

22 February 2017

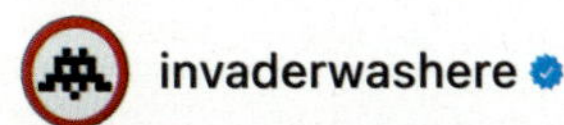

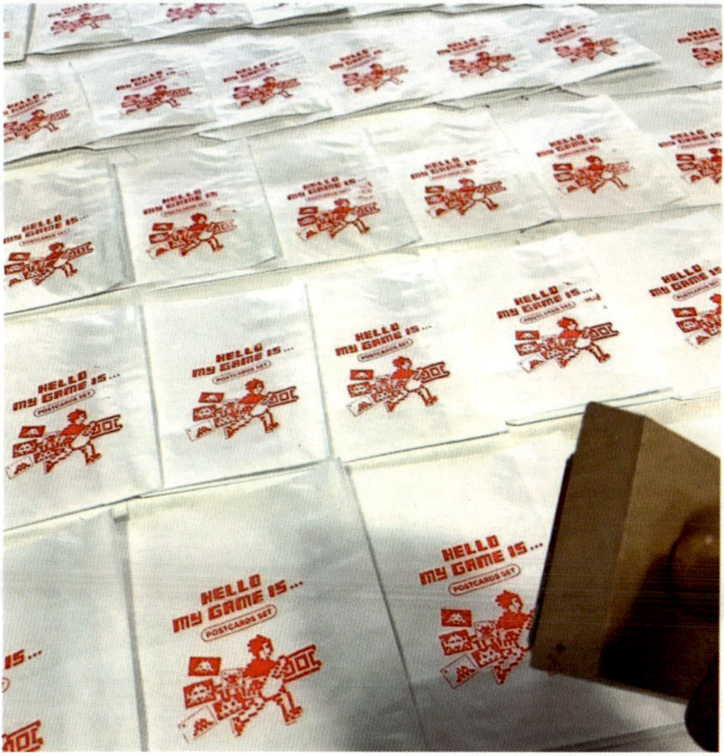

 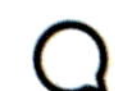  

4585 likes

invaderwashere #studiodetail Hand made stamping of the #hellomygameis postcards set. Soon online...

View all 44 comments

23 February 2017

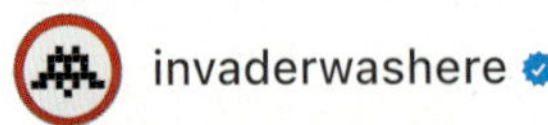

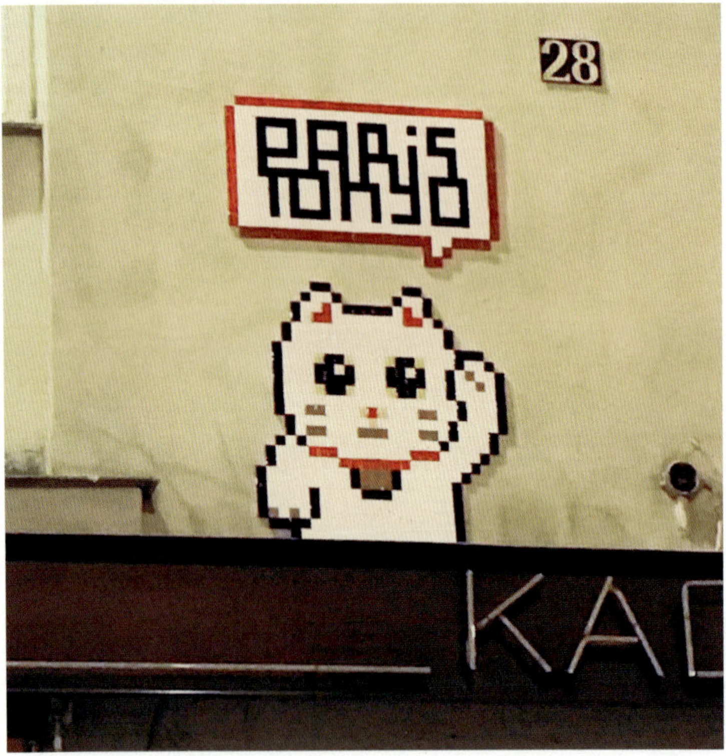

13 063 likes

invaderwashere Pa_1269 little Tokyo #manekineko #paris #bynight

View all 83 comments

23 February 2017

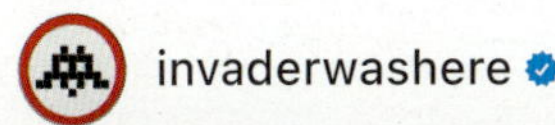

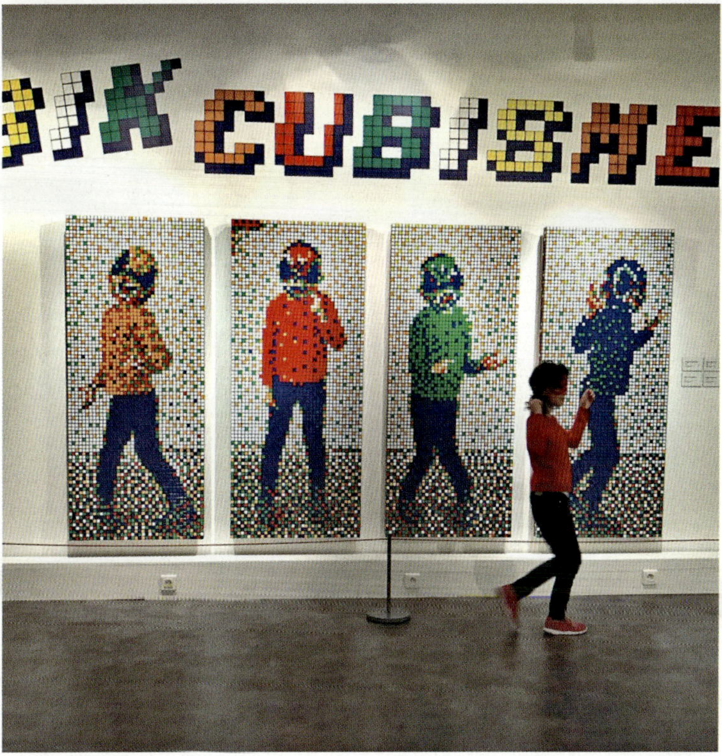

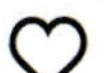   

7786 likes

invaderwashere Dancing with the RUBIK KIDS
@museeenherbe #hellomygameis #boogiewoogie
#rubikcubism #rubikcubisme

View all 33 comments

25 February 2017

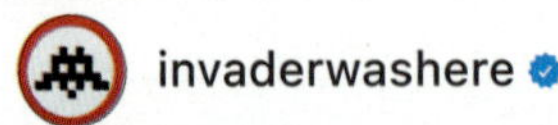

•••

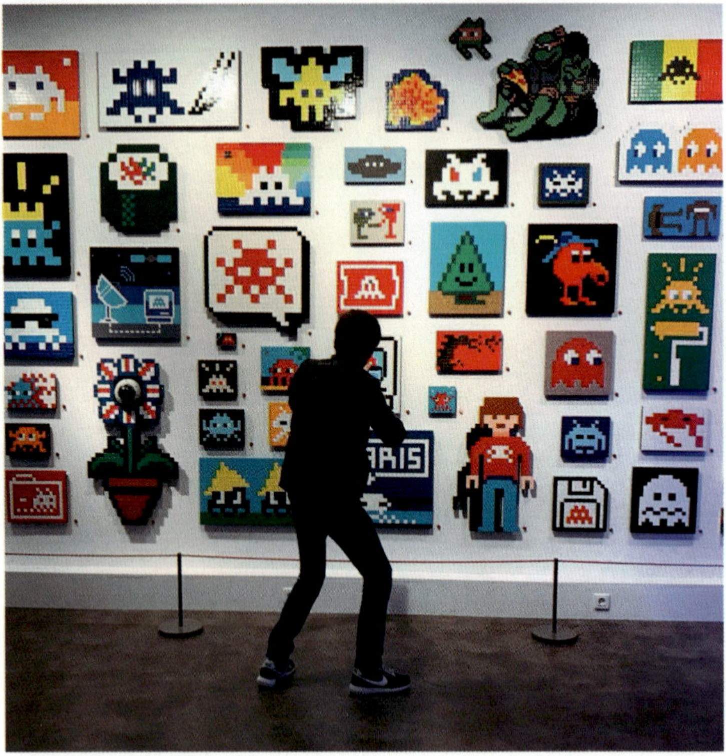

19485 likes

invaderwashere @ora_ito visiting #hellomygameis @museeenherbe Thanx for your collaboration on the #spacecontrolmachine #interactivewall

View all 91 comments

27 February 2017

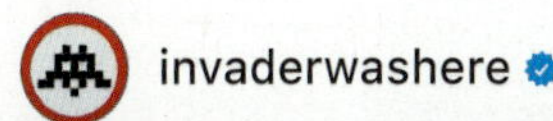

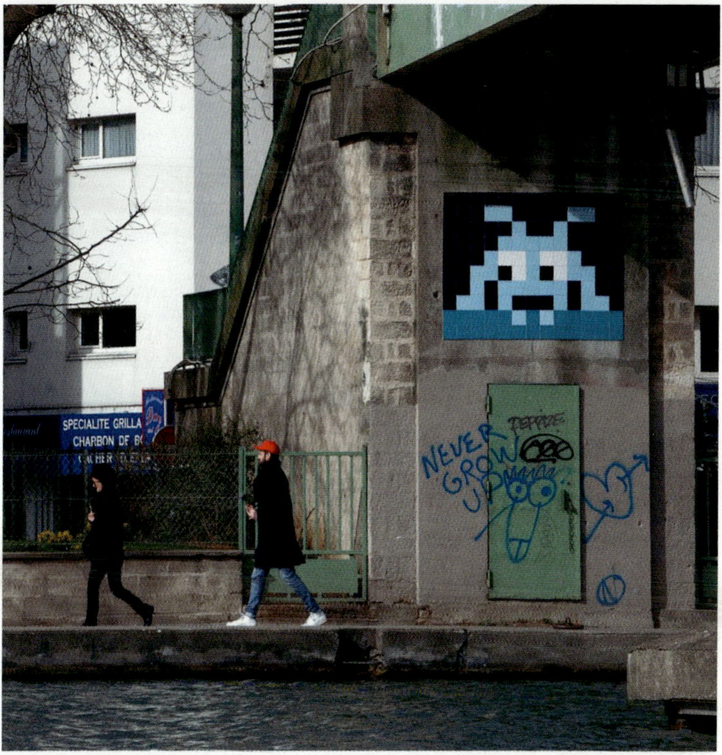

13 653 likes

invaderwashere PA_1270 by day #big #50points #NEVERGROWUP

View all 79 comments

2 March 2017

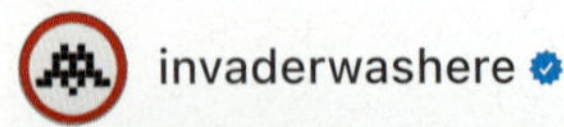

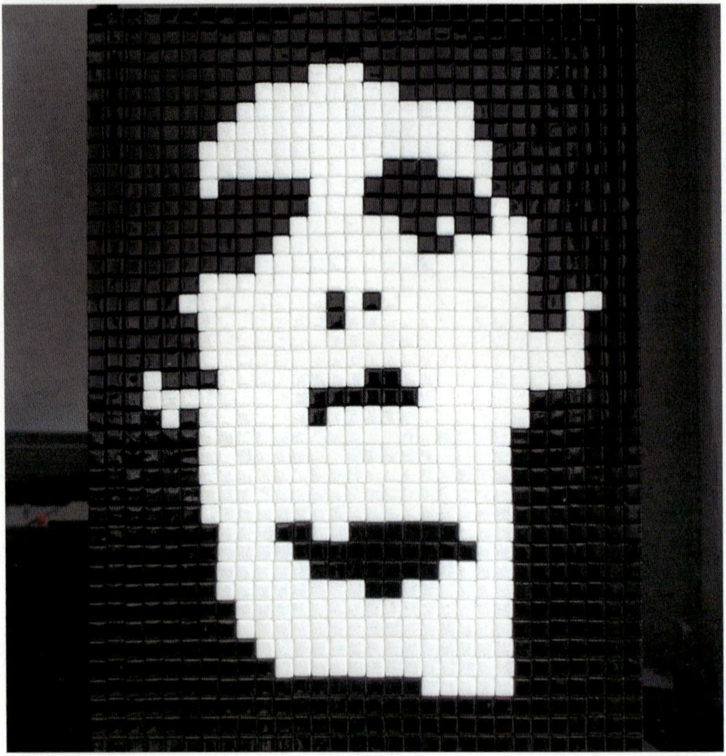

11652 likes

invaderwashere Lou, mosaic on perspex, 2005 #loureed #birthday I've been told that this piece now belongs to Steve Jones, former guitarist of the Sex Pistols 🙌

View all 108 comments

3 March 2017

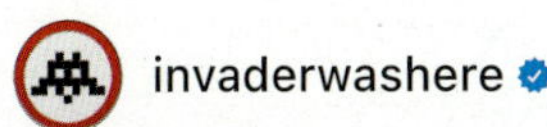

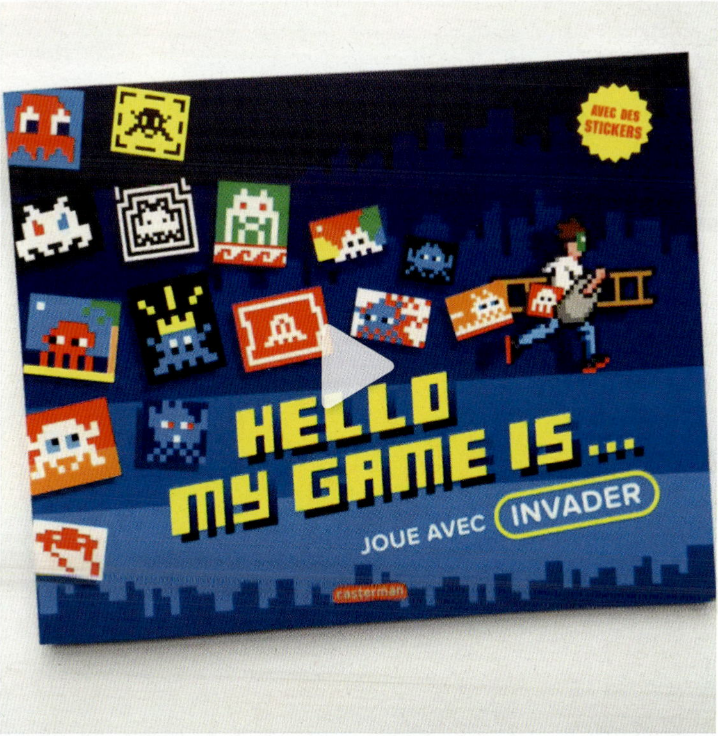

22 494 views

invaderwashere The catalogue of the exhibition "Hello my game is..." is a games book. You can find it online (link in bio) and in every good French bookstores #hellomygameis @casterman_jeunesse @museeenherbe #gamesbook #catalogue

View all 45 comments

6 March 2017

invaderwashere

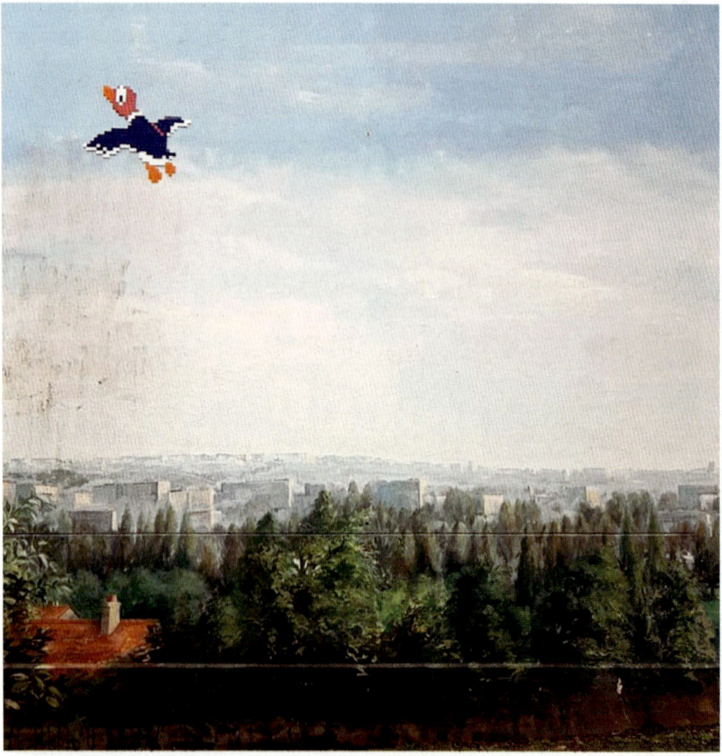

13 769 likes

invaderwashere Brand new piece, photo by @piop32
#duckhunt #pa1271

View all 114 comments

8 March 2017

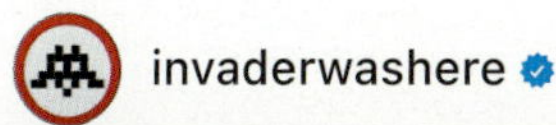

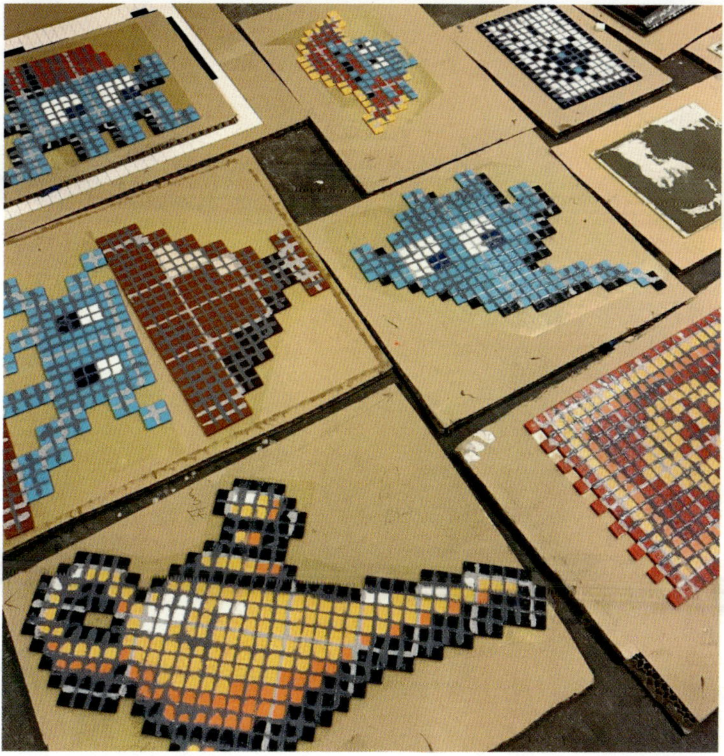

11753 likes

invaderwashere Preparing the next invasion...

View all 119 comments

10 March 2017

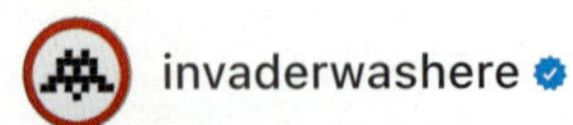

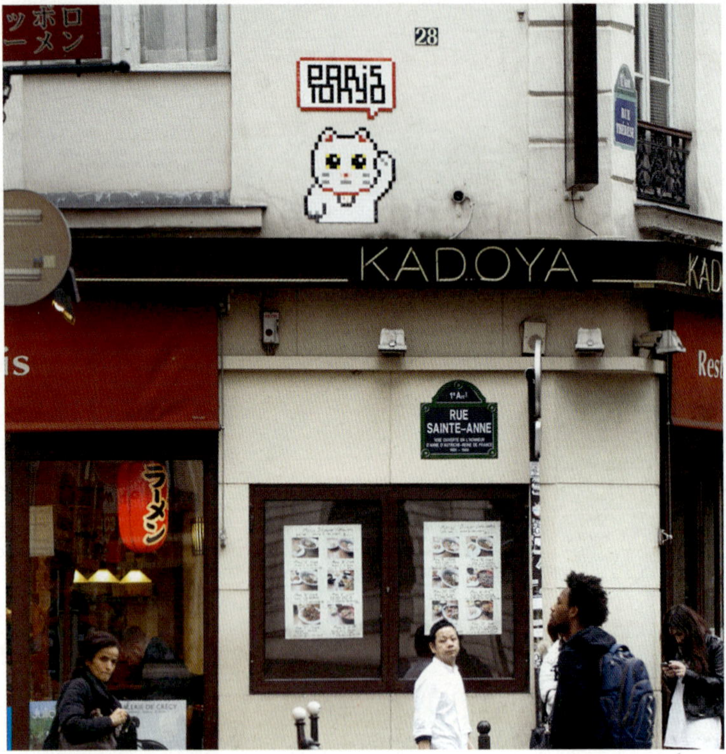

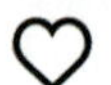  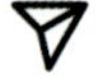 

14 302 likes

invaderwashere 🇫🇷 🇯🇵 PA_1269 by day #manekineko #paris #littletokyo

View all 51 comments

10 March 2017

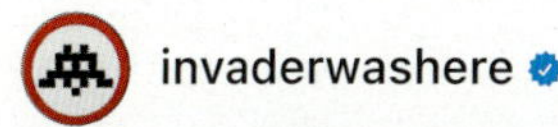

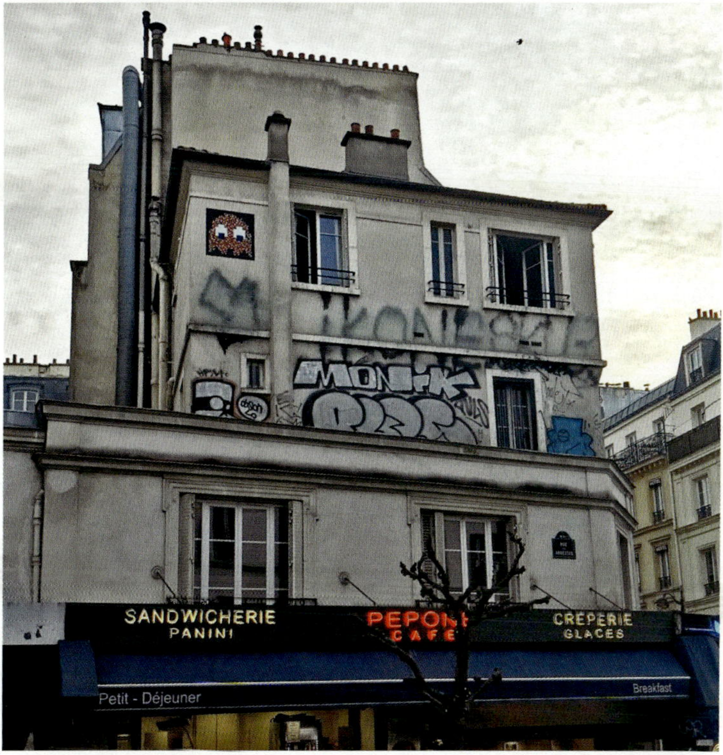

8220 likes

invaderwashere PA_1077 was not easy to put up... but I did it 🎯 #montmartre #abesses #paris #throwback #2013

View all 44 comments

11 March 2017

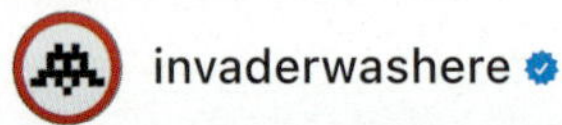

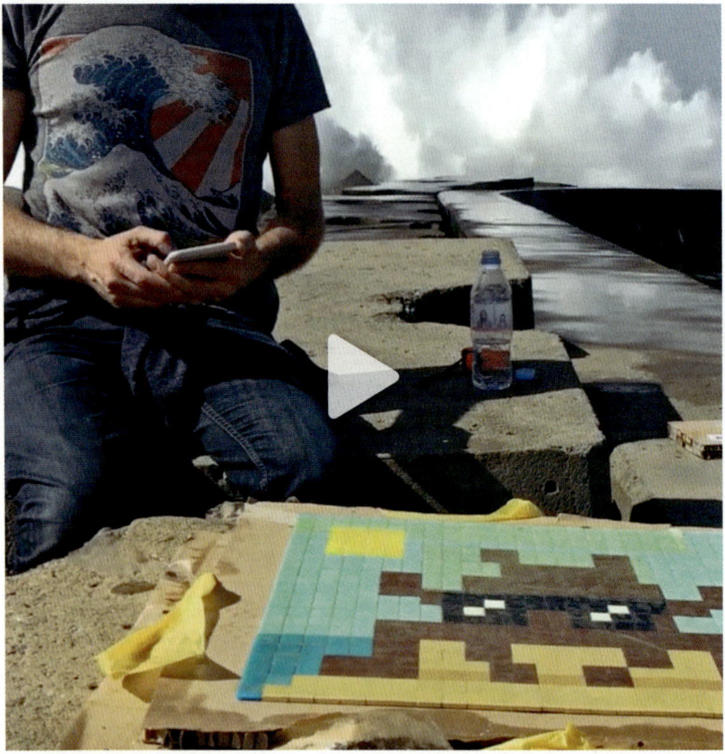

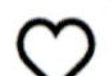   

73 147 views

invaderwashere The next one was for me... but the invasion was finally successful #bigwave 🌊

View all 78 comments

15 March 2017

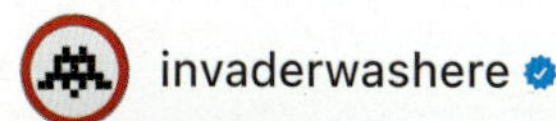

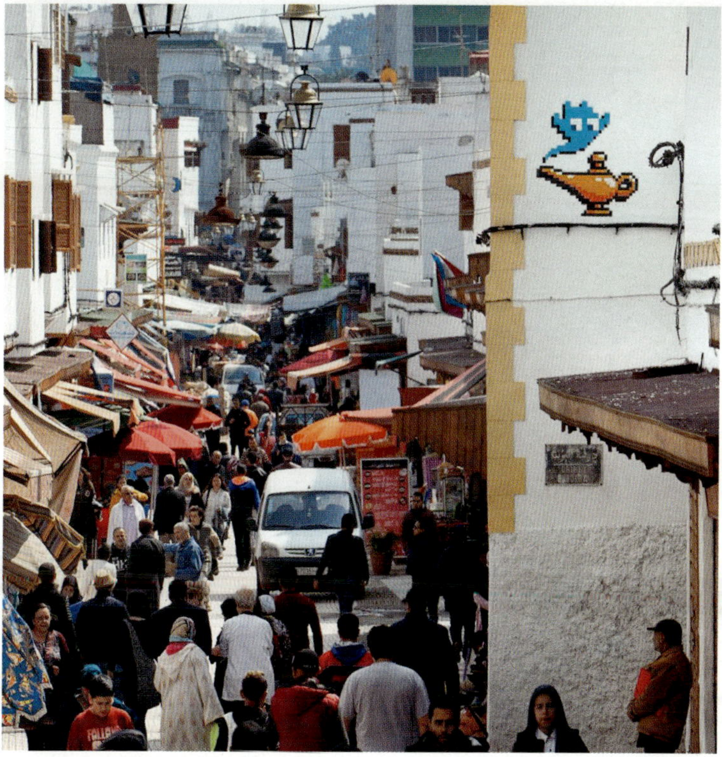

 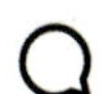  

13 302 likes

invaderwashere Back in Morocco... #photoftheday #medina

View all 127 comments

16 March 2017

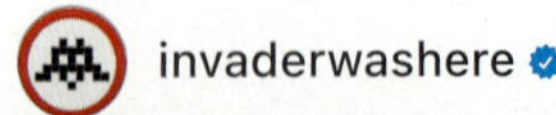

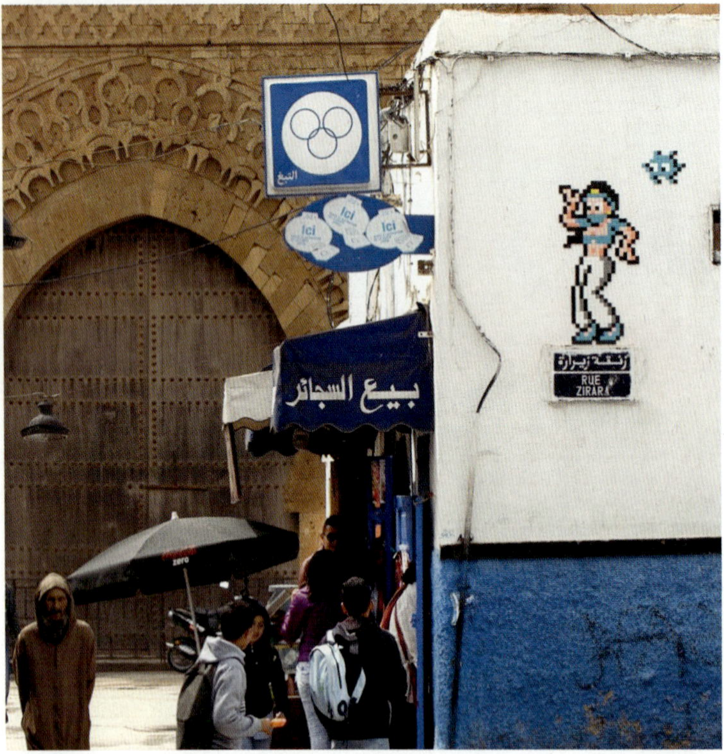

11936 likes

invaderwashere Dancing in Rabat #rabat #morroco #photooftheday

View all 101 comments

17 March 2017

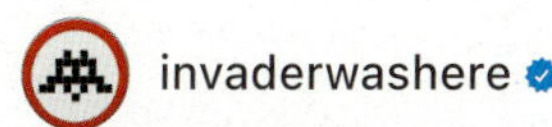

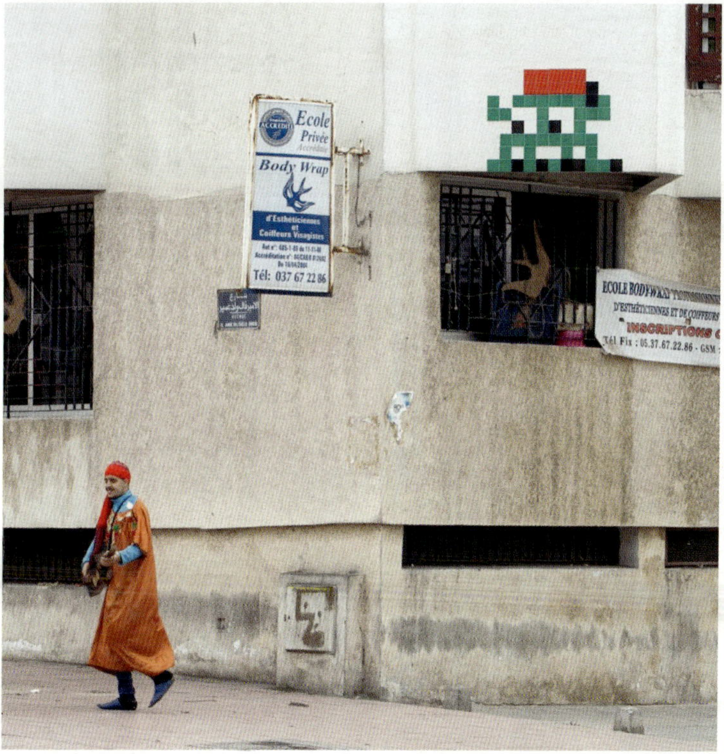

8052 likes

invaderwashere Tarboosh: a felt or cloth brimless cap resembling the fez, usually red and often with a silk tassel #GnawaStyle #tarbouche #tarboosh #rabat #morocco

View all 49 comments

18 March 2017

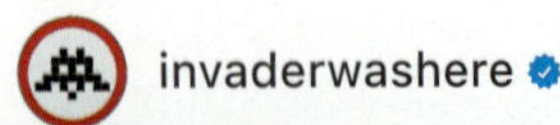

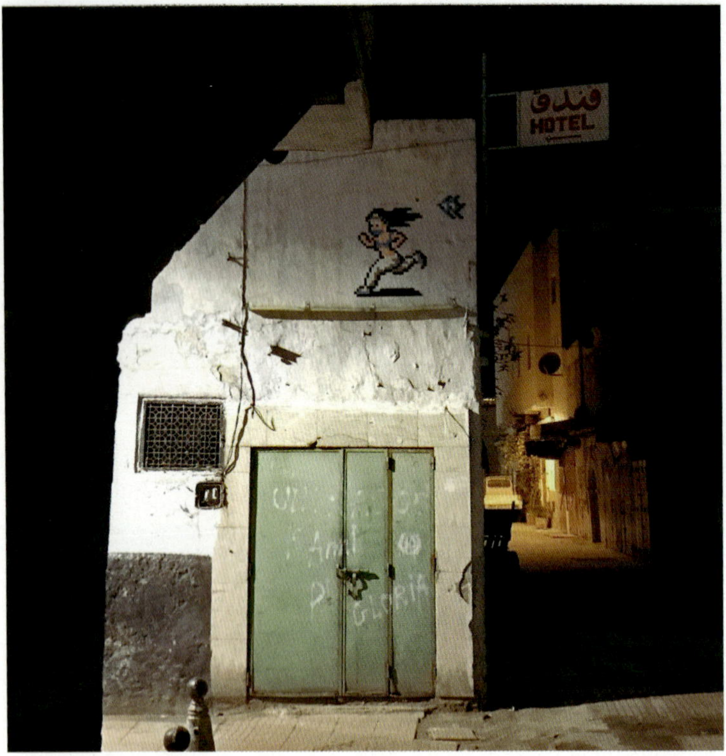

11 427 likes

invaderwashere My Space Invaders project has taken me on some memorable journeys, travelling in faraway cities in search of "spots" and secretly installing works by night in their landscapes. Each time, it's a complete geographical and cultural change of scenery, with terra incognita to conquer #RBA_19

View all 29 comments

19 March 2017

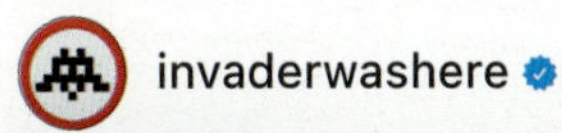

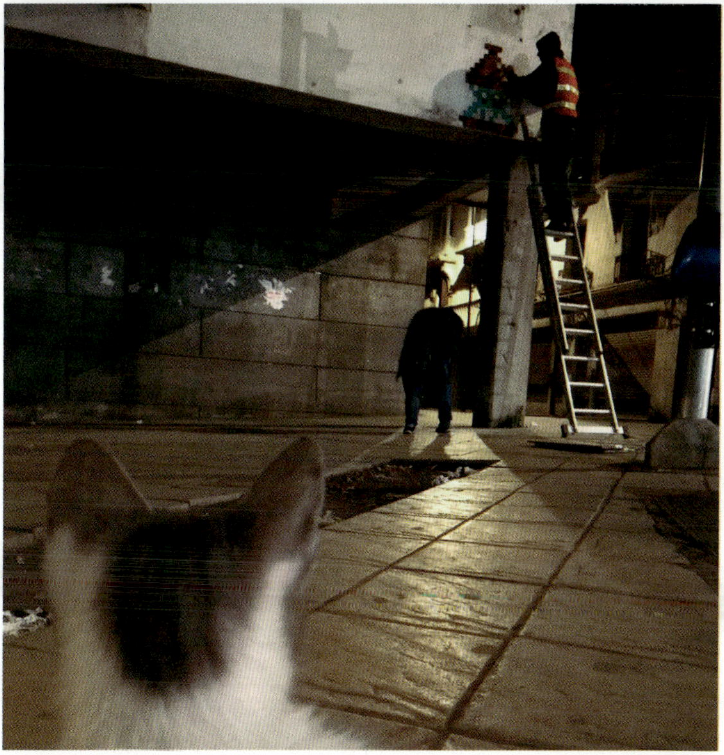

 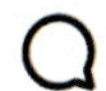  

9320 likes

invaderwashere Installation of RBA_13 🐱 👀 👾 #rabat #morocco shot by @bleditonton

View all 80 comments

20 March 2017

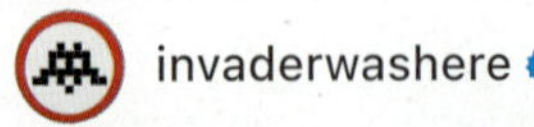

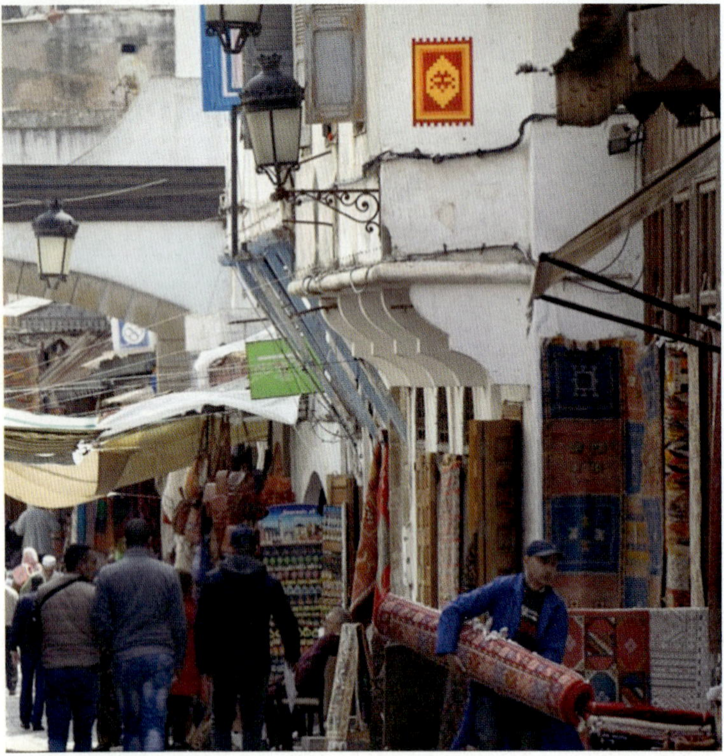

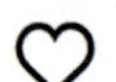   

7 550 likes

invaderwashere Souk of #rabat

View all 50 comments

21 March 2017

invaderwashere

 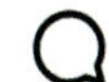  

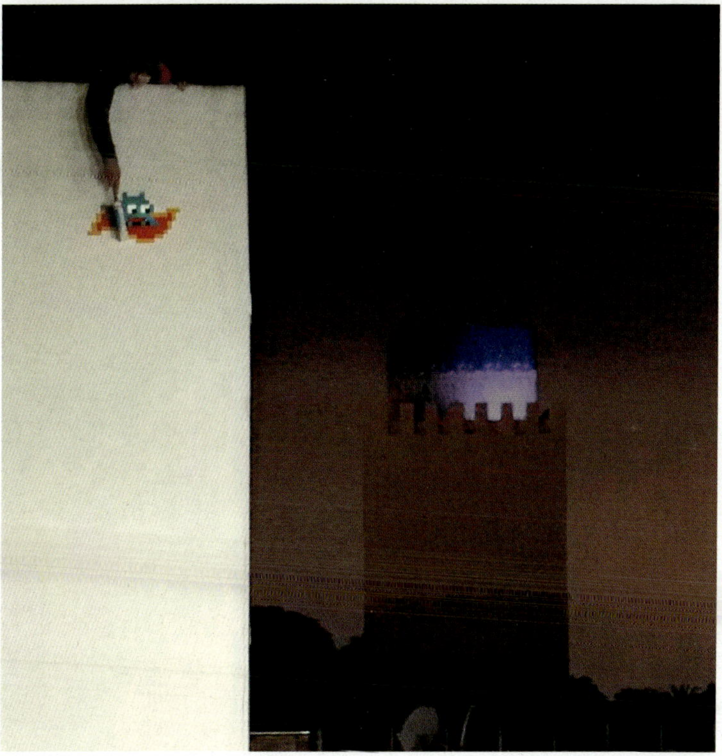

7763 likes

invaderwashere Installation of RBA_12 #flyingcarpet #bnrm #rabat #morocco photo by @bleditonton

View all 30 comments

22 March 2017

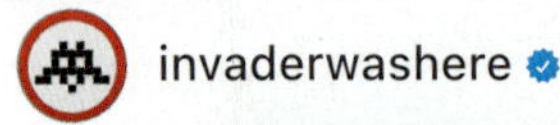

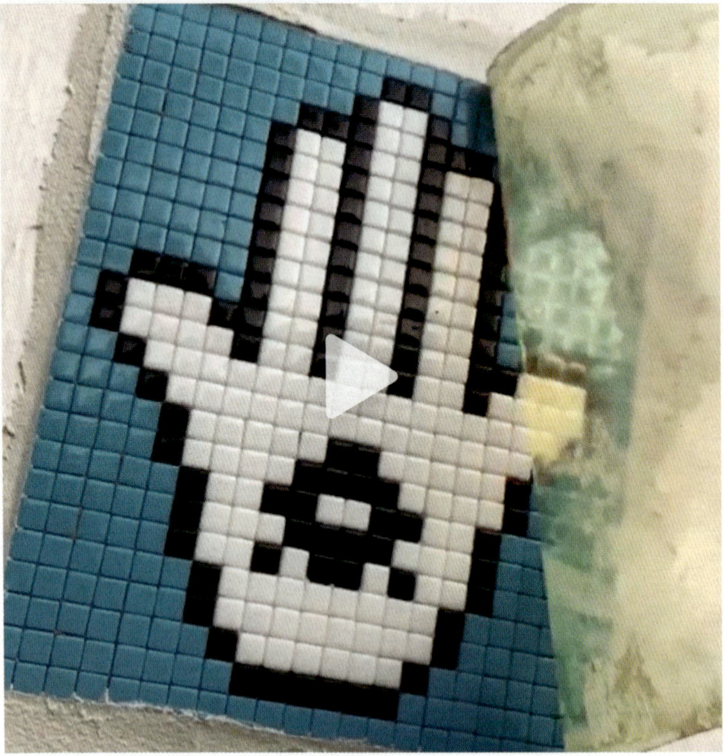

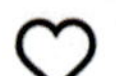  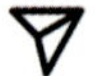 

111 980 views

invaderwashere Installing RBA_16 #khamsa into the wall

View all 121 comments

23 March 2017

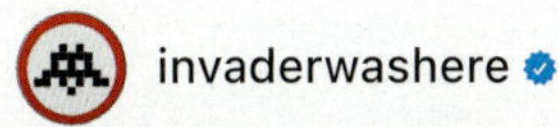

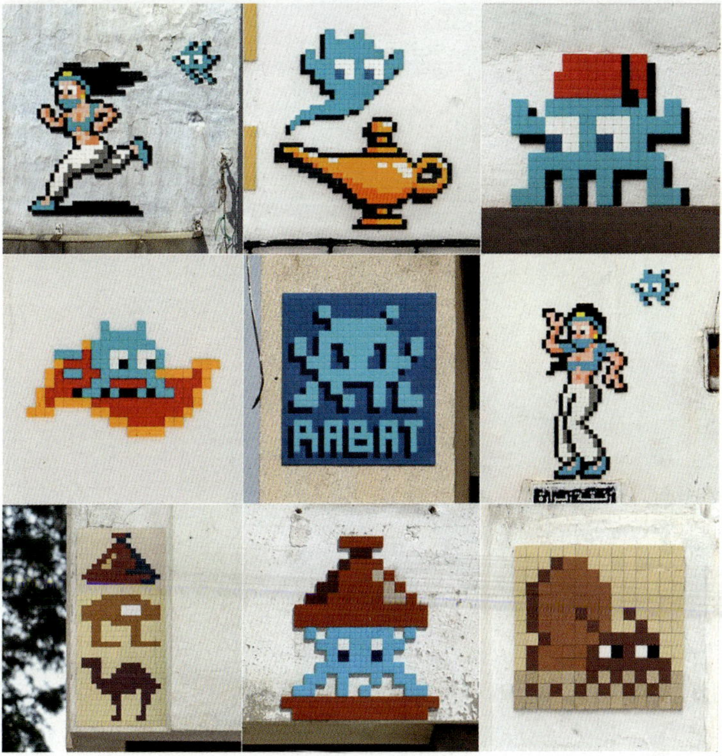

14 723 likes

invaderwashere 9 of the 20 space invaders freshly installed in Rabat / more images: link in bio / #rabat #morocco #2017 #flashinvaders

View all 122 comments

24 March 2017

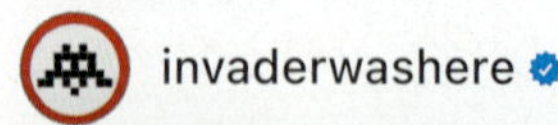

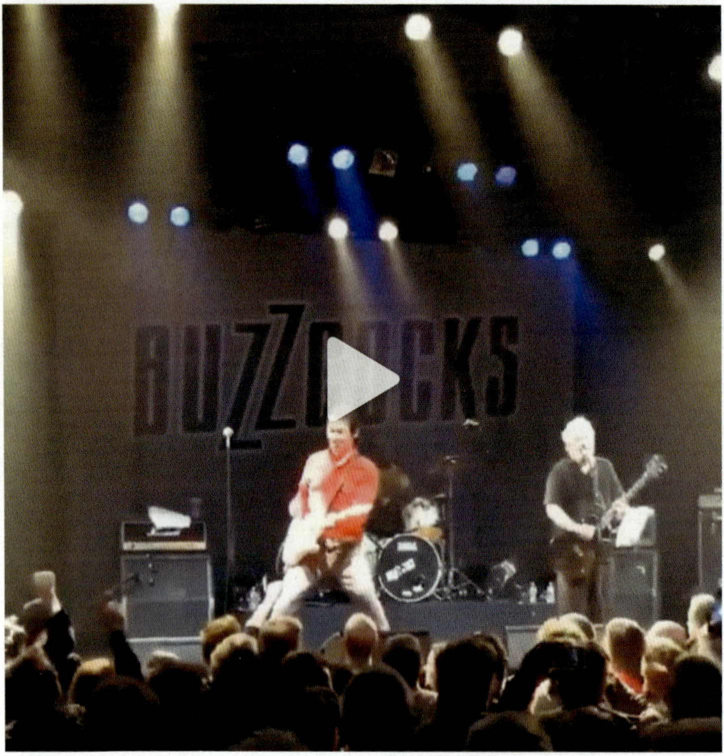

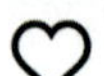   

31 948 views

invaderwashere That's worth a post! #buzzcocks #manchester #paris #whatdoiget

View all 50 comments

26 March 2017

invaderwashere

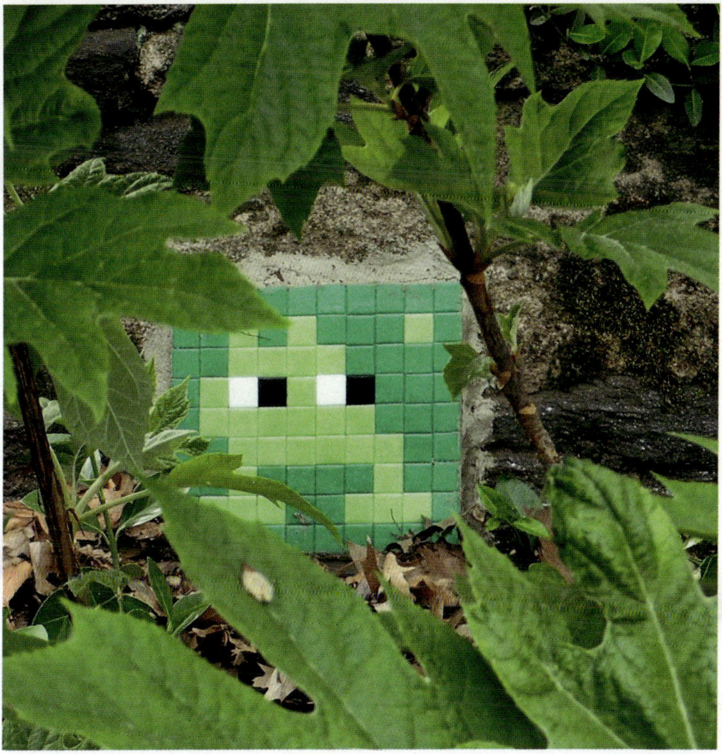

13 473 likes

invaderwashere NY_64 born in June 2003, broken in 2006, remade by a fan in April 2016, stolen and put on Ebay in March 2017! 👎⚠️ #reactivation #RegularTiles #notmine #warning #novalue #Stupid

View all 121 comments

27 March 2017

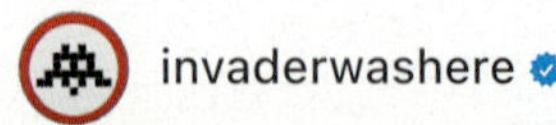

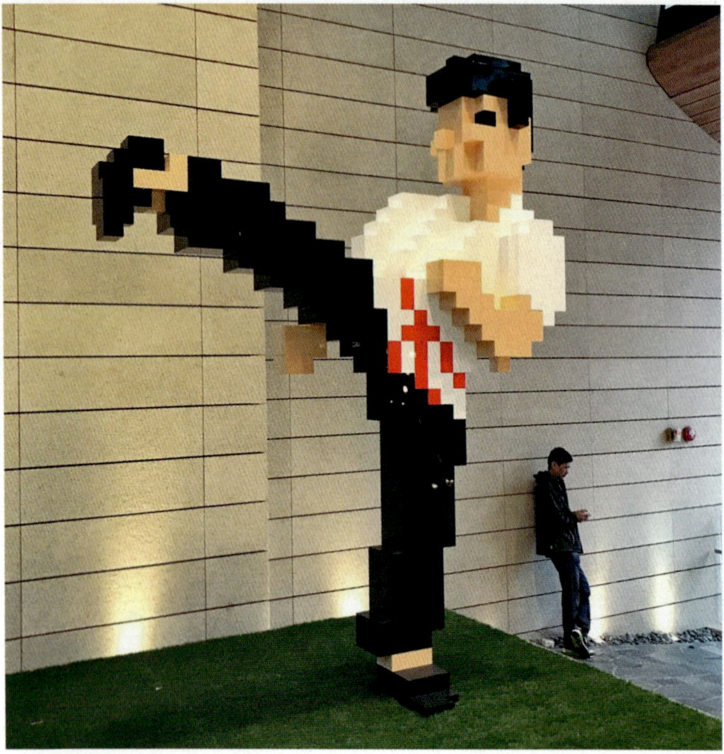

12 973 likes

invaderwashere Bruce Lee in Hong Kong #brucelee #kungfumaster #hongkong #repulsebay #sculpture #metal @hocafoundation

View all 85 comments

31 March 2017

invaderwashere

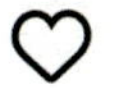  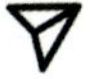 

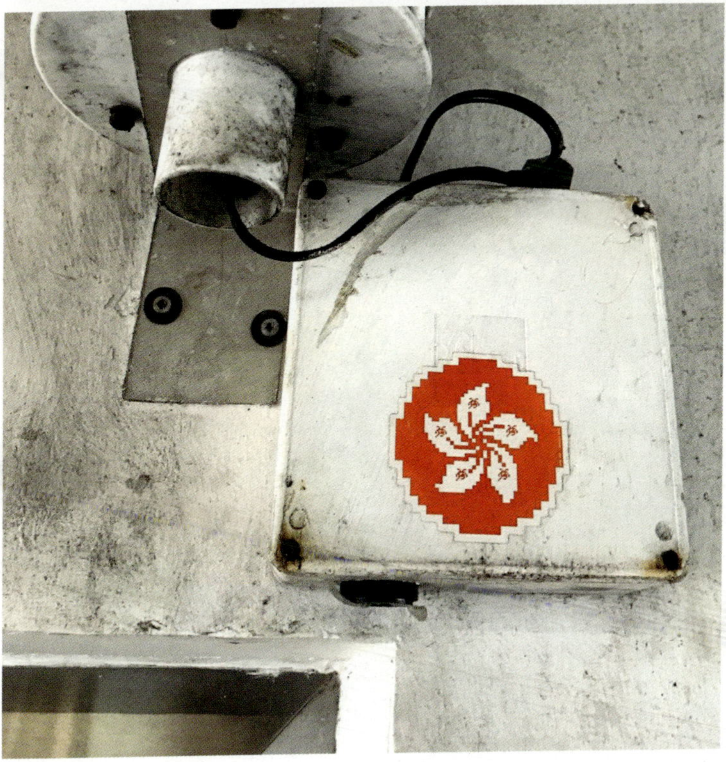

7 326 likes

invaderwashere I found back this 2 years old sticker! somewhere in #hongkong

View all 40 comments

1 April 2017

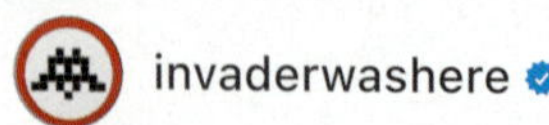

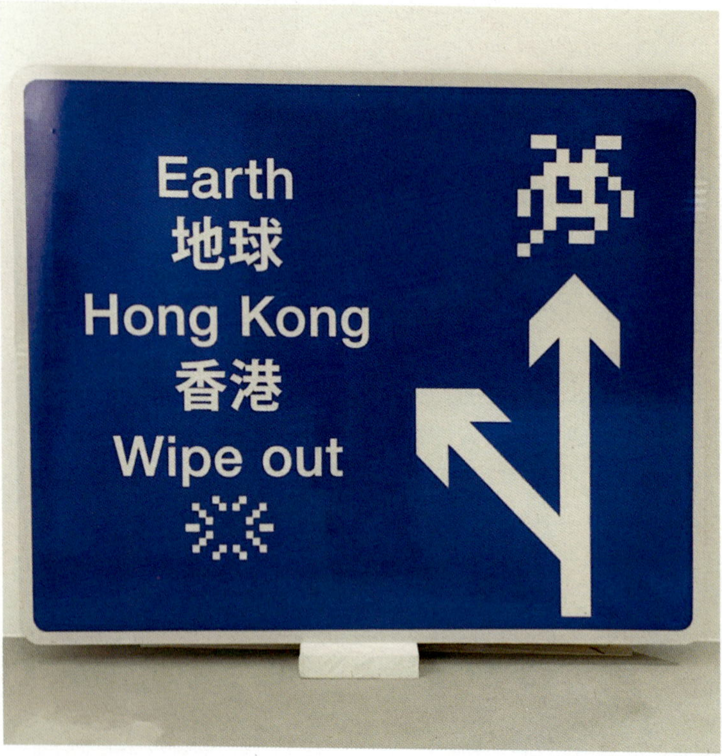

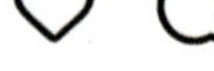

5947 likes

invaderwashere At last signed and available at @overtheinfluencehk #invadedtrafficsign #2015

View all 27 comments

1 April 2017

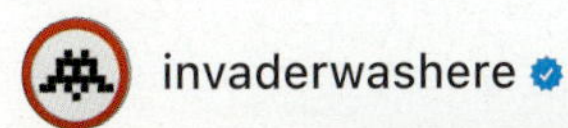

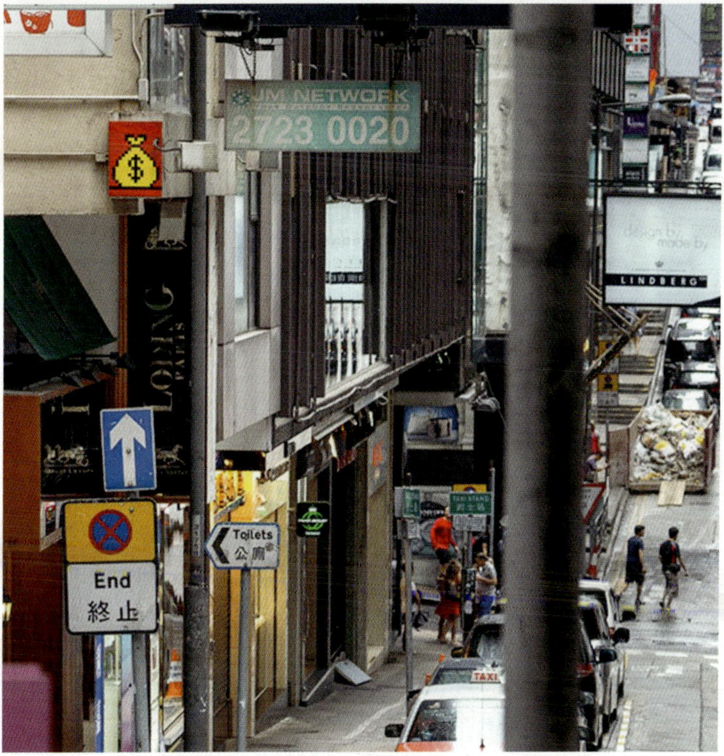

7 326 likes

invaderwashere Try to find the Hong Kong Dollars bag / HK_91 wave5 2015

View all 40 comments

2 April 2017

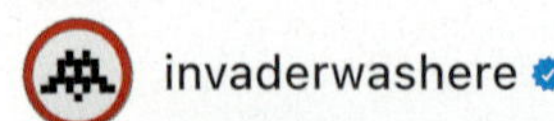

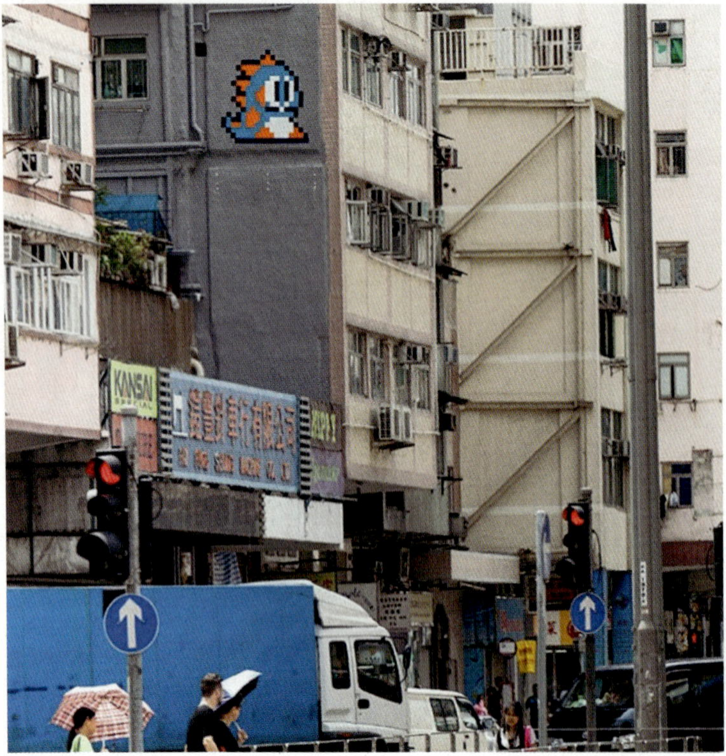

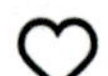   

12 485 likes

invaderwashere HK_82 #hongkong #bubblebobble lost in #mongkok @wmhostel

View all 67 comments

2 April 2017

invaderwashere

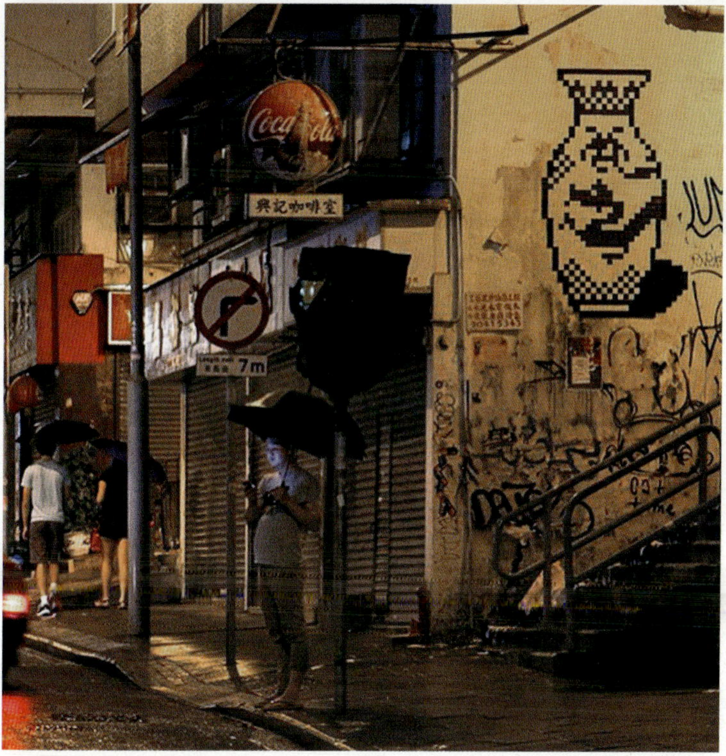

11365 likes

invaderwashere HK_98 #hongkong #mingvase #2015 #wave5 #RIP

View all 43 comments

2 April 2017

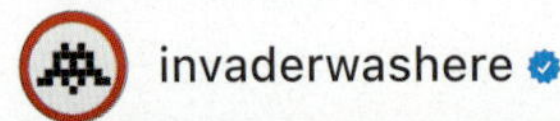

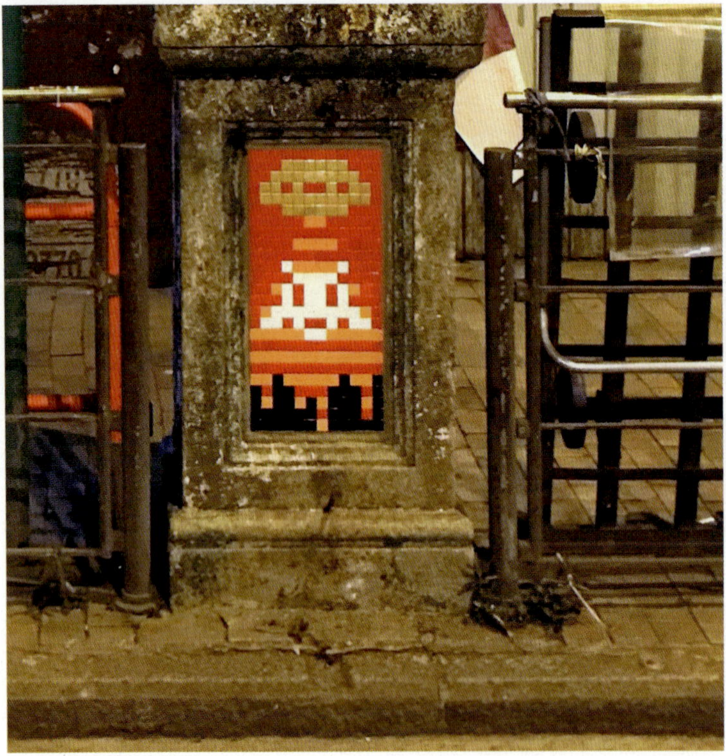

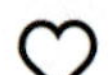 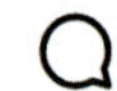  

11420 likes

invaderwashere HK_100 Fresh from last night...
#hongkong #invasion

View all 81 comments

3 April 2017

invaderwashere

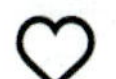   

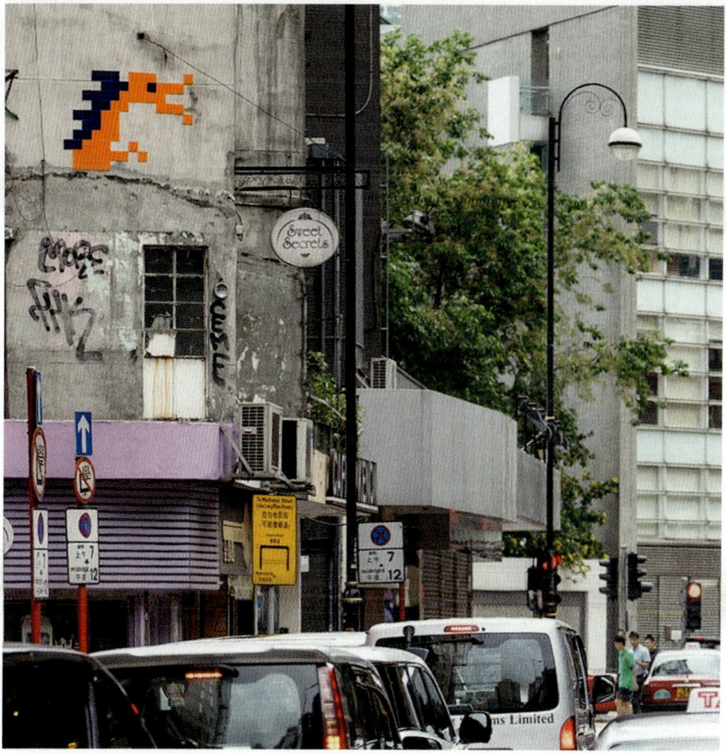

7943 likes

invaderwashere HK_85 #hongkong #lowresdragon

View all 25 comments

3 April 2017

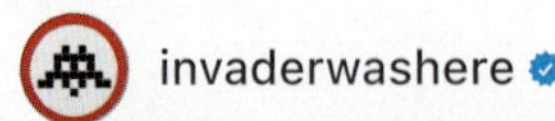

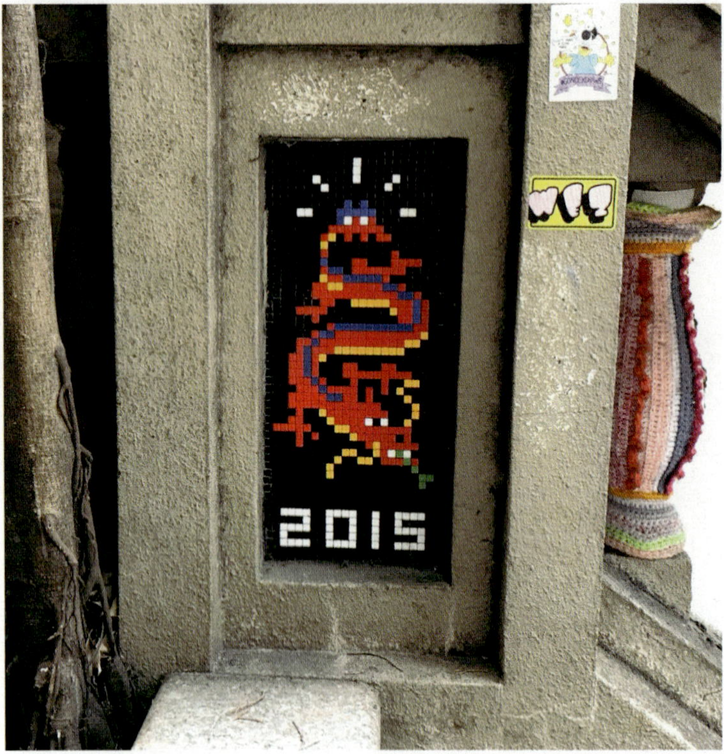

  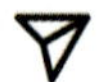 

14 220 likes

invaderwashere HK_76 #hongkong

View all 50 comments

3 April 2017

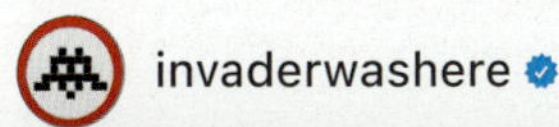

invaderwashere

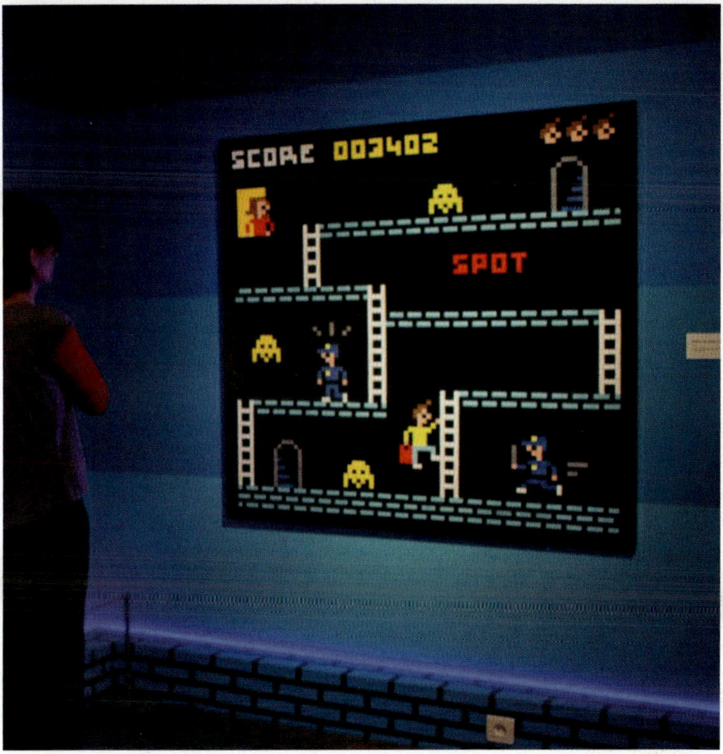

8 457 likes

invaderwashere Thank you to the 35.000 visitors who already came to see #hellomygameis @museeenherbe #paris 🙏🙏🙏🤘

View all 57 comments

5 April 2017

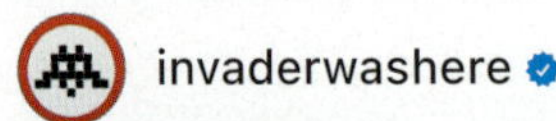

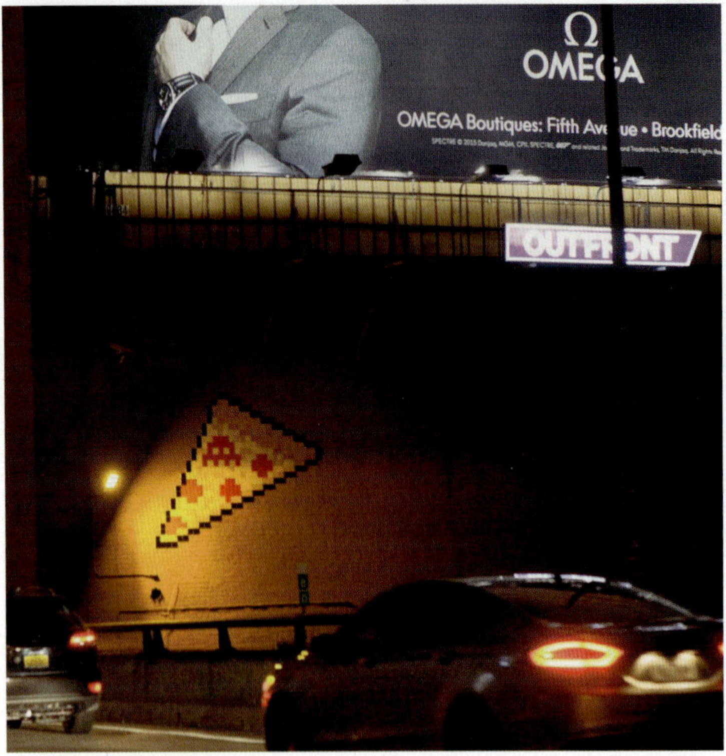

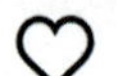   

11451 likes

invaderwashere #Before When Art and advertising shared a good pizza #NewJersey #NYC @invaderwashere @outfrontmediausa

View all 70 comments

7 April 2017

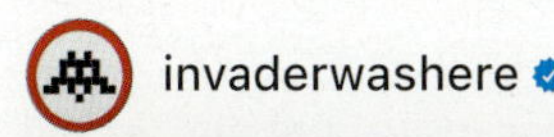

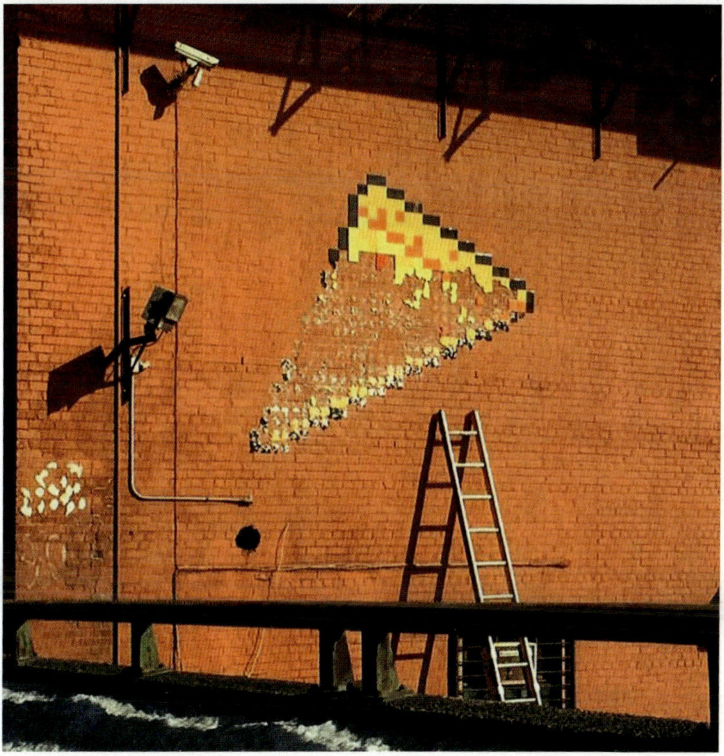

 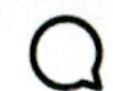  

10 691 likes

invaderwashere #After... when advertising decided to ate the pizza and only left the crust to Art 😡
@outfrontmediausa vs #art photo by @so_jojo

View all 460 comments

7 April 2017

invaderwashere •••

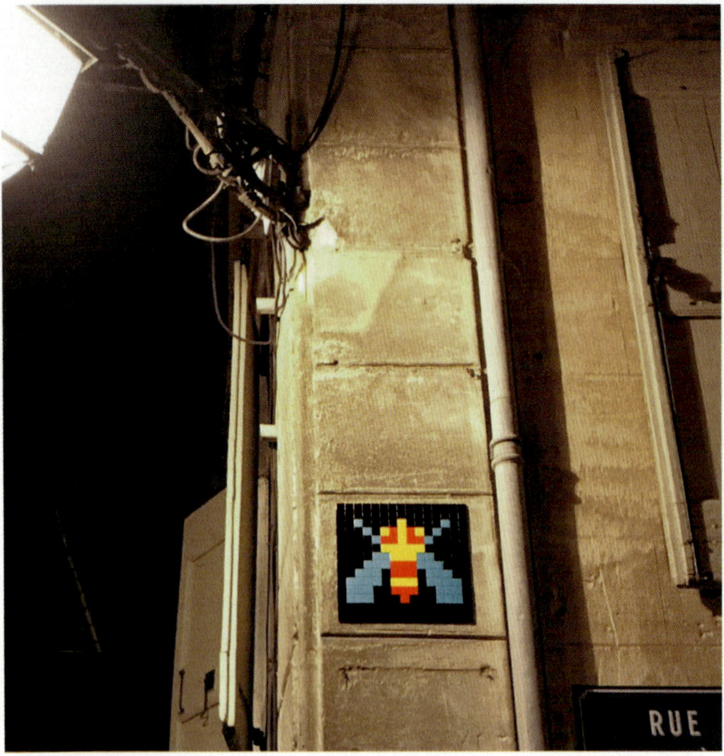

10 244 likes

invaderwashere #new #somewhere #galaga

View all 54 comments

9 April 2017

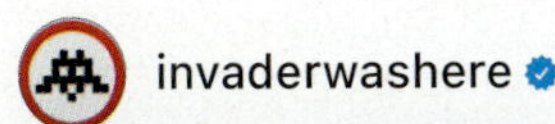

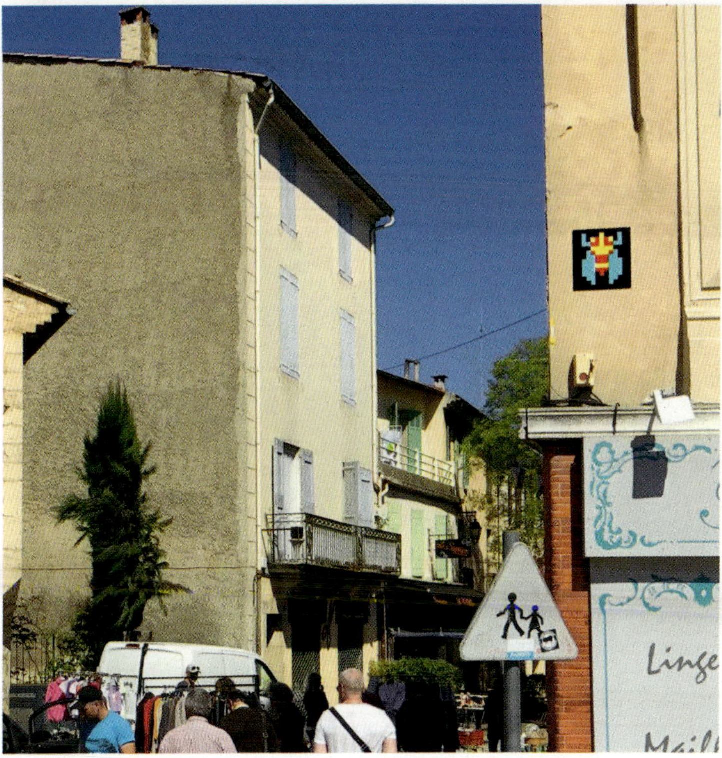

 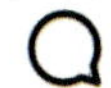  

6943 likes

invaderwashere New city invaded 👾 #forcalquier #southoffrance

View all 39 comments

10 April 2017

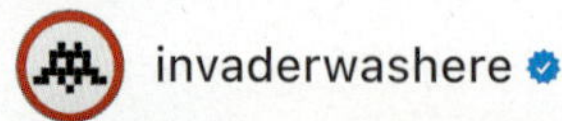

WAS
HERE

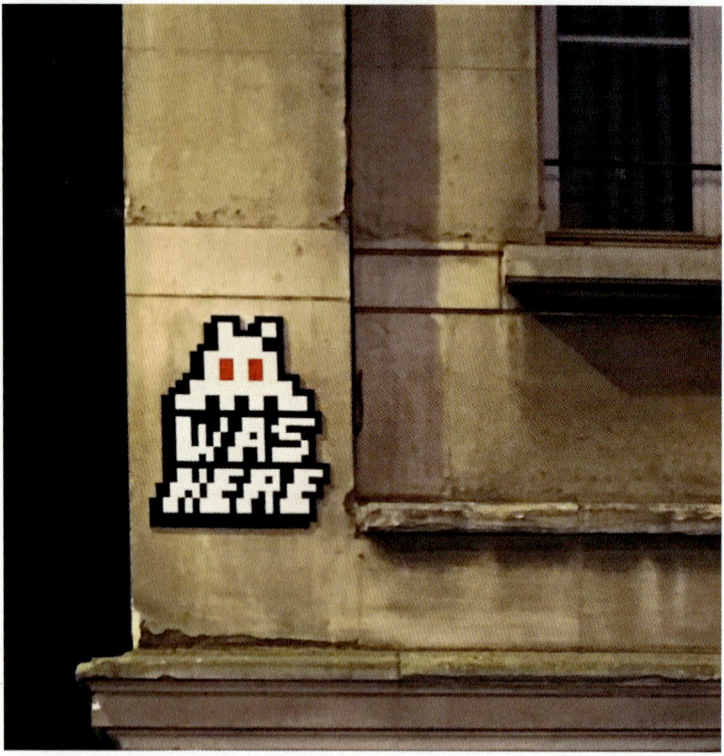

16 595 likes

invaderwashere 👾 WAS HERE!

View all 103 comments

12 April 2017

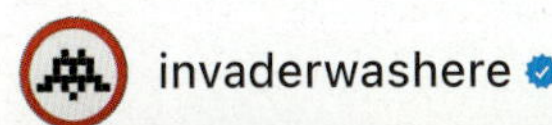

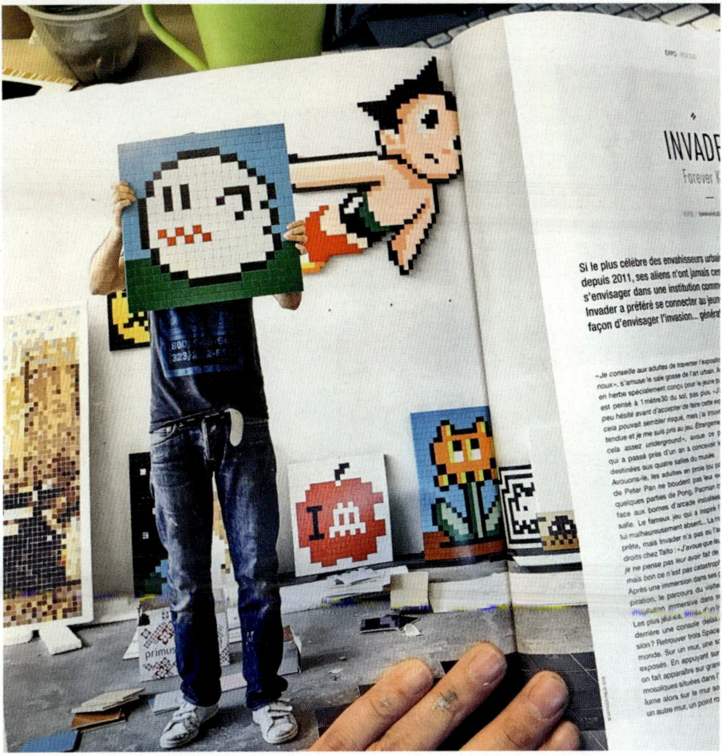

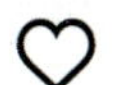   

10 721 likes

invaderwashere Thank you @graffitiartmagazine #mediainvasion #portrait #hellomygameis text: @emmanuelledreyfus photos: @kathleenfinlayphotographer & @unoeilquitraine

View all 61 comments

14 April 2017

invaderwashere

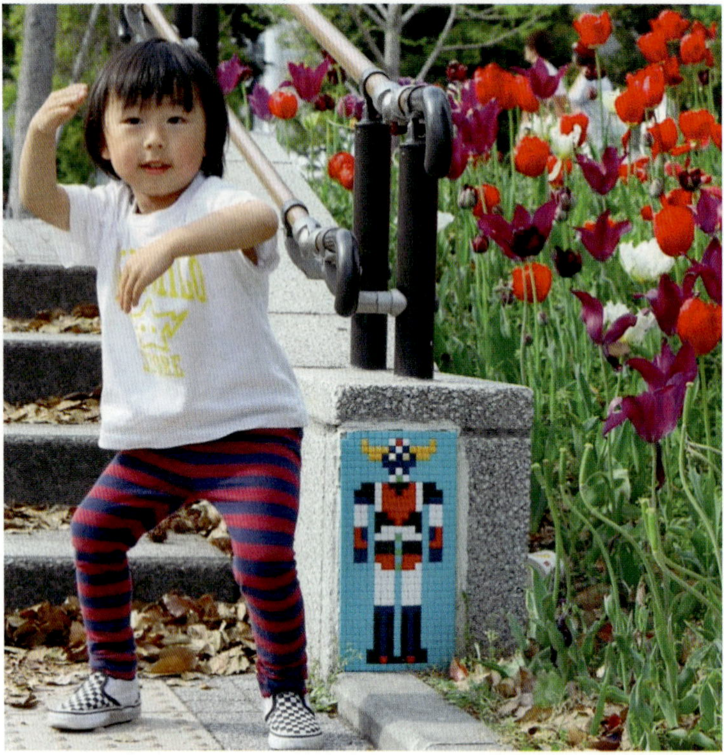

15 462 likes

invaderwashere Happy Monday! photo by: @grv1174
#tokyo #grandizer #goldorakgo

View all 110 comments

18 April 2017

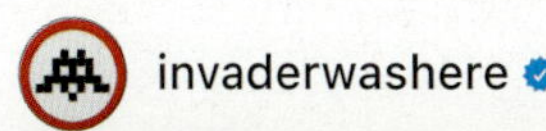

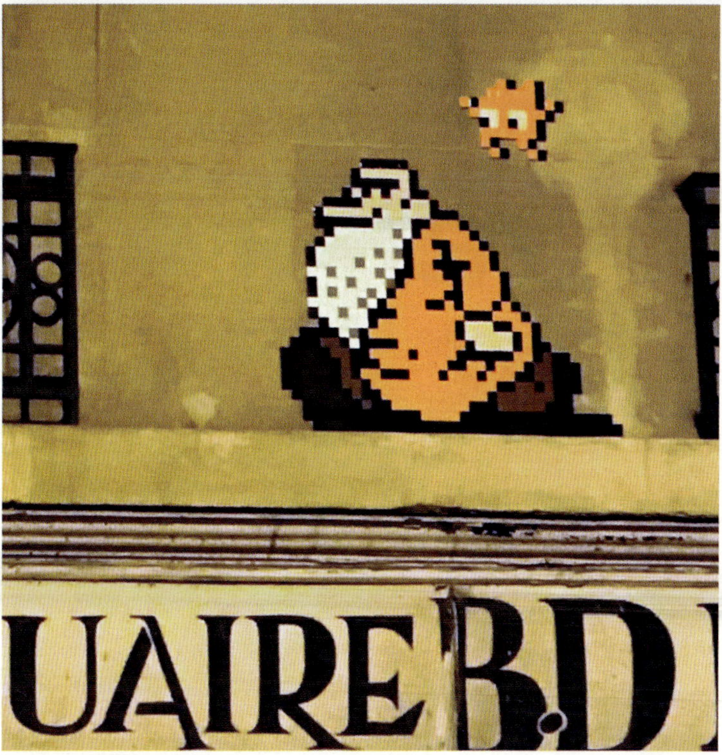

8 677 likes

invaderwashere Mister Natural! #crumb #mrnatural #freshfromlastnight #paris

View all 58 comments

20 April 2017

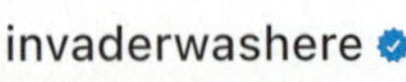

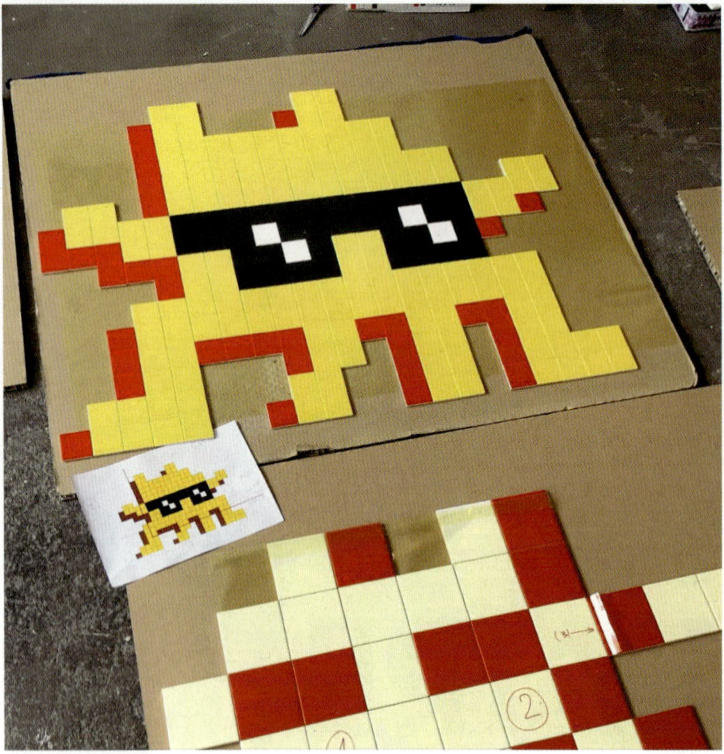

12 229 likes

invaderwashere Waiting for the sun... #studiodetail

View all 80 comments

26 April 2017

invaderwashere 

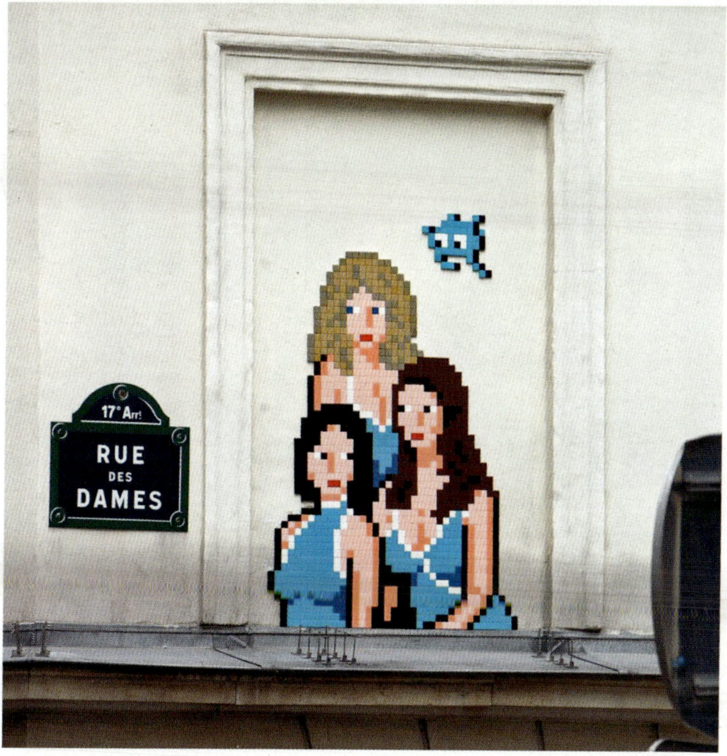

21191 likes

invaderwashere PA_1280 #50points #freshfromlastnight #goodmorningcharlie

View all 163 comments

4 May 2017

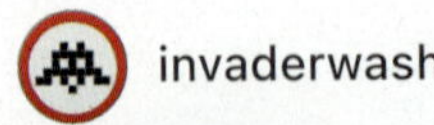

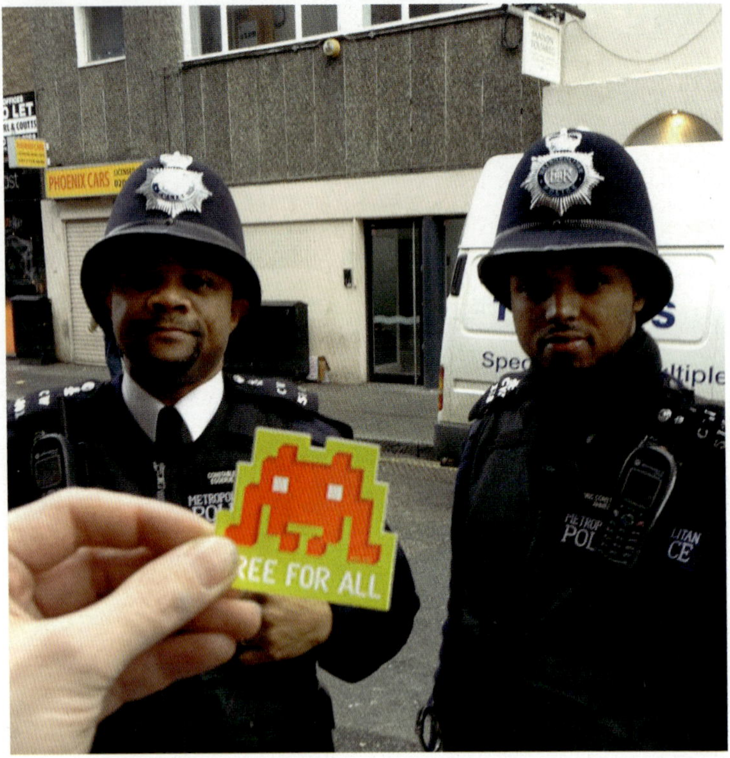

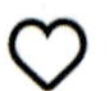   

12 510 likes

invaderwashere This is London 🇬🇧 👾

View all 60 comments

12 May 2017

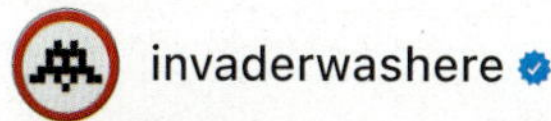

invaderwashere •••

762
publi.

444 K
abonnés

230
abos

Modifier le profil

Invader

Follow the Invasion.

space-invaders.com/

AFFICHER LA TRADUCTION

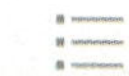

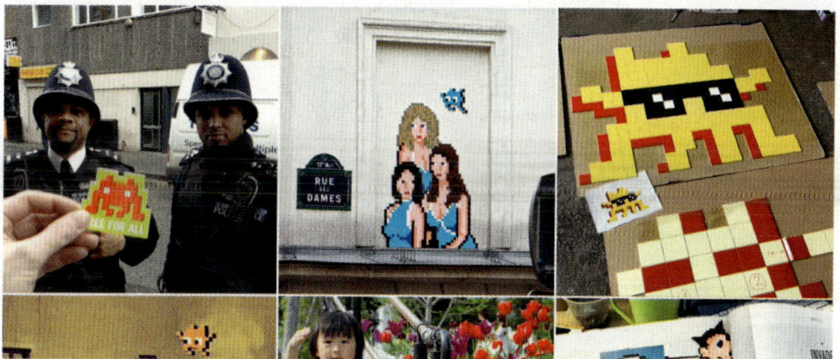

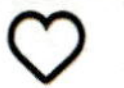  

3750 likes

invaderwashere Just scored 444k followers 
#manythanks #instagram #numbers

View all 53 comments

17 May 2017

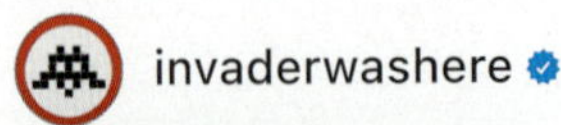

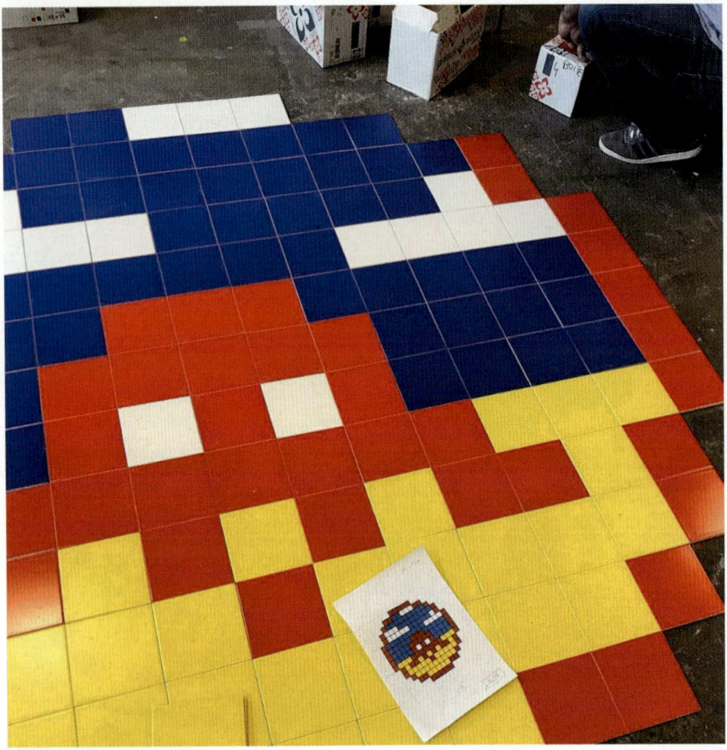

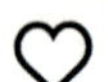   

7143 likes

invaderwashere Piece for the next city #makingof #studio

View all 24 comments

20 May 2017

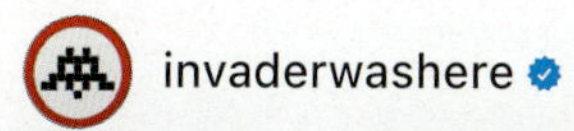

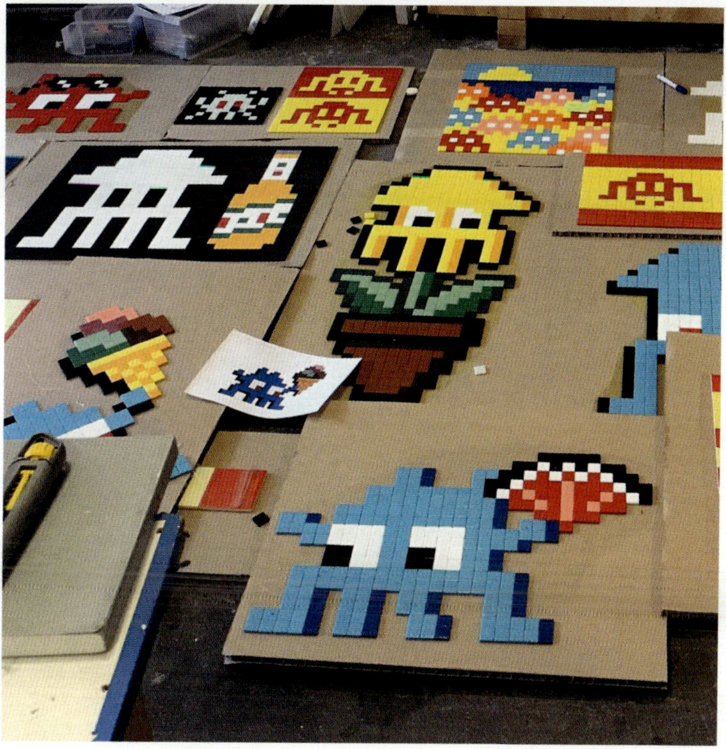

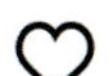 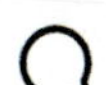  

14 151 likes

invaderwashere Pieces for the next invasion #makingof #studio

View all 112 comments

20 May 2017

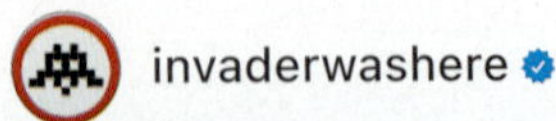

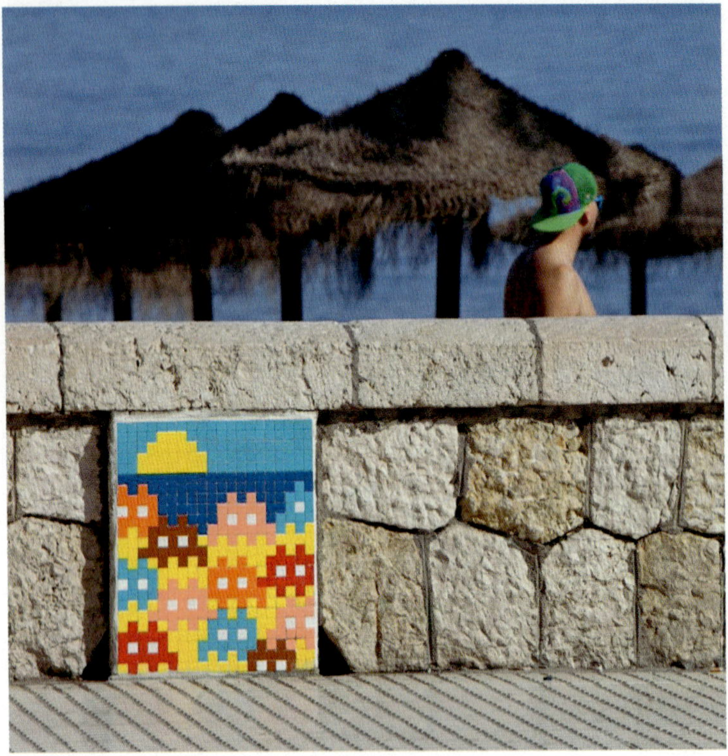

 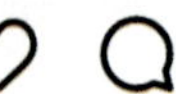 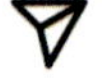 

13 463 likes

invaderwashere 1st piece of the 1st invasion wave of Málaga 👾🇪🇸🌞 #malaga #2017

View all 107 comments

20 May 2017

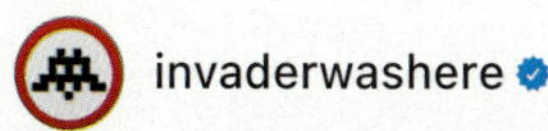

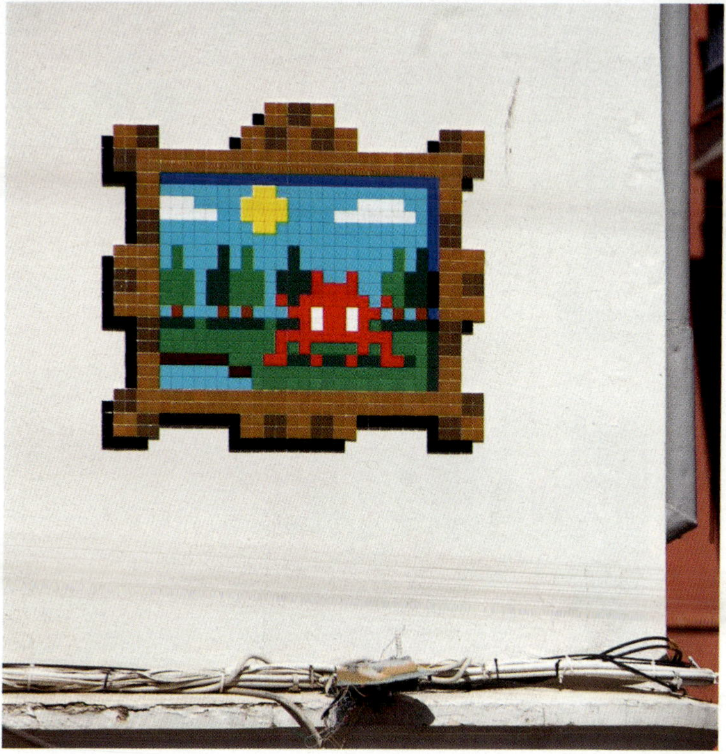

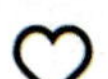 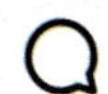  

9835 likes

invaderwashere Tonight in Málaga is the "Noche en Blanco": free entrances in the museums and lots of brand new space invaders to be discovered in the city... #malaga #art #invasion #nocheenblancomlg 🇪🇸

View all 47 comments

20 May 2017

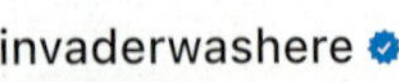

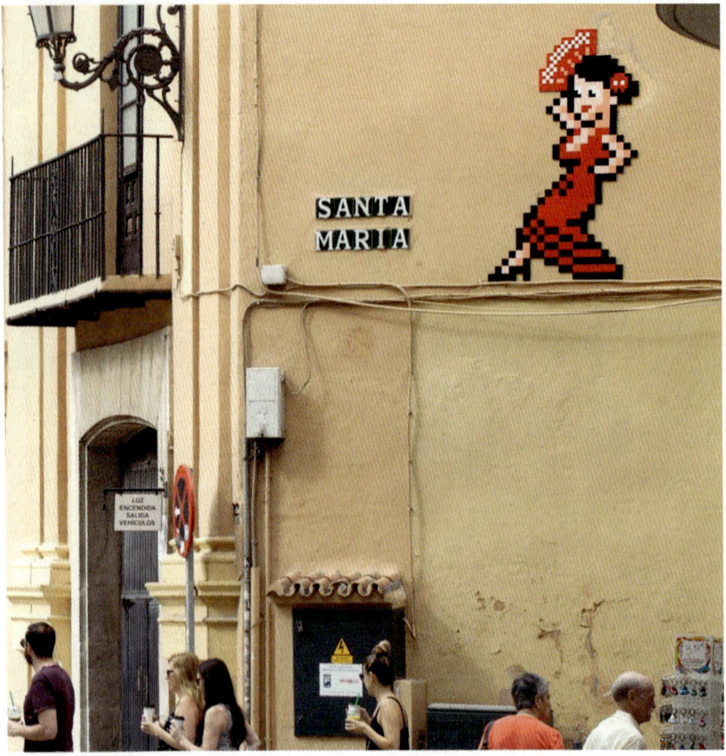

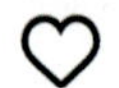   

21920 likes

invaderwashere Olé Málaga!!! 💃 👾 🇪🇸

View all 225 comments

21 May 2017

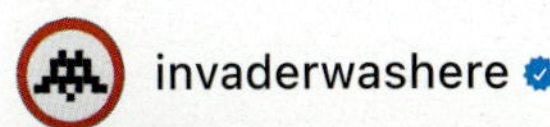

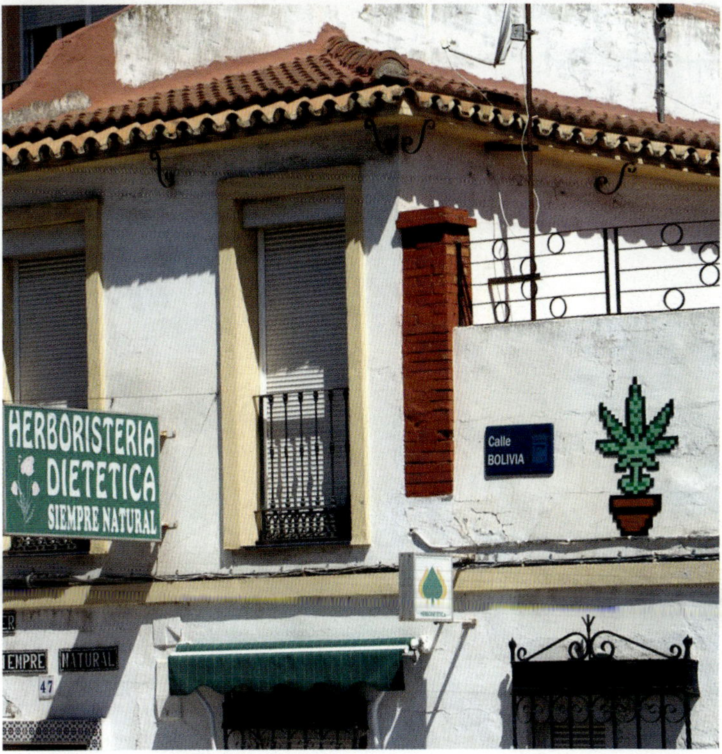

8 761 likes

invaderwashere Siempre natural! #herboristeria #malaga

View all 69 comments

21 May 2017

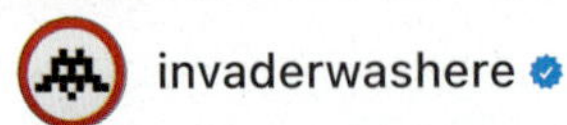

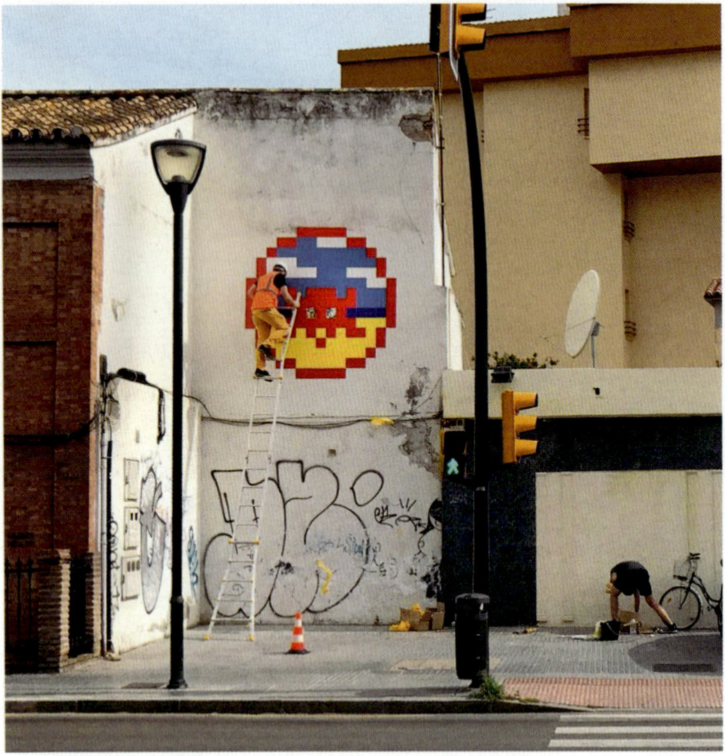

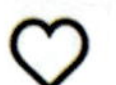   

13 717 likes

invaderwashere Greetings from Málaga 🇪🇸 👾

View all 58 comments

22 May 2017

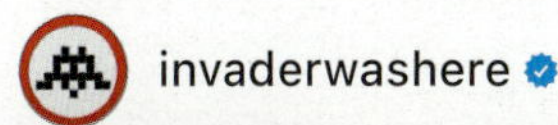

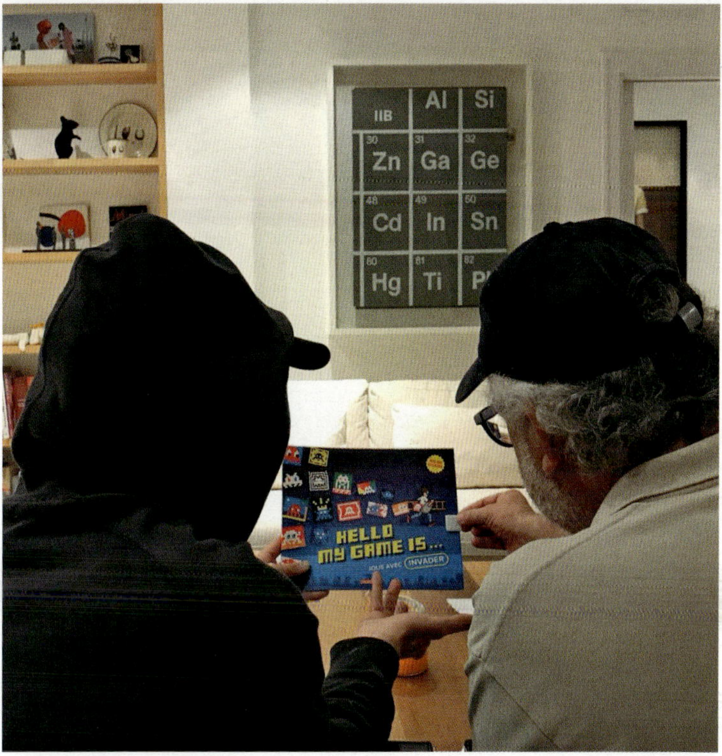

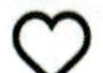   

3 799 likes

invaderwashere Speaking of art with @ferfrances Art is my passion, my obsession, my drug and my life @cacmalaga

View all 16 comments

22 May 2017

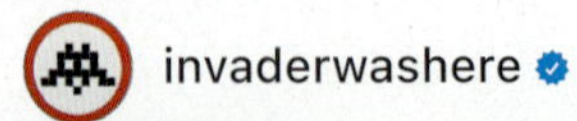

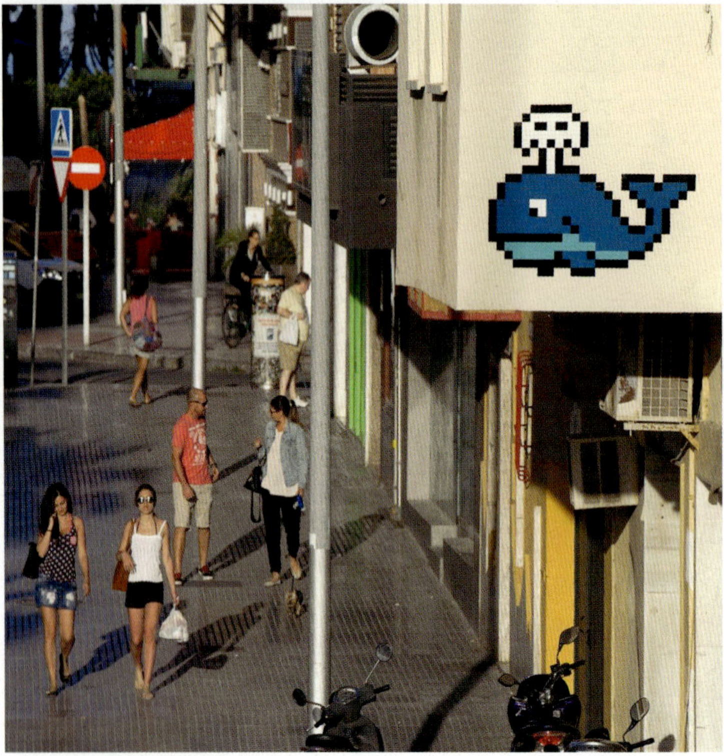

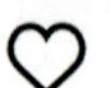   

17 078 likes

invaderwashere La ballena de Málaga #malaga #whale #bluewhale #protectwildlife 🐳 👾

View all 78 comments

24 May 2017

invaderwashere ✓ ...

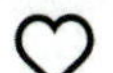   

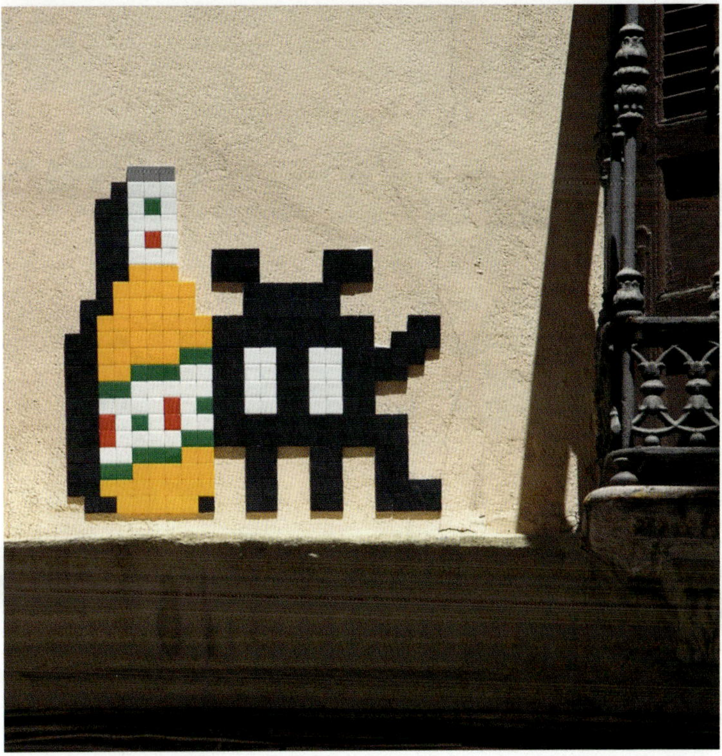

14 827 likes

invaderwashere Málaga 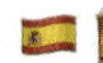 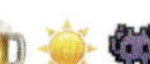

View all 60 comments

28 May 2017

invaderwashere

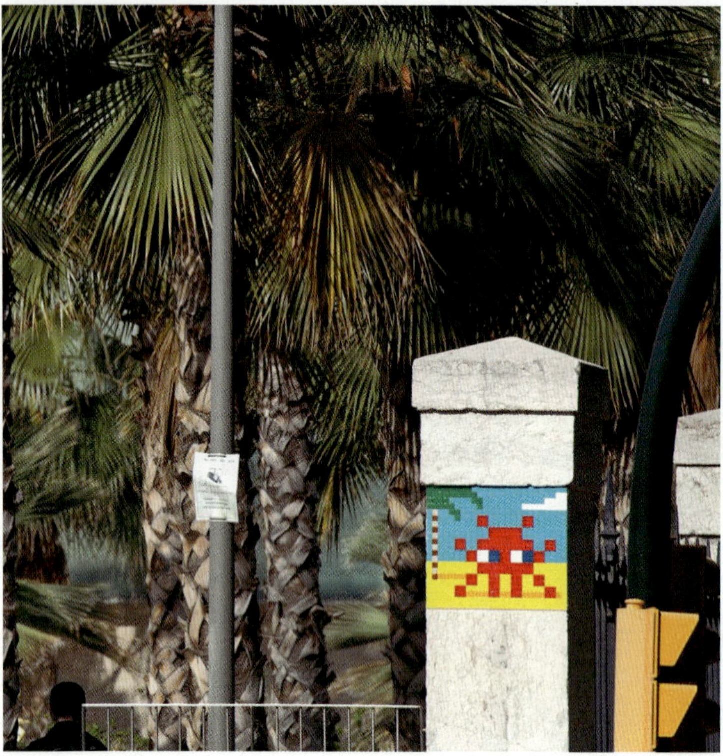

8115 likes

invaderwashere Málaga 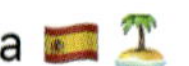

View all 33 comments

28 May 2017

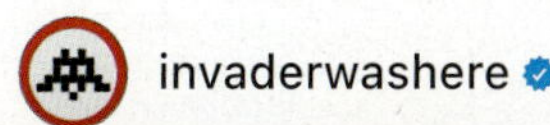
invaderwashere

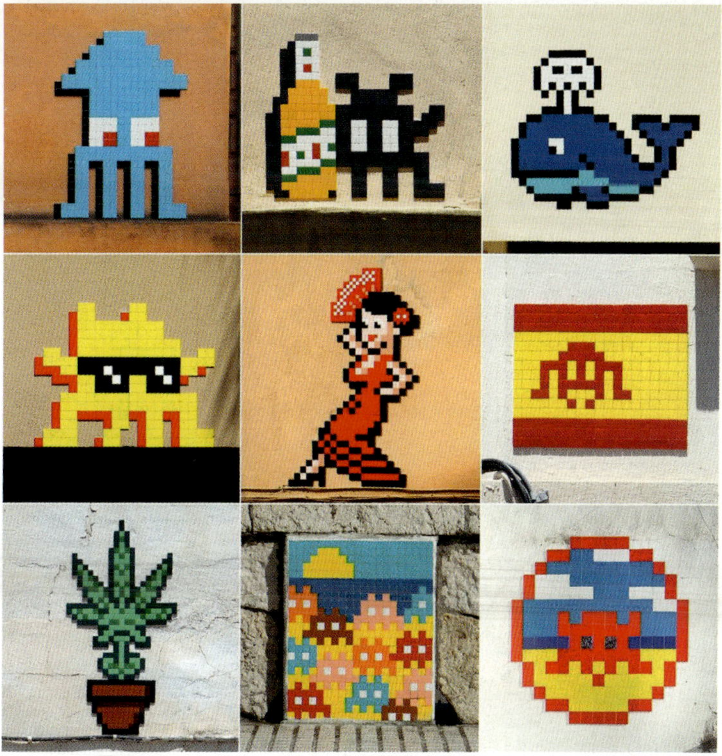

16 556 likes

invaderwashere 9 of the 29 space invaders of Málaga 🇪🇸
Total score: 1020 pts / more photos online

View all 144 comments

29 May 2017

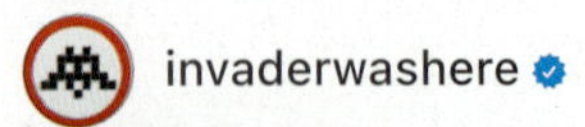

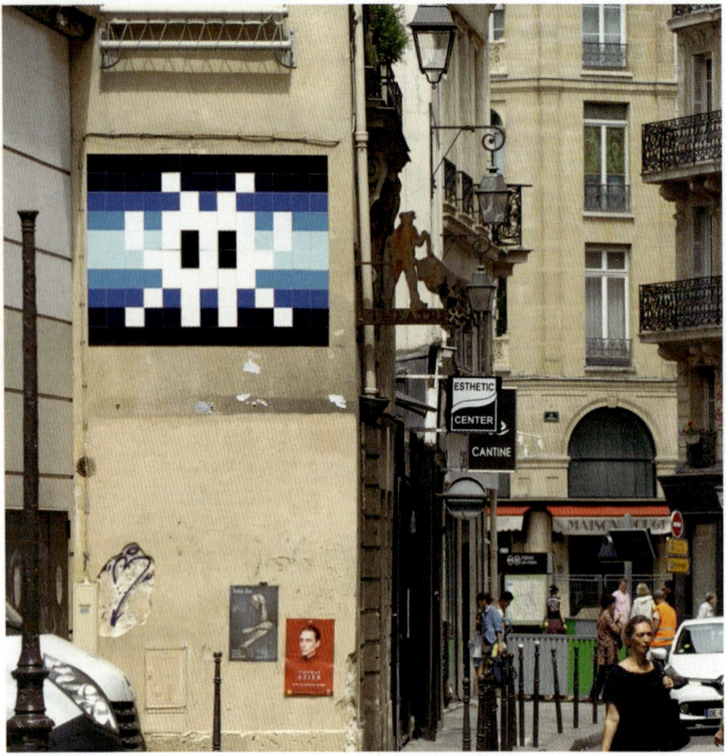

  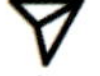 

11194 likes

invaderwashere PA_1283 #thelatest

View all 73 comments

1 June 2017

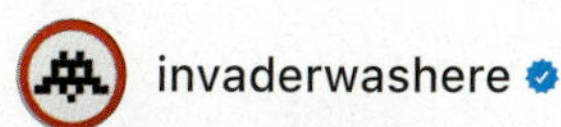

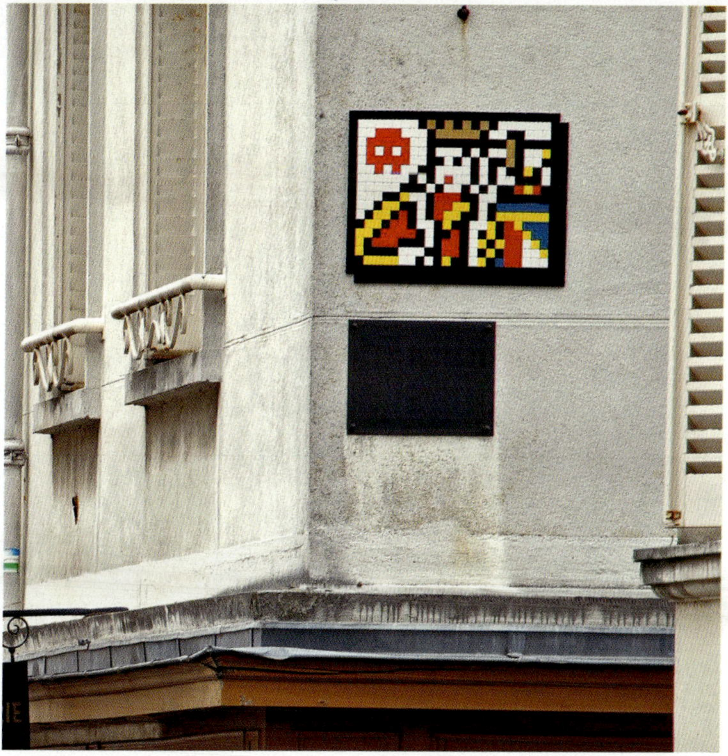

13 351 likes

invaderwashere VRS_01 Versailles #kingofspaces

View all 67 comments

8 June 2017

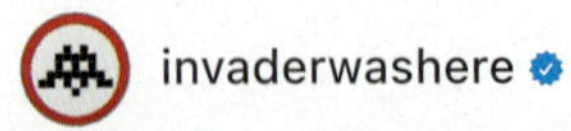

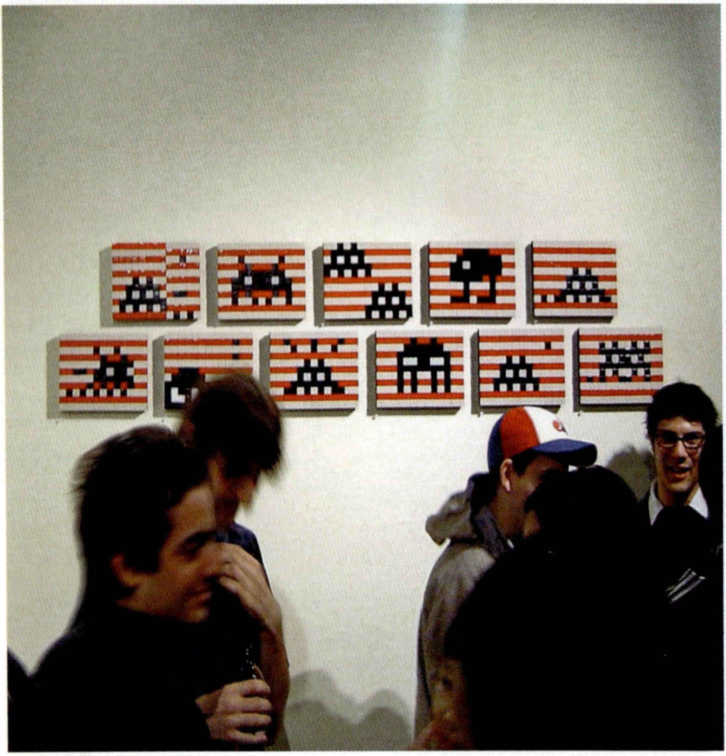

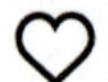  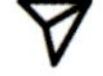 

5790 likes

invaderwashere Detail of I 👾 HO..YWO.D / May 2004 / Solo show at Subliminal Projects gallery #throwback @subliminalprojects @obeygiant

View all 10 comments

9 June 2017

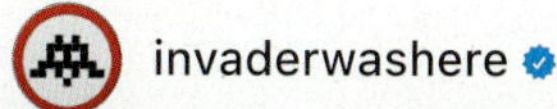

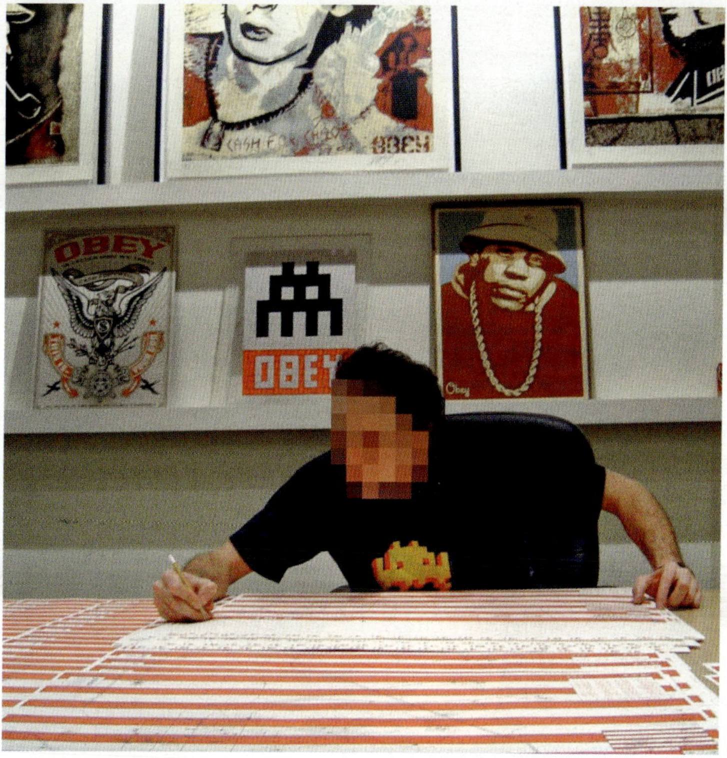

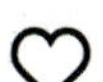 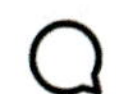  

8 337 likes

invaderwashere Signing the LA Invasion Maps / May 2004 / at Subliminal Projects gallery #throwback @subliminalprojects @obeygiant

View all 35 comments

9 June 2017

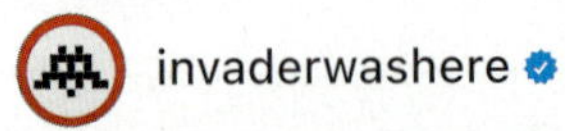

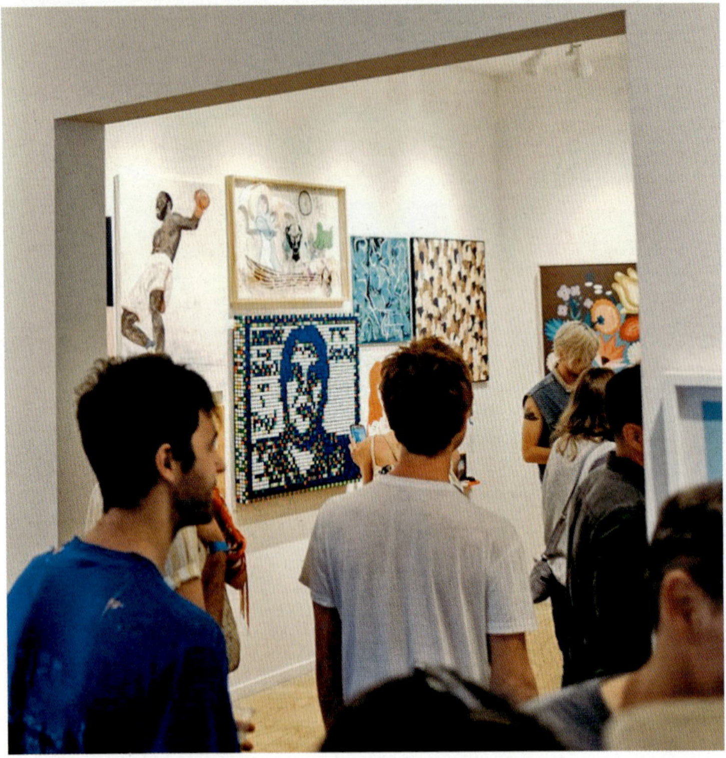

  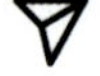 

4990 likes

invaderwashere I'm proud to be part of TWENTY-ONE, the anniversary group show of Subliminal Projects gallery featuring many great artists. Happy birthday 🎂 @subliminalprojects #losangeles #now #rubikobeyposse #rubikcubism photo by @morgnar

View all 24 comments

9 June 2017

invaderwashere

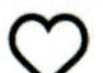   

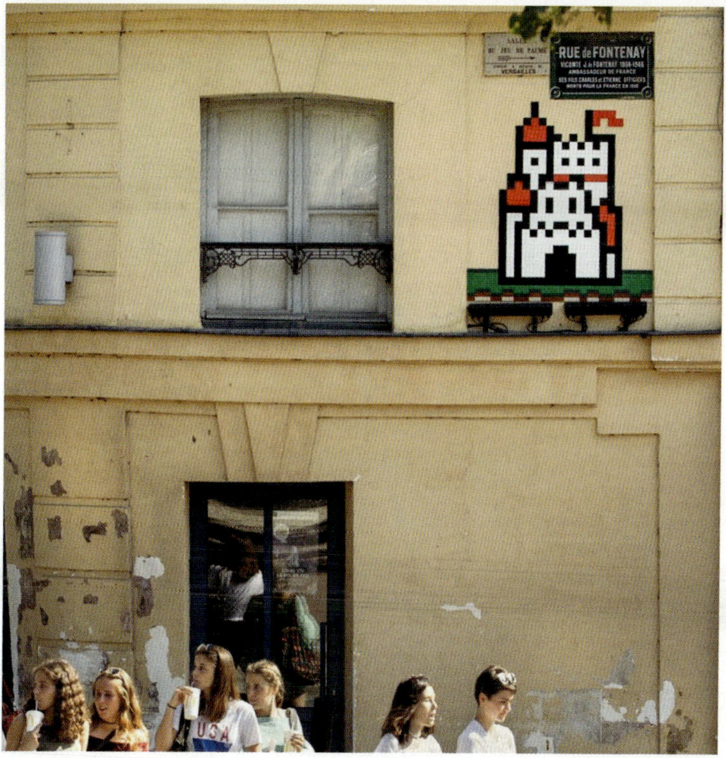

11891 likes

invaderwashere VRS_05 #versailles

View all 53 comments

15 June 2017

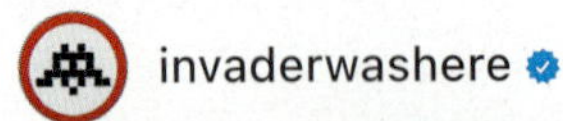

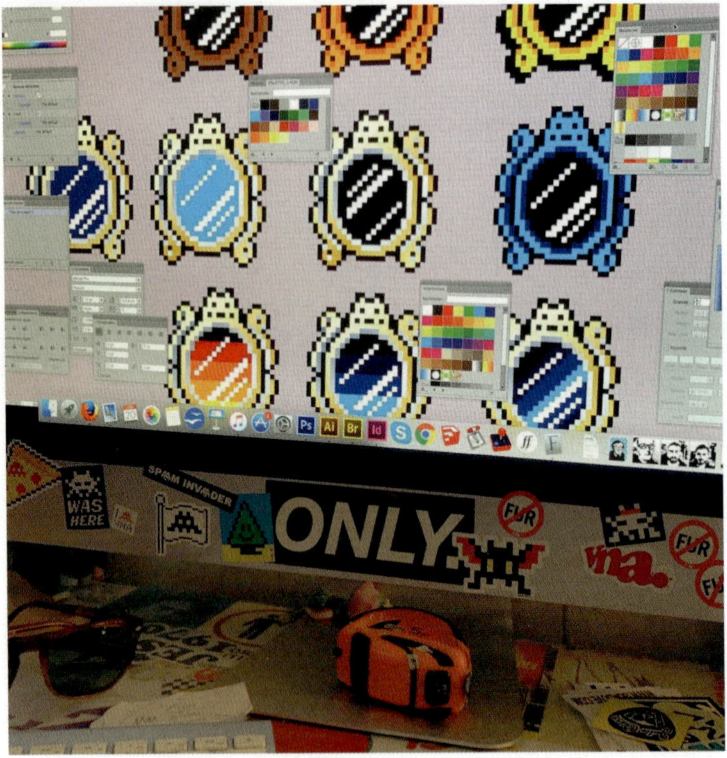

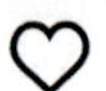   

7 913 likes

invaderwashere Mirrors, mirrors... #study #computer #8bit #pixel #mirrors

View all 61 comments

20 June 2017

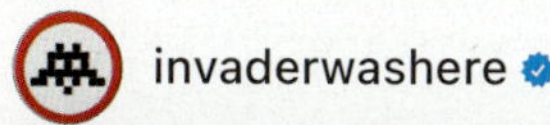

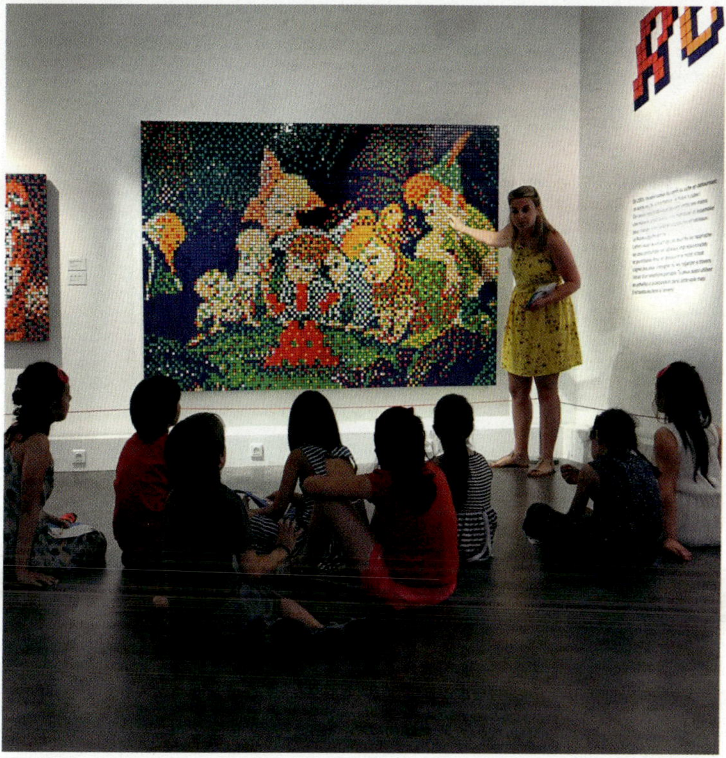

8894 likes

invaderwashere Evening guided tours @museeenherbe #hellomynameis #overtheinfluence #rubikcubism #children #neverland

View all 52 comments

25 June 2017

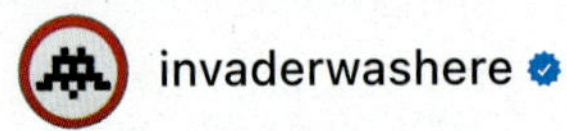

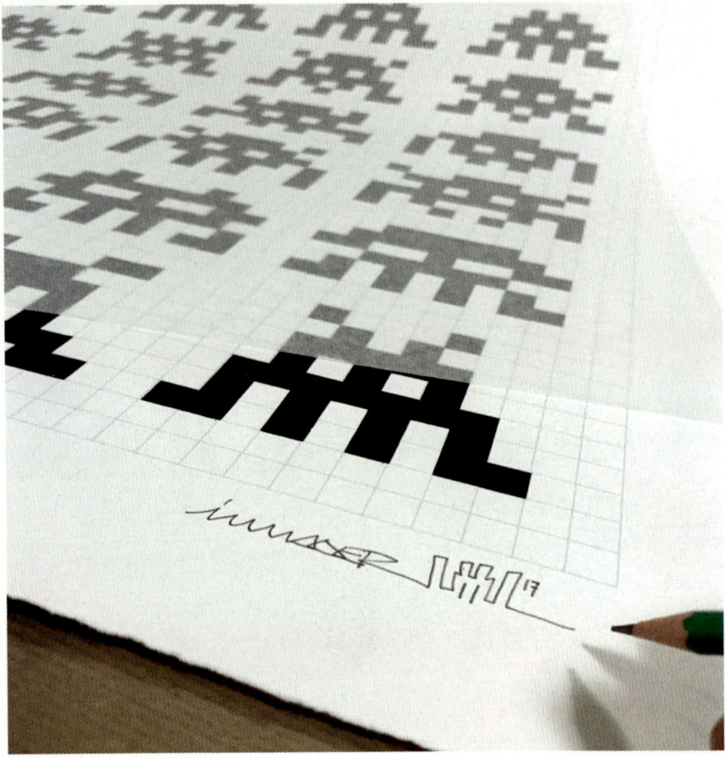

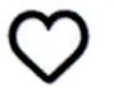   

6985 likes

invaderwashere My new print will be online today / link in bio

View all 56 comments

26 June 2017

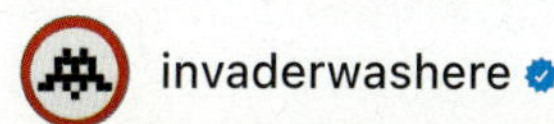

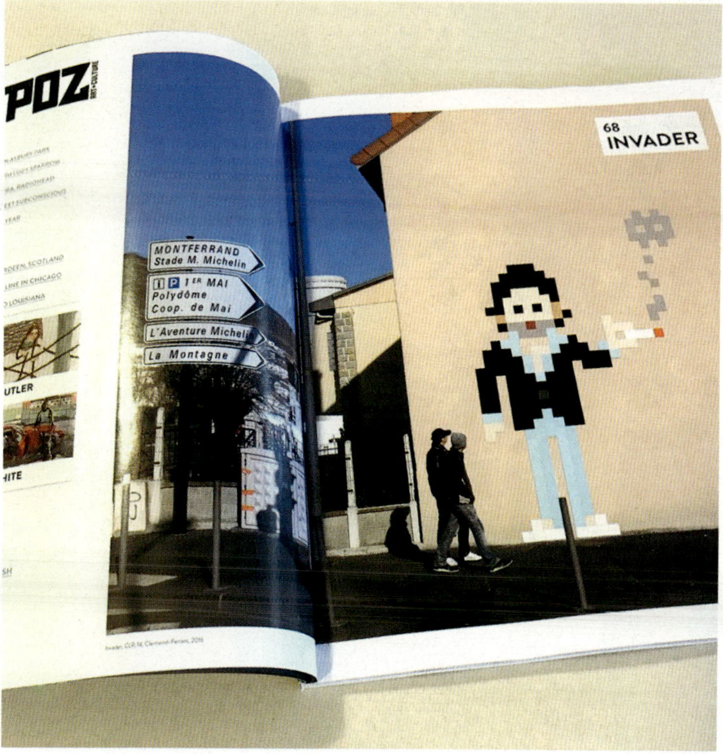

 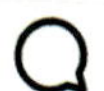  

9006 likes

invaderwashere New Juxtapoz magazine invaded! @juxtapozmag Interview by @sashabogojev #july2017 #mediainvasion

View all 37 comments

27 June 2017

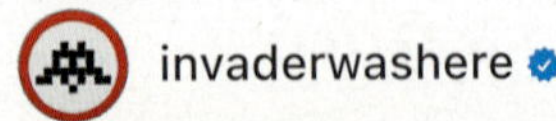

•••

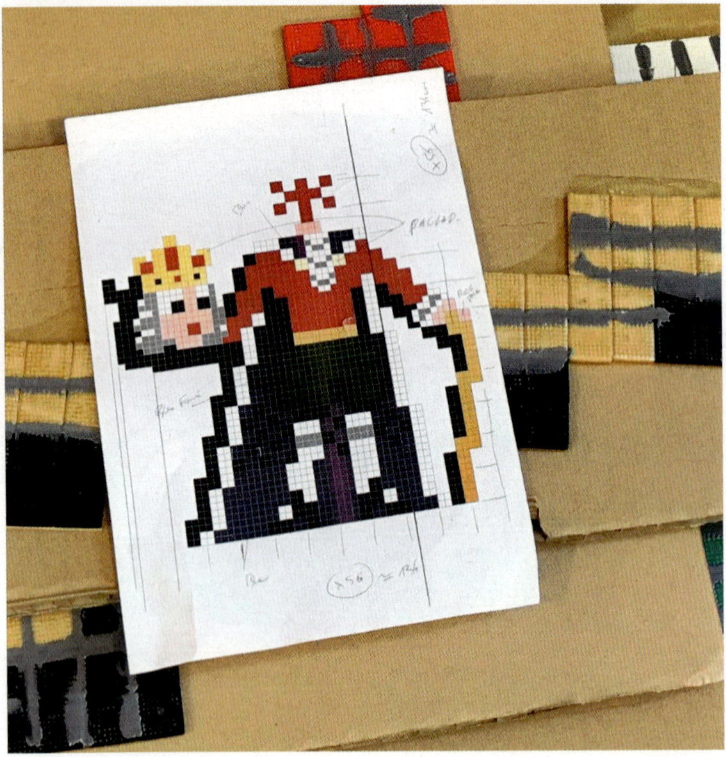

9063 likes

invaderwashere The king is dead! #sketch #makingof #studio

View all 65 comments

29 June 2017

invaderwashere

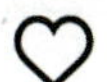   

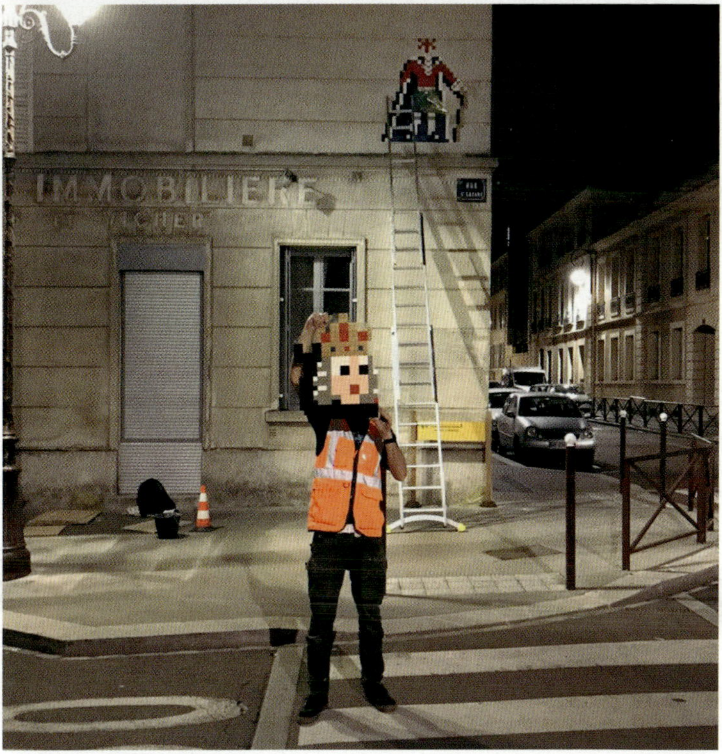

17 849 likes

invaderwashere Portrait of the week #versailles

View all 69 comments

2 July 2017

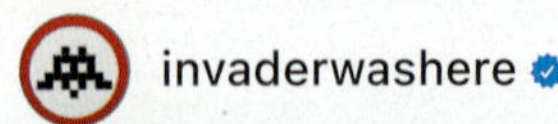

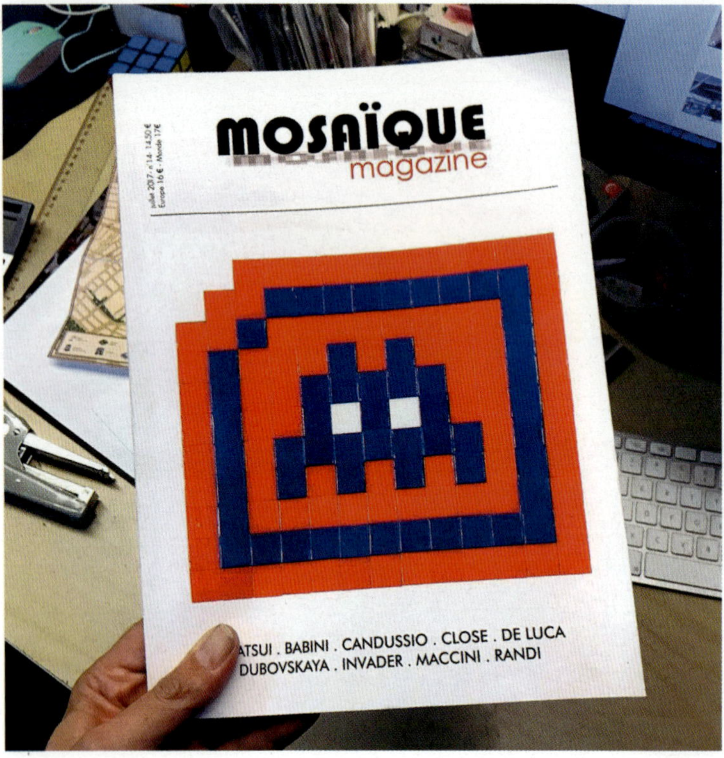

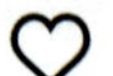   

5750 likes

invaderwashere Mosaic-art cred! #mosaiquemagazine #mosaicart #cover #mediainvasion

View all 25 comments

5 July 2017

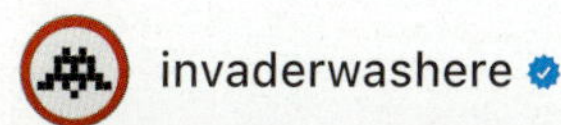
invaderwashere

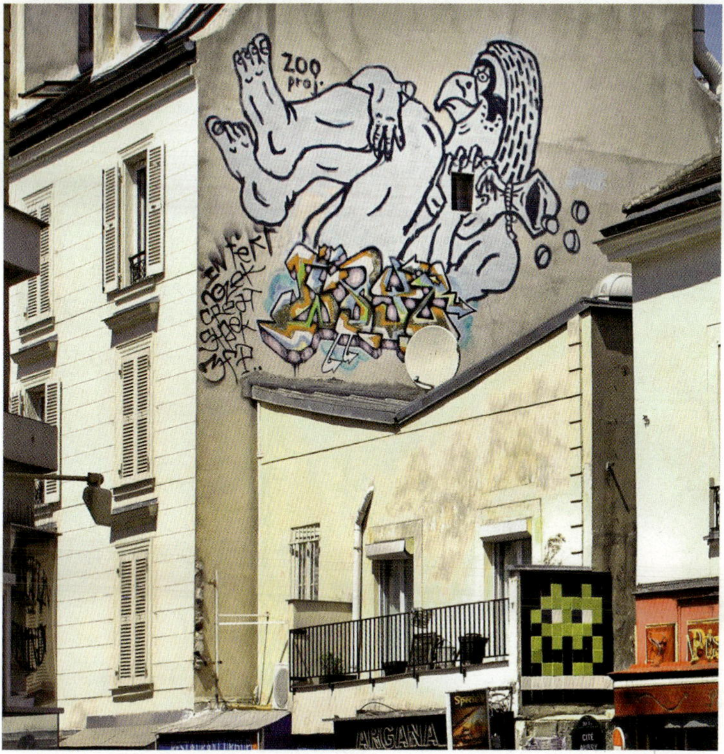

6 231 likes

invaderwashere Bilal Berreni aka Zoo Project was a young talentuous parisian artist and street fellow. He was robbed and shot during a trip to Detroit in 2013 at the age of 23. Today his friends and family want to pay a tribute to him and highlight his work. Thank you for your support: @zoo_project_hommage #crowdfunding #tribute #rip #bilalberreni 🧡🙏

View all 33 comments

6 July 2017

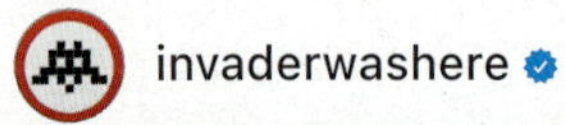

invaderwashere

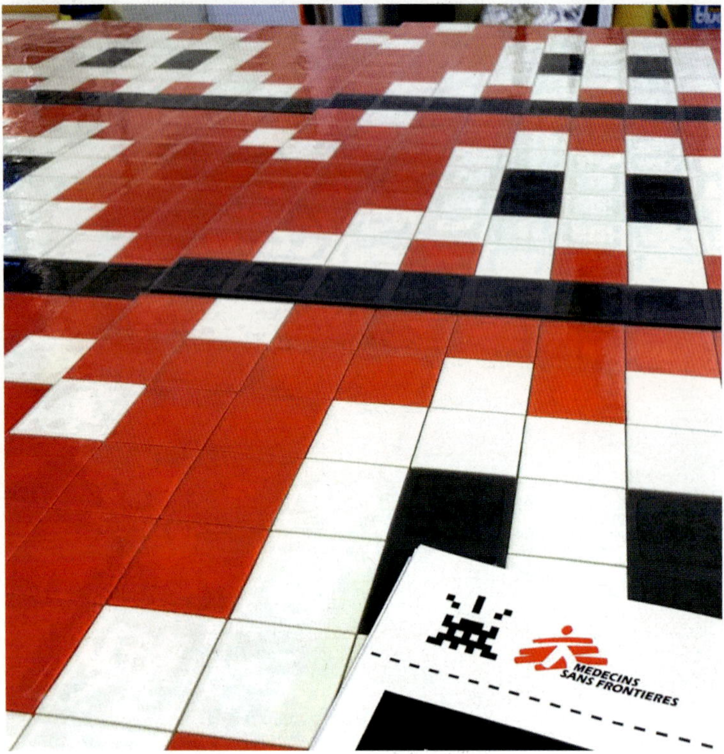

5855 likes

invaderwashere My latest Invasion Kit was specially created for "Medecins Sans Frontieres" (Doctors without borders). The whole edition has been sold by @overtheinfluencehk with 100% of the proceeds going to @doctorswithoutborders @msf_fr A really big thank to everybody who have taken part to this project and supported this great cause. #ik #invasionkit #makingof #charity

View all 42 comments

10 July 2017

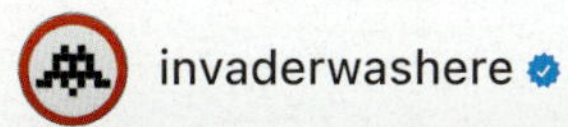

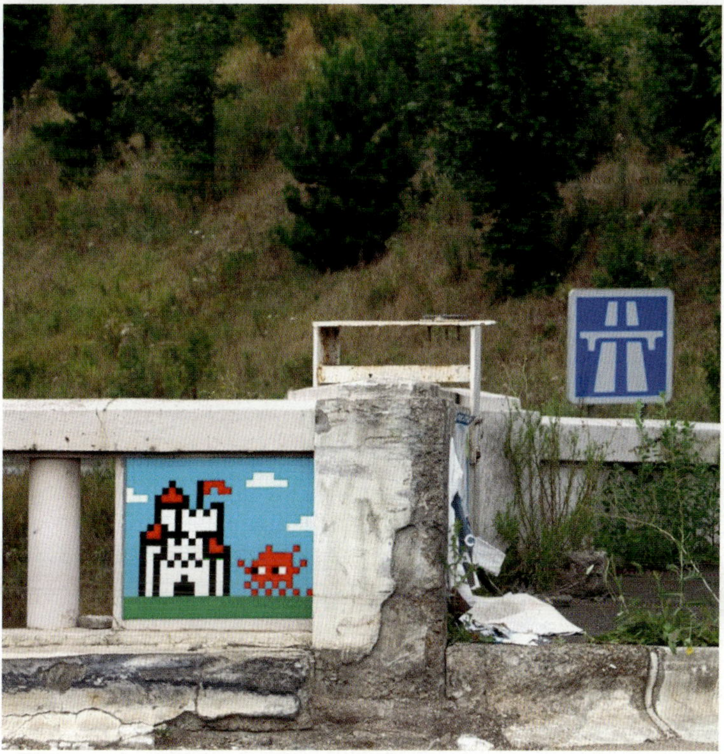

11157 likes

invaderwashere On the way to Versailles... VRS_10

View all 45 comments

16 July 2017

invaderwashere

  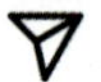 

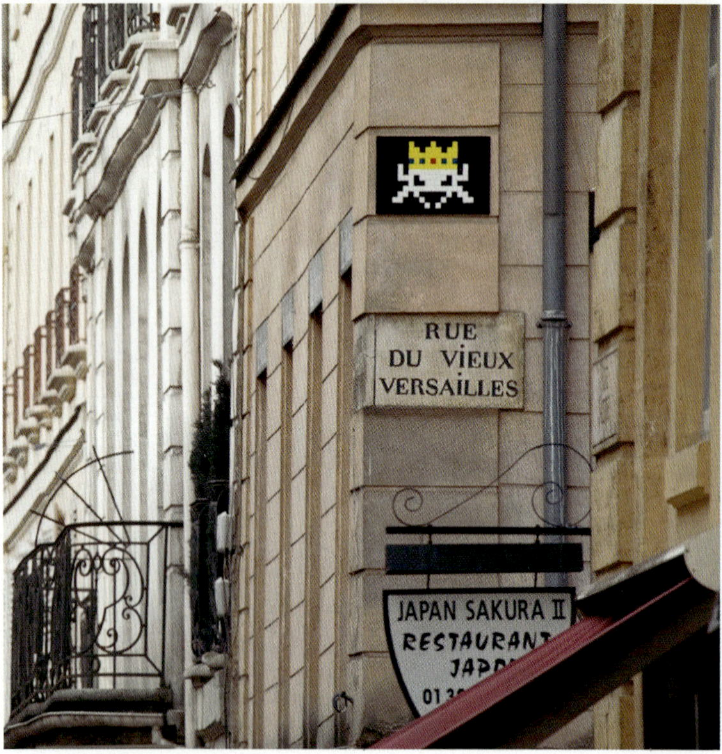

12 288 likes

invaderwashere Invader VIII 👾👑 #versailles #VRS_8

View all 41 comments

18 July 2017

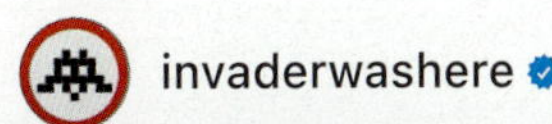

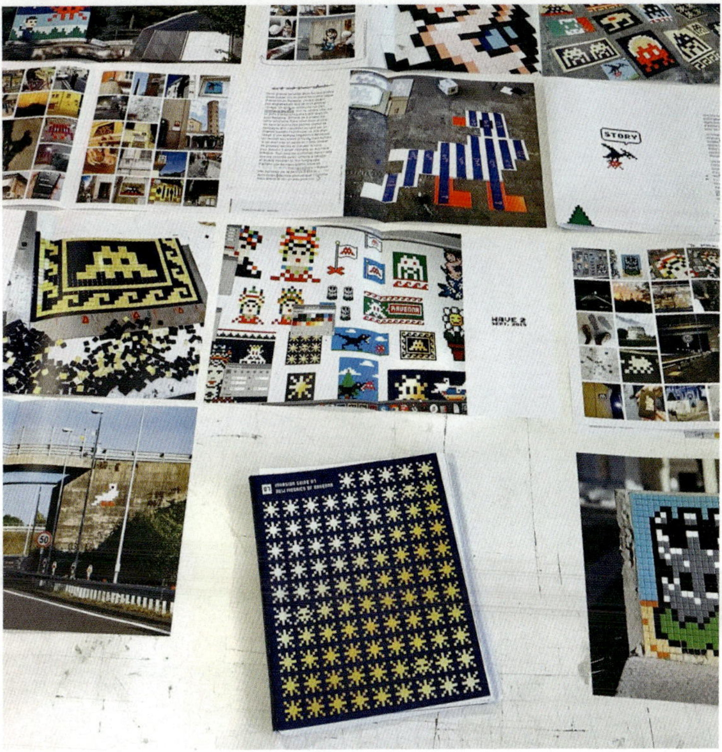

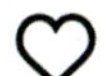 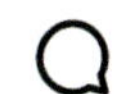  

3 619 likes

invaderwashere A new Invasion Guide should be released in September... #makingof #invasionguide07

View all 49 comments

18 July 2017

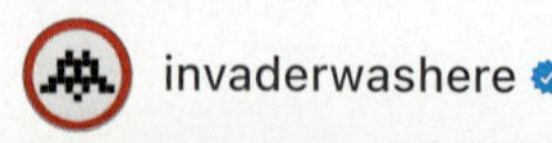

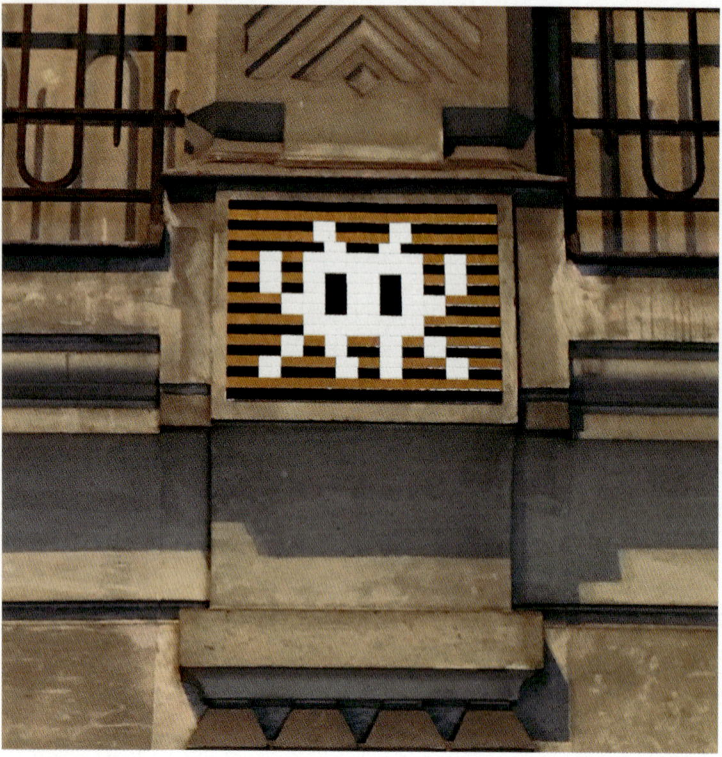

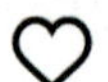   

13 737 likes

invaderwashere Just put my 3500th space invader in the world 👾 🤘 All unique! #Paris 5:25am PA_1290

View all 155 comments

21 July 2017

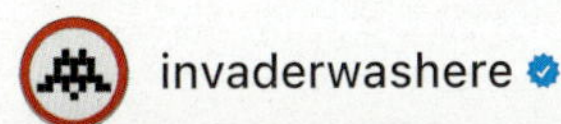

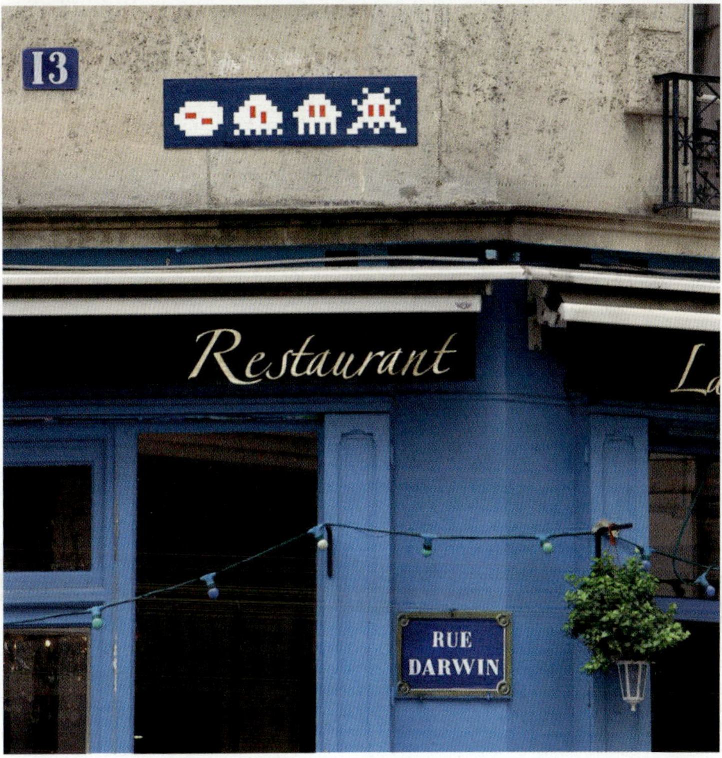

12 303 likes

invaderwashere PA_1292 #evolution #ruedarwin

View all 79 comments

26 July 2017

invaderwashere

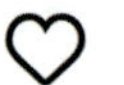

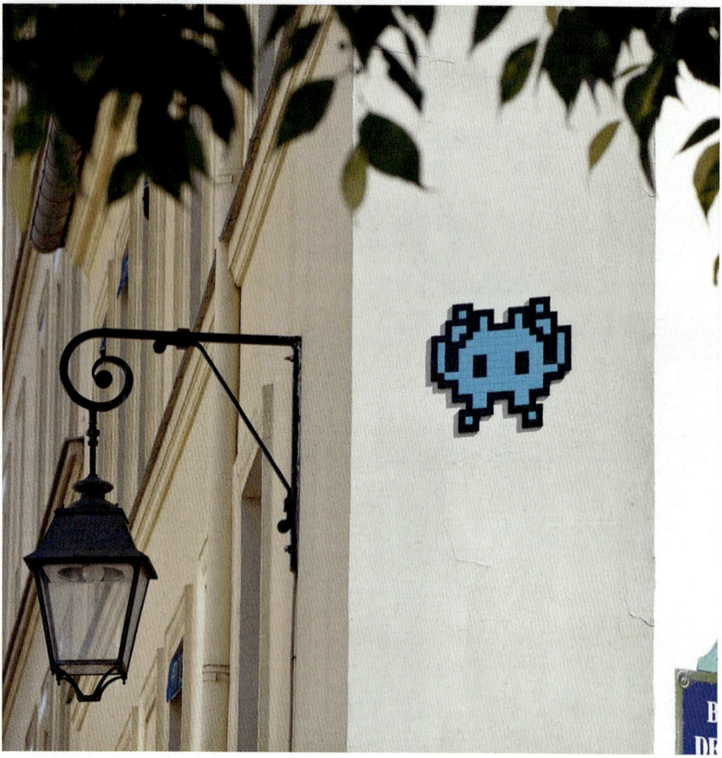

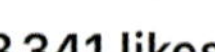

13 341 likes

invaderwashere 👾 emojinvader

View all 85 comments

27 July 2017

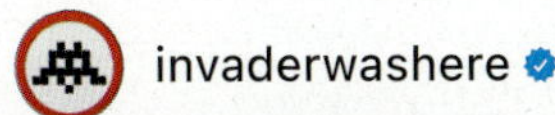

•••

   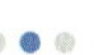 

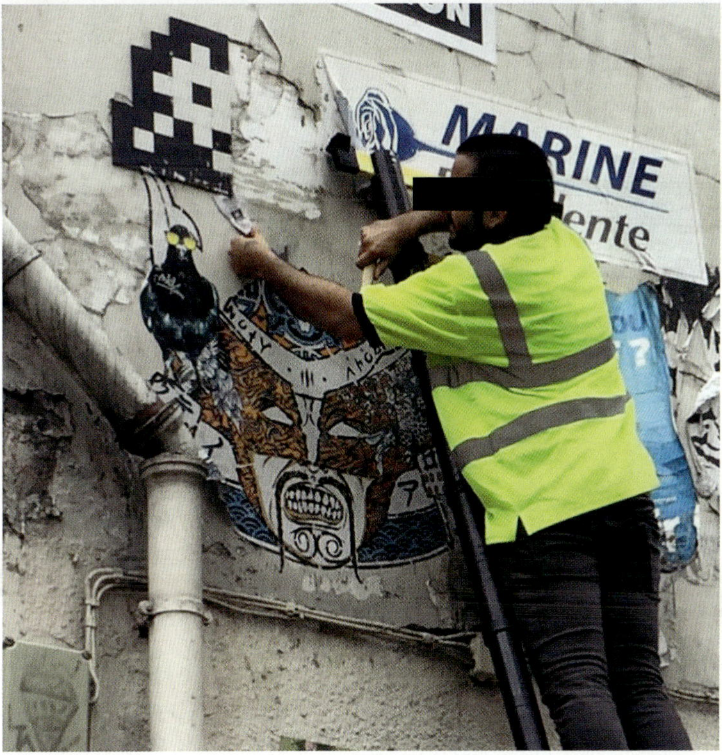

5 359 likes

invaderwashere Attention! Ils tournent dans Paris et contrairement à ce qu'ils prétendent, ils ne travaillent pas pour la Mairie. Photos et témoignage @yannlunique @olivier92300 / Those guys pretend they work for the City Council of Paris but they keep the mosaic pieces in the trunk of their Mercedes car! 👎

View all 632 comments

3 August 2017

invaderwashere

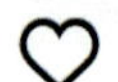

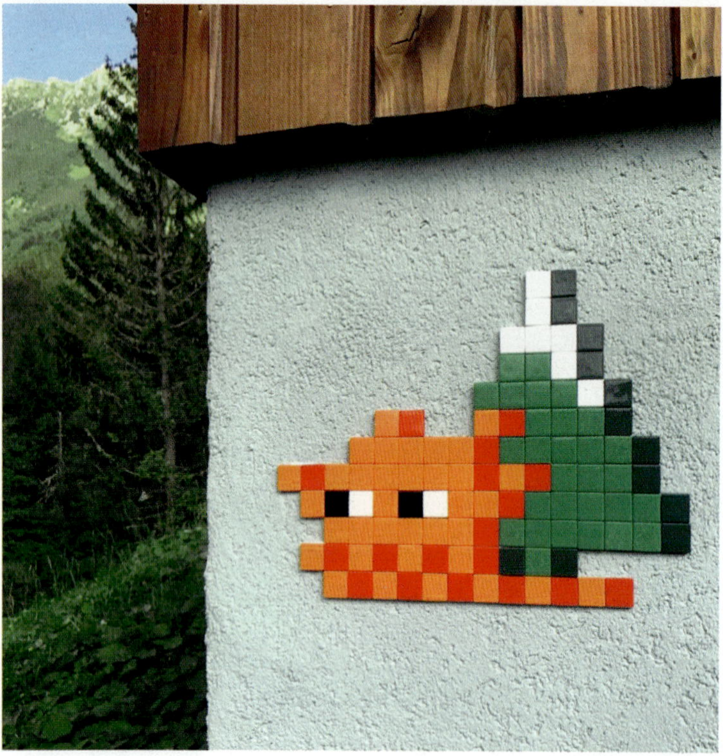

16 357 likes

invaderwashere Hidden in the mountains

View all 96 comments

5 August 2017

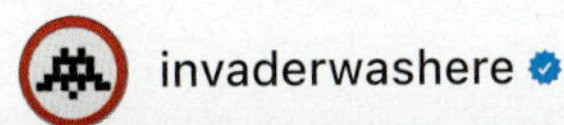

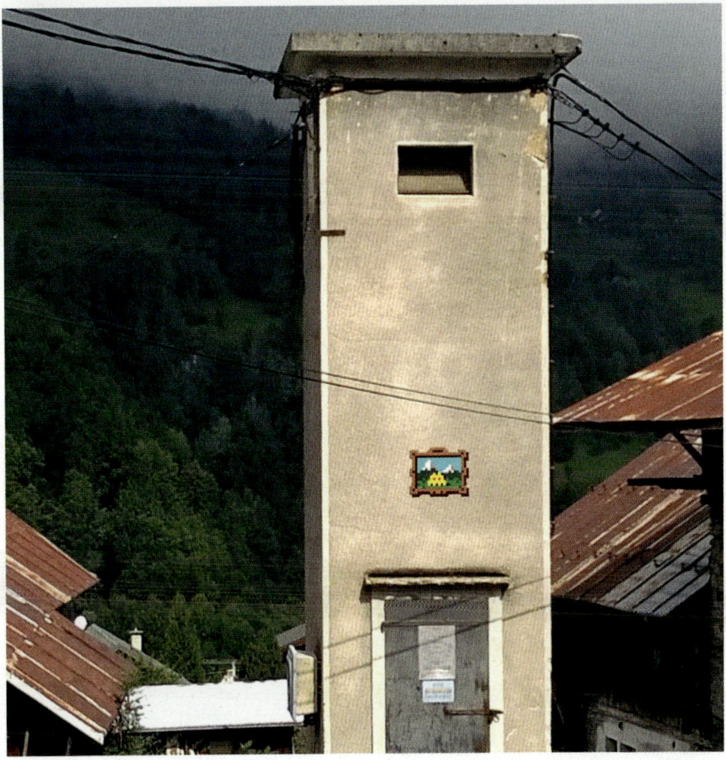

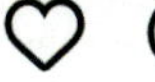    

10 640 likes

invaderwashere Between heaven and Earth

View all 69 comments

9 August 2017

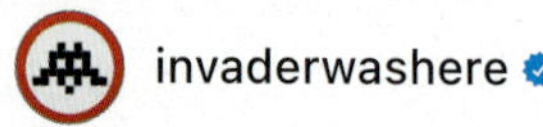

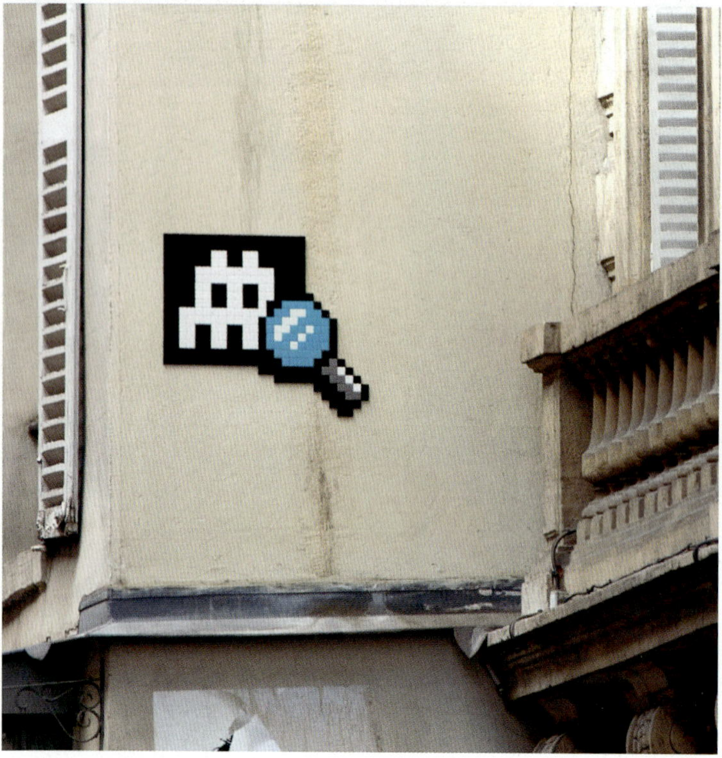

13 150 likes

invaderwashere Find them all!!! #new #Pa_1294

View all 64 comments

16 August 2017

invaderwashere

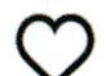   

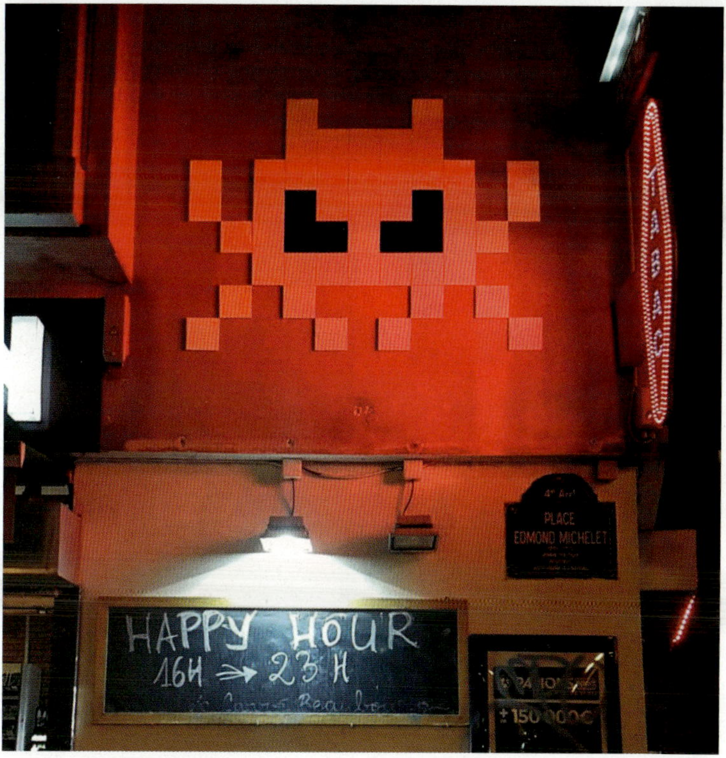

13 057 likes

invaderwashere PA_1295 under the red light #new #paris #bynight photo by @piop32

View all 63 comments

18 August 2017

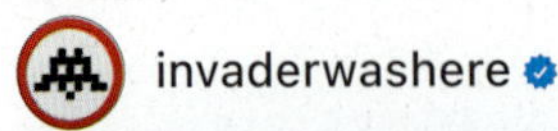

•••

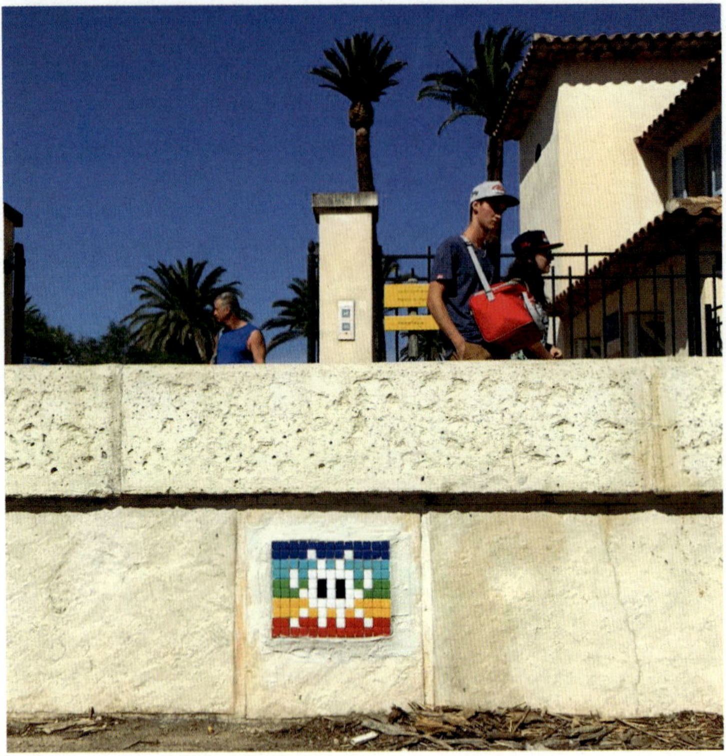

11 412 likes

invaderwashere CAZ_38 ☀️🏝️ #cotedazur #frenchriviera #island #justdone #invaderwashere

View all 45 comments

23 August 2017

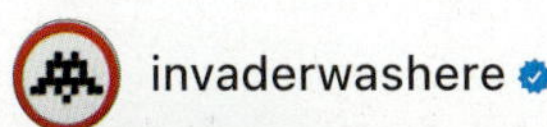

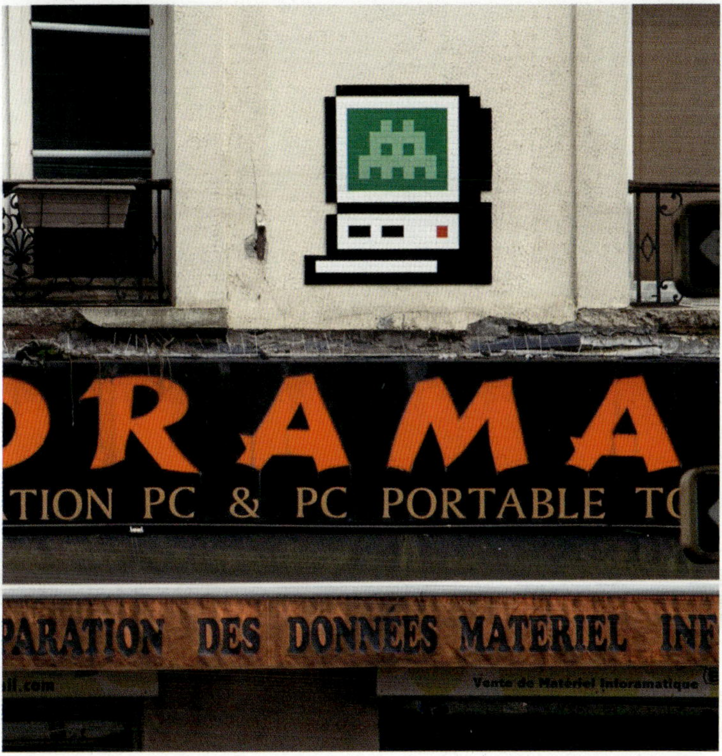

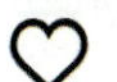   

8 325 likes

invaderwashere PA_1297 #SpaceOS #oldskoolcomputer #freshfromlastnight

View all 39 comments

25 August 2017

invaderwashere 

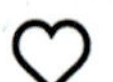   

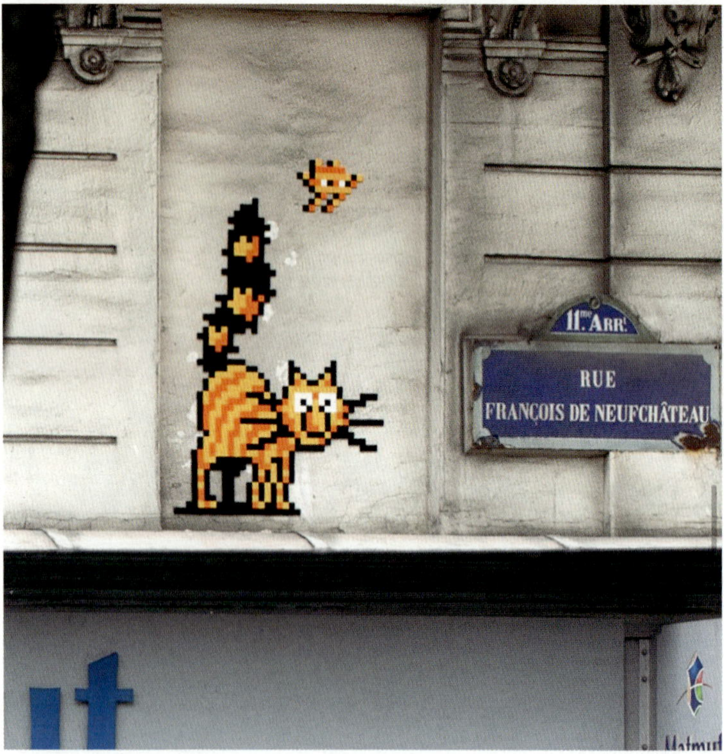

14 896 likes

invaderwashere Someone told me one day that Gilbert Shelton had his studio in that street #FatFreddyscat #freaksbrothers #gilbertshelton #undergroundcomics #PA1301 #freshfromlastnight

View all 118 comments

30 August 2017

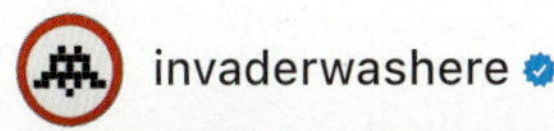

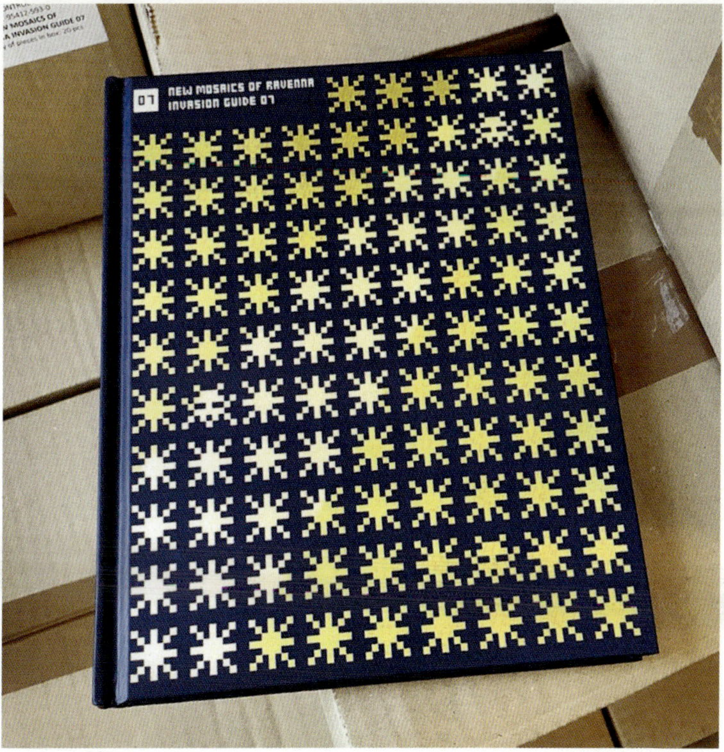

6467 likes

invaderwashere the 7th Invasion Guide will be soon available. Stay tuned... #Justoutofthebox #studiodetail #invasionguide #newmosaicsofravenna #diy #artbook #ravenna

View all 85 comments

31 August 2017

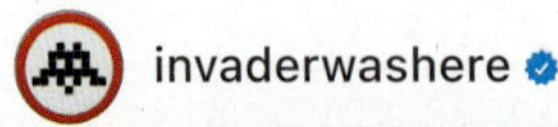

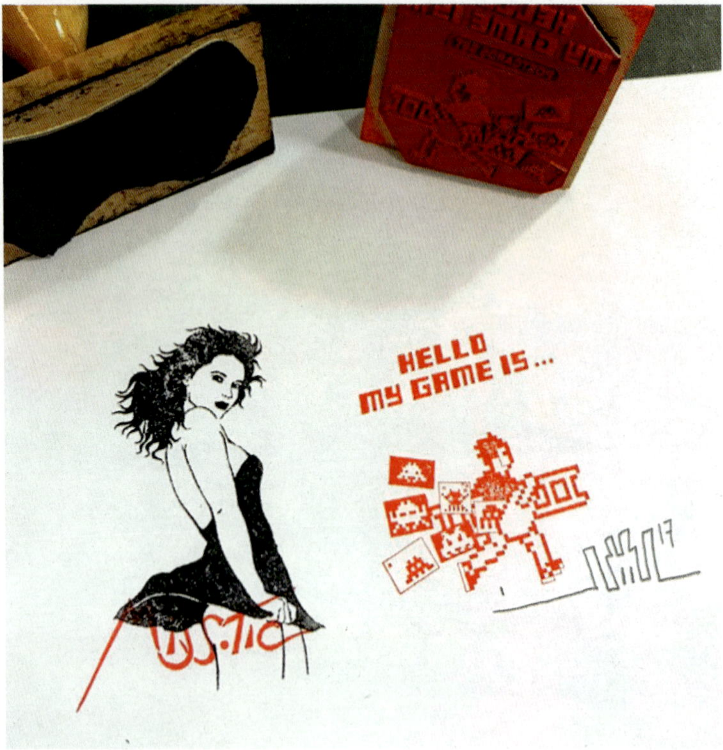

 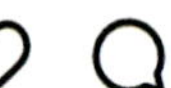  

5265 likes

invaderwashere Stamping cession with @missticofficiel
I've always been in love with the black and red stencils of Miss Tic. Her femmes fatales figures haunt the streets of Paris since the 80's. She is a great artist and a great person #misstic #rocks

View all 37 comments

3 September 2017

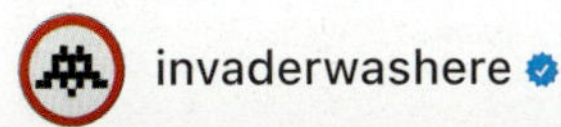

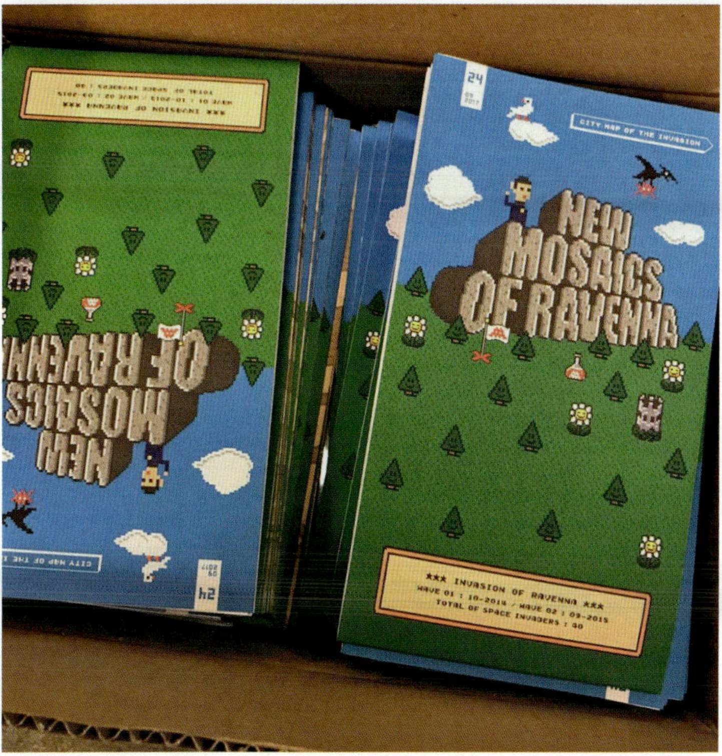

3 991 likes

invaderwashere Unpacking the Invasion Map 24. It will be soon available on the Space Shop. Stay tuned...
#invasionmap #invasionguide #ravenna

View all 55 comments

8 September 2017

invaderwashere

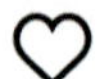   

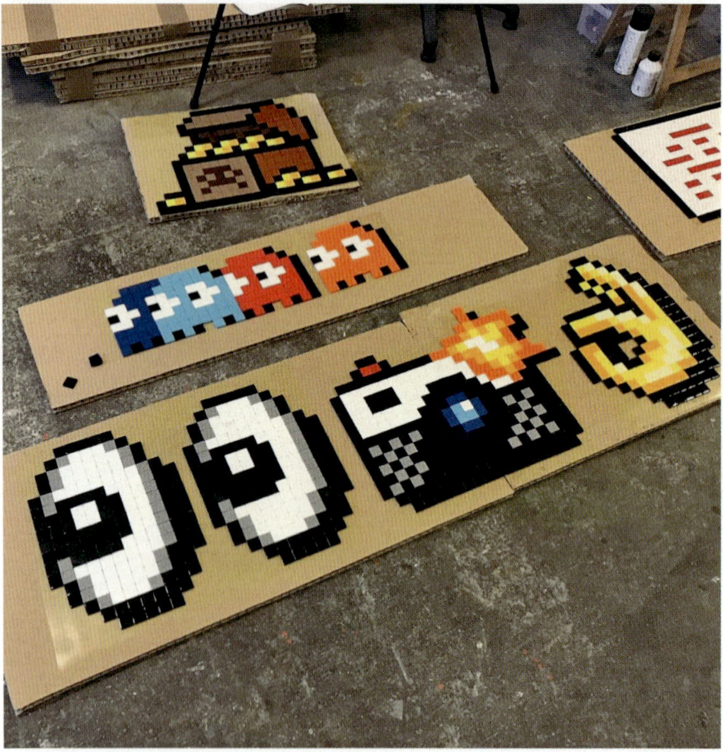

19 995 likes

invaderwashere Soon in the streeets... #makingof #treasure #ghosts #photoopportunity

View all 180 comments

12 September 2017

invaderwashere

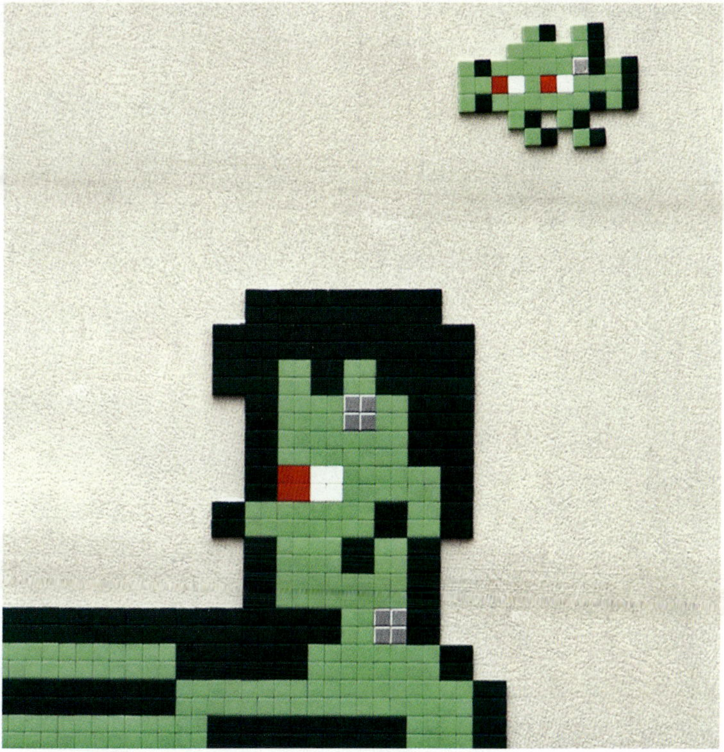

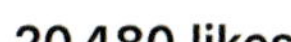

20 480 likes

invaderwashere Invaderstein 🧟 👾 #mosaicdetail

View all 172 comments

13 September 2017

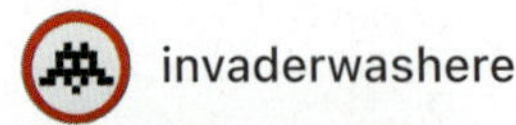

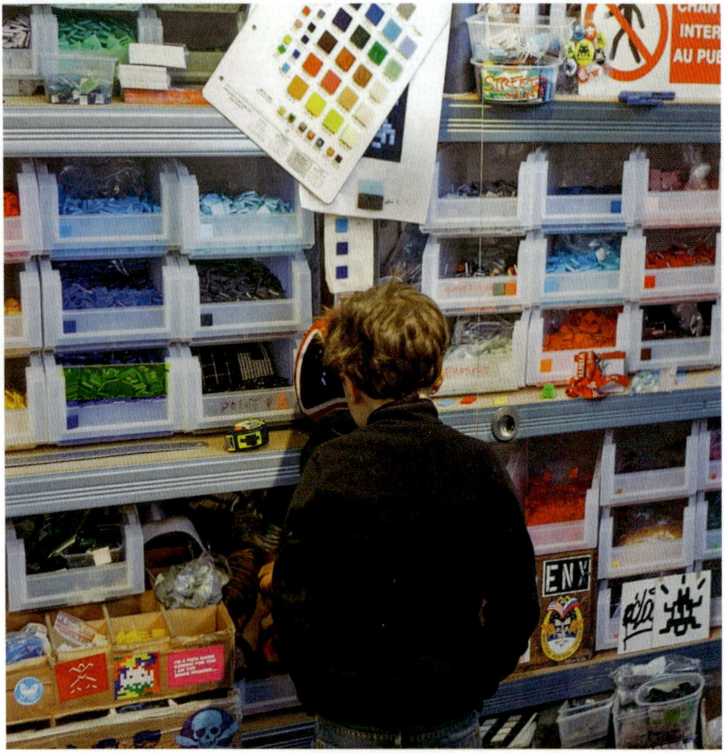

4 675 likes

invaderwashere "Hello my game is..." is prolonged until January 7th 2018 #paris #exhibition @museeenherbe

View all 55 comments

14 September 2017

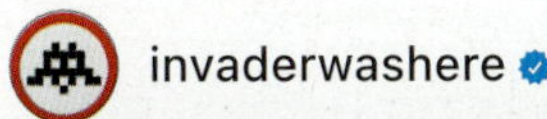

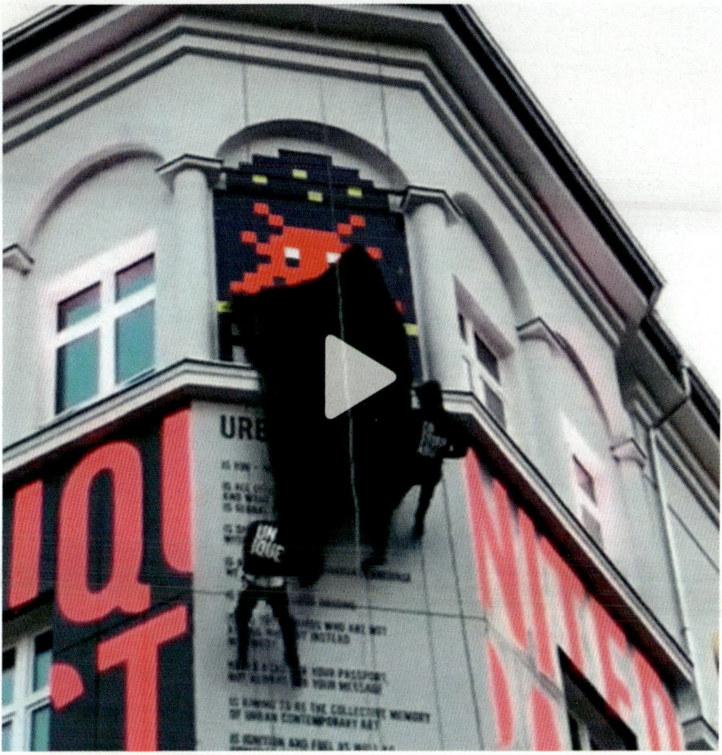

 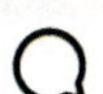  

84 784 views

invaderwashere Today in Berlin #UrbanNation #museum #opening #unstoppable #BRL12 #100Points clip by @psicosonico

View all 178 comments

16 September 2017

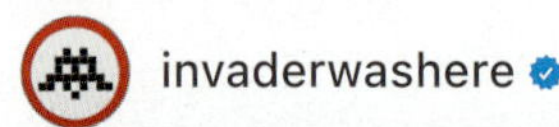

...

 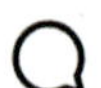  

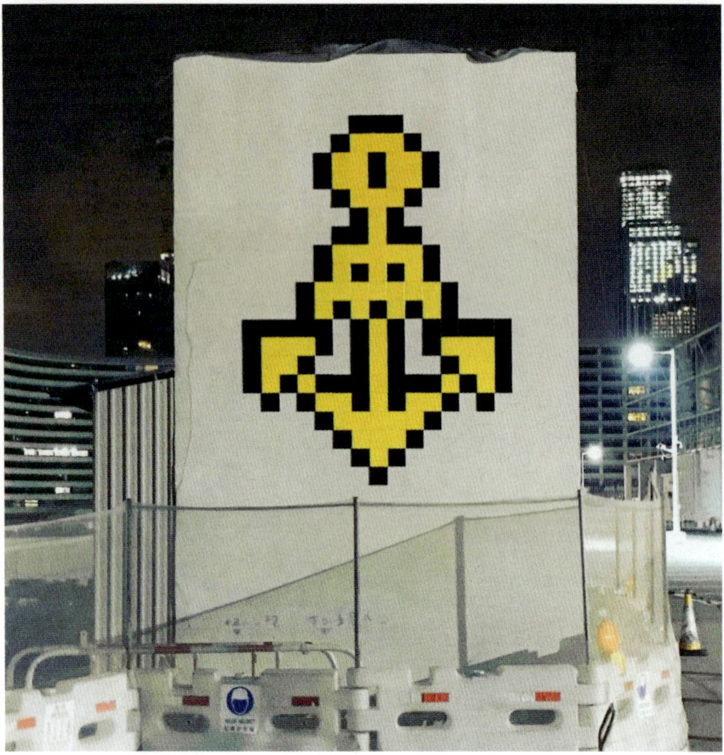

10050 likes

invaderwashere 👾⚓🌃 #backin #hongkong #justdone

View all 70 comments

20 September 2017

invaderwashere

 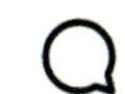  

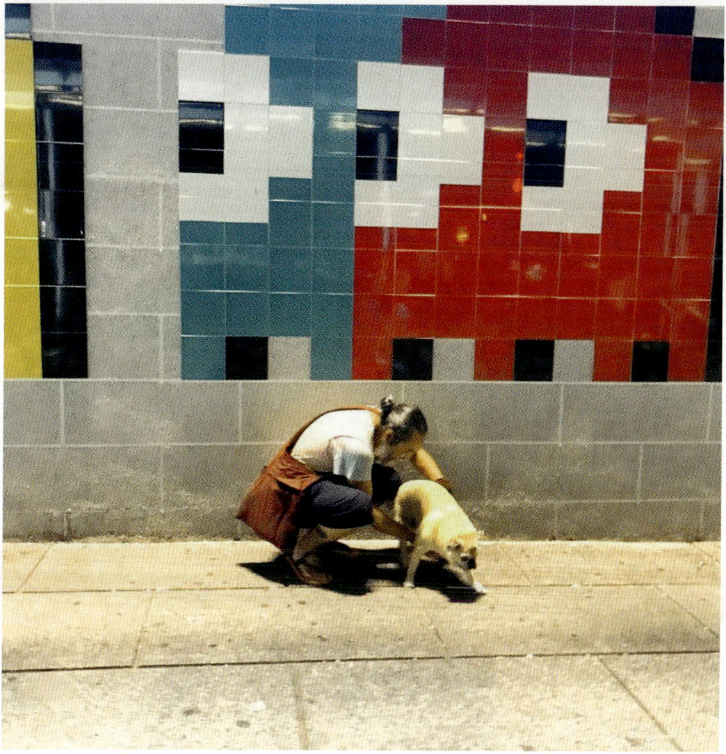

8 973 likes

invaderwashere Hanging with Syan & Gudiii #tsimshatsui

View all 63 comments

20 September 2017

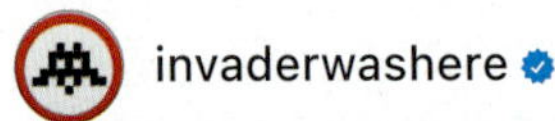

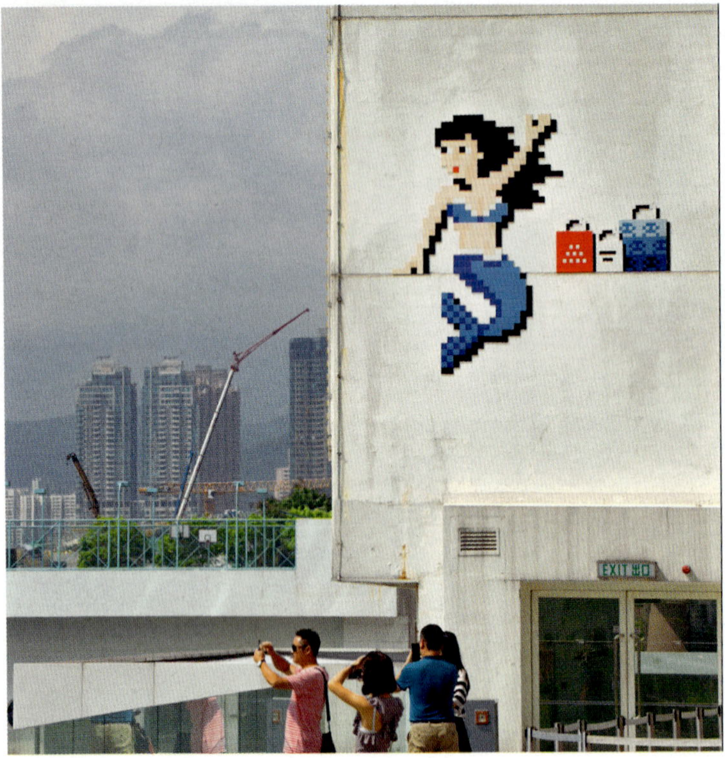

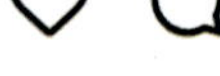

21 136 likes

invaderwashere Good morning Hong-Kong 🇭🇰
#tsimshatsui #harbourcity #whileyouweresleeping

View all 164 comments

24 September 2017

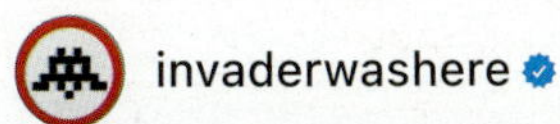

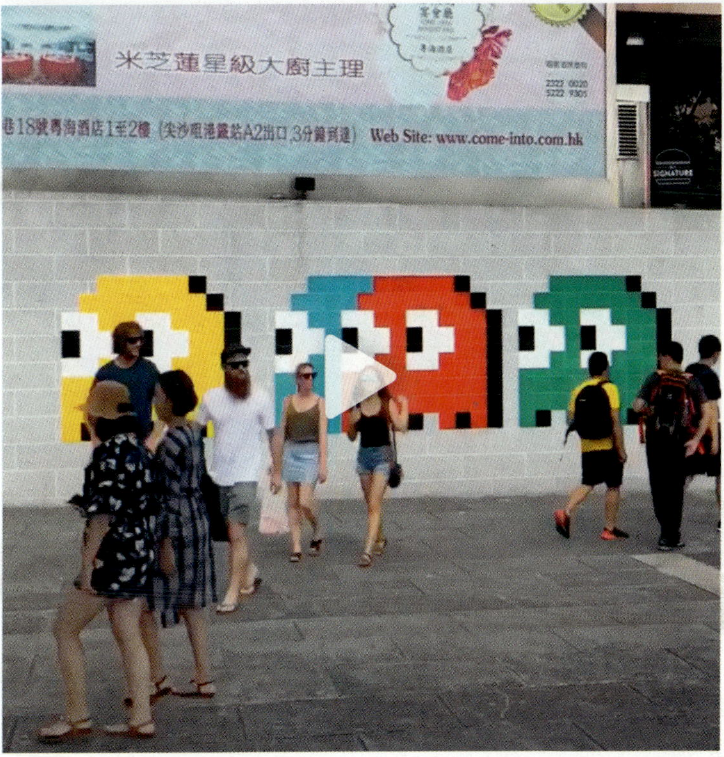

37 728 views

invaderwashere Hong Kong Ghosts Team 🇭🇰

View all 92 comments

25 September 2017

invaderwashere

   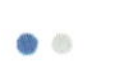 

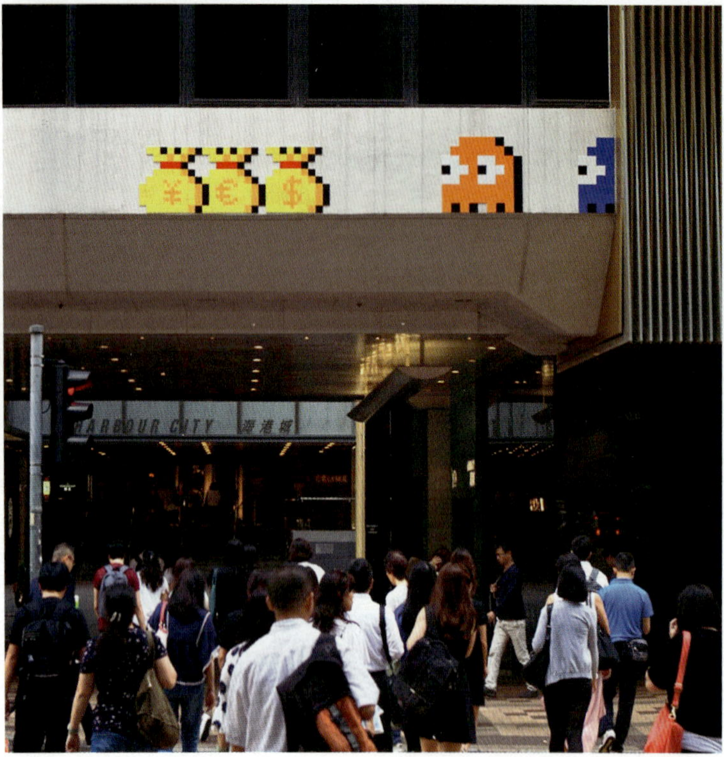

19179 likes

invaderwashere Going through the wall... ¥€$
#hongkong2017

View all 130 comments

27 September 2017

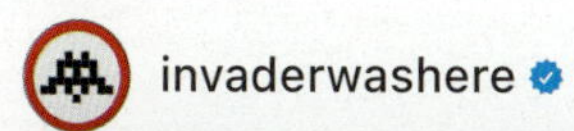

•••

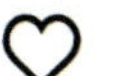    

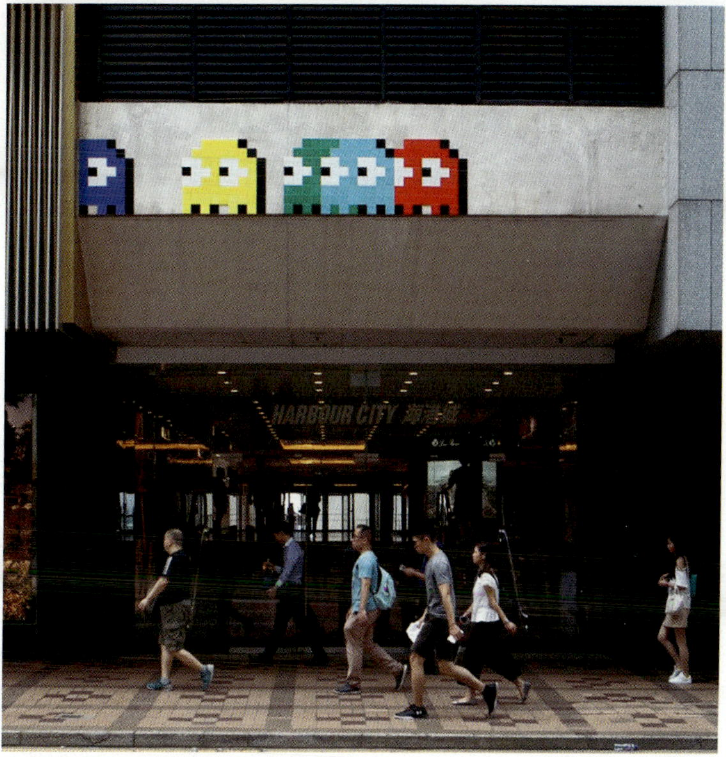

19 179 likes

invaderwashere Going through the wall... ¥€$
#hongkong2017

View all 130 comments

27 September 2017

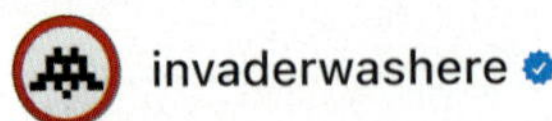

•••

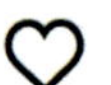   

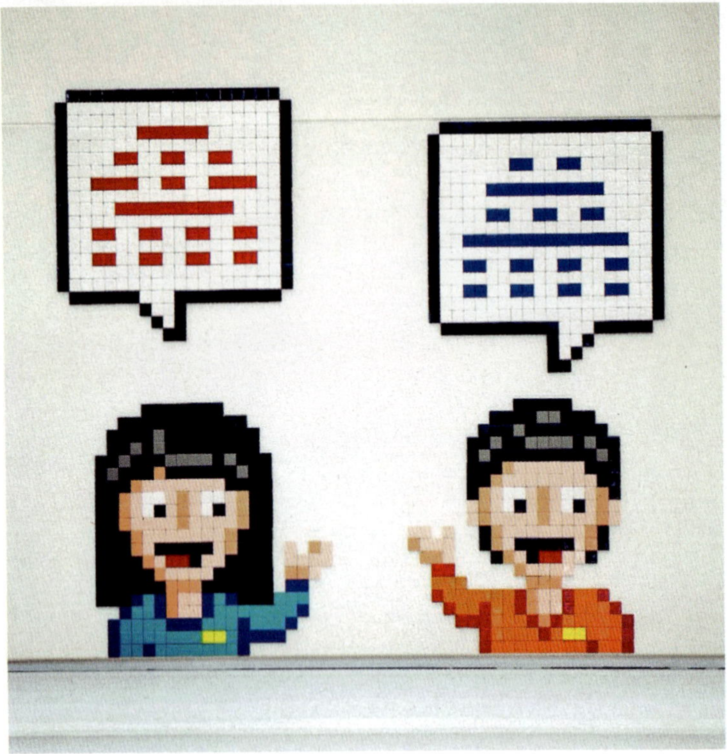

8 451 likes

invaderwashere @harbourcity #tsimshatsui #hongkong

View all 62 comments

27 September 2017

invaderwashere

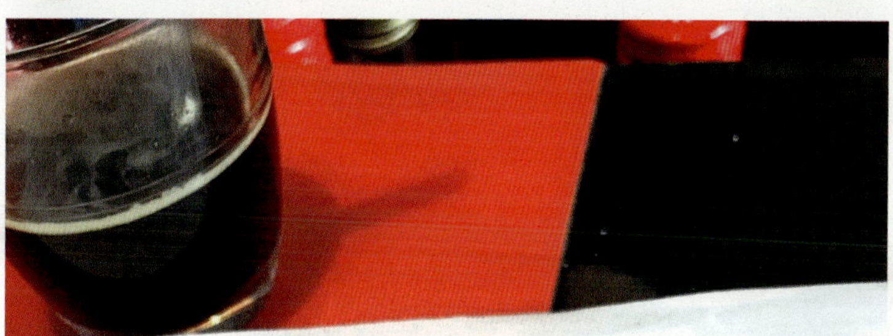

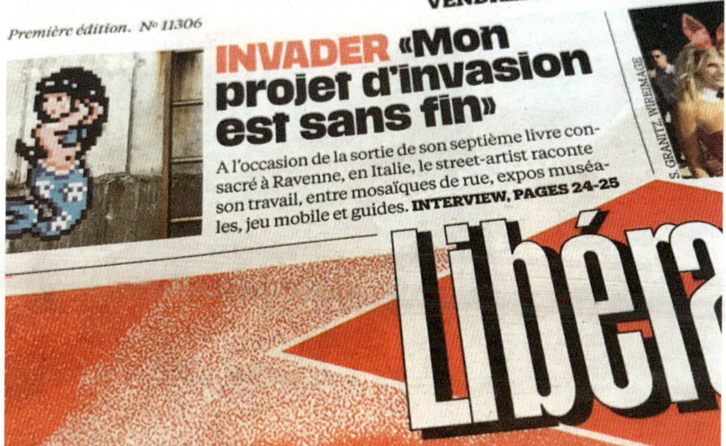

6776 likes

invaderwashere #mediainvasion of the day! Thank you @liberationfr

View all 54 comments

29 September 2017

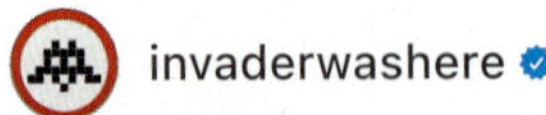

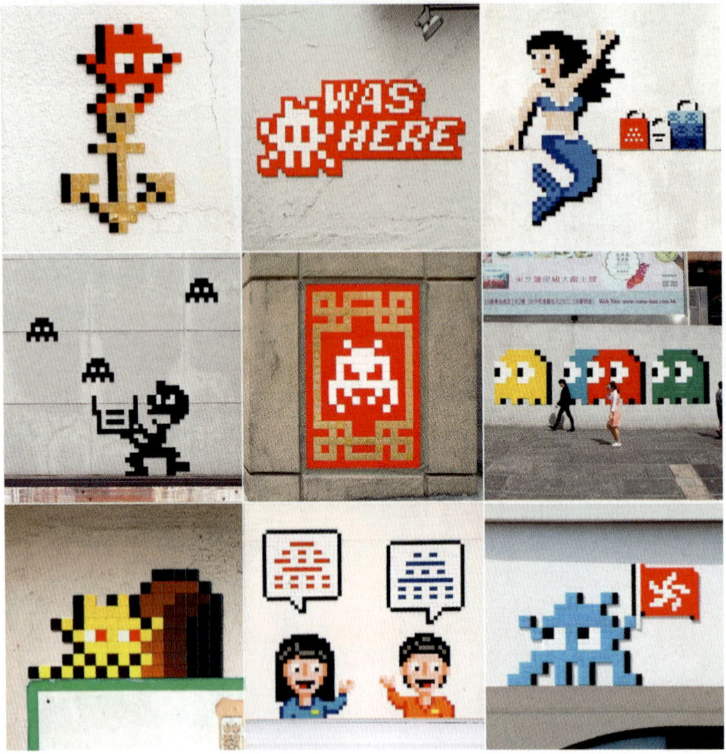

16 075 likes

invaderwashere 👆 9 of the 32 new space invaders in Hong-Kong. More info: link in bio

View all 118 comments

2 October 2017

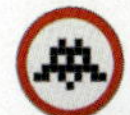

invaderwashere

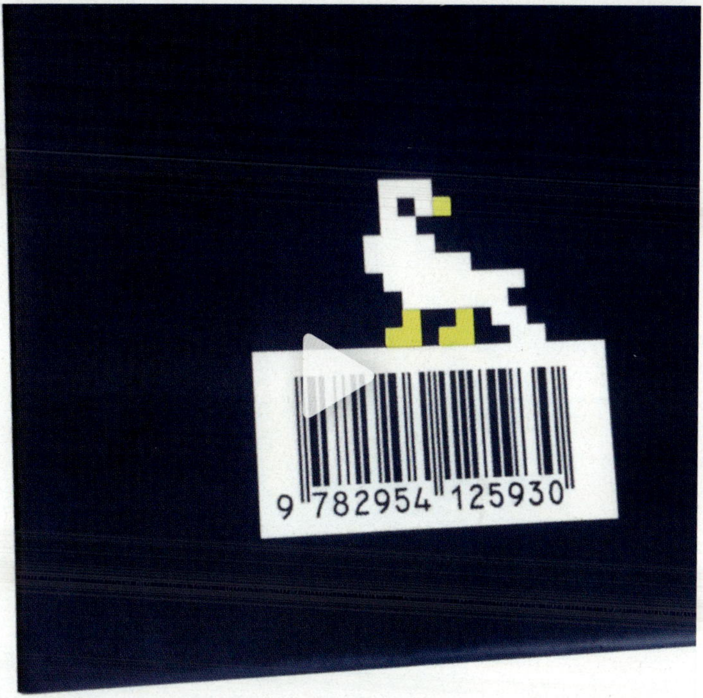

31147 views

invaderwashere "New mosaics of Ravenna" book & map are now available on the Space Shop #1stedition #invasionguide #invasionmap #ravenna Link in bio

View all 99 comments

4 October 2017

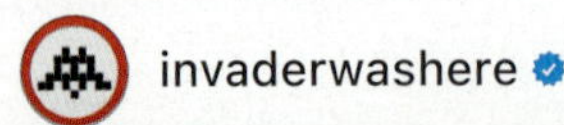

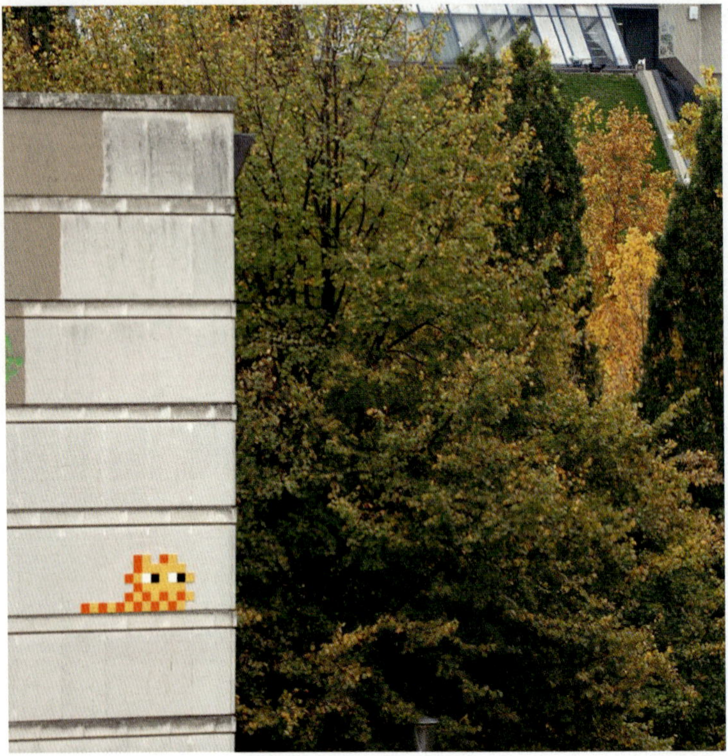

 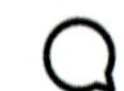  

10 852 likes

invaderwashere PA_1307 #autumn 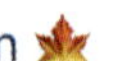

View all 45 comments

13 October 2017

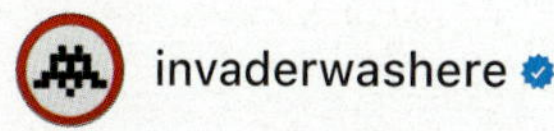

Over The Influence is proud to present
an exclusive preview of

INVADER
New Mosaics of Ravenna

Vernissage :
14th October 5-7pm

Dates :
14th October – 26th October 2017

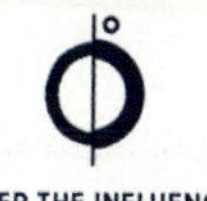

OVER THE INFLUENCE

2 387 likes

invaderwashere If you are in Hong Kong this week, don't miss the presentation of the mosaic covers of New Mosaics of Ravenna @overtheinfluencehk #Hongkong #invasionguide #ravenna #mosaiccovers

View all 36 comments

16 October 2017

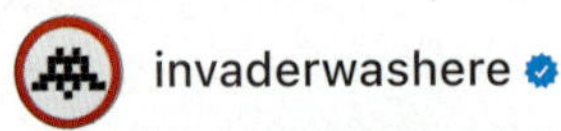

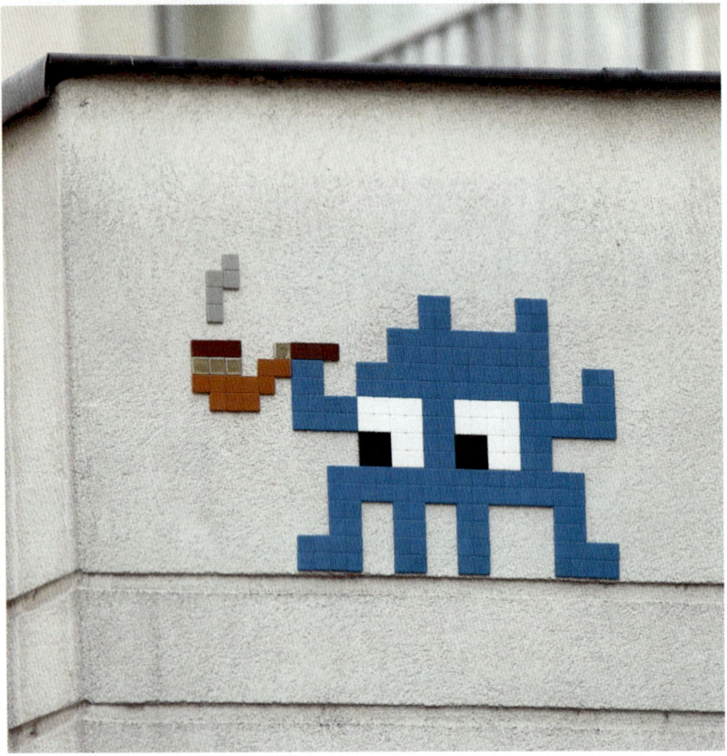

24 361 likes

invaderwashere Ceci est une pipe!

View all 165 comments

20 October 2017

invaderwashere •••

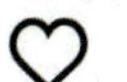   

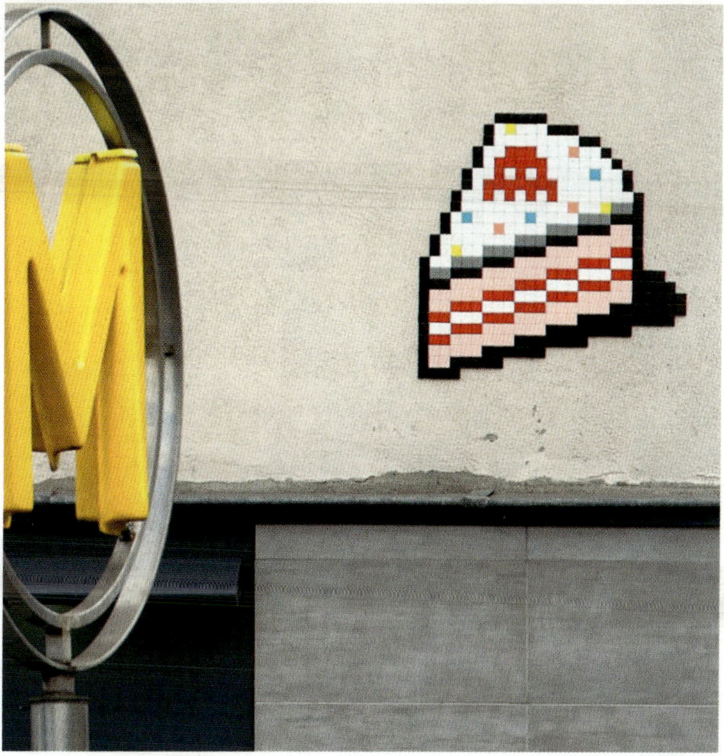

19 687 likes

invaderwashere Space cake 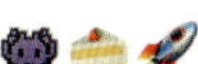

View all 131 comments

23 October 2017

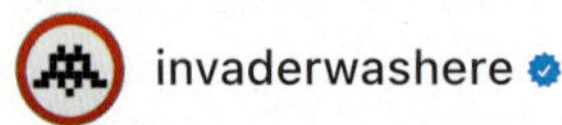

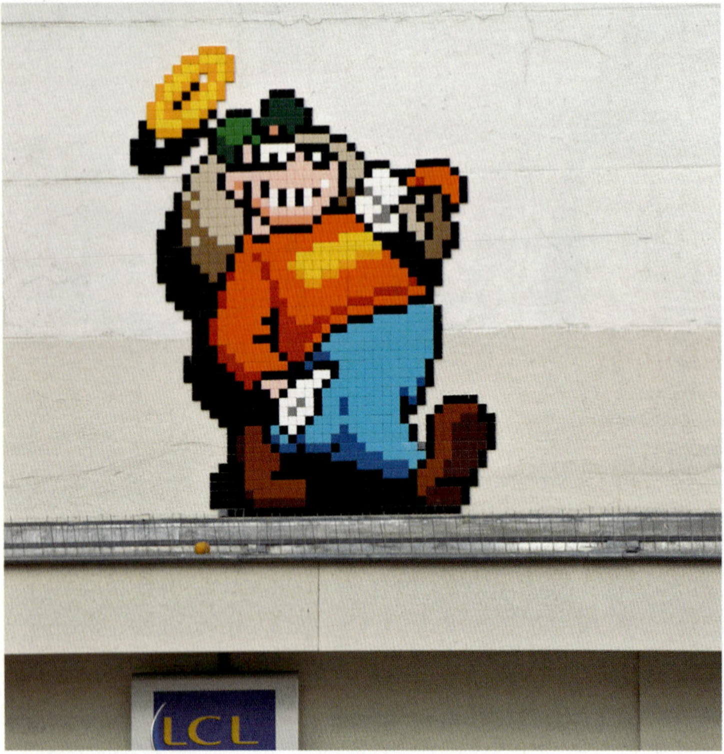

19 701 likes

invaderwashere Not seen not caught! #beagleboy #rapetou #167671 #PA1315 #bank #paris 😎 💰 👾

View all 141 comments

25 October 2017

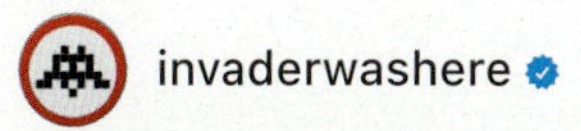

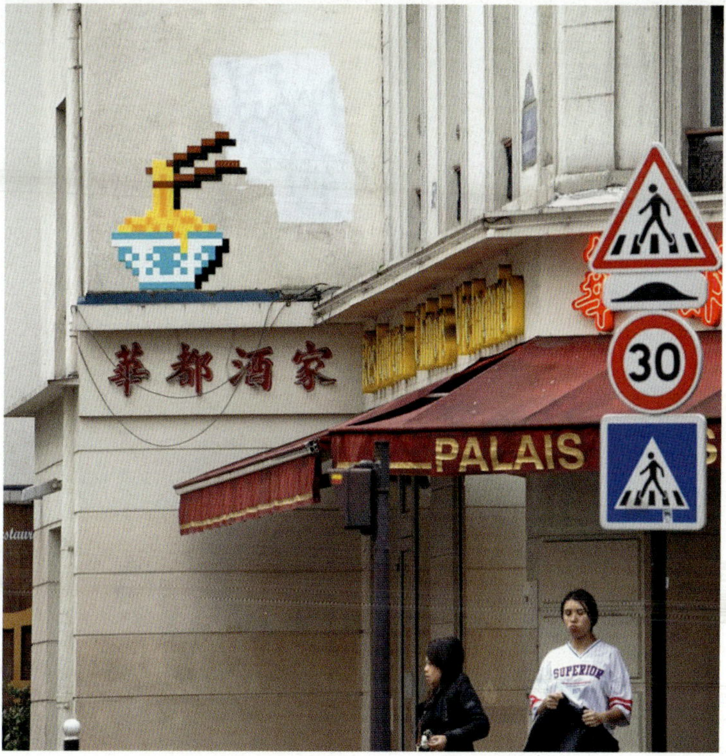

  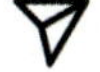 

21 790 likes

invaderwashere Space Noodles #chinatown #paris

View all 143 comments

4 November 2017

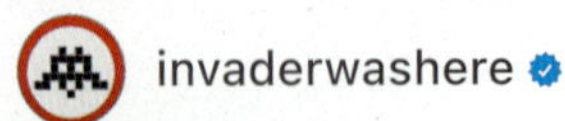

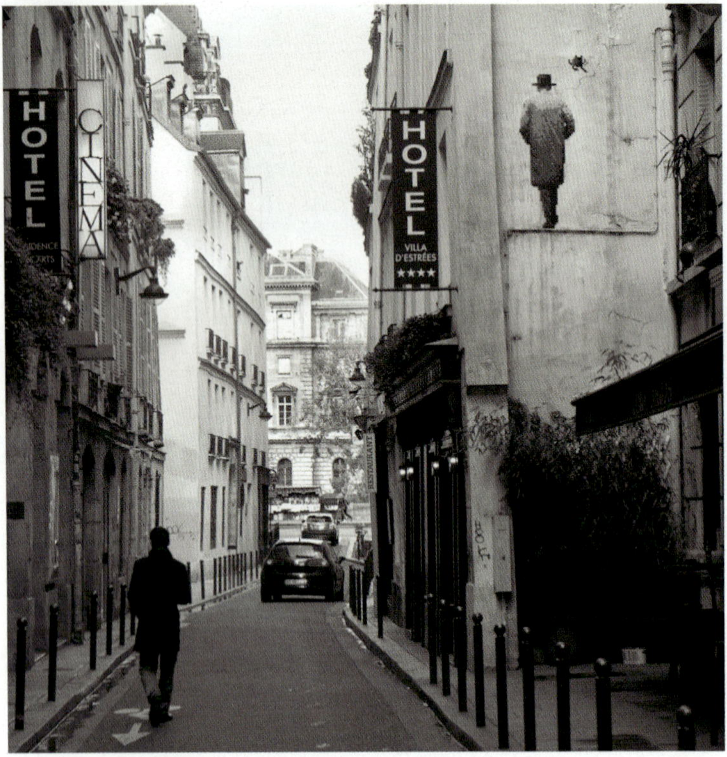

19 672 likes

invaderwashere In the late 50s the Beat generation reached its high point with Ginsberg, Kerouac and Burroughs sharing rooms in a rundown hotel rue Git-le-Cœur, a narrow medieval lane in the Latin Quarter of Paris. This piece brings back Burroughs spectrum at the entrance of the street. #Burroughs #williamburroughs #ruegitlecoeur #beathotel

View all 173 comments

6 November 2017

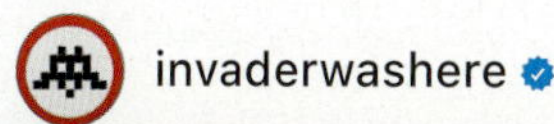

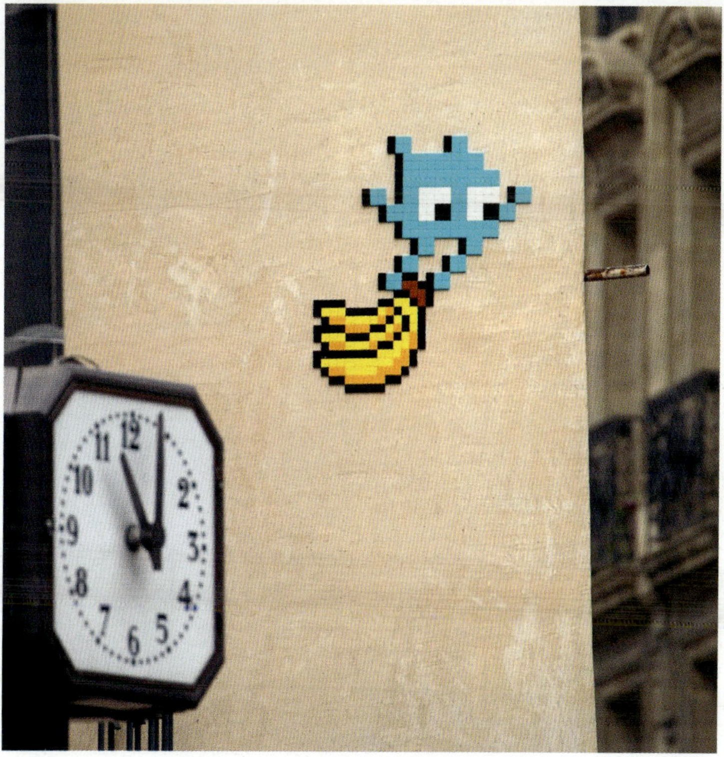

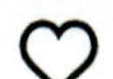   

24 418 likes

invaderwashere Bananas for Veggie Town 

View all 129 comments

8 November 2017

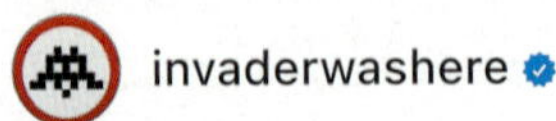

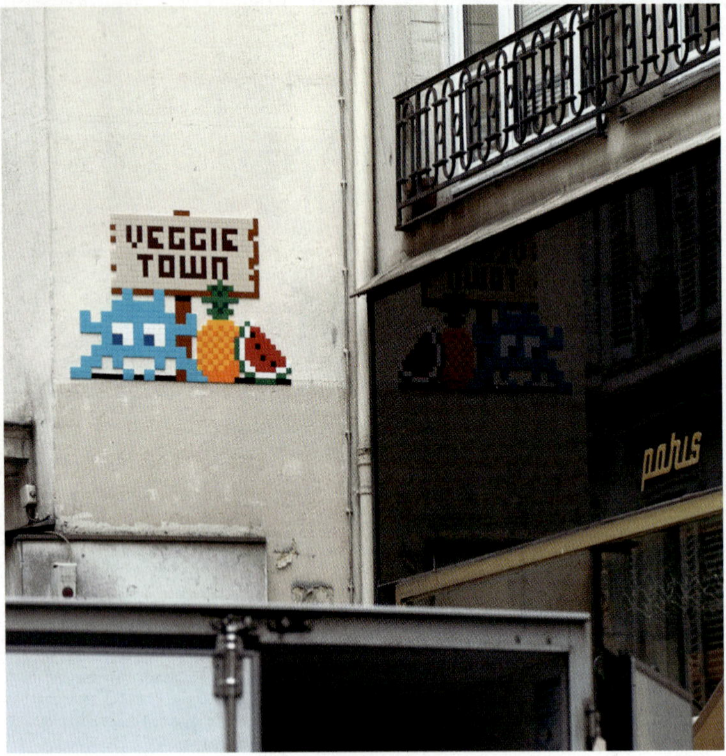

22 208 likes

invaderwashere New pieces in Veggie Town #veggietown #avf #paris #75009 #75010

View all 187 comments

15 November 2017

invaderwashere

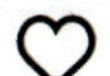   

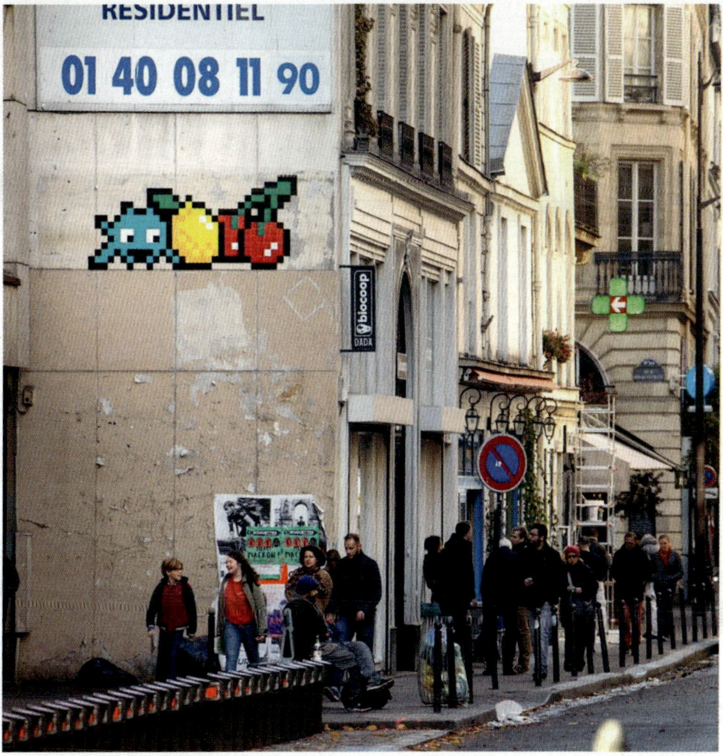

12 163 likes

invaderwashere PA_1328 #veggietown #paris

View all 48 comments

24 November 2017

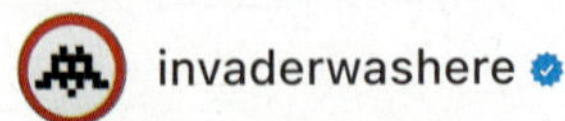

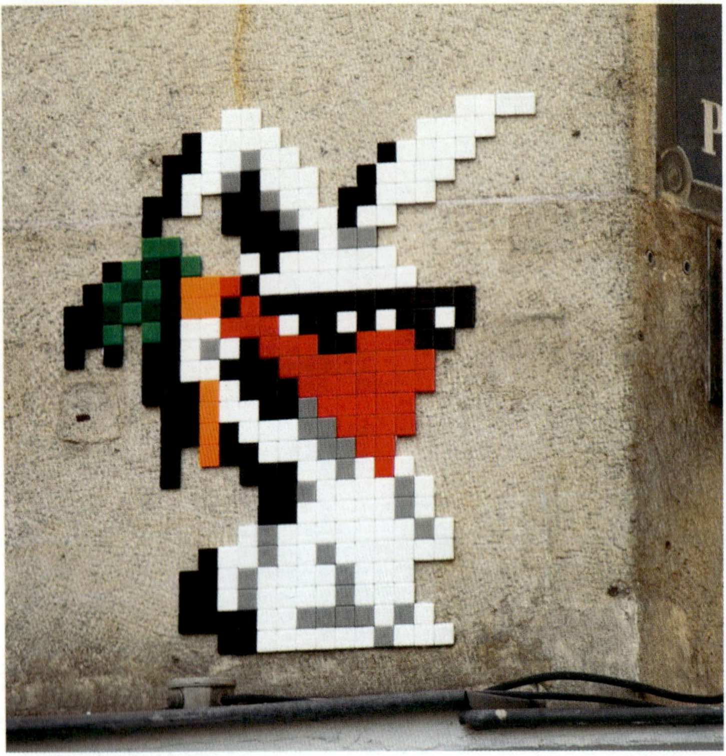

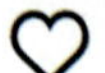   

19844 likes

invaderwashere PA_1329 #carrotpower #meatsucks #veggietown #paris

View all 112 comments

24 November 2017

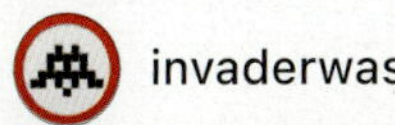

invaderwashere

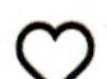  

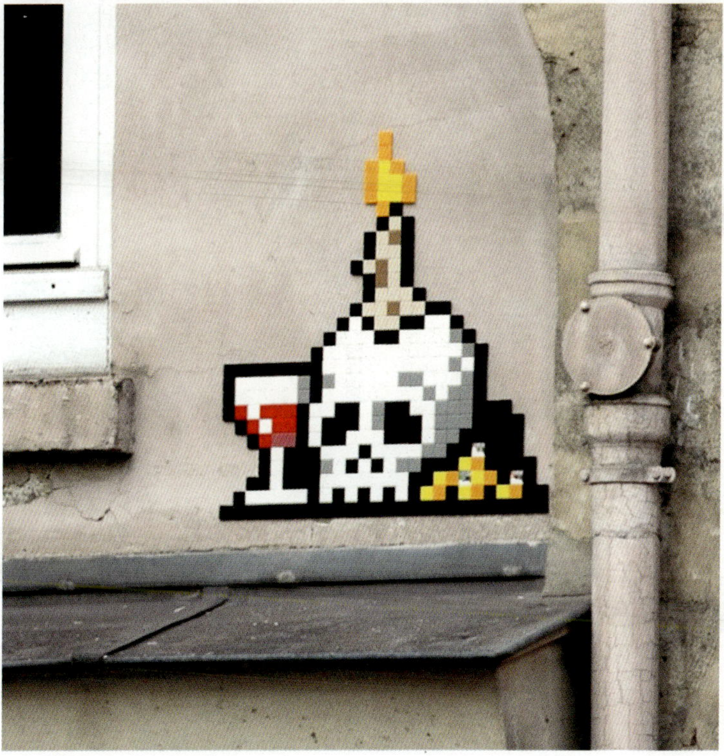

28 501 likes

invaderwashere Vanitas #stilllife

View all 171 comments

1 December 2017

invaderwashere

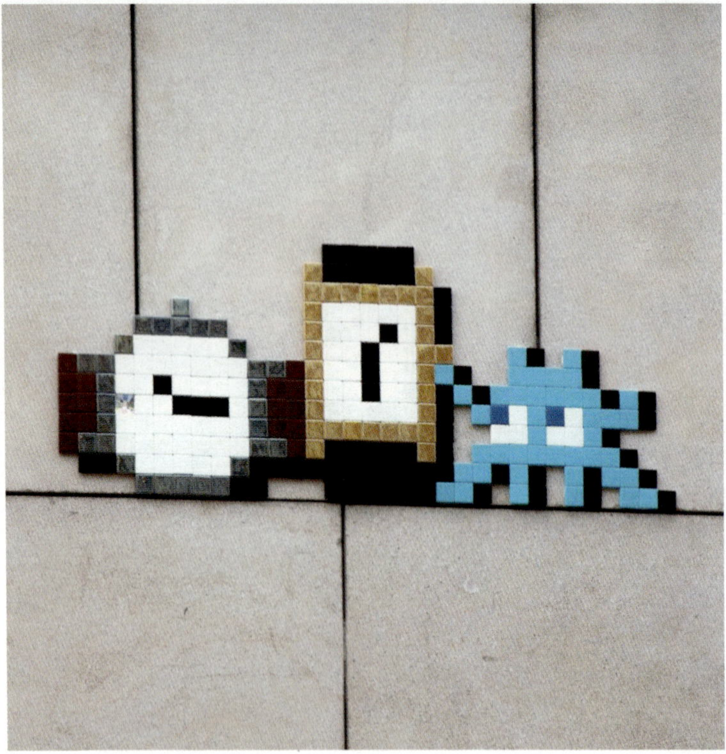

11090 likes

invaderwashere In front of Cartier above of Bretling
#PA1333 #ruedelapaix #paris

View all 39 comments

4 December 2017

invaderwashere •••

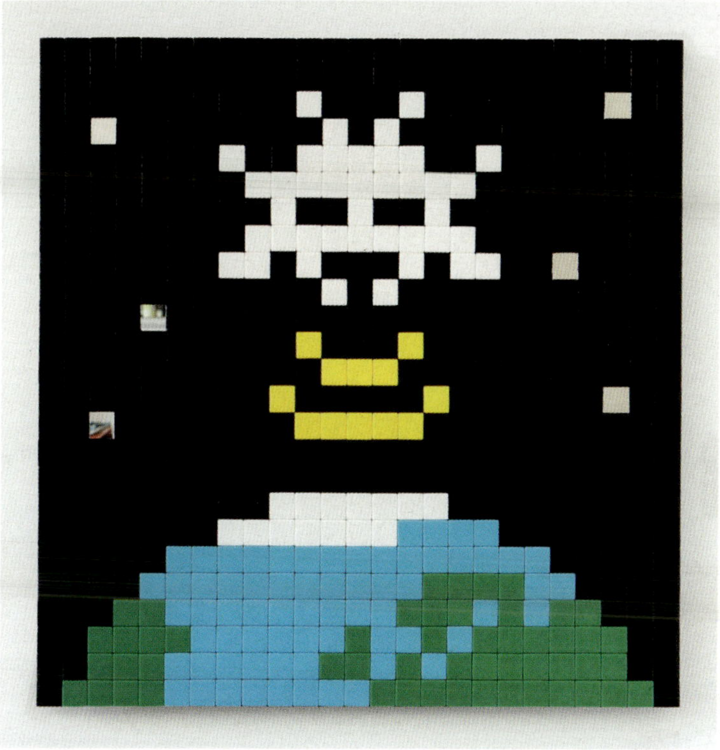

11722 likes

invaderwashere ALIAS PA_1177 is my donation to HOCA Foundation for their Annual Benefit Auction at Sotheby's Hong Kong. Link in @hocafoundation bio

View all 52 comments

5 December 2017

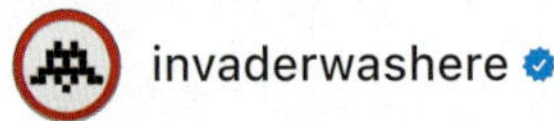

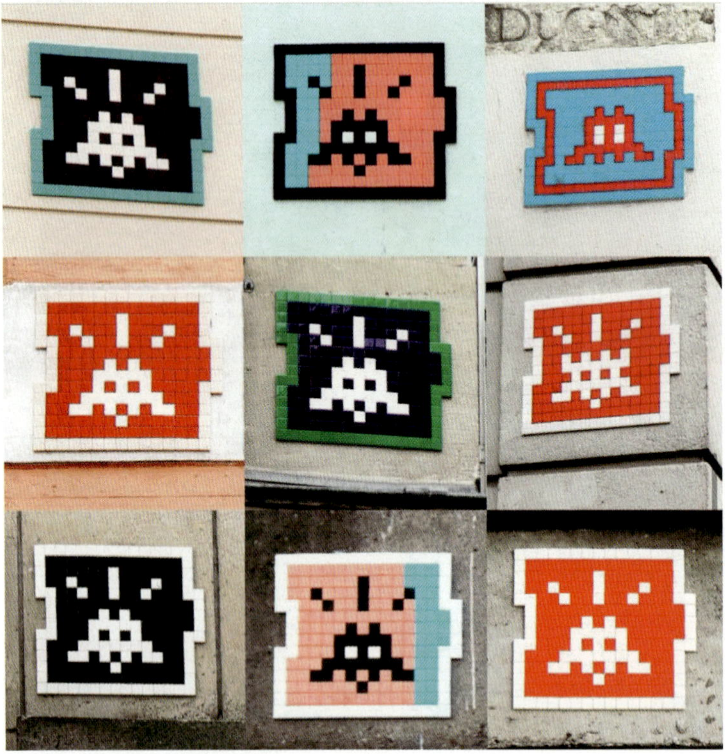

13690 likes

invaderwashere One of the amazing #invader3x3 challenge launched by @the_fox_and_the_seashells / This composition by @olivetruxi gathers some vintage Mac extension icons

View all 77 comments

6 December 2017

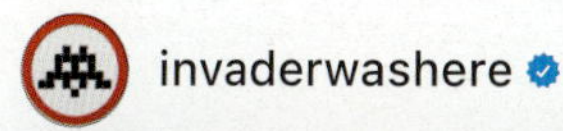

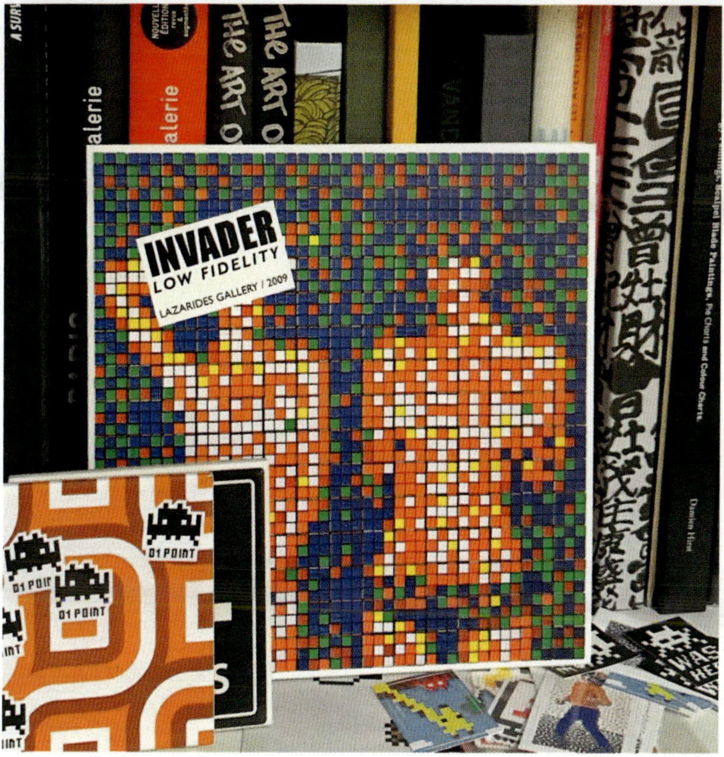

7300 likes

invaderwashere #shelfie #lowfidelity #catalog #rubikcubism #books #tiles #stickers #studiodetail #2009

View all 38 comments

12 December 2017

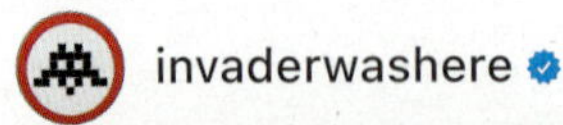

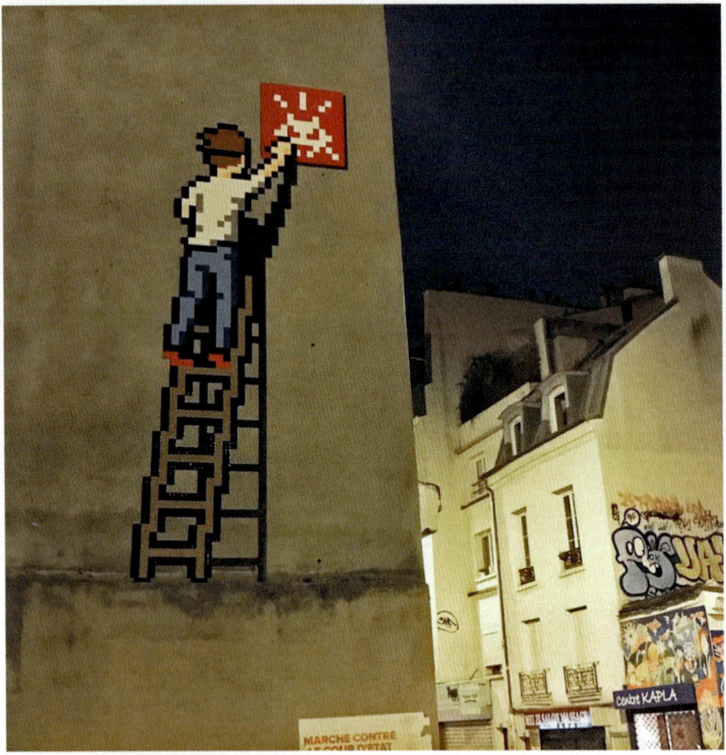

34 078 likes

invaderwashere PA_1336 Fresh from last night... The « spot » is the precise location where I install my mosaics. The process of looking for spots is a vital part of my modus operandi. This choice obeys some criteria, but is also highly subjective. In any case, when a spot catches my eye, I prepare the mosaic it's going to receive and do everything I can to reach it. I've often referred to this as urban acupuncture.

View all 284 comments

13 December 2017

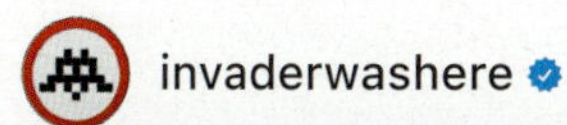

Dailymotion

Presse Communiqués Forum

Association Végétarienne de France

Adhérer Faire un don FAQ Boutique

L'association Arguments Nutrition et Santé Végé au quotidien

La lettre d'info de l'AVF

Email *

Prénom

Nom

Je m'inscris

Initiatives de l'AVF

L'invasion de Veggietown a commencé !

Actualités à la une

Des fruits et légumes venus de l'espace envahissent Veggietown

10 novembre 2017

Depuis début novembre, les habitants des 9e et 10e arrondissements découvrent sur les murs de leurs immeubles une nouvelle série de mosaïques de l'artiste Invader. On y retrouve ses célèbres personnages pixelisés [...]

Lire la suite

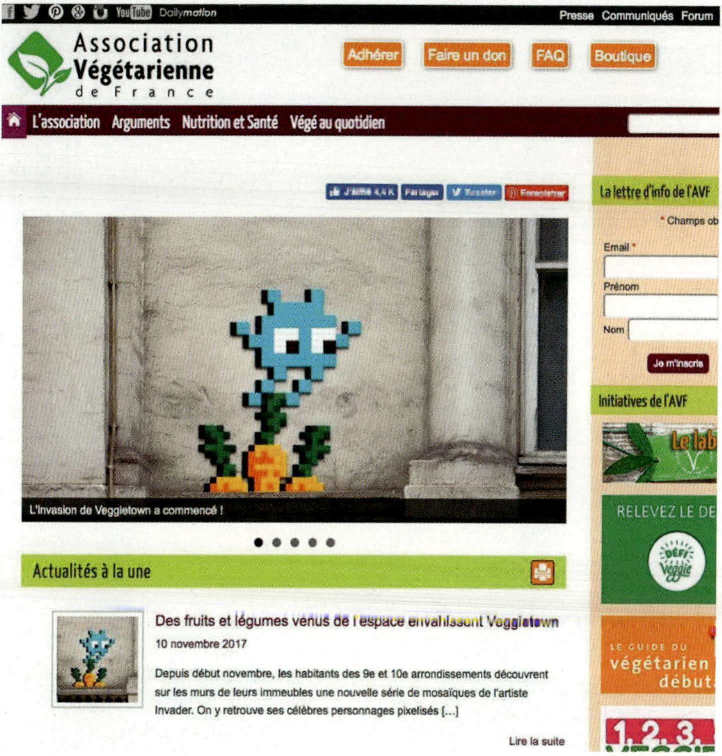

4 018 likes

invaderwashere Invasion of the French Vegetarian Association homepage. More is coming soon, stay tuned... #🥕

View all 36 comments

14 December 2017

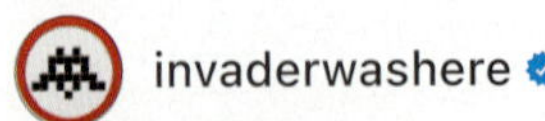

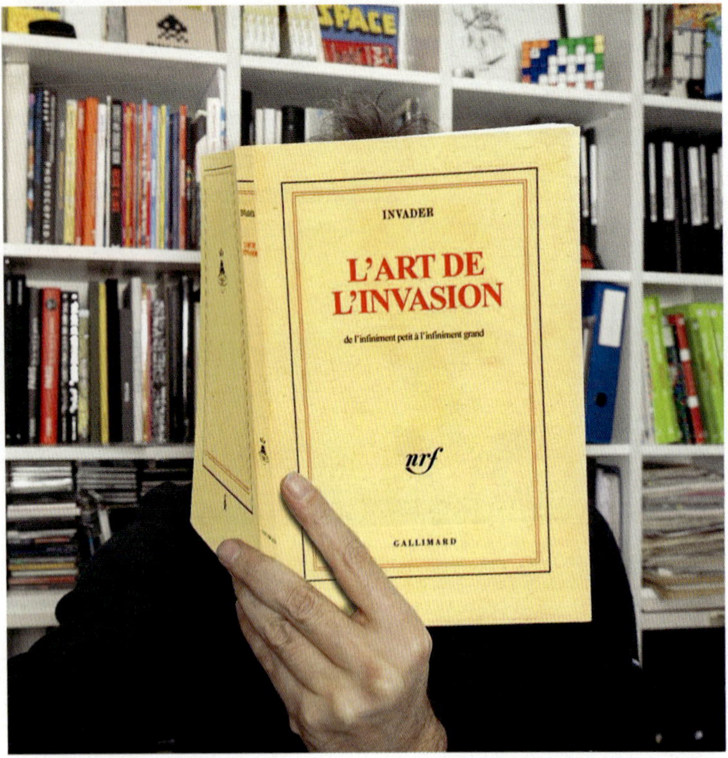

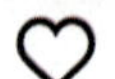   

5830 likes

invaderwashere Selfportrait for Le Monde newspaper of today #lemondedeslivres #mediainvasion @lemondefr

View all 63 comments

15 December 2017

invaderwashere

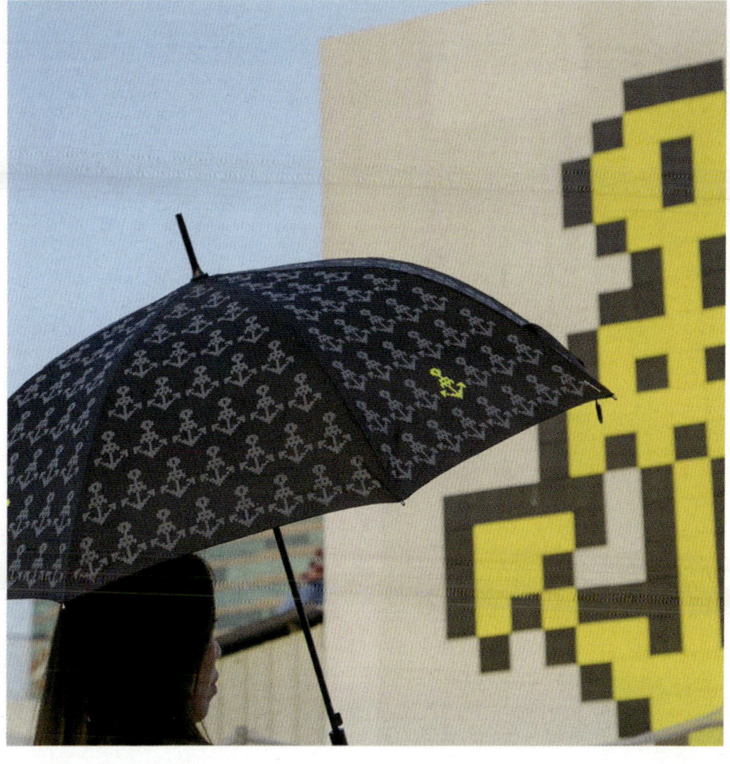

4 237 likes

invaderwashere After the invasion of @harbourcity and their will to preserve my mosaics, we have collaborated together on a Limited Edition Umbrella to raise fund for the Hong Kong Blood Cancer Foundation #harbourcity #hcart #hongkong #charityUmbrella #collector more infos: link in bio

View all 68 comments

20 December 2017

invaderwashere

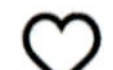   

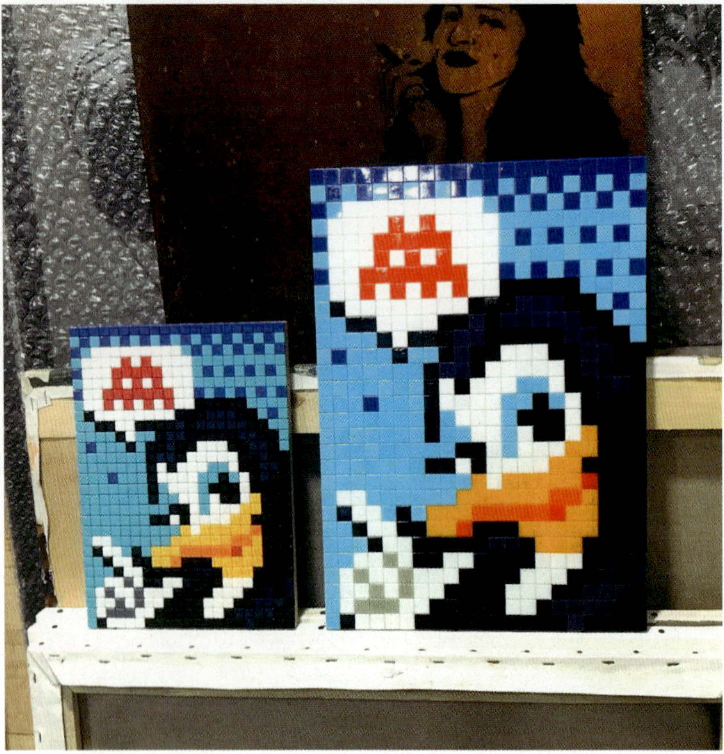

17060 likes

invaderwashere @missticofficiel #studio #misstic #magicadespell #tinytiles #pixelart

View all 87 comments

24 December 2017

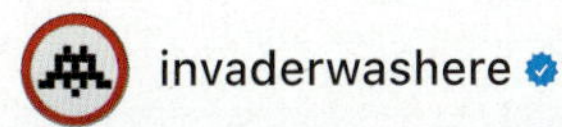

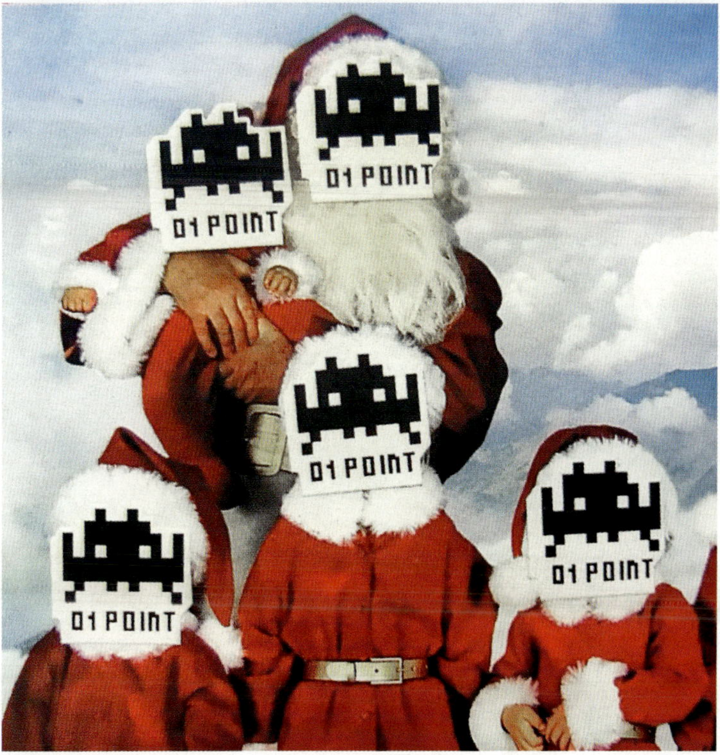

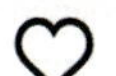   

6043 likes

invaderwashere Collage from 2005 / detail / Merry Xmas
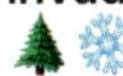

View all 37 comments

25 December 2017

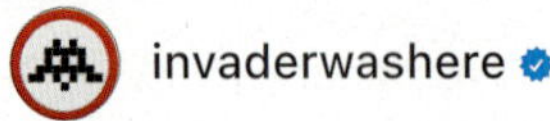

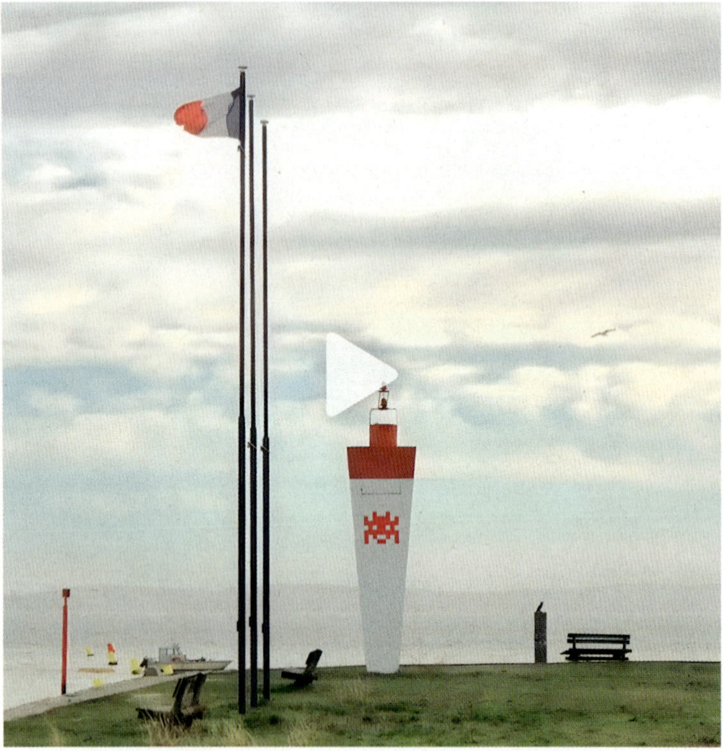

 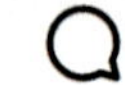  

41144 views

invaderwashere For few days, a new city has been under invasion... Bye bye 2017!

View all 100 comments

31 December 2017

2018

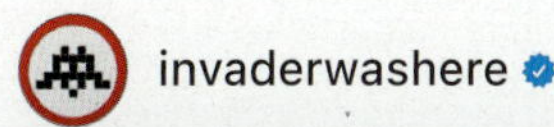

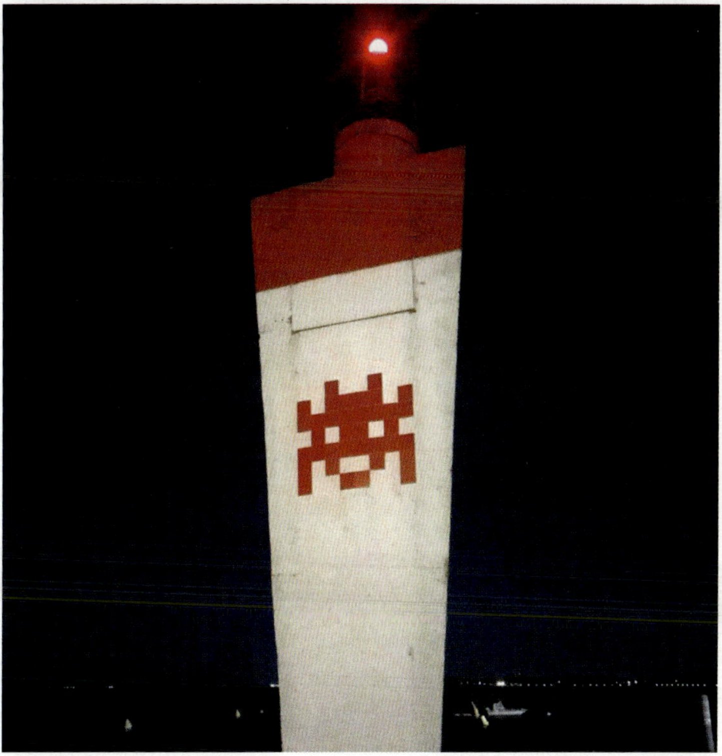

21 062 likes

invaderwashere With the invasion of Cap-Ferret I have just passed 75 invaded cities and 3600 Space Invaders installed across the World #capferret #peninsula #frenchwestcoast

View all 201 comments

4 January 2018

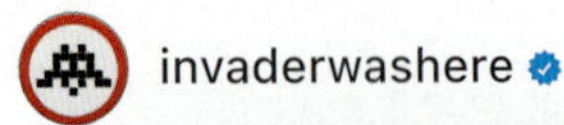

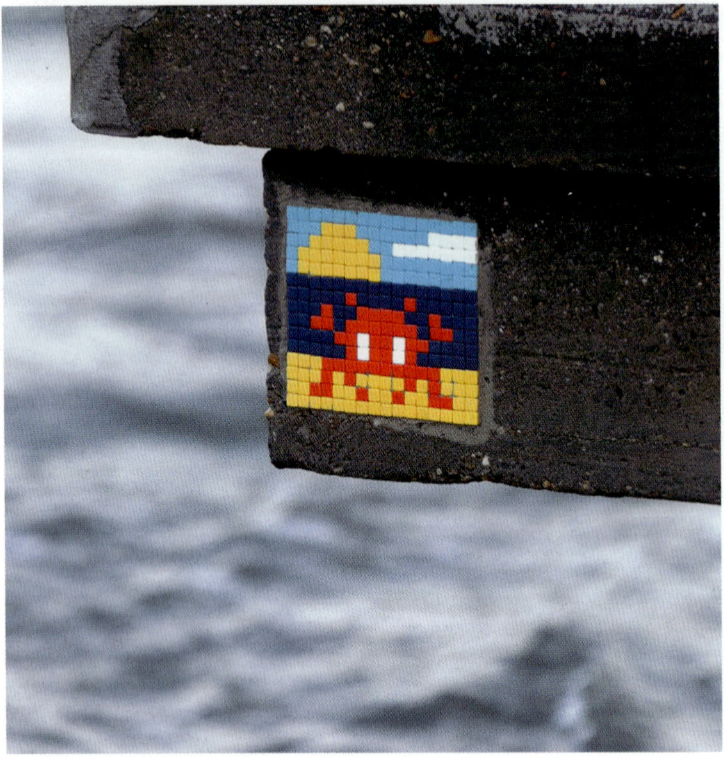

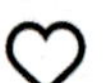    

21 062 likes

invaderwashere With the invasion of Cap-Ferret I have just passed 75 invaded cities and 3600 Space Invaders installed across the World #capferret #peninsula #frenchwestcoast

View all 201 comments

4 January 2018

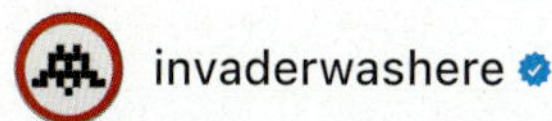

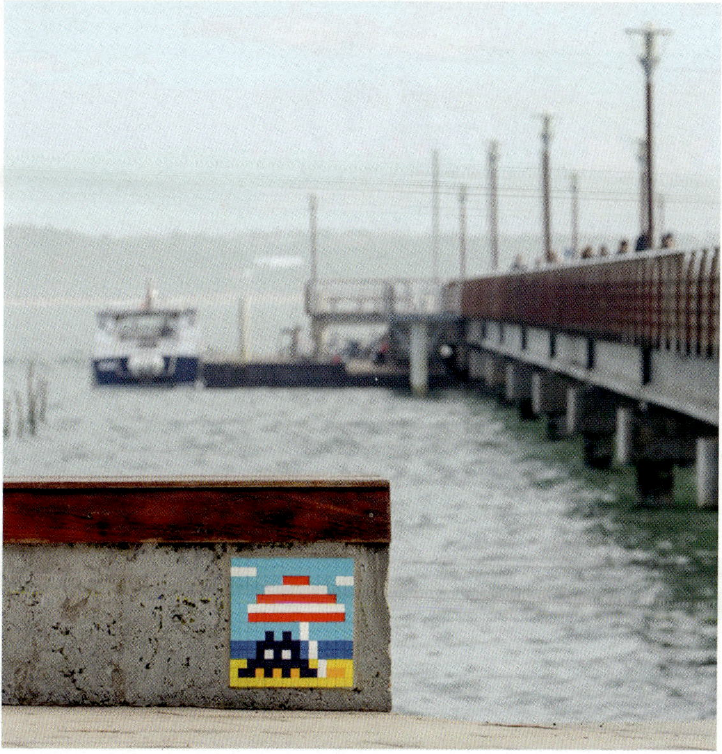

21062 likes

invaderwashere With the invasion of Cap-Ferret I have just passed 75 invaded cities and 3600 Space Invaders installed across the World #capferret #peninsula #frenchwestcoast

View all 201 comments

4 January 2018

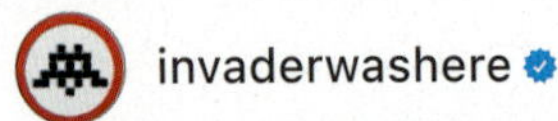

•••

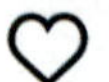  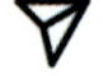 

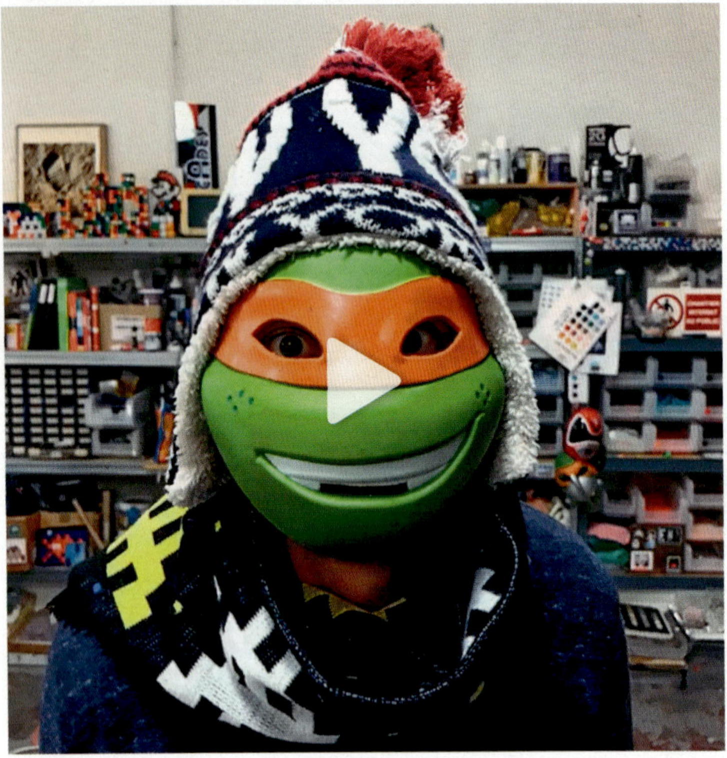

59 190 views

invaderwashere Thanks to the 129.150 visitors who came to see #Hellomygameis & a big up to @museeenherbe & @oti.official who made this exhibition possible 🙏🧡👾

View all 174 comments

12 January 2018

invaderwashere

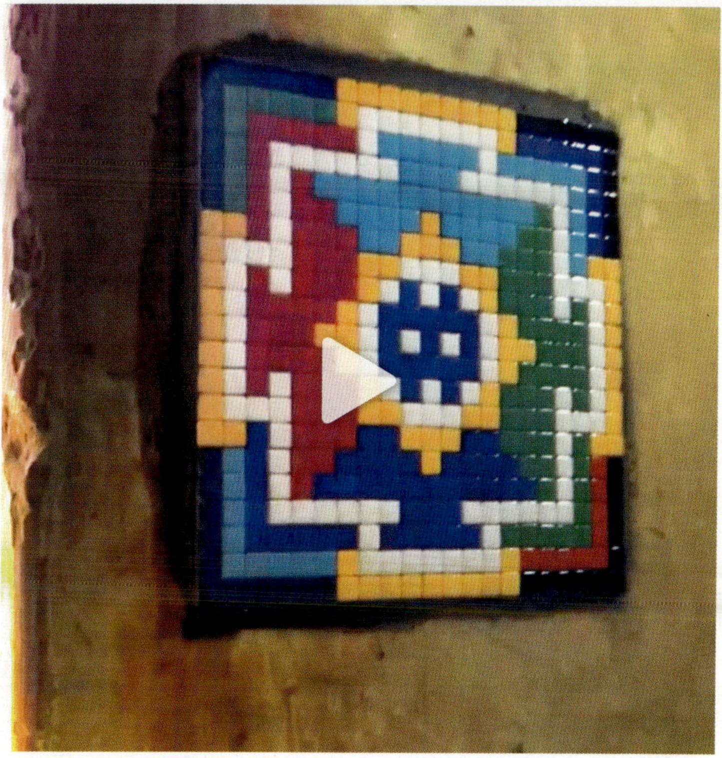

69 402 views

invaderwashere My first piece in Bhutan and my first piece inside a monastery 🙏🇧🇹 #cherigoemba #Timphu #mountains #spirituality #mandala #bhutan with the blessing of the monks!

View all 344 comments

21 January 2018

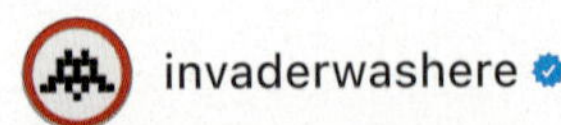

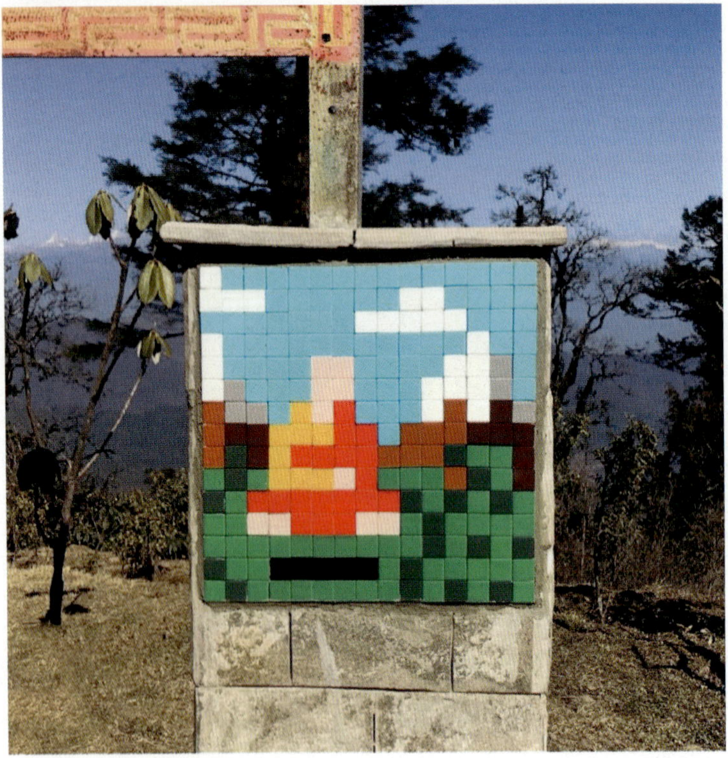

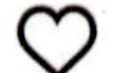   

13 501 likes

invaderwashere BT_05 Mountains and meditation #bhutan #spirituality #monk #levitation

View all 100 comments

22 January 2018

invaderwashere

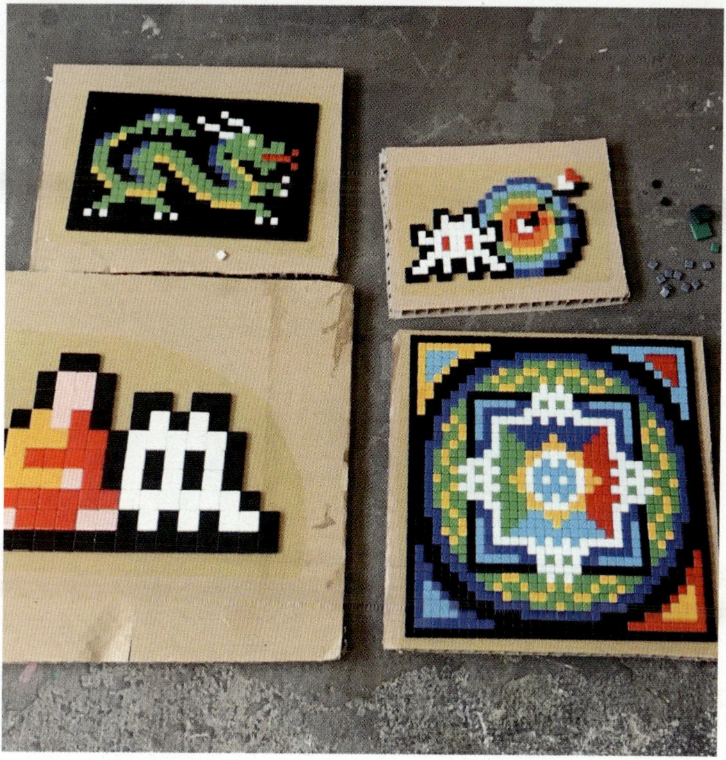

19 857 likes

invaderwashere Mosaics for Bhutan 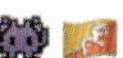

View all 201 comments

23 January 2018

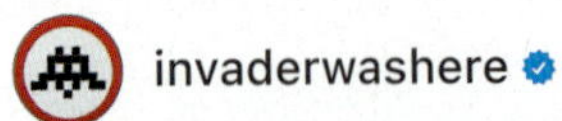

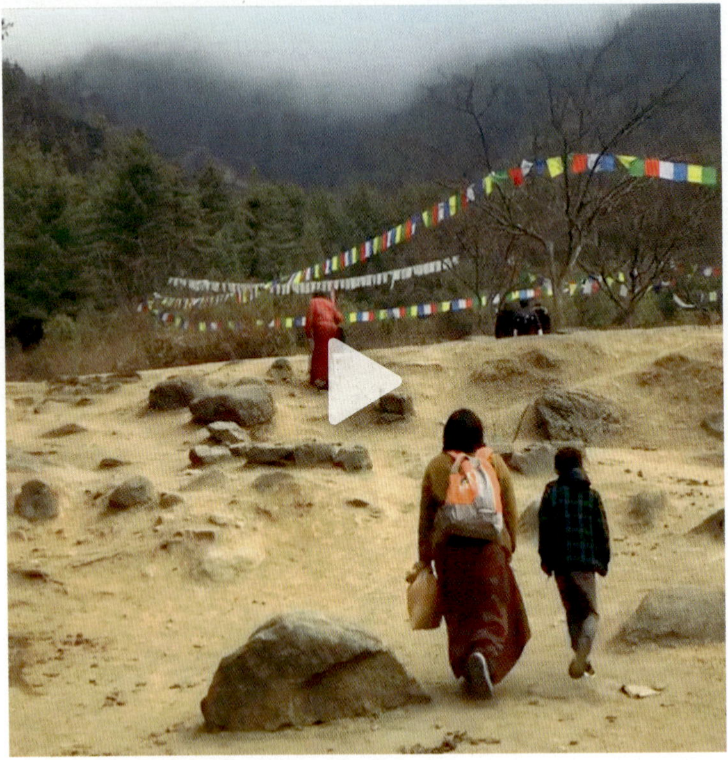

  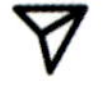

32 652 views

invaderwashere Going up... 🏔

View all 26 comments

29 January 2018

invaderwashere 

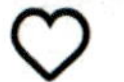   

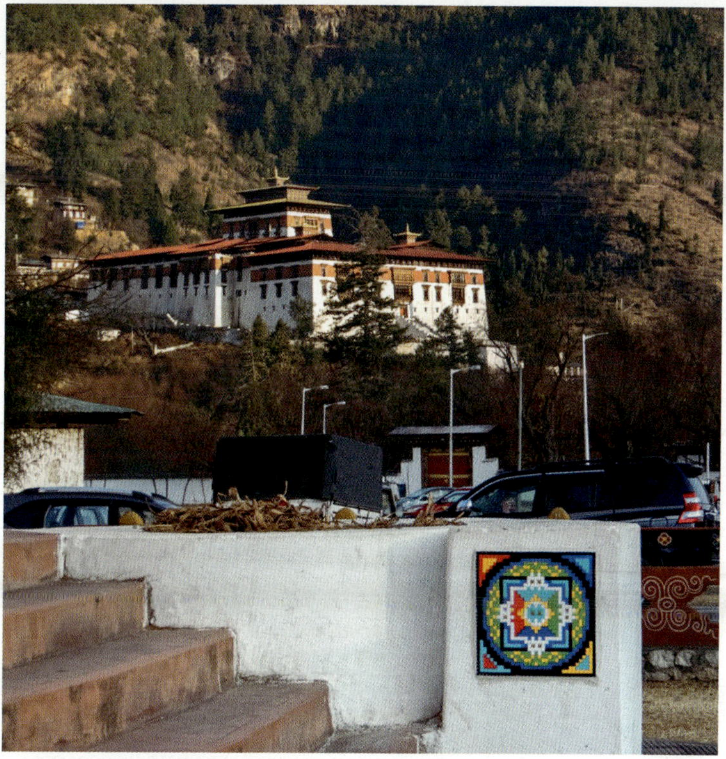

24 755 likes

invaderwashere A group of (western) people are blaming me for having practiced my art in Bhutan thinking it is outrageous and disrespectful. Personally I don't think so and that was not my intention. My practice tells a story, and I'm proud to have written some pages of it in that wonderful country. All of the Bhutanese people I've met were enchanted with it and I thanks them for their kindness and their great hospitality. Kaadinchhey la 🙏🇧🇹👾

View all 637 comments

30 January 2018

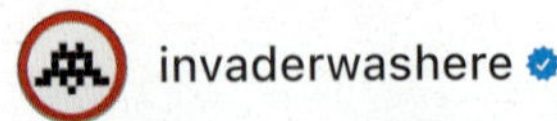

invaderwashere

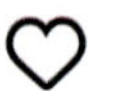  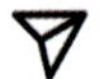 

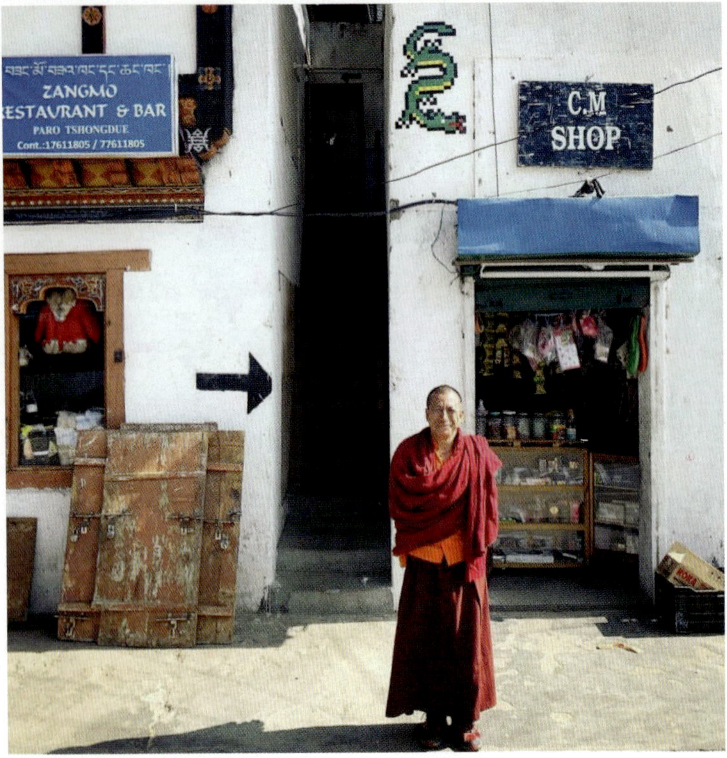

15 112 likes

invaderwashere Photo by @jttenzing 🙂 #Bhutan

View all 105 comments

2 February 2018

invaderwashere

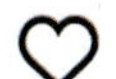
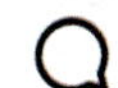

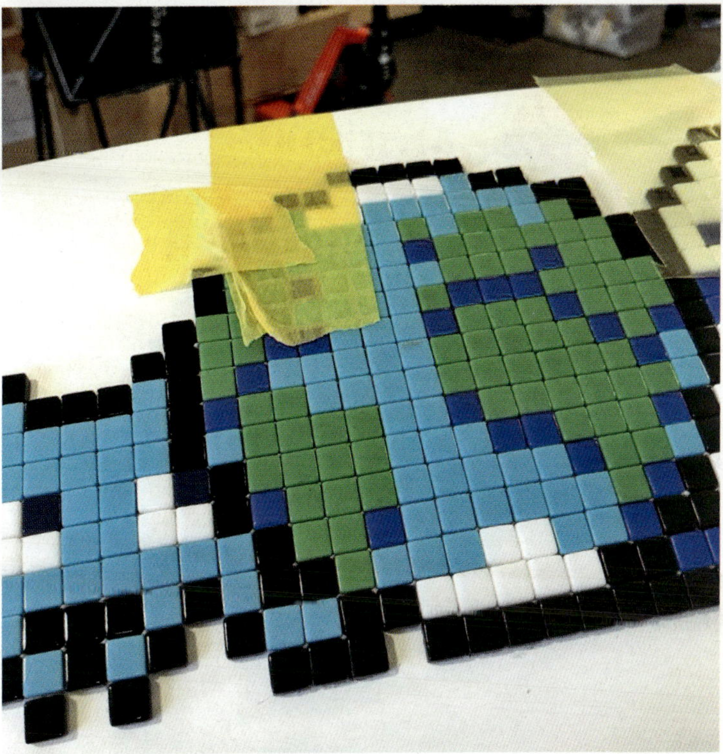

9049 likes

invaderwashere Back to the studio

View all 43 comments

5 February 2018

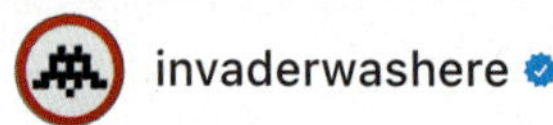

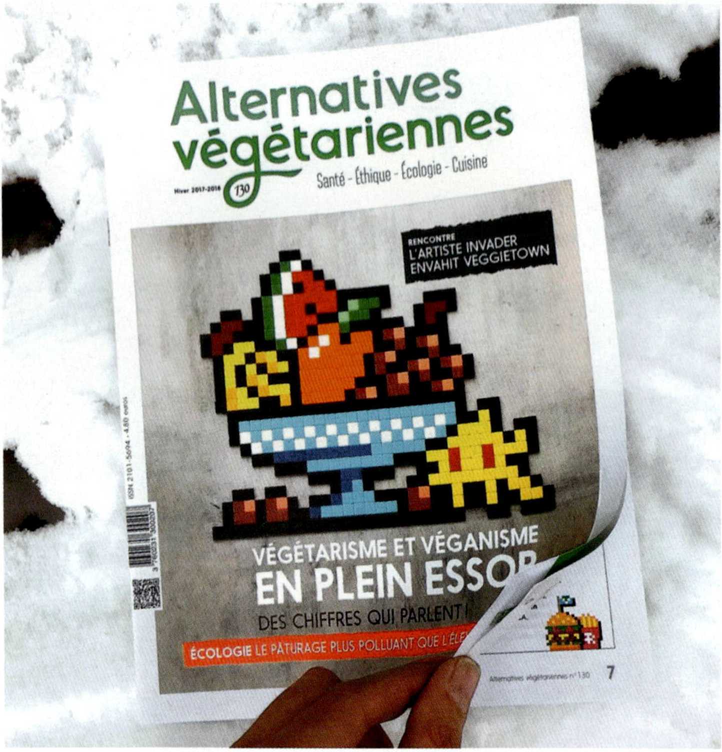

6218 likes

invaderwashere The winter issue of the « Association Végétarienne de France » newspaper is out. Cover, Interview + total invasion!!! Support the association and order it at www.vegetarisme.fr

#vegetarisme #veggie #veggieworld #govegan

View all 63 comments

7 February 2018

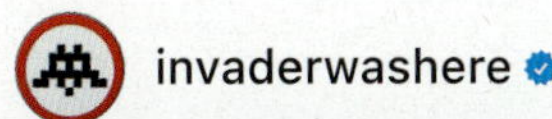

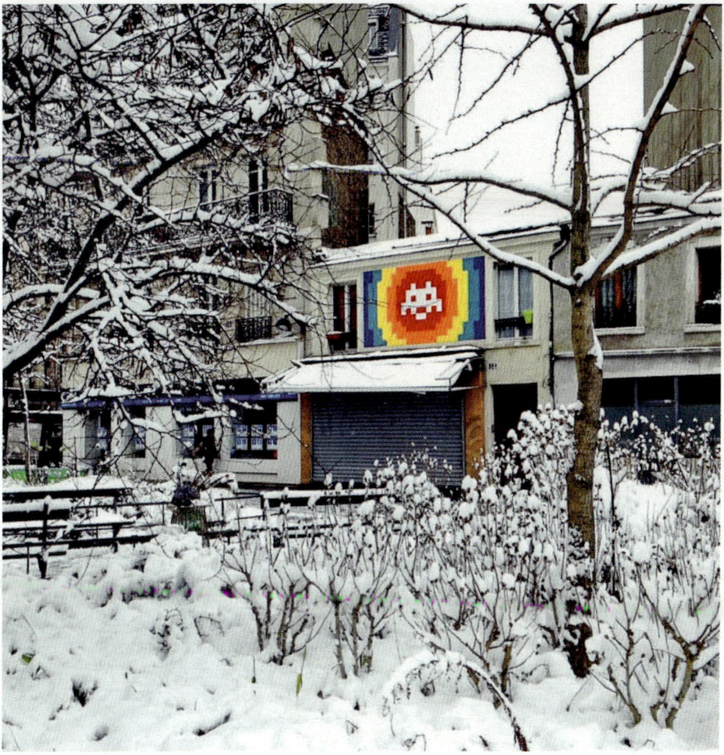

 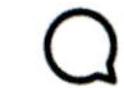  

21 656 likes

invaderwashere PA_1174 under the snow. Great photo by @virginie.f24 #paris #snow

View all 152 comments

8 February 2018

invaderwashere

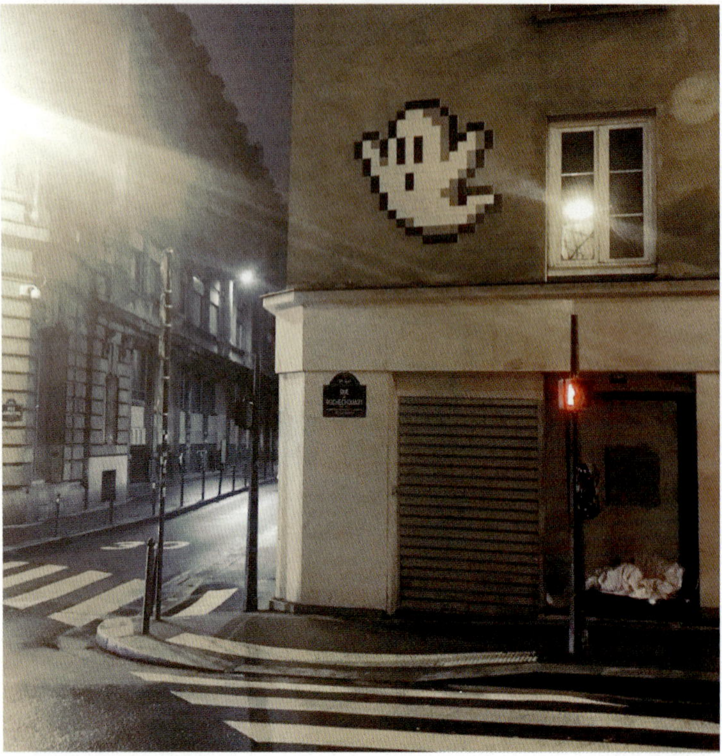

33 035 likes

invaderwashere Big ghost!!! Fresh from last night... 👻
#invaderwashere

View all 261 comments

14 February 2018

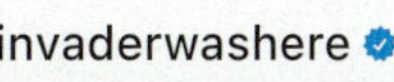

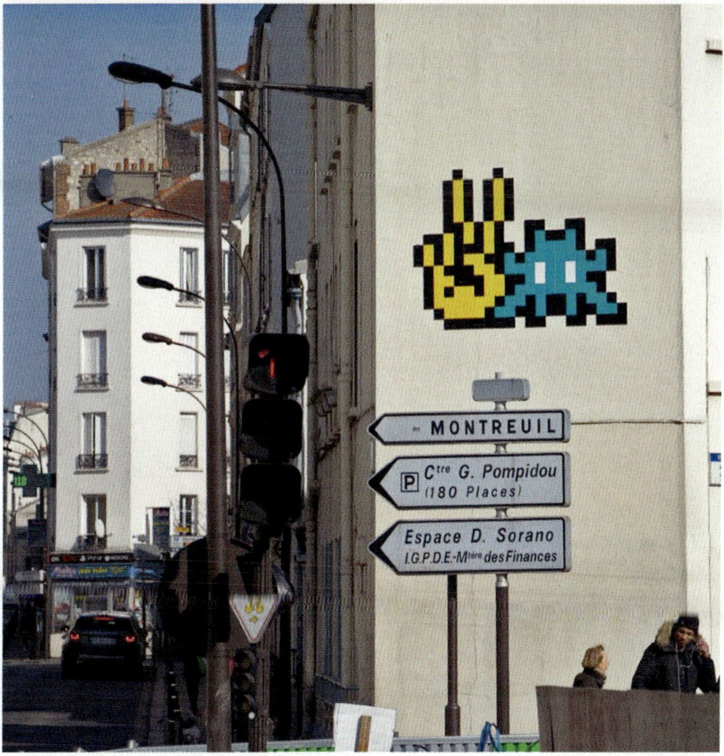

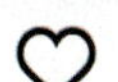   

16 561 likes

invaderwashere ✌️ 👾... New piece of the week

View all 111 comments

22 February 2018

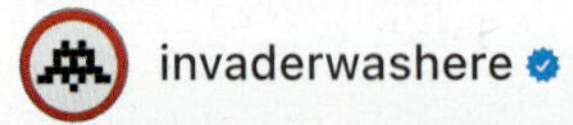

invaderwashere

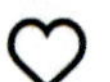   

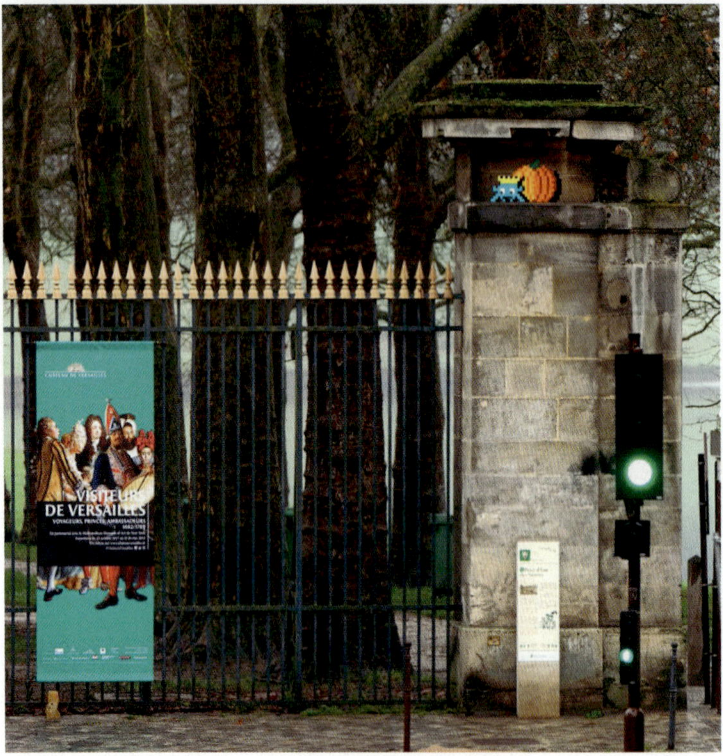

17700 likes

invaderwashere King's vegetable garden #Versailles

View all 116 comments

27 February 2018

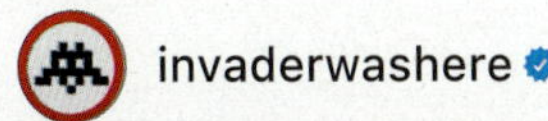

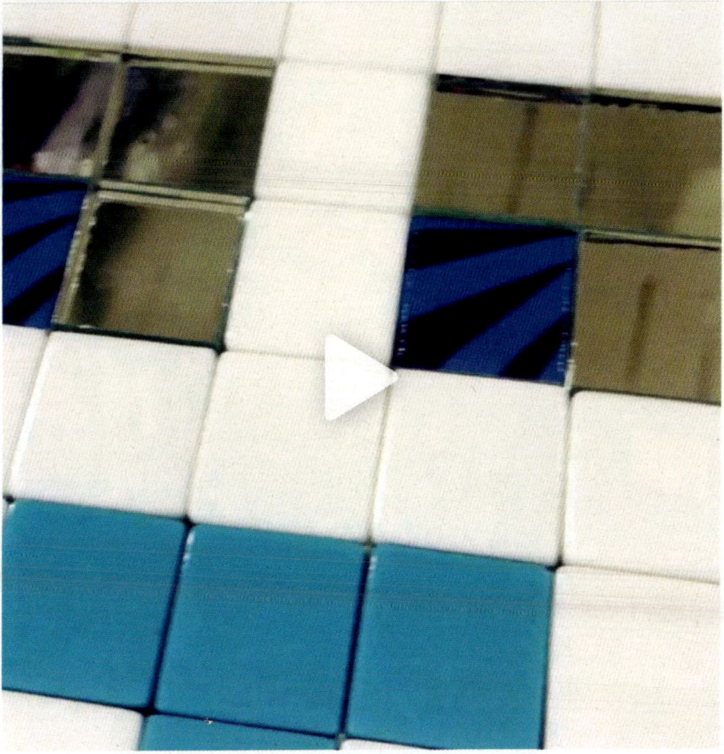

5258 likes

invaderwashere PA_1346 eyes detail 

View all 38 comments

8 March 2018

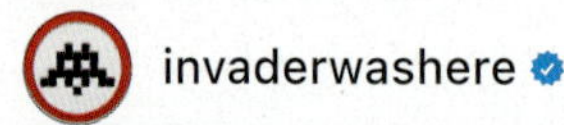

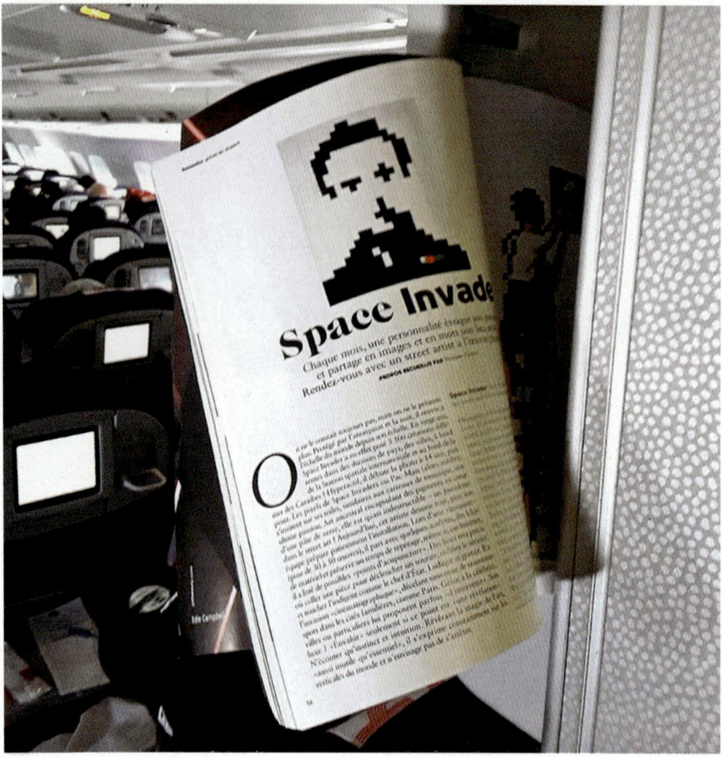

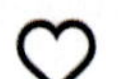

7065 likes

invaderwashere Invasion of AirFrance magazine #mediainvasion @airfrancemagazine issue 250

View all 61 comments

8 March 2018

invaderwashere

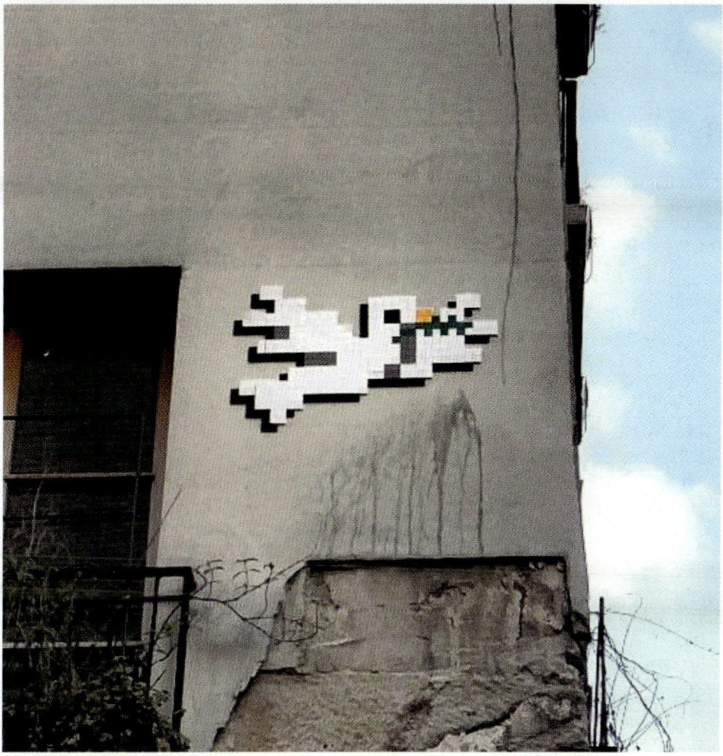

12 266 likes

invaderwashere PA_1344 #Dovestreet #Paris

View all 59 comments

11 March 2018

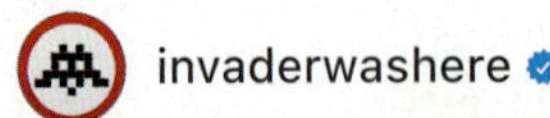

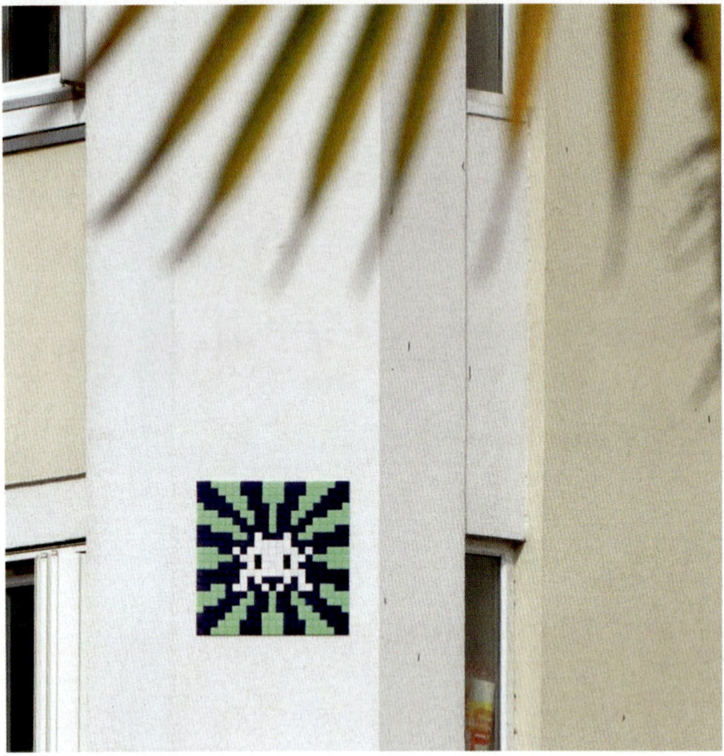

12 571 likes

invaderwashere Things turned wrong last night. I could not install a big piece I wanted to install! I finally put up this small one which actually doesn't look bad!

View all 89 comments

15 March 2018

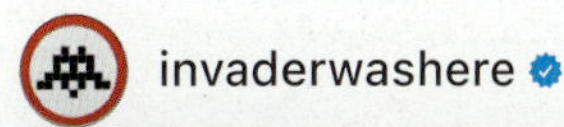

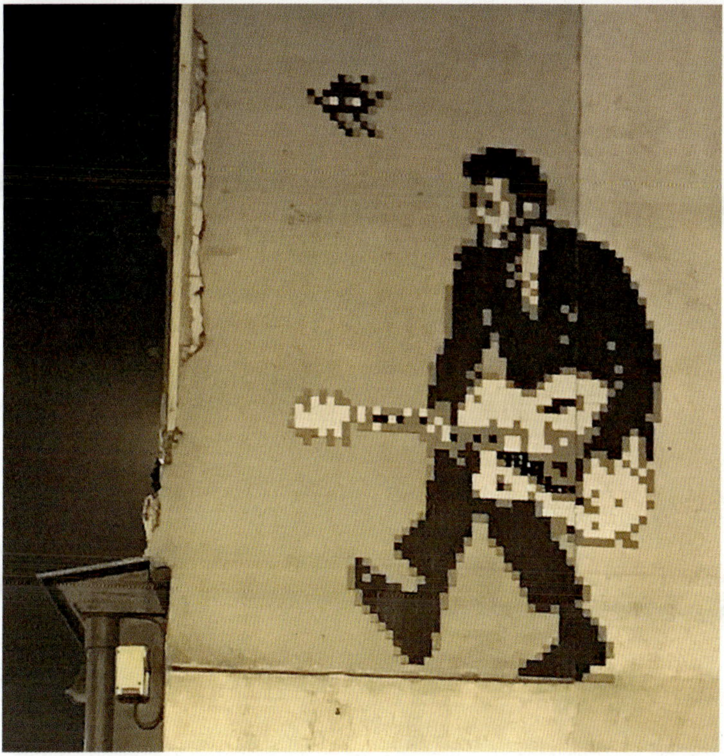

31 394 likes

invaderwashere Du rock à Duroc!!! #Paris #Duroc #3.33am #ChuckBerry #invaderwashere

View all 288 comments

21 March 2018

invaderwashere

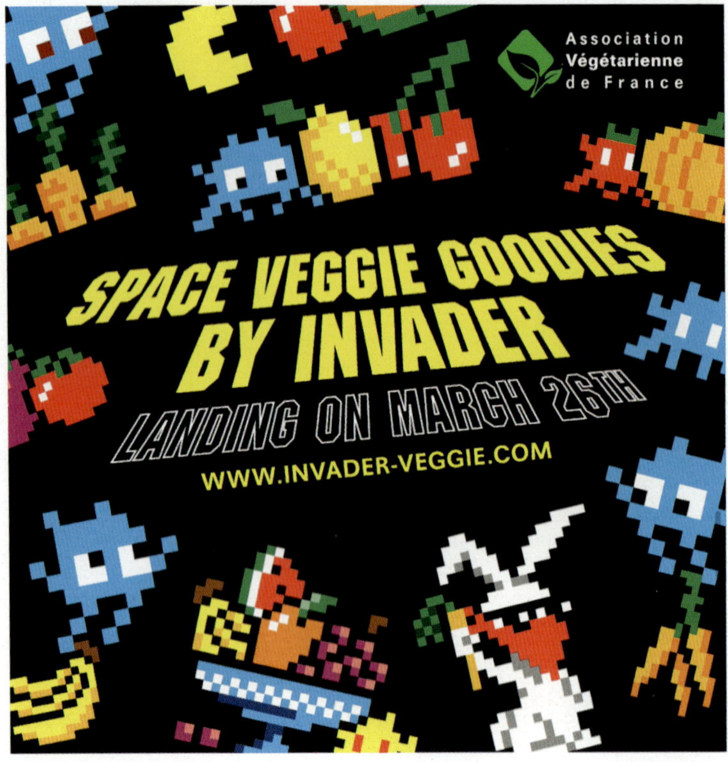

7543 likes

invaderwashere The server has crashed 💥 💥 💥 !!! Sorry for the inconvenience 😁 We will reopen tomorrow, stay tuned //////////// Invader-veggie.com presents the limited editions that I have designed for AVF (French Vegetarian Association). 100% of the benefits goes to AVF. Link in Bio @association_vegetarienne_fr #limitededitions #veggie #Tshirts #pins #stickers #govegan 🐇 👾

View all 130 comments

26 March 2018

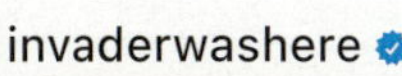

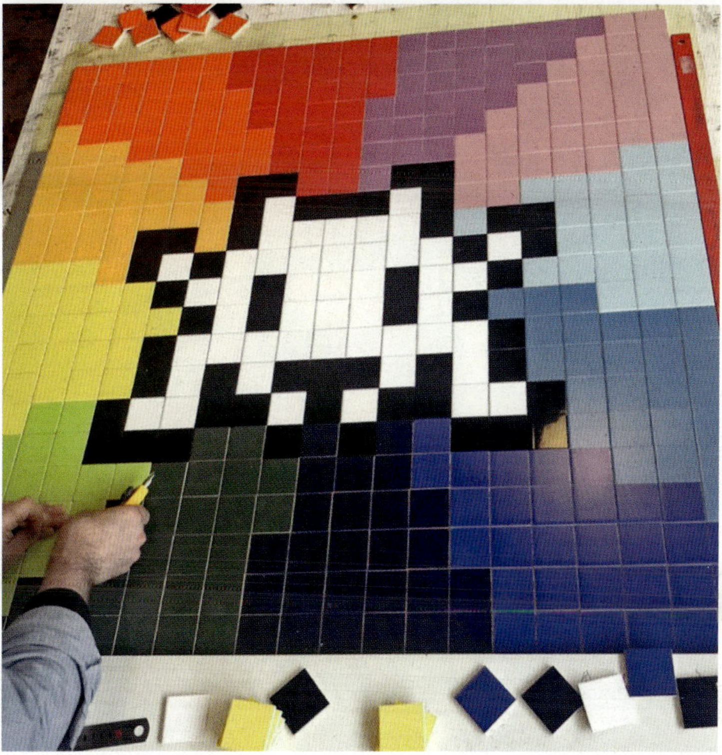

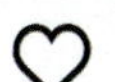

22 758 likes

invaderwashere PA_1352 Chromatic square 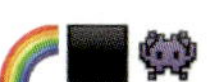

View all 163 comments

29 March 2018

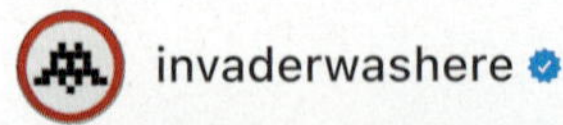

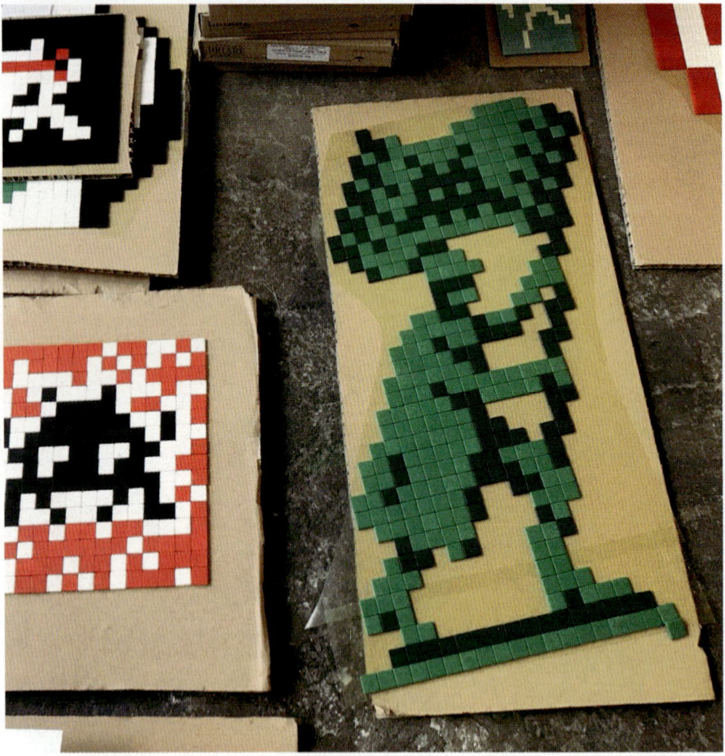

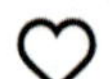  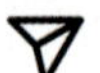 

12 290 likes

invaderwashere Studio detail, preparing the next invasion

View all 119 comments

13 April 2018

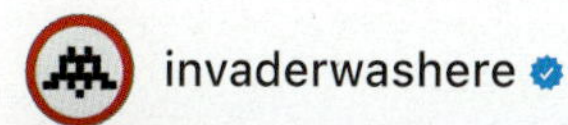

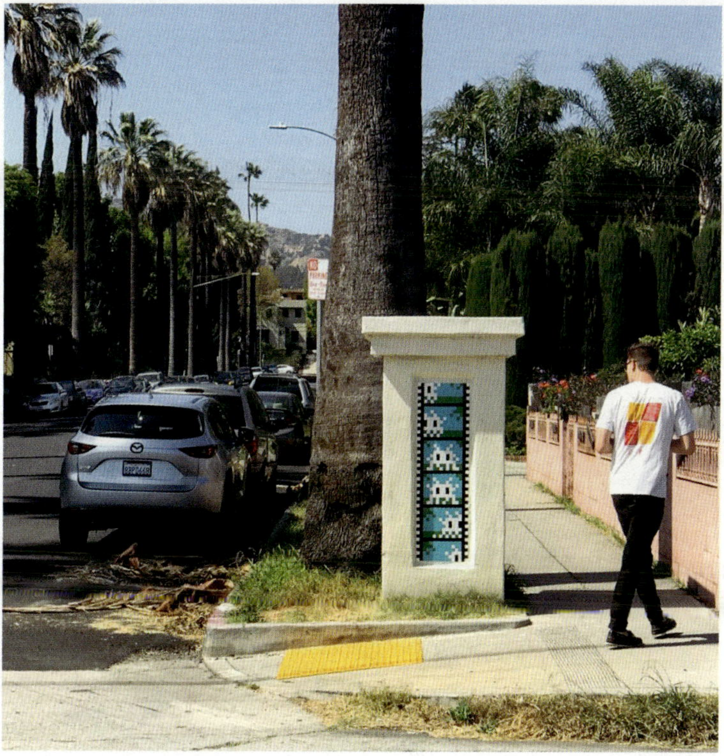

22 369 likes

invaderwashere Back in LA / first piece of wave10 #LA173 #hollywood #invaderwashere

View all 244 comments

11 May 2018

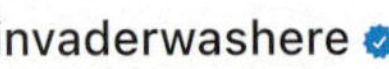

invaderwashere

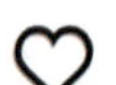  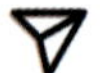 

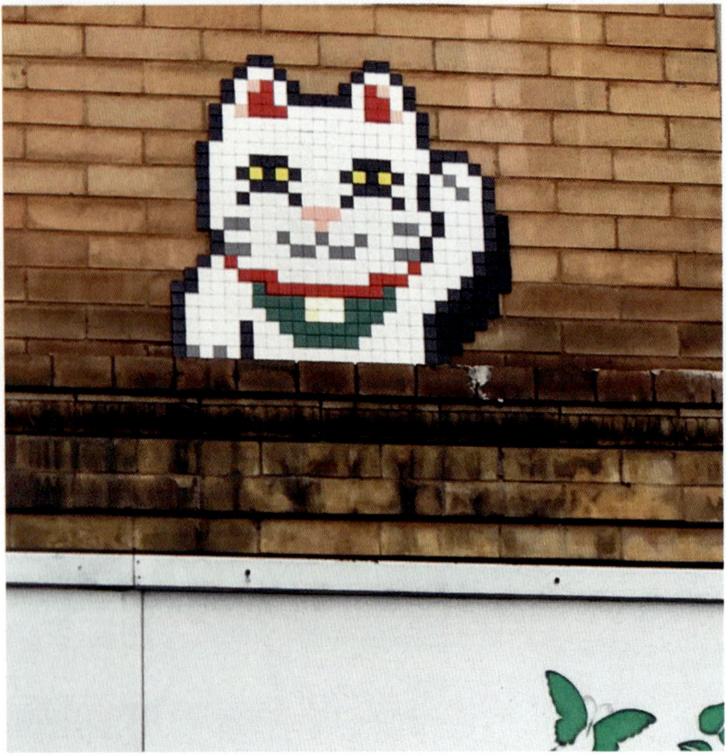

23 885 likes

invaderwashere Maneki Neko of LA #littletokyo #lookmeintheeyes

View all 189 comments

13 May 2018

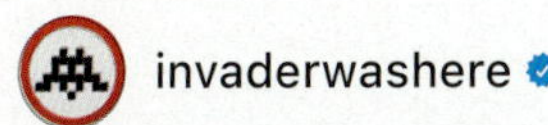

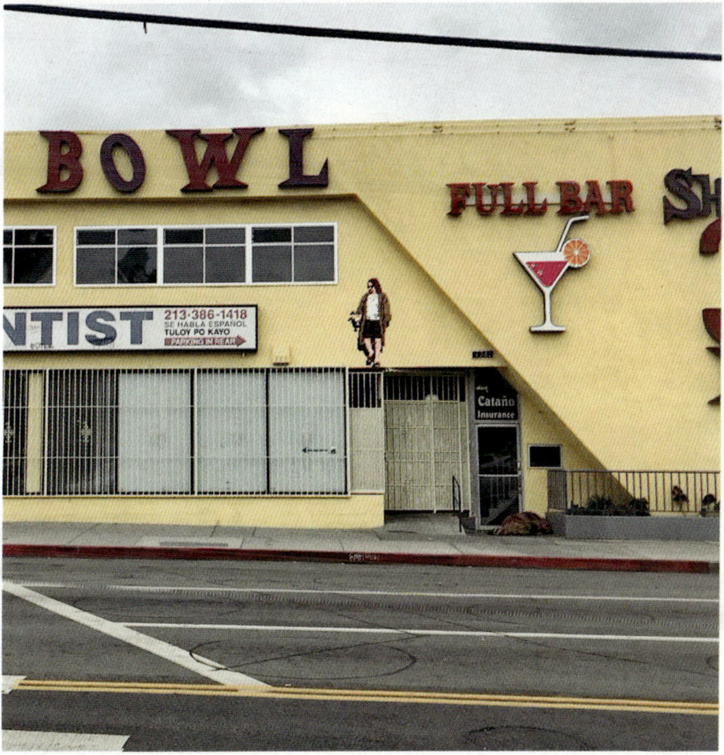

31 301 likes

invaderwashere The Dude #LA #bowling #thebiglebowski #nomorewhiterussian #100pts

View all 958 comments

13 May 2018

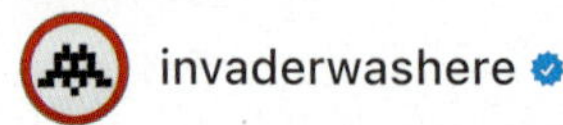

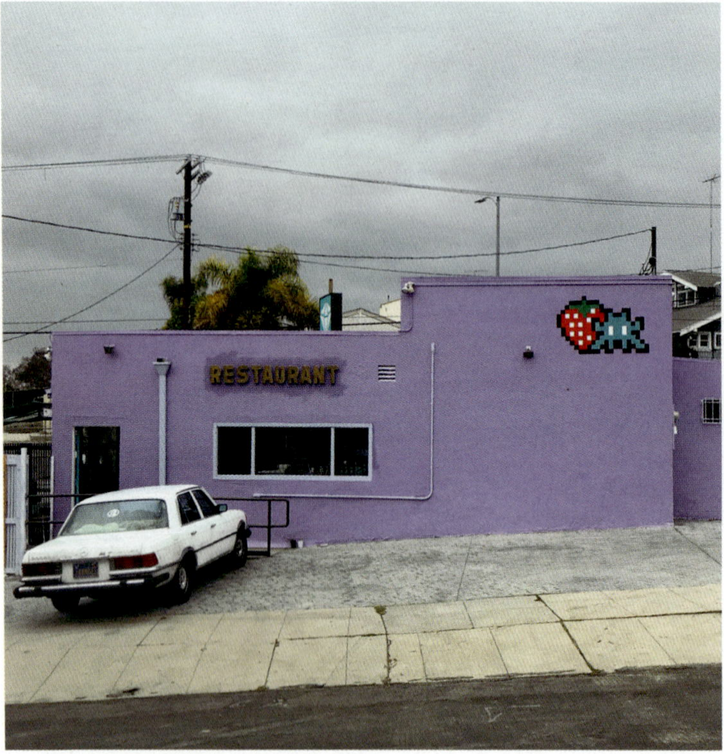

13 498 likes

invaderwashere Great spot and delicious food at Jewel restaurant #vegan #LA @eatatjewel

View all 78 comments

14 May 2018

invaderwashere

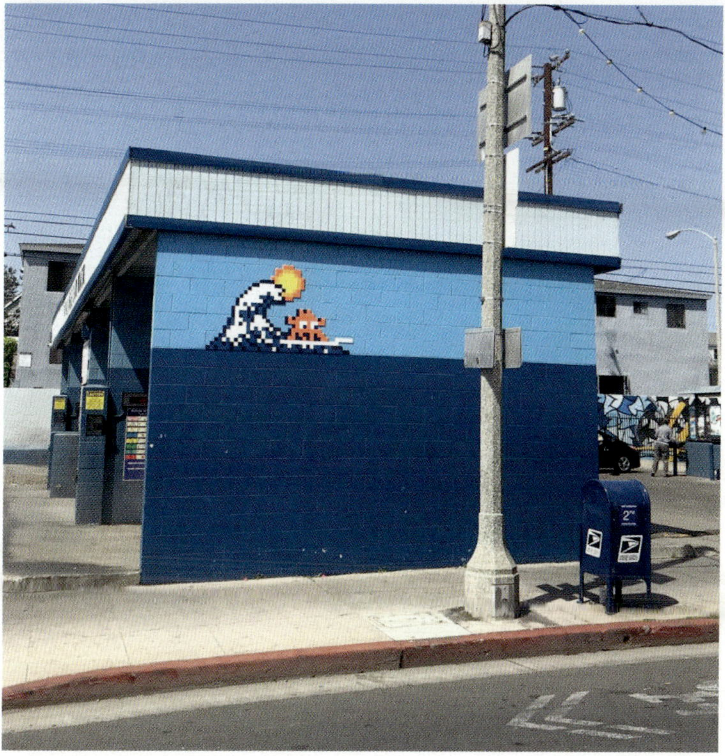

25 500 likes

invaderwashere Surfin' Santa Monica... #LA190

View all 271 comments

14 May 2018

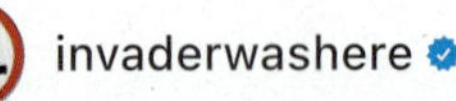

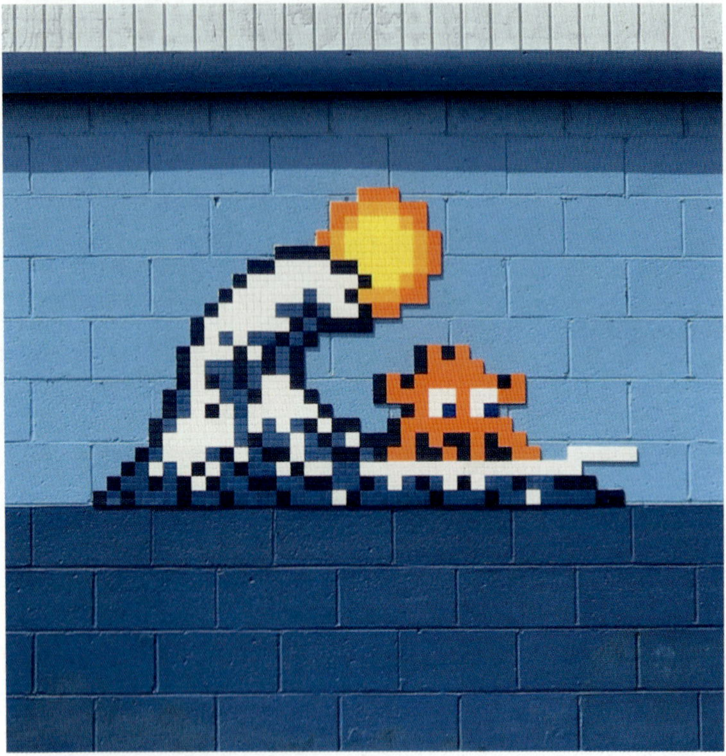

25 500 likes

invaderwashere Surfin' Santa Monica... #LA190

View all 271 comments

14 May 2018

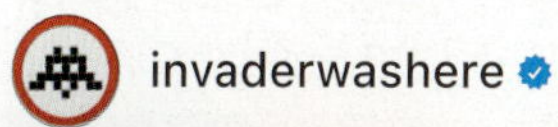

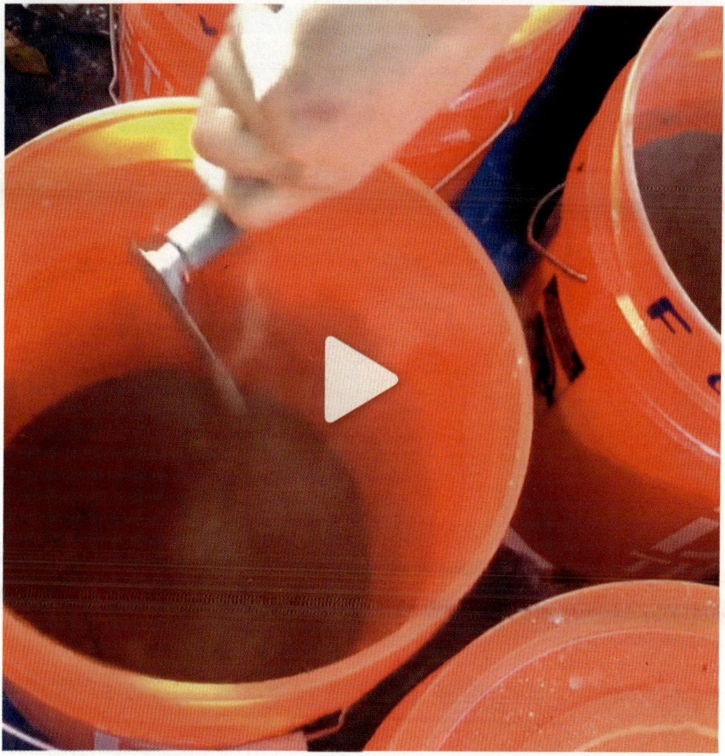

  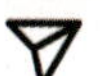 

30 596 views

View all 13 comments

15 May 2018

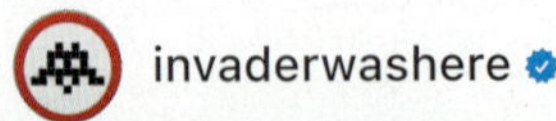

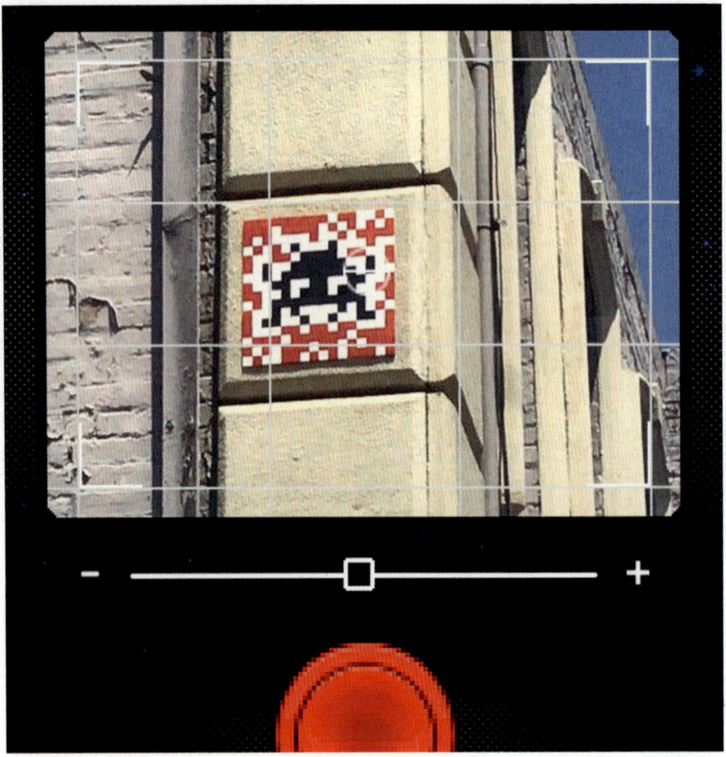

8 292 likes

invaderwashere FlashInvaders 2.3 is out today #freeapp #flashinvaders #newupdate available on appstore and googleplay. Link in bio.

View all 68 comments

15 May 2018

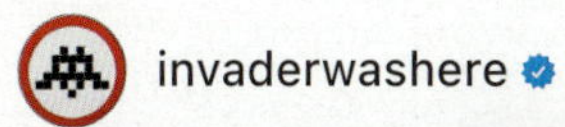

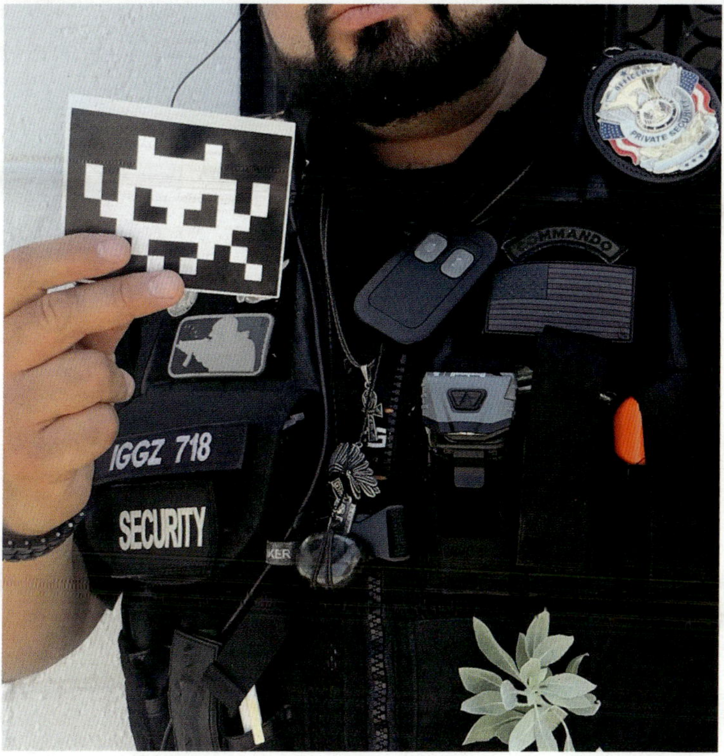

10 030 likes

invaderwashere Invaded security force

View all 76 comments

16 May 2018

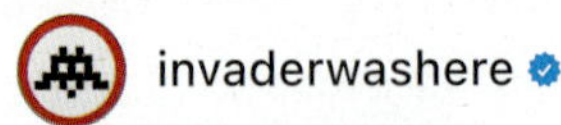

•••

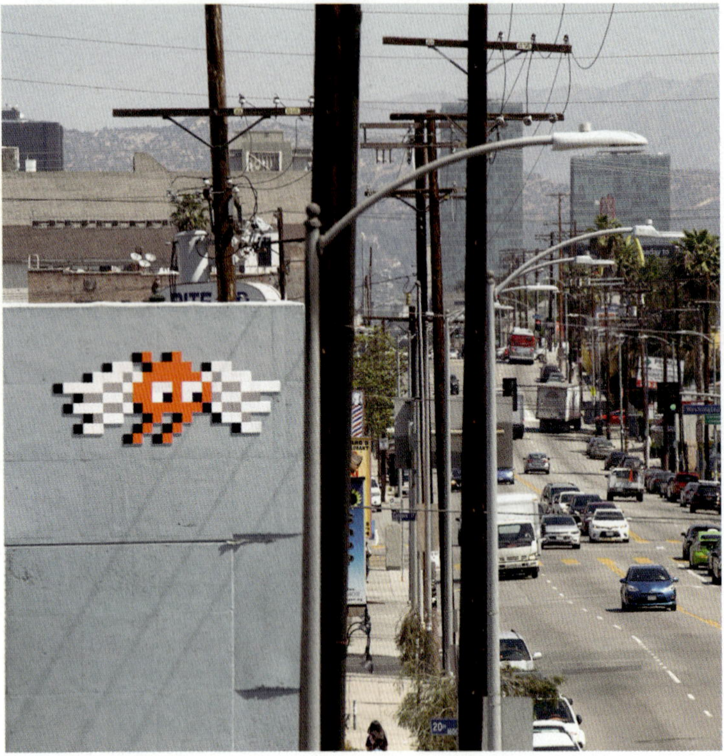

8 345 likes

invaderwashere Space Angeles 👾😇 Special thanx to @brandedarts for this great spot.

View all 61 comments

17 May 2018

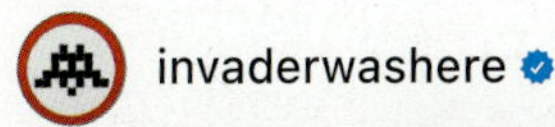

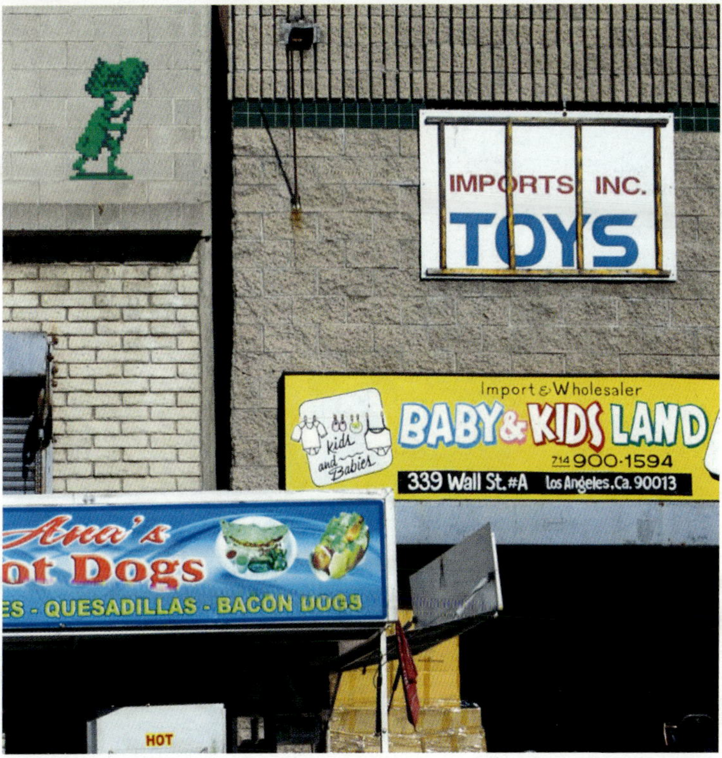

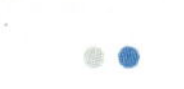

16 472 likes

invaderwashere Toys district / Downtown LA

View all 72 comments

20 May 2018

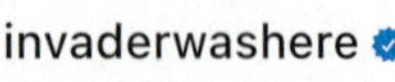

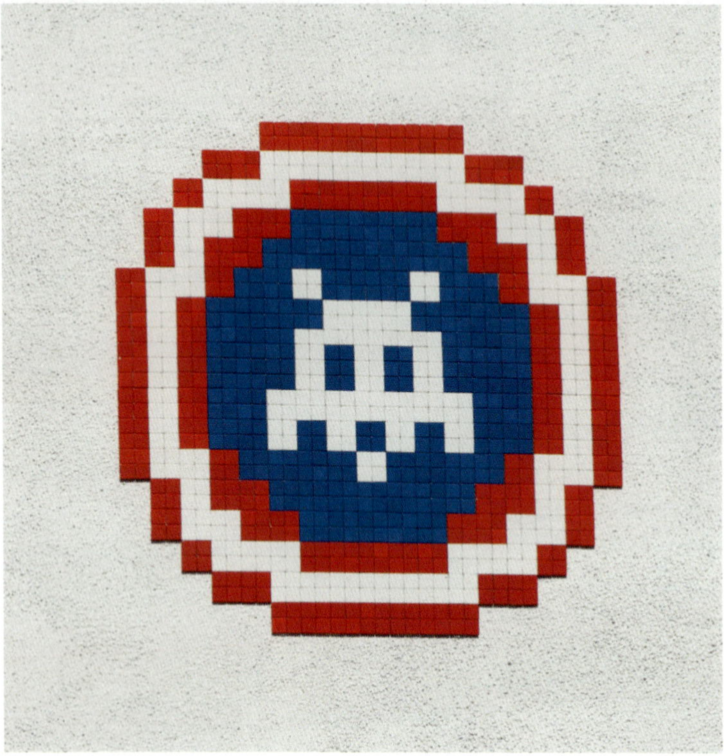

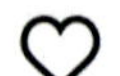 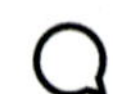   

12 714 likes

invaderwashere Captain Invader! #LA197 #melrose

View all 69 comments

21 May 2018

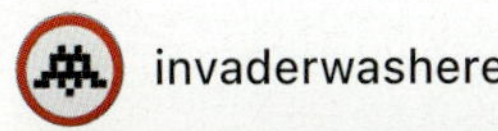

invaderwashere ...

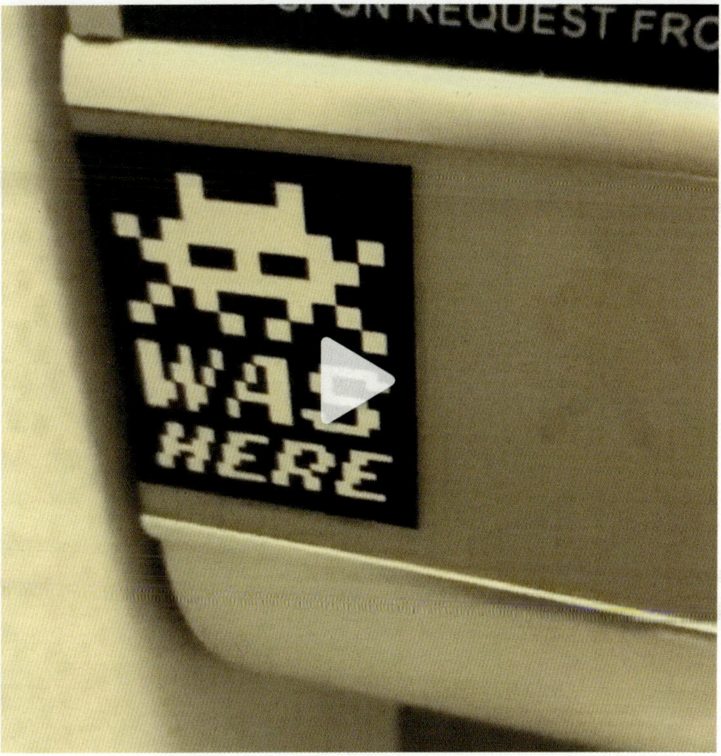

38 149 views

invaderwashere 👾✈️ I have quitted smoking in the plane lavatories, but I have not quitted putting stickers!

View all 67 comments

23 May 2018

invaderwashere

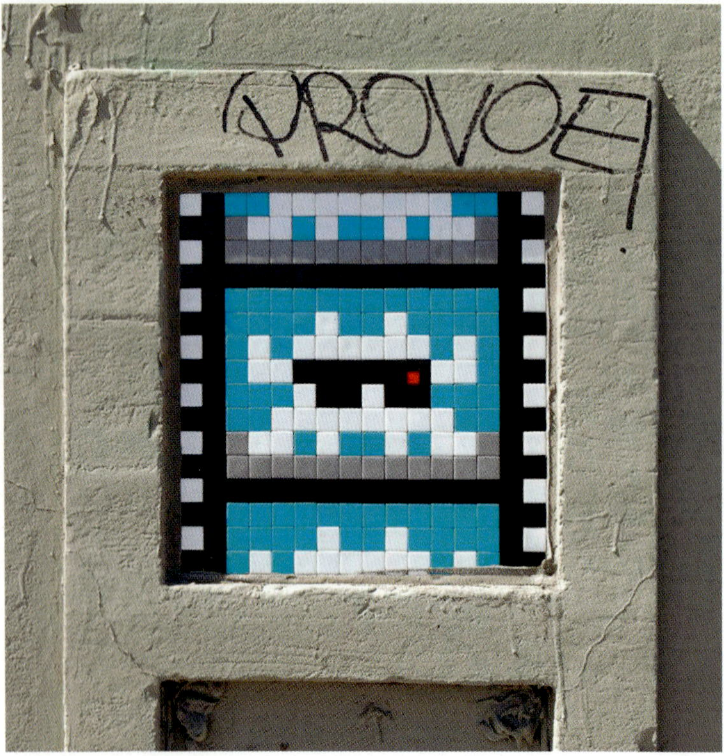

24 914 likes

invaderwashere I WAS IN LA to complete the 10th invasion wave of the city / More info and photos: link in bio

View all 219 comments

25 May 2018

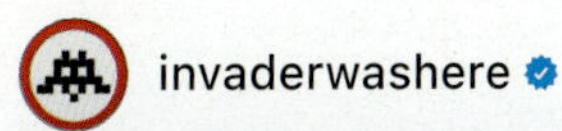

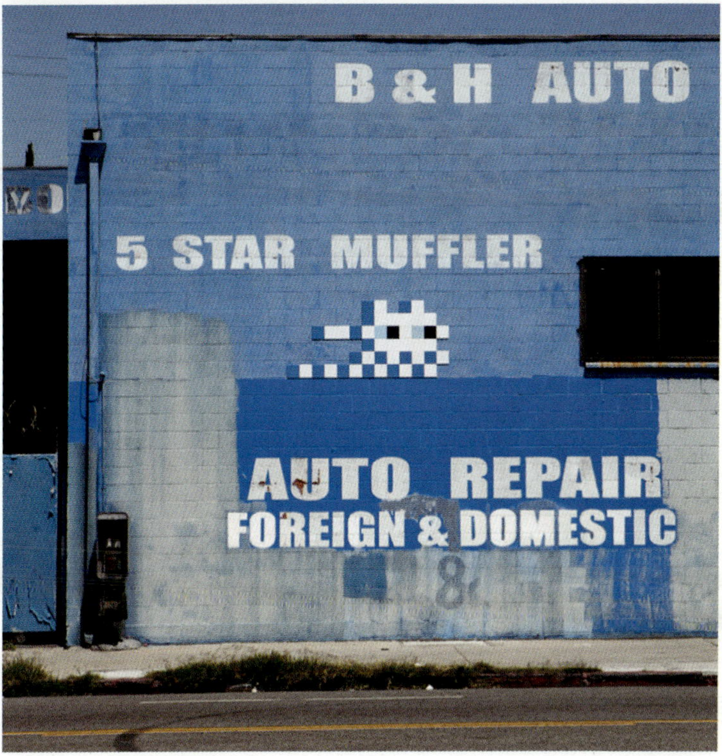

   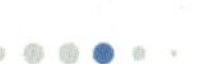 

25 417 likes

invaderwashere I WAS IN LA to complete the 10th invasion wave of the city / More info and photos: link in bio

View all 219 comments

25 May 2018

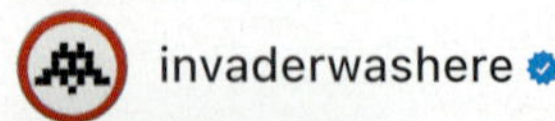

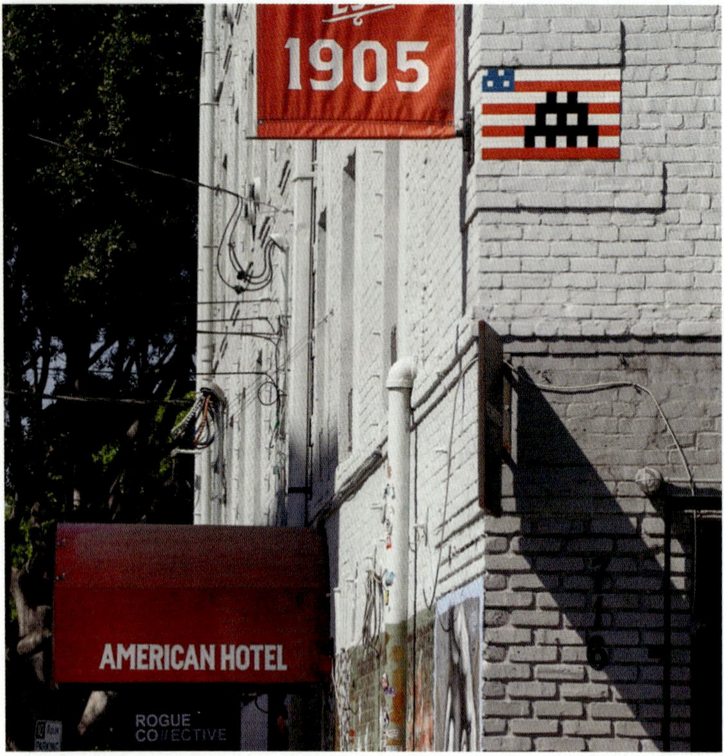

25 417 likes

invaderwashere I WAS IN LA to complete the 10th invasion wave of the city / More info and photos: link in bio

View all 219 comments

25 May 2018

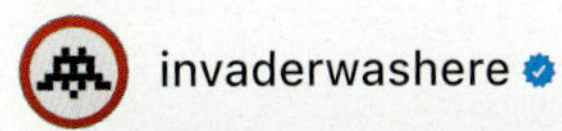

invaderwashere

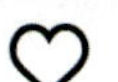    

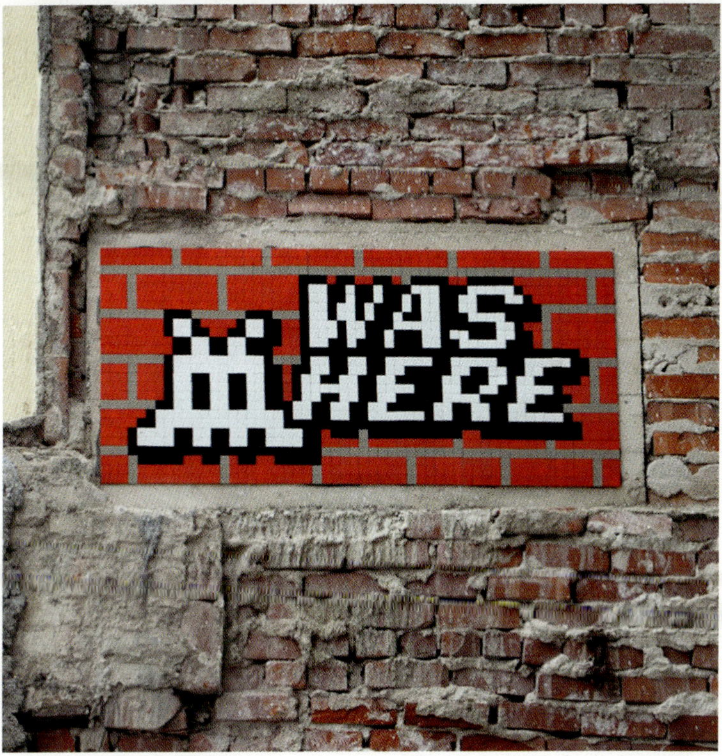

25 417 likes

invaderwashere I WAS IN LA to complete the 10th invasion wave of the city / More info and photos: link in bio

View all 219 comments

25 May 2018

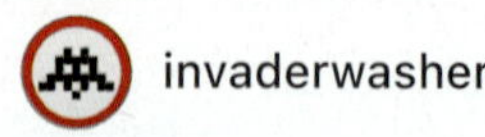

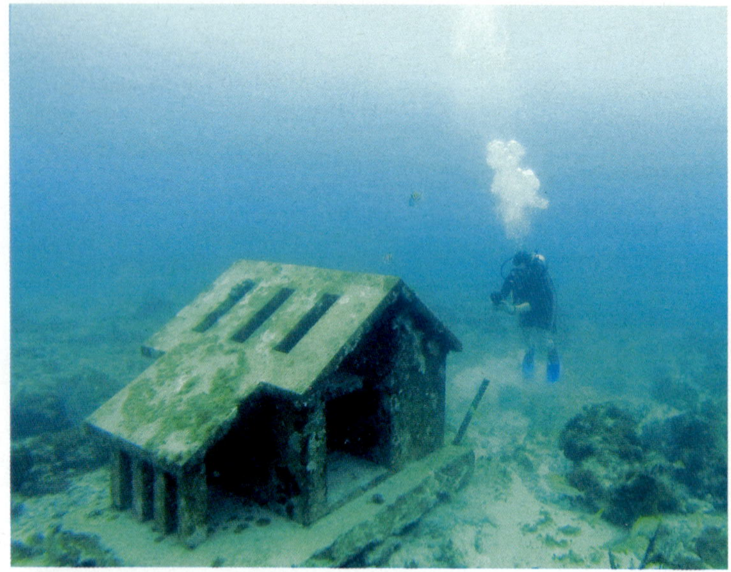

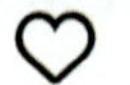   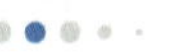 

17 907 likes

invaderwashere A flasher attempting to flash one of the most difficult space invader to flash... 🐠
#flashinvaders #cancun #underwater 2012-2018
Nature x Culture! Sculpture by @jasondecairestaylor

View all 410 comments

28 May 2018

invaderwashere

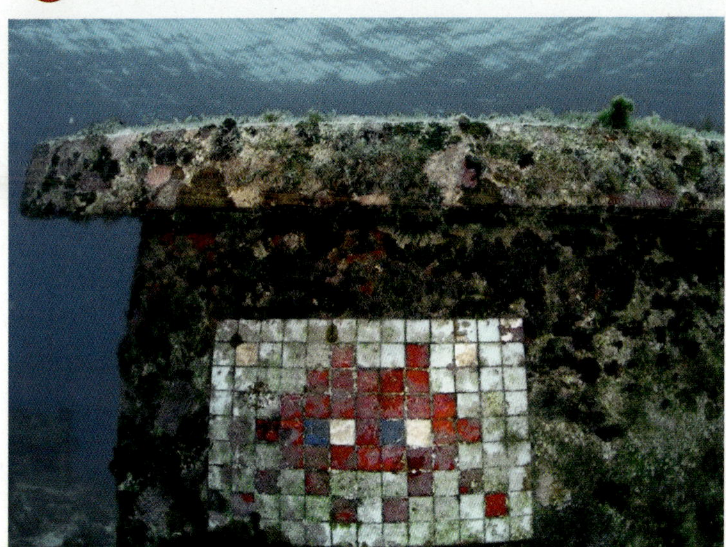

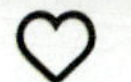   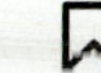

17 907 likes

invaderwashere A flasher attempting to flash one of the most difficult space invader to flash... 🐠
#flashinvaders #cancun #underwater 2012-2018
Nature x Culture! Sculpture by @jasondecairestaylor

View all 410 comments

28 May 2018

invaderwashere

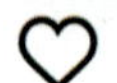
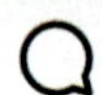

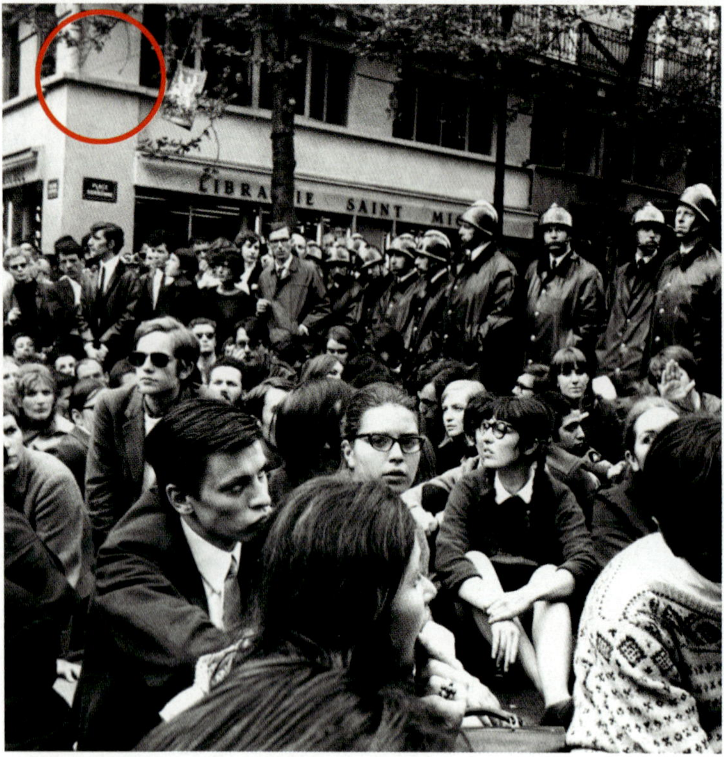

20 807 likes

invaderwashere Last day to make a May 68 anniversary tribute. I've always been a great admirer of May 68 posters. I love them for their simplicity, their unadorned designs, quickly executed in a single color, the urgency having dictated the process (screen printing), but also of course for their political effectiveness. They had a considerable influence on following generations far beyond our borders, starting with Malcolm McLaren and his graphic designer Jaimie Reid who drew inspiration from them to create the aesthetic of the Punk movement #mai68 #may68 #beforeafter #PA1359 #paris

View all 183 comments

31 May 2018

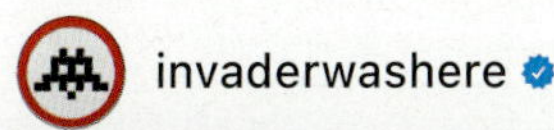

•••

   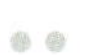 

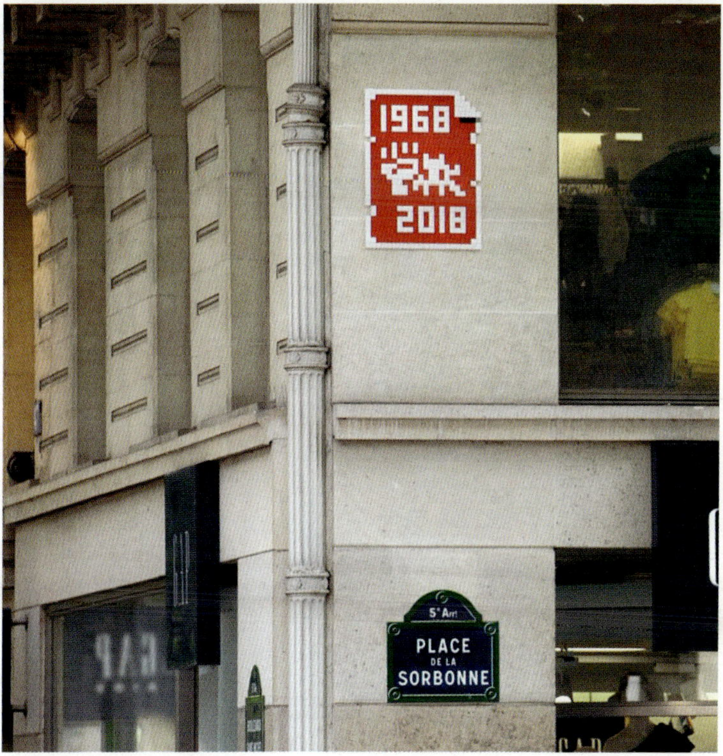

20 807 likes

invaderwashere Last day to make a May 68 anniversary tribute. I've always been a great admirer of May 68 posters. I love them for their simplicity, their unadorned designs, quickly executed in a single color, the urgency having dictated the process (screen printing), but also of course for their political effectiveness. They had a considerable influence on following generations far beyond our borders, starting with Malcolm McLaren and his graphic designer Jaimie Reid who drew inspiration from them to create the aesthetic of the Punk movement #mai68 #may68 #beforeafter #PA1359 #paris

View all 183 comments

31 May 2018

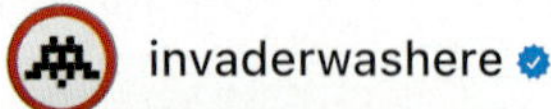

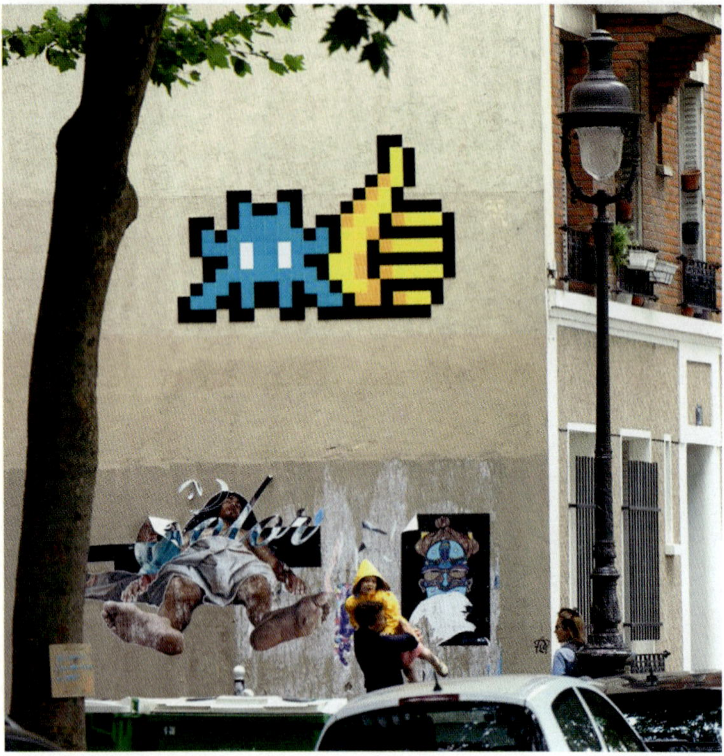

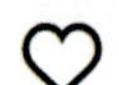   

18 402 likes

invaderwashere Tudo bom in Paris 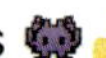

View all 106 comments

13 June 2018

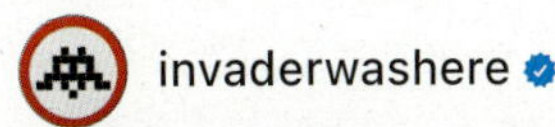

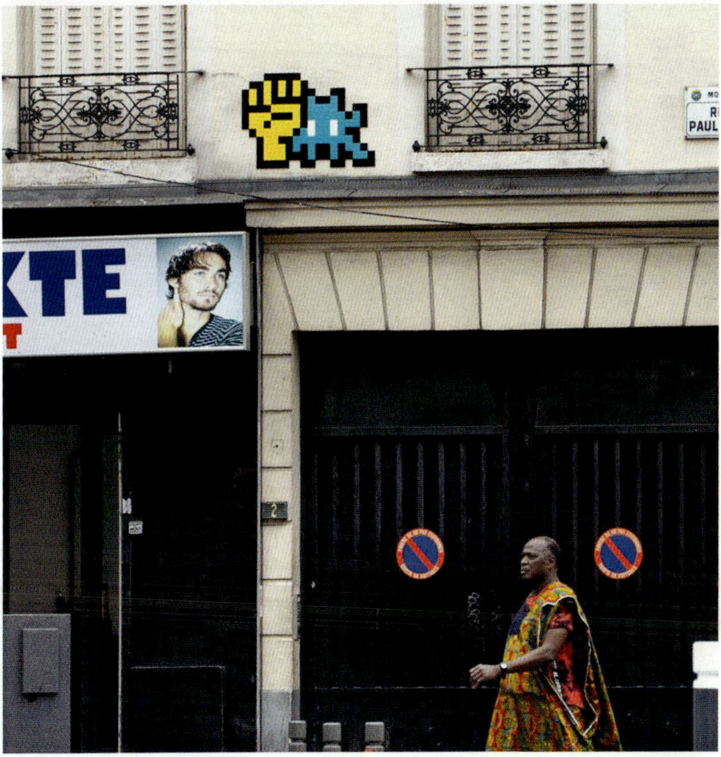

10 084 likes

invaderwashere Stand Up in Montreuil!

View all 43 comments

13 June 2018

invaderwashere

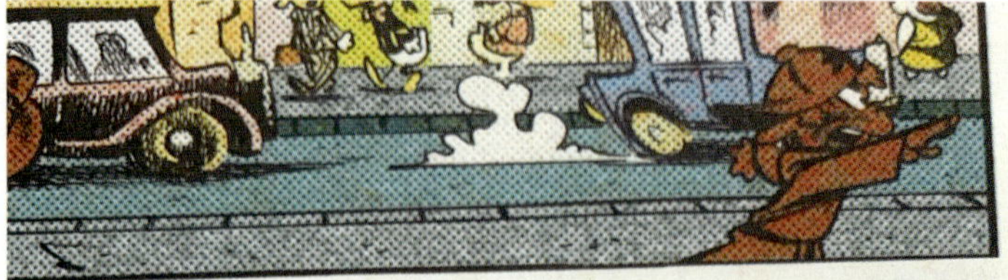

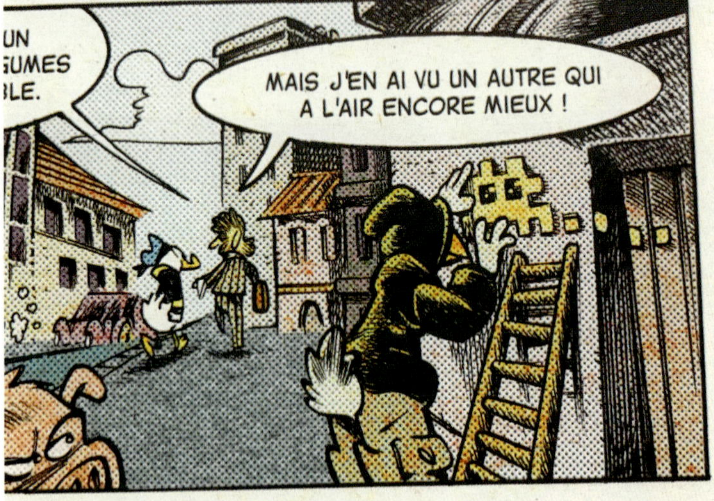

10 007 likes

invaderwashere Walt Disney Invasion! Thanx to #keramidas & #Lewistrondheim #glenat #comics 🎯

View all 153 comments

14 June 2018

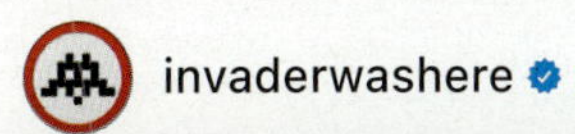

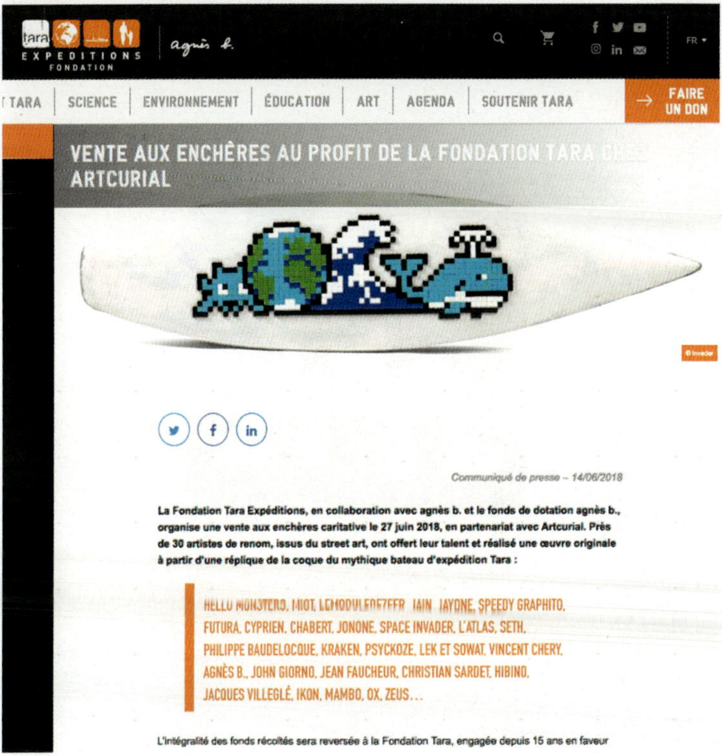

tara EXPEDITIONS FONDATION | agnès b.

FR

TARA | SCIENCE | ENVIRONNEMENT | ÉDUCATION | ART | AGENDA | SOUTENIR TARA | FAIRE UN DON

VENTE AUX ENCHÈRES AU PROFIT DE LA FONDATION TARA CHEZ ARTCURIAL

Communiqué de presse – 14/06/2018

La Fondation Tara Expéditions, en collaboration avec agnès b. et le fonds de dotation agnès b., organise une vente aux enchères caritative le 27 juin 2018, en partenariat avec Artcurial. Près de 30 artistes de renom, issus du street art, ont offert leur talent et réalisé une œuvre originale à partir d'une réplique de la coque du mythique bateau d'expédition Tara :

> HELLO MONSTERS, MIOT, LEMODULEDEZEER, IAIN, JAYONE, SPEEDY GRAPHITO, FUTURA, CYPRIEN, CHABERT, JONONE, SPACE INVADER, L'ATLAS, SETH, PHILIPPE BAUDELOCQUE, KRAKEN, PSYCKOZE, LEK ET SOWAT, VINCENT CHERY, AGNÈS B., JOHN GIORNO, JEAN FAUCHEUR, CHRISTIAN SARDET, HIBINO, JACQUES VILLEGLÉ, IKON, MAMBO, OX, ZEUS…

L'intégralité des fonds récoltés sera reversée à la Fondation Tara, engagée depuis 15 ans en faveur

9173 likes

invaderwashere Mosaic on the replica of the hull of the exploration ship Tara. All the benefice will be donated to @taraexpeditions a foundation for the preservation of the oceans. #charityauction #june27 @artcurial__

View all 80 comments

22 June 2018

invaderwashere 

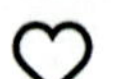   

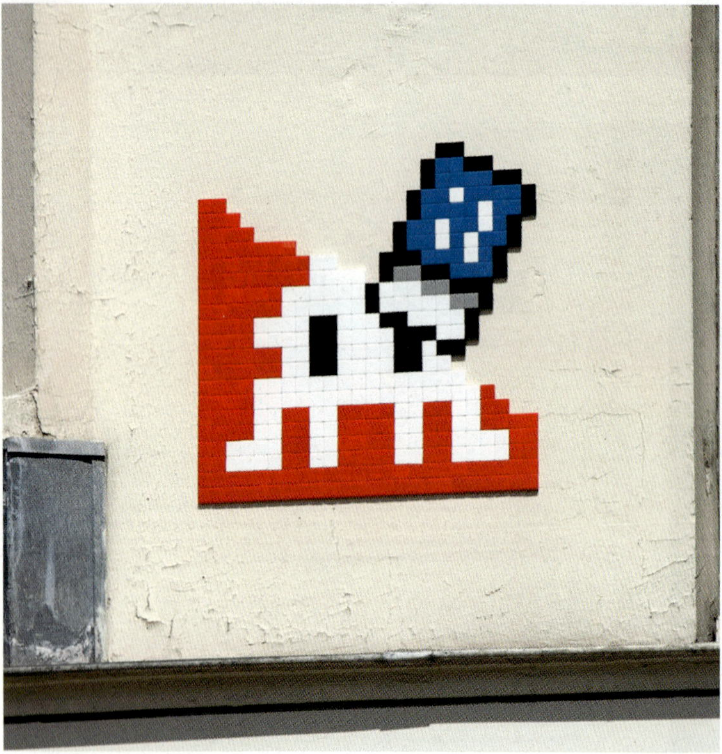

19 801 likes

invaderwashere PA_1366 the latest 👾

View all 150 comments

29 June 2018

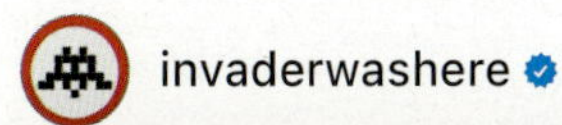

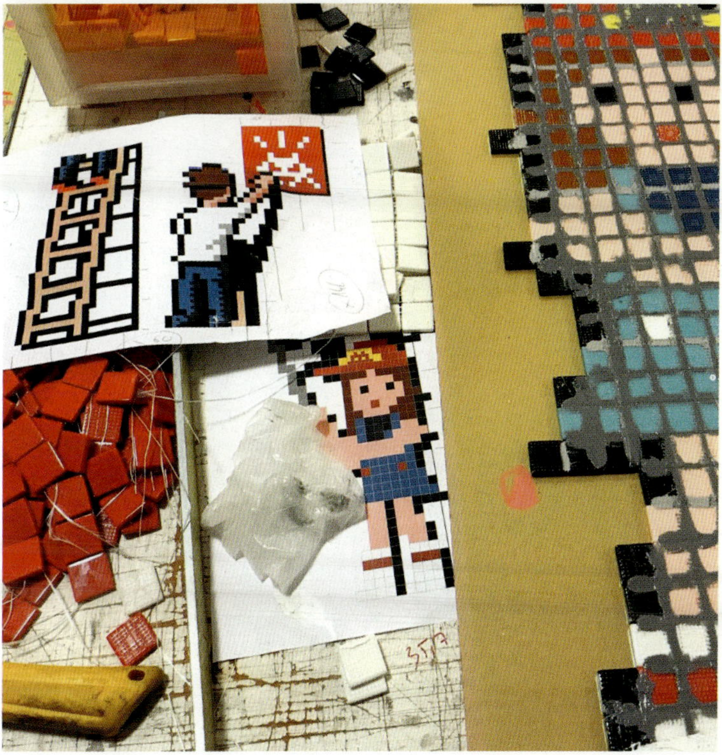

   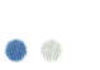 

12 396 likes

invaderwashere Studio details

View all 72 comments

8 July 2018

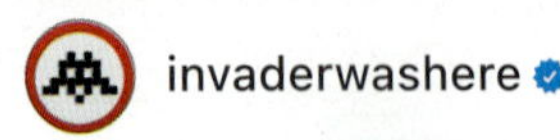

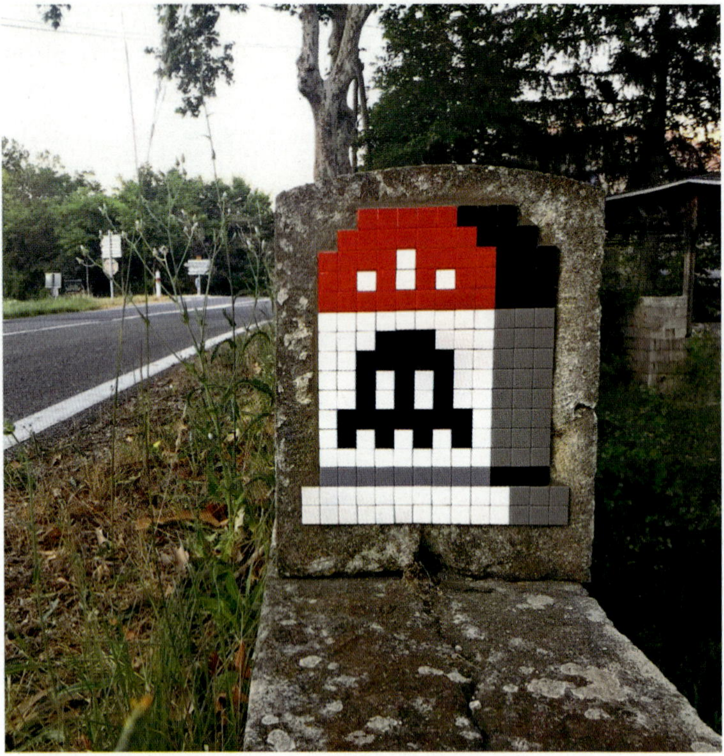

22 070 likes

invaderwashere Somewhere on the road #France #14juillet #happyholidays 🇫🇷 👾 🎇

View all 154 comments

14 July 2018

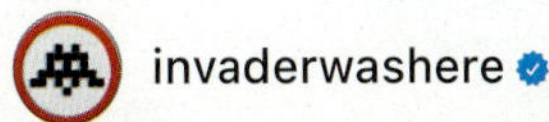

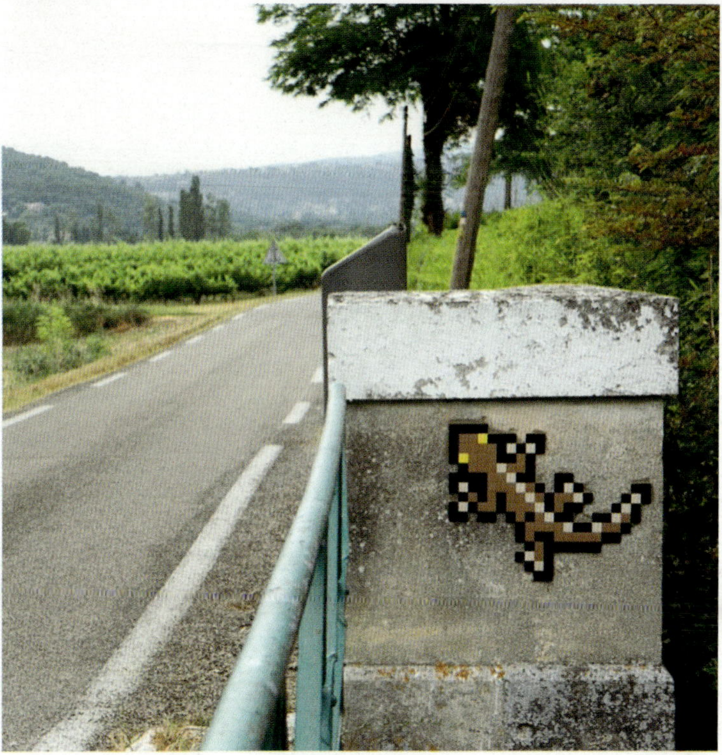

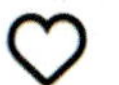 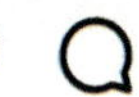  

17 309 likes

invaderwashere Vines & 🦎 LBR_03 #luberon #provence

View all 123 comments

17 July 2018

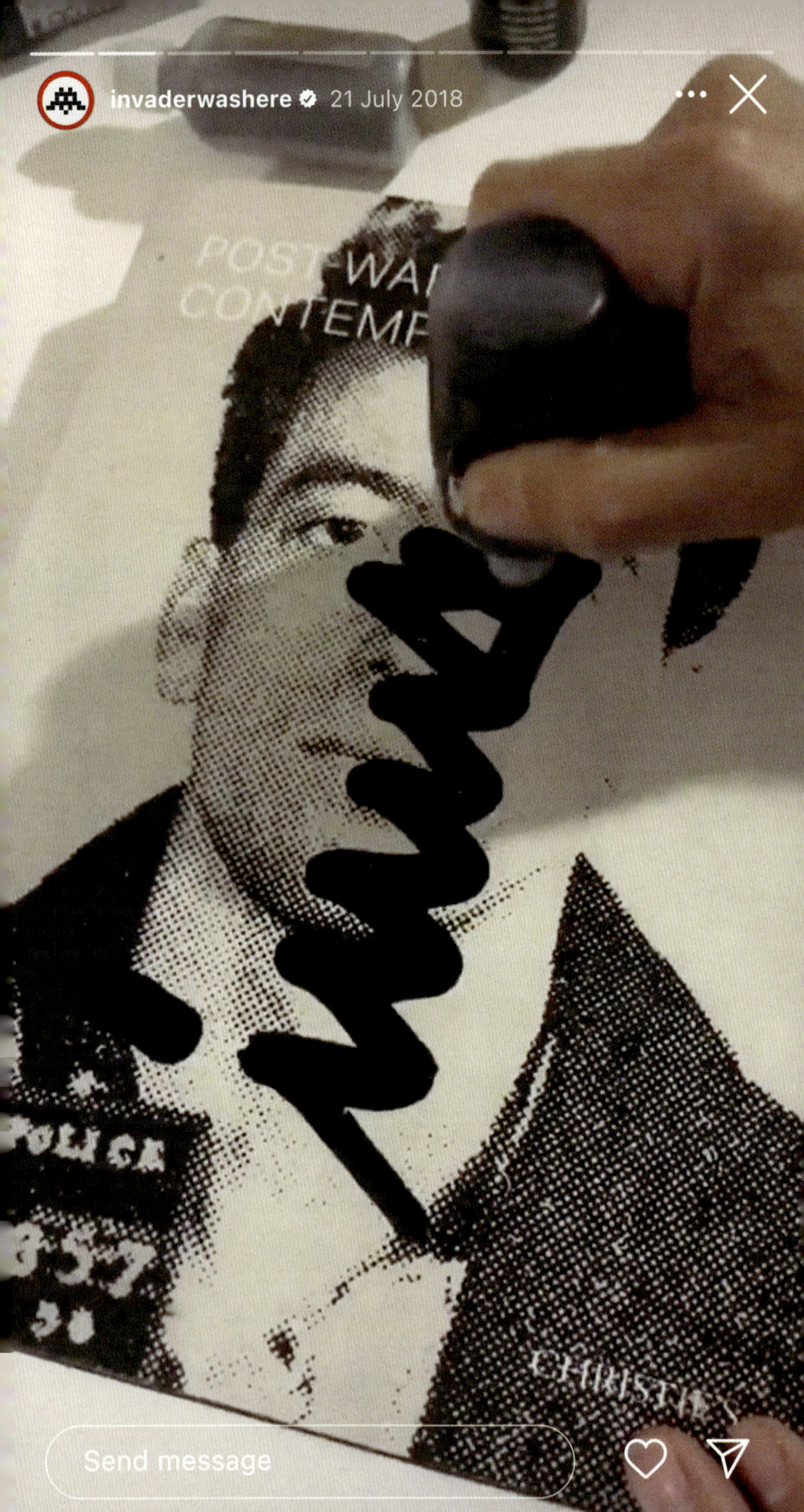
invaderwashere
21 July 2018
Send message

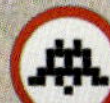

invaderwashere 21 July 2018

POST-WAR AND CONTEMPORARY

Send message

invaderwashere

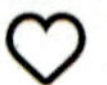  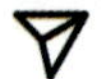 

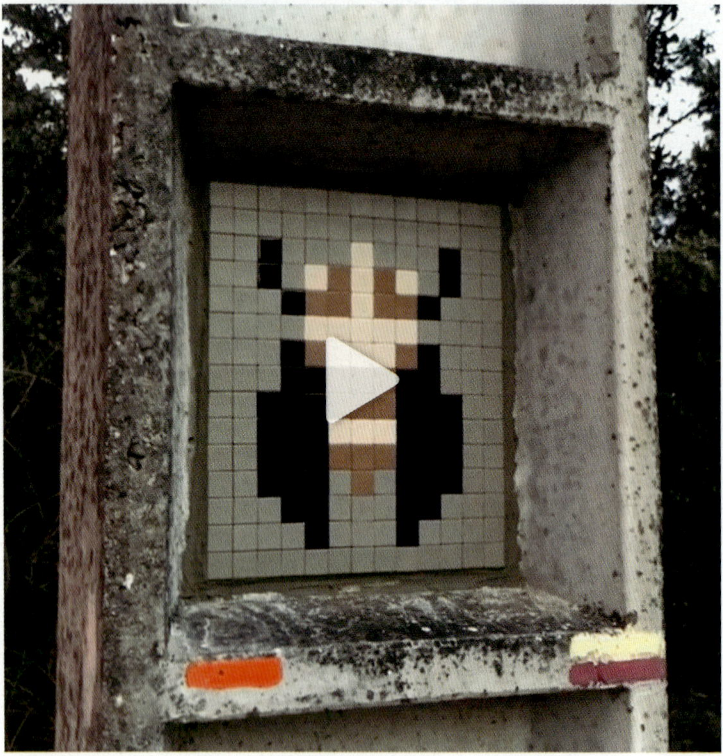

32 841 views

invaderwashere the evening song of the cicadas ♪♪

View all 83 comments

27 July 2018

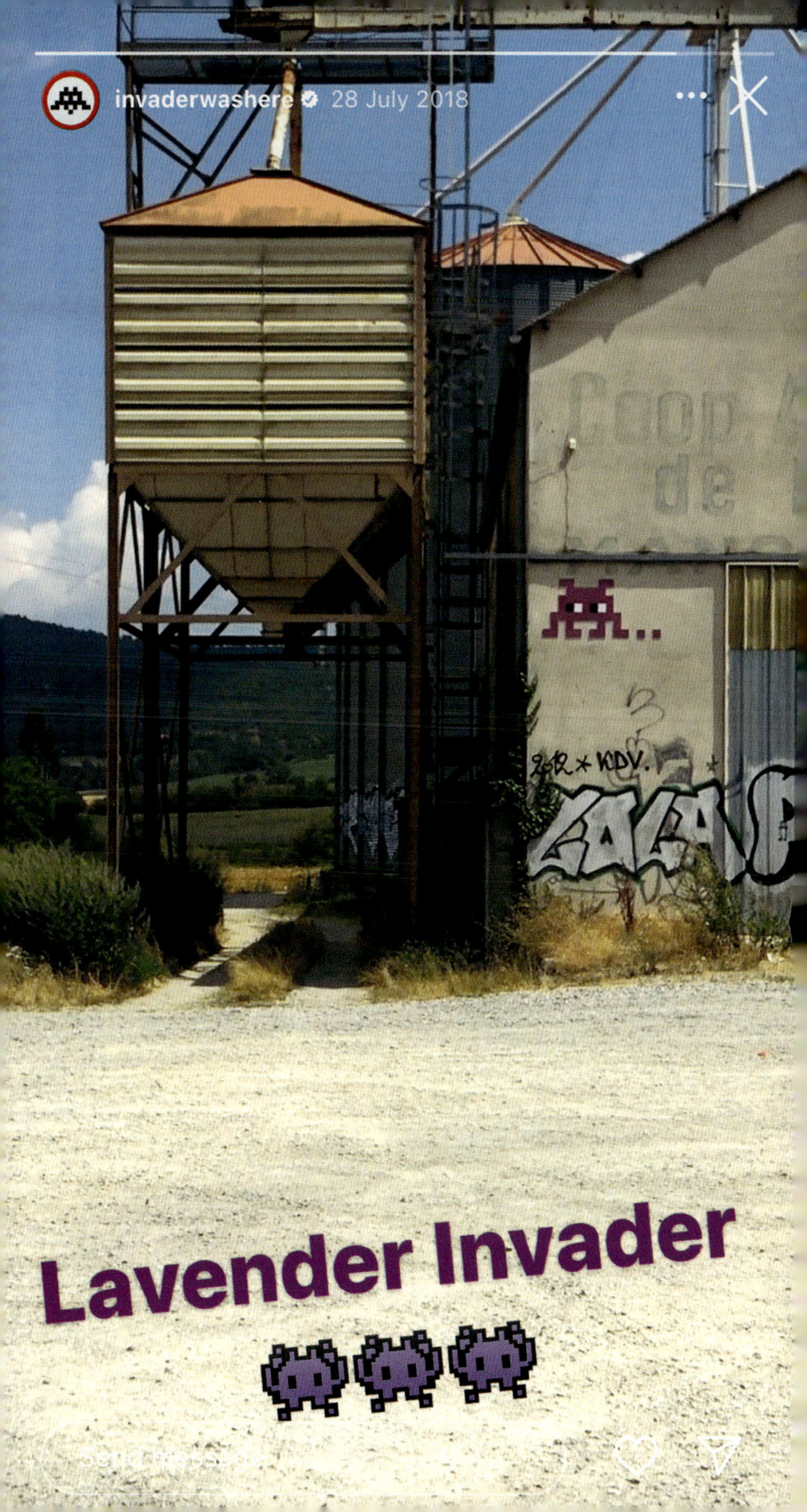

invaderwashere 28 July 2018

Lavender Invader

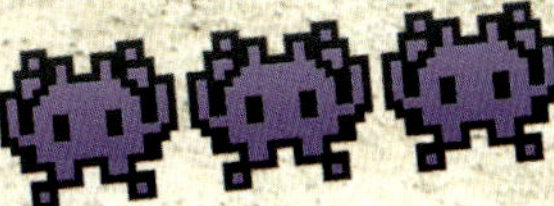

Send message

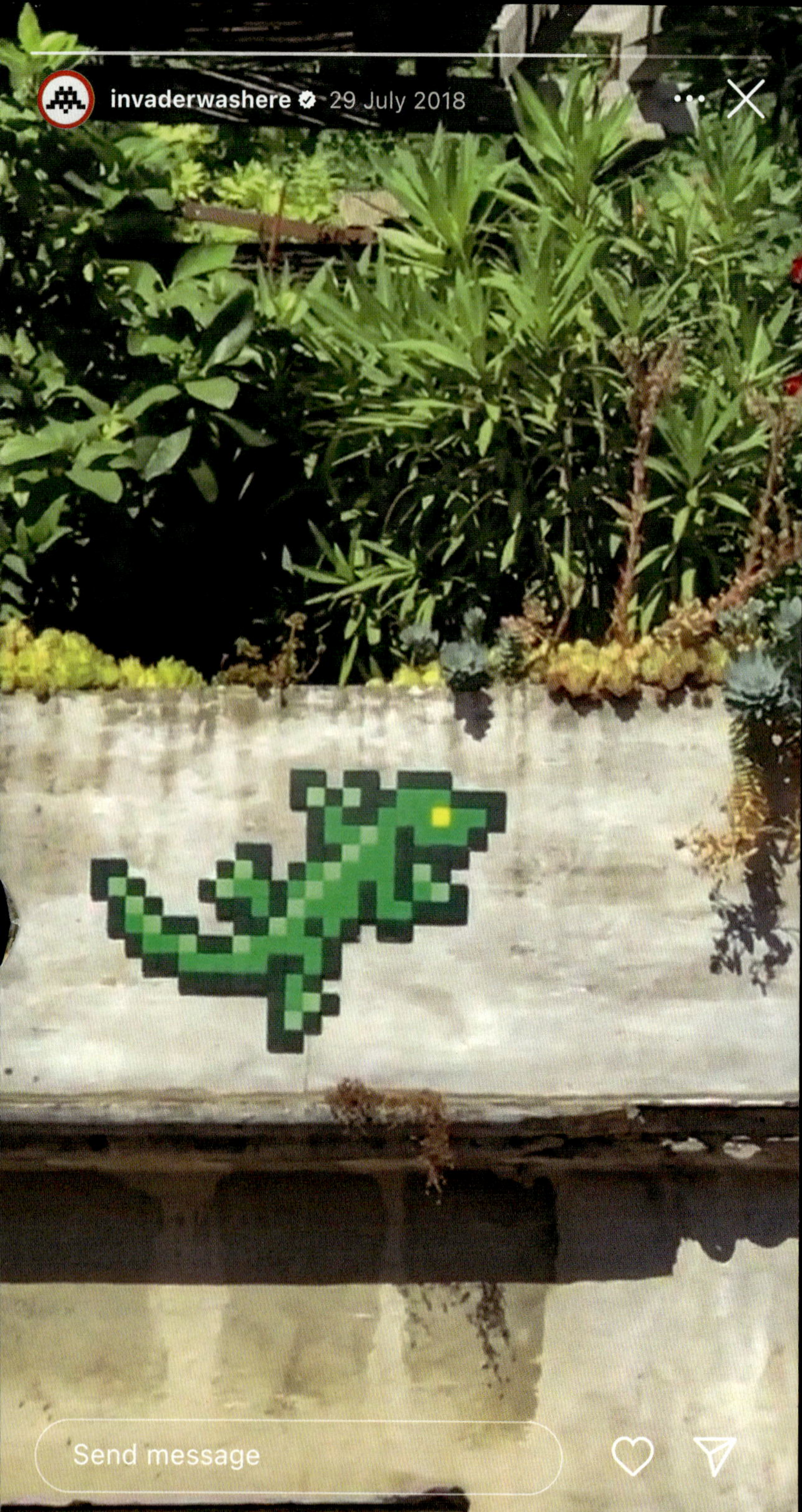
invaderwashere 29 July 2018
Send message

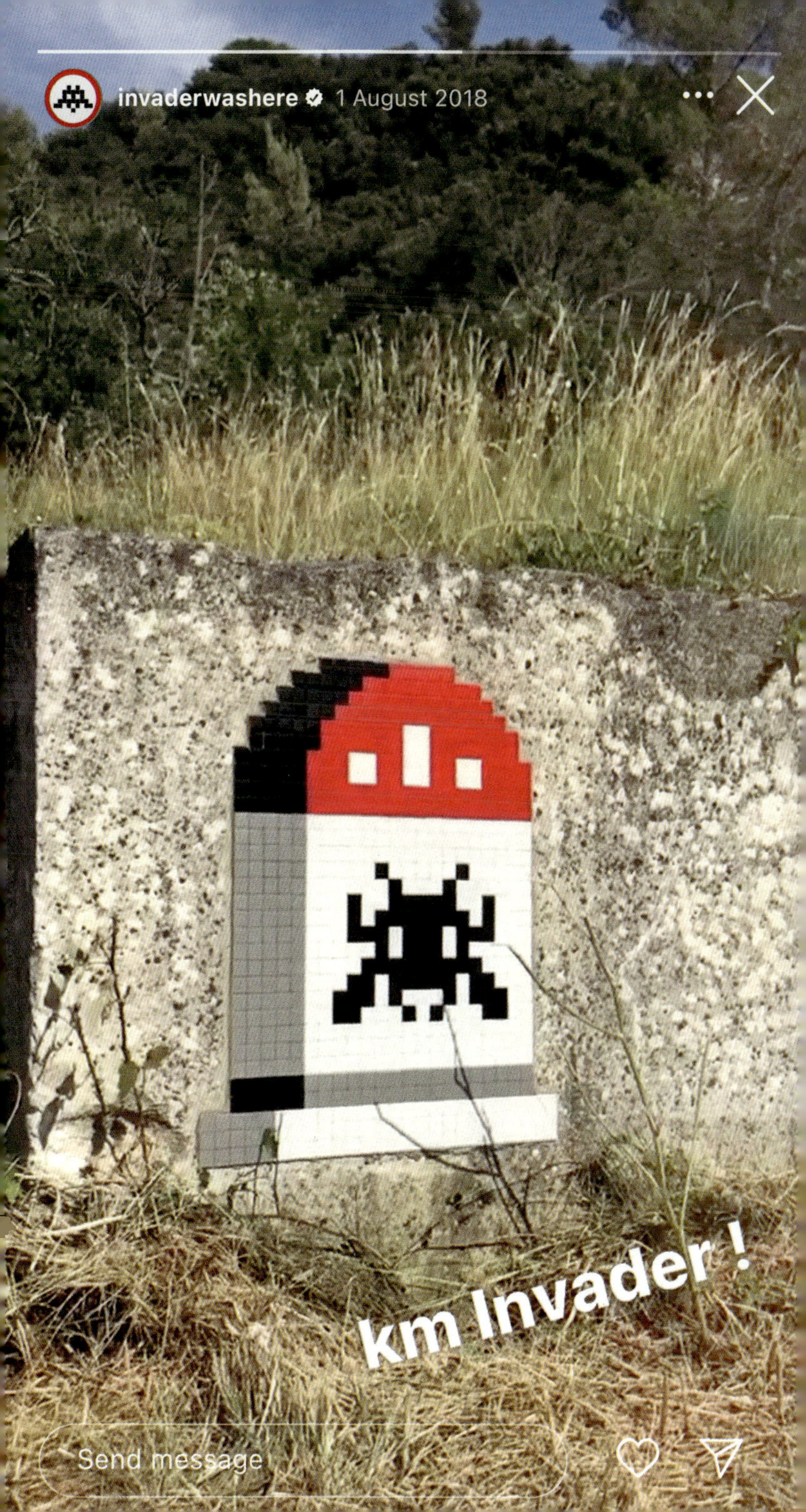
invaderwashere
1 August 2018
km Invader !
Send message

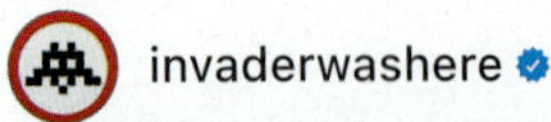

invaderwashere

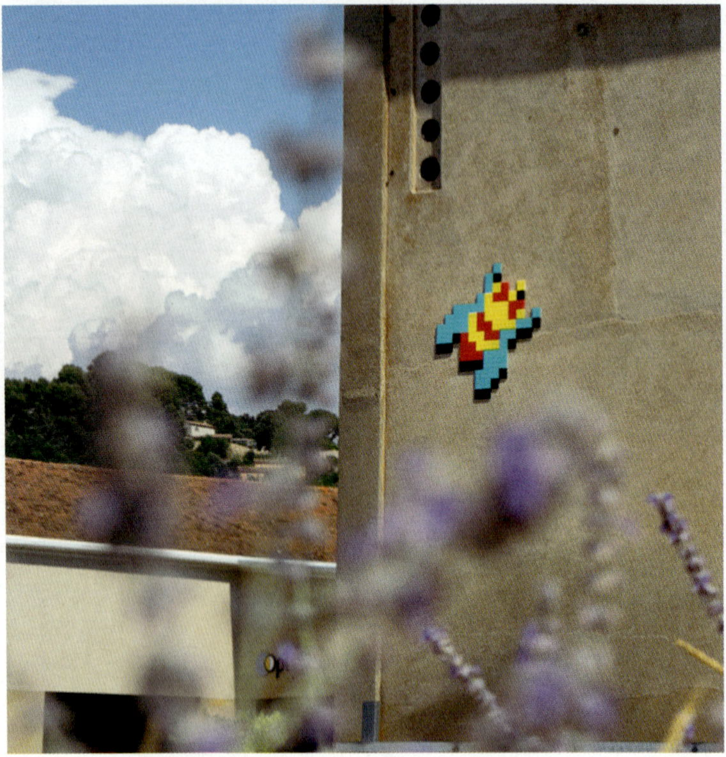

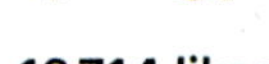

13 714 likes

invaderwashere LBR_05 #luberon #provence #galaga

View all 65 comments

11 August 2018

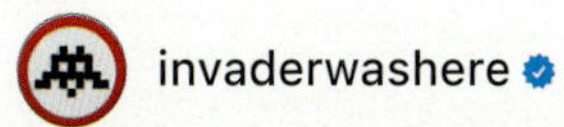

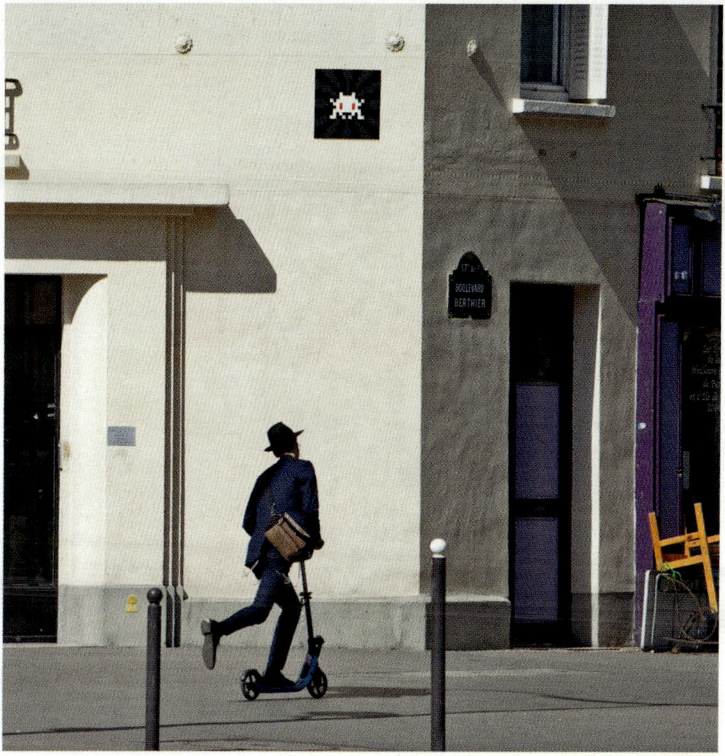

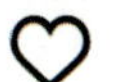   

17 438 likes

invaderwashere PA_1367 Just landed... #paris

View all 140 comments

12 August 2018

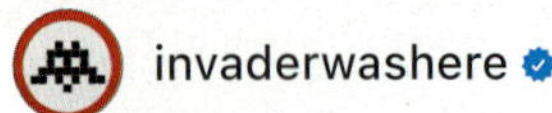

2.1 INVASION LOS ANGELES
UPDATED EDITION / 1999-2018

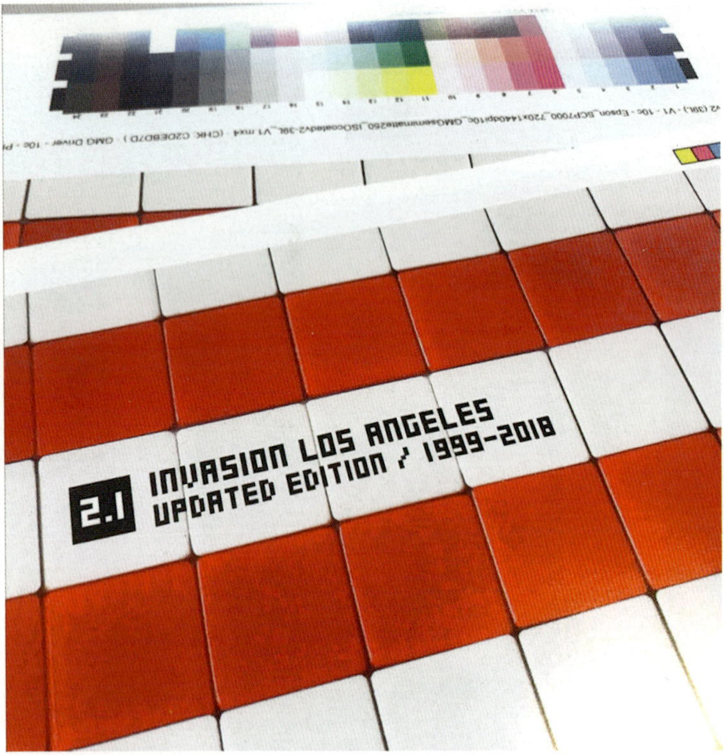

7 484 likes

invaderwashere I have been working for months on the new edition of INVASION LOS ANGELES. 📚 Release date: end of October #newbook #invasionguide #LA #cover #colorproof #2ndedition #rebuildfromscratch

View all 153 comments

4 September 2018

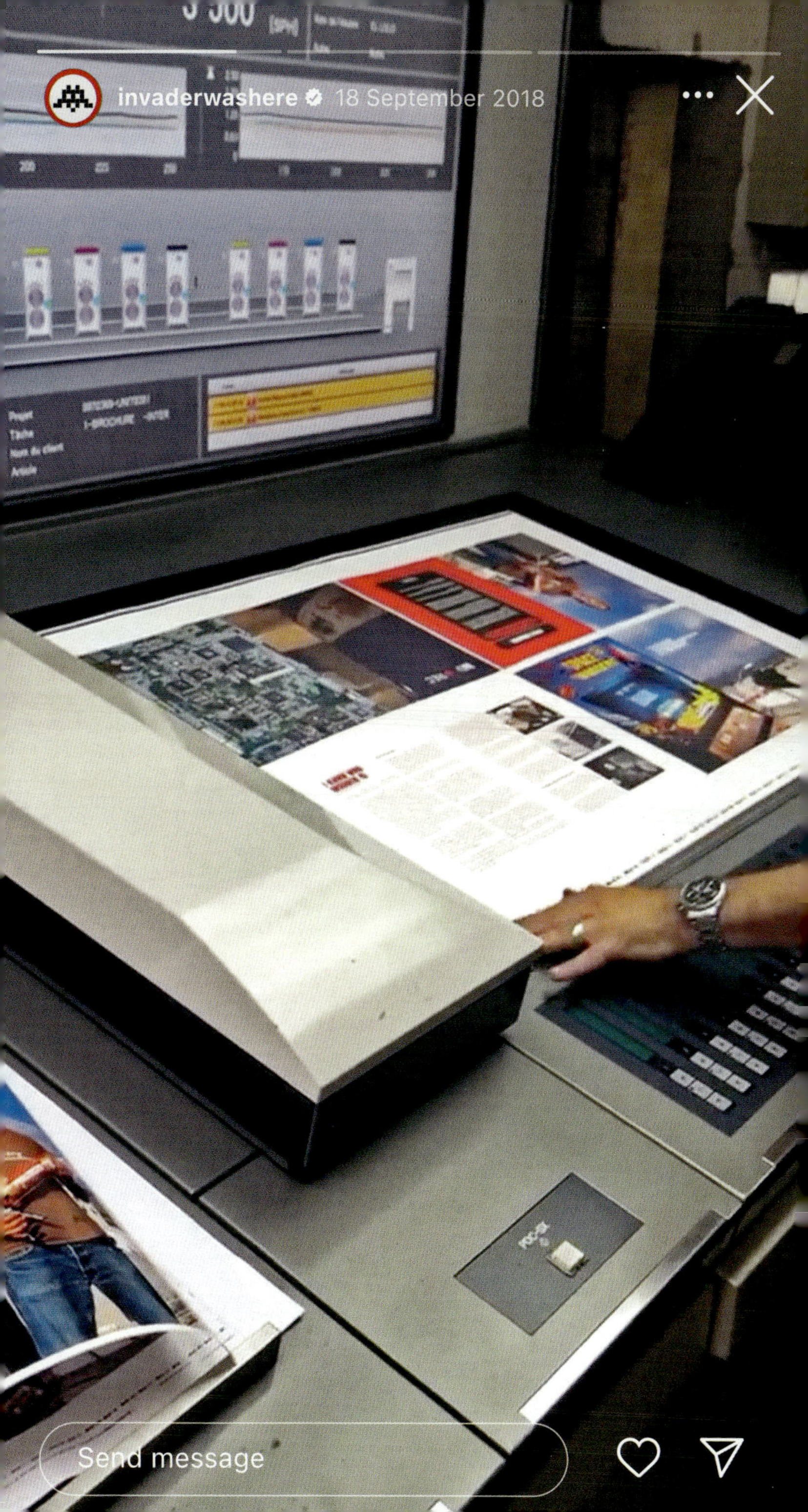
invaderwashere
18 September 2018
Send message

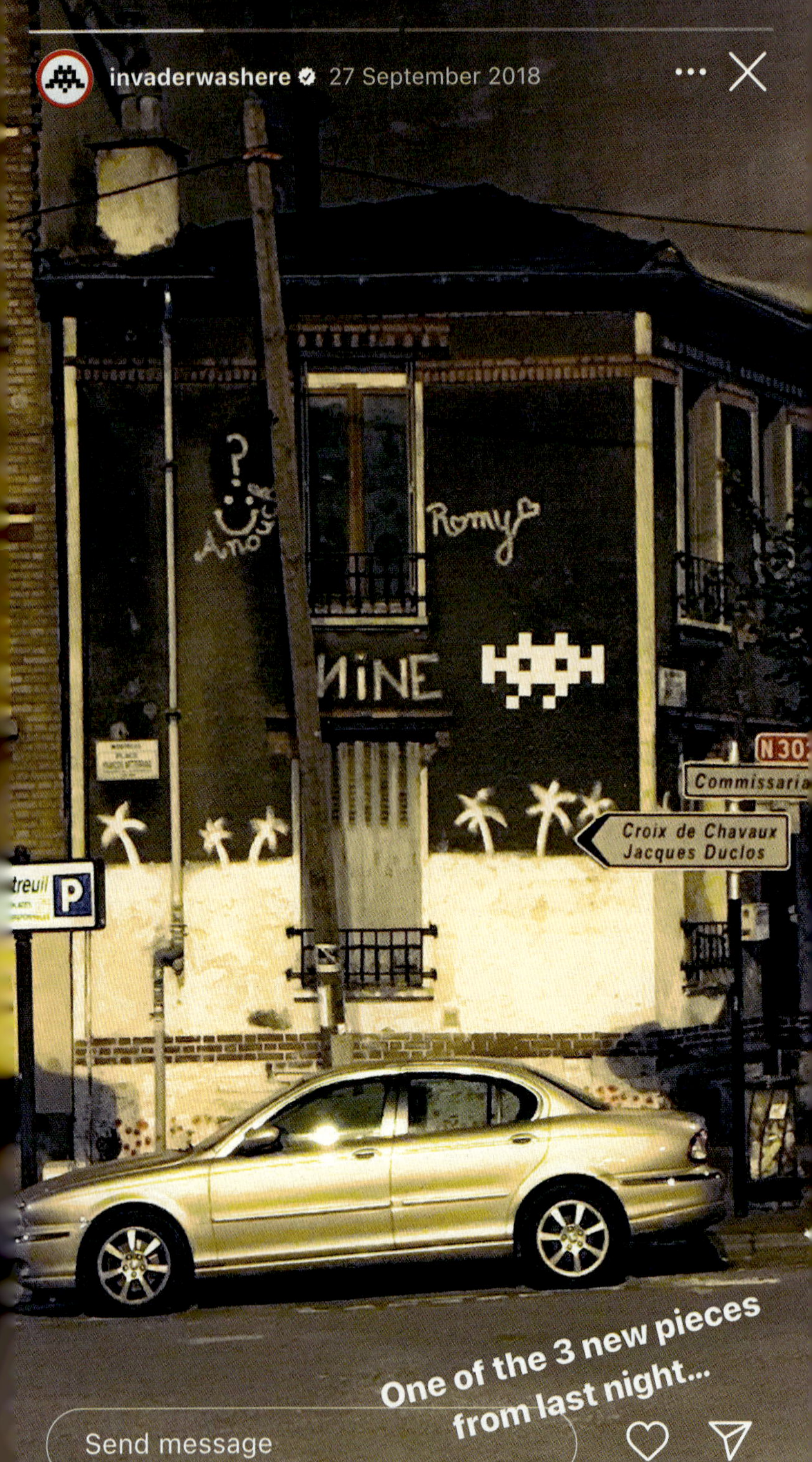
invaderwashere 27 September 2018
Romy
MINE
N 30
Commissaria
Croix de Chavaux
Jacques Duclos
treuil
P
One of the 3 new pieces
from last night...
Send message

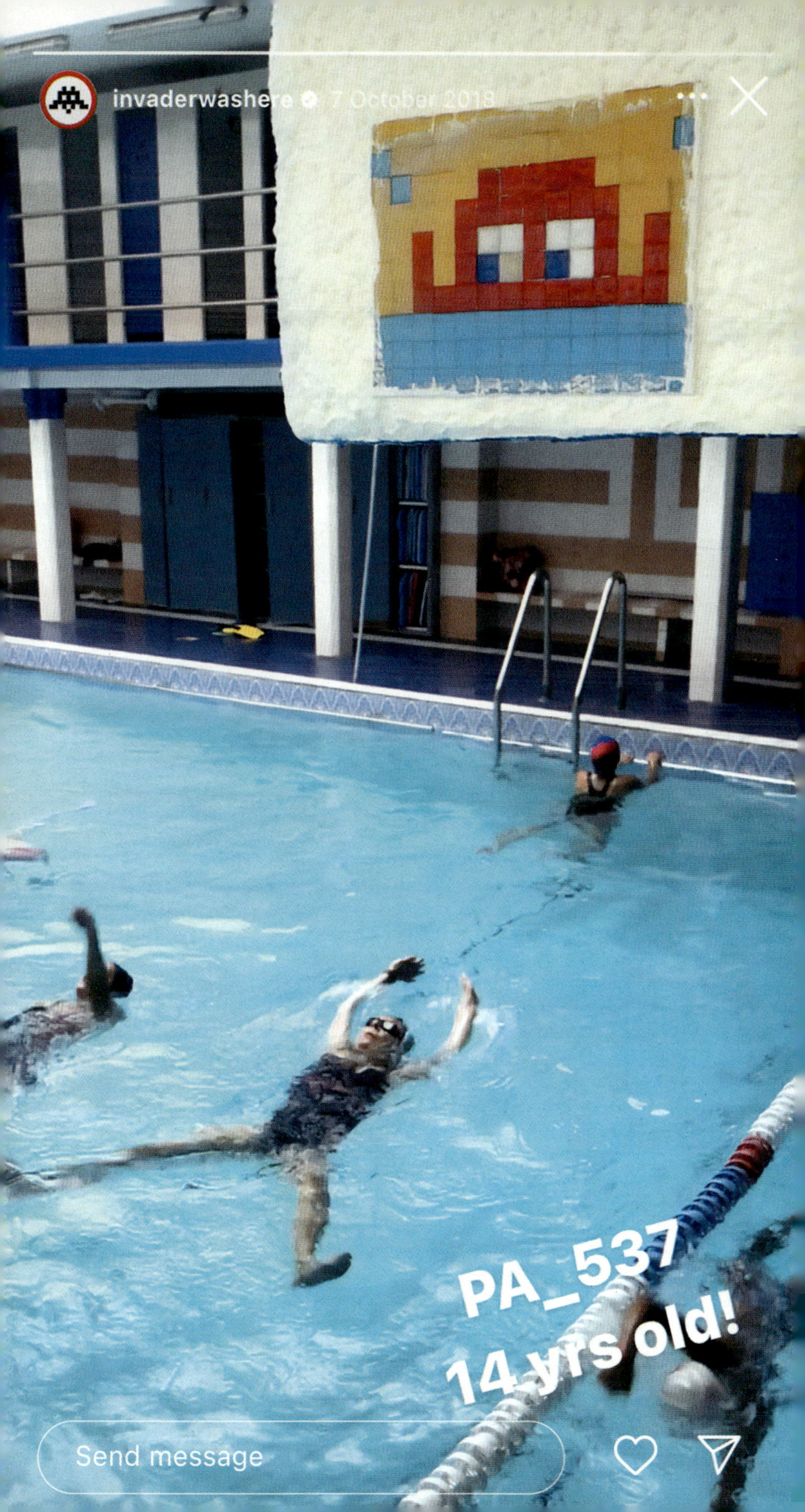
invaderwashere
7 October 2018
PA_537
14 yrs old!
Send message

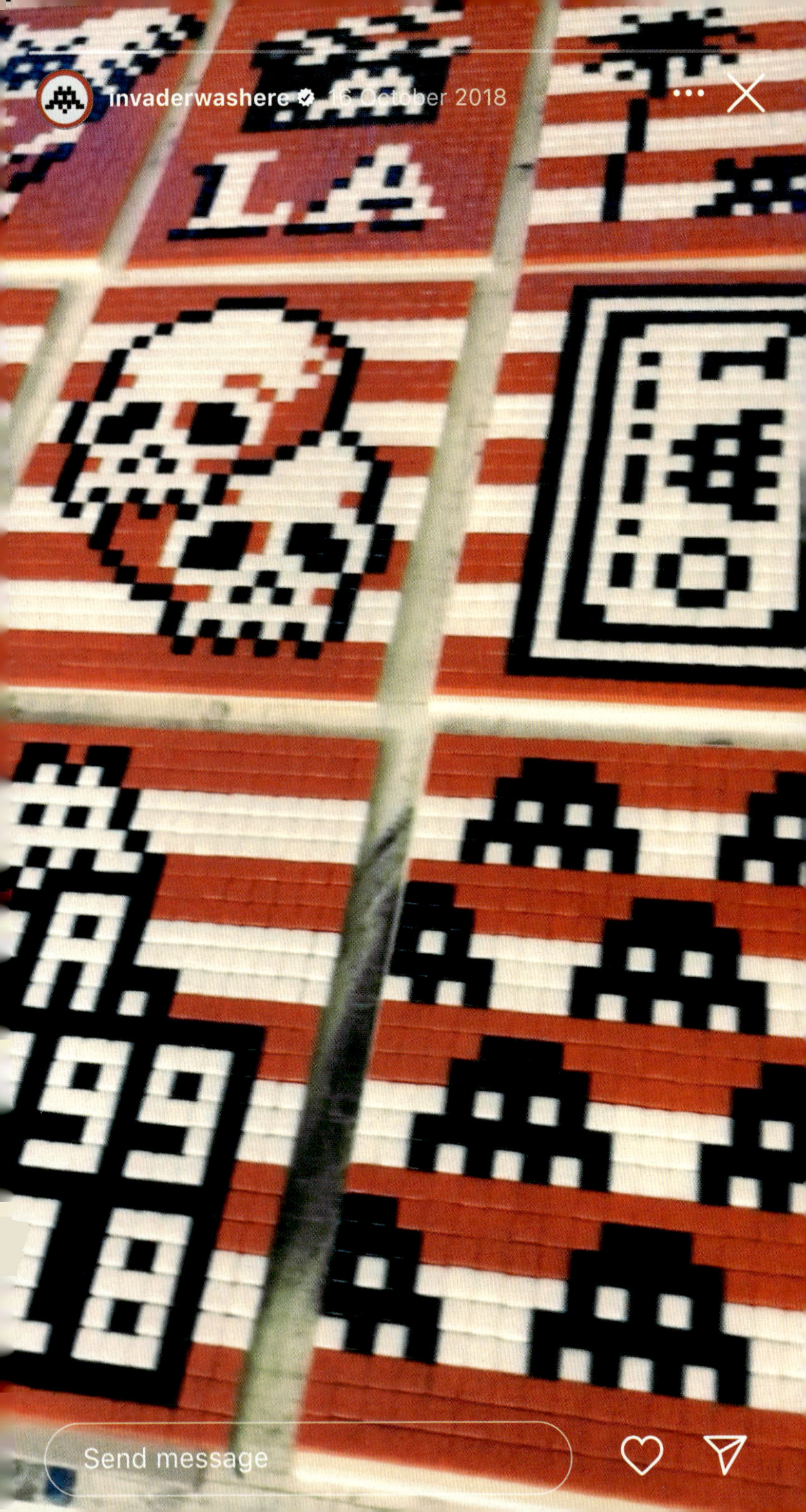
invaderwashere
16 October 2018
L.A
Send message

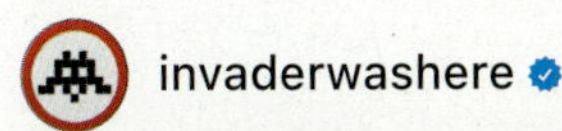

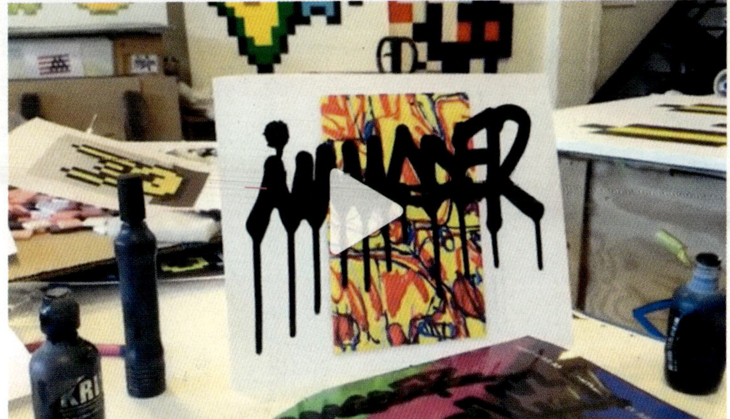

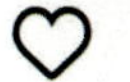  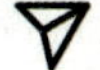 

151 891 views

invaderwashere Save the date... #teaser #T-1month #intothewhitecube @oti.official L.A. #losangeles Music: @gorillaz

View all 295 comments

17 October 2018

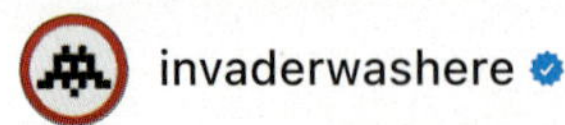

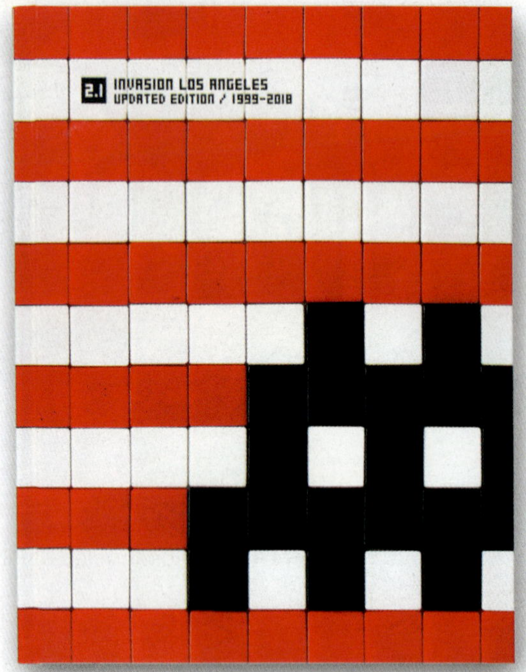

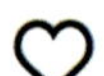    

12 149 likes

invaderwashere Invasion Los Angeles 2.1 / 1999-2018 / 304 pages / Out today in good bookstores in France and will be available next month on the Spaceshop and at @oti.official L.A. #invasionguide #losangeles

View all 163 comments

22 October 2018

invaderwashere

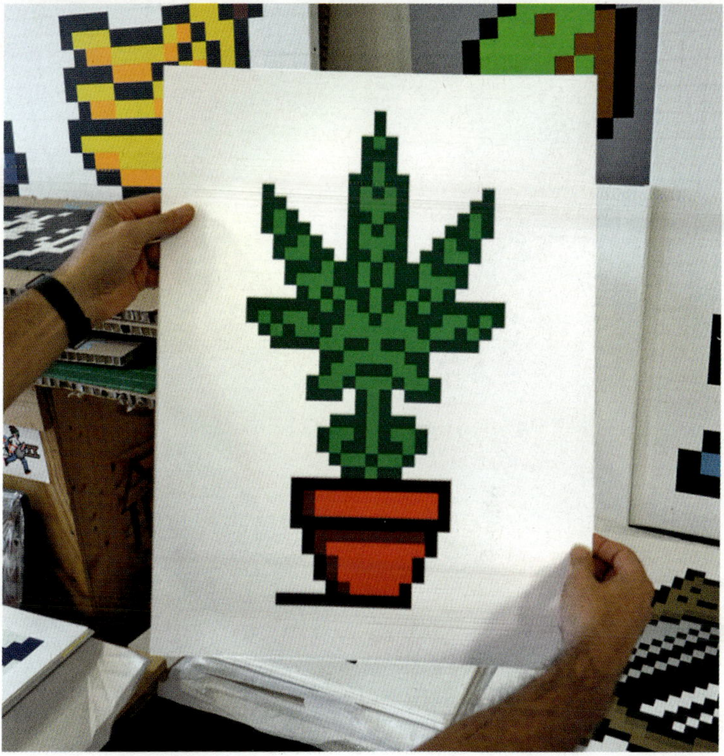

17843 likes

invaderwashere HOLLYWEED prints will be available @gareythethird @complexcon this weekend in L.A.

View all 327 comments

31 October 2018

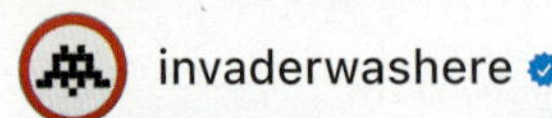

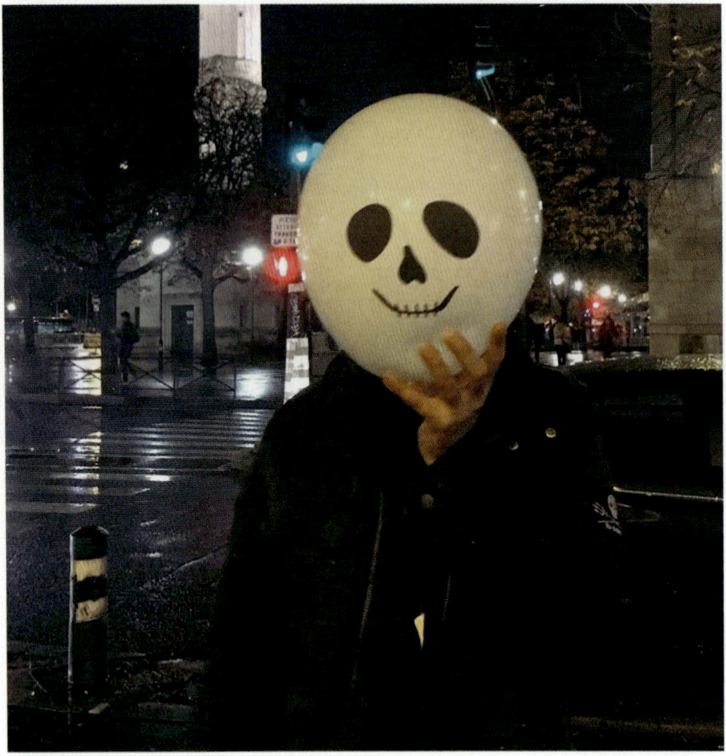

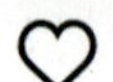   

8 073 likes

invaderwashere Street portrait #happyhalloween 

View all 53 comments

31 October 2018

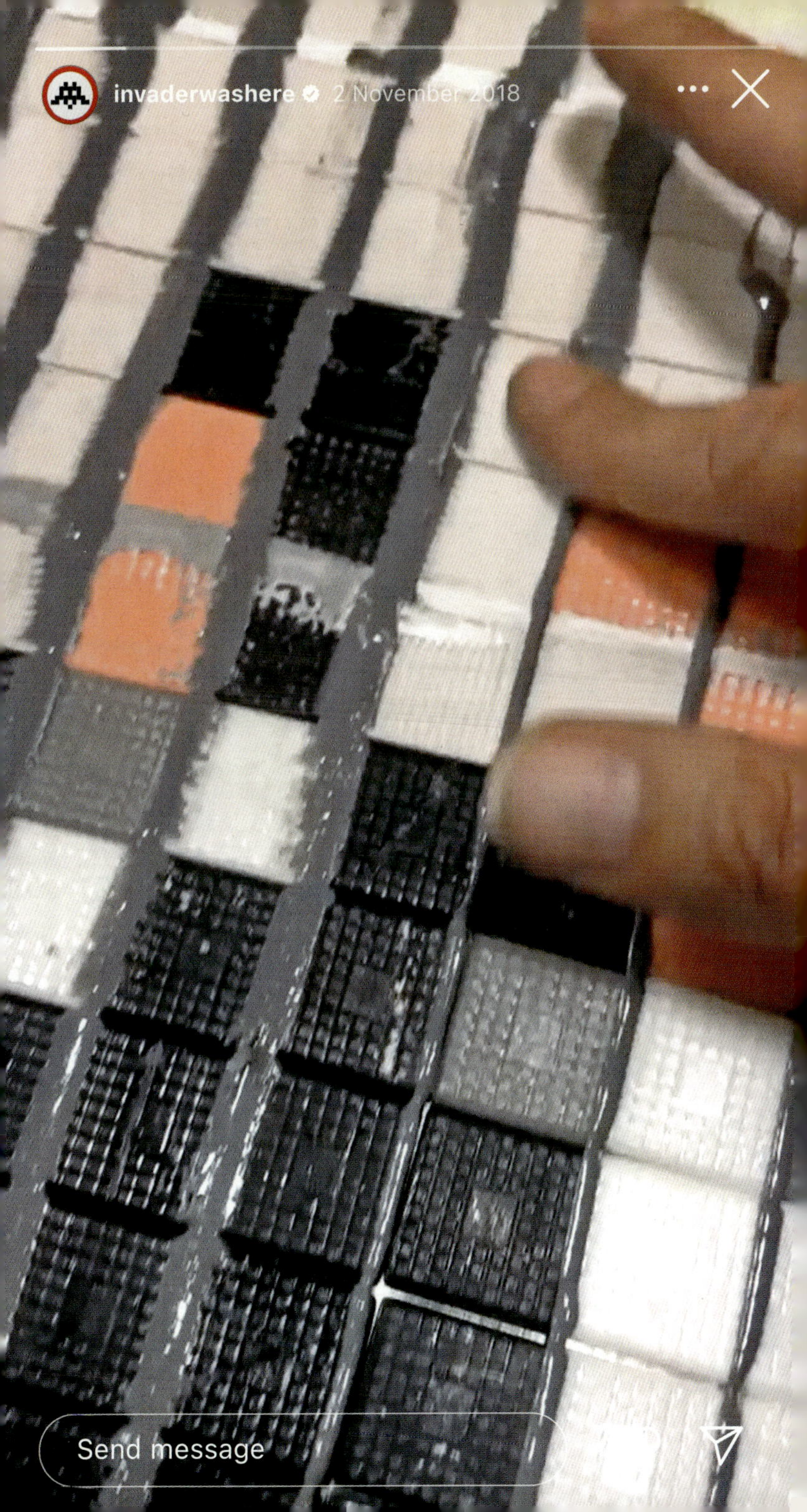
invaderwashere 2 November 2018
Send message

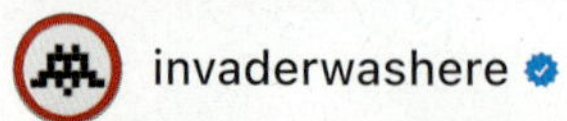

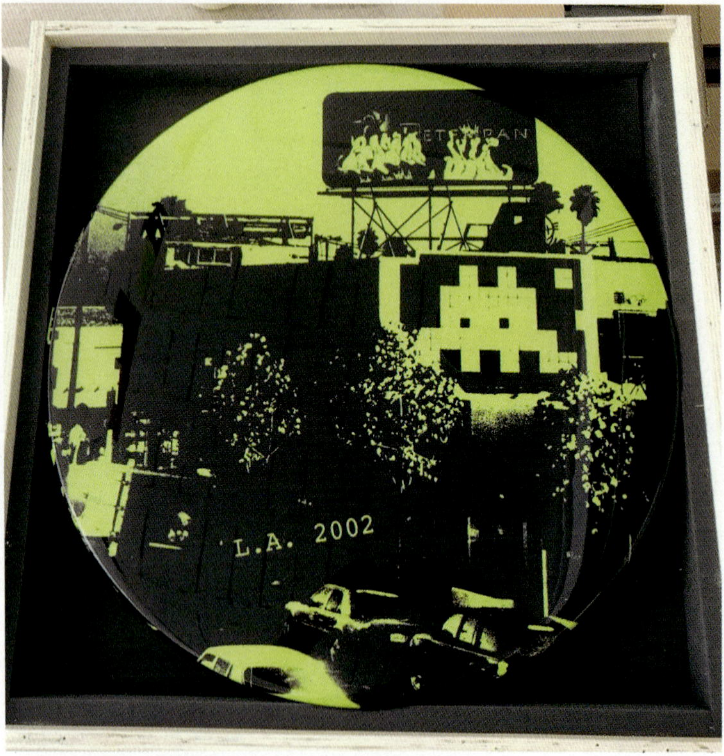

5623 likes

invaderwashere Large scale pin button

View all 21 comments

2 November 2018

invaderwashere 

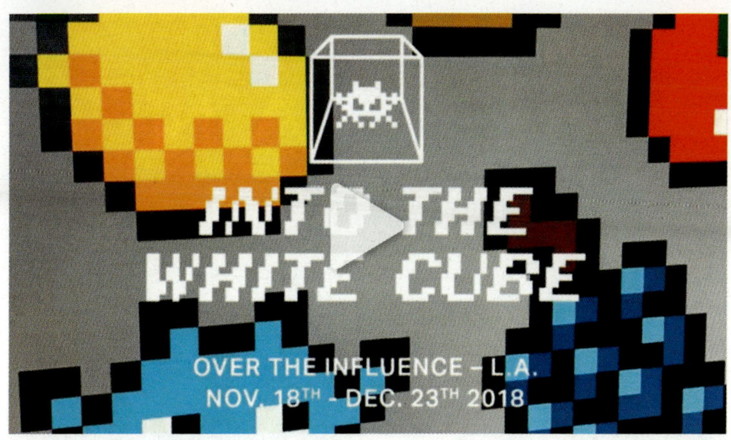

31 374 views

invaderwashere Into the white cube #teaser #savethedate #intothewhitecube @oti.official L.A. Nov 18 > Dec 23 2018 / music @gorillaz

View all 100 comments

4 November 2018

invaderwashere 

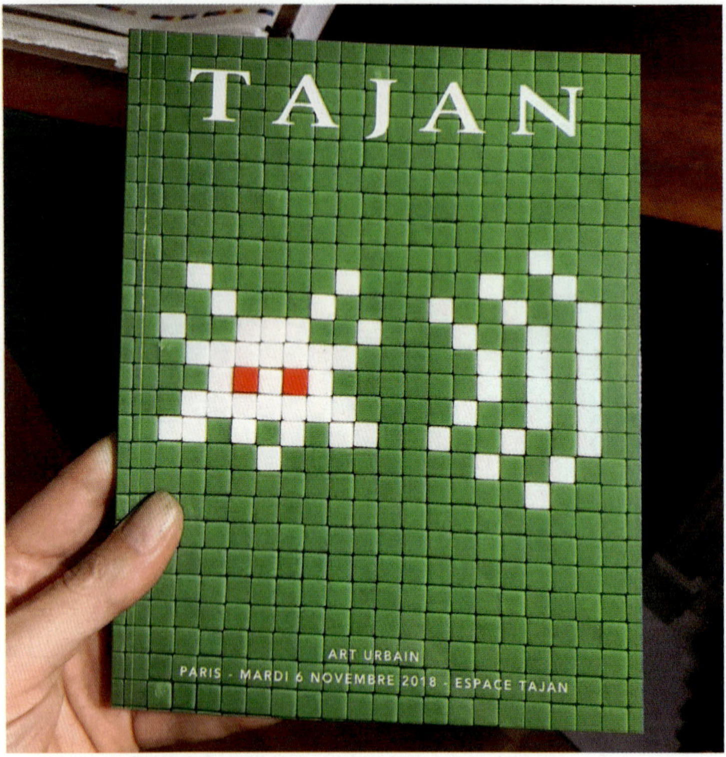

11028 likes

invaderwashere Nice cover! #auctioncatalog @tajan_auction #artworldinvasion

View all 57 comments

6 November 2018

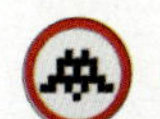 invaderwashere

 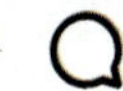  

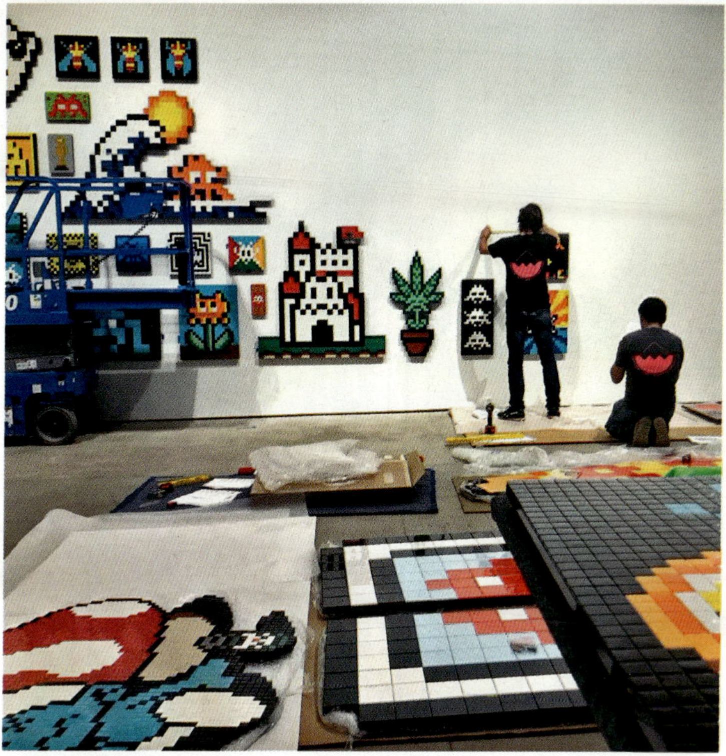

27 401 likes

invaderwashere Setting up « Into the White Cube » #exhibition @oti.official #losangeles #intothewhitecube T-3 days!!!

View all 364 comments

15 November 2018

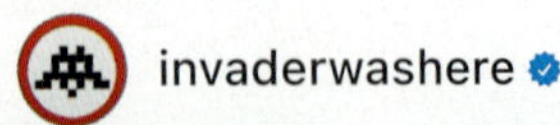

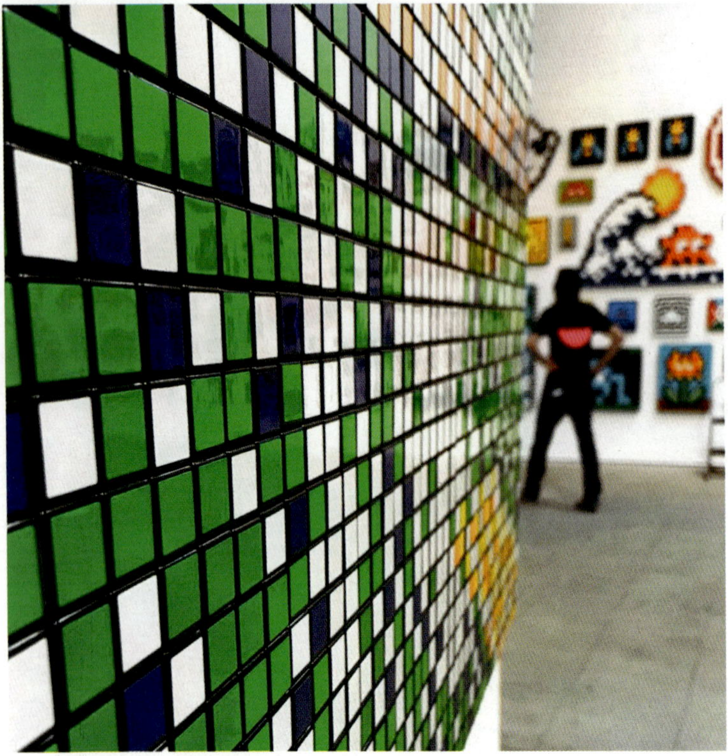

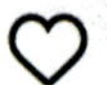   

6 848 likes

invaderwashere Setting up « Into the White Cube » #exhibition @oti.official #otila #losangeles T-3 days!!!

View all 45 comments

15 November 2018

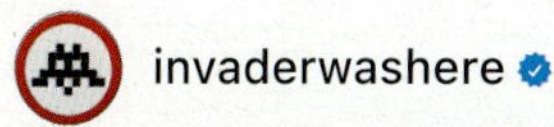

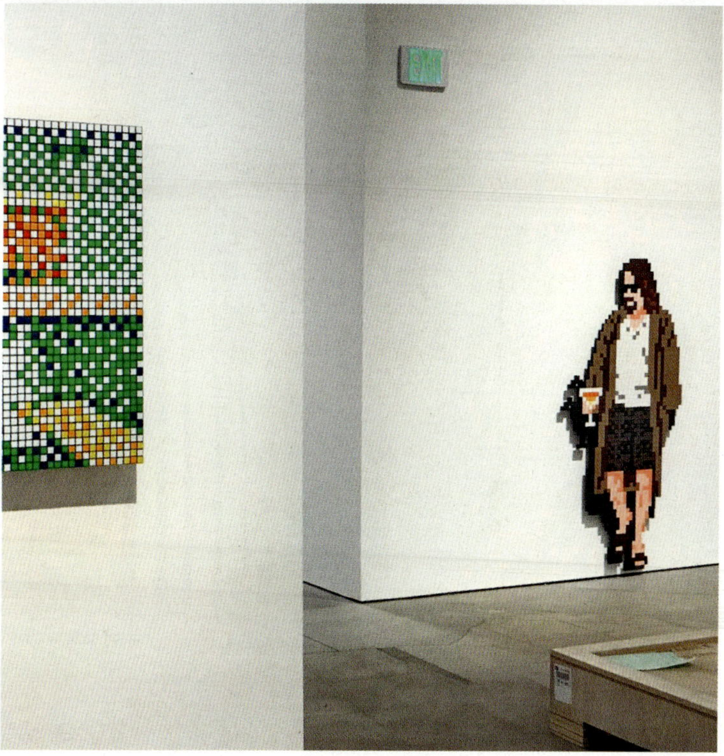

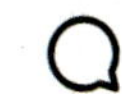

33 279 likes

invaderwashere Setting up « Into the White Cube » #exhibition @oti.official #otila #losangeles T-2 days!!!

View all 394 comments

15 November 2018

invaderwashere

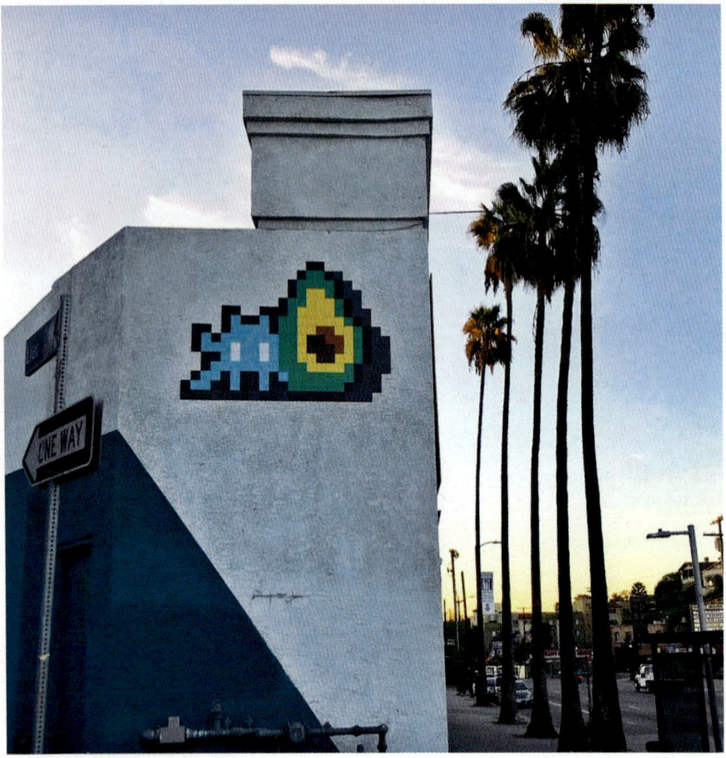

15 987 likes

invaderwashere Good Morning L.A. #LA202 #justdone #wave11 #sunsetblvd #invaderwashere

View all 153 comments

15 November 2018

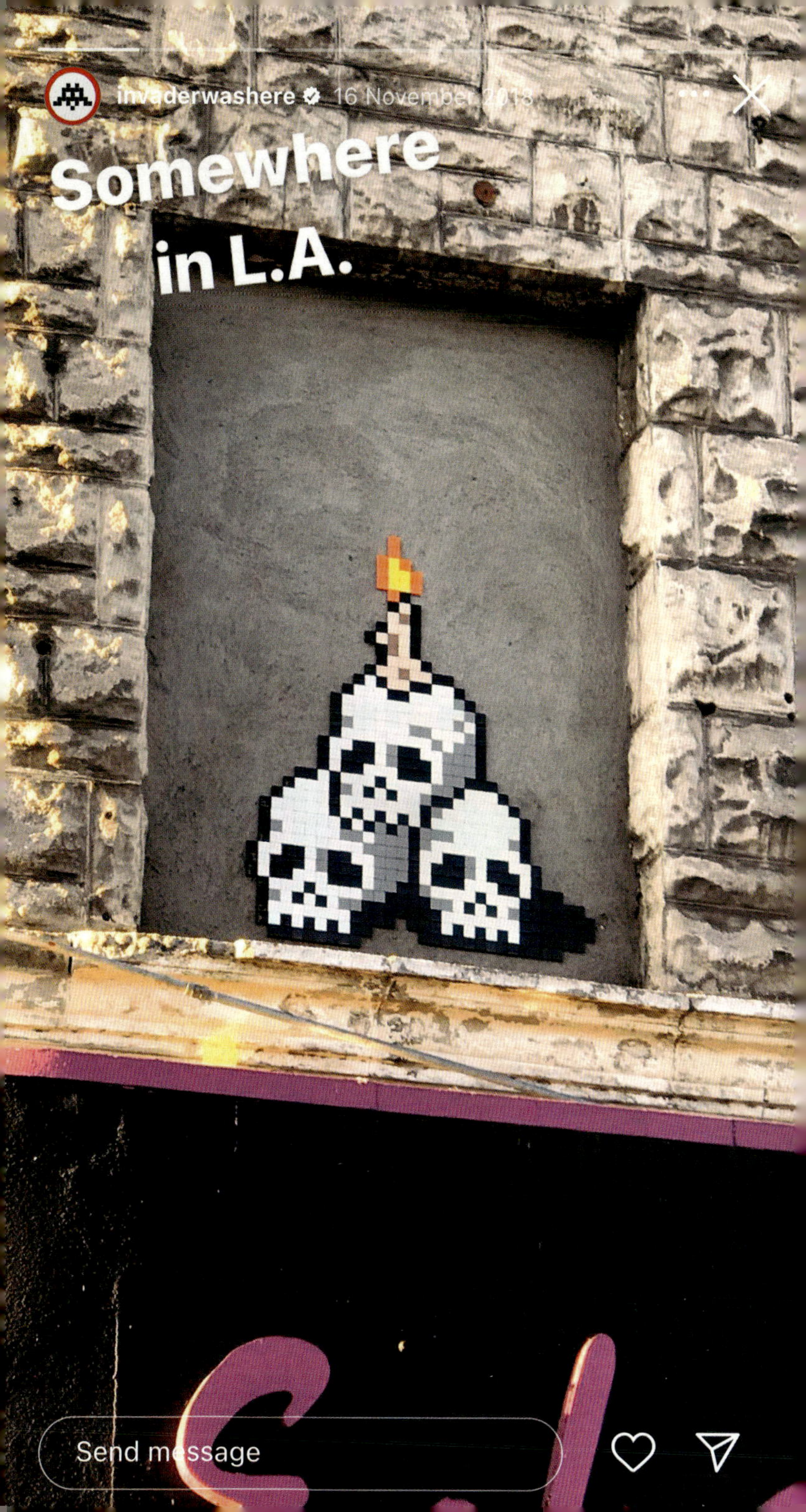

invaderwashere 16 November 2018

Somewhere in L.A.

Send message

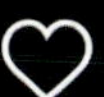

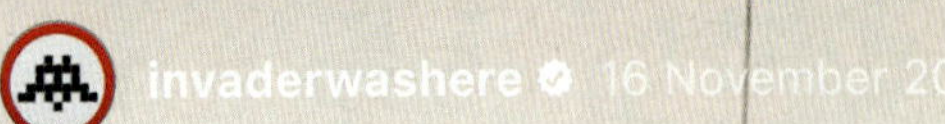

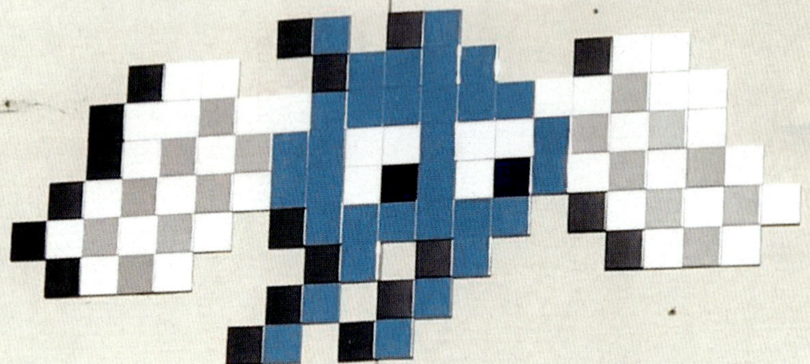

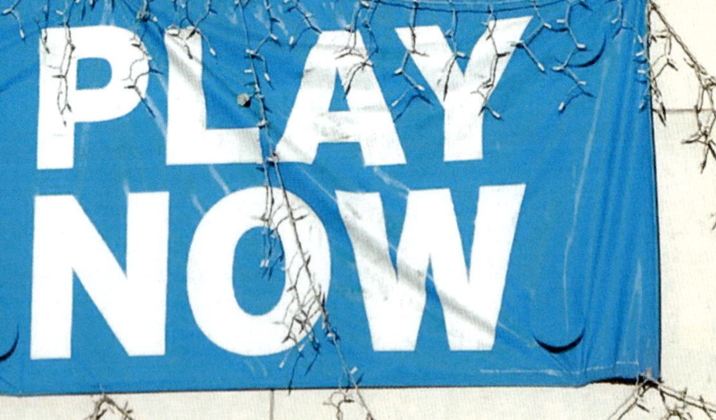

Send message

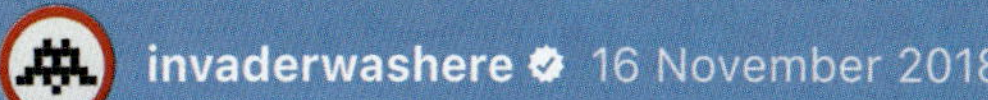

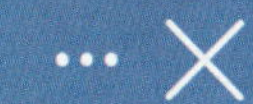
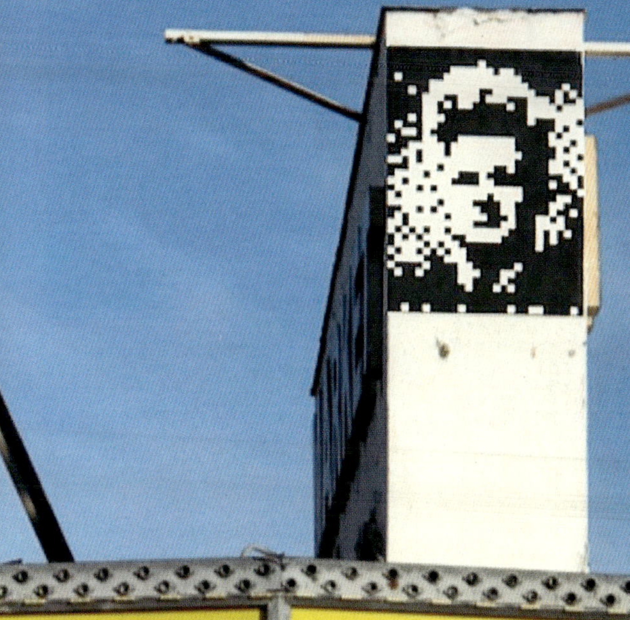

Send message

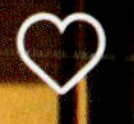
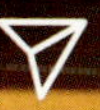

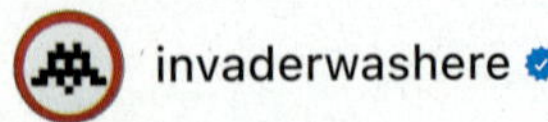

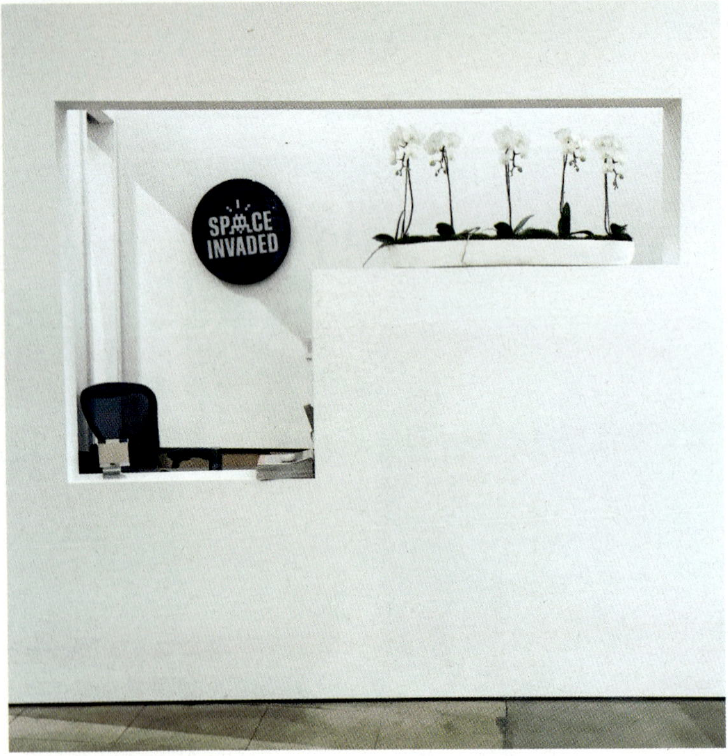

3 155 likes

invaderwashere Setting up « Into the White Cube » #exhibition #entrance @oti.official #otila #losangeles T-1 day!!!

View all 32 comments

16 November 2018

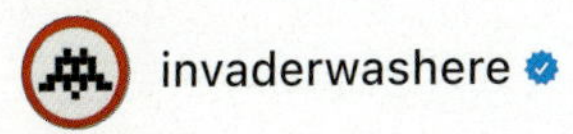

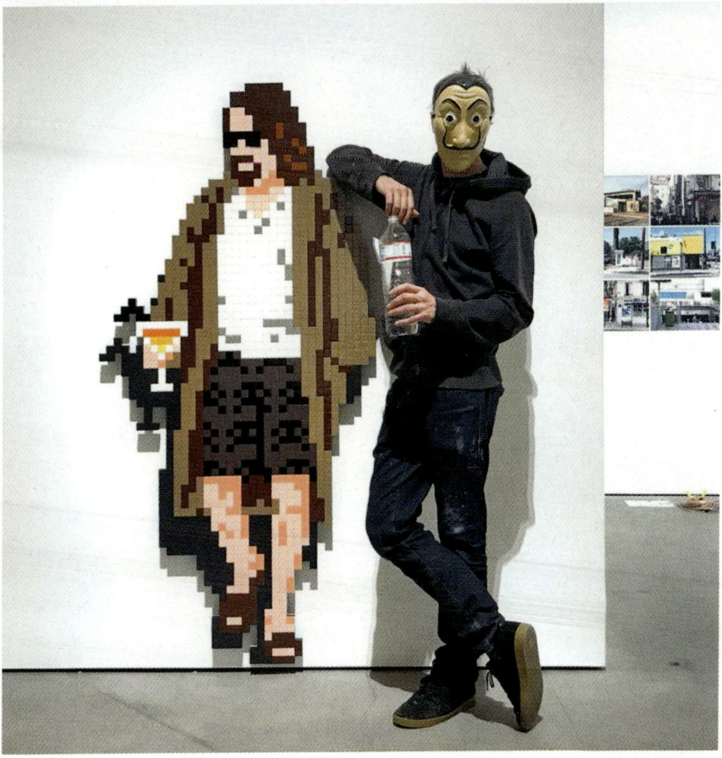

31306 likes

invaderwashere Come to join us at INTO THE WHITE CUBE opening reception tonight 🍸🍾 @oti.official #losangeles

View all 342 comments

17 November 2018

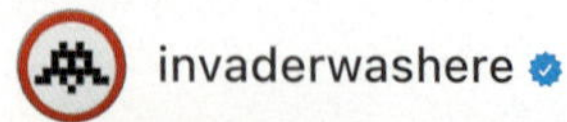

•••

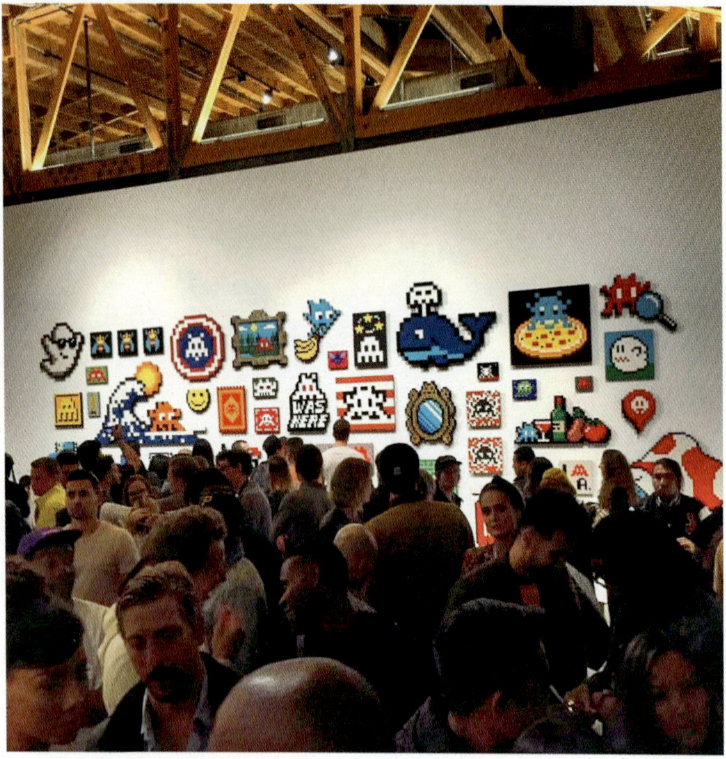

20 811 likes

invaderwashere Thank you to all who came yesterday at the opening of "Into the White Cube" / The show is now open until Dec. 23, 2018 / more infos: @oti.official / Photo: @dayinla #intothewhitecube #LA 👾

View all 163 comments

18 November 2018

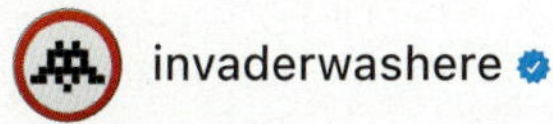

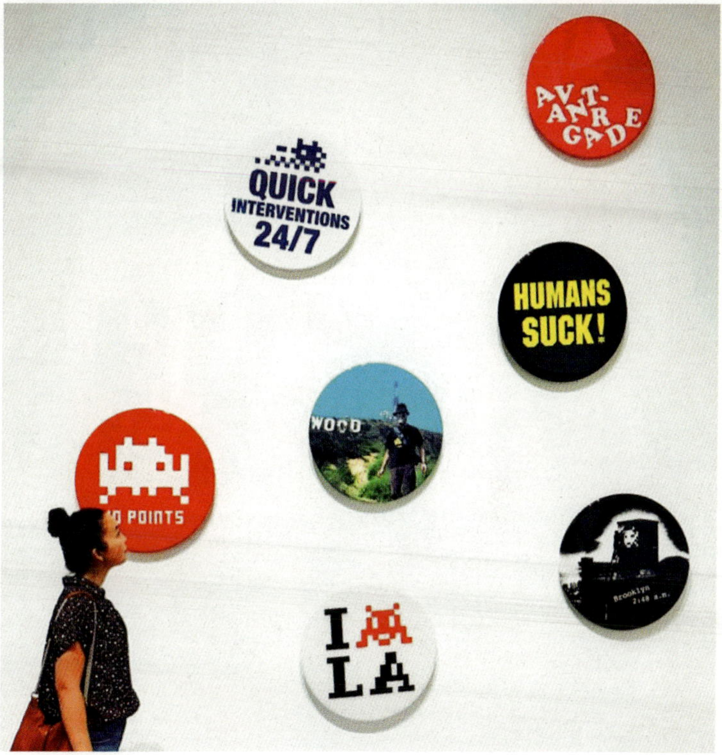

5744 likes

invaderwashere INTO THE WHITE CUBE on view through Dec. 23, 2018 #bigpins @oti.official / photo: @iireland

View all 39 comments

21 November 2018

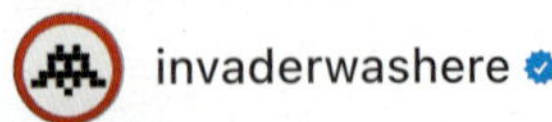

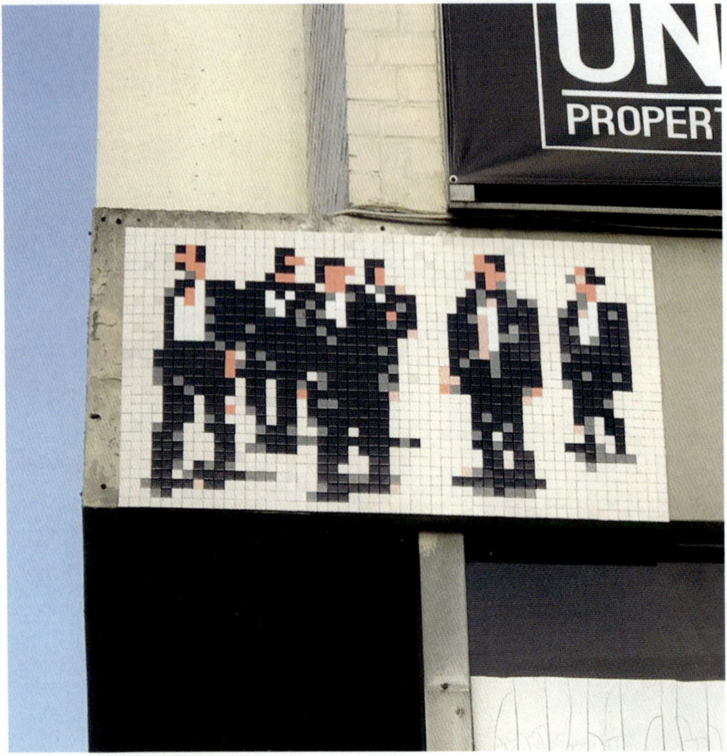

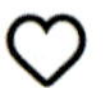  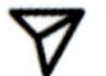 

36 996 likes

invaderwashere New piece in L.A. #LA208 #reservoirdogs

View all 479 comments

21 November 2018

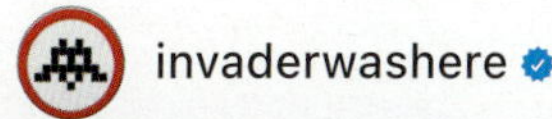

•••

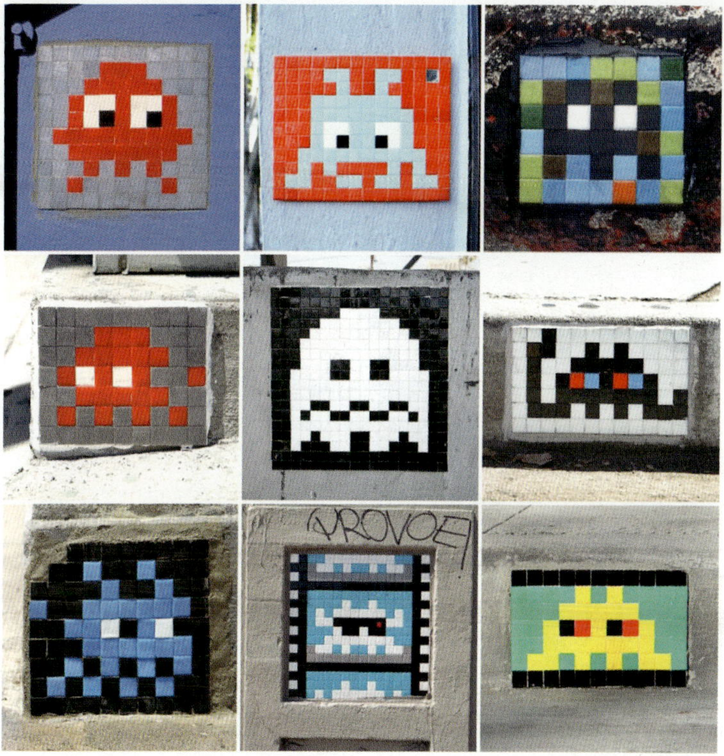

18 522 likes

invaderwashere Big Up to all the people who have reactivated some old mosaics in LA. ✨👾👏🙏
#reactivations #losangeles #backtolife #32in1week

View all 139 comments

26 November 2018

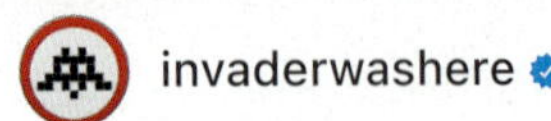

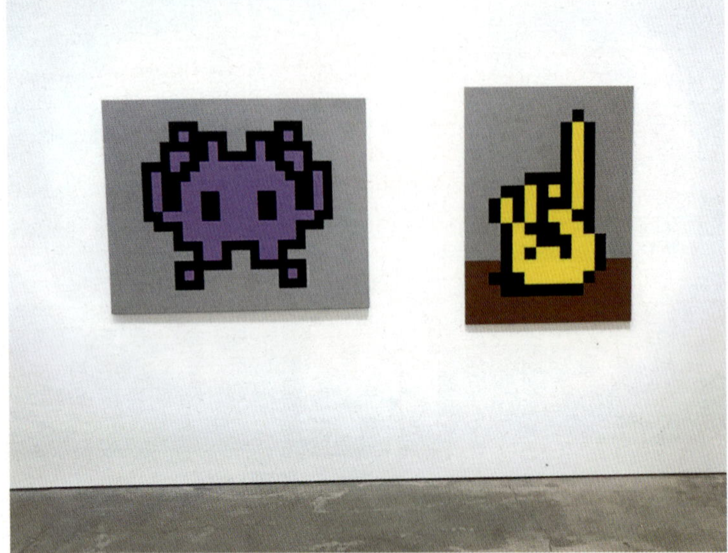

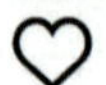   

6 384 likes

invaderwashere “My Emoji” & “What is Above”, Acrylic on canvas / Detail of #intothewhitecube @oti.official 👾 ☝️

View all 41 comments

27 November 2018

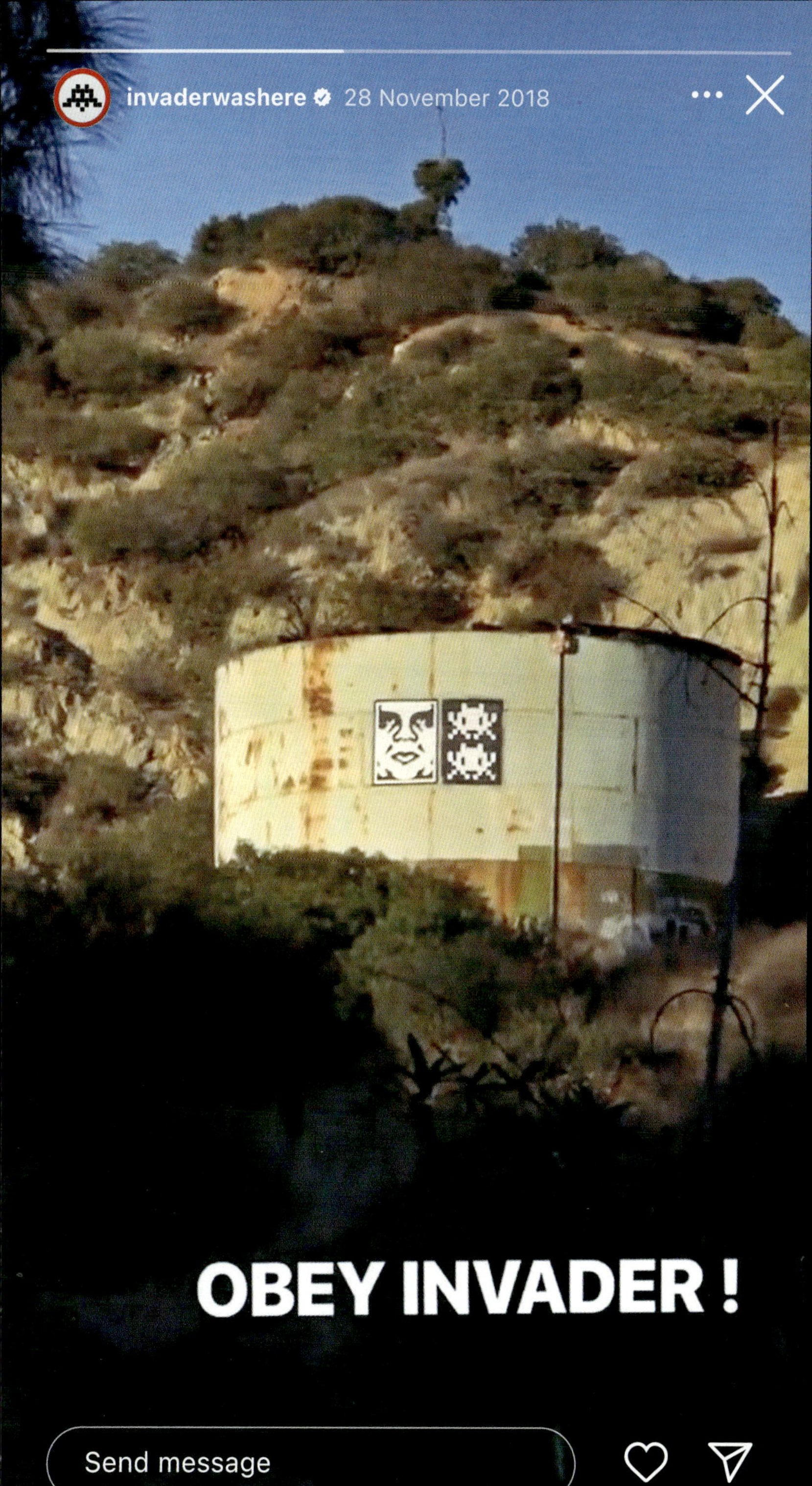

invaderwashere 28 November 2018

OBEY INVADER !

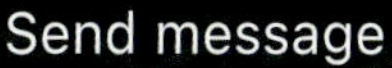

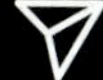

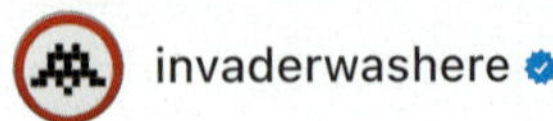

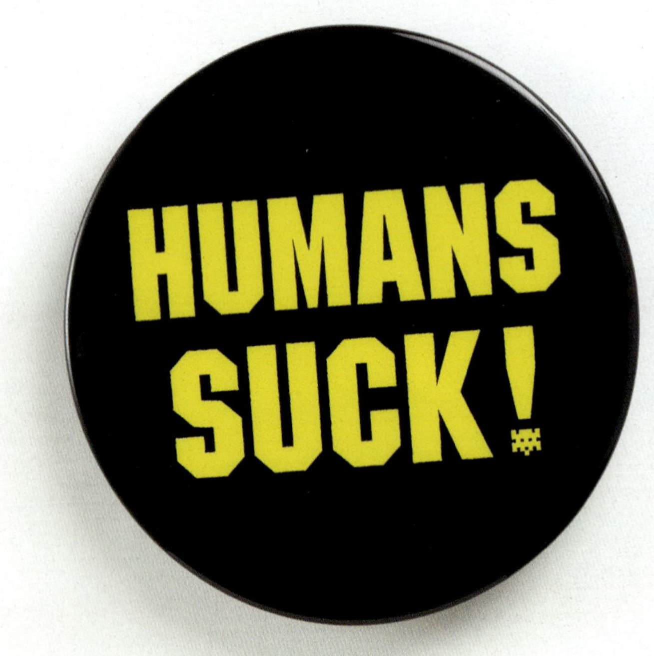

6 279 likes

invaderwashere Is the question «What planet are you going to leave to your children » or «What children are you going to leave to your planet »? 🤔👫🌎🐳

View all 101 comments

30 November 2018

invaderwashere

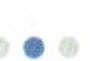

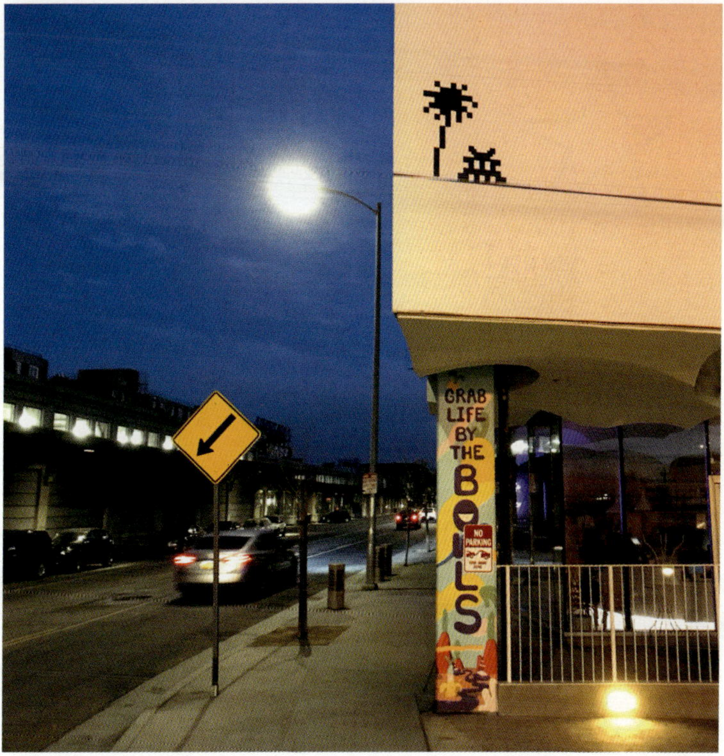

10 808 likes

invaderwashere LA_207, one of the 14 new pieces in L.A. #losangeles #Invasion #wave11 more photos: link in Bio

View all 67 comments

3 December 2018

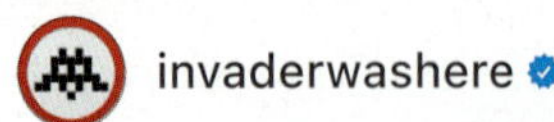

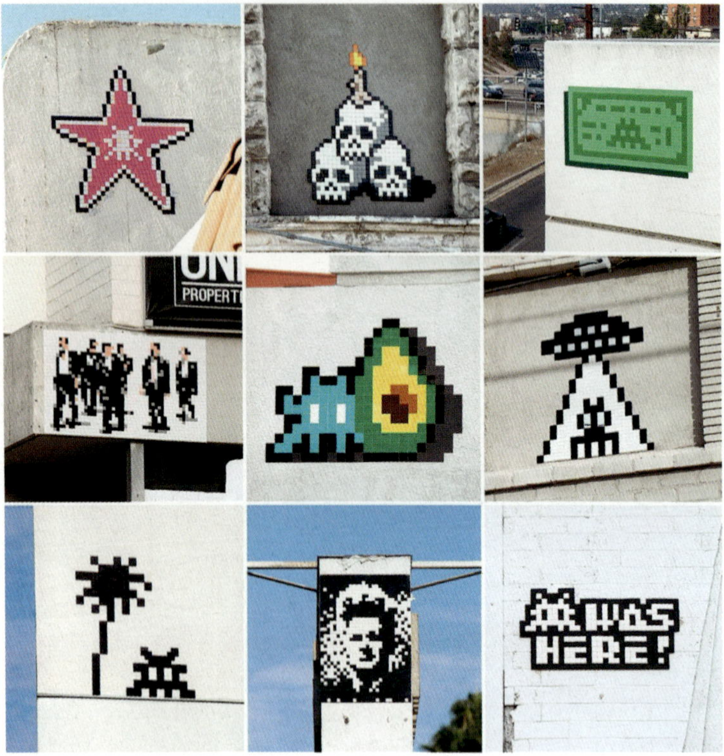

19 542 likes

invaderwashere 9 of the 14 new space invaders in L.A. / #losangeles #wave11 / More photos: Link in bio

View all 191 comments

3 December 2018

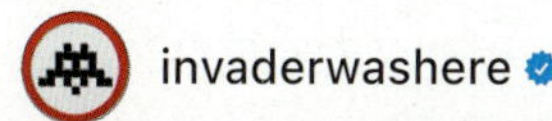

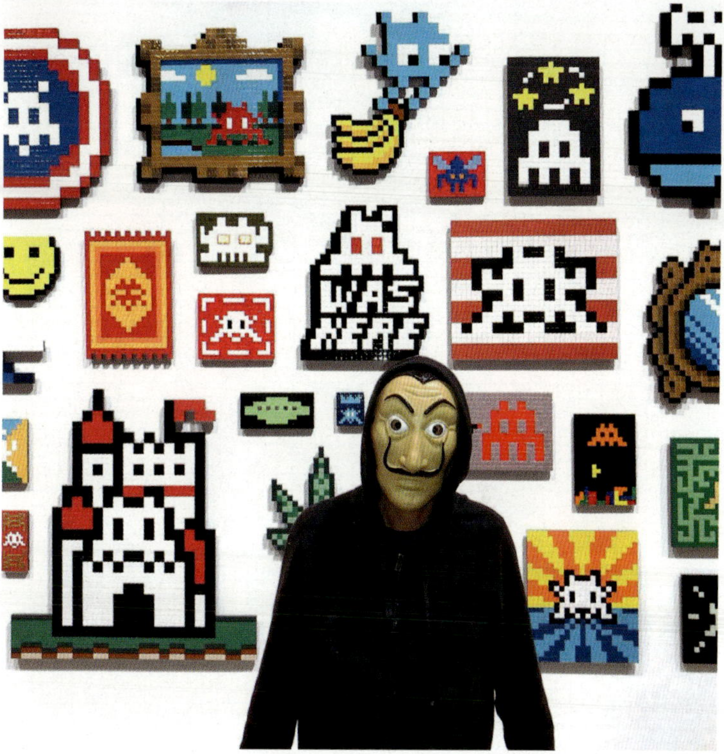

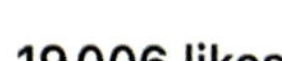

19 006 likes

invaderwashere INTO THE WHITE CUBE on view through December 23rd, 2018. I've always worked in both fields: the street and the institution. Some people think this is paradoxical, but I don't. They're two different things, but they can be complementary and I like to go back and forth between them. @oti.official #LA

View all 160 comments

5 December 2018

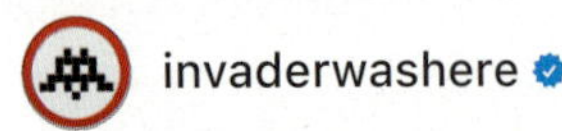

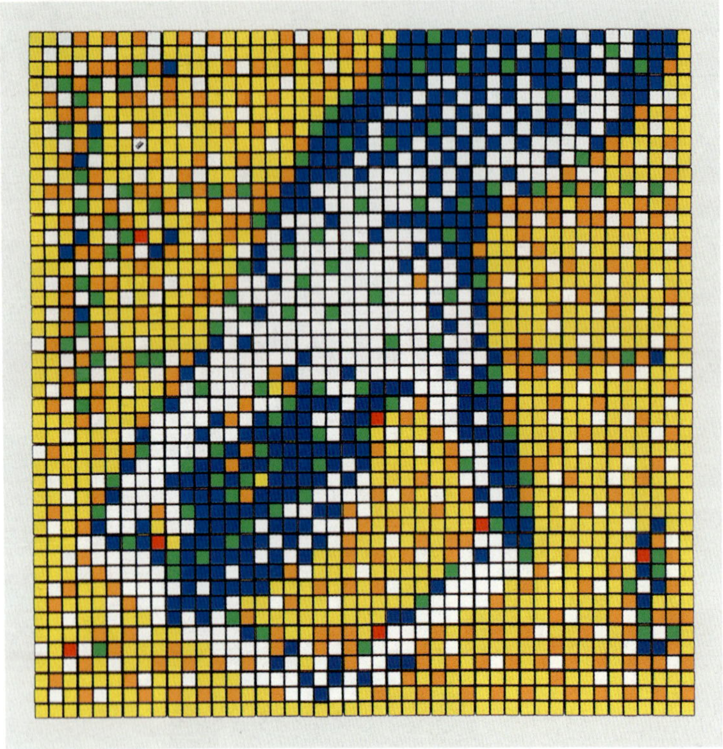

4 851 likes

invaderwashere R.I.P. Pete Shelley #peteshelley #buzzcocks #orgasmadict #cover #lindersterling #malcolmgarrett #rubikcubism #lowfidelity Rubik Orgasm Addict / 2011

View all 38 comments

7 December 2018

invaderwashere

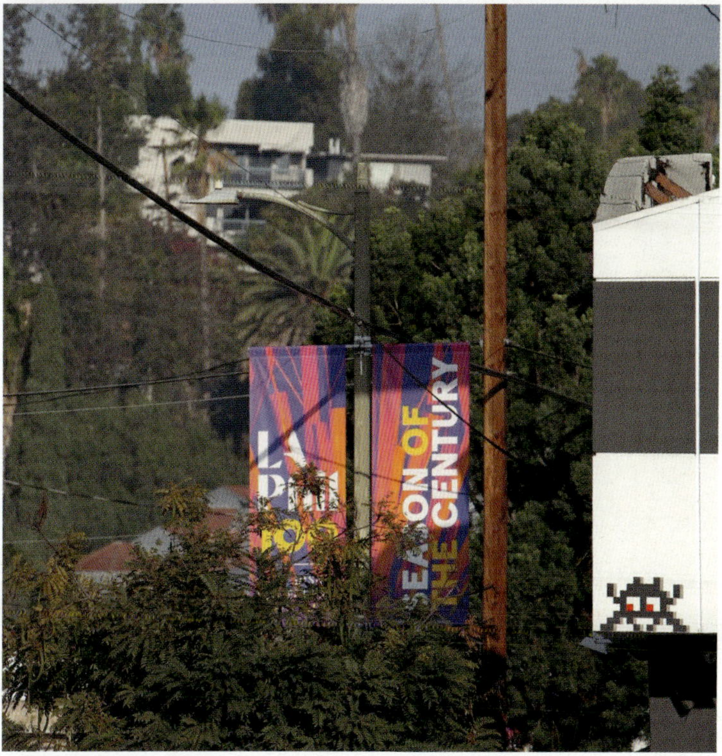

5580 likes

invaderwashere LA_211

View all 38 comments

23 December 2018

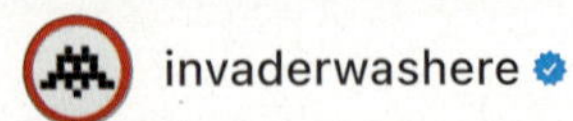

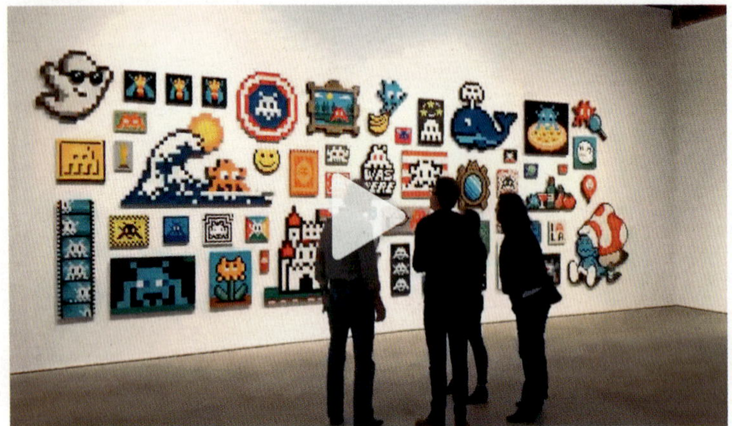

  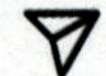 

97 493 views

invaderwashere Tomorrow will be the the last day of INTO THE WHITE CUBE @oti.official #LA #soloshow #freeentrance #quicktour

View all 244 comments

30 December 2018

2019

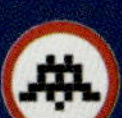
invaderwashere
3 January 2019
Happy
new year
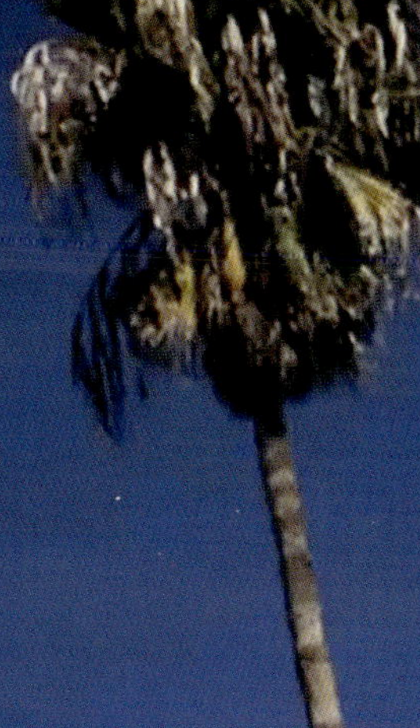
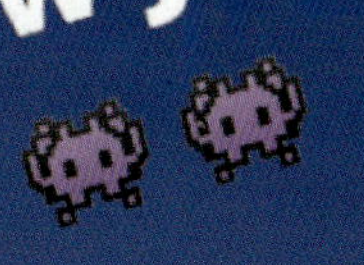

BAZAR
PAB
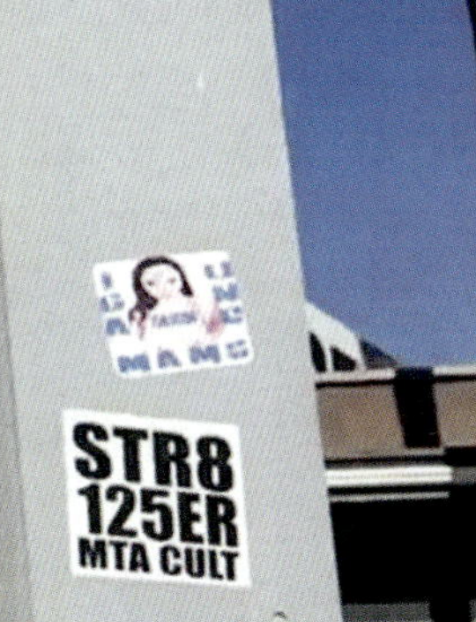
STR8
125ER
MTA CULT
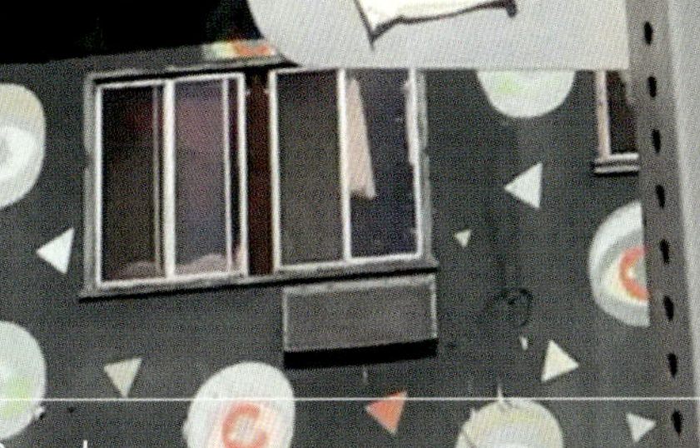
Send message
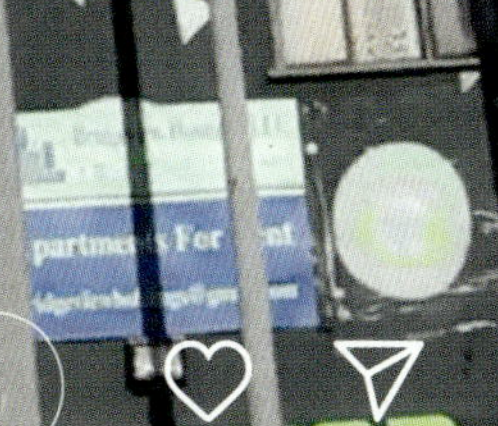

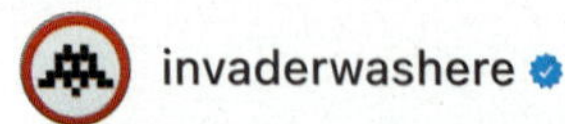

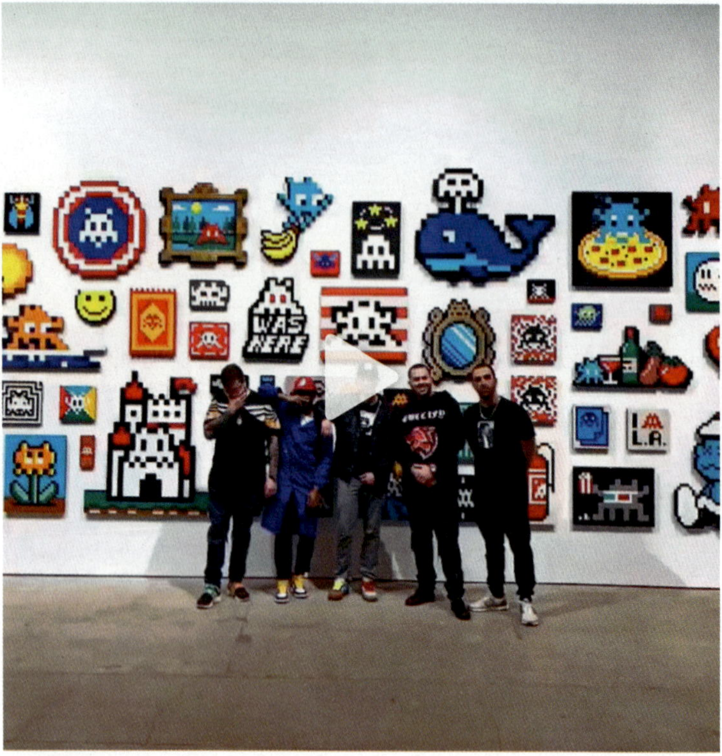

98 532 views

invaderwashere Thank you to all the earthlings who came to "Into The White Cube" #theshowisover #intothewhitecube #visitors @oti.official Photos: found on Instagram 🙏😎👾

View all 165 comments

8 January 2019

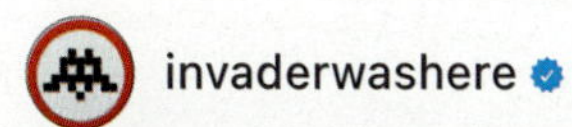

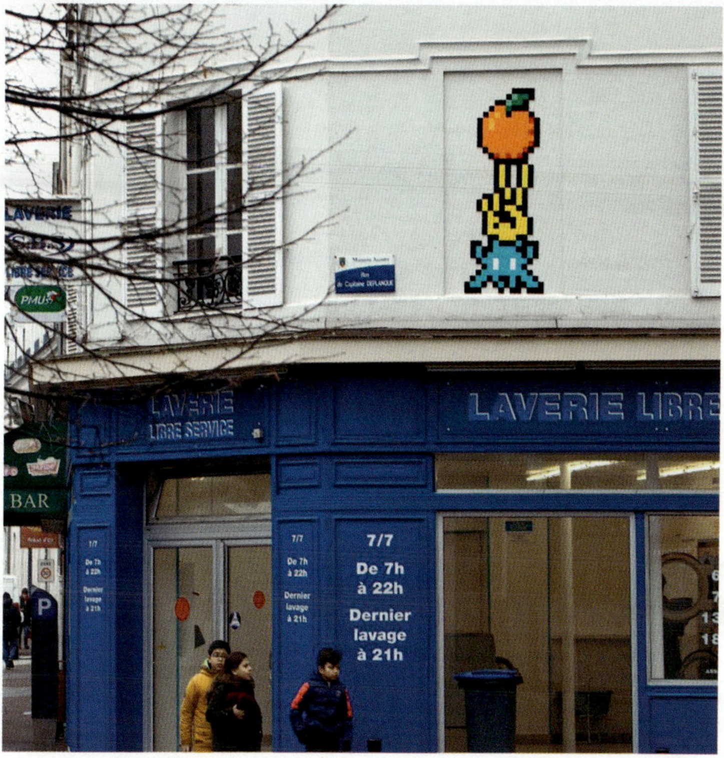

  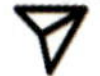 

16 198 likes

invaderwashere 1st invasion of 2019 #PA1376 #stilllife #wintervitamins #totemoji 👾 ✌️ 🍊

View all 87 comments

16 January 2019

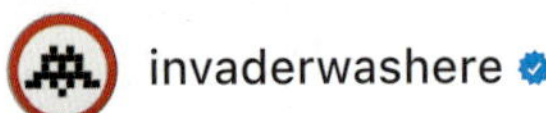

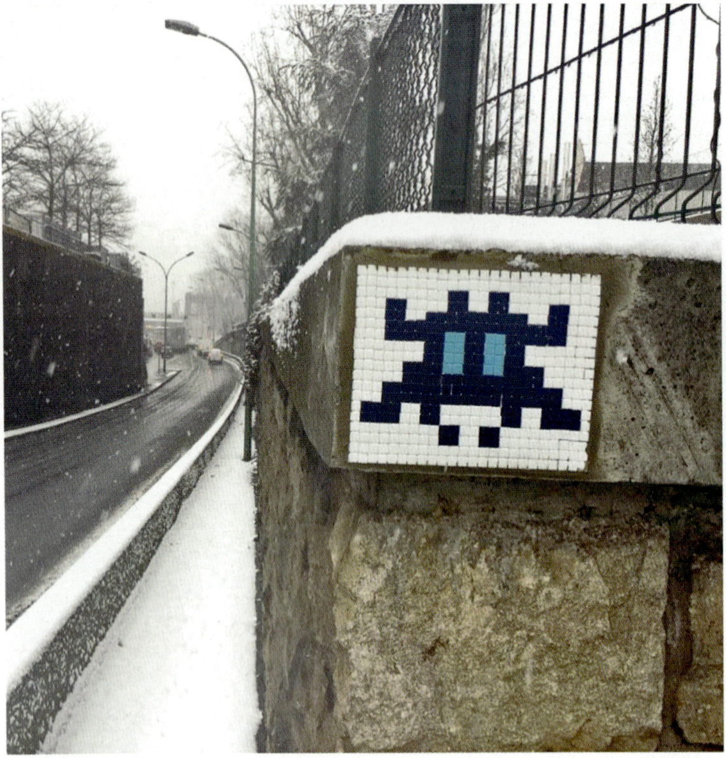

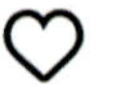  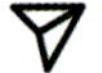 

19 275 likes

invaderwashere Snowy Paris #PA993 #reactivation photo: @xavrs78

View all 81 comments

22 January 2019

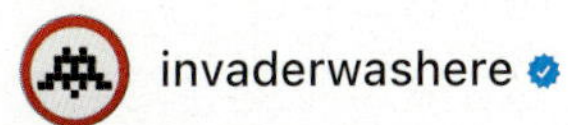

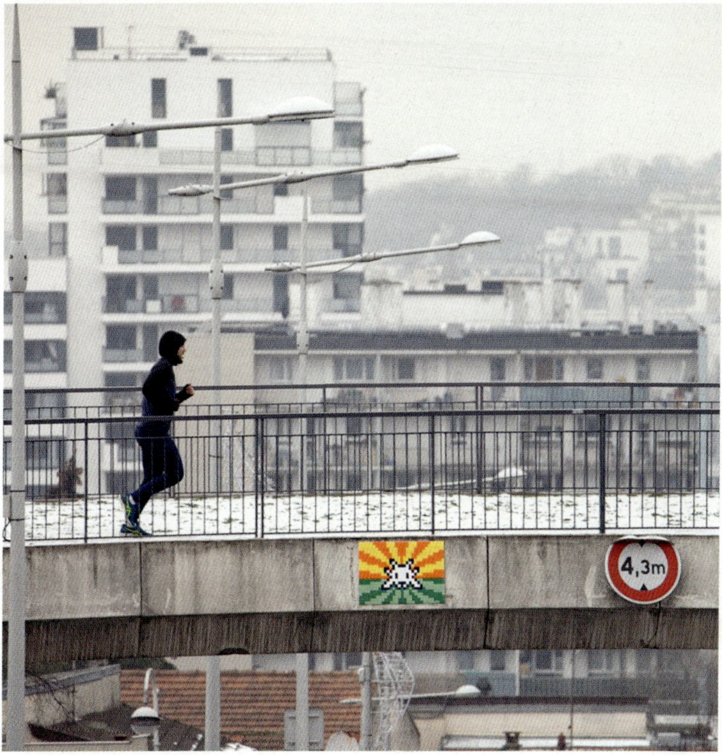

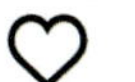   

15 570 likes

invaderwashere The latest one / Not far from Paris...
#PA_1381 #winter #waitingforthesun ❄️ ☀️

View all 100 comments

24 January 2019

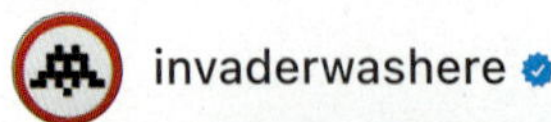

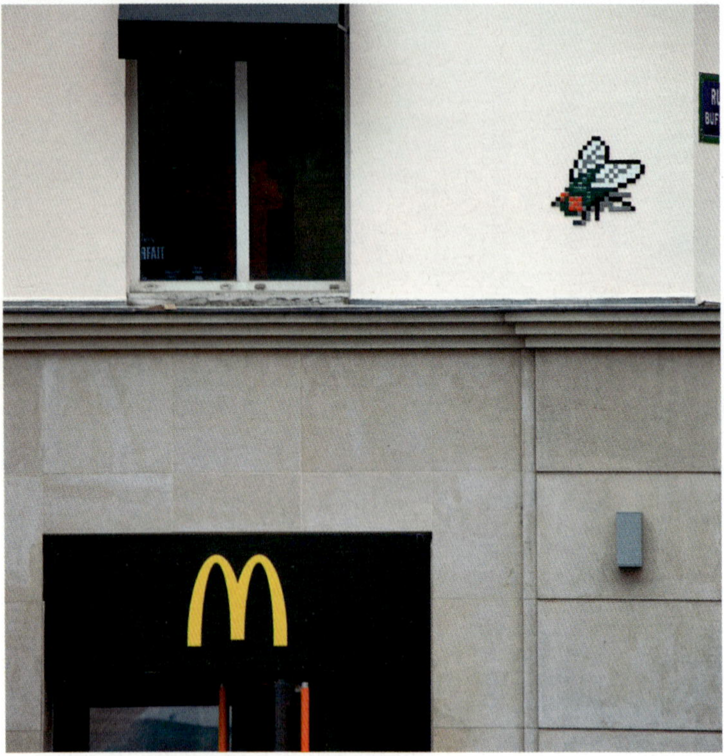

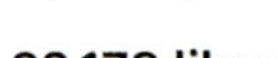

33 178 likes

invaderwashere A green fly has just landed in Paris
#yumyum #macdo #macfly

View all 306 comments

6 February 2019

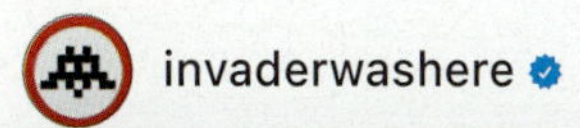

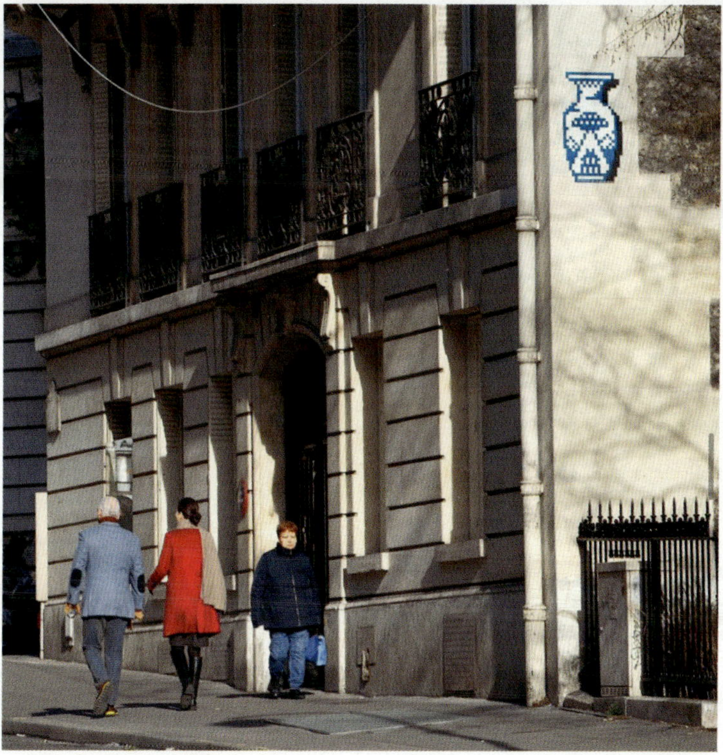

11062 likes

invaderwashere MINGINVADER beside the Musée national des arts asiatiques Guimet

View all 72 comments

14 February 2019

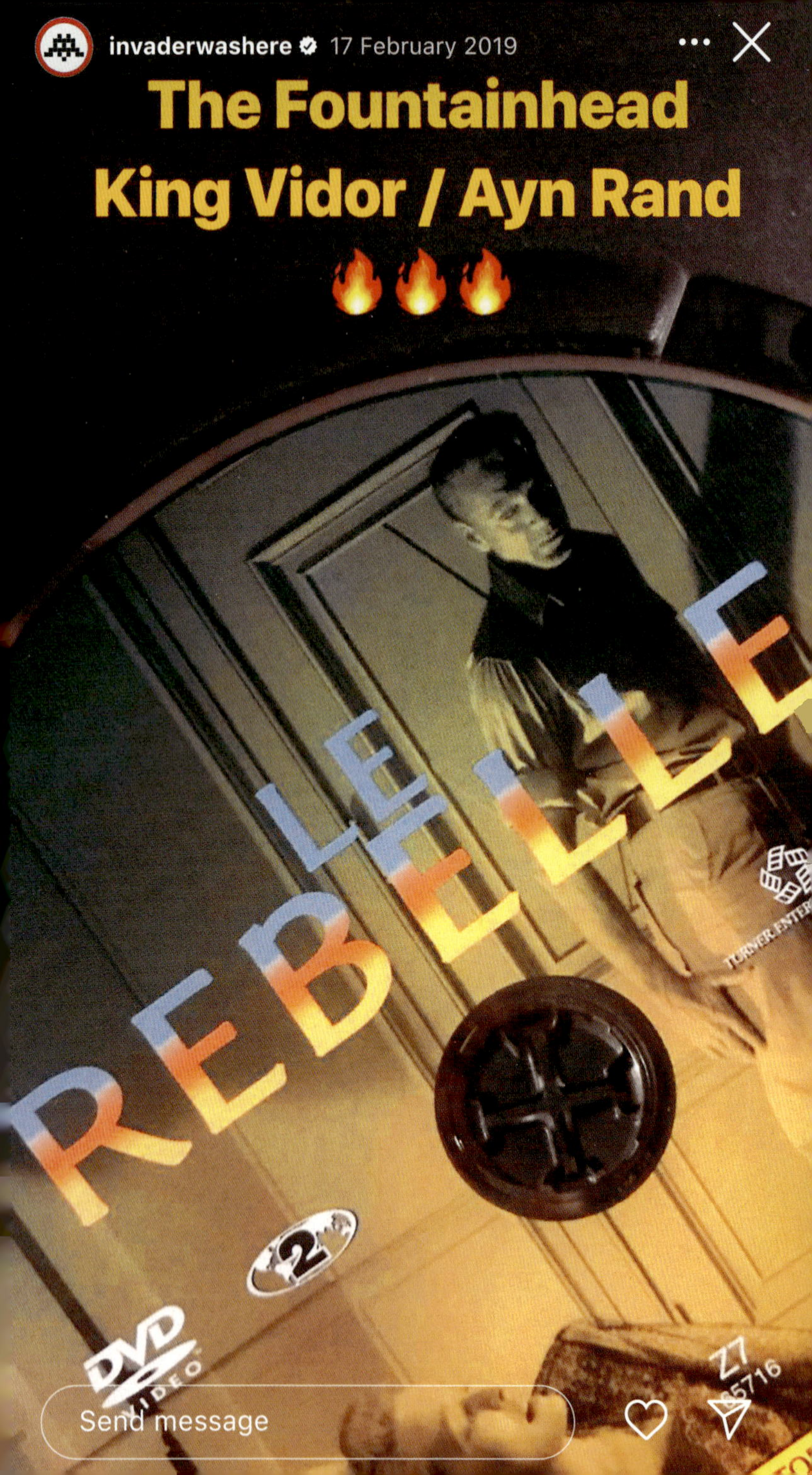

invaderwashere 17 February 2019
The Fountainhead
King Vidor / Ayn Rand
LE
REBELLE
TURNER ENTER
DVD VIDEO
2
Send message

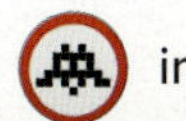 invaderwashere

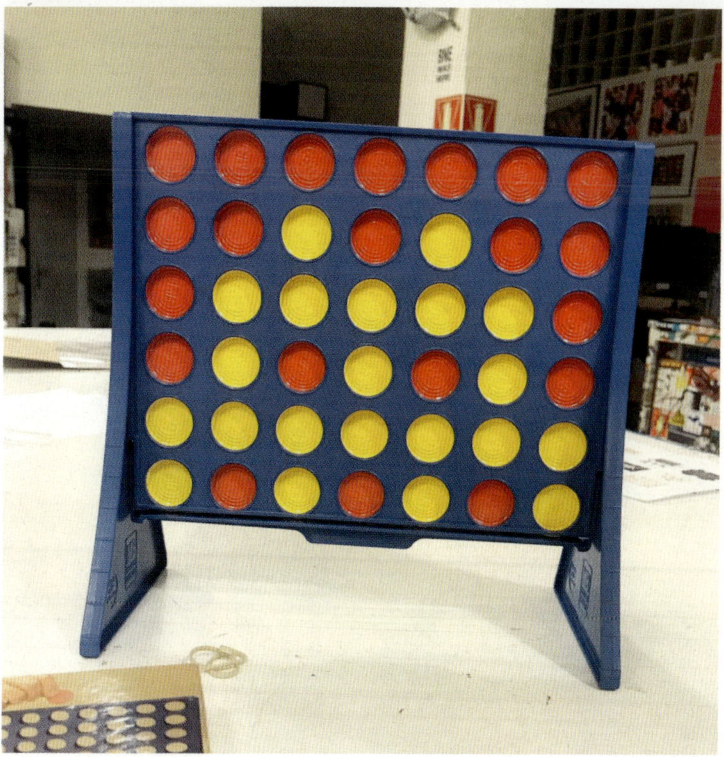

12180 likes

invaderwashere 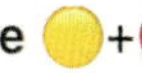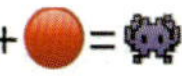

View all 119 comments

19 February 2019

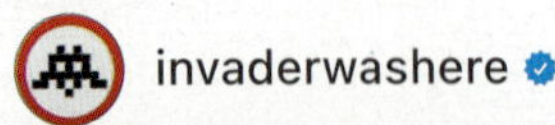

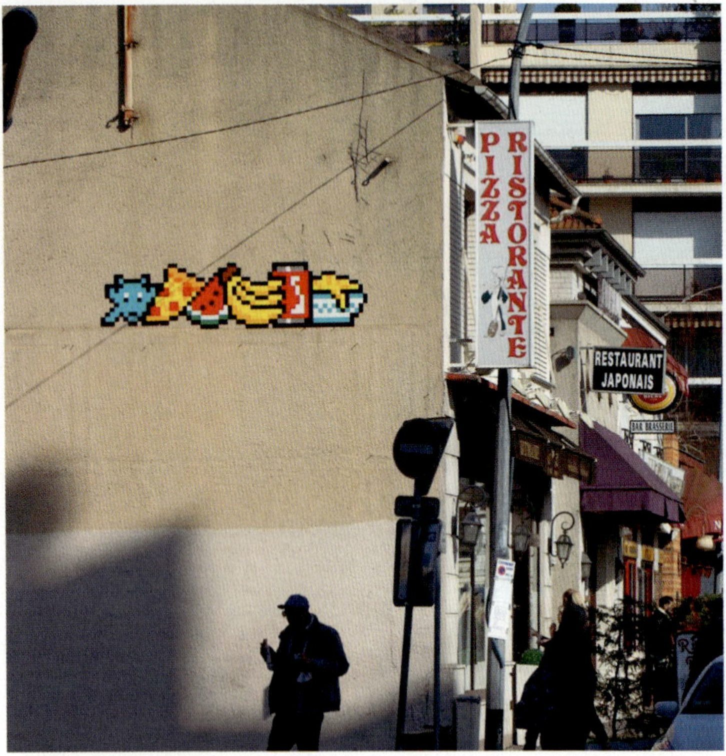

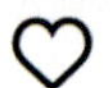  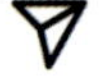 

21789 likes

invaderwashere PA_1386 #lunchtime

View all 131 comments

22 February 2019

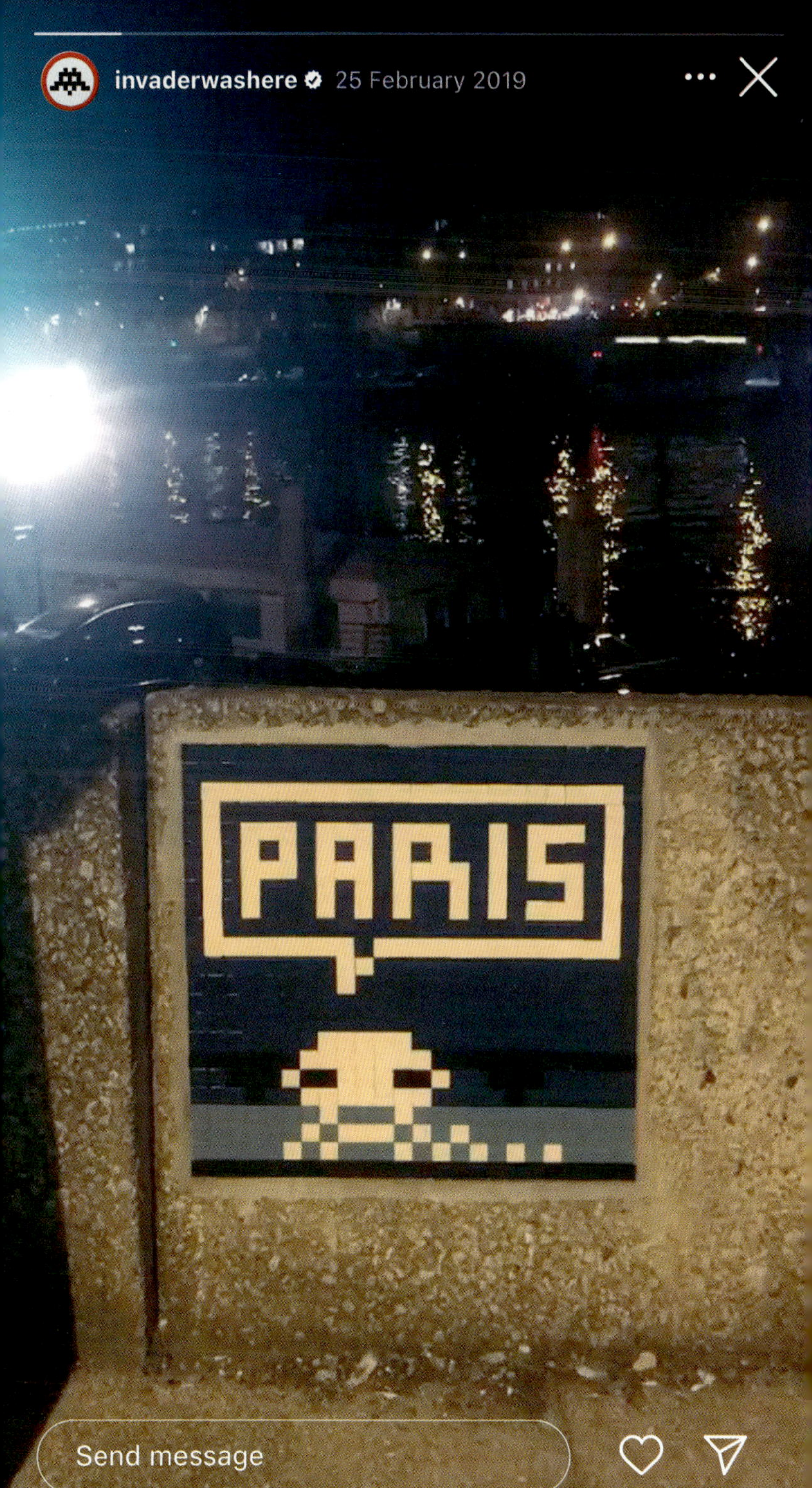
invaderwashere 25 February 2019
PARIS
Send message

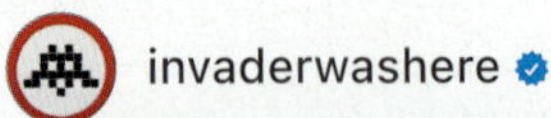

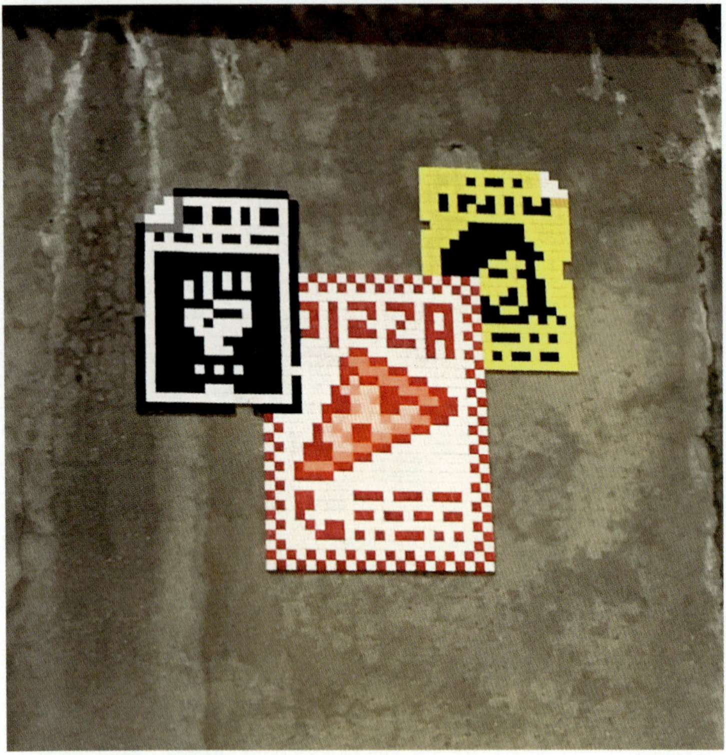

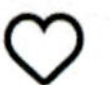    

25 387 likes

invaderwashere Can you see the 👾?

View all 264 comments

19 March 2019

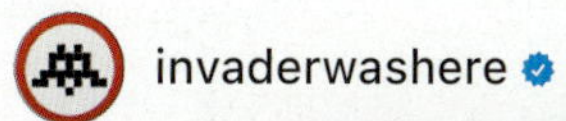

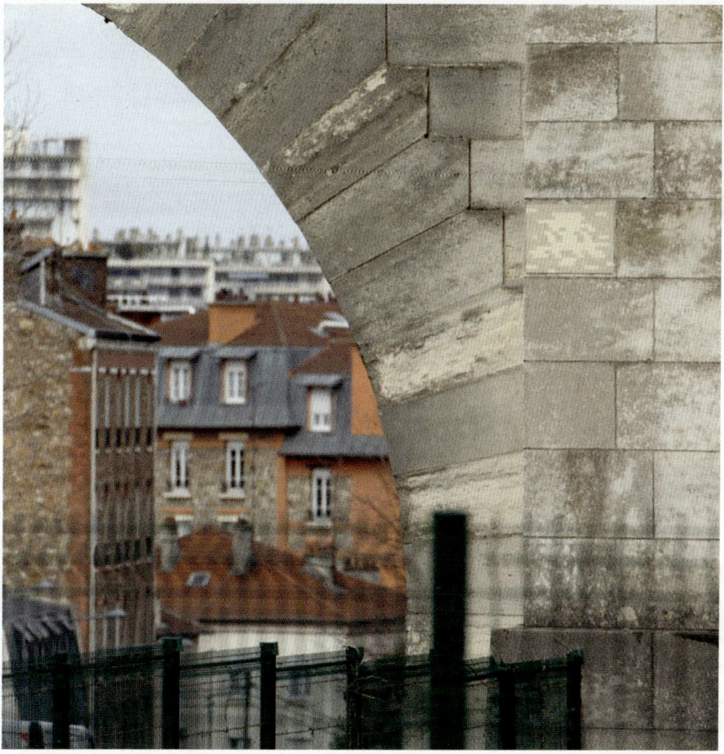

 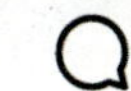  

17 246 likes

invaderwashere I usually make my pieces to be visible but sometimes I like them to be concealed. Can you see the 👾 ? #camo #glitch

View all 307 comments

21 March 2019

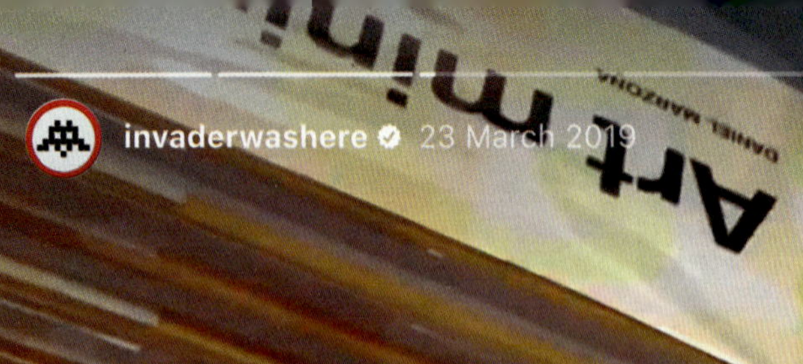
invaderwashere 23 March 2019
Art mini
DANIEL MARZONA

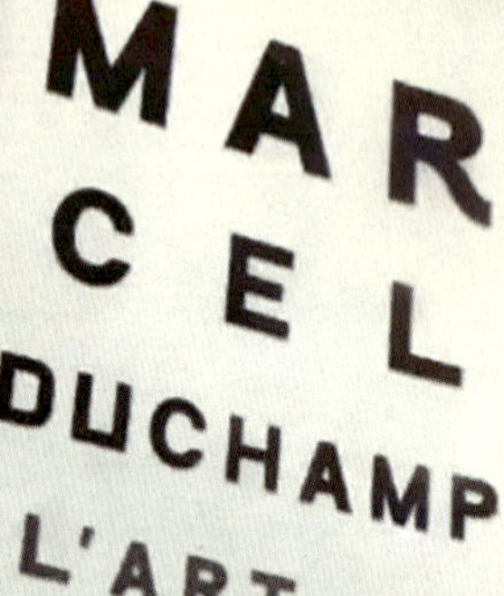
Prix éditeur:
35€
Prix Mona:
15€
MAR
CEL
DUCHAMP
L'ART A
L'ERE DE LA
REPRODUCTION
MECANISEE
Prix éditeur:
25,95€
Prix Mona:
12€

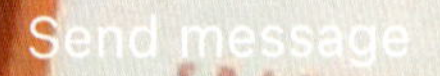
Send message

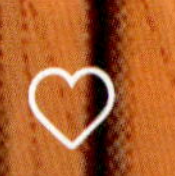

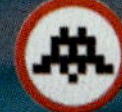

invaderwashere 23 March 2019

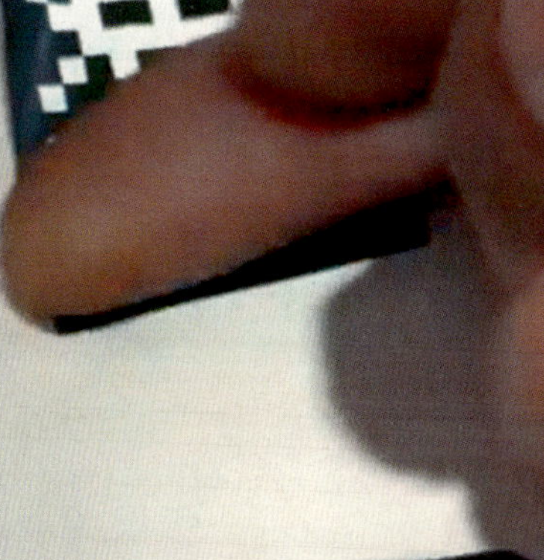

Send message

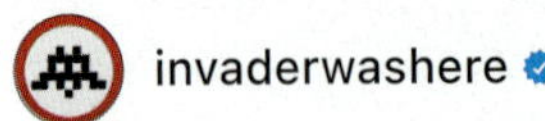

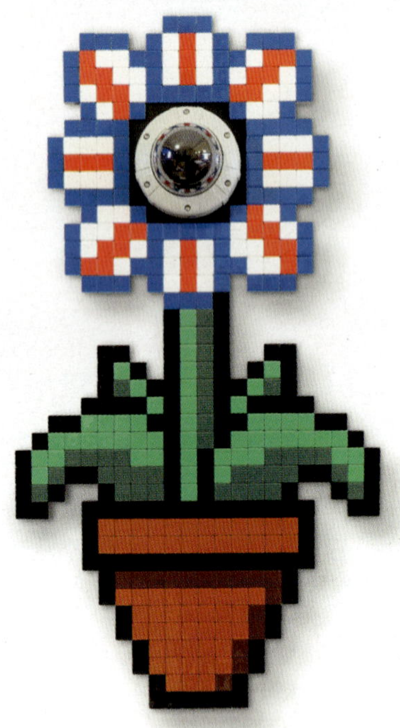

24 849 likes

invaderwashere ALIAS LDN_144, 2016
Art Central Hong Kong
Booth B08 @artcentralhk
@oti.official #otihk #cctvflower #london
VIP Opening Tuesday 26 March, 2 pm – 9 pm
Open March 27 - March 31

View all 207 comments

25 March 2019

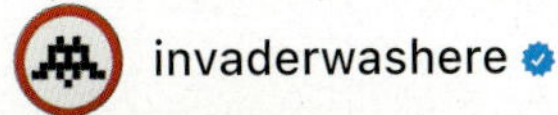

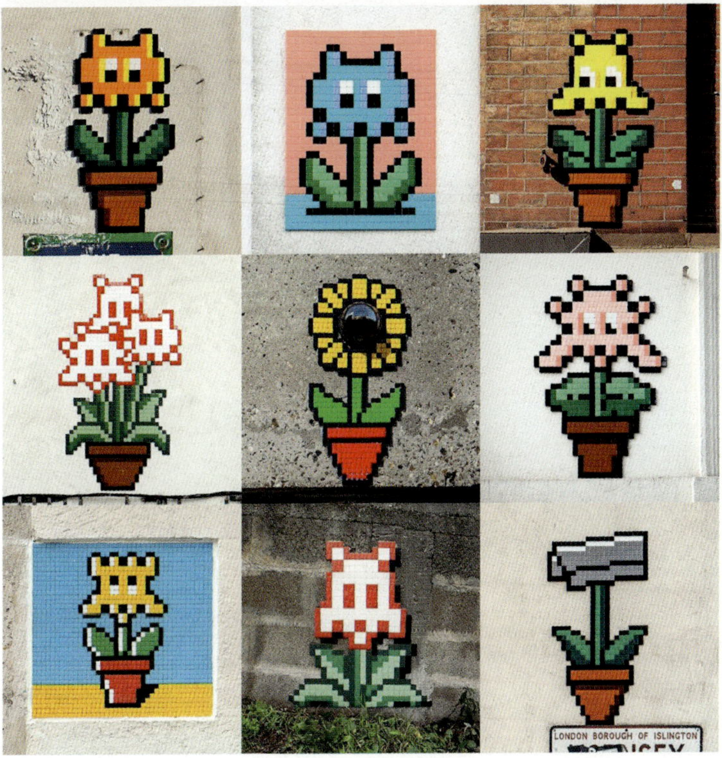

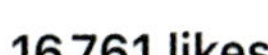

16 761 likes

invaderwashere A smell of spring... #spaceflowers

View all 113 comments

27 March 2019

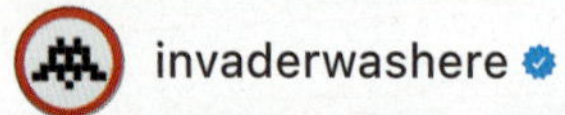

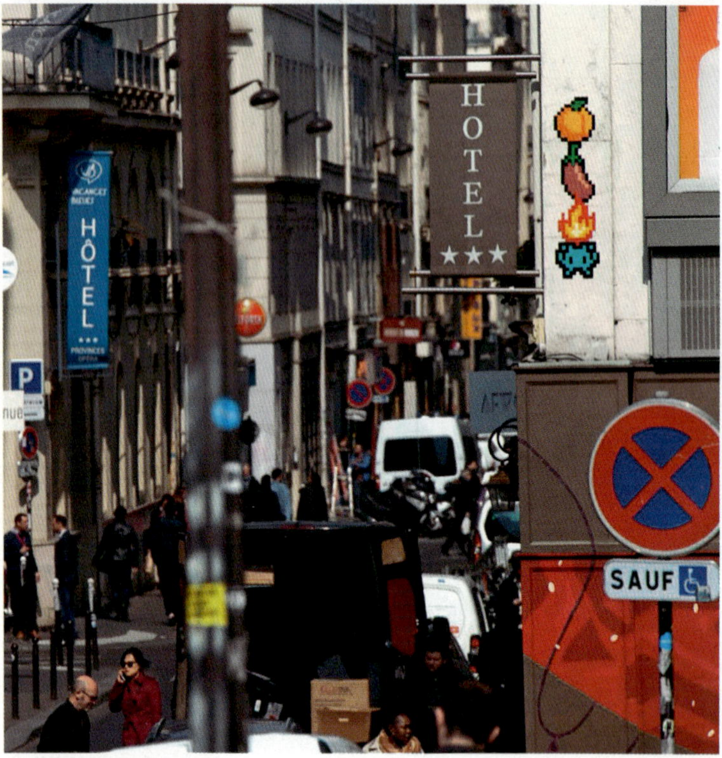

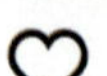   

16 608 likes

invaderwashere PA_1392 #HOT #HOTEL #latest #totemoji #paris 🇫🇷

View all 98 comments

28 March 2019

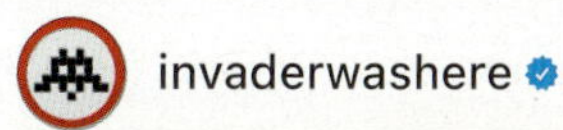

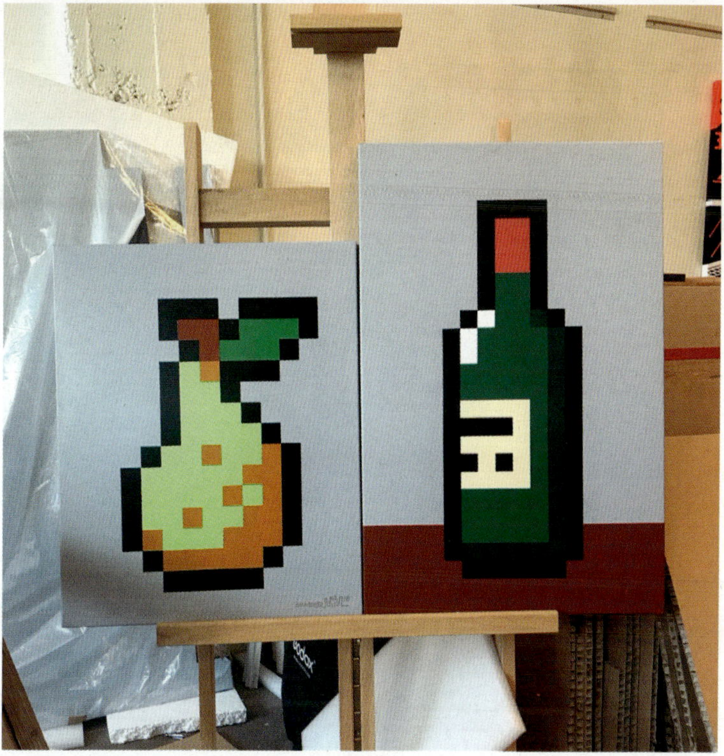

15 438 likes

invaderwashere Monday morning #studio #details

View all 145 comments

1 April 2019

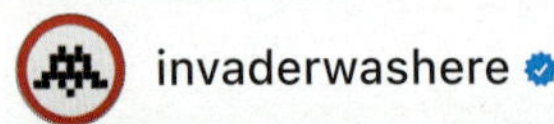

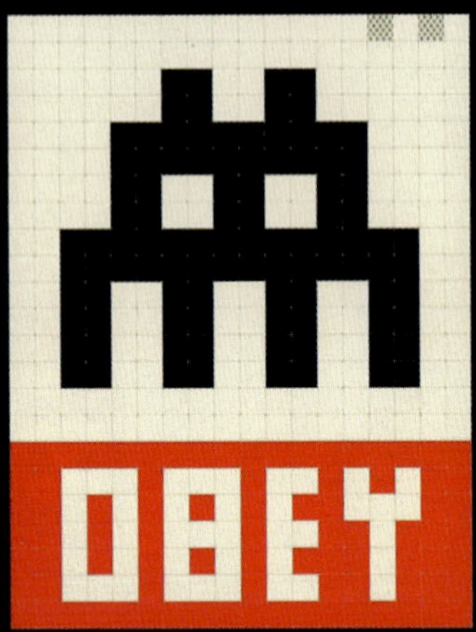

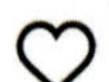 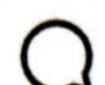  

18 073 likes

invaderwashere I've met the artist activist Shepard Fairey 20 yrs ago and since then, we always kept contact. When he asked me last year if I wanted to do something with his brand Obey Clothing I immediately accepted. We actually worked on two designs: "Water Tower" a photo of a piece we made in Griffith Park in 2018 and "LA_56" the image of a mosaic I've installed in LA in 2002. As a bonus we also edited a little print of LA_56 in situ.
More info @obeyclothing and @obeyclothingparis

View all 321 comments

2 April 2019

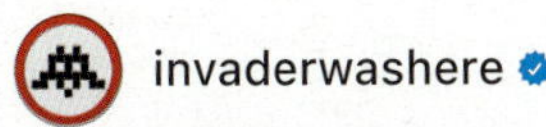

OBEY x INVADER

OBEY PARIS

13 RUE NOTRE DAME DE NAZARETH, PARIS

18 073 likes

invaderwashere I've met the artist activist Shepard Fairey 20 yrs ago and since then, we always kept contact. When he asked me last year if I wanted to do something with his brand Obey Clothing I immediately accepted. We actually worked on two designs: "Water Tower" a photo of a piece we made in Griffith Park in 2018 and "LA_56" the image of a mosaic I've installed in LA in 2002. As a bonus we also edited a little print of LA_56 in situ.

More info @obeyclothing and @obeyclothingparis

View all 321 comments

2 April 2019

invaderwashere

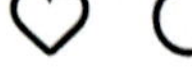
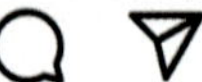

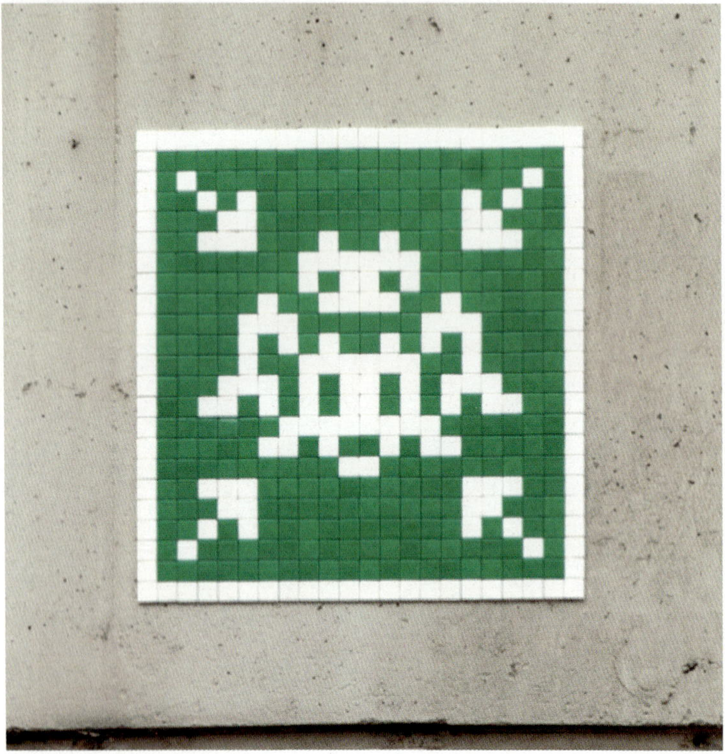

12787 likes

invaderwashere INVADERS MEETING POINT

View all 62 comments

5 April 2019

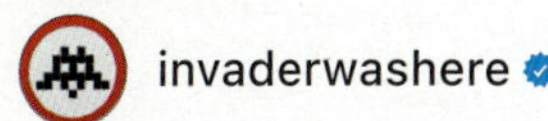
invaderwashere ...

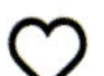 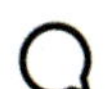  

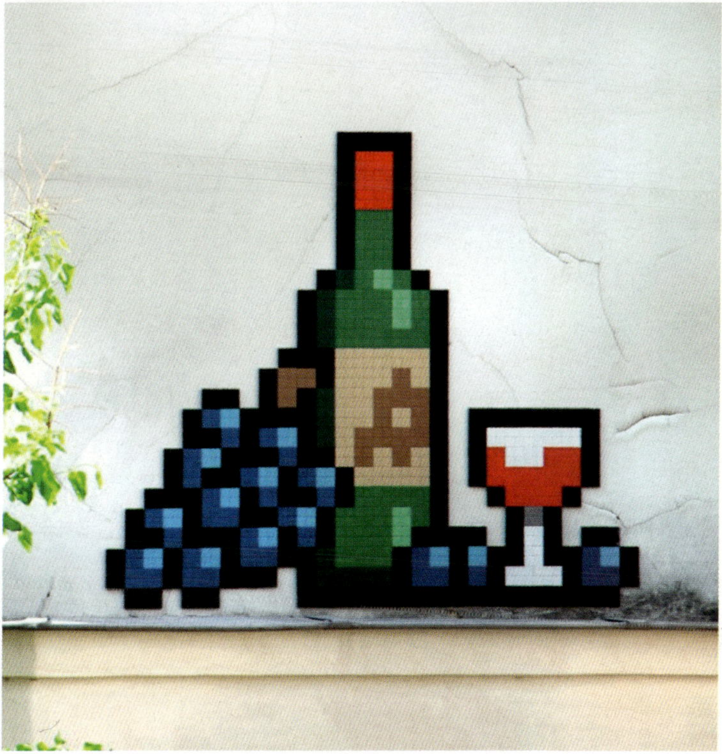

22 904 likes

invaderwashere The latest piece #stilllife #wine #grapes #findthespaceinvader #cheers 🇫🇷

View all 205 comments

14 April 2019

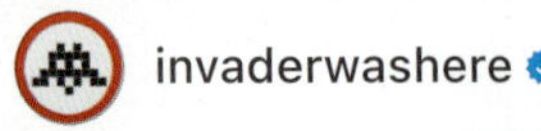

invaderwashere

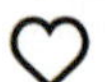   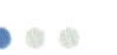 

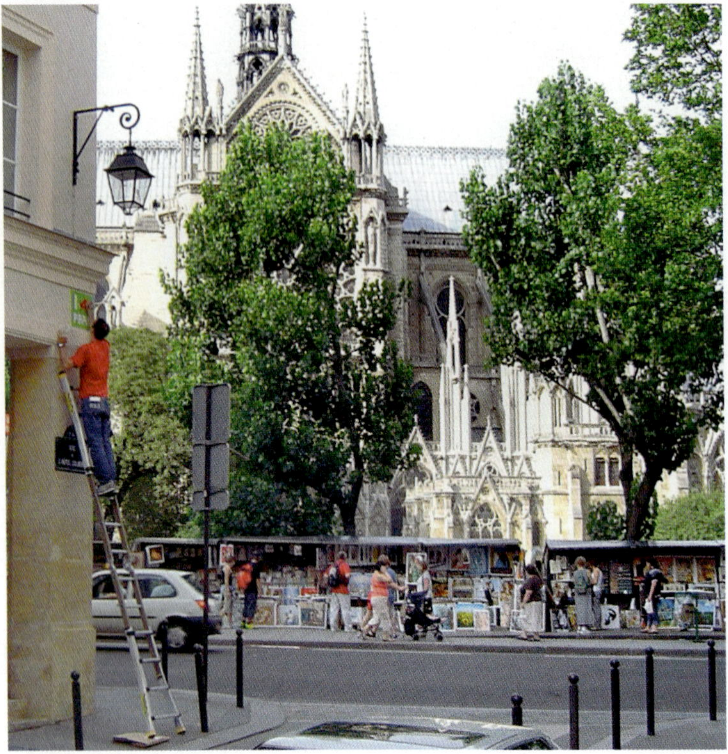

12 297 likes

invaderwashere 🔥 😢 #archive #notredame #2004 #PA556

View all 65 comments

16 April 2019

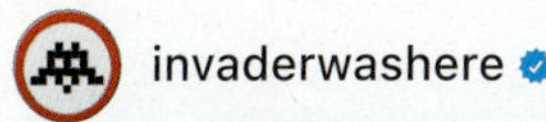

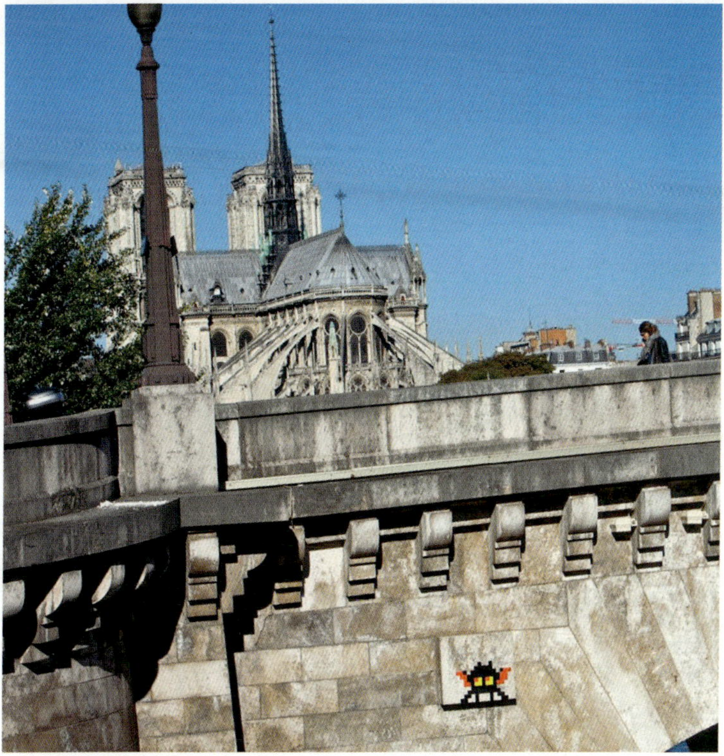

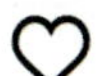   

21 218 likes

invaderwashere Sad day for Paris 🔥😢 #notredame #throwback #PA1245 #2016

View all 150 comments

16 April 2019

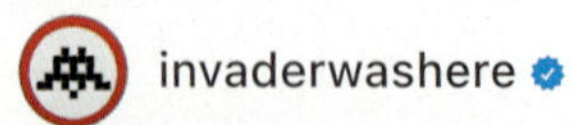

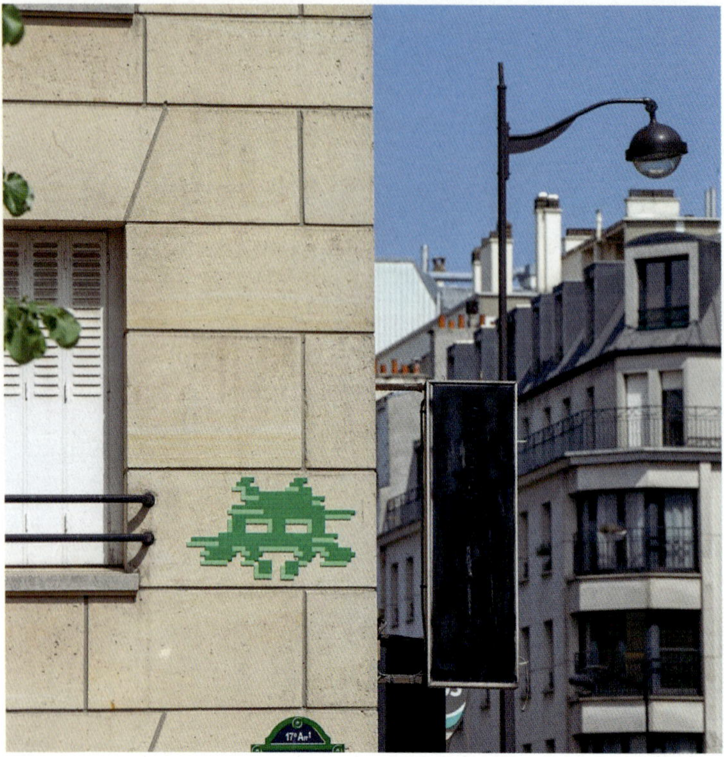

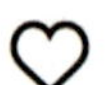   

12 076 likes

invaderwashere Glitch of Easter!

View all 49 comments

22 April 2019

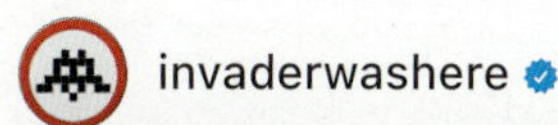

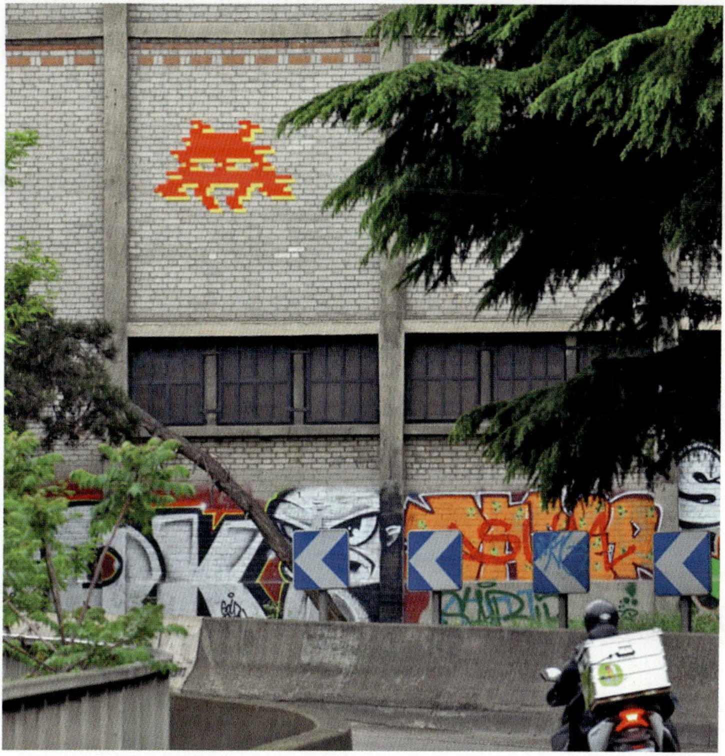

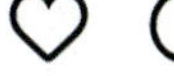

13 041 likes

invaderwashere PA_1400 Red glitch!

View all 69 comments

26 April 2019

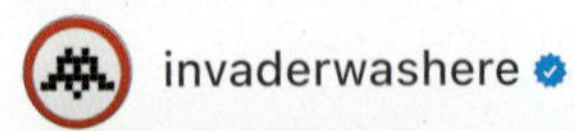

LATEST SUCCESSFUL "FLASHES"
79 836 Players / 3 988 888 Flashes

Paris, FRANCOISE2944
21 seconds ago

Paris, KIWIRORO
22 seconds ago

Cap Ferret, LENI1979
28 seconds ago

London, TCHO
30 seconds ag

Lille, _GIGI_
32 seconds ago

Amsterdam, DORIAN
33 seconds ago

Newcastle, DOUD1ER
36 seconds ago

Newcastle, BE
37 seconds ag

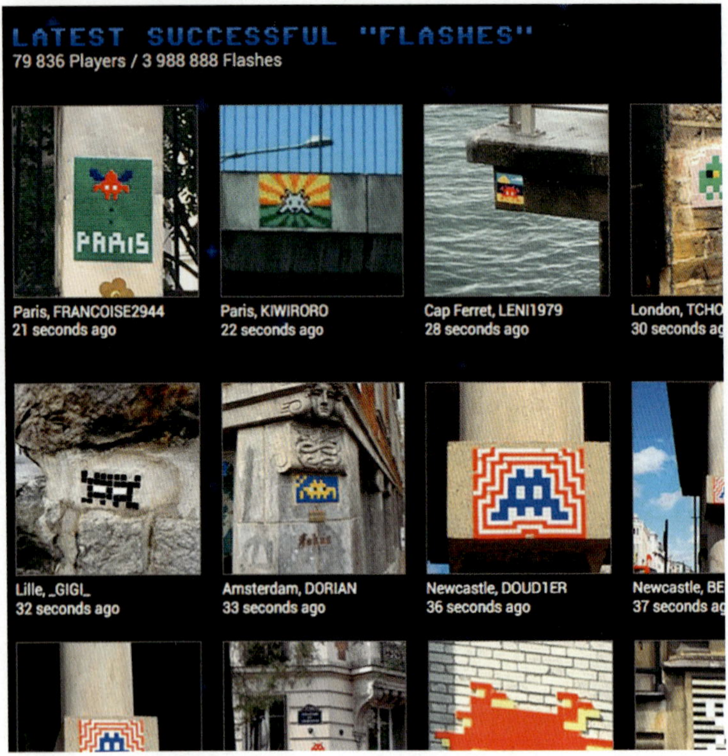

10 016 likes

invaderwashere Just reached 3.988.888 valid flashes on #Flashinvaders / Watch out the 4 Millionth one!!! Link in bio / Big Up to all the players 🙏👏👾

View all 130 comments

26 April 2019

invaderwashere ...

 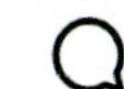   

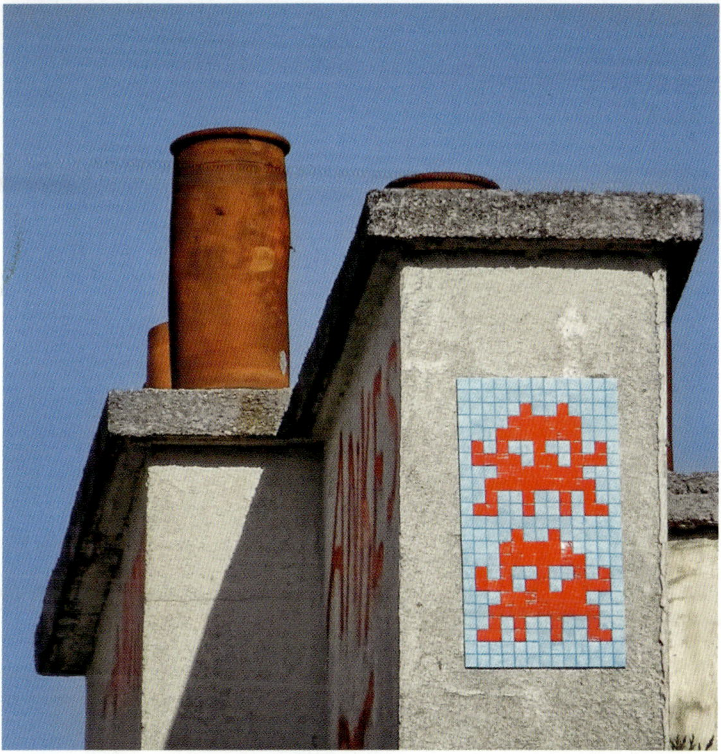

19 199 likes

invaderwashere Amazing Reactivation of PA_510 👀👏🙏
#Paris #Bastille #PA510 #reactivation Photos: @llathaly
@dark_invader_addict & @space_twinvader

View all 128 comments

28 April 2019

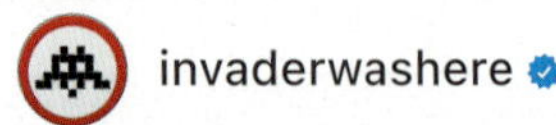

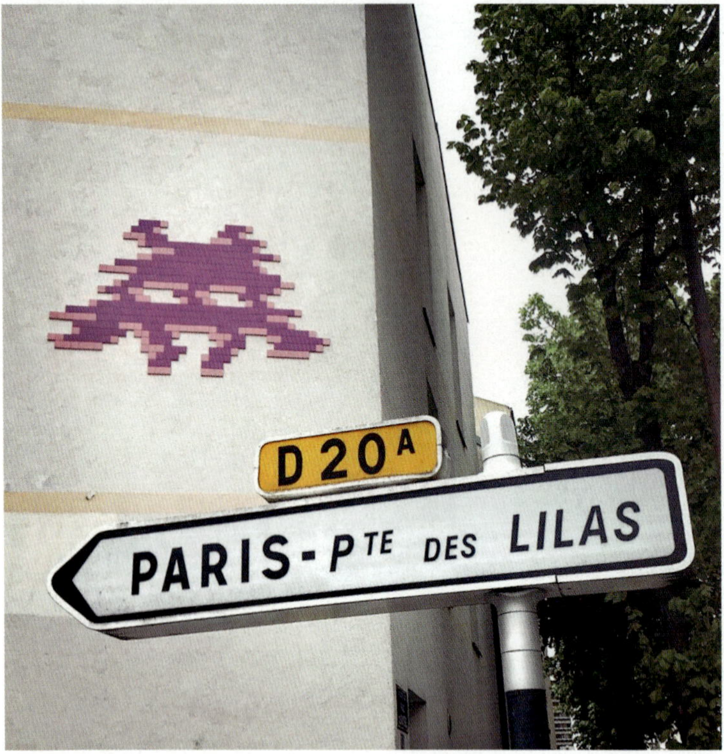

13 729 likes

invaderwashere LILAS is a color, a flower and a city near Paris #lilas #lilac #GlitchInLilas #PA1402

View all 138 comments

9 May 2019

invaderwashere

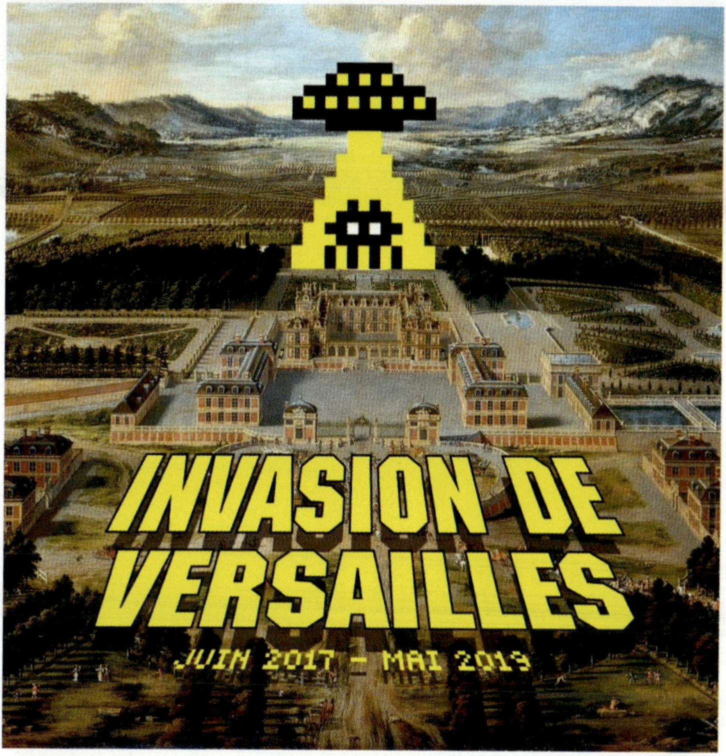

INVASION DE VERSAILLES

JUIN 2017 – MAI 2019

16 017 likes

invaderwashere INVASION DE VERSAILLES COMPLETED / More infos soon... Stay tuned... #VersaillesOFF #2017-2019

View all 337 comments

13 May 2019

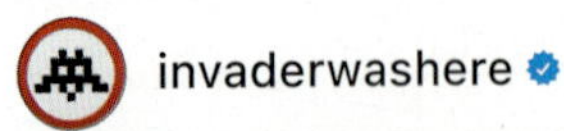

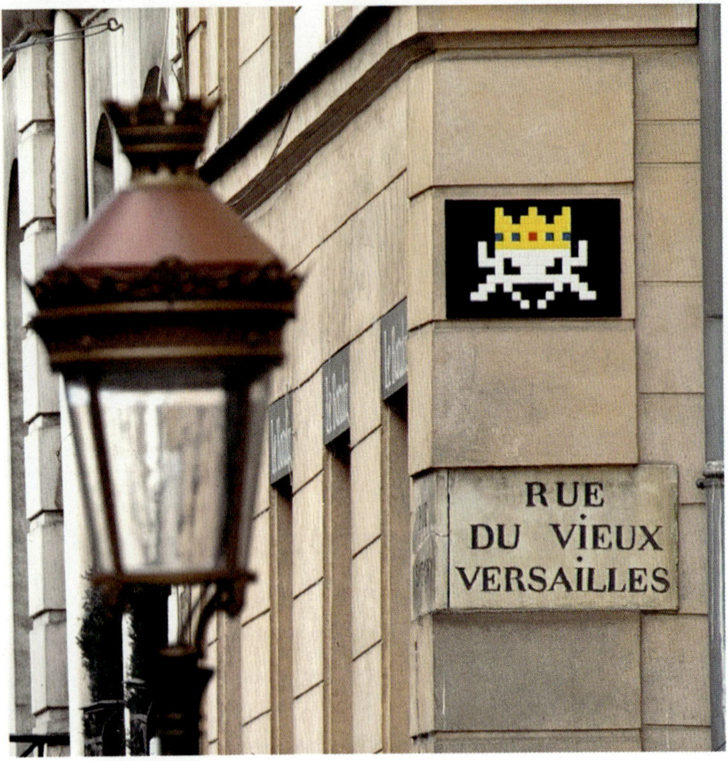

  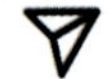 

16 221 likes

invaderwashere VRS_08 #VersaillesOff

View all 78 comments

14 May 2019

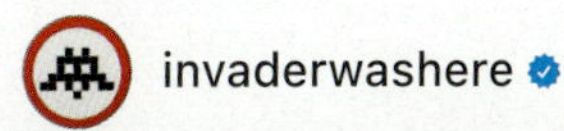

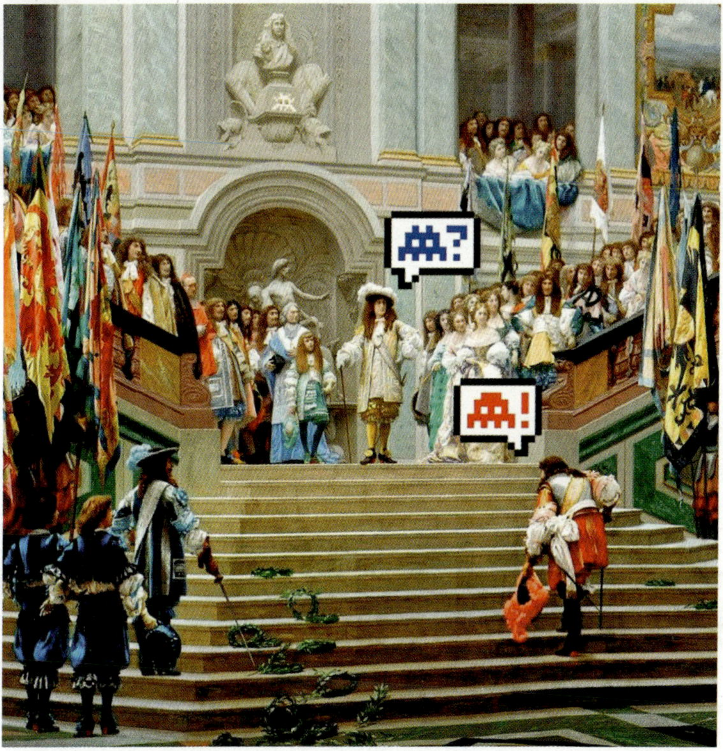

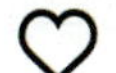   

17 424 likes

invaderwashere - WTF IS GOING ON IN MY KINGDOM?
- INVADER WAS HERE MY SIRE!

View all 126 comments

14 May 2019

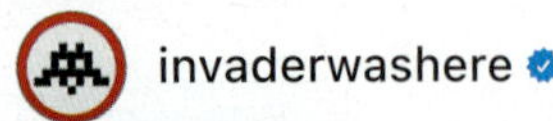

invaderwashere

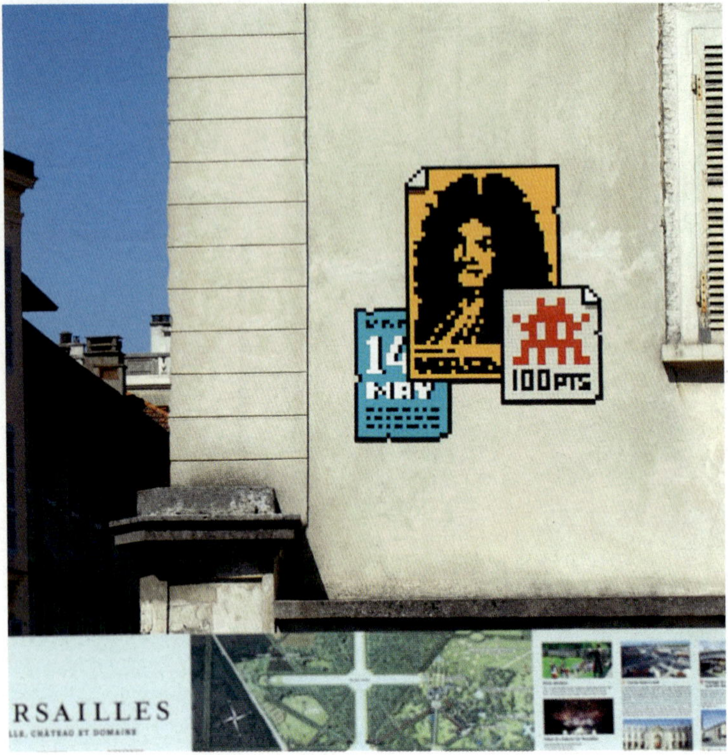

17714 likes

invaderwashere Did you know that on May 14th, 1643, Louis XIV became King of France? #VRS41 #LouisXIV #100PTS #VersaillesOff

View all 103 comments

14 May 2019

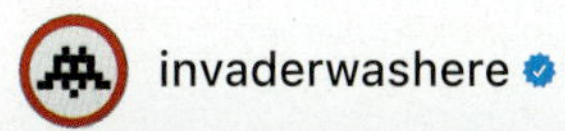

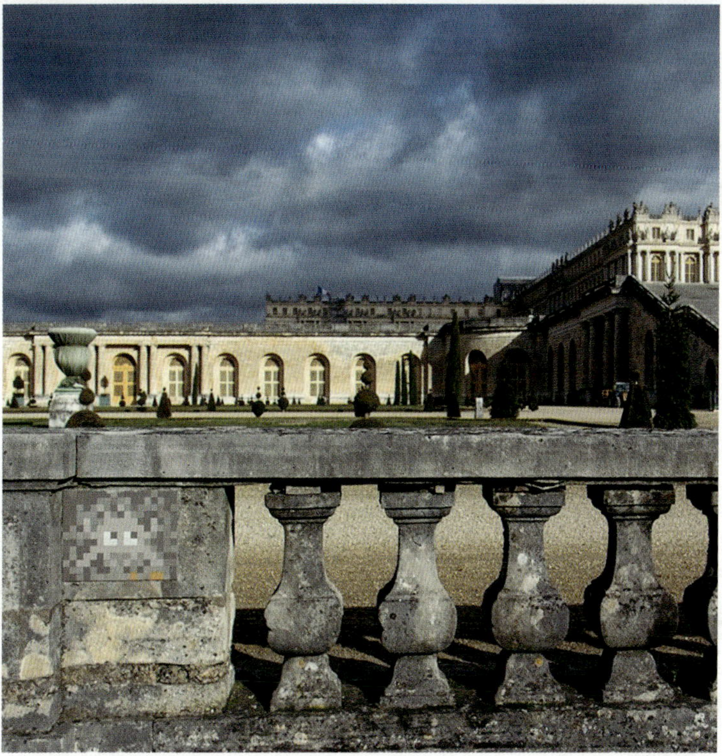

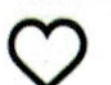

11885 likes

invaderwashere Two years of work and 12 waves of invasion were necessary to invade the city of Versailles. My main idea was to offer an alternative to the visit of the castle and to the major exhibitions of contemporary art which are regularly organized there. The end of this invasion coincides with the opening of a new group show entitled "Visible / Invisible"! And even if I'm not part of the official program, it could not be better since about 40 space invaders are now hidden in the city of Versailles. #visibleinvisible #VersaillesOff

More photos: link in Bio

View all 271 comments

14 May 2019

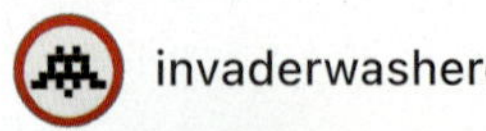
invaderwashere

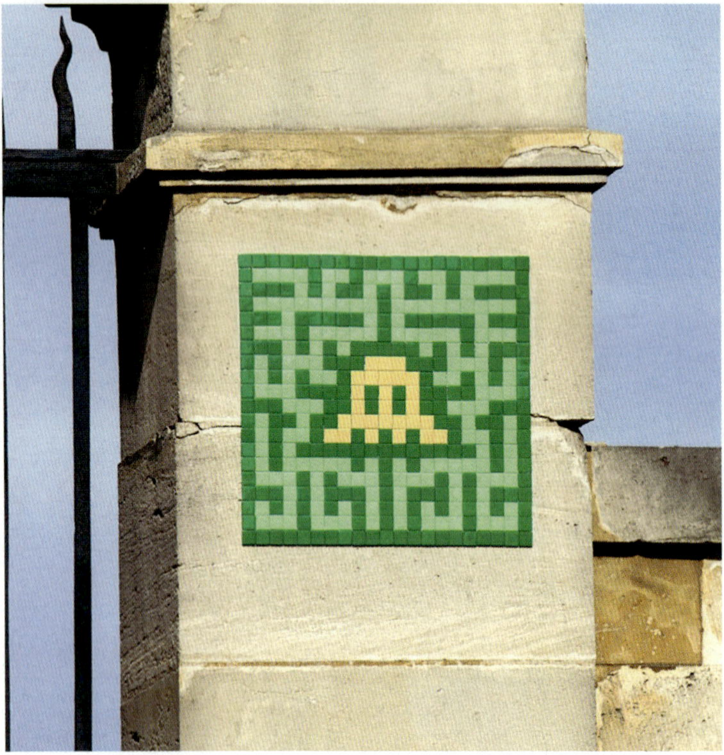

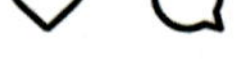

15 483 likes

invaderwashere VRS_19 #VersaillesOff

View all 79 comments

14 May 2019

invaderwashere

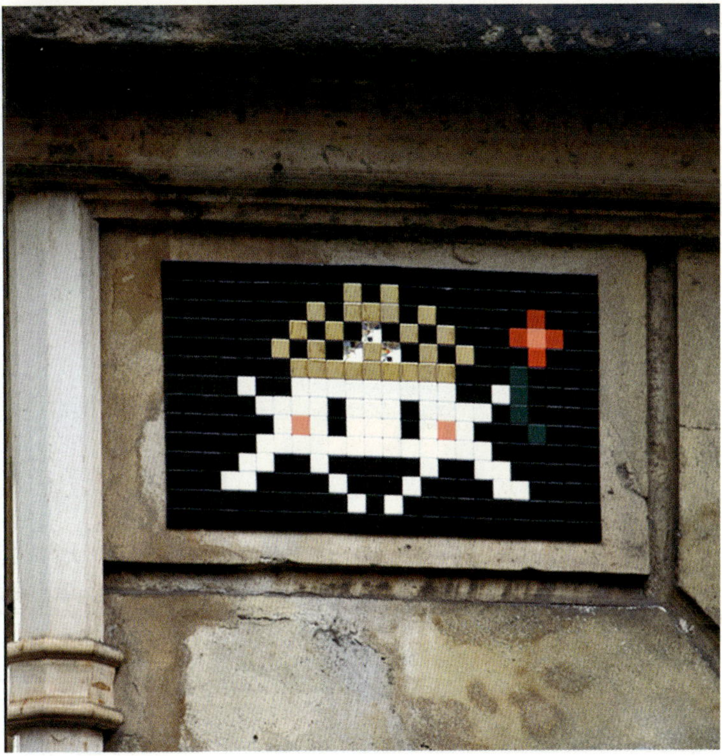

11 897 likes

invaderwashere VRS_16 #MarieAntoinette #thequeen #VersaillesOff

View all 61 comments

14 May 2019

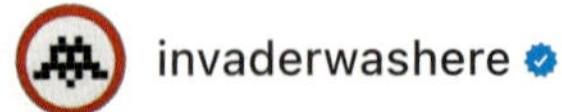

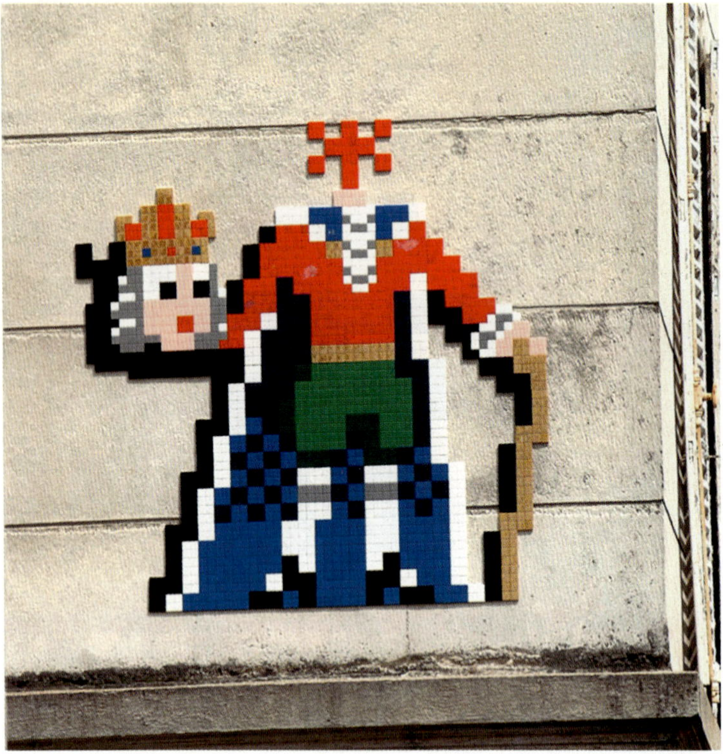

22 122 likes

invaderwashere Long live the King! #versaillesOff

View all 201 comments

15 May 2019

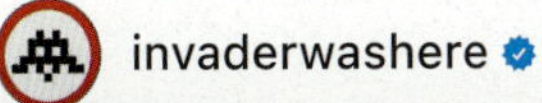

invaderwashere

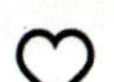   

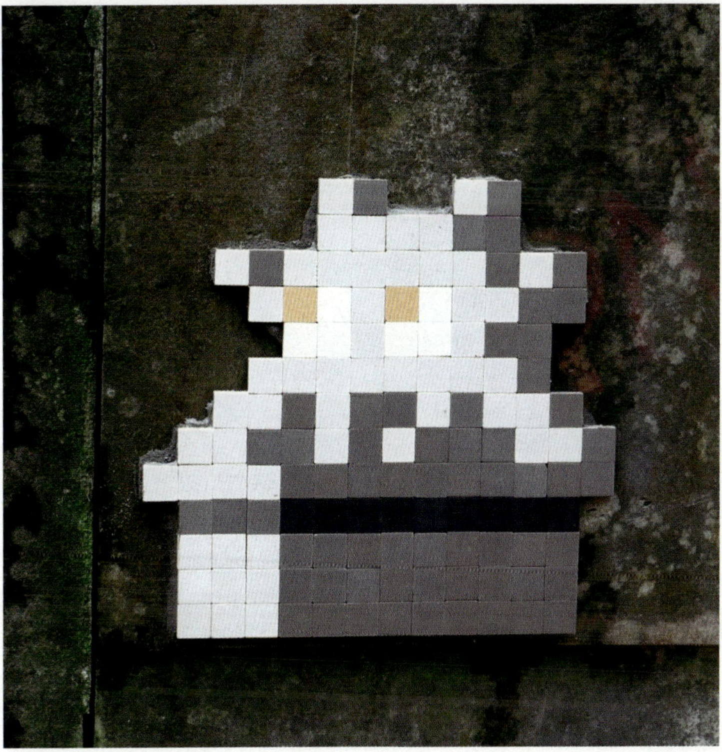

8048 likes

invaderwashere VRS_30 #VersaillesOff #visibleinvisible

View all 23 comments

16 May 2019

invaderwashere

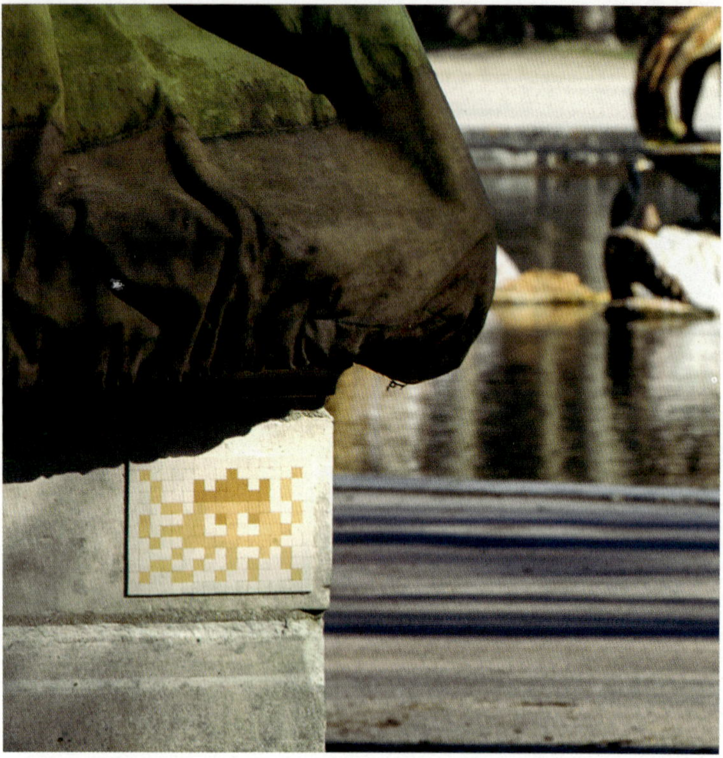

10 259 likes

invaderwashere VRS_26 #VersaillesOff #versailles #visibleinvisible

View all 43 comments

16 May 2019

invaderwashere

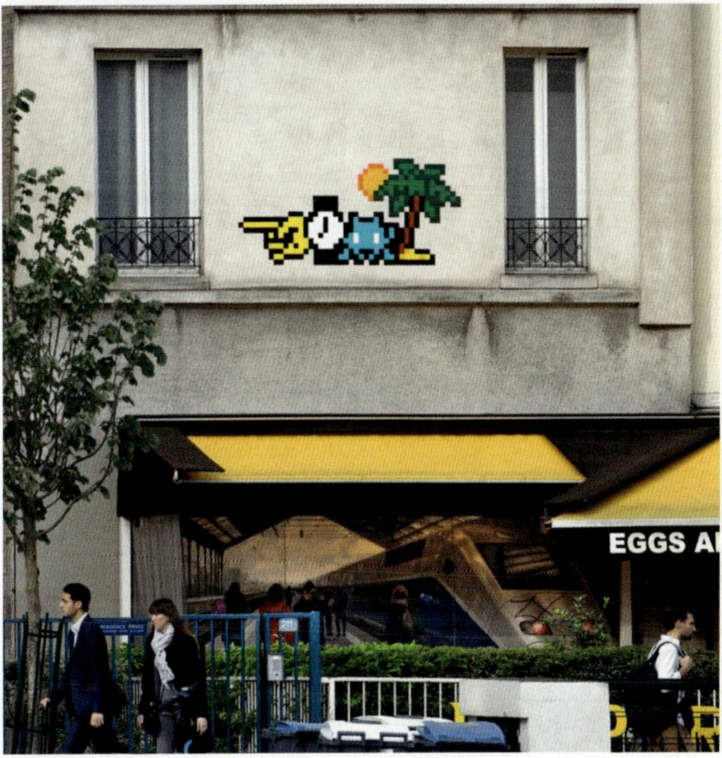

11542 likes

invaderwashere PA_1404 #GaredeLyon #dontmissthetrain #goingtosouthoffrance

View all 52 comments

24 May 2019

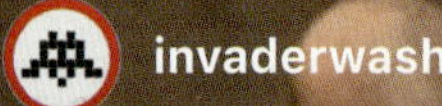
invaderwashere
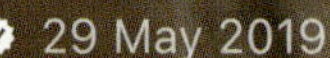
29 May 2019
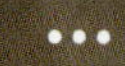
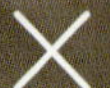
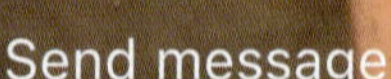
Send message
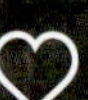
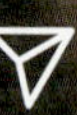

invaderwashere

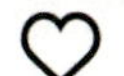   

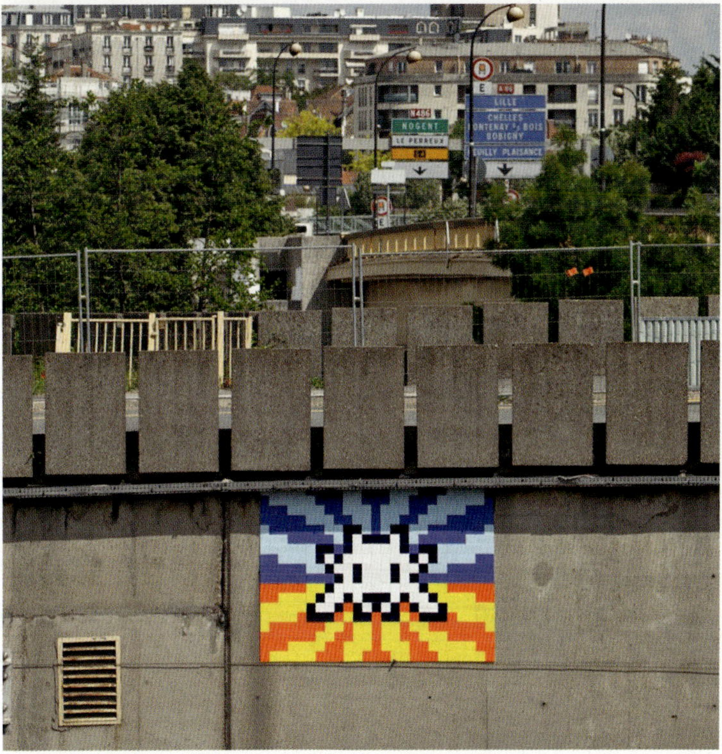

14 572 likes

invaderwashere PA_1405

View all 116 comments

29 May 2019

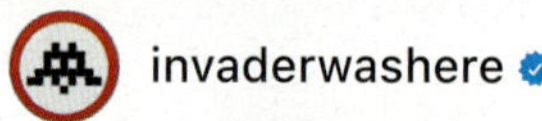

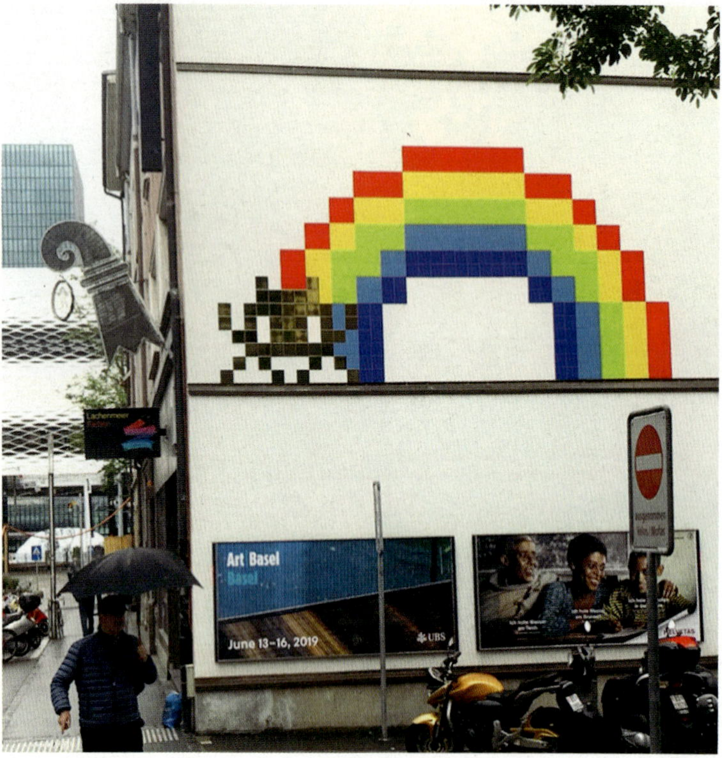

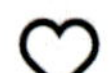   

14 583 likes

invaderwashere Art Basel, the pot of gold of the contemporary art world 🌈 🏺 👾 Thank you @artstuebli for this wonderful spot #basel #artbasel #potofgold #BSL25 #100pts

View all 130 comments

6 June 2019

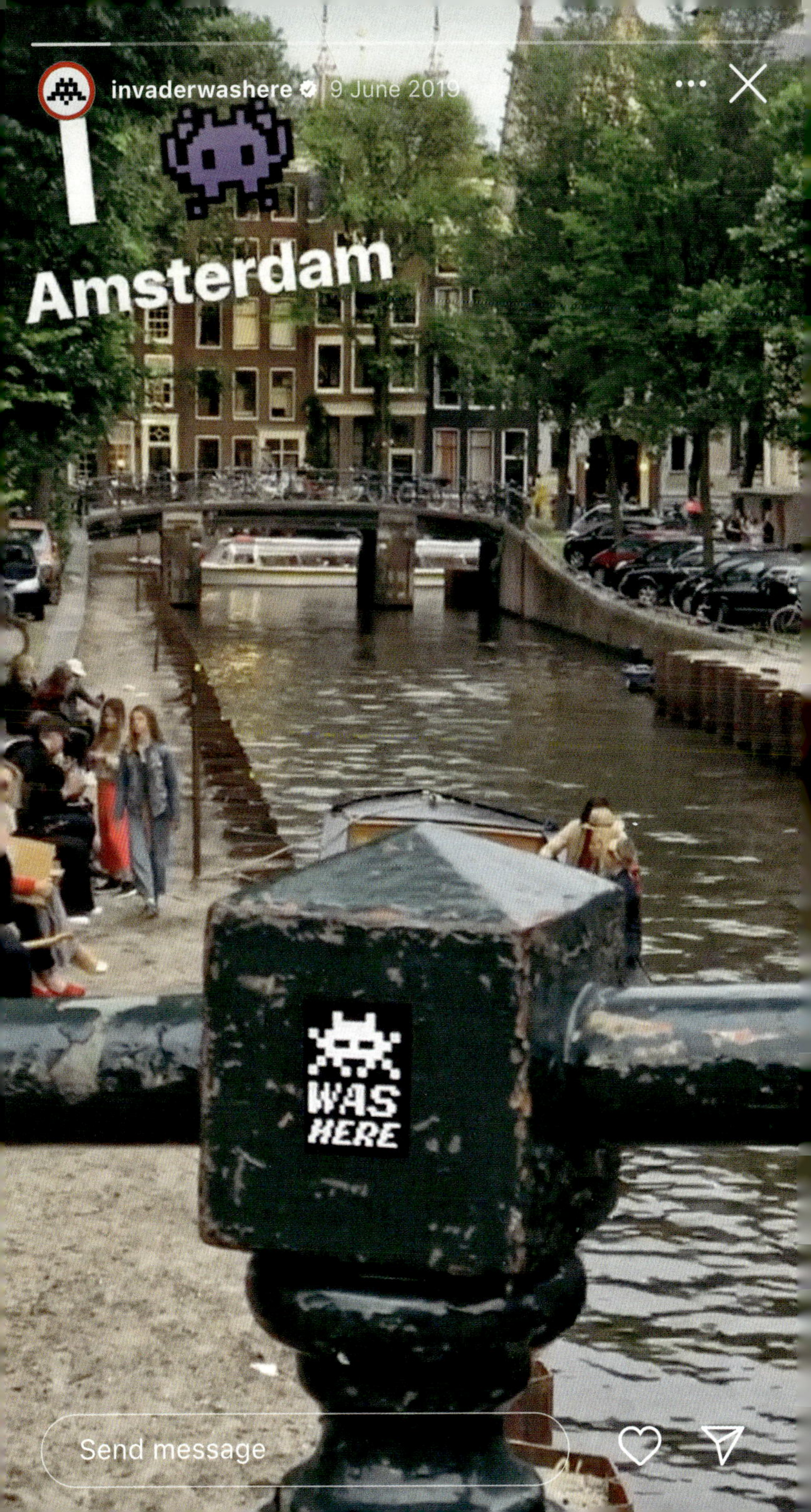

invaderwashere
9 June 2019
Amsterdam
WAS
HERE
Send message

invaderwashere

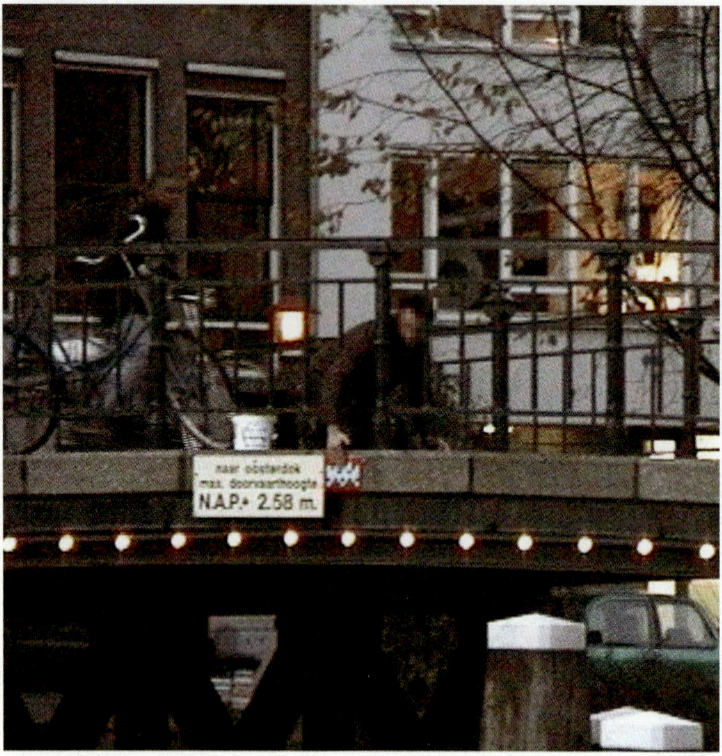

14 509 likes

invaderwashere AMS_13 #stillAlive #20yearsOld #Nov1999 #June2019 #Amsterdam #archive #throwback & #today

View all 132 comments

9 June 2019

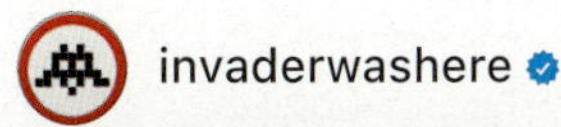

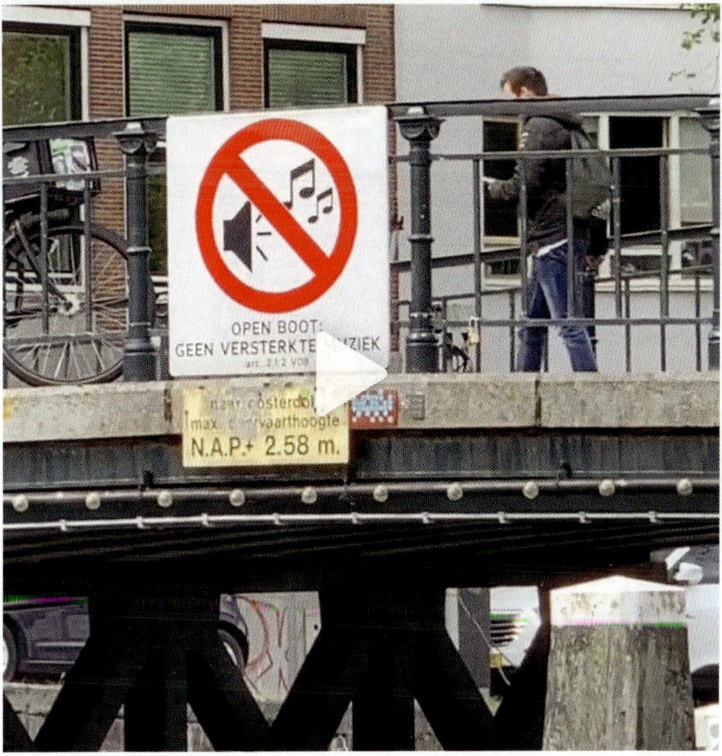

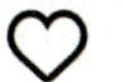   

14 494 likes

invaderwashere AMS_13 #stillAlive #20yearsOld #Nov1999 #June2019 #Amsterdam #archive #throwback & #today

View all 132 comments

9 June 2019

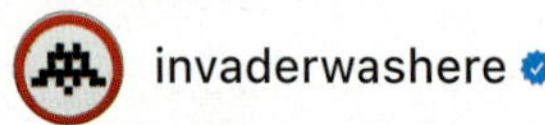

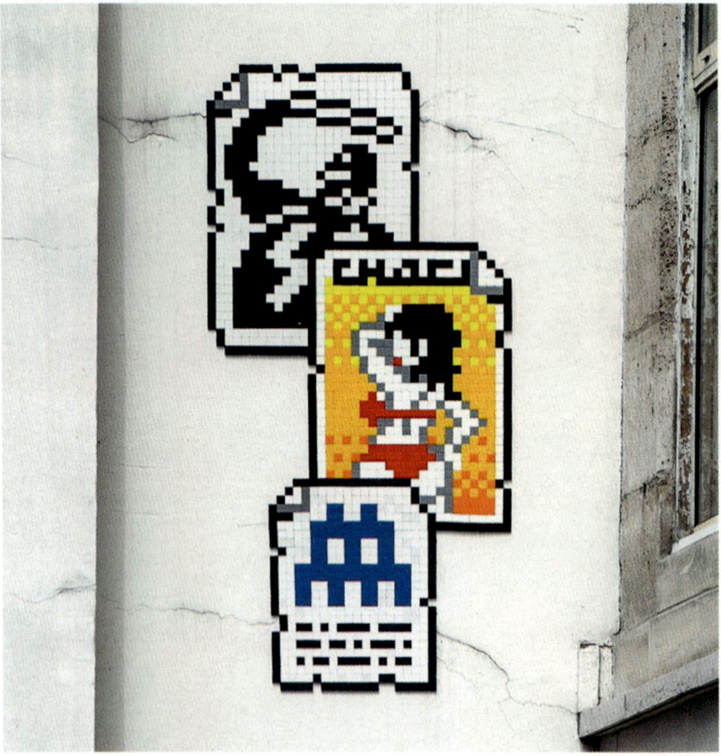

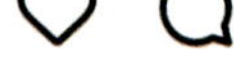

16765 likes

invaderwashere PA_1407 is done! #ceramicstreetposters #postnobills #paris #sorbonne

View all 110 comments

14 June 2019

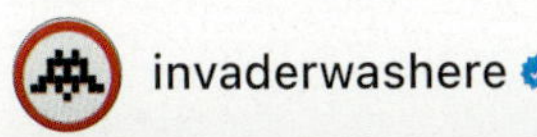

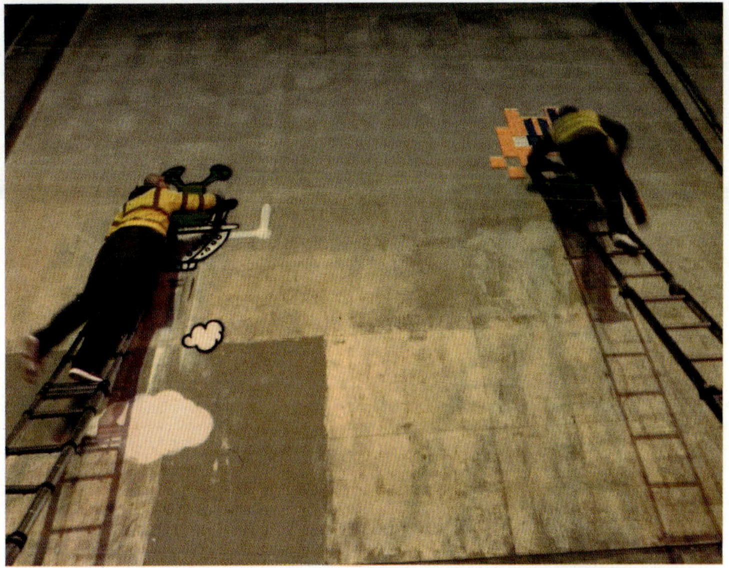

12 339 likes

invaderwashere Making of PA_1031 in company of @jaceticot #throwback #2012 #portedelavillette

View all 81 comments

18 June 2019

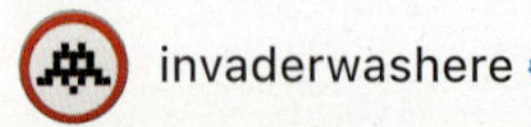

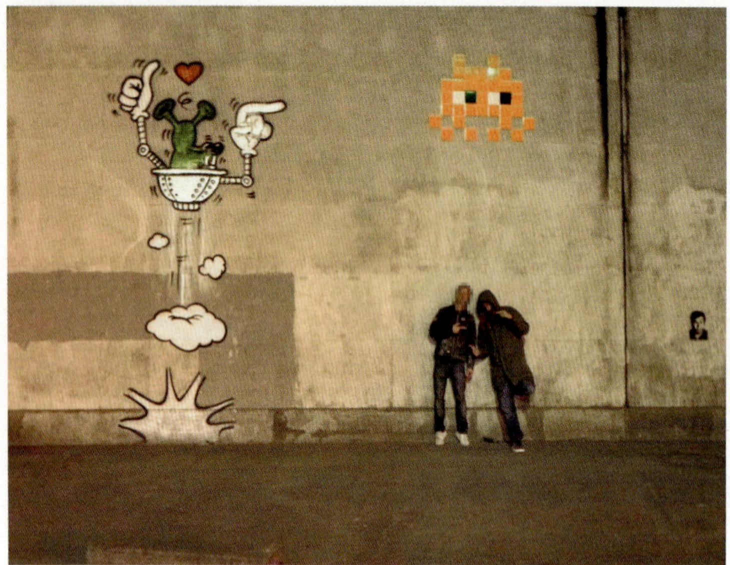

12 339 likes

invaderwashere Making of PA_1031 in company of @jaceticot #throwback #2012 #portedelavillette

View all 81 comments

18 June 2019

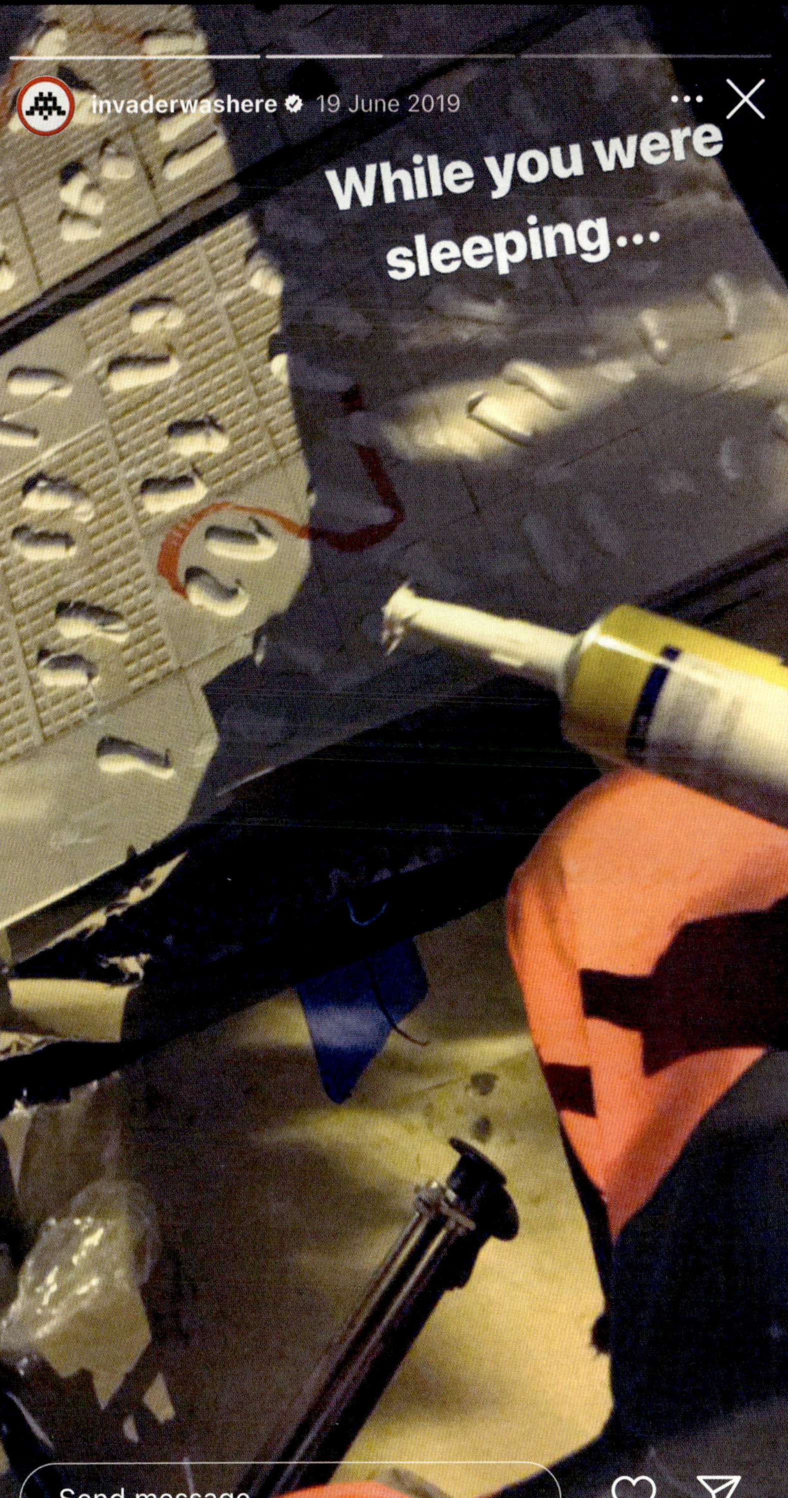
invaderwashere 19 June 2019
While you were sleeping...
Send message

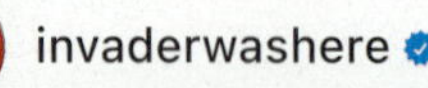

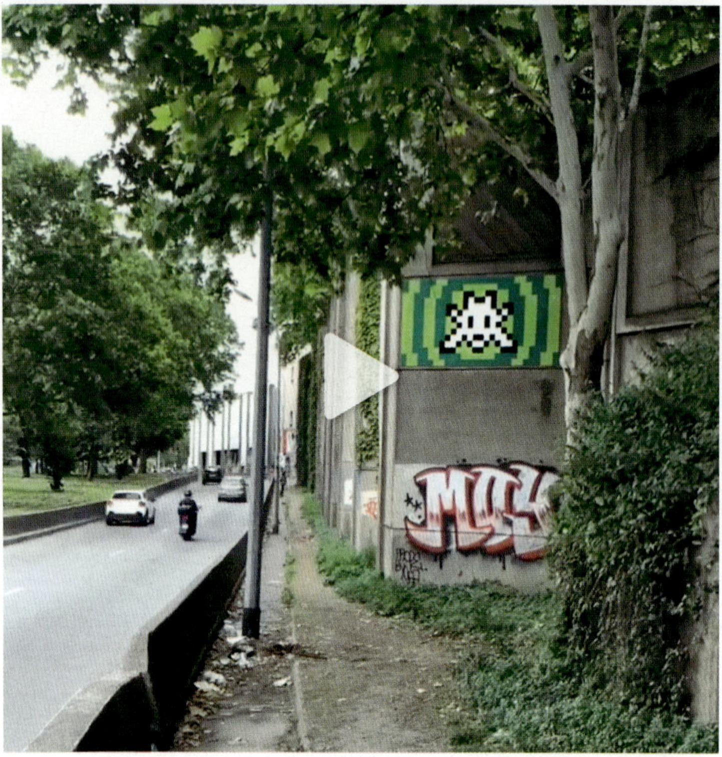

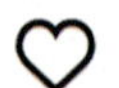   

10 949 likes

invaderwashere PA_1408 #périphériques #ring 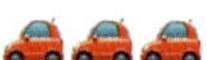

View all 85 comments

21 June 2019

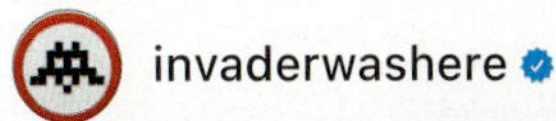

invaderwashere

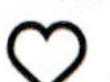    

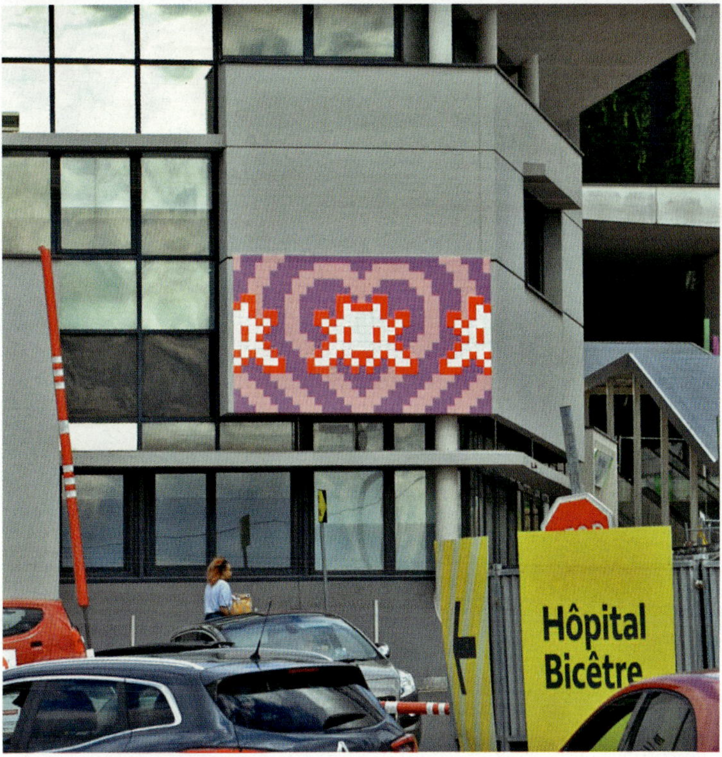

20 481 likes

invaderwashere The piece I have just made at the Kremlin Bicêtre Hospital in tribute to the organ donors will be officially unveiled today. Give organs, Give life!  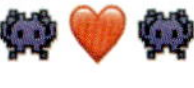 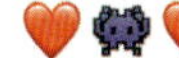 #tousdonneurs #PA1409 #100pts

View all 216 comments

24 June 2019

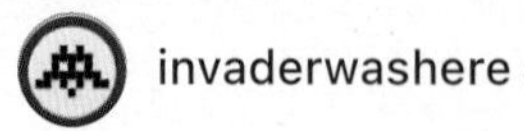

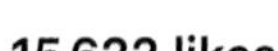

invaderwashere PA_1411 / PA_1410 #freshfromlastnight

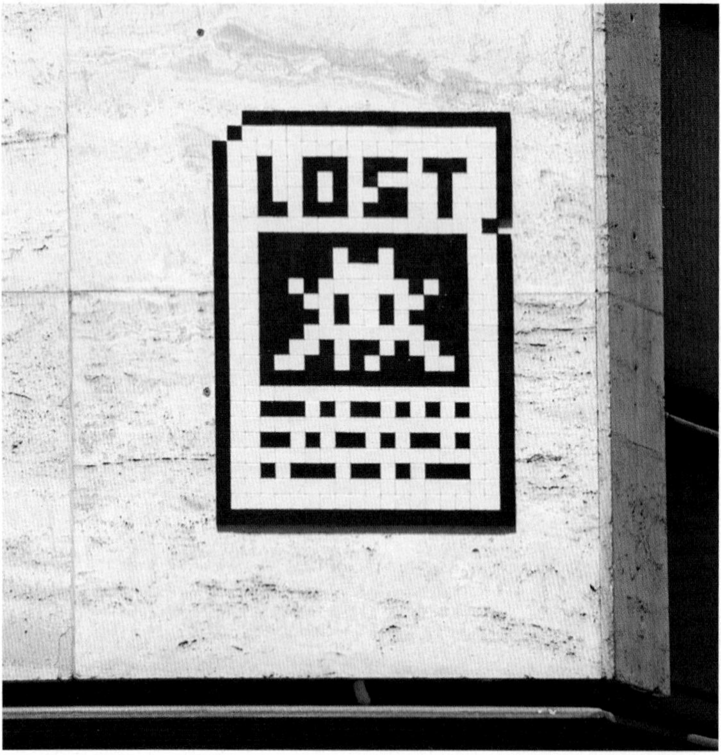

View all 71 comments

27 June 2019

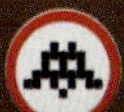

invaderwashere 2 July 2019

Material to be signed...

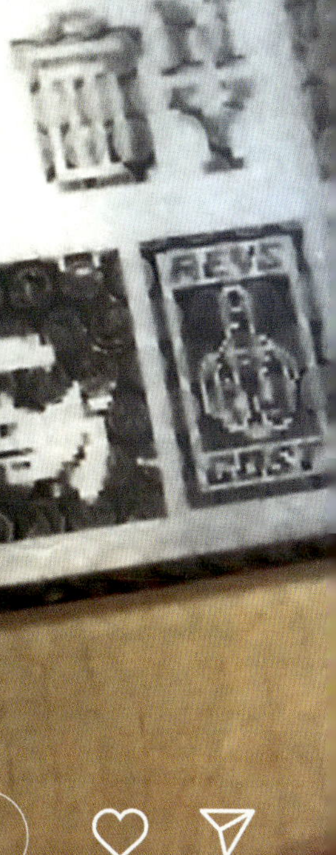

Send message

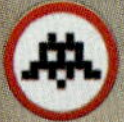

invaderwashere
2 July 2019

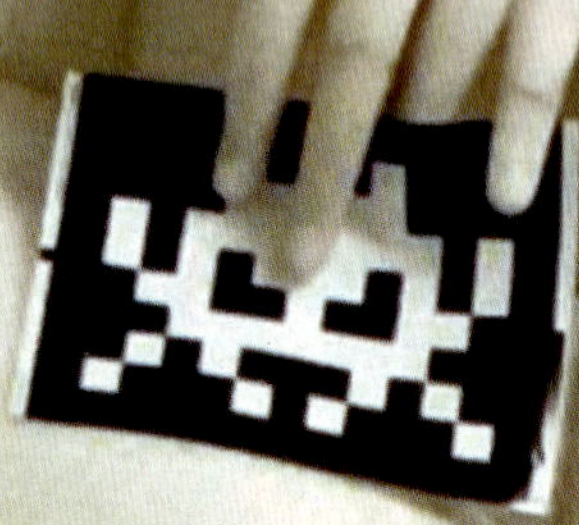

Send message

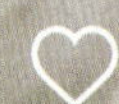

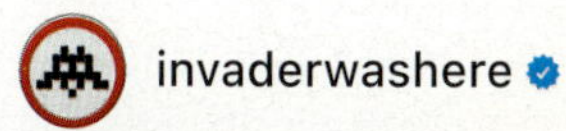

•••

 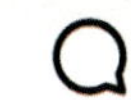  

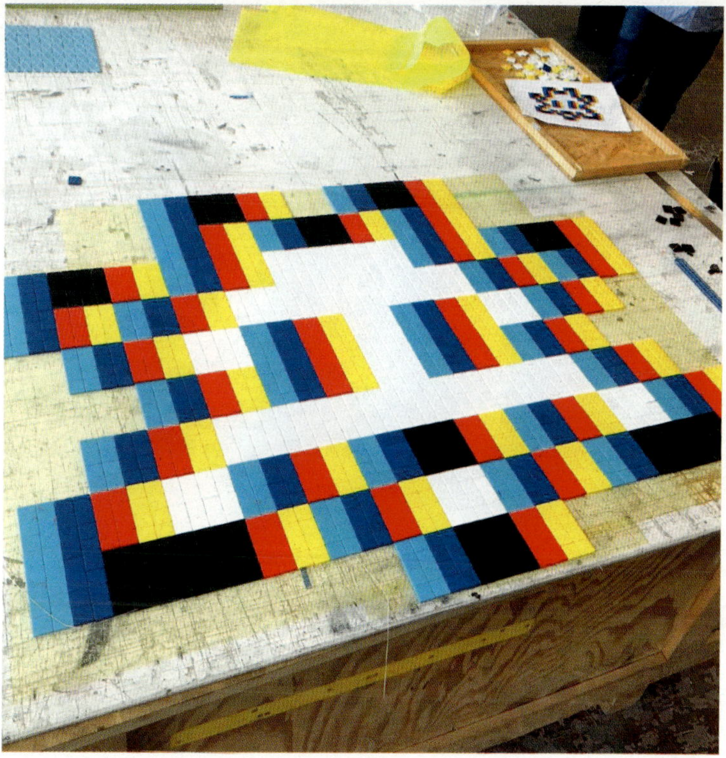

18 853 likes

invaderwashere Soon in the streets... #cmyk #vibrance

View all 257 comments

2 July 2019

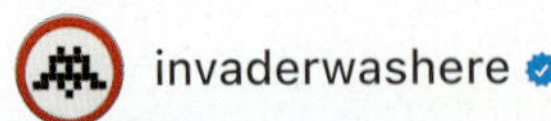

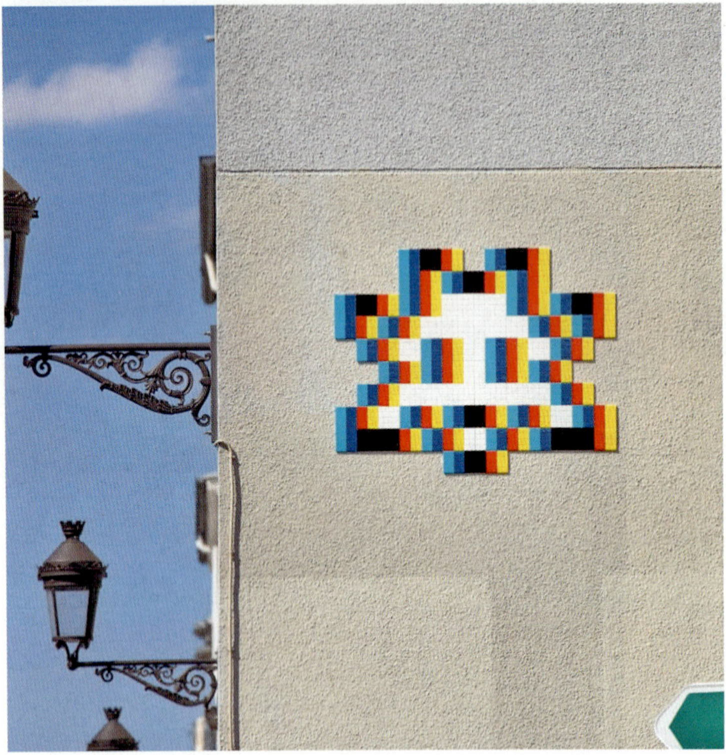

21 805 likes

invaderwashere Done! Enjoy your weekend 👾 PA_1414

View all 216 comments

5 July 2019

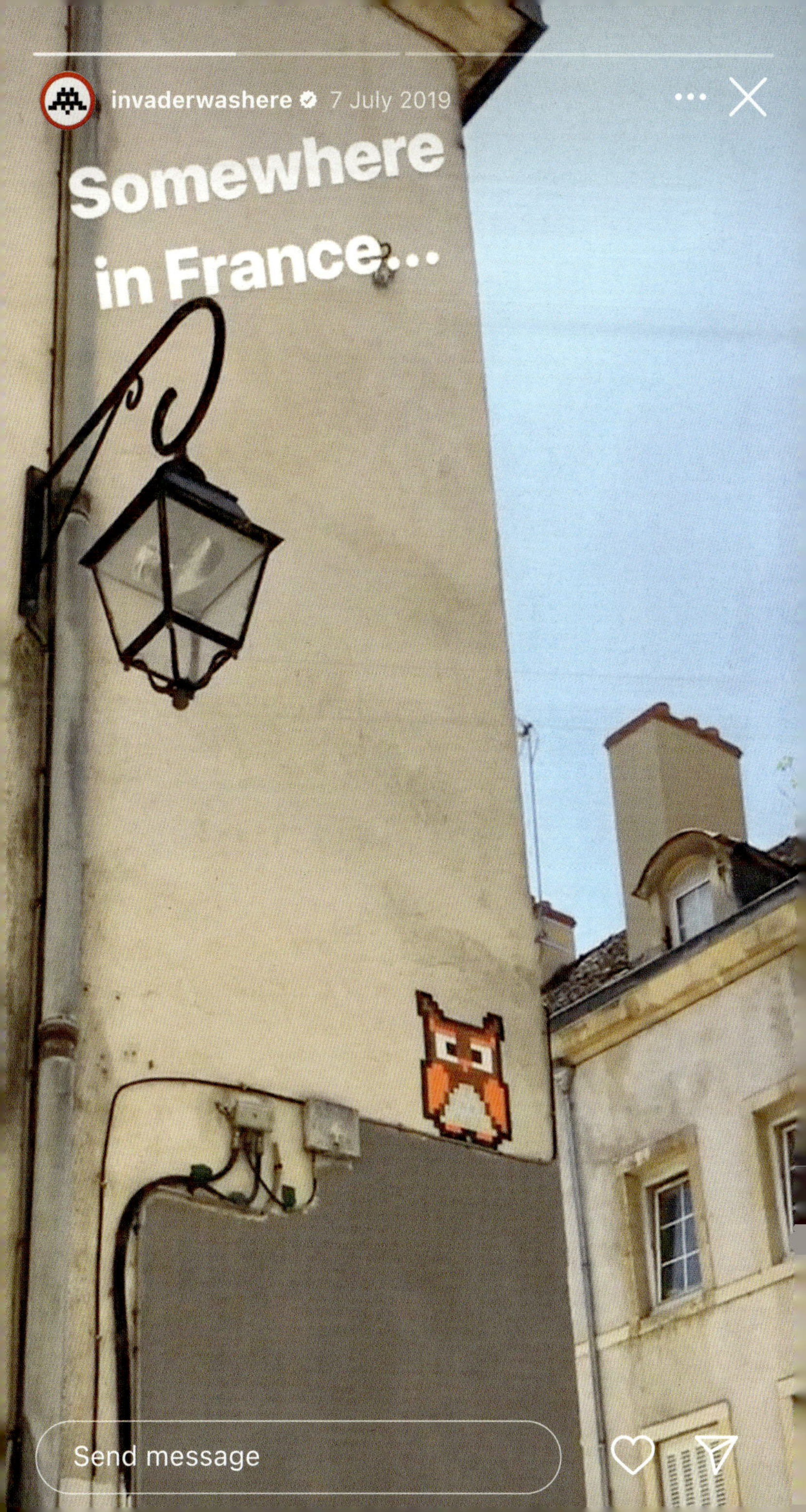
invaderwashere
7 July 2019
Somewhere in France...
Send message

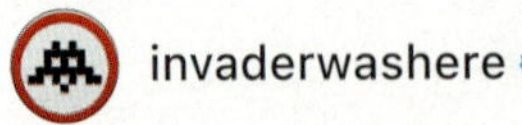

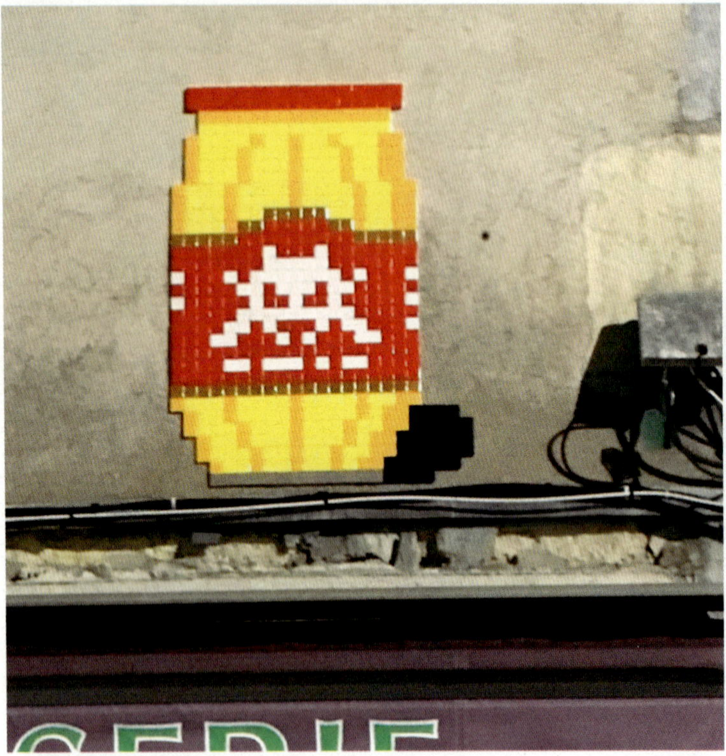

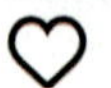  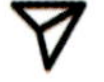 

16 733 likes

invaderwashere New city: Dijon #frenchmustard #invaderwashere

View all 222 comments

7 July 2019

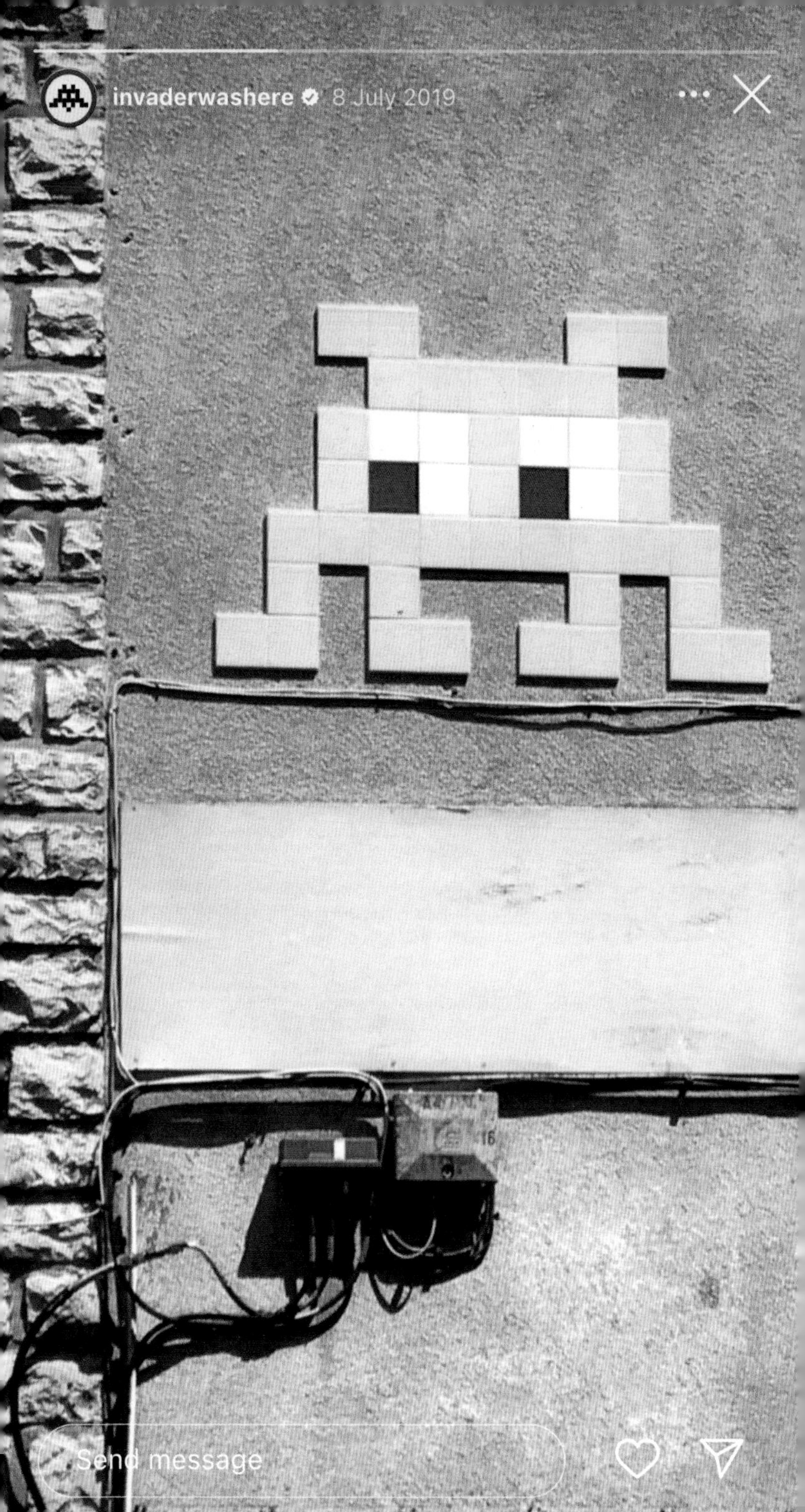
invaderwashere
8 July 2019
Send message

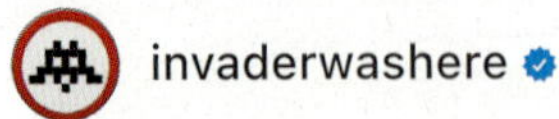

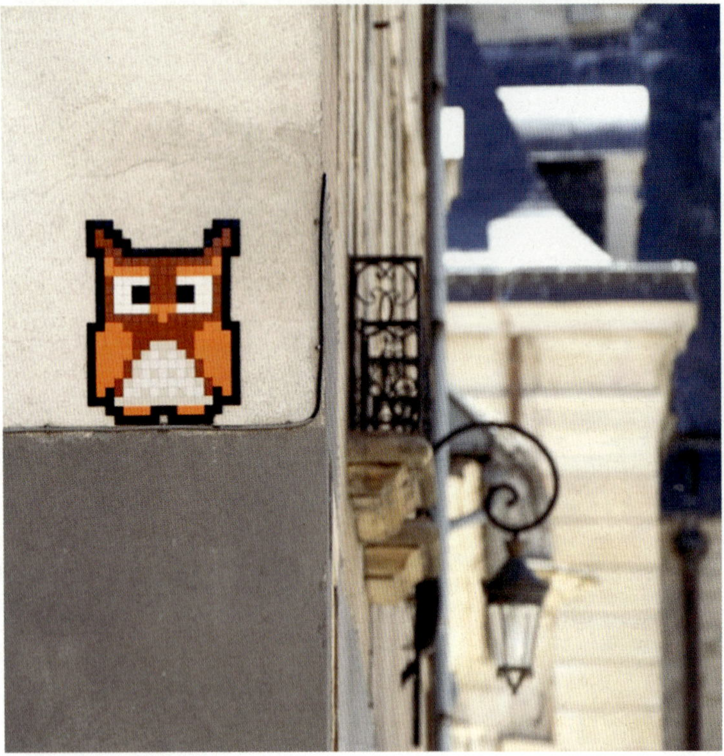

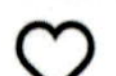   

13 841 likes

invaderwashere 🦉 👾 #dijon

View all 111 comments

13 July 2019

invaderwashere

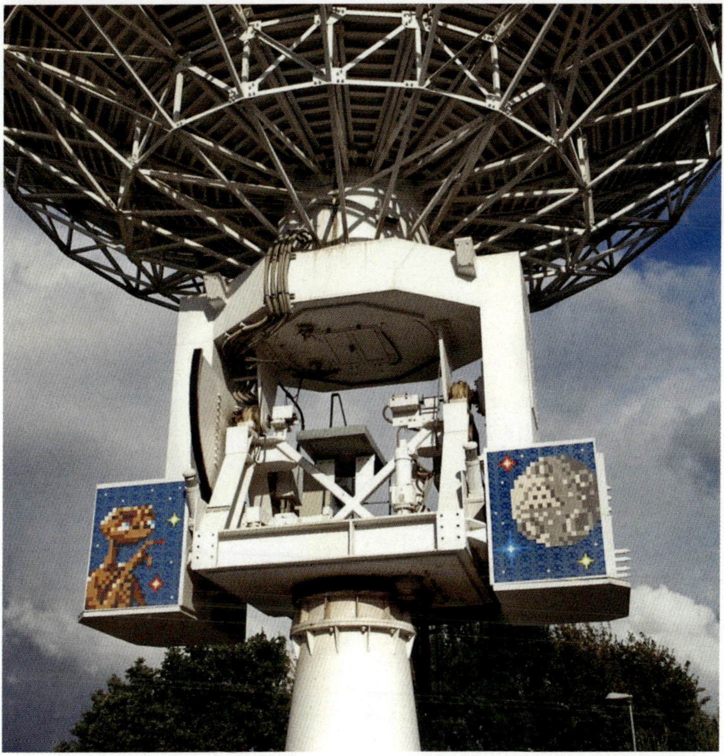

22 510 likes

invaderwashere Tribute to the first step of humans on the moon / 1969-2019 #mooninvasion #spaceconquest #rom_70 #rom_71 #esa #nasa

View all 262 comments

23 July 2019

invaderwashere

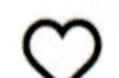   

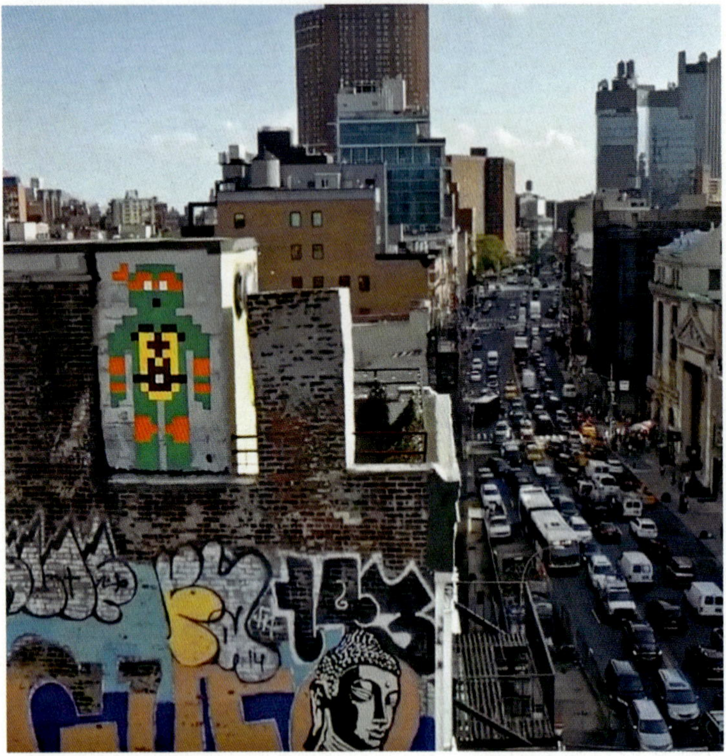

20 042 likes

invaderwashere Great shot of NY_153 / Michelangelo / by @ow.ley #drone #manhattan #bowery #goingup

View all 135 comments

3 August 2019

invaderwashere

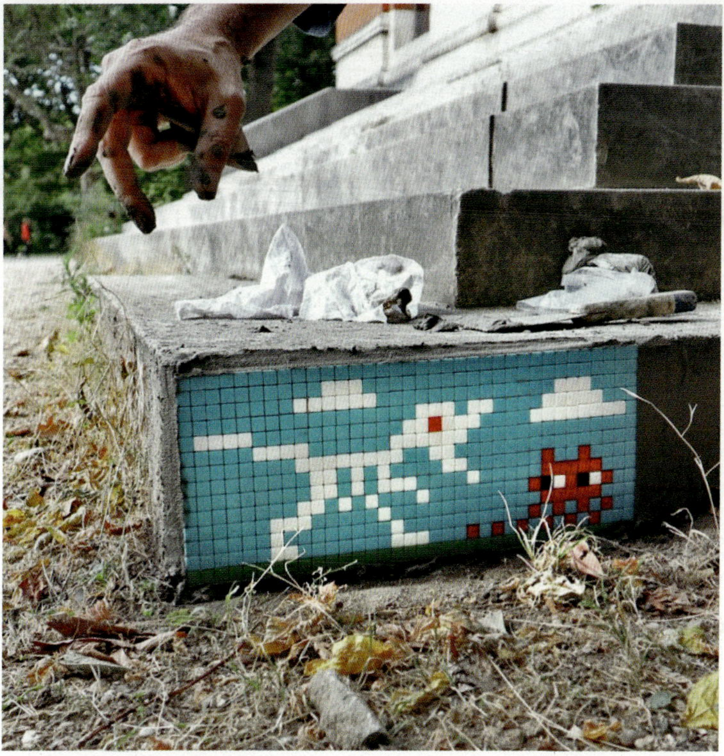

24 195 likes

invaderwashere Installing PA_1417 / T-Rex skeleton / Muséum national d'Histoire naturelle 🦴

View all 186 comments

4 August 2019

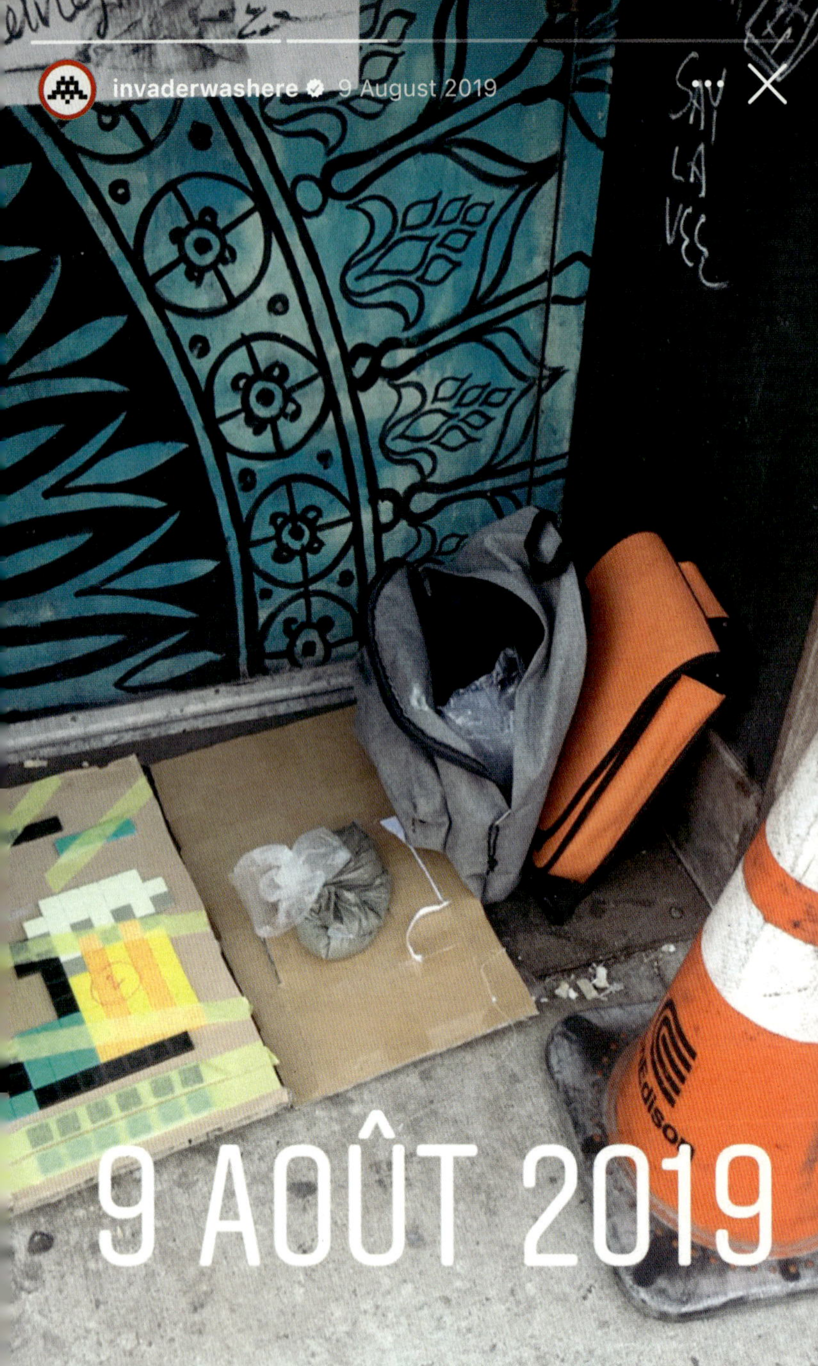

Send message

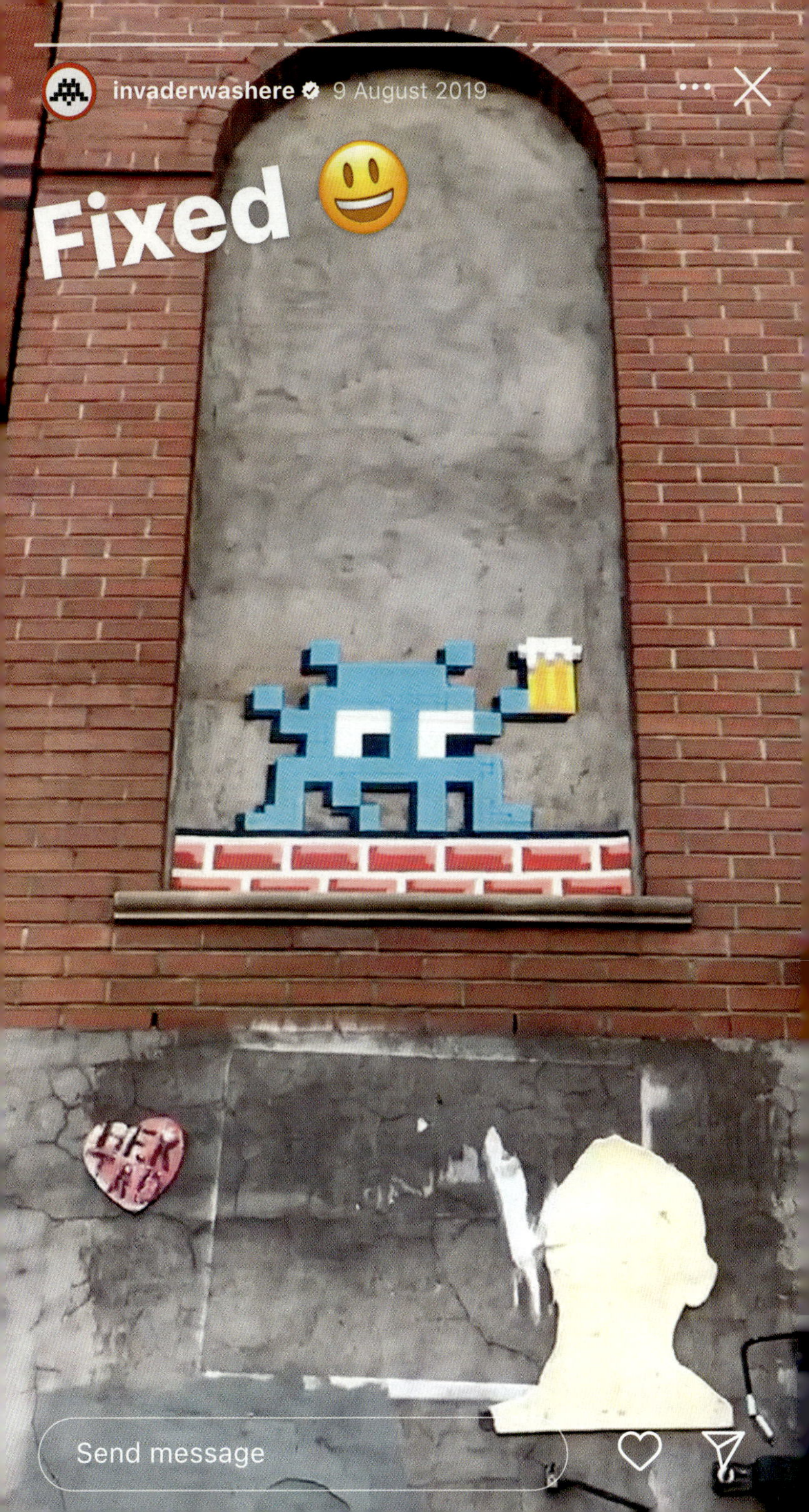

invaderwashere 9 August 2019
Fixed
Send message

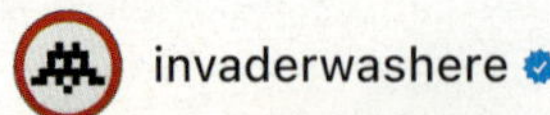

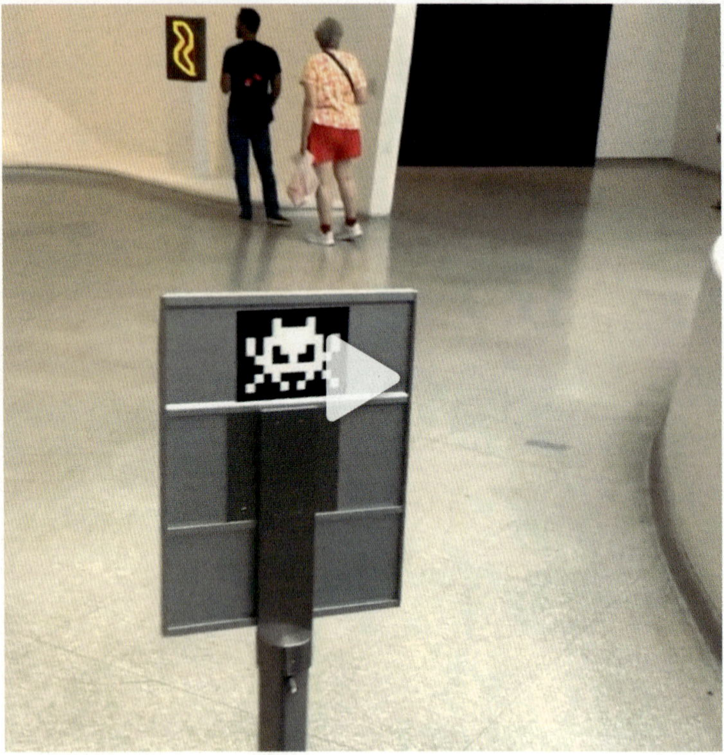

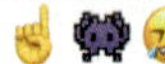

114 278 views

invaderwashere My first appearance in the #guggenheim
☝️👾🤣

View all 484 comments

11 August 2019

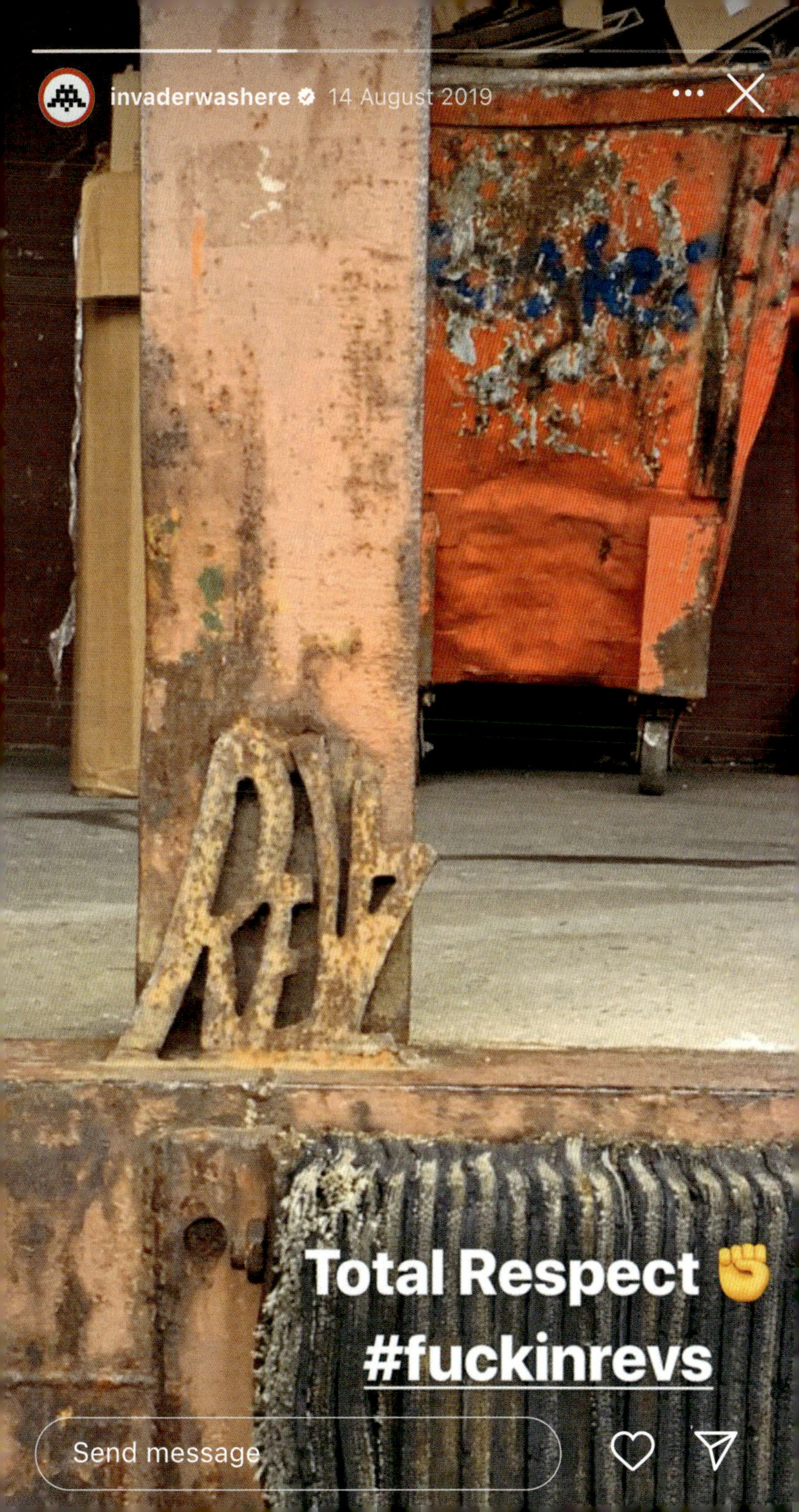
invaderwashere 14 August 2019
REV
Total Respect
#fuckinrevs
Send message

invaderwashere
14 August 2019
Send message

invaderwashere

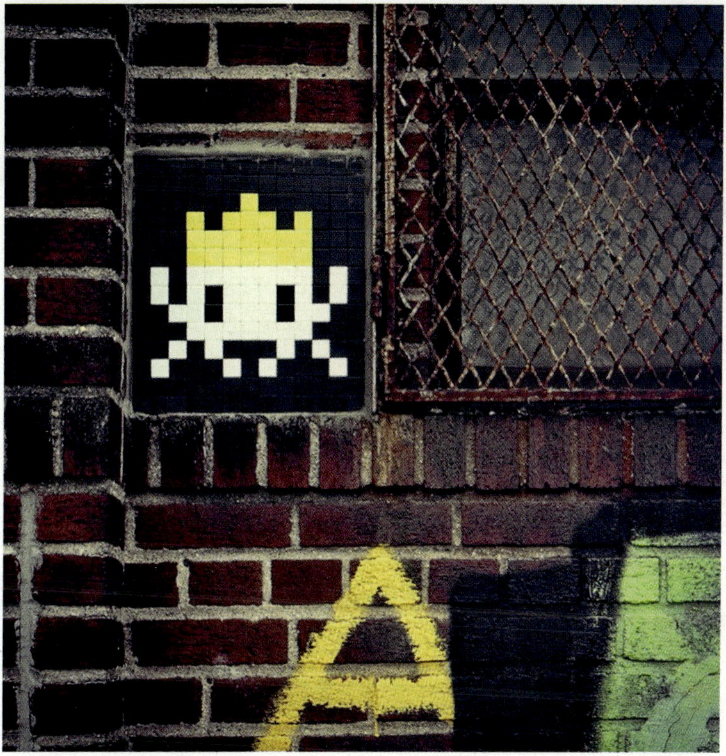

11684 likes

invaderwashere My little tribute to SAMO 👑 #NYC #2019 #SAMO #Basquiat

View all 121 comments

14 August 2019

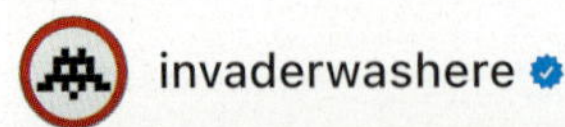

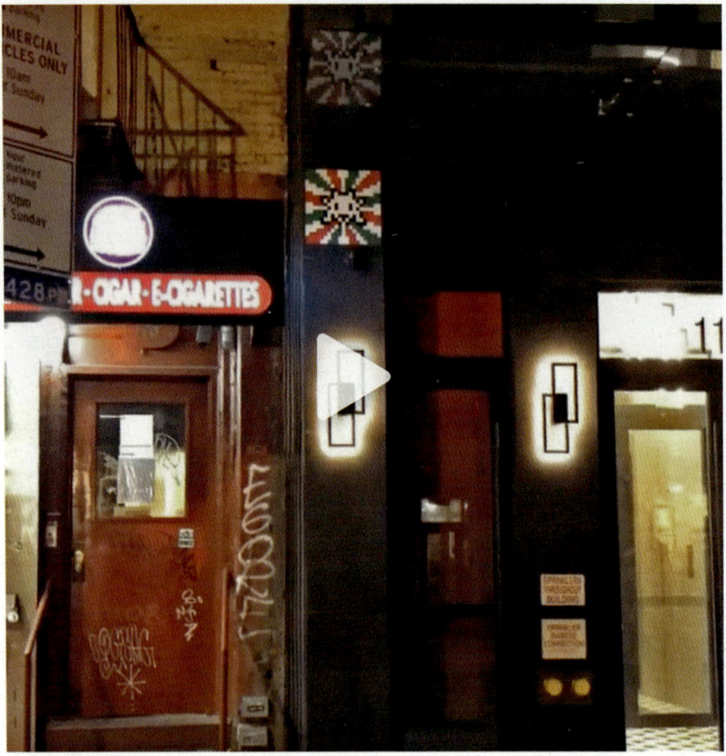

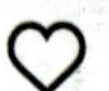   

41392 views

invaderwashere Welcome to Little Italy 🇮🇹 Big thanx to @thelisaprojectnyc #NYC #littleitaly NY_216

View all 82 comments

15 August 2019

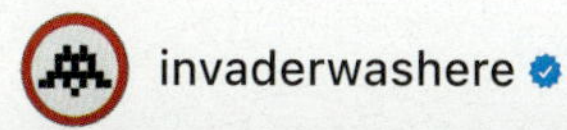

...

LATEST SUCCESSFUL "FLASHES"

96 244 Players / 5 000 000 Flashes

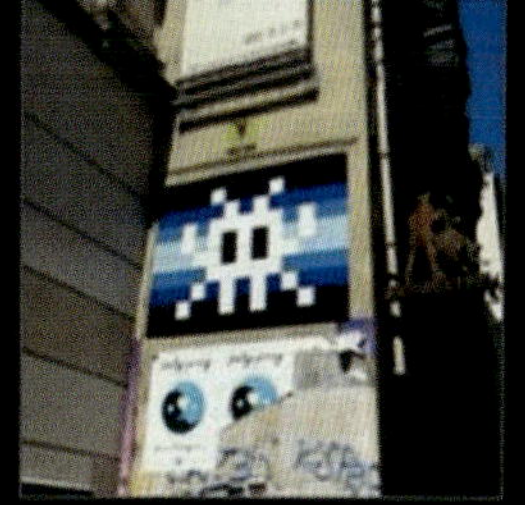

Paris, AWDE
14 seconds ago

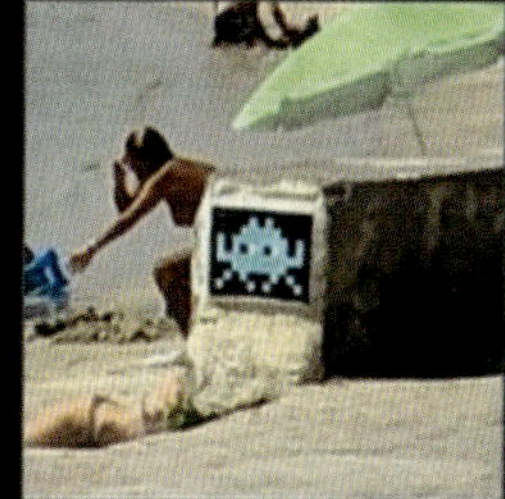

Côte d'Azur, SEINE55
21 seconds ago

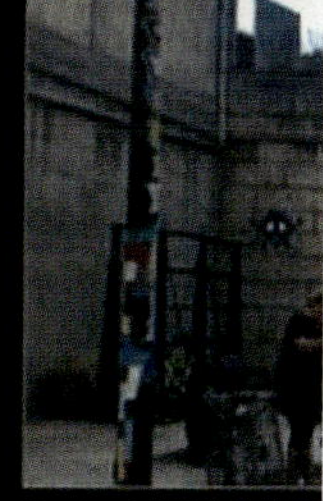

Paris, MINE DE RI
27 seconds ago

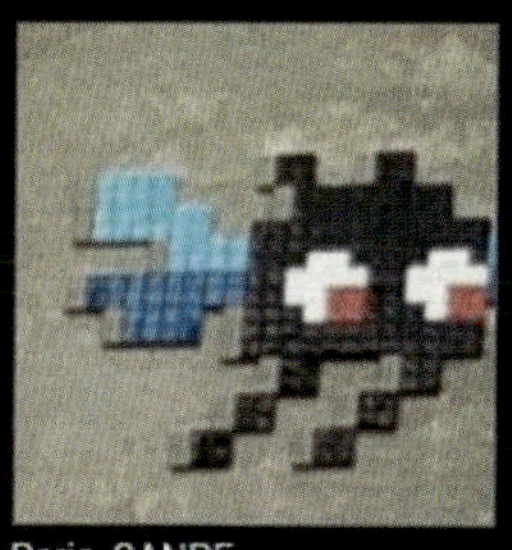

Paris, SANPE

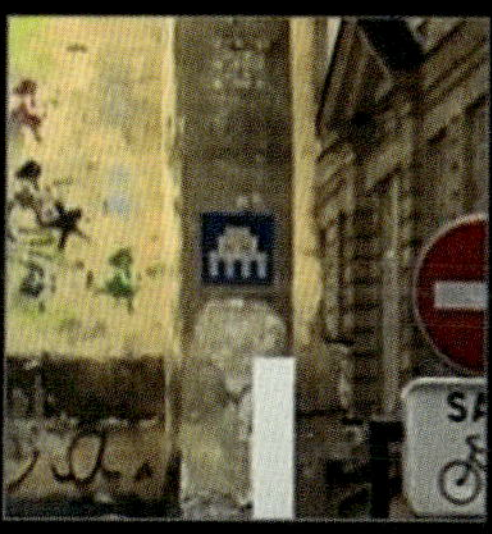

Paris, CELINESWORLD

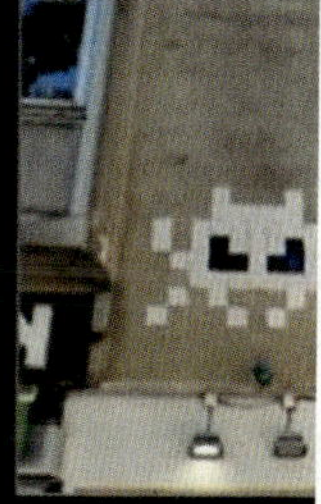

Paris, KINANIMAT

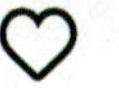   

7253 likes

invaderwashere 5 MIILIONS of successful Flashes on #FlashInvaders Big up to all the players 👏👏👏 Link in bio

View all 80 comments

17 August 2019

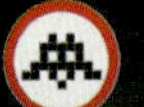

invaderwashere 19 August 2019

BEYOND THE STREETS NYC

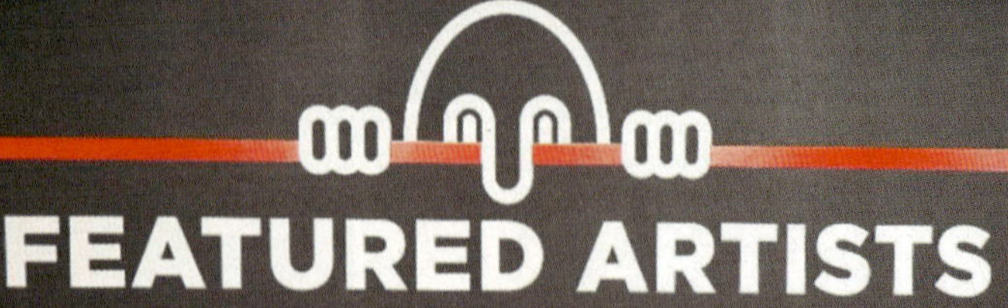

A-ONE
AIKO
Al Diaz
Alexis Ross
Alicia McCarthy
André Saraiva
Anthony Lister
Barry McGee
BAST
Beastie Boys
Bert Krak
Bill Barminski
Bill Daniel
BLADE
Broken Fingaz
Buddy Esquire
buZ blurr
Carlos Mare
Carl Weston
CES
Cey Adams
C.R. Stecyk III
Charlie Ahearn
Chaz Bojórquez
Claudia Gold
Cleon Peterson
COCO 144
Conor Harrington
Corita Kent
CORNBREAD
Craig Costello
CRASH
DABSMYLA
Dan Witz
Dash Snow
DAZE
DEFER
Dennis Hopper
Doze Green
EARSNOT
Emory Douglas
Estevan Oriol
Fab 5 Freddy
FAILE
Faith XLVII
Felipe Pantone
FREEDOM
FUTURA 2000
Gajin Fujita
Glen E. Friedman
Gordon Matta-Clark
Guerrilla Girls
Eric Haze
Henry Chalfant
Herb Migdoll
HuskMitNavn
INVADER
Jane Dickson
Jason REVOK
Jean-Michel Basquiat
Jenny Holzer
Jim Prigoff
Joe Conzo
John Ahearn
John Fekner
John Tsombikos
Jon Naar
José Parlá
Julie Reich, Ph.D
KATSU
KC Ortiz
Keith Haring
Kenny Scharf
Kilroy Was Here
LADY PINK
LAZAR
LEE Quiñones
Lisa Kahane
MADSAKI
Maripol
Mark Gonzales
Mark Mothersbaugh
Martha Cooper
Matt Weber
Maya Hayuk
Michael Lawrence
MIKE 171
MISS 17
Mister CARTOON
Nina Chanel Abney
NOC 167
Pat Riot
Patrick Martinez
Paul Insect
POSE
PRAY
Rammellzee
Randall Harrington
Richard Colman
Richard Hambleton
RIME
RISK
Ron English
Ruby Neri
SABER
Sam Friedman
SANESMITH
Sayre Gomez
Shepard Fairey
SJK 171
SLICK
SNAKE 1
snipe1
STAY HIGH 149
Stephen Powers
SWOON
Takashi Murakami
TAKI 183
TATS CRU
TENGAone
Tim Conlon
Timothy Curtis
Todd James
Trash Records
UGA
VHILS
Victor Reyes
ZESER
1UP Crew

Featuring so many great artists from the Birth of Graffiti to Street Art

Send message

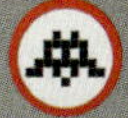

invaderwashere 19 August 2019

Don't miss it
If you are in NYC

Send message

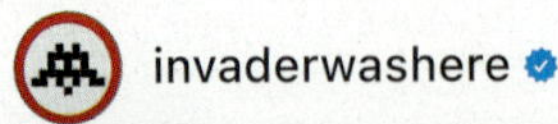

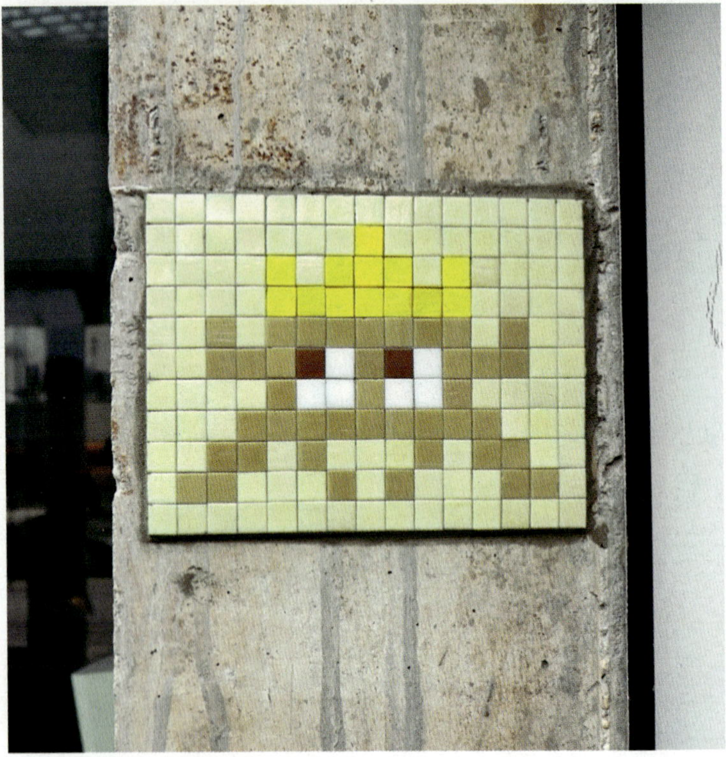

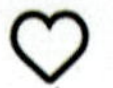  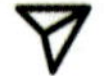 

12 587 likes

invaderwashere NY_218 Somewhere in Manhattan...

View all 95 comments

19 August 2019

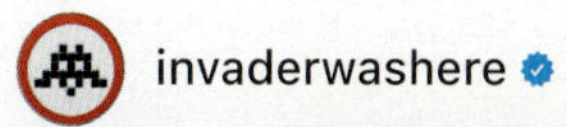

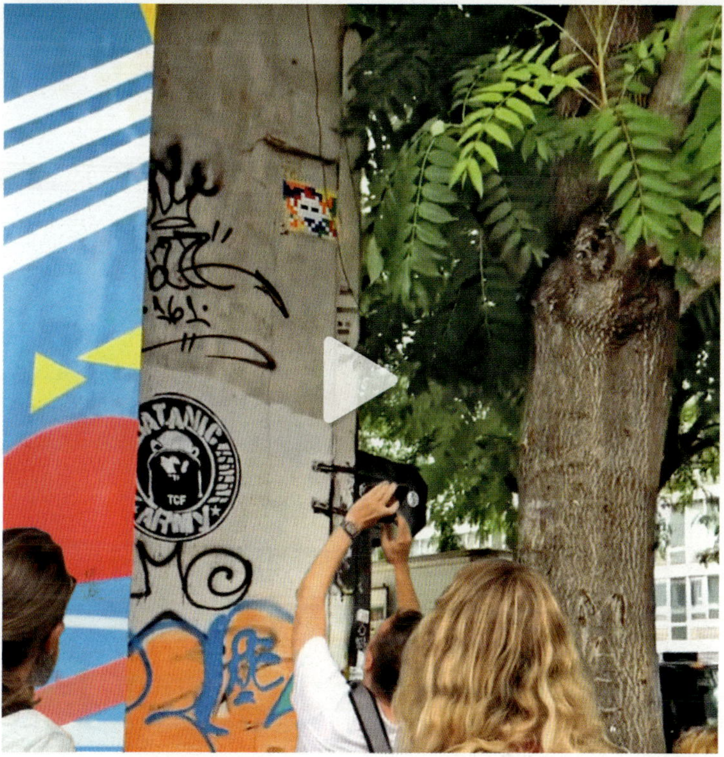

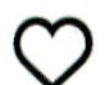  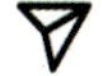 

49 878 views

invaderwashere I was lucky enough to bump into those guys 😁😂🤣 Thank you to the guide for the #flashinvaders demo and for letting me join and film the tour 👾🙏 #invaderwashere

View all 230 comments

23 August 2019

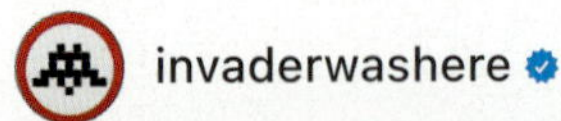

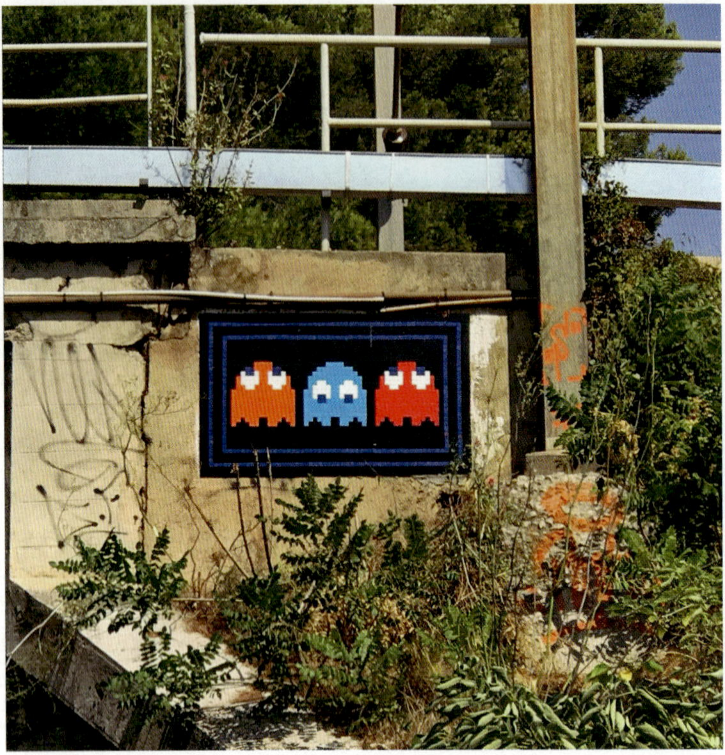

 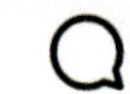  

16 210 likes

invaderwashere South of France LCT_05 ☀️ 🌿 🚂 Big up to the reactivators

View all 100 comments

26 August 2019

invaderwashere

   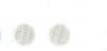 

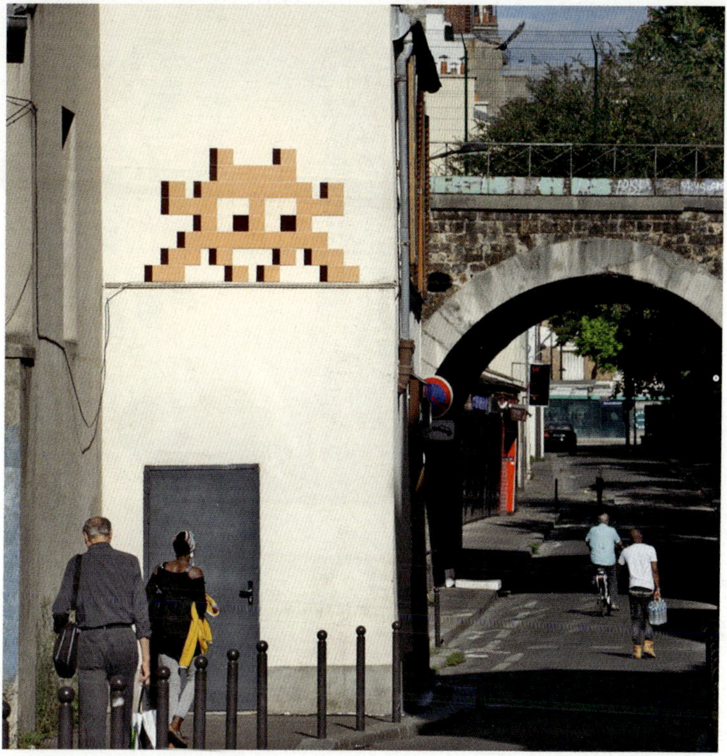

14 686 likes

invaderwashere Just landed... 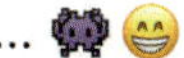

View all 128 comments

29 August 2019

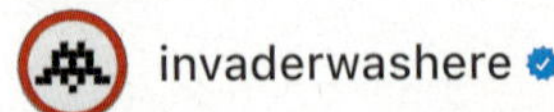

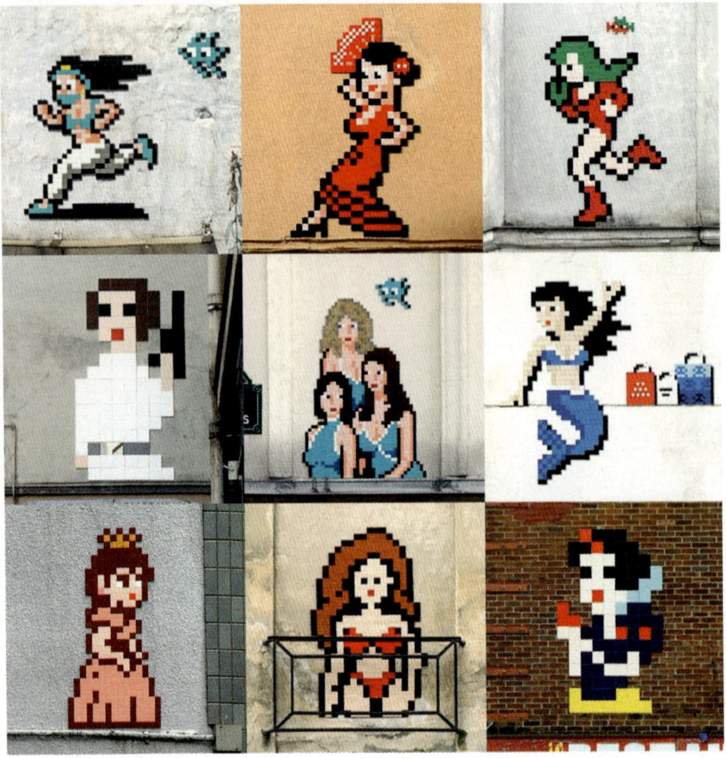

25 169 likes

invaderwashere Whether she's a princess, a warrior or a dancer, a woman dies every 2 days in France at the hands of her partner or ex-partner.
The French distress hotline number 3919 listens to and guides victims or witnesses to act against violence towards women.
Today 3 September 2019 - 3/9/19 - let's share the number that can save lives.

View all 264 comments

3 September 2019

invaderwashere

Exquisite Corpse 81

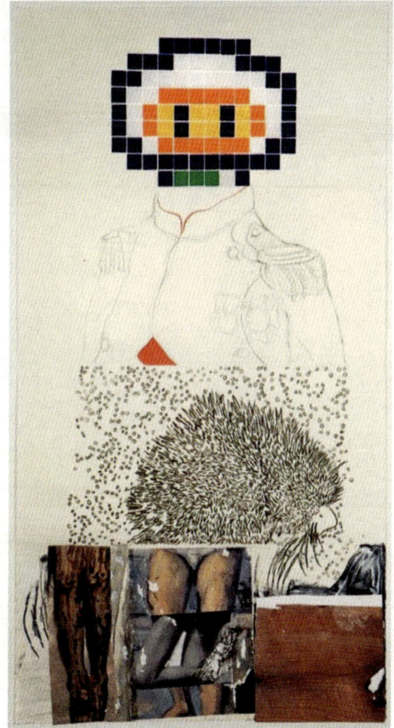

Invader
Plastic Tiles

John Baldessari
Graphite, Gouache

Robert Wilson
Graphite

Louise Fishman
Acrylic, Pencil, Paper

6082 likes

invaderwashere EXQUISITE CORPSE ARTWORK with #johnbaldessari #robertwilson & #louisefishman #throwback #workonpaper #armitagegonedance

View all 42 comments

5 September 2019

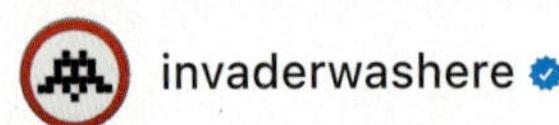

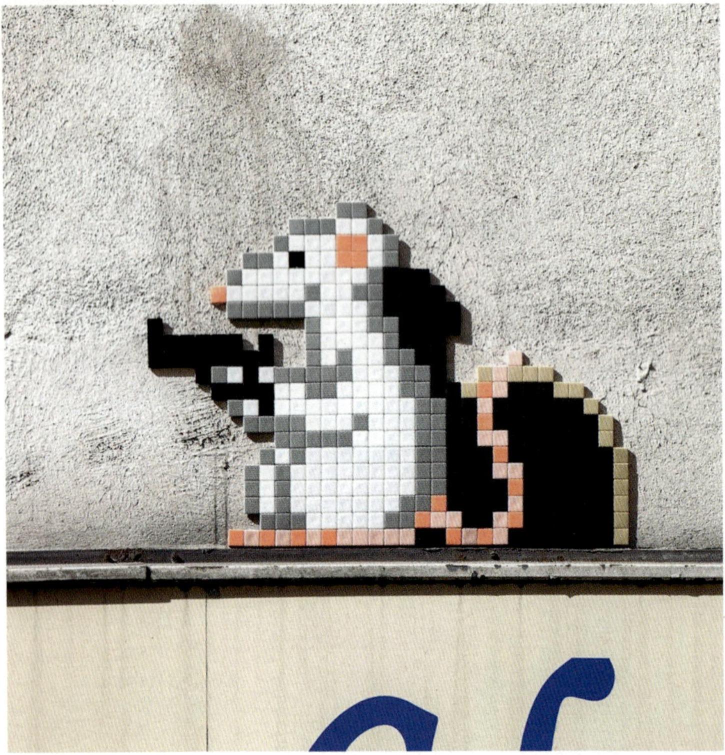

30 428 likes

invaderwashere Le Café des Chats is a cafe full of real cats #CatsKiller #ArmedLittleMouse #PA1425

View all 251 comments

13 September 2019

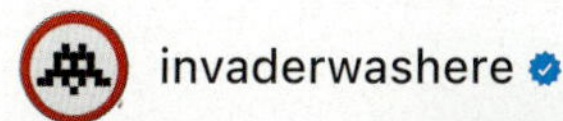

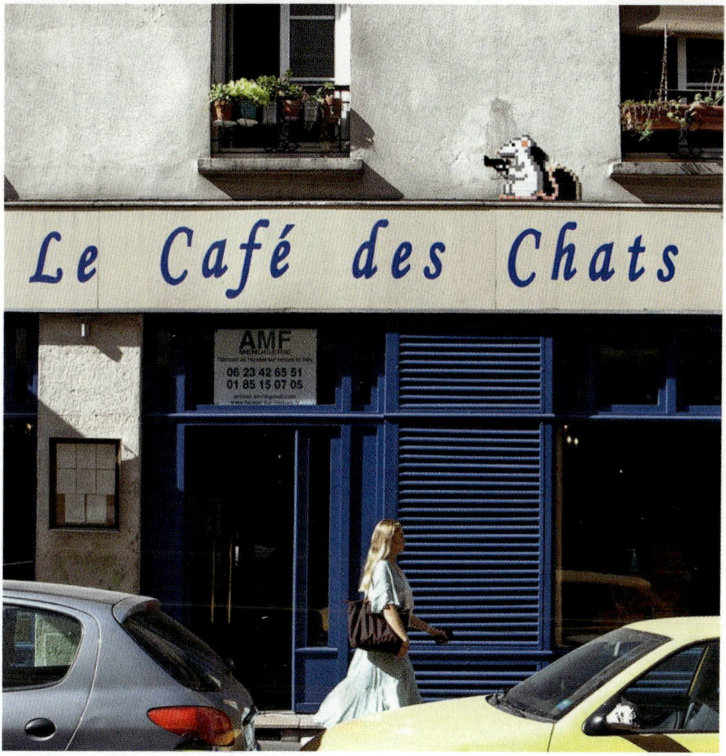

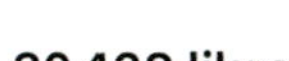

30 428 likes

invaderwashere Le Café des Chats is a cafe full of real cats #CatsKiller #ArmedLittleMouse #PA1425

View all 251 comments

13 September 2019

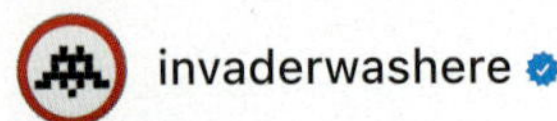

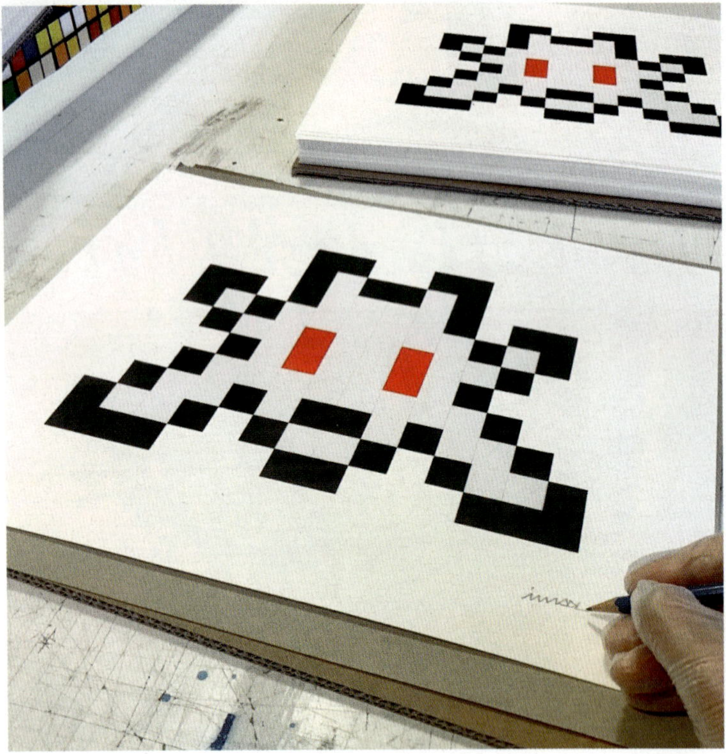

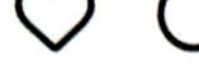

15 556 likes

invaderwashere #studiodetails

View all 272 comments

24 September 2019

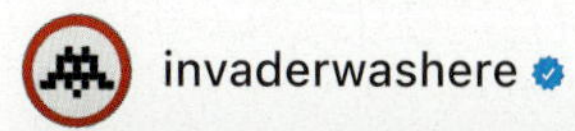

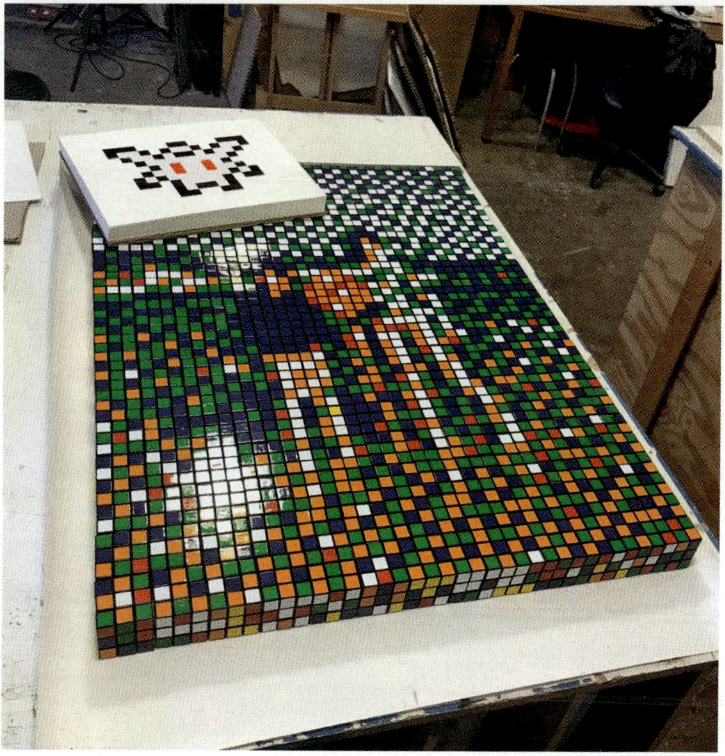

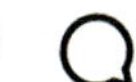

15 540 likes

invaderwashere #studiodetails

View all 269 comments

24 September 2019

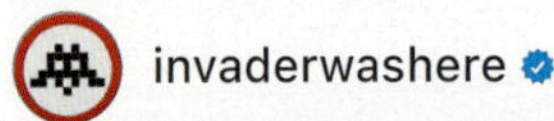

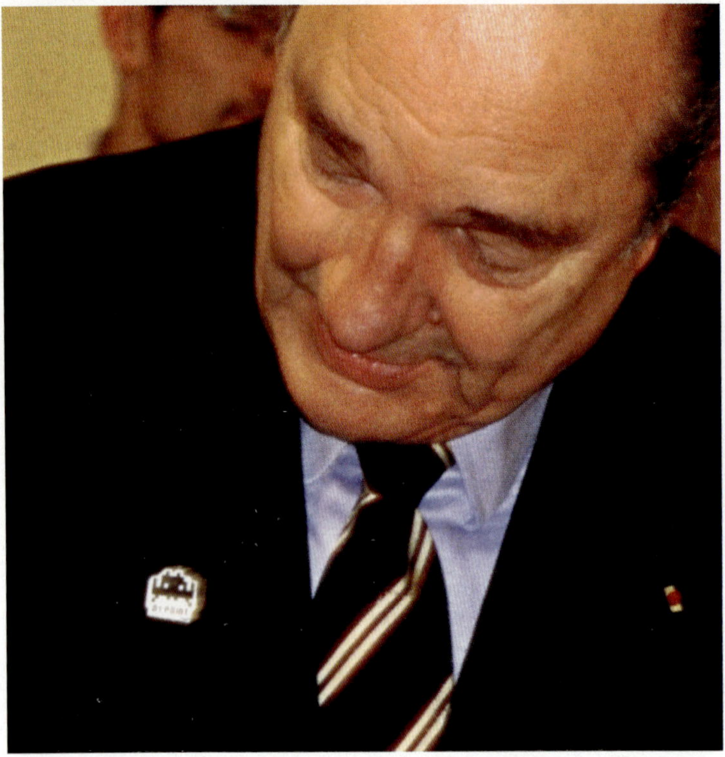

9209 likes

invaderwashere RIP Jacques Chirac #throwback #InvasionofthePresident #Fiac2000 #sticker

View all 130 comments

26 September 2019

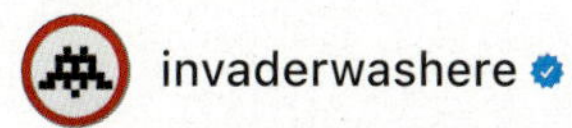

HIDDEN CHAMPION

ART & CULTURE MAGAZINE · IN STREET WE TRUST

ISSUE#54
FALL 2019
FREE

WAS HERE

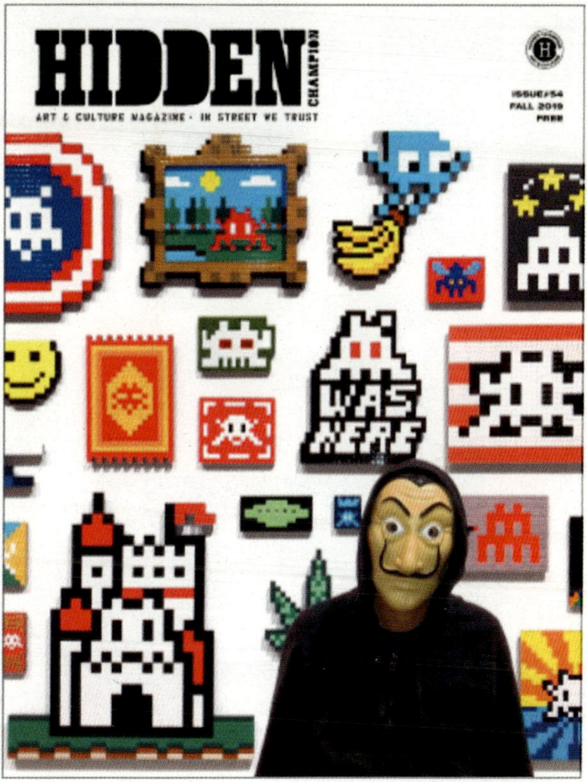

8963 likes

invaderwashere New issue of Hidden Champion Magazine #mediainvasion #japan @hidden_champion #cover 🇯🇵 👾

View all 59 comments

29 September 2019

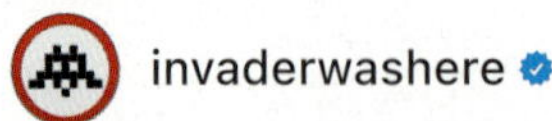

•••

  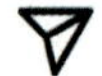 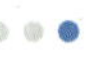 

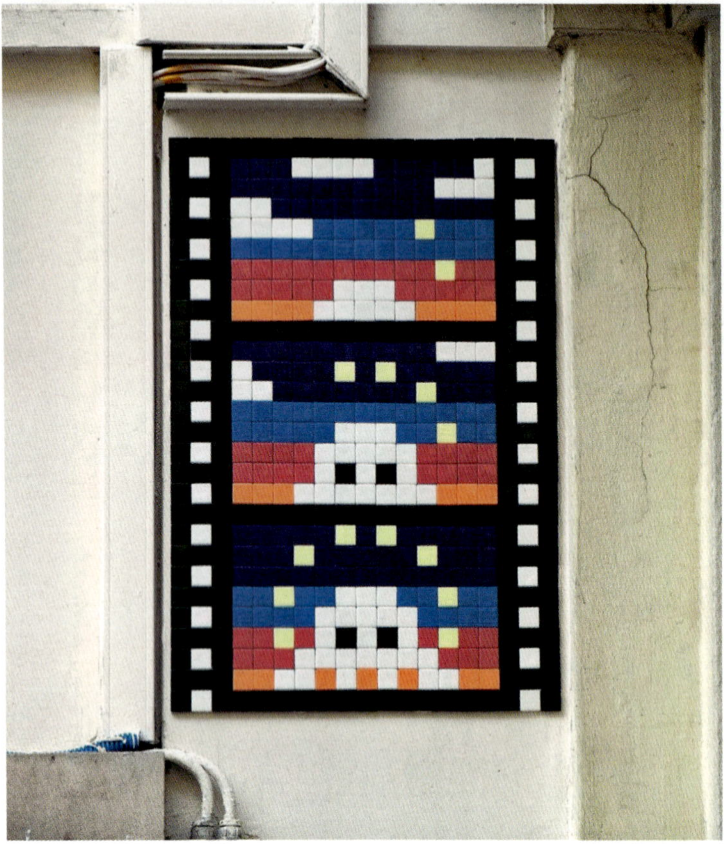

13 485 likes

invaderwashere Paramount Invader #PA1423 #cinema #grandrex #ladernieresеance

View all 144 comments

14 October 2019

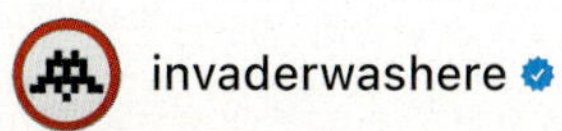

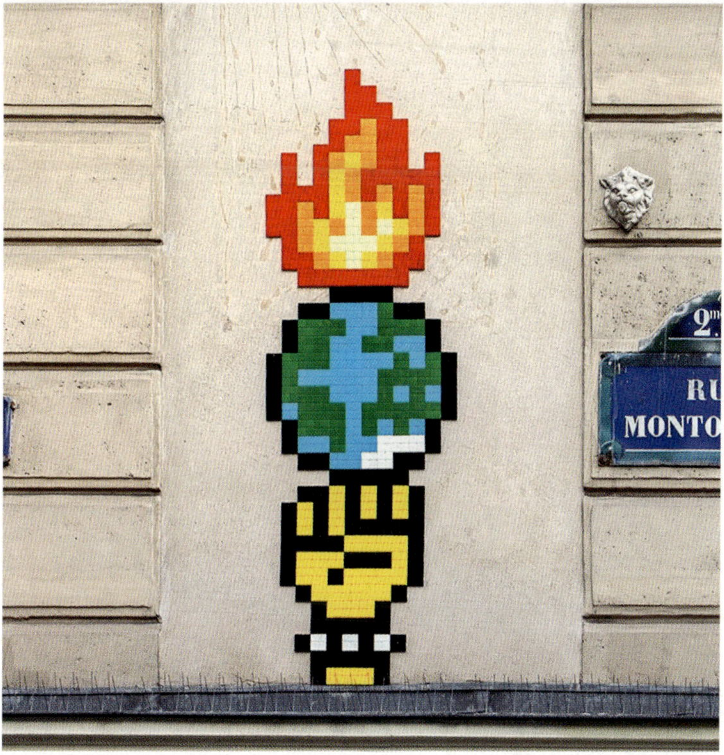

15 788 likes

invaderwashere This post to support @extinctionrebellion movement #fightforearth #protectyourplanet #educate #noviolence #noplastic #localfood #govegan #organicapparel #cleanenergy #planttrees ✊💚🌎

View all 99 comments

15 October 2019

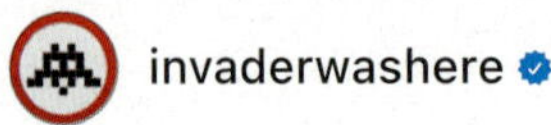

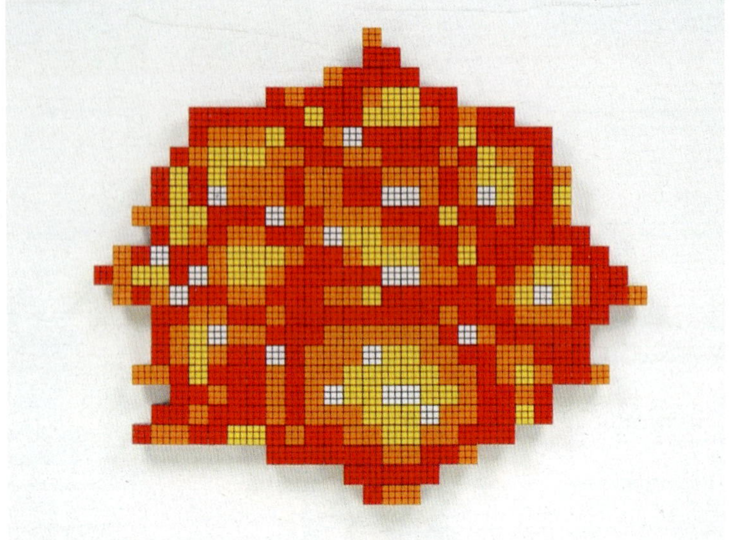

7226 likes

invaderwashere Rubik Wipe Out displayed at Open World @akronartmuseum #akron #ohio #pixelplosion #rubikcubism 💥

View all 46 comments

19 October 2019

invaderwashere

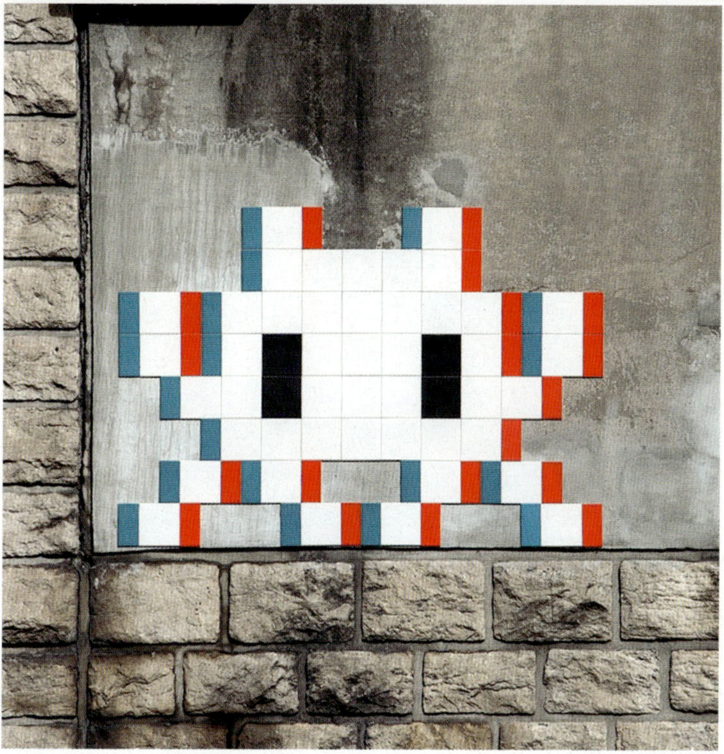

12 397 likes

invaderwashere PA_1429 Last but not least.
Photo by @_mimine

View all 57 comments

21 October 2019

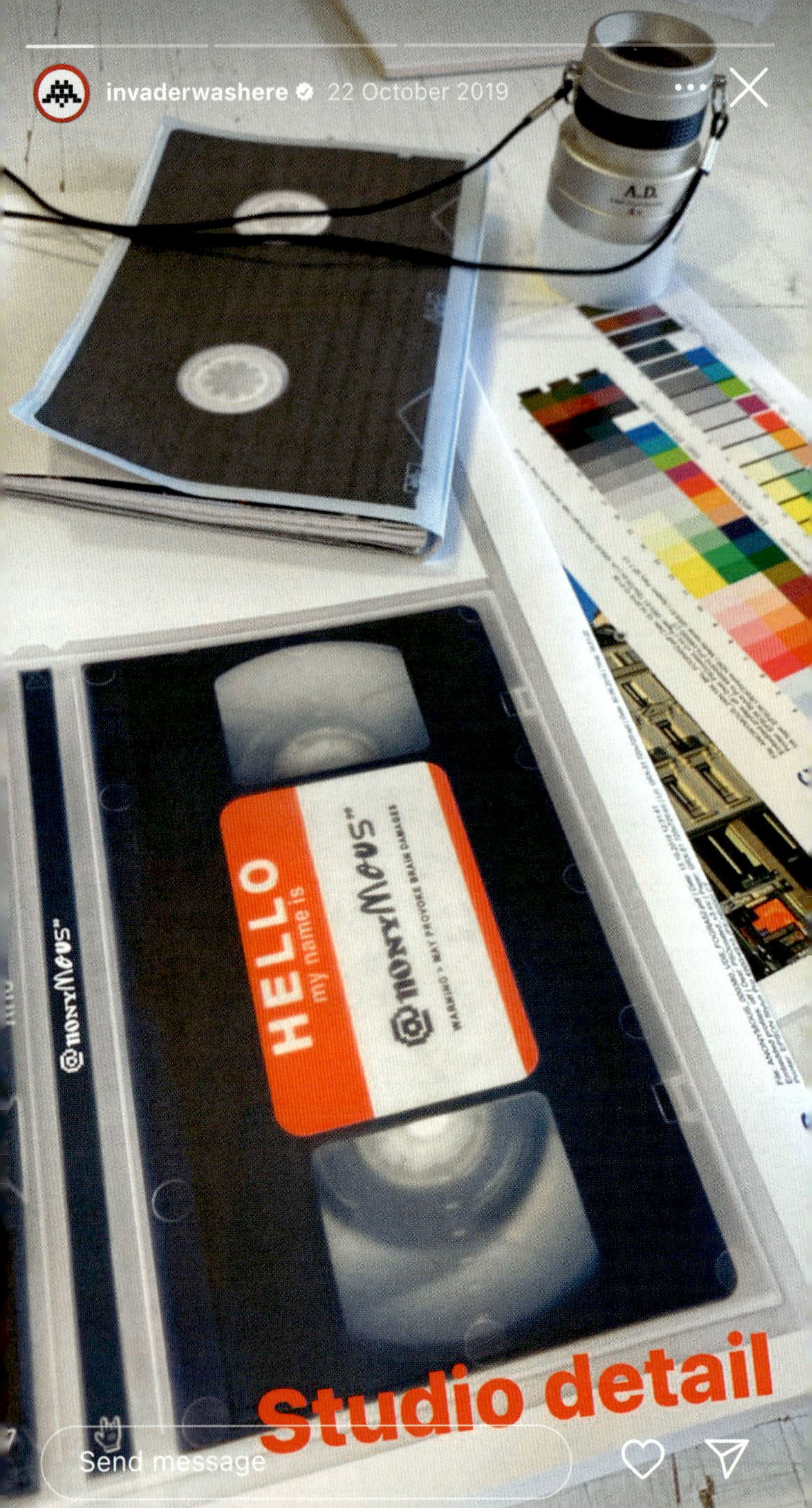
invaderwashere 22 October 2019
HELLO
my name is
@NONYMOUS
WARNING > MAY PROVOKE BRAIN DAMAGES
@NONYMOUS
Studio detail
Send message

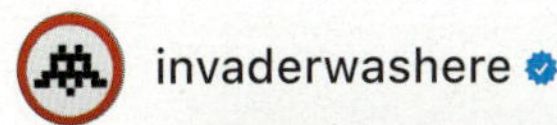

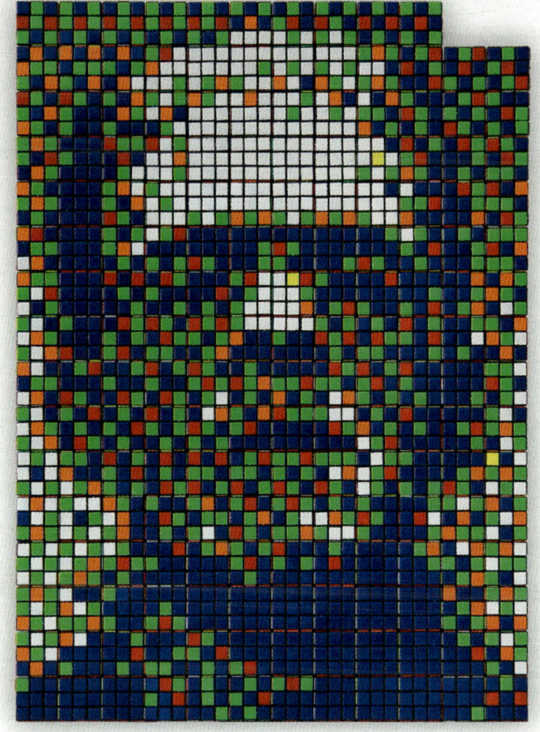

 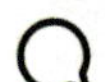 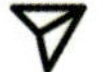 

10 948 likes

invaderwashere Happy halloween 🎃 #RubikFrankenstein #rubikcubism #throwback

View all 106 comments

31 October 2019

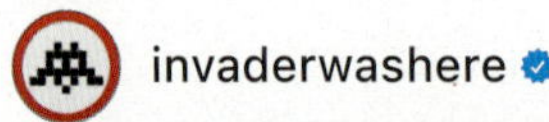

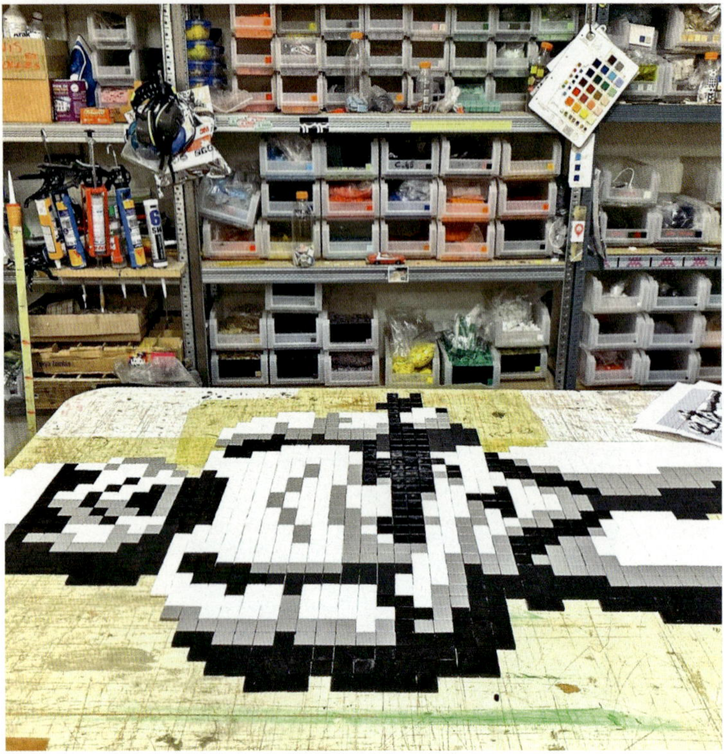

17 632 likes

invaderwashere Got a great spot for this one ☝️
#studiodetail #sooninthestreet

View all 296 comments

4 November 2019

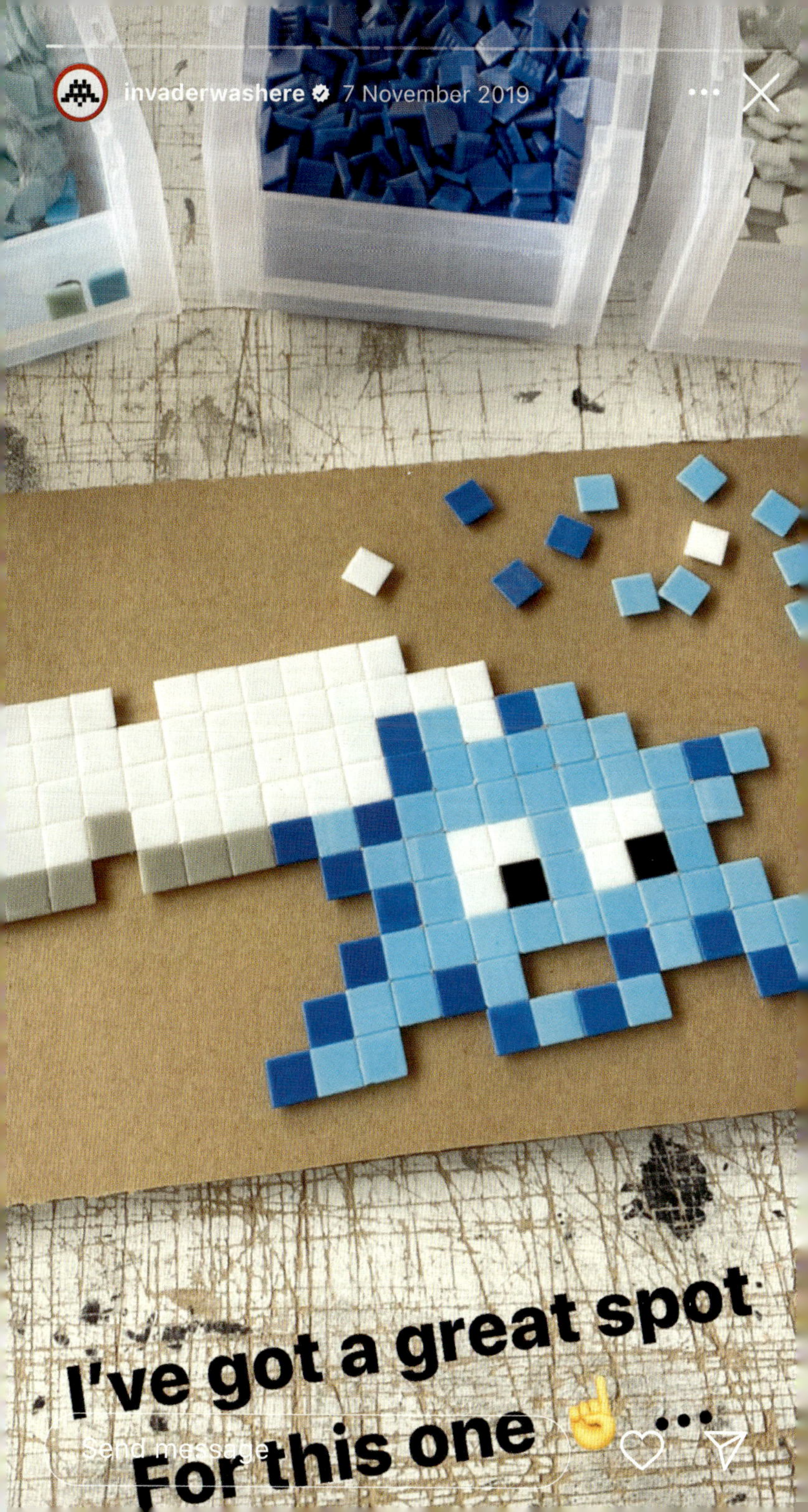
invaderwashere 7 November 2019
I've got a great spot
For this one
Send message

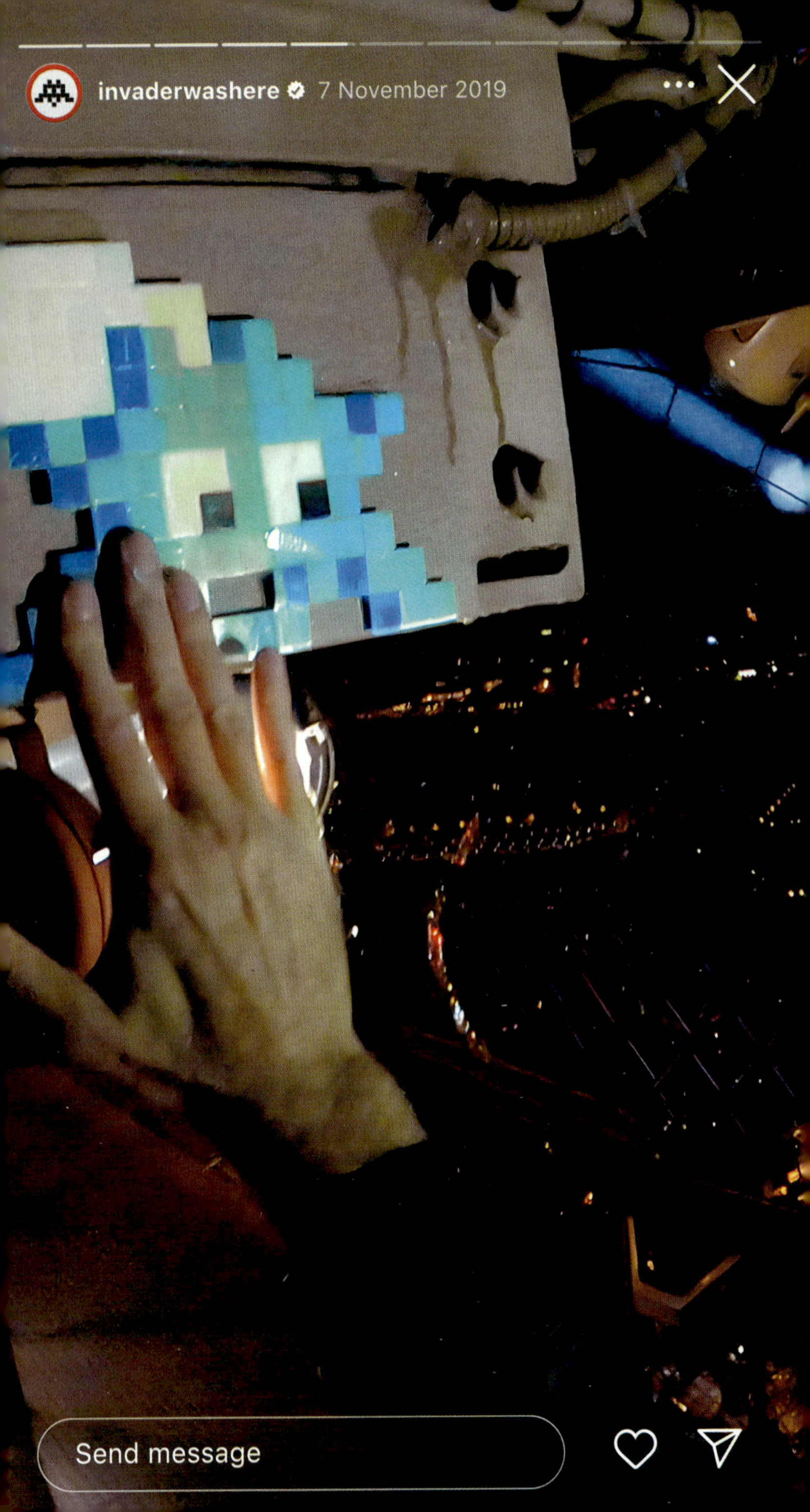
invaderwashere
7 November 2019
Send message

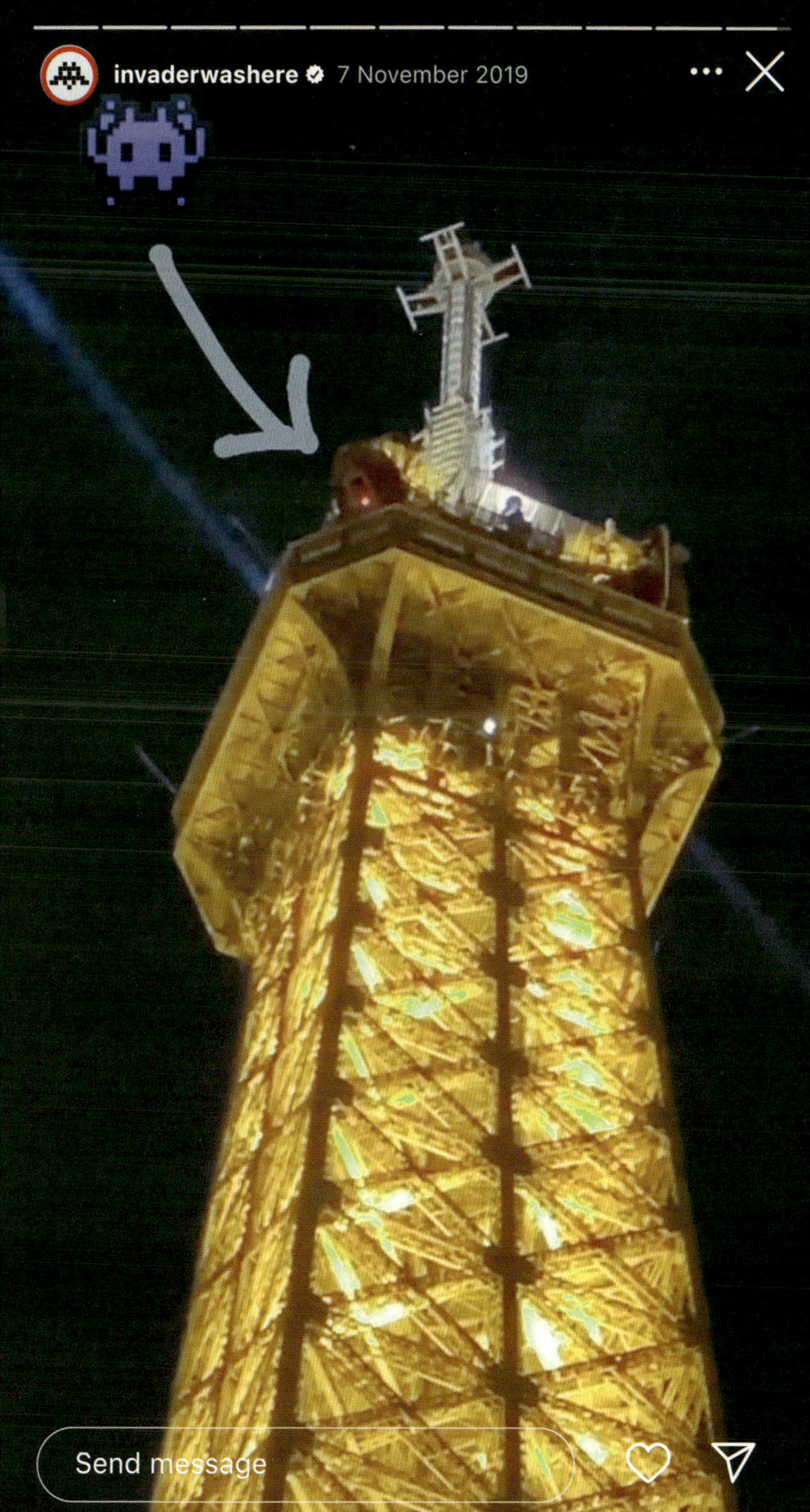
invaderwashere 7 November 2019
Send message

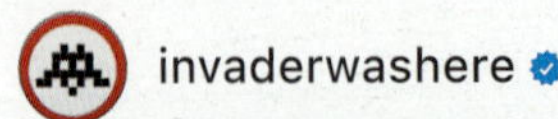

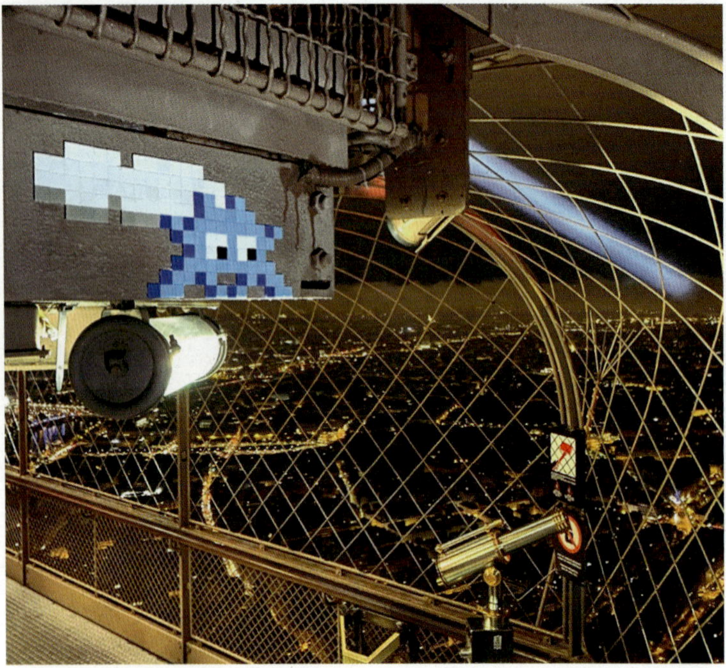

28 260 likes

invaderwashere The highest space invader of Paris is located at the top of the Eiffel Tower, the head into the clouds... #perfectspot @toureiffelofficielle

View all 593 comments

7 November 2019

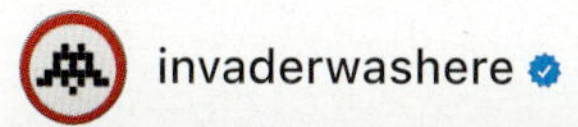

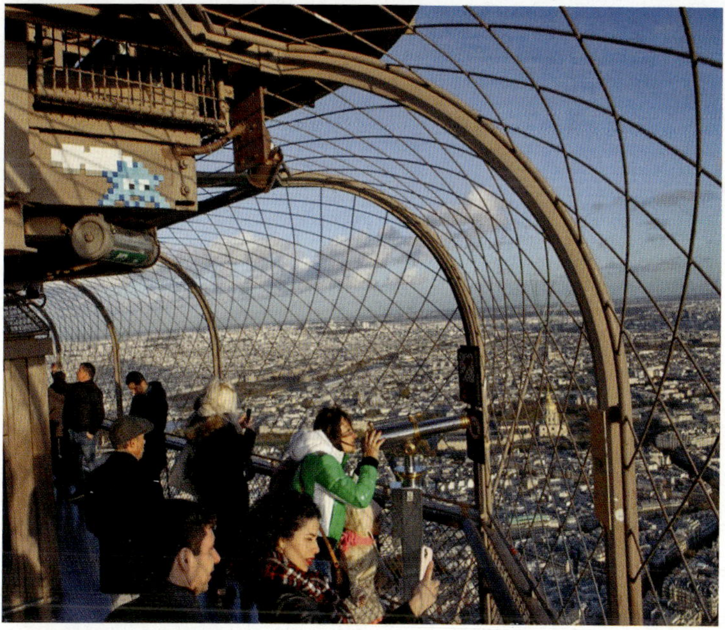

  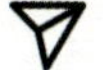 

17962 likes

invaderwashere PA_1431 / Daytime. Thank you Mr Gustave Eiffel for this great spot... ☁️ 👾

View all 186 comments

8 November 2019

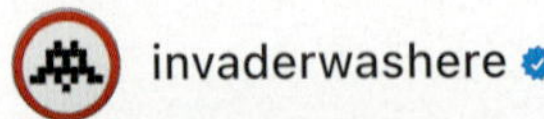

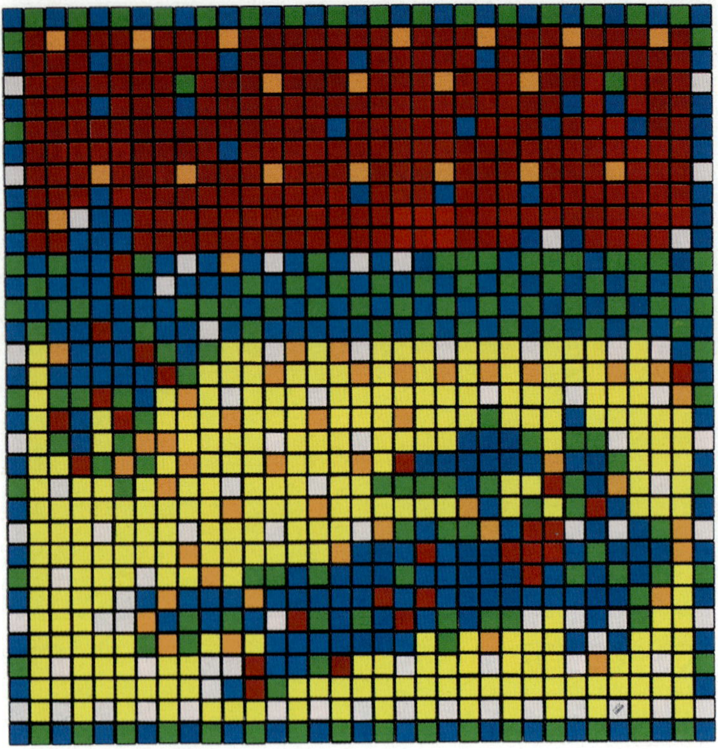

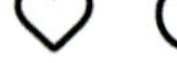    

10 073 likes

invaderwashere On this day in 1978, The Clash released their 2nd studio album « Give 'em enough rope » #RubikCubism #lowfidelity #throwback #theclash

View all 83 comments

11 November 2019

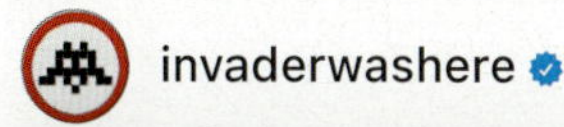

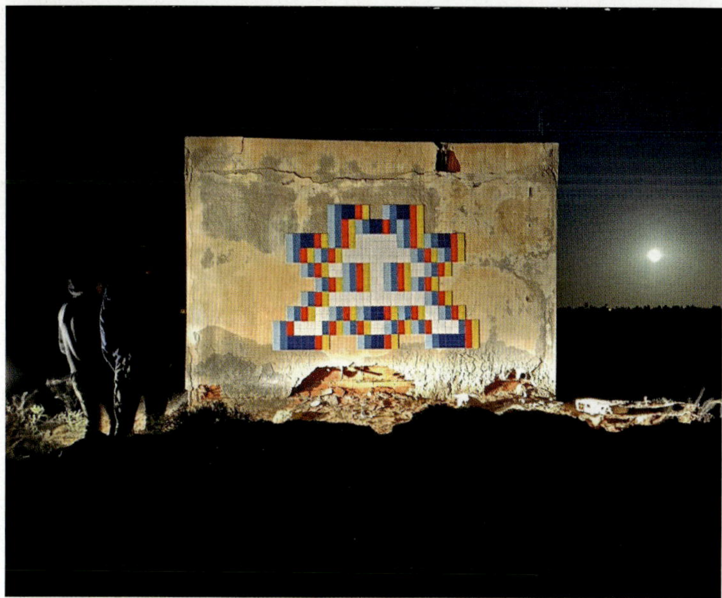

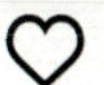  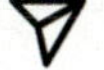 

18 289 likes

invaderwashere Just happening now... #mirage #desert #fullmoon #newcityinvasion

View all 147 comments

13 November 2019

invaderwashere

 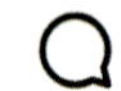  

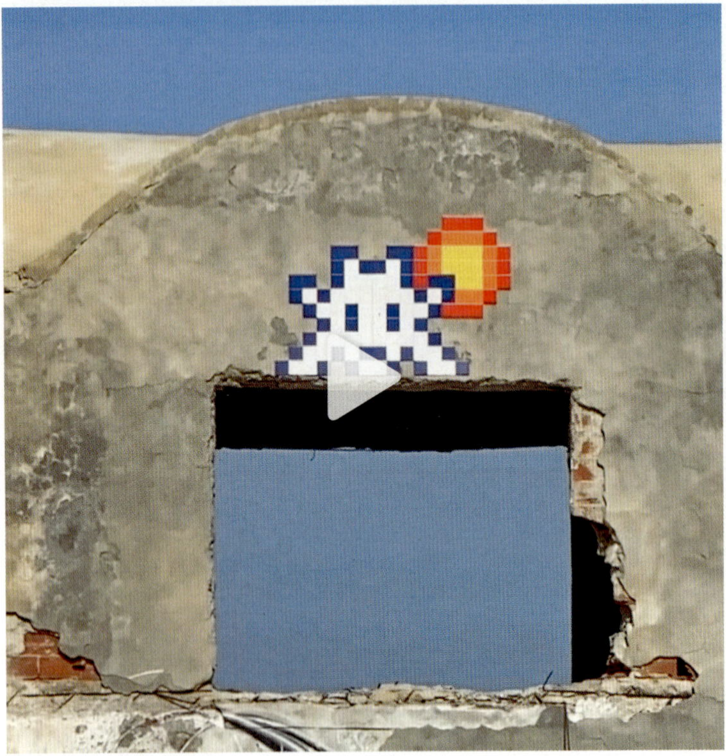

43 910 views

invaderwashere After the 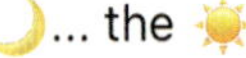 ... the

View all 112 comments

16 November 2019

invaderwashere

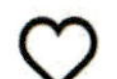   

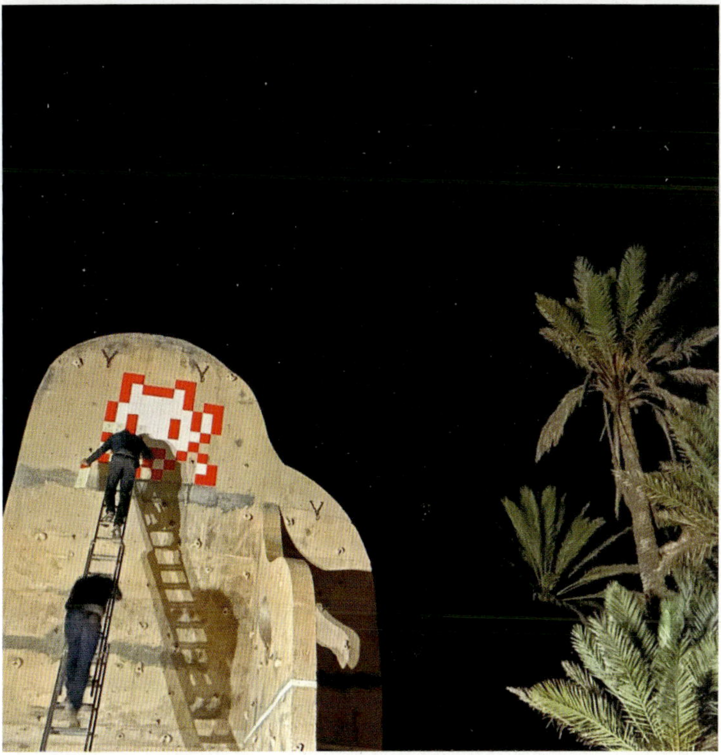

13 755 likes

invaderwashere Closer to the 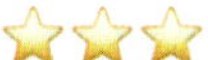

View all 72 comments

17 November 2019

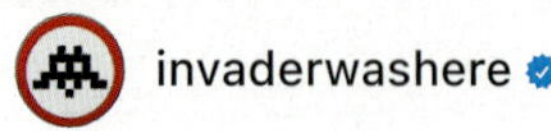

CONTEMPORARY ART DAY AUCTION

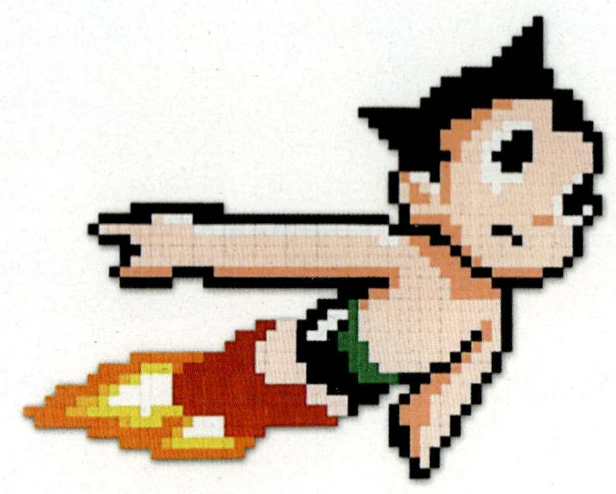

Invader

TK_119

100,000 – 150,000 USD ▾ LOT SOLD. 1,220,000 USD

16488 likes

invaderwashere Meanwhile in New York @sothebys  

View all 487 comments

17 November 2019

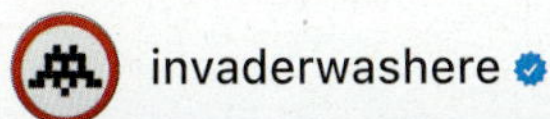

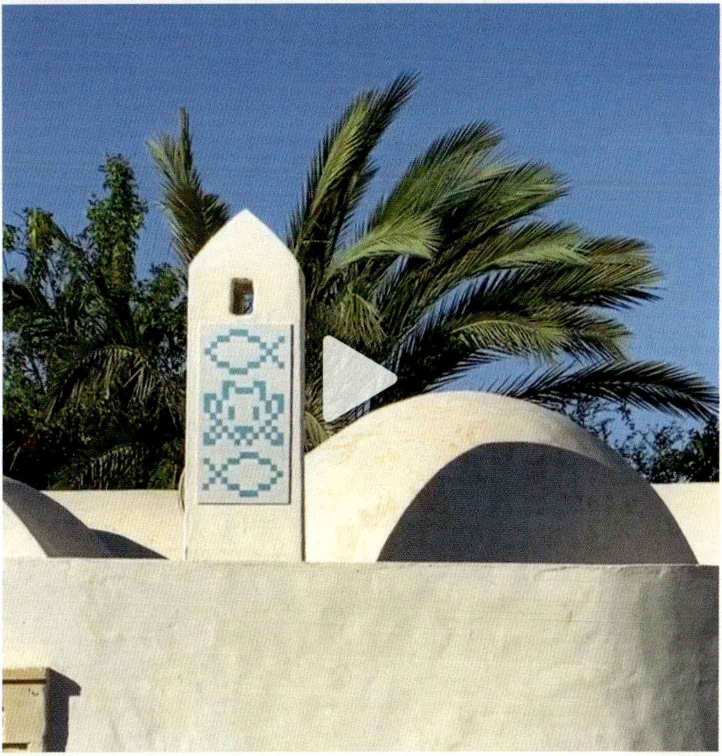

 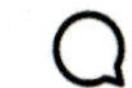  

39 255 views

invaderwashere 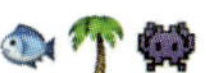

View all 103 comments

19 November 2019

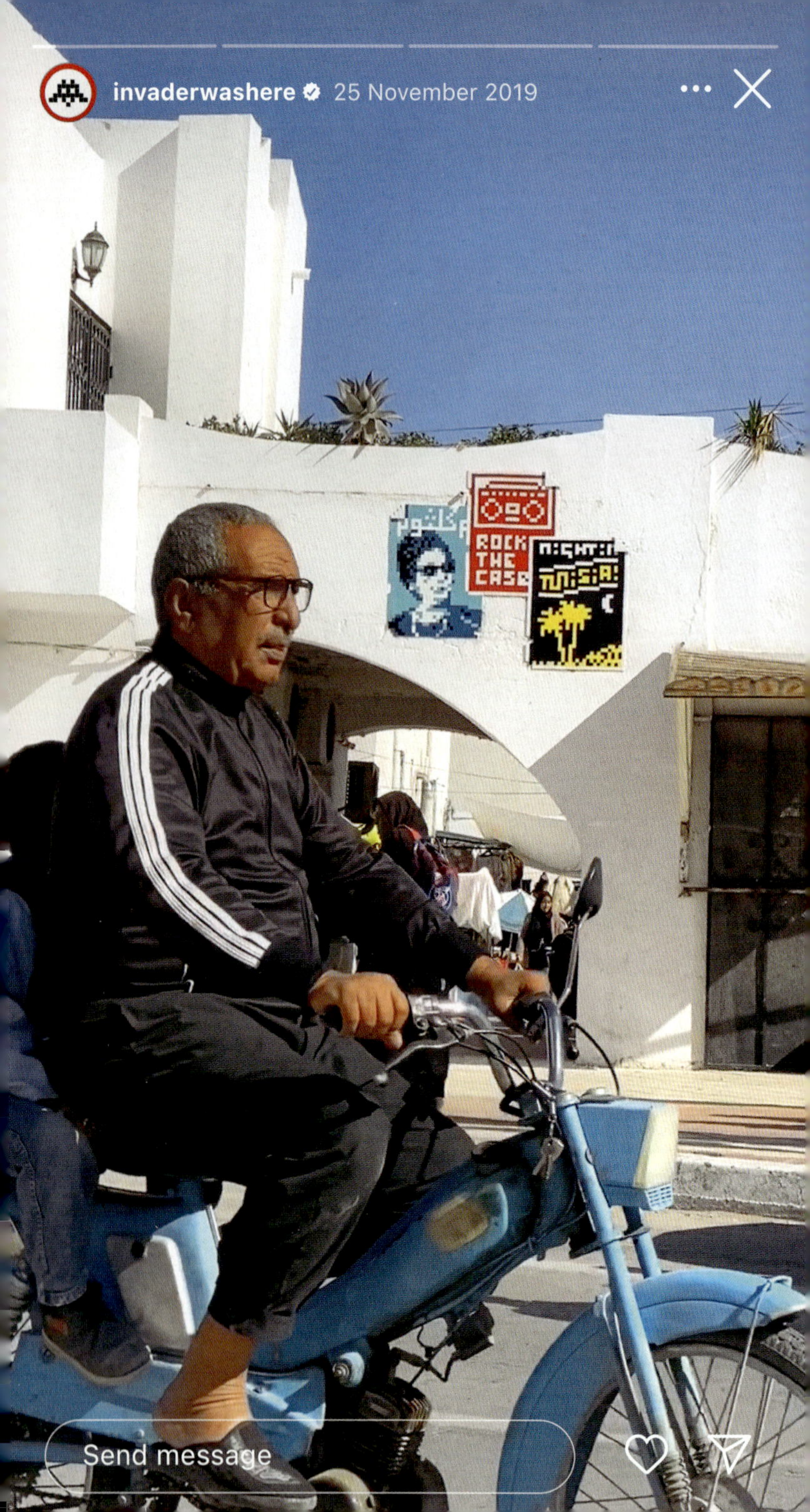
invaderwashere
25 November 2019
Send message

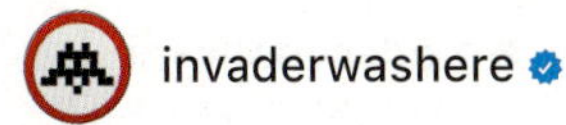

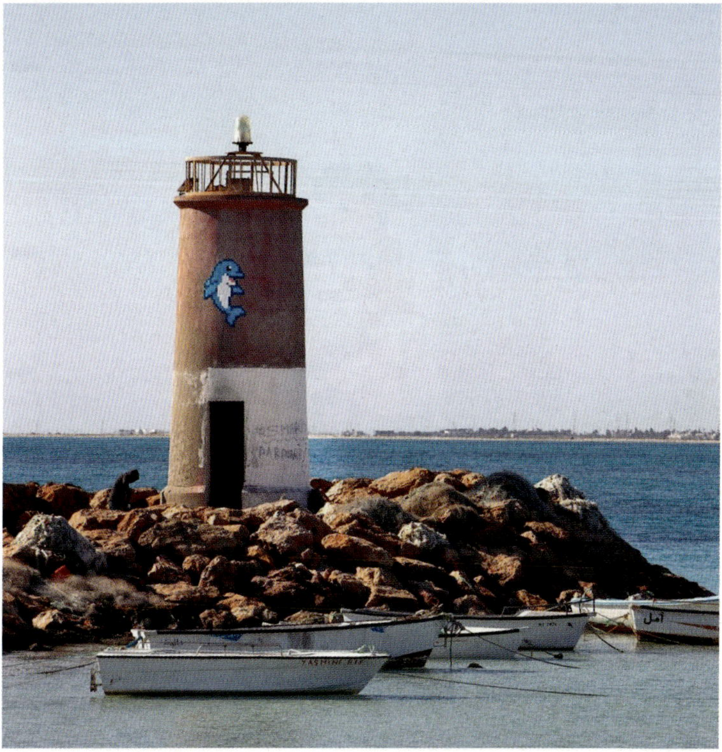

22 352 likes

invaderwashere Blue blue blue 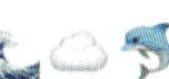

View all 188 comments

27 November 2019

invaderwashere

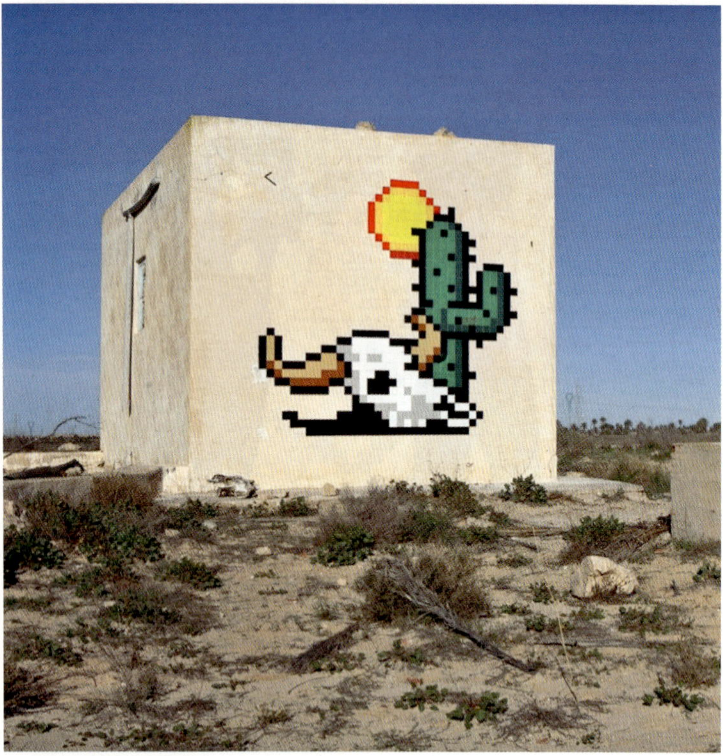

26 222 likes

invaderwashere ☀️ 💀 🌵 🦟 the most difficult point of this one were the mosquitos 🤬

View all 200 comments

29 November 2019

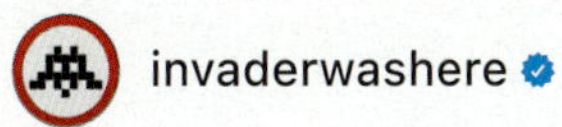

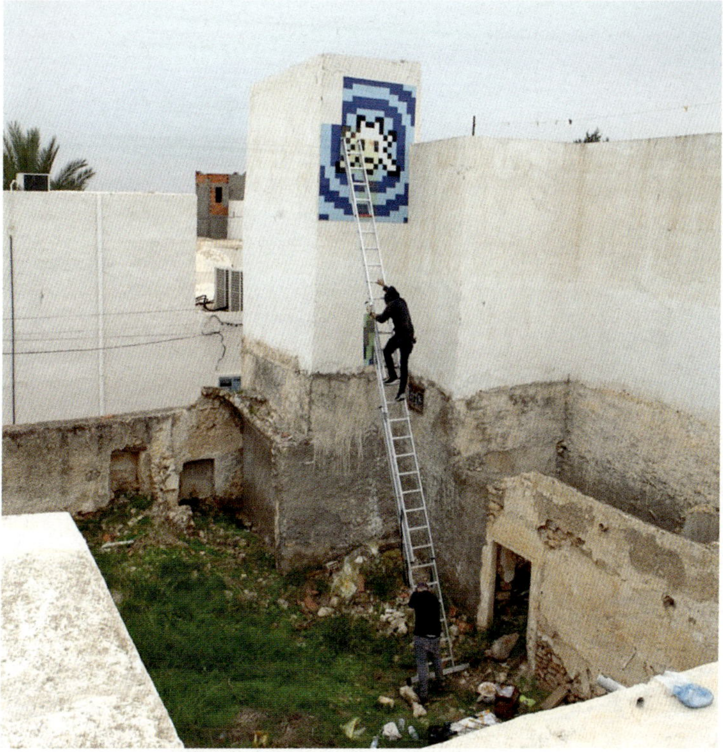

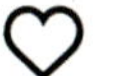   

18 913 likes

invaderwashere (((Shock Wave))) The first piece of the Invasion of Djerba. To be continued...

View all 137 comments

1 December 2019

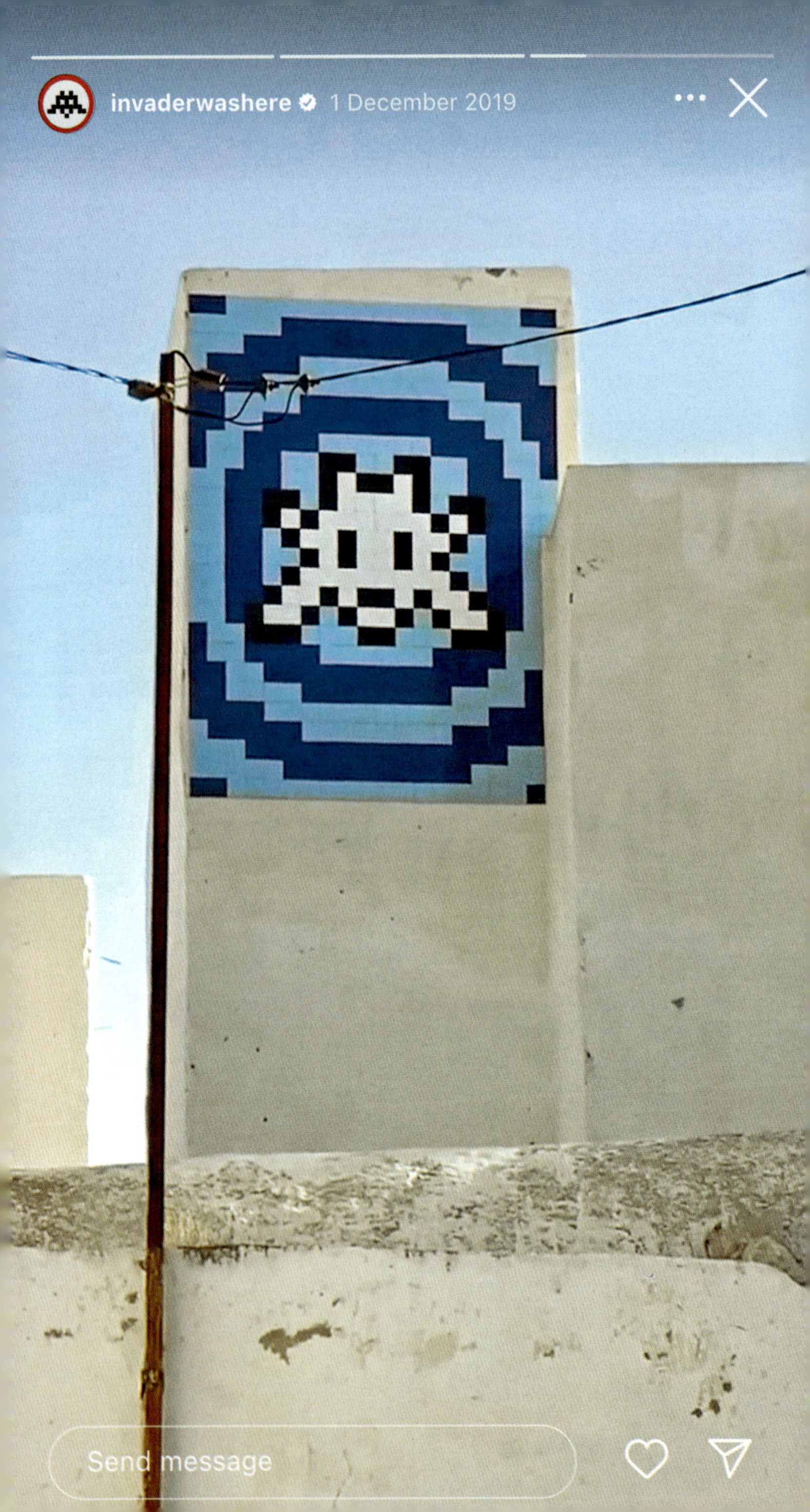

invaderwashere 1 December 2019

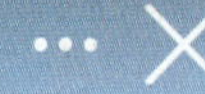

Send message

invaderwashere ✓ •••

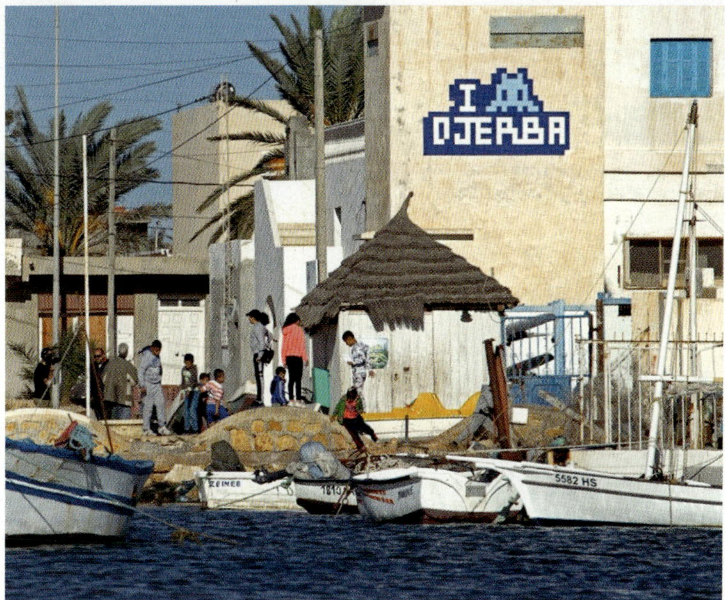

11 037 likes

invaderwashere My latest project was not about invading a city but a whole island. The Tunisian island of Djerba is the 79th invaded territory with a total score of 58 mosaics installed throughout the island. 🇹🇳 🏝️ 👾 A big thanks to @galerie_itinerrance for it precious help with this project. #djerba #tunisia #invasionsuccessful

View all 124 comments

2 December 2019

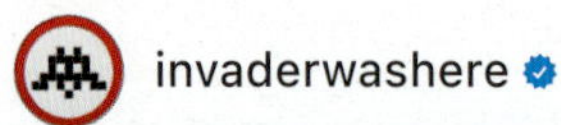

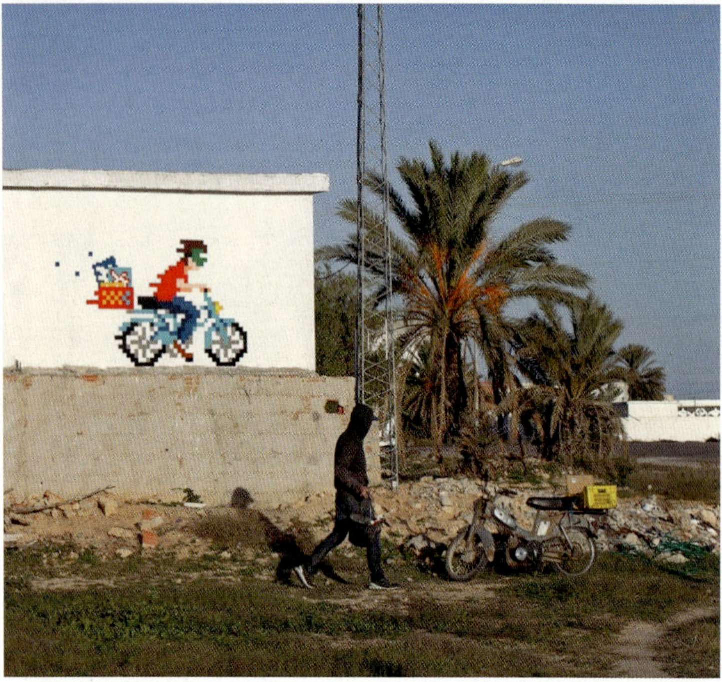

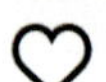   

13 695 likes

invaderwashere Self portrait with blue moped #Djerba #motobecane #DJBA45

View all 100 comments

3 December 2019

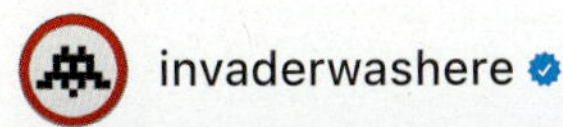

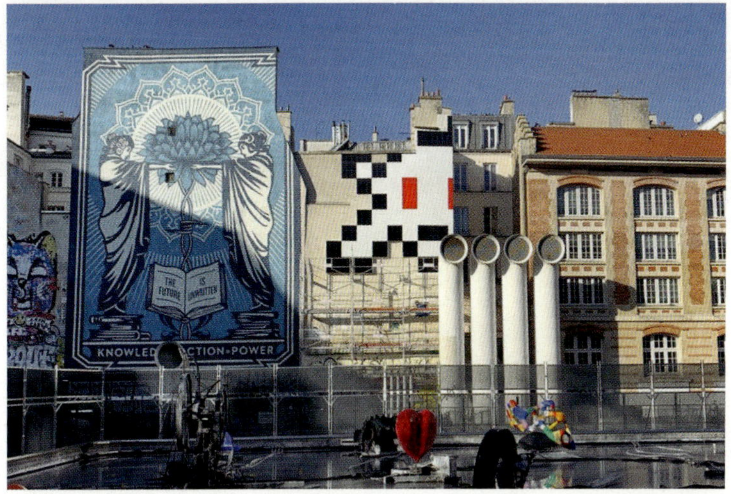

25 119 likes

invaderwashere The biggest space invader ever made has just landed Place Stravinsky, just by the Centre Pompidou. A huge thanks to Anne Hidalgo the Mayor of Paris, to the Mairie of the 4th district, to SIEMP and to the galerie Itinerrance. @annehidalgo @mairie4paris @elogiesiemp @galerie_itinerrance #GoingBigInParis #100points

View all 700 comments

4 December 2019

invaderwashere

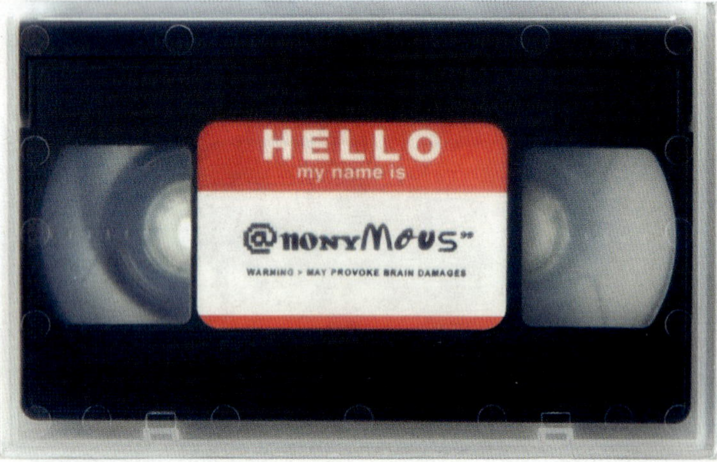

3622 likes

invaderwashere A la fin des années 90, ZEVS et moi collaborons sous le nom de code @nonymous. En 1999, nous réalisons un film qui relate nos aventures urbaines et le distribuons sous le manteau. Pour célébrer les 20 ans du film et sa réédition en DVD, il sera projeté ce Samedi 7 décembre, au cinéma LA CLEF, haut-lieu de résistance culturelle, 34 rue Daubenton, 75005 Paris / Séances à 16h, 17h, et 18h / Prix libre. NB: Malgré une bonne dose d'humour (noir!), âmes sensibles s'abstenir. @nonymous1999

View all 58 comments

5 December 2019

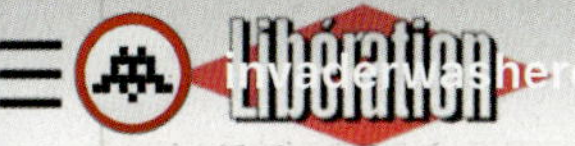

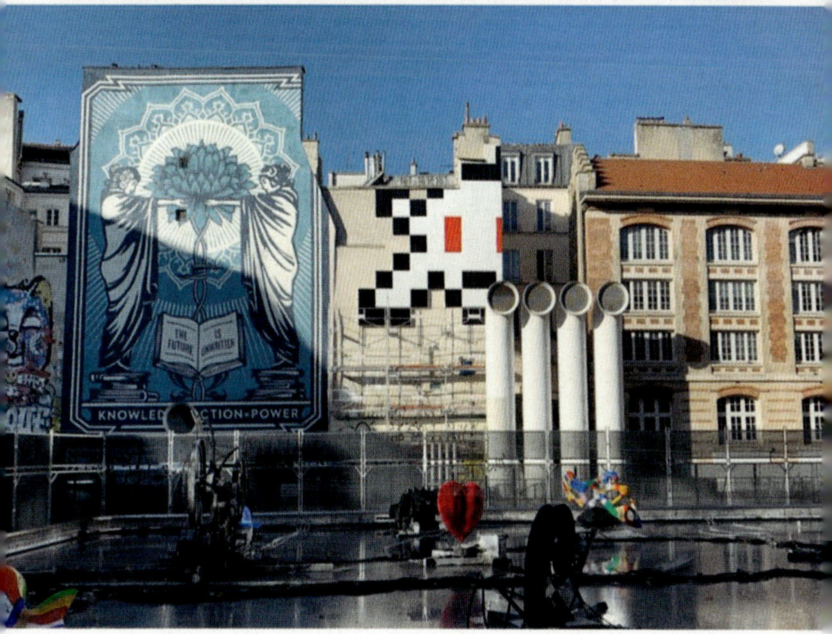

10

E DIRECT

7:00

e plus grand Invader inauguré place travinsky à Paris

treet art. Après le plus haut le mois dernier au somme e la tour Eiffel, voici venu le plus grand Space Invader mais posé. Une mosaïque géante – 70 m2 – de l'artiste ançais anonyme Invader vient d'être officiellement augurée à Paris, place Stravinsky, près de Beaubourg out à côté du «mural» de Shepard Fairey, dit Obey et d autoportrait de Jef Aerosol. *«Il a fallu refaire tout le*

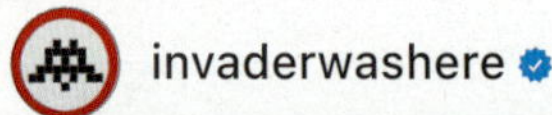

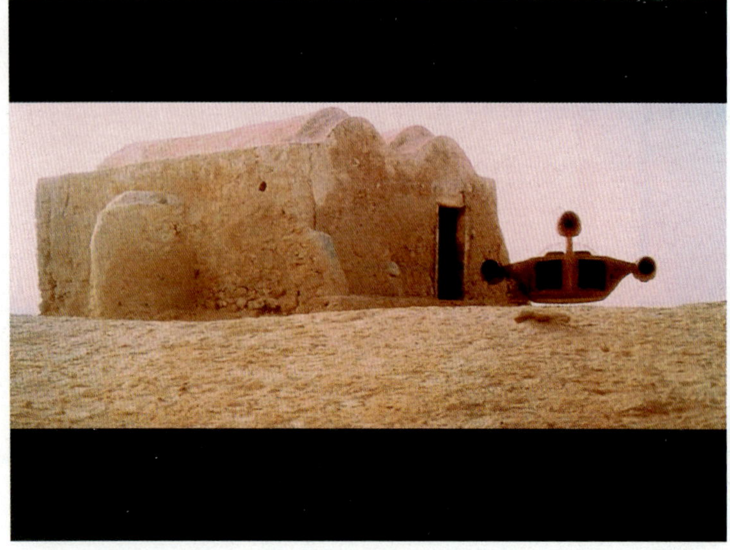

27735 likes

invaderwashere In 1976 G. Lucas went to Djerba to shoot two scenes of the first Star Wars movie. One of them was the house of Obi-Wan Kenobi. I found back the actual house and did this tribute on it. #obiwankenobi #starwars #Djerba #DJBA39 / Star Wars: A new hope / Original despecialized version 32′ 14″

View all 509 comments

10 December 2019

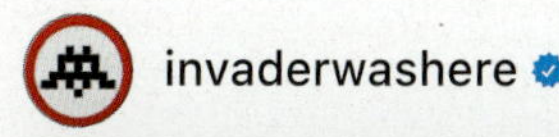

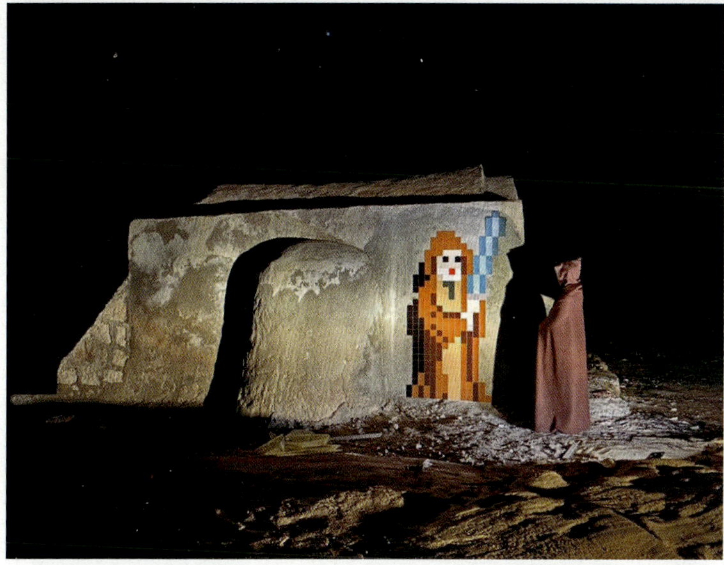

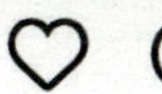

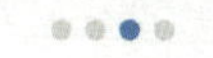

17 145 likes

invaderwashere Making of DJBA_39 on Obi-wan Kenobi house #invader #djerba #starwars

View all 218 comments

11 December 2019

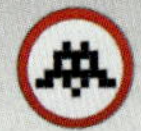

invaderwashere 13 december 2019

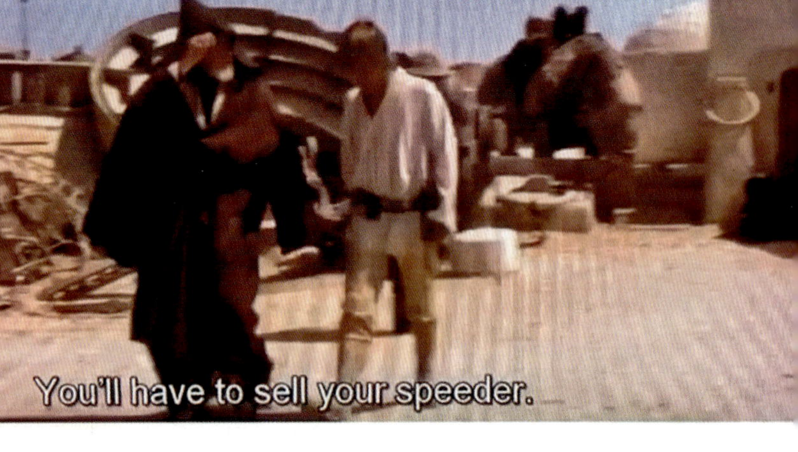

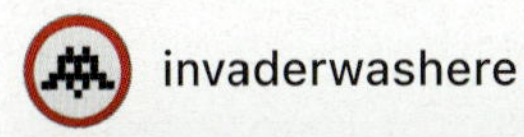

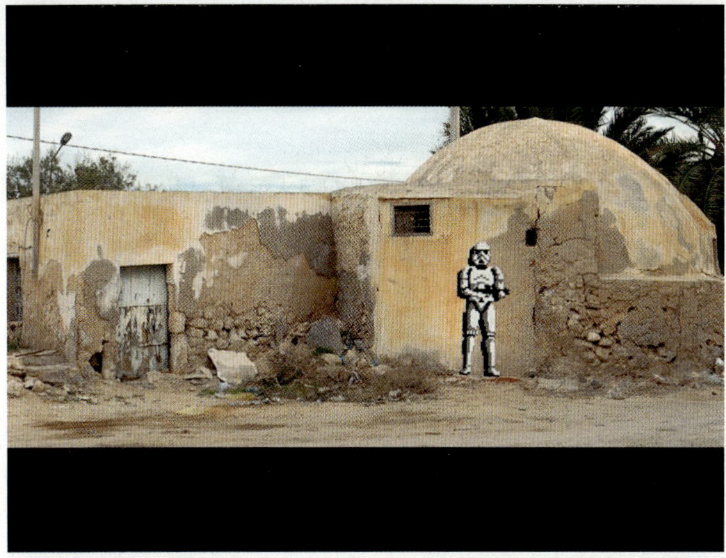

20 002 likes

invaderwashere This is the actual house where the Star Wars scene with the bar full of aliens was shot in 1976. Obi-Wan Kenobi and Luke Skywalker who are chased by some troopers meet Han Solo and Chewbacca for the first time there. One of the best scene of the movie imho! A new hope 43′ 39″ #djerba #ajim #cantina #starwars #trooper #invasion

View all 219 comments

13 December 2019

invaderwashere

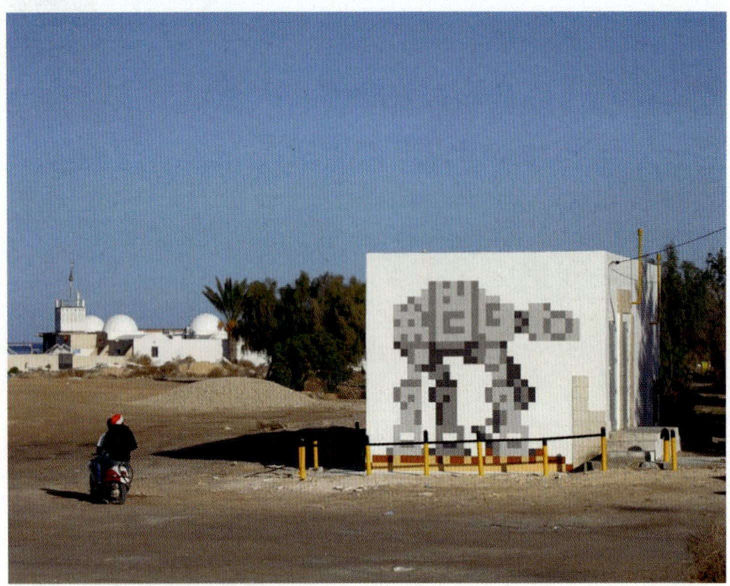

   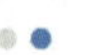 

22 546 likes

invaderwashere This is my third tribute to Star Wars in Djerba #atat #camel #big #invader #djerba 🇹🇳

View all 159 comments

16 December 2019

invaderwashere 

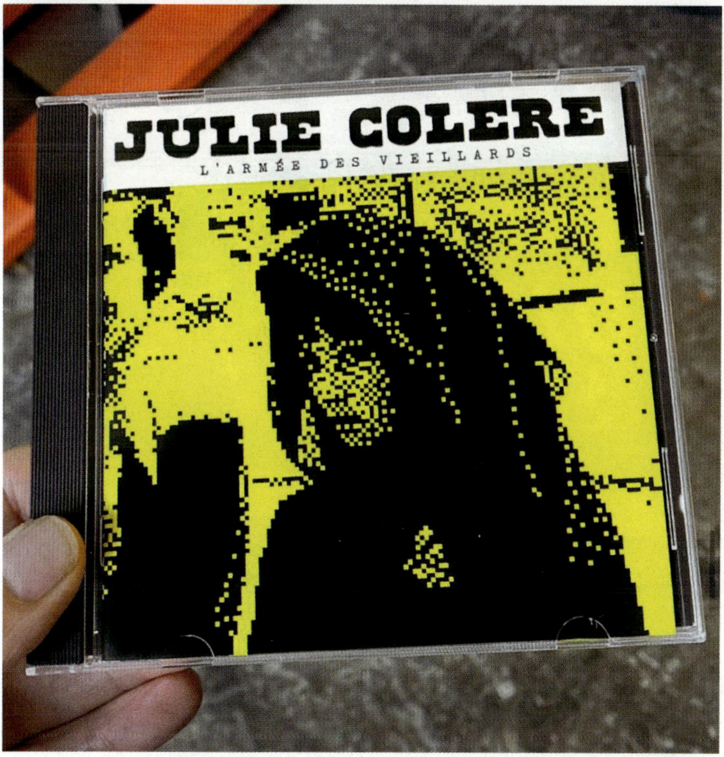

3 112 likes

invaderwashere I've just designed the cover of the new album of the french band Julie Colère. It will be available next Sunday during their live at L'Armony Bar in Montreuil. #juliecolere #newalbum #francoistruffaut #lamarieeetaitennoir

View all 30 comments

19 December 2019

invaderwashere

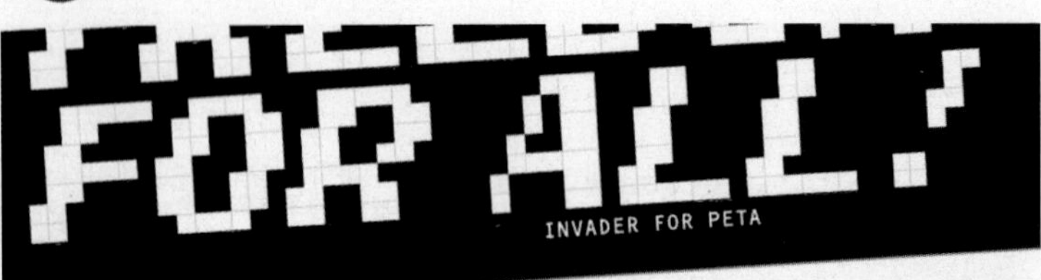

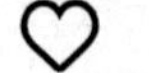    

7 339 likes

invaderwashere Visuals for the campaign I am preparing for Peta. More soon… « The greatness of a nation can be judged by the way its animals are treated ». M. Gandhi #boycottfoiegras #disgusting #meatismurder #happyholidays @peta @petafrance2019

View all 278 comments

25 December 2019

2020

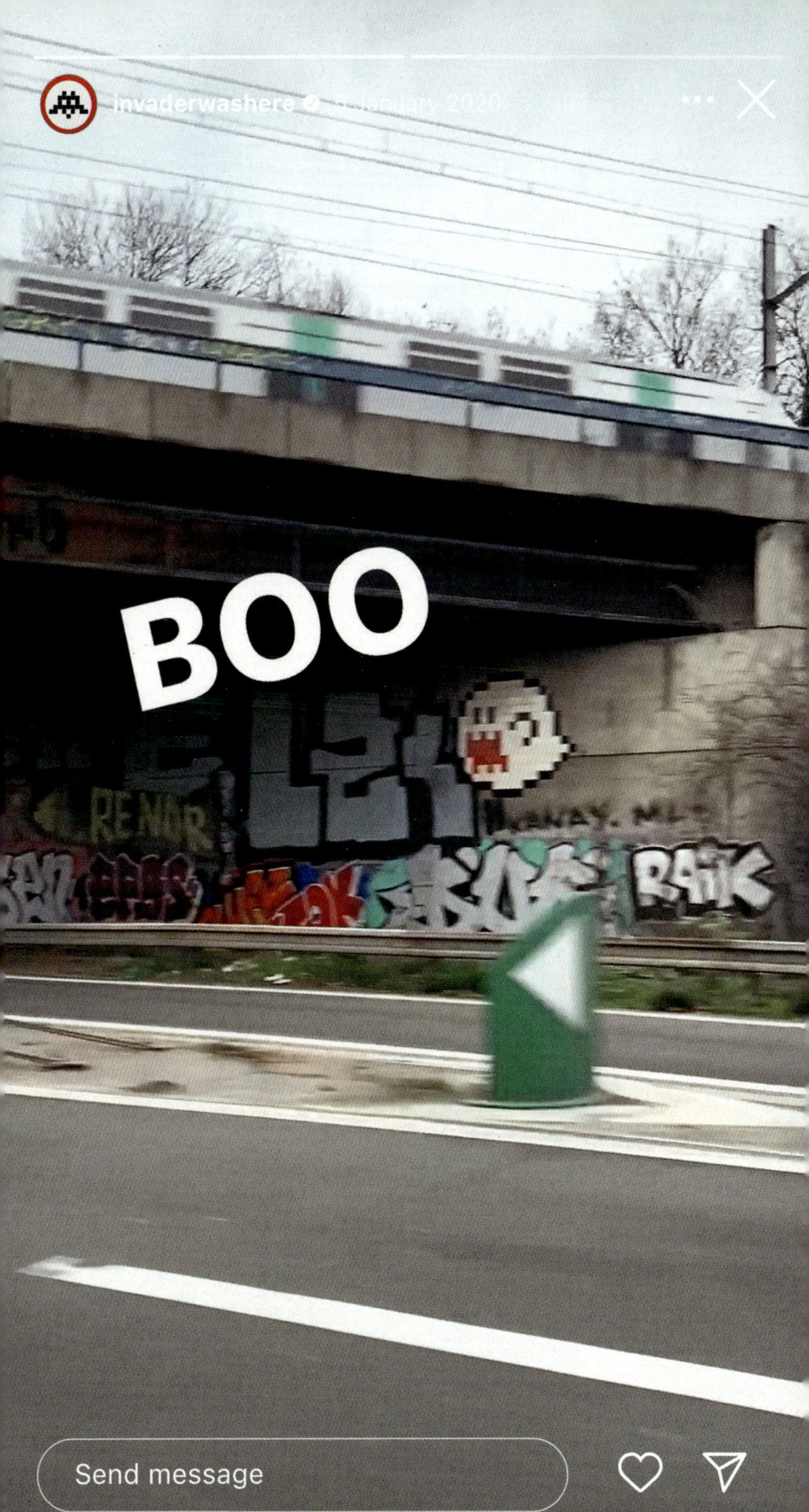
invaderwashere
5 January 2020
BOO
Send message

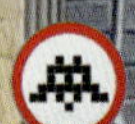
invaderwashere
6 January 2020
RIP
#JohnBaldessari

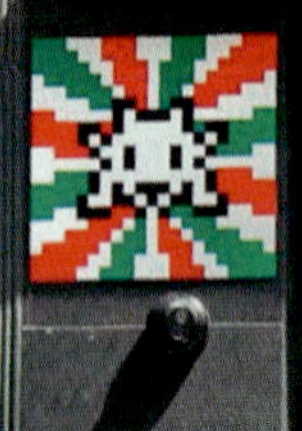
SPRINKLERS
THROUGHOUT
BUILDING
SPRINKLER
SIAMESE
CONNECTION
Send message

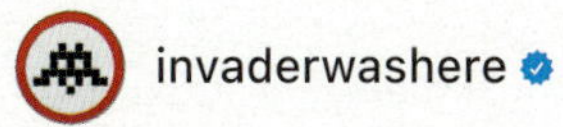

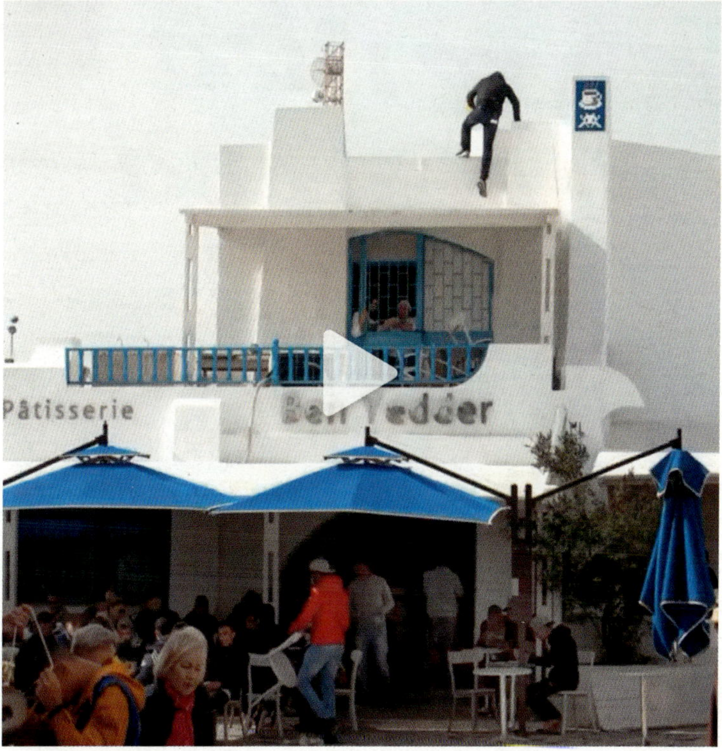

  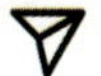 

46 698 views

invaderwashere 2019 in 41 seconds / Put the sound on
#paris #versailles #basel #dijon #ny #djerba #playfortoday

View all 144 comments

6 January 2020

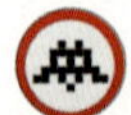

invaderwashere

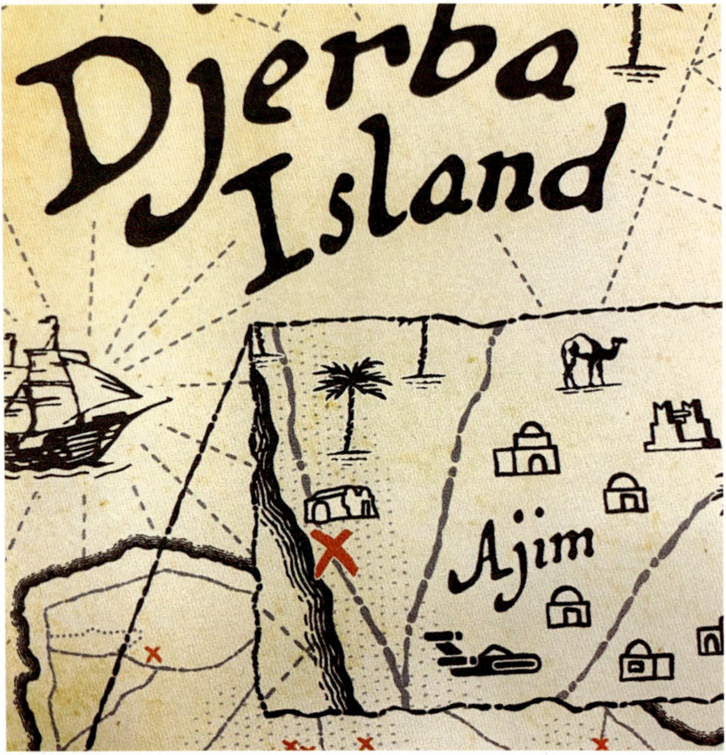

5 659 likes

invaderwashere When I invaded a city before the smartphones and GPS systems age, I used to carry its map in my pocket to note the positions of my interventions so that I could find and photograph them by daylight. These maps were an essential tool for me. I have then started redesigning and publishing some of them. Each maps is a graphic exercise in relation to the city it represents.
DJERBA ISLAND will be the 25th Invasion Map to be published. #workinprogress #treasuremap #details #djerba #staytuned...

View all 71 comments

8 January 2020

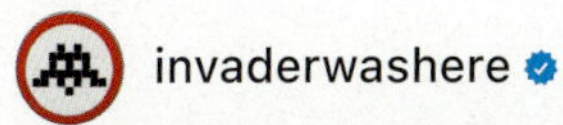

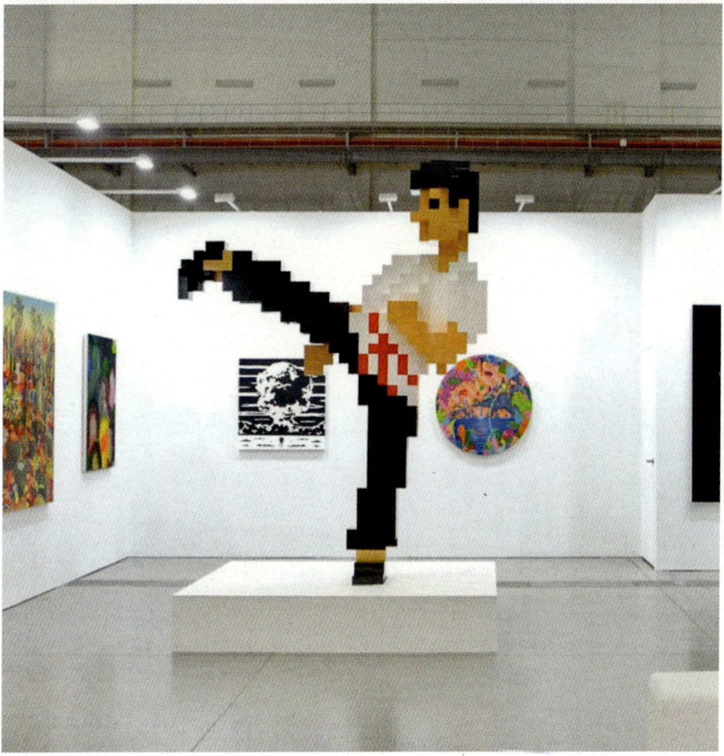

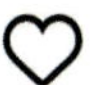   

20 458 likes

invaderwashere Bruce 💥 @taipeidangdai Art fair @oti.official booth #brucelee #kungfumaster #3D #metalsculpture

View all 175 comments

17 January 2020

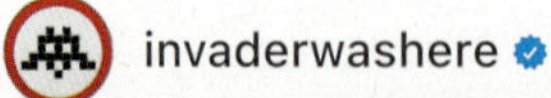

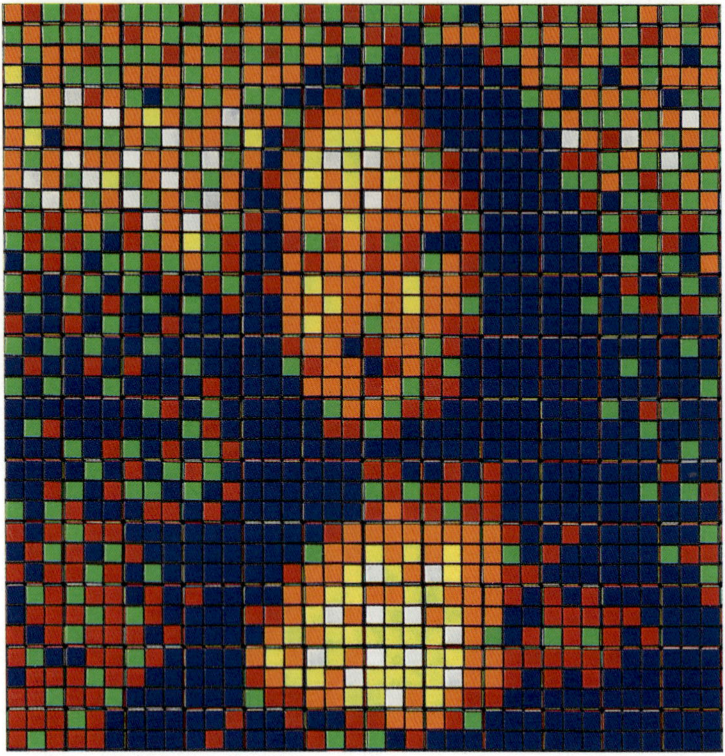

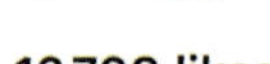

12 798 likes

invaderwashere Artcurial found back this piece from 2005. It is one of the first pieces of my Rubik Masterpieces series in which I reinterpret some works of art history that I particularly appreciate. #RubikMonaLisa #detail @artcurial__ @oliveux_artcurial_urbanart #rubikcubism #15yrsold

View all 131 comments

23 January 2020

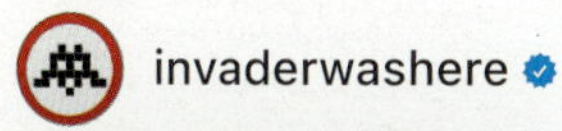

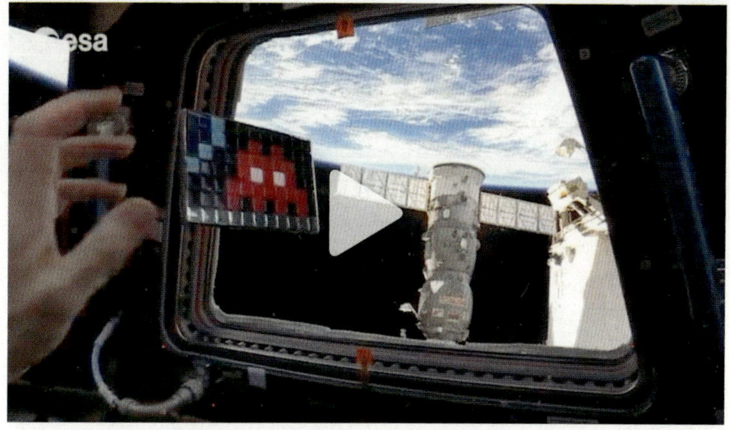

  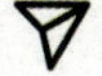 

106 625 views

invaderwashere Space2 in the ISS filmed by astronaut #samanthacristoforetti Have a good weekend 🌍🌎🌏 @europeanspaceagency @nasa #iss #backtospace #spaceinvasion #throwback

View all 665 comments

24 January 2020

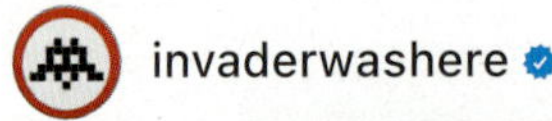

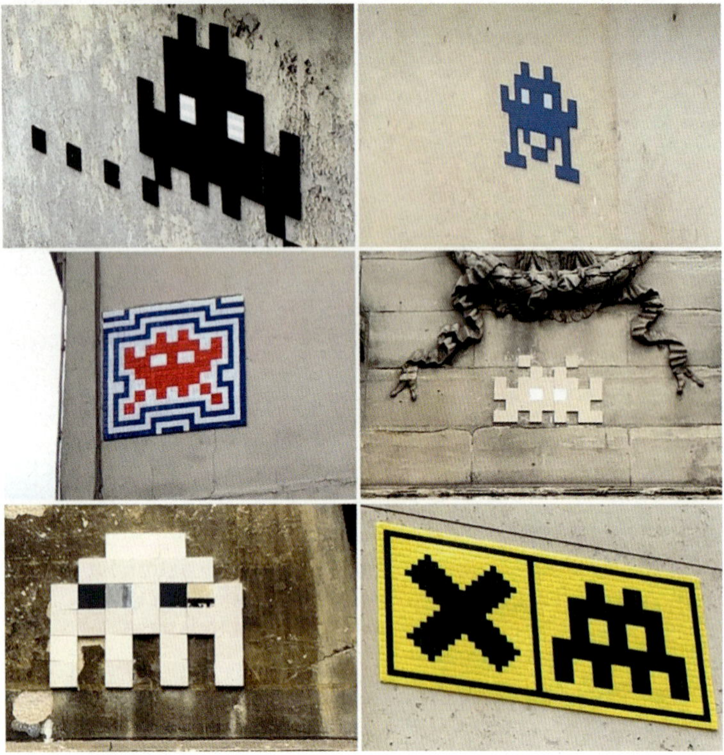

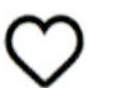  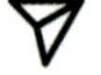 

14 078 likes

invaderwashere Some of the new reactivations in Paris 👍
#thankyou #greatjob #backtolife #reactivations Photos by
@avengers_427

View all 91 comments

26 January 2020

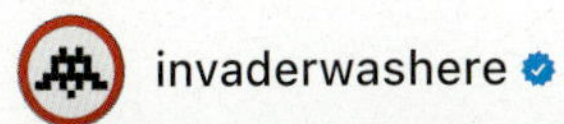

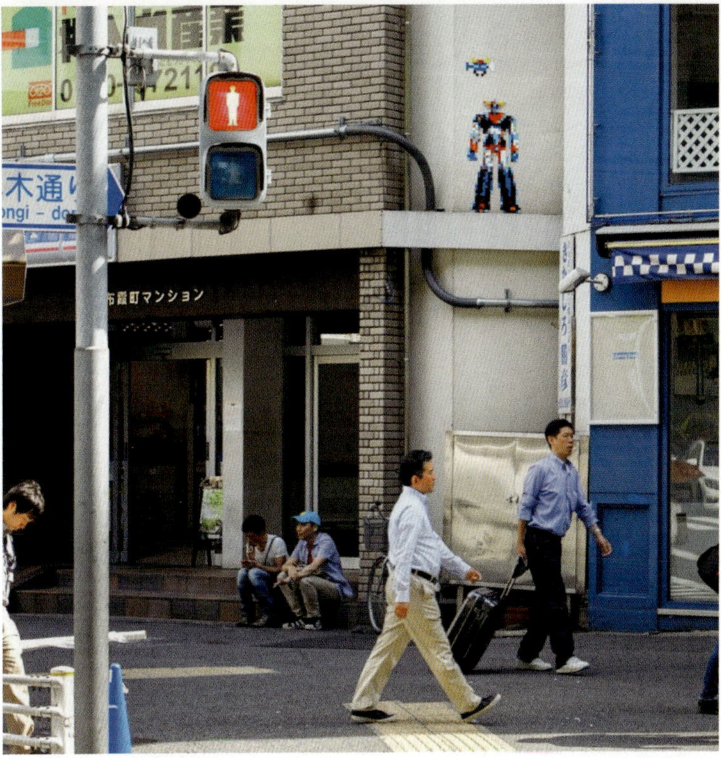

26 022 likes

invaderwashere I've installed TK_109 in Tokyo in 2014 but it had a very short life because the building owner did not like it and put it down 🙁 #tokyo #nishiazabu #grendizer #goldorak #manga #japaneseculture

View all 260 comments

26 January 2020

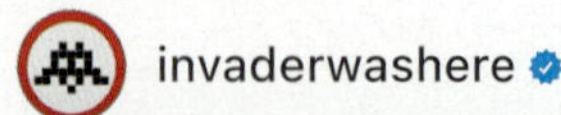

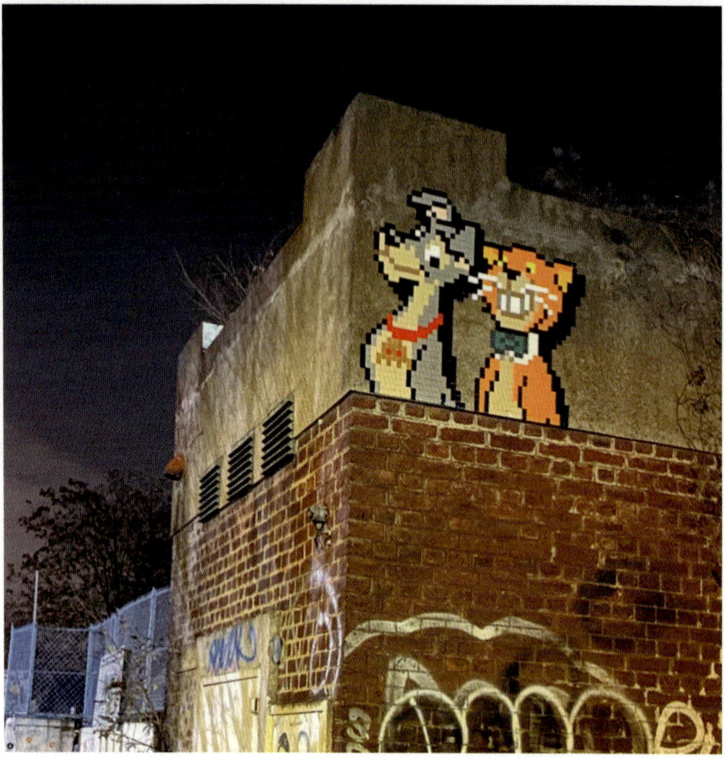

37 507 likes

invaderwashere Recently a volunteer from an animal shelter asked me if I could do something on their place to draw attention to their mission. So I did that last night. @la_spa_gennevilliers #ADOPT #adoptdontshop #SPA #PA_1435

View all 645 comments

29 January 2020

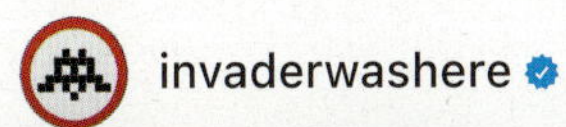

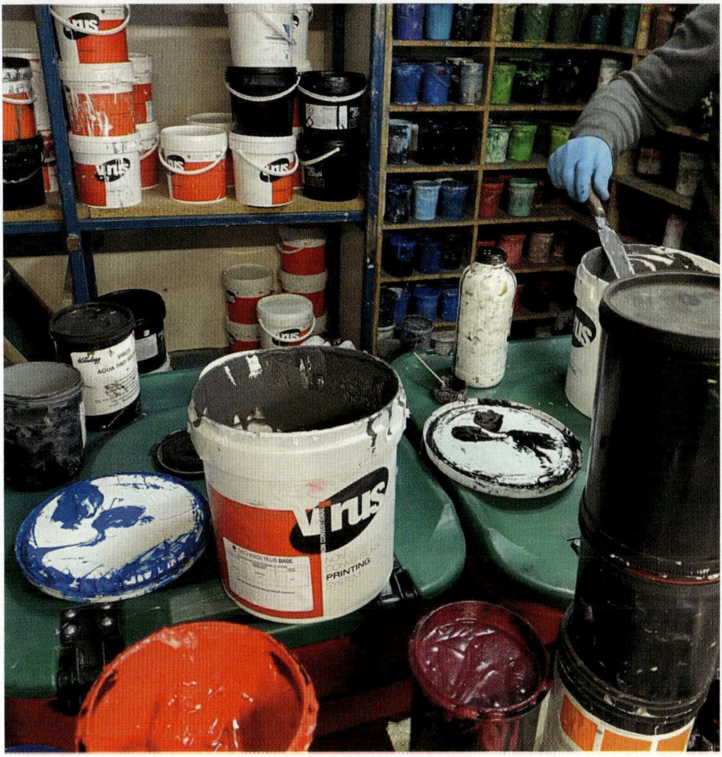

  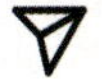  

9054 likes

invaderwashere Working on T-shirts printing today
#testprint #Vrus #handmadecolors

View all 259 comments

30 January 2020

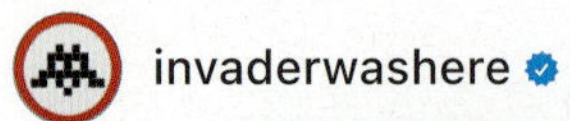

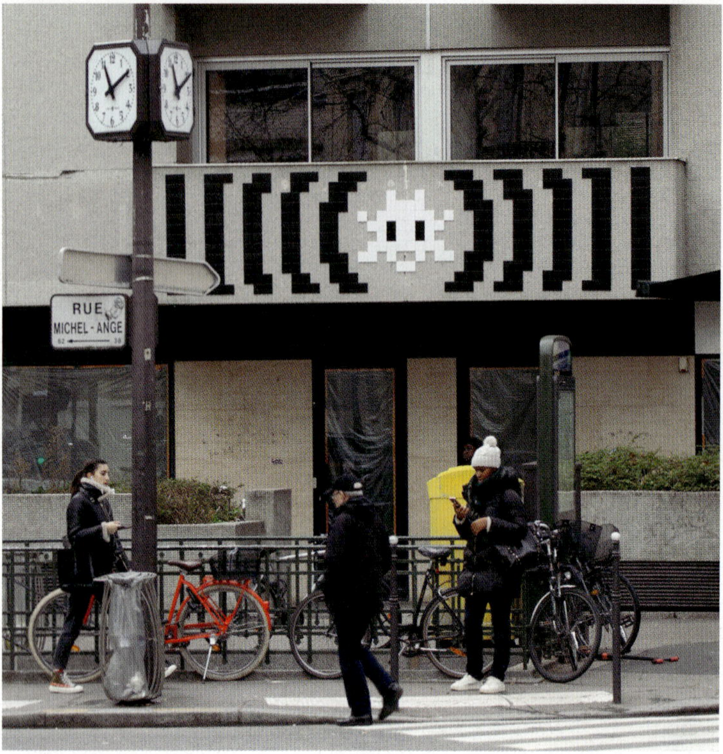

 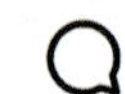  

15 457 likes

invaderwashere PA_1437 #newborn

View all 102 comments

5 February 2020

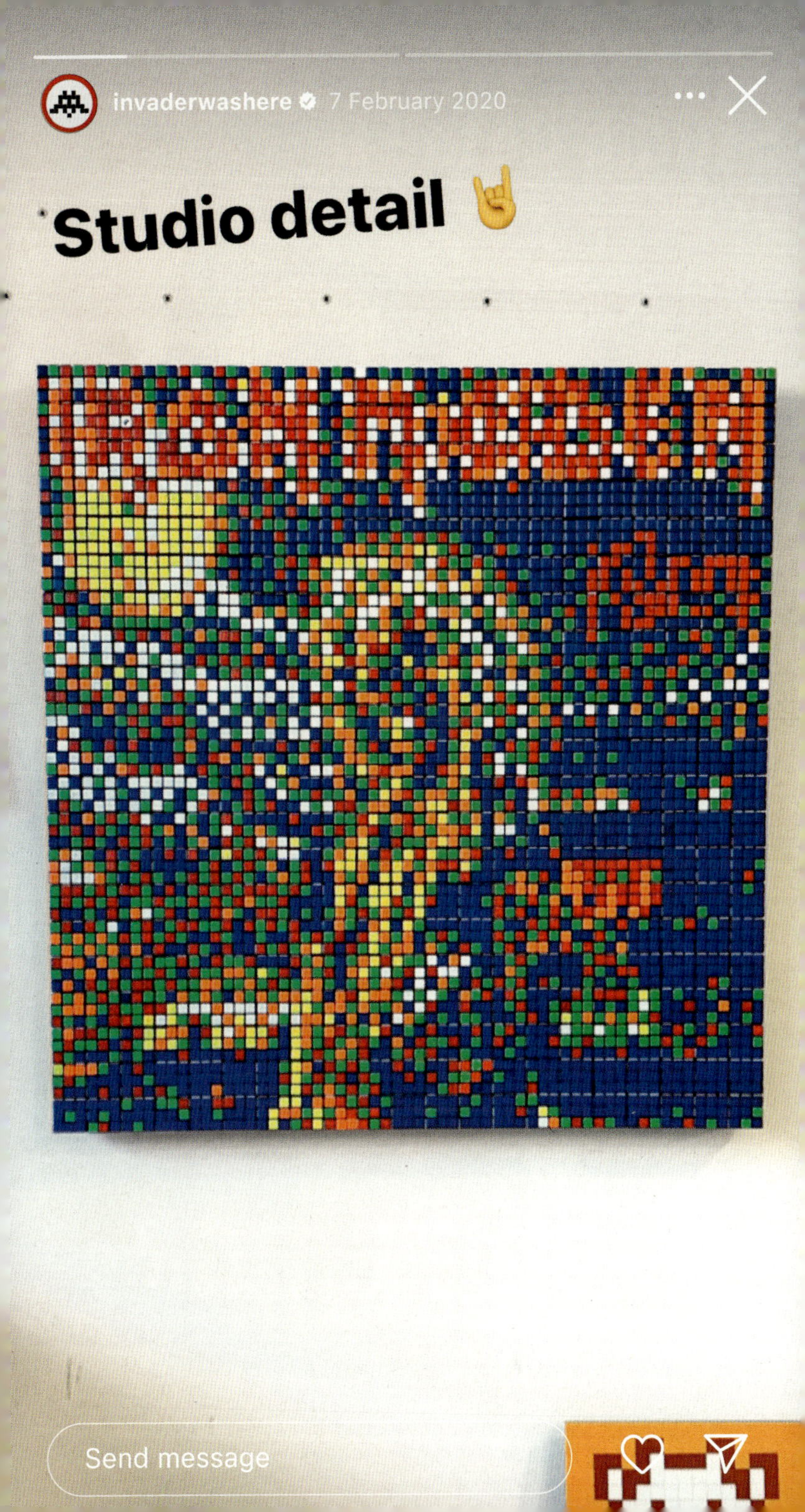

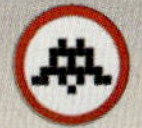

invaderwashere 7 February 2020

Studio detail

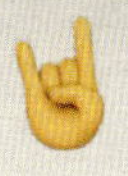

Send message

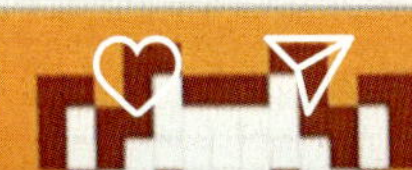

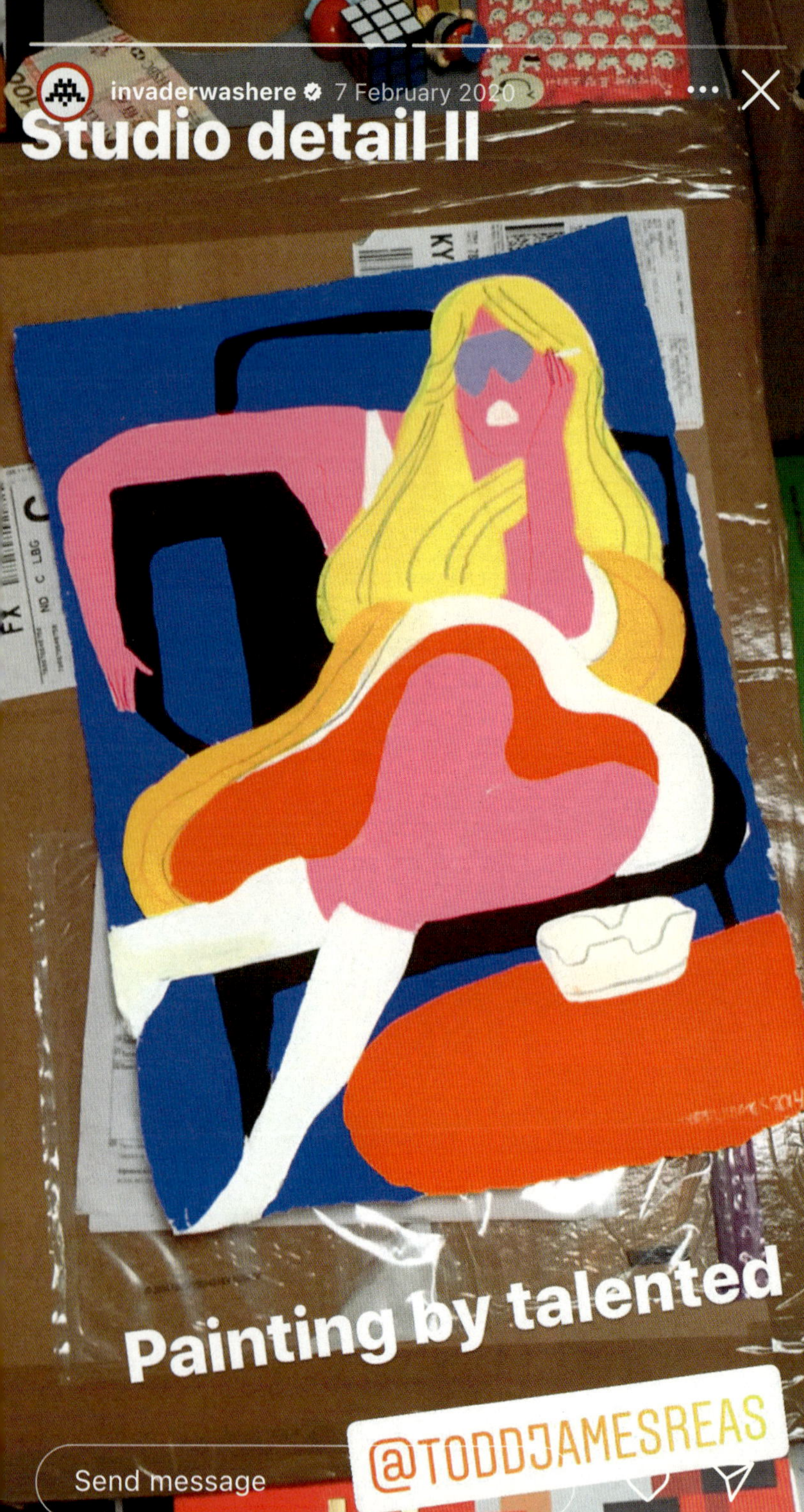
invaderwashere 7 February 2020
Studio detail II
Painting by talented
@TODDJAMESREAS
Send message

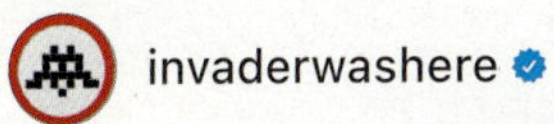

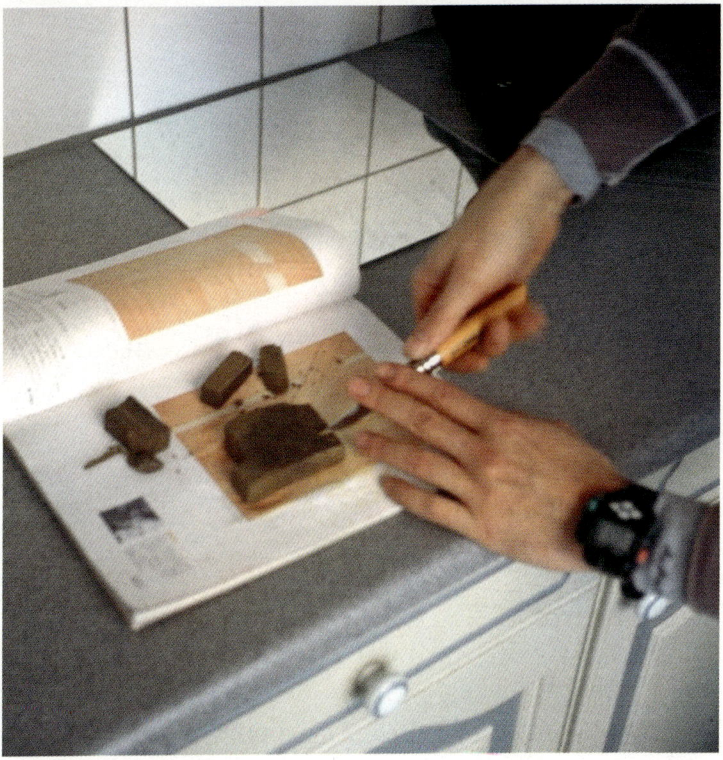

12 494 likes

invaderwashere In 2001 I was invited to participate in a group show in Rotterdam and I asked the gallery if they could find a big piece of hashish to make a sculpture. They agreed and I sculpted it in my hotel room. At the end of the show I tried to have it come to France because I thought it was now a piece of art and not a piece of drug anymore. But I've never got a feedback, I don't know what could have happened to it 🤔 #dopeart #hashishsculpture #spacespace #chocolate #mamagallery #makingof #Rotterdam

View all 332 comments

11 February 2020

invaderwashere

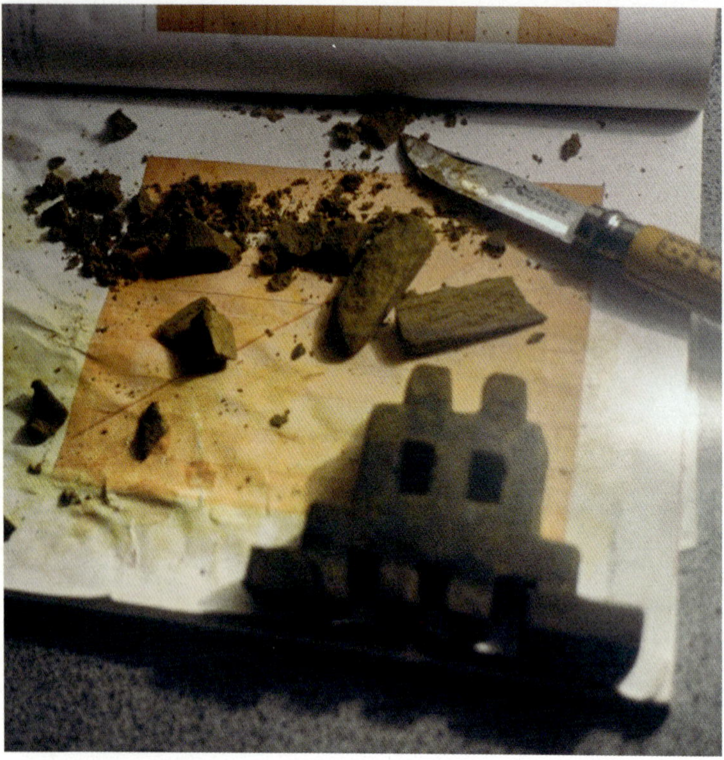

12 494 likes

invaderwashere In 2001 I was invited to participate in a group show in Rotterdam and I asked the gallery if they could find a big piece of hashish to make a sculpture. They agreed and I sculpted it in my hotel room. At the end of the show I tried to have it come to France because I thought it was now a piece of art and not a piece of drug anymore. But I've never got a feedback, I don't know what could have happened to it 🤔 #dopeart #hashishsculpture #spacespace #chocolate #mamagallery #makingof #Rotterdam

View all 332 comments

11 February 2020

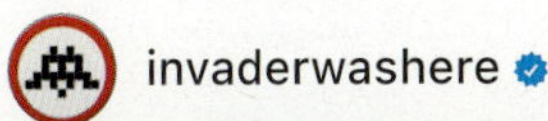

•••

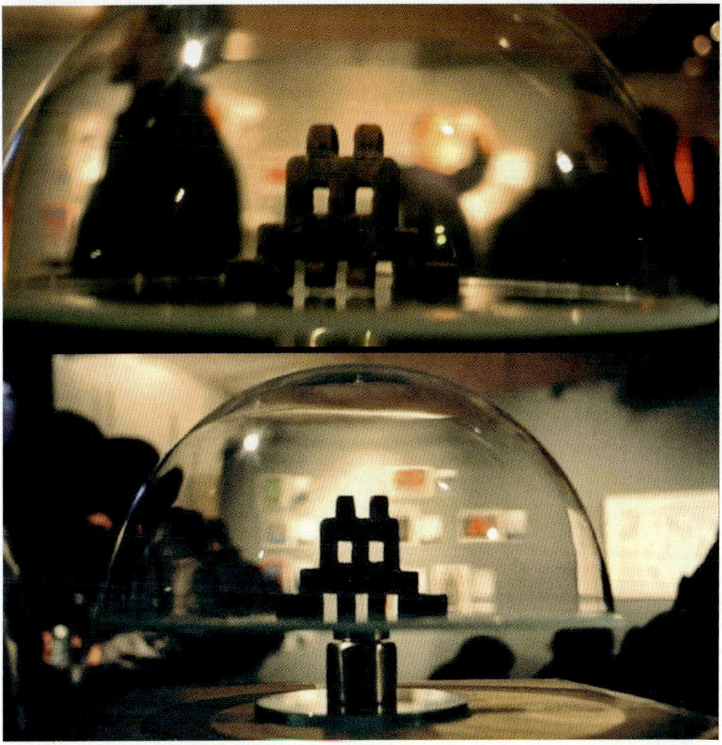

12 494 likes

invaderwashere In 2001 I was invited to participate in a group show in Rotterdam and I asked the gallery if they could find a big piece of hashish to make a sculpture. They agreed and I sculpted it in my hotel room. At the end of the show I tried to have it come to France because I thought it was now a piece of art and not a piece of drug anymore. But I've never got a feedback, I don't know what could have happened to it 🤔 #dopeart #hashishsculpture #spacespace #chocolate #mamagallery #makingof #Rotterdam

View all 332 comments

11 February 2020

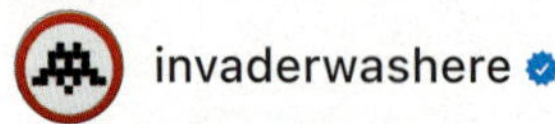

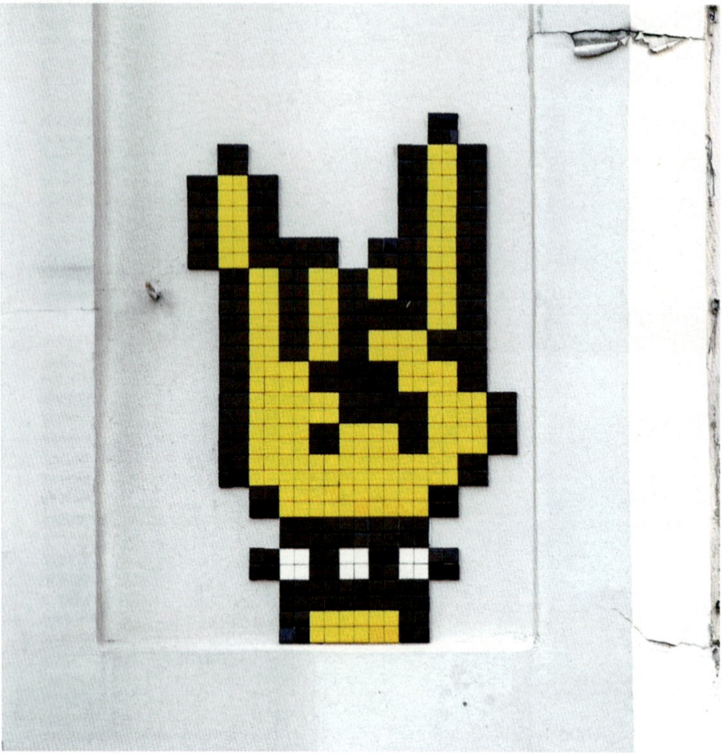

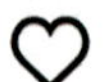   

17 374 likes

invaderwashere 666k followers! Thanks to all of you
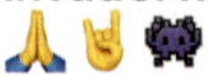

View all 199 comments

13 February 2020

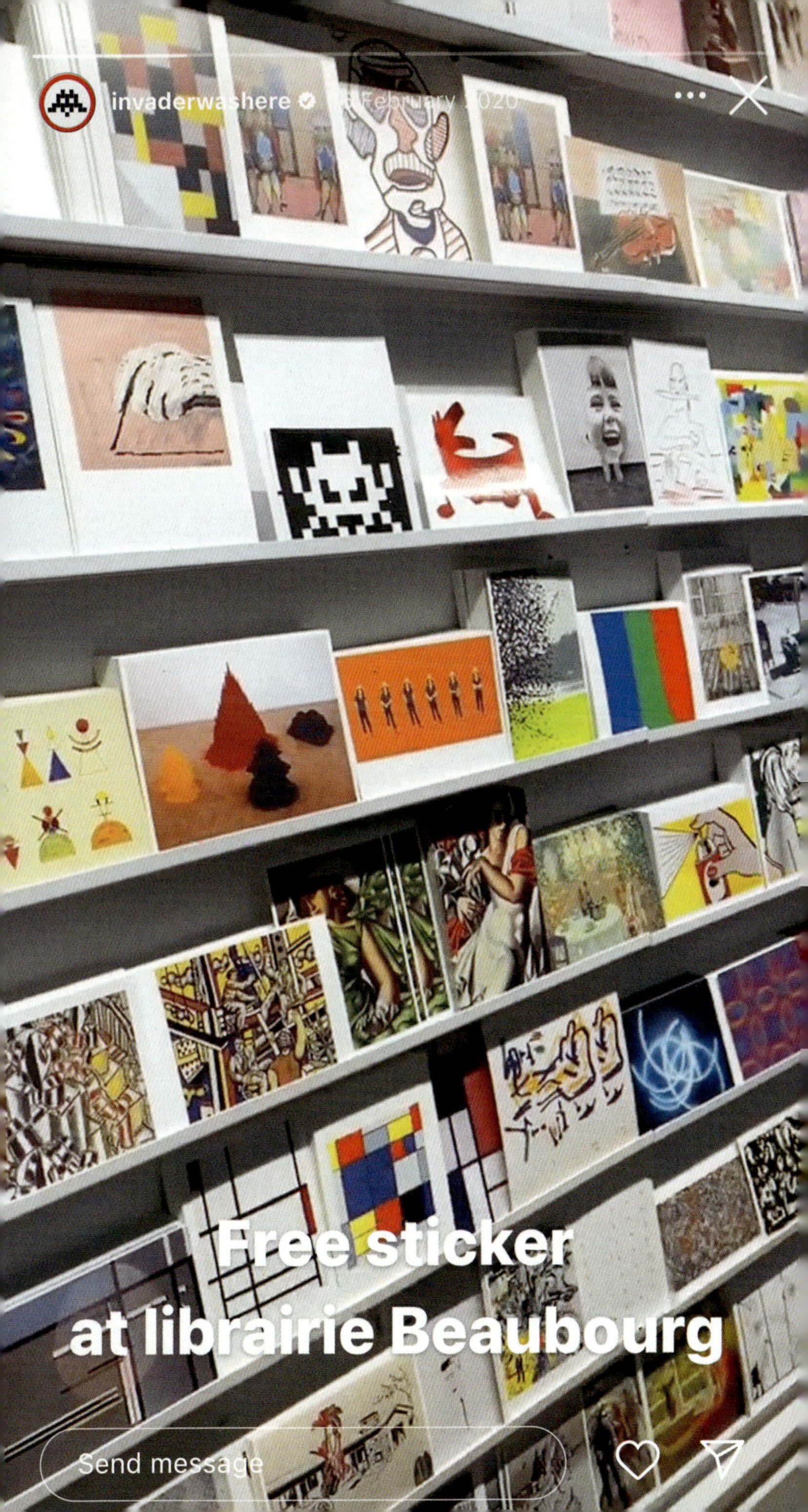
invaderwashere
February 2020
Free sticker
at librairie Beaubourg
Send message

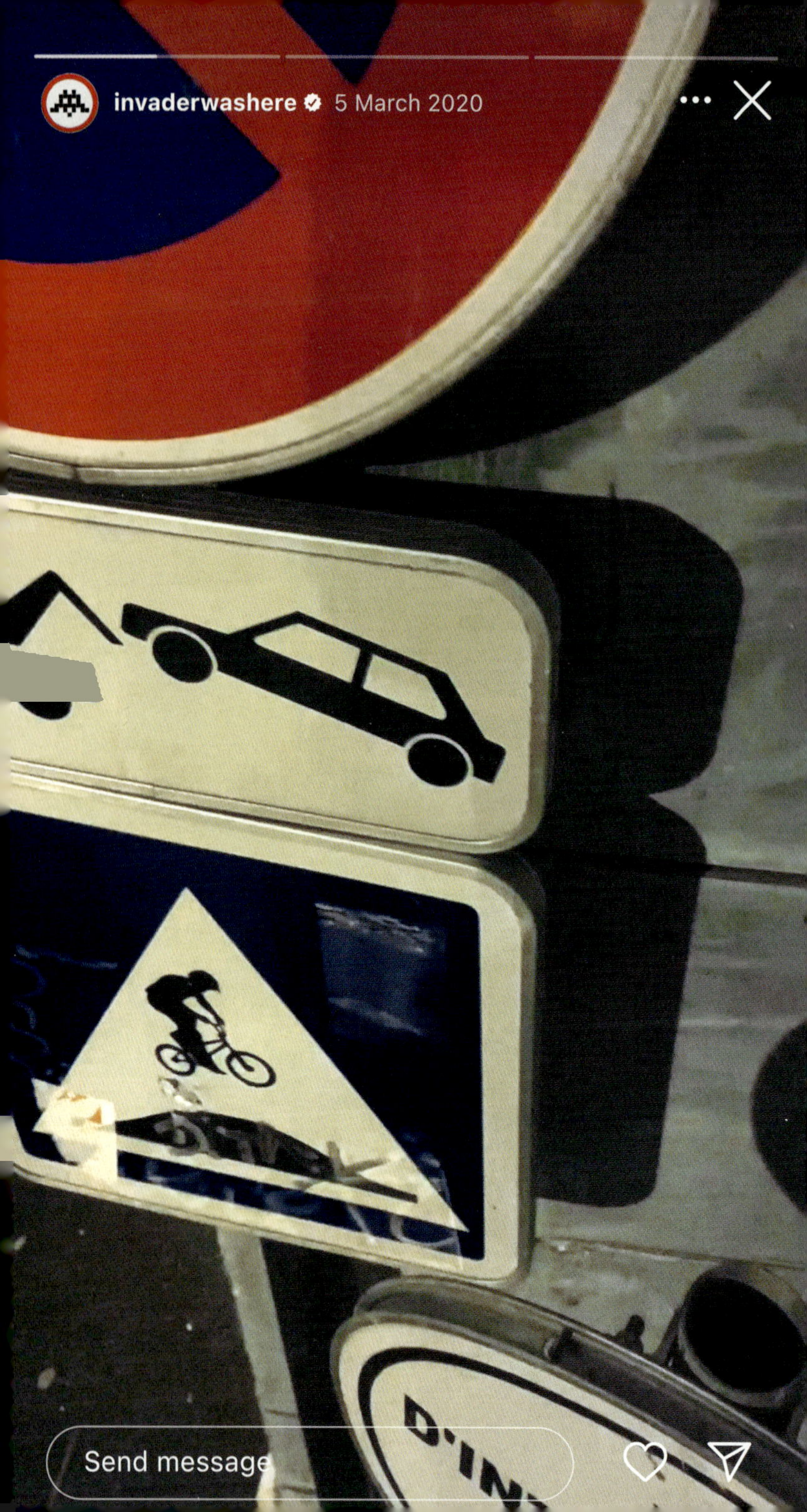
invaderwashere
5 March 2020
Send message

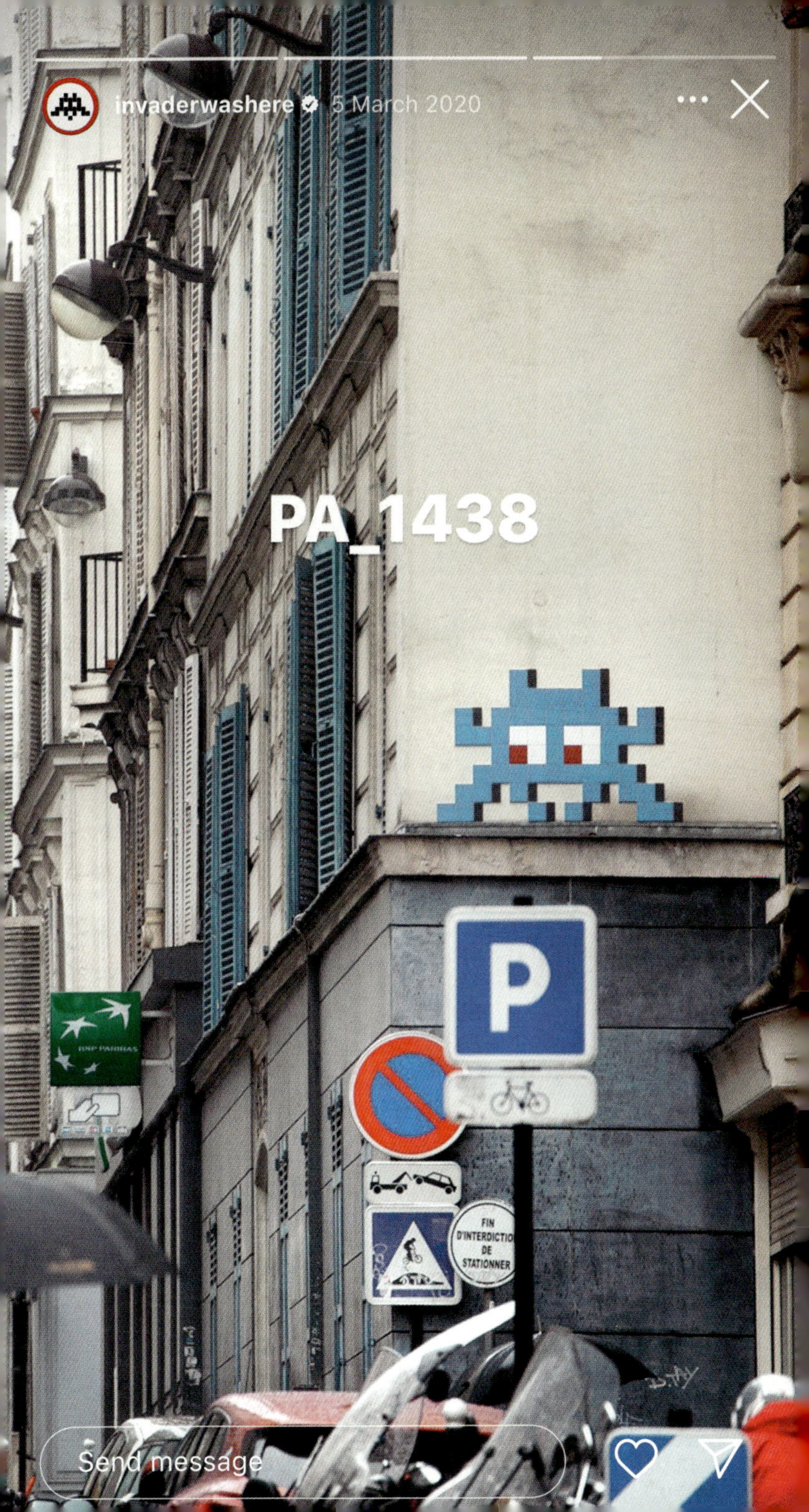
invaderwashere
5 March 2020
PA_1438
P
FIN
D'INTERDICTION
DE
STATIONNER
Send message

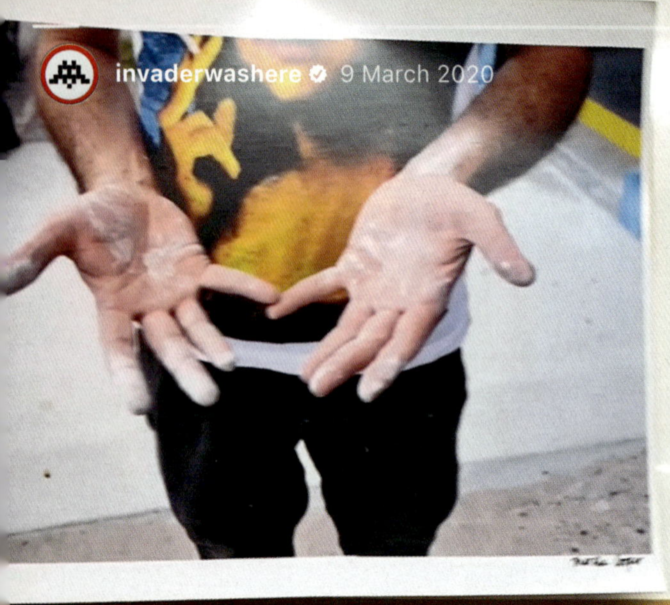

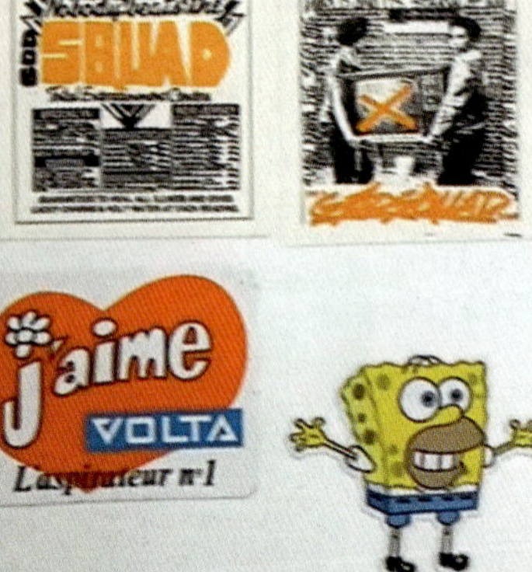

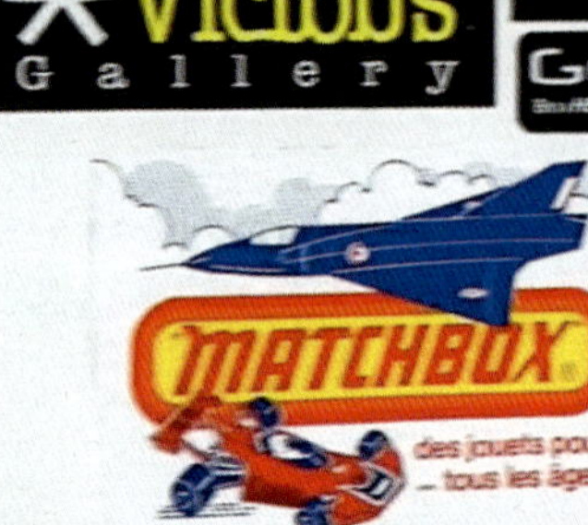

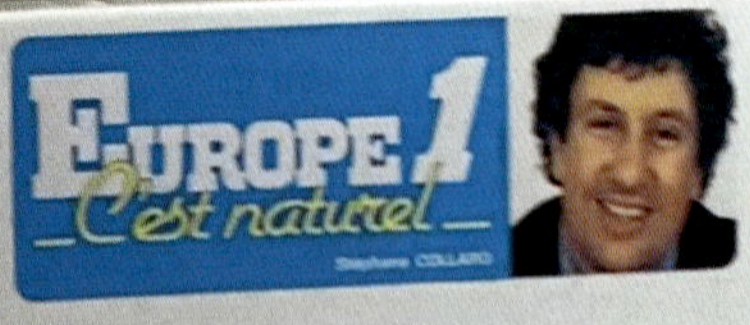

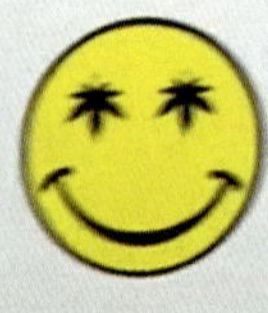

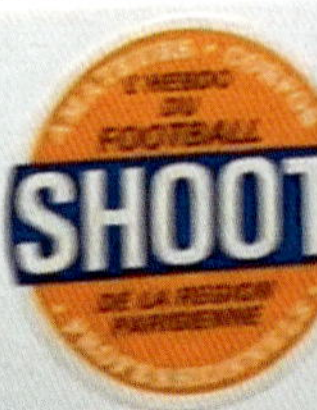

Send message

Wash your hands !

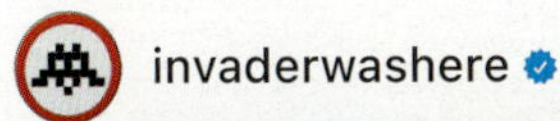

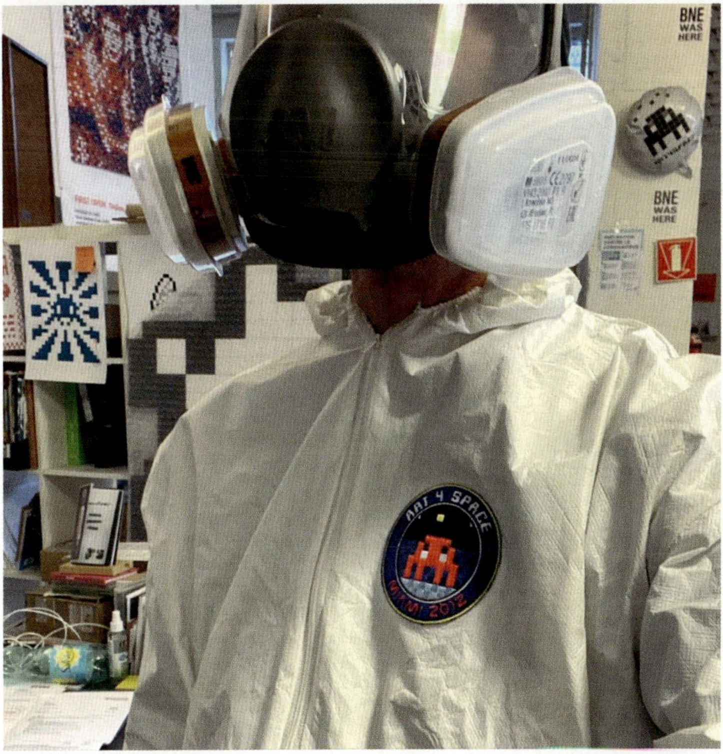

  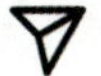 

10 595 likes

invaderwashere I'm waiting for you Covid-19... 👊 🦠

View all 114 comments

16 March 2020

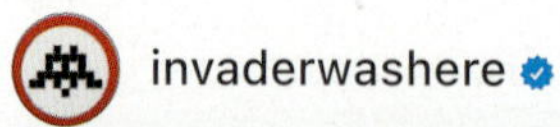

Confinement with my dear #PA_1432 @invaderwashere

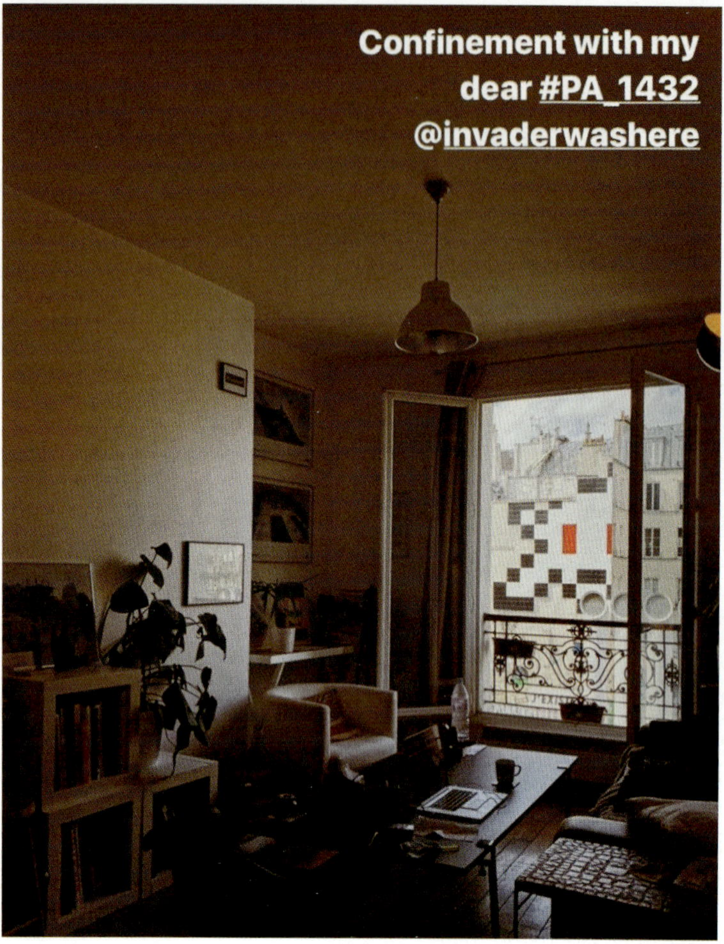

11042 likes

invaderwashere Seen on Instagram: Room with view 👀 👾 #lockdown #covid_19 #newglobalorder / photo and post by @saroufimanthony

View all 121 comments

18 March 2020

invaderwashere

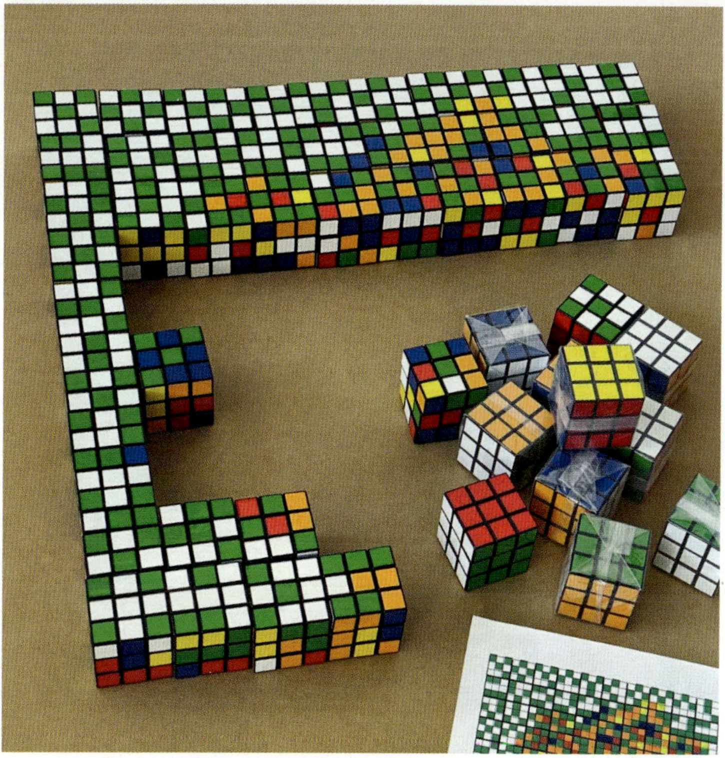

•••

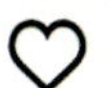   

15 078 likes

invaderwashere To create Rubikcubist artworks, I spend days in my studio twisting cubes, like painters would do mixing colors on their palette. A perfect lockdown activity! #covid_19 #newglobalorder #staysafe #rubikcubism

View all 167 comments

23 March 2020

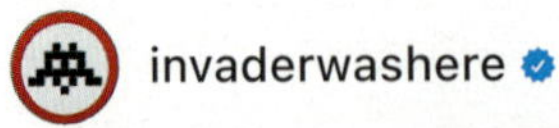

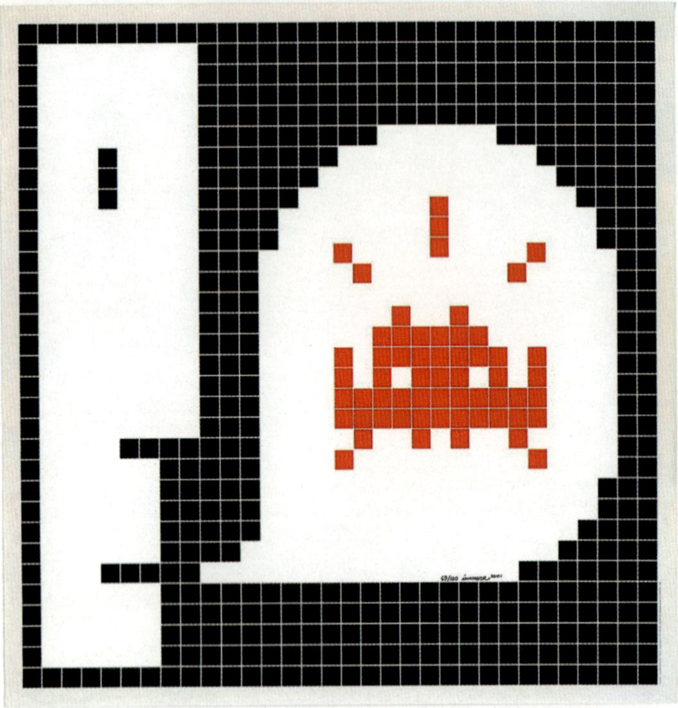

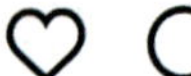

11701 likes

invaderwashere ALERT is the first print I've ever published. That was in 2001 and it was inspired by the Alert icon made by Susan Kare for the first generations of Apple computer systems. I've always regretted using an offset process rather than silkscreen, but anyway, what is done is done! #alertsystem #susankare #macOS #applecomputers #archive Thank you Susan Kare for your talent and for the inspiration 👏🙏👾

View all 105 comments

25 March 2020

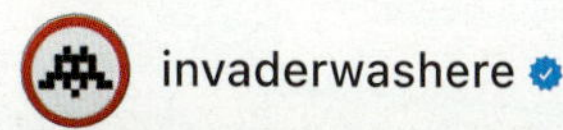

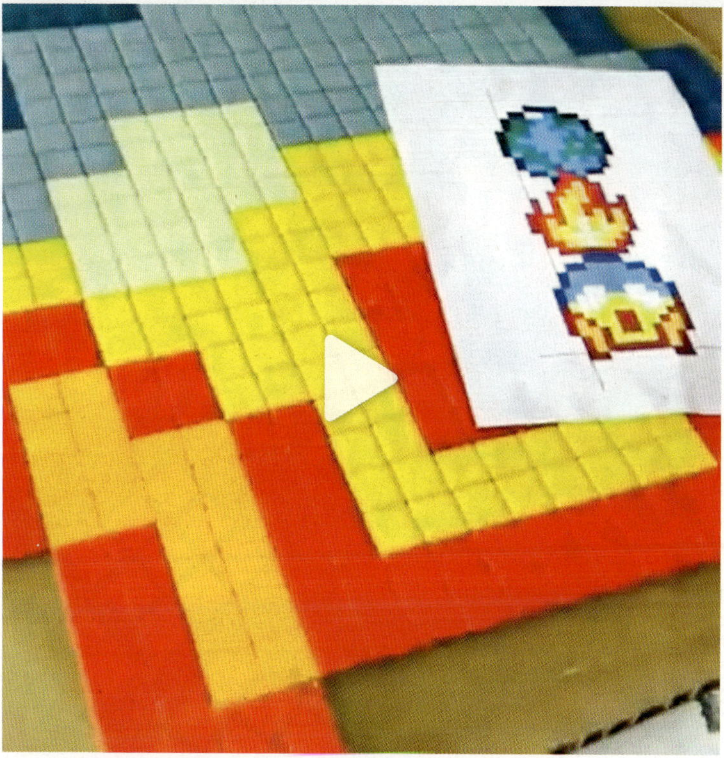

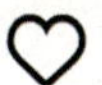  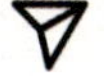 

65 521 views

invaderwashere Coincidence or premonition? That is the latest piece I was preparing for the street just before the coronavirus crisis and lockdown 😱🔥🌏 #covid19 #scream #alert #motherearth #sick #burning #studiodetail #totemoji music: Nepla relou by #lucratemilk

View all 197 comments

28 March 2020

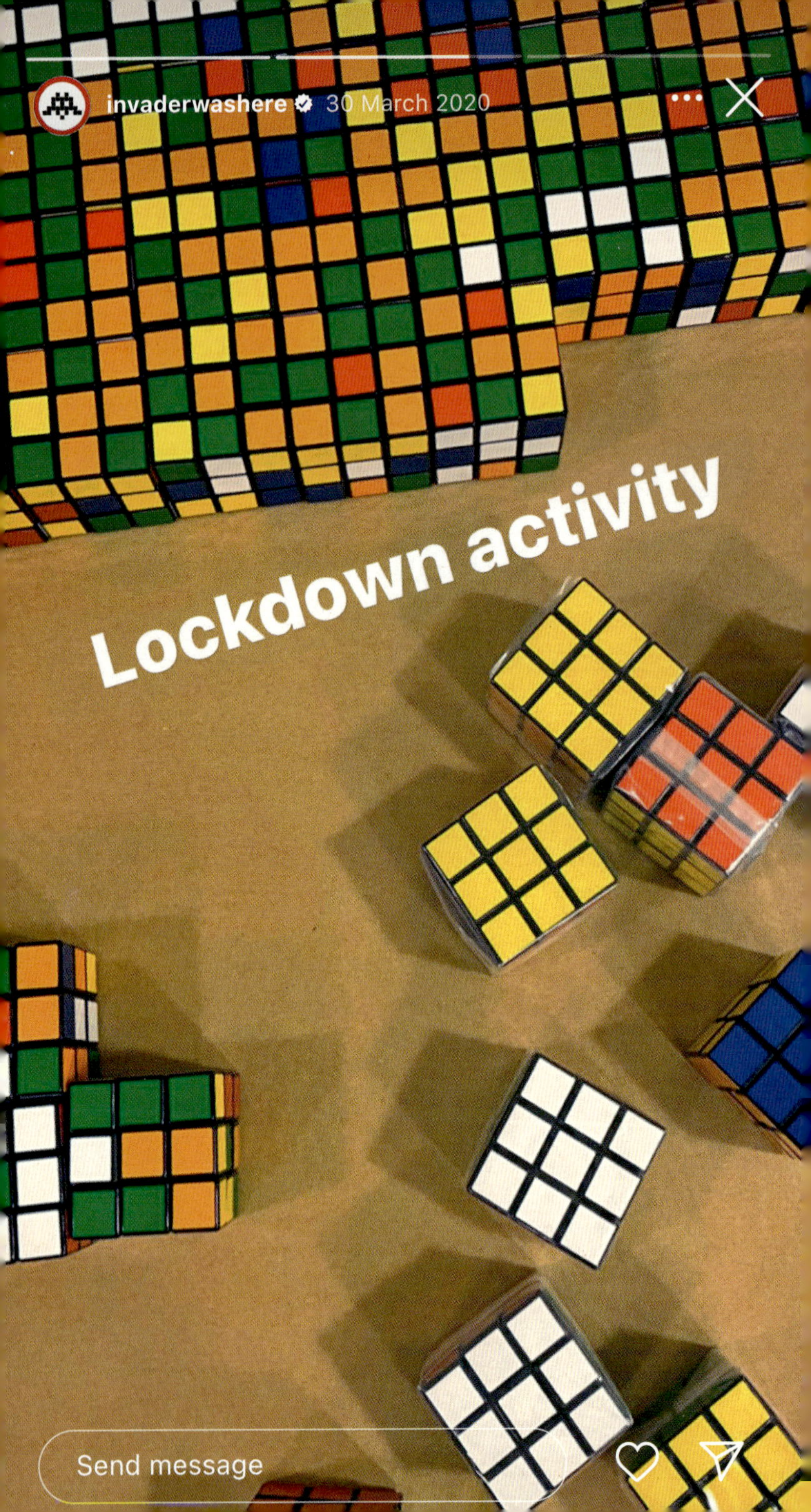
invaderwashere
30 March 2020
Lockdown activity
Send message

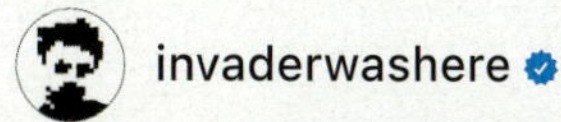

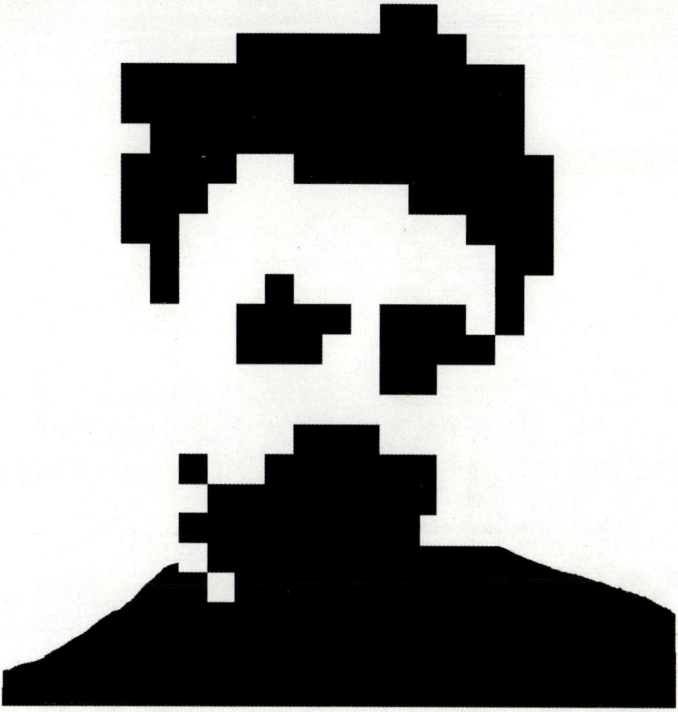

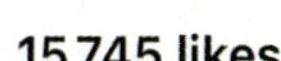
15 745 likes

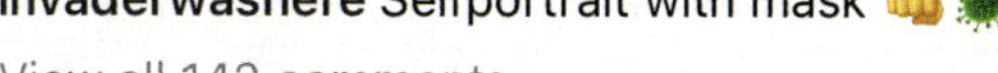
invaderwashere Selfportrait with mask 👊 🦠

View all 142 comments

30 March 2020

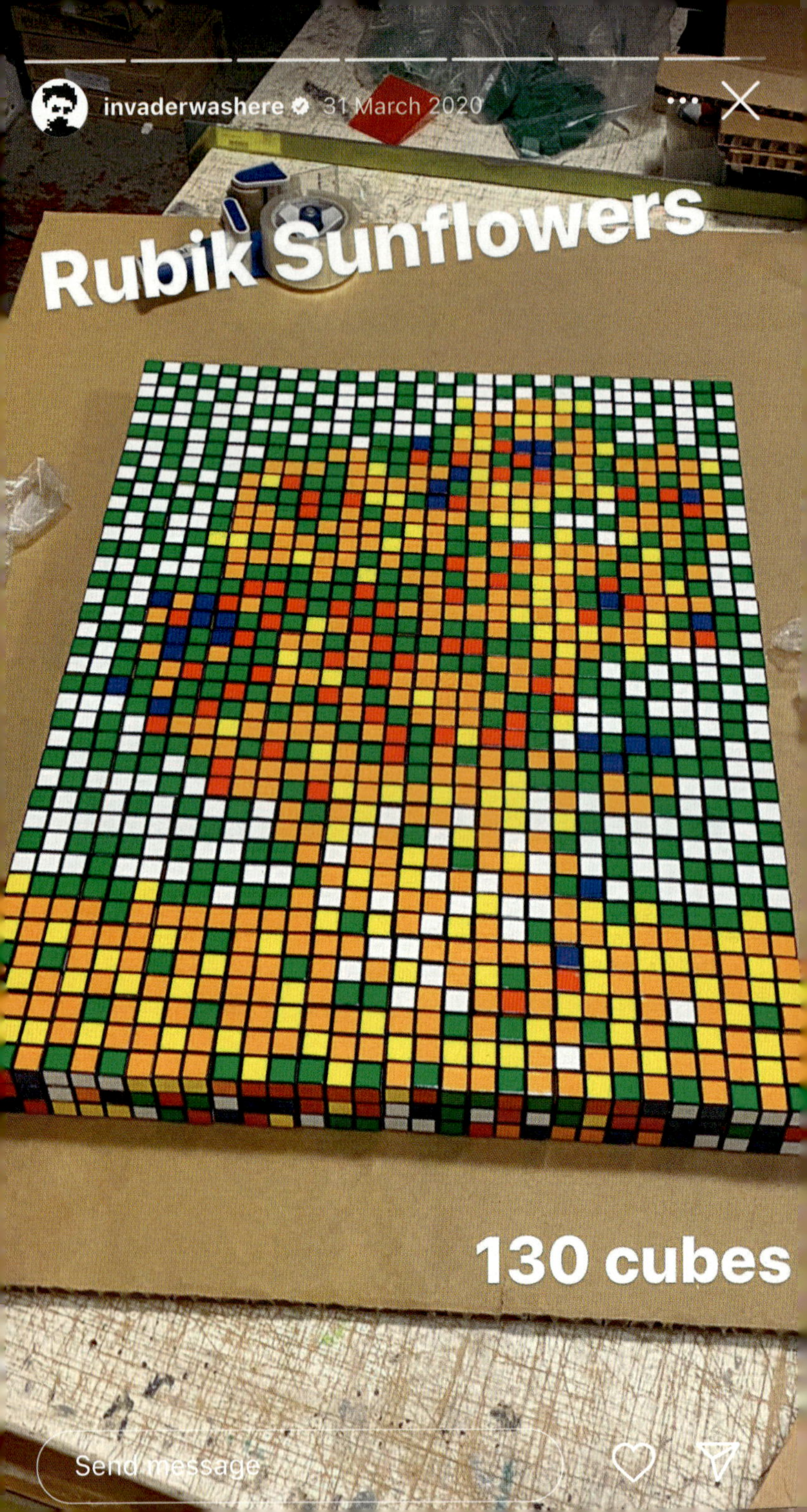
invaderwashere
31 March 2020
Rubik Sunflowers
130 cubes
Send message

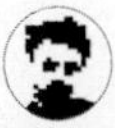

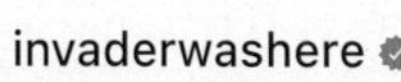

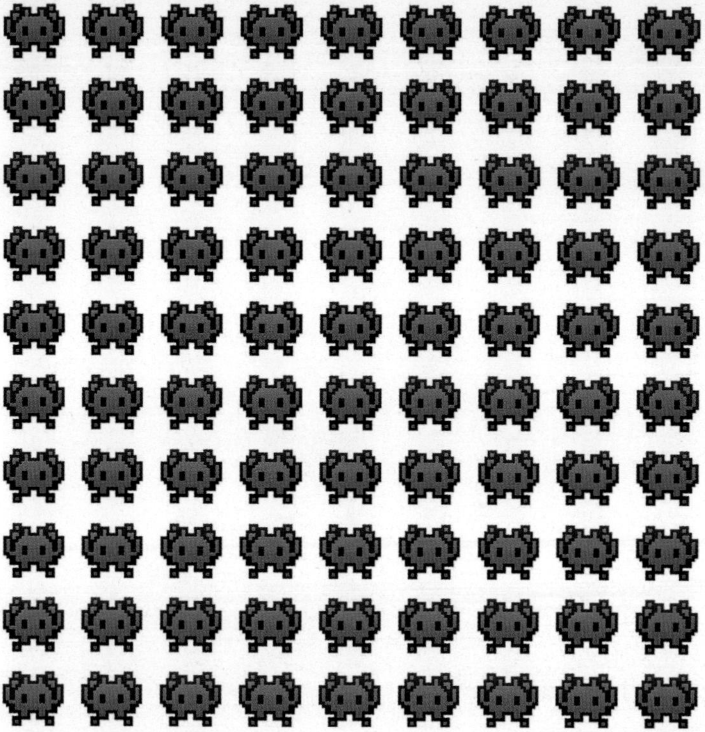

21 439 likes

invaderwashere

View all 262 comments

3 April 2020

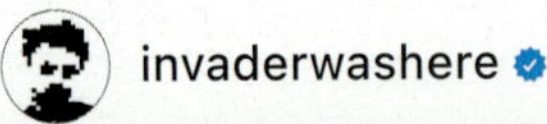

•••

The Most Dangerous Species

Steve Cutts

on Earth

 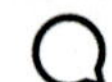  

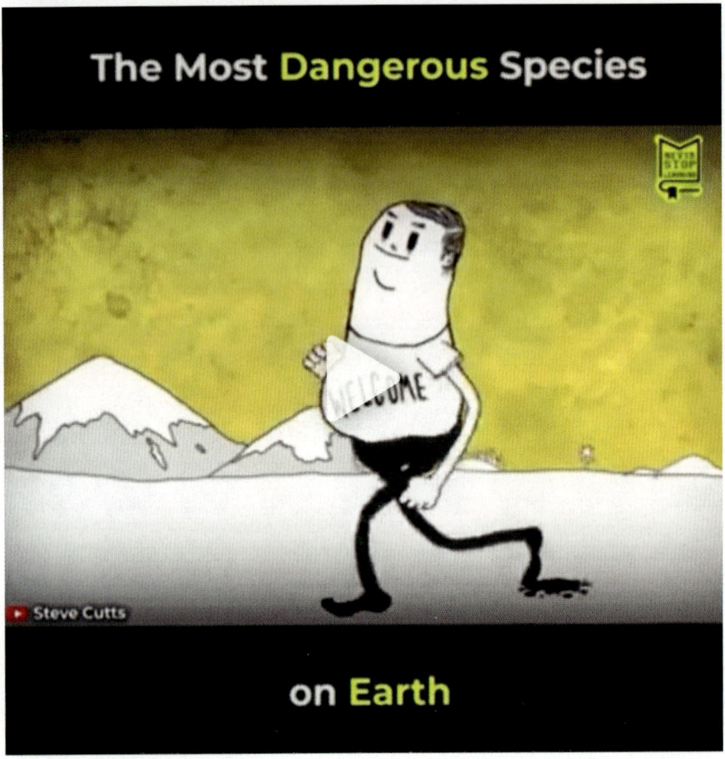

124 581 views

invaderwashere #homosapiens #foodforthought #timetochange movie by @steve_cutts_official

View all 355 comments

11 April 2020

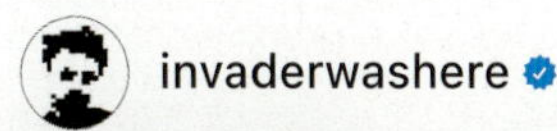

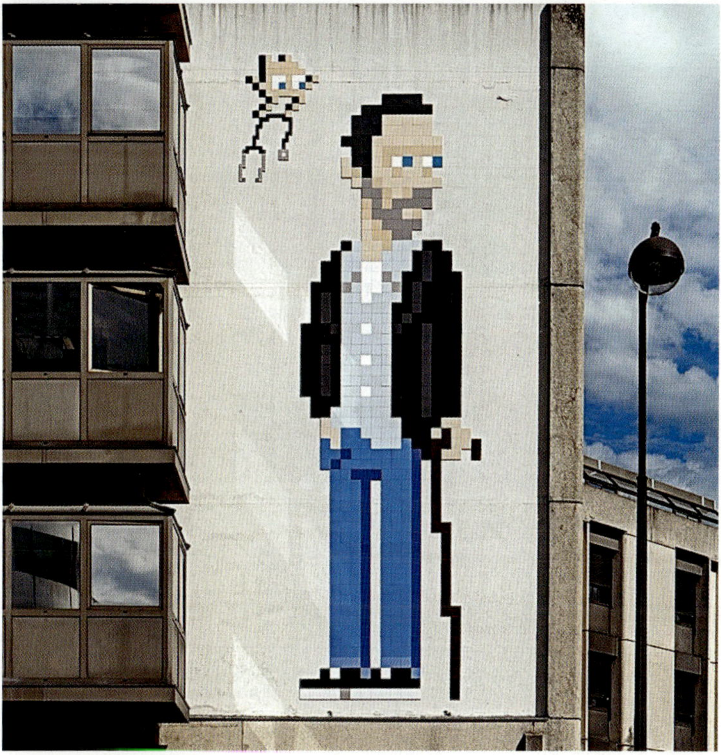

29 397 likes

invaderwashere I made this mosaic of Dr House on a Parisian hospital four years ago but it has never been as relevant as nowadays. Big up to the doctors and all the people who work in hospitals and who save lives #covid19 #pandemia #doctors #nurses #8pm 👏👏👏

View all 279 comments

13 April 2020

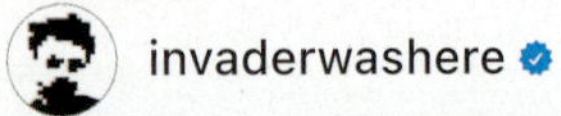

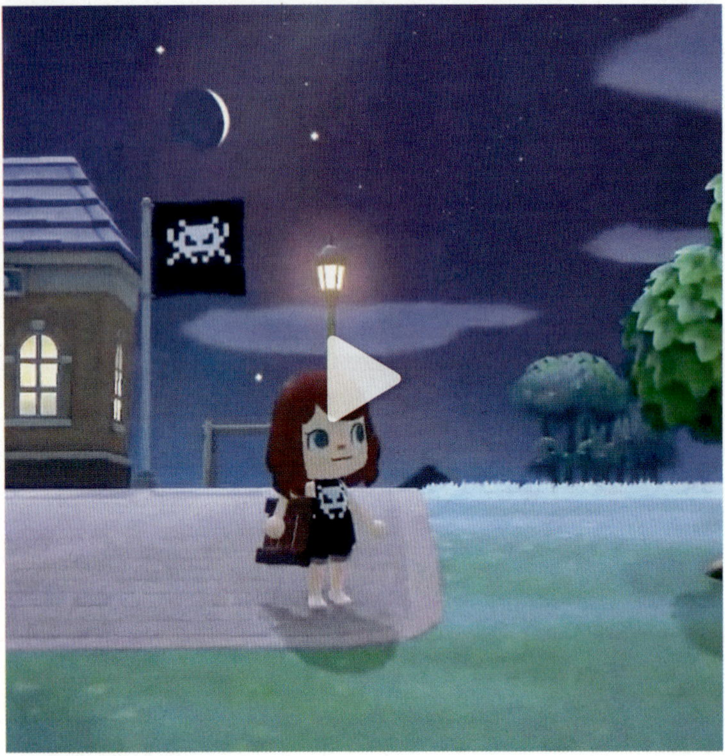

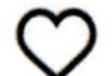   

69 565 views

invaderwashere If I can't invade the real world, then I will invade the virtual world! #quarantineactivities #lockdown #covid19 #animalcrossing #digitalinvasion #newterritories

View all 235 comments

27 April 2020

invaderwashere

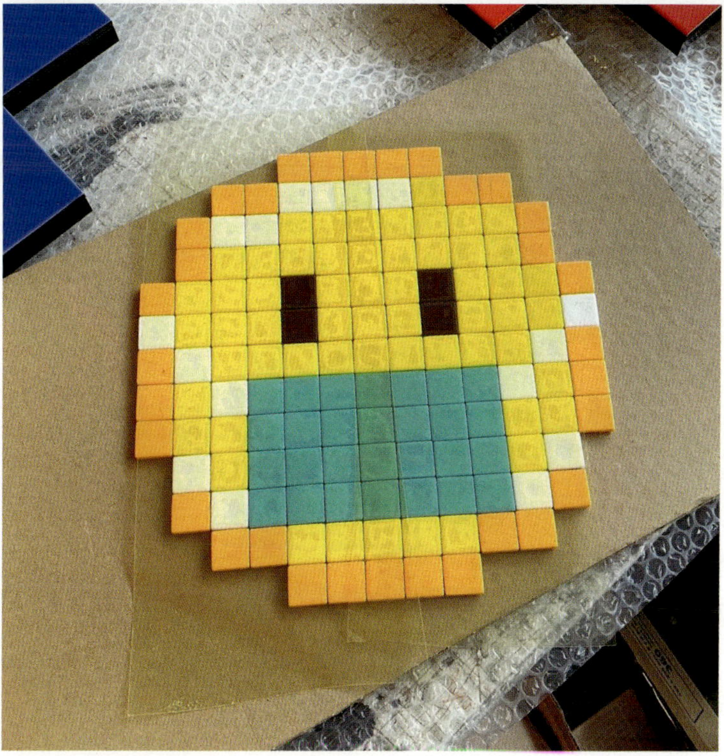

23 366 likes

invaderwashere Happy May 1st 2020 #studiodetail

View all 206 comments

1 May 2020

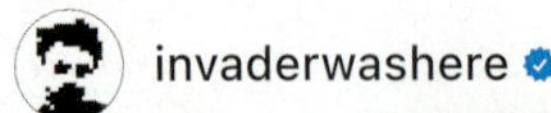

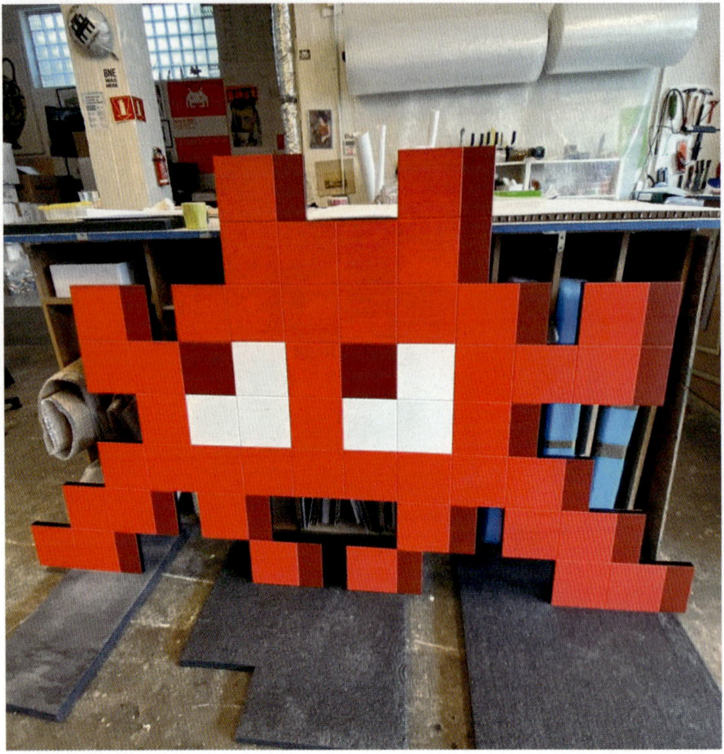

23 313 likes

invaderwashere ALIAS DJBA_33 #studiodetail

View all 171 comments

6 May 2020

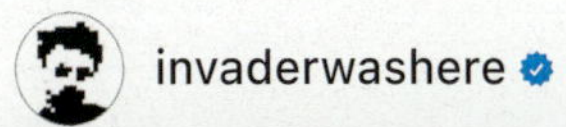

ANDREW SHARPLEY
INVADER

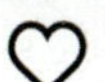    

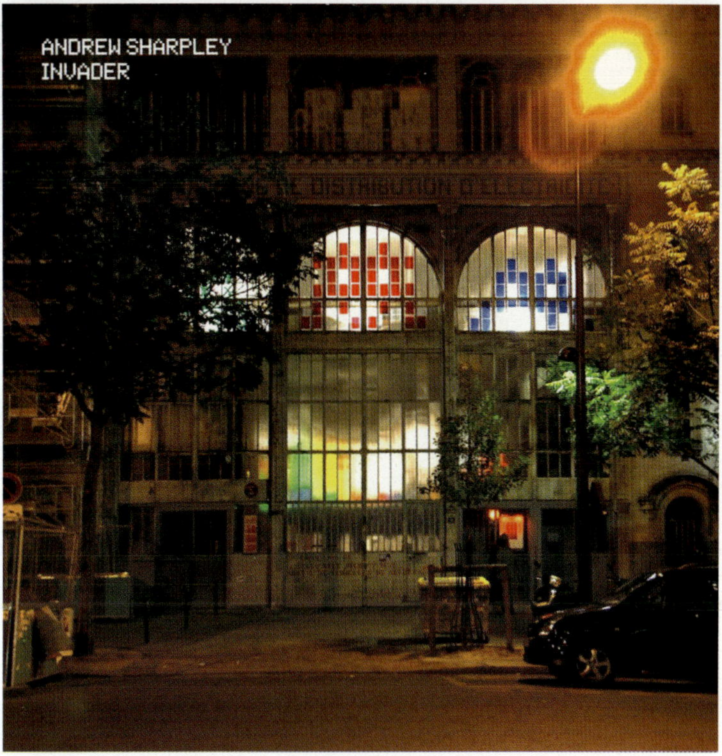

12 688 likes

invaderwashere Here is a little surprise to help you to stay home during the lockdown. This mix was made by the talented musician Andrew Sharpley for the opening of my exhibition "1000" in Paris in 2011. Dim the light, sit down comfortably and enjoy this little jem. >>> Free streaming or hi-res digital version to buy (to support the artist 🎩🙏) here: https://testrecordings.bandcamp.com #andrewsharpley #testrecordings #newalbum #invader #experimentalmusic #stockhausenandwalkman #audiocollage #electronic #archive

View all 57 comments

9 May 2020

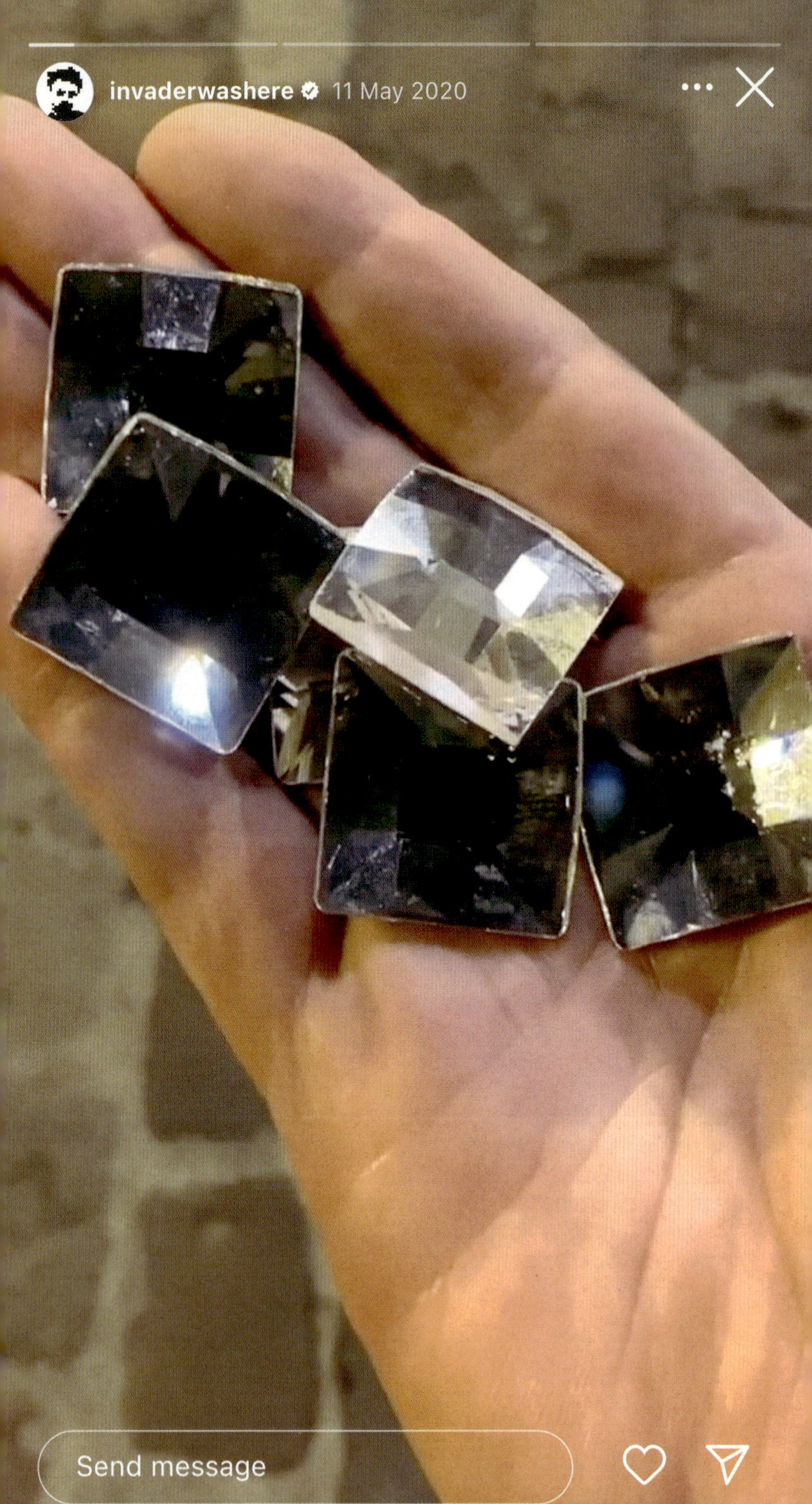
invaderwashere
11 May 2020
Send message

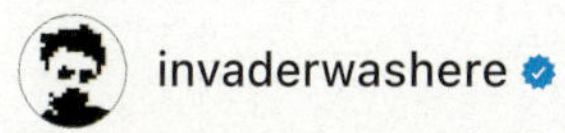

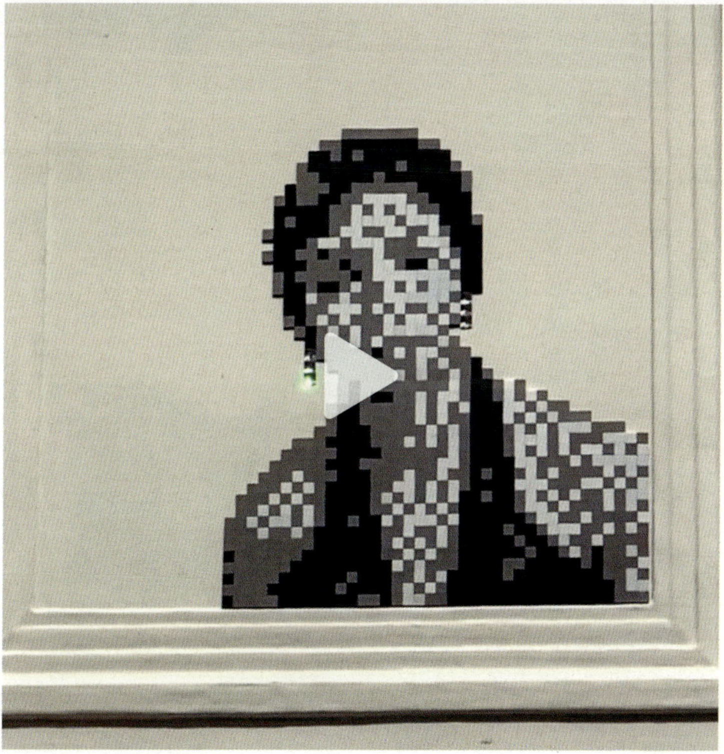

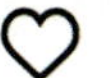

77777 views

invaderwashere Behind this wall there is a small cabaret where Nina Simone had been giving regular concerts during the winter of 1982 #quartierlatin #lestroismailletz #ninasimone #swarovskiearrings

View all 259 comments

11 May 2020

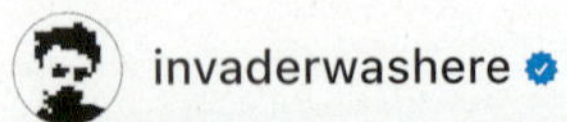

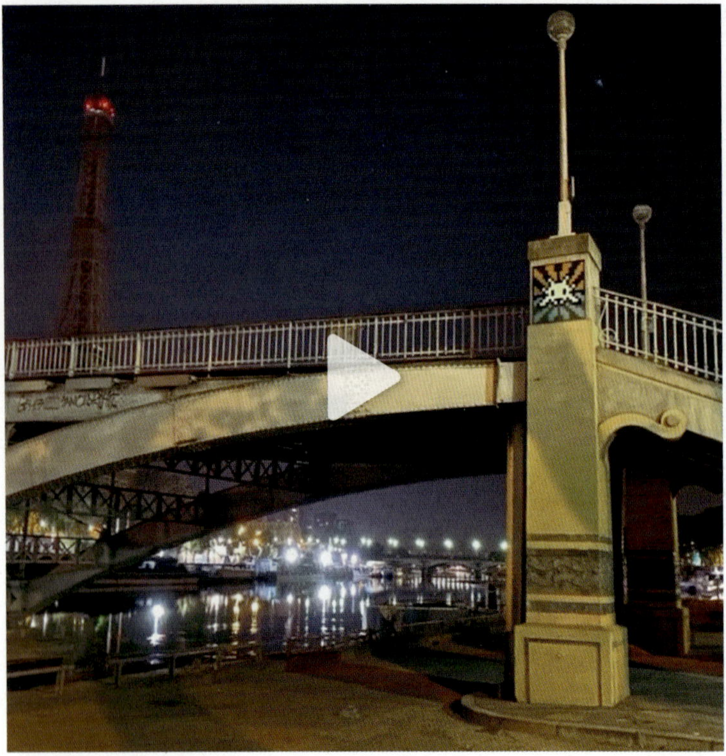

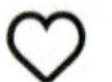   

45 526 views

invaderwashere PA_1442 alone in the night
#paris#lockdown #emptycity

View all 79 comments

13 May 2020

invaderwashere

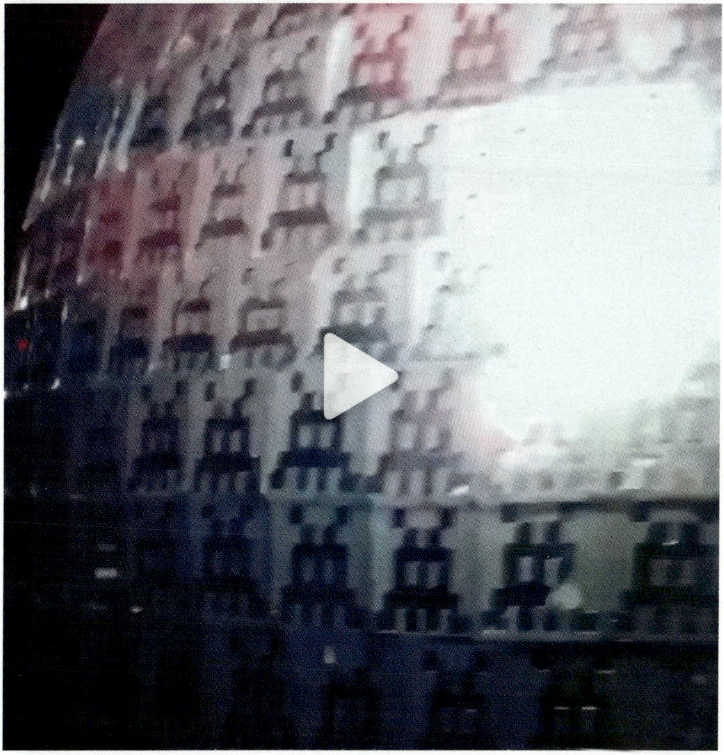

15 670 likes

invaderwashere I made this customized DISCOBALL in 2011 for the exhibition « 1000 ». It took me weeks to build it and I was far from thinking how powerful it would be until I plugged it : TOTAL SPACE INVASION : Thousands of circling space invaders screened on the walls 👾👾👾 #invadeddiscoball #spaceinvasion #1000 #archive #throwback Sound: Andrew Sharpley

View all 274 comments

13 May 2020

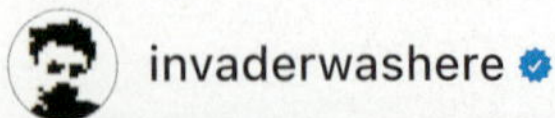

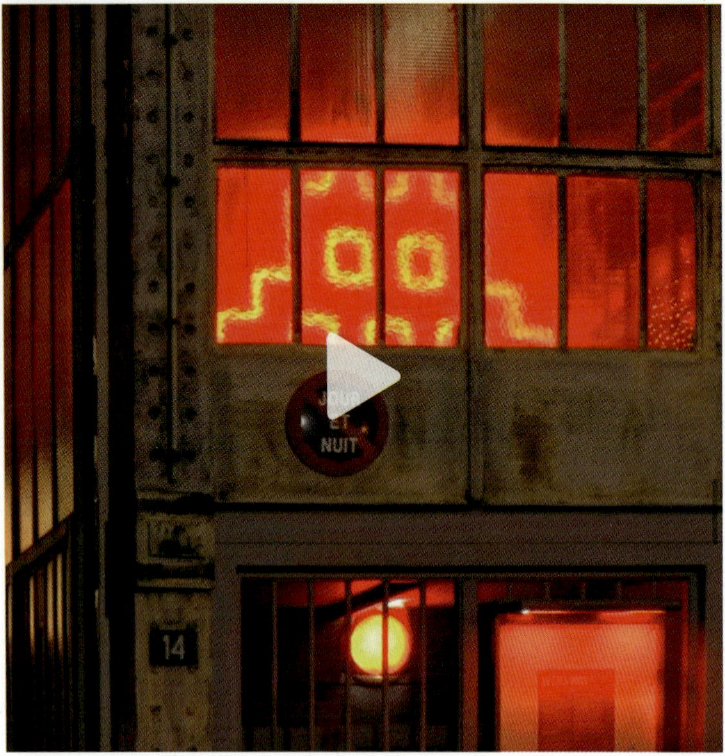

23 082 views

invaderwashere Views of the exhibition « 1000 » / 06 2011 at La Générale Paris / Sound: Andrew Sharpley see Link in bio #throwback #exhibition #1000

View all 47 comments

14 May 2020

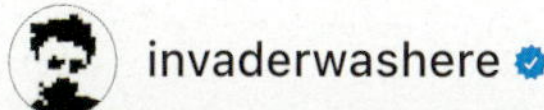

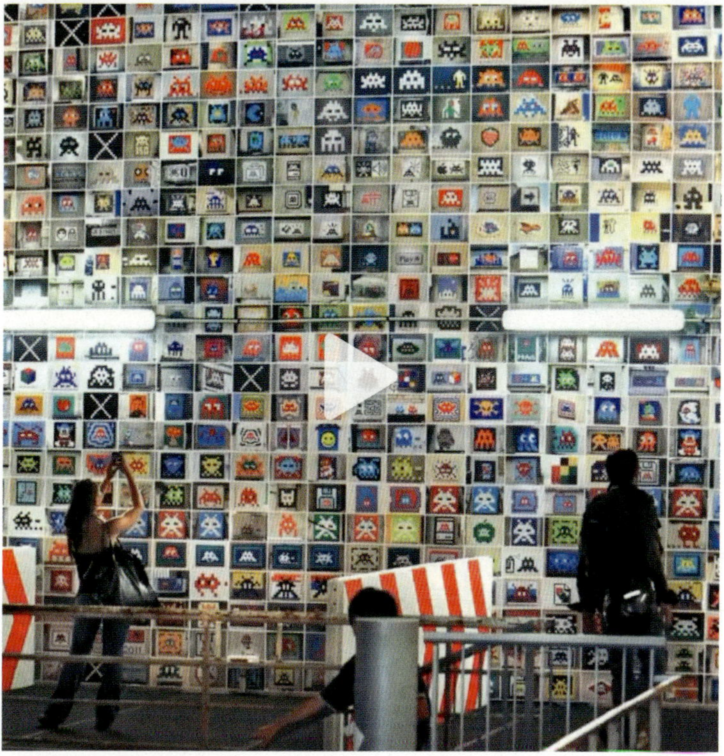

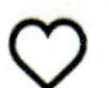  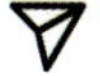 

23 082 views

invaderwashere Views of the exhibition « 1000 » / 06 2011 at La Générale Paris / Sound: Andrew Sharpley see Link in bio #throwback #exhibition #1000

View all 47 comments

14 May 2020

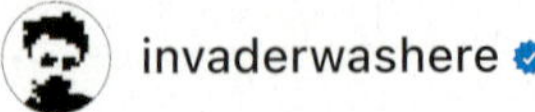

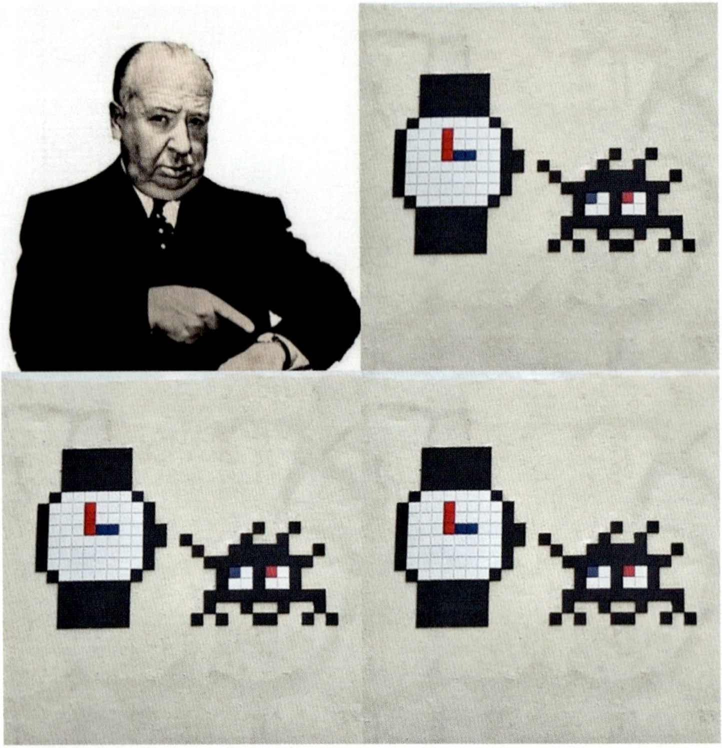

12187 likes

invaderwashere Clock district / Paris #quartierdelhorloge #reactivation #PA1049 posted by @bp78.invaders

View all 44 comments

14 May 2020

invaderwashere

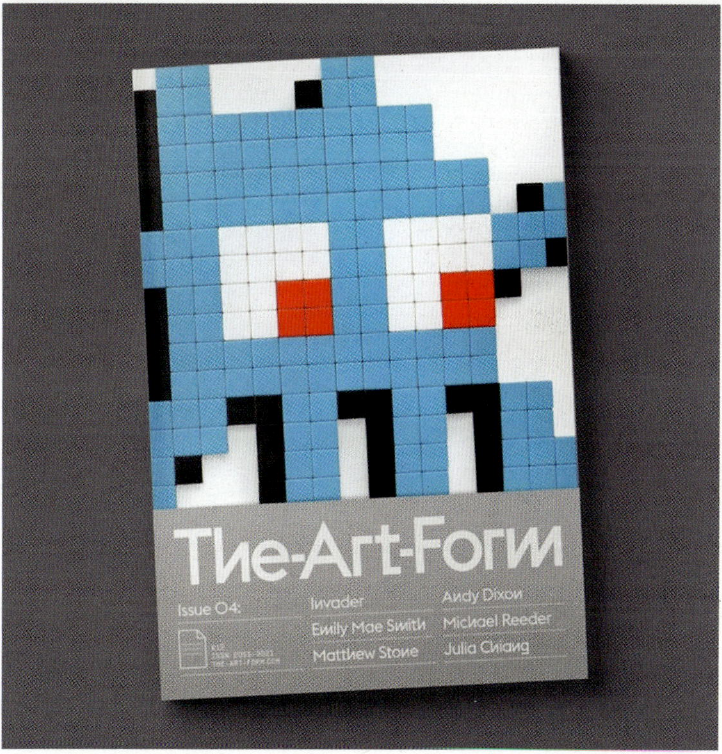

The-Art-Form

Issue 04:

Invader
Emily Mae Smith
Matthew Stone

Andy Dixon
Michael Reeder
Julia Chiang

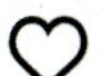    

9799 likes

invaderwashere The new issue of The-Art-Form is now available for pre-order: @the_art_form #mediainvasion #artmag #10points

View all 92 comments

19 May 2020

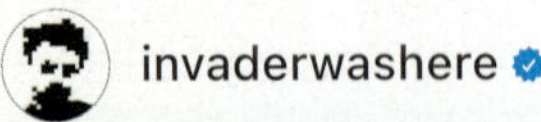

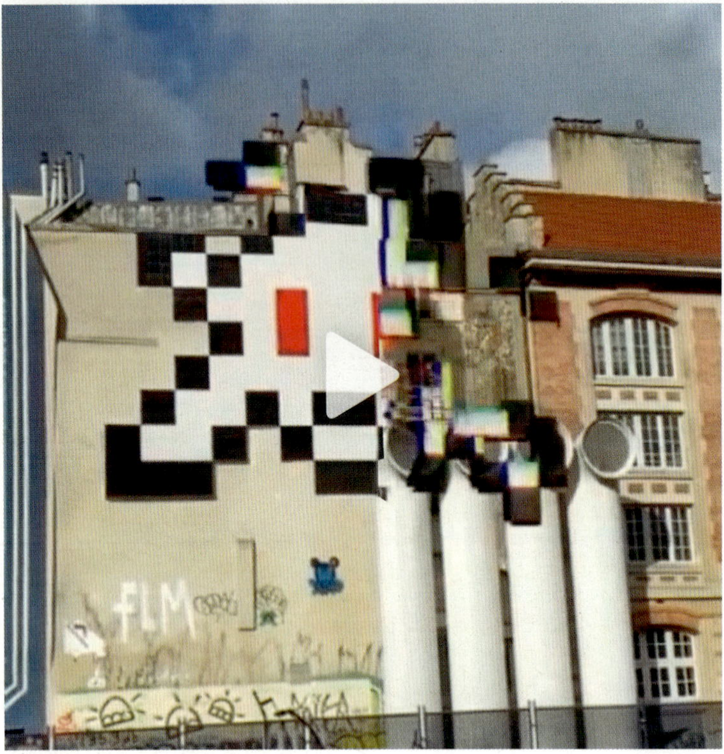

44 485 views

invaderwashere For a better understanding of #PA1432 #missingpart #appearance #sound&vision #placestravinsky #paris

View all 62 comments

30 May 2020

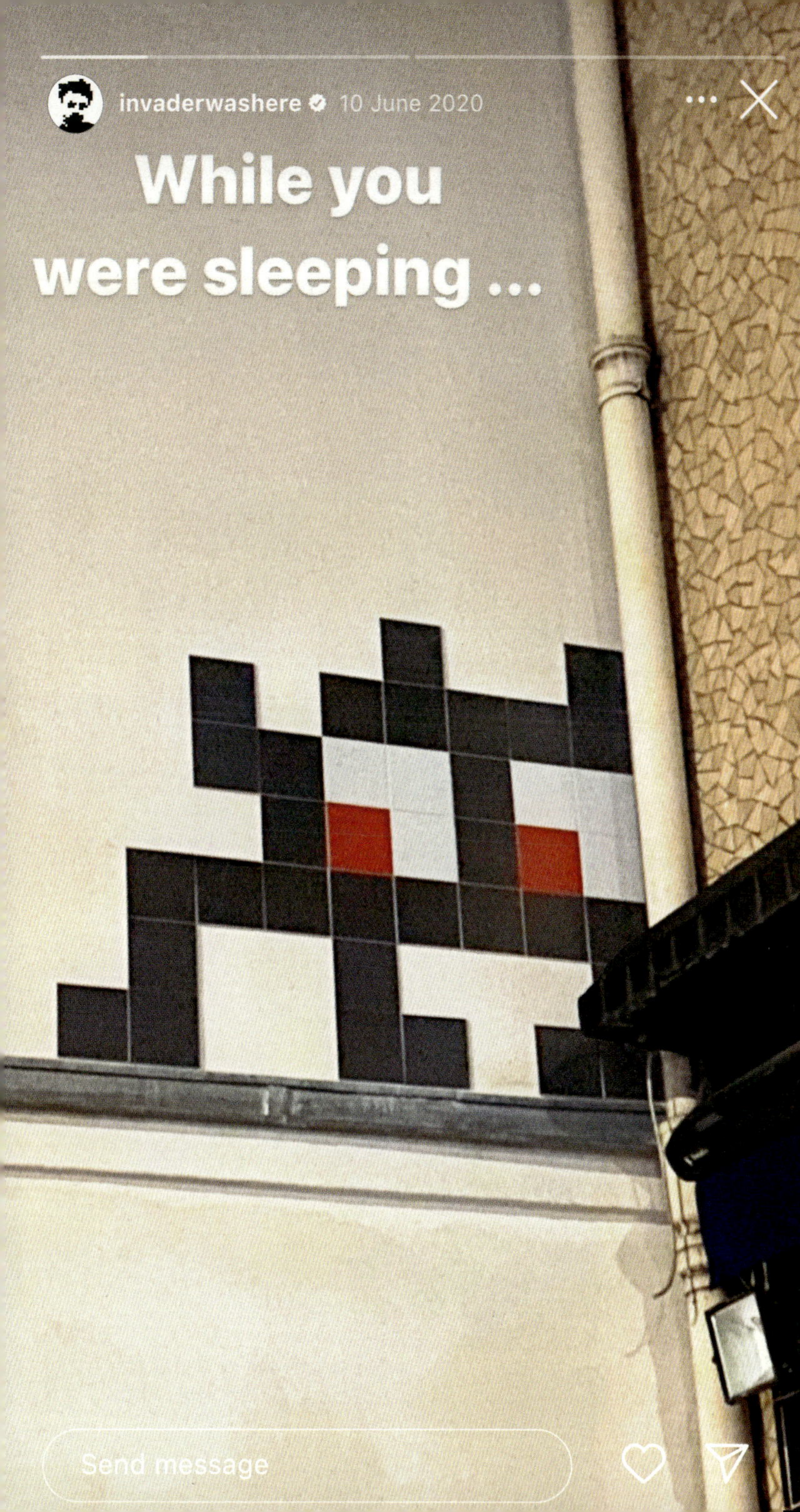
invaderwashere 10 June 2020
While you were sleeping ...
Send message

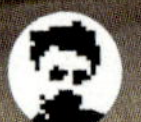

invaderwashere 10 June 2020

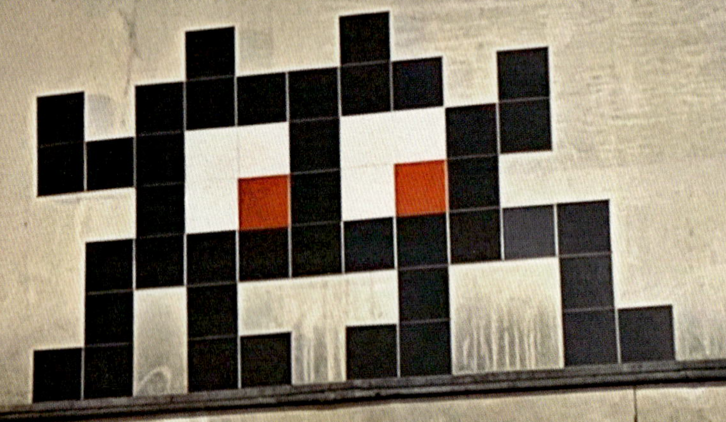

... I was invading!

Send message

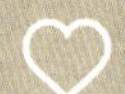

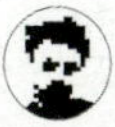

invaderwashere

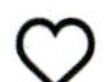    

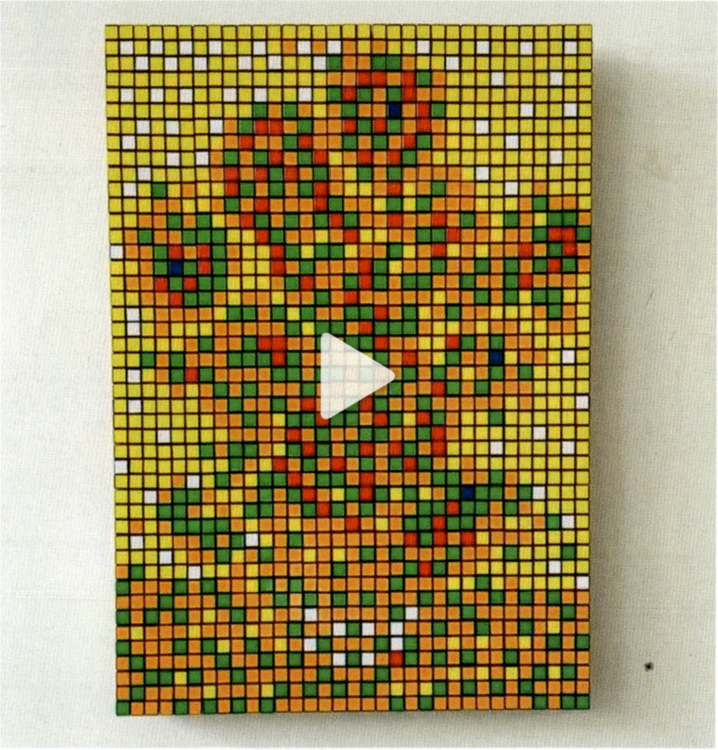

8 548 likes

invaderwashere Did you know that Van Gogh had painted 11 different canvases of sunflowers? Here are 3 of them remade in rubikcubist versions. #rubikcubism #rubikmasterpieces #vangogh #tournesols #sunflowers 🌻

View all 87 comments

16 June 2020

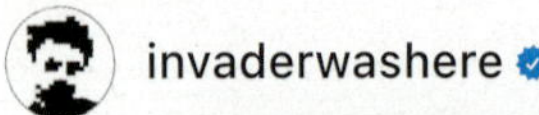

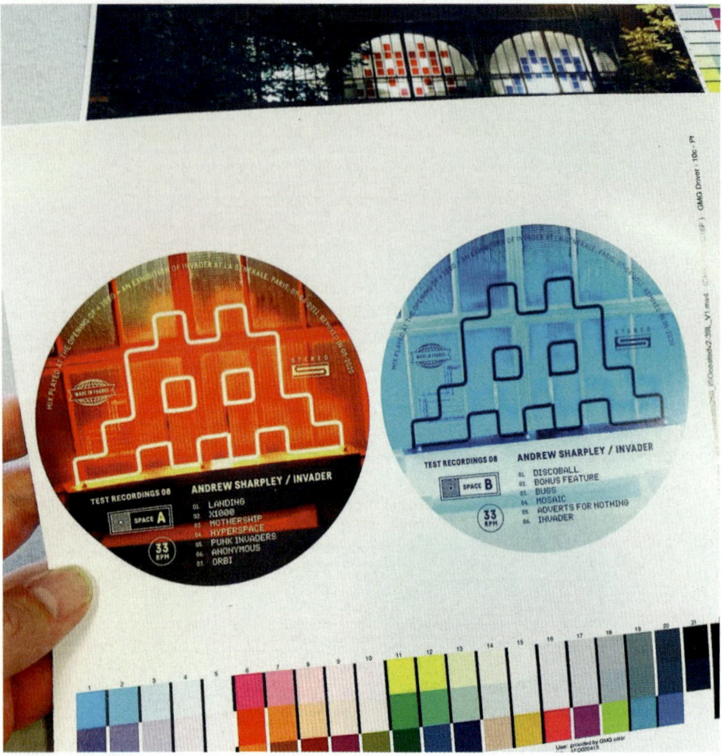

7288 likes

invaderwashere Preparing the labels for the Andrew Sharpley / Invader vinyle #33rpm #andrewsharpley #experimentalmusic #testrecordings Stay tuned...

View all 59 comments

18 June 2020

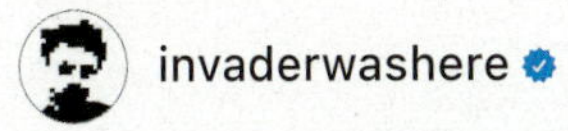

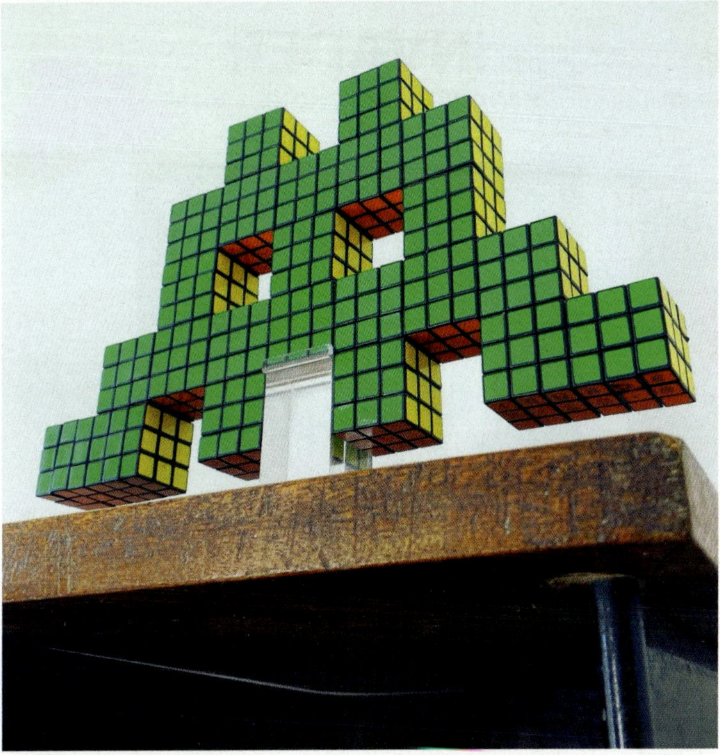

14 511 likes

invaderwashere Green Invader floating above Charlotte Perriand #charlotteperriand #furniture #rubikcubism

View all 94 comments

24 June 2020

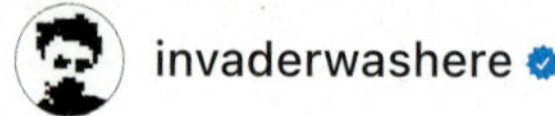

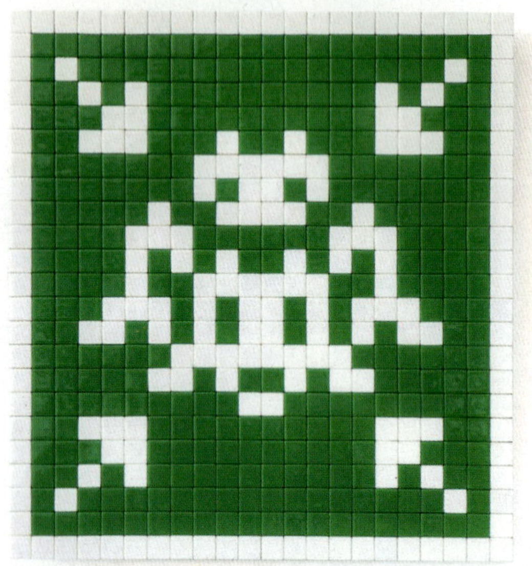

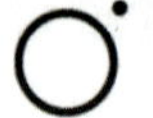

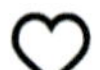   

10 464 likes

invaderwashere If you are in Hong Kong, don't miss my hanging at Over The Influence HK. Opening this Thursday 09 July from 6-8 PM. More info: @oti.official

-

Artwork: 'Alias PA_1393' 2020. Ceramic tiles on perspex. 54.3 x 51.9 cm. 21 3/8 x 20 3/8 in.

View all 134 comments

7 July 2020

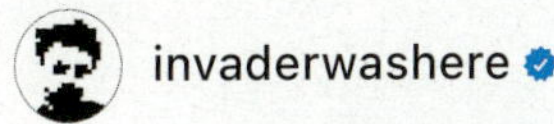

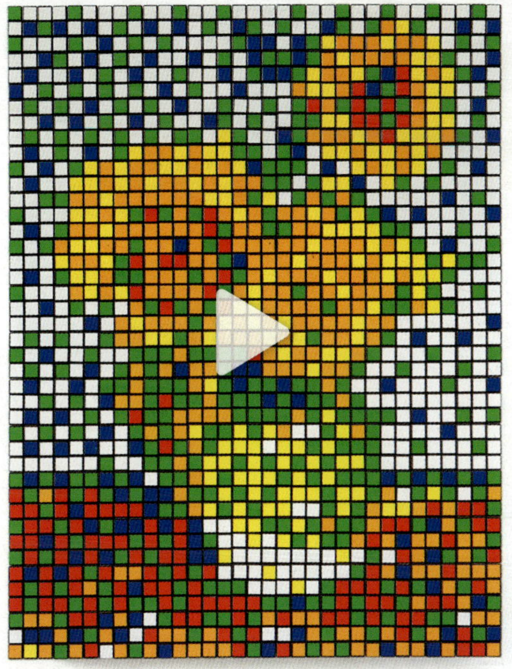

28 870 views

invaderwashere I miss you Hong Kong and I hope that this hanging will bring you a bit of joy and colors in these difficult times.
More info: @oti.official

View all 93 comments

8 July 2020

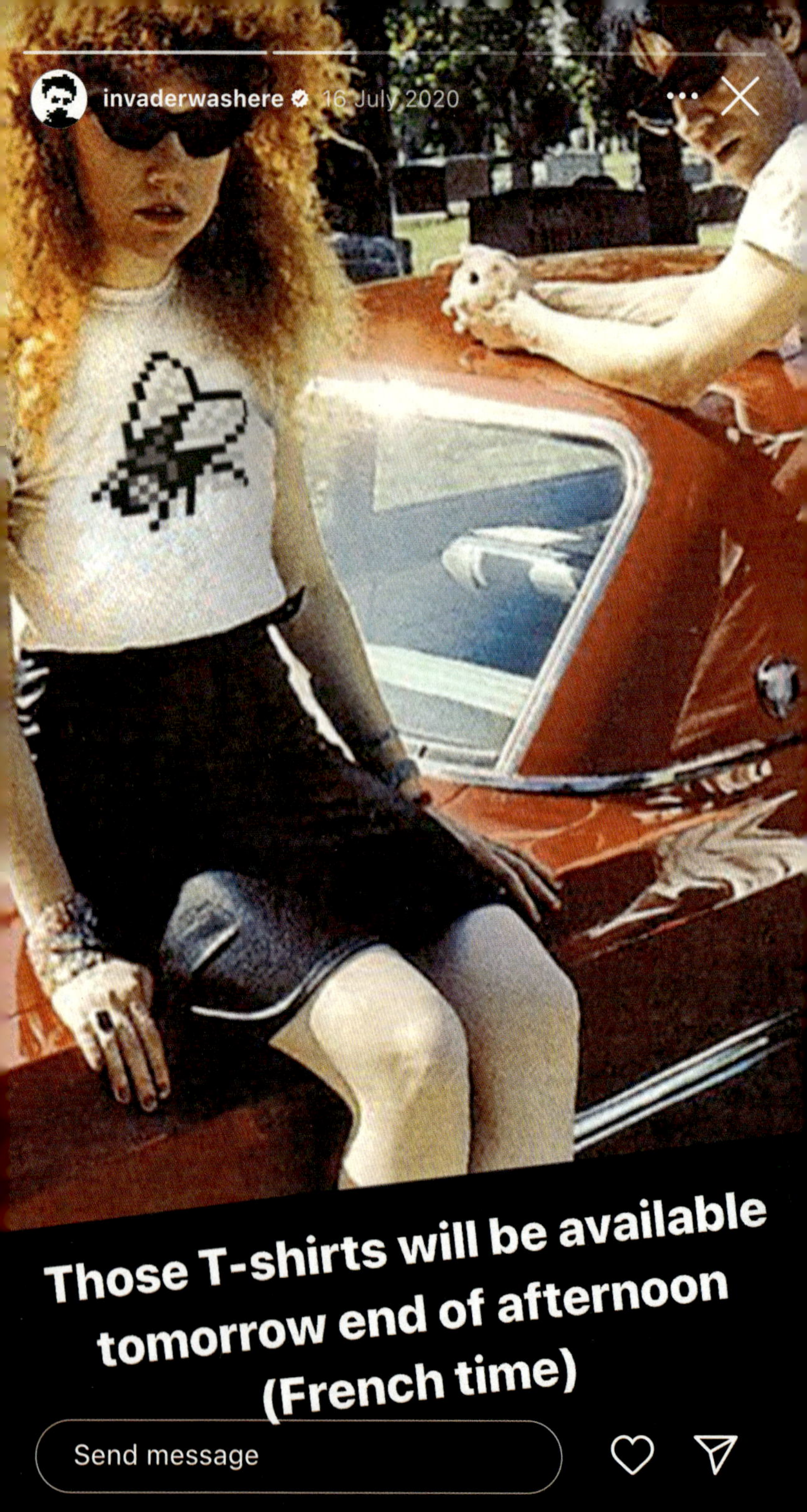

invaderwashere 16 July 2020

Those T-shirts will be available tomorrow end of afternoon (French time)

Send message

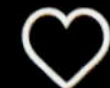

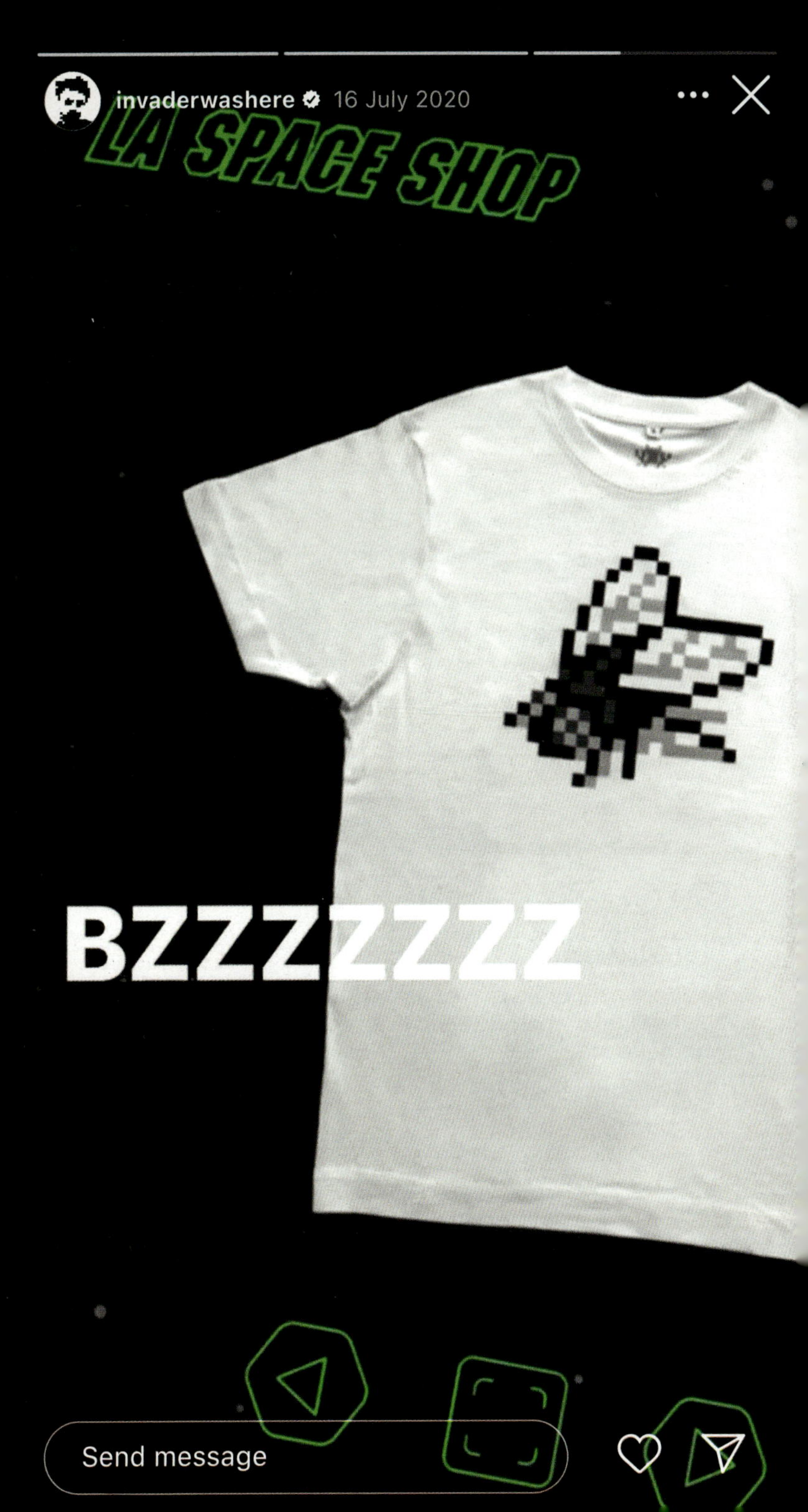

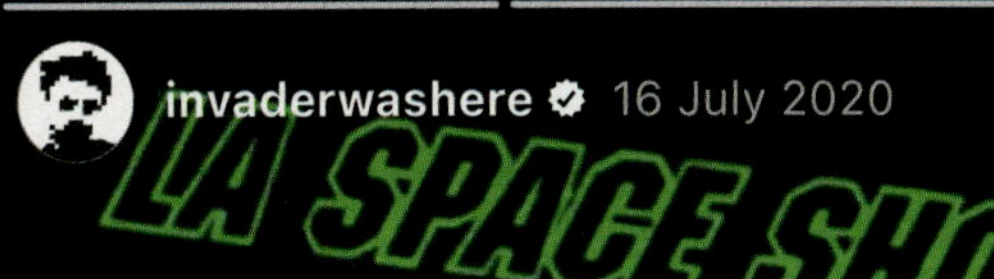

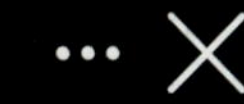

BZZZZZZZ

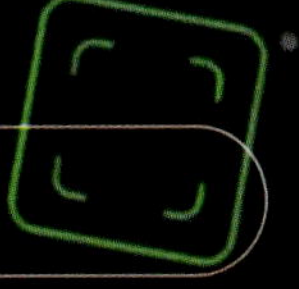

Send message

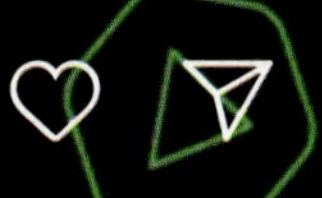

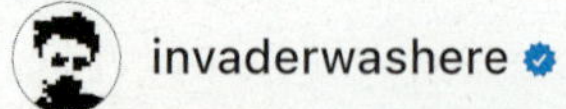

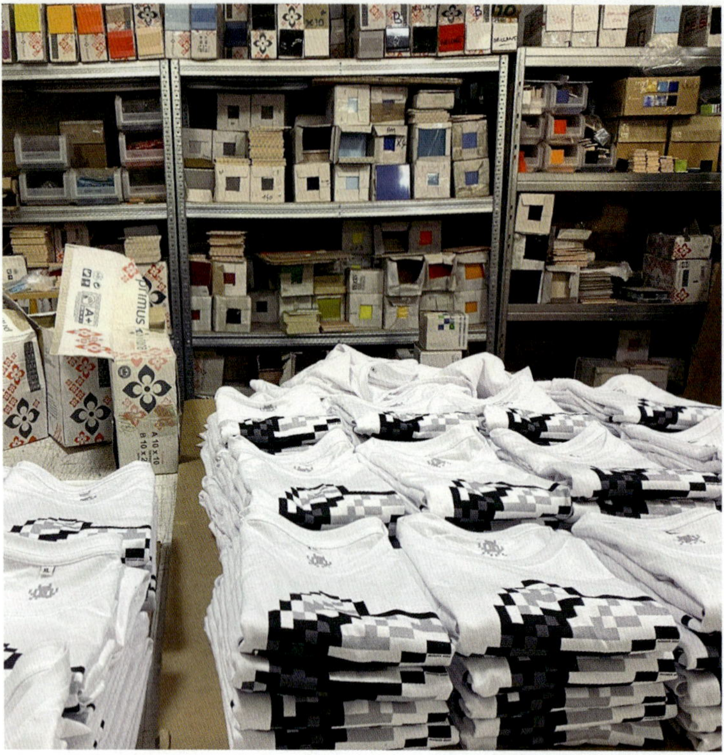

 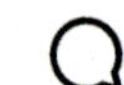   

14 689 likes

invaderwashere Studio is packed! Shipping has started but it will take weeks to send everything... Thank you for your patience ✌️ 👾

View all 244 comments

21 July 2020

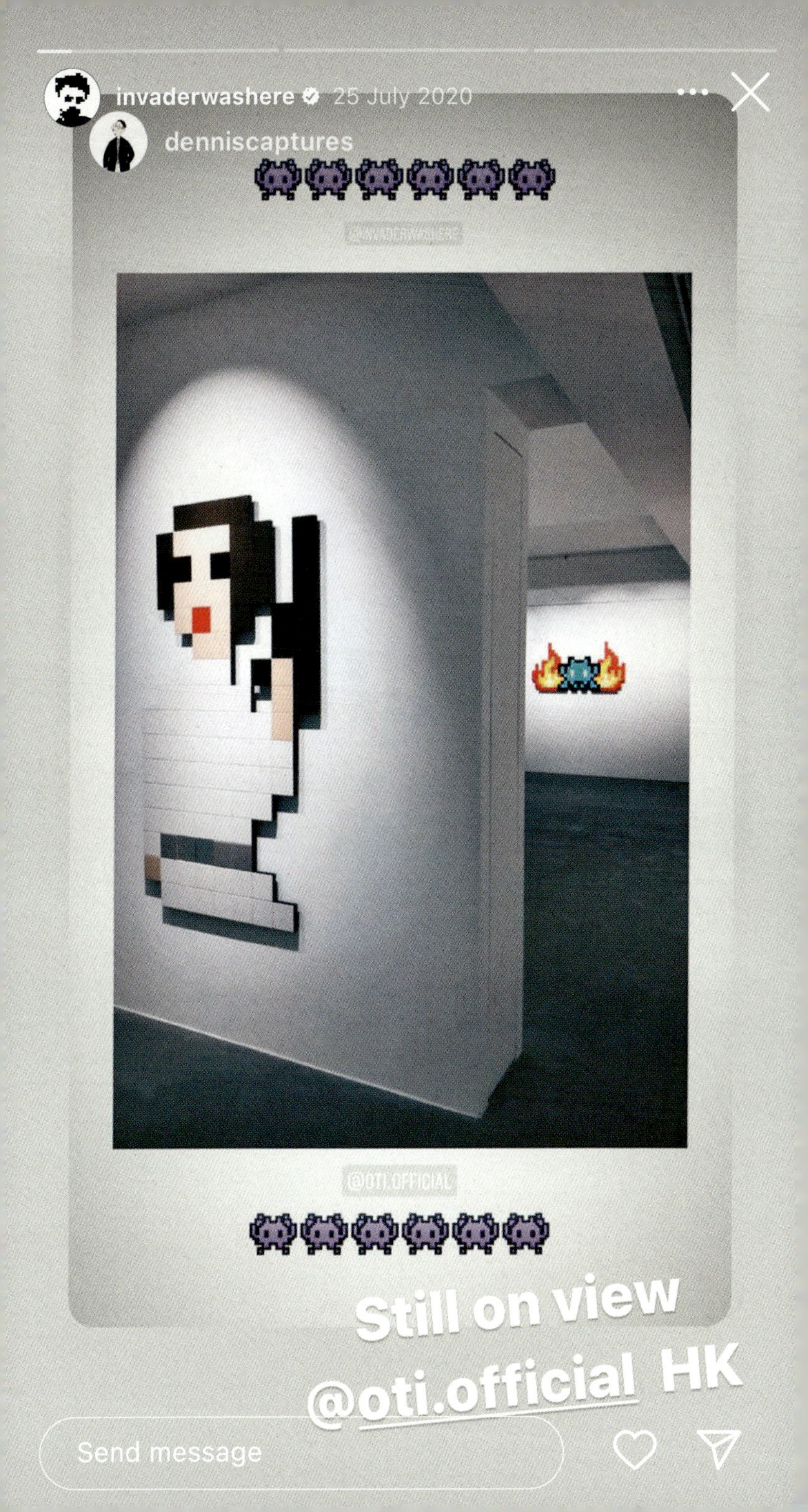

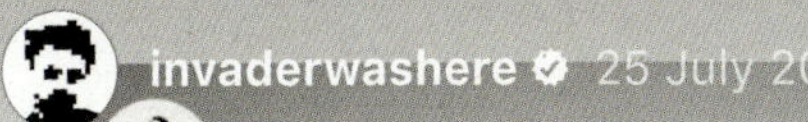

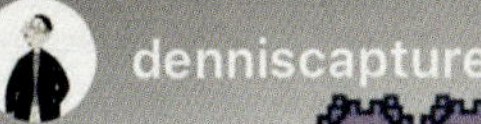

@INVADERWASHERE

@OTI.OFFICIAL

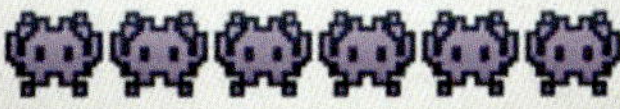

Still on view

@oti.official HK

Send message

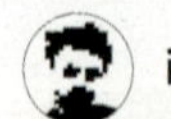

invaderwashere

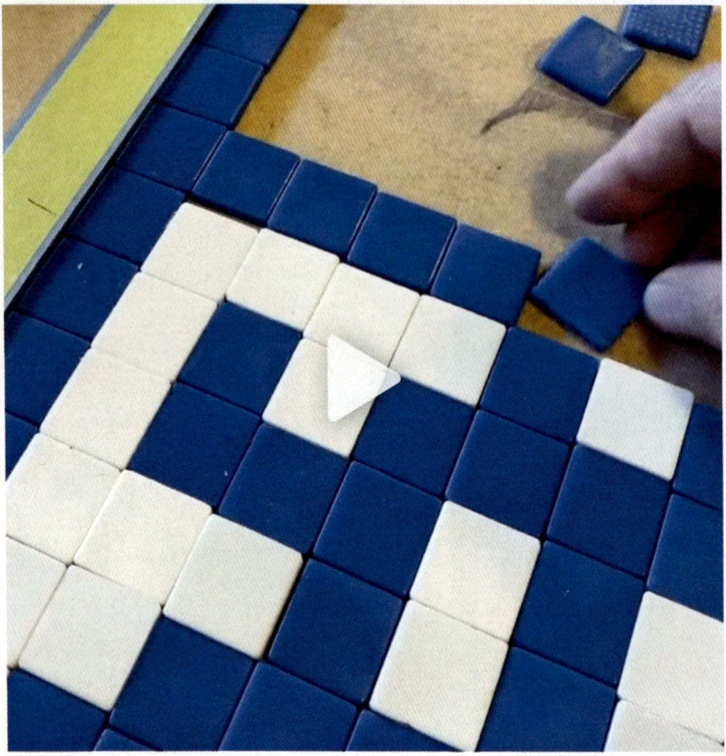

90 585 views

invaderwashere 👾👾👾👾 #oldskool #newskool #grecoromanstyle #meander #frieze #pixelart

View all 149 comments

29 July 2020

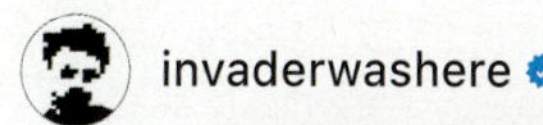

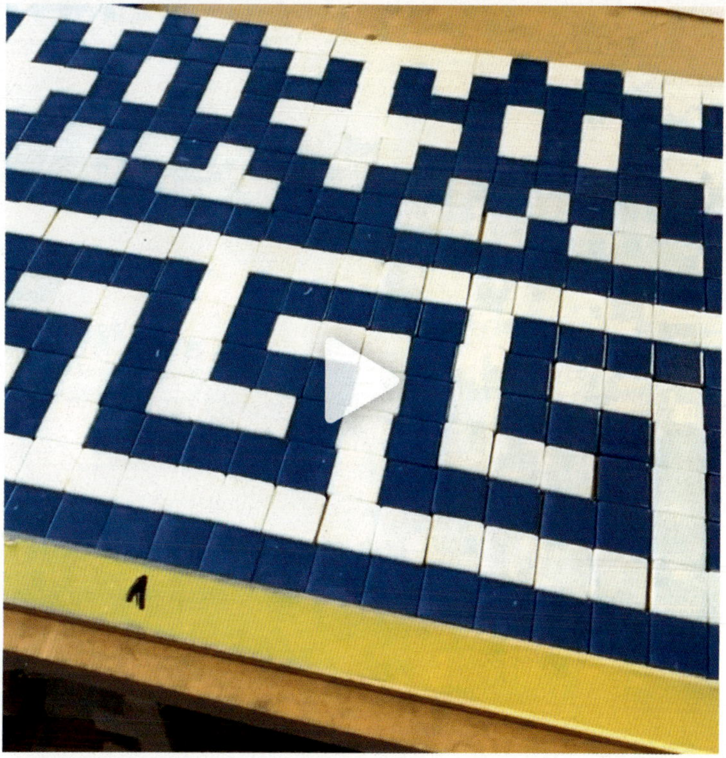

 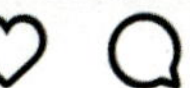  

90 585 views

invaderwashere 👾👾👾👾 #oldskool #newskool #grecoromanstyle #meander #frieze #pixelart

View all 149 comments

29 July 2020

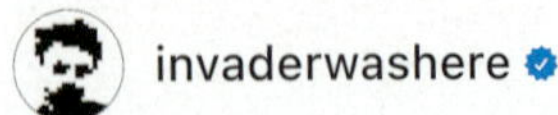

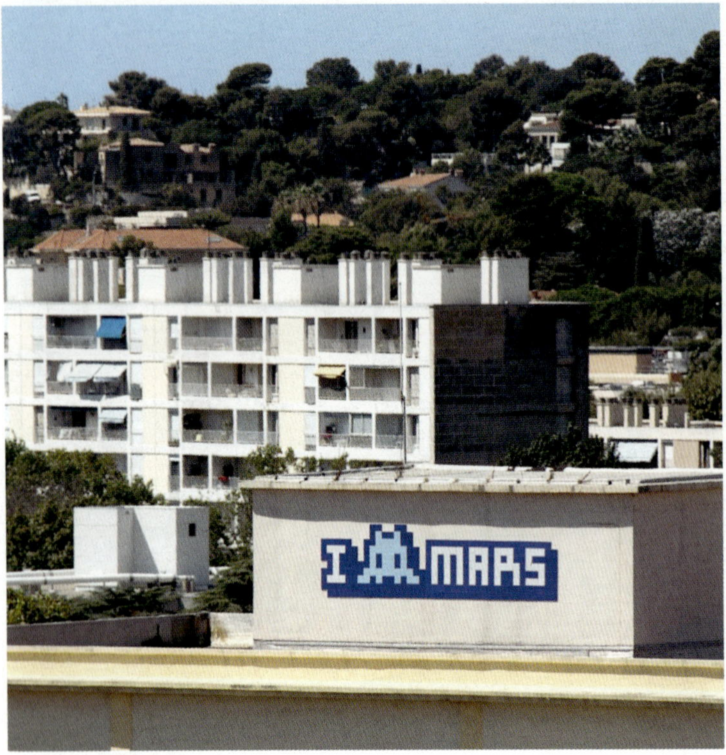

21178 likes

invaderwashere The city of MARSEILLE has just been invaded!!! More soon...

@marseillemodulor @ora_ito #mamo #marseille

\- - -

MARS_90 view from the rooftop of La Cité Radieuse / Marseille

View all 282 comments

21 August 2020

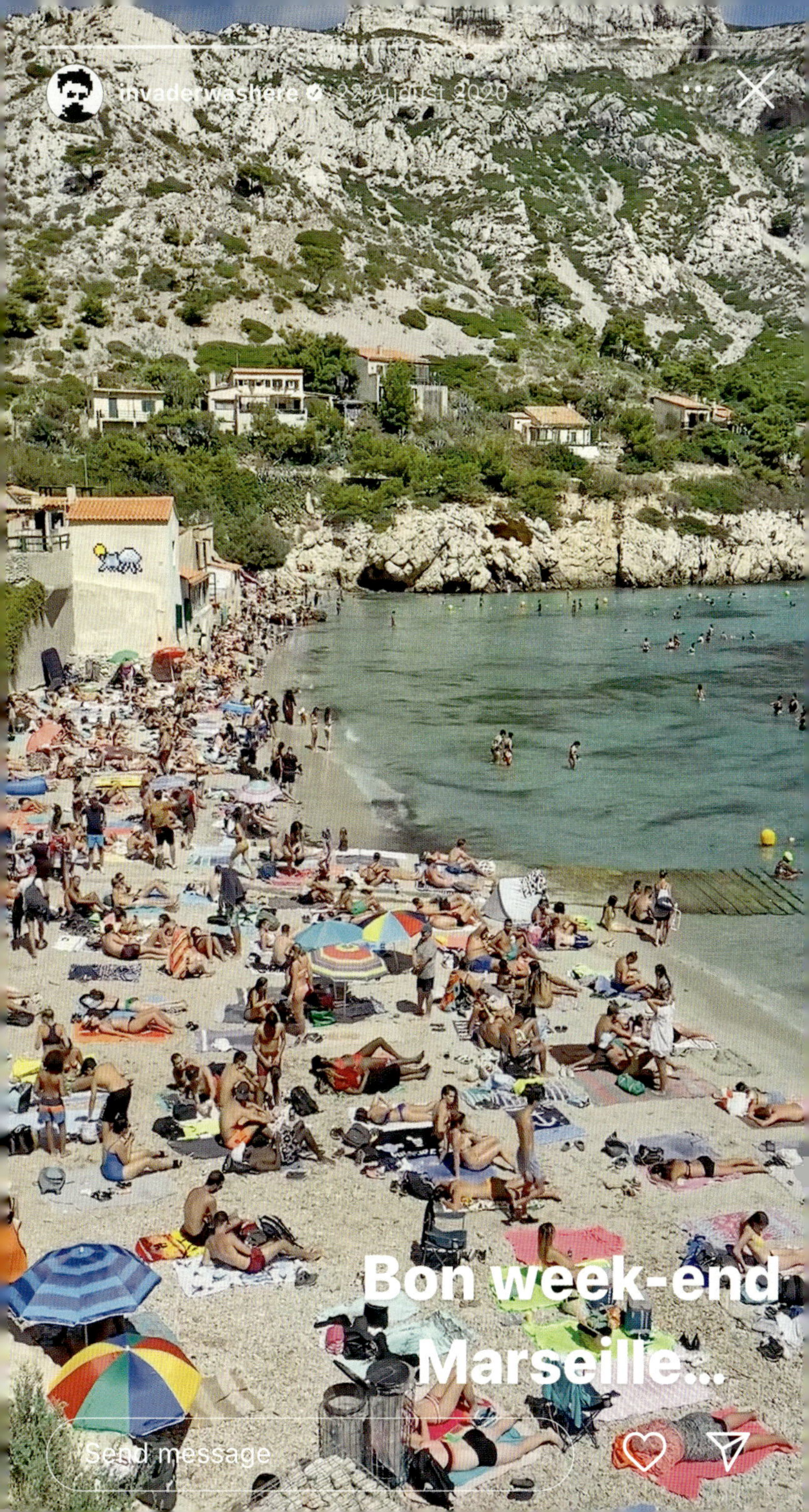
invaderwashere
22 August 2020
Bon week-end
Marseille...
Send message

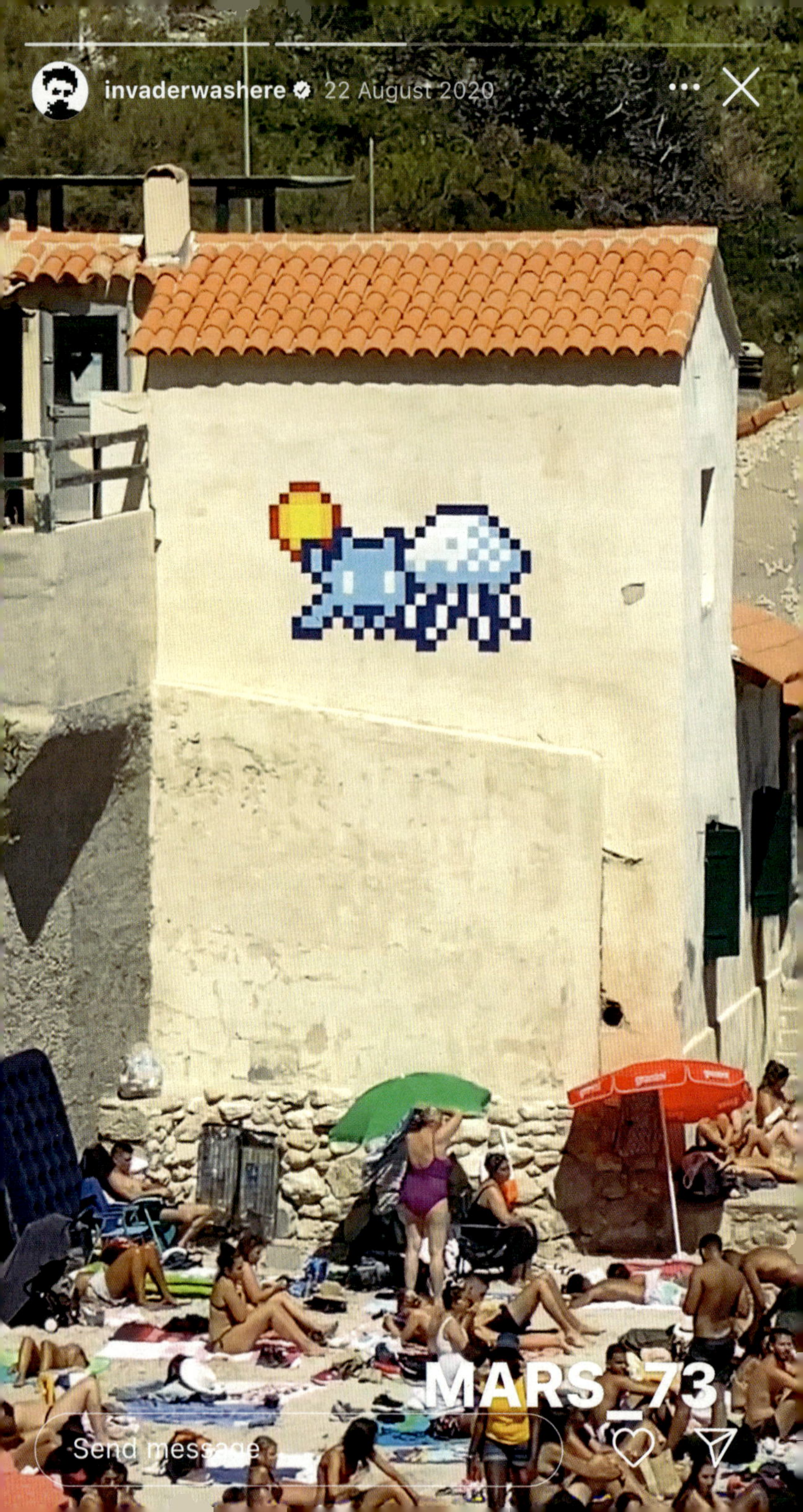
invaderwashere
22 August 2020
MARS_73
Send message

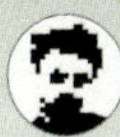

invaderwashere 25 August 2020

ora_ito

LA VICTOIRE EST À TROIS PAS

La Provence

Marseille - Aix - Aubagne

La région de Martigues à nouveau ravagée par le feu

Retour de flamme

MARSEILLE

Écoles : Rubirola fait le ménage

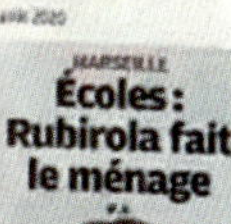

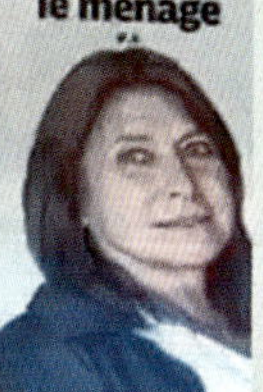

L'ÉDITO

Covid : la vérité des chiffres

Lire notre dossier page II ▸

Invader à la conquête de Mars

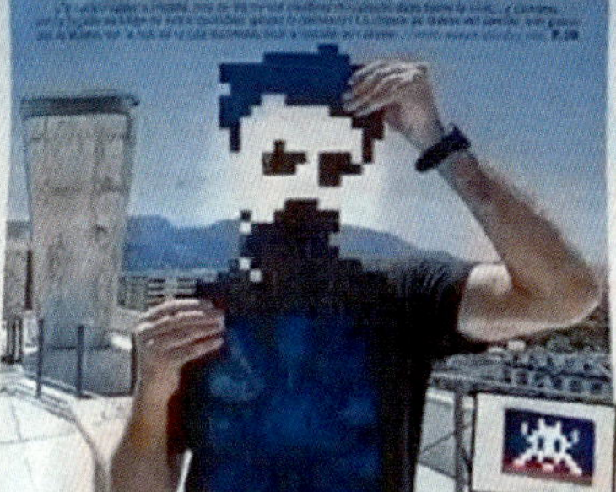

APRÈS PSG-BAYERN

Huit policiers bless[...] cinq interpellations

NOUVEAU PRÉFET

Christophe Mirman[...] pas étranger en Pa[...]

BOULES

Coup d'envoi, à 9h[...] du 103e Provençal

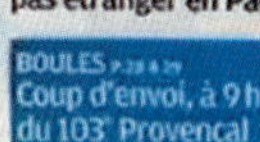

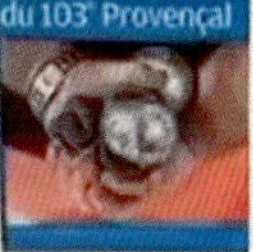

LIBAN

CMA CGM achemin[...] 2500 tonnes d'aid[...]

RACHAT DE L'OM

Boudjellal : "Ça va se faire, je sais qu'on va y arriver"

P.24 & 25

@invaderwashere

Interminables files

@marseillemodulor

@laprovence

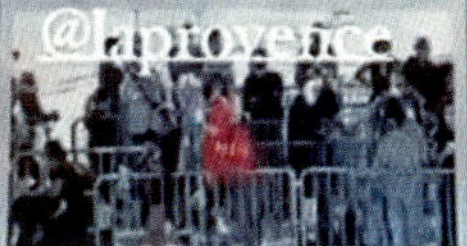

FOIRE DE MARSEILLE 25 SEPT. - 5 OCT.

Loïc Fauchon : "Nous sommes prêts"

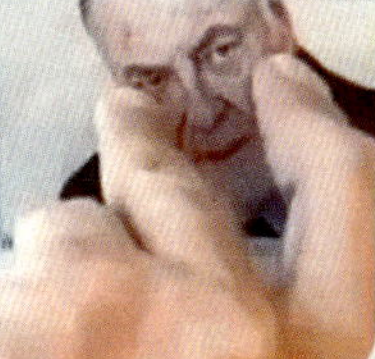

Send message

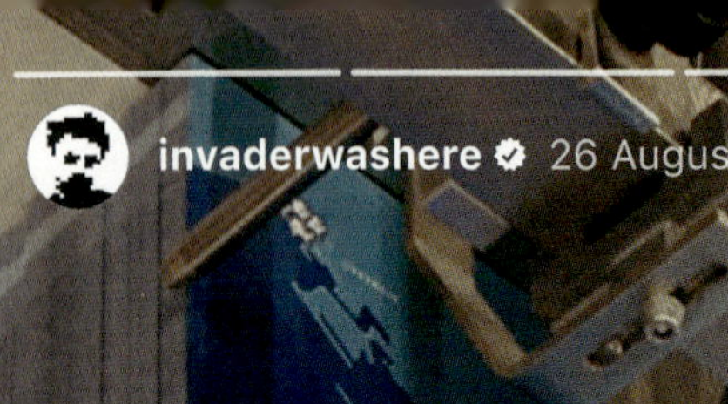

Invasion
Planete Marseille

@marseillemodulor

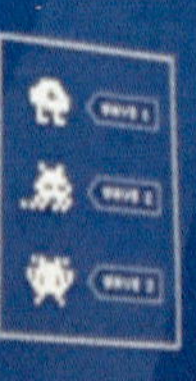

Send message

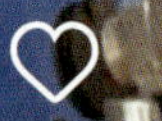

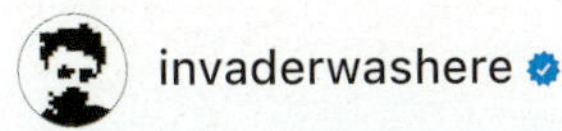

MA
MO

28/08 >
11/11/2020

MARSEILLE
MODULOR

INVADER
WAS HERE

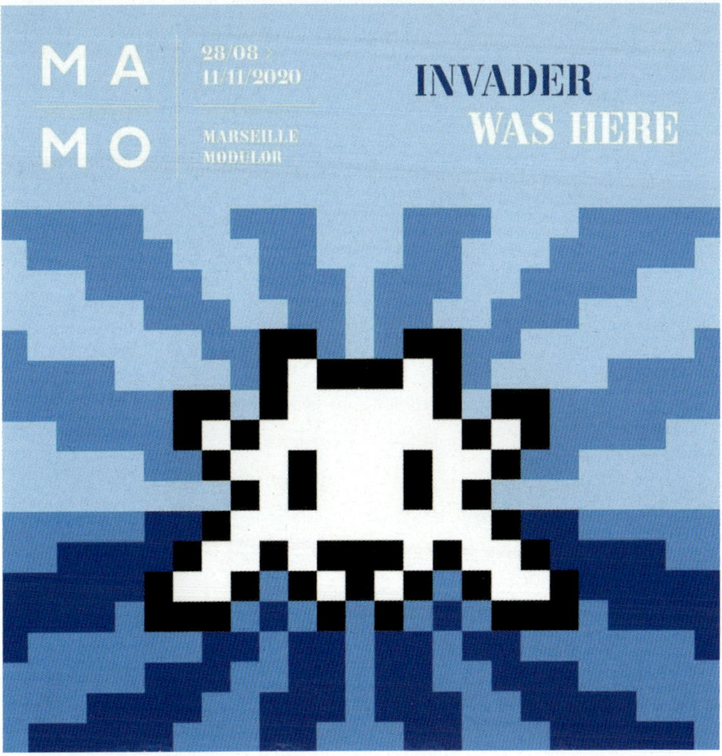

7714 likes

invaderwashere INVADER WAS HERE my new exhibition will open on August 28th at MAMO / Cité Radieuse / Marseille

- - -

August 28 > November 11 2020

Open everyday from 9 am to 6 pm

And 24 hours per day, 7 days a week in the city of MARSEILLE

- - -

@marseillemodulor @ora_ito #lciteradieuse #lecorbusier #marseille #invaderwashere

View all 131 comments

26 August 2020

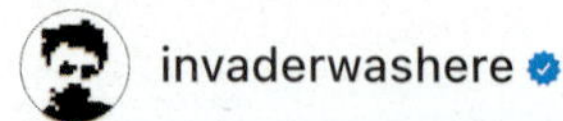

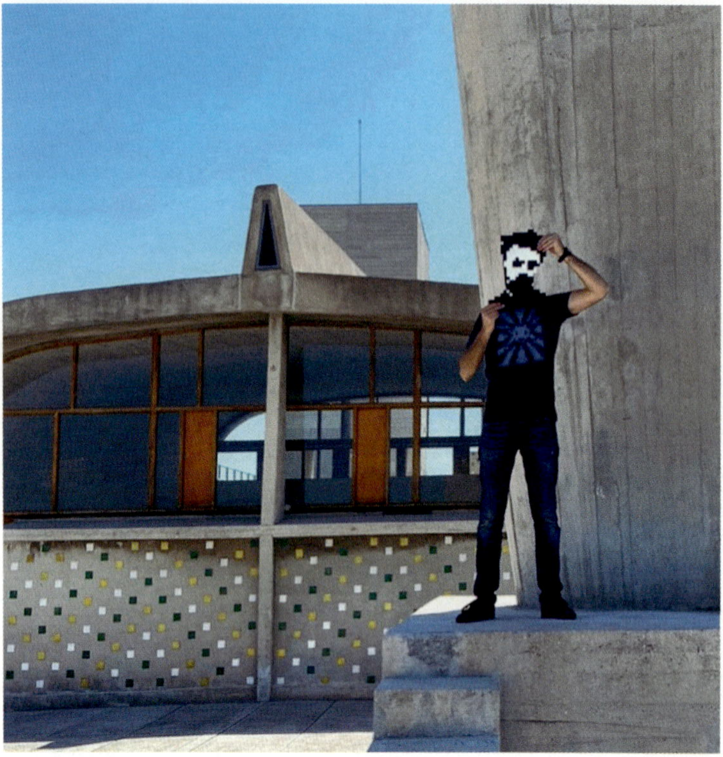

 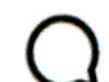  

10 024 likes

invaderwashere “INVADER WAS HERE” will open tomorrow at MAMO

@marseillemodulor @ora_ito #citeredieuse #lecorbusier #marseille #invaderwashere

View all 96 comments

27 August 2020

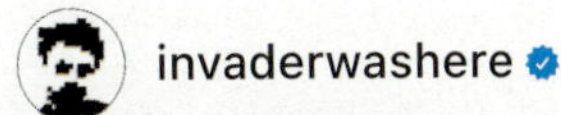

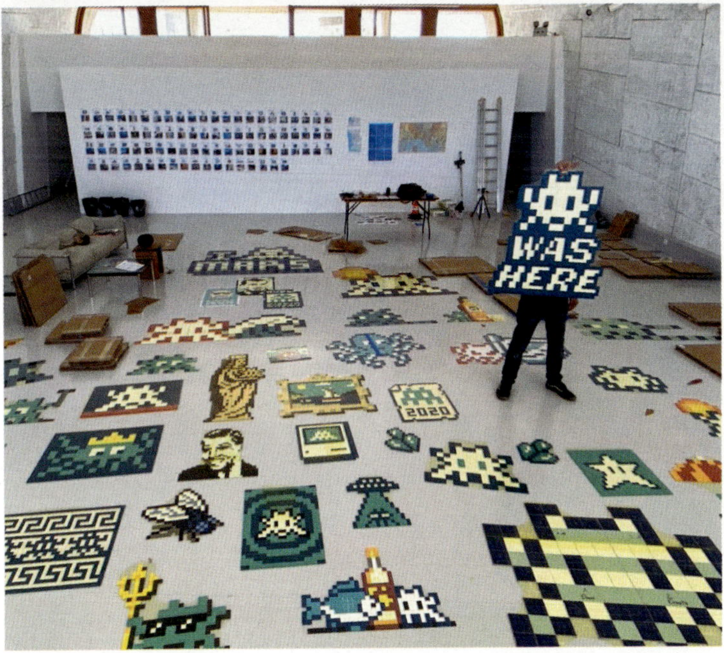

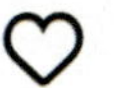   

25 981 likes

invaderwashere I'm proud to be the 8th artist invited at the MAMO art center. I've secretly turned it into an operational base for the invasion of Marseille this summer.
INVADER WAS HERE / Opening today until Nov 11th 2020
Open everyday / Free admittance

@marseillemodulor @ora_ito #citeradieuse #lecorbusier #marseille#invaderwashere

View all 256 comments

28 August 2020

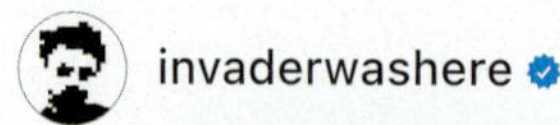

26
08
2020

CARTE RECTO/VERSO

INVASION
PLANETE
MARSEILLE

90
95
93
91
92
94
96
MAMO
CITE RADIEUSE

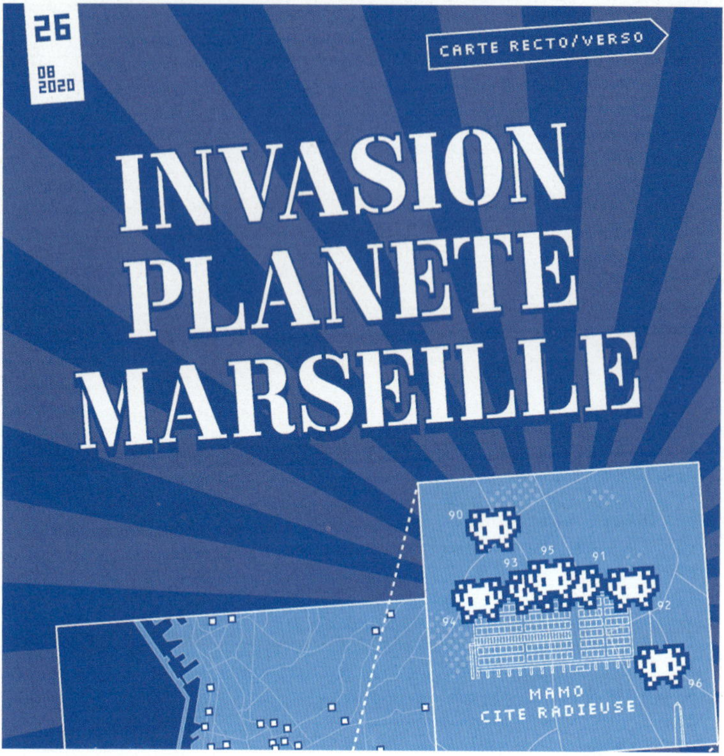

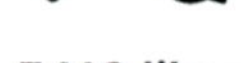

5116 likes

invaderwashere The Invasion Map of Marseille is now available @librairieimbernon (bookstore on the 3rd floor of the Cité Radieuse) and soon on the spaceshop. #invasionmap26 #marseille @marseillemodulor #citeradieuse #invaderwashere

View all 115 comments

29 August 2020

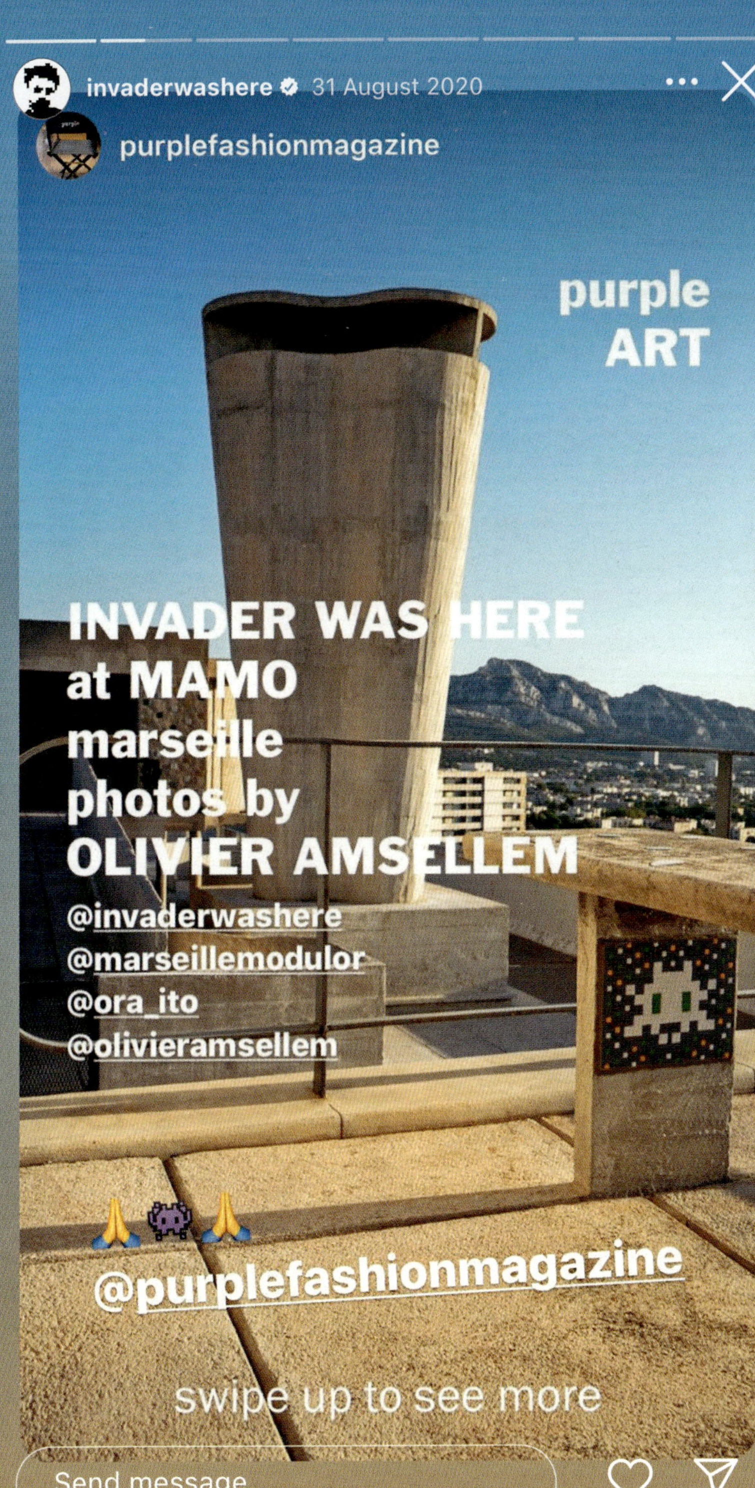
invaderwashere 31 August 2020
purplefashionmagazine
purple
ART
INVADER WAS HERE
at MAMO
marseille
photos by
OLIVIER AMSELLEM
@invaderwashere
@marseillemodulor
@ora_ito
@olivieramsellem
@purplefashionmagazine
swipe up to see more
Send message

invaderwashere 31 August 2020

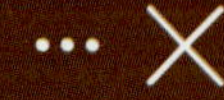

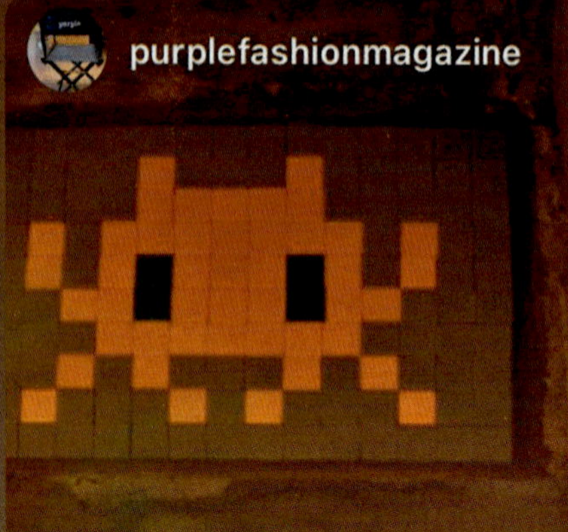

purplefashionmagazine

@invaderwashere
@marseillemodulor
@ora_ito
@olivieramsellem

Send message

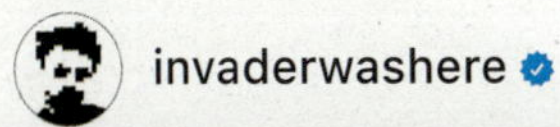

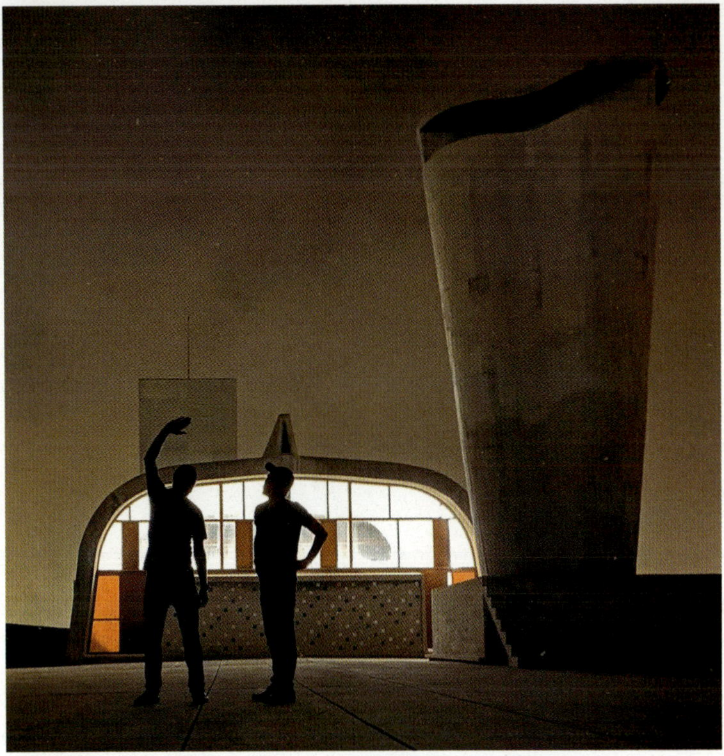

   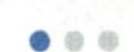 

3 709 likes

invaderwashere With Ora ïto on the roof of la Cité Radieuse in front of the MAMO
@marseillemodulor @ora_ito #citeradieuse #lecorbusier #modulor

View all 23 comments

1 September 2020

invaderwashere 2 September 2020

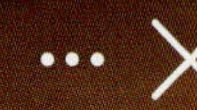

@marseillemodulor

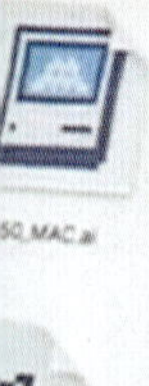

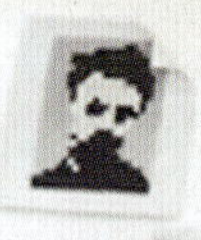

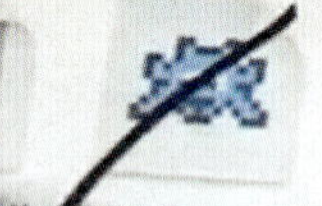

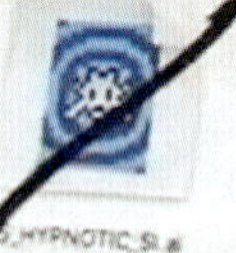

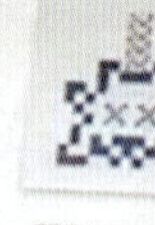

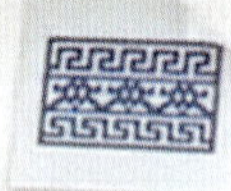

50_MAC.ai

51_PORTRAIT_WIT M ASK.ai

LITTLE_BLUE_PANIE R.ai

HYPNOTIC_SI.ai

57_PENDU_SI.ai

58_FRISE_SI.ai

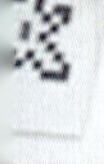

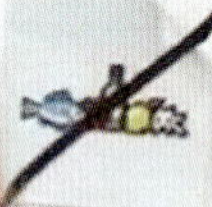

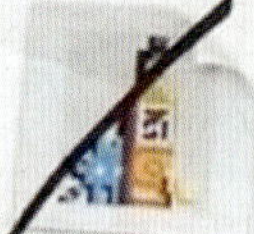

HITE.ai

NATURE_MORTE.ai

66_PASTIS_SI.ai

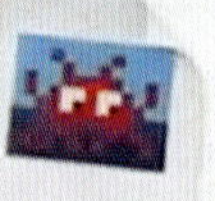

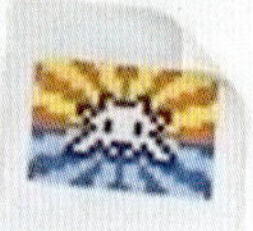

78_RED_SPACE.ai

79_SUNSET_mars.ai

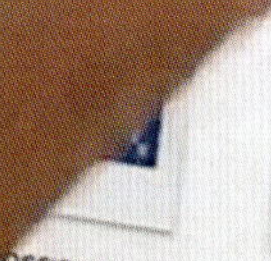

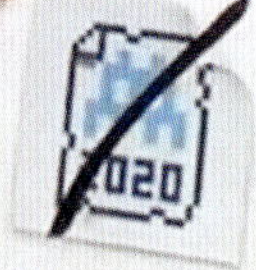

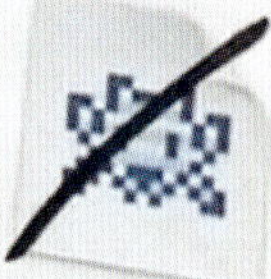

OSEIDON_SI.ai

86_POSTER_2020_SI.ai

88_BIG_BANDES_SI.ai

Send message

invaderwashere

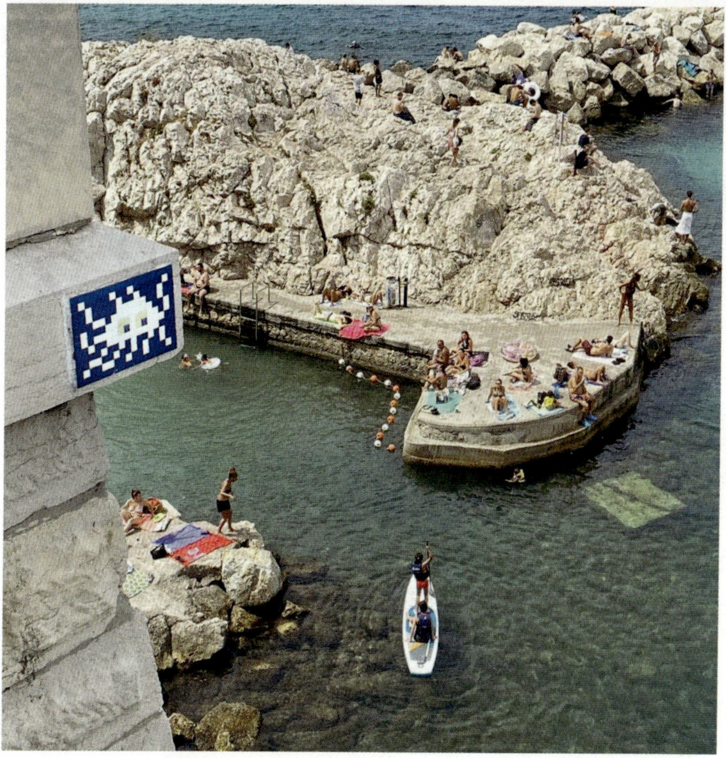

16 245 likes

invaderwashere MARS_60

Invader Was Here
@marseillemodulor #marseille

View all 101 comments

2 September 2020

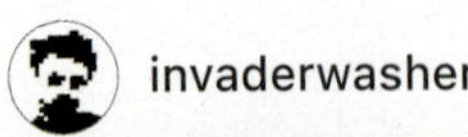

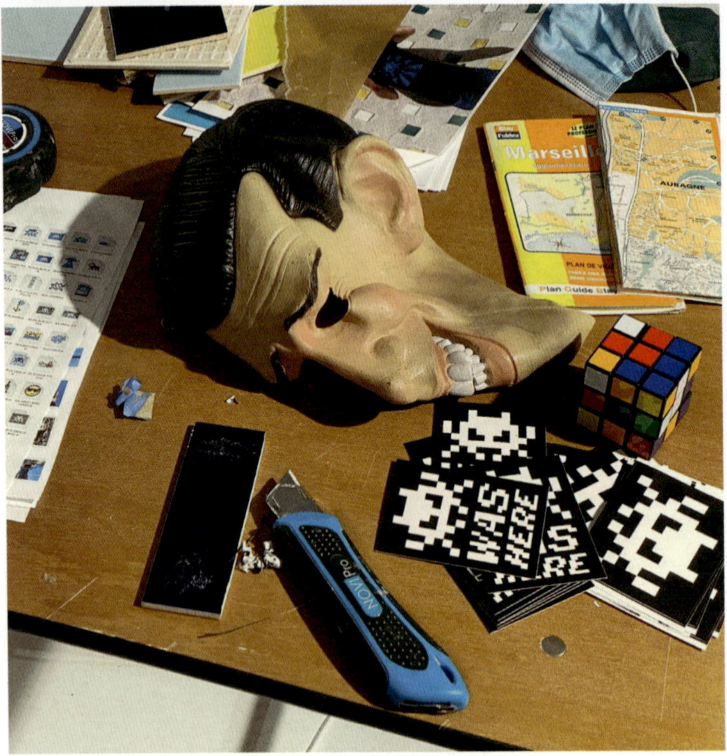

9 758 likes

invaderwashere Details of the installation on view at MAMO
@marseillemodulor #citeradieuse #marseille

View all 80 comments

6 September 2020

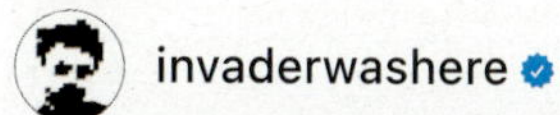

invaderwashere •••

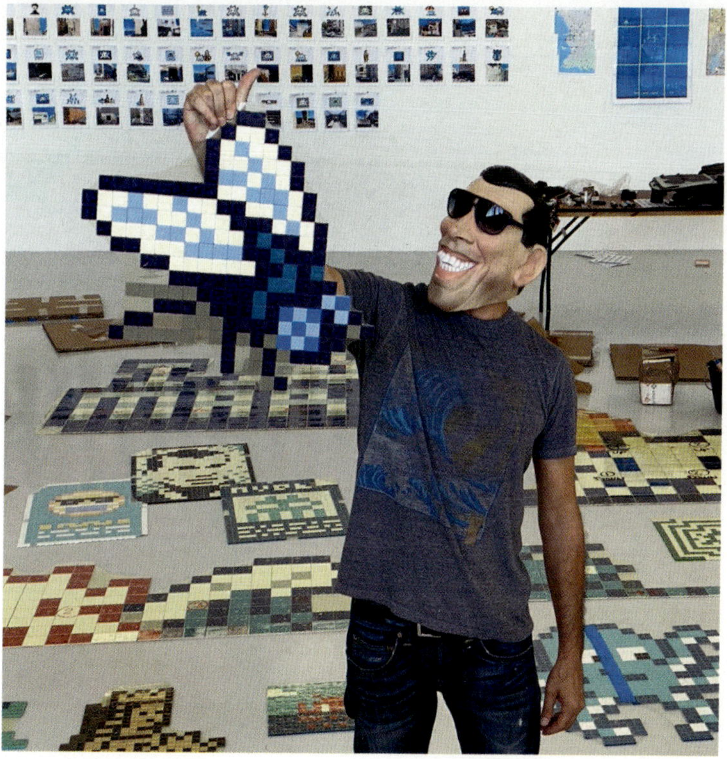

12 687 likes

invaderwashere Hello it's me 😎
#InvaderWasHere
@marseillemodulor #citeradieuse #marseille

View all 105 comments

11 September 2020

invaderwashere

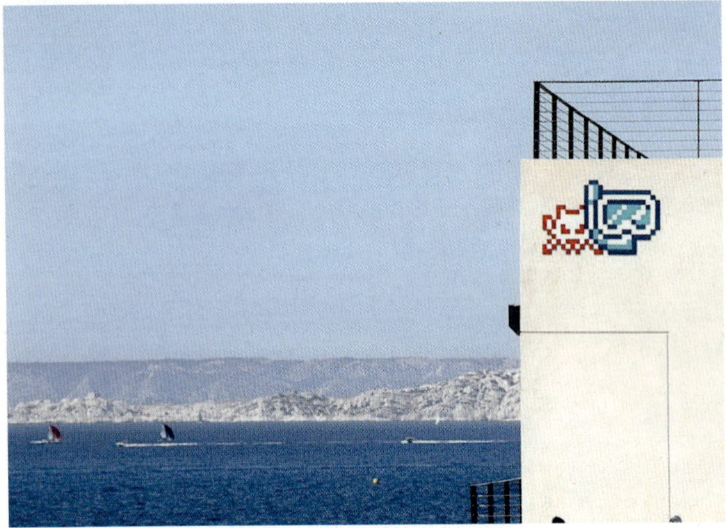

 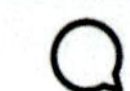   

15 205 likes

invaderwashere #marseille #invaderwashere @marseillemodulor #mars50

View all 91 comments

12 September 2020

invaderwashere 

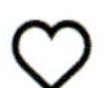   

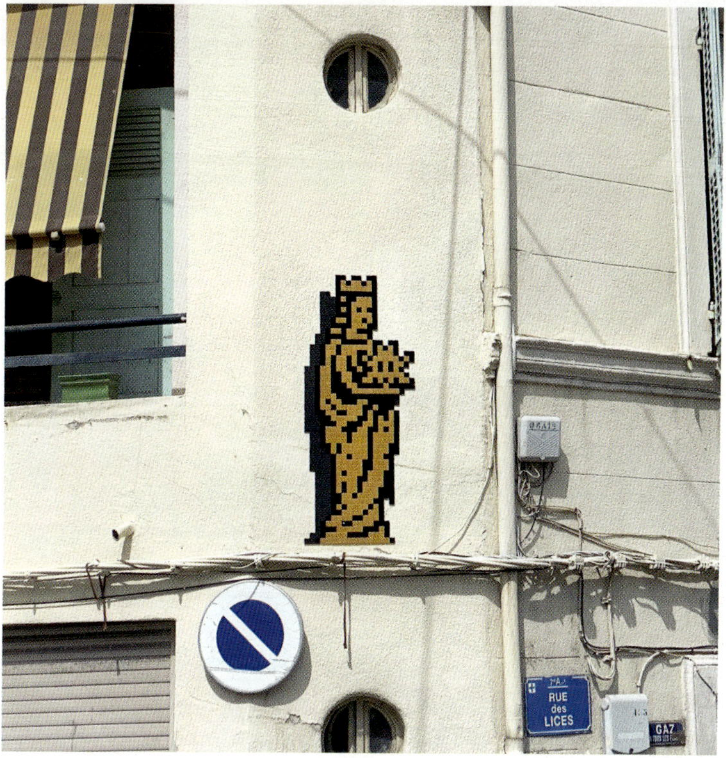

22 898 likes

invaderwashere La Bonne Mère (good mother) is one of the most famous symbol of Marseille. Perched at the top of a hill it overlooks and protects the city and the sailors. MARS_43 is located on the way down from la Bonne Mère.

#marseille #bonnemere #mars43 #invaderwashere @marseillemodulor

View all 172 comments

14 September 2020

invaderwashere 

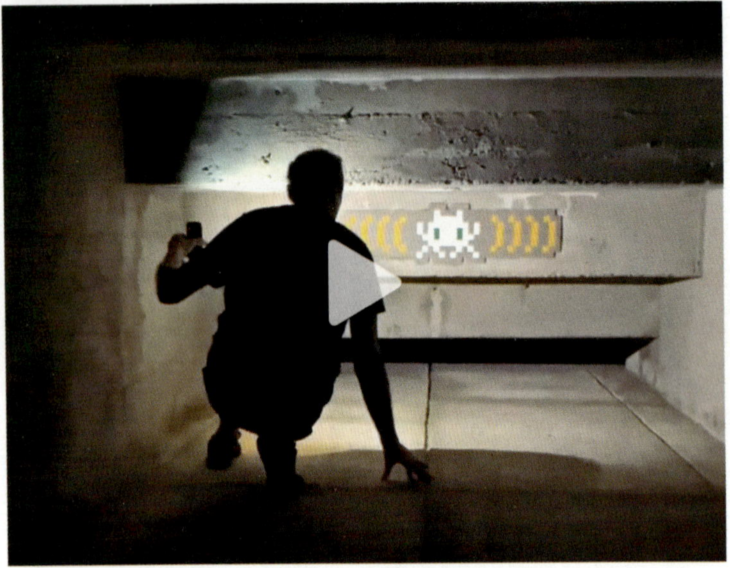

   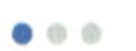 

5408 likes

invaderwashere Having lived several weeks in la Cité Radieuse and worked at Mamo on its rooftop, the opportunity was too good not to leave traces of my passage there. I tried above all to respect the place by installing my work in hidden recesses so that you have to bend down or get on all fours to see them. The point was to make these invasions funnier but also so as not to interfere with the architectural contemplation of the place. This integration is reinforced by the use of the same three colors as the earthenware tiles used by Le Corbusier to trace geometric patterns on some walls of the rooftop.
I would like to thank the Mamo for the invitation and all the inhabitants of la Cité Radieuse whom I have known during the weeks that I spent in this extraordinary place.

#invaderwashere #citeradieuse #marseille @ora_ito @marseillemodulor

View all 56 comments

16 September 2020

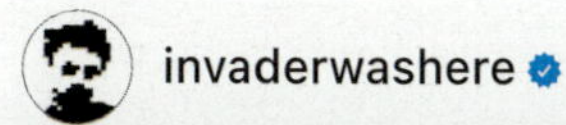

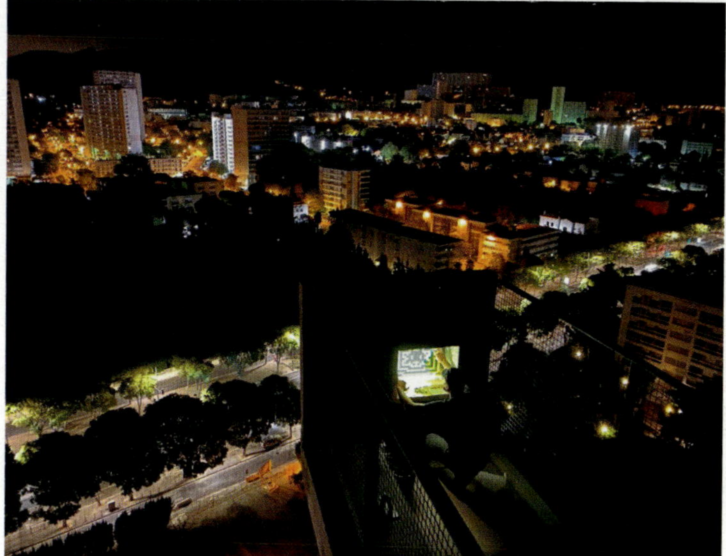

5729 likes

invaderwashere Having lived several weeks in la Cité Radieuse and worked at Mamo on its rooftop, the opportunity was too good not to leave traces of my passage there. I tried above all to respect the place by installing my work in hidden recesses so that you have to bend down or get on all fours to see them. The point was to make these invasions funnier but also so as not to interfere with the architectural contemplation of the place. This integration is reinforced by the use of the same three colors as the earthenware tiles used by Le Corbusier to trace geometric patterns on some walls of the rooftop.

I would like to thank the Mamo for the invitation and all the inhabitants of la Cité Radieuse whom I have known during the weeks that I spent in this extraordinary place.

#invaderwashere #citeradieuse #marseille @ora_ito @marseillemodulor

View all 43 comments

17 September 2020

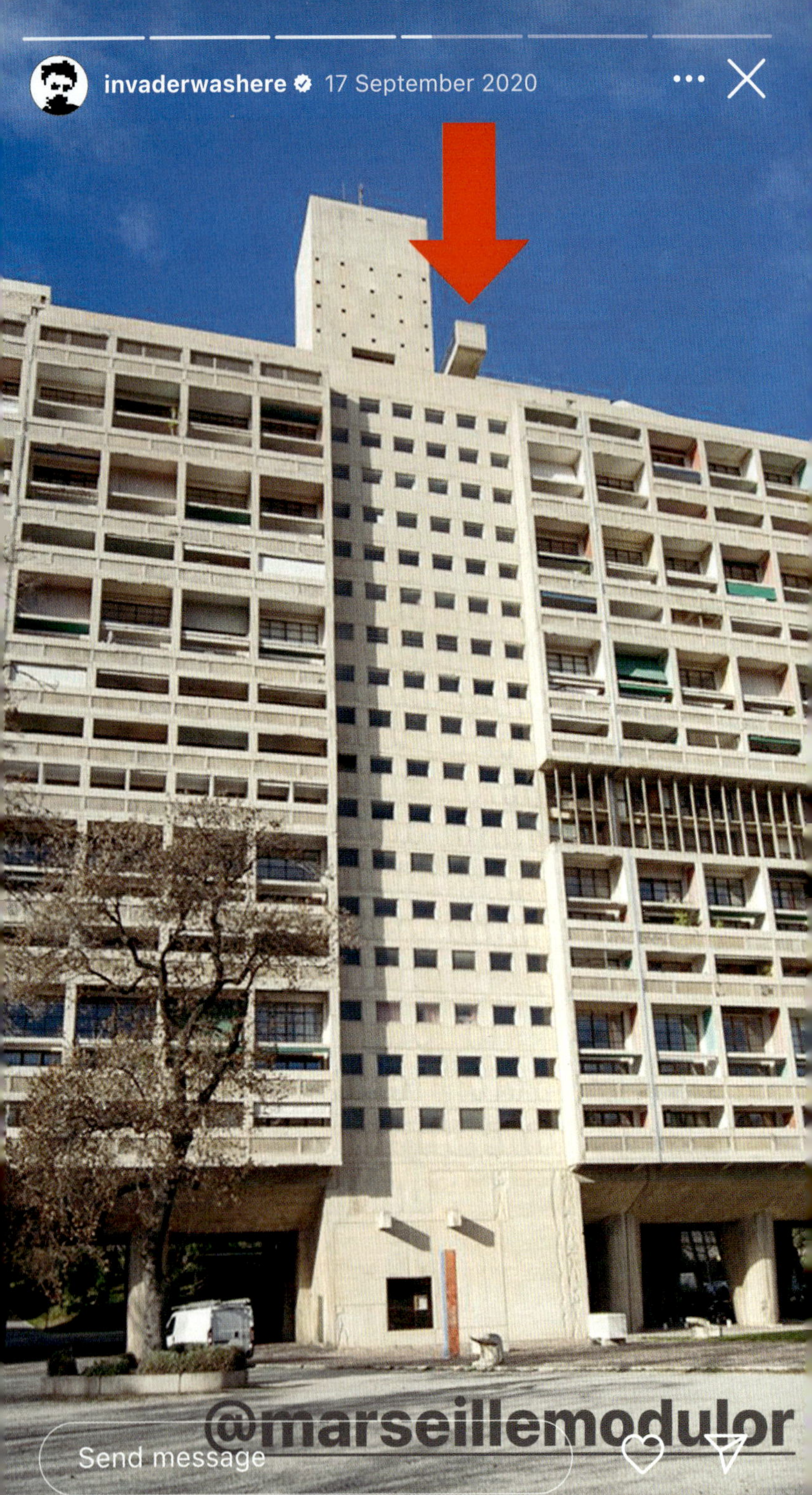
invaderwashere
17 September 2020
@marseillemodulor
Send message

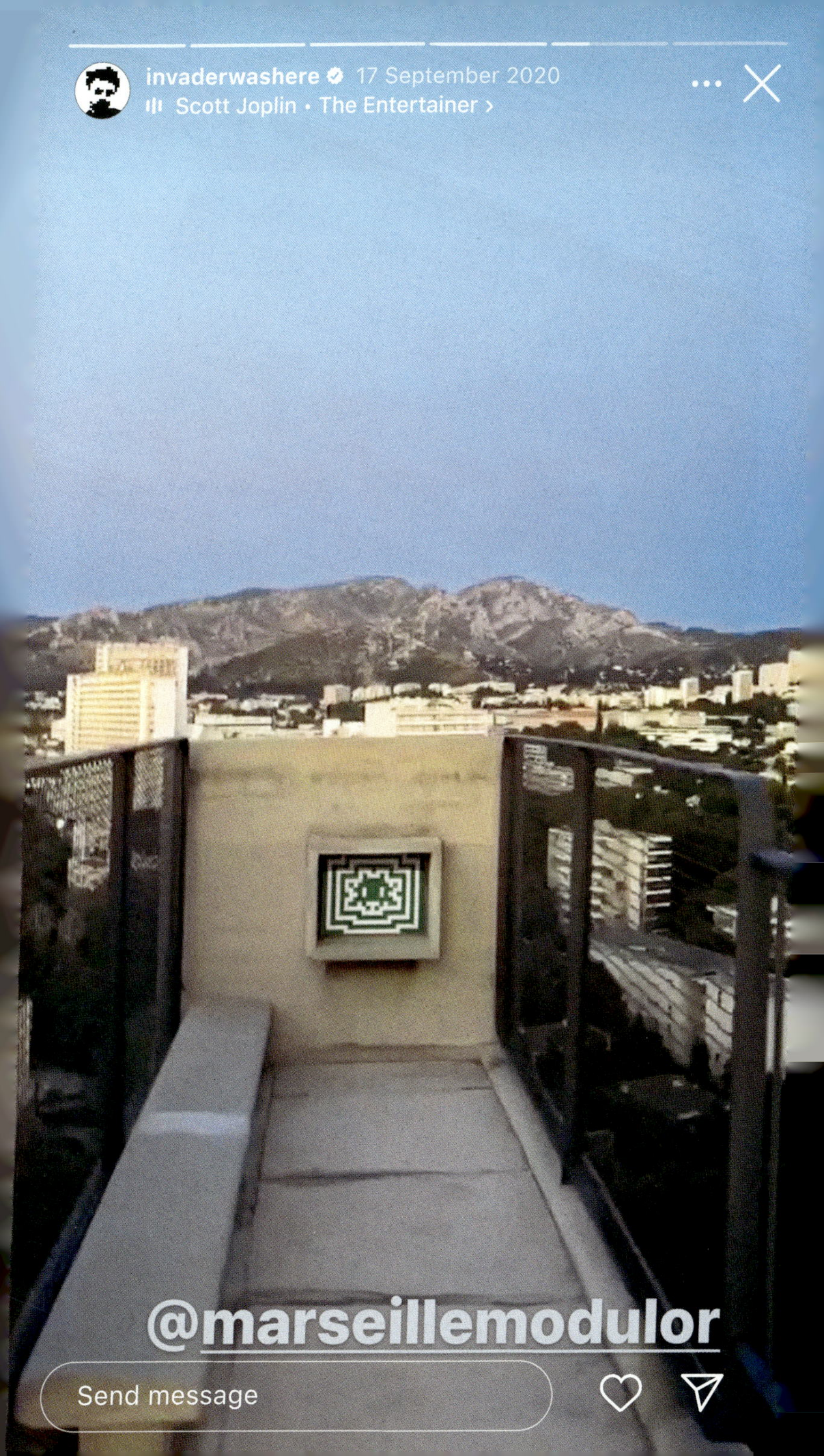

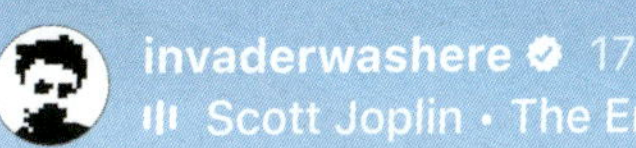
invaderwashere 17 September 2020
Scott Joplin • The Entertainer ›
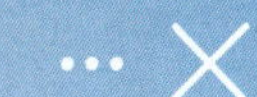
@marseillemodulor
Send message

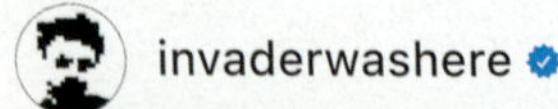

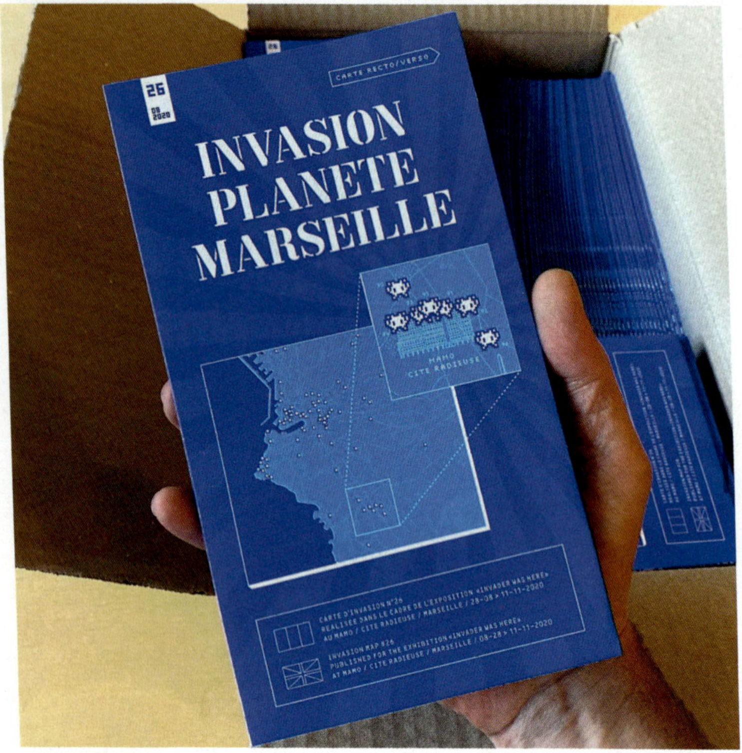

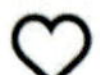    

9173 likes

invaderwashere Invasion Planète Marseille map will be available online next week #invasionmap #spaceshop #marseille

View all 231 comments

17 September 2020

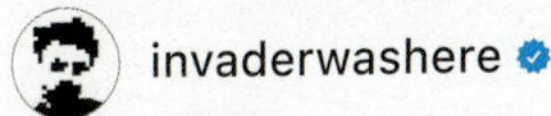

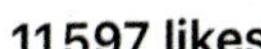

invaderwashere MARS_87 

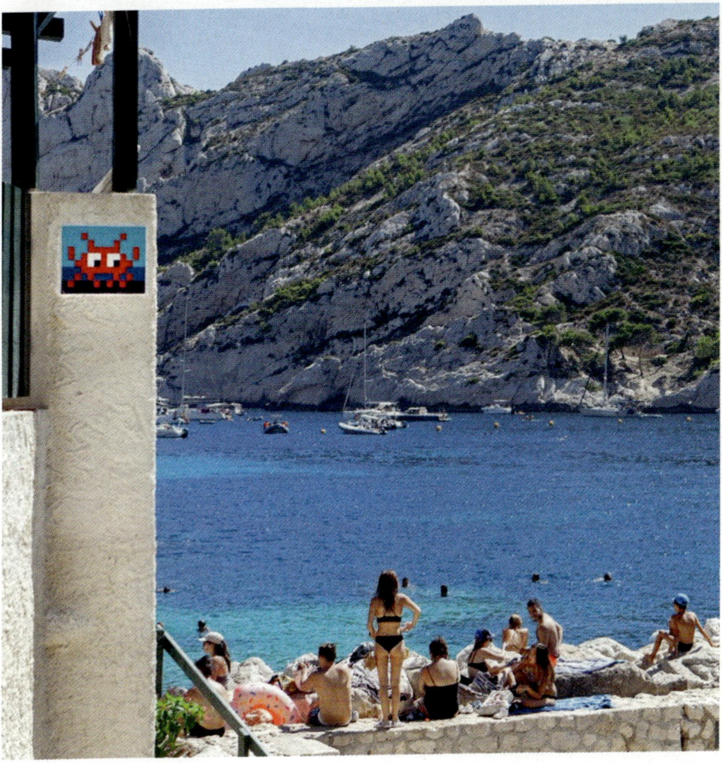

#invaderwashere #marseille @marseillemodulor

View all 56 comments

18 September 2020

invaderwashere

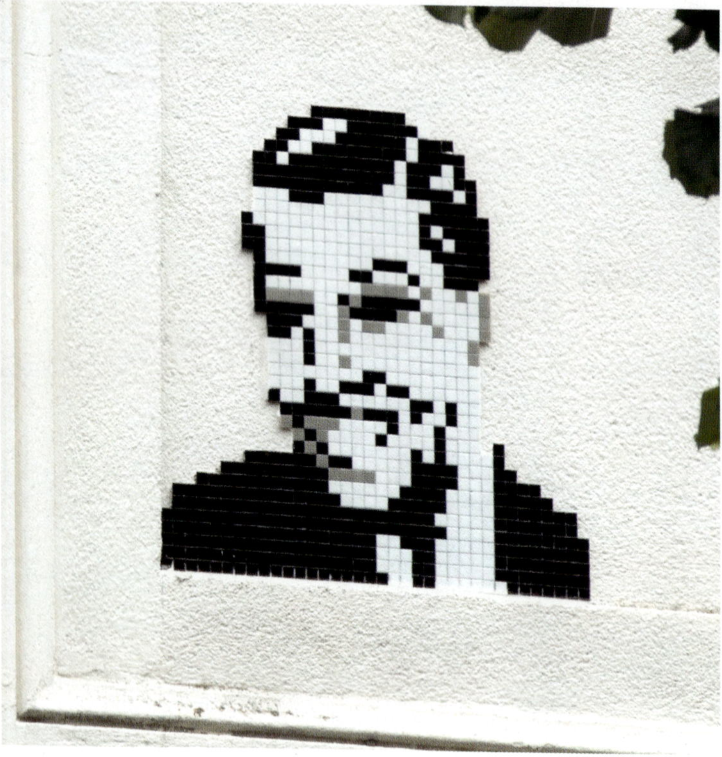

12 318 likes

invaderwashere In that house was born the French actor Fernandel #fernandel #binaryportrait #thefrenchman #legend #marseille @marseillemodulor

View all 72 comments

20 September 2020

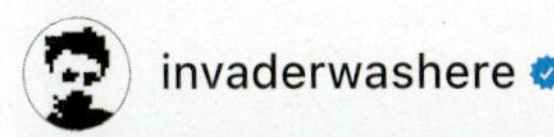

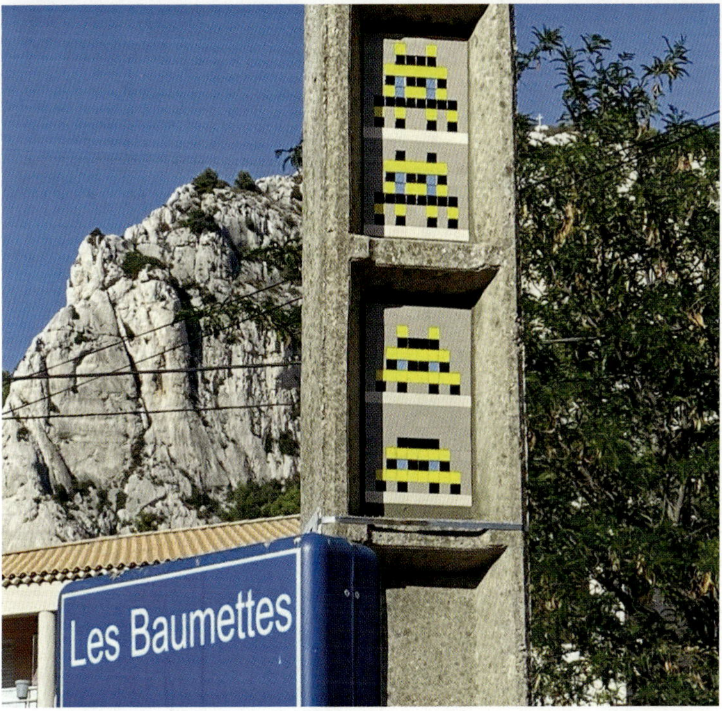

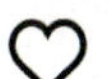    

10 881 likes

invaderwashere Les Baumettes is the infamous prison of Marseille, les Dalton brothers are the villains from Lucky Luke comic book and "22" is an old French code to say "Police is coming!" #lesbaumettes #spacedalton #escape #evasion #invasion #busstop #22 #marseille #mars_22 #invaderwashere @marseillemodulor

View all 74 comments

22 September 2020

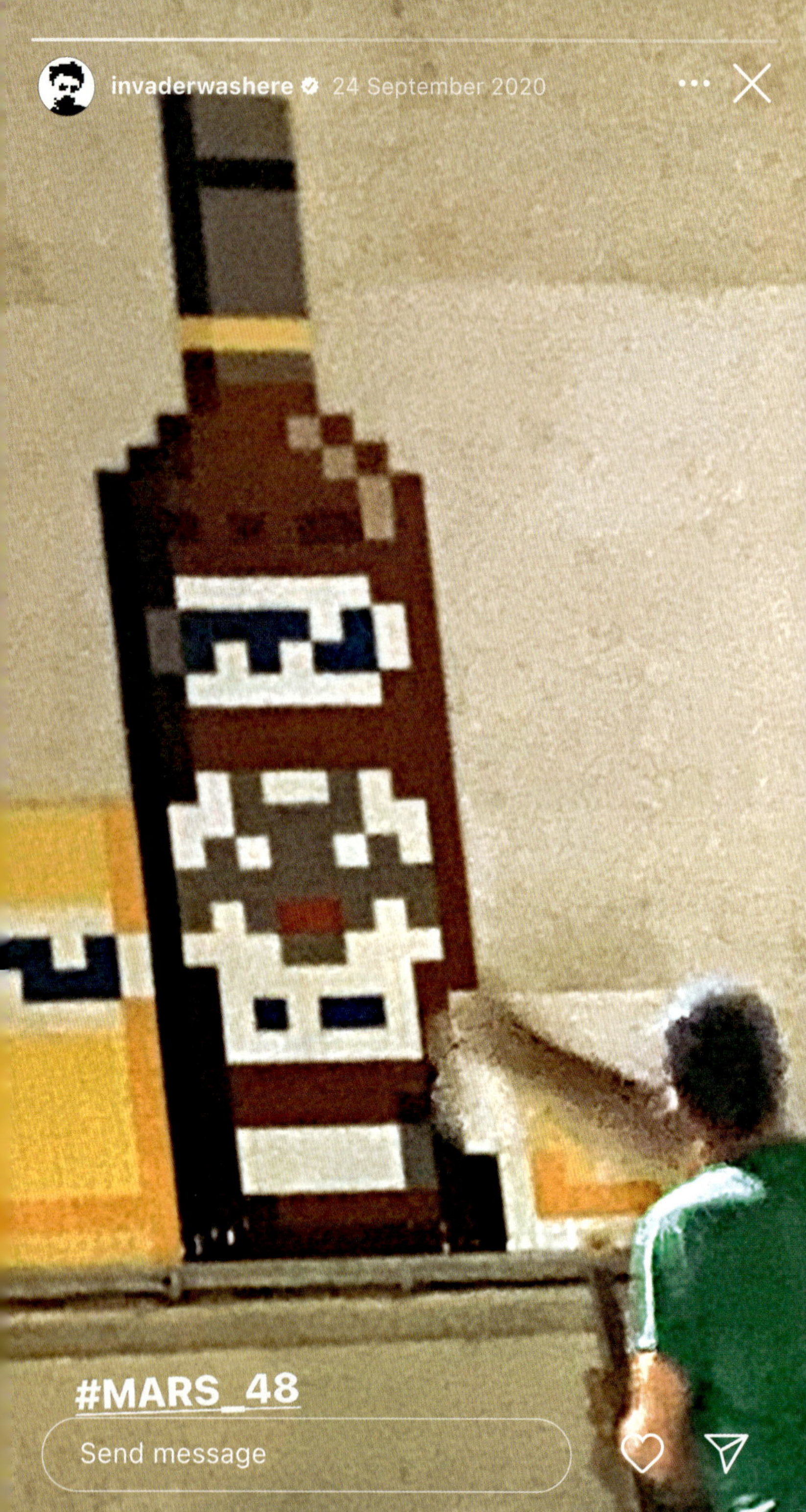
invaderwashere
24 September 2020
#MARS_48
Send message

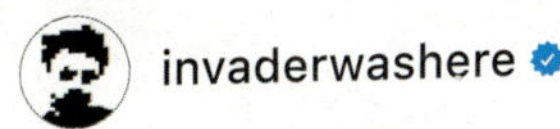

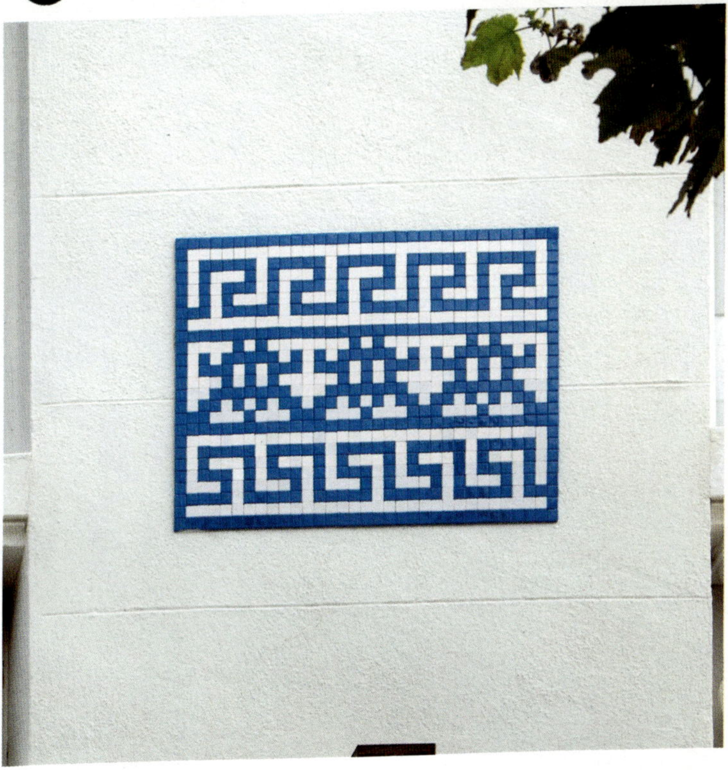

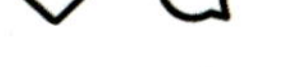

10 000 likes

invaderwashere Le Petit Nice is the only ⭐⭐⭐ restaurant of Marseille. Thank you to the chef, Gérald Passedat, for this amazing spot! @geraldpassedat #lepetitnice #3etoilesmichelin #mars_66 👾👾👾 Video shot by @ora_ito, subtitles: "How are you Gerald? / Fine, and you? / Tell me, how many 3 Michelin stars are there in the world? / Wait, there's something to eat here... / No, tell me, how many are you? / About one hundred... / Really? Only 100? So you are one of the 100 in the world"

View all 51 comments

25 September 2020

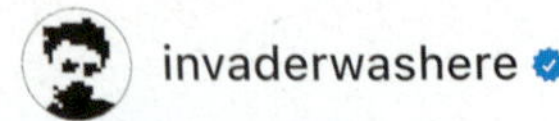

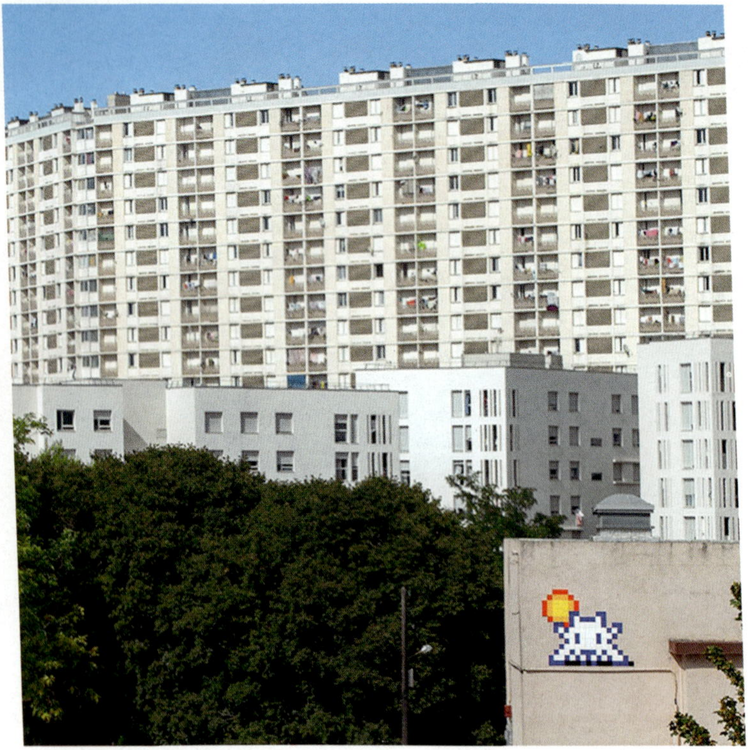

  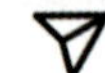  

9091 likes

invaderwashere One of the pieces in the Northern district of Marseille #quartiersnord #marseille #mars_83 #invaderwashere @marseillemodulor

View all 45 comments

28 September 2020

invaderwashere

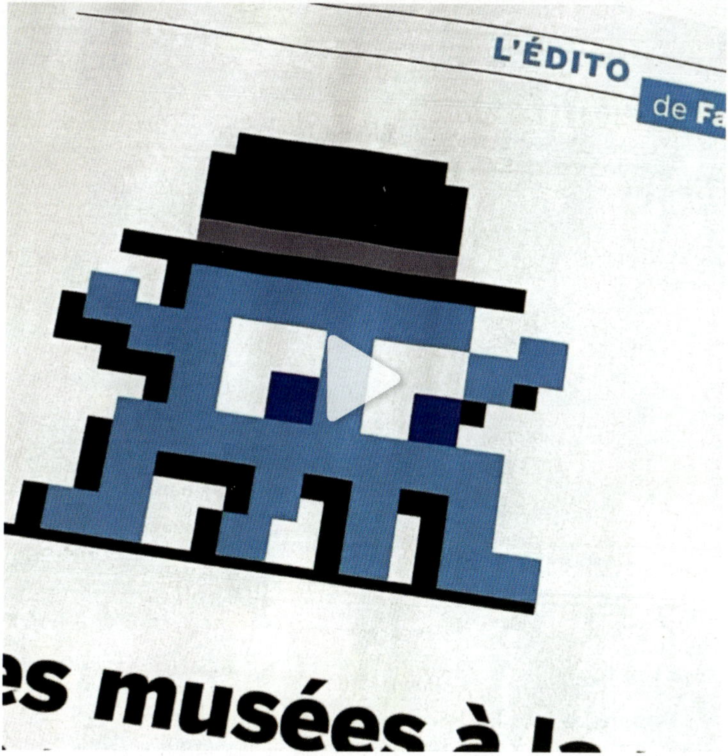

20 130 views

invaderwashere Beaux Arts Magazine invaded!!! 😎 👾
#mediainvasion @beauxarts_magazine @fabricebousteau
#invaderwashere @marseillemodulor

View all 57 comments

30 September 2020

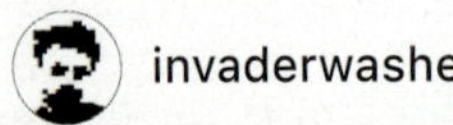

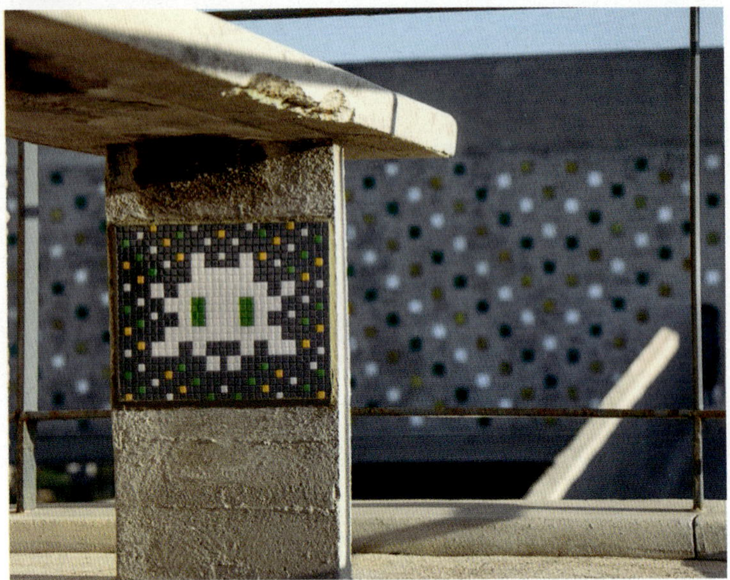

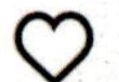    

14 134 likes

invaderwashere MARS_91 🟩⬜🟨 #citeradieuse #lecorbusier #invaderwashere @marseillemodulor @ora_ito

View all 82 comments

5 October 2020

invaderwashere 

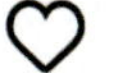 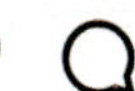  

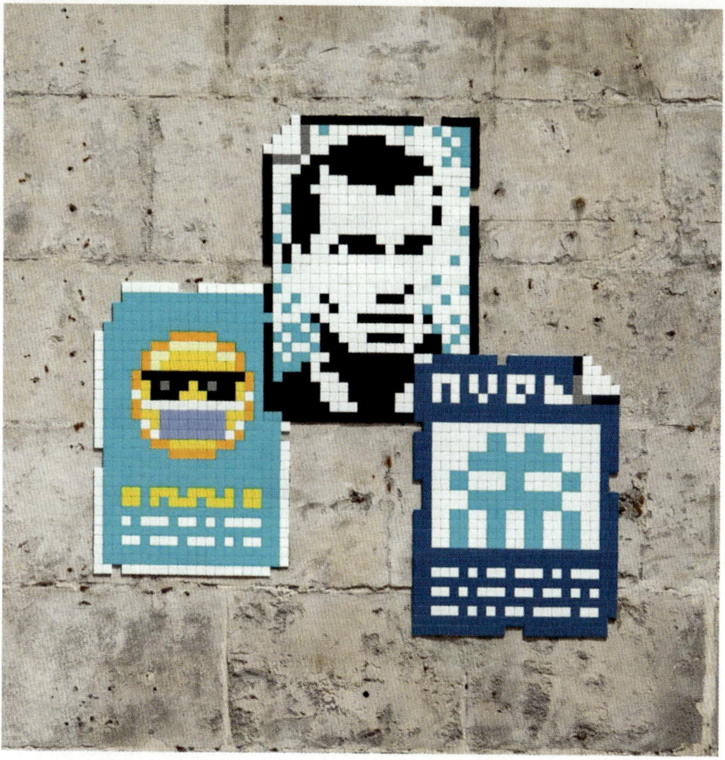

15 054 likes

invaderwashere Difficult to invade Marseille without paying tribute to Zinédine Zidane who is a real child and icon of the city #mars_39 #zinedinezidane #covid19 #signsofthetimes #ceramicposters #postersforeternity #triptych #marseille #invaderwashere @marseillemodulor @ora_ito

View all 134 comments

8 October 2020

invaderwashere

  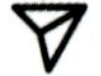 

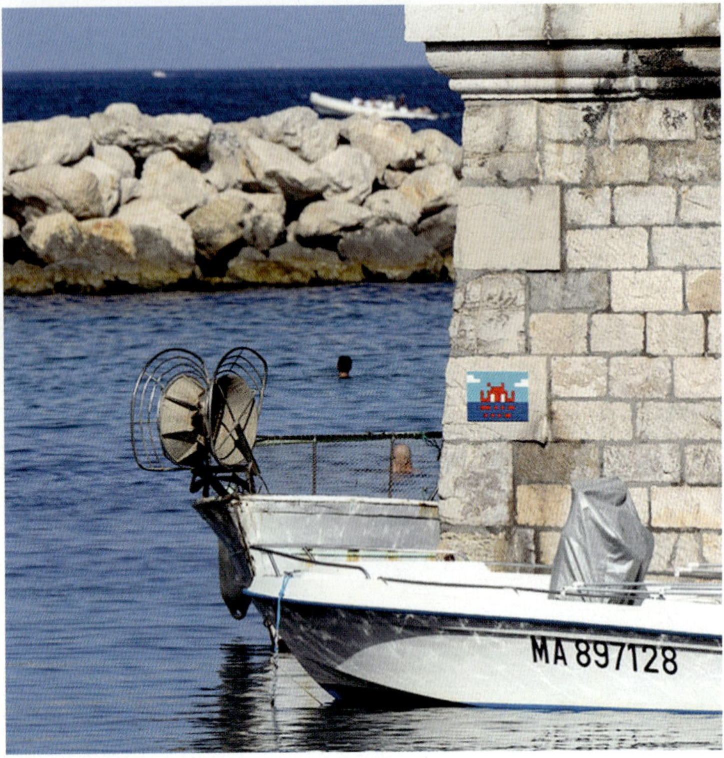

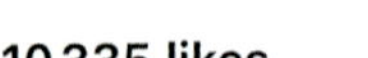

10 335 likes

invaderwashere MARS_62 🌊 👾 ☀️ 🚤
#invaderwashere #marseille #sunsetinvader
#vallondesauffes

View all 65 comments

11 October 2020

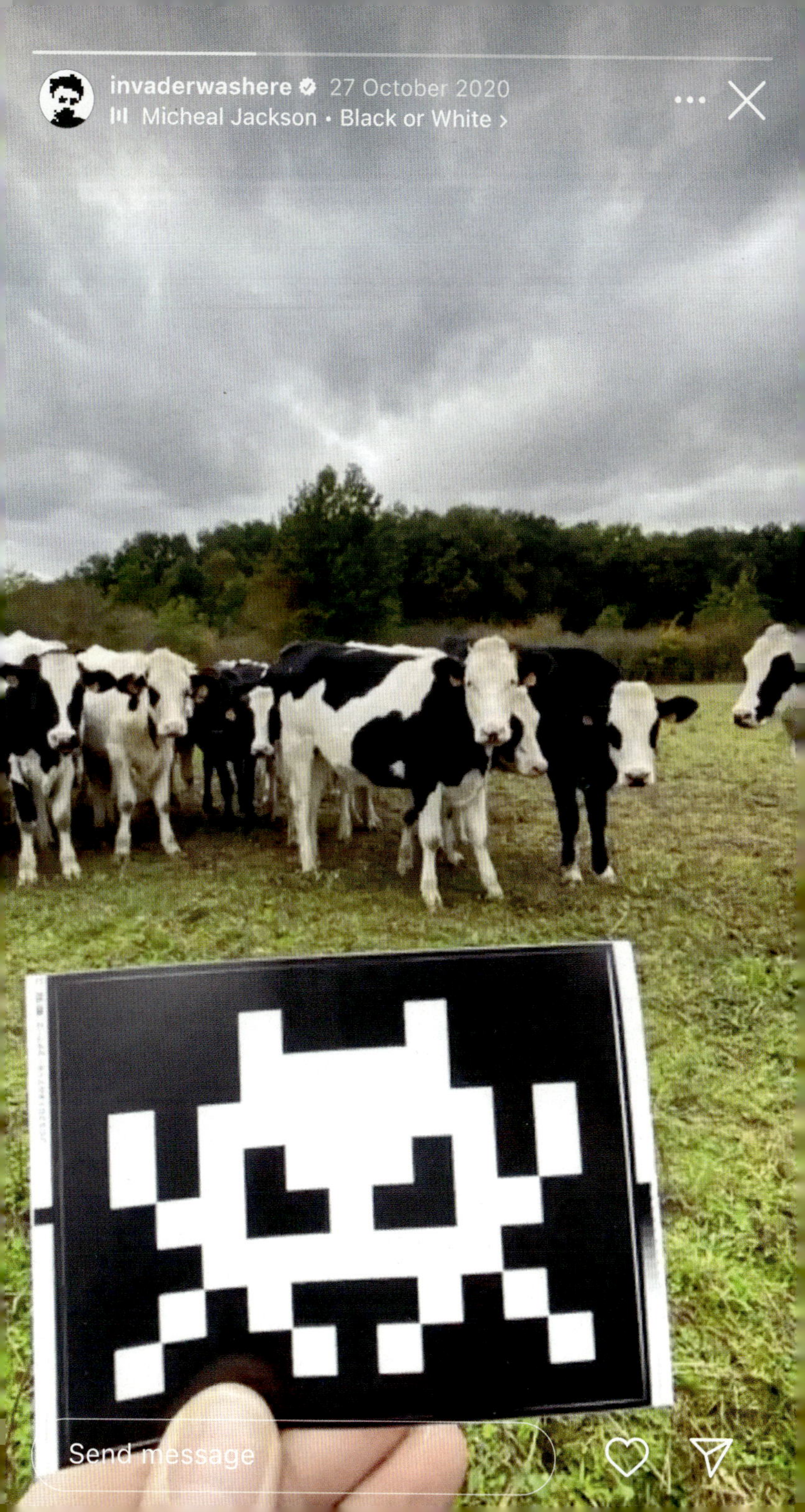

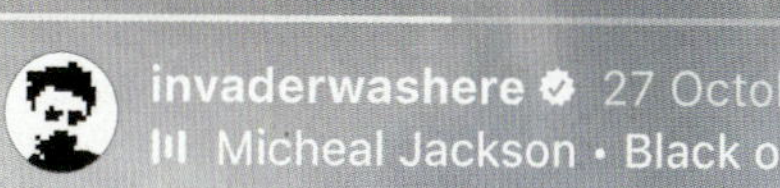
invaderwashere
27 October 2020
Micheal Jackson • Black or White ›

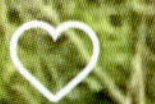
Send message

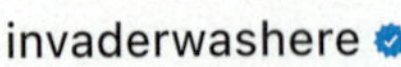

invaderwashere

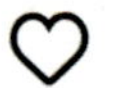   

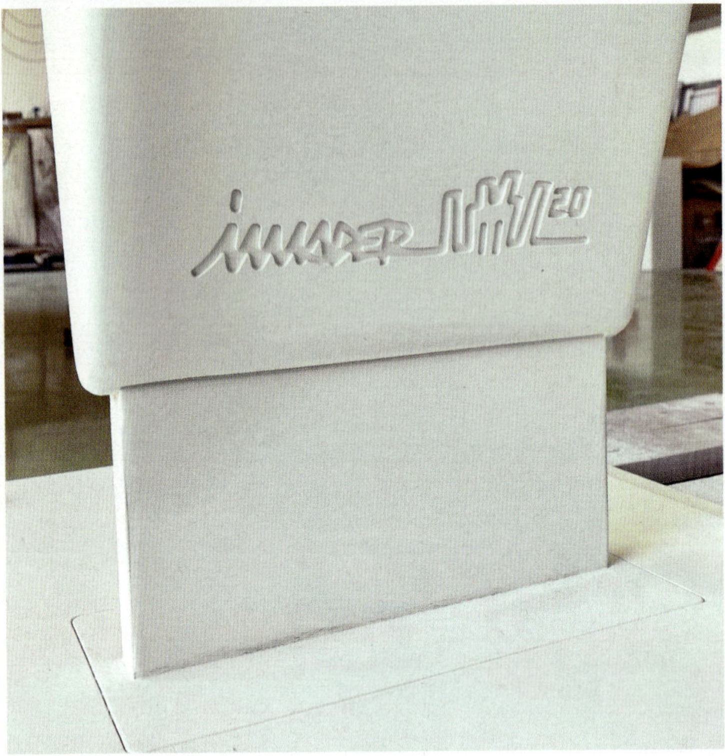

7702 likes

invaderwashere Working on a new sculpture... #metal #sculpture #detail #beforepainting

View all 102 comments

3 November 2020

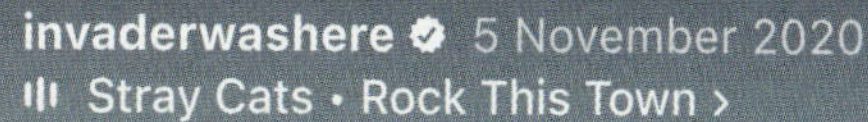

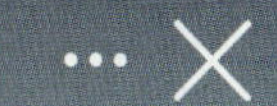

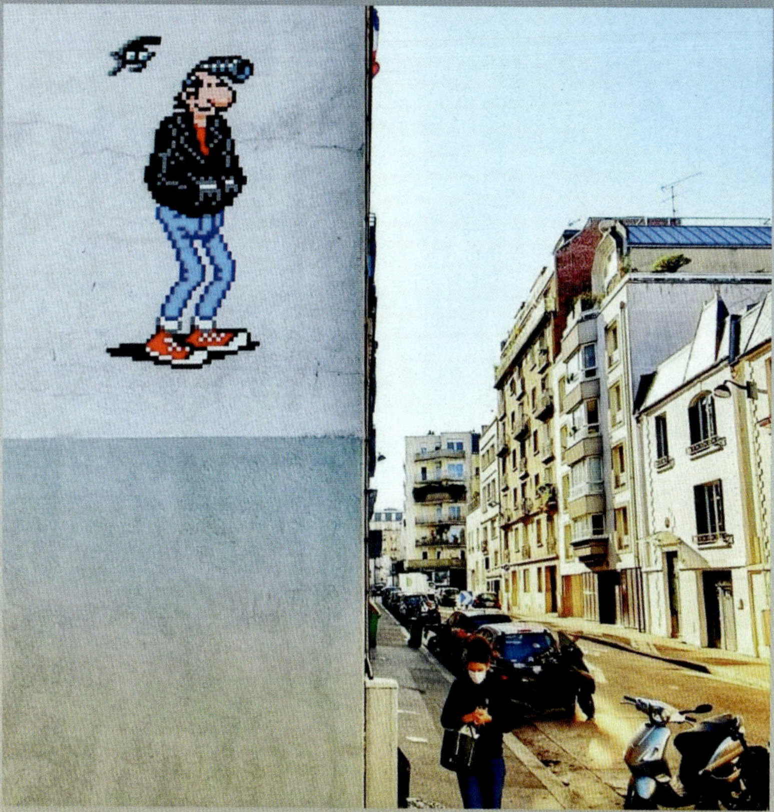

@fluide_glacial

THANK YOU #FRANKMARGERIN
FOR THE INSPIRATION
AND @FLUIDE_GLACIAL FOR THE POST

Send message

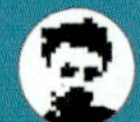

invaderwashere 7 November 2020

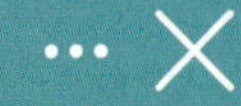

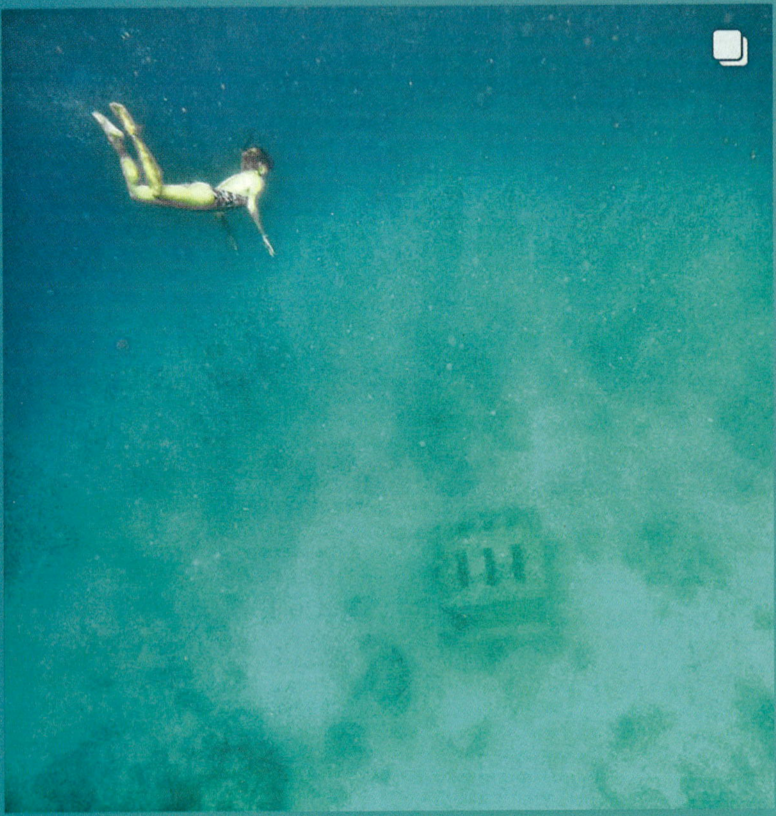

@del_arbonetta

Send message

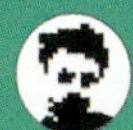

invaderwashere 7 November 2020

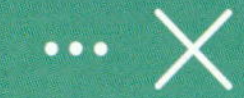

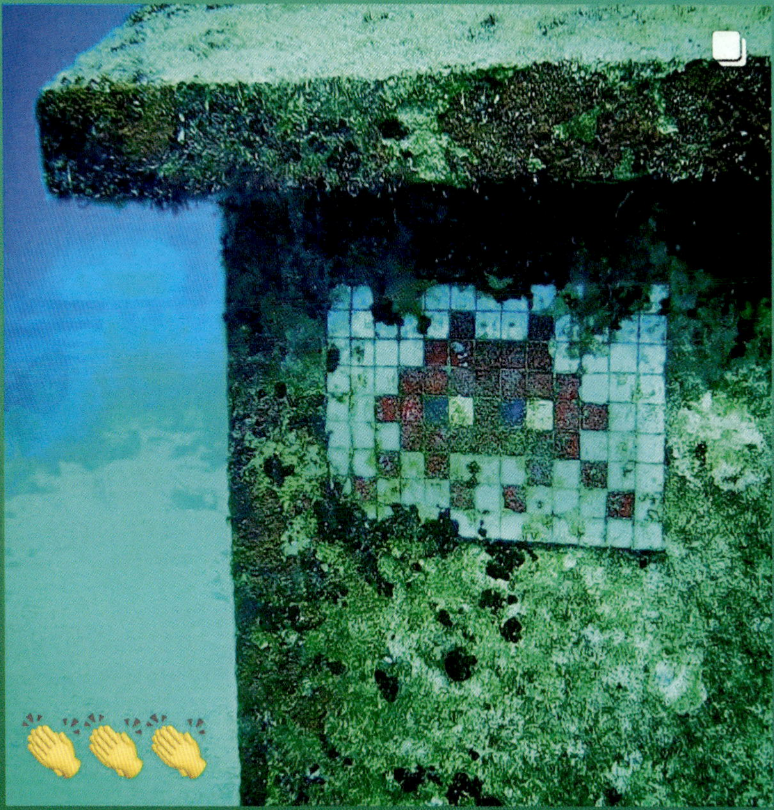

@del_arbonetta

#CCU_01
@JASONDECAIRESTAYLOR

Send message

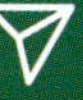

invaderwashere 

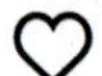 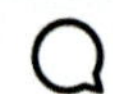  

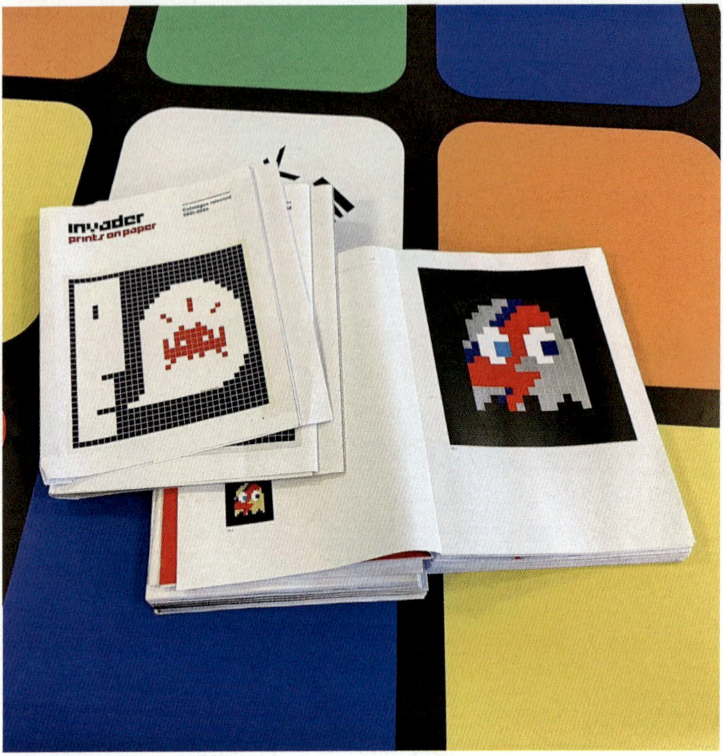

10683 likes

invaderwashere #studiodetails swipe ⬅️
Taking advantage of the lockdown to prepare many new things at the studio: #book #prints #rubikcubism #Tshirts #stickers #movie #etc...

View all 148 comments

16 November 2020

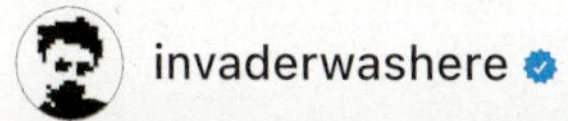

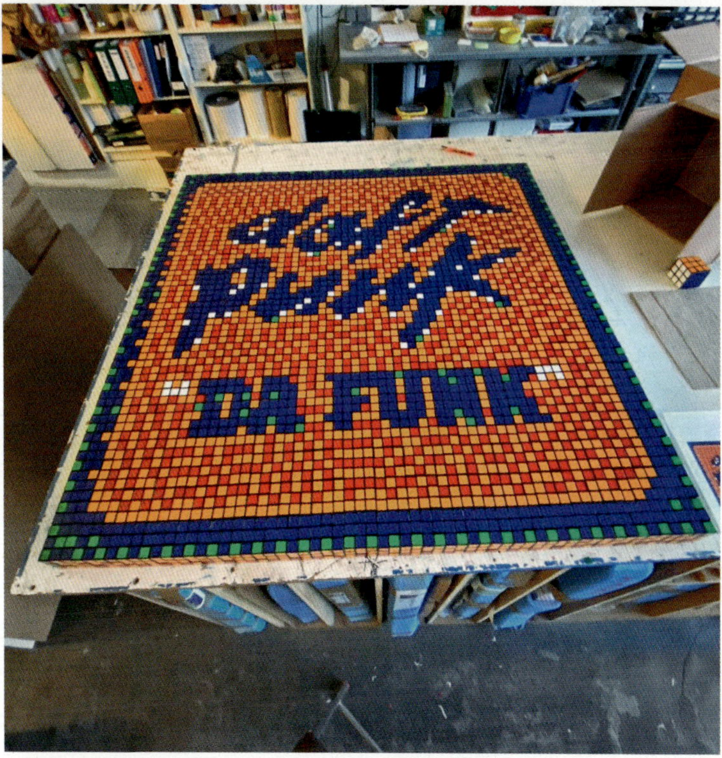

   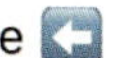 

10 703 likes

invaderwashere #studiodetails swipe ⬅️
Taking advantage of the lockdown to prepare many new things at the studio: #book #prints #rubikcubism #Tshirts #stickers #movie #etc...

View all 148 comments

16 November 2020

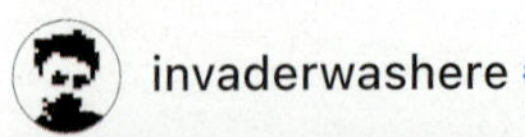

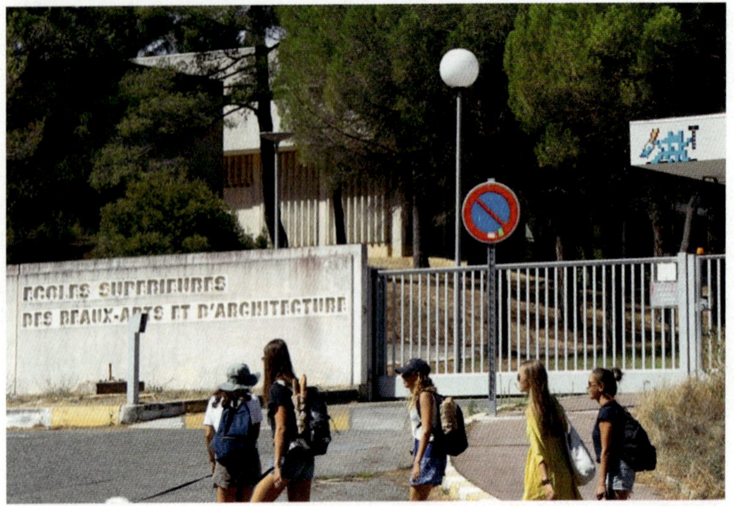

   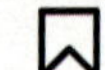

10182 likes

invaderwashere MARS_23 is located at the entrance of the schools of art and architecture of Marseille. It is also a point of departure to walk to the calanques. 🌞🌊
#marseille #invaderwashere @beaux_arts_de_marseille @archimarseille @marseillemodulor

View all 43 comments

22 November 2020

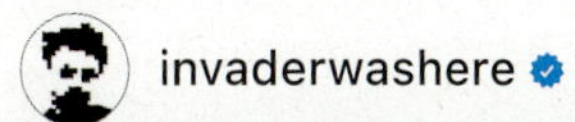

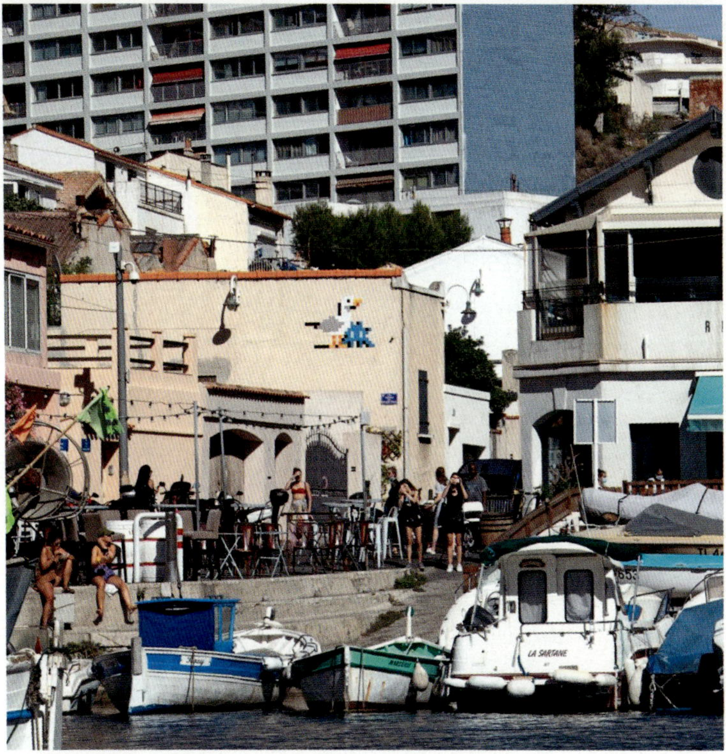

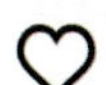   

8 290 likes

invaderwashere MARS_61 #vallondesauffes #marseille #invaderwashere @marseillemodulor

View all 59 comments

22 November 2020

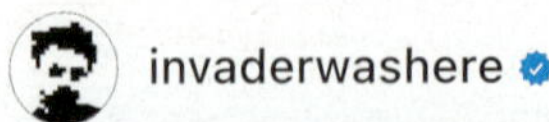

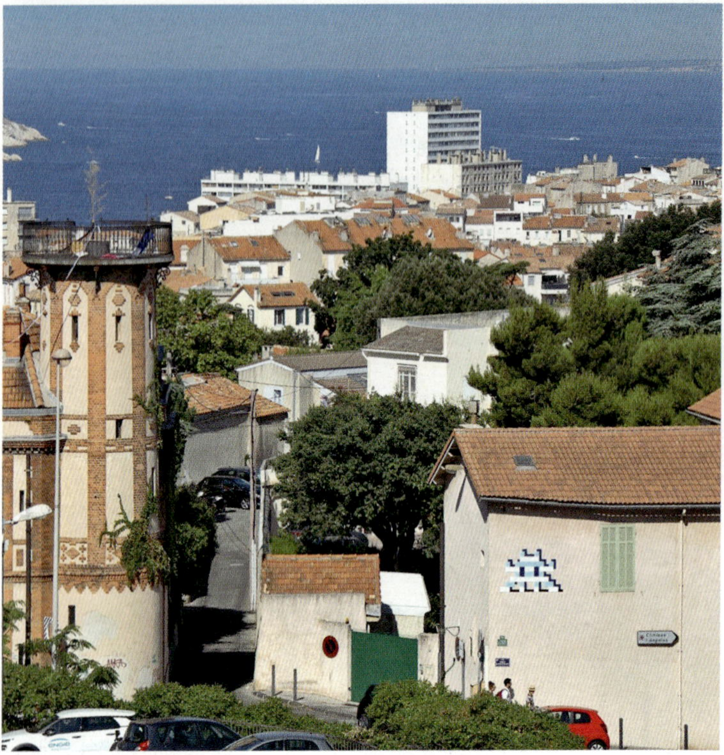

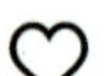 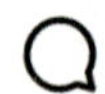  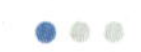 

8 308 likes

invaderwashere MARS_42 #marseille #invaderwashere @marseillemodulor

View all 48 comments

22 November 2020

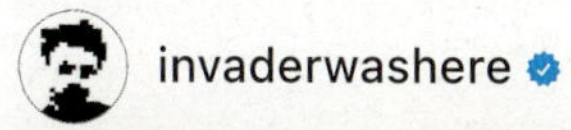

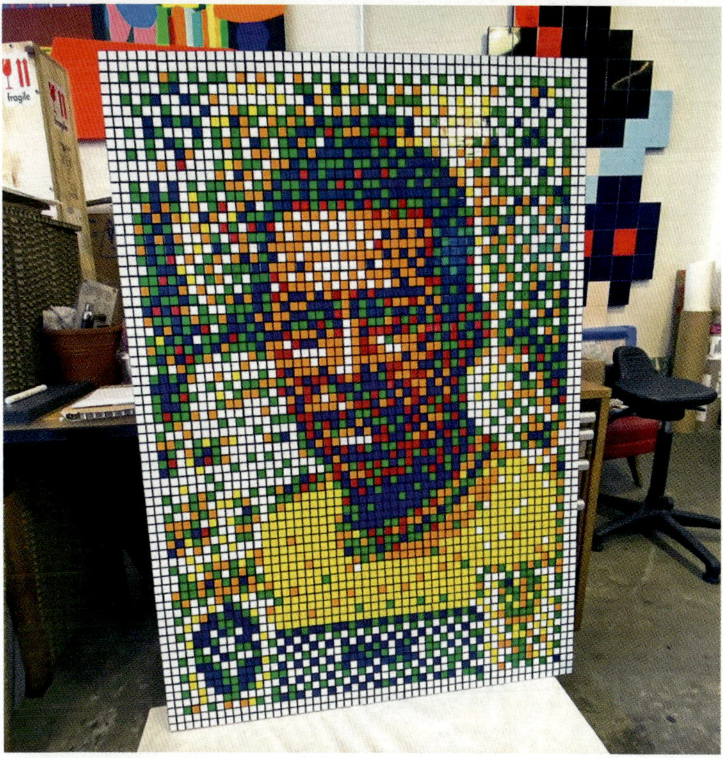

12 789 likes

invaderwashere Rubik Pelé Panini #pelé #panini #mexico70 #rubikcubism @rubiks_official

View all 253 comments

24 November 2020

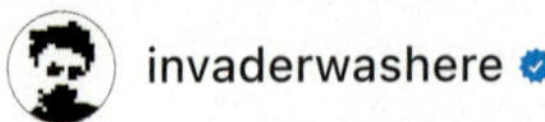

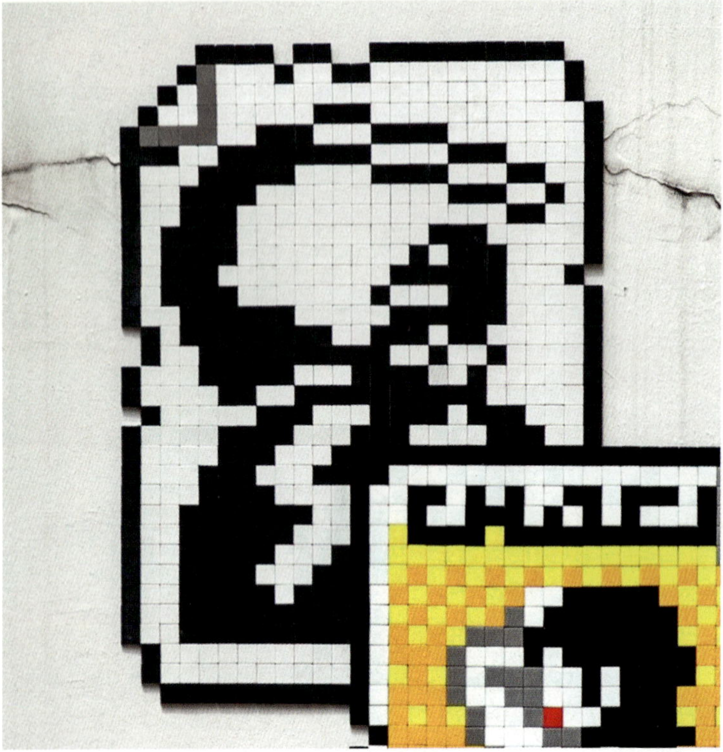

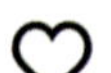 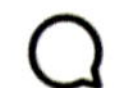  

6 664 likes

invaderwashere Detail of PA_1407 #violentcops #abuseofpower #mai68 #nov2020 #stillrelevant

View all 34 comments

27 November 2020

invaderwashere

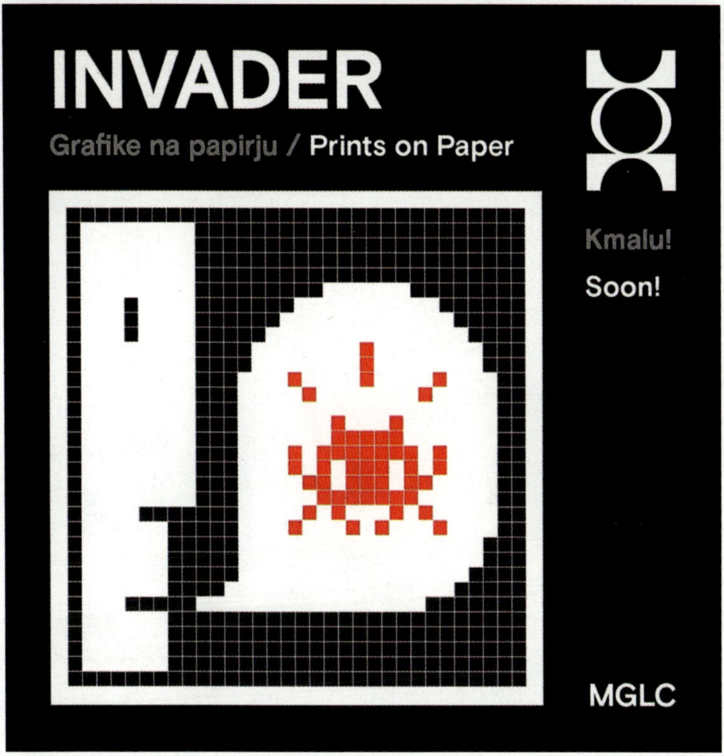

INVADER

Grafike na papirju / Prints on Paper

Kmalu!

Soon!

MGLC

  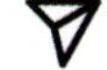 

5 380 likes

invaderwashere PRINTS ON PAPER is under installation at MGLC, Ljubljana. No date for the opening yet 🦠 😬 More info asap #Printsonpaper @mglcljubljana #ljubljana #slovenia

View all 75 comments

30 November 2020

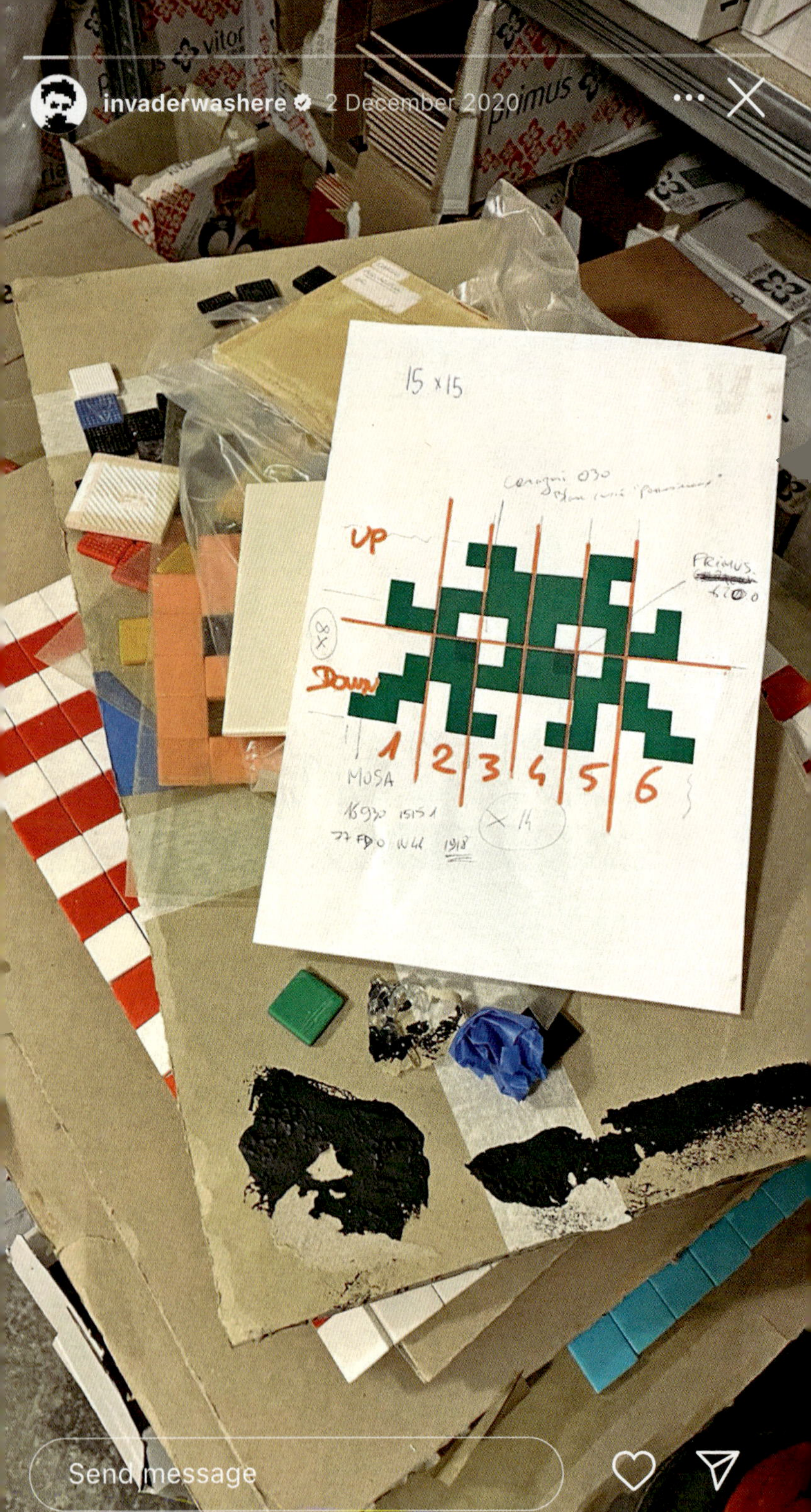
invaderwashere
2 December 2020
15 x 15
UP
Down
1 2 3 4 5 6
MOSA
PRIMUS
primus
Send message

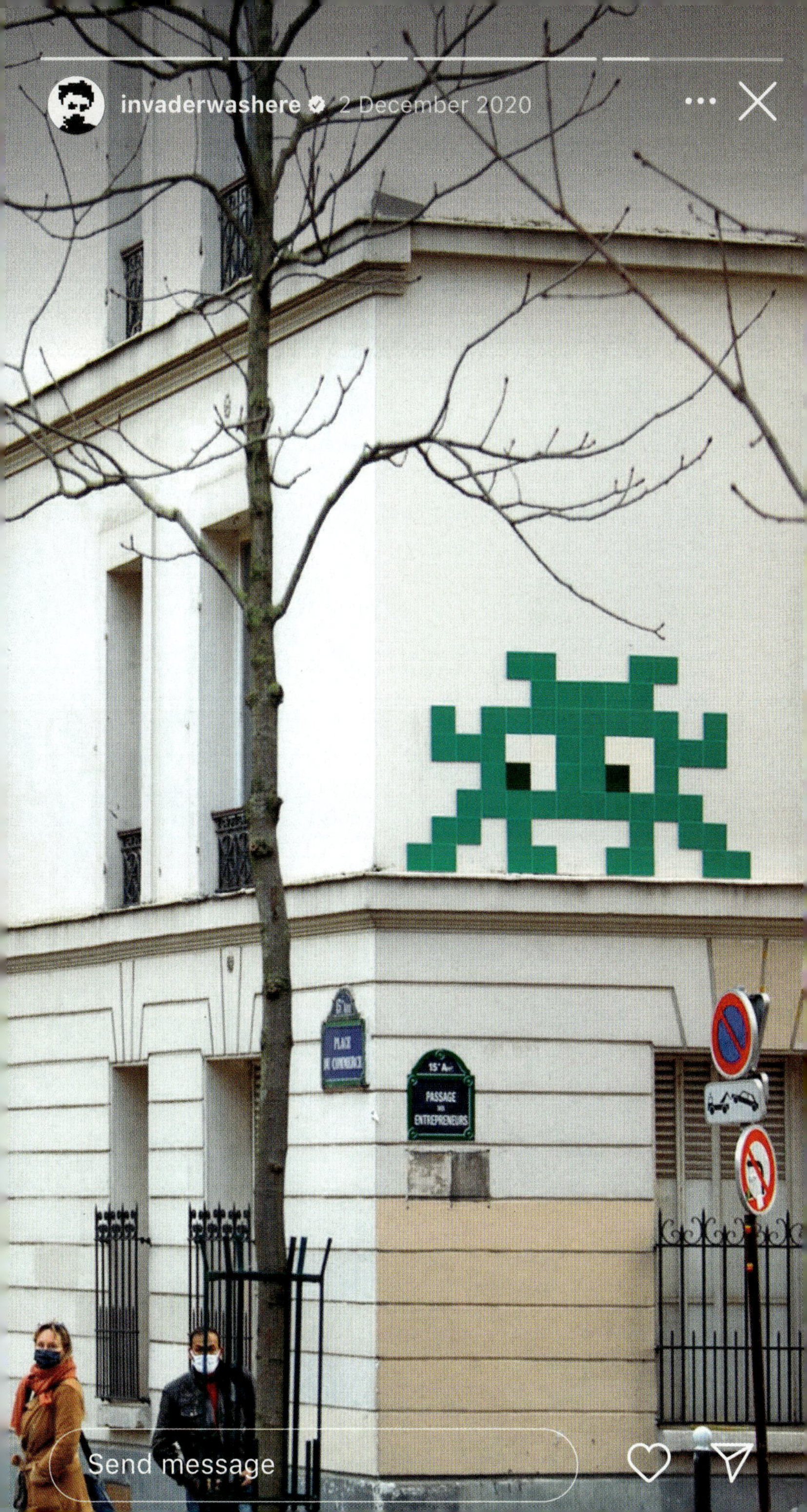
invaderwashere
2 December 2020
PASSAGE
ENTREPRENEURS
Send message

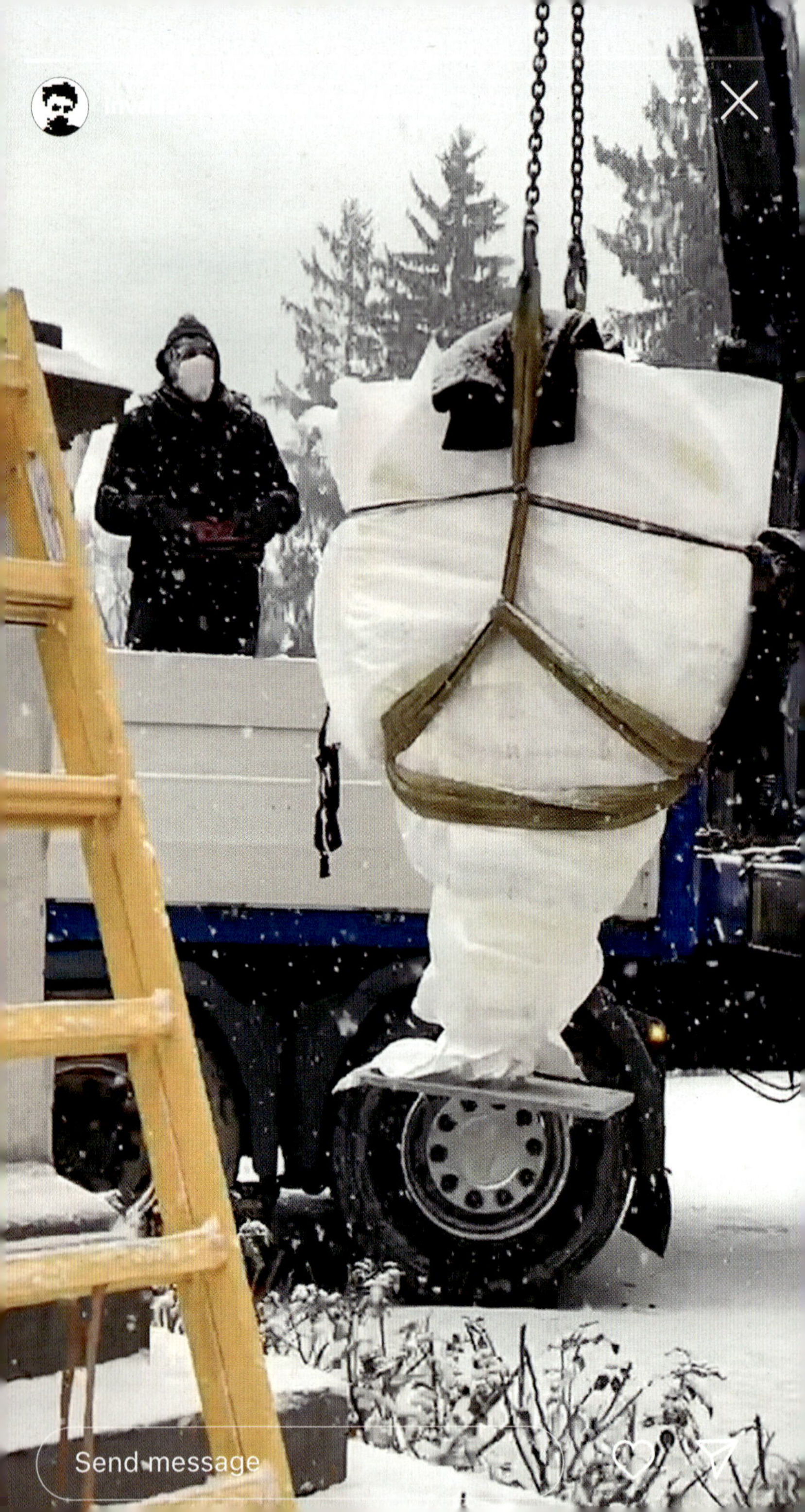
Send message

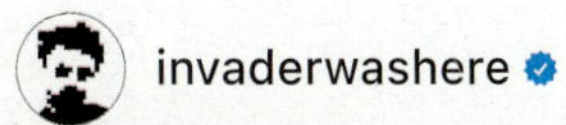

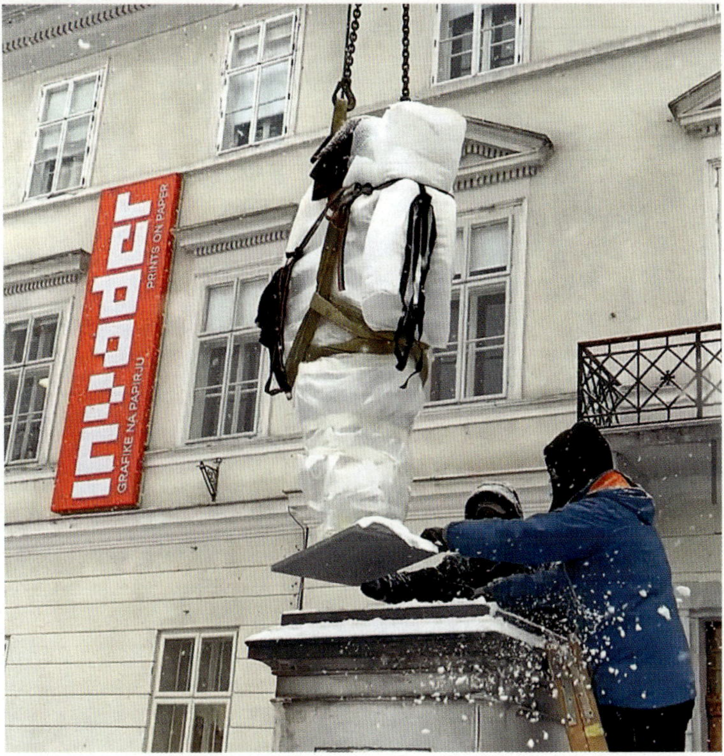

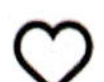   

15 934 likes

invaderwashere Installing Point of Invasion at MGLC for the coming exhibition Prints on Paper #ljubljana #POI #sculpture #printsonpaper @mglcljubljana ❄️📍👾

View all 185 comments

3 December 2020

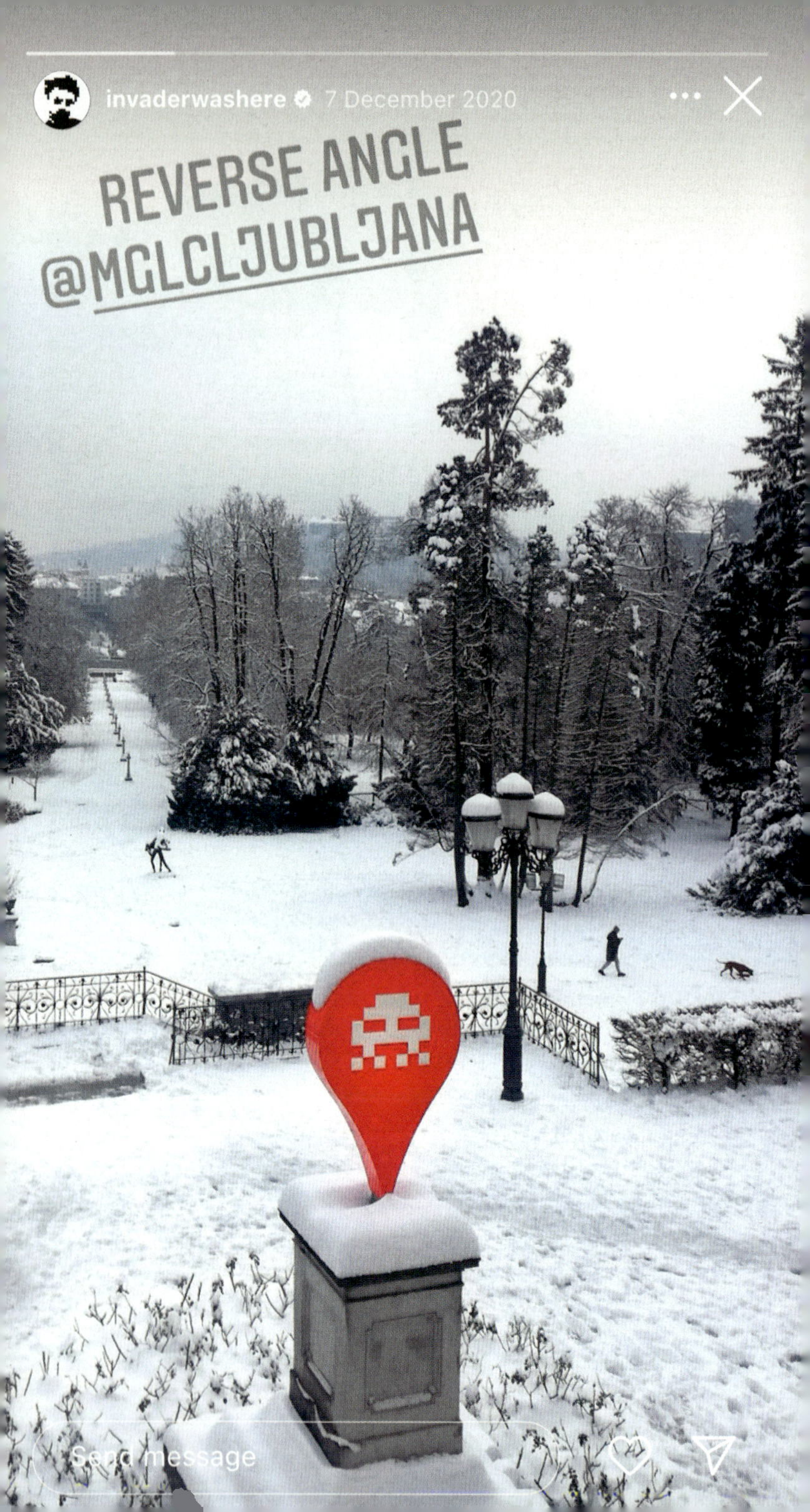

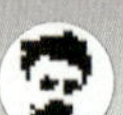

invaderwashere 7 December 2020

REVERSE ANGLE
@MGLCLJUBLJANA

Send message

invaderwashere

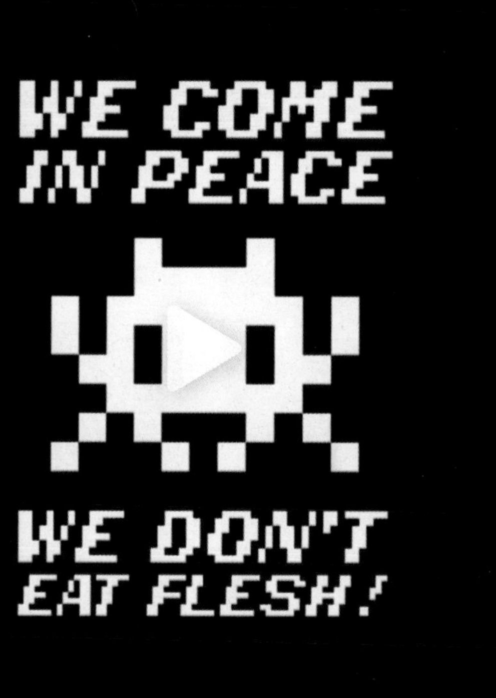

  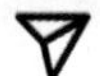 

39 005 views

invaderwashere INVADER X PETA
I am proud to have created those 12 designs to support Peta and defend animal rights. It is high time to fight the exploitation, abuse, and extermination of non-human species and end the animal-industrial complex.
Stickers and Tshirts will be available on the space-shop (link in bio) 100% of the profits will go to Peta. @peta @peta_france #invaderxpeta

View all 259 comments

16 December 2020

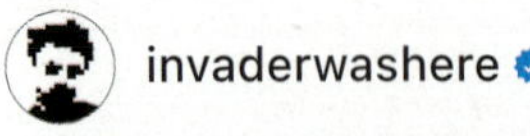

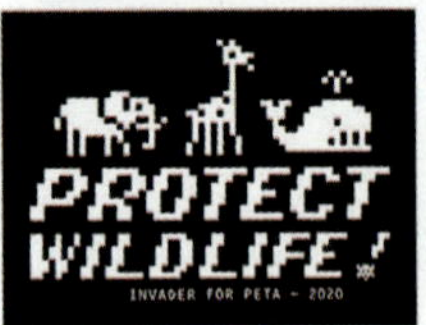

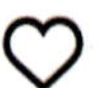    

8 998 likes

invaderwashere Invader x Peta 🦊 🐴 🦆 🐈 🐬 🐘 #stickers #Tshirts Link in bio, 100% of the profits will go to @peta @peta_france #invaderxpeta

View all 248 comments

17 December 2020

invaderwashere

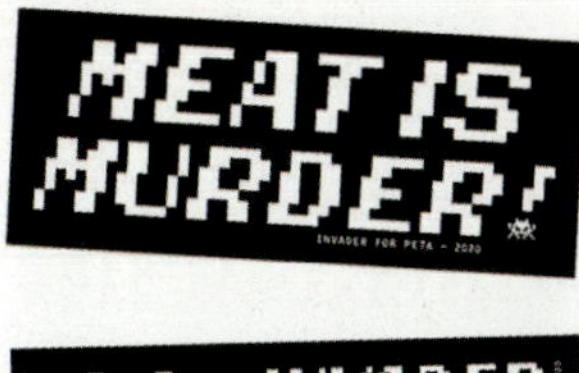

   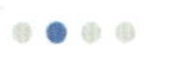 

8998 likes

invaderwashere Invader x Peta 🦊🐴🦆🐕🐬🐘
#stickers #Tshirts Link in bio, 100% of the profits will go to @peta @peta_france #invaderxpeta

View all 248 comments

17 December 2020

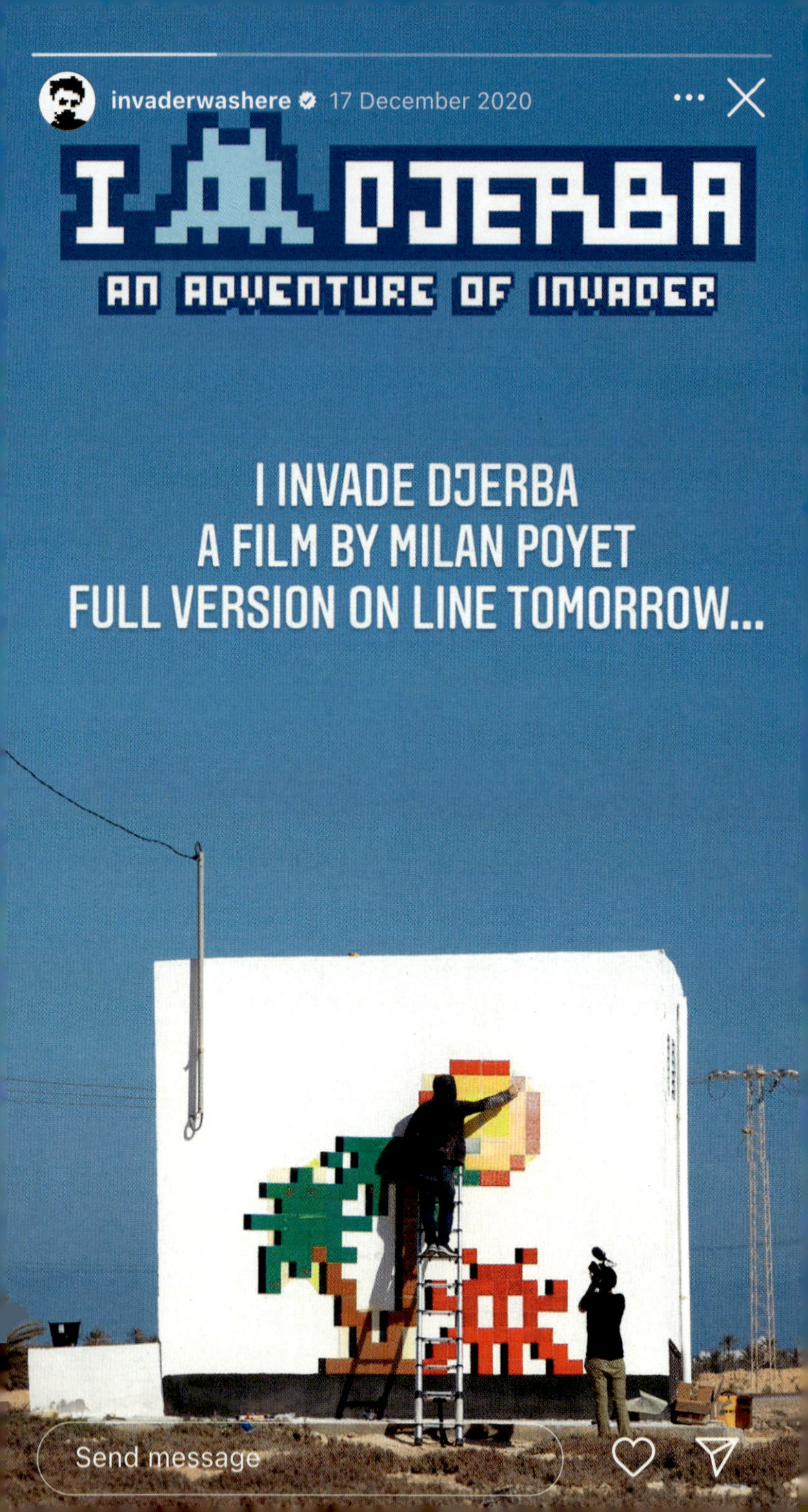

I 👾 DJERBA

AN ADVENTURE OF INVADER

I INVADE DJERBA
A FILM BY MILAN POYET
FULL VERSION ON LINE TOMORROW...

Send message

2021

invaderwashere

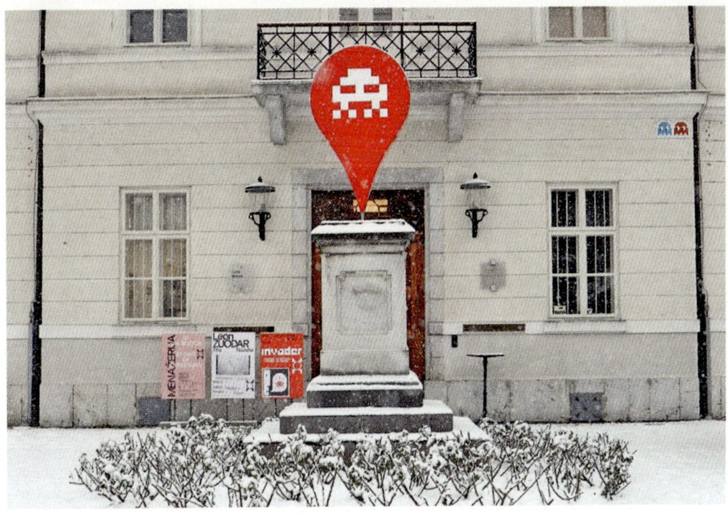

18 096 likes

invaderwashere PRINTS ON PAPER my new solo show at MGLC is only open to local public 🦠😬 But don't worry, it will run until May 18th. More infos ASAP 🤞 #printsonpaper @mglcljubljana

View all 142 comments

11 January 2021

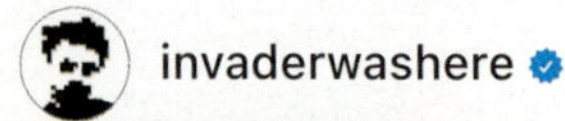

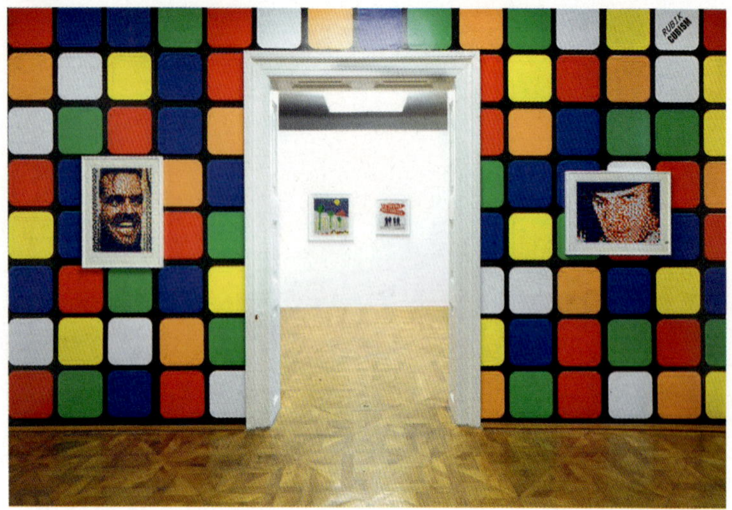

   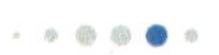 

18 096 likes

invaderwashere PRINTS ON PAPER my new solo show at MGLC is only open to local public 🦠😬 But don't worry, it will run until May 18th. More infos ASAP 🤞 #printsonpaper @mglcljubljana

View all 142 comments

11 January 2021

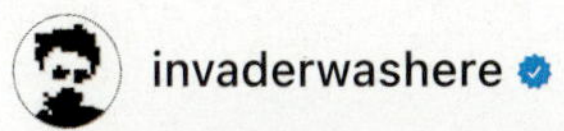

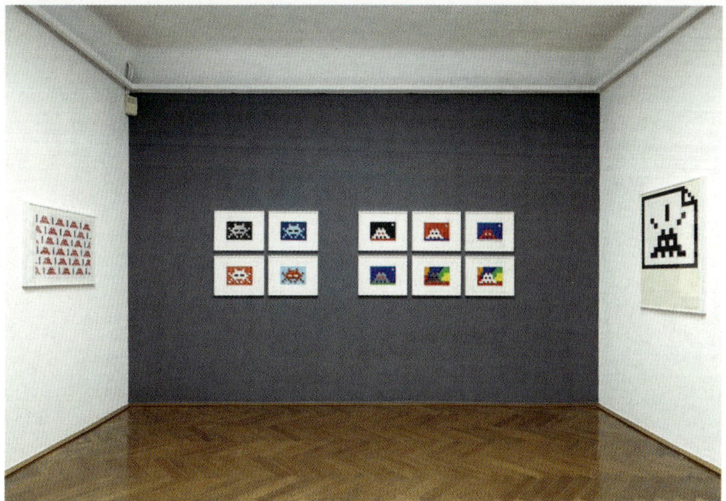

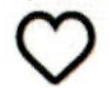   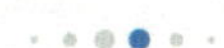 

18 096 likes

invaderwashere PRINTS ON PAPER my new solo show at MGLC is only open to local public 🦠😬 But don't worry, it will run until May 18th. More infos ASAP 🤞 #printsonpaper @mglcljubljana

View all 142 comments

11 January 2021

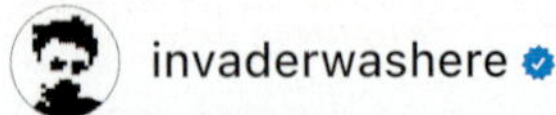

•••

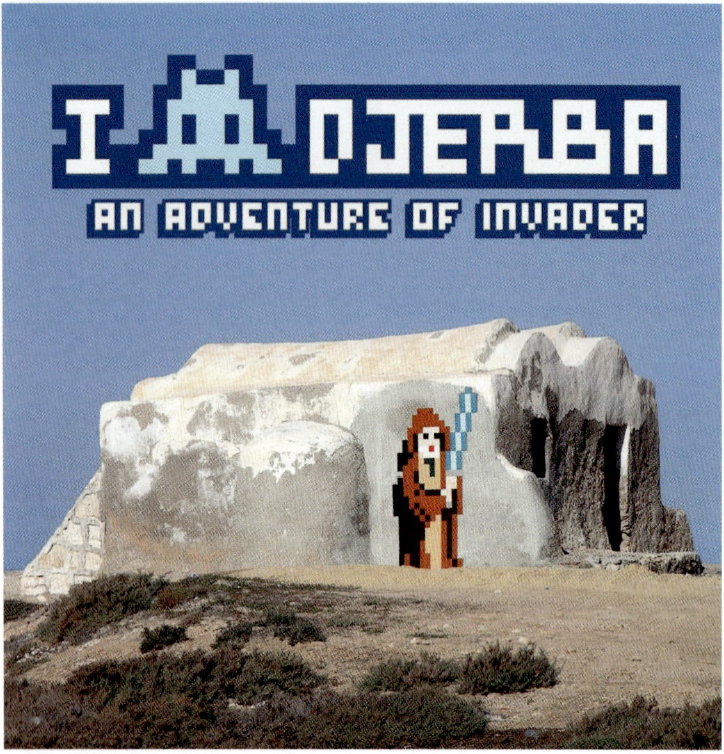

9 868 likes

invaderwashere I 👾 DJERBA the movie is online on Youtube
#youtube #invasion #djerba @vigieproduction

View all 80 comments

12 January 2021

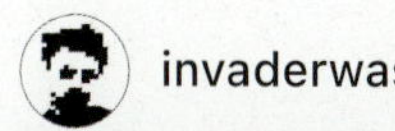

•••

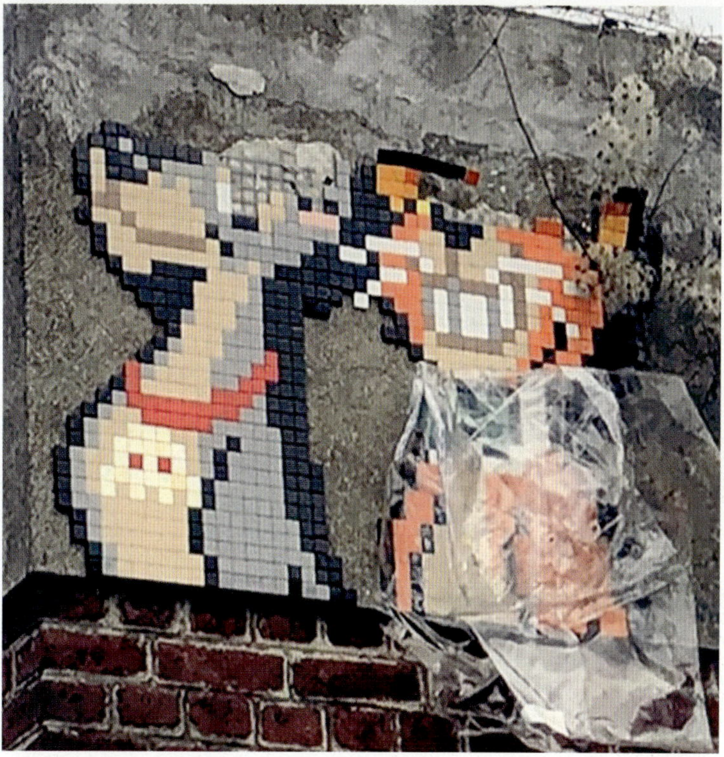

24 942 likes

invaderwashere The more I know people, the more I love dogs! #PA_1435 #animalshelter #afterBefore #shameonyou #stupid #streetartthieves Here is what happens when someone tries to steal a mosaic from a wall.

View all 330 comments

16 January 2021

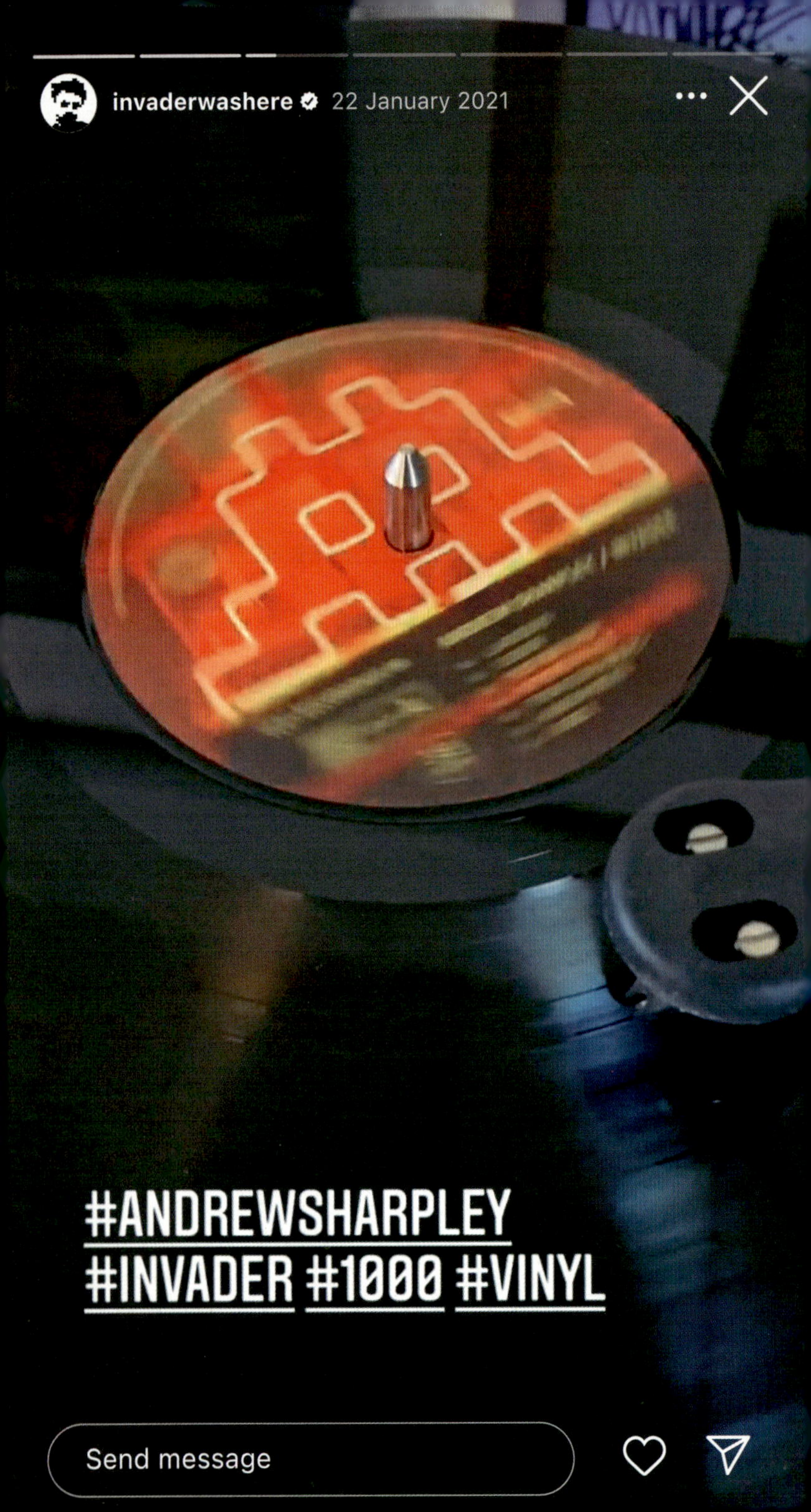

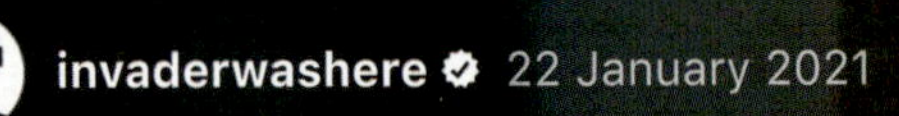

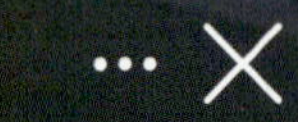

#ANDREWSHARPLEY
#INVADER #1000 #VINYL

Send message

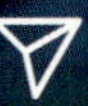

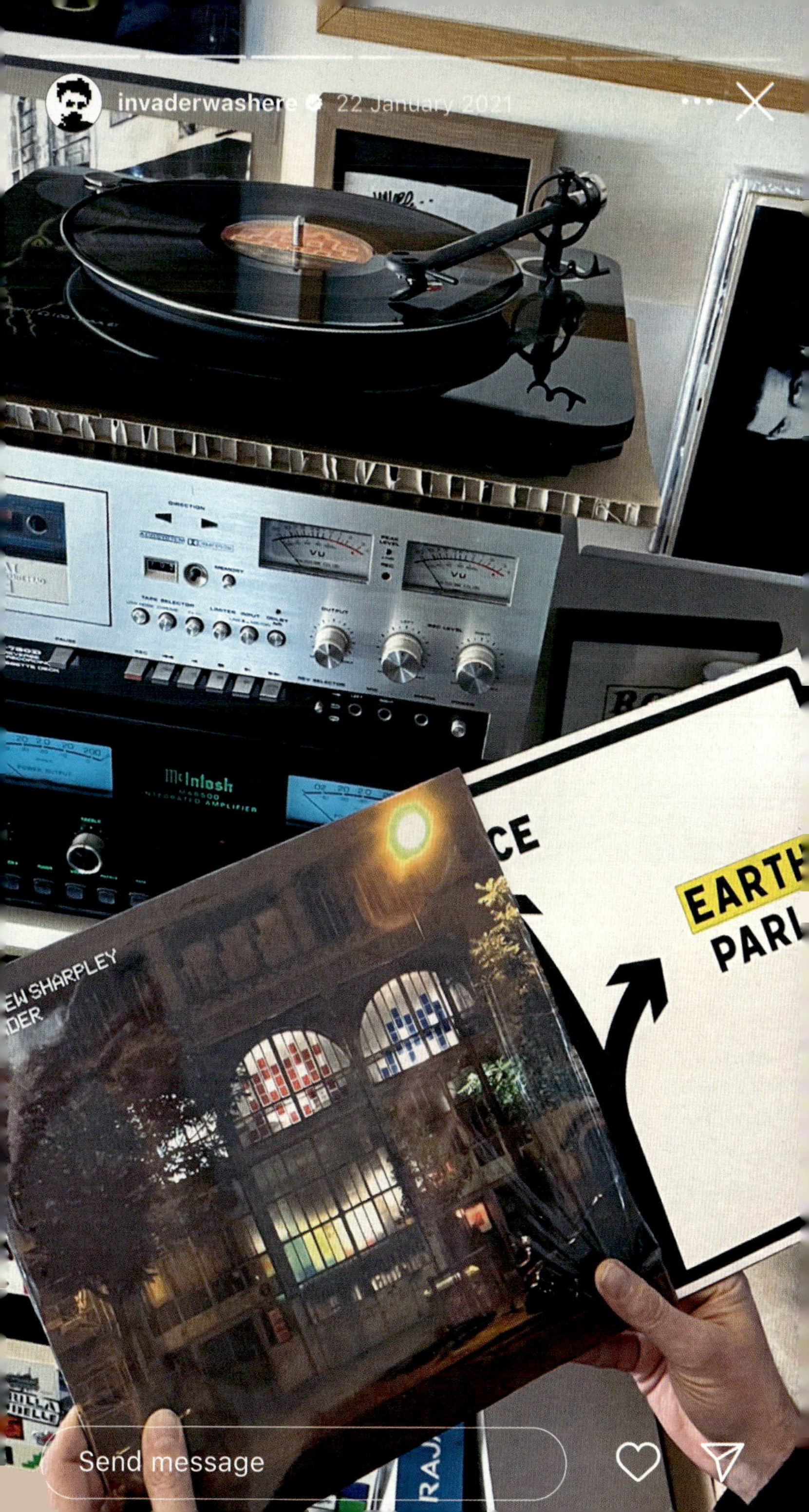
invaderwashere
22 January 2021
EW SHARPLEY
DER
CE
EARTH
PARI
Send message

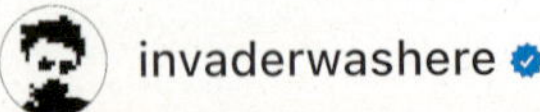

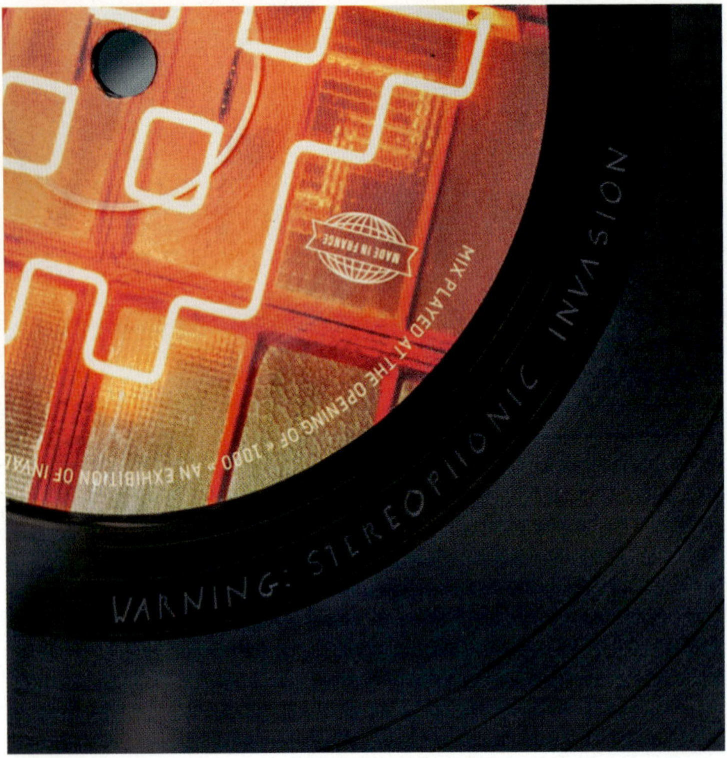

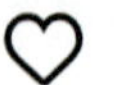    

4 390 likes

invaderwashere Invader by Andrew Sharpley / vinyl detail / a stereophonic invasion! #vinyl #detail #LP #33rpm #andrewsharpley #1000copies #testrecordings Soon on the Spaceshop

View all 95 comments

3 February 2021

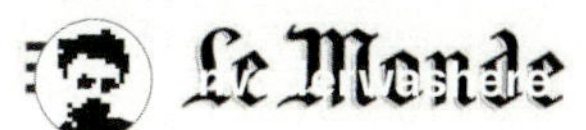

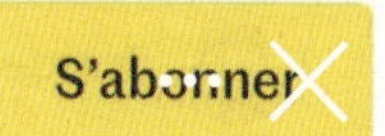

Le street-artiste Invader sur les traces de REVS dans les tunnels du métro de New York

« Un artiste regarde une œuvre » (2/6). Six peintres ou plasticiens partagent leurs coups de cœur. Aujourd'hui, le street-artiste français confie avoir une fascination particulière pour le graffeur américain.

Propos recueillis par Emmanuelle Jardonnet

Publié hier à 23h44, mis à jour à 17h13 · Lecture 4 min.

IN LE MONDE OF TODAY
@LEMONDEFR

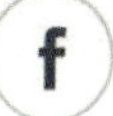

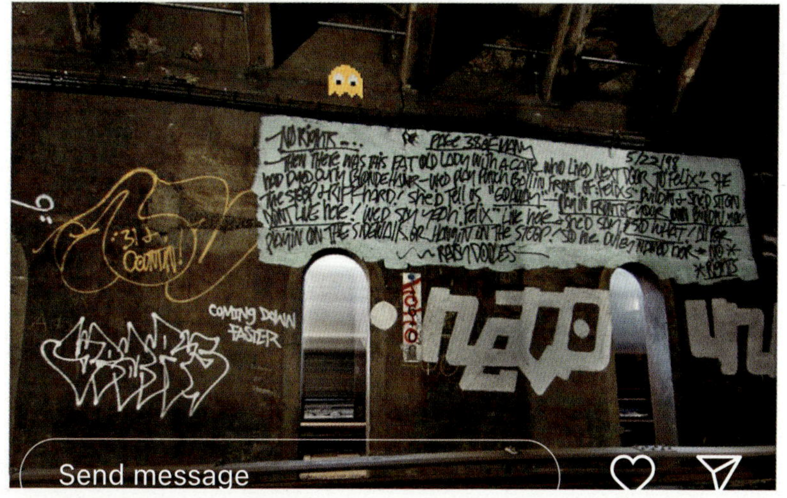

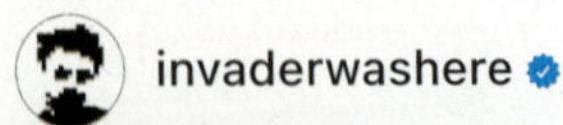

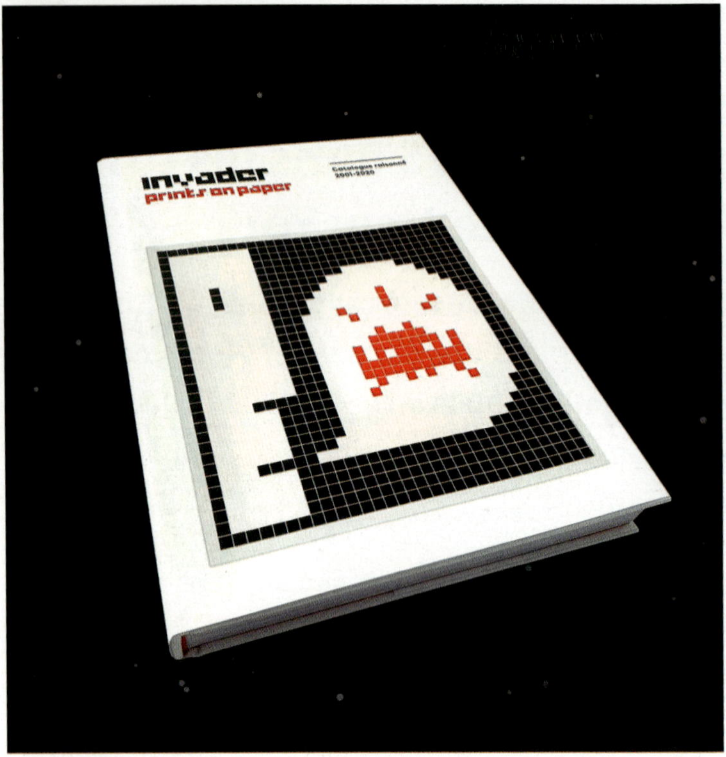

12 586 likes

invaderwashere Since the first mechanical printing processes have been invented, artists have used them to spread their creations. I have myself started printing with silkscreen process when I was a teenager and I still do. Those prints are part of my work and a great way to share it widely. The invitation from MGLC gave me the opportunity to gather and present all of my prints on paper in an exhibition but also in a eponymous catalogue raisonné. PRINTS ON PAPER / 224 p / Now on the Space shop (link in bio) and in good French bookstores #newbook #prints #catalogueraisonné #controlpeditions #mglc

View all 446 comments

17 February 2021

invaderwashere 24 February 2021

SE D'AFFICHER
PEINE D'AMENDE

POST NO BILLS !

Send message  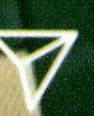

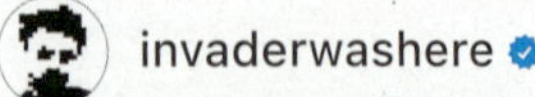

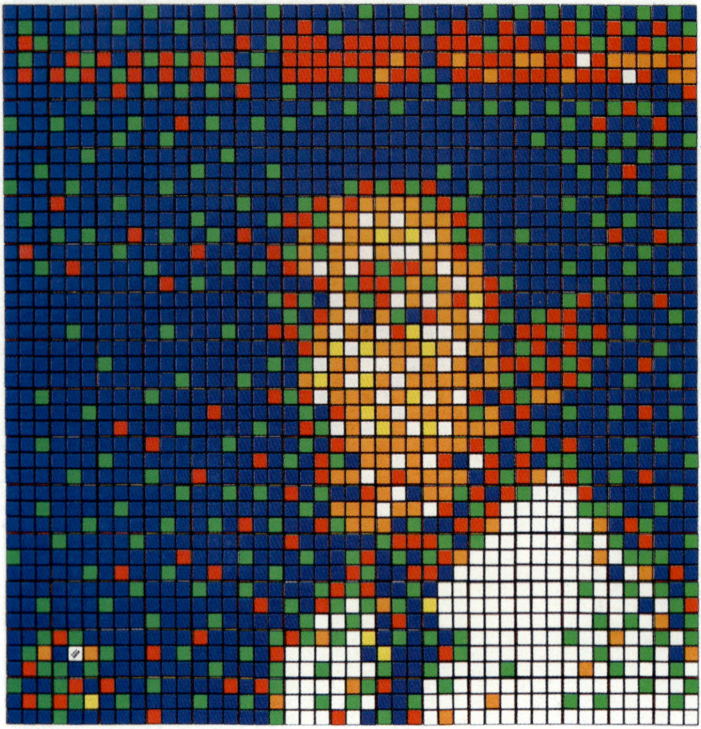

 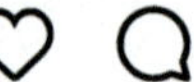   

9 859 likes

invaderwashere L'Étonnant Serge Gainsbourg / Aux Armes et cætera / Bad News from the Stars #rubikcubism #lowfidelity #3albums #gainsbourg #sergegainsbourg #30years #rip

View all 104 comments

2 March 2021

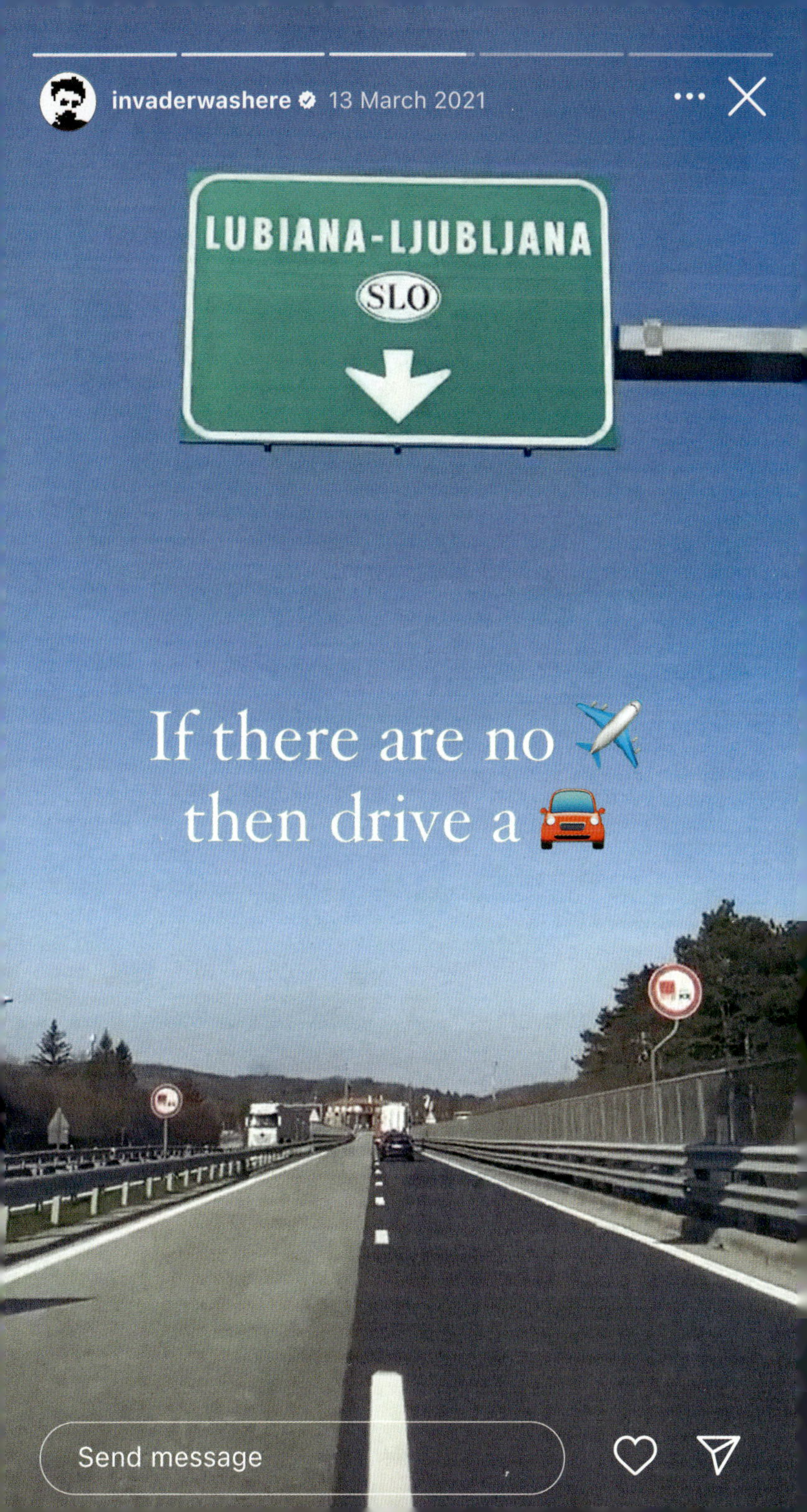

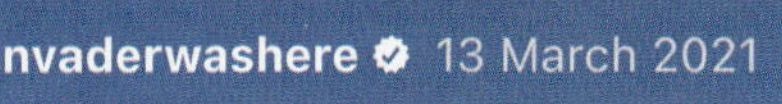

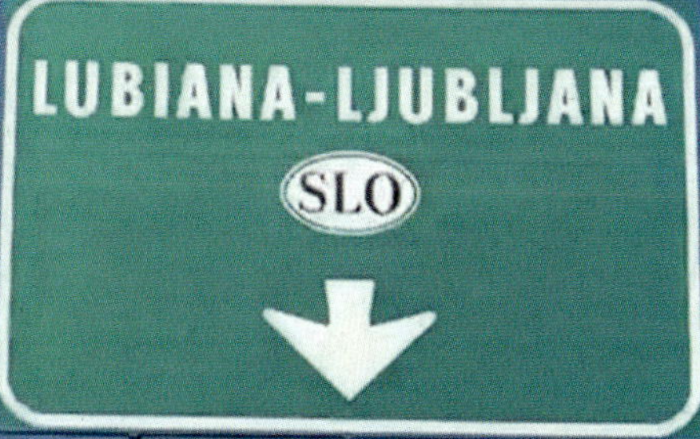

If there are no ✈️
then drive a 🚗

Send message

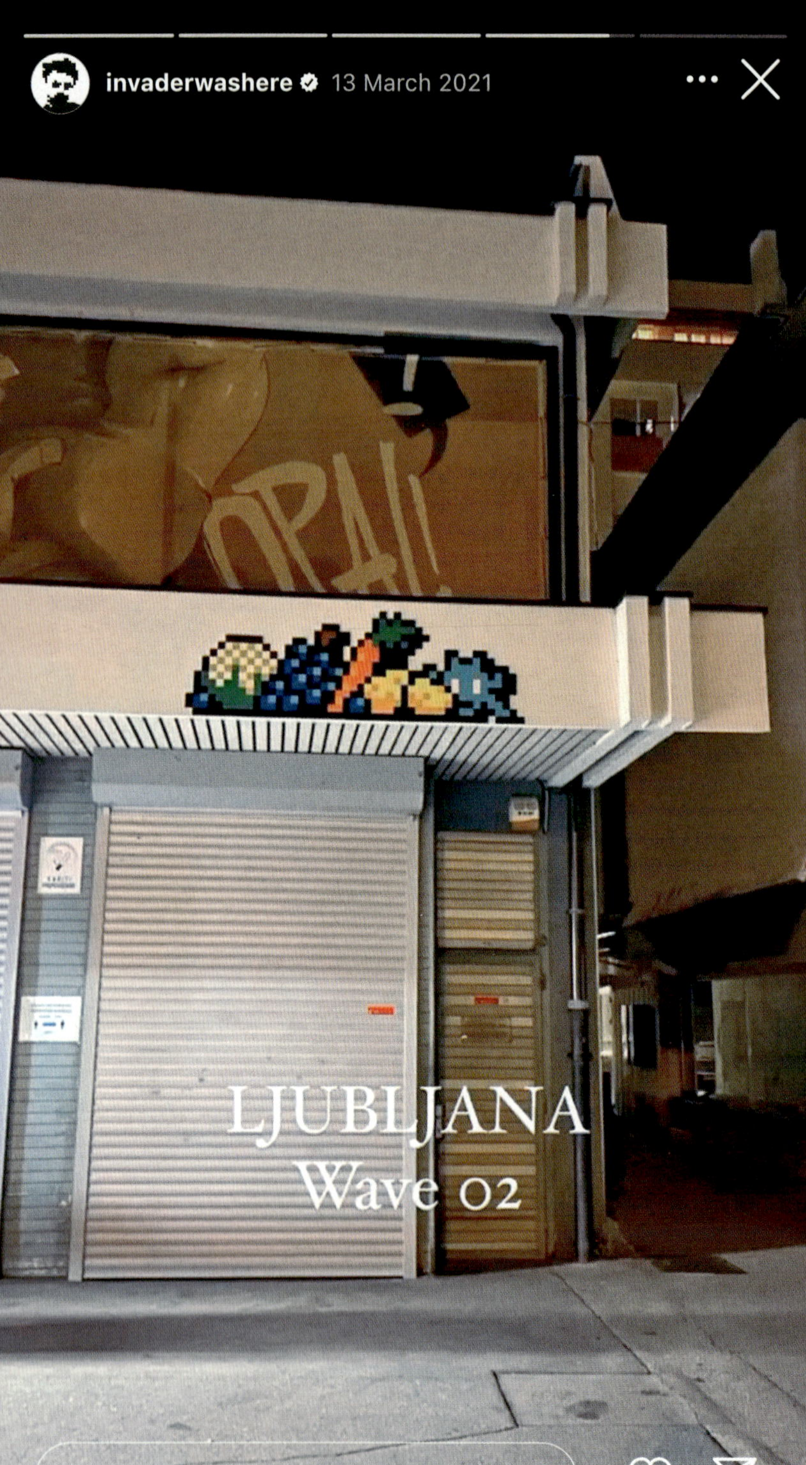

invaderwashere
13 March 2021
OPAL
LJUBLJANA
Wave 02
Send message

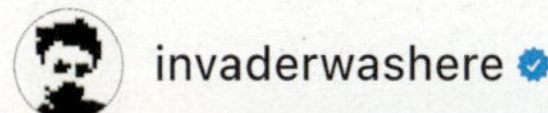

invaderwashere

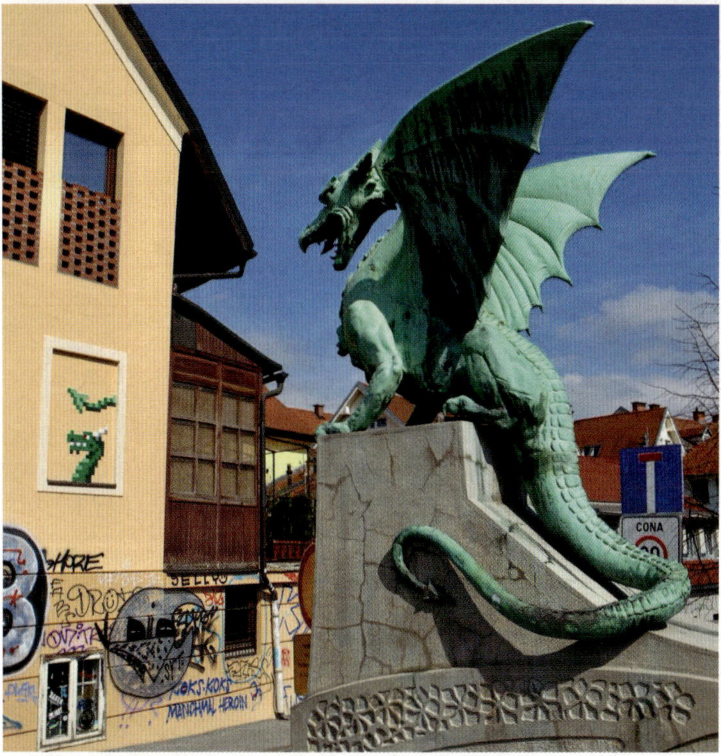

15 664 likes

invaderwashere 15 years after my first visit to Ljubljana, I'm back for a 2nd invasion wave... #ljubljana #slovenia #wave02 #dragonsbridge Photo: @alternativeljubljana

View all 134 comments

15 March 2021

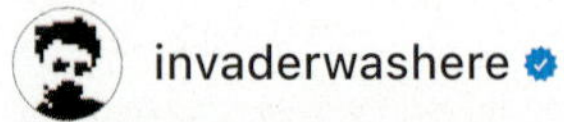

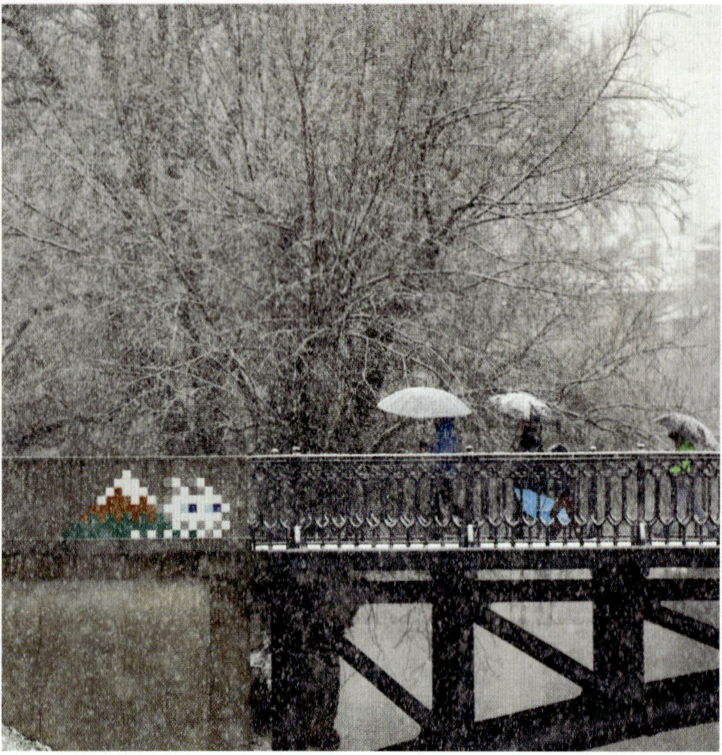

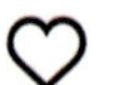 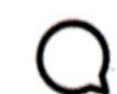 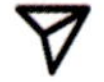 

9 410 likes

invaderwashere ❄️⬅️➡️☀️
#ljubjana #lju_25

View all 81 comments

17 March 2021

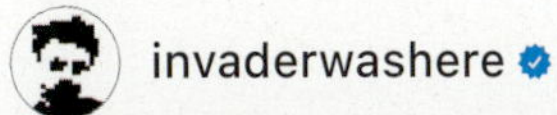

•••

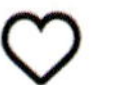  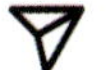 

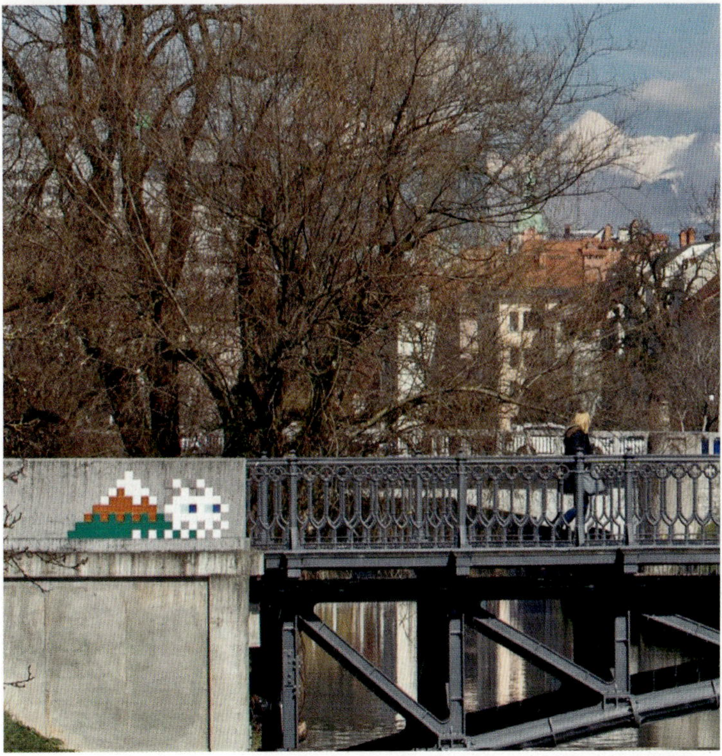

9 410 likes

invaderwashere ❄️⬅️➡️☀️
#ljubjana #lju_25

View all 81 comments

17 March 2021

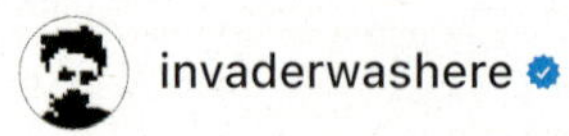

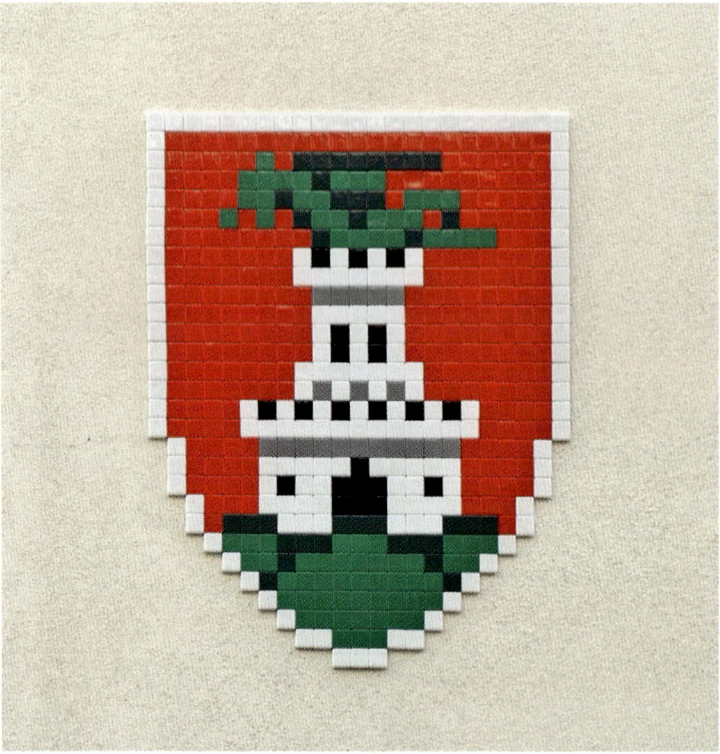

9 349 likes

invaderwashere 8-bit Ljubljana blazon #lju_34 #ljubljana
🏰🐉👾

View all 52 comments

18 March 2021

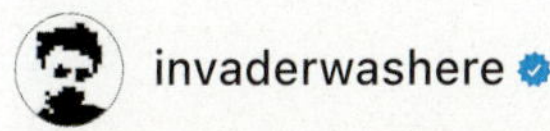

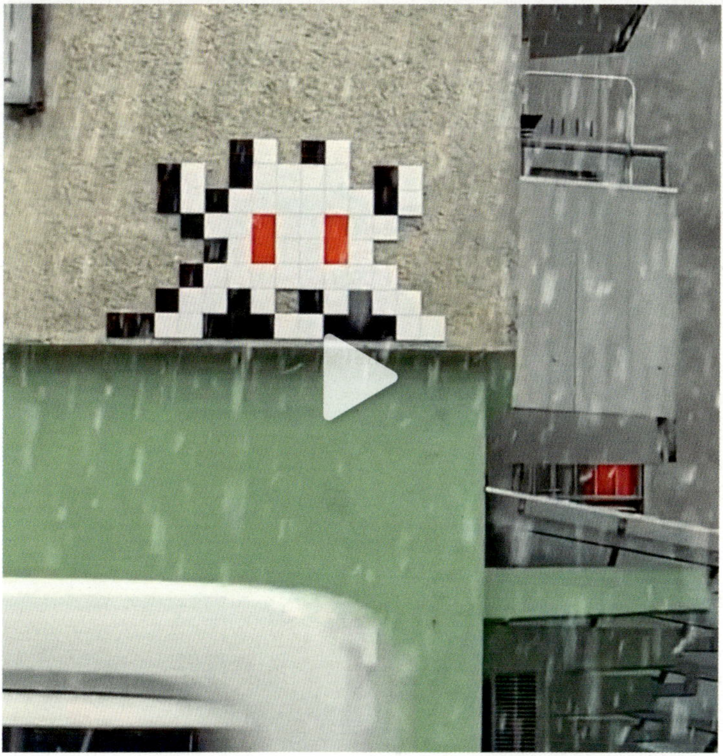

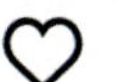  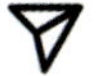 

27 926 views

invaderwashere LJU_28 ❄️ 👾 #ljubljana #wave2

View all 53 comments

19 March 2021

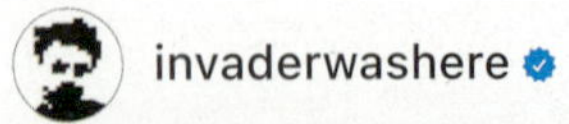

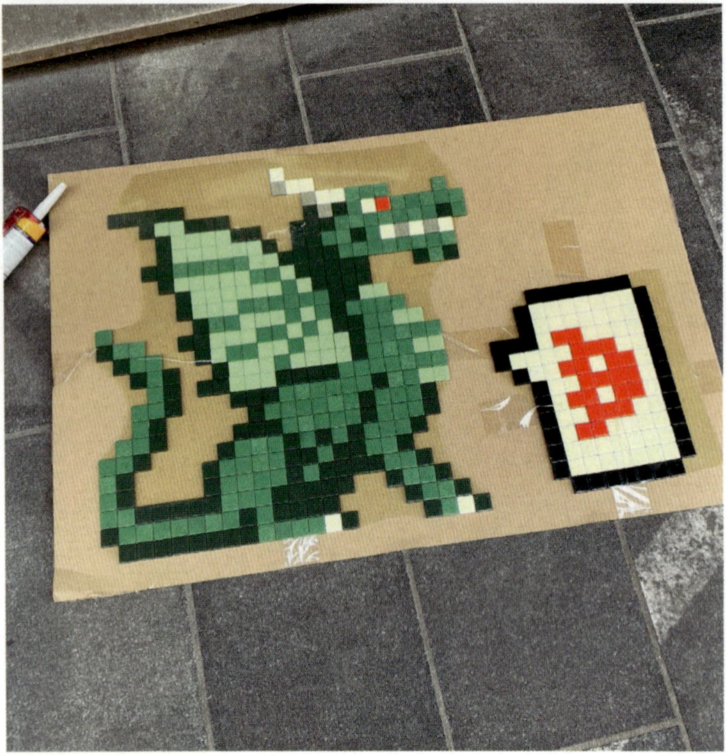

21793 likes

invaderwashere LJU_33 #ljubljana #wave2

View all 168 comments

21 March 2021

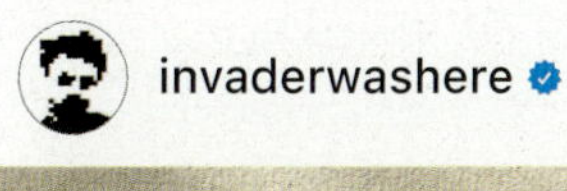

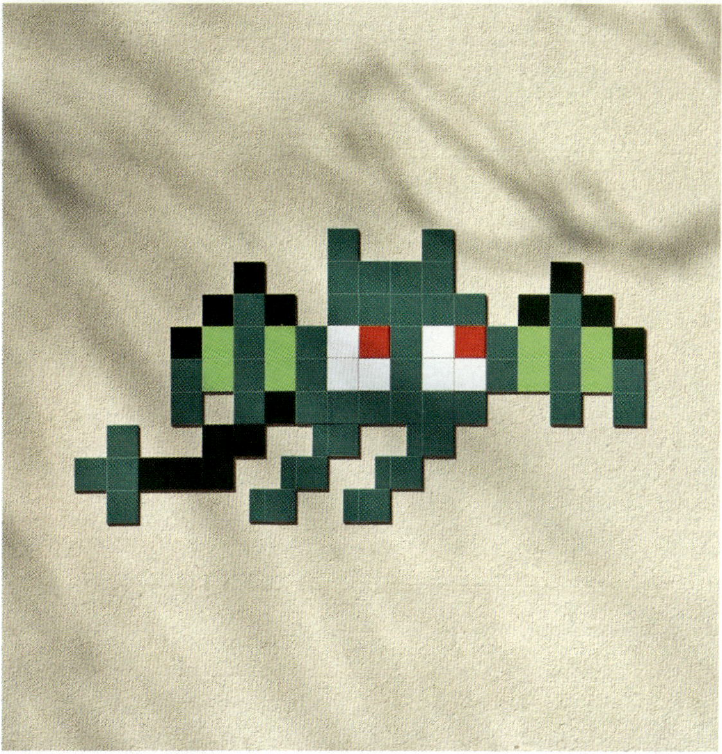

13 568 likes

invaderwashere LJU_42 🐉👾 the latest of the second wave of the invasion of Ljubljana #ljubljana #wave2 #2021

View all 78 comments

25 March 2021

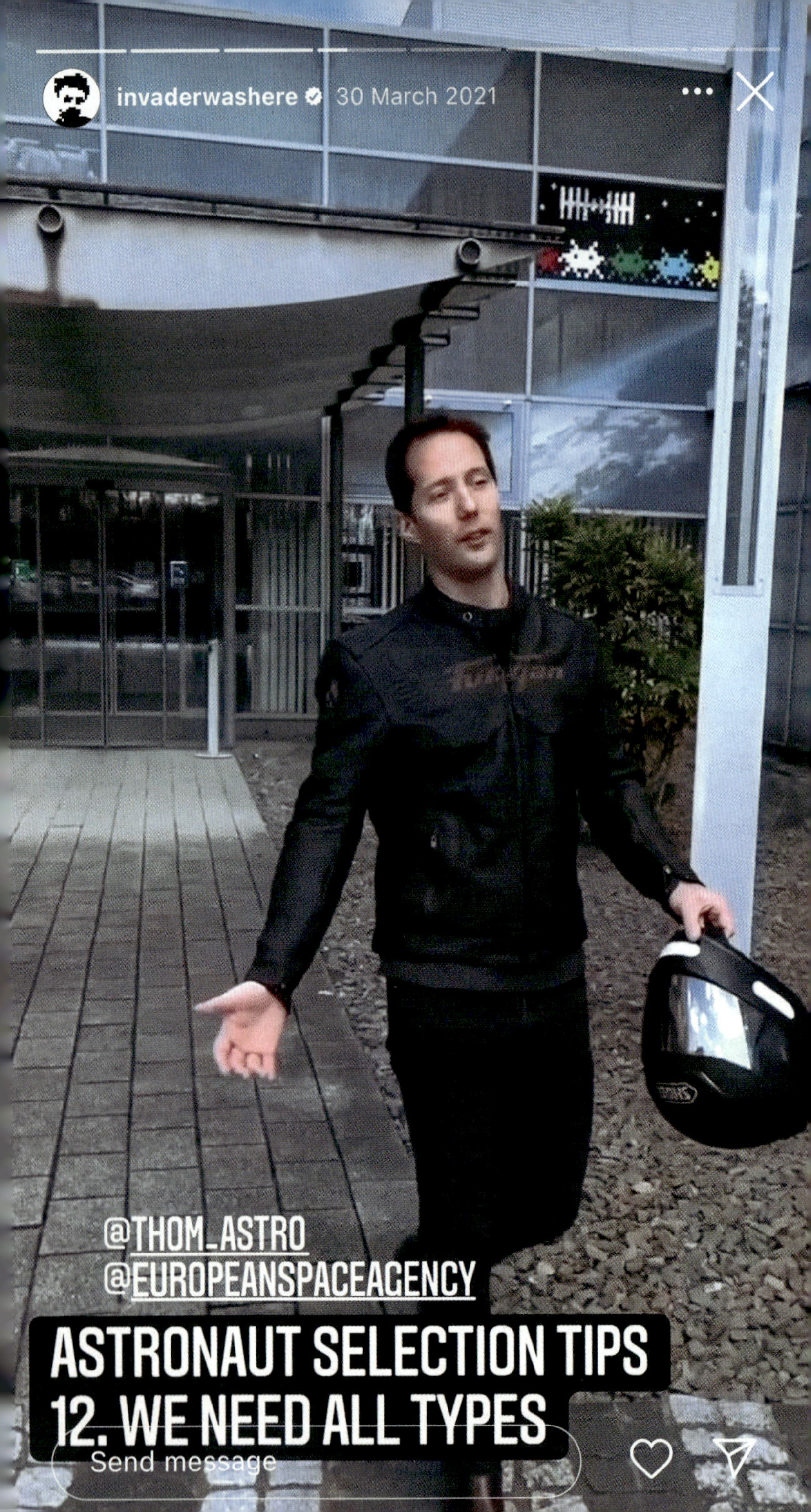
invaderwashere 30 March 2021
@THOM_ASTRO
@EUROPEANSPACEAGENCY
ASTRONAUT SELECTION TIPS
12. WE NEED ALL TYPES
Send message

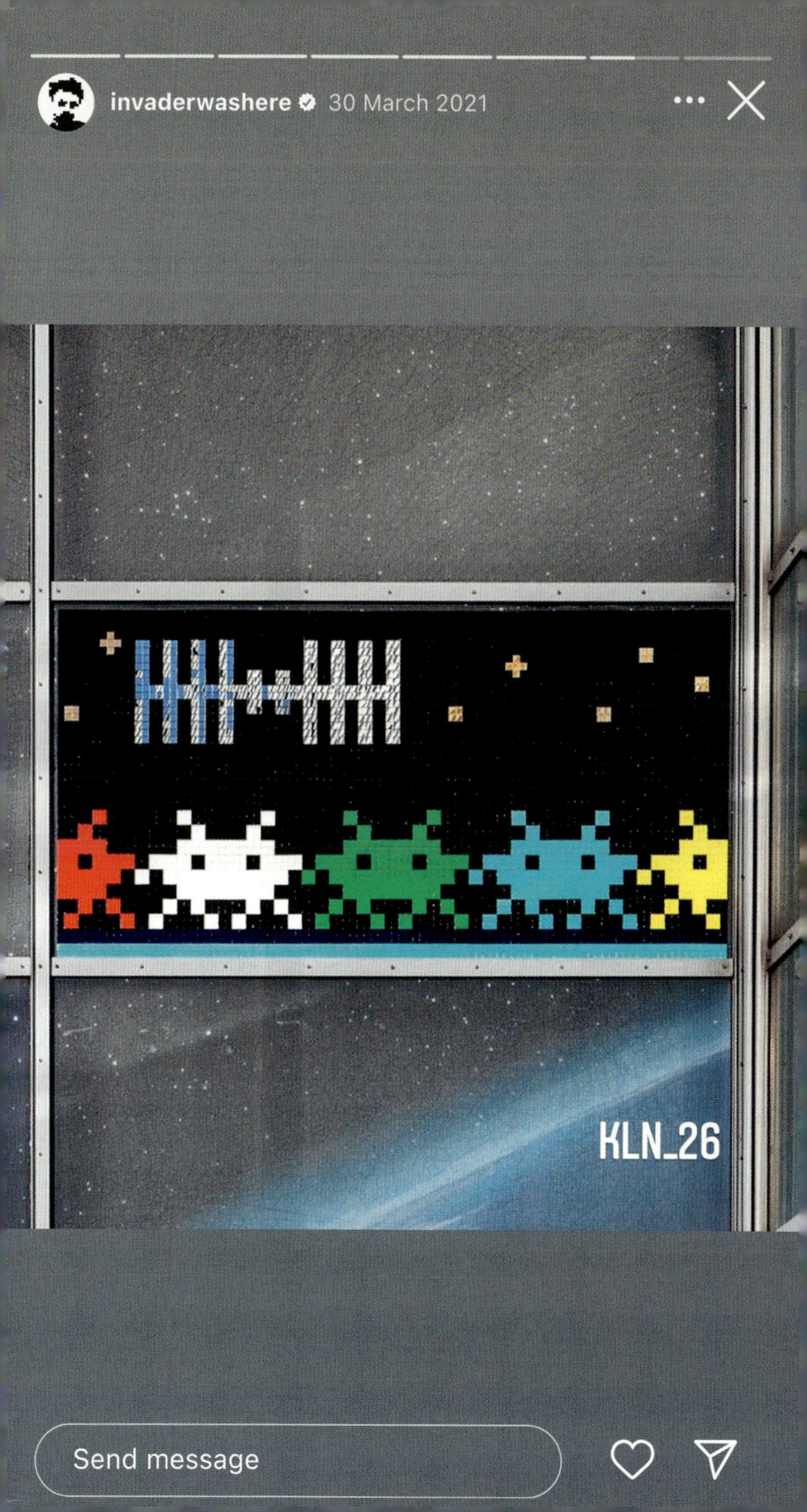

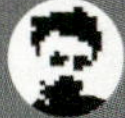

invaderwashere 30 March 2021

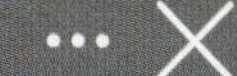

KLN_26

Send message

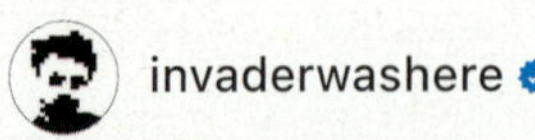

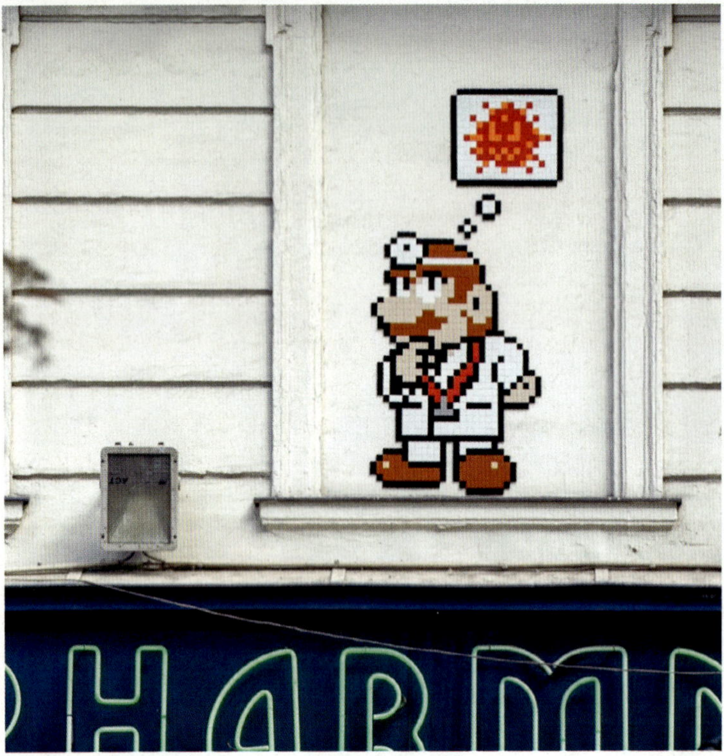

16 060 likes

invaderwashere PA_1461 / Dr Mario 2021 🦠

View all 177 comments

8 April 2021

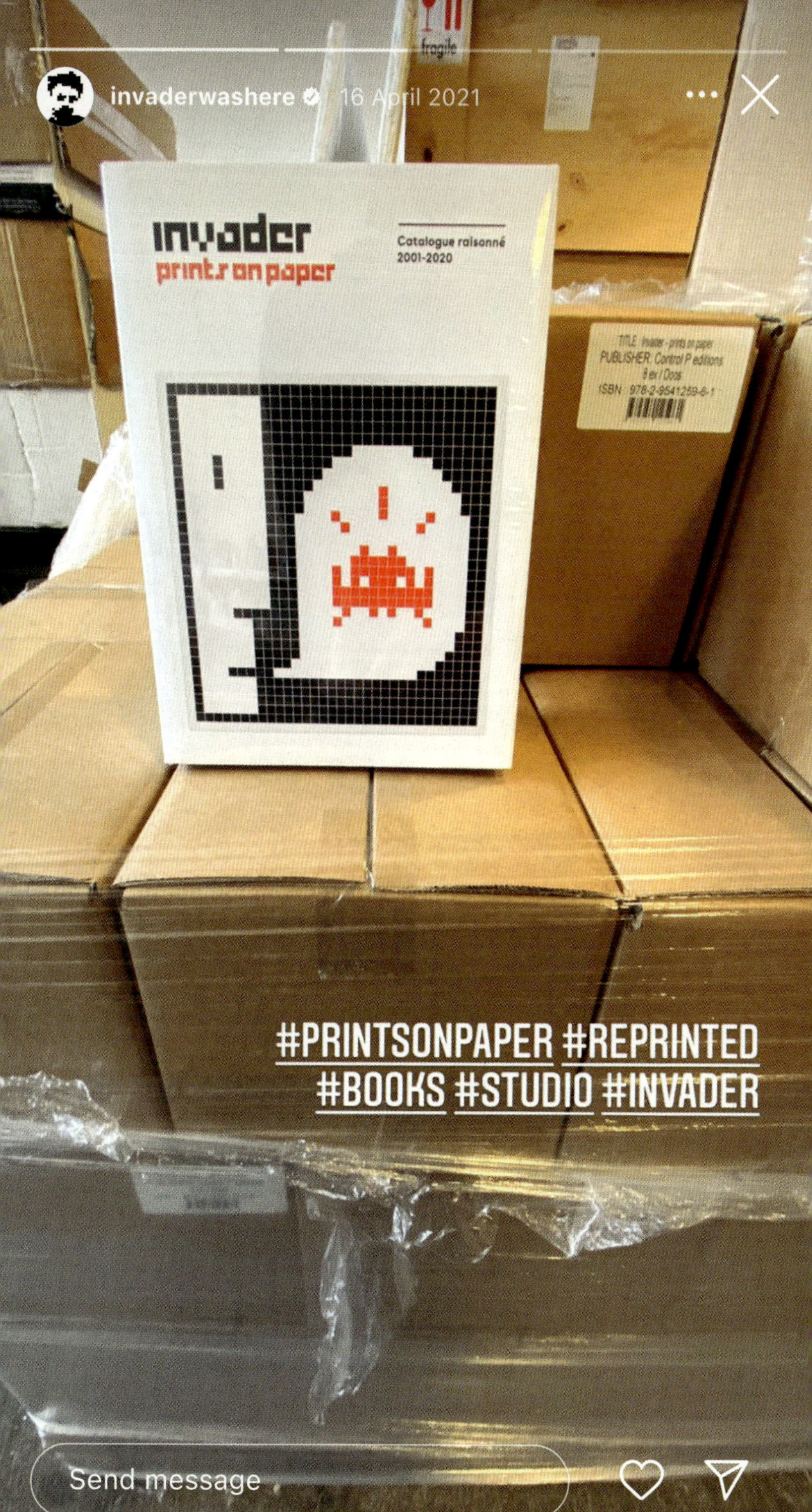

invaderwashere
16 April 2021
fragile
invader
prints on paper
Catalogue raisonné
2001-2020
PUBLISHER Control P editions
#PRINTSONPAPER #REPRINTED
#BOOKS #STUDIO #INVADER
Send message

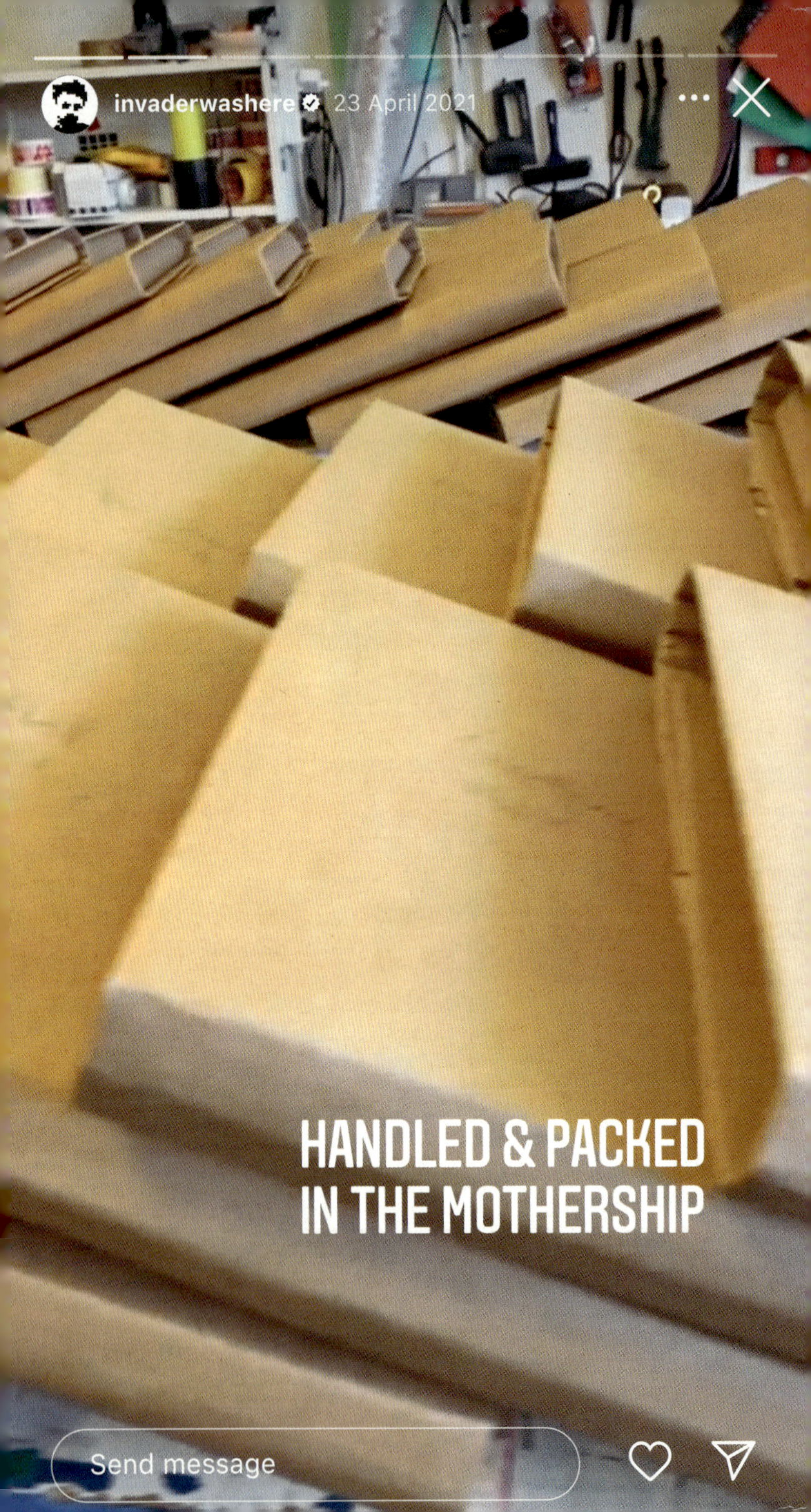
invaderwashere
23 April 2021
HANDLED & PACKED
IN THE MOTHERSHIP
Send message

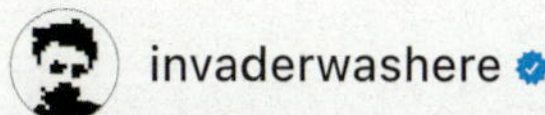

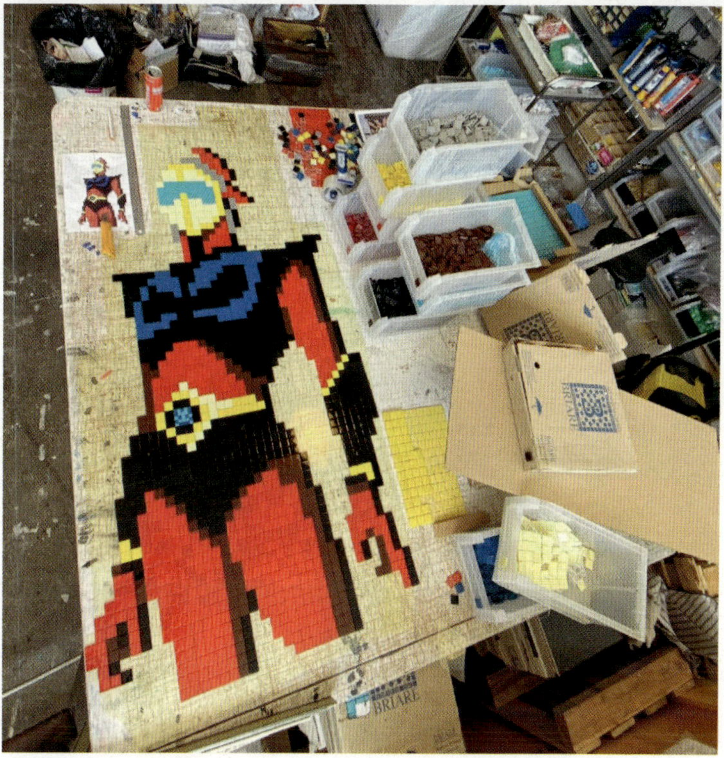

17 523 likes

invaderwashere Actarus is the main character of the japanese anime Goldorak (Grendizer). In France, he blew up the mind of all the children of my generation #actarus #goldorak #grendizer #anime #japan #manga #gonagai #childhood #legend #mygeneration

View all 422 comments

29 April 2021

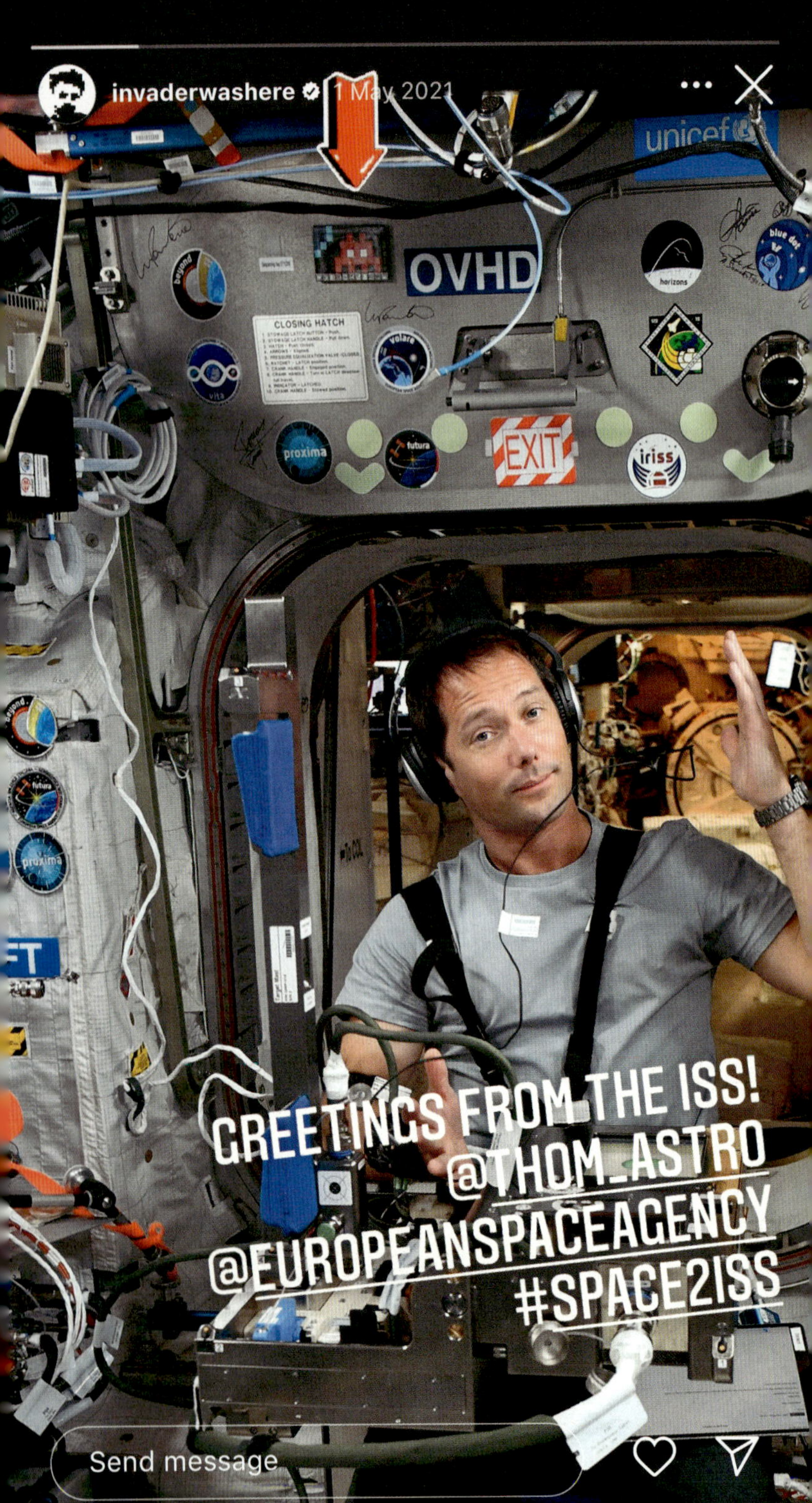
invaderwashere
1 May 2021
unicef
OVHD
CLOSING HATCH
EXIT
proxima
futura
volare
vita
beyond
horizons
iriss
blue dot
GREETINGS FROM THE ISS!
@THOM_ASTRO
@EUROPEANSPACEAGENCY
#SPACE2ISS
Send message

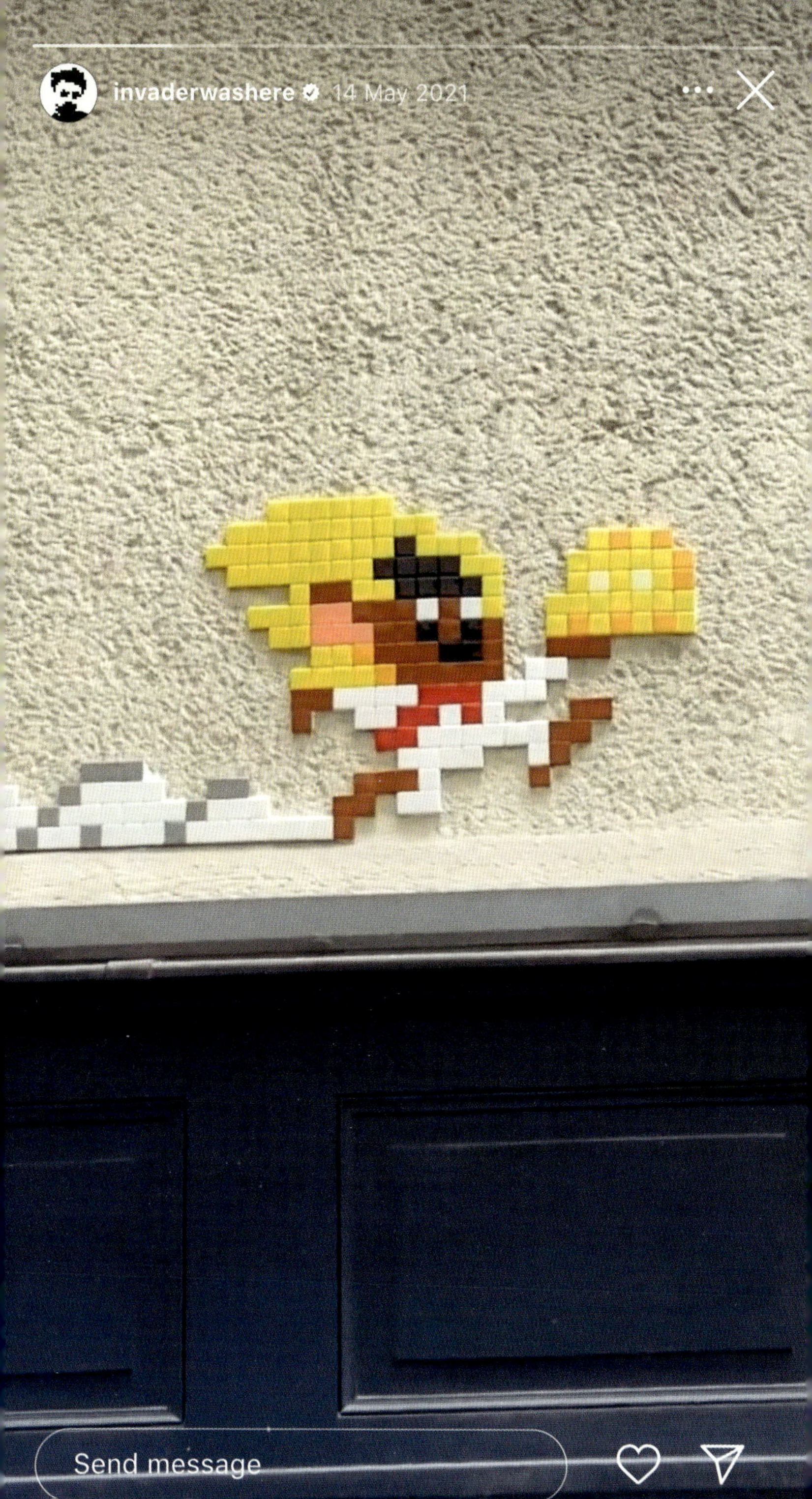
invaderwashere
14 May 2021
Send message

invaderwashere

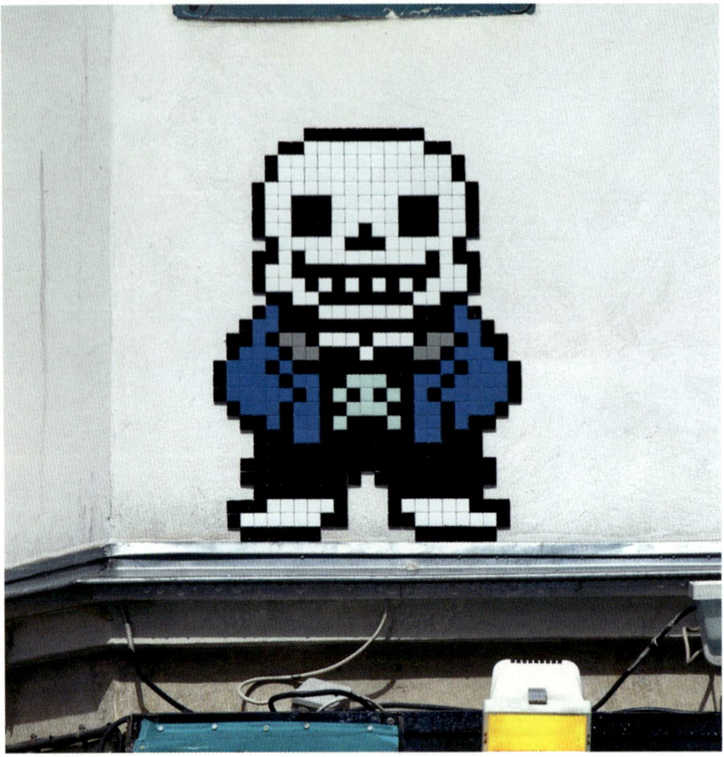

16 564 likes

invaderwashere PA_1464 appeared last night in Paris #undertale #sans #zigzag #terasse Keep safe 🖤

View all 167 comments

19 May 2021

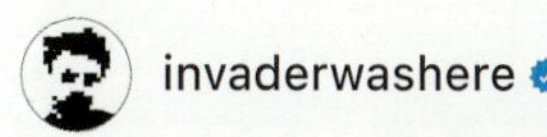

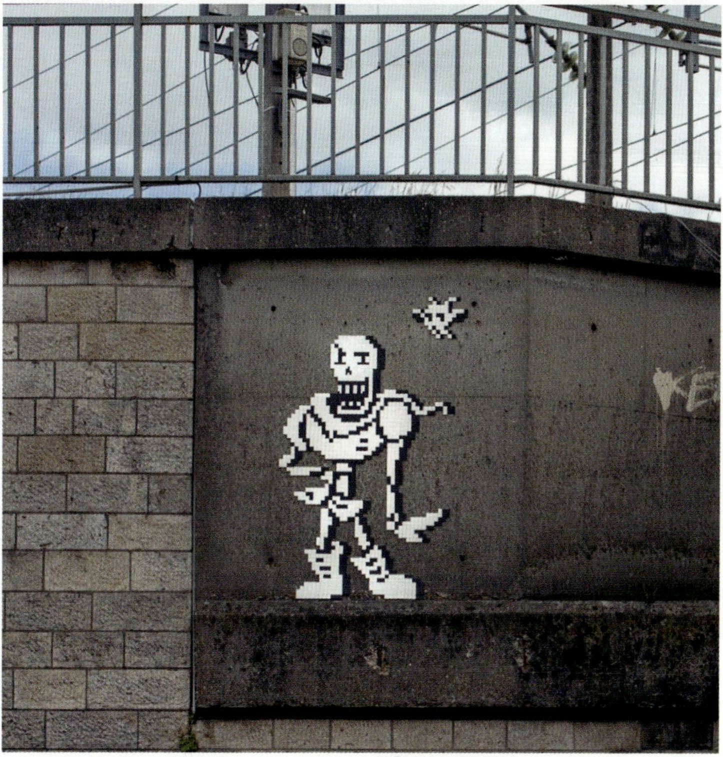

17 251 likes

invaderwashere PA_1465 💀 🦴 👾 #undertale #papyrus #skeleton #underground #videogame #reality

View all 155 comments

27 May 2021

invaderwashere 1 June 2021

our gallery, score points and compete
other players.
d luck & have fun !

ality game by INVADER

TEST SUCCESSFUL "F
675 Players / 10 000 832 Flashes

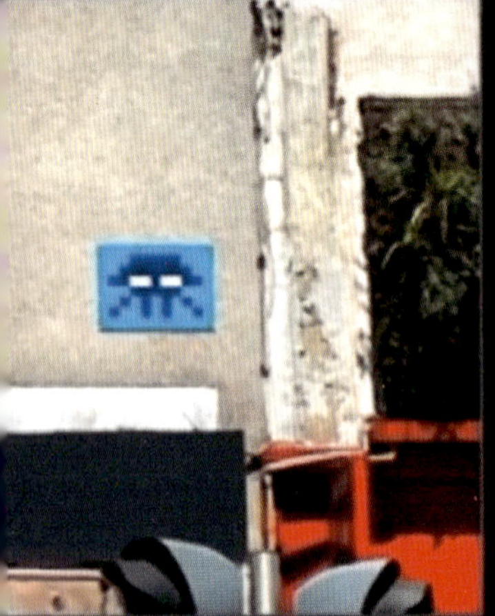

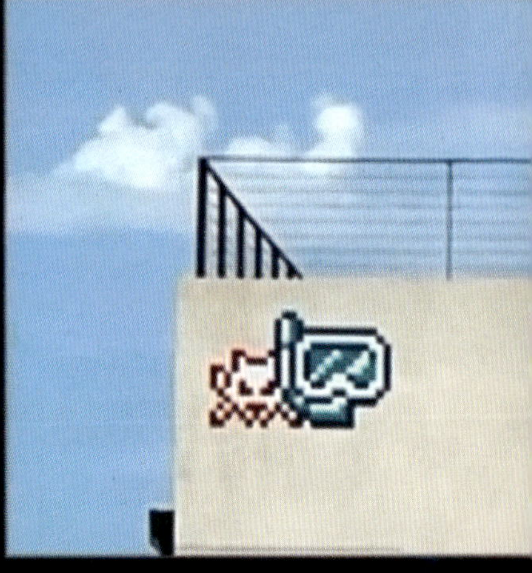

ROMAINORCHIDS
conds ago

Marseille, ANONYMOUS
16 seconds ago

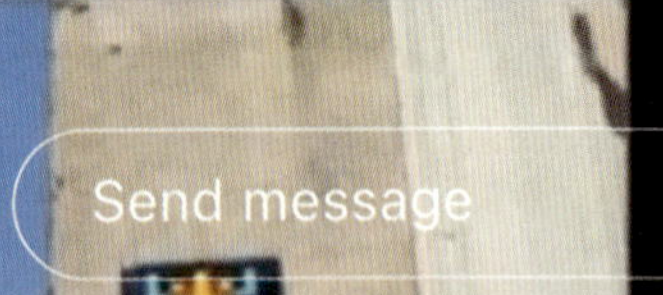

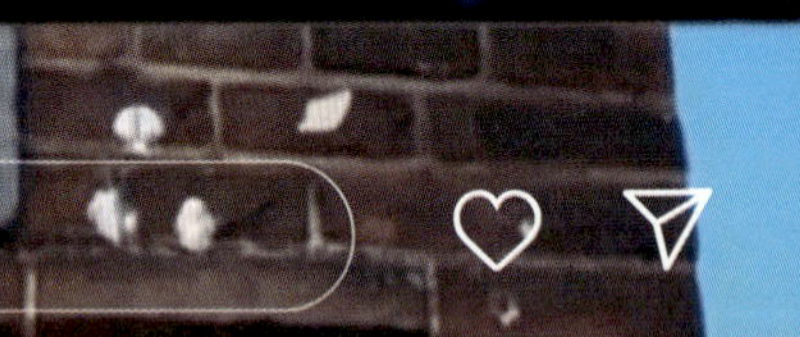

Send message

invaderwashere 1 June 2021

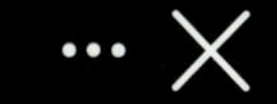

Just passed 10 Millions Flashes

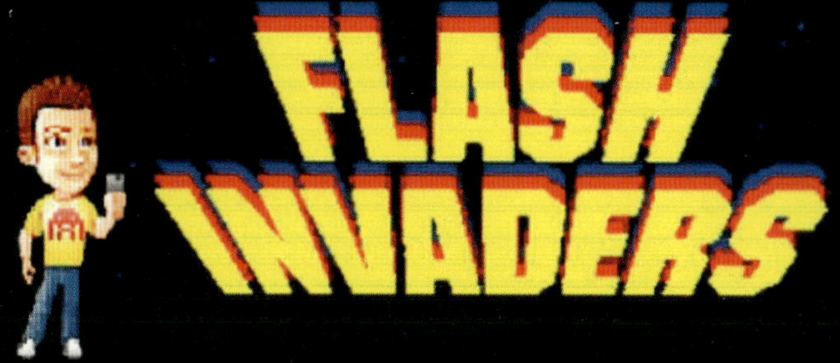

A FREE APP FOR SMARTPHONES

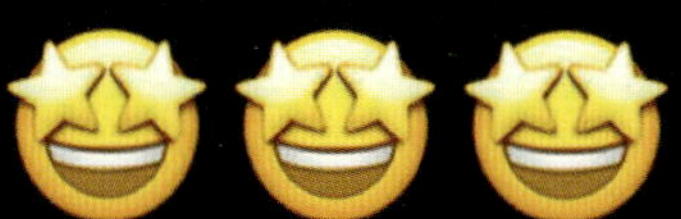

Swipe up to enter the flux

...

Send message

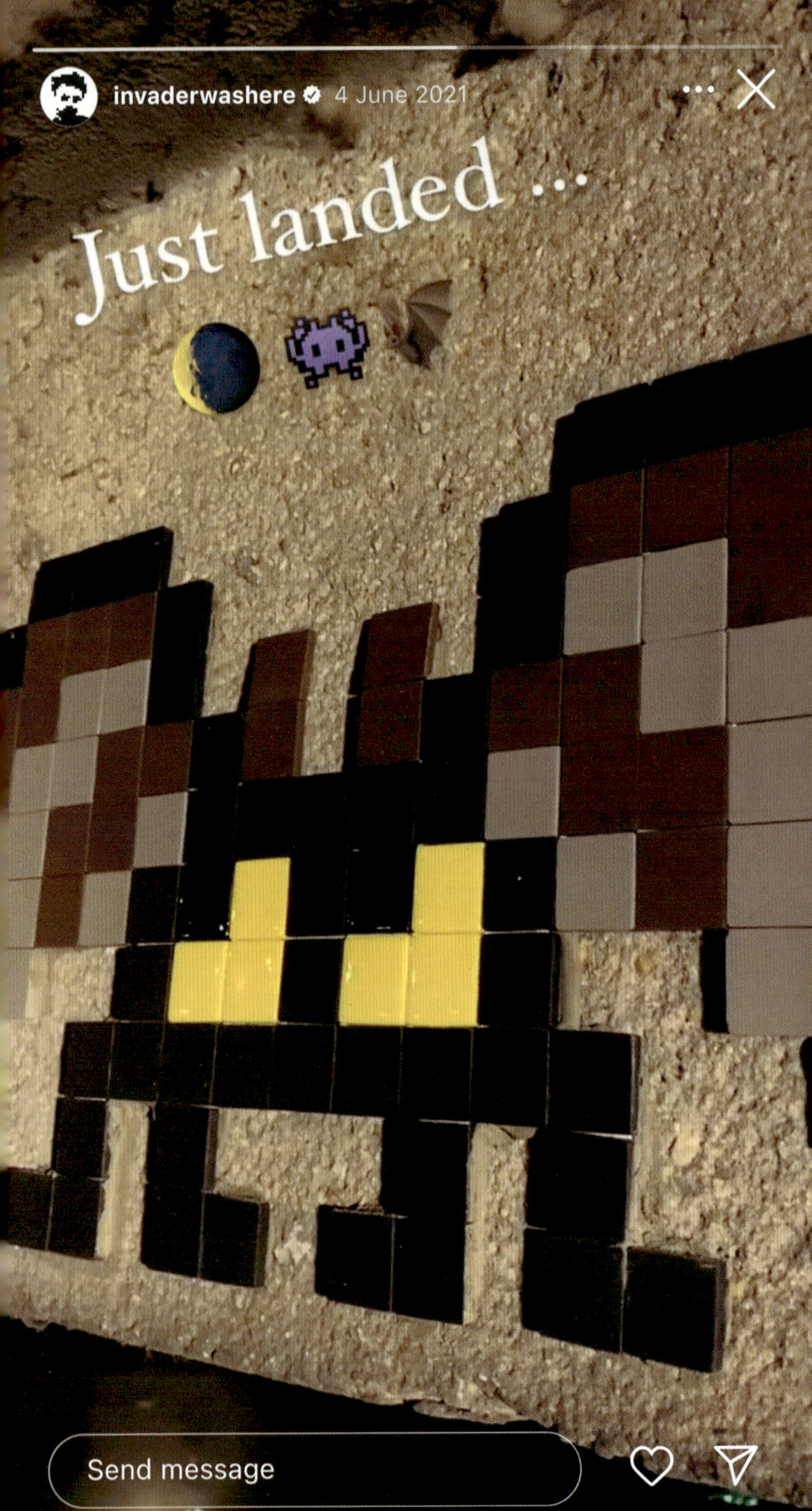
invaderwashere 4 June 2021
Just landed ...
Send message

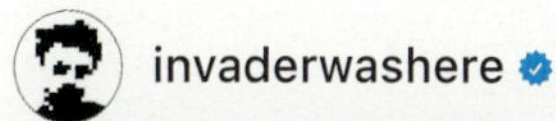

•••

 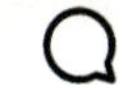 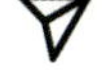 

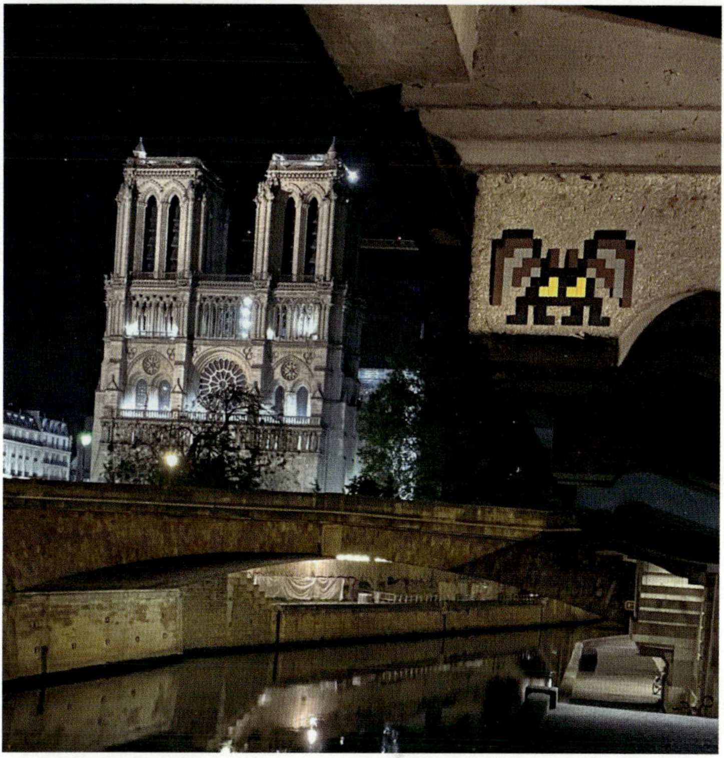

15 511 likes

invaderwashere PA_1466 the bats have left the bell tower
#batinvader #notredame #seine #paris #gargouille #goth

View all 147 comments

4 June 2021

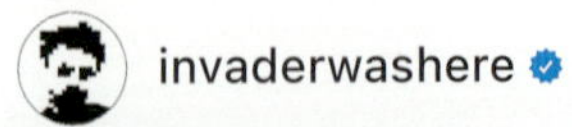

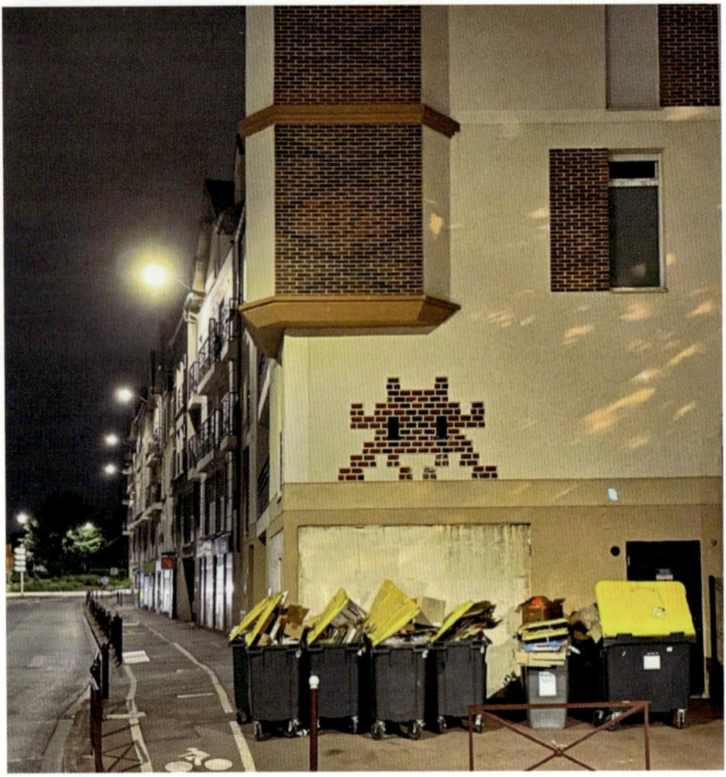

  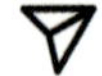 

13 962 likes

invaderwashere PA_1467 Another brick in the wall...

View all 195 comments

11 June 2021

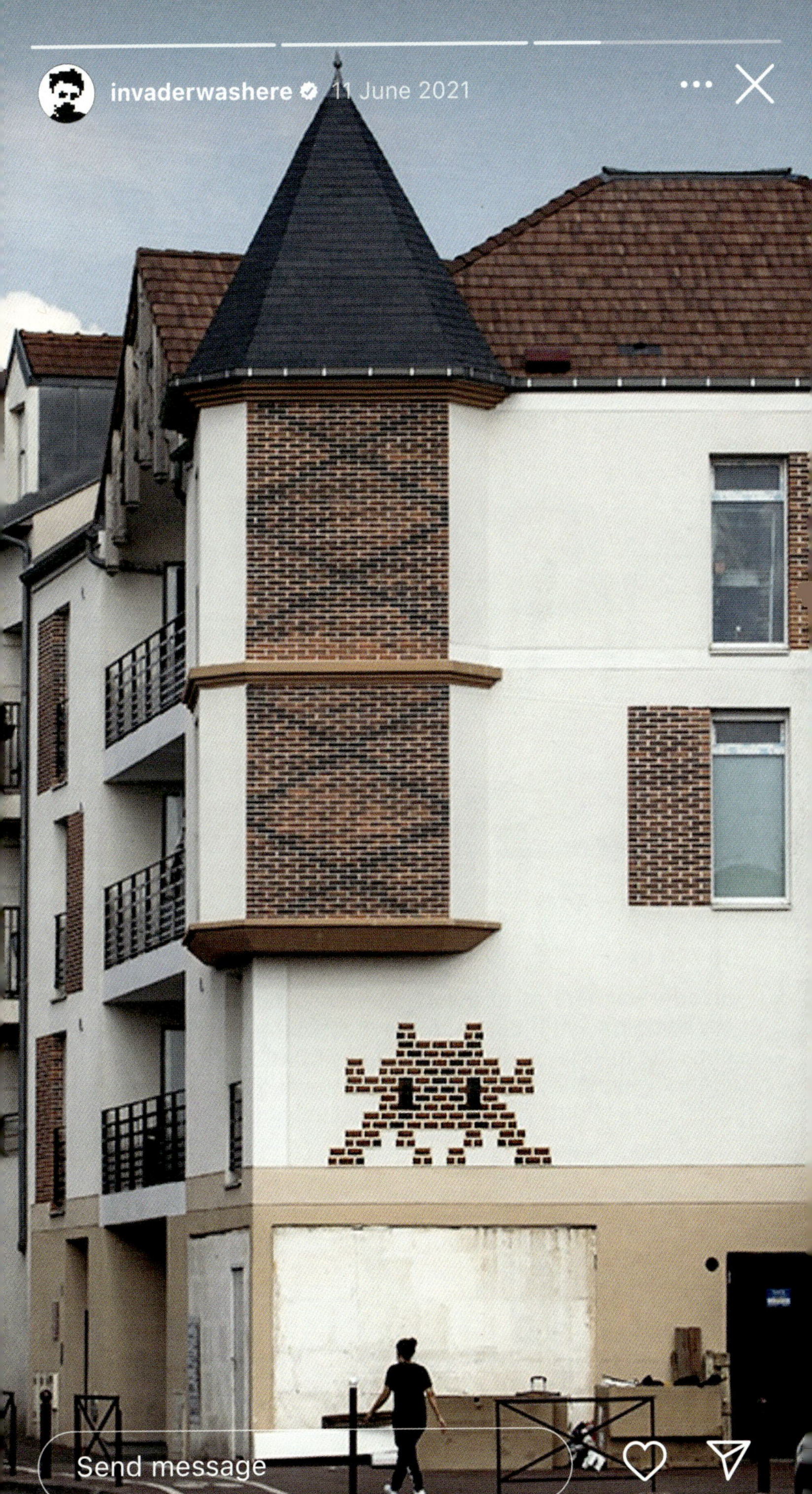
invaderwashere
11 June 2021
Send message

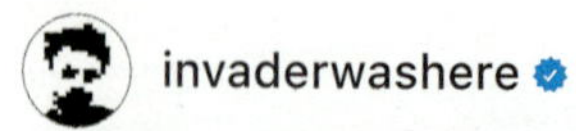

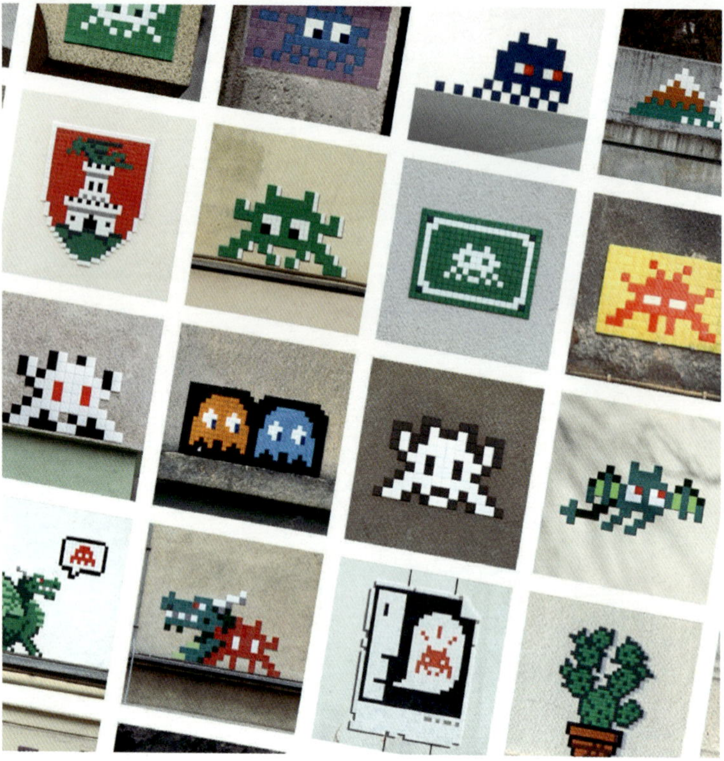

10 736 likes

invaderwashere All of the 42 space invaders of Ljubljana are back in town!!! Big up to the reactivators for putting back the missing or damaged pieces from 2006 #reactivations #fullscore #visitljubljana and if you're around don't miss "Prints on Paper" @mglcljubljana

View all 93 comments

15 June 2021

invaderwashere 20 June 2021

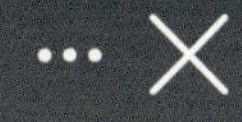

Meanwhile in
Hong Kong...

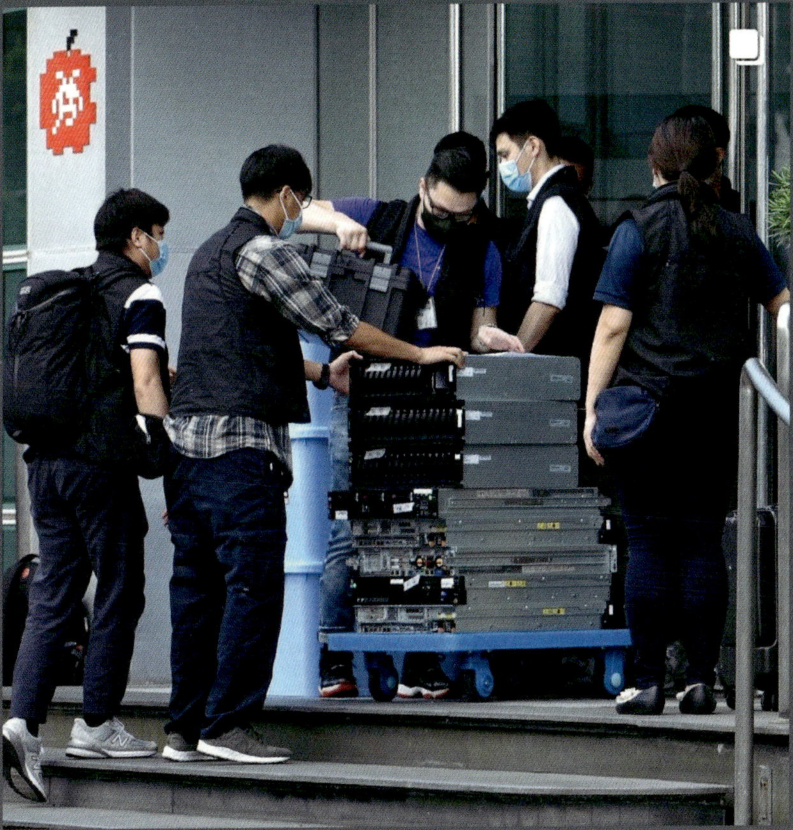

@kassy

...at the Apple Daily
newspaper office

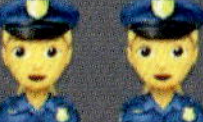 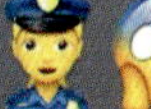 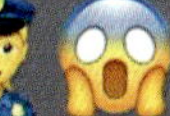

@appledailyhk

Send message

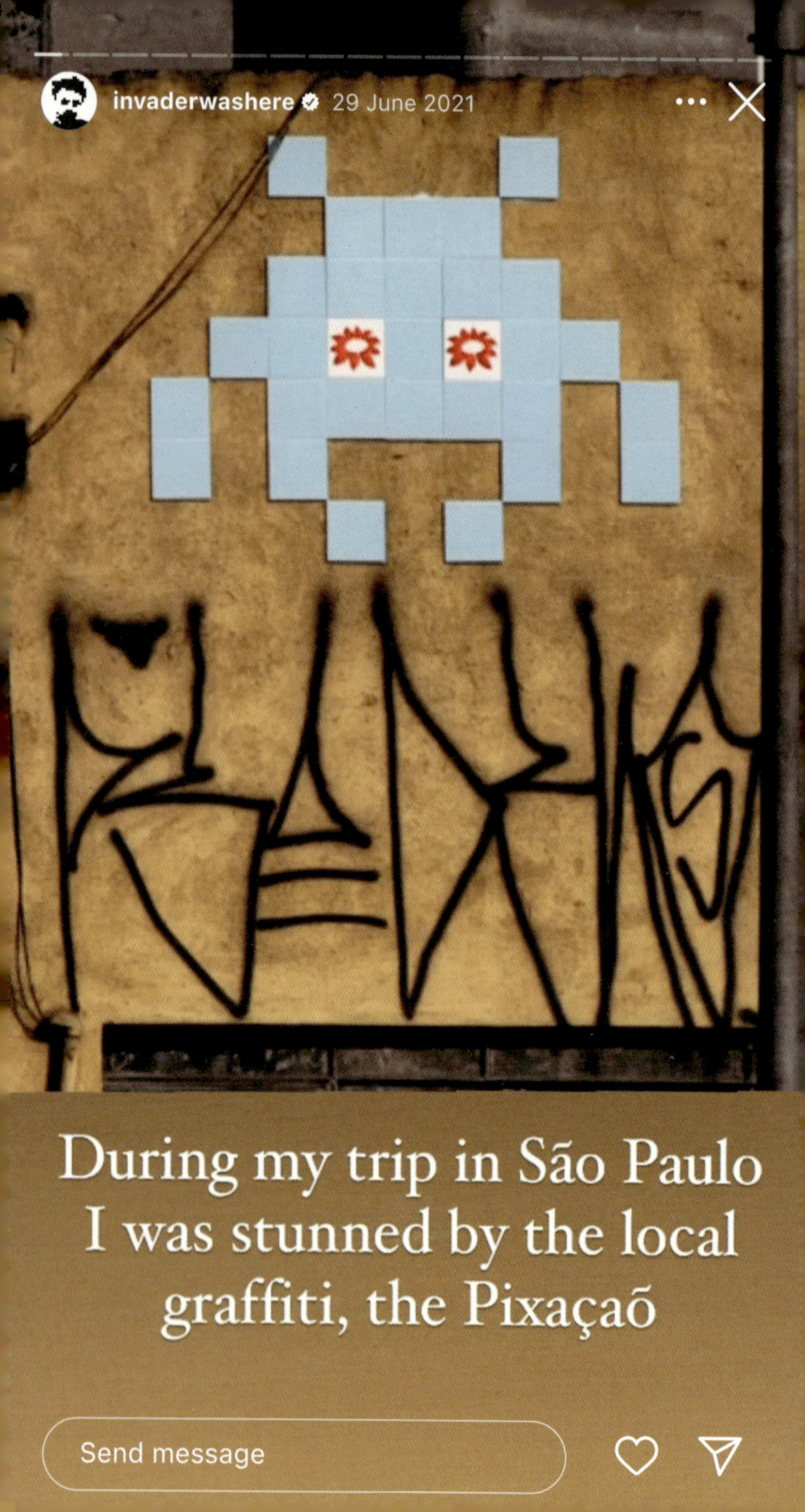

invaderwashere 29 June 2021

During my trip in São Paulo I was stunned by the local graffiti, the Pixaçaõ

Send message

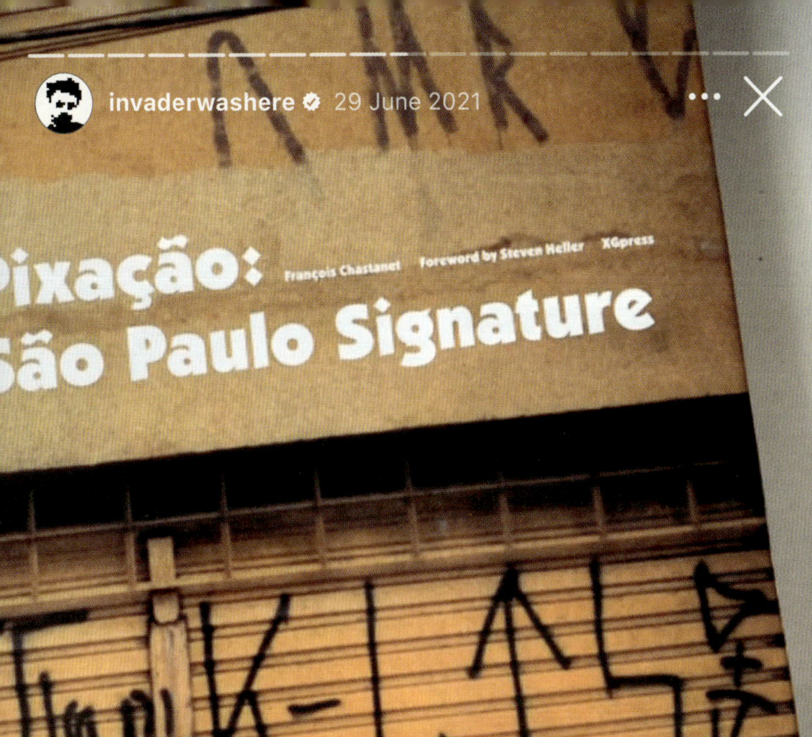

A very good study about it was made by F. Chastenet in his book “Pixaçaõ, São Paulo Signature”

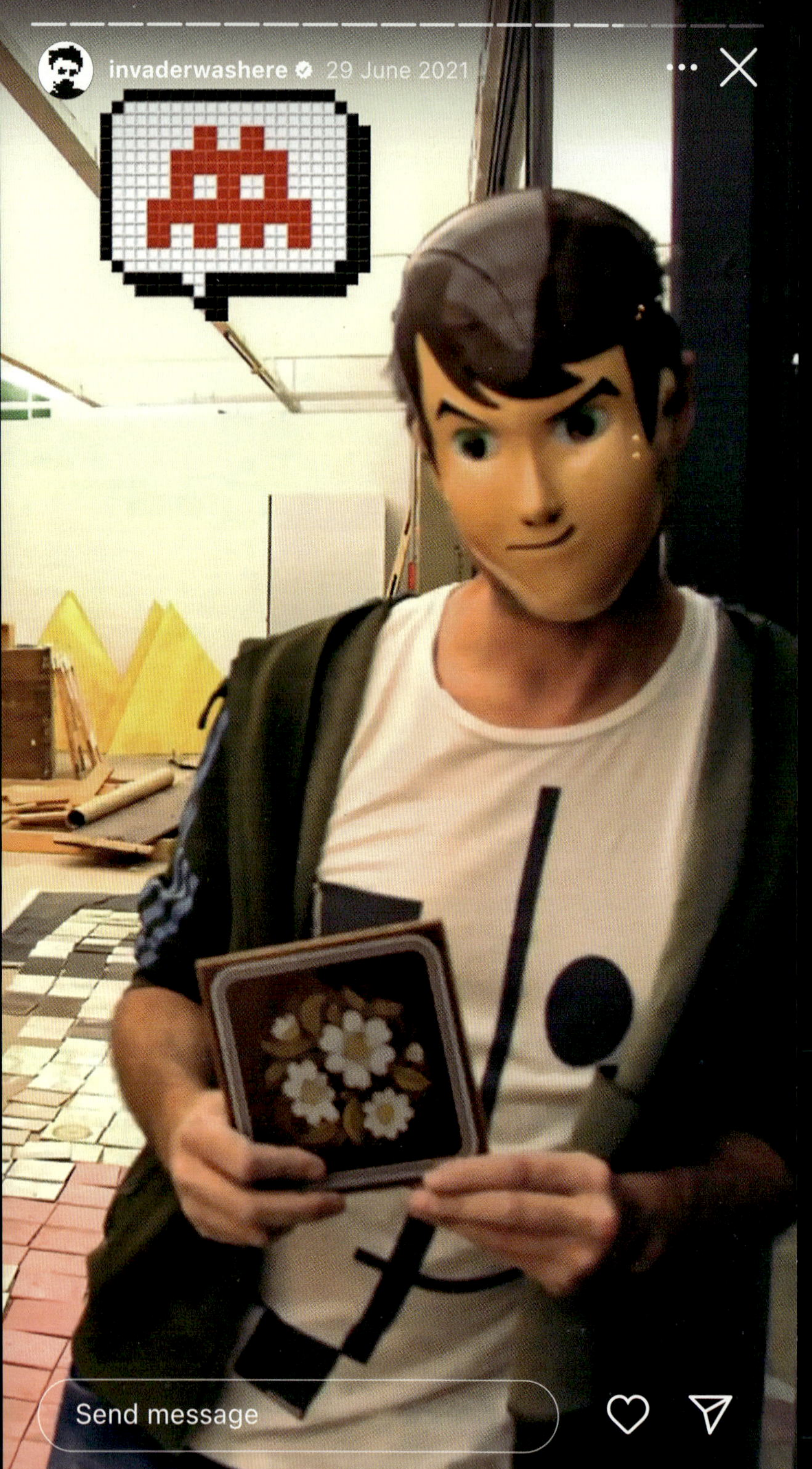
invaderwashere
29 June 2021
Send message

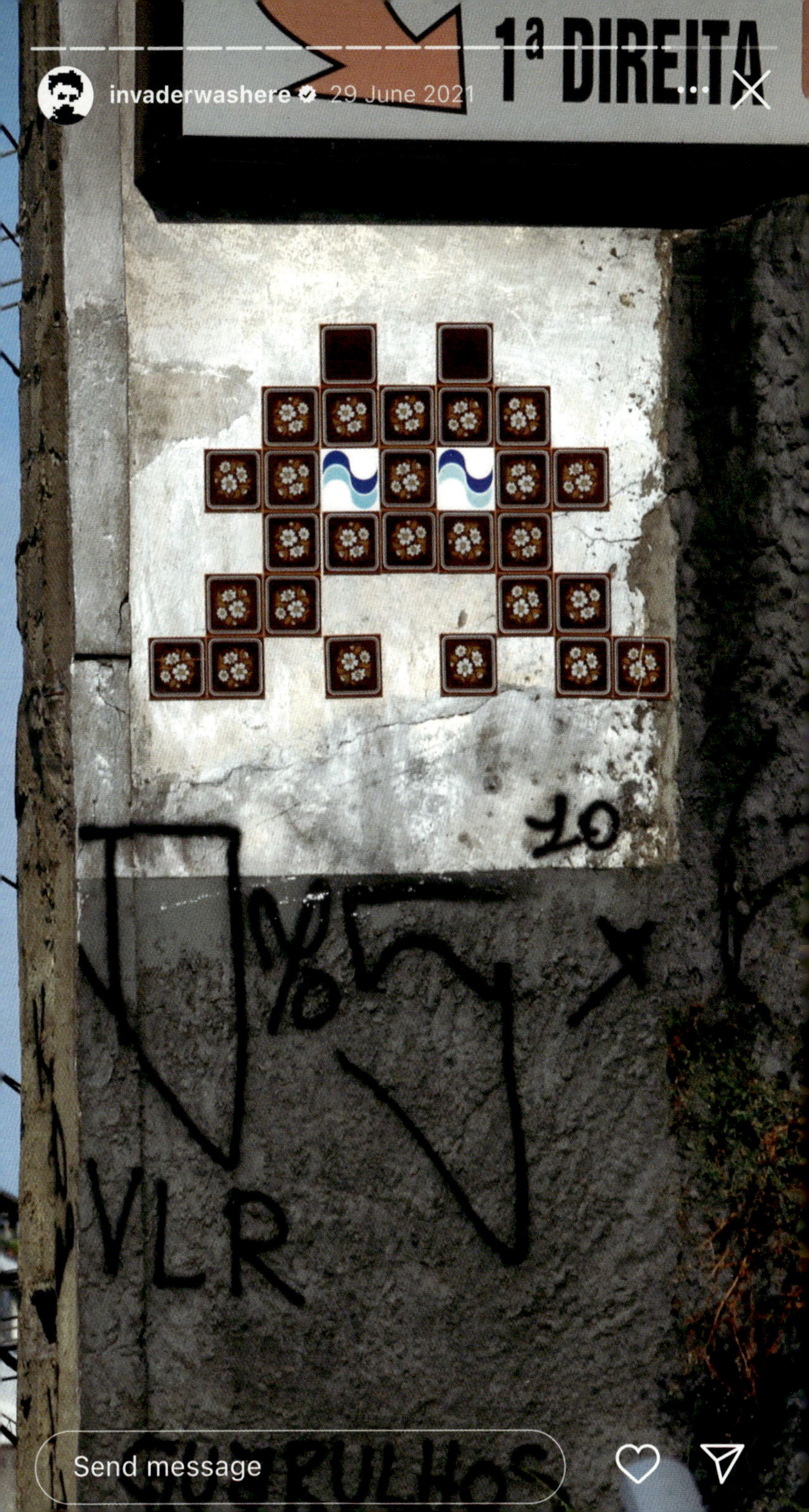
1ª DIREITA
invaderwashere
29 June 2021
VLR
Send message

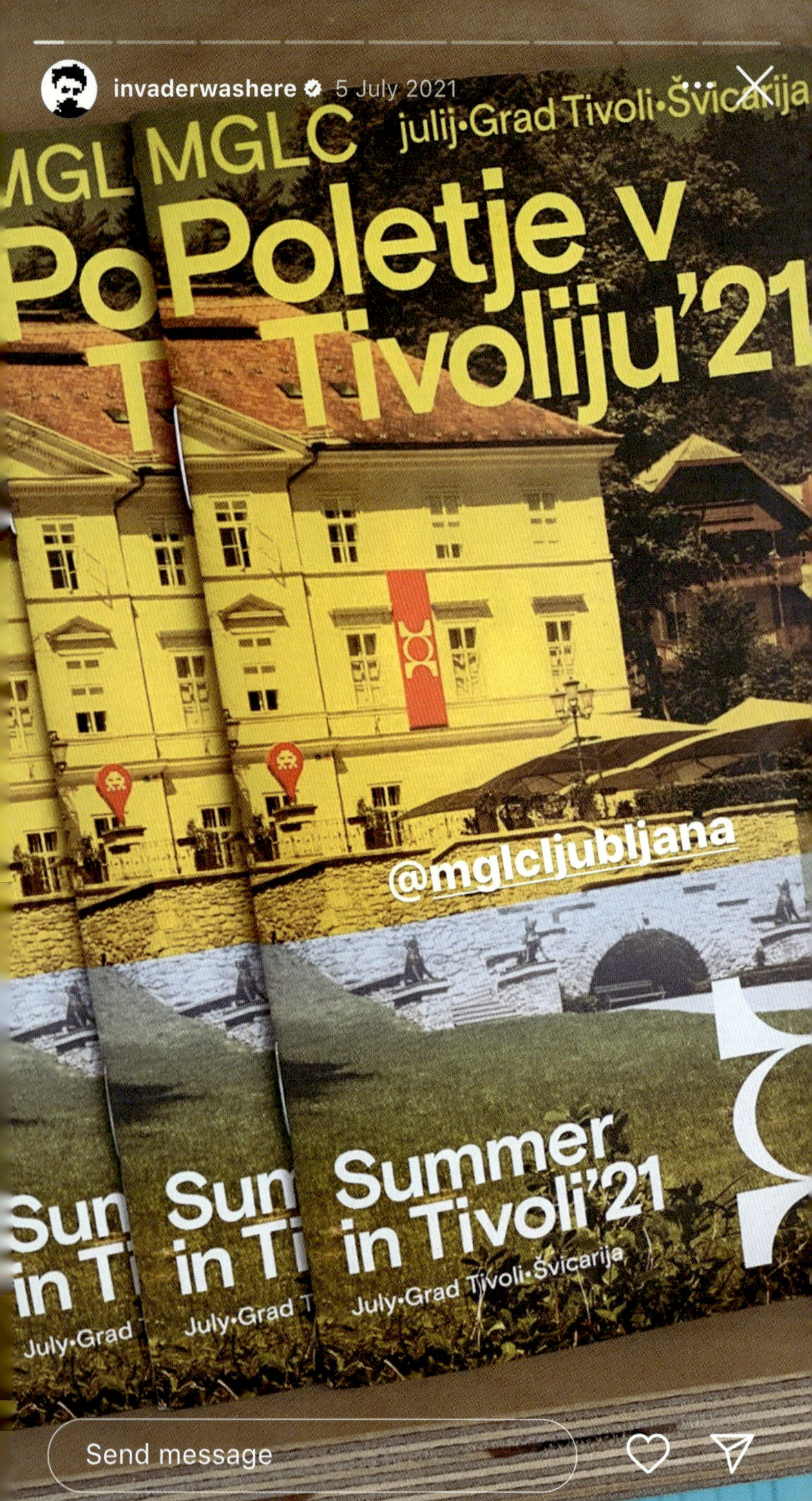
invaderwashere
5 July 2021
MGLC
julij·Grad Tivoli·Švicarija
Poletje v Tivoliju'21
@mglcljubljana
Summer in Tivoli'21
July·Grad Tivoli·Švicarija
Send message

invaderwashere 13 July 2021

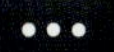

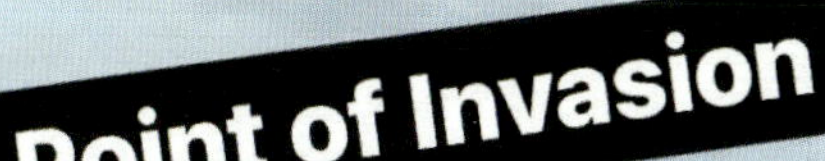

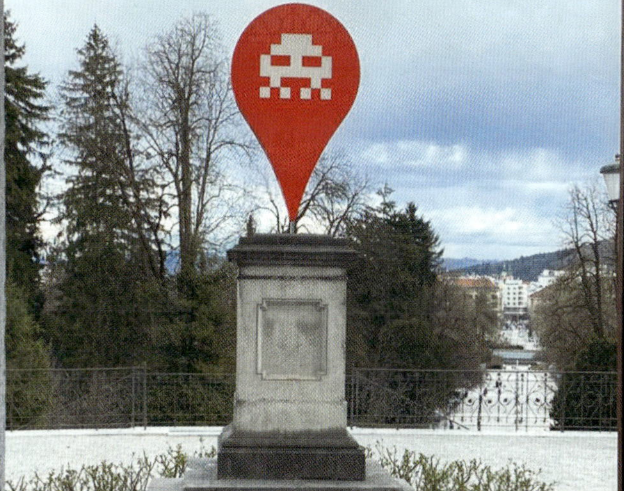

at @mglcljubljana
- Prints on paper -
EXTENDED Until
15-08-2021

Send message

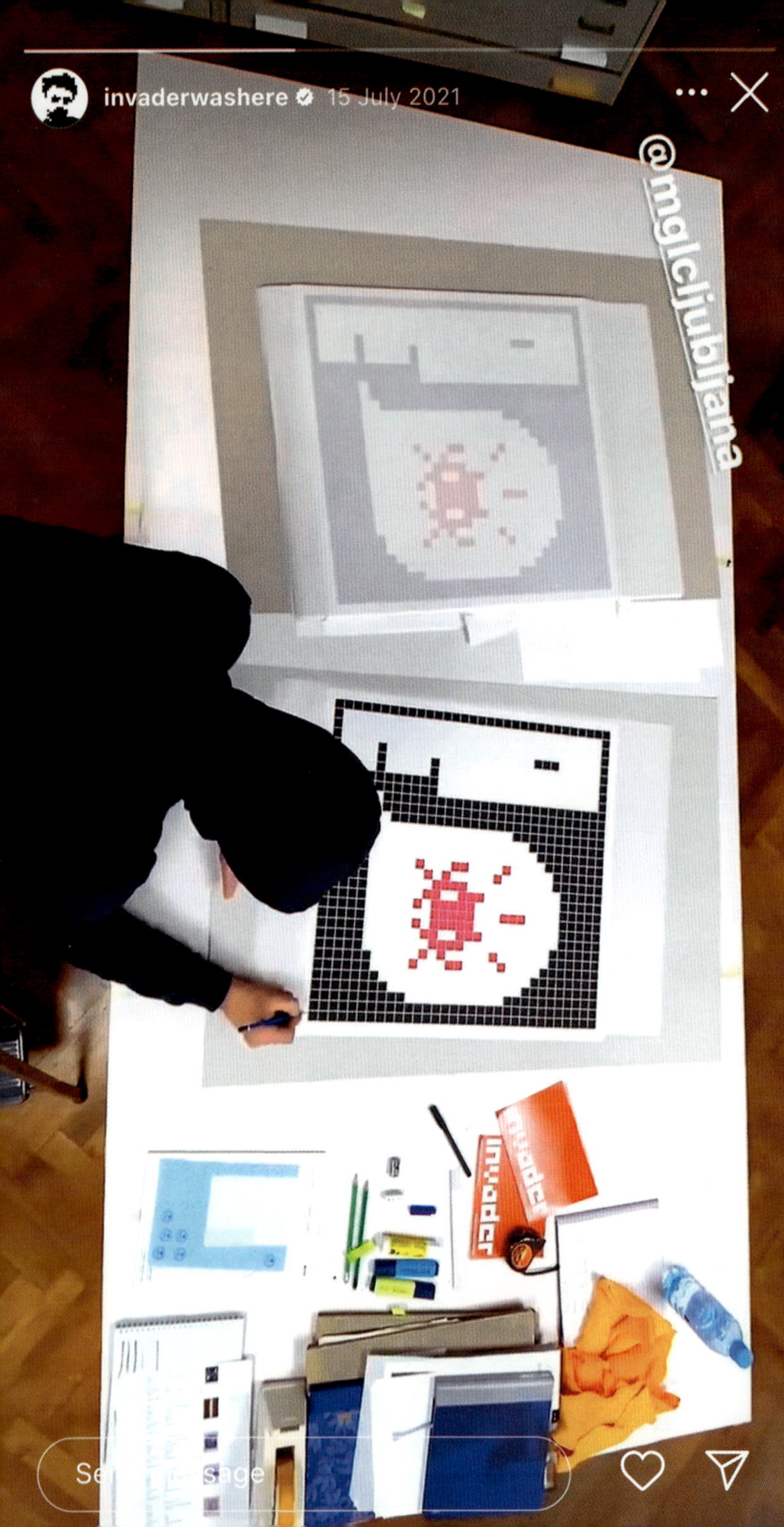
invaderwashere
15 July 2021
@mglcljubljana
invader
invader

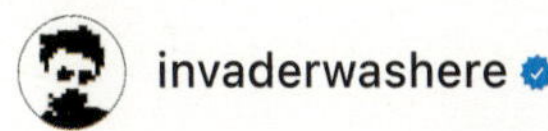

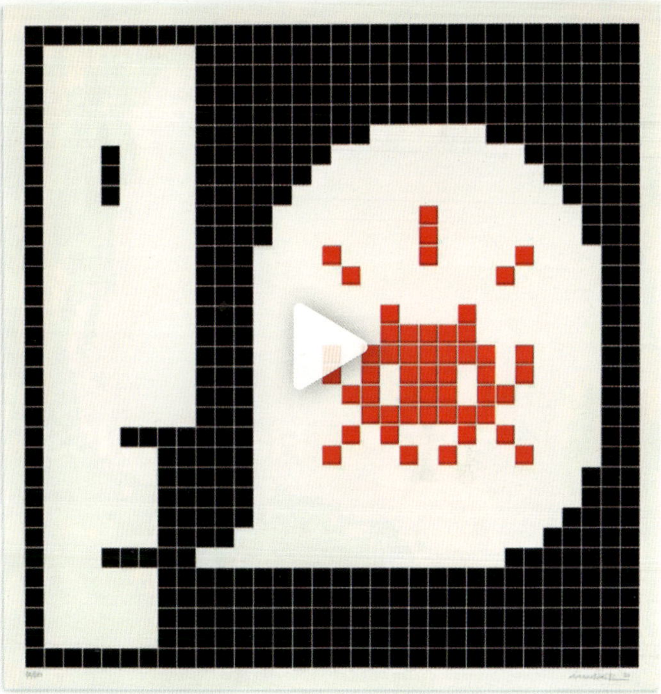

43 007 views

invaderwashere My new print, ALERT 2020, is now available at the MGLC in Ljubljana. This print is a remake of the ALERT one that I made in 2001. It was inspired by the Alert Icon created by the talented Susan Kare for the early Macintosh computer systems. The print was made at the MGLC silkscreen studio in five color variations. #alert2020 #printsonpaper #silkscreeened #susankare #bauhaus #macintosh #earlycomputers #errorsystem #virus @mglcljubljana

View all 140 comments

15 July 2021

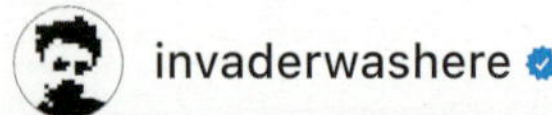

Flash the ISS

 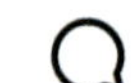  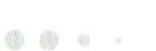 

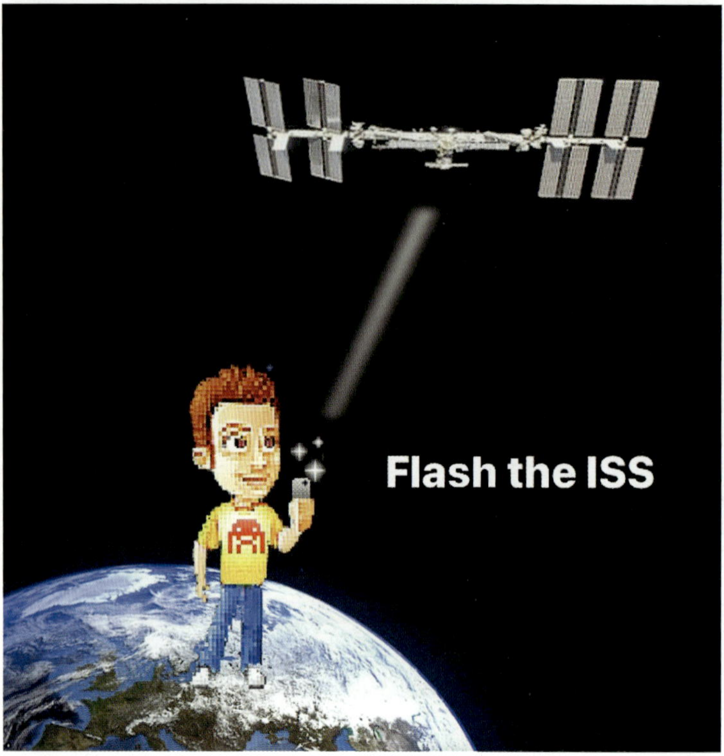

5797 likes

invaderwashere I was amazed when I looked at the valid flashes of the ISS to see that on many photos you could clearly see it in the sky 🤩. Knowing that the ISS speed is about 17,500 mph (28,000 km/h), double congrats to all the flashers who caught it! ➡️ Swipe to see some of them #flashinvaders #ISS @europeanspaceagency @thom_astro 👋

View all 131 comments

30 July 2021

invaderwashere 30 July 2021

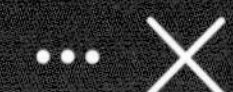

Send message

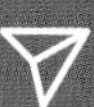

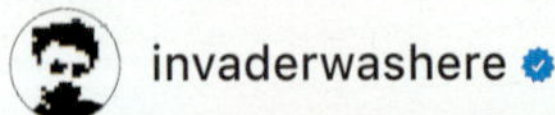

3999 INVADERS / 79 CITIES

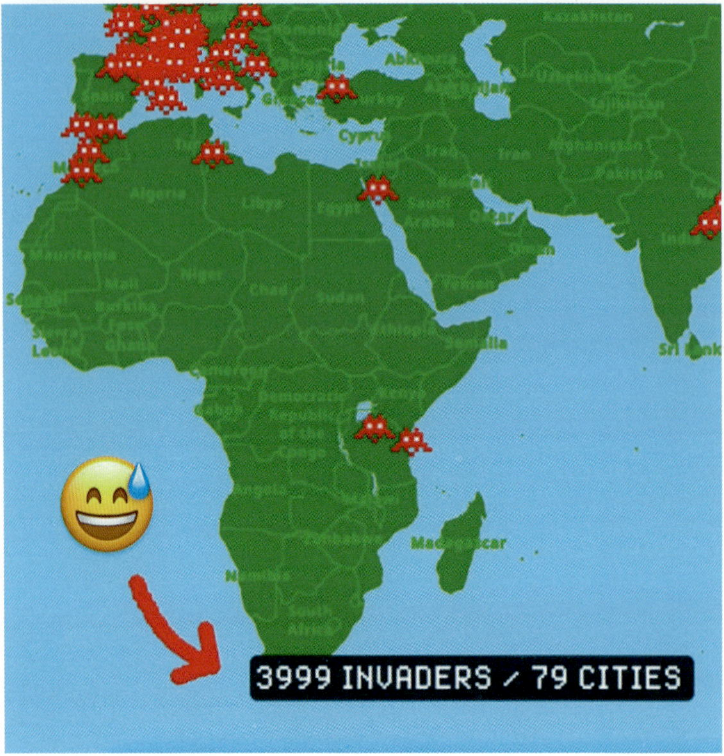

21 055 likes

invaderwashere 3999 Mosaics installed through 79 cities. Next one will be the 4000th #underpressure #4000 Don't know how, don't know where, don't know when...

View all 761 comments

2 August 2021

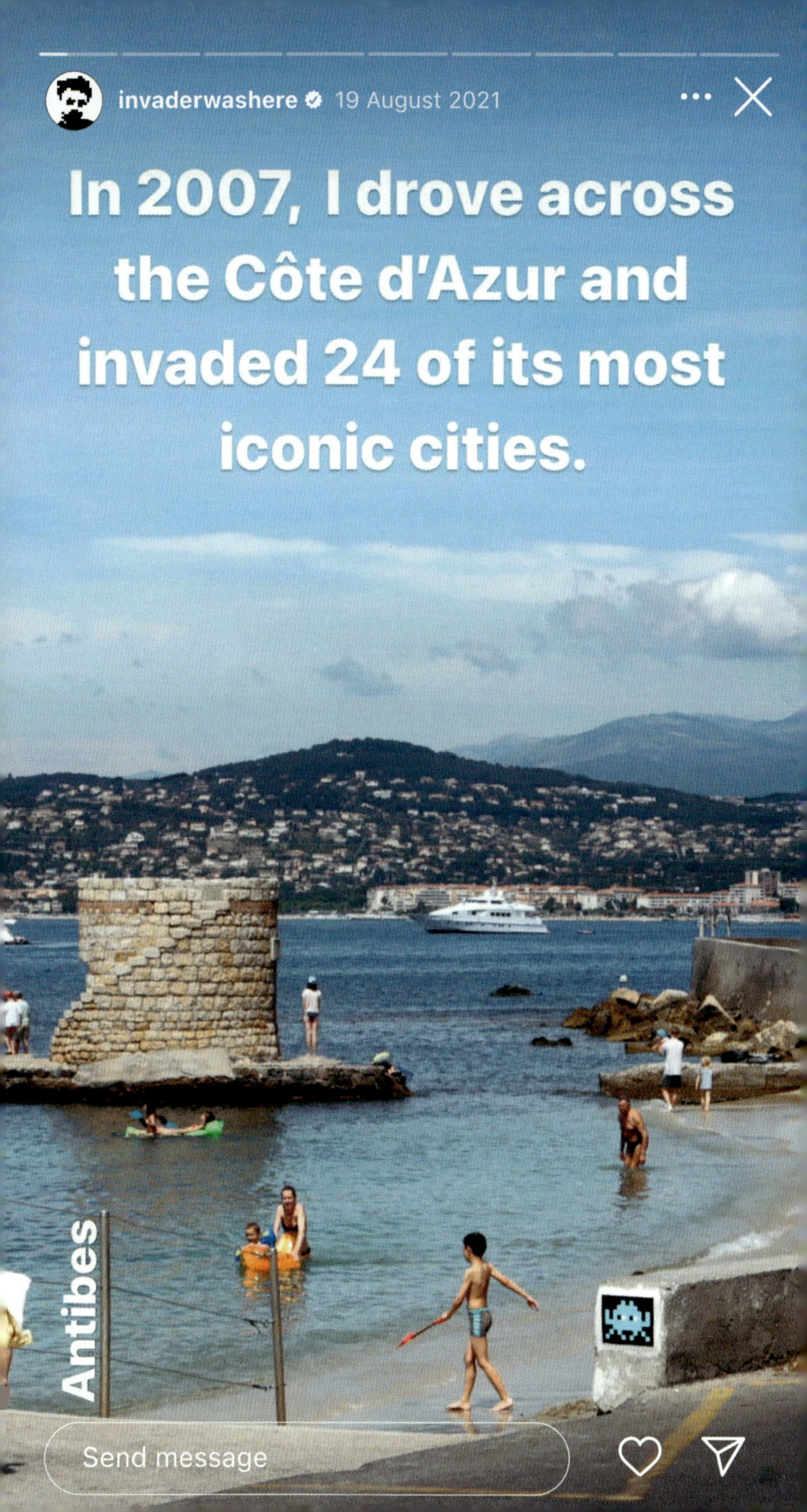

invaderwashere 19 August 2021

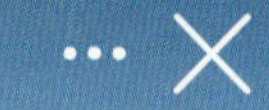

In 2007, I drove across the Côte d'Azur and invaded 24 of its most iconic cities.

Antibes

Send message

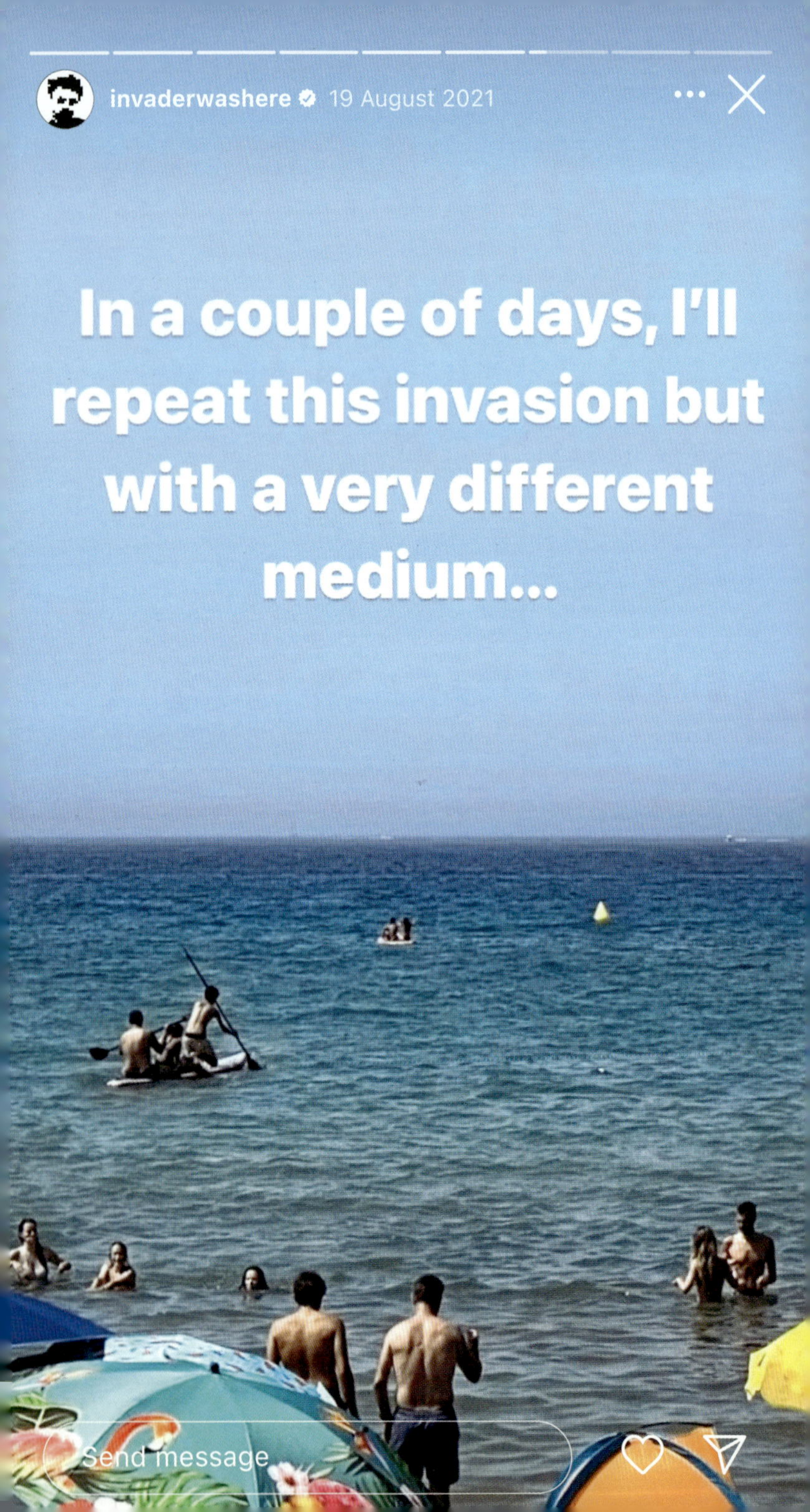

invaderwashere 19 August 2021

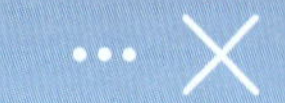

In a couple of days, I'll repeat this invasion but with a very different medium...

Send message

invaderwashere

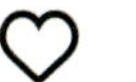  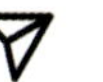 

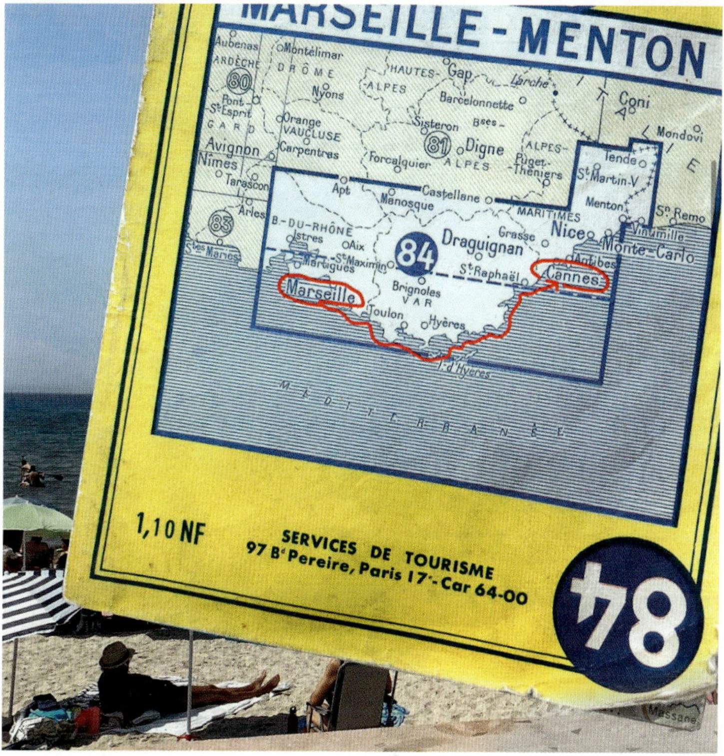

4 857 likes

invaderwashere Competition game 📸: On Saturday 21th, go to any of the beaches of the French Riviera between Marseille and Cannes and stare at the sea. If you manage to spot my new invasion, post your pics and video on Instagram and tag them @invaderwashere and #beachinvasion. The three best images will win a signed copy of my latest book. Good luck!

View all 175 comments

19 August 2021

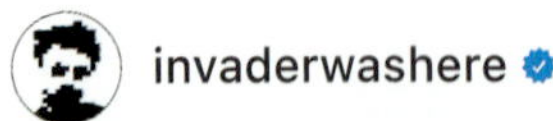
invaderwashere •••

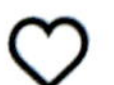  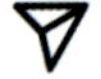 

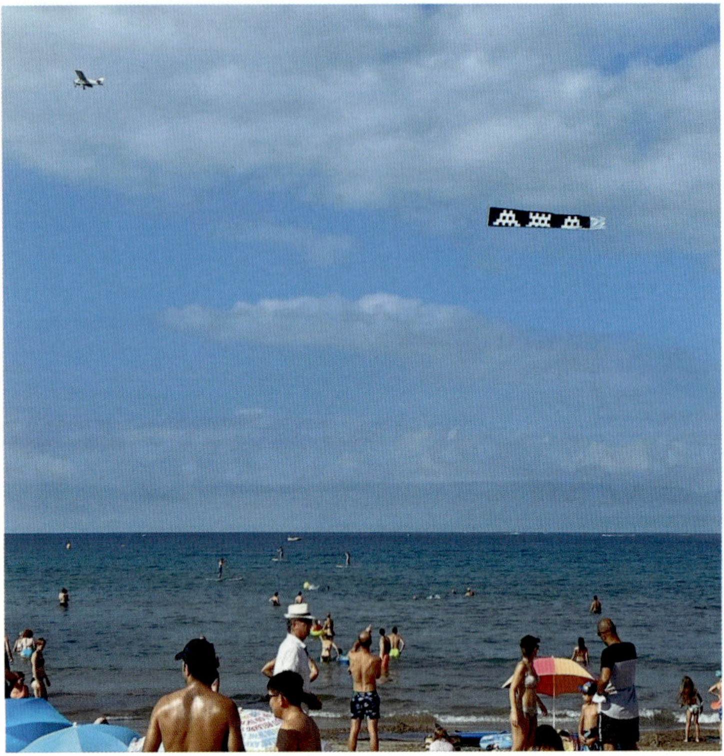

23 680 likes

invaderwashere On air... 👾👾👾✈️
#beachinvasion
#holidays #childrenmemories #beaches

View all 288 comments

21 August 2021

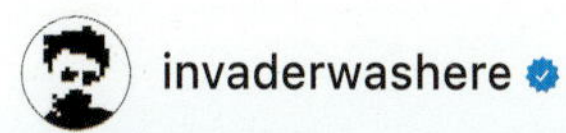

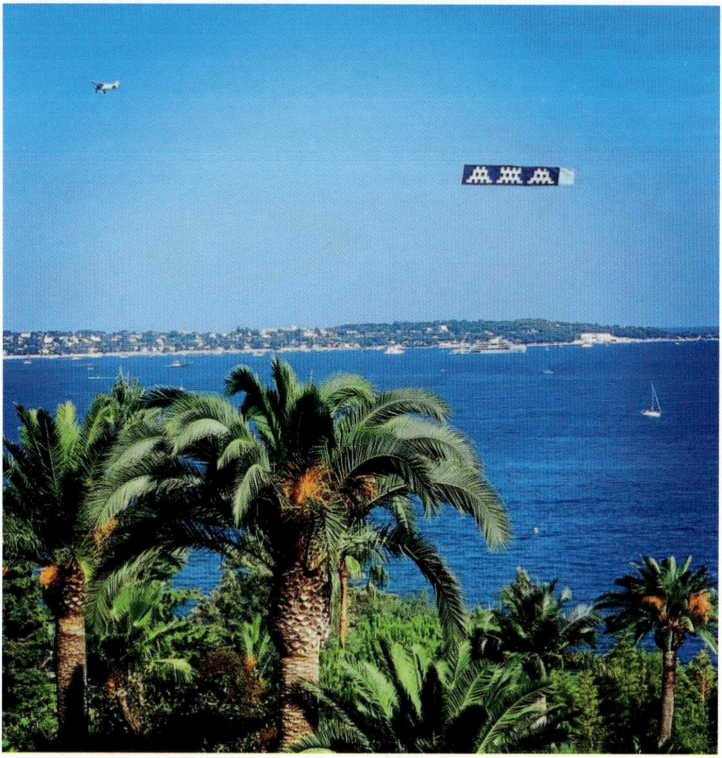

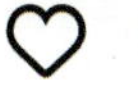    

11870 likes

invaderwashere AND THE WINNERS ARE...
I have received so many great photos of the #beachinvasion contest that I actually selected not 3 but 6 of them. Thank you to all the contributors and congratulations to the winners: @gillyeldin Cannes / @elizabethmorelle St Cyr, les Lecques / @gauquelin.thierry St Cyr / @elodie13007 Marseille / @robinm Marseille / @lililachipie_invaders_addict Hyères

View all 111 comments

24 August 2021

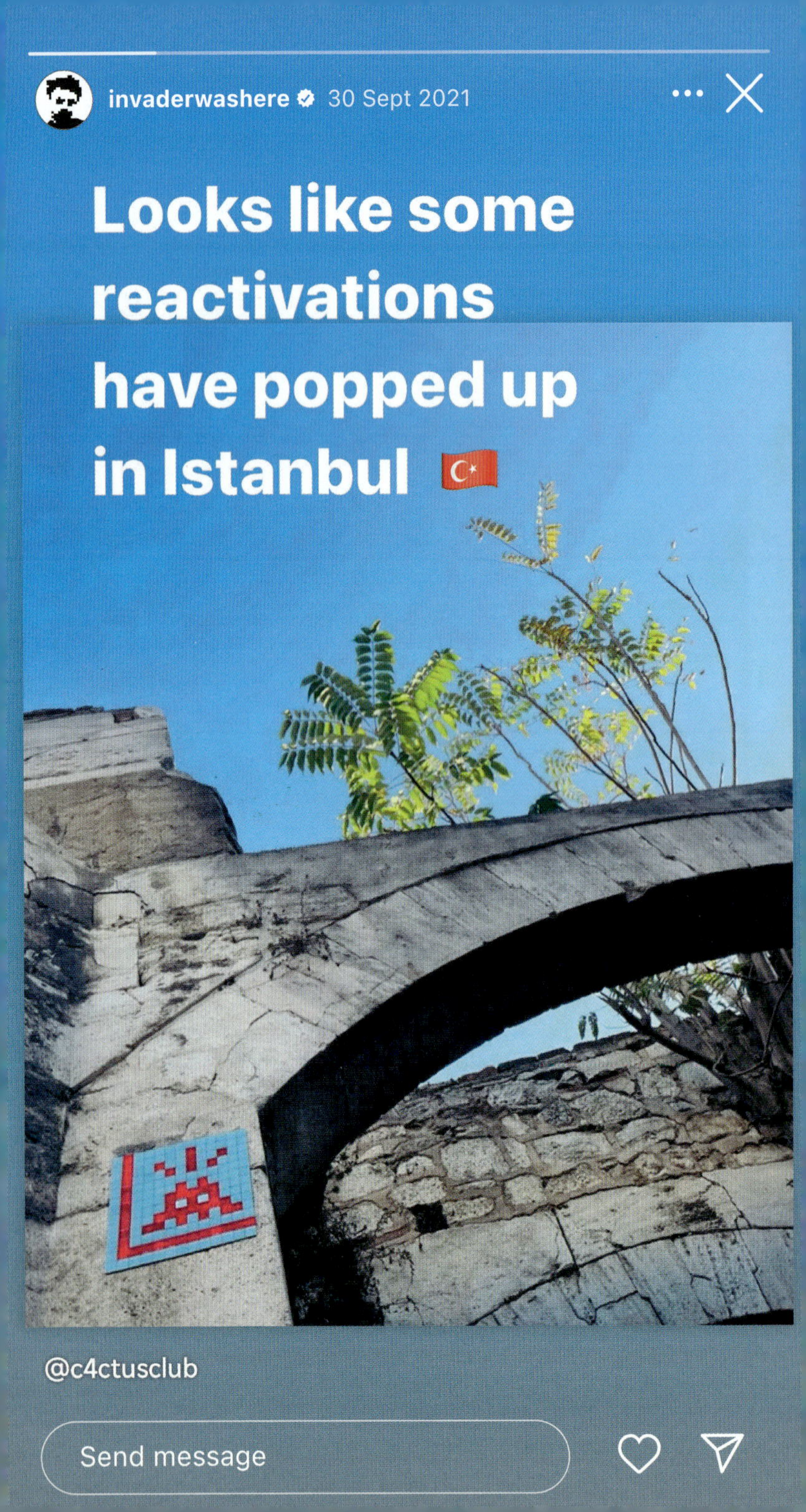

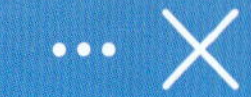

invaderwashere 30 Sept 2021

Looks like some reactivations have popped up in Istanbul 🇹🇷

@c4ctusclub

Send message

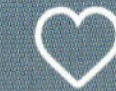

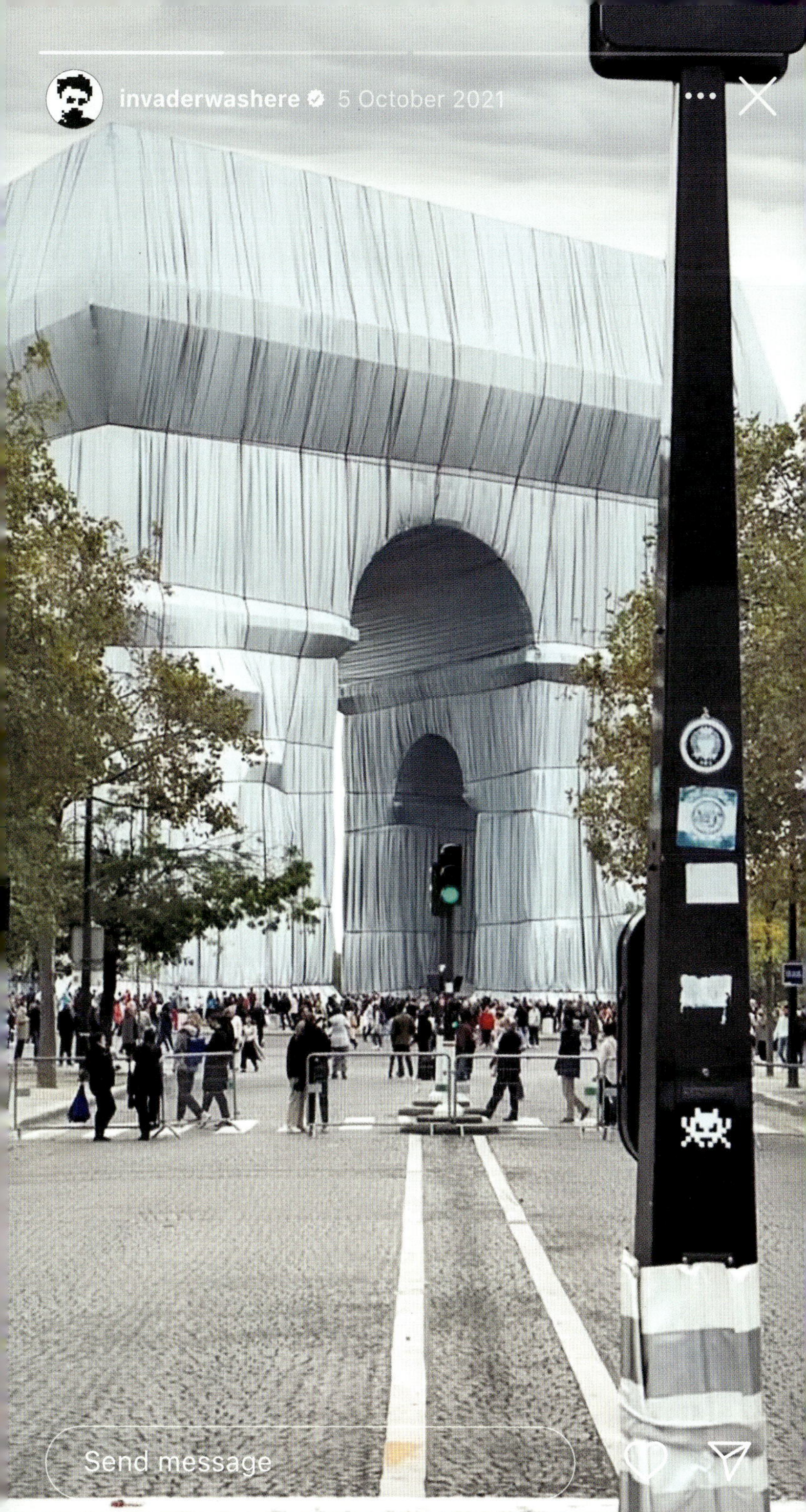
invaderwashere
5 October 2021
Send message

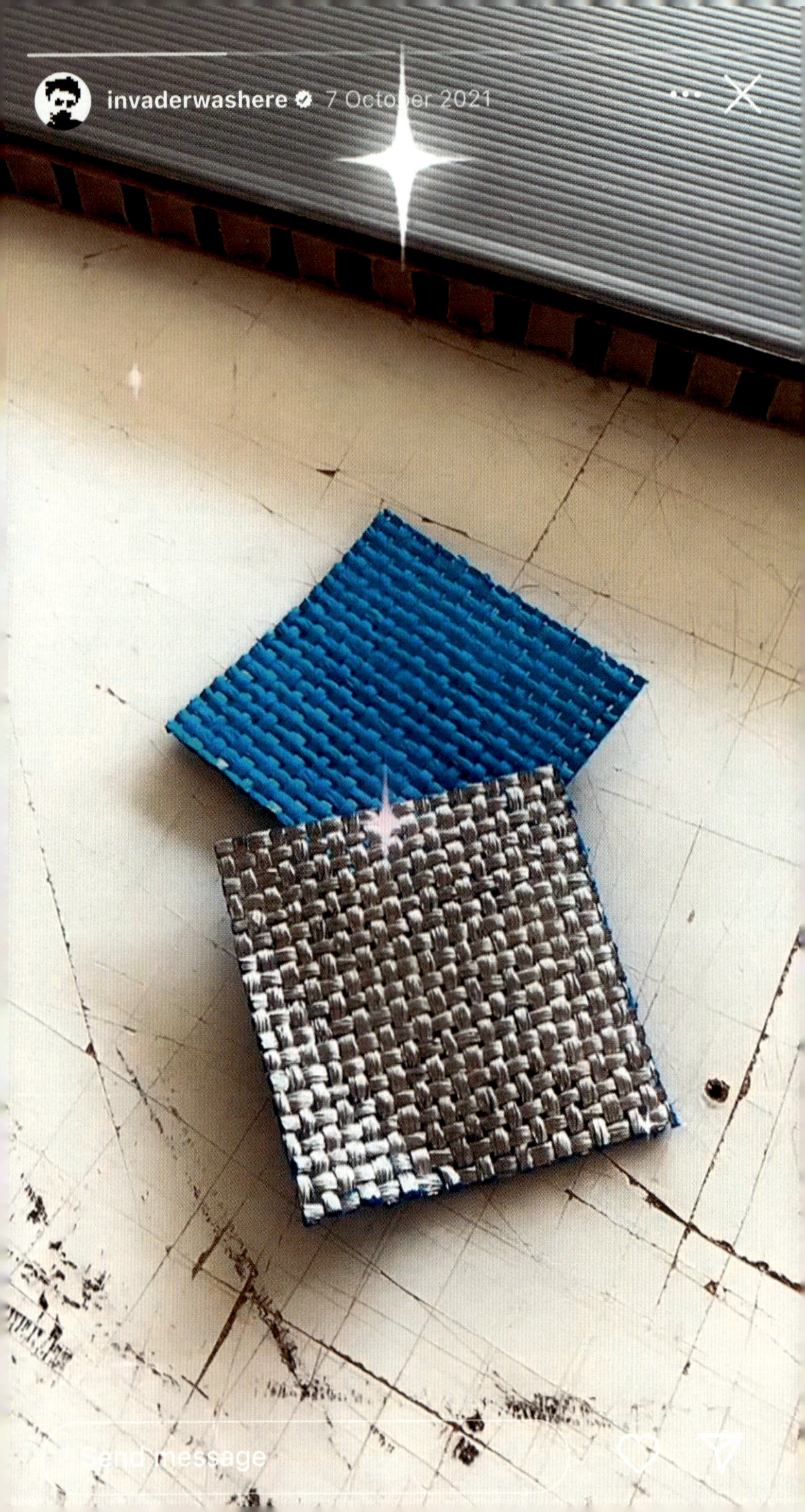
invaderwashere
7 October 2021
Send message

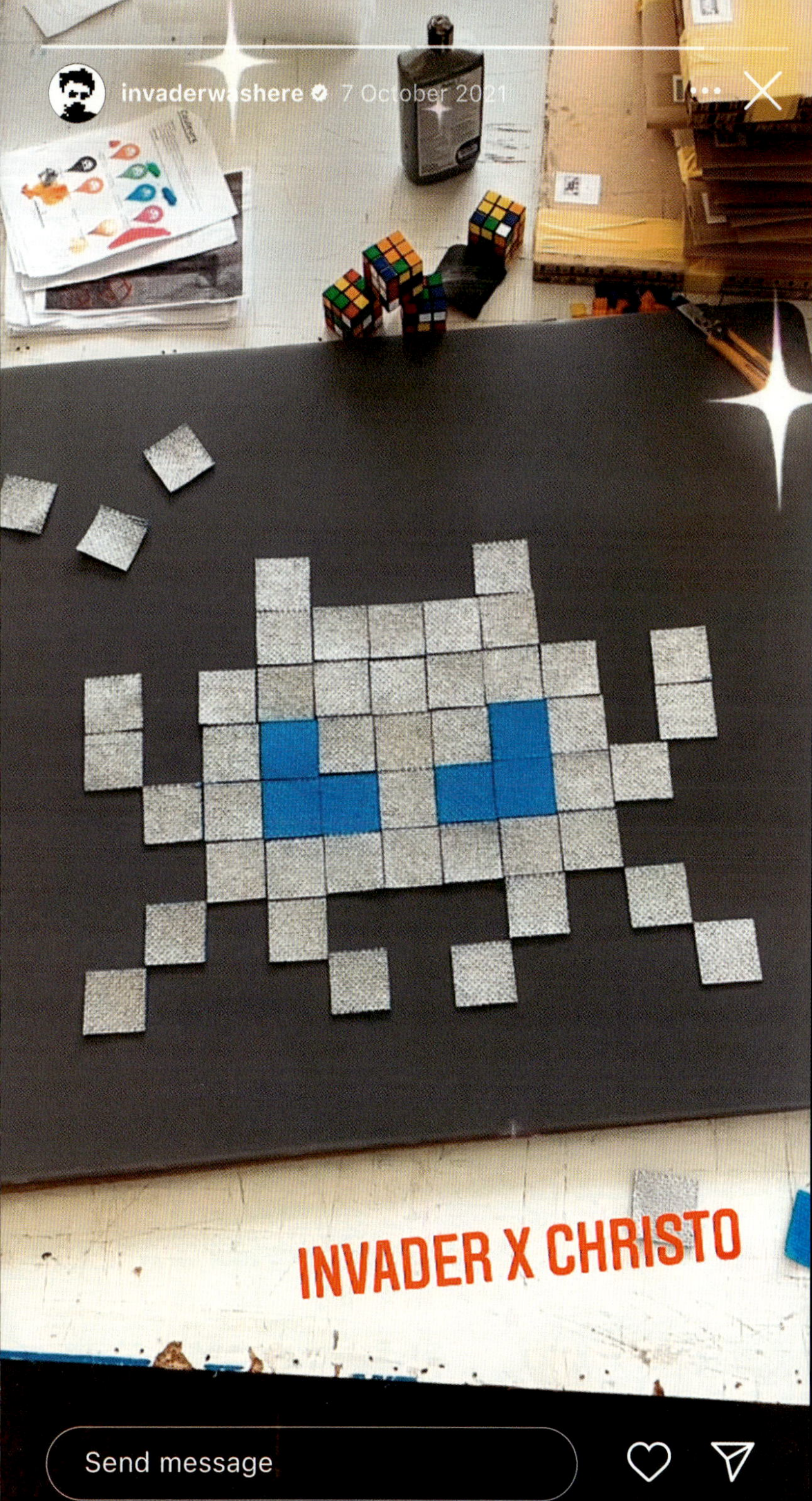
invaderwashere 7 October 2021
INVADER X CHRISTO
Send message

invaderwashere

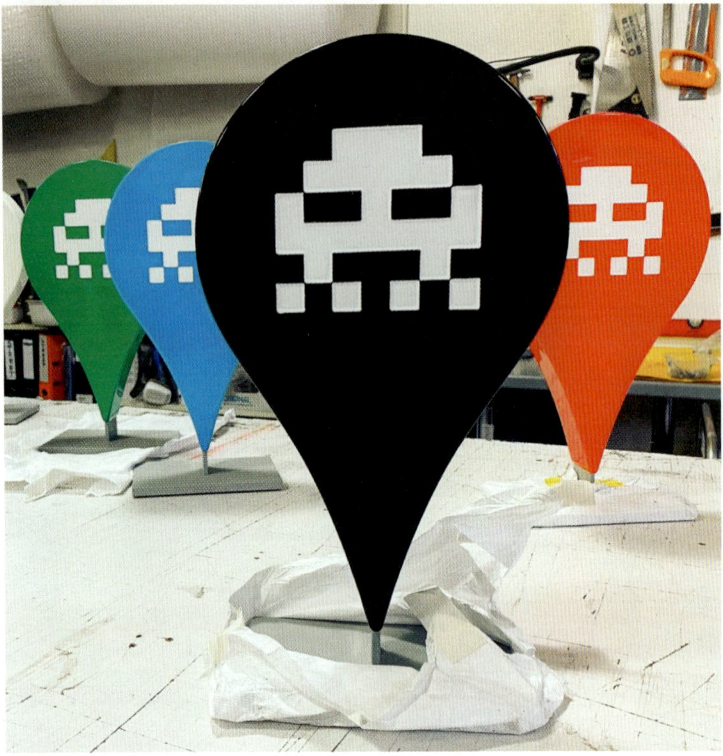

11 258 likes

invaderwashere Last check before departure ✈️
#studiodetails #POI #pointsofinvasions #bronzesculptures
#sooninLA @oti.official

View all 190 comments

14 November 2021

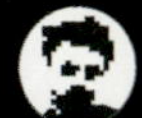

invaderwashere 21 November 2021

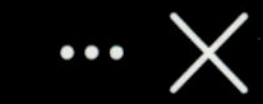

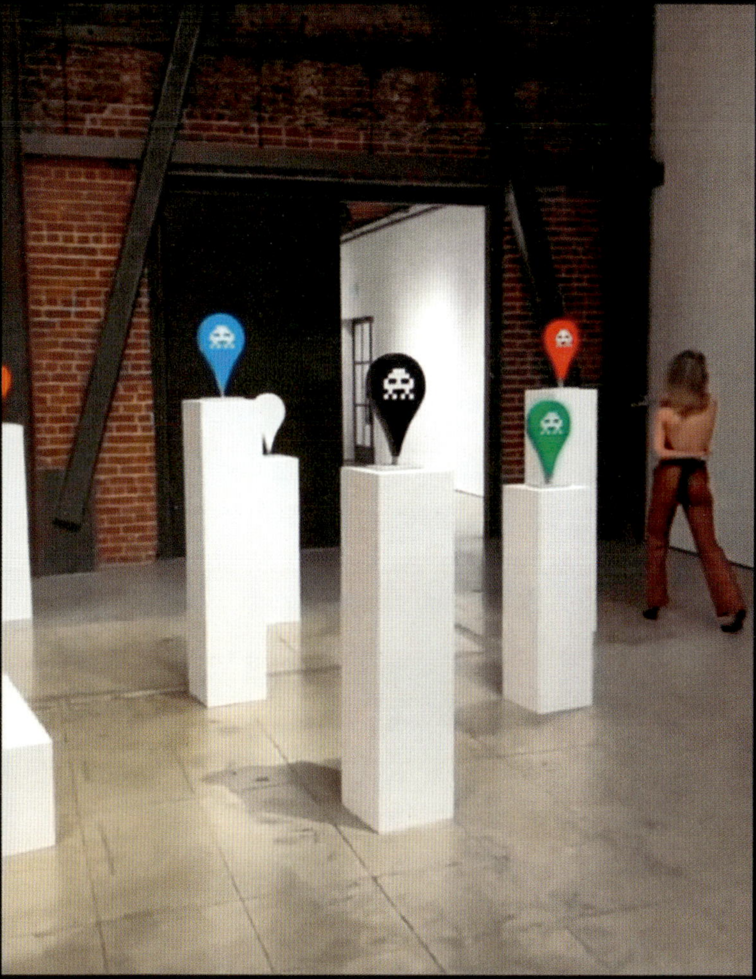

@chuang_collection

Points Of ~~Interest~~
Invasions
@oti.official L.A.

Send message

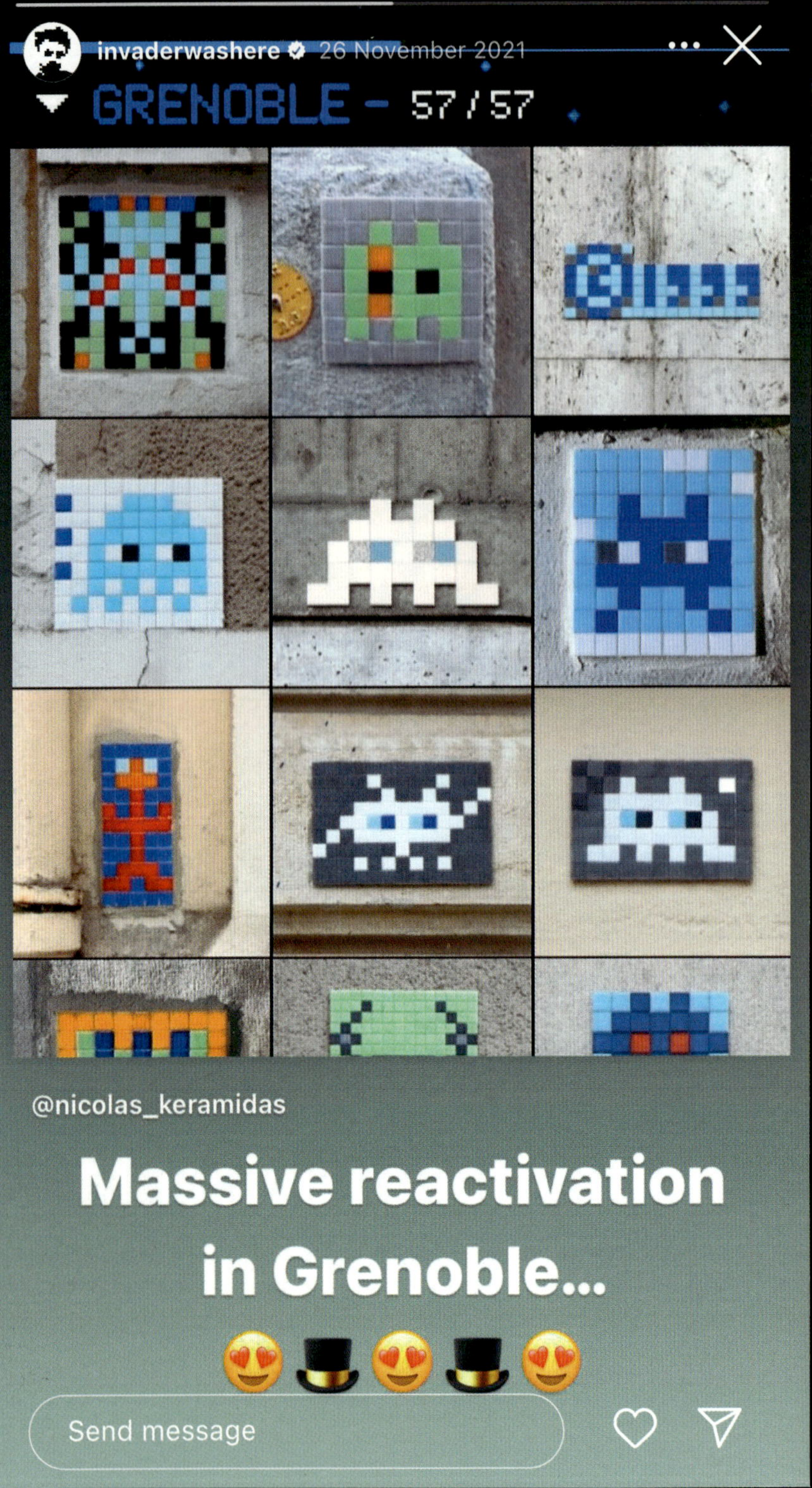

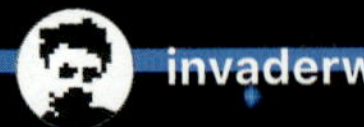

invaderwashere 26 November 2021

GRENOBLE - 57 / 57

@nicolas_keramidas

Massive reactivation in Grenoble...

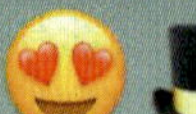 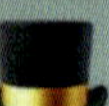 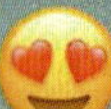 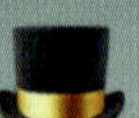 

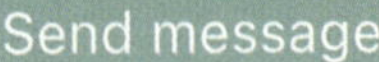

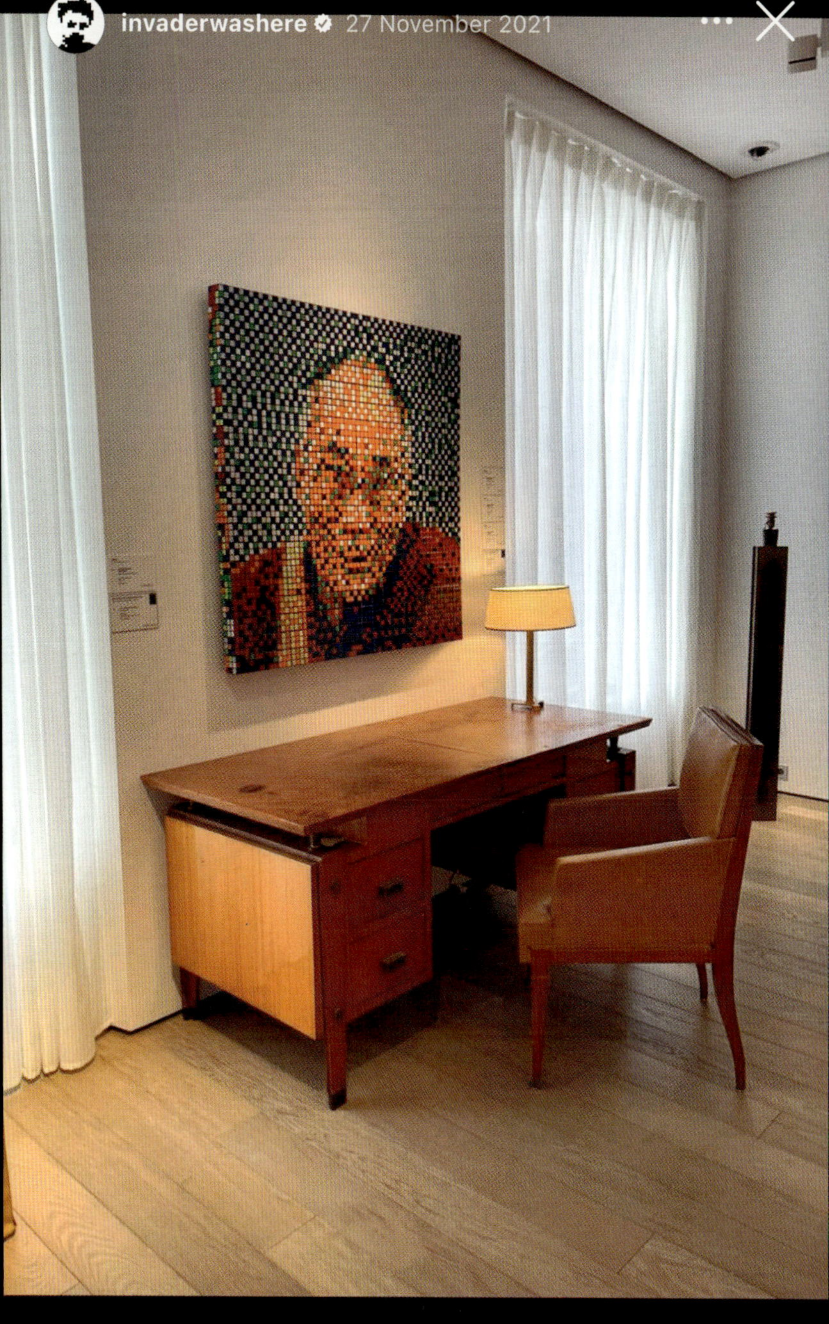
invaderwashere 27 November 2021
Shot by @guillaume_musso

invaderwashere 2 December 2021

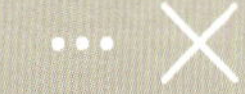

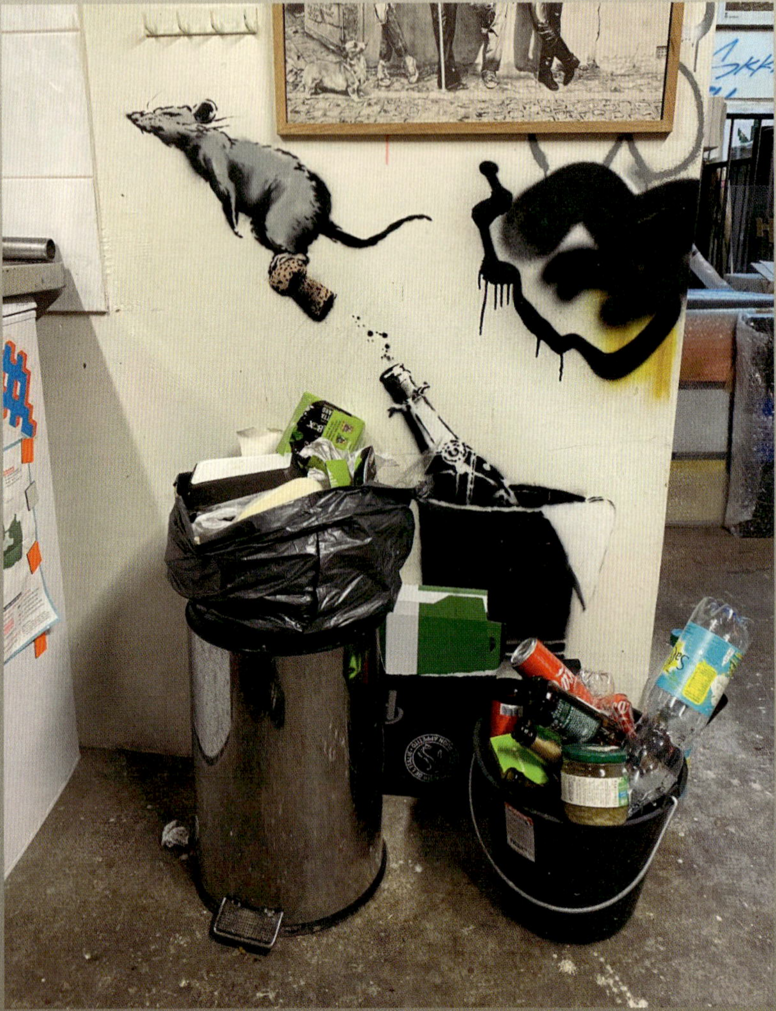

#Studiodetail!

Send message

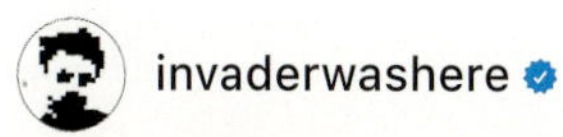
invaderwashere

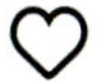   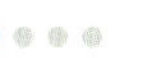 

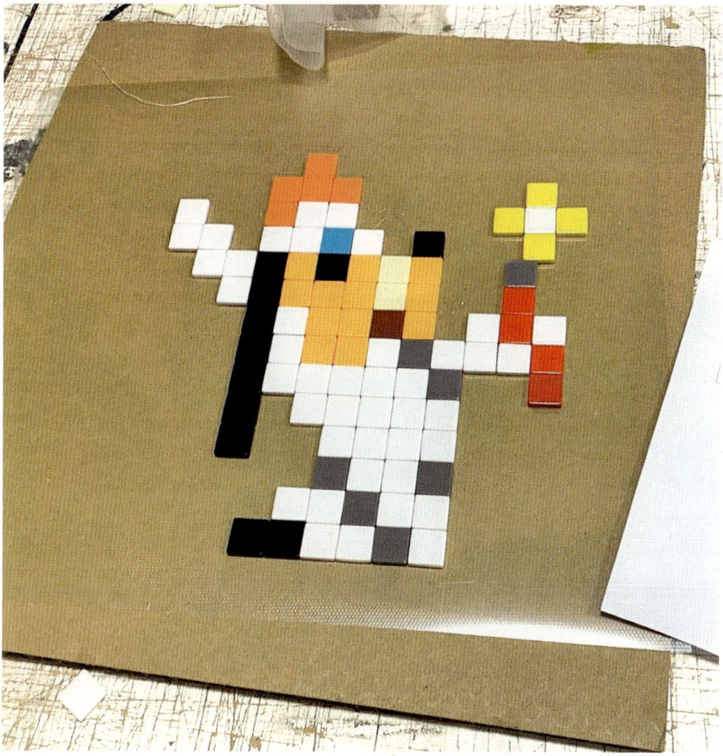

25 438 likes

invaderwashere Preparing the mosaics for my next invasion trip... #Mission4000 under construction...

View all 480 comments

2 December 2021

invaderwashere

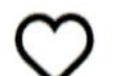
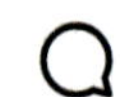

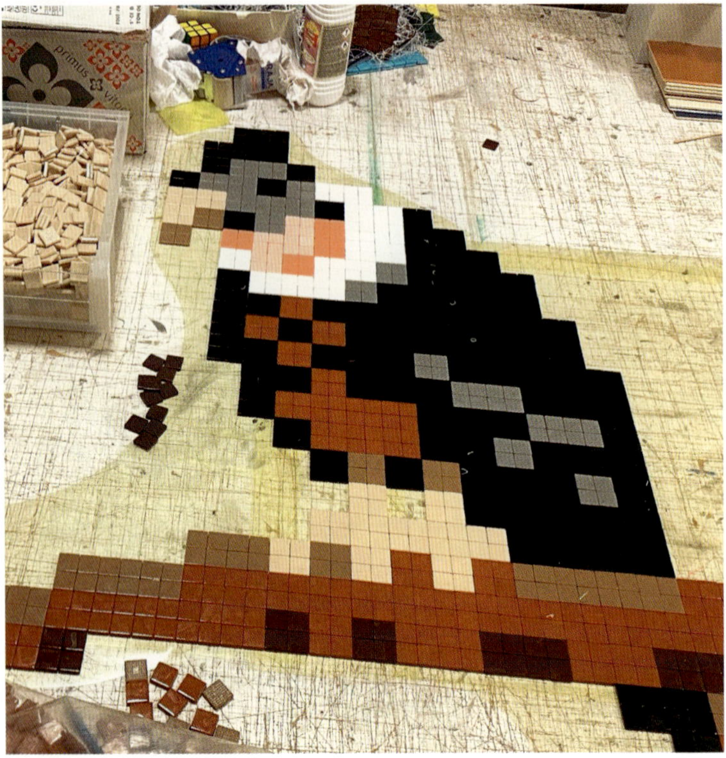

25 438 likes

invaderwashere Preparing the mosaics for my next invasion trip... #Mission4000 under construction...

View all 480 comments

2 December 2021

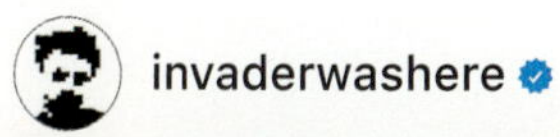

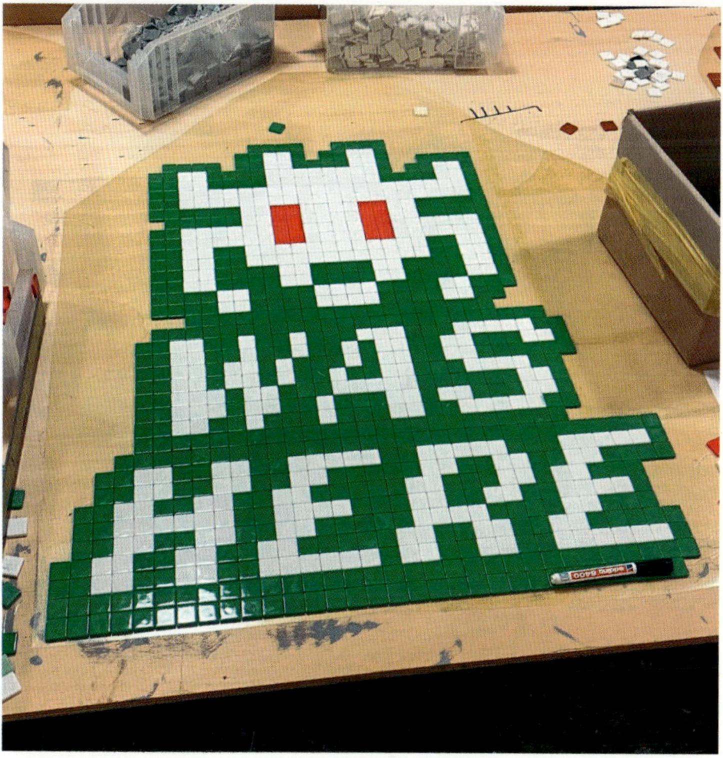

   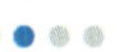 

25 438 likes

invaderwashere Preparing the mosaics for my next invasion trip... #Mission4000 under construction...

View all 480 comments

2 December 2021

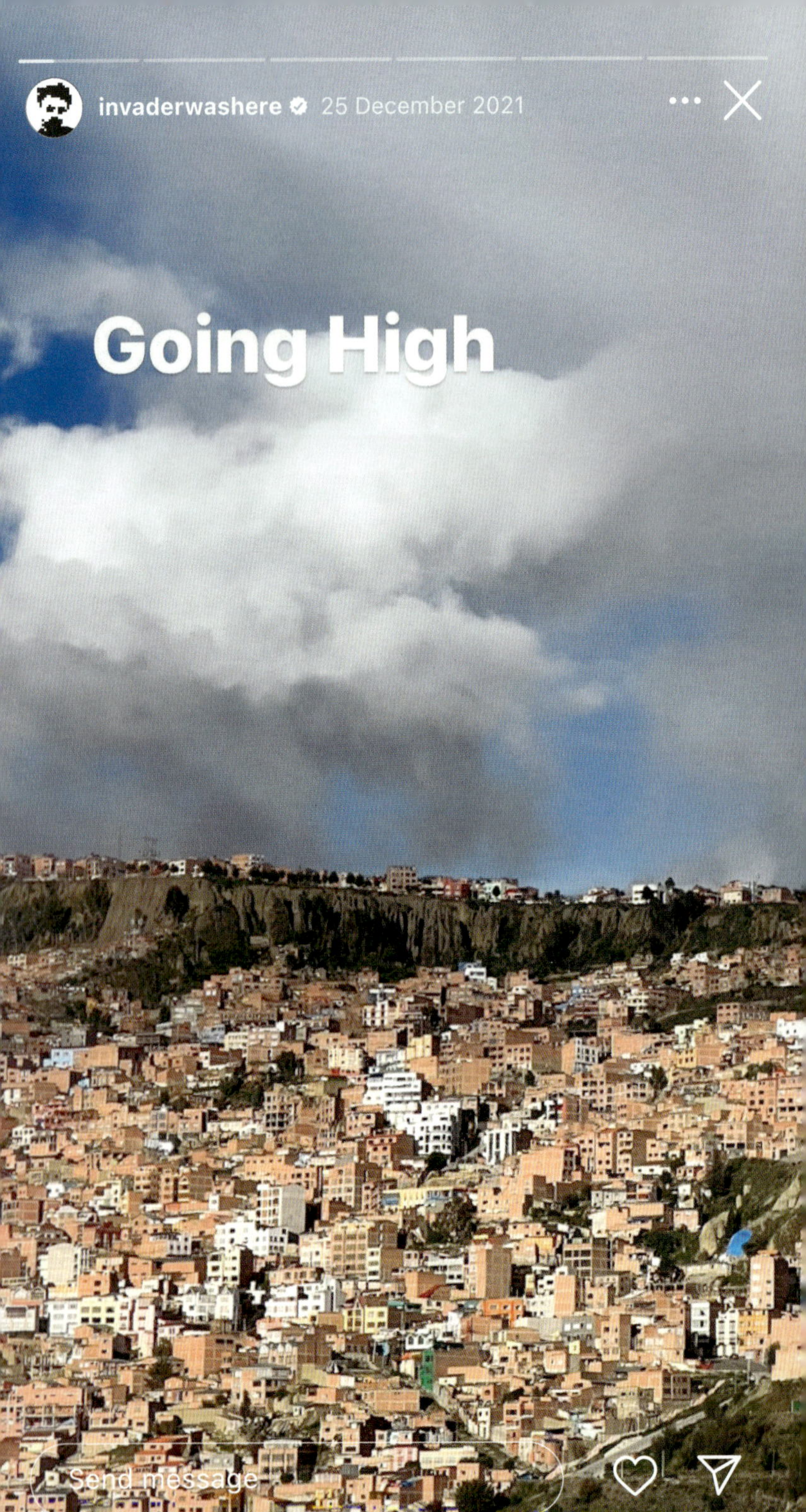
invaderwashere
25 December 2021
Going High
Send message

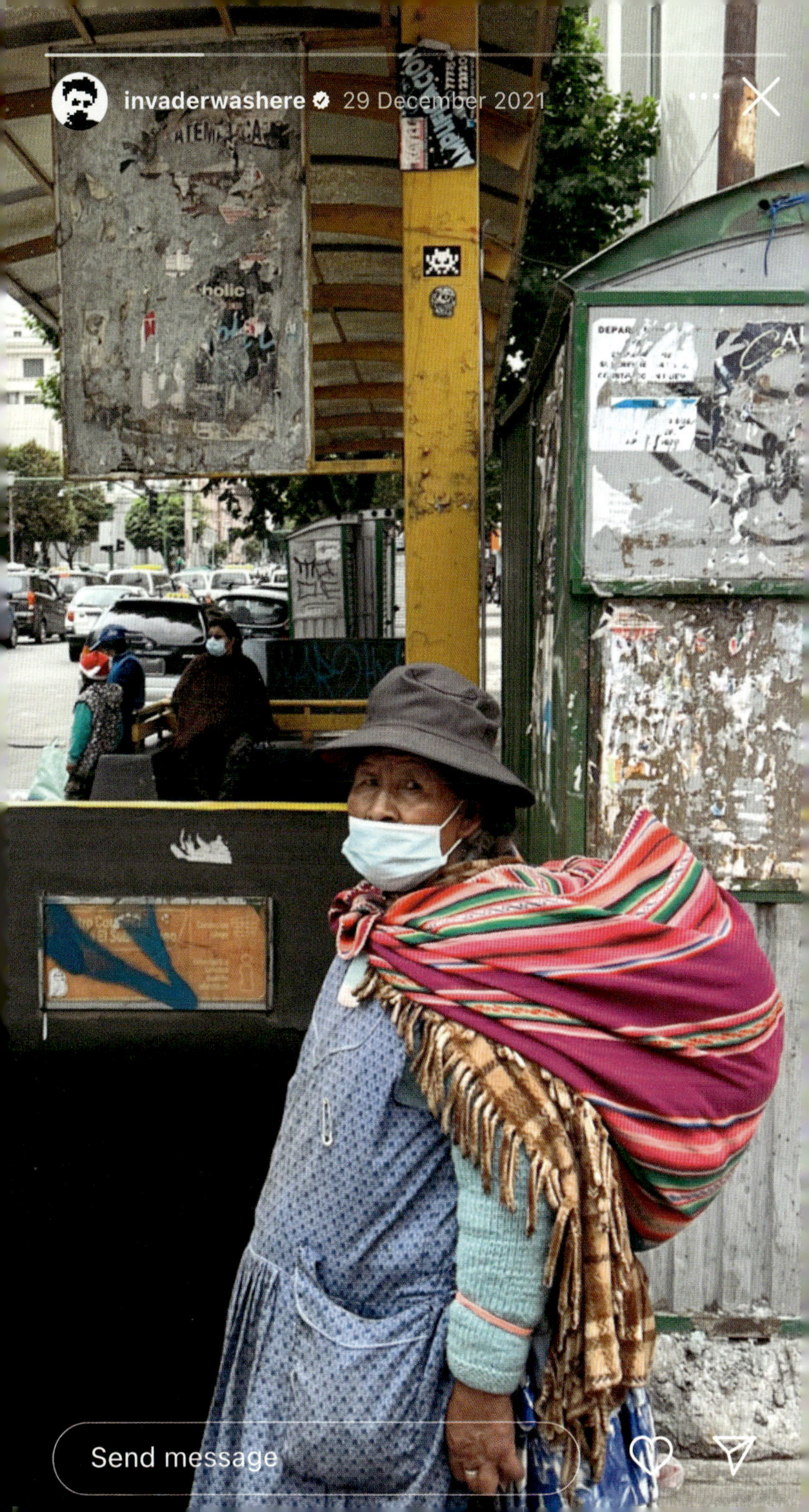
invaderwashere
29 December 2021
Send message

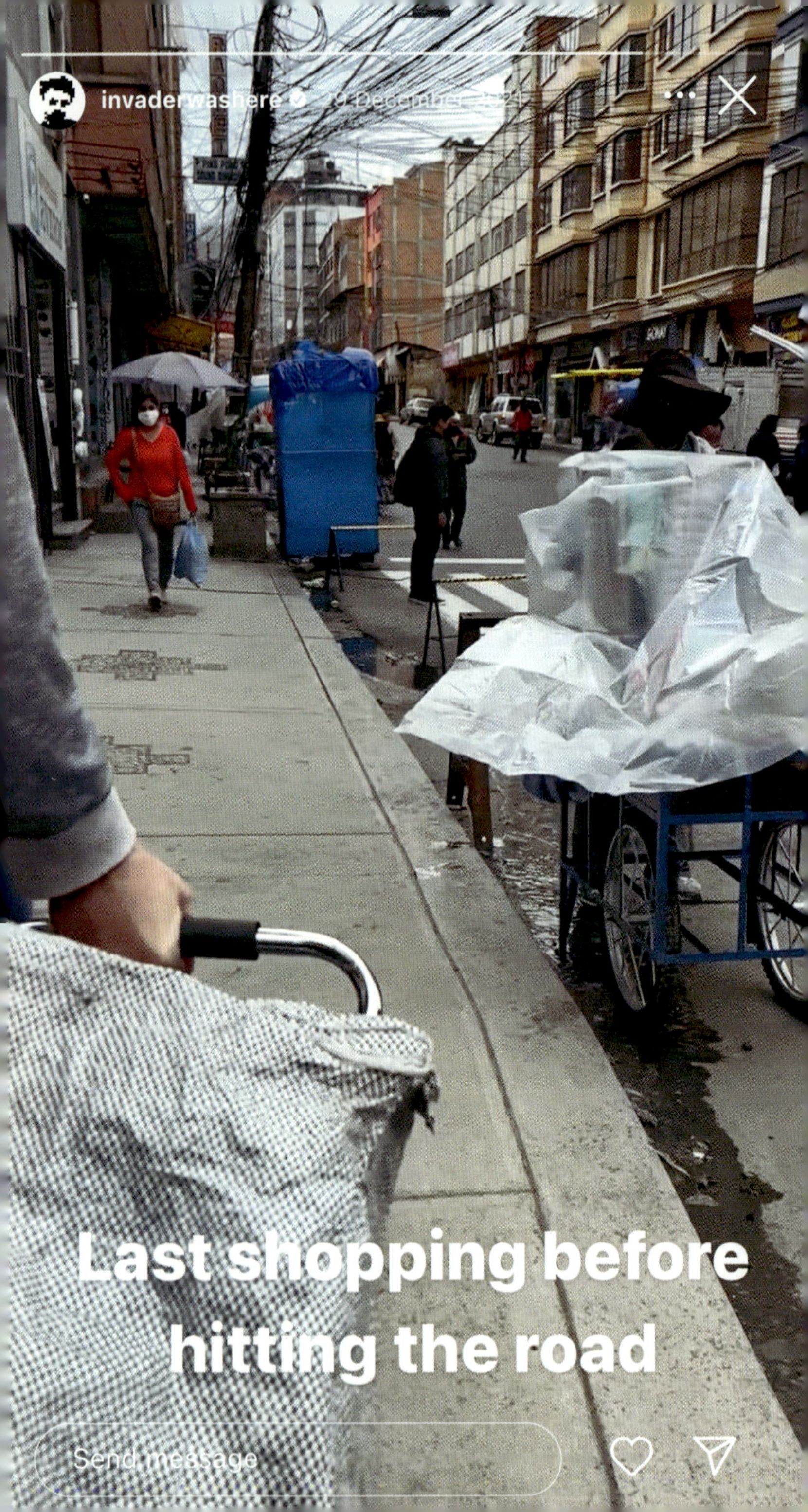
invaderwashere
20 December 2021
Last shopping before hitting the road
Send message

invaderwashere

  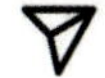 

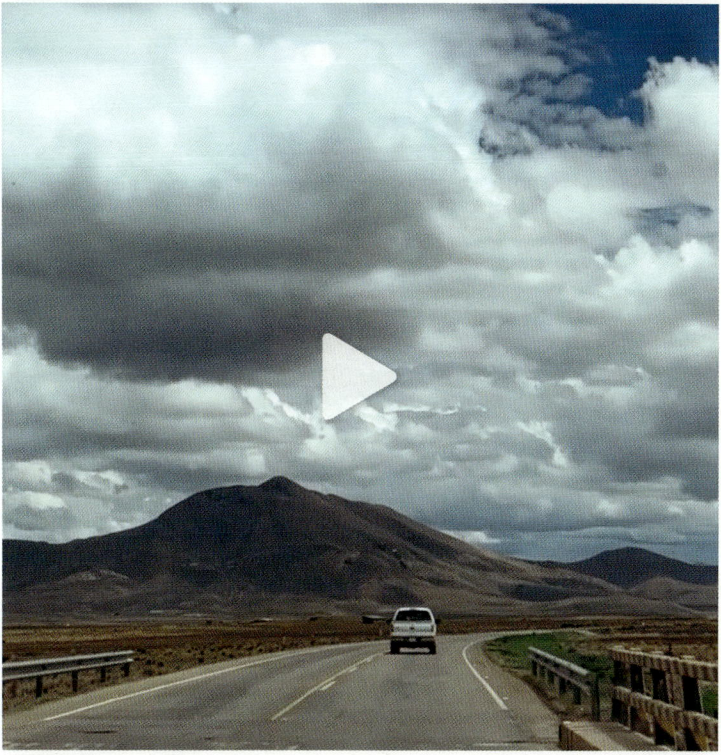

32 377 views

invaderwashere On the road... Mission #4000 👾

View all 102 comments

30 December 2021

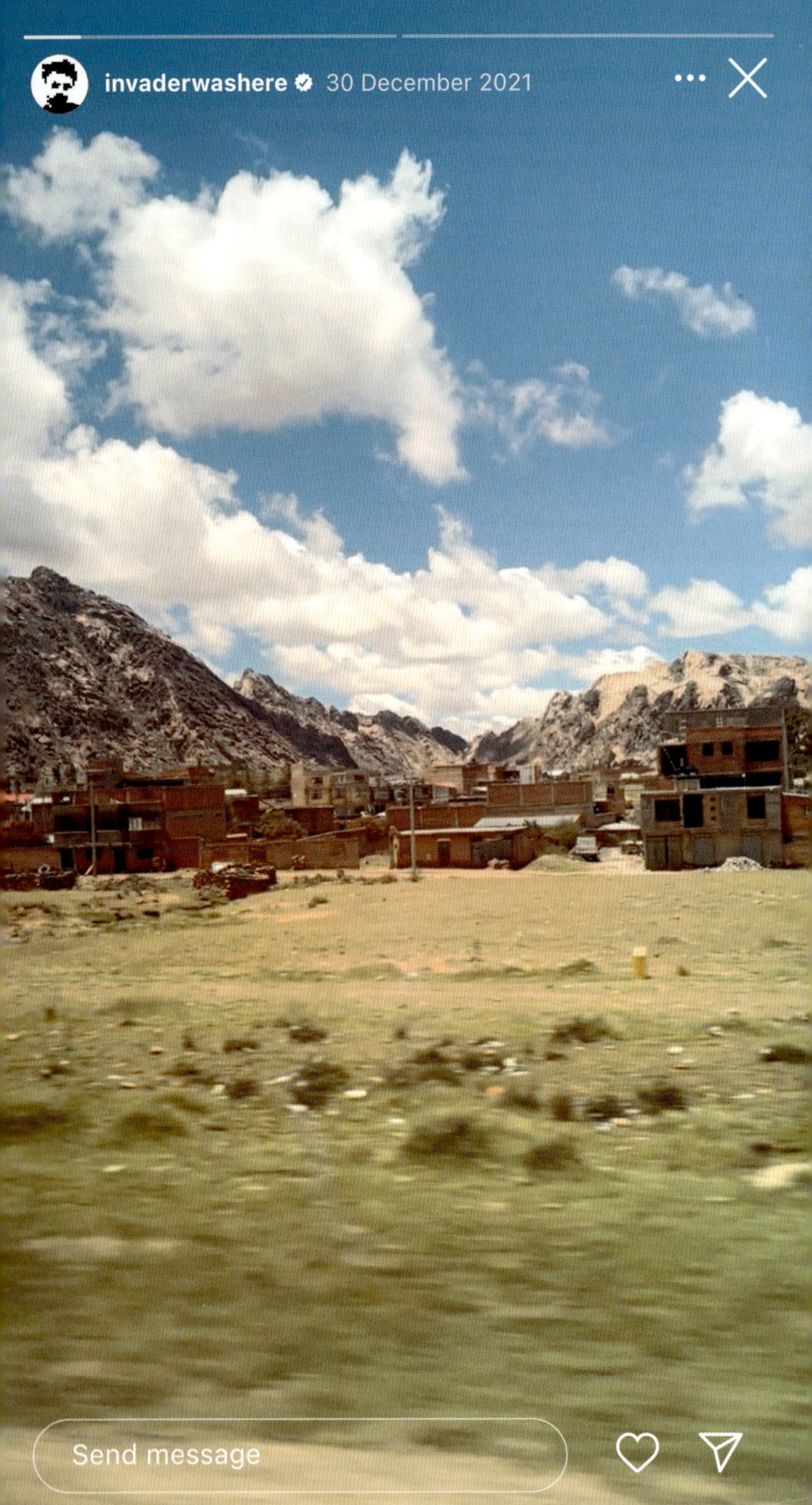
invaderwashere
30 December 2021
Send message

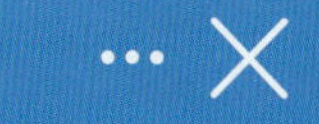

invaderwashere 30 December 2021

3495 m

Précision ± 6 m

Not high enough
Yet...

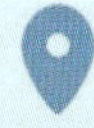

invaderwashere 

4000 m

Précision ± 3 m

15 402 likes

invaderwashere Friday Dec. 31 2021, the 4000th space invader has just landed at 4000 meters high!
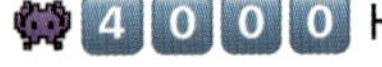 Happy new year to you all

View all 394 comments

31 December 2021

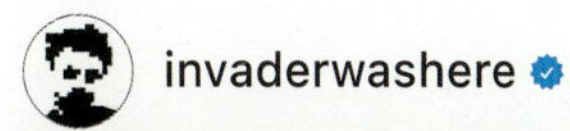

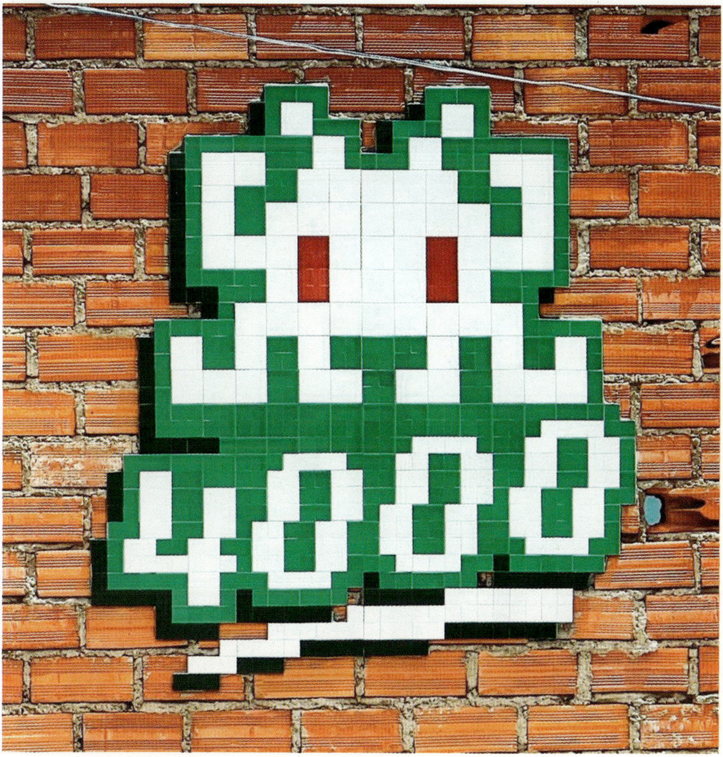

15 402 likes

invaderwashere Friday Dec. 31 2021, the 4000th space invader has just landed at 4000 meters high!
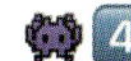 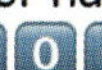 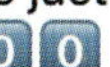 Happy new year to you all 

View all 394 comments

31 December 2021

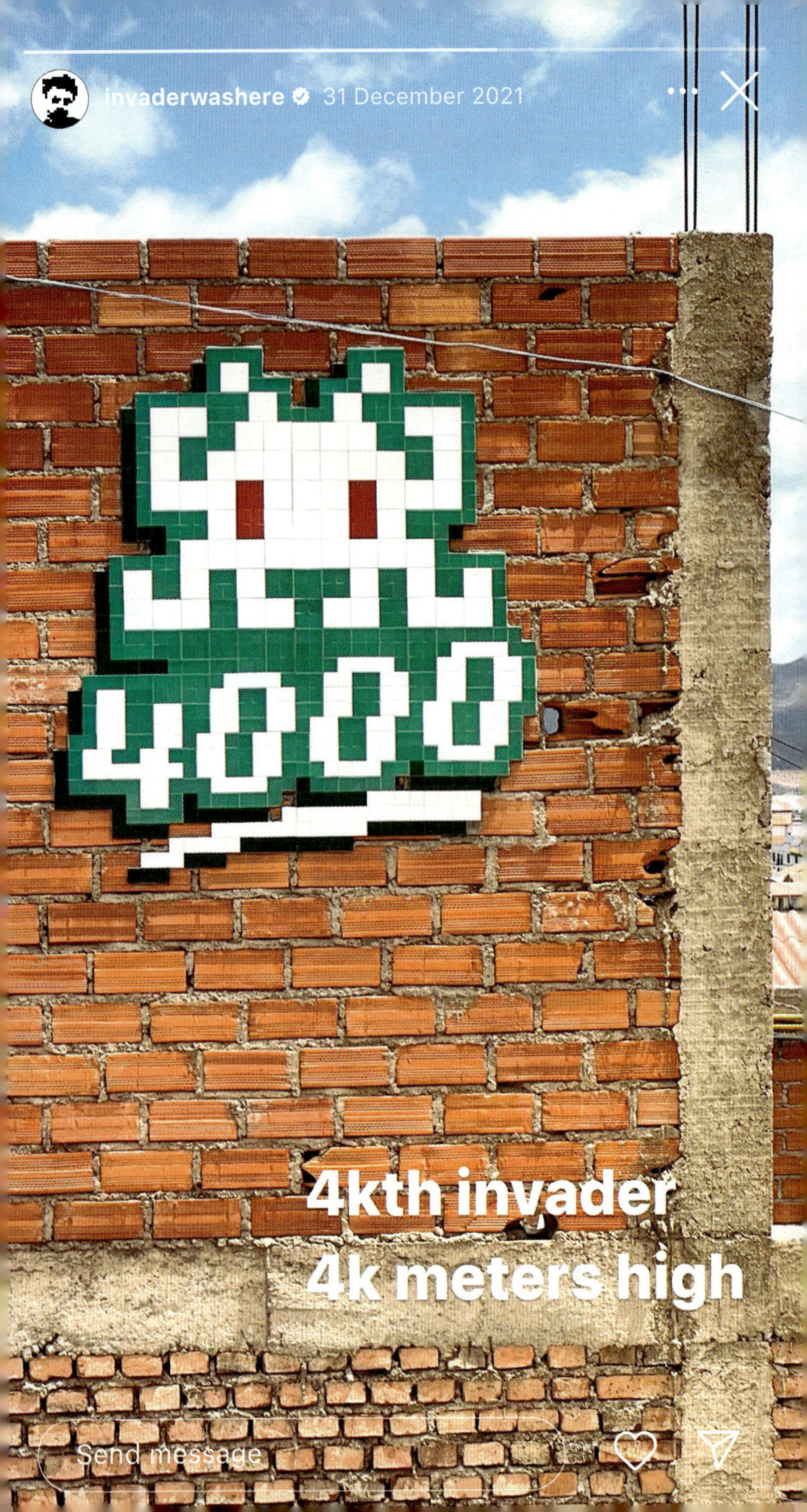

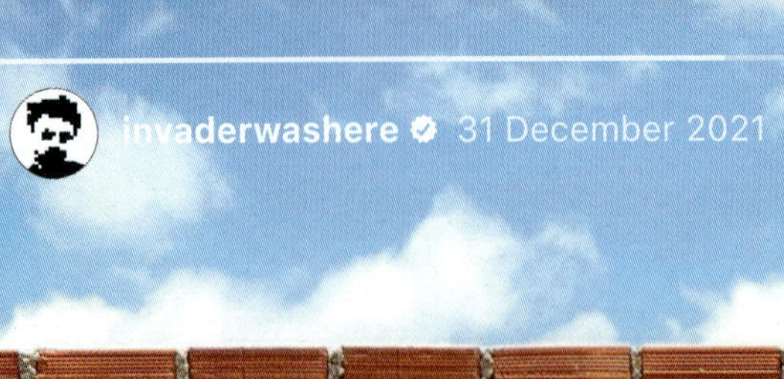

4000

4kth invader
4k meters high

Send message

2022

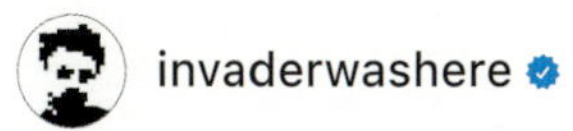

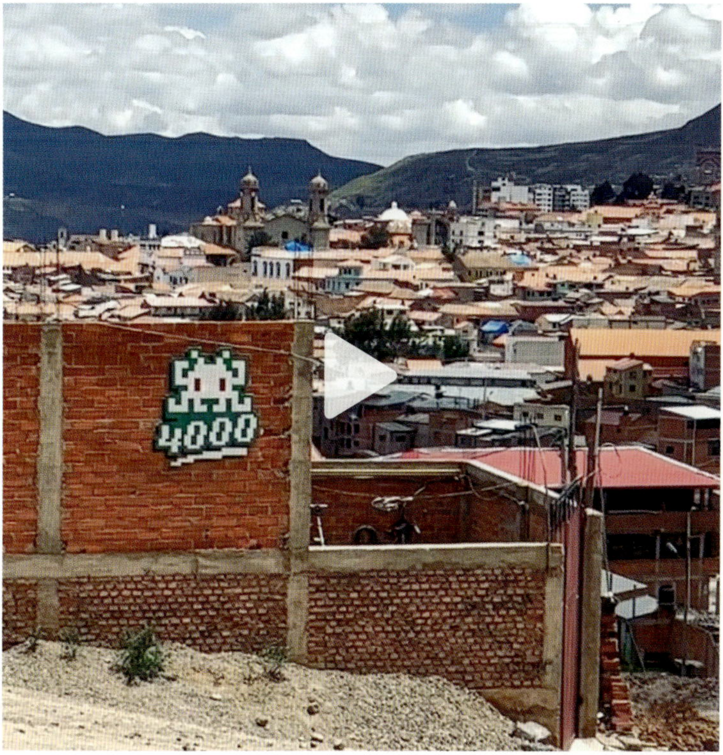

  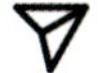 

131418 views

invaderwashere Potosí is one of the highest city in the world. POTI_01 is installed at 4000 meters above the sea level and is the 4000th space invader to land on Earth. #potosi #bolivia #4000 #gettinghigh

View all 273 comments

2 January 2022

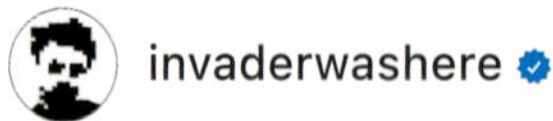

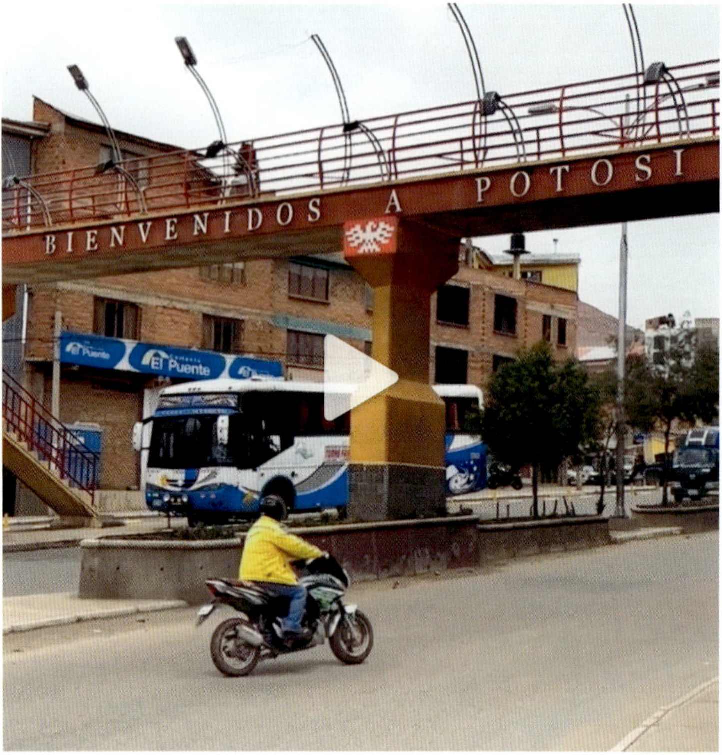

33 661 views

invaderwashere Potosí is the 80th city that I have had the opportunity to invade. Located in Bolivia at 4,000 m (13,400 ft) above sea level, I went there to install my 4,000th space invader. Once there, it would have been a shame not to install more pieces, so I brought more than half a ton of equipment with me! Its location, history and landscapes are breathtaking and it is definitely one of the most intense and amazing invasions I have been able to do so far. #POTI_02 #condor #welcometopotosí #potosi 🇧🇴

View all 109 comments

20 January 2022

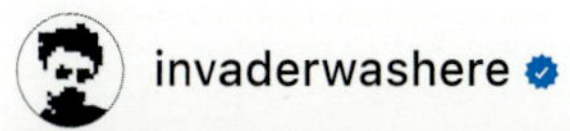

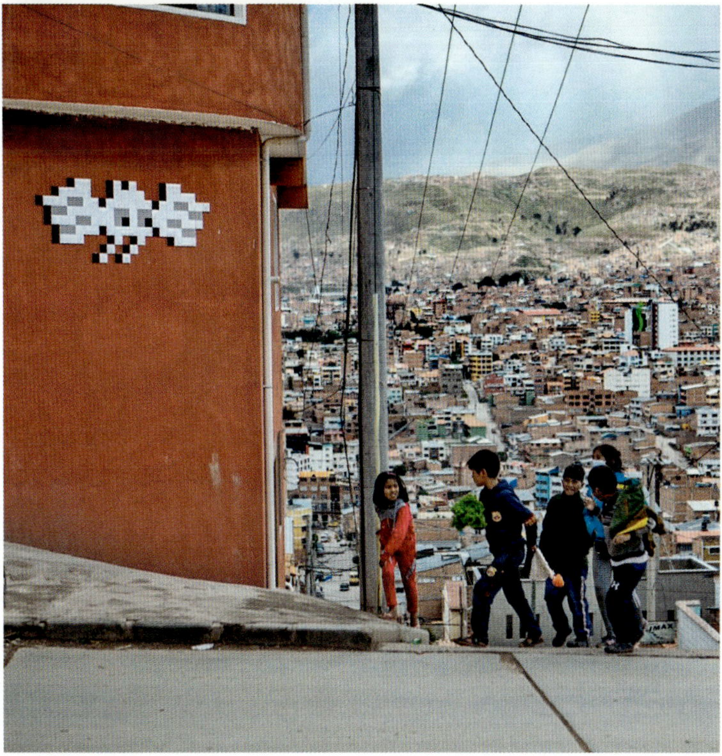

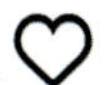   

11131 likes

invaderwashere Space-angel in Potosí...
POTI_03 photo by @henry_ponce_barco #potosí #bolivia

View all 76 comments

21 January 2022

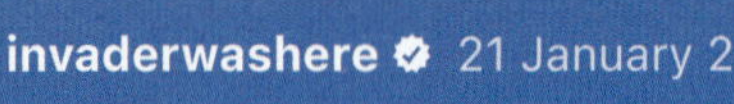

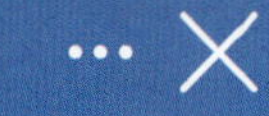

4194 m

Réception GPS

Send message
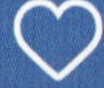

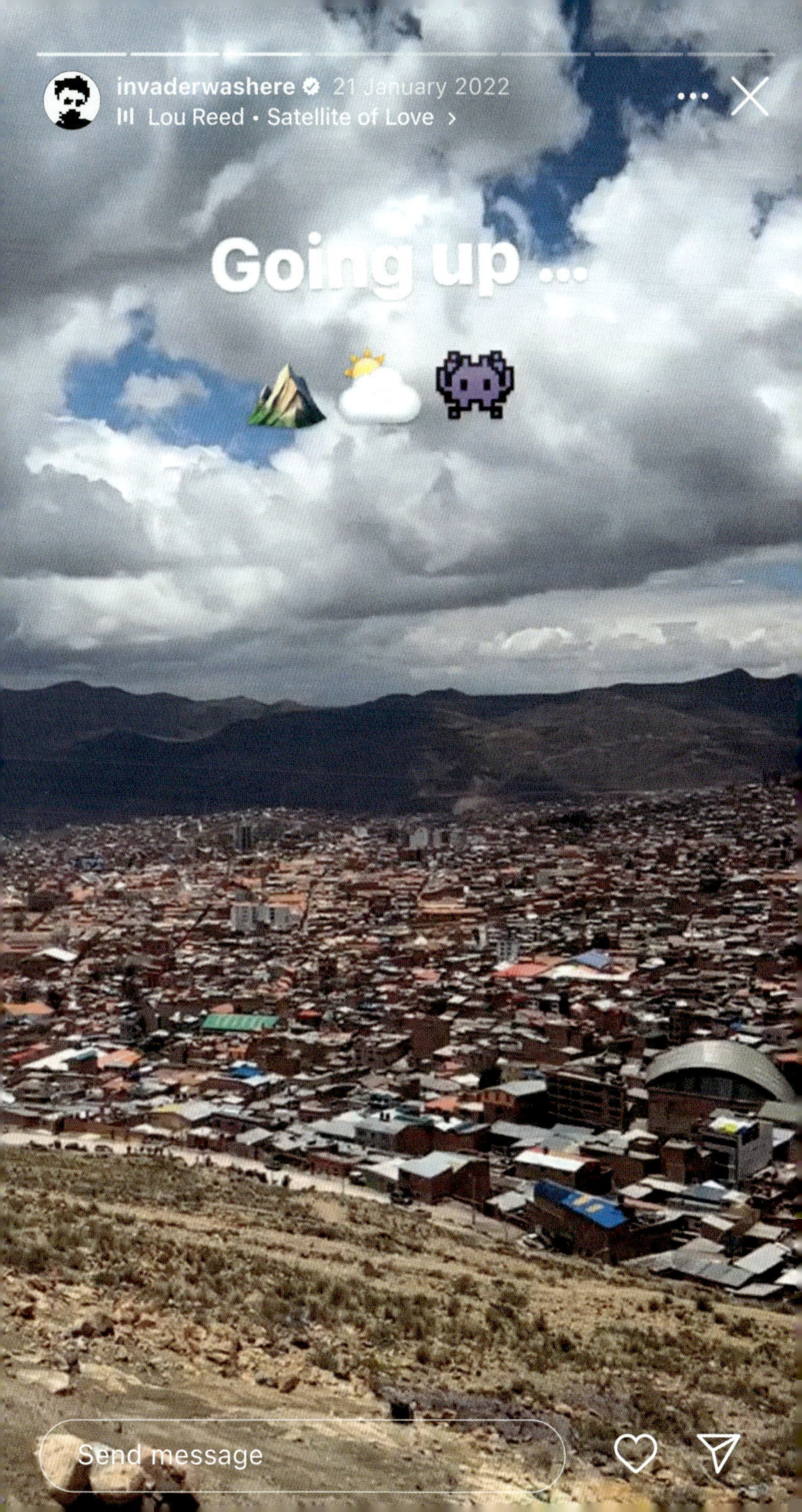
invaderwashere 21 January 2022
Lou Reed • Satellite of Love
Going up ...
Send message

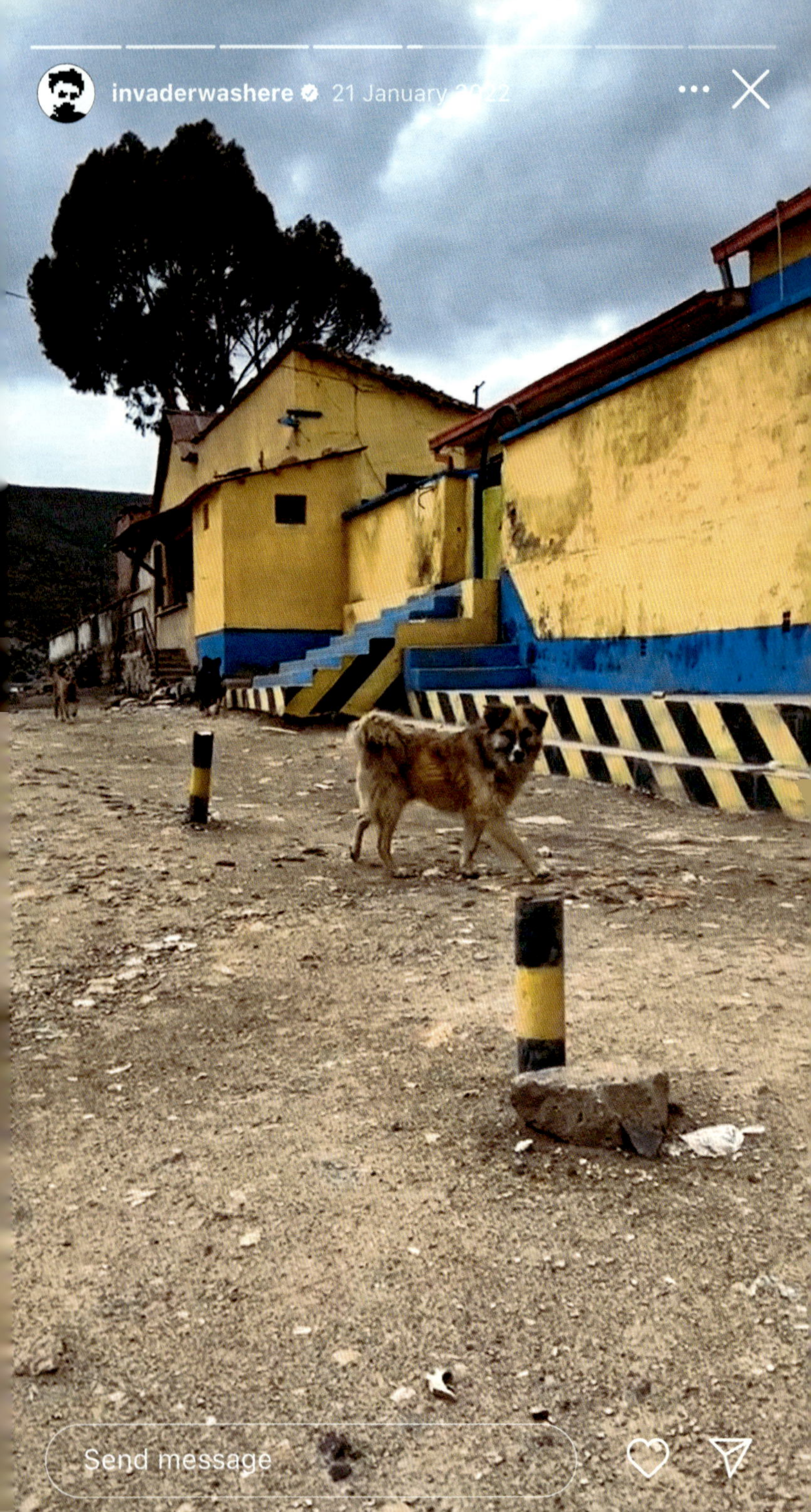
invaderwashere
21 January 2022
Send message

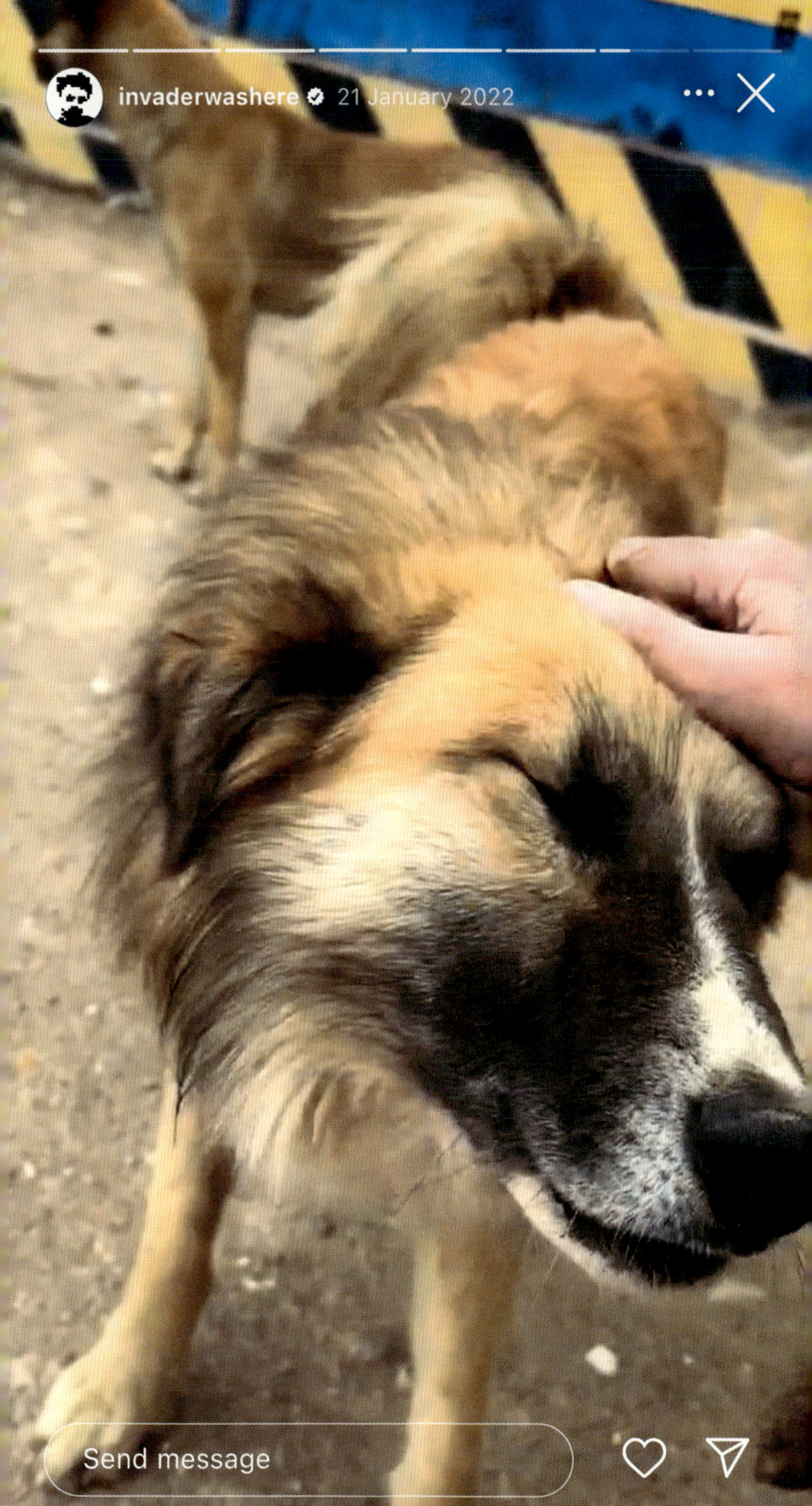
invaderwashere 21 January 2022
Send message

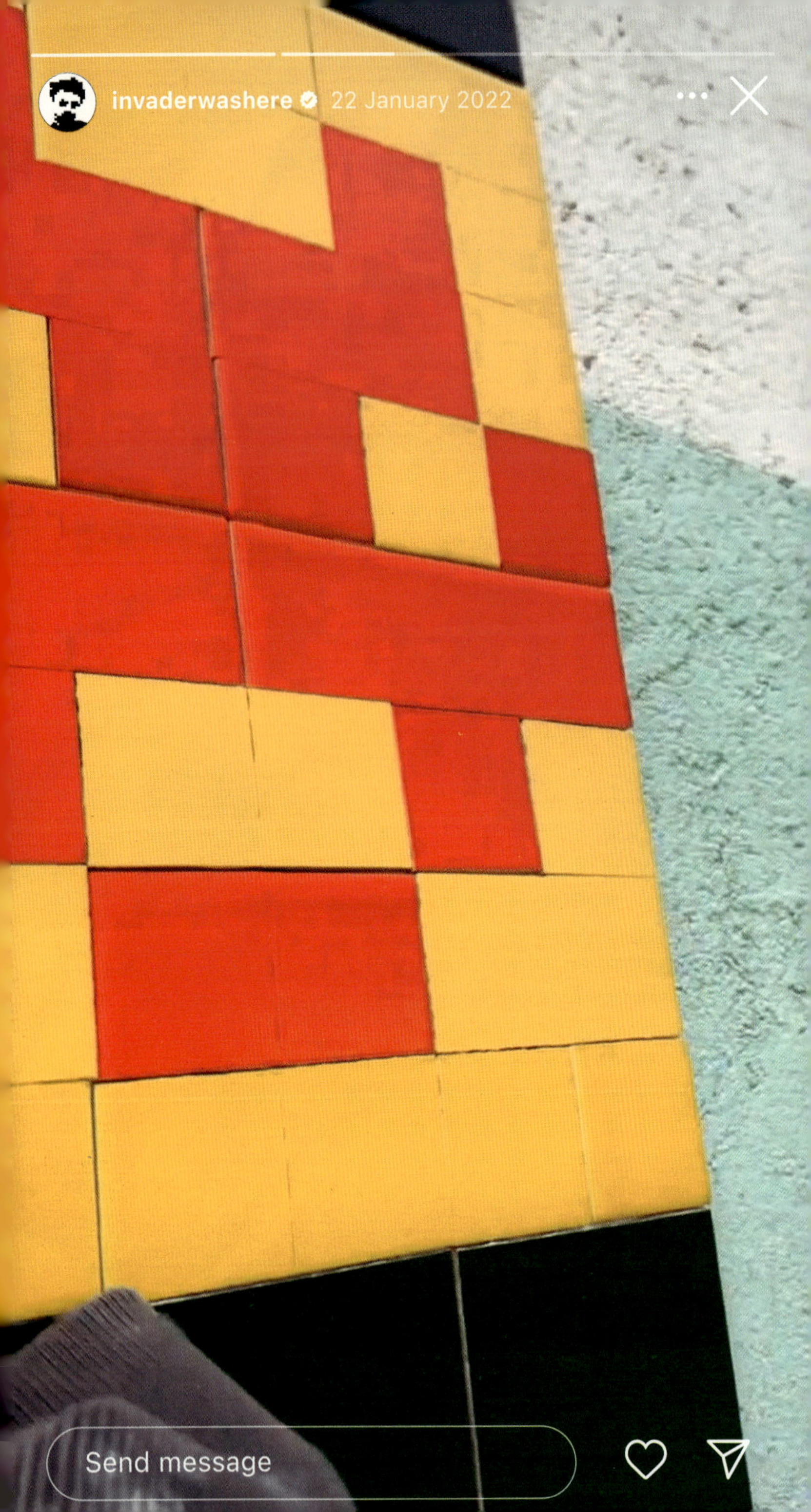
invaderwashere
22 January 2022
Send message

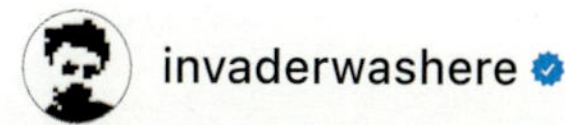

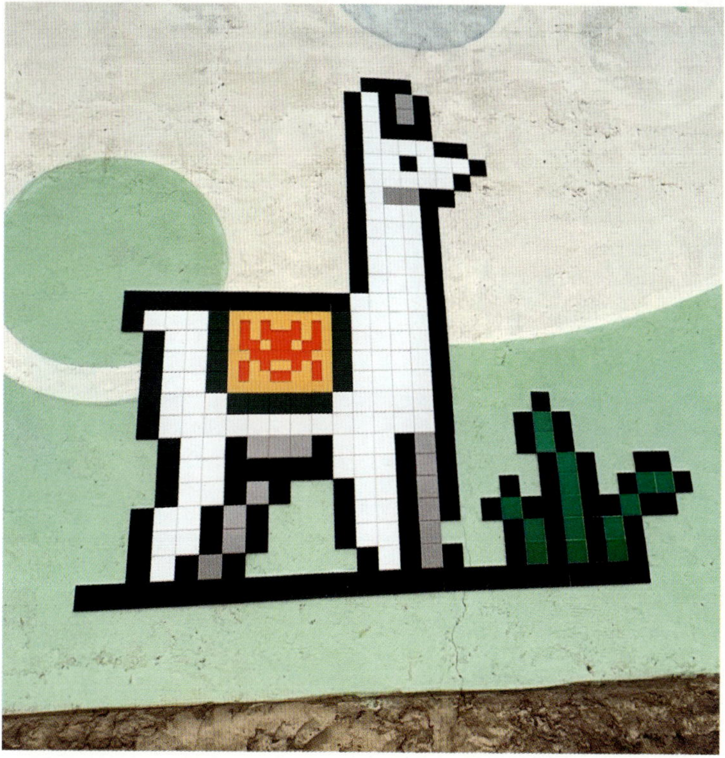

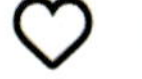   

11 454 likes

invaderwashere The Cerro Rico (Rich Mountain) of Potosí was one of the largest silver mines in the world. According to legend, it was discovered in 1545 by Diego Huallpa who was looking for his lost lama. 🏔️ 🦙 #cerrorico #lama #mine #potosi

View all 160 comments

22 January 2022

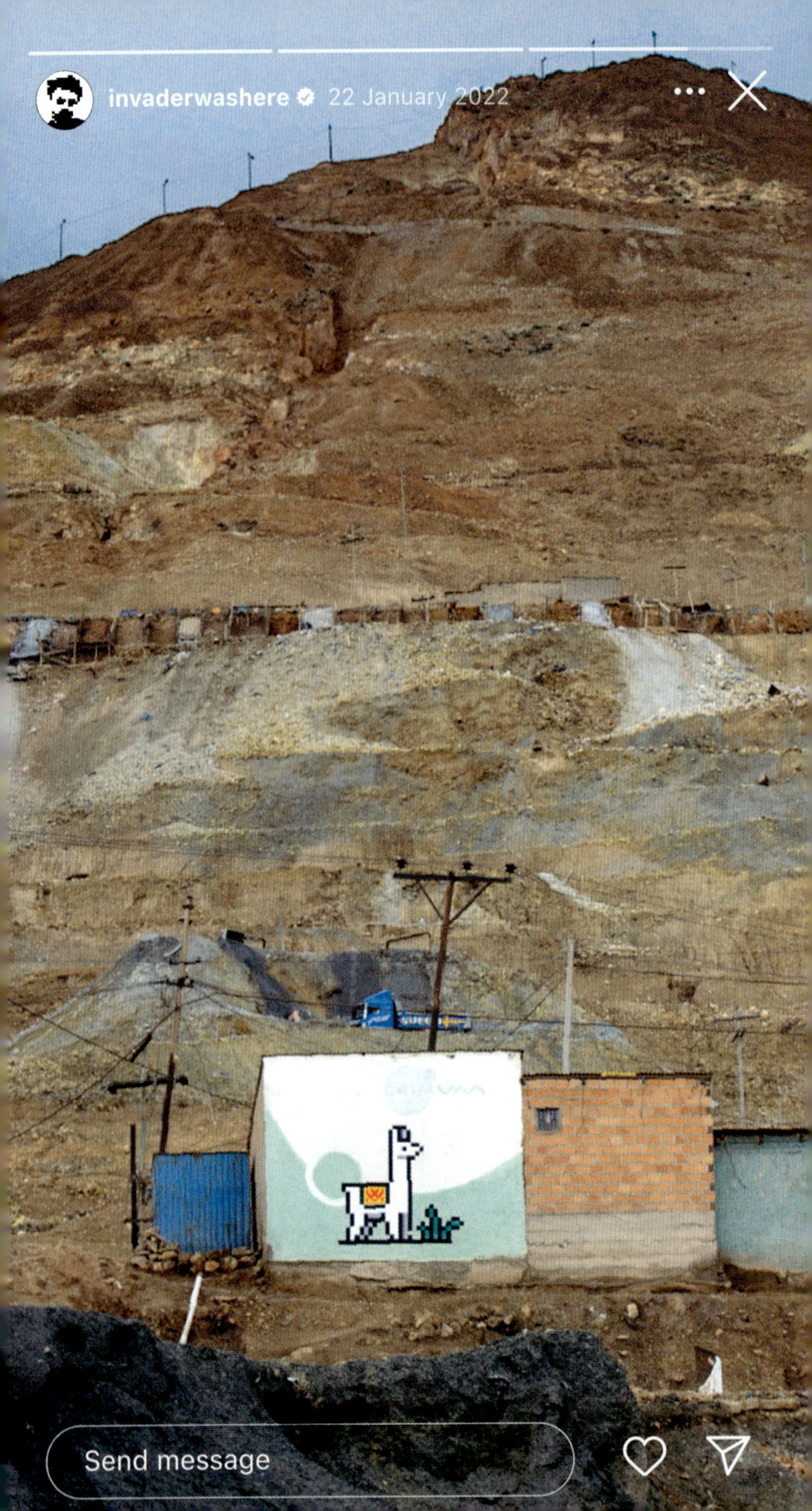
invaderwashere
22 January 2022
Send message

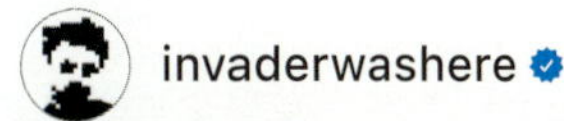

•••

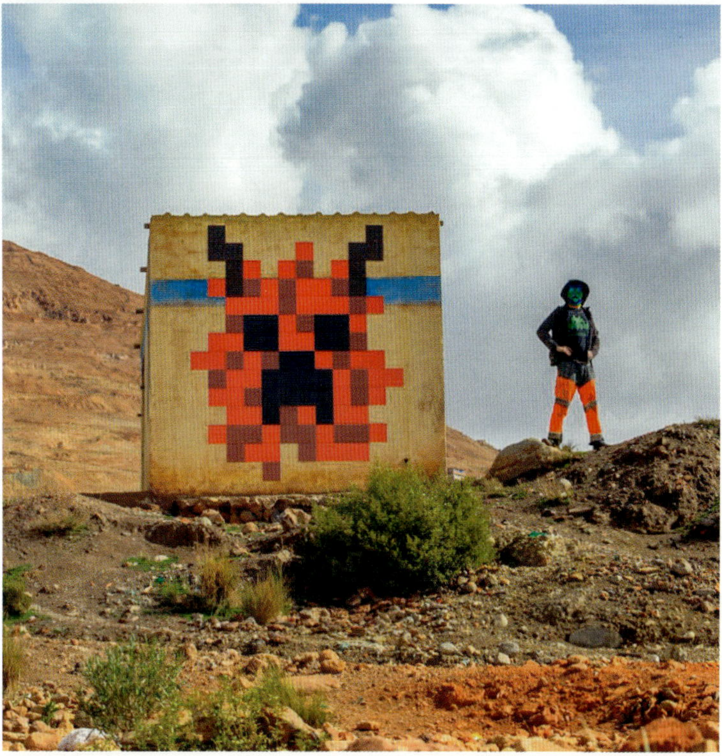

8150 likes

invaderwashere El Tio is the Lord of the underworld. He is supposed to rule over the mines of Potosí so miners bring offerings such as cigarettes, coca leaves and alcohol to its statues to get protection before entering the dark and narrow galleries of the mine #POTI_06 #tio #diablo #creeper #minecraft #cerrorico #sympathyforthedevil Invader portrait by @henry_ponce_barco

View all 107 comments

24 January 2022

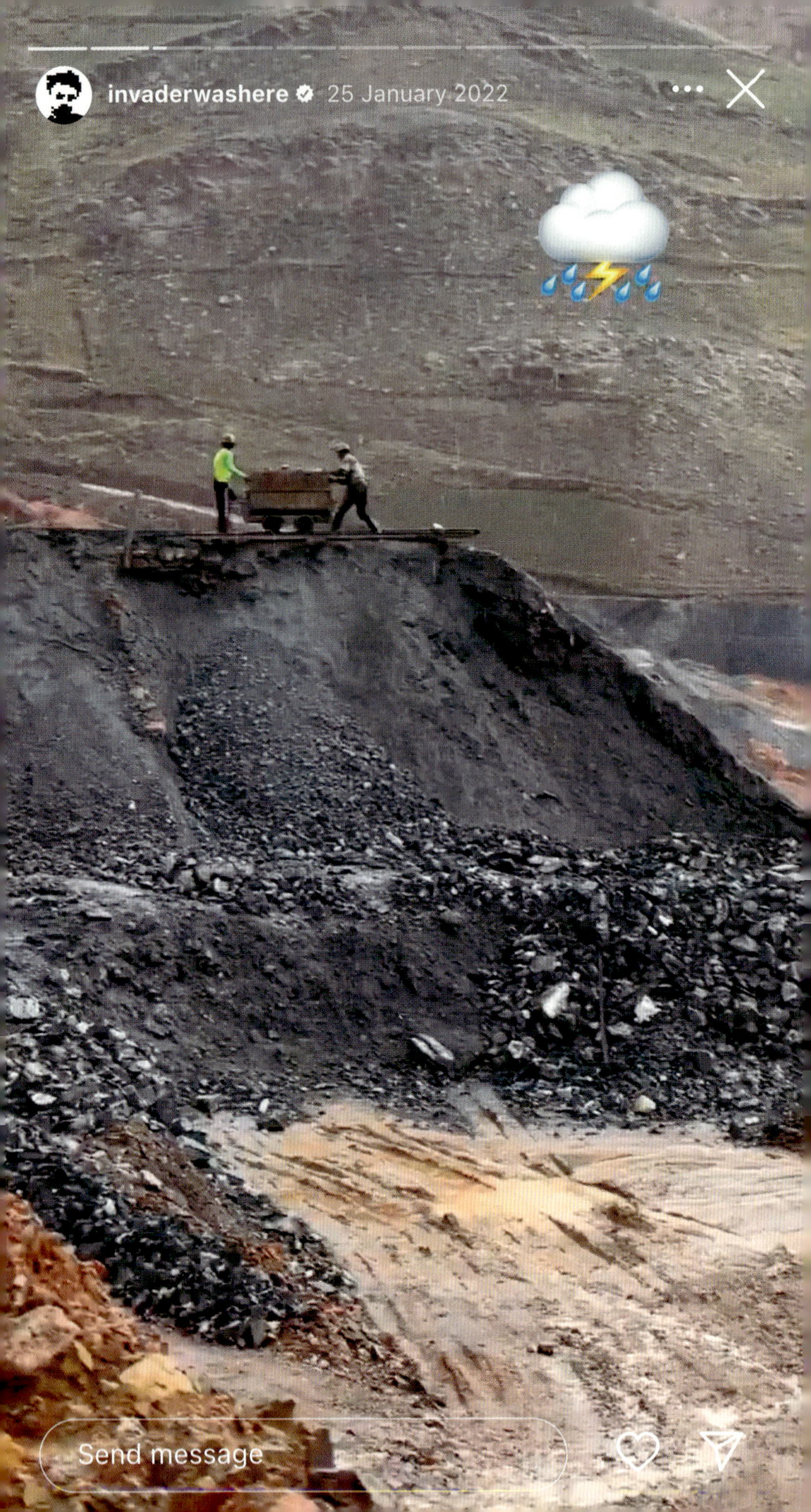
invaderwashere
25 January 2022
Send message

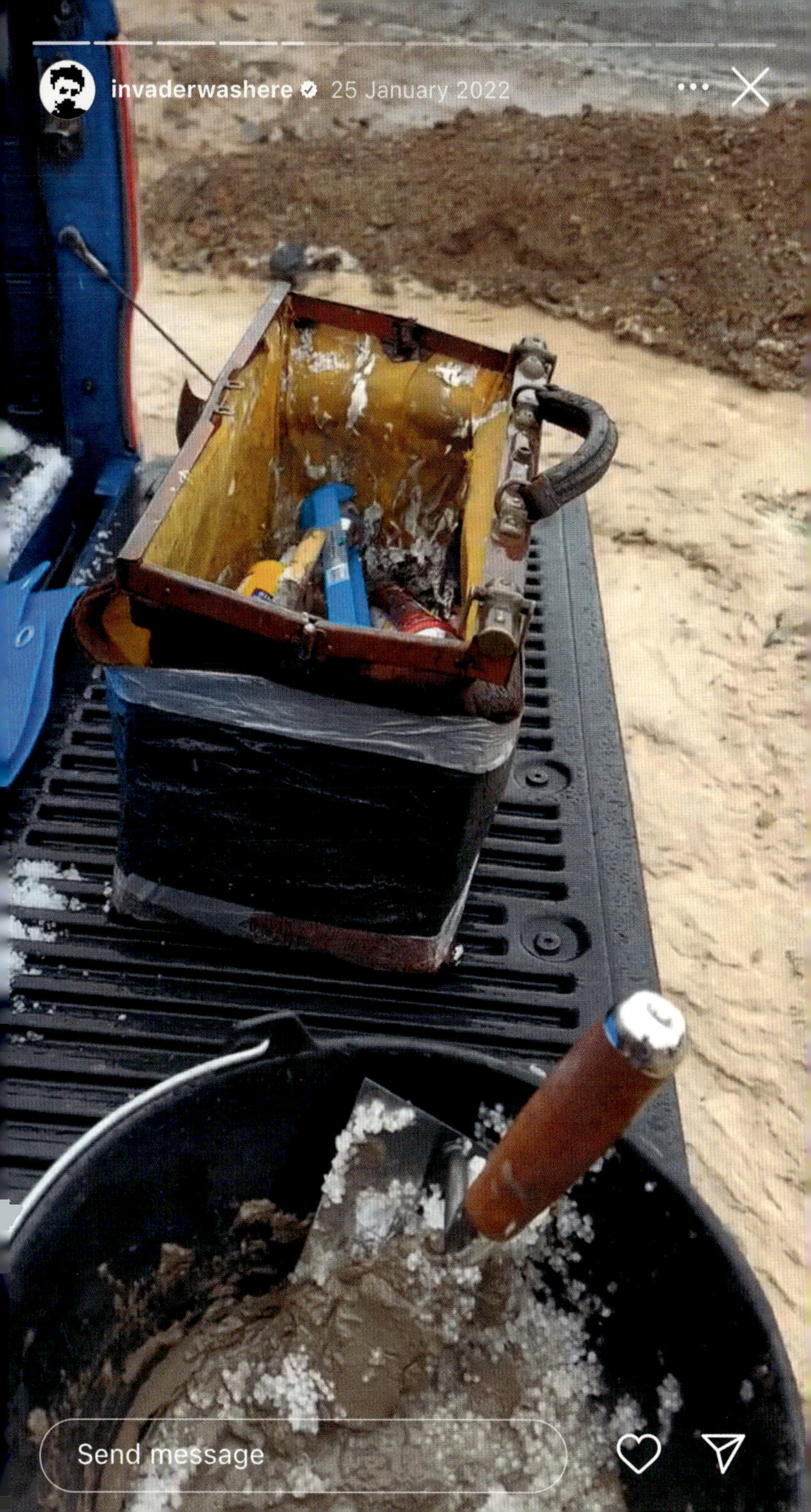

invaderwashere
25 January 2022
Send message

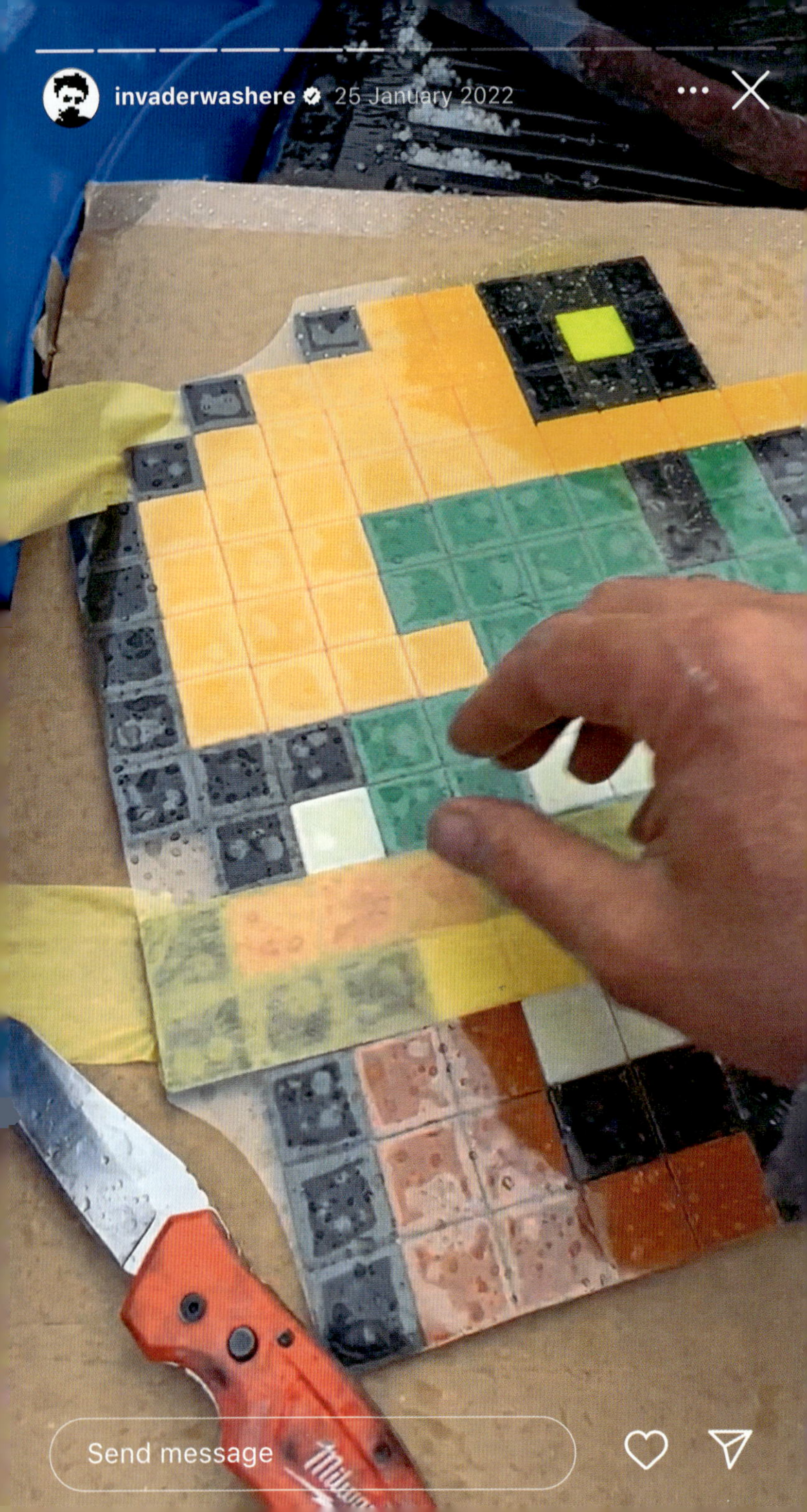
invaderwashere
25 January 2022
Send message
Milwaukee

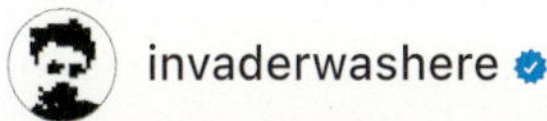

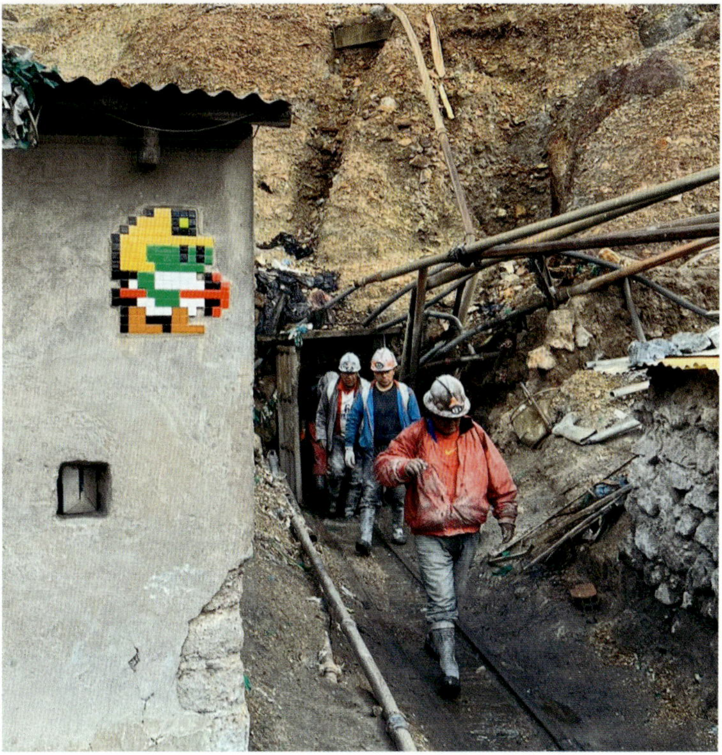

 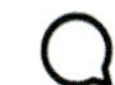   

19 519 likes

invaderwashere Dig Dug is a video game character who digs mazes underground #mines #hardwork #POTI_18 #digdug Big up to all the diggers of Potosí 🙌🙌🙌

View all 187 comments

25 January 2022

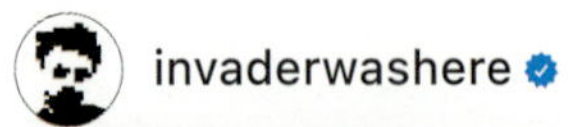

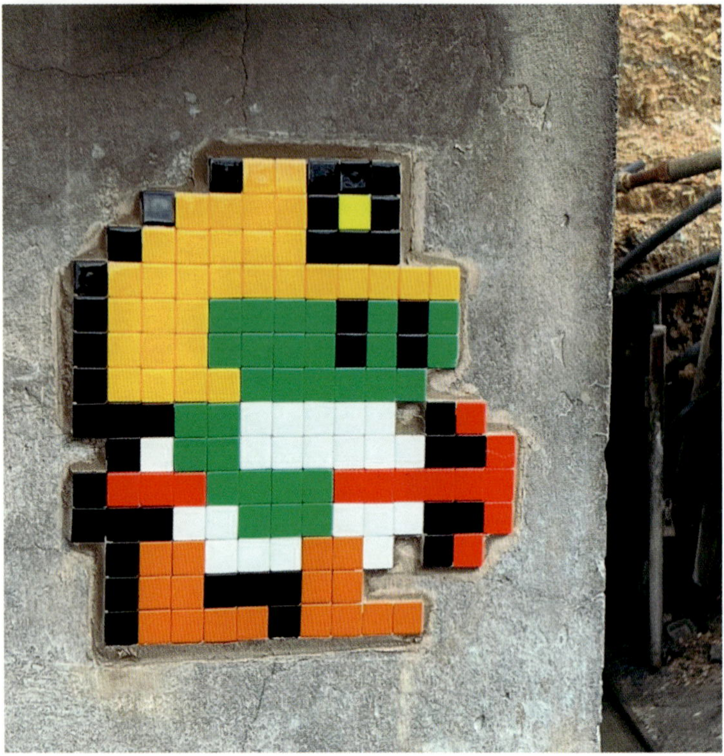

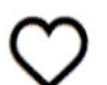   

19 519 likes

invaderwashere Dig Dug is a video game character who digs mazes underground #mines #hardwork #POTI_18 #digdug Big up to all the diggers of Potosí 🙌🙌🙌

View all 187 comments

25 January 2022

invaderwashere

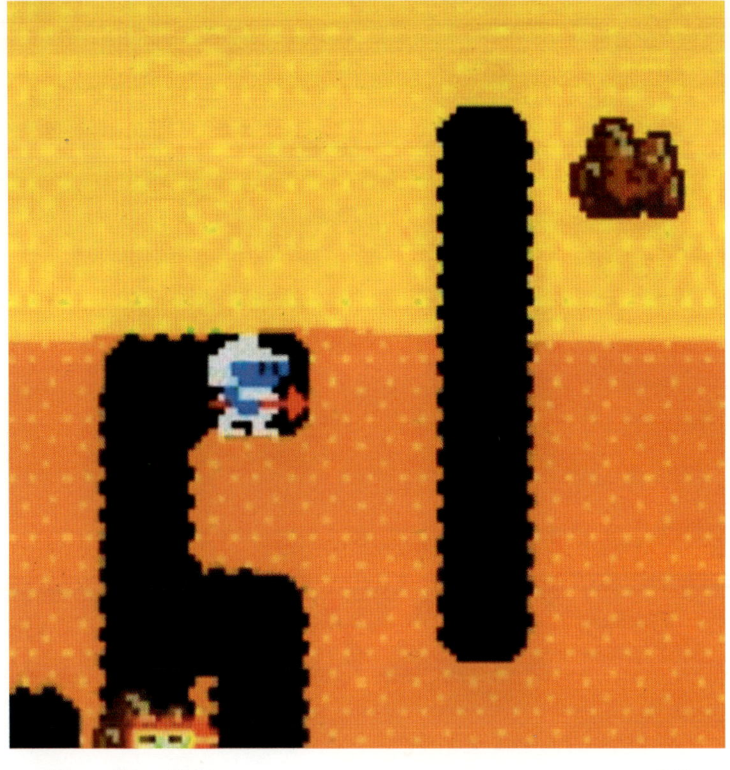

19 519 likes

invaderwashere Dig Dug is a video game character who digs mazes underground #mines #hardwork #POTI_18 #digdug Big up to all the diggers of Potosí 🙌🙌🙌

View all 187 comments

25 January 2022

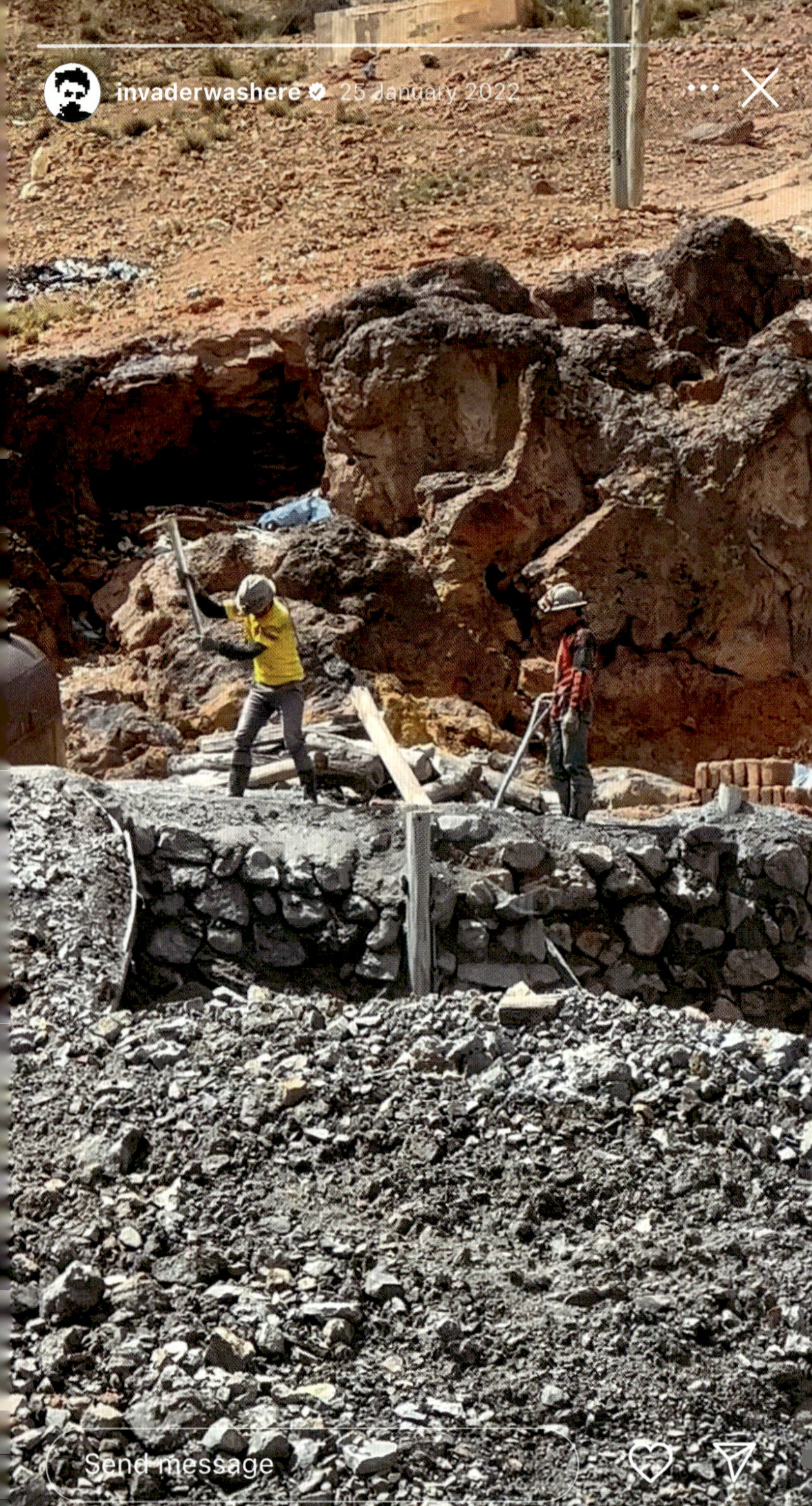
invaderwashere
25 January 2022
Send message

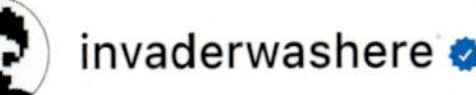

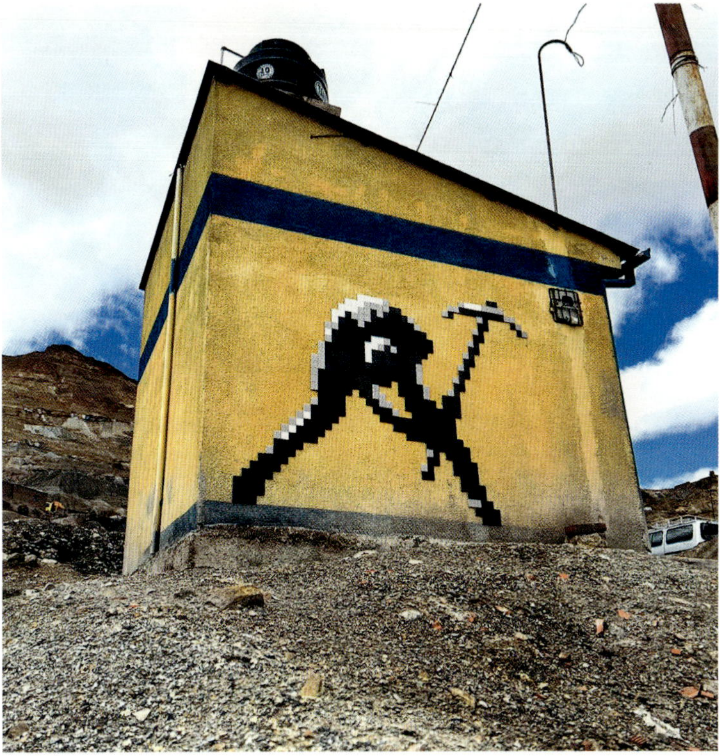

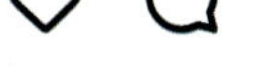

25 121 likes

invaderwashere POTOSÍ CALLING! #potosi #bolivia #cerrorico #mines #miner #theclash #rockthemines ⛏

View all 358 comments

27 January 2022

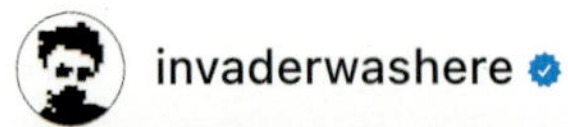

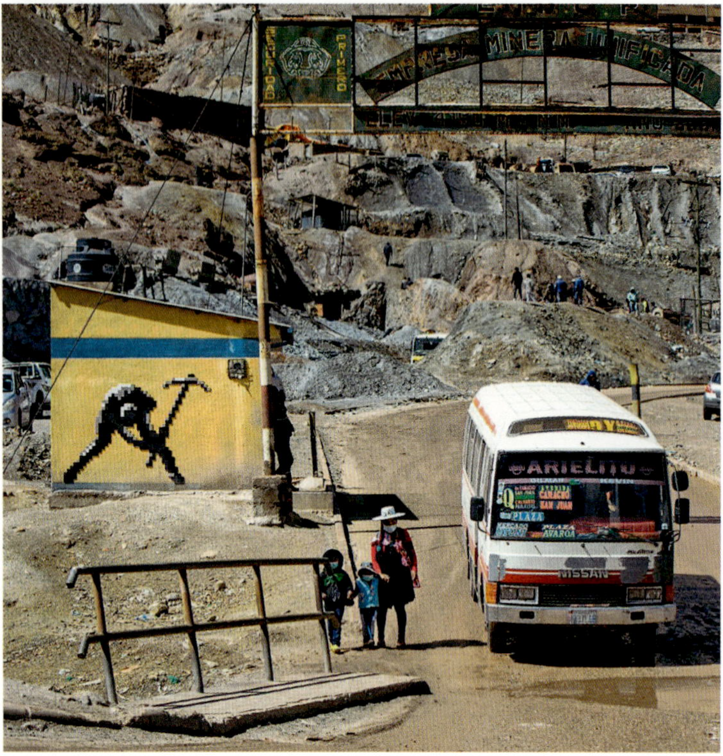

25 121 likes

invaderwashere POTOSÍ CALLING! #potosi #bolivia #cerrorico #mines #miner #theclash #rockthemines ⛏

View all 358 comments

27 January 2022

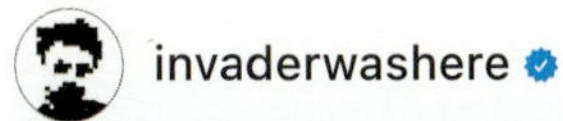

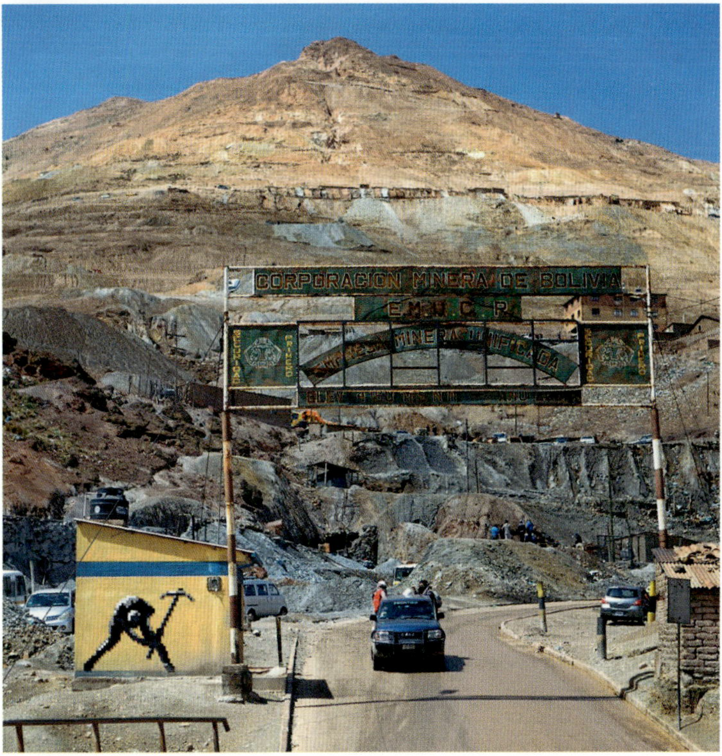

25 121 likes

invaderwashere POTOSÍ CALLING! #potosi #bolivia #cerrorico #mines #miner #theclash #rockthemines ⛏

View all 358 comments

27 January 2022

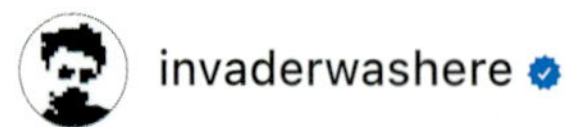

•••

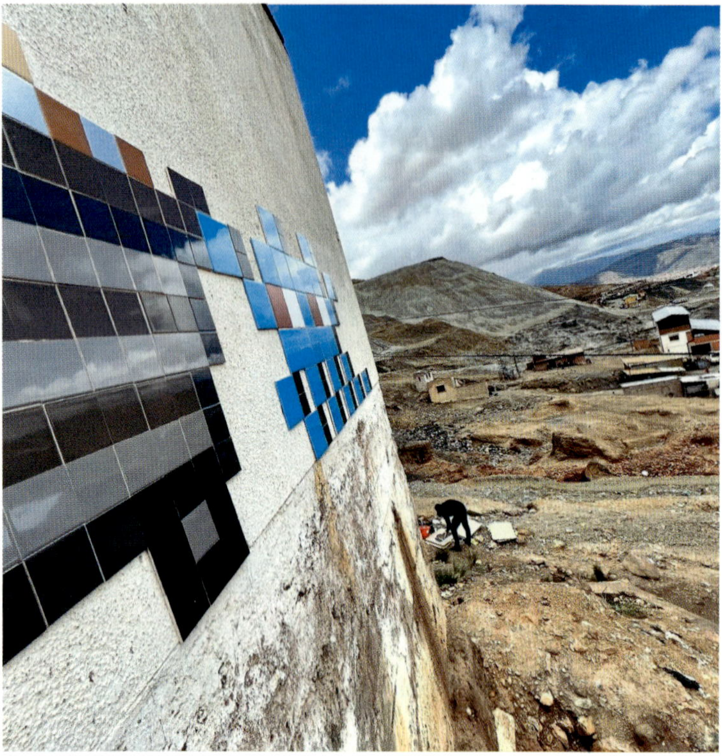

8825 likes

invaderwashere Mines of Potosí #cerrorico #potosi #bolivia Between the 16th and 18th century, 80% of the world's silver supply came out of this mine. After centuries of exploitation the mountain continues to be mined to this day. 🏔⛏🌑

View all 89 comments

30 January 2022

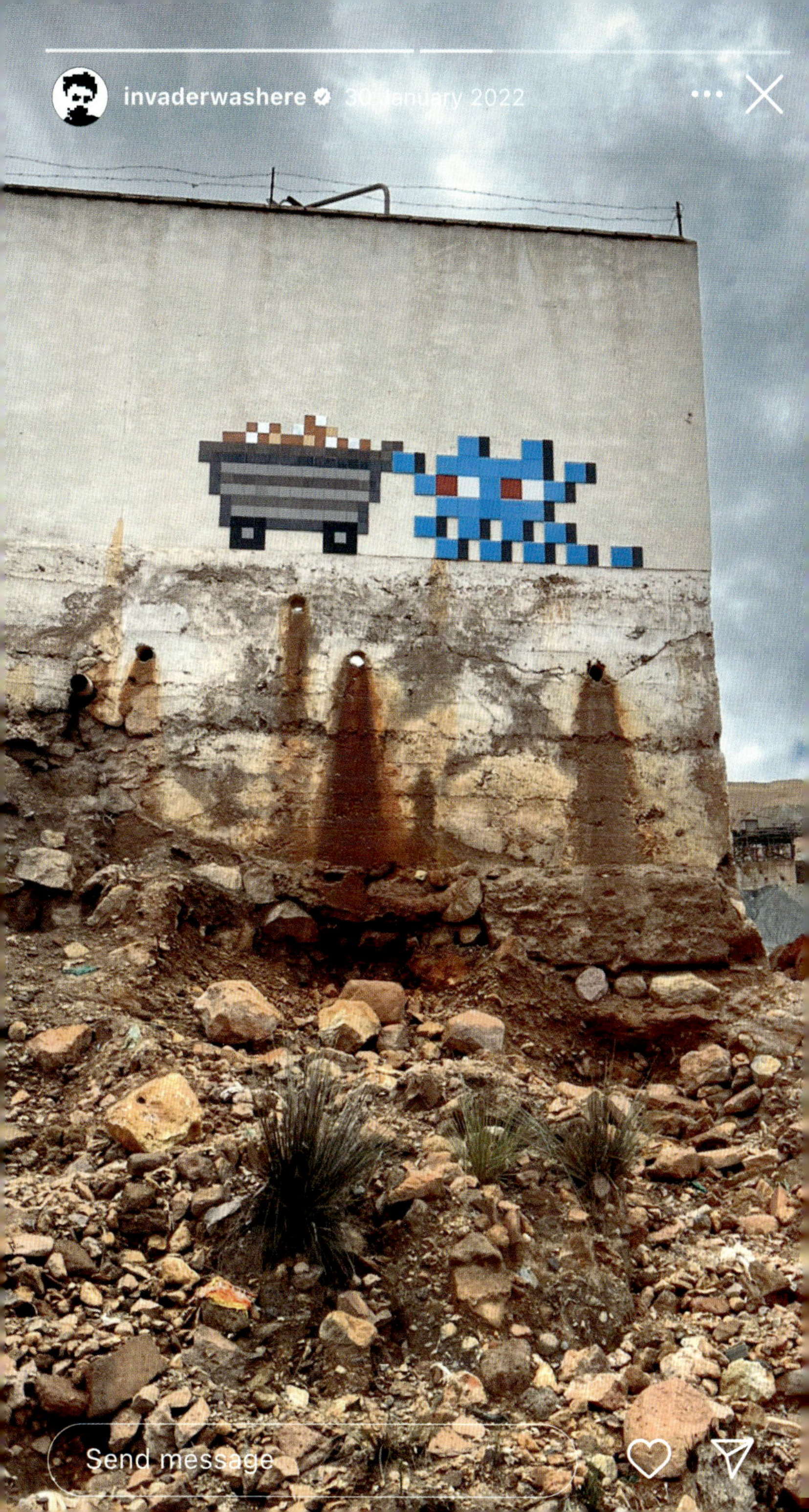
invaderwashere
30 January 2022
Send message

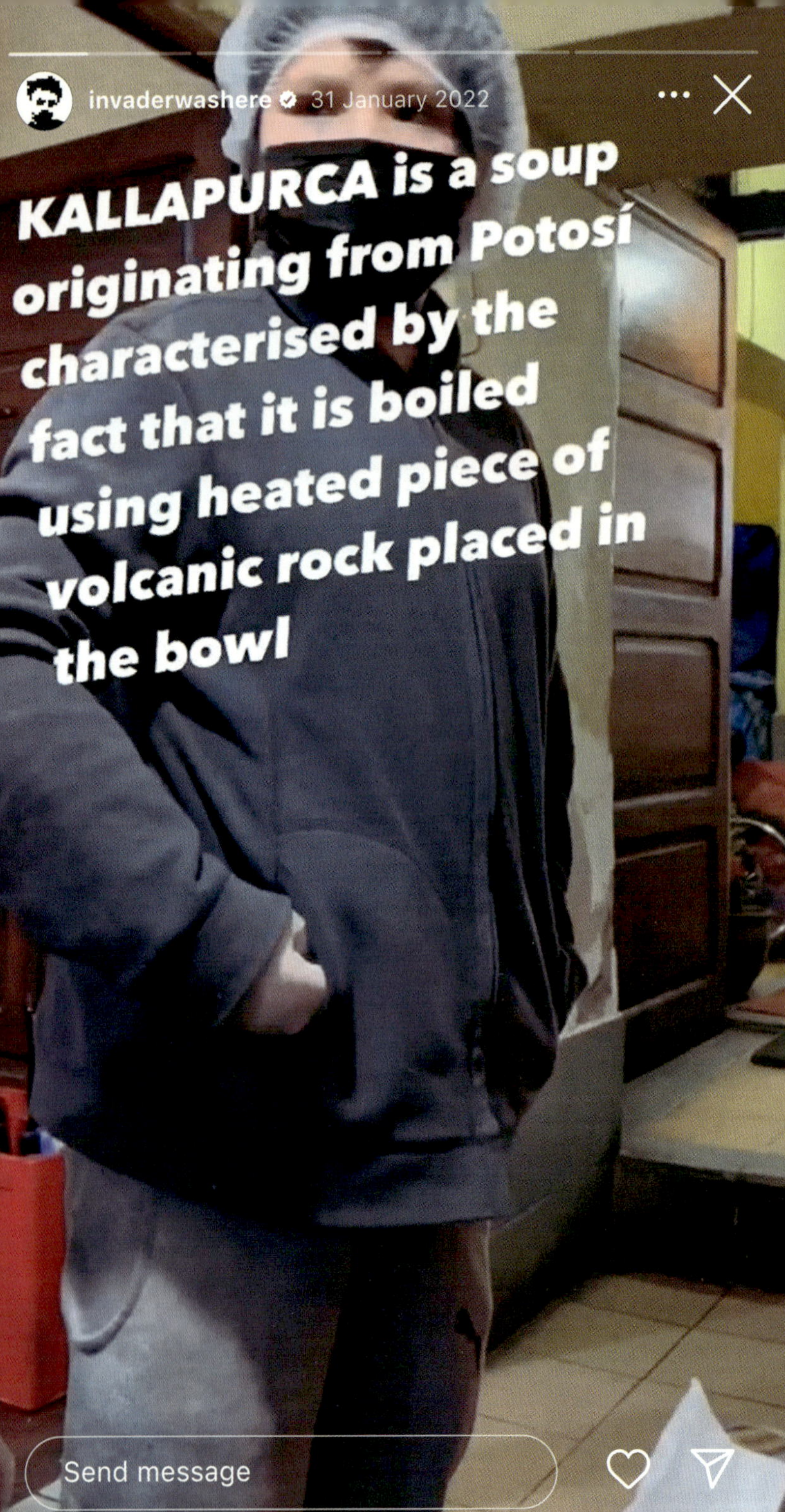
invaderwashere 31 January 2022
KALLAPURCA is a soup originating from Potosí characterised by the fact that it is boiled using heated piece of volcanic rock placed in the bowl
Send message

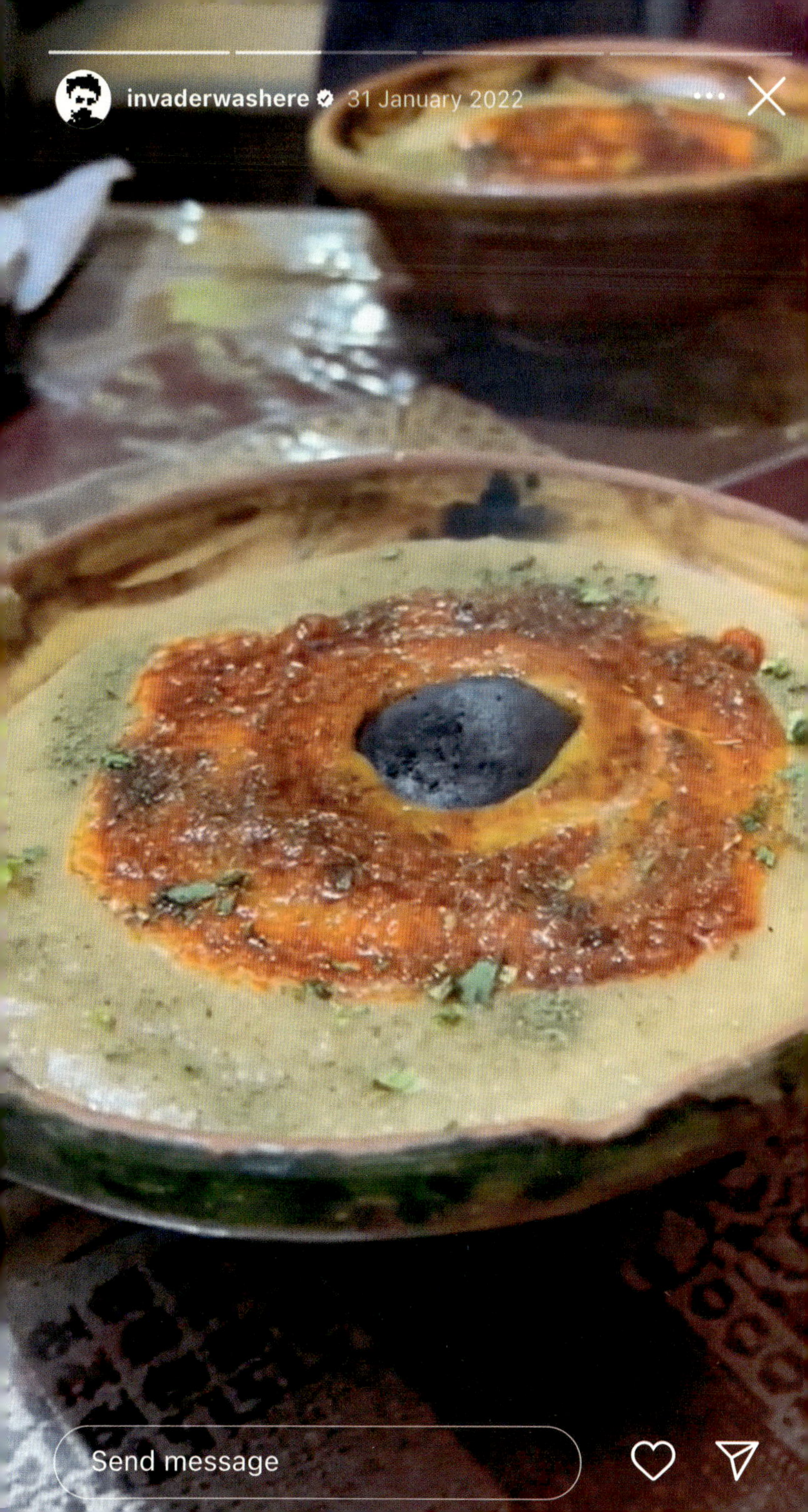
invaderwashere
31 January 2022
Send message

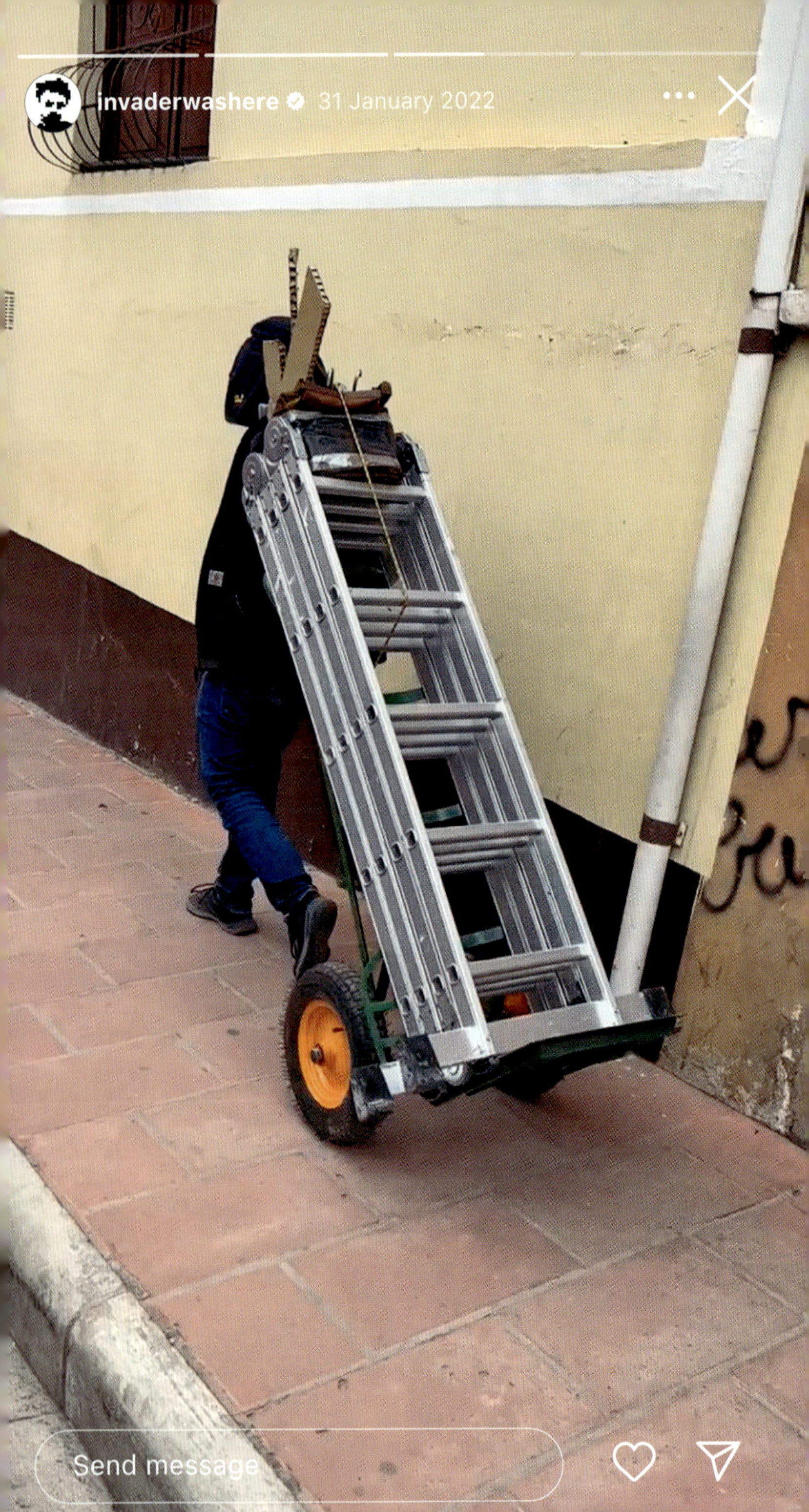
invaderwashere
31 January 2022
Send message

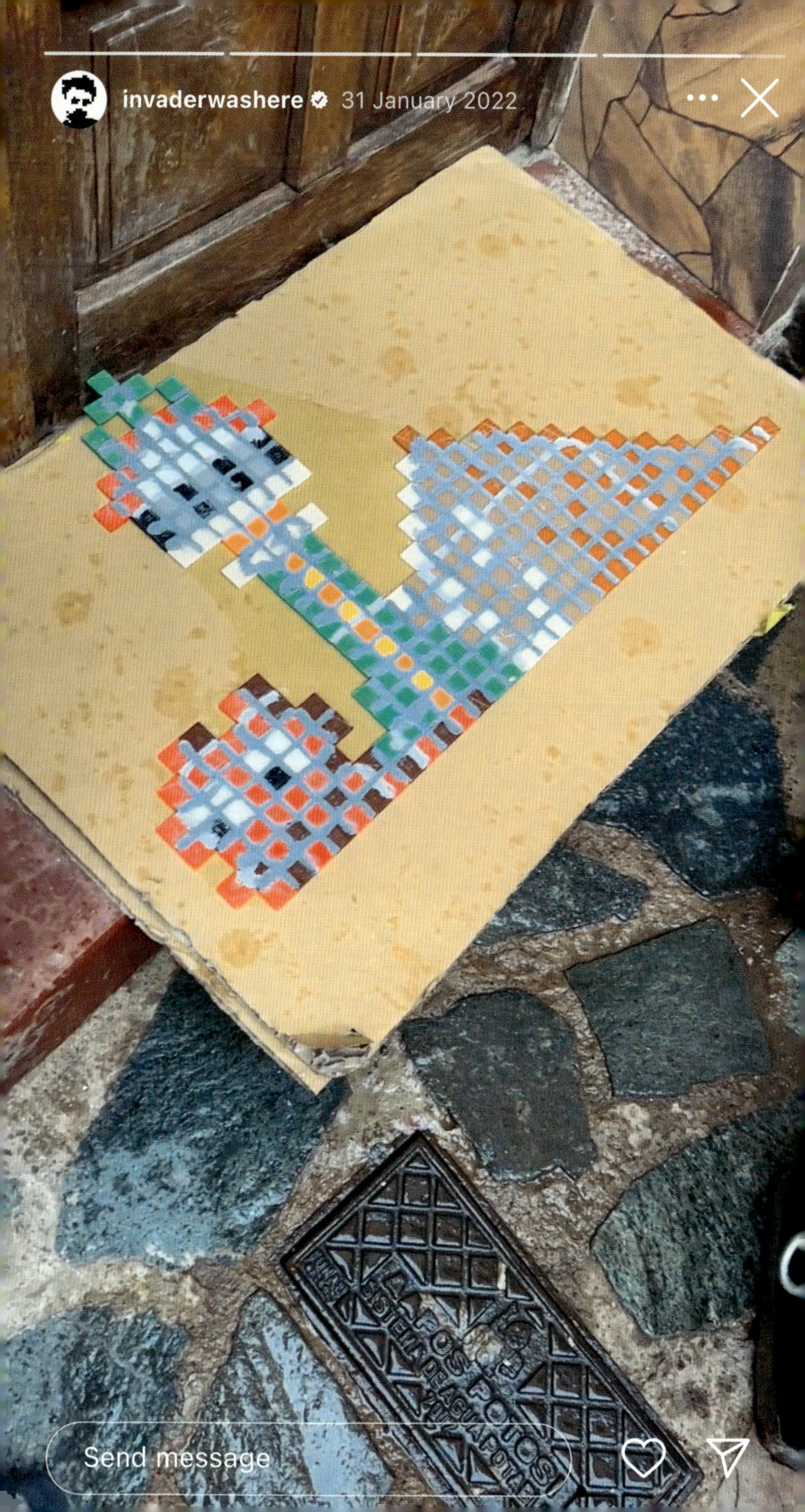
invaderwashere
31 January 2022
Send message

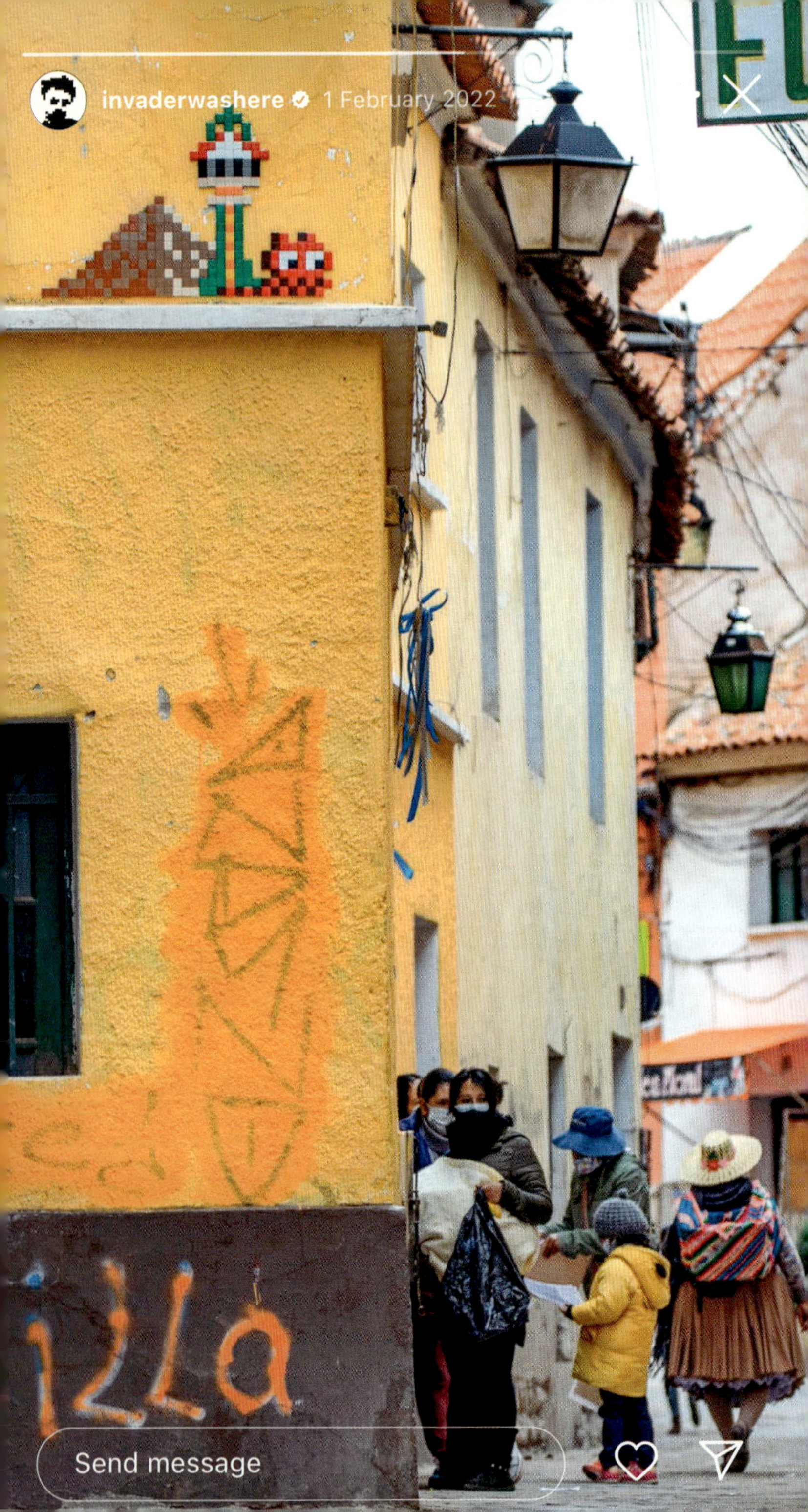
invaderwashere
1 February 2022
Send message

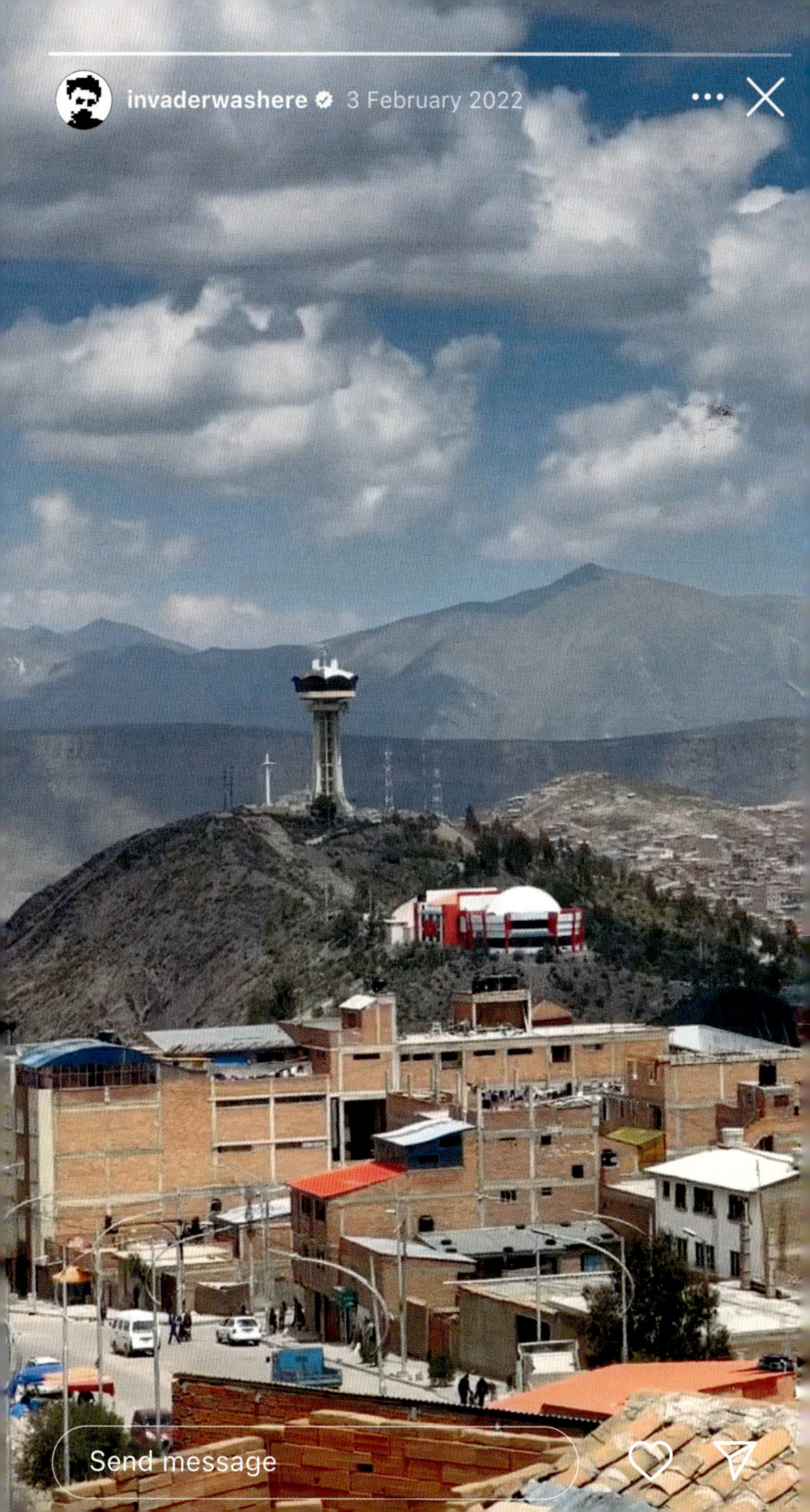
invaderwashere
3 February 2022
Send message

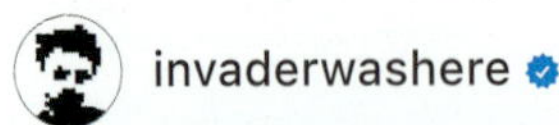

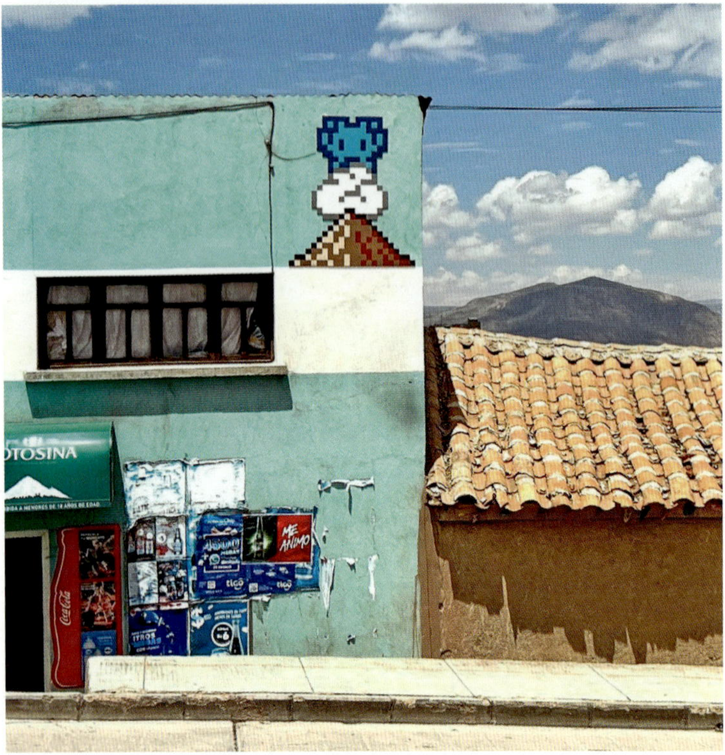

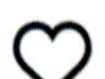    

10 467 likes

invaderwashere POTI_31

#potosi #bolivia #emojinvader #mission4000

View all 80 comments

3 February 2022

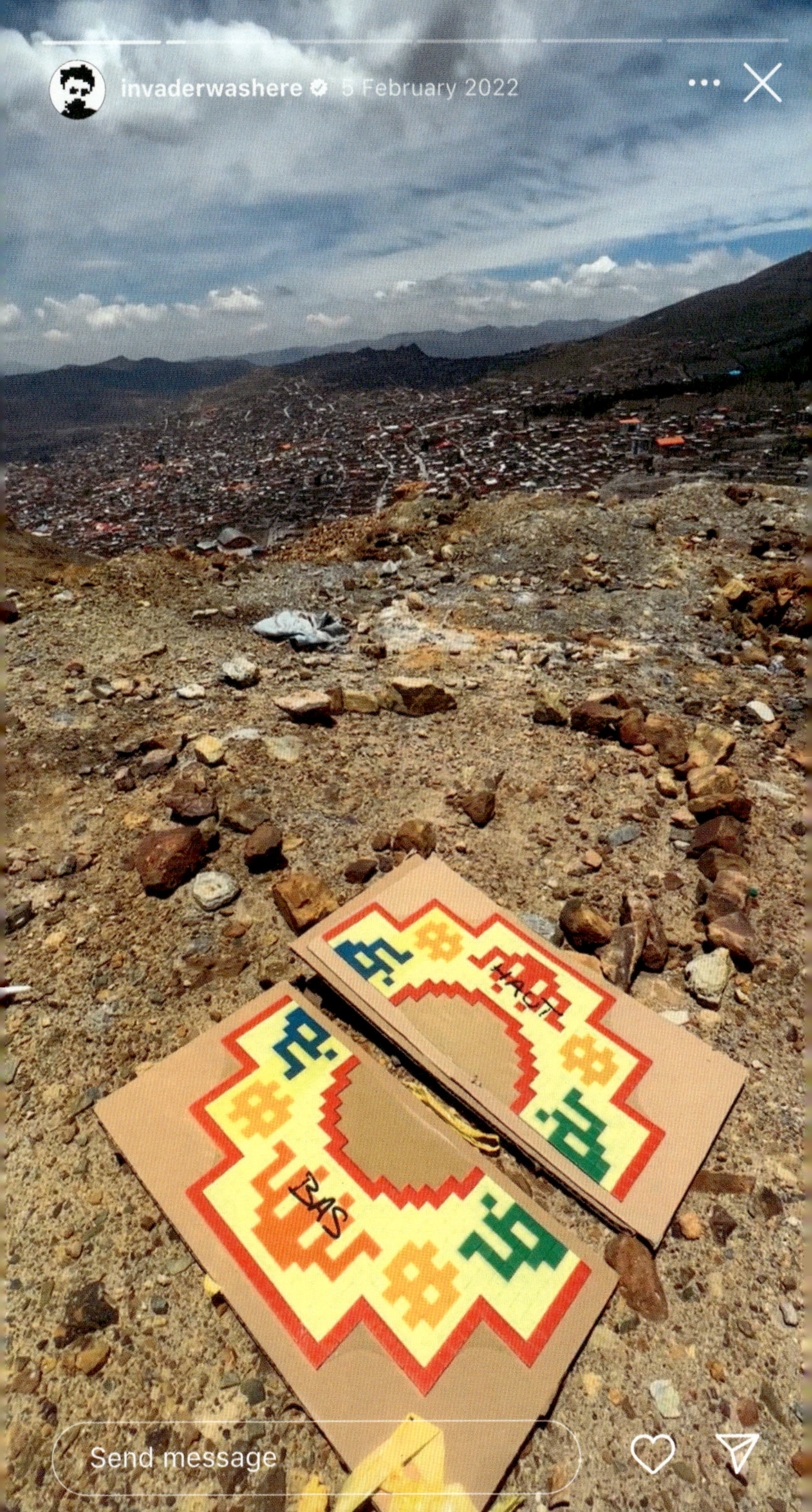
invaderwashere
5 February 2022
HAUT
BAS
Send message

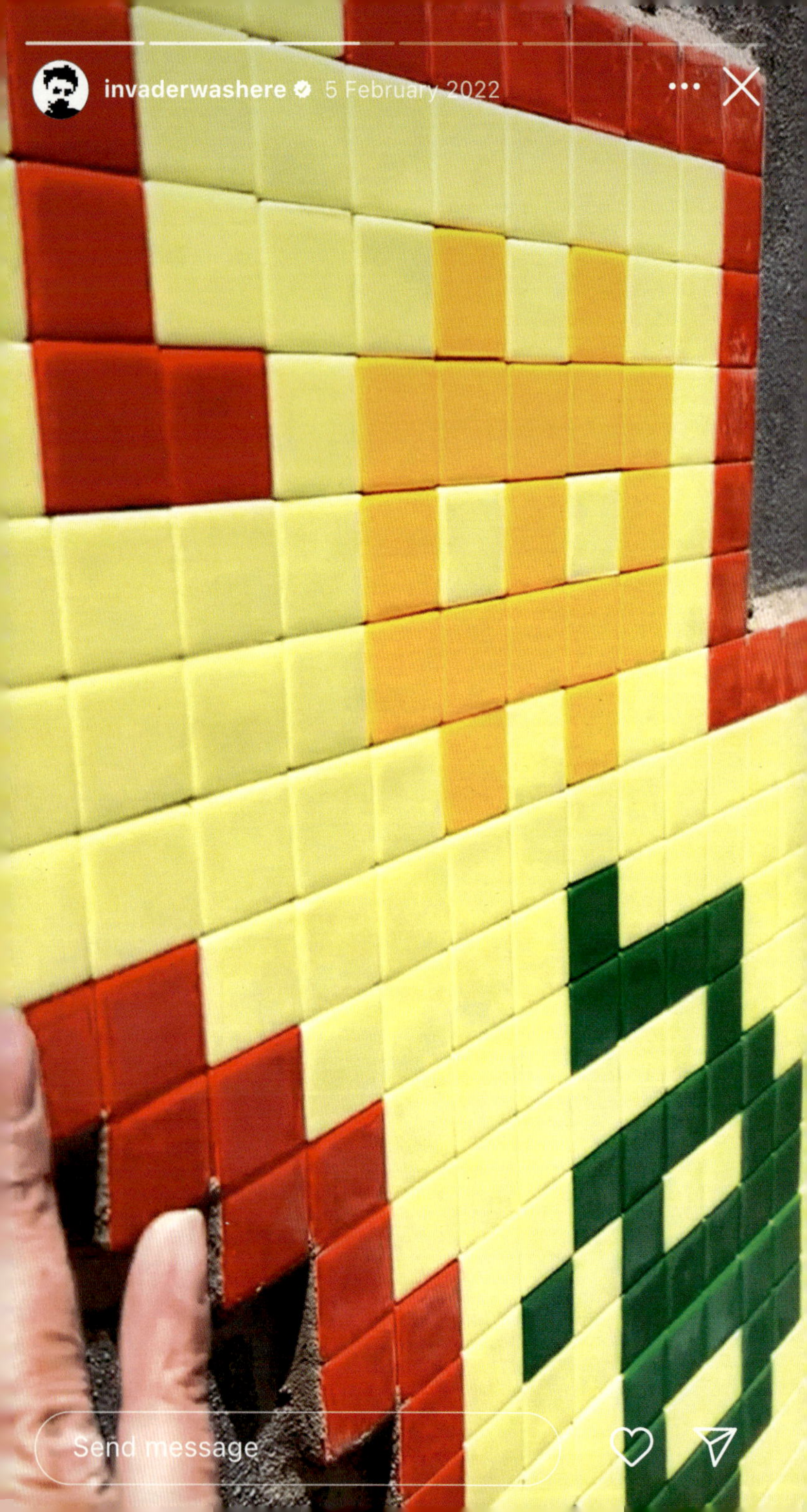
invaderwashere
5 February 2022
Send message

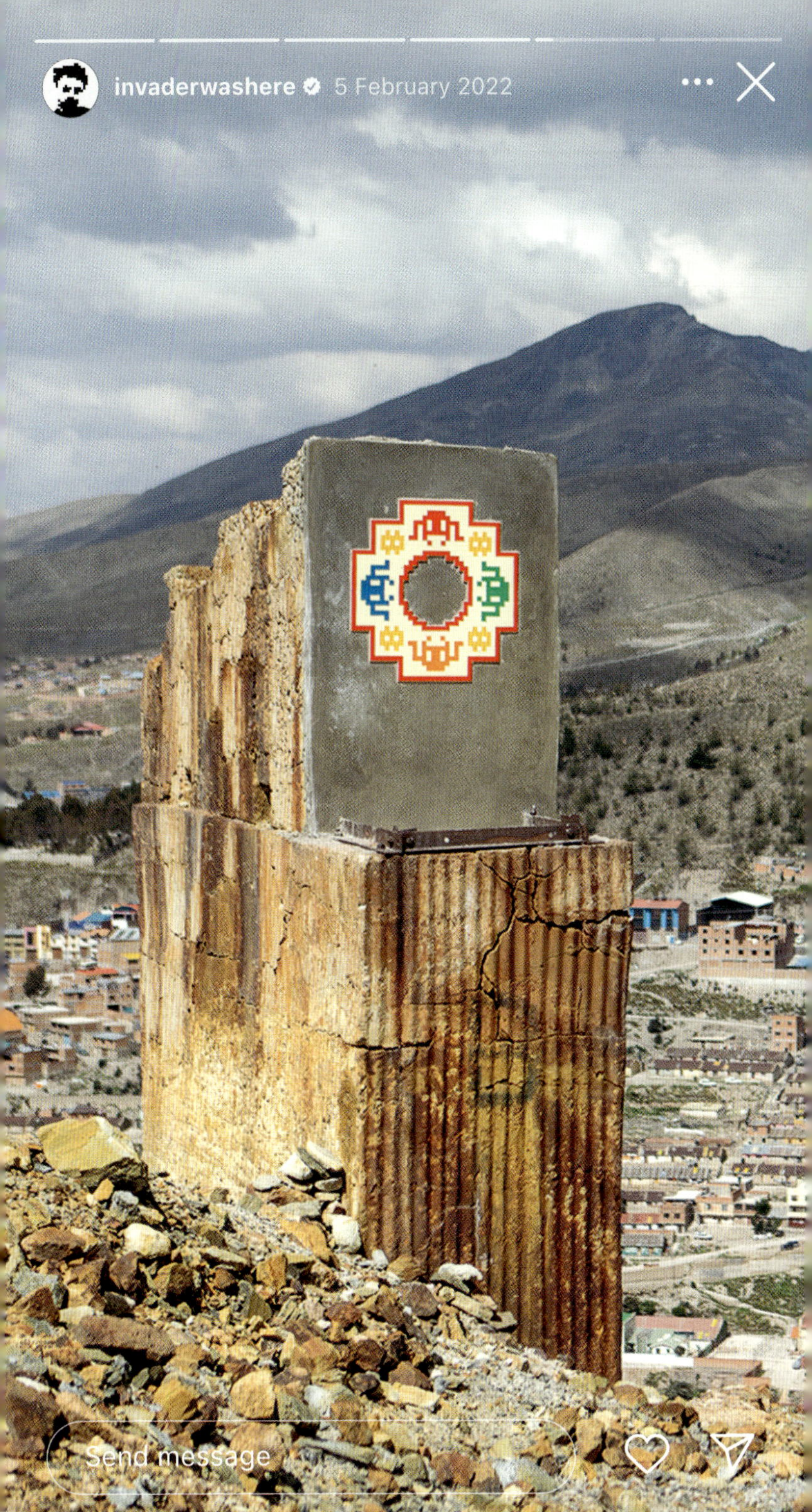
invaderwashere
5 February 2022
Send message

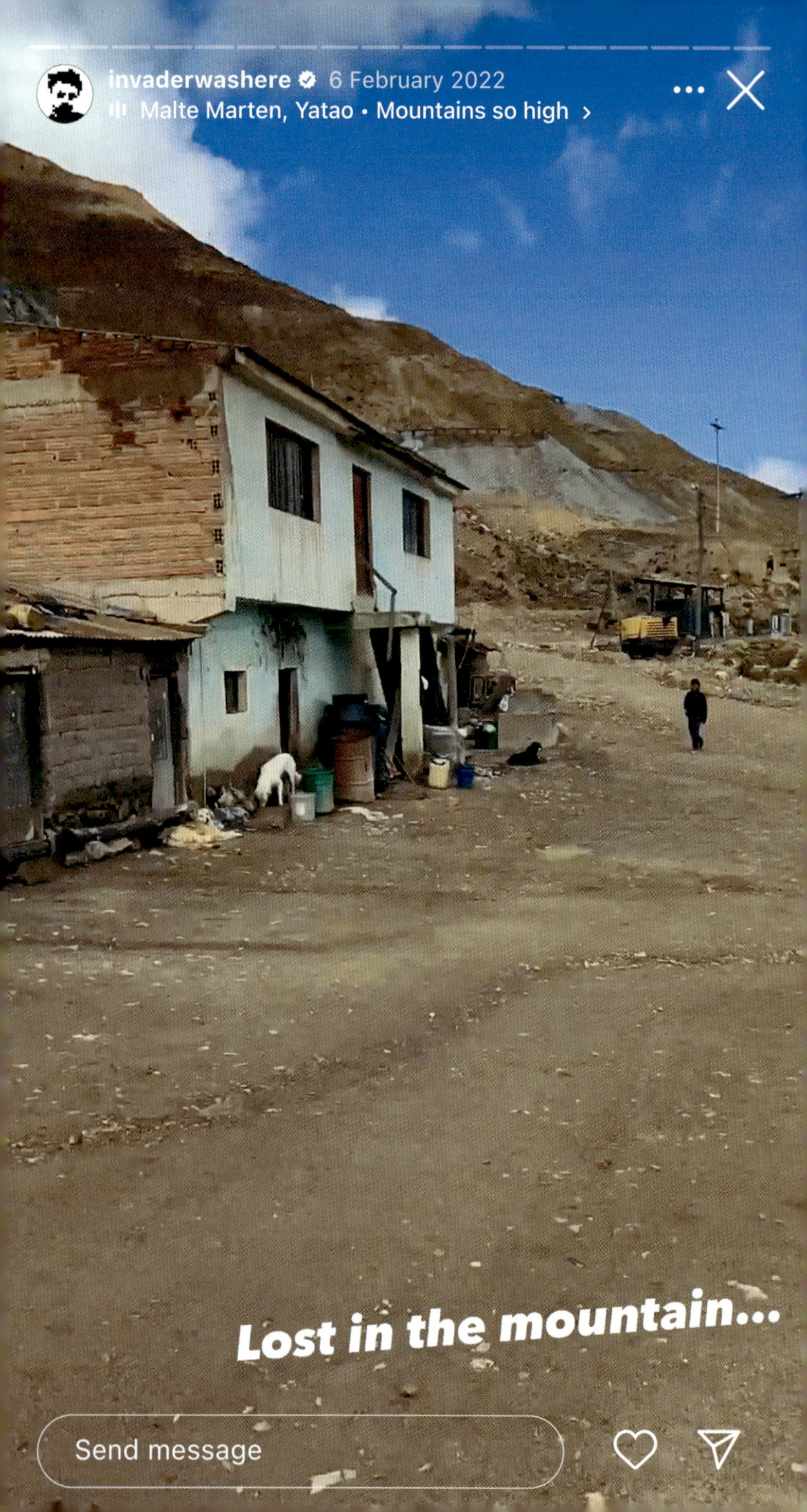

invaderwashere 6 February 2022

Malte Marten, Yatao • Mountains so high ›

Lost in the mountain...

Send message

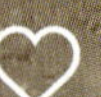
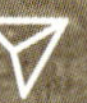

invaderwashere 6 February 2022

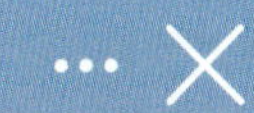

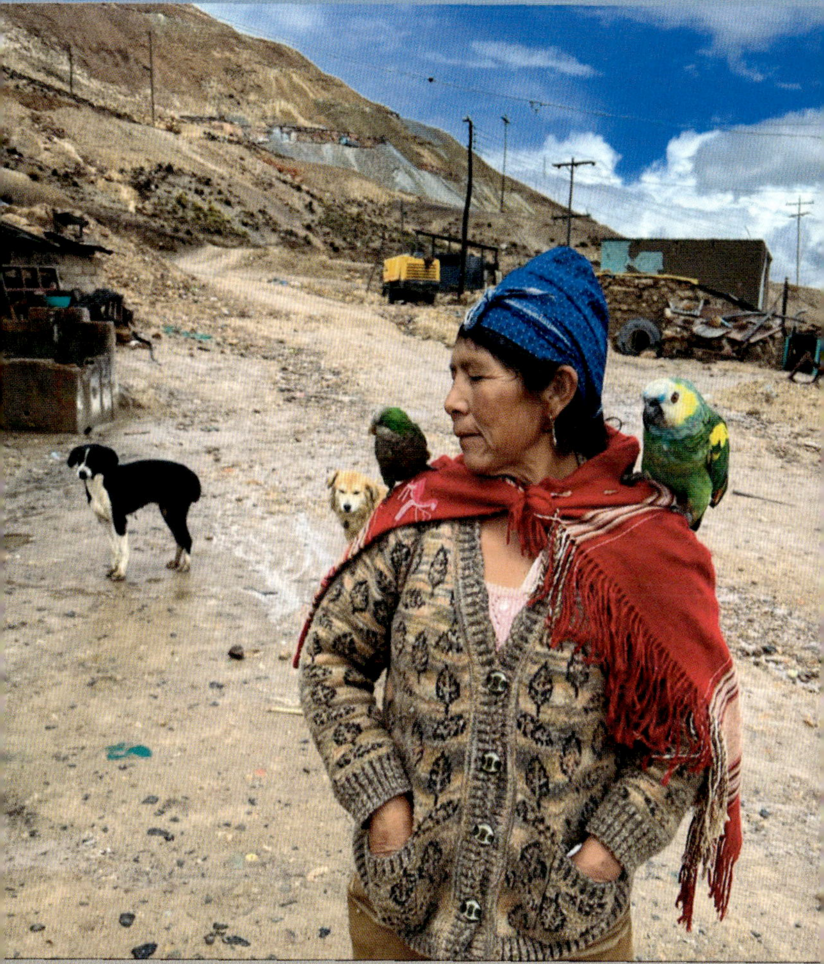

Send message

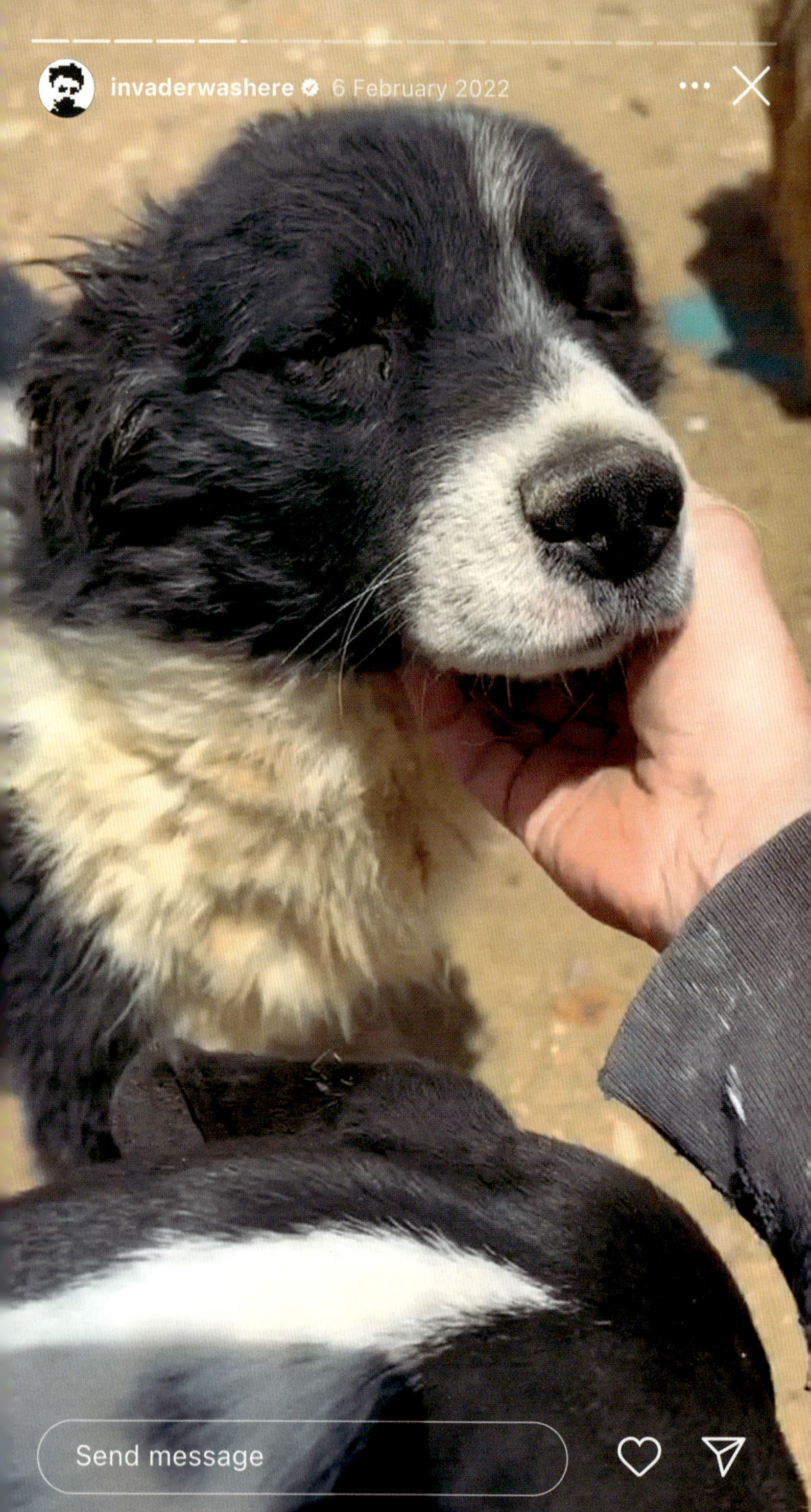
invaderwashere
6 February 2022
Send message

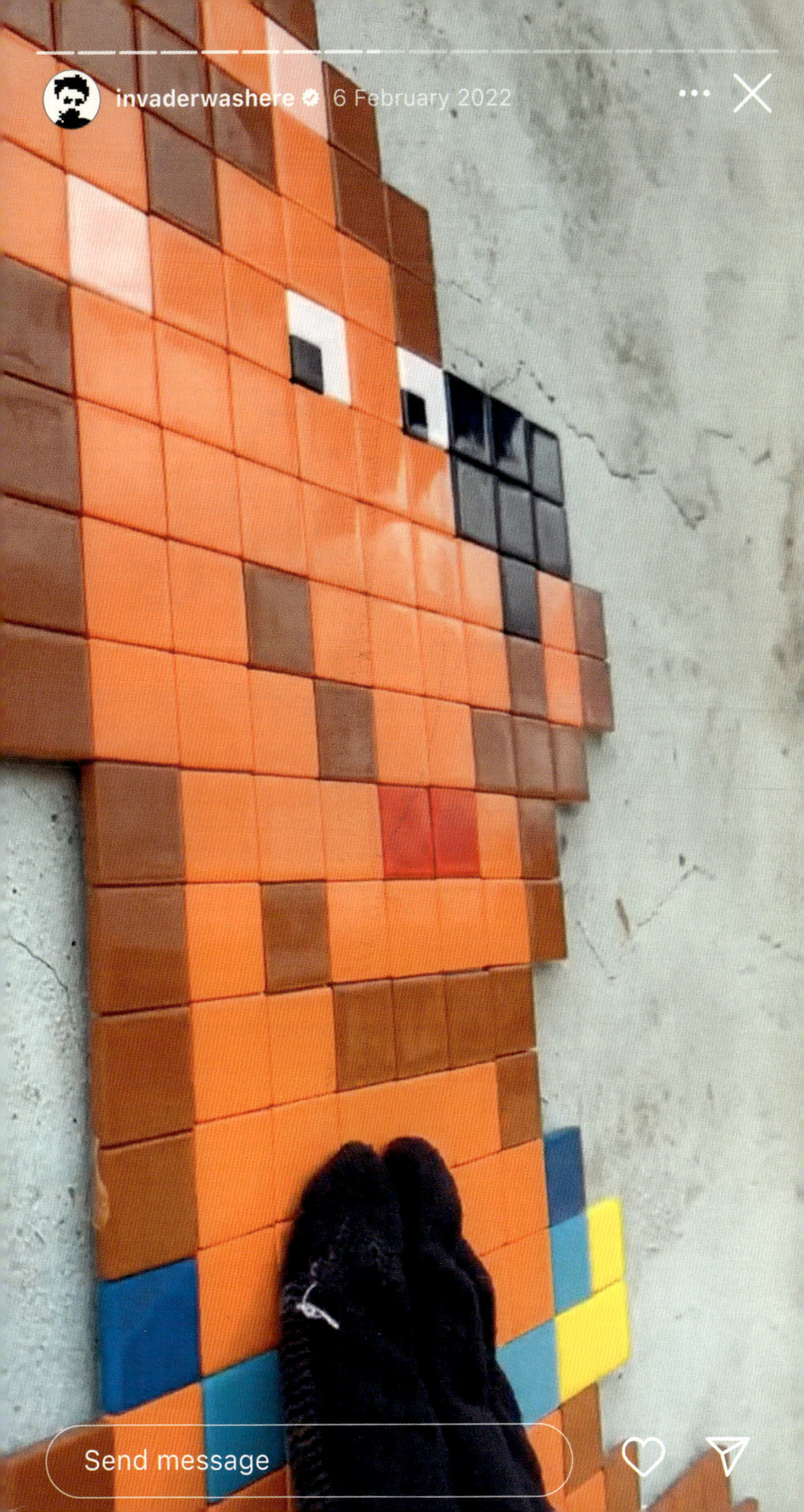
invaderwashere
6 February 2022
Send message

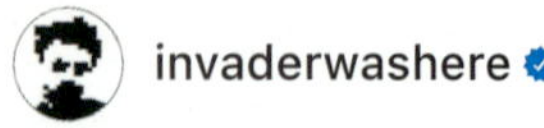

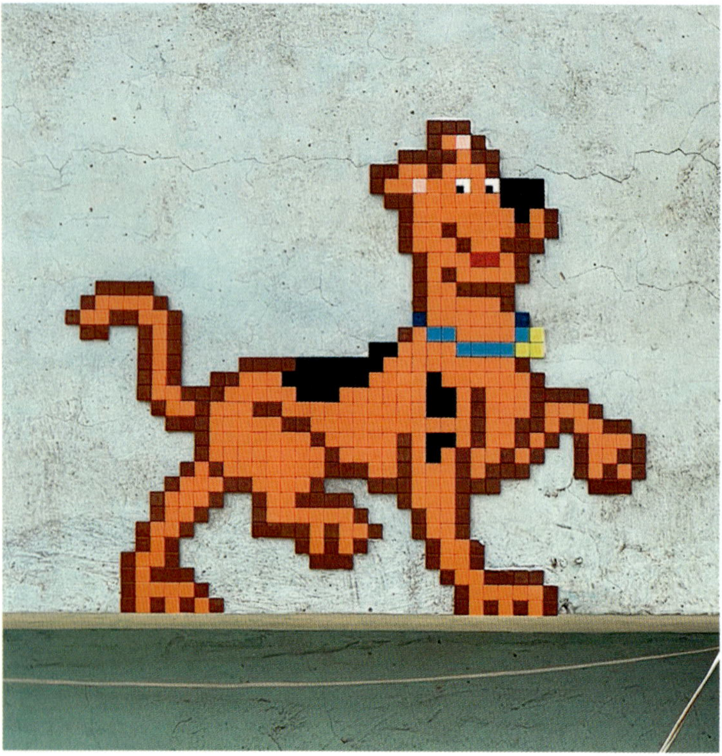

 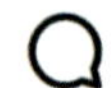  

17 223 likes

invaderwashere This one is for all the stray dogs of Potosí #dogs #perros #potosi #bolivia #mountain #cerrorico #mission4000

View all 129 comments

6 February 2022

invaderwashere

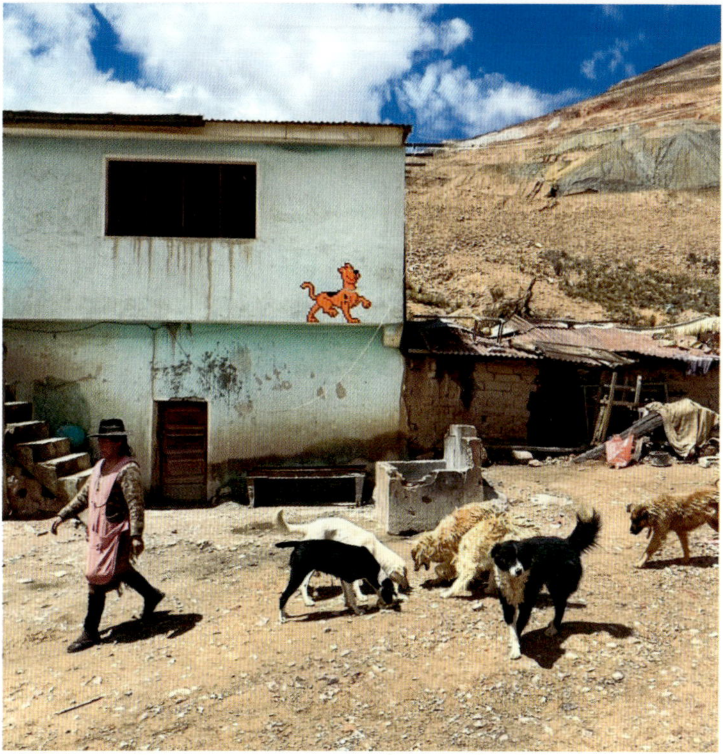

17 223 likes

invaderwashere This one is for all the stray dogs of Potosí
#dogs #perros #potosi #bolivia #mountain #cerrorico
#mission4000

View all 129 comments

6 February 2022

invaderwashere 7 February 2022

yorgotloupas

In 1999, as the art director of @crashmagazine I met @invaderwashere and started designing his invasion maps

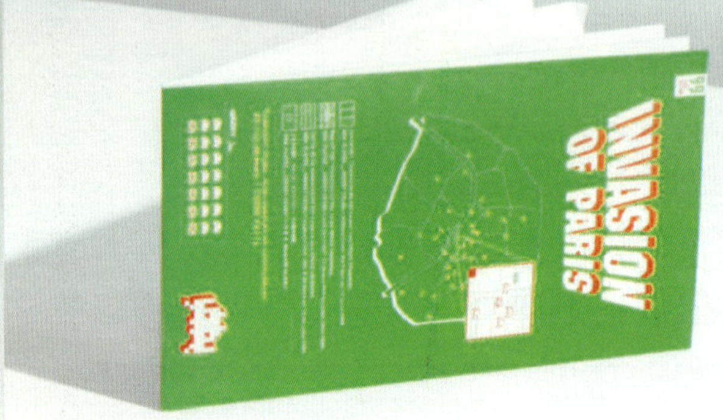

The invasion maps collection started in 1999.
The first ones were designed in collaboration with talented graphic designer @yorgotloupas
Thank you Yorgo 🙏👏👾

Send message

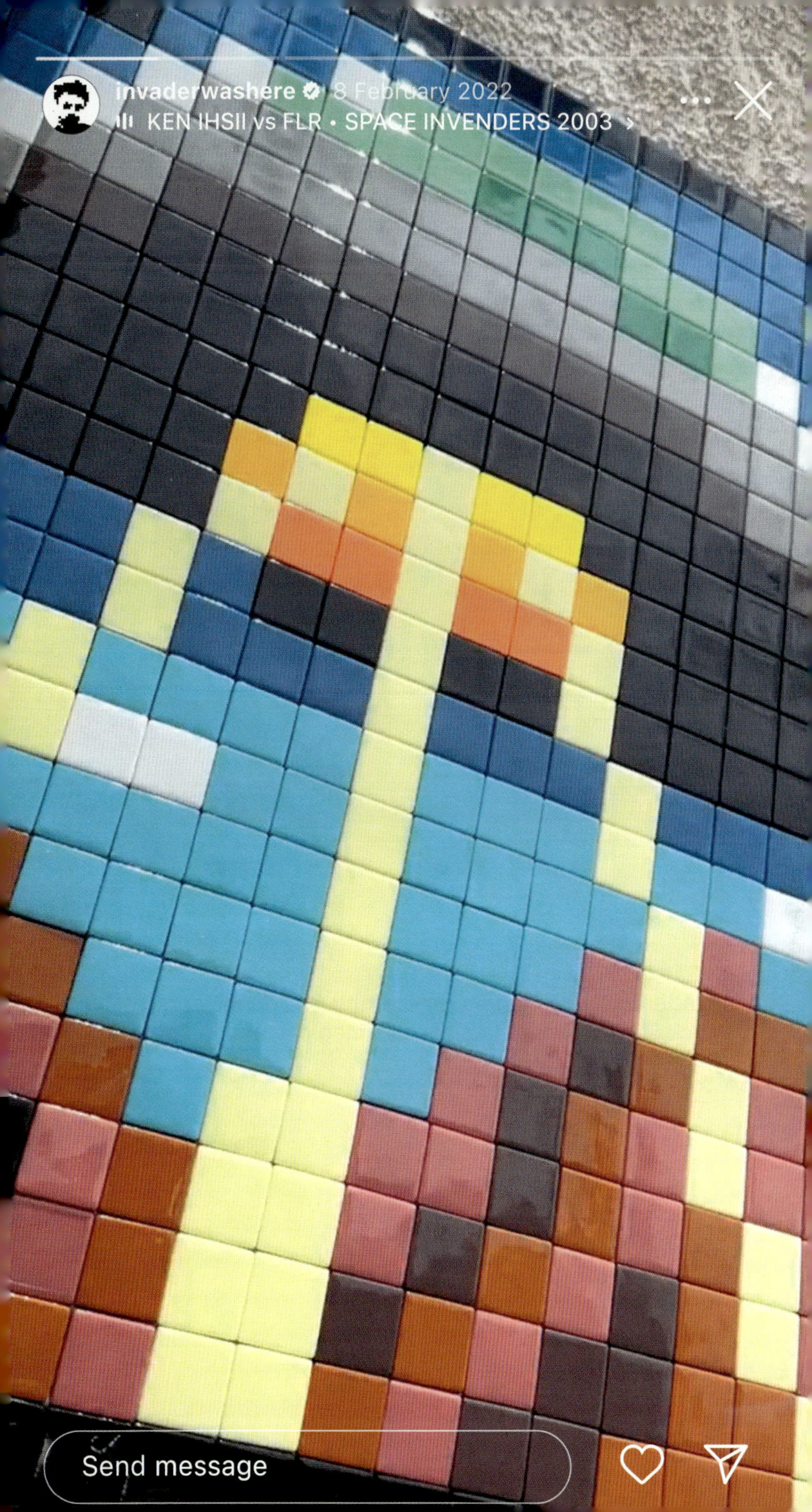
invaderwashere 8 February 2022
KEN IHSII vs FLR • SPACE INVENDERS 2003
Send message

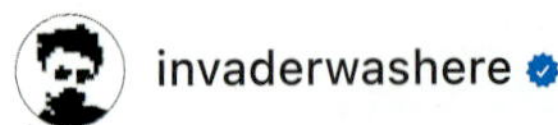

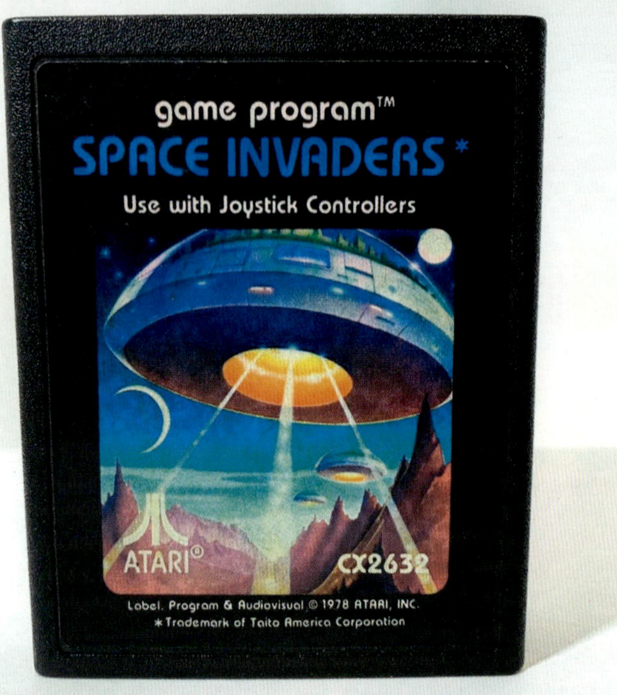

11792 likes

invaderwashere Posters for eternity #atari #minecraft #pick #creeper #ufo #cerrorico #magicmountain #potosi #mission4000

View all 100 comments

8 February 2022

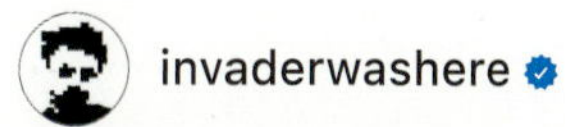

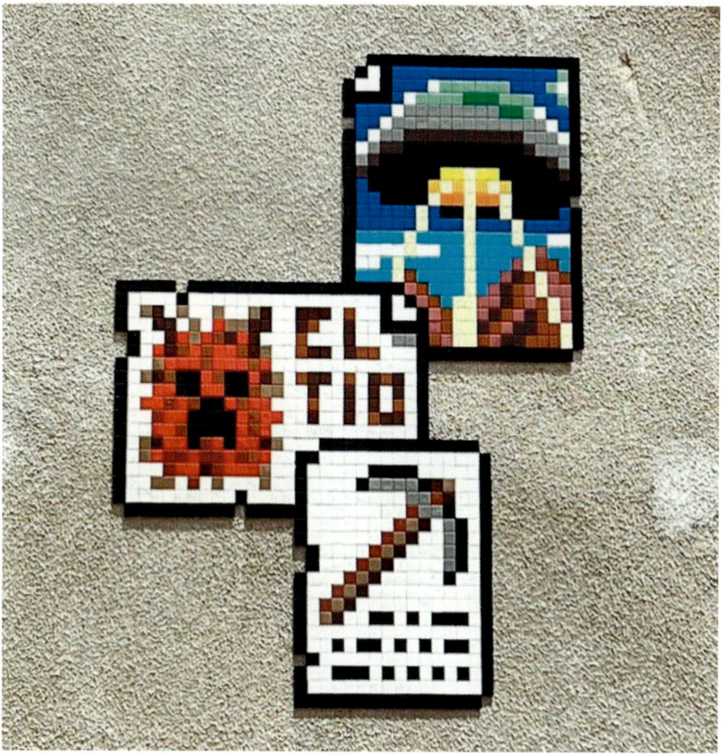

11792 likes

invaderwashere Posters for eternity #atari #minecraft #pick #creeper #ufo #cerrorico #magicmountain #potosi #mission4000

View all 100 comments

8 February 2022

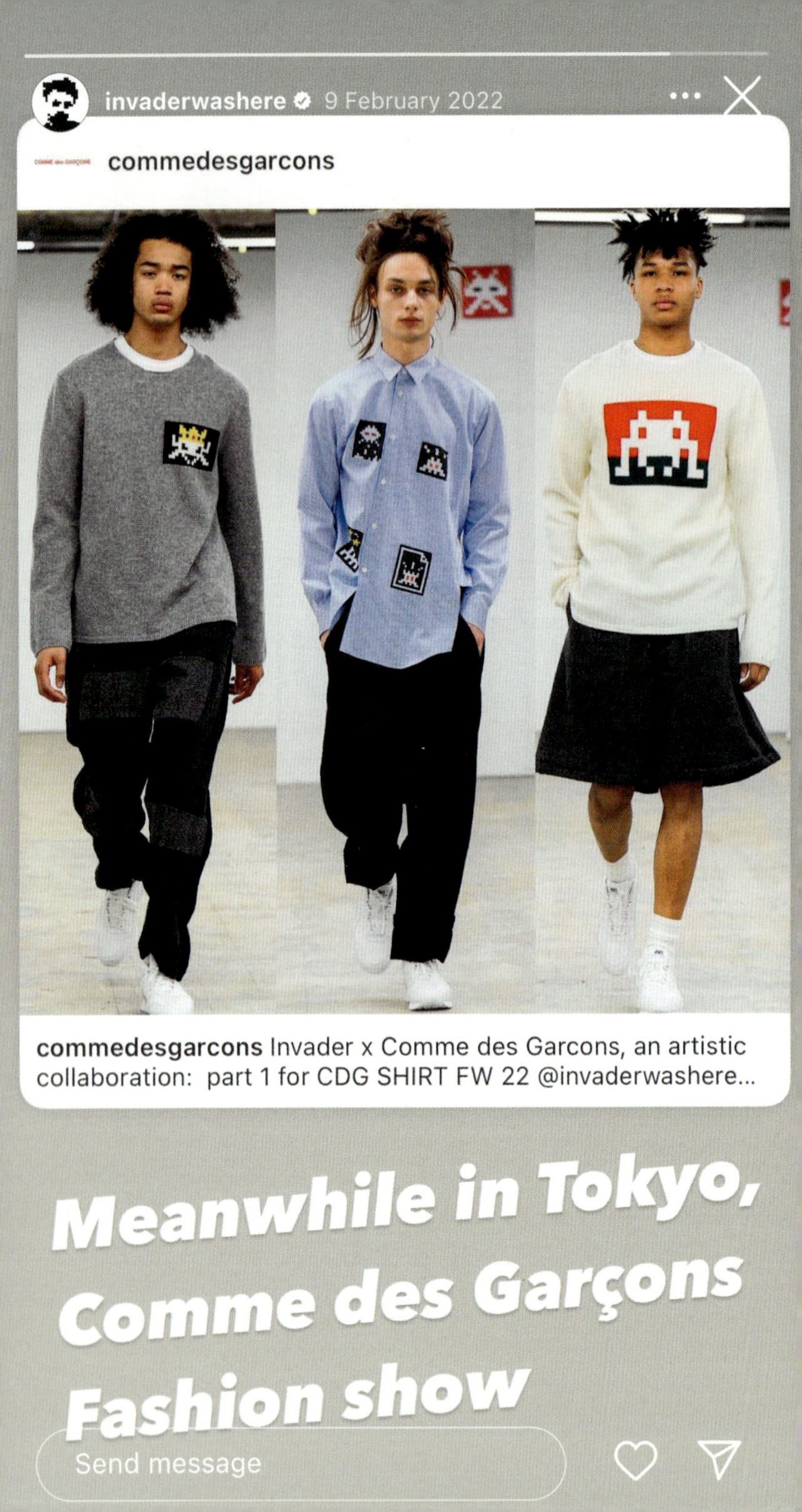

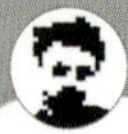

invaderwashere 9 February 2022

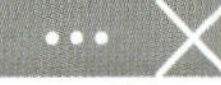

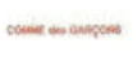

commedesgarcons

commedesgarcons Invader x Comme des Garcons, an artistic collaboration: part 1 for CDG SHIRT FW 22 @invaderwashere...

Meanwhile in Tokyo, Comme des Garçons Fashion show

Send message

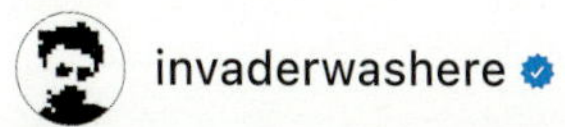

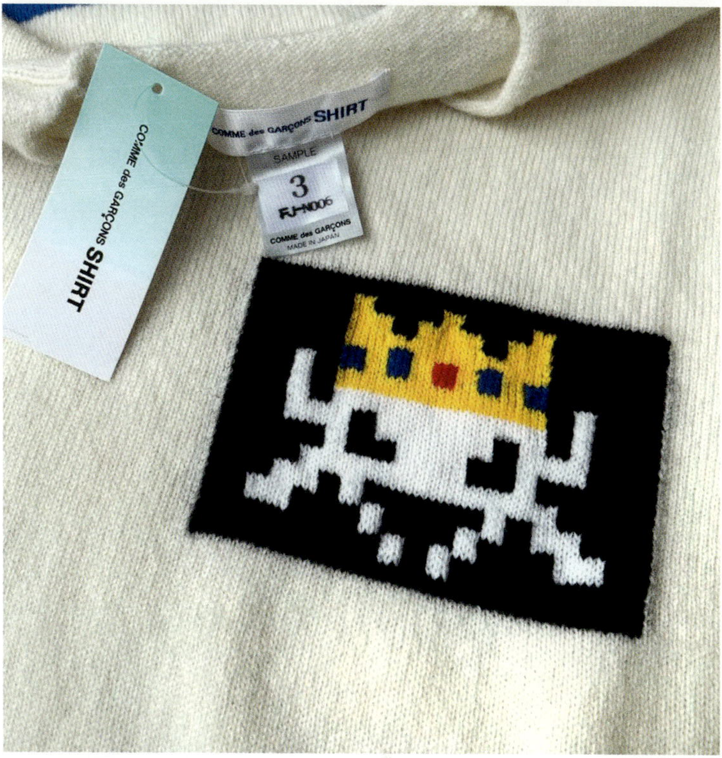

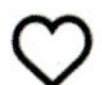    

17706 likes

invaderwashere After giving some of my designs and a carte blanche to Rei Kawakubo the creator of Comme des Garçons I've just discovered the first samples of this collection, and they look awesome 😍😍😍 #knitwear #shirt #invasion #fashion #art #collab #commedesgarcons

View all 415 comments

9 February 2022

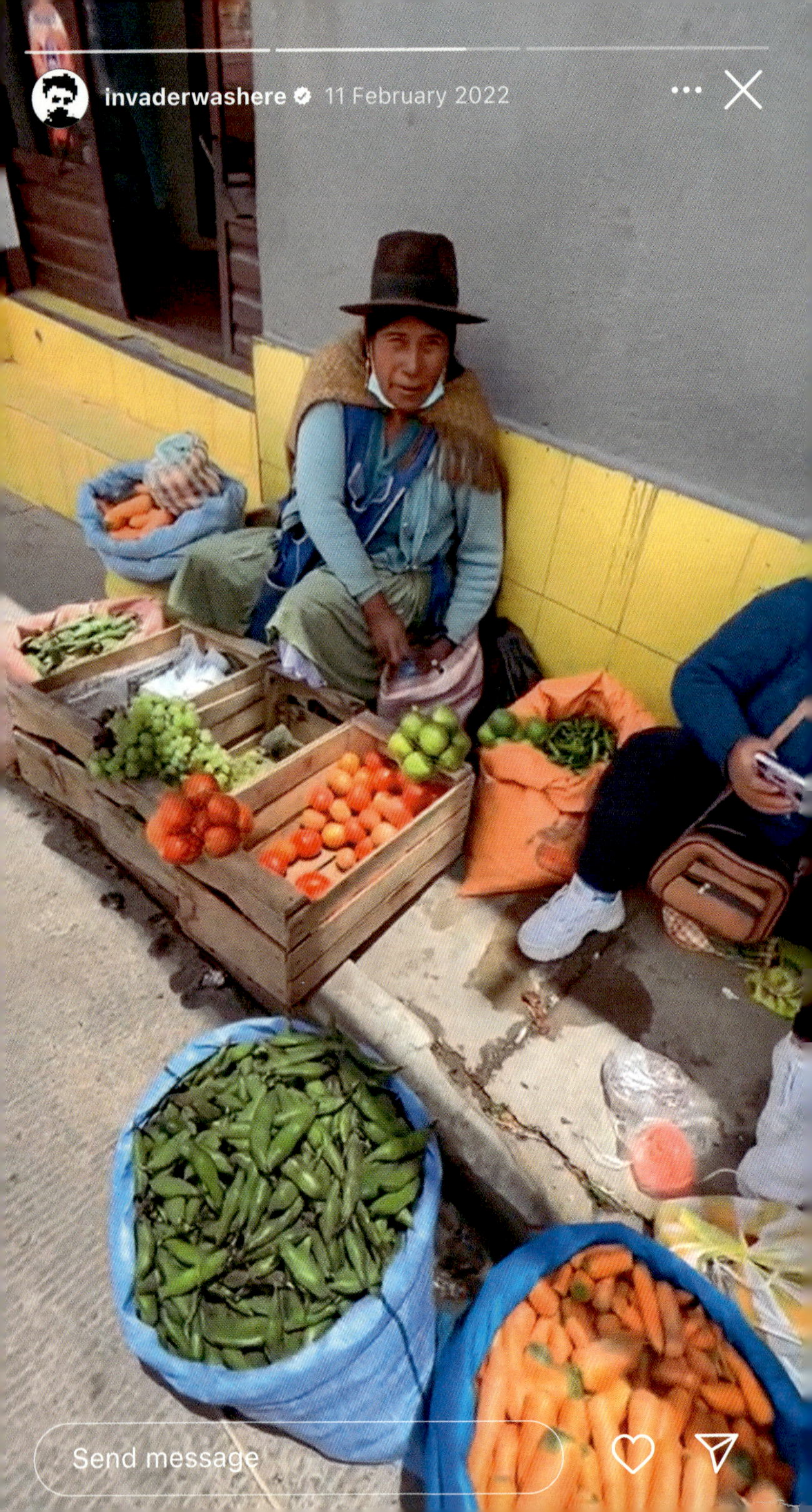
invaderwashere
11 February 2022
Send message

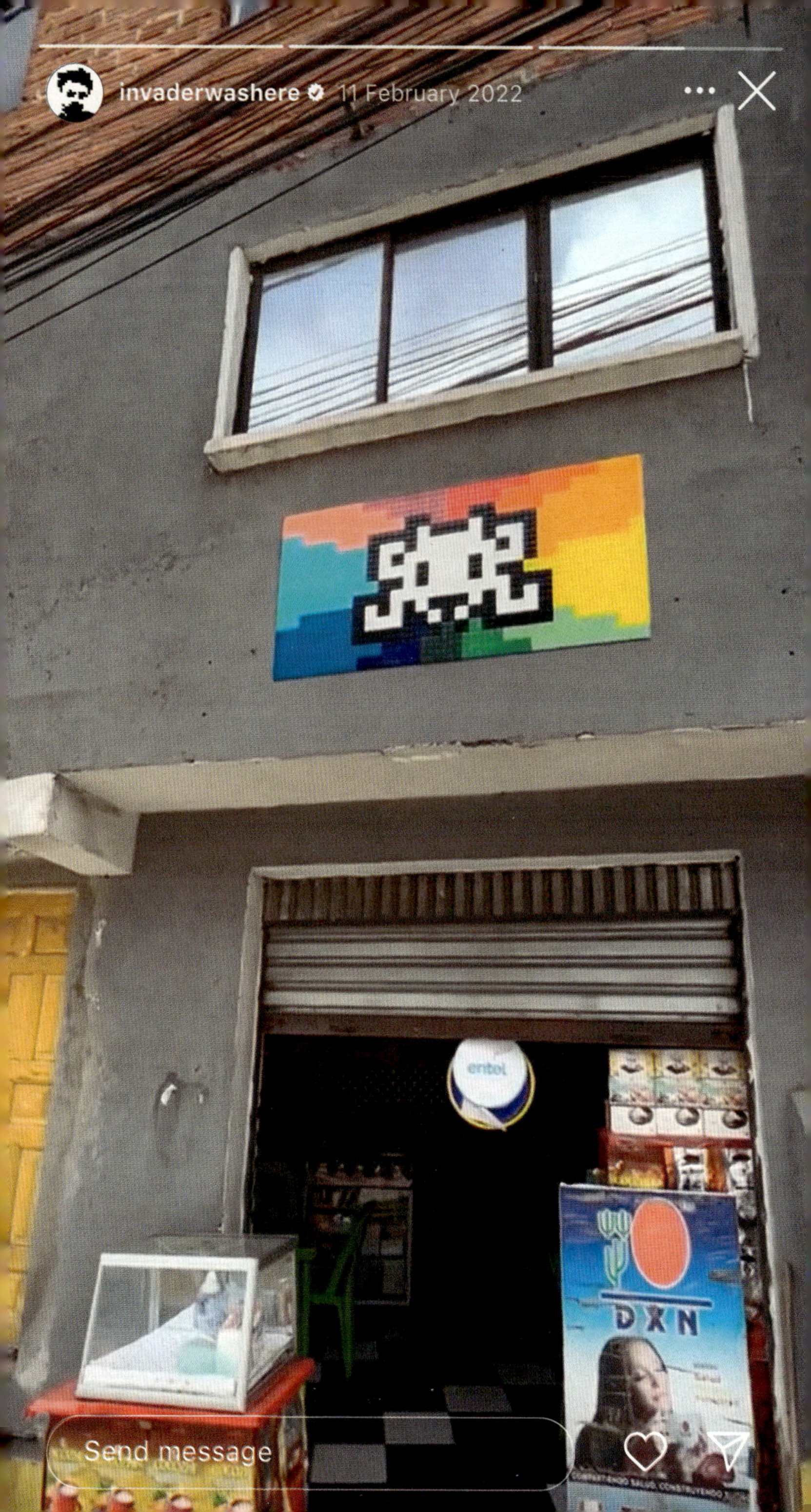
invaderwashere
11 February 2022
entel
DXN
Send message

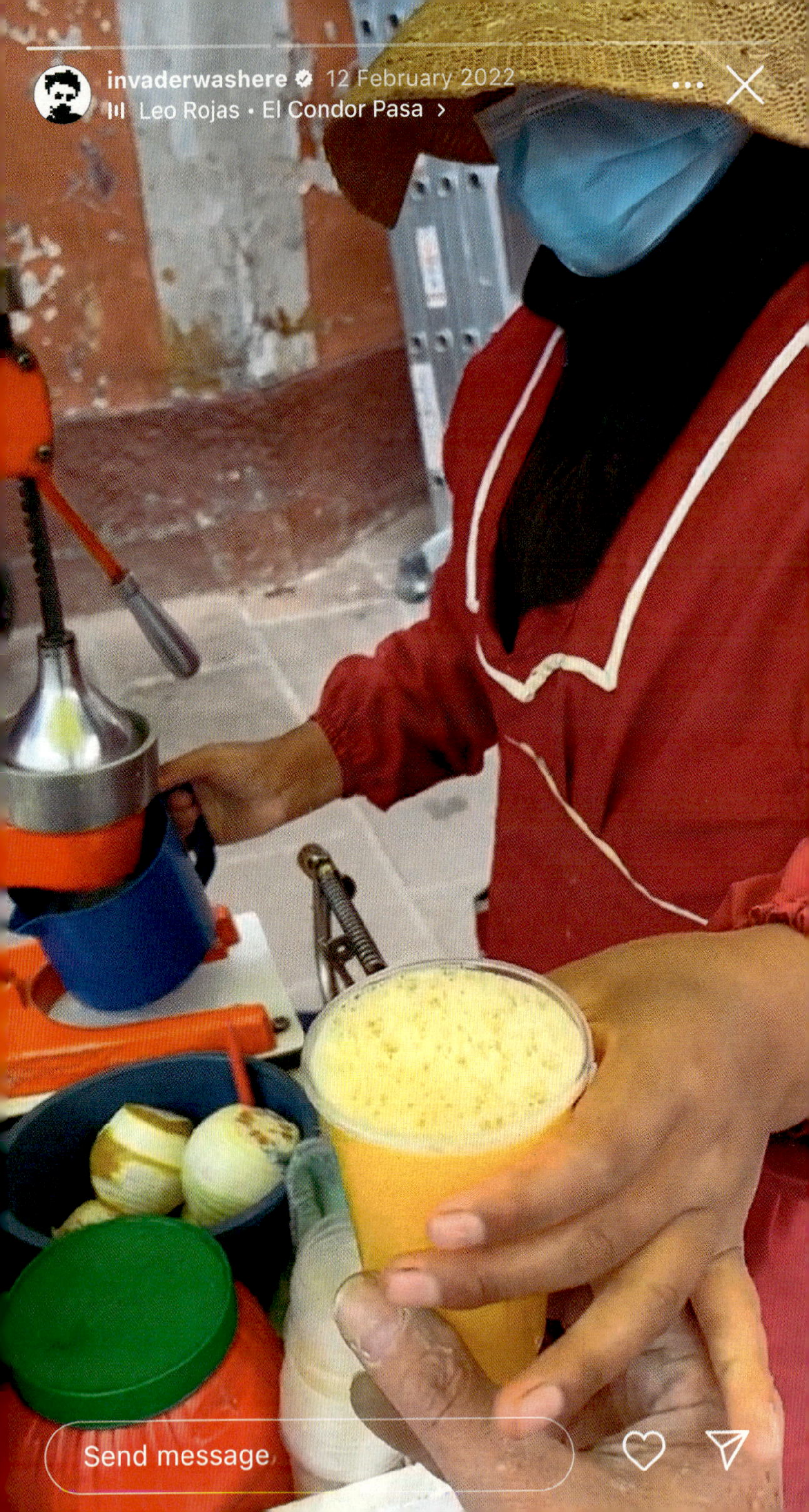
invaderwashere
12 February 2022
Leo Rojas • El Condor Pasa
Send message

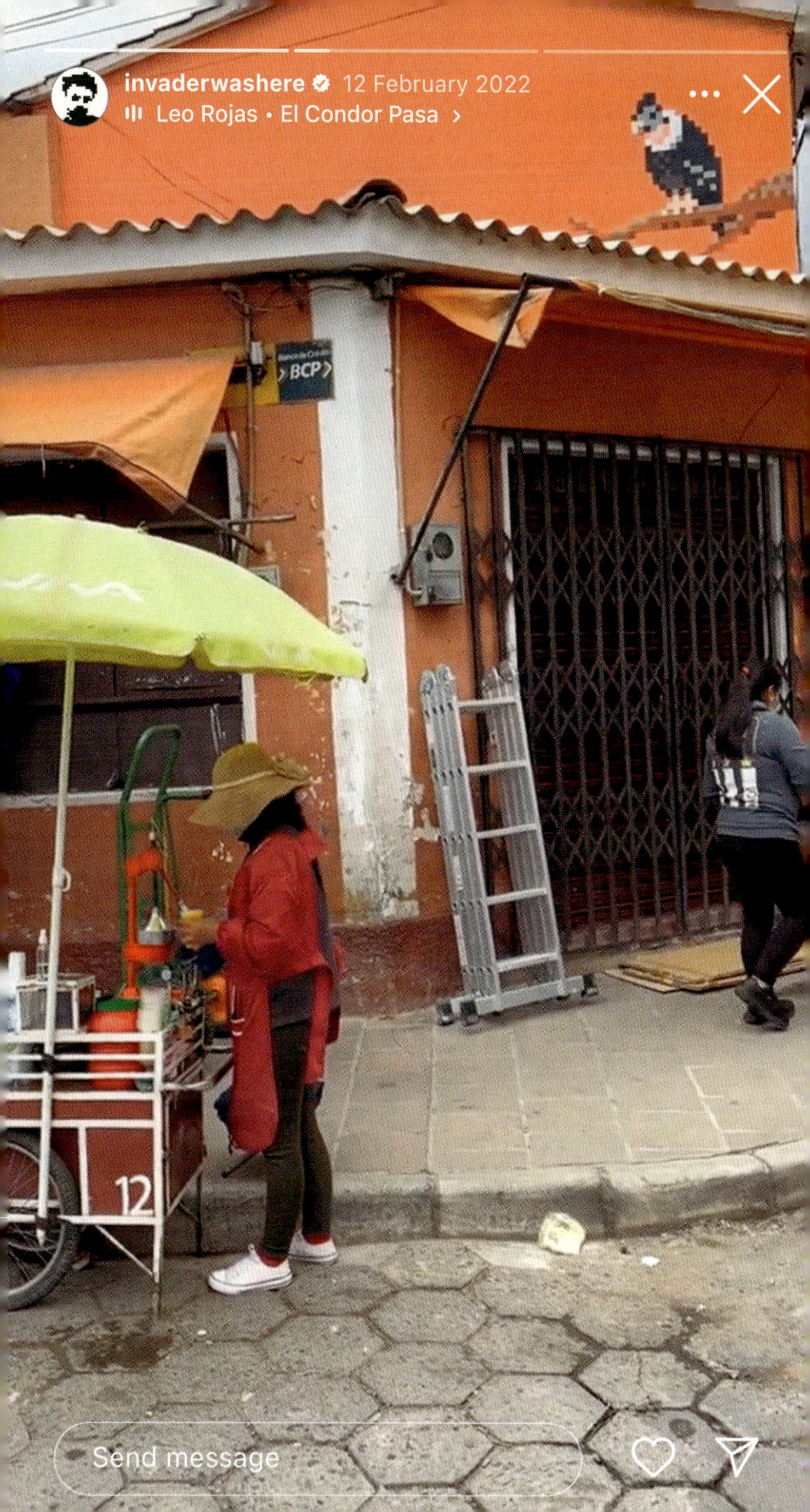
invaderwashere
12 February 2022
Leo Rojas • El Condor Pasa
BCP
12
Send message

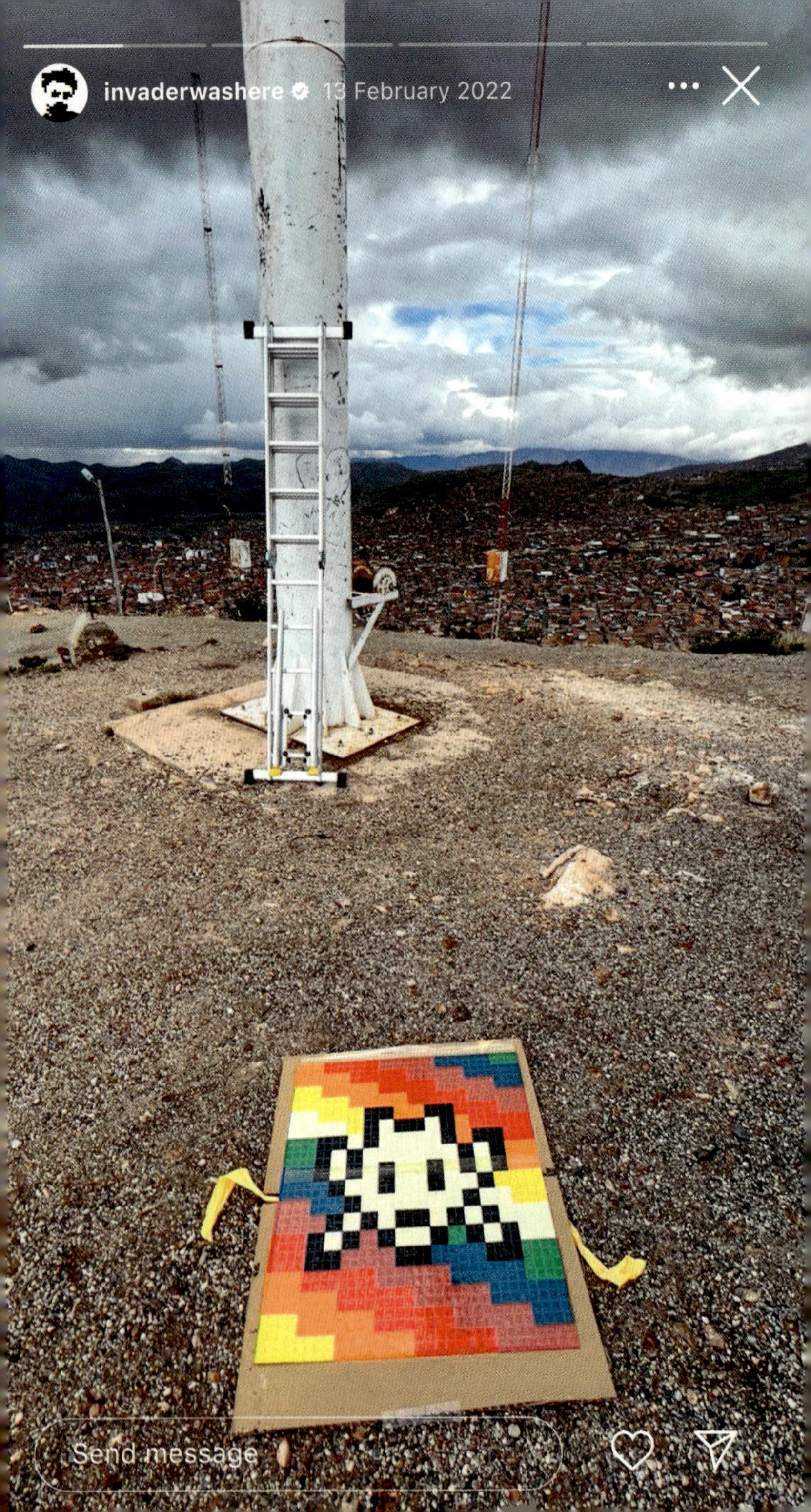
invaderwashere
13 February 2022
Send message

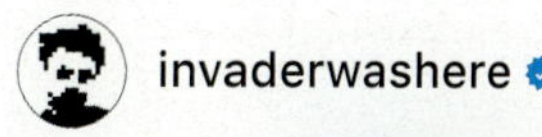

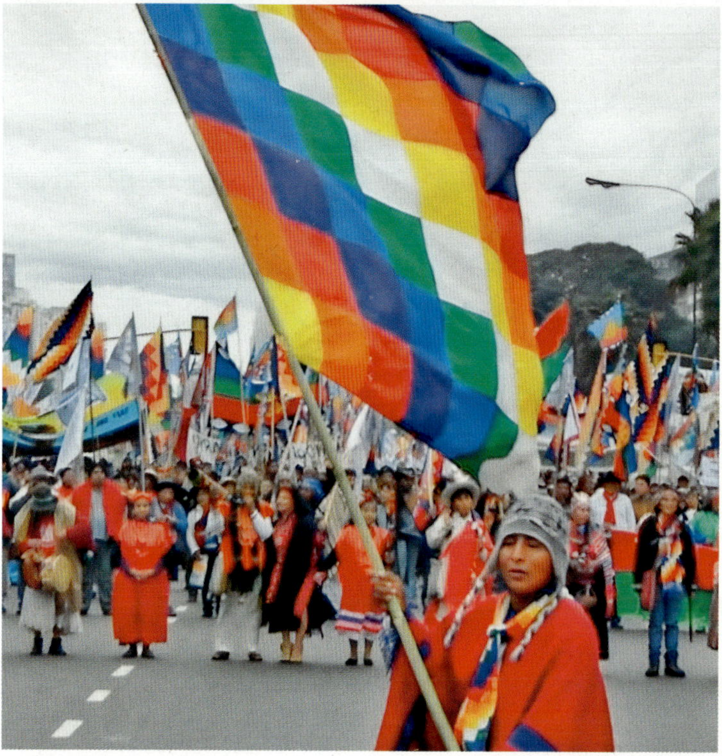

11640 likes

invaderwashere POTI_17 is inspired by the Wiphala, the colorful flag of the ethnic groups of the Andes 
 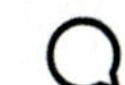  #wiphala #aymara #quechua #cerrorico #potosi #bolivia

View all 85 comments

13 February 2022

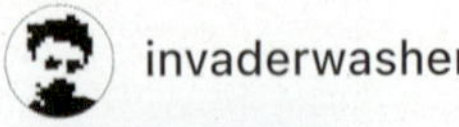

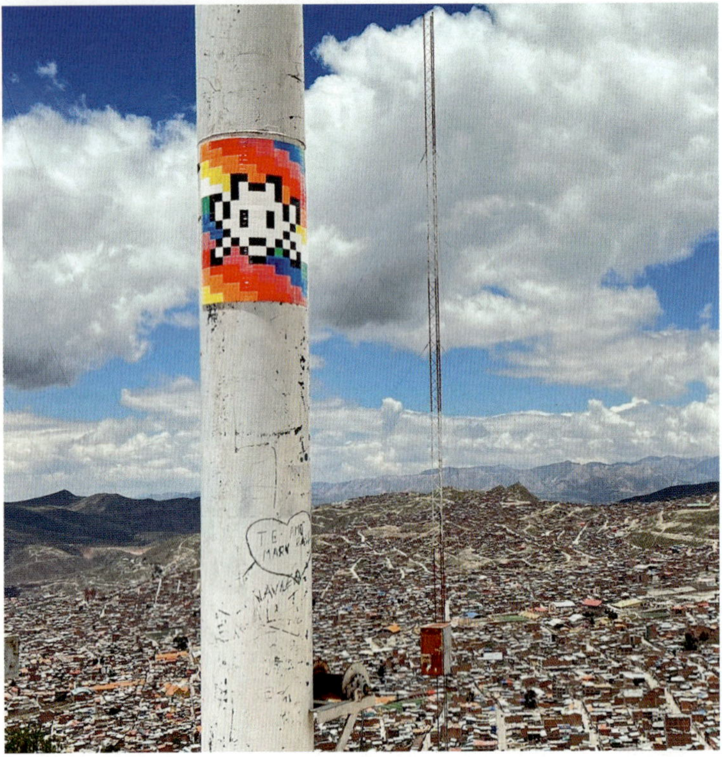

11640 likes

invaderwashere POTI_17 is inspired by the Wiphala, the colorful flag of the ethnic groups of the Andes 🟨🟧🟥🟪🟦🟩⬜ #wiphala #aymara #quechua #cerrorico #potosi #bolivia

View all 85 comments

13 February 2022

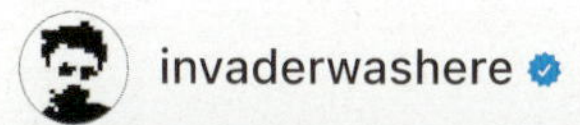

•••

   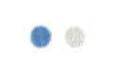 

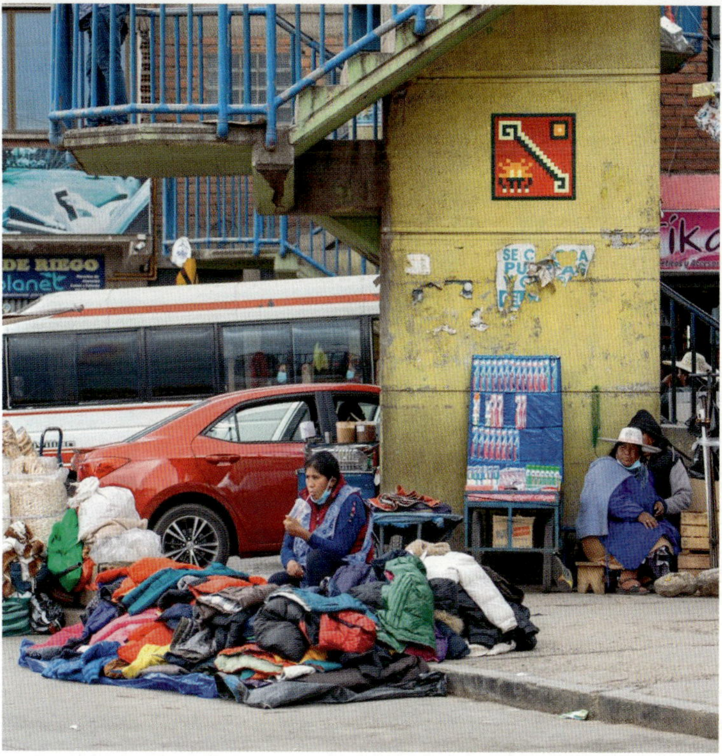

7362 likes

invaderwashere POTI_35 #potosi #bolivia🇧🇴

View all 46 comments

20 February 2022

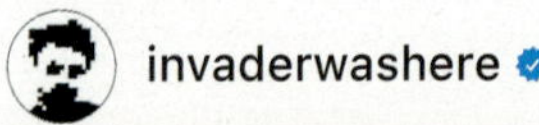

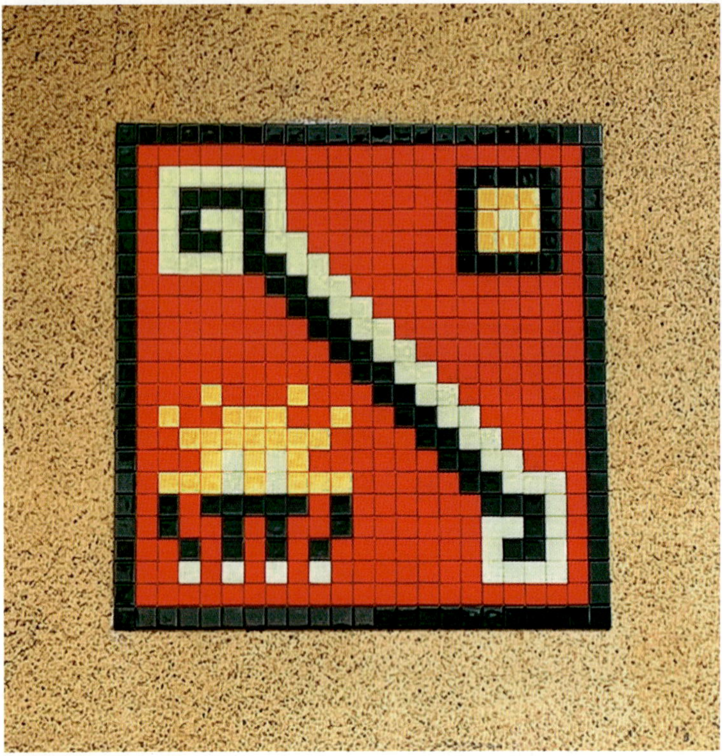

 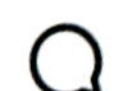  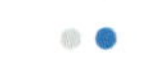 

7 362 likes

invaderwashere POTI_35 #potosi #bolivia🇧🇴

View all 46 comments

20 February 2022

invaderwashere 22 February 2022

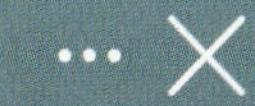

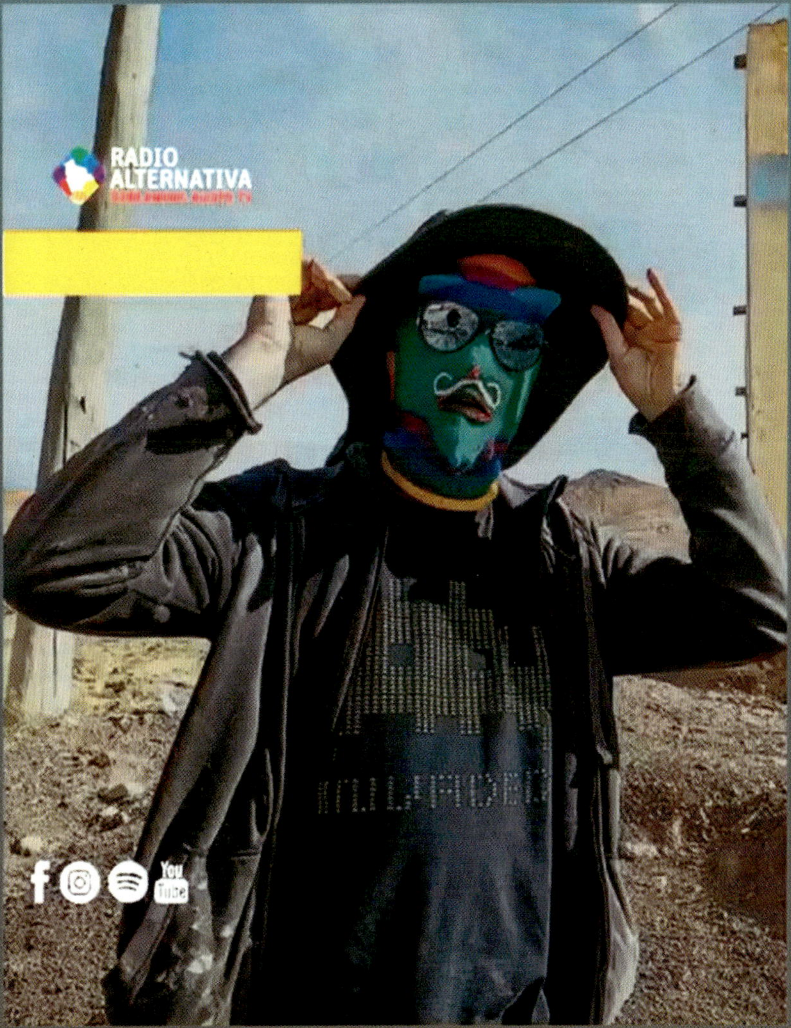

RADIO
ALTERNATIVA

@alternativaradio.com.ar

Send message

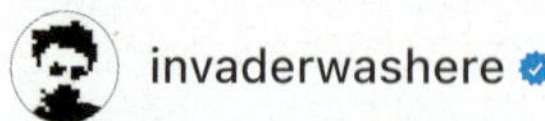

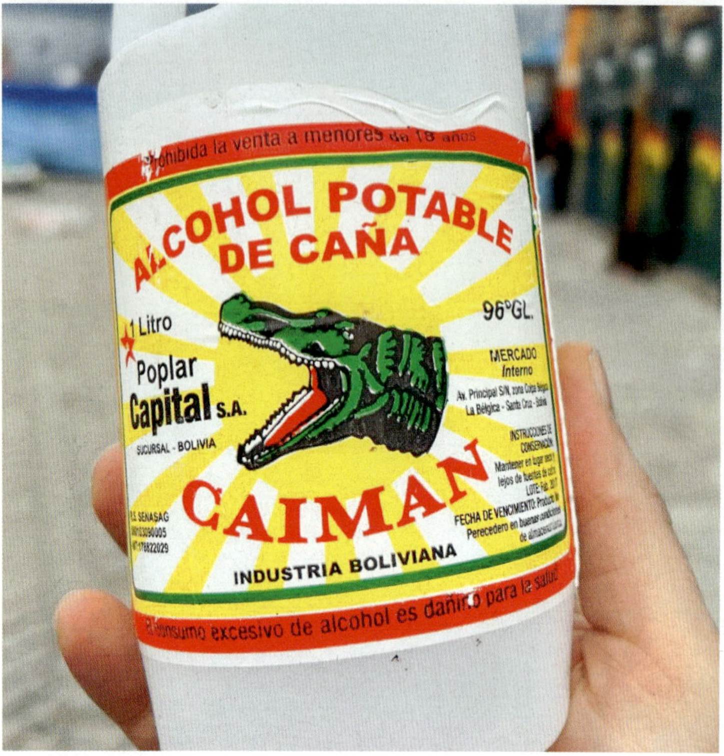

   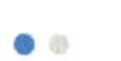 

16 458 likes

invaderwashere Caiman is the strongest booze I've ever seen... #96degrees #caiman #bolivianalcohol

View all 145 comments

22 February 2022

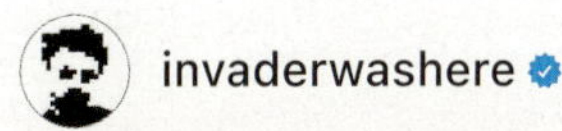

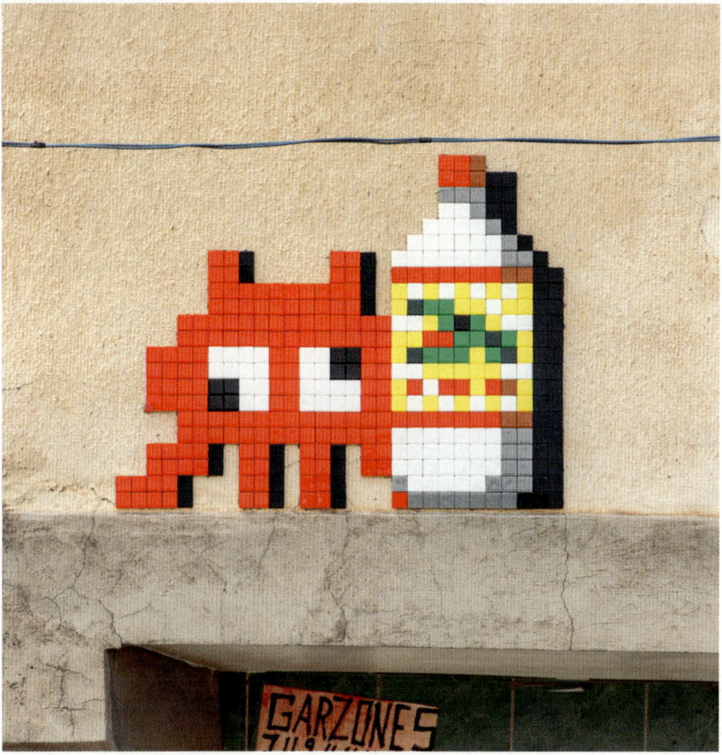

16 458 likes

invaderwashere Caiman is the strongest booze I've ever seen... #96degrees #caiman #bolivianalcohol

View all 145 comments

22 February 2022

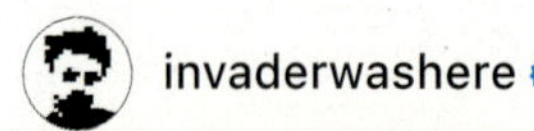

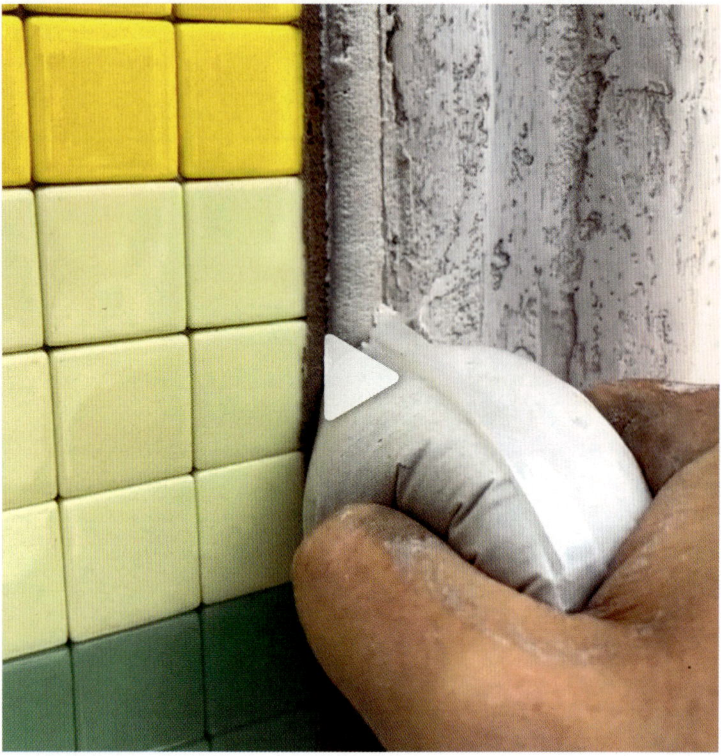

   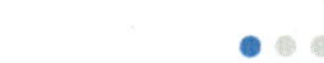 

15 519 likes

invaderwashere POTI_49 #potosi #bolivia 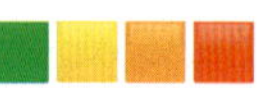

View all 169 comments

23 February 2022

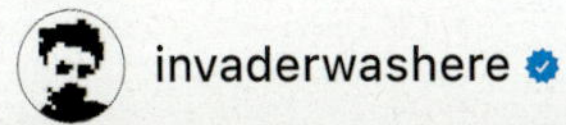

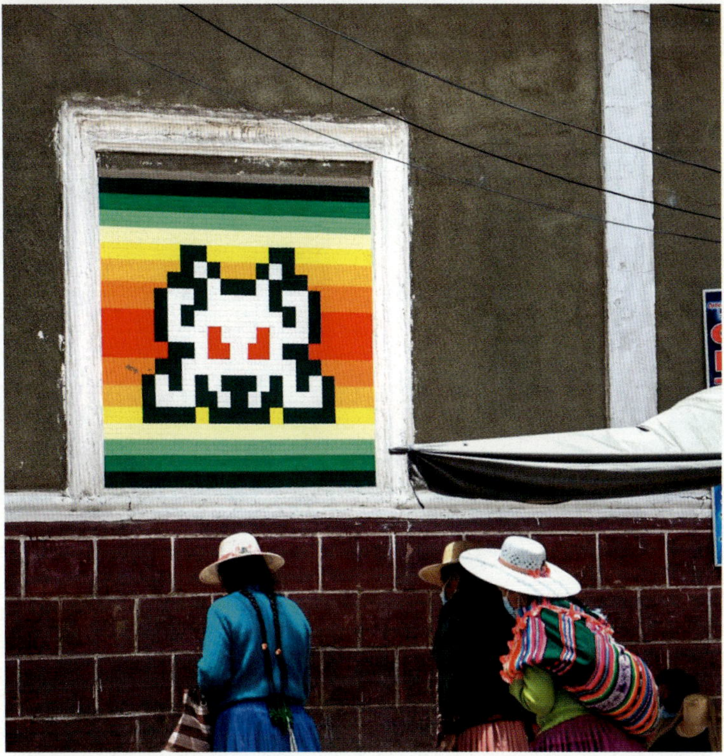

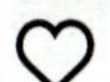

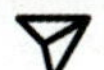

15 519 likes

invaderwashere POTI_49 #potosi #bolivia 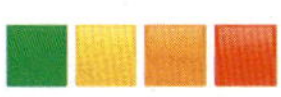

View all 169 comments

23 February 2022

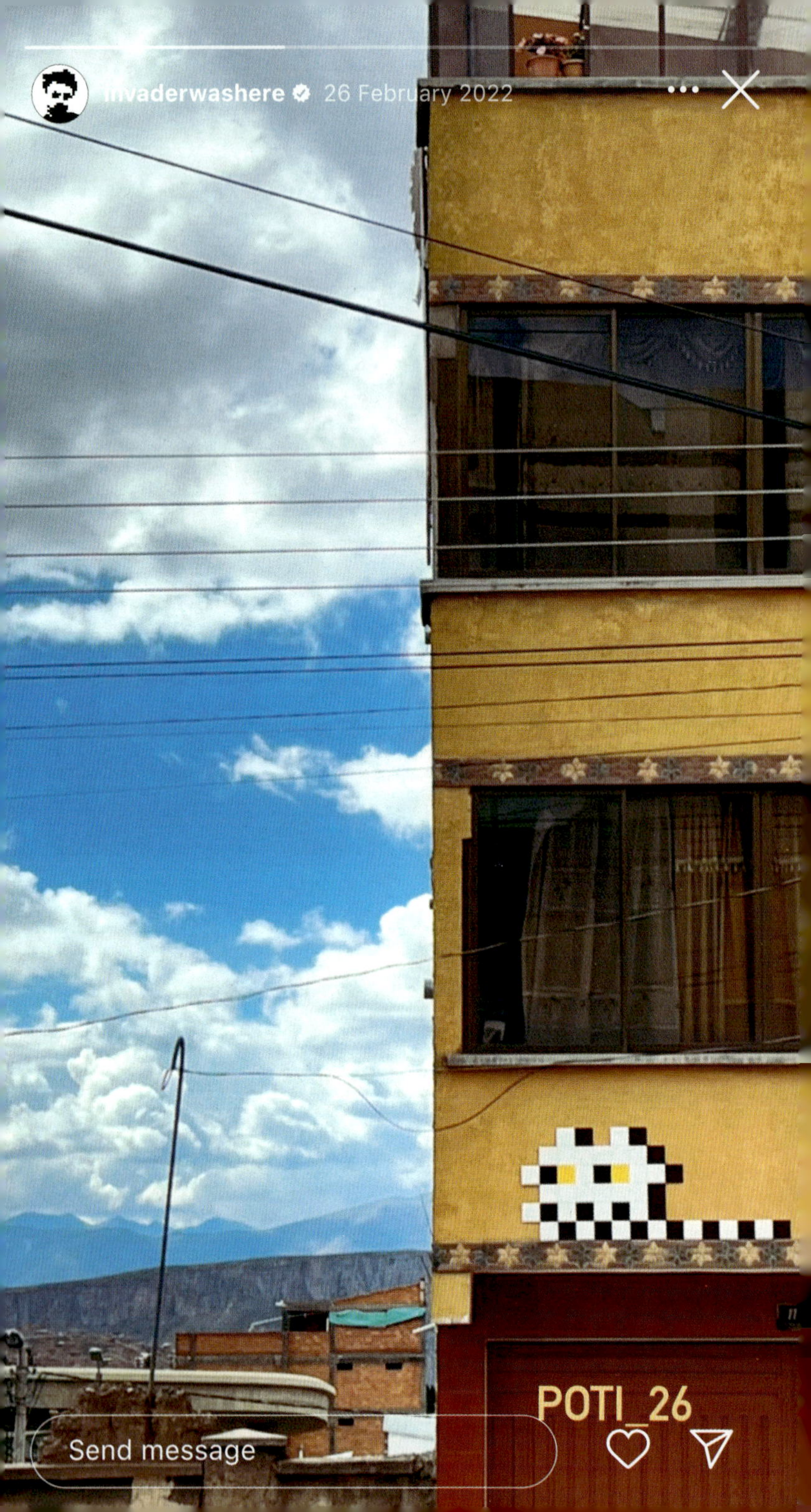
invaderwashere
26 February 2022
POTI_26
Send message

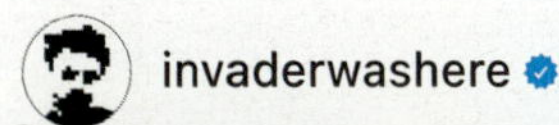

invaderwashere

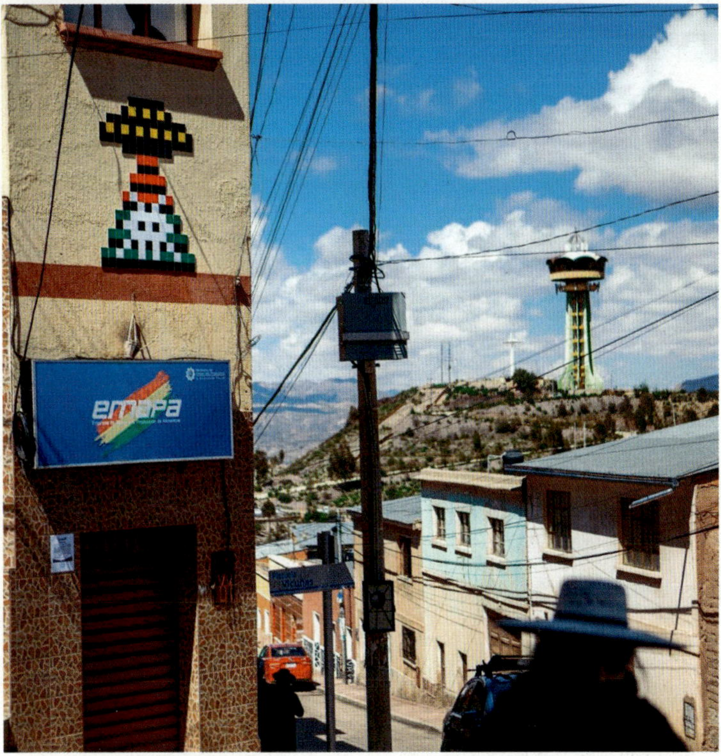

...

7628 likes

invaderwashere POTI_43 #mission4000 #potosi #bolivia 🇧🇴

View all 45 comments

26 February 2022

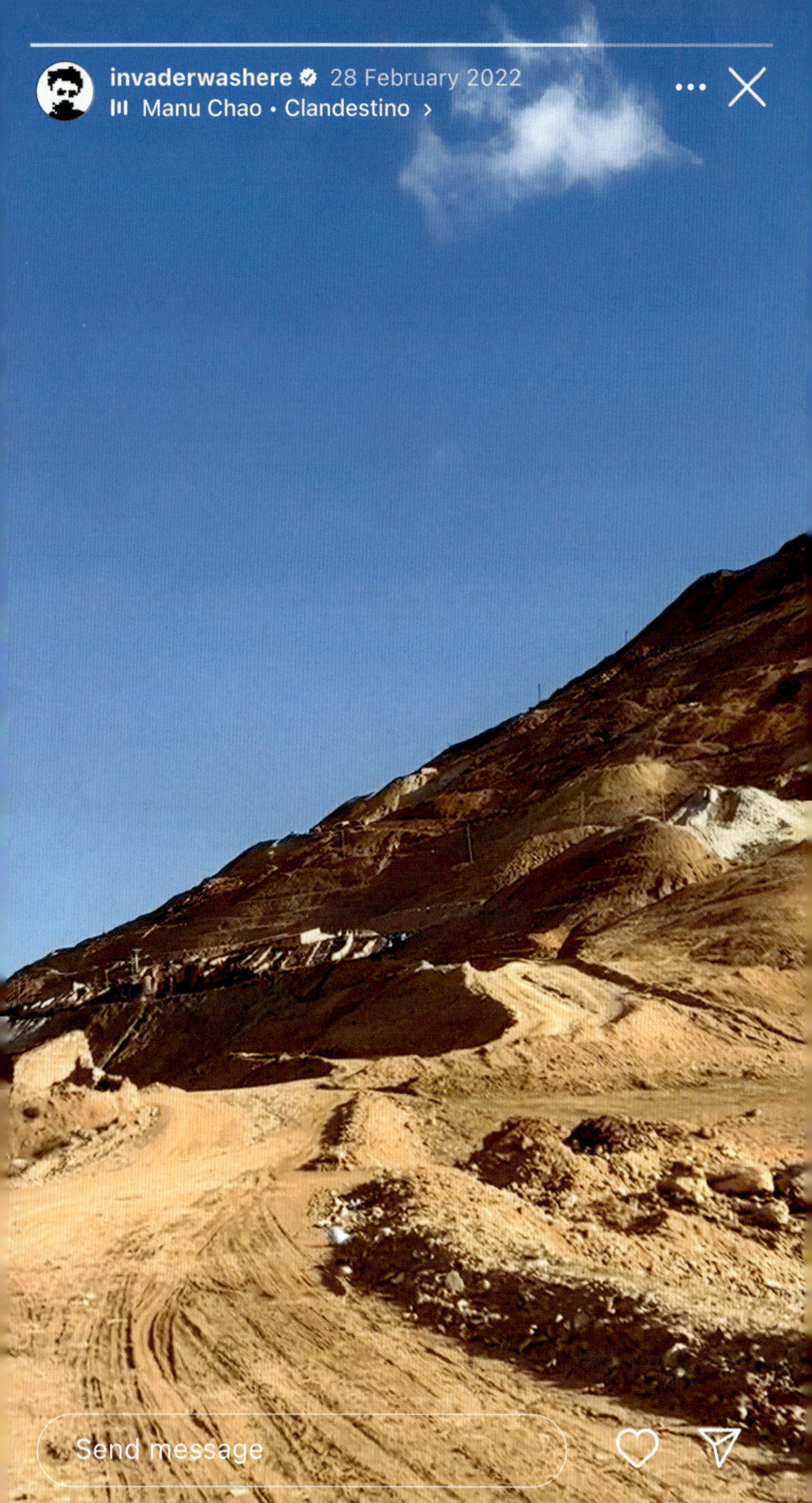
invaderwashere 28 February 2022
Manu Chao • Clandestino
Send message

invaderwashere

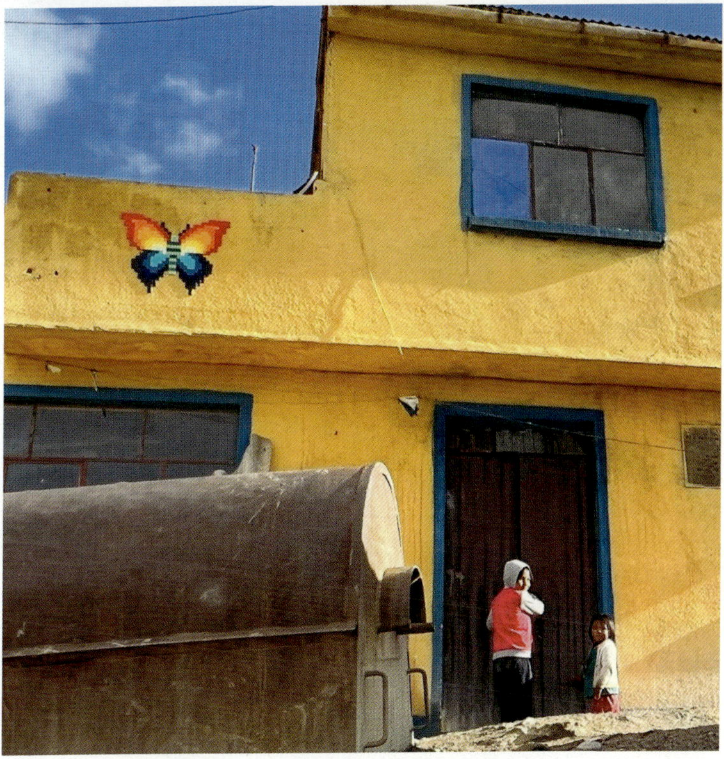

7735 likes

invaderwashere POTI_19 #mariposa #amuleto #cerrorico #mine #withview #potosi #bolivia

View all 70 comments

28 February 2022

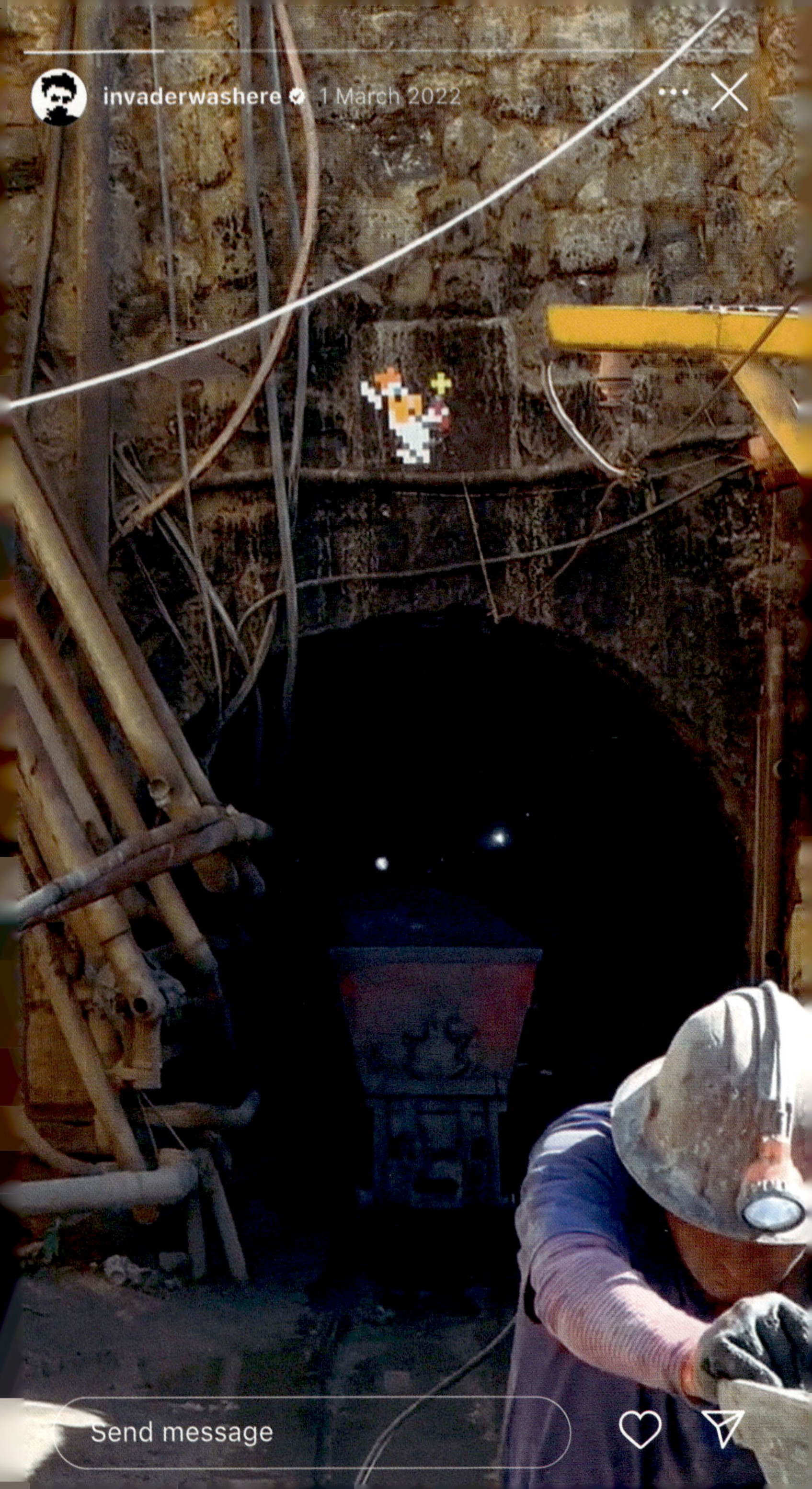
invaderwashere
1 March 2022
Send message

invaderwashere ···

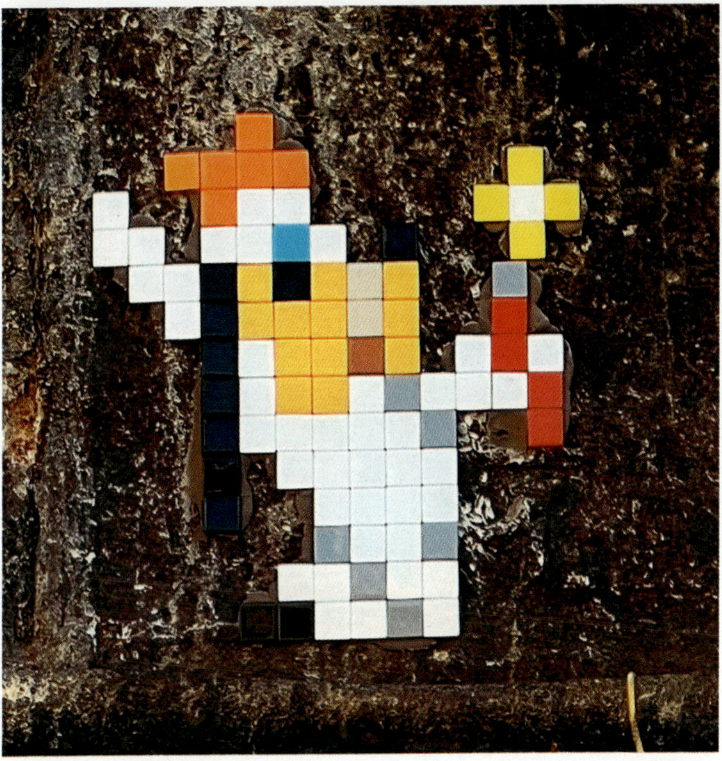

6 818 likes

invaderwashere There are two ways to dig a mine: pick or dynamite ⛏️🧨 #dynamite #droopy #miners #cerrorico #potosi #bolivia

View all 57 comments

1 March 2022

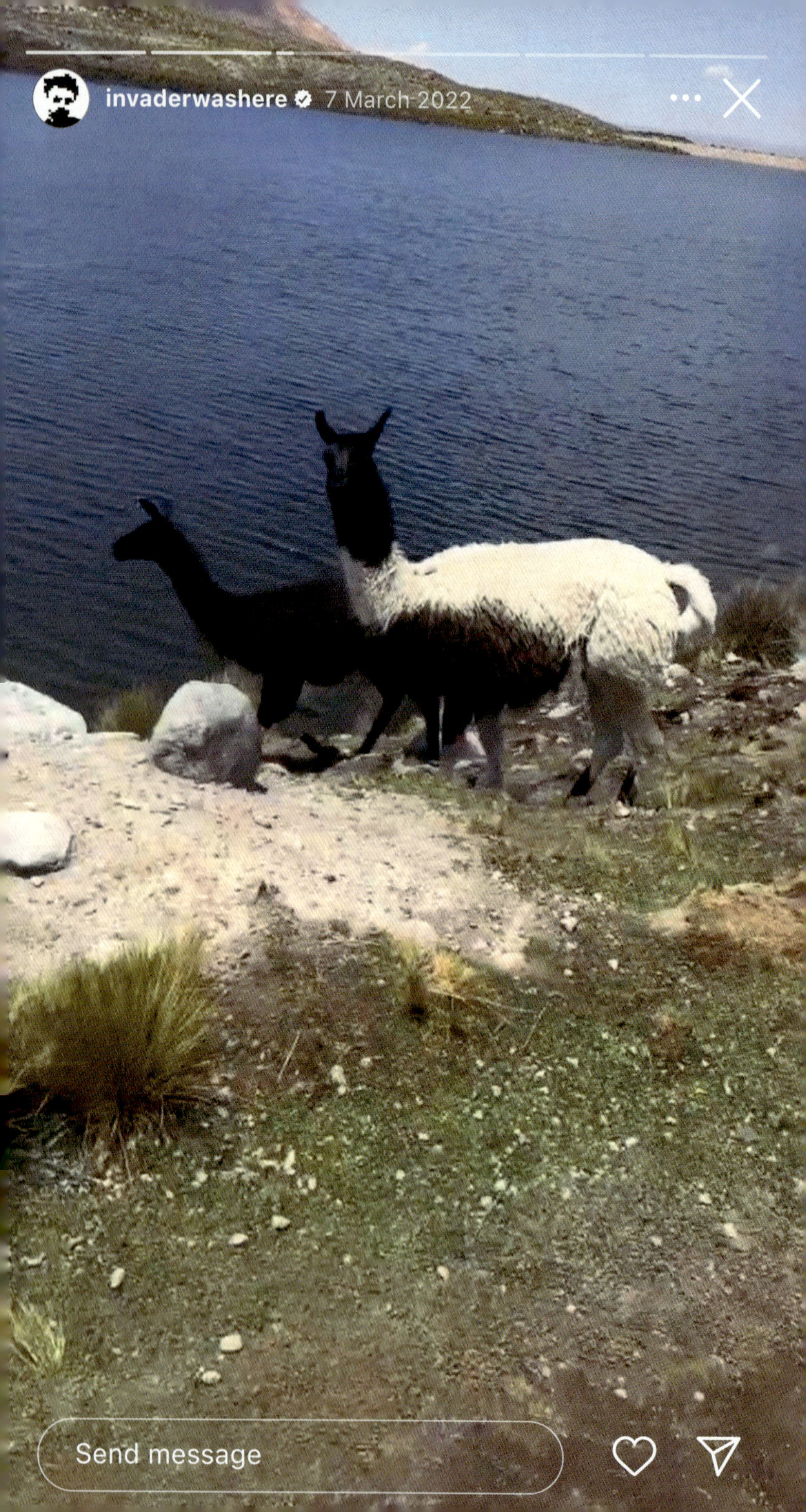

invaderwashere
7 March 2022
Send message

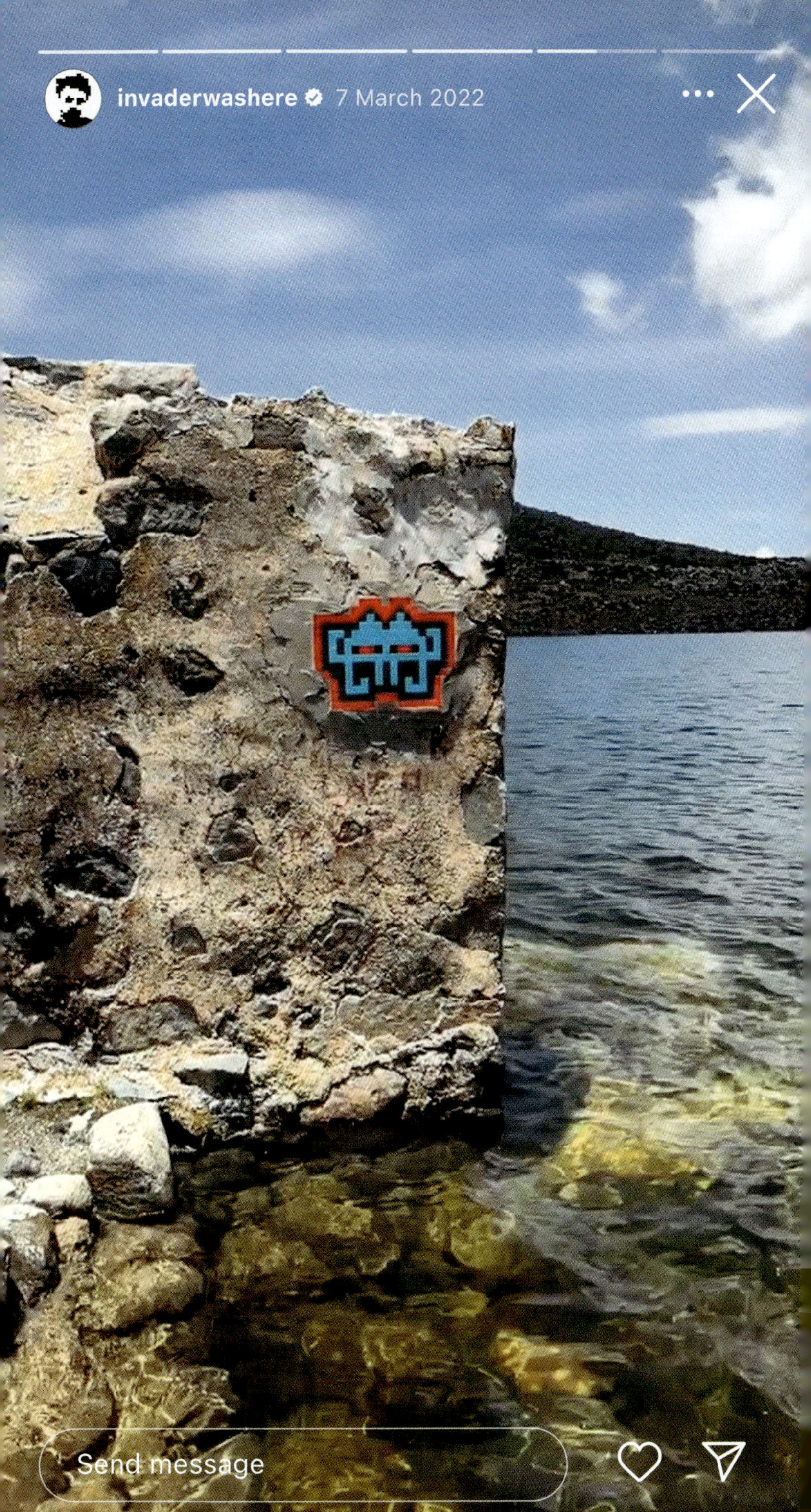
invaderwashere
7 March 2022
Send message

invaderwashere

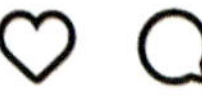
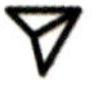

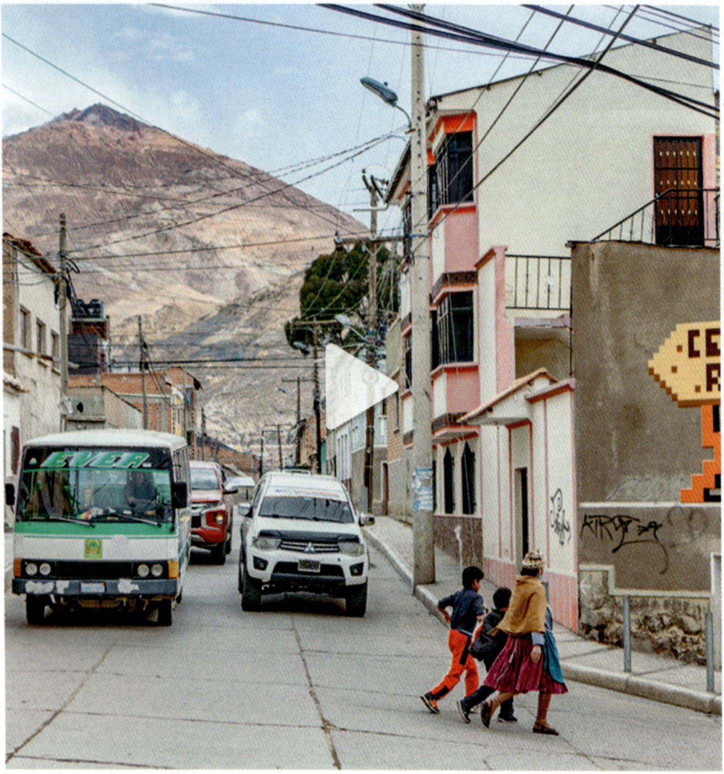

40 154 views

invaderwashere POTI_10
Photo: @henry_ponce_barco

View all 39 comments

24 March 2022

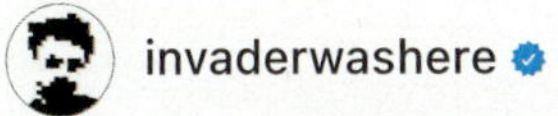

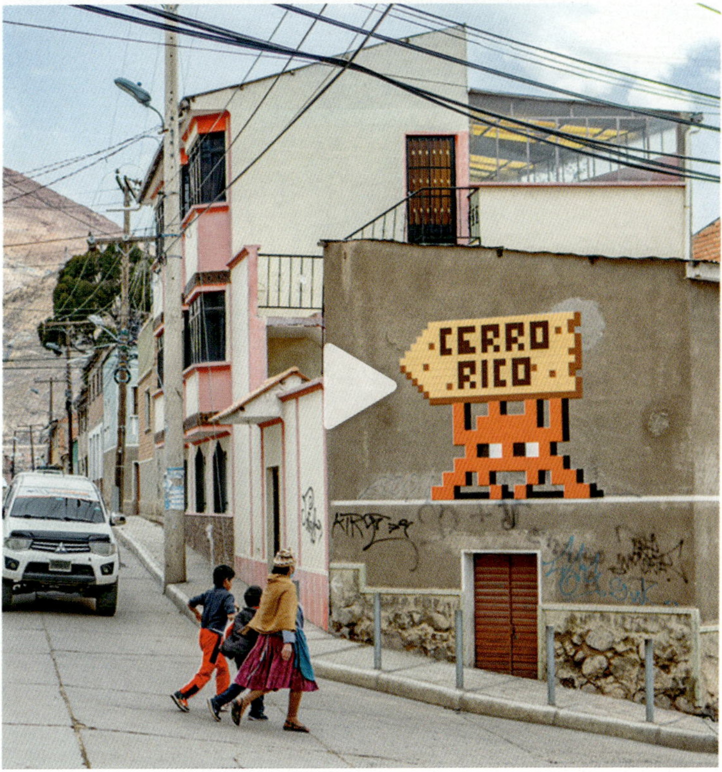

  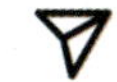

40 154 views

invaderwashere POTI_10
Photo: @henry_ponce_barco

View all 39 comments

24 March 2022

invaderwashere 

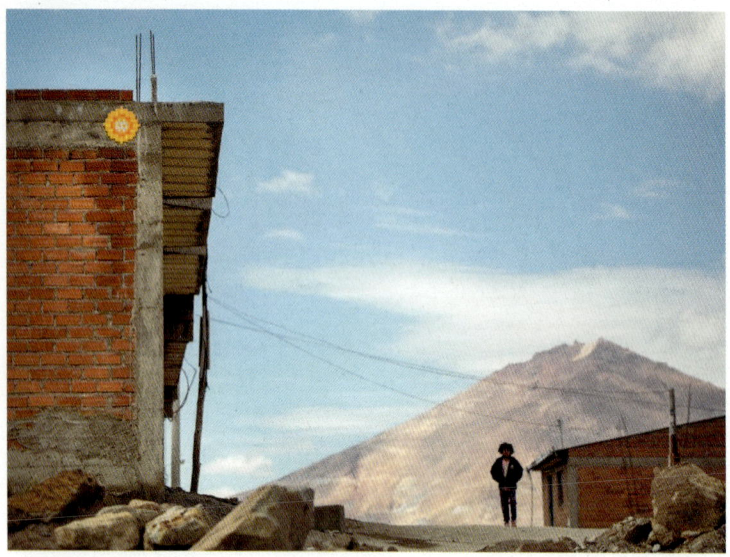

   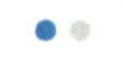 

6073 likes

invaderwashere POTI_29 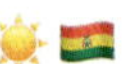

View all 35 comments

5 April 2022

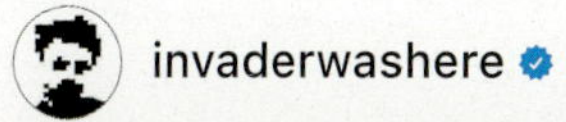

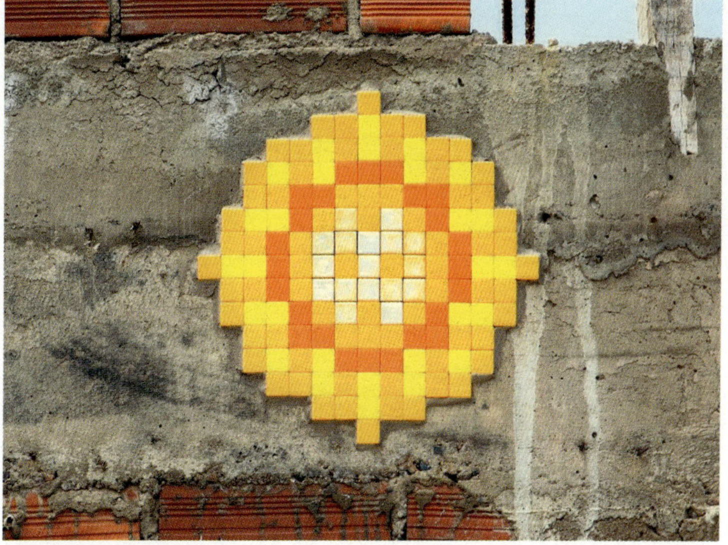

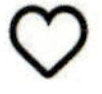    

6073 likes

invaderwashere POTI_29 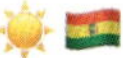

View all 35 comments

5 April 2022

invaderwashere 

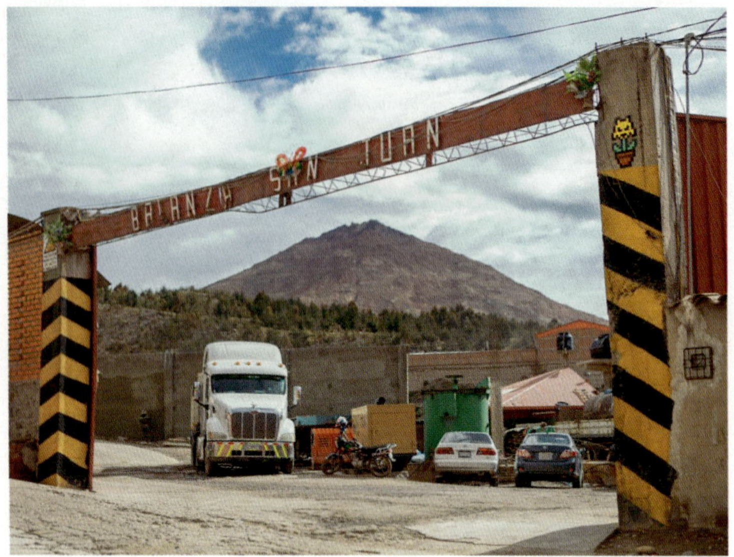

 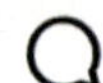  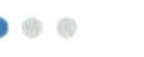 

6 321 likes

invaderwashere The Invasion of Potosí is complete with a total of 53 space invaders. I'm preparing a short movie and a new invasion map about it. Stay tuned... #mission4000 #potosi #bolivia

View all 73 comments

7 April 2022

invaderwashere 

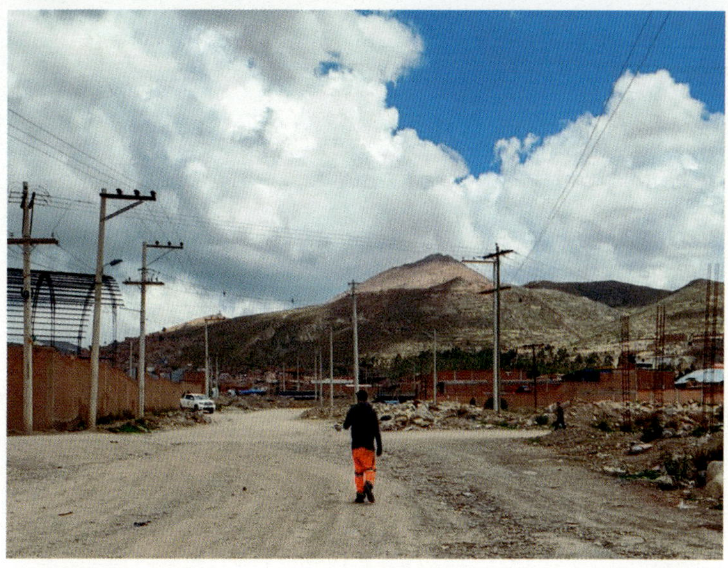

   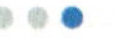 

6321 likes

invaderwashere The Invasion of Potosí is complete with a total of 53 space invaders. I'm preparing a short movie and a new invasion map about it. Stay tuned... #mission4000 #potosi #bolivia

View all 73 comments

7 April 2022

invaderwashere 9 April 2022

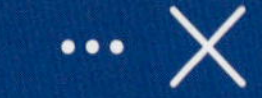

I HAVE CREATED 2 STICKERS
FOR @MIMAMUSEUM

100% OF THE PROFITS
WILL GO TO @CONSORTIUM_1212
TO HELP REGUGEES

Send message

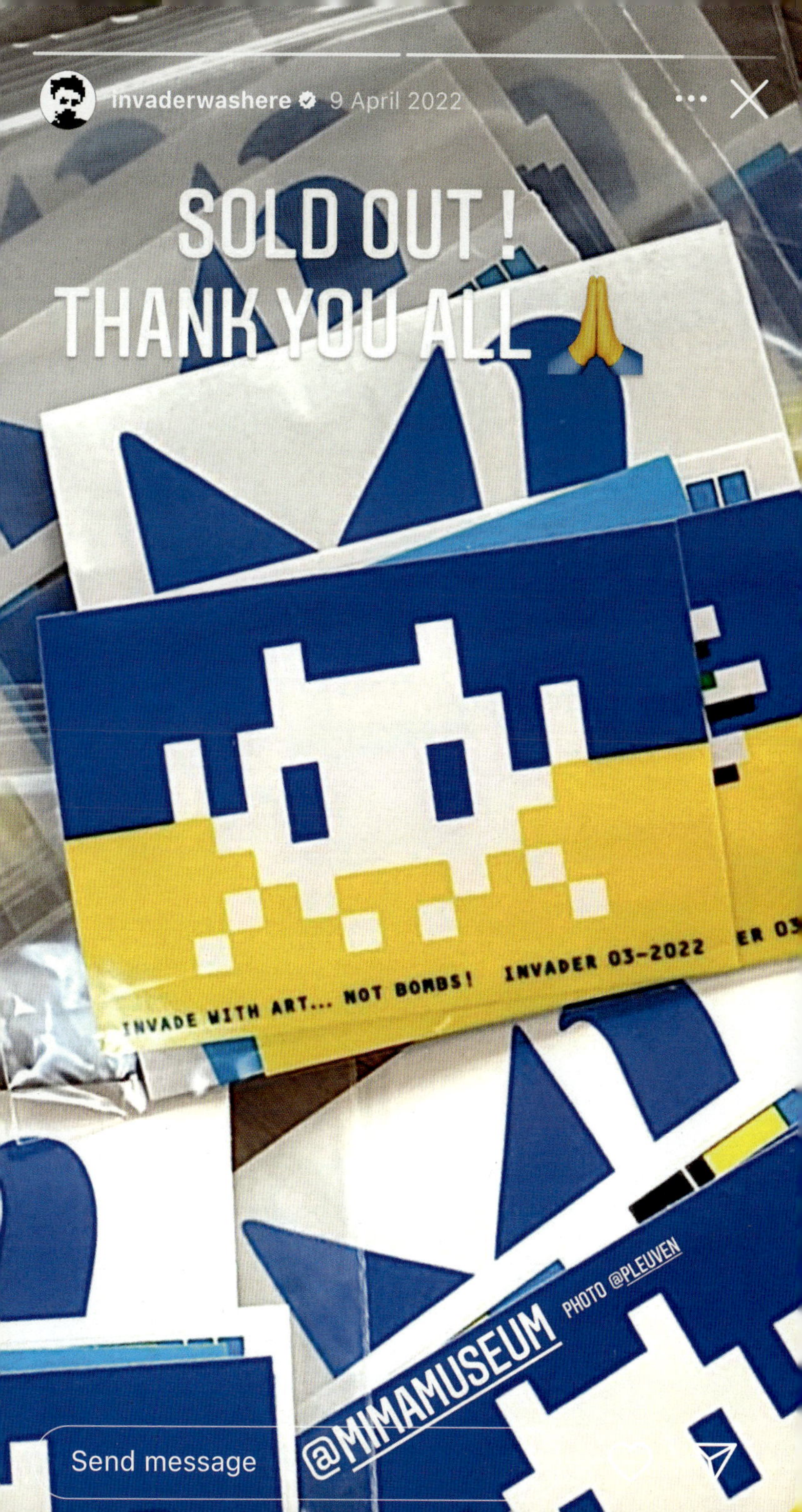
invaderwashere 9 April 2022
SOLD OUT !
THANK YOU ALL
INVADE WITH ART... NOT BOMBS! INVADER 03-2022
@MIMAMUSEUM
PHOTO @PLEUVEN
Send message

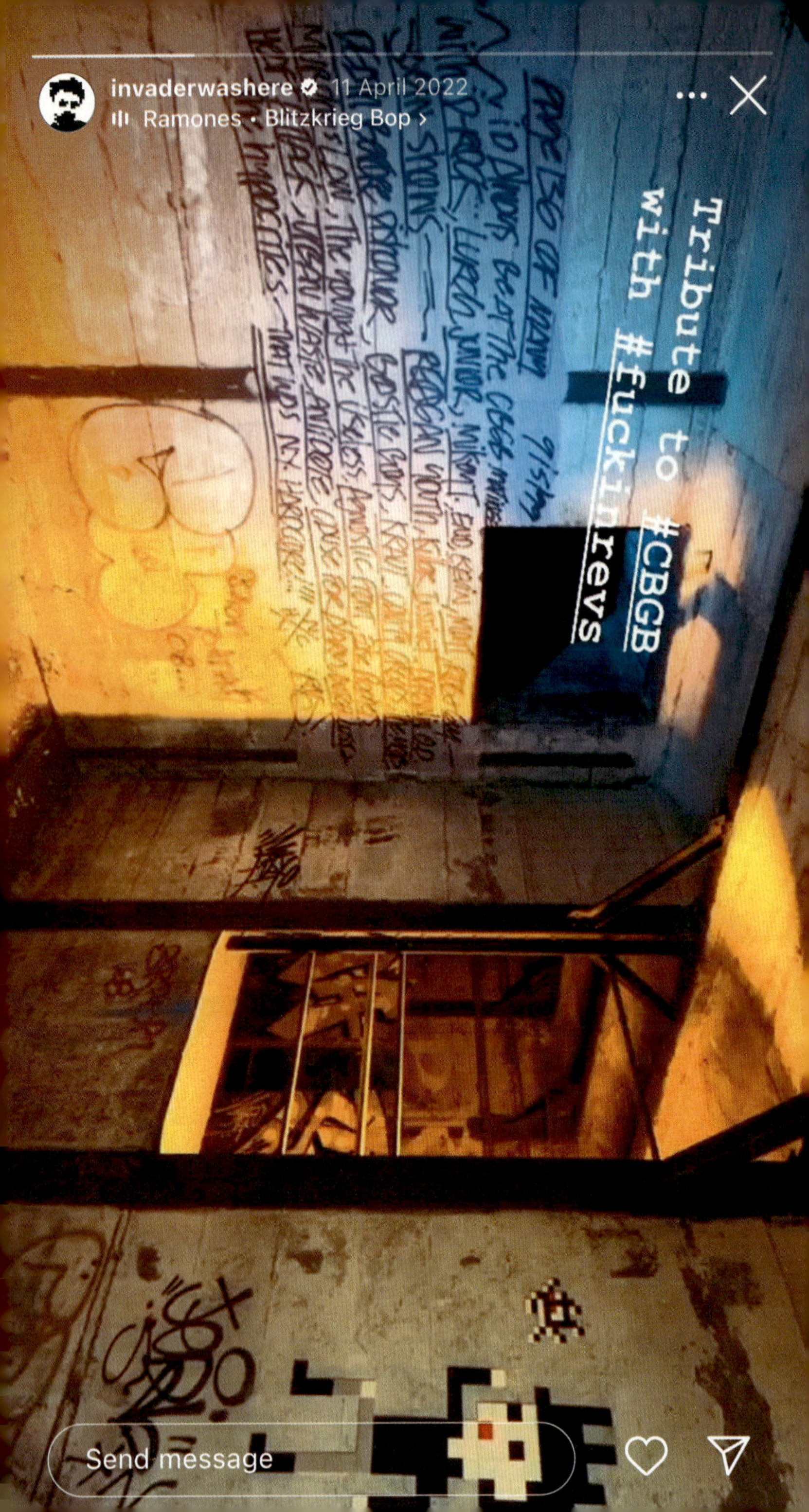
invaderwashere 11 April 2022
Ramones • Blitzkrieg Bop
Tribute to #CBGB
with #fuckinrevs
Send message

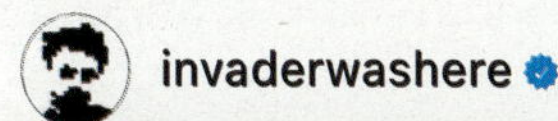

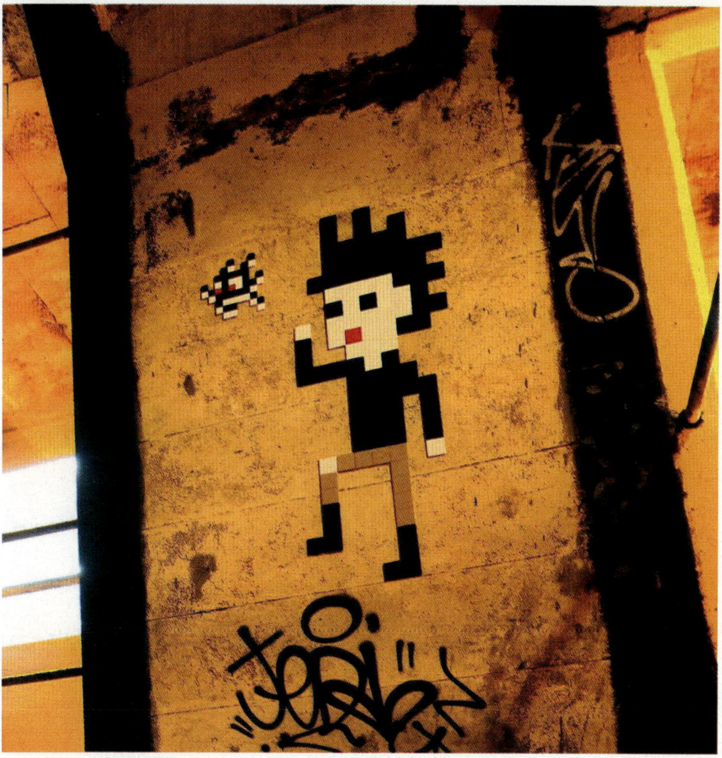

11175 likes

invaderwashere The first Cryptopunk was not a NFT!
#NY_192 #2016 #madewithtiles #underground
#subwaytunnels #cbgb #revs
Photo: @notexactlyblue

View all 109 comments

11 April 2022

invaderwashere 5 May 2022

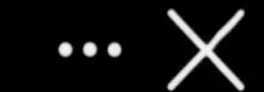

The film and the Invasion map of

POTOSÍ
Mission 4000

will be out next week

Send message

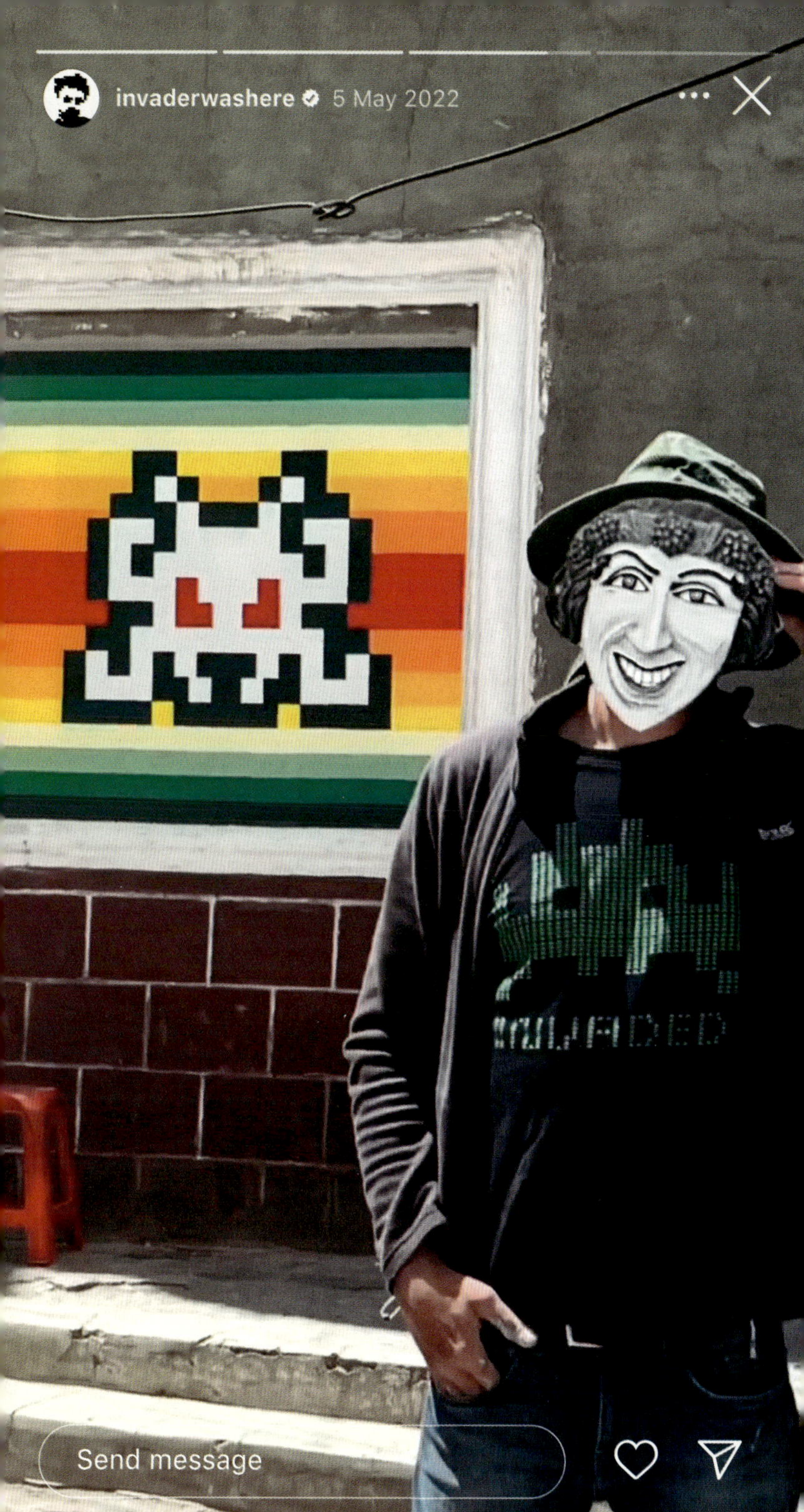
invaderwashere 5 May 2022
Send message

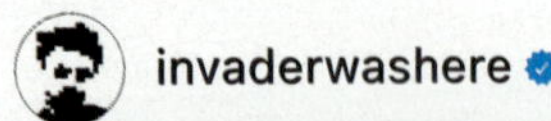

•••

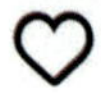   

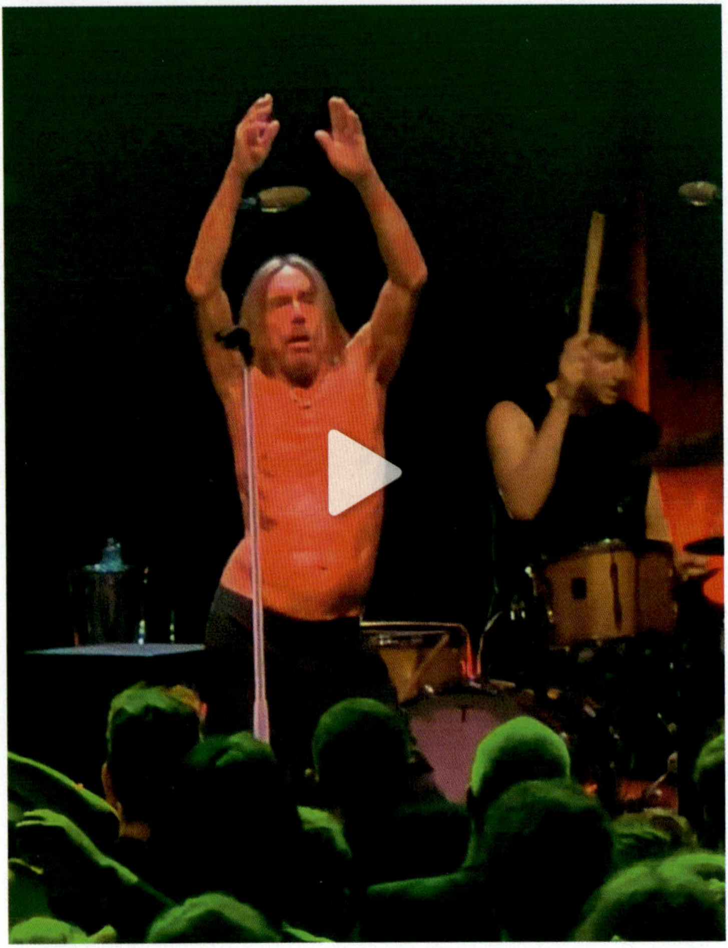

19 515 views

invaderwashere Iggy Rocks! #iggypop #paris #live #pleyel #lustforlife @iggypopofficial

View all 44 comments

8 May 2022

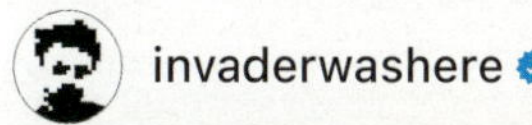

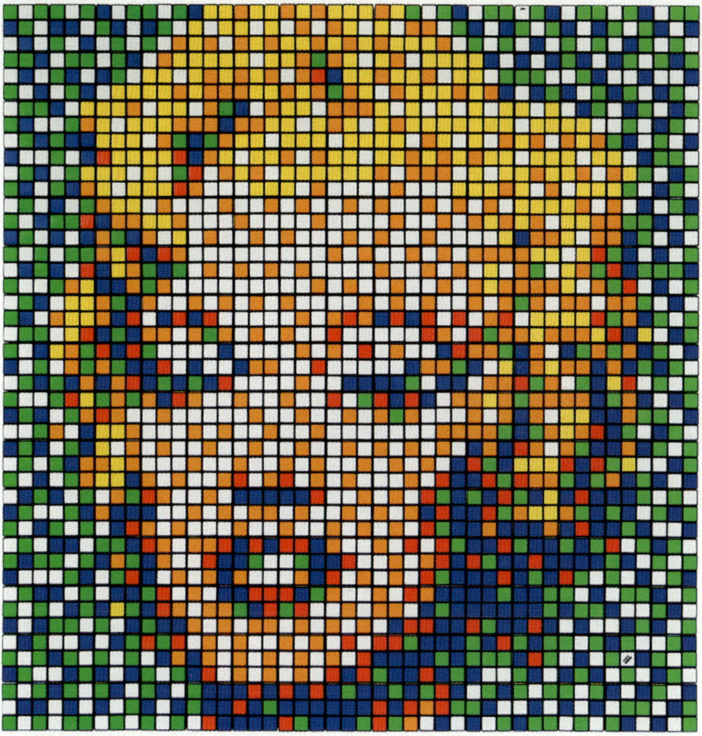

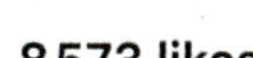

8 573 likes

invaderwashere Dear Larry, I can give you a little discount on this one 😂 #rubikcubism #rubikmarilyn #shotsagebluemarilyn @gagosian @christiesinc #195million$

View all 163 comments

10 May 2022

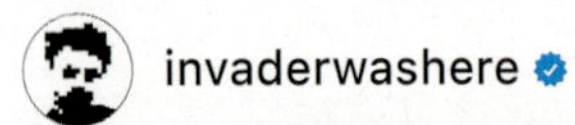

...

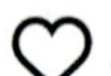   

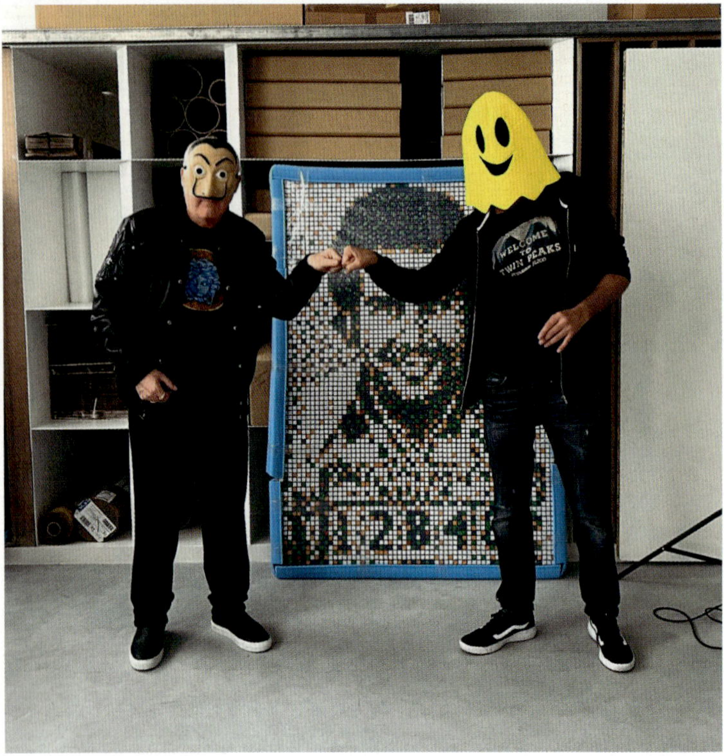

8 355 likes

invaderwashere Guess who visited the studio today...
Thanks Damien, you've always been a great inspiration to me 🦋🔴X🟧👾 @damienhirst #artmaster

View all 147 comments

11 May 2022

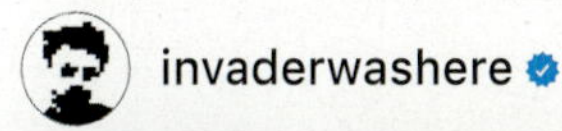

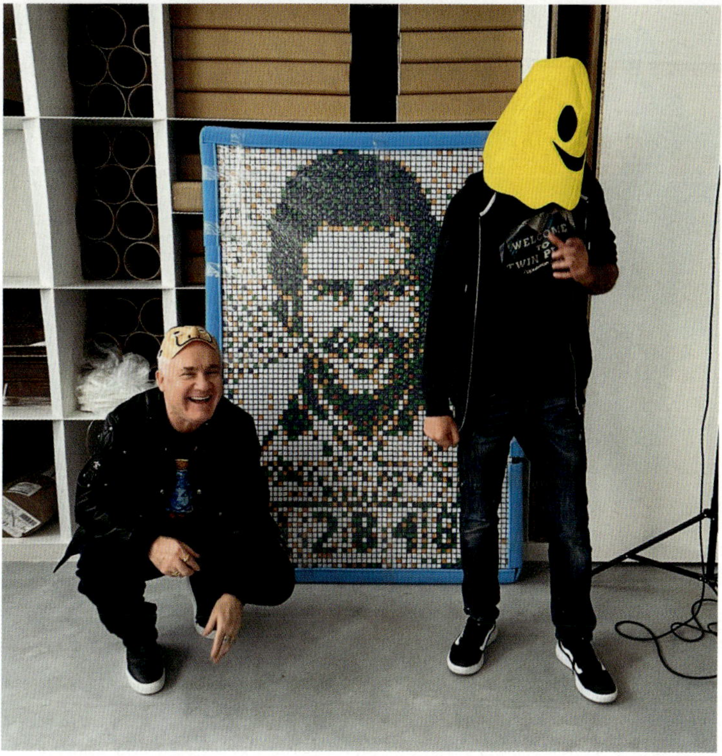

8355 likes

invaderwashere Guess who visited the studio today...
Thanks Damien, you've always been a great inspiration to me 🦋🔴X🟧👾 @damienhirst #artmaster

View all 147 comments

11 May 2022

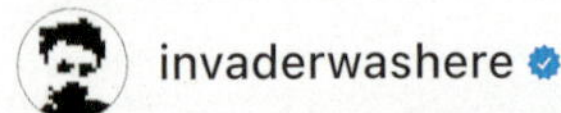

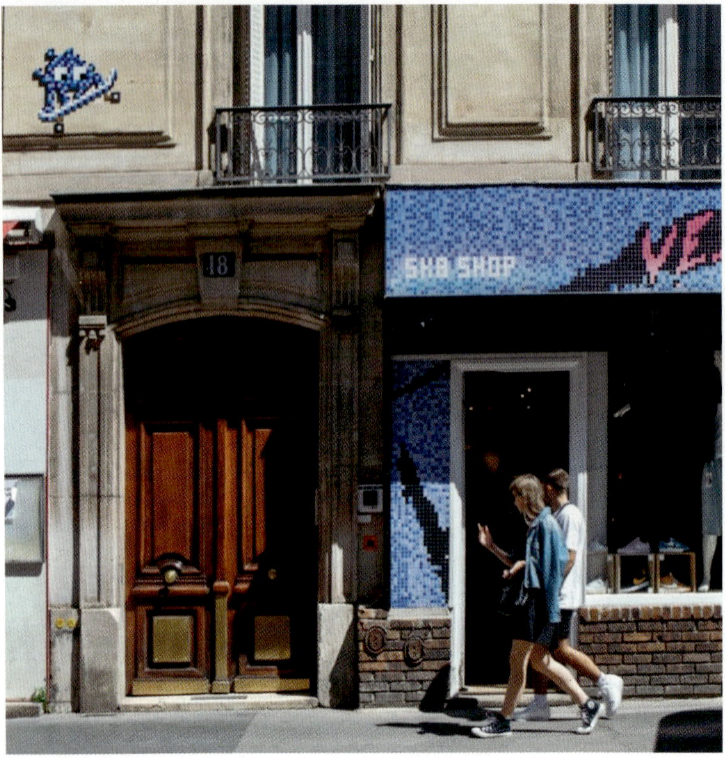

 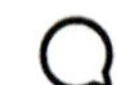  

14 352 likes

invaderwashere PA_1471 sk8 or die!

View all 201 comments

13 May 2022

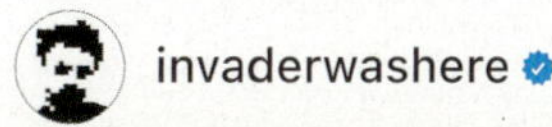

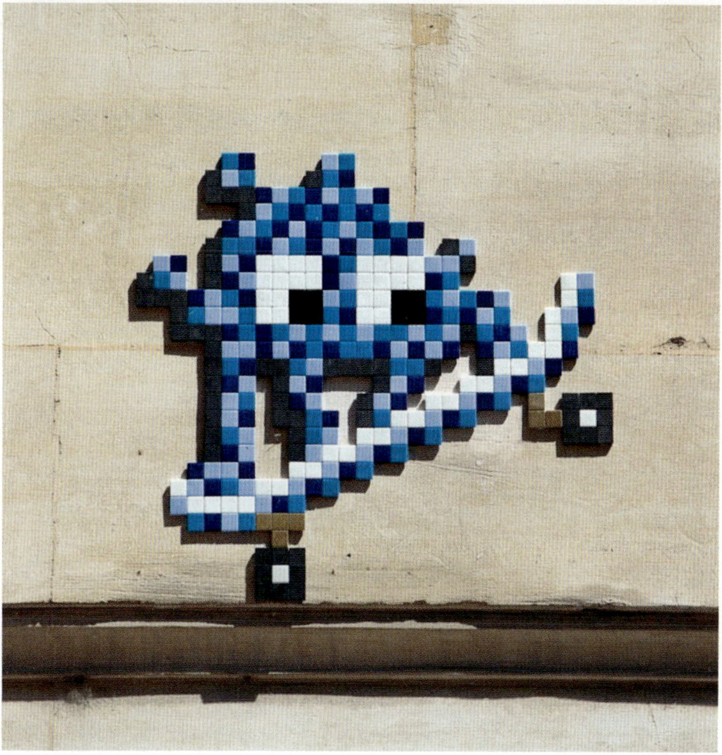

 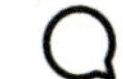  

14 352 likes

invaderwashere PA_1471 sk8 or die!

View all 201 comments

13 May 2022

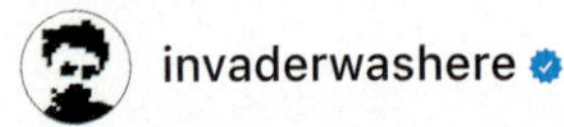

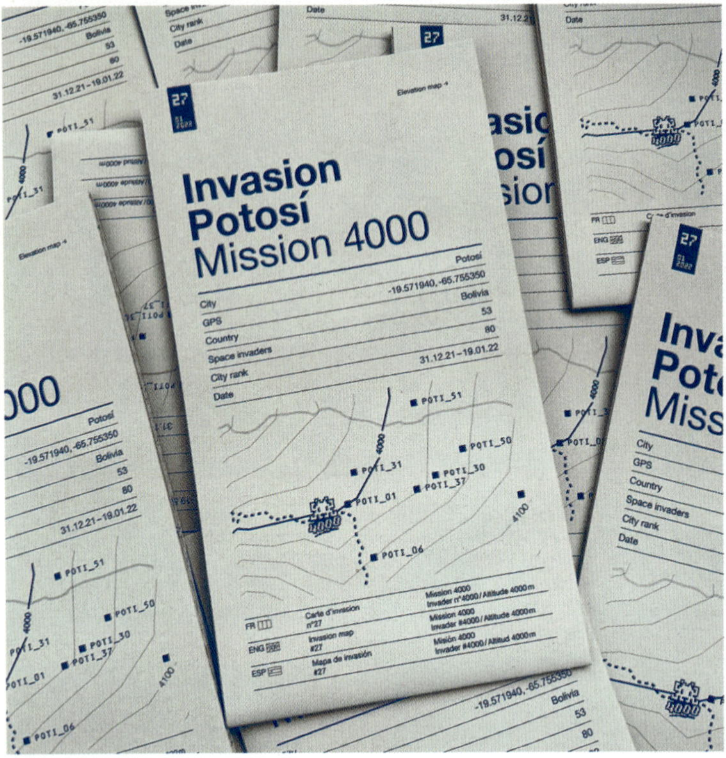

3 625 likes

invaderwashere Just received the new Invasion Map / Potosí Mission 4000. Soon on the Space Shop...
#invasionmap #27 #potosi

View all 83 comments

13 May 2022

invaderwashere

POTI_35	4034		
POTI_36	4035	14 Jan 2022	
POTI_37	4036	14 Jan 2022	30 pts
POTI_38	4037	15 Jan 2022	40 pts
POTI_39	4038	15 Jan 2022	30 pts
POTI_40	4039	15 Jan 2022	40 pts
POTI_41	4040	15 Jan 2022	30 pts
POTI_42	4041	15 Jan 2022	30 pts
POTI_43	4042	15 Jan 2022	50 pts
POTI_44	4043	16 Jan 2022	30 pts
POTI_45	4044	16 Jan 2022	20 pts
POTI_46	4045	16 Jan 2022	50 pts
POTI_47	4046	16 Jan 2022	50 pts
POTI_48	4047	17 Jan 2022	20 pts
POTI_49	4048	17 Jan 2022	50 pts
POTI_50	4049	17 Jan 2022	50 pts
POTI_51	4050	18 Jan 2022	50 pts
POTI_52	4051	18 Jan 2022	30 pts
POTI_53	4052	19 Jan 2022	20 pts

ROCK THE MINES!

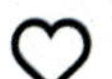   

3 625 likes

invaderwashere Just received the new Invasion Map / Potosí Mission 4000. Soon on the Space Shop...
#invasionmap #27 #potosi

View all 83 comments

13 May 2022

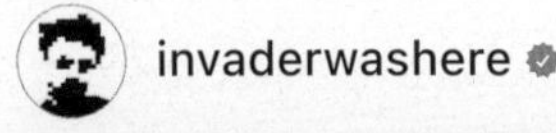

MISSION
4000

2 858 likes

invaderwashere Invasion Potosí / Mission 4000 will be on Youtube tomorrow

View all 66 comments

18 May 2022

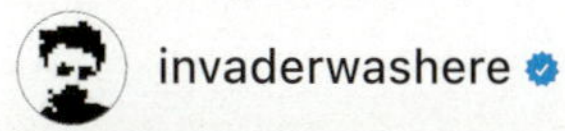

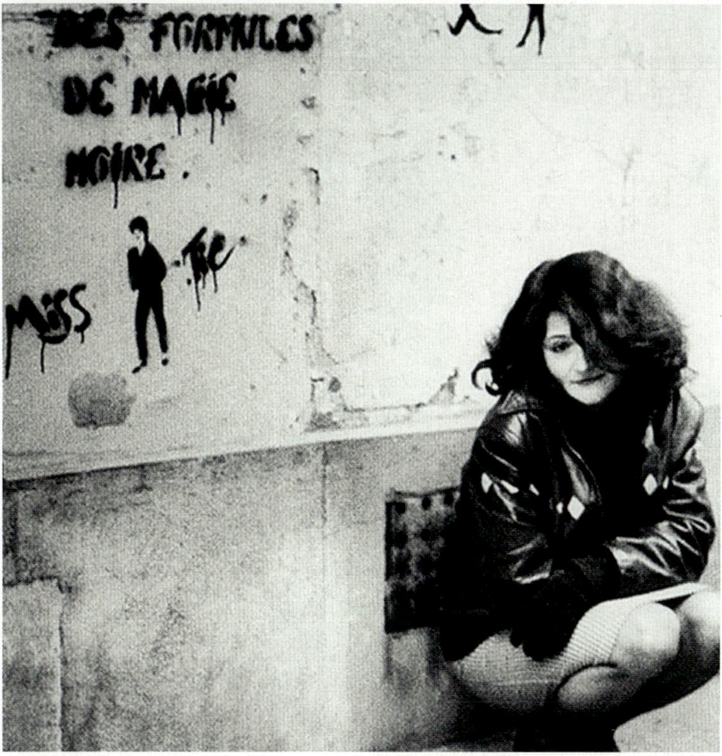

6 657 likes

invaderwashere J'ai depuis toujours aimé découvrir les pochoirs poétiques et engagés de Miss Tic dans les rues de Paris. J'ai aussi eu la chance de l'avoir connue et d'avoir partagé de beaux moments d'échange et d'amitié avec elle. Triste jour 💔 Tu vas nous manquer... Paix à ton âme Miss @missticofficiel #misstic #stencilart #femmesfatales #red #black #art #rock #icon #paris #sadsunday #rip

View all 133 comments

22 May 2022

mimamuseum and **invaderwashere**
MIMA - Museum

MIMA MUSEUM

24.06.2022
08.01.2023

WWW.MIMAMUSEUM.EU

Exhibition

INVADER RUBIKCUBIST

   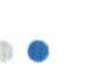 

2 314 likes

mimamuseum New Exhibition: 'INVADER RUBIKCUBIST'
24.06 > 08.01
Invader Rubikcubist is a solo exhibition by Invader entirely devoted to Rubikcubism. The term, which the artist invented in 2005, refers to his studio work around the Rubik's cube, the famous coloured puzzle with which he creates paintings and sculptures.
The exhibition at MIMA reveals more than a hundred works presented on the 4 floors of the museum and allows us to apprehend the richness of the themes tackled by the artist with nearly 20 years of creations in cubes.
#invaderwashere #mimamuseum #rubikcubism #rubikcubist

View all 59 comments

2 June 2022

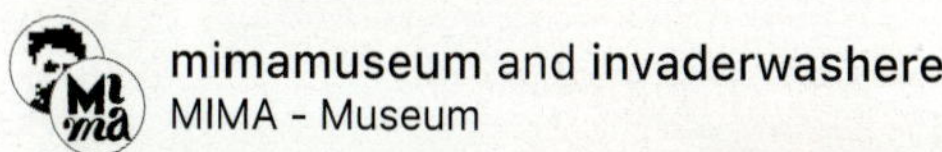

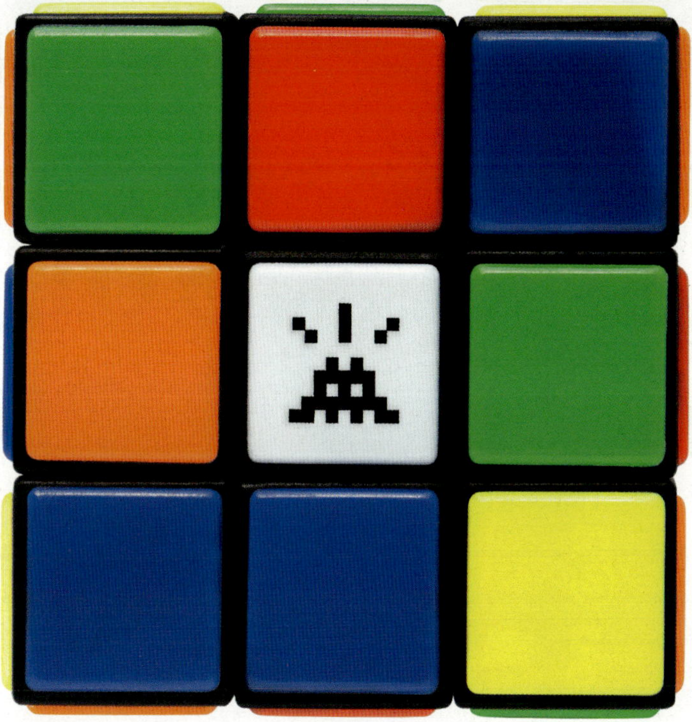

2 314 likes

mimamuseum New Exhibition: 'INVADER RUBIKCUBIST'
24.06 > 08.01
Invader Rubikcubist is a solo exhibition by Invader entirely devoted to Rubikcubism. The term, which the artist invented in 2005, refers to his studio work around the Rubik's cube, the famous coloured puzzle with which he creates paintings and sculptures.
The exhibition at MIMA reveals more than a hundred works presented on the 4 floors of the museum and allows us to apprehend the richness of the themes tackled by the artist with nearly 20 years of creations in cubes.
#invaderwashere #mimamuseum #rubikcubism #rubikcubist

View all 59 comments

2 June 2022

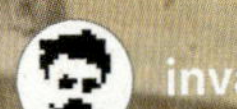

invaderwashere 3 June 2022

so nice 😍 ... thank you @geraldpassedat

2021

BANDOL

Château

SALETTES

LA CADIÈRE-D'AZUR-VAR

FRANCE

BOUTEILLE AU CHATEAU, CUVEE

PASSEDAT

Send message

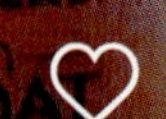

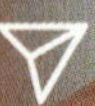

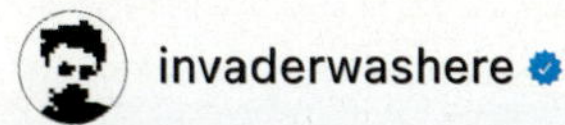

•••

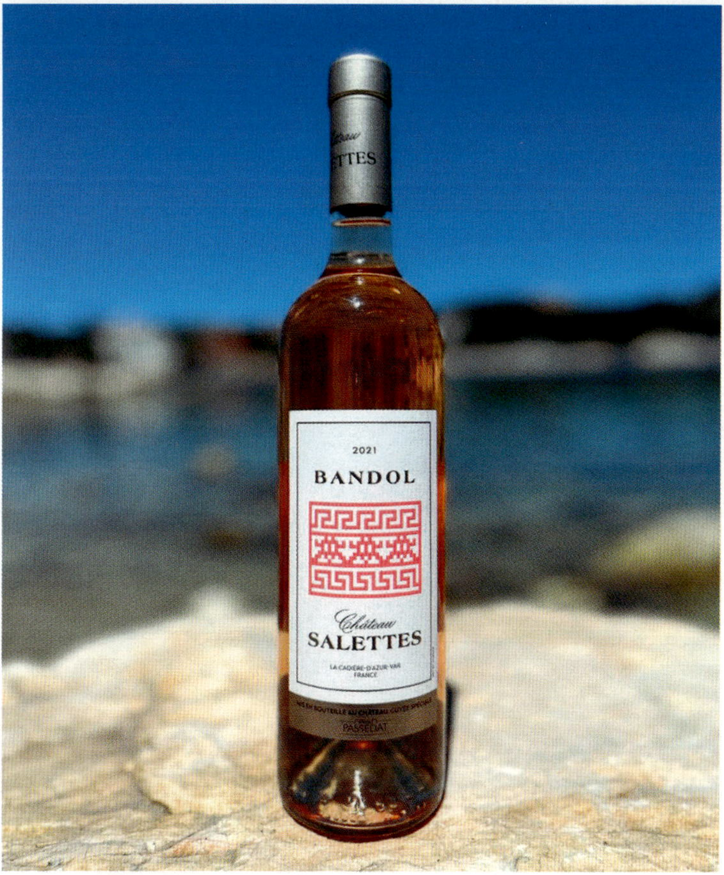

4812 likes

invaderwashere GERALD PASSEDAT X INVADER
I'm proud to have designed the label of this wine bottle for Gerald Passedat and Château Salettes.
2021 is an excellent year for the Bandol rosé and this vintage is particularly exceptional. It is limited to 1200 numbered bottles and a red and a white ones will be released soon. #wine #rosé #vin #vindegarde #wineyard #vigneron #bandol #bio #organic #firstvintage #provence #premièrecuvée #sud #southoffrance #mediterranee
More infos: @geraldpassedat @chateausalettes
View all 144 comments

3 June 2022

GET READY
FOR A NEW KIND
OF INVASION...

LANDING ON EARTH
ON JUNE 30 2022

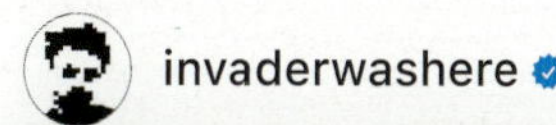

INVADER

RUBIKCUBIST

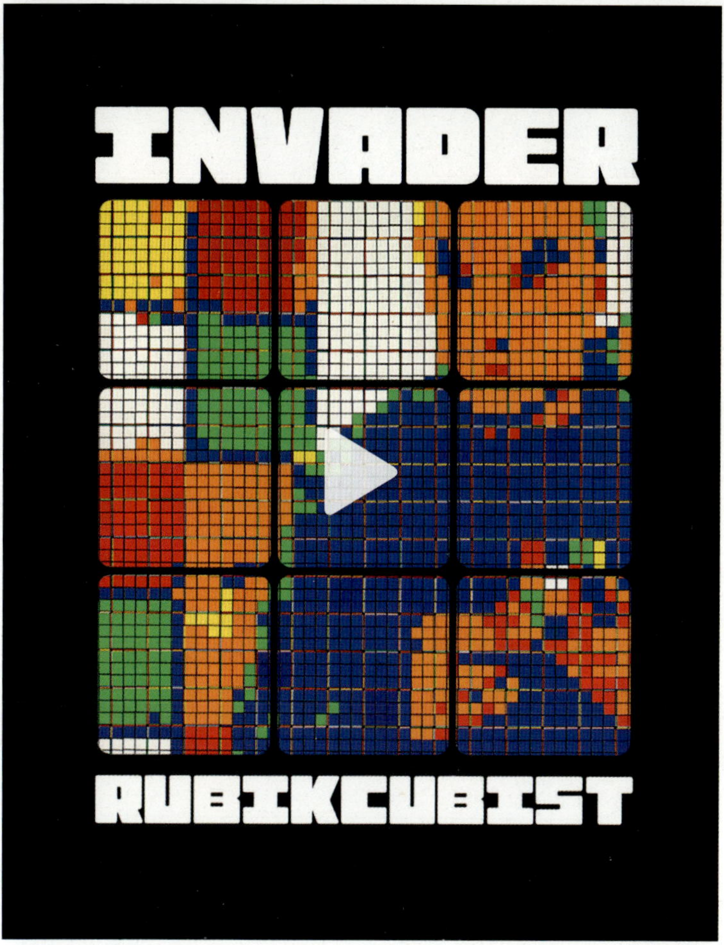

4 363 likes

invaderwashere INVADER RUBKCUBIST @mimamuseum
D-16 #rubikcubism

View all 63 comments

8 June 2022

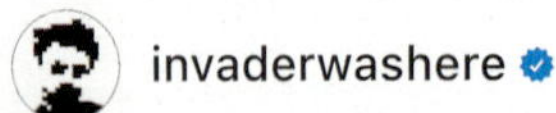

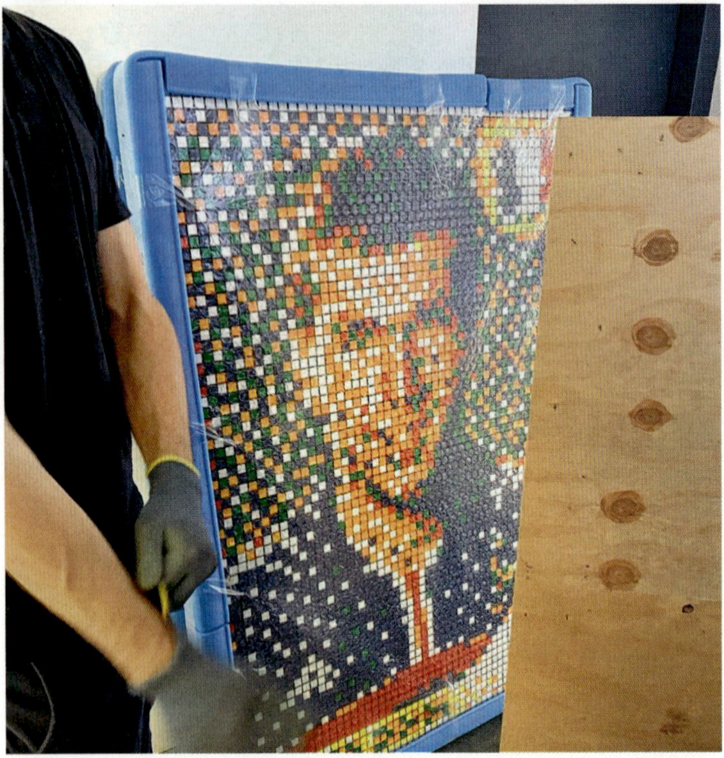

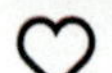   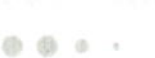 

7803 likes

invaderwashere INVADER RUBIKCUBIST D-8
@mimamuseum #rubikcubism #installation

View all 166 comments

16 June 2022

invaderwashere

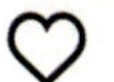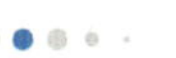

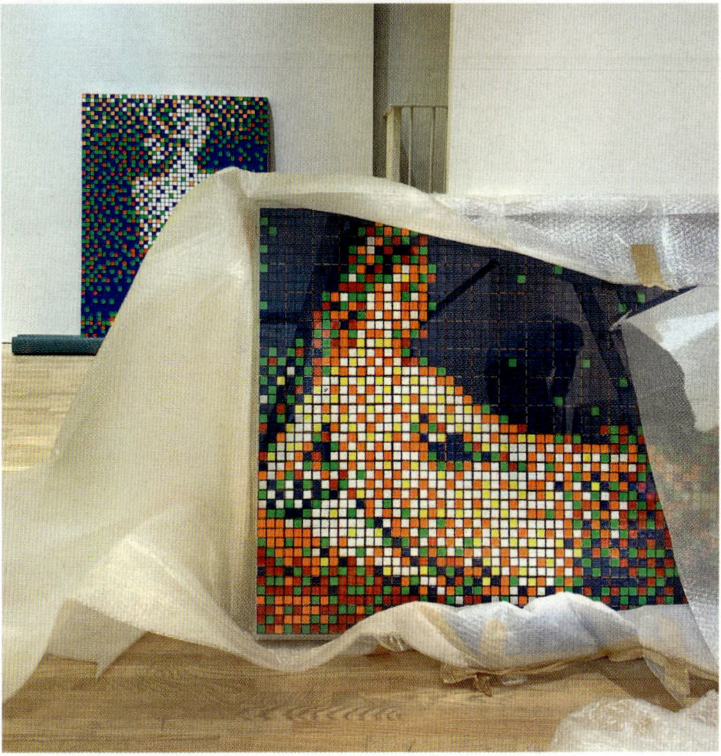

7803 likes

invaderwashere INVADER RUBIKCUBIST D-8
@mimamuseum #rubikcubism #installation

View all 166 comments

16 June 2022

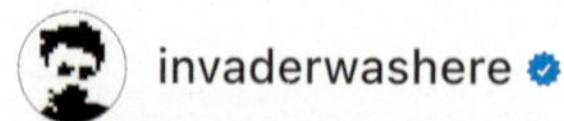

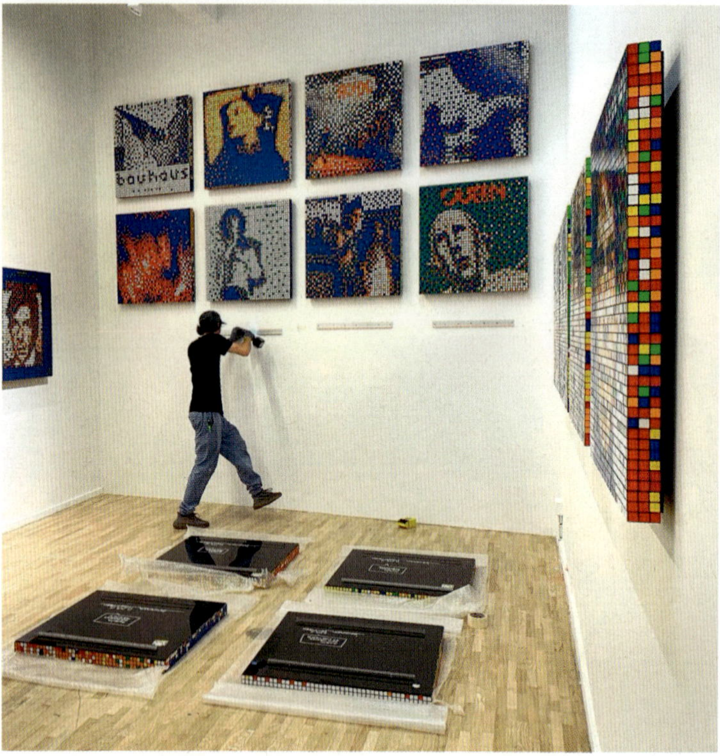

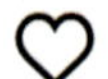 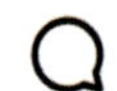  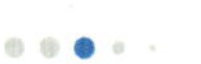 

7803 likes

invaderwashere INVADER RUBIKCUBIST D-8
@mimamuseum #rubikcubism #installation

View all 166 comments

16 June 2022

invaderwashere

  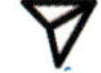 

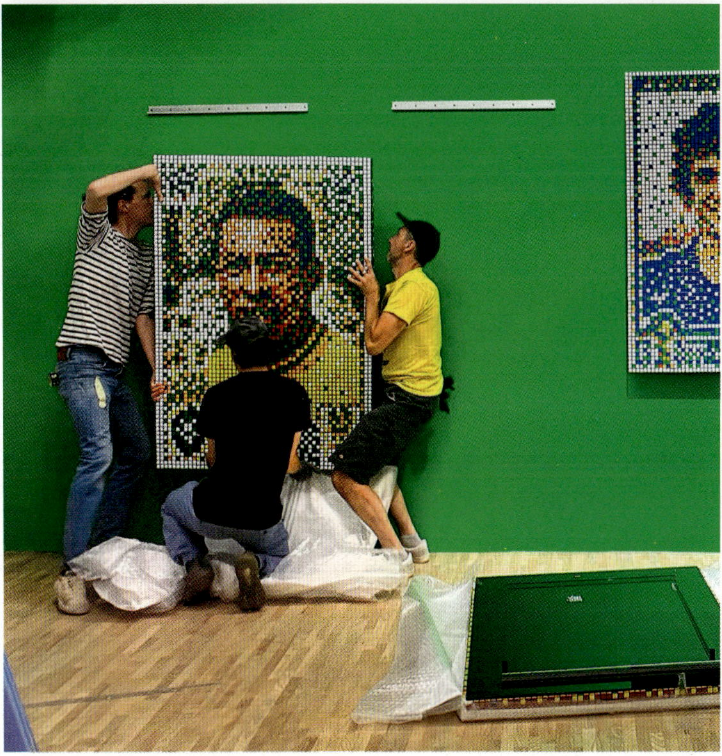

7803 likes

invaderwashere INVADER RUBIKCUBIST D-8
@mimamuseum #rubikcubism #installation

View all 166 comments

16 June 2022

invaderwashere 

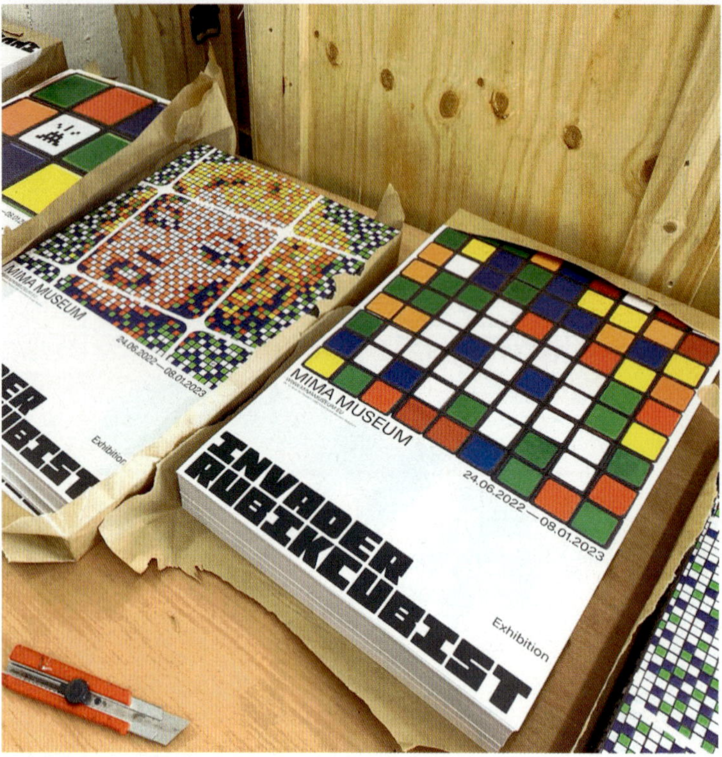

7803 likes

invaderwashere INVADER RUBIKCUBIST D-8
@mimamuseum #rubikcubism #installation

View all 166 comments

16 June 2022

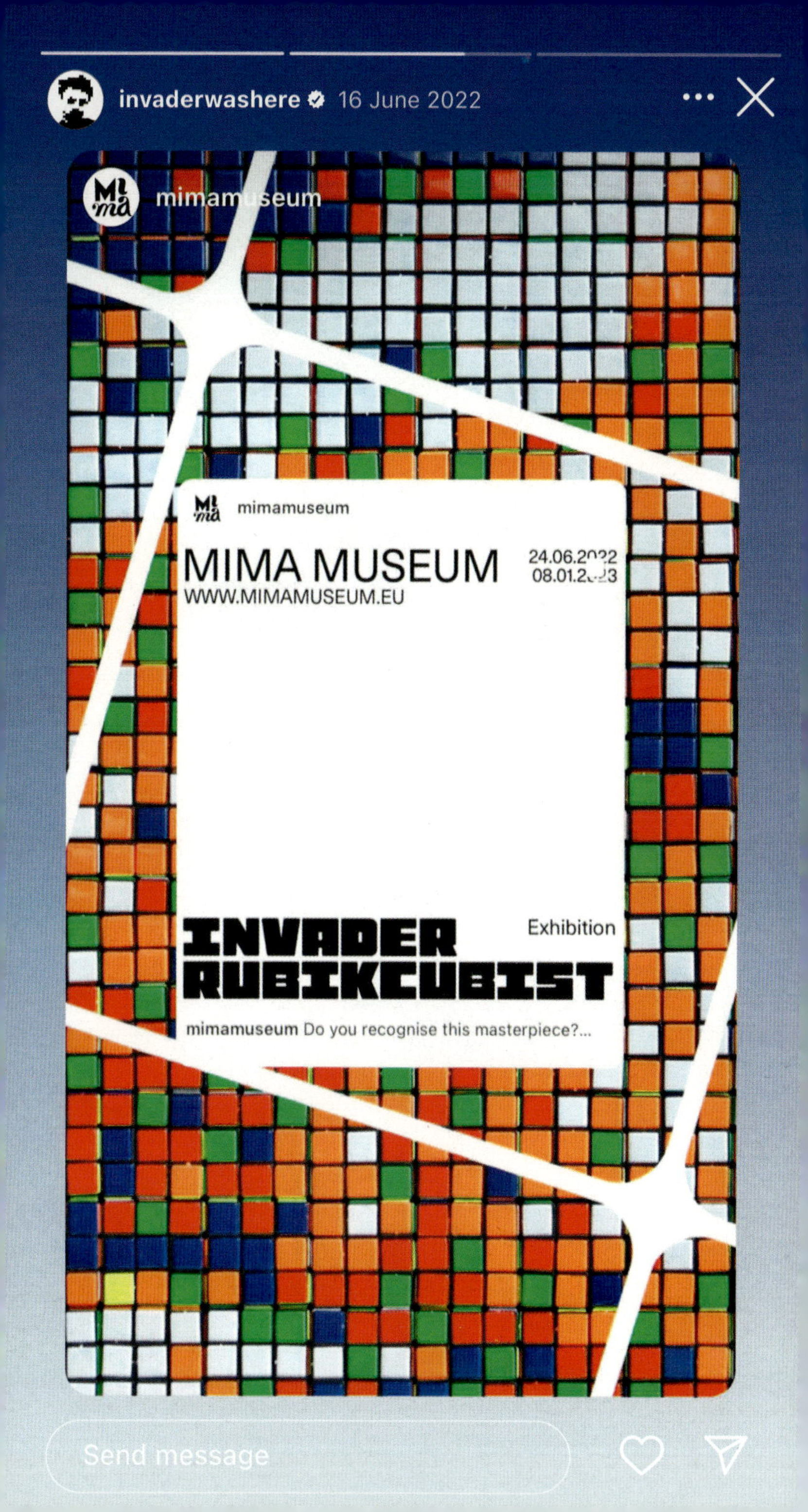

invaderwashere 16 June 2022 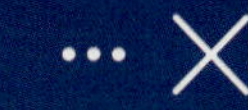

mimamuseum

mimamuseum

MIMA MUSEUM
WWW.MIMAMUSEUM.EU

24.06.2022
08.01.2023

Exhibition

INVADER
RUBIKCUBIST

mimamuseum Do you recognise this masterpiece?...

Send message

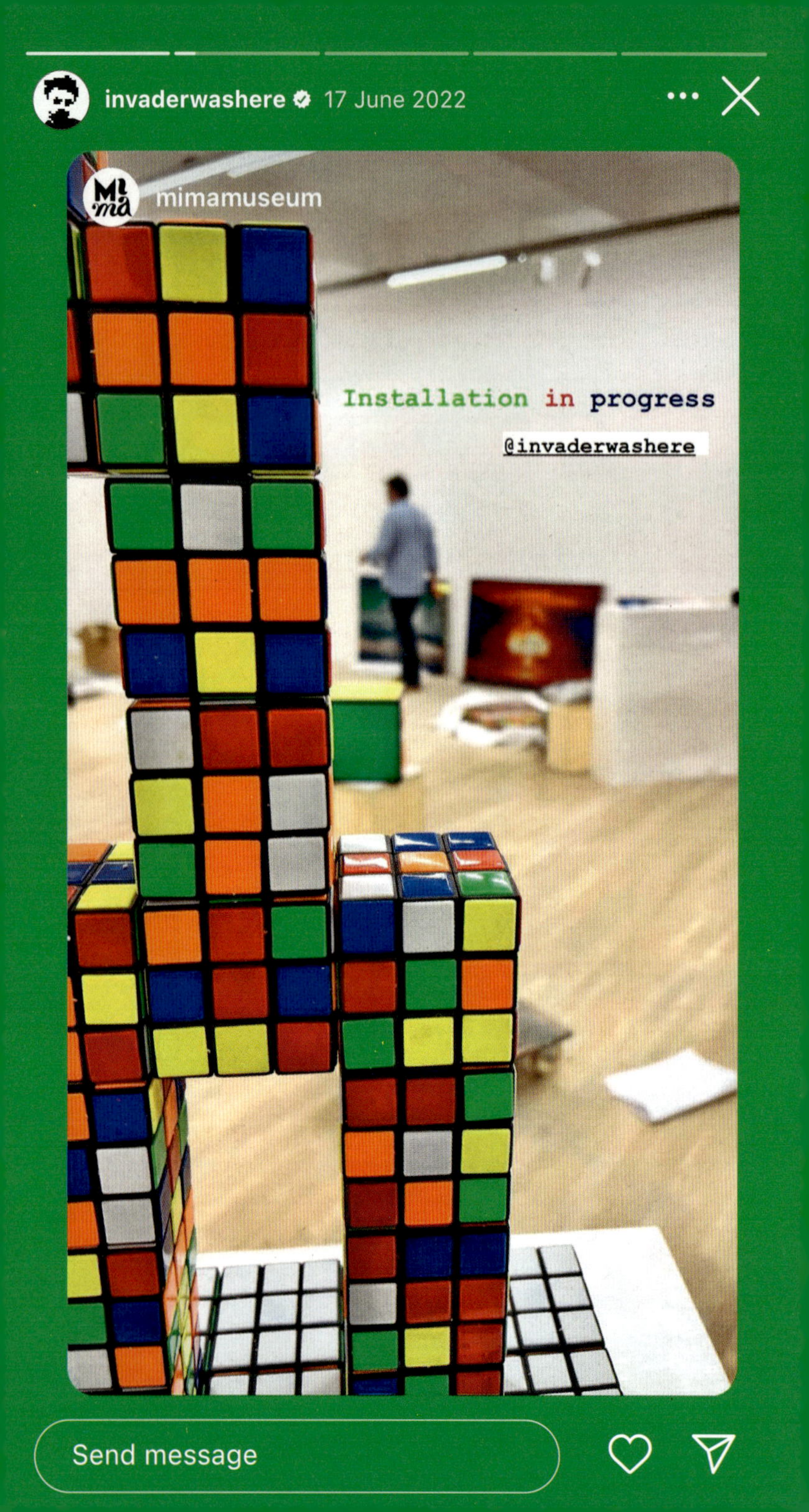

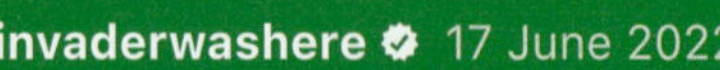

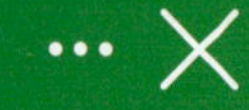

mimamuseum

Installation in progress

@invaderwashere

Send message

invaderwashere 17 June 2022

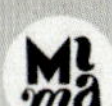

mimamuseum

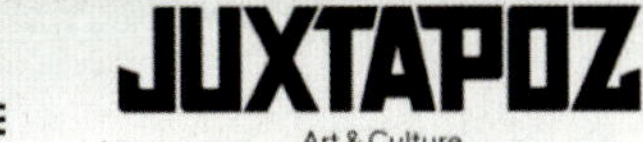

Invader is the Rubikcubist

MIMA, Brussels
June 24, 2022 - January 08, 2023

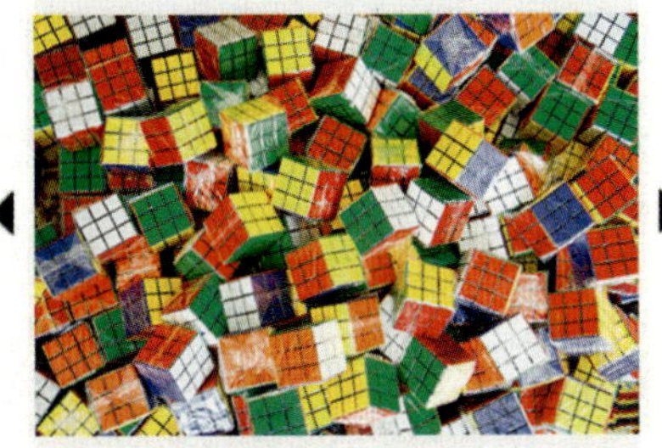

@juxtapozmag
@invaderwashere

Opening June 24, 2022, MIMA, the Millennium Iconoclast Museum of Art in Brussels, presents *Invader Rubikcubist*, a solo exhibition by Invader, the anonymous but world-famous artist who has given shape to the computer pixel with ceramic tiles that he cements on the walls of cities around the world.

READ THE ARTICLE

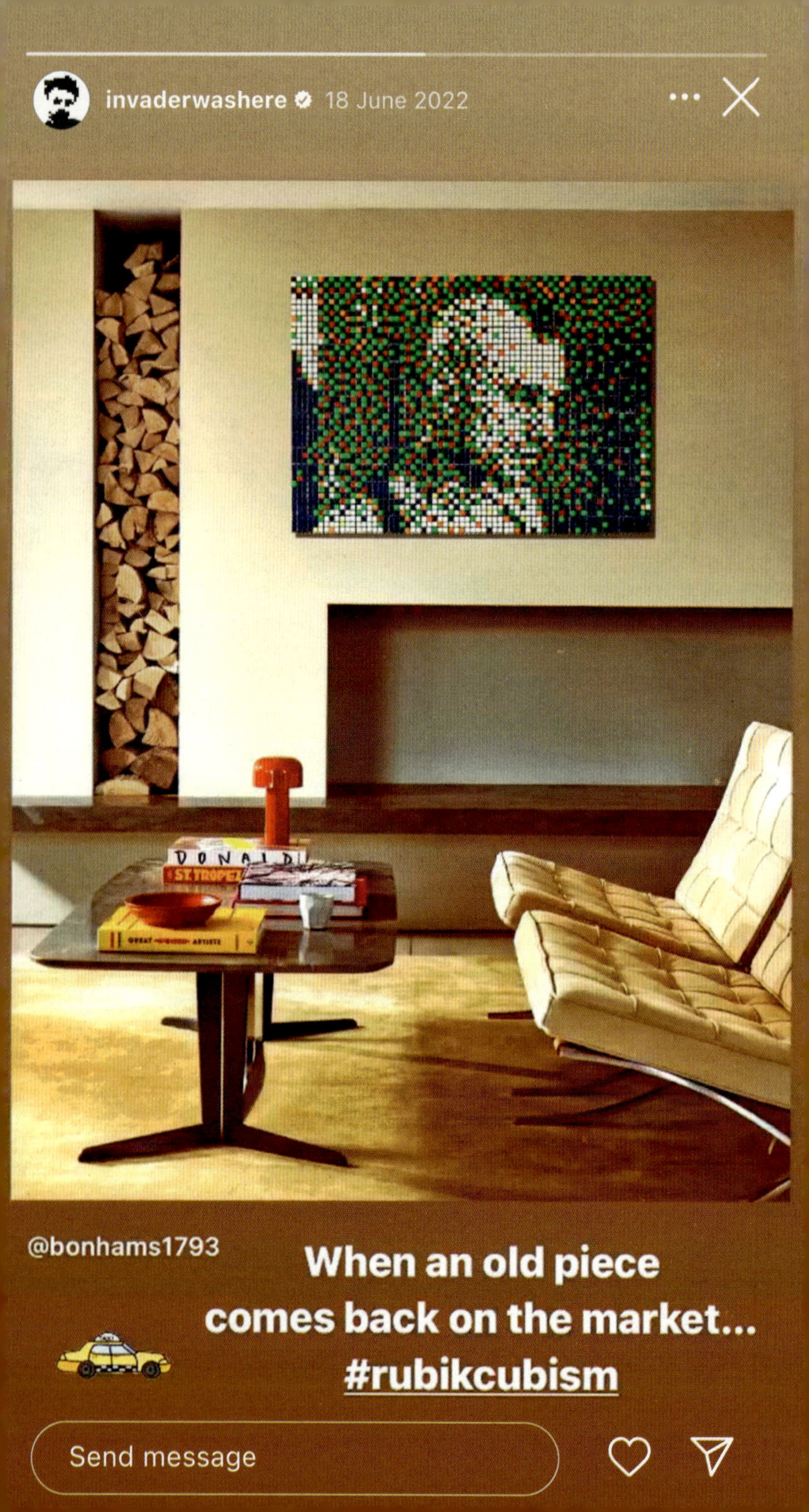

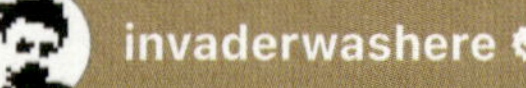

18 June 2022

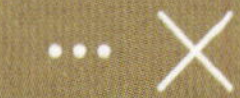

@bonhams1793

When an old piece comes back on the market...
#rubikcubism

Send message

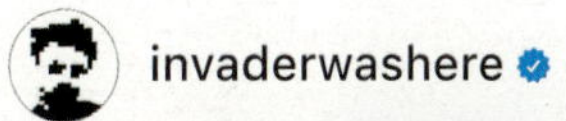

invaderwashere

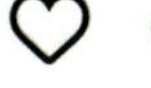

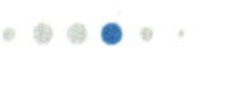

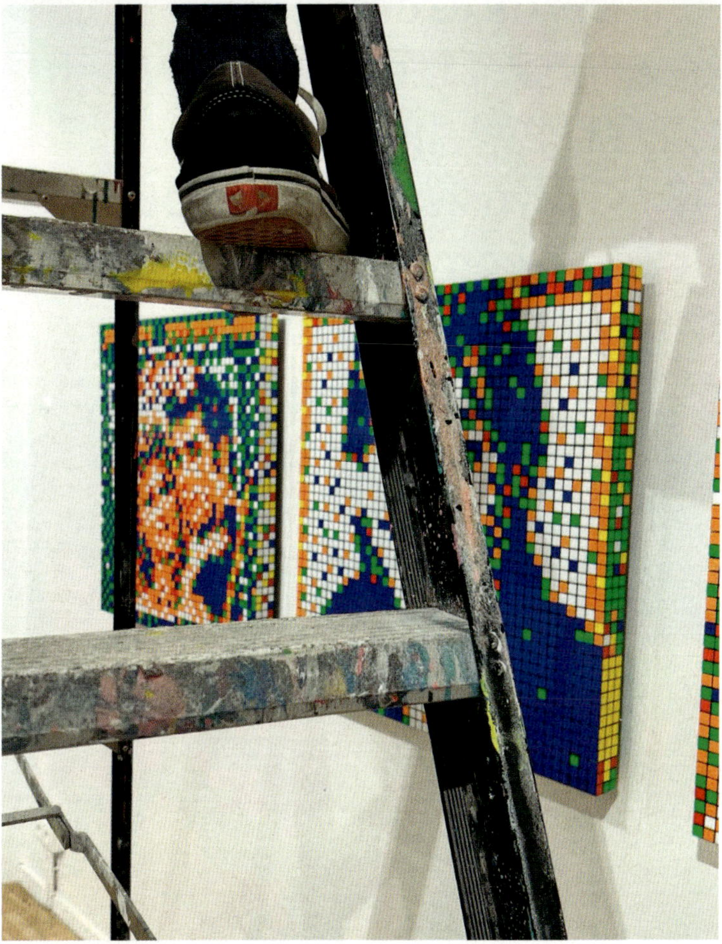

3 359 likes

invaderwashere INVADER RUBIKUBIST D-2
@mimamuseum #exhibition #rubikcubism

View all 39 comments

22 June 2022

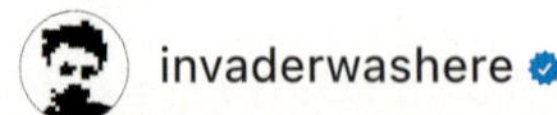

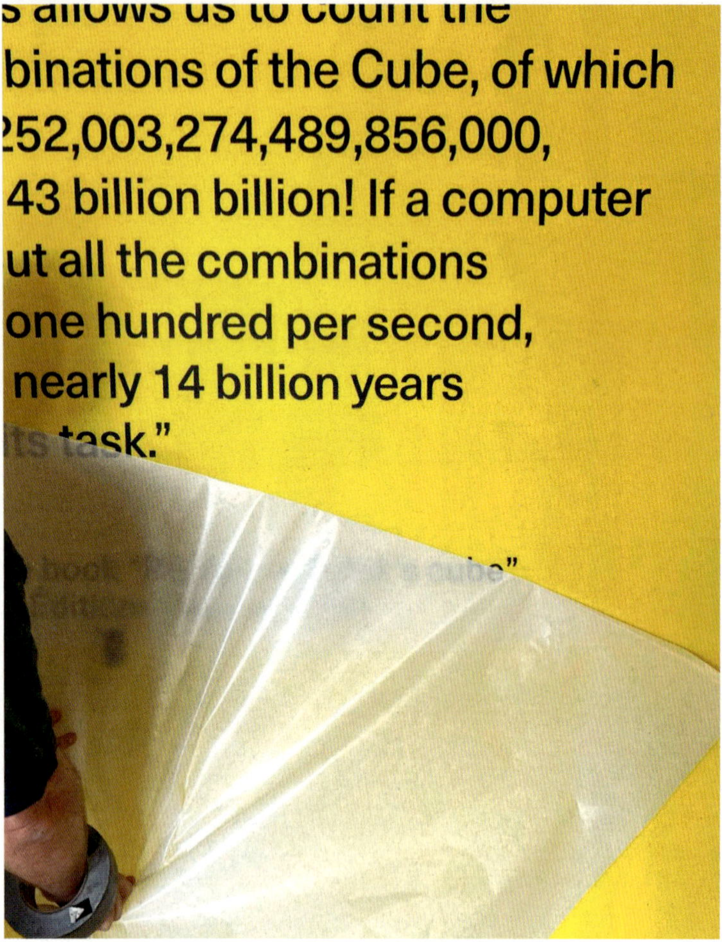

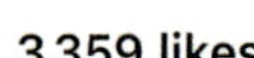

3 359 likes

invaderwashere INVADER RUBIKUBIST D-2
@mimamuseum #exhibition #rubikcubism

View all 39 comments

22 June 2022

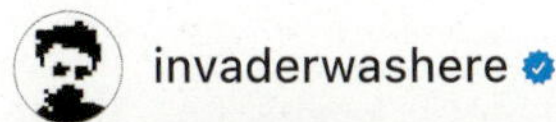

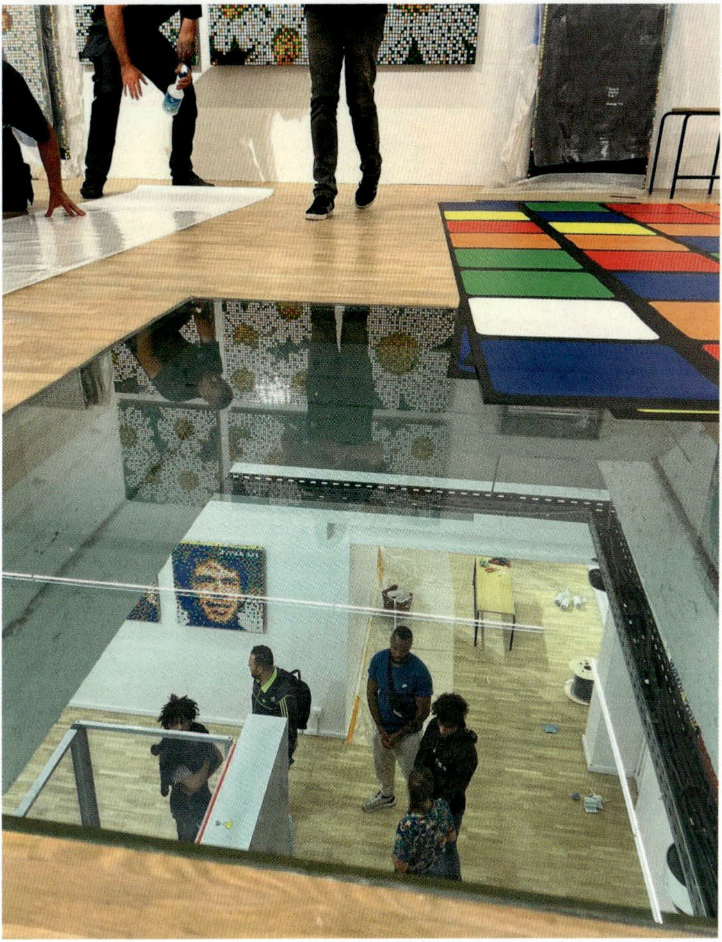

3 359 likes

invaderwashere INVADER RUBIKUBIST D-2
@mimamuseum #exhibition #rubikcubism

View all 39 comments

22 June 2022

invaderwashere

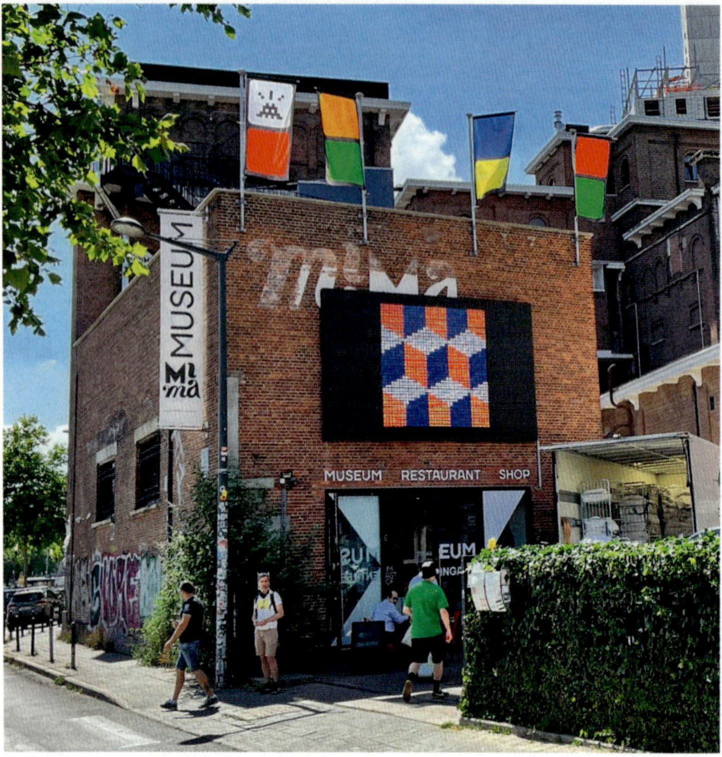

4 229 likes

invaderwashere INVADER RUBKCUBIST Press tour before public opening H-3 @mimamuseum

View all 67 comments

24 June 2022

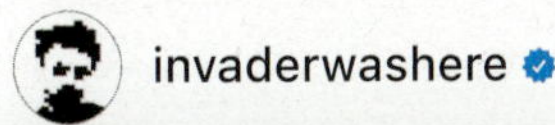

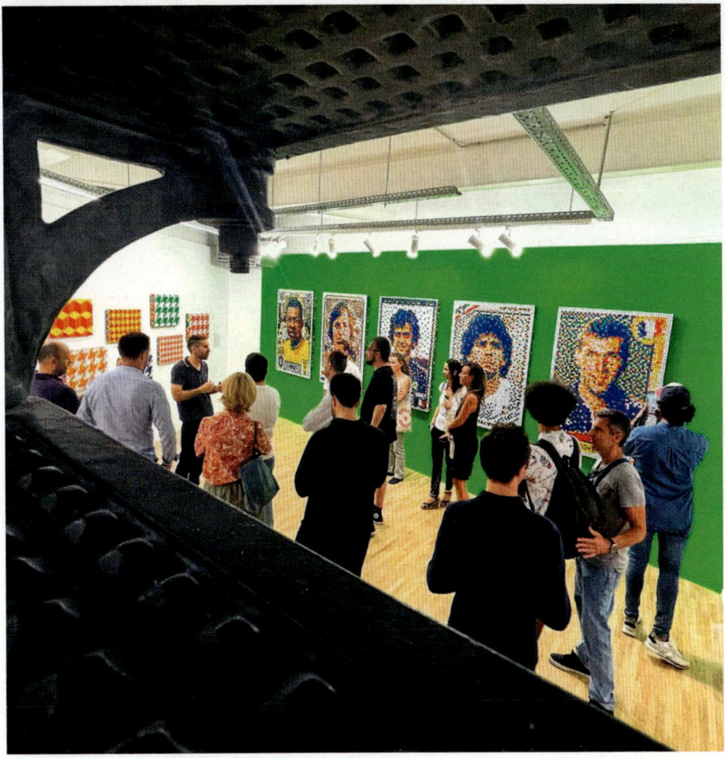

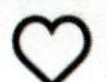

4 229 likes

invaderwashere INVADER RUBKCUBIST Press tour before public opening H-3 @mimamuseum

View all 67 comments

24 June 2022

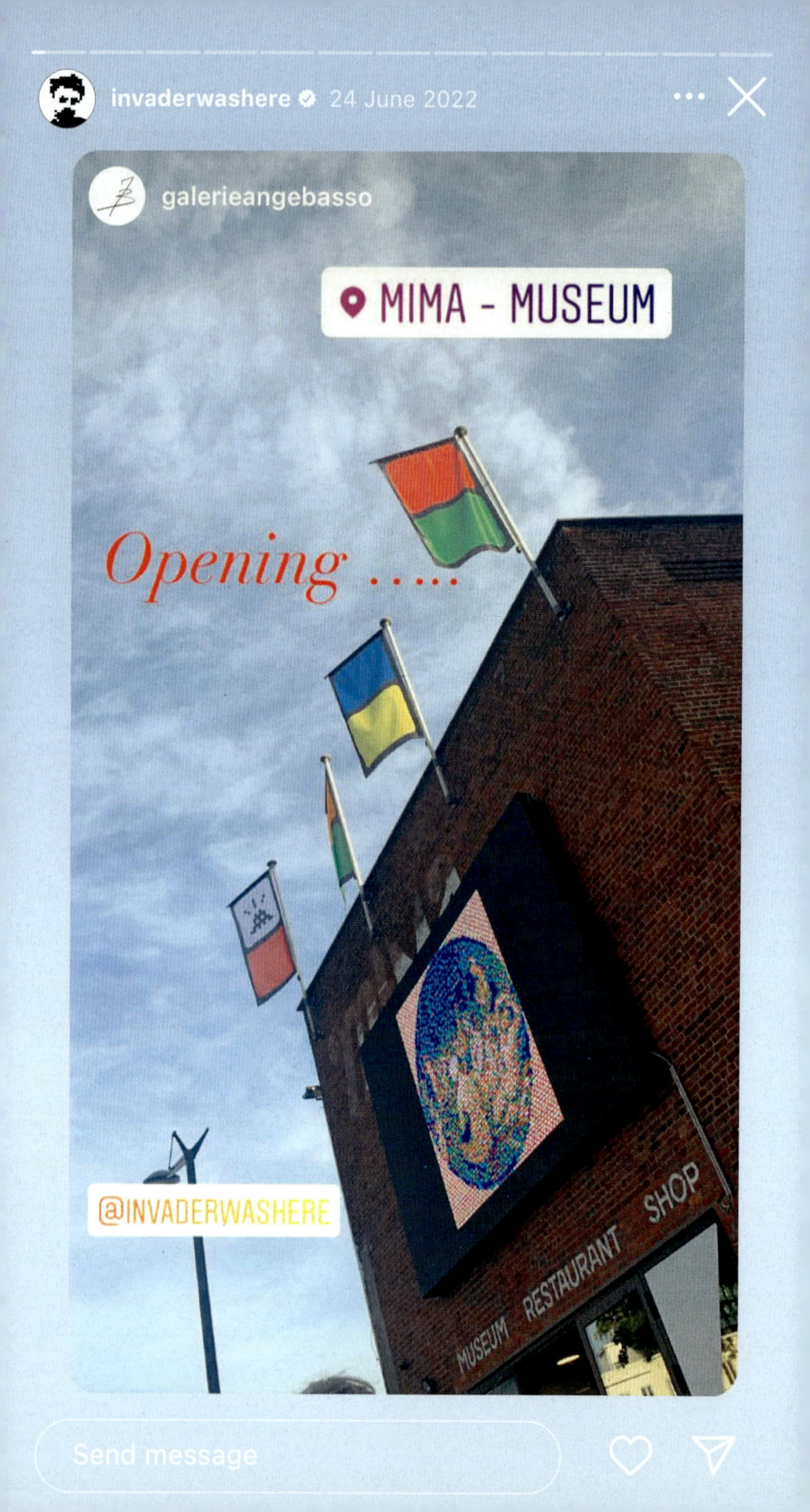

invaderwashere 24 June 2022

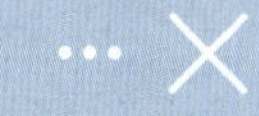

galerieangebasso

MIMA - MUSEUM

Opening .....

@INVADERWASHERE

MUSEUM RESTAURANT SHOP

Send message

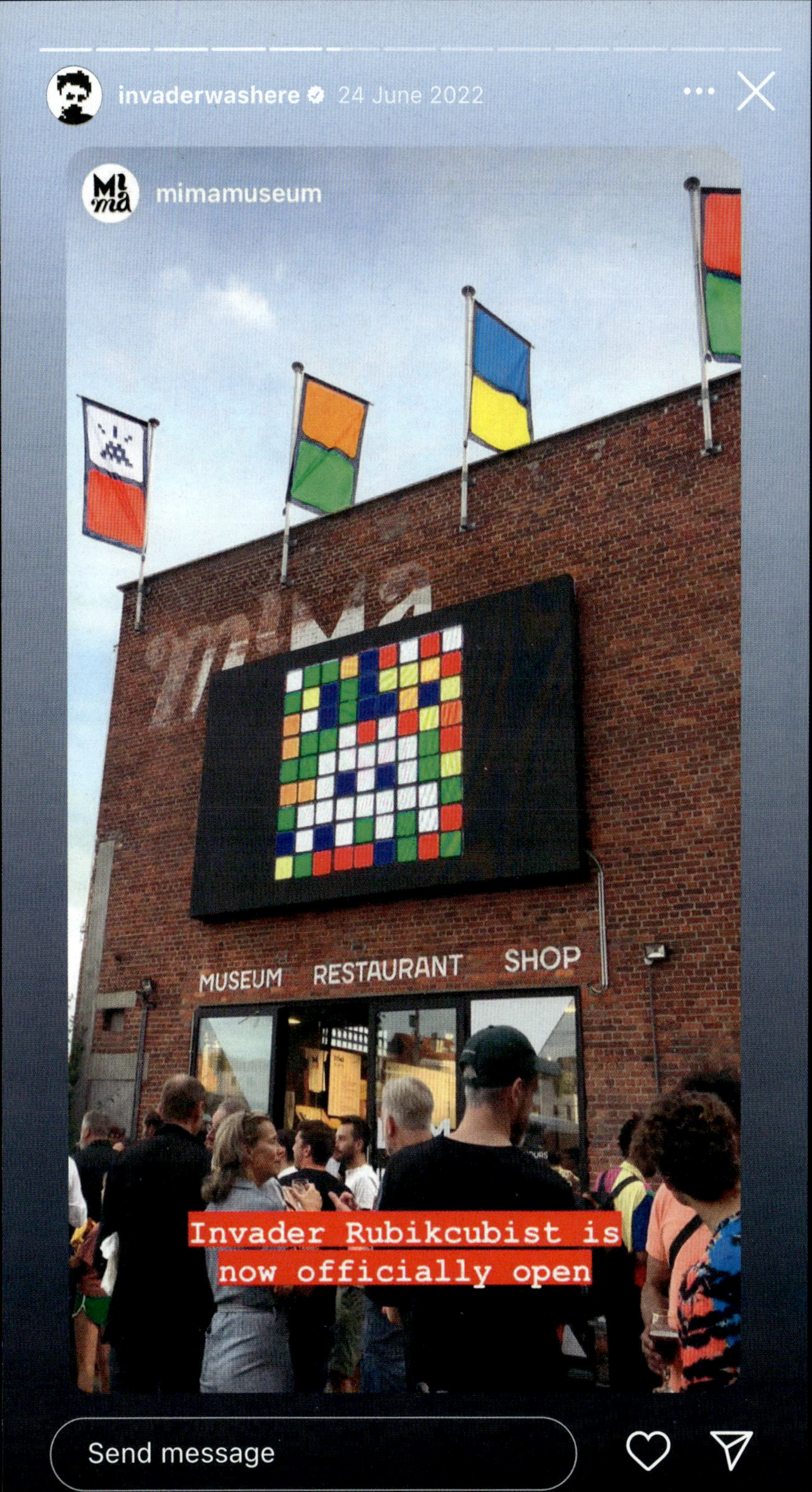

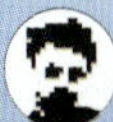

invaderwashere 24 June 2022

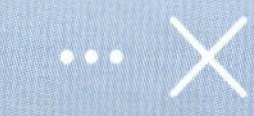

mimamuseum

MUSEUM RESTAURANT SHOP

Invader Rubikcubist is now officially open

Send message

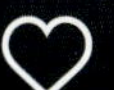

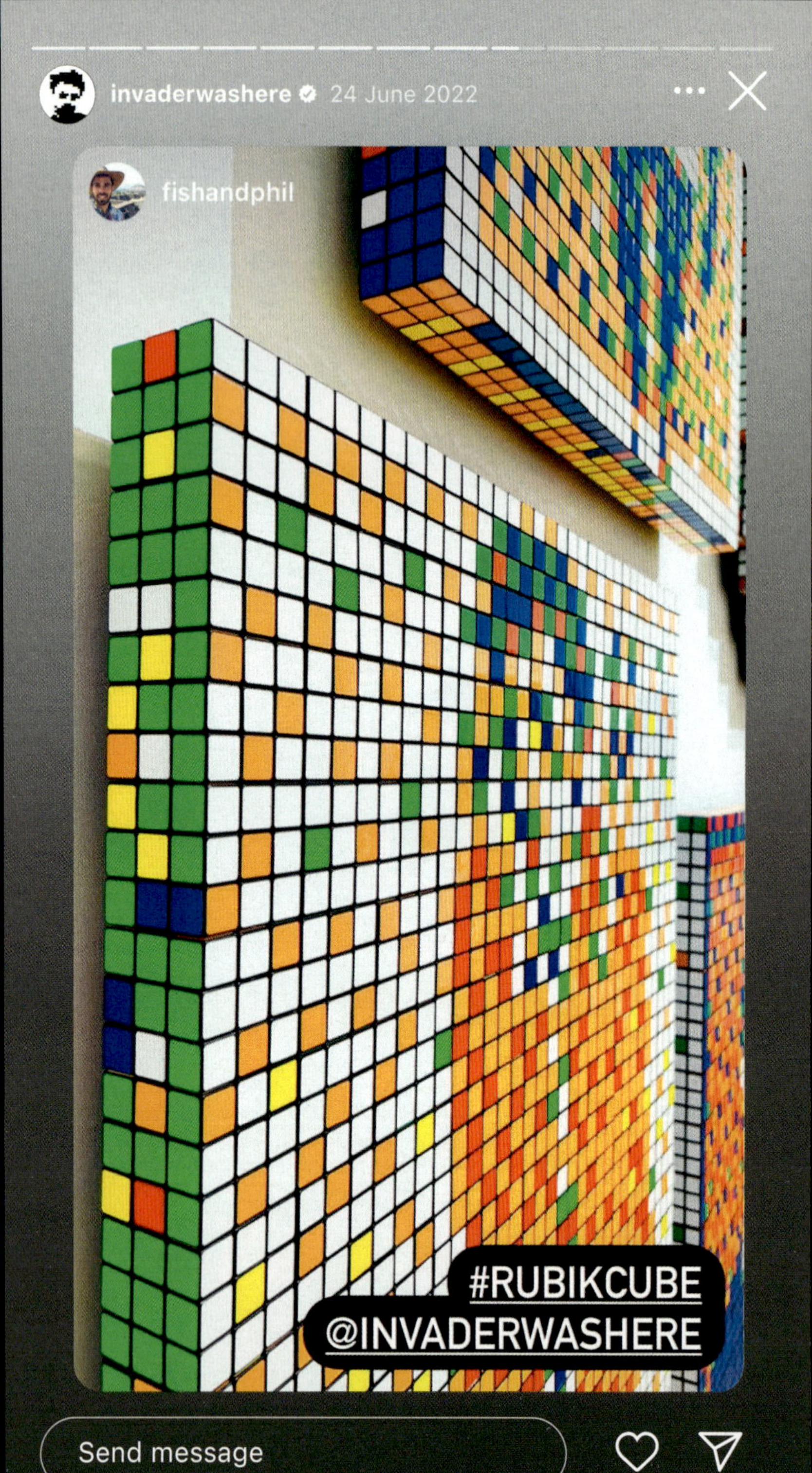

invaderwashere 24 June 2022

fishandphil

#RUBIKCUBE
@INVADERWASHERE

Send message

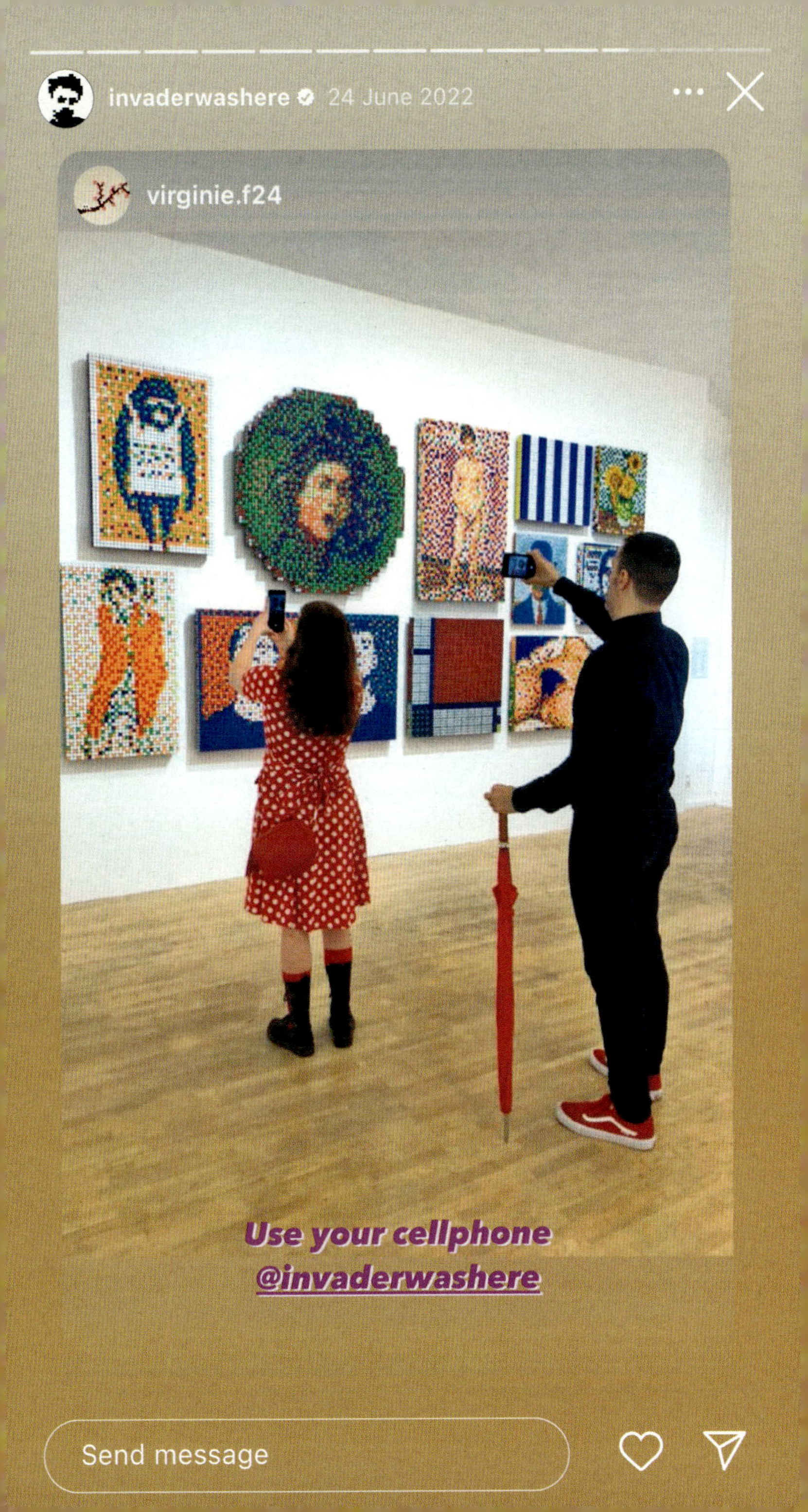

invaderwashere 24 June 2022

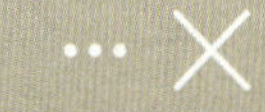

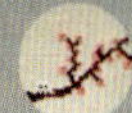

virginie.f24

Use your cellphone
@invaderwashere

Send message

invaderwashere 24 June 2022

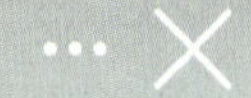

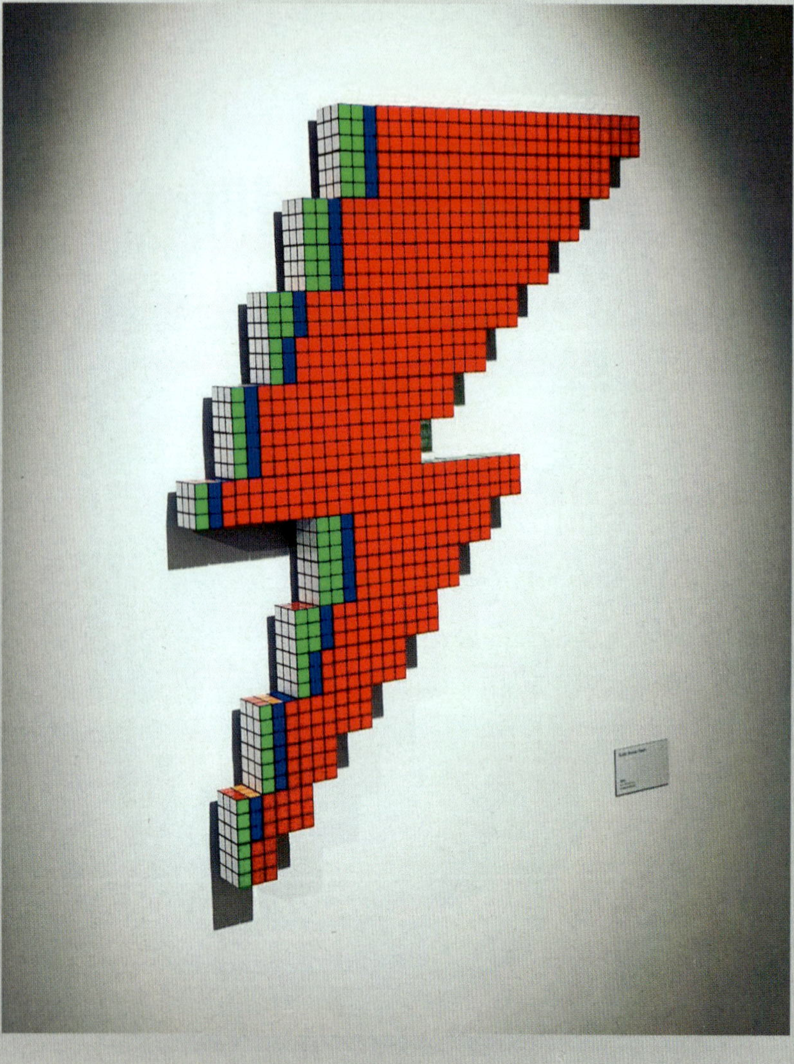

@_jvdh

Send message

invaderwashere 25 June 2022

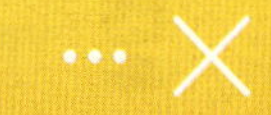

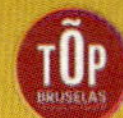

top_bruselas

@invaderwashere invade el @mimamuseum con 150 singulares obras realizadas con un objeto culto, el Rubik's cube

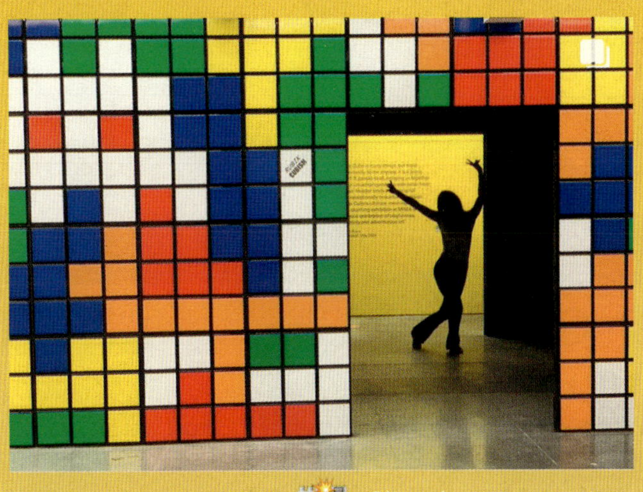

@top_bruselas

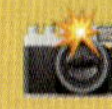

@boombartstic_magazine

Send message

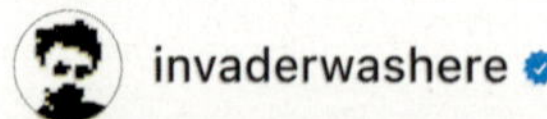

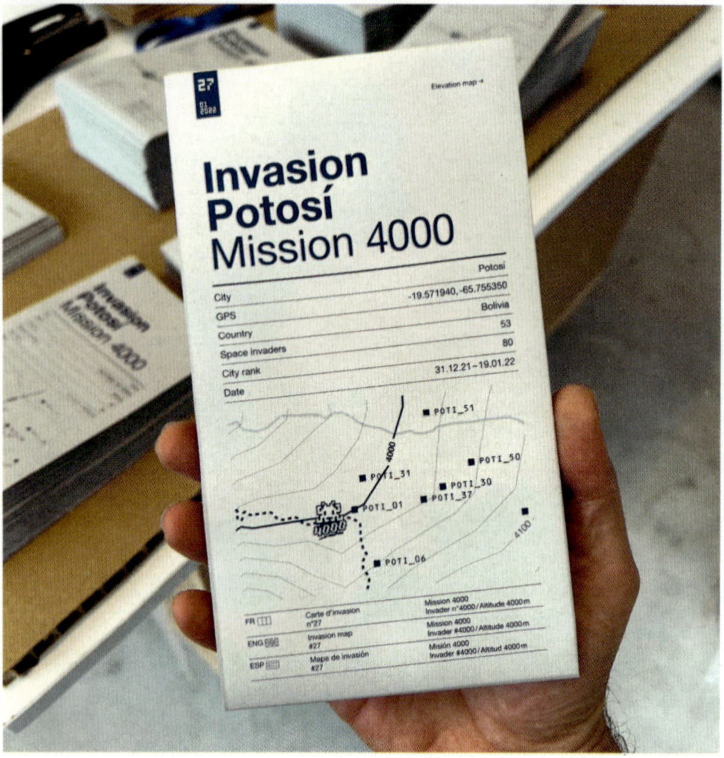

2 991 likes

invaderwashere The Invasion Map of Potosí will be online today #invasionmap #invasionmap27 #potosi #spaceshop #10€ #linkinbio

View all 94 comments

27 June 2022

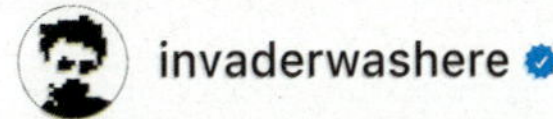

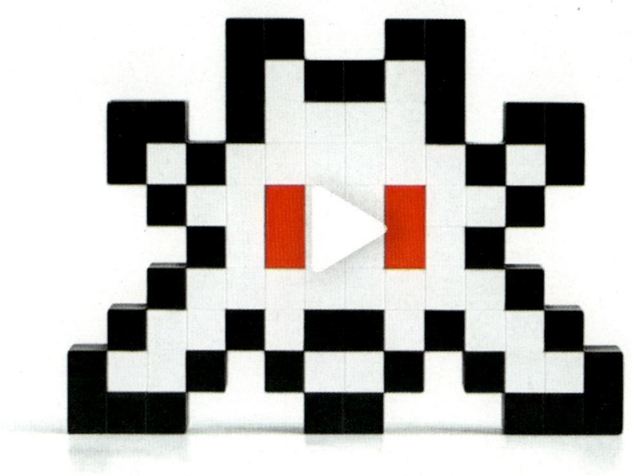

4846 likes

invaderwashere 3D Little Big Space will be released in 2 hours... @musartboutique
Thank you to @galerie_itinerrance the initiator of this project

View all 262 comments

30 June 2022

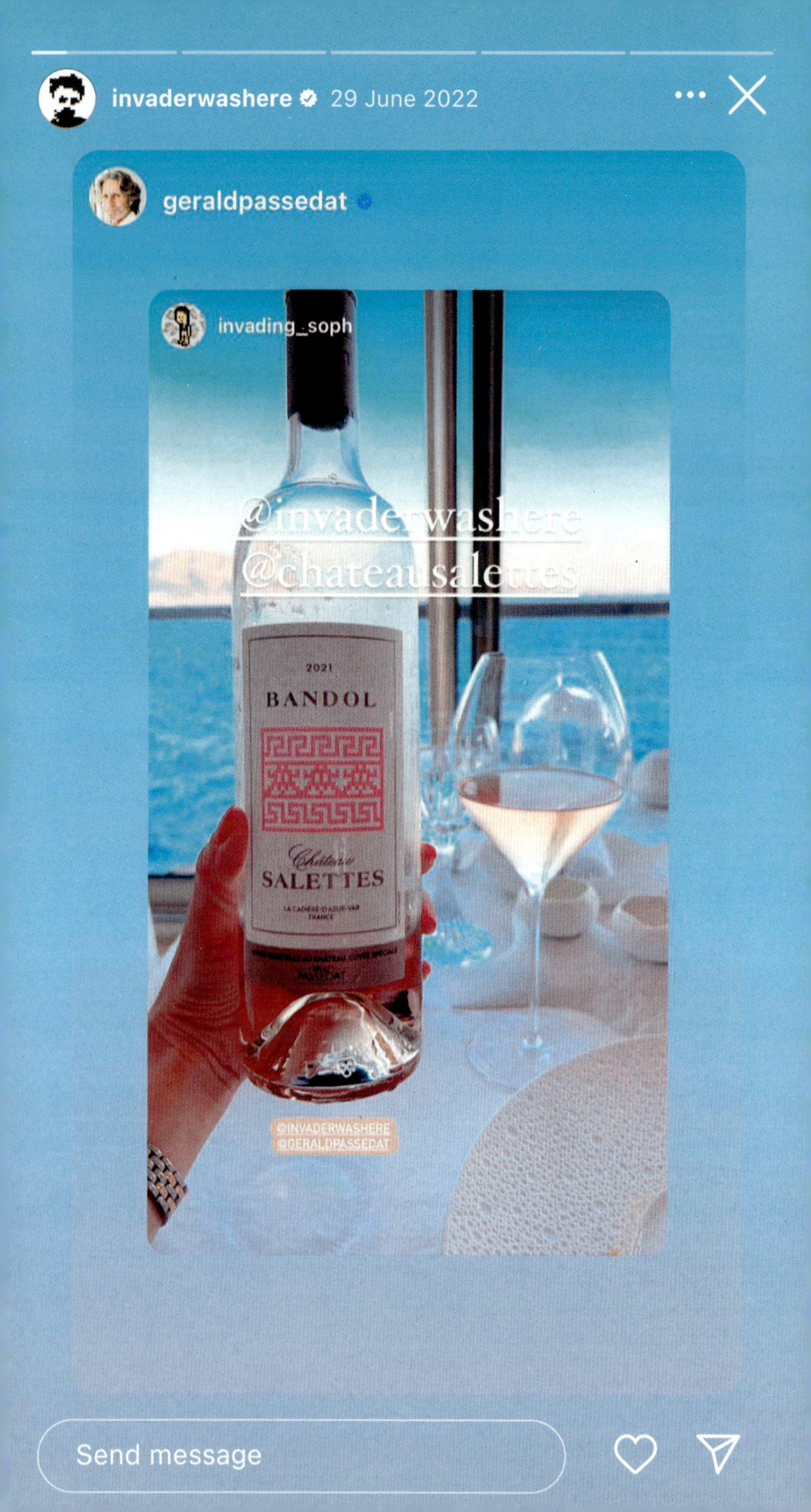

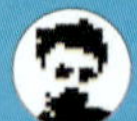

invaderwashere 29 June 2022

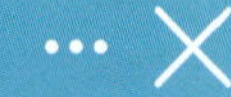

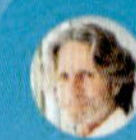

geraldpassedat

invading_soph

@invaderwashere
@chateausalettes

2021
BANDOL
Château
SALETTES
LA CADIÈRE-D'AZUR-VAR
FRANCE

@INVADERWASHERE
@GERALDPASSEDAT

Send message

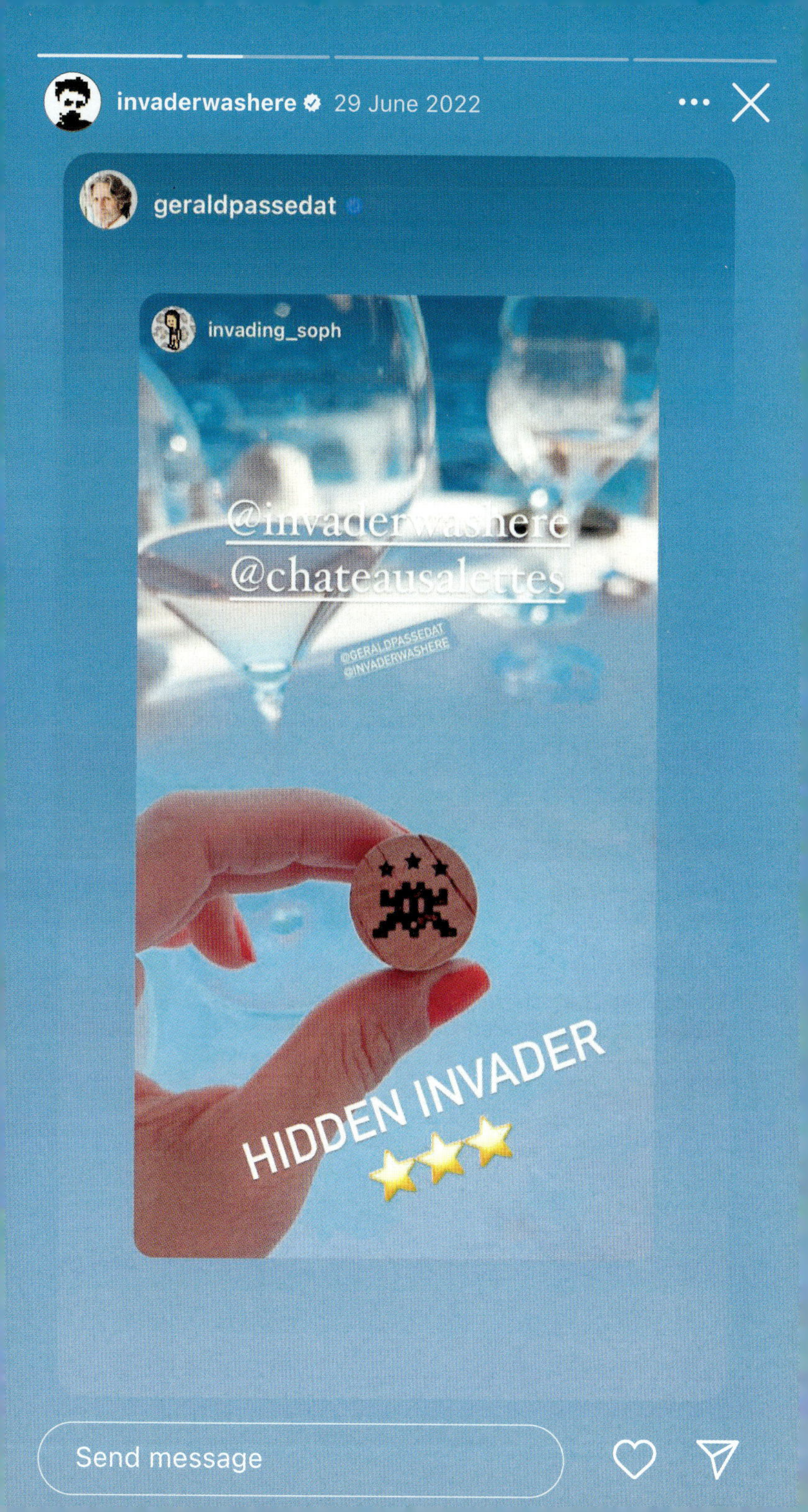

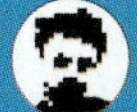

invaderwashere 29 June 2022

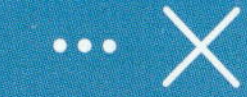

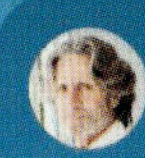

geraldpassedat

invading_soph

@invaderwashere
@chateausalettes

@GERALDPASSEDAT
@INVADERWASHERE

HIDDEN INVADER

Send message

 invaderwashere

  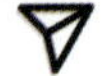  

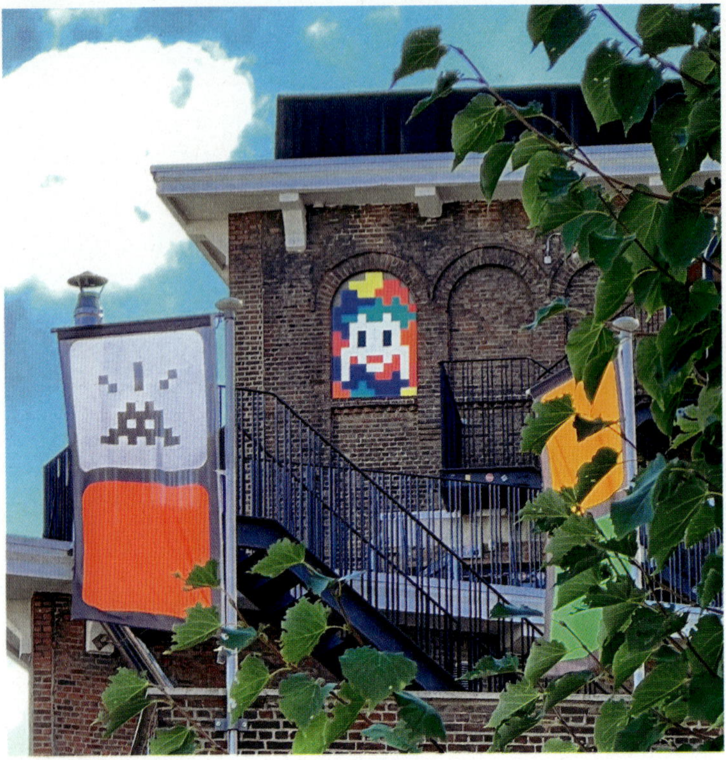

6 092 likes

invaderwashere In the Museum Invasion series, 2 new pieces have just landed @mimamuseum #brussels #rubikcubism #rubikcamo #cathedral #invaderrubikcubist

View all 65 comments

6 July 2022

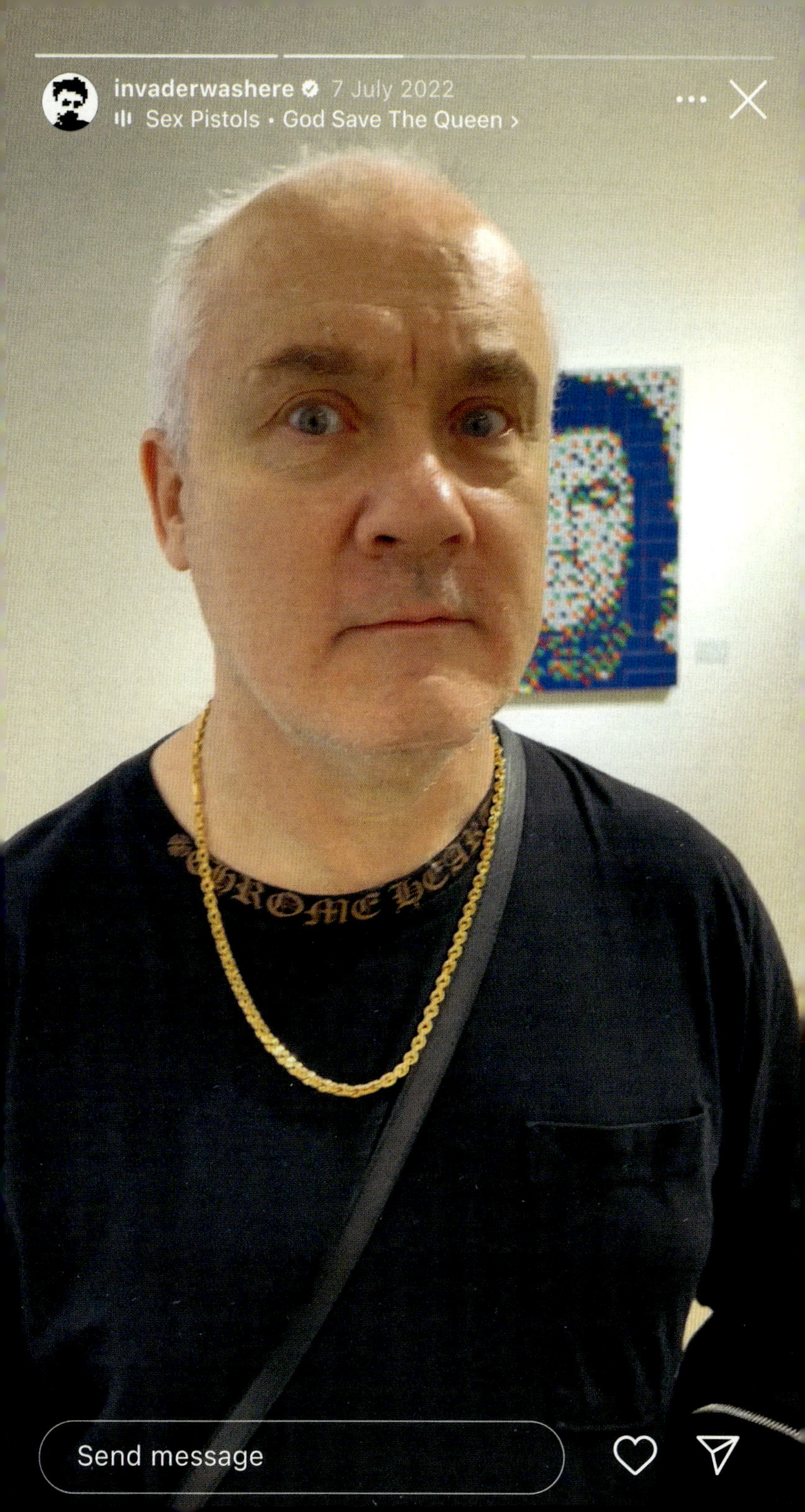

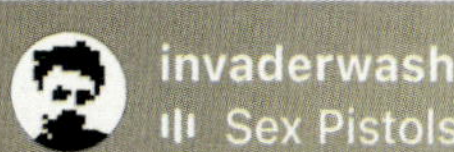
invaderwashere 7 July 2022
Sex Pistols • God Save The Queen ›
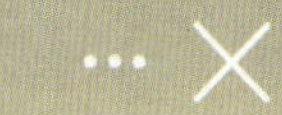

Send message
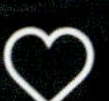
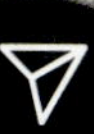

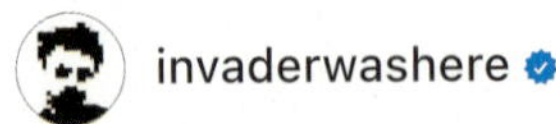

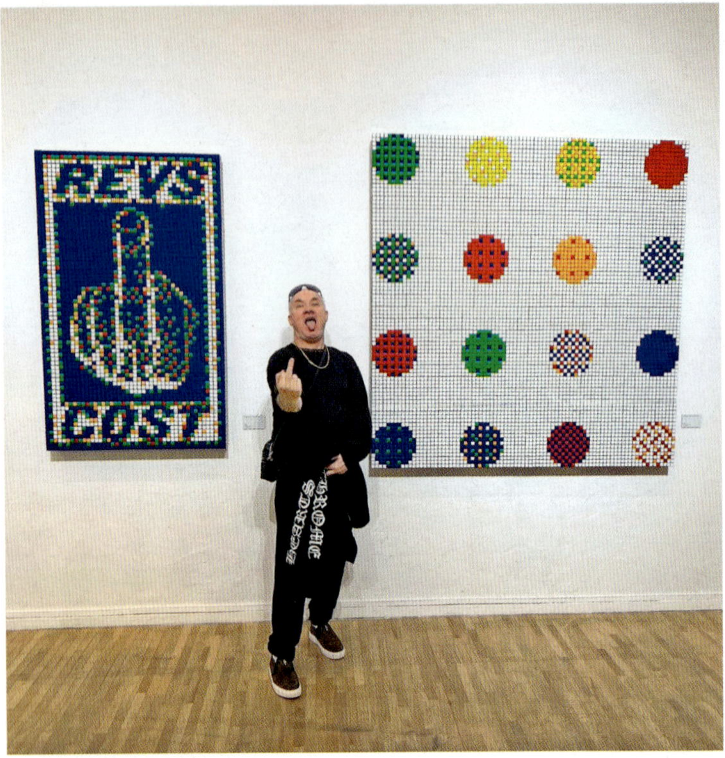

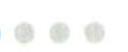

5089 likes

invaderwashere Thank you for the visit @damienhirst 🙏
💥😎😜🦋👾 @mimamuseum #invaderrubikcubist
#rubikcubism #brussels #damienhirst #artmaster

View all 78 comments

7 July 2022

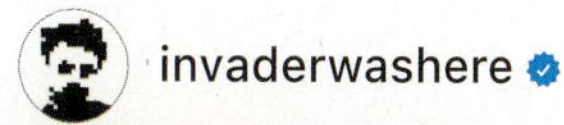

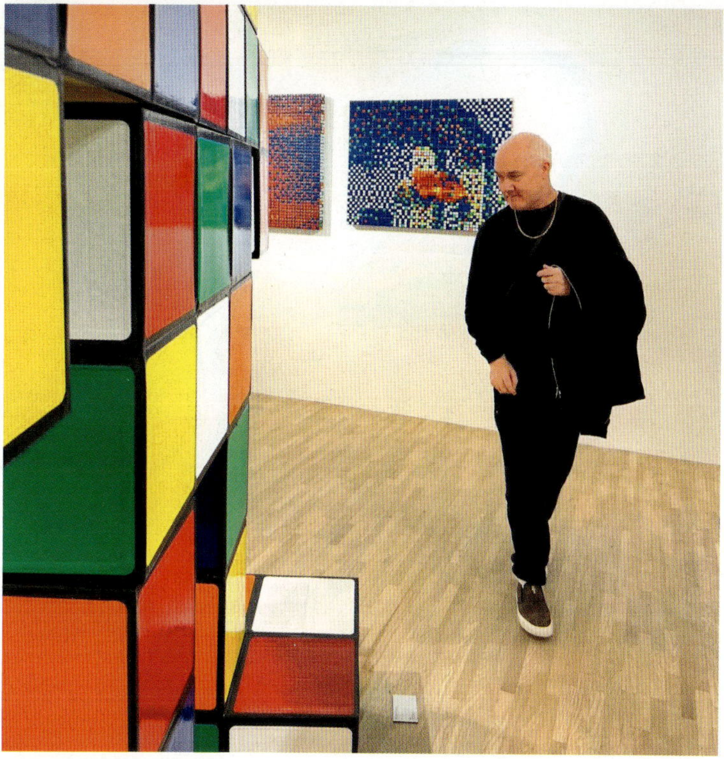

5089 likes

invaderwashere Thank you for the visit @damienhirst 
💥😎😜🦋👾 @mimamuseum #invaderrubikcubist
#rubikcubism #brussels #damienhirst #artmaster

View all 78 comments

7 July 2022

invaderwashere 

 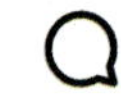  

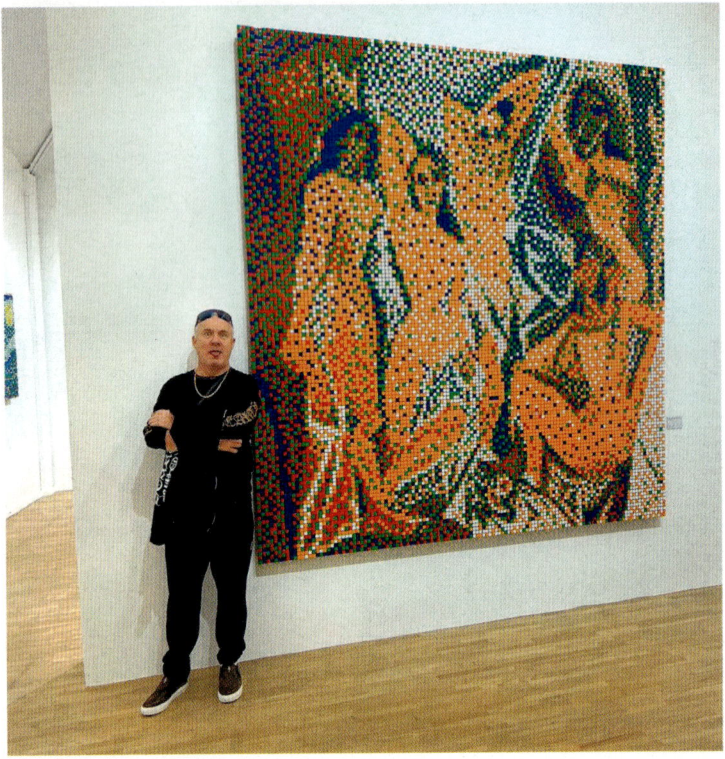

5089 likes

invaderwashere Thank you for the visit @damienhirst 
💥😎😜🦋👾 @mimamuseum #invaderrubikcubist
#rubikcubism #brussels #damienhirst #artmaster

View all 78 comments

7 July 2022

invaderwashere 12 July 2022

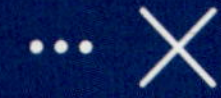

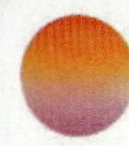

urban_life_10

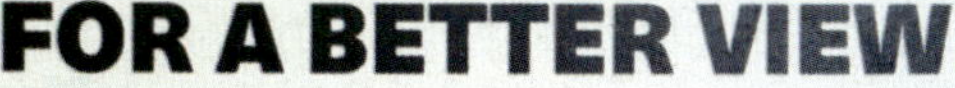

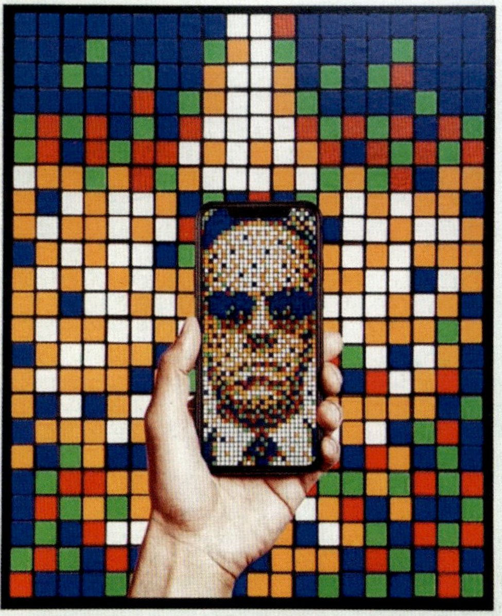

USE YOUR CELLPHONE

urban_life_10 "Invader Rubikcubist"
From the opening on 24.06.22 at Mima museum...

Send message

invaderwashere 14 July 2022

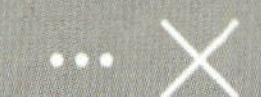

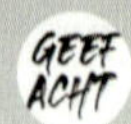

geef.acht

Whoop Whoop

Nieuwe invasion map is binnen @invaderwashere

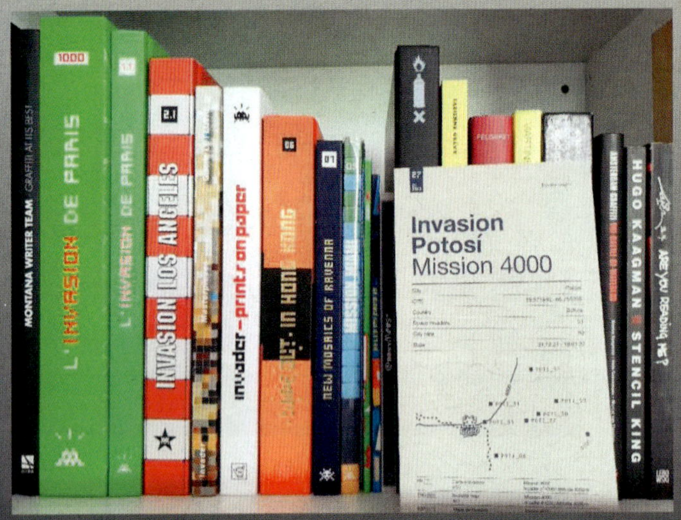

POTOSI

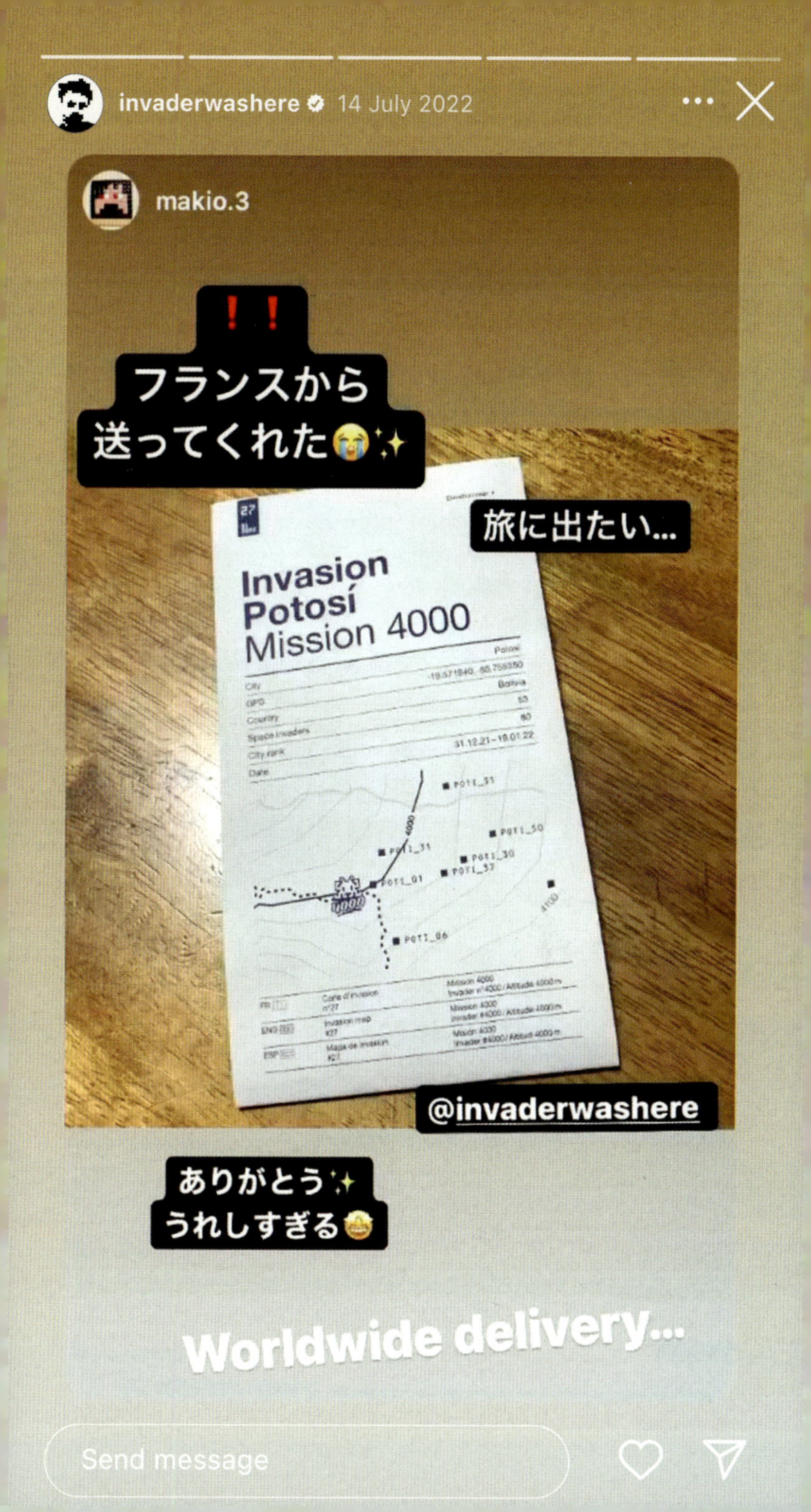

invaderwashere 14 July 2022

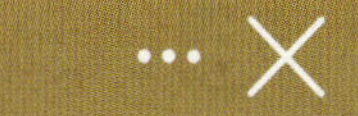

makio.3

❗❗

フランスから
送ってくれた😭✨

旅に出たい...

Invasion
Potosí
Mission 4000

City Potosí
Country Bolivia
Date 31.12.21–19.01.22

@invaderwashere

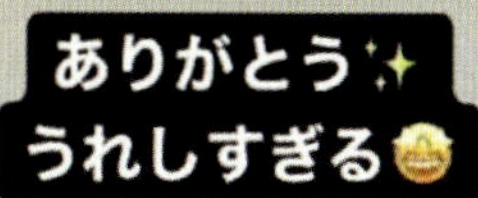

Worldwide delivery...

Send message

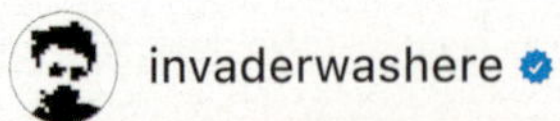

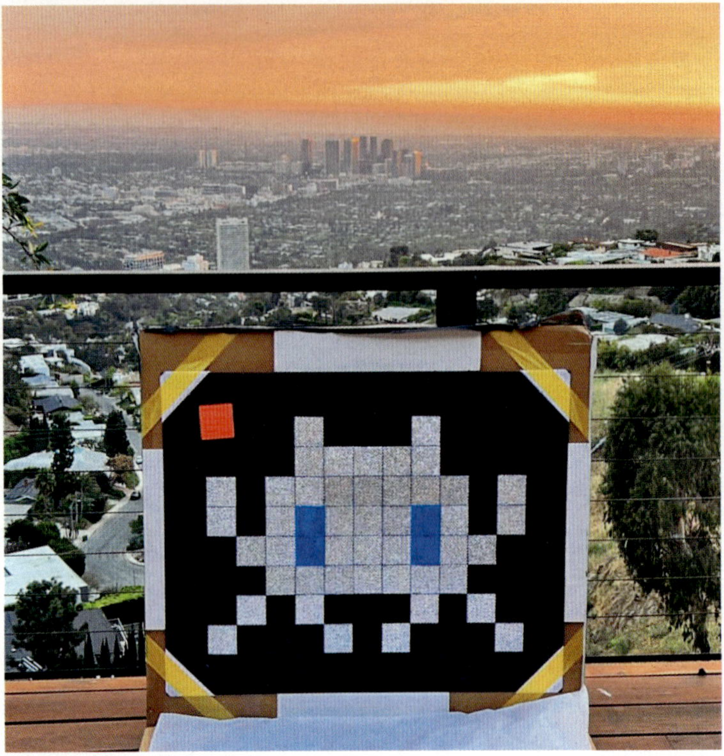

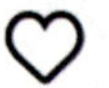   

5630 likes

invaderwashere Meanwhile in LA, from the Christo X Invader series, made with the wrapping fabric of the Arc de Triomphe #christo #christojeanneclaude #invaderwashere

View all 78 comments

14 July 2022

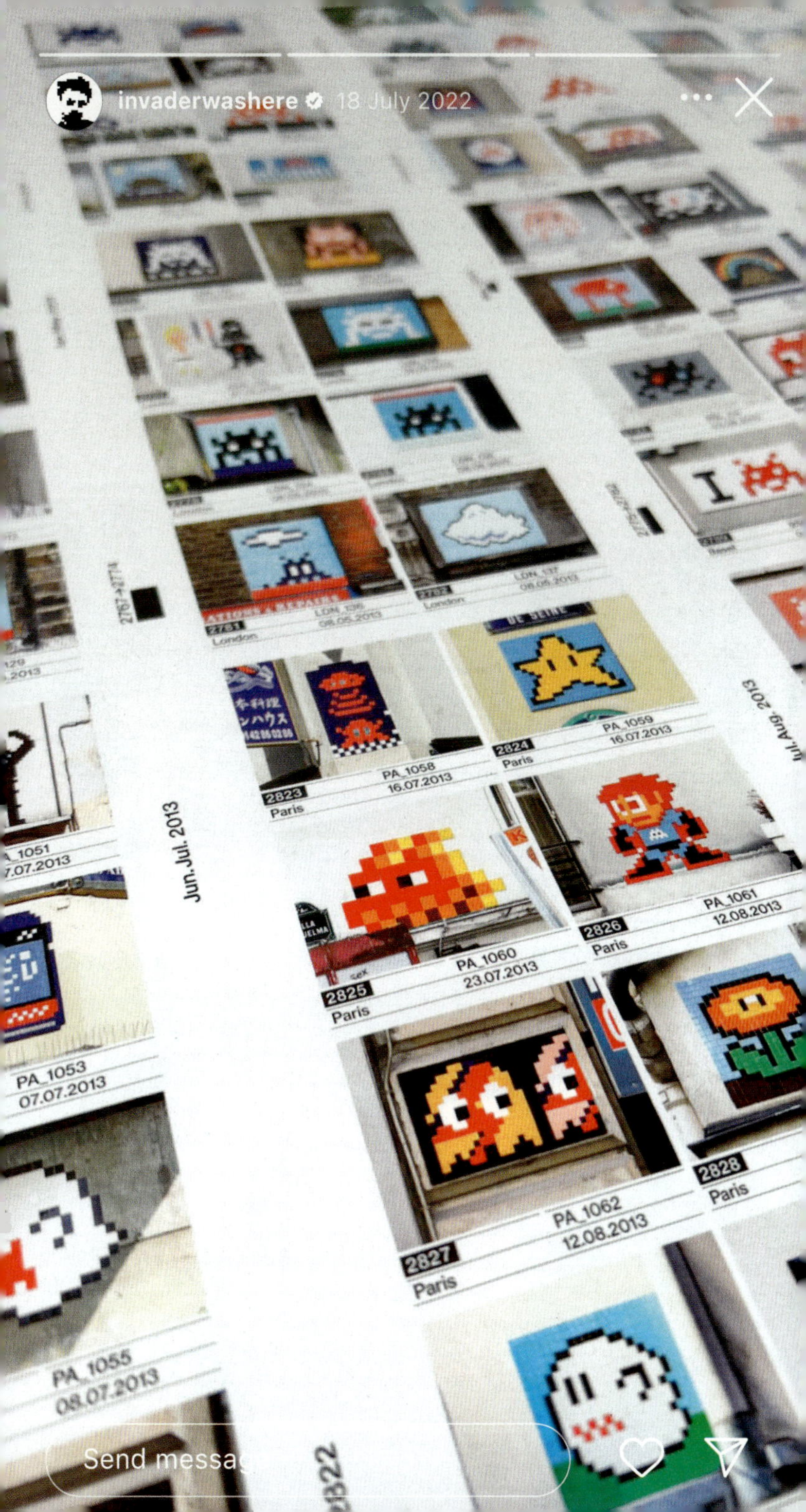
invaderwashere
18 July 2022
2781
London
LDN_136
08.05.2013
2782
London
LDN_137
08.05.2013
2787→2774
Jun.Jul. 2013
2823
Paris
PA_1058
16.07.2013
2824
Paris
PA_1059
16.07.2013
Jul.Aug. 2013
2825
Paris
PA_1060
23.07.2013
2826
Paris
PA_1061
12.08.2013
2827
Paris
PA_1062
12.08.2013
2828
Paris
PA_1051
07.07.2013
PA_1053
07.07.2013
PA_1055
08.07.2013
Send message

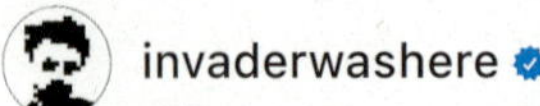

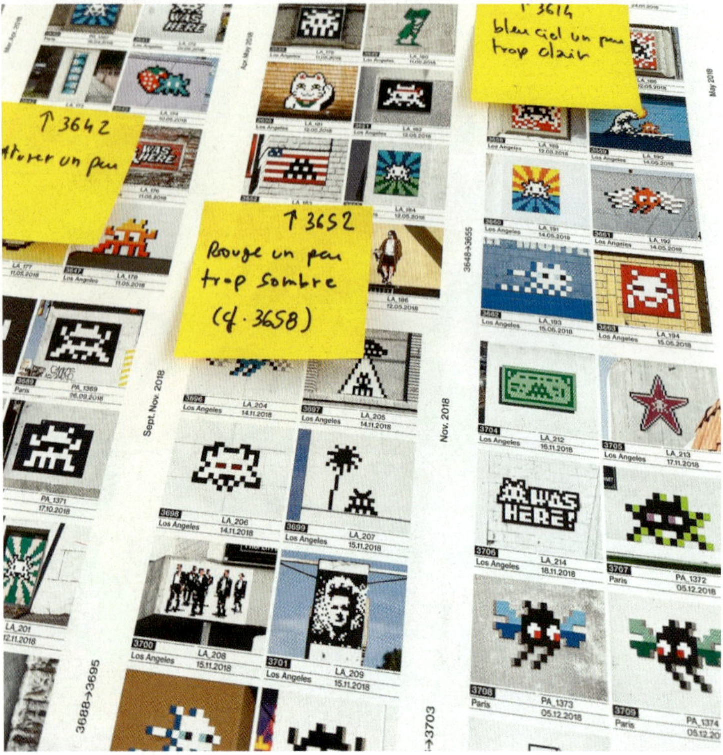

3728 likes

invaderwashere Cooking for the future... #colortest #the4000

View all 85 comments

18 July 2022

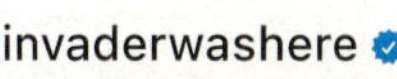

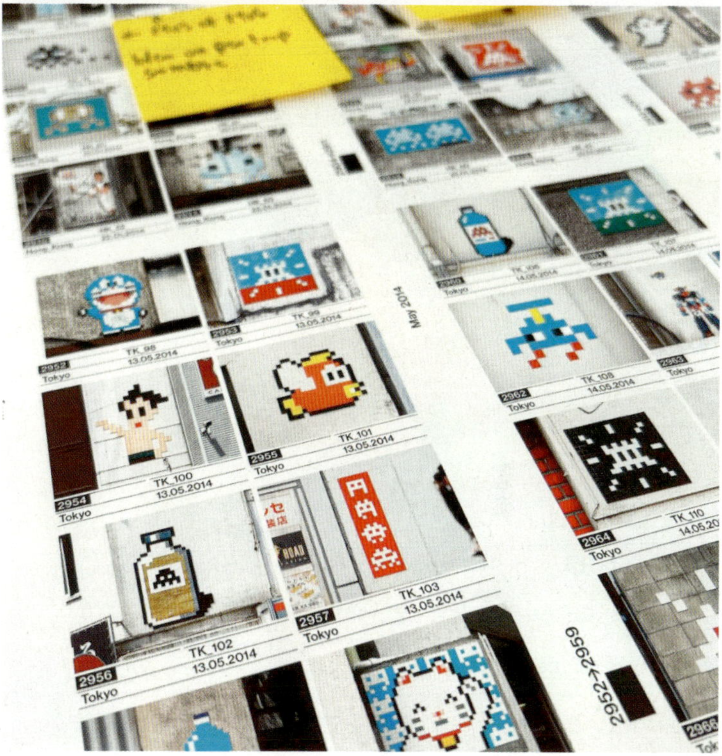

 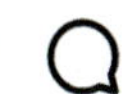  

3 728 likes

invaderwashere Cooking for the future... #colortest #the4000

View all 85 comments

18 July 2022

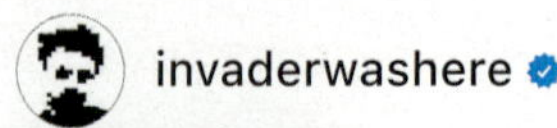

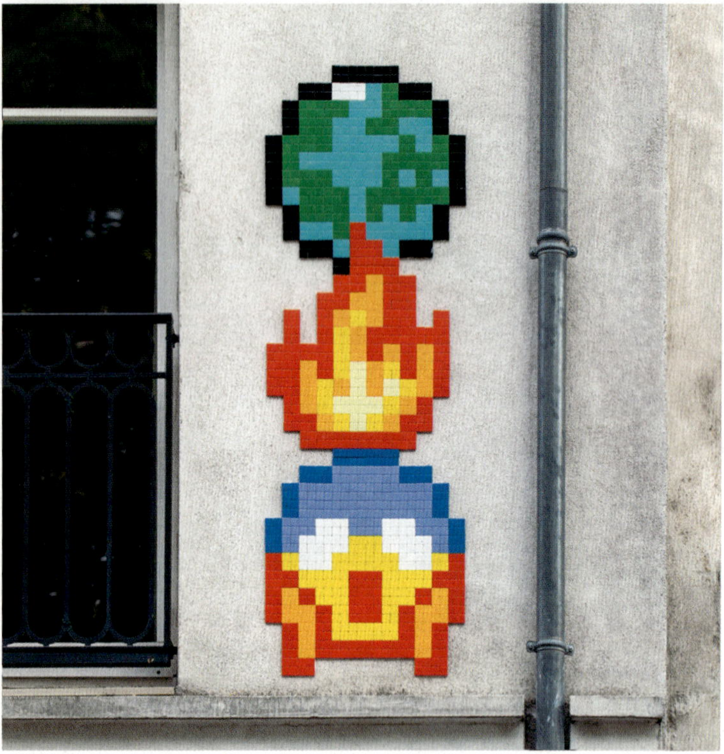

11050 likes

invaderwashere PA_1469 / Burning planet!
Scientists are unanimous, human activities are messing up the Earth.
Here are some simple tips to fight against it:
👉 Change our mode of transport 🛹🚲🚶
👉 Stop eating animals 🌱
👉 Protect forests 🌳🌳🌳
👉 Reduce water consumption 🛁
👉 Consume local 🍎🛍️📍
👉 Boycott big polluting industries 🏭💨
👉 Educate the next generations 👦👧
👉 Throw away your cellphone 😬🤪

View all 153 comments

20 July 2022

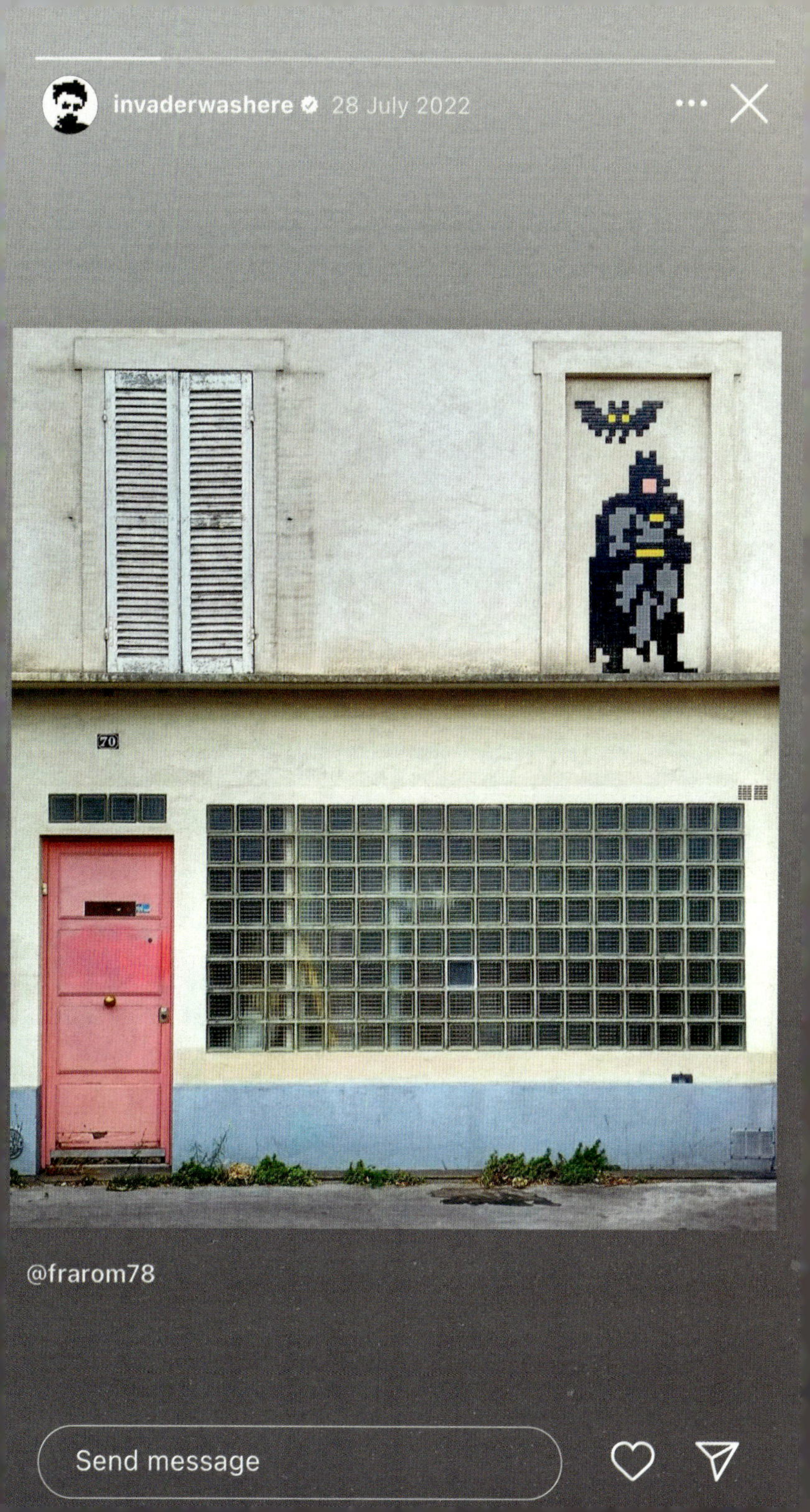

invaderwashere 28 July 2022

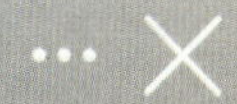

70

@frarom78

Send message

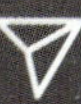

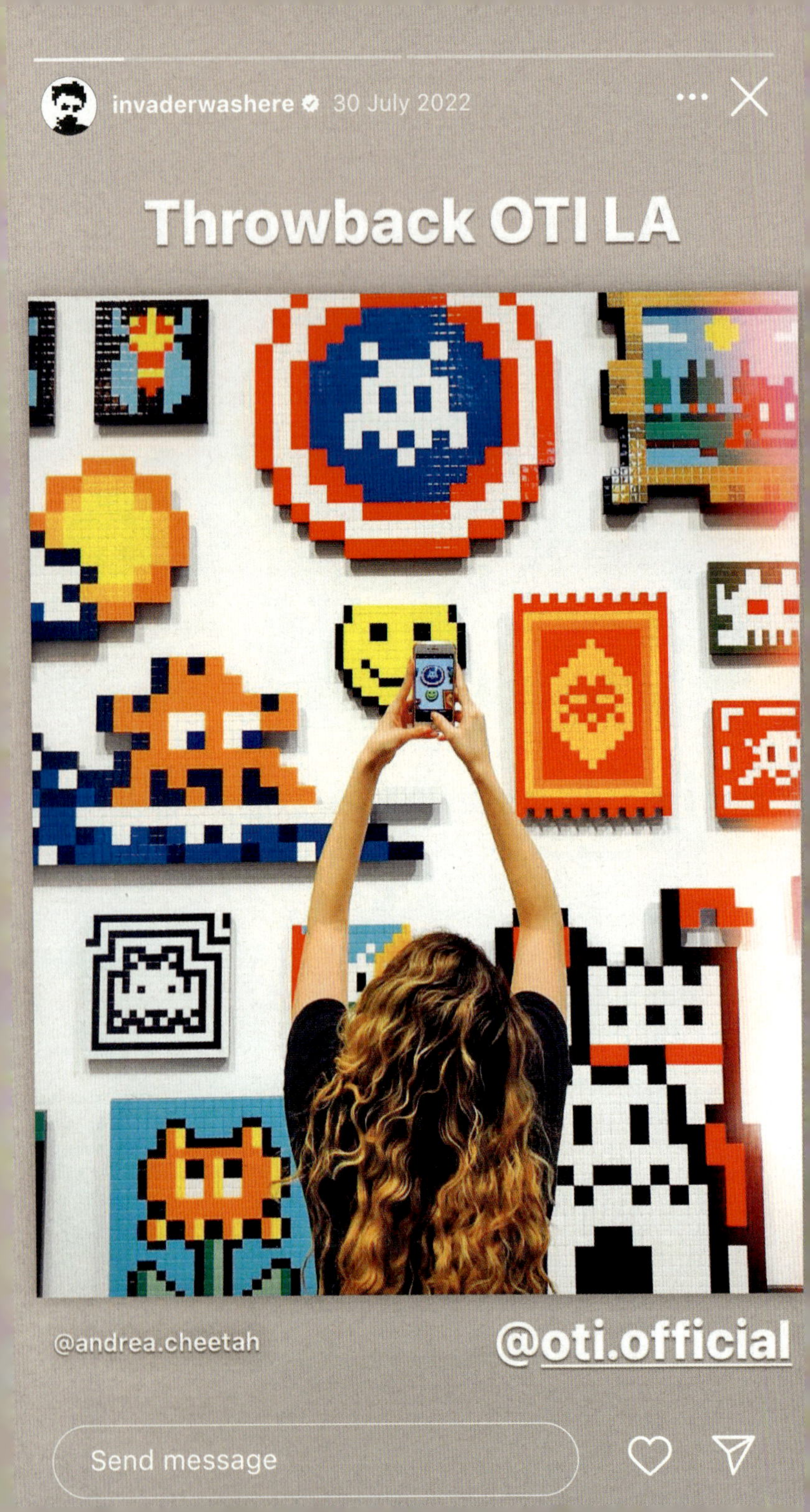

invaderwashere 30 July 2022

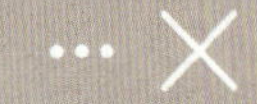

Throwback OTI LA

@andrea.cheetah

@oti.official

Send message

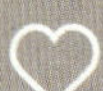

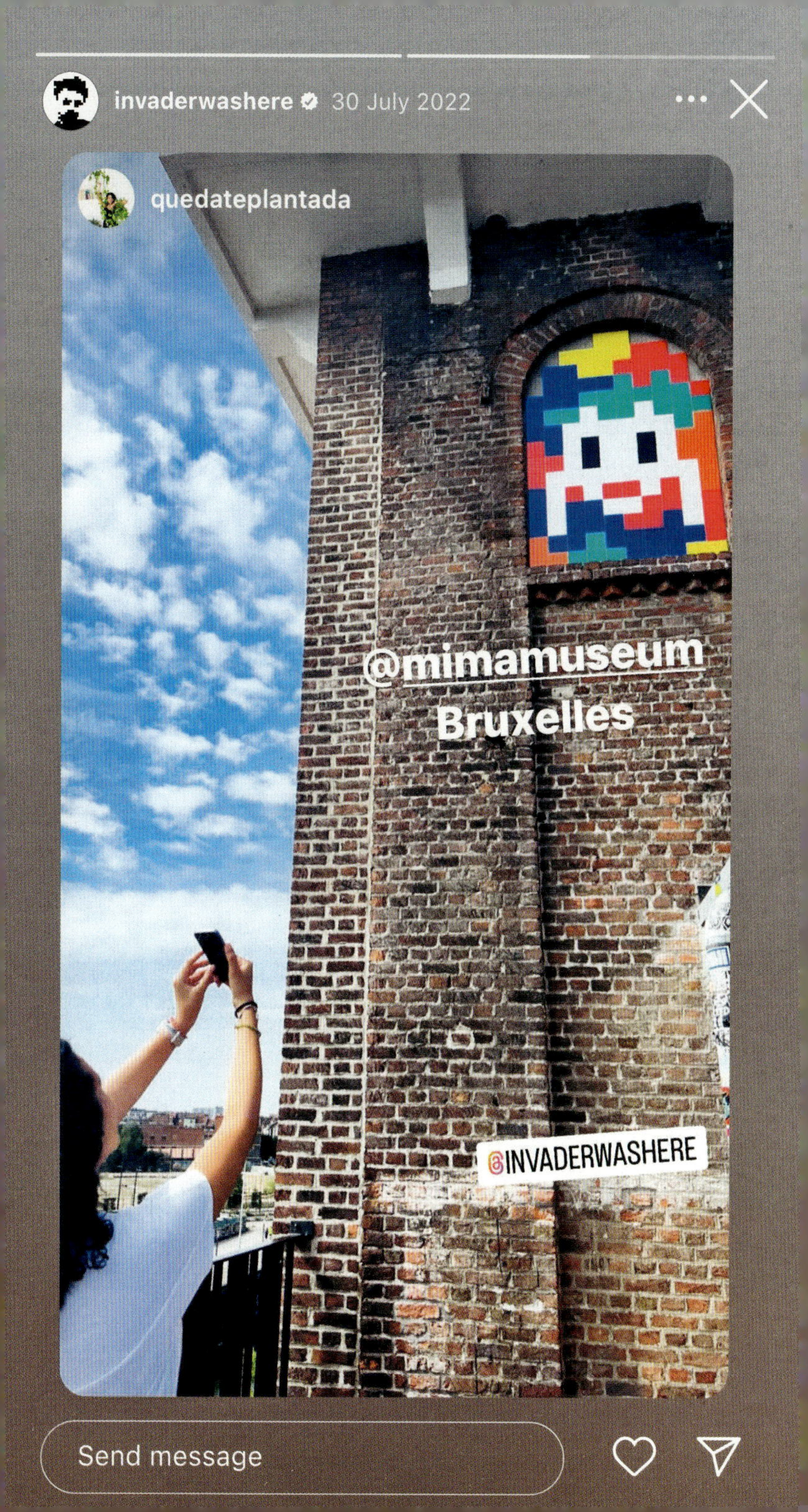

invaderwashere 30 July 2022

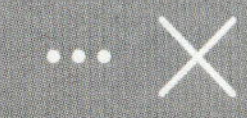

quedateplantada

@mimamuseum
Bruxelles

@INVADERWASHERE

Send message

invaderwashere 5 August 2022

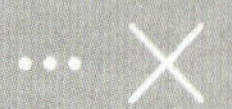

mimamuseum

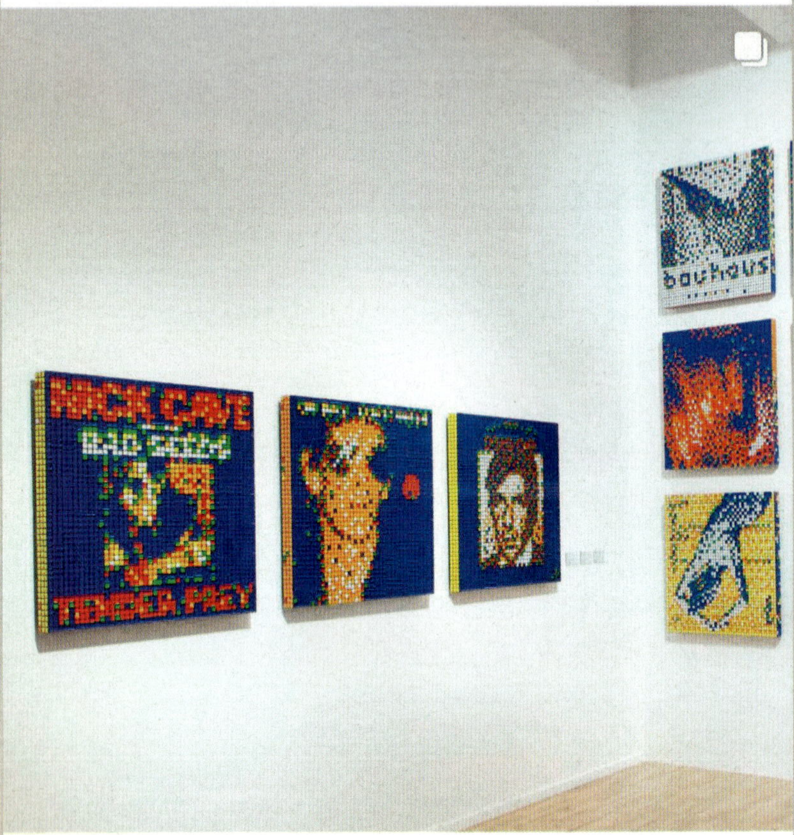

mimamuseum Unlike albums recorded in High Fidelity, @invaderwashere Rubikcubism damages the images by loweri...

Send message

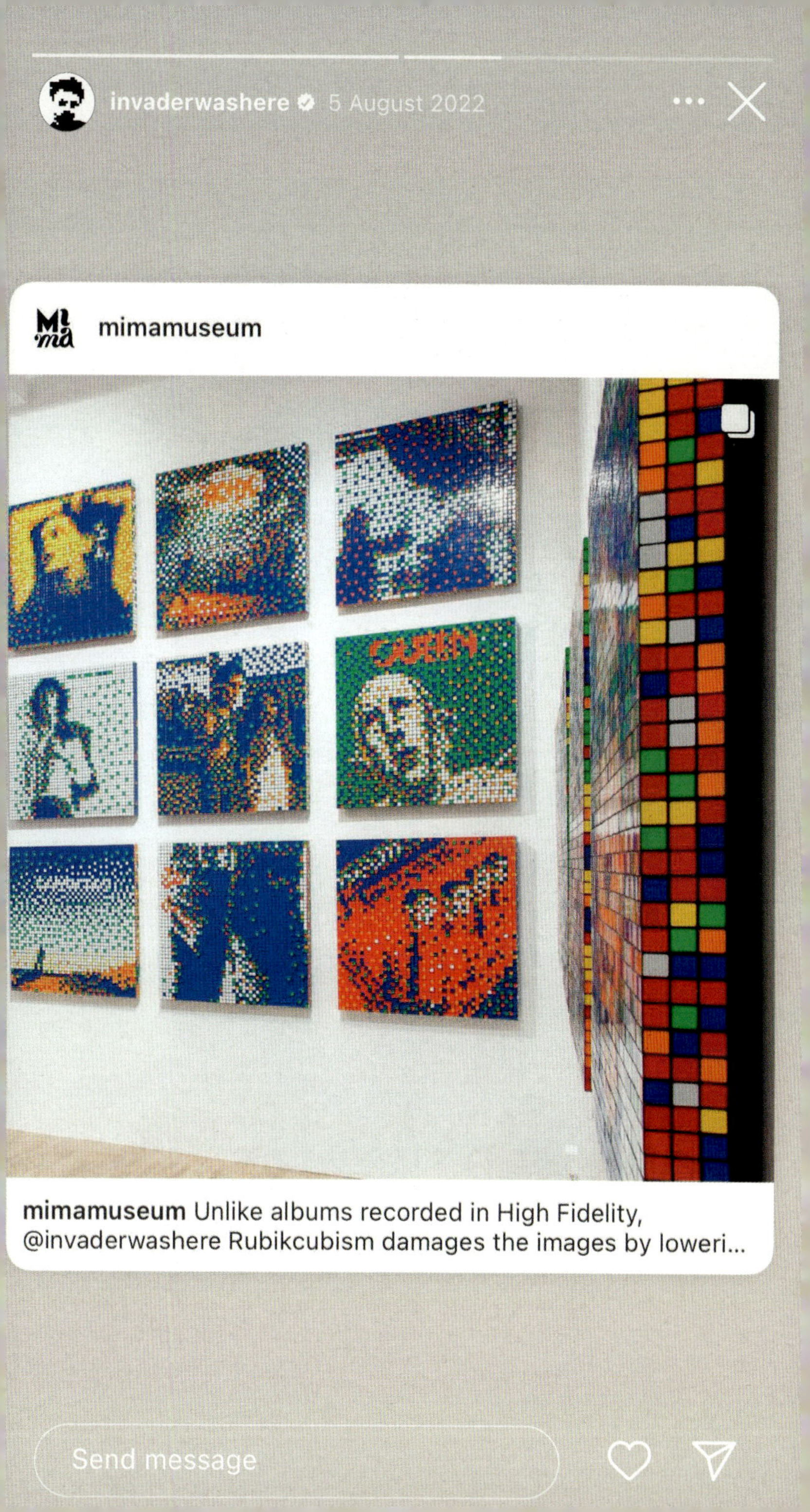

invaderwashere 5 August 2022

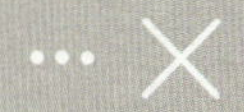

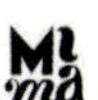

mimamuseum

mimamuseum Unlike albums recorded in High Fidelity, @invaderwashere Rubikcubism damages the images by loweri...

Send message

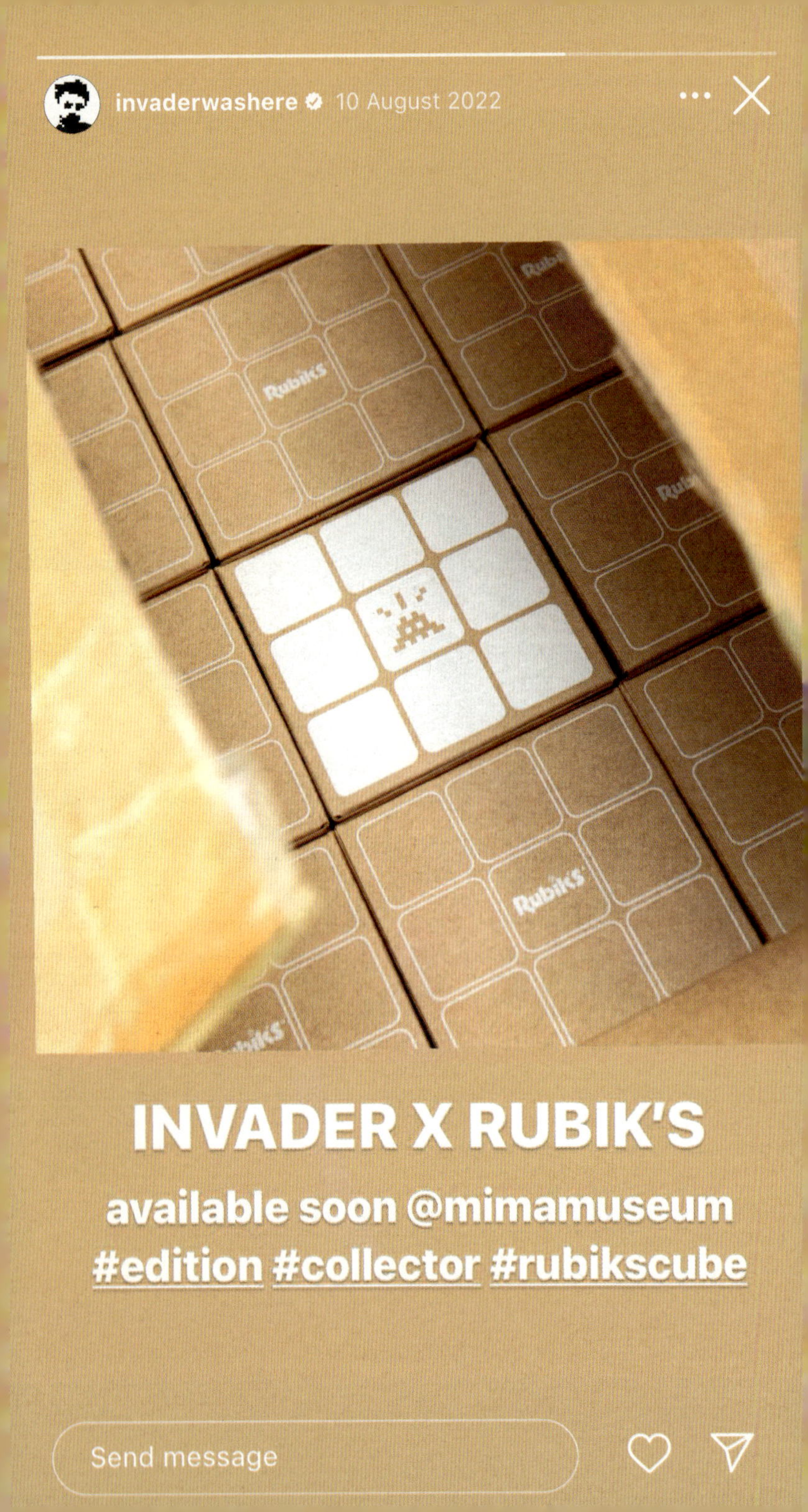

invaderwashere 10 August 2022

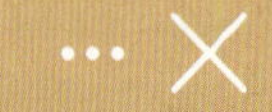

INVADER X RUBIK'S

available soon @mimamuseum
#edition #collector #rubikscube

Send message

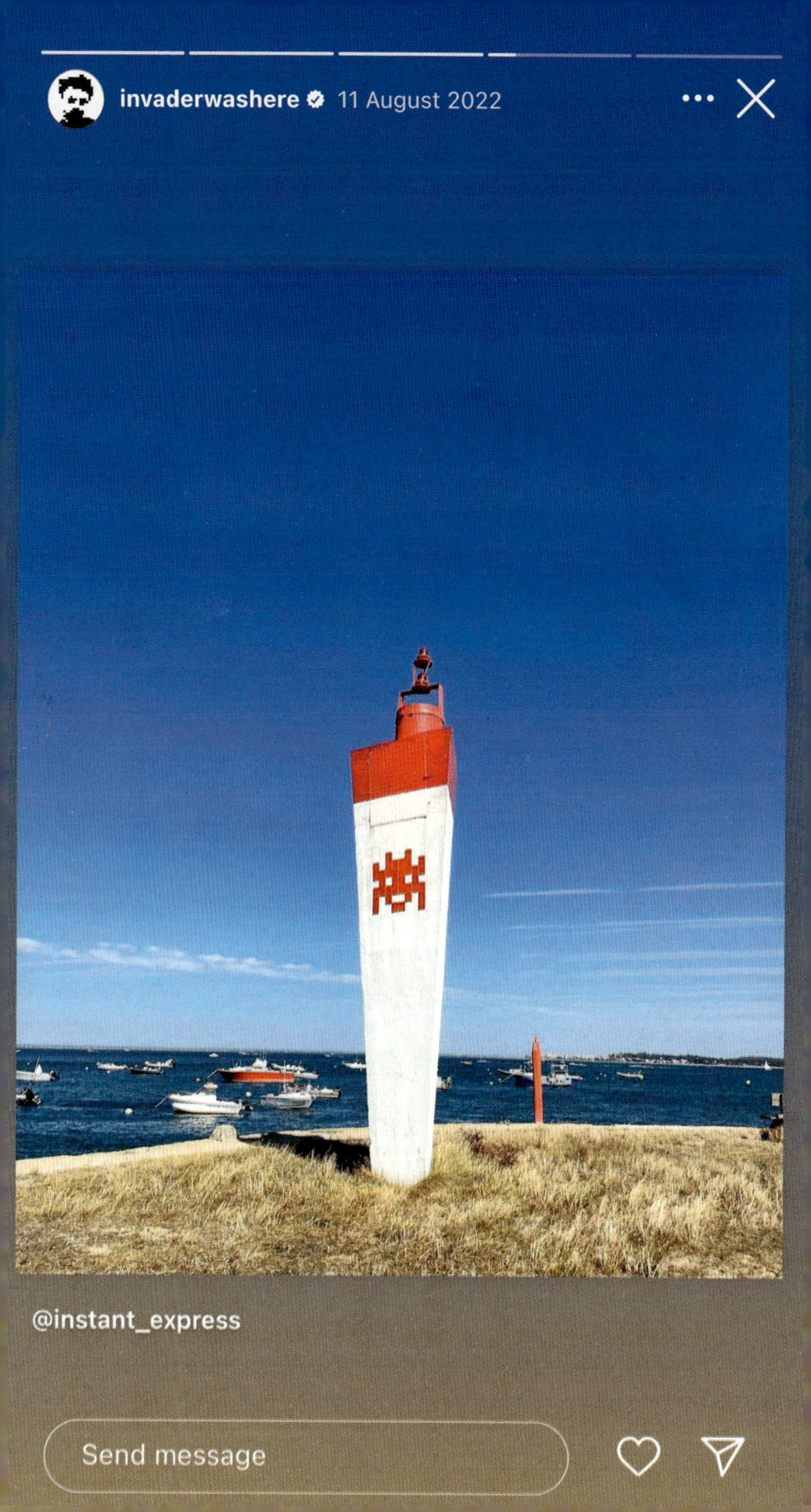

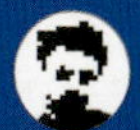

invaderwashere 11 August 2022

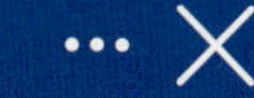

@instant_express

Send message

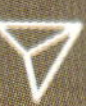

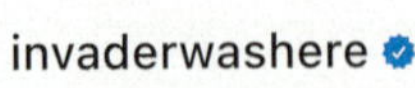

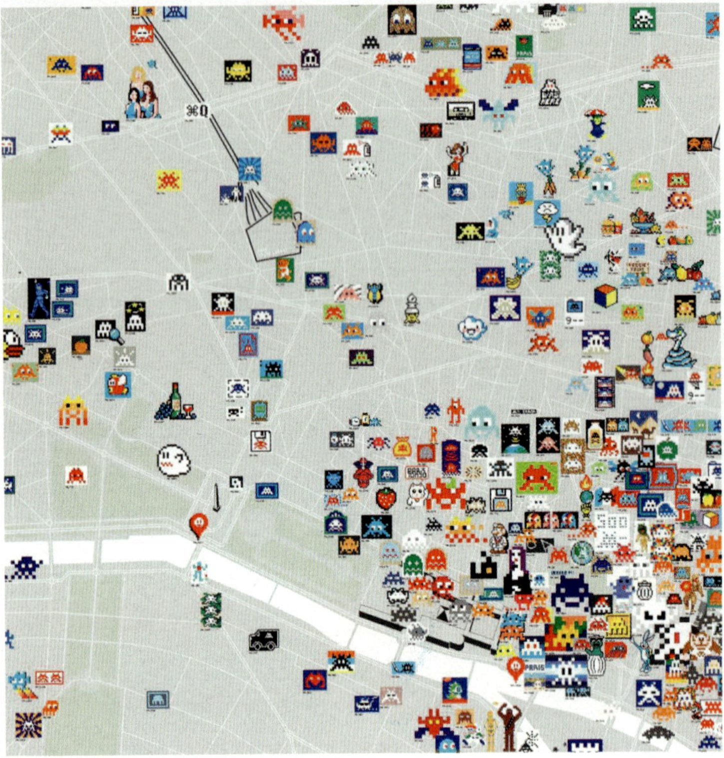

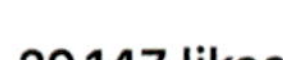

29 147 likes

invaderwashere Working on a new Invasion map of Paris 👾👾👾 #invasionmap #invasionofparis #19982022 #workinprogress #mapdetail

View all 902 comments

11 August 2022

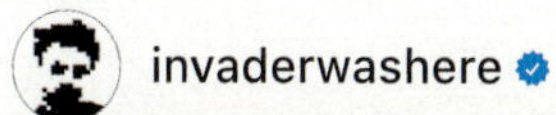

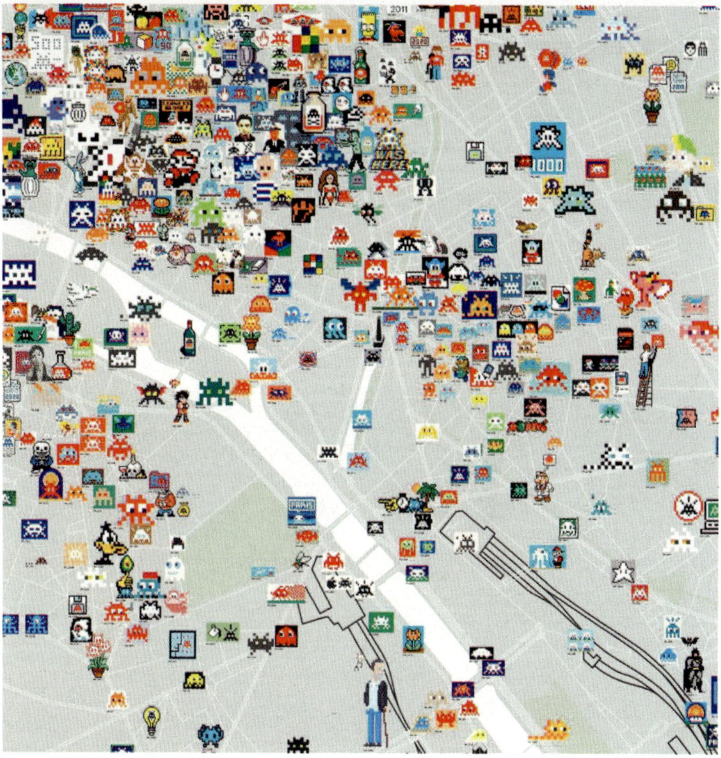

29 147 likes

invaderwashere Working on a new Invasion map of Paris 👾👾👾 #invasionmap #invasionofparis #19982022 #workinprogress #mapdetail

View all 902 comments

11 August 2022

invaderwashere 14 August 2022

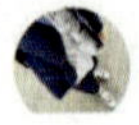
deestagramin

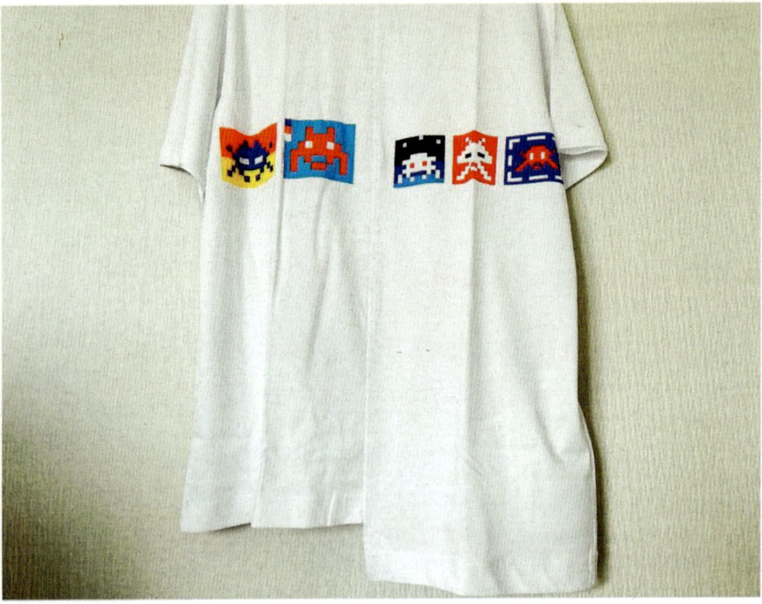

deestagramin *
COMME des GARÇONS...

Send message

invaderwashere 17 August 2022

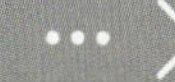

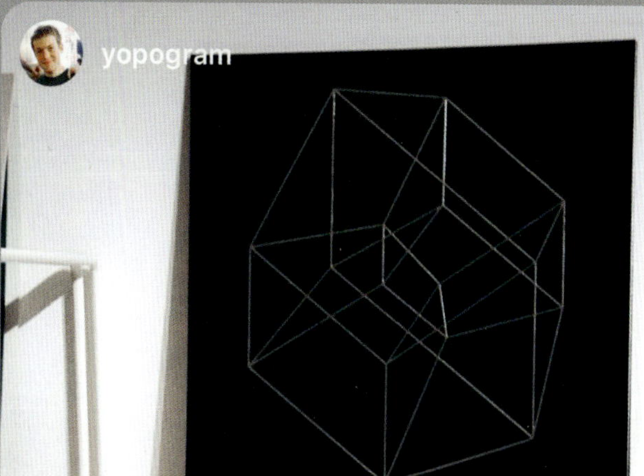

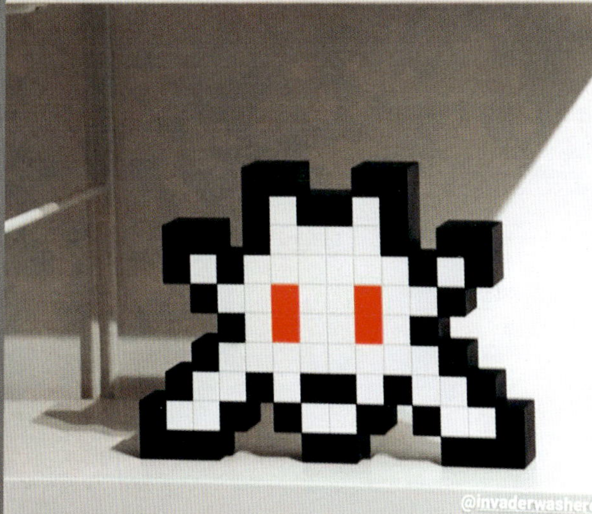

Send message

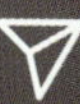

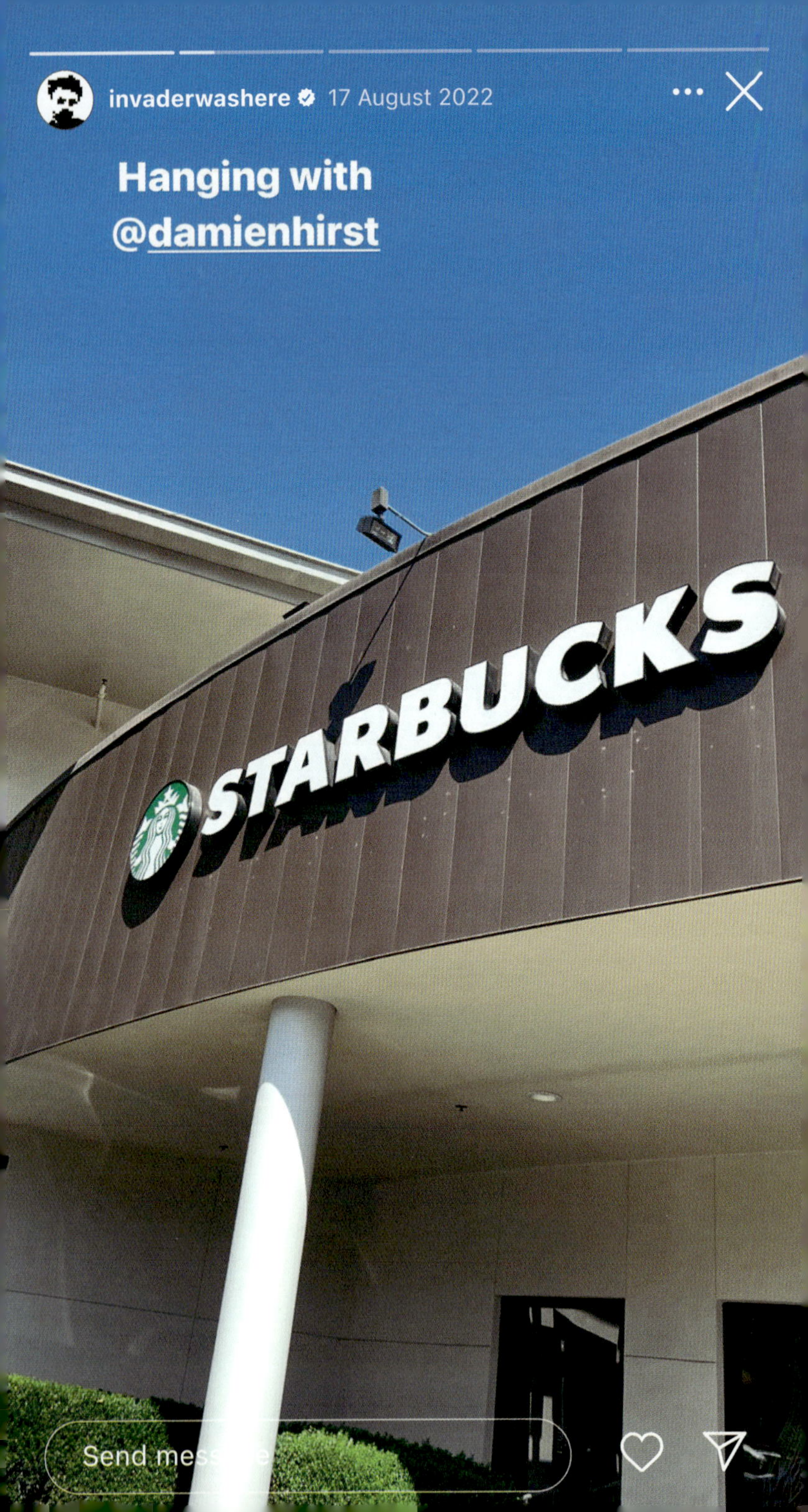

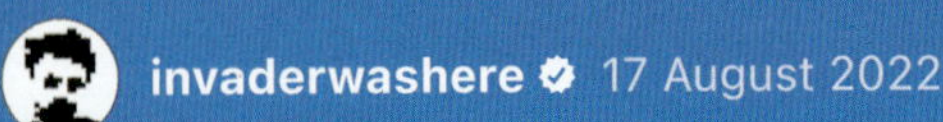
invaderwashere 17 August 2022

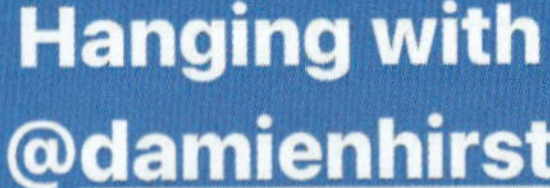
Hanging with
@damienhirst

STARBUCKS

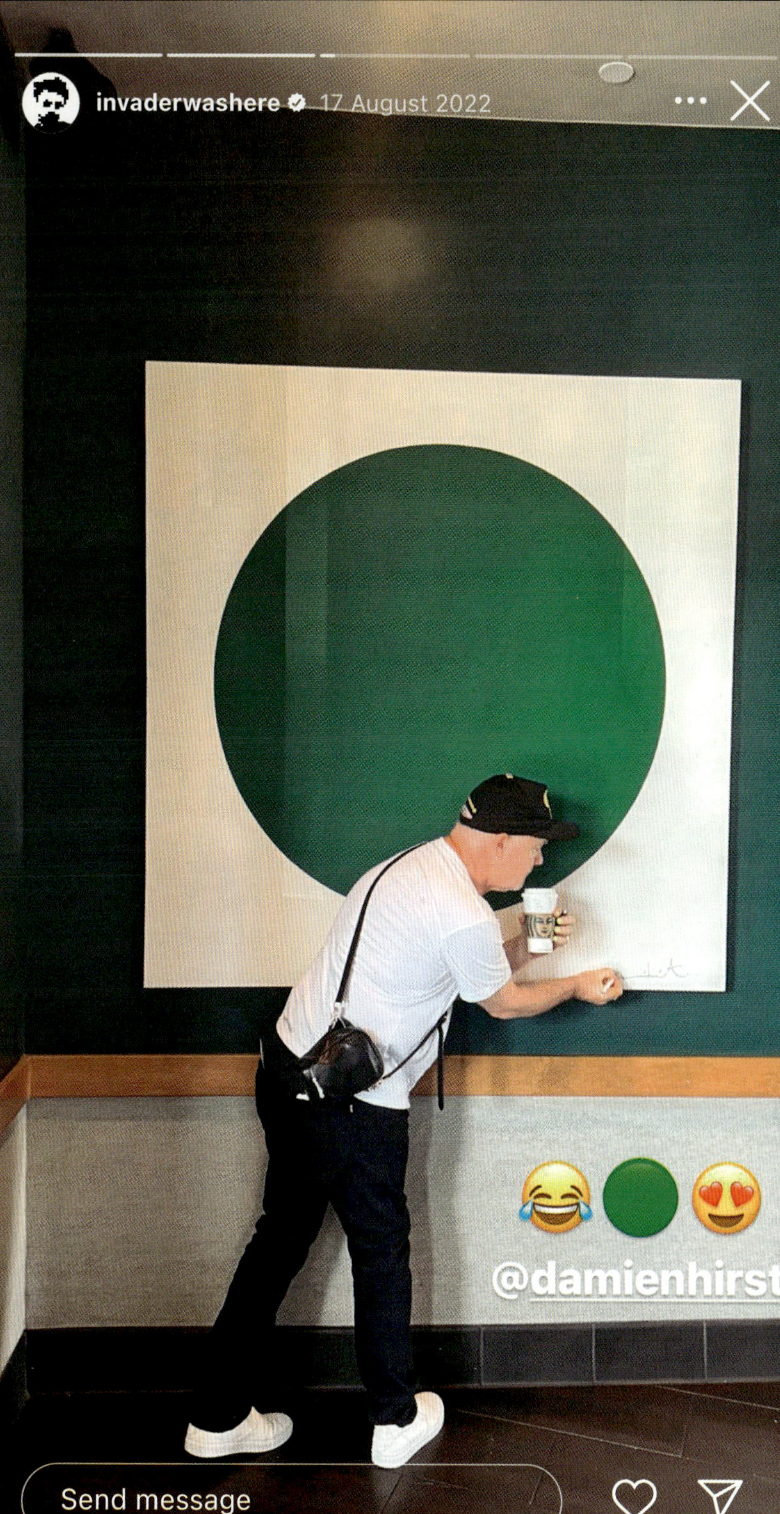
invaderwashere 17 August 2022
@damienhirst
Send message

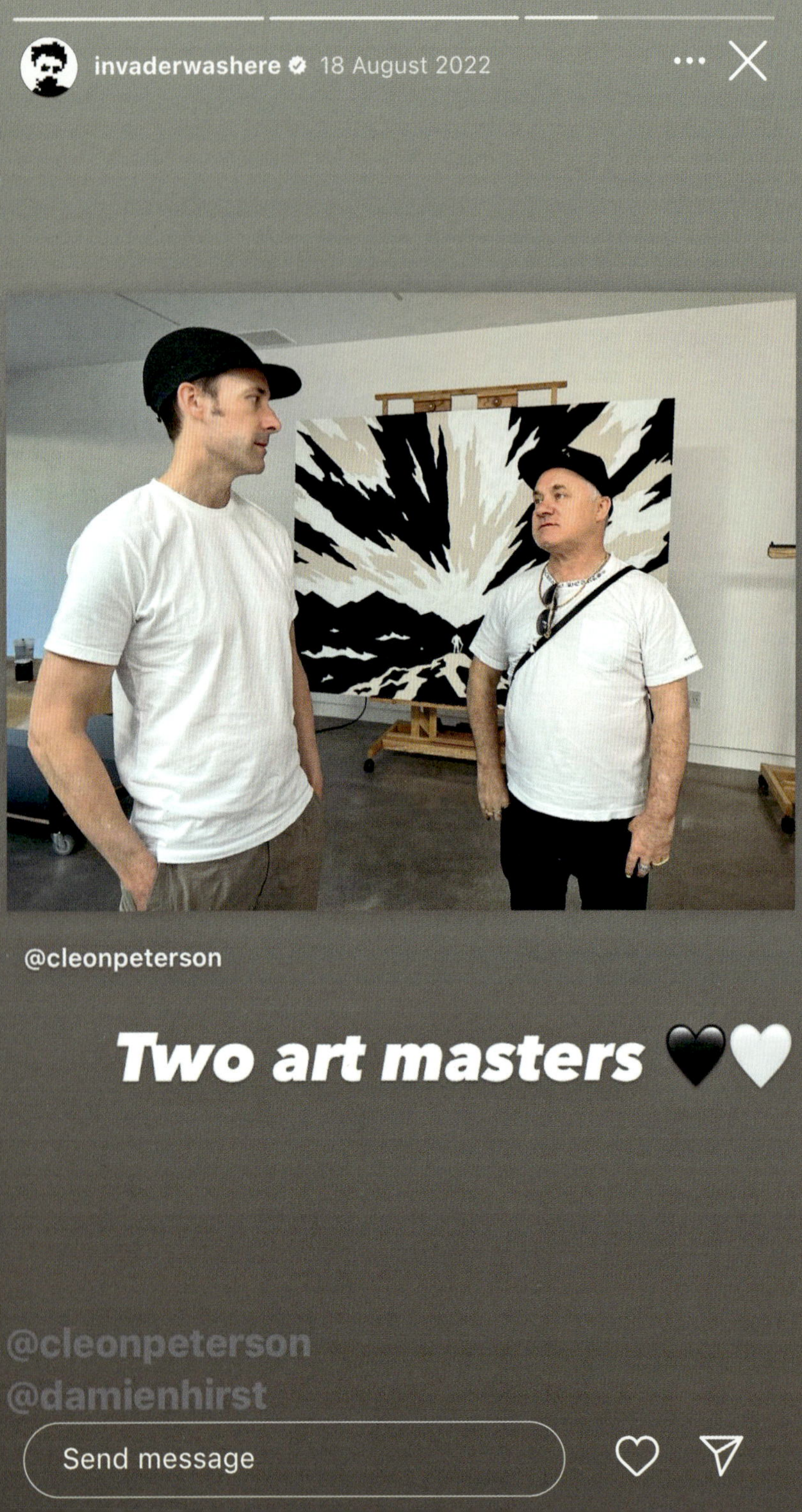

invaderwashere 18 August 2022

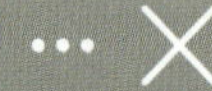

@cleonpeterson

Two art masters

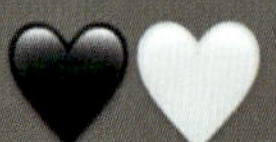

@cleonpeterson
@damienhirst

Send message

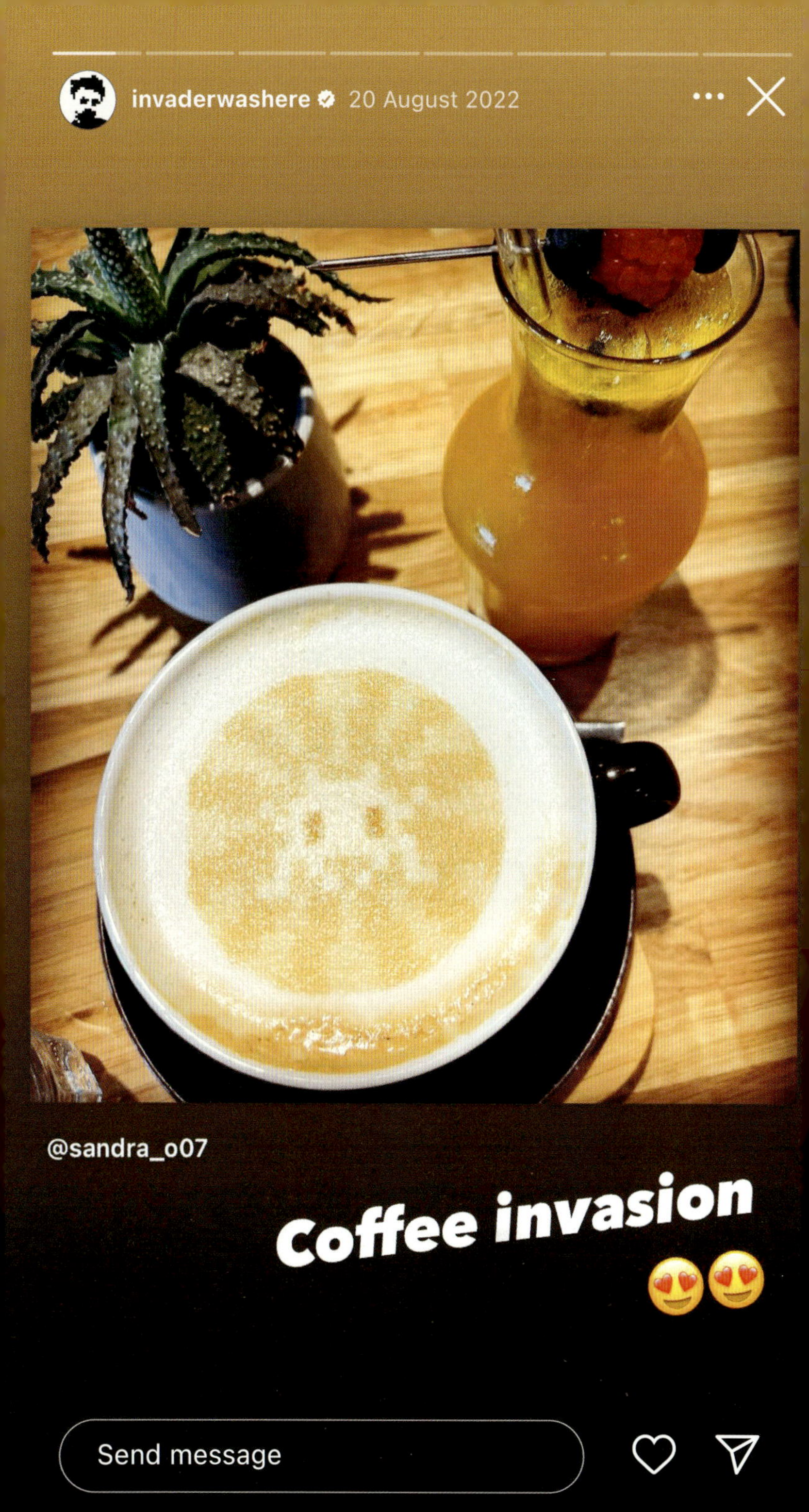

invaderwashere 20 August 2022

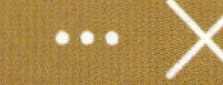

@sandra_o07

Coffee invasion

Send message

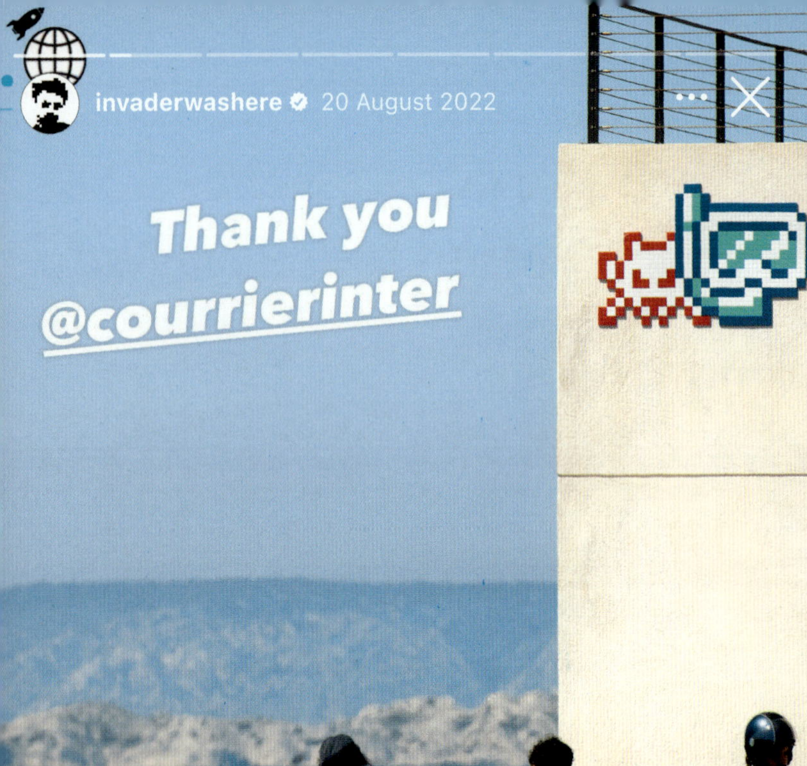

ıits)

ffel, pendant
eurs immor-
aura Fromm
e. Son zoom
te mosaïque
res, fixée sur

petits car-
des person-
e 1978 *Space*
le l'espace"].
des milliers,
irs, sous des
des villes de
ı Europe, en
e, en Asie et,

de ces enva-
Avignon et à
ompté 1675.
le chiffre de
ı'elle a télé-
" aux enva-
ders] qui lui
ıts à chaque

Invader est là

À Paris, Londres ou Tokyo, le street-artiste décline en pixels ses mosaïques. Les chercher, c'est découvrir le plaisir d'arpenter les villes autrement, écrit cette journaliste américaine.

---

qu'à Paris, on trouve ses petits envahisseurs jusque dans des librairies (Artazart, Mazarine) ou des bars et restaurants branchés (Baroom, Le Zorba, Chez Gudule, L'Abribus) et aux alentours de musées (Palais de Tokyo, Centre Pompidou).

Au fil du temps, le rapport des amoureux d'Invader à ses œuvres a évolué, et le plaisir du hasard (tomber sur une mosaïque au gré d'une promenade) a cédé la place à des chasses en règle, compteur

Une "*invasion*" née d'une révolte contre les technologies a donc fini par s'approprier la technologie du smartphone pour mieux ramener ses adeptes dans la rue, entre le bitume et le ciel – là, à l'image de Laura Fromm, ils découvrent des mégapoles hors des sentiers battus du tourisme ou profitent de ces temps de désaffection pour les voyages internationaux afin de mieux explorer les quartiers de leur ville. *"J'ai parcouru Cologne dans ses moindres recoins*

En kiosque cette semaine

de tous les temps, *"Jules-Martin"*, en a déniché 3206 à lui seul.

Le street art entretient des rapports complexes avec la loi. Invader, issu d'une formation classique en école d'art, dit avoir pensé ce projet non seulement pour lutter contre l'empiétement du numérique, mais aussi pour dénoncer le cadre rigide des musées et des institutions artistiques. Bien souvent, ses œuvres ont pris place sans autorisation, reconnaît-il, si bien qu'elles sont théoriquement illégales en France.

Mais la législation en la matière est appliquée de façon inégale. En 2016, la SNCF avait poursuivi le street-artiste M. Chat pour des dessins réalisés dans une gare. À Paris, la RATP s'empresse généralement de faire effacer les œuvres dès leur apparition.

Dans la pratique cependant, les propriétaires de sites et les municipalités cohabitent souvent bien avec le street art, notamment parce qu'ils apprécient les foules qu'il draine. L'office du tourisme de Paris a pleinement épousé la cause et propose des visites guidées thématiques. Le ministère de la Justice lui-même, tout en rappelant que les dégradations de propriété sont un délit, reconnaît que ces œuvres contribuent à la vie des rues. *"Certaines œuvres deviennent de véritables attractions populaires, conduisant à un tourisme spécifique via des parcours dans certaines municipalités"*, peut-on lire sur son site Internet.

Vols. C'est le cas de Paris, le repaire d'Invader [qui y revendique 1473 mosaïques] et l'une des villes les plus ouvertes à l'art urbain. L'artiste a parfois réalisé des collaborations avec la municipalité, dont une qui a donné naissance à sa plus grande mosaïque, un envahisseur noir, rouge et blanc de neuf mètres de haut, à deux pas du Centre Pompidou. Et si certaines œuvres ont été retirées par les propriétaires des

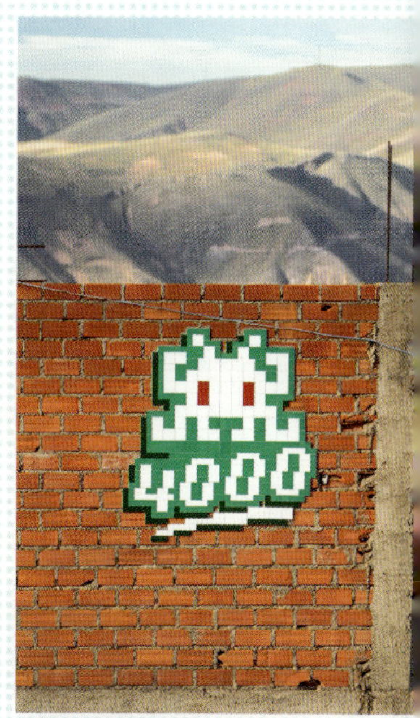

↑ À Potosí, en Bolivie, à 4000 mè

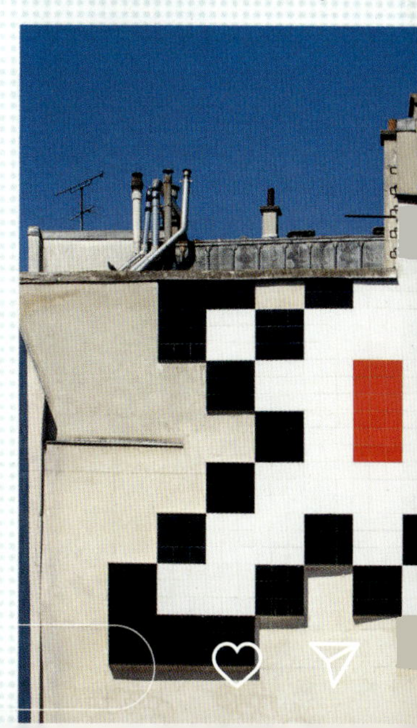

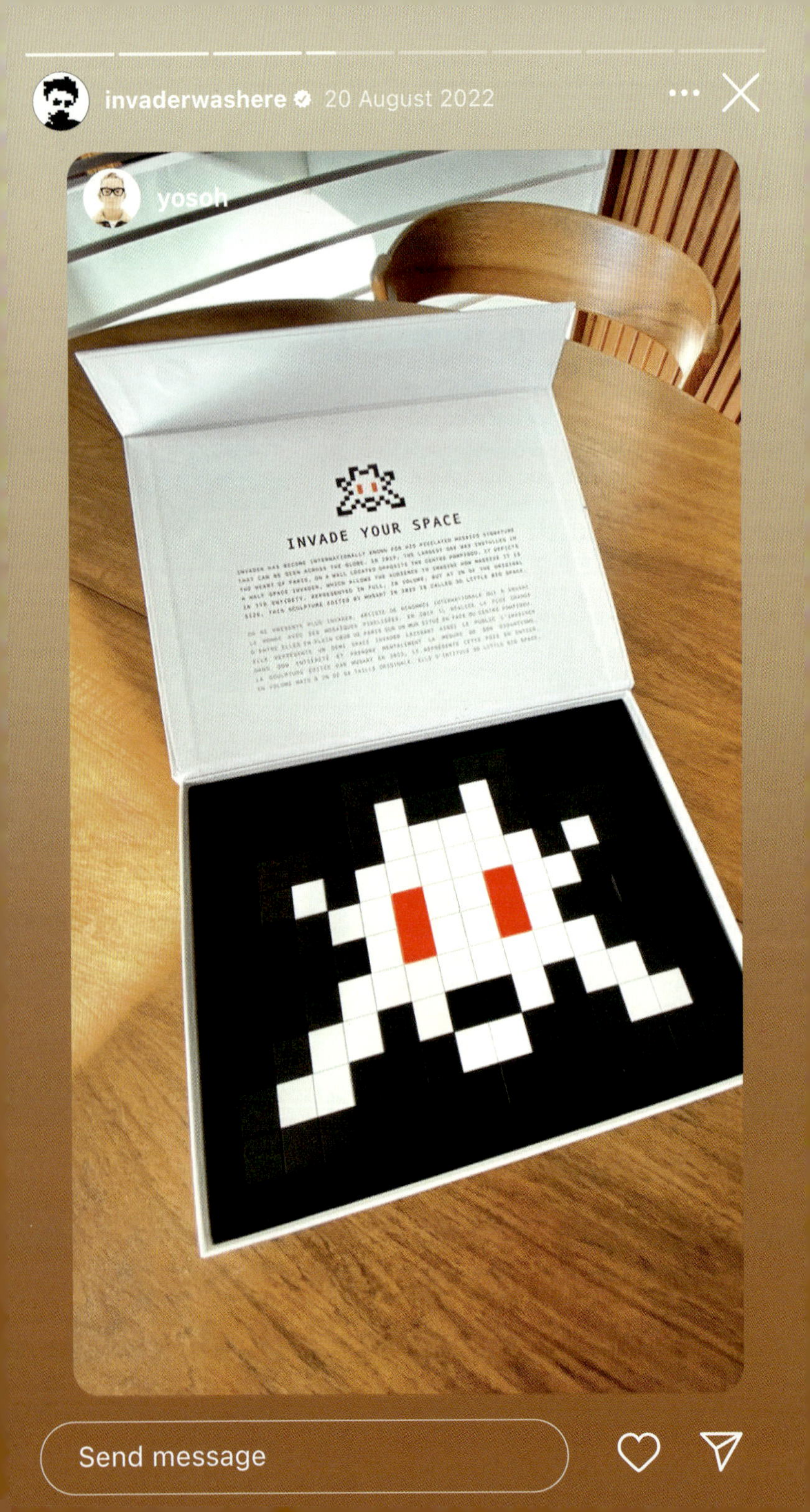

invaderwashere 20 August 2022

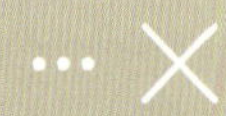

yosoh

INVADE YOUR SPACE

Send message

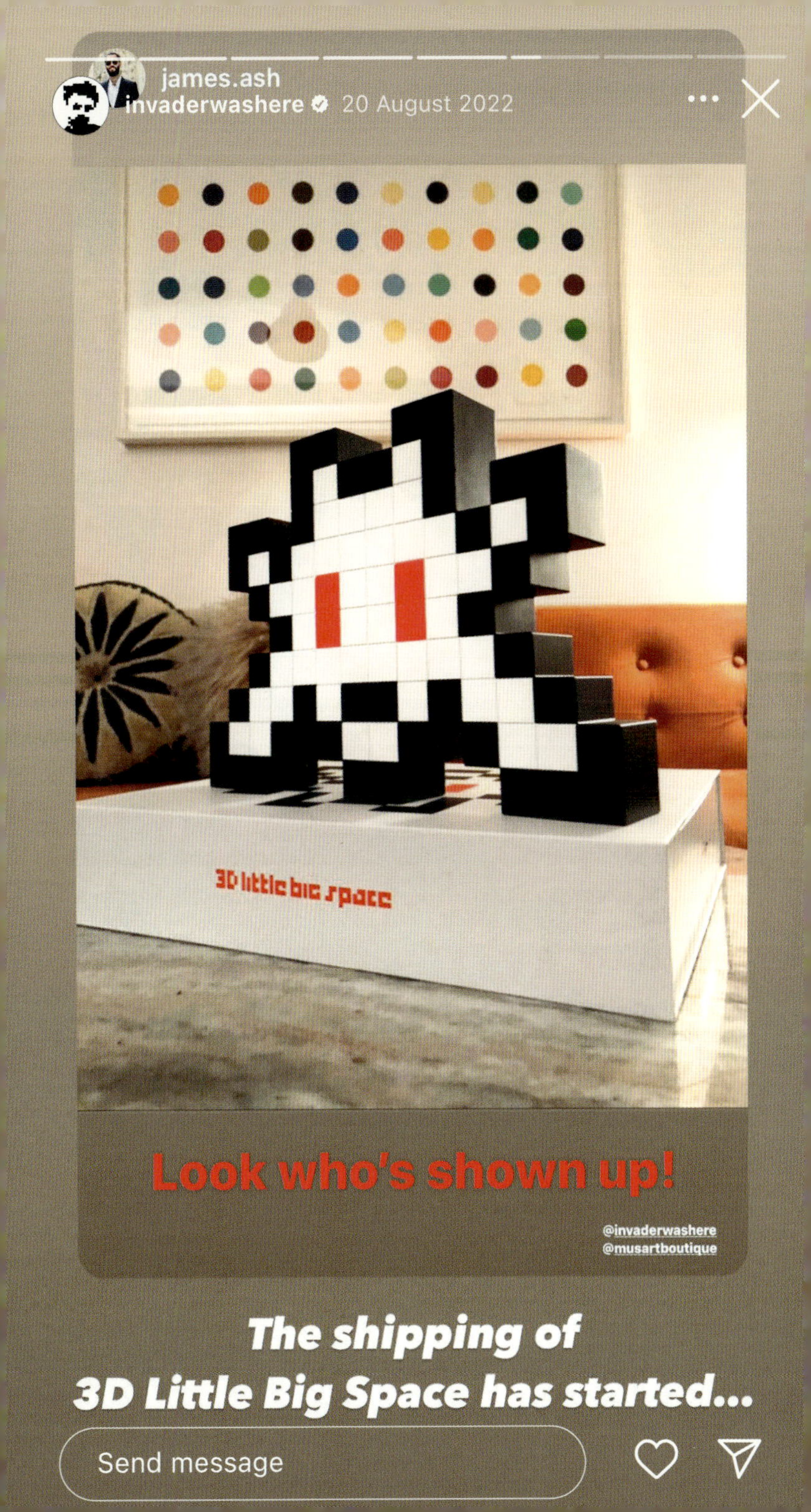

james.ash
invaderwashere 20 August 2022

3D little big space

Look who's shown up!

@invaderwashere
@musartboutique

The shipping of
3D Little Big Space has started...

Send message

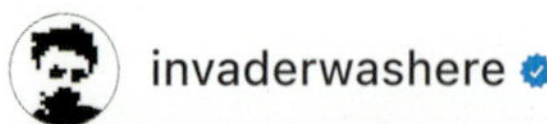

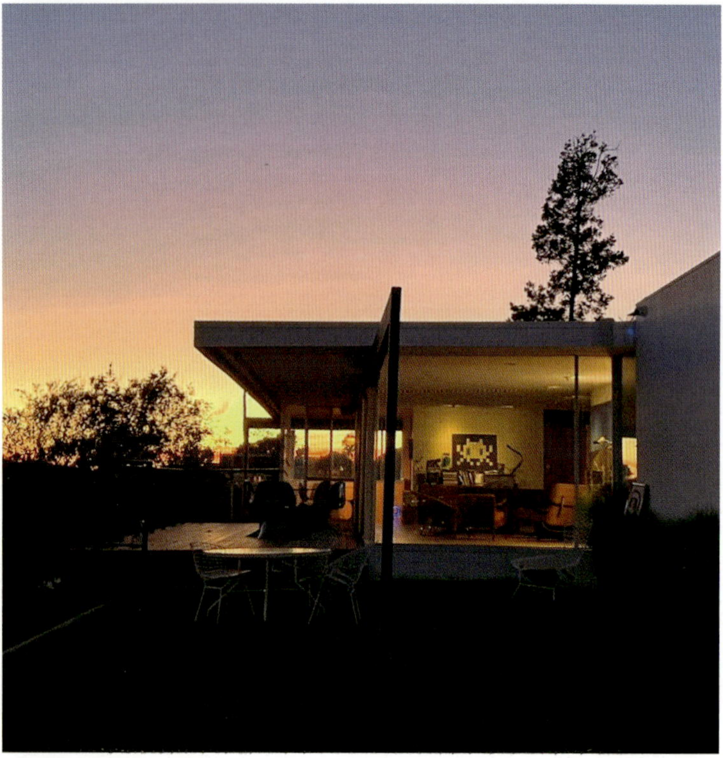

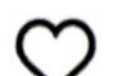 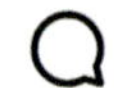  

3 726 likes

invaderwashere NEUTRA X INVADER
#richardneutra #chueyhouse #LA #architecture x #art

View all 64 comments

20 August 2022

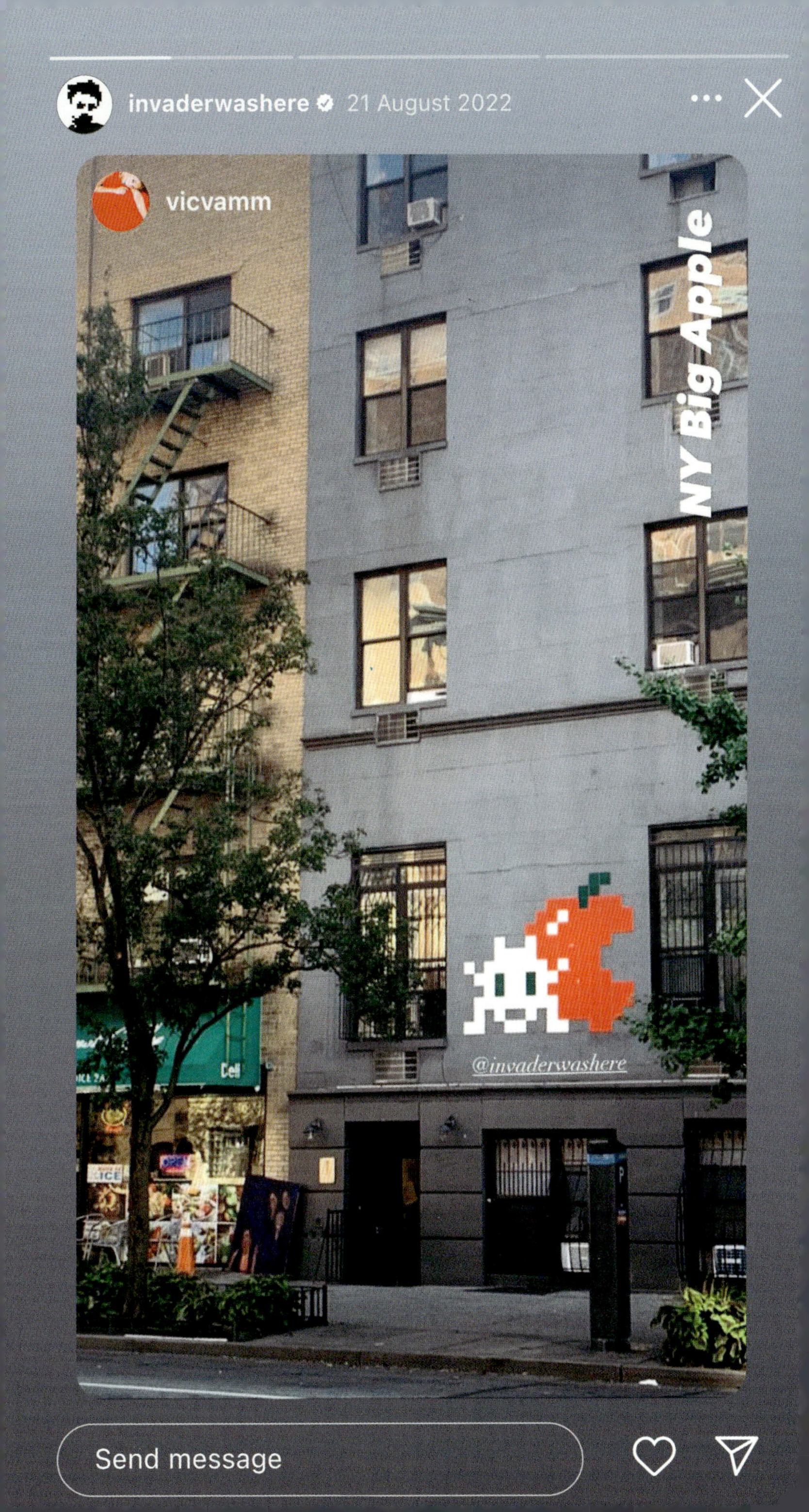

invaderwashere 21 August 2022
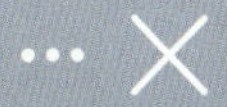

vicvamm

NY Big Apple

Deli

ICE

@invaderwashere

Send message
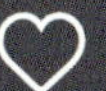
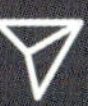

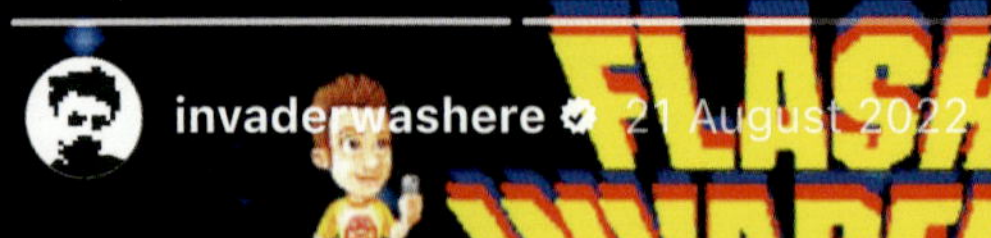

A FREE APP FOR SMARTPHONES

YOUR MISSION

Spot and "flash" the street mosaics of Invader.
Fill your gallery, score points and compete with other players.
Good luck & have fun !

A reality game by INVADER

DOWNLOAD

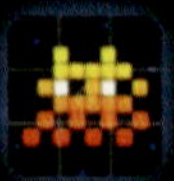

FlashInvaders is designed for iOS and Android.
Choose your version below:

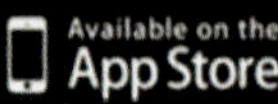

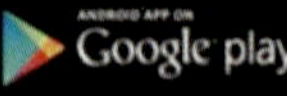

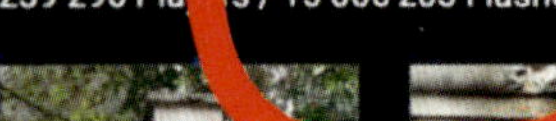

LATEST SUCCESSFUL "FLASHES"
239 296 Players / 15 000 203 Flashes

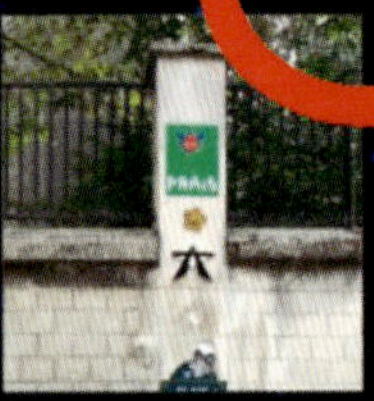
Paris
ARCADIO_FR
2 seconds ago

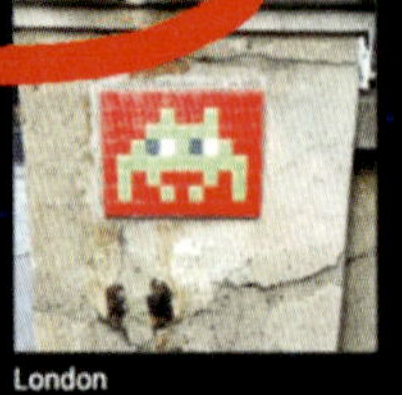

London
BALLEC
4 seconds ago

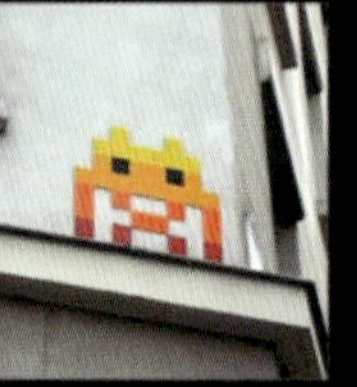
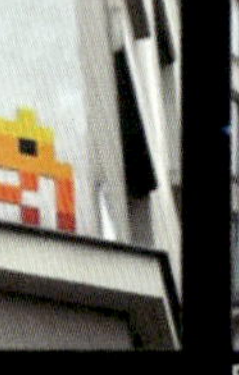
Paris
V3LDA
4 seconds ago

Paris
TYTGAT FR
5 seconds ago

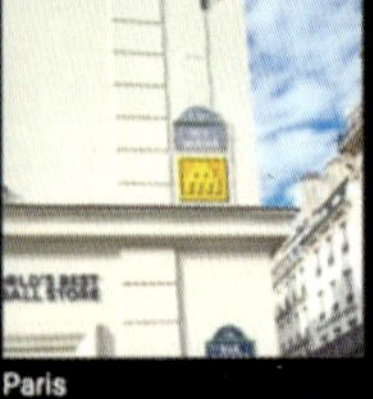
Paris
ANONYMOUS
5 seconds ago

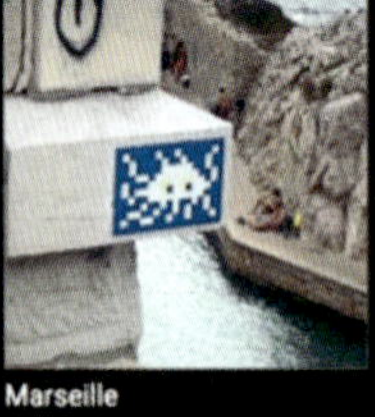
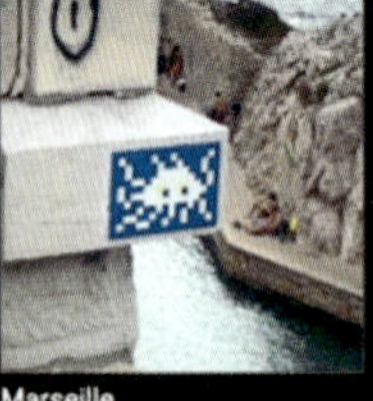
Marseille
AURELIA
8 seconds ago

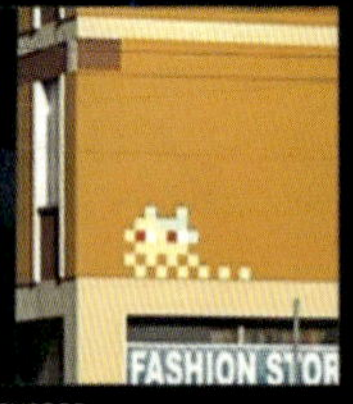

Ravenna
AYDINOVIC
10 seconds ago

New York
MARJOLALABLABLABLA
10 seconds ago

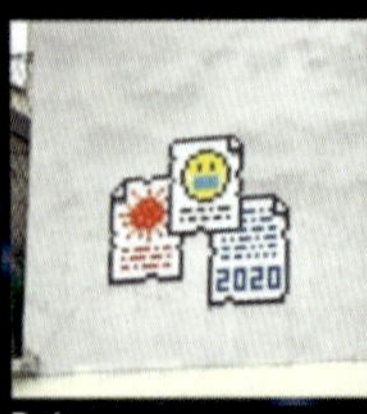

Paris
ANONYMOUS
11 seconds ago

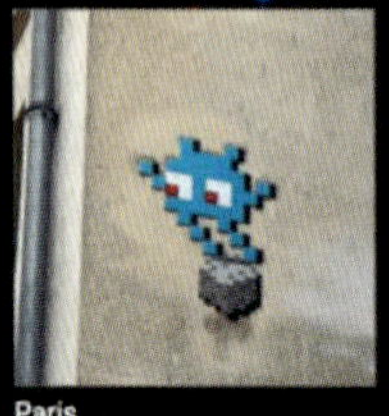
Paris
BLACKVALHY
11 seconds ago

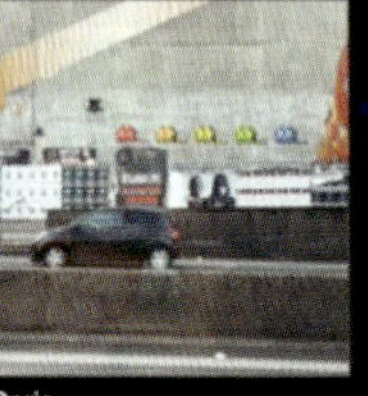
Paris
KROKMITEN
12 seconds ago

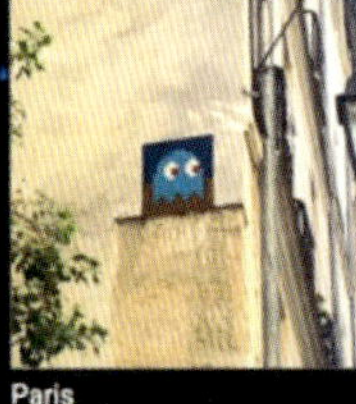
Paris
BASSLAGWELL
12 seconds ago

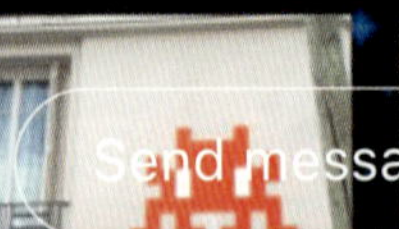

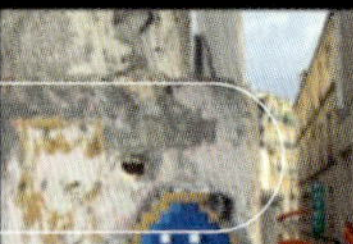

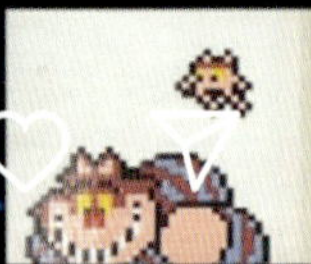

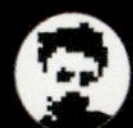

invaderwashere 21 August 2022

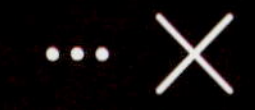

Just passed
15 000 000
Flashes

FLASHINVADERS

Send message

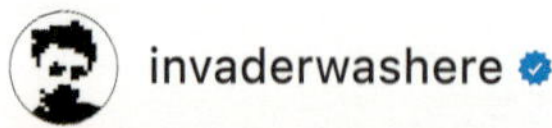

•••

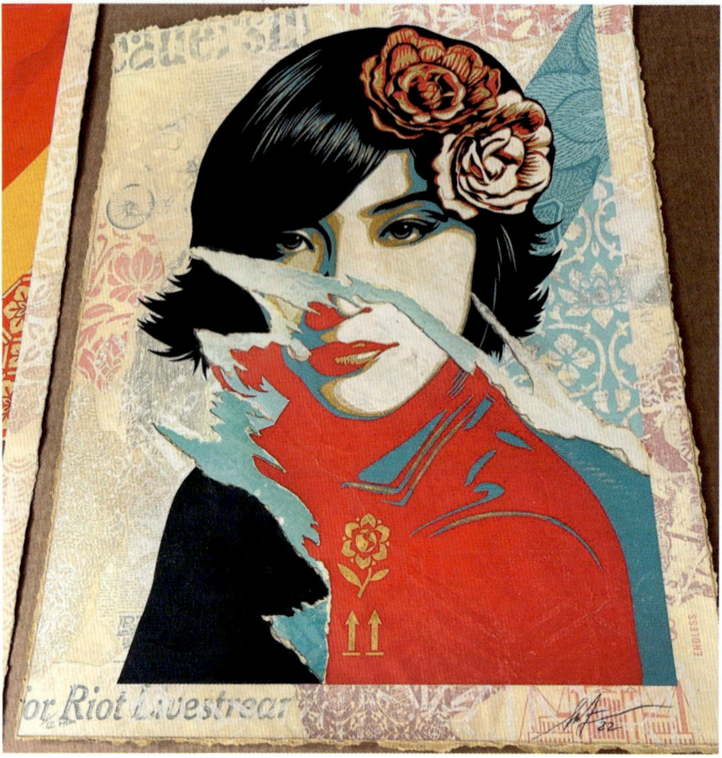

6 561 likes

invaderwashere I first met Shepard Fairey in 1999. Since then, our paths have crossed many times and we have always remained good friends. Shepard is not only a great artist, he is also a great man, smart, talented, prolific and committed to defending good causes. Thank you Shepard for your generosity, support and inspiration. Stay who you are and keep on doing your great work. #shepardfairey #obey #studiovisit #artmaster #respect 🙌

View all 78 comments

22 August 2022

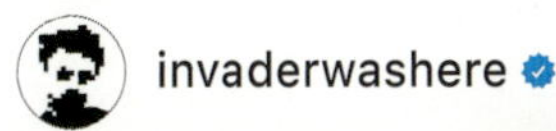

•••

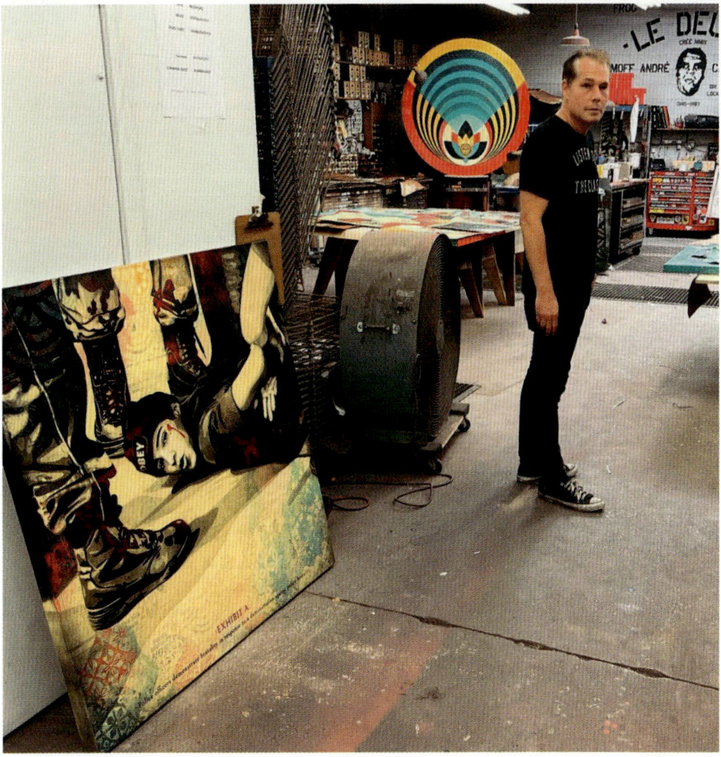

6561 likes

invaderwashere I first met Shepard Fairey in 1999. Since then, our paths have crossed many times and we have always remained good friends. Shepard is not only a great artist, he is also a great man, smart, talented, prolific and committed to defending good causes. Thank you Shepard for your generosity, support and inspiration. Stay who you are and keep on doing your great work. #shepardfairey #obey #studiovisit #artmaster #respect 🙌

View all 78 comments

22 August 2022

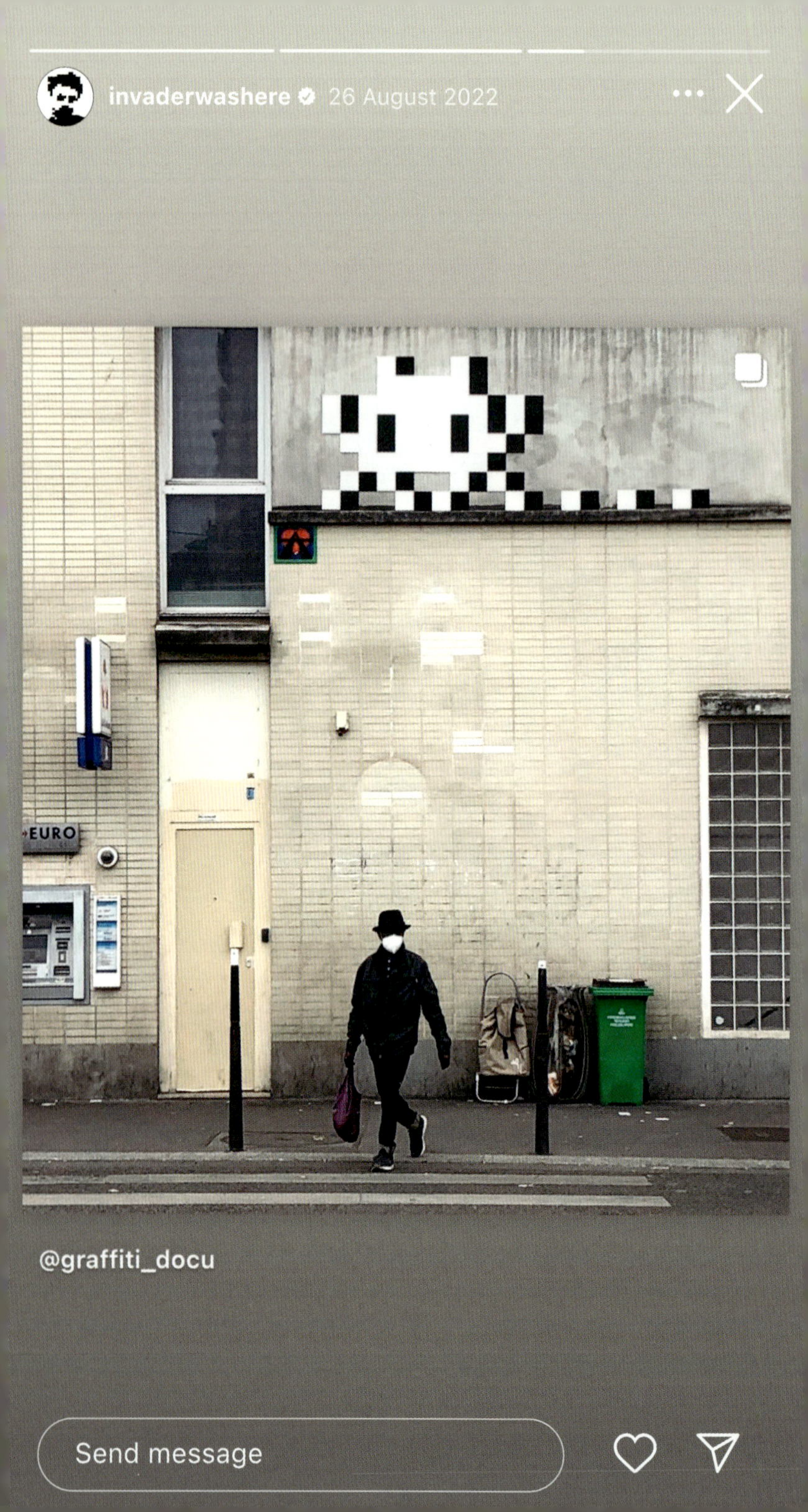

invaderwashere 26 August 2022

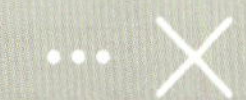

@graffiti_docu

Send message

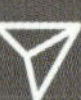

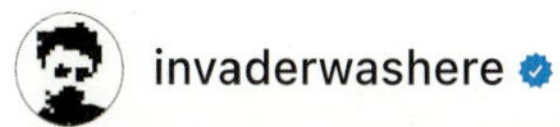

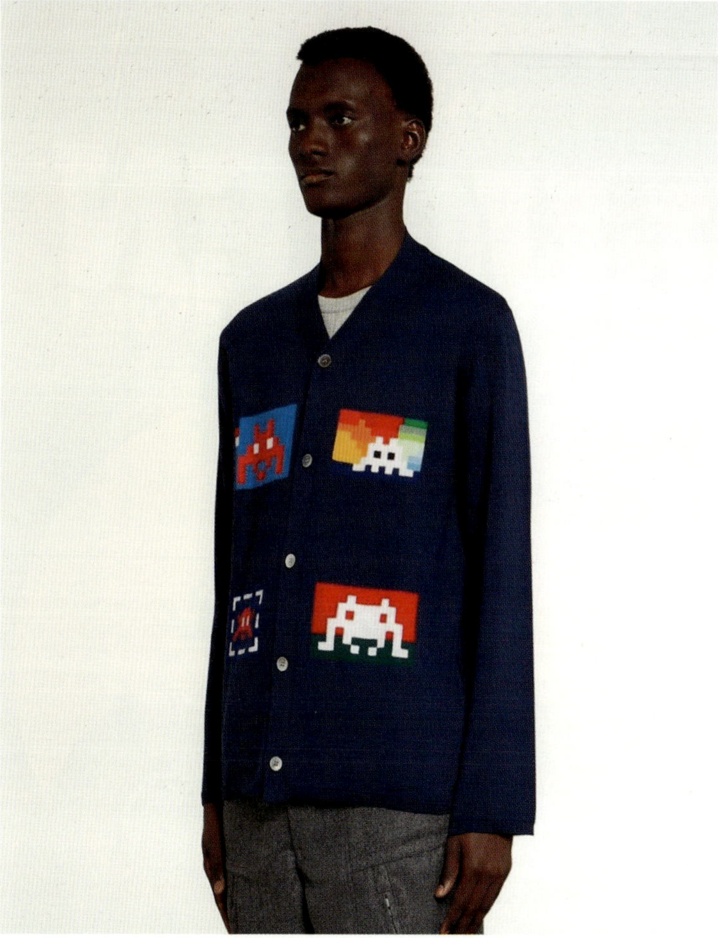

4095 likes

invaderwashere COMME DES GARÇONS X INVADER collection available now in stores and online 🚀🌎 #art x #fashion #carteblanche #reikawakubo #commedesgarcons #doverstreetmarket

Blue knit cardigan

View all 75 comments

1 September 2022

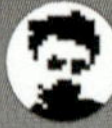

invaderwashere 4 September 2022

MARGERIN

LUCIEN

INTÉGRALE VOL.1

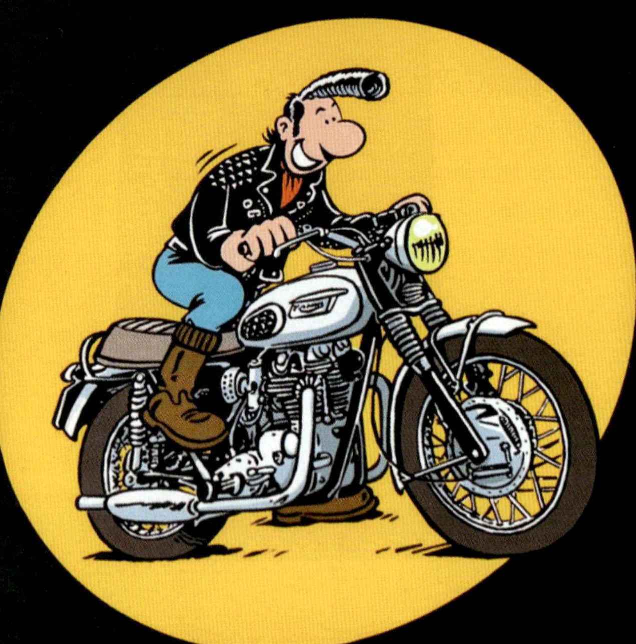

FLUIDE GLACIAL

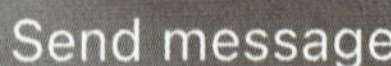

invaderwashere 4 September 2022

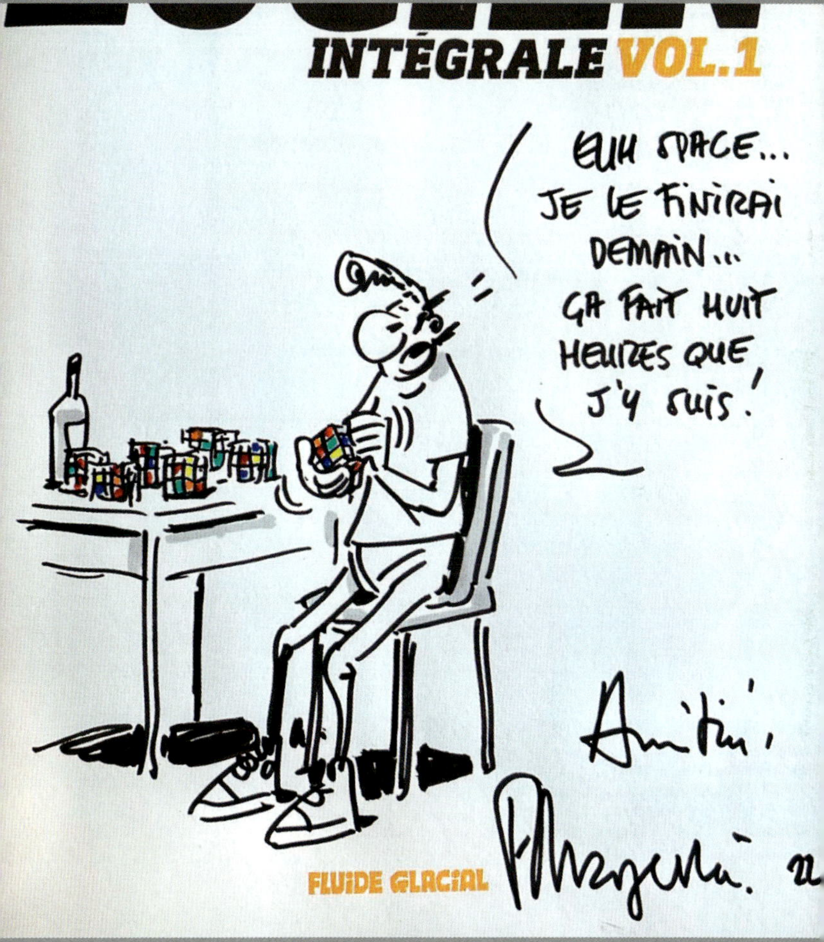

INTÉGRALE VOL.1

EUH SPACE...
JE LE FINIRAI
DEMAIN...
ÇA FAIT HUIT
HEURES QUE
J'Y SUIS!

FLUIDE GLACIAL

🙏 #frankmargerin

Send message

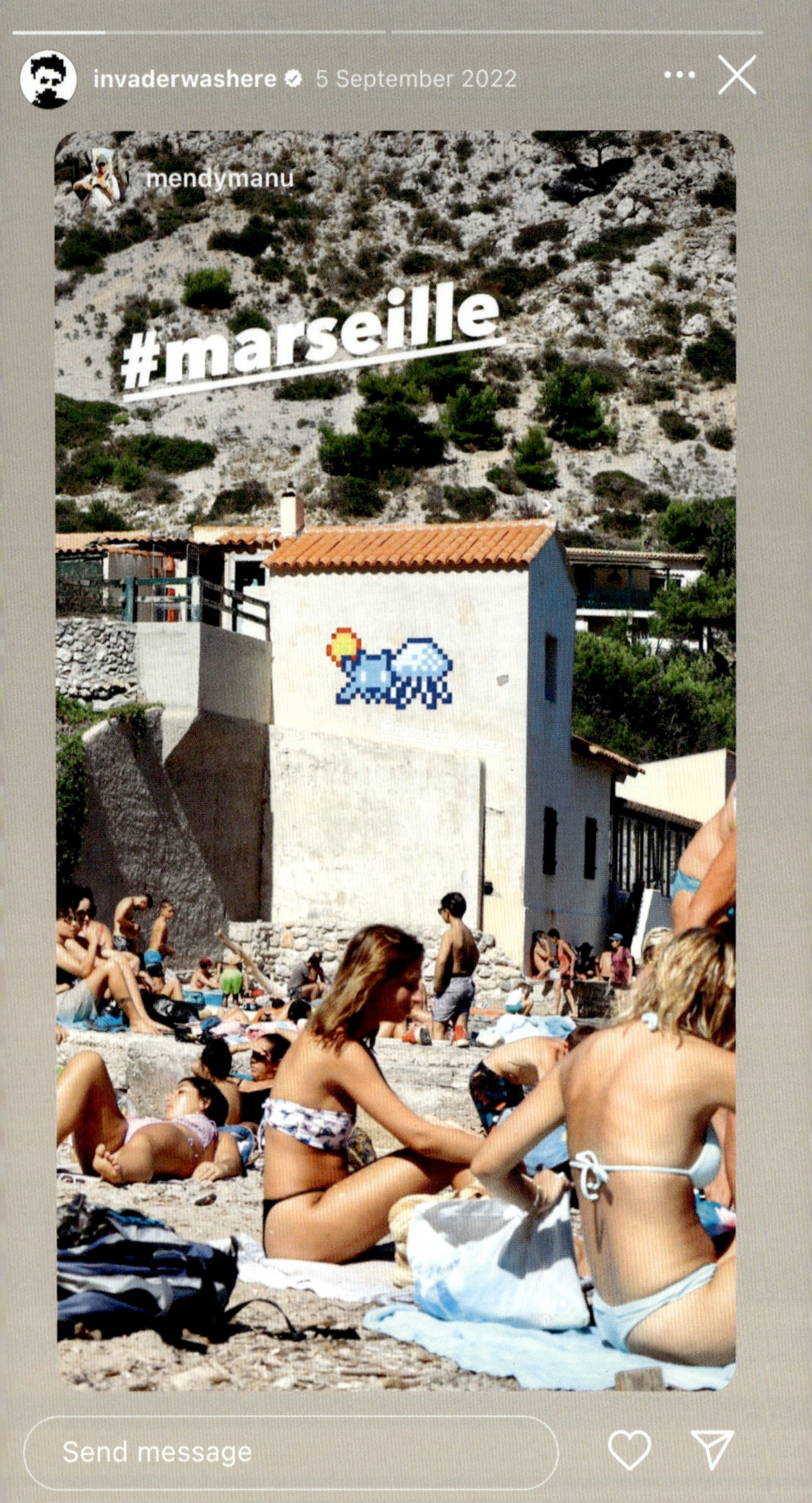

invaderwashere 5 September 2022

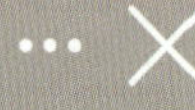

mendymanu

#marseille

Send message

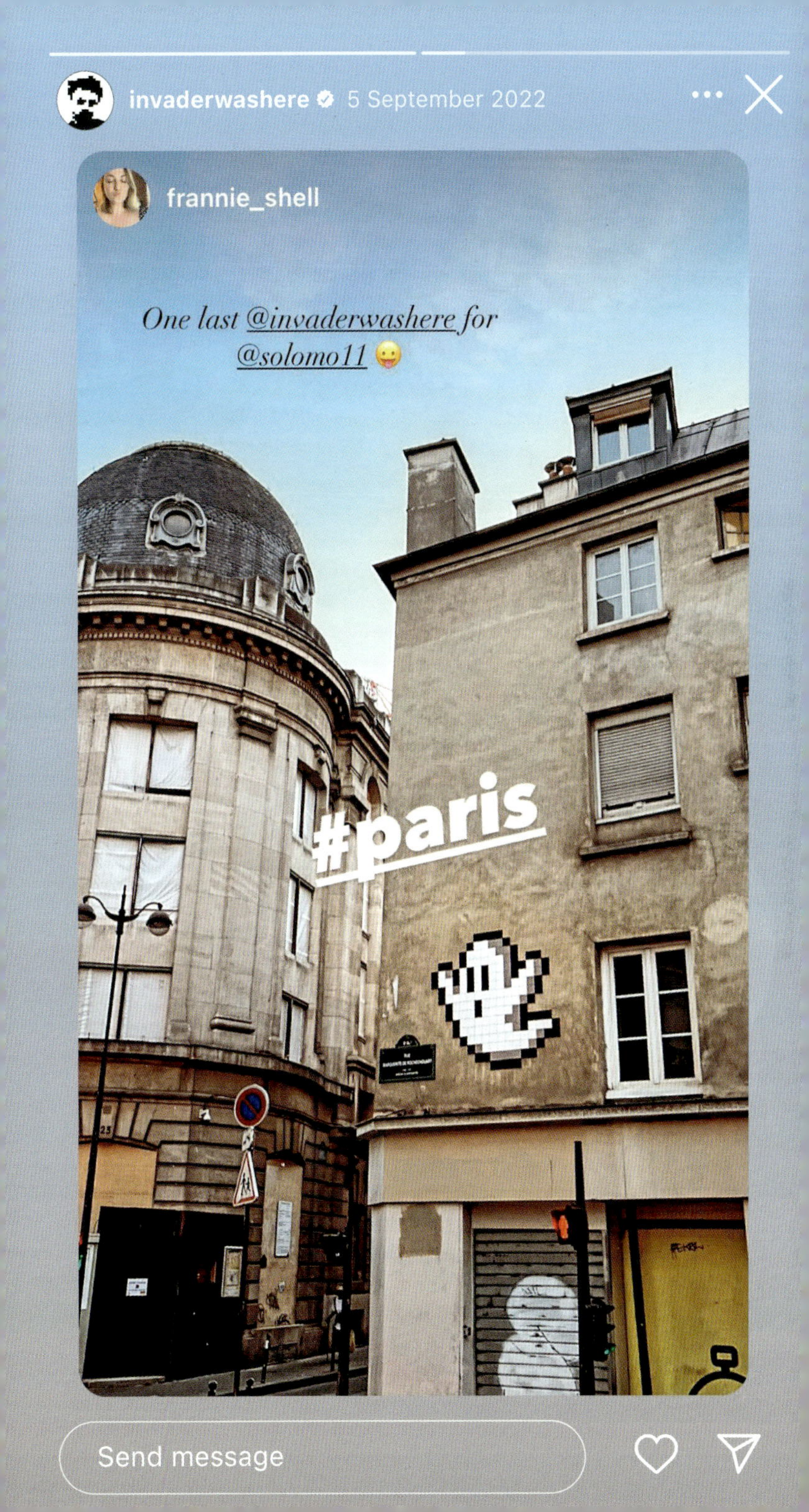

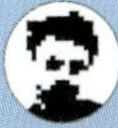

invaderwashere 5 September 2022

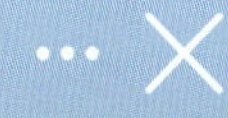

frannie_shell

One last @invaderwashere for @solomo11 😛

#paris

Send message

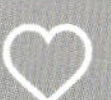

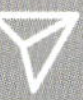

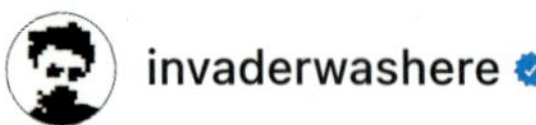

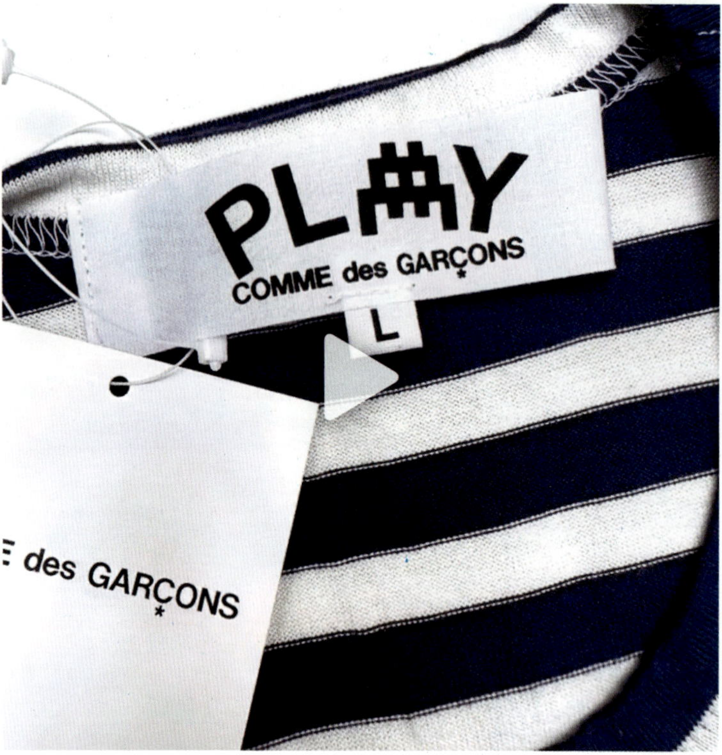

4867 likes

invaderwashere My collaboration with Comme des Garçons continues with PLAY. I've pixelated their 🧡 logo and invaded their label. Available in Japan now and from 8th September in the rest of the 🌎 at all DSM and CDG stores and CDG Pockets shops and at @doverstreetmarketginza @doverstreetmarketlondon @doverstreetmarketlosangeles @doverstreetmarketsingapore E-Shops

#madeinjapan @commedesgarcons

Music: Japanese gentlemen stand up please! by #yellowmagicorchestra

View all 84 comments

7 September 2022

invaderwashere •••

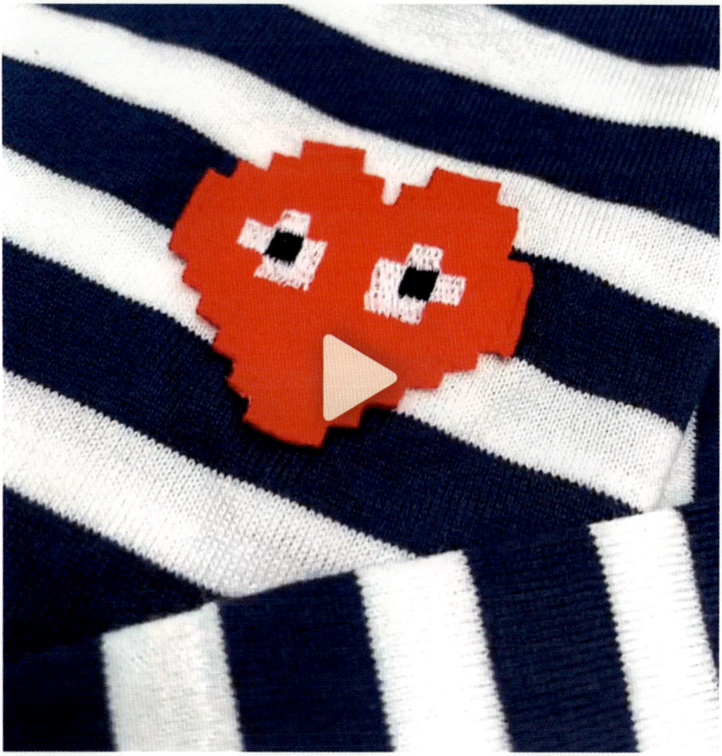

4 867 likes

invaderwashere My collaboration with Comme des Garçons continues with PLAY. I've pixelated their 🧡 logo and invaded their label. Available in Japan now and from 8th September in the rest of the 🌎 at all DSM and CDG stores and CDG Pockets shops and at @doverstreetmarketginza @doverstreetmarketlondon @doverstreetmarketlosangeles @doverstreetmarketsingapore E-Shops
#madeinjapan @commedesgarcons
Music: Japanese gentlemen stand up please! by #yellowmagicorchestra

View all 84 comments

7 September 2022

invaderwashere 11 September 2022

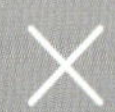

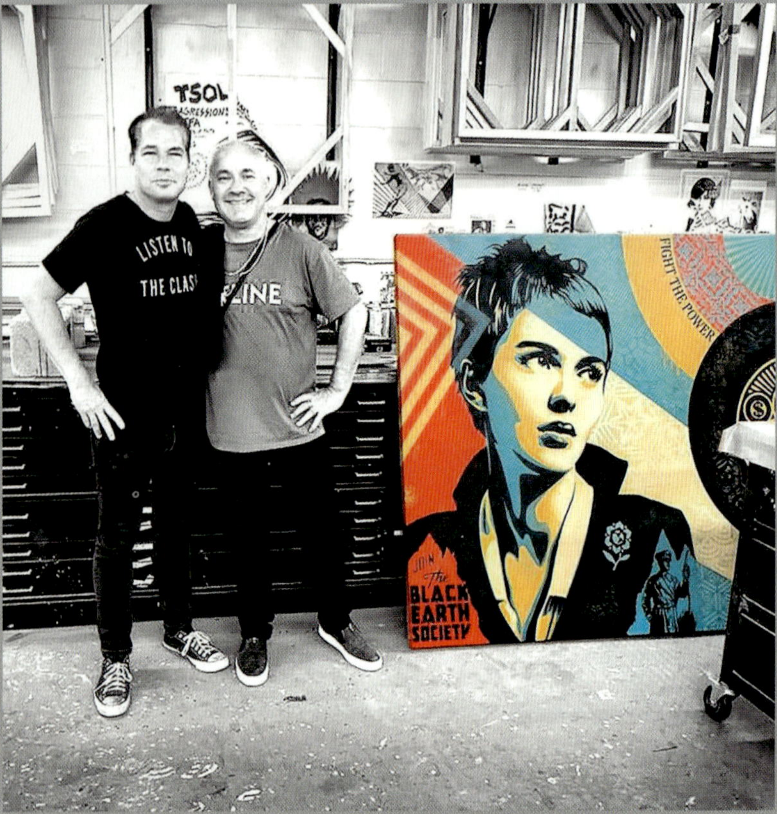

@obeygiant

2 OF MY FAV 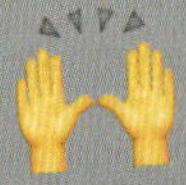

@obeygiant @damienhirst 📸 @invaderwashere

Send message

invaderwashere

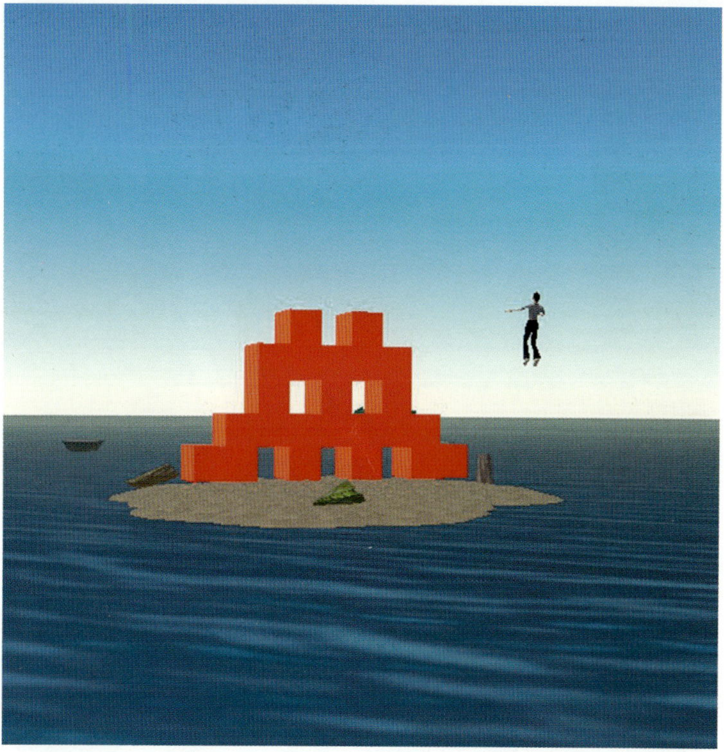

5627 likes

invaderwashere 15 years ago a friend of mine introduced me to Second Life, the ancestor of the Metaverses. Then I went there, I bought a small Island and I created a giant space invader on it. I never went back to see it, but I guess it is still there... #virtualinvasion #invaderisland #2ndlife #metaverse #throwback #archive

View all 65 comments

17 September 2022

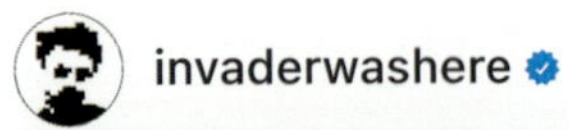

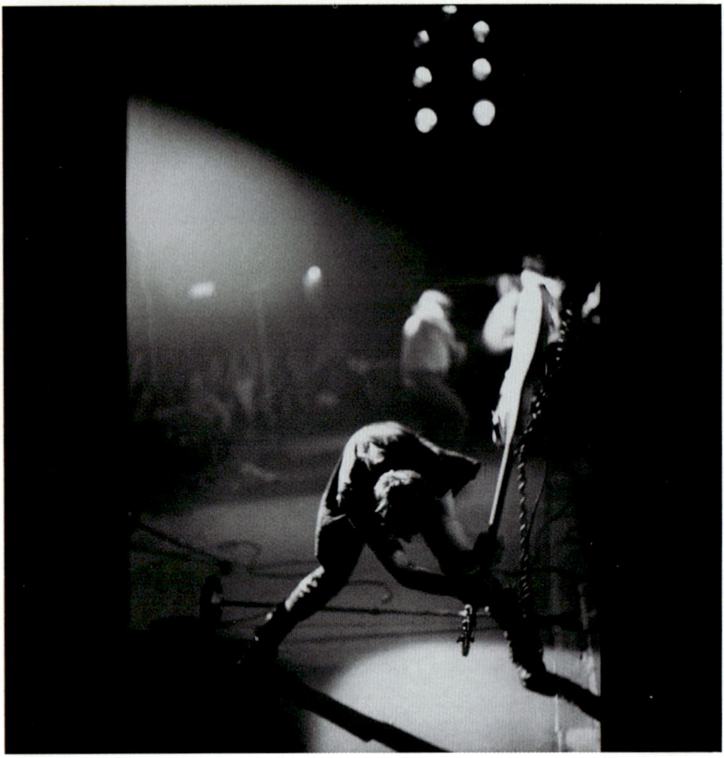

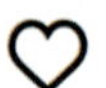

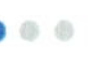

10623 likes

invaderwashere Today 43 years ago Pennie Smith took this photo during a live of the Clash at the New York Paladium. This is certainly one of the most iconic image in rock history. Last year during my trip in Potosí, Bolivia, I created this mosaic with reference to this photo. 🎸⛏️ #theclash #paulsimonon #penniesmith #punkrock #anniversary #mosaic #potosi #bolivia

View all 108 comments

20 September 2022

invaderwashere •••

   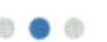 

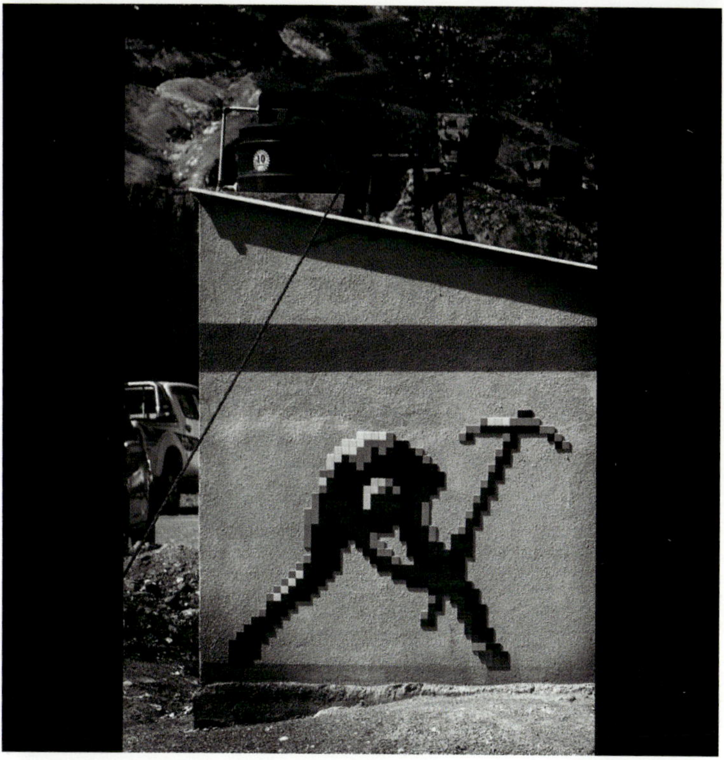

10623 likes

invaderwashere Today 43 years ago Pennie Smith took this photo during a live of the Clash at the New York Paladium. This is certainly one of the most iconic image in rock history. Last year during my trip in Potosí, Bolivia, I created this mosaic with reference to this photo. 🎸⛏️
#theclash #paulsimonon #penniesmith #punkrock #anniversary #mosaic #potosi #bolivia

View all 108 comments

20 September 2022

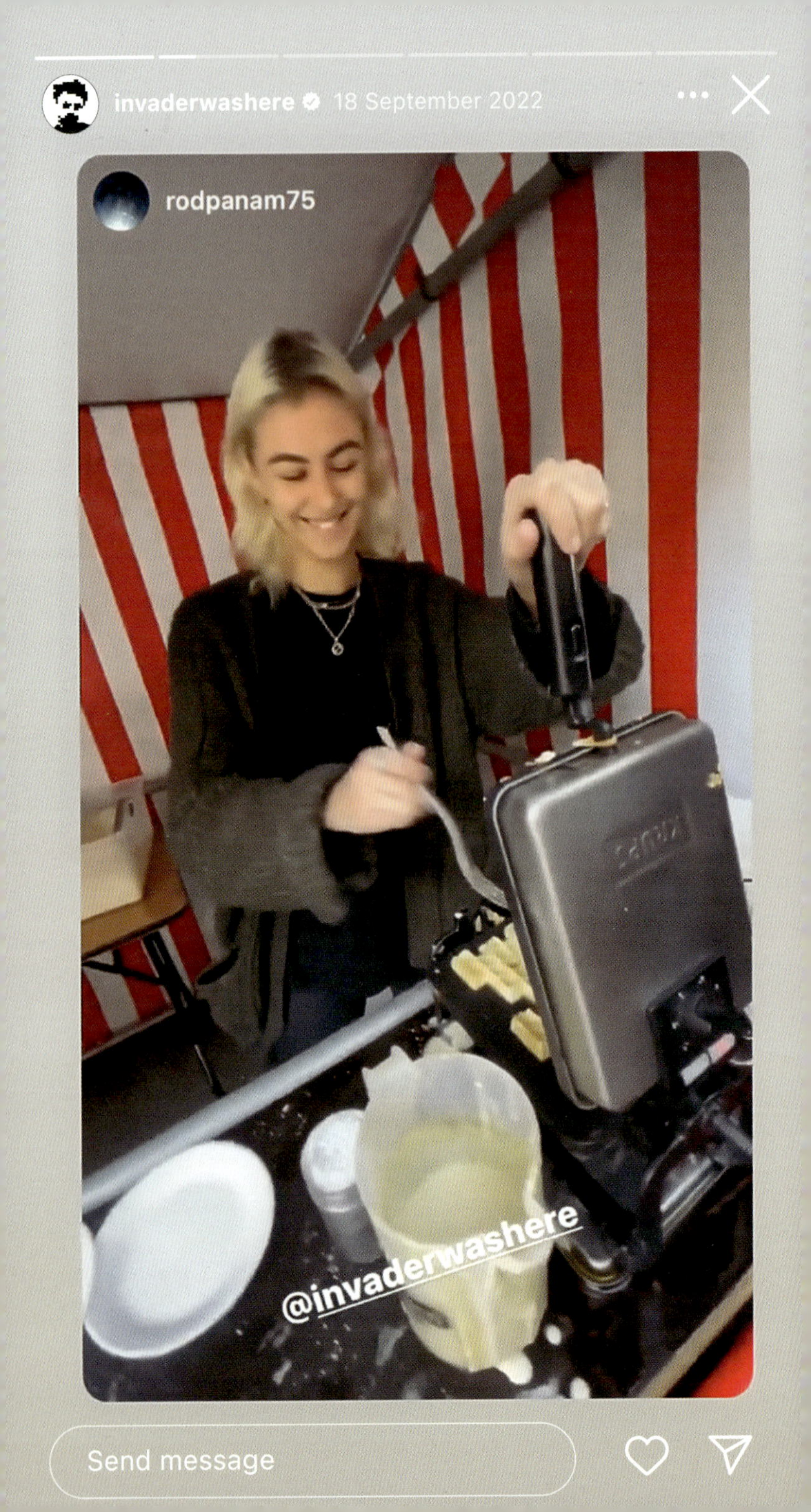

invaderwashere 18 September 2022

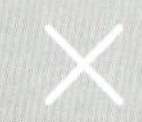

rodpanam75

@invaderwashere

Send message

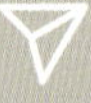

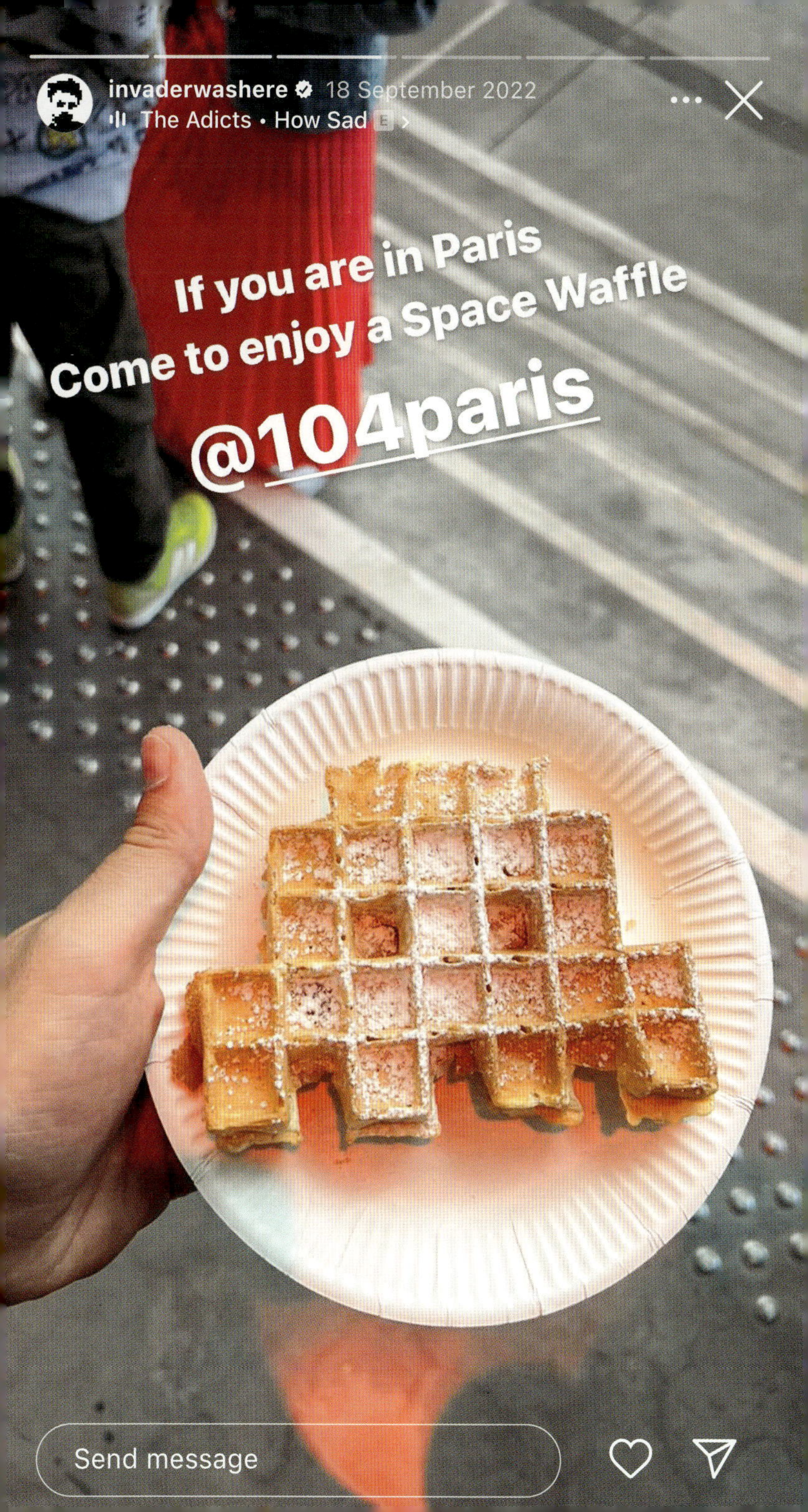

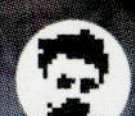

invaderwashere 18 September 2022

The Adicts • How Sad

Send message

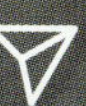

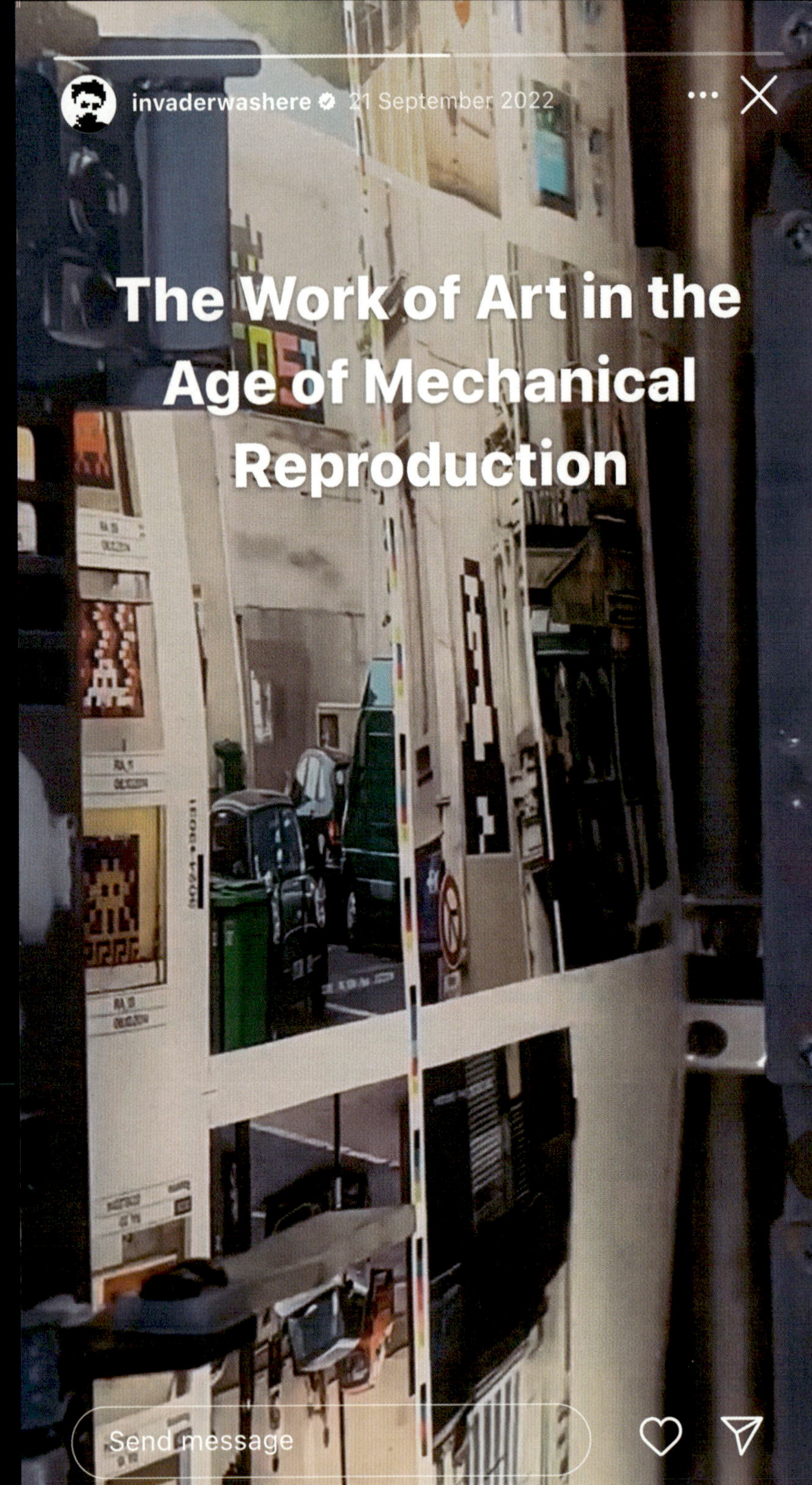
invaderwashere
21 September 2022
The Work of Art in the Age of Mechanical Reproduction
Send message

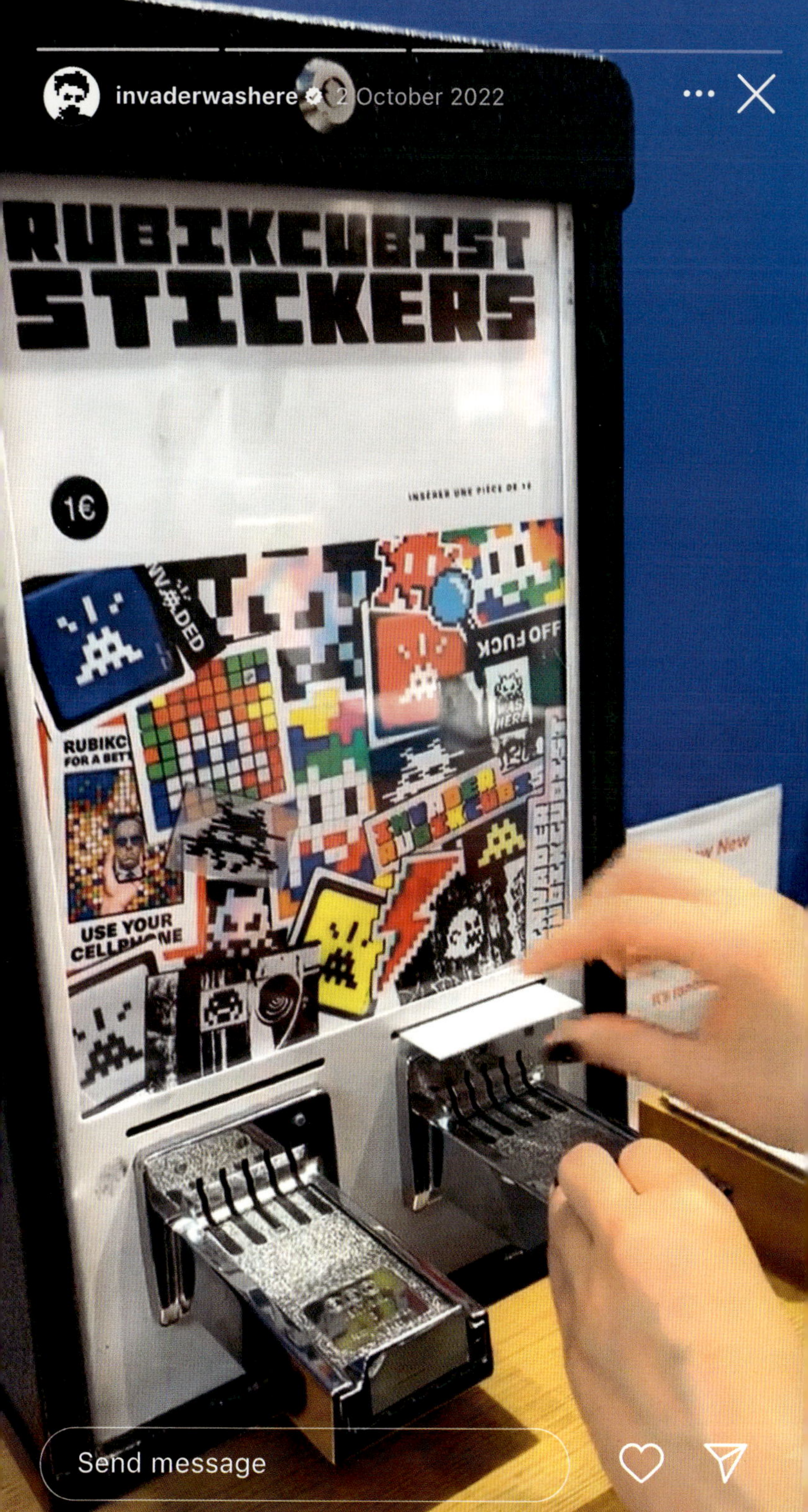
invaderwashere
2 October 2022
RUBIKCUBIST
STICKERS
1€
FUCK OFF
Send message

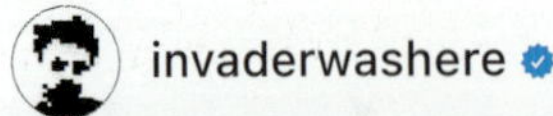

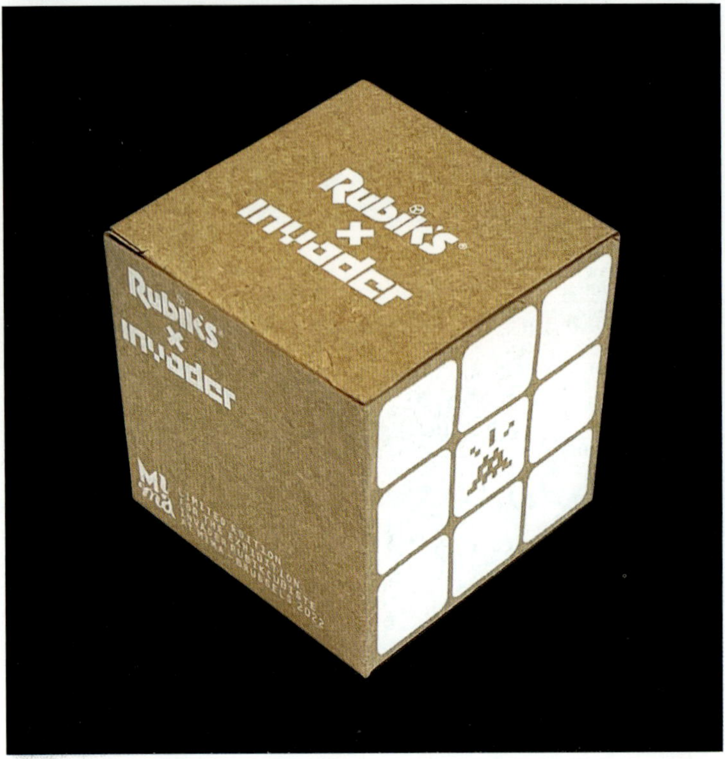

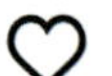   

5942 likes

invaderwashere This cube made with @rubiks_official is now available online on the SpaceShop / link in bio #rubik #rubikcubism #ltdedition

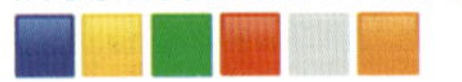

View all 218 comments

3 October 2022

invaderwashere •••

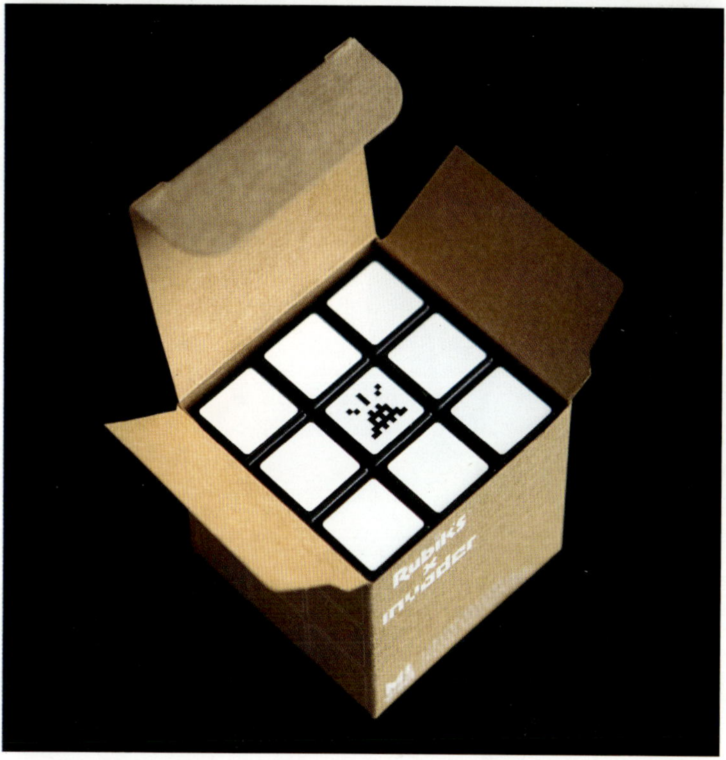

5942 likes

invaderwashere This cube made with @rubiks_official is now available online on the SpaceShop / link in bio #rubik #rubikcubism #ltdedition

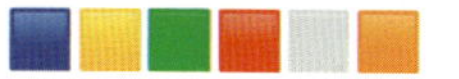

View all 218 comments

3 October 2022

invaderwashere 5 October 2022

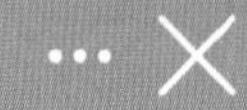

Sober, vegan and ultra limited !

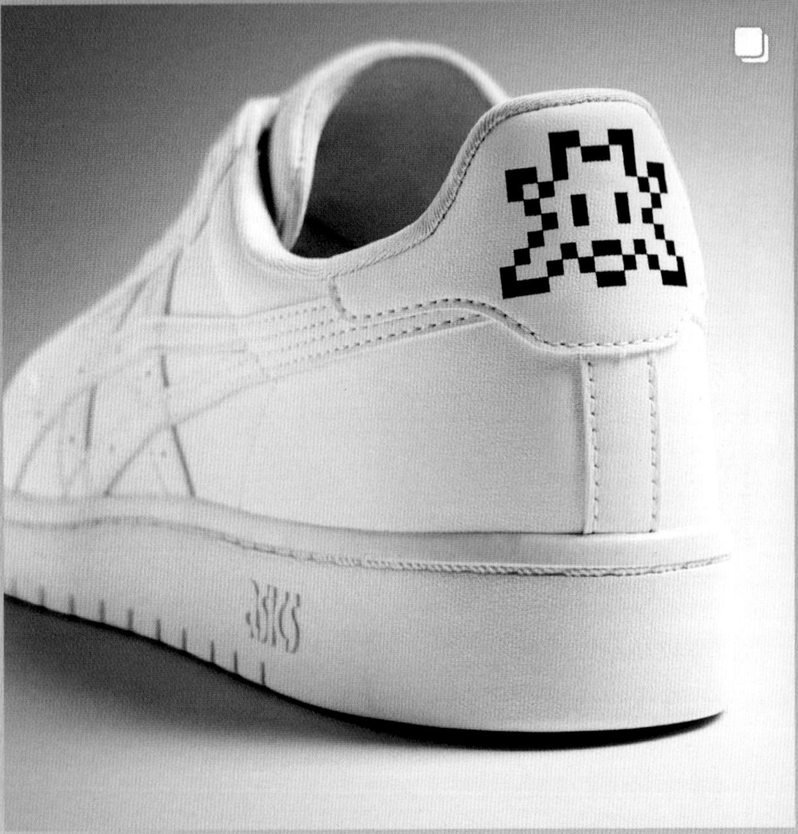

@asics_sportstyle

@invaderwashere
X @commedesgarcons
X @asics_sportstyle

Send message

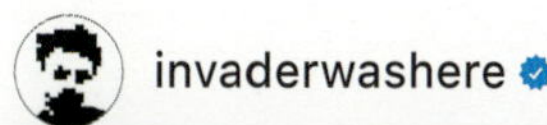

•••

EAST SIDE BURGERS
FÊTE SES 10 ANS
EDITION LIMITÉE
2012 2022
LE SPACE INBURGER
BY INVADER
100% VEGAN
AVOCAT • CHEDDAR • BACON
STEAK BEYOND MEAT • PICKLES
MAYONNAISE • BUN AU SESAME
VENDREDI 7 & SAMEDI 8 OCTOBRE
#SPACEINBURGER
RECETTE DISPO DU 7 AU 30 OCTOBRE
EAST SIDE BURGERS
60 BOULEVARD VOLTAIRE 75011 PARIS

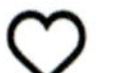

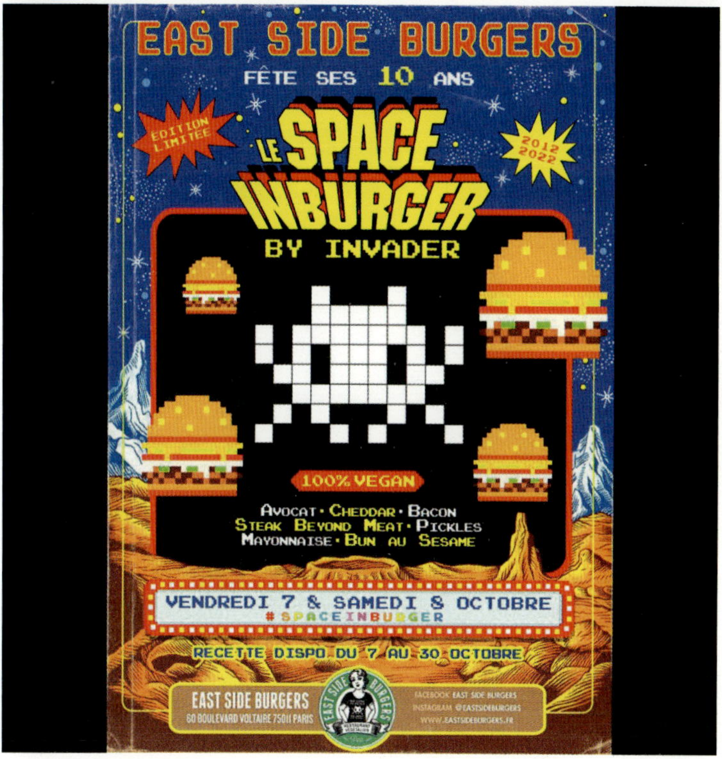

4464 likes

invaderwashere Cela fait des années que je fréquente East Side Burger un petit restaurant dans le 11e où l'on déguste les meilleurs burgers Vegan de Paris. C'est avec un grand plaisir que j'ai accepté de célébrer leur 10e anniversaire en créant avec eux la recette du Space Inburger et en revisitant leur logo. Il est disponible dès aujourd'hui et jusqu'au 30 octobre.
More infos: @eastsideburgers #spaceinburger #sticker #goodies #concourphoto #veganfood #streetfood #heyholetsgo... vegan 🎂🍔🍟🌱👾

View all 98 comments

7 October 2022

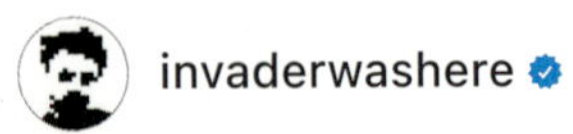

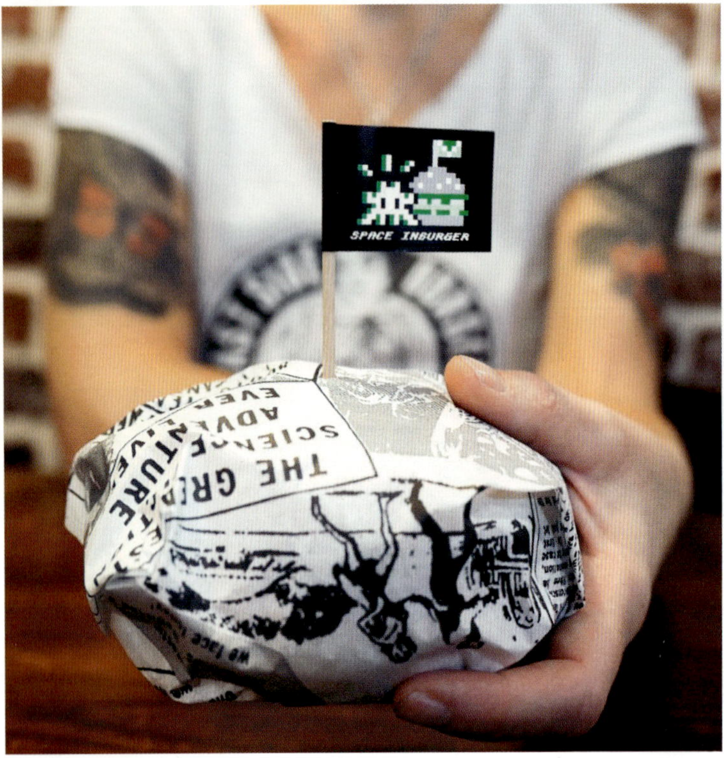

4464 likes

invaderwashere Cela fait des années que je fréquente East Side Burger un petit restaurant dans le 11e où l'on déguste les meilleurs burgers Vegan de Paris. C'est avec un grand plaisir que j'ai accepté de célébrer leur 10e anniversaire en créant avec eux la recette du Space Inburger et en revisitant leur logo. Il est disponible dès aujourd'hui et jusqu'au 30 octobre.

More infos: @eastsideburgers #spaceinburger #sticker #goodies #concourphoto #veganfood #streetfood #heyholetsgo... vegan 🎂🍔🍟🌱👾

View all 98 comments

7 October 2022

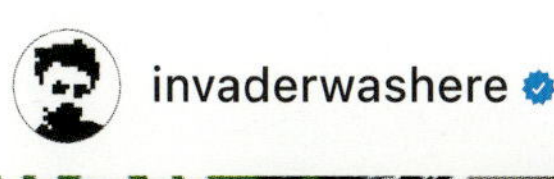

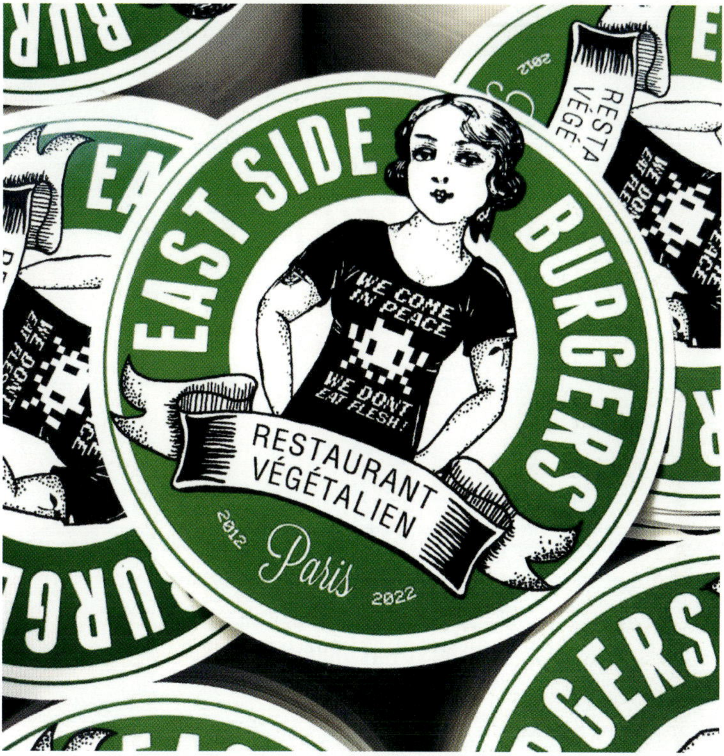

 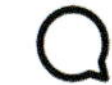   

4 464 likes

invaderwashere Cela fait des années que je fréquente East Side Burger un petit restaurant dans le 11e où l'on déguste les meilleurs burgers Vegan de Paris. C'est avec un grand plaisir que j'ai accepté de célébrer leur 10e anniversaire en créant avec eux la recette du Space Inburger et en revisitant leur logo. Il est disponible dès aujourd'hui et jusqu'au 30 octobre.

More infos: @eastsideburgers #spaceinburger #sticker #goodies #concourphoto #veganfood #streetfood #heyholetsgo... vegan 🎂🍔🍟🌱👾

View all 98 comments

7 October 2022

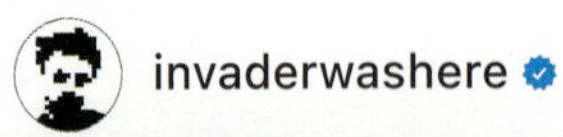

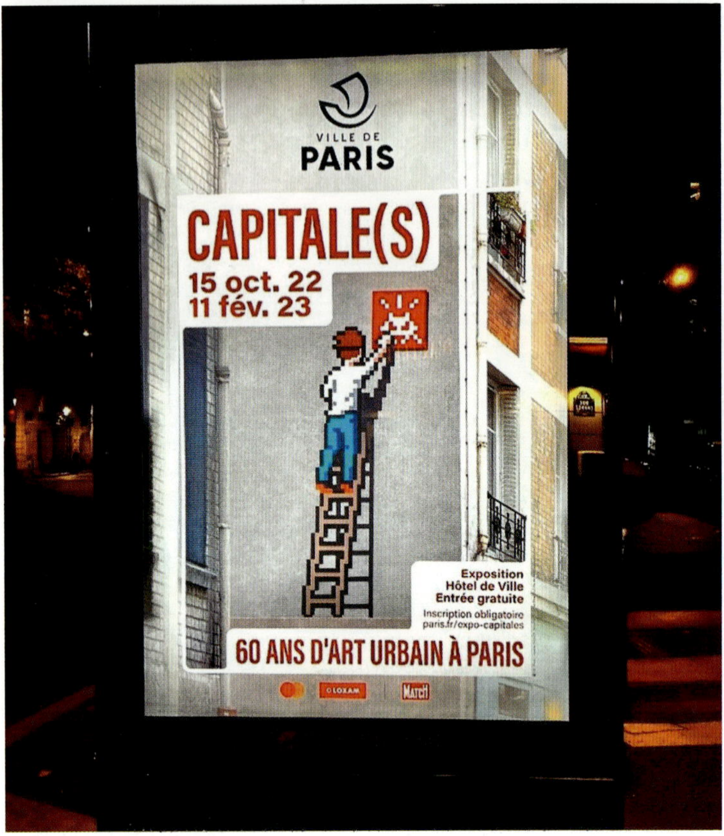

5816 likes

invaderwashere CAPITALE(S),
60 ans d'art urbain à Paris
70 artistes réunis
du 15 octobre 2022 au 11 février 2023 à l'Hotel de Ville
@Paris_maville
Exposition gratuite et accessible à tout.e.s sur réservation :
paris.fr/expo-capitales

View all 112 comments

11 October 2022

invaderwashere 15 October 2022

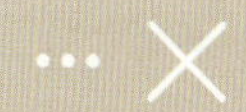

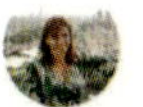

annehidalgo

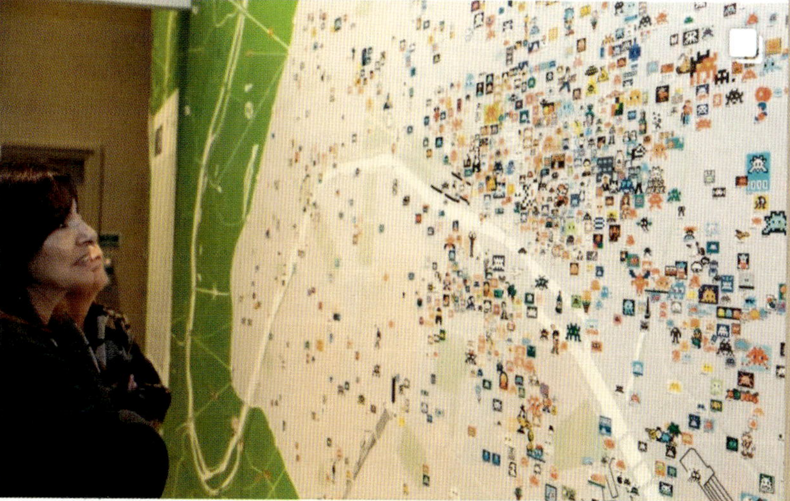

annehidalgo « Paris fait partie de l'ADN du street art » disait Madame et c'est bien vrai. Venez découvrir les créations de pl...

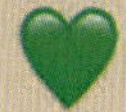

Paris 🙌 @annehidalgo

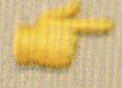

Exposition Capitale(s)

Send message

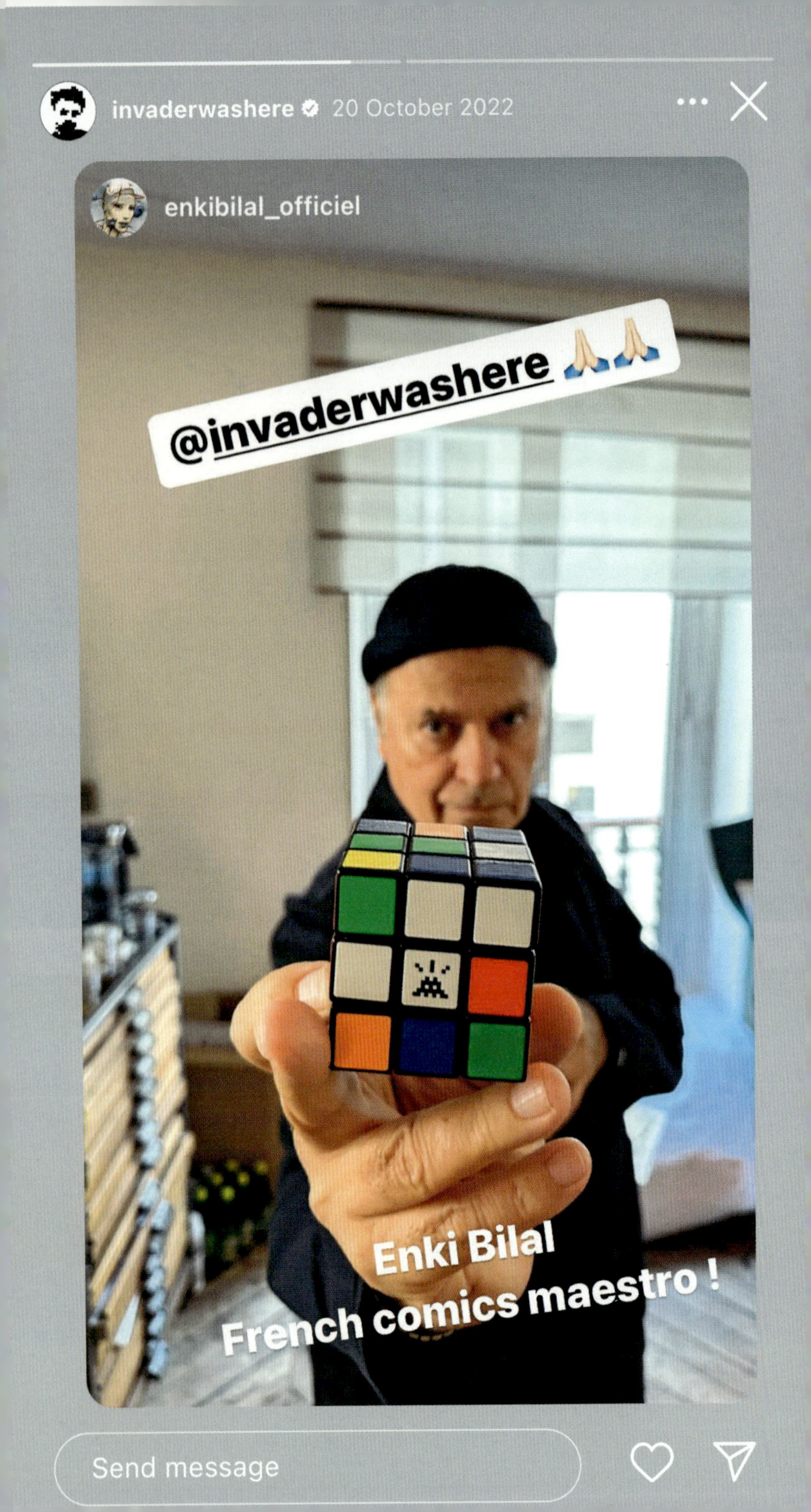

invaderwashere 20 October 2022

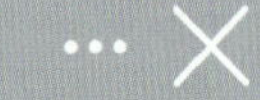

enkibilal_officiel

@invaderwashere 🙏🙏

Enki Bilal
French comics maestro !

Send message

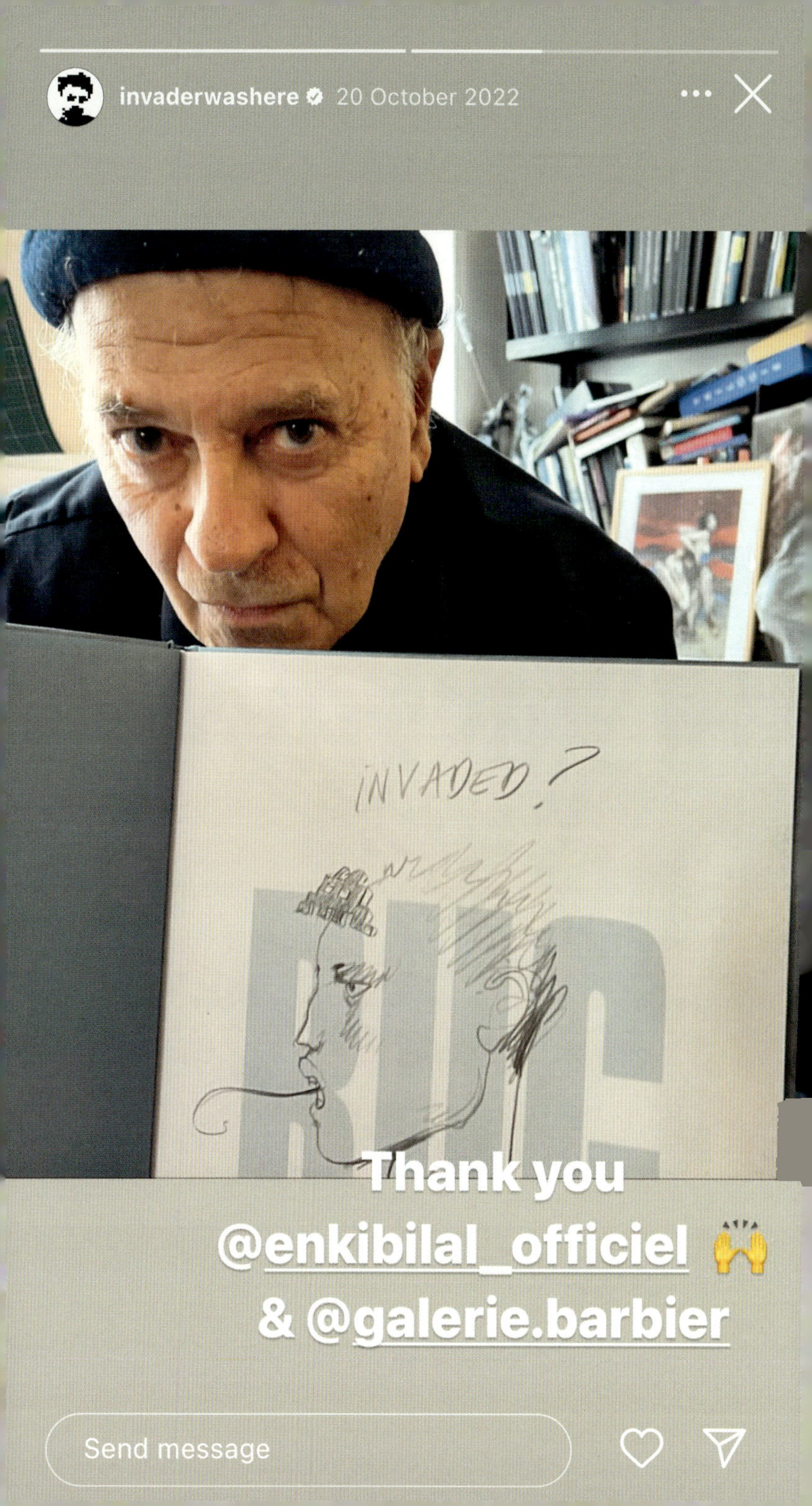

invaderwashere 20 October 2022

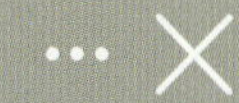

INVADED ?

Thank you
@enkibilal_officiel 🙌
& @galerie.barbier

Send message

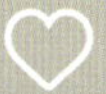

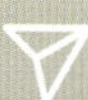

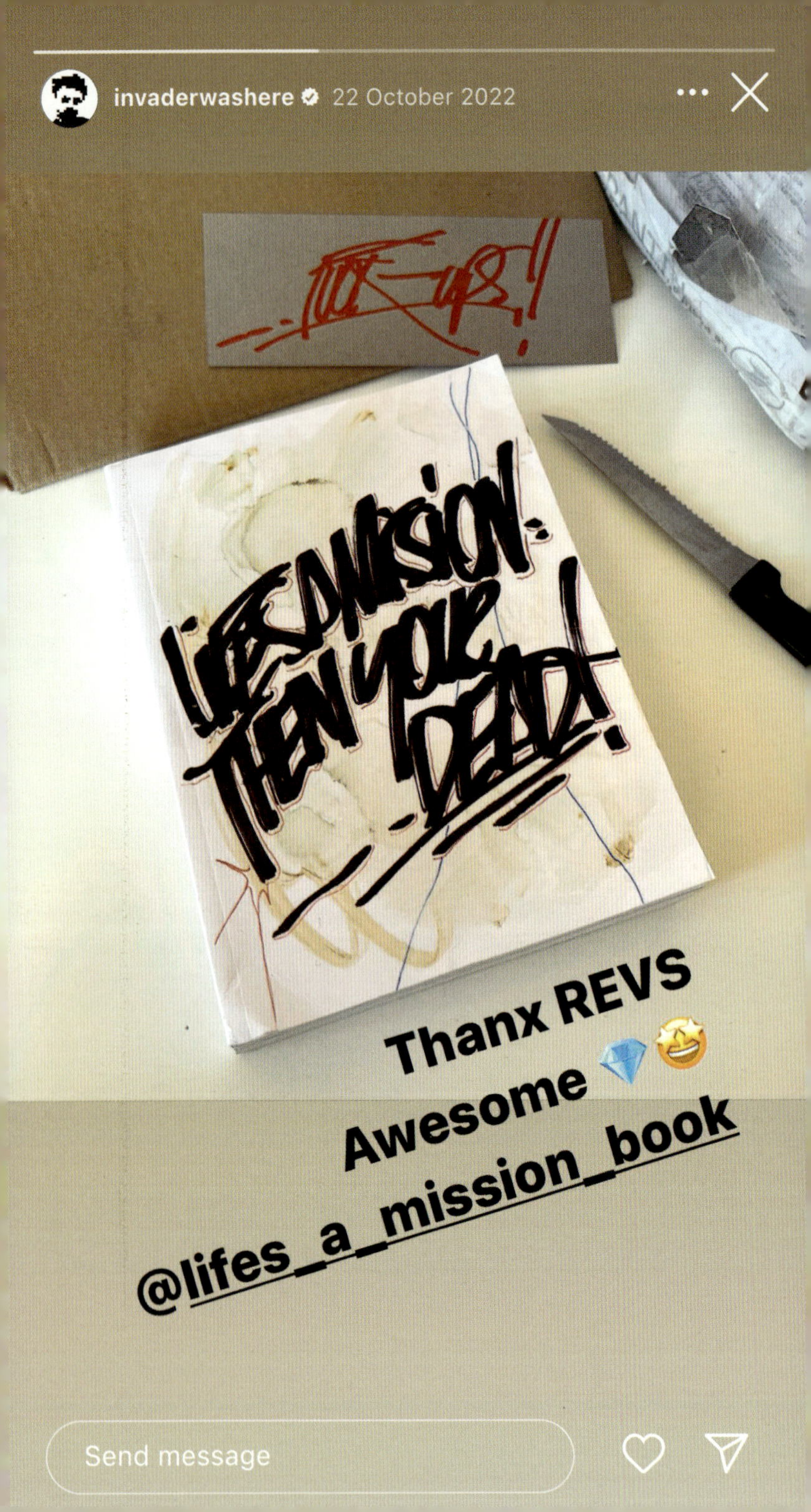

invaderwashere 22 October 2022

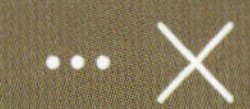

Thanx REVS
Awesome
@lifes_a_mission_book

Send message

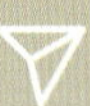

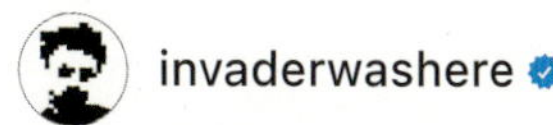

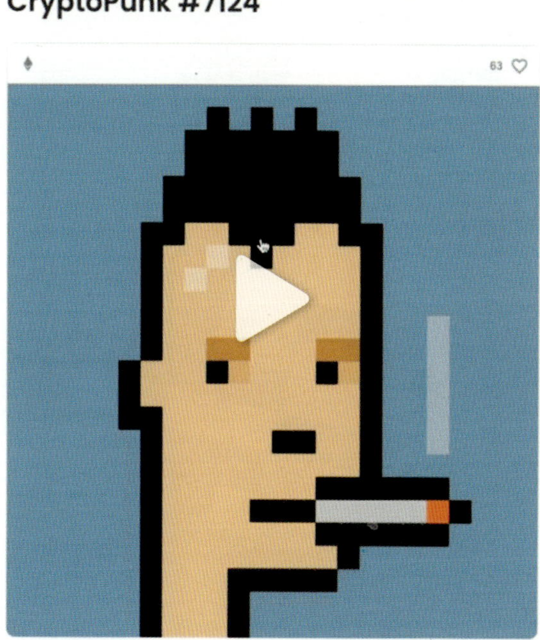

8 892 likes

invaderwashere This Cryptopunk is not a NFT anymore! He stands now on a façade in Paris, just above the place where New Rose, the legendary records shop and label was. #cryptopunks #readymade #nft #cryptoliberation #noblockchain #pixelart #virtual vs #reality #newrose #80s #paris

View all 156 comments

26 October 2022

invaderwashere

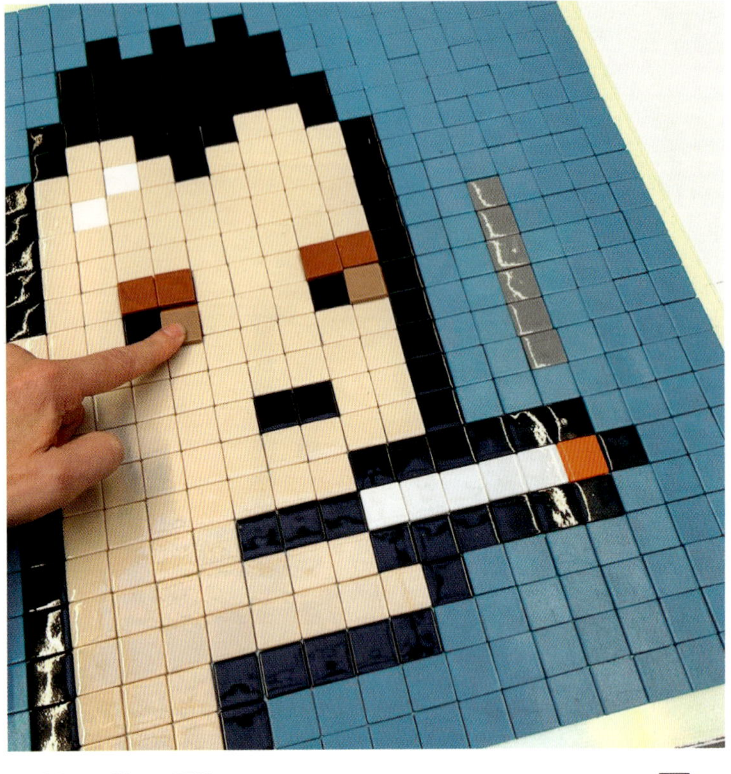

8 892 likes

invaderwashere This Cryptopunk is not a NFT anymore! He stands now on a façade in Paris, just above the place where New Rose, the legendary records shop and label was. #cryptopunks #readymade #nft #cryptoliberation #noblockchain #pixelart #virtual vs #reality #newrose #80s #paris

View all 156 comments

26 October 2022

invaderwashere

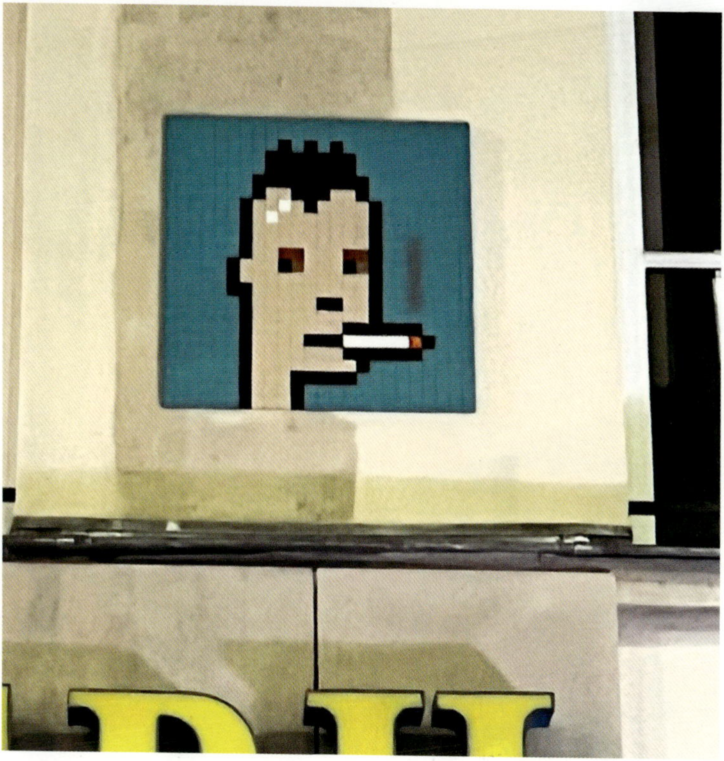

8892 likes

invaderwashere This Cryptopunk is not a NFT anymore! He stands now on a façade in Paris, just above the place where New Rose, the legendary records shop and label was. #cryptopunks #readymade #nft #cryptoliberation #noblockchain #pixelart #virtual vs #reality #newrose #80s #paris

View all 156 comments

26 October 2022

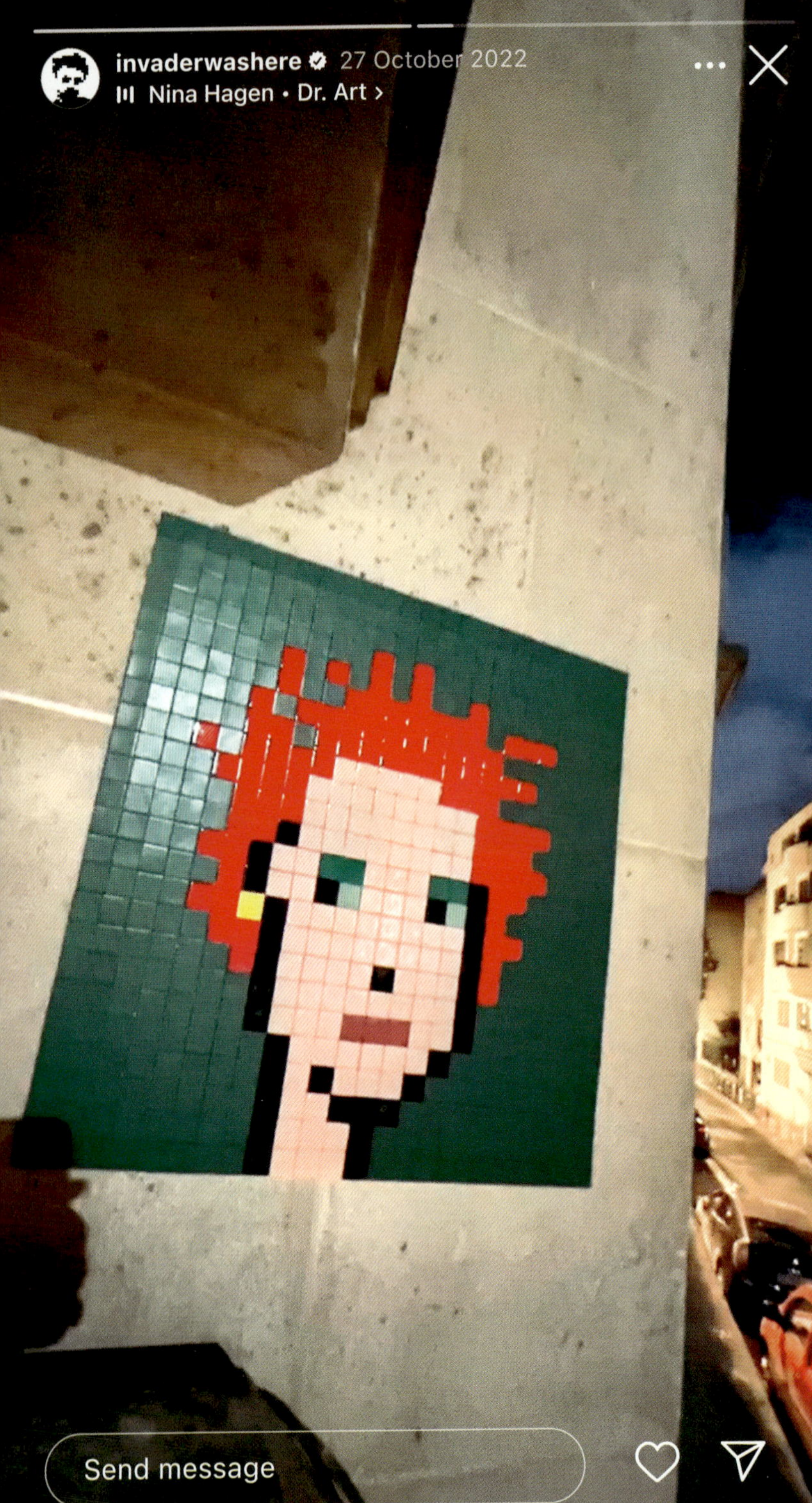

invaderwashere
27 October 2022
Nina Hagen • Dr. Art ›
Send message

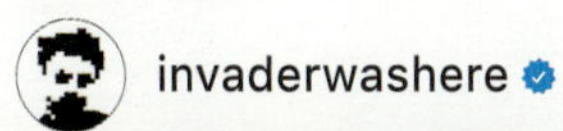

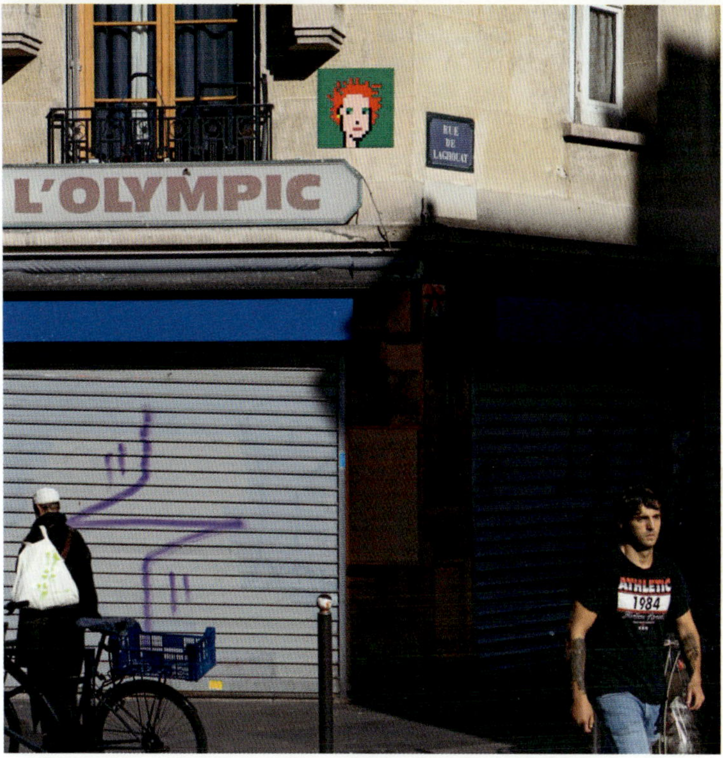

 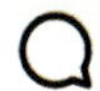  

13 073 likes

invaderwashere Second Cryptopunk to land in the real world... #cryptopunks #24x24px #nft #mosaic #virtual vs #real #digital vs #physical

View all 157 comments

27 October 2022

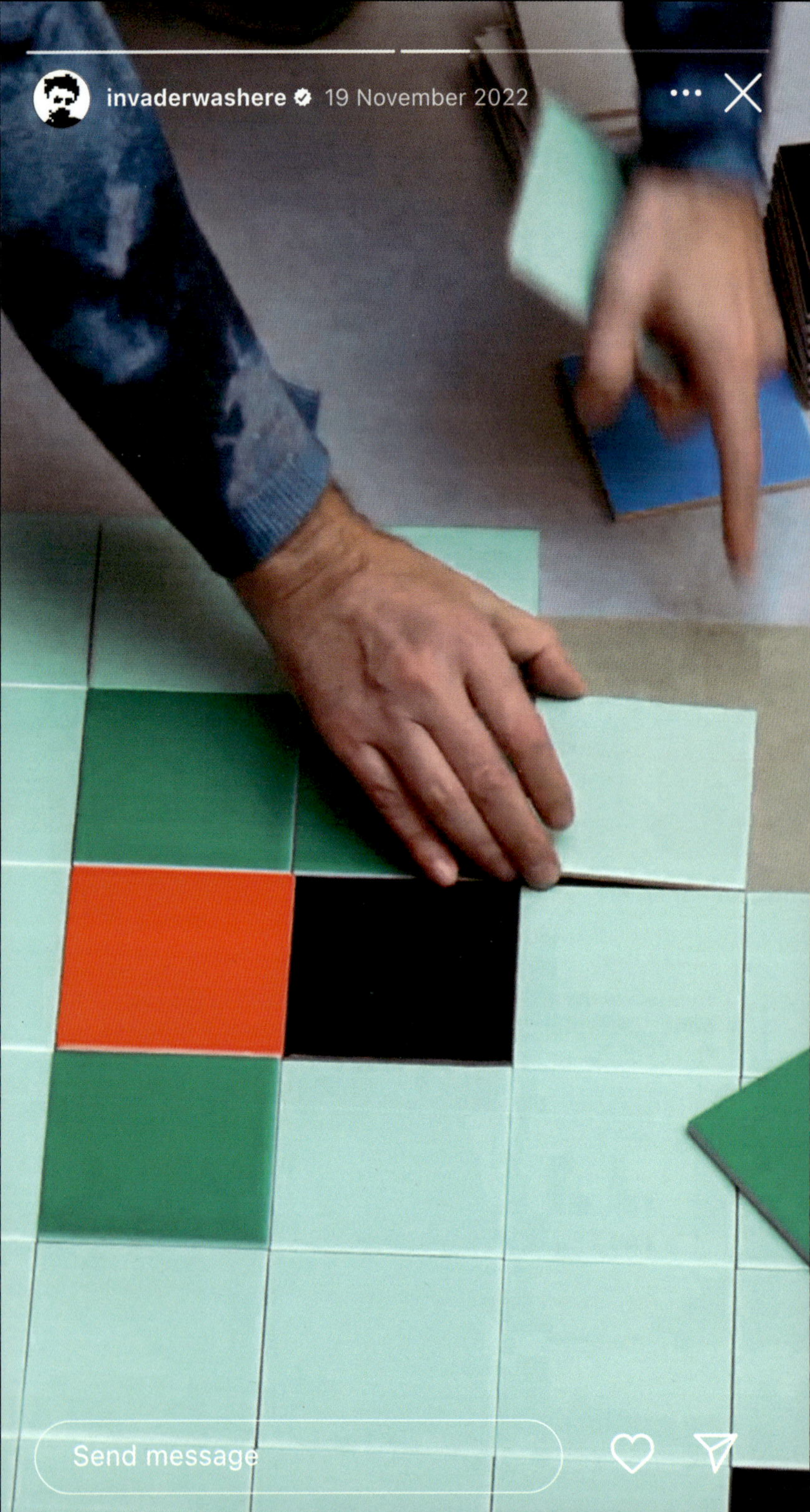

invaderwashere
19 November 2022
Send message

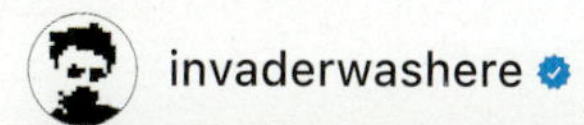

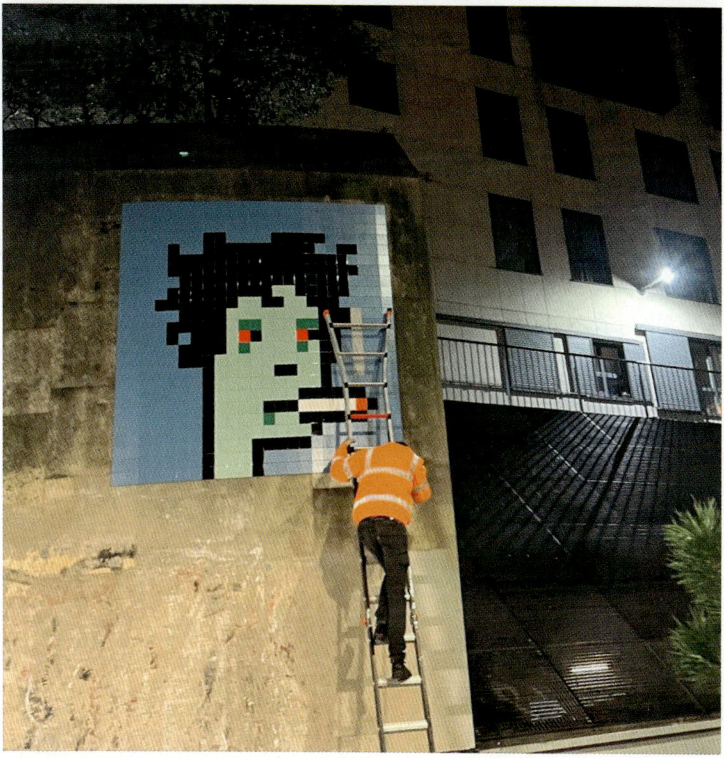

26 555 likes

invaderwashere Cryptopunks go big!!!
#cryptopunkdeshalles #zombiepunk #nonfungiblemosaic #digitalworld vs #physicalworld

View all 288 comments

19 November 2022

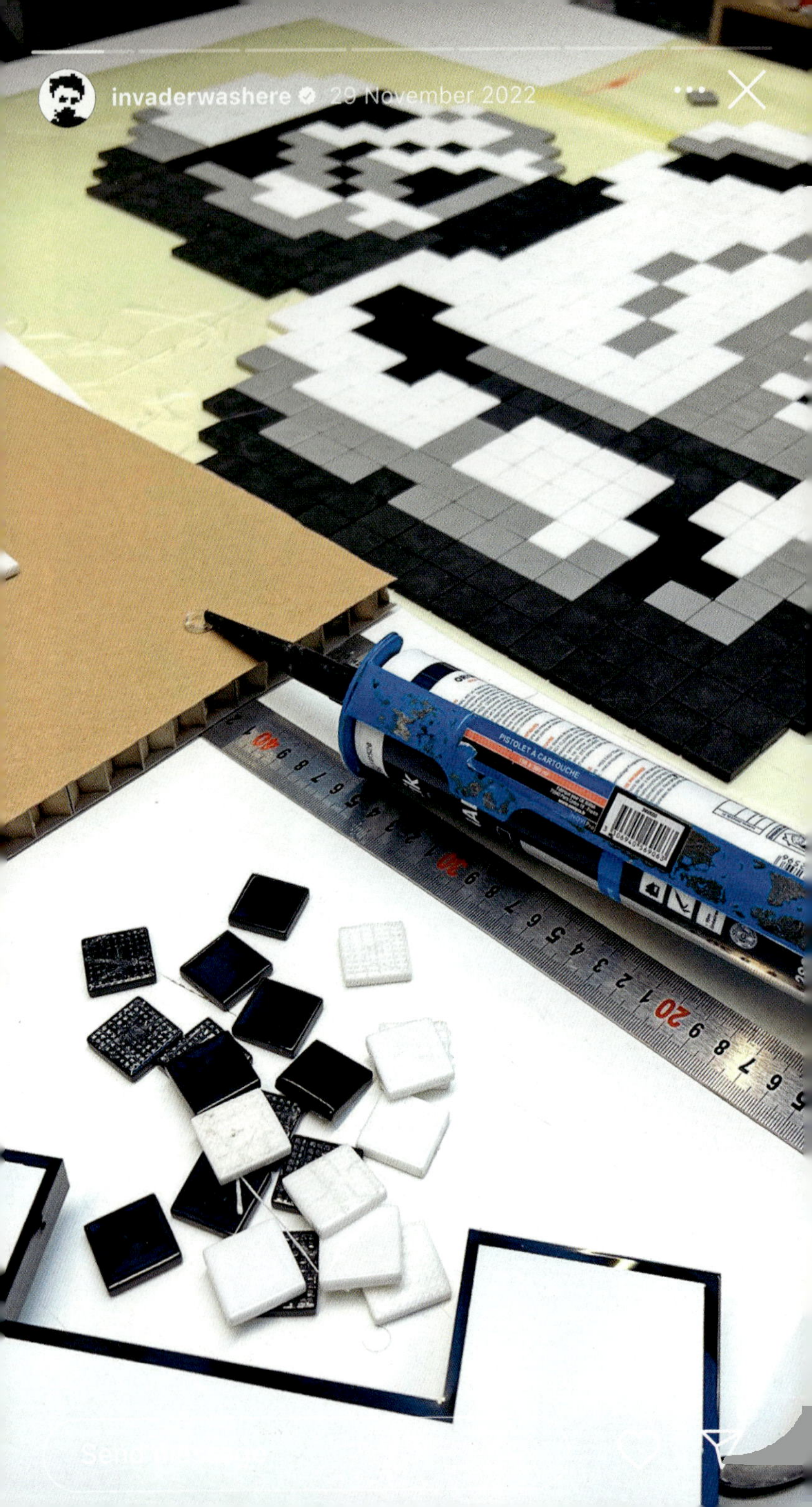
invaderwashere
29 November 2022
PISTOLET À CARTOUCHE

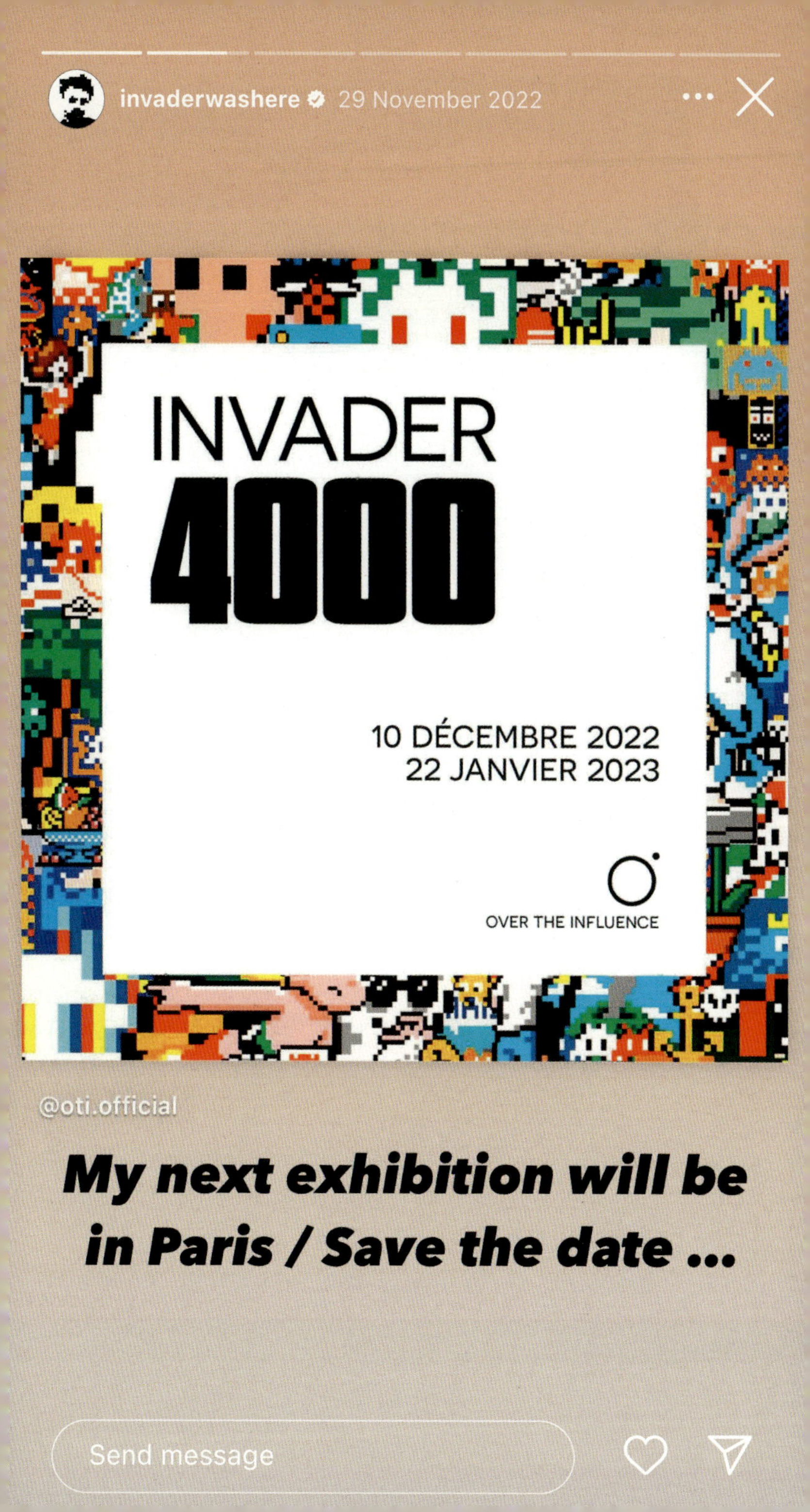

invaderwashere 29 November 2022

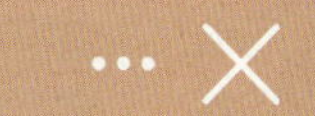

@oti.official

My next exhibition will be in Paris / Save the date ...

Send message

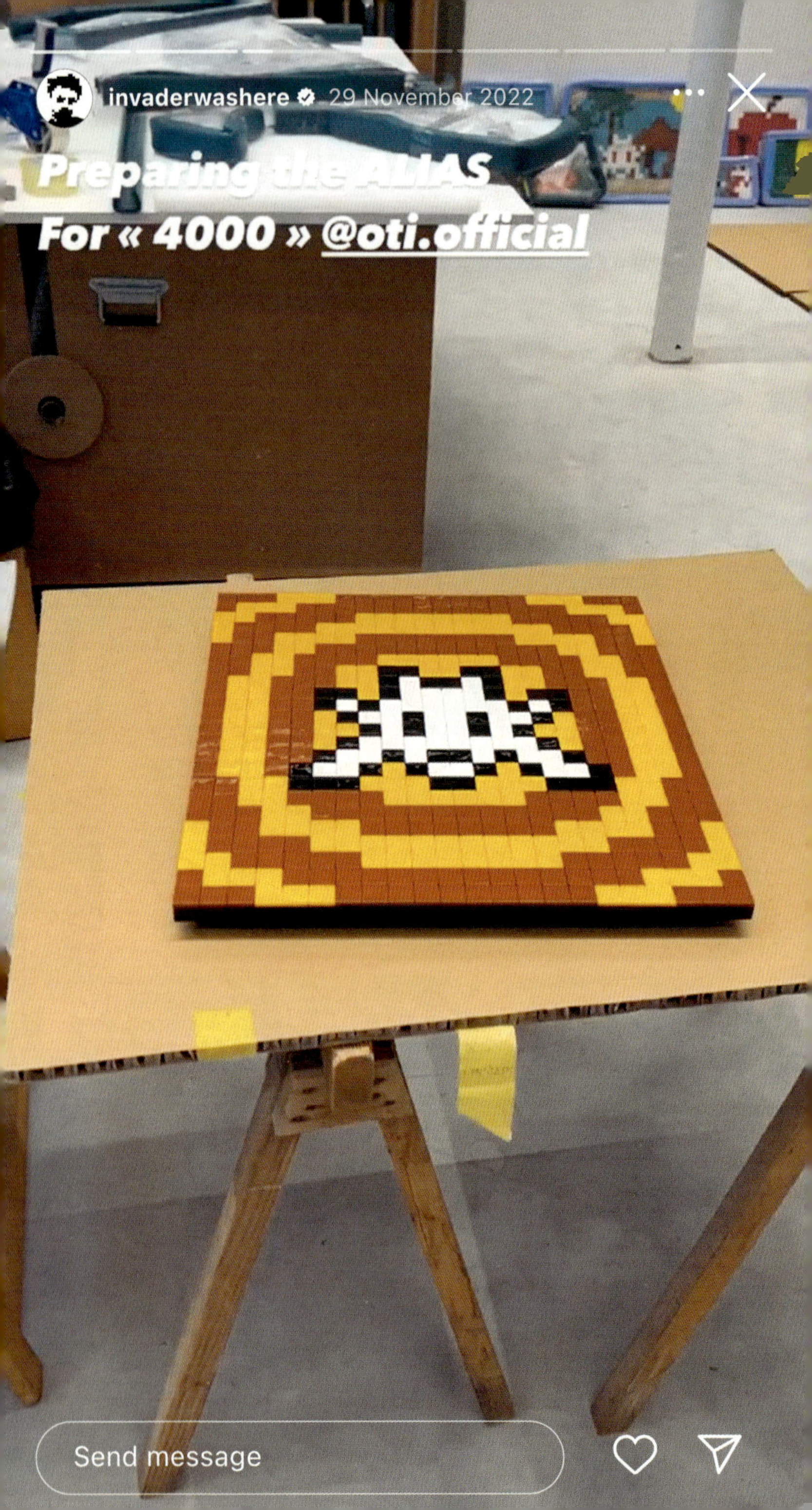
invaderwashere 29 November 2022
Preparing the ALIAS
For « 4000 » @oti.official
Send message

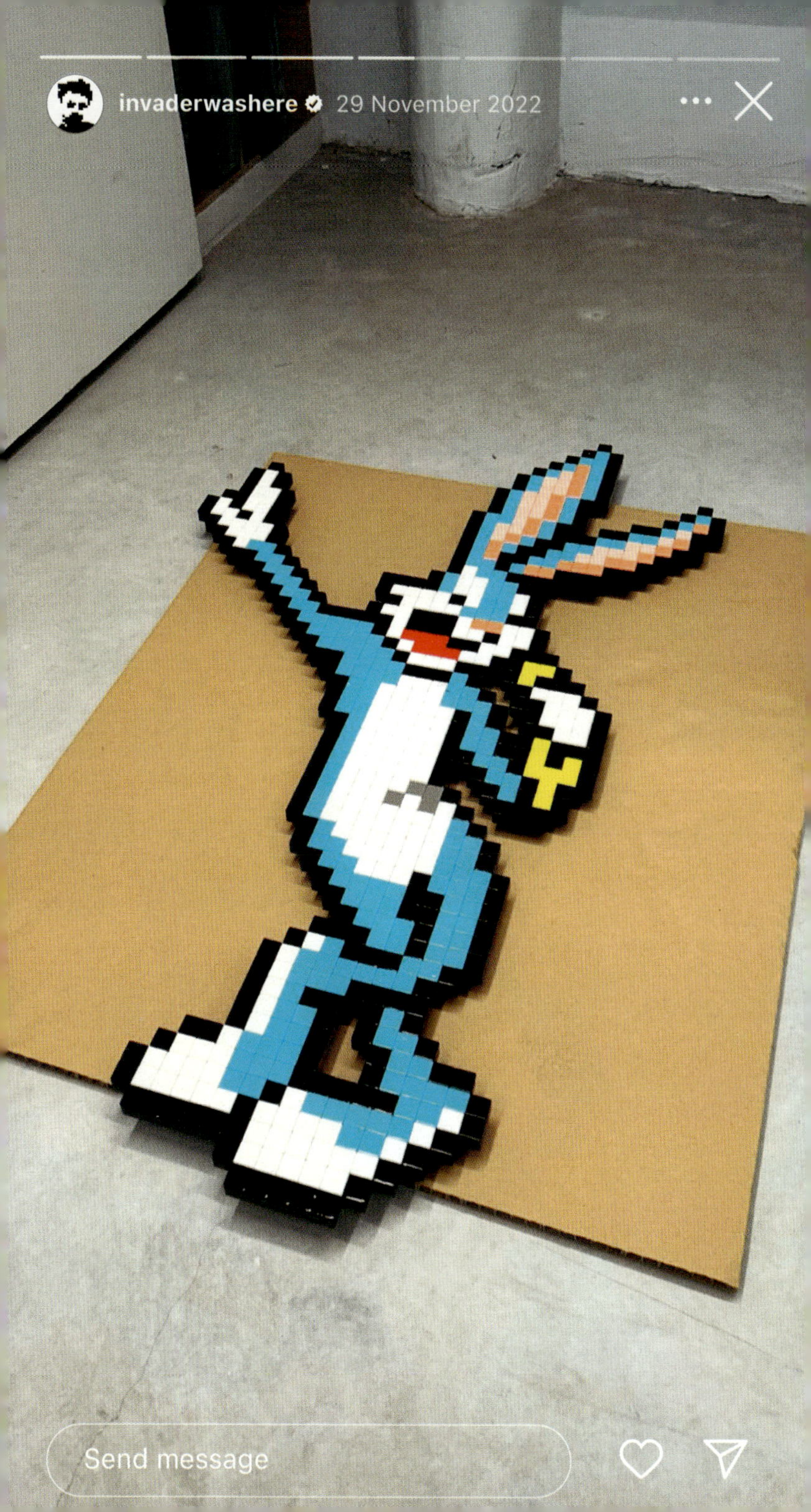

invaderwashere 29 November 2022

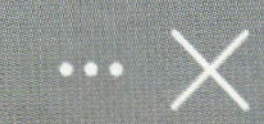

Send message

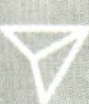

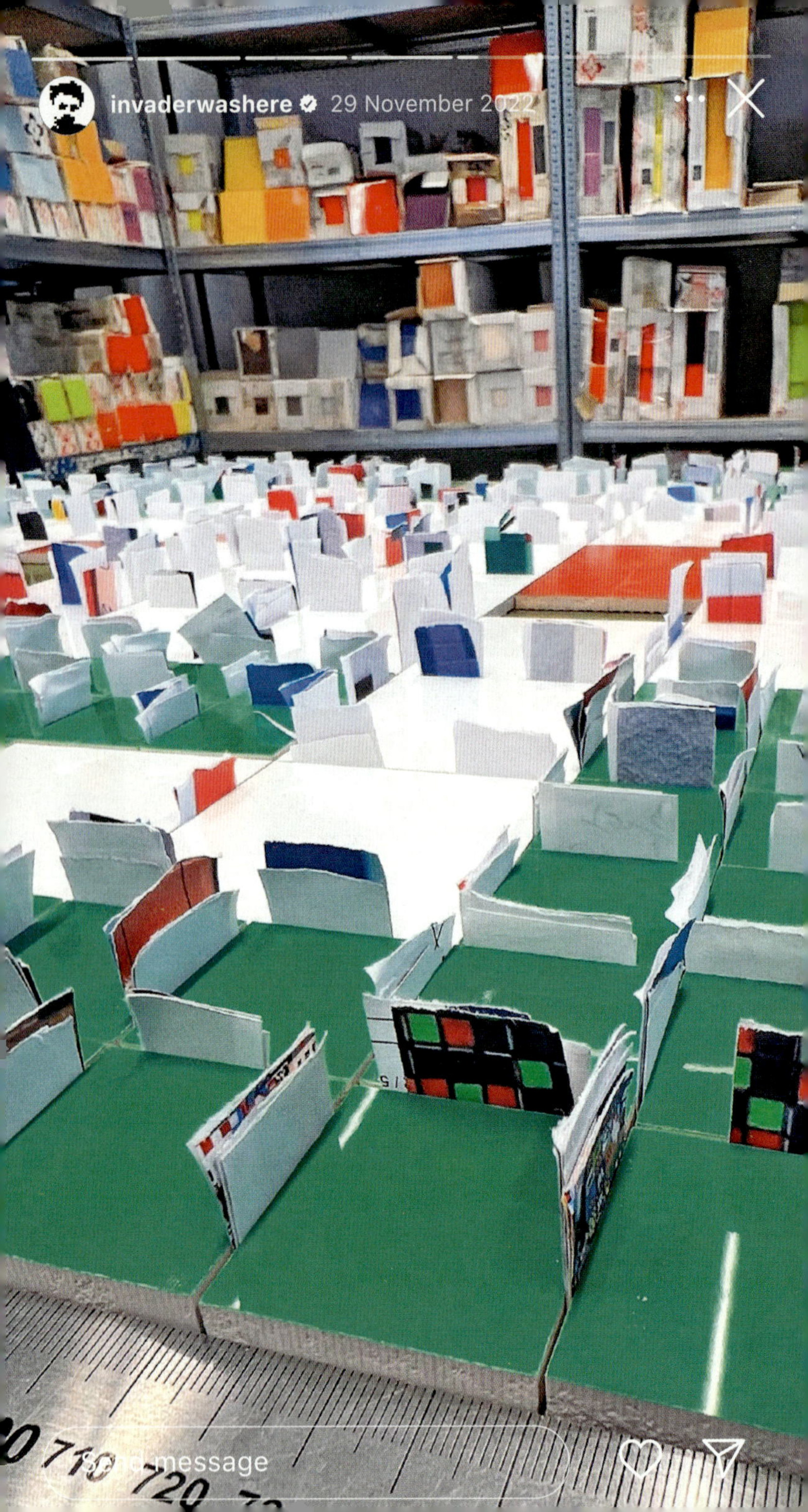
invaderwashere
29 November 2022
Send message

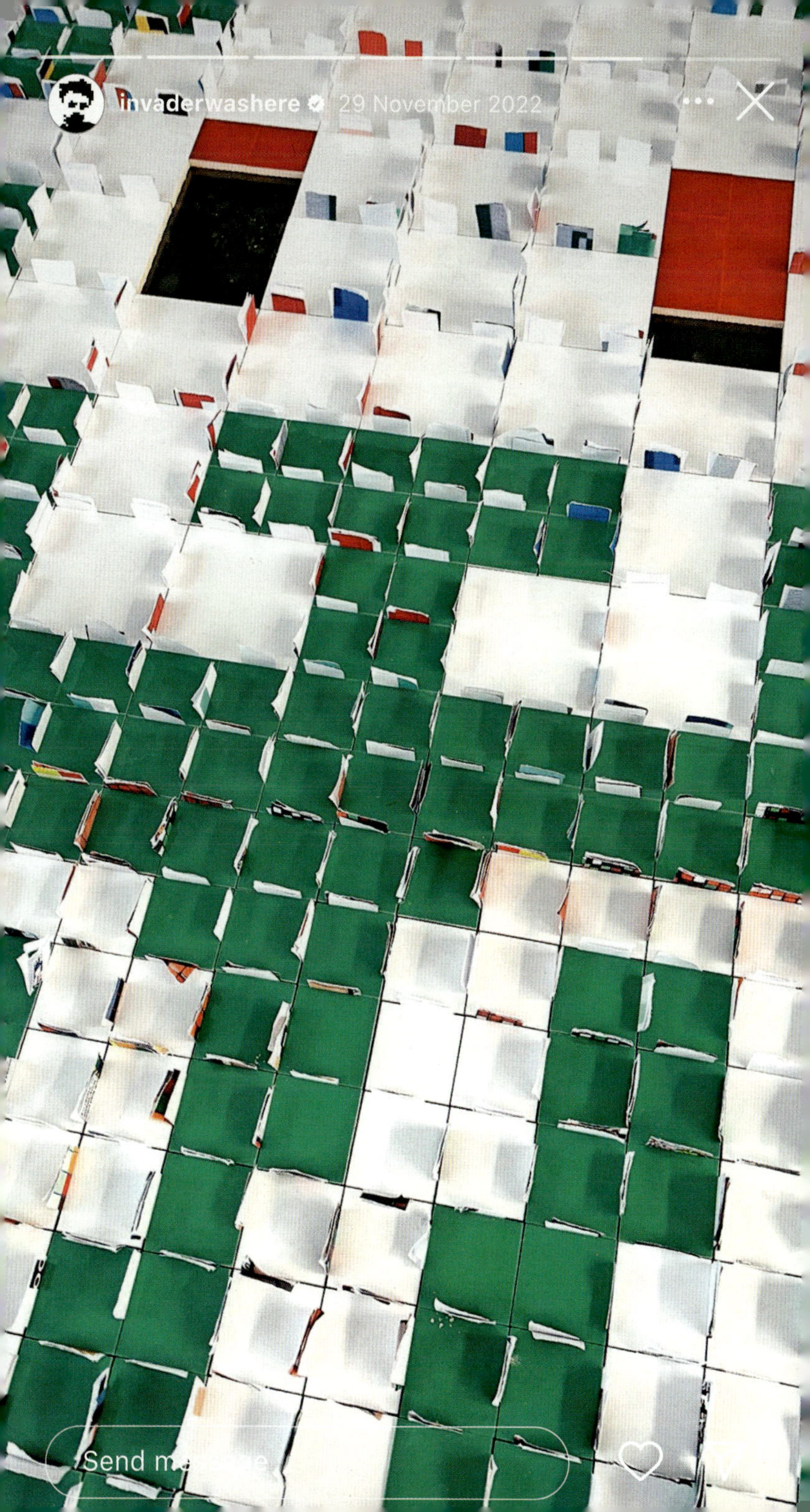
invaderwashere
29 November 2022

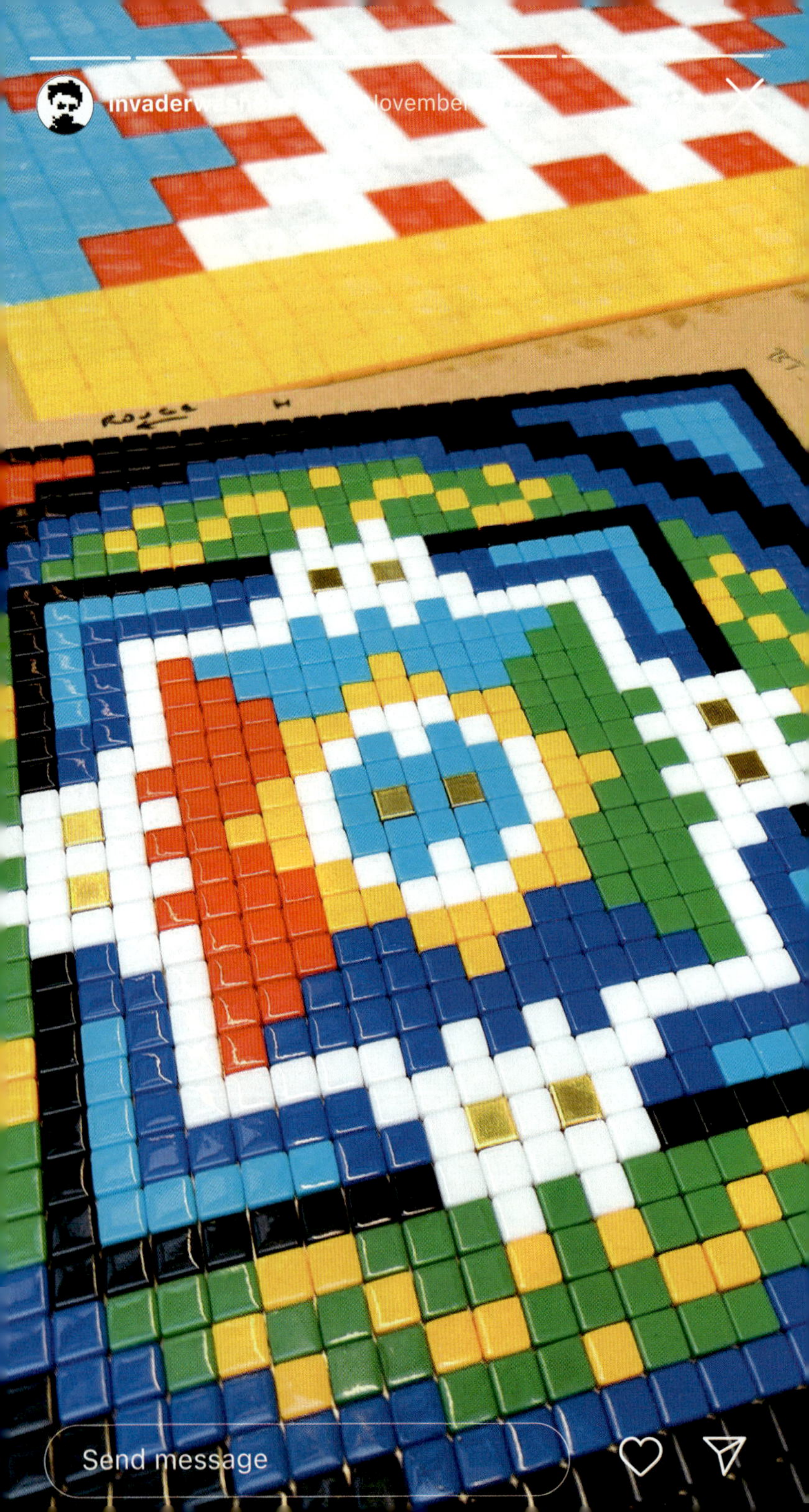
Send message

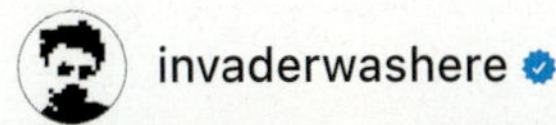

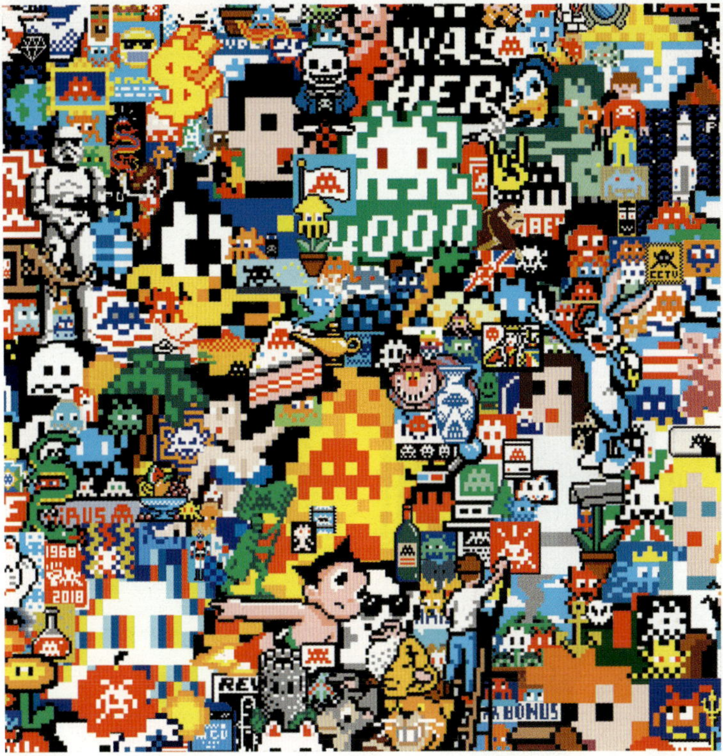

18 330 likes

invaderwashere 4000, solo show at Over The Influence, Paris / Opening: Dec 10 2022, save the date! This show is a celebration of my 4000 first mosaics installed around the world, and my return for an official exhibition in a Parisian gallery after 11 years of absence. @oti.official

View all 252 comments

29 November 2022

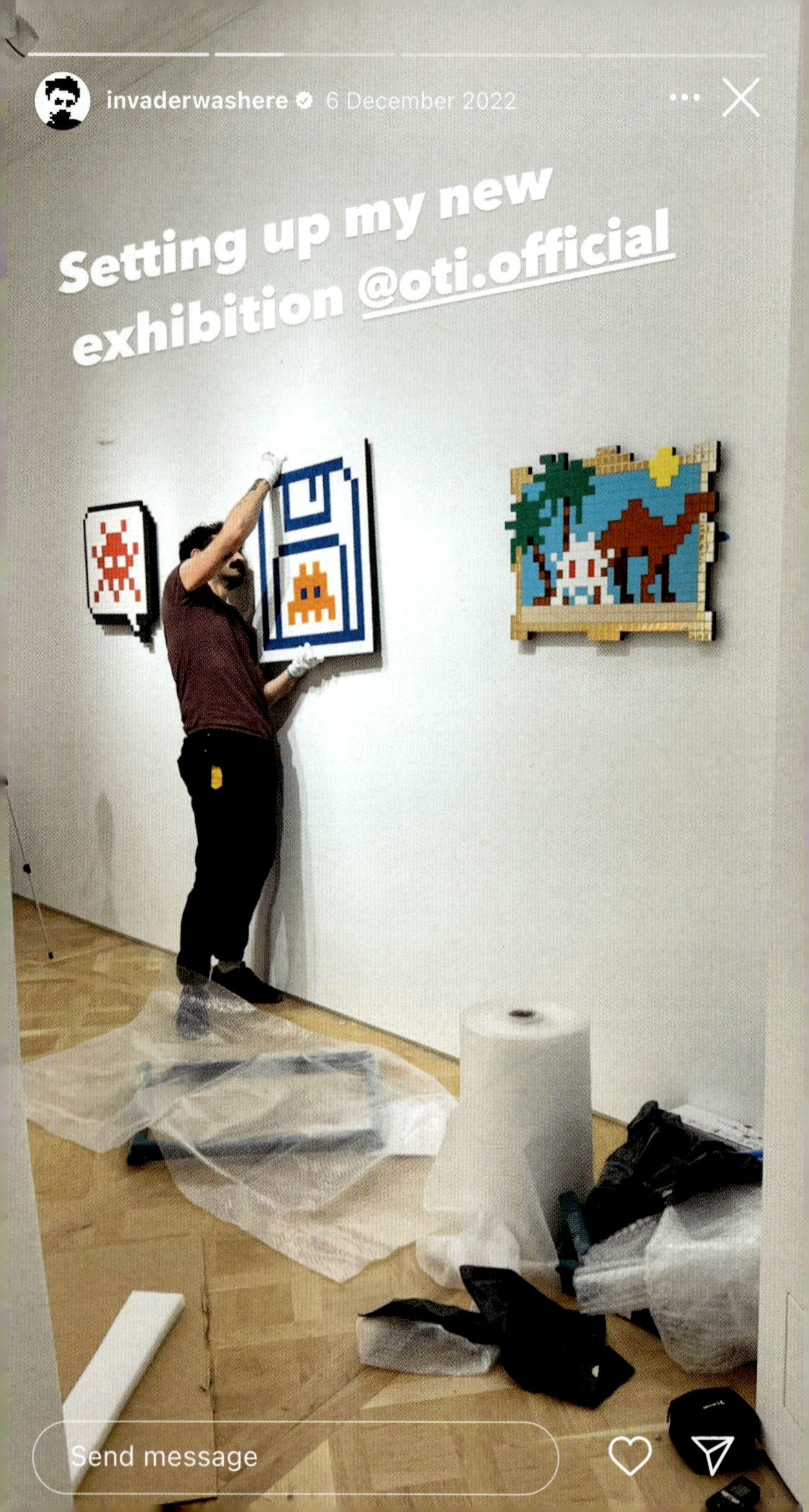

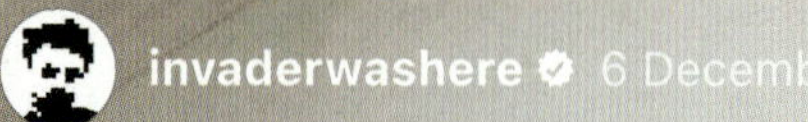

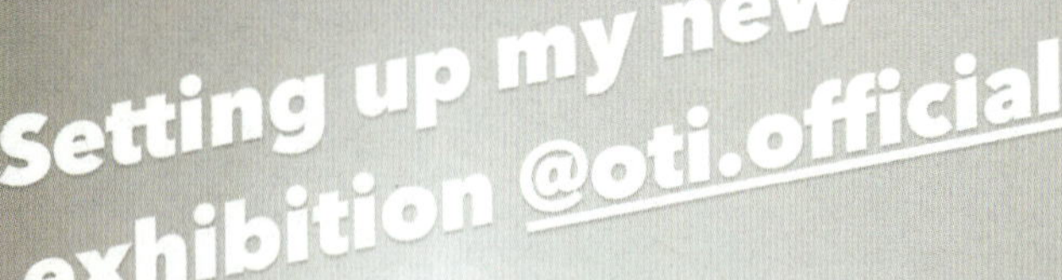

Send message

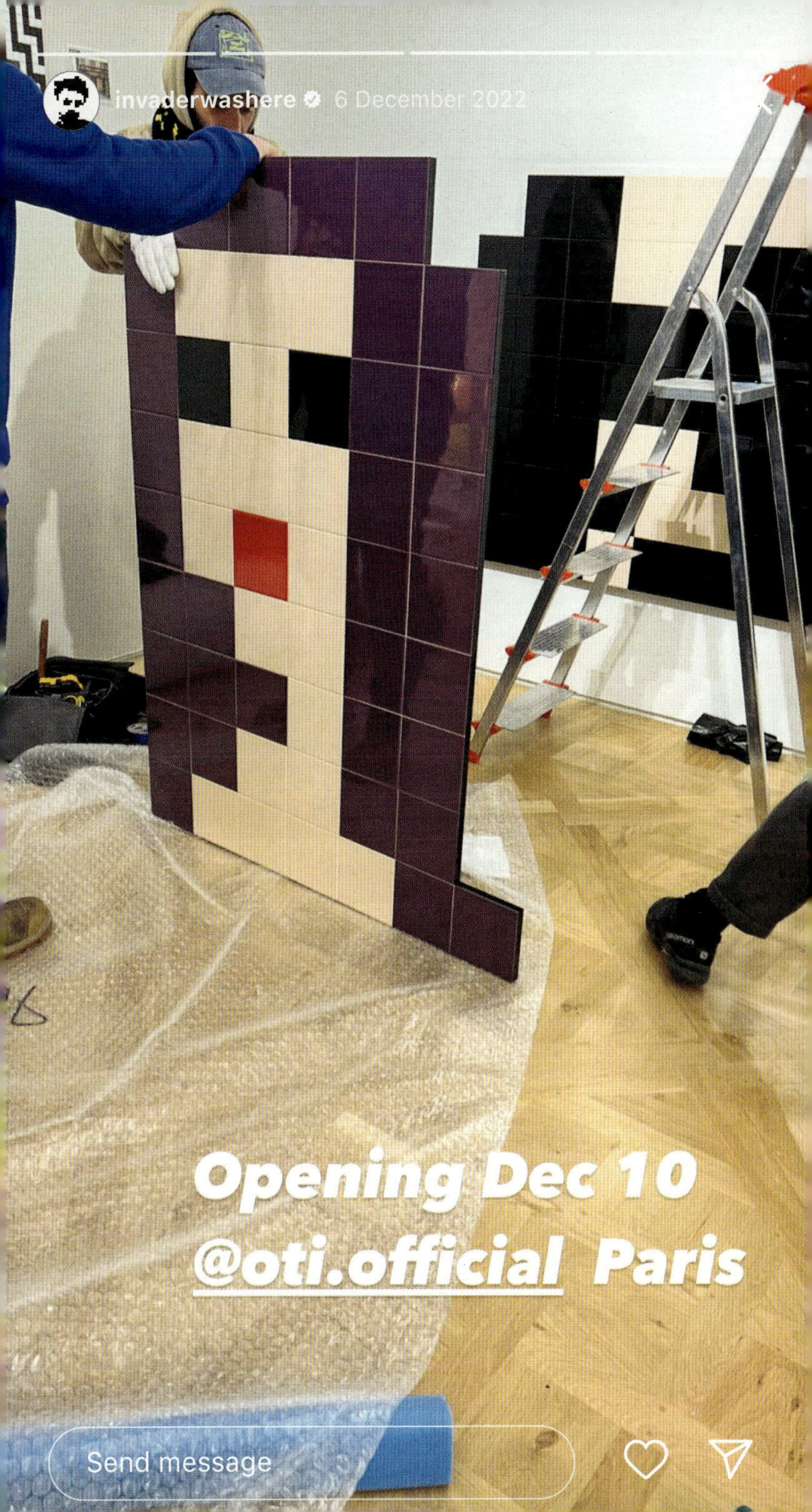
invaderwashere
6 December 2022
Opening Dec 10
@oti.official Paris
Send message

invaderwashere 9 December 2022

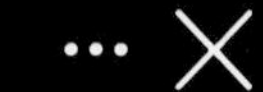

4000
The complete guide to the space invaders

Sortie demain
Samedi 10 décembre
en librarie

Send message

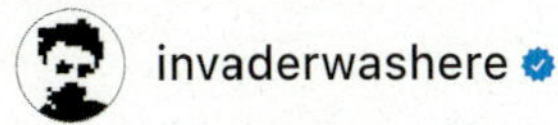

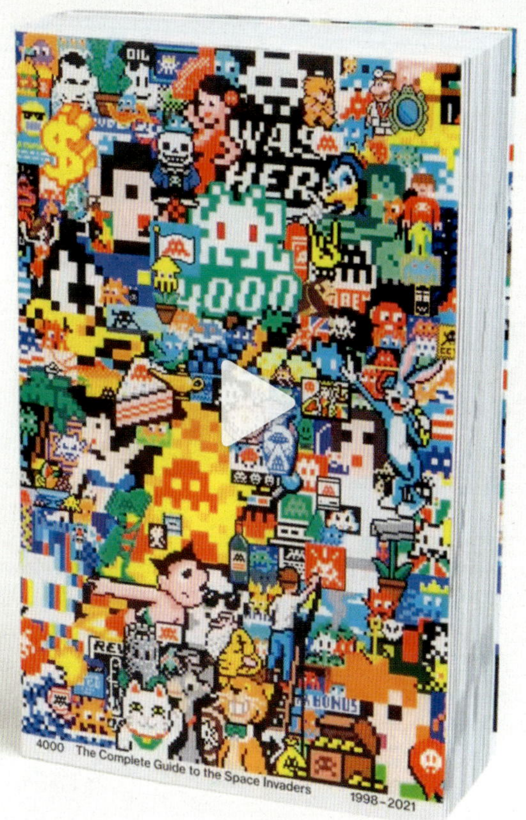

11426 likes

invaderwashere On the occasion of the «4000» exhibition, I am publishing a 1024-pages book which lists the first 4000 space invaders installed in the world. It will be available tomorrow in bookstores in France, and online in January on the Space Shop for the international.
#pocketencyclopedia #ultimateinvasionguide #invasionbible #artbook #4000

View all 298 comments

9 December 2022

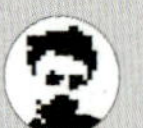

invaderwashere 10 December 2022

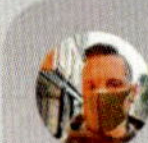

rafparis

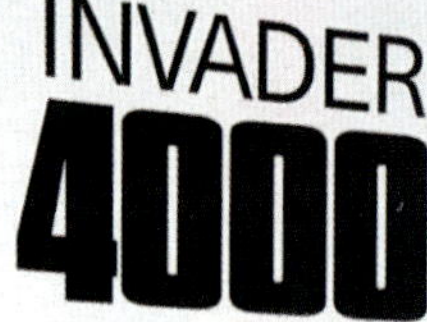

10.12.2022 — 22.01.2023

Over The Influence est fière de présenter *4000*, une exposition d'Invader, un des artistes vivants les plus énigmatiques et radicaux de notre époque.

« Plus qu'une simple pratique artistique mon projet Space Invaders est un véritable engagement et un mode de vie. Depuis plus de vingt ans, mon modus operandi consiste à parcourir le monde pour l'envahir secrètement avec mes mosaïques. Il s'agit d'une immersion totale comme dans un jeu vidéo que j'aurais transposé dans la réalité. »

Cette exposition est une célébration des 4 000 premières mosaïques installées par l'artiste, à travers le parcours d'une quarantaine d'alias de son choix. En langage informatique, un alias est un fichier qui renvoie vers un autre fichier source. Dans le cas d'Invader, il s'agit de l'unique réplique d'une mosaïque installée *in situ*, accompagnée des métadonnées liées à cette mosaïque source.

Over The Influence is proud to present *4000*, an exhibition by Invader, one of the most mysterious and radical living artist of our times.

« Much more than an artistic undertaking, my Space Invaders project is a lifetime commitment. For more than twenty years, my modus operandi has been to travel around the world and secretly invade public spaces with my mosaics. It is a full immersion just like a video game I would have transposed into reality. »

This exhibition celebrates the first 4,000 mosaics installed by Invader, through the artist's personal selection of 40 aliases. In computer terms, an alias is a small file that represents a source file to which it gives immediate access. In the case of Invader, it is the unique replica of an *in situ* mosaic, with all the metadata relating to the original artwork.

@INVADERWASHERE

@oti.official

Send message

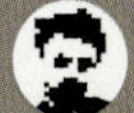

invaderwashere 10 December 2022

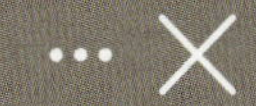

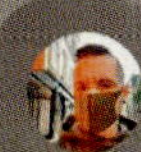

rafparis

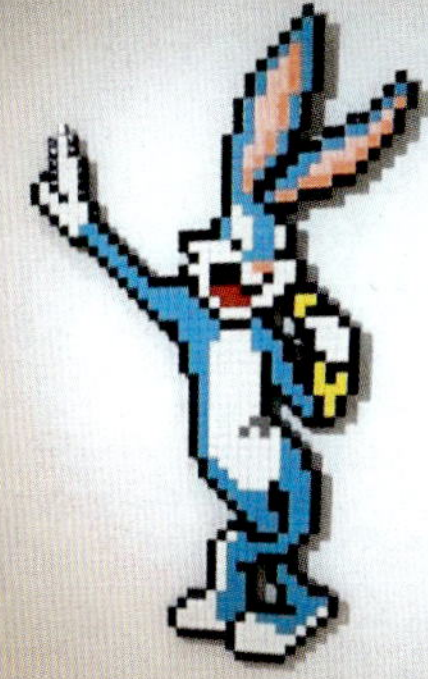

@INVADERWASHERE

Send message

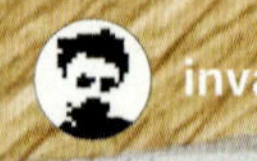

invaderwashere 12 December 2022

MARDI 13 DÉCEMBRE 2022
78e ANNÉE – N° 24241
3,20 € – FRANCE MÉTROPOLITAINE
WWW.LEMONDE.FR –
FONDATEUR : HUBERT BEUVE-MÉRY
DIRECTEUR : JÉRÔME FENOGLIO

Le Mon[…]

NOTRE BAROMÈTRE D[…]

[…]s d'Invader, à la galerie

[…] street-artiste français qui […]aïques dans le monde, à la […]ion qui lui est consacrée à Paris

foules de fans grâce à son application-jeu FlashInvaders aux quelque 265 000 participants, a franchi le cap symbolique des 4 000 mosaïques collées dans 80 villes à travers le monde. Pour ce flash-back, il a fait une sélection de 40 pièces – soit 1 % de l'ensemble –, en choisissant de panacher les lieux, les époques et les styles. On y croise l'immense *Joconde* de la rue du Louvre, le *Bugs Bunny croquant une banane* dans le quartier du Marais, à Paris, un Trooper de *Star Wars* sur un bâtiment qui a servi de décor au film à Djerba, un *Astroboy* et un petit sushi à Tokyo, un nuage londonien (issu du jeu *Mario*), un mandala au Bhoutan, mais aussi Bénarès, Perth, New York, Miami. Mar[…] révèle la carte d'identité dissimulée dans son support, avec la photo de l'œuvre prise dans son environnement urbain d'origine.

« Au début, je choisissais où j'allais coller mes mosaïques en me promenant avec ma besace la nuit.

Le 4 000e collage d'Invader à Potosi, en Bolivie, en 2021.
INVADER

Puis, peu à peu, j'ai fait des repérages en amont et imaginé des pièces sur mesure pour des emplacements. Avec un effet caméléon quant aux thèmes et aux couleurs, dans le sens […] fond dans le d[…] Ca[…] jamais été de vandaliser des lieux, c'est une invasion pacifique et artistique », détaille l'artiste. Ces im[…] mettent de ne pas se limiter aux centres-villes : *« J'essaie de comprendre les villes, et ceux qui partent à la recherche des mosaïques sont amenés à en découvrir […]rentes facettes et des lieux intéressants, mais plus à la marge. »*

vais rien de convaincant. Je me s[…] dit, quand même, tu as plus […] 600 000 personnes qui te su[…] sur Instagram, essaie de faire […] la communauté. J'ai donc […] en disant : "Vous ne de[…] où va être le 4 000e […] plus de 800 réponses. Au […] tout ça, un gars me conse[…] ler à Potosi, en Bolivie, […] altitude. […] ce nom […] fait une recherche […] là, coup de foudre : « […] réussite, isolé au-dess[…] pour […] min[…] dép[…] cle. » Il y dissém[…] 53 mosaïques. L'« […] d'inspiration in[…] […] au cœur d[…]

« Mon intention n'a jamais été […]

« Marquer le coup »

[…]he du 4 000e collage, […] fois l'ar-

Invasion du Monde… @lemondefr 🙏🙏🙏

Send message

artnet news

People

'I Wanted This Project to Have a Planetary Dimension': Street Artist Invader on Installing More Than 4,000 of His Mosaic Works Around the World

To celebrate the milestone, Over the Influence gallery in Paris is offering duplicates of some of the artist's well known public installations, priced between €38,000-€500,000.

Anna Sansom • December 12, 2022

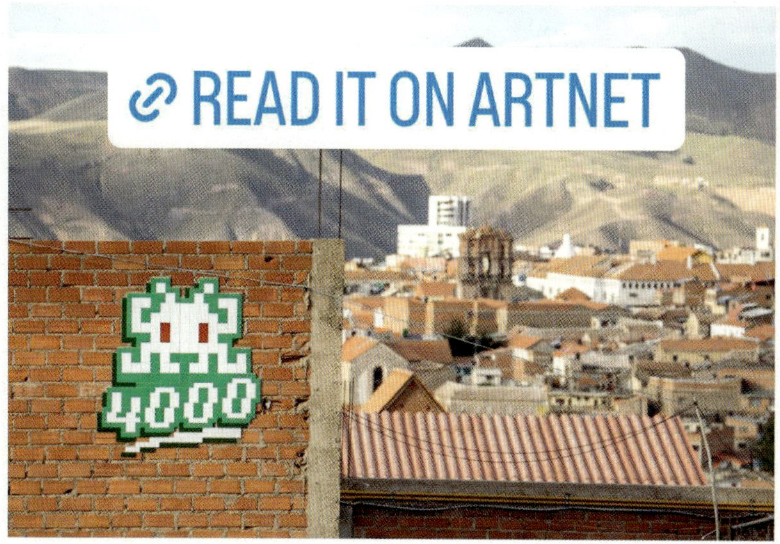

Invader's 4,000th mosaic installed last year in Potosí, Bolivia, a town 4,000 meters above sea level. Photo:

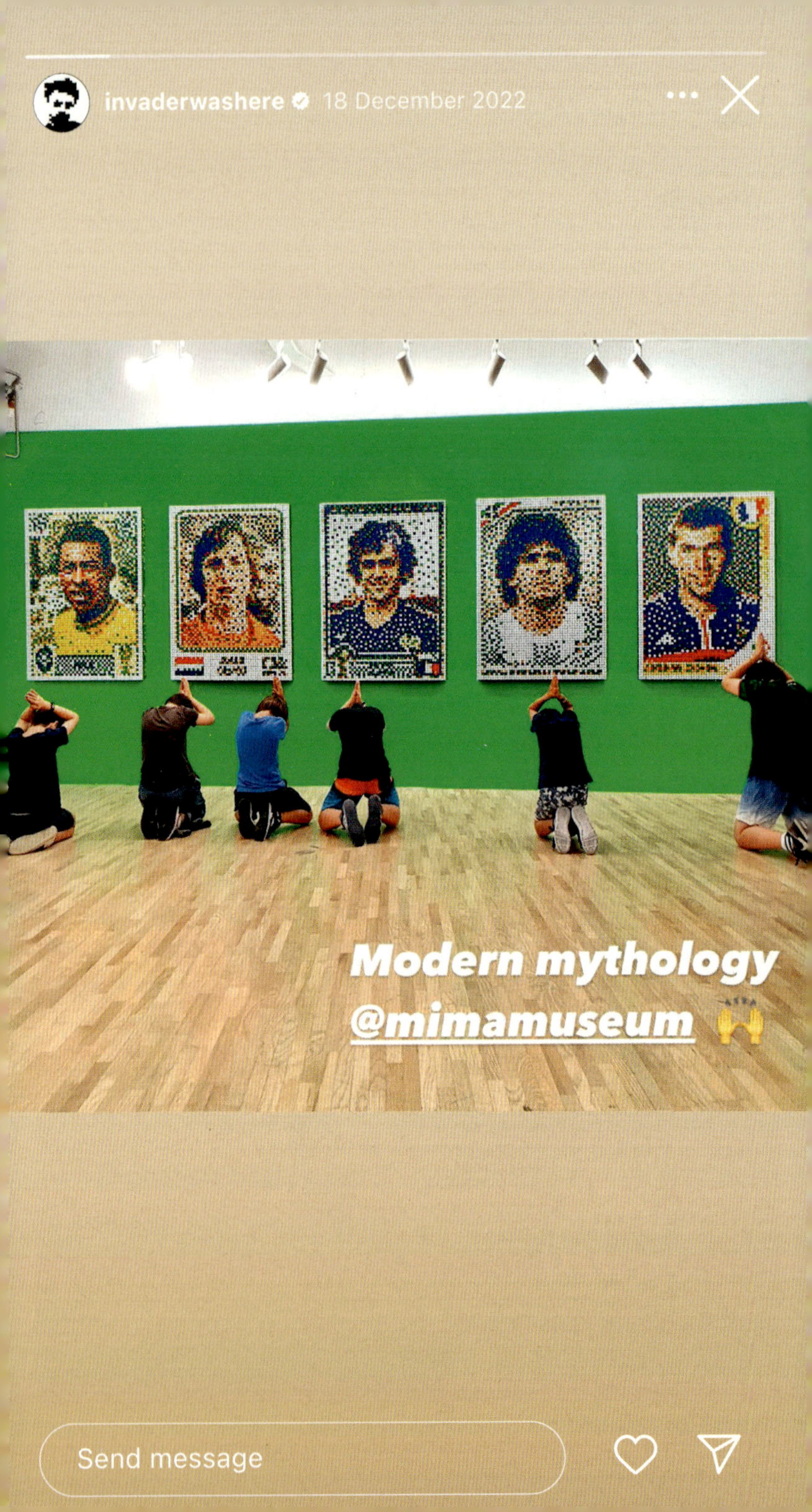

Modern mythology
@mimamuseum 🙌

Send message
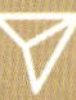

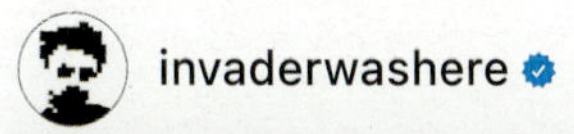

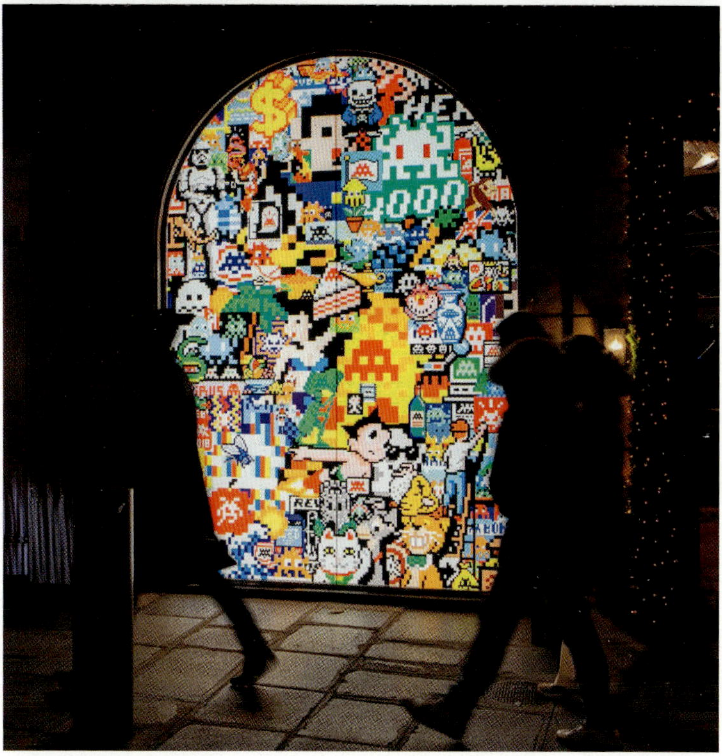

  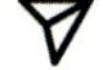  

20 010 likes

invaderwashere Some views of "4000" at Over the Influence Paris. Until Jan. 22 2023 @oti.official

View all 191 comments

20 December 2022

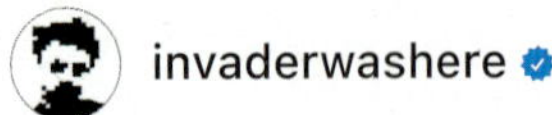

INVADER
4000
10.12.2022 — 22.01.2023

Over The Influence est fière de présenter *4000*, une exposition d'Invader, un des artistes vivants les plus énigmatiques et radicaux de notre époque.

« Plus qu'une simple pratique artistique mon projet Space Invaders est un véritable engagement et un mode de vie. Depuis plus de vingt ans, mon modus operandi *consiste à parcourir le monde pour l'envahir secrètement avec mes mosaïques. Il s'agit d'une immersion totale comme dans un jeu vidéo que j'aurais transposé dans la réalité. »*

Cette exposition est une célébration des 4 000 premières mosaïques installées par l'artiste, à travers le parcours d'une quarantaine d'alias de son choix. En langage informatique, un alias est un fichier qui renvoie vers un autre fichier source. Dans le cas d'Invader, il s'agit de l'unique réplique d'une mosaïque installée *in situ*, accompagnée des métadonnées liées à cette mosaïque source.

 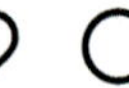  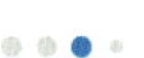 

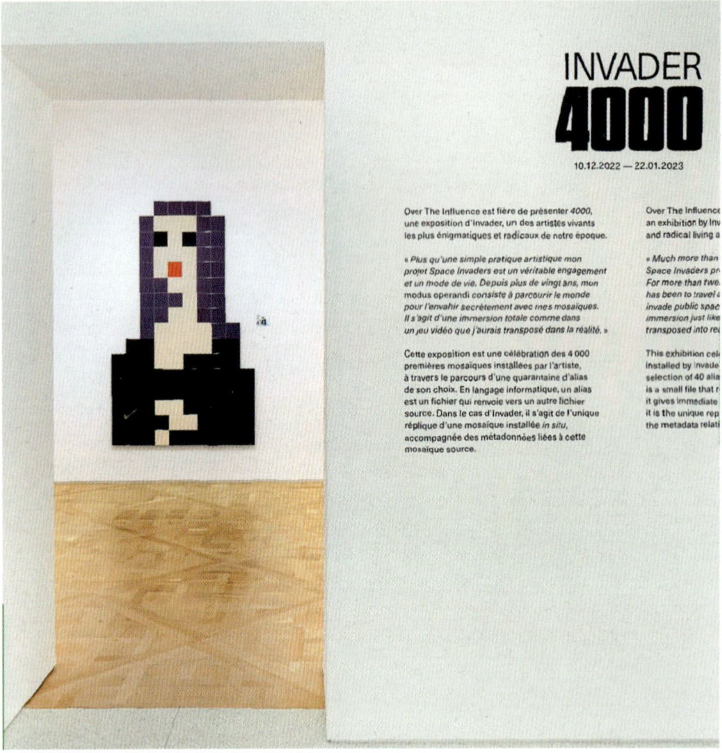

20 010 likes

invaderwashere Some views of "4000" at Over the Influence Paris. Until Jan. 22 2023 @oti.official

View all 191 comments

20 December 2022

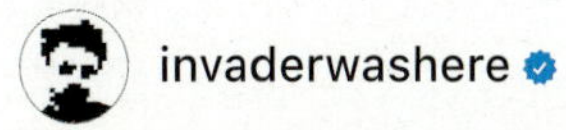

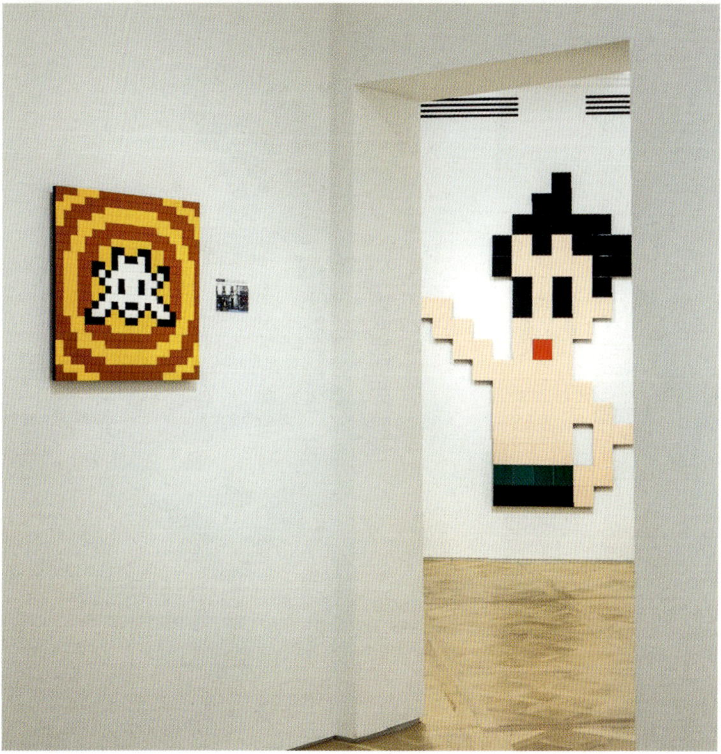

20 010 likes

invaderwashere Some views of "4000" at Over the Influence Paris. Until Jan. 22 2023 @oti.official

View all 191 comments

20 December 2022

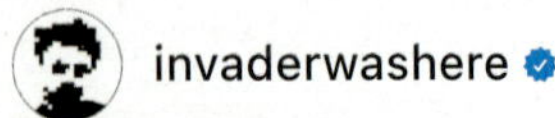

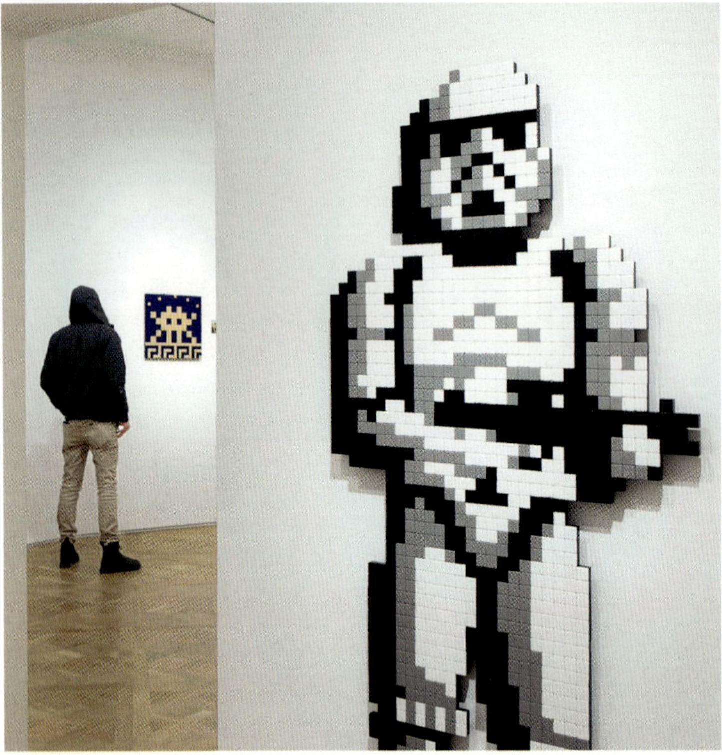

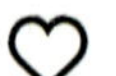 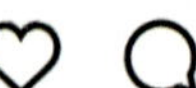  

20 010 likes

invaderwashere Some views of "4000" at Over the Influence Paris. Until Jan. 22 2023 @oti.official

View all 191 comments

20 December 2022

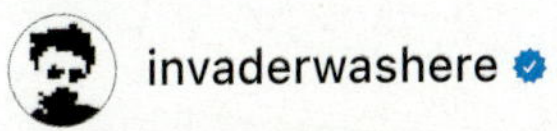

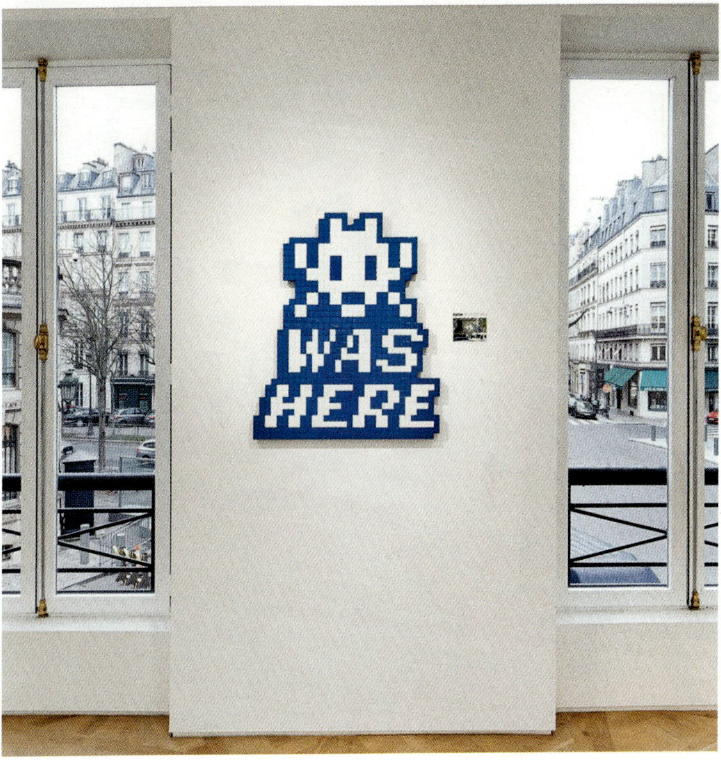

  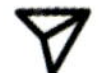 

20 010 likes

invaderwashere Some views of "4000" at Over the Influence Paris. Until Jan. 22 2023 @oti.official

View all 191 comments

20 December 2022

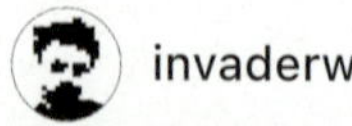
invaderwashere

   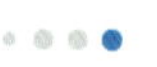 

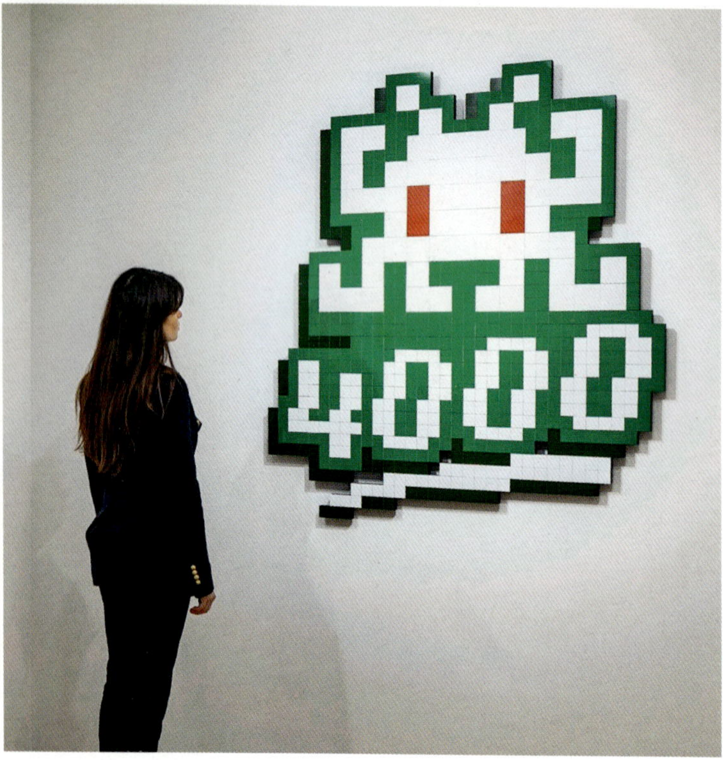

20 010 likes

invaderwashere Some views of "4000" at Over the Influence Paris. Until Jan. 22 2023 @oti.official

View all 191 comments

20 December 2022

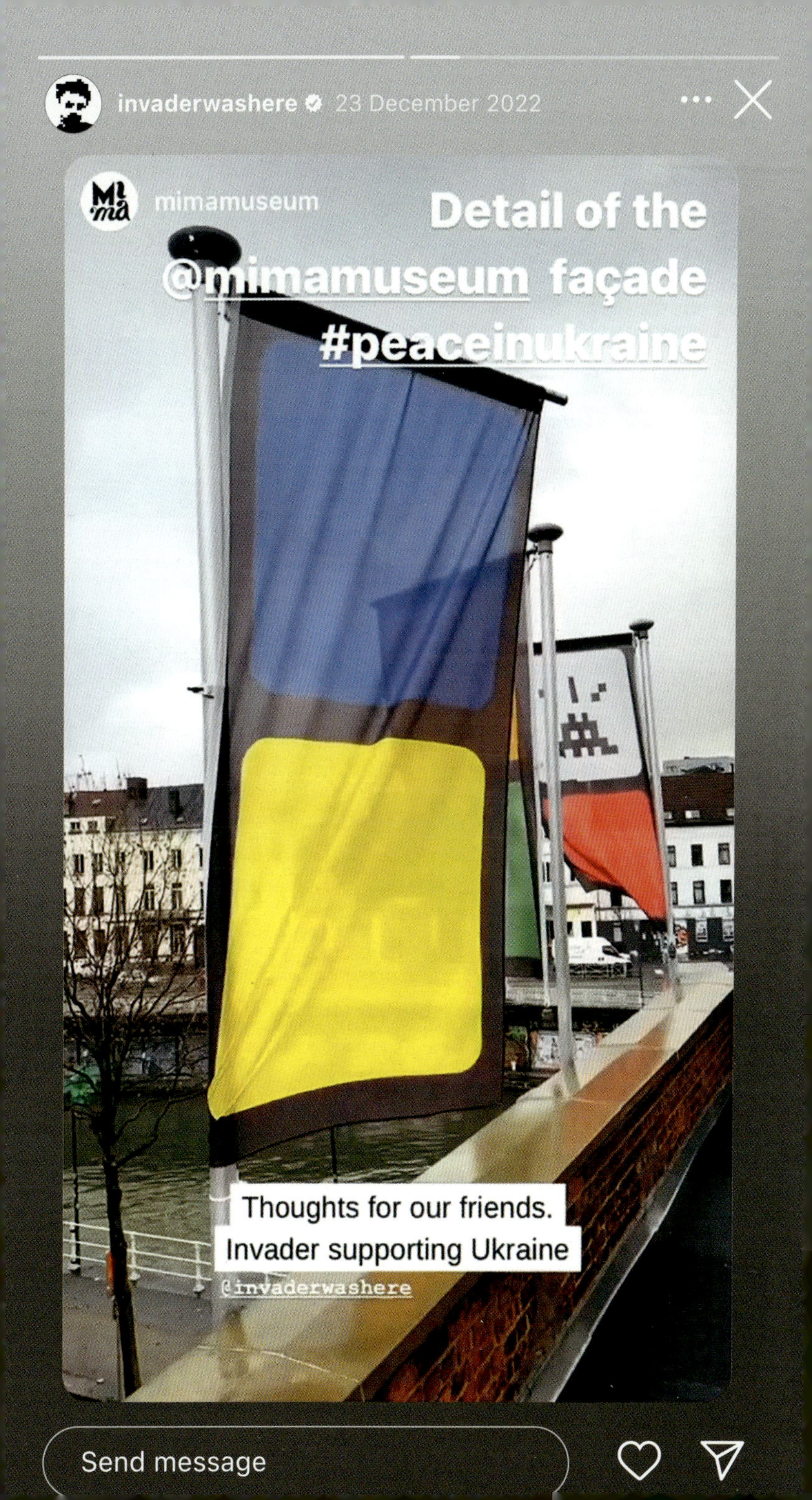

invaderwashere 23 December 2022

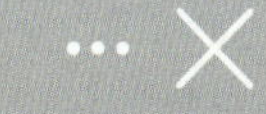

mimamuseum

Detail of the
@mimamuseum façade
#peaceinukraine

Thoughts for our friends.
Invader supporting Ukraine

@invaderwashere

Send message

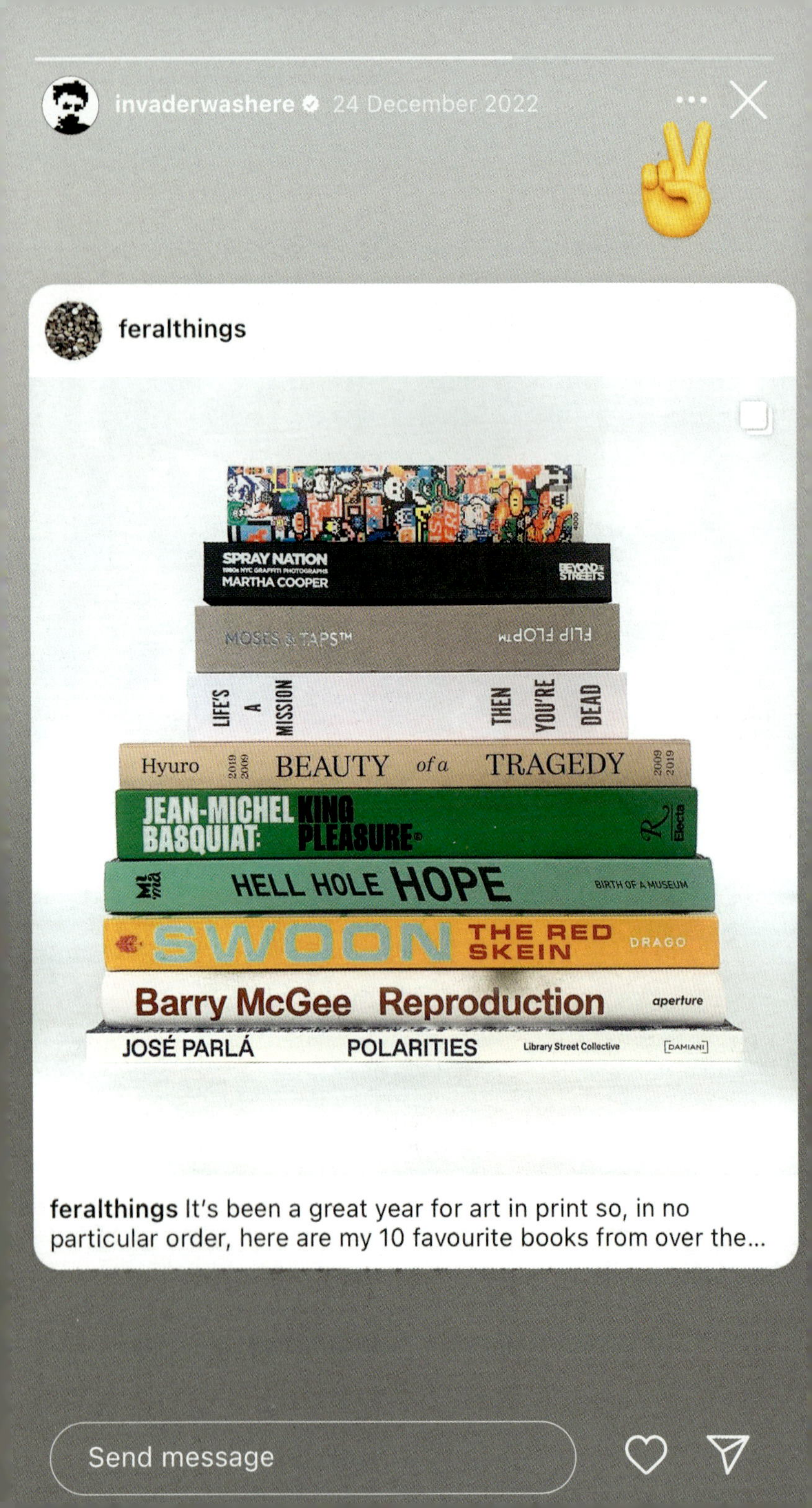

invaderwashere 24 December 2022

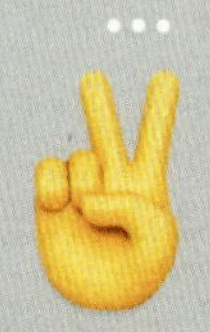

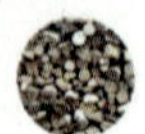

feralthings

SPRAY NATION
1980s NYC GRAFFITI PHOTOGRAPHS
MARTHA COOPER
BEYOND THE STREETS

MOSES & TAPS™ FLIP FLOP™

LIFE'S A MISSION THEN YOU'RE DEAD

Hyuro 2019 2009 BEAUTY of a TRAGEDY 2009 2019

JEAN-MICHEL BASQUIAT: KING PLEASURE©

HELL HOLE HOPE BIRTH OF A MUSEUM

SWOON THE RED SKEIN DRAGO

Barry McGee Reproduction aperture

JOSÉ PARLÁ POLARITIES Library Street Collective DAMIANI

feralthings It's been a great year for art in print so, in no particular order, here are my 10 favourite books from over the...

Send message

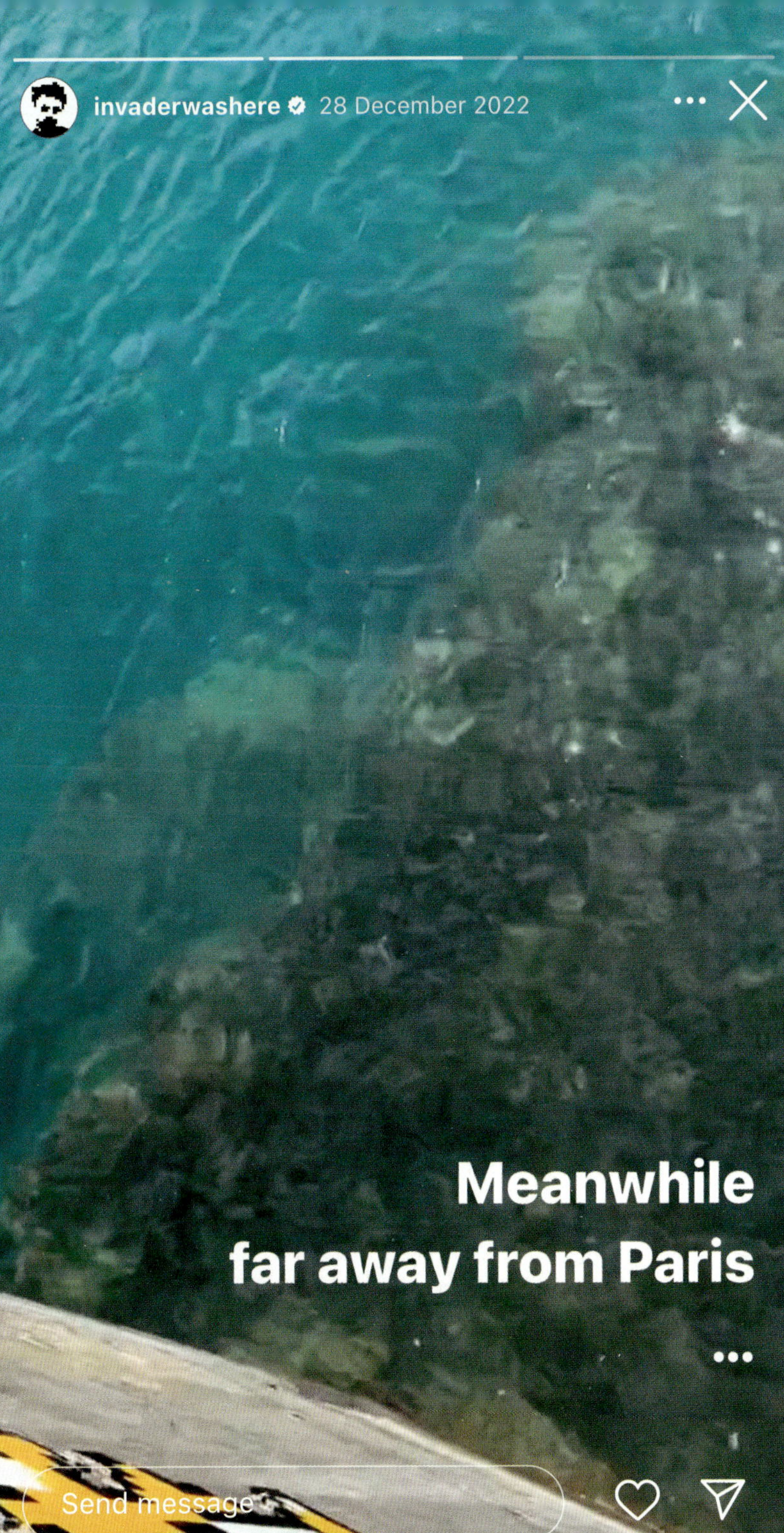
invaderwashere
28 December 2022
Meanwhile
far away from Paris
...
Send message

invaderwashere 28 December 2022

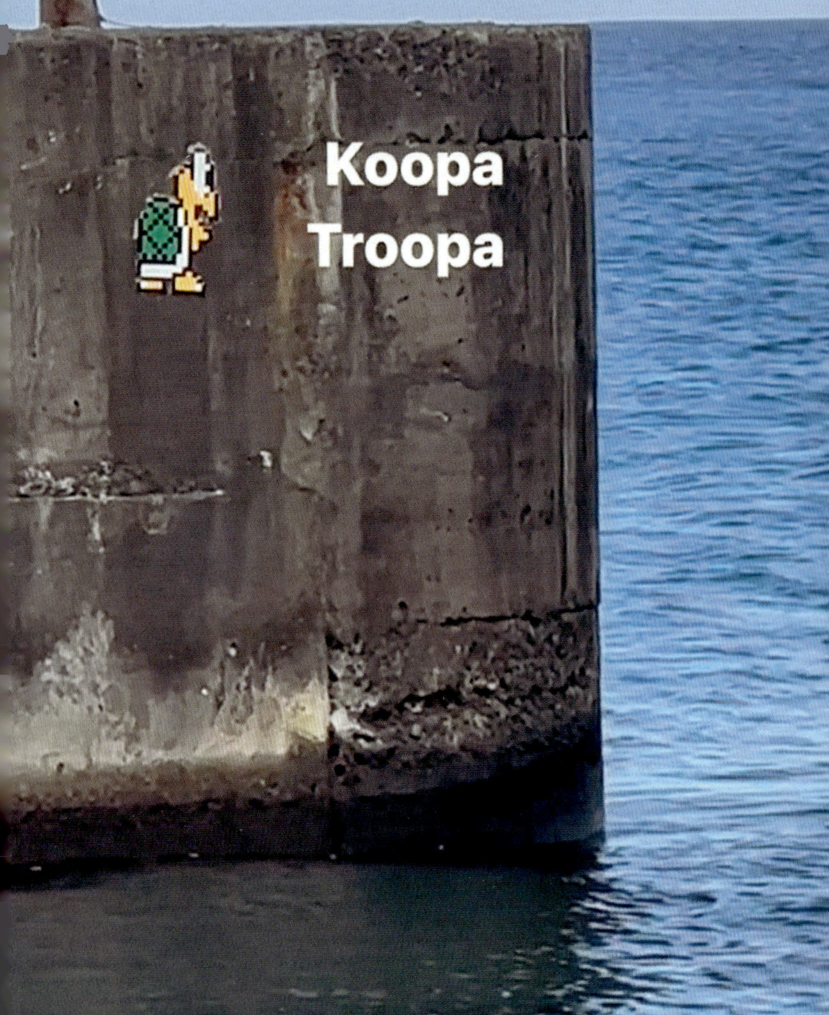

Send message

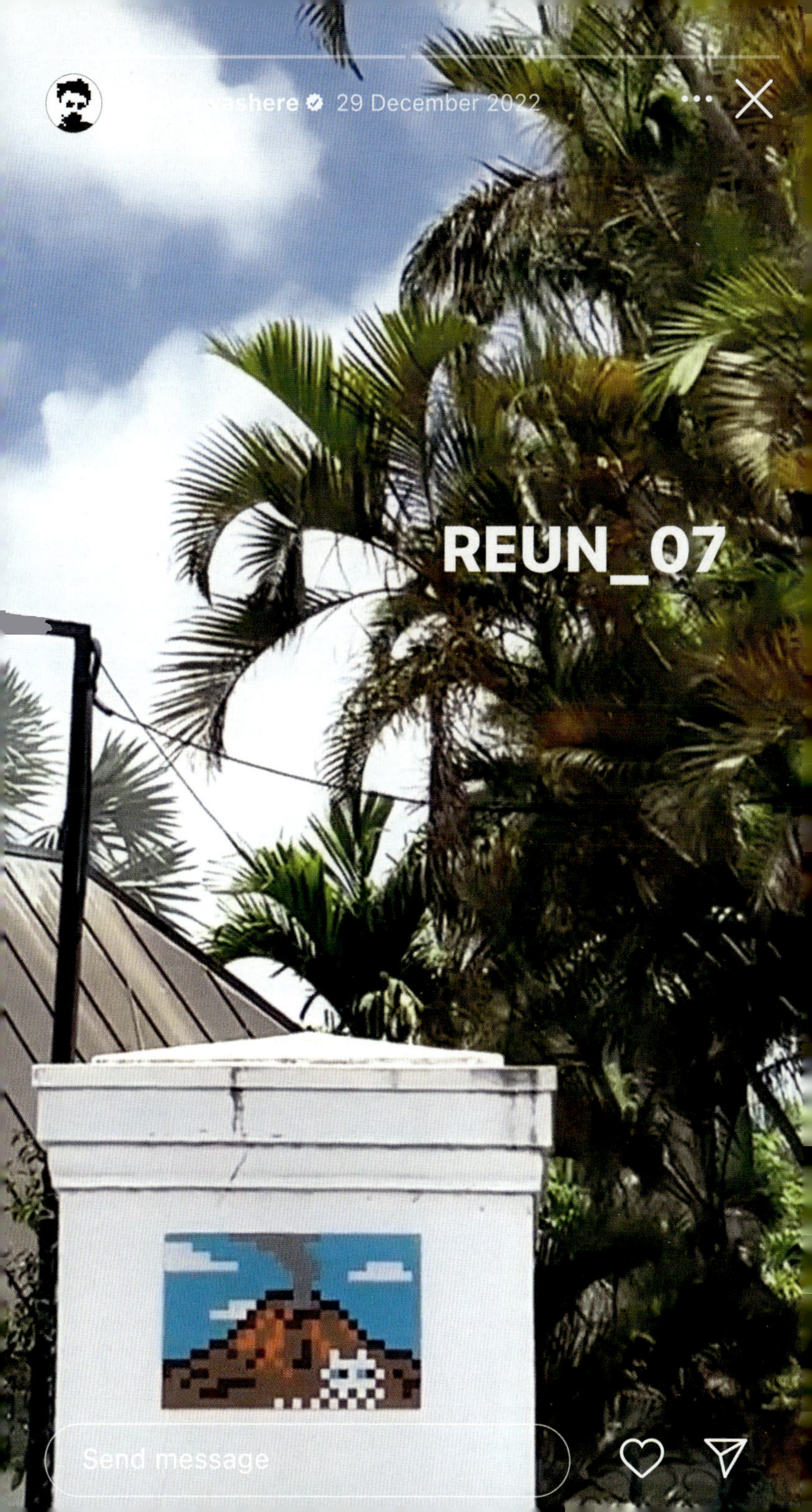
29 December 2022
REUN_07
Send message

invaderwashere 

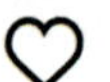   

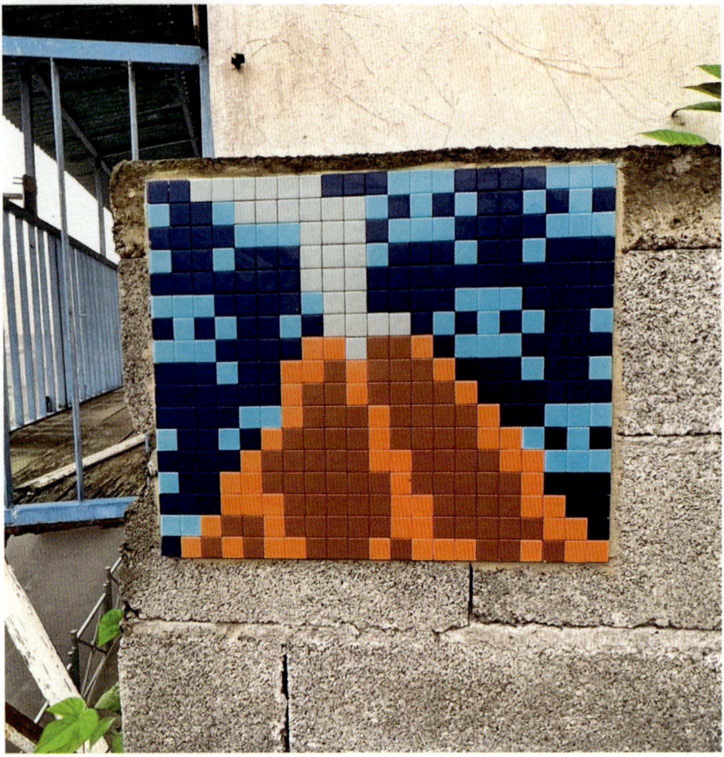

12 481 likes

invaderwashere 11 space invaders have just landed on La Réunion Island. 🌋 👾 It is the 81st territory to be invaded and the last Invasion of 2022 #REUN11 #lareunion #happynewyear

View all 138 comments

31 December 2022

2023

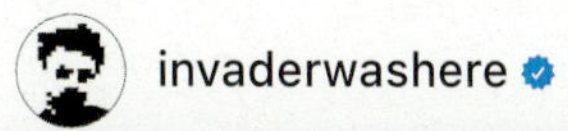

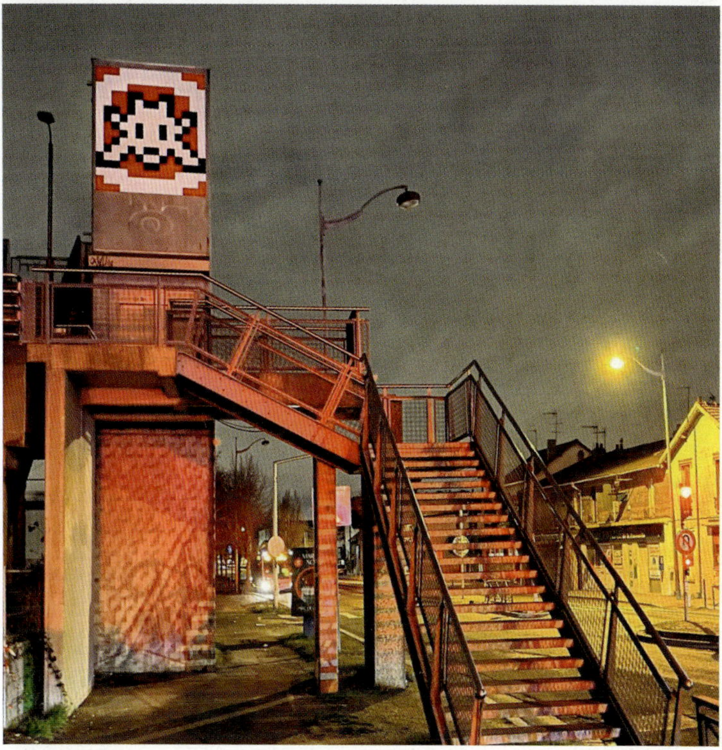

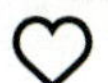   

11 488 likes

invaderwashere PA_1482, the first invasion of the year #2023 #5783 #invaderwashere #backtothebasics

View all 164 comments

6 January 2023

invaderwashere 8 January 2023
The Doors · The End ›

INVADER RUBIKCUBIST
@mimamuseum
is over !

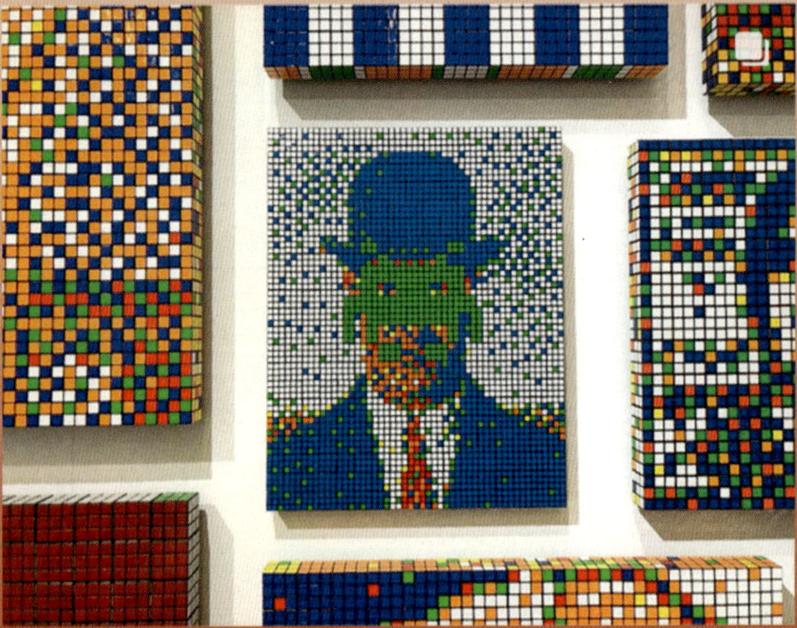

@janju31

Thank you to all visitors
who came to see it

Send message

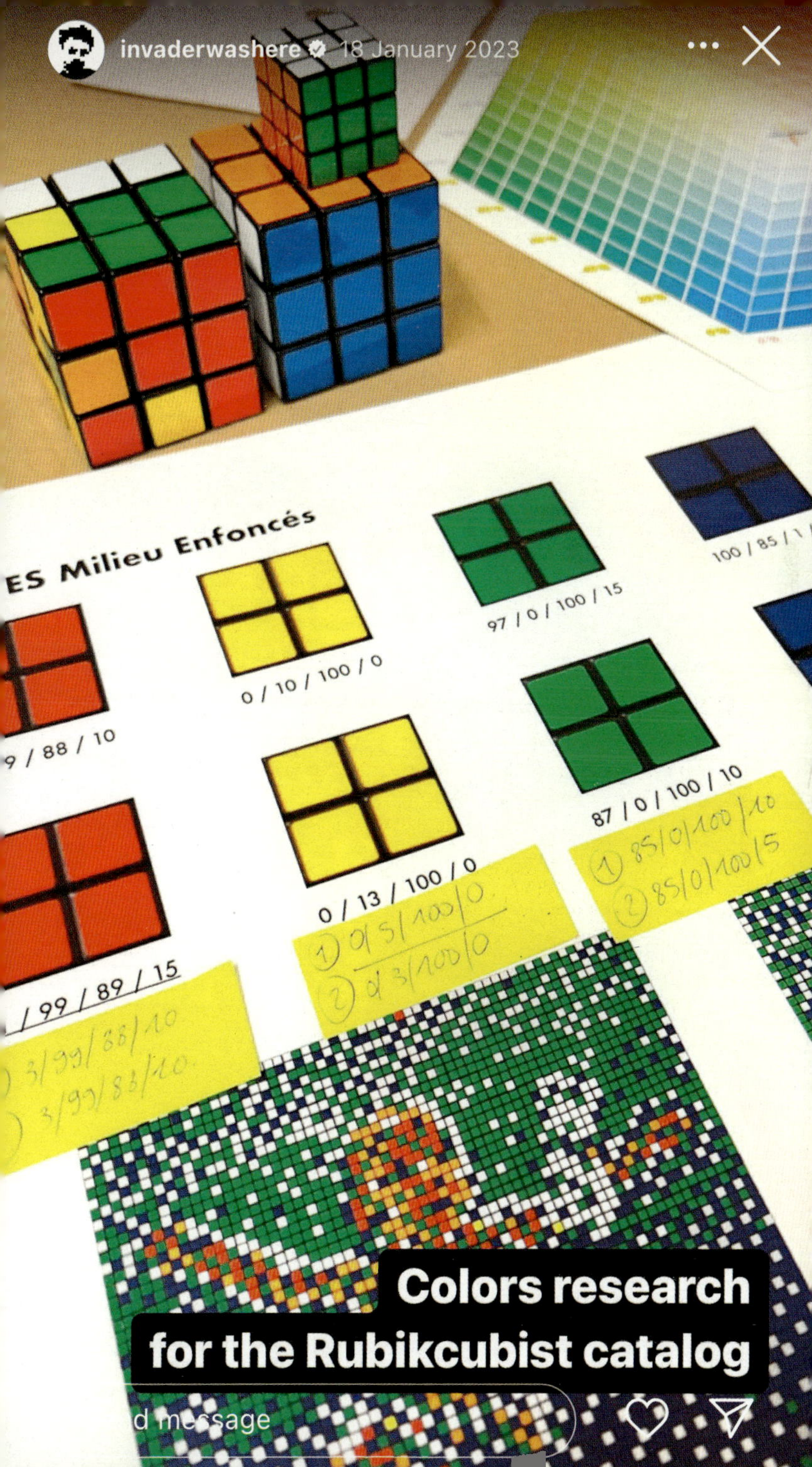
invaderwashere 18 January 2023
ES Milieu Enfoncés
0 / 10 / 100 / 0
97 / 0 / 100 / 15
100 / 85 / 1
9 / 88 / 10
87 / 0 / 100 / 10
0 / 13 / 100 / 0
/ 99 / 89 / 15
Colors research
for the Rubikcubist catalog

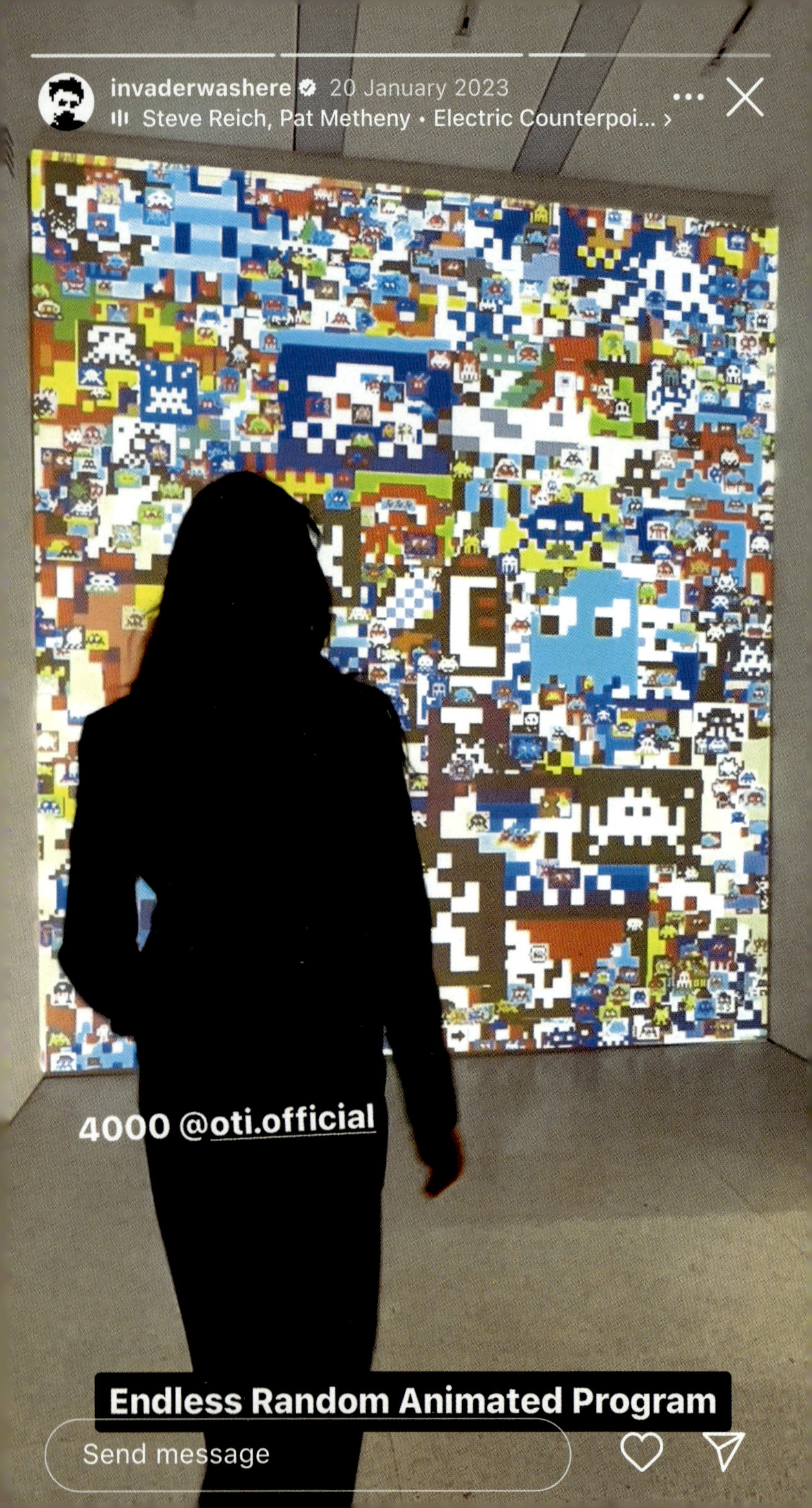

invaderwashere 20 January 2023

Steve Reich, Pat Metheny • Electric Counterpoi... ›

4000 @oti.official

Endless Random Animated Program

Send message

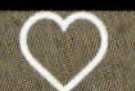

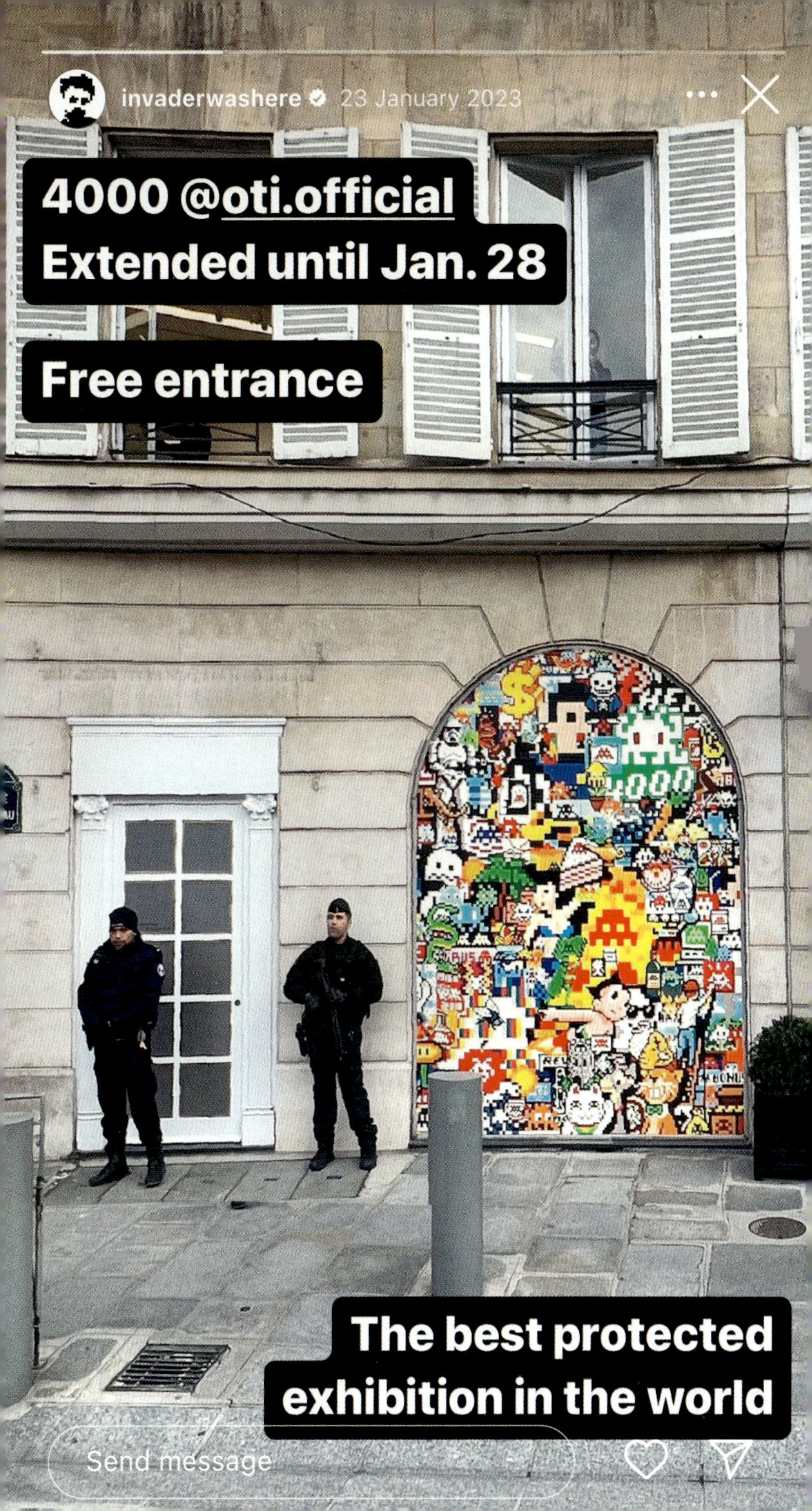
invaderwashere
23 January 2023
4000 @oti.official
Extended until Jan. 28
Free entrance
4000
The best protected
exhibition in the world
Send message

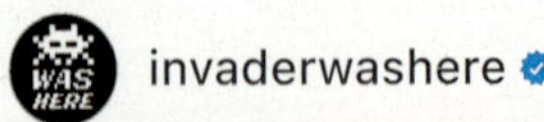

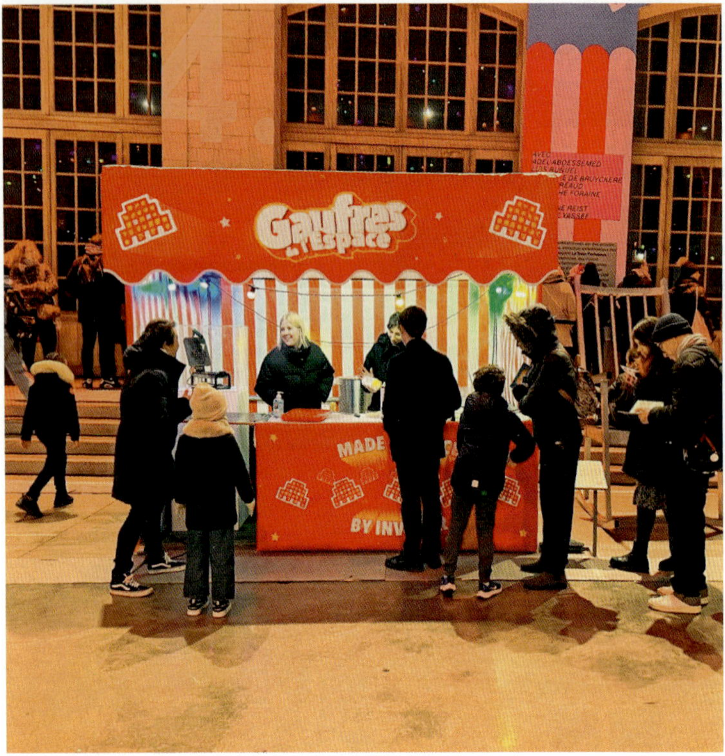

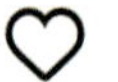   

5 478 likes

invaderwashere Derniers jours pour venir déguster une Gaufre de l'Espace à la Foire Foraine d'Art Contemporain au Cent Quatre. Nocturne ce soir, dernier week end Samedi et Dimanche. @104paris #groupshow #Paris #foodart #sculptureamanger #gaufres #waffles

View all 89 comments

26 January 2023

invaderwashere

  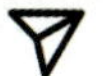 

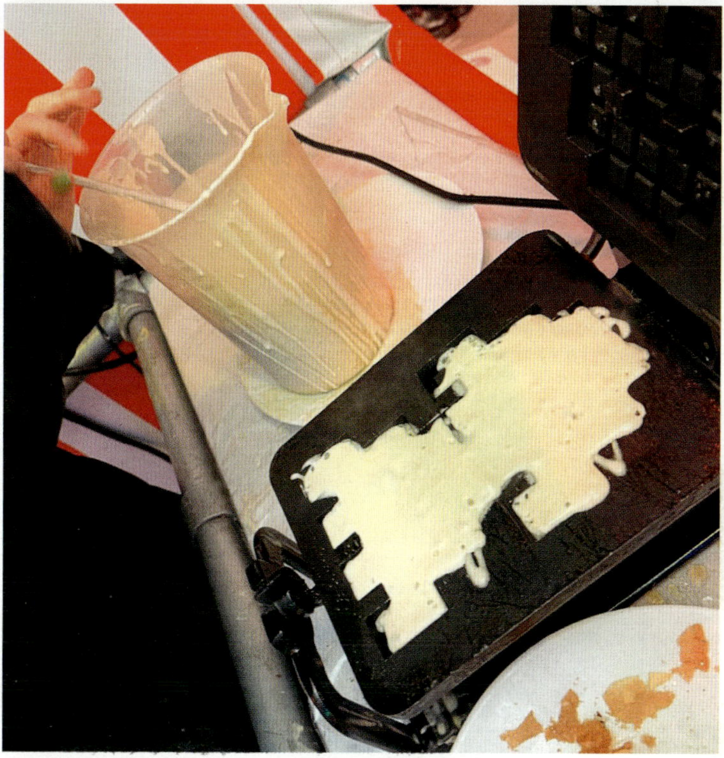

5478 likes

invaderwashere Derniers jours pour venir déguster une Gaufre de l'Espace à la Foire Foraine d'Art Contemporain au Cent Quatre. Nocturne ce soir, dernier week end Samedi et Dimanche. @104paris #groupshow #Paris #foodart #sculptureamanger #gaufres #waffles

View all 89 comments

26 January 2023

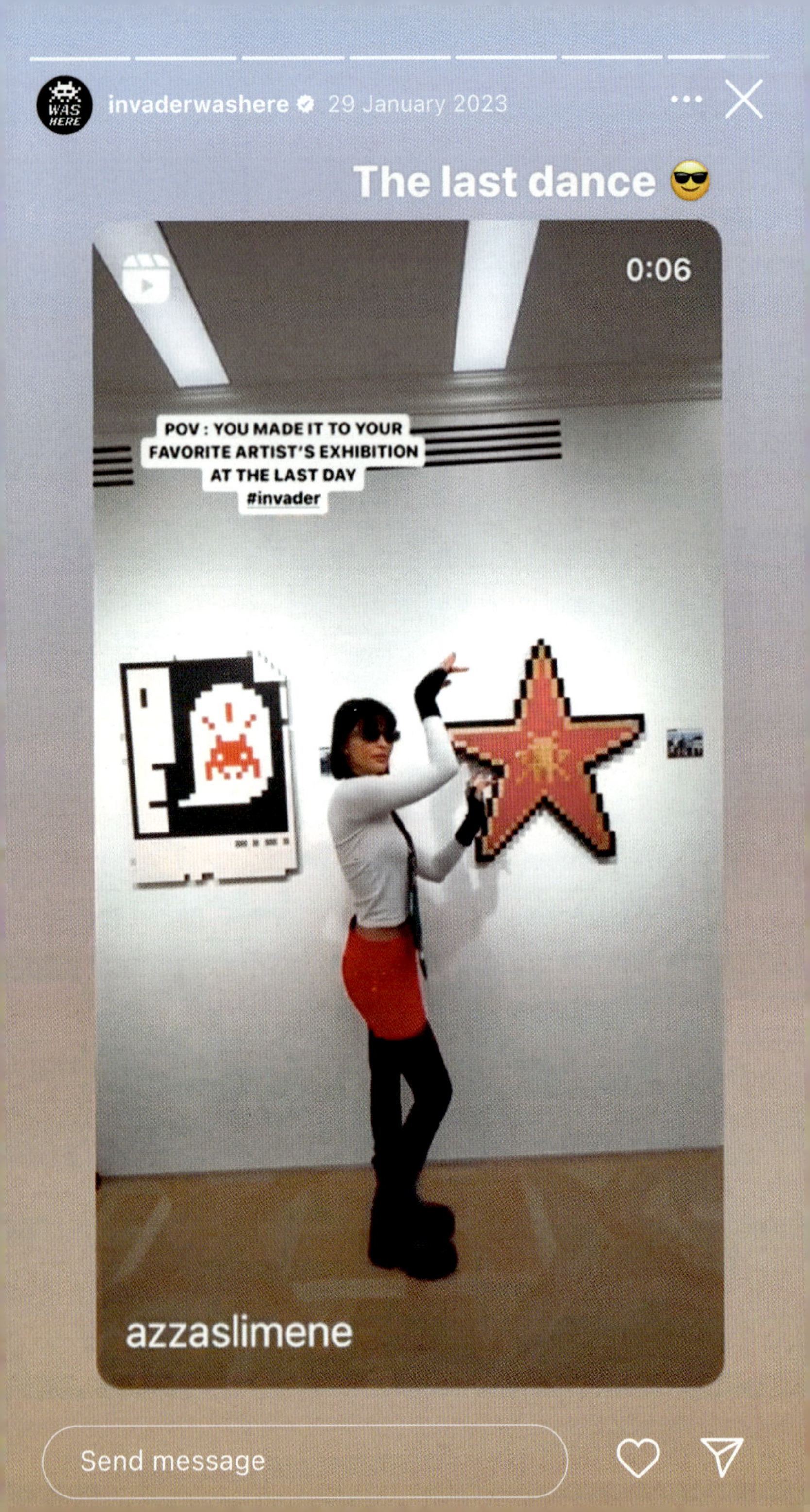

invaderwashere 29 January 2023

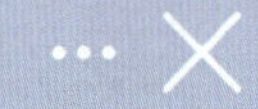

The last dance 

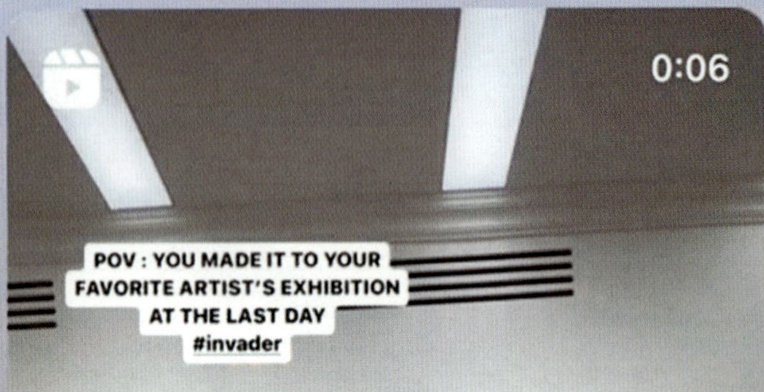

azzaslimene

Send message

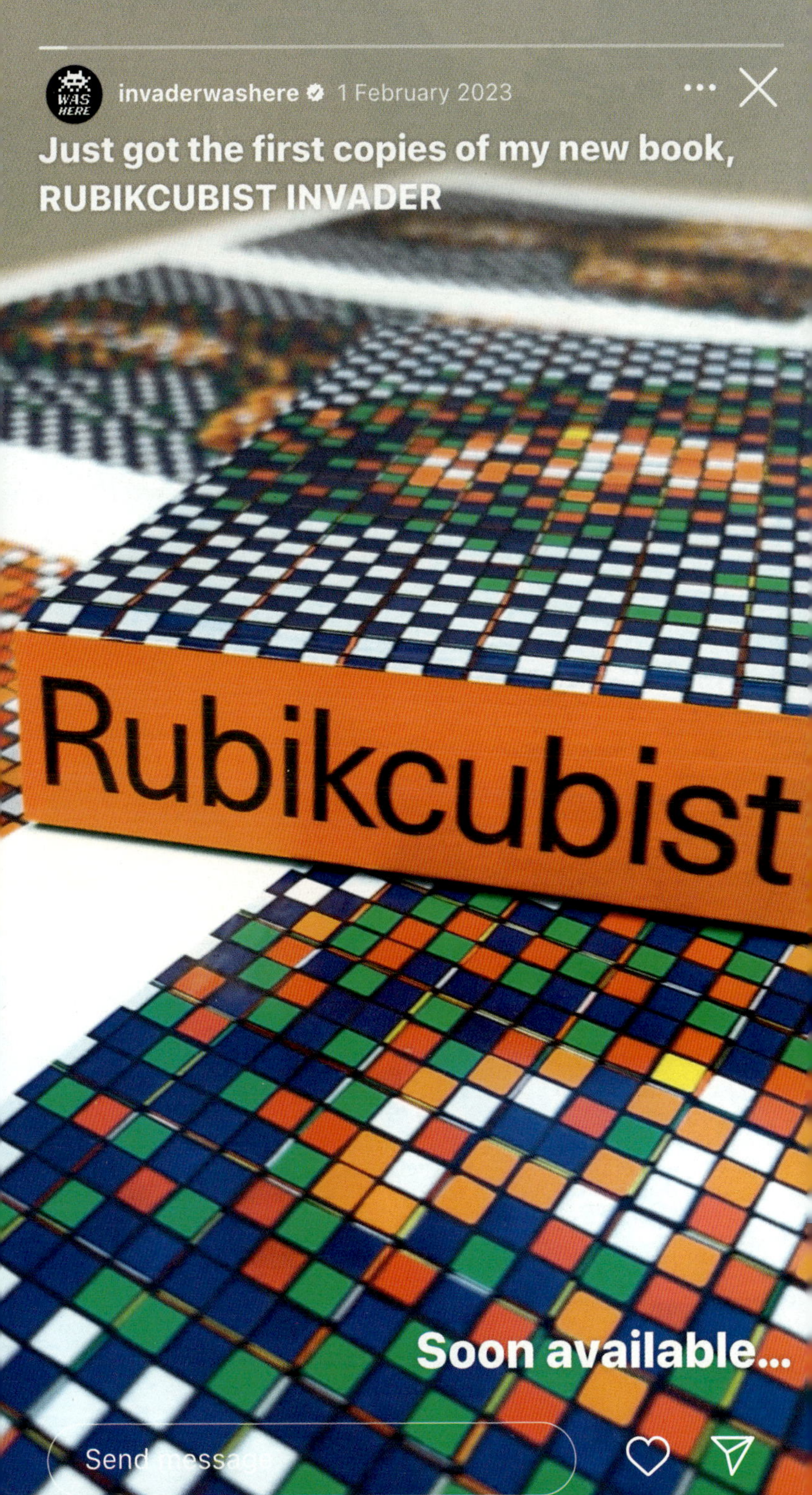
invaderwashere 1 February 2023
Just got the first copies of my new book,
RUBIKCUBIST INVADER
Rubikcubist
Soon available...
Send message

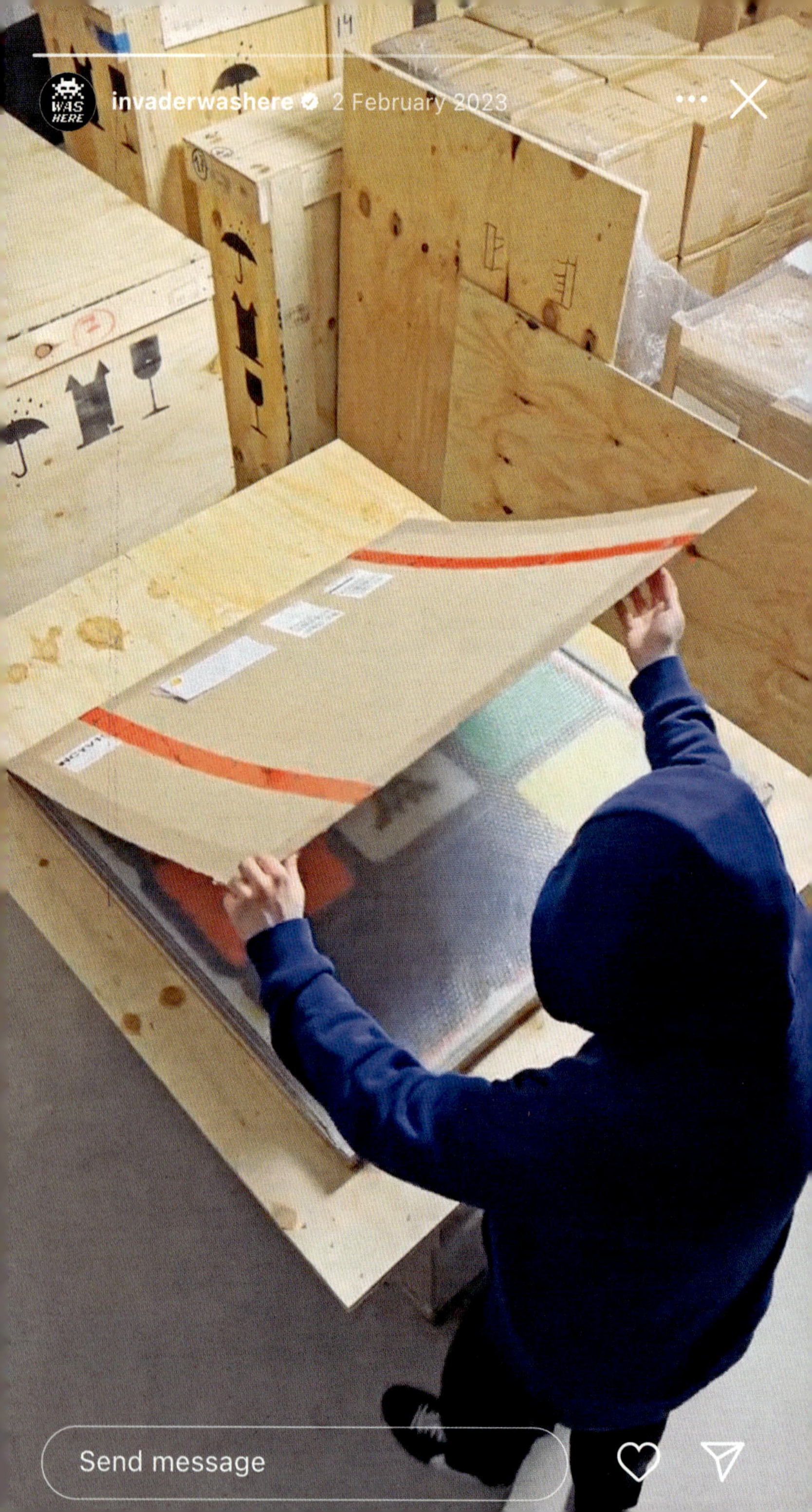
WAS HERE
invaderwashere
2 February 2023
Send message

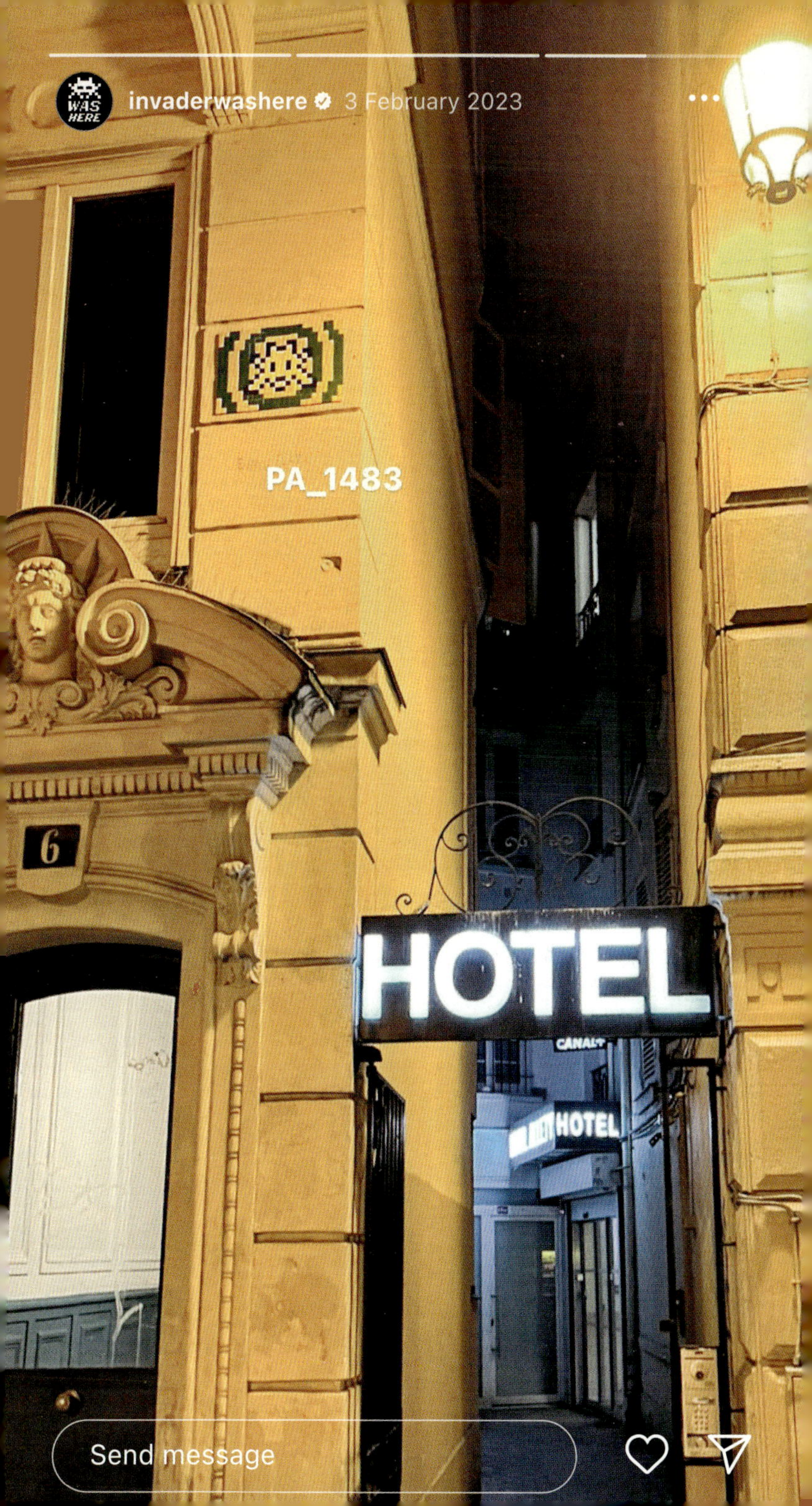
invaderwashere 3 February 2023
WAS HERE
PA_1483
6
HOTEL
CANAL+
HOTEL
Send message

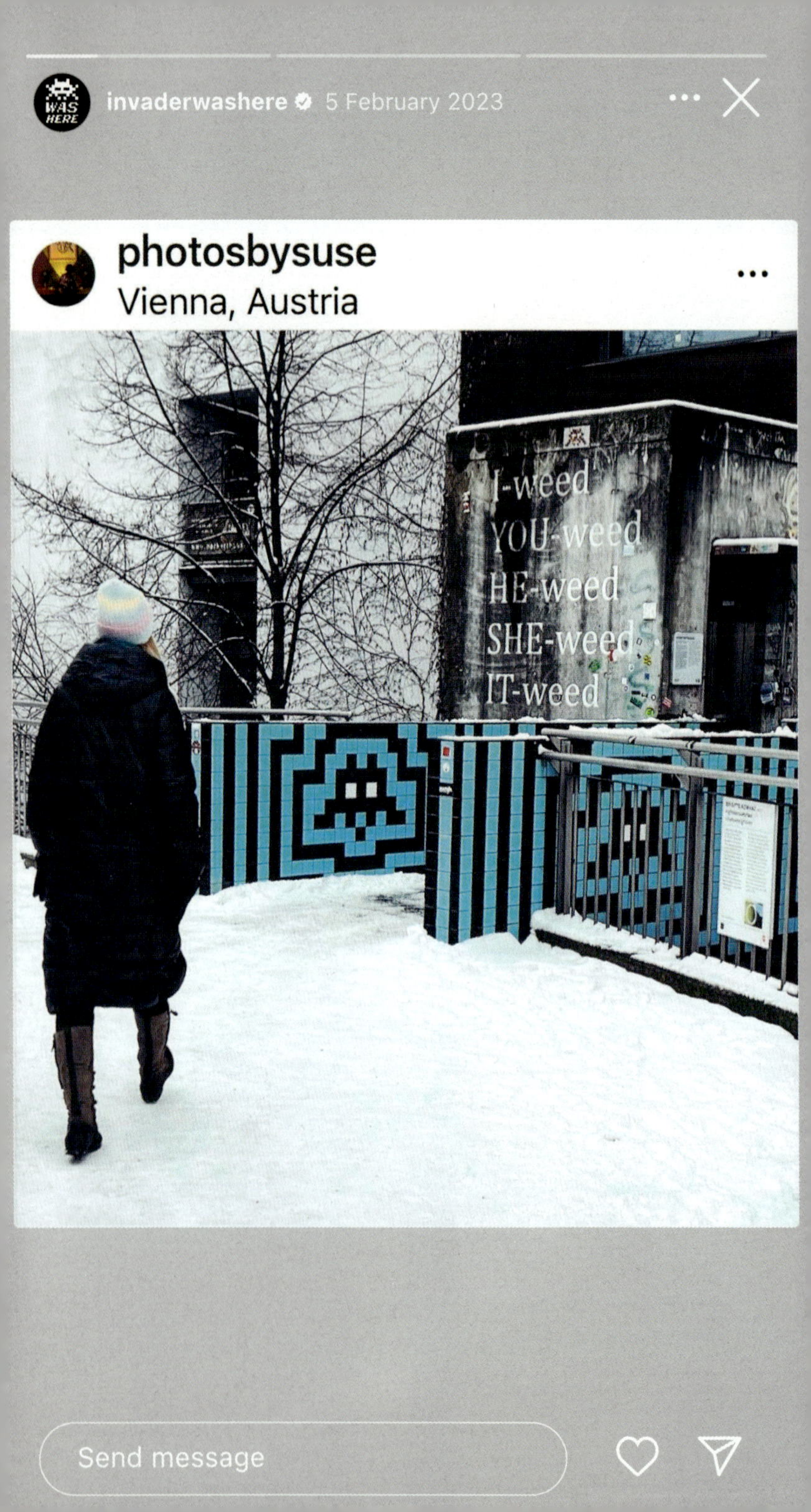

invaderwashere 5 February 2023

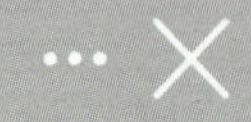

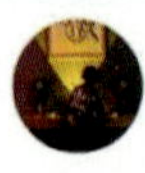

photosbysuse
Vienna, Austria

Send message

invaderwashere 5 February 2023

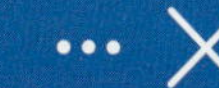

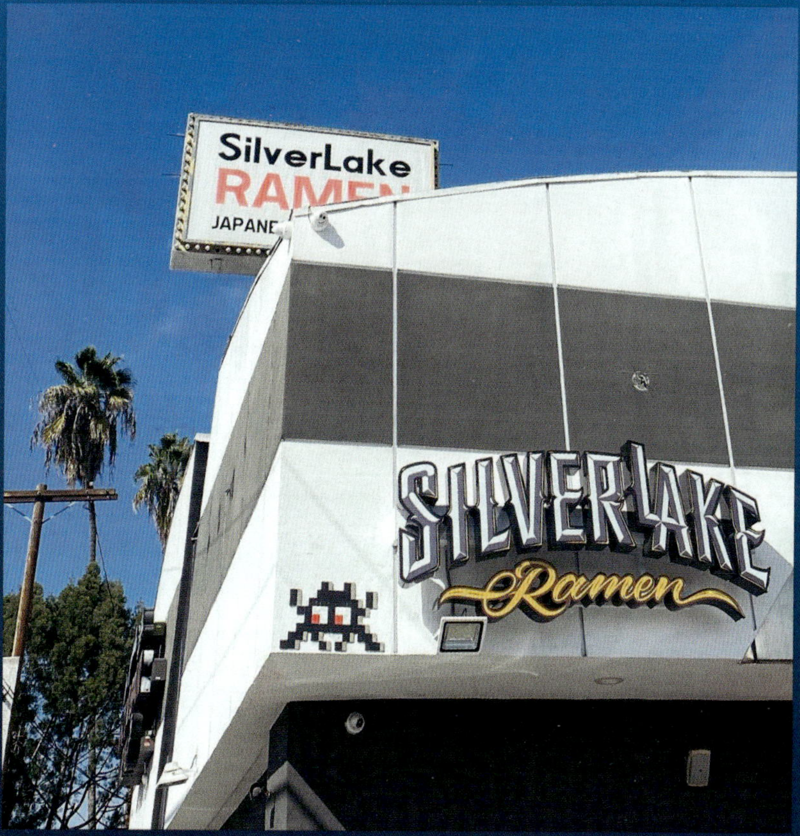

@krishaleanne

Send message

invaderwashere 5 February 2023

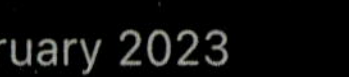

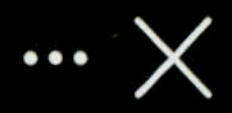

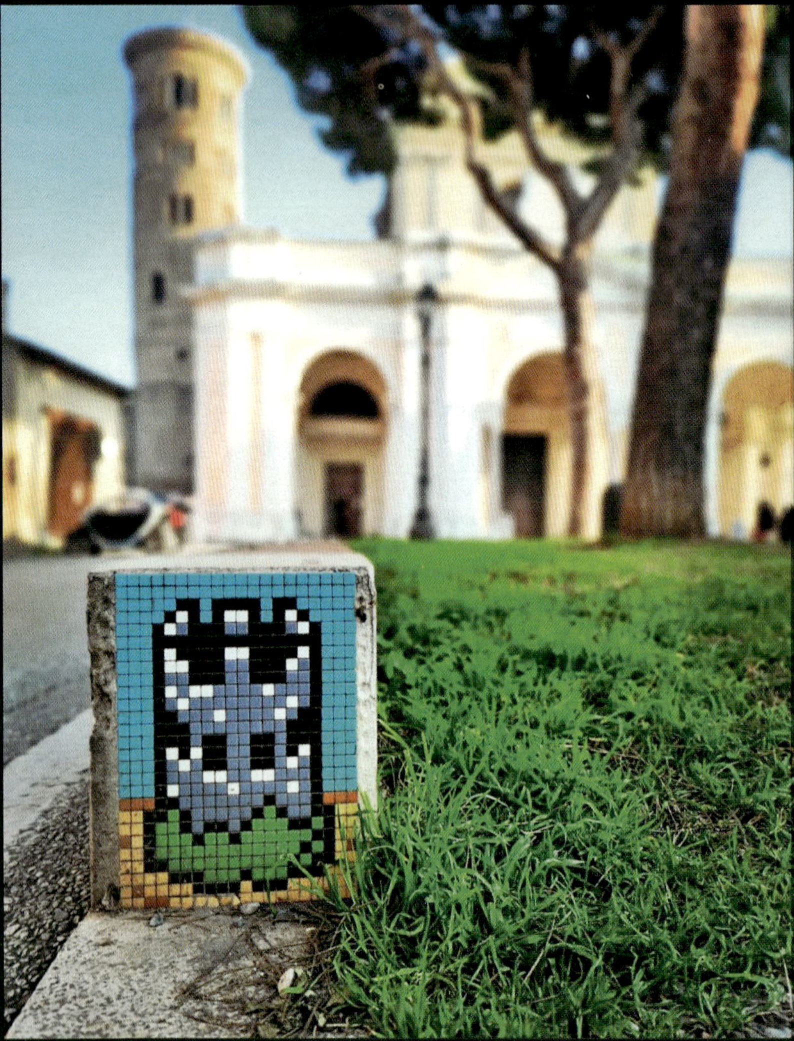

@flashvad

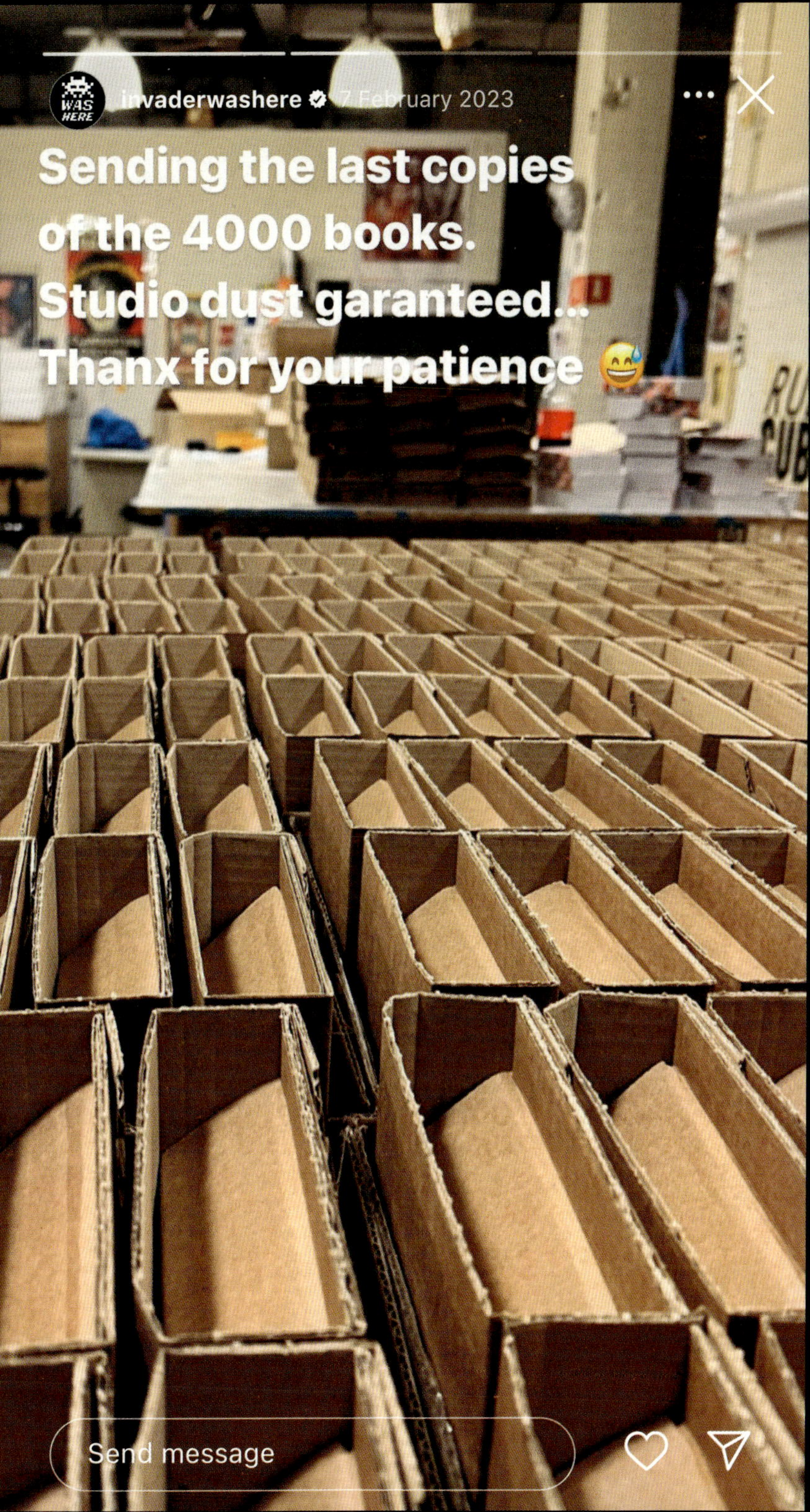
invaderwashere 7 February 2023
Sending the last copies
of the 4000 books.
Studio dust garanteed...
Thanx for your patience
Send message

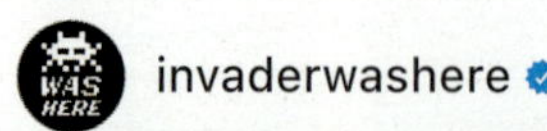

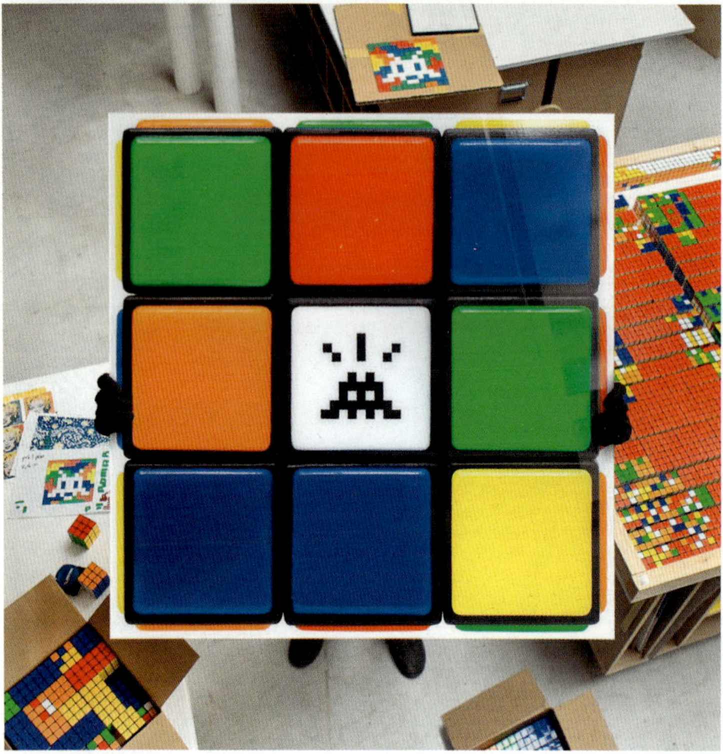

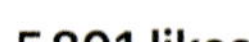

5891 likes

invaderwashere 4 Prints / Open Edition limited in time / 4 days left @heni

View all 203 comments

8 February 2023

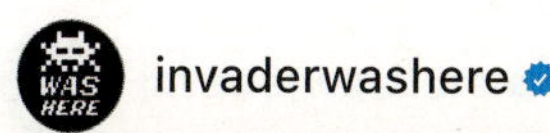

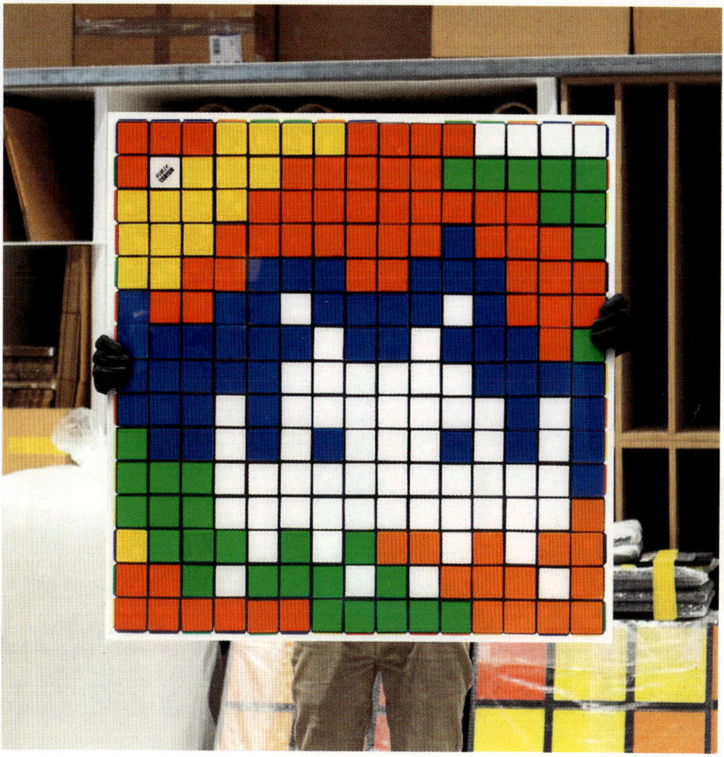

5891 likes

invaderwashere 4 Prints / Open Edition limited in time / 4 days left @heni

View all 203 comments

8 February 2023

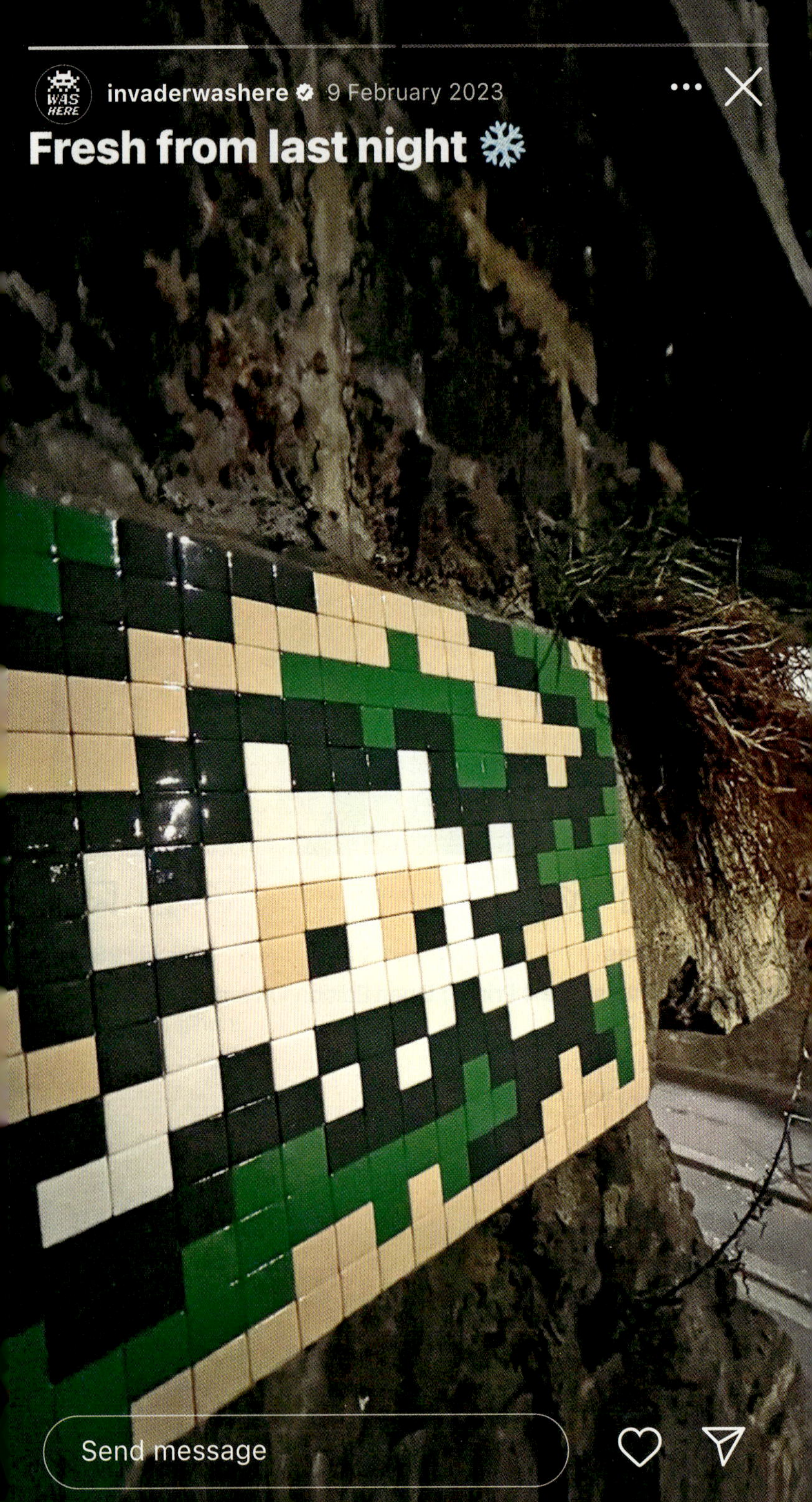

invaderwashere
9 February 2023
Fresh from last night ❄️
Send message

invaderwashere 9 February 2023

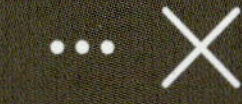

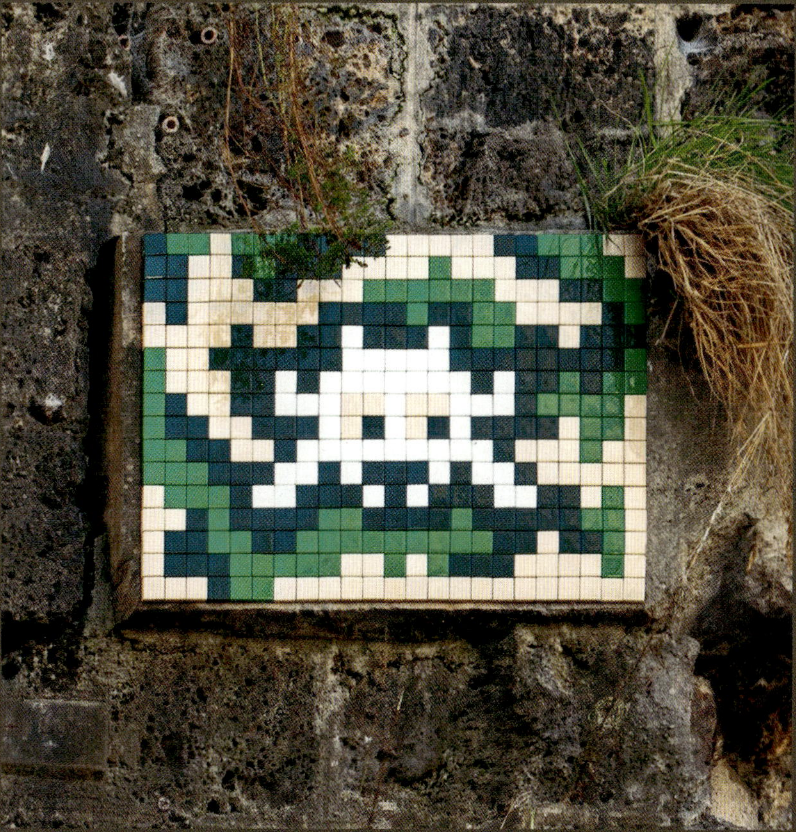

PA_1484

Send message

invaderwashere 11 February 2023

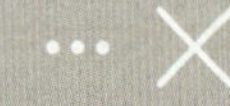

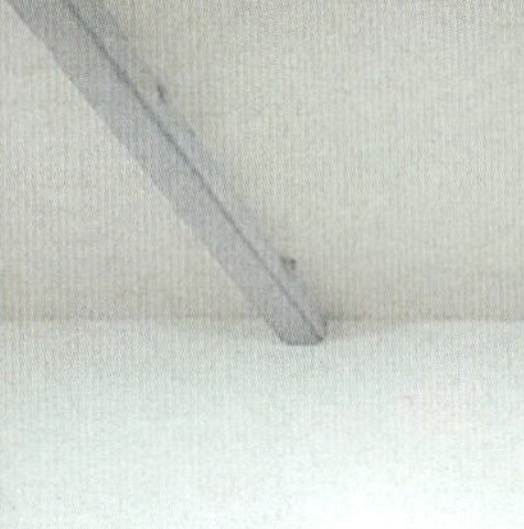

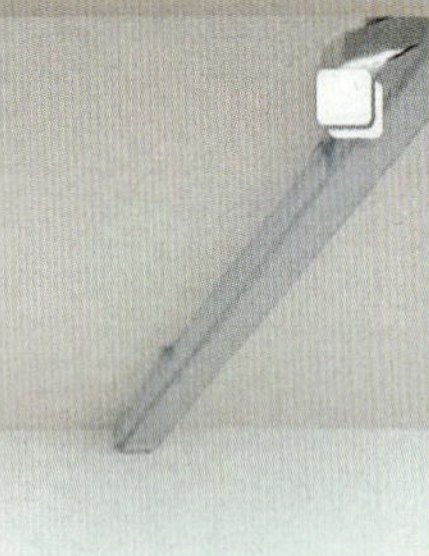

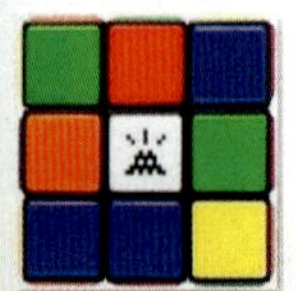

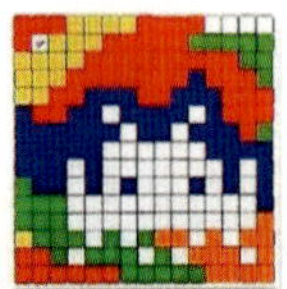

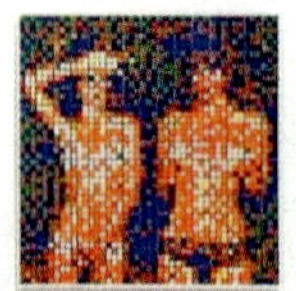

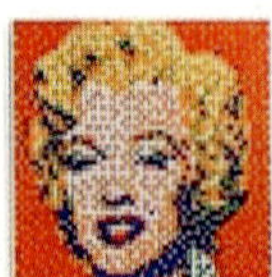

Last week end...

@heni

Send message

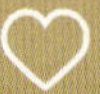

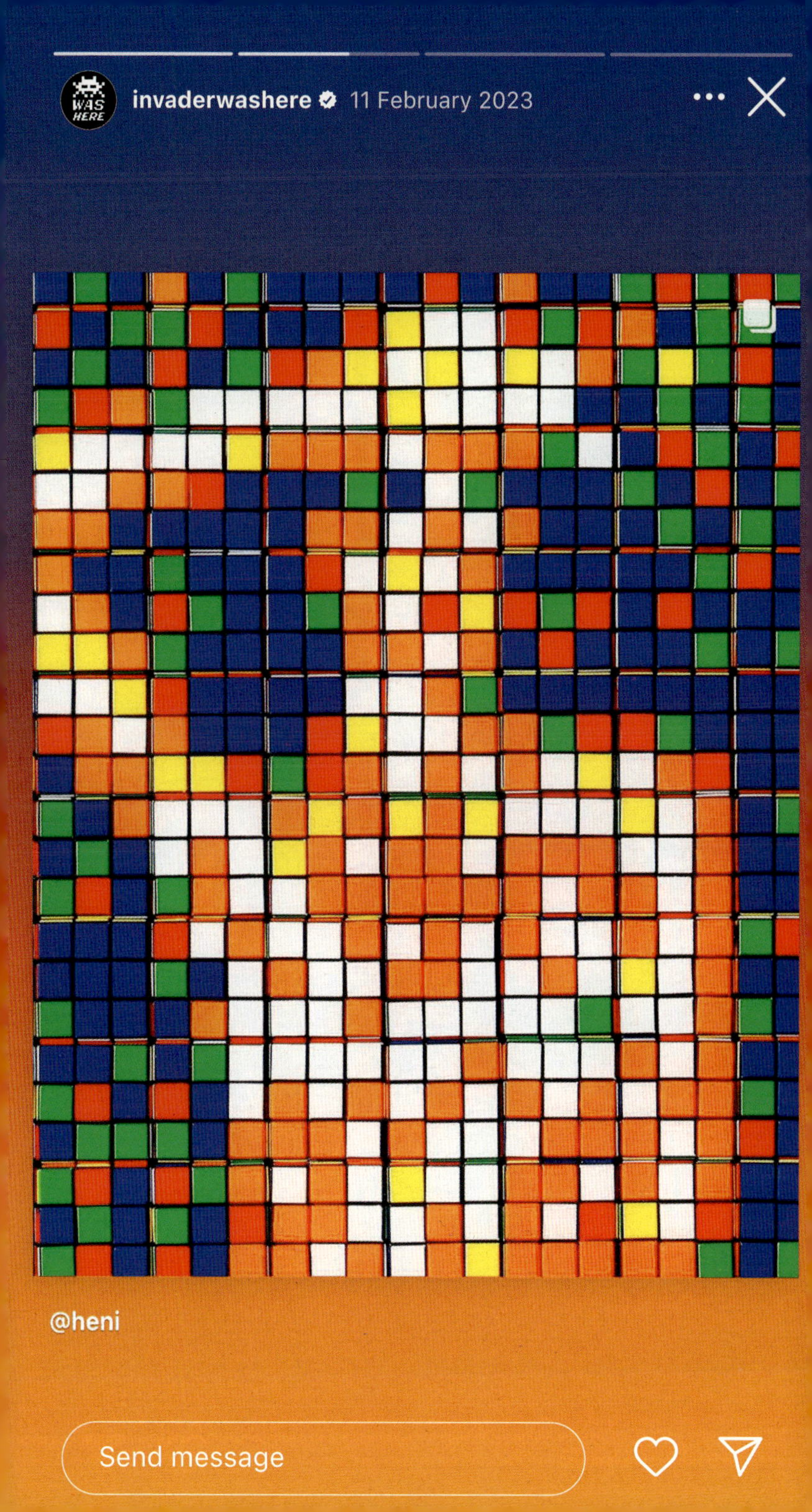

invaderwashere 11 February 2023

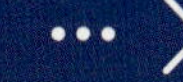

@heni

Send message

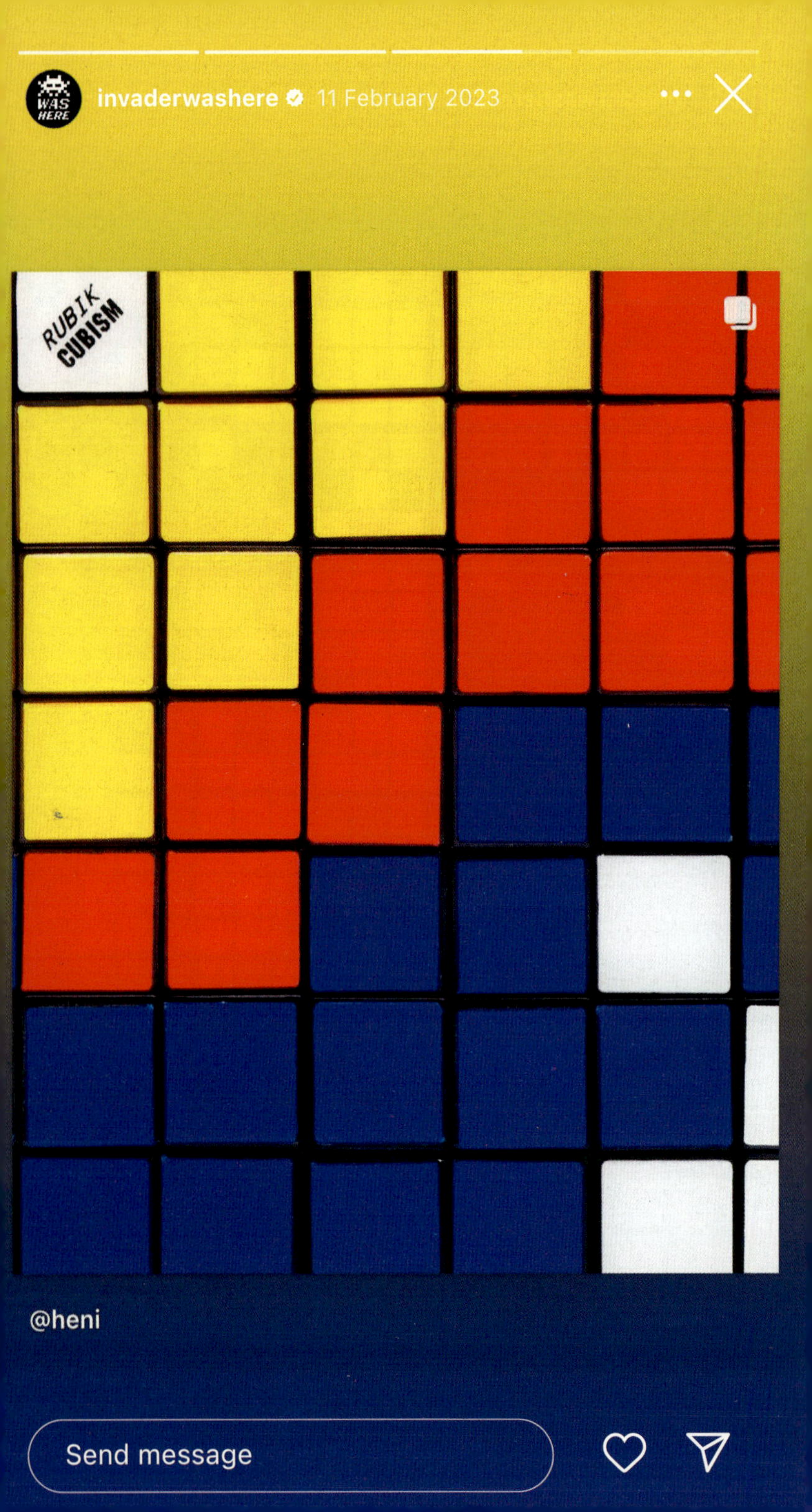

invaderwashere 11 February 2023

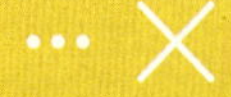

RUBIK CUBISM

@heni

Send message

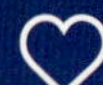

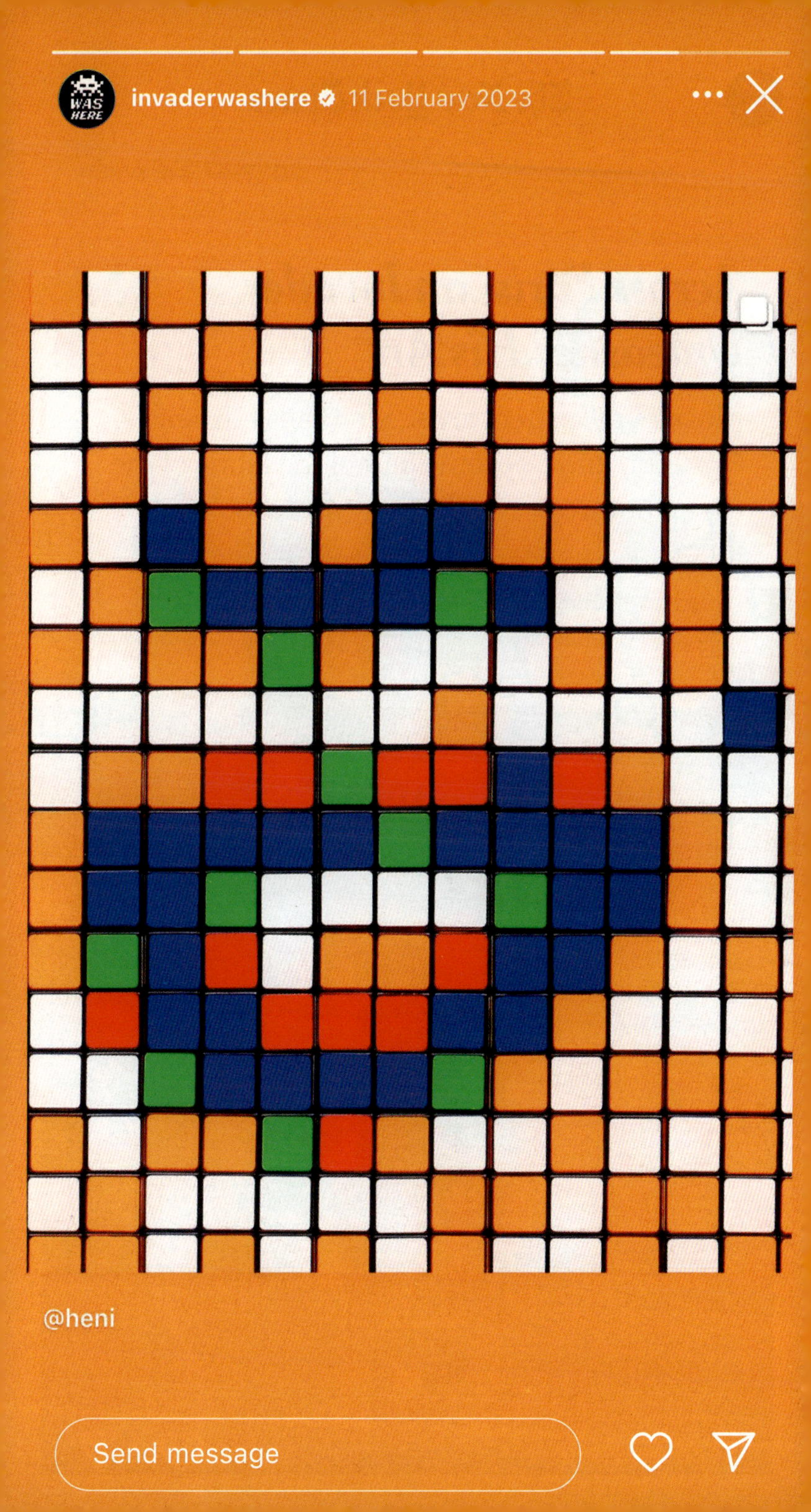

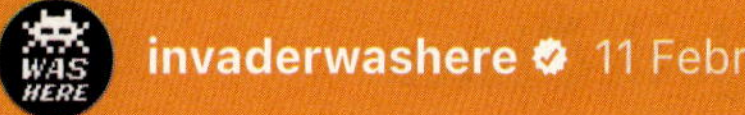

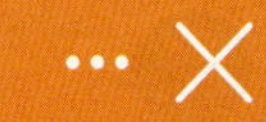

@heni

Send message

The New York Times

SUBSCRIBE FOR €0.50/WEEK

Across Paris, an Invader Unleashes His Art

Mosaics by a street artist, who calls himself "Invader," have become part of the fabric of the city. They are everywhere — if you look for them.

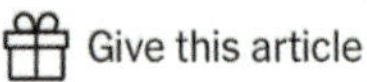

Read in app

🙌 NYT 🙌

PARIS

Send message

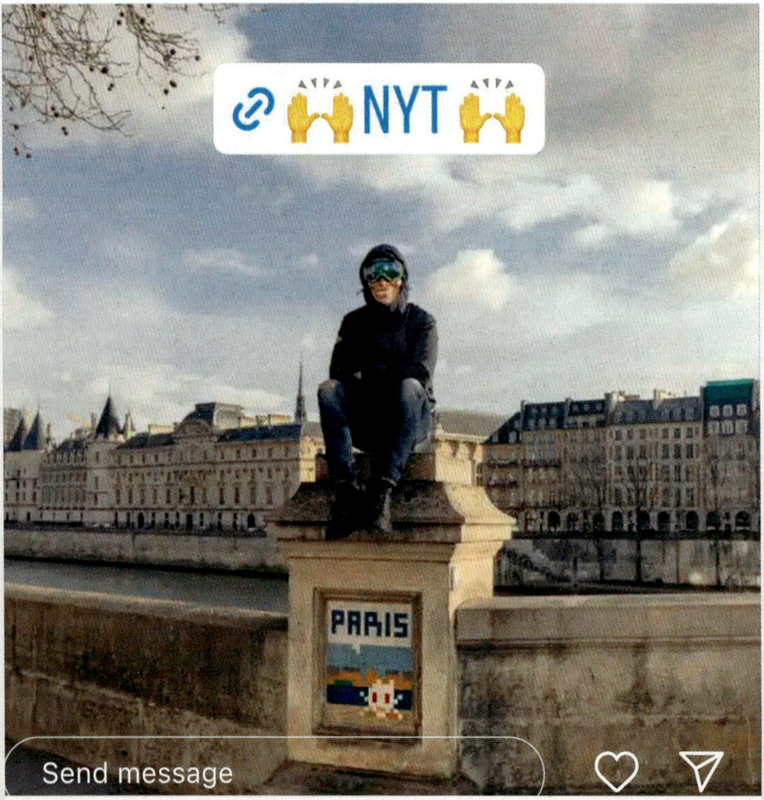

did the math on the annual carbon
of transporting Valentine's Day flowers
from Colombia alone, concluding, "Flying that much sweet-smelling cargo
burns 114 million liters of fuel and emits
approxima... ,000 metric tons of
RENKL, PA

The New Y... es publishes opinion
from a wide range of perspectives in
hopes of promoting constructive debate
about consequential questions.

P.T.A. showed no mercy, ...
ter pitch out of the scruffy park in subur-
ban Tokyo. Midway through the game,
the scorekeeper stopped counting.

Losing is nothing new for Japan's no-
torious gangsters, the yakuza. For over
a decade, they have been suffering one
defeat after another.

As late as the 1990s, yakuza numbered around 100,000. Their businesses
— scams, gambling and prostitution

rackets — were illegal, but the groups
themselves were not. Fan magazines
chronicled their exploits, sandwiching
interviews with top bosses between or-
ganizational charts and brothel reviews.
The groups had business cards and
listed addresses. They gave Halloween
candy to children and distributed relief
supplies after disasters.

But today's y...
they once were
forces wearin...
dustries have
aging popula...
find recruits
ste... are in t...
and h...s di...
demand for

Elusive, yet everywhere, for a quarter-century

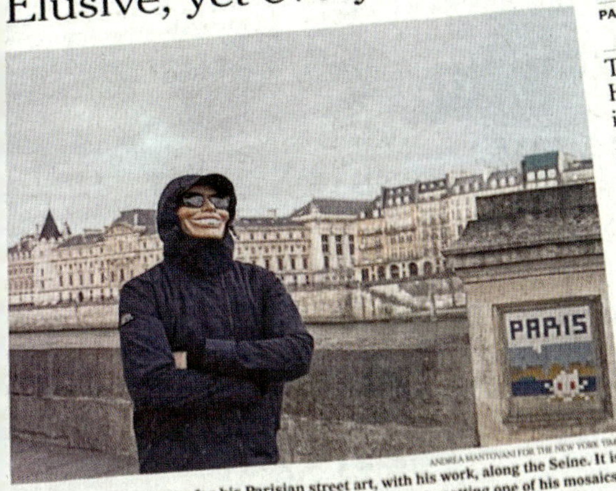

ANDREA MANTOVANI FOR THE NEW YORK TIMES

Invader, the artist known for his Parisian street art, with his work, along the Seine. It is hard to go more than a few blocks in much of Paris without spotting one of his mosaics.

PARIS

The French artist Invader: His work is still illegal, but is now part of Paris's fabric

BY CATHERINE PORTER

It all began down a narrow cobblestone road near Place de la Bastille.

An artist affixed a mosaic of a Martian from the pioneering 1978 video game Space Invaders to a wall. He used square bathroom tiles that resembled pixels.

Within the year, he had stuck 146 more on monuments, bridges and sidewalks.

He was cementing a mosaic to a church wall when the police arrested him for the first time. He was not caught when he stuck 10 up inside the Louvre.

"I was invading public space with a mosaic of a small character whose role is to invade," said the artist, who goes by the street name Invader, during an in-

terview ... hibiting ... my th... found ... A qu... more ... witho... you l... O... top ... ano... Pla... gic ... b... S...

NEWSSTAND PRICES

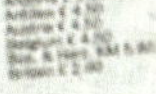

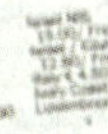

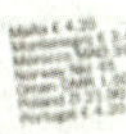

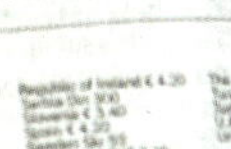

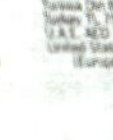

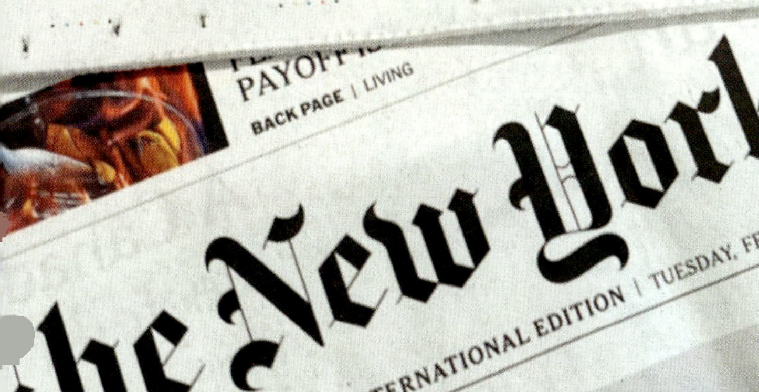

The New York Times International edition

Send message

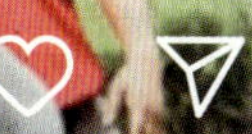

invaderwashere 17 February 2023

Rubikcubist Invader

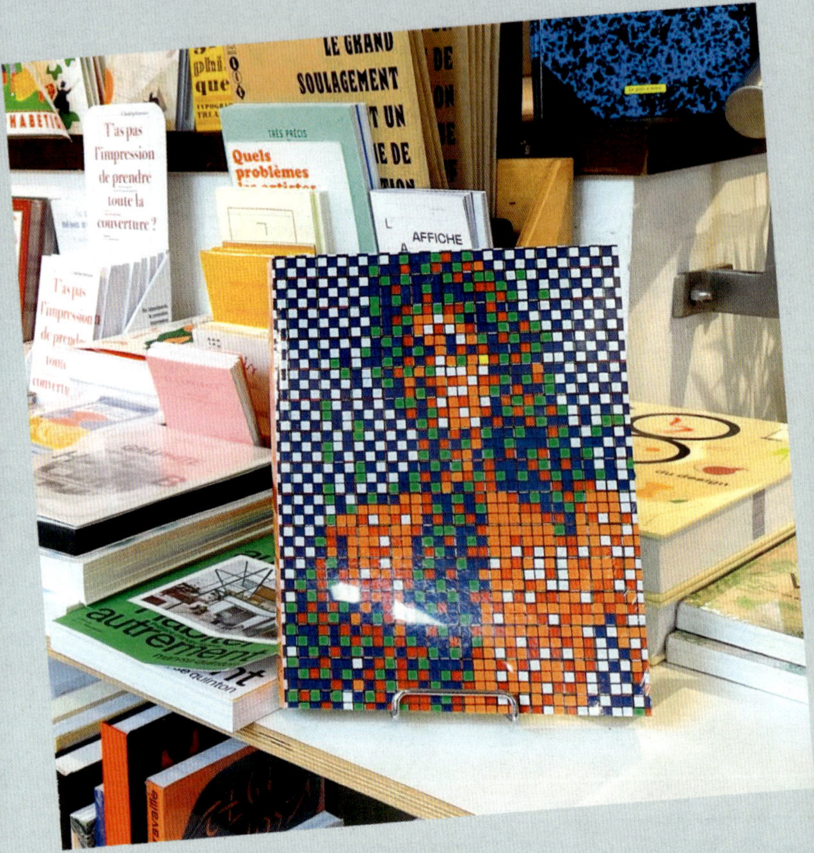

Available in French bookstores and soon online

...

Send message

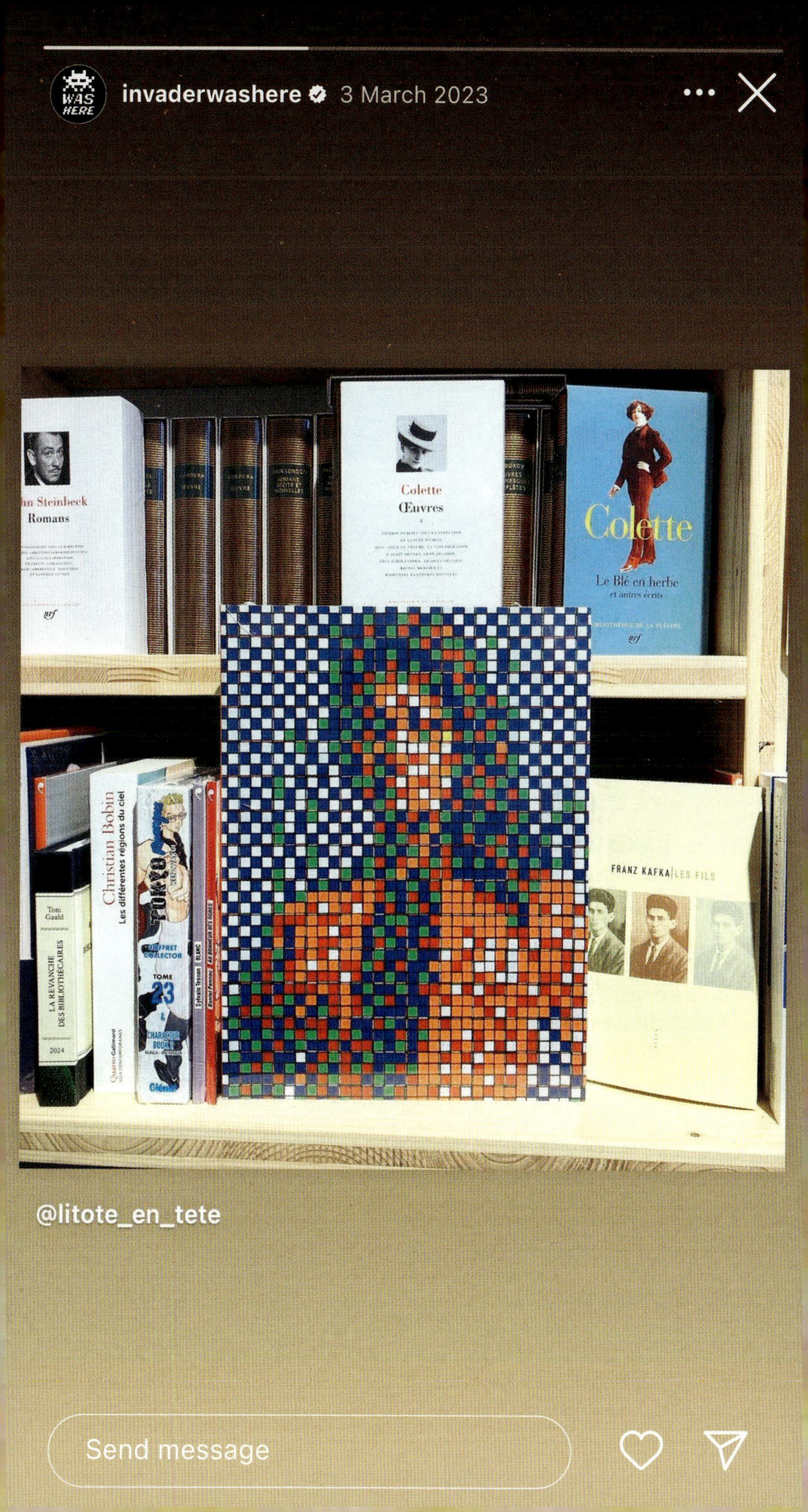

invaderwashere 3 March 2023

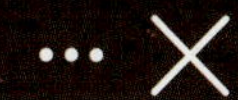

@litote_en_tete

Send message

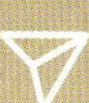

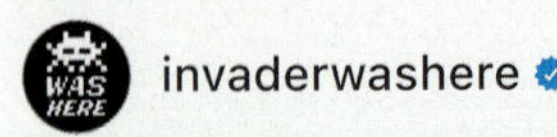

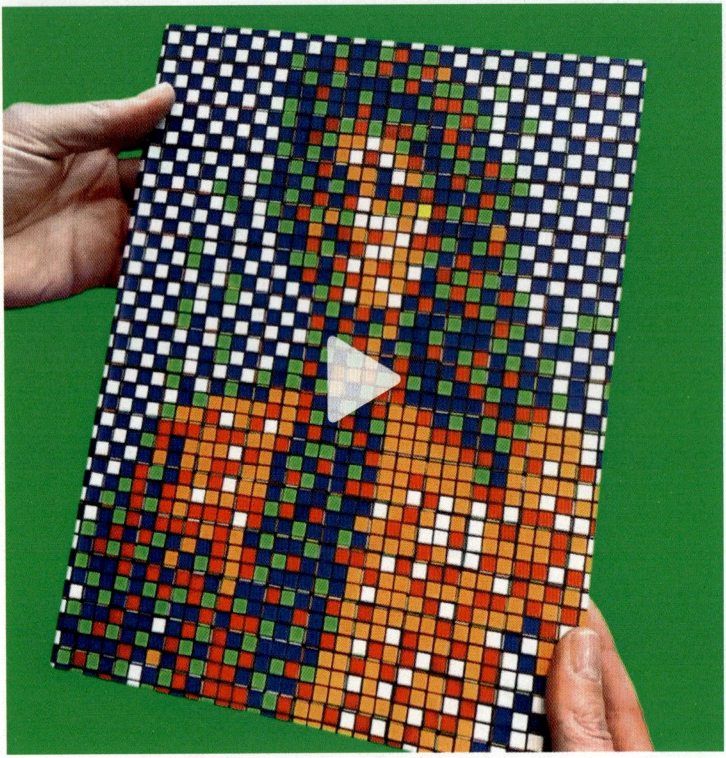

3752 likes

invaderwashere RUBIKCUBIST INVADER, 440 pages of Rubikcubism! #book #artbook #rubikcubism #rubikcubisme #controlp #online #spaceshop #plasticpassion Link in bio

View all 51 comments

9 March 2023

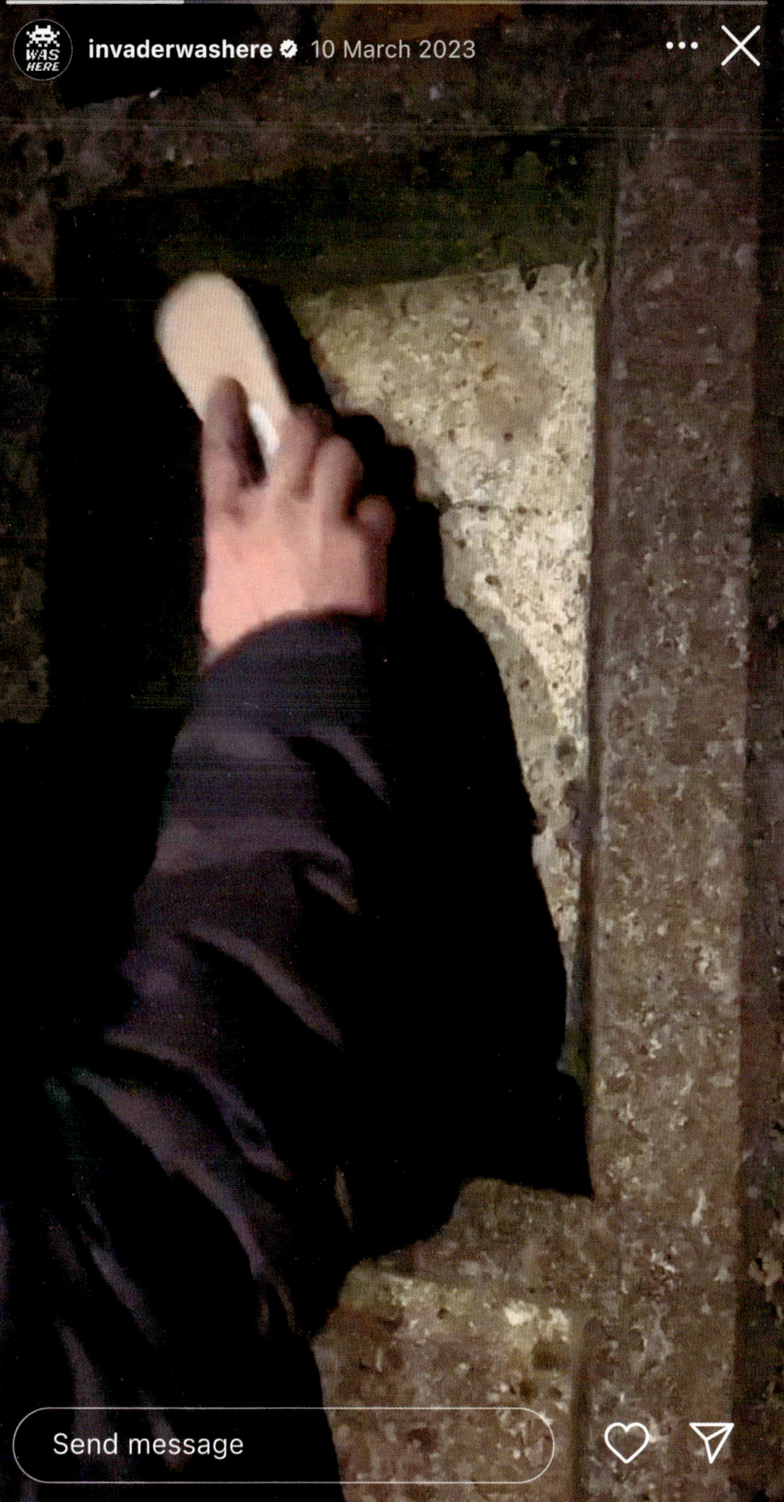

WAS HERE
invaderwashere 10 March 2023
Send message

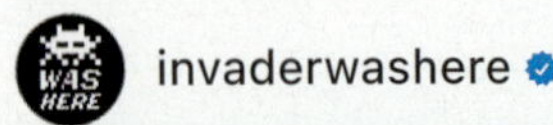

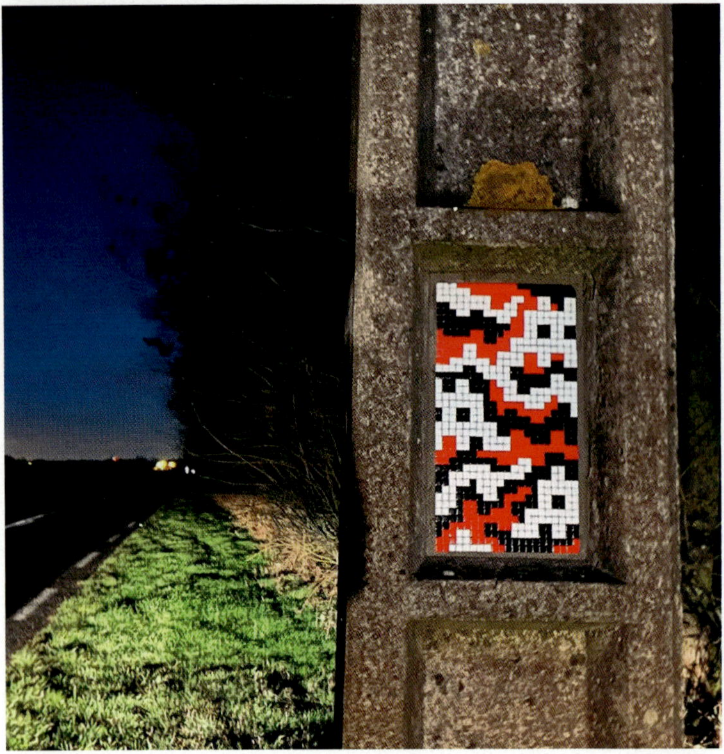

  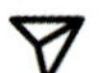 

11 382 likes

invaderwashere New territory under invasion!... #FTBL06 #fontainebleau #forest

View all 128 comments

10 March 2023

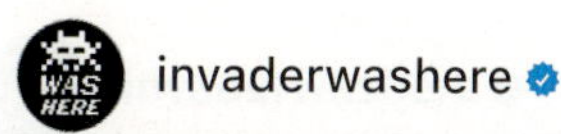

•••

  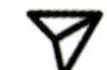 

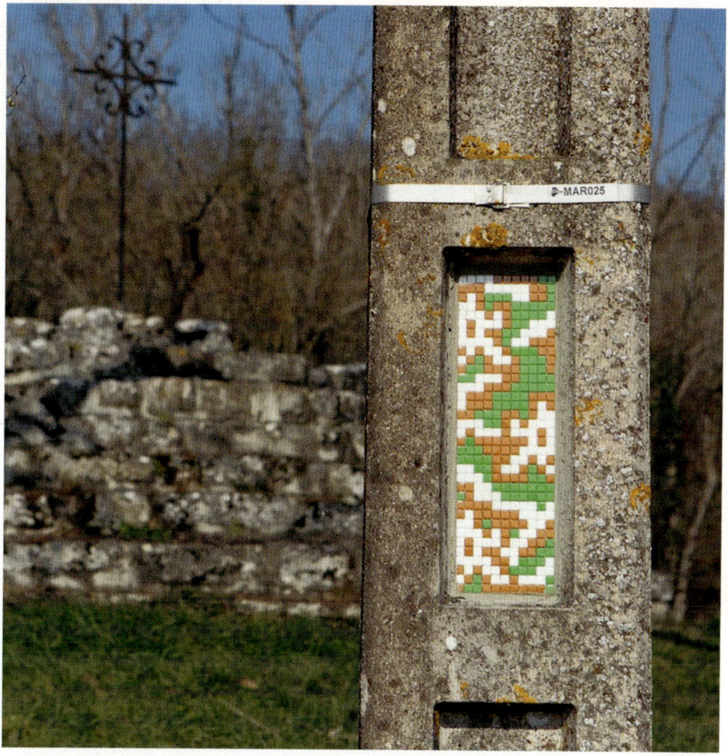

6069 likes

invaderwashere FTBL_01 #fontainebleau #larchant #forest #camouflage

View all 41 comments

12 March 2023

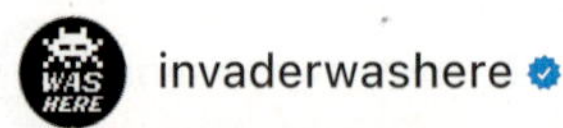

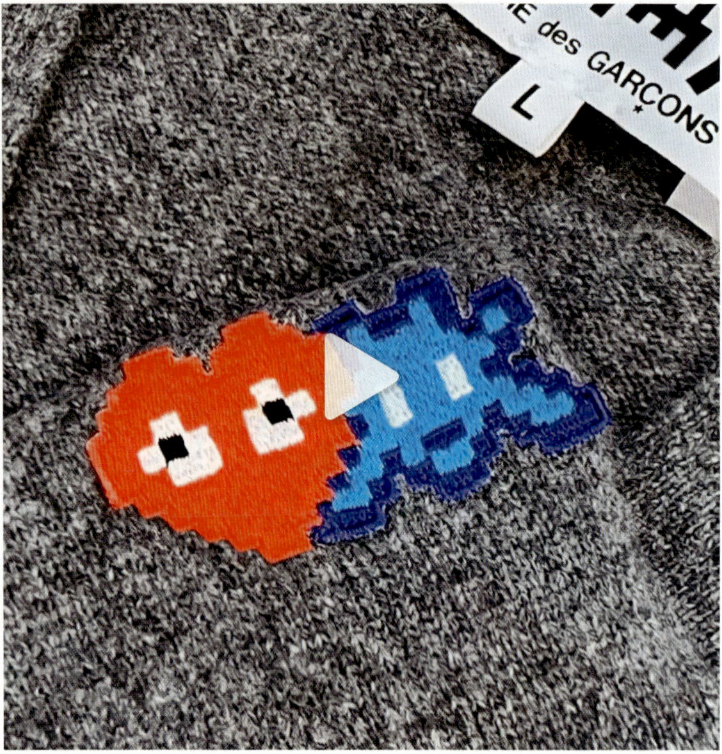

  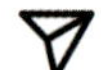 

10 456 likes

invaderwashere This is the the third part of my collaboration with Comme des Garçons / Play. The pixelated heart has now a new friend 🧡 👾 More info: @commedesgarcons

View all 100 comments

15 March 2023

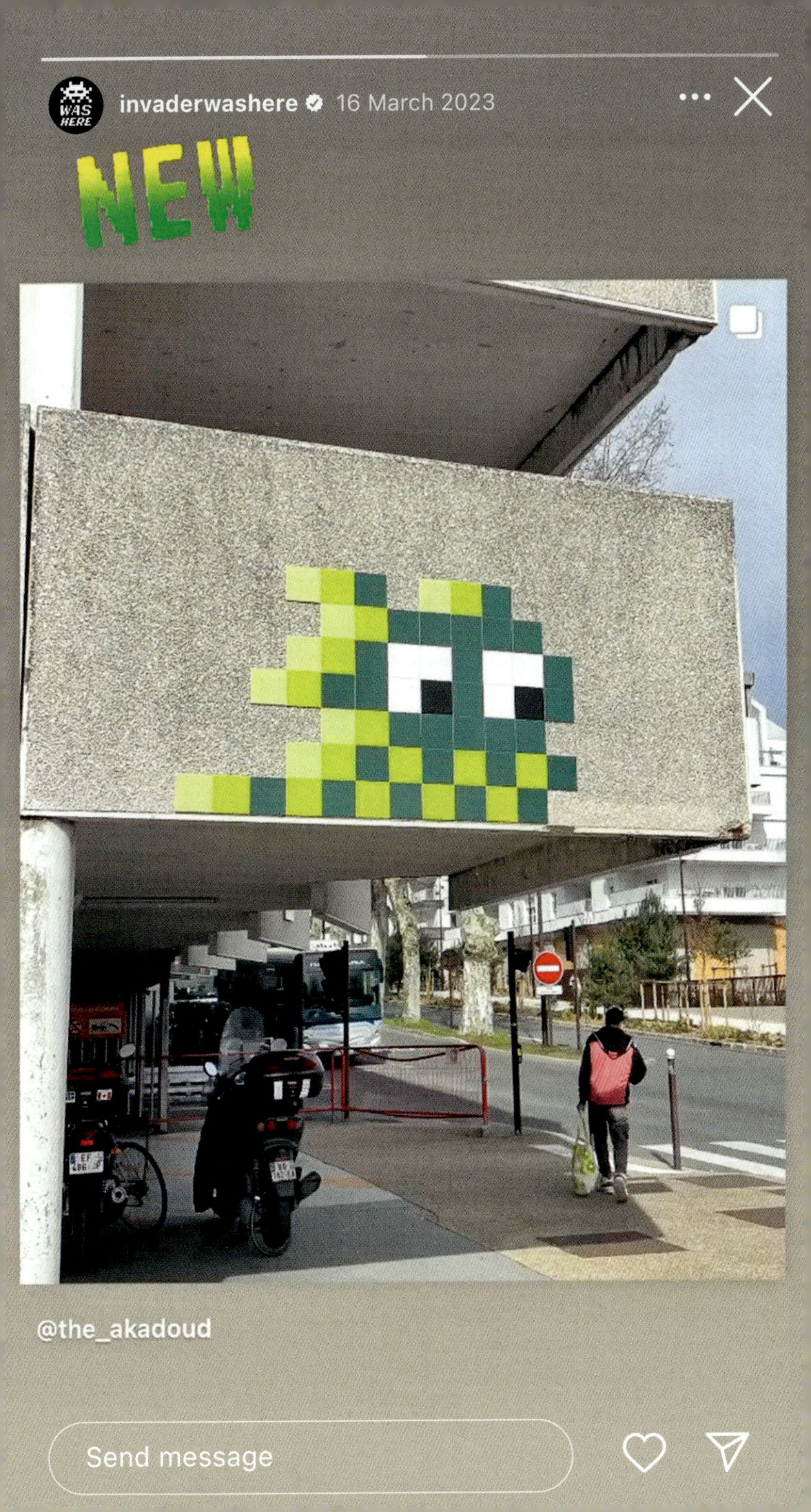

invaderwashere 16 March 2023

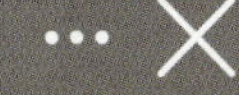

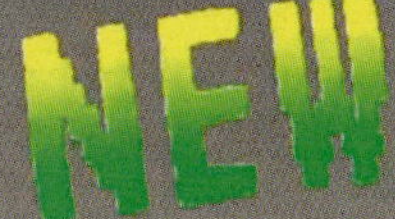

@the_akadoud

Send message

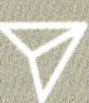

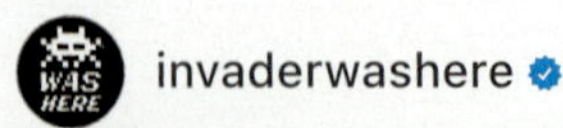

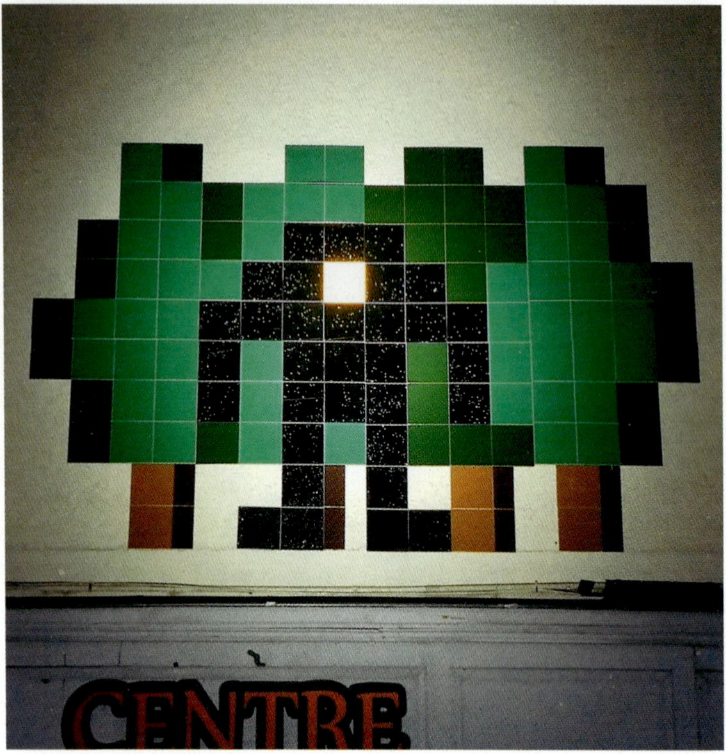

8 058 likes

invaderwashere Tribute to Le Cyclop of Tinguely & Niki de St Phalle in Milly-la-Forêt #lecyclop #tinguely #mirrors #millylaforet #fontainebleau #forest Starry night 📸 by @chesterlight75

View all 75 comments

20 March 2023

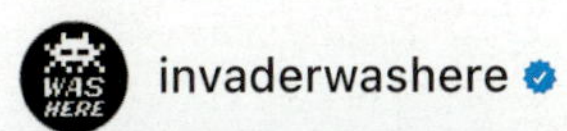

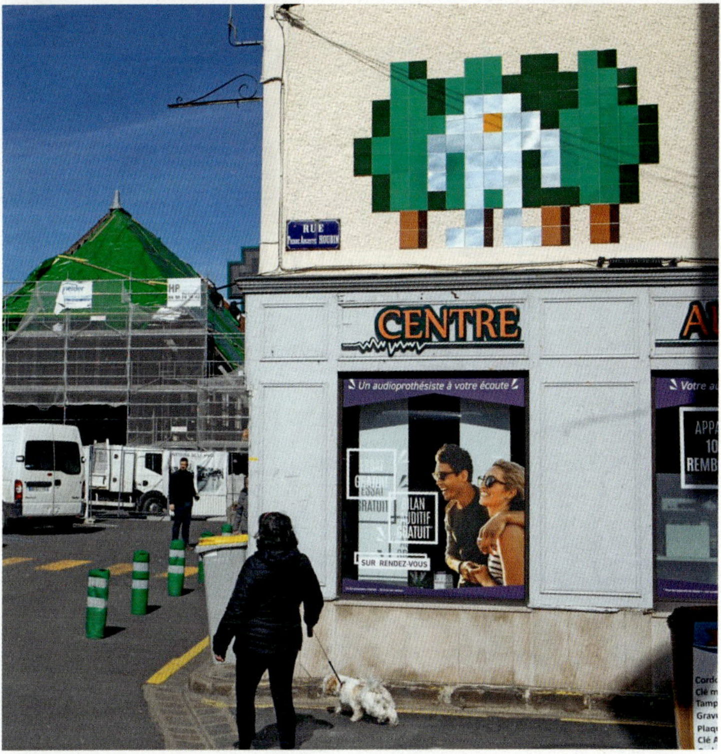

   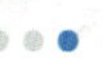 

8058 likes

invaderwashere Tribute to Le Cyclop of Tinguely & Niki de St Phalle in Milly-la-Forêt #lecyclop #tinguely #mirrors #millylaforet #fontainebleau #forest Starry night 📸 by @chesterlight75

View all 75 comments

20 March 2023

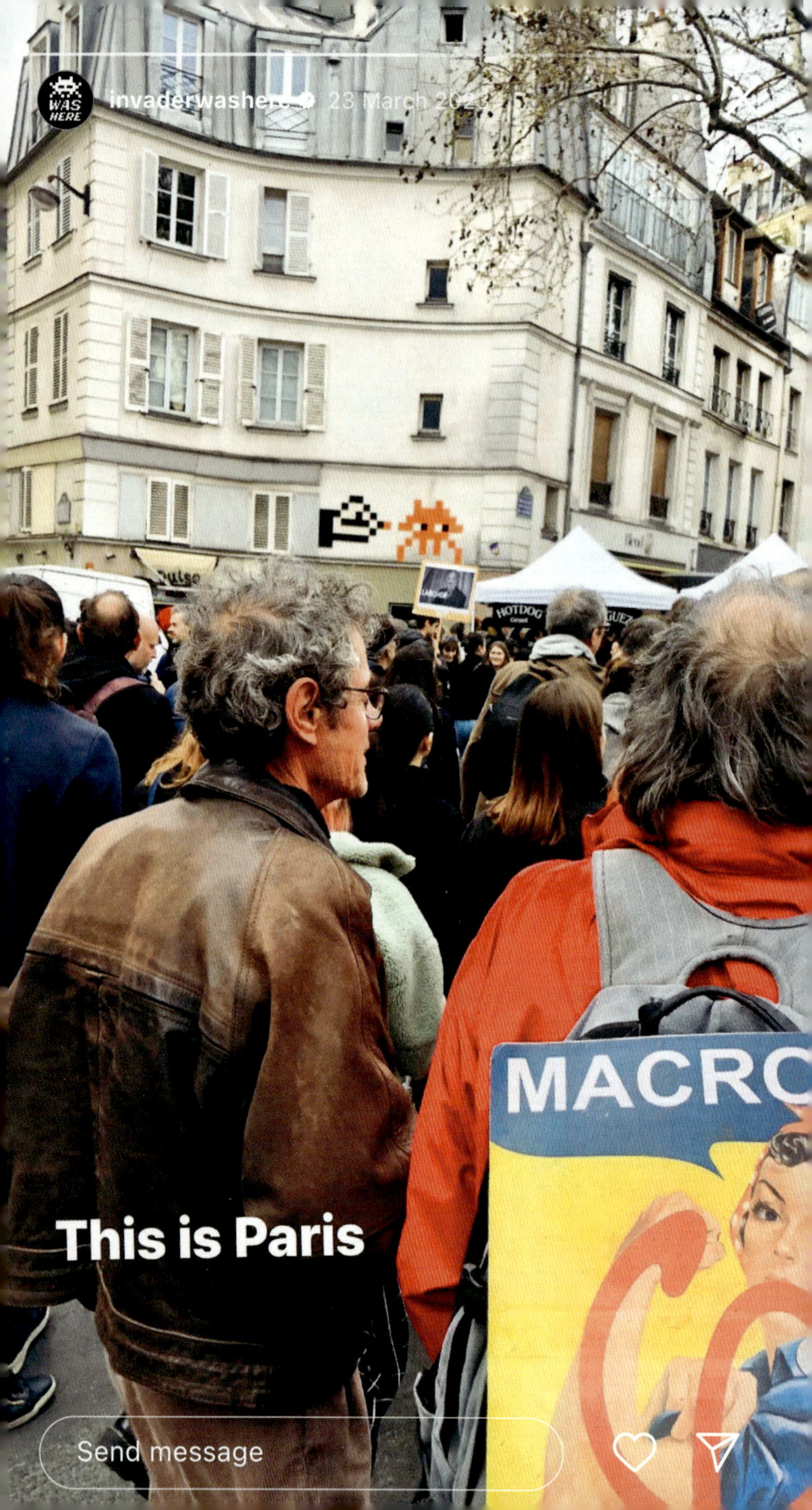
invaderwashere 23 March 2023
HOTDOG
MACRO
This is Paris
Send message

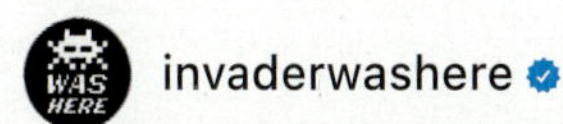

HENI

INVADER

RUBIK COUNTRY LIFE

2023
100 × 100 cm
Diasec-mounted Giclée print on aluminium composite panel
From the series Rubikcubism
Heni Editions Catalogue Number: NVDR1-3
Edition Number: 148/431

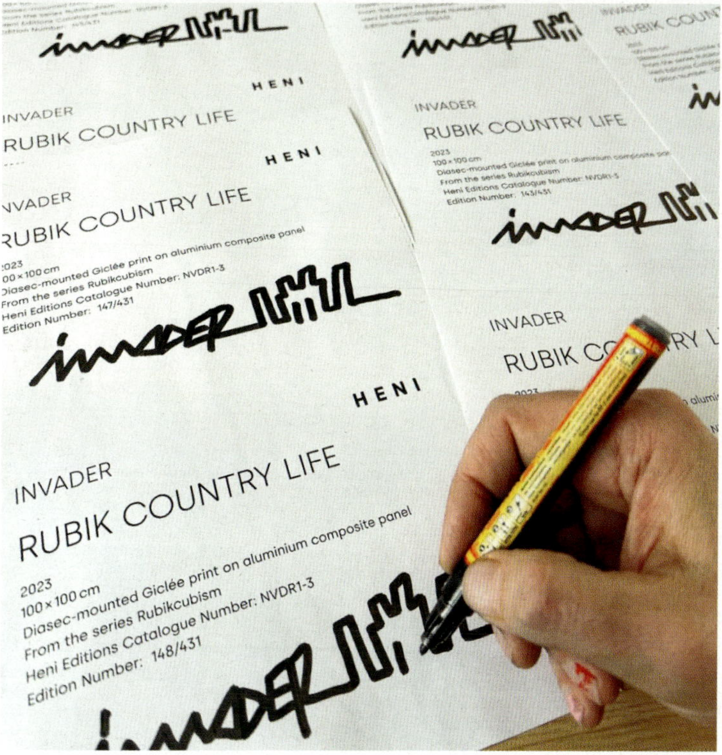

4 115 likes

invaderwashere Signing day... ✍️ @heni

View all 75 comments

24 March 2023

invaderwashere 3 April 2023
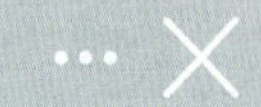

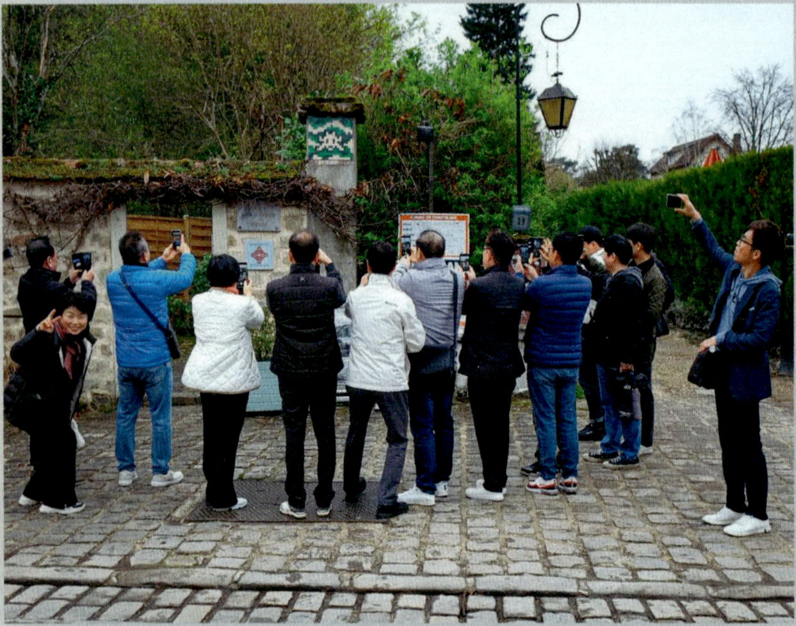

@guillaumebirraux

Corean flash tour in Barbizon 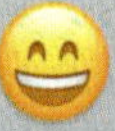

Send message  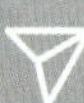

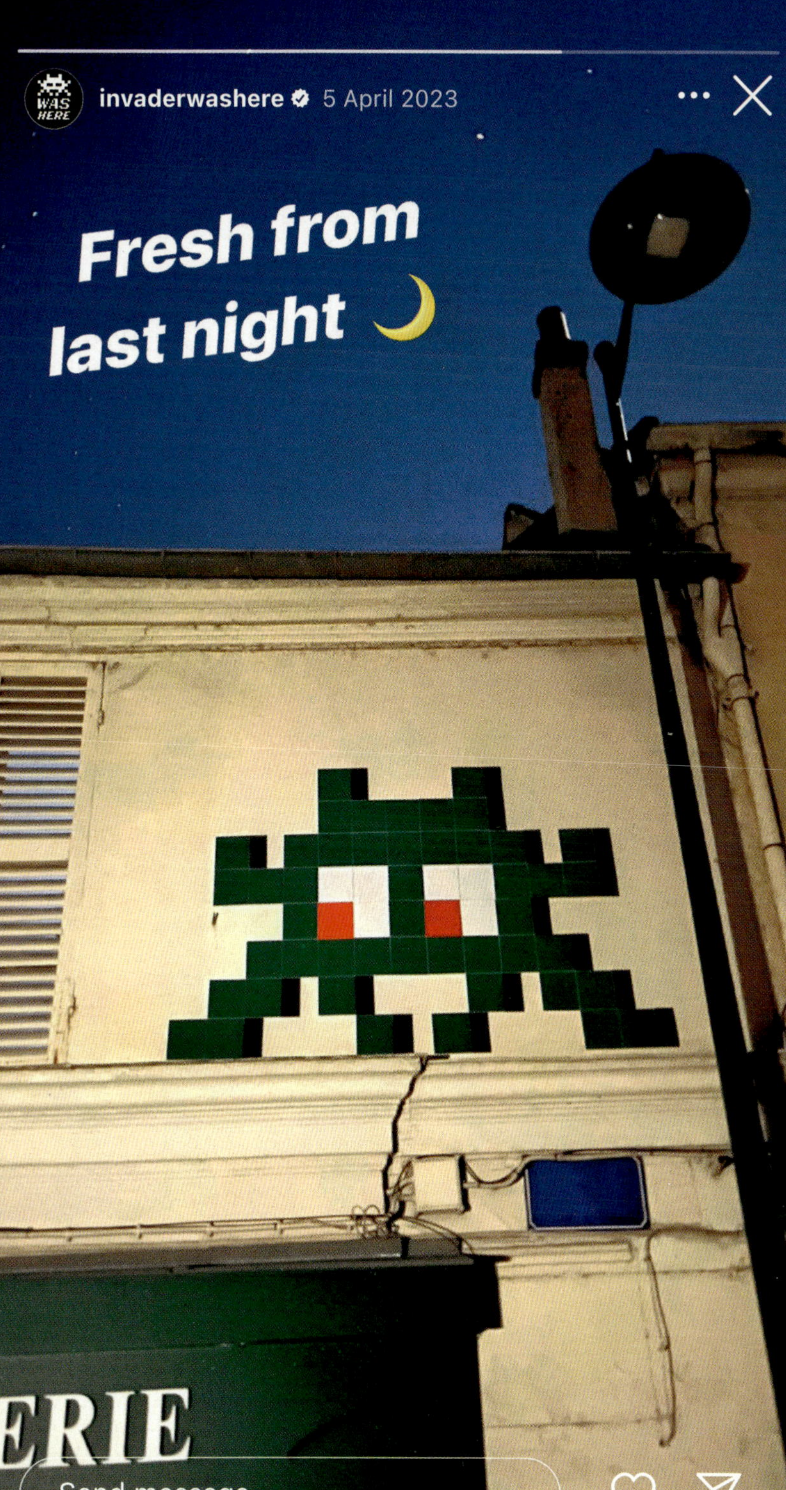

invaderwashere 5 April 2023
Fresh from last night
ERIE
Send message

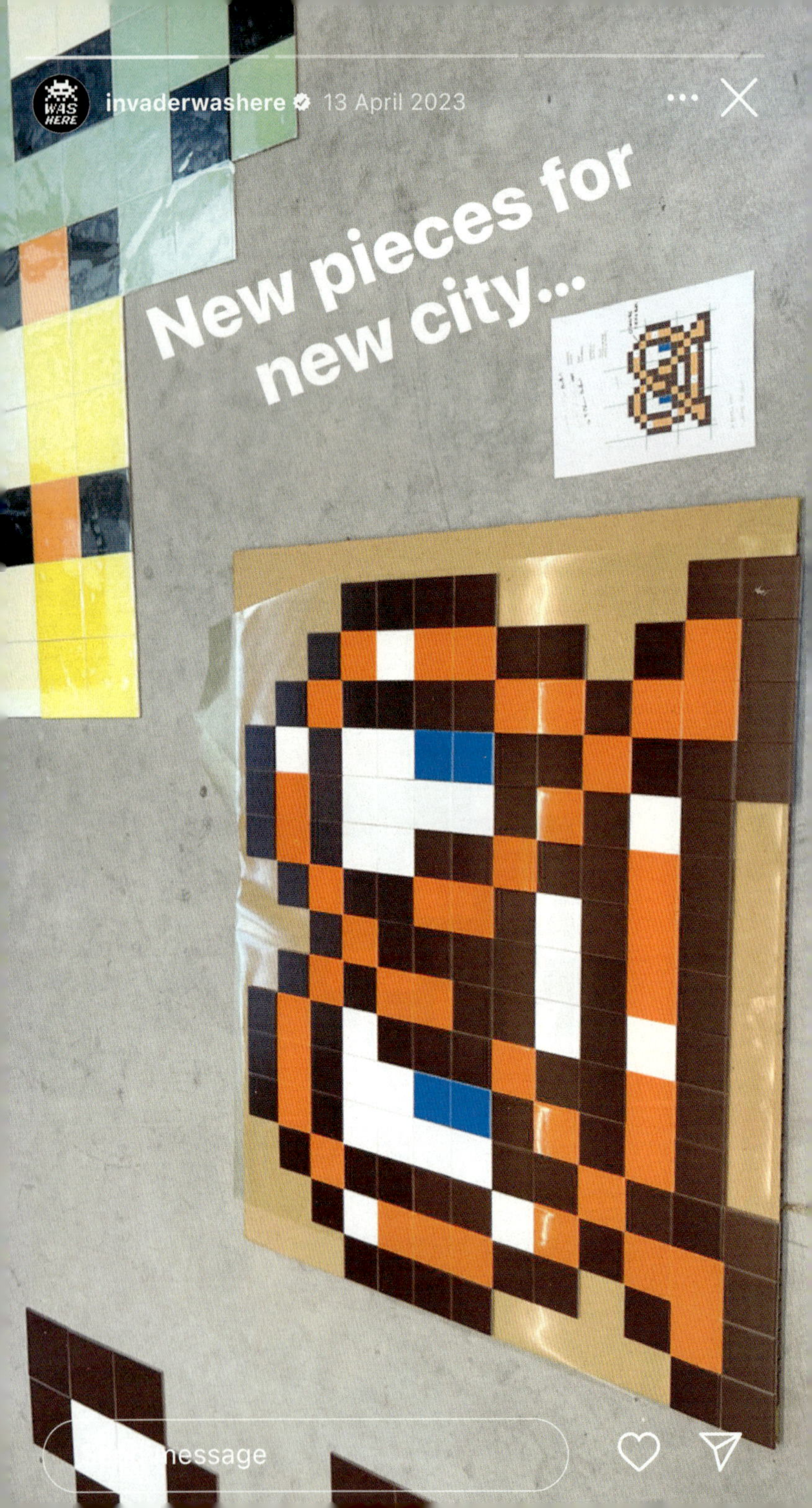

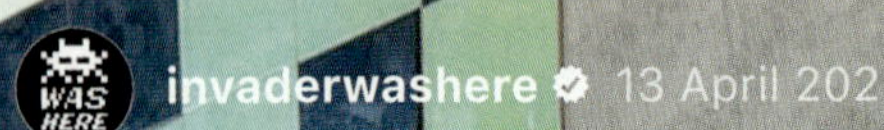

New pieces for
new city...

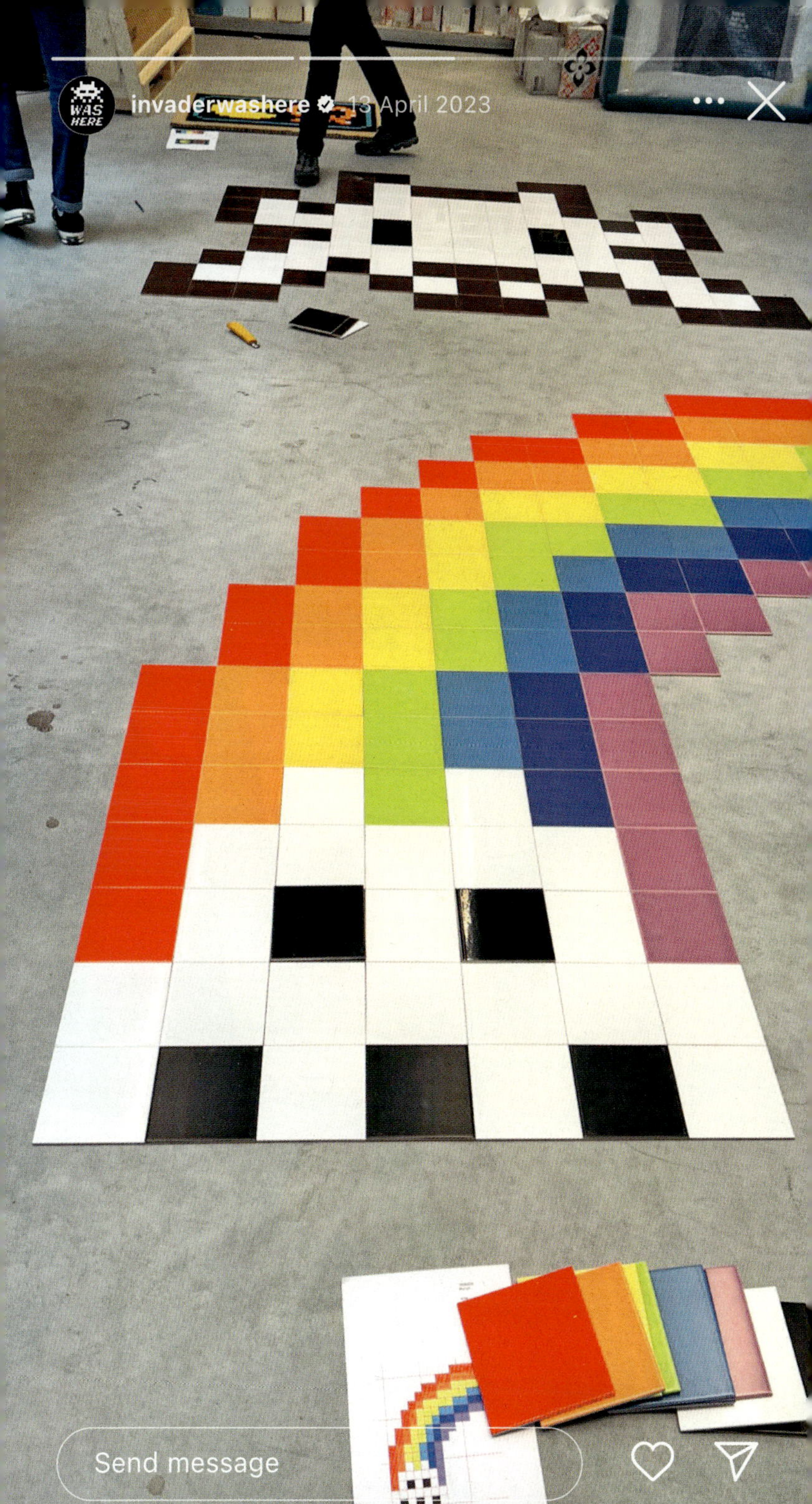
WAS HERE
invaderwashere
13 April 2023
Send message

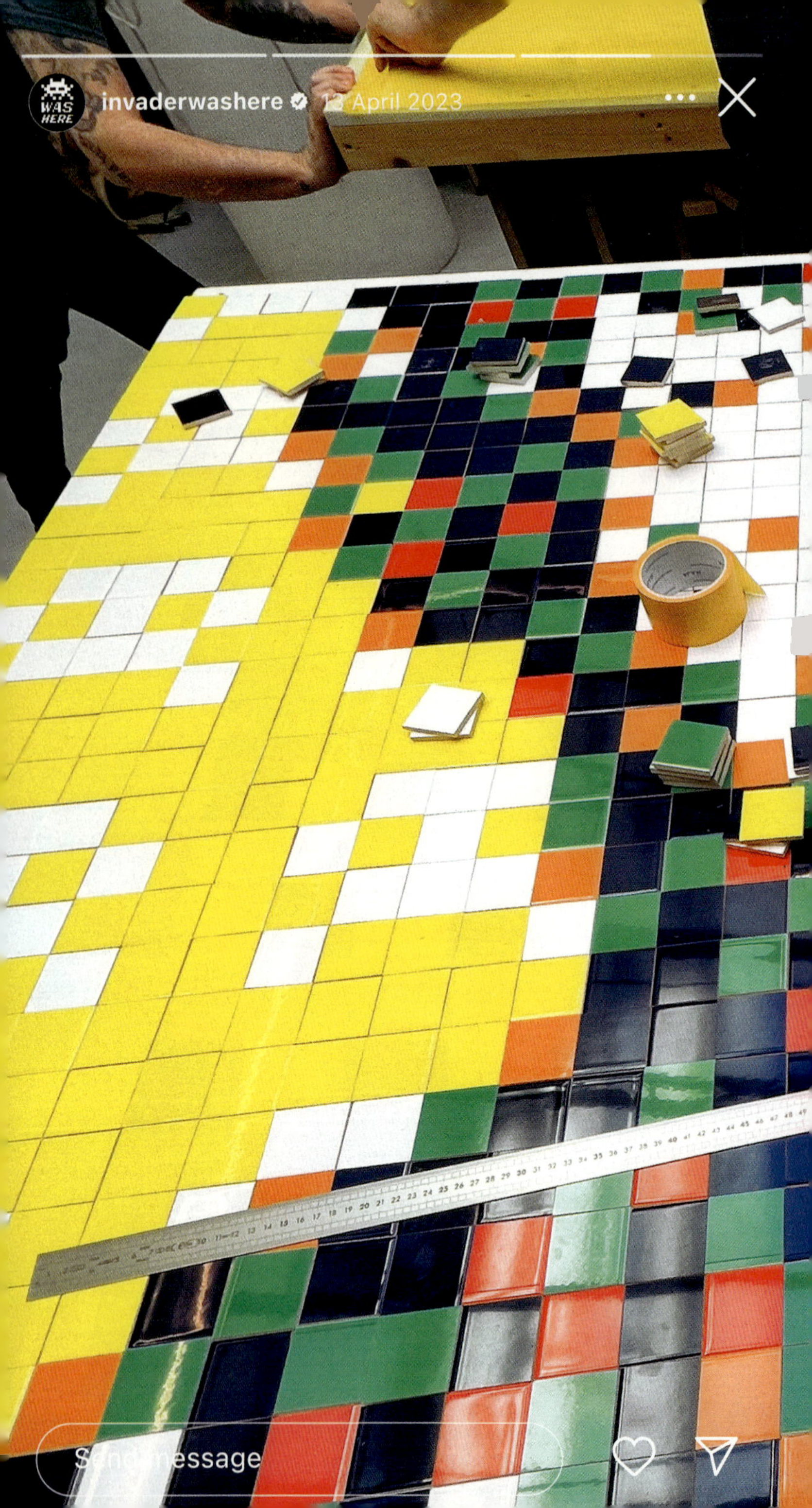

WAS HERE
invaderwashere
13 April 2023
Send message

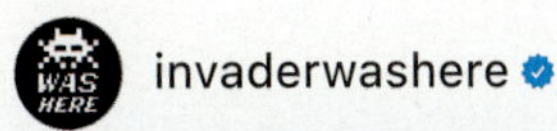

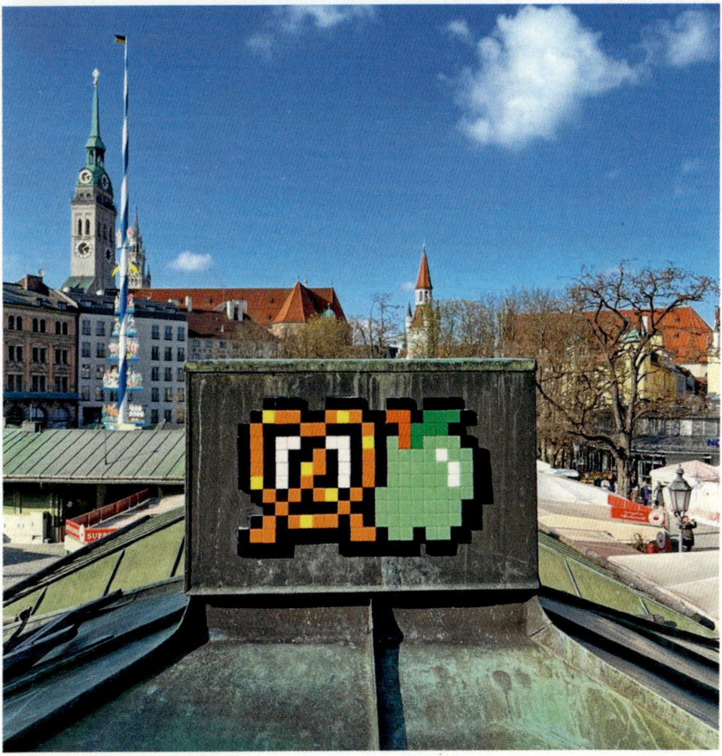

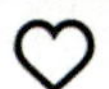   

13 770 likes

invaderwashere Munich is the new spot 🥨🇩🇪👾
#munich #münchen #bretzelinvader

View all 206 comments

14 April 2023

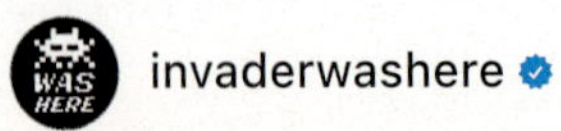

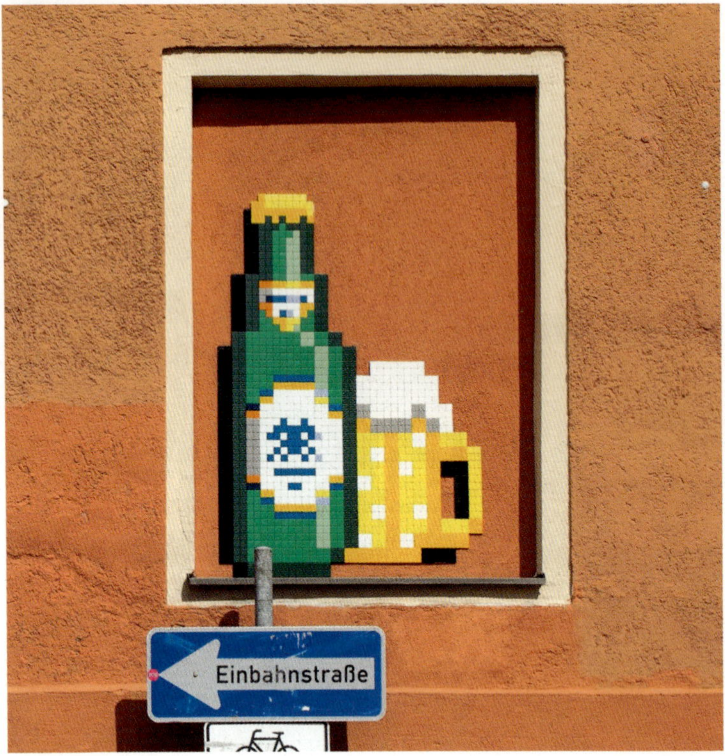

  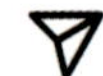 

16 598 likes

invaderwashere 👾 🍺 #munich #münchen #beer #oktoberfest #hofbrauhaus

View all 178 comments

16 April 2023

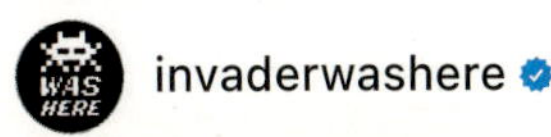

invaderwashere

  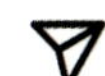 

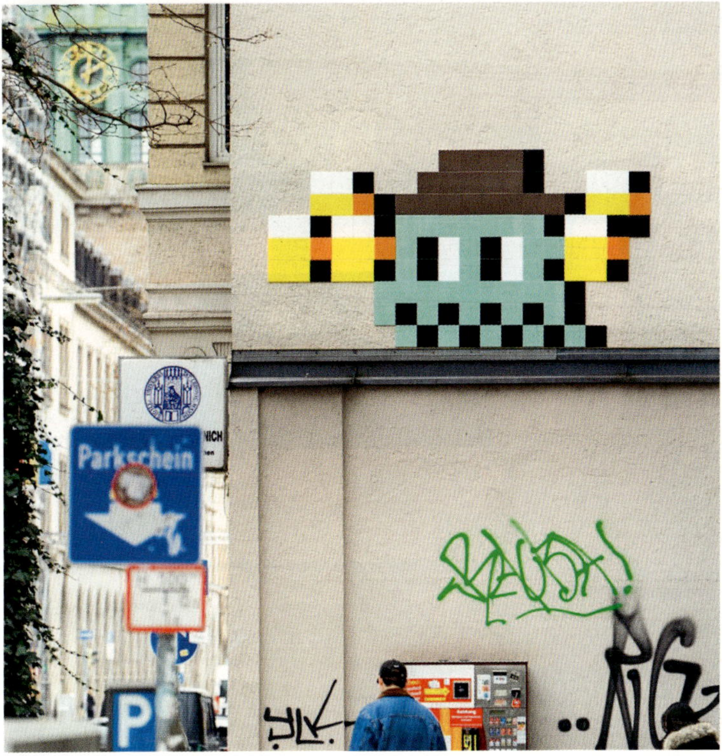

16 598 likes

invaderwashere 👾 🍺 #munich #münchen #beer #oktoberfest #hofbrauhaus

View all 178 comments

16 April 2023

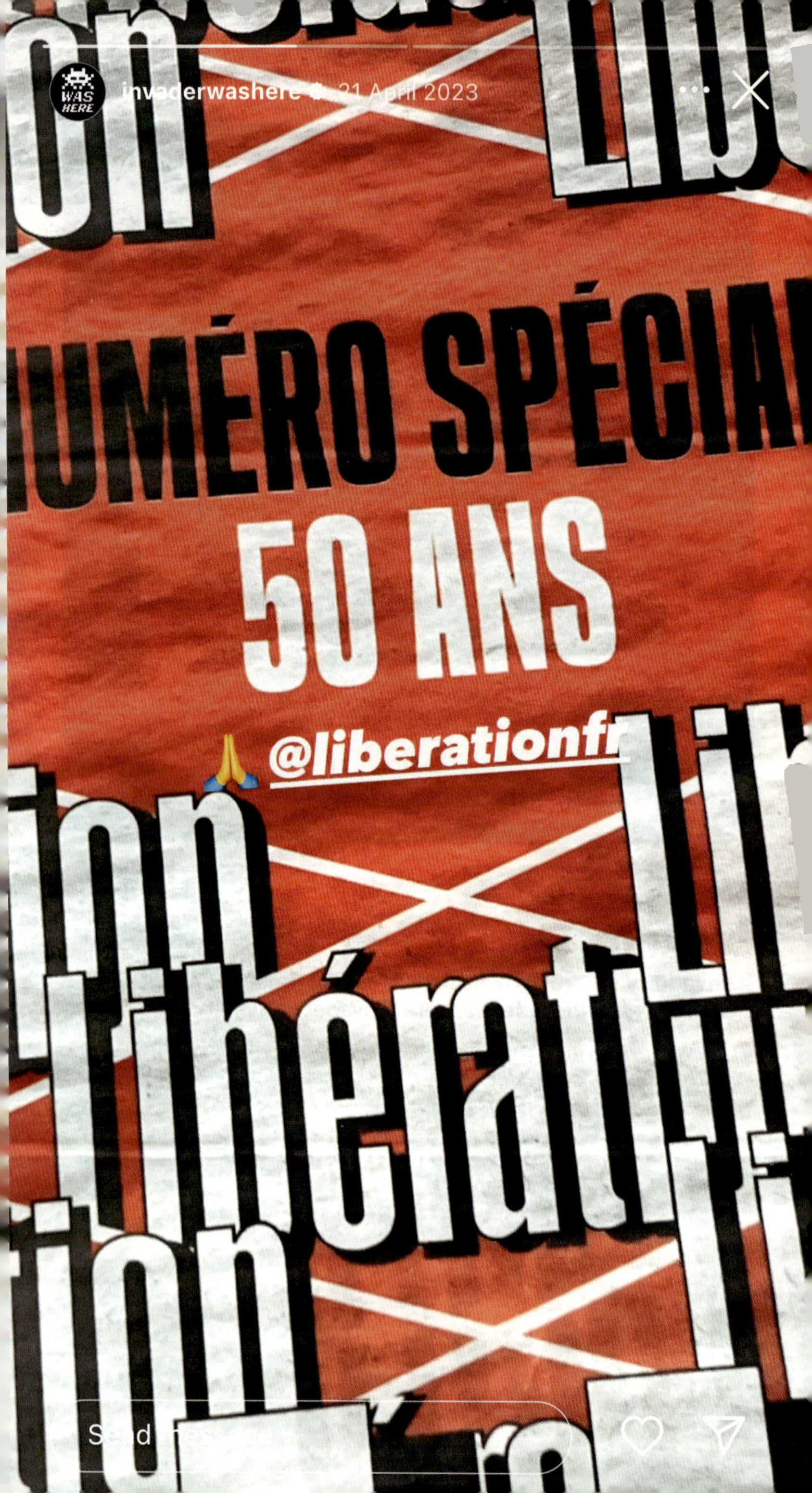
invaderwashere
21 April 2023
UMÉRO SPÉCIA
50 ANS
@liberationfr

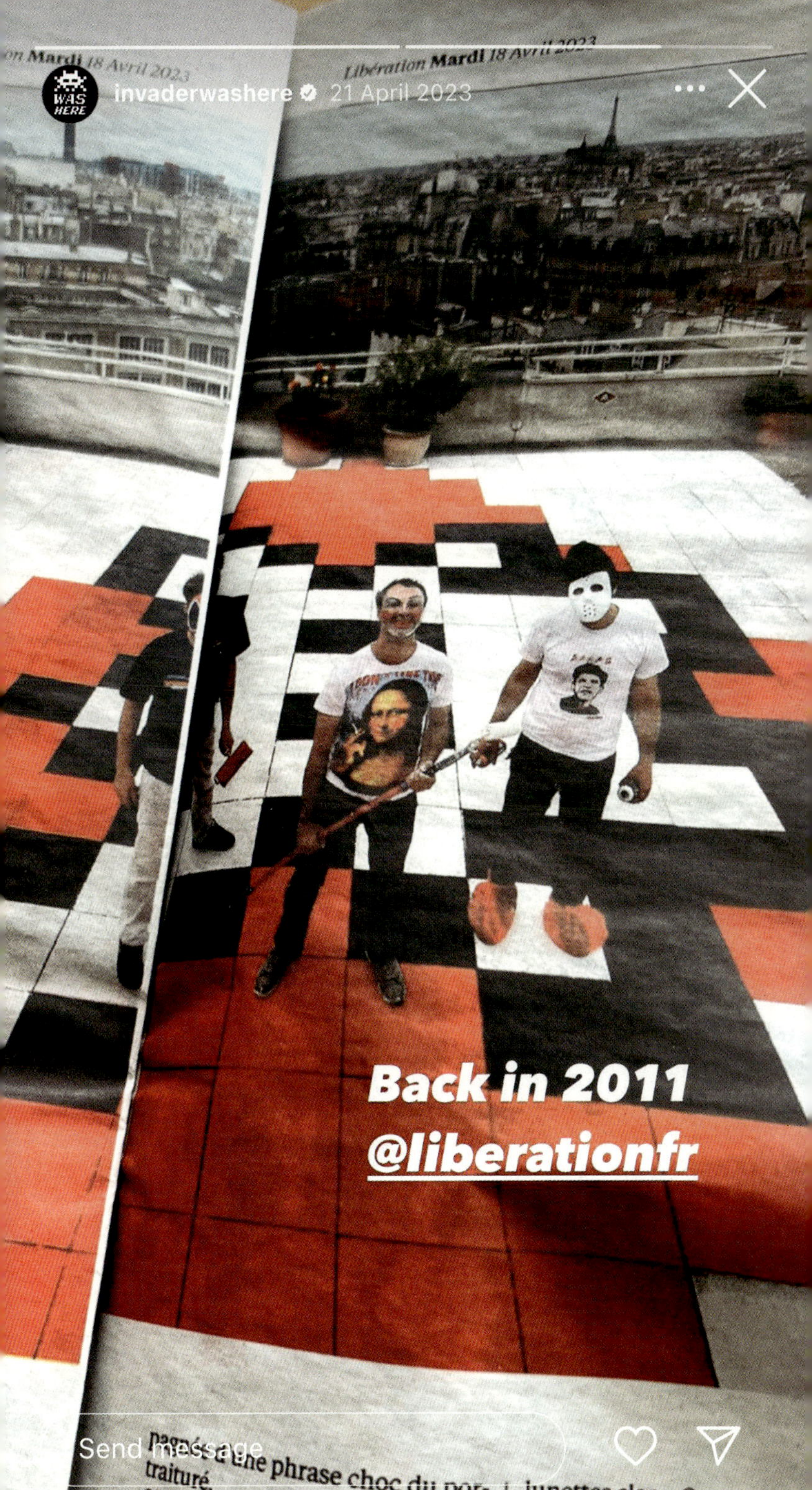

Libération Mardi 18 Avril 2023
invaderwashere
21 April 2023
WAS HERE
Back in 2011
@liberationfr
Send message

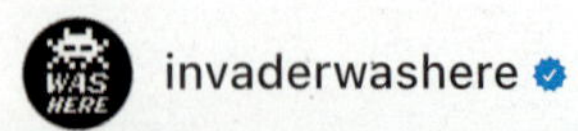

invaderwashere

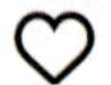   

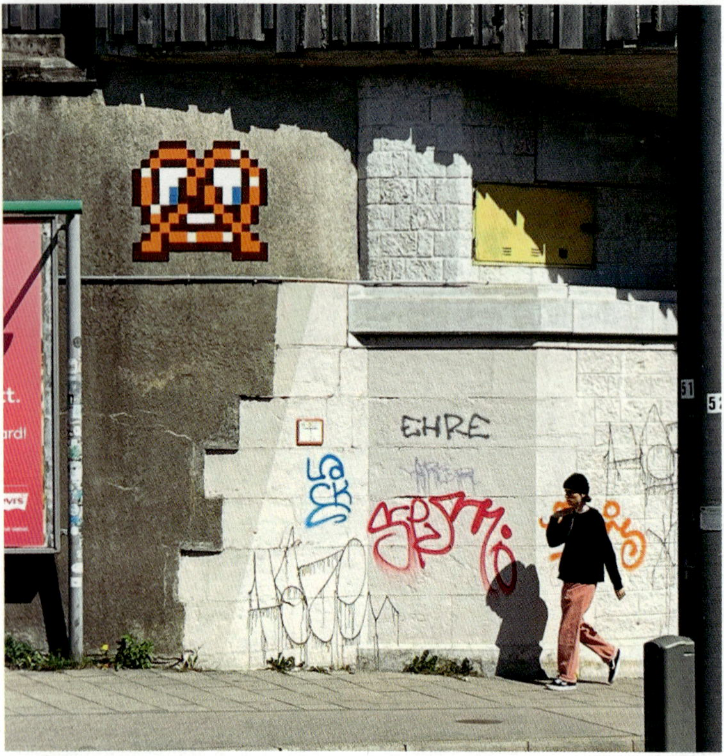

8 356 likes

invaderwashere Another 🥨 👾 in Munich

View all 58 comments

27 April 2023

invaderwashere

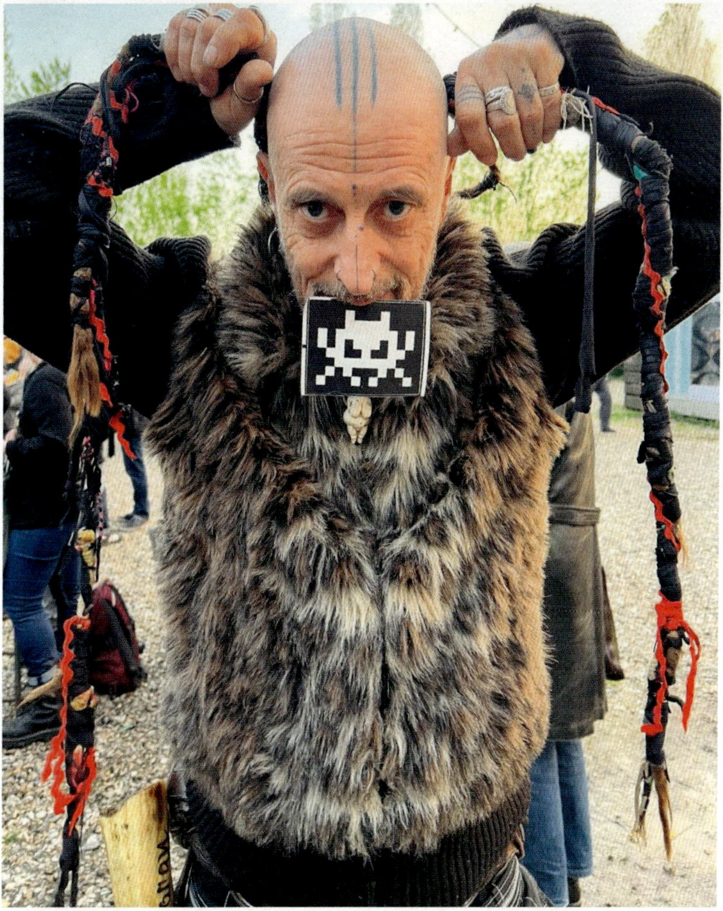

5 223 likes

invaderwashere So much respect for this guy 🙌 🙌 🙌
#loran #legend #ramoneursdemenhirs #beruriernoir
#frenchpunkrockculture

View all 72 comments

27 April 2023

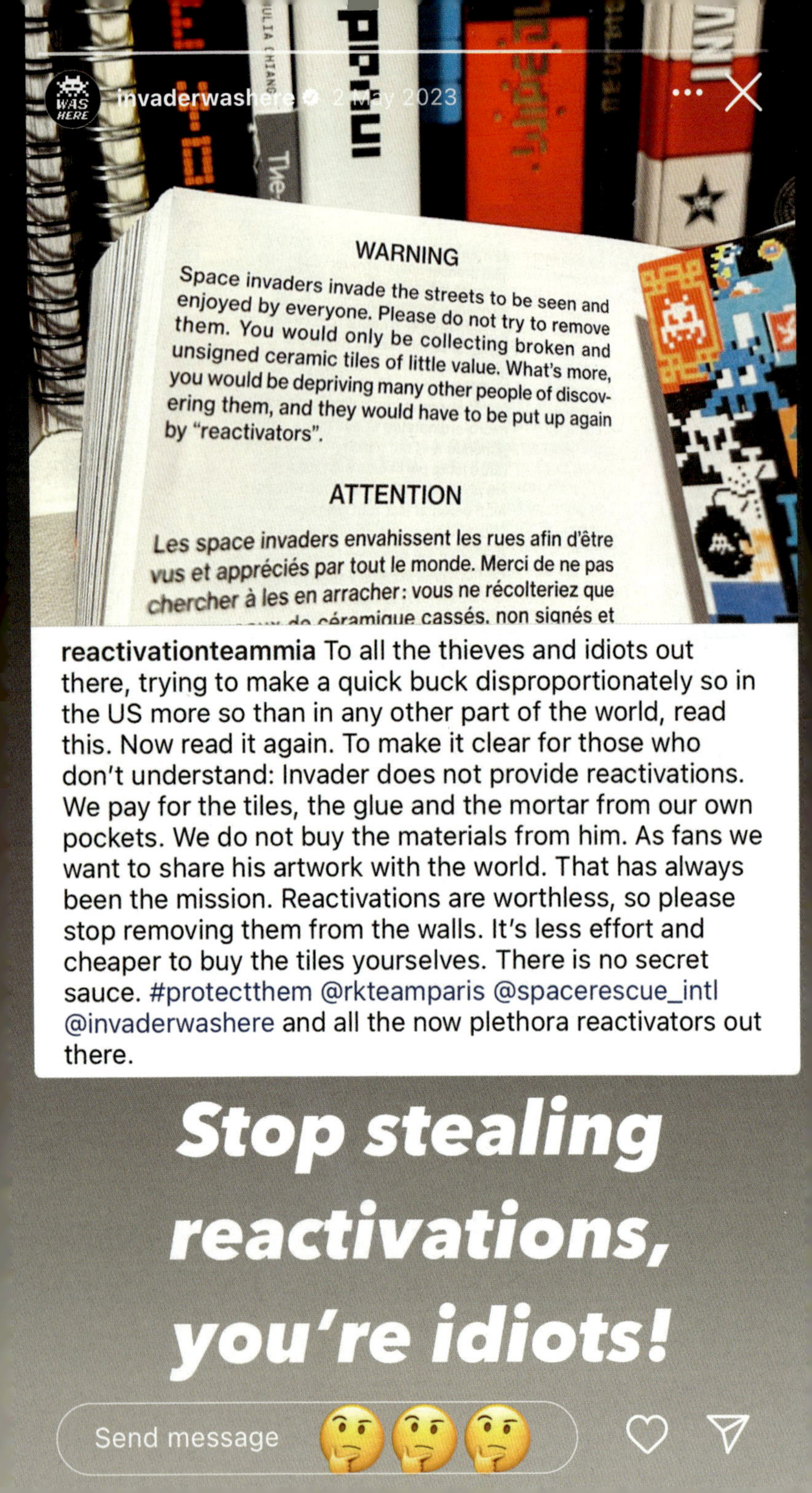

invaderwashere 2 May 2023

WARNING

Space invaders invade the streets to be seen and enjoyed by everyone. Please do not try to remove them. You would only be collecting broken and unsigned ceramic tiles of little value. What's more, you would be depriving many other people of discovering them, and they would have to be put up again by "reactivators".

ATTENTION

Les space invaders envahissent les rues afin d'être vus et appréciés par tout le monde. Merci de ne pas chercher à les en arracher : vous ne récolteriez que ... de céramique cassés, non signés et

reactivationteammia To all the thieves and idiots out there, trying to make a quick buck disproportionately so in the US more so than in any other part of the world, read this. Now read it again. To make it clear for those who don't understand: Invader does not provide reactivations. We pay for the tiles, the glue and the mortar from our own pockets. We do not buy the materials from him. As fans we want to share his artwork with the world. That has always been the mission. Reactivations are worthless, so please stop removing them from the walls. It's less effort and cheaper to buy the tiles yourselves. There is no secret sauce. #protectthem @rkteamparis @spacerescue_intl @invaderwashere and all the now plethora reactivators out there.

Stop stealing reactivations, you're idiots!

Send message

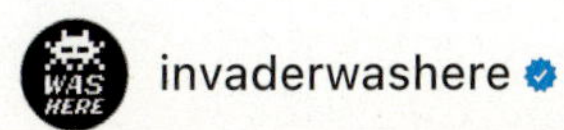

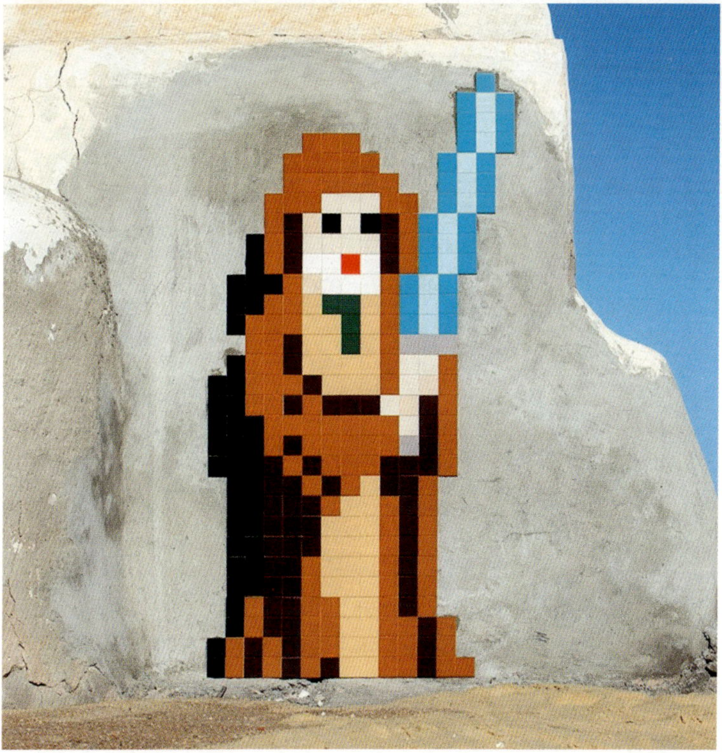

22 725 likes

invaderwashere May the 4th be with you ✨ #starwarsday #may4th #popculture #djerba #paris #roma #london

View all 161 comments

4 May 2023

invaderwashere

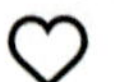    

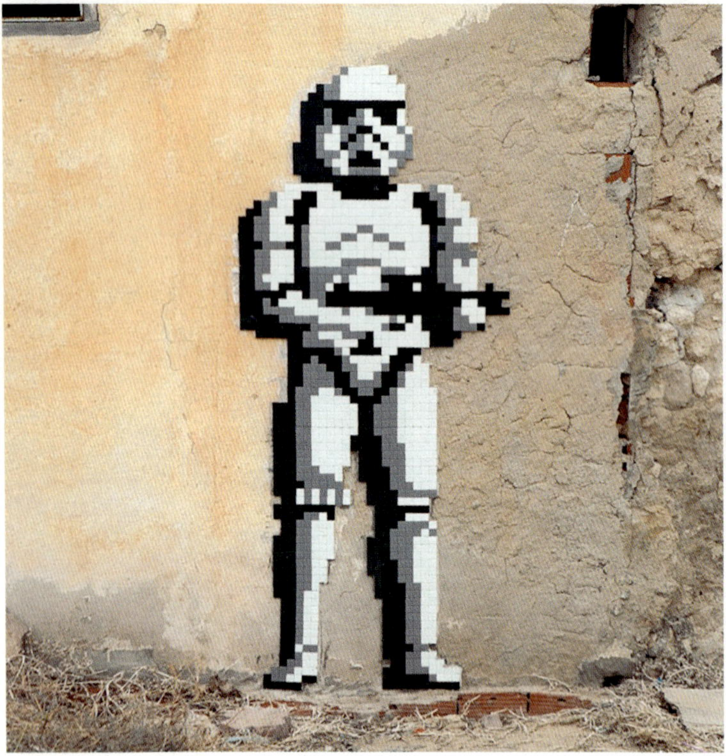

22 725 likes

invaderwashere May the 4th be with you ✨ #starwarsday #may4th #popculture #djerba #paris #roma #london

View all 161 comments

4 May 2023

invaderwashere

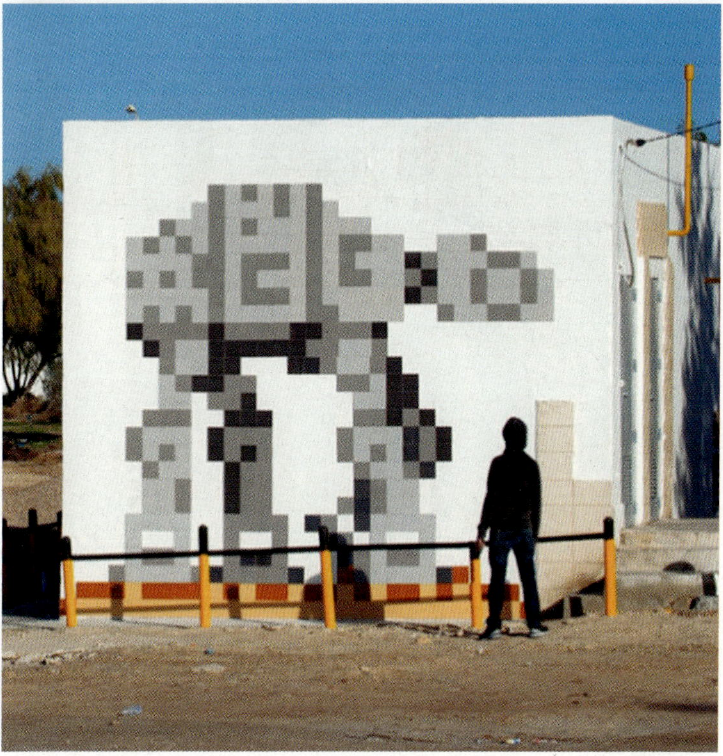

22 725 likes

invaderwashere May the 4th be with you ✨ #starwarsday #may4th #popculture #djerba #paris #roma #london

View all 161 comments

4 May 2023

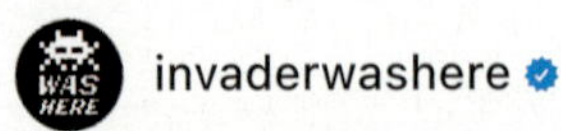

invaderwashere •••

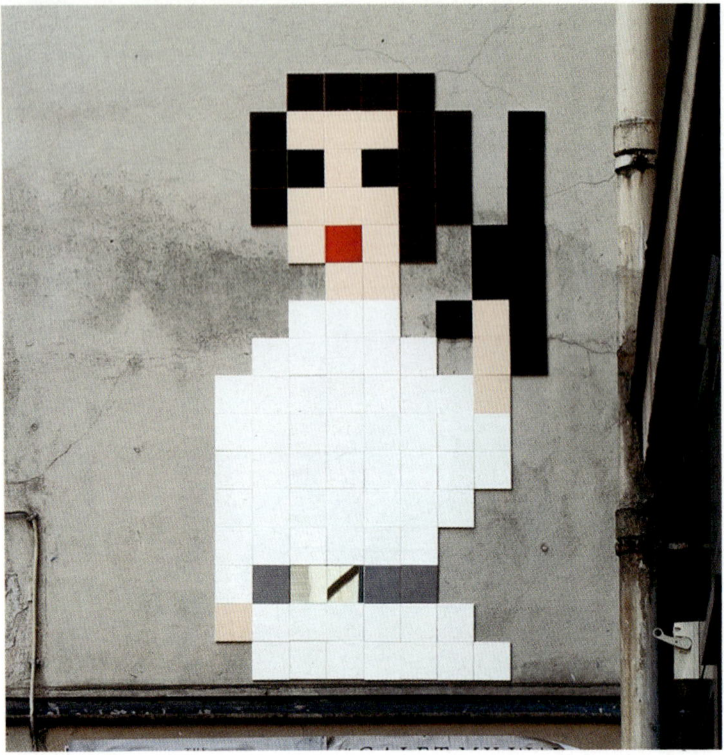

22 725 likes

invaderwashere May the 4th be with you ✨ #starwarsday #may4th #popculture #djerba #paris #roma #london

View all 161 comments

4 May 2023

invaderwashere

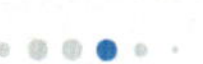

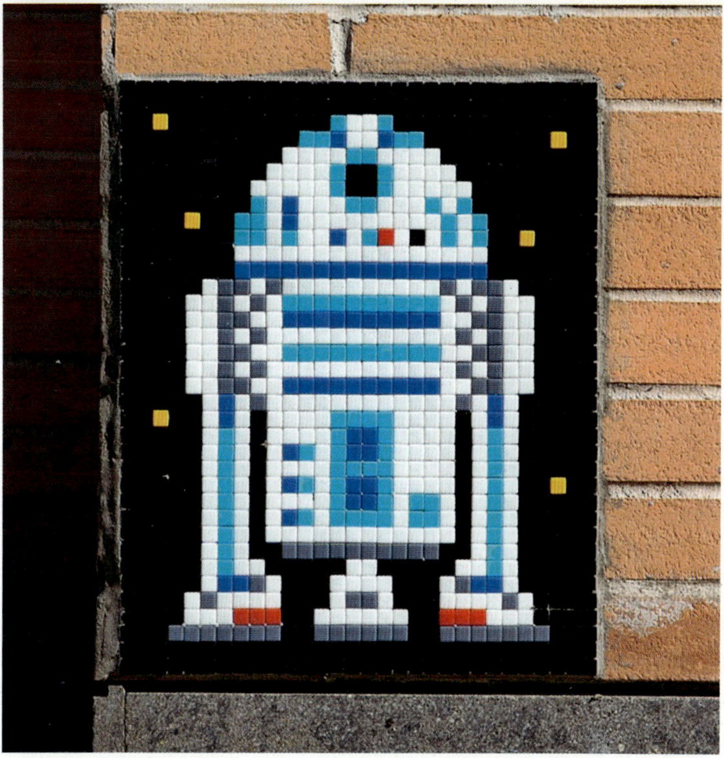

22 725 likes

invaderwashere May the 4th be with you ✨ #starwarsday #may4th #popculture #djerba #paris #roma #london

View all 161 comments

4 May 2023

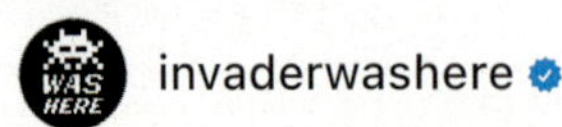

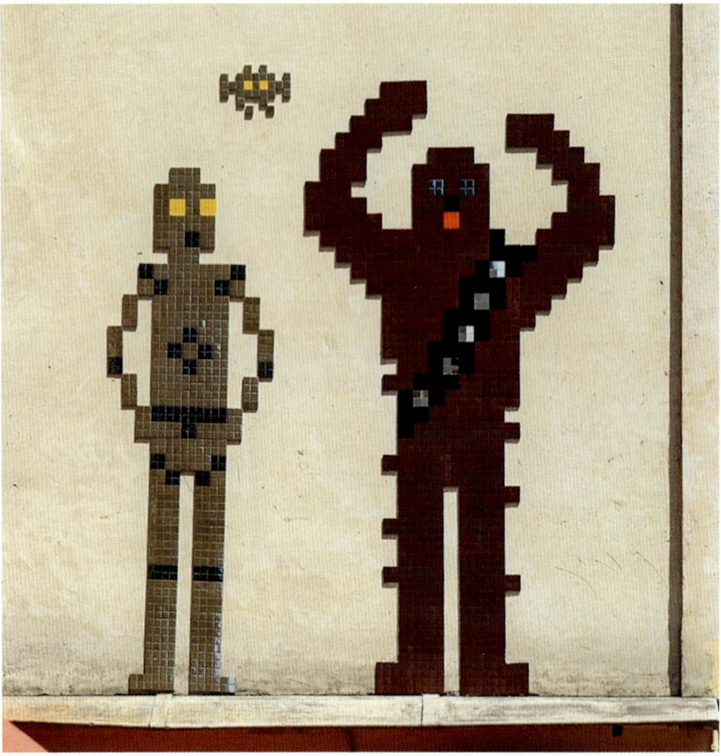

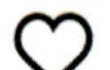    

22 725 likes

invaderwashere May the 4th be with you ✨ #starwarsday #may4th #popculture #djerba #paris #roma #london

View all 161 comments

4 May 2023

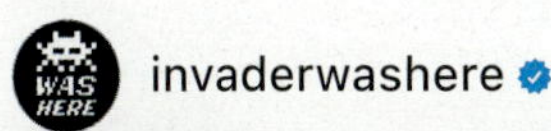

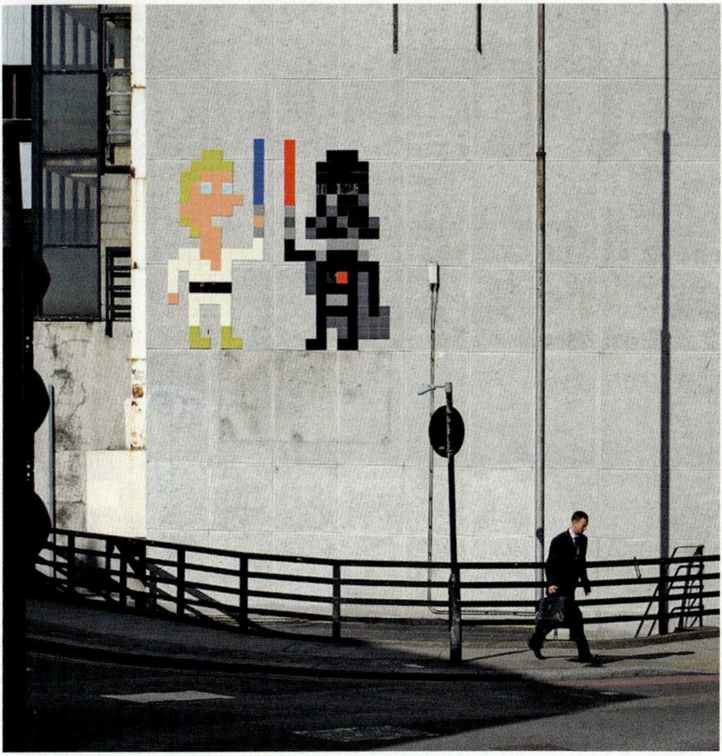

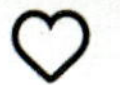   

22 725 likes

invaderwashere May the 4th be with you ✨ #starwarsday #may4th #popculture #djerba #paris #roma #london

View all 161 comments

4 May 2023

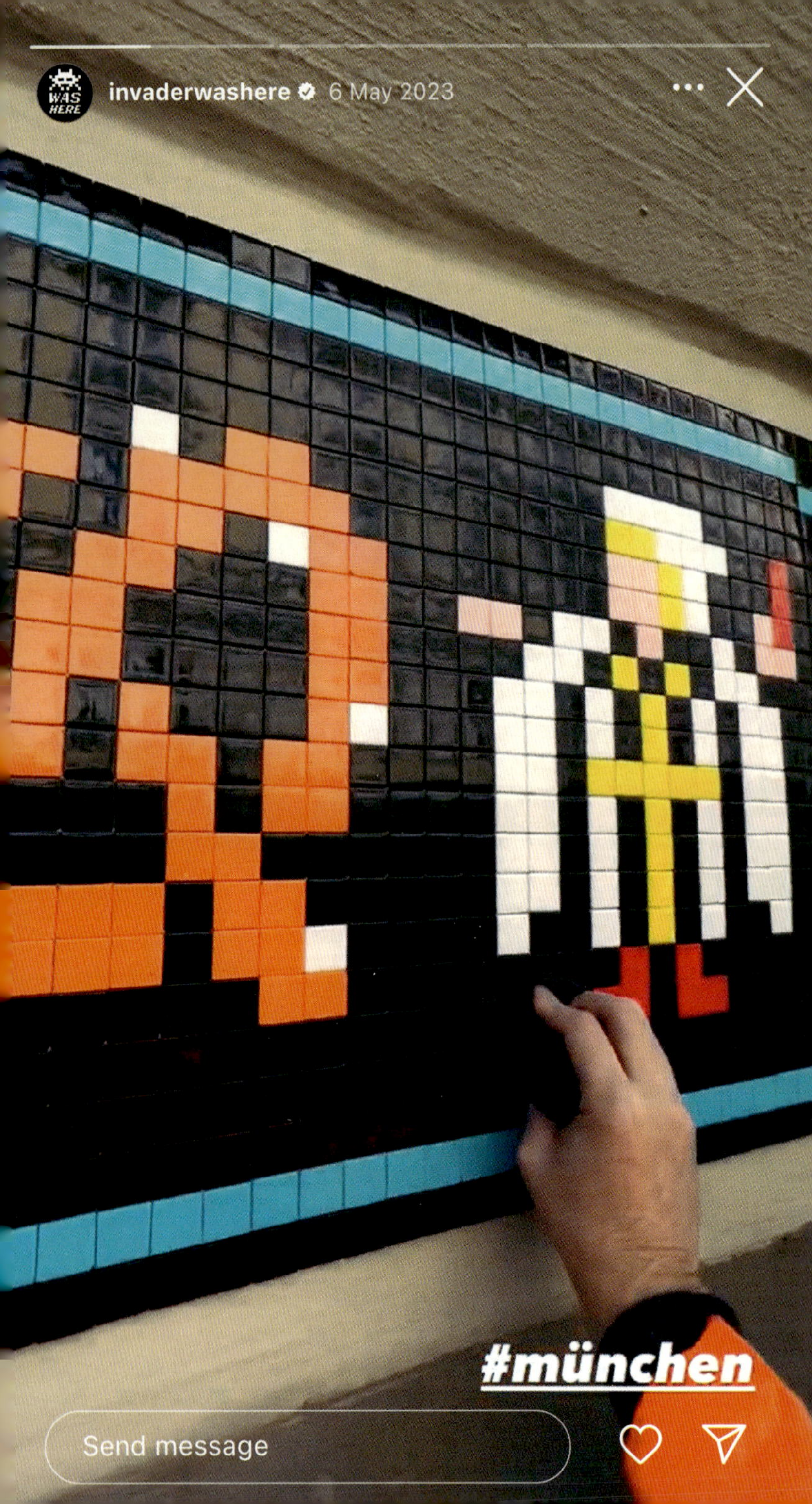

WAS HERE
invaderwashere 6 May 2023
#münchen
Send message

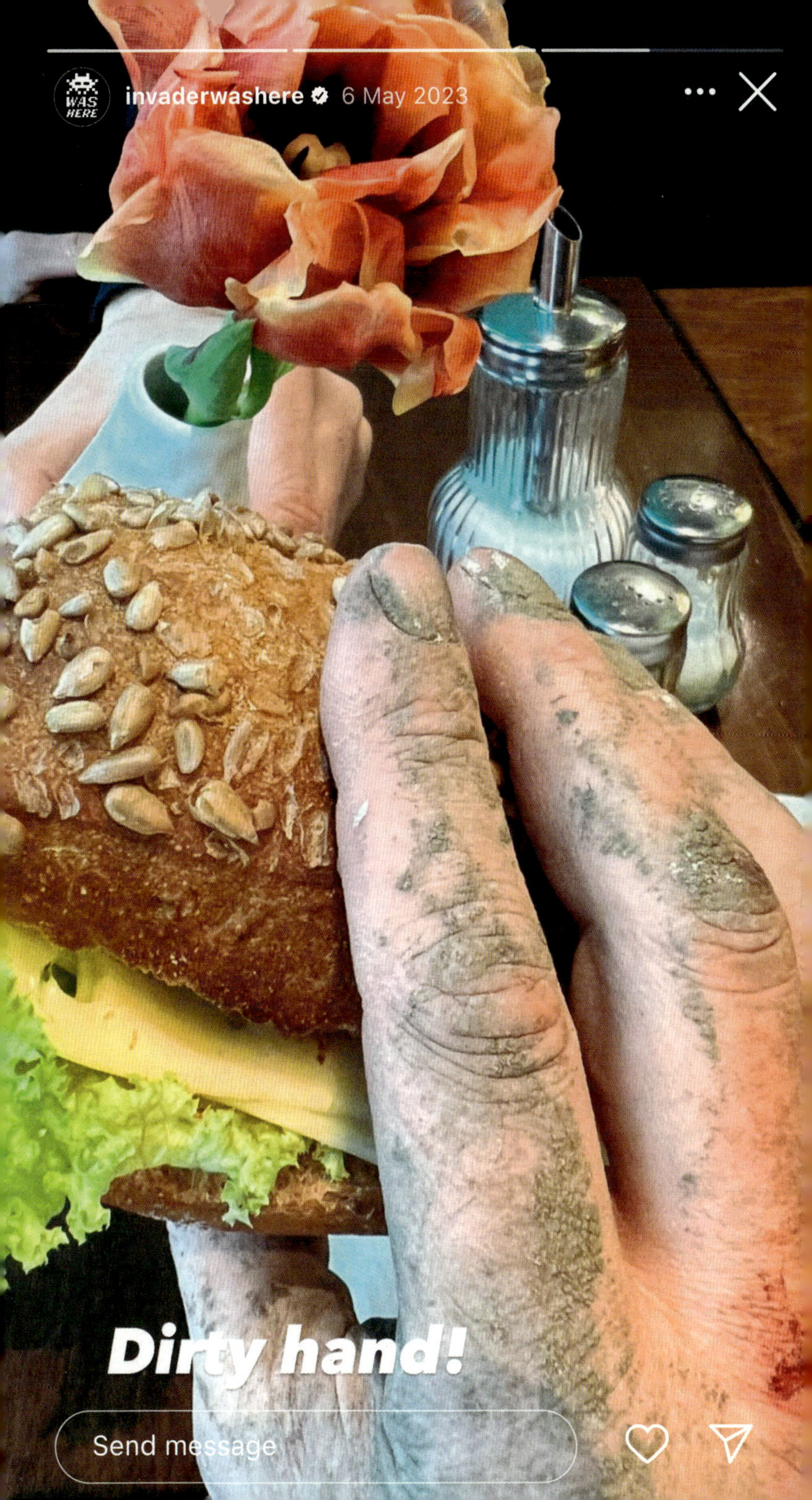
WAS HERE
invaderwashere
6 May 2023
Dirty hand!
Send message

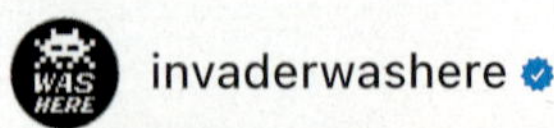

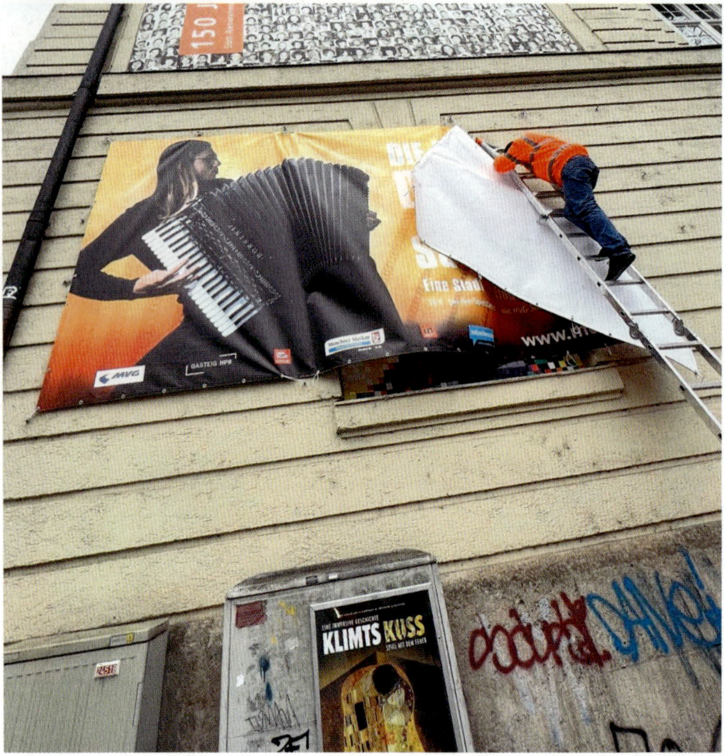

 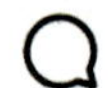  

12 719 likes

invaderwashere Guess why I've made this portrait of Edward Snowden in Munich and why it's made with Rubik's cubes colors? ⬜🟨🟧🟥🟩🟦 For the record, I had scouted this spot for a long time but two days before its installation a billboard appeared right in front of it! 😬 Fortunately I was able to remove it, to install the mosaic and then to put it back in place. 😅✌️💯 #snowden #edwardsnowden #citizenfour #munich #bnd #nsa #pixelart #rubikcubism #100pts

View all 190 comments

8 May 2023

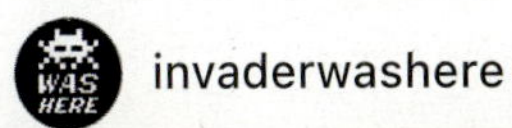

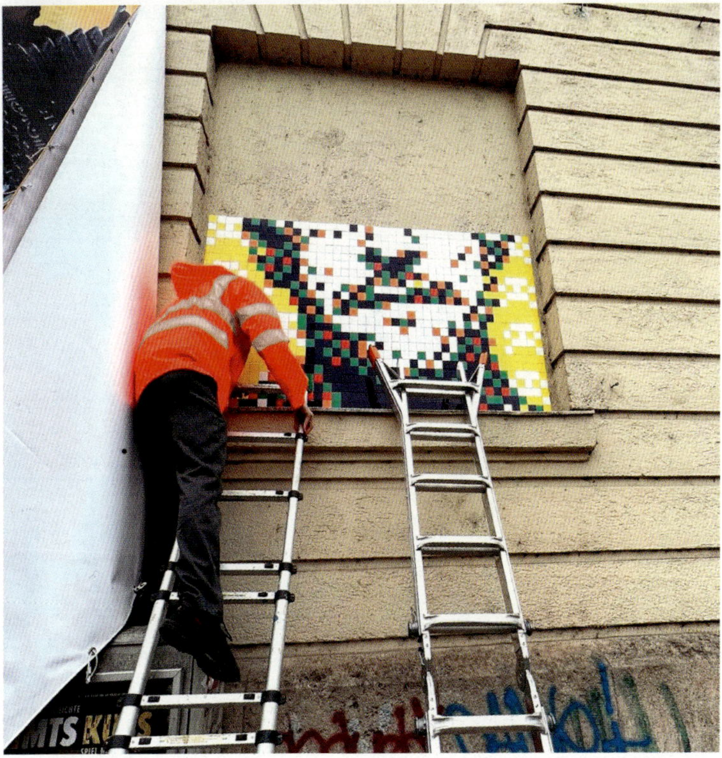

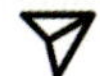

12 719 likes

invaderwashere Guess why I've made this portrait of Edward Snowden in Munich and why it's made with Rubik's cubes colors? For the record, I had scouted this spot for a long time but two days before its installation a billboard appeared right in front of it! Fortunately I was able to remove it, to install the mosaic and then to put it back in place. #snowden #edwardsnowden #citizenfour #munich #bnd #nsa #pixelart #rubikcubism #100pts

View all 190 comments

8 May 2023

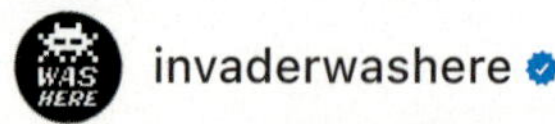

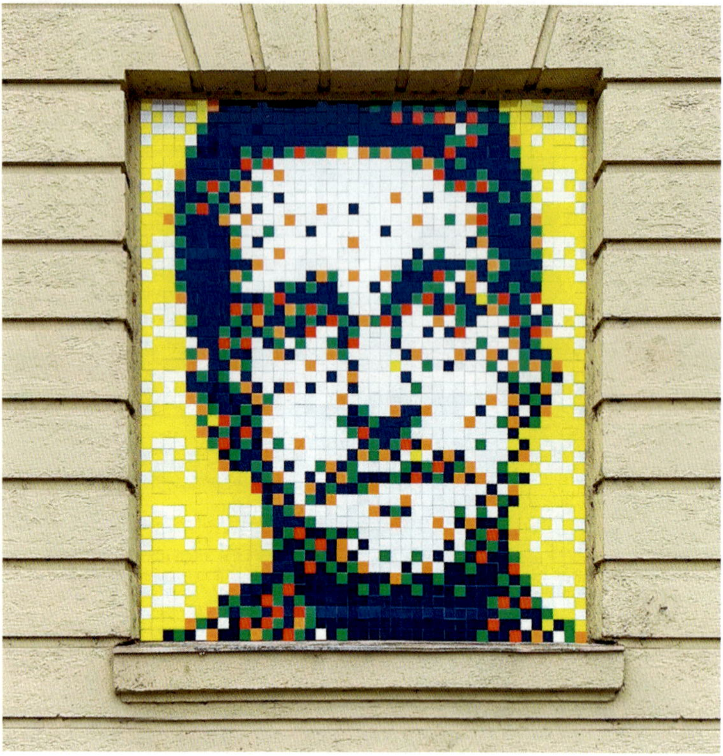

12 719 likes

invaderwashere Guess why I've made this portrait of Edward Snowden in Munich and why it's made with Rubik's cubes colors? ⬜🟨🟧🟥🟩🟦 For the record, I had scouted this spot for a long time but two days before its installation a billboard appeared right in front of it! 😬 Fortunately I was able to remove it, to install the mosaic and then to put it back in place. 😅✌️💯 #snowden #edwardsnowden #citizenfour #munich #bnd #nsa #pixelart #rubikcubism #100pts

View all 190 comments

8 May 2023

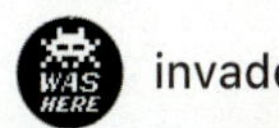

invaderwashere •••

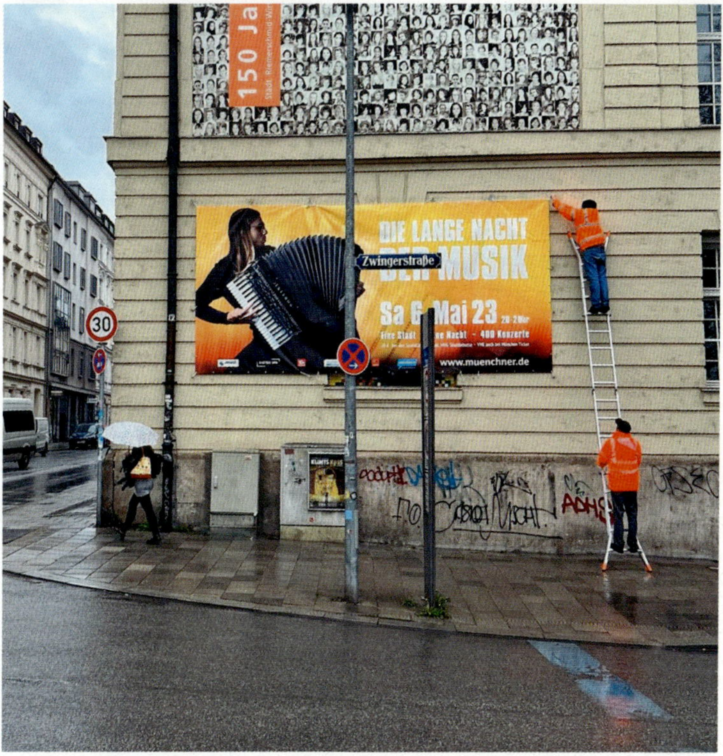

12 719 likes

invaderwashere Guess why I've made this portrait of Edward Snowden in Munich and why it's made with Rubik's cubes colors? ⬜🟨🟧🟥🟩🟦 For the record, I had scouted this spot for a long time but two days before its installation a billboard appeared right in front of it! 😬 Fortunately I was able to remove it, to install the mosaic and then to put it back in place. 😅✌️💯 #snowden #edwardsnowden #citizenfour #munich #bnd #nsa #pixelart #rubikcubism #100pts

View all 190 comments

8 May 2023

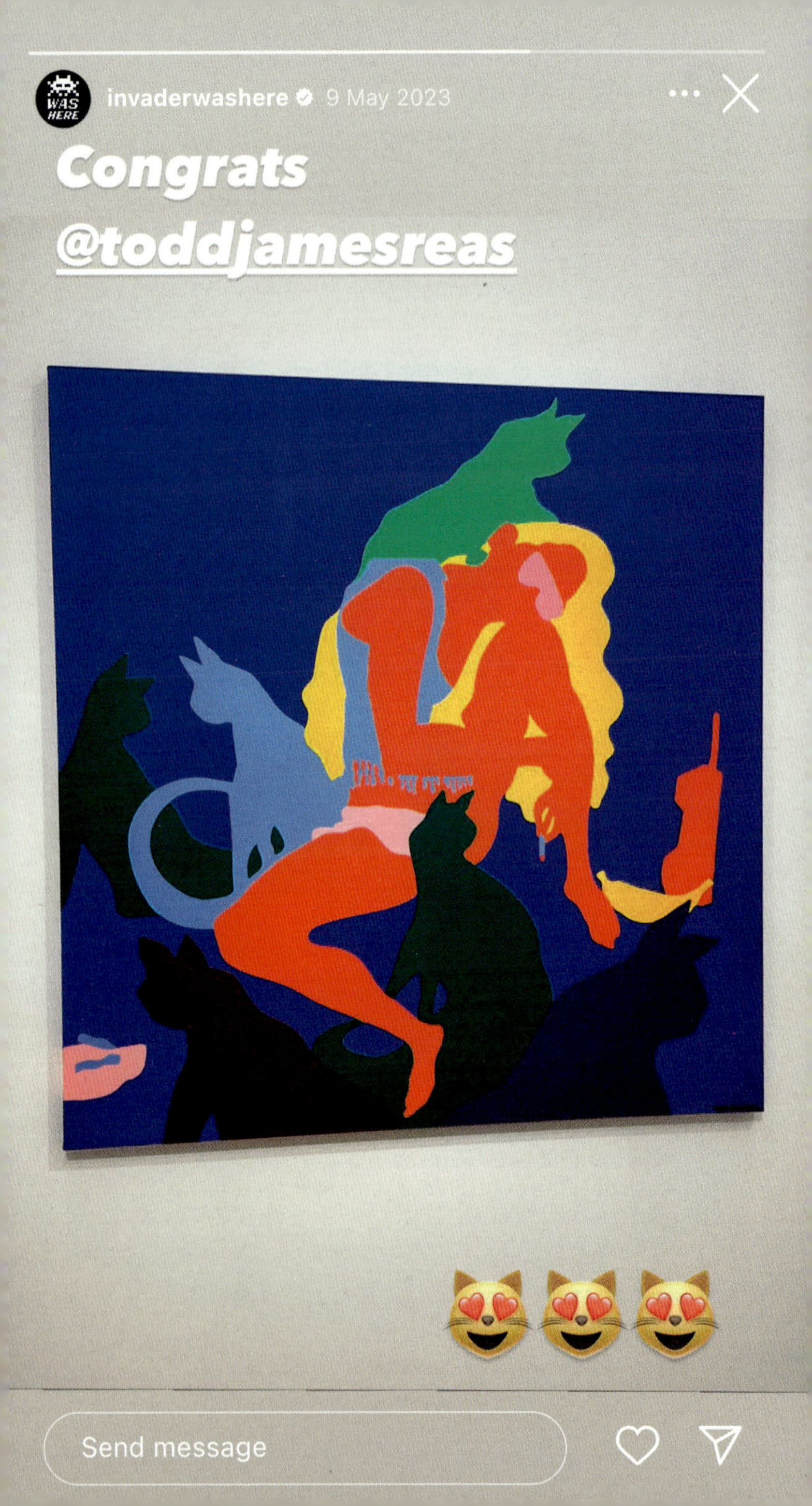

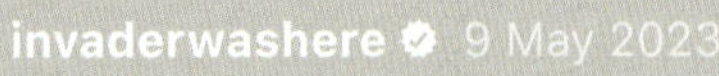

Congrats
@toddjamesreas

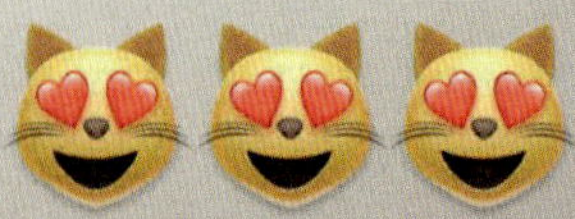

Send message

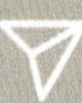

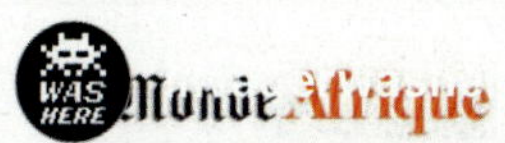

A la synagogue de la Ghriba, à Djerba, un membre de la garde nationale tunisienne ouvre le feu et fait au moins trois morts, dont un Français

La fusillade s'est déroulée lors d'un pèlerinage juif rassemblant plusieurs milliers de fidèles. Dix personnes sont blessées et l'assaillant a été abattu.

Le Monde avec AFP

Aujourd'hui à 02h12, mis à jour à 05h05. Lecture 1 min.

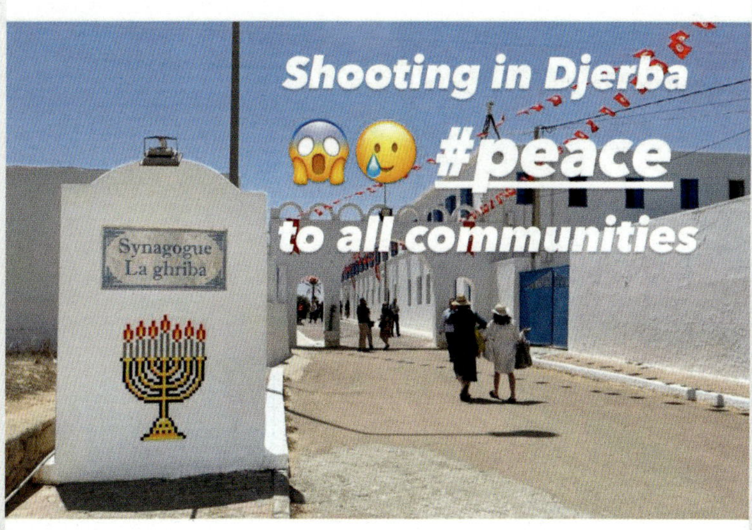

La synagogue de la Ghriba, à Djerba (Tunisie), le 18 mai 2022. JIHED ABIDELLAOUI / REUTERS

Un garde national tunisien et deux fidèles participant à un pèlerinage juif ont été tués, mardi soir 9 mai, par un autre membre de la garde invaderwashere 16 May 2023 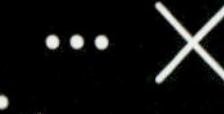

Proud to be part of it

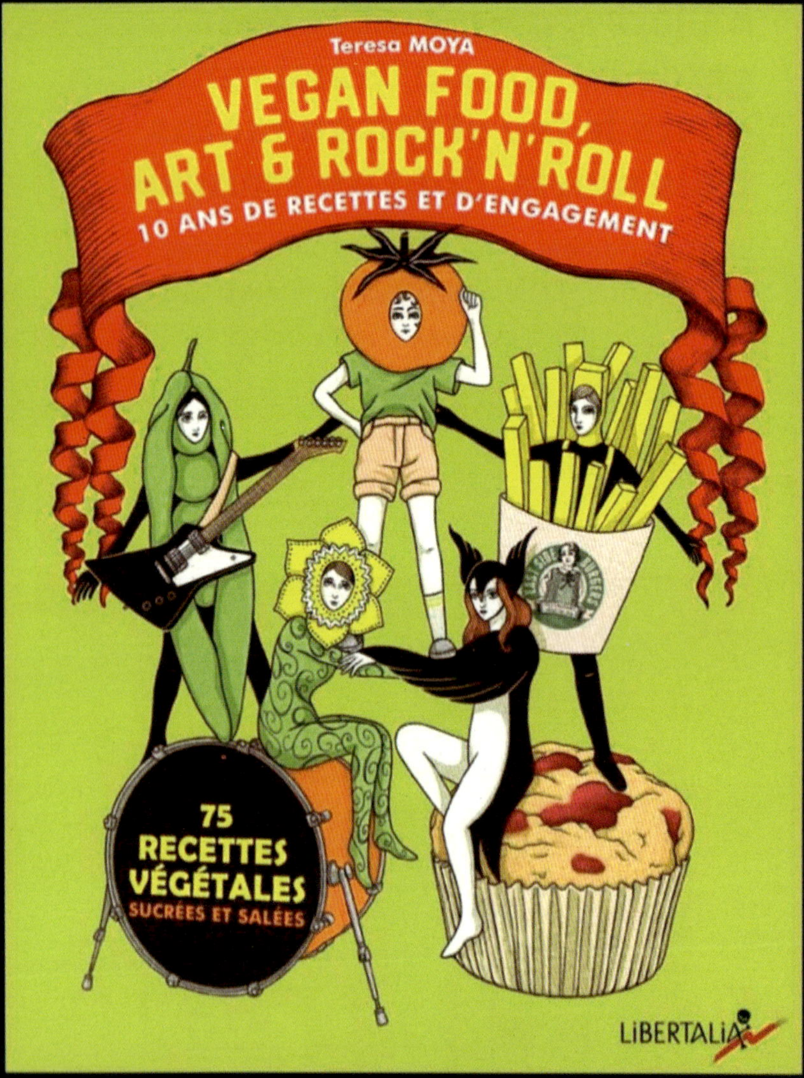

Teresa MOYA

VEGAN FOOD, ART & ROCK'N'ROLL

10 ANS DE RECETTES ET D'ENGAGEMENT

75 RECETTES VÉGÉTALES SUCRÉES ET SALÉES

LIBERTALIA

@eastsideburgers

@editionslibertalia

Send message 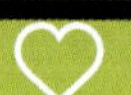 

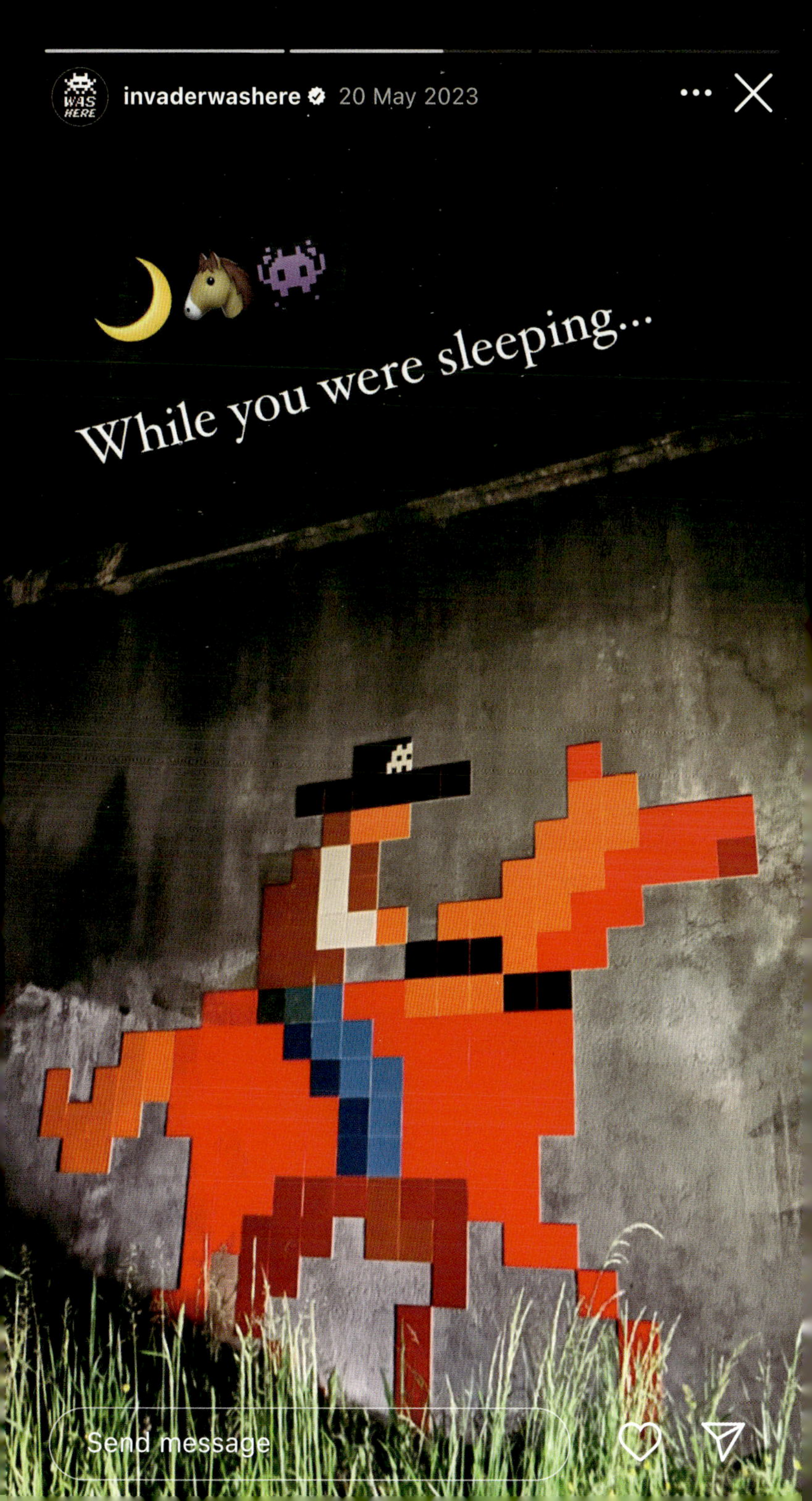

invaderwashere 20 May 2023

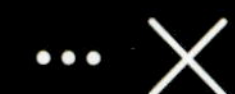

While you were sleeping...

Send message

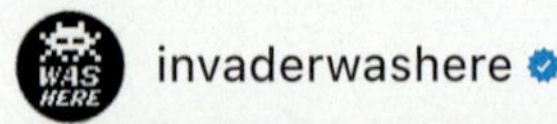

•••

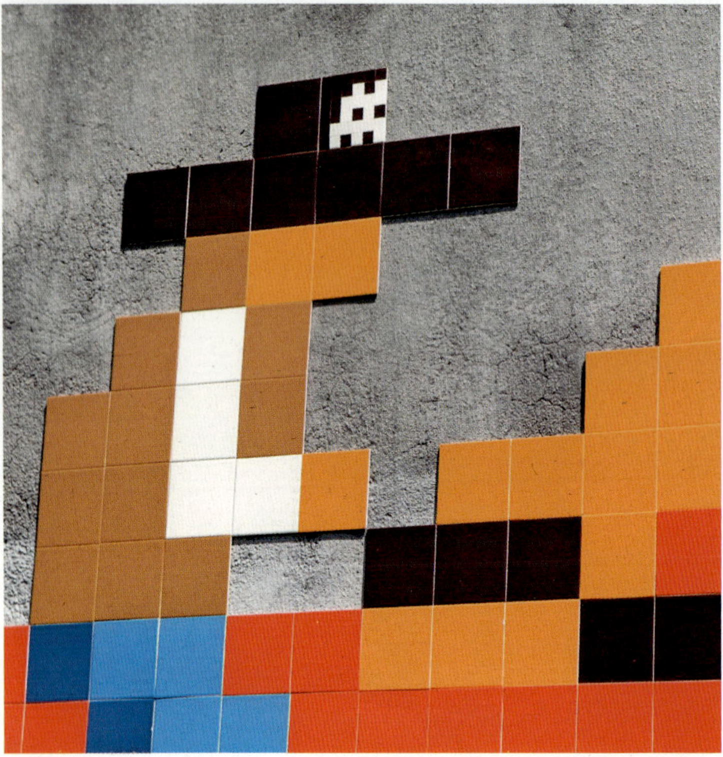

18 594 likes

invaderwashere This new piece just appeared in Fontainebleau #fontainebleau #forest #bigredhorse #spacecowboy #yeeehaw

View all 200 comments

20 May 2023

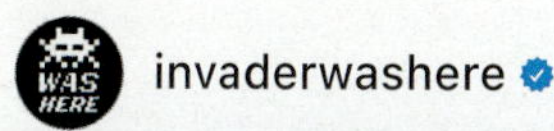

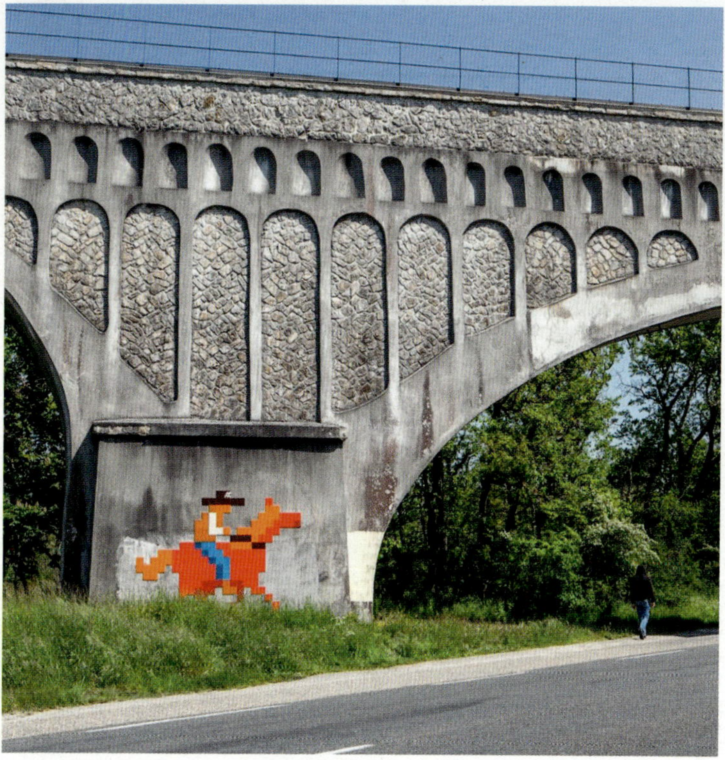

18 594 likes

invaderwashere This new piece just appeared in Fontainebleau #fontainebleau #forest #bigredhorse #spacecowboy #yeeehaw

View all 200 comments

20 May 2023

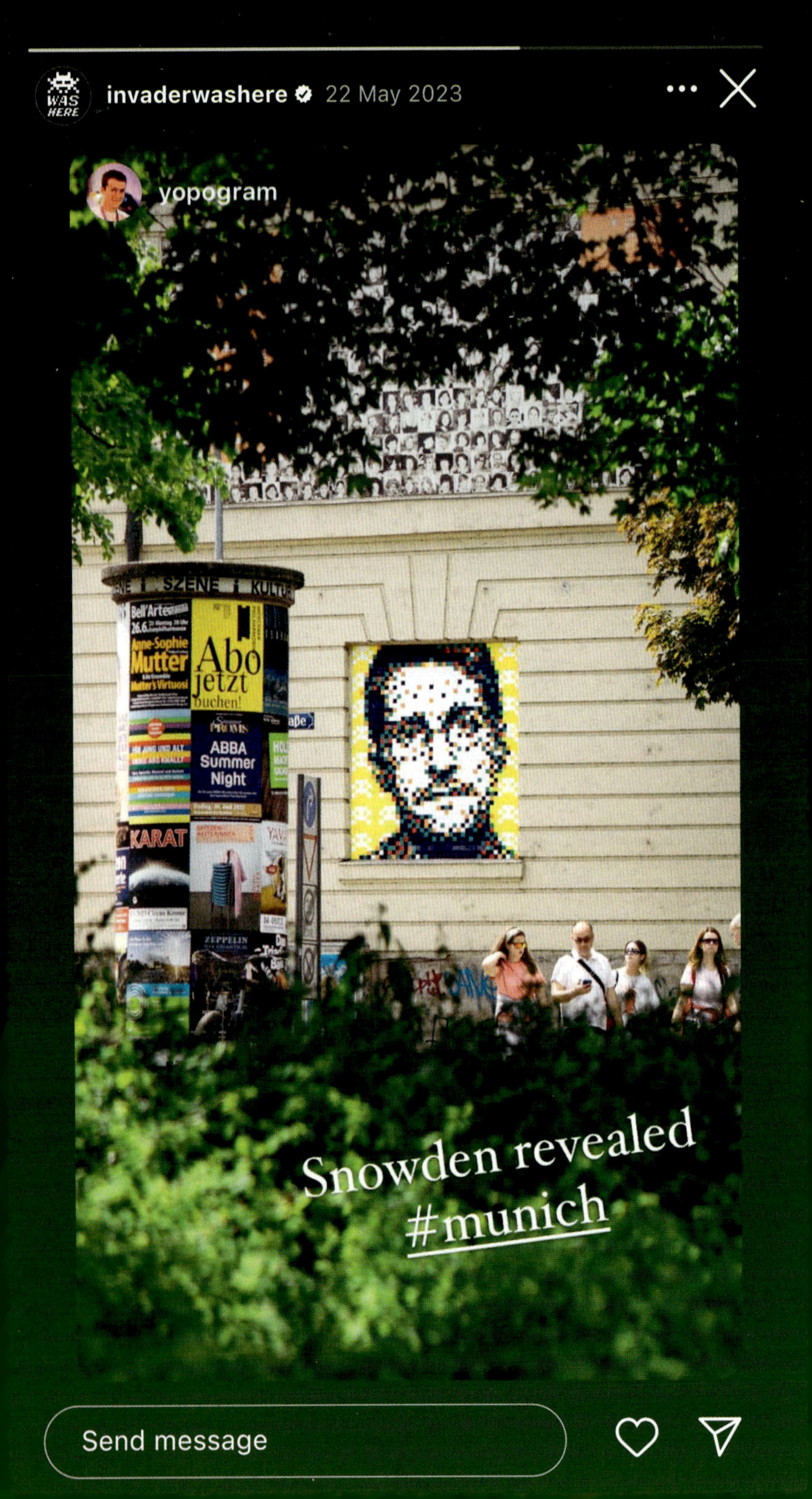

invaderwashere 22 May 2023

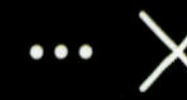

yopogram

Snowden revealed
#munich

Send message

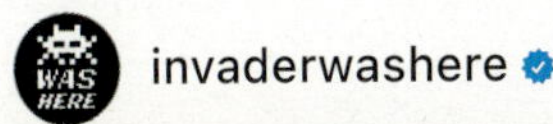

invaderwashere ···

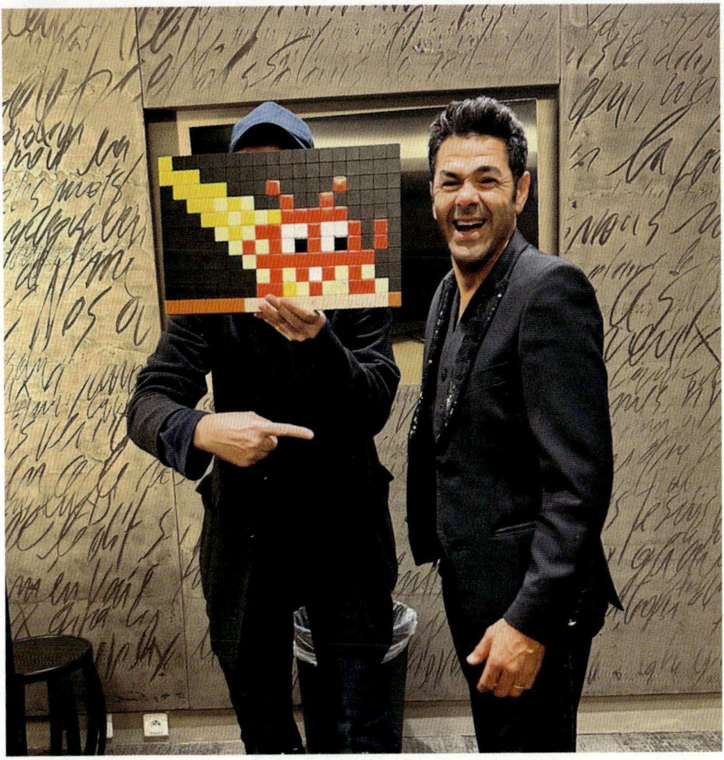

11796 likes

invaderwashere With Jamel and his Alias at Olympia yesterday. Thank you Jamel & your crew for the amazing show 👏👏👏 #kingofthestandupcomedy @jameldebbouze @jamelcomedyclub @olympiahall #jaminvader #aliasPA1470 photo: @ora_ito

View all 91 comments

26 May 2023

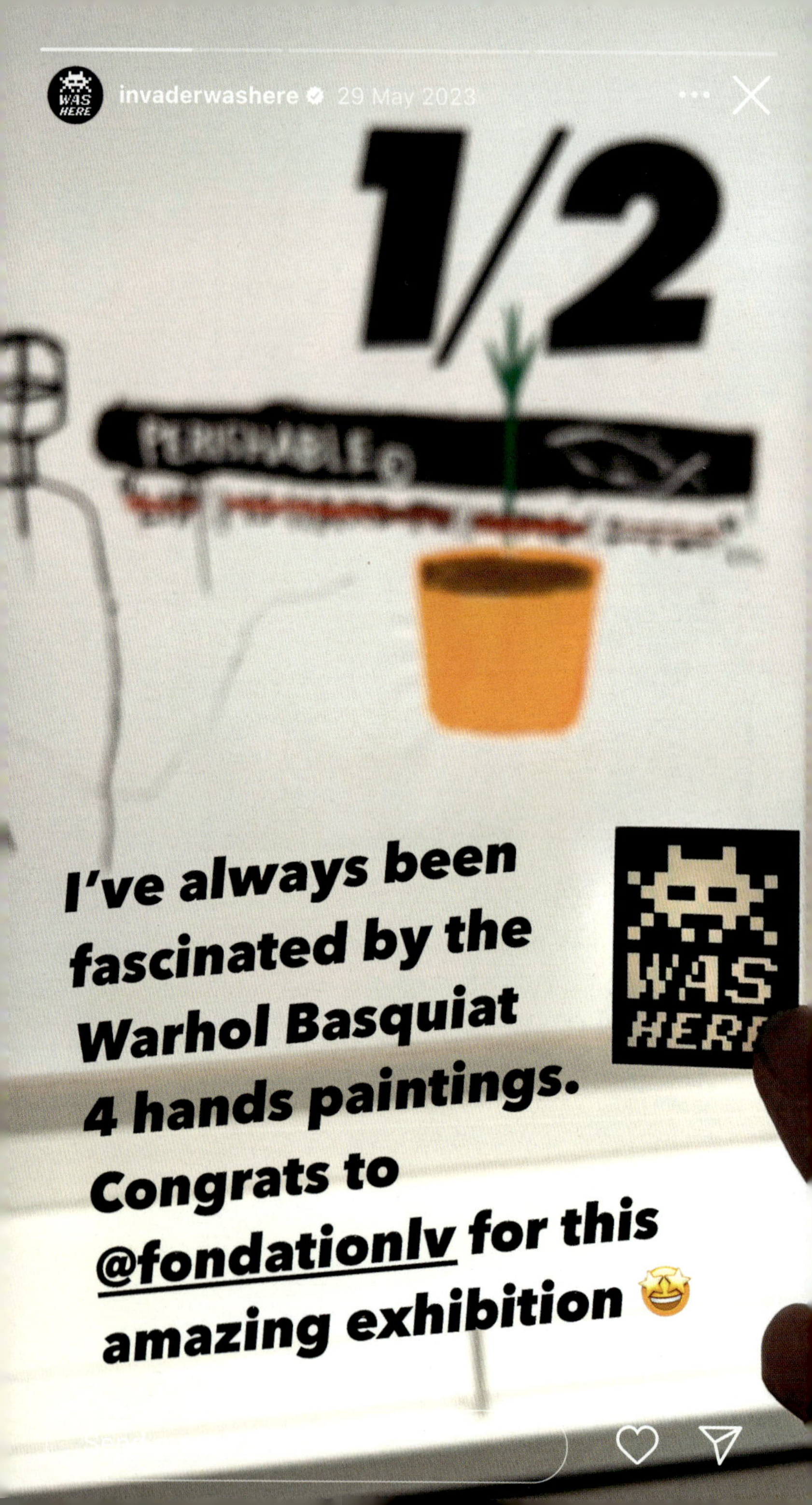

invaderwashere 29 May 2023

1/2

PERISHABLE

I've always been fascinated by the Warhol Basquiat 4 hands paintings. Congrats to @fondationlv for this amazing exhibition 🤩

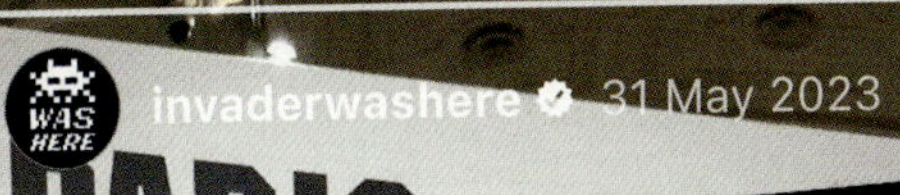

1998
2022

Last days to discover my giant Invasion Map of Paris

CAPITALE(S)
Hôtel de Ville / Paris

Send message

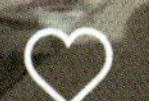
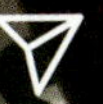

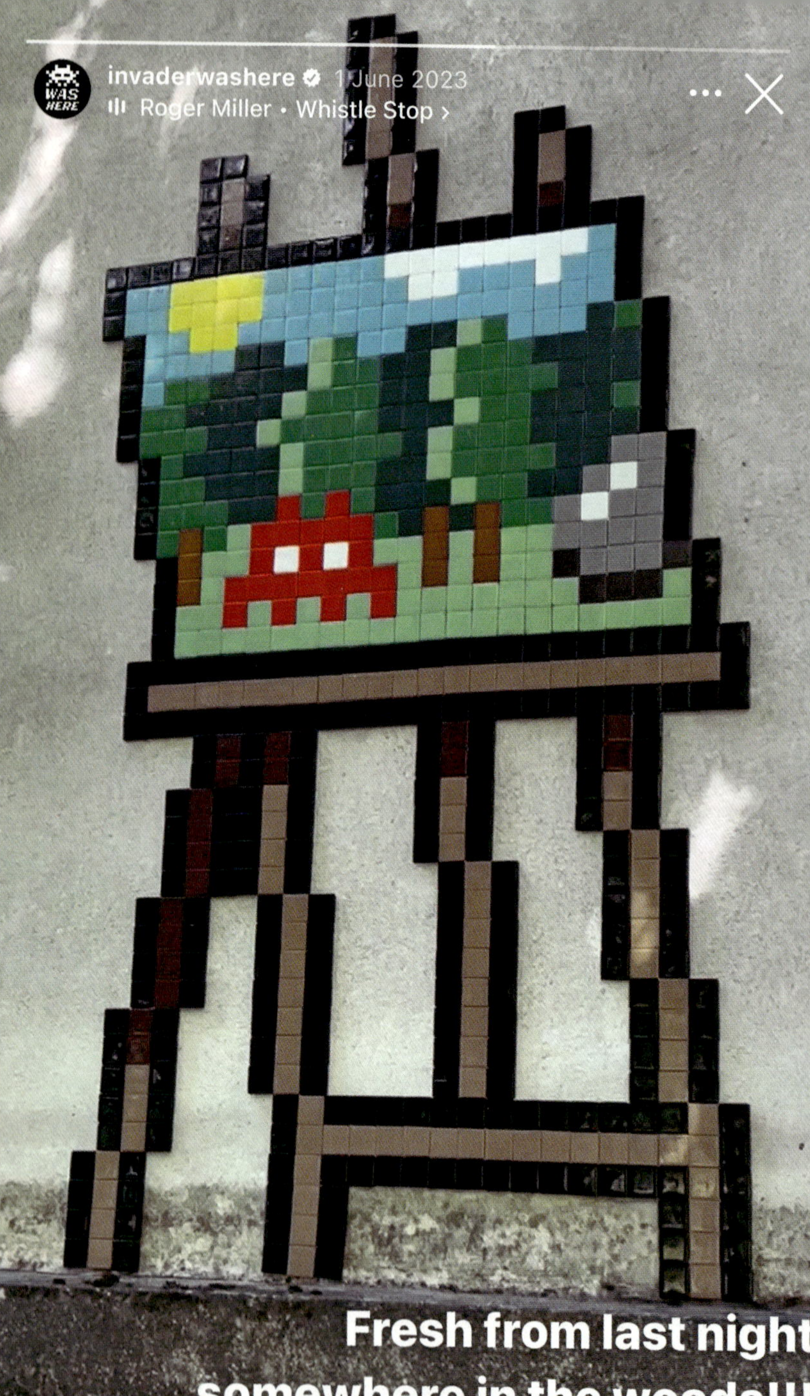
invaderwashere 1 June 2023
Roger Miller • Whistle Stop ›
Fresh from last night
somewhere in the woods!!!
Send message

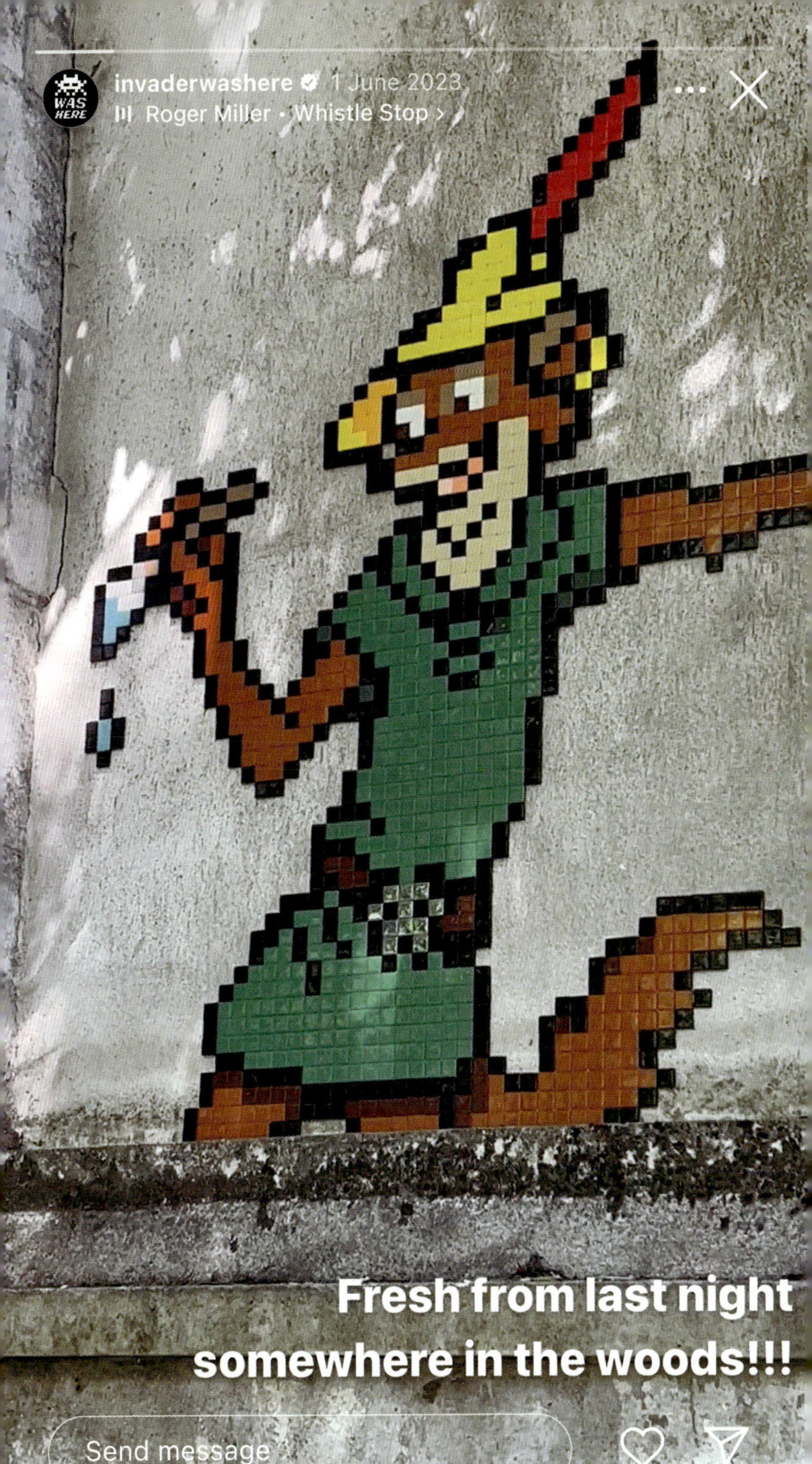
invaderwashere 1 June 2023
Roger Miller · Whistle Stop ›
Fresh from last night
somewhere in the woods!!!
Send message

invaderwashere

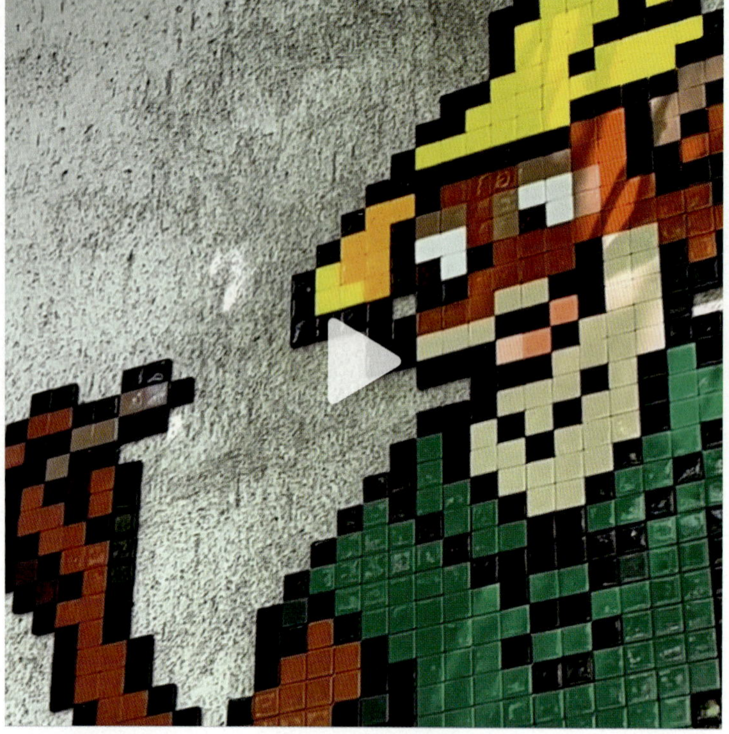

10777 likes

invaderwashere Just after installing this one a fox crossed my way! 🌙🌳🦊👾 #thepainter #barbizon #fontainebleau #forest #fox #robinvader #freshfromlastnight #50pts

View all 193 comments

1 June 2023

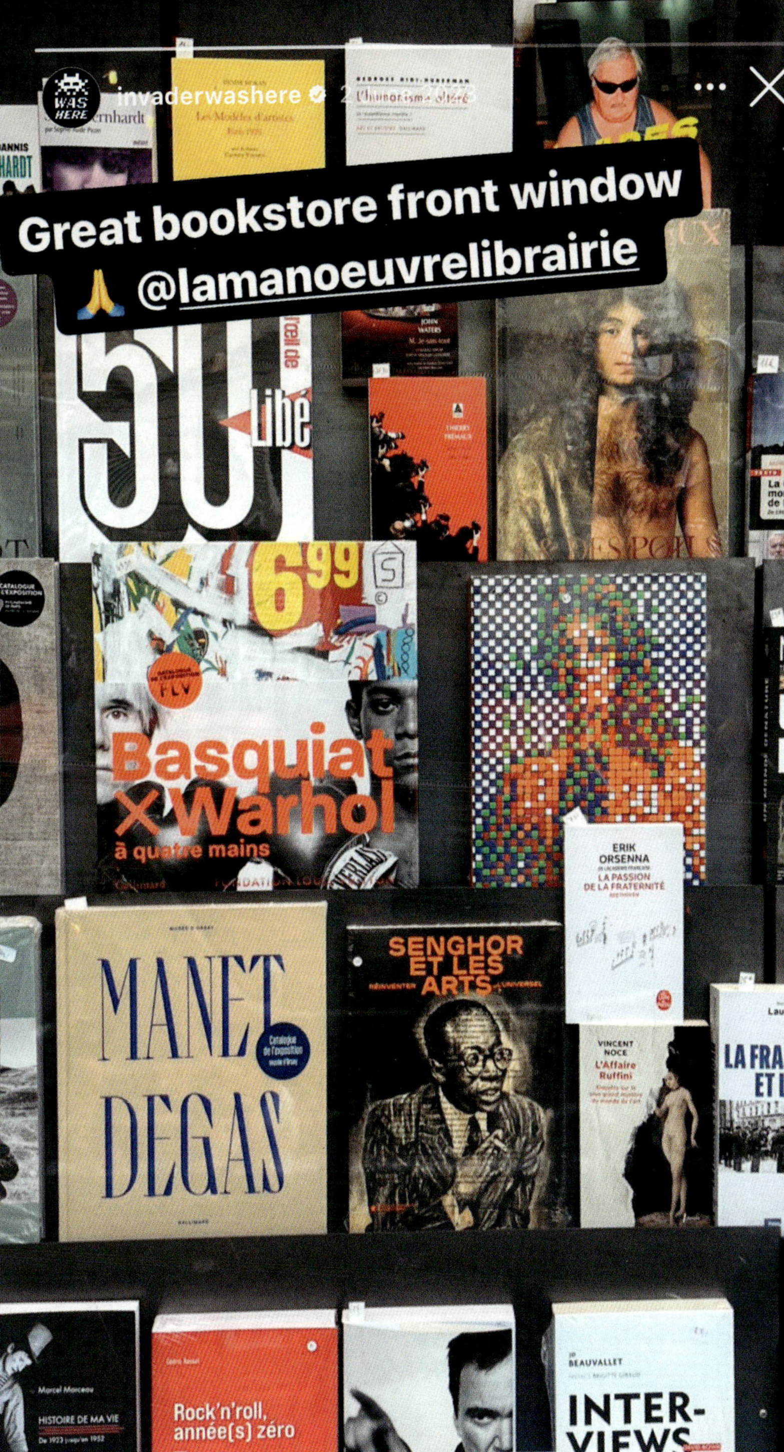

invaderwashere
Great bookstore front window
@lamanoeuvrelibrairie
L'humanisme altéré
Libé
La Guerre mondiale de la France
Basquiat x Warhol
à quatre mains
MANET DEGAS
SENGHOR ET LES ARTS
ERIK ORSENNA
LA PASSION DE LA FRATERNITÉ
VINCENT NOCE
L'Affaire Ruffini
Laurent Joly
LA FRANCE ET LA SHO
Marcel Marceau
HISTOIRE DE MA VIE
Rock'n'roll, année(s) zéro
QUENTIN TARANTINO
INTER-VIEWS
Send message

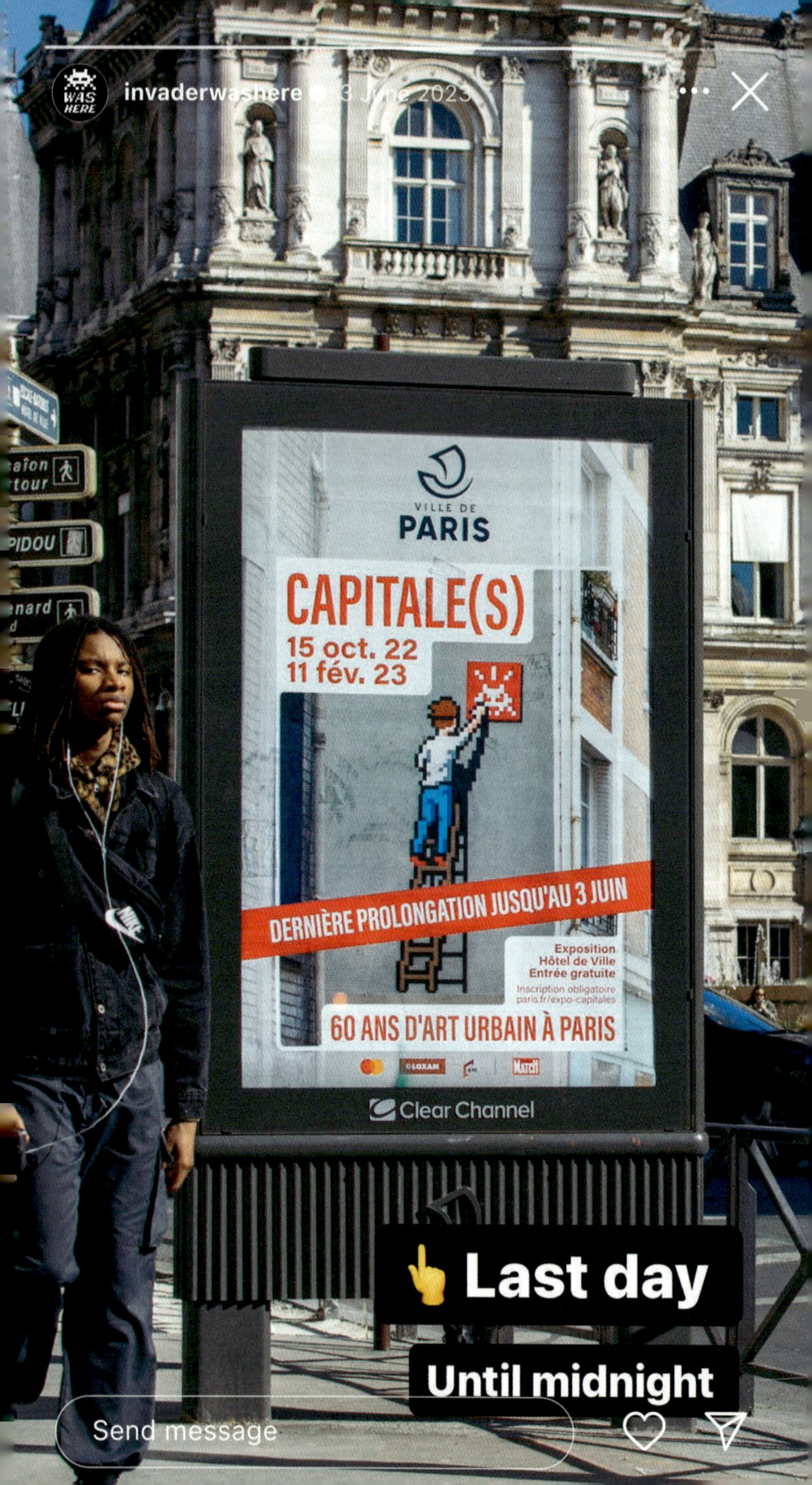
invaderwashere • 3 June 2023
VILLE DE
PARIS
CAPITALE(S)
15 oct. 22
11 fév. 23
DERNIÈRE PROLONGATION JUSQU'AU 3 JUIN
Exposition
Hôtel de Ville
Entrée gratuite
Inscription obligatoire
paris.fr/expo-capitales
60 ANS D'ART URBAIN À PARIS
Clear Channel
Last day
Until midnight
Send message

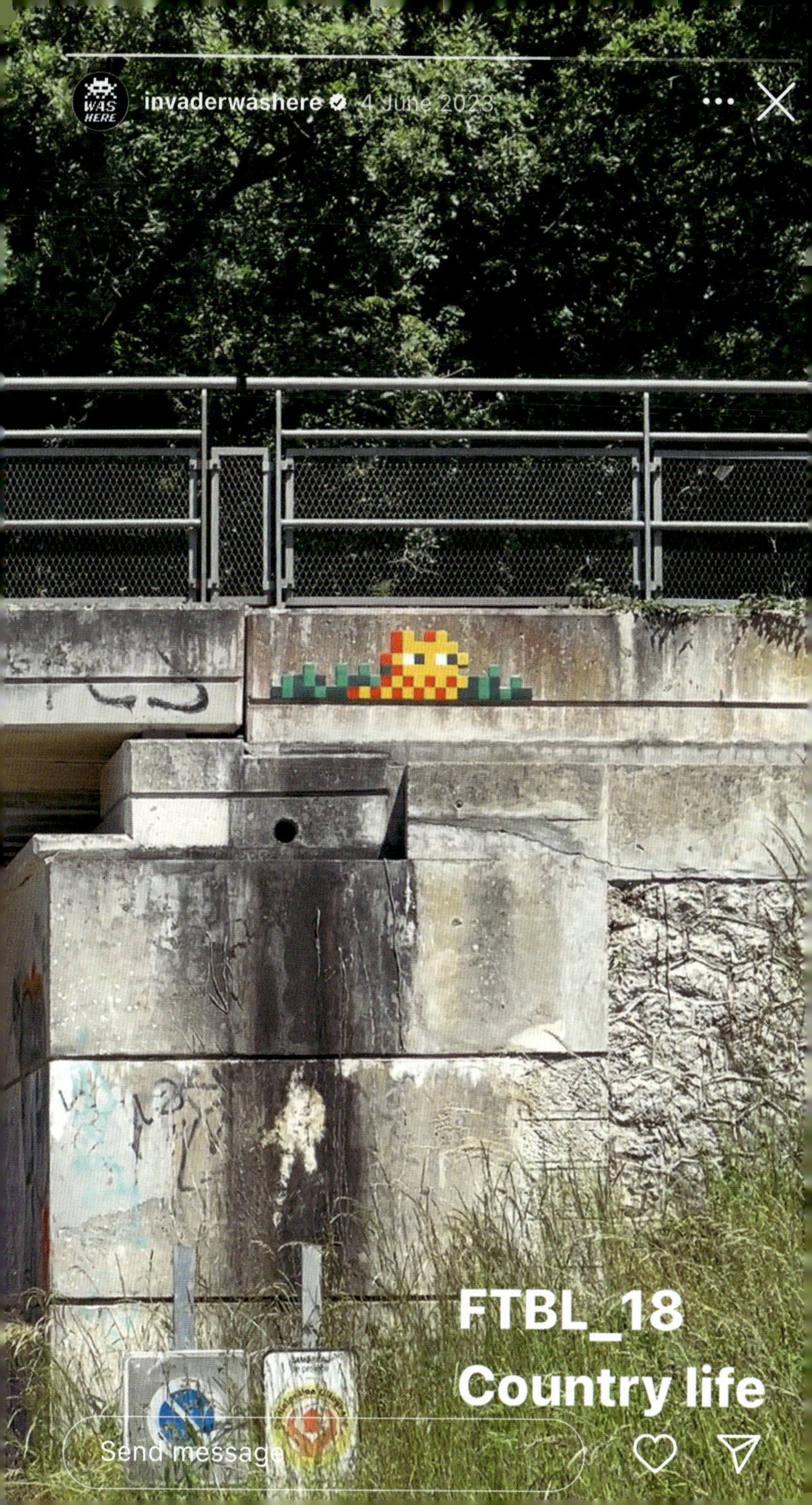

invaderwashere
4 June 2023
FTBL_18
Country life
Send message

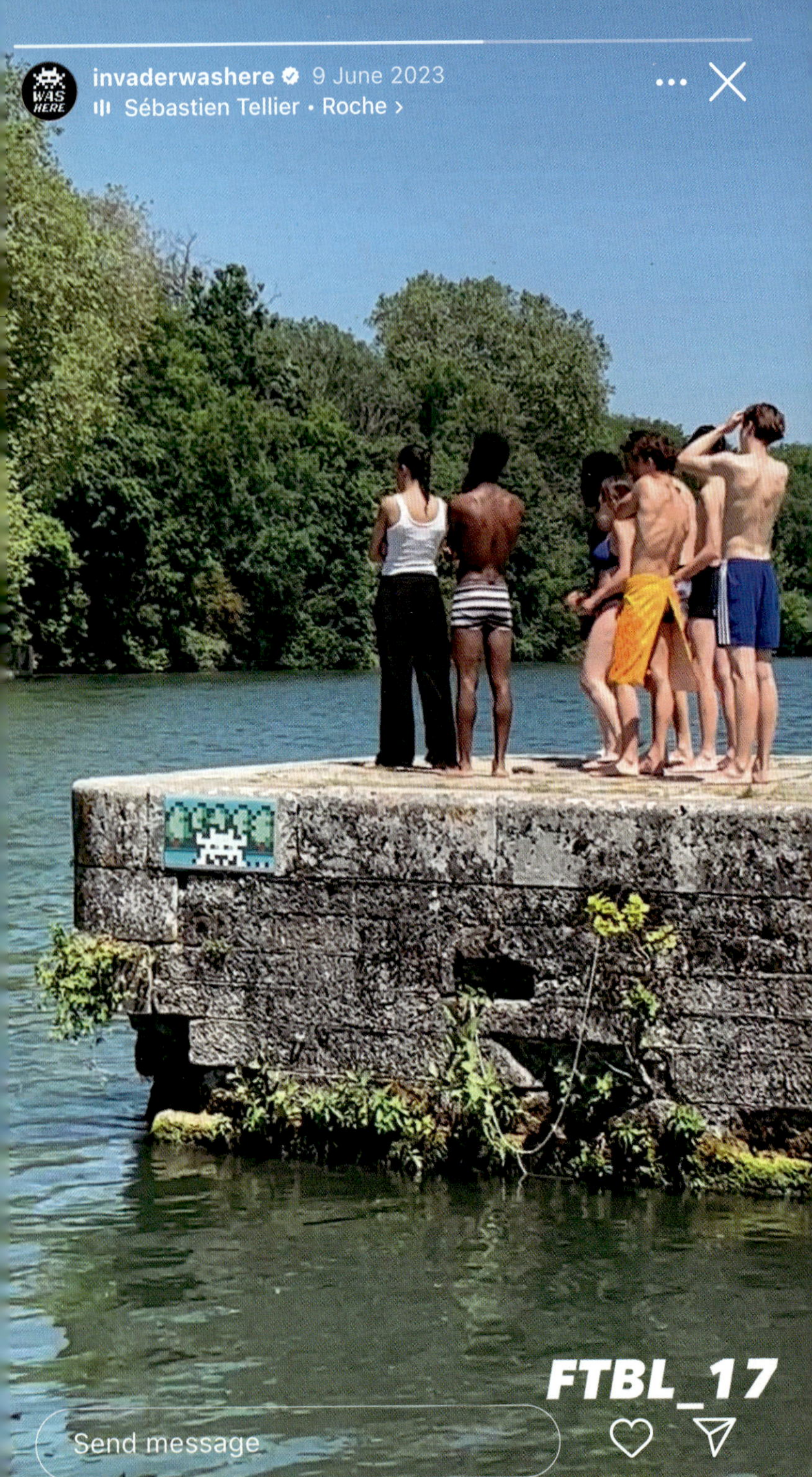
invaderwashere 9 June 2023
Sébastien Tellier • Roche
WAS HERE
FTBL_17
Send message

invaderwashere 12 June 2023

AMUSEUM PRESENTS:

Positive Propaganda

- A DECADE OF VISUAL RESISTANCE -

17. JUNE – 30. JULY 2023

BLU · ERICAILCANE · ESCIF · FAILE · INVADER · NONAME
MARK JENKINS · SKULLPHONE · SHEPARD FAIREY

AMUSEUM OF CONTEMPORARY ART · SCHELLINGSTRASSE 3, MUNICH

WWW.STREETARTMUSEUM.ORG

GEFÖRDERT UND ERMÖGLICHT DURCH: KULTURREFERAT MÜNCHEN - BAYERISCHES STAATSMINISTERIUM FÜR WISSENSCHAFT UND KUNST

@amuseum_munich

Send message

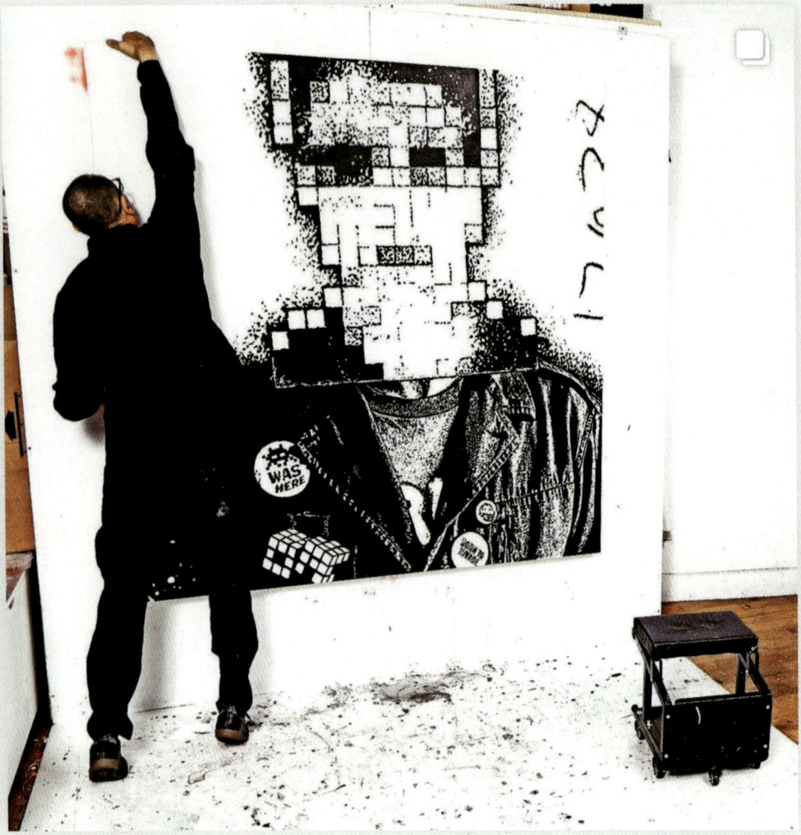

@wkinteract

from the artists portraits series by @wkinteract

Send message

invaderwashere

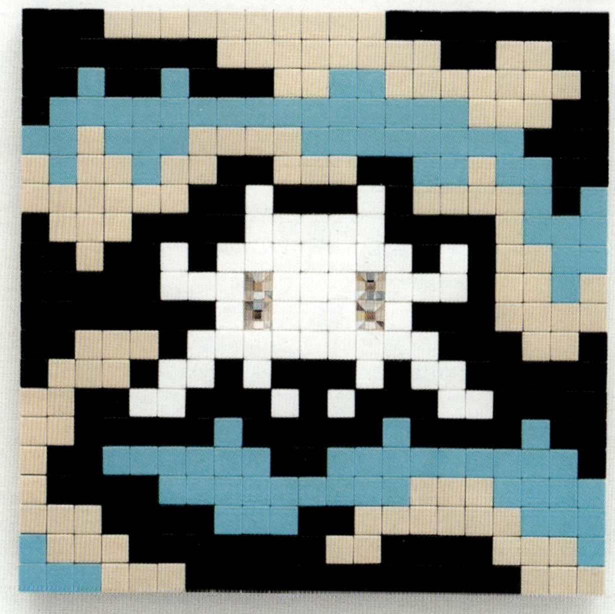

11 358 likes

invaderwashere My work "Camo for Pharrell" is on display at the "Just Phriends" auction in Paris until Saturday. It is part of a series of pixel camo works I have been working on for a little while. What a nice surprise to discover the outfit of Pharrell at Louis Vuitton fashion show, It is a perfect match! #convergence #pixelcamo #pixelartworks #artXfashion @pharrell @joopiterofficial @sarahandelman @louisvuitton

View all 134 comments

22 June 2023

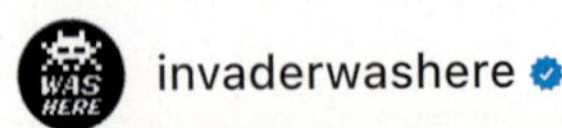

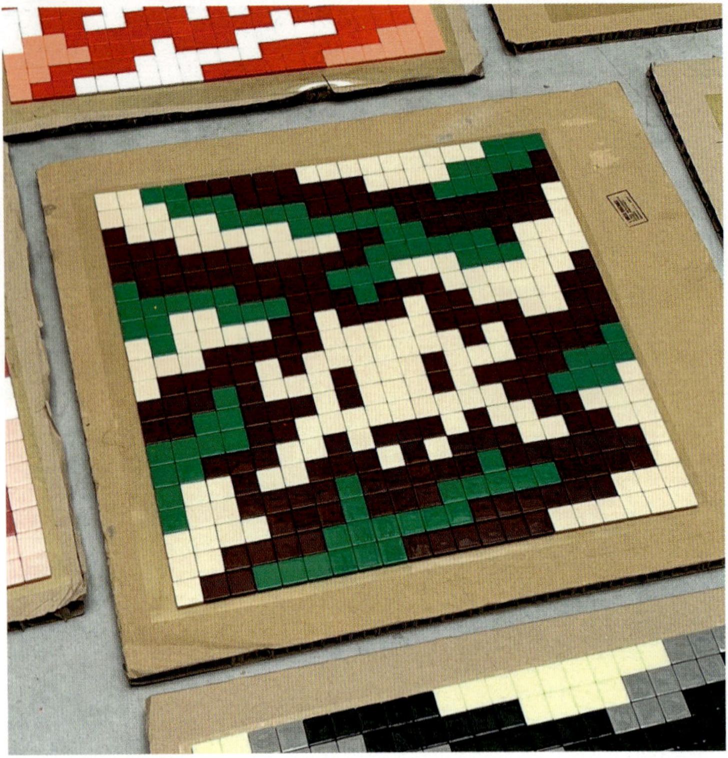

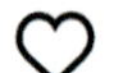   

11 358 likes

invaderwashere My work "Camo for Pharrell" is on display at the "Just Phriends" auction in Paris until Saturday. It is part of a series of pixel camo works I have been working on for a little while. What a nice surprise to discover the outfit of Pharrell at Louis Vuitton fashion show, It is a perfect match! #convergence #pixelcamo #pixelartworks #artXfashion @pharrell @joopiterofficial @sarahandelman @louisvuitton

View all 134 comments

22 June 2023

invaderwashere

 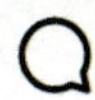 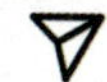 

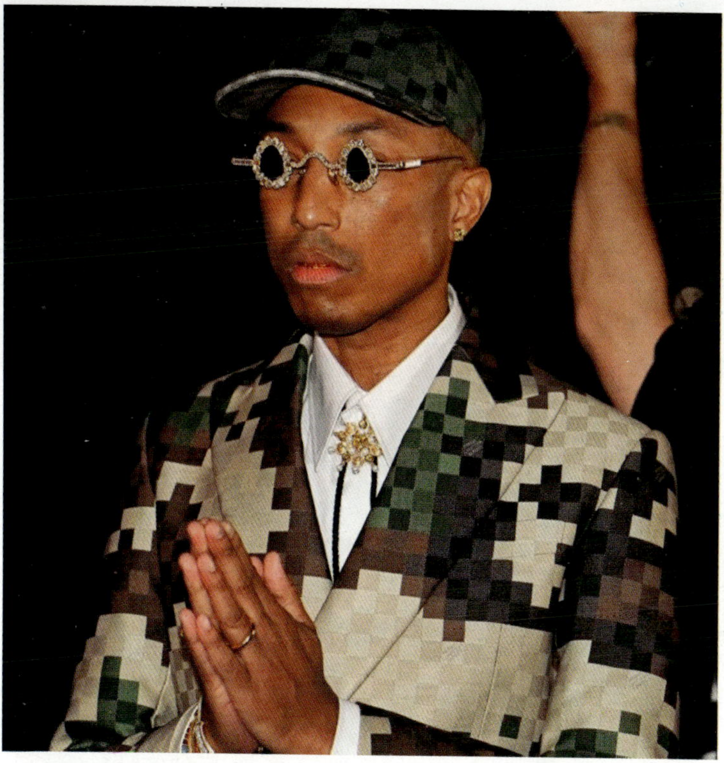

11358 likes

invaderwashere My work "Camo for Pharrell" is on display at the "Just Phriends" auction in Paris until Saturday. It is part of a series of pixel camo works I have been working on for a little while. What a nice surprise to discover the outfit of Pharrell at Louis Vuitton fashion show, It is a perfect match! #convergence #pixelcamo #pixelartworks #artXfashion @pharrell @joopiterofficial @sarahandelman @louisvuitton

View all 134 comments

22 June 2023

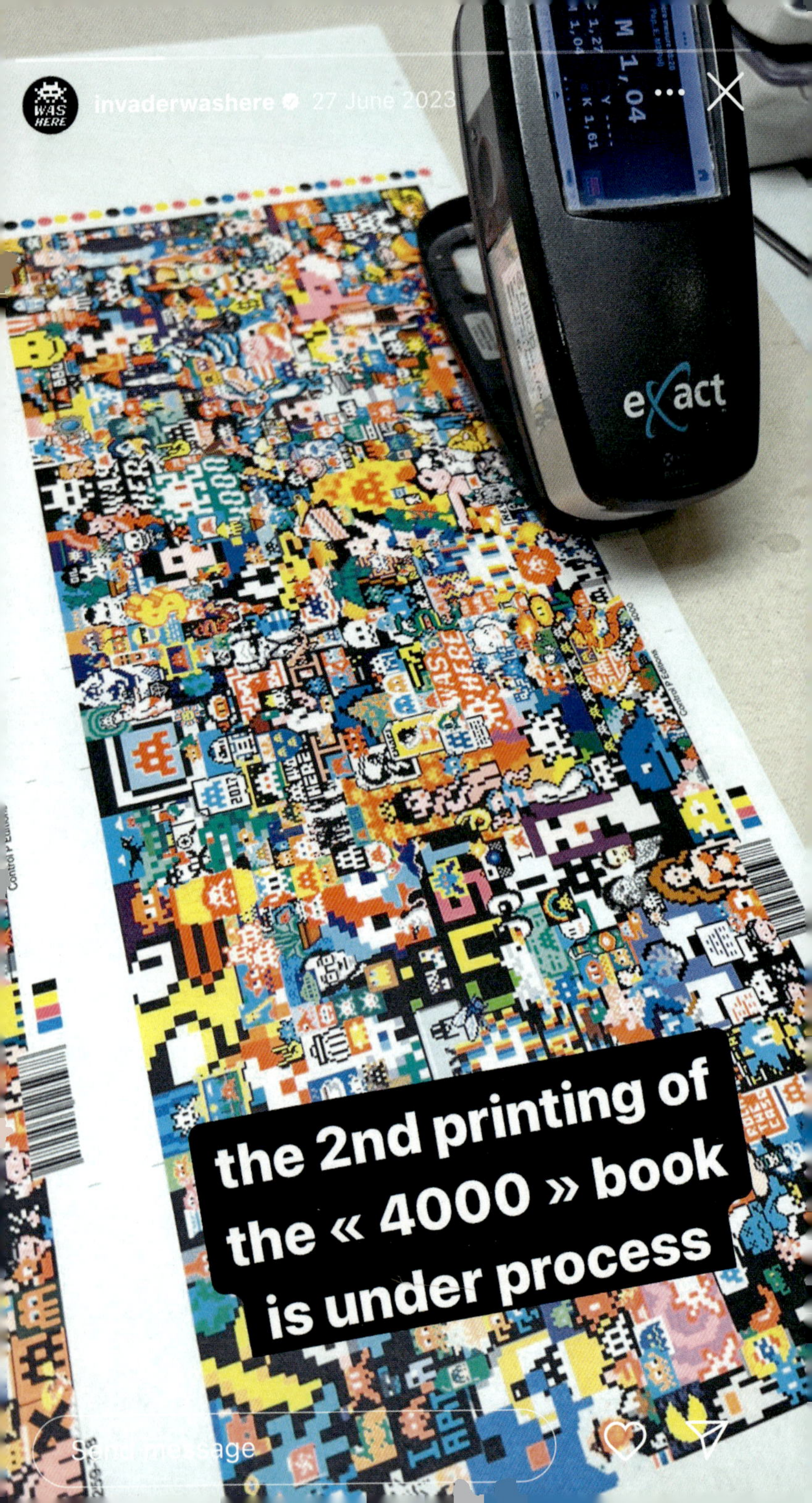
invaderwashere
27 June 2023
exact
the 2nd printing of
the « 4000 » book
is under process

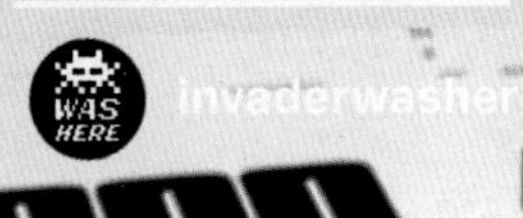

Release date:
September 2023

invaderwashere 6 July 2023

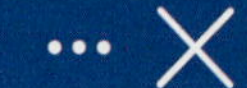

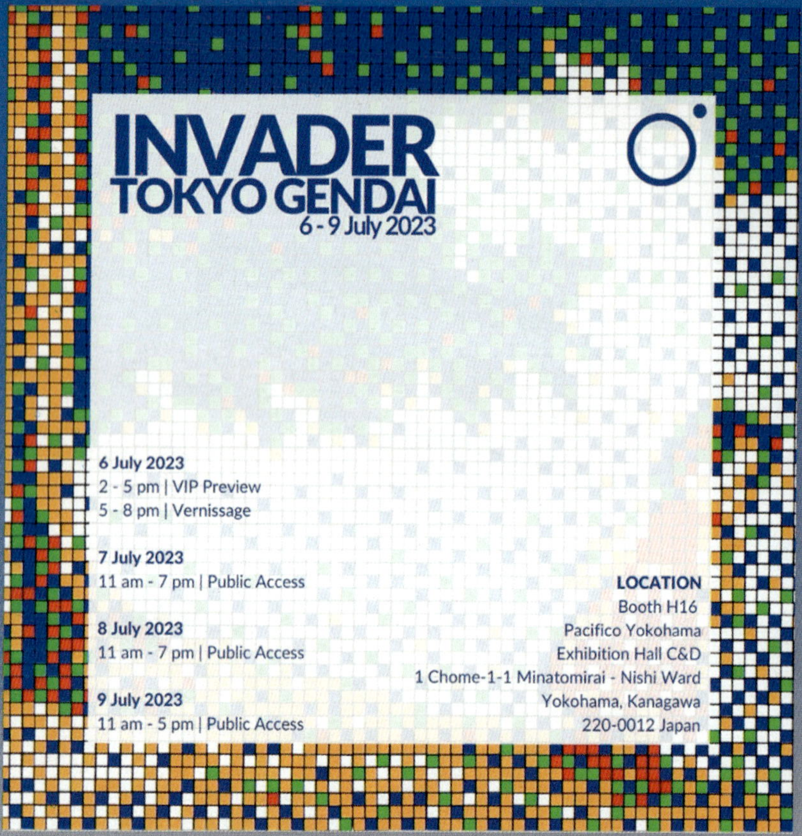

INVADER
TOKYO GENDAI
6 - 9 July 2023

6 July 2023
2 - 5 pm | VIP Preview
5 - 8 pm | Vernissage

7 July 2023
11 am - 7 pm | Public Access

8 July 2023
11 am - 7 pm | Public Access

9 July 2023
11 am - 5 pm | Public Access

LOCATION
Booth H16
Pacifico Yokohama
Exhibition Hall C&D
1 Chome-1-1 Minatomirai - Nishi Ward
Yokohama, Kanagawa
220-0012 Japan

@oti.official

Send message

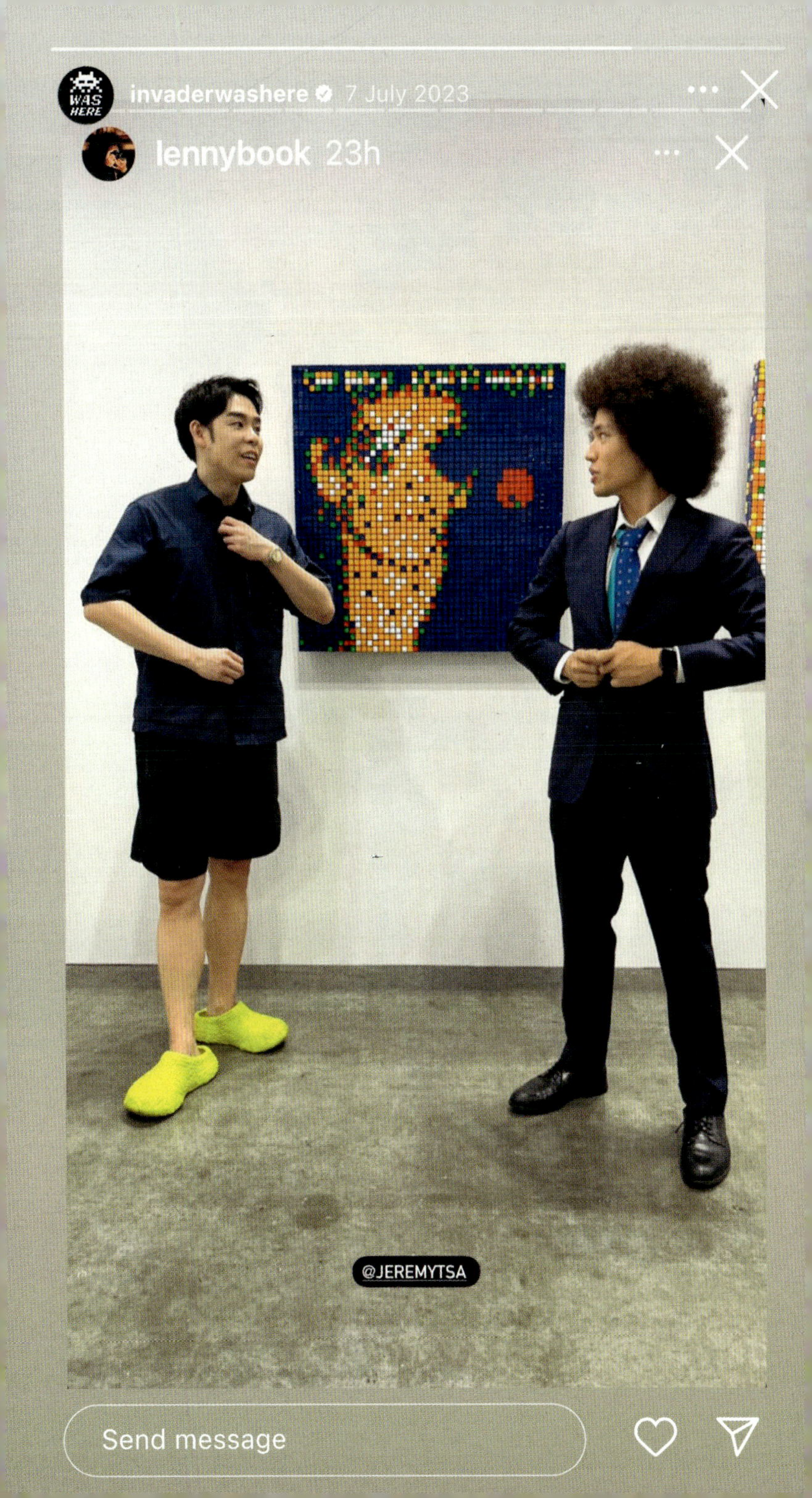

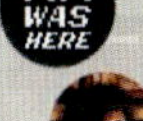
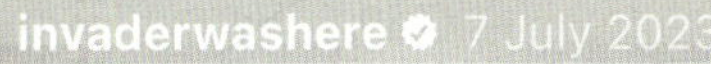

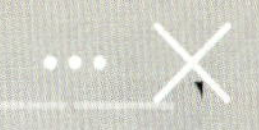
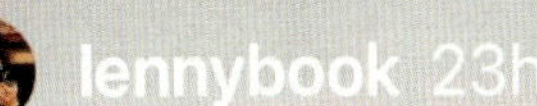

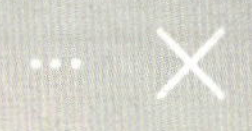

@JEREMYTSA

Send message

invaderwashere 9 July 2023

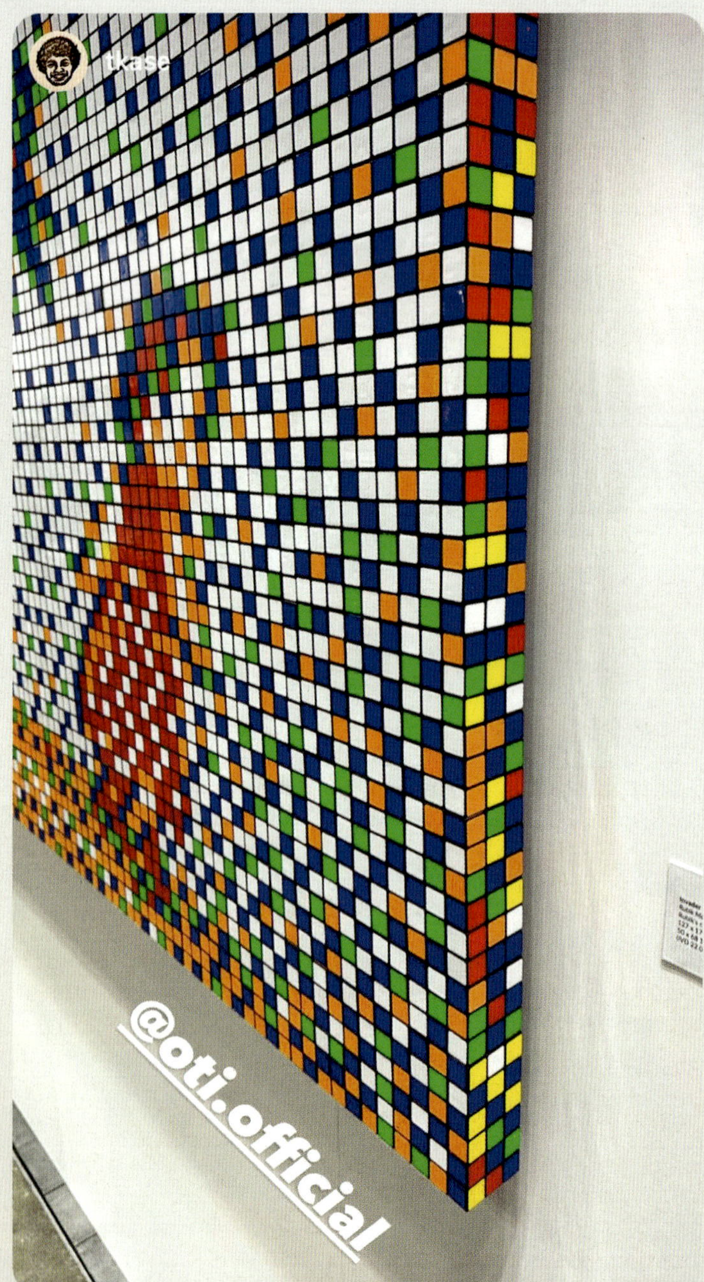

Send message

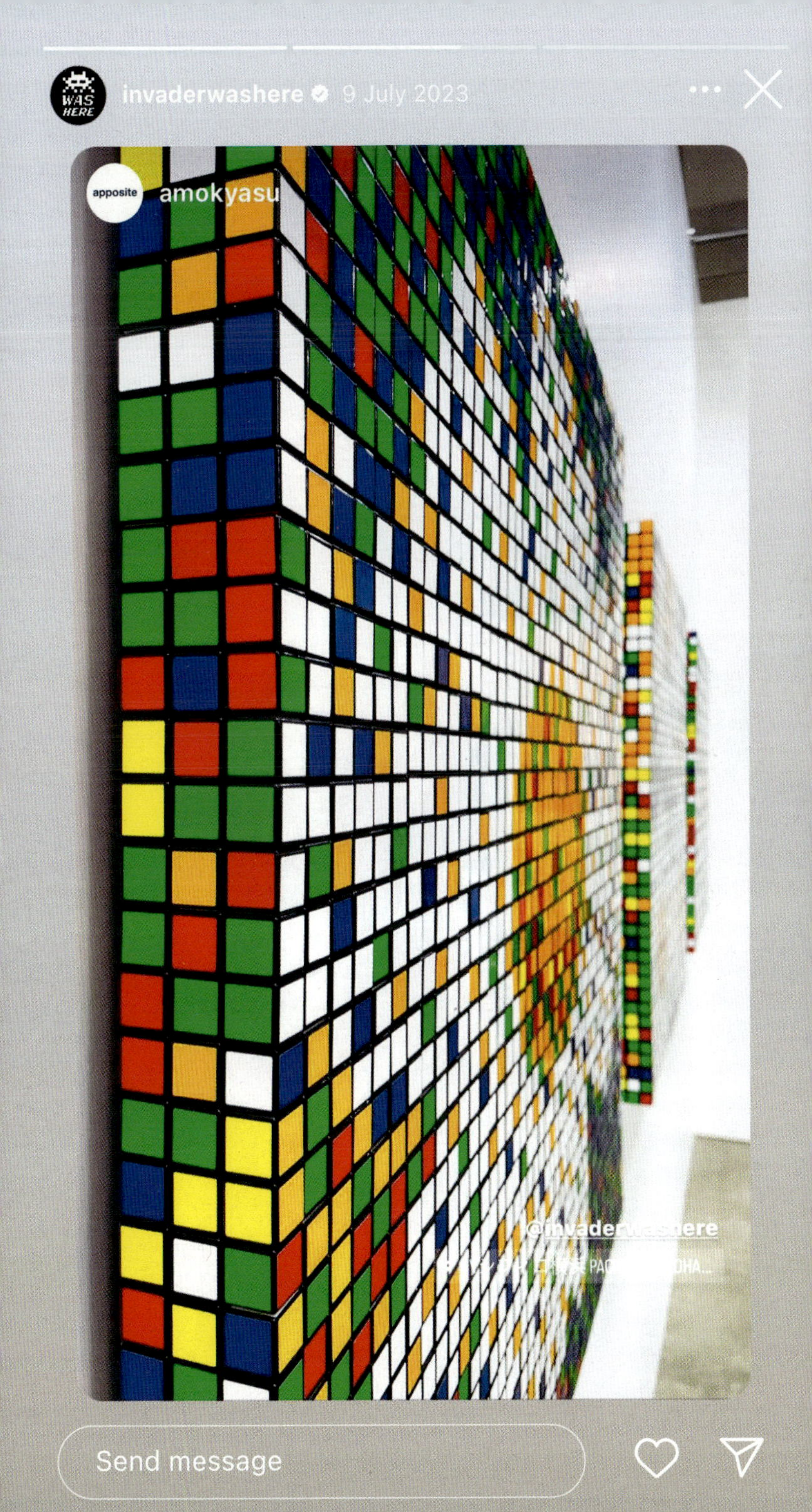

invaderwashere 9 July 2023

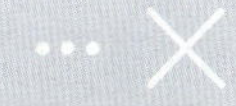

apposite amokyasu

@invaderwashere

Send message

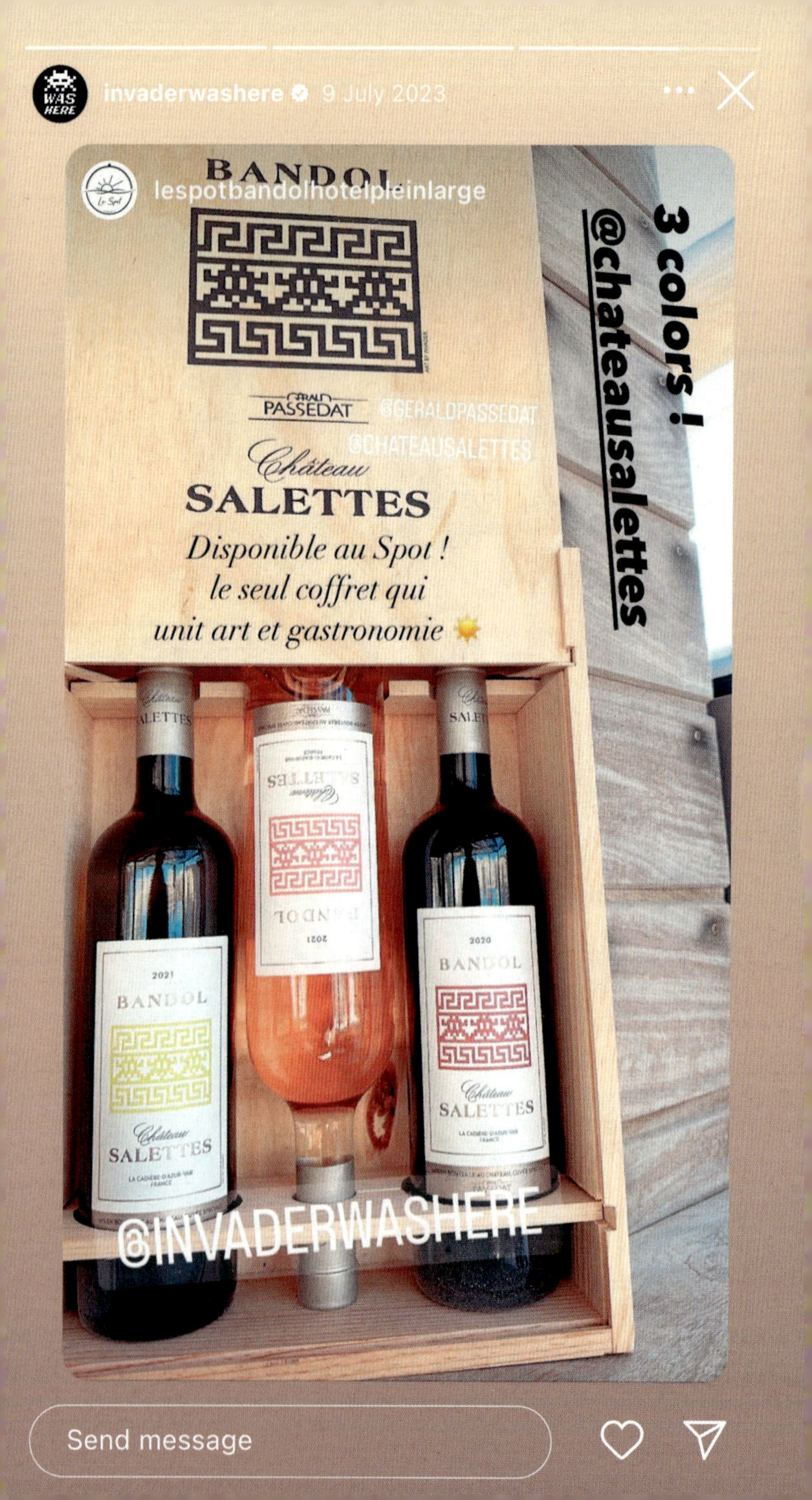

invaderwashere 9 July 2023

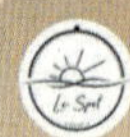

lespotbandolhotelpleinlarge

BANDOL

GERALD PASSEDAT @GERALDPASSEDAT

@CHATEAUSALETTES

Château

SALETTES

Disponible au Spot !
le seul coffret qui
unit art et gastronomie

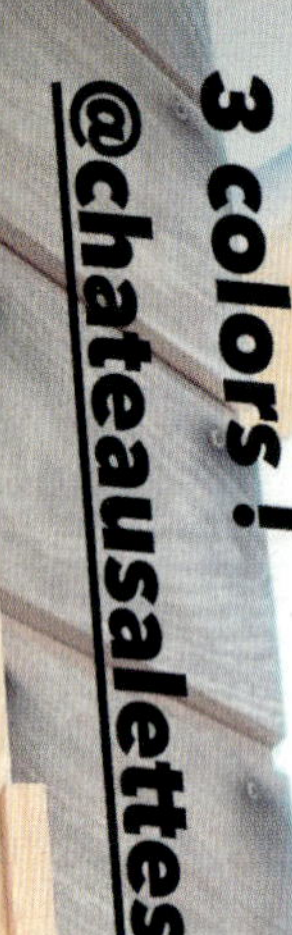

2021 BANDOL Château SALETTES

2021 BANDOL Château SALETTES

2020 BANDOL Château SALETTES

@INVADERWASHERE

Send message

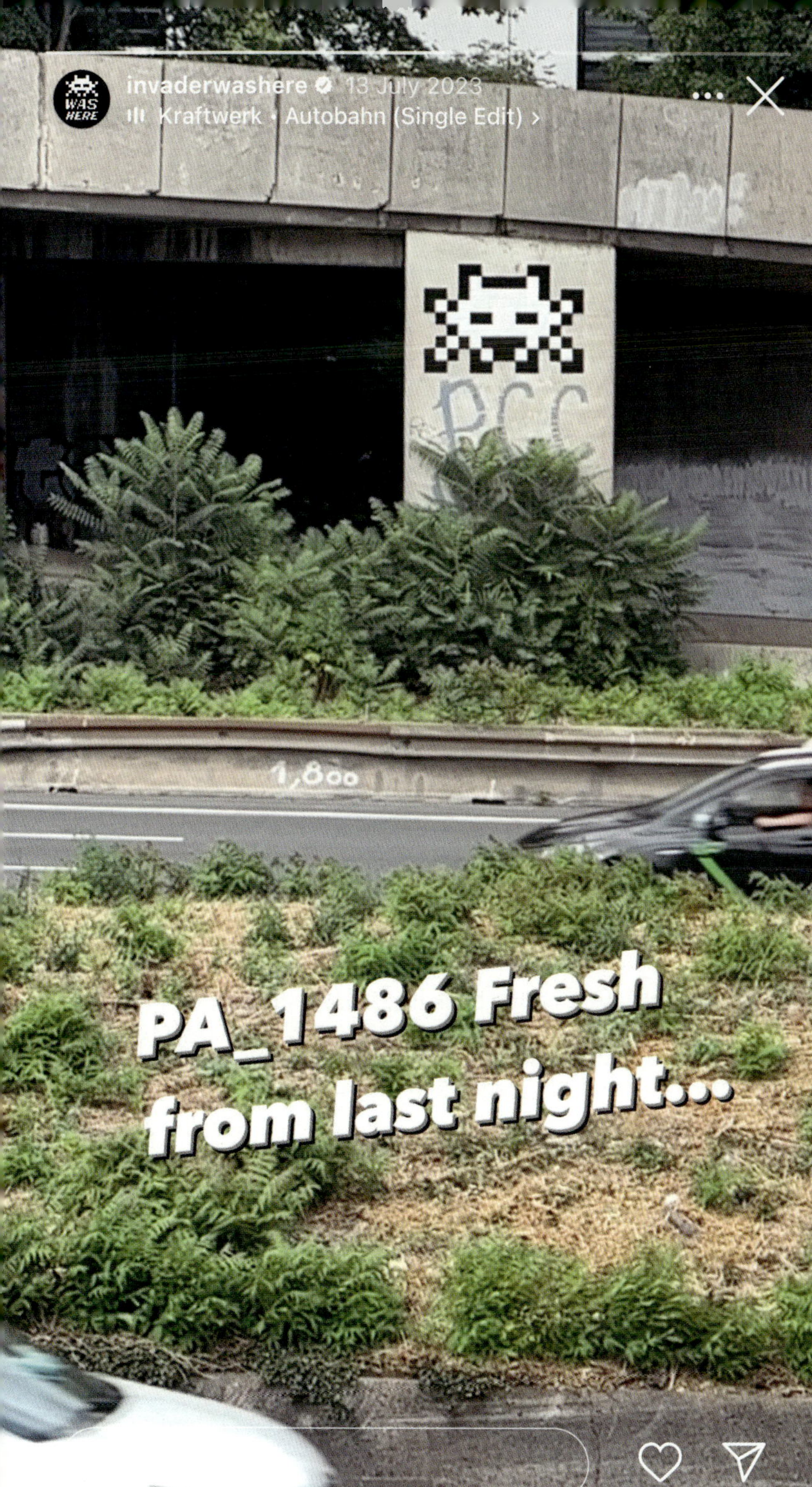

invaderwashere 13 July 2023
Kraftwerk • Autobahn (Single Edit)
PA_1486 Fresh
from last night...

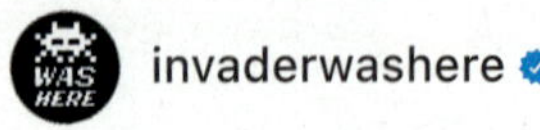

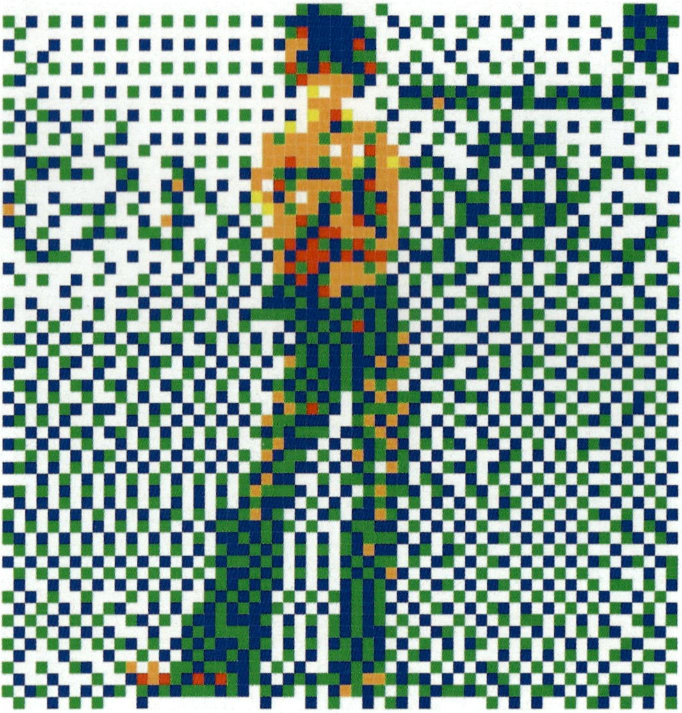

 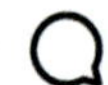  

7262 likes

invaderwashere Found back this Rubikcubism study I've made some years ago but never achieved, Rubik Histoire de Melody Nelson, RIP Jane Birkin 🌹 #janebirkin #melodynelson #gainsbourg #frenchculture #rubikcubism #lowfidelity

View all 62 comments

17 July 2023

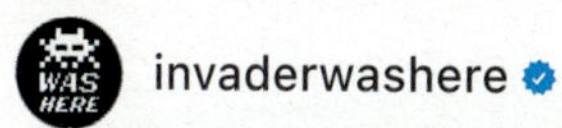

PHILIPS

histoire de melody nelson

SERGE GAINSBOURG

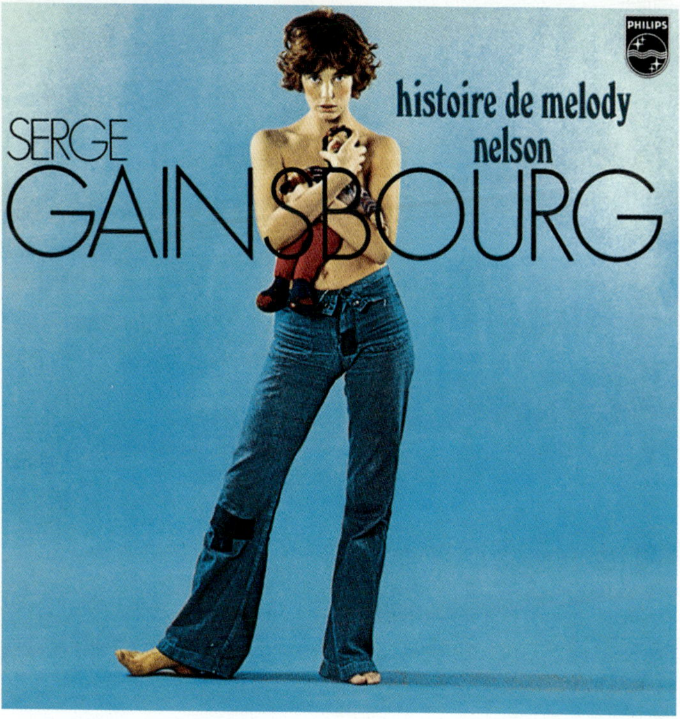

7 262 likes

invaderwashere Found back this Rubikcubism study I've made some years ago but never achieved, Rubik Histoire de Melody Nelson, RIP Jane Birkin 🌹 #janebirkin #melodynelson #gainsbourg #frenchculture #rubikcubism #lowfidelity

View all 62 comments

17 July 2023

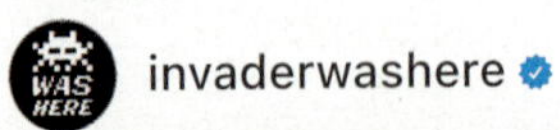

•••

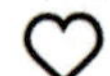   

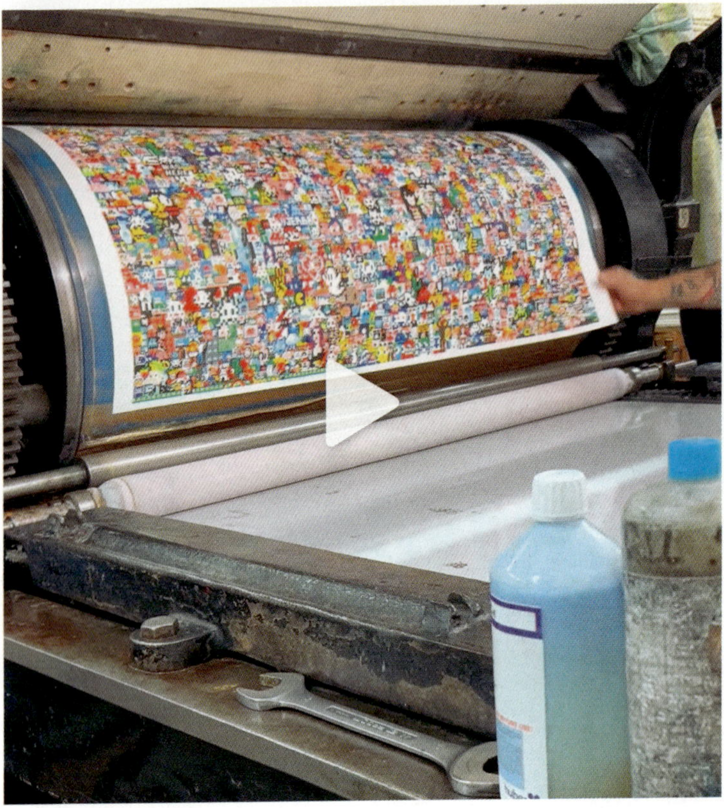

9630 likes

invaderwashere Working for months on this one... Already 110 passes but still in progress! Exceptional print made in a legendary place. #lithography @idemparis

View all 482 comments

20 July 2023

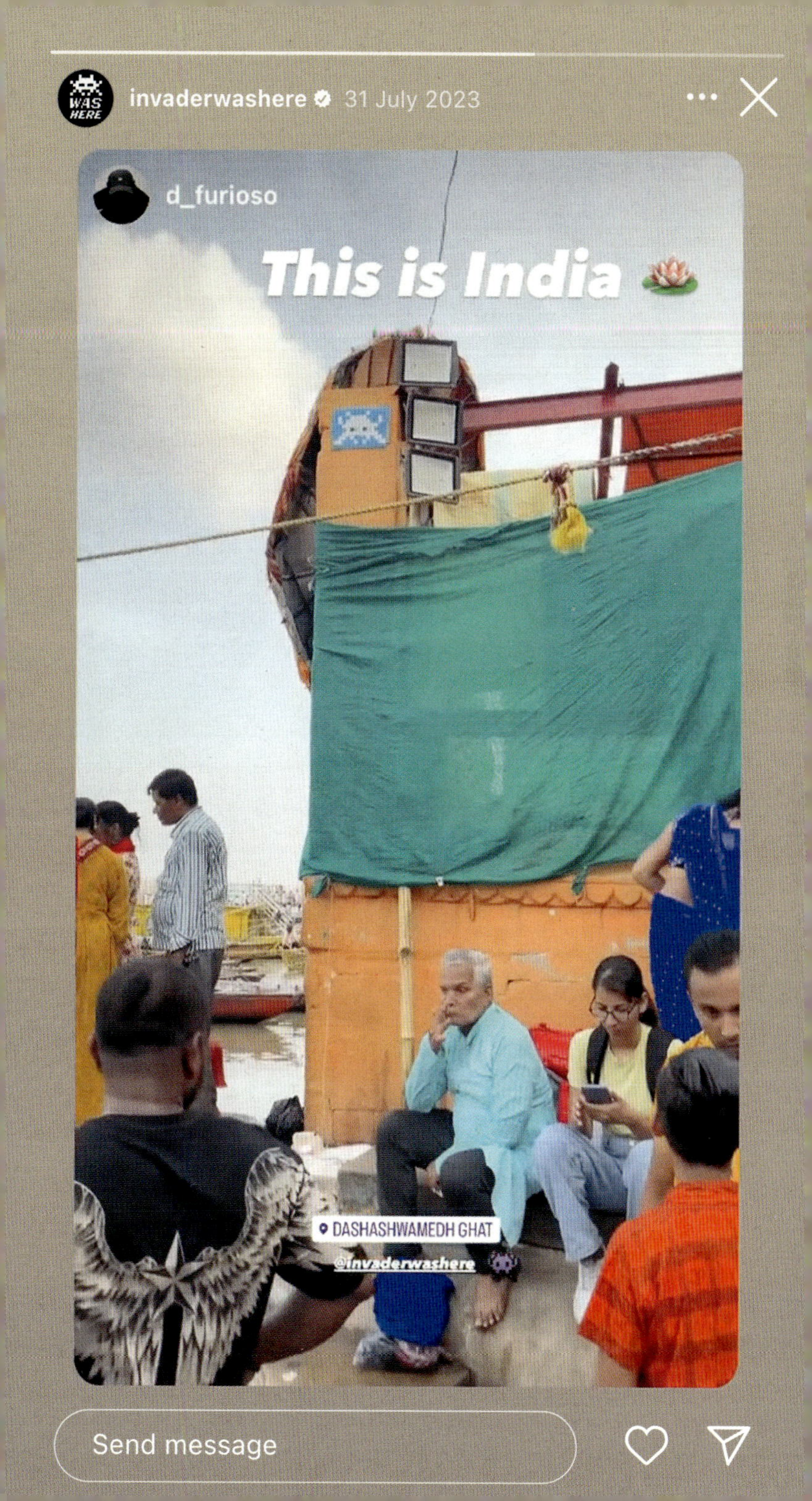

invaderwashere 31 July 2023
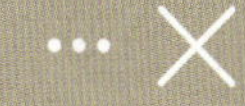

d_furioso

This is India 🪷

Send message

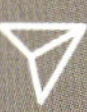

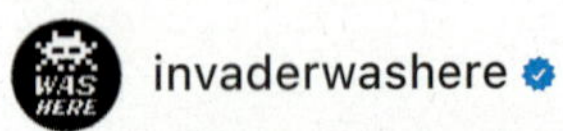

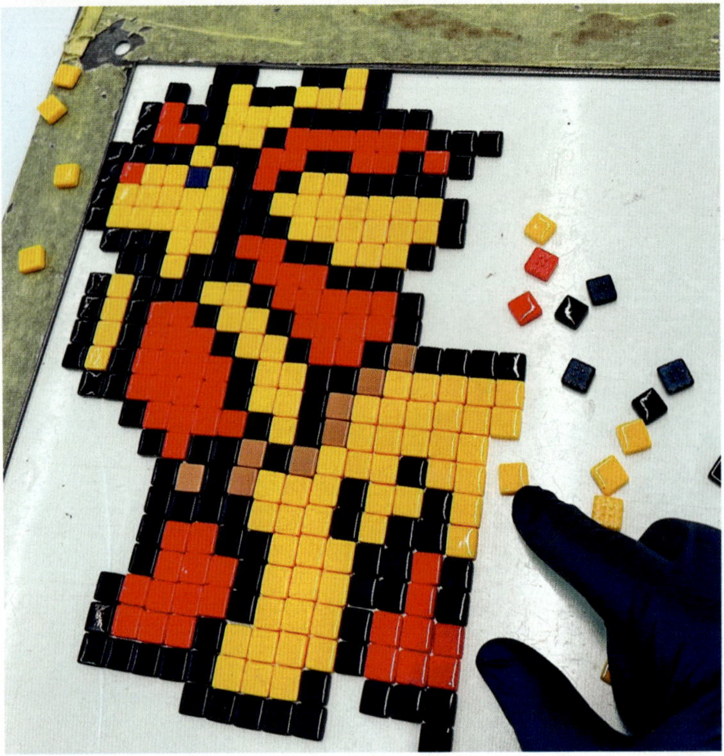

8 433 likes

invaderwashere Preparing some pieces for the next invasion... #studio #mothership #makingof #tinytiles #lion #pyroar #némélios #pokemon

View all 136 comments

1 August 2023

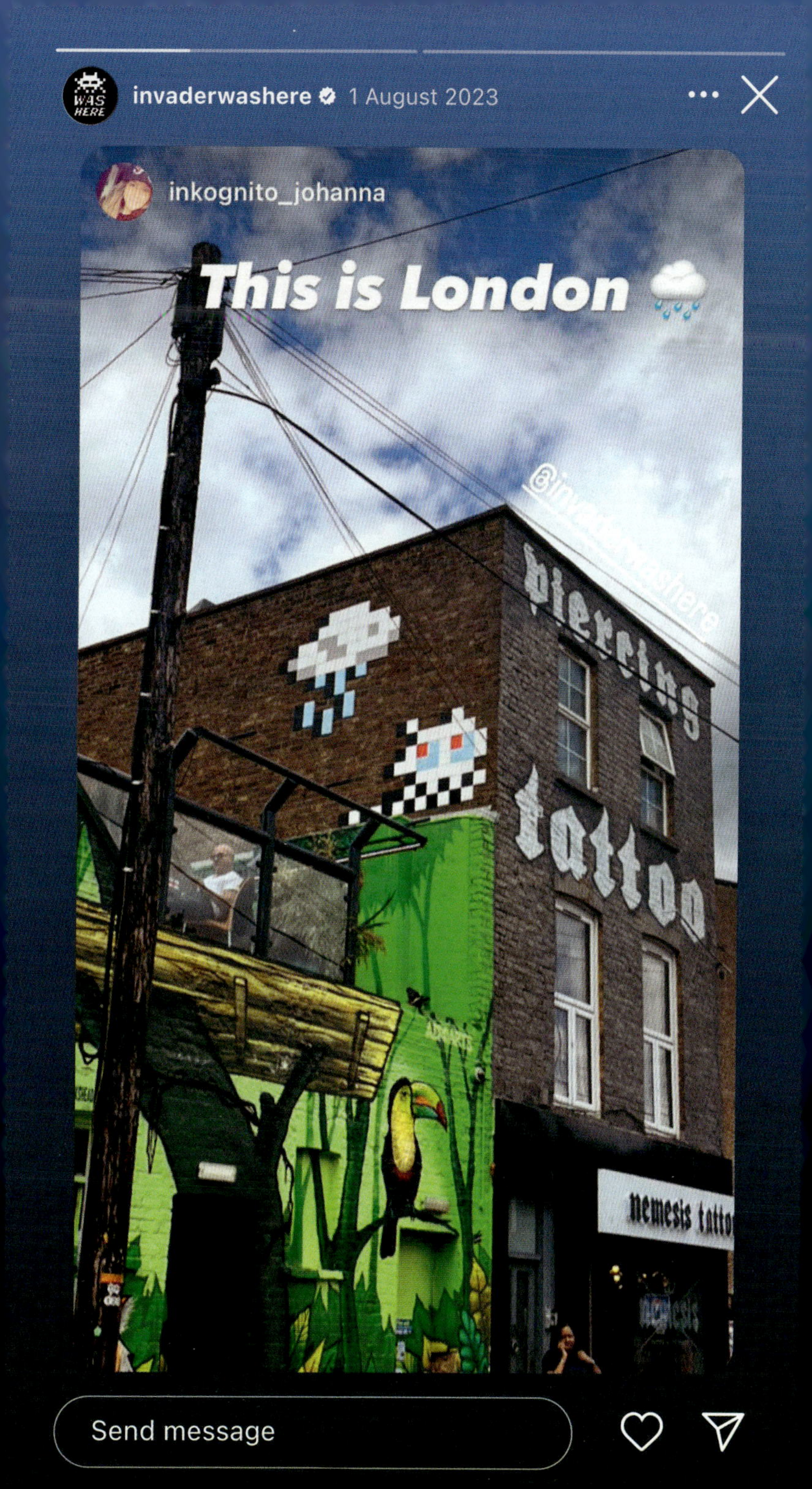

invaderwashere 1 August 2023

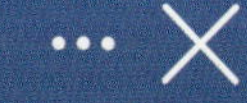

inkognito_johanna

This is London

@invaderwashere

piercing

tattoo

nemesis tatto

Send message

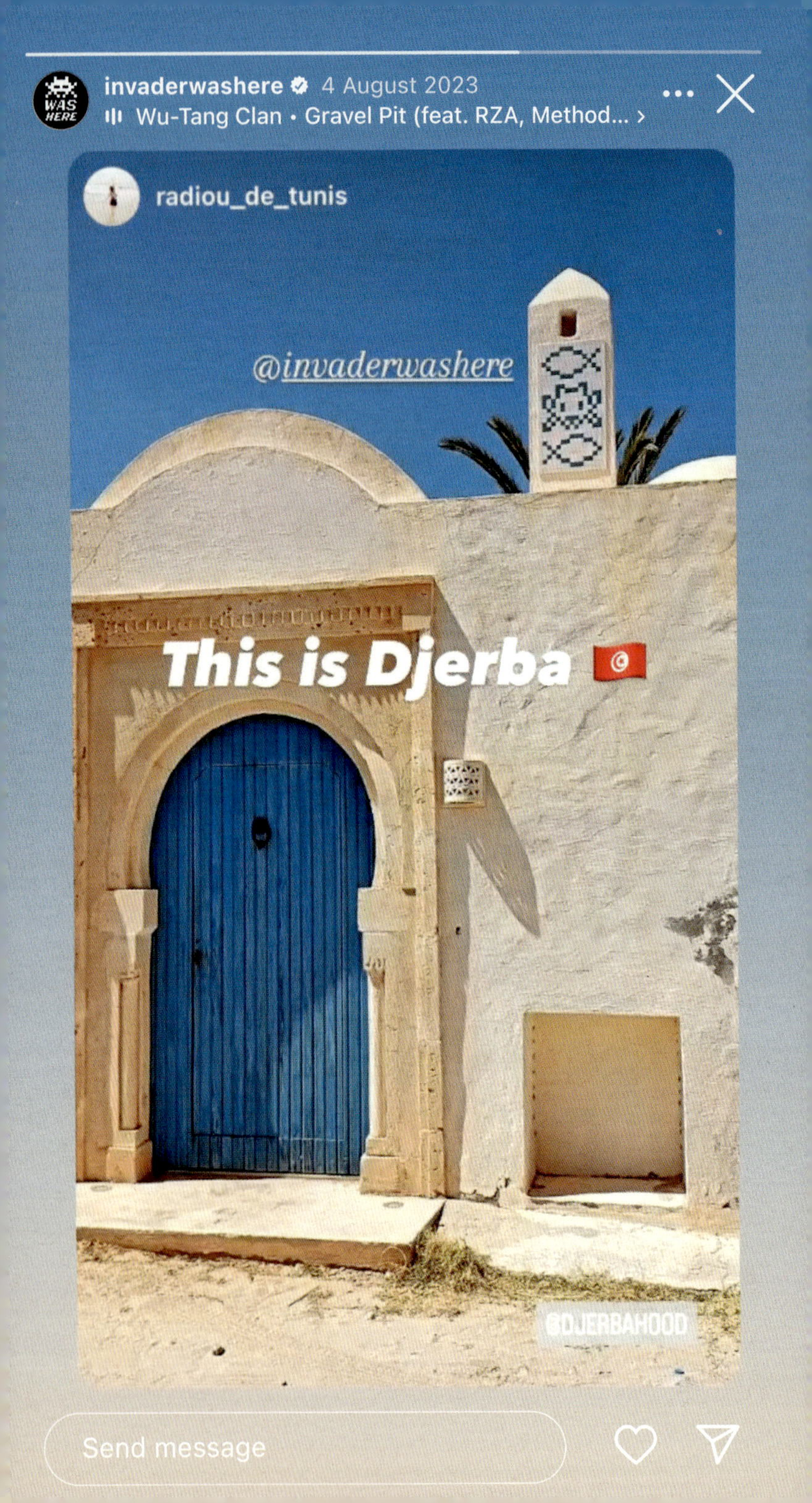

invaderwashere 4 August 2023

Wu-Tang Clan • Gravel Pit (feat. RZA, Method... >

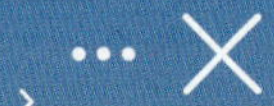

radiou_de_tunis

@invaderwashere

This is Djerba

@DJERBAHOOD

Send message

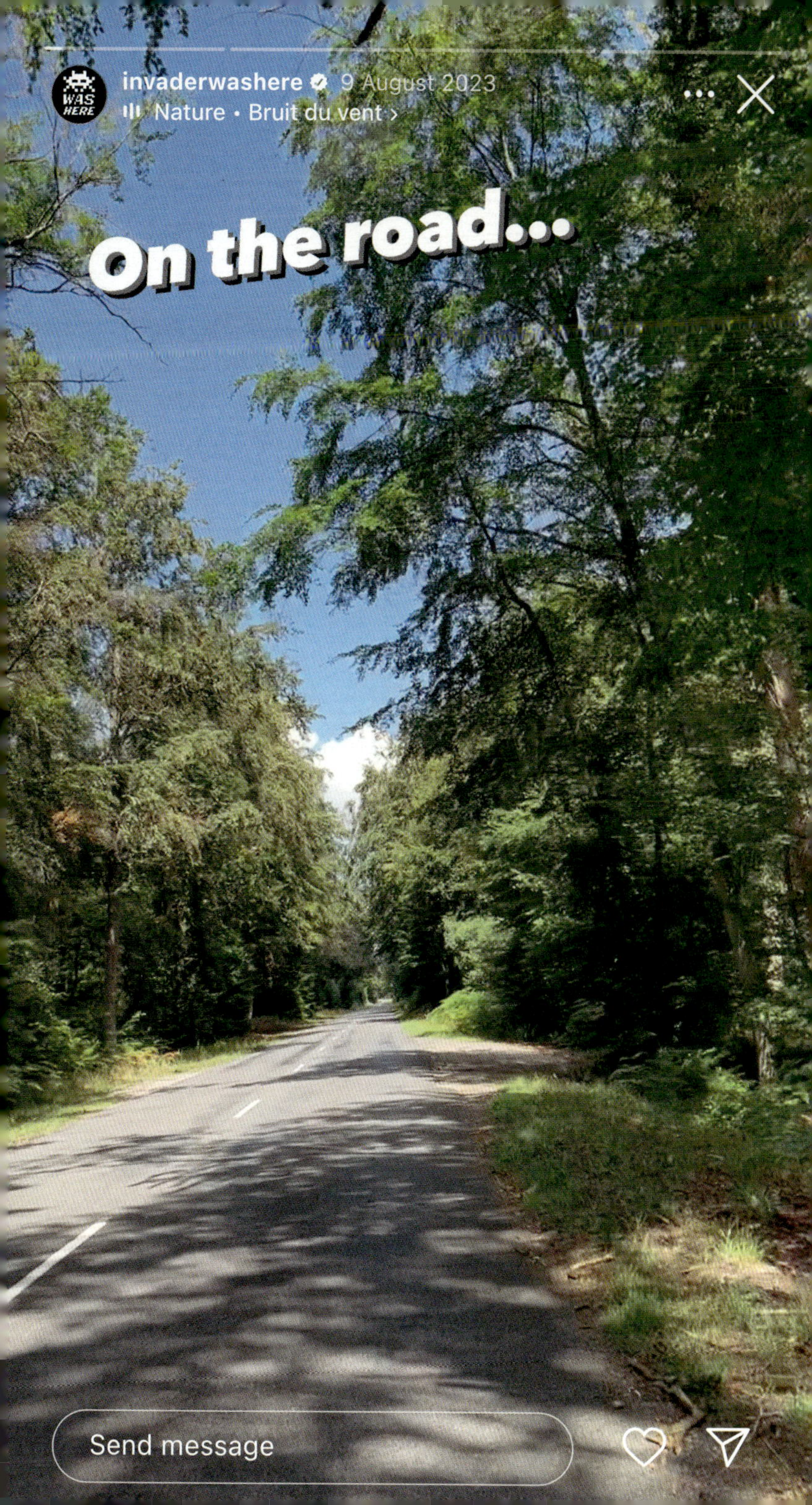
invaderwashere 9 August 2023
Nature • Bruit du vent
On the road...
Send message

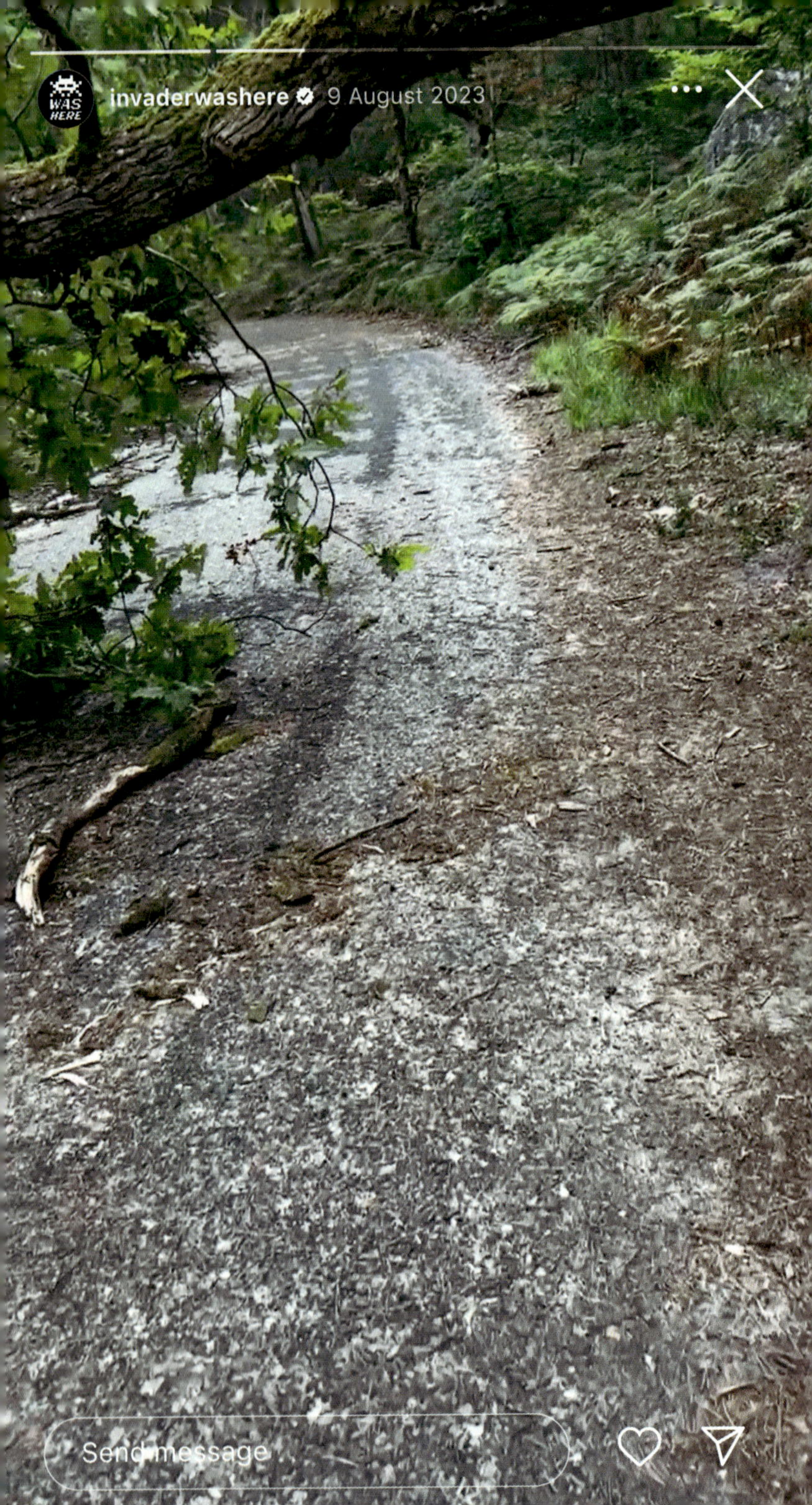
WAS HERE
invaderwashere 9 August 2023
Send message

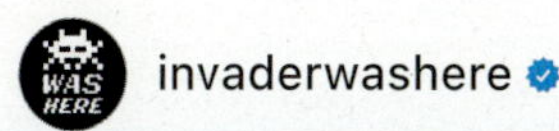

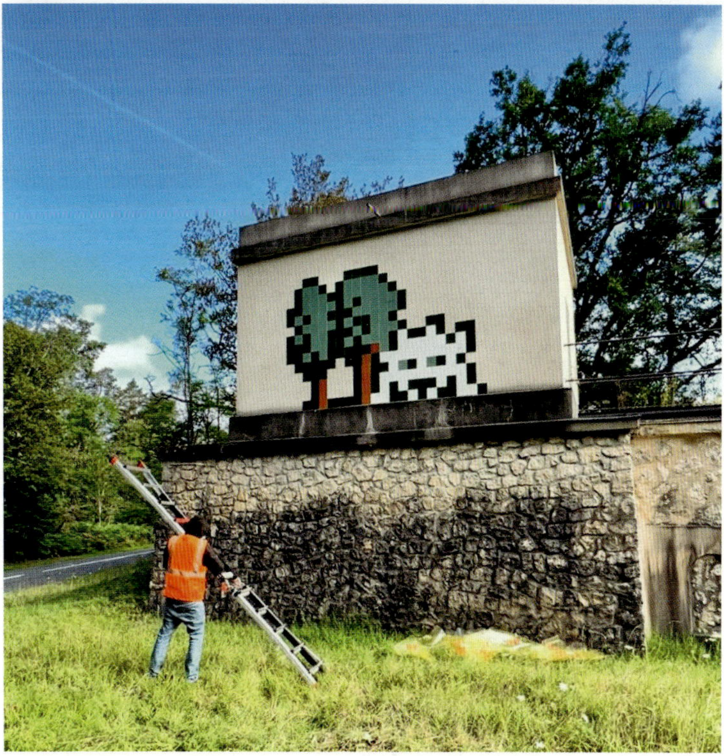

13 181 likes

invaderwashere Just finished the 7th wave of the Invasion of Fontainebleau with 28 new pieces 👾🌳 More photos soon #fontainebleau #forest #aqueduct

View all 148 comments

10 August 2023

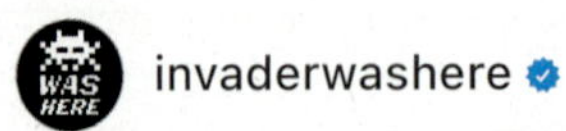

•••

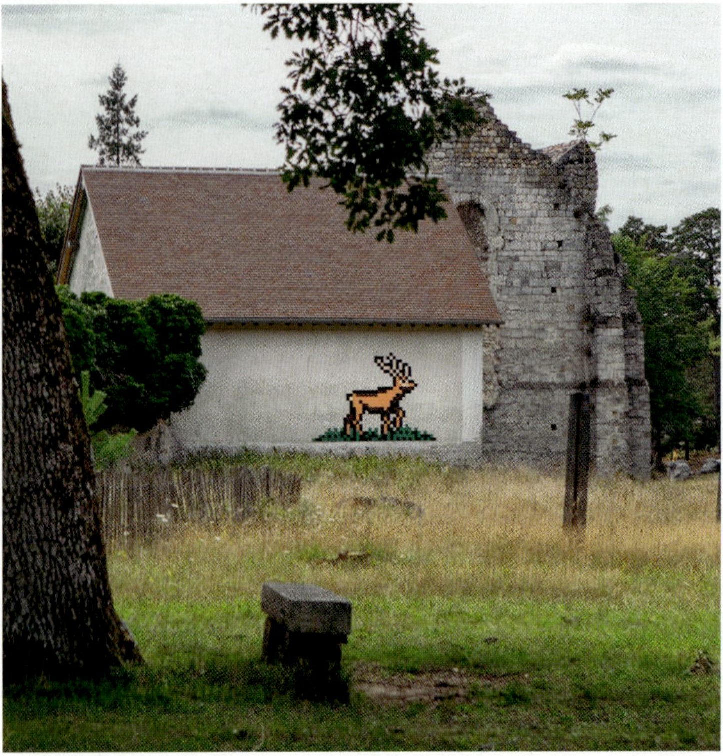

10 651 likes

invaderwashere FTBL_31 #fontainebleau #forest #wildlife

View all 88 comments

11 August 2023

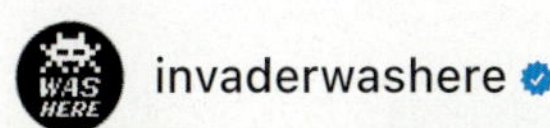

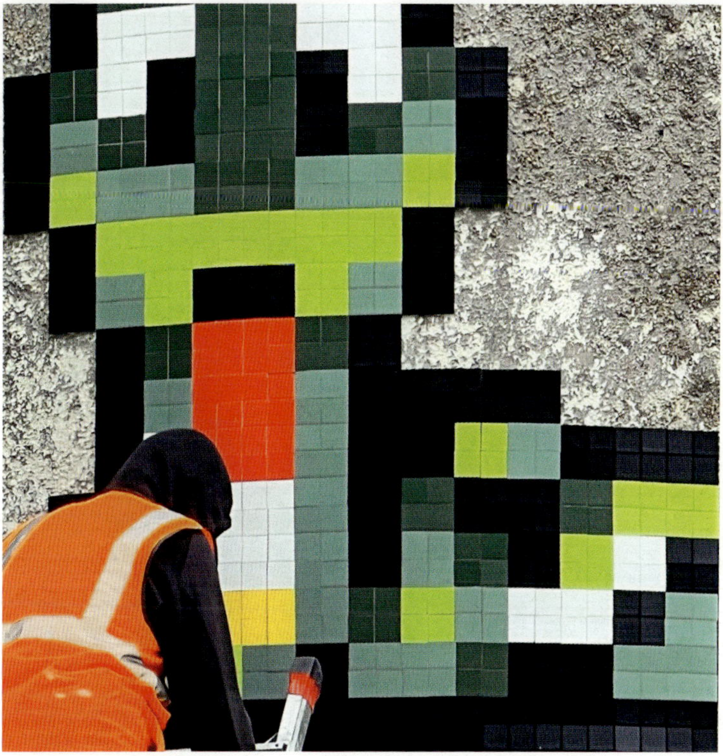

9 993 likes

invaderwashere The snake of Fontainebleau
#fontainebleau #forest #wildlife

View all 64 comments

12 August 2023

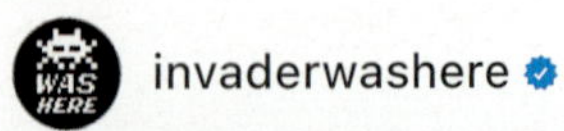

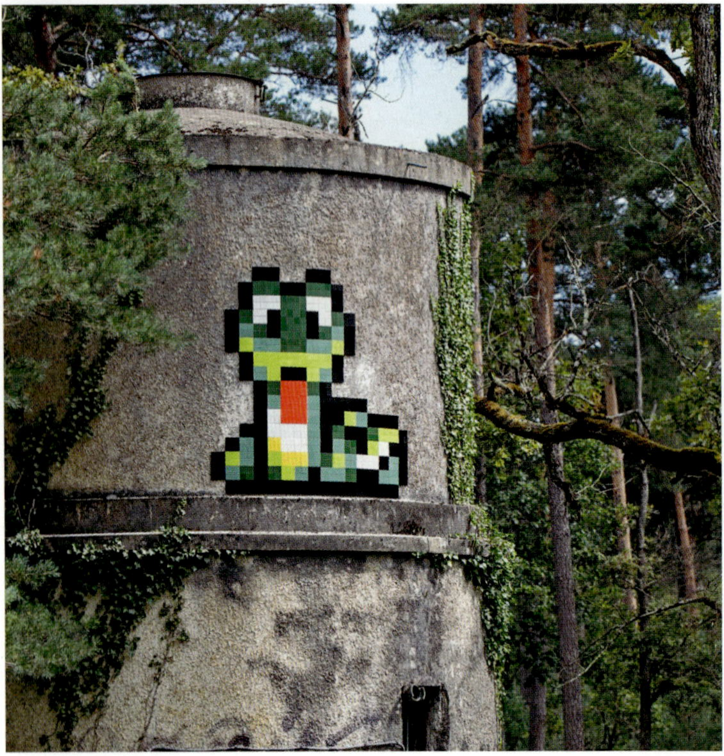

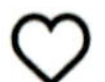   

9 993 likes

invaderwashere The snake of Fontainebleau
#fontainebleau #forest #wildlife

View all 64 comments

12 August 2023

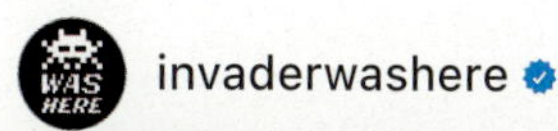

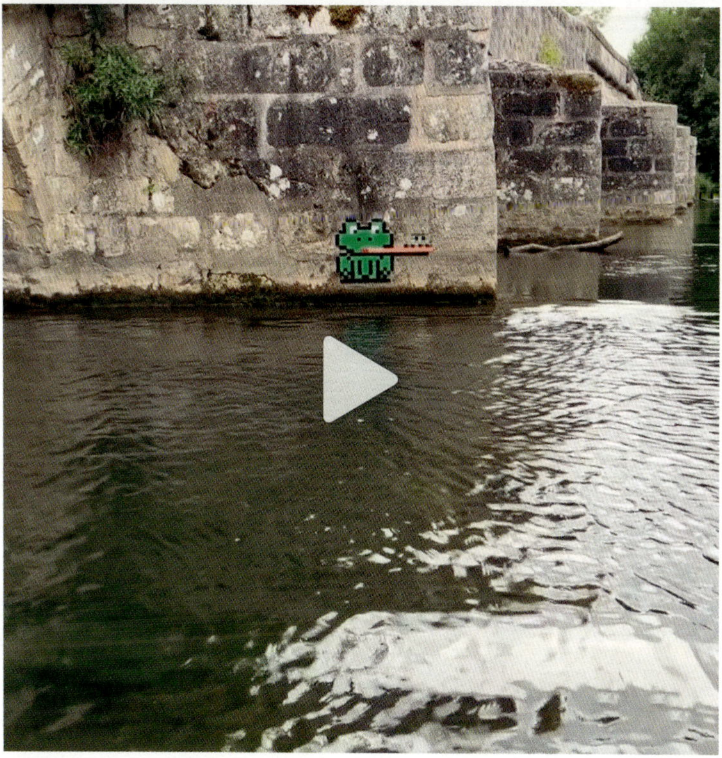

9812 likes

invaderwashere Sometimes you have to get in the water to do a good job! 🏊💦🧊🐸👾 #grezsurloing #fontainebleau #riverart

View all 114 comments

13 August 2023

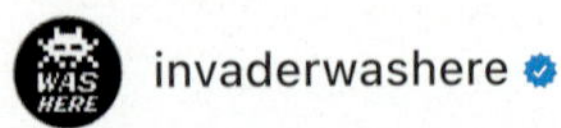

invaderwashere

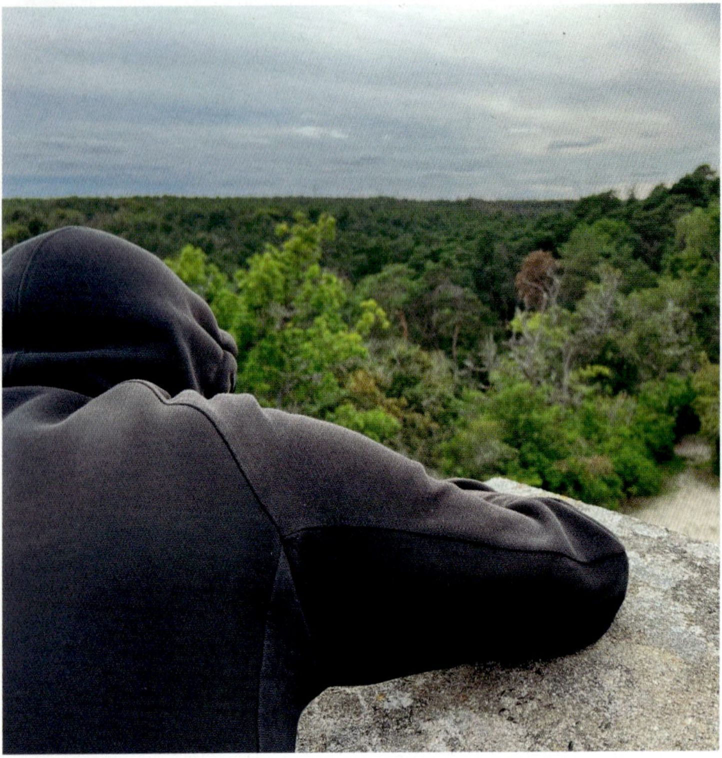

10 507 likes

invaderwashere Fontainebleau under invasion 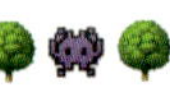
#enjoytheview #forest

View all 100 comments

14 August 2023

invaderwashere ...

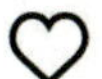   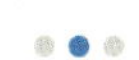 

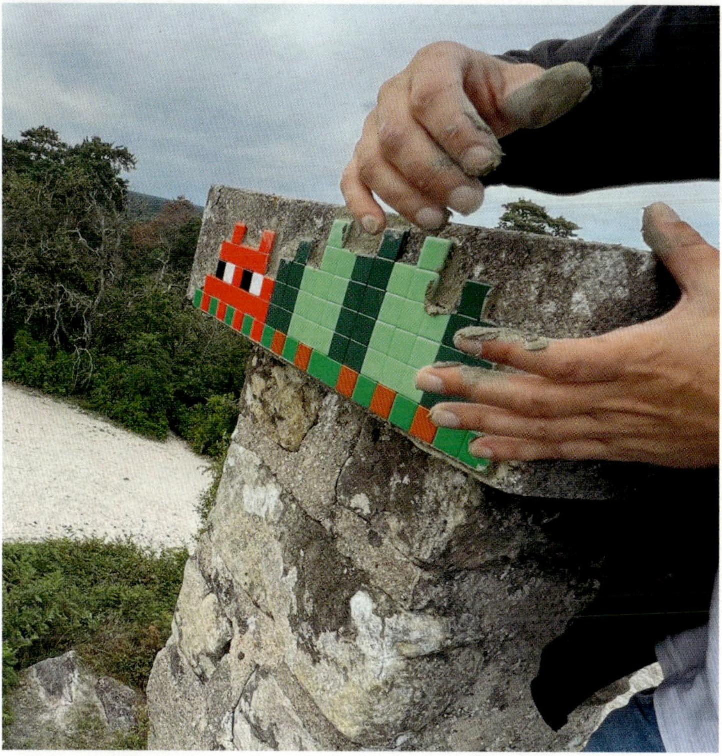

10 507 likes

invaderwashere Fontainebleau under invasion 🌳  
#enjoytheview #forest

View all 100 comments

14 August 2023

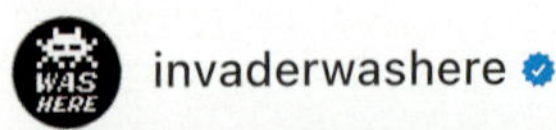

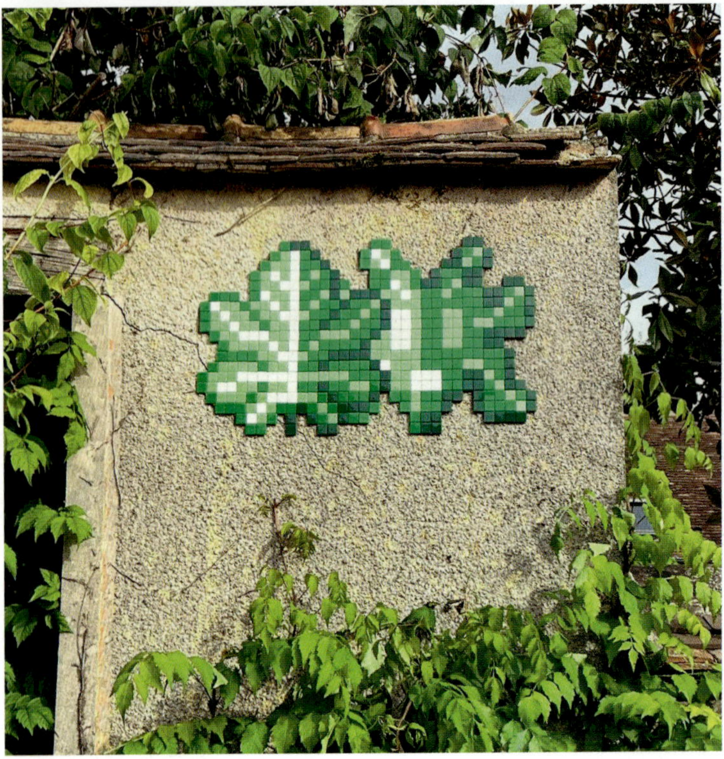

6893 likes

invaderwashere Evergreen 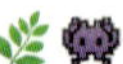

View all 49 comments

15 August 2023

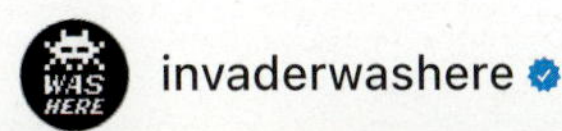

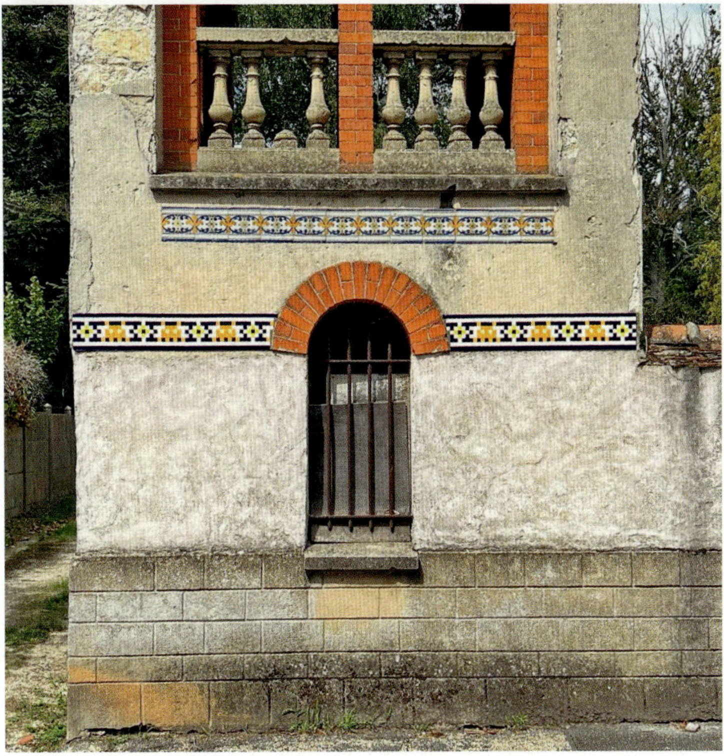

11775 likes

invaderwashere Another kind of camouflage

View all 202 comments

16 August 2023

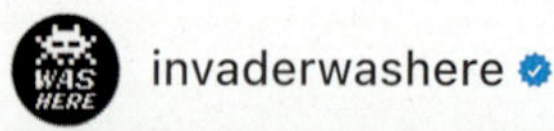

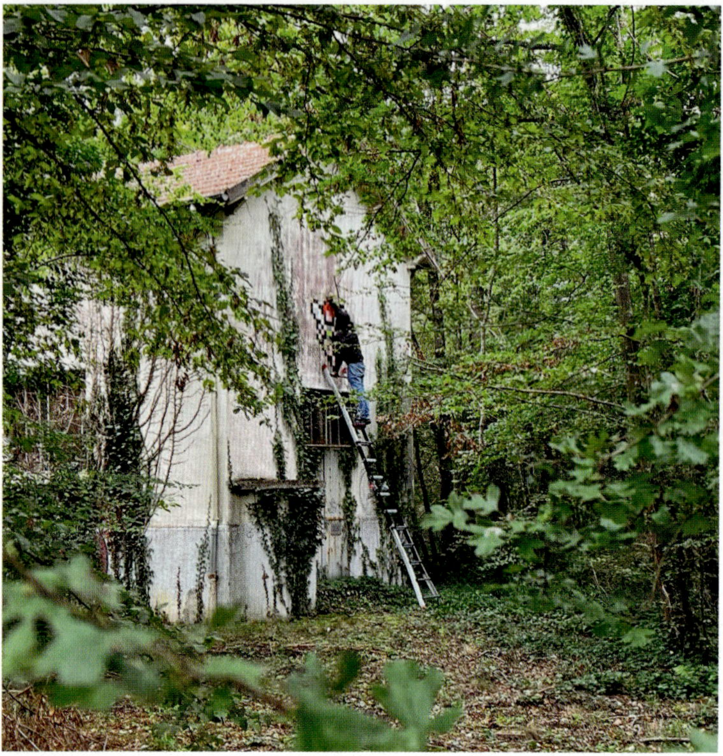

6 546 likes

invaderwashere  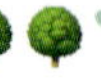 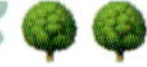

View all 73 comments

18 August 2023

invaderwashere

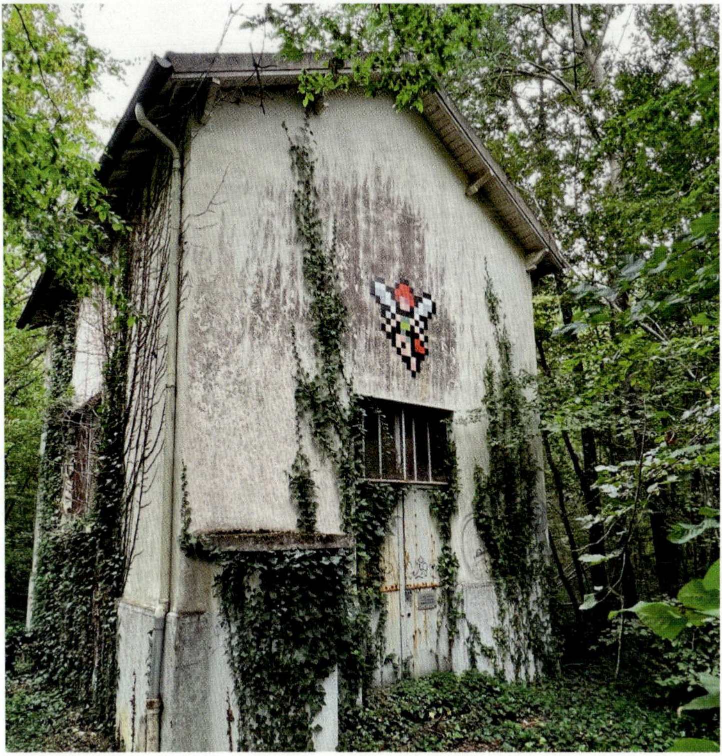

6 546 likes

invaderwashere    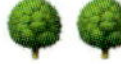

View all 73 comments

18 August 2023

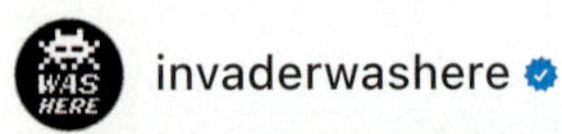

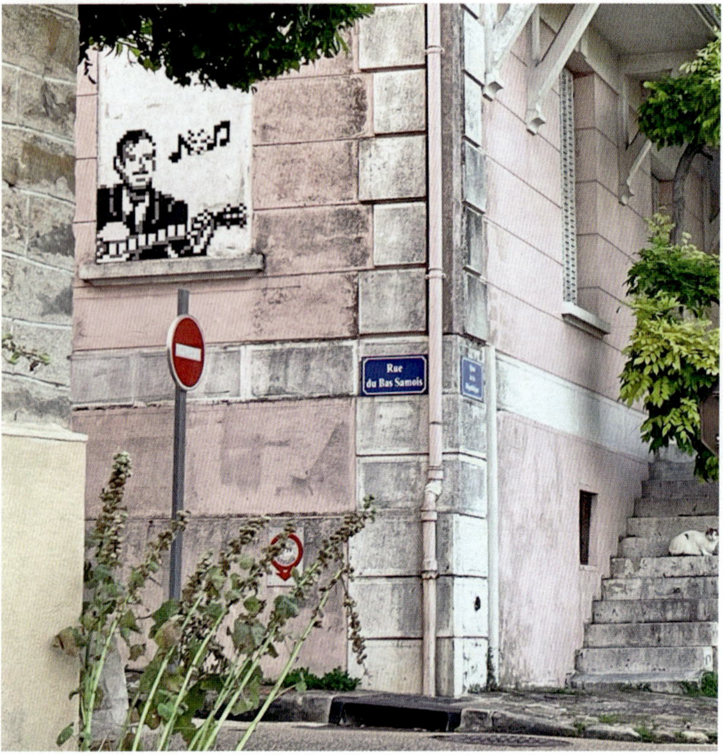

9 216 likes

invaderwashere Django Reinhardt 🎶 👾 in front of his house in Samois-sur-Seine where he retired and lived until his death #fontainebleau #djangoreinhardt #jazzvibes

View all 68 comments

20 August 2023

invaderwashere

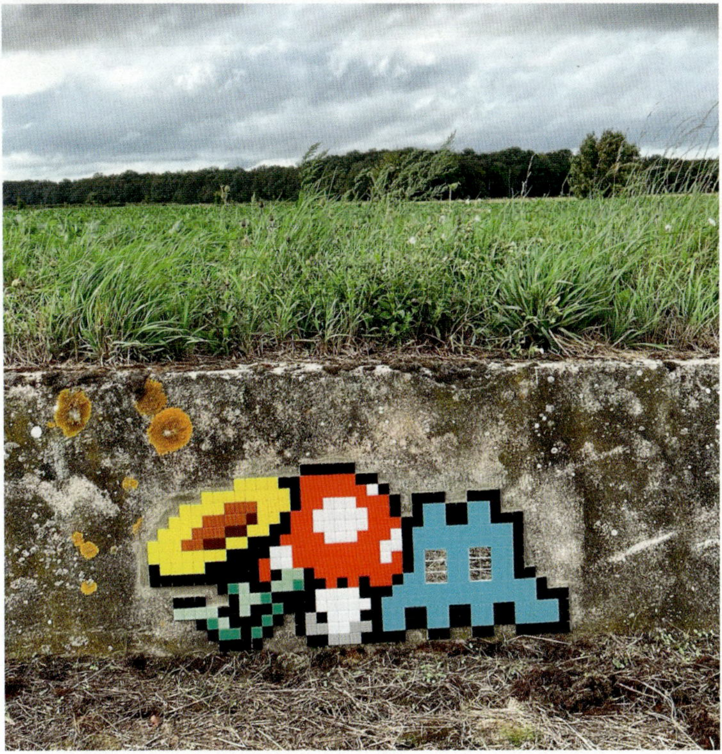

9143 likes

invaderwashere Happy Monday #fieldart #forest #fontainebleau #villages

View all 73 comments

21 August 2023

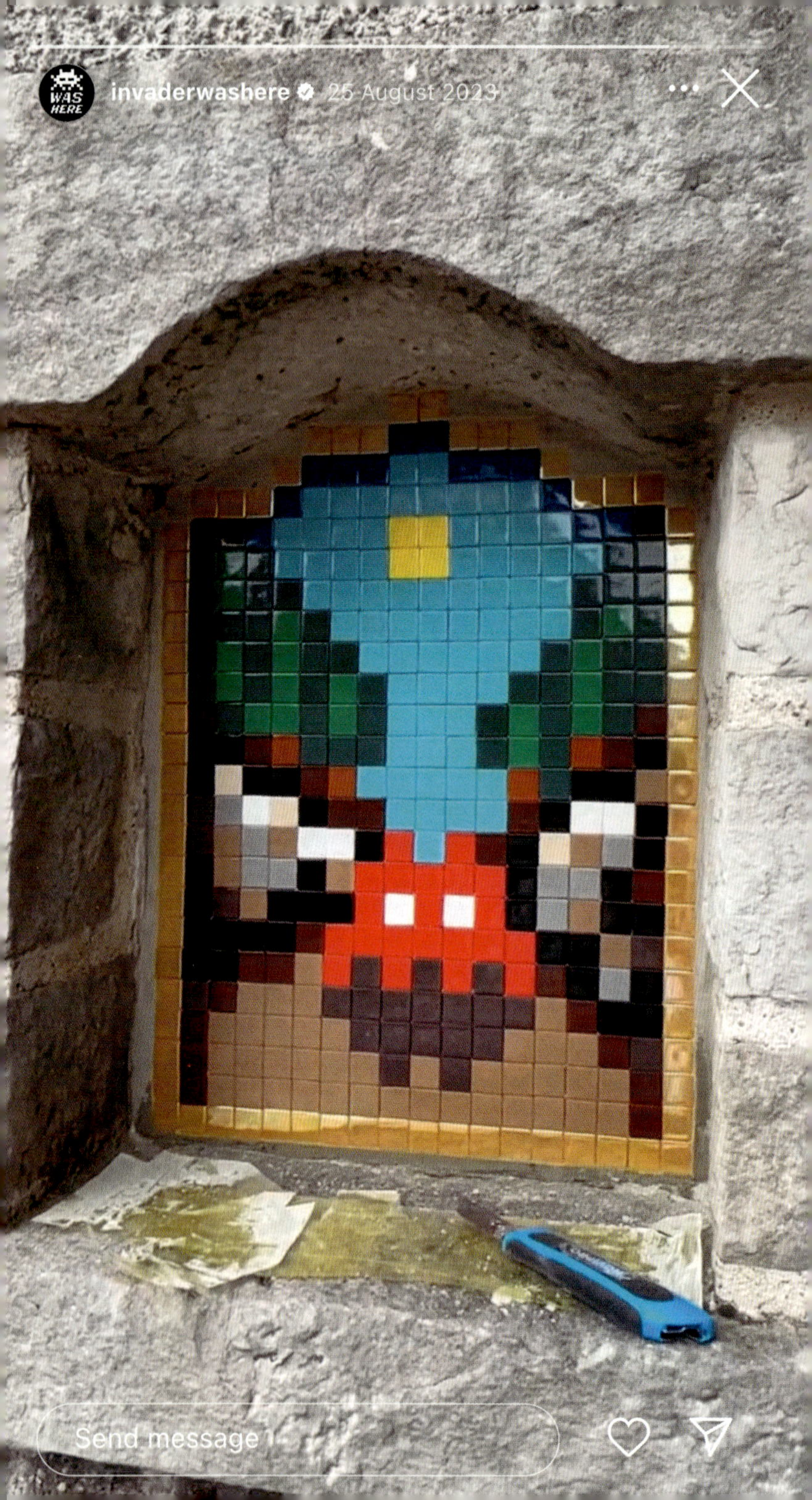
WAS HERE
invaderwashere
25 August 2023
Send message

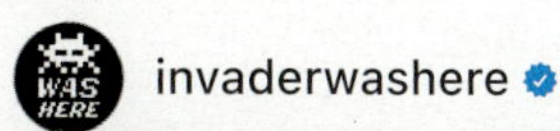

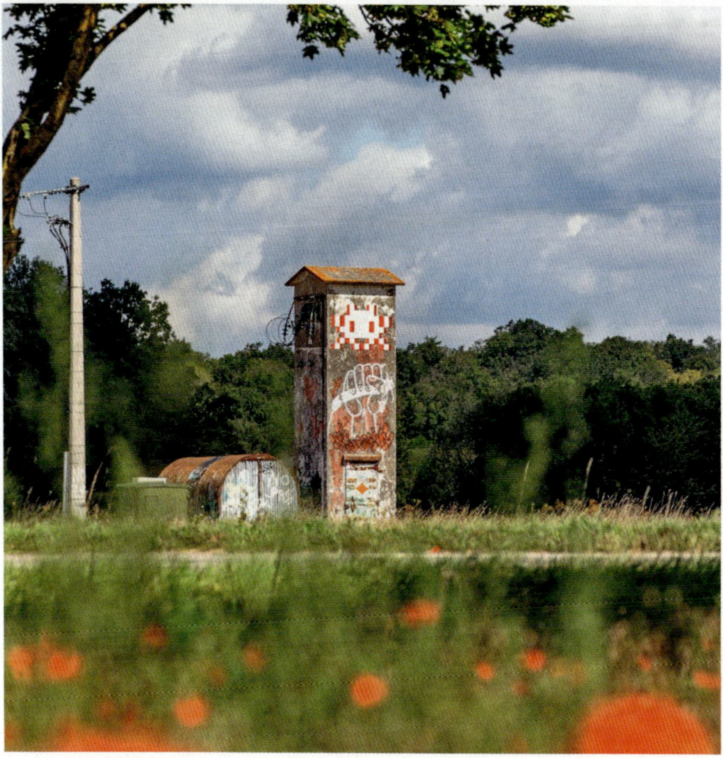

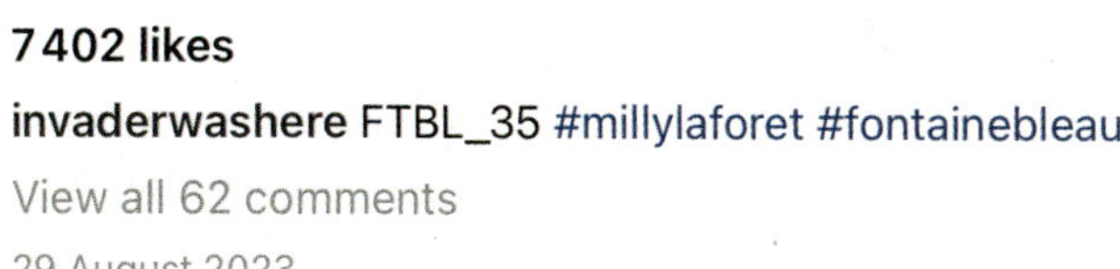

7 402 likes

invaderwashere FTBL_35 #millylaforet #fontainebleau

View all 62 comments

29 August 2023

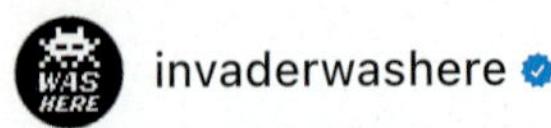

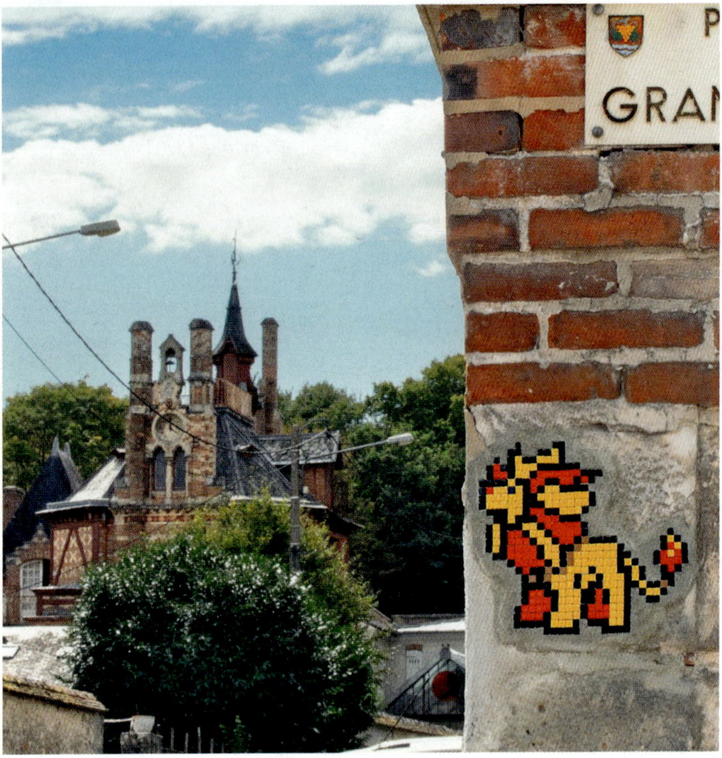

12 497 likes

invaderwashere Animal painter Rosa Bonheur lived in a small castle in Thomery surrounded by numerous animals including a pair of lions. The Pokemon lion is looking at her castle and the other one is standing on it. #rosabonheur #castle #lions #nemelios #thomery #fontainebleau

View all 80 comments

30 August 2023

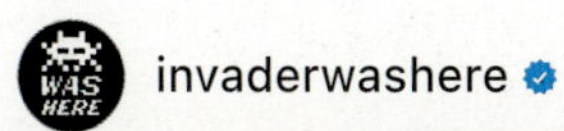

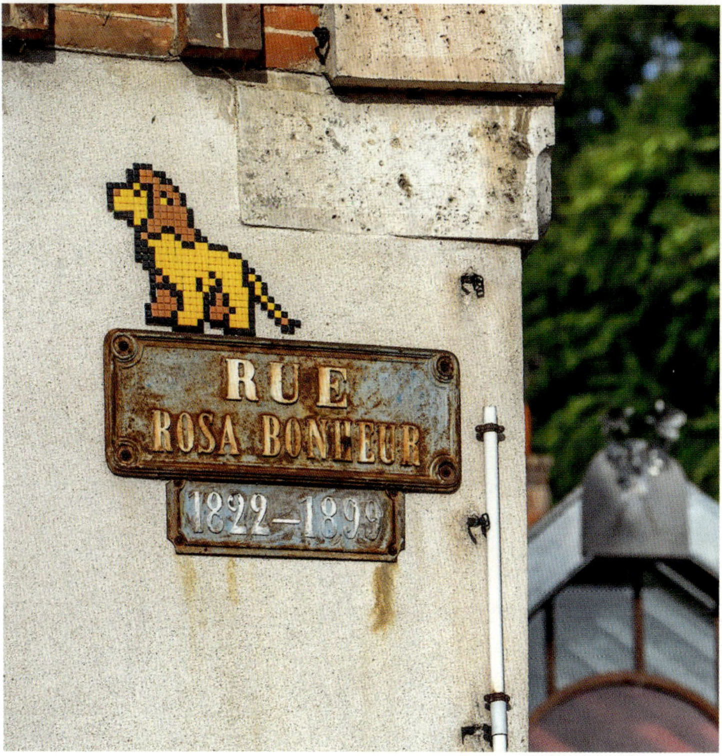

12 497 likes

invaderwashere Animal painter Rosa Bonheur lived in a small castle in Thomery surrounded by numerous animals including a pair of lions. The Pokemon lion is looking at her castle and the other one is standing on it. #rosabonheur #castle #lions #nemelios #thomery #fontainebleau

View all 80 comments

30 August 2023

invaderwashere

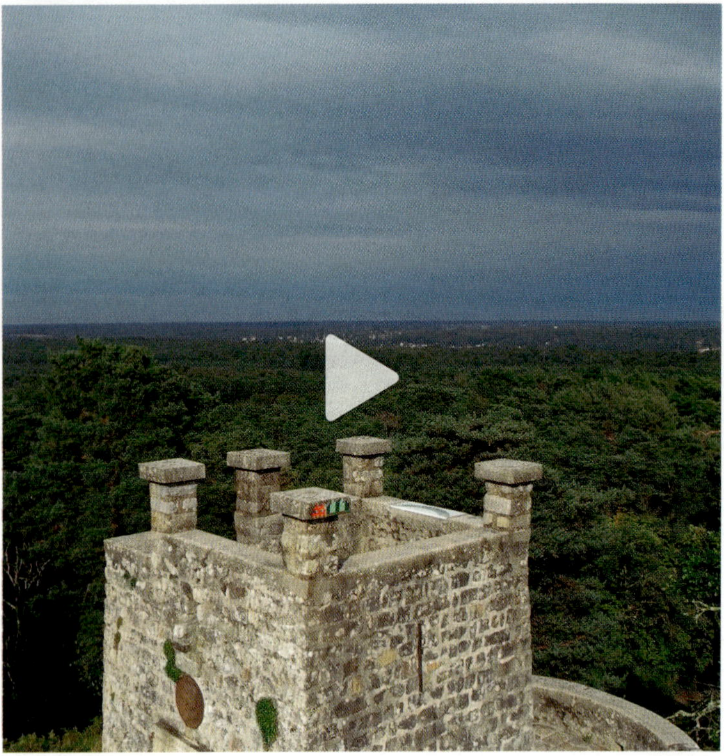

4187 likes

invaderwashere The great forest of Fontainebleau is surrounded by numerous small towns and villages with a rich historical and artistic past. I wanted to invade all this space to create a large-scale itinerary with 46 pieces already scattered across this magical and timeless territory #aforest #fontainebleau #lostinaforestallalone Drone shot by @trlelay

View all 105 comments

4 September 2023

invaderwashere

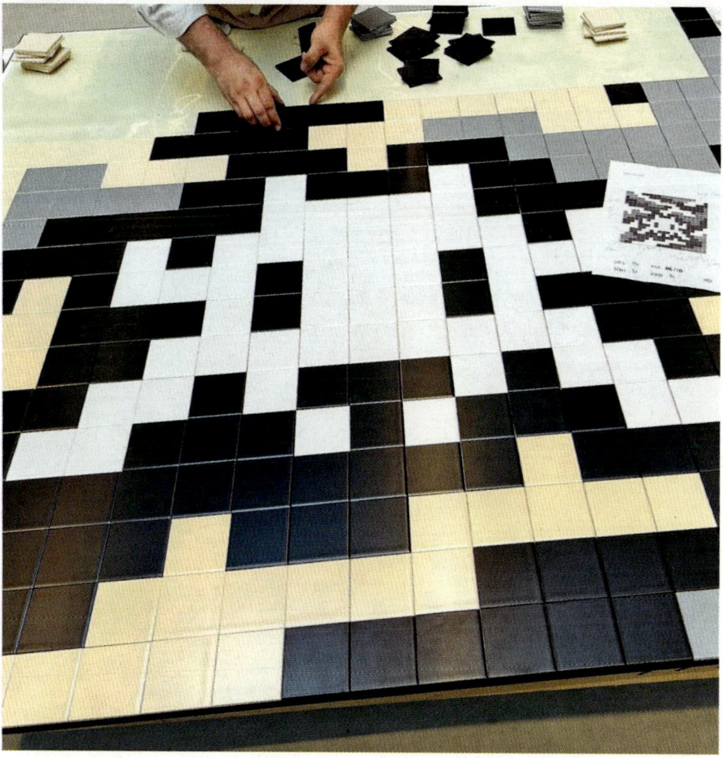

9993 likes

invaderwashere Working on my next show #studiodetails #mothership #camouflages&devilstower @oti.official Stay tuned...

View all 131 comments

7 September 2023

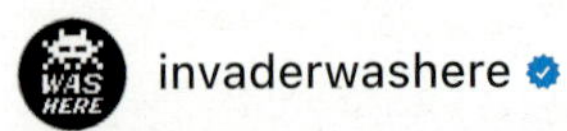

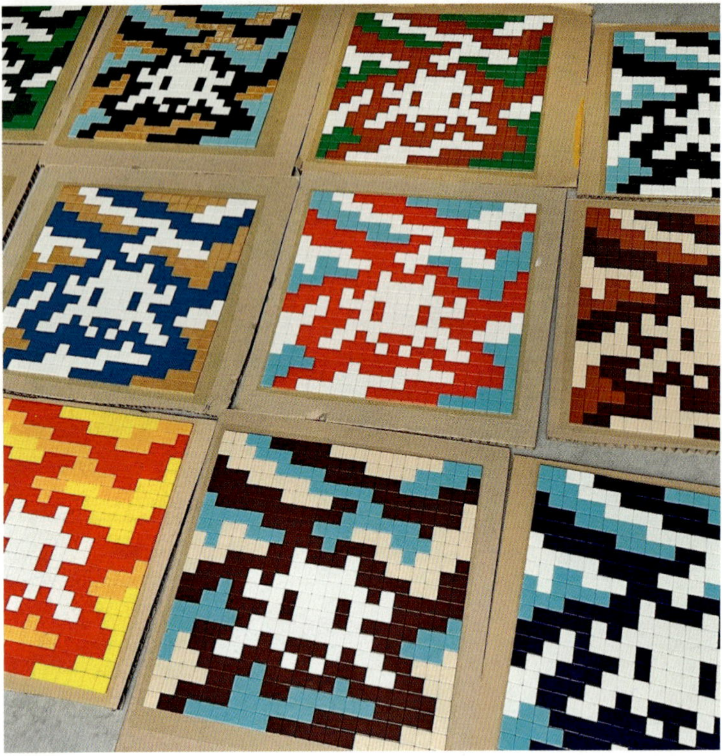

9993 likes

invaderwashere Working on my next show #studiodetails #mothership #camouflages&devilstower @oti.official Stay tuned...

View all 131 comments

7 September 2023

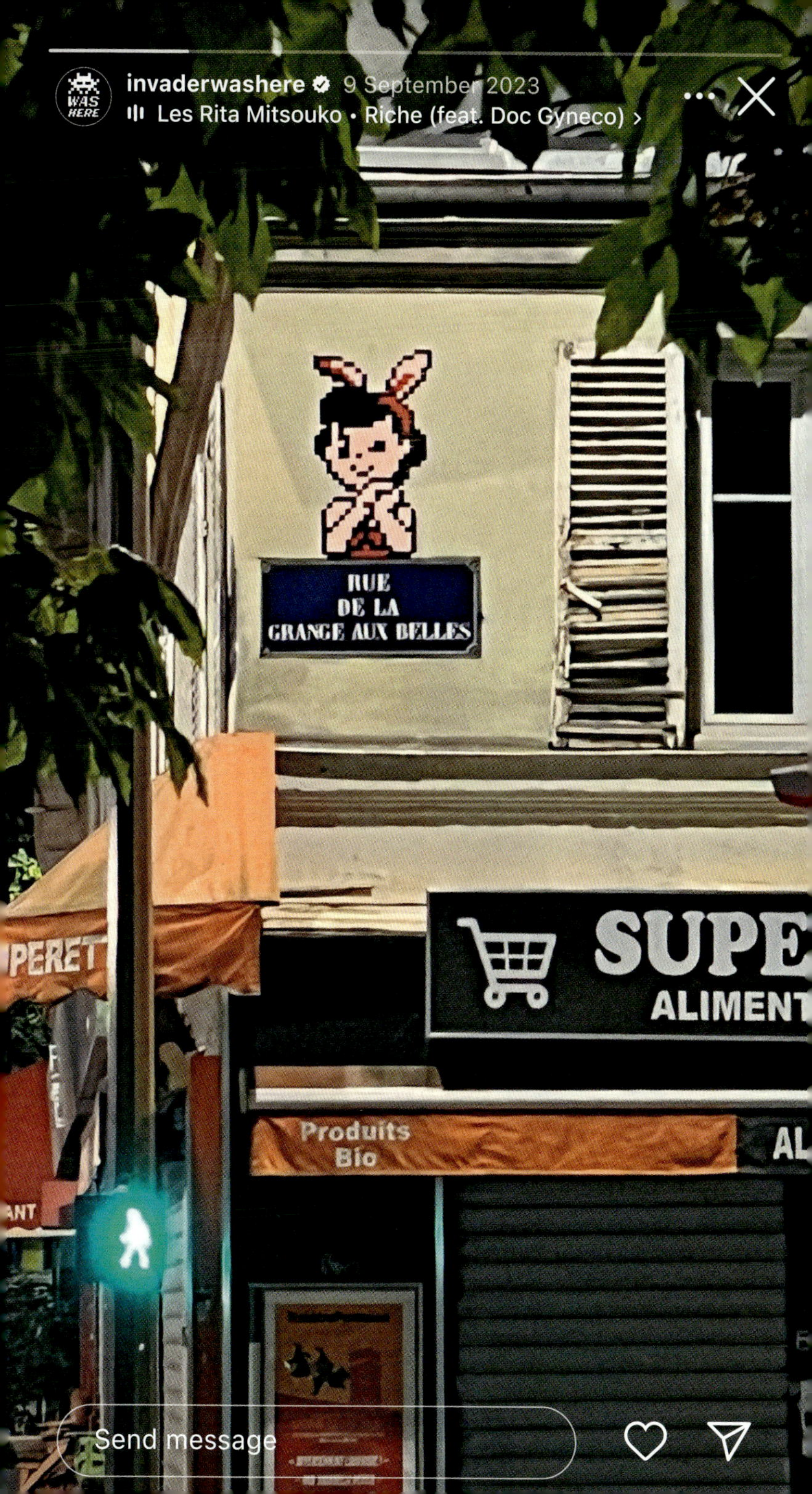

invaderwashere 9 September 2023
Les Rita Mitsouko • Riche (feat. Doc Gyneco)
RUE
DE LA
GRANGE AUX BELLES
PERET
SUPE
ALIMENT
Produits
Bio
AL
ANT
Send message

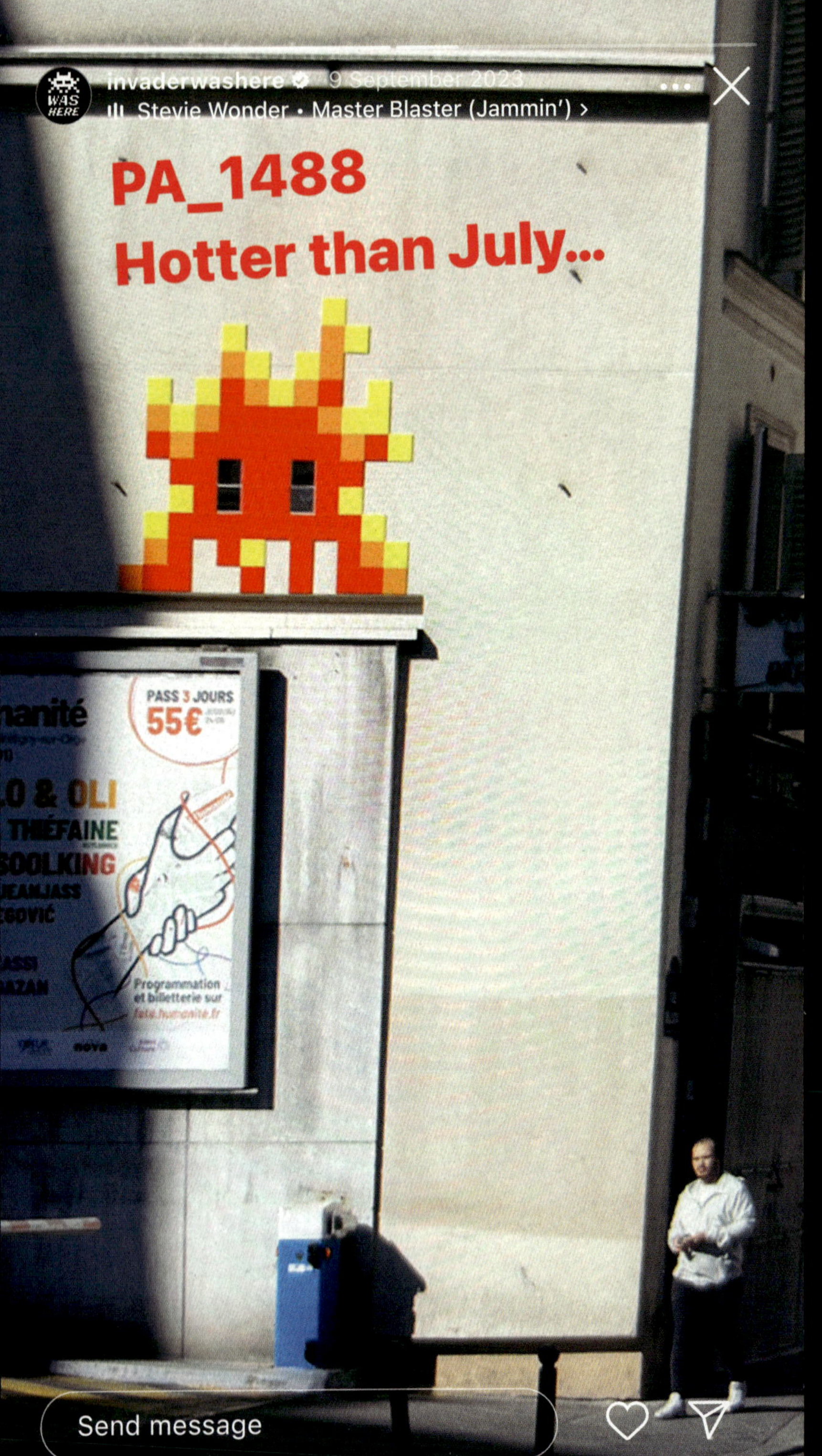
invaderwashere
9 September 2023
Stevie Wonder · Master Blaster (Jammin') ›
PA_1488
Hotter than July...
PASS 3 JOURS
55€
THIÉFAINE
SOOLKING
Programmation
et billetterie sur
fete.humanite.fr
nova
Send message

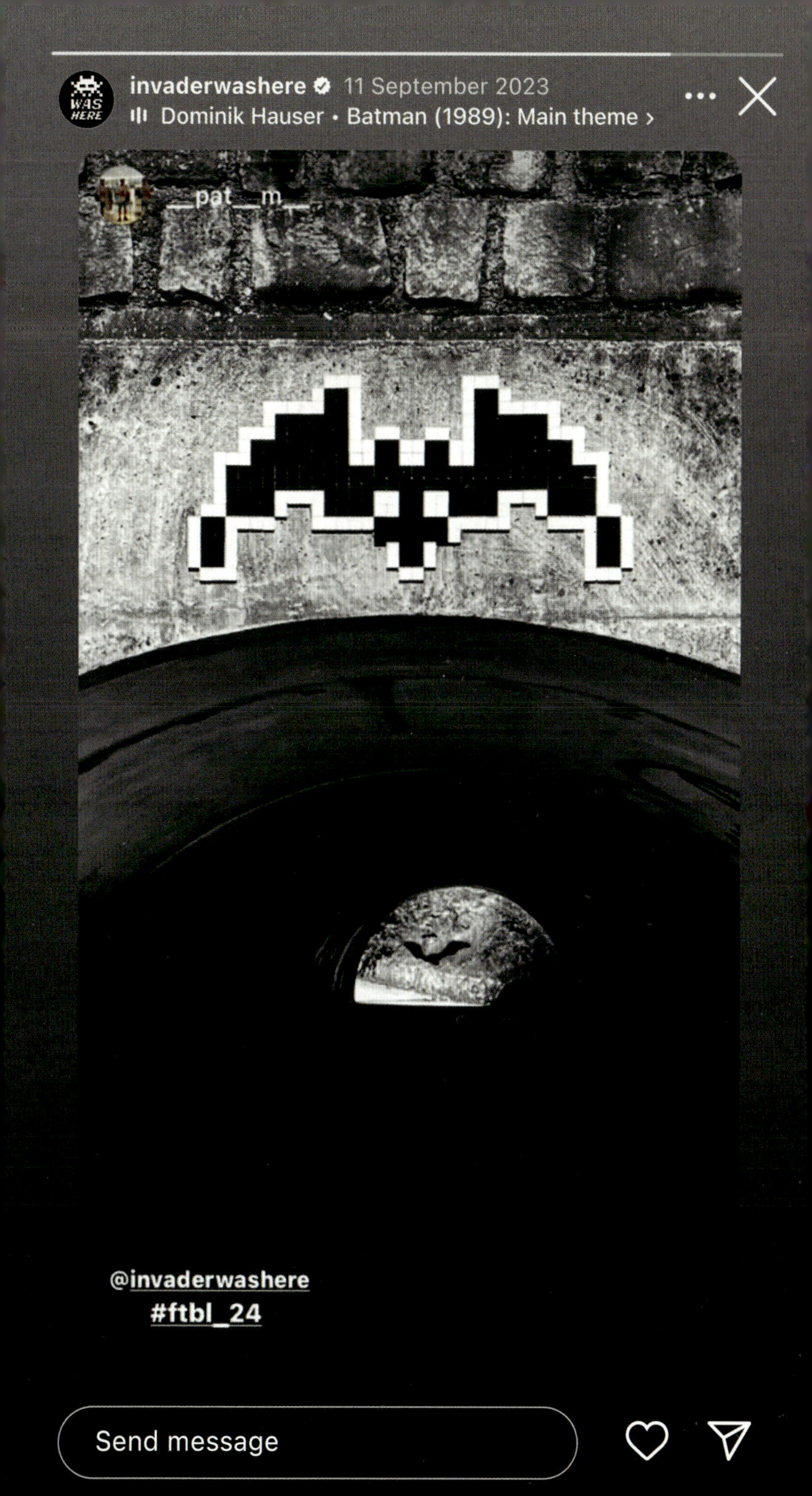

invaderwashere 11 September 2023

Dominik Hauser • Batman (1989): Main theme ›

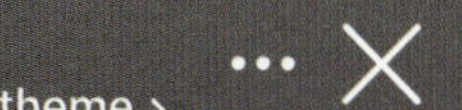

__pat__m__

@invaderwashere

#ftbl_24

Send message

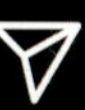

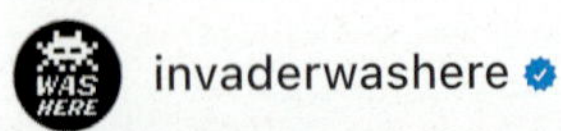

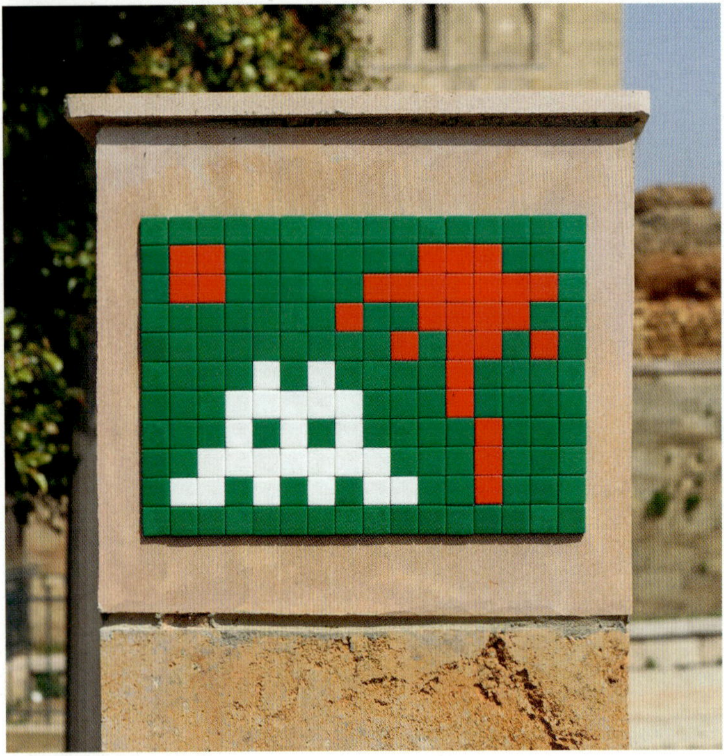

6 702 likes

invaderwashere Thoughts for Morocco in this painful event #earthquake #morocco #rabat #RBA17

View all 37 comments

12 September 2023

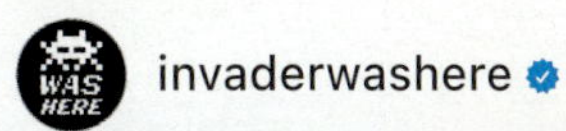

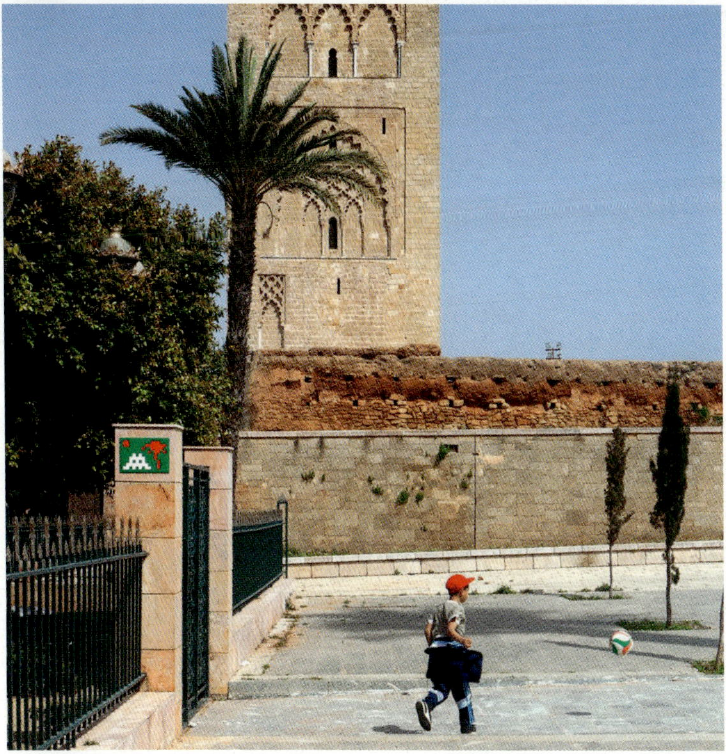

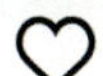    

6 702 likes

invaderwashere Thoughts for Morocco in this painful event
#earthquake #morocco #rabat #RBA17

View all 37 comments

12 September 2023

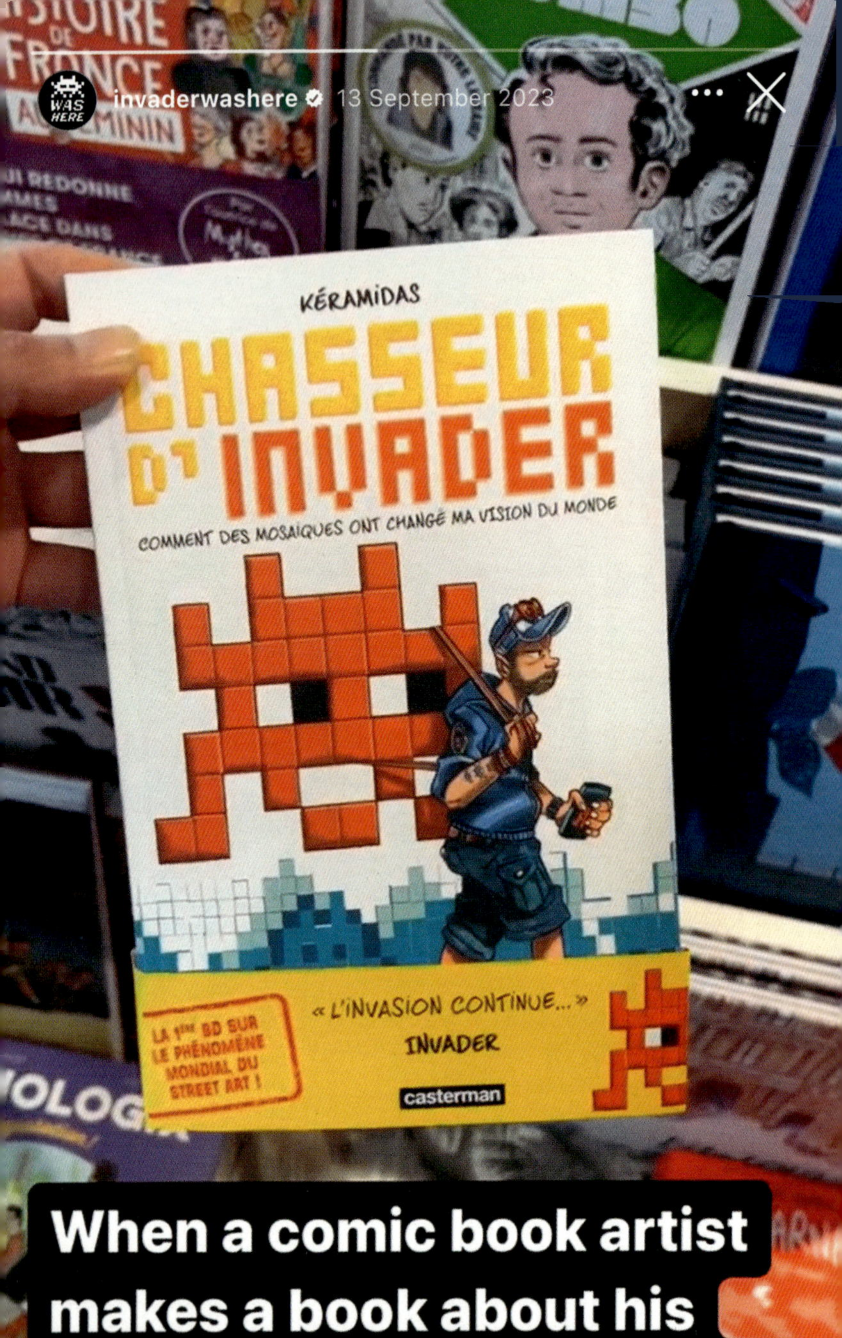

When a comic book artist makes a book about his passion: Flashing invaders

Send message

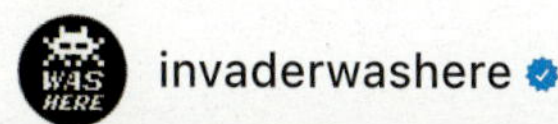

•••

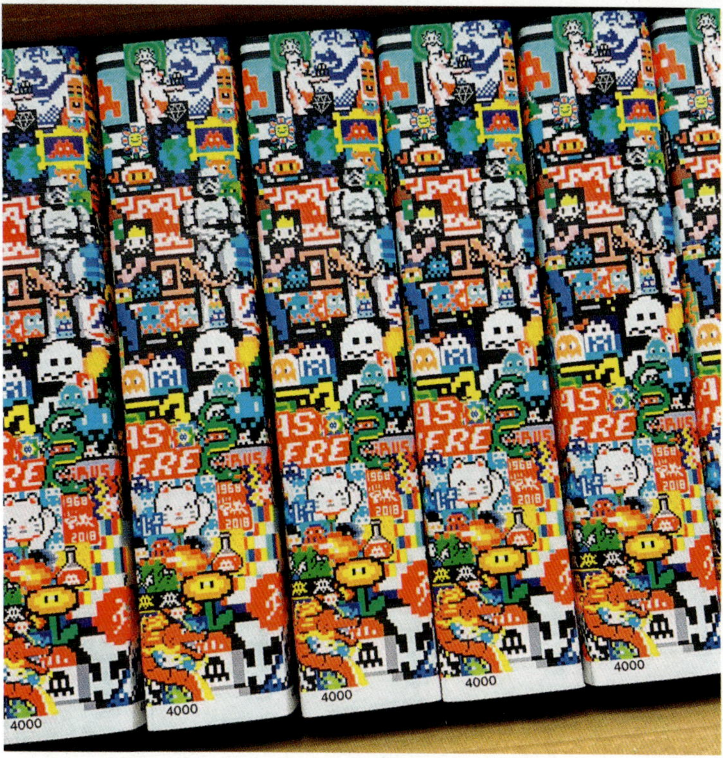

4 681 likes

invaderwashere 4000 is back in stock... This book is certainly my most ambitious to date. With its 1024 pages, it crowns 20 years of work and celebrates the first 4000 mosaics I installed around the world. They can be seen both individually and as a sprawling meta work. Available in French bookstores and on the Space-shop (link in bio) #reprint #4000mosaics #1024p Designed with @zoo_designers_graphiques Text by @jeanbaptistedepanafieu

View all 92 comments

15 September 2023

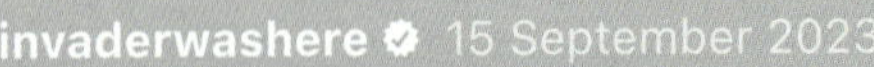

invaderwashere 15 September 2023

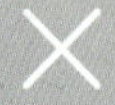

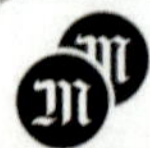

m_magazine et lemondefr

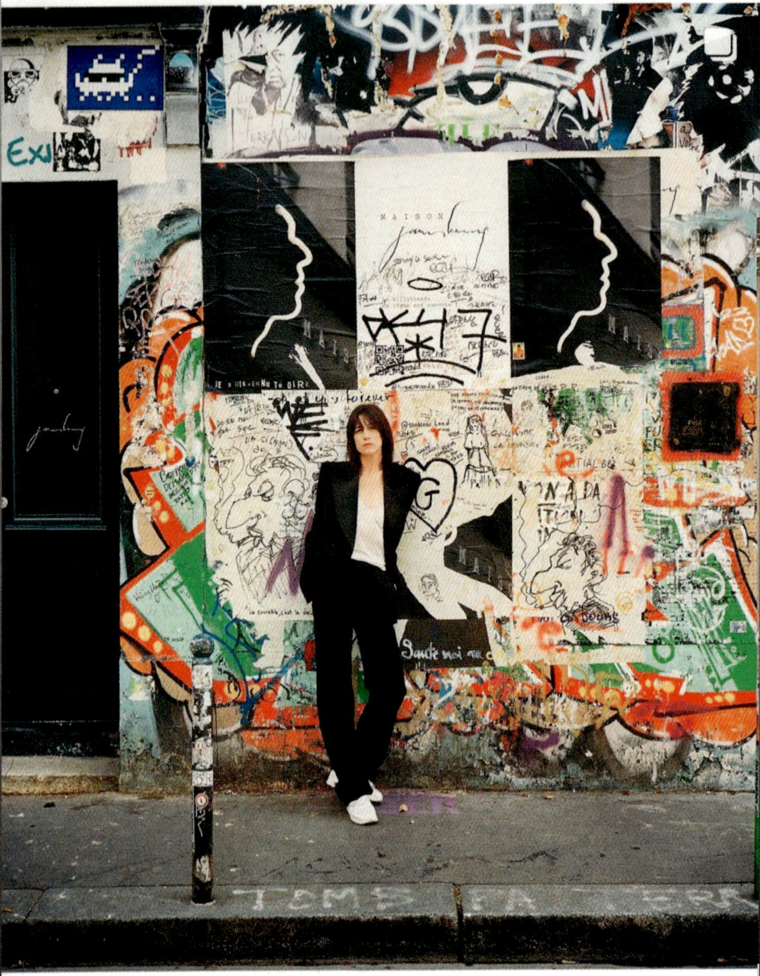

m_magazine La façade du 5 bis, rue de Verneuil, à Paris, a longtemps été le seul lieu visible de la légende Gainsbourg. À...

invaderwashere •••

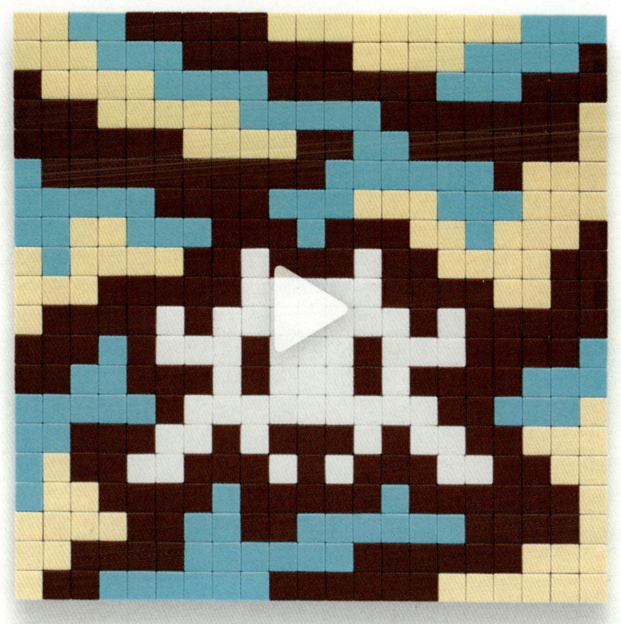

  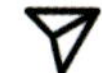 

7837 likes

invaderwashere CAMOUFLAGES & DEVILS TOWER, my new solo show at Over the Influence gallery / Los Angeles / Opening next Saturday #exhibition #LA #camo #camouflage #mosaics #pixelpieces #devilstower #rubikcubism 🎶 #kraftwerk #D-3 @oti.official

View all 99 comments

20 September 2023

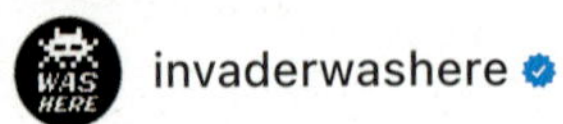

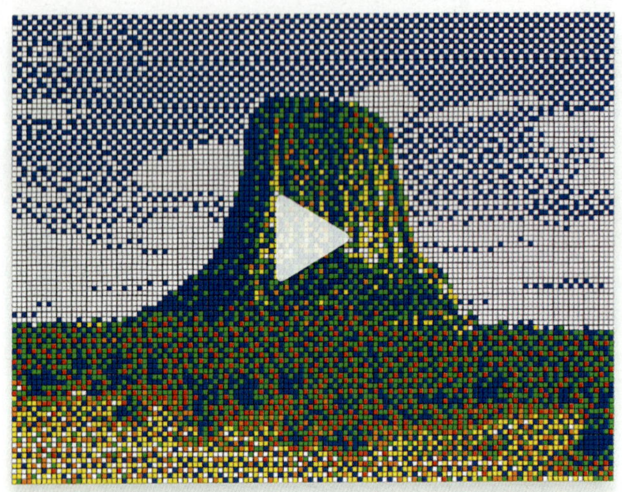

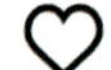

7 837 likes

invaderwashere CAMOUFLAGES & DEVILS TOWER, my new solo show at Over the Influence gallery / Los Angeles / Opening next Saturday #exhibition #LA #camo #camouflage #mosaics #pixelpieces #devilstower #rubikcubism #D-2 @oti.official

View all 99 comments

20 September 2023

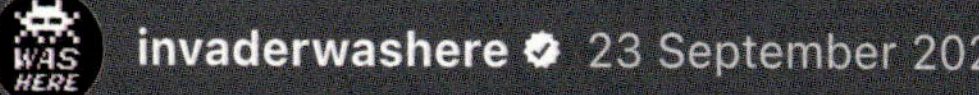
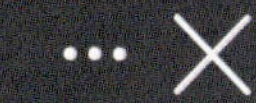
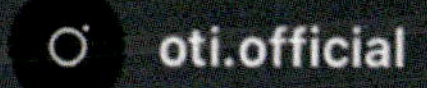
invaderwashere 23 September 2023

oti.official

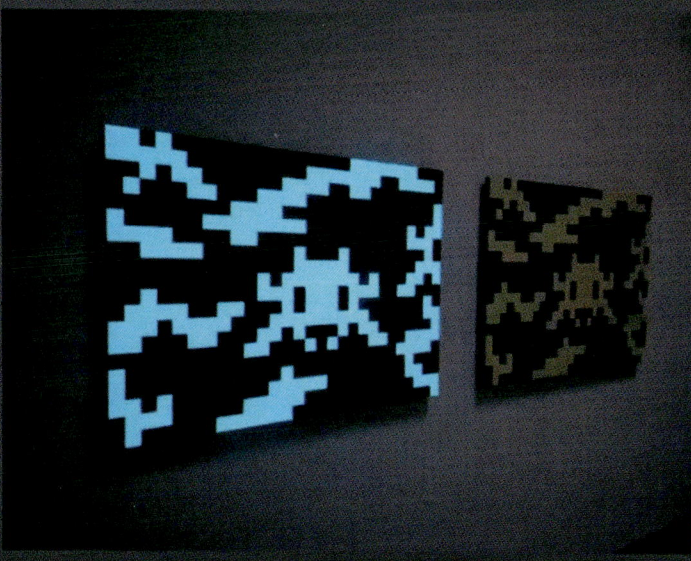

Opening tonight
@oti.official LA

Send message

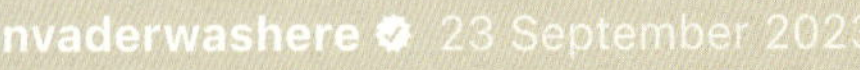
invaderwashere 23 September 2023
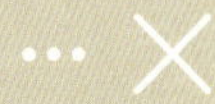
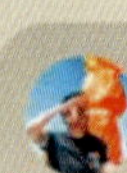
johnlendman
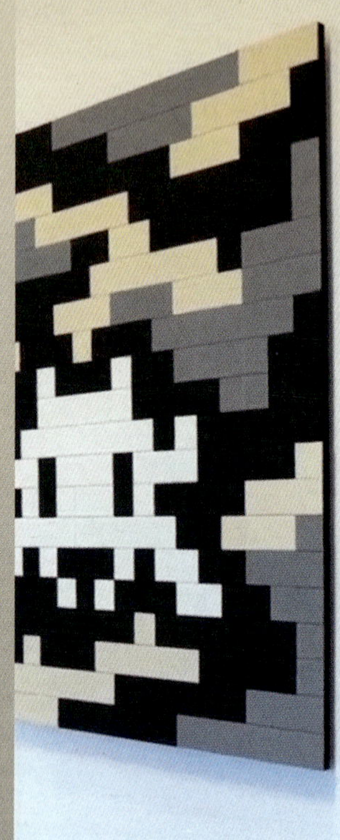
@INVADERWASHERE
OVER THE INFLUENCE LOS ANGELES
Send message

invaderwashere 23 September 2023

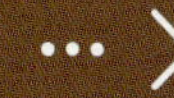

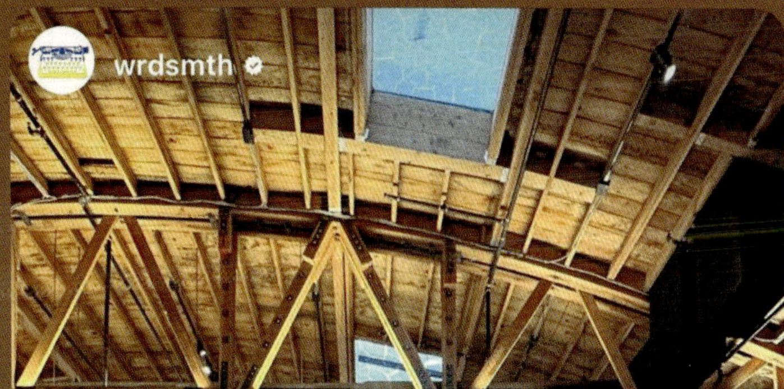

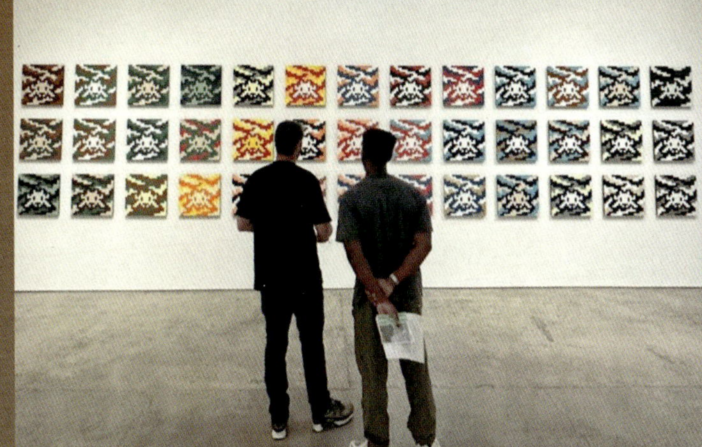

@invaderwashere
@oti.official

OVER THE INFLUENCE LOS ANGELES

Send message

invaderwashere
23 September 2023
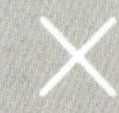
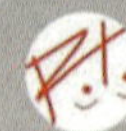
reenatolentino
ARTS DISTRICT, LOS ANGELES
No Invader wasn't here.
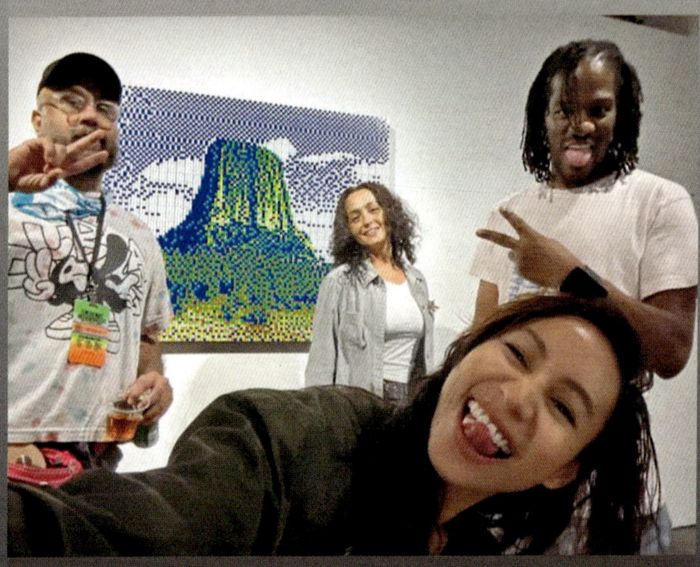
Send message

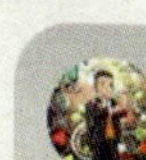

invaderwashere 1 October 2023

thekunal

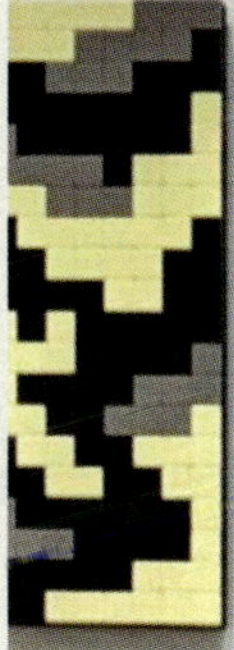

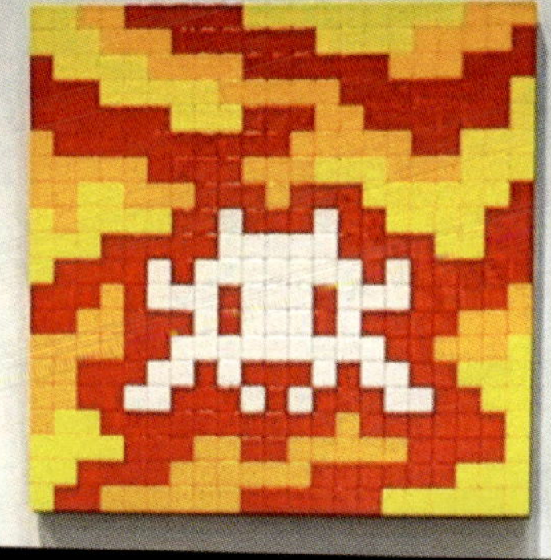

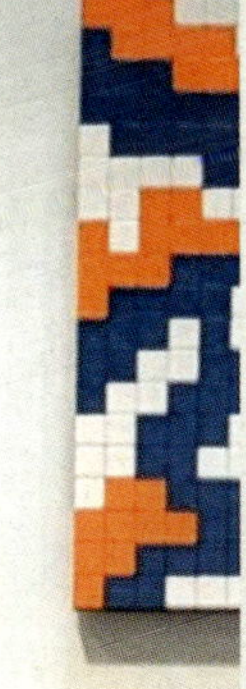

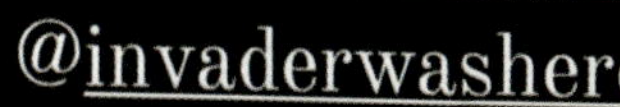

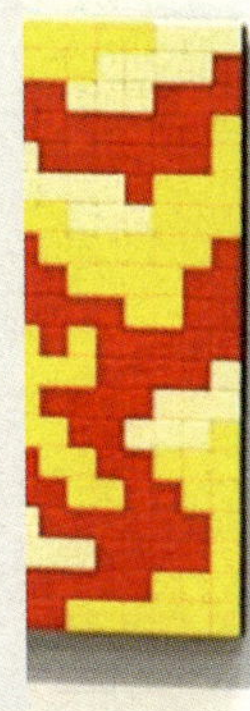

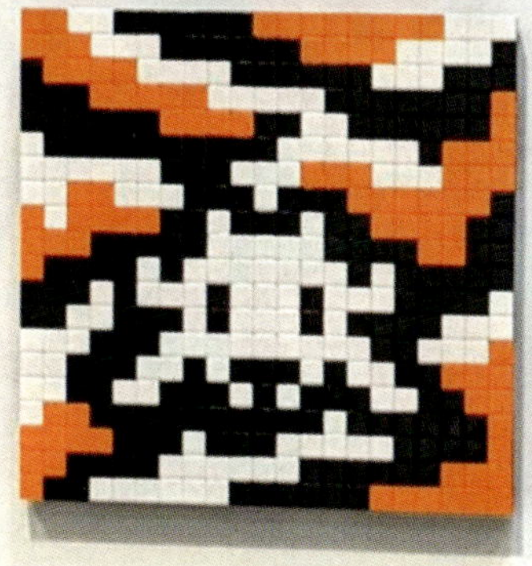

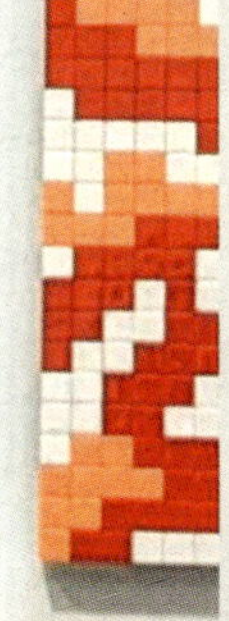

OVER THE INFLUENCE LOS ANGELES

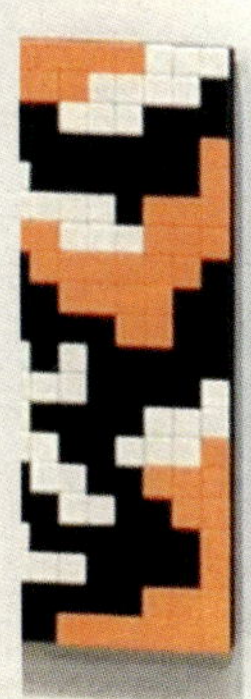

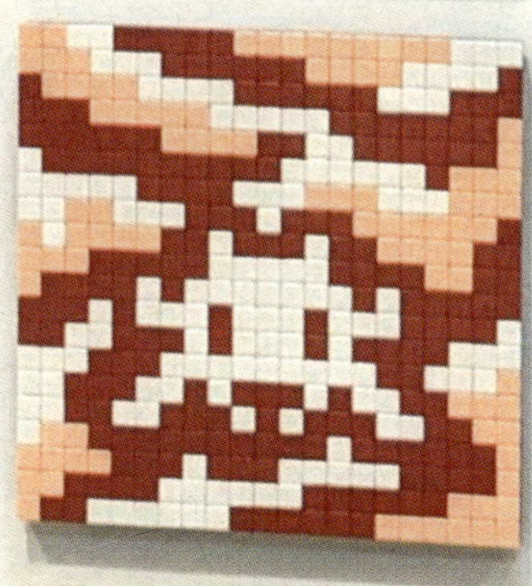

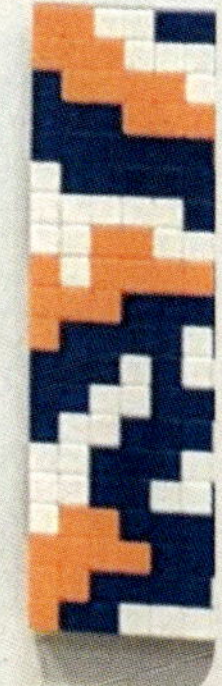

Send message

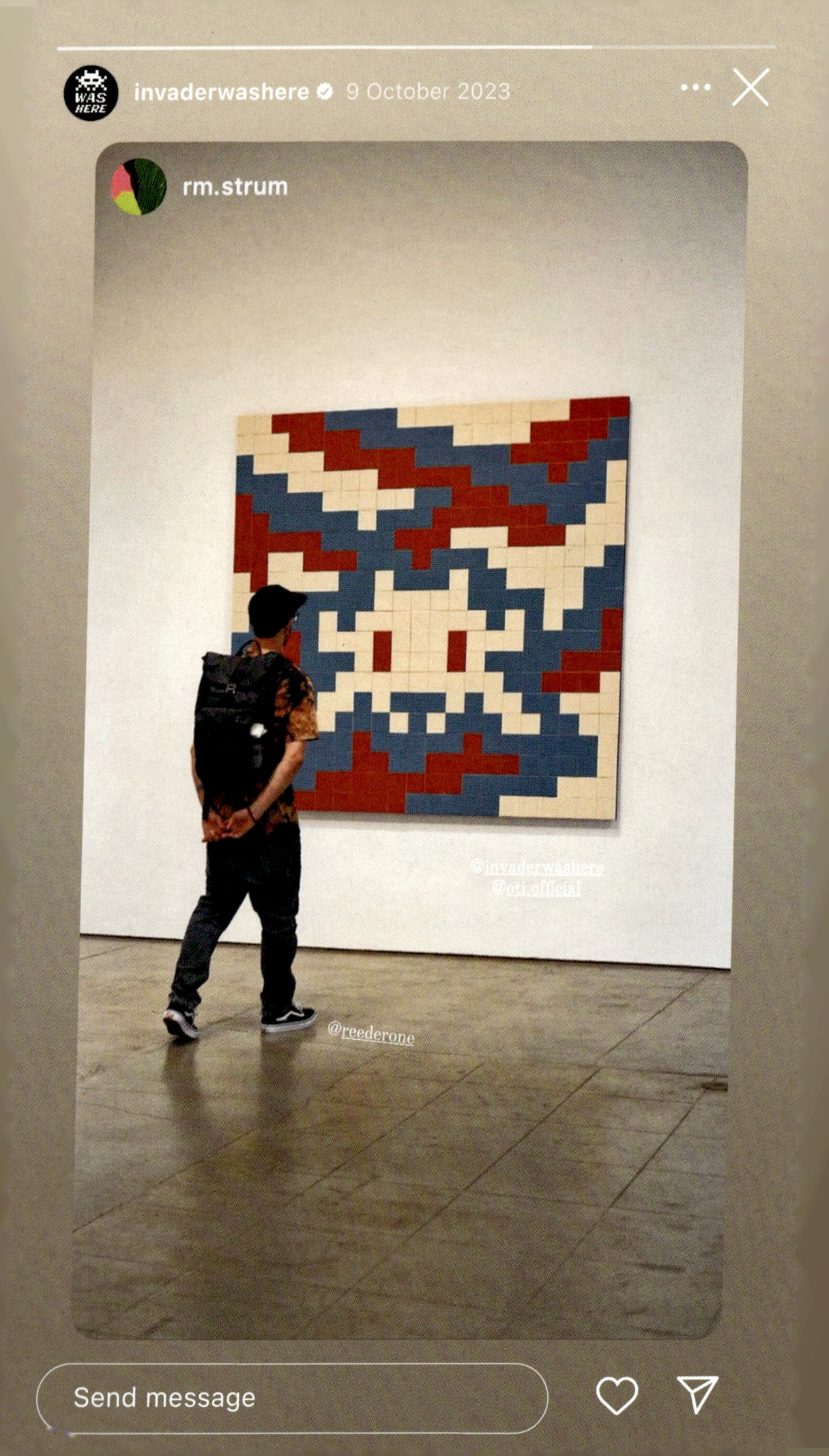

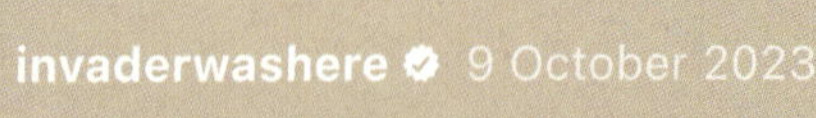

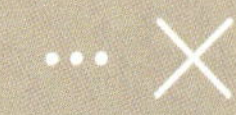

rm.strum

@invaderwashere
@oti.official

@reederone

Send message

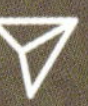

invaderwashere

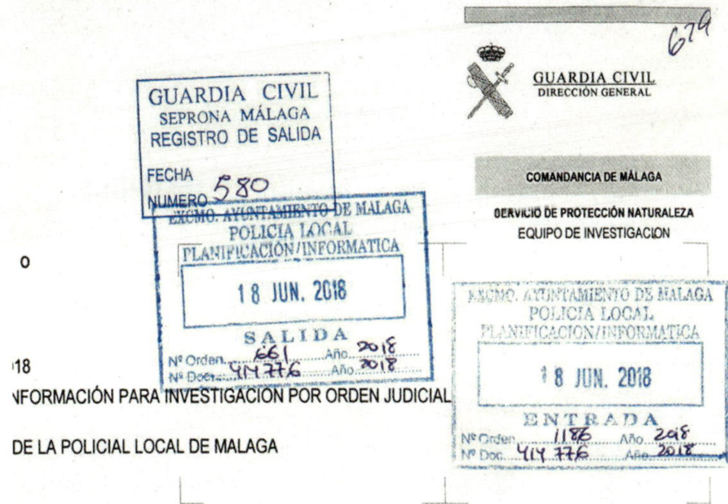

679

GUARDIA CIVIL
DIRECCIÓN GENERAL

GUARDIA CIVIL
SEPRONA MÁLAGA
REGISTRO DE SALIDA
FECHA
NUMERO 580

EXCMO. AYUNTAMIENTO DE MALAGA
POLICIA LOCAL
PLANIFICACIÓN/INFORMATICA
18 JUN. 2018
SALIDA
Nº Orden 661 Año 2018
Nº Doc. 414 776 Año 2018

COMANDANCIA DE MÁLAGA

SERVICIO DE PROTECCIÓN NATURALEZA
EQUIPO DE INVESTIGACION

EXCMO. AYUNTAMIENTO DE MALAGA
POLICIA LOCAL
PLANIFICACION/INFORMATICA
18 JUN. 2018
ENTRADA
Nº Orden 1186 Año 2018
Nº Doc. 414 776 Año 2018

o

18

NFORMACIÓN PARA INVESTIGACIÓN POR ORDEN JUDICIAL

DE LA POLICIAL LOCAL DE MALAGA

/07/2017 mediante oficio policial nº 772 y con motivo de las investigaciones que se
bo por esta Unidad por un supuesto delito contra el patrimonio histórico (colocación de
nto histórico) se solicitó a la Jefatura de la Policía Local de Málaga copia de las
ámaras de seguridad realizadas en las fechas próximas a la denominada Noche en
y 23 de mayo del 2017.

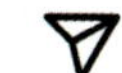

32 388 likes

invaderwashere After 5 years of proceedings, a trial and the dismantling of almost all my mosaics in Malaga, I've just been acquitted of damaging heritage ✊🥳 #malaga #artpower #notguilty

View all 875 comments

18 October 2023

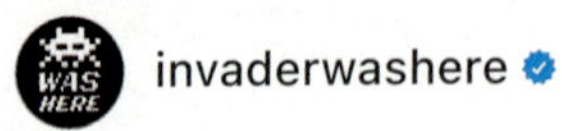

invaderwashere ...

EL PAÍS SUSCRÍBETE

Cultura

LIBROS · ARTE · CINE · MÚSICA · TEATRO · DANZA · HISTORIA · ARQUITECTURA · CÓMIC · VIDEOJUEGOS · TOROS · BABELIA · ÚLT

ARTE URBANO >

Absuelto el artista urbano Invader de un delito contra el patrimonio en Málaga

La jueza considera que el creador instaló 15 mosaicos en edificios protegidos a propuesta del gestor cultural Fernando Francés, pero que el escaso daño infligido no debe llevar una condena penal para ninguno de ellos

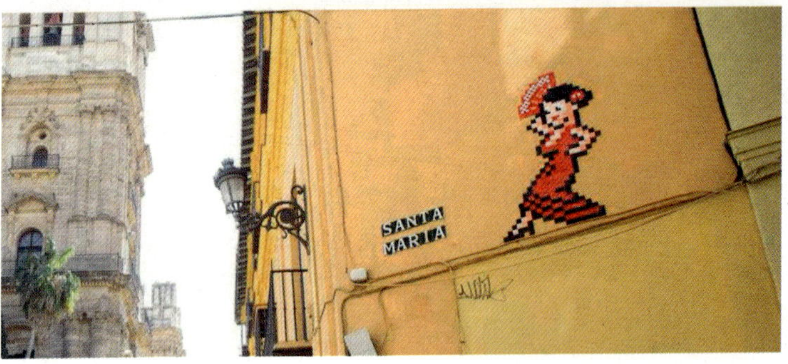

32 388 likes

invaderwashere After 5 years of proceedings, a trial and the dismantling of almost all my mosaics in Malaga, I've just been acquitted of damaging heritage ✊🥳 #malaga #artpower #notguilty

View all 875 comments

18 October 2023

invaderwashere

   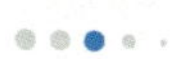 

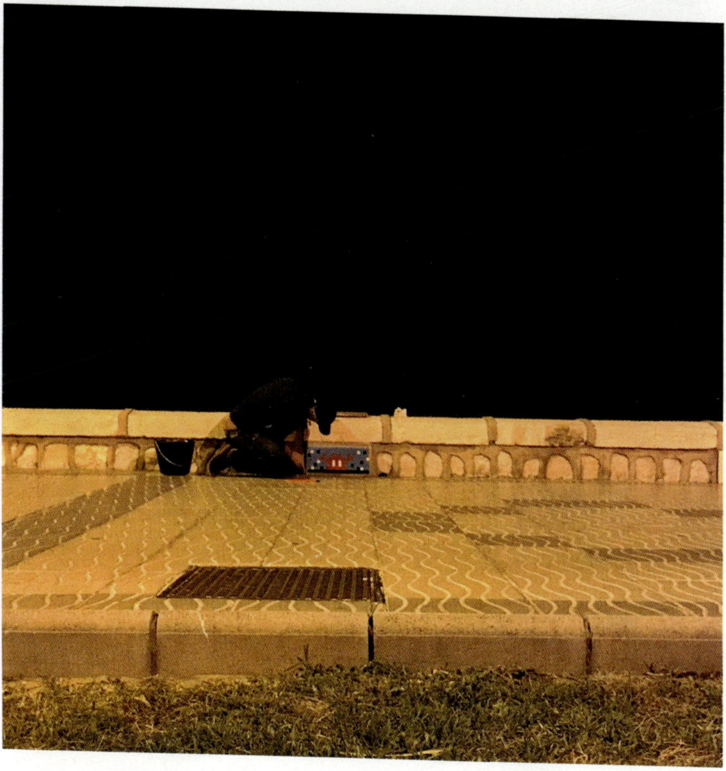

32 388 likes

invaderwashere After 5 years of proceedings, a trial and the dismantling of almost all my mosaics in Malaga, I've just been acquitted of damaging heritage ✊🥳 #malaga #artpower #notguilty

View all 875 comments

18 October 2023

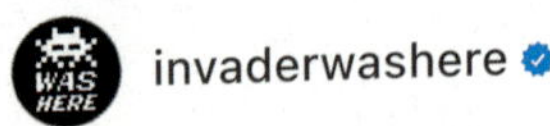

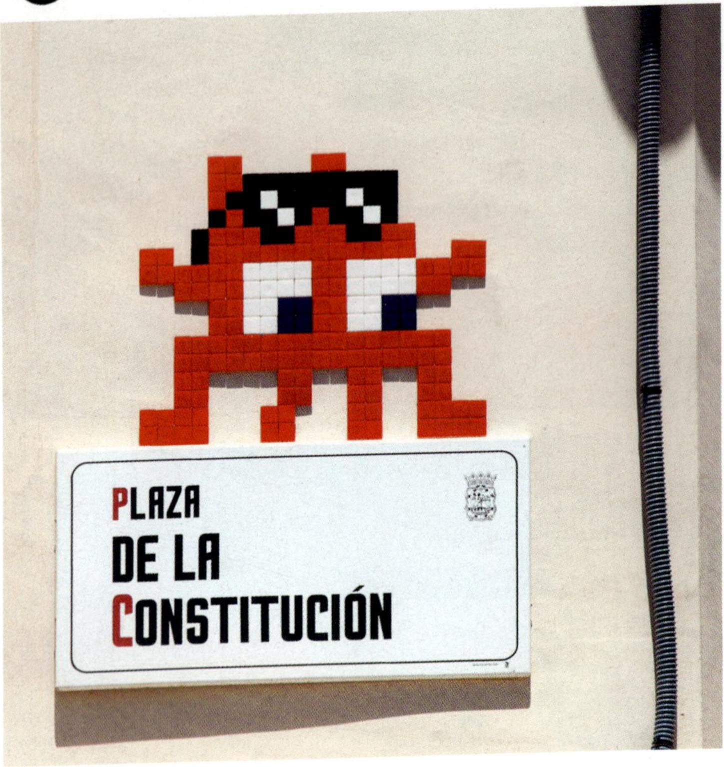

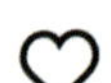   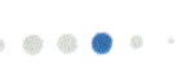 

32 388 likes

invaderwashere After 5 years of proceedings, a trial and the dismantling of almost all my mosaics in Malaga, I've just been acquitted of damaging heritage ✊ 🥳 #malaga #artpower #notguilty

View all 875 comments

18 October 2023

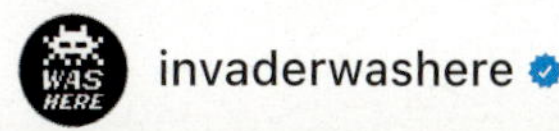

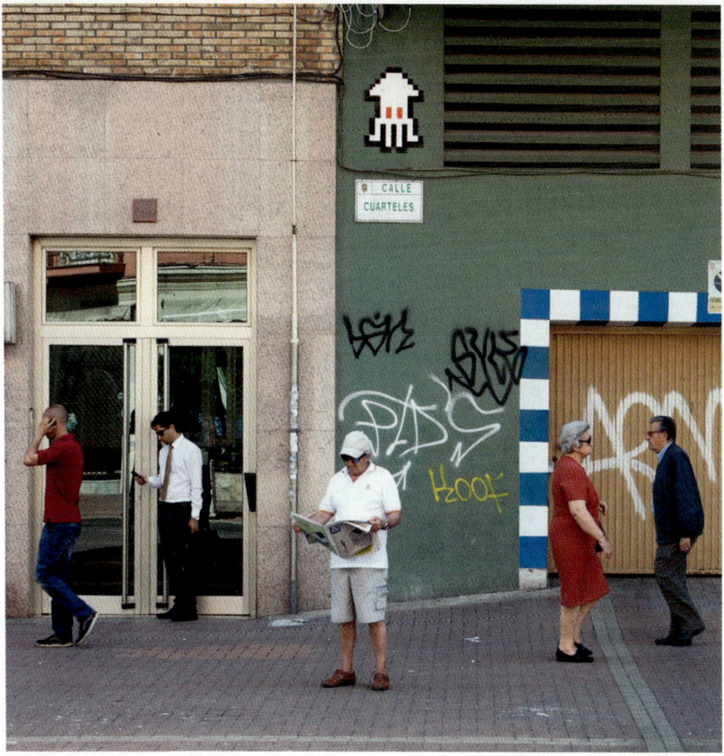

   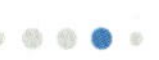 

32 388 likes

invaderwashere After 5 years of proceedings, a trial and the dismantling of almost all my mosaics in Malaga, I've just been acquitted of damaging heritage ✊ 🥳 #malaga #artpower #notguilty

View all 875 comments

18 October 2023

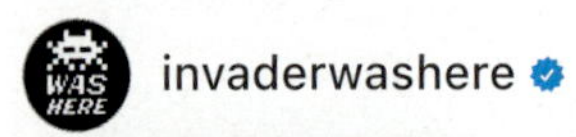

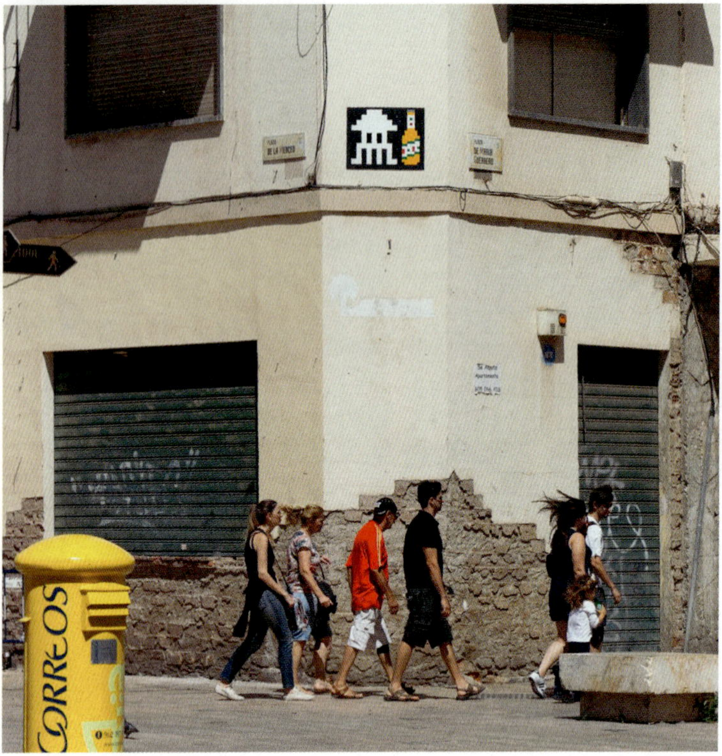

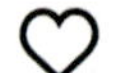 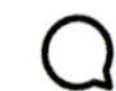  

32 388 likes

invaderwashere After 5 years of proceedings, a trial and the dismantling of almost all my mosaics in Malaga, I've just been acquitted of damaging heritage ✊ 🥳 #malaga #artpower #notguilty

View all 875 comments

18 October 2023

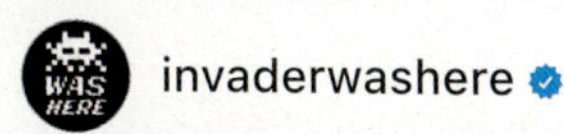

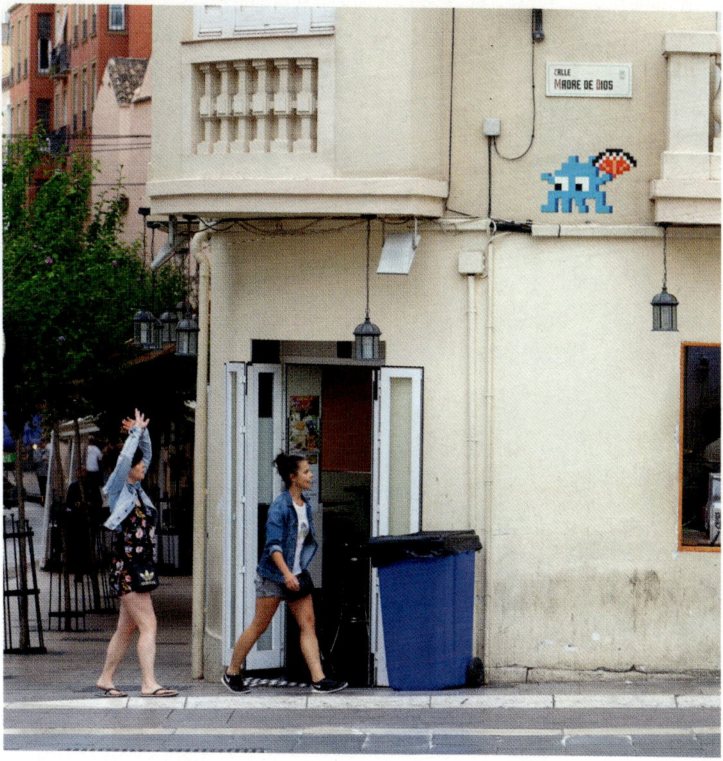

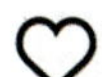   

32 388 likes

invaderwashere After 5 years of proceedings, a trial and the dismantling of almost all my mosaics in Malaga, I've just been acquitted of damaging heritage ✊🥳 #malaga #artpower #notguilty

View all 875 comments

18 October 2023

invaderwashere 

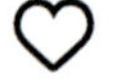   

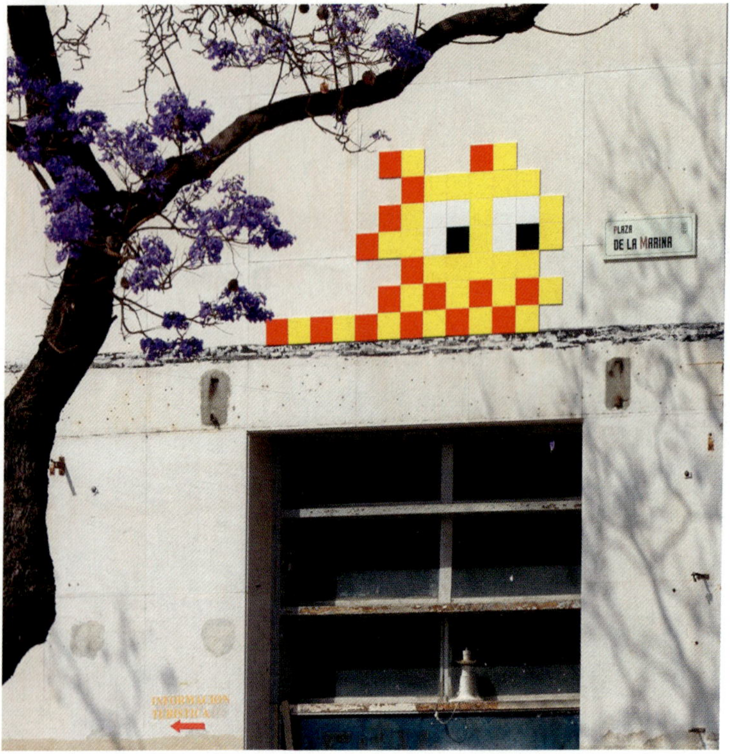

32 388 likes

invaderwashere After 5 years of proceedings, a trial and the dismantling of almost all my mosaics in Malaga, I've just been acquitted of damaging heritage ✊🥳 #malaga #artpower #notguilty

View all 875 comments

18 October 2023